Encyclopedia *of* Special Education

FOURTH EDITION

Encyclopedia *of* Special Education

A Reference for the Education of Children, Adolescents, and Adults with Disabilities and Other Exceptional Individuals

FOURTH EDITION

Volume 1: A–C

Edited by

Cecil R. Reynolds, Kimberly J. Vannest, and Elaine Fletcher-Janzen

WILEY

KH

Library of Congress Cataloging-in-Publication Data:

Encyclopedia of special education: a reference for the education of children, adolescents, and adults with disabilities and other exceptional individuals / edited by Cecil R. Reynolds, Kimberly J. Vannest, and Elaine Fletcher-Janzen.—Fourth edition.
    pages cm
  Includes bibliographical references.
  ISBN 978-0-470-64216-0 (set); ISBN 978-0-470-94938-2 (v. 1); ISBN 978-0-470-94939-9 (v. 2); ISBN 978-0-470-94940-5 (v. 3); ISBN 978-0-470-94941-2 (v. 4); 978-1-118-62830-0 (ebk.); 978-1-118-62845-4 (ebk.); 978-1-118-66058-4 (ebk.).
  1. Children with disabilities—Education—United States—Encyclopedias. 2. Special education—United States—Encyclopedias. 3. People with disabilities—Education—United States—Encyclopedias. I. Reynolds, Cecil R., 1952– editor of compilation. II. Vannest, Kimberly J., 1967– ; editor of compilation. III. Fletcher-Janzen, Elaine, editor of compilation.
  LC4007.E53 2013
    371.903—dc23   2012048628

Printed in the United States of America

10 9 8 7 6 5 4 3 2 1

3/26/14

ENCYCLOPEDIA OF SPECIAL EDUCATION ENTRIES

EDITORIAL STAFF

Heather Davis
Texas A&M University
Letters A–M

Heather Hatton
Texas A&M University
Letters N–Z

Frank E. Vannest
San Pasqual High School,
   Retired
Letters A–Z

Contributing Editors

Heather Peshak George
University of South Florida
Positive Behavior supports

Richard Parker
Texas A&M University
Single Case Research

John Davis
Texas A&M University
Single Case Research

Ben Mason
Juniper Gardens,
University of Kansas
Gifted and Talented

Mary Wagner
Principal Scientist in the
Center for Education and
Human Services
Longitudinal Studies

Stacey Smith
Texas A&M University
Reading

Ron Dumont
Fairleigh Dickinson University
Assessments

John O. Willis
Rivier College
Assessments

Kathleen Viezel
Fairleigh Dickinson University
Assessments

Jamie Zibulsky
Fairleigh Dickinson University
Assessments

Mary Capraro
Texas A&M University
Mathematics

Jennifer Ganz
Texas A&M University
Autism

Dalun Zhang
Texas A&M University
Transition

Mitchell Yell
University of South Carolina
Legal Issues in Special Education

Dave Edyburn
University of Wisconsin
Assistive Technology

Sandra Lewis
Florida State University
Visual Impairments

Pat Scherer
International Center on
Deafness and the Arts
Deaf Education

Amanda Chow
Texas A&M University
Biographies and
   Autobiographies

Lauren Williams
Texas A&M University
Organizations and
   Publications

Rose Mason
Juniper Gardens,
University of Kansas
Intelligence

Nancy Hutchins
Texas A&M University
Behavior

CONTRIBUTORS

Susanne Blough Abbott
Bedford Central School District
Mt. Kisco, New York

Marty Abramson
University of Wisconsin at Stout
Menomonie, Wisconsin

Patricia Ann Abramson
Hudson Public Schools
Hudson, Wisconsin

Salvador Hector Achoa
Texas A&M University
College Station, Texas

William M. Acree
University of Northern Colorado
Greeley, Colorado

Tufan Adiguzel
Bahcesehir Unviersity
Isantbul, Turkey

Theresa T. Aguire
Texas A&M University
College Station, Texas

Patricia A. Alexander
University of Maryland
College Park, Maryland

Vincent C. Alfonso
Fordham University
New York, New York

Nancy Algert
Texas A&M University
College Station, Texas

Bob Algozzine
University of North Carolina
    at Charlotte
Charlotte, North Carolina

Kate Algozzine
University of North Carolina
    at Charlotte
Charlotte, North Carolina

Thomas E. Allen
Gallaudet College
Washington, DC

Marie Almond
The University of Texas of the
    Permian Basin
Odessa, Texas

Anna Pat L. Alpert
Texas A&M University
College Station, Texas

Geri R. Alvis
Memphis State University
Memphis, Tennessee

Daniel G. Amen
University of California
    School of Medicine
Irvine, California

Megan Amidon
Texas State University–
    San Marcos
San Marcos, Texas

C. H. Ammons
*Psychological Reports /
Perceptual and Motor Skills*
Missoula, Montana

Song An
Texas A&M University
College Station, Texas

Carol Anderson
Texas A&M University
College Station, Texas

Cynthia Anderson
University of Oregon
Eugene, Oregon

Kari Anderson
University of North Carolina
    at Wilmington
Wilmington, North Carolina

Peggy L. Anderson
University of New Orleans,
    Lakefront
New Orleans, Louisiana

Candace Andrews
California State University,
    San Bernardino
San Bernardino, California

Karal Anhalt
Texas A&M University
College Station, Texas

Jean Annan
Massey University
New Zealand

Stephanie Anselene
University of North Carolina
    at Wilmington
Wilmington, North Carolina

J. Appelboom-Fondu
UniversitéLibre de Bruxelles
Brussels, Belgium

James M. Applefield
University of North Carolina
    at Wilmington
Wilmington, North Carolina

Pauline F. Applefield
University of North Carolina
    at Wilmington
Wilmington, North Carolina

Kimberly F. Applequist
University of Colorado at Colorado
    Springs
Colorado Springs, Colorado

Anna M. Arena
Academic Therapy Publications
Novato, California

John Arena
Academic Therapy Publications
Novato, California

Martin Argan
University of Wyoming
Laramie, Wyoming

Julie A. Armentrout
University of Colorado at Colorado
    Springs
Colorado Springs, Colorado

Laura Arnstein
State University of New York
Binghamton, New York

Patricia Ann Arramson
Hudson Public Schools
Hudson, Wisconsin

Gustavo Abelardo Arrendondo
Monterrey, Mexico

Bernice Arricale
Hunter College, City University
    of New York
New York, New York

H. Roberta Arrigo
Hunter College, City University
  of New York
New York, New York

Alfredo J. Artiles
University of California,
  Los Angeles
Los Angeles, California

Maria Arzola
University of Florida
Gainesville, Florida

Michael J. Ash
Texas A&M University
College Station, Texas

Adel E. Ashawal
Ain Shams University
Cairo, Egypt

Michelle S. Athanasiou
University of Northern Colorado
Greeley, Colorado

Shannon Atwater
Branson School Online
Branson, Colorado

William G. Austin
Cape Fear Psychological Services
Wilmington, North Carolina

Anna H. Avant
University of Alabama
Tuscaloosa, Alabama

Dan G. Bachor
University of Victoria
Victoria, British Columbia, Canada

John Baer
Rider University
Lawrenceville, New Jersey

Rebecca Bailey
Texas A&M University
College Station, Texas

Morgan Baker
Texas A&M University
College Station, Texas

Timothy A. Ballard
University of North Carolina
  at Wilmington
Wilmington, North Carolina

Melanie Ballatore
University of Texas at Austin
Austin, Texas

Tanya Y. Banda
Texas A&M University Press
College Station, Texas

Monique Banters
Centre d'Etudeet de Reclassement
Brussels, Belgium

Deborah E. Barbour
University of North Carolina
  at Wilmington
Wilmington, North Carolina

Russell A. Barkley
University of Massachusetts
  Medical Center
Worchester, Massachusetts

Charles P. Barnard
University of Wisconsin at Stout
Menomonie, Wisconsin

David W. Barnett
University of Cincinnati
Cincinnati, Ohio

Ellis I. Barowsky
Hunter College, City University
  of New York
New York, New York

Susan B. Barrett
Sheppard Pratt Health System
Towson, Maryland

Amanda L. Barth
The Chicago School of Professional
  Psychology
Chicago, IL

Lyle E. Barton
Kent State University
Kent, Ohio

Vicki Bartosik
Stanford University
Stanford, California

Paul Bates
Southern Illinois University
Carbondale, Illinois

Stacey L. Bates
University of Texas at Austin
Austin, Texas

Anne M. Bauer
University of Cincinnati
Cincinnati, Ohio

Elizabeth R. Bauerschmidt
University of North Carolina
  at Wilmington
Wilmington, North Carolina

Michael Bauerschmidt
Brunswick Hospital
Wilmington, North Carolina

Emily R. Baxter
University of Colorado
Colorado Springs, Colorado

John R. Beattie
University of North Carolina
  at Charlotte
Charlotte, North Carolina

George R. Beauchamp
Cleveland Clinic Foundation
Cleveland, Ohio

Melissa Beckham
The Citadel
Charleston, South Carolina

Pena Bedesem
Kent State University
Kent, Ohio

Ronald A. Beghetto
University of Oregon
Eugene, Oregon

Julie Bell
University of Florida
Gainesville, Florida

Karen Bender
University of Northern Colorado
Greeley, Colorado

Ana Yeraldina Beneke
University of Oklahoma
Norman, Oklahoma

Randy Elliot Bennett
Educational Testing Service
Princeton, New Jersey

Richard A. Berg
West Virginia University
  Medical Center
Charleston, West Virginia

John R. Bergan
University of Arizona
Tucson, Arizona

Dianne E. Berkell
C.W. Post Campus, Long Island
  University
Greenvale, New York

Gary Berkowitz
Temple University
Philadelphia, Pennsylvania

Shari A. Bevins
Texas A&M University
College Station, Texas

John Bielinski
AGS Publishing
St. Paul, Minnesota

Kristan Biernath
The Hughes Spalding International
  Adoption Evaluation Center
Atlanta, Georgia

Erin D. Bigler
Brigham Young University
Provo, Utah

Tia Billy
Texas A&M University
College Station, Texas

Roseann Bisighini
The Salk Institute
La Jolla, California

Kendra J. Bjoraker
University of Northern Colorado
Greeley, Colorado

Jan Blacher
University of California, Riverside
Riverside, California

Jose Blackorby
SRI International
Menlo Park, California

Jamie Bleiweiss
Hunter College, City University
    of New York
New York, New York

Gérard Bless
University of Fribourg
Fribourg, Switzerland

Richard Boada
University of Denver
Denver, Colorado

Margot Boles
Texas A&M University
College Station, Texas

L. Worth Bolton
Cape Fear Substance Abuse
    Center
Wilmington, North Carolina

Andy Bondy
Pyramid Educational Consultants
Newark, Delaware

Gwyneth M. Boodoo
Texas A&M University
College Station, Texas

Nancy Bordier
Hunter College, City University
    of New York
New York, New York

Jeannie Bormans
Center for Developmental Problems
Brussels, Belgium

Morton Botel
University of Pennsylvania
Philadelphia, Pennsylvania

Daniel J. Boudah
Texas A&M University
College Station, Texas

Michael Bourdot
Centre d'Etudeet de Reclassement
Brussels, Belgium

E. Amanda Boutot
Texas State University–San Marcos
San Marcos, Texas

Lisa Bowman-Perrott
Texas A&M University
College Station, Texas

Bruce A. Bracken
University of Memphis
Memphis, Tennessee

Mary Brady
Pennsylvania Special Education
    Assistive Device Center
Elizabethtown, Pennsylvania

Tammy Branan
University of Northern Colorado
Greeley, Colorado

Janet S. Brand
Hunter College, City University
    of New York
New York, New York

Don Braswell
Research Foundation, City
    University of New York
New York, New York

T. Berry Brazelton
Children's Hospital
Boston, Massachusetts

Adam S. Bristol
Yale University
New Haven, Connecticut

Courtney Britt
Texas State University–San Marcos
San Marcos, Texas

Warner H. Britton
Auburn University
Auburn, Alabama

Debra Y. Broadbooks
California School of Professional
    Psychology
San Diego, California

Melanie L. Bromley
California State University,
    San Bernardino
San Bernardino, California

Shannon R. Brooks
University of Minnesota
Minneapolis, Minnesota

Michael G. Brown
Central Wisconsin Center for the
    Developmentally Disabled
Madison, Wisconsin

Robert T. Brown
University of North Carolina
    at Wilmington
Wilmington, North Carolina

Ronald T. Brown
Emory University School of Medicine
Atlanta, Georgia

Tina L. Brown
Memphis State University
Memphis, Tennessee

Robert G. Brubaker
Eastern Kentucky University
Richmond, Kentucky

Catherine O. Bruce
Hunter College, City University
    of New York
New York, New York

Andrew R. Brulle
Wheaton College
Sycamore, Illinois

Virdette L. Brumm
Children's Hospital Los Angeles
Kreck/USC School of Medicine
Los Angeles, California

Laura Kinzie Brutting
University of Wisconsin at Madison
Madison, Wisconsin

Donna M. Bryant
University of North Carolina
    at Chapel Hill
Chapel Hill, North Carolina

Elizabeth A. Bubonic
Texas A&M University
College Station, Texas

Milton Budoff
Research Institute for Educational
    Problems
Cambridge, Massachusetts

Carolyn L. Bullard
Lewis & Clark College
Portland, Oregon

Melissa R. Bunner
Austin Neurological Clinic
Austin, Texas

Thomas R. Burke
Hunter College, City University
    of New York
New York, New York

Leslie Burkholder
Idea Infusion Consulting and
    Contracting
Denver, Colorado

Alois Bürli
Swiss Institute for Special Education
Lucerne, Switzerland

Matthew K. Burns
University of Minnesota
Minneapolis, Minnesota

Jason Burrow-Sanchez
University of Utah
Salt Lake City, Utah

Thomas A. Burton
University of Georgia
Athens, Georgia

Michelle T. Buss
Texas A&M University
College Station, Texas

James Button
United States Department of
    Education
Washington, DC

Glenda Byrns
Texas A&M University
College Station, Texas

Catherine M. Caldwell
University of Texas at Austin
Austin, Texas

Siglia Camargo
Texas A&M University
College Station, Texas

Claudia Camarillo-Dievendorf
Pitzer College, Claremont
Claremont, California

Anne Campbell
Purdue University
West Lafayette, Indiana

Frances A. Campbell
University of North Carolina
    at Chapel Hill
Chapel Hill, North Carolina

Mary Capraro
Texas A&M University
College Station, Texas

Robert M. Capraro
Texas A&M University
College Station, Texas

Elaine Carlson
Westat, Incorporated
Rockville, Maryland

Steven A. Carlson
Beaverton Schools
Beaverton, Oregon

Douglas Carnine
University of Oregon
Eugene, Oregon

Deborah Birke Caron
St. Lucie County School District
Ft. Pierce, Florida

Janet Carpenter
University of Oklahoma
Norman, Oklahoma

Edward G. Carr
State University of New York
    at Stony Brook
Stony Brook, New York

Nicole M. Cassidy
The Chicago School of Professional
    Psychology
Chicago, Illinois

Suzanne Carreker
Nehaus
Bellaire, Texas

Jodi M. Cholewicki-Carroll
University of South Carolina
Columbia, South Carolina

Eric Carter
Vanderbilt University
Nashville, Tennessee

Stephanie Caruthers
Texas State University–San Marcos
San Marcos, Texas

Catharina Carvalho
Texas A&M University
College Station, Texas

Tracy Calpin Castle
Eastern Kentucky University
Richmond, Kentucky

John F. Cawley
University of New Orleans
New Orleans, Louisiana

Carla C. de Baca
University of Northern Colorado
Colorado Springs, Colorado

Christine D. C. de Baca
University of Northern Colorado
Greeley, Colorado

Constance Y. Celaya
Irving, Texas

Sandra Chafouleas
University of Connecticut
Storrs, Connecticut

James C. Chalfant
University of Arizona
Tucson, Arizona

Mei-Lin Chang
Emory University
Atlanta, Georgia

Elaine A. Cheesman
University of Colorado at Colorado
    Springs
Colorado Springs, Colorado

Nina Cheng
University of Texas at Austin
Austin, Texas

Rebecca Wing-yi Cheng
The University of Hong Kong
Hong Kong, China

Robert A. Chernoff
Harbor—UCLA Medical Center
Los Angeles, California

Chris Cherrington
Lycoming College
Williamsport, Pennsylvania

Karen Elfner Childs
University of South Florida
Tampa, Florida

Robert Chimedza
University of Zimbabwe
Harare, Zimbabwe

Kathleen M. Chinn
New Mexico State University
Las Cruces, New Mexico

Mary M. Chittooran
Saint Louis University
Saint Louis, Missouri

Amanda C. Chow
Texas A&M University
College Station, Texas

Elizabeth Christiansen
University of Utah
Salt Lake City, Utah

Elaine Clark
University of Utah
Salt Lake City, Utah

Gary M. Clark
Kansas State University
Manhattan, Kansas

Deanna Clemens
College Station Independent School
    District
College Station, Texas

LeRoy Clinton
Boston University
Boston, Massachusetts

Renato Cocchi
Pesaro, Italy

Cynthia Price Cohen
Child Rights International Research
    Institute
New York, New York

Shirley Cohen
Hunter College, City University
    of New York
New York, New York

Ginga L. Colcough
University of North Carolina
    at Wilmington
Wilmington, North Carolina

Christine L. Cole
University of Wisconsin at Madison
Madison, Wisconsin

Rhonda Collins
Florida State University
Tallahassee, Florida

Sarah Compton
University of Texas at Austin
Austin, Texas

Jennifer Condon
University of North Carolina
    at Wilmington
Wilmington, North Carolina

Jane Close Conoley
University of Nebraska–Lincoln
Lincoln, Nebraska

Benjamin J. Cook
The Chicago School of Professional
    Psychology
Chicago, Illinois

Bryan Cook
University of Hawaii
Honolulu, Hawaii

Clayton R. Cook
University of California, Riverside
Riverside, California

Krystal T. Cook
Texas A&M University
College Station, Texas

Carey E. Cooper
University of Texas at Austin
Austin, Texas

Mary Corlett
University of Texas at Austin
Austin, Texas

M. Sencer Corlu
Texas A&M University
College Station, Texas

Emily Cornforth
University of Colorado
Colorado Springs, Colorado

Vivian I. Correa
University of Florida
Gainesville, Florida

Barbara Corriveau
Laramie County School District # 1
Cheyenne, Wyoming

Lawrence S. Cote
Pennsylvania State University
University Park, Pennsylvania

Kathleen Cotton
Northwest Regional Educational
    Laboratory
Portland, Oregon

Katherine D. Couturier
Pennsylvania State University
King of Prussia, Pennsylvania

Murray Cox
Southwest Adventist University
Keene, Texas

J. Michael Coxe
University of South Carolina
Columbia, South Carolina

Julia H. Coyne
The Chicago School of Professional
    Psychology
Chicago, Illinois

Anne B. Crabbe
St. Andrews College
Laurinburg, North Carolina

Lindy Crawford
University of Colorado at Colorado
    Springs
Colorado Springs, Colorado

M. Franci Crepeau-Hobson
University of Northern Colorado
Greeley, Colorado

Sergio R. Crisalle
Medical Horizons Unlimited
San Antonio, Texas

Chara Crivelli
Vito de Negrar
Verona, Italy

Jill E. Crowley
Saint Louis University
Saint Louis, Missouri

John Crumlin
University of Colorado at Colorado
    Springs
Colorado Springs, Colorado

Jack A. Cummings
Indiana University
Bloomington, Indiana

Jacqueline Cunningham
University of Texas
Austin, Texas

Susan Curtiss
University of California,
    Los Angeles
Los Angeles, California

Juliette Cutillo
Fountain–Fort Carson School
    District 8
Colorado Springs, Colorado

Rik Carl D'Amato
University of Northern Colorado
Greeley, Colorado

Amy J. Dahlstrom
University of Northern Colorado
Greeley, Colorado

Elizabeth Dane
Hunter College, City University
    of New York
New York, New York

Louis Danielson
American Institutes for Research
Washington, DC

Craig Darch
Auburn University
Auburn, Alabama

Barry Davidson
Ennis, Texas

Andrew S. Davis
University of Northern Colorado
Greeley, Colorado

Barbra L. Davis
University of Texas
Austin, Texas

Heather S. Davis
Texas A&M University
College Station, Texas

Jacqueline E. Davis
Boston University
Boston, Massachusetts

John L. Davis
Purdue University
West Lafayette, Indiana

Trina J. Davis
Texas A&M University
College Station, Texas

Raymond S. Dean
Ball State University
Indiana University School
    of Medicine
Muncie, Indiana

Lori Dekeyzer
University of Utah
Salt Lake City, Utah

Elizabeth Delaune
Texas State University–San Marcos
San Marcos, Texas

Jozi De Leon
New Mexico State University
Las Cruces, New Mexico

Bernadette M. Delgado
University of Nebraska–Lincoln
Lincoln, Nebraska

Kendra De Loach
University of South Carolina
Columbia, South Carolina

Allison G. Dempsey
The University of Health Science
    Center at Houston
Houston, Texas

Jack R. Dempsey
University of Florida
Gainesville, Florida

Randall L. De Pry
Portland State University
Portland, Oregon

Lizanne DeStefano
University of Illinois,
    Urbana-Champaign
Champaign, Illinois

S. De Vriendt
Vrije Universiteit Brussel
Brussels, Belgium

Maria Rae Dewhirst
Illinois PBIS Network
La Grange Park, Illinois

Caroline D'Ippolito
Eastern Pennsylvania Special
    Education Resources
Center King of Prussia, Pennsylvania

Mary D'Ippolito
Montgomery County Intermediate
    Unit
Norristown, Pennsylvania

Roja Dilmore-Rios
California State University,
    San Bernadino
San Bernadino, California

Jeffrey Ditterline
University of Florida
Gainesville, Florida

Marilyn P. Dornbush
Atlanta, Georgia

Amanda Jensen Doss
Texas A&M University
College Station, Texas

Susann Dowling
University of Houston
Houston, Texas

Darrell L. Downs
Mount Sinai Medical Center and
    Miami Heart Institute
Miami, Florida

Jonathan T. Drummond
Princeton University
Princeton, New Jersey

Elizabeth McAdams Ducy
Texas A&M University
College Station, Texas

Sharon Duffy
University of California, Riverside
Riverside, California

Jengjyh Duh
National Taiwan Normal University
Taipei, Taiwan

Ron Dumont
Fairleigh Dickinson University
Teaneck, New Jersey

Glenn Dunlap
University of South Florida
Tampa, Florida

Jamie Duran
Texas A&M University
College Station, Texas

V. Mark Durand
University of South Florida
Saint Petersburg, Florida

Brooke Durbin
Texas A&M University
College Station, Texas

Abbey-Robin Durkin
University of Colorado
Colorado Springs, Colorado

Mary K. Dykes
University of Florida
Gainesville, Florida

Alan Dyson
University of Manchester
Manchester, England

Peg Eagney
School for the Deaf
New York, New York

Theresa Earles-Vollrath
University of Central Missouri
Warrensburg, Missouri

Ronald C. Eaves
Auburn University
Auburn, Alabama

Lucille Eber
Illinois PBIS Network
La Grange Park, Illinois

Lauren K. Eby
The Chicago School of Professional
    Psychology
Chicago, Illinois

Jana Echevarria
California State University,
    Long Beach
Long Beach, California

Danielle Edelston
University of California, Riverside
Riverside, California

Retha M. Edens
Saint Louis University
Saint Louis, Missouri

Heather Edgel
University of Utah
Salt Lake City, Utah

Amita Edran
California State University,
    Long Beach
Long Beach, California

Dave Edyburn
University of Wisconsin–Milwaukee
Milwaukee, Wisconsin

John M. Eells
Souderton Area School District
Souderton, Pennsylvania

Cassie Eiffert
University of Florida
Gainesville, Florida

Stephen N. Elliott
University of Wisconsin at Madison
Madison, Wisconsin

Julie Ellis
University of Florida
Gainesville, Florida

Fara El Zein
Texas State University–San Marcos
San Marcos, Texas

Ingemar Emanuelsson
Goteburg University
Goteburg, Sweden

Petra Engelbrecht
University of Stellenbosch
Stellenbosch, South Africa

Carol Sue Englert
Michigan State University
East Lansing, Michigan

Chaz Esparaza
California State University,
    San Bernardino
San Bernardino, California

Christine A. Espin
University of Minnesota
Minneapolis, Minnesota

Kimberly M. Estep
University of Houston–Clear Lake
Houston, Texas

Carol Anne Evans
University of Utah
Salt Lake City, Utah

Michelle Evans
California State University,
San Bernardino
San Bernardino, California

Rand B. Evans
Texas A&M University
College Station, Texas

Rose Fairbanks
Temecula, California

Sarah Fairbanks
University of Connecticut
Storrs, Connecticut

Katherine Falwell
University of North Carolina
at Wilmington
Wilmington, North Carolina

Jennie L. Farmer
University of South Florida
Tampa, Florida

Judith L. Farmer
New Mexico State University
Las Cruces, New Mexico

Stephen S. Farmer
New Mexico State University
Las Cruces, New Mexico

Peter Farrell
University of Manchester
Manchester, England

MaryAnn C. Farthing
University of North Carolina
at Chapel Hill
Chapel Hill, North Carolina

Sharla Fasko
Rowan County Schools
Morehead, Kentucky

Lisa A. Fasnacht-Hill
Keck/USC School of Medicine
Children's Hospital of Los Angeles
Los Angeles, California

Elizabeth I. Fassig
University of Northern Colorado
Greeley, Colorado

Mary Grace Feely
School for the Deaf
New York, New York

John F. Feldhusen
Purdue University
West Lafayette, Indiana

Laurie L. Ferguson
Wright Institute
Berkeley, California
and The Children's Hospital
Denver, Colorado

John M. Ferron
University of South Florida
Tampa, Florida

Britt-Inger Fex
University of Lund
Lund, Sweden

MaryLynne D. Filaccio
University of Northern Colorado
Greeley, Colorado

Donna Filips
Steger, Illinois

Marni R. Finberg
University of Florida
Gainesville, Florida

Jeffrey Finlayson
The Chicago School of Professional
Psychology
Chicago, Illinois

Krista Finstuen
Texas A&M University
College Station, Texas

Luke W. Fischer
The Chicago School of Professional
Psychology
Chicago, Illinois

Sally L. Flagler
University of Oklahoma
Norman, Oklahoma

Dawn P. Flanagan
St. John's University
Jamaica, New York

Dennis M. Flanagan
Montgomery County Intermediate
Unit
Norristown, Pennsylvania

K. Brigid Flannery
University of Oregon
Eugene, Oregon

Kelly Ann Fletcher
Ohio State University
Columbus, Ohio

David Fletcher-Janzen
Colorado Springs, Colorado

Elaine Fletcher-Janzen
Chicago School of Professional
Psychology
Chicago, Illinois

Wendy L. Flynn
Staffordshire University
Staffordshire, United Kingdom

Cindi Flores
California State University,
San Bernardino
San Bernardino, California

Peter T. Force
International Center for Deafness
and the Arts
Northbrook, Illinois

Stephanie R. Forness
University of Northern Colorado
Greeley, Colorado

Constance J. Fournier
Texas A&M University
College Station, Texas

Rollen C. Fowler
Eugene 4J School District
Eugene, Oregon

Emily Fox
University of Michigan
Ann Arbor, Michigan

Jessica H. Franco
University of Texas at Austin
Austin, Texas

Thomas A. Frank
Pennsylvania State University
University Park, Pennsylvania

Leslie Coyle Franklin
University of Northern Colorado
Greeley, Colorado

Mary M. Frasier
University of Georgia
Athens, Georgia

Brigitte N. Fredrick
Texas A&M University
College Station, Texas

Rachel Freeman
University of Kansas
Lawrence, Kansas

Christine L. French
Texas A&M University
College Station, Texas

Joseph L. French
Pennsylvania State University
University Park, Pennsylvania

Alice G. Friedman
University of Oklahoma Health
Services Center
Norman, Oklahoma

Douglas L. Friedman
Fordham University
Bronx, New York

Douglas Fuchs
Peabody College, Vanderbilt
University
Nashville, Tennessee

Lynn S. Fuchs
Peabody College, Vanderbilt
University
Nashville, Tennessee

Gerald B. Fuller
Central Michigan University
Mt. Pleasant, Michigan

Rosemary Gaffney
Hunter College, City University
of New York
New York, New York

Marie Galan
The Chicago School of Professional
Psychology
Chicago, Illinois

Sherri L. Gallagher
University of Northern Colorado
Greeley, Colorado

Jason Gallant
University of Florida
Gainesville, Florida

Diego Gallegos
Texas A&M University
College Station, Texas

Cynthia A. Gallo
University of Colorado
Colorado Springs, Colorado

Jennifer B. Ganz
Texas A&M University
College Station, Texas

Clarissa I. Garcia
Texas A&M University
College Station, Texas

Shernaz B. Garcia
University of Texas
Austin, Texas

Roman Garcia de Alba
Texas A&M University
College Station, Texas

Katherine Garnett
Hunter College, City University
of New York
New York, New York

Jeff Garrison-Tate
Texas A&M University
College Station, Texas

Carrie George
Texas A&M University
College Station, Texas

Heather Peshak George
University of South Florida
Tampa, Florida

Melissa M. George
Montgomery County Intermediate
Unit
Norristown, Pennsylvania

Phil Bless Gerard
University of Fribourg
Fribourg, Switzerland

Verena Getahun
AGS Publishing
St. Paul, Minnesota

Violeta Gevorgianiene
Vilnius University
Vilnius, Lithuania

Harvey R. Gilbert
Pennsylvania State University
University Park, Pennsylvania

Jennifer M. Gillis
University of California, Irvine
Irvine, California

Theresa M. Gisi
Colorado Neurological Associates, PC
Denver and Colorado Springs,
Colorado

Grazina Gintiliene
Vilnius University
Vilnius, Lithuania

Elizabeth Girshick
Montgomery County Intermediate
Unit
Norristown, Pennsylvania

Joni J. Gleason
University of West Florida
Pensacola, Florida

Sharon L. Glennen
Pennsylvania State University
University Park, Pennsylvania

Dianne Goldsby
Texas A&M University
College Station, Texas

Sam Goldstein
University of Utah
Salt Lake City, Utah

Maricela P. Gonzales
Texas A&M University
College Station, Texas

Rex Gonzales
University of Utah
Salt Lake City, Utah

Rick Gonzales
Texas A&M University
College Station, Texas

Jorge Gonzalez
Texas A&M University
College Station, Texas

Suzanne Gooderham
University of Ottawa
Ottawa, Ontario, Canada

Libby Goodman
Pennsylvania State University
King of Prussia, Pennsylvania

Steve Goodman
Michigan Integrated Behavior and
Learning Support Initiative
Holland, Michigan

Fara D. Goodwyn
Texas A&M University
College Station, Texas

Carole Reiter Gothelf
Hunter College, City University
of New York
New York, New York

Elizabeth Ann Graf
University of Northern Colorado
Greeley, Colorado

Steve Graham
University of Maryland
College Park, Maryland

Shannon A. Grant
Texas A&M University
College Station, Texas

Jeffrey W. Gray
Ball State University
Muncie, Indiana

P. Allen Gray, Jr.
University North Carolina at
Wilmington
Wilmington, North Carolina

Ashley T. Greenan
The Chicago School of Professional
Psychology
Chicago, Illinois

Darielle Greenberg
California School of Professional
Psychology
San Diego, California

Jacques Grégoire
Catholic University of Louvain
Louvain, Belgium

Laurence C. Grimm
University of Illinois
Chicago, Illinois

Lindsay S. Gross
University of Wisconsin
Milwaukee, Wisconsin

Suzanne M. Grundy
California State University,
San Bernardino
San Bernardino, California

Amy R. Guerette
Florida State University
Tallahassee, Florida

Nonna Guerra
Texas A&M University
College Station, Texas

John Guidubaldi
Kent State University
Kent, Ohio

Laura A. Guli
University of Texas at Austin
Austin, Texas

J. C. Guillemard
Dourdan, France

Deborah Guillen
The University of Texas of the
   Permian Basin
Odessa, Texas

Steven Gumerman
Temple University
Philadelphia, Pennsylvania

Thomas Gumpel
The Hebrew University of Jerusalem
Jerusalem, Israel

Rumki Gupta
Indian Statistical Institute
Kolkata, India

Terry B. Gutkin
University of Nebraska–Lincoln
Lincoln, Nebraska

Kathryn L. Guy
University of Texas at Austin
Austin, Texas

Patricia A. Haensly
Texas A&M University
College Station, Texas

George James Hagerty
Stonehill College North
Easton, Massachusetts

Angelroba Hairrell
Texas A&M University
College Station, Texas

Danny B. Hajovsky
University of Kansas
Lawrence, Kansas

Robert Hall
Texas A&M University
College Station, Texas

Winnifred M. Hall
University of West Indies
Kingston, Jamaica

Lindsay Halliday
California State University,
   San Bernardino
San Bernardino, California

Richard E. Halmstad
University of Wisconsin at Stout
Menomonie, Wisconsin

Glennelle Halpin
Auburn University
Auburn, Alabama

Donald D. Hammill
PRO-ED, Incorporated
Austin, Texas

Monika Hannon
University of Northern Colorado
Colorado Springs, Colorado

Harold Hanson
Southern Illinois University
Carbondale, Illinois

Elise Phelps Hanzel
California School of Professional
   Psychology
San Diego, California

Jennifer Hargrave
University of Texas at Austin
Austin, Texas

Jennifer Harman
University of Florida
Gainesville, Florida

Janice Harper
North Carolina Central University
Durham, North Carolina

Gale A. Harr
Maple Heights City Schools
Maple Heights, Ohio

Karen L. Harrell
University of Georgia
Athens, Georgia

Frances T. Harrington
Radford University
Blacksburg, Virginia

Karen R. Harris
University of Maryland
College Park, Maryland

Kathleen Harris
Arizona State University
Tempe, Arizona

Patti L. Harrison
University of Alabama
Tuscaloosa, Alabama

Joshua Harrower
Cal State University
Seaside, California

Beth Harry
University of Miami
Miami, Florida

Stuart N. Hart
University of Victoria
Victoria, British Columbia, Canada

Lawrence C. Hartlage
Evans, Georgia

Patricia Hartlage
Medical College of Georgia
Evans, Georgia

Melissa M. Harvey
University of Colorado
Colorado Springs, Colorado

Dan Hatt
University of Oklahoma
Norman, Oklahoma

Anette Hausotter
Bis Beratungsstelle Fur Die
   Intergration
Germany

Leanne S. Hawken
University of Utah
Salt Lake City, Utah

Krista D. Healy
University of California, Riverside
Riverside, California

Lora Tuesday Heathfield
University of Utah
Salt Lake City, Utah

Kathleen Hebbeler
SRI International
Menlo Park, California

Jeff Heinzen
Indianhead Enterprise
Menomonie, Wisconsin

Floyd Henderson
Texas A&M University
College Station, Texas

Rhonda Hennis
University of North Carolina
   at Wilmington
Wilmington, North Carolina

Latanya Henry
Texas A&M University
College Station, Texas

Arthur Hernandez
Texas A&M University
College Station, Texas

Robyn S. Hess
University of Colorado
Denver, Colorado

E. Valerie Hewitt
Texas A&M University
College Station, Texas

Julia A. Hickman
Bastrop Mental Health Association
Bastrop, Texas

Meme Hieneman
Behavioral Services Program
All Children's Hospital
Tampa, Florida

Craig S. Higgins
Stonehill College
North Easton, Massachusetts

Kellie Higgins
University of Texas at Austin
Austin, Texas

Alan Hilton
Seattle University
Seattle, Washington

Delores J. Hittinger
The University of Texas of the
    Permian Basin
Odessa, Texas

Sarah L. Hoadley
Appalachian State University
Boone, North Carolina

Harold E. Hoff, Jr.
Eastern Pennsylvania Special
    Education Resources Center
King of Prussia, Pennsylvania

Elizabeth Holcomb
*American Journal of Occupational
Therapy*
Bethesda, Maryland

E. Wayne Holden
University of Oklahoma Health
    Sciences Center
Norman, Oklahoma

Andrea Holland
University of Texas at Austin
Austin, Texas

Ivan Z. Holowinsky
Rutgers University
New Brunswick, New Jersey

Kristin T. Holsker
The Chicago School of Professional
    Psychology
Chicago, Illinois

Thomas F. Hopkins
Center for Behavioral Psychotherapy
White Plains, New York

Robert H. Horner
University of Oregon
Eugene, Oregon

Najmeh Hourmanesh
University of Utah
Salt Lake City, Utah

Wayne P. Hresko
Journal of Learning Disabilities
Austin, Texas

Carolyn Hughes
Vanderbilt University
Nashville, Tennessee

Charles A. Hughes
Pennsylvania State University
University Park, Pennsylvania

Jan N. Hughes
Texas A&M University
College Station, Texas

Kay E. Hughes
The Riverside Publishing Company
Itasca, Illinois

Aimee R. Hunter
University of North Carolina
    at Wilmington
Wilmington, North Carolina

Nancy Hutchins
Texas A&M University
College Station, Texas

Nancy L. Hutchinson
Simon Fraser University
Buraby, British Columbia

Beverly J. Irby
Sam Houston State University
Huntsville, Texas

Paul Irvine
Katonah, New York

Cornelia L. Izen
George Mason University
Fairfax, Virginia

Lee Anderson Jackson, Jr.
University of North Carolina
    at Wilmington
Wilmington, North Carolina

Elisabeth Jacobsen
Copenhagen, Denmark

Markku Jahnukainen
University of Helsinki
Helsinki, Finland

Emma Janzen
University of Colorado
Colorado Springs, Colorado

Diane Jarvis
State University of New York
    at Buffalo
Buffalo, New York

Phillip Jenkins
University of Kentucky
Lexington, Kentucky

Helen G. Jenne
Alliant International University
California School of Professional
    Psychology
San Diego, California

Jenise Jensen
University of Utah
Salt Lake City, Utah

Jacqueline Jere
University of Zambia
Lusaka, Zambia

Olga Jerman
University of California, Riverside
Riverside, California

Brian D. Johnson
University of Northern Colorado
Greeley, Colorado

Judy A. Johnson
Goose Creek Consolidated
    Independent School District
Baytown, Texas

Kristine Jolivette
Georgia State University
Atlanta, Georgia

Elizabeth Jones
Texas A&M University
College Station, Texas

Gideon Jones
Florida State University
Tallahassee, Florida

Meredith Jones
Texas A&M University
College Station, Texas

Philip R. Jones
Virginia Polytechnic Institute
    and State University
Blacksburg, Virginia

Shirley A. Jones
Virginia Polytechnic Institute
    and State University
Blacksburg, Virginia

Tarcia Jones
Texas A&M University
College Station, Texas

R. Malatesha Joshi
Texas A&M University
College Station, Texas

Diana Joyce
University of Florida
Gainesville, Florida

Song Ju
Texas A&M University
College Station, Texas

David Kahn
Texas A&M University
College Station, Texas

Araksia Kaladjian
University of California, Riverside
Riverside, California

James W. Kalat
North Carolina State University
Raleigh, North Carolina

Maya Kalyanpur
Towson University
Towson, Maryland

Michele Wilson Kamens
Rider Universtiy
Lawrenceville, New Jersey

Randy W. Kamphaus
Dean, College of Education,
    Georgia State University
Atlanta, Georgia

Harrison Kane
University of Florida
Gainesville, Florida

Stan A. Karcz
University of Wisconsin at Stout
Menomonie, Wisconsin

Dilip Karnik
Children's Hospital of Austin
Austin, Texas

Austin J. Karpola
The Chicago School of Professional
    Psychology
Chicago, Illinois

Maribeth Montgomery Kasik
Governors State University
University Park, Illinois

Allison Katz
Rutgers University
New Brunswick, New Jersey

Jen Katz-Buonincontro
University of Oregon
Eugene, Oregon

Alan S. Kaufman
Yale University School of Medicine
New Haven, Connecticut

James C. Kaufman
California State University,
    San Bernardino
San Bernardino, California

Nancy J. Kaufman
University of Wisconsin at Stevens
    Point
Stevens Point, Wisconsin

Scott Barry Kaufman
Yale University
New Haven, Connecticut

Elizabeth Kaufmann
University of Texas at Austin
Austin, Texas

Kenneth A. Kavale
Regent University
Virginia Beach, Virginia

Hortencia Kayser
New Mexico State University
Las Cruces, New Mexico

Forrest E. Keesbury
Lycoming College
Williamsport, Pennsylvania

Jennifer Keith
University of Northern Colorado
Greeley, Colorado

Kristy K. Kelly
The Chicago School of Professional
    Psychology
Chicago, Illinois

Theresa Kelly
University of Northern Colorado
Greeley, Colorado

Courtney A. Kemp
The Chicago School of Professional
    Psychology
Chicago, Illinois

Barbara Keogh
University of California,
    Los Angeles
Los Angeles, California

Leanne Ketterlin-Gellar
University of Oregon
Eugene, Oregon

Kay E. Ketzenberger
The University of Texas of the
    Permian Basin
Odessa, Texas

Eve Kikas
University of Tartu
Tartu, Estonia

Paula Kilpatrick
University of North Carolina
    at Wilmington
Wilmington, North Carolina

Donald Kincaid
University of South Florida
Tampa, Florida

Peggy Kipping
PRO-ED, Incorporated
Austin, Texas

Gonul Kircaali-Iftar
Anadolu University
Eskişehir, Turkey

Bob Kirchner
University of Northern Colorado
Greeley, Colorado

Donald A. Kirson
Counseling Center, University
    of San Diego
San Diego, California

Margie K. Kitano
New Mexico State University
Las Cruces, New Mexico

Howard M. Knoff
University of South Florida
Tampa, Florida

Tim Knoster
Bloomsburg University
Bloomsburg, Pennsylvania

Brandi Kocian
Texas A&M University
College Station, Texas

Dana R. Konter
University of Wisconsin–Stout
Menomonie, Wisconsin

Peter Kopriva
Fresno Pacific University
Fresno, California

F. J. Koopmans-Van Beinum
Amsterdam, The Netherlands

Mark A. Koorland
Florida State University
Tallahassee, Florida

Peter Kopriva
Fresno Pacific University
Fresno, California

L. Koulischer
Institut de Morphologie
Pathologique Belgium

Martin Kozloff
University of North Carolina
    at Wilmington
Wilmington, North Carolina

Kathleen S. Krach
Texas A&M University
College Station, Texas

Thomas R. Kratochwill
University of Wisconsin at Madison
Madison, Wisconsin

Bob Krichner
Laramie City School District #1
Cheyenne, Wyoming

James P. Krouse
Clarion University of Pennsylvania
Clarion, Pennsylvania

Louis J. Kruger
Tufts University
Medford, Pennsylvania

Moana Kruschwitz
University of Texas at Austin
Austin, Texas

Miranda Kucera
University of Colorado at Colorado
    Springs
Colorado Springs, Colorado

Loni Kuhn
University of Utah
Salt Lake City, Utah

Alexandra S. Kutz
University of Texas at Austin
Austin, Texas

Paul G. Lacava
Rhode Island College
Providence, Rhode Island

Michael La Conte
District 11 Public Schools
Colorado Springs, Colorado

Timothy D. Lackaye
Hunter College, City University
   of New York
New York, New York

Iman Teresa Lahroud
University of Texas at Austin
Austin, Texas

Shui-fong Lam
The University of Hong Kong
Hong Kong, China

C. Sue Lamb
University of North Carolina
   at Wilmington
Wilmington, North Carolina

Gordon D. Lamb
Texas A&M University
College Station, Texas

Nadine M. Lambert
University of California, Berkeley
Berkeley, California

Russell Lang
Texas State University–San Marcos
San Marcos, Texas

Louis J. Lanunziata
University of North Carolina
   at Wilmington
Wilmington, North Carolina

Rafael Lara-Alecio
Texas A&M University
College Station, Texas

Franco Larocca
The University of Verona
Verona, Italy

Kerry S. Lassiter
The Citadel
Charleston, South Carolina

Jeff Laurent
University of Texas
Austin, Texas

Mark M. Leach
University of Southern Mississippi
Hattiesburg, Mississippi

Samuel LeBaron
University of Texas Health Science
   Center
San Antonio, Texas

Yvan Lebrun
School of Medicine
Brussels, Belgium

Jillian N. Lederhouse
Wheaton College
Sycamore, Illinois

Donghyung Lee
Texas A&M University
College Station, Texas

Linda Leeper
New Mexico State University
Las Cruces, New Mexico

Ronald S. Lenkowsky
Hunter College, City University
   of New York
New York, New York

Mary Louise Lennon
Educational Testing Service
Princeton, New Jersey

Carmen Léon
Andrés Bello Catholic University
Caracas, Venezuela

Richard Levak
California School of Professional
   Psychology
San Diego, California

J. Patrick Leverett
The Citadel
Charleston, South Carolina

Allison Lewis
University of North Carolina
   at Wilmington
Wilmington, North Carolina

Lucy Lewis
University of North Carolina
   at Wilmington
Wilmington, North Carolina

Sandra Lewis
Florida State University
Tallahassee, Florida

Tim Lewis
University of Missouri
Columbia, Missouri

Collette Leyva
Texas A&M University
College Station, Texas

Elizabeth O. Lichtenberger
The Salk Institute
La Jolla, California

Xiaobao Li
University of Houston
Houston, Texas

Ping Lin
Elmhurst College
Elmhurst, Illinois

Janet A. Lindow
University of Wisconsin at Madison
Madison, Wisconsin

Ken Linfoot
University of Western
   Sydney
Sydney, Australia

Daniel D. Lipka
Lincoln Way Special Education
   Regional Resources Center
Louisville, Ohio

Brittany Little
The Chigo School of Professional
   Psychology
Chicago, IL

Cornelia Lively
University of Illinois,
   Urbana-Champaign
Champaign, Illinois

Antolin M. Llorente
Baylor College of Medicine
Houston, Texas

Lisa A. Lockwood
Texas A&M University
College Station, Texas

Jeri Logemann
Northwestern University
Evanston, Illinois

David Lojkovic
George Mason University
Fairfax, Virginia

Charles J. Long
University of Memphis
Memphis, Tennessee

Linda R. Longley
University of North Carolina
   at Wilmington
Wilmington, North Carolina

Emilia C. Lopez
Fordham University
New York, New York

Esmerelda Lopez
Texas A&M University
College Station, Texas

Araceli Lopez-Arenas
Texas A&M University
College Station, Texas

Patricia A. Lowe
University of Kansas
Lawrence, Kansas

Michael T. Lucas
California State University,
   San Bernardino
San Bernardino, California

Emily L. Lund
Texas A&M University
College Station, Texas

Marsha H. Lupi
Hunter College, City University
   of New York
New York, New York

Ann E. Lupkowski
Texas A&M University
College Station, Texas

Teresa M. Lyle
University of Texas at Austin
Austin, Texas

Patricia S. Lynch
Texas A&M University
College Station, Texas

Loleta Lynch-Gustafson
California State University,
   San Bernardino
San Bernardino, California

Philip E. Lyon
College of St. Rose
Albany, New York

James Lyons
University of California, Riverside
Riverside, California

John W. Maag
University of Nebraska–Lincoln
Lincoln, Nebraska

Charles A. MacArthur
University of Maryland
College Park, Maryland

John MacDonald
Eastern Kentucky University
Richmond, Kentucky

Taddy Maddox
PRO-ED, Incorporated
Austin, Texas

Danielle Madera
University of Florida
Gainesville, Florida

Ghislain Magerotte
Mons State University
Mons, Belgium

Susan Mahanna-Boden
Eastern Kentucky University
Richmond, Kentucky

Charles A. Maher
Rutgers University
New Brunswick, New Jersey

Richard Mahoney
Texas State University–San Marcos
San Marcos, Texas

Kebangsaan Malaysia
Texas A&M University
College Station, Texas

Elba Maldonado-Colon
San Jose State University
San Jose, California

David C. Mann
St. Francis Hospital
Pittsburgh, Pennsylvania

Douglas L. Mann
V. A. Medical Center, Medical
   University of South Carolina
Charleston, South Carolina

Lester Mann
Hunter College, City University
   of New York
New York, New York

Denise E. Maricle
University of Wisconsin–Stout
Menomonie, Wisconsin

Donald S. Marozas
State University of New York
   at Geneseo
Geneseo, New York

Ellen B. Marriott
University of North Carolina
   at Wilmington
Wilmington, North Carolina

James E. Martin
University of Oklahoma
Norman, Oklahoma

Tamara J. Martin
The University of Texas of the
   Permian Basin
Odessa, Texas

Stephanie Martinez
University of South Florida
Tampa, Florida

Benjamin A. Mason
Texas A&M University
College Station, Texas

Patrick Mason
The Hughes Spalding International
   Adoption Evaluation Center
Atlanta, Georgia

Rose Mason
University of Kansas
Lawrence, Kansas

Margo A. Mastropieri
Purdue University
West Lafayette, Indiana

Heidi Mathie
University of Utah
Salt Lake City, Utah

Jill Mathis
Laramie School District #1
Cheyenne, Wyoming

Darin T. Matthews
The Citadel
Charleston, South Carolina

Jon Maxwell
Texas A&M University
College Station, Texas

Deborah C. May
State University of New York
   at Albany
Albany, New York

Joan W. Mayfield
Baylor Pediatric Specialty Services
Dallas, Texas

Liliana Mayo
Centro Ann Sullivan
Lima, Peru

James K. McAfee
Pennsylvania State University
University Park, Pennsylvania

Heidi A. McCallister
University of Texas at Austin
Austin, Texas

Cristina McCarthy
University of Utah
Salt Lake City, Utah

Eileen F. McCarthy
University of Wisconsin at Madison
Madison, Wisconsin

Elizabeth McClellan
Council for Exceptional Children
Reston, Virginia

Dalene M. McCloskey
University of Northern Colorado
Greeley, Colorado

George McCloskey
Philadelphia College of Osteopathic
   Medicine
Philadelphia, Pennsylvania

Laura S. McCorkle
Texas A&M University
College Station, Texas

Linda McCormick
University of Hawaii, Manoa
Honolulu, Hawaii

Ryan E. McDaniel
The Citadel
Charleston, South Carolina

Paul A. McDermott
University of Pennsylvania
Philadelphia, Pennsylvania

Breeda McGrath
The Chicago School of Professional
   Psychology
Chicago, Illinois

Kelly McGraw
The Chicago School of Professional
  Psychology
Chicago, Illinois

Kevin S. McGrew
St. Joseph, Minnesota

Stacy E. McHugh
The Children's Hospital
Denver, Colorado

Kent McIntosh
University of British Columbia
Vancouver, British Columbia,
  Canada

Phillip J. McLaughlin
University of Georgia
Athens, Georgia

James A. McLoughlin
University of Louisville
Louisville, Kentucky

James K. McMee
Pennsylvania State University
King of Prussia, Pennsylvania

Paolo Meazzini
University of Rome
Rome, Italy

Frederic J. Medway
University of South Carolina
Columbia, South Carolina

Brenda Melvin
New Hanover Regional Medical
  Center
Wilmington, North Carolina

Marissa I. Mendoza
Texas A&M University
College Station, Texas

James F. Merritt
University of North Carolina
  at Wilmington
Wilmington, North Carolina

Judith Meyers
San Diego, California

Danielle Michaux
VrijeUniversiteit Brussel
Brussels, Belgium

Jennifer Might
University of North Carolina
  at Wilmington
Wilmington, North Carolina

Stephen E. Miles
Immune Deficiency Foundation
Towson, Maryland

Susie Miles
University of Manchester
Manchester, United Kingdom

James H. Miller
University of New Orleans
New Orleans, Louisiana

Kevin Miller
University of Central Florida
Orlando, Florida

Ted L. Miller
University of Tennessee at
  Chattanooga
Chattanooga, Tennessee

Norris Minick
Center for Psychosocial Studies, The
  Spencer Foundation
Chicago, Illinois

Anjali Misra
State University of New York
Potsdam, New York

Andrew A. Mogaji
University of Lagos
Lagos, Nigeria

Lisa Monda
Florida State University
Tallahassee, Florida

Marcia L. Montague
Texas A&M University
College Station, Texas

Lourdes Montenegro
Andrés Bello Catholic University
Caracas, Venezuela

Judy K. Montgomery
Chapman University
Irvine, California

Linda Montgomery
The University of Texas of the
  Permian Basin
Odessa, Texas

Hadley Moore
University of Massachusetts
Boston, Massachusetts

Melanie Moore
University of North Carolina
  at Wilmington
Wilmington, North Carolina

Luis Benites Morales
Universidad San Martin de Porres
Lima, Peru

Susannah More
University of Texas at Austin
Austin, Texas

Marianela Moreno
Andrés Bello Catholic University
Caracas, Venzuela

Mary E. Morningstar
University of Kansas
Lawrence, Kansas

Richard J. Morris
University of Arizona
Tucson, Arizona

Amy Morrow
University of North Carolina
  at Wilmington
Wilmington, North Carolina

Lonny W. Morrow
Northeast Missouri State University
Kirksville, Missouri

Sue Ann Morrow
EDGE, Incorporated
Bradshaw, Michigan

Elias Mpofu
Pennsylvania State University
Harrisburg, Pennsylvania

Tracy A. Muenz
Alliant International University
San Diego, California

Mary Murray
Journal of Special Education
Ben Salem, Pennsylvania

Gladiola Musabelliu
University of Tirana
Tirana, Albania

Magen M. Mutepfa
Zimbabwe Schools Special Services
  and Special Education
  Department
Zimbabwe

Jack Naglieri
The Ohio State University
Columbus, Ohio

Sigamoney Naicker
Western Cape Educational SI
  Department
South Africa

Michael Nall
Louisville, Kentucky

Nicole Nasewicz
University of Florida
Gainesville, Florida

Robert T. Nash
University of Wisconsin at Oshkosh
Oshkosh, Wisconsin

Bonnie K. Nastasi
Kent State University
Kent, Ohio

Diana L. Nebel
University of Northern Colorado
Greeley, Colorado

Cameron L. Neece
University of California,
  Los Angeles
Los Angeles, California

Leslie C. Neely
Texas A&M University
College Station, Texas

Thomas Neises
California State University,
   San Bernardino
San Bernardino, California

Brett R. Nelson
University of Northern Colorado
Greeley, Colorado

Michael Nelson
University of Kentucky Louisville
Louisville, Kentucky

Joyce E. Ness
Montgomery County Intermediate
   Unit
Norristown, Pennsylvania

Ulrika Nettelbladt
University of Lund
Lund, Sweden

Lori Newcomer
University of Missouri
Columbia, Missouri

Lynn Newman
SRI International
Menlo Park, California

Jennifer Nicholls
Dysart Unified School District
El Mirage, Arizona

Robert C. Nichols
State University of New York
   at Buffalo
Buffalo, New York

Sandra Nite
Texas A&M University
College Station, Texas

Matthew K. Nock
Yale University
New Haven, Connecticut

Nancy L. Nassbaum
Austin Neurological Clinic
Austin, Texas

Etta Lee Nurick
Montgomery County Intermediate
   Unit
Norristown, Pennsylvania

Christopher Oakland
New York, New York

Thomas Oakland
University of Florida
Gainesville, Florida

Festus E. Obiakor
Emporia State University
Nigeria

Hector Salvia Ochoa
Texas A&M University
College Station, Texas

Jessica Oddi
The Chicago School of Professional
   Psychology
Chicago, Illinois

Louise O'Donnell
University of Texas Health Science
Center
San Antonio, Texas
and University of Texas at Austin
Austin, Texas

Joy O'Grady
University of Memphis
Memphis, Tennessee

Masataka Ohta
Tokyo Gakujei University
Tokyo, Japan

Ed O'Leary
Utah State University
Logan, Utah

Daniel Olympia
University of Utah
Salt Lake City, Utah

John O'Neill
Hunter College, City University
   of New York
New York, New York

Robert O'Neill
University of Utah
Salt Lake City, Utah

Ause Tugba Oner
Texas A&M University
College Station, Texas

Caitlin Onks
Bryan ISD
Bryan, Texas

Alba Ortiz
University of Texas
Austin, Texas

Samuel O. Ortiz
St. John's University
Jamaica, New York

Andrew Oseroff
Florida State University
Tallahassee, Florida

Lawrence J. O'Shea
University of Florida
Gainesville, Florida

Marika Padrik
University of Tartu
Tartu, Estonia

Doris Paez
New Mexico State University
Las Cruces, New Mexico

Ellis B. Page
Duke University
Durham, North Carolina

Kathleen D. Paget
University of South Carolina
Columbia, South Carolina

Douglas J. Palmer
Texas A&M University
College Station, Texas

Hagop S. Pambookian
Elizabeth City, North Carolina

Ernest L. Pancsofar
University of Connecticut
Storrs, Connecticut

Sara Pankaskie
Florida State University
Tallahassee, Florida

Maryann Toni Parrino
Montclair University
Upper Montclair, New Jersey

Linda H. Parrish
Texas A&M University
College Station, Texas

Daniel R. Paulson
University of Wisconsin at Stout
Menomonie, Wisconsin

Nils A. Pearson
PRO-ED, Incorporated
Austin, Texas

Mary Leon Peery
Texas A&M University
College Station, Texas

Kathleen Pelham-Odor
California State University,
   San Bernardino
San Bernardino, California

Shelley L. F. Pelletier
Dysart Unified School District
El Mirage, Arizona

Michelle Perfect
University of Texas at Austin
Austin, Texas

Olivier Périer
Université Libre de Bruxelles Centre
   Comprendreet Parler
Brussels, Belgium

Paula Perrill
University of Northern Colorado
Greeley, Colorado

Joseph D. Perry
Kent State University
Kent, Ohio

Richard G. Peters
Ball State University
Muncie, Indiana

Brooke Pfeiffer
Texas State University–San Marcos
San Marcos, Texas

Faith L. Phillips
University of Oklahoma Health
    Sciences Center
Norman, Oklahoma

Jeffry L. Phillips
University of North Carolina
    at Wilmington
Wilmington, North Carolina

Kathleen M. Phillips
University of California, Riverside
Riverside, California

Lindsey A. Phillips
University of Utah
Salt Lake City, Utah

Yongxin Piao
Beijing Normal University
Beijing, China

Diana Piccolo
Missouri State University
Springfield, Missouri

Sip Jan Pijl
Gion University of Groningen
Groningen, The Netherlands

John J. Pikulski
University of Delaware
Newark, Delaware

Casey Pilgrim
The Chicago School of Professional
    Psychology
Chicago, Illinois

Diana E. Pineda
The Chicago School of Professional
    Psychology
Chicago, Illinois

Sally E. Pisarchick
Cuyahoga Special Education Service
    Center
Maple Heights, Ohio

Anthony J. Plotner
University of South Carolina
Columbia, South Carolina

Cynthia A. Plotts
Southwest Texas State University
San Marcos, Texas

Janiece Pompa
University of Utah
Salt Lake City, Utah

Brenda M. Pope
New Hanover Memorial Hospital
Wilmington, North Carolina

John E. Porcella
Rhinebeck County School
Rhinebeck, New York

James A. Poteet
Ball State University
Muncie, Indiana

Michelle W. Potter
University of California, Riverside
Riverside, California

Shawn Powell
United States Air Force Academy
Colorado Springs, Colorado

Kristiana Powers
California State University,
    San Bernardino
San Bernardino, California

David P. Prasse
University of Wisconsin
Milwaukee, Wisconsin

Jennifer Dawn Pretorius
Vaal University of Technology
South Africa

Marianne Price
Montgomery County Intermediate
    Unit
Norristown, Pennsylvania

Elisabeth A. Prinz
Pennsylvania State University
University Park, Pennsylvania

Philip M. Prinz
Pennsylvania State University
University Park, Pennsylvania

Antonio E. Puente
University of North Carolina
    at Wilmington
Wilmington, North Carolina

Krista L. Puente
University of North Carolina
    at Wilmington
Wilmington, North Carolina

Nuri Puig
University of Oklahoma
Norman, Oklahoma

Adam C. Pullaro
California State University,
    San Bernardino
San Bernardino, CA

Elizabeth P. Pungello
University of North Carolina
    at Chapel Hill
Chapel Hill, North Carolina

Robert F. Putnam
May Institute
Randolph, Massachusetts

Shahid Waheed Qamar
Lahore, Pakistan

Cathy Huaqing Qi
University of New Mexico
Albuquerque, New Mexico

Jennifer M. Raad
University of Kansas
Lawrence, Kansas

Linda Radbill
University of Florida
Gainesville, Florida

Shannon Radcliff-Lee
University of North Carolina
    at Wilmington
Wilmington, North Carolina

William A. Rae
Texas A&M University
College Station, Texas

Paige B. Raetz
Western Michigan University
Kalamazoo, Michigan

Katrina Raia
University of Florida
Gainesville, Florida

Craig T. Ramey
University of North Carolina
    at Chapel Hill
Chapel Hill, North Carolina

Sylvia Z. Ramirez
University of Texas
Austin, Texas

Christine D. Ramos
University of Northern Colorado
Greeley, Colorado

Noe Ramos
Texas A&M University
College Station, Texas

Arlene I. Rattan
Ball State University
Muncie, Indiana

Gurmal Rattan
Indiana University of Pennsylvania
Indiana, Pennsylvania

Nancy Razo
Texas A&M University
College Station, Texas

Anne Reber
Texas A&M University
College Station, Texas

April Regester
University of Missouri
Saint Louis, Missouri

Robert R. Reilley
Texas A&M University
College Station, Texas

Fredricka K. Reisman
Drexel University
Philadelphia, Pennsylvania

Kimberly M. Rennie
Texas A&M University
College Station, Texas

Daniel J. Reschly
Peabody College, Vanderbilt
University
Nashville, Tennessee

Cecil R. Reynolds
Texas A&M University
and Bastrop Mental Health
Associates
College Station, Texas

Robert L. Rhodes
New Mexico State University
Las Cruces, New Mexico

William S. Rholes
Texas A&M University
College Station, Texas

Cynthia A. Riccio
Texas A&M University
College Station, Texas

James R. Ricciuti
United States Office of Management
and Budget
Washington, DC

Teresa K. Rice
Texas A&M University
College Station, Texas

Laura Richards
University of Utah
Salt Lake City, Utah

Paul C. Richardson
Elwyn Institutes
Elwyn, Pennsylvania

Sylvia O. Richardson
University of South Florida
Tampa, Florida

Pamela M. Richman
University of North Carolina
at Wilmington
Wilmington, North Carolina

Bert O. Richmond
University of Georgia
Athens, Georgia

Richard Rider
University of Utah
Salt Lake City, Utah

Michelle Ries
University of Memphis
Memphis, Tennessee

Catherine Hall Rikhye
Hunter College, City University
of New York
New York, New York

T. Chris Riley-Tillman
University of Missouri
Columbia, Missouri

Judy Ripsch
The Chicago School of Professional
Psychology
Chicago, Illinois

Mandi Rispoli
Texas A&M University
College Station, Texas

Selina Rivera-Longoria
Texas A&M University
College Station, Texas

Eric Roberts
Texas A&M University
College Station, Texas

Gary J. Robertson
American Guidance Service Circle
Pines, Minnesota

Kathleen Rodden-Nord
University of Oregon
Eugene, Oregon

Kimberly M. Rodriguez
Texas A&M University
College Station, Texas

Olga L. Rodriguez-Escobar
Texas A&M University
College Station, Texas

Anita M. Roginski
The Chicago School of Professional
Psychology
Chicago, IL

Matthew Roith
University of Colorado
Colorado Springs, Colorado

Dahl A. Rollins
Texas A&M University
College Station, Texas

Cassandra Burns Romine
Texas A&M University
College Station, Texas

Jean A. Rondal
University of Liege
Liege, Belgium

Sheldon Rosenberg
University of Illinois
Chicago, Illinois

Leslie D. Rosenstein
Neuropsychology Clinic, PC
Austin, Texas

Bruce P. Rosenthal
State University of New York
New York, New York

Eve N. Rosenthal
Texas A&M University
College Station, Texas

Rosalinda Rosli
Texas A&M University
College Station, Texas

Michelle Ross
The Chicago School of Professional
Psychology
Chicago, IL

Eric Rossen
University of Florida
Gainesville, Florida

Beth Rous
University of Kentucky Human
Development Institute Lexington,
Kentucky

Amy Loomis Roux
University of Florida
Gainesville, Florida

Kathy L. Ruhl
Pennsylvania State University
University Park, Pennsylvania

Elsa Cantu Ruiz
University of Texas at San Antonio
San Antonio, Texas

Joseph M. Russo
Hunter College, City University
of New York
New York, New York

Robert B. Rutherford, Jr.
Arizona State University
Tempe, Arizona

Kim Ryan-Arredondo
Texas A&M University
College Station, Texas

Daniel J. Rybicki
ForenPsych Services
Agoura Hills, California

Anne Sabatino
Hudson, Wisconsin

David A. Sabatino
West Virginia College of Graduate
Studies
Morgantown, West Virginia

Susan Sage
Dysart Unified School District
El Mirage, Arizona

Monir Saleh
Beheshti University
Tehran, Iran

Lisa J. Sampson
Eastern Kentucky University
Richmond, Kentucky

Alfred Sander
Universitat des Saarlandes
Saarbruecken, Germany

Tiffany D. Sanders
University of Florida
Gainesville, Florida

Polly E. Sanderson
Research Triangle Institute
Research Triangle Park, North
    Carolina

Therese Sandomierski
University of Florida
Tampa, Florida

Derek D. Satre
University of California
San Francisco, California

Scott W. Sautter
Peabody College, Vanderbilt
    University
Nashville, Tennessee

Robert F. Sawicki
Lake Erie Institute of
    Rehabilitation
Lake Erie, Pennsylvania

Nancy K. Scammacca
University of Texas at Austin
Austin, Texas

Walter R. Schamber
University of Northern Colorado
Greeley, Colorado

Patrick J. Schloss
Pennsylvania State University
University Park, Pennsylvania

Ronald V. Schmelzer
Eastern Kentucky University
Richmond, Kentucky

Carol Schmitt
San Diego Unified School District
San Diego, California

Carol S. Schmitt
Eastern Kentucky University
Richmond, Kentucky

Sue A. Schmitt
University of Wisconsin at Stout
Menomonie, Wisconsin

Sarah Schnoebelan
University of Texas at Austin
Austin, Texas

Lyle F. Schoenfeldt
Texas A&M University
College Station, Texas

Jacqueline S. Schon
University of Kansas
Lawrence, Kansas

Eric Schopler
University of North Carolina
    at Chapel Hill
Chapel Hill, North Carolina

Fredrick A. Schrank
Olympia, Washington

Louis Schwartz
Florida State University
Tallahassee, Florida

Adam J. Schwebach
University of Utah
Salt Lake City, Utah

Krista Schwenk
University of Florida
Gainesville, Florida

June Scobee
University of Houston,
    Clear Lake
Houston, Texas

Terrance Scott
University of Louisville
Louisville, Kentucky

Thomas E. Scruggs
Purdue University
West Lafayette, Indiana

Denise M. Sedlak
United Way of Dunn County
Menomonie, Wisconsin

Robert A. Sedlak
University of Wisconsin at Stout
Menomome, Wisconsin

Katherine D. Seelman
University of Pittsburgh
Pittsburgh, Pennsylvania

John D. See
University of Wisconsin at Stout
Menomonie, Wisconsin

Margaret Semrud-Clikeman
University of Texas at Austin
Austin, Texas

Amy Sessoms
University of North Carolina
    at Wilmington
Wilmington, North Carolina

Sandra B. Sexson
Emory University School of Medicine
Atlanta, Georgia

Susan Shandelmier
Eastern Pennsylvania Special
    Education Regional Resources
    Center
King of Prussia, Pennsylvania

Alison Shaner
University of North Carolina
    at Wilmington
Wilmington, North Carolina

Deborah A. Shanley
Medgar Evers College, City
    University of New York
New York, New York

William J. Shaw
University of Oklahoma
Norman, Oklahoma

Patricia Scherer
International Center on Deafness
    and the Arts
Northbrook, Illinois

Kaci Deauquier Sheridan
Texas A&M University
College Station, Texas

Susan M. Sheridan
University of Wisconsin at Madison
Madison, Wisconsin

Vedia Sherman
Austin Neurological Clinic
Austin, Texas

Naoji Shimizu
Tokyo Gakujei University
Tokyo, Japan

Agnes E. Shine
Barry University
Miami Shores, Florida

Erin K. Shinners
The Chicago School of Professional
    Psychology
Chicago, Illinois

Ludmila Shipitsina
Institute of Special Education and
    Psychology
Saint Petersburg, Russia

Edward A. Shirkey
New Mexico State University
Las Cruces, New Mexico

Gerald L. Shook
Behavior Analyst Certification Board
Tallahassee, Florida

Dakum Shown
University of Jos
Jos, Nigeria

Almon Shumba
University of KwaZulu-Natal
South Africa

Lawrence J. Siegel
University of Texas Medical Branch
Galveston, Texas

Jeff Sigafoos
University of Wellington at Victoria
Wellington, New Zealand

Rosanne K. Silberman
Hunter College, City University
of New York
New York, New York

Brandi Simonsen
University of Connecticut
Storrs, Connecticut

Lissen Simonsen
University of North Carolina
at Wilmington
Wilmington, North Carolina

Richard L. Simpson
University of Kansas
Lawrence, Kansas

Paul T. Sindelar
Florida State University
Tallahassee, Florida

Jessica L. Singleton
University of Northern Colorado
Greeley, Colorado

Jaime Slappey
University of North Carolina
at Wilmington
Wilmington, North Carolina

Jerry L. Sloan
Wilmington Psychiatric Associates
Wilmington, North Carolina

Jamie Slowinski
The Chicago School of Professional
Psychology
Chicago, Illinois

Julie E. Smart
Utah State University
Logan, Utah

April M. Smith
Yale University
New Haven, Connecticut

Craig D. Smith
Georgia College
Milledgeville, Georgia

E. S. Smith
University of Dundee
Dundee, Scotland

Maureen A. Smith
Pennsylvania State University
University Park, Pennsylvania

Stacey L. Smith
Texas A&M University
College Station, Texas

Judy Smith-Davis
Counterpoint Communications
Company
Reno, Nevada

Mary Helen Snyder
Devereux Cleo Wallace
Colorado Springs, Colorado

Latha V. Soorya
Binghamton University
The Institute for Child Development
Binghamton, New York

Cesar Merino Soto
University Privada San Juan
Bautista
Lima, Peru

Jane Sparks
University of North Carolina
at Wilmington
Wilmington, North Carolina

Jessica Spata
The Chicago School of Professional
Psychology
Chicago, Illinois

Barbara S. Speer
Shaker Heights City School
District
Shaker Heights, Ohio

Donna Spiker
SRI International
Menlo Park, California

Vicky Y. Spradling
Austin State Hospital
Austin, Texas

Harrison C. Stanton
Las Vegas, Nevada

Shari A. Stanton
Las Vegas, Nevada

Tilly R. Steele
National Center for Leadership in
Visual Impairment
Elkins Park, Pennsylvania

J. Todd Stephens
University of Wisconsin at Madison
Madison, Wisconsin

Bernie Stein
Tel Aviv, Israel

David R. Steinman
Austin Neurological Clinic and
Department of Psychology
University of Texas at Austin
Austin, Texas

Cecelia Steppe-Jones
North Carolina Central University
Durham, North Carolina

Linda J. Stevens
University of Minnesota
Minneapolis, Minnesota

Rachael J. Stevenson
Bedford, Ohio

Mary E. Stinson
University of Alabama
Tuscaloosa, Alabama

Roberta C. Stokes
Texas A&M University
College Station, Texas

Doretha McKnight Stone
University of North Carolina
at Wilmington
Wilmington, North Carolina

Eric A. Storch
University of Florida
Gainesville, Florida

Laura M. Stough
Texas A&M University
College Station, Texas

Michael L. Stowe
Texas A&M University
College Station, Texas

Edythe A. Strand
University of Wisconsin at Madison
Madison, Wisconsin

Elaine Stringer
University of North Carolina
at Wilmington
Wilmington, North Carolina

Dorothy A. Strom
Ball State University Indiana
School of Medicine
Muncie, Indiana

Sheela Stuart
Georgia Washington University
Washington, DC

Sue Stubbs
Save the Children Fund
London, United Kingdom

George Sugai
University of Connecticut
Storrs, Connecticut

Jeremy R. Sullivan
Texas A&M University
College Station, Texas

Kathryn A. Sullivan
Branson School Online
Branson, Colorado

Shelley Suntup
California School of Professional
Psychology
San Diego, California

Emily G. Sutter
University of Houston, Clear Lake
Houston, Texas

Lana Svien-Senne
University of South Dakota
Vermillion, South Dakota

Tricia Swan
University of Colorado
Colorado Springs, Colorado

H. Lee Swanson
University of California, Riverside
Riverside, California

Beth Sweeden
University of Wisconsin
Madison, Wisconsin

David Sweeney
Texas A&M University
College Station, Texas

Mark E. Swerdlik
Illinois State University
Normal, Illinois

Thomas G. Szabo
Western Michigan University
Kalamazoo, Michigan

Henri B. Szliwowski
HôpitalErasme, UniversitéLibre de
    Bruxelles
Brussels, Belgium

Pearl E. Tait
Florida State University
Tallahassee, Florida

Paula Tallal
University of California, San Diego
San Diego, California

Mary K. Tallent
Texas Tech University
Lubbock, Texas

Melody Tankersly
Kent State University
Kent, Ohio

C. Mildred Tashman
College of St. Rose
Albany, New York

James W. Tawney
Pennsylvania State University
University Park, Pennsylvania

Joseph R. Taylor
Fresno Pacific University
Fresno, California

Leslie Taylor
University of South Carolina
Columbia, South Carolina

Therese Tchombe
University of Yaounde
Cameroon

Ellen A. Teelucksingh
University of Minnesota
Minneapolis, Minnesota

Tirussew Teferra
Addis Ababa University
Addis Ababa, Ethiopia

Cathy F. Telzrow
Kent State University
Kent, Ohio

Yolanda Tenorio
California State University,
    San Bernardino
San Bernardino, California

David W. Test
University of North Carolina
    at Charlotte
Charlotte, North Carolina

Coleen Thoma
Virginia Commonwealth University
Richmond, Virginia

Carol Chase Thomas
University of North Carolina
    at Wilmington
Wilmington, North Carolina

Jo Thomason
Council of Administrators of Special
    Education
Fort Valley, Georgia

Bruce Thompson
Texas A&M University
College Station, Texas

Spencer Thompson
The University of Texas of the
    Permian Basin
Odessa, Texas

Sage Thornton
University of California, Riverside
Riverside, California

Eva Tideman
Lund University
Lund, Sweden

Steven R. Timmermans
Mary Free Bed Hospital and
    Rehabilitation Center
Grand Rapids, Michigan

Gerald Tindal
University of Oregon
Eugene, Oregon

Renze M. Tobin
Texas A&M University
College Station, Texas

Anne W. Todd
University of Oregon
Eugene, Oregon

Francine Tomkins
University of Cincinnati
Cincinnati, Ohio

Carol Tomlinson-Keasey
University of California, Riverside
Riverside, California

Rachel M. Toplis
Falcon School District 49
Colorado Springs, Colorado

Keith. J. Topping
University of Dundee
Dundee, Scotland

Raymond Toraille
Public Education
Paris, France

Jose Luis Torres
Texas A&M University
College Station, Texas

Audrey A. Trainor
University of Wisconsin–Madison
Madison, Wisconsin

Stanley O. Trent
University of Virginia
Charlottesville, Virginia

David M. Tucker
Austin Neurological Clinic
and University of Texas at Austin
Austin, Texas

Timothy L. Turco
Louisiana State University
Baton Rouge, Louisiana

Mary Turri
University of British Columbia
Vancouver, British Columbia,
    Canada

Lori E. Unruh
Eastern Kentucky University
Richmond, Kentucky

Susan M. Unruh
University of Kansas
Wichita, Kansas

Marilyn Urquhart
University of South Dakota
Vermillion, South Dakota

Cynthia Vail
Florida State University
Tallahassee, Florida

Greg Valcante
University of Florida
Gainesville, Florida

Hubert B. Vance
East Tennessee State University
Johnson City, Tennessee

Aryan Van Der Leij
Free University
Amsterdam, The Netherlands

Heather S. Vandyke
Falcon School District 49
Colorado Springs, Colorado

Christina E. Van Kraayenoord
The University of Queensland
Brisbane, Australia

K. Sandra Vanta
Cleveland Public Schools
Cleveland, Ohio

Juana Vaquero
Texas A&M University
College Station, Texas

Rebecca Vaurio
Austin Neurological Clinic
and University of Texas
   at Austin
Austin, Texas

Kathleen Veizel
Farliegh Dickinson University
Teaneck, New Jersey

Donna Verner
Texas A&M University
College Station, Texas

Don Viglione
California School of Professional
   Psychology
San Diego, California

Judith K. Voress
PRO-ED, Incorporated
Austin, Texas

Mary Wagner
SRI International
Menlo Park, California

Emily Wahlen
Hunter College, City University
   of New York
New York, New York

Christy M. Walcott
East Carolina University
Greenville, North Carolina

Deborah Klein Walker
Harvard University
Cambridge, Massachusetts

Donna Wallace
The University of Texas of the
   Permian Basin
Odessa, Texas

Raoul Wallenberg
International University for Family
   and Child
Saint Petersburg, Russia

James E. Walsh
The Chicago School of Professional
   Psychology
Chicago, Illinois

Marjorie E. Ward
The Ohio State University
Columbus, Ohio

Nicole R. Warnygora
University of Northern
   Colorado
Greeley, Colorado

Sue Allen Warren
Boston University
Boston, Massachusetts

John Wasserman
The Riverside Publishing
   Company
Itasca, Illinois

Sharine Webber
Laramie County School
   District #1
Cheyenne, Wyoming

Lauren M. Webster
Wake Forest University
Winston-Salem, North Carolina

Danny Wedding
Marshall University
Huntington, Virginia

Paul Wehman
Virginia Commonwealth
   University
Richmond, Virginia

Michael Wehmeyer
University of Kansas
Lawrence, Kansas

Frederick F. Weiner
Pennsylvania State University
University Park, Pennsylvania

Marjorie Weintraub
Montgomery County Intermediate
   Unit
Norristown, Pennsylvania

Bahr Weiss
University of North Carolina
   at Chapel Hill
Chapel Hill, North Carolina

Mark Weist
University of South Carolina
Columbia, South Carolina

Shirley Parker Wells
University of North Carolina
   at Wilmington
Wilmington, North Carolina

Louise H. Werth
Florida State University
Tallahassee, Florida

Catherine Wetzburger
Hôpital Erasme, Université Libre de
   Bruxelles
Brussels, Belgium

Jessi K. Wheatley
Falcon School District 49
Colorado Springs, Colorado

Larry J. Wheeler
Southwest Texas State University
San Marcos, Texas

Annika White
University of California, Riverside
Riverside, California

Michelle White
University of Florida
Tampa, Florida

Jessica Whitely
University of Ottawa
Ottawa, Ontario, Canada

Susie Whitman
Immune Deficiency Foundation
Odessa, Texas

Thomas M. Whitten
Florida State University
Tallahassee, Florida

J. Lee Wiederholt
PRO-ED, Incorporated
Austin, Texas

Lisa Wildmo
Bryan, Texas

Saul B. Wilen
Medical Horizons Unlimited
San Antonio, Texas

Karen Wiley
Universtiy of Northern Colorado
Colorado Springs, Colorado

Greta N. Wilkening
University of Colorado Health
   Sciences Center
Children's Hospital
Denver, Colorado

C. Williams
Falcon School District 49
Colorado Springs, Colorado

L. Williams
Falcon School District 49
Colorado Springs, Colorado

Lauren E. Williams
Texas A&M University
College Station, Texas

Mary Clare Williams
Ramey, Pennsylvania

Meredith Williamson
Texas A&M University
College Station, Texas

Diane J. Willis
University of Oklahoma Health
    Sciences Center
Oklahoma City, Oklahoma

John O. Willis
Rivier College
Nashua, New Hampshire

Melissa T. Willison
The Chicago School of Professional
    Psychology
Chicago, IL

Victor L. Willson
Texas A&M University
College Station, Texas

John D. Wilson
Elwyn Institutes
Elwyn, Pennsylvania

Kimberly D. Wilson
University of Texas
    at Austin
Austin, Texas

Margo E. Wilson
Lexington, Kentucky

Carol Windmill
University of Ottawa
Ottawa, Ontario, Canada

Kelly Winkels
University of Florida
Gainesville, Florida

Anna Winneker
University of South Florida
Tampa, Forida

Britt L. Winter
Western Michigan
    University
Kalamazoo, Michigan

Joseph C. Witt
Louisiana State University
Baton Rouge, Louisiana

Monica E. Wolfe
Texas A&M University
College Station, Texas

Bencie Woll
University of Bristol
Bristol, United Kingdom

Bernice Y. L. Wong
Simon Fraser University
Buraby, British Columbia

Mary M. Wood
University of Georgia
Athens, Georgia

Diane E. Woods
World Rehabilitation Fund
New York, New York

Lee L. Woods
University of Oklahoma
Norman, Oklahoma

Frances F. Worchel
Texas A&M University
College Station, Texas

Patricia Work
University of South Dakota
Vermillion, South Dakota

Eleanor Boyd Wright
University of North Carolina
    at Wilmington
Wilmington, North Carolina

Logan Wright
University of Oklahoma
Norman, Oklahoma

Karen F. Wyche
Hunter College, City University
    of New York
New York, New York

Martha Ellen Wynne
Loyola University, Chicago
Chicago, Illinois

Susan Yarbrough
Florida State University
Tallahassee, Florida

Mitchell Yell
University of South Carolina
Columbia, South Carolina

James E. Yeseldyke
University of Minnesota
Minneapolis, Minnesota

Pui-sze Yeung
The University of Hong Kong
Hong Kong, China

Roland K. Yoshida
Fordham University
New York, New York

Mantak Yuen
The University of Hong Kong
Hong Kong, China

Thomas Zane
Johns Hopkins University
Baltimore, Maryland

Ronald Zellner
Texas A&M University
College Station, Texas

Lonnie K. Zeltzer
University of Texas Health Sciences
    Center
San Antonio, Texas

Paul M. Zeltzer
University of Texas Health Sciences
    Center
San Antonio, Texas

Dulan Zhang
Texas A&M University
College Station, Texas

Xinhua Zheng
University of California, Riverside
Riverside, California

Jamie Zibulsky
Farliegh Dickinson University
Teaneck, New Jersey

Walter A. Zilz
Bloomsburg University
Bloomsburg, Pennsylvania

Elizabeth M. Zorn
The Chicago School of Professional
    Psychology
Chicago, Illinois

Kenneth A. Zych
Walter Reed Army Medical Center
Washington, DC

PREFACE TO THE FOURTH EDITION

Work on the first Encyclopedia of Special Education originated in 1982 and the first edition was published in 1987. In this 4th edition we welcome Editor Dr. Kimberly Vannest to the project team. Since the first edition of nearly 2,000 pages, this current version includes nearly 3,000. This encyclopedia both historically captures the terms, individuals, laws, and societal movements of more than 4 decades of Special Education, it also chronicles the evolution of special education.

We remain well aware of how life, research, and standards have changed for those of us who practice in special education. It is an interesting process to look back and see how the *Encyclopedia* has changed over the years and how it has really provided a mirror of the zeitgeist of the times in which we live and practice.

The first edition was full of new ideas such as profile analysis, direct instruction, and terms such as "trainable" and "educable." The field had license to imagine and try ways to rewire the brain that was having trouble in school. This fourth edition clearly marks the federal and state demands for evidence-based practices in classrooms and methodologically rigorous research, perhaps reflecting the end of imagination and the beginning of an era of proof or accountability. Hence, we see behavioral terms and behavioral-oriented credentials enjoying resurgence because they allow for documentation of behaviors that are easy to observe. Accountability is a force to be noticed as it infiltrates and guides current practice even accountability has evolved from a focus on student activities or opportunities, to student outcomes and performance and now teacher evaluation. It will be fascinating to see where we are in another decade.

The first edition was full of new and somewhat untested laws: We were still trying to interpret Public Law 94-142! Since then, we are in the reauthorization of what has evolved into IDEIA (Individuals with disabilities education Act) as Special Education Law has involved eight presidents over time. And conceptualization of disability for accessing services is under new scrutiny for learning disabilities and expanded definitions for autism to reflect the meteoric rise in prevelance. The advocacy and self-advocacy network that surrounds and includes special education students today is vast, connected, and accessible. The Internet has exponentially changed the individual's abilities to learn about support organizations and to reach out to others who have similar concerns and conditions. This movement is not just on a national level, the World Health Organization is rallying the international community to connect the daily living experiences of individuals with disabilities in the *International Classification of Functioning, Disability, and Health*. This classification system was designed to describe the *individual* with a disability, not just to classify the disability itself. Indeed, we remember that in the first edition of the *Encyclopedia*, it was acceptable to label individuals via the disability; therefore, individuals with Schizophrenia were schizophrenics and individuals with Mental Retardation were the mentally retarded. The disability came first and the individual came second. In the second edition of the *Encyclopedia*, we remember stressing heavily with all of our editors and authors that all language referring to clinical populations would have to reflect the individual first and his or her handicapping condition second. This was a major literary turn at the time! The third edition may best be characterized as disability and ability now living side by side as the 3rd edition marked a time beyond mainstreaming, beyond inclusion but of expectation for a respect of difference, and expectation for accommodation and natural adaptation of the environment or curriculum to meet the needs of people, not of the disabled. Humanness is central and our similarities outweigh our differences, even in special education.

The four editions of the *Encyclopedia* have also reflected the evolution of test construction and interpretation. The level of psychometric design is higher than ever before, providing many benefits to the population such as increased specificity in assessing executive functions, trauma, study skills, and so on. The major broadband assessment batteries that measure cognitive abilities and psychological constructs are excellent, theory-based measures that have imaginative and careful design. Therefore, our ability to include well-designed tools in the assessment process has never been better. The fourth edition of the *Encyclopedia* catalogues many new tests and revisions of old and true instruments.

The demand for "countable" accountability of special education outcomes is upon these days. For the past 20 years, the *Encyclopedia* reflected exploration, and now exploration is passé and counting and demanding results is the zeitgeist of the times. Renegades as we are, we have included more and more neuropsychological principles and terms into the various editions of the *Encyclopedia* as we have paid homage to the vast mystery of the human brain and personality that will most likely never be reduced down to accountable facts. Herein lies the rub for those with interests in brain-behavior relationships, the very thing that we seek is unattainable and therein provides continuous wonder, curiosity, and frustration! We are confident that the most important aspect of future research that seeks to improve the daily lives of children with disabilities lies in the study of the brain and its relationship to learning and daily living skills. This process will always be a study of one, and not given to group statistics. Therefore, regardless of the political zeitgeist, we have expressed our desire to support clinical excellence throughout the third edition of the *Encyclopedia* and minimize old ideas that have been parceled out as new and redesigned to fit ends that are not apolitical. The original *Encyclopedia* was bursting with curiosity and wonder about a new field. We wish to maintain this tribute in the current edition and support the continued innocence of true scientific exploration.

New to the ESE-IV were entries on Positive Behavior Supports. We would like to give many thanks to Heather Peshak George, University of South Florida, as a Contributing Editor and her amazing contribution and coverage of this topic. Areas such as autism were brought up-to-date to reflect the most recent knowledge by Jeni Ganz at Texas A&M University as a Contributing Editor and entries reflecting changes in transition services were updated by Dulan Zhang at Texas A&M University. Last but not least, the Drs. Ron Dumont and John Willis again provided a completely new thread of reviews of standardized assessments throughout the *Encyclopedia*. Joining their expertise in assessment reviews were Drs. Kathleen Viezel and Jamie Zibulsky. We once again are pleased to have them as part of our effort in updating over 100 assessment entries. Without the work of many contributing editors and authors, the Encyclopedia would not have been possible.

Please allow us to apologize to our authors if their affiliations or names have changed over the past 20 years and the most recent changes are not incorporated into the fourth edition. We have tried to keep up with the changes but are sure that we have missed a few and promise to remediate in future editions! We also had to make editorial decisions about giving credit where credit was due for updates of entries. Therefore, the reader will notice that we have taken painstaking efforts to list the authors and to which editions they contributed. Minor edits to update references, change archaic terminology, add web pages or update addresses were completed throughout the volumes. We kept a historical "chronicling of the field" approach in our edits so entries for some entities, journals, educational methods, assessments or instructional strategies were maintained in the Encyclopedia, albeit updated by "this term is no longer in use" or "this organization closed in . . . " these types of edits are not attributed to the editors In every instance but we take responsibility for any updates beyond the original contribution of the authors.

There are, as usual, many individuals to thank for assisting with the creating and preparation of this volume of work. First, let us thank the contributing editors to the previous and current editions. These individuals took on the responsibilities of looking at where the field has been and where it is going in their respective areas of expertise. They then shepherded many authors into taking on smaller parts to reflect important aspects of the basics and documenting growth. Without their commitment and dedication, we would be bereft of hope for a renovation of this size of work! We would also like to thank the individual authors for their cheerful attitude and dedication to their contributions: They are representatives of the best the field has to offer and we are very grateful for their efforts.

On a personal note - this edition comes at a time of unique personal challenges for each of us. The types of challenges where an individual may question their role in the greater societal fabric or reorder the time spent on things of value. As the newest member of the Editorial team, KV would like to express her belief that this work is not just work, it is a living contribution and documentation of the countless and untold hours of teachers, parents, students, legislators to improve the educational experiences and outcomes of students with disabilities. For every biography there are thousands who dedicate their lives in service. This encyclopedia represents so much more than the sum of the entries, it represents a commitment of people and our culture to improve the lives of others In a way that makes us unique as living organisms on this planet. This work was and is of great value and I'm privileged to be a part of the project.

Cecil would like to thank Julia, as he does so untiringly, for her support in so many ways, and his long-deceased Dad, who gave him the gift of a model of service. Elaine would like to thank Cecil for the opportunity that he gave her many years ago to be a part of this historical project: Words cannot reflect the depth of appreciation. Elaine would also like to thank Kimberly for taking up the baton and continuing the Encyclopedia of Special Education standard of excellence—it is in the best of hands! Kimberly would like to express deep appreciation for the work of her colleagues Cecil and Elaine, and express enduring thankfulness for her father Frank Vannest, who painstakingly checked references and web links for the 3,000-page manuscript. Thanks also to staff and students Heather Davis, Heather Hatton, Amanda Chow, and Erica Strickland for your excellent work. Finally, a personal thank you to Jack—your cheerful patience shooting baskets while I edited from the bleachers, your piano concerts in the background, and most compelling, learning the Aggie war hymn on the bass. Thank you all for the support.

Lastly, we would like to thank the editors at John Wiley & Sons, Inc., Marquita Flemming, Sherry Wasserman, and Kim Nir. What started as a description of the field of special education became a history of special education and a chronicle of its life and times. We have been honored to witness this process and, as always, look forward to future growth.

A

AAAS, AMERICAN ASSOCIATION FOR THE ADVANCEMENT OF SCIENCE

The American Association for the Advancement of Science (AAAS) was founded in Philadelphia in 1848, making it one of the oldest professional societies in the United States. AAAS is a nonprofit society dedicated to the advancement of scientific and technological quality across all fields of science, and to increasing the general public's understanding of science and technology. The mission of the organization, according to its Constitution, is to "further the work of scientists, facilitate cooperation among them, foster scientific freedom and responsibility, improve the effectiveness of science in the promotion of human welfare, advance education in science, and increase the public's understanding and appreciation of the promise of scientific methods in human progress" (AAAS, 2011).

Today AAAS's membership is international, and is composed of over 143,000 scientists, science educators, engineers, and interested others; membership is open to anyone interested in scientific and technological progress. There are 285 scientific and engineering societies that have chosen to affiliate themselves with the AAAS, and they include 238 other societies, 44 state and regional academies of science, and 3 city academies. AAAS is thus the world's largest federation of professional scientific organizations. The association is organized into 24 sections which represent the various fields of interest of members, and four regional divisions. Programs fall into one of three directorates: Education and Human Resources, International, and Science and Policy.

The Association publishes many science books and reference works, the most prestigious being the weekly *Science*, a highly respected publication which disseminates state-of-the-art scientific research.

1200 New York Avenue NW, Washington, DC 20005. Tel.: (202) 326-6400.

REFERENCE

American Association for the Advancement of Science (AAAS). (2011). *General information.* Retrieved http://www.aaas.org/aboutaaas/

KAY E. KETZENBERGER
The University of Texas of the Permian Basin

AMERICAN ASSOCIATION OF INTELLECTUAL AND DEVELOPMENTAL DISABILITIES

The American Association of Intellectual and Developmental Disabilities (AAIDD), formerly American Association on Mental Retardation (AAMR), was founded in 1876, and claims over 5,000 members in the United States and 55 countries. Its membership is composed of professionals from a large variety of academic disciplines who are interested in the field of what is now known as intellectual disabilities, as well as nonprofessionals who are involved in and care of same. The primary goals of the AAIDD are to enhance the capacity of professionals who work with individuals with intellectual and developmental disabilities, participate in the development of a society that fully includes individuals with intellectual and developmental disabilities, and build an effective, responsive, well-managed, responsibly governed, and sustainable organization.

The AAIDD offers strong support to research in ID in the service of increasing the knowledge and skills of all who are involved in the field of ID, through the publication of two professional journals and the Association's newspaper *News and Notes*. The *American Journal on Intellectual and Developmental Disabilities* or *AJIDD*, reports current and critical research in biological, behavioral, and educational sciences, it is also a resource in the causes, treatment, and prevention of intellectual disability. The *Intellectual and Developmental Disabilities (IDD)* is a clinical and applied journal that ranks consistently among the top journals in special education and rehabilitation. *IDD* is a journal of policy, practices, and perspectives for professionals, clinicians, and other support staff interested in intellectual disabilities and related developmental disabilities. The AAIDD also provides an Early Career Professional page which allows students and professionals alike to connect through web-based trainings, blog entries, and future events.

The AAIDD is organized into 10 regions that cover the United States, Canada, and parts of the Pacific, and contains over 85 local, state, or provincial chapters. There are different areas you can choose to be affiliated with when becoming a member. These groups are divided into categories called divisions, special interest groups (SIGS), and action groups. There are many topics available within these groups; some examples are administrative division, communication disorder division, community service division, creative arts therapy SIG, criminal justice action group, direct support professionals division, education division, families SIG, genetics (SIG), gerontology division, health and wellness action network, humanism action network, hurricane disaster preparedness for persons with ID, and legal process and advocacy division. Membership in the AAIDD is open to anyone concerned about intellectual and developmental disabilities.

AAIDD plays a critical role in setting policy and priorities by working closely with federal agencies such as the Office of Special Education and Rehabilitative Services, the Administration on Developmental Disabilities, and the Division of Maternal and Child Health. AAIDD has taken a stand in recent U.S. Supreme Court cases on everything from medical decisions affecting newborns, school exclusion, and exclusionary zoning of group homes to the rights of defendants charged in criminal cases.

American Association on Intellectual and Developmental Disabilities, 501 Third Street NW, Suite 200, Washington, DC 20001. Tel.: (202) 387-1968, website: www.aaidd.org

KAY E. KETZENBERGER
The University of Texas of the Permian Basin
Third edition

SHANNON GRANT
Texas A&M University
Fourth edition

AAIDD (AMERICAN ASSOCIATION ON INTELLECTUAL DEVELOPMENTAL DISABILITIES) CLASSIFICATION SYSTEMS

Founded in 1876 as the American Association on Mental Retardation (AAMR) and now called the AAIDD, this organization is the world's oldest and largest interdisciplinary organization of professionals concerned about Intellectual Development Disabilities. With headquarters in Washington, DC, the AAIDD has a constituency of more than 50,000 people and an active core membership in the United States and in 55 other countries. The mission is to promote progressive policies, sound research, effective practices, and universal rights for people with intellectual disabilities. The AAIDD has led the field of developmental disabilities by officially defining the condition known as *Intellectual Developmental Disabilities*. A diagnostic and classification system remains important in today's society because it is used to determine who can access publicly funded services and supports.

The AAIDD has updated the definition of *Mental Retardation* 10 times since 1908. Changes in the definition have occurred when there is new information, or there are changes in clinical practice or breakthroughs in scientific research. The 11th edition of *Mental Retardation: Definition, Classification, and Systems of Supports* (AAIDD, 2010) contains a comprehensive update to the landmark 1992 system and provides important new information, tools, and strategies for the field and for anyone concerned about people with intellectual and developmental disabilities. The 11th edition discusses the 2010 AAIDD definition and classification system in great detail. It presents the latest thinking about Intellectual Disabilities and includes important tools and strategies to determine if an individual has IDD along with detailed information about developing a personal plan of individualized supports. It is available from the AAIDD through their website at http://www.AAIDD.org/bookstore/ or by calling (301) 604-1340.

The overall AAIDD definition of *Intellectual Developmental Disablties* is that it is a disability characterized by significant limitations both in intellectual functioning and in adaptive behavior as expressed in conceptual, social, and practical adaptive skills. This disability originates before the age of 18. The AAIDD considers five assumptions that are essential to the application of this definition:

1. Limitations in present functioning must be considered within the context of community environments typical of the individual's age peers and culture.

2. Valid assessment considers cultural and linguistic diversity as well as differences in communication, sensory, motor, and behavioral factors.

3. Within an individual, limitations often coexist with strengths.

4. An important purpose of describing limitations is to develop a profile of needed supports.

5. With appropriate personalized supports over a sustained period, the life functioning of the person with Intellectual Developmental Disabilities generally will improve (AAIDD, 2010).

A complete and accurate understanding of AAIDD involves realizing that *Intellectual Developmental Disabilities* refers to a particular state of functioning that begins in childhood, has many dimensions, and is affected positively by individualized supports. As a model of functioning, it includes the contexts and environment within which the person functions and interacts and requires a multidimensional and ecological approach that reflects the interaction of the individual with the environment and the outcomes of that interaction with regards to independence, relationships, societal contributions, participation in school and community, and personal well-being.

Table A.1.

Botswana	700,000
Ethiopia	15,600,000
Eritrea	1,600,000
Kenya	12,100,000
Lesotho	600,000
Malawi	3,200,000
Namibia	700,000
Tanzania	8,700,000
Uganda	10,500,000
Zambia	2,900,000
Zimbabwe	3,200,000

Table A.2.

WORD TYPE	EXAMPLE
CVC words that begin with a continuous phoneme	mat, sat, fat, hat
CVC words that begin with a stop phoneme	big, top, dip
CVCC words that end with a consonant blend or double consonants	sand, bend, toss
CCVC words beginning with a consonant blend	trip, slam, drop
CCVCC, CCCVC, CCCVCC	still, drink, truck
Compound words with CVC word or CVC variants	catnip

Adaptive behavior is the collection of conceptual, social, and practical skills people use to function in their everyday lives. Significant limitations in adaptive behavior impact a person's daily life and affect the ability to respond to a particular situation or to the environment. Limitations in adaptive behavior can be determined by using standardized tests that are normed on the general population, including people with disabilities and people without disabilities. On these standardized measures, significant limitations in adaptive behavior are operationally defined as performance that is at least two standard deviations below the mean of either (1) one of the following three types of adaptive behavior: conceptual, social, or practical, or (2) an overall score on a standardized measure of conceptual, social, and practical skills (AAIDD, 2010). Table A.1 includes some specific examples of adaptive behavior skills.

The concept of supports originated in the 1970s with the AAIDD, and it has revolutionized the way habilitation and education services are provided to persons with Intellectual Developmental Disabilities. Rather than mold individuals into preexisting diagnostic categories and force them into existing models of service, the supports approach evaluates the specific needs of the individual and then suggests strategies, services, and supports that will optimize individual functioning. The supports approach also recognizes that individual needs and circumstances will change over time. Supports were an innovative aspect of the 1992 AAMR manual, and they remain critical in the present system. *Supports* are defined as the resources and individual strategies necessary to promote the development, education, interests, and personal well-being of a person with Intellectual Disabilities. Supports can be provided by a parent, friend, teacher, psychologist, or doctor or by any appropriate person or agency. Providing individualized supports can improve personal functioning, promote self-determination and societal inclusion, and improve personal well-being of a person with Intellectual Developmental Disabilities. Focusing on supports as the way to improve education, employment, recreation, and living environments is an important part of person-centered approaches to providing supports to people with Intellectual Developmental Disabilities.

The AAIDD recommends that an individual's need for supports be analyzed in at least nine key areas: human development, teaching and education, home living, community living, employment, health and safety, behavioral, social, and protection and advocacy. Some specific examples of supports areas and support activities can be found in Table A.2.

The AAIDD publishes the Supports Intensity Scale (SIS), a planning tool that assesses the practical supports requirements of a person with an intellectual disability. The SIS is directly related to the 2002 classification system and therefore allows seamless transition from assessment to intervention (AAIDD, 2005). Contact information for the AAIDD is as follows: American Association on Intellectual Developmental Disabilities, 501 3rd St. NW, Ste. 200, Washington, DC 20001-1512. Tel.: (202) 387-1968 or (800) 424-3688, fax: (202) 387-2193, website: http://www.AAIDD.org

REFERENCES

American Association on Intellectual Developmental Disabilities (AAIDD). (2010). *Mental Retardation: Definition, classification, and systems of supports* (11th ed.). Washington, DC: Author.

American Association on Intellectual Developmental Disabilities (AAIDD). (2010). Definition. Retrieved from http://www.AAIDD.org

KIMBERLY J. VANNEST
Texas A&M University

See also AAIDD, American Association on Intellectual Developmental Disabilities

Acknowledgment: Please note that the information contained in this entry was taken from the AAIDD website with gracious permission from the AAMR. Personal communications with Anu Prabhala (June 15 through June 23, 2005) in the AAMR office of publications greatly enhanced the original breadth and depth of this entry, and we thank her for her time and consideration.

ABILITY TRAINING, EARLY EFFORTS IN

Many educators believe that most academic and social learning is based on factors such as student aptitudes or abilities, instructional environment, and teaching methodology. While these three variables do not form a complete structure capable of containing all those factors contributing to learning, they certainly account for many of the variables educators would agree are important to success in school.

Learner aptitudes or abilities are those personological variables that frequently are called intelligence(s), traits, gifts, and characteristics. Frequently, educators will talk about a child's potential to learn, using the term ability as if it were a predetermined factor waiting to be drawn on at some point. The logic, then, is that if learning is a result of the presence and development of certain mental abilities, school failure (both academic and social) may be the result of disabilities, with disability implying an academic or social handicap.

If regular (elementary and secondary) educators teach to the abilities of students to learn, then special educators may direct more of their instruction to the disabilities that inhibit learning, hence the term and concept of ability training. How valid is this construct of ability training? A short response to that question is impossible. Any field involving relatively newly defined services to persons, especially children, in particular children with disabilities, will generate professional controversy. Any field struggling with the pressures associated with economic, political, social, legislative, litigative, and basic human rights and values will face diversity. Any field that requires its many disciplines to unite in purpose will experience communicative stress. But, few professionals will purposely question their field's major methodology to the degree special and remedial educators have, for the period of time they have done so, and in the face of such a degree of controversy.

Some special educators believe avidly in ability training of all types; some reject it totally; but almost all, no matter what they believe, practice ability training. The truth in that observation is displayed when we recognize that the value of ability training to individuals with disabilities has been questioned repeatedly for over the past 100 years. What then is in ability training that has caused the field of special education to tenaciously and steadfastly support its methods? Ability training is routed in the historic search for the structure and function of the mind. Educators, in particular special educators, seek to diagnose specific abilities and provide remediation to those abilities, or disabilities as the case may be.

Mental ability (aptitude), concerns those components that are assumed to constitute the mind, and therefore explain learning. Mental-ability structures, in more scientific parlance, may be referred to as information-processing behaviors. Mental processes or information processes are those theoretical or conceptual acts (processes) by which information is transmitted from the peripheral (to the central nervous system) sensory organs (i.e., eyes, ears, fingers [tactile], muscles [kinesthetic]) perceived, labeled, stored, provided mediated meaning, conceptually associated, and expressed as language or motoric responses. It is not unusual for practitioners to reference most psychological functions synonymously with mental abilities. Hence, the very definition of learning disabilities refers to "basic psychological processes."

The history of man, at least those aspects related to the structures of the mind, how it works, and therefore how these processes can be measured, begins with the early Greek philosophers. Pythagoras placed the "mind" in the brain in the sixth century B.C.E. Most of the processes described then were hypotheoretical, related to this assumed function. Therefore, the names given these processes sometimes sound as if they had been isolated neurologically or psychoneurologically. The truth is that the majority of the commonly referenced mental processes, that is, perception and language, are not simple, easily explained constructs. They are complex concepts that may contain hundreds of component subparts. The major issues relating to ability training have been the long-standing arguments regarding the mind, its disabilities, and the habilitation or rehabilitation needed. A case in point is that while simple tests are designed to ascertain visual perceptual-motor development, visual perception is not a simple discriminate function. In a general sense, perception requires the discrimination of distinctive features, wherein a specific symbolic meaning can be assigned each distinct stimuli. Logically then, once perceptual information has been discriminated, it may be stored for some short-term reference, or it may be assigned a permanent symbolism, then converted to a language concept. Logically then, too, there may be both visual and auditory perception. These two processes may need to be coordinated when auditory and visual information is presented in an integrated manner. Perception, however, is not logically complex in contrast to the explanations of the structure and function of language.

A mental ability may also be referred to as a faculty. Mann (1979) credits Aristotle for establishing the basis for modern faculty psychology. The Romans further refined and added descriptors such as intellect, attention, and language. St. Thomas Aquinas, during the Middle Ages, although poorly credited, began to amplify and extend faculty psychology by dividing it into two parts: the *intellectus*, which carries out abstractions and functions of the possible intellect; and the *ratio*, which is directed toward understanding, judgment, and reasoning. The intellect is active and creative, the ratio is passive and receptive—that is, sensory stimuli must be perceptually assigned symbolic meaning/value before they have intellectual meaning.

Faculty psychology, the theoretical basis for mental process, was soundly criticized by many of the 17th-, 18th-, and 19th-century scholars. Hobbes (1588–1679) displaced it with his theories of automotion in the brain set off by sensory stimulation. Locke (1632–1704) was a sensationalist, and an arch antifaculist. Hume (1715–1776), also a sensationalist in the British tradition, condemned faculties, basing mental response solely in sensory stimulation. By the mid 19th century, the psychologist and educator Herbart attempted to destroy for all time the residual of faculty psychology.

One of the predominate figures in mental measurement, Spearman, writing in 1927, notes that faculty psychology seems to persist, no matter what the criticism.

One curious feature about these formal faculties has yet to be mentioned. The doctrine loses every battle—so to speak—but always wins the war. It will bend to the slightest breath of criticism; but not the most violent storm can break it. The attacks made long ago by the Herbartians appeared to be irresistible; no serious defense was even attempted. Yet the sole permanent effect of these attacks was only to banish the word "faculty," leaving the doctrine represented by this word to escape scot-free (pp. 38–39). However, other early individuals in the field such as Thorndike continued to be critical. As a quote from Mann (1979) notes,

> The science of education should at once rid itself of its conception of the mind as a sort of machine, different parts of which sense, perceive, discriminate, imagine, remember, conceive, associate, reason about, desire, choose, form habits, attend to.... There is no power of sense discrimination to be delicate or coarse.... There are only the connections between separate sense stimuli and our separate senses and human judgments thereof.... There is no memory to hold in a uniformly tight and loose grip the experiences of the past. There are only the particular connections between particular mental events and others. (Klein, 1970, p. 662)

Though an out-and-out antifaculist, Thorndike, interestingly enough, could not shake the ingrained habit of his times of speaking about "faculties." Thus, he described his bonds as faculties in the 1903 edition of *Education Psychology* (p. 30): "the mind is a host of highly particularized and independent faculties" (Spearman, 1927, p. 36).

Yet, it is faculty psychology that provided the definition for 20th-century mental measurement. On the basis of his inquiries, Galton described what, in essence, is a superfaculty, which he called "general ability," assigning to this faculty the name intelligence (a term popularized by Spencer). Galton distinguished this superfaculty from special aptitudes. He was more interested in the first, since he believed that general ability inevitably set a limit to accomplishment of any kind. He complained that most writers emphasized specific aptitudes or skill, that they

> lay too much stress upon apparent specialties, thinking that because a man is devoted to some particular pursuit, he could not have succeeded in anything else; they might as well say that, because a youth has fallen in love with a brunette, he could not possibly have fallen in love with a blonde. He may or may not have had any more natural liking for the former type of beauty than for the latter; but it is as probable as not that the affair was mainly or wholly due to a general amorousness. It is just the same with intellectual pursuits. (Burt, 1955, p. 85)

Galton most certainly did not deny the existence of special capacities or their potential importance. He cited instances in which memory, musical ability, and artistic and literary talent ran within several members of the same family. Home environment or family tradition could not explain all such cases, for example, "prodigies of memory." However, his studies in the main had convinced him "in how small a degree intellectual eminence can be considered as due to purely special powers" (Burt, 1955, p. 85).

As to the measurement of both general and special abilities, Galton suggested that individual differences in both are distributed in accordance with the normal curve, much as other human characteristics such as size or height are distributed. He printed a tabular classification of frequencies which he held "may apply to special just as truly as to general ability" (Burt, 1955, p. 85). Thus we see the beginnings of psychometric assessment of both general ability and specific abilities.

About 1880, the German psychiatrist Kraeplin, one of Wundt's students, began to use different tests to describe higher cognitive functions (Guilford, 1967). His testing interests were directed to such processes as general memory, specific memory, attention, and task-directed behaviors. However, it was James McKeen Cattell who first formulated the term "mental tests." Cattell's extension of Galton's simple tests began the modern practice of psychometrics as we know it today. Others such as DeSanctis attacked the realms of higher cognitive functioning. DeSanctis published a series of six tests including (1) memory for colors, (2) recognition of forms, (3) sustained attention, (4) reasoning involving relations, (5) following instructions, and (6) thinking.

At the turn of the 20th century, the French Minister of Public Instruction was still wrestling with an age-old problem: how to consistently identify the individuals with disabilities. Having agreed on the terminology to be used (idiot for the lowest level; imbecile for the intermediate level; and moron for the mildly mentally retarded), a psychologist, Alfred Binet, and physician, Theodore Simon, were commissioned to develop a consistent means of classifying children. Binet and Simon (1905, 1908) produced, through a standardized procedure of observation, a psychological classification of quantifiable differences in children's intellectual characteristics (traits). By 1905 Binet and Simon had developed 29 such tests designed to measure specific traits; by 1908 they had developed a classification of tests beginning at age three and continuing through age 13. Thus, the work preceding 1905 established human intelligence as a comprehensive integration of several traits including memory, attention, comprehension, muscular coordination, spatial relations, judgment, initiative, and ability to adapt. Further, the criteria for measurement of these traits were standardized at various chronological age levels. From this procedure the measurement of human performance took a great leap forward.

Binet carried his interest in higher processes into his work of developing mental tests for use in Paris schools. He and his associates criticized tests of the Galton type as being too simple, too sensory-motor, and too dependent on associationistic dogma. They expressed their own preference for the complex cognitive functions, proposing that 10 categories be explored by mental tests: (1) memory, (2) imagery, (3) imagination, (4) attention, (5) comprehension, (6) suggestibility, (7) aesthetic appreciation, (8) moral sentiment, (9) muscular force, force of will, and motor skill, and (10) judgment of visual space.

Modern psychoeducational assessment and remedial practices, indeed the very content of most perceptual, motor, language, vocational, and academic remedial curricula, are based on Binet's work. Two of the major issues are the specificity with which mental ability processes can reliably be ascertained and the desirability of remediating the specific perceptual or language processes in terms of their transferability and ultimate academic and social learning transfer.

But, it is clear that abilities had been identified by tests and that ability training was to become a crucial issue facing the 20th century. The main philosophic question is, do mental abilities really exist in nature? The second question is, do they respond to specific training once they are described, measured, observed, and, in short, isolated as specific mental abilities? These two questions constitute the major issues facing special educators today. Since mental abilities are developmentally linked to chronological growth, culture, and experience, they may be encouraged by structured educational experiences. Conversely, when developmentally delayed, culturally neglected, or separated from sequenced experiential practice, ability may degenerate. Mental ability deficiencies may then be the principal characteristics associated with disabling conditions such as learning and emotional or behavioral disorders. The entire nervous system develops only successfully decoding information or perceiving symbolic features providing a language construct and a mechanism to communicate. Therefore, specific reference is made in the definition of intellectual disability and learning disabilities, two of the largest categories of special education service categories, to dysfunction of perceptual, perceptual-motor, or language abilities.

Philosophically, then, it appears that a leap in logic is *not* required to assume that if a disability exists, and interferes with functioning, it should be corrected. That is exactly what ability training implies. It would appear that it was incorrectly named to begin with. The history of ability training parallels that of the field of special education. The pioneers in ability training were the pioneers of the field. Itard, Howe, Sequin, Montessori, Binet, Wepman, Kirk, Strauss, Fernald, Frostig, and Cruickshank were all advocates of special education as it grew, and responsible for advancing ability training simultaneously. Tests used to describe a disability were followed by commercially prepared curricula to minimize the disability by improving ability. The logic is obvious. The problem is in the scientific validation, or lack of it.

The early 1960s brought with it a concern for neurological impairment with children. The mid 1960s added the term learning disabled as a category of disabling conditions. Both of these conditions required an increased emphasis on psychoneurological and psychoeducational assessment. Those that developed psychoeducational and psychoneurological tests to diagnose these conditions fueled the fire for ability training by describing conditions which, by their description, must exist.

Curricula designed to modify and treat patterns of disability were soon commercially available. Whole classes of children were exposed to Montessori, Frostig, and Fernald techniques, and administered Frostig, Kephart, and Delaccato assessment procedures. Tests such as the Illinois Test of Psycholinguistic Abilities became commonplace, much as the Woodcock-Johnson test batteries of today. The prevailing belief was that specific mental processes must be diagnosed in order for modification of a specific disability to result in quantum jumps in academic remedial achievement and potential normalization. Thus, the so-called diagnostic-prescriptive process is one aspect of ability training.

What then is the difficulty with visual and auditory perceptual training, perceptual motor training, language training, and the other forms of sensory, motor, perceptual, and language ability training? The problem is that data arrived at through quasi-scientific means lead to controversial results. There are data to support ability training, if the objective to be achieved is a change in an ability, and that ability alone. There are few data to support that training of a perceptual or cognitive ability will transfer to an academic achievement skill, for instance reading.

The overall interaction among these abilities includes the stimulus provided during physical or auditory training and how the information is interpreted and organized (Hammill, 2004). Language training seemingly has the greatest transference to academic remediation. But even the search for generalities would produce only controversy. The fact is, ability training makes sense logically but has not been sufficiently researched devoid of other educational practices with school-age children to permit definitive statements. And yet, the practice does not only continue, it continues to thrive.

REFERENCES

Binet, A., & Simon, T. (1905). Methodes nouvelles pour le diagnostic du niveau intellectuel des anomaux. *L'anne psychologique*, *11*, 191–244.

Binet, A., & Simon, T. (1908). Le developpement de l'intelligence chez les infants. *L'anne psychologique, 14*, 1–94.

Burt, C. (1955). The evidence for the concept of intelligence. *British Journal of Educational Psychology, 25*, 158–177.

Hammill, D. (2004). What we know about correlates of reading. *Exceptional Children, 70*(4), 453–468.

Klein, D. B. (1970). *A history of scientific psychology.* New York, NY: Basic Books.

Mann, L. (1970). *On the trail of process.* New York, NY: Grune & Stratton.

Spearman, C. (1927). *The abilities of man: Their nature and measurement.* London, UK: Macmillan.

DAVID A. SABATINO
West Virginia College of Graduate Studies
Third edition

See also Diagnostic Prescriptive Teaching; Fernald Method; Illinois Test of Psycholinguistic Abilities; Intelligence; Remediation, Deficit-Centered Models of

ABNORMALITIES, NEUROPHYSIOLOGICAL

The human nervous system consists of the brain, the spinal cord, and an intricate network of nerve fibers projecting from the brain and spinal cord. Structurally, the brain is differentiated into the two cerebral hemispheres, the brain stem, and the cerebellum. The brain, together with the spinal cord, traditionally has been conceptualized as the central nervous system (CNS). The entire network of nerve fibers is then referred to as the peripheral nervous system (PNS). The brief discussion regarding normal neurological structure and function that follows is meant as an aid in the appreciation of neurophysiological disorders. The intent here is to offer an overview; for a more detailed account of the nervous system, the reader is referred to one of a number of neurophysiological texts (e.g., Bickerstaff, 1978; Lindsley & Holmes, 1984; Swaiman & Ashwal, 2006).

Peripheral nerves are referred to by the direction the impulses flow and the site of their termination. Specifically, the direction of the impulses carried in relation to the CNS, the originating structure, or final destination of the impulse, and the nature of the impulse itself, are used to classify peripheral nerves. For instance, the PNS contains sensory nerves that carry impulses from the sense organs (eyes, ears, nose, etc.) to the CNS. By way

of contrast, the motor nerves travel from the CNS to the periphery, exciting both skeletal (voluntary) and smooth (involuntary) muscle into movement. Included in PNS, the cranial nerves arise from or travel to the brain stem (connecting structure between spinal cord and cerebrum). Similarly, the spinal nerves travel to or from the spinal cord. The group of peripheral nerves that carry impulses to smooth muscle (causing involuntary movements of the intestines, heartbeat, constriction of the pupils, etc.) and those that incite the secretion of glands cause automatic changes in the body. These peripheral nerves are sometimes referred to collectively as the autonomic nervous system.

Functionally, the fundamental building block of the nervous system is the neuronal circuit. The simplest neuronal circuit contains only two interconnected nerve cells, involving an input and an output cell (e.g., simple knee-jerk reflex). Local circuits exist at all levels of the nervous system and, in fact, such circuits in the spinal cord connect the cerebral cortex, brain stem, and cerebellum. These connections can function as modules in more complex circuits. Indeed, these integrated networks are capable of sustaining complex behavior (Gaddes, 1985; Kandel, Schwartz, & Jessell, 1991).

As an example, sensory impulses traveling from the various sense organs to the brain are integrated, recorded, recognized, stored, or remembered, as interpreted by the cerebral cortex. Moreover, skeletal movement may be affected by motor nerves traveling by way of the spinal cord. Generally, the entire system works to regulate and coordinate bodily responses to both internal and external changes in the environment (Taber, 1970). A malfunctioning neurological system results in an impaired capacity for responding adaptively to a changing environment.

Neurophysiological abnormality may occur by means of many agents and during various stages of the life process; some stages offer more vulnerability than others. Antenatal agents (occurring before birth) described by Nelson (1969) include genetic factors, chromosomal aberrations, placental disease, maternal complications, number of previous pregnancies, age of both mother and father, intrauterine infection, toxic agents (including certain drugs and alcohol), and radiation. Various organ systems begin and end their prenatal development at different times, therefore their sensitivity to agents varies with maturity of the fetus. The most vulnerable period for the brain is from 15 to 25 days of gestation but, clearly, damage can occur at any time during the development of the nervous system (Hetherington & Parke, 1979).

Perinatal (occurring just before or after birth) vulnerability to neurological insult is accentuated by premature birth. Inadequate oxygen during this stage, hemorrhage, trauma, and infection are the principal offenders (Nelson, 1969). Postnatal (occurring after birth) damage to the neurological system may include damage incurred after birth, during childhood, or throughout the various stages of adulthood. Infections, principally meningitis and encephalitis, injuries, and degenerative neurological disease have also been implicated (Nelson, 1969).

Weller, Swash, McLellan, and Scholtz (1983) estimated that 40% of developmental malformations of the CNS arise from genetic abnormality. The most common genetic abnormality is Down syndrome. This disorder is associated with a group of chromosomal aberrations involving the 21st chromosome pair. In the great majority of cases, a failure to join occurs during the meiosis process, resulting in a trisomy (additional chromosome) of the 21st chromosome pair. Translocation and mosaician represent less frequently occurring aberrations of the 21st chromosome pair, also associated with Down syndrome (Kopp & Parmelee, 1979).

The incidence of Down syndrome is between one and two per thousand live births for all races and ethnic groups (Gillberg, 1995; Norman, 1963). Although there is some variability in incidence, most researchers cite an increase in relation to maternal age (Benda, 1960; Lawrence, 1981; Weller et al., 1983). A gradual increase begins with maternal age of 35 and escalates drastically after 40. Metabolic or environmental factors in the mothers' ovaries have been suggested as causes for the syndrome (Benda, 1960; Lawrence, 1981; Nelson, 1969; Norman, 1963; Weller, Swash, McLellan, & Scholtz, 1983). Structural inspection of the Down syndrome brain suggests impairment of both growth and differentiation (Benda, 1960). The brain is generally low in weight and the normal convolutional pattern of the brain is simplified. The density of the nerve cells in the cerebral cortex is reduced (Weller et al., 1983).

Rate of mental development is not only slower than normal but also deteriorates progressively with age in Down syndrome (Cornwell & Birch, 1969; Dicks-Mireaux, 1972; Gillberg, 1995). Many explanations, including neurophysiologic changes, have been offered as an explanation for this progressive deterioration. Weller et al. (1983) noted that the microscopic study of brain tissue of Down syndrome victims during autopsy reveals patterns of neurofibrillary tangles, senile plaques, and granulovacular degeneration such as are found in Alzheimer's disease (deteriorative disease of the elderly involving degeneration of the smaller blood vessels of the brain). Kopp and Parmelee (1979) suggest that the severe limitations in higher level integrative abilities evident in Down syndrome may cause deficits in information processing (e.g., use of language) that could have progressive detrimental effects on the child's intellectual development over time. The child's capacity for responding adaptively to changing stimulus conditions, a necessity for proper intellectual development, may be impaired directly by the nature of the syndrome. However, the nature of the environment in which these children find themselves, whether it is enriched or impoverished, also can affect development.

In contrast to Down syndrome, which is genetically related, spina bifida seems to be more influenced by environmental factors. Although genetic factors are suggested by the higher incidence in infants born to parents with a family history of such lesions, it seems that racial, geographical, and even seasonal factors also may be implicated (Kopp & Parmelee, 1979; Weller et al., 1983). Clearly, the interaction of genetic and environmental factors has recently been given prominence. Genetic predisposition combined with certain environmental factors may be the causal condition for spina bifida occurrence (Carter, 1974).

Spina bifida is a birth defect that involves the incomplete development of the spinal cord or its coverings. Spina bifida occurs at the end of the first month of pregnancy when the two sides of the embryo's spine fail to join together, leaving an open area. In some cases, the spinal cord or other membranes may push through this opening in the back. The condition usually is detected before a baby is born and treated right away. The contents of the spinal column (nerve fibers, meninges, and fluid) may protrude from the lower back in a sac (meningomyelocele). Individual defects vary depending on the extent of damage to the nerve fibers and the existence of other associated conditions (Kleinberg, 1982). The spinal cord is frequently abnormal above and below the level of the spina bifida (Weller et al., 1983). Hydrocephalus, abnormal accumulation of cerebral spinal fluid, frequently is associated with spina bifida. Untreated hydrocephalus creates severe enlargement of the head, increased pressure, and subsequent damage to the brain (Kleinberg, 1982).

Intellectual levels of individuals with spina bifida are variable, ranging from an IQ of 137 to severe subnormality (Gillberg, 1995; Hunt, 1981). More specifically, Spain (1974) associates intellectual disability with protrusion of a portion of the brain (cranial meningocele and cephalocele), whereas infants with other forms are considered to have potentially normal intellect. Many individuals with spina bifida are incontinent, and have weakness of their legs with sensory loss below the level of the lesion (Kleinberg, 1982). Owing to the presence of the typical locomotor problems in spina bifida, it is unclear whether some deficits are due to neurological impairment or environmental influence. Spain's (1974) longitudinal spina bifida studies have revealed significant deficits in spatial and manipulative development. The fact that the disorder limits the individual's experience may, in fact, cause or influence the specific deficits in spatial and manipulative development. Among the educational problems noted are difficulties with arithmetic and perseveration in language, as well as emotionality and poor motivation (Kopp & Parmelee, 1979).

Primary disorders of the CNS, like Down syndrome and spina bifida, represent a relatively small proportion of the neurological problems in infants (Horwitz, 1973). More frequently, the genetic programs for potentially normal neurological development are subverted by adverse prenatal or birthing conditions such as lack of oxygen (hypoxia). Cerebral hemorrhage often occurs during prolonged hypoxia. The accumulation of stagnate blood that follows circulatory collapse may cause bleeding and ultimate damage to brain tissue (Weller et al., 1983). Premature infants are especially vulnerable to hypoxia. Since the respiratory system is not fully perfected until the last 4 to 6 weeks of gestation, these infants are often born without an optimally functioning respiratory system. Postmortem studies on premature children show that the bleeding usually occurs within one of the cavities of the brain or the space below the arachnoid membrane that contains cerebrospinal fluid (subarachnoid space [Horwitz, 1973]). Later complications of such subarachnoid hemorrhage involve epilepsy, dementia, and hydrocephalus (Weller et al., 1983). Full-term infants are more likely to suffer from hemorrhage in the mid-brain stem (pons) and the posterior portion of the cerebral cortex (hippocampus). The location and size of brain lesions at or soon after birth are the primary determinants of the extent of nervous system impairment. The results may range from a gross alteration of brain organization to more minimal effects such as motor overactivity, shortened attention span, or slight muscle impairment (Pincus & Tucker, 1974; Teberg et al., 1982). Large injuries in infants tend to produce more widespread deficits in intellectual abilities than similar injuries in adults. Dulling of many areas of intellectual functioning, as opposed to having an effect in specific functioning (e.g., language development, visual-spatial relationship comprehension), is also a hallmark effect of the diffuse damage that follows hypoxia (Rapin, 1982).

Neurological deficiencies from early injury are difficult to predict. The nervous system of the newborn infant is extremely immature, functioning largely at brain stem and spinal cord level. The neurologic reflexes such as Moro, grasping, and stepping represent primitive neuronal function that is largely uninhibited by higher cerebral control. Changes in these reflexes are usually not helpful in localizing the lesion, and may occur with either cortical or subcortical dysfunction (Horwitz, 1973). Damage to the cerebral cortex, for instance, may not be evident until the age when behavior dependent on the damaged part makes its developmental appearance. Thus, pathology of fine motor coordination, speech, and cognition is unlikely to be diagnosed in infancy (Rapin, 1982). However, changes in reflexes and disorganized activity of the subcortical structures expressed as a movement disorder or spasticity continue to be used as indicators of neurological damage. In Teberg et al.'s study of low birth weight infants (1982), spastic quadriplegia did, in fact, emerge as the indicative diagnosis of neurological handicap. Churchill, Masland, Naylor, and Ashworth (1974) support this finding.

Turkewitz (1974) contended that the standard methods used for the early identification of neurologic handicaps are insensitive to many forms of neurological involvement.

Infants who have had difficulties shortly before or during the birth process frequently appear to recover in a few days. However, abnormalities in motor, language, and intellectual functioning become apparent later in infancy and childhood. Studies using indicators of higher levels of neurological organization (e.g., left/right preference) are being investigated in an effort to identify infants who have experienced neurological damage that is normally not expressed until later in life. However, normative patterns of left/right preference for infants must be established first, before atypical patterns can be interpreted.

The possibilities for neurophysiological dysfunction are limitless; the pathologies presented should not be considered as inclusive by any means. However, it is hoped that an appreciation of the complexity of cerebral neural structure and the corresponding intricacies of impairment resulting from neurophysiological dysfunction will encourage the reader to treat each impaired patient as a unique individual, for heterogeneity of outcome is common (Gaddes, 1985; Goldstein & Reynolds, 1999; Kopp & Parmelee, 1979).

REFERENCES

Benda, C. E. (1960). *The child with mongolism (congenital acromicria)*. New York, NY: Grune & Stratton.

Bickerstaff, E. R. (1978). *Neurology* (3rd ed.). Bungay, UK: Chaucer.

Carter, C. O. (1974). Clues to the aetiology of neural tube malformations: Studies in hydrocephalus and spina bifida. *Developmental Medicine and Child Neurology, 16*(Suppl. 32), 3–15.

Churchill, J. A., Masland, R. L., Naylor, A. A., & Ashworth, M. R. (1974). The etiology of cerebral palsy in pre-term infants. *Developmental Medicine and Child Neurology, 16*, 143–149.

Cornwell, A. C., & Birch, H. G. (1969). Psychological and social development in home-reared children with Down's syndrome (mongolism). *American Journal of Mental Deficiencies, 74*, 341–350.

Dicks-Mireaux, M. J. (1972). Mental development of infants with Down's syndrome. *American Journal of Mental Deficiencies, 77*, 26–32.

Gaddes, W. H. (1985). *Learning disabilities and brain function: A neuropsychological approach* (2nd ed.). New York, NY: Springer-Verlag.

Gillberg, C. (1995). *Clinical child neuron psychiatry*. Cambridge, UK: Cambridge University Press.

Goldstein, S., & Reynolds, C. R. (1999). *Handbook of neurodevelopmental and genetic disorders of children*. New York, NY: Guilford Press.

Hetherington, E. M., & Parke, R. D. (1979). *Child psychology: A contemporary viewpoint* (2nd ed.). New York, NY: McGraw-Hill.

Horwitz, S. J. (1973). Neurologic problems. In M. H. Klaus & A. A. Fanaroff (Eds.), *Care of the high-risk neonate* (pp. 287–300). Philadelphia, PA: Saunders.

Hunt, G. (1981). Spina bifida: Implications for 100 children at school. *Developmental Medicine and Child Neurology, 23,* 160–172.

Kandel, E., Schwartz, J., & Jessell, T. (1991). *Principles of neural science.* New York, NY: Elsevier.

Kleinberg, S. B. (1982). *Educating the chronically ill child.* Rockville, MD: Aspen Systems.

Kopp, C. B., & Parmelee, A. H. (1979). Prenatal and perinatal influences on infant behavior. In J. D. Osofsky (Ed.), *Handbook of infant development* (pp. 29–75). New York, NY: Wiley.

Lawrence, K. M. (1981). Abnormalities of the central nervous system. In A. P. Norman (Ed.), *Congenital abnormalities in infancy* (pp. 21–81). Oxford, UK: Blackwell.

Lindsley, D. F., & Holmes, J. E. (1984). *Basic human neurophysiology.* Amsterdam: Elsevier Science.

Nelson, W. E. (Ed.). (1969). *Textbook of pediatrics* (9th ed.). Philadelphia, PA: Saunders.

Norman, A. P. (1963). *Congenital abnormalities in infancy.* Philadelphia, PA: Davis.

Pincus, J. H., & Tucker, G. J. (1974). *Behavioral neurology.* New York, NY: Oxford University Press.

Rapin, I. (1982). *Children with brain dysfunction: Neurology, cognition, language and behavior.* New York, NY: Raven.

Spain, B. (1974). Verbal performance ability in pre-school children with spina bifida. *Developmental Medicine and Child Neurology, 16,* 773–780.

Swaiman, K. F., & Ashwal, S. (2006). *Pediatric neurology principles and practice* (4th ed.). St. Louis: Mosby.

Taber, C. W. (1970). *Taber's cyclopedic medical dictionary* (11th ed.). Philadelphia, PA: Davis.

Teberg, A. J., Wu, P. Y. K., Hodgman, J. E., Mich, C., Garfinkle, J., Azen, S., & Wingert, W. A. (1982). Infants with birth weight under 1500 grams: Physical, neurological, and developmental outcome. *Critical Care Medicine, 10,* 10–14.

Turkewitz, G. (1974). The detection of brain dysfunction in the newborn infant. In D. P. Purpura & G. P. Reaser (Eds.), *Methodological approaches to the study of brain maturation and its abnormalities* (pp. 125–130). Baltimore, MD: University Park Press.

Weller, R. O., Swash, M., McLellan, D. S., & Scholtz, C. L. (1983). *Clinical neuropathology.* New York, NY: Overwallop; Great Britain: BAS.

DOROTHY A. STROM
RAYMOND S. DEAN
Ball State University
Indiana University School of Medicine

See also Adapted Physical Education; Health Maintenance Procedures; Physical Anomalies

ABPP (*See American Board of Professional Psychology*)

ABROMS, KIPPY I. (1942–1987)

Kippy I. Abroms received her BA in psychology from the University of New Hampshire in 1962, MEd in reading from Tulane University in 1973, and PhD in special education from the University of South Mississippi in 1977. Abroms also completed postdoctoral training at the University of California, Riverside in 1977 where she worked with Jane Mercer on the System of Multiple Pluralistic Assessment (SOMPA). Abroms worked as an associate professor at Tulane University beginning in 1975. She directed several projects for the Office of Special Education and Rehabilitation Services and the Bureau of Education for the Handicapped.

Abroms conducted research with J. W. Bennett (1981) that dispelled the well-entrenched notion of exclusive maternal etiology in Down syndrome. Abroms and Bennett found that in a significant number of cases the extra 21st chromosome, the immediate cause of Down syndrome, comes from the sperm. Thus there can be a maternal or paternal contribution to the etiology of Trisomy 21.

Her research included a longitudinal study on the social development of preschool gifted children, and, as a member of the craniofacial team at Tulane University Medical Center, she has been involved in investigations of the relationship between cognitive functioning, self-concept, and craniofacial intervention. She has also become interested in how genetic disorders are manifested in children, and especially in facial deformities that are obvious in the classroom (Abroms, 1987).

REFERENCES

Abroms, K. (1987). Genetic disorders underlying facial deformities. *Topics in early childhood special education, 6,* 92–100.

Abroms, K. I., & Bennett, J. W. (1981). Parental contributions to Trisomy 21: Review of recent cytological and statistical findings. In P. Mittler (Ed.), *Frontiers of knowledge in mental retardation, Vol. 2. Biomedical aspects* (pp. 149–157). Baltimore, MD: University Park.

ELAINE FLETCHER-JANZEN
Chicago School of Professional Psychology

See Speech, Absence of

ABSENCE SEIZURES

Absence seizures (previously referred to as *petit mal epilepsy*) are characterized by impaired consciousness that is unaccompanied by large convulsive movements. Individuals with absence seizures describe them as "brief flashes of blackouts," "like in a daze," or "getting into a trance" (Panayiotopoulos et al., 1992). While absence seizures are nonconvulsive during the seizure, some movement (e.g., eye-blinking, staring) and other minor facial movements (e.g., twitching) may be present. An observer also may notice body limpness and the arrest of activity, such as the dropping of an item.

There is a lack of aura (i.e., a sensation that it is about to occur) prior to the onset of an absence seizure as well as an absence of a postictal period (post-seizure confusion) following the seizure's termination. Absence seizures are characterized by their brevity; although they may last up to 1 minute, they typically last for 5 to 10 seconds. The term *pyknolespy* (*pyknos* refers to overcrowding) is frequently used to describe absence seizures as they have a tendency to occur in rapid succession. Prolonged periods of impaired consciousness due to consecutive absence seizures may lead to considerable dysfunction in school activities and others that require concentration and comprehension. For example, if absence seizures occur while a teacher is discussing novel material, impaired consciousness may cause the child to miss important instructional objectives that may not be addressed again during the academic school year (Leppik, 2000). Therefore, academic deficits are not uncommon in children who experience absence seizures.

Absence seizures are generalized. They involve abnormal activity throughout the brain, and their genesis is not in a discrete (focus) part of the brain. A distinction is made between typical and atypical absence seizures. Electroencephalograms (EEGs) show that typical absence seizures are characterized by an abrupt and synchronous onset and termination of both hemispheres and by a characteristic three-cycle-per-second spike and wave pattern. Structural abnormalities typically are not noted during neurological exams or the use of computerized axial tomographic scans.

Absence seizures occur in 2% to 10% of children with epilepsy. The age of onset typically is between 5 and 15 and is more common in girls. Typical absence seizures are frequently idiopathic (genetic) and remit in 40% of patients (Leppik, 2000). Hyperventilation, and, less commonly, photic stimulation may facilitate the spike discharges associated with absence seizures (Panayiotopoulos et al., 1992).

Atypical absence seizures are more complex than typical absence seizures. During atypical absence seizures, children can retain some ability for purposive movement and speech. Electroencephalogram results show a gradual onset and offset with less symmetrical synchrony between the hemispheres (Nolan, Bergazar, Chu, Cortez, & Snead, 2005). Furthermore, the predominant frequency tends to be less than a three-cycle-per-second wave pattern (Nolan et al., 2005). Like typical absence seizures, atypical absence seizures occur more frequently in females and present prior to adolescence. However, compared to typical absence seizures, atypical absence seizures tend to occur with greater frequency, are more prolonged, and commonly are combined with other seizure types. Children with atypical absence seizures demonstrate significantly higher rates of intellectual disability and tend to have a higher incidence of global cognitive deficits. This seizure type tends to be expressed as a nonspecific symptom of brain injury during development.

Valproate (Depakene) and ethosuximide are the most commonly prescribed drugs for absence seizures. Childhood absence seizures are frequently benign, therefore, ethosuximide usually is recommended first; valproate is reserved for when ethosuximide is insufficient or when the child also has generalized tonic-clonic seizures. Lamotrigine formerly was considered a second line drug; however, its use has increased significantly over time (Posner, Mohamed, & Marson, 2005).

REFERENCES

Leppik, I. L. (2000). *Contemporary diagnosis and management of the patient with epilepsy*. Newton, PA: Handbooks in Health Care.

Meeren, H., van Luijtelaar, G., Lopes da Silva, F., & Coencen, A. (2005). Evolving concepts of pathophysiology of absence seizures. *Archives of Neurology, 62*, 371–376.

Nolan, M., Bergazar, M., Chu, B., Cortez, M. A., & Snead, O. C. (2005). Clinical and neurophysiologic spectrum associated with atypical absence seizures in children with intractable epilepsy. *Journal of Child Neurology, 20*(5), 404–410.

Panayiotopoulos, C. P., Chroni, E., Daskslopoulos, C., Baker, A., Rowlinson, S., & Walsh, P. (1992). Typical absence seizures in adults: Clinical EEG, video-EEG findings and diagnostic/syndromic considerations. *Journal of Neurology, Neurosurgery, and Psychiatry, 55*, 1002–1008.

Posner, E. B., Mohamed, K., & Marson, A. G. (2005). A systematic review of treatment of typical absence seizures in children and adolescents with ethosuximide, sodium valproate, or lamotrigine. *Seizure, 14*, 116–122.

NICOLE NASEWICZ
University of Florida

See also Electroencephalograph; Seizure Disorders

ABSENTEEISM/ATTENDANCE OF CHILDREN WITH DISABILITIES

Compulsory school attendance laws have been enacted by all states. These laws have been narrowed in most states by the introduction of exemption clauses excusing students with significant physical or mental disabilities from school attendance if an alternate environment is a better fit for the student; however, the laws also ensure students with disabilities do have the right to attend school regardless of the severity or type of disability if able.

Legal challenges concerning children with disabilities for extension and protection of the right established under state law of equal access to educational opportunity was ensued during the early 1970s. Federal and state laws mandating a free appropriate public education (FAPE) to children with disabilities followed these cases. Under IDEA and Section 504 of the Rehabilitation Act of 1973, a child with a disability must be educated in the most least restrictive environment (LRE) that his or her needs allow. Federal law recognizes that there are instances when, because of the nature or severity of a child's disability, the child must be educated in a setting other than the regular classroom. However, the least restrictive environment provisions prohibit placement of a child on homebound instruction or other exclusion from the regular educational environment solely because the child has disabilities.

Children with serious, often chronic, health impairments who require special education and related services may receive instruction in hospitals or in the home. Schools use various approaches, including home visitations, school-to-home telephone communication, and interactive television to connect a homebound or hospitalized student with the classroom.

There have been a few studies of program and school attendance as a factor in the achievement of students with disabilities. The National Center for Education Statistics established that some risk factors for attendance difficulties might include students of English Language Learner status, eligibility for free and reduced lunch, and the receipt of special education services (2006). There is some evidence suggesting that students with disabilities who are attending regular, public schools are no more likely to be absent from school than students without disabilities students (Sullivan & McDaniel, 1983). High rates of school attendance do not necessarily ensure high rates of program attendance or achievement. Sullivan and McDaniel concluded that children served in resource rooms may be receiving up to one-quarter less schooling time than is prescribed in their individualized education programs because of competing school activities and absences of either the resource room teacher or the student during a scheduled period (1983). In various studies involving children with and without disabilities investigators in the area of academic learning time as it relates to academic achievement have found a positive correlation between the learning of basic skills and the number of minutes students spend on academically relevant tasks (Ivarie, Hogue, & Brulle, 1984; Rosenshine, 1979). Another study reported that 15.6% of the school day was spent on academic instruction while the rest of the day was consumed with tasks such as paperwork, personal

time, supervision and planning (Vannest & Hagan-Burke, 2010). Researchers are continuing their study of increased active learning time as a powerful intervention technique for all students. In addition the reduction of absenteeism is present in policy such as the Elementary and Secondary Education Act of 1965 and the more recent No Child Left Behind Act of 2001 (Redmond & Hosp, 2008).

Under the IDEA and Section 504, mandatory procedural safeguards exist that allow parents to challenge school disciplinary actions that would interrupt the education of a student with disabilities. Expulsions, suspensions, and transfers to settings outside a regular classroom or school are considered placement changes because such measures remove students from their current school program or curtail attendance (Simon, 1984). A series of court decisions on this sensitive area have provided important guidelines for determining when and for what length of time the student with disabilities may be expelled or suspended under federal law (Reschly & Bersoff, 1999; Simon, 1984).

REFERENCES

Ivarie, J., Hogue, D., & Brulle, A. (1984). Investigation of mainstream teacher time spent with students labeled learning disabled. *Exceptional Children, 51,* 142–149.

National Center for Education Statistics. (2006). *Student effort and educational progress: Student absenteeism.* Retrieved from http://nces.ed.gov/pubs2002/2002025_3.pdf

Redmond, S. M., & Hosp, J. L. (2008). Absenteeism rates in students receiving services for CD's LD's and ED's: A macroscopic view of the consequences of disability. *Language, Speech, and Hearing Services in Schools, 39,* 97–103.

Reschly, D., & Bersoff, D. (1999). Law and school psychology. In C. R. Reynolds & T. B. Gutkin (Eds.), *The handbook of school psychology* (3rd ed., pp. 1077–1112). New York, NY: Wiley.

Rosenshine, B. V. (1979). Content, time, and direct instruction. In P. L. Peterson & H. J. Walberg (Eds.), *Research on teaching* (pp. 28–56). Berkeley, CA: McCutchan.

Simon, S. G. (1984). Discipline in the public schools: A dual standard for handicapped and nonhandicapped students. *Journal of Law & Education, 13,* 209–237.

Sullivan, P. D., & McDaniel, E. A. (1983). Pupil attendance in resource rooms as one measure of the time on task variable. *Journal of Learning Disabilities, 16,* 398–399.

Vannest, K. J., & Hagan-Burke, S. (2010). Teacher time use in special education. *Remedial and Special Education, 31,* 126–142.

SHIRLEY A. JONES
Virginia Polytechnic Institute and State University
Third edition

LAUREN E. WILLIAMS
Texas A&M University
Fourth edition

ABSTRACTION, CAPACITY FOR

Abstract reasoning refers to the ability to identify common features of two or more concepts, and has been considered an essential component of intelligence (e.g., Thorndike, 1927). Abstract reasoning ability can be assessed through at least three types of tasks: those that require a person to identify a general concept common to several exemplars, for example, sorting objects according to categories; to state common features among different concepts, for example, the Similarities subtest of the Wechsler Intelligence Scale for Children–IV, or to state examples or features of a given concept (Burger, Blackman, Clark, & Reis, 1982).

While general abstraction ability varies across persons, ability to reason abstractly in specific tasks appears to vary with subject area expertise. For example, in studying the superior memory of chess masters for the configuration of briefly presented game arrangements, Chi, Glaser, and Rees (1981) suggest that experts form abstract, organized representations of the field of play, while novices retain only the surface features of the problem. Adelson (1984) found that novice computer programming students actually had better recall for the details of a briefly presented program than did expert programmers, but that the experts had better recall for what the programs were designed to do. Ability to make abstractions about information seems to improve with experience; as one gains more experience with an area of knowledge, one becomes familiar with the organization of it, and is able to integrate new information with greater success.

Burger et al. (1982) found that adolescents with intellectual disabilities could be trained to improve their abstract reasoning abilities. Context and instructional support also influence the application of abstract thinking skills (Alexander & Murphy, 1999; Chiesi, Primi, & Morsanyi, 2011; Gopnik, Glymour, Sobel, Schulz, Kushnir, & Danks, 2004).

REFERENCES

Adelson, B. (1984). When novices surpass experts: The difficulty of a task may increase with expertise. *Journal of Experimental Psychology: Learning, Memory, and Cognition, 10*, 483–495.

Alexander, P. A., & Murphy, P. K. (1999). What cognitive psychology has to say to school psychology: Shifting perspectives and shared purposes. In C. R. Reynolds & T. B. Gutkin (Eds.), *The handbook of school psychology* (3rd ed., pp. 167–193). New York, NY: Wiley.

Burger, A. L., Blackman, L. S., Clark, H. T., & Reis, E. (1982). Effects of hypothesis testing and variable format training on generalization of a verbal abstraction strategy by EMR learners. *American Journal on Mental Deficiency, 86*, 405–413.

Chi, M. T. H., Glaser, R., & Rees, E. (1981). Expertise in problem solving. In R. Sternberg (Ed.), *Advances in the psychology of human intelligence* (Vol. 1, pp. 7–75). Hillsdale, NJ: Erlbaum.

Chiesi, F., Primi, C., & Morsanyi, K. (2011). Developmental changes in probalistic reasoning: The role of cognitive capacity, instructions, thinking styles, and relevant knowledge. *Thinking and Reasoning. 17*(3), 315–350.

Gopnik, A., Glymour, C., Sobel, D. M., Schulz, L. E., Kushnir, T., & Danks, D. (2004). A theory of causal learning in children: Causal maps and Bayes nets. *Psychological Review, 1*, 3–32.

Thorndike, E. L. (1927). *The measurement of intelligence.* New York, NY: Bureau of Publications, Teachers College, Columbia University.

JOHN MacDONALD
Eastern Kentucky University

See also Intelligence Testing; Mental Retardation

ABSTRACT THINKING, IMPAIRMENT IN

A theory of abstract reasoning hinges on the notion that human thinking is a process of conceptualization. Concept formation is the organization of data into categories. To know a concept is to know the characteristics of an entity that either include it or exclude it from a category. To know the concept of "dog" is to know that animals with four legs, hair, and the ability to bark belong together in a category. Some argue that forming a concept is a process of abstracting. To learn the concept of dog requires noticing common characteristics of different dogs, as well as noticing that cats have some characteristics that eliminate them from that category. However, not all concepts are created equally. Some are based on immediate, sensory experience or represent the concrete. For example, a child may form a category of "doggy" by directly experiencing dogs and pictures of dogs. This is considered to be a concrete concept. On the other hand, there are concepts that are built from other concepts, for example, the notion of "mammal." A concept even further removed from direct experience is "democracy." The more removed the concept from the concrete, the more abstract it is. The term *abstract*, then, is used in two different ways. On the one hand, it is used to mean the process by which the salient characteristics of entities are identified in order to form concepts. On the other hand, it is used in contrast with the term *concrete* to indicate the role of direct experience.

Another factor related to abstract reasoning is the role of symbolization. Luria (1961) stated that the development of more abstract concepts was dependent on symbolization—more specifically the use of language. In fact, he felt that higher-level concept formation was probably dependent on the mediation of language. For example, Luria would contend that a concept such as democracy more than likely requires language for acquisition.

Teachers with children with learning problems are interested in the role of conceptualization and symbolization in the development of abstract reasoning. Johnson and Myklebust (1967) asserted that some children have difficulties in the process of concept formation itself. They argued that any deficit in the processes of perception, imagery, symbolization, or abstracting could interfere with conceptualization. Others have difficulty not so much in the process of conceptualization as in dealing with the more abstract concepts. As Johnson and Myklebust point out, an individual with disturbances in the processes of abstracting or conceptualizing may be identified as a concrete thinker.

Myers and Hammill (1982) note that children who cannot form abstract concepts often have learning impairments that require repetitive instruction. Children with learning disabilities are often described as having "concrete behavior characterized by a dependence upon immediate experience as opposed to abstract behavior that transcends any given immediate experience and results in the formation of conceptual categories" (p. 39). Many would argue that the difficulty exhibited by children with a learning disability is caused by a developmental lag and is not a permanent problem. In the case of children with intellectual developmental delays, however, the conceptualization problem may be permanent. Further, a body of research has been dedicated to trying to determine whether the conceptual behavior of children with intellectual developmental delays represents simply a delay or difference (Zigler & Balla, 1982; Robinson, Zigler, & Gallagher, 2000). To understand this problem researchers may, for example, look at how children with intellectual developmental delays use the role of language as a mediation device for concept formation (Field, 1977).

It is not uncommon for those working with hearing-impaired children to describe their cognitive behavior as concrete (Johnson & Myklebust, 1967). There are several difficulties with this notion, however children with hearing impairments may simply not have had a sufficient experiential base to adequately form concepts that would be expected of children with hearing. Another problem in understanding children with hearing impairments conceptualization is that these children live in a visual linguistic world. What may appear to be concrete behavior on the part of the child may simply be an artifact of one of the underlying rules of natural sign language systems. The rule is that the structure of an utterance cannot violate the visual world. For example, the word order of the structure "I finished my work, then watched television" is directly translatable into American Sign Language. "I watched television after I finished my work" is not, because it violates the visual sequence of events. Difficulties that children with hearing impairments have with the latter structure, when encountering it in English, are sometimes interpreted as evidence that the child is a concrete thinker. In truth, it may be simply that the child is having difficulty in dealing with a structure that violates the child's linguistic rules (also see Braden, 1994).

It is important to note that the relationship between sensory information, concept formation, and symbolization is not well understood. Research gives us only the most sketchy idea of what the relationship among the three might be. One field of philosophy, epistemology, has been dedicated to trying to understand these relationships. Introspection and logical reasoning remain the most powerful tools available to both psychology and philosophy for describing concept development and abstract reasoning.

In summary, the notion of abstract reasoning is used in two different ways. It can mean the process by which one identifies the salient characteristics in entities for purposes of categorization. Abstract reasoning can also be the process by which individuals deal with concepts that are based on other concepts, rather than concepts that are based on direct experience. Children with learning problems can have difficulties with either type of abstract reasoning. When difficulties are exhibited, the question arises as to whether the difference is simply developmental delay or a difference in cognitive processing. Some people working with learning-disabled children contend that they eventually outgrow problems in these areas. Children with intellectual disability may not necessarily do so. Children who are hearing impaired have also been described as "concrete" learners. However, their difficulties may be a result of too little experience and their use of visually based linguistic rules.

REFERENCES

Braden, J. P. (1994). *Deafness, deprivation, and IQ*. New York, NY: Plenum Press.

Field, D. (1977). The importance of verbal content in the training of Piagetian conversation skills. *Child Development*, 1583–1592.

Johnson, D. J., & Myklebust, H. R. (1967). *Learning disabilities: Educational principles and practices*. New York, NY: Grune & Stratton.

Luria, A. R. (1961). *The role of speech in the regulation of normal and abnormal behavior*. New York, NY: Liveright (Pergamon Press).

Myers, P. I., & Hammill, D. D. (1982). *Learning disabilities: Basic concepts, assessment practices, and instructional strategies*. Austin, TX: PRO-ED.

Robinson, N. M., Zigler, E., & Gallagher, J. J. (2000). Two tails of the normal curve: Similarities and differences in the study of mental retardation and giftedness. *American Psychologist, 55*, 1413–1424.

Zigler, E., & Balla, D. (1982). *Mental retardation: The developmental-difference controversy*. Hillsdale, NJ: Erlbaum.

CAROLYN BULLARD
Lewis & Clark College
Third edition

See also Concrete Operations; Deaf; Learning Disabilities

ABUSED CHILDREN, PSYCHOTHERAPY WITH

Today abused children are typically regarded as suffering from a primary illness (Quirk, 1980). A primary illness refers to the notion that living with a certain circumstance for a prolonged period of time creates a situation in the victim requiring primary treatment. The primary illness of child abuse has identifiable symptoms and etiology along with an official diagnosis and prescribed treatments.

Systematic comprehensive treatment for abused children, and adults who were abused as children, involves the ability of the clinician to identify and diagnose properly the dilemma and its ramifications and to facilitate the natural healing process from trauma. Thus the first step in treatment is the proper identification of child abuse as the problem to be treated.

Children who have been abused relive their abuse over and over in clear or symbolic ways. They dream abusive dreams, remember abusive situations, and in adulthood go so far as to recreate abusive relationships. The abuse manifests negative effects in interpersonal relationships, dissociative symptoms, problems with intimacy, and express difficulty in trusting others (Herman, 1981; Thomas, 2005). They are depressed and have difficulty in developing meaningful relationships or experiences in their lives. Adults who were abused children are often defensive, suspicious, nervous, and overly alert. They may be preoccupied with their bodily functions and may be labeled hypochondriacs. Insomnia is another frequently reported symptom, even in the absence of distressing nightmares. Abused children are also guilt-ridden, and experience much shame and self-hatred. Concentrating and following a task through to its completion is another problem area for this population (American Psychiatric Association, 1994; Mrazek & Kempe, 1981; Williams & Money, 1980).

Acting out the abuse in self-destructive ways such as drug abuse is frequently observed in this population, which is disproportionately represented in chemical and other addiction dependency treatment facilities. As teenagers, abused children often become runaways and act out their rage in criminal behavior. Abused children are also disproportionately represented in facilities for delinquents. A disproportionately large group in this population may attempt suicide, hallucinate, manifest seizures, and ultimately be placed in psychiatric hospitals. While these obvious problematic behaviors will occur at high rates, another observed phenomena of this population is the frequency with which they become quiet, good children who then marry an abusive partner. Other compulsive behaviors are frequently manifested by these children and subsequently they will be found as adults in Al-Anon, Alcoholics Anonymous, Narcotics Anonymous, Overeaters Anonymous, Gamblers Anonymous, and other self-help treatment programs.

Abused children as adults have difficulty with parenting. Appropriate discipline is difficult for them because it is too restimulating. Consequently, they will abdicate their parenting until the children eventually become abusive toward them (Justice & Justice, 1976). This promotes another likely place for adult abused children to reflect inadequacies—as parents of children in trouble. On the other hand, adult abused children may become abusive parents themselves. The inordinate numbers of child abusers that were themselves abused has been widely documented.

Because young and abused children live and grow with a wounded and fragmented personality, they often need intensive treatment efforts. The client who clings or annoys the clinician, reporting that something is missing from treatment, will often be a person who was abused. This person will often complain about the deficiencies of treatment and report that he or she has not been responded to reasonably. This type of reporting should be expected in view of the fact that abused children are wounded people who will have difficulty objectifying their relations: after all, their primary objects, Mom or Dad, abused them.

Treatment programs and clinicians should routinely be sensitive in recognizing and treating child abuse. When working with clients the following questions should be a routine part of the interview. What was your childhood like? How did your parents treat you? How were you disciplined? What were the punishments employed by your parents? Were you ever raped or seduced? Those who report having difficulty recalling all or crucial parts of their childhood should definitely be regarded as potentially having been abused. This self-induced amnesia, or dissociation, is a primitive form of defense against the pain and discomfort resulting from recall of an abusive situation. Naturally, this needs to be dealt with in a sensitive manner by the clinician, and the client should not be prematurely pushed into acknowledging information or feelings they are not prepared to confront.

Abused children often feel at fault for their experience of child abuse. They live with much guilt, shame, self-blame, and self-loathing. Often their abusers told them it was their fault. Child molesters use guilt as a tool with their victims in order to keep the secret, while parents who physically beat their children do so in the name of discipline. Yet, abused children mentally make their parents correct and good. Generally, therapists should enjoy relationships with people, but it is even more important for therapists of abused children to like their clients: While one might think that all therapists would like their clients, fragile clients often find themselves disliked by their therapists. Since they do not grow as the therapist expects, they experience rejection in the context of the therapeutic relationship.

Adults who were abused in childhood have unusual difficulty in establishing trust with the therapist, identifying and discussing feelings, and cooperating with the therapeutic process. Because their tormentors were often people they trusted (e.g., parents), abused children may recoil at the need to trust the therapist. Therefore, an unusually long working-through process is frequently required. This is often difficult for the novice therapist, educator, or other professional lacking information about child abuse and its symptoms.

Most children learn to cope by making decisions separate from the influence of their parents. Abused children have more to cope with, and fewer skills to do so. Reparenting applies here also. Regardless of age, abused children need to learn to live and cope in the real world, and come to recognize that not all people are as threatening as their abusive parents. Therefore, learning coping skills is essential to any successful treatment program. The following are examples of important coping skills to be addressed: learning to trust one's own instincts; learning to identify one's own needs; and learning to proceed to satisfy those needs. Another essential component to treatment is the development of an ability to identify and avoid close contact with abusive people.

Because abuse occurs in the context of an interpersonal relationship, the environment of a therapeutic group has proven itself a particularly helpful treatment modality. In view of the characteristics of this population, the following are important considerations for the leader of a group of abused children. The group should be initially supportive, gentle, homogeneous, and closed to new members after the group has begun. These elements are necessary to address the difficulty in trusting manifested by this population. The group needs to project an image of safety and members must be monitored from inappropriately expressing the rage some may possess. Confrontation must be kept well managed to further reduce regression that may be promoted by some of the more fragmented members. The group leader must monitor the development of any situation that may resemble the childhood abuse of any member in the group. A primary goal of the group is to develop understanding of the personal dynamics of abuse and coping skills that may prevent the development of similar abusive situations in the future.

REFERENCES

American Psychiatric Association. (1994). *Diagnostic and statistical manual of mental disorders* (4th ed.). Washington, DC: Author.

Herman, J. L. (1981). *Father-daughter incest*. Cambridge, MA: Harvard University Press.

Justice, B., & Justice, R. (1976). *The abusing family*. New York, NY: Human Sciences.

Mrazek, P. B., & Kempe, C. H. (Eds.). (1981). *Sexually abused children and their families*. New York, NY: Pergamon.

Quirk, J. P. (Ed.). (1980). *Readings in child abuse*. Guilford, CT: Special Learning.

Thomas, P. M. (2005). Dissociation and internal models of protection: Psychotherapy with child abuse survivors. *Psychotherapy: Theory, Research, Practice, Training, 42,* 20–36.

Williams, J. W., & Money, J. (Eds.). (1980). *Traumatic abuse and neglect of children at home*. Baltimore, MD: Johns Hopkins University Press.

CHARLES P. BARNARD
University of Wisconsin at Stout

See also Acting Out; Child Abuse; Etiology

ACADEMIC ASSESSMENT

The global function of achievement testing is to assess a student's attainment of academic content areas. Reading, written language, and mathematical functioning are the major domains under the rubric of academic achievement. Anastasi (1982) notes that traditionally academic assessment has been differentiated from aptitude/ability testing by the degree to which a measure is designed to assess uniform versus diverse antecedent experiences. To be categorized as a measure of academic achievement, a measure is designed to test a fairly uniform previous experience (e.g., first-grade instruction in reading). In contrast, an aptitude test would be designed to assess the impact of multiple or diverse antecedent experiences. Contemporary measurement specialists recognize that both achievement and aptitude tests assess acquired knowledge, but differ on the degree of specificity and abstraction.

Salvia and Ysseldyke (1981) have described four functions that achievement tests fulfill within the schools. They are used for screening students who may need more in-depth assessment to determine whether special services are appropriate; determining whether a child is eligible for placement in a special education class based on local criteria; assessing a child's strengths and weaknesses to facilitate decisions regarding his or her placement in an instructional sequence; and determining the impact of educational intervention on a class or group of students.

Achievement testing may be conceptualized along several lines: norm-referenced versus criterion referenced; individual versus group administered; and informal teacher-constructed versus standardized instruction. Each of these dimensions will be discussed to highlight the multifaceted construct of academic achievement assessment.

Norm-referenced testing (NRT) began to play a prominent role in American education after World War I. Army Alpha and Beta tests were used for the classification of recruits during the war. The Otis Group Intelligence Scale was published in 1918 by the World Book Company. This scale employed such advances as multiple-choice questions, answer sheets, test booklets, and improved normative sampling procedures (Cunningham, 1986). These advances were adapted for the first norm-referenced, standardized measure of academic achievement, the Stanford Achievement Test, published in 1923.

The most salient characteristic of norm-referenced achievement tests is that an examinee's performance on the test is interpreted by comparing his or her relative standing to a given reference group. The reference group or standardization sample is usually composed of representative peers of the same chronological age, or peers in the same grade placement. Performance on a norm-referenced test is typically expressed in scores based on the normal curve such as stanines, T-scores, and/or standard scores (which usually have a mean of 100 and a standard deviation of 15, or sometimes 16). Performance on a norm-referenced test may also be expressed in percentiles, which tell a student's standing relative to a hypothetical group of 100 children. For instance, a score at the 86th percentile indicates that the examinee scored better than 86 out of 100 of his or her hypothetical same-aged peers.

The major norm-referenced group achievement tests include the California Achievement Test (CTB/McGraw-Hill, 1985); the Comprehensive Test of Basic Skills (CTB/McGraw-Hill, 1981); the Iowa Test of Basic Skills (Hieronymus, Lindquist, & Hoover, 1983); the Metropolitan Achievement Test (Barlow, Farr, Hogan, & Prescott, 1978); and the Standard Achievement Test (Gardner, Rudman, Karlsen, & Merwin, 1982).

These group-administered tests have multiple levels, each designated for a specified grade range. For instance, the Stanford Achievement Test series has six levels: Primary Level 1 for grades 1.5–2.9; Primary Level 2 for 2.5–3.9; Primary Level 3 for 3.5–4.9; Intermediate Level 1 for 4.5–5.9; Intermediate Level 2 for 5.5–7.9; and Intermediate Level 3 for 7.0–9.9. Generally, these tests have gone through several revisions. The Stanford Achievement Test, for example, is in its seventh revision and has been in use in the public schools for over 60 years.

A primary difference between norm-referenced and criterion-referenced tests lies in the way they are interpreted. As noted, the norm-referenced achievement test is designed to give information on a given student's performance relative to a representative group of same-aged peers. In contrast, the criterion-referenced achievement test is designed to give information on a given student's performance in terms of whether he or she has learned a given concept or skill. Thus, the criterion-referenced measure is designed to tell what the student can and cannot do. For instance, the student can add single digit numerals with sums less than 10, but has not learned to regroup or perform simple subtraction problems. Since discrimination among students is not the purpose of a criterion-referenced test, the difficulty level of items and the power of items to separate students are not as important as they are in norm-referenced measures. The major issue in criterion-referenced measurement is whether items reflect a specified instructional domain. Most of the major group-administered achievement tests

have been adapted to yield criterion-referenced information. The problem with adapting norm-referenced tests is that there are a multiplicity of instructional objectives (Cunningham, 1986). Since each objective requires several test items to achieve an adequate level of reliability, the length of the test becomes unmanageable.

Up to this point group-administered measures have been used to illustrate the norm- versus criterion-referenced dimensions of academic assessment. Academic achievement testing may also be examined from the viewpoint of the administration format, either individual or group. While group achievement tests are usually given to a whole class by the regular education teacher, individual achievement measures are administered by specially trained personnel (special education teachers, educational diagnosticians, and school psychologists) to a child on a one-to-one basis. Typically, the child has been referred for testing because of academic or behavioral problems manifested in the regular classroom. A general distinction between group and individual measures relates to their use in the decision-making process. Group measures are designed to make decisions about groups, while individual tests are more appropriate for decisions concerning an individual. Therefore, caution must be exercised when attempting to interpret the results of a single child's performance on a group-administered measure. There are many variables that may influence a child's performance on a group-administered measure and result in an inaccurate portrayal of that child's academic skills. Misunderstanding instructions, fatigue, random guessing, class distractions, looking on a neighbor's response sheet, and so on, may invalidate a child's scores. When a child is being considered for placement in a special education program, a poor performance on a group-administered measure should be followed up with an individual assessment.

Finally, the academic achievement test may be approached by examining the degree to which the directions to students are standardized. The standardized test is one where the instructions and test questions are presented in the same manner to all examinees. On the other hand, in the teacher-constructed test, there is unlimited latitude in the construction and administration of test items. Both standardized and informal teacher-made tests have advantages and disadvantages. However, they should share certain attributes, that is, clear directions to students, careful development of items based on a table of specifications, and the type or format of test items.

Whether the directions to an achievement test are standardized or constructed by the teacher, building a table of specifications represents the first step in test construction. A table of specifications contains a listing of instructional objects as well as the relative emphasis to be assigned to each objective. For standardized measures of achievement, the table of specification is based on an examination of major textbook series used across the country. For instance, when reading subtests are constructed, the most widely used basal reading series are reviewed by the test developer. Note is taken at what point in the curricula various concepts are introduced. Invariably, decisions and compromises have to be made regarding content, because all basal reading series are not identical. As such, the consumer of both individual and group standardized achievement tests must examine the available measures, not just in terms of quality of standardization and reliability, but also with respect to the match between the concepts assessed by the test and those taught within the framework of the local curriculum.

A major difference between standardized and informal, teacher-developed tests is that the former usually represents many more hours of item development, refinement, empirical trials, and final selection of test items. In developing standardized achievement tests, considerable weight is placed on both content validity (the representativeness of the items to the domain being tested, and the appropriateness of the format and wording of items relative to the age level of the prospective examinees), and the empirical tryout of the items in terms of reliability. The advantage of the standardized test lies in its documented reliability (presented in an accompanying technical manual), and its ability to compare a student's performance with that of a reference group or specified criterion. Whereas standardized tests measure content that is common to reading and mathematics programs from around the country, the teacher-constructed tests can be specifically targeted to the content of the local curriculum, or to a specific teacher's class.

In addition to defining informal assessment as the administration of a teacher-constructed measure, the term may also be applied to diagnostic processes. These include error analysis, behavioral observation, and the learner's relations to various instructional strategies (Sedlak, Sedlak, & Steppe-Jones, 1982). This last process is flexible and dynamic. A psychoeducational examiner presents tasks to the student in a branching manner similar to the operation of a branching computer-assisted instructional program. Information about the student's mastery of various skills is gleaned from analysis of his or her errors. Error analysis has been applied to reading, writing, mathematics, second language learning, and spelling (Bejar, 1984). The analysis is usually conducted within a "content" framework, such as an educational taxonomy.

Mathematical functioning is a key area where error analysis has been profitably employed (Brown & VanLehn, 1982). Ashlock (1976) offers useful exercises in a semiprogrammed text to help detect common error patterns in computation. Lankford (1974) demonstrated the value of having a student think aloud while solving arithmetic problems. Thus, when an error is made, the computation strategy used by the student becomes apparent. Roberts (1968) has noted four common error categories for arithmetic computation: selecting the wrong operation; erring in recalling a specific arithmetic fact; attempting the correct operation but using an inappropriate algorithm; and random responding that has no apparent relationship to the problem.

Another strategy that has a long history of success for assessment of academic skills is curriculum-based assessment (CBA; Fuchs, Fuchs, Prentice, Hamlett, Finelli, & Courey, 2004). CBA attempts to link assessment more directly to classroom instruction and to provide a more direct assessment of a student's instructional needs (Shapiro & Elliott, 1999). Although touted as an alternative to traditional norm-referenced testing, CBA and NRT are seen best as complementary models, and not as competitive ones as alternatives implies.

In summary, academic achievement assessment is used to make decisions about students. These decisions may be made from a normative perspective or in terms of students' mastery of a specified skill. Depending on the administration, format decisions can be made for an individual student or for groups of students. Norm-referenced achievement tests provide information about a student's relative standing compared with that of a reference group, while criterion-referenced tests and informal assessments may be used to make informed decisions about a student's future instructional needs. Specific achievement tests are described throughout this work.

REFERENCES

Anastasi, A. (1982). *Psychological testing* (5th ed.). New York, NY: Macmillan.

Ashlock, R. B. (1976). *Error patterns in computation: A semiprogrammed approach* (2nd ed.). Columbus, OH: Merrill.

Barlow, I. H., Farr, R., Hogan, T. P., & Prescott, G. A. (1978). *Metropolitan Achievement Tests* (5th ed.). New York, NY: Psychological Corp.

Bejar, I. I. (1984). Educational diagnostic assessment. *Journal of Educational Measurement, 21,* 175–189.

Brown, J. S., & VanLehn, K. (1982). Toward a generative theory of "bugs." In T. P. Carpenter, J. M. Moser, & T. A. Romberg (Eds.), *Addition and subtraction: A cognitive perspective.* Hillsdale, NJ: Erlbaum.

CTB/McGraw-Hill. (1981). *The Comprehensive Tests of Basic Skills.* New York, NY: Author.

CTB/McGraw-Hill. (1985). *California Achievement Tests.* New York, NY: Author.

Cunningham, G. K. (1986). *Educational and psychological measurement.* New York, NY: Macmillan.

Fuchs, L. S., Fuchs, D., Prentice, K., Hamlett, K., Finelli, R., & Courey, S. J. (2004). Enhancing mathematical problem solving among third-grade students with schema-based instruction. *Journal of Educational Psychology, 96,* 635–647.

Gardner, E. G., Rudman, H. C., Karlsen, B., & Merwin, J. C. (1982). *Stanford Achievement Test* (1982 ed.). New York, NY: Psychological Corp.

Hieronymus, A. N., Lindquist, E. F., & Hoover, H. D. (1983). *Iowa Tests of Basic Skills.* Chicago, IL: Riverside.

Jastak, S., & Wilkinson, G. S. (1984). *The Wide Range Achievement Test–Revised* (1984 revised ed.). Wilmington, DE: Jastak Associates.

Lankford, F. G. (1974). What can a teacher learn about a pupil's thinking through oral interviews? *Arithmetic Teacher, 21,* 26–32.

Roberts, G. H. (1968). The failure strategies of third-grade arithmetic pupils. *Arithmetic Teacher, 15,* 442–446.

Salvia, J., & Ysseldyke, J. E. (1981). *Assessment in special and remedial education* (2nd ed.). Boston, MA: Houghton-Mifflin.

Sedlak, R. A., Sedlak, D. M., & Steppe-Jones, C. (1982). Informal assessment. In D. A. Sabatino & L. Mann (Eds.), *A handbook of diagnostic and prescriptive teaching*. Rockville, MD: Aspen Systems.

Shapiro, E., & Elliott, S. N. (1999). Curriculum-based assessment and other performance based assessment strategies. In C. R. Reynolds & T. B. Gutkin (Eds.), *The handbook of school psychology* (3rd ed., pp. 383–408). New York, NY: Wiley.

JACK A. CUMMINGS
Indiana University
Third edition

See also Achievement Tests; Criterion-Referenced Testing; Curriculum-Based Assessment; Norm-Referenced Testing; specific test names

ACADEMIC LANGUAGE

Academic language (instructional discourse, cognitive-academic language, or school language) is the way teachers and students organize their communication interactions within educational environments. The purpose is to transmit knowledge and skills related to academics. In contrast, everyday discourse (conversation, social discourse, or basic interpersonal communication) has as its general purpose the regulation of social interaction or interpersonal functions (Chamot & O'Malley, 1994; Wallach & Butler, 1994; Wallach & Miller, 1988; Westby, 1985).

Comprehending and producing academic language requires more cognitive and linguistic complexity than using social language. The transition from oral communication to literate communication marks the need for increased cognitive and linguistic complexity in the teaching-learning process (Cummins, 1983; Larson & McKinley, 1995; Merritt & Culatta, 1998; Naremore, Densmore, & Harman, 1995; Nelson, 1998; Ripich & Creaghead, 1994; Westby, 1997, 1998). Major cognitive, linguistic, and contextual characteristics of academic language include:

Cognitive: abstract concepts; cognitively demanding tasks (critical thinking [analytical and creative],

problem solving, decision making); language-thinking and executive functions that are stabilizing (Nelson, 1998; Wallach & Butler, 1994; Wallach & Miller, 1988; Westby, 1998).

Linguistic: complex morphological markers, syntactic transformations, and semantic relationships and networks with explicit vocabulary, resulting in increased oral and text cohesion and coherence; the ability to project, predict, and infer; increased demand for oral and text *form* (pronunciation, spelling, punctuation, organization), *content* (accuracy, synthesis cohesion, and coherence), and *style* (advanced narrative levels and expository genres) (Hedberg & Westby, 1993; Hughes, McGillivray, & Schmidek, 1997; Naremore et al., 1995; Nelson, 1998; Tough, 1979; Wallach & Butler, 1994; Wallach & Miller, 1988).

Contextual: reduced contextual clues; indeterminate audience diffuse in time and space; often physical and temporal separation between sender (writer, speaker) and receiver (listener, reader) (Merritt & Culatta, 1998; Nelson, 1998; Wallach & Butler, 1994; Wallach & Miller, 1988).

Academic communication-learning problems are associated with many developmental and acquired disorders. Academic language use and rules vary from culture to culture (Solomon & Rhodes, 1996) and are now also influenced by technology (Cummins, 2000). However, the consensus is that to succeed in mainstream educational settings in the course of life students must be able to understand and use the cognitive, linguistic, and contextual conventions associated with academic language.

REFERENCES

Chamot, A. U., & O'Malley, J. M. (1994). *The CALLA handbook: Implementing the cognitive academic language learning approach*. Reading, MA: Addison-Wesley.

Cummins, J. (1983). Language proficiency and academic achievement. In J. W. Oller, Jr. (Ed.), *Issues in language testing research*. Rowley, MA: Newbury House.

Cummins, J. (2000). Academic language learning, transformative pedagogy, and information technology: Toward a critical balance. *TESOL Quarterly, 34,* 537–547.

Hedberg, N. L., & Westby, C. E. (1993). *Analyzing storytelling skills: Theory to practice*. Tucson, AZ: Communication Skill Builders.

Hughes, D., McGillivray, L., & Schmidek, M. (1997). *Guide to narrative language*. Eau Claire, WI: Thinking Publications.

Larson, V. L., & McKinley, N. (1995). *Language disorders in older students: Preadolescents and adolescents*. Eau Claire, WI: Thinking Publications.

Merritt, D. D., & Culatta, B. (1998). *Language intervention in the classroom*. San Diego, CA: Singular Publishing Group.

Naremore, R. C., Densmore, A. E., & Harman, D. R. (1995). *Language intervention with school-aged children: Conversation, narrative, and text*. San Diego, CA: Singular Publishing Group.

Nelson, N. W. (1998). *Childhood language disorders in context: Infancy through adolescence* (2nd ed.). Boston, MA: Allyn & Bacon.

Ripich, D. N., & Creaghead, N. A. (Eds.). (1994). *School discourse problems* (2nd ed.). San Diego, CA: Singular Publishing Group.

Solomon, J., & Rhodes, N. (1996). Assessing academic language: Results of a survey. *TESOL Journal, 5*, 5–8.

Tough, J. (1979). *Talk for teaching and learning*. Portsmouth, NH: Heinemann.

Wallach, G. P., & Butler, K. G. (1994). *Language learning disabilities in school-age children and adolescents: Some principles and applications*. New York, NY: Merrill/Macmillan College Publishing.

Wallach, G. P., & Miller, L. (1988). *Language intervention and academic success*. San Diego, CA: College-Hill/Little, Brown.

Westby, C. E. (1985). From learning to talk to talking to learn: Oral-literate language differences (pps 191–213). In C. Simon (Ed.), *Communication skills and classroom success: Therapy methodologies for language-learning disabled students*. San Diego, CA: College-Hill.

Westby, C. E. (1997). There's more to passing than knowing the answers. *Language, Speech and Hearing Services in the Schools, 28*, 274–287.

Westby, C. E. (1998). Communicative refinement in school age and adolescence. In W. O. Haynes & B. B. Shulman (Eds.), *Communication development: Foundations, processes, and clinical applications* (pp. 311–360). Baltimore, MD: Williams and Wilkins.

STEPHEN S. FARMER
New Mexico State University

See also Discourse; Language Assessment

ACADEMIC SKILLS

While to some individuals the definition of academic skills conjures up the three Rs, to others the delineation of the academic skills most important to the process of special education is a task that poses an awesome definitional problem. To the preschool special educator, for example, certain fine motor skills may be defined as important academic skills. On the other hand, for the special educator working at the secondary level, the ability to accept positive and negative feedback (social skills), driving skills, or home economics may be considered important academic skills that warrant inclusion in the secondary special education curriculum.

A comprehensive sourcebook on research on teaching presents detailed analyses of seven academic skill areas: written composition, reading, mathematics, natural sciences, arts and aesthetics, moral and values education, and social studies (Wittrock, 1986). At least a few of these areas would be considered by most individuals to be core or basic academic skills. The fact that these academic skill areas have entire chapters devoted to them also indicates that there is enough research, theory, or perhaps controversy regarding them as to allow them to be studied and discussed extensively.

Beyond the issue of defining academic skills are the related issues of the rise and fall of skills across generations (which is constantly addressed by the popular media), and equally important, the procedures by which these skills are taught and acquired by students in special education. Cartwright, Cartwright, and Ward (1981) list several approaches used by special education teachers to impart academic skills; these include the diagnostic teaching model, remedial and compensatory education models, direct instruction, task analysis, perceptual-motor training, inquiry, modeling, media-based instruction, education games, and computer-assisted and computer-managed instruction. Two additional instructional approaches that were popularized in the 1970s include mastery learning and cooperative learning (Stallings & Stipek, 1986). In any case, current instructional methodology requires evidence-based instruction for any academic skill and in any setting (Lerman, Vorndran, Addison, & Contrucci, 2004; Odom, Brantlinger, Gersten, Horner, & Thompson, 2005).

With regard to learner characteristics that affect the acquisition of academic skills, Wittrock (1986) suggests the following broad categories for consideration: students' perceptions and expectations, attention, motivation, learning and memory, comprehension and knowledge acquisition, learning strategies, and metacognitive processes. In summary, special educators must first define the academic skills that their students must acquire and then consider instructional, student, and other variables in planning for the optimal acquisition of academic skills.

REFERENCES

Cartwright, P. G., Cartwright, C. A., & Ward, M. E. (1981). *Educating special learners*. Belmont, CA: Wadsworth.

Lerman, D. C., Vorndran, C. M., Addison, L., & Contrucci, S. (2004). Preparing teachers in evidence-based practices for young children. *School Psychology Review, 34*, 510–526.

Odom, S. L., Brantlinger, E., Gersten, R., Homer, R. H., & Thompson, B. (2005). Research in special education: Scientific methods and evidence-based practices. *Exceptional Children, 71*, 137–148.

Stallings, J. A., & Stipek, D. (1986). Research on early childhood and elementary school teaching programs. In M. C. Wittrock (Ed.), *Handbook of research on teaching*. New York, NY: Macmillan.

Wittrock, M. C. (1986). Students' thought processes. In M. C. Wittrock (Ed.), *Handbook of research on teaching*. New York, NY: Macmillan.

RANDY W. KAMPHAUS
University of Georgia

See *also* Achievement Tests; Memory Disorders; Metacognition

ACADEMIC THERAPY

Academic Therapy was the first journal designed for specialists (special education teachers, educational diagnosticians, psychologists, resource room specialists, practitioners in speech, language, communication, vision, and hearing) who are in direct contact with children manifesting learning, language, and communication difficulties. Since 1965, it has established a reputation for easy-to-read and practical articles that focus on "what works" in the special clinical, therapeutic, or classroom setting. Contributors are teachers, professors, and specialists. Articles are short and are selected on the basis of their usefulness and ability to be put into immediate use by the journal reader. Each issue includes listings of new materials, current news on the national level, and ideas for home management. *Academic Therapy* is published five times during the year: September, November, January, March, and May.

JOHN ARENA
Academic Therapy Publications

ACADEMIC THERAPY PUBLICATIONS

A family-owned company since 1965, Academic Therapy Publications (ATP) offers a range of assessments and supplementary educational materials for teachers of general education, special education, and English as a second language; parents; speech-language pathologists; occupational and educational therapists; school psychologists; and specialists working with persons who have reading, learning, and communication deficits or disabilities. ATP is separated into four divisions and publishes two free biannual catalogs: one for tests, assessments, and interventions, the other for readers.

Academic Therapy Publications/ATP Assessments provides a broad range of testing, evaluation, and intervention materials. These include professional reference books, standardized assessments of various academic skills and processing abilities, supplemental curricula, and a variety of teacher and parent resources such as skill-building games and workbooks (http://www.academictherapy.com).

Ann Arbor Publishers specializes in materials and workbooks that develop letter recognition and eye movement skills, two fundamental components of basic reading ability (http://www.academictherapy.com/support/arbor .tpl).

Arena Press publishes the Consortium On Reading Excellence's (CORE) *Literacy Library* series, a research-based reading assessment and instruction program, as well as a line of high interest literature and word search puzzle games (http://www.arenapressbooks.com/).

High Noon Books provides reading intervention programs, workbooks, and a selection of paperbacks, graphic novels, and audio read-along books designed for struggling readers and those learning English as a second language. These fiction and nonfiction chapter books are written at first through fourth grade reading levels yet are designed to engage students of all ages with subject material that is more appealing to their maturity level (http://www.HighNoonBooks.com).

The office address of Academic Therapy Publications is 20 Commercial Boulevard, Novato, CA 94949. TEL.: (800) 422-7249.

ANNA M. ARENA
Academic Therapy Publications
First edition

RACHEL M. TOPLIS
Falcon School District 49, Colorado Springs,
    Colorado
Third edition

AUSTIN J. KARPOLA
The Chicago School of Professional Psychology,
    Chicago, IL
Fourth edition

ACALCULIA

The ability to complete calculations often is impaired in individuals with traumatic brain injury (TBI) or other focal brain damage (Ardila & Rosselli, 1994) and represents a loss in function rather than a failure to develop. For example, consider a fourth grader who has already mastered basic operations and basic facts, can do grade-appropriate calculation, and is meeting expectancy in the classroom. An accident occurs, and there is brain damage, and one of the residual problems from the brain damage is that the child can no longer recall basic facts or complete basic computational problems. Originally referred to in this way by Henschen in 1925 (Ardila & Rosselli, 2002), this loss of ability attributed to brain injury or damage is called *acalculia* (Loring, 1999).

Although calculation abilities are routinely included as part of psychoeducational and neuropsychological assessments, there is limited research specific to acalculia. Ardila and Rosselli (2002) reviewed the existing research and offered a conceptualization of acalculia that is dissociated from language disorders. They concluded that arithmetic skills are associated with a range of other ability domains, including verbal memory, visuospatial ability, visual perception, constructional abilities, as well as language. Each of these is associated, in turn, with differing structures of the brain, as such the location(s) of the injury or damage result(s) in a variety of calculation disorders. Most often indicated in calculation are the left prefrontal areas and posterior superior temporal gyrus (Burbaud et al., 1995; Sakurai, Momose, Iwata, Sasaki, & Kanazawa, 1996). Further, calculation ability is highly related to overall intellectual functioning and the ability to manipulate acquired knowledge (Mandell, Knoefel, & Albert, 1994); functional magnetic resonance imaging (MRI) and positron emission tomography (PET) reveal a complex pattern of brain activity to be involved in completing arithmetic operations (Burbaud et al., 1995; Sakurai et al., 1996).

There are different forms of acalculia (e.g., Ardila & Rosselli, 1990; Grafman, 1988). *Primary acalculia* is said to occur when the primary deficit is in arithmetic skills. In contrast, acalculia that is secondary to some other disorder, such as a language disorder, is referred to as *secondary acalculia* (Ardila & Rosselli, 1990). Individuals with primary acalculia have difficulty with numerical concepts, with the concept of quantity, with numerical signs, with magnitude estimation, and with syntactic operations (e.g., regrouping, borrowing). For primary acalculia, the deficits are evident regardless of modality of presentation of the math task or output. Abilities such as counting and rote fact learning may not be impaired (Ardila & Rosselli, 1994). Primary acalculia is associated with damage to the left angular gyrus (e.g., Gerstmann, 1940; Levin et al., 1993) or the left parietal area (Rosselli & Ardila, 1989). Acalculia frequently co-occurs with acquired language disorder or aphasia. In particular, individuals with acalculia also may evidence difficulty in anomia, word-finding difficulties, and language comprehension problems. This is not surprising in that numbers are encoded verbally, and some mathematical tasks (e.g., word problems) require language.

Assessment for acalculia is intended to determine (a) if the individual is experiencing significant difficulty in calculation following brain injury or damage, (b) to determine the pattern of difficulties (i.e., through error analysis) the individual is evidencing, (c) to identify any collateral or related deficits, and (d) to develop a rehabilitation program (Ardila & Rosselli, 2002). Available measures for such assessment are limited to specific subtests of broad measures of cognitive ability and achievement tests.

Curriculum-based measures of mathematical skills also may be helpful in identifying subtle deficits. In all, assessment for acalculia should include a variety of tasks such as counting, enumeration, reading numbers, writing numbers, reading and writing arithmetical signs, rote learning, magnitude comparison (i.e., which is greater?), arithmetic operations, aligning numbers in columns, mental calculation, and so on (Ardila & Rosselli, 2002). Determination of the types of errors (e.g., errors in signs, errors in algorithms, errors in borrowing or carrying over) can be useful in determining the intervention plan. Multiple techniques have been used successfully to address acalculia (see Ardila & Rosselli, 2002).

REFERENCES

Ardila, A., & Rosselli, M. (1990). Acalculias. *Behavioral Neurology, 3,* 39–48.

Ardila, A., & Rosselli, M. (1994). Spatial acalculia. *International Journal of Neuroscience, 78,* 177–184.

Ardila, A., & Rosselli, M. (2002). Acalculia and dyscalculia. *Neuropsychology Review, 12,* 179–231.

Burbaud, P., Degreze, P., Lafon, P., Franconi, J. M., Bouligand, B., Bioulac, B., et al. (1995). Lateralization of prefrontal activation during internal mental calculation: A functional magnetic resonance imaging study. *Journal of Neurophysiology, 74,* 2194–2200.

Gerstmann, J. (1940). The syndrome of finger agnosia, disorientation for right and left, agraphia, and acalculia. *Archives of Neurology and Psychiatry, 44,* 398–404.

Grafman, J. (1988). Acalculia. In F. Boller, J. Grafman, G. Rizzolatti, & H. Goodglass (Eds.), *Handbook of neuropsychology* (Vol. *1,* pp. 121–136). Amsterdam: Elsevier.

Levin, H. S., Goldstein, F. C., & Spiers, P. A. (1993). Acalculia. In K. M. Heilman & E. Valenstein (Eds.), *Acalculia in clinical neuropsychology* (pp. 91–122). New York, NY: Oxford University Press.

Loring, D. W. (Ed.). (1999). *INS dictionary of neuropsychology.* New York, NY: Oxford University Press.

Mandell, A. M., Knoefel, J. E., & Albert, M. L. (1994). Mental status examination in the elderly. In A. L. Albert & J. E. Knoefel (Eds.), *Clinical neurology of aging* (pp. 277–313). New York, NY: Oxford University Press.

Rosselli, M., & Ardila, A. (1989). Calculation deficits in patients with right and left hemisphere damage. *Neuropsychologia, 27,* 607–618.

Sakurai, Y., Momose, T., Iwata, M., Sasaki, Y., & Kanazawa, J. (1996). Activation of prefrontal and posterior superior temporal areas in visual calculation. *Journal of Neurological Science, 39,* 89–94.

CYNTHIA A. RICCIO
Texas A&M University

See also Arithmetic Remediation; Dyscalculiad; Traumatic Brain Injury; Traumatic Brain Injury in Children

ACCELERATION OF GIFTED CHILDREN

Acceleration has been defined as "progress through an educational program at rates faster or at ages younger than conventional" (Pressey, 1949, p. 2). Acceleration of gifted children is employed to allow students to engage in academics at the appropriate individual pace and level of complexity. Acceleration is a broad term that encompasses multiple programs and service delivery models for gifted students (Southern & Jones, 2004), but is typically conceptualized in one of two ways. In the first, within-class methods or beyond class methods are considered (VanTassell-Baska & Sher, 2011).

Within-class methods include:

- Diagnostic assessment
- Cluster grouping (aggregating students with similar interests and abilities within the same curricular activity)
- Follow-up curricular intervention

Beyond-class methods include:

- Early admission to postsecondary coursework
- Content acceleration
- Grade advancement

In the second model, acceleration is conceptualized as either grade-based or subject-based. While grade-based acceleration shortens the progression through traditional schooling, subject-based acceleration involves exposure to more advanced content and skills within a specific subject. Grade-based acceleration can be performed in a variety of ways, including the following options:

- Early admission to kindergarten or first grade
- Grade advancement (e.g., "grade skipping") of 2 or more years
- Grade telescoping, which involves the compression of academic content into atypically small time frames (e.g., 4 years of high school into 2 years)

Various methods of subject-based acceleration may include the following:

- Use of a self-paced curriculum (*compacted curriculum*) in which progress is determined by content mastery rather than a predetermined pace.
- Concurrent enrollment, in which students enroll in classes across grade levels.
- Mentorship by a content area expert (Siegle, McCoach, & Wilson, 2009).
- Credit by examination to show readiness for more advanced curricula.

- Delivery of content via distance learning, which allows for a wide array of learning opportunities for gifted students, particularly as asynchronous delivery has advanced to allow coursework to be completed at irregular times.

Acceleration is a practice that has been considered to be controversial due to common belief that the practice is detrimental for social development despite little supportive evidence. In fact, multiple longitudinal studies have supported multiple forms of acceleration (e.g., early college entrance, early school entrance, grade skipping) as being positive for social development, self-esteem, and motivation (Kulik, 2004; Neihart, 2007; Rogers, 2002; Sayler & Brookshire, 1993; Shepard, Nicpon, & Doobay, 2009; Wai, Lubinski, Benbow, & Steiger, 2010).

REFERENCES

Kulik, J. A. (2004). Meta-analytic studies of acceleration. In N. Colangelo, S. Assouline, & M. U. M. Gross (Eds.), *A nation deceived: How schools hold back America's brightest students* (Vol. 2, pp. 13–22). Iowa City: University of Iowa, The Connie Belin & Jacqueline N. Blank International Center for Gifted Education and Talent Development.

Neihart, M. (2007). The socioaffective impact of acceleration and ability grouping: Recommendations for best practice. *Gifted Child Quarterly, 51*, 330–341.

Pressey, S. L. (1949). *Educational acceleration: Appraisals and basic problems* (Ohio State University Studies, Bureau of Educational Research Monograph No. 31). Columbus: Ohio State University Press.

Rogers, K. B. (2002). Effects of acceleration on gifted learners. In M. Neihart & S. Reis (Eds.), *The social and emotional development of gifted children: What do we know?* (pp. 3–12). Waco, TX: Prufrock Press.

Sayler, M. F., & Brookshire, W. K. (1993). Social, emotional, and behavioral adjustment of accelerated students, students in gifted classes, and regular students in eighth grade. *Gifted Child Quarterly, 37*, 150–154.

Shepard, S. J., Nicpon, M. F., & Doobay, A. F. (2009). Early entrance to college and self-concept: Comparisons across the first semester of enrollment. *Journal of Advanced Academics, 21*(4), 40–57.

Siegle, D., McCoach, D. B., & Wilson, H. E. (2009). Extending learning through mentorships. In F. A. Karnes, & S. M. Bean (Eds.), *Methods and materials for teaching the gifted* (pp. 519–563). Waco, TX: Prufrock Press.

Southern, W. T., & Jones, E. D. (2004). Types of acceleration: Dimensions and issues. In N. Colangelo, S. Assouline, & M. U. M. Gross (Eds.), *A nation deceived: How schools hold back America's brightest students* (Vol. 2, pp. 5–12). Iowa City: The University of Iowa, The Connie Belin & Jacqueline N. Blank International Center for Gifted Education and Talent Development.

VanTassel-Baska, J., & Sher, B. T. (2011). Accelerating learning experiences in core content areas. In J. VanTassel-Baska, &

C. A. Little (Eds.), *Content-based curriculum for high-ability learners* (pp. 49–69). Waco, TX: Prufrock Press.

Wai, J., Lubinski, D., Benbow, C. P., & Steiger, J. H. (2010). Accomplishment in science, technology, engineering, and mathematics (STEM) and its relation to STEM educational dose: A 25-year longitudinal study. *Journal of Educational Psychology*, *102*(4), 860–871. doi:10.1037/a0019454

Wells, R., Lohman, D., & Marron, M. (2009). What factors are associated with grade acceleration? An analysis and comparison of two U.S. databases. *Journal of Advanced Academics*, *20*(2), 248–273.

Benjamin A. Mason
Texas A&M University
Fourth edition

See also **Gifted and Talented Children; Gifted Children**

ACCESS BOARD

The Access Board (formerly the Federal Architectural and Transportation Barriers Compliance Board) is a federal commission responsible for accessibility issues of federal facilities. According to their statement of purpose, the Access Board is an independent federal agency devoted to accessibility for people with disabilities. Created in 1973 to ensure access to federally funded facilities, the Board is now a leading source of information on accessible design. The Board develops and maintains design criteria for the built environment, transit vehicles, telecommunications equipment, and for electronic and information technology. It also provides technical assistance and training on these requirements and on accessible design and continues to enforce accessibility standards that cover federally funded facilities (United States Access Board, 2007).

The Access Board was instituted as a result of an increasing need for federal coordination of access issues in communication, architecture, and transportation settings. In recent years, many of its efforts have focused on information, specifically communications accessibility. In 2007, the Access Board published a set of communication guidelines that covered the accessibility of software applications and operating systems, web-based intranet and Internet information and applications, telecommunications products, video and multimedia products, self-contained or closed products, and desktop and portable computers. Of particular interest are the web-based accessibility guidelines.

In 2010, the Board's vision is to "achieve a fully accessible America for all" and "lead to the development, advancement, and implementation of accessibility requirements." Four goals create the foundation for the work implemented by the Access Board: (1) develop and maintain accessibility requirements, (2) educate stakeholders about accessibility, (3) enforce compliance with the ABA, and (4) anticipate opportunities for accessibility in our changing environment.

In addition to ensuring Americans with Disabilities have access to public areas, transportation, and housing, the Access Board also raises awareness for the public to engage in topics or issue of concern. Awareness campaigns were established to implement projects and programs to improve infrastructures, transportation, energy efficiency, education, and healthcare. All information was retrieved from: http://www.access-board.gov/about/par.htm (August 1, 2011).

For additional information on the Access Board, please contact: *ADA Accessibility Guidelines* Access Board, tel.: (800) 872-2253 (voice), (800) 993-2822 (TTY), website: http://www.access-board.gov/contact.htm

REFERENCES

About the Access Board. Retrieved from http://www.access-board.gov/about.htm

United States Access Board. (2007b). Telecommunications Act Accessibility Guidelines. Retrieved from http://www.access-board.gov/guidelines-and-standards/communications-a-it/about-the-telecommunications-act-guidelines/section-255-guidelines/preamble/summary?highlight=WyJ0ZWxlY29tbXVuaWNhdGlvbnMiLCJhY3QiLCJ0ZWxlY29tbXVuaWNhdGlvbnMgYWN0Il0=

United States Access Board. (2007c). Transportation vehicles. Retrieved from http://www.access-board.gov/transit/index.htm

David Sweeney
Texas A&M University
Third edition

See also **Accessibility of Programs; Americans With Disabilities Act**

ACCESSIBILITY

Accessibility refers to the qualities of a product that support, or inhibit, its use by people with disabilities. Accessibility is related to, but different from, usability, which is the evaluation of user's efficiency and effectiveness with a product. Accessibility is a core construct in the field of assistive technology because of the limitations inherently associated with disabilities. The very nature of a disability frequently interferes with how a task is completed. However, awareness of the impact of disabilities is not always common knowledge as product designers make assumptions about the characteristics of the intended user.

The transition from inaccessible design to universally accessible design will involve awareness training,

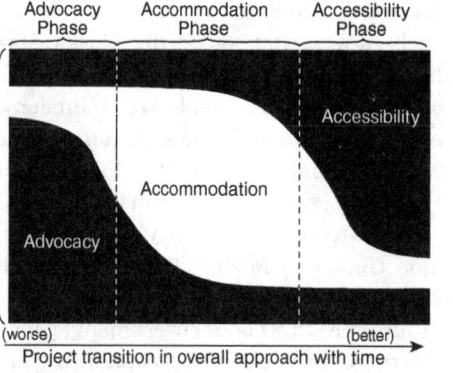

Advocacy Phase   Accommodation Phase   Accessibility Phase

A System's Overall Approach at any point in time (expressed as the proportions of the three strategies used to meet the needs of people with disabilities)

Accessibility

Accommodation

Advocacy

(worse)   (better)

Project transition in overall approach with time

Figure A.1. Model and transition of approach.
The A3 Model illustrates the dynamic nature of advocacy, accommodations, and accessibility in three developmental phases. The differential impact of the three components in terms of time, effort, and focus are illustrated by the waves across phases.
Source: Copyright © 2000, 2001 by Schwanke, Smith, and Edyburn.

new technical development, and time. The A3 Model (Schwanke, Smith, & Edyburn, 2001) illustrates the ebb and flow of concurrent interactions between advocacy, accommodation, and accessibility across a three-phase developmental cycle required to achieve universal accessibility (see Figure A.1).

Advocacy efforts raise awareness of inequity and highlight the need for system change to respond to the needs of individuals with disabilities. *Accommodations* are the typical response to advocacy. Inaccessible environments and materials are modified and made available. In most cases, accommodations are provided upon request (i.e., reactive). While this represents a significant improvement over situations found in the earlier phase, accommodations tend to maintain inequality since there may be a delay (i.e., time needed to convert a handout from print to braille), it may require special effort to obtain (i.e., call ahead to schedule), or it may require going to a special location (i.e., the only computer with text enlargement software is in the library). *Accessibility* describes an environment where access is equitably provided to everyone at the same time. Often this is accomplished through outstanding design (i.e., ergonomic furniture, software with accessibility, and performance supports built-in). All three factors are present in each phase. However, the differential impact of the three components in terms of time, effort, and focus are illustrated by the waves across phases that reflect a change in how time, effort, and resources are allocated. The A3 Model is believed to be relevant for describing the change process experienced by both individuals and organizations as they work toward achieving universal accessibility.

The issue of accessibility manifests itself in three ways in special education: (1) advocating for accessible design, (2) providing assistive technology and accommodations to compensate for an impairment, and (3) developing technical standards for making products accessible. The goal of universal accessibility involves the design of products

that can be used by the widest possible array of people (Vanderheiden & Henry, 2003).

Advocating for Accessible Design

Accessible design does not happen naturally. In fact, researchers have hypothesized that the default model of design is known as "ego design," that is, designing a product with assumptions that everyone is like me (Molenbroek & de Bruin, 2006). This is a powerful explanation for why there are inherent barriers found in mass-market products such as digital textbooks (Wiazowski, 2010), ebook readers (Parry, 2010), online learning systems (Brunvand & Abadeh, 2010; Burgstahler, 2006; Erath & Larkin, 2004), and software (Golden, 2002), that are discovered to be inaccessible to some individuals with disabilities after the product has been commercially released.

A powerful approach for advocating for accessible design involves helping others understand the special needs of individuals with disabilities, and how the interventions that will help not only this subgroup of the population, can also be made available to others for their benefit (such as senior citizens who are experiencing limitations as a result of the aging process). Indeed, this tactic was first successfully used in the mid-1990s in helping the computer industry understand the benefit of building accessibility features into computer operating systems (Atkinson, Neal, & Grechus, 2003; Niemeijer, 2005) rather than require accessibility interventions to be provided as an after-market add-on.

Advocating for accessible design involves raising awareness of the need for equal access (i.e., access to all the same information, at the same time, as nonhandicapped peers). There is considerable technical knowledge on how to design information and products so they are universally accessible (discussed below). However, such knowledge is not always readily available to nonspecialists. As a result, the literature provides a number of advocacy strategies, including: Assistive technology self-advocacy (Arizona Center for Disability Law, 2008), the use of an advocate (Edyburn, 2009), and training all stakeholders to be committed to accessible design (Thompson, 2003). Advocacy has also occurred in the context of arguments for digital equity (Norris, Sullivan, Poirot, & Soloway, 2003; Solomon, 2002).

Providing Assistive Technology and Accommodations to Compensate for an Impairment

In describing barriers to access associated with augmentative communication interventions, Beukelman and Mirenda (1998) developed a framework that is useful for understanding the nature of barriers. They suggest there are two types of barriers. Access barriers result from an individual's impairments. Assistive technology can be used to overcome and workaround access barriers. However, they identified five types of opportunity barriers:

Policy barriers, practice barriers, attitude barriers, knowledge barriers, and skill barriers that are more formidable to overcome.

The need for accommodations and modifications emerges when there is a mismatch between the abilities of the user and the requirements of a product or device. For example, when an instructional designer creates an audio file, and fails to understand that a deaf individual would like to have access to the information, a barrier is created. Or, when a designer assumes that everyone can use a standard computer keyboard, access barriers are created that prevent individuals with physical or cognitive limitations from interacting with the computer. Similarly, when curriculum developers assume that all students can read at grade level, the language, vocabulary, and sophistication of argument that they use, can create barriers for some struggling students that prevents them from accessing the general curriculum.

Assistive technologies generally focus on overcoming barriers related to mobility, sensory perception and processing, and cognitive functioning by providing individuals with an alternative means of completing a task. In this context, access to computer hardware, both alternative input (alternatives to the keyboard and mouse such as switch access, touch access) and alternative output (alternatives to text, audio, video, and multimedia). Generally, it is desirable to provide information in multiple formats so that the user may select their preferred format.

The concept of accessibility has also been applied to the K-12 curriculum. Beginning with the reauthorization of *the Individuals with Disabilities Act* (IDEA) in 1997 (Public Law 105-17), access to the curriculum has been a predominant theme. The research has examined a number of issues, including: access to the curriculum for individuals with intellectual disabilities (Agran, Alper, & Wehmeyer, 2002; Soukup, Wehmeyer, Bashinski, & Bovaird, 2007) and for individuals with high incidence disabilities (Edyburn, 2000; Maccini, Strickland, Gagnon, & Malmgren, 2008; Schumaker, Deshler, Bulgren, Davis, Lenz, & Grossen, 2002). Recently, the issue of accessible assessment has taken center stage in the context of creating a new generation of accessible high-stakes tests (Ketterlin-Geller & Tindal, 2007; Russell, Hoffman, & Higgins, 2009; Salend, 2009).

Developing Technical Standards for Accessible Design

The disability community has recognized that while advocacy is an important strategy for change, efforts to develop technical standards may have greater impact on the development of accessible products. As a result, technical experts have convened work groups to create standardized protocols for ensuring that technologies are universally accessible.

Federal law has been used to mandate accessibility (Skylar, 2007) (see also Assistive Technology Legislation).

Technical standards cover a wide array of technologies such as lifts (Balmer, 2010), kiosks (Vasiliadis & Angelidis, 2005), mobile devices (Baker & Moon, 2008), and of course the World Wide Web (Gunderson, 1999). Interested readers are encouraged to learn more by visiting a web page maintained by the federal government (http://standards.gov/assistiveTechnology.cfm).

Research on accessibility policy is becoming more common (Baker & Moon, 2008; Blair, Goldman, & Relton, 2004). However, research has consistently documented the failure of K-12 schools, government agencies, and universities to create accessible websites as required by federal law (Flowers, Bray, & Algozzine, 1999; Krach, 2007; Krach & Jelenic, 2009; Opitz, Savenye, & Rowland, 2003; Wells & Barron, 2006).

Standards have been slow to emerge to inform the accessible design of classroom instruction. However, the literature features a number of promising investigations on how to bridge the gap between assistive technology and the universal design of learning materials (Abell, Bauder, & Simmons, 2005; Auchincloss & McIntyre, 2008; Doyle & Giangreco, 2009; Hoffman, Hartley, & Boone, 2005; Pisha & Coyne, 2001).

One relatively new area of accessibility is the concept of accessible instructional materials (AIM). This construct was officially added to IDEA in the 2004 reauthorization. Teachers and administrators must be aware of their responsibilities concerning the provision of accessible instructional materials (Zabala & Carl, 2010). The statute is as follows:

Sec. 300.172 Access to instructional materials.

(a) General. The State must—

(1) Adopt the National Instructional Materials Accessibility Standard (NIMAS), published as appendix C to part 300, for the purposes of providing instructional materials to blind persons or other persons with print disabilities, in a timely manner after publication of the NIMAS in the Federal Register on July 19, 2006 (71 FR 41084); and

(2) Establish a State definition of "timely manner" for purposes of paragraphs (b)(2) and (b)(3) of this section if the State is not coordinating with the National Instructional Materials Access Center (NIMAC) or (b)(3) and (c)(2) of this section if the State is coordinating with the NIMAC.

(b) Rights and responsibilities of SEA.

(1) Nothing in this section shall be construed to require any SEA to coordinate with the NIMAC.

(2) If an SEA chooses not to coordinate with the NIMAC, the SEA must provide an assurance to the Secretary that it will provide instructional

materials to blind persons or other persons with print disabilities in a timely manner.

(3) Nothing in this section relieves an SEA of its responsibility to ensure that children with disabilities who need instructional materials in accessible formats, but are not included under the definition of blind or other persons with print disabilities in Sec. 300.172(e)(1)(i) or who need materials that cannot be produced from NIMAS files, receive those instructional materials in a timely manner.

(4) In order to meet its responsibility under paragraphs (b)(2), (b)(3), and (c) of this section to ensure that children with disabilities who need instructional materials in accessible formats are provided those materials in a timely manner, the SEA must ensure that all public agencies take all reasonable steps to provide instructional materials in accessible formats to children with disabilities who need those instructional materials at the same time as other children receive instructional materials.

(c) Preparation and delivery of files. If an SEA chooses to coordinate with the NIMAC, as of December 3, 2006, the SEA must—

(1) As part of any print instructional materials adoption process, procurement contract, or other practice or instrument used for purchase of print instructional materials, must enter into a written contract with the publisher of the print instructional materials to—

(i) Require the publisher to prepare and, on or before delivery of the print instructional materials, provide to NIMAC electronic files containing the contents of the print instructional materials using the NIMAS; or

(ii) Purchase instructional materials from the publisher that are produced in, or may be rendered in, specialized formats.

(2) Provide instructional materials to blind persons or other persons with print disabilities in a timely manner.

(d) Assistive technology. In carrying out this section, the SEA, to the maximum extent possible, must work collaboratively with the State agency responsible for assistive technology programs.

(e) Definitions.

(1) In this section and Sec. 300.210—

(i) Blind persons or other persons with print disabilities means children served under this part who may qualify to receive books and other publications produced in specialized formats in accordance with the Act entitled "An Act to provide books for adult blind," approved March 3, 1931, 2 U.S.C. 135a;

(ii) National Instructional Materials Access Center or NIMAC means the center established pursuant to section 674(e) of the Act;

(iii) National Instructional Materials Accessibility Standard or NIMAS has the meaning given the term in section 674(e)(3)(B) of the Act;

(iv) Specialized formats has the meaning given the term in section 674(e)(3)(D) of the Act.

(2) The definitions in paragraph (e)(1) of this section apply to each State and LEA, whether or not the State or LEA chooses to coordinate with the NIMAC. (Authority: 20 U.S.C. 1412(a)(23), 1474(e))

Accessibility Trends and Issues

For many years, some types of assistive technology were necessary to work-around input and output barriers intrinsic to some technologies. Increased awareness about accessible design has improved the accessibility and usability of many mainstream devices by people with disabilities (e.g., use of text messaging on cell phones has almost extinguished the market for TTY devices). However, the popularity of other types of media (e.g., video) continues to increase the demand for captioning and text descriptions that have typically been labor-intensive and expensive interventions to provide and have yet to be fully automated. Proponents of accessible design argue that barrier-free design, or mainstream design with the application of universal design, can yield products that benefit everyone. Therefore the costs should be considered across the entire population rather than viewed as expense that benefits only a small number of users.

Recently the U.S. Department of Justice, Office of Civil Rights has become more active in enforcing federal accessibility laws associated with the Americans with Disabilities Act (ADA) and Section 504 of the Rehabilitation Act (i.e., the University of Michigan football stadium remodeling, OCR, 2007), the adoption of inaccessible e-book readers by postsecondary institutions (Parry, 2010), and inaccessible web pages (Kincaid, 2009). As of this writing, it is widely expected that recommendations will be made to update the ADA to address web and mobile device accessibility issues.

Finally, only recently have researchers begun to focus on issues of cognitive accessibility (Davies, Stock, & Wehmeyer, 2001; Davies, Stock, King, & Wehmeyer, 2008; Edyburn, 2002, 2006) and accessibility requirements for invisible disabilities (Edyburn, 2000, Yalon-Chamovitz, 2009). These issues are expected to become more predominant in the future and physical and sensory barriers are more routinely addressed.

REFERENCES

Abell, M. M., Bauder, D. K., & Simmons, T. J. (2005). Access to the general curriculum: A curriculum and instruction perspective for educators. *Intervention in School and Clinic, 41*(2), 82–86.

Agran, M., Alper, S., & Wehmeyer, M. (2002). Access to the general curriculum for students with significant disabilities: What it means to teachers. *Education and Training in Mental Retardation and Developmental Disabilities, 37*(2), 123–133.

Arizona Center for Disability Law (2008). *Assistive technology: A self-advocacy guide.* Retrieved from http://www.acdl.com/New%20Logo%20Guides/AT1New%20Logo.pdf

Atkinson, T., Neal, J., & Grechus, M. (2003). Microsoft Windows XP accessibility features. *Intervention in School and Clinic, 38*(3), 177–180.

Auchincloss, C., & McIntyre, T. (2008). iPod teach: Increased access to technological learning supports through the use of the iPod Touch. *Journal of Special Education Technology, 23*(2), 45–49.

Baker, P. M., & Moon, N. W. (2008). Wireless technologies and accessibility for people with disabilities: Findings from a policy research instrument. *Assistive Technology, 20*(3), 149–156.

Balmer, D. C. (2010). Impact of the A18.1 ASME standard on platform lifts and stairway chairlifts on accessibility and usability. *Assistive Technology, 22*(1), 46–50.

Beukelman, D. R., & Mirenda, P. (1998). *Augmentative and alternative communication: Management of severe communication disorders in children and adults* (2nd ed.). Baltimore, MD: Brookes.

Blair, M. E., Goldman, H., & Relton, J. (2004). Accessibility of electronically mediated education: Policy issues. *Assistive Technology, 16*(2), 85–93.

Brunvand, S., & Abadeh, H. (2010). Making online learning accessible: Using technology to declutter the web. *Intervention in School and Clinic, 45*(5), 304–311.

Burgstahler, S. (2006). Ten indicators of distance learning program accessibility to students with disabilities. *Closing the Gap, 25*(5), 1, 7.

Davies, D. K., Stock, S. E., & Wehmeyer, M. L. (2001). Enhancing independent Internet access for individuals with mental retardation though use of a specialized web browser: A pilot study. *Education and Training in Mental Retardation and Developmental Disabilities, 36*, 107–113.

Davies, D. K., Stock, S. E., King, L. R., & Wehmeyer, M. L. (2008). *Moby Dick* is my favorite: Evaluating a cognitively accessible portable reading system for audiobooks for individuals with intellectual disability. *Intellectual and Developmental Disabilities, 46*(4), 290–298.

Doyle, M. B., & Giangreco, M. F. (2009). Making presentation software accessible to high school students with intellectual disabilities. *Teaching Exceptional Children, 41*(3), 24–31.

Edyburn, D. L. (2000). Assistive technology and mild disabilities. *Focus on Exceptional Children, 32*(9), 1–24.

Edyburn, D. L. (2002). Cognitive rescaling strategies: Interventions that alter the cognitive accessibility of text. *Closing the Gap, 21*(1), 1, 10–11, 21.

Edyburn, D. L. (2006). Cognitive prostheses for students with mild disabilities: Is this what assistive technology looks like? *Journal of Special Education Technology, 21*(4), 62–65.

Edyburn, D. L. (2009). Assistive technology advocacy. *Special Education Technology Practice, 11*(2), 15–17.

Edyburn, D. L. (2010). Would you recognize universal design for learning if you saw it? Ten propositions for new directions for the second decade of UDL. *Learning Disability Quarterly, 33*(1), 33–41.

Erath, A. S., & Larkin, V. M. (2004). Making distance education accessible for students who are deaf and hard-of-hearing. *Assistive Technology, 16*(2), 116–123.

Flowers, C. P., Bray, M., & Algozzine, R. F. (1999). Accessibility of special education program home pages. *Journal of Special Education Technology, 14*(2), 21–26.

Golden, D. C. (2002). Instructional software accessibility: A status report. *Journal of Special Education Technology, 17*(1), 57–60.

Gunderson, J. (1999). W3C web accessibility initiative guidelines. *Closing the Gap, 17*(6), 1, 14–15.

Hoffman, B., Hartley, K., & Boone, R. (2005). Reaching accessibility: Guidelines for creating and refining digital learning materials. *Intervention in School and Clinic, 40*(3), 171–176.

Ketterlin-Geller, L. R., & Tindal, G. (2007). Embedded technology: Current and future practices for increasing accessibility for all students. *Journal of Special Education Technology, 22*(4), 1–15.

Kincaid, J. M. (2009) Highlights of ADA/Section 504 Decisions as applied to institutions of higher education. Available from: http://ebookbrowse.com/highlights-of-court-and-agency-rulings-higher-ed-6-1-08-doc-doc-d15417499

Krach, S. K. (2007). Snapshot—Ten years after the law: A survey of the current status of university web accessibility. *Journal of Special Education Technology, 22*(4), 30–40.

Krach, S. K., & Jelenic, M. (2009). The other technological divide: K-12 web accessibility. *Journal of Special Education Technology, 24*(2), 31–37.

Maccini, P., Strickland, T., Gagnon, J.C., & Malmgren, K. (2008). Accessing the general education math curriculum for secondary students with high-incidence disabilities. *Focus on Exceptional Children, 40*(8), 1–32.

Molenbroek, J. F., & de Bruin, R. (2006). Anthropometry of a friendly rest room. *Assistive Technology, 18*(2), 196–204.

Niemeijer, D. (2005). Accessing Mac OS X Tiger: Apple and third party solutions. *Closing the Gap, 24*(4), 23–24, 26.

Norris, C., Sullivan, T., Poirot, J., & Soloway, E. (2003). No access, no use, no impact: Snapshot surveys of educational technology in K-12. *Journal of Research on Technology in Education, 36*(1), 15–27.

Office of Civil Rights. (2007). Enforcing the ADA: A status report from the Department of Justice. Available from: http://www.ada.gov/octdec07.pdf

Opitz, C., Savenye, W., & Rowland, C. (2003). Accessibility of state department of education home pages and special education pages. *Journal of Special Education Technology, 18*(1), 17–27.

Parry, M. (2010). Inaccessible e-readers may run afoul of the law, feds warn colleges. *Chronicle of Higher Education*. Retrieved from http://chronicle.com/blogs/wiredcampus/inaccessible-e-readers-may-run-afoul-of-the-law-feds-warn-colleges/25191

Pisha, B., & Coyne, P. (2001). Smart from the start: The promise of universal design for learning. *Remedial and Special Education, 22*, 197–203.

Russell, M., Hoffman, T., & Higgins, J. (2009). NimbleTools: A universally designed test delivery system. *Teaching Exceptional Children, 42*(2), 6–12.

Salend, S. (2009). Using technology to create and administer accessible tests. *Teaching Exceptional Children, 41*(3), 40–51.

Schumaker, J. B., Deshler, D. D., Bulgren, J. A., Davis, B., Lenz, K. L., & Grossen, B. (2002). Access of adolescents with disabilities to general education curriculum: Myth or reality? *Focus on Exceptional Children, 35*(3), 1–16.

Schwanke, T. D., Smith, R. O., & Edyburn, D. L. (2001). A3 model diagram developed as accessibility and universal design instructional tool. *RESNA 2001 Annual Conference Proceedings, 21*, pp. 205–207. Arlington, VA: RESNA Press.

Skylar, A. A. (2007). Section 508: Web accessibility for people with disabilities. *Journal of Special Education Technology, 22*(4), 57–62.

Solomon, G. (2002). Digital equity: It's not just about access anymore. *Technology and Learning, 22*(9), 18–26.

Soukup, J. H., Wehmeyer, M. L., Bashinski, S. M., & Bovaird, J. A. (2007). Classroom variables and access to the general curriculum for students with disabilities. *Exceptional Children, 74*(1), 101–120.

Thompson, T. (2003). The interdependent role of all players in making technology accessible. *Journal of Special Education Technology, 18*(4), 21–27.

Vanderheiden, G. C., & Henry, S. L. (2003). Designing flexible, accessible interfaces that are more usable by everyone. Retrieved from http://www.sigchi.org/chi2003/docs/t10.pdf

Vasiliadis, T., & Angelidis, P. (2005). Methodology and guidelines for the evaluation of accessibility of public terminal devices by people with visual or hearing disabilities: Sound, audio and speech design considerations. *Technology and Disability, 17*(1), 11–24.

Wells, J. A., & Barron, A. E. (2006). School websites: Are they accessible to all? *Journal of Special Education Technology, 21*(3), 23–30.

Wiazowski, J. (2010). (in)accessible digital textbooks. *Closing the Gap, 29*(3), 17–22.

Yalon-Chamovitz, S. (2009). Invisible access needs of people with intellectual disabilities: A conceptual model of practice. *Intellectual and Developmental Disabilities, 47*(5), 395–400.

Zabala, J. S., & Carl, D. (2010). The AIMing for achievement series: What educators and families need to know about accessible instructional materials. Part one: Introduction and legal context. *Closing the Gap, 29*(4), 11–14.

DAVE EDYBURN, PHD
University of Wisconsin-Milwaukee
Fourth edition

ACCESSIBILITY OF WEBSITES (*See Web Accessibility*)

ACCESSIBILITY RESOURCES IN STANDARD COMPUTER SYSTEMS

In addition to being able to incorporate a wide range of special accessibility hardware and software resources, today's major computer operating systems (Windows and Mac OS) contain a number of built-in options to provide accessibility in relation to a variety of disabilities. The two major platforms available in schools have similar assistive features to help empower many students with disabilities without the need for additional expense, hardware, or materials.

Apple OS X Accessibility

Macintosh OS X Snow Leopard provides features for individuals with vision, hearing, and motor skills disabilities. Universal Access provides numerous modification capabilities that work with basic computer functions as well as with many applications. Because OS X allows settings for multiple users, the same computer can be preset to provide personalized interaction for any number of individual students or groups with similar needs.

Vision

Numerous options are provided to help individuals see the screen contents. The screen text, graphics, and even video can be easily magnified up to 40 times without distracting pixilation. As the cursor is moved about, the screen adjusts and follows to automatically display the desired content. The cursor itself is resizable to help the viewer keep oriented. The screen contrast and color range can also be adjusted to any individual preferences.

The Mac is also equipped with speech technologies including talking alerts, a talking calculator, a talking clock, and Text to Speech (TTS) function that reads selected or typed text aloud for students with learning, mobility, or visual disabilities. VoiceOver is an integrated screen reader that narrates any activity on the screen to the user in natural intonation—even at very fast speaking rates—to provide a full verbal description of the actions. The audio narration content can also be displayed simultaneously in a fully configurable, large-print text caption panel. The system also reads the content of documents and provides full keyboard navigation (without requiring mouse) for control of the computer. Improved object navigation and positional cues help students with reduced motor skills or visual disabilities more easily move around the Mac and remember the location of items on the screen.

Hearing

For hearing difficulties, the system can be set to flash the screen to alert the user as an alternative to the audio alerts. Quick-access key commands can also be used to adjust the system volume, choose a custom system beep alert, set the alert beep volume independent of the system volume setting, and play unique sounds that identify various system events. Mac OS X can also help students, who are missing some of the music or audio contained in one of the channels of stereo recordings, by playing play both left and right audio channels in both left and right speakers.

Motor Skills

Students having difficulty with motor skills will often have problems using the mouse. MouseKeys let you adapt the numeric keypad to move the mouse cursor, click, double-click, and drag. The StickyKeys option lets the student create multiple key controls, such as Shift-Option-8, as a sequence of key presses. Key commands can be used to navigate menus, windows, the Dock, and other interface elements using Full Keyboard Access; this feature can also be assigned to work within specific applications. A parallel assistive function uses the built-in speech recognition system to allow the student to speak commands instead of having to type them. Standard features include keyboard control over key repeat and delay rates and control of the mouse tracking and double-click speeds. Individualization of all key shortcuts is also available. Handwriting recognition capability is also built-in using Ink and can be used for text input. Most dialog boxes have buttons that can be selected and activated by keystrokes instead of by the standard mouse click.

Windows 7 Accessibility Features

Windows 7 contains a number of built-in accessibility features and is compatible with more than a dozen assistive technology products by working closely with assistive technology vendors to serve the needs of users with vision, hearing, mobility, and cognitive disabilities. The Ease of Access Center provides a convenient, centralized place to locate and modify these accessibility settings and programs to make it easier to see the computer, use the mouse and keyboard, and use other input devices.

Vision

Windows 7 has Magnifier, a display utility that makes the screen more readable by students with vision problems by magnifying a portion of the screen, the area around the mouse pointer, or full screen. The screen display can be customized by changing features such as position, size, and window color. The magnification level and magnifier tracking options can also be controlled. Narrator is a TTS utility for individuals who are blind or have limited vision. Using its built-in internal driver, TTS engine, it reads the contents of the active window, menu options, or text that has been typed. Narrator has many options that allow the user to customize the way screen elements are read by setting them to announce events on the screen, to read typed characters, to move the mouse pointer to active item, and to adjust voice options. The user can select alternate voices and control the speed, volume, and pitch of the narration.

ToggleKeys provides audio cues when certain keys are pressed. A predefined set of mouse pointers can be chosen to increase visibility of the cursor location. Windows 7 can be set to display pointer trails and change the length of the pointer trail for better visibility of mouse pointer. When working with a document while typing with an enlarged mouse pointer, the user can hide mouse pointer for better visibility. The relative speed of the cursor movement can also be adjusted. A SnapTo feature moves the cursor to the default button and selected by the Enter key.

Hearing

Windows 7 provides a feature, SoundsEntry, to change the settings to generate visual warnings, such as a blinking title bar or screen flash for people who have difficulty hearing computer system sounds. Visual warnings can be chosen for sounds made by windowed programs or full-screen text programs. The Show Sounds feature instructs programs that usually convey information only by sound to also provide all information by displaying text captions or informative icons.

Motor Skills

On-Screen Keyboard, one of the built-in utilities, displays a virtual keyboard on the computer screen that allows students with mobility disabilities to type data by using a pointing device or joystick. Different options can be accessed by resizing the keyboard screen to make it easier to see, enabling text prediction to display a list of words that students might be typing, changing font settings of the keys to make them more legible, using Click Sound to add an audible click, using Clicking Mode to select the on-screen keys to type text, and enabling Hovering Mode to use a mouse or joystick to point to a key image for a predefined period of time to type the character. Such students can also command their computers with their voices including the capability to dictate into almost any application with built-in Speech Recognition function in Windows 7. StickyKeys allows users to press keys one at a time in sequence rather than need to hold them all at once. FilterKeys adjusts the keyboard repeating rate. Also, Windows 7 can be set to display pointer trails and change the length of the pointer trail for better tracking and visibility of the mouse pointer. Additionally, Mouse

Keys can be activated to provide use of the numeric keypad for both navigation and data entry.

REFERENCES

Apple Computer, Inc. (2011). *Accessibility in Apple-Mac OS X*. Retrieved from http://www.apple.com/macosx/accessibility/

Microsoft Corporation. (2011). *Accessibility in Windows 7*. Retrieved from http://www.microsoft.com/enable/products/windows7/

TUFAN ADIGUZEL
Bahcesehir University

RON ZELLNER
Texas A&M University
Fourth edition

ACCOMMODATION

Accommodation is one of two complementary processes proposed by Jean Piaget to account for an individual's adaptation to the environment; its counterpart is assimilation. Accommodation involves changing or transforming cognitive or sensorimotor schemes according to the demands of the environment; assimilation involves incorporating external elements into existing conceptual schemes.

The difference between accommodation and assimilation can be illustrated by an example of an infant's response to a rattle (Ginsburg & Opper, 1969). When a rattle suspended from an infant's crib begins to shake after the infant's arm movement causes it to move, the infant looks at and listens to the toy rattling, assimilating the event into his or her schemes of looking and listening. To repeat the movement of the rattle, the infant must make the necessary hand and arm movements, accommodating his or her actions according to the demands of the situation.

Assimilation and accommodation were viewed by Piaget as inseparable aspects of a single process of adaptation, separable only for purposes of discussion (Brainerd, 1978). Assimilation and accommodation occur simultaneously; a balance between the two is necessary for adaptation. A scheme must accommodate itself to the specific characteristics of the object or event it is attempting to assimilate; accommodation guides the eventual change in structures (Gelman & Baillargeon, 1983).

REFERENCES

Brainerd, C. J. (1978). *Piaget's theory of intelligence*. Englewood Cliffs, NJ: Prentice Hall.

Gelman, R., & Baillargeon, R. (1983). A review of some Piagetian concepts. In P. H. Mussen (Ed.), *Handbook of child psychology*: *Vol. III. Cognitive development* (pp. 167–230). New York, NY: Wiley.

Ginsburg, H., & Opper, S. (1969). *Piaget's theory of intellectual development: An introduction*. Englewood Cliffs, NJ: Prentice Hall.

LINDA J. STEVENS
University of Minnesota

See also Assimilation; Cognitive Development; Piaget, Jean

ACCOMMODATIONS VERSUS ACADEMIC ADJUSTMENT

Accommodations change the way instruction is provided or assessment tasks are administered to students with disabilities. These changes reduce the impact of physical, cognitive, or sensory barriers that may prevent students from gaining access to the targeted domain or expressing their knowledge and skills. For example, a student with a hearing impairment may need test directions presented in sign language to understand the information. Without this accommodation, the student would not be able to perform the tasks necessary to demonstrate his or her abilities. As such, accommodations allow students with disabilities to meaningfully interact with curricular materials, thereby increasing their participation in the general education environment.

Changes to the presentation, response, setting, and timing of materials are acceptable accommodations provided they do not change or interfere with the targeted construct. Maintaining the integrity of the construct allows for valid interpretations of student knowledge and skills. If the construct is altered, however, similar interpretations of student ability are not possible.

Presentation accommodations change the format of information that is presented to the student. Such accommodations include, but are not limited to, presenting material in braille, sign language, high or low contrast, and visual magnification of text or response forms. Other presentation accommodations include reading the directions or questions aloud to students, simplifying the language used in the directions or questions, or reducing the amount of text on a page. Testing accommodations must be carefully constructed or written. Accommodations that are made without consideration to the test can alter the reliability and validity of the test.

Response accommodations change the format in which responses are recorded or the method in which the student responds to questions or tasks. Format changes include allowing students to use additional space on the paper; record answers directly on a test booklet; or use different types of paper, such as graph or lined paper. Examples of changes to the method of response include providing assistive devices such as word processors or braillers. Scribes as well as audio recording responses for transcription are also classified as response accommodations. Allowing students to check spelling or grammar is appropriate as long as these skills are not part of the targeted construct.

Setting accommodations change the environment in which instruction is presented or assessment tasks are administered. Setting accommodations include working with the student in a separate location or in a small group, reducing the distractions in a typical setting, or providing assistive furniture. Finally, timing accommodations change the amount of time allocated to the tasks. Examples include providing additional time to complete tasks, allowing the student to complete work during multiple short sessions within or across days, providing frequent breaks, presenting materials at specific times of the day, or changing the schedule to accommodate special needs. Again, it is important to note that any of these accommodations are appropriate if they do not interfere with the targeted construct. Carefully considering the test construct when accommodations are implemented helps to avoid changes which can alter the reliability and validity of the construct.

Accommodated materials are created by retrofitting existing activities or embedding changes within the design of new materials. Retrofitting materials allows teachers and other educators to use already created instructional activities and assessment tasks, thereby avoiding the costs of designing new forms. However, changing existing materials can be costly and may result in less than ideal conditions, which may compromise the goal of the accommodation. As an example, imagine creating a braille version of an existing science test that included multiple graphical representations. Each image would be redesigned in order to be converted to braille, or the image would be omitted from the braille version. In any case, the student would not receive the same materials as sighted students.

To avoid the drawbacks incurred when retrofitting existing materials, accommodations can be embedded during the design and construction phases of materials development (Ketterlin-Geller, 2003). For example, the science test discussed in the previous example would be created with simple graphic images that display only the necessary information. When a braille version is created, the images are easily converted so that all students receive the same materials. By considering the characteristics of the target population when materials are created, developers can include accommodations from the beginning. This circumvents the costs associated with accommodating existing materials.

Once accommodated materials are created, students with disabilities are assigned accommodations that will reduce the sources of error that are caused by the disability. An individualized educational program (IEP) team is responsible for making decisions about assignment of accommodations for an individual student. Input from a variety of sources including parent preference, teacher's experience and observations, and inferences about student performance is considered when determining the use of accommodations (Fuchs & Fuchs, 1999). Care must be taken to assign appropriate accommodations based on the student's characteristics. For accommodations to be beneficial, format changes must be specific to the individual's characteristics and needs (Helwig & Tindal, 2003). For example, a student with a visual impairment may benefit from information presented in large text or braille. However, this same student may be distracted or confused by materials constructed using simplified language.

Additionally, for accommodations to effectively support students with disabilities and provide meaningful opportunities for these students to participate in the general education curriculum, they must be applied in both instructional and assessment settings. Without the use of accommodations in instruction, students are denied the opportunity to learn the material and are subsequently penalized on assessments. When unfamiliar accommodations are introduced during testing, they may provide additional sources of irrelevant variance in the students' score.

REFERENCES

Fuchs, L. S., & Fuchs, D. (1999). Fair and unfair testing accommodations. *School Administrator, 56*(10), 24–29.

Helwig, R., & Tindal, G. (2003). An experimental analysis of accommodation decisions on large-scale mathematics tests. *Exceptional Children, 69,* 211–225.

Ketterlin-Geller, L. R. (2003). *Establishing a validity argument for universally designed assessments.* Unpublished doctoral dissertation, University of Oregon, Eugene.

LEANNE KETTERLIN-GELLER
University of Oregon

See also American Sign Language; Test Anxiety

ACETYLCHOLINE

Acetylcholine (ACh) is a neurotransmitter, a chemical that is released from one neuron to pass a message to another neuron. Acetylcholine is naturally synthesized in living cells in cholinergic nerve terminals that are located primarily in the autonomic nervous system. It also is evident at parasympathetic postganglionic synapses, and at neuromuscular junctures (Cooper, Bloom, & Roth, 1982).

The autonomic nervous system is involved in what appears to be functionally reflexive responses directed toward energy conservation or preparation for possible trauma. Thus, with cholinergic stimulation, pupils contract, heart rate slows, and muscular contraction is facilitated (Katzung, 1982). Experimental work by Deutsch (1984) suggests the possibility of an indirect, environmental role for ACh in the development of memories. Results of animal studies indicate that drugs that block cholinergic action tend to increase low rates of response and decrease high rates of response among behaviors that were maintained through food reinforcers (Seiden & Dykstra, 1977). Such findings are consistent with the likelihood that ACh plays a role in creating a chemical environmental context for learning by mediating autonomic responsiveness and attention (Himmelheber, Sarter, & Bruno, 2001). A role in pain perception also has been postulated (Cooper et al., 1982). Myasthenia gravis, a disease characterized by fluctuating muscle weakness, especially in muscles innervated by the motor nuclei of the brain stem (Adams & Victor, 1981), is a model of ACh dysfunction. Observed involvement of cholinergic systems in tardive dyskinesia, Huntington's chorea, and Alzheimer's dementia has led to experimental administration of drugs that facilitate ACh; however, no consistent results have been observed in such studies (Cooper et al., 1982).

REFERENCES

Adams, R. D., & Victor, M. (1981). *Principles of neurology*. New York, NY: McGraw-Hill.

Cooper, J. R., Bloom, F. E., & Roth, R. H. (1982). *The biochemical basis of neuropharmacology*. New York, NY: Oxford University Press.

Deutsch, J. A. (1984). Amnesia and a theory for dating memories. In G. Lynch, J. L. McGaugh, & N. M. Weinberger (Eds.), *Neurobiology of learning and memory* (pp. 105–110). New York, NY: Guilford Press.

Himmelheber, A., Sarter, M., & Bruno, J. P. (2001). *Cognitive Brain Research, 12*, 353–370.

Katzung, B. G. (1982). *Basic and clinical pharmacology*. Los Altos, CA: Lange Medical Publications.

Seiden, L. S., & Dykstra, L. A. (1977). *Psychopharmacology: A biochemical and behavioral approach*. New York, NY: Van Nostrand Reinhold.

ROBERT F. SAWICKI
Lake Erie Institute of Rehabilitation

See also **Central Nervous System; Neurological Organizations**

ACHENBACH CHILD BEHAVIOR CHECKLIST

The purpose of the Child Behavior Checklist (CBCL 6–18, 2001) is to quickly (in 15 to 20 minutes) collect standardized ratings on a broad spectrum of competencies and problems for children ages 6 to 18 years as reported by the child's parent or others that are involved with the child within the home environment. For the 120 behavioral, emotional, and social problem statements, the respondent is directed to answer all items as best as possible even if they do not seem applicable to the child. The instructions to the respondent are located on the CBCL booklet and are written on a fifth-grade reading level. If the respondent cannot read, the CBCL can be administered in an alternate format where the examiner reads the items and records responses of the respondent.

The CBCL measures competencies using a Total Competence Score, which represents a parent's perception of their child's performance on an Activities scale, Social scale, and School scale.

Problems are measured on the CBCL's Syndrome Scales. These represent the parents' perception of their child's behavior based on eight statistically derived categories (factors): Anxious/Depressed, Withdrawn/Depressed, Somatic Complaints, Social Problems, Thought Problems, Attention Problems, Rule-Breaking Behavior, and Aggressive Behavior.

The Anxious/Depressed, Withdrawn/Depressed, and Somatic Complaints scales constitute the Internalizing Problems scale score, and the Rule-Breaking Behavior and Aggressive Behavior scales combine to yield the Externalizing Problems scale scores. Adding the Social Problems, Thought Problems, and Attention Problems scales with the Internalizing and Externalizing Problem scales generates a Total Problem scale score.

In addition, problems on the CBCL have been categorized into six DSM-Orientated Scales: Affective Problems, Anxiety Problems, Somatic Problems, Attention Deficit/Hyperactivity Problems, Oppositional Defiant Problems, and Conduct Problems.

Scoring the CBCL is easy and responses are directly recorded from the CBCL booklet. Scoring can be done in one of three ways: hand-scored, computer-scored, or scored by scanner. The hand-scoring method is time consuming and the many calculations leave room for frequent errors. Although the computer-scoring or scanning methods are initially more costly, they reduce time spent scoring and are more accurate.

Males and females have separate norms based on age. The two age ranges used for each gender are 6–11 and 12–18. The 2007 revision of the scales offers a variety of norms based on culture. Normative data is only provided on the hand-scoring profiles. No other printed norm tables are available at this time. The computer generated profile does not provide the examiner with such data.

T-scores and Percentiles are calculated for each scale for comparative purposes. For each scale T-Scores are further categorized as within normal limits, within the Borderline range, or within the Clinical range. The value of T-Scores for each range varies depending on the scale. On the Competence Scales and Total Competence scale, higher T-Scores are associated with normal functioning. On the syndrome scales, Internalizing, Externalizing, Total Problem, and DSM-Orientated scales, lower T-Scores are associated with normal functioning.

The CBCL also allows for multiple respondent comparisons to be made using another CBCL, TRF, or YSR.

The CBCL sample consisted of 1753 children. The demographics in the manual indicate that 914 boys and 839 girls were used. There were 387 boys in the 6–11 age group and 527 boys in the 12–18 age group. There were 390 girls in the 6–11 age group and 449 girls in the 12–18 age group. The number of participants for each year (i.e., number of 6-year-olds, number of 7-year-olds, etc.) was not presented in the manual. For the sample, SES was broken down to three levels with the following results: Upper (33%), Middle (51%), and Lower (16%). In terms of ethnicity, 60% were Non-Latino White, 20% were African American, 9% were Latino, and 12% were Mixed/Other. There were 100 sampling sites in 40 states and the District of Columbia. 17% were from the Northeast, 20% were from the Midwest, 40% were from the South, and 24% were from the West. Overall the sample procedures appear to be adequate and fairly representative.

Internal consistency or "split-half reliability" were moderately high and ranged from .55 to .75. For the empirically based problem scales (syndromes, Internalizing, Externalizing, and Total Problem) reliabilities were high, ranging from .78 to .98. In all cases, Total scores have the highest internal consistency. For the DSM-Orientated Scales, alphas were high as they ranged from .72 to .91. Test-Retest reliability was high for most of the scales with a range of .80 to .94. The test-retest interval was 8–16 days and the sample included children that had been referred for mental health services and those who were not.

The CBCL is very user friendly. It is easy to administer and take. A big drawback for the examiner is related to the time and accuracy of hand-scoring procedures. If the computer-scoring system is used, scoring is also relatively easy.

REFERENCES

Achenbach System of Empirically Based Assessment. http://www.aseba.org/

Belter, R. W., Foster, K. Y., & Imm, P. S. (1996). Convergent validity of select scales of the MMPI and the Achenbach Child Behavior Checklist—Youth Self-Report. *Psychological Reports, 79*, 1091–1100.

Biederman, J., Monuteaux, J. C., Greene, R. W., Braaten, E., Doyle, A. E., & Faraone, S. V. (2001). Long-term stability of the Child Behavior Checklist in a clinical sample of youth with attention deficit hyperactivity disorder. *Journal of Clinical Child Psychology, 30*, 492–502.

Impara, J. C., & Plake, B. S. (Eds.). (1998). *The thirteenth mental measurements yearbook.* Lincoln, NE: Buros Institute of Mental Measurements.

Youngstrom, E., Youngstrom, J. K., & Starr, M. (2005). Bipolar diagnoses in community mental health: Achenbach Child Behavior Checklist profiles and patterns of comorbidity. *Biological Psychiatry, 58*, 7, 569–575.

JOHN DUMONT
Fairleigh Dickinson University

JOHN O. WILLIS
Rivier College

KATHLEEN VIZEL
Fairleigh Dickinson University

JAMIE ZIBULSKY
Fairleigh Dickinson University
Fourth edition

ACHIEVEMENT NEED

Achievement need is also known as achievement motivation, the need for achievement, and *n:Ach*. The concept was first defined by Murray (1938) as the need "to overcome obstacles, to exercise power, to strive to do something difficult as well and as quickly as possible" (pp. 80–81). Murray, however, chose not to attempt to conduct applied research in achievement motivation and the concept did not receive much attention until McClelland (1951) developed a cognitive theory of motivation in which the need for achievement is one element. McClelland's theory states that a person's tendency to approach a task (effort) is a function of the strength of the achievement need, the strength of the need to avoid failure, the person's subjective belief about the probability of success or failure, and the value of the incentives associated with either success or failure. According to McClelland (1951) and Atkinson (1964), achievement need is intrinsic. It is not associated with extrinsic rewards that accrue as a result of achievement. Achievement need is generally measured through the Thematic Apperception Test (TAT), although Hermans (1970) developed a paper and pencil test for this purpose called *n:Ach*.

Many researchers have attempted to determine how achievement need develops. Crandall (1963) discovered that children with high achievement needs had mothers who rewarded achievement and achievement activities at an early age. These mothers also did not attend to their children's pleas for help when the children faced a difficult problem. Crandall further concluded that middle- and upper-class parents were more likely to engage in behaviors that develop achievement motivation than were parents of lower economic status. Currently, parental involvement to assist achievement need is taking center stage as an educational improvement strategy (Jeynes, 2005; Fan & Chen, 2001).

A number of studies have been conducted to determine the effects of achievement on task performance and personality. Weiner (1970) found that high-need achievement persons persist in the face of failure while low-need achievement persons become more inhibited in their responses. He further found that low-need achievement persons will engage in achievement activity when success and reinforcement rates approach 100%, but high-need achievement persons work best when reinforcement is attained approximately 50% of the time. Weiner and Kukla (1970) related achievement need research to Rotter's (1966) research in locus of control. Using elementary school children, they concluded that high-need achievement children viewed their successes as resulting from their effort. Both high- and low-achievement need children attributed failure to themselves, but high-need achievement children attributed failure to lack of effort while low-achievement children attributed it to lack of ability.

REFERENCES

Atkinson, J. W. (1964). *An introduction to motivation.* Princeton, NJ: Van Nostrand.

Crandall, V. J. (1963). Achievement. In H. W. Stevenson (Ed.), *Child psychology* (pp. 416–459). Chicago, IL: University of Chicago Press.

Hara, S. R., & Burke, D. J. (1998). Parent involvement: The key to improved student involvement. *School Community Journal, 8,* 9–19.

Hermans, H. J. M. A. (1970). A questionnaire measure of achievement motivation. *Journal of Applied Psychology, 54,* 353–363.

McClelland, D. C. (1951). *Personality.* New York, NY: Dryden.

Fan, X., & Chen, M. (2001). Parental involvement and students' academic achievement: A meta-analysis. *Educational Psychology Review, 13*(1), 1–22.

Jeynes, W. H. (2005). A meta-analysis of the relation of parental involvement to urban elementary school student academic achievements. *Urban Education, 40*(3), 237–269.

Murray, H. A. (1938). *Exploration in personality.* New York, NY: Oxford University Press.

Rotter, J. B. (1966). Generalized expectancies for internal versus external control of reinforcement. *Psychology Monographs, 80.*

Weiner, B. (1970). New conceptions in the study of achievement motivation. In B. A. Maher (Ed.), *Progress in experimental personality research* (Vol. 5). New York, NY: Academic Press.

Weiner, B., & Kukla, A. (1970). An attributional analysis of achievement motivation. *Journal of Personality and Social Psychology, 15,* 1–20.

JAMES K. MCAFEE
Pennsylvania State University
Third edition

See also Learned Helplessness; Motivation; Self-Concept; Self-Control Curriculum

ACHIEVEMENT TESTS

Achievement tests are individually or group-administered standardized instruments intended to measure the effectiveness of former training. Achievement tests are the dominant form of standardized assessment in education. Measures of achievement have been used to evaluate student performance, school instruction efficacy, candidates for scholarship awards, admission to academic programs, and applicants for industrial and government employment. Group administered achievement tests are more likely to be employed for the evaluation of a scholastic program, whereas individually administered achievement tests are typically used to assist in appropriate grade placement in schools and the identification and diagnosis of learning disabilities.

Traditional achievement tests were based on the principle of comparing examinees to their peers, or normative testing (classical test theory). Some more contemporary achievement tests are based on the premise that a prediction can be made about the performance of a person with a specified ability in regard to that person's probable success or failure on an item of specified difficulty (Anastasi, 1988). In other words, as the level of ability increases, the probability that an examinee will give a correct response increases (Hambleton, Swaminathan, & Rogers, 1991). Given the special characteristics of item response theory (IRT), computer adaptive testing is a desirable method to select different sets of items for each subject.

Some examples of commonly used normative achievement tests and their publishers include: Comprehensive Tests of Basic Skills (CTB/McGraw-Hill), Iowa Tests of Basic Skills (Riverside Publishing Company), Kaufman–Test of Educational Achievement Second Edition (American Guidance Service), Stanford Test of Academic Skills (Psychological Corporation), and Tests of General Educational Development (GED Testing Service of the American Council on Education).

The use of computer aided testing and IRT represents a new era in achievement testing. For example, the ACCU-PLACER (College Board online administration) computerized battery of achievement tests for college level placement is implemented in the placement of hundreds of thousands of students during each school year (Cole, Muenz, & Bates, 1998).

REFERENCES

Anastasi, A. (1988). *Psychological testing* (6th ed.). New York, NY: Macmillan.

Cole, J. C., Muenz, T. A., & Bates, H. G. (1998). Age in correlations between ACCUPLACER's reading comprehension subtest and GPA. *Perceptual and Motor Skills, 86*, 1251–1256.

Hambleton, R. K., Swaminathan, H., & Rogers, H. J. (1991). *Fundamentals of item response theory*. London, UK: Sage.

TRACY A. MUENZ
California School of Professional Psychology

See also Criterion-Referenced Tests; Norm-Referenced Tests

ACHONDROPLASIA

Achondroplasia, also called chondrodystrophy, refers to a defect in the formation of cartilage in the epiphyses of long bones, such that a type of dwarfism results. This most common form of dwarfism is usually inherited as an autosomal dominant trait, or it may result from spontaneous mutation (Avioli, 1979; Magalini, 1971). Clinical features of achondroplasia include absolute diminution of extremities; normal trunk and head size; a prominent, bulging forehead; and a flattened, saddle nose. Hands and feet typically are short, and fingers tend to be nearly equal in length (trident hands). Adult height generally does not exceed 1.4 meters. Achondroplasia occurs with equal frequency in females and males and affects approximately 1 in 25,000 children in the United States (Toplis, 2003).

The intelligence of affected persons is reported to be normal (Avioli, 1979; Lubs, 1977), although there is evidence of occasional neurologic complications during early adulthood (Magalini, 1971). The fertility of achondroplastic dwarfs or a little person is reported to be 30% of normal. Of offspring of two affected persons, two-thirds will exhibit the syndrome (Lubs, 1977). In educational settings, afflicted children may require adaptive equipment to accommodate their short stature. While there is no evidence to suggest that achondroplasia places individuals at increased risk for learning problems, a multifactored evaluation is appropriate for children who experience difficulty in school.

REFERENCES

Avioli, L. V. (1979). Diseases of bone. In P. B. Beeson, W. McDermott, & J. B. Wyngaarden (Eds.), *Cecil textbook of medicine* (pp. 2225–2265). Philadelphia, PA: Saunders.

Lubs, M. (1977). Genetic disorders. In M. J. Krajicek & A. I. Tearney (Eds.), *Detection of developmental problems in children* (pp. 55–77). Baltimore, MD: University Park Press.

Magalini, S. (1971). *Dictionary of medical syndromes*. Philadelphia, PA: Lippincott.

Toplis, R. (2003). Achondroplasia. In E. Fletcher-Janzen & C. R. Reynolds (Eds.), *Childhood disorders diagnostic desk reference* (p. 3). Hoboken, NJ: Wiley.

CATHY F. TELZROW
Kent State University

See also Congenital Disorders; Minor Physical Anomalies

ACNE VULGARIS

Acne vulgaris (AV) is a skin disorder seen primarily in adolescents (Burkhart, Burkhart, & Lehmann, 1999). It is the most common skin disease treated by physicians (Krowchuk, 2000). AV is characterized by a pilosebaceous follicular eruption of the comedo that starts an inflammatory reaction. A pilosebaceous follicle consists of a follicle or pore, the sebaceous gland, and a hair. These specialized follicles are concentrated on the face, chest, and back. Formation of papules, pustules, and cysts can result from the inflammation. AV is a chronic condition that may last for years and may cause emotional distress and permanent facial scarring (Krowchuk, 2000). Clinical characteristics of AV vary with age, stage of puberty attained, gender, and race (White, 1998).

There are four basic reasons that adolescents are at risk for AV: hormonal surges that take place both before and during puberty, bacteria, comedogenesis, and genetic predisposition (Krowchuk, 2000). In adolescents, cycling hormones cause gonadal development and adrenal maturation, which increases androgen production, leading to sebaceous gland enlargement and higher sebum. Higher levels of androgen dehydroepiandrosterone sulfate (DHEAS) cause more sebum to be produced, which leads to the oily face and chin with scattered comedones that are the hallmark of puberty production (White, 1998). Bacteria are also involved with increased acne production. Krowchuk (2000) reports that Propionibacterium acnes (P. acnes) begin to colonize after sebum production increases. This bacteria uses the sebum as a nutrient that allows this normal facial bacteria to multiply so that it increases the inflammatory reaction that causes the pustules, papules, and cysts characteristic of AV. Finally, although it is not possible to predict the severity of AV based on genetic factors, there does appear to be a genetic predisposition for AV (Krowchuk, 2000).

AV affects an estimated 17 million people in the United States, affecting 85% of adolescents and young adults

(Krowchuk, 2000), although a higher percentage of teenage boys than teenage girls are affected by AV (White, 1998). Krowchuk (2000) reports that AV severity correlates with sebum secretion, which is caused by adrenal and gonadal androgens. Therefore, both sebum secretion and AV peaks during adolescence and begins to decline after age 20.

Characteristics

1. Obstructive lesions are blackheads or whiteheads. Blackheads are open comedones, or follicles with a wide, dark opening. Whiteheads are closed comedones, or small, white papules. They are follicles that have become dilated with cellular and lipid debris but have only a microscopic opening into the skin.
2. Some patients with acne will develop scars or cysts when inflammatory lesions have resolved.

The first step in treating AV is conducting a global assessment of acne severity that states the number, size, location, and extent of lesions and scarring (Krowchuk, 2000). Next, the patient should be given information that will help him or her avoid behaviors and factors that worsen AV. This information list should include advice such as do not pick at acne, avoid wearing athletic gear over areas with acne, avoid cosmetics and moisturizers containing oils, use only noncomedogenic or nonacnegenic products, and avoid working in an environment where one comes into contact with grease.

Acne is a chronic condition, and treatment efforts generally take 6–8 weeks before therapeutic benefit is seen (Krowchuk, 2000). Both topical and systemic treatments are recommended for AV. Topical therapies include benzoyl peroxide, topical antibiotics, and azelaic acid, which when used alone or in combination with each other have an antibacterial effect on mild to moderate inflammatory acne. Topical retinoids (Retin-A) and salicylic acid are indicated in the treatment of mild to severe obstructive lesions. Severe inflammatory acne is best treated with oral antibiotics, such as erythromycin or tetracycline. Other treatments include isotretinoin (Accutane), which can help in some severe cases of inflammatory lesions that do not respond to milder treatments, because Accutane can have adverse effects. Oral contraceptives are generally seen as adjunctive therapy and should be utilized in combination with other treatments for AV.

In the classroom, AV can affect student performance because of the emotional distress that generally accompanies active lesions on the face. These adolescents may be distracted from learning because of a preoccupation with their face. In addition, these students may be vulnerable to peer teasing. Therefore, teachers should be sensitive to adolescents who may have severe cases of AV, and a referral to the school counselor may be appropriate.

There are several areas of future research in the area of AV. Certain forms of AV may be resistant to oral and topical antibiotics. According to Krowchuk (2000), researchers in the United Kingdom found that cases of acne resistant to antibiotics rose from 34.5% in 1991 to 60% in 1996. Because multiple factors influence effectiveness of antibiotic treatment, studies clarifying what strains of AV are actually treatment resistant are needed. New treatments or therapies for treatment-resistant AV are also needed. Another area for future research is investigating and clarifying the exact relationship between microbial organisms and the inflammation that creates AV. P. acnes is the predominant microorganism in the pilosebaceous follicle, and although P. acnes is not pathogenic, it is the main target of oral and topical antibiotic treatments. Burkhart et al. (1999) suggest that future research should clarify how P. acnes and other microorganisms are involved in acne inflammation via its interaction with other chemical properties.

REFERENCES

Burkhart, C. G., Burkhart, C. N., & Lehmann, P. F. (1999). Acne: A review of immunologic and microbiologic factors. *Postgraduate Medical Journal, 75*(884), 328–331.

Krowchuk, D. P. (2000). Treating acne: A practical guide. *Adolescent Medicine, 84*(4), 811–828.

White, G. M. (1998). Recent findings in the epidemiologic evidence, classification, and subtypes of acne vulgaris. *Journal of the American Academy of Dermatology, 39*(2/3), S34–S37.

JENNIE KAUFMAN SINGER
*California Dept. of Corrections,
Region 1 Parole Outpatient Clinic*

ACROCALLOSAL SYNDROME

Acrocallosal syndrome (ACS) is a genetic disorder that is apparent at birth. The disorder is typically characterized by underdevelopment or absence of the corpus callosum and by intellectual disability. However, other associated symptoms may be variable, even among affected members of the same family.

ACS is believed to be a rare condition, but prevalence is unknown and has not been studied in detail. Considered at first to be sporadic, the syndrome has more recently been ascribed to an autosomal recessive gene, on the basis of its observation in two siblings (Schinzel, 1988) and in two unrelated patients, each born to consanguineous parents (Salgado, Ali, & Castilla, 1989; Temtamy & Meguid, 1989). True and confirmed etiology remains unknown.

There have been no reports of prenatal diagnosis of this syndrome. However, certain manifestations such as polydactyly and cerebral malformations can be detected by ultrasound examination during the second trimester (Hendricks, Brunner, Haagen, & Hamel, 1990). In view of the variability of the major clinical manifestations, prenatal detection of this syndrome may not be possible in all cases.

Characteristics

1. Macrocephaly, large anterior fontanel, epicanthal folds, prominent occiput, and bulging forehead
2. Low-set posteriorly rotated ears
3. Down-slanting palpebral fissures, exotropia, protruding eyeballs, and hypertelorism
4. Broad and short nose and anteverted nostrils
5. Short upper lip and high arched cleft palate
6. Umbilical and inguinal hernia
7. Postaxial polydactyly of the fingers and toes, bifid terminal phalanges of the thumbs, and tapered fingers
8. Hypotonia
9. Hypoplasia or agenesis of corpus callosum, seizures, and hyperreflexia
10. Hypospadias and hypogonadism
11. Mental, motor, and speech impairments

REFERENCES

Greig, D. M. (1926). Oxycephaly. *Edinburgh Medical Journal, 33,* 189–218.

Hendricks, H. J. E., Brunner, H. G., Haagen, T. A. M., & Hamel, B. C. J. (1990). Acrocallosal syndrome. *American Journal of Medical Genetics, 35,* 443–446.

Salgado, L. J., Ali, C. A., & Castilla, E. E. (1989). Acrocallosal syndrome in a girl born to consanguineous parents. *American Journal of Medical Genetics, 32,* 298–300.

Schinzel, A. (1982). Acrocallosal syndrome. *American Journal of Medical Genetics, 12,* 201–203.

Schinzel, A. (1988). The acrocallosal syndrome in first cousins: Widening of the spectrum of clinical finding and further indication of autosomal recessive inheritance. *Journal of Medical Genetics, 25,* 332–336.

Temtamy, S. A., & Meguid, N. A. (1989). Hypogentialism in the acrocallosal syndrome. *American Journal of Medical Genetics, 32,* 301–305.

CAREY E. COOPER
University of Texas at Austin

See also Acrodysostosis

ACRODYSOSTOSIS

Acrodysostosis is also called acrodysplasia, Arkless-Graham syndrome, or Maroteaux-Malamut syndrome. It is an extremely rare disease in which bones and skeleton are deformed. The hands and feet are short with stubby fingers and toes (National Organization for Rare Disorders [NORD], 2000; PDR, 2000). The cause of the disease is unknown at this time (Medlineplus, 2000; PDR, 2000).

Both sexes are equally likely to be affected. It tends to occur with older parental age (Medlineplus, 2000).

Characteristics

1. Abnormally short and malformed bones of the hands and feet (peripheral dysostosis).
2. Underdevelopment of the nose (nasal hypoplasia)—short nose with low bridge, broad and dimpled tip, anteverted nostrils, long philtrum, and epicanthal folds.
3. Mild to moderate growth deficiency—short stature and unusual head and facial (craniofacial) features.
4. Characteristic facial features may include a flattened, underdeveloped (hypoplastic) pug nose, an underdeveloped upper jaw bone (maxillary hypoplasia), widely spaced eyes (ocular hypertelorism), and an extra fold of skin on either side of the nose that may cover the eyes' inner corners (epicanthal folds).
5. Mental deficiency in approximately 90% of affected children.
6. Short head, measured front to back (brachycephaly).
7. Other abnormalities of the skin, genitals, teeth, and skeleton.
8. It frequently co-occurs with middle ear infections.

(Medlineplus, 2000; National Library of Medicine [NLM] 1999; NORD, 2000).

There is no treatment or cure for this syndrome. It is recommended that the child be referred to a geneticist (specialist in inherited diseases) and the child should be monitored by a medical professional (NORD, 2000). If the skeletal deformities are severe enough to interfere with academic progress, children with this disorder would receive services under orthopedically impaired. Depending on the extent of the cognitive deficiency, the child may receive services for Learning Disability, Mental Retardation, or both. Services could include resource classes, physical therapy, and occupational therapy. If the child's cognitive or physical impairment is not severe enough, the 504 modifications with technology to modify the regular curriculum might be sufficient.

The prognosis of the children who have acrodysostosis varies depending on the degree of skeletal involvement and intellectual disability (Medlineplus, 2000). The treatment should be provided according to the child's condition.

REFERENCES

Medlineplus. (2000). Acrodysostosis condition. Retrieved from http://medlineplus.adam.com/ency/article/001248.htm

National Library of Medicine. (1999, October 27). Acrodysostosis condition. Retrieved from http://www.nlm.nih.gov/mesh/jablonski/syndromes/syndrome005.html

NORD. National Organization for Rare Disorders. (2000). Acrodysostois. Retrieved from http://www.rarediseases.org/rare-disease-information/rare-diseases/byID/613/viewAbstract

NINA CHENG
University of Texas at Austin

ACROMEGALY

Acromegaly is characterized by excessive growth due to oversecretion of growth hormone, which is produced in the liver and other tissues and is secreted by the anterior pituitary gland. Oversecretion of growth hormone is often caused by the presence of a benign pituitary tumor (adenoma) but can also be caused by lung and pancreas tumors that stimulate the excessive production of substances similar to growth hormone (Berkow, Beers, & Fletcher, 1997).

The prevalence of acromegaly is approximately 50–70 cases per million. Three or four infants who will develop acromegaly are born per million births (Novartis Pharmaceuticals Corporation, 1999). It has been estimated that there are 15,000 cases of acromegaly within the United States. Its onset most commonly occurs between the ages of 30 and 50 years (Berkow et al., 1997), but it is not usually diagnosed until 10 years after increased hormone secretion has begun (Novartis Pharmaceuticals Corporation, 1999). Reasons accounting for this delay of diagnosis include slow development of symptoms, a variety of clinical signs and symptoms, and the need to rule out other medical conditions with similar signs and symptoms (Novartis Pharmaceuticals Corporation, 1999). If excessive growth of the same nature occurs by the age of 10 years, it is referred to as gigantism (accelerated growth). Acromegaly is diagnosed through the presence of elevated blood levels of growth hormone (GH) or insulin-like growth factor I (IGF-I). X rays confirm the thickening of bones. Pituitary tumors are the cause of acromegaly in 90% of cases (Tierny, McPhee, & Papadakis, 2000). A CT scan or magnetic resonance imaging (MRI) examines the site and size of possible tumors. If there is no tumor, these same tests can be used to detect the enlargement of organs or the source of excessive growth hormone excretion.

Additional symptoms associated with acromegaly include carpal tunnel syndrome, sleep apnea, goiter, colon polyps, and hypertension. Weight gain is frequent and largely attributable to muscle and bone growth. Diabetes sometimes occurs due to insulin resistance, and arthritis and joint pain are common. The heart may become enlarged, increasing the chance of heart failure. Headaches are common due to pressure caused by the tumor. As tissues enlarge, they may compress nerves including the optic nerve, sometimes resulting in loss of vision.

Characteristics

1. Enlarged hands, feet, jaw, facial features, and internal organs
2. Coarsening facial features and deeper voice
3. Excessive perspiration
4. Amenorrhea
5. Sweaty handshake

Treatment of acromegaly is primarily medical. Initially, the tumor is either removed through surgery or destroyed through radiation therapy. Medication such as octreotide or bromocriptine slow or block the production of growth hormone (Berkow et al., 1997). When surgical treatment is successful, normal pituitary function returns, resulting in the decrease of soft tissue swelling. Bone enlargement, however, is permanent (Tierney et al., 2000). In children, because excessive growth hormone is secreted before the bones stop growing, the result is abnormal height and excessive bone growth.

Acromegaly, referred to as gigantism when seen in children, is not necessarily accompanied by cognitive deficiencies. Special education issues are most often related to physical accommodations or services such as occupational therapy.

Unlike adults with acromegaly, children who are treated for gigantism do not become deformed. Other symptoms persist, however, such as swollen tissue around bones, delayed puberty, and incomplete development of the genitals (Berkow et al., 1997). One study has shown that the life expectancy of individuals with acromegaly is approximately 10 years lower than that of nonacromegalic individuals (Novartis Pharmaceuticals Corporation, 1999).

REFERENCES

Berkow, R., Beers, M. H., & Fletcher, A. J. (Eds.). (1997). *Merck manual of medical information: Home edition.* Whitehouse Station, NJ: Merck Research Laboratories.

Novartis Pharmaceuticals Corporation. (1999). The acromegaly infosource. Retrieved from http://www.acromegalyinfo.com

Tierney, L. M., Jr., McPhee, S. J., & Papadakis, M. A. (Eds.). (2000). *Current medical diagnosis and treatment* (39th ed.). New York, NY: Lange Medical Books/McGraw-Hill.

KATHRYN L. GUY
University of Texas at Austin

NANCY L. NUSSBAUM
Austin Neurological Clinic

ACROMESOMELIC DYSPLASIA (ACROMESOMELIC DWARFISM)

Acromesomelic dysplasia is a form of dwarfism characterized by premature fusion of the areas of growth (epiphyses) in the long bones of the arms and legs. Affected individuals have severely shortened forearms, lower legs, and short stature (short-limbed dwarfism).

Acromesomelic dysplasia is extremely rare. It is inherited in an autosomal recessive manner. Two distinct clinical forms, distinguished by different X-ray and biochemical findings, have been described. The Maroteaux type is caused by an abnormal gene in Chromosome 9. The Hunter-Thompson type has been traced to Chromosome 20.

Characteristics

1. Prominent forehead, slightly flattened face, and short nose
2. Short limbs, especially the forearms and lower leg below the knee
3. Progressive inward curving of the lower spine (kyphosis) as the child ages
4. Linear growth deficiency that becomes more obvious with increasing age
5. Short, broad hands and feet
6. Mild lag in motor development
7. Normal intelligence

There is no specific treatment or cure for this disorder. In the future, therapy directed toward correcting the defective gene offers some promise.

Children with acromesomelic dysplasia may benefit from modifications in the classroom, such as provision of an appropriately sized desk and chair. Evaluation and treatment by occupational and physical therapists may be needed to address the lag in the motor development. These children should be treated in an age-appropriate manner and not according to their short stature.

Evaluation of a small number of adults with this problem showed that they had normal intelligence. Final heights in these individuals ranged from 38 to 49 inches.

Families may benefit from additional emotional support as they learn coping strategies and problem solving abilities to help integrate their child into society. For more information and support, please contact:

Restricted Growth Association, P.O. Box 8, Countesthorpe, Leicestershire, LE8-5ZS, United Kingdom. Tel. (44) 116-2478913.

Little People of America, Inc.: P.O. Box 745, Lubbock, TX 79408. Tel.: (888) 572-2001, e-mail: lpadatabase@juno.com.

International Center for Skeletal Dysplasia: Saint Joseph's Hospital, 7620 York Road, Towson, MD 21204. Tel.: (410) 337-1250.

REFERENCES

Jones, K. L. (1997). *Smith's recognizable patterns of human malformation* (5th ed.). Philadelphia, PA: W. B. Saunders.

National Organization for Rare Disorders (1999). Acromesomelic dysplasia. Retrieved from http://rarediseases.org/rare-disease-information/rare-diseases/byID/1087/viewAbstract

BARRY H. DAVISON
Ennis, Texas

JOAN W. MAYFIELD
*Baylor Pediatric Specialty Services
Dallas, Texas*

ACROMICRIC DYSPLASIA

Initially described by Spranger (1971), acromicric dysplasia is a rare bone deformity mainly characterized by reduced bone growth; this results in facial anomalies, short limbs, and abnormally limited growth. It is very closely linked to geleophysic dysplasia, sharing many of the same characteristics, and there has been speculation as to whether these two are in fact the same disorder but have different methods of inheritance. It is possible that acromicric dysplasia is inherited through a dominant gene: There have been a few cases in which the disorder was present in multiple family members; however, these cases were the minority, and the possibility of genetic inheritance is still debated.

Biochemically speaking, acromicric dysplasia is caused by disorganization at the site of bone growth—abnormal cells, isolated clusters of cells, and abnormal levels of collagen forming rims around the cells (Maroteaux, Stanescu, Stanescu, & Rappaport, 1986).

Characteristics

1. Facial deformities
2. Shortened limbs
3. Abnormally short stature
4. Cell disorganization at growth sites

Children with acromicric dysplasia display normal intelligence levels. Accordingly, these children will most likely be placed in inclusive programming if chronic health issues and treatment do not prevent regular school attendance.

REFERENCES

Jones, K. L. (1997). *Smith's recognizable patterns of human malformation*. Philadelphia, PA: W. B. Saunders.

Maroteaux, P., Stanescu, R., Stanescu, V., & Rappaport, R. (1986). Acromicric dysplasia. *American Journal of Medical Genetics, 24*, 447–459.

Spranger, J. W. (1971). Geleophysic dwarfism: A "focal" mucopolysaccharidosis? *Lancet, 2*, 97.

ALLISON KATZ
Rutgers University

ACTING OUT

Acting out has been defined by Harriman (1975) as the "direct expression of conflicted tensions in annoying or antisocial behavior in fantasies" (p. 30). A child who exhibits acting-out behavior is one who cannot easily accept structural limits and is difficult to manage in the classroom. Acting-out behaviors are similar to conduct disorders or externalizing behaviors, but not necessarily as severe. One reason for the similarity is that acting-out behavior is one of the characteristics clustered under the broader grouping of conduct disorders. Acting-out behaviors usually are of high frequency and of significant duration, and do not include minor daily misbehavior.

Usually, when a behavior is identified as an acting-out behavior, it is operationally defined, observed, and recorded by the classroom teacher in specific and observable terms. Some of the behaviors that can be identified as acting-out behaviors include fighting, lying, temper tantrums, pouting, stealing, hyperactivity, threatening, and bullying (Quay, 1979).

Acting out, or externalizing behaviors are linked to persistent poverty (Eamon, 2000) and observed more frequently in males (Wicks-Nelson & Israel, 2000).

REFERENCES

Eamon, M. K. (2000). Structural model of the effects of poverty on externalizing and internalizing behaviors of four to five-year-old children. *Social Work Research, 24*, 143–154.

Harriman, P. L. (1975). *Handbook of psychological terms*. Totowa, NJ: Littlefield, Adams.

Quay, H. C. (1979). Classification. In H. C. Quay & J. S. Werry (Eds.), *Psychopathological disorders of childhood* (2nd ed.). New York, NY: Wiley.

Wicks-Nelson, R., & Israel, A. C. (2000). *Behavior disorders of childhood*. Upper Saddle River, NJ: Prentice Hall.

MARIBETH MONTGOMERY KASIK
Governors State University

See also Applied Behavior Analysis; Conduct Disorder

ADAPTED PHYSICAL EDUCATION

Adapted physical education is a diversified program of developmental activities, games, sports, and rhythms suited to the interests, capacities, and limitations of students with disabilities who may not safely and successfully engage in unrestricted participation in vigorous activities of the general physical education program (Hurley, 1981, p. 43).

The focus of adapted physical education is on the development of motor and physical fitness and fundamental motor patterns and skills in a sports-like environment (Sherrill, 1985).

Adapted physical education implies the modification of physical activities, rules, and regulations to meet existing limiting factors of specific handicapped populations. By definition, adapted physical education includes activities planned for persons with learning problems owed to mental, motor, or emotional impairment, disability, or dysfunction; planned for the purpose of rehabilitation, habilitation, or remediation; modified so the handicapped can participate; and designed for modifying movement capabilities.

Adapted physical education primarily occurs within a school setting, but it may also occur in clinics, hospitals, residential facilities, daycare centers, or other centers where the primary intent is to influence learning or movement potential through motor activity (AAHPER, 1952).

In the school setting, adapted physical education differs from regular physical education in the following manner. It has a federally mandated base through IDEA 2004. It serves students who are primarily identified as having a handicapping condition but may serve students such as the obese, who are not identified as handicapped but are in need of physical activity modification within a restricted environment. Adapted physical education classes are usually separate and educationally distinct from regular physical education owing to the need to modify the curriculum to suit the individual interests and capabilities of the student.

The basic elements in curriculum planning are individuality, flexibility, and educational accountability. Because of the intra- and intervariability of individual differences within and across handicaps, activities must be designed and programmed to fit each child's motor capabilities. For instance, children within a particular handicapped group may be able to throw a ball, but each within the group, because of motor limitations, may throw the ball differently while still achieving the objective of distance and accuracy. Second, adapted physical education activities are designed to be flexible enough to achieve educational goals. For instance, for basketball, a smaller ball is provided and baskets are lowered so that students may be able to score more baskets in a game, thereby increasing their enjoyment in the sport (Auxter & Pyer, 1985).

Adapted physical education for students classified as handicapped implies accountability via the individualized educational plan (IEP). Objectives stated on an IEP ensure that the student is receiving instruction in activities where there is the greatest physical, motor, and social need. The student is evaluated periodically to assess progress toward the short- and long-term goals stated in the IEP.

REFERENCES

AAHPER. (1952, April). *Guiding principles for a physical education journal of health, physical education, recreation.* Author.

Auxter, D., & Pyer, J. (1985). *Adapted physical education.* St. Louis, MO: Mosby.

Hurley, D. (1981). Guidelines for adapted physical education. *Journal of Health, Physical Education, Recreation, and Dance,* 43–45.

Sherrill, C. (1985). *Adapted physical education and recreation* (3rd ed.). Dubuque, IA: Brown.

THOMAS R. BURKE
Hunter College, City University of New York

See also **Motor Learning; Physical Education for Students With Disabilities**

ADAPTIVE BEHAVIOR

Adaptive behavior includes skills used by an individual to meet personal needs, deal with the natural and social demands in one's environment, skills to care for him or herself, and to relate to others (Nihira, Leland, & Lambert, 1993). These skills also include independently caring for one's personal health and safety, the ability to dress, bathe, communicate, display socially appropriate behaviors and academic skills, engagement in recreation, work, and in community life (Ditterline & Oakland, 2010). The American Association on Intellectual and Developmental Disabilities (AAIDD) has developed a model of adaptive behavior that consists of 10 skills: communication, community use, functional academics, home and school living, health and safety, leisure, self-care, self-direction, social, and work (Ditterline, Banner, Oakland, & Becton, 2008). Adaptive behavior is an integral part of the evaluation and planning for individuals with and without disabilities. Increased emphasis is now placed on the use of adaptive behavior concepts in special education and programs for individuals with disabilities (Meyers, Nihira, & Zetlin, 1979).

Edgar Doll was among the first researchers to propose the use of adaptive behavior when diagnosing individuals with intellectual disabilities. It was not until 1959 that the American Association on Mental Deficiency published its official manual and formally included deficits in adaptive behavior, in addition to low intelligence, as an integral part of the definition of intellectual disabilities (Heber, 1961). Subsequent editions of the manual have further emphasized the importance of adaptive behavior. Several issues in the 1960s and 1970s precipitated an upsurge of interest in adaptive behavior and adaptive behavior assessment (Witt & Martens, 1984). A concern arose about "6-hour retarded children" or minority group and low socioeconomic status children who were labeled as "retarded" in the public schools but exhibited adequate adaptive behavior at home and in the community (Mercer, 1973).

This concern eventually led to litigation such as the Guadalupe and Larry P. cases and court decisions that indicated that results of intelligence tests cannot be the primary basis for classifying children as having an intellectual disability and that adaptive behavior must be assessed. The 1960s and 1970s saw a trend toward the normalization of individuals with disabilities and the awareness that effective programs for teaching adaptive skills allow individuals with disabilities to participate as fully as possible in normal environments. A third issue was the need for a nonbiased and multifaceted assessment of all children with disabilities to facilitate the fairness of decisions based on the results of tests and to investigate functioning in all areas related to a particular handicap.

The passage of the Education of All Handicapped Children Act of 1975 (Public Law 94-142) represented the culmination of the issues of the 1960s and 1970s. Public Law 94-142 and its latest revision, the current Individuals with Disabilities Education Act, commonly known as IDEIA, 2004, have stringent guides for the assessment of children with disability and stipulates that deficits in adaptive behavior must be substantiated before a child is classified as having an intellectual disability. Further, it recognizes the importance of adaptive behavior assessment for children with disabilities other than the intellectual disabilities. Since the passage of the law, most states have developed guidelines for adaptive behavior assessment (Patrick & Reschley, 1982) and many have strict criteria for the types of adaptive behavior instruments and scores to be used.

Traditionally adaptive behavior assessments have been used to identify individuals with intellectual disabilities. Information on adaptive behavior is increasingly being used for comprehensive assessment, treatment planning, intervention, and program evaluation for individuals with various disorders. Research is now being done on the adaptive behavior skills of individuals with disabilities including: Down syndrome, autism spectrum disorders developmental delay, hearing and visual impairments, fragile X syndrome, Williams syndrome, externalizing problems, psychological disturbances, and learning disabilities (Ditterline, Banner, Oakland, & Becton, 2008).

Ditterline, Banner, Oakland, and Becton (2008) researched adaptive behavior profiles of students with disabilities. They found that children with different disabilities display varying adaptive skills. Those diagnosed as emotionally disturbed displayed deficits in socialization, communication, and daily living skills. Children diagnosed with autism spectrum disorders showed deficits in communication and socialization and those diagnosed with learning disabilities displayed deficits in academic skills. Principles from applied behavior analysis guide many adaptive behavior training programs (Neidert, Dozier, Iwata, & Hafen, 2010).

Sparrow, Balla, and Cicchetti (1984, 2005) discuss several characteristics that are inherent in concepts of adaptive behavior. Adaptive behavior is an age-related construct; as normally developing children grow older, adaptive behavior increases and becomes more complex. Adaptive behavior is determined by the standards of other people, those who live, work, play, teach, and interact with an individual. Finally, adaptive behavior is defined as what an individual does day by day, not by an individual's ability or what he or she can do. If a person has the ability to perform a daily task, but does not do it, adaptive behavior is considered to be inadequate. An important issue in the description of adaptive behavior is the distinction between adaptive behavior and intelligence (Meyers, Nihira, & Zetlin, 1979). Adaptive behavior and intelligence have several important differences. First, adaptive behavior focuses on everyday behavior and intelligence on thought processes. Adaptive behavior is based on concrete environmental demands while intelligence focuses on academic demands. Adaptive behavior assessment involves common, typical, and everyday behaviors, whereas intelligence scales attempt to measure a person's potential, or his or her best possible performance. Negative reinforcement has been shown to play a critical role in the development of adaptive behavior (Neidert, Dozier, Iwata, & Hafen, 2010).

Since the passage of Public Law 94-142, a large number of adaptive behavior scales have been published. Most adaptive behavior scales are administered to a respondent such as a parent or teacher who is familiar with the daily activities of the person. Some are administered directly to the person whose adaptive behavior is being assessed. The Vineland Adaptive Behavior Scales (Sparrow, et al., 1984, 2005) measure adaptive behavior in the areas of communication, daily living skills, socialization, motor skills, and maladaptive behavior. The Adaptive Behavior Inventory for Children (Mercer & Lewis, 1977) assessed a child's adaptation to family, community, and peer social systems. The AAIDD Adaptive Behavior Scale (Lambert, Nihira, & Leland, 1993) evaluates personal sufficiency, social sufficiency, responsibility, and personal and social adjustment. The Scales of Independent Behavior revised (Bruininks, Woodcock, Weatherman, & Hill, 1996) include measures of motor skills, social interaction and communication, personal and community independence, and problem behaviors. The Children's Adaptive Behavior Scale (Richmond & Kicklighter, 1980) contains scales for language, independent functioning, family roles, economic vocational activity, and socialization. The Adaptive Behavior Assessment System—Second Edition (Harrison & Oakland, 2003) assesses conceptual social and practical areas of adaptive behavior cited by the AAIDD.

REFERENCES

Bruininks, R. J., Woodcock, R. W., Weatherman, R. F., & Hill, B. K. (1996). *Scales of Independent Behavior Revised*. Itasca, IL: Riverside Publishing.

Ditterline, J., Banner, D., Oakland, T., & Becton, D. (2008). Adaptive behavior profiles of students with disabilities. *Journal of Applied School Psychology, 24*, 191–208.

Ditterline, J., & Oakland, T. (2010). Adaptive behavior. In E. Mpofu & T. Oakland (Eds.), *Assessment in Rehabilitation and Health*. Boston, MA: Allyn & Bacon.

Harrison, P. L. (1985). *Vineland Adaptive Behavior Scales, Classroom Edition Manual*. Circle Pines, MN: American Guidance Service.

Harrison, P., & Oakland, T. (2003). *Adaptive Behavior System—Second Edition*. San Antonio, TX: PsychCorp.

Heber, R. F. (1961). A manual on terminology and classification in mental retardation (Monograph Suppl.). *American Journal of Mental Deficiency*.

Nihira, K., Leland, H., & Lambert, N. (1993). *AAMR Adaptive Behavior Scale—Residential and Community* (2nd ed.). Austin, TX: PRO-ED.

Mercer, J. R. (1973). *Labeling the mentally retarded.* Berkeley: University of California Press.

Mercer, J. R., & Lewis, J. E. (1977). *Adaptive Behavior Inventory for Children.* New York, NY: Psychological Corporation.

Meyers, C. E., Nihira, K., & Zetlin, A. (1979). The measurement of adaptive behavior. In N. R. Ellis (Eds.), *Handbook of mental deficiency: Psychological theory and research* (2nd ed., pp. 215–253). Hillsdale, NJ: Erlbaum.

Neidert, P. L., Dozier, C. L., Iwata, B. A., & Hafen, M. (2010). Behavior analysis in intellectual and developmental disabilities. *Psychological Services*, 7, 103–113.

Patrick, J. L., & Reschley, D. J. (1982). Relationship of state educational criteria and demographic variables to school system prevalence of mental retardation. *American Journal of Mental Deficiency*, 86, 351–360.

Richmond, B. O., & Kicklighter, R. H. (1980). *Children's Adaptive Behavior Scale.* Atlanta: Humanities Limited.

Sparrow, S. S., Balla, D. A., & Cicchetti, D. V. (1984). *Vineland Adaptive Behavior Scales.* Circle Pines, MN: American Guidance Service.

Sparrow, S. S., Balla, D. A., & Cicchetti, D. V. (2005). *Vineland Adaptive Behavior Scales–II.* Circle Pines, MN: AGS.

Witt, J. C., & Martens, B. K. (1984). Adaptive behavior: Test and assessment issues. *School Psychology Review*, 13, 478–484.

PATTI L. HARRISON
University of Alabama

See also AIDD Classification Systems; Mental Retardation; *Vineland Adaptive Behavior Scales—Second Edition*

ADAPTIVE BEHAVIOR ASSESSMENT SYSTEM—SECOND EDITION

The Adaptive Behavior Assessment System—Second Edition (ABAS-II) evaluates a variety of adaptive skills in individuals from birth to 89 years of age. There are five rating forms which allow for assessment from multiple respondents and settings: The Parent/Primary Caregiver Form (ages 0–5), Parent Form (ages 5–21), the Teacher/Daycare Provider Forms (ages 2–5), the Teacher Form (5–21) and an Adult Form (ages 16–89) which can be completed by another individual or, with adult populations, through self-report. The forms appropriate for infants and preschoolers are new to the Second Edition of the ABAS. The Parent/Primary Caregiver, Parent, and Teacher/Daycare Provider Forms are available in Spanish; however, the manual urges caution when interpreting the Spanish forms due to lack of psychometric information.

The manual contains clear and thorough instructions for administration and scoring. On all ABAS-II Scales, respondents rate the frequency with which individuals correctly perform a behavior on a Likert scale ranging from 0 ("Is Not Able") to 3 ("Always When Needed"). The respondent can also indicate if they guessed on an item. Examiners should interpret scores with caution if the respondent indicated guessing on four or more items in a skill area. Each rating form takes approximately 20 minutes to complete and 5–10 minutes to hand-score. The ABAS is designed to measure skills consistent with how adaptive behavior is defined by the American Association on Mental Retardation (AAMR; 1992, 2002) and the *Diagnostic and Statistical Manual of Mental Disorders*—Fourth Edition—Text Revision (DSM-IV-TR), making it useful in the diagnosis and classification of several disorders, including intellectual disability. Ratings derived from each ABAS-II form are used to generate standard scores for a General Adaptive Composite (GAC) and three domain scores: Conceptual, Social, and Practical. Ratings on each form are also used to generate scaled scores for individual skill areas appropriate for the designated age and setting. For example, the Teacher/Daycare Provider Form includes the following skill areas: Communication, Functional Pre-Academics, School Living, Health and Safety, Leisure, Self-Care, Self-Direction, Social and Motor. Percentile ranks and confidence intervals are available for the standard scores, and the user can easily calculate an individual's strengths and weaknesses. Finally, the ABAS-II manual provides test-age equivalents of raw scores and descriptive classifications. Admirably, the authors describe the strengths and limitations inherent in using various types of scores.

The ABAS-II was normed on a standardization sample which was stratified by sex, race/ethnicity, and educational levels according to U.S. Census data (from 1999 for the school age and adult forms, and from 2000 for the infant/preschool forms). Efforts also were made to gather participants from the four major geographical regions in the United States as defined by the Census. Individuals with a variety of clinical diagnoses were included. Detailed information about the normative sample for each form is provided in the manual.

The manual provides evidence for internal consistency, test-retest reliability, interrater reliability, and cross-form consistency, as well as standard errors of measurement. Reliability coefficients were mostly above .90 and reflected a high degree of internal consistency. The test-retest coefficients were also generally good, ranging from the upper .80s and .90s for the GAC and domains, and the .70s (infant-preschool) to .90s for the skill areas. As young children are in the midst of myriad developmental changes that occur over a short period of time, it is unsurprising the test-retest for infants and toddlers would be somewhat lower than those derived from older populations. The interrater reliability coefficients for the GAC scores on the various forms fell in the .80s or .90s. For domain areas, the interrater coefficients were in the high .70s or .80s. For skill areas, the coefficient averages were generally in the

.70s, but reached .82 for the Adult form. The consistency between two raters of the same individual was more varied, but still higher than some previous adaptive behavior scales. Additionally, difference between respondents could at least be partially explained by the variation of behavior across settings and with raters who may also have different levels of familiarity with the target individual.

The theoretical basis of items as well as results of field testing provide evidence for content validity, and the intercorrelation data support the theoretical structuring of domains. Confirmatory factor analysis also supports the structure of the ABAS-II. Comparisons with several other tests which measure adaptive, behavioral, cognitive, and achievement skills argue for convergent and discriminant validity. Finally, the ABAS-II manual presents several clinical validity studies which indicate the test can adequately discriminate between those with and without adaptive skill deficits.

Overall, the ABAS-II appears to be a theoretically and psychometrically sound instrument. The manual is thorough and user-friendly. Particularly impressive are the guidelines for interpretation, which even include suggestions for intervention planning. Reviews of the instrument are generally positive, with minor reservations including interpreting the individual skill areas with more caution than the domains (Burns, 2005), and some concern about the size of the standardization sample (Meikamp, 2005).

REFERENCES

Burns, M. K. (2005). Review of the Adaptive Behavior Assessment System—Second Edition. In R. A. Spies & B. S. Plake (Eds.), *The sixteenth mental measurements yearbook*. Lincoln, NE: Buros Institute of Mental Measurements.

Meikamp, J. (2005). Review of the Adaptive Behavior Assessment System—Second Edition. In R. A. Spies & B. S. Plake (Eds.), *The sixteenth mental measurements yearbook*. Lincoln, NE: Buros Institute of Mental Measurements.

Richardson, R., & Burns, M. (2005). Adaptive Behavior Assessment System—Second Edition) by Harrison, P. L, & Oakland, T. (2002). San Antonio, TX: Psychological Corporation. *Assessment for Effective Intervention*, 30(4), 51–54.

KATHLEEN VIEZEL
Fairleigh Dickinson University

JAMIE ZIBULSKY
Fairleigh Dickinson University
Fourth edition

ADAPTIVE BEHAVIOR SCALE (See *Vineland Adaptive Behavior Scales*—Second Edition)

ADAPTIVE DEVICES (See *Assistive Devices*)

ADAPTIVE TECHNOLOGIES AND PROGRAMS, WEBSITES RELATED TO

American Association of People with Disabilities (AAPD) URL: http://www.aapd.com/

The AAPD is a national organization dedicated to promoting the economic and political empowerment of all people with disabilities. The AAPD is "the largest national nonprofit cross-disability member organization in the United States, dedicated to ensuring economic self-sufficiency and political empowerment for the more than 58 million Americans with disabilities." The AAPD mentoring effort promotes nationwide career development for students and job seekers with disabilities through job shadowing and hands-on career exploration. The Disability Vote Project addresses the fundamental inequalities faced by this nation's voters with disabilities and works in a nonpartisan manner to ensure they are provided full accessibility to all polling places and voting equipment. The AADP promotes bipartisan legislation and policy that will further the ability of people with disabilities to live independently, contribute to society, pursue meaningful careers, and enjoy self-determination and maintains a Listserv dedicated to this purpose.

Apple Computer Accessibility in Education URL: http://www.apple.com/education/special-education/

The Apple site provides resources for educators in relation to a number of accessibility issues. The site provides five sections that focus on specific areas: vision, hearing, physical and motor, literacy and learning, and language and communication. While much of the information is related to features of Apple's hardware and software accessibility resources, links are readily available that lead to related philosophical, research, funding, and general support resources. The main strength of the site is that it organizes the technical information around the various categories of disability solutions. Each area leads to expanded pages that provide detailed information on the resources and solutions related to that topic. In many instances, PDF files are available for download to provide more detailed information. In addition, links to third-party hardware and software are provided to present a full range of resources available in any of the disability areas. Both hardware and software components are presented with brief descriptions and links to the appropriate manufacturer's website. The literacy and learning and language and communication pages provide more academic, skill-building resources. There is also a section that is devoted to web accessibility concerns and features information on a server-based application that automatically converts and renders web pages into text-only pages to make them more accessible and easier to navigate. This section also provides technical information as well as links to general implementation resources.

Assistive Tech Net URL: http://assistivetech.net/

Assistive Tech Net provides "a diverse resource for assistive technology (AT) and disability-related information." Assistivetech.net maintains an online searchable database that helps the user target solutions, determine costs, and find vendors of AT products for people with disabilities, family members, service providers, educators, and employers. The database can be searched by function, activity, or vendor. Searches can also be associated with specific discussion groups or Assistive Technology Act of 1998 projects. The assistivetech.net site is supported by the Center for Assistive Technology and Environmental Access, the National Institute on Disability and Rehabilitation Research, and the Rehabilitation Services Administration.

Center for Applied Special Technology (CAST) URL: http://www.cast.org/

Founded in 1984, CAST "has earned international recognition for its development of innovative, technology-based educational resources and strategies based on the principles of Universal Design for Learning (UDL)." The CAST is a nonprofit organization focused on expanding learning opportunities for all individuals, especially those with disabilities. The CAST's research and development of innovative, technology-based educational resources and strategies is conducted by specialists in education research and policy, neuropsychology, clinical or school psychology, technology, engineering, curriculum development, kindergarten through 12th-grade professional development, and more. The CAST supports universal design for learning, which includes multiple means of representation, multiple means of expression, and multiple means of engagement. The CAST has been involved in the creation or codevelopment of initiatives to develop and promote a National Instructional Materials Accessibility Standard (NIMAS), as well as innovative software such as Thinking Reader, WiggleWorks, and Bobby. Also, NIMAS provides a guide to the production and electronic distribution of curricular materials in accessible, student-ready versions, including braille and digital talking books. The NIMAS Development Center is focused on improving the standard by monitoring relevant research and technological advances. The NIMAS Technical Assistance Center advises educators and publishers on the production and distribution of NIMAS-compliant materials. Teachers and administrators can access support through The CAST UDL Center, which provides access to a professional development network, consultation, publications, and online resources.

Center for Assistive Technology and Environmental Access (CATEA) URL: http://www.catea.org/

The CATEA, a unit of the College of Architecture at the Georgia Institute of Technology, maintains research projects on accessibility and usability through two research foci:

> Development, evaluation, and utilization of assistive technology
> Design and development of accessible environments

The CATEA supports individuals with disabilities of any age through expert services, research, design and technological development, information dissemination, and educational programs.

Council for Exceptional Children (CEC) URL: http://www.cec.sped.org/

The CEC "is the largest international professional organization dedicated to improving educational outcomes for individuals with exceptionalities, students with disabilities, and/or the gifted." In addition to a number of general programs and resources for special education in general, CEC has the Technology and Media Division (TAM; http://www.tamcec.org/) that "addresses the need, availability and effective use of technology and media for individuals with disabilities and/or who are gifted." The TAM hosts a national conference and publishes the *Journal of Special Education Technology* (JSET) and the *TAM Connector* newsletter. The TAM is focused on providing mentoring, technical assistance, and relevant information. Development of technical standards and advocating for funds and policies is also stressed. The site provides access to a number of publications, products, and links to websites providing information on the selection and use of ATs. The JSET is an e-journal: an online publication of the Technology and Media Division of the CEC (http://www.jset.unlv.edu). The JSET is a refereed professional journal presenting information and opinions about issues, research, policy, and practice related to the use of technology in the field of special education. Articles are indexed by publication date and accessed as web pages.

The International Center for Disability Resources on the Internet (ICDRI) URL: http://www.icdri.org/

The ICDRI is a nonprofit center based in the United States that is focused on "the equalization of opportunities for persons with disabilities." The center is organized by and for people with disabilities and seeks to increase opportunities for people with disabilities by "identifying barriers to participation in society and promoting best practices and universal design for the global community." The ICDRI gathers and maintains a collection of disability resources and best-practices. This collection is available on their website to provide education, outreach, and training opportunities. The ICDRI also provides disability rights education and customized programs to the international community for public policy strategic planning.

Job Accommodation Network (JAN)
URL: http://www.askjan.org/

The JAN is a free service of the Office of Disability Employment Policy, U.S. Department of Labor, that offers assistance "designed to increase the employability of people with disabilities by: (a) providing individualized worksite accommodations solutions, (b) providing technical assistance regarding the ADA and other disability related legislation, and (c) educating callers about self-employment options." The JAN offers assistance to employers, people with disabilities, rehabilitation professionals, and people affected by disability. The JAN website offers a small business and self-employment service, a searchable online accommodation resource, a library of presentations on specific topics, and an online newsletter and consultant resources. A variety of downloadable resources and publications are available that provide information or materials related to accommodation needs and services. Links to several employment and informational websites are also provided. In addition, links related to specific disability legislation, specific disability resources, and all levels of government resources are presented.

National Association for State Directors of Special Education, Inc. (NASDSE)
URL: http://www.nasdse.org/

The NASDSE is "dedicated to, and focused on, continuously improving educational services and outcomes while ensuring a balance of procedural guarantees for our children and youth with disabilities and their families." The NASDSE provides support in the delivery of quality education to children and youth with disabilities through training, technical assistance, research, policy development, and powerful collaborative relationships with other organizations. The NASDSE markets a number of publications and assistive technology instruction to professionals through either distance (online) education or face-to-face (on-site) instruction. Its website describes these products in detail and also provides links to a wide range of related organizations and resources.

National Center to Improve Practice (NCIP)
URL: http://www2.edc.org/NCIP/

The NCIP was funded by the U.S. Department of Education, Office of Special Education Programs from 1992 to 1998. Its goal is to "promote the effective use of technology to enhance educational outcomes for students with sensory, cognitive, physical and social/emotional disabilities."

To support this goal, the NCIP has worked to facilitate the exchange of information and build knowledge through collaborative dialogue, particularly through a series of facilitated discussion forums and online workshops.

The NCIP has gathered, synthesized, and disseminated information about technology, disabilities, practice, and implementation through a variety of efforts:

NCIP Library. A collection of resources about technology and special education

Video Profiles. Short videos with supporting print materials that illustrate students using assistive and instructional technologies to improve their learning

NCIP Guided Tours: Early Childhood. Presents tours of two exemplary early childhood classrooms

Spotlight on Voice Recognition. Demonstrates the use of voice recognition technology to address writing difficulties

Online Workshops and Events. Contains archives of NCIP's online workshops and events held from 1996 to 1998

The NCIP site provides links to other special education and technology resources with a focus on relevant organizations and technology companies. Links to sites for special education and universities with special education resources are also provided. The disability resources highlighted include those for sensory, physical, and speech impairments as well as learning disabilities, cognitive or developmental disabilities, Asperger Syndrome, ayperlexia, autism, Attention Deficit Disorder, and Attention Deficit/Hyperactivity Disorder. Family and parent support resources are also identified.

National Institute on Disability and Rehabilitation Research (NIDRR) URL: http://www.ed.gov/about/offices/list/osers/nidrr/

The NIDRR is a national leader in sponsoring research and is intended to generate, disseminate, and promote new knowledge to improve the options available to persons with disabilities. The NIDRR is a component of the United States Department of Education Office of Special Education and Rehabilitative Services (OSERS). The NIDRR conducts programs of research and related activities for the benefit of individuals of all ages with disabilities. Their goal is to maximize their full inclusion, social integration, employment, and independent living. The NIDRR's focus includes research in areas such as employment, health, and function as well as technology for access and function, independent living, and community integration. The NIDRR attempts to support the scientific community in relation to rehabilitation medicine, engineering, psychosocial rehabilitation, integration, vocational outcomes, and the virtual and built environments. The NIDRR's consumer support is based in its efforts to integrate disability research into national policies.

Quality Indicators for Assistive Technology (QIAT) URL: http://natri.uky.edu/assoc_projects/qiat/

The QIAT Consortium is a "nationwide grassroots group that includes hundreds of individuals who provide input into the ongoing process of identifying, disseminating, and implementing a set of widely-applicable Quality Indicators for Assistive Technology Services in School Settings." The resources are intended for use by school districts to provide quality AT services, AT service providers to evaluate and improve their services, consumers of AT services to find adequate AT services, universities and professional developers to develop AT service competencies, and policy makers. The QIAT Consortium provides quality indicators for AT services in school settings and forums for professional involvement, sharing, and discussion.

Rehabilitation Engineering and Assistive Technology Society of North America (RESNA) URL: http://www.resna.org/

The RESNA is an "interdisciplinary association of people with a common interest in technology and disability" dedicated to the use of technology for the improvement of the potential of people with disabilities so they may achieve their goals. The RESNA promotes research, development, education, advocacy, and provision of technology and also supports the people who are engaged in such activities.

The RESNA publishes the *Assistive Technology Journal*, hosts annual conferences, and maintains active international affiliations. To ensure consumer safeguards and increase consumer satisfaction, the RESNA maintains a credentialing program for professionals in three applied areas:

1. *Assistive Technology Practitioner (ATP)*. For service providers who are involved in analysis of a consumer's needs and training in the use of a particular AT device
2. *Assistive Technology Supplier (ATS)*. For service providers who are involved with the sale, including determination of consumer needs and service of rehabilitation equipment, of AT and commercially available products and devices
3. *Rehabilitation Engineering Technologist (RET)*. For service providers who apply engineering principles to the design, modification, customization or fabrication of AT for persons with disabilities

AbleData URL: http://www.abledata.com/

AbleData serves the nation's disability, rehabilitation, and senior communities by providing objective information on AT and rehabilitation equipment available from domestic and international sources. The most significant resource offered by AbleData is the database of AT, which contains objective information on almost 40,000 assistive products. For each product, a detailed description of the product's functions and features, price information, and contact information for the product's manufacturer and/or distributors are provided. Several other types of resources on the AbleData site are: (a) links to web resources that provide information on AT and other disability-related issues (b) the AT Library, a searchable list of books, articles, papers, and other paper and electronic publications that deal with AT (c) AbleData's own publications that aid in selecting assistive products; (d) product reviews and classified ads in the Consumer Forum; (e) conferences and other events on AT and disability; and (f) news items on AT and disability issues.

Rehabilitation Services Administration (RSA) URL: http://www.ed.gov/about/offices/list/osers/rsa/

The RSA is a component of the U.S. Department of Education of Special Education and Rehabilitative Services (OSERS). The RSA "oversees formula and discretionary grant programs that help individuals with physical or mental disabilities to obtain employment and live more independently through the provision of such supports as counseling, medical, and psychological services, job training, and other individualized services." One of the RSA's major goals is enhancing the connection between vocational rehabilitation agencies and employers.

REFERENCES

AbleData. (2011). *AbleData*. Retrieved from http://www.abledata.com/

American Association of People with Disabilities. (2011). *American Association of People with Disabilities*. Retrieved from http://www.aapd.com/

Apple Computer, Inc. (2011). *Accessibility in education*. Retrieved from http://www.apple.com/education/special-education/

Assistive Tech Net. (20011). *Assistivetech.net: Your global assistive technology explorer*. Retrieved from http://assistivetech.net/

Center for Applied Special Technology. (2011). *Center for Applied Special Technology (CAST)*. Retrieved from http://www.cast.org/

Center for Assistive Technology and Environmental Access. (2011). *Center for Assistive Technology and Environmental Access (CATEA)*. Retrieved from http://www.catea.org/

Council for Exceptional Children. (2011). *Council for Exceptional Children*. Retrieved from http://www.cec.sped.org/

Education Development Center, Inc. (2011). *National Center to Improve Practice*. Retrieved from http://www2.edc.org/NCIP/

The International Center for Disability Resources on the Internet. (2011). *The International Center for Disability Resources on the Internet (ICDRI)*. Retrieved from http://www.icdri.org/

Job Accommodation Network. (2011). *Job Accommodation Network*. Retrieved from http://www.askjan.org/

National Association for State Directors of Special Education, Inc. (2011). *National Association for State Directors of Special Education*. Retrieved from http://www.nasdse.org/

The Office of Special Education and Rehabilitative Services. (2011a). *National Institute on Disability and Rehabilitation Research*. Retrieved from http://www.ed.gov/about/offices/list/osers/nidrr/

The Office of Special Education and Rehabilitative Services. (2011b). *The Rehabilitation Services Administration*. Retrieved from http://www.ed.gov/about/offices/list/osers/rsa/

QIAT Consortium. (2011). *Quality Indicators for Assistive Technology (QIAT)*. Retrieved from http://natri.uky.edu/assoc_projects/qiat/

Rehabilitation Engineering and Assistive Technology Society of North America. (2011). *RESNA*. Retrieved from http://www.resna.org

TUFAN ADIGUZEL
Bahcesehir University

RONALD ZELLNER
Texas A&M University
Fourth edition

ADDERALL

Adderall is a stimulant medication that is a different mixture of amphetamine isomers than the common stimulants such as dexedrine, benzedrine, methamphetamine, methylphenidate, and magnesium pemoline. It is available in 5, 10, 20, and 30 mg tablets. Adderall is used primarily in the treatment of attention-deficit hyperactivity disorder (ADHD) and narcolepsy. It has also been used in the treatment of obesity (Konopasek, 2003). Adderall has been shown in clinical trials to increase alertness, improve attention span, decrease distractibility, and increase the ability to follow directions among children ages 3 years and up.

Adderall is popular among many children and families because it may need to be taken only once or twice a day, eliminating the need for dosing at school. Since it is a different chemical preparation, Adderall has been found to be effective with patients who do not respond to more popular stimulant treatments, such as Ritalin. However, Adderall may take as long as 3 to 4 weeks to become effective, while other stimulants tend to take effect more immediately. Adderall has a similar side-effect profile to other common stimulants, the most common of those being appetite suppression, growth retardation, insomnia, and headache. Less frequent side effects of this drug class include tics, dry mouth, irritability, cardiovascular acceleration, and, at high dosages, hallucinations and a disorder characterized as amphetamine psychosis. Adderall also interacts

with a variety of drugs used in the treatment of depression and with drugs used to treat psychotic symptoms. Certain foods, especially those at extremes of acidity or alkalinity, may also alter dosage effects of Adderall.

Adderall may be habit-forming and has a high potential for abuse (Konopasek, 2003). Monitoring of dose response, side effects, and polypharmacy by a physician is crucial to safe use of Adderall and other drugs in its class. Additional information is available in Arky (1998) and Cahill (1997).

REFERENCES

Arky, R. (1998). *Physicians desk reference*. Montvale, NJ: Medical Economics Data Production.

Cahill, M. (Ed.). (1997). *Nursing 97 drug handbook*. Springhouse, PA: Springhouse Corporation.

Konopasek, D. E. (2003). *Medication fact sheets*. Longmont, CO: Sopris West.

CECIL R. REYNOLDS
Texas A&M University

See *also* Stimulant Drugs; Attention Deficit/Hyperactivity Disorder

ADDISON'S DISEASE

First described by Dr. Thomas Addison in the mid-1800s, Addison's disease (adrenocortical insufficiency, hypocortisolism) is an endocrine disorder characterized by a lack of production of the hormones cortisol and aldosterone, both of which are produced by the adrenal cortex. Each individual has two adrenal glands, one above each kidney. Each adrenal gland has two parts. The inner part is called the medulla, and the outer part is called the cortex. Thus, the outer part of the adrenal gland is responsible for producing the hormones cortisol and aldosterone. Cortisol has many effects on the body, including maintaining blood pressure, maintaining cardiovascular functions, and slowing the immune system's inflammatory response. In addition, cortisol balances the effects of insulin in breaking down sugar for energy and regulating the metabolism of proteins, carbohydrates, and fats. Aldosterone helps the body maintain blood pressure, water, and salt balance. Together these two hormones have a role in the proper functioning of our major organs. Thus, Addison's disease has a significant impact on the body's functions.

Although there are no exact statistics on the incidence of Addison's disease, most studies report that this disease effects between 1 and 4 individuals per 100,000 (Merck Research Laboratories, 1992). Addison's disease occurs in all age groups and occurs slightly more frequently in females than in males (Marguiles, 1998). In approximately

70% of the cases, onset is due to the gradual destruction of the adrenal cortex by the body's own immune system. Tuberculosis is the second leading cause, accounting for another 20% of the cases. The remainder of cases are caused by chronic infections (especially fungal and cytomegalovirus infection in association with AIDS), cancer metastasis, and surgical removal of the adrenal glands.

Characteristics

1. Fatigue that may steadily worsen
2. Loss of appetite
3. Weight loss
4. Low blood pressure
5. Lightheadedness, especially upon standing
6. Nausea
7. Vomiting
8. Diarrhea
9. Muscles that are weak and spasm
10. Irritability
11. Depression
12. Craving for salty foods
13. Darkening of the skin in exposed and unexposed areas of the body

---

Treatment of Addison's disease consists of hormone replacement therapy. Cortisol is replaced orally in the form of hydrocortisone tablets divided into morning and afternoon doses. Aldosterone is replaced by fludrocortisone (a synthetic steroid) tablets taken daily. The doses of each of these hormones are adjusted for the individual's size and any coexisting medical conditions. Because the disease is chronic, replacement hormones must be taken for life.

Children with this disorder may be classified under Other Health Impairment. They may need a school schedule that includes rest periods, a shortened school day, or both. Peer helpers may be needed to assist students during the day. Also, easy access to restrooms and the health or nurse's office should be available to the student. In addition, psychological services may be needed to deal with chronic health concerns and other mental health issues. Parents should consult with the school psychologist in their district to discuss any academic needs with respect to chronic illness.

The prognosis for Addison's disease is good, and patients can lead a normal, crisis-free life as long as replacement hormones are taken properly and absorbed. Individuals with Addison's disease should wear an identification bracelet or necklace to ensure proper treatment in an emergency because additional doses of hydrocortisone may be needed so the body can effectively deal with the additional stress associated with trauma.

REFERENCES

Marguiles, P. (1997–1998). National Addison's Disease Foundation. Retrieved from www.nadf.us/index.htm

Merck Research Laboratories. (1992). *Addison's disease.* Merck manual (16th ed.). Whitehouse Station, NJ: Merck Research Laboratories.

MARYLYNNE D. FILACCIO
University of Northern Colorado

RIK CARL D'AMATOR
University of Northern Colorado

ADDITIVE-FREE DIETS

Feingold (1976), a pediatrician and allergist, reported an observed decrease in hyperactivity in many of the adults and children who adhered to his strict additive-free Kaiser-Permanente diet. The Kaiser-Permanente diet was designed to eliminate salicylates (which are related to compounds in aspirin) and synthetic, and thus nonnutritive, food dyes and flavors from the diets of people who showed adverse somatic reactions to the additives (e.g., rashes). Feingold inferred that some nonnutritional food dyes and flavors, as well as the salicylates, may have an effect similar to pharmacological compounds and alter the brain's chemistry of those that ingest them. He suggested these alterations in neurological functioning may result in behavioral changes, including increases in hyperactive behavior. Thus, Feingold believed that an additive-free diet, in which children avoid all foods with artificial dyes, flavors, and salicylates (i.e., features that characterize the Feingold diet), may be an appropriate intervention for children that demonstrate hyperactive behavior.

The Feingold diet recommends that parents with concerns about their children's hyperactive behavior should eliminate all artificial colors, flavors, sweeteners, and preservatives as well as salicylates that can be found in many fruits and vegetables (e.g., raisins and berries) from their diet. Recommendations include avoiding the use of products (e.g., toothpastes, vitamins, medications, food and beverage items) that contain any of the nonnutritive additives or salicylates. After a child has strictly adhered to the diet for 4 to 6 weeks and demonstrates improvements in behavior, food items containing salicylates can be added slowly back into the diet.

Studies that have examined the effectiveness of the Feingold diet on hyperactive behavior in children have produced mixed results. For instance, many studies have produced results that suggest that the Feingold diet is an effective intervention for children with hyperactive behavior. Feingold (1976) found that children that adhered to an additive-free diet demonstrated marked decrease in hyperactive behavior and improvement in scholastic achievement, according to teacher report, within 3 weeks of beginning the diet. Bateman and colleagues (2004) found that a diet that eliminated artificial food coloring and preservatives significantly reduced hyperactive behavior in 3-year-old children, regardless of whether they met criteria for a diagnosis of Attention-Deficit/Hyperactivity Disorder (ADHD).

In contrast, Holborow, Elkins, and Berry (1981) found that when the diet was administered to children with and without hyperactive behavior, children with hyperactive behavior did not show significant levels of decreased hyperactivity. However, children who ingested the highest levels of synthetic food colors and flavors before beginning the diet showed greater improvements in behavior than their peers, regardless of whether they demonstrated significant levels of hyperactivity before the diet.

However, many researchers have been unable to produce findings in support of the Feingold diet. Mattes (1983) conducted multiple studies and did not find the diet significantly improved behavior in hyperactive children. Thus, he concluded that, while the diet may be effective for a small percentage of children, it is not an effective intervention to treat the majority of hyperactive children.

Critics of the Feingold diet argue that Feingold and other researchers who found support of the additive-free diet did not utilize rigorous scientific methods to measure changes in behavior and instead relied on anecdotal observations from parents and teachers. Furthermore, they attribute the reported decreases in hyperactivity to the increased attention parents focused on their children during the implementation phase, instead of the direct effects of the diet. Some scholars attribute the lack of consistent findings to support the Feingold diet to the methods implemented in the research studies.

Thus, these findings suggest that the Feingold diet may be an effective treatment for a small proportion of children who demonstrate hyperactive behavior, perhaps 10% to 15%, but is not an effective intervention for the majority of children with hyperactive behavior (Schnoll, Burshteyn, & Cea-Aravena, 2003). Additionally, the diet seemingly is more effective for children in early childhood rather than during the elementary years and older.

REFERENCES

Bateman, B., Warner, J. O., Hutchinson, E., Dean, T., Rowlandson, P., Gant, C.,...Stevenson, J. (2004). The effects of a double blind, placebo controlled artificial food colorings and benzoate preservative challenge on hyperactivity in a general population sample of preschool children. *Archives of Disease in Childhood, 89,* 506–511.

Feingold, B. F. (1976). Hyperkinesis and learning disabilities linked to artificial food flavors and colors. *Journal of Learning Disabilities, 9,* 551–559.

Holborow, P., Elkins, J., & Berry, P. (1981). The effect on the Feingold diet on "normal" school children. *Journal of Learning Disabilities, 14,* 143–147.

Mattes, J. A. (1983). The Feingold diet: A current reappraisal. *Journal of Learning Disabilities, 16,* 319–323.

Rimland, B. (1983). The Feingold diet: An assessment of the reviews by Mattes, by Kavale and Forness and others. *Journal of Learning Disabilities, 16,* 331–333.

Schnoll, R., Burshteyn, D., & Cea-Aravena, J. (2003). Nutrition in the treatment of Attention-Deficit/Hyperactivity Disorder: A neglected but important aspect. *Applied Psychophysiology and Biofeedback, 28,* 63–75.

ALLISON G. DEMPSEY
University of Florida
Third edition

See also **Attention-Deficit/Hyperactivity Disorder; Feingold Diet; Hyperactivity**

ADJUSTMENT OF INDIVIDUALS WITH DISABILITIES

Individuals with disabilities and their families lead as fulfilling and satisfying lives as the families without disabilities. Adjustment to disability is typically related to adjustment before disability. A part of adjustment may be involved with seeking and obtaining appropriate care and services.

Another necessary adjustment requires recognizing and dealing with influences of a disability on all aspects of the individual's development. For example, a physical disability affects social development and interactions in ways that have only recently been addressed scientifically and professionally, but have long been sources of confusion and frustration.

It has become fashionable among educators and developmental psychologists to refer to the "whole child" in nurturing and/or describing the development of "normal," that is, nondisabled, children. Some (e.g., Shontz, 1980) have advocated this integrated approach in understanding the development of children and adolescents. However, two factors make it especially difficult to grasp specific implications of particular handicapping conditions for domains not directly affected by the conditions. One difficulty is that the interrelationships among the various developmental domains are subtle and complex; another is that the exceptional child's development is affected by special social and internal forces. Therefore, our ability to recommend theoretically based prescriptions for professional and parenting practices that will promote maximal development in indirectly affected domains is limited by the lack of empirical evidence comparing particular approaches to raising, treating, and educating the "whole" child.

The development of the child with a disability occurs along the same lines as that of the child without a disability. However, an individual child's development will exhibit qualitative variations from the norm. The specific deviations from typical development depend both on the nature and severity of the condition and on the level of adjustment achieved by the child and his or her family and teachers.

Normal personal-social development includes the emergence of the individual's self-concept and self-esteem. These beliefs about one's characteristics, relative worth, and competence are acquired by internalizing an image of one's self as it is reflected by important adults and peers. Bartel and Guskin (1980) emphasize that the feedback one receives from the social environment is a crucial factor in the development of a positive self-concept and high self-esteem, for it creates an expectation and interpretive schema for self-evaluation of one's abilities and efforts. The self-concept of a child with disabilities is at risk because society's negative evaluations of individuals who are different from the norm are systematically, if unconsciously, transmitted to him or her (Gliedman & Roth, 1980). Because the development of high self-esteem is based on what an individual *can* do, a handicapping condition may endanger a child's self-esteem by focusing attention on what the child cannot do.

A disability may limit a child's or adolescent's physical activities. The handicap may impose restrictions owing to physical limitations or medical complications that limit freedom to get about in the environment. Physical and/or medical limitations may reduce opportunities for interaction and exploration in both the physical and social realms and thus curtail experiences that stimulate and promote cognitive growth and personal-social development. Children with disabilities must be encouraged not to retreat from any activities that are accessible, although inconvenient, because of physical restrictions. Professionals and others can help them to participate in an adapted way, if necessary, in order not to deprive them of beneficial experiences.

Children with disabilities may have to adjust medical interventions or therapies such as drugs, braces, physical therapy, surgical procedures, hearing appliances, and so on. The child's adjustment to the medical aspect of his or her program is absolutely essential because the child must cooperate in order to achieve the maximum benefits of the prescribed treatment(s).

An exceptional child is very likely to have to make an adjustment involving his or her educational programs. The adjustment may range from simply modifying his or her study habits or methods to full-time participation in a special self-contained program. Professionals who work with the child should strive to minimize whatever educational disadvantage(s) may be imposed by the handicap. The goals of the child's educational program should emphasize activities to compensate for and/or overcome his or her disability.

The effectiveness of the child's program will be amplified by the active involvement of parents in consistently following through on behavioral and educational interventions in the home environment. Concrete benefits are derived from the parents' participation. Parents are able to provide additional reinforcement and practice for skills learned during the school day, helping their child consolidate gains more rapidly. In addition, their involvement is a signal to the child of their commitment to his or her development and the high value they place on educational achievement. These attitudes are highly motivating and will help see the child through difficult periods.

Parents who do not accept and adjust to the child's handicap escalate their child's difficulties. Maladaptive behavior patterns that emerge in the relationship between parents and their handicapped child can arise from either of two opposite, but equally harmful, reactions. Parents may either overestimate or underestimate their child's abilities and potential. Overestimates may be due to parents' denial of their child's problems. Such parents are prone to establish unreasonably high standards for their child's behavior or development. Because the child wants to please the parents but is not capable of fulfilling their expectations, he or she continually faces feelings of frustration, inadequacy, and other negative emotions such as guilt, disappointment, and uncertainty as to his or her place in the affections of the parents. On the other hand, some parents seem to overcompensate for their handicapped child. Some typical behaviors of these parents include setting goals that are too easily attained, praising or rewarding the child for work that is below his or her level of functioning, and intervening unnecessarily when the child is working on difficult tasks. Such behaviors convey the message, albeit indirectly, that the parents do not recognize or appreciate the child's actual abilities. These signals undermine the development of high self-esteem and a positive self-concept. Of course professionals helping parents of children with disabilities need to make sure that support programs are culturally sensitive (Lian & Fantanez-Phelan, 2001).

Adjusting to the child's disability is difficult, but Kogan (1980) has shown that parents can learn and use techniques for interacting with their child in ways that promote an adaptive relationship. General guidelines for parents in nurturing optimum development include realistically accepting the child, including abilities and disabilities. Parents should be sympathetic, but must encourage independence in order to enhance the child's self-esteem and promote his or her success in the "real" world.

Parents also have a crucial role in setting the stage for good sibling relationships. They must not show favoritism toward any of their children. Although they may enjoy different activities with their individual children, they should not give their attention preferentially to any single child. In particular, parents must avoid making comparisons among their children, and instead emphasize each child's individual strengths. All children will benefit when parents provide experiences and delegate responsibilities in accordance with each child's developmental level and needs.

Due to increasing recognition of social and emotional problems that may be secondary to other disabilities, the IDEIA requires a behavioral assessment of all children with a disability, regardless of their handicapping condition. It has become commonplace to use objective behavior rating scales and personality assessments during the initial referral and evaluation process (e.g., Reynolds & Kamphaus, 2004). Also, as a direct result of recognition of behavioral and emotional concomitants of various disabilities, IDEIA now requires a behavioral assessment prior to disciplining a child with a disability, so that it can be determined whether the behavior of concern is a result of the child's disability. When behavioral problems are disability-related, children must be treated, not punished. Teachers will have the primary role to play in such interventions at school.

Over and above the special methods and materials teachers use in working with the handicapped child, perhaps the most important element of the handicapped child's educational experience is a positive social climate. Teachers can provide a model for accepting individual differences in general and specifically valuing each child's, including the child with disabilities, abilities, and contributions. The child's classmates will imitate the teacher and assimilate the underlying nondiscriminatory attitudes (Hunt, Doering, Hirose-Hatae, Maier, & Goetz, 2001). Being accepted by one's teachers and classmates nourishes the handicapped child's self-concept and self-esteem, thereby promoting not only social development, but also cognitive growth and educational achievement.

REFERENCES

Bartel, N. R., & Guskin, S. L. (1980). A handicap as a social phenomenon. In W. M. Cruickshank (Ed.), *Psychology of exceptional children and youth* (pp. 45–73). Englewood Cliffs, NJ: Prentice Hall.

Gliedman, J., & Roth, W. (1980). *The unexpected minority: Handicapped children in America*. New York, NY: Harcourt Brace Jovanovich.

Hunt, P., Doering, K., Hirose-Hatae, A., Maier, J., & Goetz, L. (2001). Across-program collaboration to support students with and without disabilities in a general education classroom. *Journal of the Association of Persons with Severe Handicaps*, 26, 240–256.

Kogan, K. L. (1980). Interaction systems between preschool handicapped or developmentally delayed children and their parents. In T. Field, S. Goldberg, D. Stern, & A. M. Sostek (Eds.), *High risk infants and children: Adult and peer interactions* (pp. 227–247). New York, NY: Academic Press.

Lian, M. J., & Fantanez-Phelan, S. M. (2001). Perceptions of Latino parents regarding cultural and linguistic issues and advocacy for children with disabilities. *Journal of the Association for Persons with Severe Handicaps*, 26, 189–194.

Novak, M. A., Olley, G., & Kearney, D. S. (1980). Social skills of children with special needs in integrated separate preschools. In T. Field, S. Goldberg, D. Stern, & A. M. Sostek (Eds.), *High risk infants and children: Adult and peer interactions* (pp. 327–346). New York, NY: Academic Press.

Reynolds, C. R., & Kamphaus, R. W. (2004). *Behavior assessment system for children-2*. Circle Pines, MN: American Guidance Service.

Shontz, F. C. (1980). Theories about adjustment to having a disability. In W. M. Cruickshank (Ed.), *Psychology of exceptional children and youth* (pp. 3–44). Englewood Cliffs, NJ: Prentice Hall.

Wang, M., & Brown, R. (2009). Family quality of life: A framework for policy and social service provisions to support families of children with disabilities, *Journal of Family Social Work*, 12(2), 144–167.

PAULINE F. APPLEFIELD
University of North Carolina at Wilmington
Third edition

See also Adaptive Behavior; Behavior Assessment System for Children; Family Counseling; Family Response to a Child with Disabilities; Handicapism; Individuals With Disabilities Education Improvement Act of 2004 (IDEIA); Teacher Expectancies

ADLER, ALFRED (1870–1937)

Alfred Adler, an Austrian psychiatrist, severed an early connection with Freudian psychoanalysis to develop his more socially oriented Individual Psychology, which was a powerful influence in the development of the field of social psychology. Adler's work in education and child guidance is less well known, but it contributed greatly to the development of school services in Austria and it had worldwide significance for the education and treatment of children.

At the Pedagogical Institute of the City of Vienna, he helped to train thousands of teachers and established the first child guidance clinics in the Vienna school system. In 1935, with the coming of a fascist regime in Austria, Adler left Vienna for the United States, where he established a private practice and served as professor of medical psychology at the Long Island College of Medicine.

REFERENCES

Ansbacher, H. L., & Ansbacher, R. (1956). *The individual psychology of Alfred Adler*. New York, NY: Basic Books.

Watson, R. I. (1963). *The great psychologists.* New York, NY: Lippincott.

PAUL IRVINE
Katonah, New York
Third edition

ADMINISTRATION OF SPECIAL EDUCATION

Prior to the advent of public school programs for individuals with disabilities in the late 19th and early 20th centuries, administration of special education programs was usually executed by persons who were not administrators. Because many of the early programs were provided by religious organizations (Hewett & Forness, 1977), the earliest administrators were probably monks, nuns, or other religious figures (e.g., Pedro Ponce deLeon, a Spanish monk who worked with the deaf in the 16th century). During the late 18th and early 19th centuries, philosophical changes and a new attention to science changed attitudes toward individuals with disabilities and their treatment. These changes, evidenced in the French and American revolutions, created a reverence for the individual and a belief that the lives of individuals with disabilities could be significantly improved through the application of science. Thus a new wave of administrators arose. These administrators were not interested primarily in running a program, but in teaching, scientific inquiry, and having an impact on contemporary thought through their writings. Thus a time was born in which most programs were managed by scientists, physicians, and philosophers such as Edouard Sequin, Valentin Hauy, and Samuel Gridley Howe. During the 19th century a great number of public and private residential schools/institutions were developed. For the most part, these institutions (which remained the dominant force in special education until the middle of the 20th century) were administered by physicians. This was especially true for institutions for the intellectually and developmentally delayed, the emotionally disturbed, and the physically disabled.

Public school services for exceptional children began early in the 19th century largely because of the efforts of Elizabeth Farrell in New York Public Schools and the common school movement in the New York area. By the middle of the 20th century, public school classes became the primary mode of education for exceptional children. With this change, the administration of special education programs fell to educators and school psychologists. Although special education programs were held in public school buildings, frequently they included immigrant populations for purposes of culturation and they were usually separated from the general population. Writers of the time advocated separate administration and supervision systems (Ayer & Barr, 1928).

The rise of special education administration as a discipline occurred simultaneously with the rise of segregated public school programs. Special education administrators during the first quarter of the 20th century were not trained generally as administrators; it was not until 1938 that any professional identity was established. In that year, the National Association of State Directors of Special Education was founded (Burrello & Sage, 1979). In 1951 the Council of Administrators of Special Education (CASE) convened as a special interest group within the Council for Exceptional Children (Burrello & Sage, 1979).

During the 1950s, 1960s, and 1970s, special education administration grew as a result of the increase in public special-education programs brought about by the increased federal role in programs for the handicapped individuals with disabilities. In the 1950s, the U.S. Office of Education conducted several large-scale studies of special education and special-education administration (Mackie & Engel, 1956; Mackie & Snyder, 1957). These studies helped to establish the roles of administrators of programs for exceptional children and the need for professional training. Many more studies were conducted during the 1960s and 1970s (e.g., Kohl & Marro, 1971; Sage, 1968; Wisland & Vaughan, 1964). It was, however, the passage of PL 94-142, The Education of All Handicapped Children Act of 1975, that brought special education administration to its current state. This legislation, and others that followed, together with numerous lawsuits, created a demand for administrators who were specifically trained to manage special-education programs, a demand that has grown with subsequent programs (e.g., IDEA).

Although special education administration has developed a uniqueness and identity, there is considerable variety within the discipline. This variety is expressed across governmental levels and organizational arrangements. There are three governmental levels in special education administration: federal, state, and local. Within each level the tasks of the administrator may vary considerably depending on the specific role of the administrator, the organization of the agency for which the administrator works, and the ways in which the agency delivers services.

Presently, the federal role in special education administration is executed primarily by the Office of Special Education and Rehabilitation of the U.S. Department of Education. The administrative roles of this office include monitoring state compliance with IDEIA; generating research; providing public information; formulating regulations; promoting personnel development; and drafting legislation. As a result of PL 94-142, IDEA, and IDEIA the federal role in administration of special education has grown substantially. Nearly every administrative decision in special education must be made with consideration for the regulations propagated by IDEIA. Because of this, the majority of the administrators at the federal level are involved in activities related to providing services to the states in order that they may carry out the provisions of IDEIA, or in evaluating/monitoring the state's efforts.

Administration of special education programs at the state level occurs in three places: at the state education agency (SEA); at state-operated schools; and at state-operated regional centers. At the SEA, the roles of administration are to develop legislation; to develop state plans; to obtain and administer financial resources; to develop personnel preparation systems and standards; to develop plans for improving instruction; to enforce and monitor regulations; and to develop public relations (Podemski, Price, Smith, & Marsh, 1984). The SEAs also directly administer programs such as state schools for the deaf or blind (e.g., Pennsylvania). These programs are usually for low-incidence populations. In Georgia, the SEA administers both state schools and regional centers that provide direct service to low-incidence populations, especially in rural areas. Regional centers also serve as resource centers for local education agencies (LEAs).

Some state-operated programs in special education are not administered by the SEA. These programs usually serve persons with intellectual disability or emotional disturbance and may be managed by state agencies such as a department of mental health, and juvenile services. Such programs are generally subject to the same regulations as programs operated by the SEA. In many instances, however, the programs are not managed by educators. The practice of employing physicians, psychologists, or social workers to manage state residential programs is a vestige of a tradition in state institutions and is justifiable for programs that are not chiefly educational.

At the local level, there are a number of different administrative arrangements and even more varied service delivery arrangements (Burrello & Sage, 1979). The simplest administrative arrangement is the LEA. The LEA, also known as the local school district, provides direct services to exceptional children through various delivery systems. Administration at the local level may be centralized or decentralized. In a centralized system, persons (i.e., teachers) who provide services to exceptional children are managed by a district-wide special education director (coordinator). The special education director in a centralized system exercises a great amount of control over special education personnel and programs. In a decentralized system, the special education administrator serves in a coordinating/supporting/advising role. This administrator may have some authority over personnel but it is generally a building administrator (principal) who oversees daily operations.

More complex local administrative arrangements include intermediate educational units (IEU) and cooperative programs. Intermediate units exist in approximately 35 states (Podemski et al., 1984). In some states (e.g., Georgia) these units may be state-operated regional programs. In other states (e.g., New York, Texas, Wisconsin,

Pennsylvania) the intermediate units are administered as a separate level of education agency. Intermediate units may be known by several names (e.g., Board of Cooperative Educational Services in New York, Regional Education Service Centers in Texas). According to Podemski et al. (1984), intermediate units were developed to pool resources and to share costs. In some states (e.g., Pennsylvania) intermediate units provide more than special education services and were developed for political as well as educational reasons during a time of district consolidation. Intermediate units have been criticized as arrangements that violate the principle of least restrictive environment because their services often require removing a child from his or her home school. Among the problems facing administrators of intermediate units are competition with LEAs for funds and students, potential conflict in lines of authority, communication gaps with the LEA, and salary variations that influence competition with LEAs for teachers.

Many rural school systems and suburban systems enter into cooperative agreements in order to provide more cost-effective programs, especially for low-incidence populations (Howe, 1981). Cooperative programs engender the same problems as do IEUs. Additionally, they must often contend with long distances for busing students.

The competencies of LEA and IEU special education administrators are similar. The differences are probably in terms of the amount of time devoted to different tasks rather than the tasks themselves. This may be true also for administrators of state-operated direct service programs (e.g., state schools). The competency areas for such administrators include organization theory and behavior, budget development, curriculum development, supervision, personnel administration, community relations, community resources, change processes, physical plant management, research, professional standards, and policy development.

Specialized graduate training for administrators of programs for exceptional children began in 1965. The impetus for such training was provided by a journal article by Milazzo and Blessing (1964). Subsequent to the publishing of that article, the U.S. Office of Education awarded grants to universities for the purpose of developing training programs (Burrello & Sage, 1979). Although most states do have certification requirements for special education leadership positions, requirements can be met with a general administrative certificate or a collection of courses and experience.

Special education administrators now have organized to promote and shape special education policies. The Council of Administration of Special Education (CASE) promotes leadership and provides special education administrators with opportunities for personal and professional advancement. CASE is a special interest division of the Council for Exceptional Children (CEC; 2005). The website for CASE has extensive resources for administrators and reflects an international presence.

REFERENCES

Ayer, F. C., & Barr, A. S. (1928). *The organization of supervision.* New York, NY: Appleton.

Burrello, L. C., & Sage, D. D. (1979). *Leadership and change in special education.* Englewood Cliffs, NJ: Prentice Hall.

Council for Exceptional Children (CEC). (2005). *Special interest divisions.* Retrieved from http://www.cec.sped.org/dv/

Gearheart, B. R., & Wright, W. S. (1979). *Organization and administration of educational programs for exceptional children* (2nd ed.). Springfield, IL: Thomas.

Hewett, F. M., & Forness, S. R. (1977). *Education of exceptional learners.* Boston, MA: Allyn & Bacon.

Howe, C. (1981). *Administration of special education.* Denver, CO: Love.

Kohl, J. W., & Marro, T. D. (1971). *A normative study of the administrative position in special education.* Grant No. OEG-0-70-2467 (607), U.S. Office of Education, Pennsylvania State University.

Mackie, R. P., & Engel, A. M. (1956). *Directors and supervisors of special education in local school systems.* U.S. Office of Education Bulletin 1955, No. 13. Washington, DC: U.S. Government Printing Office.

Mackie, R. P., & Snyder, W. E. (1957). *Special education personnel in state departments of education.* U.S. Office of Education Bulletin 1956, No. 6. Washington, DC: U.S. Government Printing Office.

Milazzo, T. C., & Blessing, K. R. (1964). The training of directors and supervisors of special education programs. *Exceptional Children, 31,* 129–141.

Podemski, R. S., Price, B. J., Smith, T. E. C., & Marsh, G. E. (1984). *Comprehensive administration of special education.* Rockville, MD: Aspen.

Sage, D. D. (1968). Functional emphasis in special education administration. *Exceptional Children, 35,* 69–70.

Wisland, M. V., & Vaughan, T. D. (1964). Administrative problems in special education. *Exceptional Children, 31,* 87–89.

JAMES K. MCAFEE
Pennsylvania State University
Third edition

See also **Individuals With Disabilities Education Improvement Act of 2004 (IDEIA); Politics and Special Education; Special Education Programs; Supervision in Special Education; Child Guidance Clinic**

ADOPTEES

The practice of adoption is centuries old, but our understanding of the impact of this form of child care continues to be without definitive answers. At the theoretical level, adoption has often been associated with increased risk for psychological maladjustment. Psychoanalytic theory, for example, suggests that the experience of adoption sets the stage for disturbances in personality and identity development. This is especially true because of doubt surrounding the true circumstances of the child's origins, and because the child has two sets of parents instead of one with whom to identify. Bowlby's work (1969) suggests that adopted children are at risk for emotional problems, but only in cases where there is disruption in the development and continuity of primary attachment relationships. Consequently, infants adopted soon after birth and cared for continually by affectionate and competent parents would not be viewed as being at risk in terms of possible maladjustment. However, individuals raised by multiple caregivers, or separated from caregivers after a secure attachment has developed, would be perceived as being at risk.

In contrast to the theoretical literature, the results of empirical research have produced an inconsistent picture of the effects of adoption on an individual's psychological development. After reviewing the social work literature on the success of adoption placements, both Mech (1973) and Kadushin (1974) concluded that the majority of placements were satisfactory and this has been supported in recent studies (Feigelman, 2001) of domestic adoptions but not so much with international adoptions (Tieman, van der Ende, & Verhulst, 2005). However, an examination of the records of mental-health clinics reveals that adopted children are referred to these clinics at disproportionate rates. Mech (1973) reported that while adopted children reared by nonrelatives constitute approximately 1% of the population, they account for over 4% of the children seen in clinics. Researchers have also reported that there are differences in types of problems presented by adopted children versus those who are nonadopted. Adopted children typically manifest more aggressive and acting-out problems, as well as learning-related difficulties (Simmel, Brooks, Barth, & Hinshaw, 2001). Some studies have stated that adopted females are more likely to display symptoms of conduct disorder that those that are not adopted (Nilsson et al., 2011). In fact, a study has even reported an elevated number of pediatric health conditions among adopted children (Dalby, Fox, & Haslam, 1982). Adoption satisfaction has been tied as the cause of many of these displays of aggression, conduct disorder, and so forth and were proven based on calculating Person correlations, the DISC, the level of conduct problems, the MTF survey, and domains of adoption satisfaction (Nilsson et al., 2011). Children who have low levels of adoption satisfaction will manifest unwanted behaviors and aggression, while those with higher adoption acceptance and security will be more successful in integrating with their new family as well as behaviorally (Nilsson et al., 2011). When adoptive family members are content with the contact they have with the adopted child, the child is more likely to thrive positively and manifest less problems in the long run throughout his/her life.

While there are those studies available that validate these findings, there are also those such as Aumend and

Barrett's (1984) that provide a contrary set of findings. In their study of adult adoptees they reported the following: the majority of those in their study scored above the 60th percentile on the Tennessee Self Concept Scale; had positive scores on the Attitude Toward Parents Scales; were happy growing up, with only 12% reporting that they were unhappy; and did not report revelation of their adoptive status as being disruptive or traumatic. These findings were consistent with those of Norvell and Guy (1977), who determined there were no significant differences between self-concepts of an adopted and nonadopted population, aged 18 to 25. They concluded that problems of a negative identity seemed to stem more from problems within the home, rather than an association with adoption.

Because of a lack of definitive empirical information, the issue of open records, or allowing adopted children to learn about their biological parents at a particular point in time, continues to be controversial. There have been recent calls for unconditional release of records (Miall & March, 2005). Grotevant et al. (2010) concluded that there is not a relationship between contact with a child's birth mother, adoptive parent's discussing adoption-related issues, and the manifestation of externalizing behaviors. The largest factor in the success of an adopted child succeeding is the satisfaction the family has with the child and vice versa (Grotevant, et al., 2010). While this is still a topic that needs considerably more research, it is a topic to be considered in the well-being of a child who has been adopted and his/her family. Another issue unique to adoption is when children should be informed of their adoptive status. Currently, most specialists on adoption advocate telling children before they are 5 years of age. The specialists believe this promotes the development of a trusting relationship within the context of a warm and supportive family and eliminates the possibility that the child will hear of his or her unique family status from nonfamily members under less-than-desirable conditions. While many advocate telling the child during the preschool years, recent studies such as that by Brodzinsky, Schechter, Braff, and Singer (1984) suggest that a child's cognitive development during the preschool years may mitigate against his or her understanding of the nature of adoption. Their concern is that parents may relate this information to children and then feel the "job is done," failing to understand that advanced stages of cognitive development call for further explanations and sequential exploration of concerns the child might harbor. Finally, the most sensational adoption issue is currently being debated and that is of gay adoption. At this time, large surveys questioning same-sex adoption indicate approximately half for and half against (Miall & March, 2005).

While the data are not as definitive as might be liked, it certainly seems that adoption is a legitimate way of building families and caring for young children. It is superior to alternatives such as serial placements in a number of homes, or large-scale institutional care. Assuming the family is capable of providing a stable environment that is free of debilitating or otherwise pathological features, and relates the information on adoption in a facilitative fashion, there seems to be little reason to expect greater childhood problems than experienced in biologically created families. In families where psychological attachment between adoptee and parent fails, increased emotional and behavioral problems will occur (Ziegler, 1994).

REFERENCES

Aumend, S. A., & Barrett, M. C. (1984). Self-concept and attitudes toward adoption: A comparison of searching and nonsearching adult adoptees. *Child Welfare, 63*, 251–259.

Bowlby, J. (1969). *Attachment and loss: Volume 1 attachment*. New York, NY: Basic Books.

Brodzinsky, D. M., Schechter, D. E., Braff, A. M., & Singer, L. M. (1984). Psychological and academic adjustment in adopted children. *Journal of Consulting and Clinical Psychology, 52*, 582–589.

Dalby, J. T., Fox, S. L., & Haslam, R. H. (1982). Adoption and foster care rates in pediatric disorders. *Developmental and Behavioral Pediatrics, 3*, 61–64.

Feigelman, W. (2001). Comparing adolescents in diverging family structures: Investigating whether adoptees are more prone to problems than their nonadopted peers. *Adoption Quarterly, 5(2)*, 5–37

Grotevant, H. D., Rueter, M., Von Korff, L., Gonzalez, C. (2010). Post-adoption contact, adoption communicative openness, and satisfaction with contact as predictors of externalizing behavior in adolescence and emerging adulthood. *Journal of Child Psychology, 52(5)*, 529–536.

Howard, J. A., Smith, S. L. MSSW, LCSW, Ryan, S. D. (2004). A comparative study of child welfare adoptions with other types of adopted children and birth children. *Adoption Quarterly, 7(3)*, 1–30.

Kadushin, A. (1974). *Child welfare services*. New York, NY: Macmillan.

Mech, E. V. (1973). Adoption: A policy perspective. In B. Caldwell & H. Ricuitti (Eds.), *Review of child development research* (Vol. 3). Chicago, IL: University of Chicago Press.

Miall, C. E., & March, K. (2005). Social support for changes in adoption practice: Gay adoption, open adoption, birth reunions and the release of confidential identifying information. *Families in Society, 86*, 83–92.

Nilsson, R. Rhee, S. H., Corley, R. P., Rhea, S., Wadsworth, S. J., DeFries, J. C. (2011). Conduct problems in adopted and nonadopted adolescents and adoption satisfaction as a protective factor. *Adoption Quarterly, 14(3)*, 181–198.

Norvell, M., & Guy, R. F. (1977). A comparison of self-concept in adopted and nonadopted adolescents. *Adolescence, 12*, 443–448.

Simmel, C., Brooks, D., Barth, R. P., & Hinshaw, P. (2001). Externalizing symptomatology among adoptive youth: Prevalence and preadoptive risk factors. *Journal of Abnormal Child Psychology, 29*, 57–69.

Tieman, W., van der Ende, J., & Verhulst, C. (2005). Psychiatric disorders in young adult Intercountry Adoptees: An epidemiological study. *American Journal of Psychiatry, 162*, 592–598.

Ziegler, D. (1994). Adoption and adjustment. In B. James (Eds.), *Handbook for treatment of attachment-trauma problems in children* (pp. 256–266). New York, NY: Lexington Books.

CHARLES P. BARNARD
University of Wisconsin at Stout

See *also* Post-Institutionalized Children

ADRENAL HYPERPLASIA, CONGENITAL

Congenital adrenal hyperplasia is a family of inherited disorders that result from the inability of the adrenal glands to sufficiently synthesize hormones known as corticosteroids. The various types of congenital adrenal hyperplasia are caused by enzyme deficiencies in different stages of hormone production. The most common enzyme deficiency is 21-hydroxylase, which is necessary for the production of two adrenal steroid hormones, cortisol and aldosterone. Cortisol is responsible for maintaining the body's energy supply, blood sugar level, and reaction to stress. Aldosterone is a salt-retaining hormone, which maintains the balance of salt and water in the body. In response to the low cortisol levels, the anterior pituitary gland produces high amounts of adrenocorticotropin hormone (ACTH) to activate the adrenal glands to produce cortisol. The high levels of ACTH result in the overproduction of cortisol precursors, which are used to produce an excessive amount of androgens. Excess androgens cause abnormal sexual development, such as masculinized external genitalia in female newborns. An additional defect in aldosterone synthesis may be present, resulting in the inability to conserve urinary sodium. Deficient aldosterone in addition to insufficient cortisol production is labeled the salt-wasting form of the disorder. Individuals with only deficient cortisol production have the non-salt-wasting form of congenital adrenal hyperplasia. The third type of congenital adrenal hyperplasia is the milder, nonclassic form, which has a later onset between early childhood and puberty (McKusick, 1994; Plum & Cecil, 1996).

About 95% of cases of congenital adrenal hyperplasia are caused by 21-hydroxylase deficiency, affecting one in 13,000–15,000 births in the general population. About half the cases have the salt-wasting form of the disorder (McKusick, 1994). Nonclassical adrenal hyperplasia affects approximately 1 in 20 Ashkenazi Jews, 1 in 40 Hispanic persons, 1 in 50 Yugoslavians, and 1 in 300 Italians. Congenital adrenal hyperplasia is an autosomal recessive disorder. The defective gene that causes 21-hydroxylase deficiency is located on the short arm of Chromosome 6 (Carlson, Obeid, Kanellopoulou, Wilson, & New, 1999).

Characteristics

1. Symptoms include muscle weakness, nausea, vomiting, anorexia, irritability, depression, hyperpigmentations of the skin, hypotension, lack of tolerance to cold temperatures, and the inability of the body to effectively respond to stress (Pang, 2000).
2. A child will grow rapidly and develop pubic hair during early childhood.
3. Female newborns may have an abnormally enlarged clitoris and joining labial folds, resulting in ambiguous external genitalia. In rare cases females are raised as males.
4. Male newborns do not exhibit physical signs except for pigmentation around the genitalia (Wynbrandt & Ludman, 2000).
5. An infant with the salt-wasting form may experience vomiting, poor weight gain, poor feeding, drowsiness, diarrhea, dehydration, and circulatory collapse. Without treatment the infant will go into shock and die (Plum & Cecil, 1996).
6. During puberty girls with the mild form of the disorder will develop excess body hair, acne, menstrual irregularity, and in some cases infertility and polycystic ovaries.

Early diagnosis and treatment of congenital adrenal hyperplasia is extremely important, especially for the salt-wasting form of the disorder, which is life threatening. Treatment is aimed at providing the body with the ability to maintain energy, normal growth, and a balance between salt and water. In the non-salt-wasting form of the disease, only cortisol replacement is needed. In the salt-wasting form, it is necessary to replace cortisol, aldosterone, and salt with synthetic hormones such as hydrocortisone and fludrocortisone (Florinef), a salt-retaining hormone. Extra doses of hydrocortisone are important when the child experiences injury, infection, or surgery because the body cannot respond to stress without cortisol (Pang, 2000).

With treatment, children with congenital adrenal hyperplasia can have normal growth and development. However, they must continue receiving cortisol therapy. Without treatment, the child may experience dehydration, electrolyte imbalance, and adrenal crisis. Children under stress such as high fever, serious injury, or vomiting usually need additional cortisol treatment and possibly emergency care (Pang, 2000). Thus, medication may need to be managed at school. Special education services may be available to children with congenital adrenal hyperplasia under Other Health Impairment. A health care plan should be implemented in the child's individual educational plan so that school personnel understand the necessary actions during an emergency (Plumridge, Bennett, Dinno, & Branson, 1993).

If congenital adrenal hyperplasia continues to be treated and monitored throughout life, an individual with the disorder is expected to have a normal life expectancy and live a healthy, productive life. Many individuals do not reach the height potential indicated by family height because they have premature growth spurts and bone aging. The effectiveness and safety of certain drug treatments continue to be investigated. Female fetuses affected with the 21-hydroxylase deficiency form of congenital adrenal hyperplasia may be treated with dexamethasone, a long-acting corticosteroid, early in the pregnancy until birth. As a result, the adrenal glands are suppressed and the external genitalia develop normally (Carlson et al., 1999). In the future researchers will investigate whether enzyme replacement by gene therapy is possible.

REFERENCES

Carlson, A. D., Obeid, J. S., Kanellopoulou, N., Wilson, R. C., & New, M. I. (1999). Congenital adrenal hyperplasia: Update on prenatal diagnosis and treatment. *Journal of Steroid Biochemistry and Molecular Biology, 69*, 19–29.

McKusick, V. A. (Ed.). (1994). *Mendelian inheritance in man: A catalog of human genetic disorders* (11th ed.). Baltimore, MD: Johns Hopkins University Press.

Pang, S. (2000). Congenital adrenal hyperplasia. Retrieved from http://www.magicfoundation.org/www

Plum, F., & Cecil, R. L. (Eds.). (1996). *Cecil textbook of medicine* (20th ed., Vol. 2). St. Louis, MO: W. B. Saunders.

Plumridge, D., Bennett, R., Dinno, N., & Branson, C. (1993). *The student with a genetic disorder.* Springfield, IL: Charles C. Thomas.

Wynbrandt, J., & Ludman, M. D. (2000). *The encyclopedia of genetic disorders and birth defects* (2nd ed.). New York, NY: Facts on File.

SUSANNAH MORE
University of Texas at Austin

ADRENOCORTICOTROPIC HORMONE (ACTH) DEFICIENCY

Adrenocorticotropic hormone (ACTH) deficiency, sometimes referred to as secondary adrenal insufficiency, is a rare (affecting fewer than 1 in 100,000) and potentially life-threatening form of adrenocortical failure in which there is partial or complete lack of ACTH production and secretion by the anterior pituitary gland (Schmidli, Donald, & Espiner, 1989). ACTH acts to stimulate release of cortisol from the adrenal cortex during both the diurnal rhythm and exposure to stressors. Onset may occur throughout the life span.

Characteristic signs and symptoms of ACTH deficiency include weight loss, anorexia (lack of appetite), vomiting, hyponatremia (sodium deficiency), hypoglycemia, postural hypotension, muscular fatigue or stiffness, hypotonia (loss of muscle tone), muscle weakness, lethargy, general fatigue, and subtle attentional or memory deficits (Brown, 1994). In contrast to Addison's disease, abnormal skin pigmentation and aldosterone hyposecretion are not present (Schmidli et al., 1989). More easily diagnosed in conjunction with various other conditions (see later discussion), ACTH deficiency is more difficult to diagnose when isolated; across a number of studies, a sizable minority of cases display an idiopathic etiology. Additionally, clinician awareness may not be high, and some complex diagnostic work may require referral to specialists (Schmidli et al., 1989).

A number of tests may be administered to diagnose ACTH deficiency. The insulin-induced hypoglycemia test is sometimes considered the gold standard, but it requires close supervision and may not be as safe for children as the metyrapone test (Erturk, Jaffe, & Barkan, 1998). The metyrapone test is very effective, but it may induce adrenal crisis, it requires overnight hospitalization, and metyrapone is at times difficult to obtain for diagnostic use. See Rose et al. (1999) for an outstanding comparison of the metyrapone, high-dose ACTH, and low-dose ACTH tests. Hypothyroidism may mask ACTH deficiency, and it may not be revealed by the aforementioned tests until L-thyroxine therapy has been initiated (Nanao, Miyamoto, Anzo, Tsukuda, & Hasegawa, 1999). The cause of ACTH deficiency may be of hypothalamic (rather than pituitary) origin, and a corticotropin-releasing hormone (CRH) test may be indicated. CT scans or other imaging procedures are often employed as a check for tumors, lesions, or trauma.

There are many likely causes of ACTH deficiency. It has been observed in association with familial history of ACTH deficiency, hypopituitarism (and short stature), pituitary or brain tumor, head trauma, benign intracranial hypertension, cranial radiation therapy, long-term pharmacologic steroid therapy, intermittent high-dose steroid therapy, autoimmune disorders, diabetes mellitus, a likely cleavage enzyme defect, hypothalamic and pituitary lesions, birth injury, infection, and neurosurgery (Rose et al., 1999).

Characteristics

1. Weight loss, anorexia, or vomiting
2. Hypocortisolism, hypoglycemia, or hyponatremia
3. Postural hypotension
4. Muscular fatigue or stiffness, hypotonia, or muscle weakness
5. Lethargy and general fatigue
6. Subtle attentional or memory deficits.

Treatment of ACTH deficiency involves replacing cortisol that the adrenal cortex is not being stimulated to produce; this is most often done with daily oral administration of hydrocortisone and additional "stress dosing" as required (Rose et al., 1999). In partial ACTH deficiency, only stress dosing may be needed. In severe cases, intravenous injections of hydrocortisone may be needed during high stress or other crises.

Although treatment is quite effective and many treated children will require no special education support, the period during which ACTH deficiency was untreated may have generated some conditions requiring such services and support (Rose et al., 1999; Schmidli et al., 1989). Being of short stature, underweight, and physically weaker, as well as experiencing delayed growth and development, may require both educational and psychological support. Cognitive (attentional and memory) deficits in the past or present may generate some special educational considerations. Finally, educators should be somewhat knowledgeable about daily and stress dosing requirements, should crises arise in the educational setting. All of these concerns can be exacerbated by the presence of other diseases or conditions with which ACTH deficiency is often associated.

Further research continues on ACTH deficiency and hypothalamic-pituitary-adrenal function across the fields of psychology, psychiatry, neurology, endocrinology, and immunology. The greatest promise of such research is further insight into the etiology and prompt, precise diagnosis of the condition, especially in cases of isolated ACTH deficiency.

REFERENCES

Brown, R. E. (1994). *An introduction to neuroendocrinology*. New York, NY: Cambridge University Press.

Erturk, E., Jaffe, C. A., & Barkan, A. L. (1998). Evaluation of the integrity of the hypothalamic-pituitary-adrenal axis by insulin hypoglycemia test. *Journal of Clinical Endocrinology and Metabolism, 83*(7), 2350–2354.

Nanao, K., Miyamoto, J., Anzo, M., Tsukuda, T., & Hasegawa, Y. (1999). A case of congenital hypopituitarism: Difficulty in the diagnosis of ACTH deficiency due to high serum cortisol levels from a hypothyroid state. *Endocrine Journal, 46*(1), 183–186.

Rose, S. R., Lustig, R. H., Burstein, S., Pitukcheewanont, P., Broome, D. C., & Burghen, G. A. (1999). Diagnosis of ACTH deficiency. *Hormone Research, 52*, 73–79.

Schmidli, R. S., Donald, R. A., & Espiner, E. A. (1989). ACTH deficiency: Problems in recognition and diagnosis. *New Zealand Medical Journal, 102*, 255–257.

Jonathan T. Drummond
Princeton University

ADRENOLEUKODYSTROPHY

Adrenoleukodystrophy (ALD) is an inherited, serious, progressive neurological disorder affecting the adrenal gland and white matter of the nervous system. The defective gene is located within the Xq28 region (Moser, 1997) and is inherited in an X-linked, recessive fashion; only males demonstrate the classic disease. The biochemical defect, an abnormal accumulation of very long chain fatty acids (VLCFA) is common to all forms of the disease, although there are multiple presentations (phenotypes) of the disorder.

Estimates of the incidence of ALD vary, with a range of 1.1 to 1.6 per 100,000 live births (Bezman & Moser, 1998). There is not complete agreement regarding the relative frequency of the different phenotypes of ALD (also discussed in this section), although the childhood cerebral phenotype and adrenomyeloneuropathy (AMN) are consistently found to be the most frequently occurring (Bezman & Moser, 1998). It is reported that up to two thirds of those who have the genetic abnormality escape the most severe phenotype, childhood cerebral form of ALD (CCALD) (Moser, 1997) The rate of occurrence appears to be the same worldwide. ALD has been identified in many ethnic groups, and there appears to be no racial predilection.

Characteristics

1. Childhood cerebral form of andrenoleukodystrophy (CCALD):

   Most common (40% of all cases) and severe form (Melhem, Barker, Raymond, & Moser, 1999).

   Male child, normal until 4–8 years of age when he presents with attentional and behavioral difficulties and school failure. Poor coordination may be noted.

   Symptoms rapidly progress, with evidence of increasing motor deficits (progressive ataxia and spasticity, including loss of ambulation), swallowing problems, visual loss (cortical blindness), personality changes, seizures, and dementia. Ongoing deterioration results in a vegetative state, generally within 2 to 3 years of the emergence of initial symptoms.

2. Adolescent cerebral form of adrenoleukodystrophy:

   Signs and symptoms of cerebral involvement, as in the childhood cerebral form, but are evident between 10 and 21 years.

3. Adult cerebral form of adrenoleukodystrophy:

   Rapid regression of neurological status presenting after 21 years of age, including dementia, psychiatric disturbances, and spasticity (more in the lower extremities than in the upper extremities (Garside, Rosebush, Levinson, & Mazurek, 1999).

Often present with symptoms that are similar to multiple sclerosis; differentiation is important for identification of at-risk family members.

4. Adrenomyeloneuropathy:

This is a more indolent form of the disorder, with later age of onset, generally between 20 and 30 years of age.

Neurological changes are generally preceded by symptoms of adrenal insufficiency (inability to tolerate mild illnesses, hyperpigmentation; Brett & Lake, 1998)

Primary pathology is the white matter of the spinal cord (Sakkubai, Theda, & Moser, 1999). Patients present with progressive spastic paraplegia, sphincter disturbances, peripheral neuropathy, and ataxia (Melhem et al., 1999).

Progression is slower than in CCALD; the interval from onset to vegetative state or death is more than 13 years (Brett & Lake, 1998).

5. ADL with Addison's disease only, asymptomatic patients with the biochemical defect of ADL, symptomatic heterozygotes

Five of eight patients followed for Addison's disease only have the biochemical marker for ADL but do not have neurological deterioration (Sakkubai et al., 1999). Identification is important for counseling purposes. Asymptomatic children with ALD (identified biochemically because of their genetic relationship to a known patient) may have evidence of neuropsychological deficits and have MRI changes prior to disease progression (Riva, Mova, & Brussone, 2000). Women who are carriers of the gene may have neurological symptoms (20%, Melhem et al., 1999)—generally motor involvement—late in life (Sakkubai et al., 1999), and up to 50% have abnormalities on neurobehavioral testing (Melhem et al., 1999). The results of treatment of ADL have been disappointing. The adrenal insufficiency is readily responsive to treatment with oral corticosteroids (Melhem et al., 1999). The neurological manifestations of the disease have not been responsive. Documentation of raised VLCFAs in patients with ALD raised hopes that neurological deterioration could be altered via dietary restriction. Dietary restriction of VLCFAs were unsuccessful in decreasing serum levels of VLCFAs or in halting disease progression (Moser, 1997). Use of Lorenzo's oil, a mixture of glyceryl trioleate (GTO) and glyceryl trierucate (GTE), proved successful in lowering plasma levels of VCLA but has no efficacy upon the neurological progression of the disease in individuals already demonstrating neurological progression (Moser, 1997). There are ongoing attempts to evaluate the efficacy of preventative treatment via Lorenzo's oil in presymptomatic effected individuals. Given the variability of the progression of the disease (e.g., the multiple phenotypes that occur both within and among families), this research is difficult and requires long term follow-up. Initial results indicate that the treatment is not an absolute preventative (Moser, 1997). Bone marrow transplantation (BMT) has been utilized in treating patients with overt, rapid deterioration secondary to ALD. Initial attempts revealed that transplantation was contraindicated in these individuals, with yet more rapid progression of the disease subsequent to transplantation (Moser, 1997). More recent reports of improved neurological outcome in ALD patients' post-BMT has renewed hope that this treatment can be successful for individuals who show early evidence of cerebral involvement (Moser, 1997). Immunosuppression, as a treatment for ALD, has been attempted to reduce the inflammatory brain response that is thought to be a major pathogenic factor in cerebral ALD. This treatment has been unsuccessful to this point (Moser, 1997).

It is difficult to know how best to provide education to children with a severe degenerative neurological disease. Identification is currently important for genetic purposes and presumably will ultimately be important for treatment. Overt, persistent deterioration (loss) in skills and behavior requires medical evaluation. It is important to remember that after the genetic abnormality associated with ALD is identified, the outcome is not clear or predictable.

REFERENCES

Bezman, L., & Moser, H. W. (1998). Incidence of X-linked adrenoleukodystrophy and the relative frequency of its phenotypes. *American Journal of Medical Genetics, 76,* 415–419.

Brett, E., & Lake, B. D. (1997). Progressive neurometabolic brain diseases. In E. Brett (Ed.), *Pediatric neurology* (3rd ed.). New York, NY: Churchill Livingstone.

Garside, S., Rosebush, P. I., Levinson, J. J., & Mazurek, M. F. (1999). Late-onset adrenoleukodystrophy associated with long-standing psychiatric symptoms. *Journal of Clinical Psychiatry, 60,* 460–468.

Melhem, E. R., Barker, P. B., Raymond, G. V., & Moser, H. W. (1999). X-linked adrenoleukodystrophy in children: Review of genetic, clinical and MR imaging characteristics. *American Journal of Roentgenology, 173*(6), 1575–1581.

Moser, H. W. (1997). Adrenoleukodystrophy: Phenotype, genetics, pathogenesis, and therapy. *Brain, 120,* 1485–1508.

Riva, D., Mova, S. M., & Brussone, M. G. (2000). Neuropsychological testing may predict early progression of asymptomatic adrenoleukodystrophy. *Neurology, 54,* 1651–1655.

Sakkubai, N., Theda, C., & Moser, H. W. (1999). Perioxisomal disorders. In Swaiman & Ashwal (Eds.), *Pediatric neurology: Principle and practice* (3rd ed.). St. Louis, MO: Mosby.

GRETA N. WILKENING
*University of Colorado Health Sciences Center,
The Children's Hospital*

Baron-Cohen, S., Wheelwright, S., Skinner, R., Martin, J., & Clubley, E. (2001). The autism spectrum quotient (AQ): Evidence from Asperger syndrome/high functioning autism, males and females, scientists and mathematicians. *Journal of Autism and Developmental Disorders, 31,* 5–17.

MEGAN AMIDON
RUSSELL LANG
Texas State University–San Marcos

APRIL REGESTER
*University of Missouri–St. Louis
Fourth edition*

ADULT ASPERGER ASSESSMENT

The Adult Asperger Assessment (AAA) is an electronic data-based instrument, designed to aid in diagnosing Asperger syndrome (AS) or autism in adults who are high functioning (Baron-Cohen, Wheelwright, Robinson, & Woodbury-Smith, 2005). The assessment consists of four sections designed to identify the presence of diagnostic criteria found in the Diagnostic and Statistical Manual of Mental Disorders, fourth edition (DSM-IV): deficits in social interaction, the presence of stereotyped and repetitive behaviors, and delays in language, as well as impairment in imagination. Adults that do not exhibit language delays in childhood and meet all other criteria are diagnosed with AS. Adults that meet the criteria and do exhibit language delays, or reportedly did in childhood, are diagnosed with autism (Baron-Cohen et al., 2005). Adults suspected to have AS or autism are asked to complete the Autism Spectrum Quotient (AQ) questionnaire (Baron-Cohen, Wheelwright, Skinner, Martin, & Clubley, 2001) and the Empathy Quotient (EQ) questionnaire (Baron-Cohen & Wheelwright, 2004). The results from these questionnaires are then used as components within the AAA (Baron-Cohen et al., 2005). During the interview process, an informant (i.e,. someone who can attest to the client's developmental history), must contribute to the information gathered. Data gathered from the AQ, the EQ, the informant, and the patient themselves, are used in the AAA. A validity study on the AAA found that diagnosed individuals scored significantly higher than nondiagnosed individuals on the AQ ($t = 3.1$, $p = .004$) and significantly lower than nondiagnosed individuals on the EQ ($t = -2.5$, $p = .015$), as expected (Baron-Cohen et al., 2005).

REFERENCES

Baron-Cohen, S., Wheelwright, S., Robinson, J., & Woodbury-Smith, M. (2005). The Adult Asperger Assessment (AAA): A diagnostic method. *Journal of Autism and Developmental Disorders, 35,* 807–819.

Baron-Cohen, S., & Wheelwright, S. (2004). The empathy quotient (EQ). An investigation of adults with Asperger syndrome or high functioning autism, and normal sex differences. *Journal of Autism and Developmental Disorders, 34,* 163–175.

ADULT PROGRAMS FOR INDIVIDUALS WITH DISABILITIES

There are numerous programs of several types that serve adults with disabilities. Many such programs are financed by federal, state, and local governments; many others are funded by private business, private nonprofit organizations, and charities. The following is a summary of major programs organized by function and financing source. It will not capture the complexity and breadth of these programs, especially at the state and local level.

The Social Security Act authorizes several major programs providing cash payments and health insurance to adults on the basis of disability. The disability insurance (DI) program replaces in part income lost when a person with a work history can no longer work because of a physical or mental impairment. Many individuals, of course, have separate commercial disability insurance policies provided by an employer or purchased on their own. After receiving Social Security DI benefits for 24 months, regardless of age, an individual becomes eligible for government-provided health insurance under the Medicare program, which normally covers persons 65 and over. The Social Security Act also contains the Supplemental Security Income (SSI) program, which provides cash income support payments to needy individuals who are aged, blind, or disabled. Income is provided regardless of work history to those who meet means and asset requirements. In most states, with SSI eligibility comes eligibility for the Medicaid program (federal-state matching required), which provides health insurance for low-income individuals. Included in Medicaid is support for intermediate care facilities for the intellectually disabled (ICFs/MR), which provide residential care and service programs. Many disabled individuals benefit from programs for which they may be eligible without regard to their disability, for example, Social Security Old Age and Survivors insurance payments and Medicare (persons 65 and older).

Finally, there are four other major federal programs of this type for special groups of disabled individuals. Veterans with service-connected disabilities are eligible for special cash payments under the Veterans Compensation program. Veterans of wartime service with nonservice-connected disabilities are eligible for a special pension program. Coal miners disabled by black lung or other lung disease are eligible for one of two separate special payment programs (one administered by the Social Security Administration, the other by the Labor Department), depending on circumstances.

Special programs of postsecondary education for the deaf and hearing impaired, supported with significant federal funding, are provided at Gallaudet University, the National Technical Institute for the Deaf, and four special regional postsecondary institutions. In addition, educational programs that are recipients of federal financial assistance at public and private colleges and universities must be accessible to and usable by individuals with disabilities of all types. Some schools are making adaptations and providing support services that go beyond legal requirements.

Rehabilitation and job training services are available from a number of sources. Under Title I of the Rehabilitation Act, the federal government and the states provide vocational rehabilitation services such as physical restoration, job training, and placement to persons with mental and physical disabilities, regardless of prior work history. Physical rehabilitation is covered by most accident and health insurance policies; vocational rehabilitation is sometimes covered. Rehabilitation is available and in fact required under some state workers' compensation laws. Rehabilitation services financed by various forms of insurance are provided by private, for-profit companies and facilities, private nonprofit agencies, and state agencies. Provision of rehabilitation services by private, profit-making (proprietary) firms has been a growing phenomenon (Taylor et al., 1985) for many years now.

Private nonprofit entities play a significant role in providing job training, rehabilitation, and other skill development to adults with disabilities. Included in this group are organizations such as the ARC (formerly the Association for Retarded Citizens), Easter Seals, Goodwill Industries, and United Cerebral Palsy. Some activities of these organizations are financed by the government; others are funded by contracts with businesses for work performed.

Major employers, faced with rising costs of disability, will find it in their interest to pay greater attention to management, rehabilitation, and disability prevention (Schwartz, 1984). Many are increasing efforts in these areas, including rehabilitation, job, and work-site modification efforts to facilitate entry or return to jobs by individuals with disabilities. Contracts with the federal government of more than $2,500 must operate with an affirmative action program to employ and advance individuals with disabilities.

Self-help, referral, and training services are available to people with very severe disabilities to improve their capacity for independent living. These services are available through a network of community-based nonprofit centers and from state rehabilitation agencies. In addition, supported employment is an important new program for individuals with disabilities so severe they were previously thought incapable of working. These individuals (especially those with mental impairments) are likely to need continual support, but they are able to work on regular jobs in integrated settings if given a highly structured training program and some support on the job site (Mank, 1986).

Special housing and transportation programs are available for individuals with disabilities, financed by both the federal government and states and localities. The same is true for special recreation programs for the disabled, in which local governments, service organizations, charities, and private businesses play a large role. Therapeutic recreation is also part of some rehabilitation programs. In addition, many local recreation facilities and organizations, including those involved with the arts, are adapting programs so that people with disabilities can participate or attend with the general public.

REFERENCES

General Services Administration. (1985). *Catalog of federal domestic assistance*. Washington, DC: U.S. Government Printing Office.

Mank, D. (1986). Four supported employment alternatives. In W. Kiernan & J. Stark (Eds.), *Pathways to employment for developmentally disabled adults*. Baltimore, MD: Brooks.

National Council on the Handicapped. (1986). *Toward independence: An assessment of federal laws and programs affecting persons with disabilities*. Washington, DC: U.S. Government Printing Office.

Schwartz, G. (1984, May). Disability costs: The impending crisis. *Business and Health*, 25–28.

Taylor, L. J., Golter, M., Golter, G., & Backer, T. (Eds.). (1985). *Handbook of private sector rehabilitation*. New York, NY: Springer.

JAMES R. RICCIUTI
United States Office of Management and Budget
Third edition

See also **Accessibility of Programs; Americans With Disabilities Act; Habilitation of Individuals With Disabilities; Rehabilitation**

ADVANCED PLACEMENT PROGRAM

The Advanced Placement Program was established in 1955 as a program of college-level courses and examinations for secondary school students. It is administered by the College Board, a nonprofit membership organization composed of public and private secondary schools, colleges, and universities. This program gives high school students the opportunity to receive advanced placement and/or credit on entering college.

The essential premise of the Advanced Placement Program provides college-level courses on high school campuses to provide curriculum to students who wish to acquire college credits before leaving high school (College Entrance Examination Board, 2010). Descriptions and examinations on 34 introductory college courses in 19 fields are disseminated. These fields include art, biology, chemistry, computer science, English, French, German, government and politics, history, Latin, mathematics, music, physics, and Spanish. Course descriptions are prepared, with the help of the Educational Testing Service, by working committees of school and college teachers appointed by the College Board. Exams are administered by the Educational Testing Service.

Most participating high schools, offering one or more advanced placement courses (called AP courses) are larger schools with enough students to qualify for a class. Smaller schools usually provide independent study for those students wishing to take advanced placement exams. The AP course teachers are provided with course descriptions and teachers' guides that state curricular goals and suggest strategies to achieve them. Teachers are not required to follow a detailed plan of assignments and classroom activities; however, seven Advanced Placement Regional Offices and Advanced Placement Program conferences are available to assist teachers.

The 7th Annual AP Report to the Nation indicates minority students who successfully completed AP programs have doubled over the past decade, while numbers of significantly increased in the number students who successfully completed AP math and science placement tests. Taking tests and courses in areas such as math and science often lead to higher education degrees in these specific areas. For more information, please contact: The College Board, 45 Columbus Ave, New York, NY 10023–8052. Website: www.collegeboard.org/

REFERENCE

College Entrance Examination Board (2011). *About AP*. Retrieved June 1, 2011, from http://www.collegeboard.org

MARY K. TALLENT
Texas Tech University
Third edition

See also **Acceleration of Gifted Children; Gifted and Talented Children**

ADVANCE ORGANIZERS

Advance organizers are general overviews or conceptual models of new information presented to learners immediately prior to receiving new information. Ausubel (1960) originally proposed the concept of the advance organizer for use with reading material. The principle of advance organizers is that learning is enhanced when information is linked to learners' existing cognitive structures, thereby enabling the learner to organize and interpret new information (Mayer, 1979). Thus advance organizers prepare the learner for the meaningful reception of new learning. They can either present salient prerequisite knowledge not known to the learner (known as expository organizers), or help the learner establish connections between relevant dimensions of existing knowledge and the new information (known as comparative organizers; Ausubel, Novak, & Hanesian, 1979).

Expository organizers draw the learner's attention to the internal organization of the body of new information by means of a rough overview that briefly presents general topics and concepts and how they are related. Outlines, models, and introductory paragraphs may serve this purpose. With comparative organizers, students' previous experiences or prior learning is tapped in such a way as to identify major points or dimensions of similarity between the new information and existing understandings. By providing external organization, or demonstrating how new information is related to what students already know, comparative organizers establish a meaningful learning set.

Advance organizers may be either verbal or graphic, and can take a variety of formats, including overviews, outlines, analogies, examples, thought-provoking questions, concrete models, and figures such as cognitive maps (Alexander, Frankiewicz, & Williams, 1979; Mayer, 1984; Zook, 1991). Although originally conceptualized as abstract introductions, advance organizers tend to be more effective if they are concrete and if they are both familiar to the learner and well-learned. In this way, advance organizers provide frameworks or cognitive maps for new content. Corkill (1992) also emphasizes the importance of using examples that enable learners to identify the relationship between ideas in the organizer and the new information.

Eggen and Kauchak (1996) use the following example of an advance organizer from an elementary social studies lesson on governments.

> The organization of a government is like a family. Different people in the government have different responsibilities and roles. When all the people work together, both families and governments operate efficiently. (p. 214)

Current schema theory provides a theoretical basis for advance organizers, whose function can be viewed as both activating relevant schemata for to-be-learned material and revising the activated schemata to promote assimilation of the new material (Derry, 1984; Glover, Ronning, & Bruning, 1990). Advance organizers will benefit learners most when students lack the prerequisite knowledge for understanding, and when the transfer of learning to new problems is the desired outcome. To be maximally effective, they should be easy to acquire, as concrete as possible, integrated with technology, and offer an integrated overview or model of the new material (Jordan School District, 2005; Mayer, 1987).

Advance organizers are commonly found in the KU learning challenges material at the University of Kansas and free examples are readily available in a variety of online sources at www.kucrl.org/about/research-focus/

REFERENCES

Alexander, L., Frankiewicz, R., & Williams, R. (1979). Facilitation of learning and retention of oral instruction using advance and post organizers. *Journal of Educational Psychology, 71,* 701–707.

Ausubel, D. P. (1960). The use of advance organizers in the learning and retention of meaningful verbal material. *Journal of Educational Psychology, 51,* 267–272.

Ausubel, D. P., Novak, J. D., & Hanesian, H. (1979). *Educational psychology: A cognitive view* (2nd ed.). New York, NY: Holt, Rinehart & Winston.

Corkill, A. (1992). Advance organizers: Facilitators of recall. *Educational Psychology Review, 4,* 33–67.

Derry, S. J. (1984). Effects of an organizer on memory for prose. *Journal of Educational Psychology, 76,* 98–107.

Eggen, P. D., & Kauchak, D. P. (1996). *Strategies for teachers: Teaching content and thinking skills* (3rd ed.). Boston, MA: Allyn & Bacon.

Glover, J. A., Ronning, R. R., & Bruning, R. H. (1990). *Cognitive psychology for teachers.* New York, NY: Macmillan.

Jordan School District. (2005). *Transforming teaching through technology.* Retrieved from www.jordandistrict.org

Mayer, R. E. (1979). Can advance organizers influence meaningful learning? *Review of Educational Research, 49,* 371–383.

Mayer, R. E. (1984). Aids to text comprehension. *Educational Psychologist, 19,* 30–42.

Mayer, R. E. (1987). *Educational psychology: A cognitive approach.* Boston, MA: Little, Brown.

Zook, K. B. (1991). Effects of analogical processes on learning and misrepresentation. *Educational Psychology Review, 3,* 41–72.

JAMES M. APPLEFIELD
University of North Carolina at Wilmington
Third edition

See *also* Diagnostic Prescriptive Teaching; Direct Instruction

ADVENTITIOUS DISABILITIES

Disabilities may present themselves at birth or be acquired through disease or accident. Those acquired later in life are known as adventitious disabilities. Among these is brain damage produced by extremely high and consistent temperatures or a lack of needed oxygen to the brain. Adventitious disabilities may also be a consequence of trauma to the brain or injury to other parts of the body. A major cause of adventitious disabilities is child abuse (Gilles, 1999). Child abuse is emotionally or physically damaging and can cause durable learning problems. An area of childhood exceptionality often associated with an adventitious disability is hearing impairment or deafness (Rapin, 1999). Hearing losses may be present at birth or adventitiously acquired later on in life through disease or accident. Adventitious disabilities and congenital disabilities that appear similar (but are obviously of different etiologies) may well have different outcomes.

REFERENCES

Gilles, E. E. (1999). Nonaccidental head injury. In K. F. Swaiman & S. Ashwal (Eds.), *Pediatric neurology* (3rd ed., pp. 898–914). St. Louis, MO: Mosby.

Rapin, I. (1999). Hearing impairment. In K. F. Swaiman & S. Ashwal (Eds.), *Pediatric neurology* (3rd ed., pp. 77–95). St. Louis, MO: Mosby.

STAFF

See *also* Brain Damage/Injury; Child Abuse;
    Post-Institutionalized Children

ADVOCACY FOR CHILDREN WITH DISABILITIES

Advocacy for children with disabilities has become a strong force in today's world due to concern regarding the legal rights of those with disabilities. Advocacy is vital to sustaining and improving the lives of children with disabilities (The Arc of the United States, 2010). The term advocacy has a variety of meanings, but at the most fundamental level it is the role that is assumed by anyone who cares (Lippman & Goldberg, 1973). In its essence, advocacy refers to the attempts made to guarantee the rights of children with disabilities by persons with disabilities, friends and family of people with disabilities, as well as numerous professionals including educators, lawyers, and social workers. According to The Arc of the United States (2010), advocacy must occur at both the individual and systems levels to be successful. The origins of the advocacy movement can be traced back to the 1920s and the early 1930s when parents of children with disabilities began to band together to combat the inappropriate and neglectful actions by professionals who claimed to be helping the children and their families. Frustrated with the professionals' responses, parents turned to each other for help.

Founded in 1921, the National Society for Crippled Children was the first national parent group in the United States. Shortly thereafter, in 1933, parents in Ohio founded the Cuyahoga County Council for the Retarded Child, establishing the first parent-supported community classes for the "gravely" retarded (Winzer, 2009). At the same time, grassroots organizations began to spring up in different communities across the country. In 1950 the various parent organizations joined together to form the National Association for Retarded Children, which was renamed in 1992 to the Arc of the United States (Arc of the United States, 2010). The Arc of the United States was the first organization to fund research on intellectual and developmental disabilities and played a key role in the enactment of laws that increased the rights of people with disabilities (Arc of the United States, 2010). In addition, the Arc of the United States provided emotional support to families with disabled children, developed preschool, school-age, and adult programs that became the models for voluntary agencies and public education, and helped reduce the stigma of having a disabled child by bringing the issues of intellectual disabilities, into the public view (Lippman & Goldberg, 1973). Therefore, once united, the early parent movements formed a base on which later societal, judicial, and governmental action would be built.

In recent years, the breadth of advocacy groups has expanded beyond the Arc of the United States to include groups advocating the interests of children with learning disabilities, children who are deaf or blind, and children with autism, as well as children with a variety of medical and physical disabilities. As a result, the role of the Arc of the United States, as a direct service provider has significantly declined since its inception in the 1950s. The Arc of the United States now places greater emphasis on providing information and public education services, advocacy, legislation, and funding (Arc of the United States, 2010). Subsequently, professionals and volunteers have joined with parents to change the makeup of many groups formerly consisting of exclusively of parents with disabled children. Various advocacy groups and professional associations have formed coalitions to increase their political and public influence, with many organizations maintaining full-time or part-time offices in Washington, DC, as well as in state capitals (Consortium for Citizens with Disabilities, 2010). These groups are often closely linked with legal advocacy agencies and are represented by members of the state and national advisory panels, accrediting boards, and monitoring bodies, due in large part to federal and state regulations along with court orders. Furthermore, advocacy groups have been instrumental in the initiation of legislation, often through the use of class-action suits to guarantee the existing rights of disabled persons are safeguarded, to obtain new rights and services, or to enhance currently available programming (Consortium for Citizens with Disabilities, 2010; Arc of the United States, 2010).

Today, advocacy for people with disabilities is a spreading force in the United States and abroad (Herr, 1983). Moreover, as long as having a disability leads to exclusion and disregard for a person's human dignity and legal rights, advocating forces such as the Arc and other coalitions will not fade away (Herr, 1983). Therefore, advocacy continues to be the place "...for crusader and technician, linking professional skills to the aspirations of self-advocates, volunteers, family members, and other activists. By one means or another they will animate advocacy models and develop the networks to implement hard-won rights" (Herr, 1983).

REFERENCES

Arc of the United States,. (2010). *The History of The Arc*. Retrieved from http://www.thearc.org/page.aspx?pid=2338

Consortium for Citizens with Disabilities. (2010). *About CCD*. Retrieved from http://www.c-c-d.org/about/about.htm

Herr, S. S. (1983). *Rights and advocacy for retarded people*. Lexington, MA: Lexington Books.

Lippman, L., & Goldberg, I.I. (1973). *Right to education: Anatomy of the Pennsylvania case and its implications for exceptional children*. New York, NY: Teachers College Press.

Winzer, M. A. (2009). *From integration to inclusion: A history of special education in the 20th century*. Washington, DC: Gallaudet University Press.

MEREDITH WILLIAMSON
Texas A&M University
Fourth edition

See also AAIDD, American Association on Intellectual Developmental Disabilities; Consortium for Citizens With Disabilities

ADVOCACY GROUPS, CITIZEN

A citizen advocacy group is defined, in general, as any organization that focuses on increasing the quality of life for a specific handicapped population. Two examples of citizen advocacy groups containing both parents and professionals include the Association for Children With Learning Disorders (ACLD) and the American Association on Mental

Deficiency. These two groups have national headquarters organized state by state, having local chapters at county, city, or regional levels. Although grass-roots advocacy groups relate to citizen advocacy groups, their classifications are different.

An example of an informal organization is Youth Advocacy, centralized in the Washington, DC area. This organization consists of a group of citizens (nonparents), with paid professional leadership, that provide services for adjudicated youths. These individuals offer an alternative to incarceration, providing community-based rehabilitation and supporting school, work, and living arrangements for youths in the area. Another example of a grassroots nationally organized group is the Association for Autistic Children. Important features of this type of group include that the organization of these local support groups is informal and consists mostly of parents, while the leadership has national consolidation. There are formal and informal advocacy groups at national, regional, and local levels serving handicapped students and providing representation for a variety of disability groups. The purposes for each group may differ considerably, depending on the perceived needs of the group.

The work of advocacy groups includes seeking federal or state legislation, developing ordinances at the community level, supporting parental work, and intervening directly for the benefit of the students. One example of a community-based advocacy group is the Lions Club, which supports the visually handicapped. Other social clubs support the hearing impaired (Rotary), the intellectually disabled (Civitan), or orthopedically impaired (Shriners) by paying for services, prostheses, or therapy. Another example is the Junior Chamber of Commerce, which is a group that promotes the support of group homes, sheltered employment centers, and day schools for the emotionally disturbed.

Two of the major purposes of advocacy organizations include providing funds toward services and the development of a community-support base. The objective of a community-support base varies depending on the particular advocacy group and needs of the community. In addition, it is imperative to provide emotional support to the parents. Obtaining legislation for the handicapped is another primary function because parents, as opposed to professionals, provide it. Advocacy groups may purchase or provide direct services to those with disabilities and their families. Although this has not been their major role in the past, it is becoming increasingly prominent and represents a trend toward advocacy in the United States.

David A. Sabatino
West Virginia College of Graduate Studies

Kimberly M. Rodriguez
Texas A&M University–College Station
Fourth edition

ADVOCACY ORGANIZATIONS

Advocacy organizations are groups (generally nonprofit) whose efforts are devoted to influencing public policy (Boris & Mosher-Williams, 1998) and who may advocate on behalf of marginalized groups. An advocacy organization represents a particular group (e.g., ethnic minorities, people with disabilities) and engages in educational and service activities related to that particular group and its issues (Andrews & Edwards, 2004). Advocacy organizations strive to improve the welfare of individuals who share similar needs and who are unable to effectively advocate for themselves (Sage & Burrello, 1986). The need for advocacy organizations on behalf of people with disabilities began in the early 20th century as a reaction to the inequalities that people with disabilities faced (Pfeiffer, 1993). Several of the services currently available to children and adolescents with disabilities can be credited to the efforts put forth by advocacy organizations. Advocacy organizations may include groups such as churches, parents, educational, health, and/or charitable organizations. Some advocacy organizations include the American Association of People with Disabilities (AAPD) and the American Foundation for the Blind (AFB). The AAPD formed as a national voice in advocating and implementing the goals of the Americans with Disabilities Act (American Association of People with Disabilities, n.d.), while the AFB focuses on ensuring that the rights and interests of individuals with vision loss are represented in public policy. The AFB also focuses on broadening access to technology along with promoting independent and healthy living among individuals with vision loss by providing them and their family with resources (American Foundation for the Blind, n.d.). Yet another advocacy organization is the World Institute on Disability (WID). The WID is internationally recognized and its public policy issues focus on issues related to individuals' abilities to live full and independent lives. They do so by creating programs and tools, conducting research, public education, training and advocacy campaigns, and providing technical assistance, all in an effort to eliminate barriers regarding social integration, employment, economic security, and health care for persons with disabilities (World Institute on Disability, n.d.).

Advocacy organizations engage in activities that advance the well-being of the people they serve through various services such as advocacy, research, public policy, professional development, and general educational information and support. Advocacy organizations vary greatly in the areas in which they specialize, including housing; employment; assuring equal access and opportunity to services; education; transportation; accessibility; and legal services; and general human rights for people with disabilities. Furthermore, advocacy organizations vary in the populations that they serve, including persons who are deaf, blind, or visually impaired; persons with physical disabilities, and veterans, among others.

The number of advocacy organizations is vast. In general, each organization composes a mission statement that gives direction to the services and advocacy that they provide. Advocacy organizations will also discuss their philosophy, provide a brief history of how the organization developed, and provide a means to contact the organization and become involved. For a complete list of additional advocacy organizations on disabilities, see http://www.access-board.gov/links/disability.htm

REFERENCES

American Association of People with Disabilities. (n.d.). About us. Retrieved from http://www.aapd.com/site/c.pvI1IkNWJqE/b.5555493/k.C88C/About_Us.htm

American Foundation for the Blind. (n.d.). About AFB. Retrieved from http://www.afb.org/section.asp?SectionID=42

Andrews, K. T., & Edwards, B. (2004). Advocacy organizations in the U.S. political process. *Annual Review of Sociology, 30,* 479–506.

Boris, E., & Mosher-Williams, R. (1998). Nonprofit advocacy organizations: Assessing the definitions, classifications, and data. *Nonprofit and Voluntary Sector Quarterly, 27,* 488–506.

Pfeiffer, D. (1993). Overview of the disability movement: History, legislative record, and political implications. *Policy Studies Journal, 21,* 724–734.

Sage, D. D., & Burrello, L. C. (1986). *Policy and management in special education.* Englewood Cliffs. NJ: Prentice Hall.

World Institute on Disability. (n.d.). About WID. Retrieved from http://www.wid.org/about-wid

LESTER MANN
Hunter College, City University of New York
First edition

ARACELI LÓPEZ-ARENAS
Texas A&M University
Fourth edition

AFFECTIVE DISORDERS

Affect is the externally observable, immediately expressed component of human emotion (e.g., facial expression, tone of voice). Mood is considered to be a sustained emotion that pervades an individual's perception of the world. Affective disorders, as defined by the American Psychiatric Association (2002) are the class of mental disorders where the essential feature is a disturbance of mood.

Emotions and their expression are an integral part of human experience. It is only under certain conditions that the expression of emotion is considered maladaptive; in some instances, in fact, a lack of affect might be viewed as abnormal. It is only when an emotional reaction is disproportionate to the event, when the duration of the reaction is atypical, or when it interferes with a person's psychological, social, or occupational functioning that an emotional response may be labeled symptomatic of an affective disorder.

Affective disorders are comprised of two basic elements, depression and mania, which can be conceptualized as opposite ends of a continuum paralleling the normal happiness/sadness continuum. Both depression and mania have their counterparts in everyday life: The parallels for depression are grief and dejection; the experience corresponding to mania is less clear-cut, but probably could be described as the feverish activity with which people sometimes respond to stress.

Formally, both mania and depression can be characterized by symptoms at the emotional, cognitive, and somatic/motivational levels. The major emotional components of depression are sadness and melancholy, often accompanied by feelings of guilt and worthlessness. These emotions permeate the individual's total experience of life. Cognitively, depressed persons are characterized by a negatively distorted view of themselves, the world, and the future. Their outlook is generally one of unrealistic hopelessness. In terms of their physical functioning, depressed persons frequently suffer appetite and sleep disturbances, fatigue, apathy, and a general loss of energy.

In certain aspects, the symptoms of mania could be viewed as opposite to those of depression. For instance, people suffering a manic episode often are in a highly elevated mood, seeming to experience life with an intense euphoria. However, it generally takes little frustration to shift this elated enthusiasm to irritability or tears, which suggests that mania may be closer to depression than initially seems apparent. In fact, it has been suggested by a number of theorists that mania is a defense against depression, that it is an attempt to ward off depressive feelings through feverish activity.

Cognitively manic individuals characteristically show wildly inflated self-esteem, believing themselves to be capable of great accomplishments or possessed of exceptional talent. Manic individuals act on their high opinion of themselves. They behave recklessly, involving themselves in unwise business deals or sexual liaisons, wasting large sums of money on shopping sprees or gambling. When experiencing a manic episode, individuals often have a decreased need for sleep, sometimes going for days without rest.

Within the affective disorders, there are two major syndromes: major depression (or unipolar depression as it has traditionally been called) and bipolar disorder (formerly manic-depressive disorder). In unipolar depression, an individual experiences one or more episodes of depression without ever experiencing an episode of mania. Approximately half of the people who suffer major depression will undergo only one episode of depression: Their first episode will be their last. In general, even without intervention, most people will recover from an occurrence of unipolar depression within 3 to 6 months.

In bipolar disorder, an individual experiences both manic and depressive episodes. In rare cases, an individual vacillates between manic and depressive episodes without an intervening period of normal functioning. More often, there are periods of normality interspersed between the manic and/or depressive episodes. There is no separate diagnostic category for persons who experience only manic episodes; this occurs only rarely. In such instances, an assumption is made that the person will ultimately experience a depressive episode, and a diagnosis of bipolar disorder will be made.

Of the two disorders, bipolar disorder is typically, but not always, the more serious and debilitating. People with bipolar disorder, in comparison with those with unipolar disorder, experience more episodes, and their interepisode functioning is worse. Further, such people are more likely to have serious alcohol abuse problems and attempt and commit suicide at a higher rate than persons with unipolar disorder.

Mood disorders have long been the most common of mental illnesses, but they are on the increase in modern society (Johannessen et al., 2001; Keller & Baker, 1992). Depression has been referred to as the common cold of mental illness. Around 10% of the males and perhaps 22% of the females living in the United States will at some point in their lives experience an episode of major depression. This one-to-two ratio has been found in many different cultures, in Europe and Africa as well as North America. (There are, however, a few notable exceptions such as the Amish in Pennsylvania.) It has been hypothesized that more women experience depression than men because it is more socially acceptable for women to respond to negative life experiences with passive, depressive symptoms. Men may be less likely to experience or express depressive symptoms because they may receive more social rejection (or less social reinforcement) than women for acting depressed. Instead, men may respond to stressful events more actively, with substance abuse (e.g., alcoholism) or antisocial behavior.

Bipolar disorder is much less common than unipolar disorder; slightly less than 1% of the U.S. population will experience bipolar disorder at some point in their lives. Unlike unipolar disorder, bipolar disorder occurs with approximately the same frequency in men as in women. Both unipolar and bipolar disorder tend to run in families, though bipolar disorder probably has a significantly larger genetic component than unipolar disorder. At present, the nature of the genetic mechanisms underlying the affective disorders is not clear. It is known, however, that in both mania and depression there are abnormalities in the level of neurotransmitters in the brain.

Beyond the possibility noted that mania is a defense against depression, there has been relatively little psychological theorizing about the causes of mania and bipolar disorder. This is not the case with unipolar depression, for which a number of etiological theories have been developed. From a Freudian perspective, depression is viewed as the punishment an overly punitive superego inflicts on the ego for the ego's failure to properly treat a lost love. The superego's harshness is seen also as a means of preventing the ego's feelings of anger and aggression from being expressed (Freud, 1917).

From a more behavioral perspective, Lewinsohn (1974) has hypothesized that depression is the result of a low rate of response-contingent reinforcement, caused by either a lack of social skills or a deficient environment, which results in the person experiencing behavioral extinction. Rather than being a function of the rate of reinforcement, Seligman and colleagues (Abramson, Seligman, & Teasdale, 1978) believe that it is the individual's lack of control over his or her environment and the attributions that this person makes about this lack of control that result in depression. Seligman believes that a lack of control that is attributed to causes that are internal (the self), global (some general quality), and stable (not likely to change) will result in depression.

Most theorists believe that the cognitions that depressed persons experience are a consequence of depression. Beck (1967), however, believes that negative cognitions and thought patterns are the cause of unipolar depression rather than a consequence of depression. He has proposed that individuals prone to depression have negative schema that are activated by stress. Once activated, the individual tends to interpret his or her experience in the worst possible light, using errors of logic (e.g., drawing sweeping conclusions based on one or two events) to do so. This negative interpretation occurs even when more plausible explanations for experiences are available; the person chooses his or her explanation on the basis of its negativity rather than its validity.

From the viewpoint of the individual working with children, what may be most important regarding affective disorders is an awareness of and ability to recognize signs of childhood affective disorders. It should be noted first that it is rare for children, particularly prior to puberty, to experience manic episodes. When a young child exhibits overactive behavior that appears manic, it is probably more appropriately considered a symptom of hyperactivity. (It is also possible for overactive behavior to result from an endocrine dysfunction.) Depressivelike syndromes, on the other hand, have been reported in children 3 years of age and younger. The symptoms of these syndromes vary in part as a function of age; the older a depressed child, the more closely his or her symptoms will parallel those of adults. Consequently, this discussion will focus on the symptoms of younger school-aged children (i.e., approximately ages 6 to 14).

A major distinction between depressed children and adults is that children, in contrast to adults, seldom seek help or complain about feelings of depression. Instead, they may become apathetic regarding school or socially withdrawn, sometimes preferring to remain in their rooms at home rather than playing with friends. They may make vague physical complaints about head or stomach pains, seem overly self-conscious, and cry inexplicably. Older children may see themselves as bad kids—incompetent in school and unworthy of the love of adults or the friendship of other children. Some, but not all, depressed children may simply look sad, particularly in their facial expressions, for extended periods of time with little apparent fluctuation in mood. Overall, a child will usually exhibit only some of the symptoms noted, and the symptom pattern may vary across a period of weeks.

Such symptoms are expressed in what is essentially a passive manner. Though there is far from universal agreement on the issue, certain professionals believe that in some instances children may express depression through aggressive misbehavior. While it is usually difficult to distinguish between genuine misbehavior and misbehavior that is an expression of so-called masked depression, children who are acting out as a symptom of depression often are more responsive to firm (but not overly authoritarian) limit-setting than children who are misbehaving for other reasons.

A technique that is sometimes useful in determining if a child is feeling depressed is to ask the child where he or she stands on a scale of 1 to 10, with 10 being children who are very happy, and 1 being children who are very sad. (This technique presupposes a certain level of cognitive development in the child.) On an informal level, there are several things a teacher can do for a depressed child. With children who appear apathetic and low in self-esteem, it may be useful to set lower standards for praising their accomplishments in school, or to praise them for their efforts in addition to their finished products. It is important, however, to strike a balance between setting criteria that allow an increase in praise and avoiding reinforcement of the child's symptoms. The latter may lead to the child using the symptoms as an excuse to perform at a level significantly below his or her ability level. Children may also respond to messages from the teacher that suggest that the child is an important, valued person. Overall, it is important to make sure that such interactions with the child are honest and nonpatronizing; if it is not possible to do something in this manner, it is probably better not to do it. Psychologists use a variety of objective testing methods to assess the presence, absence, and degree of depression. Objective testing is necessary for accurate diagnosis.

If a teacher feels that a child needs more assistance than the teacher has the training or experience to render, there is a wide range of professional treatments for depression, many with proven efficacy (though the majority of treatment research has focused on adults rather than children). These treatments range from medication to psychotherapy and behavior therapy. Antidepressants are often prescribed in the treatment of unipolar depression, and they tend to be quite effective. Lithium carbonate is usually prescribed for bipolar disorder in adults; it has an effect on both the depressive and manic symptoms, and is probably the treatment of choice for bipolar disorder. The exact mechanism for lithium's action is unknown. In a few instances, lithium may be used to successfully treat adult unipolar depression.

The variety of psychological and behavioral therapies used in the treatment of depression is vast. Techniques such as social skills training, modification of negative cognitions through cognitive restructuring and reality testing, and the teaching of self-control strategies (to name just a few) have been used. Treatment may occur individually or in groups and many of the therapies have been empirically tested, often with results supporting their value as treatments for depression. Cognitive-behavioral therapies have the greatest support in the scientific literature (e.g., Knell, 1998).

REFERENCES

Abramson, L. Y., Seligman, M. E. P., & Teasdale, J. D. (1978). Learned helplessness in humans: Critique and reformulation. *Journal of Abnormal Psychology, 87*, 49–74.

American Psychiatric Association. (2000). *Diagnostic and statistical manual of mental disorders* (4th ed., text rev.). Washington, DC: Author.

Beck, A. T. (1967). *Depression: Clinical, experimental, and theoretical aspects.* New York, NY: Harper & Row.

Freud, S. (1976). Mourning and melancholia. In J. Strachey (Ed. and Trans.), *The complete psychological works.* New York, NY: Norton. (Original work published 1917).

Johannessen, J. O., McGlashan, T. H., Larsen, T. K., Horneland, M., Joa, I., Mardal, S., … Opjordsmoen, S. (2001). Early detection strategies for untreated first-episode psychosis. *Schizophrenia Resource, 51*, 39–46.

Keller, M., & Baker, L. (1992). The clinical course of panic disorder and depression. *Journal of Clinical Psychiatry, 53*, 5–8.

Knell, S. M. (1998). Cognitive-behavioral play therapy. *Journal of Clinical Child Psychology, 27*, 28–33.

Lewinsohn, P. M. (1974). A behavioral approach to depression. In R. J. Friedman & M. Katz (Eds.), *The psychology of depression: Contemporary theory and research.* Washington, DC: Winston-Wiley.

BAHR WEISS
*University of North Carolina at Chapel Hill
Third edition*

See *also* **Childhood Neurosis; Childhood Psychosis; Depression, Childhood and Adolescent; Psychoneurotic Disorders**

AFFECTIVE EDUCATION

Affective education promotes emotional development by educating students about attitudes, thoughts, values, feelings, beliefs, and interpersonal relationships (Morse, Ardizzone, Macdonald, & Pasick, 1980; Saarni, 2000). Through it, students are provided experiences in which cognitive, motor, social, and emotional elements are inter-related and balanced (Morse et al., 1980), leading to the enhancement of self-concept (what one is) and self-esteem (how one feels about what one is) and the development of social skills essential to meeting basic needs in a satisfying and socially responsible way (Wood, 1982). Affective education helps youngsters to establish value systems, morals, independence, a sense of responsibility, and self-direction (Morse et al., 1980; Wood, 1982). In addition, affective education focuses on promoting emotional competency which includes a set of emotional skills such as emotional awareness, emotion expressions, empathy, understanding other's emotions based on context and cues, use of emotional regulation strategies, and emotional self-efficacy (Saarni, 2000). Although the need for affective education is not limited to students in special education programs, it is especially relevant for them because social skills are essential for success in mainstream placements.

Although most educators agree on the importance of affective education and understand its general purpose, there is less agreement among them on the specific objectives or how best to realize them. In part, this ambiguity derives from the persistent difficulty of defining such terms as self-concept, self-esteem, affect, and attitude. The general lack of systematic programming should not, however, be an indication that affective goals are unimportant (Francescani, 1982). Affective education is commonplace in regular education classrooms and is routinely addressed in teacher education programs (e.g., Woolfolk, 1995). Morse et al. (1980) have argued that affective education represents serious obligation and is an essential component of special education. Essentially, all children deserve the right to more "systematic assistance with their affective growth" (Morse et al., 1980, p. 6).

Recently, affective education has been transformed into school programming with the concept of social and emotional learning (SEL). According to Collaborative for Academic, Social, and Emotional Learning (CASEL), an organization founded in 1994 by the author of *Emotional Intelligence*, Daniel Goleman, social and emotional learning is a process for helping children and even adults develop the fundamental skills for life effectiveness. SEL skills include "recognizing and managing our emotions, developing caring and concern for others, establishing positive relationships, making responsible decisions, and handling challenging situations constructively and ethically" (CASEL, 2005). They are the skills that allow children to calm themselves when angry, make friends, resolve conflicts respectfully, and make ethical and safe choices.

With the federal support (HR 4223: The Academic, Social, and Emotional Learning Act) authorized in 2009, National Technical Assistance and Training Center for Social and Emotional Learning was established to provide technical assistance and training to states, local educational agencies, and community-based organizations to identify, promote, and support evidence-based SEL standards and programming in elementary and secondary schools. Interventions or programs to promote SEL have been widely accepted and implemented in many states (Durlak, Weissberg, Dymnicki, Taylor, & Schellinger, 2011). For example, Illinois became the first state to mandate every school district to develop a plan for the implementation of SEL programming in their schools. The New York State Department of Education has also developed Social/Emotional Development and Learning (SEDL) standards.

Nonetheless, affective goals are often subordinated to academic objectives, as the following example (Reinert, 1982) illustrates. Ann, age 10, was known by her teacher to display many different types of inappropriate behavior in the classroom. She talked out loud, pushed and shoved other children, would not share, and cried for no apparent reason. During evaluation, it was discovered that Ann was reading and spelling on a kindergarten level and her arithmetic skills were 2 years below grade level. In addition, Ann's parents were divorced and she was often absent from school because she had to babysit for her younger sister while her mother worked. She seldom came to school appropriately groomed or attired. Ann was either unwilling or unable to speak to adults or peers in a normal, conversational tone of voice; she had a poor self-concept and relatively few friends. Upon staffing, her Individual Education Plan (IEP) prescribed 60 minutes in a resource room for remedial help in arithmetic and reading skills, but no emphasis on affective problems. Although affective needs should be a part of an IEP, they are seldom systematically delineated.

Systematic instruction in the affective domain is especially important for emotionally handicapped students like Ann. Emotionally handicapped students include those who have not learned essential skills for social and emotional growth, or how to control their behavior in times of stress, how to communicate their feelings and needs in a socially acceptable manner, how to bring interpersonal problems to a satisfying solution, or how to encounter others without conflict (Francescani, 1982). It is difficult to imagine how a student with deficits as pervasive as these can survive in an environment for which he or she is so poorly equipped. Yet it is in the highly socialized classroom world in which affective education must occur, and most proponents recognize the need to integrate affective learning into everyday classroom life.

Integrated affective learning lies at one end of the intrinsic/extrinsic dimension of affective education. Morse et al. (1980) defined this dimension as the extent "to which (affective education) grows naturally out of what is going on in the educational life space versus how much is added as a special function" (p. 16). Ideally, affective lessons should derive naturally from school activities, using materials already in the curriculum in harmony with the philosophy of the program (Morse et al., 1980; Schlindler, 1982). Teachers should capitalize on naturally occurring opportunities spending time motivating the uninvolved student, resolving peer conflicts, encouraging a reluctant student to join in group activity, or trying to enliven a depressed student. A teacher should not rely on an added-on or extrinsic curriculum to accomplish affective goals.

Affective educators stress the need for developing empathetic relationships between teachers and students in order to convey fundamental human relationships where the "sense of relationship dominates authoritarianism" (Morse et al., 1980, p. 15). Teachers and students share responsibilities, goals, and rules for living together (Morse et al., 1980; Reinert, 1982; Sarason, 1971). Positive teacher-student relationships support student growth both in social and cognitive development (Davis, 2003; Davis & Lease, 2007). Moreover, teachers serve as a socializing role. They help children to acquire emotion display rules and opportunities to practice regulating their emotions (Thompson, 1991). Even as they age, the task of helping children to regulate their emotion experiences and emotion displays becomes no less complex for teachers of preadolescents and adolescents. In the teacher-student relationships, teachers may be engaged in productive emotional labor such as making their genuine attempts to get to know their students and systematically reflecting on their relationships/emotions (Chang & Davis, 2009). Moreover, teachers can help students to develop an understanding of emotions and teach them self-regulatory strategies like learning to label their emotions and to re-evaluate what happened in daily encounters.

However, to expect all teachers to act at all times with the spontaneity, sensitivity, and astuteness that the ideal intrinsic approach requires is unrealistic. This expectation belies the human limitations of teachers and assumes a degree of training that is rare if not unknown in teacher preparation programs. The lack of training on emotional understanding or emotional regulation in teacher preparation programs or in-service teacher education places teachers at high risk for emotional exhaustion. Teachers who work with children of special needs have experienced higher emotional exhaustion among the teacher workforce (Chang, 2009). Teachers often feel emotionally drained or burned out from teacher-student relationships if they do not regulate their own emotions appropriately (Chang, 2009; Chang & Davis, 2009; Carson, 2007). Intervention programs such as Cultivating Awareness and Resilience in Education (CARE; Jennings, Snowberg, Coccia, & Greenberg, 2011) have shown significant improvements promoting teachers' well-being.

Affective education has grown out of the school mental health movement, and gradually it has evolved to promoting SEL for all students. In early years, one of the most popular and widely used curricula for affective education is DUSO (Developing Understanding of Self and Others). It is designed to be used by teachers or counselors as an add-on to the academic curriculum. Throughout the school year, eight themes (e.g., Developing Self-Concept, Understanding Peers) are explored through listening, modeling, discussion, and role-playing activities. Everyday problems of classroom life are described through pictures, stories, and puppetry, and solutions are discussed, modeled, and role-played. The elements of the lessons are carefully prescribed and the materials are attractive and engaging to a primary-aged audience. Although the curriculum is extrinsic, it does provide a structure through which problems may be simulated and the values of alternative solutions weighed.

Recently, more intervention programs to promoting social and emotional learning have been implemented in recent decade. Durlak et al. (2011) conducted a meta-analysis of 213 school-based, universal social and emotional learning (SEL) programs involving 270,034 kindergarten through high school students. The research team documented that SEL participants demonstrated significantly improved social and emotional skills, attitudes, behavior, and academic performance.

Affective education has grown out of the school mental health movement, and it has gradually evolved into well-formulated programs such as SEL. However, it is not intrinsic to the ongoing school process (Morse, 1980). Instead it tends to be relegated to the periphery of the basic curriculum. If affective education is to realize its potential, deliberate efforts must replace the haphazard, casual, and indirect approaches currently in operation.

REFERENCES

Carson, R. L. (2007). *Emotional regulation and teacher burnout: Who says that the management of emotional expression doesn't matter?* Paper presented in the annual meeting of American Educational Research Association, Chicago, IL.

Chang, M.-L. (2009). An appraisal perspective of teacher burnout: Examining the emotional work of teachers. *Educational Psychology Review, 21*, 193–218.

Chang, M.-L., & Davis, H. A. (2009). Understanding the role of teacher appraisals in shaping the dynamics of their relationships with students: Deconstructing teachers' judgments of disruptive behavior/students. In P. A. Schutz & M. Zembylas, M. (Eds.), *Advances in teacher emotion research: The impact on teachers' lives.* New York, NY: Springer.

Collaborative for Academic, Social, and Emotional Learning [CASEL]. (2005). Safe and sound: An educational leader's guide to evidence-based social and emotional learning programs—Illinois edition. Retrieved from http://www.casel.org

Davis, H. A. (2003). Conceptualizing the role and influence of student-teacher relationships on children's social and cognitive development. *Educational Psychologist, 38*(4), 207–234.

Davis, H. A., & Lease, A. M. (2007). Perceived organizational structure for teacher liking: The role of peers' perceptions of teacher liking in teacher-student relationship quality, motivation, and achievement. *Social Psychology in Education: An International Journal, 10,* 403–427.

Durlak, J. A., Weissberg, R. P., Dymnicki, A. B., Taylor, R. D., & Schellinger, K. (2011). The impact of enhancing students' social and emotional learning: A meta-analysis of school-based universal interventions. *Child Development, 82,* 474–501.

Durlak, J. A., Weissberg, R. P., & Pachan, M. (2010). A meta-analysis of after-school programs that seek to promote personal and social skills in children and adolescents. *American Journal of Community Psychology, 45,* 294–309.

Francescani, C. (1982). M A R C: An affective curriculum for emotionally disturbed adolescents. *Teaching Exceptional Children, 14,* 217–222.

Jennings, P. A., Snowberg, K. E., Coccia, M. A., & Greenberg, M. T. (2011). Improving classroom learning environments by Cultivating Awareness and Resilience in Education (CARE): Results of two pilot studies. *Journal of Classroom Interaction, 46,* 37–48.

Morse, W. C., Ardizzone, J., Macdonald, C., & Pasick, P. (1980). *Affective education for special children and youth.* Reston, VA: Council for Exceptional Children.

Reinert, H. R. (1980). *Children in conflict* (2nd ed.). St. Louis, MO: Mosby.

Reinert, H. R. (1982). The development of affective skills. In T. L. Miller & E. E. Davis (Eds.), *The mildly handicapped student* (pp. 421–451). New York, NY: Grune & Stratton.

Saarni, C. (2000) Emotional competence: A developmental perspective. In R. Bar-On and J. D. A Parker (Eds.), *The handbook of emotional intelligence: Theory, development, assessment, and application at home, school, and in the workplace* (pp. 68–91). San Francisco, CA: Jossey-Bass.

Sarason, S. B. (1971). *The culture of schools and the problem of change.* Boston, MA: Allyn & Bacon.

Schlindler, P. J. (1982). Affective growth in the preschool years. *Teaching Exceptional Children, 14,* 226–232.

Thompson, R. A. (1991). Emotional regulation and emotional development. *Educational Psychology Review, 3,* 269–307.

Wood, F. H. (1982). Affective education and social skills training. *Teaching Exceptional Children, 14,* 212–216.

Woolfolk, A. E. (1995). *Educational psychology* (6th ed.). Boston, MA: Allyn & Bacon.

LOUISE H. WERTH
PAUL T. SINDELAR
Florida State University

MEI-LIN CHANG
Emory University
Fourth edition

AFIBRINOGENEMIA, CONGENITAL

Congenital afibrinogenemia is a rare blood disorder that causes improper clotting of the blood. It is also referred to as hypofibrinogenemia. Afibrinogenemia is an inherited condition that is caused by an autosomal recessive gene. It is found in both males and females.

Congenital afibrinogenemia is characterized by problems with the functionality of fibrinogen, a protein in the body that is necessary for the clotting of blood. This condition can be due to a lack of fibrinogen or to a defect in existing fibrinogen.

Diagnosis at birth is common because uncontrollable bleeding from the umbilical cord is often found. Later in life, bleeding in the cerebrum and spleen areas is also found to be common (Neerman-Arbez, Honsberger, Antonarakis, & Morris, 1999).

Patients diagnosed with congenital abrinogenemia show no major mutations or deletions in the vicinity of the gene responsible for the production of fibrinogen (Duga et al., 2000). It is most likely that this disorder is caused by missense mutations in the gene and the corresponding problems with fibrinogen secretion. It is also likely that there are multiple mutations causing the condition. Affected people tend to respond well to fibrinogen replacement techniques, and the breakdown times of this substance in the body are normal.

Characteristics

1. Failure of blood to clot
2. Absence or malfunction of fibrinogen
3. Possible uncontrolled bleeding from umbilical cord at birth
4. Possible spontaneous bleeding in areas of the cranium, spleen, or both

---

Treatment for congenital afibrinogenemia is usually preventive. Patients may be transfused with plasma (the liquid portion of the blood) or cryoprecipitate (a blood product containing concentrated fibrinogen) to treat bleeding episodes or in preparation for surgery needed to treat other conditions. Children with this condition should be immunized with the hepatitis B vaccine because of the increased risk of developing hepatitis due to transfusion. Because this disorder is genetic, children born with the condition will most likely be born into families in which multiple people have the disorder; from a psychological standpoint, this may be much better for the child's mental outlook. Seeing others who are affected could help normalize the situation for someone with a disorder this rare and this unusual. Children who are in school must of course take many precautions against routine cuts and scrapes that could begin to bleed excessively. Additionally, teachers, nurses, and other responsible adults in the school system should be made aware of the situation. However, much worry can be eliminated with preventive care and the administration of fibrinogen on a regular basis so that there is always some present in the patient's system. However, some patients may develop antibodies (inhibitors) to fibrinogen with treatment, or they may develop other complications such as gastrointestinal bleeding, cranial bleeding, or bleeding from the mucous membranes. Therefore, the prognosis for children with this condition is dependent on consistent and appropriate medical management. Genetic counseling may be helpful for families and the child when he or she reaches childbearing age.

REFERENCES

Duga, S., Asselta, R., Santagostino, E., Zeinali, S., Simonic, T., Malcovati, M., & Tenchini, M. L. (2000). Missense mutations in the human beta brinogen gene cause congenital abrinogenemia by impairing brinogen secretion. *Blood, 95,* 1336–1341.

Neerman-Arbez, M., Honsberger, A., Antonarakis, S. E., & Morris, M. A. (1999). Deletion of the brogen alpha-chain gene (FGA) causes congenital afibrogenemia. *Journal of Clinical Investigation, 103,* 215–218.

ALLISON KATZ
Rutgers University

AFRICA: EAST AND SOUTHERN SPECIAL EDUCATION

A brief history, statements on current status, and the future prospects of special education in 12 East and Southern African countries are presented here. The countries discussed include Botswana, Ethiopia, Eritrea, Kenya, Lesotho, Malawi, Namibia, Swaziland, Tanzania, Uganda, Zambia, and Zimbabwe. The availability of information on the aforementioned topics and between these countries differs widely. Thus, some countries are discussed in greater detail (Tanzania, Uganda, and Zimbabwe) than others (Eritrea, Malawi, and Swaziland).

Incidence of Handicapping Conditions Within This Region

Reliable data on the incidence of childhood disorders within this region are unavailable. Various problems associated with incidence surveys preclude obtaining accurate data. Parents may need to register their disabled children in special centers, and they often are reluctant to admit their children display handicapping conditions (Kisanji,

1997; Whyte & Ingstad, 1995). Also, community attitudes toward the handicapped often are negative (Devlieger, 1995; Jackson & Mupedziswa, 1989). These and other qualities are believed to contribute to grossly underestimated incidence figures for handicapping conditions.

This large region in East and Southern Africa is home to an estimated 59,800,000 children. Population details for children ages 5 to 16 years for the year 1996 are provided in the the table below (UNICEF, 1996):

Population Details for African Children Aged 5 to 16 Years, 1996 Data

Botswana	700,000
Ethiopia	15,600,000
Eritrea	1,600,000
Kenya	12,100,000
Lesotho	600,000
Malawi	3,200,000
Namibia	700,000
Tanzania	8,700,000
Uganda	10,500,000
Zambia	2,900,000
Zimbabwe	3,200,000

If we accept the World Health Organization's general incidence estimate that 10% of a country's population is likely to be handicapped, almost 6 million children in this region can be expected to have one or more handicapping conditions. We believe this estimate substantially underestimates the number of handicapped children, given the region's substandard medical, health, and early childhood education facilities. Among children with handicaps, less than 1% attend formal school (Kann, Mapolelo, & Nleya, 1989; Tungaraza, 1994).

General History of Educational Services for Handicapped Children

The availability of special education services and other resources for children with physical, sensory, and cognitive disabilities occurred recently. Historically, native African societies integrated learning and other developmental activities within their everyday home and community activities (Kisanji, 1997). Home- and community-based activities provide various advantages: a favorable ratio between the young and elders, accommodations to match the child's developmental levels, and utilization of the child's natural milieu within which to promote development and transfer of training. The extent to which homes and communities provide appropriate adaptations to accommodate children with disabilities is unknown. The beneficial effects that professional services can have on children with disabilities are well-established.

The introduction and evolution of professional services for these children in East and Southern Africa closely follows a pattern found in other developing areas:

first, national or regional institutions, often residential in nature and initiated by religious, humanitarian, and philanthropic agencies, are established. Professional services for middle-class children then develop in metropolitan centers. The widespread provision of services to children with disabilities in public schools occurs only after general education services, at least through the elementary level, are well-developed and nationally available. Children with handicapping conditions who reside in rural areas are least likely to receive professional services. Stronger special education services generally are found in countries with stronger and well-established regular education programs (Saigh & Oakland, 1989).

The majority of countries in this region have inadequate basic education programs (UNICEF, 1991, 1994), lack formal special education policies, and experience school dropout rates in the range of 15% to 60% involving disadvantaged children, which includes those with disabilities (Kann et al., 1989; Stubbs, 1997; UNICEF, 1994).

The Role of Missionaries

Christian missionaries, often from Western Europe, initiated and provided almost all formal education within African communities during the colonial period. The development of special education services in this region is closely associated with their work. Trends in the development of special education facilities within individual countries generally followed a consistent pattern: Services were provided first for those with visual handicaps, and then for those with auditory, physical, and mental handicaps. This trend probably reflected the missionaries' beliefs as to the resources (like teaching expertise and materials) needed to serve each of these groups, as well as the family's willingness to admit one or more members have a disability. Because of their normal hearing ability, persons with visual impairments may have been thought to respond more favorably to the use of conventional instructional methods.

In Botswana, German missionaries opened special schools for the visually handicapped at Linchwe (in Mochudi) and the hearing impaired at Ramotswa (in Ramotswa) in the 1950s. A German couple opened residential centers named Rankoromane based on the Waldorf School model to educate children with mental handicaps in a number of towns in the late 1960s (Ingstad, 1995).

In Ethiopia, the Christofeblinden Mission opened a school for the blind and a training program for teachers of the visually handicapped in the early 1950s. Finnish missionaries were involved in developing Ethiopia's special education programs, and they opened a school for the deaf at Keren in the 1950s. The Church of Christ established the Mekanissa School for the Deaf in 1964. The Baptist Mission created the Alpha School for the Deaf in Addis Ababa in 1967. The Ethiopian Evangelical Mekaneyesus Church started the Hossana School for the Deaf in 1981.

In Eritrea, French Catholic, Swedish Lutheran, and Italian Catholic churches provided school education to the natives since 1890 (Miran, 1998). The role of these organizations in founding schools for persons with disabilities could not be established. Eritrea, now an independent nation, was once a province of Ethiopia.

The first school in Kenya for the visually impaired, the Thika School, was opened by the Salvation Army in 1946 (Kristensen, 1987). Kenya's first full-time program to prepare teachers of students with visual handicaps and a school for deaf-blind children were founded by the Christofeblinden Mission in the 1980s.

In Malawi, education for the blind was started during the early 1940s when two primary residential special schools were established by missionaries at Kasungu and Lulwe. The Catholic Order of the Immaculate Conception (of the Netherlands) developed a program in 1964 that integrated students with and without visual impairments into regular classrooms within ordinary schools; resource rooms provided supportive services to the visually impaired. Fourteen resource rooms serving about 100 blind students were in operation by 1983 (Ross, 1988). The program at Montfort College, organized by the Catholic teaching brothers of the Order of the Immaculate Conception, prepared teachers for students with auditory and visual impairments for Malawi and some neighboring countries (namely, Lesotho, Swaziland, Tanzania, Zimbabwe, and Zambia) in the 1970s.

Tanzania established its first special education facility in 1950 when the Anglican Church opened a school for the blind, the Buigiri School. Two additional schools for the blind followed this school, one opened by the Swedish Free Mission, the Furaha, in 1962, and another by the Lutheran Church, the Irente School, in Lushoto in 1963. The first Tanzanian school for the hearing impaired, the Tabora Deaf-Mute Institute, was opened by the Roman Catholic Church in 1963. The Salvation Army opened the first school in Tanzania for the physically handicapped in 1967.

In Zambia, missionaries again pioneered special education services in the region (Csapo, 1987a). The Dutch Reformed Church established the first school for the deaf (Sichula, 1990) and one for the blind (Csapo, 1987a) at Magwero Mission in 1955. The Christian Mission of Zambia opened another school for the blind at Mambiling soon after. Other special schools were opened by missionaries and continue to exist today.

In Zimbabwe, the Dutch Reformed Church opened the Margaret Hugo School for The Blind, at Masvingo in 1927 (Peresuh, Adenigba, & Ogonda, 1997). Two schools for the hearing impaired opened in 1947, one in Loreto and another in Pamushana, founded by the Catholic Dominican Sisters and the Dutch Reformed Church respectively (Chimedza, 1994).

Information on missionary work and the opening of special education facilities in Lesotho, Namibia,

Swaziland, and Uganda could not be located. However, the Dutch Reformed Church appears to have been involved in Namibia, and the Roman Catholic Church and Church of Uganda may have been involved in Uganda. Margaret Brown of the Church Missionary Society initiated Uganda's in-service teacher education for children with hearing impairment in 1962. Although Islam has a substantial following in some East African countries (namely, Tanzania, Uganda, Kenya, and Ethiopia), its role in establishing special education facilities in these countries could not be ascertained.

The Role of International Nongovernmental Organizations and Local Organizations

International nongovernmental organizations and local organizations advocating on behalf of students with disabilities also have had strong roles in developing and providing special education services. Their importance exceeds that of the colonial governments. The Danish International Development Agency (DANIDA), UNESCO Sub-Regional Project for Special Education in Eastern and Southern Africa, Swedish International Development Agency (SIDA), Royal Commonwealth Society for the Blind (now called the Sight Savers), International League for Persons with Mental Handicaps, and the British Red Cross are among the international agencies that have played significant roles in establishing special education programs in East and Southern Africa. DANIDA has been actively involved in promoting special education advising in Kenya, Uganda, and Zimbabwe for at least the past decade. SIDA has been involved in developing special education programs in all 12 Eastern and Southern African countries which comprise the focus of this paper. It helped establish braille printing presses in Tanzania in 1971 (Tungaraza, 1994) and in Zimbabwe in 1994. In the early 1960s the Royal Commonwealth Society for the Blind started a rehabilitation center at Salama (in Uganda) for adults with visual impairments (Onen & Njuki, 1998).

Information on the involvement of local organizations in founding special education facilities in the East and Southern African countries is quite sparse. The Botswana Red Cross, with support from the Norwegian Red Cross, established a vocational training center for persons with physical disabilities in 1981. The Botswana Council for the Disabled has been unable to implement programs that enable children with disabilities to attend school (Ingstad, 1995). In Ethiopia, the Haile Selassie One Foundation established two special schools for blind students. They became government schools in the 1980s.

In Kenya, local voluntary organizations established two special schools for the mentally handicapped at St. Nicholas and Aga Khan in the late 1950s. These schools amalgamated in 1968 to form the Jacaranda School (Ross, 1988). The Kenya Society for the Mentally Handicapped and The Parents and Friends of Handicapped Children

were formed by parents of children with disabilities to promote the education of persons with disabilities, improve the preparation for teachers of children with disabilities, and consolidate schools. The Tanzania Society for the Deaf established the first school for the hearing impaired at Buguruni in 1974. In 1955, the first school for children with visual impairment and blindness was started at Madera in Eastern Uganda by the joint effort of the then-local education committee (Teso education committee), the Ministry of Education, and Uganda Foundation for the Blind. The Uganda government later asked the Catholic Church to administer the school.

With the assistance of the Uganda Society for the Deaf, Sherali Bendali Jafer, Peter Ronald, and Mr. Semmpebwa were closely involved in developing awareness throughout Uganda of the need to educate children with hearing impairment (Onen & Njuki, 1998). As a result of their efforts, an integration unit for children with hearing impairment was started at Mengo Primary School. Subsequently, the Uganda School for the Deaf was started on Namirembe Hill in 1968. The following year, Ngora School for the Deaf was established.

Ugandan educational services for children with physical disabilities and mental handicaps both began in 1968, and both were largely the results of efforts of local self-help organizations. For instance, the Uganda Spastic Society was formed in 1968. Its membership consisted mainly of parents of children with spastic conditions and polio, and medical professionals. The society played a key role in the establishment of a school for the physically handicapped at Mengo (Onen & Njuki, 1998). Services for children with mental disabilities were available through the Uganda Association for Mental Health (UAMH). This association, established in 1968 by the Ministry of Health, had a short life due to the political turmoil in the country at the time and in subsequent years. In 1983, the Uganda Association for the Mentally Handicapped was founded, and it has been instrumental in the founding of many resource units for children with mental handicaps.

In Zimbabwe, the Jairos Jiri Association founded the Narran Center School for the Deaf and the Blind in Gweru in 1968, a school for the visually impaired at Kadoma in 1981, and a number of other schools for children with various physical, mental, and multiple handicaps at Bulawayo, Gweru, and Harare in the 1970s (Farquar, 1987). Zimbabwe's Council for the Blind has been involved in providing structural facilities and equipment to school-based integration units for children with visual disabilities since about 1980. Its Zimcare Trust has been actively involved in providing education for Zimbabwean children with mental handicaps since the 1980s.

Zambia's Council for the Handicapped has conferred with teachers and the Zambian government to promote effective ways of teaching children with disabilities since the 1970s. However, its role in the establishment of special education facilities in that country is unclear.

Information on the involvement of international non-governmental agencies and local organizations advocating for those with disabilities and the establishment of special education facilities in Eritrea, Malawi, Namibia, and Swaziland could not be located.

The Role of Postcolonial Governments

Support for the development of special education by the postcolonial governments in each of the 12 East and Southern African countries differs widely. Support is strongest when elementary and secondary education is widely available and a commitment to the principle of universal education is widely held. Countries recently ravaged by civil war (Uganda, Eritrea, Ethiopia) currently are attempting to reestablish basic elementary and secondary education programs. Their programs in special education are in initial stages of development and support. In contrast, countries that have enjoyed relative political stability (Kenya, Tanzania, Zimbabwe) tend to have stronger regular education programs, as well as a longer history and stronger support for special education programs.

Although Botswana's National Development Plans (1973–1978; 1991–1997) identify the needs of disabled persons as a national priority (Ingstad, 1995), the government historically has viewed educational support to children with disabilities as a family responsibility rather than a state obligation (Ingstad, 1995; Kann et al., 1989). Children with disabilities are conspicuous in their absence from Botswana schools (Kann et al., 1989). Nonetheless, a special education unit was established within the Botswana Ministry of Education in 1984 with the support of SIDA. The University of Botswana has complemented government efforts by offering a 2-year diploma course for specialist teachers for children with mental, visual, hearing, and learning handicaps, and is expected to launch a bachelor's degree in special education in August, 1998 (C. Abosi, pers. comm., February 2, 1998).

The Kenya government, through the Kenya Institute of Education, launched special needs teacher education programs at Jacaranda and Highridge Teachers Colleges in 1966–1967 (Peresuh et al., 1997). The Kenya Institute of Special Education (KISE), founded by the Kenyan government with the assistance of DANIDA, has assumed responsibility for these programs. More than one thousand teachers have graduated from the KISE teacher education programs since 1987. KISE also is responsible for the educational placement of children with disabilities, community education, and teacher in-service education programs on disabilities.

Lesotho's government became involved in special education in 1987 when its Ministry of Education, with the financial support from the United States Agency for International Development (USAID), commissioned a comprehensive study of its special education programs and accompanying guidelines for its development (Csapo,

1987b). The report recommended the infusion of special needs components to both pre- and in-service teacher preparation programs, adoption of an integration (resource room) model for educating children with special needs, and full community involvement in establishing and supporting special education facilities. The Lesotho Ministry of Education, Lesotho National Federation of Disabled People, Ministry of Social Welfare and Health, and Save the Children Fund (UK) created 10 integration units. A special education unit was established in the Lesotho Ministry of Education in 1991 to coordinate the opening of integration units. The Lesotho National Teacher Training College assumed responsibility for introducing special education components in its pre-service programs in 1996, and the previously mentioned special education unit within the Ministry of Education assumed responsibility for in-service education programs for teachers (Pholoho, Mariga, Phachaka, & Stubbs, 1995).

Namibia became politically independent in 1990 after a legacy of colonial rule under apartheid from South Africa, which left most of its Blacks with little or no education. Thus, the history of educating children with disabilities in Namibia is recent and short. According to Bruhns et al. (1995), Namibia established its first school for children with disabilities, the Dagbreek Special School, in 1970 as a racially segregated facility for White children. The school opened its doors to disabled students of other races after Namibia become independent. The Eluwa School for blind and deaf students was established at Ongwdiva in 1973 with 20 deaf and 20 blind students. By 1995 the school enrolled 172 deaf, 70 blind, and 8 physically disabled students. The Moreson School for children with severe learning difficulties was established by the Association of the Handicapped in 1976 and became a government school in 1990. It had 60 students along with seven teachers in 1995.

The Tanzania government, with the help of the Royal Commonwealth Society for the Blind, established the country's first integrated education program for children with visual handicaps, Uhuru Co-education School, in 1966, followed by a similar program for children with mental handicaps in 1982 (Tungaraza, 1994). The government also established a diploma-level teacher education program in 1976 and one for teachers of pupils with mental handicaps in 1983 at the Tabora Teacher Training College. In addition, the Mpwapwa Teacher Training College prepares teachers to work with students with visual handicaps. The number of special needs teachers who have graduated from the two Tanzania colleges could not be established.

Uganda's government involvement in special education came earlier than others in the region because of the lobbying efforts of Sr. Andrew Cohen, then-Governor of Uganda, to educate a blind relative (Atim, 1995). Government support to educate the blind was established through an act of Parliament in 1952. The first trial to integrate children with visual impairment was launched in 1962 at Wanyange Girls School in Eastern Uganda. In July 1973, a department of special education was established at the Uganda Ministry of Education headquarters in Kampala. This department was created to coordinate special education services in the Ministry and to work with other governmental and nongovernmental organizations providing services for persons with disabilities. The head start Uganda enjoyed in developing its special education programs was severely thwarted during two decades of dictatorships and civil war. Special education programs in Uganda began to rebuild after 1991.

The Ugandan government, with the help of DANIDA, founded the Uganda National Institute of Special Education (UNISE) in 1991 and gave it the responsibility for coordinating the country's special education programs and teacher education programs at certificate, diploma, and degree levels. So far, about 255 teachers have received specialist training and attended awareness seminars, which are offered to ordinary primary school teachers in the districts throughout the country. The Special Education/Educational Assessment and Resource Services of Uganda (EARS-U) was formed in 1992. EARS-U, a division within the Uganda Ministry of Education, is responsible for evaluating programs for children with hearing, speech, learning, visual, mental, and physical impairments. EARS-U also is responsible for coordinating educational placements of children with disabilities, counseling services to their parents, community education, and prevention programs.

The Zimbabwe government, with the assistance of SIDA, established a Department of Special Education within the Ministry of Education in 1982, with its primary responsibility being educational placement of children with disabilities, pre-service and in-service training of teachers on special educational needs, and community education programs on disabilities. A teacher education program for teachers of children with visual, mental, hearing, and speech and language impairments was established by the government at the United College of Education in Bulawayo in 1983. About 300 special needs teachers graduated from the United College of Education since the establishment of its special education teacher education program. A 2-year, post-diploma bachelor's degree in special education was launched at the University of Zimbabwe in 1993 and has graduated about 75 teachers of special needs children. The Zimbabwe Ministry of Education also has issued a number of documents to guide special education programs in the schools (Mpofu & Nyanungo, 1998).

Government involvement in special needs programs in Zambia, Ethiopia, Eritrea, Malawi, and Swaziland could not be ascertained. However, respondents to a recent survey of special needs experts in these countries suggested that special education facilities in these countries are quite limited (Mpofu, Zindi, Oakland, & Peresuh, 1997).

Current Status of Special Education in East and Southern Africa

Special education services in East and Southern Africa generally follow a functional integration (resource room) model in which children with disabilities attend class part-time to full-time with their nondisabled peers and receive support of a full-time specialist teacher (Charema & Peresuh, 1997). Specialist teachers maintain the resource room, provide intensive individualized instruction to children with disabilities, and work closely with mainstream teachers in planning and effecting integration strategies for children with disabilities. A functional integration model generally is preferred for children with mild to moderate sensory, physical, and cognitive handicaps. Children with more severe handicaps generally attend special schools and rehabilitation centers, typically those residential in nature, which provide more specialized resources. With few exceptions, most integration units for the visually handicapped and hearing impaired are residential, whereas those for children with moderate to mild physical and cognitive handicaps are nonresidential.

Compared to current needs and potential demand, special education facilities in the 12 East and Southern countries of this survey are severely limited. Botswana has approximately 20 special schools and resource units for children with visual, auditory, mental, and physical handicaps (C. Abosi, pers. comm., February 2, 1998). Current enrollment figures by handicapping condition were unavailable. However, previous enrollment was vision (35 students), hearing (88), mental (176), and physical (18) (Kann et al., 1989). There are no facilities in the country for children with severe disabilities.

Lesotho has twelve special schools (Stubbs, 1997). Enrollment figures by handicapping condition were unavailable. Lesotho's Ministry of Education, with support from international nongovernmental organizations and United Nations agencies, recently opened integration units for children with a variety of handicaps in 8 of the country's 10 districts.

Namibia's school for children with visual impairments has 71 students and its school for the hearing impaired has 185 students (Bruhns et al., 1995). Twenty-four specialist teachers work in these schools. Two schools and 15 specialist teachers serve 125 children with severe learning disabilities. Two additional schools staffed by 67 teachers provide instruction to 733 children with mild learning difficulties. Twelve schools and 16 teachers offer remedial education to 385 children with specific learning disabilities. Namibia also has 28 integration units attended by 507 children with moderate to mild disabilities and taught by 40 teachers.

In Tanzania, services for students with visual impairments are provided in twelve special schools and 23 integrated (18 primary, 5 secondary) schools that offer education to 979 children with visual disabilities (Possi

& Mkaali, 1995; Tungaraza, 1994). Sixty-four specialist teachers and 157 regular education teachers provide education to children with visual handicaps. Services for children with auditory impairments are provided through 14 special schools and three integrated primary (one residential and two nonresidential) schools to approximately 980 pupils and staffed by 100 specialist and 26 regular class teachers. In addition, six schools serve 305 deaf-blind students. About 930 children with physical disabilities attend 61 specialist and integration units staffed by 185 specialist and regular class teachers. The vast majority of children with physical disabilities either attend schools in their communities or do not attend school at all. Tanzania also has four residential special schools for children with moderate mental handicaps and 15 nonresidential integrated units that serve 980 children with moderate to mild mental handicaps. Sixty-seven specialist and 128 regular class teachers teach these children. Twelve children with autism and 14 with cerebral palsy attend four units taught by six specialist teachers. Thousands of children with severe mental handicaps do not receive any schooling. In contrast, more than 90% of Tanzanian children with epileptic conditions attend ordinary schools (Whyte, 1995).

Uganda has at least six special schools and one integration unit which serve about 500 children with visual impairments, two special schools for 150 children with hearing impairments, and one special school for 124 students with physical handicaps (Ross, 1988). An estimated 32,134 children with mild to moderate disabilities are attending ordinary schools (Onei & Njuki, 1998). The Ugandan government's goal was to have the country's estimated 325,000 children with disabilities attend school in 1997 (Kristensen, 1997; Uganda Ministry of Education, 1992). However, the country lacked the resources for meeting this highly ambitious target then, and it still does today (Mpofu et al., 1997).

Zimbabwe's 20 special schools provide educational and rehabilitation services to 5,000 children with visual, hearing, physical, and mental disabilities. The country also has 162 integrated resource units: 69 for those with hearing disabilities, 46 with mental disabilities, and 47 with visual disabilities. A total of 1,315 children with disabilities are served by the integrated resource units: 552 with hearing impairments, 409 with mental impairments, and 354 with visual impairments. Additionally, about 4,300 children with moderate to mild generalized learning difficulties attend 270 part-time special classes in regular education settings. At least 50,000 children with learning difficulties receive part-time remedial education in classes or clinics in general education schools.

The current status of special education programs in Swaziland, Eritrea, Kenya, and Zambia is unknown. However, information from respondents to a survey on school psychology practices in these countries (Mpofu et al., 1997) suggests special education programs may be better established in Kenya than in other East and Southern African countries. Such programs generally are limited to urban areas in Zambia, and may not exist to any significant degree in Swaziland and Eritrea.

Although the need for more special education facilities in all of the East and Southern African countries is quite apparent, a paradox exists in that attendance is below capacity in many existing special education schools and units in some countries, including Tanzania and Lesotho (Kisanji, 1995; Stubbs, 1997). This under-utilization exists because the facilities are not well-known to parents of children with disabilities and parents in some rural communities are suspicious of their intended purposes. In addition, government departments and international aid agencies often established special education schools and units in certain communities in response to requests by local politicians or parochial interest groups, but without adequate consultation with traditional and other community leaders. Thus, resistance to utilizing these facilities often occurs regardless of their need.

Some countries in this region have mounted comprehensive community outreach programs aimed at educating citizens on the nature of disabilities, their prevention, and appropriate educational interventions. In addition, teachers have walked from village to village to locate children with disabilities to attend school (Kisanji, 1995). The teachers' door-to-door, village-to-village approach can effectively reach families and significant community leaders, and it often yielded larger enrollments of children with disabilities in areas that seem to have few if any such children.

Future Prospects of Special Education in East and Southern Africa

Nearly all countries in East and Southern Africa provide some forms of special education programs. The work of Christian missionaries and nongovernmental agencies often resulted in the establishment of special education programs. The continued involvement of missionaries, although desired, is unlikely to match prior levels of involvement. Nongovernmental agencies increasingly are recognized by international agencies (like the United Nations and the World Bank) as effective implementers of needed social programs. Although their involvement is likely to continue for some years, their resources also are limited in time. Thus, special education programs in this large and important region must depend more heavily, if not exclusively, on local and regional resolve and resources.

A government's involvement in special education programs and teacher preparation programs (through policies enacted and funded by its legislature and implemented by its ministries of education) provides demonstrable evidence that they support special education as an essential component of its national education program. Although the degree to which federal governments are involved in special education programs differs among the 12 countries within this region, all are involved to some degree. However, beneficial policies often are enacted and are either not funded or not implemented by ministries of education. For example, the governments of Uganda and Botswana both established policy underscoring the importance of school attendance among children with disabilities as a national priority. However, this policy remains to be implemented.

The adoption of the principle of universal primary education by these governments implicitly recognizes children with disabilities as having the right to education. This, and other positive trends in educational thinking, eventually can be expected to translate into more favorable policies and practices governing special education programs. Moreover, most governments continue to support the further development of their elementary and secondary regular education programs—conditions prerequisite to the strong support of special education programs. Thus, prospects for the continued growth and availability of special education programs in these countries are somewhat encouraging.

However, one should not underestimate impediments to the further development of sustainable special education programs in East and Southern Africa. These impediments include inadequate personnel and financial resources for the provision of basic and regular education and inadequate leadership from advocacy groups.

Given other pressing responsibilities, federal governments in this region are unlikely to prioritize special education programs without some form of external support. Uncertainty exists as to the willingness and commitment of some governments to fund special education programs at current or higher levels than that currently provided by international development agencies (like DANIDA and SIDA).

The sustainability of donor-supported special education programs in East and Southern Africa will depend on the extent to which donor agencies build into their aid packages policies and practices that cultivate a cadre of local personnel willing to lobby for future programs, to implement genuine partnerships with federal and regional government to establish and maintain special education programs, to employ phased donor-funding withdrawal, and to help developing vibrant self-advocacy organizations at the local and national levels. For example, the Swedish Federation for the Blind has financed an advisory project in Eastern Africa aimed at improving the organization and self-advocacy of persons with disabilities (Ross, 1988).

Greater involvement of parents and community members in founding special education schools and integration units would strengthen a sense of ownership for special education facilities in communities, leading to greater attendance and school retention. In addition, the importance of community education programs on disabilities to the future of special education programs in East and Southern Africa cannot be overemphasized. Most parents

of children with disabilities are not involved with any special interest groups or agencies providing special education services (Kisanji, 1995; Ross, 1988).

The significantly limited material and manpower resources within most of these countries constrain the establishment and growth of special education programs (Ross, 1988; Tungaraza, 1994). Most countries are grappling with the provision of basic education and health facilities. The countries have very few personnel specifically prepared to work with children with disabilities in either special or mainstream school settings. The future of special education programs in the region could be considerably enhanced if countries pooled resources to promote professional preparation and research on effective methods to promote basic education of students in special education.

REFERENCES

Atim, S. (1995). *Special education in Uganda*. Paper presented at the South-South–north Workshop. Kampala, Uganda.

Bruhns, B., Murray, A., Kanguchi, T., & Nuukuawo, A. (1995). *Disability and rehabilitation in Namibia: A national survey*. Windhoek: The Namibian Economic Policy Research Unit.

Charema, J., & Peresuh, M. (1997). Support services for special needs educational needs: Proposed models for countries south of the Sahara. *African Journal of Special Needs Education, 1*, 76–83.

Chimedza, R. (1994). Bilingualism in the education of the hearing impaired in Zimbabwe: Is this the answer? *Zimbabwe Bulletin of Teacher Education, 4*, 1–11.

Csapo, M. (1987a). *Perspectives in education and special education in southern Africa*. Vancouver, British Columbia, Canada: Center for Human Development and Research.

Csapo, M. (1987b). *Basic, practical, cost-effective education for children with disabilities in Lesotho*. Vancouver, Canada: University of British Columbia.

Devlieger, P. (1995). Why disabled? The cultural understanding of physical disability in an African society. In B. Ingstad & S. R. Whyte (Eds.), *Disability and culture* (pp. 94–106). Berkeley: University of California Press.

Farquhar, J. (1987). *Jairos Jiri—The man and his works*. Gweru, Zimbabwe: Mambo.

Ingstad, B. (1995). Public discourses on rehabilitation: From Norway to Botswana. In B. Ingstad & S. R. Whyte (Eds.), *Disability and culture* (pp. 174–195). Berkeley: University of California Press.

Jackson, H., & Mupedziswa, R. (1989). Disability and rehabilitation: Beliefs and attitudes among rural disabled people in a community based rehabilitation scheme in Zimbabwe. *Journal of Social Development in Africa, 1*, 21–30.

Kann, U., Mapolelo, D., & Nleya, P. (1989). *The missing children: Achieving basic education in Botswana*. Gaborone: NIR, University of Botswana.

Kisanji, J. (1995). Interface between culture and disability in the Tanzania context: Part 1. *International Journal of Disability, Development and Education, 42*, 93–108.

Kisanji, J. (1997). The relevance of indigenous customary education principles in the education of special needs education policy. *African Journal of Special Needs Education, 1,* 59–74.

Kristensen, K. (1997). School for all: A challenge to special needs education in Uganda—A brief country report. *African Journal of Special Needs Education, 2,* 25–28.

Miran, J. (1998). *Missionaries, education and the state in the Italian colony of Eritrea 1980–1936.* Paper presented at the Third Annual Midwest Graduate Student Conference in African Studies. University of Wisconsin-Madison, February 27–March 1.

Mpofu, E., & Nyanungo, K. R. (1998). Educational and psychological testing in Zimbabwean schools: Past, present and future. *European Journal of Psychological Assessment.*

Mpofu, E., Zindi, F., Oakland, T., & Peresuh, M. (1997). School psychological practices in East and Southern Africa. *Journal of Special Education, 31,* 387–402.

Murray, J. L., & Lopez, A. D. (1996). *Global health statistics: A compendium of incidence, prevalence and mortality estimates for over 200 conditions.* Cambridge, MA: Harvard University Press.

Onen, N., & Njuki, E. P. (1998). *Special education in Uganda.* Unpublished manuscript.

Peresuh, M., Adenigba, S. A., & Ogonda, G. (1987). Perspectives on special needs education in Nigeria, Kenya, and Zimbabwe. *African Journal of Special Needs Education, 2,* 9–15.

Pholoho, K., Mariga, L., Phachaka, L., & Stubbs, S. (1995). Schools for all: National planning in Lesotho. In B. O'Tootle & R. McConkey (Eds.), *Innovations in developing countries for people with disabilities.* Lancashire, UK: Lisieux Hall Publications.

Possi, M. K., & Mkaali, C. B. (1995). *A brief report on special education services in Tanzania.* Paper presented at the South-South–north Workshop. Kampala, Uganda.

Ross, D. H. (1988). *Educating handicapped young people in Eastern and Southern Africa.* Paris: UNESCO.

Saigh, P. A., & Oakland, T. (Eds.). (1989). *International perspectives on school psychology.* Hillsdale, NJ: Erlbaum.

Sichula, B. (1990). *East African sign language report.* Helsinki, Finland: Finnish Association of the Deaf.

Stubbs, S. (1997). Lesotho integrated education programme. *African Journal of Special Needs Education, 1,* 84–87.

Tungaraza, F. D. (1994). The development and history of special education in Tanzania. *International Journal of Disability, Development, and Education, 41,* 213–222.

Uganda Ministry of Education. (1992). *Government white paper on the education policy review commission report.* Kampala, Uganda: Author.

UNICEF. (1991). *Children and women in Zimbabwe: A situation analysis update, July 1985–July 1990.* Republic of Zimbabwe: Author.

UNICEF. (1994). *The state of the world's children: 1994.* Oxford, UK: Oxford University Press.

UNICEF. (1996). *The state of the world's children: 1996.* Oxford, UK: Oxford University Press.

Whyte, S. R. (1995). Constructing epilepsy: Images and contexts in East Africa. In B. Ingstad & S. R. Whyte (Eds.), *Disability and culture* (pp. 226–245). Berkeley: University of California Press.

Whyte, S., & Ingstad, B. (1995). Disability and culture: An overview. In S. Whyte & B. Ingstad (Eds.), *Disability and culture* (pp. 3–22). Berkeley: University of California Press.

ELIAS MPOFU
Pennsylvania State University

THOMAS OAKLAND
University of Florida

ROBERT CHIMEDZA
University of Zimbabwe

AFRICA, SPECIAL EDUCATION

Special education is relatively new in most African countries. The need for a major commitment to special education by African countries to provide handicapped learners with a variety of programs and services has been recognized for some time now (Anderson, 1983; Joy, 1979; Shown, 1980; UNESCO, 1979, 1986), though progress toward realization has been slow and halting. The UNESCO definition of special education is one that generally adheres to western European and American expectations. Thus the Nigerian National Policy on Education (1981) has defined special education as "education of children and adults who have learning difficulties as a result of not coping with the normal school organization and methods" (Nigerian Year Book, 1984). In Nigeria's Plateau State (Nigeria), special education is defined as including "the course and content of education, including specially defined classroom, material, and equipment designed to meet the unique needs of a handicapped child" (Shown, 1986).

Despite such broad perspectives, special education in Africa is more likely to be concerned with children who are physically and sensorially handicapped rather than suffering from mild cognitive deficits. Children with more severe cognitive deficits are likely to be cared for in other contexts than those of formal special education. Expressing this fact, Shown observes: "To acquire education in the modern sense one must possess and make full use of all his senses. This is beside being fully mobile" (Shown, 1980). Sambo (1981) has pointed out "when one loses two or more of these senses, then the acquisition of education in the normal sense becomes a problem entirely different from those problems normally encountered in the acquisition of education. For such a person, there is a need for a viable alternative for educating him."

Anderson (1973) observed that the majority of African teachers were not familiar with the special techniques and methods required to assist handicapped students to become educationally competent. Furthermore, as Shown (1986) has pointed out, a lack of clear educational objectives has hampered the delivery of educational services to handicapped learners.

Because most African nations have faced major fiscal difficulties for many years, improvements in special education have been difficult to achieve. Nations like Nigeria have, however, made serious efforts at both federal and local levels to teach the elements of special education in teacher training institutions (Nigeria Federal Ministry, 1977). Nigeria has established training programs at the universities of Jos and Ibadan. These universities provide training and research on scientific education of the handicapped at undergraduate and graduate levels.

In most places in Africa, there are not likely to be clearly defined admission policies for the handicapped or age limits for education of the handicapped as it now exists in Africa. It is not uncommon, therefore, to find a handicapped adult in a special education class with much younger students. Furthermore, the personnel providing special education services are likely to come from the middle or lower ranks of school staffs rather than the higher. The burden of education for handicapped students is thus frequently carried by less well-trained aides and members of the local community, rather than by highly skilled teachers.

Special education teachers working in regular school settings have been reported to be facing emotional and psychological problems (Joy, 1972). They may face neglect and even hostility on the part of other teachers who resent having handicapped students and special education teachers in regular schools. Also, nonspecialist teachers are often resentful of the fact that special education teachers receive extra pay.

Many of the special education services provided in Africa on a noninstitutional basis must be on an itinerant basis because of the scarcity of educational facilities able to serve handicapped students. A dearth of itinerant teachers has limited the extent and effectiveness of such education. Recent efforts have been made in certain African countries to mainstream handicapped students. Thus the Federal Ministry of Information, Lagos, Nigeria (1977) mandates that handicapped school children, where possible, should be mainstreamed along with their nonhandicapped peers. Some African educators have expressed disagreement with this policy (Shown, 1980). There is concern about the dangers that the physical hazards of African terrain may pose for mainstreamed handicapped students who are not carefully supervised, for example, most parts of Nigeria have dangerous structures and hazards such as rocks, forests, and rivers. Also, the application of mainstreaming policies in Africa places an inordinate burden on most handicapped students unless they are able to use the same materials as their nonhandicapped peers or can be assisted to achieve comparable levels of attainment; this is difficult to achieve in light of the current dearth of trained professionals and the lack of proper facilities and materials. As UNESCO has pointed out (1979), mere physical placement in a mainstreamed school environment is not an answer to providing services to handicapped African children. Provisions at African colleges for handicapped students are essentially nonexistent. There are no ramps, suitable steps elevators, or toilet facilities with special accommodations.

Despite efforts to improve the education of the handicapped, the outlook of Africans respecting the needs of handicapped students and adults is not such as to raise hopes for serious concern regarding their transition into productive roles in society. As Shown has observed regarding the largest nation in Africa, "Nigerians are immensely practical people calling something or someone only if it is seen to be economically useful. With this in mind, the outlook for the handicapped would seem to be bleak" (Shown, 1980).

REFERENCES

Anderson, E. (1983). *The disabled school child*. A study in integration. Open University Set Book, Jos, Nigeria.

Federal Government of Nigeria. (1984). *Nigerian year book*. Lagos, Nigeria: Author.

Joy, D. C. (1979, August 9). Experiment with blind children. New Nigerian.

Nigeria Federal Ministry of Information. (1977). *The republic of Nigeria national policy on education*. Lagos, Nigeria: Author.

Sambo, E. W. (1981, April). *What is special education?* Paper presented at the workshop on the integration of elements of special education into teachers education curriculum in Plateau State, University of Jos, Jos, Nigeria.

Shown, D. G. (1980). *A study of effectiveness of mainstreaming of visually handicapped children in Plateau State of Nigeria with a view toward determining quality education for these children*. Jos, Nigeria: University of Jos.

Shown, D. G. (1986, April). *Integrating handicapped children in Plateau State*. Paper presented at the workshop on the integration of elements of special education into teachers education curriculum in Plateau State, University of Jos, Jos, Nigeria.

UNESCO. (1979, October 15–20). Expert meetings of special education, UNESCO headquarters, Paris. *Final Report*.

UNESCO. (1981, July 20–31). *Sub-regional seminar on planning for special education*. Nairobi, Kenya.

UNESCO. (1986, April). *Expert meeting on special education*. Plateau State, Nigeria: University of Jos.

DAKUM SHOWN
University of Jos, Nigeria

See also **Nigeria, Special Education in**

AFRICA, SUB-SAHARAN, SPECIAL EDUCATION IN

Special education is a recognized educational service by a majority of the national governments of the 36 countries of sub-Saharan Africa. National governments in sub-Saharan Africa consider special education as the provision of access to the regular educational curriculum through the adaptation or modification of methods, equipment, and physical environment to meet the unique learning needs of students with disabilities (Mpofu, Oakland, & Chimedza, 2000). They also define *special education* to include the provision of special or modified curriculum and appropriate intervention to modify the social structure and emotional climate in which education takes place (Jere, 2005).

Definitions of *special educational needs* by the national governments in sub-Saharan African countries tend to be inclusive of the effects of socioeconomic deprivation experienced by millions of African children who may not necessarily have physical, sensory, or cognitive impairments. For example, the South African Department of Education has adopted barriers to learning and development as a perspective to understanding special educational needs. The barriers to learning perspective focus on person-environment interactions to special needs education. It considers special educational needs to be located in the child (e.g., a disability), within the school (e.g., lack of resources, lack of trained teachers) or within the broader social, economic, and political context (e.g., poverty; Department of Education, 1997; Engelbretcht, 2005; Muthukrishna & Schoeman, 2000).

The governments of Cameroon and Ethiopia consider special needs to include the habilitation and rehabilitation of children in poverty, including street children (Tchombe, 2005; Teferra, 2005). However, regardless of any differences in the definition of *special educational needs* among African countries, students with physical, sensory, or cognitive impairments are more likely to receive special needs education in school and other community settings (Mpofu et al., 2000). Children with emotional-behavioral disorders or giftedness tend to not be recognized by the national governments as having special educational needs and are not well served (Jere, 2005; Mpofu, Mutepfa, Chireshe, & Kasayira, 2007; Mpofu, Peltzer, Shumba, Serpell, & Mogaji, 2005; Tchombe, 2005).

There are no reliable national disability prevalence data in all countries in sub-Saharan Africa (Mpofu et al., 2000). We estimate that less than 1% of students with disabilities in sub-Saharan Africa receive special education services. For example, about 14,000 of 1.5 million children of school-going age receive special education services in Zambia, 70,000 of about 3 million students in Zimbabwe, and 5,000 of 1.2 million students in Cameroon. Sub-Saharan Africa has an estimated total population of 682 million people, about two-thirds (or about 400 million) of which are children under the age of 15 (United Nations Population Division, 2004). The World Health Organization (WHO; 1980) estimates that 10% of the general population or 70 million citizens of sub-Saharan Africans have significant disabilities. At least 42 million of people with disabilities in sub-Saharan are children under the age of 15.

A majority of the national governments in sub-Saharan Africa have adopted policies on special needs education. Variability among the countries in this region in the development of special needs policies is considerable. Countries that have relatively more advanced formal education systems (e.g., Kenya, Nigeria, South Africa, Zimbabwe) tend to have more elaborate special education policies than those with relatively less-developed education systems (e.g., Angola, Democratic Republic of the Congo, Somalia; Mpofu, Zindi, Oakland, & Peresuh, 1997; Mpofu et al., 2005). None of the countries in sub-Saharan Africa has special education or other legislation mandating that students with special educational needs receive the services they need. Thus, despite the fact that national governments in sub-Saharan Africa have adopted special education policies, special education services are not available to the vast majority of children in the region.

Assessment services for special educational needs are barely available to children with special needs in sub-Saharan Africa (Mpofu, 2001, 2004; Mpofu et al., 1997). The few children born at hospitals may have their disability noted by a physician. However, that information may not be available to the teachers at school enrollment, and, often, the physician's diagnosis does not address any education related issues. Traditional midwives in the villages deliver the vast majority of children born in sub-Saharan Africa, and the children's special education needs may go unnoticed or be ascribed by family to metaphysical forces that require spiritual assistance (Mpofu, 2003). A tiny minority of children with disabilities in countries with more-developed special education services (e.g., South Africa, Zambia, Zimbabwe) receive psychoeducational assessment from professionals (Mpofu, 1996, 2004; Mpofu et al., 1997, 2005; Mpofu & Nyanungo, 1998). Parents of students with special education needs are often minimally involved in both the assessment and subsequent education intervention (Mpofu et al., 1997; Oakland, Mpofu, Glasgow, & Jumel, 2003). In many cases, the parents defer to the special education and allied professionals who they accord the same respect as medical doctors or traditional healers (Mpofu, 2000, 2001, 2003).

Where special education services are available, they are offered at special day schools, residential special schools, special classes in regular schools, integrated schools, or other inclusive settings (Mpofu et al., 1997, 2000; Teferra, 2005). The schools and the classes are typically overcrowded, ill equipped, and understaffed (Mutepfa, 2005; Teferra, 2005; Tchombe, 2005). The vast majority of teachers providing education to children with special educational needs in sub-Saharan Africa are not trained in special needs education. Most of the countries in sub-Saharan Africa have no teacher education programs in special needs education, and those that do (e.g., Ethiopia, Kenya, Nigeria, South Africa, Zambia, and Zimbabwe) qualify a very small number relative to need. A good starting point in making special needs education training available to a majority of teachers in sub-Saharan Africa would be through the infusion of special needs education into all preservice teacher education programs and provision of certificate courses in special education to teachers already in service.

Special education services in sub-Saharan Africa barely exist. The limited services available are likely to be found in the few countries with better-developed educational infrastructures. The fact that most national governments in the region have special education policies suggests that the long-term prospects for the development of special education in sub-Saharan Africa are good.

REFERENCES

Department of Education. (1997). *Quality education for all. Overcoming barriers to learning and development. Report of the National Commission on Special Needs in Education and Training (NCSNET) and National Committee on Education Support Services (NCESS).* Pretoria, South Africa: Government Printers.

Engelbretcht, P. (2005). *Inclusive education in South Africa.* Unpublished manuscript.

Jere, J. (2005). *Special education in Zambia.* Unpublished manuscript.

Kasonde-Ng'andu, S., & Moberg, S. (2001). *Moving toward inclusive education: A baseline study of the special educational needs in the North-Western and Western provinces of Zambia.* Lusaka, Zambia: Ministry of Education and Ministry for Foreign Affairs of Finland.

Mpofu, E. (1996). The differential validity of standardized achievement tests for special educational placement purposes: Results and implications of a Zimbabwean Study. *School Psychology International, 17,* 81–92.

Mpofu, E. (2000). Rehabilitation in international perspective: A Zimbabwean experience. *Disability and Rehabilitation, 23,* 481–489.

Mpofu, E. (2001). Mental retardation in cross-cultural perspective: Implications for education. In R. Chimedza & S. Peters (Eds.), *Special education in an African context: Putting theory into practice from the perspective of different voices* (pp. 98–136). Harare, Zimbabwe: College Press.

Mpofu, E. (2003). Conduct Disorder: Presentation, treatment options and cultural efficacy in an African setting. *International Journal of Disability, Community and Rehabilitation, 2,* 44–49. http://www.ijdcr.ca/VOL02_01_CAN/articles/mpofu.shtml

Mpofu, E. (2004). Learning through inclusive education: Practices with students with disabilities in sub-Saharan Africa. In C. de la Rey, L. Schwartz, & N. Duncan (Eds.), *Psychology: An introduction* (pp. 361–371). Cape Town, South Africa: Oxford University Press.

Mpofu, E., Mutepfa, M., Chireshe, R., & Kasayira, J. M. (2007). School psychology in Zimbabwe. In S. Jimerson, T. Oakland, &

P. Farrell (Eds.), *Handbook of international school psychology* (pp. 437–451). Thousand Oaks, CA: Sage.

Mpofu, E., & Nyanungo, K. R. L. (1998). Educational and psychological testing in Zimbabwean schools: Past, present and future. *European Journal of Psychological Assessment, 14,* 71–90.

Mpofu, E., Oakland, T., & Chimedza, R. (2000). Special education in East and Southern Africa: An overview. In C. R. Reynolds & E. Fletcher-Janzen (Eds.), *Encyclopedia of special education* (pp. 1678–1686). New York, NY: Wiley.

Mpofu, E., Peltzer, K., Shumba, A., Serpell, R., & Mogaji, A. (2005). School psychology in sub-Saharan Africa: Results and implications of a six country survey. In C. R. Reynolds & C. Frisby (Eds.), *Comprehensive handbook of multicultural school psychology* (pp. 1128–1151). Hoboken, NJ: Wiley.

Mpofu, E., Zindi, F., Oakland, T., & Peresuh, M. H. (1997). School psychology practices in East and Southern Africa: Special educators' perspective. *Journal of Special Education, 31,* 387–402.

Mutepfa, M. M. (2005). Special education in Zimbabwe. Unpublished manuscript.

Muthukrishna, N., & Schoeman, M. 2000. From "special needs" to "quality education for all": A participatory, problem-centered approach to policy development in South Africa. *International Journal of Inclusive Education, 4*(4), 315–335.

Oakland, T., Mpofu, E., Glasgow, K., & Jumel, B. (2003). Diagnosis and administrative interventions for students with Mental Retardation in Australia, France, United States and Zimbabwe 98 years after Binet's first intelligence test. *International Journal of Testing, 3*(1), 59–75.

Tchombe, T. (2005). *Special education in Cameroon.* Unpublished manuscript.

Teferra, T. (2005). *Special education in Ethiopia.* Unpublished manuscript.

United Nations Population Division. (2004). Sub-Saharan Africa demographic trends. Retrieved from http://www.un.org/popin/

World Health Organization (WHO). (1980). *International classification of impairments, disability and handicaps: A manual of classifications relating to the consequences of disease.* Geneva, Switzerland: Author.

ELIAS MPOFU
Pennsylvania State University

PETRA ENGELBRETCHT
University of Stellenbosch

JAQUELINE JERE
University of Zambia

MAGEN M. MUTEPFA
Zimbabwe Schools Special Services and Special Education Department

ALMON SHUMBA
University of KwaZulu-Natal

THERESE TCHOMBE
University of Yaounde 1

TIRUSSEW TEFERRA
Addis Ababa University

AGAMMAGLOBULINEMIAS

Primary agammaglobulinemias are a group of rare immune deficiencies characterized by a lack of antibodies to fight disease and by dysfunction of B lymphocytes (specialized white blood cells that produce antibodies). Other names for this syndrome include antibody deficiency, gammaglobulin deficiency, and immunoglobulin deficiency. There are many subdivisions of primary agammaglobulinemia that describe the specific deficiency in a given patient. Acquired immunodeficiency syndrome (AIDS) is perhaps the most well known of these subdivisions.

Antibodies, which are vital to the body's ability to fight disease, are responsible for killing any foreign cells that enter the body, such as bacteria, viruses, and other toxic substances. Thus, they protect the body from disease and form the basis of the immune system. These antibodies are composed of immunoglobulins—proteins that are produced internally by cells such as B lymphocytes. These B lymphocytes, in addition to T lymphocytes (better known as killer T cells), search out these foreign cells and produce antibodies that are tailored to kill the specific invading cell. When the function of these lymphocytes is suppressed due to an immunoglobulin deficiency such as in the case of primary agammaglobulinemia, the body is increasingly subject to infection.

In some cases, this condition has been linked to genetic inheritance (Smart & Ochs, 1997). It can also be caused by the presence of a secondary condition that impairs the immune system, by an autoimmune disease, or by abnormally excessive cell growth.

Characteristics

1. Weakened immune system
2. Susceptibility to infection and illness
3. Lack of gammaglobulins
4. Inability to produce antibodies

Treatment for primary agammaglobulinemia ranges with the specific subdivision of the disease. The overall goal, however, is to reduce the number and severity of infections—without treatment, a minor infection can become severe and eventually fatal. Patients are usually given gamma globulins to supplement the immune system. These may come in injection form, or in cases in which gamma globulins are needed quickly, they may be given by plasma transfusion directly into a vein, because many antibodies are contained in plasma. In cases in which an infection is already in progress, patients can be given high-titer gamma globulin in high doses and antibiotics in the case of bacterial infections. The lives of many people with primary agammaglobulinemia have been improved with proper treatments.

Schoolchildren with primary agammaglobulinemia will need special care and special precautions. These children may be undergoing regular treatments to receive gamma globulins to boost their immune systems; therefore, they may need to miss abnormally large amounts of school for doctor's appointments, tests, and hospital stays. However, perhaps more important is that the parents and teachers of children with primary agammaglobulinemia will have to be extraordinarily vigilant to minimize the chances of exposure to sickness and infection for the child; this is indeed a very daunting task. Additionally, it requires the child to be aware of his or her condition, to be able to explain it, to have the confidence to refuse contact with peers who may be sick, and to be able to take steps to prevent infections in day-to-day life. Peers of a child with primary agammaglobulinemia may need to be educated about the disorder, and an affected child will most certainly need family support and counseling to aid in attempts to normalize day-to-day life.

REFERENCE

Smart, B. A., & Ochs, H. D. (1997). The molecular basis and treatment of primary immunodeficiency disorders. *Current Opinions in Pediatrics, 9,* 570–576.

ALLISON KATZ
Rutgers University

AGE-APPROPRIATE CURRICULUM

An age-appropriate curriculum is the concept of matching educational activities to both a student's chronological age and developmental or skill levels. Teachers sometimes face difficulties when applying this concept to older students with significant intellectual delay and developmental disabilities (IDD). Students with significant IDD often function at preschool ability levels and require training in fine motor, cognitive, and language skills. Acquiring skills that can be used immediately and will transfer to later community and vocational placements (Bruce, Campbell, & Sullivan, 2009; Drew, Logan, & Hardman, 1984) is important for students with signficant intellectual disabilities. Preschool "looking" materials such as cartoons or early childhood references are not always appropriate for older students and may be stigmatizing. Teachers must expose students to environments and settings that promote acquisition of skill deficits while planning and modifying age-appropriate curriculums to meet the student at his or her current functioning level.

The Education for All Handicapped Children Act (P.L. 94-142), and its successors, the Individuals with

Disabilities Education Improvement Act (IDEIA, 2004), both mandate an appropriate education for all students with disabilities, but wide differences remain when defining this term. Students with significant intellectual disabilities are often expected to be educated with nondisabled peers in general education settings (McSheehan, Sonnenmeier, Jorgensen, & Turner, 2006). Many concerns arise when focusing on the rigorous curriculum and peer cultures which both increase at rapid rates causing students with significant disabilities to sometimes get teased or "left out" of social groups (Carter & Kennedy, 2006). Teachers at the secondary level struggle to create a age-appropriate curriculum that equals access to the typical life experiences of the nondisabled peers at home, in the community, and during vocational and recreational pursuits (Carter & Kennedy, 2006). Although it may appear unrealistic to teach age-appropriate behaviors to students with severe developmental delays, Larsen and Jackson (1981) argue that this is the mission of special education: "No, we will not be completely successful (but)...our goals for students will stress skills relevant to the general culture, rather than skills that have a proven value only in special-education classrooms" (p. 1).

Our current knowledge of developmental milestones, task analysis procedures, and behavior modification principles can be used in adopting this approach by examining the age appropriateness of the materials, skills, activities, environments, and reinforcers used during instruction. For example, in learning visual discrimination of shapes, elementary-age students may use form boards and shape sorters, while older students use community signs and mosaic art activities. For other skills, calculators may be used instead of number lines, colored clothing can be sorted rather than colored cubes, and the assembly of vocational products may replace peg boards and beads (Bates, Renzaglia, & Wehman, 1981).

Because certain skills are difficult for older students with intellectual developmental disabilities to acquire (e.g., reading a newspaper or independently buying groceries), curriculum should focus on related abilities that can be learned (e.g., reading survival signs or following directions) to enhance future vocational and community skills. To identify these skills for each group of students, Brown et al. (1979) employs an ecological inventory approach listing the environments and subenvironments where the students currently (or will eventually) function. An inventory of the activities in each environment and a listing of skills needed to participate in those activities provide the framework for selecting curriculum goals. In this approach, for example, the basic skill of matching pictures leads to finding grooming items in a drugstore. Identifying different foods can lead to ordering in a restaurant with picture menus.

Students may experience extremely slow learning rates and much difficulty in generalizing learning skills to new situations. Therefore, the education of students with signficant disabilities must include teaching critical skill clusters and providing opportunities to practice functional skills in natural settings, such as: employment or vocational simulations, supermarkets, and accessing public transportation. For a more-detailed description of curricular approaches to teaching functional skill clusters, see Guess and Noonan (1982).

REFERENCES

Bates, P., Renzaglia, A., & Wehman, P. (1981). Characteristics of an appropriate education for severely and profoundly handicapped students. *Education & Training of the Mentally Retarded, 16*, 142–149.

Brown, L., Branston, M. B., Homre-Nietupski, S., Pumpian, I., Certo, N., & Grunewald, L. (1979). A strategy for developing chronological age appropriate and functional curriculum content for severely handicapped adolescents and young adults. *Journal of Special Education, 13*, 81–90.

Bruce, S. M., Campbell, C., & Sullivan, M. (2009) Supporting children with severe disabilities to achieve means-end. *TEACHING Exceptional Children Plus, 6*(1), article 2.

Carter, E. W., & Kennedy, C. H. (2006). Promoting access to the general curriculum using peer support strategies. *Research and Practice for Persons with Severe Disabilities, 31*, 284–292.

Drew, C. J., Logan, D. R., & Hardman, M. L. (1984). *Mental retardation: A life-cycle approach* (3rd ed.). St. Louis, MO: Times Mirror/Mosby.

Guess, D., & Noonan, M. J. (1982). Curricula and instructional procedures for severely handicapped students. *Focus on Exceptional Children, 14*, 9–10.

Individuals with Disabilities Education Improvement Act of 2004. 108–446, 118 Stat. 2647 (2004).

Larsen, L. A., & Jackson, L. B. (1981). Chronological age in the design of educational programs for severely and profoundly impaired students. *PRISE Reporter, 13*, 1–2.

McSheehan, M., Sonnenmeier, R. M., Jorgensen, C. M., & Turner, K. (2006). Beyond communication access: Promoting learning of the general curriculum by students with significant disabilities. *Topics in Language Disorders, 26*, 266–290.

KATHERINE D. COUTURIER
Pennsylvania State University
Second edition

KIMBERLY F. APPLEQUIST
University of Colorado at Colorado Springs
Third edition

HEATHER S. DAVIS
Texas A&M University
Fourth edition

See also Adaptive Behavior; Functional Instruction; Functional Skills Training; Mental Retardation

AGE AT ONSET

Age at onset refers to the point in an individual's life when a specific condition began. Age at onset can be compared with a child's chronological age to establish the duration of a condition. It is a significant variable in making diagnostic judgments and prognostic statements. Within a school setting, age at onset is typically a consideration in: (1) understanding behavioral disorders; (2) understanding the prognosis for adequate intellectual and learning performance in children with neurologic and chronic medical conditions; and (3) assessing and programming for children with learning disabilities.

In the assessment of behavioral difficulties, it is important to have an adequate history of the disorder, including an estimate of when the child began experiencing difficulties. Knowledge of age at onset allows one to assess the relationship between changes and other significant occurrences in the child's life (e.g., Did difficulties start when a sibling was born? When the child entered school?). Some psychopathologic conditions typically occurring at age of onset, and significance. For example, infrequent nightmares are not pathognomonic, in fact, they are normal in a 3-year-old child (Lowrey, 1978). Infantile autism, by definition, has an age of onset prior to 18 months of age (Barbaro & Dissanayake, 2009). For many disorders, age of onset will influence diagnostic decisions, treatment choices, and prognostications.

REFERENCES

American Psychiatric Association. (2000). *Diagnostic and statistical manual of mental disorders—Text revision* (4th ed., text rev.). Washington, DC: Author.

Barbaro, J., & Dissanayake, C. (2009). Autism spectrum disorders in infancy and toddlerhood: A review of the evidence on early signs, early identification tools, and early diagnosis. *Journal of Developmental & Behavioral Pediatrics, 30,* 447–459.

Lowrey, G. H. (1978). *Growth and development of children.* New York, NY: Year Book Medical.

GRETA N. WILKENING
Children's Hospital
Third edition

See also Medical History; Mental Status Exams

AGENESIS OF THE CORPUS CALLOSUM

Agenesis of the corpus callosum (ACC) is a congenital disorder characterized by partial to complete absence of the corpus callosum. The incidence of the disorder is difficult to estimate because many individuals with ACC are relatively asymptomatic and may never present for evaluation. However, Ashwal (1994) reports that ACC occurs in approximately 1 to 3 births per 1,000.

Characteristics

1. The central diagnostic features on magnetic resonance imaging (MRI) or CT scan are partial to total absence of the corpus callosum. The septum pellucidum is also typically absent. The lateral ventricles are shifted laterally, leaving a large subarachnoid interhemispheric space. The third ventricle is enlarged. The occipital horns of the lateral ventricles are dilated, creating an appearance resembling rabbit ears or teardrops.

2. Commissural fibers that form remain ipsilateral, creating large bundles of Probst.

3. In isolation, ACC is not life threatening and may produce little if any clinically significant symptomatology.

4. ACC is often associated with or the consequence of other congenital anomalies that can result in a wide variety of symptoms ranging from mild cognitive dysfunction to intellectual disability to failure to thrive and death.

Multiple etiologies have been reported for ACC. Sporadic cases may result from vascular or inflammatory lesions; those occurring prior to the 10th to 12th week of gestation result in complete agenesis, whereas later occurring lesions result in partial dysgenesis (Gupta & Lilford, 1995). Sporadic cases have also been found in association with fetal alcohol syndrome, Dandy-Walker syndrome, Leigh's syndrome, Arnold-Chiari II syndrome, maternal toxoplasmosis, maternal rubella, and inborn errors of metabolism (Gupta & Lilford, 1995). Callosal lipoma has been reported to mechanically block the decussation of callosal fibers. Factors affecting neuronal differentiation and migration can affect callosal development as well (Utsunomiya, Ogasawara, Hayashi, Hashimoto, & Okazaki, 1997). ACC can be transmitted as an autosomal dominant or sex-linked trait, or by means of genetic abnormalities of Chromosomes 8, 11, and 13–15. Given these multiple etiologies, ACC can be found to occur (a) in isolation, (b) in combination with other CNS and somatic anomalies, or (c) as a central feature of another syndrome.

When ACC occurs in isolation (Type I), it is relatively asymptomatic. Often, the diagnosis is made as a coincidental finding. However, on very detailed cognitive tasks, subtle difficulties with bimanual coordination and interhemispheric transfer of sensorimotor information have been reported (Klaas, Hannay, Caroselli, &

Fletcher, 1999; Sauerwein & Lassonde, 1994). In keeping with Rourke's theory of white matter dysfunction as a potential cause of nonverbal learning disability (NVLD), an association between ACC and NVLD has been suggested, but thus far, a causal association has not been substantiated (Smith & Rourke, 1995). Several mechanisms have been suggested for the relative lack of symptoms in these individuals, including (a) less hemispheric specialization, leading to bilateral representation of cognitive functions; (b) simple behavioral compensation (e.g., "crossed" self-cueing); (c) greater reliance on ipsilateral pathways; (d) greater reliance on subcortical pathways (e.g., collicular, thalamic, etc.); and (e) greater reliance on the anterior and posterior commissures (Smith & Rourke, 1995).

ACC can also occur in combination with a variety of other congenital anomalies (Type II). Gupta and Lilford (1995) report that up to 85% of postmortem cases of ACC also show other CNS abnormalities. Seizures occur in approximately 42% of Type II cases. Associated neurological problems include hydrocephalus, heterotopias, cortical dysplasia, porencephaly, pachygyria, and micrencephaly (Utsunomiya et al., 1997). ACC is a characteristic feature of Aicardi, Andermann, and Sharpiro syndromes (Ashwal, 1994). In general, the constellation of neurological and neuropsychological findings in the Type II group is more dependent on the comorbid abnormalities than on ACC per se.

ACC and associated anomalies can be identified prenatally by transvaginal sonography and CT scan. After ACC is identified, genetic testing and counseling are recommended. Children identified with ACC in isolation have an excellent prognosis for normal intellectual development and for living a normal and productive life. When severe CNS and somatic abnormalities are identified, difficult questions regarding continuation of pregnancy may arise (Gupta & Lilford, 1995). Often, symptoms of Type II ACC are easily observable at birth and are generally diagnosed by the age of 2 years. Children who manifest developmental delays and seizures should also be screened for metabolic disorders (National Institute of Neurological Disorders and Stroke [NINDS], 2000). Treatment and special education considerations of ACC are largely dependent on the nature and severity of the associated anomalies in a given individual.

REFERENCES

Ashwal, S. (1994). Congenital structural defects. In S. Manning (Ed.), *Pediatric neurology: principles and practice* (pp. 440–442). St. Louis, MO: Mosby.

Gupta, J. K., & Lilford, R. J. (1995). Assessment and management of fetal agenesis of the corpus callosum. *Prenatal Diagnosis, 15*, 301–312.

Klaas, P. A., Hannay, J. H., Caroselli, J. S., & Fletcher, J. M. (1999). Interhemispheric transfer of visual, auditory, tactile, and visuomotor information in children with hydrocephalus and partial agenesis of the corpus callosum. *Journal of Clinical and Experimental Neuropsychology, 21*(6), 837–850.

National Institute of Neurological Disorders and Stroke. (2000, August 1). Agenesis of the corpus callosum. Retrieved from http://www.ninds.nih.gov/

Sauerwein, H. C., & Lassonde, M. (1994). Cognitive and sensorimotor functioning in the absence of the corpus callosum: Neuropsychological studies in callosal agenesis and callosotomized patients. *Behavioural Brain Research, 64*, 229–240.

Smith, L. A., & Rourke, B. P. (1995). Callosal agenesis. In B. P. Rourke (Ed.), *Syndrome of nonverbal learning disabilities: Neurodevelopmental manifestations* (pp. 45–92). New York, NY: Guilford Press.

Utsunomiya, H., Ogasawara, T., Hayashi, T., Hashimoto, T., & Okazaki, M. (1997). Dysgenesis of the corpus callosum and associated telencephalic anomalies: MRI. *Neuroradiology, 39*, 302–310.

DAVID M. TUCKER
REBECCA VAURIO
Austin Neurological Clinic and
University of Texas at Austin

AGE OF MAJORITY

The age of majority is important in special education because the rights to make educational decisions transfers from a parent to their student. The transfer of rights is explained in the Code of Federal Regulations (CFR) under 34 CFR 300.520, the section dealing with Procedural Safeguards and 34 CFR 300.320, the section dealing with individualized education programs (IEPs).

These rights are explained to parents and students in the Procedural Safeguards of each state as directed by 34 CFR 300.520. This section of the Code of Federal Regulations address the fact that both the parent and child should be notified of the transfer of parental rights listed under Part B of IDEA at the age of majority. In addition, this section also explains that regardless of the age of majority set by each state, parental rights transfer to the student if the student is incarcerated in an adult or juvenile, state, or local correctional institute, and the child and parent must be notified of the transfer of parental rights to the child. Finally, this regulation requires each state to detail a process by which a parent or other appropriate individual may acquire the parental rights listed under Part B of IDEA when a student has been judged to be incompetent or not to be able to give informed consent at the age of majority.

The transfer of parental rights at age of majority is also discussed in 34 CFR 300.320, the definition of individualized education programs. This part of the Federal Code adds that the transfer of parental rights at age of majority must be included in an IEP not later than 1 year before the child reaches the age of majority. Furthermore, a statement in the IEP must detail which rights transfer.

The age of majority is not defined in the CFR, however most states set the age of majority at 18 (Kochar-Bryant, Bassett, & Webb, 2009). Alabama, Delaware, and Nebraska set the age of majority at 19, while Arkansas, Nevada, Ohio, Tennessee, Utah, Virginia, and Wisconsin set the age of majority at the later of 18 or graduation from high school (Goldberg, 2010).

Given that students will retain the rights formerly given to the parents, it is incumbent upon both school and parents to involve youth in a meaningful way in IEP transition planning. Research indicates that students of all cognitive levels can be involved in the transition process in meaningful ways but often are not included (Walker & Child, 2008). Students who are included in the transition process become trained in self-determination, which has been shown to lead to better post school outcomes (Whemeyer & Palmer, 2003). One method of planning that may facilitate self-determination is person centered planning, in which a lead role is taken by the student or family and authority is lessened for a teacher or service provider (Holburn, Jacobson, Schwartz, Flory, & Vietze, 2004).

To review, CFR 300.520 and CFR 300.320 define the requirements for all states regarding transfer of rights at the age of majority. States are required to send parents notice of the transfer of rights at least 1 year before the student's age of majority, which varies from state to state. Upon age of majority all rights under Part B of the Individuals with Disabilities Education Act transfer to the student, unless it is determined that the student is incompetent or is determined not to have the ability to give informed consent as determined by a process decided by each state. The transfer of rights before the age of majority can occur if a student is incarcerated in a juvenile or adult facility; the parents must be notified of the transfer of rights. Rights which transfer to the student at the age of majority include placement, evaluation, programming, mediation and due process (Test, Aspel, & Everson, 2006) and must be included in the IEP. Again, for a parent to retain educational rights, a student must either be declared incompetent or determined to not have the ability to give informed consent. It is important for parents to understand that rights transfer regardless of disability.

Parents may retain educational rights by seeking guardianship through legal means. A guardian is empowered to make all decisions for the student, and under limited guardianship, students may retain certain rights (Test, Aspel, & Everson, 2006). Other options to guardianship include: Power of Attorney, Durable Power of Attorney, Durable Power of Attorney over Health Care, Directive to Physician, Management of Community Property, Money Management, Social Security Representative Payment program, Trusts, and Consent to Authorize Advocacy (Guardianship, n.d.). It is important to understand the alternatives to guardianship because some argue that guardianship is disability-based discrimination (Salzman, 2010) and guardianship is diametrically opposed to self-determination (Millar, 2007).

REFERENCES

Definition of individualized education program, 34 C. F. R. pt. 320 (2011).

Goldberg. D. (2010). How the Age of Majority affects an IEP. *Special Education Advisor*. Retrieved from http://www.specialeducationadvisor.com/how-the-age-of-majority-affects-an-iep/comment-page-1/#comment-388

Guardianship. (n.d.). Retrieved from http://www.texasprojectfirst.org/Guardianship.html

Holburn, S., Jacobson, J. W., Schwartz, A. A., Flory, M. J. & Vietze, P. M. (2004). The Willowbrook futures project: A longitudinal analysis of person-centered planning. *American Journal on Mental Retardation, 109*(1), 63–76.

Kochar-Bryant, C., Bassett, D. S., & Webb, K. W. (2009). *Transition to postsecondary education for students with disabilities*. Thousand Oaks, CA: Corwin Press.

Millar, D. S. (2007). I never put it together: The disconnect between self-determination and guardianship—implications for practice. *Education and Training in Developmental Disabilities, 42*(2), 119–129.

Procedural Safeguards Due Process Procedures for Parents and Children, 34 C.F.R. pt. 520 (2011).

Salzman, L. (2010). Rethinking guardianship (again): Substituted decision making as a violation of the integration mandate of Title II of the Americans with Disabilities Act. *University of Colorado Law Review, 81*(1), 157–245.

Test, D. W., Aspel, N. P., & Everson, J. M. (2006). *Transition methods for youth with disabilities*. Columbus, OH: Merrill Prentice Hall.

Walker, J. S., & Child, B. (2008). *Involving youth in planning for their education, treatment and services: Research tells us we should be doing better*. Portland, OR: Research and Training Center on Family Support and Children's Mental Health, Portland State University.

Wehmeyer, M. L., & Palmer, S. B. (2003). Adult outcomes for students with cognitive disabilities three-years after high school: The impact of self-determination. *Education and Training in Development Disabilities, 38*, 131–144.

JAMIE DURAN
Texas A&M University
Fourth edition

AGGRESSION

Research investigating aggression offers various overlapping definitions of the word *aggression*. Many accept the definition of aggression to be a form of behavior directed toward the goal of harming or injuring another living being who is motivated to avoid such treatment. (Baron & Richardson, 2004).

Different forms of aggression exist (Kempes, 2011). Direct, overt aggression occurs when both the perpetrator and the victim are present (e.g., acts of physical aggression as when a child physically hits another child). Indirect, covert aggression includes the presence of a third person who acts as a facilitator of the aggressive act (e.g., a child who starts a rumor about another child; Juvonen & Graham, 2001). Physical aggression may be thought of as reactive or proactive aggression. Proactive aggression is defined as behavior that anticipates a reward, while reactive aggression derives from the frustration-aggression model of Berkowitz (Kempes, 2011). Specifically, reactive physical aggression refers to an immediate display of violent behavior in response to another's actions. It does not involve premeditated planning. Proactive physical aggression is planned aggression (Clarke, 2004; Conner, Steingard, Anderson, & Melloni, 2003; Vitaro, Brendgen, & Tremblay, 2002).

Aggression may also be thought of as including physical, relational, or verbal. Physical aggression includes acts completed with physical force (e.g., to hit someone, to throw something, to kick something, or to push someone). Verbal aggression includes acts of saying something harmful directly to someone (e.g., insulting someone or saying "I hate you!"). Relational aggression uses peer relationships as ammunition for the aggressive act (e.g., telling someone that he or she cannot be one's friend; Juvonen & Graham, 2001; Monks, Ruiz, & Val, 2002). Turngay (2009) found verbal aggression to be more common in patients with Oppositional Defiant Disorder (ODD). Many patients with ODD have mild physical aggression but do not meet the criteria for Conduct Disorder (CD). Serious, ongoing physical aggression is more commonly associated with CD (Turgay, 2009).

Those who engage in physical aggression are more likely to be males (Juvonen & Graham, 2001; McEvoy et al., 2003; Monks et al., 2002), older, and physically larger than their victims. However, controversy exists regarding the extent to which victims are physically weaker than their attackers (Juvonen & Graham, 2001; Monks et al., 2002). Some research found that victims of physical aggression are not physically weaker than nonvictims (Monks et al., 2002), while other studies found that victims are physically weaker than nonvictims (Juvonen & Graham, 2001).

Aggressive acts are common among very young children. Childhood aggression is a behavioral characteristic associated with different psychosocial problems. These problems often continue into adulthood and have negative effects on society (White, 2011). Aggressive and violent behavior could lead to a diagnosis of and are characteristic of Disruptive Behavior Disorders (DBD) or juvenile delinquency. During childhood, aggression is more severe within the home. By the time children reach adolescence aggressive behavior can also become severe in school (Turgay, 2009).

ODD behaviors are more severe and frequent than typical childhood disobedience, and CD behaviors are more severe than those associated ODD. The rate of ODD in children and adolescents has been reported to be between 2% and 16% (Turgay, 2009). In early childhood, ODD is characterized by frequent, severe temper tantrums and an intolerance of frustration. Children who have been diagnosed with ODD commonly exhibit severe and frequent aggression (Lumley, McNeil, Herschell, & Bahl, 2002). ODD is more common in males than in females.

Young children engage in physical aggression the most between the ages of 2 and 4 (Burt, 2011.) Young females often exhibit more relational aggression than physical or verbal aggression (e.g., verbal threats). Females are more physically aggressive than verbally aggressive. Likewise, males engage in physical aggression most often and verbal aggression least often (Monks et al., 2002). After age 3, boys are more likely than girls to engage in both aggressive and nonaggressive antisocial behaviors (National Institute of Mental Health, 2006).

Perpetrators and victims of aggression are at risk for negative outcomes. For example, young children who engage in aggressive acts tend to be less socially accepted than their less aggressive peers (Monks et al., 2002). Similarly, according to the National Institute of Mental Health (NIMH), one's peer group influences his or her engagement in youth violence. Home factors also can contribute to youth violence (http://www.nimh.nih.gov).

Aggression is more common among individuals with disabilities than the general population. (Brosnan, 2010). It is also one of the most difficult behaviors to treat (Matson, 2005). Aggression reflects social and personal problems that have the potential for serious negative outcomes. Aggression imposes a grave personal cost to the individual and a great expense to the community and society. Some aggressive children and adolescents with ODD are likely to be associated with low self-esteem, low frustration tolerance, temper outbursts, poor peer relations and, eventually, poor school performance (Turgay, 2009). Aggression can have serious short-term and long-term consequences to the quality of life experienced by the individual exhibiting aggressive behavior. Thus, aggressive behaviors are most likely to be identified for intervention (Brosnan, 2010) since 16% of the school age population are identified with problems in the area of aggression (Reynolds, Kamphause, 2004).

REFERENCES

Baron, R. A., & Richardson, D. R. (2004). *Human aggression.* New York, NY: Plenum Press.

Brosnan, J., & Healy, O. (2011). A review of behavioral interventions for the treatment of aggression in individuals with developmental disabilities. *Research in Developmental Disabilities, 32,* 437–446.

Burt, A. S., Donnellan, M. B., Iacono, W. G., & McGue, M. (2011). Age-of-onset or behavioral subtypes? A prospective comparison of two approaches to characterizing the heterogeneity within antisocial behavior. *Journal of Abnormal Child Psychology, 39,* 633–644.

Clarke, N. M. (2004). Aggression and antisocial behavior in children and adolescents: Research and treatment. *Bulletin of the Menninger Clinic, 68*(2), 192.

Conner, D. F., Steingard, R. J., Anderson, J., & Melloni, R. H. (2003). Gender differences in reactive and proactive aggression. *Child Psychiatry and Human Development, 33*(4), 279–294.

Juvonen, J., & Graham, S. (Eds.). (2001). *Peer harassment in the schools: The plight of the vulnerable and victimized.* New York, NY: Guilford Press.

Kempes, M., Matthys, W., Bries, H., & Engeland, H. (2010). Children's aggressive responses to neutral peer behavior: A form of unprovoked reactive aggression. *Psychiatry Research, 176,* 219–223.

Lavigne, J. V., Cicchetti, C., Gibbons, R. D., Binns, H. J., Larsen, L., & DeVito, C. (2001). Oppositional Defiant Disorder with onset in preschool years: Longitudinal stability and pathways to other disorders. *Journal of American Academy of Child and Adolescent Psychiatry, 40*(12), 1393–1400.

Lumley, V. A., McNeil, C. B., Herschell, A. D., & Bahl, C. B. (2002). An examination of gender differences among young children with Disruptive Behavior Disorders. *Child Study Journal, 32*(2), 89–99.

Matson, J. L., Dixon, D. R., & Michael, M. L. (2005). Assessing and treating aggression in children and adolescents with developmental disabilities: A 20-year overview. *Educational Psychology, 25,* 151–181.

McEvoy, M. A., Estrem, T. L., Rodriguez, M. C., & Olson, M. L. (2003). Assessing relational and physical aggression among preschool children: Intermethod agreement. *Topics in Early Childhood Special Education, 23*(2), 53–64.

Meyer, H. A., Astor, R. A., & Behre, W. J. (2002). Teacher's reasoning about school violence: The role of gender and location. *Contemporary Educational Psychology, 27*(4), 499–528.

Monks, C., Ruiz, R. O., & Val, T. (2002). Unjustified aggression in preschool. *Aggressive Behavior, 28,* 458–476.

National Institute of Mental Health. (2005). *NIMH: Child and Adolescent Violence Research at the NIMH.* Retrieved from http://www.nimh.nih.gov/

Reynolds, C. R., & Kamphaus, R. W. (2004). *BASC-2: Behavior assessment system for children—Second Edition manual.* Circle Pines, MN: American Guidance Service.

Taylor, J., Iacono, W. G., & McGue, M. (2000). Evidence for a genetic etiology of early-onset delinquency. *Journal of Abnormal Psychology, 109,* 634–643.

Turgay, A. (2009). Psychopharmacological treatment of oppositional defiant disorder. *CNS Drugs, 23,* 1–17.

Vitaro, F., Brendgen, M., & Tremblay, R. E. (2002). Reactively and proactively aggressive children: Antecedent and subsequent characteristics. *Journal of Child Psychology and Psychiatry, 43*(4), 495–506.

White, B. A., & Kistner, J. A. (2011). Biased self-perceptions, peer rejection, and aggression in children. *Journal of Abnormal Child Psychology, 39,* 645–656.

JENNIFER HARMAN
LINDA RADBILL
University of Florida
Third Edition

See also Behavior Disorder

AGORAPHOBIA

Agoraphobia (Greek for fear of the market) is fear of being alone in places or situations in which the individual believes that escape might be difficult or embarrassing or in which help may not be available in the event that the individual experiences panic-like symptoms. The fear leads to an avoidance of a variety of situations that could include riding a bus, going into a school building, maintaining attendance for the complete school day, being on a bridge or in an elevator, and riding in cars or attendance at special events like field trips or performances. Children in particular may come up with their own "treatment" for the disorder, in the form of rules—not riding in other people's cars, not waiting in lines, not going to birthday parties, and so on—that are difficult for family members to accommodate.

The 1-year prevalence rate for anxiety disorders in children ages 9–17 is 13% (U.S. Department of Health and Human Services, 2000). In 95% of clinical populations, agoraphobia is frequently diagnosed with a concurrent panic disorder. Two thirds of individuals with agoraphobia are female. Symptoms typically develop in later adolescence (ages 17–18) into midadulthood, so agoraphobia is infrequently diagnosed in young children. The median age for onset of agoraphobia is 27 years of age. The onset may be sudden or gradual in nature. People with agoraphobia often develop the disorder after first experiencing one or more panic attacks without warning; this makes it impossible for them to predict what situation will trigger such a reaction, so the fear is often tied to many possible situations.

Characteristics

1. Focus of anxiety is on being in situations or places from which escape may not be available in the event an individual experiences incapacitating

or extremely embarrassing panic-like symptoms.
Fears typically involve clusters of situations.

2. Situations are endured under great duress or with
anxiety associated with the fear of experiencing
a panic attack. The individual may require the
presence of a companion in order to move about
normally.

3. Symptoms are not due to the direct physiological
effects of medications or other substances or to a
medical condition.

4. If an associated medical condition is present (e.g.,
severe allergy), the fear of being incapacitated or
embarrassed by the development of symptoms is
clearly in excess of that usually associated with
the condition.

(Adapted from American Psychiatric Association, 1994)

The most widely used treatments for phobias consist
of behavioral, cognitive-behavioral, and pharmacological
interventions. There is relatively little research on the
efficacy of traditional psychotherapy in the treatment
of agoraphobia (Kendall et al., 1997). The most recent
large sample trials of treatments for all anxiety disorders
point to the efficacy of behavioral and cognitive-behavioral
therapy (CBT). For childhood-onset phobias, contingency
management was the only intervention deemed to be
well established. Other therapies showing good support
in the literature include systematic desensitization, modeling and observational learning, and several cognitive-
behavior therapies (CBT). These treatments often incorporate the individual's progressive exposure to fear- or
anxiety-provoking stimuli. Graduated exposure, response
prevention, and relaxation training have shown consistent
positive treatment effects for the disorder. Cognitive therapy, which addresses patterns of cognitive distortions and
their relationship to worsening symptoms, has also been
effective when the child or adolescent is motivated and
able to identify his or her own thoughts and feelings and
when extended time is available for treatment. Recently, a
parent-training component added to CBT intervention significantly enhanced treatment outcomes when compared
with CBT alone (Barrett, Dadds, & Rapee, 1996).

Medical treatments for agoraphobia may involve the
use of selective serotonin reuptake inhibitors (SSRIs) such
as Prozac, Paxil, Celexa, Zoloft, and Luvox. They generally
require 6–8 weeks to achieve effectiveness and need to be
periodically monitored for effectiveness. Neither trycyclic
antidepressants (Aventyl, Norpramine, and imipramine)
nor benzodiazepines have been shown to be more effective
than placebo in children, although they may be used to a
lesser extent for relief of multiple symptoms.

Special education services may be available to students
diagnosed with agoraphobia under specific categories of
Other Health Impaired, Severe Emotional Disurbance, or
Behavior Disorder if an impact on the child's education
can be established; this may be particularly important if
the disorder is chronic in nature. Accommodations may
also be requested and provided under Section 504 of the
Rehabilitation Act of 1973. Due to the nature and scope of
the disorder, school attendance may become problematic.
Families can benefit from additional counseling and support to effectively implement a treatment plan across both
school and home settings.

There is some speculation that early onset of separation anxiety disorder in children is associated with the
development of agoraphobia in adolescence and adulthood.
Although data on the course of agoraphobia are lacking,
retrospective patient accounts indicate that it appears to
be a chronic condition that waxes and wanes in severity.
Unfortunately, the chronicity of the disorder may be due
in part to the lack of appropriate treatment.

REFERENCES

American Psychiatric Association. (1994). *Diagnostic and statistical manual of mental disorders* (4th ed.). Washington, DC:
Author.

Barrett, P. M., Dadds, M. R., & Rapee, R. M. (1996). Family
treatment of childhood anxiety: A controlled trial. *Journal of
Consulting and Clinical Psychology, 64*, 333–342.

Kendall, P. C., Flannery-Schroeder, E., Panicelli-Mindel, S. M.,
Southam-Gerow, M., Henin, A., & Warman, M. (1997). Therapy for youths with anxiety disorders: A second randomized
clinical trial. *Journal of Consulting and Clinical Psychology,
65*, 366–380.

U.S. Department of Health and Human Services. (1999). *Children
and mental health in mental health: A report of the Surgeon
General*. Rockville, MD: Author.

DANIEL OLYMPIA
Utah

AGRAPHIA

The *Encyclopedia of Education* (1915) defined *agraphia* as
a disorder of the associations of speech in which there is
a partial or complete inability to express ideas by means
of written symbols in an individual who had previously
acquired this mode of speech expression. More recent
definitions describe agraphia as the loss or impairment of
the ability to produce written language and is the result of
a central nervous system dysfunction (Acree & Johnson,
2003). Agraphia is often associated with apraxia and with
so-called motor aphasia.

Orton (1937) distinguished between motor agraphia
and development agraphia, or special writing disability.
Orton defined motor agraphia as the loss of ability to
write restricted to the motor component of writing. Orton

attributed this problem to dysfunction in relevant motor control areas of the brain without accompanying dysfunction in nearby speech functioning areas. Developmental agraphia was said to manifest itself in one of two ways: the first instance characterized by an unusually slow rate of writing; the second characterized by quality of writing. Orton suggested that "shifted sinistrals," or enforced training of the right hand in left-hand children, may result in slow writing. In other cases, the lack of dominant handedness was said to result in writing problems.

Strauss and Werner (1938) suggested that finger agnosia (inability to recognize one's own fingers) may be related to agraphia. Terms such as agraphia have declined in popularity in recent years, partly as a result of a trend toward the use of more educationally relevant orientations (see Hallahan, Kauffman, & Lloyd, 1985, for a historical overview). Deficits in writing performance are best defined and remediated in terms of task-specific behaviors (Mercer, 1979). Recent and future trends in remediation and adoption include neuroimaging to identify different types of agraphia and technology to assist writing abilities (Acree & Johnson, 2003).

REFERENCES

Acree, W. M., & Johnson, B. D. (2003). Agraphia. In E. Fletcher-Janzen & C. R. Reynolds (Eds.), *Childhood disorders diagnostic desk reference* (pp. 17–19). Hoboken, NJ: Wiley.

Cyclopedia of education (1915). New York, NY: Macmillan.

Hallahan, D. P., Kauffman, J. M., & Lloyd, J. W. (1985). *Introduction to learning disabilities*. Englewood Cliffs, NJ: Prentice Hall.

Mercer, C. (1979). *Children and adolescents with learning disabilities*. Columbus, OH: Merrill.

Orton, S. T. (1937). *Reading, writing, and speech problems in children*. New York, NY: Norton.

Strauss, A. A., & Werner, H. (1938). Deficiency in finger schema in relation to arithmetic disability (finger agnosia and acalculia). *American Journal of Orthopsychiatry, 8*, 719–724.

THOMAS E. SCRUGGS
Purdue University

MARGO A. MASTROPIERI
Purdue University

See also Dysgraphia; Handwriting

AICARDI SYNDROME (CALLOSAL DYSGENESIS)

Aicardi syndrome is a rare genetic disorder that was first reported in 1965 by Jean Aicardi (Steinman, 2003). Aicardi Syndrome is the most common of syndromes involving agenesis or dysgenesis of the corpus callosum and is sometimes used interchangeably with the designation *callosal dysgenesis*. The corpus callosum is the largest of the cerebral commissures and is the major communication link between the left and the right hemispheres of the brain.

Depending upon the level of dysgenesis, symptoms may vary considerably in their severity but among the most common are: intellectual disability, autistic syndromes, severe obsessive compulsive disorders, seizure disorder, and macrocephaly (Gillberg, 1995). When limited to the extreme posterior portions of the corpus callosum, ADHD is a more common result. Girls tend to be overrepresented in callosal dysgenesis syndromes and in Aicardi Syndrome proper, only girls occur since it is an X-linked, dominant mutation. AS, among the callosal dysgenesis syndromes, is among the most severe and typically results in moderate to severe intellectual disability and numerous physical abnormalities, especially of the spine and the orofacial area. Diagnosis is by CAT scan or MRI. Neuropsychological testing is recommended due to the possible range of reaction.

Treatment is entirely symptomatic and virtually all such children will require special education services and may qualify under multiple areas of disability. In less severe cases of callosal dysgenesis, asymptomatic presentations have been reported, emphasizing the need for ongoing neuropsychological follow-up and periodic reassessment of intervention plans. Symptoms not appearing by puberty typically do not occur and the disorder is not progressive. In the most severe forms of callosal agenesis, death in infancy is common.

REFERENCES

Gillberg, C. (1995). *Clinical child neuropsychiatry*. Cambridge, UK: Cambridge University Press.

Steinman, D. (2003). Aicardi syndrome. In E. Fletcher-Janzen, & C. R. Reynolds (Eds.), *Childhood disorders diagnostic desk reference* (pp. 19–20). Hoboken, NJ: Wiley.

CECIL R. REYNOLDS
Texas A&M University

See also Neurological Organization

AIDES TO PSYCHOLINGUISTIC TEACHING

Psycholinguistic training requires the evaluator to determine difficulties in auditory, visual motor reception, integeration, and expressive abilities on the interactions and psychological functions underlying communication.

It attends to the processes by which a speaker or writer emits signals or symbols, and the interpretation of those signals by the receiver (Hammill & Larsen, 1974; Kavale & Forness, 2001).

Language programs and assessment techniques have been derived from these psycholinguistic principles and have been applied to education. A basic tenet of psycholinguistics is that language is made up of discrete components that may be identified and measured; further, it is assumed that if one is deficient in a given component, the deficiency can be remediated. This leads to two more assumptions, that a child's failure to learn stems from his or her own weaknesses, and that strengthening weak areas will result in improved classroom learning (Hammill & Larsen, 1974). If these assumptions are valid, programs aimed at mitigating psycholinguistic weaknesses are both necessary and desirable. If the assumptions are invalid, however, a great deal of time and money is being wasted on the application of these programs in educational settings.

In their review of research, Hammill and Larsen (1974) showed that the efficacy of psycholinguistic training had not been adequately demonstrated. They pointed out that many exceptional children are being provided with training programs aimed at increasing their psycholinguistic competencies. On the basis of their review, the authors claimed that it is essential to determine whether the constructs are trainable by present programs. It is also necessary, they said, to identify the children for whom such training would prove worthwhile.

Arter and Jenkins (1977), in their examination of the benefits and prevalence of modality considerations in special education, concluded that research evidence failed to support the practice of basing instructional plans on modality assessment. Thirteen of the 14 studies they reviewed indicated that students were not differentially assisted by instruction congruent with their modality strengths. Further, they stated that "increased efforts in research and development of test instruments and techniques may be warranted but, as far as the practitioner is concerned, advocacy of the (modality) model cannot be justified" (p. 295).

Kavale and Glass (1982) refer to a meta-analysis performed by Kavale in 1981 that investigated the effectiveness of psycholinguistic training. Kavale's studies yielded 240 effect sizes with an overall ES of 0.39. Kavale and Glass conclude by asserting that there are specific situations where psycholinguistic training is effective and that it should be included within a total remedial program. The findings from this research should be qualified, however, because of the lack of consideration of research methodologies across the different investigations empirical statements of the efficacy of psycholingustic training should be interepreted with caution. Furthermore outcome measures were based on performance of the process tests (i.e., Illinois Test of Psycholinguistic Abilities—ITPA), not on academic tests. Further analyses of studies using

achievement outcomes have found negligible effect sizes. It remains open to question whether such improvement on psycholinguistic process tasks would translate into improved performance on academic tasks in the classroom.

More recently Kavale (2001) found psycholinguistic training to have moderate mean effect sizes (.39) through evaluation of effective practices using meta-analytical techniques. Burns and Ysseldyke (2009) investigated evidence-based instructional practices in special education and found psycholinguistic training to be one of the least reported approaches being implemented in classrooms. Further examination of a survey of respondents and effectiveness evaluated by Kavale and Forness (2001) revealed that of eight interventions reviewed, psycholinguistic training was rated seventh by special education teachers and school psychologists. Data in the more recent study only reported the prevalence of various interventions and did not give information on teacher choice of selection and implementation (Burns & Ysseldyke, 2009). While psycholingustic teaching has been found to demonstrate moderate effects, attention should continue to be devoted to intervention selection and the fidelity of implemention. Concerns still exist within instructional research regarding implementation fidelity and the effects of the intervention when chosen and implemented without empirical evidence (Burns & Ysseldyke, 2009).

REFERENCES

Arter, J. A., & Jenkins, J. R. (1977). Examining the benefits and prevalence of modality considerations in special education. *Journal of Special Education, 11*(3), 281–298.

Burns, M. K., & Ysseldyke, J. E. (2009). Reported prevalence of evidence-based instructional practices in special education. *The Journal of Special Education, 43*(1), 3–11.

Forness, S. R. (2001). Special education and related services: What have we learned from meta-analysis? *Exceptionality, 9,* 185–197.

Hammill, D. D., & Larsen, S. C. (1974). The effectiveness of psycholinguistic training. *Exceptional Children, 41,* 5–14.

Kavale, K. A., & Forness, S. R. (2000). Policy decisions in special education: The role of meta-analysis. In R. Gersten, E. P. Schiller, & S. Vaughn (Eds.), *Contemporary special education research: Synthesis of the knowledge base on critical instructional issues* (pp. 281–326). Mahwah, NJ: Erlbaum.

Kavale, K. A., & Glass, G. V. (1982). The efficacy of special education interventions and practices: A compendium of meta-analysis findings. *Focus on Exceptional Children, 15*(4), 1–16.

KATHLEEN RODDEN-NORD
GERALD TINDAL
University of Oregon

See also **Fernald Method; Orton-Gillingham Method; Psycholinguistics**

AIDS (*See* Pediatric Acquired Immune Deficiency Syndrome)

AIDS DYSMORPHIC SYNDROME

The National Organization for Rare Disorders (2009) describes AIDS dysmorphic syndrome (ADS) as a rare disorder of infancy that can result from a mother's infection with the human immunodeficiency virus (HIV) during pregnancy. HIV is the retrovirus that causes acquired immune deficiency syndrome (AIDS). This syndrome has many synonyms, such as dysmorphic AIDS, fetal AIDS infection, HIV embryopathy, and perinatal AIDS. ADS is caused by the transmission of HIV-1 or HIV-2, both forms of the human immunodeficiency virus. The transmission can occur during fetal development or during the birth of the child. Current data suggest that the most likely time for transmission of HIV between mother and infant occurs late in pregnancy or during delivery (Milosevic, 1998).

Most infants born to HIV-positive mothers have passively acquired maternal antibodies against this virus. An infant with passive antibodies is protected because the antibodies help fight the infection by neutralizing or destroying certain foreign proteins called antigens, thus fighting off HIV. If the antibodies prevent the infant from getting ADS, they will no longer be present in the infant's bloodstream by about 12 to 16 months of age. ADS can be accurately diagnosed when the infant is 18 months of age and the presence or absence of the passive antibodies can be clearly tested (National Organization for Rare Disorders [NORD], 2000). NORD (2009) reports that current estimates suggest that the risk of an infant's contracting HIV from his or her infected mother is approximately 13% to 39% of infants who are born to HIV-positive mothers in developed countries who have not undergone treatment with antiviral medications during pregnancy. Milosevic (1998) reports that the incidence of perinatal transmission of ADS varies from 25% to 48% for developing countries. ADS is believed to affect equal numbers of male and female infants (NORD, 2009). Statistics provided from Centers for Disease Control and Prevention (CDC) show that in the early 1990s, approximately 1,000–2,000 new cases of ADS were contracted each year in the United States. Between 1992 and 1998, these numbers have declined 75% in the United States, largely because of utilized preventive measures unknown prior to the later 1990s. CDC (2009) also reports that HIV transmission from infected mother to infant during pregnancy, during labor, during delivery, or by breastfeeding has accounted for 91% of reported AIDS cases in children in the United States. These children are differentially affected by racial background. CDC (2009) reports that 84% of children with AIDS were African American and Hispanic. This number is particularly concerning because only 31% of the U.S. population of children are African American or Hispanic.

Characteristics

1. Unusually small head (microencephaly with a prominent boxlike forehead)
2. Prominent and widely set eyes (ocular hypertelorism)
3. Flattened nasal bridge and shortened nose
4. An unusual bluish tint to the tough, outermost layer of the eyes (sclerae)
5. An unusually pronounced vertical groove (philtrum) in the center of an abnormally prominent upper lip

---

The best treatment for ADS is the use of preventive measures (CDC, 2009; Milosevic, 1998; NORD, 2009). These measures would include utilizing or creating programs that would work to prevent infection in women. These programs would dispense knowledge of how to have safe sex and avoid activities such as needle sharing if a woman is an intravenous drug user. After a woman is infected with HIV, education can help her understand the risks of pregnancy and help with birth control methods. If a woman is both infected with HIV and pregnant, the best treatment is early prenatal care, which would include HIV testing, counseling, and treatment with AZT and additional antiviral medications. In addition, delivery by cesarean section may reduce the risk of transmission of HIV to the newborn. The mother would also be told to refrain from breast-feeding her child, and the child would receive AZT during the first 6 weeks of life.

HIV-infected mothers with newborns should consult specialists in infants and children with HIV. Specific drug therapies suggested for the child may include AZT, didanosine (ddI), or lamivudine (3TC; nucleoside analog reverse transcriptase inhibitors) in combination with protease inhibitors. The child will need continued monitoring to assess the effectiveness of the drug therapy.

Teachers working with students affected with ADS will have to be aware of these children's potential for lowered intelligence and problems in psychomotor functioning. Special education teachers should help students with ADS learn skills that will help them with activities requiring a coordination between physical and mental tasks. Children with ADS who are performing below grade level would be good referrals to school psychologists who could assess the child's intellectual, psychomotor, and psychological functioning. The psychological reports can aid teachers in developing a better learning program by utilizing a child's strengths to combat his or her weaknesses.

Children with ADS may look smaller and more immature than their classmates; they may also need a referral to a school counselor or social worker in order to help them develop better social skills so that they can fit in better with same-age peers. Aside from their potentially small stature, their facial abnormalities may prompt severe teasing from their peers. Teasing can be extremely hurtful, and counseling may help the child build necessary coping skills.

Children with ADS are at chronic risk for developing life-threatening illnesses such as non-Hodgkins B-cell lymphoma, brain lymphoma, and Pneumocystis carinii pneumonia (NORD, 2009). An exact percentage of how many ADS children survive into adulthood and older age is unknown. Survival depends on medication therapy and individual treatment for all infections that are likely to assault the child's immune system. Future research should also focus on exactly how and when transmission occurs and on improving methods for preventing transmission between HIV-positive mothers and their infants. Most beneficially, however, future research should focus on continued efforts to find better treatment medications until a cure or vaccine for HIV is developed.

REFERENCES

Center for Disease Control and Prevention (CDC). (2009). *HIV in the United States*. Atlanta, GA: Author.

Milosevic, S. (1998). Perinatal infection with the human immunodeficiency. *Medicinski Pregled, 51*, 325–328.

National Organization for Rare Disorders (NORD). (2009). *AIDS dysmorphic syndrome*. New Fairfield, CT: Author.

JENNIE KAUFMAN SINGER
*California Department of Corrections,
Region 1 Parole Outpatient Clinic
Sacramento, California*

AKINETON

Akineton is the proprietary name of *biperiden*, a skeletal muscle relaxant used in the treatment of Parkinson's disease (Modell, 1985). It is available in tablet and ampule form. Akineton is used in the treatment of all forms of parkinsonism, and it helps reduce movement disorders associated with this condition. It also is used in conjunction with antipsychotic drugs such as the phenothiazines to control extrapyramidal disturbances. Safe, effective use in children has not been established. Possible side effects associated with Akineton include dryness of the mouth, drowsiness, blurred vision, and urinary retention. Extreme adverse effects include mental confusion, agitation, and disturbed behavior. Teachers who have students with juvenile Parkinsonism may encounter those side effects in their students.

REFERENCES

Modell, W. (Ed.). (1985). *Drugs in current use and new drugs* (31st ed.). New York, NY: Springer.

Physician's desk reference (59th ed.). (2005). Oradell, NJ: Thomson.

CATHY F. TELZROW
Kent State University

See also Chorea; Phenothiazine

AL-ANON

Al-Anon (which includes Alateen for younger members) originally was an adjunct of Alcoholics Anonymous, but in 1954 it incorporated as a separate fellowship. The central headquarters, known as the World Service Office (WSO), serves Al-Anon groups all over the world. The WSO is guided by a voluntary board of trustees, a policy committee, and an executive committee that makes administrative decisions. There is a paid staff with an executive director. Although there is a central headquarters, all local groups operate autonomously. The only requirement for membership is the belief that one's life has been or is being deeply affected by close contact with a problem drinker.

Al-Anon groups help those affected by someone else's drinking to:

Learn the facts about alcoholism as a family illness

Benefit from contact with members who have had the same problem

Improve their own attitudes and personalities by the study and practice of the "twelve steps"

Reduce tensions and improve the attitudes of the family through attendance at Al-Anon meetings

Al-Anon is primarily a self-help/support group that focuses on assisting family members in dealing with the problems that an alcoholic brings to the family. It is based on anonymity and sharing.

Al-Anon is not allied with any sect denomination, political entity, organization or institution; does not engage in any controversy; and neither endorses nor opposes any cause except to help families of alcoholics (Al-Anon, 2011).

REFERENCE

Al-Anon. (2011). *Al-Anon at a glance*. Retrieved from http://www.al-anon.alateen.org/for-professionals/al-anon-at-a-glance

PHILIP E. LYON
College of St. Rose

ALATEEN

Alateen is a self-help, self-support group for young Al-Anon members whose lives have been affected by someone else's drinking. Each Alateen group has an active, adult member of Al-Anon who serves as a sponsor and who is responsible for guiding the group and sharing knowledge of the twelve steps and traditions. The basic purpose of this group is to help Alateens to cope with the turmoil created in their lives by someone else's drinking. Meetings are voluntary and generally are held in community buildings. Alateen members openly discuss their problems, share experiences, learn effective ways to cope with their problems, encourage one another, and help each other to understand the principles of the Al-Anon program.

In a survey conducted by World Service Office it was found that 46% of the Alateens held membership for between 1 and 4 years, 57% were female, most were children of alcoholics, 27% were the brother, sister, or other relative of an alcoholic, and the average age of a member was 14, with 71% between the ages of 13 and 17. Furthermore, 31% of the Alateen members had participated in treatment/counseling before or since coming to Alateen. Fully 94% of the Alateen respondents indicated that personal influences were responsible for their attendance at their first Alateen meeting, with Alcoholics Anonymous members, Al-Anon/Alateen members, or family members being the most frequently identified influence.

REFERENCE

Alateen. (2011). *Alateen's purpose*. Retrieved from http://www.al-anon.alateen.org/for-professionals/al-anon-at-a-glance

PHILIP E. LYON
College of St. Rose

See also Al-Anon; Alcohol and Drug Abuse; Substance Abuse

ALBANIA, SPECIAL EDUCATION

Special education in Albania began in 1963 with the opening of an institute for children with visual and auditory disorders in Tirana, the capital of Albania, and remains the only institute that provides services to children with this disability. After 1970, the first schools for children with mental disorders (mainly mild and moderate levels of intellectual disability) were opened in some of the cities where psychiatric hospitals already existed. Special schools for children with intellectual disabilities were opened in Durres in 1974, in Tirana in 1979, in Vlore in 1983, and in Elbasan in 1984. Other schools were opened after 1990. Albania has two national institutions, six special schools, and four day centers. These 12 institutions have 77 classes whose 184 teachers serve 800 students (35% female) with special needs in three categories: visual, auditory, or mental disorders (i.e., only intellectual disabilitiy).

Most (75%) teachers completed a 4-year university teacher education program, while others completed a high school teacher preparation program. None specialized in working with special needs children except for very few professionals who obtained a psychology degree from a university abroad. Years of experience and their desire and will to help these children have guided their work.

In 1996, a law Normative Provisions of Public Education outlined expectations of inclusion services to be offered to children from ages 6 through 19. Children with Intellection Developmental Delays may enroll in public nurseries and kindergartens. However, their numbers are small. Parents generally do not want to publicly admit that their child has a problem and prefer to keep them at home. In addition, teachers of young children are not prepared to work with children with special needs. While the law was implemented to move Albanian schools toward inclusive education, the International Bureau of Education found very few children with significant disabilities were being educated in public schools (Nano, 2007). Many students drop-out by the fourth grade even though pressure is given to parents to enroll children with intellectual developmental disabilities in public schools.

The Ministry of Education and Science is responsible for creating special schools. All special schools are public. Some nongovernmental organizations in the larger cities have opened a few day centers for special needs children and provide community-based services, which include counseling with family members, raising awareness in the community about the needs of these children, educating disabled children, and integrating them in public schools and community. A change in attitudes from teachers and other students toward students with disabilities has been seen in Albania and often does not present a problem for the classes of 35–40 students on average in the cities of Albania (Nano, 2007).

The Institute of Curriculum and Standards continues to improve the National Curriculum in Albania. Curricula changes used for students in special education generally are consistent with those used in the normal schools with some changes and adoptions according to the disability of the child. Individual Educational Plans (PEIs) are developed to assist teachers with selection and appropriate adjustments that should be made to the curriculum for each student identified with a disability (Nano, 2007). Training and curriculum development continues in Albania with the general consensus that children with disabilities are best educated in the public school system. With further training and development of curricula and PEIs which are effective, the movement toward inclusive education will hopefully continue for students with disabilities in Albania.

REFERENCES

Ministry of Education and Science. (1996). *Normative Provisions of Public Schools*. Tirane: MES.

Nano, V. (2002). *Albanian Schools in the Integration Process: A study on the integration of children with disability in regular schools*. Tirane: Albanian Disability Rights Foundation.

Nano, V. (2007, June). Albania: Regional Preparatory Workshop on Inclusive Education. Workshop presented at the Organizacion de las Naciones Unidas para la Educaion la Ciencia y la Cultura, Sinaia, Romania. Retrieved from: http://www.ibe.unesco.org/fileadmin/user_upload/Inclusive_Education/Reports/sinaia_07/albania_inclusion_07.pdf

GLADIOLA MUSABELLIU
University of Tirana

ALBERS-SHÖNBERG DISEASE (OSTEOPETROSIS, MARBLE BONE DISEASE)

Albers-Schönberg disease is one form of osteopetrosis, which is a hereditary disorder affecting bone density and formation. In persons with osteopetrosis, decreased skeletal resorption leads to improper bone formation inside the bone marrow space, which leads to increased bone density (Carolino, Perez, & Popa, 1998). Osteopetrosis can have onset in infancy, childhood, or adulthood, with childhood and infant onset leading to the most serious forms of the disease. Which form of osteopetrosis is technically called Albers-Schönberg disease is not always consistent in the literature (i.e., www.osteopetrosis.org and Bénicho et al., 2001). For this reason, the childhood and infant forms of the disease will be referred to as simply osteopetrosis for this article. The forms affecting children are autosomal recessive, meaning that both parents must carry the gene for osteopetrosis in order for the disease to manifest in the child. In the less serious adult form, the disease is autosomal dominant (Carolino et al., 1998). The location of the gene that causes Albers-Schönberg disease has been mapped to Chromosome 16p.13.3 (Bénicho et al., 2001).

Because osteopetrosis is autosomal recessive, it is a rare disorder. It is estimated that it affects only 1 in 200,000 children (www.stjude.org). There have been no epidemiological studies performed on osteopetrosis (Manusov, Douville, Page, & Trivedi, 1993).

Characteristics

1. Child is usually diagnosed by age 1 year, after having multiple fractures, having multiple infections, or being diagnosed with failure to thrive (Manusov et al., 1993).
2. Child may experience thickening at the base of the skull, which can lead to vision loss, deafness, and hydrocephalus (Carolino et al., 1998). Vision loss is also caused by retinal degeneration (Manusov et al., 1993).
3. Child may have bone marrow failure, leading to more frequent infections and severe anemia. Because other systems are attempting to compensate for the bone marrow failure, a child with osteopetrosis may have an enlarged spleen and liver (Carolino et al., 1998).
4. Other symptoms may include growth retardation, "rugger jersey" spine, brittle bones, delayed dentition, and psychomotor retardation (Manusov et al., 1993).

The only known cure for autosomal recessive osteopetrosis is bone marrow transplant (Carolino et al., 1998). Transplants from siblings are the most successful, and the child must have the transplant early in life to avoid permanent, irreversible effects of osteopetrosis (www.stjude.org). Because bone marrow transplants are expensive and donors can be difficult to find in time, other forms of treatment are being researched.

Special education concerns for children with osteopetrosis will revolve around physical concerns and the physical safety of the child. Because they are prone to bone fractures, children with osteopetrosis may need special supervision in certain situations to help them avoid injury. Special testing situations and classroom setup may need to be considered for children with vision or hearing loss. Children with osteopetrosis may miss many days of school because of their medical problems.

Without successful treatment of the disease, autosomal recessive osteopetrosis is usually fatal within the first 10 years of life. Children with osteopetrosis usually die of severe anemia or infections. Current research is examining the effectiveness of a drug called interferon-gamma on osteopetrosis (www.stjude.org). Some researchers have also tried a nutritional supplement called 1,25 dihydroxy vitamin D, with limited results (Carolino et al., 1998). As research on the location of the gene that causes osteopetrosis continues, gene therapy is also an option that many hope will be available in the future (www.stjude.org).

REFERENCES

Bénicho, O., Cleiren, E., Gram, J., Bollerslev, J., de Vernejoul, M., & Van Hul, W. (2001). Mapping of autosomal dominant osteopetrosis type II (Albers-Schöenberg Disease) to chromosome 16p13.3. *American Journal of Human Genetics, 69,* 647–654.

Carolino, J., Perez, J. A., & Popa, A. (1998). Osteopetrosis. *American Family Physician, 57,* 1293–1296.

Manusov, E. G., Douville, D. R., Page, L. V., & Trivedi, D. V. (1993). Osteopetrosis ("marble bone" disease). *American Family Physician, 47,* 175–180.

Osteopetrosis. (n.d.). Retrieved from http://www.osteopetrosis.org/

Osteopetrosis. (n.d.). Retrieved from http://www.stjude.org/

Whyte, M. P. (1995). Chipping away at marble bone disease. *The New England Journal of Medicine, 332,* 1639–1640.

MARY HELEN SNIDER
Devereux Cleo Wallace Colorado Springs, Colorado

See also Myelofibrosis, Idiopathic; Osteopetrosis

REFERENCES

Barsh, G. S. (1996). The genetics of pigmentation: From fancy genes to complex traits. *Trends in Genetics, 12,* 299–305.

Brondum-Nielsen, K., Chitayat, D., Fukai, K., Lee, S., Lipson, M. H., . . . Weleber, R. G. (1997). Novel mutations of the P gene in Type II oculocutaneous albinism (OCA2). *Human Mutation, 10,* 175–177.

King, R. A., & Oetting, W. S. (1999). Molecular basis of albinism: Mutations and polymorphisms of pigmentation genes associated with albinism. *Human Mutation, 13,* 99–115.

Kodsi, S. R., Rubin, S. E., & Wolf, A. B. (2005). Comparison of clinical findings in pediatric patients with albinism and different amplitudes of nystagmus. *Journal of the American Association for Pediatric Ophthalmology and Strabismus, 9,* 363–368.

SELINA RIVERA-LONGORIA
Texas A&M University

See also Congenital Disorders; Visual Acuity; Visual Impairment

ALBINISM

Albinism encompasses a group of disorders that are inherited and characterized by lack of or not enough melanin production. It does not only affect the pigmentation of the skin but also may evidence itself in the skin, hair, and eyes (oculocutaneous albinism) or may affect only the eyes (ocular albinism; Kodsi, Rubin, & Wolf, 2005). Of the variations of albinism, four types are common. In Type I albinism, the body cannot metabolize tyrosine. This deficit blocks the channel for the conversion of tyrosine, an amino acid, to melanin (Barsh, 1996). Type II albinism is an autosomal recessive disorder of pigmentation set apart by a reduced amount of pigmentation in the skin, hair, and eyes. This type of albinism is usually considered less severe than Type I albinism (Brondum-Nielsen et al., 1997). In oculocutaneous albinism, there is a lack of melanin production in the skin, hair, and eyes as stated earlier. People with this type of albinism have an increased sensitivity to ultraviolet light and a predisposition to skin cancer (King & Oetting, 1999). Ocular albinism is when only the eyes are affected by a lack of melanin production. In turn, the lack of melanin in the developing eye contributes to abnormal routing of the optic nerves. This abnormal form of routing is the cause of nystagmus, strabismus, and reduced visual acuity common to all types of albinism (King & Oetting, 1999). The needs of a person with albinism are dependent on their type of albinism. However, the most common special services needed are related to their visual acuity. Some may benefit from counseling if they are experiencing emotional sensitivity or psychological stress due to their phenotypical traits.

ALBRIGHT'S HEREDITARY OSTEODYSTROPHY (PSEUDOHYPOPARATHYROIDISM)

Albright's hereditary osteodystrophy (AHO) is believed to be an X-linked inherited disorder that results in a low level of calcium and a high level of phosphorus in the blood. Varying degrees of intellectual disability, ranging from slight to severe, are associated with the condition, and hearing and vision problems are found in a number of afflicted children. At times, hyperthyroidism is associated with Albright's, therefore alterations in personality and behavior may be seen (Carter, 1978).

Children with this condition are usually short and stocky with skeletal abnormalities often observed in both upper and lower extremities and prominent foreheads. Calcium deposits may be present in the brain, skin, and organs. Calcification is often found in hands, wrists, and feet. Toes and fingers are short and stubby. There may be impairment in the sense of sour and bitter taste and the sense of smell. Glandular disorders may be seen and sexual glands may be poorly developed (Lemeshaw, 1982).

AHO is a rare disorder and the incidence is unknown at this time. There is a female-to-male sex ratio of 2:1 (Davidson & Mayfield, 2003). Neurological, sensory, and motor problems often accompanying this syndrome will require related attention. Developmental and mental status evaluations will be necessary to measure the degree of disability each child has. Because seizures may be present, drug therapy may be necessary and must be known and monitored.

REFERENCES

Carter, C. (Ed.). (1978). *Medical aspects of mental retardation* (2nd ed.). Springfield, IL: Thomas.

Davidson, B. H., & Mayfield, J. W. (2003). Albright hereditary osteodystrophy. In E. Fletcher-Janzen & C. R. Reynolds (Eds.), *Childhood disorders diagnostic desk reference* (pp. 23–24). Hoboken, NJ: Wiley.

Lemeshaw, S. (1982). *The handbook of clinical types in mental retardation.* Boston, MA: Allyn & Bacon.

Stonburg, J., & Wyngaarden, J. (1978). *Metabolic basis of inherited disease.* New York, NY: McGraw-Hill.

SALLY L. FLAGLER
University of Oklahoma

See also **Hyperthyroidism; Physical Anomalies**

ALCOHOL AND DRUG ABUSE PATTERNS

Alcohol and drug abuse patterns in contemporary American society should be viewed from multiple perspectives in an effort to understand the multidimensional nature of the problem. Patterns of alcohol and drug use, abuse, and dependence, particularly among adolescents, have changed radically in past years. Rates of use, abuse, and dependence have all increased at an alarming rate, as has the variety of substances indulged in by young and old alike. Satre (2003) states that prevalence increases with age, leveling off in the early 20s. For example, a large national survey conducted in 2000 found that 14% of eighth graders and 30% of 12th graders reported binge drinking in the preceding 2 weeks. Many theories have been developed as social scientists seek to understand and explain the upsurge in adolescent alcohol and drug use.

To explore and explain fully the complex nature of alcohol and drug use among youths, one must look at the theoretical constructs of anthropology, economics, medicine, politics, psychology, and sociology. In a review of the many determinants of alcohol and drug use, Galizio and Maisto (1985) call for a "biopsychosocial" model. Given the alarming rate of acceleration in alcohol and drug use and the complexity of the issue, such a model would allow theorists and scientists from varying disciplines to study and collaborate in an effort to understand and intervene in this escalating social issue.

The fourth edition of the *Diagnostic and Statistical Manual of Mental Disorders* (American Psychiatric Association, 2000) clearly distinguishes among the terms *use, abuse,* and *dependence.* Although each category of psychoactive drug use (e.g., alcohol, barbiturate, opioid, cocaine, amphetamine, phencyclidine, hallucinogen, cannabis, and tobacco) is separated within the manual, the more general term *substance use* is employed when referencing the disorder as a whole. Substance use is defined as a pattern of consumption of a psychoactive substance (i.e., one that has a mechanism of action in the brain) that does not meet the definitive criteria that follow for abuse or dependence. Substance abuse is a pattern of pathological use (i.e., impairment in social or occupational functioning that is related to the use of the substance) that lasts at least 1 month. Substance dependence is defined by the presence of body tolerance to the drug, or evidence of withdrawal symptoms (e.g., runny nose, goose flesh, fevers and chills, gastrointestinal discomfort, muscle cramping) after cessation of use. Tolerance is defined as a state of use in which larger and larger amounts of the particular substance are required to produce the user's desired outcome. Withdrawal symptoms can be physiological, psychological, or both; several drugs, notably alcohol, heroin, opioids, barbiturates, sedatives, and some types of stimulants, frequently create both. This point is significant regarding the establishment and maintenance of specific patterns of alcohol and drug use. Cessation of use by a chemically dependent person may create such great discomfort that the user feels compelled to return to use for relief.

Patterns of alcohol and drug use among adolescents are strongly linked with delinquent behavior. Indeed, delinquent behavior and substance abuse are consistently correlated (Elliott & Ageton, 1976). At the least, use of alcohol, illicit drugs, or prescription drugs not prescribed for the individual using them is illegal. Further, other unconventional or nonconforming actions such as sexual experiences, attenuated academic performance, and flagrant violations of minor and major laws often precede involvement with illicit substances. Not all youths who experiment with alcohol and other drugs will manifest the problems associated with chronic or continued substance abuse, but current research supports a high correlation between continuing drug and alcohol use and delinquent behavior (Clayton, 1981). Initial, or trial, use of alcohol and drugs is likely to occur in youths who have already participated in other minor deviant activities; those who choose a high level of peer group involvement; and those who have seen both parent and peer use. Huba, Wingard, and Bentler (1980) found that prior behavior is a much stronger predictor of intended drug behavior than is either expressed interest or desire. This factor is significant in understanding the causal relationship between criminal behavior and drug and alcohol use. Initial research suggested that drug use precedes other forms of juvenile delinquent behavior (Single & Kandel, 1978), but more recent studies indicate that delinquent subgroups establish group acceptance of continued alcohol and drug use beyond the level of what could be considered normal adolescent experimentation and curiosity (Clayton, 1981).

Initiation of alcohol and drug use can be seen as either a developmental issue of adolescence (Kandel, 1975; NIAAA,

2011) or as an abnormal adaptation to frustration (Hendin, 1980), among other possibilities. Numerous theories have been posited about the initial or trial stage of drug use. However, consensus has been reached as to the critical role of peer-group pressure and the addictive nature, physically and/or psychologically, of the substances used in maintaining drug use. Thus regardless of the reason for beginning drug use, acceptance and support by peers to continue use, tolerance, and aversive withdrawal symptoms are essential factors in understanding the use, abuse, and dependence continuum. The addictive potential of the substance used, amount used, frequency and duration of use, and route of administration are key factors influencing adolescent's ability to start and stop their alcohol and drug use.

Adolescents seem to follow a predictable pattern in their continued alcohol and drug use. The use of legal drugs usually precedes the use of illegal drugs, irrespective of what age the use of illegal drugs is begun. Similarly, the use of illicit drugs like marijuana rarely takes place without prior experimentation or use. However, no evidence indicates that anything inherent in the pharmacologic properties of any substance necessarily leads from use of one to the use of another (the stepping-stone theory of addition). That is, the use of tobacco leads to alcohol, alcohol to marijuana, marijuana to stronger drugs, and finally addiction and dependency. Factors such as parental role models, peer pressure, and availability and access seem to be more important than anything pharmacological (Kandel, 1975; NIAAA, 2011).

A further complication is that adolescents who use and abuse substances that can produce tolerance may suffer the biomedical consequences of lifelong chemical affinity for continued abuse and dependency (Cohen, 1981). Also, evidence of a biogenetic predisposition to drug dependency can be seen in patterns of use and abuse in the offspring of alcoholics and, to a lesser degree, other substance-addicted parents (Crabbe, McSwigan, & Belknap, 1985). Children of addicted parents may become addicted with fewer episodes of intoxication, smaller amounts of substances, and fewer of the factors noted previously for adolescents. A word of caution is offered by Schuckit (1980), who states that even when a predisposition or affinity for substances is noted in an adolescent, the final picture must involve not only genetics but also the careful consideration of environment, culture, and other social factors.

The range and variation of the adolescent experience is an important final concern in understanding adolescent patterns of alcohol and drug use. The period of chronological growth beginning at age 12 and continuing through age 21 is marked by great physical, emotional, and intellectual development. Early-, middle-, and late-phase adolescents respond differently to issues such as opportunity for first use, continued use, decision making, the ability to make choices, stress and anxiety, and prevalent patterns of communication within a given peer network. Cohen (1983) and Kandel (1975) substantiate concerns about the impact of the age of first use moving downward. Data on age of admission to treatment centers and survey responses both suggest that a large number of adolescents will become dependent at an earlier age. Further research is needed to determine the impact of this trend on the rapidly developing, but fragile, systems of young people. Although some studies suggest a decline in the frequency of adolescent drug and alcohol use in this society (Johnston, Bachman, & O'Malley, 1982), more specific information is needed about high-risk youths from isolated populations that are not routinely surveyed in national studies (e.g., high school dropouts, younger members of the armed forces, and residents of college dorms). Miller (1981) indicates that the "surveillance function of epidemiological research" will best be served by closer attention to special "pockets" of substance-abusing youths who have escaped close scrutiny in the recent past, and research that points to effective prevention (Satre, 2003).

REFERENCES

American Psychiatric Association. (2000). *Diagnostic and statistical manual of mental disorders* (4th ed.). Washington, DC: Author.

Clayton, R. R. (1981). The delinquency and drug use relationship among adolescents: A critical review. In D. J. Lettieri & J. P. Lundford (Eds.), *Drug abuse and the American adolescent* (pp. 82–98). Rockville, MD: National Institute on Drug Abuse.

Cohen, S. (1981). Adolescence and drug abuse: Biomedical consequences. In D. J. Lettieri & J. P. Ludford (Eds.), *Drug abuse and the American adolescent* (pp. 104–109). Rockville, MD: National Institute on Drug Abuse.

Cohen, S. (1983). *The alcoholism problems*. New York, NY: Haworth.

Crabbe, J. C., McSwigan, J. D., & Belknap, J. K. (1985). The role of genetics in substance abuse. In M. Galizio & S. A. Maisto (Eds.), *Determinants of substance abuse* (pp. 13–54). New York, NY: Plenum Press.

Elliott, J. D. S., & Ageton, A. R. (1976). The relationship between drug use and crime among adolescents. In Research Triangle Institute, *Appendix to drug use and crime: Report of the Panel on Drug Use and Criminal Behavior* (pp. 297–322). Springfield, VA: National Technical Information Service.

Galizio, M., & Maisto, S. A. (1985). Toward a biopsychosocial theory of substance abuse. In M. Galizio & S. A. Maisto (Eds.), *Determinants of substance abuse* (pp. 425–427). New York, NY: Plenum Press.

Hendin, H. (1980). Psychosocial theory of drug abuse. In D. J. Lettieri, M. Sayers, & H. W. Pearson (Eds.), *Theories on drug abuse* (pp. 195–200). Rockville, MD: National Institute on Drug Abuse.

Huba, G. J., Wingard, J. A., & Bentler, P. M. (1980). Framework for an interactive theory of drug use. In D. J. Lettieri, M. Sayers, & H. W. Pearson (Eds.), *Theories on drug abuse* (pp. 95–101). Rockville, MD: National Institute on Drug Abuse.

Johnston, L. D., Bachman, J. G., & O'Malley, P. M. (1982). *Student drug use, attitudes, and beliefs: National trends 1975–1982.* Detroit, MI: Institute of Social Research.

Kandel, D. (1975). Stages in adolescent involvement in drug use. *Science, 190,* 912–914.

Lettieri, D. J., Sayers, M., & Pearson, H. W. (Eds.). (1980). *Theories on drug abuse: Selected contemporary perspectives.* Rockville, MD: National Institute on Drug Abuse.

Maisto, S. A., & Caddy, G. R. (1981). Self-control and addictive behavior: Present status and prospects. *International Journal of the Addictions, 16,* 109–133.

Miller, J. D. (1981). Epidemiology of drug use among adolescents. In D. J. Lettieri & J. P. Ludford (Eds.), *Drug abuse and the American adolescent* (pp. 25–35). Rockville, MD: National Institute on Drug Abuse.

National Institute on Alcohol Abuse and Alcoholism (NIAAA). (2011). *Frequently asked questions.* Retrieved from http://www.niaaa.nih.gov/alcohol-health/overview-alcohol-consumption/alcohol-use-disorders

Roebuck, J., & Kessler, R. (1972). *The etiology of alcoholism.* Springfield, IL: Thomas.

Satre, D. D. (2003). Alcohol abuse. In E. Fletcher-Janzen & C. R. Reynolds (Eds.), *Childhood disorders diagnostic desk reference* (p. 24). Hoboken, NJ: Wiley.

Schuckit, M. A. (1980). A theory of alcohol and drug abuse: A genetic approach. In D. J. Lettieri, M. Sayers, & H. W. Pearson (Eds.), *Theories on drug abuse* (pp. 297–302). Rockville, MD: National Institute on Drug Abuse.

Single, E., & Kandel, D. (1978). The role of buying and selling in illicit drug use. In A. Trebach (Ed.), *Drugs, crime and politics.* New York, NY: Praeger.

L. WORTH BOLTON
Cape Fear Substance Abuse Center

See also Chemically Dependent Youths; Drug Abuse; Substance Abuse

ALEXANDER GRAHAM BELL ASSOCIATION FOR THE DEAF

The Alexander Graham Bell Association for the Deaf is a nonprofit membership organization established in 1890. The Association's mission is to empower persons who are hearing impaired to function independently by promoting universal rights and optimal opportunities to learn, use, maintain, and improve all aspects of their verbal communications, including their abilities to speak, speechread, use residual hearing, and process both spoken and written language. Toward this end, the association strives to promote (a) better public understanding of hearing loss in children and adults, (b) detection of hearing loss in early infancy, (c) prompt intervention and use of appropriate hearing aids, (d) dissemination of information on hearing loss, including causes and options for treatment, and (e) inservice training for teachers of children who are deaf or hard of hearing. The organization also collaborates on research relating to auditory/verbal communication and with physicians, audiologists, speech/language specialists, and educators to promote educational and social opportunities for individuals of all ages who are hearing impaired.

To accomplish these objectives, a wide variety of member-oriented programs, publications, and financial aid programs are offered, including school-age financial aid awards, scholarships, aid to parents of infants diagnosed with moderate to profound hearing loss, and arts and sciences awards.

Alexander Graham Bell Association for the Deaf and Hard of Hearing, 3417 Volta Place NW, Washington, DC 20007. Tel.: (202) 337–5220 (voice) or (202) 337–5221 (TTY), fax: (202) 337–8314, e-mail: info@agbell.org, website: www.agbell.org

REFERENCES

Alexander Graham Bell Association for the Deaf. (1996). Washington, DC: Author.

Alexander Graham Bell Association for the Deaf and Hard of Hearing. (2011). Retrieved from http://www.listeningandspokenlanguage.org/

TAMARA J. MARTIN
The University of Texas of the Permian Basin

ALEXIA

Alexia is an acquired neuropsychological disorder of reading in which premorbidly literate adults exhibit severe reading impairments in the absence of other obvious language deficits (McKeeff & Behrmann, 2004). This disorder has been characterized as occurring secondary to a lesion in the left occipito-temporal region. The hallmark of this deficit is the word-length effect: the naming latencies of patients increase dramatically with increasing numbers of letters in the word (Montant & Behrmann, 2000). Alexia also may be known by other names, such as *letter-by-letter reading, alexia without agraphia, spelling dyslexia, verbal dyslexia, word blindness,* or *letter-by-letter dyslexia.*

There are several types of alexic disorders, which are characterized by the types of paralexias (incorrect production of words in oral reading) produced and by the properties of words that tend to affect reading performance. These properties include letter length, orthographic regularity, part of speech, concreteness, and familiarity (Friedman & Lott, 2000). The alexic disorders that have been identified and commonly agreed upon are pure alexia, surface alexia, phonological alexia, and deep alexia.

Pure alexia was first described by Déjerine. Déjerine described pure alexia as a disconnection syndrome that isolates the "center for the optic images of letter," situated in the left angular gyrus, from both visual cortices. Because this language center cannot be accessed through visual stimulation, the patients cannot read (Montant & Behrmann, 2000). Individuals with this condition are able to write (thus no agraphia) but are unable to read anything (alexia). This includes words that they have just finished writing; they almost always have a right homonymous hemianopia as well (Nolte, 1993). Although patients with pure alexia have great difficulty recognizing written words, they are able to identify words that are spelled aloud to them. These individuals retain their ability to speak, write, and understand speech because the lesion, or combination of lesions, affects input from the visual cortex to the left angular gyrus, which itself remains intact. As a result, the language areas (in particular the left angular gyrus) are cut off from all visual input, the destroyed left visual cortex can supply no visual input, but the language areas remain undamaged and still connected to the motor cortex; therefore, verbal and written languages can still be produced (Nolte, 1993). Alexia without agraphia occasionally results following a stroke that involves the left posterior cerebral artery if it causes destruction of the left visual cortex (hence the hemianopia) and of the splenium of the corpus callosum (Nolte, 1993).

Surface alexia has been identified as a variant of alexia. Individuals with surface alexia appear to rely upon the pronunciations of written words in order to ascertain their meanings (Friedman, 2005). Patients with this disorder display an inability to distinguish between homophonic words, such as *threw, through,* and *thru.* The ability to correctly pronounce the words remains intact, but there is an inability to denote which word is on the page.

Phonological alexia is sometimes viewed as the antithesis to surface alexia. While patients with surface alexia tend to depend upon a sounding-out process for reading, patients with phonological alexia are unable to read via this mechanism (Friedman & Lott, 2000). This disorder is characterized by the ability of individuals to recognize and read words that are known well, but unknown words and unpronounceable words cannot be read.

Deep alexia features the production of semantic paralexias when reading aloud. A semantic paralexia is a type of reading error in which the word produced is related in meaning to the written target word (Friedman, 2005). Friedman notes that individuals with deep alexia demonstrate difficulty in reading words with affixes, and derivational paralexias are produced in which word endings are added, deleted, or substituted for one another (Friedman & Glosser, 1998).

REFERENCES

Friedman, R. B. (2005). *Alexia by R. B. Friedman*. Retrieved from http://neurology.georgetown.edu/facultylisting/391891.html

Friedman, R. B., & Glosser, G. (1998). Aphasia, alexia, and agraphia. In H. S. Friedman (Ed.), *Encyclopedia of mental health* (pp. 137–148). San Diego, CA: Academic Press.

Friedman, R. B., & Lott, S. N. (2000). Rapid word identification in pure alexia is lexical but not semantic. *Brain and Language, 72,* 219–237.

McKeeff, T. J., & Behrmann, M. (2004). Pure alexia and covert reading: Evidence from stroop tasks. *Cognitive Neuropsychology, 21,* 443–458.

Montant, M., & Behrmann, M. (2000). Pure alexia. *Neurocase, 6,* 265–294.

Nolte, J. (1993). *The human brain* (3rd ed.). St. Louis, MO: Mosby Year Book.

CYNTHIA RICCIO
FLOYD HENDERSON
Texas A&M University

See also Dyslexia; Traumatic Brain Injury

ALGOZZINE, BOB (1946–   )

After receiving a BS in economics in 1968 from Wagner College in New York, Bob Algozzine earned his MS in educational psychology from the State University of New York, Albany, in 1970 and his PhD in the education of exceptional children from Pennsylvania State University in 1975. He was a professor at the University of Florida where he was involved with training regular class teachers to work with exceptional students. Currently, he is professor at the University of North Carolina Charlotte, in the Department of Educational Leadership and project codirector of the U.S. Department of Education–supported Behavior and Reading Improvement Center.

Algozzine's main interest began in working with students who fail to profit in regular classes. Much of his work was focused on the similarities between learning-disabled (LD) and low-achieving students. Algozzine contended that LD was a sophisticated term for low achievement and that it represented an oversophistication of a concept (Algozzine, Ysseldyke, & Shinn, 1982). He has shown that few differences exist in test profiles of LD and low-achieving students and that performance profiles of many normal students evidence significant discrepancies as well. He believes that schools need to spend less energy trying to identify exceptional students and place more effort on determining what to do with all students who fail to profit from their current educational placement (Algozzine & Ysseldyke, 1983).

Currently Algozzine's interests include: effective teaching, behavior instruction, positive behavior supports, data-based decision making, and progress monitoring of children with emotional and behavioral problems (Retrieved from http://coedpages.uncc.edu/rfalgozz/MAIN/bavita.pdf on December 16, 2011). Algozzine has written over 250 articles, research reports, monographs, final reports, and books. He has been a member of the Council for Exceptional Children, the American Educational Research Association, and the North Carolina Council for Children with Behavior Disorders.

He currently serves as the Executive Editor for *Multicultural Learning and Teaching* while also coediting journals within the field of special education that include: *Career Development for Exceptional Individuals*, *The Journal of Special Education*, and *Teacher Education and Special Education*. Algozinne previously served as a coeditor of Exceptional Children and as a column editor for *Preventing School Failure*.

REFERENCES

Algozzine, B., & Ysseldyke, J. E. (1983). Learning disabilities as a subset of school failure: The oversophistication of a concept. *Exceptional Children*, 50, 242–246.

Algozzine, B., Ysseldyke, J. E., & Shinn, M. (1982). Identifying children with learning disabilities: When is a discrepancy severe? *Journal of School Psychology*, 20, 299–305.

Algozzine, B. (2011). Curriculum vitae. Retrieved from http://coedpages.uncc.edu/rfalgozz/MAIN/bavita.pdf

E. VALERIE HEWITT
Texas A&M University
First edition

KAY E. KETZENBERGER
The University of Texas of the Permian Basin
Second edition

RACHEL M. TOPLIS
Falcon School District 49 Colorado Springs, Colorado
Third edition

ALLERGIC DISEASES

An allergy is a hypersensitivity to a specific substance (an antigen) that in a similar quantity does not affect other people. The abnormal reactions are usually in the form of asthma, hay fever, eczema, hives, or chronic stuffy nose (allergic rhinitis). Technically, the use of the term should be limited to those conditions in which an immunological mechanism can be demonstrated (Hourmanesh & Clark, 2003). Allergies are common to 10% of the children in the United States and are inherited (NIAID, 2011). The tendency to develop allergies is present at birth but may appear at any age. Food allergies occur in 5% of children under the age of 5 and 4% of children ages 5 to17 (NIAID, 2011).

Allergies can be classified into two types: immediate hypersensitivity (such as allergic rhinitis, asthma, and food allergies) and delayed hypersensitivity (such as reactions to poison ivy). Patients with the former have more of the antibody IgE in their systems. This antibody reacts with whatever patients are allergic to, whether it is something that they breathe, eat, or have skin contact with. This reaction causes certain cells in the body to release chemical mediators such as histamine and serotonin. These chemicals cause the dilation of the small blood vessels, increased secretion from the mucous glands, and smooth muscle contractions that produce the allergy symptoms.

Allergic rhinitis is the commonest cause of nasal congestion in children. Epidemiological data indicate that in the United States alone allergic rhinitis occurs in 59.7 cases per 1,000, accounting for 2 million days lost from school (Shapiro, 1986). An important complication of perennial allergic rhinitis is otitis media with effusion, an accumulation of fluid behind the eardrum in the middle ear. Patients usually have at least an intermittent loss of hearing and may complain of a sensation of fullness or popping and cracking noises.

Allergies often play a role in the etiology of asthma, especially in childhood (Hourmanesh & Clark, 2003). The chemical mediators released upon the allergic reaction cause contraction of the smooth muscles in the walls of the bronchial airways, swelling of the bronchial tubes, and an increase in the rate of secretion of mucus by submucosal glands. This produces obstruction and causes the characteristic wheezing and shortness of breath. Asthma may be mild (one or two mild attacks per year) or severe with intractable wheezing daily. The severe form may greatly restrict physical activity and make school attendance difficult for school-age children. Physical exertion may precipitate wheezing and become a problem in physical education classes.

Skin allergies are common, especially in younger children. Atopic dermatitis (eczema) may occur in 3% to 4% of infants and result in a dry, scaly, itchy rash involving the cheeks and extremities. While most children outgrow the rash, over 50% of them tend to develop respiratory allergies. Another common rash with an allergic origin is urticaria or hives. Possible causes are allergies to drugs like aspirin or penicillin and to foods.

Food allergies are perhaps the most controversial area of allergy study. Some allergists feel that allergic reactions to foods are rare, while others feel they are a common cause of illness. The frequency of food allergy seems to decrease as children grow older. The most common symptoms of food allergy include gastrointestinal symptoms such as abdominal pain, vomiting and diarrhea, and rashes such as hives. Food may play a role in other allergic conditions such as allergic rhinitis, asthma, and eczema, especially during the first 3 or 4 years of life. The most serious allergic reaction to foods and drugs is an anaphylactic one, in which the person experiences a shocklike reaction that can result in death. Any food can cause an allergic reaction, but the foods most apt to cause one in children include milk, eggs, fish, wheat, corn, peanuts, soy, pork, and chocolate. In December 2010, Guidelines for Diagnosis and Management of Food Allergies in the United States was published to better inform parents and personnel working with children about the signs and reactions to food allergies (NIAID, 2011).

Stinging insect allergies may cause a severe anaphylactic reaction to the sting of a bee, wasp, hornet, or yellow jacket. The reaction may occur within minutes after the sting and allergic persons need immediate medical attention.

A thorough history and physical examination are important components of a diagnosis. Seasonal patterns of symptoms, exposure to animals, and usual diet are useful information in identifying causes. Laboratory analysis of nasal secretions, sputum, and blood may establish the presence of eosinophil cells that appear in increased numbers with allergic reactions. Pulmonary function tests are also helpful. Scratch and intradermal skin tests for the suspected allergens can confirm a diagnosis. Another tool is the radio-allergoabsorbant (RAST) test, which measures the level of IgE in the blood for a particular allergen (Hourmanesh & Clark, 2003). The elimination-challenge diet is used for suspected food allergies; after avoiding a particular food for 2 to 3 weeks, the patient consumes it and is observed for reactions. Awareness of environmental conditions from change of seasons, foliage in different parts of the country, and environmental factors in homes, schools, and the work place also assists the diagnostician.

While there is no cure for allergies, symptoms may be controlled in a variety of ways. First, symptomatic treatment involves using medication. Antihistamines are the most commonly prescribed drugs for the treatment of allergic reactions. They inhibit some of the actions of histamine but frequently have negative side effects such as sedation, excitation, and insomnia. Antihistamines are often combined with decongestant drugs. Asthmatics are usually treated with bronchodilator drugs that cause relaxation of the smooth muscle surrounding the bronchial tubes. Acute asthmatic attacks and anaphylactic reactions are frequently treated with epinephrine. Both drugs may have negative side effects. For severe allergic problems, corticosteroids may be used, but on a limited basis because of adrenal suppression and limitation of physical growth in children.

The second method of treatment is environmental control, that is, removal of troublesome antigens such as pet hair, dust, and pollen. Good housekeeping practices, use of air conditioning at home and in the car, and other careful planning can prevent many allergic problems. A third and related approach is to teach self-regulation strategies to persons with asthma and other types of allergies. They include relaxation training, biofeedback procedures to modify physiological reactions, and general education about the medical condition (Creer, Marion, & Harm, 1988). A fourth treatment is immunotherapy, which involves injecting the patient with small amounts of an antigen that has been processed into a dilute form. These injections stimulate the immune system to produce another type of antibody that inhibits the reaction between the allergic antibody and the antigen. While initially the shots are taken once or twice a week, the regimen is gradually phased out over a 2- to 3-year period (Patterson et al., 1978).

Allergies have been connected with specific learning disabilities through analyses of case studies (Rapaport & Flint, 1976). Allergic children are rated lower in reading, auditory perception, and visual perception (Harvard, 1975). Teacher and parent ratings as well as test scores indicated lower proficiency among allergic students in some areas (Rawls, Rawls, & Harrison, 1971). Learning-disabled students with recurrent otitis media may have more problems with allergies and verbal skills than nondisabled children (Loose, 1984). Geschwind and Behan (1982) associate left-handedness with reports of learning problems and immunological diseases such as thyroid and bowel disorders.

However, McLoughlin et al. (1983) found no differences in parent reports concerning academic achievement, diagnosis for disabilities, and behavioral problems of allergic and nonallergic students. There was a tendency for children with asthma and chronic rhinitis to be rated lower in listening skills. Additionally, a comparison of group achievement scores of allergic and nonallergic students indicated no interaction of exceptional conditions and allergies (McLoughlin, Nall, & Petrosko, 1985). Some lower estimates of allergic children's school performance seem confused with the effects of socioeconomic factors.

Higher rates of school absenteeism are reported for asthmatic children and those with chronic rhinitis (Shapiro, 1986). Asthmatic children may be absent 10% of the time; such absenteeism is a direct cause of school problems. Additionally, the seasonal occurrence of allergic reactions (especially in the fall) and the typical pattern of frequent, brief absences are disruptive to classroom performance, attending skills, and social development. Milder forms of allergies may not cause significant school absenteeism, particularly with improved medical treatment, self-management programs, and parent education (McLoughlin et al., 1985). Furthermore, some previous estimates of higher absenteeism of allergic children may have been confused with the effects of socioeconomic status.

Hearing difficulties are frequently associated with otitis media resulting from allergies (Northern, 1980). Among allergic students, Szanton and Szanton (1966) found many cases of intermittent hearing loss that had been undetected on screening measures. Articulation and/or vocal quality problems have also been reported among allergic students (Baker & Baker, 1980). Recurrent otitis media among 3-year-olds has been associated with lower speech and language performance (Rapin, 1999; Teele et al., 1984).

Allergy history seems present among cases of behavioral and emotional disorders (Mayron, 1978). King (1981) estimated that 70% of students with such disorders have personal or family allergy histories; cognitive-emotional symptoms were noted after allergic exposure under double-blind conditions. Psychological and personality changes are frequently reported by asthmatic children and their parents (Creer, Marion, & Creer, 1983). However, comparisons of reports and ratings of behavioral problems, placement in services for behavior disorders, and school suspensions between allergic and nonallergic students have not yielded significantly different profiles (McLoughlin et al., 1985).

Allergy medication may have adverse effects on behavior and exacerbate existing behavioral problems (Hourmanesh & Clark, 2003; McLoughlin et al., 1983). Theophylline has been significantly correlated with inattentiveness, hyperactivity, irritability, drowsiness, and withdrawal behavior; the negative side effects increase with length of use. Furakawa and his colleagues (1984) found decreased test performances under the influence of theophylline. Terbutaline created socially inappropriate behavior in a comparison group (Creer, 1979), and corticosteroids negatively affected academic performance (Suess & Chai, 1981). Ladd, Leibold, Lindsey, and Ornby (1980) also reported euphoria, insomnia, and visual disturbances with corticosteroids. Antihistamines may cause sedation, dry mouth, and irritability (Weinberger & Hendeles, 1980). Visual hallucinations occur among some children receiving decongestants (Sankey, Nunn, & Sills, 1984).

Allergic disorders have important implications for the professional assessment and intervention of exceptionalities as well as for parental involvement. Certain types of allergies and/or the side effects of medication may be contributing factors in behaviors of concern and may require special consideration when designing special services. The self-monitoring and management skills taught in special education may be mutually beneficial in coping with this medical condition.

REFERENCES

Baker, M., & Baker, C. (1980). Difficulties generated by allergies. *Journal of School Health, 50*, 583–585.

Creer, T. L. (1979). *Asthma therapy*. New York, NY: Springer.

Creer, T. L., Marion, R. J., & Creer, P. P. (1983). The asthma problem behavior checklist: Parental perceptions of the behavior of asthmatic children. *Journal of Asthma, 20*, 97–104.

Creer, T. L., Marion, R. J., & Harm, D. L. (1988). Childhood asthma. In D. K. Routh (Ed.), *Handbook of pediatric psychology* (pp. 162–189). New York, NY: Guilford Press.

Furakawa, C. T., Shapiro, G. G., DuHamel, T., Weimer, L., Pierson, W. E., & Bierman, C. W. (1984, March). Learning and behavior problems associated with theophylline therapy. *Lancet, 621*.

Geschwind, N., & Behan, P. (1982). Left-handedness: Association with immune disease, migraine, and developmental learning disorders. *Proceedings of the National Academy of Science, USA, 79*, 5097–5100.

Harvard, J. G. (1975). Relationship between allergic conditions and language and/or learning disabilities. *Dissertation Abstracts International, 35*, 6940.

Hourmanesh, N., & Clark, E. (2003). Allergy disorders. In E. Fletcher-Janzen & C. R. Reynolds (Eds.), *Childhood disorders diagnostic desk reference* (pp. 27–28). Hoboken, NJ: Wiley.

King, D. S. (1981). Can allergic exposure provoke psychological symptoms? *Biology Psychiatry, 16*, 3–19.

Ladd, F. T., Leibold, S. R., Lindsey, C. N., & Ornby, R. (1980). RX in the classroom. *Instructor, 90*, 58–59.

Loose, F. F. (1984). *Educational implications of recurrent otitis media among children at risk for learning disabilities*. Unpublished doctoral dissertation, Michigan State University.

Mayron, L. (1978). Ecological factors in learning disabilities. *Journal of Learning Disabilities, 11*, 40–50.

McLoughlin, J. A., Nall, M., Isaacs, B., Petrosko, J., Karibo, J., & Lindsey, B. (1983). The relationship of allergies and allergy treatment to school performance and student behavior. *Annals of Allergy, 51*, 506–510.

McLoughlin, J. A., Nall, M., & Petrosko, J. (1985). Allergies and learning disabilities. *Learning Disability Quarterly, 8*, 255–260.

NIAID. (2011). *National Institute of Allergy and Infectious Diseases allergy statistics*. Retrieved from http://www.niaid .nih.gov/topics/allergicDiseases/Pages/default.aspx

Northern, J. L. (1980). Diagnostic tests of ear disease. In C. Bierman & D. Pearlman (Eds.), *Allergic diseases of infancy, childhood and adolescence* (pp. 492–501). Philadelphia, PA: Saunders.

Patterson, R., Lieberman, P., Irons, J., Pruzansky, J., Melam, H., Metzger, W. J., & Zeiss, C. R. (1978). Immunotherapy. In E. Middleton, Jr., C. Reed, & E. Ellis (Eds.), *Allergy principles and practice* (Vol. 2, pp. 877–897). St. Louis, MO: Mosby.

Rapaport, H. G., & Flint, H. (1976). Is there a relationship between allergy and learning disabilities? *Journal of School Health, 46*, 139–141.

Rapin, I. (1999). Hearing impairments. In R. F. Swaiman & S. Ashwal (Eds.), *Pediatric neurology* (pp. 77–95). St. Louis, MO: Mosby.

Rawls, D. J., Rawls, J. R., & Harrison, D. W. (1971). An investigation of 6- to 11-year-old children with allergic disorders. *Journal of Consulting and Clinical Psychology, 36*, 260–264.

Sankey, R. J., Nunn, A. J., & Sills, J. A. (1984). Visual hallucinations in children receiving decongestants. *British Medical Journal, 288*, 1369.

Shapiro, G. (1986). Understanding allergic rhinitis. *Pediatrics in Review, 7*, 212–218.

Suess, W. M., & Chai, H. (1981). Neuropsychological correlates of asthma: Brain damage or drug effects? *Journal of Consulting and Clinical Psychology, 49*, 135–136.

Szanton, V. J., & Szanton, W. C. (1966). Hearing disturbances in allergic children. *Journal of Asthma Research, 4*, 25–28.

Teele, D. W., Klein, J. O., Rosner, B. A., & the Greater Boston Otitis Media Study Group. (1984). *Pediatrics, 74*, 282–287.

Tuft, L. (1973). *Allergy management in clinical practice.* St. Louis, MO: Mosby.

Weinberger, M., & Hendeles, L. (1980). Pharmacologic management. In C. Bierman & D. Pearlman (Eds.), *Allergic diseases of infancy, childhood and adolescence* (pp. 311–332). Philadelphia, PA: Saunders.

JAMES A. MCLOUGHLIN
University of Louisville

MICHAEL NALL
Louisville, Kentucky

See also Asthma; Chronic Illness in Children

ALLEY, GORDON R. (1934–1999)

Gordon R. Alley received his BA (1959) from Augustina, Illinois, later earning his MA (1961) in Psychology and his doctorate (1967) in Special Education and School Psychology from the University of Iowa. Alley's contributions to the field of education include his service as teacher of the intellectually disabled, school psychologist, and director of special education. He taught at the University of Utah (1967–1970), and was professor of special education and a lecturer in pediatrics at the University of Kansas from 1970. Alley was invited to present his papers to regional and national gatherings on numerous occasions.

Alley's work emphasized learning strategies associated with the developmental characteristics of adolescents, with his research promoting alternatives to the traditional tutorial and remedial approaches to interventions for students with learning disabilities. As a cofounding member of the Institute for Research in Learning Disabilities at the University of Kansas, Alley published many of his writings pursuant to his interests, including a chapter in *Instructional Planning for Exceptional Children* (1979). Other important publications are his 1979 work, *Teaching the*

Learning Disabled Adolescent and *The Effect of Advance Organizers on the Learning and Retention of Learning Disabled Adolescents within the Context of a Cooperative Planning Model*, a study conducted by Alley and Keith Lenz in 1983. Alley's study investigated whether advance organizers would help learning disabled adolescents process information on selected academic tasks more effectively. Results of the research indicated the efficacy of their use in secondary classrooms.

REFERENCES

Alley, G., & Deshler, D. D. (1979). *Teaching the learning disabled adolescent: Strategies and methods.* Denver, CO: Love.

Alley, G., & Foster, C. (1979). *Instructional planning for exceptional children.* Denver, CO: Love.

Lenz, B. K., & Alley, G. R. (1983). *The effect of advance organizers on learning and retention of learning disabled adolescents within the context of a cooperative planning model.* Lawrence, KS: Florida Atlantic University/Kansas University.

ROBERTA C. STOKES
Texas A&M University

TAMARA J. MARTIN
The University of Texas of the Permian Basin
Third edition

ALOPECIA AREATA

Alopecia areata is an unpredictable autoimmune skin disease resulting in the loss of hair on the scalp and sometimes elsewhere on the body. The affected hair follicles are mistakenly attacked by the person's own immune system (white blood cells), impeding hair growth. Heredity plays a role in the development of this condition. At least one in five persons with alopecia areata have a family member with the condition. Alopecia areata often occurs in families whose members have asthma, hay fever, atopic eczema, or other autoimmune diseases such as thyroiditis.

Alopecia areata occurs in males and females of all ethnicities and ages. Onset is often in childhood. Approximately 1.7% of the overall population is affected by this condition (more than 4 million U.S. citizens).

Characteristics

1. Alopecia areata usually starts in childhood with one or more small, round, smooth bald patches on the scalp.
2. Progression to total scalp hair loss (alopecia totalis) or complete body hair loss (alopecia universalis) is possible.

3. In some people, the nails develop stippling that looks as if a pin had made rows of tiny dents.

4. The hair can grow back even after years of hair loss. However, it can also fall out again at a later date.

Several treatments are available, and choice of treatment depends upon the individual's age and extent of hair loss. Treatments available for mild hair loss include such things as cortisone injections into the areas of the scalp affected by hair loss. Or solutions (e.g., topical minoxidil or anthralin cream) can be applied to the affected areas. For more severe cases, cortisone pills, topical immunotherapy (which consists of producing an allergic rash to trigger hair growth), or wigs can be used.

Because the general public is still generally unfamiliar with this disorder, students diagnosed with alopecia areata may find that this disease can have a profound impact upon their school life (e.g., Smith, 2001). Due to its sudden onset, recurrent episodes, and unpredictable course, alopecia areata can be life-altering. Therefore, students may require counseling to be able to come to terms with this disorder. School personnel may benefit from information about this disorder to help them understand the condition and support the student. Contact with other individuals with this condition may help to bolster student's self-esteem.

The prognosis for someone with this condition is varied. For some individuals, hair growth can return to normal. For some people, however, recurring hair loss can occur. The National Alopecia Areata Foundation (NAAF) funds research into this disorder and holds research workshops to exchange knowledge and further alopecia areata research in the field. For more information, contact: NAAF, P.O. Box 150760, San Rafael, CA 94915. Tel.: (415) 456–4644; National Organization for Rare Disorders, P.O. Box 8923, New Fairfax, CT 06812–8923

REFERENCE

Smith, J. A. (2001). The impact of skin disease on the quality of life of adolescents. *Adolescent Medicine, 12*(2), 343–353.

RACHEL TOPLIS
University of Northern Colorado

See also Monilethrix

ALPHA-1-ANTITRYPSIN DEFICIENCY

Alpha-1-antitrypsin deficiency (A-1-AD) is caused by an inadequate amount of the enzyme alpha-1-antitrypsin in the blood. Affected individuals have 10–20% of normal levels of this serum protein. As a result, they experience early-onset emphysema (blebs and cysts replacing normal lung tissue), usually in the third or fourth decade. A-1-AD can also cause liver disease in infants and children.

Alpha-1-antitrypsin inactivates protreases, which are substances released from dead bacteria and white blood cells. Accumulation of proteases in the lung leads to destruction of normal architecture and emphysema.

A-1-AD is an hereditary disorder. Symptomatic individuals are homozygous for the abnormal gene. A-1-AD is one of the most common fatal genetic diseases in people of European descent. The incidence in white populations is 1:200–1:4,000.

Characteristics

1. Highly variable course of liver disease in infants. Jaundice and liver enlargement may occur in the first week of life. These findings may resolve completely or progress to chronic liver disease with diffuse scarring (cirrhosis) and liver failure.

2. Lung disease in childhood is rare. A few pediatric patients experience chronic cough, wheezing, or shortness of breath. Passive smoke exposure enhances early development of emphysema.

3. Symptoms of chronic lung disease usually do not begin until the third or fourth decade.

General therapy includes aggressive treatment of lung infections, immunization with pneumococcal and influenza vaccines, inhaled medications for wheezing, and avoidance of smoke exposure as well as other environmental irritants. Intravenous administration of alpha-1-antitrypsin can raise blood levels into the normal range, at least temporarily.

Children with A-1-AD may meet eligibility criteria to receive support services as Other Health Impaired if an educational need is demonstrated. There is no research to indicate cognitive delay as a result of this disease; however, the child's ability to function in the classroom may be impaired by his or her illness. Providing additional emotional support to help the child develop age-appropriate coping mechanisms would be helpful.

A-1-AD patients have a guarded prognosis. Liver transplantation can be curative for young children with cirrhosis and liver failure, but that procedure is no stroll through the park. Older patients with chronic lung disease must deal with their illness every day. They are susceptible to pneumonia and bronchitis, which can cause swift, catastrophic deterioration in their respiratory status. In the future, gene insertion therapy offers the best hope for prolonged survival and improved quality of life.

For more information and support, contact the Alpha 1 National Association at: Tel.: (800) 521-3025, e-mail AIN@alpha1.org.

REFERENCES

Balistreri, W. F. (2000). Metabolic disease of the liver. In R. E. Behrman, R. M. Kleigman, & H. B. Jenson (Eds.), *Nelson's textbook of pediatrics* (16th ed., pp. 1207–1212). Philadelphia, PA: W. B. Saunders.

Orenstein, D. M. (2000). Emphysema and overinflation. In R. E. Behrman, R. M. Kleigman, & H. B. Jenson (Eds.), *Nelson's textbook of pediatrics* (16th ed., pp. 1302–1305). Philadelphia, PA: W. B. Saunders.

What is alpha 1? (n.d.). Retrieved from http://www.alpha2alpha. org/whatisalpha1.htm

BARRY H. DAVISON
Ennis, Texas

JOAN W. MAYFIELD
Baylor Pediatric Specialty Services
Dallas, Texas

As the English language evolved, letter names no longer directly represented speech sounds; therefore, children became more and more confused as they tried to read modern literature by simply reciting the names of the letters. Realizing that this confusion hindered efforts to teach reading effectively, the alphabetic method was gradually replaced by phonetically based methods of reading instruction. By the beginning of the 20th century, the classic alphabetic method was seldom used.

REFERENCES

Huey, E. B. (1908). *The psychology and pedagogy of reading.* New York, NY: Macmillan.

Matthews, M. M. (1966). *Teaching to read.* Chicago, IL: University of Chicago Press.

CHRIS CHERRINGTON
Lycoming College
Fourth edition

See also Distar; Reading Remediation; Whole Word Teaching

ALPHABETIC METHOD

The alphabetic method of teaching children to read is historically connected with the development of an alphabet. Once letters and sounds were fixed in a structure (an alphabet), a method to master this structure emerged. The first recorded use of the alphabetic method was in ancient Greek and Roman civilizations. Reading instruction began by teaching children all the letters in their proper alphabetical order. After a complete mastery of the alphabet, children learned to group the letters to form syllables, words, and finally sentences. Reading instruction was considered primarily an oral process; the child recited the spelling of each syllable or word and then pronounced it. This progression of teaching letters, syllables, words, and sentences was the predominant method of teaching reading from Greek and Roman times until the late 1800s (Huey, 1908).

In using this method, 16th- and 17th-century teachers drilled children unmercifully on the names of the letters (Matthews, 1966). Instructional materials that presented lists of letters, syllables, and words to be memorized before advancing to the text were developed. The *New England Primer* was one of the most widely used reading texts in 17th-century America. Each reading selection focused on a moral or religious lesson, and was preceded by an alphabet, lists of the vowels and consonants, and lists of syllables such as *ab*, *eb*, and *ib*. The lists of words for spelling began with one-syllable words and progressed to two- and three-syllable words (Huey, 1980).

ALPHABETIC PRINCIPLE/PHONICS

The National Reading Panel (2000) identified five critical features of an effective reading curriculum. These five features are phonemic awareness, alphabetic principle or phonics, reading fluency, vocabulary development, and comprehension. Alphabetic principle is "the recognition that there are systematic and predictable relationships between written letters and spoken sounds" (Armbruster, Lehr, & Osborn, 2001, p. 11). Not only must this relationship between the written letters (graphemes) and spoken sounds (phonemes) be established, but students must be able to automatically apply this knowledge to decode unfamiliar words while reading. Phonemic awareness is the precursor to developing alphabetic principle or phonics.

Different terminology is often used to describe this relationship between letters and sounds, including graphophonemic relationships, letter-sound correspondence, phonics, and sound-symbol correspondence. Systematic and explicit instruction in alphabetic principle/phonics teaches students the relationship between the 26 graphemes (letters of the alphabet) and the 41 to 44 phonemes used in the English language. Systematic alphabetic principle/phonics instruction positively influences spelling skills in kindergarten and first-grade students (NRP).

There is a logical sequence of skills necessary to achieving mastery in alphabetic principle/phonics. Short vowel sounds (phonemes) should be taught first along with selected consonant phonemes. It is critical at this initial point that the student masters the idea of a phoneme being represented by a grapheme. Once students are able to associate the most common phoneme to the appropriate grapheme then words can be formed. Words are introduced through word "families" where one consonant (C) varies and the vowel (V) and additional consonants (C) remain constant. This instructional sequence is explained in the following table (Bursuck & Damer, 2011).

Word Type	Example
CVC words that begin with a continuous phoneme	mat, sat, fat, hat
CVC words that begin with a stop phoneme	big, top, dip
CVCC words that end with a consonant blend or double consonants	sand, bend, toss
CCVC words beginning with a consonant blend	trip, slam, drop
CCVCC, CCCVC, CCCVCC	still, drink, truck
Compound words with CVC word or CVC variants	catnip

Once students are able to read words and groups of words and apply the alphabetic principle to unknown words, high-frequency irregular words can be introduced. By introducing some high-frequency words students are able to read beginning text. These high-frequency words are also known as Dolch sight words.

More advanced skills used in teaching the alphabetic principle/phonics include the influence of other languages, pattern recognition, affixes, morphology, and the six basic syllable types used in English. The six syllable types are explained in the table below.

Syllable type	Definition	Example
Closed	A syllable with a short vowel (spelled with one letter) and ending with one or more consonants	cat, ho•tel
Open	A syllable that ends with a long vowel sound (spelled with one letter)	fly, re•sign
Vowel-Consonant +e	A syllable with a long vowel sound (spelled with one letter), followed by a consonant, and a final silent e	kite, pre•cede
Vowel team	Syllables were the vowel sound is spelled using a combination of vowel letters	boat, re•peat
Vocalic –r	A syllable with a single vowel letter followed by an -r. The vowel sound changes because of the influence of the -r	for, sup•per
Consonant +le	An unaccented final syllable consisting of a consonant + l + silent e	ap•ple, can•dle

The two main goals of phonics instruction are to provide students with essential knowledge and skills of the relationship between graphemes and phonemes and to ensure they know how to apply these concepts when reading and writing.

REFERENCES

Armbruster, B., Lehr, F., & Osborn, J. (2001). *Put reading first: The research building blocks for teaching children to read.* Washington, DC: Partnership for Reading.

Bursuck, W. D., & Damer, M. (2011). *Teaching reading to students who are at risk or have disabilities* (2nd ed.). Upper Saddle River, NJ: Pearson Education.

Moats, L.C. (2010). *Speech to print: Language essentials for teachers* (2nd ed.). Baltimore, MD: Paul H. Brookes.

National Early Literacy Panel. (2008). *Developing early literacy: Report of the National Early Literacy Panel*. Washington, DC: National Institute for Literacy.

National Institute of Child Health and Human Development. (2000). *Report of the National Reading Panel. Teaching children to read: an evidence-based assessment of the scientific research literature on reading and its implications for reading instruction: Reports of the subgroups* (NIH Publication No. 00–4754). Washington, DC: U.S. Government Printing Office.

GLENDA BYRNS, PHD, CCC-SLP
Texas A&M University
Fourth edition

ALPORT SYNDROME

Alport syndrome is an inherited (usually X-linked) disorder. It involves damage to the kidneys, blood in the urine, and loss of hearing in some families—and in some cases, loss of vision. In cases in which there is no family history of kidney disease, Alport syndrome is caused by a mutation in a collagen gene.

This uncommon disorder affects about 2 out of 10,000 people (MEDLINE Plus Health Information, 2000). Although approximately 1 in 50,000 Americans carry the Alport Syndrome gene, twice as many females as males carry the gene. However, a greater percentage of males with the gene have symptoms. Before the age of 50, nearly all of the males carrying the gene show symptoms. They eventually develop chronic renal failure and end-stage renal disease (ESRD), which is the final stage in chronic renal failure. Even though most females with the gene manifest the same symptoms, the progression and severity of the disease is less severe. Only about 20% of the females carrying the gene will develop ESRD, but usually at an older age (National Organization for Rare Disorders [NORD], 2001).

Alport syndrome is classified by mode of inheritance, age, and features other than kidney abnormalities. The age of onset of ESRD determines whether Alport Syndrome is classified as a juvenile form or an adult form of the disease. If ESRD occurs before the age of 31, it is classified as the juvenile form; after the age of 31, it is classified as the adult form (NORD, 2001).

There are six subtypes of Alport syndrome:

1. Type I is a dominantly inherited juvenile form. The symptoms include kidney disease, nerve deafness, and eye abnormalities.

2. Type II is an X-linked dominant juvenile form. Symptoms are the same as in the Type I subtype.

3. Type III is an X-linked dominant adult form. Symptoms include kidney disease and nerve deafness.

4. Type IV is an X-linked dominant adult form. It primarily involves kidney disease. There are no vision or hearing impairments.

5. Type V (Epstein syndrome) is an autosomal dominant form of the disease. Symptoms include nerve deafness and thrombocytopathia (disorders of blood platelets). It is so rare that it has not been classified as either adult or juvenile. The incidence of ESRD in the reported cases seems to be the same for males and females.

6. Type VI is an autosomal juvenile form. Symptoms include kidney disease, nerve deafness, and eye abnormalities (NORD, 2001).

Characteristics

1. Abnormal urine color
2. Blood in the urine
3. Loss of hearing (more common in males)
4. Decrease or loss of vision (more common in males)
5. Cough
6. Ankle, feet, and leg swelling
7. Swelling, overall
8. Swelling around the eyes
9. Upset stomach
10. Peculiar-smelling breath
11. Fatigue and excessive need for sleep
12. Shortness of breath
13. Dry, often itchy skin

Source: MEDLINE Plus Health Information (2000).

Treatment of Alport syndrome includes vigorous treatment of the chronic renal failure. Hemodialysis may be used to treat this problem. This treatment would involve removing blood from the patient's artery, cleaning it of unwanted substances that would be normally excreted in the urine, and returning the cleansed blood to a vein (NORD, 2001). It is also important to aggressively treat urinary tract infections and control blood pressure; this can be done through diet by restricting salt and protein intake. High blood pressure can also be controlled with medication. Cataracts may be surgically repaired (MEDLINE Plus Health Information, 2000). Genetic counseling is also recommended.

Hearing loss may be permanent. It is therefore important to learn new skills such as sign language or lip reading. Hearing aids are helpful, and it is recommended that young men use hearing protection in noisy environments. Counseling and education can help to increase coping skills (MEDLINE Plus Health Information, 2000).

If diagnosed during school age, the child may be eligible for special education services under the classification of Hearing Impaired, Visually Impaired, or Other Health Impaired. They may benefit from services to address these impairments.

Prognosis for females is that they usually have a normal life span with little or no manifestation of the disease. Some complications may arise during pregnancy. Males, however, are likely to develop permanent deafness, a decrease in or total loss of vision, chronic renal failure, and ESRD by the age of 50. Investigational therapies include the use of a new drug, calcium acetate, during ESRD, to treat hyperphosphatemia.

REFERENCES

MEDLINE Plus Health Information. (2000, September 5). Alport syndrome. Retrieved from http://medlineplus.adam.com/ency/article/000504.htm

National Organization for Rare Disorders. (2001, January 30). Alport syndrome. Retrieved from http://www.rarediseases.org

VEDIA SHERMAN
Austin Neurological Clinic

ALSTRÖM SYNDROME

Alström syndrome is an autosomal recessive genetic disorder characterized primarily by retinitis pigmentosa beginning during infancy and progressive sensorineural hearing loss beginning in early childhood. There is typically infant or childhood obesity that may normalize somewhat later, and individuals with this disorder frequently develop diabetes mellitus by early adulthood. In contrast to Bardet-Biedl syndrome, which shares several symptoms, in Alström syndrome there are normal intelligence and normal extremities (Online Mendelian Inheritance in Man, 2000).

Characteristics

1. Retinitis pigmentosa from infancy; nystagmus and photosensitivity
2. Mild to moderate sensorineural hearing loss, starting in childhood
3. Cardiomyopathy, in infancy or later
4. Moderate obesity in infancy and childhood, possibly normalizing
5. Insulin resistance syndrome, with associated acanthosis nigricans
6. Diabetes mellitus (non-insulin-dependent diabetes mellitus), typically juvenile onset
7. Renal disease; early signs of urine retention, incontinence, or both
8. Possible hepatic disease
9. Possible short stature, scoliosis, and hypothyroidism
10. Normal intellectual range

Other symptoms of Alström syndrome can include progressive renal disease, hepatic dysfunction, congestive heart failure (appearing at any age), growth retardation, and insulin resistance syndrome along with its related dark pigmentation of skin flexures (acanthosis nigricans). Alström syndrome in childhood is typically difficult to recognize without the presence of infantile cardiomyopathy, and it is often not identified until the development of diabetes in the second or third decade. Homozygotic carriers appear to be asymptomatic.

First described in 1959 by Swedish physician and researcher Carl-Henry Alström, the syndrome is quite rare. To date there have been only about 76 cases of Alström syndrome reported in the medical literature. Current incidence is estimated as about 117 worldwide, including cases in 18 countries (Jackson Laboratory, 2000). The disorder occurs in males and females with equal probability. It has relatively increased frequency in French Acadian or Amish groups in which couples often have common ancestors. The largest numbers of diagnosed cases have been in the United States and the United Kingdom, likely due to increased availability of informed health care.

The degeneration of the retina (retinitis pigmentosa) may be apparent in the first year of life. Nystagmus and photosensitivity (so-called photophobia) can be early indicators. There is early loss of central vision, in contrast to initial loss of peripheral vision as is typically seen with other pigmentary retinopathies. The electroretinogram is absent or attenuated, with better-preserved rod than cone function early on. The retinal dystrophy is progressive, leading to total blindness. Visual acuity is typically 6/60 or less by age 10 and absence of light perception occurs by about age 20. When a patient presents with infantile cone and rod retinal dystrophy—especially if the weight is above the 90th percentile or there is infantile cardiomyopathy—then the diagnosis of Alström syndrome should be considered (Russell-Eggitt et al., 1998).

Because of the syndrome's effects on endocrine functioning, growth can be stunted, leading to short stature, and there may be scoliosis and hypothyroidism (Alter & Moshang, 1993). Renal and hepatic dysfunction can lead to serious complications. Screening for bladder dysfunction signs of urinary retention and/or incontinence has been suggested to help identify renal disease earlier and allow more timely preventive care (Parkinson & Parkinson, 2000).

General intelligence is not affected. Although some studies suggest there may be developmental delays, such effects seem most likely secondary to the visual and aural deficits. Intellectual functioning is typically within the normal range, and the prognosis to lead full productive lives is very good. Special education services may be available to children with Alström syndrome under the classification of Other Health Impaired or Physical Disability. Classroom modifications for visual and hearing deficits should be made (including for the photophobia). Most children can be mainstreamed if accommodations are made successfully and supported with appropriate supplemental programming. It is suggested that braille be learned early to prevent the child from falling behind in school as vision deteriorates. Incorporating regular physical activity is very important in regulating weight and managing diabetes.

Alström syndrome has been linked to Chromosome 2p13, but the gene has not yet been identified (Collin et al., 1999). Study of the Alström gene may contribute to knowledge about the regulation of body weight and blood glucose and about how these processes may be related to maintenance of sight and vision.

At present there is no prenatal screening for Alström syndrome available. Diagnosis is typically made on the basis of presenting features. There is no cure; treatment is focused on ameliorating the symptoms. Interventions include monitoring and controlling metabolism, weight, and diabetes and providing compensatory audiovisual aids.

REFERENCES

Alter, C., & Moshang, T. (1993). Growth hormone deficiency in two siblings with Alström syndrome. *American Journal of Disabled Children, 147*(1), 97–99.

Collin, G., Marshall, J., Boerkoel, C., Levin, A., Weksberg, R., Greenberg, J.,...Nishina, P. M. (1999). Alström syndrome: Further evidence for linkage to human chromosome 2p13. *Human Genetics, 105*, 474–479.

Jackson Laboratory. (2000, December 14). Alström. Retrieved from http://www.jax.org/alstrom

Online Mendelian Inheritance in Man. (2000, December 14). Alström syndrome. Retrieved from www.ncbi.nlm.nih.gov

Parkinson, J., & Parkinson, K. (Eds.). (2000, September 5). Alström UK Newsletter, No. 7. Retrieved from http://www.alstrom.org.uk

Russell-Eggitt, I., Clayton, P., Coffey, R., Kriss, A., Taylor, H., & Taylor, J. (1998). Alström syndrome: Report of 22 cases and literature review. *Ophthalmology, 105*(7), 1274–1280.

VICKY Y. SPRADLING
Austin State Hospital

ALTERNATING HEMIPLEGIA OF CHILDHOOD

Alternating hemiplegia of childhood (AHC) is a rare but serious neurological disorder. The hallmark of AHC is the onset of frequent, recurrent, transient episodes of hemiplegia (paralysis of a body part). Hemiplegia manifestations run the gamut from numbness to complete loss of movement and feeling. Hemiplegia may affect either side of the body and may occasionally affect both sides simultaneously. These attacks may last a few minutes or may go on for days. In most cases, sleep induces resolution of a hemiplegia episode.

AHC is a relatively new addition to the list of neurological diseases. Fewer than 100 cases have been reported in the United States. Worldwide, there appear to be only about 250 cases. The exact cause of AHC is not known. However, the appearance of more than one in sibling groups suggests that—at least in some situations—there may be an autosomal dominant mode of transmission.

Characteristics

1. Onset of symptoms no later than 18 months of age.
2. Episodic hemiplegia affecting both sides of the body.
3. The existence of other paroxysmal neurological abnormalities not related to hemiplegia. This list includes dystonia (exaggerated muscle contraction), choreoathetosis (sudden, involuntary movement of limb or facial muscles), and temporary paralysis of muscles that control eye movement.
4. Autonomic abnormalities (excessive sweating, changes in skin color, and changes in body temperature).
5. Diminished intellectual function.
6. Exclusion of other causes responsible for recurrent neurological deficits.

AHC has no known cure. Because the frequency and duration of attacks appear to have a cumulative damaging effect on the brain, therapy is directed toward ameliorating their severity. Because sleep usually ends an episode, one strategy is to use sedatives. Seizures, which frequently complicate the clinical picture, respond to anticonvulsants.

A few clinical trials, involving small groups of patients, show that the drug flunarizine may decrease the severity of hemiplegic episodes. However, the results of these studies have been deemed inconclusive.

Children with AHC will require support services from an early age. Because of the delay in development, children will be eligible to receive support services from the early childhood intervention (ECI) program. Therapy services provided through ECI in the areas of occupational, physical, and speech therapy may help the child attain developmental milestones. As the child develops and the deficits become more evident, support services will need to be modified to meet the changing needs of the child. There also may be cognitive deficits as a result of the medication needed to help control the seizure activity. Careful monitoring of the educational strategies will be required to continue to help the child attain his or her academic potential.

AHC is a serious neurological disorder with a rather poor prognosis. There is no evidence that the disease shortens life expectancy, but there are insufficient data from long-term follow-ups of affected children to be confident about that assumption. Symptoms persist into adulthood, but as many of these patients grow older, they tend to handle attacks better. The younger the child is at the time of diagnosis, the more likely he or she is to acquire permanent neurological impairment and arrested intellectual development as he or she approaches maturity.

For more information and support, please contact: International Foundation for Alternating Hemiplegic of Childhood (IFAHC), 239 Nevada Street, Redwood City, CA 94062. E-mail:laegan@aol.com, website: http://www.ahckids.org; NIH/National Institute of Neurological Disorders and Stroke, 31 Center Drive MSC 2540, Building 31, Room 8806, Bethesda, MD 20892. Tel.: (301) 496-5751 or (800) 352-9424, website: http://www.ninds.nih.gov

REFERENCES

Haslam, R. H. A. (2000). Acute stroke syndromes. In R. E. Behrman, R. M. Kleigman, & H. B. Jenson (Eds.), *Nelson's textbook of pediatrics* (16th ed., pp. 1854–1856). Philadelphia, PA: W. B. Saunders.

National Organization for Rare Disorders. (1996). Alternating hemiplegia of childhood. Retrieved from http://www.stepstn.com/cgi-win/nord.exe?proc=GetDocument&rectype=0&recnum=1027

Roach, E. S., & Riela, A. R. (1995). *Pediatric cerebrovascular disorders* (2nd ed.). New York, NY: Futura.

Silver, K., & Andermann, F. (1993). Alternating hemiplegia of childhood: A study of 10 patients and results of flunarizine treatment. *Neurology, 43*, 36–41.

What is AHC? (n.d.). Retrieved from http://www.ahckids.org/ahc_whatis.htm

BARRY H. DAVISON
Ennis, Texas

JOAN W. MAYFIELD
*Baylor Pediatric Specialty Services
Dallas, Texas*

See also Hemiplegia

ALTERNATING TREATMENTS DESIGN
(*See* Single Case Research Designs)

ALTERNATIVE ASSESSMENTS (*See* Assessments, Alternative)

ALTERNATIVE FORMATS OF INFORMATION

An alternative format is produced when information in one medium is transformed into a different medium while maintaining as much of the original meaning as possible. The form and format of the information may change, but the conservation of the original information is usually the goal of such conversions. For example, a printed textbook (original medium) may be converted into a braille book or audio book (new medium). When applied to special education, alternative formats usually refer to media conversions done to make information available to a student with a disability. Although *alternative formats* have traditionally referred to media used to accommodate students with sensory impairments (e.g., braille, taped texts, tactile graphics, refreshable braille), the term is today being applied to alternative formats used to accommodate students who require differentiation in the formatting of learning materials.

Students with disabilities frequently take advantage of taped text materials, text-to-speech technology, cognitive mapping technology, audio files of text materials, and others. "Enlarged print materials, enlarged screen text, speech synthesizers and braille technologies provide students with visual impairments access to general education. Learning Ally's audiobooks provide print access to educational materials through the human voice." (Retrieved from: http://www.learningally.org/About-Us/The-Community-We-Serve/The-Myths-and-Realities-of-Print-Disabilities/149/ on December 16, 2011). Learning Ally works to provide students with varying disabilities access to reading materials. Accomodations such as audible text help provide students with disabilities equal opportunities to curriculum materials.

Advances in technology such as e-readers and apps for technological devices increases the availability and accessibility of information in alternate formats. Additional information on alternative format materials available to students with disabilities can be found at www.learningally.org. Learning Ally continues to focus on creating an organization which provides alternate formatted media to students with disabilities. Learning Ally publishes a newsletter *The Download* and coordinates annual conferences.

Learning Ally National Headquarters, 20 Roszel Road, Princeton, NJ 08540. Website: www.learningally.org

REFERENCE

Learning Ally formerly known as Recording for the Blind and Dyslexic. (2011). Reading Ally: Making reading accessible for all. Retrieved from http://www.learningally.org/

DAVID SWEENEY
Texas A&M University

HEATHER DAVIS
*Texas A&M University
Fourth edition*

See also Braille; Recording for the Blind

ALTERNATIVE SETTINGS, POSITIVE BEHAVIOR SUPPORTS

The success of school-wide positive behavior support (SWPBS) in public school settings across the United States has generated mounting interest in its potential for alternative settings, including those serving youth whose challenging behavior causes them to be excluded from public schools. These settings include alternative education programs, residential schools and treatment programs, and juvenile detention and correctional facilities. In addition to the demonstrated effectiveness of SWPBS in schools, impetus for pursuing an approach to discipline that is positive, proactive, and instructional in alternative settings is the poor outcomes experienced by youth in these settings, outcomes that include failure to complete a high school education, arrest and incarceration, and recidivism rates for incarcerated youth that average over 50% (Keith & McCray, 2002; Snyder & Sickmund, 2006). In addition to their histories of school failure, substantial proportions of youth in these settings also have educational disabilities, mental health needs, and histories of substance, physical, and emotional abuse (Gagnon & Richards, 2008; Nelson, Sprague, Jolivette, Smith, & Tobin, 2009). The relationship between academic failure, antisocial behavior, and juvenile incarceration is so well established that researchers and advocates refer to this pattern as the "school-to-prison pipeline" (American Civil Liberties Union, 2009; Nelson, Jolivette, Leone, & Mathur, 2010; Southern Poverty Law Center, 2009).

Initial efforts to adapt SWPBS in these settings have been encouraging (Jolivette & Nelson, 2010; Nelson et al., 2009). Farkas et al. (in press) found that grades improved and discipline referrals decreased for students with emotional and behavioral disorders and other health impairments when SWPBS was implemented with fidelity in an alternative education junior-senior high school. Simonsen, Britton, and Young (2010) reported a decrease in serious problem behavior and the use of physical restraint, and an increase in the percentage of students who refrained from physical aggression following the implementation of universal SWPBS in an alternative education program for students with significant problem behavior. Jolivette, Kennedy, Patterson, Houchins, and McDaniel (2010) found that behavioral incidents among students with emotional and behavioral disorders in a residential facility decreased when SWPBS was implemented with fidelity (as measured by the School-wide Evaluation Tool). Implementation in secure juvenile facilities has been reported by a number of authors (e.g., Nelson et al., 2009; Nelson, Scott, Gagnon, Jolivette, & Sprague, 2008; Sidana, 2006), and similar reductions in problem behavior and increases in prosocial behavior and academic performance have been reported. However, to date no scientifically rigorous studies of SWPBS or large-scale evaluations or efficacy studies have been completed in these settings. The absence of a national database on SWPBS in alternative settings also hampers efforts to assess the scope of adoption.

Need for Adaptation

As noted above, the characteristics and needs of youth in alternative settings require adjustments in SWPBS structure and methodology. Youth characteristics include a high prevalence of disabilities, mental health diagnoses, issues involving substance, physical, and sexual abuse, as well as ingrained patterns of antisocial behavior (Gagnon & Barber, 2010; Nelson et al., 2009). The prevalence of youth with mental health disorders in the juvenile justice

system is so high that it has been referred to as the *de facto* children's mental health system (Grizzo, 2007).

Characteristics of Alternative Settings

The nature of alternative settings requires modifications to the structure and implementation of SWPBS. These settings tend to be isolated from typical public schools, staffed by professionals and paraprofessionals representing a variety of disciplines, and concerns regarding safety and security may dominate therapeutic programming. Many alternative education programs are designed to serve students who are at-risk of school failure or unable to succeed in regular classrooms because of their behavior; others operate as day treatment programs under the auspices of mental health agencies or as diversion programs sponsored by juvenile courts. In residential facilities, implementation in a 24/7 environment involving multiple shifts of staff constitutes another distinction, and the primacy of security in juvenile justice facilities requires further adaptations in training and implementation.

Staff Attitudes

A relatively common attitude toward youth in these settings is that they are all "red zone" students, meaning that as a group, they are characterized by the highest rates of problem behavior and need for support. This suggests that a greater proportion of youth will require secondary and tertiary level interventions. Staff who already feel overextended by the demands of reacting to behavioral challenges may be resistant to entreaties to redirect their focus to prevention. Related to this is the attitude that because youth are in an alternative setting (especially if it is correctional), punishment should be the primary disciplinary mode. Such attitudes invite the common wisdom that the most difficult part of implementing SWPBS (or any innovation, for that matter) is changing the behavior of adults. That punitive attitudes and behavior patterns are deeply ingrained in the staff of alternative (and especially correctional) settings magnifies the difficulty of changing the culture to teaching and supporting desired behavior.

Use of Data

Another barrier to implementation in alternative settings is that typically, decisions regarding youth behavior are not data-driven. That is, staff do not routinely collect, review, and systematically analyze data regarding youth behavior as a basis for making decisions regarding policies, staff training, or interventions. Whereas a plethora of discipline data typically exists in these settings, seldom are these data used to make programmatic decisions. Furthermore, because of a history of advocates and media using behavior data against secure facilities, administrators are reluctant to have such data available for potential public scrutiny, and may even restrict dissemination among staff internally. Furthermore, security staff typically manages major behavioral events in these settings, with legislatively or administratively prescribed sanctions for rule violations. Staff may simply ignore minor behavioral incidents until they escalate into major infractions. Redirecting staff to record and respond to minor behavior events not only is a major change in the culture, but also may require additional data entry and management.

Implementation

Fortunately, a steady increase in the number of alternative education programs and residential facilities that are implementing SWPBS is occurring, and the knowledge gained from these implementation efforts has helped to guide subsequent initiatives. One particularly useful observation is that, unless a program or facility is in crisis, youth behavior tends to follow the same proportions as in public schools. As one juvenile corrections education administrator put it, "20% of the kids cause 80% of the problems" (M. Clarida, personal communication, July, 2005). When appropriate and effective universal preventions are in place, the great majority of youth are successful. The proportions of those who need secondary and tertiary support follow the SWPBS percentages, and the same response to intervention (RtI) logic can be used to their needs. Further, when staff no longer spend large amounts of time dealing with fairly minor problem behavior, they are able to respond more constructively (and effectively) to more challenging misbehavior. Staff also are able to focus on doing their jobs (e.g., teaching) as opposed to responding to misbehavior.

Adaptations for Alternative Settings

Five basic implementation steps comprise the SWPBS framework: (1) formation of a PBIS leadership team; (2) getting buy-in by a majority of staff, which generally is considered to be a minimum of 80%; (3) establishing a data-based action plan, consisting of agreed-upon expectations, procedures for teaching and encouraging compliance, and for addressing failure; (4) ensuring implementation with fidelity; and (5) establishing formative data-based monitoring of youth behavior and outcomes (Simonsen, 2010). The implementation of this framework is as important in alternative settings as in public schools; however, some adaptations in methodology are necessary. Because alternative education programs generally function as educational institutions, these adaptations are less marked than in residential treatment or juvenile justice settings. The major considerations tend to be lower teacher to student ratios, the presence of staff from other disciplines, and an increased focus on security. The nature of residential treatment and juvenile justice settings raises a number of considerations for adaptation: whether to implement PBIS within a single program in a facility (e.g., education) or facility-wide; training staff across disciplines and shifts; gaining staff consensus regarding expectations for behavior, teaching and supporting desired behavior, and responding to behavioral errors. Jolivette and Nelson (2010) offer the following suggestions for adapting SWPBS in alternative education and residential settings.

Leadership and Buy-In. In selecting participants for the leadership team, it is important to ensure that key stakeholders are represented. These persons include personnel from disciplines not typically found in regular public schools, such as specialized treatment staff, court workers, security officers, and facility administrators. Even if implementation is planned for only one system in a facility, such as education, staff from other disciplines will be affected to varying degrees and should be familiar with the structure and process. The support and participation of program or facility administration is particularly important. Teams also must secure a commitment by a majority of staff to adopt SWPBS, and to implement it with fidelity. In public schools, a criterion of 80% staff buy-in is the standard; however, staffing configurations and logistics in alternative settings suggest that a higher level of sustained commitment (e.g., 90% to 95%) may be necessary.

Staff Training. When implementing SWPBS in alternative settings, the logistics of staff training are important to consider. Particularly in residential programs, strategies for training staff across shifts and roles must be thought out. These may include arranging for staff to receive compensation for participating in training when they are off duty, providing substitutes to relieve staff for training, or having members of the SWPBS Leadership Team coach staff through the process. Extra coaching and modeling may be required for staff accustomed to using punishment as the primary (or only) tool for addressing behavior. Staff also may access training via Internet linkages, but hands-on coaching and mentoring to ensure fidelity of implementation must supplement such training.

In the majority of states, public school districts may access training in SWPBS through state leadership teams, as well as through the national technical assistance center (www.pbis.org). It is not likely that state or national trainers will be familiar with the idiosyncrasies of alternative settings outside of the education domain. One way to compensate for the shortage of trainers who have knowledge of alternative settings is to use a trainer-of-trainers approach, in which designated local staff receive training from regional or national trainers who have knowledge of SWPBS content and the features of the settings where SWPBS is to be implemented. Ideally, local trainers shadow or co-train with qualified mentors as they gain proficiency, and then move on to train program or facility staff independently. Implementation of SWPBS with fidelity is much more successful when leadership teams are guided by both external and internal coaches. The former provide an objective frame of reference and the latter first-hand knowledge of the workings of the program or facility. External coaches must be carefully selected and trained. They may be staff from other programs in the system, in which case they must receive released time for working outside their settings. Internal coaches also must have adequate time released from other duties to fulfill this vital function. The Texas Youth Commission is addressing staff SWPBS training by providing centralized training to facility leadership teams and following this with training of facility trainers by external SWPBS coaches (who were recruited from a university SWPBS training program and facilitated teams in the centralized training).

Obviously, the selection of local trainers and coaches is critical. These persons must be highly skilled, readily available, and capable of communicating with staff from various disciplines and with differing philosophies regarding youth behavior. They also must receive adequate support. In addition to providing these personnel with adequate time for these duties, program and facility administrators must give their full and active support.

Action Planning. To maintain focus and function proactively, SWPBS leadership teams should work from data-based action plans. Such plans include strategies for (a) reaching consensus on behavioral expectations; (b) teaching expectations; (c) reinforcing youth for meeting expectations; and (d) responding to behavioral errors. The approach to implementation of SWPBS taken in public schools may be alien to the culture of alternative settings, in that expectations are stated positively, and the emphasis is on rewarding and encouraging youth compliance as opposed to punishing noncompliance. The selection and use of reinforcers also may be problematic, in that items may be deemed contraband by some staff or in some locations.

Phasing In. Residential settings in which PBIS has been implemented (especially those housing a relative large number of youth) generally have opted to begin with one system. Since the vast majority of experience with SWPBS has come from schools, the education program is the logical place to begin. Adding to this logic, education staff should be better prepared to develop lesson plans and instructional procedures for teaching expectations, providing reinforcement, and correcting errors in a way that does not involve institutional punishment, such as seclusion or restraint. Education staff can model and teach implementation procedures to other staff, and data that demonstrate improvements in youth (and staff) behavior can promote implementation in other systems within a facility. Youth also may advocate for SWPBS in other systems; Jolivette et al. (2010) reported that youth in a residential treatment facility persuaded dormitory staff to extend implementation from the facility's education program to housing units.

Conclusion

Implementation of SWPBS in alternative settings may seem a daunting task requiring much thought and adaptation, and it is. However, the benefits of a positive, proactive, and accountable system for addressing and improving the behavior of youth and staff in alternative settings are worth the effort. Because of their histories of school failure, educational disabilities, mental health conditions, and abuse issues, the majority of youth in these settings are substantially more vulnerable to lifelong failure. A milieu where they can succeed and learn more adaptive ways to interact with their environments is a path forward that previously has not been widely available. With increasing implementation of data reports and new research underway to demonstrate the efficacy of SWPBS in alternative settings, the momentum will shift toward a more positive future.

REFERENCES

American Civil Liberties Union. (2009). *School-to-prison pipeline: Talking points*. Retrieved from http://www.aclu.org/racial-justice/school-prison-pipeline-talking-points

Gagnon, J. C., & Barber, B. (2010). Characteristics of and services provided to youth in secure care facilities. *Behavioral Disorders, 36,* 7–19.

Gagnon, J. C., & Richards, C. (2008). *Making the right turn: A guide about youth involved in the juvenile corrections system* (pp. 1–61). Washington, DC: National Collaborative on Workforce and Disability for Youth, Institute for Educational Leadership.

Farkas, M. S., Simonsen, B., Migdole, S., Donovan, M. E., Clemens, K., & Cicchese, V. (in press). Schoolwide positive behavior support in an alternative schools setting: An evaluation of fidelity, outcomes, and social validity of tier I implementation. *Journal of Emotional and Behavioral Disorders.*

Grisso, T. (2007). Progress and perils in the juvenile justice and mental health movement. *Journal of the American Academy of Psychiatry and the Law, 35,* 158–167.

Jolivette, K., Kennedy, C., Patterson, D. P., Houchins, D. E., & McDaniel, S. C. (in press). A 24/7 case study: The effects of facility-wide positive behavioral interventions and supports on the social behaviors of students with emotional and behavioral disorders in a residential facility.

Jolivette, K., & Nelson, C. M. (2010). Adapting positive behavioral interventions and supports for secure juvenile justice settings: Improving facility-wide behavior. *Behavioral Disorders, 36,* 28–42.

Keith, J. M., & McCray, A. D. (2002). Juvenile offenders with special needs: Critical issues and bleak outcomes. *Qualitative Studies in Education, 15,* 691–710.

Nelson, C. M., Jolivette, K., Leone, P. E., & Mathur, S. R. (2010). Meeting the needs of at-risk and adjudicated youth with behavioral challenges: The promise of juvenile justice. *Behavioral Disorders, 36,* 70–80.

Nelson, C. M., Scott, T. M., Gagnon, J. C., Jolivette, K., & Sprague, J. R. (May, 2008). Positive behavior support in the juvenile justice system. *Positive Behavioral Interventions and Supports Newsletter, 4*(3). Retrieved from http://www.pbis.org/news/New/Newsletters/Newsletter4-3.aspx

Nelson, C. M., Sprague, J. R., Jolivette, K., Smith, C. R., & Tobin, T. J. (2009). Positive behavior support in alternative education, community-based mental health, and juvenile justice settings. In W. Sailor, G. Dunlap, G. Sugai, & R. Horner (Eds.), *Handbook of positive behavior support* (pp. 465–496). New York, NY: Springer.

Sidana, A. (2006). *PBIS in juvenile justice settings*. Washington DC: The National Evaluation and Technical Assistance Center for the Education of Children and Youth Who are Neglected, Delinquent, or At-Risk. Retrieved from http://www.neglecteddelinquent.org/nd/resources/spotlight/spotlight200601b.asp

Simonsen, B. (2010). School-wide positive behavior support. In M. M. Kerr & C. M. Nelson, *Strategies for addressing behavior problems in the classroom* (6th ed., pp. 36–68). Upper Saddle River, NJ: Pearson.

Simonsen, B., Britton, L., & Young, D. (2010). School-wide positive behavior support in a non-public school setting: A case study. *Journal of Positive Behavior Interventions, 12*, 180–191.

Snyder, H. N., & Sickmund, M. (2006). *Juvenile offenders and victims: 2006 national report*. Washington, DC: U.S. Department of Justice, Office of Justice Programs, Office of Juvenile Justice and Delinquency Prevention.

Southern Poverty Law Center. (2009). *Legal action: Stopping the school-to-prison pipeline by enforcing special education law*. Retrieved from http://www.splcenter.org/legal/schoolhouse.jsp

Michael Nelson
University of Louisville

Kristine Jolivette
Georgia State University
Fourth edition

AMAROUTIC FAMILIAL IDIOCY (*See* Tay-Sachs Syndrome)

AMBLYOPIA

Amblyopia, also called suppression blindness (Harley & Lawrence, 1977), is a visual condition that occurs when an anatomically healthy eye cannot see because of some other defect (Eden, 1978). Amblyopia is commonly called "lazy eye"; however, this is a misnomer (Eden, 1978) because it implies that amblyopia results from a muscular problem. Actually, amblyopia can have a number of causes. For example, strabismus (a condition in which the two eyes are not parallel when viewing an object) can lead to amblyopia. The brain ignores the visual signals of one of the two eyes to reduce the annoyance of double vision. Other factors such as astigmatism can also lead to amblyopia.

The degree of visual impairment associated with amblyopia can vary a great deal from losses that are just below normal to those in which only large objects can be identified. Treatment of amblyopia consists of treating the causal factors. It must be accomplished early in life (before the age of 6) because the child is likely to permanently lose the ability to process a 20/20 image from the affected eye.

REFERENCES

Eden, J. (1978). *The eye book*. New York, NY: Viking.

Harley, R. K., & Lawrence, G. A. (1977). *Visual impairment in the schools*. Springfield, IL: Thomas.

Toplis, R. (2003). Amblyopia. In E. Fletcher-Janzen & C. R. Reynolds (Eds.), *Childhood disorders diagnostic desk reference* (pp. 33–34). Hoboken, NJ: Wiley.

Thomas E. Allen
Gallaudet College

See also Blind; Cataracts

AMERICAN ACADEMY FOR CEREBRAL PALSY AND DEVELOPMENTAL MEDICINE

The American Academy for Cerebral Palsy, founded in 1947, changed its name in 1976 to the American Academy for Cerebral Palsy and Developmental Medicine (AACPDM). The Academy expanded their scope of interests from an initial focus on cerebral palsy into related areas of developmental medicine, including spina bifida, neuromuscular disease, traumatic brain injury and other acquired disabilities, genetic disorders, communication problems, and specific learning disabilities. The AACPDM is a professional organization whose membership is open to all who have training and experience in relevant fields.

The AACPDM promotes prevention, diagnosis, care, and quality of life primarily through continuing education, advocacy, and research grants. The Academy provides information, services, and resources via their website, peer-reviewed journal, newsletter, broadcast e-mails, live instructional tutorials, webinar lectures, and annual meeting. Patient and family resources are also available through their website. The office address of AACPDM is 555 East Wells Street, Suite 1100, Milwaukee, WI 53202. Tel.: (414) 918-3014, fax: (414) 276-2146, e-mail:

info@aacpdm.org, website: www.aacpdm.org Office hours: 8:00 a.m.–5:00 p.m. CST.

SHIRLEY A. JONES
Virginia Polytechnic Institute and State University
First edition

KAY KETZENBERGER
The University of Texas of the Permian Basin
Second edition

RACHEL M. TOPLIS
Falcon School District 49 Colorado Springs,
*   Colorado*
Third edition

AUSTIN J. KARPOLA
The Chicago School of Professional Psychology,
*   Chicago, IL*
Fourth edition

annual reference issue, a comprehensive listing of schools and programs in the United States and Canada for students who are deaf or hard of hearing and their teachers, is also published by the *Annals*. In addition to the listings, the reference issue provides demographic, audiological, and educational data regarding students who are deaf and hard of hearing and the schools they attend. The data are compiled annually by the Center for Assessment and Demographic Studies, a component of the Gallaudet Research Institute.

REFERENCE

American Annals of the Deaf. (2011). Retrieved from http://gupress.gallaudet.edu/annals/

DIANA E. PINEDA
The Chicago School of Professional Psychology
Fourth edition

AMERICAN ANNALS OF THE DEAF

The *American Annals of the Deaf* is a professional journal dedicated to quality in education and related services for children and adults who are hearing impaired. First published in 1847, the publication is the oldest and most widely read English language journal dealing with deafness and the education of people who are deaf. The *Annals* is the official organ of the Council of American Instructors of the Deaf (CAID) and of the Conference of Educational Administrators of Schools and Programs for the Deaf (CEASD). Members of the executive committees of both organizations form the Joint *Annals* Administrative Committee charged with the direction and administration of the publication.

For over 150 years, the *Annals* has primarily focused on the education of students who are deaf as well as dissemination of information for professionals associated with the educational development of this population. Concurrently, the *Annals* extends its range of topics beyond education, incorporating the broad interests of educators in the general welfare of children and adults who are deaf, and representing the diverse professional readership of the publication. Topics covered include communication methods and strategies, language development, mainstreaming and residential schools, parent-child relationships, and teacher training and teaching skills.

Four literary issues are published by the journal each year in the spring, summer, autumn, and winter. Individuals and institutions can obtain membership to the *Annals* through various levels of monetary support. An

AMERICAN ART THERAPY ASSOCIATION

Founded in 1969, The American Art Therapy Association, Inc. (AATA) is an organization that maintains the belief that creating art can be a therapeutic and healing process for individuals of any age who may be experiencing physical, mental, or emotional concerns. The creative process of self-expression can assist in areas such as reducing stress, resolving conflicts, managing behavior, or increasing self-awareness. The association supports over 5,000 members and the general public by providing (a) educational opportunities, (b) public awareness, (c) therapeutic advancement, (d) research development, (e) criteria for training future therapists, (f) opportunities for communication among professionals and the general public, (g) scholarships and research grants, and (h) institutional and private practice settings. The association's mission is to advance art therapy and enhance lives by maintaining standards of professional competence and expanding the art therapy knowledge base. AATA is committed to public service, social justice, and advocacy for self-respect and creative potential in individuals. The association is also committed to diversity, exceptional service, maintaining high ethical standards, and providing financial and educational support.

AATA is composed of 36 statewide chapters. Membership is open to anyone, including practicing art therapists, students, educators, and related practitioners in addition to individuals who present an interest in the process of art therapy around the world. Members receive benefits in career advancement, practical support, and the latest research by utilizing resources such as the Practice Center, the Career Center, and the ART Clearinghouse. Members also gain access to the association's publication, *Art Therapy: Journal of the American Art Therapy Association*, which provides peer-reviewed, empirical research, theory and practice papers, viewpoints, reviews of cultural literature in art therapy, and best practices. Conferences are held annually around the United States and may include themes such as Weaving a Tapestry. For additional information on AATA, visit www.americanarttherapyassociation.org or contact the association at info@arttherapy.org. Association headquarters are located at 225 North Fairfax Street, Alexandria, VA 22314. Tel.: (888) 290-0878.

Jessica Spata
The Chicago School of Professional Psychology

are held throughout the United States and Canada for continued learning and professional development in marriage and family therapy. Updated information and resources are available at www.aamft.org. The website also has additional links and directories such as TherapistLocator.net, which allow potential clients to search from a directory of over 15,000 marriage and family therapists who have met training requirements set forth by the AAMFT. The association offices are located at 112 South Alfred Street, Alexandria, VA 22314-3061. Tel.: (703) 838-9808, fax: (703) 838-9805, website: http://www.aamft.org/iMIS15/AAMFT/

Linda M. Montgomery
The University of Texas of the Permian Basin
Third edition

Luke W. Fischer
The Chicago School of Professional Psychology
Fourth edition

AMERICAN ASSOCIATION FOR MARRIAGE AND FAMILY THERAPY (AAMFT)

The American Association for Marriage and Family Therapy (AAMFT), founded in 1942, is the national organization representing marriage and family therapists. The association seeks to (a) advance marriage and family therapy through increased understanding, research, and treatment; (b) establish and maintain standards for the education and training of marriage and family therapists; and (c) promote professional development, ethics, and conduct among marriage and family therapists. The AAMFT has over 24,500 members in the United States, Canada, and abroad. Clinical, Associate, and Student members are mental health therapists or therapists-in-training who have met varying levels of AAMFT credential standards. Affiliate members are individuals in allied mental health professions who are interested in staying informed about developments in marriage and family therapy.

The AAMFT publishes periodicals and directs practitioners to a variety of books, DVDs, brochures, and other resources. The *Journal of Marital and Family Therapy* (the official journal of the association) offers current research findings in marriage and family therapy. *Family Therapy Magazine* provides the latest updates in the field of marriage and family therapy.

Each year the AAMFT sponsors an annual conference in early fall for training in family systems theory, practice, and research. The 2011 Annual Conference held in Fort Worth, Texas, was a four-day event with over 100 available sessions. Also, division conferences and training events

AMERICAN ASSOCIATION FOR THE SEVERELY HANDICAPPED (See TASH)

AMERICAN ASSOCIATION OF COLLEGES FOR TEACHER EDUCATION

The American Association of Colleges for Teacher Education (AACTE) is a national, voluntary association of colleges and universities with undergraduate and/or graduate programs committed to the preparation of professional educators, including teachers and other educational personnel. The Association is composed of over 700 member institutions representing both private and public colleges and universities of every size and located in every state, the District of Columbia, Puerto Rico, the Virgin Islands, and Guam. As a group, the AACTE institutions produce more than 85% of new educators each year.

The Association encourages major initiatives and innovations in teacher education, and serves as advocate for the profession on issues of interest to the membership, particularly in areas of certification, accreditation, and assessment. AACTE is a major influence in helping form federal and state educational policy, and is recognized as the primary representative of teacher education interests before Congress, state legislatures, other governmental agencies, and the media. The Association continues to advise the National Council for Accreditation of Teacher Education (NCATE) on issues of institutional standards and accreditation. AACTE publishes the biweekly newsletter *Briefs*, which reports on current happenings in the education, public policy, and government arenas to the teacher education community.

AACTE offices are located at 1307 New York Ave. N.W., Suite 300, Washington, DC 20005. Tel.: (202) 293-2450. For additional information, please visit the website: http://www.aacte.org

KAY E. KETZENBERGER
The University of Texas of the Permian Basin

AMERICAN BOARD OF PROFESSIONAL NEUROPSYCHOLOGY

The American Board of Professional Neuropsychology (ABPN) is a credentialing board that examines doctoral-level psychologists with specialized training in the field of clinical neuropsychology and awards diplomas if examination performance is satisfactory. Examinations consist of an essay exam concerning clinical casework, a work sample examination (wherein examinees submit for scrutiny two actual cases from their practice), and a 3-hour oral examination. Additionally, documentation of appropriate credentials and training is required. Incorporated in 1982, ABPN was the first (and as of this writing, the only) psychology credentialing board that has applied to be approved and certified by the National Commission of Certifying Agencies, the certification arm of the National Organization for Competency Assurance, an organization charged by the federal government with oversight and accreditation of health care certification bodies. The ABPN central office address is Care of the Executive Director, Dr. Michael Raymond, John Heinz Institute of Rehabilitation Medicine, Neuropsychology Services, 150 Mundy Street, Wilkes-Barre, PA 18702.

CECIL R. REYNOLDS
Texas A&M University

AMERICAN BOARD OF PROFESSIONAL PSYCHOLOGY

Originally named the American Board of Examiners in Professional Psychology, this organization was renamed the American Board of Professional Psychology (ABPP) in 1968. Founded in 1947 with the support of the American Psychological Association, it consists of a board of 15 trustees with headquarters in Savannah, Georgia. This certification board conducts oral examinations and awards specialty certification in eleven specialties: behavioral

psychology, clinical psychology, clinical neuropsychology, counseling psychology, family psychology, forensic psychology, health psychology, industrial/organizational psychology, psychoanalysis in psychology, rehabilitation psychology, and school psychology. Necessary for certification is 5 years of qualifying experience in psychological practice.

The ABPP annually presents the Distinguished Professional Achievement Award. This and other awards are presented at the annual convention of the American Psychological Association in August. Publications of the ABPP include the *Specialist* newsletter and the *Directory of Diplomats* (biannual).

MARY LEON PEERY
Texas A&M University
First edition

KAY E. KETZENBERGER
The University of Texas of the Permian Basin
Second edition

AMERICAN CANCER SOCIETY (ACS)

The American Cancer Society (ACS) is a voluntary organization committed to the elimination and control of cancer. This nationwide effort is conducted through 12 chartered geographic Division affiliates throughout the United States, more than 900 local offices nationwide, and a presence in more than 5,100 communities. The ACS effort is accomplished through four major activities: (1) the public education program, which emphasizes regular, preventative care for adults, attention to specific warning signals, and information regarding positive outcomes when prompt diagnosis and preventative measure are adopted; (2) a comprehensive professional education program designed to stimulate health professionals to use the best cancer detection, diagnostic, and patient management techniques available, to exchange knowledge on the latest cancer-fighting techniques, and to disseminate new ideas and developments in the community; (3) a wide range of volunteer-based service and rehabilitation programs to assist cancer patients and their families with the necessary practical and emotional support so vital to coping with the wide-ranging effects of the disease; and (4) research into all aspects of cancer, from direct clinical investigations and training to prospective cancer prevention studies.

The ACS began in 1913, when 15 physicians and business leaders gathered in New York City and founded the American Society for the Control of Cancer (ASCC). The Society's founders were aware that the disease, steeped in a climate of fear and denial, must be brought to the attention of the people. Articles were written for popular magazines and professional journals, a monthly bulletin providing information about the cancer was published, and physicians were recruited throughout the United States in an attempt to increase public awareness.

In 1936, Marjorie G. Illig, an ASCC field representative and chair of the General Federation of Women's Clubs Committee on Public Health, proposed the creation of a legion of volunteers, with the sole purpose of waging war on cancer. The Women's Field Army, as this organization came to be known, was the driving force behind the agency's move to the forefront of voluntary health organizations.

Today, the core of the organization's effort resides in more than 3 million volunteers who implement the society's public and professional education programs, service programs for patients and families, and raise funds for research programs.

The ASCC was reorganized in 1945, becoming the American Cancer Society (ACS), today's leader in the fight against cancer through its programs in research, patient services, prevention, detection and treatment, and advocacy. The Society strives to achieve this goal by promoting the early detection of cancer through education, intervention, and programs such as the Breast Cancer Network and Man to Man, a prostate cancer education and support group. In conjunction with these efforts, the ACS has increased its effort to protect children through comprehensive school health education and similar programs designed to discourage tobacco and promote healthy living.

Scientists supported by ACS have successfully established the link between cancer and smoking, demonstrated the effectiveness of the Pap smear, developed cancer-fighting drugs and biological response modifiers, dramatically increased the cure rate for leukemia, and proved the safety and effectiveness of mammography. The American Cancer Society has committed almost $3.5 billion to research and funded 44 Nobel Prize winners.

REFERENCE

American Cancer Society (ASC). (2011). Retrieved from http://www.cancer.org

CRAIG S. HIGGINS
Stonehill College
First edition

TAMARA J. MARTIN
The University of Texas of the Permian Basin
Second edition

ANITA M. ROGINSKI
The Chicago School of Professional Psychology
Fourth edition

AMERICAN COUNCIL ON RURAL EDUCATION (ACRES)

The American Council on Rural Special Education (ACRES) was founded in 1981 by a group of individuals interested in the unique challenges of rural students and individuals needing special services. The five goals of ACRES are to (1) foster quality education and services for individuals with exceptional needs living in rural America; (2) promote cultural diversity and the empowerment of minorities and members of traditionally underrepresented groups in providing services to individuals with exceptional needs, their families, and service providers; (3) promote national recognition for rural special education, health, and human services; (4) promote collaborative partnerships with organizations interested in special education, health, and human services; and (5) disseminate information concerning promising practices and research for improving education and services for individuals with disabilities living in rural communities.

Today, ACRES is the only national organization devoted entirely to special education issues that affect rural America. The geographically diverse membership of ACRES is representative of all regions of the country and comprises special educators, general educators, related service providers, administrators, teacher trainers, researchers, and parents who are committed to the enhancement of services to students and individuals living in rural America. This fact is especially important as rural issues are not only different from urban issues but also may vary among specific rural settings. The members of ACRES strive to provide leadership and support to enhance services for individuals with exceptional needs, their families, the professionals who work with them, and for the rural communities in which they live.

The ACRES publishes the only national scholarly journal solely devoted to rural special education issues, *Rural Special Education Quarterly* (*RSEQ*). The purpose of *RSEQ* is to disseminate information and research concerning rural special education, federal, and other events relevant to rural individuals with disabilities, progressive service delivery systems, reviews of relevant publications, and resources for rural special educators.

Each year, ACRES sponsors an annual conference in March. It is the only national conference devoted entirely to rural special education issues. Topic strands include administration, at-risk issues, collaborative education models, early childhood, gifted and talented, multicultural issues, parents and families, professional development, technology, transition, and related services. Annually, ACRES awards a scholarship to provide a practicing rural teacher an opportunity to pursue education and training that would not otherwise be affordable within his or her district and presents the Exemplary Rural Special Education Program Award to exemplar programs providing services in rural settings. Additional information on the

American Council on Rural Special Education is provided on the website at http://acres-sped.org.

KEVIN J. MILLER
University of Central Florida

AMERICAN COUNSELING ASSOCIATION (ACA)

The American Counseling Association (ACA) was begun in 1952 through a collaboration of the National Vocational Guidance Association (NVGA), the Student Personnel Association for Teacher Education (SPATE), the National Association of Guidance and Counselor Trainers (NAGCT), and the American College Personnel Association (ACPA). The ACA, originally known as the American Personnel and Guidance Association (APGA) and then later (1983) reorganized as the American Association of Counseling and Development, is presently composed of 19 divisions and 56 branches, representing multiple interests and practice areas in the United States and in multiple other countries. It functions to "enhance the quality of life in society by promoting the development of professional counselors, advancing the counseling profession, and using the profession and practice of counseling to promote respect for human dignity and diversity" (http://www.counseling.org/aboutus, para. 4).

Counselors work in the bio-psycho-social realm to promote health, growth, and wellness. Presently a comprehensive definition of counseling has been proposed. "Counseling is a professional relationship that empowers diverse individuals, families, and groups to accomplish mental health, wellness, education, and career goals" (http://www.counseling.org/resources, para. 6). Within this definition and within the ACA, school counselors, formerly known as guidance counselors, are most germane to serving the needs of the special education population. These counselors strive to help students develop in personal, social, academic and career areas. Many other ACA members are counselors, who are prepared to work, not only with the students, but also with their families and their communities.

Further information about the ACA, and the multiple journals it publishes, can be obtained from American Counseling Association, 5999 Stevenson Ave., Alexandria, VA 22304, 800-347-6647, or from the website http://www.counseling.org/

JUDY RIPSCH, PHD
The Chicago School of Professional Psychology
Fourth edition

AMERICAN EDUCATIONAL RESEARCH ASSOCIATION

The American Educational Research Association (AERA) was founded in 1916 as the National Association of Directors of Educational Research. AERA is the most prominent international professional organization, with more than 25,000 members. Members include educators; administrators; directors of research; persons working with testing or evaluation in federal, state and local agencies; counselors; evaluators; graduate students; and behavioral scientists.

The objectives of AERA include improving education process by encouraging scholarly inquiry related to education and evaluation and by promoting the dissemination and practical application of research results. There are 12 divisions within AERA. These 12 divisions range from administration and curriculum to teacher education and education policy and politics. AERA also proves Special Interest Groups (SIGs) for the involvement of individuals drawn together by a common interest in a field of study, teaching, or research. The Association provides SIGs program time at the Annual Meeting, publicity, scheduling, staff support, viability, and the prestige of AERA affiliation.

Journals published by the AERA include the *American Educational Research Journal, Educational Evaluation and Policy Analysis, Journal of Educational and Behavioral Statistics, Review of Educational Research, Educational Researcher, Review of Research in Education* (annual), *Qualitative Inquiry, Sociological Method & Research, Encyclopedia of Educational Research,* and *Handbook of Research on Teaching* (both revised every 10 years).

The AERA holds an annual convention for the presentation of reports, papers, and awards. It also holds research training programs and monitors federal educational research activities.

REFERENCE

American Educational Research Association. *About AERA*. Retrieved July 27, 2011, from http://www.aera.net/

SHANNON GRANT
Texas A&M University
Fourth edition

AMERICAN FOUNDATION FOR THE BLIND

The American Foundation for the Blind (AFB), a nonprofit organization, was founded in 1921 to serve as the national partner of local services for the blind and visually impaired. The organization is a leading national resource for people who are blind or visually impaired, the organizations that serve them, and the general public. The mission of the organization is to enable people who are blind or visually impaired to achieve equality of access and opportunity in order to ensure freedom of choice in their lives.

AFB traces its origins to a meeting of a group of professionals in Vinton, Iowa, in the summer of 1921 (Koestler, 1976). This meeting primarily included officers of the American Association of Workers for the Blind (AAWB). The meeting resulted in the recognition of the pressing need for a national organization that was not affiliated with special interest groups, professional organizations, or any local, regional, or state organizations currently serving the needs of the blind (Hagerty, 1987).

Helen Keller was closely identified with AFB from the early 1920s until her death. The organization is recognized as her cause in the United States. Working with AFB for over 40 years, Keller represented the organization in their efforts to educate legislators and the public about services needed for people who are blind.

AFB also publishes books, pamphlets, videos, and periodicals about blindness for professionals and consumers. This includes the leading professional journal of its kind, *Journal of Visual Impairment and Blindness*. In addition, the organization is responsible for maintaining and preserving the Helen Keller archives, a collection of personal material donated by her. AFB also houses the M. C. Migel Memorial Library, one of the world's largest collections of print materials on blindness.

Additionally, AFB conducts, evaluates, and publishes policy research that positively affects the quality of life for people who are blind or visually impaired. The organization also serves as an advocate for and evaluator of the development of assistive products and technology. A group of individuals from an organization called the Maintenance of the Careers & Technology Information Bank serve as mentors through AFB. Mentors from this organization consist of blind individuals from all 50 states and Canada who use assistive technology in multiple aspects of their lives.

In the accomplishment of its mission, AFB also strives to educate policymakers and the public in the needs and capabilities of people who are blind or visually impaired. AFB accomplishes this goal by consulting on legislative issues and representing blind and visually impaired persons before Congress and government agencies. AFB also produces books and other audio materials such as duplicated *Talking Books* under contract to the Library of Congress. The organization records and duplicates annual reports and other publications for various corporations and nonprofit organizations, thus making them accessible to print-handicapped employees, clients, and shareholders.

The AFB website (www.afb.org) provides links to reader-friendly blogs and materials for families, career seekers/employers, seniors and other professionals. For example, the senior page provides helpful home repair tips from an AFB retiree. The career connect page offers career advice from mentors such as Erik Weihenmayer, the first blind man ever to reach the summit of Mt. Everest. AFB's family site links families to leading experts through blogs for interactive question-and-answer format dialogues. The family site also lists information about nationwide programs on topics such as braille penpals and early childhood programs for blind children. AFB's site offers a plethora of information on topics relating to all aspects of living with vision loss.

The website also holds information regarding AFB's Blind Center on Vision Loss. The center utilizes unique presentations of information to support and accommodate people with vision loss. Its staple is Esther's Place, a fully furnished 1,800-square-foot model home in Dallas, Texas. The home is fitted with adaptations and products to assist individuals with vision loss in activities of daily living. Visitors can walk through the model apartment, test out the various technologies in Esther's Place and gain ideas and information about modifications they can make in their own homes.

For more information about the American Foundation for the Blind, contact the offices: 2 Penn Plaza, Suite 1102, New York, NY 10121. Tel.: (800) AFB-LINE (232–5463) or (212) 502–7600 (in New York state), e-mail: afbinfo@afb.net

REFERENCES

Hagerty, S. J. (1987). American foundation for the Blind. In C. R. Reynolds & L. Mann (Eds.), *Encyclopedia of special education* (1st ed.). New York, NY: Wiley.

Koestler, F. A. (1976). *The unseen minority*. New York, NY: McKay.

TAMARA J. MARTIN
The University of Texas of the Permian Basin
Third edition

AMANDA L. BARTH
The Chicago School of Professional Psychology
Fourth edition

AMERICAN GUIDANCE SERVICE

American Guidance Service, Inc. (AGS) is an educational publishing company founded in 1957, and is an employee-owned company that encourages partnership and ongoing dialogue with the professionals that use its products. AGS publishes a wide variety of norm-referenced assessment instruments for the identification of special needs students, focusing primarily on cognitive ability, achievement, behavior, and personal and social adjustment, with many publications also available in Spanish. Their better-known tests include the Peabody Picture Vocabulary Test (PPVT-III), Vineland adaptive behavior scales—Second Edition (Vineland II), Kaufman Assessment Battery for Children—Second Edition (K-ABC II), Kaufman Test of Educational Achievement—Second Edition (K-TEA II), the Developmental Indicators for the Assessment of Learning, third edition (DIAL III), and the Behavioral Assessment System for Children—Second Edition (BASC 2).

In addition to testing materials, AGS publishes a great many instructional materials, including over 900 textbooks, as well as programs for parenting and family living. Much of their material is focused on children with learning/emotional problems or in special education, though they also publish material geared to all ages. AGS can be reached at 4201 Woodland Road, Circle Pines, MN 55014-1796. Tel.: (800) 328-2560 or (651) 287-7220.

TAMARA J. MARTIN
The University of Texas of the Permian Basin

AMERICAN INSTITUTE—THE TRAINING SCHOOL AT VINELAND

The American Institute—The Training School at Vineland is located in Vineland, New Jersey (Main Road and Landis Avenue, Vineland, NJ 08360). The school and training facility were founded in 1887; they are under the supervision and administrative management of Elwyn Institutes. The facility serves children and adults who are intellectually disabled, brain damaged, emotionally disturbed, physically handicapped, and learning disabled (Sargent, 1982).

The school programs are ungraded at the elementary and secondary levels. The school features education and training programs that are designed to train young people to return to the community. The programs serve intellectually disabled. The range of educational programs and vocational training experiences are developed with individualized educational plans and rehabilitation services. The facility is internationally recognized for the pioneering works of Binet and Doll. The Stanford Binet tests were translated and norms were developed at the school. Dr. Edward Doll is recognized as the pioneer in the development of the Vineland Social Maturity Scale.

REFERENCE

Sargent, J. K. (1982). *The directory for exceptional children* (9th ed.). Boston, MA: Porter Sargent.

PAUL C. RICHARDSON
Elwyn Institutes

AMERICAN JOURNAL OF MENTAL RETARDATION

Originally known as the *American Journal of Mental Deficiency*, *AJMR* then the American Association on Mental Retardation (AAMR) is now the AJIDD American Journal of Intellectual and Developmental Disabilities. The original title reflected the original name of the sponsoring organization, which was changed from the American Organization on Mental Deficiency (AOMD) and then (AAIDD). The primary purpose of the journal is to publish theoretical manuscripts and research in the area of intellectual disability, with an emphasis on material of an objective, scientific, and experimental nature. Book reviews are included. The journal address is P.O. Box 1897, Lawrence, KS 66044. Tel.: (785) 843-1235, e-mail: AJMR@allenpress.com.

STAFF

AMERICAN JOURNAL OF OCCUPATIONAL THERAPY

The *American Journal of Occupational Therapy* (*AJOT*) is an official publication of the American Occupational Therapy Association. *AJOT* is published monthly except for July/August and November/December, when it appears in bimonthly issues. Manuscripts are subjected to anonymous peer review. Accepted articles pertain to occupational therapy and may include reports of research, educational activities, or professional trends; descriptions of new occupational therapy approaches, programs, or services; review papers that survey new information; theoretical papers that discuss or treat theoretical issues critically; descriptions of original therapeutic aids, devices, or techniques; case reports that describe occupational therapy for a specific clinical situation; or opinion essays that discuss timely issues or opinions and are supported by cogent arguments. In addition, the journal contains letters to the editor, publication reviews, and product advertising.

AJOT is abstracted or indexed by Applied Science Index and Abstracts, Behavioral Medicine Abstracts, Cumulative Index to Nursing and Allied Health Literature, Exceptional Child Education Resources, Excerpta Medica, Inc., Hospital Literature Index, Index Medicus, Institute for Scientific Information, MEDLINE, OT BibSys, Psychological Abstracts, and Social Sciences Citation Index. Microfilms of complete volumes can be obtained from University Microfilms, Inc.

ELIZABETH HOLCOMB
American Journal of Occupational Therapy

AMERICAN JOURNAL OF ORTHOPSYCHIATRY

The *American Journal of Orthopsychiatry (AJO)*, is the quarterly journal of the American Orthopsychiatric Association. The association was founded in 1926 and began publication of *AJO* in 1930. The *AJO* is a quarterly, refereed, scholarly journal written from a multidisciplinary perspective. The *AJO* is dedicated to public policy, professional practice, and information that relates to mental health and human development. Clinical, theoretical, research, review, and expository papers are published in *AJO*. These papers are essentially synergistic and directed at concept and theory development, reconceptualization of major issues, explanation, and interpretation.

The *AJO* concentrates on many topics of concern to special educators. During its lifetime, *AJO*'s articles have centered around the topics of social issues and the handicapped, childhood psychosis, psychopharmacology, school phobia, depression, suicide, child abuse, intellectual disability, and treatment of all of these disorders. The contributors' list and editorial board have, over the years, featured some of the finest scholars from developmental medicine, developmental psychopathology, child development, school psychology, clinical psychology, special education, neurology, psychiatry, and related mental health fields. The *AJO* is an influential journal that publishes top scholars' writing on special education.

CECIL R. REYNOLDS
Texas A&M University

See also American Orthopsychiatric Association

AMERICAN JOURNAL OF PSYCHIATRY

The *American Journal of Psychiatry* began publication in 1844 as the *American Journal of Insanity*, changing to its current title in 1921. It is the official journal of the American Psychiatric Association, and is the most widely read psychiatric journal in the world. Published monthly, the *American Journal of Psychiatry* publishes peer-reviewed research studies and articles that focus on developments in the biological aspects of psychiatry, on treatment issues and innovations, and on forensic, ethical, social, and economic topics. Letters to the editor, book reviews, and official American Psychiatric Association reports are also included. Of special interest to many readers are the overview and special lead articles, which address major psychiatric syndromes and issues in depth.

KAY E. KETZENBERGER
The University of Texas of the Permian Basin

AMERICAN OCCUPATIONAL THERAPY FOUNDATION

The American Occupational Therapy Foundation was founded in 1965 as the American Occupational Therapy Association's (AOTA) philanthropic sister organization. The foundation has devoted its energies to raising funds and resources in three program areas—publications, research, and scholarships—associated with the profession of occupational therapy and health-care delivery.

The foundation's publication program aims to increase public knowledge and understanding of the occupational therapy profession. In addition to various reports and documents, it publishes *The Occupational Therapy Journal of Research*, and has produced a major bibliography of completed research in the field. The foundation supports the Occupational Therapy Library, which supplies requested materials through interlibrary loan.

A research program is conducted through the foundation's Office of Professional Research Services. Program services include the Academy of Research, support of researchers through grant awards (in association with the AOTA), and doctoral and postdoctoral fellowship awards to support researchers. The foundation widely disseminates scholarship information for undergraduate and graduate students in occupational therapy publications and through occupational therapy schools.

The American Occupational Therapy Foundation is located at 4720 Montgomery Lane, P.O. Box 31220, Bethesda, MD 20824.

SHIRLEY A. JONES
Virginia Polytechnic Institute and State University
First edition

KAY KETZENBERGER
The University of Texas of the Permian Basin
Second edition

AMERICAN ORTHOPSYCHIATRIC ASSOCIATION

The American Orthopsychiatric Association (Ortho) was formed at the invitation of Herman Adler and Karl Menninger at the Institute for Juvenile Research in Chicago in 1924 under the name of the Association of American Orthopsychiatrists. The group operated informally, debating its name and purpose and finally founding Ortho a year later. In 1926 Ortho amended its constitution, which limited membership to physicians, to redefine membership to include psychiatrists, psychologists, social workers, and other professional persons "whose work and interests lie in the study and treatment of conduct disorders." According to Eisenberg and DeMaso (1985), the first published membership roster, published October 1, 1927, included 45 psychiatrists, 12 psychologists, 5 social workers, and several lawyers and penologists. Ortho had as its purpose the centralization of the techniques, objectives, and aspirations of psychiatrists, psychologists, and related mental health workers whose primary interests were in the area of human behavior, providing a common meeting ground for students of behavior problems and for fostering scientific research and its dissemination. The early membership included names familiar to special educators, including such notables as Edgar Doll, Lightner Witmer, and Carl Murchison.

Lightner Witmer, noted among historians of psychology as the man who coined the term clinical psychology, founded school psychology and established the first psychological clinic; he also coined the term orthogenics and established the team approach to children's problems when he invited neurologists to collaborate on case studies (Eisenberg & DeMaso, 1985). Ortho subsequently became a major force in the establishment of the child guidance movement in the early 1900s. In 1930 Ortho established the *American Journal of Orthopsychiatry*, a widely read and respected journal that in its early years vigorously debated the roles and functions of various professionals (e.g., psychiatrists, psychologists, social workers, etc.) in the treatment of childhood mental health disorders.

Presently, many special educators belong to Ortho. It is a large, robust organization of more than 10,000 members. It is involved in social, scientific, and public policy issues, including diagnosis, evaluation, and treatment, relevant to the improvement of the lives of the handicapped. The *American Journal of Orthopsychiatry* is provided as a benefit of membership; it contains many articles of interest to special educators. The association is located at Department of Psychology, Box 871104, Arizona State University, Tempe, AZ 85287. Tel.: (480) 727-7518.

REFERENCES

American Orthopsychiatric Association (Ortho). (1998). *About Ortho*. Retrieved from http://aoatoday.com/

Eisenberg, L., & DeMaso, D. R. (1985). Fifty years of the *American Journal of Orthopsychiatry*: An overview and introduction. In E. Flaxman & E. Herman (Eds.), *American Journal of Orthopsychiatry: Annotated index: Vols. 1–50. 1930–1980*. Greenwich, CT: JAI.

CECIL R. REYNOLDS
Texas A&M University

See *also* American Journal of Orthopsychiatry; Witmer, Lightner

AMERICAN PHYSICAL THERAPY ASSOCIATION

The American Physical Therapy Association (APTA) endeavors to improve physical therapy services and education by accrediting academic programs in physical therapy, assisting states in preparing certification examinations, and offering workshops and continuing education courses for therapists at the national and local levels. There are seven membership types available through APTA: physical therapist/physical therapist assistant, physical therapist postprofessional student, student of physical therapy, foreign-educated physical therapist (living within the United States), international partner (foreign-educated living outside the United States), retired/life membership, and faculty partner.

Benefits for physical therapists and assistants include APTA healthcare advocacy in Washington DC, access to public relations marketing tools, professional resources, and evidence-based practices. Physical therapists also receive networking opportunities, conference discounts, publications, and continuing education opportunities. Benefits for student members include access to educational resources, networking opportunities, and financial assistance such as scholarships, grants, and award opportunities. Benefits for employers sponsoring membership for their staff include attracting clients, decreasing professional development expenses, improving recruitment, and retaining current employees.

Information is available through APTA about careers in physical therapy, accredited preparation programs, sources of student financial aid, and employment opportunities. A variety of pamphlets are available on prevention of injuries and chronic or degenerative conditions. APTA has a published newsletter and journal. Bibliographies have been prepared on topics including resources for stroke victims, quadriplegics, paraplegics, amputees, parents, and educators. Members benefit from information regarding practice and disabilities. The association also serves as a referral source for individuals who require physical therapy services. Association offices are located at 1111 North Fairfax Street, Alexandria, VA 22314-1488. Tel.: (800) 999-2782, website: www.apta.org.

PHILIP R. JONES
*Virginia Polytech Institute
and State University*
Third edition

AMANDA L. BARTH
*The Chicago School of Professional
Psychology*
Fourth edition

AMERICAN PRINTING HOUSE FOR THE BLIND

The American Printing House for the Blind (APH), the oldest private, nonprofit institution for the blind in the United States, was founded in Louisville, Kentucky, in 1858. It is the world's largest company devoted solely to creating products and services for people who are visually impaired. The Act to Promote the Education of the Blind, mandated by Congress in 1879, enabled the APH to receive grants for education texts and aids for those with visual impairments from the federal government. Funds appropriated under the Act are used by each state to purchase educational materials from APH for their blind students below the college level (APH, 1998).

The Company's mission is to promote the independence of blind and visually impaired persons by providing special media, tools, and materials needed for education and life. A wide variety of products and services are available through APH, including braille, large type, recorded, computer disk, and tactile graphic publications as well as a wide assortment of educational and daily living products. Various services designed to assist consumers and professionals in the field of vision are also offered, including *Louis*, a database listing materials available from accessible media across North America and *Patterns*, a reading instruction program developed through APH research.

APH's Talking Books on cassette tape, produced in agency recording studios, are a popular reading medium for blind and visually impaired people of all ages. Fiction and nonfiction topics, ranging from romance to cookbooks, are produced by professional narrators who are also teachers, actors, and media personalities. Most Talking Books can be obtained on a free loan basis from the National Library for the Blind and Physically Handicapped, a division of the Library of Congress. Three magazines are offered by APH directly to eligible blind readers. They include *Readers Digest, Newsweek*, and *Weekly Reader*.

In addition to the publications and products provided to those who are visually impaired, APH maintains a national center for research and development, focusing on the creation of products for blind students and adults, and a museum, offering a look at the history of education of blind people.

REFERENCE

American Printing House for the Blind (APH). (1998). *What is the American Printing House for the Blind?* Louisville, KY: Author.

TAMARA J. MARTIN
The University of Texas of the Permian Basin

AMERICAN PSYCHIATRIC ASSOCIATION

The American Psychiatric Association was founded in 1844 as the Association of Medical Superintendents of American Institutions for the Insane, and changed to its current name in 1921. The Association is a national medical specialty society that had over 35,000 U.S. and international members in 2005; members are physicians who specialize in the diagnosis and treatment of mental, emotional, and substance-abuse disorders. The Association's major focus areas include mental health, psychopharmacology, psychotherapy, and health professions development, and its primary objectives include the advancement and improvement of care for people with mental illnesses through the provision of nationwide education, public information, and awareness programs and materials.

The Association publishes the *American Journal of Psychiatry* (its official monthly journal), *Hospital and Community Psychiatry* (monthly), and *Psychiatric News* (twice monthly). The Association offers many continuing education workshops, seminars, and courses, as well as library services for members. The Association can be contacted at their national offices at 1000 Wilson Boulevard, Suite 1825, Arlington VA 22209. Tel.: (703) 907-7322 or (800) 368-5777.

KAY E. KETZENBERGER
The University of Texas of the Permian Basin

AMERICAN PSYCHOLOGICAL ASSOCIATION

The American Psychological Association (APA) is the nation's major psychology organization. The APA works to advance psychology as a science and a profession, and to promote human welfare. When the APA was established in 1892, psychology was a new profession and the organization had fewer than three dozen members. Over the years the organization has grown rapidly: In 1998 the APA had more than 155,000 members, 51 divisions in specialized subfields and interest areas, and 58 affiliated state, provincial, and territorial psychological associations.

The growth of the science and profession of psychology is reflected in the development of diverse programs and services administered by the association. These programs aim to disseminate psychological knowledge, promote research, improve research methods and conditions, and develop the qualifications and competence of psychologists through standards of education, ethical conduct, and professional practice.

The program and business activities of the APA are coordinated at the association's central office in Washington, DC. These offices are headquarters for APA's programs in governance affairs, national policy studies, public affairs, communications, and financial affairs. Through these programs, the central office staff provides information to members, other professionals, students, and the public through the publication of books, major journals, pamphlets, the monthly APA *Monitor* newspaper, and a growing spectrum of bibliographic and abstracting services covering the literature of psychology.

The affairs of the association are administered by the Board of Directors, which is responsible for the work of an executive officer who administers the affairs of the central office. The Board of Directors is composed of a president, past president, and president-elect, all of whom are elected by APA members at large, and a treasurer, a secretary, and six board members who are elected by the Council of Representatives. The Council of Representatives is composed of members of the association who are elected by their division and state members in proportion to the annual assignment of seats by the membership. The Council of Representatives sets policy for the association, and those policies are administered by the Board of Directors through the executive officer and the staff of the central office.

The governance affairs office of the association coordinates and directs psychology programs and activities such as accreditation of doctoral programs in professional psychology and predoctoral internship sites; supervision of educational affairs aimed at identifying and analyzing developments in higher education and training of psychologists; setting standards for scientific and professional ethics, professional affairs, scientific affairs, social and ethical responsibility of psychologists, and overseeing special issues concerning minority groups and women's programs.

The national policy studies of APA help to formulate and implement federal policy and legislative activities of the association. The Public Policy Office develops advocacy positions, informs Congress and federal agencies of psychology's concerns, keeps the APA membership and governance structure informed of related policy issues, and develops working coalitions with outside organizations on common legislative issues.

The Public Affairs Office works to provide overall direction on the ways organized psychology is presented to its national and international public. The office works with television, radio, and print media to demonstrate the contributions psychologists make to society and to improve public understanding of psychology's broad scope and application.

The APA publishes more than 30 periodicals and a variety of books, brochures, and pamphlets. Among these are *American Psychologist*, the official journal of the association, and *Psychological Abstracts*, which contains abstracts of the world's literature on psychology and related disciplines.

Each year more than 12,000 psychologists and other individuals attend the APA convention in late summer. This is the world's largest meeting of psychologists and one of the largest professional conventions in the United States. The week-long program features more than 3,000 presentations through symposiums, lectures, invited addresses, specialized workshops, and other forums. Through the convention, practitioners and the public are given the opportunity to learn of the latest findings from psychological research, their applications in society, and other professional, scientific, and educational issues.

From energy conservation and industrial productivity to child development, aging, and prevention of stress and related illness, hardly a personal or national problem exists that does not demand an understanding of human behavior. Even modern technological innovations emerge from the ability of the mind to transform observations and data into action. Because of their fundamental understanding of behavior, psychologists are increasingly consulted for ways to increase human progress and well-being. APA can be contacted at 750 First St., N.E., Washington, DC 20002. Tel.: (800) 374-2721.

NADINE M. LAMBERT
University of California, Berkeley

AMERICAN PSYCHOLOGIST

American Psychologist is the official journal of the American Psychological Association. Published monthly, it is the most widely circulated psychological journal in the world, going out to more than 155,000 members of the Association around the globe. It is a primary source of discussion on cutting-edge issues in psychology, and it publishes empirical, theoretical, and practical articles on broad aspects of psychology. It is indexed in over 20 abstracting/indexing services, including: PsychINFO, Index Medicus, Academic Index, Social Sciences Index, and Applied Social Science Index & Abstracts, thereby making its contents easily discoverable and highly available to users. As the official journal of the Association, it contains but is not limited to: the annual report of the Association, council minutes, the Presidential address, editorials, other reports of the Association, ethics information, surveys of the membership, employment data, obituaries, calendars of events, announcements, selected award addresses, and (in each year's December issues) a listing of all APA-approved doctoral training programs in clinical, counseling, and school psychology in the United States and Canada.

In setting forth general editorial policy for the *American Psychologist*, past and present editors have agreed that the journal should (a) contribute to enlightened participation in the profession of psychology and thereby to effective function of the association; (b) provide a forum for the examination of the relationship between psychology and society, especially as historical, cultural, and societal influences have an impact on the science and practice of psychology; (c) foster the development of the diverse applications of psychological knowledge; and (d) present and disseminate psychological knowledge in a form and style suitable to the general membership and to the interested public.

The current editor is Norman B. Anderson. The journal's offices are housed within the American Psychological Association's national headquarters, located at 750 First Street, NE, Washington, DC, 20002. The e-mail address of the editorial office of the *American Psychologist* is APeditor@apa.org.

Nadine M. Lambert
University of California
First edition

Kay E. Ketzenberger
The University of Texas of the Permian Basin
Second edition

Cortney A. Kemp
The Chicago School of Professional Psychology
Fourth edition

AMERICAN SIGN LANGUAGE

American Sign Language (ASL), Pidgin Signed English (PSE), and Signed Exact English (SEE) are a few of the many alternative forms of sign communication taught to either deaf or hearing individuals (Marschark, 1997). Only ASL is discussed in detail.

American Sign Language is a complex visual-spatial language used by the deaf community (Daniels, 2001; Drasgow, 1998; Marschark, 1997; Moores, 2001). American Sign Language is a complete nonauditory yet verbal language that is independent of English (Drasgow, 1998; Marschark, 1997; Moores, 2001), one that is linguistically complete and natural (Daniels, 2001; Drasgow, 1998; Moores, 2001). American Sign Language is the native language of many individuals who are deaf as well as some hearing children born into deaf families (Moores, 2001; Nakamura, 2000). As many as 15 million people in North America communicate to some degree using ASL, thus making it the third most commonly used language in the country (Daniels, 2001).

Like other verbal languages, ASL contains many properties (e.g., phonology, morphology). Its structure can be divided into five components: phonology, morphology, syntax, space, and nonmanual characteristics (Daniels, 2001). The first three will be compared to the English language.

In English, phonology refers to the use of vocal organs. In contrast, the phonological properties of ASL require manual expression and movement that are significant to the visual system.

The four gestural components are location (i.e., the placement of the produced signs at approximately 20 distinct locations on the signer's body), hand shapes (i.e., the shape of each hand when producing the approximate 40 handshapes), movement (i.e., the motion of the hands from one point to another in the signing space), and orientation (i.e., the direction of the hands in relation to approximately 10 distinct orientations to the body; Daniels, 2001; Drasgow, 1998).

Morphology refers to the structure of word, including changes in them by adding prefixes or suffixes. In English, this process generally emerges in a sequential manner (Daniels, 2001; Drasgow, 1998). For example, the letter /s/ at the end of a noun generally makes it plural. In contrast, morphology in ASL is organized in a simultaneous rather than a sequential fashion. That is, rather than adding prefixes or suffixes to a word stem, ASL morphology operates by nesting the sign stem within active movement contours (Daniels, 2001; Drasgow, 1998). For example, the word *improve* (a verb) requires a single slow movement, while the word *improvement* (a noun) requires a faster, more dynamic movement (Daniels, 2001; Drasgow, 1998).

Syntax refers to word order. The word order in English usually is subject-verb-object. Word order is important in English because there are few inflections to show grammatical relationships (Daniels, 2001; Drasgow, 1998). In contrast, ASL is more variable in word order. Although ASL often uses a subject-verb-object sequence, this sequence does not dominate and instead grammatical facial expressions, spatial syntax, and other nonmanual features are used (Daniels, 2001; Drasgow, 1998). *Topicalization*, the process of using facial expressions and head position to alter word order by putting the most important information at the beginning of the sentence, is common in ASL.

The final two components of ASL, space and nonmanual characteristics, are not evident in English. In ASL, space plays a large and complex role as it is used to indicate verb tenses and for indexing (Daniels, 2001; Drasgow, 1998). The notion of tense is represented by an imaginary time line that surrounds the signer's body, where the past is represented by the space behind the signer, the future is represented by the space in front of the signer, and the present is represented by the space nearest to the signer's upper body (Daniels, 2001). *Indexing* refers to pointing to designated locations within the signing space. A signer may place a referent, such as a person or object, in a designated space and then refer to that space later in time (Daniels, 2001; Drasgow, 1998).

Nonmanual characteristics in ASL involve movements of the eyes, mouth, face, hand, and body posture. The purpose of these characteristics is to serve as intonation acts in a spoken language or as punctuation acts in a written language (Daniels, 2001). Alterations in the behavior of the body determine the meaning or emphasis of a specific sign (Daniels, 2001).

Children can acquire and retain considerable knowledge by learning ASL and spoken English simultaneously (Daniels, 1997). Gallaudet believed that employment of sign language as an additional sensory channel provided a stronger language base for young hearing learners (Daniels, 1997). The basic motor control of one's hands occurs before the use of one's voice. Therefore, the use of sign language with young children has various advantages (Bonvillian & Floven, 1993). For example, the use of both a written alphabet and sign language provides an early and convenient form of writing for young children "who are able to finger spell far sooner than they acquire the manual dexterity to write words with paper and pencil" (Daniels, 1997, p. 29). In addition, as Daniels (1997) states, using sign language "literally allows a child to feel language" (p. 29).

American Sign Language has been incorporated in many programs and research studies that have investigated language acquisition and development (Birke, 2003; Carney, Cioffi, Raymond, & Floven, 1985; Daniels, 1993, 1994, 1996a, 1996b; deViveiros & McLaughlin, 1982; Griffith, 1985; Holmes & Holmes, 1980; Orlansky & Bonvillian, 1985; Prinz & Prinz, 1981; Weller & Mahoney, 1983). Findings show that learning ASL and spoken English simultaneously allows children to acquire a greater language base (Daniels, 1997); basic motor control of the child's hands occurs before the voice; therefore, the use of ASL by young children is favored over the use only of voice (Bonvillian & Floven, 1993); signing helps children expand their vocabulary (Stewart & Luetke-Stahlman, 1998); and ASL improves receptive and expressive language of hearing kindergarten children with no hearing impairments (Birke, 2003; Daniels, 1996b; deViveiros and McLaughlin, 1982).

The literature supports the premise that simultaneously presenting words visually, kinesthetically, and verbally enhances vocabulary development in kindergarten students. The assumption that the use of various modalities when teaching language, including ASL, enriches the language acquisition is reasonable (Birke, 2003; Daniels, 1997). Moreover, their simultaneous use holds promise as an effective multisensory method to use with language-delayed children.

REFERENCES

Birke, D. E. (2003). The effect of exposure to American Sign Language on receptive and expressive vocabulary skills of hearing kindergarten children. Unpublished master's thesis, University of Florida, Gainesville.

Bonvillian, J. D., & Floven, R. J. (1993). Sign language acquisition: Developmental aspects. In M. Marschark & M. D. Clark (Eds.), *Psychological perspectives on deafness* (pp. 229–265). Hillsdale, NJ: Erlbaum.

Carney, J., Cioffi, G., Raymond, M., & Floven, R. (1985). Using sign language for teaching sight words. *Teaching Exceptional Children, 17*(3), 170–175.

Daniels, M. (1993). ASL as a factor in acquiring English. *Sign Language Studies, 78,* 23–29.

Daniels, M. (1994). Words more powerful than sound. *Sign Language Studies, 83,* 156–166.

Daniels, M. (1996a). Bilingual, bimodal education for hearing kindergarten students. *Sign Language Studies, 90,* 25–37.

Daniels, M. (1996b). Seeing language: The effect over time of sign language on vocabulary development in early childhood education. *Child Study Journal, 26*(3), 193–208.

Daniels, M. (1997). Teacher enrichment of prekindergarten curriculum with sign language. *Journal of Research in Childhood Education, 12*(1), 27–33.

Daniels, M. (2001). *Dancing with words: Signing for hearing children's literacy.* Westport, CT: Bergin & Garvey.

deViveiros, C. E., & McLaughlin, T. F. (1982). Effects of manual sign use to the expressive language of four hearing kindergarten children. *Sign Language Studies, 35,* 169–177.

Drasgow, E. (1998). American Sign Language as a pathway to linguistic competence. *Exceptional Children, 64*(3), 329–343.

Griffith, P. L. (1985). Mode switching and mode finding in a hearing child of deaf parents. *Sign Language Studies, 35,* 195–222.

Holmes, K. M., & Holmes, D. W. (1980). Signed and spoken language development in a hearing child of hearing parents. *Sign Language Studies, 28,* 239–254.

Marschark, M. (1997). *Raising and educating a deaf child: A comprehensive guide to the choices, controversies, and decision faced by parents and educators.* New York, NY: Oxford University Press.

Moores, D. F. (2001). *Educating the deaf: Psychology, principles, and practices* (5th ed.). Princeton, NJ: Houghton-Mifflin.

Nakamura, K. (2000). The deaf resource library. Retrieved from http://www.deaflibrary.org

Orlansky, M. D., & Bonvillian, J. D. (1985). Sign language acquisition: Language development in children of deaf parents and implications for other populations. *Merrill-Palmer Quarterly, 31*(2), 127–143.

Prinz, P., & Prinz, E. (1981). Acquisition of ASL and spoken English by a hearing child of a deaf mother and a hearing father: Phase II, Early combinatorial patterns. *Sign Language Studies, 30,* 78–88.

Stewart, D., & Luetke-Stahlman, B. (1998). *The signing family: What every parent should know about sign communication.* Washington, DC: Gallaudet University Press.

Weller, E. L., & Mahoney, G. J. (1983). A comparison of oral and total communication modalities on the language training of young mentally handicapped children. *Education and Training of the Mentally Retarded, 18*(2), 103–110.

DEBORAH BIRKE CARON
St. Lucie County School District,
St. Lucie County, Florida

See *also* Alternative Communication Methods in Special Education; Deaf; Gallaudet College

AMERICAN SOCIETY FOR DEAF CHILDREN

The American Society for Deaf Children (ASDC) is a national nonprofit organization dedicated to providing support, information and access to resources to parents and families of children who are deaf or hard of hearing. Founded in 1967, ASDC's stated mission is to educate parents of deaf and hard of hearing children while advocating for high quality services and programs. The ASDC advocates for four core values: deaf and hard of hearing children are entitled to have full access to communication in their home and school settings, deaf and hard of hearing children should be exposed to sign language and English to have optimal social-emotional development and academic success, deaf and hard of hearing children should have access to early identification and interventions in order to become self-advocating independent adults, and parents should be the primary decision makers of their deaf or hard of hearing children's lives.

Individuals, families, and organizations can obtain membership to ASDC through various levels of monetary support. ASDC keeps parents informed about current issues, such as access to various articles regarding deaf and hard of hearing children, information about American Sign Language (ASL), opportunities for scholarships, various coalitions and partnerships, information about the Individuals with Disabilities Act (IDEA), access to the ASDC lending library, and provides parents with Spanish resources. The ASDC also furnishes individuals with useful links to multiple websites that provide information about relevant topics related to the deaf and hard of hearing community as well as provides individuals with up to date news regarding this population. A list of all the state organizations that support the education of the deaf and hard of hearing and have become members of ASDC can be accessed on the ASCD website. The ASDC also publishes *The Endeavor*, a magazine sent out four times a year to ASDC members, containing relevant articles, personal stories, and advertisements of organizations supporting individuals who are deaf or hard of hearing. Every two years a conference known as the ASDC Biennial Conference is hosted at different schools of the deaf around the country. This 5-day conference provides families with the opportunity to attend workshops, meet other families with deaf or hard-of-hearing children, and partake in entertaining recreational activities. Parents who have demonstrated exceptional dedication, service, and leadership to the deaf or hard of hearing community are recognized with the Lee Katz Award at this conference.

The ASDC headquarters are located at 800 Florida Avenue NE, #2047, Washington, DC 20002-3695. Tel.: (800) 942-2732 (Parent Information Hotline), fax: (410) 795-0965, e-mail asdc@deafchildren.org.

REFERENCE

American Society for Deaf Children (ASDC). (2010). Retrieved from http://www.deafchildren.org/

KAY E. KETZENBERGER
The University of Texas of the Permian Basin
First edition

DIANA E. PINEDA
The Chicago School of Professional Psychology
Fourth edition

AMERICAN SPEECH-LANGUAGE-HEARING ASSOCIATION

The American Speech-Language-Hearing Association (ASHA) is the professional, scientific, and credentialing association for more than 140,000 speech-language pathologists, audiologists, and speech, language, and hearing scientists in the United States and international community. For over 75 years, ASHA works with these professionals in the development of national standards for speech-language pathologists and for audiologists. ASHA's vision statement of "Making effective communication, a human right, accessible and achievable for all" is advanced by its mission to advocate on behalf of persons with communication and related disorders, to advance communication science, and to promote effective human communication.

In 1925, a small group of people met at an informal meeting of the National Association of Teachers of Speech (NATS) in Iowa City, Iowa. These individuals, who were primarily teachers of rhetoric, debate, and theater, were interested in communication disorders and wanted to create an organization devoted entirely to the study and treatment of communication disorders. As a result of this meeting the American Academy of Speech Correction was established in December 1925. The current name of the organization, American Speech-Language-Hearing Association, was adopted in 1978.

As the nation's leading professional, credentialing, and scientific organization for speech-language pathologists, audiologists, and speech/language/hearing scientists, ASHA initiated the development of national standards. These national credentialing standards, the Certificate of Clinical Competence in Speech Pathology (CCC-SP) and Audiology (CCC-A), have been in use by ASHA since 1952. The professionals who have achieved ASHA certification have the knowledge, skills, and expertise to provide high quality clinical services, and actively engage in ongoing professional development.

ASHA has five major publications for their members: *The ASHA Leader*, the *American Journal of Audiology*, the *American Journal of Speech-Language Pathology*, the *Journal of Speech, Language, and Hearing Research*, and *Language, Speech, and Hearing Services in Schools*. Resources to help understand communication and communication disorders can be found at http://asha.org

The ASHA offices are located in Rockville, Maryland. Tel.: (800) 638-8255 (voice) or (301) 296-5650 (TTY), e-mail: actioncenter@asha.org.

REFERENCES

American Speech-Language-Hearing Association, downloaded from http://asha.org

Paden, E. P. (1970). *A history of the American Speech and Hearing Association, 1925–1958*. Washington, DC: American Speech and Hearing Association.

FREDERICK F. WEINER
Pennsylvania State University
First edition

KAY E. KETZENBERGER
The University of Texas of the Permian Basin
Second edition

GLENDA BYRNS
Texas A&M University
Fourth edition

AMERICANS WITH DISABILITIES ACT

The Americans with Disabilities Act of 1990 (ADA) is a comprehensive civil rights law designed to prohibit discrimination against people with disabilities. The ADA is a civil rights law; therefore, it preempts any other local, state, or federal law that grants lesser rights to individuals with disabilities (National Association of State Directors of Special Education [NASDSE], 1992), although states may in some instances grant rights in excess of those mandated by the ADA. Federal funding is not provided to carry out the ADA mandates; however, a wide range of public and private institutions, including educational institutions, are required to comply with the ADA provisions. The four purposes of the ADA are

1. to provide a clear and comprehensive national mandate for the elimination of discrimination against individuals with disabilities
2. to provide clear, strong, consistent, enforceable standards addressing discrimination against individuals with disabilities

3. to ensure that the federal government plays a central role in enforcing the standards established in this Act on behalf of individuals with disabilities; and
4. to invoke the sweep of congressional authority, including the power to enforce the 14th Amendment, to address the major areas of discrimination faced by people with disabilities. (42 U.S.C. §§ 12101 Sec 2 [b][1–4])

The ADA derives its substance from Section 504 of the Rehabilitation Act of 1973, but its procedures from Title VII of the Civil Rights Act of 1964, amended in 1991 (First & Curcio, 1993).

In 1988, the ADA bill was first introduced in Congress in response to mounting evidence that Americans with disabilities, over 40 million strong, faced an inordinate number of inequities in different spheres of life (Jacob-Timm & Hartshorne, 1995). Moreover, congressional testimony had documented a strong link between disability and economic and social hardships and limited educational opportunities (Burgdorf, 1991). Based on these inequities and disadvantages, congressional legislative action was taken to bring individuals with disabilities into the American social and economic mainstream through the enactment of the ADA. The U.S. Congress approved the final version of the bill on July 13, 1990, and President George Bush signed it into law on July 26, 1990.

The ADA consists of five titles. The areas addressed in these five titles include employment, public services, public accommodations, telecommunications, and miscellaneous provisions. Title I prohibits discrimination in employment of persons with disabilities. Under this title, employers must reasonably accommodate the disabilities of the otherwise qualified applicants or employees unless undue hardship would result. An example of an undue hardship would be a significant difficulty or excessive expense to the employer associated with making alterations or modifications at the job site to accommodate a qualified applicant who is also an individual with a disability. All school districts, regardless of the number of personnel employed, are subject to Title I standards.

Title II prohibits discrimination in programs, activities, and services provided by state and local governments and their instrumentalities. Title II applies to all public entities, including public schools, regardless of federal funding status. Under Title II, school facilities, whether existing facilities or under construction, must meet accessibility requirements for individuals with disabilities consistent with Section 504 of the Rehabilitation Act (First & Curcio, 1993). Public transportation, like buses and rail vehicles, must also meet accessibility requirements. Title II requires school districts to provide appropriate aids so that individuals with disabilities have equal opportunities to participate in available programs and services. Likewise, districts are required to give primary consideration to disabled individuals' requests and to ensure that individuals with hearing or visual impairments receive information in an appropriate and understandable format about available programs and services. Examples of public school programs, services, and activities covered by Title II include public entertainment or lectures sponsored by the school district, after-school activities and social events offered by the schools, parent-teacher conferences, classroom activities, field trips, and any other service provided for students or staff (Office of Civil Rights [OCR], 1996).

Title III prohibits discrimination based on disability in privately owned public accommodations. Nonsectarian private schools and school bus transportation, as well as other privately owned public accommodations, must make reasonable alterations in policies, practices, and procedures to avoid discrimination. Nonsectarian private schools must provide auxiliary aids and services to individuals with visual or hearing impairments. In addition, physical barriers must be removed unless readily unachievable. If not readily achievable, alternate methods of providing services must be offered. All new construction and alterations in existing facilities must be handicap accessible. School bus transportation services, such as bus routes, must be comparable in duration and distance for disabled and nondisabled individuals.

Title IV requires telephone companies to provide telecommunication relay services for hearing- and speech-impaired individuals. Closed-captioned public service announcements must also be provided. Under Title IV, schools must ensure that communication with disabled individuals is just as effective as communication with nondisabled individuals.

Title V consists of a variety of provisions. The title identifies the federal agencies responsible for the enforcement and technical assistance related to the ADA. The federal agency responsible for the enforcement of Title II, Subtitle A, programs, activities, and services provided by state and local governments and their instrumentalities, which extends to all public school systems, is the Office of Civil Rights (OCR) in the Department of Education. The OCR not only enforces the ADA provisions under Title II, Subtitle A but it also handles complaints filed with regard to alleged violations of this title. Title V also dictates that state governments are not immune from legal actions related to the ADA. In addition, individuals with disabilities have the right to accept or reject accommodations and services offered under the ADA. Furthermore, individuals with or without disabilities cannot be coerced or retaliated against for exercising their rights under the ADA. The title also addresses the relationship between the ADA and other laws and its impact on insurance providers and benefits.

In examining the relationship between the ADA and other federal laws affecting persons with disabilities, ADA is viewed as a complementary law (Cunconan-Lahr, 1991). The ADA does not diminish any of the rights of disabled individuals under the Civil Rights Act of 1964, as amended in 1991, Individuals with Disabilities Education Act (IDEA), or Section 504 of the Rehabilitation Act of 1973 (NASDSE, 1992).

Section 504 and the ADA espouse the same underlying principle, which is that entities under their jurisdiction cannot discriminate against individuals with disabilities in their programs, activities, and services (Cunconan-Lahr, 1991). To eliminate discrimination, both laws stress the importance of equal opportunity, not just equal treatment, for disabled and nondisabled individuals. However, the ADA does create a higher standard of nondiscrimination than does Section 504 in several respects. First, Section 504 applies only to recipients of federal funding, whereas the ADA applies to employment, public services, public accommodations, and transportation, regardless of whether federal funding is received. Second, Section 504 covers qualified individuals with disabilities, whereas the ADA extends protection to a person without a disability who is related to or associated with an individual with a disability (OCR, 1996).

With the aforementioned exceptions, Title II of the ADA, which extends to public schools, does not impose any new major requirements on school districts (OCR, 1996). Much of the language in Title II and Section 504 are similar, and school districts that receive federal funding have been required to comply with Section 504 for over 30 years. In the area of education, nondiscrimination requirements related to disabled individuals are detailed more specifically under Section 504 than under Title II. However, Title II requirements are not to be interpreted as applying a lesser standard or degree of protection for disabled individuals. In fact, if a rule issued under Section 504 imposes a lesser standard than the ADA regulation, the language in the ADA statute replaces the language in Section 504 (NASDSE, 1992).

The ADA statute does not directly specify procedural safeguards related to special education, evaluation and placement procedures, due process procedures, and responsibility and requirements under the provision of a free, appropriate public education (FAPE) as does Section 504 and IDEA. The ADA incorporates the specific details of these concepts from Section 504 and IDEA into Title II, Subtitle A. The ADA also provides additional protection in combination with the actions brought under Section 504 and IDEA. For example, reasonable accommodations must be made for eligible individuals with disabilities to perform essential functions of a job. Special education programs that are community-based and involve job training or placement are covered under the ADA statute. The ADA protections are also applicable to nonsectarian private schools but not to organizations or entities controlled by religious affiliations (Henderson, 1995).

Section 504 and IDEA provide specific details regarding procedural safeguards, whereas the ADA does not. Procedural safeguards involve notification to parents regarding identification, evaluation, and placement of a child in special education programs and related services. The ADA, on the other hand, specifies administrative requirements, complaint procedures, and consequences for noncompliance related to services (Henderson, 1995).

The ADA does not specify evaluation and placement procedures as does Section 504 and IDEA. However, the ADA does require reasonable accommodations for individuals with disabilities across educational settings and activities. Reasonable accommodations are not limited to, but may include, modifying equipment, hiring one-on-one aids, modifying tests, providing alternate forms of communication, relocating services in more accessible areas, altering existing facilities, and constructing new facilities (Henderson, 1995).

The ADA does not delineate specific due process procedures; however, IDEA and Section 504 do. Section 504 and IDEA require local educational agencies (LEAs) to provide hearings for parents who disagree with the identification, evaluation, or placement of a child. With the passage of the 1997 Amendments to IDEA, parents and LEAs or state educational agencies (SEAs) are strongly encouraged to participate in voluntary mediation to resolve disputes prior to conducting due process hearings. According to the ADA, individuals with disabilities who are discriminated against in an educational setting have the same recourse that is available under Title VII of the Civil Rights Act of 1964, as amended in 1991. Individuals may file complaints with the OCR or sue in federal court. The OCR encourages informal mediation and voluntary compliance (Henderson, 1995). However, administrative remedies do not have to be exhausted prior to filing a lawsuit (28 C.F.R. § 35.172). Federal funds may be removed from schools for noncompliance with the ADA mandates, and individuals with disabilities may be awarded attorney fees if they prevail in any action filed under the ADA (28 C.F.R. § 35.175).

Title II, Subtitle A of the ADA is the section of the statute pertaining to public schools. The statute prohibits discrimination against any "qualified individual with a disability." The ADA's definition of an *individual with a disability* is essentially the same as Section 504's definition. The ADA definition of a *disability* consists of three prongs. The ADA defines a *disability*, with respect to an individual, as "a physical or mental impairment that substantially limits one or more of the major life activities of such individual, a record of such an impairment, or being regarded as having such an impairment" (42 U.S.C. § 12102 [2]).

The first prong of the ADA definition, which is a physical or mental impairment, includes physiological disorders, cosmetic disfigurement, or anatomical loss that affects body systems as well as mental or psychological disorders (28 C.F.R. § 35.104 [1][i]). Examples of physical or mental impairments under the ADA definition of a *disability* are epilepsy; muscular dystrophy; multiple sclerosis;

cancer; heart disease; diabetes; intellectual disability; emotional illness; specific learning disabilities; drug addiction; HIV disease (symptomatic or asymptomatic); alcoholism; and orthopedic, visual, speech, and hearing impairments (OCR, 1996). The preceding examples are not an exhaustive list of physical and mental impairments under the ADA definition of a *disability*.

Another key concept in the ADA definition of a *disability* is "a substantial limitation in a major life activity." A major life activity refers to a basic activity that the "average person performs with little or no difficulty" such as walking, speaking, seeing, breathing, working, and learning (28 C.F.R. § 35.104). A person who has a substantial limitation that is determined by the nature, severity, duration, and long-term or permanent impact of the impairment on a major life activity is protected under the ADA (OCR, 1996).

In the second prong, a person with a record or history of an impairment that substantially limits a major life activity also meets the ADA's definition of an *individual with a disability* (28 C.F.R. § 35.104 [3]). Examples include a person who has a history of a mental or emotional illness, drug addiction, alcoholism, heart disease, or cancer. An individual who has been misclassified as having an impairment (such as a person misdiagnosed as being intellectually disabled or emotionally disturbed) is also protected under the ADA (OCR, 1996).

The third prong of the definition of a *disability* under ADA protects a person who has an impairment that does or does not substantially limit a major life activity but is perceived by the public or public entity as being substantially limiting (28 C.F.R. § 35.104 [13]). For example, a girl who walks with a limp but is not substantially limited in her ability to walk is not allowed to participate on the school's soccer team out of fear by school personnel that she will be injured. Under the ADA, the third prong of the definition of an *individual with a disability* applies and thus protects the girl. The third prong of the definition of a *disability* also protects an individual who does not have an impairment but who the public or public entity perceives as having an impairment (28 C.F.R. § 35.104 [3]).

An individual who is covered under the second or third prong of ADA's definition of a *disability* is not necessarily entitled to special education and related services or regular education with supplementary services. If a student is protected under the second or third prong, but not under the first prong, then the student is not eligible for special education and related services. For example, if a student has an Attention Deficit Disorder (ADD) but is performing well in the classroom, then an evaluation for special education and related services at the present time is not needed. On the other hand, if a student's mental or physical impairment substantially limits the student's ability to learn in the classroom, then the student would be entitled to an evaluation, and special education and related services or regular education with supplementary services may follow (OCR, 1996).

Title II and Section 504 use the three-prong definition of a *disability*, whereas IDEA uses the 13 recognized disability categories and the *need* criteria. In other words, there must be a need for special education and related services. Based on these differences in the definition of a *disability*, there may be some students who qualify for regular or special education and related services under Section 504 and Title II but do not have one of the 13 disabilities recognized by IDEA (OCR, 1996).

Protection under Title II, Subtitle A is afforded to qualified individuals with disabilities. An individual with a disability is qualified to receive services or participate in an elementary and secondary education program if the student meets the eligibility requirements of a qualified individual with a disability established under Section 504. As previously mentioned, Title II incorporates the more specific details and standards in Section 504. A qualified individual with a disability is an individual who has a disability and is of the appropriate age (school-aged), and who, with or without reasonable modifications to rules, policies, or practices, the removal of architectural, communication, or transportation barriers, or the provision of auxiliary aids and services, meets the essential eligibility requirements for the receipt of services or the participation in programs or activities provided by a public entity (28 C.F.R. § 35.104).

Parents or other associates of a student who are disabled themselves and who are invited to attend a school event or choose to participate in a school event open to the public are also qualified as individuals with disabilities and are protected under the ADA. Under these circumstances, the school district must ensure program accessibility and provide auxiliary aids and services to ensure effective communication for these individuals with disabilities. For example, if a parent is deaf and is invited to attend a parent-teacher conference for his or her child, who may or may not be a student with a disability under the ADA, then the school is responsible for providing an interpreter at the parent's request in order for the parent to participate in the meeting (OCR, 1996).

Title II also extends protection to, but does not provide accommodations for, an individual who is not disabled but who assists or lives with someone with a disability (28 C.F.R. § 35.130 [g]). Family members, friends, or any other person or entity who associates with an individual with a disability are protected under this federal regulation. Likewise, Title II extends protection to an individual with or without a disability who takes action to oppose any act or practice prohibited by the statute or assists or encourages others to exercise their rights under the ADA regulations (28 C.F.R. § 35.134). For example, if an educator encourages a family to exercise their rights under the ADA regarding a school policy, then the educator and the family, including the individual with the disability, are protected under ADA from any coercion or retaliation from the school district.

To bring a school district into compliance with the ADA statute, five action steps must be taken by the district. First, the school district must designate a responsible employee to coordinate ADA compliance. Under Title II, if the school district has 50 or more employees, then at least one coordinator must be designated (28 C.F.R. § 35.107 [a]). The ADA coordinator's role includes planning and coordinating compliance efforts, implementing and ensuring completion of the five action steps, and receiving and investigating complaints of possible discrimination against individuals with disabilities. Second, the school district, regardless of size, must provide notice of the ADA requirements to all interested parties including participants, beneficiaries, employees, applicants, and the public. Specific information on how Title II requirements apply to particular programs, services, and activities must be included (28 C.F.R. § 35.106). Appropriate methods to disseminate this information include publications, public posters, or media broadcast. The most effective methods for making people aware of their rights and protections under the ADA, however, are determined by the head of the school district or delegated to the ADA coordinator. Third, school districts with 50 or more employees must adopt and publish grievance procedures providing for prompt and equitable resolution of complaints alleging violations of the ADA (28 C.F.R. § 35.107). These grievance procedures are available to school district employees, students, or the public. Fourth, every school district, regardless of size, must conduct a self-evaluation of its policies and practices, including communications and employment, and correct any inconsistencies in its policies and practices in relation to the ADA statute (28 C.F.R. § 35.105 [a]). However, if the school district has received federal funding and has conducted a self-evaluation as required under Section 504, then only those programs and new or modified policies or practices since the Section 504 self-evaluation must be reviewed and corrections made to be consistent with the ADA regulations (28 C.F.R. § 35.105 [c]). School districts should have completed Title II self-evaluations by January 26, 1993 (28 C.F.R. § 35.105 [c]) for current programs, policies, and practices in existence at that time. Fifth, a transition plan must be developed to bring existing facilities into structural compliance with the ADA statute. A transition plan is needed to ensure that programs, services, or activities are accessible to individuals with disabilities (28 C.F.R. § 35.150 [di [1]). Structural changes outlined in the transition plan should have been completed by January 26, 1995 for existing facilities (28 C.F.R. § 35.150 [c]).

Nondiscrimination requirements are used to analyze the policies, programs, and practices of a public school district. Specific nondiscrimination requirements imposed on a school district under Section 504 are applicable under Title II. According to Section 504, a school district is obligated to provide a free, appropriate public education (FAPE) to school-aged children with disabilities. The school district's responsibilities are specifically described under Section 504 and are incorporated into the general provisions of Title II (28 C.F.R. § 35.130; 28 C.F.R. § 35.103 [a]; see 34 C.F.R. §§ 104.31-104.37).

Title II also requires a school district to ensure that qualified individuals with disabilities are not excluded from participation in or denied any benefits from the district's programs, services, or activities based on their disability (28 C.F.R. § 35.130 [a]). This requirement applies to programs, services, and activities operated or provided directly by the district as well as those operated or provided by another entity on behalf of the district under contractual agreement or other arrangements (28 C.F.R. § 35.130 [h]). For example, if a student with a disability is excluded from bus service by a private school bus company that is under contract with the school district to provide this service, then the school district would be liable for the alleged discriminatory act under Title II (OCR, 1996).

The school district must also ensure that qualified individuals with disabilities have an equal opportunity to participate in the district's programs as do nondisabled individuals. Likewise, individuals with disabilities must have an equal opportunity to benefit from any aids, benefits, or services provided by the school district as do nondisabled individuals. For example, if a student with a severe visual impairment is evaluated and it is determined, in order to provide FAPE, visual aids and services must be provided, and the school district refuses to pay for the visual aids, citing expenses, then under these circumstances, the school district is in violation of Title II standards because the district has denied related aids and services to the student. As a result, the student does not have an equal opportunity as does a nondisabled student to participate in or receive benefits from the school program (OCR, 1996). Similarly, a school district's benefits and services must be effective enough to afford equal opportunity to obtain the same results, benefits, or levels of achievement for both individuals with and without disabilities.

Under Title II, a school district may not operate different or separate programs or provide different or separate benefits or services, unless the programs, benefits, or services are needed to provide equal benefits to individuals with disabilities (28 C.F.R. § 35.103 [a]; 28 C.F.R. § 35.130 [b1[1] [iv]). If separate or different programs, services, or benefits are needed, then the school district must provide them in the most integrated setting for individuals with disabilities (28 C.F.R. § 35.103 [a]; 28 C.F.R. § 35.130 [d]). However, in the establishment of separate or different programs, services, or benefits, individuals with disabilities may not be denied participation in the regular programs or access to regular benefits and services.

Another nondiscrimination requirement under Title II includes the prohibition of surcharges. A school district is

not allowed to place a surcharge on an individual with a disability to cover the costs of measures that are necessary to provide nondiscriminatory treatment (28 C.F.R. § 35.130 [f]). For example, if an evaluation is conducted and it is determined that a student with a disability should be placed in a regular education program with related aids and services, including a computer, then the school district cannot charge the student or his or her parents for the use of the computer as the computer is a necessary aid in order to provide FAPE. Similarly, modifications that would fundamentally alter a specific benefit, program, service, or activity are prohibited. On the other hand, if failure to modify a specific benefit, program, service, or activity results in the denial of FAPE, then the school district must make modifications. However, a school district is not required to provide a personal device, such as a wheelchair, or service of a personal nature, such as toileting, unless the device or service is necessary to provide FAPE to the student.

Nondiscriminatory requirements also apply to eligibility criteria. A school district may not use eligibility criteria to screen out individuals with disabilities from participation in its programs or receipt of its benefits or services (28 C.F.R. § 35.103 [a]; 28 C.F.R. § 35.130 [b][8]). However, a school has the right to impose legitimate safety requirements needed for the safe operation of its services, benefits, or programs, but these safety requirements must be based on actual risks, not stereotypes. For example, if a school offers a course in scuba diving and demonstrates that a certain level of swimming ability is needed for safe participation in the class, then those individuals who cannot pass a swimming test, including some individuals with disabilities, could be screened out without violating the law (OCR, 1996).

Besides nondiscriminatory requirements, a school district must ensure that their programs, services, and activities are accessible to individuals with disabilities. This includes not only students, but also parents, guardians, and members of the public with disabilities. According to Title II, two standards are used to determine program accessibility. One standard deals with existing facilities and the other standard deals with new construction and alterations. For existing facilities, when viewed in their entirety, the program or activity must be accessible to and usable by individuals with disabilities, unless a fundamental alteration in the program or undue financial or administrative burden would result (28 C.F.R. § 35.130). The burden of proof, according to Title II, is placed on the school district. For new or altered facilities, the same standard applies; however, the fundamental alteration or undue burden is not applicable.

Based on the program accessibility standard, numerous misconceptions have evolved, such as the view that buildings must be completely accessible and barrier free. As long as the program, class, or function is accessible, Title II does not require that existing buildings offer a barrier-free environment. In other words, if the program can be held in another classroom or building, and this classroom or building meets accessibility requirements, then the school district's fundamental alteration in the program is in compliance with the standards set forth under Title II (OCR, 1996).

In addition to program accessibility requirements, transition services are also addressed under Title II as well as Title III of ADA. Transition services are defined as "a set of coordinated activities that promote movement from school to postschool activities" (Jacob-Timm & Hartshorne, 1995, p. 379). Transition services for youth with disabilities are provided in more specific details under IDEA. The enactment of the ADA is expected to lead to the expansion of opportunities for youth with disabilities in their transition to postschool activities (American Council on Education, 1993). Postschool activities may include vocational training, continuing education, integrated employment, independent living, community participation, and postsecondary education.

For postsecondary education, the enactment of the ADA has translated into renewed attention focused on disability access to facilities and programs as well as employment and promotion issues. In addition, the ADA has resulted in a greater number of opportunities for students with disabilities due to increased access to employment, public accommodations, transportation, and telecommunications. Thus, an expanded pool of qualified college-educated disabled workers is expected in the future to address anticipated manpower shortages in the next decade (American Council on Education, 1993).

Numerous implications exist for education officials under Title II. First, local agencies may witness an increase in the number of requests for public hearings to determine student eligibility for special education. A potential increase in the number of students served may occur. Second, parents and other adults' requests to participate in school activities may increase. Because public schools offer programs and opportunities to the community, many adults with disabilities may desire greater participation due to the enactment of the statute. As a result, the public school's responsibilities may increase in meeting program accessibility, service, and benefit requirements. Third, the ADA encourages full participation in society of individuals with disabilities. Thus, parents' requests for their children with disabilities to participate in school activities (e.g., athletic events, field trips, recreational offerings, etc.) may increase, and transportation issues will also need to be addressed (NASDSE, 1992).

The implementation of the ADA has expanded the role of the schools in the preparation of students with disabilities to take full advantage of employment opportunities, to participate more fully in school programs, to achieve greater independence through the use of public transportation, and to learn and to communicate more effectively through the use of telecommunication systems (First & Curcio, 1993). The ADA encourages the education system to become more actively involved in the lives of individuals with disabilities and to assist in the empowerment of students with disabilities. Educators and parents are challenged to bring real meaning into the lives of students with disabilities and to the school environment, not only for the students' benefit, but also for the benefit of all people.

REFERENCES

American Council on Education. (1993). *Americans with Disabilities* (Report No. H030C3002-94). Washington, DC: HEATH Resource Center. (ERIC Reproduction Document Service No. ED 381 919)

Americans with Disabilities Act of 1990, 28 C.F.R. § 35; 34 C.F.R. §§ 104.31–404.37 (1993).

Americans with Disabilities Act of 1990, 42 U.S.C. § 12101 *et seq.* (West 1994).

Burgdorf, R. L. (1991). The Americans with Disabilities Act: Analysis and implications of a second-generation civil rights statute. *Harvard Civil Rights—Civil Liberties Law Review, 26*, 413–522.

Cunconan-Lahr, R. (1991). *The Americans with Disabilities Act: Educational implications and policy considerations.* (ERIC Document Reproduction Service No. ED 333 665)

First, P. F., & Curcio, J. L. (1993). *Individuals with disabilities: Implementing the newest laws.* Newbury Park, CA: Corwin.

Henderson, K. (1995). *Overview of ADA, IDEA, and Section 504* (Report No. EDO-EC-94-8). Washington, DC: Office of Educational Research and Improvement. (ERIC Document Reproduction Service No. ED 389 142)

Jacob-Timm, S., & Hartshorne, T. (1995). *Ethics and law for school psychologists.* Brandon, VT: Clinical Psychology.

National Association of State Directors of Special Education (NASDSE). (1992). The Americans with Disabilities Act: New challenges and opportunities for school administrators. *Liaison Bulletin, 18*(4), 1–11.

Office of Civil Rights (OCR). (1996). *Compliance with the Americans with Disabilities Act: A self-evaluation guide for public elementary and secondary schools.* Washington, DC: U.S. Government Printing Office.

PATRICIA A. LOWE
CECIL R. REYNOLDS
Texas A&M University
Second edition

KIMBERLEY F. APPLEQUIST
University of Colorado at Colorado Springs
Third edition

See also Architectural Barriers; Individuals With Disabilities Education Improvement Act of 2004 (IDEIA); Rehabilitation Act of 1973, Section 504

AMES LOUISE BATES (1908–1996)

Born in Portland, Maine, Louise Ames received her BA in 1930 from the University of Maine. She then went on to receive her MA in 1933 and PhD in 1937 in experimental psychology from Yale University, where she studied with Arnold Gesell. Her relationship with Gesell resulted in the founding of the Gesell Institute in 1950, a project where Dr. Ames collaborated with Dr. Frances Ilg and Dr. Janet Learner. Ames was also an instructor. She was assistant professor at Yale Medical School (1936–1950) and curator of the Yale Films of Child Development (1944–1950).

Working with Frances Ilg and Arnold Gesell, Dr. Ames developed the important developmental theory that patterned, predictable behaviors are associated with chronological age, with the explicit implication that human development unfolded in discrete, recognizable stages. Such ideas were relatively novel at the time and have had great impact since their development. Her career interests and research in the behavior and development of normal children resulted in the development of standard references for psychologists working with children, and served to educate nonprofessionals as well through its coverage by the popular media.

Dr. Ames' greatest impact was in teaching parents and teachers about the course of child development, primarily through her prolific publications, which included *Infant and Child in the Culture of Today* (1940), *School Readiness* (1956), the syndicated newspaper column "Child Behavior" in collaboration with her colleagues (which later became a weekly half-hour television show in the 1950s), *Child Behavior* (1981), and *Don't Rush Your Preschooler* (1980), coauthored with her daughter Joan Ames Chase. Ames also had a strong interest in projective assessment and provided normative data in *Child Rorschach Responses* (1974). This interest extended to assessment of the elderly (*Rorschach Responses in Old Age*) and a series of articles developing test batteries for assessing deterioration of functions in old age.

Over her long career, Dr. Ames authored some 300 articles and monographs, coauthored/collaborated on 25 books, and received honorary degrees and many awards for service. One of the most publicized women in psychology, Louise Bates Ames died of cancer in November, 1996, at the age of 88.

REFERENCES

Ames, L. B. (1940). *Infant and child in the culture of today.* New York, NY: Harper & Row.

Ames, L. B. (1974). *Child Rorschach responses.* New York, NY: Brunner/Mazel.

Ames, L. B. (1981). *Child behavior.* New York, NY: Harper Perennial.

Ames, L. B., & Chase, J. A. (1980). *Don't rush your preschooler.* New York, NY: Harper & Row.

Ames, L. B., & Ilg, F. (1956). *School readiness.* New York, NY: Harper & Row.

Ames, L. B., Metraux, R. W., Rodell, J. L., & Walker, R. W. (1973). *Rorschach responses in old age.* New York, NY: Brunner/Mazel.

ELAINE FLETCHER-JANZEN
Chicago School of Professional Psychology
First edition
Third edition

KAY E. KETZENBERGER
The University of Texas of the Permian Basin
Second edition

AMNESIA

Amnesia is a disorder of memory that occurs in the absence of gross disorientation, confusion, or dementia. Amnesia may be retrograde, where the individual has difficulty remembering events and information learned prior to the onset of the amnesia, or it may be anterograde, where the individual is unable to learn new information from the point of onset of the amnesia. Amnesics do not have difficulty with immediate memory. Digit span and immediate repetition are intact. Rather, individuals with amnesia are unable to remember after a delay filled with interference.

Amnesia is fascinating because observation of amnesics may help us understand how new information is learned (e.g., what brain structures are involved and what processes facilitate new learning). Amnesics are also of interest because the sense of continuity and time passing, remembering experiences, and hence, self-identity (Walton, 1977) depend on continuous access to information about the remote and recent past. The difficulties that amnesic patients encounter in awareness of their own experiences emphasizes just how important memory is.

Amnesia as an isolated neurologic symptom can be mistaken for a psychiatric disorder (DeJong, Itabashi, & Olson, 1969). There are hysterical amnesias that are a consequence of psychiatric distress alone. Fugue states are 20 dissociative episodes during which an individual forgets his or her identity and past. Hysterical amnesia is discriminable from neurologic conditions causing amnesia in that the total loss of self-identity rarely occurs in neurologically based amnesias, and because the end of the fugue state is abrupt. In the neurologically based amnesias that remit, the cessation of memory loss is gradual, with the period of time for which the individual is amnesic shrinking only gradually.

Transient amnesia is a known consequence of electroconvulsive therapy (ECT shock treatment). Individuals receiving ECT have both retrograde amnesia for events occurring just prior to treatment, and anterograde amnesia for what happens subsequent to treatment. When compared with their own performance after recovery from amnesia, patients who are amnesic after receiving ECT forget more easily and at an abnormal rate (Squire, 1981). This suggests a deficit in consolidation and elaboration of memory. There is some disagreement as to whether memory loss secondary to ECT is cumulative. Transient amnesia also may occur when an individual receives general anesthesia.

Anterograde amnesia that gradually remits is a frequent occurrence after closed head injuries (Levin, Benton, & Grossman, 1982; Reynolds & Fletcher-Janzen, 1997). There often is a more limited retrograde amnesia for the period just prior to the injury. Anterograde amnesia secondary to closed head injury (also called posttraumatic amnesia) is a good index of the severity of the injury and useful in the prediction of long-term recovery. After the amnesia has remitted, there is often a residual memory disorder.

Transient global amnesia is a neurologic condition that is now assumed to be a consequence of transient ischemia (Heathfield, Croft, & Swash, 1973). The presentation of an individual with transient global amnesia is characteristic. There is an abrupt onset of amnesia, both retrograde and anterograde, with perhaps only initial, mild clouding of consciousness, and no change in cognition or speech. Episodes typically last for several hours only, and the retrograde amnesia gradually shrinks, leaving individuals amnesic only for the period during which they had anterograde amnesia (Hecaen & Albert, 1978).

Amnesia is the hallmark of Korsakoff's disease (an entirely adult disease induced by alcohol consumption). Patients with Korsakoff's have a profound anterograde amnesia. Though immediate repetition is intact, remembering what they have been told after an interference (e.g., a brief conversation) is impossible. Patients hospitalized with Korsakoff's often reintroduce themselves to their physicians when the physician who has been caring for them reenters the room after a short interval. Korsakoff's patients are notable for their tendency to confabulate (i.e., fill in the blanks in their memory with imaginary accounts). The most common etiology of Korsakoff's is thiamine deficiency as a consequence of alcoholism. Head injury, anoxia, carbon monoxide poisoning, tumors, and other pathologies involving the same brain structure are other causes of the disorder (Walton, 1977).

A great deal has been learned about amnesia and memory through the study of groups of patients with unremitting forms of amnesia: amnesia secondary to Korsakoff's syndrome, amnesia secondary to neurosurgery for control of epilepsy, traumatic brain lesions resulting in amnesia, and generalized dementing processes (especially Huntington's disease and Alzheimer's disease) in which memory deficits are disproportionately problematic (at least during specific stages of the disease). Careful investigation of

these patients clearly reveals that though the average clinician thinks of memory as a unitary phenomenon, memory loss is a multidimensional symptom with different etiologies resulting in characteristic, discriminable patterns of memory loss and skill (Butters, 1984). One pattern of amnesia reflects hemispheric differences. Individuals with amnesia secondary to isolated damage to the right hemisphere have deficient skills in nonverbal memory when the information is presented visually. Those amnesic secondary to isolated left hemisphere damage have greater difficulty with verbal memory. Verbal memory deficits are seen regardless of the sensory modality used to present the information; for example, visual presentation of verbal information (Hecaen & Albert, 1978).

The pattern of retrograde amnesia is not the same across all amnesic populations. Butters (1984) compared remote memory functioning in Huntington's disease, Korsakoff's disease, and normal subjects by assessing their ability to recall famous people and events from past decades. Korsakoff's patients had more severe difficulties recalling past events, but there was a normal gradation in their ability to remember, with events that occurred further in the past recalled better than more recent past experiences. The Huntington's disease patients demonstrated a flat pattern. They were equally unable to remember any past event. This pattern of remote recollection occurs across the stages of Huntington's disease, though the severity increases as the disease progresses.

Amnesic patients of differing etiologies demonstrate differential responses to manipulations aimed at facilitating memory. For example, Korsakoff's amnesics are assisted in memorization by increasing rehearsal time, intertrial rest intervals, and a structured orientation procedure. They are not aided, however, by the provision of verbal mediation. Conversely, Huntington's disease patients are not assisted as are Korsakoff's patients; neither increased rehearsal time, increased intertrial intervals, nor does general orientation aid their performance. They are assisted, however, by verbal mediation. Patients with Alzheimer's disease are not assisted by verbal mediation.

Another difference between amnesic syndromes is related to the ability to acquire procedural versus declarative memories (Squire, 1982). Declarative memory pertains to specific facts and data. Procedural memory refers to the rules for completing a specific type of task. Studies of amnesic patients indicate that patients with amnesia secondary to Korsakoff's disease acquire procedural information but have great difficulty in learning declarative data. Huntington's disease patients do not remember procedural rules, but do learn (or at least recognize) previously presented data of a declarative type.

The study of patient populations with known etiologies has been useful in increasing our understanding of what brain structures are involved in the elaboration and retrieval of memory. Evidence from neurosurgical intervention to control severe epilepsy has demonstrated that damage to the medial aspects of both temporal lobes, especially the hippocampus, results in profound amnesia (Hecaen & Albert, 1978; Squire, 1982). This amnesia is distinguished by rapid and abnormal forgetting. Other amnesics appear to have diencephalic damage with some disagreement as to exactly which structures are affected. The mammillary bodies and dorsal-medial nucleus of the thalamus are involved, though the relative contributions of either structure are not known. Damage to the dorsal-medial nucleus appears sufficient to cause amnesia (Squire, 1982). Amnesia secondary to diencephalic damage is notable for a normal forgetting curve, but difficulty with encoding. Identification of structures involved in memory is useful not only in terms of understanding specific syndromes, but also in considering pharmacologic manipulations to assist in treatment.

With the exception of posttraumatic amnesia, amnesia in its pure form is not reported to occur in children. Subsequent to head injuries, children do exhibit posttraumatic amnesia and have difficulty learning new information in school and remembering what they learned just prior to their injuries. Consequently, they will be confused in the school setting. Posttraumatic amnesia generally will remit. Such children should be allowed to recover after their injuries (with the most rapid recovery occurring in the first 6 months; Pompa, 2003) without the expectation that by studying harder they will remember significantly better. Once the major recovery period is over (after 6 to 9 months), cognitive rehabilitation programs aimed at providing strategies to assist in memory may be useful. There are limited data available on how generalizable the effect of cognitive rehabilitation is in the adult population, and less data regarding children.

It should be clear that the short-term memory impairments described in the learning of disabled children bear little resemblance to amnesic disorders. Amnesic patients are capable of short-term memory performance. Children with severe brain injury may become amnesic, but it is most often within the context of general dementia with difficulties in a variety of areas.

REFERENCES

Butters, N. (1984). The clinical aspects of memory disorders: Contributions from experimental studies of amnesia and dementia. *Journal of Clinical Neuropsychology, 6*, 17–36.

DeJong, R. N., Itabashi, H. H., & Olson, J. R. (1969). Memory loss due to hippocampal lesion. *Archives of Neurology, 20*, 339–348.

Heathfield, K. W. G., Croft, P. B., & Swash, M. (1973). The syndrome of transient global amnesia. *Brain, 96*, 729–731.

Hecaen, H., & Albert, M. L. (1978). *Human neuropsychology.* New York, NY: Wiley.

Levin, H. S., Benton, A. L., & Grossman, R. G. (1982). *Neurobehavioral consequences of closed head injury.* New York, NY: Oxford University Press.

Milner, B., Corkin, S., & Teuber, H. L. (1968). Further analysis of the hippocampal amnesic syndrome: A 14-year follow-up study of H.M. *Neuropsychologia, 6*, 215–234.

Pompa, J. (2003). Amnesia. In E. Fletcher-Janzen & C. R. Reynolds (Eds.), *Childhood disorders diagnostic desk reference* (pp. 34–35). Hoboken, NJ: Wiley.

Reynolds, C. R., & Fletcher-Janzen, E. (Eds.). (1997). *Handbook of clinical child neuropsychology.* New York, NY: Plenum Press.

Squire, L. (1981). Two forms of human amnesia: An analysis of forgetting. *Journal of Neurosciences, 1*, 635–640.

Squire, L. (1982). The neuropsychology of human memory. *Annual Review of Neurosciences, 5*, 241–273.

Walton, J. N. (1977). *Brain's diseases of the nervous system.* Oxford, UK: Oxford University Press.

GRETA N. WILKENING
Children's Hospital

See also Memory Disorders; Traumatic Brain Injury

AMNIOCENTESIS

Amniocentesis is the sampling of amniotic fluid surrounding a fetus. A physician anesthetizes a small area of the pregnant woman's abdomen, inserts a small needle through the abdominal wall, and, with the aid of ultrasonography, enters the amniotic sac and removes 20 ml (approximately 1 oz) of fluid. It is performed most frequently between 15 and 18 weeks gestation to detect hereditary disease or congenital defects in the fetus. One disadvantage is that analysis of the fluid takes 2 to 4 weeks. Damage to the fetus also may occur, but the risk is small—.06% or 1 in 1600 (Eddleman, Malone, & Sullivan, 2006; March of Dimes, 2005).

Midtrimester amniocentesis plays an important role in genetic and other prenatal counseling by providing potential parents with reproductive options. It should be considered when the pregnant woman is over 35, or a family history of genetic or congenital disorders is apparent (Kaback, 1979; March of Dimes, 2005). Cytogenetic analysis of fetal fluid leads to prevention of birth of approximately 15,000 chromosomally abnormal infants each year in the United States alone (Pritchard, MacDonald, & Gant, 1985).

Amniocentesis allows identification of about 300 chromosomal, single-gene, and other congenital abnormalities (Pritchard et al., 1985). The list grows with the discovery of new markers. Chromosomally based disorders are identified through karyotyping and resultant abnormal appearance of one or more chromosomes; other disorders are identified through elevated or reduced levels of particular substances. Among the disorders that can be reliably diagnosed are (a) all chromosomally based disorders such as Down syndrome and cri du chat; (b) about 75 inborn errors of metabolism, including galactosemia, Tay-Sachs disease, and Lesch-Nyhan syndrome (X-linked), but not phenylketonuria; (c) some central nervous system defects including meningocele (a form of spina bifida) and anencephaly; (d) some fetal infections (cytomegalovirus, herpes simplex, and rubella); (e) and some hematologic disorders (e.g., sickle-cell anemia; Pritchard et al., 1985).

The widespread availability of amniocentesis forces many women to confront the decision to terminate an advanced pregnancy. Attachment grows throughout pregnancy, and confronting the decision of choosing termination at a late stage can be emotionally painful (Brewster, 1984). Many women are unprepared for the anxiety associated with both waiting several weeks for results of their amniocentesis and choosing between life and quality of life. Optimally, women in high-risk groups should weigh this decision and discuss other reproductive options with a genetic counselor prior to conception. Some counselors suggest that health caregivers be sensitive to pregnant women's emotional reactions and not use measures such as a doppler to hear the fetus's heartbeat or ultrasonography to take pictures of the fetus, that promote maternal attachment prior to amniocentesis (Brewster, 1984).

A new diagnostic technique, chorion-villus biopsy, usable as early as 8 weeks gestation, may be preferable in some cases, but risks include 1 in 100 pregnancies being at risk for miscarriage.

REFERENCES

Brewster, A. (1984). After office hours: A patient's reaction to amniocentesis. *Obstetrics & Gynecology*, *64*, 443–444.

Eddleman, K. A., Malone, F. D., & Sullivan, L. (2006). Pregnancy loss rates after midtrimester amniocentesis. *Obstet Gynecol*, *108*(5), 1067–72. doi:10.1097/01.AOG.0000240135.13594.07. PMID 17077226.

Kaback, M. M. (1979). Predictors of hereditary diseases or congenital defects in antenatal diagnosis (National Institute of Child Health and Human Development, U.S. Department of HEW, NIH Publication No. 79-1973). *Antenatal Diagnosis*, 39–42.

March of Dimes. (2005). *What's inside*. Retrieved from http://www.marchofdimes.com/pnhec/159_520.asp

Pritchard, J. A., MacDonald, C., & Gant, N. F. (Eds.). (1985). *Williams obstetrics* (17th ed., pp. 267–293). Englewood Cliffs, NJ: Appleton-Century-Crofts.

BRENDA M. POPE
New Hanover Memorial Hospital

See *also* Chronic Villus Sampling; Genetic Counseling; Inborn Errors of Metabolism

AMPHETAMINE PSYCHOSIS

Amphetamine psychosis results from the neurochemical and behavioral interaction of large doses of amphetamines. The toxic reaction, induced by chronic amphetamine abuse or by an acute overdose, leads to transitory symptoms that are clinically indistinguishable from those of paranoid schizophrenia. Such symptoms, occurring as early as 36 to 48 hours after a large dosage, include vivid auditory, visual, and tactile hallucinations, changes in affect, loosening of associations with reality, and paranoid thought processes (Gilman, Goodman, & Gilman, 1980). Affected individuals may also show behavioral stereotypes such as continuous rocking or polishing motions, repetitive grooming activities (rubbing or picking of the skin), and other locomotor irregularities. Biochemical correlates of amphetamine psychosis, including increased dopaminergic activity, are similar to those of schizophrenia (Kokkinidis & Anisman, 1980).

In addition to reducing amphetamine intake, treatment includes sedatives, psychotherapy, and custodial care. Acidification of the urine will speed excretion of the amphetamines. The psychotic state usually clears in about a week after beginning treatment, with hallucinations being the first symptom to disappear (American Medical Association, 1980). However, some confusion, memory loss, and delusional ideas commonly persist for months (Merck, 2005).

REFERENCES

American Medical Association. (1980). *AMA drug evaluations* (4th ed.). New York, NY: Wiley.

Gilman, A. G., Goodman, L. S., & Gilman, A. (1980). *Goodman and Gilman's pharmacological basis of therapeutics* (6th ed.). New York, NY: Macmillan.

Kokkinidis, L., & Anisman, H. (1980). Amphetamine models of paranoid schizophrenia: An overview and elaboration of animal experimentation. *Psychological Bulletin*, *88*, 551–579.

Merck Manual. (2005). *Amphetamine dependence*. Retrieved from http://www.merck.com/mrkshared/mmanual/section15/chapter195/195g.jsp

VICKI BARTOSIK
Stanford University

See *also* Childhood Schizophrenia; Drug Abuse; LSD; Psychotropic Drugs

AMSLAN (See American Sign Language)

AMYOPLASIA CONGENITAL DISRUPTIVE SEQUENCE (ARTHROGRYPOSIS MULTIPLEX CONGENITAL)

Amyoplasia congenital disruptive sequence (ACDS) is a congenital neuromuscular disease. Patients with ACDS are born with markedly diminished muscle mass and multiple joint contractures that are generally symmetrical. These malformations usually affect all four extremities, but they may involve only the arms or only the legs.

The etiology of ACDS is unclear. One plausible explanation for this unique set of anomalies is poor blood flow to the developing fetal spinal cord.

The occurrence of this disorder is sporadic. Its frequency is higher than expected in identical twins, although only one of the pair is affected. This disorder is considered rare; however, more than 500 case reports of ACDS have appeared in the medical literature.

Characteristics

1. Diminished muscle mass and severe, symmetrical joint contractures present at birth.
2. Round face, small jaw, small upturned nose.
3. Rounded, sloping shoulders with decreased muscle mass.
4. Elbows are fully extended. Severe contractures of the wrists, hands and fingers are usually present.
5. Lower extremity findings include fixed dislocation of the hips and bilateral clubfoot.
6. The spine is usually straight and stiff, but scoliosis is common as children age.

Therapy for ACDS patients requires multiple orthopedic procedures to obtain the best functional results. With good physical therapy, almost all of these individuals become ambulatory and self-supportive. However, treatment must be started early to mobilize and strengthen what muscle mass there is. Casting and splinting may be necessary to correct clubfeet and knee contractures.

A child with ACDS may require modifications in the physical environment such as assistive devices or technology of the classroom to allow them to achieve their academic potential in light of their physical limitations. There is no research to support cognitive deficits. Providing a positive environment that builds good self-images will facilitate peer relationships.

The prognosis for this disorder is generally favorable. Intelligence is usually normal. There may be diminished bone growth in affected extremities. Occasionally the joint contractures worsen with age. However, with aggressive management of the orthopedic abnormalities, ACDS patients can achieve a considerable degree of self-sufficiency.

REFERENCES

Jones, K. (1997). *Smith's recognizable patterns of human malformations* (5th ed.). Philadelphia, PA: W. B. Saunders.

Thompson, G. H., & Scoles, P. V. (2000). Arthrogryposis. In R. E. Behrman, R. M. Kleigman, & H. B. Jenson (Eds.), *Nelson's textbook of pediatrics* (16th ed., pp. 2094–2095). Philadelphia, PA: W. B. Saunders.

BARRY H. DAVISON
Ennis, Texas

JOAN W. MAYFIELD
*Baylor Pediatric Specialty Services
Dallas, Texas*

ANASTASI, ANNE (1908–2001)

Anne Anastasi obtained her BA from Barnard College in 1928 and her PhD from Columbia University in 1930 at the age of 21. Influenced by H. L. Hollingworth and articles about early precursors of factor analysis by C. Spearman, Anastasi changed her orientation from mathematics to psychology. She also extended her study of individual differences to include major group differences. These changes began her association with the development of differential psychology. Her major areas of study are the nature and identification of psychological traits, test construction and evaluation, and interpretation of test results with specific reference to the role of cultural factors in individual and group differences.

Anastasi's publication of *Psychological Testing*, in the most recent edition, continues to stress the responsibility of the test administrator in selecting appropriate tests and methods of testing, interpreting test scores, and using and communicating test results. Other major publications include *Differential Psychology* and *Fields in Applied Psychology*. She has published more than 170 journal articles and monographs and was the only author who has contributed to every edition of the *Mental Measurements Yearbook* since its inception in 1938.

Anastasi received several honorary degrees and many awards such as the 1977 Educational Testing Service Award for Distinguished Service to Measurement, the E. L. Thorndike Award for Distinguished Psychological Contributions to Education (from APA Division 15), the American Psychological Association Distinguished Scientific Award for the Application of Psychology, the American Psychological Foundation Gold Medal, and the AERA award for Distinguished Contributions to Research in Education. In 1987 she was presented with the National Medal of Science by President Ronald Reagan. Anastasi was also professor emeritus at Fordham University and was esteemed as the third female president of the American Psychological Association. Anne Anastasi was known and seen by her peers as the most prominent woman in psychology up until her death in the year 2001.

REFERENCES

Anastasi, A., & Urbina, S. (1997). *Psychological testing* (7th ed.). Upper Saddle River, NJ: Prentice Hall.

Anastasi, A. (1979). *Fields of applied psychology* (2nd ed.). New York, NY: McGraw-Hill.

Anastasi, A. (1958). *Differential psychology* (3rd ed.). New York, NY: Macmillan.

ELAINE FLETCHER-JANZEN
Chicago School of Professional Psychology
First edition

DEBORAH B. GUILLEN
The University of Texas of the Permian Basin
Second edition

RACHEL M. TOPLIS
Falcon School District 49, Colorado Springs, Colorado
Third edition

ANASTASIOW, NICHOLAS J. (1924–   )

Though he retired as Thomas Hunter professor at Hunter College, City University of New York, in 1992, Nicholas Anastasiow maintains his principal interest in early childhood special education and child development. He began his career as an elementary school teacher in the early 1950s and garnered various educational certifications until he received his PhD in child development and guidance from Stanford University in 1963. In 1967, he completed postdoctoral courses in neurology at Columbia University.

Anastasiow believes that "many at-risk children can lead normal lives when they are provided remediation as well as support and education for their parents" (personal communication, August 2, 1985). This belief is well represented in the 200 articles, reports, and books he has published on a vast array of subjects such as language development. Some of his titles are *Language and Reading Strategies for Poverty Children* (Anastasiow, Hanes, & Hanes, 1982), *The At-Risk Infant* (Harel & Anastasiow, 1984), and *Development and Disabilities* (Anastasiow, 1986). He currently has finished the 11th revision of the classic textbook *Educating Exceptional Children*, which he coauthors with Samuel Kirk and Jim Gallagher.

Anastasiow is also interested in the "prevention of at-risk children by educating future parents in knowledge of child development and the skills and strategies of parenting before they become parents" (personal communication, August 2, 1985). He has encouraged schools to establish child development courses for sixth and seventh graders in publications such as *The Adolescent Parent* (1982).

Anastasiow has served as a consultant to the Assistant Secretary on Human Development, the White House Conference on the Handicapped, and the President's Council for Exceptional Children—Early Childhood Division, and as an exchange delegate to the USSR.

REFERENCES

Anastasiow, N. J. (1982). *The adolescent parent*. Baltimore, MD: Brookes.

Anastasiow, N. J. (1986). *Development and disabilities*. Baltimore, MD: Brookes.

Anastasiow, N. J., Hanes, M. L., & Hanes, M. (1982). *Language and reading strategies for poverty children*. Austin, TX: PRO-ED.

Anastasiow, N. J., & Harel, S. (Eds.). (1993). *The at-risk infant*. Baltimore, MD: Brookes.

Harel, S., & Anastasiow, N. J. (Eds.). (1984). *The at-risk infant*. Baltimore, MD: Brookes.

ELAINE FLETCHER-JANZEN
Chicago School of Professional Psychology

ANDERSON, META L. (1878–1942)

Meta L. Anderson, while a teacher in the New York City public schools, enrolled in a course in the education of children with intellectual disabilities at "The Training School" at Vineland, New Jersey. There, Edward R. Johnstone and Henry H. Goddard, recognizing her unusual ability, recommended her to the Newark, New Jersey, Board of Education, which employed her to begin special classes for children with intellectual disabilities. In 1910 she established two special classes and Newark joined the handful of school systems that provided special programs for handicapped students.

Anderson developed an instructional approach based on careful analysis of the abilities and limitations of each student and devised trade classes and a work experience program to provide vocational preparation. Her book, *Education of Defectives in the Public Schools* (1917), described the program and added impetus to the growing special class movement in the United States. In the closing months of World War I, Anderson was appointed head of reconstruction aid in Europe. After the war she served for a year in Serbia. She returned to the Newark schools in

1920 to become director of the city's comprehensive special education program. She received her PhD from New York University in 1922. She served as president of the American Association on Mental Deficiency in 1941.

REFERENCES

Anderson, M. L. (1917). *Education of defectives in the public schools*. Yonkers, NY: World Book.

Whitney, E. A. (1953). Some stalwarts of the past. *American Journal of Mental Deficiency, 57,* 345–360.

PAUL IRVINE
Katonah, New York

ANEMIA, APLASTIC

There are various types of anemias that differ in severity and etiology (e.g., aplastic, sickle cell, and Fanconi). The first description of aplastic anemia was offered by Ehrlick in 1888 and later named by Vaquez in 1904 (Young, 1995). In general, aplastic anemia is the failure of bone marrow to reproduce new blood cells. Specifically, there is a low production of (a) red blood that carries the oxygen to all parts of the body, (b) white blood cells that help the body fight off infection, and (c) platelets that involve the controlling of bleeding by forming blood clots. Production of new blood is of critical importance because blood cells have very limited life spans (e.g., red about 120 days, platelets about 6 days, and white less than 24 hours). The diagnosis of aplastic anemia is usually done through blood and bone marrow tests, and as blood count decreases, severity and morbidity increase.

Aplastic anemia is a rare disorder; about 2 per 1 million individuals are diagnosed each year in the United States. The incidence of aplastic anemia varies; more cases are identified in Asia (e.g., Thailand about 4 per 1 million new cases each year) than on other continents. Both males and females are equally affected. Although the median age of onset is 20–25 years, newborns have been diagnosed with the disorder. The underlying etiology in about 50% of the cases is unknown, and the other known 50% may be due to physical or chemical damage to the bone marrow, viral infection, cytotoxic drugs used in chemotherapy, prescription and over-the-counter drugs, or heredity.

Characteristics

1. Fatigue
2. Bleeding of the mucous membranes
3. Headaches
4. Dizziness
5. Nausea
6. Shortness of breath
7. Heart palpitations
8. Underside of eyelids, nails, and lips may become very pale
9. May bruise easily
10. High risk for infection

Aplastic anemia is generally considered a medical emergency, and the individual is immediately hospitalized. In cases in which the cause is known, the cause is removed if possible, and the individual is given a transfusion. For more severe cases and for children, the first line of treatment is bone marrow transplantation. The bone marrow of one person is extracted and then grafted into the bone marrow of the affected individual; the ideal donor is a sibling.

If a sibling donor is not viable, other individuals in the family or community may potentially become donors. While waiting for a donor, the child may be given a blood transfusion (not from family or any potential donor) and is carefully monitored because such children are highly susceptible to infections. The transplantation is successful if the recipient's body does not reject the transplant and new blood is reproduced. If a donor cannot be found, treatment with immunosuppressant drugs is prescribed. Immunosuppressant drugs such as cyclosporine are often used with bone marrow transplantations to lessen the possibility of rejection (March & Gordon-Smith, 1998).

Children diagnosed with aplastic anemia may need special education services, including home-based tutoring and psychological services. They may be classified as Other Health Impaired. The classroom and school of the child may also need psychological services with a focus on supportive peer and family counseling.

In the past, for individuals with severe aplastic anemia, prognosis has been grim—about 30% to 50% of individuals died within 6 months of diagnosis. Therefore, research on aplastic anemia has focused on understanding the underlying physiological structure of the disorder and on developing new treatment protocols that can increase survival rate (Fouladi et al., 2000). For example, in an 8-year follow-up study of children with aplastic anemia treated with bone marrow transplant or a regiment of immunosuppressant drugs, the survival rate was 80% (Pitcher, Hann, Evans, & Veys, 1999). The educational or psychological effects of the diagnosis of aplastic anemia have not been adequately addressed in the literature.

REFERENCES

Aplastic Anemia Foundation of America. Retrieved from http://www.teteport.com/nonprofit/aafa

Aplastic Anemia & MDS International Foundation, Inc. Retrieved from http://www.aplastic.org

Fouladi, M., Herman, R., Rolland-Grinton, M., Jones-Wallace, D., Blanchette, V., Calderwood, S.,...Freedman, M. H. (2000). Improved survival in severe acquired aplastic anemia in childhood. *Bone Marrow Transplant*, *26*(11), 1149–1156.

March, J. C., & Gordon-Smith, E. C. (1998). Treatment options in severe aplastic anemia. *Lancet*, *351*(9119), 1830–1831.

Pitcher, L. A., Hann, I. M., Evans, J. P., & Veys, P. (1999). Improved prognosis for acquired aplastic anemia. *Archives of Disease in Childhood*, *80*(2), 158–166.

Young, N. S. (1995). Aplastic anemia. *Lancet*, *346*(8969), 228–238.

AGNES E. SHINE
Barry University

DARRELL L. DOWNS
Mount Sinai Medical Center and Miami Heart Institute

ANEMIA, DIAMOND-BLACKFAN

Diamond-Blackfan anemia (DBA) is a congenital deficiency in the precursor mechanism of red blood cells causing failure or low production rates of new blood cells in the bone marrow. The disease is usually present at birth or develops during the first year of life, with 50% of males developing the disease by 2 months of age and 3 months for females. The ratio of males to females is 1.1 to 1.

The etiology and pathogenesis of DBA is unknown. Researchers have studied the possible link between DBA and mutations of ribosomal protein RPS 19; the presence of a second gene on Chromosome 8p (Willig, Gazda, & Sieff, 2000) and Chromosome 19. The characteristics of individuals with DBA vary, and a consistent pattern has not been established due to the small number of cases seen.

Characteristics

1. Weakness and fatigue
2. Slow growth
3. Webbing or shortness of the neck
4. Hand deformities
5. Congenital heart defects
6. At risk for developing leukemia
7. Facial dysmorphic features such as wide-set eyes, thick upper lip, micro- or macrocephaly
8. Upper limb malformations
9. Cataracts, epicanthal folds
10. Renal structural anomalies
11. Short stature

Individuals with DBA are usually treated with corticosteroids such as prednisone (DeCosta, Willig, Fixer, Mohandas, & Tchernia, 2001). Side effects of prednisone therapy may include growth retardation, hypertension, diabetes, fluid retention, gastric ulcers, cataracts, and weight gain. For individuals who do not positively respond to prednisone, red blood cell transfusion may be an option. Transfusions are generally needed every 3 weeks. Side effects associated with transfusion include adverse reactions and the possibility of contracting hepatitis. Bone marrow transplantation may be utilized in cases in which the individual does not response to other forms of treatment. With advances in bone marrow transplantation and immunosuppressant drug therapy, survival rates after transplantation have increased. However, because the child's bone marrow is destroyed prior to transplantation, rejection or poor functioning of the new grafted bone marrow generally results in death. In about 15% of the individuals with DBA, spontaneous remission occurs, and the median age of survival for individuals with DBA is approximately 31 years.

Educational needs of children with DBA change dependent upon their general health and treatment protocol. Children may receive special education services under the Other Health Impaired category. At times, homebound services may be needed. Children who received successful bone marrow transplantation (i.e., a child has not rejected the marrow and the new marrow is normally functioning) may be considered cured and may only need minimal medical supervision. Predisone treatment or blood transfusion involves many more risks, and frequency of the treatment (3–6 hours for blood transfusion) may result in missed educational opportunities. Fatigue, physical problems, and treatment side effects can have a negative impact on the child's physical and cognitive growth. Because children with DBA may be very fragile, their ability to engage in age-appropriate play and to interact with age mates may be limited.

REFERENCES

DeCosta, L., Willig, T. N., Fixer, J., Mohandas, N., & Tchernia, G. (2001). Diamond-Blackfan anemia. *Current Opinion in Pediatrics*, *13*(1), 10–15.

Diamond Blackfan Anemia Online. Retrieved from http://www.Diamondblackfan.com

National Organization for Rare Disorders. Retrieved from http://www.rarediseases.org

Willig, T. N., Gazda, H., & Sieff, C. A. (2000). Diamond-Blackfan anemia. *Current Opinion in Hematology*, 7(2), 85–94.

DARRELL L. DOWNS
Mount Sinai Medical Center and Miami Heart Hospital

AGNES E. SHINE
Barry University

ANEMIA, FANCONI

Fanconi anemia (FA) was first reported by Guido Fanconi, a Swiss pediatrician, in 1927. Because FA is an autosomal recessive disorder that leads to bone marrow failure, both parents must carry the recessive gene for the child to have the disorder. People with FA do not produce a protein necessary for cell functioning; as the cells die and are not reproduced, the individual develops aplastic anemia. Because FA is a recessive gene disorder, after a sibling is diagnosed with FA, all siblings should be tested for FA.

FA occurs equally in males and females and can affect all ethnic groups. The prevalence rate is unknown, but there are about 3,500 known cases; estimates of carrier frequency are approximately 1 in 600. Birth defects occur in approximately 75% of the children born with FA, and the disorder affects all body systems (Alter, 1996). Of major concern for children with FA is the high rate of aplastic anemia, leukemia, and cancers (DeKerviler, Guermazi, Zagdanski, Gluckman, & Frija, 2000). Although FA may be diagnosed at birth, age of onset is typically between 3 and 12 years of age, and in rare cases, adults may be diagnosed with FA. Children with the disorder rarely live to adulthood; their life expectancy is about 22 years.

Characteristics

1. Short stature
2. Anomalies of the thumb and arm
3. Skeletal anomalies (e.g., hip and spine)
4. Structural renal malformations
5. Mental or learning disabilities
6. Gastrointestinal difficulties
7. Heart defects, cancer, and leukemia
8. Hyperpigmentation of the skin (café-au-lait spots)
9. Urinary malformations

In children with FA, treatment is usually bone marrow transplantation, androgen therapy, synthetic growth factor therapy, and gene therapy. Androgen and synthetic growth therapies (drug therapies) are used to stimulate blood growth and can be very effective (Frohnmayer & Frohnmayer, 2000). They are not a cure, and most FA patients eventually fail to respond to drug therapy. Bone marrow transplantation is an effective therapy; the best prognosis is seen in young children who are relatively healthy and have received no or few blood transfusions. Five years after transplantation with a sibling donor, the survival rate is about 70%, whereas the survival rate with nonrelated donors is negligible (Bosch, 2000). At the present time, researchers are investigating at least eight different genes involved in FA.

Children with FA should be allowed to engage in age-related activities as much as possible. Some children may need special education services such as hospital or homebound instruction, individualized instruction focusing on learning problems, or support given through classes for Other Health Impaired children. Children with FA and their families need psychological support, and the child must feel accepted and cared for while attending school. Because about 50% of children with FA are short in stature, care should be given that they are treated as any other child their age and not treated as if they were much younger children.

REFERENCES

Alter, B. P. (1996). Aplastic anemia, pediatric aspects. *Oncologist*, 1(6), 361–366.

Bosch, X. (2000). Setbacks and hopes for patients with Fanconi's anaemia. *Lancet*, 355(9200), 291–295.

DeKerviler, E., Guermazi, A., Zagdanski, A. M., Gluckman, E., & Frija, J. (2000). The clinical and radiological features of Fanconi's anaemia. *Clinical Radiology*, 55(5), 340–345.

Fanconi Anemia Research and Family Support Network, Fact Sheet. Retrieved from http://www.fanconi.org/

AGNES E. SHINE
Barry University

DARRELL L. DOWNS
Mount Sinai Medical Center and Miami Heart Institute

ANEMIA, HEREDITARY NONSPHEROCYTIC HEMOLYTIC

Hereditary nonspherocytic hemolytic anemia describes a group of blood disorders that may result from defects in red blood cell membranes, chemical abnormal metabolism, and approximately 16 enzyme deficiencies in the cells, such as glucose-6-phosphate dehydrogenase deficiency (Fiorelli, Martinez di Montemuros, & Cappellini, 2000). The shape of the red blood cell is not changed as a result of the disorder. The two most common disorders are Glucose-6-Phosphate Dehydrogenase deficiency and Pyruvate Kinase Deficiency.

Glucose-6-phosphate dehydrogenase deficiency (G-6-PD) is a hereditary X-linked recessive enzyme disorder. When an individual with the disorder is exposed to stress of infection or some drugs, the G-6-PD enzyme in the red blood cells is reduced and the red blood cells begin to break down. The incidence for G-6-PD is higher in African Americans; 10–14% of African American males are affected. Individuals with the disorder can remain undiagnosed until their red blood cells are exposed to infections or oxidants such as antimalarial drugs and antibiotics. However, new blood cells do not have decreased levels of G-6-PD and so episodes of anemia may be brief.

Characteristics

1. Fatigue
2. Pale color
3. Shortness of breath
4. Rapid heart rate
5. Yellow skin tone
6. Dark urine
7. Enlarged spleen

If the decrease in red blood cell G-6-PD is a result of infection, the infections is treated, and if the cause is drugs, the drugs are stopped. This form of treatment generally returns the individual to a more normal healthy state.

Pyruvate kinase deficiency is the second most common cause of enzyme related nonspherocytic hemolytic anemia and is an inherited autosomal recessive trait which results in a decrease of the enzyme pyruvate kinase in red blood cells. Evidence of pyruvate kinase deficiency can be found in all ethnic groups, but it appears to affect some groups of people more than others (e.g., Amish). The deficiency can cause mild to severe hemolysis (cell death) and anemia and can be identified in infancy.

Characteristics

1. Family history
2. Pallor
3. Jaundice

Treatment for the disorder depends on severity; some individuals experience few if any symptoms, whereas others may need blood transfusions and a splenectomy to decrease the destruction of red blood cells.

For individuals with G-6-PD or pyruvate kinase deficiency, family and genetic counseling may be appropriate. Children and adolescents with these disorders may not need any additional special educational support unless they develop chronic anemia, which may restrict their activities and result in missed school days. The category of Other Health Impaired may need to be considered if the student's activities are restricted. Providing the individual with information about their disorder is important, since the individual may need emotional support when dealing with life-long conditions. Additional research is needed to understand etiology and treatment.

REFERENCES

Fiorelli, G., Martinez di Montemuros, F., & Cappellini, M. D. (2000). Chronic nonspherocytic haemolytic disorders associated with glucose-6-phosphate dehydrogenase variants. *Best Practices in Research Clinical Haematology*, *13*(1), 39–55.

Medline Plus Medical Encyclopedia. Retrieved from http://www.nlm.nih.gov/medlineplus/encyclopedia.html

Rare Disease Database. Retrieved from http://www.stepstn.com/cgi-win/nord

Vanderbilt University Medical Center. Retrieved from http://www.mc.vanderbilt.edu/peds/

AGNES E. SHINE
Barry University

DARRELL L. DOWNS
Mount Sinai Medical Center and Miami Heart Institute

ANEMIA, HEREDITARY SPHEROCYTIC HEMOLYTIC

The blood cells in individuals with hereditary spherocytic hemolytic anemia (HSHA) are sphere-shaped due to a defect within the blood cell as a result of a metabolic defect. Because of the cells' shape, they are not readily passed through the small blood vessels of the spleen and are often prematurely destroyed by the spleen. The incidence rate of HSHA in the United States is estimated to be approximately 1 in 5,000 individuals and usually affects Caucasian individuals of northern European ancestry; it is rarely found in other racial groups. The disorder is autosomal dominant, with 50% of the siblings affected. However, in a small number of cases, neither parent has the defect and the expression of the disorder may be due to a recessive form of the disorder or to spontaneous mutation. The severity of the disorder depends upon whether the individual can compensate for the loss of red blood cells by producing more cells. If the bone marrow temporarily halts production of new blood cells due to infection, the individual may experience an aplastic crisis as a result of the loss of blood.

Characteristics

1. Jaundice, causing skin and whites of the eyes to turn yellow
2. Fatigue
3. Enlarged spleen

Treatment for the disorder for a young child consists of folic acid supplements, and in emergencies transfusions may be provided. For individuals older than 5 years of age, a splenectomy (removal of the spleen, which allows the blood cells to live longer) may be needed (Beutler & Luzzatto, 1999). However, removal of the spleen is not considered a cure, and the individual must take precautions to prevent serious infections that may increase the risk of anemia.

The educational and social-emotional needs of the individual will depend upon the severity of the disorder. In mild cases, the individual may need to avoid infections and stress-related activities. In more severe cases, physical activities may be restricted and the individual may constantly feel fatigued. Children and adolescents should be instructed about their condition and play a vital role in the management of their care. Special education services may need to be provided in the Other Health Impaired category. Psychological counseling and education may also be needed.

REFERENCES

Beutler, E., & Luzzatto, L. (1999). Hemolytic anemia. *Seminar in Hematology, 36*(4 Suppl. 7), 38–47.

Medline Plus Medical Encyclopedia. Retrieved from http://medlineplus.nlm.nih.gov/medlineplus/ency

Rare Disease Database. Retrieved from http://rarediseases.org/

Vanderbilt University Medical Center. Retrieved from http://www.mc.vanderbilt.edu/peds/

AGNES E. SHINE
Barry University

DARRELL L. DOWNS
Mount Sinai Medical Center and Miami Heart Institute

ANENCEPHALY

Anencephaly is a congenital disorder marked by the absence of the cerebral cortices. It belongs to a class of disorders that are termed neural tube defects (NTD) and results from the failure of the neural tube to close during embryogenesis. The neural tube, which is the precursor to the brain and spinal cord, usually closes by the 28th day after conception (Kloza, 1985). If this does not occur completely, various defects to the central nervous system (CNS) become manifest. If this occurs "lower" on the neural tube, spina bifida will be present. However, if the "top" of the neural tube remains open, anencephaly results. Anencephaly with spina bifida rarely occurs (Swaiman & Wright, 1973).

As anencephaly is ostensibly marked by the absence of the cerebral cortices; the centers of higher cognitive functioning are absent. Therefore, while certain subcortical structures may remain intact (producing the reflex patterns and responses often indicative of neonates), higher cerebral activity is precluded by the absence of structures subserving those functions. Many anencephalics are stillborn, as they lack the brain structures necessary to maintain respiration and other functions vital to survival. On the occasion that the newborn is physiologically viable, it should be remembered that associative processes, reasoning, and cognitive and language development are not possible. Therefore, educational services are not a practical consideration and absolute custodial supervision and care are indicated. Ethical considerations pertaining to care must also come into play.

The development of anencephaly and other NTDs is believed to be multifactorial. The second most common group of congenital anomalies, with environment, intrauterine environment, and genetic factors implicated in their development are NTDs. Kandel, Schwartz, and Jessell (1991) provide a detailed review of the development of NTDs, including anencephaly. Geographically, anencephaly appears to be a more common occurrence on the East Coast of the United States and in the Rio Grande Valley of Texas. It is found more frequently in female births than male (2:1). It has been suggested that a higher prevalence of anencephaly is found in lower socioeconomic class families (James, Nevin, Johnston, & Merrett, 1981; Nevin, Johnston, & Merrett, 1981).

Treatment of anecephaly consists of surgically closing the opening of the sac that encloses the brain. This is a very high-risk procedure and still does not prevent infant fatality upon birth due to the complications of anencephaly. With NTDs, a substance called alpha fetoprotein (AFP) occurs in higher concentration in the amniotic fluid surrounding the fetus (Adinolfi, 1985; Kloza, 1985). The AFP enters the mother's circulation either by the amniotic fluid or the placenta; it can then be measured in the mother's blood. Higher levels of AFP in the mother's blood at certain times in fetal gestation indicate NTDs. This method of identifying anencephaly has been shown to be 99% reliable, with a reliability of similar magnitude for other NTDs such as spina bifida.

REFERENCES

Adinolfi, M. (1985). The development of the human blood-csf-brain barrier. *Developmental Medicine and Child Neurology, 27*(4), 532–537.

James, W. H., Nevin, N. C., Johnston, W. P., & Merrett, J. D. (1981). Influence of social class on the risk of recurrence of anencephaly and spina bifida. *Developmental Medicine and Child Neurology, 23*(5), 661–662.

Kandel, S., Schwartz, J., & Jessell, T. (1991). *Principles of neural sciences* (3rd ed.). New York, NY: Elsevier.

Kloza, E. M. (1985). Prenatal screening: Neural tube defects. In *Disorders of brain development and cognition.* Boston, MA: Eunice Kennedy Shriver Center and Harvard Medical School.

Nevin, N. C., Johnston, W. P., & Merrett, J. D. (1981). Influence of social class on the risk of recurrence of anencephaly and spina bifida. *Developmental Medicine and Child Neurology, 23*(2), 151–154.

Swaiman, K. F., & Wright, F. S. (1973). Neurologic diseases due to developmental and metabolic defects. In A. B. Baker & L. H. Baker (Eds.), *Clinical neurology.* New York, NY: Harper & Row.

ELLIS I. BAROWSKY
Hunter College, City University of New York
Third edition

See also **Baby Doe; Congenital Disorders**

ANGELMAN SYNDROME

Angelman syndrome (formally Happy Puppet syndrome) is an emerging disorder, little studied, with no good population studies completed to allow proper prevalence or incidence estimates. However, it is roughly estimated to be 1 in 10,000 to 1 in 20,000 (Steinman, 2003). Many, but not all, Angelman syndrome individuals have deletions on chromosome 15 in maternally related regions (q11–q12) while others are of unknown pathogenic origin. The disorder is characterized by physical, motoric, and behavioral features. Physical features include a wide mouth, prominent lower jaw, and microbrachycephalia. Motor problems are related to diverse, jerky, sometimes rhythmic movements. Some children experience particular difficulties with inadequate control of chewing and swallowing, which creates feeding problems. However, these problems abate after infancy in most cases. Acquisition of walking is delayed, and mild to severe ataxia after learning to walk is common.

A variety of behavioral and cognitive problems are evident. Most children with Angelman syndrome have severe to profound levels of intellectual disability, although some patients may reach moderate and, rarely, mild levels of ID. Spoken language is absent in 75–80% of children with Angelman syndrome, but receptive language is typically superior to expressive language. Some do develop skills in sign language but normal levels of communication have not been seen in any published case. Behavioral presentation of Angelman syndrome often includes hyperactivity, impulsivity, episodic pica, random bursts of laughter (in nearly all cases), jerky nighttime movements, and a generally happy disposition.

Diagnosis is sometimes very difficult, as Angelman has similarities of presentation to Rett syndrome and to Prader-Willi syndrome in a number of cases. Detailed cytogenic studies are often necessary for proper diagnosis and even then the diagnosis may still be only inferred rather than confirmed. EEG is helpful as a common pattern with posterior slow wave activity used as a marker variable. CT and MRI are normal in 30–35% of cases, and others show mixed results with diffuse atrophy, deep white matter lesions (periventricular leukomalacia), and cerebellar growth retardation all having been documented in various cases.

At present 100% of children with Angelman syndrome are believed to require special education services, typically as children with intellectual disability, although numerous related services may be required (Steinman, 2003). Intervention is largely related to symptom management and the teaching of fundamental adaptive behavior and communication skills. Sheltered employment is possible in many but not all cases. However, more and better longitudinal studies of Angelman syndrome individuals are needed to document the long-term effects of interventions and general life outcomes.

REFERENCE

Steinman, D. R. (2003). Angelman syndrome. In E. Fletcher-Janzen & C. R. Reynolds (Eds.), *Childhood disorders diagnostic desk reference* (pp. 41–42). Hoboken, NJ: Wiley.

CECIL R. REYNOLDS
Texas A&M University

See also **Prader-Willi Syndrome; Rett Syndrome**

ANGIOEDEMA (HEREDITARY)

Occupational therapy may help fine motor and oral motor control. Because expressive speech is very limited, speech or communication therapy is important for developing nonverbal communication methods. Incorporating communication aids, such as picture boards, at the earliest appropriate time is advisable. Consistency in techniques used at school and home facilitates development of skills for activities of daily living (National Angelman Syndrome Foundation, 2000).

Additional research is needed for better understanding and control of seizures. Future research in genetics holds promise for reversing the abnormal gene processes that cause Angelman syndrome and other disorders with similar etiology.

REFERENCES

Angelman, H. (1965). "Puppet" children: A report on three cases. *Developmental Medicine and Child Neurology*, 7, 681–688.

Laan, L. A. E. M., Haeringen, A. V., & Brouwer, O. F. (1999). Angelman syndrome: A review of clinical and genetic aspects. *Clinical Neurology and Neurosurgery*, 101, 161–170.

National Angelman Syndrome Foundation. (2000). Facts about Angelman syndrome. Retrieved from http://www.angelman .org/

Williams, C. A., Angelman, H., Clayton-Smith, J., Driscoll, D. J., Hendrickson, J. E., Knoll, J. H. M.,...Whidden, E. M. (1995). Angelman syndrome: Consensus for diagnostic criteria. *American Journal of Medical Genetics*, 56, 237–238.

DAVID R. STEINMAN
Austin Neurological Clinic and Department of Psychology, University of Texas at Austin

ANIMALS FOR INDIVIDUALS WITH DISABILITIES

Today, animals are being used to assist individuals with disabilities with daily living. For centuries, the blind have used dogs to assist them in ambulation. Recently, pilot programs using domesticated monkeys to assist moderately to severely disabled persons in the home to perform rote chores has been a successful innovation. Horseback riding has emerged as a leisure-time pursuit for many types of disabled persons.

The benefits of human/animal interaction are now being realized, especially for special education purposes. Lowered blood pressure has been documented in studies where the participants had regular contact with dogs. In another study, Friedman (1980) found that the survival rate of hypertensive persons increased dramatically with pet ownership. Pets have been considered effective agents in the reduction of everyday stress. They provide a sense of relaxation (Kidd, 1981). They also provide a chance to exercise, and for many a sense of security (White & Watson, 1983).

Animals provide the opportunity to communicate. This is probably the most valuable attribute of the human/animal relationship. Levinson (1969) states that an animal can have a "very positive effect on a family and that they have the potential to bridge the gap between children and adults by providing a common object of responsibility."

According to Levinson (1969), the introduction of animals into a residential setting for the disabled indicates that the staff believes that anything of possible treatment value to the disabled can and should be used. It reveals an awareness of the potential healing properties of pet ownership, even if those benefits have not been scientifically documented in the laboratory.

A child with disabilities is not constantly reminded of his or her disability in the interaction with a pet. A deaf child can care for a dog competently and receive all of the rewards that a hearing child would for the same efforts. The same is true for a variety of handicaps; only the type of pet might have to be changed. A child confined to a wheelchair may interact well with a rabbit or an aquarium and achieve a sense of purpose and responsibility previously unrealized.

The teaching of the emotionally disturbed child provides a setting in which the use of animals may be especially beneficial. Typically, motivating this student to participate in class can be a difficult task for the teacher. Often, these students have never learned to care for or share with others. The animal in the class may provide both the subject matter and the motivation to learn. The child who had previously trusted no one can begin to trust the teacher for the first time when he or she sees the teacher's concern in dealing with the classroom pet. This could be the first step by the child in accepting the structure of the class (Levinson, 1969).

REFERENCES

Friedman, E. (1980, July/August). Animal companions and one year survival of patients after discharge from a coronary care unit. *Public Health Reports*, 44(4), 37–42.

Kidd, A. (1981). Dogs, cats, and people. *Mills Quarterly*, 23(8), 23–28.

Levinson, B. (1969). *Pet-oriented child psychotherapy*. Springfield, IL: Thomas.

White, B., & Watson, T. (1983). *Pet love, how pets take care of us*. New York, NY: Pinnacle.

THOMAS R. BURKE
Hunter College, City University of New York

See also Equine Therapy
Therapeutic Recreation

ANIRIDIA CEREBELLAR ATAXIA MENTAL DEFICIENCY

Aniridia cerebellar ataxia mental deficiency, also known as Gillespie syndrome, is characterized by intellectual disability, partial absence of the iris of the eye (partial aniridia), and incoordination of voluntary movements due to underdevelopment of the brain's cerebellum (cerebellar ataxia; National Organization of Rare Disorders, 1998).

Aniridia cerebellar ataxia mental deficiency is an extremely rare autosomal recessive condition, with approximately 16 cases reported in the literature (McKusick, 1997). It affects males and females equally.

Characteristics

1. Child may have slow and halting speech, hypotonia, and an unsteady gait (Nevin, 1990).
2. Child may show developmental delays with certain motor skills, such as walking or speaking.
3. Intellectual disability is usually present.
4. The pupillary margin of the iris and the sphincter pupillae may be absent, resulting in poor vision and photophobia (Wittig, Moreira, Freire-Maia, & Vianna-Morgante, 1988).
5. Child may develop glaucoma, which could lead to loss of vision.

Treatment for aniridia cerebellar ataxia mental deficiency depends on the individual's symptoms. A team of ophthalmologists and optometrists is necessary to treat visual problems. Surgery may be required for the child's visual difficulties, such as diplopia. Glasses or contact lenses may be necessary to alleviate problems caused by partial aniridia. The child should also be monitored for glaucoma to prevent possible vision loss. Physical therapists may assist the child with gross motor skills, and speech therapists may be necessary to address speech delays. In rare cases, individuals with the disorder have heart abnormalities or skeletal malformations that require treatment (McKusick, 1997).

Children with aniridia cerebellar ataxia mental deficiency have intellectual disability, cerebellar ataxia, visual impairments, health problems, and possible speech delays that may interfere with their education. To help them reach their maximum learning potential, most children with this disorder need special education services and early intervention programs. The services required depend on the child's symptoms and needs. Psychoeducational assessments can help school personnel develop an appropriate individual educational plan for each child. Physical therapy and speech therapy may also be necessary for young children with motor impairments or speech delays (Plumridge, Bennett, Dinno, & Branson, 1993).

Individuals with aniridia cerebellar ataxia mental deficiency may require some form of assisted living, depending on the severity of their symptoms. There does not appear to be a decrease in functioning with age, and in some cases motor performance improves (McKusick, 1997). Future research is focusing on the etiology, prevention, and treatment of this disorder.

REFERENCES

McKusick, V. A. (Ed.). (1997, August). Online Mendelian inheritance in man: A catalog of human genes and genetic disorders. Retrieved from http://www.ncbi.nlm.nih.gov

National Organization for Rare Disorders. (1998, February 28). Aniridia cerebellar ataxia mental deficiency. Retrieved from http://www.rarediseases.org

Nevin, N. C., & Lim, J. H. (1990). Syndrome of partial aniridia, cerebellar ataxia, and mental retardation—Gillespie syndrome. *American Journal of Medical Genetics, 35,* 468–469.

Plumridge, D., Bennett, R., Dinno, N., & Branson, C. (Eds.). (1993). *The student with a genetic disorder.* Springfield, IL: Charles C. Thomas.

Wittig, E. O., Moreira, C. A., Freire-Maia, N., & Vianna-Morgante, A. M. (1988). Partial aniridia, cerebellar ataxia, and mental deficiency (Gillespie syndrome) in two brothers. *American Journal of Medical Genetics, 30,* 703–708.

SUSANNAH MORE
University of Texas at Austin

ANNALS OF DYSLEXIA

Originating in 1950 as the *Bulletin of the Orton Society* under the editorial leadership of June Lyday Orton, the annual periodical of the Orton Dyslexia Society was renamed the *Annals of Dyslexia* in 1981. It was designed as a means for enhancing communication among the members of the Orton Dyslexia Society, an organization founded in 1949 whose aim was to further research and work with children with specific language disabilities.

The journal was aimed at professional multidisciplinary membership, consisting of neurologists, psychologists, pathologists, psychiatrists, educators, and social workers. Through concrete illustration of the practical applications of new knowledge, *Annals* served as a bridge between the researcher and the field worker.

The Orton Dyslexia Society was renamed the International Dyslexia Association in 1997. The International Dyslexia Association publishes the *Annals of Dyslexia* in partnership with Springer Publishing. Currently, the *Annals of Dyslexia* is a peer-reviewed journal that prints studies of evidence-based effective practices related to the study of dyslexia and other related language disorders.

International Dyslexia Association, 40 York Road, Suite 400, Towson, MD 21204. Tel.: (410) 296-0232, ext. 409, e-mail: info@interdys.org (monitored daily), website: www.interdys.org (L. Marston, personal communication, May 26, 2011).

ELIZABETH DANE
Hunter College, City University of New York
First edition

KAY E. KETZENBERGER
The University of Texas of the Permian Basin

ANNUAL DIRECTORY OF EDUCATIONAL FACILITIES FOR THE LEARNING DISABLED
(*See* Biennial Directory of Educational Facilities for the Learning Disabled)

ANNUAL GOALS

Annual goals describe expected student performance as part of an individual education plan (IEP), and are in compliance with the Individuals with Disabilities Education Improvement Act of 2004. Annual goals originated with PL-94-142 in 1975 requiring each IEP to contain a statement of annual educational goals, with specific objectives, conditions under which desired performance should occur, description of the desired performance, and a listing of the criteria for adequate performance. The proportion of IEP objectives achieved by each student at the end of the term divided by the total number written at the start of the term has been used as a measure of educational progress (Brinker & Thorpe, 1984). Progress of annual goals are to be reported at least as frequently as other grade reporting periods.

Public Law 94-142 mandated that pupils' rates of progress be continuously monitored so that educational programs can be reassessed and improved as students move toward goals. A common assessment method used in instruction is the pretest, teach, posttest design. Teachers in special education commonly rely on observation and develop curriculum-based measurement systems matched to annual goals.

Findings indicate that the use of more systematic measurement and evaluation systems than those currently in use result in better student achievement toward goals (Fuchs, Deno, & Mirkin, 1984). Another finding is that public goal setting between student and teacher is more effective than private goal setting in increasing on-task behavior in the classroom (Lyman, 1984). One suggested system is the Goal Attainment Scale (GAS; Kiresuk & Sherman, 1968), a method that can help special educators to become more accountable and effective and increase the likelihood that curricula will become student centered rather than method centered.

The method involves devising a set of goals with the involved persons, developing a set of expected outcomes for each goal, scoring the outcomes on a five-point continuum from worse than expected to better than expected, and calculating a summary score of outcomes across the goals. Mutual determination of goals and their importance by the persons involved ensures relevance and meaning to parents, students, and educators. This mutual determination also helps students to learn about alternative behaviors and helps to clarify expectations for both students and teachers. GAS is independent of theoretical predispositions and can be used by teachers to clarify specific problems, sharpen goal setting, and point out directions for action (Carr, 1979). Setting objective, observable goals and evaluating outcomes is crucial to student progress (Martens, Witt, Daly, & Vollmer, 1999), and this position continues in the latest reauthorization of the Individuals with Disabilities Education Improvement Act (IDEIA) of 2004. While benchmarks and objectives for annual goals have been eliminated from the latest legislation, it remains to be seen how progress toward annual goals will be determined.

REFERENCES

Brinker, R. P., & Thorpe, M. E. (1984). Integration of severely handicapped students and the proportion of IEP objectives achieved. *Exceptional Children, 51*, 168–175.

Carr, R. A. (1979). Goal Attainment Scaling as a useful tool for evaluating progress in special education. *Exceptional Children, 46*, 88–95.

Fuchs, L. S., Deno, S. L., & Mirkin, P. K. (1984). The effects and frequent curriculum-based measurement and evaluation on pedagogy, student achievement and student awareness of learning. *American Education Research Journal, 21*, 449–460.

Gerardi, R. J., Grohe, B., Benedict, G. C., & Collidge, P. G. (1984). IEP—more paperwork and wasted time. *Contemporary Education, 56*, 39–42.

Jaffe, M. J., & Snelbecker, G. E. (1982). Evaluating independent education programs: A recommendation and some programmatic implications. *Urban Review, 14*(2), 73–81.

Kiresuk T. J., & Sherman R. E. (1968). Goal attainment scaling: A general method for evaluating comprehensive community mental health programs. *Community Mental Health Journal, 4*(6), 443–453.

Lyman, R. D. (1984). The effect of private and public goal setting on classroom on-task behavior of emotionally disturbed children. *Behavior Therapy, 15*, 395–402.

Martens, B., Witt, J., Daly, E., & Vollmer, T. (1999). Behavior analysis: Theory and practice in educational settings. In C. R. Reynolds & T. B. Gutkin (Eds.), *The handbook of school psychology* (3rd ed., pp. 638–663). New York, NY: Wiley.

CATHERINE O. BRUCE
Hunter College, City University of New York

See *also* Individual Education Plan; Individuals With Disabilities Education Improvement Act of 2004 (IDEIA)

ANNUAL REPORT TO CONGRESS ON THE IMPLEMENTATION OF THE INDIVIDUALS WITH DISABILITIES EDUCATION ACT, TWENTY-NINTH EXECUTIVE SUMMARY OF THE

The 29th Annual Report to Congress (2007) focuses on IDEIA results and accountability. The 29th Annual Report to Congress on the Implementation of the Individuals with Disabilities Education Act, 2007 focuses on key state performance data following recommendations of the President's Commission on Excellence in Special Education.

National Data

Infants and Toddlers Served Under IDEA, Part C

- In 2005, under *IDEA*, Part C, there were 298,150 eligible infants and toddlers birth through age 2 who received early intervention services. Of these, 293,816 were served in the 50 states and the District of Columbia. This number represents 2.4% of the birth-through-2 population in the 50 states and the District of Columbia (page 14).
- From 1996 through 2005, the percentage of the general population of infants and toddlers who were served under *IDEA*, Part C, increased for each of the age years served. The increase continued to be largest for 2-year-olds. In 1996, Part C served 2.4% of 2-year-olds. By 2005, Part C served 3.9% of 2-year-olds (page 15).
- In 2004, approximately four-fifths of infants and toddlers being served under *IDEA*, Part C, received their early intervention services primarily in the *home* (82.7%). The next most common setting category was *service provider location* (5.6%) followed by *program designed for typically developing children* (4.4%) and *program designed for children with developmental delay or disabilities* (4.4%). Less than three percent (2.9%) of infants and toddlers received early intervention services in the setting categories presented as "Other" (page 19).

- In 2004–2005, about two-thirds (68.6%) of children served under *IDEA*, Part C, who exited Part C when they reached age 3 were determined to be *Part B eligible*. Other children who exited Part C when they reached age 3 did so with their *Part B eligibility not determined* (14%). Of the children who exited Part C when they reached age 3 and who were not eligible for Part B (17.4%), approximately 12% exited with referrals to other programs, and about 6% exited with no referrals (page 22).
- In 2004–2005, for every racial/ethnic group, more than 60% of children exiting Part C when they reached age 3 were eligible for Part B preschool services (page 24).

Children Ages 3 Through 5 Served Under IDEA, Part B

- In 2005, Part B served 704,087 children ages 3 through 5 with disabilities. Of these, 698,938 were served in the 50 states, the District of Columbia, and Bureau of Indian Affairs (BIA) schools. This number represents 5.8% of the U.S. population ages 3 through 5 (page 43).
- The percentage of 3-year-olds in the general population who received special education and related services increased from 2.8% in 1996 to 3.8% in 2005. The percentage of 4-year-olds in the general population who received special education and related services increased from 4.7% in 1996 to 6.5% in 2003 and decreased slightly to 6% in 2005. The percentage of 5-year-olds in the general population who received special education and related services increased from 6.1% in 1996 to 6.6% in 2001, then increased yearly to 7.7% in 2005 (pages 44–45).
- In 2005, American Indian/Alaska Native and White (not Hispanic) children ages 3 through 5 both had risk ratios above 1 (1.5 and 1.3, respectively). This indicates that they were more likely to be served under Part B preschool programs than were children 3 through 5 years of age of all other racial/ethnic groups combined. Black (not Hispanic) children ages 3 through 5, with a risk ratio of 1, were just as likely to be served under Part B preschool programs as same-age children of all other racial/ethnic groups combined. Asian/Pacific Islander and Hispanic children ages 3 through 5 were less likely to be served under Part B preschool programs than same-age children of all other racial/ethnic groups combined (both with risk ratios of 0.7) (pages 47–48).
- In 2005, about one-third of children ages 3 through 5 served under *IDEA*, Part B, received all of their special education and related services in *early childhood* environments (34.1%). Only 2.9% of children ages 3 through 5 served under *IDEA*, Part B, received special education and related services in *home* environments (page 49).

- According to the Pre-Elementary Education Longitudinal Study (PEELS), in 2003–2004, nearly three-fourths of children ages 3 through 5 served under *IDEA*, Part B, were identified as having one of two primary disabilities—speech or language impairments (46.4%) or developmental delay (27.8%) (page 54).

- In 2003–2004, children identified as having orthopedic impairments, *other health impairments* or intellectual disability typically started receiving services from a professional at younger ages (13 months of age, 18 months of age and 19 months of age, respectively) than children identified as having other types of disabilities, according to PEELS (page 55).

Students Ages 6 Through 21 Served Under IDEA, Part B

- In 2005, a total of 6,109,569 students ages 6 through 21 were served under *IDEA*, Part B. Of these, 6,021,462 were served in the 50 states, the District of Columbia, and Bureau of Indian Affairs (BIA) schools. This number represents 9.1% of the U.S. general population ages 6 through 21 (page 58).

- In 2005, the largest disability category among students ages 6 through 21 served under *IDEA*, Part B, was specific learning disabilities (45.5%). The next most common disability category was speech or language impairments (18.9%), followed by *other health impairments* (9.2%), intellectual disability (8.9%) and emotional disturbance (7.7%) (page 61).

- For most disability categories, annual change in the percentage of the population ages 6 through 21 served under *IDEA*, Part B, was negligible from 1996 through 2005 (page 62).

- In 2005, American Indian/Alaska Native students ages 6 through 21 and black (not Hispanic) students ages 6 through 21 were about 1.5 times more likely to be served under *IDEA*, Part B, than same-age students in all other racial/ethnic groups combined (1.54 and 1.47, respectively); Asian/Pacific Islander students, white (not Hispanic) students and Hispanic students, ages 6 through 21, were less likely to be served under Part B than same-age students of all other racial/ethnic groups combined (0.51, 0.89 and 0.92, respectively) (page 71).

- In 2005, 96% of students ages 6 through 21 served under *IDEA*, Part B, were educated in regular classes. However, the amount of time they spent in regular classrooms varied. More than half of all students served under *IDEA*, Part B (53.6 percent) were educated for most of the school day in regular classes; that is, they were *outside the regular class for less than 21 percent of the school day* (page 72).

- In 2005, the percentage of students served under *IDEA*, Part B, receiving special education in each environment varied by disability category (page 75).

- In 2005, 43.9 percent of Black (not Hispanic) students ages 6 through 21 served under *IDEA*, Part B, were educated in the regular class for most of the school day compared to 59.1 percent of White (not Hispanic) students with disabilities (page 77).

- From 1995–1996 through 2004–2005, the rate at which students with disabilities *graduated with a regular high school diploma* improved for students in all disability categories. The largest gains were made by students with speech or language impairments (22.7 percentage point increase) and autism (19.2 percentage point increase). Notable gains were also made by students with emotional disturbance (15 percentage point increase) and specific learning disabilities (11.4 percentage point increase) (page 80).

- From 1995–1996 through 2004–2005, the dropout rate declined for students in all disability categories except deaf-blindness. The improvement was most notable for students with speech or language impairments (25.2 percentage point decrease), emotional disturbance (21.7 percentage point decrease), autism (13 percentage point decrease) and specific learning disabilities (17.6 percentage point decrease) (page 82).

- In 2004–2005, the rate at which students served under *IDEA*, Part B, *graduated with a regular high school diploma* was highest for Asian/Pacific Islander (66.7%) and White (61.5%) students served under *IDEA*, Part B. The graduation rate was lowest for Black students served under *IDEA*, Part B (39.2%). The graduation rate for all students served under *IDEA*, Part B, was 54.4% (page 83).

- According to the Special Education Elementary Longitudinal Study (SEELS), in 2004, the vast majority of students in all disability categories participated in their state accountability systems through standardized or alternate assessments. Between one-half and three-fourths of students with most disabilities participated in standardized tests with accommodations or modifications. The fraction was closer to two-fifths of students with intellectual disability (43%), autism (37%) and multiple disabilities (40%) (page 85).

All reports can be found at: http://www2.ed.gov/about/reports/annual/osep/index.html. Information retrieved on August 10, 2011.

HEATHER DAVIS
Texas A&M University
Fourth edition

ANOMALIES, PHYSICAL
(See Physical Anomalies)

ANOREXIA NERVOSA

Anorexia nervosa (starvation due to nerves) is a condition in which an individual eats little or no food for prolonged periods. No physical basis for the abnormal eating can be found. This disorder can be life-threatening, is increasing in incidence, and is a serious problem for medical and psychological professionals.

Although famous and tragic cases such as that of singer Karen Carpenter have made anorexia familiar, little can confidently be said about specific etiology or overall effective treatment. Anorexics share certain personality characteristics and frequently have families with a particular complex of unhealthy attitudes and behaviors. The physical appearance of anorexics is emaciated.

Anorexia is largely a disorder of middle- and upper-class adolescent females. It occurs approximately nine times more often in women than in men, and may affect one in one hundred white women between the ages of 12 and 18 years (Newman & Halvorson, 1983). The most common age of onset for anorexia is early adolescence (Newman & Halvorson, 1983).

Diagnostic criteria for anorexia nervosa may be summarized as involving intense fear of becoming obese, which does not diminish as weight loss progresses; disturbed body image (e.g., feeling fat even when emaciated); refusal to maintain normal body weight; and in postmenarcheal females, amenorrhea (i.e., the absence of at least three consecutive menstrual cycles; American Psychiatric Association, 1994).

Anorexics are subject to numerous additional complications, including malnutrition, edema, loss of hair, hyperactivity, hypoglycemia, vitamin deficiencies, constipation, weakness, and fatigue. In extreme cases, death may result from starvation, electrolyte depletion, or cardiac arrhythmia (Newman & Halvorson, 1983).

Anorexic sufferers share many behaviors and concerns among each other. They are terrified of becoming obese and measure their worth and self-esteem by how much they weigh and how much their stomachs protrude. They tend to be perfectionists, overdemanding of themselves, and very success-oriented. Low self-esteem and fear of rejection, especially by the opposite sex, are common. They have difficulty allowing anyone to become emotionally close to them.

Many anorexics were model children who were "people pleasers." They tend to be introverted, well-behaved, compulsive, self-critical, and very conscientious. As the disorder progresses, anorexics frequently become suspicious, indecisive, stubborn, unsociable, and disliking of any change. Phobic, depressive, or hysterical features are also common. Perceptions of events often become very distorted.

Studies indicate that children as young as 8 to 10 years old may be likely to be concerned with weight and body esteem. Shapiro, Newcomb, and Loeb (1997) found that 8- to 10-year-old children admitted to concern with their body weight and dieting. The investigators concluded that eating disorders or disregulated-restrained eating in vulnerable children and adolescents might be both expressed and internalized at an extremely early age. Brumberg (1997) report that studies have demonstrated that as many as 53% of 13-year-olds and 78% of 17-year-olds are dissatisfied with their bodies. *Seventeen* magazine in 1995 ran a headline in the July 1995 issue which asked: "Do You Hate Your Body? How to Stop." Although the article offered adolescents ways to stop hating their bodies, the author confessed that it is very difficult to do so in a culture where your body is very important. Wolf (1994) stated that the world never gives girls the message that their bodies are valuable simply because they themselves are inside them. Until our culture tells young girls that they are welcome in any shape—that women are valuable with or without the excuse of beauty—girls will continue to starve.

The specific etiologies of anorexia nervosa are not known, but are thought to be biopsychosocial diseases. Unknown biological predispositions may interact with both individual psychological states and needs and our culture's emphasis, especially for females, on thinness as a worthy or desirable characteristic (Wooley & Wooley, 1985). Several etiological factors can be described:

1. According to Bruch (1985), in the past 20 years the average female under 30 years of age has become heavier; at the same time, the ideal shape for women has been in the direction of being thinner. To be thin is to increase women's desirability both in their eyes and the eyes of others. The result is demonstrated in the mushrooming of the weight reduction industry and the numerous books and magazine articles that have appeared on losing weight and dieting.

2. Wooley and Wooley (1985) quote from Ambrose Bierce's *Devil's Dictionary*: "To men a man is but a mind, who cares what face he carries? Or what form he wears? But woman's body is the woman." For many centuries females' cultural conditioning has tied self-esteem to physical attractiveness. Many therapists think that recent cultural emphasis on "thinness is beautiful and good" has contributed to the increased incidence of eating disorders (Wooley & Wooley, 1985). The message to woman in particular is that in order to be popular, attractive, accepted, sexy, healthy, and desired in the world of work, they must be thin. The ideal of feminine beauty increasingly conforms each year to the adolescent male physique, implying emulation of men both behaviorally and physically (Wooley & Wooley, 1985). This change may be due to broader social changes involving competition between women and men for prestige and power. Also involved for many young women is the resolution of intense identification

conflicts with their parents. Young women today are the first generation raised by extremely weight-conscious mothers who additionally view themselves as failures by current social standards of beauty.

3. Bruch (1985) says that a cultural emphasis for slimness as a determining factor does not explain the more severe disturbance of "frantic preoccupation with excessive slenderness of the anorexic." She believes that the changing status of expectations for women is important in understanding the etiology. Females, says Bruch, who have been raised as "clinging vines" and future wives, and who find themselves during their teens with the expectation to demonstrate that they are women of achievement, may find that they are filled with self-doubt and uncertainty. By bowing to the dictum to be thin, they are validating that they deserve respect.

Anorexia can begin with a stressful life situation for which the young woman does not possess appropriate coping skills. Real or perceived perfection, sexual engagements, or loss of some kind frequently precedes development of the disorder. Any change can be catastrophic for an anorexic. Worrying about performing perfectly and being socially accepted often results in situations in which anorexics find themselves out of control. Magical thinking is common.

According to Bemis and colleagues, who have studied hypothalamic functions in anorexics, starvation may actually damage the hypothalamus, and emotional stress may interfere with hypothalamic functioning. Further, psychological aberrations associated with anorexia may be relatively independent expressions of a primary hypothalamic deficiency that is of unknown origin (Bemis, 1978).

Women may be biologically more susceptible to eating disorders than men because women tend to demonstrate greater appetite fluctuations when confronted by stress. Also, through socialization, women are more likely than men to inhibit expression of negative feelings, leading to internal stress. This internal stress may exacerbate a biological predisposition.

Certain family factors facilitate the development of anorexia. If a parent has had the disorder or is either extremely thin or obese, the chances of a young woman becoming anorexic increase (Neuman & Halvorson, 1983). In families of anorexics, food is usually a primary issue. The family may use food for other than nutritional purposes. For example, eating may be a way of dealing with personal problems or negative or positive feelings, or it may be a method of presenting the appearance of a happy family. Power struggles over eating are extremely common.

Families of anorexics show certain personality patterns, although no one pattern appears consistently. Mothers are frequently intrusive and dominating and have experienced clinical depressions, whereas fathers appear passive and aloof from the family. Less frequently, these patterns may be reversed (Newman & Halvorson, 1983).

Family interpersonal dynamics are a significant contributing factor. Features that appear to be correlated with the development of the disorder are rigidity, lack of conflict resolution, overprotectiveness, and enmeshment (appearing to be a very close family). Keeping the peace at any cost is a high priority in these families; conflicts are not dealt with openly. In many families of anorexics, the anorexic generally feels powerless and ineffective, and behaves primarily on the basis of what other people want or need. Often the family has not encouraged or allowed the young woman to develop her autonomy or individuality. Only compliance is tolerated. Anorexia may develop as a result of a young woman's attempt to take control of her own life and achieve her own sense of identity. She learns that one thing she can control is her weight. Families must realize that this is an emotionally based disorder with the attempt to control, hide, avoid, and forget emotional pain. Nobody can make these anorexics eat, therefore it is important not to immediately focus on the food (http://www.something-fishy.org/).

In some cases the family unconsciously does not want the child to grow up. This message is received by the child, who in turn exhibits anorexic behavior, which then leads to failure to develop secondary sexual characteristics. Some anorexics enjoy being viewed as special by their families. Thus being anorexic can bring a great deal of attention, leading to self-perpetuation of the disorder.

Adolescent peer memberships are viewed as being critical in making the transition from childhood to adulthood. Some investigators have noted that anorexics have few if any close peer friendships (Neuman & Halvorson, 1983). Adolescent anorexics' overdependence and involvement with their families may prevent the formation of normal adolescent peer relationships. Thus, these youngsters may be at great disadvantage in making the essential developmental transition to adulthood.

Fifty percent of women diagnosed and treated for anorexia nervosa can be expected to recover completely within 2 to 5 years. Nutritional improvement or recovery can be expected in approximately two thirds of treated cases. Usually, after adequate body weight has been attained, menstruation will resume within a year.

As many as half of all anorexics experience a relapse. Approximately 38% may be re-hospitalized at some point during the next 2 years. Three to 25% of anorexia nervosa cases end in death from medical complications or suicide. This disorder has the highest death rate in psychiatry.

No consensus exists regarding the most effective form of treatment for anorexia nervosa (Vandereycken & Meermann, 1984). The course of treatment typically begins with stabilizing the patient's health, and then it is important that a course of therapy takes place (http://www.something-fishy.org/). Current treatment is aimed at first normalizing body weight, correcting the irrational thinking about weight loss, and finally preventing relapse. To obtain these goals, one must be admitted to a hospital or a day treatment program where the disorder can be monitored (Walsh & Devlin, 1998).

Many forms of treatment for anorexia are used. Therapists have used behavioral therapy, diet counseling, cognitive therapy, cognitive-behavioral treatment, drug treatment, and family therapy with varying degrees of success (Garner & Garfinkel, 1985). Whatever the treatment approach, the usual goals are aimed at increasing confidence and self-esteem, challenging irrational or "anorexic" thinking, developing autonomy, and teaching coping skills. Further, Vandereycken and Meermann (1984, p. 219) suggest that the "best guarantees of success in therapy are a constructive patient/therapist working relationship and an explicit but consistent treatment plan/contract." In the case of drug treatment, the therapist is not trying to treat the eating disorder with medication, but the emotional disorder that they are suffering from that causes the eating disorder (http://www.something-fishy.org/).

Hospitalization becomes necessary when outpatient therapy fails to reverse an impasse or a deteriorating physical or psychological course. The therapist assumes considerable physical and psychological control and responsibility for the care of the hospitalized anorexic. A weight restoration program is usually initiated in which the anorexic is expected to gain at least 1 pound a week until she achieves a target weight consisting of 95% of her ideal weight (Anderson, Morse, & Santmyer, 1985).

Psychotherapy combined with the restoration of weight through direct management of the anorexic's eating is effective in varying degrees. The anorexic has, through her disorder, avoided dealing with several important issues that need to be addressed in psychotherapy. These include individuation, assuming responsibility, separation, becoming an adult, making career and other decisions, and dealing with the loss of one's own life. A key factor in treating eating disorders is to develop a framework for intervention. One should begin prevention of eating disorders to help control the problem. Prevention should be aimed at the students who are susceptible to develop this disorder (Schwitzer, Bergholz, Dore, & Salimi, 1998). Prevention relies on educating individuals about anorexia nervosa. Educating these individuals by giving them facts increases knowledge, and that will likely change their attitude toward anorexia. If the individual continues to develop anorexia, it is assumed that this education will intrigue them to seek help for their existing problem.

Certain beliefs and values seem very important in the maintenance of these conditions. One of these is the belief that weight and shape are extremely important and need to be closely controlled at all cost. A change in these psychopathological beliefs and values concerning body weight and shape may be necessary for complete recovery. Self-help and support groups may be valuable. According to Garrett (1997), anorexics claim that events, people, and processes outside therapy were the most relevant things toward their recovery.

Because eating-disordered individuals are usually perfectionists, teachers can help by advising and encouraging them to take fewer courses and to balance academic loads by combining difficult classes with classes that are less demanding. If hospitalization becomes necessary, and the anorexic student expresses fear that she will be unable to maintain her academic standing, the teacher can point out that usually hospital personnel are more than willing to assist the patient by insuring that the patient will be provided the opportunity to continue uninterrupted with academic requirements. Major treatment centers as well as many hospitals have educational components and academic teachers on their staff.

REFERENCES

American Psychiatric Association. (1994). *Diagnostic and statistical manual of mental disorders* (4th ed.). Washington, DC: Author.

Anderson, A. E., Morse, C., & Santmyer, K. (1985). Inpatient treatment for anorexia nervosa. In D. M. Garner & P. E. Garfinkel (Eds.), *Handbook of psychotherapy for anorexia nervosa and bulimia* (pp. 311–343). New York, NY: Guilford Press.

Bemis, K. M. (1978). Current approaches to the etiology and treatment of anorexia nervosa. *Psychological Bulletin, 35,* 395–617.

Bruch, H. (1985). Four decades of eating disorders. In D. M. Garner & P. E. Garfinkel (Eds.), *Handbook of psychotherapy for anorexia and bulimia* (pp. 7–18). New York, NY: Guilford Press.

Brumberg, J. J. (1977). *The body project: An intimate history of American girls.* New York, NY: Vintage.

Garner, D. M., & Garfinkel, P. E. (Eds.). (1985). *Handbook of psychotherapy for anorexia nervosa and bulimia.* New York, NY: Guilford Press.

Garrett, C. J. (1998). Recovery from anorexia nervosa: A sociological perspective. *International Journal of Eating Disorders, 21,* 261–272.

Halmi, K. A. (1983). Advances in anorexia nervosa. In M. Wolrich & D. K. Routh (Eds.), *Advances in development and behavioral pediatrics* (Vol. 4, pp. 1–23). Greenwich, CT: JAI Press.

Hart, K. J., & Ollendick, T. H. (1985). Prevalence of bulimia in working and university women. *American Journal of Psychiatry, 142,* 851–854.

Johnson, C., & Flach, A. (1985). Family characteristics of 105 patients with bulimia. *American Journal of Psychiatry, 142,* 1321–1324.

Mitchell, J. E., Halsukami, D., Eckert, E. D., & Pyle, R. L. (1985). Characteristics of 275 patients with bulimia. *American Journal of Psychiatry, 142,* 251–255.

Newman, P. A., & Halvorson, P. S. (1983). *Anorexia nervosa and bulimia: A handbook for counselors and therapist.* New York, NY: Van Nostrand Reinhold.

Schwitzer, A. M., Bergholz, K., Dore, T., & Salimi, L. (1998). Eating disorders among college women: Prevention, education, and treatment responses. *College Health, 45*, 199–207.

Shapiro, S., Newcomb, M., & Loeb, T. B. (1997). Fear of fat, disregulated-restrained eating, and body-esteem: Prevalence and gender differences among eight- to ten-year-old children. *Journal of Clinical Psychology, 26*(4).

Vandereycken, W., & Meermann, R. (1984). *Anorexia nervosa: A clinician's guide to treatment*. Berlin, Germany: de Gruyter.

Walsh, B. T., & Devlin, M. (1998). Eating disorders: Progress and problems. *Science, 280*, 1387–1391.

Wooley, S. C., & Wooley, O. W. (1985). Intensive outpatient and residential treatment for bulimia. In D. M. Garner & P. E. Garfinkel (Eds.), *Handbook of psychotherapy for anorexia nervosa and bulimia* (pp. 391–430). New York, NY: Guilford Press.

C. Sue Lamb
University of North Carolina at Wilmington

Wendy L. Flynn
Staffordshire University

See also **Bulimia Nervosa; Eating Disorders; Obsessive-Compulsive Disorders**

ANOSMIA

The term *anosmia* derives from the Greek *an* (without) and *osme* (odor); it refers to the absence or impairment of the sense of smell. Hyposmia refers to diminished olfactory functioning (Mannella, 1999). Synonyms for this condition include anodmia, anosphrasia, and olfactory anesthesia (*Dorland's*, 1981). Organic forms of anosmia are categorized as afferent (related to impaired conductivity of the olfactory nerve), central (due to cerebral disease), obstructive (related to obstruction of the nasal fossae), and peripheral (due to diseases of peripheral olfactory nerves; *Blakiston's*, 1979).

The most common cause of anosmia is a severe head cold or respiratory infection, which intranasal swelling blocks the nasal passages, preventing odors from reaching the olfactory region. This type of anosmia is temporary. Other organic causes of this condition include neoplasms (tumors), head injuries, or chronic rhinitis associated with granulomatous diseases (Levin, Benton, & Grossman, 1982; Mennella, 1999; *Mosby's*, 1983; Thomson, 1979). Anosmia also is a characteristic of olfactogenital dysplasia, also known as *Kallman's syndrome* or anosmia-eunuchoidism. This condition, more prevalent in males, is associated with lack of development of secondary sexual characteristics and anosmia. The apparently X-linked

autosomal dominant or recessive inheritable condition is associated with dysfunction of the hypothalamus and the pituitary (Magalini, 1971). Anosmia with these etiologies typically is a permanent condition. Decreased sense of smell, microsmia, is also common with aging and among smokers.

Psychological forms of anosmia, while less common, may occur. Phobias or fears have been identified as precipitating such forms of anosmia (*Mosby's*, 1983). Specific types of anosmia include anosmia gustatoria (loss of the ability to smell foods) and preferential anosmia (loss of the ability to smell certain odors; *Dorland's*, 1981). Mennella (1999) provides a detailed description of conditions associated with a disturbance of olfaction and excellent clinical analyses with children.

REFERENCES

Blakiston's Gould medical dictionary (4th ed.). (1979). New York, NY: McGraw-Hill.

Dorland's illustrated medical dictionary (26th ed.). (1981). Philadelphia, PA: Saunders.

Levin, H. A., Benton, A. L. M., & Grossman, R. G. (1982). *Neurobehavioral consequences of closed head injury*. New York, NY: Oxford University Press.

Magalini, S. (1971). *Dictionary of medical syndromes*. Philadelphia, PA: Lippincott.

Mennella, J. A. (1999). Taste and smell. In K. F. Swaiman & S. Ashwal (Eds.), *Pediatric neurology* (pp. 105–113). St. Louis, MO: Mosby.

Mosby's medical and nursing dictionary. (1983). St. Louis, MO: Mosby.

Thomson, W. A. R. (1979). *Black's medical dictionary* (32nd ed.). New York, NY: Barnes & Noble.

Cathy F. Telzrow
Kent State University

See also **Traumatic Brain Injury**

ANOXIA

Anoxia literally means an absence of oxygen, a condition that is incompatible with life. Recent terminology more correctly uses the term hypoxia to refer to a condition of lowered oxygen intake. Although hypoxia is compatible with life, long-term sequelae may result depending on the degree and duration of the condition.

Anoxia may be a rare cause of mortality in individuals experiencing status epilepticus (Pellock, 1999) carbon monoxide poisoning, placental insufficiency, microcephaly, or micrencephaly (De Meyer, 1999).

REFERENCES

De Meyer, W. (1999). Microcephaly, micrencephaly, megalocephaly and megalencephaly. In K. F. Swaiman & S. Ashwal (Eds.), *Pediatric neurology* (pp. 301–311). St. Louis, MO: Mosby.

Pellock, J. M. (1999). Status epilepticus. In K. F. Swaiman & S. Ashwal (Eds.), *Pediatric neurology* (pp. 683–691). St. Louis, MO: Mosby.

BRENDA M. POPE
New Hanover Memorial Hospital

See also Asphyxia; Hypoxia

ANTECEDENT

An antecedent is a stimulus that precedes a behavior and may exert discriminative control over that behavior (Heward, 2006; Liauspin, Nelson, & Jolivetter, 2003). Antecedents are implemented by structuring the environment to prevent behavior problems and increasing motivation (Kern & Clemens, 2007). Isolating a specific behavior and defining it in observable and measurable terms allows the antecedents and consequences to be identified. The behavior that is being analyzed is often referred to as the *target behavior* (Alvero & Austin, 2004; Pierangelo & Giuliani, 2006). By manipulating either an antecedent that leads to the target behavior or a consequence of the behavior, modifications can be made to the target behavior. In this way, the teacher or researcher may increase a desired behavior or decrease an undesirable behavior (Scott, Liauspin, Nelson, & Jolivette, 2003).

Following the preceding procedure, if there is a student that is engaging in disruptive behaviors, the first step is to define those behaviors. For example, a student's disruptive behaviors may be operationally defined as repeatedly tapping his pencil on his desk hard enough to produce noise. We then monitor these behaviors recording not only their frequency but also the events that occur before (antecedents) and after (consequences) the behaviors.

Antecedents can be divided into three categories: (1) antecedents that occur in the environment of the target behavior, sometimes called *fast triggers*, (2) antecedents that occur outside of the environment of the target behavior, sometimes called *setting events* or *slow triggers*, and (3) conditions that increase or decrease the likelihood of the behavior occurring, sometimes called *establishing operations*. An antecedent that occurs immediately before the specific, or target, behavior is the easiest to identify and manipulate. When this occurs, the link from antecedent to behavior may become obvious if systematic observation of the target behavior is implemented (Magg, 1999; Scott et al., 2003; Taylor, 2006; Heward, 2006).

We may find that the tapping behavior described previously increases after the teacher has asked for a volunteer or when instructions are given to read silently. By knowing these events trigger the target behaviors, they can be manipulated to reduce the occurrence of the target behaviors. The teacher may ask that the students to put all materials away, including pencils, before asking the class to get out silent reading books.

When an antecedent is removed from the specific environment (occurring before the behavior, but not in the same environment) it is referred to as a *setting event*, as it sets the stage for the event (target behavior) to occur (Heward, 2006; McLoughlin & Lewis, 2005; Taylor, 2006). Because of the separation in time from the antecedent to the target behavior, this form of antecedent is more difficult to connect to the target behavior. However, this form of antecedent is important to identify in order to understand why the behavior is occurring. It is therefore necessary to monitor and accurately record the events that occur regarding a student in all environments so that accurate information can be used to analyze a behavior.

Using the example of the pencil-tapping behavior, a teacher may discover that the behavior increases whenever the student has missed the bus that day or on the days that the student goes to speech therapy. These events are outside of the immediate classroom environment but are affecting the behavior. Knowing this, the teacher may choose to have silent reading on a different day instead of one of the days the student has speech therapy.

The final form of antecedent that may affect the target behavior is an establishing operation or ecological event. This type of antecedent is a condition that affects the likelihood that the student or subject will perform the target behavior (Heward, 2006; Taylor, 2006). Some examples of such conditions include the student or subject being tired, rested, full, hungry, cold, or hot. Because these conditions are intangible, this form of antecedent is the most difficult to monitor; however, once they are identified, they can be controlled.

Continuing to use the example of the student that taps his pencil, by examining all the factors that could be contributing to the tapping behavior, it is possible that intangible patterns may be discovered. It is possible that the teacher, using systematic monitoring of the behavior, discovers that the behavior escalates as the day goes on and then drops again in the afternoon. In this example, it is possible that hunger is adding to the frequency of the tapping. Decreasing the level of hunger in the student may decrease the behavior.

REFERENCES

Alvero, A. M., & Austin, J. (2004). The effects of conducting behavioral observations on the behavior of the observer. *Journal of Applied Behavior Analysis, 37,* 457–468.

Haager, D., & Klinger, J. K. (2005). *Differentiating instruction in inclusive classrooms: The special educator's guide*. New York, NY: Allyn & Bacon.

Heward, W. L. (2006). *Exceptional children: An introduction to special education* (8th ed.). Upper Saddle River, NJ: Pearson Prentice Hall.

Kern, L., & Clemens, N. H. (2007). Antecedent strategies to promote appropriate classroom behavior. *Psychology in the Schools, 44*, 65–75. doi: 10.1002/pits.20206

Magg, J. (1999). *Behavior management: From theoretical implications to practical applications*. San Diego, CA: Singular.

McLoughlin, J. A., & Lewis, R. B. (2005). *Assessing students with special needs* (6th ed.). Upper Saddle River, NJ: Pearson Prentice Hall.

Pierangelo, R., & Giuliani, G. A. (2006). *Assessment in special education: A practical approach* (2nd ed.). New York, NY: Allyn & Bacon.

Scott, T. M., Liaupsin, C. J., Nelson, C. M., & Jolivette, K. (2003). Ensuring student success through team-based functional behavioral assessment. *Teaching Exceptional Children, 35*, 16–21.

Taylor, R. L. (2006). *Assessment of exceptional students: Educational and psychological procedures* (7th ed.). New York, NY: Allyn & Bacon.

WALTER A. ZILZ
Bloomsburg University

ANTECEDENT TEACHING

Antecedent stimuli are those events that occur before a desired response that affect the probability of the occurrence of that response. In *Science and Human Behavior*, Skinner (1953) describes the response sequence as having three parts: the antecedent events, the response, and the consequences. Although much of operant conditioning focuses on the use of consequences to shape learning, antecedent events are equally important in this process. Antecedent teaching involves the use of both antecedent stimuli and antecedent responses in order to increase the frequency of the desired response (Ormrod, 2003). Examples of antecedent stimuli include cueing (or prompting), setting events, generalization, and discrimination. An example of an antecedent response is behavioral momentum.

Cueing involves verbal and nonverbal signals that remind students of expected behaviors. Directing a class to put away their reading materials before lining up to get a drink is an example of a verbal form of cueing. Placing a finger over one's lips in order to quiet a class is an illustration of nonverbal cueing. Setting events involve creating environments whereby the desired response is more likely to occur. An example of a setting event is increasing students' social interaction by having them complete projects in small groups.

Generalization occurs when a learner recognizes that certain responses are expected in similar types of settings. After learning that one must speak quietly in a school library, one recognizes that similar behavior is expected in public libraries. The final component, discrimination, occurs when one recognizes the conditions or circumstances when certain behaviors are expected and when they are not. One raises a hand to ask a question during school but not at home during dinner.

Behavioral momentum, an antecedent response, is the phenomenon of continuing to make appropriate responses based on prior responses. This is more likely to occur if tasks are arranged from least difficult to most difficult. Adding a column of four-digit numbers is more likely to occur after successfully adding a series of two- and three-digit number columns.

Researching the effects of antecedent stimuli on student behavior has been particularly helpful in assisting students with special needs in inclusive settings (Flood & Wilder, 2002; Harrell, 1996; Scott, Liaupin, Nelson, & Jolivette, 2003). Scott et al. (2003) analyzed teachers' directives that triggered inappropriate verbal outbursts in a middle-school student. By examining patterns in verbal antecedent stimuli, student responses, and resulting consequences, the team was able to identify the types of antecedents that worked effectively in facilitating appropriate student behavior. Whereas directions that required extensive peer interaction resulted in disrespectful comments, instructions that allowed for individually completed assignments resulted in compliance and significant achievement. By subsequently allowing the student to complete all group assignments independently, teachers were able to interact effectively with the student, and the student was able to remain in the general education setting.

Research involving antecedent stimuli has also focused on increasing student achievement and teacher effectiveness. Comparing various types of antecedent stimuli enables educators to determine more effective methods when working with students with special needs. Singleton, Schuster, Morse, and Collins (1999) found that students with intellectual disability mastered grocery vocabulary more rapidly when utilizing an antecedent prompt and testing approach. However, students retained the information longer and were able to make generalizations more effectively when utilizing simultaneous prompting procedures.

Research of antecedent stimuli has also focused on teacher effectiveness. Wolfe (1990) found that utilizing visual prompts enhanced teacher questioning strategies and directives when teaching music. Britton, Raizen, Kaser, and Porter (2002), in seeking to close the current achievement gap that exists in mathematics between White and urban minority schools, call for more ethnographic studies that focus on the antecedent instructional conditions that facilitate or frustrate the development of proficiency in quantitative problem solving.

Teachers exert tremendous control over the antecedents to which their students are exposed. These include not only methodological approaches but also curriculum, materials, and classroom atmosphere. The area of antecedent teaching is both broad and important. For more information on how this strategy blends with the area of behavioral teaching, the reader is referred to Skinner (1953, 1968) and Repp (1983).

REFERENCES

Britton, E., Raizen, S., Kaser, J., & Porter, A. (2002). *Open questions in mathematics education.* (ERIC Digest ED 478719).

Flood, W. A., & Wilder, D. A. (2002). Antecedent assessment and assessment based treatment of off-task behavior in a child diagnosed with Attention-Deficit/Hyperactivity Disorder. *Education and Treatment of Children, 25,* 331–338.

Harrell, C. (1996). *General classroom structural interventions for teaching students with Attention-Deficit/Hyperactivity Disorder.* (ERIC Document Reproduction Service No. ED399699).

Ormrod, J. E. (2003). *Educational psychology: Developing learners* (4th ed.). Upper Saddle River, NJ: Merrill Prentice Hall.

Repp, A. C. (1983). *Teaching the mentally retarded.* Englewood Cliffs, NJ: Prentice Hall.

Scott, T. M., Liaupsin, C. J., Nelson, C. M., & Jolivette, K. (2003). Ensuring student success through team-based functional behavior assessment. *Teaching Exceptional Children, 35*(5), 16–21.

Singleton, D. K., Schuster, J. W., Morse, T. E., & Collins, B. C. (1999). A comparison of antecedent prompt and test and simultaneous prompting procedures in teaching grocery words to adolescents with Mental Retardation. *Education and Training in Mental Retardation and Developmental Disability, 34,* 182–199.

Skinner, B. F. (1953). *Science and human behavior.* New York, NY: Macmillan.

Skinner, B. F. (1968). *The technology of teaching.* New York, NY: Appleton-Century-Crofts.

Wolfe, D. E. (1990). Effect of a visual prompt on changes in antecedents and consequents of teaching behavior. *Music Education, 44*(1), 9–13.

Andrew R. Brulle
Jillian N. Lederhouse
Wheaton College

See also **Advance Organizers; Applied Behavior Analysis**

ANTHROPOSOPHIC MOVEMENT

The anthroposophic movement was founded by Rudolf Steiner (1861–1925). Steiner defined anthroposophy as knowledge produced by the higher self in man, and a way of knowledge that undertakes to guide man's spirit to communion with the spirit of the cosmos (Wannamaker, 1965). Anthroposophy postulates a spiritual world beyond man's sensory experiences. Steiner proposed that, through proper training, each person could develop an enhanced consciousness that would restore values and morality to materialistic society.

Steiner became involved in the education of both adults and children. Anthroposophic education for adults took place at the Goetheanum, a school for physical science, near Basel, Switzerland. The Waldorf School, founded in Stuttgart, Germany, in 1919, was the first of several schools for children that sought to reach the inner nature of the child and provide guidance to maturity. By 1965, 80 Waldorf Schools had been attended by more than 25,000 children in the United States and Europe (Wannamaker, 1965). Eurythmy (movement of speech and music) was used to develop concentration, attention, imitation, and an awareness of position in space (Ziegler, 1979). The schools included programming for the emotionally disturbed, socially maladjusted, and other exceptional children.

During a residential tutorship, Steiner began to apply anthroposophic training to the mentally handicapped. Karl Konig, a student of Steiner's, continued the application of Steiner's techniques in an approach known as curative education (Payne & Patton, 1981). In 1939 Konig founded the first integrated community for the intellectually disabled, founded on the anthroposophic philosophy and based in Aberdeen, Scotland (Payne & Patton, 1981). This "Camphill movement" formulated anthroposophy into the following four bases of curative education:

1. A right to education for all children
2. A humanistic/developmental perspective
3. An accepting milieu, providing the disabled with stability and support
4. Group and individual instruction, providing the disabled with a sense of integration with mankind

Camphill communities are comprised of approximately equal numbers of disabled and normal citizens. These self-sufficient, monasticlike communes are comprised of "families" of no more than 15 persons, about half of whom are disabled. Criteria for admission include the ability to care for personal needs and adequate physical health (Zipperlen, 1975). Presently, there are communities in 21 countries in the world (Camphill, 2005).

REFERENCES

Camphill. (2005). *Global directory.* Retrieved from http://www.camphill.org.uk

Payne, J. S., & Patton, J. R. (1981). *Mental retardation*. Columbus, OH: Merrill.

Steiner, R. (1972). *Outline of occult science*. New York, NY: Anthroposophical Society.

Wannamaker, O. D. (1965). *The anthroposophical society: The nature of its objectives*. New York, NY: Anthroposophical Society.

Ziegler, E. F. (1979). *A history of physical education and sport*. Englewood Cliffs, NJ: Prentice Hall.

Zipperlan, H. R. (1975). Normalization. In J. Wortis (Ed.), *Mental retardation and developmental disabilities. Volume VII*. New York, NY: Brunner/Mazel.

ANNE M. BAUER
University of Cincinnati

See also Camphill Community Movement; Humanism and Special Education

ANTICONVULSANTS

Anticonvulsants are medications used to control seizure activity. The appropriate anticonvulsant is chosen on the basis of its safety record, side effects, and the type of seizures that need treatment (Kutscher, 2005). Investigation of the possible effects of anticonvulsant medications on a person's ability to function has been complicated by certain methodological difficulties, including the use of only normal controls, the interaction of a placebo with an active agent, and the use of a limited number of performance measures. Studies tend to fall into three different groups: those that have not distinguished among different drugs, those examining the effects of specific drugs, and those that have included the measurement of serum (blood) anticonvulsant levels (Corbett & Trimble, 1983).

Phenobarbital is perhaps one of the most widely investigated anticonvulsants with regard to effects on cognitive functioning. Lennox (1940) assessed the causes of mental deterioration in 1,245 individuals with epilepsy and determined that in 15% of the cases, the anticonvulsant medication was the cause. In a later publication, Lennox and Lennox (1960) reduced this number to 5%. Relatively few studies on the effects of multiple drugs on children have been carried out. Of the investigations reported, the results have been conflicting. Chaudhry and Pond (1961) examined the causes of intellectual deterioration in 28 children with epilepsy and found no evidence to suggest that anticonvulsant medications were responsible for the noted declines in functioning. Rather, these authors suggested that such declines were related to seizure frequency. In a study of 117 children with seizures in regular public school classes, Holdsworth and Whitmore (1976) reported no differences in academic achievement depending on whether or not phenobarbital had been prescribed. These findings lend support to an earlier study that assessed the psychological performance of 26 epileptic patients over a 3-month period and found little effect on total environmental adjustment caused by the use of anticonvulsants (Loveland, Smith, & Forster, 1957). There were, however, no controls in the study and the majority of patients had been receiving anticonvulsant medication for several years prior to the study.

Conversely, a number of studies of multiple drug effects have reported learning impairments with specific deficits noted in visual-spatial perception and performance (Cepeda, 1997; Rayo & Martin, 1959; Tchicaloff & Gaillard, 1970). In a study by Hutt, Jackson, Belsham, and Higgins (1968), phenobarbital was administered to normal subjects with serum level control. Decreases in abilities were noted that were related to phenobarbital blood serum levels. These effects were seen most prominently on tasks requiring sustained attention, psychomotor performance, and spontaneous speech. The drug effects became more prominent as the tasks became longer and more difficult and as the degree of external constraint (having the examiner in the room) was decreased. It was concluded that phenobarbital has effects maximally evident on tasks requiring attention and concentration, but that it also may have pronounced effects on motor coordination.

Unfavorable behavioral changes have been estimated to occur in 20% to 75% of children receiving phenobarbital as prophylaxis for febrile convulsions in infancy (Bennett & Ho, 1997; Heckmatt, Houston, & Dodds, 1976; Thorn, 1975; Wolf & Forsythe, 1978). Although no significant IQ differences were reported for groups of toddlers receiving an 8- to 12-month period of phenobarbital or placebo, there were effects on memory that were related to blood serum levels and effects on comprehension that were related to the duration of treatment (Camfield et al., 1979). There was no evidence of hyperactivity, although 15 of the 315 children on phenobarbital in the study did demonstrate an increase in "daytime fussiness and irritability."

Phenytoin (Dilantin) is the most widely used anticonvulsant in the world (Bennett & Ho, 1997; Dodrill, 1981; Hartlage & Hartlage, 1997). It has been shown to be effective with a broad range of attacks including generalized tonic-clonic seizures, most types of partial seizures, and some other less frequently observed seizure types. Acute intoxication with phenytoin leads to a confusional state, occasionally referred to as encephalopathy, which is associated with neurological symptoms of toxicity, especially ataxia and nystagmus (Corbett & Trimble, 1983). It also has been demonstrated that prolonged use of this medication, even in low doses (Logan & Freeman, 1969; Vallarta, Bell, & Reichert, 1974), may result in a clinical picture of a progressive degenerative disorder that may occur without the classic signs of such a disorder. Rosen (1968) and Stores (1975) have both reported impaired intellectual performance on long-term treatment with phenytoin. Dodrill

(1975) reports that phenytoin has behavioral effects specifically related to motor performance decrements.

Ethosuximide (Zarontin), an anticonvulsant used with children for control of absence (petit mal) seizures, has been shown to impair memory and speech as well as result in affective disturbances (Guey et al., 1967). Soulayrol and Roger (1970) reported intellectual impairment in children treated with this medication; however, other studies have not confirmed this (e.g., Brown et al., 1975).

Carbamazepine (Tegretol) has been reported to have psychotropic effects. About half of 40 studies cited by Dalby (1975), in a major review of the literature, reported a beneficial psychologic effect. Typically, improvements in mood and behavior have been noted, as manifested by greater cooperativeness, reduced irritability, and a possible decrease in aggression. Increases in cognitive skill levels have been reported as well (Bennett & Ho, 1997). There have been no reported studies of the effects of primidone (Mysoline) on behavior in children, although adults occasionally have been reported to develop a florid confusional state on doses within the normal therapeutic range (Booker, 1972). It is well recognized that the drug initially may cause drowsiness and have effects similar to phenobarbital in causing restlessness in some children.

Trimble and Corbett (1980a, 1980b) studied the relationship between anticonvulsant drug levels and the behavior and cognitive performance of 312 children with seizures. The drug most commonly prescribed was phenytoin, followed by carbamazepine, valproic acid, primidone, and phenobarbital. A decrease in IQ was noted in 15% of the 204 children studied; these children had significantly higher mean phenytoin and primidone levels than other subjects. A distinct relationship between an increase in serum drug levels and a decline in nonverbal skills was reported.

Newer anticonvulsants such as gabapentin (Neurontin), topiramate (Topamax), tiagabine (Gabatril), and lamotrigine (Lamictal) are generally used as add-on therapy for partial seizures in children under the age of 12 (Kutscher, 2005). Despite these side effects associated with anticonvulsants, they are recognized as essential in the management of epilepsy. According to Dodrill (1981), when anticonvulsant blood serum levels fall within therapeutic ranges and when there are no overt signs of toxicity, the chances of deleterious effects are minimal if detectable at all. Furthermore, the deleterious effects are distinctly offset by decreased seizure frequency, which has known effects on the deterioration of mental functions. It is far preferable to have modest drug side effects than seizures. Other, low incidence drugs used as anticonvulsants are reviewed in detail by Bennett and Ho (1997).

REFERENCES

Bennett, T., & Ho, M. (1997). The neuropsychology of pediatric epilepsy and antiepileptic drugs. In C. R. Reynolds & E. Fletcher-Janzen (Eds.), *Handbook of clinical child neuropsychology* (2nd ed., pp. 517–538). New York, NY: Plenum Press.

Booker, H. E. (1972). Primidone toxicity. In D. M. Woodbury, J. K. Penry, & R. P. Schmidt (Eds.), *Antiepileptic drugs* (pp. 169–204). New York, NY: Raven.

Brown, T. R., Dreifuss, F. E., Dyken, P. R., Goode, D. J., Penry, J. K., Porter, R. J., White, B. J., & White, P. T. (1975). Ethosuccimide in the treatment of absence (petit mal) seizures. *Neurology, 25,* 515–525.

Camfield, C. S., Chaplin, S., Doyle, A. B., Shapiro, S. H., Cummings, C., & Camfield, P. R. (1979). Side effects of phenobarbitone in toddlers: Behavioral and cognitive effects. *Journal of Pediatrics, 95,* 361–365.

Cepeda, M. (1997). Nonstimulant psychotropic medication: Desired effects and cognitive/behavioral adverse effects. In C. R. Reynolds & E. Fletcher-Janzen (Eds.), *Handbook of clinical child neuropsychology* (2nd ed., pp. 573–586). New York, NY: Plenum Press.

Chaudhry, M. R., & Pond, D. A. (1961). Mental deterioration in epileptic children. *Journal of Neurology, Neurosurgery, & Psychiatry, 24,* 213–219.

Corbett, J. A., & Trimble, M. R. (1983). Epilepsy and anticonvulsant medication. In M. Rutter (Eds.), *Developmental neuropsychiatry* (pp. 112–129). New York, NY: Guilford Press.

Dalby, M. A. (1975). Behavioral effects of carbamazepine. In J. K. Penry & D. D. Daley (Eds.), *Advances in neurology* (Vol. 11, pp. 130–149). New York, NY: Raven.

Dodrill, C. B. (1975). Diphenylhydantoin serum levels, toxicity, and neuropsychological performance in patients with epilepsy. *Epilepsia, 16,* 593–600.

Dodrill, C. B. (1981). Neuropsychology of epilepsy. In S. B. Filskov & T. J. Boll (Eds.), *Handbook of clinical neuropsychology* (pp. 366–395). New York, NY: Wiley.

Guey, J., Charles, C., Coquery, C., Roger, J., & Soulayrol, R. (1967). Study of the psychological effects of ethosuccimide on 25 children suffering from petit mal epilepsy. *Epilepsia, 8,* 129–141.

Hartlage, R. L., & Hartlage, L. C. (1997). The neuropsychology of epilepsy: Overview and psychosocial aspects. In C. R. Reynolds & E. Fletcher-Janzen (Eds.), *Handbook of clinical child neuropsychology* (2nd ed., pp. 506–516). New York, NY: Plenum Press.

Heckmatt, J., Houston, A., & Dodds, K. (1976). Failure of phenobarbitone to prevent febrile convulsions. *British Medical Journal, 1,* 559–561.

Holdsworth, L., & Whitmore, K. (1976). A study of children with epilepsy attending ordinary schools. *Developmental Medicine & Child Neurology, 16,* 746–758.

Hutt, S. J., Jackson, P. M., Belsham, A., & Higgins, G. (1968). Perceptual motor behavior in relation to blood phenobarbitone levels: A preliminary report. *Development Medicine & Child Neurology, 10,* 626–632.

Kutscher, M. L. (2005). *Diagnostic tests and treatment.* Retrieved from http://www.pediatricneurology.com/treatment.htm

Lennox, W. G. (1940). Brain injury, drugs, and environment as a cause of mental decay in epilepsy. *American Journal of Psychiatry, 99,* 174–180.

Lennox, W. G., & Lennox, M. A. (1960). *Epilepsy and related disorders*. Boston, MA: Little, Brown.

Logan, W. J., & Freeman, J. M. (1969). Pseudodegenerative diseases due to diphenylhydantoin intoxication. *Archives of Neurology, 21*, 631–637.

Loveland, N., Smith, B., & Forster, F. (1957). Mental and emotional changes in epileptic patients on continuous anticonvulsant medication. *Neurology, 7*, 856–865.

Rayo, D., & Martin, F. (1959). Standardized psychometric tests applied to the analysis of the effects of anticonvulsant medication on the proficiency of young epileptics. *Epilepsia, 1*, 189–207.

Rosen, J. A. (1968). Dilantin dementia. *Transactions of the American Neurological Association, 93*, 273–277.

Soulayrol, R., & Roger, J. (1970). Effects psychiatriques defovorables des medications antiepileptiques. *Revue de Neuropsychiatrie Infantile* (English abstract), *18*, 599–603.

Stores, G. (1975). Behavioral effects of anticonvulsant drugs. *Developmental Medication & Child Neurology, 17*, 547–658.

Tchicaloff, M., & Gaillard, F. (1970). Quelques effets indesirables des medicaments antiepileptiques sur les rendements intellectuels. *Revue de Neuropsychiatrie Infantile* (English abstract), *18*, 599–603.

Thorn, I. (1975). A controlled study of prophylactic longterm treatment of febrile convulsions with phenobarbital. *Acta Neurologica Scandinavica, 60*, 67–70.

Trimble, M. R., & Corbett, J. A. (1980a). Anticonvulsant drugs and cognitive function. In J. A. Wada & J. K. Penry (Eds.), *Advances in epileptology: The X International Symposium*. New York, NY: Raven.

Trimble, M. R., & Corbett, J. A. (1980b). Behavioral and cognitive disturbances in epileptic children. *Irish Medical Journal, 73*, 21–28.

Vallarta, J. M., Bell, D. B., & Reichert, A. (1974). Progressive encephalopathy due to chronic hydantoin intoxication. *American Journal of Diseases of Children, 128*, 27–34.

Wolf, S. M., & Forsythe, A. (1978). Behavior disturbance, phenobarbital, and febrile seizures. *Pediatrics, 61*, 728–730.

RICHARD A. BERG
West Virginia University Medical Center

See also **Dilantin; Medication; Phenobarbital; Seizure Disorders; Tegretol**

ANTIHISTAMINES

Antihistamines are a class of pharmaceutical agents that block the effect of histamine. Histamine is a naturally occurring body substance that is released in certain allergic reactions. Typically, antihistamines are more effective in preventing rather than in reversing the action of histamine. For pediatric populations, antihistamines may be effective in the treatment of hay fever or mild recurrent hives of unknown etiology. Some antihistamines, particularly Atarax and Vistaril, are used as safe, alternative antianxiety medications without withdrawal (Cepeda, 1997). Some research also has suggested the potential efficacy of antihistamines in the prevention of motion sickness in children (Macnair, 1983).

Typically, antihistamines are found in cold preparations prescribed for children (Pruitt, 1985). Children who are treated with antihistamines are likely to have less severe runny noses, yet the other features of the common cold are not significantly affected by this class of drugs. Antihistamines have atropine like effects that diminish the amount of secretions produced by the irritated lining of the nose or bronchial passages. Although some antihistamines have been marketed as cough suppressants, a number of studies have shown that antihistamines are no better than placebos in relieving children of the symptoms of the common cold (Markowitz, 1983).

Because the use of minor and major tranquilizers carries significant disadvantages in the treatment of behavioral and anxiety disorders in children (Popper, 1985), it has been suggested that antihistamines be used short term for calming acutely anxious children (Cepeda, 1997) and for controlling agitation in severely psychotic children (Popper, 1985). Risks of recreational abuse, management abuse, tolerance, and dependence are also lower than for anti-anxiety agents and major tranquilizers (Cepeda, 1997; Popper, 1985), making this class of drugs more appealing for use by the practicing physician. The enduring cognitive effects of antihistamines are not well documented in the empirical literature, although some recent research has suggested an amelioration of behavioral difficulties and improved academic performance in response to antihistamine therapy (McLoughlin et al., 1983). Further, some investigators (Mattes, 1979; Millichap, 1973) have found antihistamines to be efficacious in the treatment and management of hyperactivity. While the effects of antihistamines on cognitive and learning outcome appear to be somewhat promising, more research must be mounted before any definitive conclusions can be made in this area. Moreover, while the use of antihistamines in the treatment of psychiatric disorders of children may provide a safer alternative than the use of other psychotropic agents, including neuroleptic agents and antianxiety drugs, it still entails some of the same risks and the physician must carefully weigh the potential benefits against any possible risks.

Although the long-term effects of antihistamines have received little systematic study, the use of these agents appears to provide primarily short-term benefits. They are typically safe and consequently are often sold without a prescription. They may have adverse effects, although these usually occur with higher doses. Sedation is the most common side effect in children, but some tolerance may develop. These negative side effects are associated mostly with the first-generation oral antihistamines. Second-generation antihistamines cause little or no sedation effect due to their low lipophilicity, their large molecular size, their greater affinity for peripheral H_1 receptors, and their relative lack of affinity for neuroreceptors (NIAID, 2003).

Combinations of anthistamines with other central nervous system depressants (e.g., alcohol) should be avoided. In high doses, or for children who are particularly sensitive to these agents, antihistamines may cause undesirable side effects. These may include excitation, nervousness, palpitations, rapid heartbeat, dryness of the mouth, urinary retention, and constipation. In rare instances, red blood cells can burst (hemolytic anemia) or bone marrow can be depleted of blood-forming cells (agranulocytosis; Markowitz, 1983). Sustained antihistamine usage with pediatric populations may be associated with persistent daytime drowsiness, "hangover," or mild enduring effects on cognition (Popper, 1985). Although such side effects are better tolerated by younger children than by adolescents, the occurrence of these effects should result in the prompt cessation of antihistamine therapy.

REFERENCES

Cepeda, M. (1997). Nonstimulant psychotropic medication: Desired effects and cognitive/behavioral adverse effects. In C. R. Reynolds & E. Fletcher-Janzen (Eds.), *Handbook of clinical child neuropsychology* (2nd ed., pp. 573–586). New York, NY: Plenum Press.

Macnair, A. L. (1983). Cinnarizine in the prophylaxis of car sickness in children. *Current Medical Research Opinion, 8*, 451–455.

Markowitz, M. (1983). Immunity, allergy, and related diseases. In R. E. Behrman & V. C. Vaughn (Eds.), *Nelson textbook of pediatrics* (pp. 497–594). Philadelphia, PA: Saunders.

Mattes, J. (1979). Trial of diphenpyraline in hyperactive children (letter). *Psychopharmacology Bulletin, 15*, 5–6.

McLoughlin, J., Nall, M., Isaacs, P., Petrosko, J., Karibo, J., & Lindsey, B. (1983). The relationship of allergies and allergy treatment to school performance and student behavior. *Annals of Allergy, 51*, 506–510.

Millichap, J. G. (1973). Drugs in management of minimal brain dysfunction. *Annals of the New York Academy of Science, 205*, 321–334.

National Institute of Allergy and Infectious Diseases (NIAID). (2005). *Current trends.* Retrieved from http://www.nih.gov/

Popper, C. W. (1985). Child and adolescent psychopharmacology. In R. Michels & J. O. Cavenar (Eds.), *Psychiatry* (Vol. 2, pp. 1–23). New York, NY: Lippincott.

Pruitt, A. W. (1985). Rational use of cold and cough preparations. *Pediatric Annals, 14*, 289–291.

RONALD T. BROWN
Emory University School of Medicine

See *also* Tranquilizers

ANTISOCIAL BEHAVIOR

A study by Peterson (1961) considered a sampling of many behaviors of children that could be considered as antisocial. More than 400 representative case folders from files of a child-guidance clinic were inspected and the referral problems of each child noted. Peterson's results indicated that the interrelationship among 58 items could be reduced to two independent clusters: conduct problems and personality problems. The two dimensions of problems most frequently reported among the public school students in these two major clusters were aggression and withdrawal. Each child could be placed somewhere in these two dimensions regardless of the number of problem behaviors or other dimensions the child manifested. Children's behaviors differ quantitatively not qualitatively. The degree of quantitative difference between normal and abnormal is usually slight.

Definitions are particularly difficult to generate when context is general and critical, as is the case when the word "social" is used. While there is a need to convey with words what is meant by antisocial behavior, the intensity, timeliness, and impact of a behavior on others in the culture/society/group where the behavior is experienced determines the definition; therefore, a static meaning is not effective. Antisocial behaviors or misbehaving (disliked performances) are accepted daily by society. A behavior is labeled antisocial when the tolerance level of an observer is exceeded with respect to that observer's interpretation of societal rules.

For example, aggressive antisocial behavior is manifested when a student stands and yells a phrase of profanity during a school assembly. The consequences of such behavior could be removal from the audience (peer group), immediate verbal reprimand by adult authorities, a quick trip to the administrator's office, or dismissal from a school. In contrast, if the same pupil were to stand during a professional ball game and yell the same phrase of profanity, not only might the audience approve of the behavior, it might even reward the verbal expressiveness.

Variables in the environment that define the tolerance level of observers when a behavior is judged antisocial are many: time, social status, money, event, location, age, reputation, intensity, duration, frequency, and group expectations. When the cumulative effect of these variables is negative, exceeding the dynamic acceptable definition of the moment, a person's behavioral performance is judged antisocial. For example, when a behavior is poorly timed, appropriate social status is not recognized, intensity is high and loud, the behavior is against school rules, reputation is known, duration is long, frequency is perceived as too often, and other students are conforming to rules of the environment, an antisocial behavior is said to exist. To identify specific factors related to perceptions of antisocial behavior, recent investigation has emphasized those behaviors that teachers and students find most disturbing. Aggressive behavior is most often primary, but withdrawal behaviors such as fear, anxiety, and tension are also defined as antisocial.

This second type of antisocial behavior is reported to be more tolerable to society. The child suffering from withdrawal may be in deeper pain, despair, or depression than an aggressive individual; however, such a child is less aversive to adults and peers, and less likely to excite the environment into action. These children have too little behavior rather than too much. Characteristics accompanying withdrawal are feelings of inferiority and self-consciousness, social withdrawal, shyness, anxiety, weeping, hypersensitivity, infrequent social smiles, nail chewing, depression and chronic sadness, drowsiness, sluggishness, daydreaming, passivity, short attention span, preoccupation, and somber quietness. These children are also picked on by others.

The term antisocial behavior is often applied when behaviors remain inflexible, or frozen, and the person performing the behaviors continues to react to the environment in a manner judged by the group to be displeasing, inappropriate, and uncomfortable. The label antisocial behavior is attached to the person displaying the behavior and the definition itself magnifies the individual's differences. Not only does the behavior classify a person, but the antisocial definition itself accentuates differences. Only if classification leads to positive action through school programs on the behalf of the child is this definition constructive.

Characteristics

Patterns, for example, of antisocial behavior have received a variety of labels, for example, unsocialized aggressive, conduct disorder, aggressive, unsocialized psychopathic, psychopathic delinquent, antisocially aggressive, and sadistically aggressive. Children exhibiting antisocial behaviors apparent to school officials and teachers may demonstrate one or more of the following characteristics.

1. An inability to learn that cannot be explained by conventional intellectual, sensory, or health factors. A learning-disabled child seldom escapes recognition. He or she is frequently labeled learning disabled, thus lowering self-esteem. The inability to learn is perhaps the single most significant characteristic of antisocial children, with the learning disability manifested as the inability to profit from social experiences and/or academic instruction.

2. An inability to build and maintain satisfactory interpersonal relationships with peers and teachers; to demonstrate sympathy and warmth toward others; to stand alone when necessary; to have close friends; to be aggressively constructive; to enjoy working and playing with others as well as working and playing alone. Children who are unable to build and maintain satisfactory interpersonal relationships are easily defined as different by teachers and peers.

3. "Inappropriate" behaviors or feelings that occur under normal conditions. What is appropriate is judged by the teacher and the student's peers. This judgment is sensed by children because of their ability to profit from school experiences and relate to their teachers. Children classified as antisocial often cannot learn what is appropriate because of their inability to relate to and profit from cultural experiences. This amplifies the daily failures of children who fail to conform to social/cultural rules and exacerbates their lack of socialization.

4. Lack of flexibility. When behaviors become frozen into patterns of inappropriateness of such intensity, duration, and frequency that they interfere with social activities of a group, those behaviors are identified as antisocial.

5. Depression and general moods of unhappiness, characteristics of withdrawal. When children seldom smile and express unhappiness in play, art work, group discussions, and language arts, the observer should watch for antisocial expression.

6. A tendency to develop physical symptoms, pains, or fears, especially in reaction to school situations or authority figures. These symptoms may indicate potential antisocial behaviors.

7. Disobedience, disruptiveness, fighting, temper tantrums, irresponsibility, impertinence, jealousy, anger, bossiness, the use of profanity, attention-seeking behavior, boisterousness, defiance of authority, feelings of guilt and inadequacy, irritability, and quarrelsomeness. These descriptors are often associated with antisocial phenomena.

Behaviors described by these characteristics may formulate a pattern of active antisocial behavior that results in conflict with parents, peers, and social institutions. Children and adolescents who represent extreme patterns of antisocial behaviors are likely to have difficulty with law-enforcement agencies. Extreme antisocial behavior will be defined as criminal conduct and result in arrest, incarceration, recidivism, and failure to become a good citizen.

Acquisition

The possibility of hereditary or predispositional factors cannot be ignored, neither can the contributions of organic factors be ruled out. Prematurity (birth weight less than 5 pounds), is regarded as an important cause of brain damage in children. Epilepsy and cerebral palsy studies report higher prevalances of antisocial behaviors among those with known brain lesions. Situations where trait patterns of deviant behavior can be studied along with the mechanisms by which the acquisition of the traits occurs is very revealing. Sociological literature has emphasized social class, deviant social organization, and social inequalities as influential. The family is also a setting where deviant behavior has been studied. It is obvious in making the acquisition of principal behavioral patterns of antisocial behavior more probable. Psychiatric illness in parents reflects an increased rate of behavior problems in children. Antisocial parents tend to rear antisocial children. Childhood behavior problems are more common among lower socioeconomic classes. To what extent the influence of parents' disturbances on the child's behavior is genetic and to what extent it is environmental, is speculative.

Children with antisocial behaviors are most visible when required to pay strict attention, follow directions, demonstrate control, exhibit socially acceptable behavior, and master academic skills. School, the primary socializing agency for society, emphasizes conformity and educational achievement. These expectations are basic to the order of formal training. When children are unable to meet these expectations, concerns frequently arise among teachers. Questions educators pose may include: How many children are there? How do they behave? How can they be controlled and managed in the classroom? How should they be classified to reduce effects created by labels? What support systems can provide these children with needed programs?

Terms used in educational settings to describe children with antisocial behaviors are emotionally disturbed, socially maladjusted, minimally neurologically impaired, culturally disadvantaged, behavior disordered, educationally handicapped, and conduct disturbed. Such labels represent different orientations that exist among educators confronted with the task of providing educational programs for children with antisocial behaviors. All these labels could be used collectively for a single child experiencing difficulty in school. For qualification for programs, labels and treatments should be closely related to how the antisocial child (in classroom, community, or at home) is perceived (by educators, social groups, or family). Educational offerings frequently depend on how a child is perceived and the attitude of the referring school toward the child.

Treatment

When an individual has appropriate behavioral responses in his or her repertoire and exhibits these responses under appropriate circumstances, antisocial behavior is interpreted. Through systematic and explicit application of the principles of learning, behavior management can be applied in educational settings to treat antisocial behaviors.

The individual can be helped to change deficient or maladaptive behavior by receiving assistance to modify his or her responses to specific sound cues. In the case of maladaptive behavior, for example, aggression could be modified to be elicited or emitted under appropriate circumstances only. This type of behavioral learning, unlearning, or relearning is known as behavior management. The teacher or behaviorist operates on the assumption that the behavior can be modified without understanding why the behavior is antisocial. The antecedents to the behavior need not be reconstructed to initiate corrective action. Teaching the child to react more appropriately is the only relevant issue, not finding out how the child came to behave antisocially. The focus during behavior therapy is on teaching new behaviors and eliminating old ones. The first task of the therapist (teacher) is to decide which behavior should be modified. Once a target behavior is defined, the treatment goal can be specified. Treatments are based on principles of learning: respondent learning, operant conditioning, interrelationships of operation and respondent factors, social reinforcement, desensitization, and aversive and contingency control. The treatment goal is assessed when the antisocial behavior has become adapted. If in the process of identifying target behaviors the teacher discovers antecedents as causes, the organization of the classroom environment, stimuli, and consequences can be arranged so that the learning situation supports the child's development. An engineered, structured classroom with clear-cut expectations and rewarding consequences for appropriate behavior and academic accomplishment can result in definite academic and behavioral gains. Primary or tangible rewards, teacher attention, "game" approaches, and high-interest activities can become successful interventions for adapting antisocial behaviors. Precision teaching involves selecting a behavior, charting it on a graph, recording changes and occurrences, analyzing the child's performance, and changing the program according to program effects. Some schools use a resource room concept, in which the child participates part time in a special program and part time in a regular class program.

Completely self-contained classrooms for children with more severe learning and behavioral problems can be successful. The engineered classroom directs attention to the establishment of specific goals or develops a sequence of behavioral objectives, for example, attention, response, order, exploration, social activity, mastery, and achievement. This engineering translates behavior modification strategy into realistic use in the classroom. There is constant manipulation of stimuli and intervention in the class to assure a child's continued success.

There are limitless behaviors that can disturb, interfere, or interrupt. There are as many interventions to attempt to modify disturbing behaviors. The range of children's behaviors that are judged negatively is extensive, especially in the complex social system called school. Our tendency is to cause a child to internalize his or her problematic characteristics through inadvertent reinforcement.

Reactors classify, define, program, analyze, label, and provide some services to those identified as aggressive when threatening behaviors become a serious concern. Seldom do educators recognize the responder as a contributor to the disturbances. The child judged as antisocial is the one who violates a large number of behavioral codes, yet some of the most seriously troubled go unrecognized and untreated as passive aggressors.

The intensity of observer reaction may be related to the observer's own social tolerance and his or her difficulty in controlling comparable tendencies. Certainly, the observer's tolerance plays a significant role in determining the services to be received by the antisocial performer.

If a tree crashes in the forest but there is no human ear to hear it, is there a noise? When an individual behaves in an antisocial fashion, does the disturbance exist without a reactor to register the event? Does the disturbance reside in the child or the reactor, or is it a product of both?

REFERENCE

Quay, H. C., & Werry, J. S. (1972). *Psychopathological disorders of childhood*. New York, NY: Wiley.

ANNE SABATINO
Hudson, Wisconsin

See also Conduct Disorder; Emotional Disorders; Seriously Emotionally Disturbed

ANTISOCIAL PERSONALITY

The antisocial personality is characterized by a recurring pattern of antisocial behaviors and a general disregard for the rights of others. This pattern of behavior has, in the past, been referred to as psychopathy or sociopathy. It emerges during childhood in the form of truancy and other school-related academic and behavior problems such as delinquency, lying, fighting, sexual promiscuity, substance abuse, and running away from home. The *DSM-IV* (American Psychiatric Association [DSM-IV-TR], 2000) requires at least four of the following nine manifestations of the disorder be present before a diagnosis of antisocial personality disorder (APD) is made: inability to sustain consistent work behavior; lack of ability to function as a responsible parent; failure to accept social norms with respect to lawful behavior; inability to maintain enduring attachment to a sexual partner; irritability or aggressiveness; failure to honor financial obligations; failure to plan ahead, or impulsivity; disregard for the truth; and

recklessness. Cleckley (1976) has identified other characteristics such as lack of remorse or shame, failure to learn from experience, poor judgment, and absence of anxiety.

The diagnosis of APD is typically reserved for individuals age 18 and over. Younger children and adolescents who manifest signs of APD are diagnosed as conduct disorder. There are four subtypes of conduct disorder depending on the presence or absence of normal social attachments and aggressive behavior. Many, but not all, children who manifest conduct disorder go on to develop an antisocial personality disorder (Loeber, 1982). Research has identified five factors that appear to play a role in the etiology of APD including heredity, brain abnormalities, autonomic nervous system underarousal, and family and environmental influences.

REFERENCES

American Psychiatric Association. (2000). *Diagnostic and statistical manual of mental disorders* (4th ed., text rev.). Washington, DC: Author.

Cleckley, H. M. (1976). *The mask of sanity* (5th ed.). St. Louis, MO: Mosby.

Loeber, R. (1982). The stability of antisocial and delinquent behavior: A review. *Child Development, 53*, 1431–1446.

ROBERT G. BRUBAKER
Eastern Kentucky University

See also Aggression; Conduct Disorder

ANTISOCIAL PERSONALITY DISORDER

Antisocial Personality Disorder (ASPD) falls under the broadband heading of *Personality Disorders* found in the *Diagnostic and Statistical Manual of Mental Disorders*, fourth edition (*DSM-IV;* American Psychiatric Association, 2000). According to the *DSM-IV*, to be diagnosed with ASPD an individual must demonstrate a pervasive pattern of disregard for and violation of the rights of others occurring since age 15, as evidenced by three or more of the following seven characteristics: (1) a failure to conform to social norms with respect to lawful behaviors such as by repeatedly engaging in acts that are grounds for arrest; (2) a pattern of deceitfulness exhibited by the use of aliases, repeated lying, or surreptitiously depriving others out of personal profit or pleasure; (3) impulsivity or failure to plan ahead; (4) behaving in an irritable and aggressive manner, as documented by repeated physical fights or assaults; (5) showing reckless disregard for the safety of others or one's self; (6) consistent irresponsibility, as documented by a failure to honor financial obligations or being unable to maintain consistent work or employment over time; and (7) demonstrating an aloofness or lack of remorse toward having hurt, mistreated, or stolen from someone.

In addition, the individual must be at least 18 years of age at the time of ASPD diagnosis; there must be evidence of a diagnosis of Conduct Disorder (CD) with onset before age 15 years; and the individual's antisocial behavior cannot occur exclusively during the course of Schizophrenia or a Manic Episode. As the *DSM-IV* points out, the core feature of ASPD is the pervasive pattern of disregard for and violation of the rights of others that often begins in childhood or early adolescence. The use of deceit and manipulation are constant themes in the life and behavior of such individuals (American Psychiatric Association, 1994).

Educational practitioners need to be aware that just as there is a developmental progression or link between Oppositional Defiant Disorder (ODD) and CD, there is also a developmental progress, or strong link, between CD in childhood or adolescence and ASPD in adulthood (Hinshaw & Lee, 2003; for a broader understanding of developmental issues related to ODD or CD, child psychopathology, and antisocial behavior, the reader is directed to the work of Cicchetti & Nurcombe, 1993; Dishion, French, & Patterson, 1995; Mash & Dozois, 2003). Adults diagnosed with ASPD have almost always been diagnosed with CD earlier in life, with the predicted poor outcome of ASPD being increased significantly if Substance Abuse is involved (Hinshaw & Lee, 2003). Moreover, official court record evidence shows that 50% to 70% of youths with CD, or youths who have been arrested for delinquent acts during childhood or adolescence, are arrested in adulthood (Lahey & Loeber, 1997). Longitudinal sample studies have documented that 40% to 43% of children or youth with CD who had either been reared in institutional or group home settings or who had been receiving treatment in psychiatric clinics for severe Antisocial Behavior met criteria for ASPD in adulthood (Harrington, Fudge, Rutter, Pickles, & Hill, 1991; Zoccolillo, Pickles, Quinton, & Rutter, 1992). Kratzer and Hodgins (1997) study also supports these findings in which a large birth cohort of over 12,700 males and females were followed up at age 30. By age 30, 76% of the males and 30% of the females who met criteria for childhood CD had either a criminal record, a mental disorder (i.e., severe Substance Abuse), or both.

Although, as the preceding data suggests, not all children or youth with CD end up with a diagnosis of ASPD, it still begs the question of what predicts whether a child with CD will be diagnosed with later adult ASPD. To date, relatively few predictive studies have been carried out; however, some researchers have found that (a) children with CD with a biological parent with ASPD are more likely to meet the criteria of ASPD than children with CD who do not have a biological parent with ASPD, (b) lower intelligence is associated with the persistence of juvenile

delinquency and CD into adulthood, and (c) a history of ASPD in a biological parent is the most powerful predictor of *persistence* of CD from childhood into adolescence, but this predictive relationship is affected by whether youths have strong verbal abilities (i.e., verbal IQ score above 100), such that if a child or youth with CD possesses a verbal IQ score of above 100 and does not have a biological parent with ASPD, then there is a substantially lower risk of persistent CD than for all other children or youth with CD (Lahey & Loeber, 1997).

The preceding data and information make it clear that adults who meet criteria for ASPD will have started their antisocial lifestyle earlier in life, before age 15, in fact, as the diagnosis of ASPD requires an individual to have previously met criteria for CD (Hinshaw & Lee, 2003; Kratzer & Hodgins, 1997). Interestingly, and while rare, there are small subgroups of adults who engage in antisocial activities without any noteworthy childhood patterns of behavior indicative of CD (Hinshaw & Lee, 2003). Children and youth who display CD are highly likely to become substance abusers, juvenile delinquents, and adult criminals; as adults with ASPD, these poor and negative outcomes continue to exacerbate, leading to further troubles such as marital discord or divorce; mental health or psychiatric difficulties of all types; premature death; holding multiple jobs over a short time span; unemployment; having no confiding relationships; persistent friction with friends, workmates, and neighbors; domestic violence; inept parenting; drug and alcohol addiction; and so on (Dishion et al., 1995; Kratzer & Hodgins, 1997). These poor adult outcomes have their genesis in childhood, making it abundantly clear that in order to prevent such outcomes, early intervention and treatment at home and school is critical and may be the best and only opportunity these children have to lead successful lives as adults (Farmer, Compton, Burns, & Robertson, 2002; Walker, Colvin, & Ramsey, 1995).

REFERENCES

American Psychiatric Association. (2000). *Diagnostic and statistical manual of mental disorders* (4th ed., text rev.). Washington, DC: Author.

Cicchetti, D., & Nurcombe, B. (Eds.). (1993). Toward a developmental perspective on Conduct Disorder [special issue]. *Developmental Psychopathology, 5*, 518–537.

Dishion, T. J., French, D. C., & Patterson, G. R. (1995). The development and ecology of Antisocial Behavior. In D. Cicchetti & D. J. Cohen (Eds.), *Developmental psychopathology* (Vol. 2, pp. 421–471). New York, NY: Wiley.

Farmer, M. Z., Compton, S. N., Burns, B. J., & Robertson, E. (2002). Review of the evidence base for treatment of childhood psychopathology: Externalizing disorders. *Journal of Consulting and Clinical Psychology, 70*, 1267–1302.

Harrington, R., Fudge, H., Rutter, M., Pickles, A., & Hill, J. (1991). Adult outcome of childhood and adolescent depression:

I. Links with Antisocial Disorder. *Journal of the American Academy of Child and Adolescent Psychiatry, 30,* 434–439.

Hinshaw, S. P., & Lee, S. S. (2003). Conduct and Oppositional Defiant Disorders. In E. J. Mash & R. A. Barkley (Eds.), *Child psychopathology* (2nd ed., pp. 144–198). New York, NY: Guilford Press.

Kratzer, L., & Hodgins, S. (1997). Adult outcomes of child conduct problems: A cohort study. *Journal of Abnormal Child Psychology, 25,* 65–81.

Lahey, B. B., & Loeber, R. (1997). Attention-Deficit/Hyperactivity Disorder, Oppositional Defiant Disorder, Conduct Disorder, and Adult Antisocial Behavior: A life span perspective. In D. M. Stoff, J. Breiling, & J. D. Maser (Eds.), *Handbook of antisocial behavior* (pp. 51–59). New York, NY: Wiley.

Mash, E. J., & Dozois, D. J. A. (2003). Child psychopathology: A developmental-systems perspective. In E. J. Mash & R. A. Barkley (Eds.), *Child psychopathology* (2nd ed., pp. 3–71). New York, NY: Guilford Press.

Walker, H. M., Colvin, G., & Ramsey, E. (1995). *Antisocial behavior in school: Strategies and best practices.* Pacific Grove, CA: Brooks/Cole.

Zoccolillo, M., Pickles, A., Quinton, D., & Rutter, M. (1992). The outcome of Childhood Conduct Disorder: Implications for defining adult Personality Disorder and Conduct Disorder. *Psychological Medicine, 22,* 971–986.

ROLLEN C. FOWLER
Eugene 4J School District, Eugene, Oregon

ANTLEY-BIXLER SYNDROME

This syndrome is a rare hereditary disorder. It causes distinctive deformities of the head and face. There are also other skeletal anomalies of the extremities.

Only a few cases have appeared in the medical literature. One instance of affected siblings suggests an autosomal recessive pattern of inheritance.

Characteristics

1. High, arched skull with flattening of the back of the skull
2. Craniosynostotis (premature closure of the sutures between the skull bones)
3. Protruding forehead
4. Flattened, underdeveloped midfacial area, including the bridge of the nose and the eye sockets
5. Choanal atresia (very small nasal openings)
6. Lowset, malformed ears; bulging eyes
7. Limb deformities, including fusion of the bones of the forearm (radioulnar synostosis), joint contractures, arachnodactyly (long, thin fingers) and femoral bowing (curvature of the thigh bone)

These infants have a very dysmorphic appearance. However, plastic surgeons who specialize in the repair of craniofacial anomalies can transform their appearance in an almost magical way. Several operations may be necessary to achieve acceptable cosmetic results. Babies who survive past the first few months of life may need tracheostomy to relieve severe upper airway obstruction and gastrostomy (a surgical opening into the stomach through the abdominal wall) to overcome feeding difficulties. Joint contractures usually improve with age and respond to physical therapy.

There is no research to support the need for educational modifications due to the rarity of the disorder and the poor prognosis.

Prognosis for the disorder is rather dismal. There is an 80% mortality rate in the first few months, secondary to breathing difficulties, including apneic episodes. After these patients survive infancy, their outlook improves. One 10-year-old child with this problem is currently a normal fifth grader who functions well both socially and intellectually.

For more information, please contact FACES: The National Craniofacial Association, P.O. Box 11082, Chattanooga, TN 37401. Tel.: (423) 266-1632 or (800) 332-2373, website: http://www.faces-cranio.org

REFERENCE

Jones, K. (1997). *Smith's recognizable patterns of human malformations* (5th ed.). Philadelphia, PA: W. B. Saunders.

BARRY H. DAVISON
Ennis, Texas

JOAN W. MAYFIELD
*Baylor Pediatric Specialty Services
Dallas, Texas*

ANXIETY

We live in an "age of anxiety" (Spielberger & Rickman, 1990, p. 69). People have become more anxious and worried than ever before (Twenge, 2000). In recent years, children and adolescents have reported higher levels of anxiety than individuals in decades past (Twenge, 2000). Twenge suggests that a decrease in social connectedness and an increase in environmental threat may be responsible for the increased levels of anxiety reported among our nation's youth.

Anxiety is a basic emotion that humans have experienced since the beginning of mankind (McReynolds, 1985). Anxiety is a unique emotion as it may be viewed in both a positive and negative light. From a positive perspective, anxiety occurs normally in a child's development, and its presence indicates that one's development is progressing at an expected rate (Huberty, 1997). For example, toddlers typically show signs of anxiety in the presence of strangers, preschoolers and elementary school–age children usually become anxious in the presence of animals, children in middle school typically show signs of anxiety when they visit a dentist's or principal's office, and adolescents usually become anxious when they are required to give a speech in front of a class (Barrios & Hartmann, 1997). Anxiety may also be adaptive and alert a child to a real threat or potentially dangerous situation (Huberty, 1997). The child may react to the real threat or potentially dangerous situation with a fight-or-flight response. Besides being a normative indicator of development or an adaptive response to a potentially threatening environmental event or cue, anxiety may motivate and facilitate a child's performance so that the child performs optimally on a task or an activity (Huberty, 1997). Research has suggested that a moderate level of anxiety (i.e., not too much or not too little) may boost a child's performance. In contrast, very low and very high levels of anxiety are more likely to be associated with poorer performance (Yerkes & Dodson, 1908). Most researchers in the field of anxiety believe a curvilinear relationship (i.e., an inverted U-shaped relationship) exists between anxiety and performance. From a negative perspective, anxiety may be "a destructive and debilitating force in human behavior" (Richmond, 2000, p. 124). At extremely high levels, anxiety may interfere with a child's academic, behavioral, emotional, and social functioning. As a result, clinic- or school-based interventions may be required to treat the devastating effects of anxiety.

Anxiety is somewhat portentous and may manifest itself in many different ways. As mentioned earlier, anxiety may be a simple reaction to an environmental event, or it may represent a symptom in and of itself. Anxiety may be a symptom in another disorder, or it may represent a disorder of various types (American Psychiatric Association 2000; Lowe & Reynolds, 2000; Reynolds, 1998). Anxiety consists of feelings of uneasiness, tension, and worry which can be further examined through observation or self-report of an individual's reactions to stress, performance on tasks, behavior, or other manifestations of physical signs (Lowe & Reynolds, 1998). People may experience thoughts of avoidance, fear, dizziness, sweating, or perform rituals to cope with the overwhelming thoughts or fears (DSM-IV; American Psychiatric Association, 2000).

Defining the boundary between normal and pathological anxiety has been a struggle within the field. Wakefield (1992) proposed that normal and pathological anxiety can be distinguished from each other based on a harmful dysfunction account of the disorder. According to Wakefield, two interrelated criteria must be met in order for pathological anxiety to exist: (1) a psychobiological mechanism must malfunction, and (2) the malfunctioning of the psychobiological mechanism must result in suffering, maladaptation, or both (Evans et al., 2005). In contrast, Evans and colleagues proposed that normal and pathological anxiety can be distinguished from each other based on three clinical features: distress, dysfunction, and symptom inflexibility. Although Wakefield (1992) and Evans and colleagues (2005) have suggested criteria for distinguishing normal and pathological anxiety, it is not known at the present time whether their criteria represent the ideal criteria in making this distinction.

Anxiety is viewed as a multidimensional construct and consists of three dimensions—cognitive, behavioral, and physiological. These three components may be manifested by a child in varying degrees. The cognitive component may consist of ruminative thoughts, excessive worries, and attention and memory difficulties. Behavioral manifestations may include fidgety behaviors, motor restlessness, and avoidance or escape behaviors in the presence of anxiety-provoking stimuli. The physiological component may consist of rapid heartbeat, perspiration, muscle tension, headaches, and stomachaches (Huberty, 1997).

One of the most prevalent conceptualizations of anxiety is provided by the state-trait model of anxiety. Spielberger (1972) viewed state anxiety as a transitory condition that varied across individuals and situations, whereas trait anxiety was viewed as a more permanent condition. Spielberger (1972) defined *state anxiety* as "feelings of tension, apprehension, nervousness, and worry, with associated activation or arousal of the autonomic nervous system" (p. 29). State anxiety occurs when a child perceives a situation as threatening, resulting in a complex set of emotional reactions that may vary in degree and intensity to a real or imagined threat (Reynolds & Richmond, 1985). In contrast, trait anxiety is viewed as a stable personality characteristic. A child with a high level of trait anxiety has a propensity to feel anxious (Spielberger, 1972). The child frequently experiences anxiety even when anxiety-provoking stimuli are relatively weak (Reynolds & Richmond, 1985).

Prevalence rates of various anxiety symptoms in community samples of children have been difficult to estimate. Kashani and Orvaschel (1990) reported that the prevalence of anxiety symptoms in community samples of children and adolescents have ranged as high as 67%. In contrast, Puskar, Sereika, and Haller (2003) examined anxiety symptoms in a community sample of 466 adolescents and found that 20% of their sample reported elevated levels of anxiety. Vannest, Harrison, & Reynolds

(2010) identified anxiety as a "top ten problem" in students nationwide as rated by teachers and parents. Puskar and colleagues also found that females reported more anxiety than males. This finding of a gender difference in anxiety symptoms reported is consistent with the literature. However, it is unclear at the present time whether females experience more anxiety symptoms than males or whether females recognize more readily their anxieties than males (Reynolds, 1998). Additional research is needed to explore this issue. Few studies have examined racial or ethnic differences in anxiety symptoms among children. Of the few studies conducted to date, findings suggest that ethnic majority and minority children may have more similarities than differences in the levels and types of anxieties reported (Ginsburg & Silverman, 1996; Neal, Lilly, & Zakis, 1993). Although additional studies need to be conducted to obtain a better understanding of the relationship between anxiety and different demographic variables, it is clear, based on the prevalence rates reported, that anxiety is a major problem experienced by many children and that early detection is needed to reduce anxiety and its negative effects in the child population.

Early detection of anxiety in children typically involves the use of different assessment techniques. A multimethod approach is strongly advocated in the assessment of anxiety in children. In the multimethod approach, a variety of measures are used, including clinical interviews, direct observations, behavior rating scales, personality measures, and possibly psychophysiological measures (Lowe & Reynolds, 2006). Behavior rating scales, including self-report measures, are popular and effective techniques used in the early detection of anxiety in children.

Because other emotional, behavioral, and social concerns often accompany anxiety problems in children, it is useful to use both broadband and narrowband behavioral rating scales. Broadband instruments allow a more global assessment of a child's behavior. With broadband measures, different dimensions of personality may be assessed, such as depression and withdrawn behavior, in addition to anxiety. Broadband instruments may include different forms for different raters such as parents, teachers, and the child. This allows information to be collected from multiple sources in multiple settings in which a child's behavior is observed. One of the most widely used broadband measures is the Achenbach System of Empirically Based Assessment (ASEBA; Achenbach & Rescorla, 2001). The ASEBA consists of three scales: a parent rating scale, a teacher rating scale, and a self-report scale. The ASEBA is used to assess social competencies, adaptive functioning, and problematic behaviors, including anxiety, in children and adolescents, ages 1.5 to 18. Another widely used broadband instrument is the Behavior Assessment System for Children—Second Edition (BASC-2; Reynolds & Kamphaus, 2004). The BASC-2 assesses behavioral and emotional difficulties, including anxiety, in children and adolescents, ages 2 to 25. Like the ASEBA, the BASC-2

consists of multiple forms that are completed by multiple raters. The BASC-2 includes a parent rating scale, a teacher rating scale, and a self-report scale. Finally, the Beck Youth Inventories—Second Edition (BYI-II; Beck, Beck, Jolly, & Steer, 2005) measures emotional and social difficulties in children and adolescents, ages 7 to 18. The BYI-II is a self-report measure and consists of five scales assessing symptoms across several domains, including anxiety.

When assessing anxiety in children, it is also useful to include one or more narrowband measures of anxiety. Whereas broadband instruments measure a wide array of psychological dimensions, narrowband measures focus on a specific domain such as anxiety. One of the most widely used narrowband instruments is the State-Trait Anxiety Inventory (STAI; Spielberger, Gorsuch, & Lushene, 1970). This scale provides a measure of both state and trait anxiety and can be used with high school students and adults. A children's version of the STAI, the State-Trait Anxiety Inventory for Children (STAI-C; Spielberger, Edwards, Lushene, Montuori, & Platzek, 1973), is also available for individuals in Grades 4 through 6. Another popular measure used to assess anxiety in children and adolescents is the Revised Children's Manifest Anxiety Scale (RCMAS; Reynolds & Richmond, 1978). The RCMAS is a self-report measure designed to assess the level and nature of anxiety in children and adolescents, ages 6 to 19. The RCMAS consists of a Total Anxiety scale, which provides a global measure of chronic manifest anxiety, and three anxiety subscales (Worry/Oversensitivity, Social Concerns, and Physiological Anxiety). The Multidimensional Anxiety Scale for Children (MASC; March, 1997) is another self-report measure used to assess anxiety in individuals between the ages of 8 and 19. The MASC consists of four scales: Physical Symptoms, Harm Avoidance, Social Anxiety, and Separation/Panic. Several MASC scales also include subscales. The Fear Survey Schedule for Children–Revised (FSSC-R; Ollendick, 1983) is a narrowband instrument used to measure the number of fears and the overall level of fearfulness in children, ages 7 to 18. The Social Anxiety Scale for Children, Revised (SASC-R; LaGreca & Stone, 1993) and the Social Anxiety Scale for Adolescents (SAS-A; LaGreca & Lopez, 1998) are self-report measures used to assess a child or adolescent's anxiety in social situations. Both the SASC-R and the SAS-A include a Total Social Anxiety scale as well as three subscales: Fear of Negative Evaluation (FNE), Social Avoidance and Distress of New Situations or People (SAD-New), and Social Avoidance and Distress of General Situations or People (SAD-General). Finally, the Social Phobia Anxiety Inventory for Children (SPAIC; Beidel, Turner, & Morris, 1998) and the Social Phobia Anxiety Inventory (SPAI; Turner, Dancu, & Beidel, 1996) are measures used to assess anxiety and fears related to social situations in individuals, ages 8 to 14 and 15 and older, respectively. These broadband and narrowband measures are widely used in the schools and clinical settings by mental health professionals to specify the nature of anxiety along with other concerns. Results obtained with these assessment tools are then directly linked to intervention strategies when needed in an attempt to reduce a child's anxiety and collateral concerns.

REFERENCES

Achenbach, T. M., & Rescorla, L. A. (2001). *Achenbach system of empirically based assessment.* Burlington: University of Vermont, Research Center for Children, Youth, and Families.

American Psychiatric Association. (2000). *Diagnostic and statistical manual of mental disorders* (4th ed., text rev.). Washington, DC: Author.

Barrios, B. A., & Hartmann, D. P. (1997). Fears and anxieties. In E. J. Mash & R. A. Barkley (Eds.), *Treatment of childhood disorders* (pp. 249–337). New York, NY: Guilford Press.

Beck, J. S., Beck, A. T., Jolly, J. B., & Steer, R. A. (2005). *The Beck Youth Inventories* (2nd ed.). San Antonio, TX: Psychological Corporation.

Beidel, D. B., Turner, S. M., & Morris, T. L. (1998). *The Social Phobia and Anxiety Inventory for Children.* North Tonawanda, NY: Multi-Health Systems.

Evans, D. L., Foa, E. B., Gur, R. E., Hendin, H., O'Brien, C. P., Seligman, M. E. P., & Walsh, B. T. (2005). *Treating and preventing adolescent mental health disorders: What we know and what we don't know.* New York, NY: Oxford University Press.

Ginsburg, G. S., & Silverman, W. K. (1996). Phobic and anxiety disorders in Hispanic and Caucasian youth. *Journal of Anxiety Disorders, 10,* 517–528.

Harrison, J., Vannest, K., Davis, J. L. & Reynolds, C. R. (2012). Most common behavior problems in the United States. *Journal of Emotional and Behavioral Disorders.*

Huberty, T. J. (1997). Anxiety. In G. Bear, K. Minke, & A. Thomas (Eds.), *Children's needs II: Development, problems and alternatives* (pp. 305–314). Bethesda, MD: National Association of School Psychologists.

Kashani, J. H., & Orvaschel, H. (1990). A community study of anxiety in children and adolescents. *American Journal of Psychiatry, 147,* 313–318.

LaGreca, A. M., & Lopez, N. (1998). Social anxiety among adolescents: Linkages with peer relations and friendships. *Journal of Abnormal Child Psychology, 26,* 83–94.

LaGreca, A. M., & Stone, W. L. (1993). Social Anxiety Scale for Children–Revised: Factor structure and concurrent validity. *Journal of Clinical Child Psychology, 22,* 17–27.

Lowe, P. A., & Reynolds, C. R. (2000). Exploratory analysis of the latent structure of anxiety among older adults. *Educational and Psychological Measurement, 60,* 100–116.

Lowe, P. A., & Reynolds, C. R. (2006). Examination of the psychometric properties of the Adult Manifest Anxiety Scale–Elderly scores. *Educational and Psychological Measurement.*

March, J. S. (1997). *Multidimensional Anxiety Scale for Children.* North Tonawanda, NY: Multi-Health Systems.

McReynolds, P. (1985). Changing conceptions of anxiety: A historical review and a proposed integration. *Issues in Mental Health Nursing, 7,* 131–158.

Neal, A. M., Lilly, R. S., & Zakis, S. (1993). What are African American children afraid of? A preliminary study. *Journal of Anxiety Disorders, 7,* 129–139.

Ollendick, T. H. (1983). The reliability and validity of the Revised Fear Survey Schedule for Children (FSSC-R). *Behaviour Research and Therapy, 21,* 685–692.

Puskar, K., Sereika, B., & Haller, L. (2003). Anxiety, somatic complaints, and depressive symptoms in rural adolescents. *Journal of Child and Adolescent Psychiatry, 2,* 265–273.

Reynolds, C. R. (1998). Need we measure anxiety differently for males and females? *Journal of Personality Assessment, 70,* 212–221.

Reynolds, C. R., & Kamphaus, R. W. (2004). *Behavior Assessment Scale for Children* (2nd ed.). Circle Pines, MN: American Guidance Services.

Reynolds, C. R., & Richmond, B. O. (1978). What I think and feel: A revised measure of children's manifest anxiety. *Journal of Abnormal Child Psychology, 6,* 271–280.

Reynolds, C. R., & Richmond, B. O. (1985). *Revised Children's Manifest Anxiety Scale manual.* Los Angeles: Western Psychological Services.

Richmond, B. O. (2000). Anxiety. In C. R. Reynolds & E. Fletcher-Janzen (Eds.), *Encyclopedia of special education* (2nd ed., pp. 124–125). New York, NY: Wiley.

Spielberger, C. D. (1972). Anxiety as an emotional state. In C. D. Spielberger (Ed.), *Anxiety: Current trends in theory and research* (pp. 24–49). New York, NY: Academic Press.

Spielberger, C. D., Edwards, C. D., Lushene, R. E., Montuori, I., & Platzek, D. (1973). *The State-Trait Anxiety Inventory for Children.* Palo Alto, CA: Consulting Psychologists Press.

Spielberger, C. D., Gorsuch, R. L., & Lushene, R. E. (1970). *The State-Trait Anxiety Inventory.* Palo Alto, CA: Consulting Psychologists Press.

Spielberger, C. D., & Rickman, R. L. (1990). Assessment of state and trait anxiety. In N. Sartorius, V. Andreoli, G. Cassano, L. Eisenberg, P. Kielholz, P. Pancheri, & Racagni, G. (Eds.), *Anxiety: Psychobiological and clinical perspectives* (pp. 69–83). New York, NY: Hemisphere.

Turner, S. M., Dancu, C. V., & Beidel, D. B. (1996). *The Social Phobia and Anxiety Inventory.* North Tonawanda, NY: Multi-Health Systems.

Twenge, J. M. (2000). The age of anxiety? Birth cohort change in anxiety and neuroticism, 1952–1993. *Journal of Personality and Social Psychology, 79,* 1007–1021.

Wakefield, J. C. (1992). The component of mental disorder: On the boundary between biological facts and social values. *American Psychologist, 47,* 373–388.

Yerkes, R. M., & Dodson, J. D. (1908). The relation of strength of stimulus to rapidity of habit-formation. *Journal of Comparative and Neurological Psychology, 18,* 459–482.

PATRICIA A. LOWE
JENNIFER M. RAAD
University of Kansas

ANXIETY DISORDERS

Anxiety is a common mental health concern found among many children. *Anxiety* is defined as "an unpleasant emotional state or reaction that is distinguished from other states by a unique combination of experiential qualities and physiological changes" (Spielberger & Rickman, 1990, p. 69). Anxiety consists of multiple cognitive, physiological, and behavioral phenomena. The cognitive component may include worry, concentration difficulties, and memory and attention problems. Physiological manifestations may consist of muscle tension, perspiration, heart palpitations, headaches, and stomachaches, whereas the behavioral patterns may include motor restlessness and fidgety behaviors (Huberty, 1997). Mild anxiety problems found in children are typically short-lived. However, severe anxiety problems experienced by some children are typically chronic, interfere with their adaptive functioning, and persist into adulthood (Keller et al., 1992; Ollendick & King, 1994; Vasey & Ollendick, 2000).

Pathological anxiety in children is determined by three clinical features: degree of distress and dysfunction and symptomatic inflexibility. Degree of distress and dysfunction varies in importance as a function of an individual's age, whereas symptomatic inflexibility is relevant, regardless of a person's age (Evans et al., 2005). Children with Anxiety Disorders experience a high degree of distress, severe dysfunction, and symptomatic inflexibility.

There are 15 types of Anxiety Disorders specified in the *Diagnostic and Statistical Manual of Mental Disorders—4th Edition, Text Revision (DSM-IV-TR;* American Psychiatric Association, 2000). These disorders include Generalized Anxiety Disorder, Separation Anxiety Disorder, Specific Phobia, Social Anxiety Disorder, Obsessive-Compulsive Disorder, Posttraumatic Stress Disorder, Acute Stress Disorder, Anxiety Disorder Not Otherwise Specified, Panic Attack, Panic Disorder with and without Agoraphobia, Agoraphobia without a History of Panic Disorder, Anxiety Disorder Due to a General Medical Condition, and Substance-Induced Anxiety Disorder. Of these 15 types of Anxiety Disorders, the most common Anxiety Disorders found among children are Separation Anxiety Disorder, Generalized Anxiety Disorder, and Specific Phobia (Silverman & Kurtines, 2001).

Although there are different types of Anxiety Disorders, these disorders share several common features. These features include sympathetic activation, faulty threat perception, attentional hypervigilance, chronic worry, and escape and avoidance behaviors. Activation of the sympathetic nervous system is an adaptive response to a potential threat. Most anxiety states result in the activation of the sympathetic nervous system, producing physiologic changes in the body such as increased muscle tension, respiration, cardiac output, and sweating. However, in the case of Anxiety Disorders, the system is activated in the absence of a real or potential threat. Faulty threat perception is another common feature found among individuals with Anxiety Disorders. Individuals with Anxiety Disorders erroneously perceive situations as threatening when, in fact, they are not. The third common feature is attentional hypervigilance. Individuals with Anxiety Disorders attend excessively to what they perceive as threat cues. The excessive attention to these perceived threat cues reduces attentional resources to process corrective threat disconfirming information. As a result, attentional hypervigilance may exacerbate anxiety because these individuals continue to perceive the cues as threatening when in reality they are not. A fourth feature is chronic worry. Individuals with Anxiety Disorders worry about current and future events. Avoidance and escape behaviors are additional features shared among individuals with Anxiety Disorders. Escape or avoidance behaviors are likely to be demonstrated when a perceived threat cue is present (Telch, Smits, Brown, & Beckner, 2002).

Prevalence rates for any Anxiety Disorder found in children range from 5.78% to 17.7% (Silverman & Kurtines, 2001). According to Merrell (2001), Anxiety Disorders may be the largest group of internalizing disorders found among children. Gender differences have been reported among children, with girls more likely than boys to have an Anxiety Disorder (Costello, Egger, & Angold, 2004). Of the few studies conducted to date, there is little evidence to suggest differences in the pattern of childhood Anxiety Disorders across different racial groups (Safren et al., 2000). In contrast, age differences have been noted in Anxiety Disorders across the child and adolescent life span, with an increase in the prevalence of Anxiety Disorders reported with an increase in age. However, Separation Anxiety Disorders do not follow this age trend (Silverman & Kurtines, 2001).

Examination of Anxiety Disorders from a developmental perspective reveals that Specific Phobias and Separation Anxiety Disorders have the earliest onset. Both disorders have an onset in early childhood. Generalized Anxiety Disorders are likely to appear slightly later, around the age of 8 to 10. In contrast, the onset for Social Anxiety Disorders, Panic Disorders with and without Agoraphobia, and Obsessive-Compulsive Disorders typically occurs in adolescence (Saavedra & Silverman, 2002).

Children diagnosed with an Anxiety Disorder are likely to have another comorbid condition (American Psychiatric Association, 2000). High rates of comorbidity exist between Anxiety Disorders and depression. The rate of comorbidity reported between these two internalizing disorders is as high as 60% to 70% (Wilmshurst, 2005). There is much discussion in the field as to whether anxiety and depression are separate disorders. Some researchers believe that the two disorders are distinct, whereas other researchers believe that the two disorders are related. Watson and Clark (1984) proposed a tripartite model to explain the relationship between anxiety and depression. According to the tripartite model, negative affectivity (emotional distress) is the underlying trait shared by both disorders, whereas low positive affectivity (anhedonia) is unique to depression, and physiologic arousal is unique to anxiety (Watson & Clark, 1984). Other researchers have suggested a sequential link between the two disorders, with anxiety serving as an early precursor to a Depressive Disorder (Costello, Mustillo, Erkanli, Keeler, & Angold, 2003). Comorbidity rates between different types of Anxiety Disorders are also high. Children who have been diagnosed with an Anxiety Disorder as their primary diagnosis often present with another Anxiety Disorder (Wilmshurst, 2005). Besides depression and Anxiety Disorders, other common comorbid disorders include Attention-Deficit/Hyperactivity Disorder, Oppositional Defiant Disorder, and Conduct Disorder (Costello et al., 2004).

The costs of Anxiety Disorders are high (Greenberg et al., 1999). Greenberg and colleagues conducted one of the most comprehensive studies of the monetary costs of Anxiety Disorders. Greenberg et al. reported the total costs of Anxiety Disorders were $63.1 billion. This figure is based on the monetary value of the dollar in 1998. Nonpsychiatric and psychiatric treatment were identified as the major costs.

Many children with Anxiety Disorders experience difficulty in the school setting. Impairments in social (Beidel, Turner, & Morris, 2000; Caster, Inderbitzen, & Hope, 1999) and academic functioning (Ialongo, Edelsohn, Werthamer-Larsson, Crockett, & Kellam, 1994, 1995; Woodward & Fergusson, 2001) have been reported. Ialongo et al. (1994) assessed 1,197 children in the first grade and found an inverse relationship between anxiety and academic performance. Ialongo and colleagues reported that children with higher levels of anxiety were 2.4 times more likely than their same-age peers to perform in the lowest quartile of reading achievement. These same children were 7.7 times more likely to perform in the lowest quartile of math achievement in comparison to their peers. Four years later, these children with higher levels of anxiety were 10 times more likely than their same-age peers to be in the lower one-third of their class academically.

Besides academic difficulties, many children with Anxiety Disorders experience poor peer relationships. These children are more likely than their peers to have negative perceptions about themselves and their relationships with others (Huberty, 1997). These negative perceptions about their relationships with others reduce the likelihood of these children's interactions with others and may result in social isolation.

Most schools are cognizant of the negative effects anxiety has on the socioemotional and academic functioning of children (Cohen, 1999). Children with an Anxiety Disorder may qualify for special education and related services under the emotional disturbance (ED) category of the *Individuals with Disabilities Education Improvement Act of 2004* (IDEIA). To meet the eligibility criteria, a child must exhibit one or more of the following five conditions, and the condition(s) must have occurred over a long period of time and to a marked degree and must adversely affect the child's educational performance:

1. An inability to learn that cannot be explained by intellectual, sensory, or health factors.
2. An inability to build or maintain satisfactory interpersonal relationships with peers and teachers.
3. Inappropriate types of behavior or feelings under normal circumstances.
4. A general pervasive mood of unhappiness or depression.
5. A tendency to develop physical symptoms or fears associated with personal or school problems (34 C.F.R. § 300.8).

Different theories exist about the origin of an Anxiety Disorder. According to the psychoanalytic approach, anxiety results from the conflict between a child's ego and impulses unacceptable to it. The child's ego defends itself by forcing the impulses out of consciousness. In the conflict, anxiety is displaced or transferred to some other form or idea, giving rise to one of the Anxiety Disorders (Freud, 1924). Learning theories suggest that anxiety is acquired through and maintained by classical and operant conditioning or possibly modeling (Dashiell, 1935). In classical conditioning, a neutral stimulus becomes associated with an aversive stimulus (an unconditioned stimulus) and acquires the properties of the unconditioned stimulus. The neutral stimulus is designated the conditioned stimulus. The conditioned stimulus then produces fear, which may generalize to other neutral stimuli. In operant conditioning, fear of an object or a situation is maintained by a negative reinforcement contingency. The feared object or situation is avoided or attempts are made to escape from the situation. Escape or avoidance behavior is maintained because it reduces a child's anxiety. In modeling, the child observes other's reactions to aversive stimuli and situations. The child then models the behavior of others in response to similar aversive stimuli and situations (Vasey & Ollendick, 2000). The cognitive approach to Anxiety Disorders assumes aberrant cognitions underlie symptom expression. Cognitive researchers suggest that a child who is anxious exhibits threat-related attentional and interpretive biases. That is, the child selectively attends to threat-related stimuli and interprets ambiguous stimuli in a threatening manner (Evans et al., 2005). Biological explanations of Anxiety Disorders have focused on structural regions of the brain, genetic transmission, neurotransmitter functions, immunology, and autonomic nervous system activity. Abnormalities of autonomic regulation, with greater activation in the right frontal area of the brain (Gorman & Sloan, 2000), perturbations in the hypothalamic-pituitary-adrenal axis (Essex, Klein,

Cho, & Kalin, 2002), and abnormalities in the immune system (Kagan, Snidman, McManis, & Woodward, 2001) have been reported in individuals with Anxiety Disorders or the offspring of individuals with Anxiety Disorders. Recent studies in behavioral genetics have suggested that childhood anxiety symptoms are moderately inheritable, accounting for about one-third of the variance in most cases (Eley, 1999; Silverman & Kurtines, 2001). Examination of epidemiological findings and genetic data strongly imply distinct biological profiles for the different types of Anxiety Disorders. Many of these biological profiles suggest neurochemical processes are the underlying factor in many of these disorders (Evans et al., 2005). Behavioral inhibition, another biological factor, has received attention as a risk factor in the development of childhood Anxiety Disorders (Vasey & Ollendick, 2000). Emotional factors and family factors may also predispose a child to an Anxiety Disorder. Deficits in emotional regulation and overcontrolling parents low in affection who demonstrate inconsistent parenting styles are believed to put a child at risk for an Anxiety Disorder (Vasey & Ollendick, 2000).

A multimethod, multisetting, multitrait approach has been recommended in the assessment of children with an Anxiety Disorder (Huberty, 1997). A multimethod, multisetting, multitrait approach involves obtaining information from multiple sources (parent, teacher, and child) and settings (home and school) and assessing multiple traits or characteristics (internalizing, externalizing, and social behaviors) to pinpoint problematic areas of concern. As part of the assessment process, behavior observations are performed; parent, teacher, and child interviews are conducted; rating scales are completed by the parent, teacher, and child if applicable; and multidimensional personality scales are administered. If cognitive or academic difficulties exist, standardized measures of intelligence and academic achievement as well as informal measures such as curriculum-based measures may be administered. Other areas that may need to be assessed include a child's self-esteem, coping skills, and peer relationships. Family functioning may be another area to examine as well as a child's thoughts, beliefs, and attributions about anxiety (Huberty, 1997).

Once an evaluation has been conducted, the results of the assessment are linked to intervention strategies to address the areas of concern. For children with Anxiety Disorders, pharmacotherapy, cognitive-behavior therapy, or a combination of the two are effective strategies to treat Anxiety Disorders in children (Evans et al., 2005). Other treatment strategies may be needed to address related concerns and comorbid conditions.

Specific information about the common Anxiety Disorders (Generalized Anxiety Disorder, Obsessive-Compulsive Disorder, Panic Disorder, Posttraumatic Stress Disorder, Separation Anxiety Disorder, Specific Phobia, and Social Anxiety Disorder) found in children follows. Although not listed as a separate disorder in the

DSM-IV-TR, School Phobia is also included because of its prevalence among children. Controversy exists as to whether School Phobia is a Specific Phobia, Social Anxiety Disorder, Separation Anxiety Disorder, or a behavioral outcome, resulting from one of the Anxiety Disorders. A description, prevalence, comorbidity, etiology, and treatment of each Anxiety Disorder are discussed.

Generalized Anxiety Disorder

Generalized Anxiety Disorder, which now includes Overanxious Disorder of Childhood, is characterized by an excessive and chronic state of worry about a variety of events, circumstances, or situations such as friends, family, health, schoolwork, appearance, money, or one's future. Another central characteristic of a Generalized Anxiety Disorder is a child's inability to control his or her worry. Children with a Generalized Anxiety Disorder may experience restlessness, fatigue, irritability, concentration difficulties, muscle tension, or sleep problems. These symptoms must be present for at least 6 months (American Psychiatric Association, 2000). Lifetime prevalence of a Generalized Anxiety Disorder is between 2% and 5% (Wilmshurst, 2005). Prevalence estimates reported for an Overanxious Disorder in children range from .5% to 7.1% (Evans et al., 2005). Comorbid disorders found among children with a Generalized Anxiety Disorder include Separation Anxiety Disorder, depression, Specific Phobia, and Social Anxiety Disorder (Evans et al., 2005). Genetics may play an important role in the development of a Generalized Anxiety Disorder in children. Cognitive factors may also explain the development of Generalized Anxiety Disorder as children may attend to and interpret ambiguous stimuli negatively. Finally, familial factors such as parenting and behavior modeling may increase the risk for a Generalized Anxiety Disorder in children (Wilmshurst, 2005). Cognitive-behavioral therapy can help children cope with and reduce their levels of anxiety. For children of anxious parents, it is most effective to involve the entire family in cognitive-behavioral therapy as reinforcement and modeling of appropriate behavior at home is important. Medication has also been shown to be effective in the treatment of a Generalized Anxiety Disorder in children (Evans et al., 2005).

Obsessive-Compulsive Disorder

Obsessive-Compulsive Disorder usually develops during adolescence and consists of obsessions or compulsions. Obsessions are recurrent thoughts or worries that cause distress or interfere with one's ability to function normally. These obsessions then may lead to compulsions, which are repetitive behaviors or rituals that the individual performs in order to relieve the distress caused by obsessions or prevent dreaded events or situations from occurring (American Psychiatric Association, 2000). Obsessions and compulsions in children often center on four primary areas: contamination (hand washing), safety (checking), preoccupations with orderliness and symmetry (aligning), and counting or touching rituals. An Obsessive-Compulsive Disorder may cause severe difficulties in children's lives, as they may feel embarrassed by their rituals or the need to follow rigid routines. In addition, many children experience problems in school because of concentration problems, preoccupations, or perfectionist tendencies (Wilmshurst, 2005). Prevalence estimates for an Obsessive-Compulsive Disorder in children have ranged from 1% to 4% (Evans et al., 2005; Wilmshurst, 2005). Co-occurring disorders include depression (Evans et al., 2005), behavior disorders (Geller et al., 2001), and Tic Disorders (Evans et al., 2005). A number of etiologies have been offered to explain an Obsessive-Compulsive Disorder, including genetics, neurotransmitters (i.e., low levels of serotonin), highly critical and overinvolved parents, and maladaptive thinking patterns (Wilmshurst, 2005). Treatment strategies to address an Obsessive-Compulsive Disorder in children include medication and cognitive-behavior therapy involving repeated exposure and response prevention (Evans et al., 2005).

Panic Disorder

A Panic Disorder consists of recurrent, unexpected Panic Attacks. Each attack is followed by a concern about having another attack, worry about the consequences of an attack, or change in behavior related to the attack. The concern, worry, or change in behavior lasts at least 1 month (American Psychiatric Association, 2000). These attacks consist of an extreme fear of imminent danger along with associated somatic symptoms such as heart palpitations, difficulty breathing, sweating, and choking (Evans et al., 2005). Cognitive symptoms include feelings of depersonalization, urge to leave the situation, and feelings of losing control or going crazy. To meet the diagnostic criteria for a Panic Attack, at least four somatic or cognitive symptoms must be present (Wilmshurst, 2005). Attacks have an acute onset and often last for approximately 10 minutes. This disorder is relatively rare in children before puberty. When a Panic Disorder follows a progressive pattern, it often develops in puberty with attacks becoming more frequent and often evolving into Agoraphobia (fear of public places) in adulthood. Community samples have reported lifetime prevalence rates as high as 3.5%, with onset typically occurring in later adolescence to early adulthood. Panic Disorders occur more frequently in females (Wilmshurst, 2005). This disorder is often comorbid with Agoraphobia, other Anxiety Disorders, and depression. The etiology of Panic Disorders suggests that genetics plays a role as well as the neurotransmitter norepinephrine. One treatment option is the use of antidepressant medication. Many antidepressant medications increase the level of norepinephrine in the

brain. Another treatment option is the use of cognitive-behavioral techniques, with an emphasis on increasing coping skills, reevaluating cognitive appraisals, and systematic desensitization (Wilmshurst, 2005). Studies conducted using cognitive and cognitive-behavioral strategies appear promising (Evans et al., 2005).

Posttraumatic Stress Disorder

Posttraumatic Stress Disorder is a disorder in which an individual reexperiences a traumatic event along with a state of heightened physiological arousal and the avoidance of stimuli associated with the event. The traumatic event may involve the experience of a serious injury or witnessing a serious injury or a death. The response to the traumatic event consists of fear or helplessness and, in children, agitation or disorganized behavior. The symptoms must last for at least 1 month; if less than 1 month, an Acute Stress Disorder may be present. There must also be significant distress or impairment in social, school, or other important areas of functioning (American Psychiatric Association, 2000). Reexperiencing the trauma is another central characteristic and may manifest itself in several ways, including flashbacks, nightmares, or images (Evans et al., 2005). Young children may also reenact the trauma through play (Wilmshurst, 2005). High comorbidity rates with Social Anxiety Disorder, Disruptive Behavior Disorders, depression, and Panic Disorder have been reported (Evans et al., 2005). A common reaction to trauma in adolescents is to increase risk-taking behaviors, which can lead to additional stress (Wilmshurst, 2005). Community-based studies suggest that the lifetime prevalence rate for a Posttraumatic Stress Disorder is approximately 8% (American Psychiatric Association, 2000). Community violence is a variable that is strongly correlated with a Posttraumatic Stress Disorder, and there is a high rate of Posttraumatic Stress Disorder in those that have experienced Sexual Abuse (Wilmshurst, 2005). Factors that can influence a person's vulnerability for a Posttraumatic Stress Disorder include gender (i.e., being female), history of Physical or Sexual Abuse, exposure to violence, separation from parents before the age of 10, and existence of an Anxiety Disorder, Depressive Disorder, or another psychiatric disorder. Evidence indicates that stressful events can lead to physiological changes in the body. Abnormal levels of the neurotransmitter norepinephrine and increases in the hormone cortisol have been found in children with a Posttraumatic Stress Disorder as well as alternations in the hippocampus's ability to regulate stress hormones (Wilmshurst, 2005). Limited use of medication has been reported in the treatment of a Posttraumatic Stress Disorder in children (Evans et al., 2005). Studies conducted using cognitive-behavioral strategies have found significant increases in adaptive functioning and a decrease in Posttraumatic Stress Disorder symptoms in groups of children who have experienced Sexual

Abuse, war, earthquakes, and exposure to community violence and crime (Evans et al., 2005).

School Phobia

School Phobia is generally described as frequent absences from school, which are not due to an actual illness or truancy. Several other terms such as *school avoidance* and *school refusal* have also been used to describe the same behavior (Paige, 1993). Common symptoms of a School Phobia are somatic complaints and excessive fears, although the fears do not have to be excessive in a child. The somatic complaints disappear once school has been avoided for the day (Paige, 1993). Research on the prevalence rate of School Phobia varies from 1.7% to 5%, with a similar prevalence rate for males and females (Paige, 1997). Typical age of onset for a School Phobia is between 6 and 10 years of age. Theories about the etiology of a School Phobia vary and include anxious mothers who want to keep their child at home, separation anxiety, school factors such as bullying, or the occurrence of a significant event such as an accident or a death. A School Phobia is maintained by the positive reinforcement and reduction of fear a child receives for staying home (Paige, 1993). Children with a School Phobia are also more likely to exhibit another Specific Phobia, Social Anxiety Disorder, Separation Anxiety Disorder, or depression (Paige, 1997). One of the key components of treatment of a School Phobia is that it must occur quickly before a pattern of school avoidance becomes ingrained and reinforced. Research indicates that behavioral techniques such as systematic desensitization, contingency management programs, and behavioral contracting have been successful in the treatment of a School Phobia. Medications which help children to relax or reduce depression might be helpful as an adjunct to a behavioral approach. A team approach involving parents and school personnel working together is recommended (Paige, 1993).

Separation Anxiety Disorder

Separation Anxiety Disorder involves unrealistic worry or anxiety that accompanies separation from home or a caretaker to such a degree that it interferes with appropriate behavior. The unrealistic worry or distress must be present for at least 4 weeks. A Separation Anxiety Disorder usually develops before adolescence, and is one of the earliest-occurring Anxiety Disorders (Evans et al., 2005). Children may experience nightmares involving the theme of separation as well as physical symptoms such as headaches, stomachaches, nausea, or vomiting. The excessive worry may stem from a child's fear of harm coming to the caregiver or fear of being separated from or losing the caregiver. Children with a Separation Anxiety Disorder may refuse to be separated from the caregiver, to be alone without the caregiver, or even to sleep separately from the caregiver (American Psychiatric Association, 2000).

Children with a Separation Anxiety Disorder are often described by parents as being demanding and intrusive (Wilmshurst, 2005). A Separation Anxiety Disorder affects approximately 4% of the general population (Wilmshurst, 2005). Comorbid disorders found among children with a Separation Anxiety Disorder include a Generalized Anxiety Disorder, Specific Phobia, Social Anxiety, and possibly Panic Disorder (Evans et al., 2005). Many children with a Separation Anxiety Disorder also have a mother with a history of an Anxiety Disorder, suggesting either a genetic link or other familial factors, such as overprotectiveness, modeling of avoidant behavior, or reinforcement of the child's avoidant behavior. Other familial factors that play an important role are maternal depression and family dysfunction. In these situations, the child may be reluctant to leave the home for fear that he or she will not be able to care for or protect the primary caregiver (Wilmshurst, 2005). Finally, from a cognitive perspective, children with a Separation Anxiety Disorder may experience distorted, maladaptive, catastrophic, and ruminative thoughts, which lead them to misinterpret ambiguous stimuli as threatening. Treatment of a Separation Anxiety Disorder includes cognitive-behavior techniques and behavioral strategies such as contingency management programs or behavioral contracts. Additionally, if familial factors are involved, it is often most effective to involve the entire family with the chosen intervention (Wilmshurst, 2005).

Specific Phobia

Specific Phobia is one of the earliest occurring Anxiety Disorders (Wilmshurst, 2005). Symptoms of a Specific Phobia include an extreme or irrational fear or anxiety that is associated with specific animals or insects, aspects of the natural environment (e.g., storms, heights, or water), blood (e.g., seeing an injury or receiving an injection), situations (e.g., crossing bridges or being in enclosed places), or other stimuli (e.g., loud sounds or costumed characters). This fear causes extreme distress and significant impairment in normal functioning and may be expressed in children by crying, tantrumming, freezing, clinging, or experiencing physiological reactions such as dizziness, shortness of breath, increased heart rate, and fainting (American Psychiatric Association, 2000; Wilmshurst, 2005). Children may often feel a strong desire to escape from or avoid the fear-inducing object or situation, which may result in even more intense feelings of anxiety and panic when they are unable to escape or avoid the feared object or situation. Prevalence rates for a Specific Phobia among children are estimated to be around 15% (Silverman & Nelles, 2001). Comorbid conditions associated with a Specific Phobia include another phobia, Depressive Disorder, Generalized Anxiety Disorder, Separation Anxiety Disorder, and Social Anxiety Disorder (Evans et al., 2005; Wilmshurst, 2005). The development of a Specific Phobia is best understood as an interaction between the child's temperament, characteristics of the child's family, and the child's exposure to traumatic or frightening experiences. Most commonly, a Specific Phobia is linked to conditioning experiences, wherein a child develops anxious or fearful reactions in response to a frightening or stressful experience (i.e., classical conditioning). Other theories suggest that a Specific Phobia may result from family characteristics. For example, children may learn to react in certain ways by observing a parent's fearful behavior (Wilmshurst, 2005). Behavioral and cognitive-behavioral techniques such as participant modeling, reinforced practice, systematic desensitization, and self-instructional training have been suggested as useful techniques in the treatment of a Specific Phobia in children (Ollendick & King, 1998).

Social Anxiety Disorder

Social Anxiety Disorder, also known as *Social Phobia*, is characterized by an extreme worry over ridicule, humiliation, or embarrassment in social situations, which may include speaking in class, talking to authority figures, conversing with peers, eating, drinking, or writing in public (American Psychiatric Association, 2000). Children with a Social Anxiety Disorder tend to respond to social or performance situations with avoidant or escape behavior and increased physiological arousal (Wilmshurst, 2005). These individuals often have poor social skills. A Social Anxiety Disorder usually develops during adolescence (American Psychiatric Association, 2000). Prevalence estimates of 1% to 2% have been reported for children with a Social Anxiety Disorder (Wilmshurst, 2005). Children with a Social Anxiety Disorder are at an increased risk for depression, Substance Abuse, Specific Phobia, Separation Anxiety Disorder (Evans et al., 2005), and Generalized Anxiety Disorder (Wilmshurst, 2005). A Social Anxiety Disorder is strongly linked with children's temperament styles (Biederman et al., 1993). Biederman and colleagues found that children with behavioral inhibition were at an increased risk for a Social Anxiety Disorder. Children who are at a higher risk of developing a Social Anxiety Disorder are more likely to have a first-degree biological relative with the disorder, suggesting a genetic component (American Psychiatric Association, 2000). Treatment for a Social Anxiety Disorder includes social skills training (Wilmshurst, 2005), cognitive-behavior therapy, family therapy, and medication (Evans et al., 2005).

Anxiety Disorders are chronic and debilitating conditions that impact a large number of children with mental health disorders. The costs associated with Anxiety Disorders are exorbitant to the child, family, and society. After two decades of research, medication, cognitive-behavior therapy (CBT), and a combination of the two strategies have been shown to be effective in treating most Anxiety Disorders in children (Evans et al., 2005). However, it is unclear at the present time whether the combination of CBT and medication is more effective in treating Anxiety Disorders in children than either treatment alone (Evans et al., 2005). Empirically supported treatments (ESTs) are available to treat Anxiety Disorders. Empirically supported treatments consist of education, cognitive restructuring, relaxation training, and exposure. Future research is still needed to identify the most essential components of these multitreatment packages.

REFERENCES

American Psychiatric Association. (2000). *Diagnostic and statistical manual of mental disorders* (4th ed., text rev.). Washington, DC: Author.

Beidel, D. C., Turner, S. M., & Morris, T. L. (2000). Behavioral treatment of childhood Social Phobia. *Journal of Consulting and Clinical Psychology, 68*, 1072–1080.

Biederman, J., Rosenbaum, J. F., Boldue-Murphy, E. A., Faraone, S. V., Chaloff, J.,...Kagan, J. (1993). A 3-year follow-up of children with and without behavioral inhibition. *Journal of the American Academy of Child and Adolescent Psychiatry, 32*, 814–821.

Caster, J. B., Inderbitzen, H. M., & Hope, D. (1999). Relationship between youth and parent perceptions of family environment and social anxiety. *Journal of Anxiety Disorders, 13*, 237–251.

Cohen, J. (1999). *Educating the minds and hearts: Social emotional learning and the passage into adolescence.* New York, NY: Teachers College Press.

Costello, E. J., Egger, H. L., & Angold, A. (2004). The developmental epidemiology of Anxiety Disorders. In T. Ollendick & J. March (Eds.), *Phobic and Anxiety Disorders in children and adolescents* (pp. 61–91). New York, NY: Oxford University Press.

Costello, E. J., Mustillo, S., Erkanli, A., Keeler, G., & Angold, A. (2003). Prevalence and development of psychiatric disorders in childhood and adolescence. *Archives of General Psychiatry, 60*, 837–844.

Dashiell, J. F. (1935). A survey and synthesis of learning theories. *Psychological Bulletin, 32*(4), 261–275.

Eley, T. C. (1999). Behavioral genetics as a tool for developmental psychology: Anxiety and depression in children and adolescents. *Clinical Child and Family Psychology Review, 2*, 21–36.

Essex, M. J., Klein, M. H., Cho, E., & Kalin, N. H. (2002). Maternal stress beginning in infancy may sensitize children to later stress exposure: Effects on cortisol and behavior. *Biological Psychiatry, 52*, 776–784.

Evans, D. L., Foa, E. B., Gur, R. E., Hendin, H., O'Brien, C. P., Seligman, M. E. P., & Walsh, B. T. (2005). *Treatment and preventing adolescent mental health disorders: What we know and what we don't know.* New York, NY: Oxford Press.

Freud, S. (1924). *Collected papers* (Vol. *1*). London, UK: Hogarth Press.

Geller, D. A., Biederman, J., Farapme, S., Agranat, A., Cradlock, K., Hagermoser, L.,...Coffey, B. (2001). Disentangling chronological age from age of onset in children and adolescents with Obsessive-Compulsive Disorder. *International Journal of Neuropsychopharmacology, 4*, 69–178.

Gorman, J. M., & Sloan, R. P. (2000). Heart rate variability in Depressive and Anxiety Disorders. *American Heart Journal, 140*, 77–83.

Greenberg, P. E., Sisitsky, T., Kessler, R. C., Finkelstein, S. N., Berndt, E. R., Davidson, J. R. T., ... Fyer, A. (1999). The economic burden of Anxiety Disorders in the 1990s. *Journal of Clinical Psychiatry, 60*, 427–235.

Huberty, T. J. (1997). Anxiety. In G. Bear, K. Minke, & A. Thomas (Eds.), *Children's needs II: Development, problems and alternatives* (pp. 305–314). Bethesda, MD: National Association of School Psychologists.

Ialongo, N., Edelsohn, G., Werthamer-Larsson, L., Crockett, L., & Kellam, S. (1994). The significance of self-reported anxious symptoms in first-grade children. *Journal of Abnormal Child Psychology, 22*, 441–455.

Ialongo, N., Edelsohn, G., Werthamer-Larsson, L., Crockett, L., & Kellam, S. (1995). The significance of self-reported symptoms in the first-grade children: Prediction to anxious symptoms and adaptive functioning in fifth grade. *Journal of Child Psychology Psychiatry, 36*, 427–437.

Individuals with Disabilities Education Improvement Act of 2004 (Public Law 108-446). (2004). *Federal Register, 70*(118). Retrieved from http://www.ed.gov/policy/speced/guid/idea/idea 2004.html

Kagan, J., Snidman, N., McManis, M., & Woodward, S. (2001). Temperamental contributions to the affect family of anxiety. *Psychiatric Clinics of North America, 24*, 677–688.

Keller, M. B., Lavori, P. W., Wunder, J., Beardslee, W. R., Schwartz, C. E., & Roth, J. (1992). Chronic course of Anxiety Disorders in children and adolescents. *Journal of the American Academy of Child and Adolescent Psychiatry, 31*, 595–599.

Merrell, K. W. (2001). *Helping students overcome depression and anxiety: A practical guide*. New York, NY: Guilford Press.

Ollendick, T. J., & King, N. J. (1991). Origins of childhood fears: An evaluation of Rachman's theory of fear acquisition. *Behaviour Research and Therapy, 29*, 117–123.

Ollendick, T. J., & King, N. J. (1994). Diagnosis, assessment, and treatment of internalizing problems in children. *Journal of Consulting and Clinical Psychology, 6*, 918–927.

Ollendick, T. J., & King, N. J. (1998). Empirically supported treatment for children with Phobic and Anxiety Disorders: Current status. *Journal of Clinical Child Psychology, 27*, 156–167.

Paige, L. Z. (1993). *The identification and treatment of School Phobia*. Silver Spring, MD: National Association of School Psychologists.

Paige, L. Z. (1997). School Phobia, school refusal, and school avoidance. In G. G. Bear, K. M. Minke, & A. Thomas (Eds.), *Children's needs II: Development, problems and alternatives* (pp. 339–347). Bethesda, MD: National Association of School Psychologists.

Saavedra, L. M., & Silverman, W. K. (2002). Classification of Anxiety Disorders in children: What a difference two decades make. *International Review of Psychiatry, 14*, 87–101.

Safren, S. A., Gonzalez, R. E., Horner, K. J., Leung, A. W., Heimberg, R. G., & Juster, H. R. (2000). Anxiety in ethnic minority youth: Methodological and conceptual issues and review of the literature. *Behavior Modification, 24*(2), 147–183.

Silverman, W. K., & Kurtines, W. M. (2001). Anxiety Disorders. In J. N. Hughes, A. M. LaGreca, & J. C. Conoley (Eds.), *Handbook of psychological services for children and adolescents* (pp. 225–244). New York, NY: Oxford University Press.

Silverman, W. K., & Nelles, W. B. (2001). The influence of gender on children's ratings of fear and self and same-aged peers. *The Journal of Genetic Psychology, 148*, 17–21.

Spielberger, C. D., & Rickman, R. L. (1990). Assessment of state and trait anxiety. In N. Sartorius, V. Andreoli, G. Cassano, L. Eisenberg, P. Kielholz, P. Pancheri, & G. Racagni (Eds.), *Anxiety: Psychobiological and clinical perspectives* (pp. 69–83). New York, NY: Hemisphere.

Telch, M. J., Smits, J. A., Brown, M., & Beckner, V. (2002). Treatment of Anxiety Disorders: Implications for medical cost offset. In N. Cummings, W. T. O'Donohue, K. E. Ferguson (Eds.), *The impact of medical cost offset on practice and research: Making it work for you* (pp. 167–200). Reno, NV: Context Press.

Vasey, M. W., & Ollendick, T. H. (2000). Anxiety. In A. J. Sameroff, M. Lewis, & S. M. Miller (Eds.), *Handbook of developmental psychopathology* (2nd ed., pp. 511–529). New York, NY: Kluwer Academic/Plenum Press.

Watson, D., & Clark, L. A. (1984). Negative affectivity: The disposition to experience aversive emotional states. *Psychological Bulletin, 96*(3), 465–490.

Wilmshurst, L. (2005). *Essentials of child psychopathology*. Hoboken, NJ: Wiley.

Woodward, L. J., & Fergusson, D. A. (2001). Life course outcomes of young people with Anxiety Disorders in adolescence. *Journal of the American Academy of Child and Adolescent Psychiatry, 40*, 1086–1093.

Patricia A. Lowe
Jennifer M. Raad
Jacqueline S. Schon
University of Kansas
Third edition

Carrie George
Texas A & M University

APECED SYNDROME

APECED is also known as autoimmune polyglandular disease Type I or autoimmune-polyendocrinopathy-candidias. APECED stands for autoimmune polyendocrinopathy (APE), candidiasis (C), and ectodermal dysplasia (ED). It is a very rare genetic syndrome that involves the autoimmune system. It is a combination of several distinct disorders and is defined as the subnormal functioning of several endocrine glands at the same time (National Organization for Rare Disorders [NORD], 2000; Tierney, McPhee, & Papadakis, 2000; Ward et al., 1999). There are three types of APECED: polyglandular autoimmune syndrome, Type I; polyglandular autoimmune syndrome, Type II; and polyglandular autoimmune syndrome, Type III. Type I affects children and adults younger than age 35. Type II more frequently strikes adults, with peak incidence at about 30 years.

APECED syndrome affects people of all ages. It usually begins in childhood. However, it can develop as late as the fifth decade. The syndrome affects equal numbers of males and females. It is a very rare disease that occurs in only about 170 persons worldwide. The majority of the affected persons live in Finland (NORD, 2000).

APECED is defined as a combination of at least two of the following disorders: hypoparathyroidism (a disorder that causes lower than normal levels of calcium and phosphate in the blood), candidiasis (harmless yeast infection that occurs in the mouth, intestinal tract, skin, nails, and genitalia), ectodermal dysplasia (a group of hereditary nonprogressive syndromes that affects tissues derived from the ectodermal germ layer).

Characteristics

1. Children with hypoparathyroidism have symptoms such as weakness, muscle cramps, and abnormal sensations such as tingling, burning, and numbness of the hands. Excessive nervousness, loss of memory, headaches, and uncontrollable cramping muscle movements of the wrists and feet are also present.

2. Children with hypoparathyroidism may have inability to adequately absorb nutrients (malabsorption), and diarrhea can result. Anemia and autoimmune thyroid disease may also occur.

3. Children with candidasis have the symptoms of yeast infection of either the mouth or nails.

4. Dystrophy of the teeth and nails.

The treatment of APECED syndrome is directed toward the specific diseases that are apparent in each patient. Hypoparathyroidism (low plasma levels of calcium and phosphate) is treated with calcium, ergocalciferol, or dihydrotachysterol (forms of Vitamin D). There is no known cure for ectodermal dysplasia. Treatment is directed at symptoms. Over-the-counter creams may relieve skin discomfort. Dentures, hearing aids, and so forth may be required. Heat and overexercise are to be avoided due to impaired sweating. Cleft lip and palate, syndactyly, and other limb deformations are treated by surgery (NORD,

1999). Genetic counseling is important for patients with APECED and for their relatives.

This syndrome would probably not necessitate special education services. Classification under Section 504 of the Vocational Rehabilitation Amendment of 1973 would be appropriate to release the child from physical education requirements. Furthermore, modifications can be made if the child is frequently absent from school.

The researchers showed that mutations in the gene AIRE (autoimmune regulator) are responsible for the pathogenesis of APECED. The identification of the gene defective in APECED should facilitate finding a potential treatment for the disease. Some studies (Ward et al., 1999) have supported the use of cyclosporine (CyA) therapy for the treatment of severe APECED.

REFERENCES

National Organization for Rare Disorders. (November 30, 1999). APECED syndrome. Retrieved from http://rarediseases.org/

Tierney, E. M., McPhee, S. J., & Papadakis, M. A. (2000). *Current medical diagnosis and treatment* (39th ed.). Los Altos, CA: Lange Medical Publications.

Ward, L., Paquette, J., Seidman, E., Huot, C., Alvarez, F., Crock, P.,…Deal, C. (1999). Severe autoimmune polyendocrinopathy-candidiasis-ectodermal dystrophy in an adolescent girl with a novel AIRE mutation: Response to immunosuppressive therapy. *Journal of Clinical Endocrinology and Metabolism, 84*, 844–852.

NINA CHENG
University of Texas at Austin

See also **Ectodermal Dysplasia**

APERT SYNDROME

Apert syndrome is a genetic defect that is classified as a craniofacial and limb anomaly. It can be either inherited or sporadically occurring. Apert is one of four autosomal dominant disorders and is a result of de novo mutations (Ferreira et al., 1999). It results in specific distortions of the head, face, hands, and feet during fetal development, including abnormal skull development (craniosynostosis), concave face (midface hypoplasia), and fusion of the fingers and toes (syndactyly). The presence of syndactyly separates Apert syndrome from other similar syndromes.

Apert syndrome is caused by a mutation of fibroblast growth-factor receptor-2 (FGFR2; Wilkie et al., 1995). Ninety-nine percent of patients identified with Apert syndrome had mutations on chromosomes S252W or P253R of the fibroblast growth factor gene. Infants with P253R mutations generally have better craniofacial appearance after surgery than do infants with S252W mutations.

In a study involving 53 affected children, approximately 50% of fathers were over the age of 35, whereas in approximately 20% of cases, both parents were over 35 (Tolarova, Harris, Ordway, & Vargervik, 1997). This finding suggested that mutations may be more associated with paternal alleles. Rare cases in offspring of healthy couples can be explained by germinal mosaicism (Allanson, 1986).

Since its discovery in the late 19th century, more than 300 cases of Apert syndrome have been reported (Cohen, 1991). The prevalence was found to be 12.4 cases per million births (Tolarova et al., 1997). Asians were found to have the highest prevalence rate (22.3 per million live births), and Hispanics had the lowest prevalence rate (7.6 per million live births). Both genders seem to be affected equally.

Characteristics

1. At birth or during sonogram, the following features are found:

   Craniosynostosis—distortions of the head and face, primarily with a large skull, widely spaced and slanted eye sockets, and crowding of the teeth

   Midface hypoplasia

   Syndactyly of the hands and often the feet—webbed or "mitten" hands

2. Brain scans reveal malformations of the corpus callosum, limbic system, gyral abnormalities, hypoplastic white matter, and heterotopic gray matter.

3. Cleft palate occurs in 30% of cases.

For infants with Apert syndrome, premature fusion of plates in the skull restricts brain growth and causes increased pressure in the brain as it develops. Early surgery can detach the plates to relieve the pressure. Craniofacial surgery results in some healing of features (vonGernet, Golla, Ehrenfels, Schuffenhauer, & Fairley, 2000). Surgery is needed to separate the fingers to maximize functionality, but this procedure is performed on the feet only if walking will otherwise be impaired. Surgery normally takes place between 5 and 8 months.

In the past, diagnosis was made at birth, but advances within the last decade have made prenatal diagnosis possible. In mothers with Apert syndrome, detection as early as 20 weeks has been made (Lyu & Ko, 2000). In unaffected mothers, prenatal diagnosis is typically in the third trimester (Kaufmann, Baldinger, & Pratt, 1997). Prenatal diagnosis is generally based on findings of

craniosynostosis and syndactyly originally using fetoscopy and more recently using sonograms (Lyu & Ko, 2000).

Although cases of normal cognitive functioning are common, varying degrees of intellectual disability are found in 50% of patients (Sarimski, 1998). Psychosocial functioning of children with Apert syndrome is similar to that of children with facial disfigurement in general, with children with more severe cognitive deficits experiencing more severe psychosocial impairment (Sarimski, 1998). Twenty percent of patients were found to suffer from emotional lability, social competence deficits, hyperactivity, or attentional problems. Psychosocial intervention is implicated for children with Apert syndrome as well as their parents, but little research on specific interventions has been conducted.

Prognosis and complications vary between patients. Additional reconstructive surgeries may be needed and congenital abnormalities may exist that require additional treatment. More research is needed in order to improve treatment and early detection of Apert syndrome.

REFERENCES

Cohen, M. M., & Kreiborg, S. (1991). Genetic and family study of the Apert syndrome. *Journal of Craniofacial Genetic Developmental Biology*, *11*, 7–17.

Ferreira, J. C., Carter, S. M., Bernstein, P. S., Jabs, E. W., Glickstein, J. S., Marion, R. W., ... Gross, S. J. (1999). Second-trimester molecular prenatal diagnosis of sporadic Apert syndrome following suspicious ultrasound findings. *Ultrasound in Obstetrics and Gynecology*, *14*, 426–430.

Kaufmann, K., Baldinger, S., & Pratt, L. (1997). Ultrasound detection of Apert syndrome: A case report and literature review. *American Journal of Perinatology*, *14*, 427–430.

Lyu, K. J., & Ko, T. M. (2000). Prenatal diagnosis of Apert syndrome with widely separated cranial sutures. *Prenatal Diagnosis*, *20*, 254–256.

Sarimski, K. (1998). Children with Apert syndrome: Behavioural problems and family stress. *Developmental Medicine and Child Neurology*, *40*, 44–49.

Tolarova, M. M., Harris, J. A., Ordway, D. E., & Vargervik, K. (1997). Birth prevalence, mutation rate, sex, ratio, parents' age, and ethnicity in Apert syndrome. *American Journal of Medical Genetics*, *72*, 394–398.

vonGernet, S., Golla, A., Ehrenfels, Y., Schuffenhauer, S., & Fairley, J. D. (2000). Genotype-phenotype analysis in Apert syndrome suggests opposite effects of the two recurrent mutations on syndactyly and outcome of craniofacial surgery. *Clinical Genetics*, *57*, 137–139.

Wilkie, A. O. M., Slaney, S. F., Oldridge, M., Poole, M. D., Ashworth, G. J., Hockley, A. D., ... Rutland, P. (1995). Apert syndrome results from localized mutations of FGFR2 and is allelic with Crouzon syndrome. *Nature and Genetics*, *9*, 165–172.

ELIZABETH KAUFMANN
University of Texas at Austin

APGAR RATING SCALE

The Apgar Rating Scale was specifically designed to assess medical distress in newborns. Ratings are made by attending nurses or physicians at 1 minute after birth, with possible further ratings at 3, 5, and 10 minutes. Five vital signs, heart rate, respiratory effort, reflex irritability, muscle tone, and color, are rated on a 3-point scale: 2 if present, 1 if not fully present, and 0 if absent. Thus the range of possible scores is 0–10, with scores greater than 7 (about 70% of all newborns) indicating excellent condition, 3–7 (24% of all newborns) indicating a moderately depressed condition, and less than 3 (6% of all newborns) indicating a severely depressed condition (Apgar, 1953; Apgar, Holaday, James, & Weisbrott, 1958; NCEMI, 2005).

The Apgar Scale has been used extensively in research in anesthesiology, obstetrics, pediatric neurology, and developmental psychology. Apgar scores are predictive of infant mortality: 15% of neonates with severely depressed scores die within 7 months, compared with 0.13% of those receiving scores of 10 (Apgar et al., 1958). There is also a moderate relationship between Apgar scores and intellectual and motor development: Edwards (1968), for example, found an Apgar correlation of 0.251 with Stanford-Binet IQ, 0.456 with a battery of fine-motor tasks, and 0.480 with gross-motor tasks at age 4. The 5-minute postnatal Apgar scores were more predictive than 1-minute scores in Edwards' study.

REFERENCES

Apgar, V. (1953). A proposal for a new method of evaluation of the newborn infant. *Current Researches in Anesthesia and Analgesia, 32*, 260–267.

Apgar, V., Holaday, D., James, L., Weisbrott, I., & Berrien, C. (1958). Evaluation of the newborn infant—second report. *Journal of the American Medical Association, 168*, 1985–1988.

Edwards, N. (1968). The relationship between physical condition immediately after birth and mental and motor performance at age four. *Genetic Psychology Monographs, 78*, 257–289.

NCEMI. (2005). *National Center for Emergency Medicine Apgar Score*. Retrieved from http://www.ncemi.org

JOHN MACDONALD
Eastern Kentucky University

See also Low Birth Weight Infants; Neonatal Behavioral Assessment; Prematurity/Preterm

APHASIA

Everyone with the diagnosis of aphasia has an acquired language disorder, but the type of language disorder (problems understanding talking, problems talking, problems reading, problems writing) and the severity of these difficulties vary, reflecting the different locations and the extent of the damage to the brain. For most people, damage to the left side (hemisphere) is responsible for the aphasia. Aphasia usually has a sudden onset such as a result from a brain injury or stroke, but some individuals have a slower onset as with the development of a brain tumor (NIDCD, 2005).

There also are similarities in the type of problems using language among persons whose brains have been damaged in the same location. Aphasiologists are persons who study aphasia and attempt to provide a structure for understanding and diagnosing this language disorder upon the basis of these variations and similarities. As a result of their studies, there are many different definitions of aphasia and many different classification systems offering a means of subdividing aphasia (Chapey, 1994; Davis, 1993).

Literature within the past decade reflects a general agreement on the following: The term aphasia (acquired language disorder due to brain damage) applies to persons who formerly had intact, developed language functioning and, therefore, the term aphasia does not apply to language disorders experienced by children (Davis, 1993). Some aphasiologists (Darley, 1982; Schuell, 1972) set forth arguments against subdividing or classifying aphasia according to differences or similarities of symptoms. In the opinion of these experts, the variations in symptoms reflect degrees of problems in the total, integrated brain function.

However, if classification is considered, one common basis is nonfluent versus fluent. In this case, separation is made on the basis of whether the symptoms of a person's language disorder result in a disruption of fluency (Hegde, 1994). Rosenbek, Wertz, and LaPointe (1989) define being fluent as producing five or more connected words. Obviously, persons who have aphasia and who cannot produce five or more connected words have nonfluent aphasia. Further common subdivision types within nonfluent aphasia include Broca's, global, isolation, and transcortical motor. Subdivisions of fluent aphasia include Wernicke's transcortical sensory and conduction.

Other common perspectives seen in the literature for defining symptoms of aphasia are those in terms of cognitive impairments (Chapey, 1981; Davis, 1993) and linguistic analysis of the disordered language (Caplan, 1991; Jakobsen, 1971). Cognitive definitions of aphasia are based on the idea that cognition underlies language and that if language is impaired, some aspects of cognition also must be impaired. Descriptions of symptoms are reported as impairments in long- and short-term memory for words, phrases, and sentences and as impairments in processing linguistic information (Hegde, 1994). Research done from the linguistic point of view is called "neurolinguistic," and it analyzes the symptoms from a perspective of whether a patient shows difficulties in linguistic units if they are shorter or longer, simple or complex, active or passive, embedded or unembedded, and so forth (Hegde, 1994).

The types of language disorders encountered by persons with aphasia include difficulties in comprehending spoken language (for example, the patient cannot point to a picture or object named, or the person may not know the meaning of ordinary words) and difficulties in talking (the patient may substitute sounds or words and create new words that do not mean anything to the listener, or the person may omit sounds within words or whole words). Persons with aphasia may struggle to get out any words and speak very little, or they may talk a great deal with ease, but the words and grammar do not have meaning for the listener. Persons with aphasia may also experience difficulties in reading or writing and doing number calculations (Hegde, 1994). In addition, there are often many related disorders that occur from the damage to the overall neurological network, such as motor speech problems or paresis of the oral structure and/or arm and leg.

Over one million people in the United States suffer from aphasia and each day almost 300 new cases occur. Rehabilitation requires commitment and support from professionals and family. In an effort to provide a better understanding of this disorder, a national organization, the National Aphasia Association has been formed (LaPointe, 1997).

National Aphasia Association, 350 Seventh Avenue, Suite 902, New York, NY 10001. Tel.: (800) 922-4622, e-mail: responsecenter@aphasia.org, website: http://aphasia.org/index.html.

REFERENCES

Caplan, D. (1991). Agrammatism is a theoretically coherent aphasic category. *Brain and Language, 40,* 274–281.

Chapey, R. (1981). Assessment of language disorders in adults. In R. Chapey (Ed.), *Language intervention strategies in adult aphasia* (pp. 31–84). Baltimore, MD: Williams & Wilkins.

Chapey, R. (1994). *Language intervention strategies in adult aphasia* (3rd ed.). Baltimore, MD: Williams & Wilkins.

Darley, F. (1982). *Aphasia.* Philadelphia, PA: W. B. Saunders.

Davis, G. (1993). *A survey of adult aphasia and related language disorders* (2nd ed.). Englewood Cliffs, NJ: Prentice Hall.

Hegde, M. (1994). *A coursebook on aphasia and other neurogenic language disorders.* San Diego, CA: Singular.

Jakobsen, R. (1971). Two aspects of language and two types of aphasic disturbances. In R. Jakobson & M. Halle (Eds.), *Fundamentals of language* (2nd ed.). The Hague, Netherlands: Mouton.

LaPointe, L. (1997). *Aphasia and related neurogenic language disorders* (2nd ed.). New York, NY: Thieme.

National Institute on Deafness and Other Communication Disorders (NIDCD). (2005). *Aphasia.* Retrieved from http://www.nidcd.nih.gov/health/voice/aphasia.asp

Rosenbek, J., LaPointe, L., & Wertz, R. (1989). *Aphasia: A clinical approach.* Austin, TX: PRO-ED.

Schuell, H. (1972). *The Minnesota Test of Differential Diagnosis of Aphasia.* Minneapolis: University of Minnesota Press.

SHEELA STUART
George Washington University

See also Childhood Aphasia; Developmental Aphasia; Language Disorders

APHASIA, BROCA'S

Often called expressive or motor aphasia, Broca's aphasia is characterized by difficulties with the motor production of speech, problems with articulation, and a paucity of spoken language. Broca's aphasia can vary in severity from a slight difficulty in the reproduction of a spoken word to a complete inability to produce spoken language.

Broca's aphasia occurs in children who either fail to or have difficulty in expressing themselves despite normal cognitive abilities and normal linguistic comprehension. Developmental language disorders and intellectual disability should be ruled out when screening for this disorder. The main cause is a traumatic brain injury resulting in a lesion to the left hemisphere of the brain in either the frontal operculum or the corticocortical association pathways in the white matter of the temporal, parietal, and frontal lobes that relate to the motor speech areas (Martin, 1989).

Characteristics

1. Difficulties in the production of spoken language, accompanied by a varying impairment in language comprehension.

2. Verb forms are often reduced to the infinitive or participle; nouns are usually expressed in singular form and conjunctions; and adjectives, adverbs, and articles are often omitted. This type of speech is often labeled telegraphic speech (Goodwin, 1989).

3. Speech tends to be slow, nonfluent, effortful, and poorly articulated.

4. Repetition of single words is effortful but usually accomplished.

5. Although Broca's aphasia is associated with language expression, difficulties in language reception and comprehension may accompany this disorder. This symptom can be observed in deficits in comprehension, reading, naming, and memory (Hynd & Willis, 1988).

6. May be associated with hemiplegia, a weakness or paralysis on the right side of the body. This tends to be manifested by motor weakness and sagging or drooping of the lower right side of the face. There also may be weakness in the right arm and leg (Goodwin, 1989).

The treatment of Broca's aphasia focuses on retraining the child to recover or gain the ability to produce spoken language; this is done by addressing the child's deficits by symptom, such as intense retraining using picture cards to improve naming ability. It is hoped that retraining will have the effect of shifting language expression to an area of the brain that is not impaired. Because Broca's aphasia tends to be associated with left-hemisphere damage, the expectation is that the right hemisphere will assume the responsibility of producing expressive language.

The effect of treatment on Broca's aphasia in children can vary greatly. Children tend to have greater success in recovery than do adults, due to their increased brain plasticity. Many predictive factors can influence a child's level of recovery. The size and type of lesion in the brain is the most critical variable. For example, a minor closed head injury that results in slight swelling of the brain could produce signs and symptoms of Broca's aphasia that could later disappear completely. A traumatic brain injury that involves extensive bilateral damage could produce a case of Broca's aphasia resulting in a complete loss of language expression, from which the child would never recover.

Another major predictive recovery factor is the age of the child when the lesion occurs. It is thought that younger children have increased plasticity of the brain, the ability to reorganize actions within levels of functioning, and the ability to shift functioning to different areas of the brain that have not been impaired (Goodwin, 1997). A problem can emerge, however, with shifting functions from one area of the brain to another. It may be that when an area of the brain not yet specialized in function assumes a new responsibility, a compromise in meeting later developmental milestones may emerge (Fletcher-Janzen & Kade, 1997).

Special education placement can be a very important issue for children with Broca's aphasia. If their impairment is severe, they will probably be classified as a child with a traumatic brain injury. If their difficulties are related to academic problems, they could be served as children with learning disabilities or as children needing speech and language services. Difficulties with expression of language can inhibit many educational, emotional, and social aspects of a child's development. The special education teacher will need to be cognizant of a number of special considerations that these children require. For example, the ability to learn to read can be severely affected by Broca's aphasia, even if the child's receptive language skills are intact. The child may have difficulty exchanging and expressing thoughts and ideas and asking questions; this could result in a significantly reduced vocabulary and an inability to obtain phonemic awareness of words and rules of grammar. The child's social skills can also be affected because the child may have problems with positive, normal peer interactions; this can also lead to a deficit in the development of social skills and nuances as well as the development of appropriate behavior. Children with Broca's aphasia may demonstrate signs of depression, especially those children with localized impairment, because they have no other cognitive difficulties and are fully aware of their deficits.

The future for children with Broca's aphasia appears to be promising. Improved technology helps emergency services respond more quickly to accidents involving brain trauma and new medical technology such as the positron-emission tomography (PET) scan is helping neurologists understand more about how the brain operates. Although prognosis for recovery still remains guarded for children with severe lesions and diffuse damage, improved understanding of Broca's aphasia is offering increasing amounts of hope for children with expressive language problems.

REFERENCES

Fletcher-Janzen, E., & Kade, H. D. (1997). Pediatric brain injury rehabilitation in a neurodevelopmental milieu. In C. R. Reynolds & E. Fletcher-Janzen (Eds.), *Handbook of clinical child neuropsychology* (2nd ed., pp. 452–481). New York, NY: Plenum Press.

Goodwin, D. M. (1989). A dictionary of neuropsychology. New York, NY: Springer-Verlag.

Hynd, G. W., & Willis, W. G. (1988). *Pediatric neuropsychology*. Orlando, FL: Grune & Stratton.

Martin, J. H. (1989). *Neuroanatomy: Text and atlas*. Norwalk, CT: Appleton and Lange.

ANDREW S. DAVIS
University of Northern Colorado

APHASIA, DEVELOPMENTAL (*See Childhood Aphasia, See also Language Disorders*)

APHASIA, JARGON

Jargon aphasia (JA) is an acquired language disorder in the comprehension and use of words, in which patients use incorrect words or sounds in place of intended words. The speech jargon in JA can be (a) paraphasic—grammatically intact with the inclusion of misused, semantically related words; (b) asemantic—intact speech with the inclusion of nonsense words, or neologisms; and (c) phonemic, a stream of nonsense syllables. Given the intact ability to produce speech, JA is considered a form of fluent aphasia.

In children and adults, JA results from brain damage due to infection, tumors, cerebrovascular disturbance, or head trauma. Although early conceptualizations assumed a right-hemisphere damage bias in childhood aphasias, more recent analyses have found that childhood aphasias are usually the result of left-hemisphere damage, which is consistent with the etiology of adult aphasias (Woods & Teuber, 1978). The trauma responsible for the acquired aphasias may initially lead to other symptoms, such as headaches, muscle weakness or paralysis, visual field deficits, and personality changes. It is important to note that children with JA may have difficulties in auditory comprehension, despite their ability to produce speech.

```
┌─────────────────────────────────────────────┐
│              Characteristics                  │
│                                               │
│  1. Language disorder involving use of        │
│     incorrect words or sounds and auditory    │
│     comprehension                             │
│  2. Result of severe brain damage             │
│  3. Prognosis is good, but some language      │
│     and educational deficiencies persist      │
└─────────────────────────────────────────────┘
```

Recovery from JA depends on a number of interrelated factors, such as etiology, the site and size of the brain damage, age at which the brain insult occurred, and the presence of other neurological disturbances (Murdoch, 1990). It is generally believed that younger children show more complete and rapid recovery from acquired aphasias, reflecting the plasticity of the developing brain. However, several reports have documented slow (months to years) and incomplete recovery in children, resulting in persistent language deficits. There are numerous treatments available for JA and other aphasias, such as speech or writing therapies, but their efficacy is variable. Often, language ability exhibits spontaneous recovery, in which the natural healing of the brain restores some speech capacity—that is, in the absence of any intervention, children with acquired aphasias show improvement over time. This tendency underscores the fact that the defining symptoms of a form of acquired aphasia (such as the jargon in JA) may subside as the recovery process unfolds, but that other subtle language and cognitive impairments may persist.

In general, children with JA and other acquired aphasias show lower levels of scholastic achievement due at least in part to persistent language impairments. Cooper and Flowers (1987) tested individuals on a variety of language and academic achievement tests 1 to 10

years after suffering childhood aphasias. They found that although these individuals were competent verbal communicators, they performed more poorly than did age-matched controls on tasks of word, sentence, and paragraph completion, naming, production of complex sentences, and word fluency. Other academic difficulties included arithmetic and spelling skills. Accordingly, two thirds of the group were receiving special education services at the time of testing. Thus, regular monitoring of JA children after apparent clinical recovery is crucial for supporting educational achievement.

REFERENCES

Cooper, J. A., & Flowers, C. R. (1987). Children with a history of acquired aphasia: Residual language and academic impairments. *Journal of Speech and Hearing Disorders, 52,* 251–262.

Murdoch, B. E. (1990). *Acquired speech and language disorders: A neuroanatomical and functional neurological approach.* London, UK: Chapman and Hall.

Woods, B. T., & Teuber, H. L. (1978). Changing patterns of childhood aphasia. *Annals of Neurology, 3,* 273–280.

ADAM S. BRISTOL
Yale University

JENNIFER M. GILLIS
University of California, Irvine

APHASIA, TRANSCORTICAL

Three types of transcortical aphasia were identified by Goldstein in 1948, including transcortical sensory aphasia, transcortical motor aphasia, and mixed transcortical aphasia. In transcortical motor aphasia, the damage occurs in the frontal lobe, anterior to Broca's area along the motor speech cortex. The lesion is often deep in the cortical matter. In transcortical sensory aphasia, the damage occurs in the occipito-temporal area, posterior to Wernicke's area. Some authorities believe the two types are actually deficits to the same semantic accessing system and that they simply differ in the anatomical levels that are involved (Rothi, 1998). They can result from trauma, stroke, or disease. In mixed transcortical aphasia, the damage can occur in both areas or in the association cortex; it often occurs as a result of diffuse damage (i.e., carbon monoxide poisoning, dementia, multiple infarctions). The incidence of transcortical aphasia is not reported in the literature, and prevalence likely depends on the etiology of the disorder. However, in children it is considered rare.

Characteristics

Transcortical motor aphasia:

1. Able to maintain a simple conversation.
2. Speech may be somewhat disfluent as a result of lack of connector words and is often characterized as having phonemic and global paraphasias.
3. The ability to repeat is very good; often they are echolalic and visual and auditory comprehension is adequate.

Transcortical sensory aphasia:

1. Often have anosognosia, meaning it is difficult for children to recognize that they have deficits.
2. Speech is often quite fluent but may have paraphasias.
3. Often able to repeat and may be echolalic, which distinguishes them from Wernicke aphasia.
4. The primary concern is the very poor comprehension.

Mixed transcortical aphasia:

1. The speech is often disfluent.
2. Diminished quantity of speech.
3. Poor comprehension.
4. Adequate ability to repeat.
5. Individuals with the mixed variety may be able to correct syntactic errors but not semantic errors.

Treatment of aphasias generally follows one of two major regimes, including restoration of functioning or development of compensatory strategies. The treatment of transcortical motor aphasias tends to follow the restoration philosophy, often because the transcortical variety is believed to be a less severe form of aphasia and more likely to show improvement. For example, treatment may focus on restoring volitional initiation of motor acts through practice and self-cueing techniques. The use of pharmacology has also been reported to improve functioning in some individuals. The treatment of transcortical sensory aphasia is highly dependent on the etiology of the aphasia. For example, when the aphasia results from dementia, therapy is different from that used to treat aphasia resulting from a stroke. Rothi (1998) reported that therapy of transcortical sensory aphasia has received no attention in the rehabilitation literature. Treatment of the mixed variety has also not been discussed in the literature.

In children, the terms acquired aphasia and developmental aphasia must be distinguished. Acquired aphasia refers to language disorders that are the result of identifiable neurological insults (tumor, stroke, trauma, etc.).

Developmental aphasia, also known as developmental language disorders, has no known neurological etiology, but the child fails to develop language and speech in an expected manner (Aram, 1998). Depending on the degree of deficit and concomitant problems, the child will likely qualify for special education. Acquired aphasia will likely be identified in the schools under the Traumatic Brain Injury or Physical or Other Health Disorders labels, but depending on the presence of other symptoms, it could be identified as a Speech and Language Disorder. If the disorder is acquired, revision of the child's educational plans should parallel gains. Developmental aphasia will likely be treated under the category of Speech and Language Disorder. Special education plans should be reviewed at least annually, and monitoring of academic progress is highly encouraged.

Generally, the best prognosis is reserved for transcortical motor aphasia, followed by sensory aphasia, and then by mixed transcortical aphasia. Based on several single-case studies, the prognosis for TMA is good; however, with studies that have larger sample sizes, the results have been less encouraging. Wernicke aphasia patients often recover into a condition of transcortical sensory aphasia. When this occurs, the prognosis is considered favorable. Future research dealing with treatment efficacy and future theoretical models will add much to the knowledge based in aphasiology.

REFERENCES

Aram, D. M. (1998). Acquired aphasia in children. In M. T. Sarno (Ed.), *Acquired aphasia* (pp. 451–480). New York, NY: Academic Press.

Rothi, L. J. G. (1997). Transcortical motor, sensory, and mixed aphasia. In L. I. LaPointe (Ed.), *Aphasia and related neurogenic language disorders* (2nd ed., pp. 91–111). New York, NY: Thieme.

DALENE MCCLOSKEY
University of Northern Colorado

APHASIA, WERNICKE (SENSORY APHASIA)

Wernicke aphasia is characterized by the inability to comprehend speech or to produce meaningful speech following lesions to the posterior cortex. Individuals with Wernicke aphasia rarely experience muscular weakness affecting one side of the body, or hemiparesis. In most cases, its etiology involves a lesion affecting the dominant temporal lobe, particularly the auditory association cortex of the posterior-superior portion of the first temporal gyrus (Benson, 1993; Kolb & Whishaw, 1990).

Although anyone can acquire Wernicke aphasia, it most often affects people in their middle to late years of life. It has been estimated that 80,000 adults and 1,400 children acquire some type of aphasic disorder each year; this results in an estimated 1 million Americans who currently live with some type of aphasia. Although the exact prevalence of Wernicke aphasia is unknown, Wernicke is one of the more commonly recognized aphasic syndromes. Men and women appear to be equally affected, and common causes include stroke, severe head trauma, brain tumors, and infections (National Institute on Deafness and Other Communication Disorders, 2000).

Characteristics

1. This disorder is acquired following a period of normal language functioning.

2. The key feature of the disorder is a striking disturbance in comprehension of verbal and/or written language.

3. Deficits in the ability to repeat information (e.g., when patients are instructed to repeat "no ifs, ands, or buts") and to name common objects are frequently noted.

4. Verbal output is fluent, but it is almost always contaminated by unintended syllables, words, or phrases (paraphasias) and by made-up words (neologisms).

Some individuals with Wernicke aphasia will experience a spontaneous recovery within a few hours to a few days following the injury, and no additional treatment will be necessary. In most cases, however, language recovery is neither quick nor complete. In these instances, the most common treatment involves some form of language therapy. Although there are various approaches to conducting language therapy, all approaches attempt to help individuals utilize remaining abilities, restore impaired abilities, compensate for lost abilities, and learn alternative methods of communicating. It is widely believed that language therapy is most effective early in the recovery process. Additional treatment modalities may include medications, such as the anticoagulant Heparin, and in some instances, surgery (Richman & Wood, 1999).

Children with Wernicke aphasia will likely require speech and language services and frequently qualify for special education services for individuals with speech and language impairments, traumatic brain injuries, or learning disabilities. For severely impaired children, compensatory strategies intended to maximize the amount of communication they can regain will be indicated. Children with less severe deficits will probably have phonemic segmentation weaknesses. They may benefit from reading instruction that focuses on phonemic awareness and synthesis activities such as being presented with the same and different sounds through headphones in a repetitive manner. Placement in the regular education classroom with full inclusion will probably be problematic. Individual services in a special education resource room will probably be needed. Some children may have such difficulty with phonemic awareness activities that whole-word approaches will be necessary for reading instruction. Deficits in listening or reading comprehension are also likely to be present, and instructional modifications will probably be necessary (Richman & Wood, 1999).

Children with significant language deficits have also been found to be at increased risk for both internalizing and externalizing behavior problems (Cantwell & Baker, 1991). Consequently, children with Wernicke aphasia may also qualify for special education services under the Serious Emotional Disturbance or Other Health Impaired categories. Treatment for these comorbid psychological and behavioral problems will probably need to be addressed in order for speech and language therapy to be effective. Due to problems with language comprehension, traditional "talk therapies" are likely to be of limited benefit. Behavior modification techniques and highly structured, and repetitive exercises that address specific topics (e.g., social skills training, impulse control) may be most beneficial for managing the comorbid behavior problems associated with language deficits in children (Richman & Wood, 1999). Parent training and parent education will also probably be important treatment interventions.

In general, the prognosis for recovery from Wernicke aphasia is influenced by a number of factors. The first is related to the severity and location of the lesion. The more isolated and limited the lesion, usually the better the prognosis. The age of the individual is also an important factor. Younger patients—usually no older than early adulthood—tend to recover prior levels of functioning more fully than do older patients. Healthier patients also tend to recover more fully. Finally, the time at which educational interventions are initiated also appears to be important. The sooner services can be provided, the better the outcome.

Research activities that investigate new combinations of medications to improve recovery or decrease the risk of the vascular accidents that frequently result in Wernicke aphasia are currently in progress. Research activities that investigate the use of new gene therapies to actually regenerate neural pathways are on the horizon. Studies investigating new diagnostic devices such as positron-emission tomography (PET) and functional magnetic resonance imaging (fMRI) are ongoing. It is hoped that with these new devices, more accurate diagnostic techniques will be identified. Investigations concerning which language therapy techniques work best and how computer-aided interventions can help aphasic patients are also currently underway.

REFERENCES

Benson, D. F. (1993). Aphasia. In K. M. Heilman & E. Valenstein (Eds.), *Clinical neuropsychology* (3rd ed., pp. 17–36). New York, NY: Oxford University Press.

Cantwell, D. P., & Baker, L. (1991). *Behavior problems and developmental disorders in children with communication disorder.* Washington, DC: American Psychiatric Press.

Kolb, B., & Whishaw, I. Q. (1990). *Fundamentals of human neuropsychology* (3rd ed.). New York, NY: W. H. Freeman.

National Institute on Deafness and Other Communication Disorders. (2000, September 20). Aphasia. Retrieved from http://www.nidcd.nih.gov/Pages/default.aspx

Richman, L. C., & Wood, K. M. (1999). Psychological assessment and treatment of communication disorders: Childhood language subtypes. In S. D. Netherton, D. Holmes, & C. E. Walker (Eds.), *Child and adolescent psychological disorders* (pp. 51–75). New York, NY: Oxford University Press.

BRIAN D. JOHNSON
University of Northern Colorado

APNEA, INFANTILE

Apnea is defined as a lack of respiration for a period of 20 to 30 seconds with or without an accompanied decrease in heart rate. Infant apnea is defined as resulting in a blue or purplish color of the skin. Twenty-five percent of infants in premature nurseries, but only a small percentage of full-term infants, exhibit apnea (Nemours Foundation, 2005). Apnea, therefore, appears in most cases to stem from actual immaturity of the neural mechanism responsible for regulation of respiration. When immature, this mechanism is vulnerable to metabolic disturbances in calcium and blood-sugar levels, changes in body temperature, or disturbances in brain-wave patterns that occur during seizures or normal REM (rapid eye movement) sleep. The association between apnea and sleep is significant because premature infants sleep up to 80% of the time and REM sleep is the predominant sleep state of these infants (Parry, Baldy, & Gardner, 1985). Apnea is less frequently caused by actual obstruction of the airway itself either from excessive mucus or improper body positioning, as premature infants have very flexible tracheas.

Apnea owed to immaturity or genetic influences appears to be a possible cause of sudden infant death syndrome (SIDS). The fact that SIDS occurs most frequently in children less than 1 year of age supports this theory. Treatment focuses on prevention and involves general measures to promote adequate respiration until the infant "outgrows" the condition. Correction of existing chemical imbalances may be all that is required. Theophylline, a respiratory stimulant drug, decreases apnea and is widely used. Most infants reinstitute breathing with gentle tactile stimulation such as stroking or jostling, but at times they require manual ventilation to prevent prolonged anoxia and to restore breathing. Occasionally apnea becomes so severe that the child has to be temporarily placed on a respirator (Volpe & Koenigsberger, 1981). Generally, the heart and respiratory rates of premature infants should be closely monitored for signs of apnea. A home monitor may be necessary for infants with persistent apnea. Full-term infants who are at high risk for SIDS should also be monitored for apnea (Spitzer & Fox, 1984).

Prognosis is generally good for infants who do not experience prolonged apnea and who are otherwise healthy. It becomes less favorable with increased frequency and duration of apneic episodes (Parry et al., 1984). However, at least one study suggests that infantile apnea may be associated with deficiencies in later gross motor, and perhaps some cognitive, functions and behavior (Deykin, Bauman, Kelly, Hsieh, & Shannon, 1984). Since apnea produces transient hypoxia, it can, when extensive, cause many of the problems associated with that disorder.

Patients and family members may find assistance with the American Sleep Apnea Association located at 1424 K Street NW, Suite 203203, Washington, DC 20005. Tel.: (202) 293-3650, website: http://sleepapnea.org/

REFERENCES

Deykin, E., Bauman, M., Kelly, D., Hsieh, C., & Shannon, D. (1984). Apnea of infancy and subsequent neurologic, cognitive and behavioral status. *Pediatrics, 73,* 638–645.

Nemours Foundation. (2005). *Apnea of prematurity.* Retrieved from http://www.nemours.org

Parry, W., Baldy, M., & Gardner, S. (1985). Respiratory diseases. In G. B. Merenstein & S. L. Gardner (Eds.), *Handbook of neonatal intensive care.* St. Louis, MO: Mosby.

Spitzer, A., & Fox, W. (1984). Infant apnea, an approach to management. *Clinical Pediatrics, 23,* 374–380.

Volpe, J., & Koenigsberger, R. (1981). Neurologic disorders. In G. B. Avery (Ed.), *Neonatology: Pathophysiology and management of the newborn* (2nd ed., pp. 920–923). Philadelphia, PA: Lippincott.

BRENDA M. POPE
New Hanover Memorial Hospital

See also Anoxia; Infant Stimulation

APPLIED BEHAVIOR ANALYSIS

Applied Behavior Analysis (ABA) is a known and effective treatment for autism spectrum disorders (ASD; National

Standards Project, 2009; Simpson, 2005) and others who desire approaches to changing behavior. There is not a single manualized approach that is called ABA. Rather, there are several approaches and strategies that fall under the ABA umbrella. While several manualized programs that are based in ABA do exist (e.g., STAR, LEAP, PECS), some of which also have efficacy, several programs for ASD that utilize a variety of strategies including those under the ABA umbrella, as well as those not falling under this umbrella (e.g., visual schedules, story-based interventions) also have efficacy (see National Autism Center, 2009).

Definition of ABA

Applied Behavior Analysis is defined as "the process of applying sometimes tentative principles of behavior to the improvement of specific behaviors, and simultaneously evaluating whether or not any changes noted are indeed attributed to the process of application" (Baer, Wolf, & Risley, 1968, p. 91). In practice, ABA utilizes the principles of behavior to assess, shape, and modify socially important behaviors with the aim of generalization of success to the real world (Boutot & Hume, 2010). To be considered to be ABA, Baer, Wolf, and Risley (1968, 1987) recommend that interventions and research be judged according to six criteria:

1. Intervention/Research should be *applied*, meaning that it must address socially important, functional skills and behaviors.

2. Intervention/Research should be *behavioral*, meaning that behaviors addressed are observable and measurable.

3. Intervention/Research should be *analytic and conceptual*, meaning that a functional relation should be established between the intervention and any behavioral change through the use of data collection and the interventions should be conceptually sound.

4. Intervention/Research should be *technological*, meaning that procedures should include clarity and details to allow for replication.

5. Intervention/Research should be *effective*, meaning that noticeable and meaningful changes in the individual's natural environment are key to determining true success of an intervention.

6. Intervention/Research should have *generality*, meaning that changes should last over time and after the intervention is withdrawn.

(Boutot & Hume, 2010)

When these six criteria are met, then ABA is said to be in place. In the absence of these six criteria, regardless of strategies used, ABA is not in place.

Strategies Based on ABA

Similar to the field of medicine, where "medicine" is a term used for both the science and the treatment (e.g., pharmacology), ABA is both a science and a collection of treatments or strategies (Choutka, Doloughty, & Pirkel, 2004). Such strategies include discrete trial training (DTT), incidental teaching, task analysis and chaining, functional behavioral assessment, shaping, and prompting. ABA strategies may be used in natural environments such as home, schools, and communities, or in clinics (Boutot & Hume, 2010). While research supports each of these strategies, it is important to recognize that what is appropriate for individuals may vary (Simpson et. al., 2005).

One ABA strategy that is frequently used with students with ASD is discrete trial training (Choutka, et al., 2004). Though many laypersons mistakenly believe that DTT is synonymous with ABA, DTT is only one component of an effective intervention package based on the principles of ABA (National Autism Center, 2009). This strategy is used to teach single-step skills through a three-term contingency. The three-term contingency involves an antecedent (which may be thought of as the instructional cue; also called the discriminative stimulus or S^D), a behavior (the student's response), and a consequence (such as a positive reinforcer designed to increase the likelihood that in the future, in the presence of this same S^D the student will engage in this behavioral response; Olive, Boutot, & Tarbox, 2011). For example, a teacher may present a field of three color cards, red, blue, and yellow, and say to the child, "Give me blue" (S^D), the child then hands the teacher the blue card (behavior), and is rewarded with a high five (reinforcing consequence). DTT may be conducted in either massed (multiple) trials of 3–5 or more or in single trials and should be used as part of a comprehensive treatment approach to ASD, not viewed as the sole treatment option (Boutot & Hume, 2010). For more information on applied behavior analysis and certification programs, please access the website: http://www.abainternational.org/

REFERENCES

Baer, D., Wolf, M., & Risley, T. (1968). Some current dimensions of applied behavior analysis. *Journal of Applied Behavior Analysis, 1*, 91–97.

Baer, D., Wolf, M., & Risley, T. (1987). Some still-current dimensions of applied behavior analysis. *Journal of Applied Behavior Analysis, 20*, 313–327.

Boutot, E. A. & Hume, K. (2010). Beyond time out and table time: Today's applied behavior analysis for students with autism. Division on Autism and Developmental Disabilities of The Council for Exceptional Children Critical Issues Paper. Retrieved from http://daddcec.org/

Choutka, C. M., Doloughty, P. T., & Pirkel, P. A. (2004). The "discrete trials" of applied behavior analysis for children with autism: Outcome-related factors in the case law. *The Journal of Special Education, 38*, 95–103.

National Autism Center. (2009). *The National Standards Report.* http://www.nationalautismcenter.org/affiliates/model.php

Olive, M., Boutot, E. A., & Tarvox, J. (2011). Teaching students with autism using the principles of applied behavior analysis. In Boutot & Myles (Eds), *Autism spectrum disorders: Foundations, characteristics, and effective strategies* (pp. 141–162). Boston, MA: Pearson.

Simpson, R. L., deBoer-Ott, S., Griswold, D., Myles, B. S., Byrd, S., Ganz, J. B., . . . Adams, L. (2005). *Autism spectrum disorders: Interventions and treatments for children and youth.* Thousand Oaks, CA: Corwin Press.

E. Amanda Boutot
Texas State University
Fourth edition

APPLIED PSYCHOLINGUISTICS

Applied Psycholinguistics publishes original articles on the psychological processes involved in language. Articles address the development, use, and impairment of language in all its modalities, including spoken, signed, and written. *Applied Psycholinguistics* is of interest to professionals in a variety of fields, including linguistics, psychology, speech and hearing, reading, language teaching, special education, and neurology. Specific topics featured in the journal include language development (the development of speech perception and production, the acquisition and use of sign language, studies of discourse development, second language learning); language disorders in children and adults (including those associated with brain damage, intellectual disability and autism, specific learning disabilities, hearing impairment, and emotional disturbance); literacy development (early literacy skills, dyslexia and other reading disorders, writing development and disorders, spelling development and disorders); and psycholinguistic processing (bilingualism, sentence processing, lexical access).

In addition to research reports, theoretical reviews will be considered for publication, as will short notes, discussions of previously published papers, and book reviews. The journal will occasionally publish issues devoted to special topics within its purview. *Applied Psycholinguistics* is published by Cambridge University Press, The Edinburgh Building, Shaftesbury Road, Cambridge CB2 2RU UK.

Philip M. Prinz
Pennsylvania State University
First edition

Rachel M. Toplis
Falcon School District 49, Colorado Springs, Colorado
Third edition

APPLIED VERBAL BEHAVIOR

Applied verbal behavior (AVB) is a type of behavioral intervention that focuses primarily on increasing functional verbal communication in children with autism and related disorders (LeBlanc, Esch, Sidener, & Firth, 2006). AVB is based in a Skinnerian approach to language (see Skinner, 1957). Thus, in AVB, language is viewed not in terms of words but rather in terms of operational units of language, which are based on the function or purpose of the communication, such as "mands" and "tacts." A mand, derived from the word "demand," is a word or phrase that can achieve a desired response by the speaker and is unique in its ability to produce a desired result whereas a tact, which is a comment or label, describes language and lacks the direct purpose of a mand (Skinner, 1957). AVB promotes the use of language by rewarding the use of mands and tacts and by using operant conditioning principles to teach that specific mands can lead to certain specific and desired outcomes, such as the receipt of a desired item (LeBlanc et al., 2006).

For children who do not yet have a large number of mands, AVB promotes the use of mands through the use of establishing operations (EOs) (LeBlanc et al., 2006). As described by Michael (1993, 2000), EOs increase the desirability of a reward (e.g., using food restriction as an EO to increase the potency of food as a reward). This can involve either direct, unconditioned EO relationships (e.g., food deprivation and hunger) or conditioned EO relationships established through classical conditioning by pairing an unconditioned EO with an initially neutral stimulus.

Theoretically, the use of an EO during AVB will entice a child to establish some sort of mand (e.g., manual sign, spoken word) in order to receive the desired reward (e.g., food or drink). The mand can be further shaped and reinforced through subsequent operant conditioning and further use of EOs (LeBlanc et al., 2006). Use of tacts, on the other hand, may be trained through intraverbal techniques (e.g., pairing a tact with a question where the tact would be an appropriate response) and maintained through general social reinforcement (LeBlanc et al., 2006). AVB initially focuses more heavily on mands, given their functional use and natural development through the use of EOs.

Although AVB can be used in naturalistic settings, it differs from other verbal and language therapies in that it places greater value on establishing a direct, "pure" relationship between a mand and a response than it does on naturalistic training settings (LeBlanc et al., 2006). In other words, while generalization is a goal of AVB, the principles of the intervention hold that creating a pure operant relationship between specific mands and specific outcomes should come before attempts to teach and promote the use of verbal behavior in naturalistic settings (LeBlanc et al., 2006). For example, the relation between the mand "cookie" and the presentation of a chocolate chip cookie should be directly and firmly established before the mand is used in a preschool setting where the result of the mand may be less explicit and consistent.

REFERENCES

LeBlanc, L. A., Esch, J., Sidener, T. M., & Firth, A. M. (2006). Behavioral language interventions for children with autism: Comparing applied verbal behavior and naturalistic teaching approaches. *Analysis of Verbal Behavior, 22,* 49–60.

Michael, J. (1993). Establishing operations. *The Behavior Analyst, 16,* 191–206.

Michael, J. (2000). Implications and refinements of the establishing operation concept. *Journal of Applied Behavior Analysis, 33,* 401–410.

Skinner, B. F. (1957). *Verbal behavior.* Cambridge, MA: Prentice Hall.

EMILY M. LUND
Texas A&M University
Fourth edition

APRAXIA, DEVELOPMENTAL

Developmental apraxia refers to a sensory integration problem that involves praxis and motor planning deficits. It can affect gross and fine motor performance as well as speech. The disorder is one of higher cortical process and results in problems with planning and executing learned, volitional movements. These children, however, show normal strength, tone, reflex, sensation, and coordination. Developmental apraxia can affect a broad range of functioning, including self-care and academic performance. There are also social implications for children with this disorder (Ripley, Daines, & Barrett, 1997).

Extensive searching of the literature failed to provide prevalence data. There is, however, evidence to suggest that developmental apraxia is a function of immature brain development, or fewer connections between nerve cells (Portwood, 1999). There is also evidence of low weight gain during pregnancy and infant feeding problems. In these cases, neural pathways may be poorly developed, causing problems with neurosynaptic transmission.

The Diagnostic and Statistical Manual of Mental Disorders–Fourth Edition (DSM-IV) uses the term *Developmental Coordination Disorder* to refer to developmental apraxia (American Psychiatric Association [APA], 1994). Children with this disorder may qualify for special education services under the Individuals with Disabilities Education Act (IDEA). Typically, these services are provided under the category of Other Health Impaired. In order to qualify for services, the child must demonstrate a marked impairment in the development of motor coordination that significantly interferes with academic achievement or activities of daily living. Coordination difficulties cannot be due to a general medical condition, such as cerebral palsy, muscular dystrophy, or hemiplegia. Furthermore the diagnosis is not made when problems with sensory integration are a function of a pervasive developmental disorder (PDD). It can, however, be made concurrent with a diagnosis of intellectual disability (ID); however, motor difficulties must be in excess of those found in children with MR. Associated features include phonological disorder, expressive language disorder, and mixed receptive-expressive disorder (APA, 1994). Developmental apraxia has also been found among children diagnosed with attention-deficit/hyperactivity disorder and specific learning disorders such as dyslexia, dyspraxia, and dyscalculia (House, 1999). According to House, it is important to consider developmental apraxia as a possible comorbid diagnosis in children with dyscalculia or mathematics disorder, both of which are linked to nonverbal learning disabilities.

Characteristics

1. Delayed development of motor skills, with tasks performed slowly and inefficiently
2. Visuospatial deficits and a poor sense of body and objects in space
3. A tendency to fall and bump into objects
4. Heightened sensitivity to sensory input (e.g., noise and lights)
5. Difficulty carrying out a sequence of movements causing oral production (articulation) and fine and gross motor problems (illegible handwriting)
6. Associated problems with attention, concentration, hyperactivity, following directions, and interacting socially

Depending on the severity and nature of the problem, a number of professionals may be involved in the assessment process; this includes the school psychologist, speech-language pathologist, and occupational (and sometimes physical) therapists. Pediatric neurologists may also be involved in order to rule out alternative explanations for the apraxia (e.g., acute or degenerative central nervous system disorder). Tools that are used to evaluate developmental apraxia include the Sensory Integration and Praxis Tests, Bruininks-Oseretsky Test of Motor Proficiency, Comprehensive Apraxia Test, and the Movement Assessment Battery for Children (see Portwood, 1999). In addition to administering standardized measures such as these, it is important to obtain an in-depth developmental history and comprehensive evaluation of the child's cognitive skills and academic performance. Behavioral observations should be a part of the assessment process in order to identify specific deficits that might interfere with the child's classroom performance and extracurricular activities (e.g., recreation).

Treatment often includes speech and language services and occupational therapy involving sensory integration techniques. There are a number of classroom accommodations that may prove beneficial, including allowing extra time to complete assignments, requiring smaller amounts of information to be worked on at any given time, providing extra structure and organization (e.g., line up columns for math assignments), and offering alternative tests and assignments such as dictated rather than written homework.

With appropriate accommodations and services, the prognosis should be good. Further research, however, is needed to provide information about the incidence of this disorder and ways to best remedy the problem.

REFERENCES

American Psychiatric Association. (2000). *Diagnostic and statistical manual of mental disorders* (4th ed., text rev.). Washington, DC: Author.

House, A. E. (1999). *DSM-IV diagnosis in the schools*. New York, NY: Guilford Press.

Portwood, M. (1999). *Developmental dyspraxia: Identification and intervention: A manual for parents and professionals* (2nd ed.). London, UK: David Fulton.

Ripley, K., Daines, B., & Barrett, J. (1997). *Dyspraxia: A guide for teachers and parents*. London, UK: David Fulton.

LINDSEY A. PHILLIPS
ELAINE CLARK
University of Utah

APRAXIA, OCULAR MOTOR COGAN TYPE

Ocular motor apraxia, Cogan type (OMA) is a rare congenital eye disorder. This is also referred to as congenital oculomotor apraxia (COMA). Cogan (CaF Directory, 1997) first reported this disorder in 1952. It is thought to be inherited as an autosomal recessive genetic trait. However, school-age children, as a secondary problem to neurological and metabolic diseases, may acquire this condition. Ocular motor apraxia can be associated with a wide array of brain malformations, metabolic disorders, and perinatal problems (OMA Homepage, 2000).

Ocular motor apraxia effects the mechanism that controls horizontal eye movement, both voluntary and responsive. This disorder is characterized by defective or absent horizontal ocular attraction movements or absence of horizontal voluntary or responsive eye movements.

Infants with the disorder may appear to be blind at first because they do not seem to respond to visual stimuli, but later they may develop head movements to shift their gaze (Kearney, Groenveld, Sargent, & Poskitt, 1998). In addition, there have been some reports of infants with the disorder having colic during their first few months of life. Many children fail hearing tests when there is nothing wrong with their hearing because traditional hearing tests do not account for the impact of visual impairment on a child's responses.

The condition and its causes are relatively unexplored because of the rarity of its occurrence. Additionally, due to the rarity of this congenital disorder, its epidemiology was difficult to obtain. The National Organization for Rare Disorders (2000) stated that there were only 50 reported cases in the medical literature.

Characteristics

1. Infant may seem visually unresponsive from birth, behaving as if he or she were blind.
2. There is difficulty with horizontal eye movement. The child will develop a jerking of the head or excessive blinking, which helps to break and then realign focus.
3. The child will have to turn his or her head for side vision instead of using peripheral vision.
4. Low muscle tone is common but is usually due to the secondary condition of being developmentally delayed.
5. The child may reach developmental milestones more slowly than do his or her peers.

There is no direct treatment for ocular motor apraxia. Most treatment is related to the secondary effects of the disorder. Regular visits to a physiotherapist to assist in the development of muscle tone and the use of special toys and equipment in an attempt to correct the effects of ocular motor apraxia are examples of treatments for this condition (CaF Directory, 1997; OMA Homepage, 2000). Parents of children with OMA may find a valuable support system by registering with the OMA organization (http://www.oma.org/). This is a helpful site to interact with other families and gather information regarding this disorder.

Children with OMA may be eligible for special services at school. These children, due to the nature of their disorder, typically have poor reading skills that require remedial assistance. Many of these individuals also display speech apraxia and require speech and language services. Secondary to OMA itself, there may be gross and fine motor difficulties that may make the child appear clumsy. In an effort to cope with such clumsiness, a child may develop behavior problems.

OMA is not a progressive disease. Generally it is thought that the prognosis of this disorder is good and has a developmental resolution. This disorder typically improves or disappears between the ages of 5 and 10. However, there are cases still apparent in adulthood (Prasad & Nair, 1994).

REFERENCES

CaF Directory. (1997, December). Congenital ocular motor apraxia. Retrieved from http://www.cafamily.org.uk

Kearney, S., Groenveld, M., Sargent, M., & Poskitt, K. (1998). Speech, cognition, and imaging studies in congenital ocular motor apraxia. *Developmental Medicine and Child Neurology, 40*, 95–99.

National Organization for Rare Disorders. (2000). *Apraxia, ocular motor, Cogan type.* Retrieved from http://www.rarediseases.org

OMA Homepage. (2000, July). *Investigating and dealing with ocular motor apraxia.* Retrieved from http://www.ocularmotorapraxia.net/Home.html

Prasad, P., & Nair, S. (1994). Congenital ocular motor apraxia: Sporadic and familial: Support for natural resolution. *The Journal of Neuroophthalmology, 14*, 102–104.

THERESA KELLY
WILLIAM M. ACREE
University of Northern Colorado

APRAXIA (*See Developmental Apraxia*)

APTITUDE TESTING

The term *aptitude test* has been traditionally employed to refer to tests designed to assess the level of development attained by an individual on relatively homogenous and clearly defined segments of ability, such as spatial visualization, numerical aptitude, or perceptual speed. Aptitude tests measure the effects of learning under the relatively uncontrolled and unknown conditions of daily living. In this sense, they differ from achievement tests that measure the effects of a relatively standardized set of experiences encountered in an educational program. The two types of tests differ in use as well. Achievement tests generally represent a terminal evaluation of an individual's status on the completion of training. Aptitude tests serve to predict subsequent performance. They are employed to estimate the extent to which an individual will profit from a specific course of training, or to predict the quality of achievement in a new situation.

The term *special aptitude* originated at a time when the major emphasis in testing was placed on general intelligence. Traditional intelligence tests were designed primarily to yield a single global measure of an individual's general level of cognitive development such as an IQ. Although they were comprised of a heterogeneous grouping of subtests, both practical and theoretical analysis soon revealed that intelligence tests were limited in their coverage of abilities, and that more precise measures were required. This development led to the construction of separate tests for measuring areas of ability that were not included in the intelligence batteries. Traditional intelligence tests oversampled abstract functions involving the use of verbal or numerical symbols; therefore, a particular need was felt for tests covering the more concrete or practical abilities. The earliest aptitude tests were those measuring mechanical aptitude, but soon tests to measure clerical, musical, and artistic aptitude were developed. These special aptitudes were regarded as supplementary to the IQ in a description of an individual, and were usually administered in conjunction with a standard intelligence battery.

A strong impetus to the construction of special aptitude tests was provided by the problems of matching job requirements with the specific pattern of abilities that characterize each individual, a task commonly faced by psychologists in career counseling or in the classification of industrial and military personnel. Intelligence tests were not designed for this purpose. Aside from the limited representation of certain aptitudes discussed earlier, their subtests or item groups were often too unreliable to justify the sort of intra-individual analysis required for classification purposes. To respond to this need, the testing field turned to the development of multiple aptitude batteries.

Like intelligence tests, multiple aptitude batteries measure a number of abilities, but instead of a total score, they yield a profile of scores, one for each aptitude; thus they provide a suitable instrument for making intra-individual analysis (Anastasi, 1997). In addition, the abilities measured by multiple aptitude batteries are often different than those measured by intelligence batteries. Aptitude batteries tend to measure more concrete skills, such as arithmetic reasoning, numerical aptitude, perceptual speed, and spatial visualization, thereby placing less emphasis on verbal skills than intelligence tests.

Nearly all multiple aptitude batteries have appeared since 1945. Much of the test research and development began in the armed forces during World War II, when the Air Force designed special batteries to select training candidates to be pilots, bombardiers, radio operators, and range finders. The armed services still sponsor a considerable amount of research in this area, but a number of multiple aptitude batteries have been developed for civilian use in educational and vocational counseling and in personnel selection and classification (Murphy, 1994).

The application of factor analysis to the study of trait organization provided the theoretical basis for the construction of multiple aptitude batteries. Factor analysis identified, sorted, and defined the abilities that were loosely grouped under the definition of intelligence. The tests that best measured the factors identified in the analysis were then included in the multiple aptitude battery. The Chicago Test of Primary Mental Abilities (1941) represents the first attempt to construct a battery based on factor analysis using the pioneer factor analytic work of Thurstone (1938). Most multiple aptitude batteries developed since that time have employed the use of factor analysis in construction.

About a dozen multiple aptitude batteries have been developed for use in a number of fields. These instruments vary widely in approach, technical quality, and the amount of available validation data. In business and industry, data gained from the administration of multiple aptitude test batteries may be used for institutional decisions regarding the assignment of personnel to different jobs. In education, multiple aptitude batteries such as the SRA Primary Mental Abilities Test (Hanna, 1992) are used to guide the admission of students to different educational curricula (Schutz, 1972). The armed services use aptitude data to assign specific job classifications to personnel after screening with a more general instrument (Weitzman, 1985). The Air Force pioneered this practice, but all branches of the armed services now use the Armed Services Vocational Aptitude Battery (ASVAB; Bayroff, 1968).

A number of multiple aptitude batteries have been designed for use with high school students to aid in the transition from high school to work or postsecondary training (e.g., Ball Foundation, 2002). The most widely used of these tests is the Differential Aptitude Test (DAT; Bennett, Seashore, & Wesman, 1990). Based on the factor analytic work of Thurstone (1938), the DAT is used in the educational and vocational counseling of students. It provides a profile of scores on eight subtests: Verbal Reasoning, Numerical Ability, Abstract Reasoning, Clerical Speed and Accuracy, Mechanical Reasoning, Spatial Relations, Spelling, and Language Usage. In the most recent fifth edition of the DAT, significant changes have occurred in the battery of tests. The fifth edition is divided into two parallel forms for grades 7–9 and 10–12. New items have been added, old items have been revised and updated, and the overall testing time has been shortened by reducing the length of some tests. Using the student's profile in conjunction with an interest inventory, a counselor can use a computer or casebook to predict the student's success in postsecondary education, or generate a list of potential careers. A vast amount of validity data is available for the DAT. The predictive validity coefficients are high, indicating that the DAT serves as a good predictor of high school achievement in academic and vocational programs (Schmitt, 1995). However, the differential validity of the separate tests is quite poor. The DAT should therefore be used cautiously for classification purposes (such as to identify possible fields of educational or occupational specialization; Hattrup, 1995; Wise, 1995).

In 1987 the Computerized Adaptive Testing (CAT) edition of the DAT was developed, which allowed the test to be administered via Apple II or DOS-based IBM-compatible systems. However, the CAT has not been revised in light of recent technological innovations, and has therefore become somewhat obsolete (White, 1985). The Comprehensive Ability Battery (Hakstian & Cattell, 1977) and the Guilford-Zimmerman Aptitude Survey (Guilford & Zimmerman, 1956) are other multiple aptitude batteries that are often used in transition and vocational education (Biskin, 1995).

Many aptitude tests have been designed explicitly for counseling purposes in which classification decisions are preeminent. In a counseling situation, the profile of test scores is used to aid the counselor in choosing among several possible fields of educational or occupational specialization. The General Aptitude Test Battery (GATB; U.S. Department of Labor, 1980) was developed by the U.S. Employment Services (USES) for use by employment counselors in state employment services offices. The GATB is comprised of 12 tests that combine to yield nine factor scores: Intelligence, Verbal Aptitude, Numerical Aptitude, Spatial Aptitude, Form Perception, Clerical Perception, Motor Coordination, Finger Dexterity, and Manual Dexterity. The profile of these subtest scores can then be compared with profiles corresponding to a huge number of job categories. An alternative form is available for nonreading adults and there is also an addition for use with individuals who are deaf. A host of studies have been conducted on the GATB, which have consistently shown that the test is a reasonable predictor of performance across a range of jobs (Bemis, 1968).

Unlike the multiple aptitude batteries, special aptitude tests typically measure a single aptitude. Certain areas such as vision, hearing, motor dexterity, and artistic talents are often judged to be too specialized to justify inclusion in standard aptitude batteries, yet often these abilities are vital to a certain task. Special aptitude tests were designed to measure such abilities. They are often administered in conjunction with an aptitude battery, either to assess a skill not included in the battery or to further probe a skill or interest. Special aptitude tests may also be custom-made for a particular job, and be constructed using a simulation of the requisites of the job, such as the Minnesota Clerical Test (The Psychological Corporation, 1992), the Meier Art Judgment Test (Meier, 1942), or the Seashore Measure of Musical Talents (Seashore, 1938). Despite wide use in education, counseling, and industry, the development of aptitude tests has been slow (Murphy, 1994). Many of the aptitude tests currently in use were developed in the 1940s and 1950s and have been revised and reissued in subsequent years.

REFERENCES

Anastasi, A. (1997). *Psychological testing* (7th ed.). Saddle River, NJ: Prentice Hall.

Ball Foundation. (2002). *Ball Career System technical manual.* Glen Ellyn, IL: Author.

Bayroff, A. G., & Fuchs, E. F. (1968). The armed forces vocational aptitude battery. *Proceedings of the 76th annual convention of the American Psychological Association, 3*, 635–636.

Bemis, S. E. (1968). Occupational validity of the General Aptitude Test Battery. *Journal of Applied Psychology, 52*, 240–244.

Bennett, G. K., Seashore, H. G., & Wesman, A. G. (1990). *Fifth edition manual for Differential Aptitude Tests, Forms S and T*. New York, NY: Psychological Corporation.

Biskin, B. H. (1995). Review of the Guilford-Zimmerman Interest Inventory. In J. C. Conoley & J. C. Impara (Eds.), *The twelfth mental measurements yearbook* (pp. 442–443). Lincoln, NE: Buros Institute of Mental Measurements.

Guilford, J. P., & Zimmerman, W. S. (1956). *The Guilford-Zimmerman Aptitude Survey*. New York, NY: McGraw-Hill.

Hakstian, A. R., & Cattell, R. B. (1977). *The Comprehensive Ability Battery*. Champaign, IL: Institute for Personality and Ability Testing.

Hanna, G. S. (1992). Review of the SRA Achievement Series Forms 1 & 2 and survey of Basic Skills Form P & Q. In J. J. Kramer & J. C. Conoley (Eds.), *The eleventh mental measurements yearbook* (pp. 859–861). Lincoln, NE: Buros Institute of Mental Measurements.

Hattrup, D. (1995). Review of Differential Aptitude Tests: Fifth Edition. In J. C. Conoley & J. C. Impara (Eds.), *The twelfth mental measurements yearbook* (pp. 302–304). Lincoln, NE: Buros Institute of Mental Measurements.

Meier, N. C. (1942). *Art in human affairs*. New York, NY: McGraw-Hill.

Murphy, K. R. (1994). Aptitude interest measurement. In D. J. Keyser & R. C. Sweetland (Eds.), *Test critiques: Volume 10* (pp. 31–38). Austin, TX: PRO-ED.

The Psychological Corporation. (1992). *Minnesota Clerical Test*. New York, NY: Author.

Schmitt, N. (1995). Review of Differential Aptitude Tests: Fifth Edition. In J. C. Conoley & J. C. Impara (Eds.), *The twelfth mental measurements yearbook* (pp. 304–305). Lincoln, NE: Buros Institute of Mental Measurements.

Schutz, R. E. (1972). S.R.A. primary mental abilities. *Seventh mental measurements yearbook* (Vol. 11, pp. 1066–1068). Highland Park, NJ: Gryphon.

Seashore, C. E. (1938). *Psychology of music*. New York, NY: McGraw-Hill.

Thurstone, L. L. (1938). Primary mental abilities. *Psychometric Monographs*. No. 1.

U.S. Department of Labor, Employment, and Training Administration. (1980). *Manual, USES General Aptitude Test Battery*. Washington, DC: U.S. Government Printing Office.

Weitzman, R. A. (1985). Review of the Armed Services Vocational Battery. In J. V. Mitchel (Ed.), *The ninth mental measurements yearbook* (Vol. 1, pp. 83–84). Lincoln, NE: Buros Institute of Mental Measurements.

White, K. R. (1985). Review of the Comprehensive Ability Battery. In J. V. Mitchel (Ed.), *The ninth mental measurements yearbook* (Vol. 1, pp. 377–379). Lincoln, NE: Buros Institute of Mental Measurements.

Wise, S. L. (1995). Review of Differential Aptitude Tests: Computerized Adaptive Edition. In J. C. Conoley & J. C. Impara (Eds.), *The twelfth mental measurements yearbook* (pp. 300–301). Lincoln, NE: Buros Institute of Mental Measurements.

LIZANNE DeSTEFANO
University of Illinois

See also Achievement Tests; Assessment, Curriculum-Based; Criterion-Referenced Testing; Vocational Education

APTITUDE-TREATMENT INTERACTION

Aptitude-treatment interaction refers to an educational phenomenon in which students who are dissimilar with regard to a particular aptitude perform differently under alternate instructional conditions. The alternate instructional conditions are specifically designed to reflect the students' aptitude differences. Thus, if a significant performance difference between the groups results under alternate instructional conditions, an aptitude by treatment interaction has occurred.

Aptitude-treatment interactions have been discussed at length by Bracht (1970), who defines an aptitude-treatment interaction as "a significant disordinal interaction between alternate treatments and personological variables" (p. 627). A personological variable is any measure of an individual characteristic such as learning style, intelligence, achievement anxiety, or locus of control. Disordinal interactions refer to performance differences between groups that denote the significantly better performance of one group under one set of conditions and the significantly better performance of the second group under alternate conditions. Figure A.2 graphically displays a disordinal aptitude-treatment interaction.

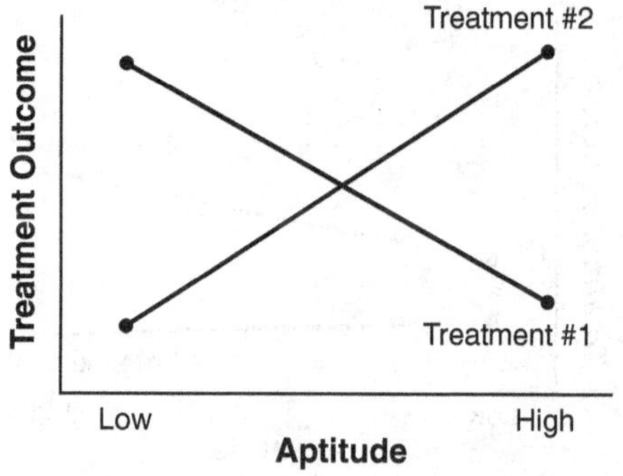

Figure A.2. Disordinal experimental outcome that is not indicative of an aptitude-treatment interaction.

Source: Bracht, G. H. (1970). Experimental factors related to aptitude-treatment interactions. *Review of Educational Research, 40*(50), 627–645.

Figure A.2 depicts hypothetical data for two groups of students who differ on a particular aptitude, one group being high and the other being low. Alternate treatments, matched to the students' aptitude, were provided. Students with low aptitude performed better under treatment number 1. Students with high aptitude performed better under treatment number 2. The data confirm the occurrence of an aptitude-treatment interaction and support the use of different instructional approaches for these two groups of students.

Figures A.3 and A.4, respectively, display hypothetical experimental outcomes that are not indicative of an aptitude-treatment interaction. In Figure A.3, both groups of students, despite the aptitude difference, performed better under treatment number 1. In Figure A.4, treatment number 1 was again superior for both groups of students. However, the differences for the low-aptitude students under treatment conditions number 1 and number 2 were not significant. The aptitude difference does not suggest the use of different treatments for the two groups; other factors may dictate the use of one or the other treatment for both groups. In this instance, the aptitude dimension did not clarify the choice between treatments.

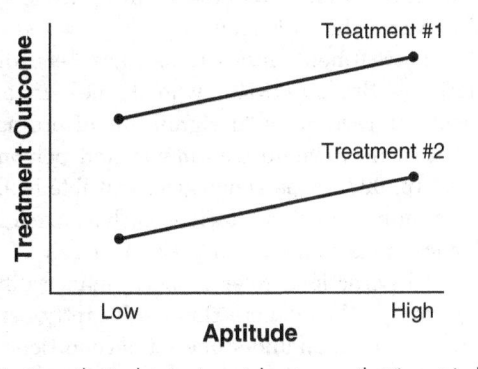

Figure A.3. Hypothetical experimental outcome that is not indicative of an aptitude-treatment interaction.
Source: Bracht, G. H. (1970). Experimental factors related to aptitude-treatment interactions. *Review of Educational Research, 40*(50), 627–645.

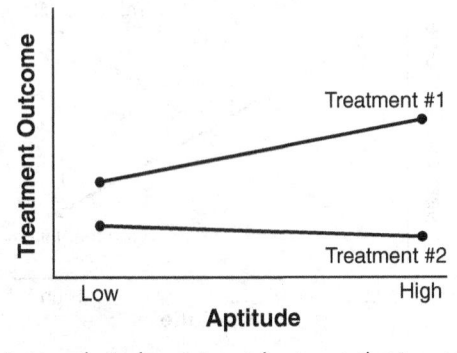

Figure A.4. Hypothetical experimental outcome that is not indicative of an aptitude-treatment interaction.
Source: Bracht, G. H. (1970). Experimental factors related to aptitude-treatment interactions. *Review of Educational Research, 40*(50), 627–645.

Interest in aptitude-treatment interactions is fueled by the widely espoused commitment to individualization of instruction and the quest for teaching adaptations that enhance individual student performance. Appreciation for individual differences is a relatively recent development (Snow, 1977). Snow believes that the "recognition that individual differences in aptitude not only predict learning outcomes but also often interact with instructional treatment variations" (p. 11). This concept makes adaptive instruction a possibility. Teachers have long recognized individual differences and have accommodated such differences in a myriad of ways. Nowhere is the concern for individual differences greater than in special education. The Individual Educational Program requirement of PL 94-142 and its revisions has mandated individualized educational planning for all exceptional children. Adaptation and accommodation to individual learner needs and characteristics is at the heart of the special education instructional process. Corno and Snow (1986), in a discussion of adapted teaching, view adaptations as involving either direct aptitude development or circumvention of inaptitude. In special education, the adage "teach to the strengths and remediate the weaknesses" prevails. Teachers generally seek intact or relatively strong abilities as avenues for instruction. Accompanying remediation is most often focused on specific skill or knowledge deficits that impede academic performance or independent functioning. Unfortunately, the commitment among educators, particularly teachers of the exceptional, to individualized instruction in practice is not matched by a strong commitment to educational research. "While it is clear that teachers adapt their behavior to students' individual differences at virtually all levels of education, what is less clear is the underlying logic and intentionality that governs these adaptations" (Corno & Snow, 1986, p. 614).

The systematic experimental investigation of teaching adaptations in relation to student characteristics is the focus of aptitude-treatment interaction research. However, the research to date underscores the difficulties associated with investigations of this kind. Bracht's review of 90 aptitude-treatment interaction studies yielded only five in which disordinal interactions were found. However, Bracht's review did help to clarify the nature of the aptitude and treatment variables and to identify the variables that increase the probability of significant aptitude-treatment interactions. Bracht's review included five studies that involved handicapped learners; none of the studies yielded significant interactions. Bracht notes that the subjects in these five studies bore categorical labels such as intellectually disabled and emotionally disturbed. Such broad categories tend to mask the considerable heterogeneity that exists within the groups—a factor that works against the probability of aptitude-treatment interactions. In another review, Ysseldyke (1973) discussed five aptitude-treatment interaction studies involving handicapped learners grouped for instruction according to modality differences. Auditory and/or visual functioning were the modalities under consideration. Instruction matched to modality strengths or preferences failed to yield evidence of significant interactions across a variety of academic outcome measures (e.g., reading achievement and word recognition skills) in any of these studies.

Another review of research specifically involving modality-instructional matching was reported by Arter and Jenkins (1977). Preset criteria limited the number of studies reviewed in depth to 14. In all of the studies, the students were assigned to a modality group based on a statistical difference in modality functioning (modality assessments had adequate test-retest reliability and validity). Alternate instructional methods had a clear modality emphasis and outcome measures were constant across the groups. Only one study (Bursuk, 1971) demonstrated a significant modality-instruction interaction. This study involved tenth-grade below-average readers who were given instruction in listening and reading comprehension (reading comprehension lessons were given to the visual modality preference group only) over an entire school semester. The authors point out the specificity and control of subjects, treatments, and outcome measures that distinguish the Bursuk study from the remaining 13 research reports.

The results from studies specifically designed to demonstrate the interaction between modalities and instruction have not been a deterrent to practitioners. Despite the lack of supportive research, instruction based on the modality concept has been used for many years. The modality model of instruction is founded on aptitude-treatment interaction theory, but the applicability of aptitude-treatment interaction theory to modality-based instruction has yet to be demonstrated and validated to this day.

Aptitude-treatment interaction research is by no means confined to special education or to investigations of modality-based instruction. Aptitude-treatment interaction research has been conducted in other academic areas such as math (Holton, 1982) and reading (Blanton, 1971). The results generally have been disappointing.

The number of research studies that have successfully demonstrated aptitude-treatment interactions is limited, but the research has provided considerable insight into the complexities of the interaction phenomenon and the conditions that favor the occurrence of aptitude-treatment interactions (Veeman & Elshout, 1994). Bracht (1970) found that disordinal interactions were related to the degree of control over treatment tasks, the factorial makeup of the specific personological variables, and the nature of the dependent outcome variables. Controlled treatments, factorially simple personological variables, and specific, rather than complex, outcome variables favor aptitude-treatment interaction (Mills, Dale, Cole, & Jenkins, 1995). Snow (1977) stresses the "essential importance of detailed description of specific instructional variables and specific groups of people" (p. 12) to aptitude-treatment interaction research. In retrospect, the research reports that documented significant aptitude by treatment interactions displayed the prerequisite degree of control and specificity of critical variables that seem essential for aptitude-treatment interactions to occur.

The research findings to date suggest that each aptitude-treatment interaction, when found, will be valid only in a specific context. Each finding will pertain to a particular group of students under particular instructional conditions. Generalizations, if made at all, will be limited. Educators should not anticipate general educational theories with potential for broad application to emerge from aptitude-treatment interaction research. Rather, aptitude-treatment interaction theory implies ongoing evaluation of student and instructional variables and a constant readiness to adjust to meet changing conditions.

REFERENCES

Arter, J. A., & Jenkins, J. R. (1977). Examining the benefits of modality considerations in special education. *Journal of Special Education, 11*(3), 281–298.

Berliner, C. D., & Cohen, L. S. (1973). Trait-treatment interaction and learning. In F. N. Kerlinger (Ed.), *Review of research in education* (Vol. 1). Ithasca, IL: Peacock.

Blanton, B. (1971). Modalities and reading. *Reading Teacher, 25*(2), 210–212.

Bracht, G. H. (1970). Experimental factors related to aptitude-treatment interactions. *Review of Educational Research, 40*(50), 627–645.

Bursuk, L. A. (1971). Sensory mode of lesson presentation as a factor in the reading comprehension improvement of adolescent retarded readers. (ERIC Document Reproduction Service No. ED 047 435).

Corno, L., & Snow, R. E. (1986). Adapting teaching to individual differences among learners. In M. C. Wittrock (Ed.), *Handbook of research on teaching* (3rd ed.). New York, NY: Macmillan.

Holton, B. (1982). Attribute-treatment-interaction research in mathematics education. *School Science & Mathematics, 82*(7), 593–601.

Mills, P. E., Dale, P. S., Cole, K. N., & Jenkins, J. R. (1995). Follow-up of children from academic and cognitive preschool criteria at age 9. *Exceptional Children, 61*, 378–393.

Snow, R. E. (1977). Individual differences and instructional theory. *Educational Researcher, 6*(10), 11–15.

Snow, R. E. (1984). Placing children in special education: Some comments. *Educational Researchers 13*(3), 12–14.

Veeman, M. V., & Elshout, J. J. (1994). Differential effects of instructional support on learning in simulation environments. *Instructional Science, 22*, 363–383.

Ysseldyke, J. E. (1973). Diagnostic-prescriptive teaching: The search for aptitude-treatment interactions. In L. Mann &

D. A. Sabatino (Eds.), *The first review of special education.*
Philadelphia, PA: JSE Press.

LIBBY GOODMAN
Pennsylvania State University

See also Diagnostic Prescriptive Teaching; Direct
Instruction; Remediation, Deficit-Centered Models;
Teacher Effectiveness

ARACHNOID CYSTS

Arachnoid cysts are benign cerebrospinal fluid-filled sacs
that develop between the surface of the brain and cranial
base or attach to the arachnoid membrane (National Institute of Neurological Disorders and Stroke [NINDS], 2000).
The cysts may develop anywhere along the cerebrospinal
axis but have a predilection for the Sylvian fissure. Arachnoid cysts account for approximately 1% of all intracranial
space-occupying lesions (Wester, 1999). Although most
are slow growing and asymptomatic at first, if untreated,
they can have devastating effects as a result of increased
intracranial pressure.

Symptoms are often dependent on the size and location of the cyst. Common symptoms, however, include
headache, vomiting, and papilloedema (i.e., problems associated with hypertension). Other symptoms associated
with increased pressure include hydrocephalus and subsequent changes in the cranial vault. Gait can also be
disturbed, and both endocrine problems and seizures can
occur (Adan et al., 2000). Although epilepsy occurs more
often in adults than children with cysts, in 20% of pediatric
cases a seizure disorder is diagnosed (compared to 80% in
adults; Artico, Cervoni, Salvati, Fiorenza, & Caruso, 1995).

Most arachnoid cysts are congenital; however, they can
be acquired. Head injury is often responsible for acquired
cysts. Ultrasound is often used to make the diagnosis,
even in utero. Males seem to be more prone to developing
arachnoid cysts, and the cysts most often occur in the left
temporal lobe (Wester, 1999). No sex differences have been
found for other cyst locations.

Characteristics

1. Common symptoms include those associated with
   hypertension (headache, vomiting, papilloedema)
2. Less common problems include gait disturbance,
   endocrine abnormalities, and epilepsy
3. Cognitive problems are often associated with etiology (e.g., head injury causing poor verbal memory,
   visuo-spatial deficits, difficulty shifting sets, and
   slowed processing)

Arachnoid cysts must be treated in order to avoid severe
brain damage from increased pressure, hemorrhaging, or
both. Treatment depends on the size and location of the
cyst, but most interventions are intended to drain the cyst
and prevent the accumulation of fluid. Surgical procedures
typically include cyst fenestration and shunt placement.
Although fenestration appears to be preferred over shunt
placements (i.e., to avoid shunt dependency and infection),
when arachnoid cysts communicate with the subarachnoid
space to cause increased pressure (and hydrocephalus),
shunts are used (Artico et al., 1995).

Although there is little indication that these cysts have
any long-term physical or cognitive sequelae, some problems appear to be associated with the cause of the cyst (e.g.,
traumatic brain injury). Other symptoms, however, that
have been related to arachnoid cysts include problems
such as verbal memory and learning, visual-perceptual
skill, cognitive flexibility, and psychomotor speed (Soukup,
Patterson, Trier, & Chen, 1998). The impact on learning,
beyond the acute phase, is unclear. Neuropsychological
assessments are, therefore, in order to identify potential
deficits in order to design effective interventions. Special
education may in these cases be necessary and provided
under the category of Other Health Impaired. In cases in
which a traumatic brain injury causes the cyst, however,
services may be more appropriately provided under that
category. More often than not, Section 504 services or
classroom accommodations will suffice (e.g., assistance to
catch up on missed assignments or reduction of homework
to assist the child in completing work in a reasonable time
frame).

Prognosis appears to be good when arachnoid cysts are
treated early—that is, before they cause further neurological damage (NINDS, 2000). Research, however, is needed
to better diagnose the cyst in utero and in infants. Further investigations of preferred treatment strategies are
also needed in order to maximize treatment outcome and
reduce negative side effects (e.g., problems associated with
shunts).

REFERENCES

Adan, L., Bussieres, L., Dinand, V., Zerah, M., Pierre-Kahn, A.,
& Brauner, R. (2000). Growth, puberty and hypothalamic-
pituitary function in children with supresellar arachnoid cyst.
European Journal of Pediatrics, 159(5), 348–355.

Artico, M., Cervoni, L., Salvati, M., Fiorenza, F., & Caruso, R.
(1995). Supratentorial arachnoid cysts: Clinical and therapeutic remarks on 46 cases. *Acta Neurochirurgica, 132,*
75–78.

National Institute of Neurological Disorders and Stroke. (2000,
September 16). NINDS arachnoid cysts information page.
Retrieved from http://www.ninds.nih.gov/

Soukup, V., Patterson, J., Trier, T., & Chen, J. (1998). Cognitive
improvement despite minimal arachnoid cyst decompression.
Brain Development, 20(8), 589–593.

Wester, K. (1999). Peculiarities of intracranial arachnoid cysts: Location, sidedness distribution in 126 consecutive patients. *Neurosurgery, 45*(4), 775–779.

WENDY WOLFE
ELAINE CLARK
University of Utah

ARC, THE

The Arc was founded in 1950 by a group of parents and other individuals to assist in the development and care of children and adults with intellectual disabilities and or to help support families. The organization has undergone several name changes, but its mission has remained constant: The Arc promotes and protects the human rights of people with intellectual and developmental disabilities. It actively supports their full inclusion and participation in the community throughout their lifetime. Throughout its 60-year history, the Arc has taken a leadership role in encouraging research into the causes and prevention of intellectual disability, and in educating the public in the results of that research. Some of the research projects and developments funded by the Arc include a new screening test for phenylketonuria (PKU) in 1961, the Bioengineering Program launched in 1982, and ongoing research on fetal alcohol syndrome. The Arc has also spearheaded efforts to influence federal policy toward children and adults with intellectual disabilities. Some of its successes include the expansion of Medicaid to finance residential programs, Supplemental Security Income, the passage of Public Law 94-142, the passage of the "Baby Doe" Amendments to the Child Abuse Act protecting newborns with disabilities from the withdrawal of medical care, and the Fair Housing Act Amendment of 1988, which prohibits housing discrimination based on disability. One of the national initiatives of the Arc is the "Autism NOW: The National Autism Resource and Information Center," which helps to provide evidence-based resources and support for individuals with Autism Spectrum Disorder.

The Arc also serves as a clearinghouse for information on subjects important in the field of intellectual and developmental disabilities, from medical advances to education to setting up financial trusts. It funds numerous publications, many of which can be downloaded from its website. The Arc is considered one of the nation's leading advocates for people with intellectual and developmental disabilities. Having its national office located in Washington, DC affords it the opportunity to lead legislative changes.

Among the supports and services the Arc provides for individuals with intellectual and developmental disabilities and their families are:

- Early intervention
- Availability of healthcare
- Assisting with employment, including help with job skills and help with finding a job
- Ensuring a free and appropriate public education for all children with intellectual and development disabilities
- Supports for families, including respite care
- Assisting with independent living
- Advocacy

The Arc has 700 state and local chapters, with over 140,000 members. Information on membership, publications, and topics of interest can be obtained from The Arc National Headquarters, 1825 K Street NW, Suite 1200 Washington, DC 20006. Tel.: (202) 534-3700 or (800) 433-5255, fax: (202) 534-3732, e-mail: info@thearc.org.

REFERENCE

Arc of the United States, The. [Organization website]. Retrieved November 5, 2011, from http://thearc.org/

DONNA WALLACE
The University of Texas of the Permian Basin

DONNA VERNER
Texas A&M University, College Station, Texas
Fourth edition

See also AAIDD, American Association of Intellectual Developmental Disabilities; Intellectual Developmental Disabilities

ARCHITECTURAL BARRIERS

Efforts to fully integrate individuals with disabilities into the societal mainstream have demanded the elimination of physical barriers that impede access to facilities, work (Stark, 2004), and the surrounding environment. Common barriers to facility or service accessibility confronted by handicapped citizens include constricted entranceways, ill-equipped public facilities (e.g., restrooms and parking areas), limited passageways, poor room spacing and layout, inadequate lighting, and limitations in the availability of supplementary mediums for providing public information (e.g., Braille directions, visual warning or evacuation alarms).

Prior to the 1960s, the vast majority of buildings and thoroughfares were designed for the "ideal user" (i.e., an able-bodied young adult). However, with the passage of the Architectural Barriers Act of 1968 which mandated all buildings being accessible, the National Center for Law and the Handicapped (1978) and the U.S. Department of Housing and Urban Development (1983) the confluence of federal and state legislation, judicial pronouncements, and publicly accepted standards of accessibility brought about significant and permanent changes in the architectural design of structures and thoroughfares. These changes prompted the removal of barriers that inhibited the accessibility (e.g., mobility and orientation) of physically and sensorily impaired citizens.

The American National Standards Institute (ANSI) specifications, originally adopted in 1961 and updated in the 1970s, establish barrier-free criteria for buildings, entranceways, and thoroughfares. These standards are designed to eliminate all architectural barriers that have historically impeded the access of the following populations:

Nonambulatory Disabled. People with physical impairments that confine them to wheelchairs.

Semiambulatory Disabled. People with physical impairments that cause them to walk with insecurity or difficulty and require the assistance of crutches, walkers, or braces.

Coordination Disabled. Those with impairments of muscle control that result in faulty coordination and that create an increased potential for personal injury.

Sight Disabled. Those with impairments that affect vision, either totally or partially, to the extent that an individual functioning in the environment is insecure or liable to injury.

Hearing Disabled. People with impairments that affect hearing, either totally or partially, to the extent that an individual functioning in the environment is insecure or liable to injury.

Modifications that may be required to eliminate architectural barriers in facilities and along public accessways include, but are not limited to, the construction of ramps, wheelchair lifts, and curbing cutouts; the improvement of transfer areas and enlarged spaces for parking facilities; the enhancement of public facilities such as restrooms, telephones, physical education facilities, and dining areas; and the improvement of passageways, entrances (e.g., doors, doorways), room designs (e.g., spacing and layout), facility lighting, and public/user information systems.

The Americans with Disabilities Act of 1990 extended all of the architectural barrier-free activities of state and local governments and businesses whether they were receiving federal funding or not. Regularly updated guidelines are published and the minimal requirements for accessibility include guidelines for new construction, additions, alteration, and historic buildings. The full guidelines can be seen at the ADA website: http://www.access-board.gov/adaag/html. The guidelines are extensive in breadth and depth and include subjects such as platform lifts, sinks, signage, telephones, and drinking fountains.

The last update was in 2002. Direct inquiries can be answered by tel.: (800) 872-2253 (voice) or (800) 993-2822 (TTY), or e-mail: ta@access-board.gov.

REFERENCES

National Center for Law and the Handicapped. (1978, July/August). *Moving toward a barrier free society: Amicus.* South Bend, IN: Amicus.

Stark, S. (2004). Removing environmental barriers in the homes of older adults with disabilities improves occupational performance. *Occupation, Participation, & Health, 24,* 32–39.

U.S. Department of Housing and Urban Development. (1983). *Access to the environment.* Washington, DC: U.S. Government Printing Office.

GEORGE JAMES HAGERTY
Stonehill College

See also Accessibility; Americans With Disabilities Act; Architecture and Individuals With Disabilities

ARCHITECTURE AND INDIVIDUALS WITH DISABILITIES

The 2000 National Census results state that 77,429,844 individuals have a sensory, physical, mental, or self-care disability in the United States (U.S. Census Bureau, 2003). Just over 6.8 million Americans living outside of institutions use assistive devices to help them with mobility. The use of wheelchairs, canes, and other devices is influenced by age, ethnicity, and gender (Kaye, Kang, & LaPlante, 2000).

Apart from the visually handicapped/blind, hearing impaired/deaf, and physically/orthopedically impaired, are those individuals who have health impairments involving cardiopulmonary disorders or neuromuscular diseases. These disorders may permit some mobility but may result in diminished stamina, poor coordination, or limited grasping and manipulative capacity.

Architectural considerations vary and are dependent on whether the handicap is physical, visual, or aural. In fact, such considerations can involve competing requirements that necessitate the establishment of unique environments for the physically handicapped in comparison with the visually handicapped. For example, a physically handicapped person confined to a wheelchair may function best in spaces that are open and large. In contrast, individuals who are blind may do better in smaller spaces where key elements of the sensory environment are within close range. Similarly, an environment that reflects noises may be advantageous for the blind but a disadvantage to the hearing impaired, who have difficulty in attenuating to multiple acoustical cues.

There are a number of general factors to be considered in designing or adapting environments:

1. Many handicapped persons may be smaller or weaker than average; therefore, slopes, reach distances, and forces necessary to open and close objects should be reduced.
2. A number of individuals who use mobility-assist devices (e.g., wheelchairs) may have secondary disabilities that involve difficulty in strength, grasping, and so forth.
3. Most persons blind at birth, or shortly after birth, know braille, while those adventitiously blind often do not know braille.
4. Tactile signals and signs should be few in number and their location carefully considered to ensure uniformity of placement throughout a building.
5. Audible signals should be in the lower frequencies, because persons lose the capacity to hear higher frequencies with increasing age.
6. Many deaf and blind persons can hear and see in favorable environments such as acoustically "dead" surroundings for the deaf and well-lit and magnified print environments for the blind.
7. Visual and aural signals are best to provide redundancy of cues and to accommodate deaf or blind persons (Sorensen, 1979, p. 2).

Through the use of mobility training programs provided through special education classes or rehabilitation efforts, the blind are able to go virtually anywhere. While guide dogs are used by a small proportion of the blind population, most blind people are initially guided through a building and later follow a memorized route. As might be expected, the primary impediments for the blind are unanticipated hazards such as people or objects moving across their paths or objects placed temporarily in a familiar area. Some specific building modifications that can be of assistance to the blind include:

Providing steps and stairs that are not open and do not have square, extended nosings on each step.

Using sound-reflecting walls since such walls allow the blind to better use their sense of hearing as a guide (moreover, sounds reflected from surfaces assist in orienting the blind to their position in an area).

Changing the construction materials in walking surfaces to denote entrances, restrooms, stairs, and other potentially hazardous areas.

Identifying doors leading to dangerous areas by door knobs that are distinctive from that of hardware used throughout the remainder of a building.

Placing all signs and letters/numbers at a consistent height, usually between 5 feet and 5 feet, 6 inches from the floor, so that the blind will know where to find them.

Of all those having auditory deficits, few are totally deaf. Even with a large hearing loss, many of those who are legally deaf can hear and comprehend if the environment is devoid of ambient noises. Modifications that can be of assistance to the deaf include:

Warning and direction devices equipped with visual indicators, as well as audible signals.

Telephones equipped with amplifiers for the hard of hearing and telephone typewriters for those who cannot use a standard phone even with amplification.

Clear signs so the deaf do not have to ask for directions since some deaf individuals have a difficult time talking and being understood.

Those individuals who have physical disabilities can be divided into those who are ambulant (able to walk with canes, crutches, or braces) and the chair-bound. The architectural requirements for those two groups, while similar, differ in some respects.

The ambulant disabled frequently have difficulty in stooping or bending. Consequently, modifications may include:

Placing handles, controls, switches, etc., within the reach of a standing person so stooping is unnecessary.

Placing ramps with a maximum gradient of slope of 1:12.

Using steps and stairs with nonprotruding nosings so individuals with restricted joint movement or braces will not catch their toes as they climb.

Placing hand rails on both sides of steps and stairs that extend beyond the first and last steps.

Chairbound individuals evidencing high degrees of independence use collapsible adult-size wheelchairs. Apart from the greater space needed for wheelchair movement, the chair-bound individual may need:

Grab bars to transfer via the front of the wheelchair to the shower, bed, and so on.

Space alongside a chair or bed.

The placement of countertops, control devices, and so on within the low to middle range of a standing person's areas of reach.

Much of the impetus for the modification of buildings and facilities for the physically handicapped began with the Architectural Barriers Act of 1968 (PL 90-480) and its subsequent amendments. The act specifies that buildings financed with federal funds must be designed and constructed to be accessible to the physically handicapped. In addition, the Rehabilitation Act of 1973 (PL 93-112 and its amendments) created the Architectural and Transportation Barriers Compliance Board, which has as its mission, in part, to:

Ensure compliance with the Architectural Barriers Act, as amended.

Examine alternative approaches to barriers that confront handicapped individuals in public settings.

Determine the measures that federal, state, and local governments should take to eliminate barriers.

Many states, by state statute, require that accessibility for the physically handicapped be provided in newly constructed, privately funded buildings that are open to the public. All states require that publicly funded buildings be accessible to the handicapped. A number of states require that when extensive remodeling is undertaken, such remodeling will include making the building accessible.

The Americans with Disabilities Act of 1990 requires accessibility, and its subsequent revisions have provided up-to-date and consistently revised guidelines for removing and preventing architectural barriers for individuals with disabilities. An ADA technical assistance center has an extensive list of resources and can be found at http://www.adaportal.org.

REFERENCES

Americans with Disabilities Act of 1990, 42 U.S.C. §§ 12101 et seq.

Harkness, S. P., & Groom, J. N. (1976). *Building without barriers for the disabled*. New York, NY: Whitney Library of Design.

Kaye, H. S., Kang, T., & LaPlante, M. P. (2000). *Mobility device use in the United States*. San Francisco: University of California, San Francisco, Disability Statistics Center.

Moe, C. (1977). *Planning for the removal of architectural barriers for the handicapped*. Monticello, IL: Council of Planning Librarians.

Sorensen, R. J. (1979). *Design for accessibility*. New York, NY: McGraw-Hill.

U.S. Census Bureau. (2003). American community survey summary tables. Retrieved from http://www.factfinder.census.gov

PATRICIA ANN ABRAMSON
Hudson Public Schools, Hudson, Wisconsin

See also Accessibility of Buildings; Americans with Disabilities Act; Mobility Instruction; Mobility Trainers

ARCHIVES OF CLINICAL NEUROPSYCHOLOGY

Archives of Clinical Neuropsychology (*ACN*) is the official journal of the National Academy of Neuropsychology (NAN), a 4,000+ member organization composed primarily of practicing clinical neuropsychologists. The journal was founded in 1985 under the NAN Presidency of Raymond Dean, who became its first editor. Originally a quarterly, the journal increased to eight times a year in 1996, and also enlarged its page format to accommodate more articles. It is free as a benefit of membership in the Academy and available by subscription to nonmembers. The present editor is W. D. Gouvier of Louisiana State University. The journal is owned by the Academy and published by Elsevier Science, the largest scientific publisher in the world today.

The journal publishes original research dealing with psychological aspects of the etiology, diagnosis, and treatment of disorders arising out of dysfunction of the central nervous system. Manuscripts that provide new and insightful reviews of existing literature or raise professional issues are also accepted on occasion. The journal reviews books and tests of interest to the field, and publishes the abstracts of the annual meeting of the Academy. A Grand Rounds section is also included that provides in-depth information about individual or small groups of patients with unique, unusual, or low incidence disorders. According to impact factors calculated by the Social Science Citation Index, the journal is one of the most influential in the field of clinical neuropsychology.

CECIL R. REYNOLDS
Texas A&M University

ARGENTINA, SPECIAL EDUCATION SERVICES FOR YOUNG CHILDREN IN

Among the countries of Latin America, Argentina has a well-established record of providing educational services to its citizens. Mandatory school attendance was established in 1884 and Argentina has the highest literacy rate (84%) in Latin America (UNESCO, 1984). The National Directorate of Special Education is responsible for the special instruction of mentally, physically, and socially handicapped students. Services are provided from preschool through adulthood.

Early intervention services for children from birth to age 3 were scarce in Argentina and poorly organized (UNESCO, 1981). There was a need for early educational intervention services for children and their families prior to enrolling a child in a nursery school or special center. As a result, services were developed for early stimulation and education. These services are divided by handicapping condition and are provided in infant consultation units. For children with slight to moderate mental handicaps, services focus on sensory and motor stimulation, socialization skills, and speech development. Parents are involved in these activities so that follow through can be done at home. For children with physical handicaps (blind, partially sighted, deaf or hard of hearing), the education is divided into two stages. The first stage is early neurological and sensory stimulation; it is continued until the child has reached a developmental level of 18 months (UNESCO, 1981). The next stage involves stimulation of sensorimotor activities, language development, and the development of self-care and socialization skills. Guidance and educational services also are given to the families.

The primary goal of these intervention programs is to raise the child's level of developmental functioning so that he or she can enter a prenursery special education program. Along with outreach to parents is the involvement and continuing education of special education teachers. There is a central registry of handicapped children so that they may be referred to the appropriate resources. Primary prevention programs are initiated via the media, with special programs for or articles on handicapped children. Public meetings on issues relating to handicapped students constitute an ongoing effort at general education as to the needs of handicapped children.

REFERENCES

UNESCO. (1981). *Handicapped children: Early detection, intervention and education in selected case studies from Argentina, Canada, Denmark, Jamaica, Jordan, Nigeria, Sri Lanka, Thailand, and the United Kingdom* (Report No. ED/MD/63). Paris: Author.

UNESCO. (1984). Wastage in primary education from 1970 to 1980. *Prospects, 14*, 348–367.

KAREN F. WYCHE
Hunter College, City University of New York

See also **Peru, Special Education in**

ARITHMETIC REMEDIATION

Remediation in arithmetic has evolved into an instructional system consisting of goals and objectives; tests at various levels and of kinds that assess the objectives; instructional activities that represent curriculum at the concrete, pictorial, and abstract levels; and summative evaluations. Instructional goals are based on the general mathematics goals of a school district or similar educational agency. These goals usually emerge from curriculum groups of teachers, supervisors, administrators, and content specialists from outside the school district. In some cases, goals are determined by available textbooks. Objectives are translations of the goals into observable performance statements.

According to the National Council of Supervisors of Mathematics (NCSM, 1979), the goal of the mathematics curriculum that was determined in 1977 (NCSM, 1977) should be to ensure that each student is able to

1. Solve problems
2. Apply mathematics to everyday situations
3. Determine if results are reasonable
4. Estimate
5. Compute
6. Use geometry
7. Measure
8. Read, interpret, and construct tables, charts, and graphs
9. Use mathematics to predict
10. Understand the role of computers

Objectives used to assess each of the NCSM goals might be to

1. Generate a list of possible solutions for finding the difference between two integers
2. Purchase items from a store and use the correct amount of money
3. State whether a series of answers make sense
4. State whether a quantity is reasonable for a specified purpose
5. Add with renaming
6. Find the circumference of a circle
7. Find the volume of a container
8. Interpret a graph showing income of teachers compared to inflation rates over time
9. Use a graph to predict direction of a group of stocks over time
10. Describe the use of the computer as a mathematics tutor

Diagnostic assessments may include survey tests, concept tests, interviews, attitude scales, and learning style inventories. Survey tests tap broad ranges of mathematics competence and serve to present an overview of students' strengths and weaknesses. Survey tests also are referred to as screening tests, where there are relatively few items for each of a great number of objectives. Survey tests have the following characteristics:

1. They may be group or individually administered
2. Test items are usually sequenced from easy to difficult

3. They are usually not timed
4. They may be machine scored
5. Test results indicate further areas of investigation in terms of student strengths and weaknesses

Concept tests may be used for diagnosing in more depth weaknesses identified in the survey test. Concept tests tap objectives with a greater number of items than survey tests. There may be five items on the concept test as compared with two on the survey test for each objective. Furthermore, a greater number of objectives are assessed on achievement or concept tests.

Interviews are crucial to diagnostic assessment, which is the foundation for designing, developing, implementing, and evaluating remedial programs in mathematics. Interviews occur after the paper-pencil assessments and may accompany additional diagnosis at concrete and pictorial levels. Interviews provide a structure for probing how and what a student is thinking. The following types of data may emerge from interviews: (1) what the student is thinking; (2) the student's thought processes, for example, whether the thinking is concrete or simplistic, whether cause-effect relations are apparent; (3) the problem-solving strategies being used by the student; (4) the mode of representation that appears most comfortable for the student: concrete, pictorial, or abstract; (5) how the student's performance compares with age peers as well as with other things that the student can do, for example, science, writing, art, music, sports, and social interaction. Interviews may be organized around topics such as whole numbers, fractions, geometry, measurement, and mathematical applications. The purpose of the interview is to collect data in a manner that is more thorough than from written tests. It is important to probe during an interview and to avoid correcting errors and instructing. If the student gets stuck, rephrase questions and move to a lower but related objective. The interview should allow the diagnostic teacher to identify error patterns, understand the student's thinking in regard to isolated errors, and observe whether the student's performance differs on the same objective with concrete models, or pictorial and abstract representations. Data from interviews should clarify performance on written assessments. The following matrix serves as a structure for selecting interview activities in terms of mode of representation of probe items:

The following are guidelines for conducting an interview:

1. Establish rapport to get to know the student and allow the student to relax.
2. Explain the purpose of the meeting as well as what you wish to learn. Ask the student whether he or she has any questions about the meeting.
3. Probe and learn about the student's strengths and weaknesses; do not teach.

4. Check to determine whether the student can perform prerequisite as well as corequisite skills. Prerequisites are subskills or components of a task; corequisites are parallel tasks. Multiplication and division may be considered corequisites by the time the student is in grade five; addition is prerequisite to multiplication, while subtraction is prerequisite to division.
5. Look for generic patterns of performance that may be trouble spots. Most errors in arithmetic are not random but represent patterns of misunderstanding.
6. Ask questions that serve different purposes to help identify different styles of thinking. Include divergent and convergent types such as "How many different ways can you use these materials to help you find an answer?" or "What is your favorite color?"

Attitude scales provide information about the student's interest in, fear of, or enjoyment of arithmetic. Often those students who do not do well in mathematics have high anxiety toward the subject and do not like mathematics. Thus because attitude often interacts with performance, it is necessary to gather information about the student's attitude as part of the diagnostic process. The following are some instruments that assess attitude toward mathematics: (1) Aiken Mathematics Attitude Scale (Aiken, 1972); (2) Dutton Mathematics Attitude Scale (Dutton, 1956); and (3) Mott Mathematics Student Survey (Mott, 1984).

Learning style inventories provide another view of how the student learns best. This type of inventory may assess preferences by the student such as grouping (e.g., small group, large group, or individual), or preferences concerning instruction (e.g., teacher explanations, peer tutoring, or self-instruction).

Cawley (1985), Reisman and Kauffman (1980), and Reisman (1981), presented a number of remedial instructional strategies. These include the following:

1. Present small amounts of a sequence to be learned in an organized format
2. Use visual or auditory cues that highlight what is to be learned
3. Use separating and underlining as cues
4. Emphasize patterns
5. Teach rehearsal strategies such as repetition, verbal elaboration, systematic scanning, and grouping material to be remembered
6. Reinforce attention to a relevant dimension
7. Point out relevant relationship
8. Emphasize differences in distinctive features of stimuli
9. Control irrelevant stimuli

10. Replace incidental learning tasks with structured intentional learning tasks

11. Reduce complexity of task

12. Use consistent vocabulary

13. Use a model whose competency in the task has been established

14. Encourage deferred judgment during problem solving

15. Use peer-team learning

16. Provide immediate knowledge of results

17. Plan for transfer in learning

18. Use short, simple sentences when giving directions

19. Use concrete examples of spatial and quantitative relationships

20. Use prompting

Summative evaluation should include broad objectives that allow students to demonstrate their ability to compare, summarize, classify, interpret, judge, imagine, hypothesize, and engage in decision making. Remediation is an integrated system of assessment and instruction. The concept of remediation described here goes beyond the diagnose-prescribe model that focuses on fixing with a remedy, to the preventive model that implies doing it right the first time.

The NCSM has called for schools to have designated mathematics program leaders to help meet the current challenges in mathematics education (NCSM, 1998).

REFERENCES

Aiken, L. R. (1972, March). Research on attitudes toward mathematics. *Arithmetic Teacher, 19*(3), 229–234.

Brown, J. S., & Burton, R. R. (1978). Diagnostic models for procedural bugs in basic mathematical skills. *Cognitive Science, 2,* 155–192.

Cawley, J. F. (1985). *Cognitive strategies and mathematics for the learning disabled.* Rockville, MD: Aspen.

Dutton, W. H. (1956). Attitudes of junior high school pupils toward arithmetic. *School Review, 64,* 18–22.

Mott, T. (1984). *Mott mathematics student survey.* Unpublished doctoral dissertation, University of Pittsburgh.

NCSM. (1977). *NCSM position paper on basic mathematical skills.* Retrieved from http://www.ncsmonline.org

NCSM. (1998). *The case for designated mathematics program leaders.* Retrieved from http://www.ncsmonline.org

Reisman, F. K. (1981). *Teaching mathematics: Methods and content.* Boston, MA: Houghton-Mifflin.

Reisman, F. K. (1982). *A guide to the diagnostic teaching of arithmetic.* Columbus, OH: Merrill.

Reisman, F. K., & Kauffman, S. H. (1980). *Teaching mathematics to children with special needs.* Columbus, OH: Merrill.

Suydam, M. N. (1979, February). The case for a comprehensive mathematics curriculum. *Arithmetic Teacher, 26,* 10–13.

FREDRICKA K. REISMAN
Drexel University

See also Acalculia; Mathematics, Learning Disabilities In

ARMITAGE, THOMAS RHODES (1824–1890)

Thomas Rhodes Armitage, an English physician forced by failing sight to leave the practice of medicine, founded the British and Foreign Blind Association in 1868. This organization, which became the Royal National Institute for the Blind, had as its major purposes the establishment of an effective educational program for the blind and the elimination of the existing confusion over printing systems for the blind.

Armitage established the Royal Normal College and Academy of Music to provide vocational preparation for blind students. Eighty percent of its graduates became self-supporting, a unique accomplishment in that time. After conducting an extensive study of printing systems for the blind, Armitage and his association became the leading English proponents of braille. They were instrumental in the ultimate adoption of that system throughout Britain.

REFERENCES

Armitage, T. R. (1886). *Education and employment for the blind* (2nd ed.). London, UK: Harrison.

Ross, I. (1951). *Journey into light.* New York, NY: Appleton-Century-Crofts.

PAUL IRVINE
Katonah, New York

ARMSTRONG V. KLINE (1979)

Armstrong v. Kline was filed on behalf of children with disabilities seeking special education services during the summer term. The plaintiffs argued that handicapped children needed continuous, year-round programming in order to receive an appropriate education. The state countered that summer school was beyond the needs of these children and was not made available to nonhandicapped children free of charge and therefore was not required. In finding that some handicapped children are in need of year-round services, the court used the reasoning that "the normal child, if he or she has had a loss, regains lost skills in a few weeks, but for some handicapped children, the interruption in schooling by the summer recess may result in substantial loss of skills previously learned."

The court was referring principally to the severely handicapped, concluding that they would most likely require summer sessions. Of particular importance is that the court's finding seems to shift the burden of proof from the parents (to show need) to the school district (to show a lack of necessity for year-round programming). This ruling has been upheld in the appeals process and subsequent court cases (e.g., *Battle v. Commonwealth of Pennsylvania*, 1980). The court did not issue a blanket requirement for summer sessions for all handicapped children but, rather, required a determination to be made on the basis of the needs of the individual child. This ruling ultimately forced the development of better techniques for assessing retention and regression among disabled students and helped pave the way for later federal regulations relating to extended school year services.

REFERENCES

Armstrong v. Kline, 476 F. Supp. 583 (E.D. Pa. 1979), aff'd CA78-0172 (3rd Cir. 1980).

Battle v. Commonwealth of Pennsylvania, 629 F. 2d 269 (3rd Cir. 1980).

Cecil R. Reynolds
Texas A&M University
Second edition

Kimberly F. Applequist
University of Colorado at Colorado Springs
Third edition

See also **Extended School Year for Students With Disabilities**

ARMY GROUP EXAMINATIONS

The Group Examination Alpha, better known as the Army Alpha, was the first group test of intelligence for adults. The examination was one of a battery of tests developed as a result of the armed forces's need during World War I to have an objective means of classifying vast numbers of recruits for military service.

The original examination, consisting of 13 subtests, was developed between June and September 1917 by the Committee on the Psychological Examining of Recruits. The committee was chaired by R.M. Yerkes and included W.V. Bingham, H.H. Goddard, A.S. Otis, T.H. Haines, L.M. Terman, F.L. Wells, and G.M. Whipple. Although experience among measurement experts with group examination procedures was rare, the committee relied heavily on A.S. Otis's group adaptation to the Binet scales for content and standards for administration (Yoakum & Yerkes, 1920). The committee worked continuously for almost a month developing, selecting, and adapting methods for the test content, and another month thoroughly testing the efficacy methods in military stations across the United States. The resulting version of the test consisted of eight subtests: (1) oral directions, (2) disarranged sentences, (3) arithmetic reasoning, (4) information, (5) Otis synonyms and antonyms, (6) practical judgment, (7) number series complete, and (8) analogies. There were five alternative forms provided and the average administration time was 40 to 50 minutes for groups of up to 500 recruits (Linden & Linden, 1968).

Between April 1 and December 1, 1918, Army Alpha was administered to approximately 1,250,000 military recruits. Contributing to its reliability and concurrent validity, the Army Alpha correlated with other ability measures as follows:

0.50 to 0.70 with officer ratings

0.80 to 0.90 with Stanford-Binet

0.72 with Trabue B and LC completion test combined

0.80 with Beta

0.94 with composite of Alpha, Beta, and Stanford-Binet.

Army Beta

The Army Alpha had more than adequately addressed the need for an instrument with which large numbers of individuals could be evaluated in a short period of time, but another problem quickly emerged. Army psychologists did not know what to do about the approximately 30% of the draftees who either could not read English or read so slowly that they could not perform on the Army Alpha. The Army Group Examination Beta, or Army Beta, was prepared to meet this need. The development of an instrument that could be group-administered without a heavy emphasis on reading or understanding verbal language presented special problems. These problems were mainly eliminated through the use of demonstration charts and pantomime to convey instructions (Yoakum & Yerkes, 1920).

The final version of the examination consisted of seven subtests: (1) maze test, (2) cube analysis, (3) X-O series, (4) digit symbol, (5) number checking, (6) pictorial completion, and (7) geometrical completion. The Beta also took approximately 50 minutes to administer and yielded the same type of numerical scores as the Alpha. Although the ability scores obtained on the Beta were somewhat less accurate than on the Alpha for the higher range of intelligence, the data obtained revealed the following correlations:

0.80 with the Alpha

0.73 with the Stanford-Binet

0.91 with the Stanford-Binet, Alpha, and Beta

The general administration procedure for the Army examinations soon became routine. Groups of draftees (100 to 500) reported to a special building to take the mental test(s). Based on whether the draftees could speak and/or write English, they were assigned to take either the Army Alpha for literates or Army Beta for illiterates or foreign-born recruits. Depending on the individual's performance on one of these tests, a decision was made regarding classification in the military or on the need for further testing to ascertain mental capacity for military service. Individuals failing the Alpha exam were automatically administered the Beta exam to factor out the possible role of reading and oral language in their poor performance. Anyone failing the Alpha exam and the Beta exam initially was given one of three individual performance examinations. Thus, no individual was designated as mentally incompetent solely based on performance on the group examinations.

The Army Alpha and the Army Beta yielded numerical scores of ability ranging from 0 to 212, which for military classification purposes were translated into the letter grades A, B, C, D, or E. Classifications were assigned as in the following examples:

Intelligence Grade	Probable Classification	Definition	Score (Alpha)
A	High officer type	Very superior	135–212
B	Commissioned/ Noncommissioned officer	Superior	105–134
D–	Considered fit for regular duty; rarely suited for tasks requiring special skill or alertness	Very inferior	0–14

The scores on the Alpha showed a high correlation with the individual's social status. The data also seemed to indicate a high correlation between an individual's Alpha score and level of occupational responsibility (Yoakum & Yerkes, 1920). These data were at least partially responsible for the soon to be widespread use of tests to predict vocational success, but as Matarazzo (1972) points out in reporting this data, there was a failure to highlight the considerable overlap in the scores obtained by individuals in the various occupational groups. More important,

the vast amounts of data generated from the Army Alpha exams provided glimpses of the full range of adult abilities, confirming Galton's assumption that intelligence test scores are normally distributed in the population at large. Additionally, these data were largely responsible for the practice of using a fixed mental age for calculating adult intelligence.

The practical utility of the entire battery is expounded in terms of the number of men discharged from military service before the country wasted vast amounts of money, effort, and time training them. Yoakum and Yerkes (1920) reported that between April and November 1918, 45,653 draftees were found deficient to serve in the military. From a measurement or psychometric perspective, the subtests and techniques developed and used for the army group examinations paved the way for the tremendous growth of group and individual testing in education and industry. Subtests developed for the army examinations are very much in evidence on most current tests of intelligence. For example, the Wechsler scales are composed of subtests that are in many respects identical to the subtests on the Army Alpha and Beta. This is not surprising: The author of these scales, David Wechsler, participated in the army testing program during World War I.

The influence of the army group examinations is not all positive. Anastasi (1976) reminds us that often tests modeled after the army examinations failed to acknowledge and account for the limitations of the technical properties of the group examination methods. This failure resulted in much of the negative sentiment toward ability testing in the United States. That sentiment threatened the demise of psychological testing. Thus the army examinations may have done as much to retard as to advance the progress of psychological tests. The ease and efficiency of these group techniques also created a preference for impersonal testing as opposed to the more clinical, individual testing methods promoted by pioneers such as Binet (Matarazzo, 1972).

REFERENCES

Anastasi, A. (1976). *Psychological testing* (4th ed.). New York, NY: Macmillan.

Linden, K. W., & Linden, J. D. (1968). *Modern mental measurement: A historical perspective*. Boston, MA: Houghton-Mifflin.

Matarazzo, J. D. (1972). *Wechsler's measurement and appraisal of adult intelligence* (5th ed.). Baltimore, MD: Williams & Wilkins.

Yoakum, C. S., & Yerkes, R. M. (1920). *Army mental tests*. New York, NY: Holt.

JULIA A. HICKMAN
Bastrop Mental Health Association

See also Intelligence Testing; Measurement

ARTERIOVENOUS MALFORMATIONS

Arteriovenous malformations (AVMs) of the central nervous system are a set of vascular abnormalities. These congenital lesions are typified by the failure of development of the capillary network normally separating arteries and veins. Lack of a capillary bed allows exaggerated blood flow through the malformation, shunting and stealing blood from other areas of the vascular system, potentially hemorrhaging, and at times growing, so as to lead to obstructive hydrocephalus. The clinical features of the malformation depend on the site, size, and integrity of the malformation. The most common presentation is related to the hemorrhage of an AVM (Humphreys, 1999). Less than 15% of children with AVMs present with seizures, and the remainder are identified secondary to symptoms that include evidence of ischemia, congestive heart failure, developmental delay, or chronic headaches (Humphreys, 1999). AVMs may be divided into three subtypes: true AVMs, AVMs involving the vein of Galen (aneurysms of the vein of Galen), and cavernous hemangiomas (Brett, 1997).

Arteriovenous malformations of the brain or spinal cord are reported to be rare (Hubbard & Meyer, 1998). Prevalence and incidence rates are not reported, however, probably because these lesions are identified only when there is a clinical event (e.g., hemorrhage or seizure). Humphreys (1999) reported that AVMs are rarely discovered as an incidental finding, except in the context of trauma.

Characteristics

1. True AVMs
   - These are structural defects in the formation of the capillary network.
   - The etiology of the abnormality is unclear.
   - Classic AVMs may expand their bulk, causing obstructive hydrocephalus. They may present when they hemorrhage. The gliotic cortex may become a seizure focus.
2. AVMs involving the vein of Galen
   - AVMs involving the vein of Galen are marked by direct communication between the cerebral arterial circulation and the vein of Galen.
   - Congestive heart failure is the usual presentation in infants and occurs when massive amounts of blood are shunted to the malformation leading to progressive high-output heart failure.
   - In toddlers, presentation is frequently that of obstructive hydrocephalus. A reversible hemiplegia, secondary to a steal effect (blood being shunted away from one hemisphere), may be present.
   - Older children may present with headaches, pyramidal and cerebellar signs, hydrocephalus, or intellectual disability.
3. Cavernous hemangiomas
   - Cavernous malformations (also called angiographically occult vascular malformations) are comprised of dilated thin-walled vascular channels.
   - Cavernous angiomas may be inherited as an autosomal dominant disorder. The genetic abnormality is not the same between pedigrees (e.g., there is genetic heterogeneity; Labauge, Lagerge, Brunereau, Levy, & Tournier-Lasserve, 1998).

AVMs are treated when they become symptomatic. Treatment goals are to preserve life and limit neurologic compromise while achieving complete removal of the AVM and maintaining cerebral circulation (Humphreys, 1999). AVMs can be ablated via surgical resection, intravascular embolization, radiosurgery, or a combination of these modalities. The choice of modality is dependent on the size and site of the lesion. Seizures, which often persist after surgical resection, are treated with anticonvulsant medication but may require repeat surgery for seizure control (Humphreys, 1999). The natural history of cavernous angiomas is less clear, so treatment decisions are difficult (Humphreys, 1999; Labauge et al., 1998).

Educational needs are dependent on the degree of neurologic dysfunction. A full neuropsychological evaluation is required to identify current needs and establish areas of deficit and strength. The mechanism of damage (e.g., hemorrhage vs. hydrocephalus vs. ischemia, etc.), as well as location and age of symptom onset, will mediate educational needs. There is some suggestion that the less invasive nature of radiosurgery will mitigate cognitive consequences for those children in whom it is an appropriate treatment modality (Humphreys, 1999).

Prognosis depends on the type of AVM involved. Eighty percent of children who have symptomatic AVMs will require neurosurgery (Humphreys, 1999). History of a previous bleed, a single draining vein, and diffuse AVM morphology are the most important risk factors predicting additional hemorrhage in those with classic AVMs (Kondziolka, Pollack, Lunsford, 1999). There is some suggestion that mortality from hemorrhage is higher in children than in adults (Kondziolka et al., 1999). The risk of hemorrhage in children with cavernous angiomas is unclear (Humphreys, 1999). Functional outcome depends on the site of a cavernous lesion (Labauge et al., 1998). Vein-of-Galen malformations are associated with high morbidity, and treatment is difficult (DeVeber, 1999). Progress in imaging and treatment of AVMs has decreased mortality and morbidity and will be the focus of continued investigation (Humphreys, 1999).

REFERENCES

Brett, E. M. (1997). Vascular disorders of the nervous system in childhood. In E. M. Brett (Ed.), *Pediatric neurology*. New York, NY: Churchill Livingstone.

DeVeber, G. (1999). Cerebrovascular disease in children. In K. F. Swaiman & S. Ashwal (Eds.), *Pediatric neurology: Principles and practice* (3rd ed.). St. Louis, MO: Mosby.

Hubbard, A. M., & Meyer, J. S. (1998). Magnetic resonance imaging of the fetus. In A. Milunsky (Ed.), *Genetic disorders and the fetus: Diagnosis, prevention and treatment*. Baltimore, MD: Johns Hopkins Press.

Humphreys, R. P. (1999). Vascular malformations: Surgical treatment. In A. L. Albright, I. F. Pollack, & P. D. Adelson (Eds.), *Principles and practice of pediatric neurosurgery*. New York, NY: Theime Medical.

Kondziolka, D. S., Pollack, B. E., & Lunsford, L. D. (1999). Vascular malformations: Conservative management, radiosurgery, and embolization. In A. L. Albright & I. F. Pollack (Eds.), *Principles and practice of pediatric neurosurgery*. New York, NY: Theime Medical.

Labauge, P., Lagerge, S., Brunereau, L., Levy, C., & Tournier-Lasserve, E. (1998). Hereditary cerebral cavernous angiomas: Clinical and genetic features in 57 French families. *Lancet, 352*, 1892–1897.

GRETA N. WILKENING
*University of Colorado Health Sciences Center
The Children's Hospital,*

ARTHRITIS, JUVENILE

Juvenile rheumatoid arthritis (JRA) is a systemic disease that causes inflammation of one and usually more joints. The manifestations of JRA vary considerably among patients. The most common symptoms include joint swelling, warmth, tenderness, and pain, which may lead to stiffness, contractures, and retardation of growth. This disease is usually accompanied by fever bursts, rash, and visceral symptoms.

This form of arthritis is the most common connective tissue disease in children and is the most prevalent of the arthritic diseases. It has been estimated that around 250,000 Americans have JRA with an incidence of 1.1 cases per year in 1,000 school-age children (Varni & Jay, 1984). The disease affects more girls than boys. It is similar to adult rheumatoid arthritis except that it typically appears before puberty and is more likely to stay in remission.

The causes of JRA are only recently known. Infection, autoimmune disorders, trauma, psychological stress, and heredity all have been considered, but evidence now supports the ideas that JRA is primarily an autoimmune disorder (Rennebohm, 1994). As there are no known causes, there are also no known cures. The most common treatment is the administration of nonsteroidal anti-inflammatory drugs such as aspirin. Other common drug treatments include gold salts, antimalarial drugs, corticosteroids, and penicillamine. Immune system medications such as methotrexate and azathiprine may also be employed (Arthritis Foundation, 2005). Special exercises and sometimes periods of rest may also be employed. Different kinds of heat may be applied to reduce stiffness and pain, and a variety of other pain-control measures have been tried. Splints are often used to prevent deformity and enhance function. Surgery, including total joint replacement, may sometimes be necessary and can be beneficial.

There are basically three forms of JRA: systemic, polyarticular, and pauciarticular. The systemic form accounts for approximately 20% of the population with JRA. High fevers, rashes, stomach pains, and severe anemia are usually present in this type. Pauciarticular accounts for 30% to 40% of the cases. It begins by affecting only a few joints, usually the large ones (knees, ankles, or elbows). Polyarticular is the most common type, accounting for 40% to 50% of children with JRA. This type affects several joints (five or more), usually small joints of the fingers and hands (Arthritis Foundation, 1983).

The long-term effects of JRA vary greatly depending on the type as well as the individual. There is no way to know the outcome of the disease in its early stages. However, the overall prognosis for children with JRA is good. Most will be able to go through adulthood without any severe physical limitations. Only about 25% will suffer any significant disability (Jay, Helm, & Wray, 1982). In most cases the disease will go into permanent remission but structural damages and functional limitations will remain. In other cases the disease may continue to be active throughout the individual's life (Rennebohm, 1994).

In addition to physical considerations, certain psychological aspects of JRA are also important. McAnarney, Pless, Satterwhite, and Friedman (1974) found that children who have JRA but no disabilities have more emotional problems than disabled arthritics. They also found that parents of the nondisabled children had a poorer understanding of the disease and were less likely to acknowledge its impact on the child's behavior, schooling, and social relations. Litt, Cuskey, and Rosenburg (1982) found that good self-image and greater autonomy coincided with higher compliance in treatment.

Wilkinson (1981) studied the emotional and social behavior of adolescents with chronic rheumatoid arthritis.

She found that one of the major complaints among these adolescents was people's tendency to treat them as younger than their age because of their smaller size. She also reported a high anxiety level because of restricted mobility and fears about an uncertain future. Children with JRA are at increased risk of emotional and behavioral problems but there is considerable variability in the response to the disorder psychologically (Varni, Rapoff, & Waldrov, 1994).

Schaller (1982) stressed the need to avoid an image of chronic invalidism. It is important to account for the limitations experienced by individuals with JRA; however, when not specifically restricted by the disease, they should be expected to perform as well as their peers.

The way children are treated by others affects their self-image; therefore, those working with these children should help them to avoid feelings of inferiority. Wilkinson (1981) reported that the adolescents in her study expressed a desire for more social contacts with able-bodied individuals and a desire to be in regular rather than special classes.

In the classroom as well as at home, children should not be unnecessarily restricted from activities. They should be encouraged to find alternatives when they cannot participate in regular play. Periodically calling on the child to do an activity requiring movement may help relieve stiffness whenever the child is not in pain. Beales, Keen, and Holt (1983) stressed the importance of being aware of the child's perception of pain. Children may be less likely to interpret internal sensations as pain and therefore may fail to recognize it as a warning sign. Often, even when children know they are in pain they may not complain and may even try to conceal it. Some visible signs that may help determine the presence of pain are walking with a stiff gait, taking short steps, tense muscles, and inability to perform certain tasks. Cognitive behavior therapies may be useful in controlling chronic pain in JRA (see Arthritis Foundation, 2005; Varni et al., 1994).

REFERENCES

Arthritis Foundation. (1983). *Arthritis in children and when your student has childhood arthritis.* Atlanta, GA: Patient Services Department.

Arthritis Foundation. (2005). *Medications.* Retrieved from http://www.arthritis.org/

Beales, J. G., Keen, J. H., & Holt, P. L. (1983). The child's perception of the disease and the experience of pain in juvenile arthritis. *Journal of Rheumatology, 10*(1), 61–65.

Jay, S., Helm, S., & Wray, B. B. (1982). Juvenile rheumatoid arthritis. *American Family Physician, 26*(2), 139–147.

Litt, I. F., Cuskey, W. R., & Rosenberg, A. (1982). Role of self-esteem and autonomy in determining medication compliance among adolescents with juvenile rheumatoid arthritis. *Pediatrics, 69*(1), 15–17.

McAnarney, E. R., Pless, I. B., Satterwhite, B., & Friedman, S. B. (1974). Psychological problems of children with chronic juvenile arthritis. *Pediatrics, 53*, 523–528.

Rennebohm, R. M. (1994). Juvenile rheumatoid arthritis: Medical issues. In R. Olson, L. Mullins, J. Gillman, & J. Chang (Eds.), *The sourcebook of pediatric psychology* (pp. 70–74). Boston, MA: Allyn & Bacon.

Schaller, J. G. (1982). Juvenile rheumatoid arthritis. *Pediatric Annals, 11*(4), 375–382.

Varni, J., Rapoff, M., & Waldron, S. (1994). Juvenile rheumatoid arthritis: Psychological issues. In R. Olson, L. Mullins, J. Gillman, & J. Chang (Eds.), *The sourcebook of pediatric psychology* (pp. 75–89). Boston, MA: Allyn & Bacon.

Varni, J. W., & Jay, S. M. (1984). Biobehavioral factors in juvenile rheumatoid arthritis: Implications for research and practice. *Clinical Psychology Review, 4*, 543–560.

Wilkinson, V. A. (1981). Juvenile chronic arthritis in adolescence: Facing the reality. *International Rehabilitation Medicine, 3*, 11–176.

DAN HATT
NURI PUIG
LOGAN WRIGHT
University of Oklahoma

See also **Physical Disabilities**

ARTICULATION DISORDERS

Articulation involves the study of (1) the phonemes in a given language, (2) the manner in which they are produced, (3) the order in which they are acquired by the members of a culture, and (4) the disorders which may occur. There are 40 phonemes in the English language, consisting of 26 consonants and fourteen vowels (Bernthal & Bankson, 1998). A phoneme is defined as the smallest difference conveying a change of meaning. This is in contrast to an allophone which includes all of the acceptable productions of a given phoneme. Allophonic variations do not impact meaning.

The consonant sounds may be differentiated on the basis of three distinctive features: place, manner, and voicing. A vowel varies according to tongue height, placement, and whether the tongue is tense or lax. There are also other characteristics of phonemes, known as suprasegmentals, that cause variations in sounds but do not signal a difference of meaning in English. Suprasegmentals are distinctive in some languages. For example, in tonal languages, the pitch of a phoneme signals a change in meaning.

If a traditional view of articulation development is taken, the age of emergence of specific phonemes may be identified. For example, /p/, /b/, and /m/ are early developmental phonemes and are typically in a child's repertoire by age 3. In contrast, the /s/ phoneme may not emerge until a child is 8 years of age or older. Numerous studies, including one by Sander (1972), have examined the age of emergence of various phonemes. All children have articulation errors when they are young and are moving through the normal developmental process. The errors decrease in number as the child matures. Generally, articulation development is thought to be complete by age 8, although some children continue to develop articulation skills beyond this age.

When a child or adult has an articulation disorder, it is characterized by sound production errors, usually involving less than 10 phonemes. The individual's underlying rule system for combining sounds into words is thought to be intact. That is, the speaker understands how sounds are put together to make words which convey meaning, but the speaker is having trouble making individual sounds. The errors can further be classified as phonetic or phonemic in nature.

A listener will generally understand a person with articulation errors, although speech production will attract the listener's attention. The misarticulations may vary in severity from a mild distortion to omission. The least noticeable error is a mild distortion. The listener will recognize the sound as an /s/, for example, but its production will be just outside of the acceptable allophonic range. Only the skilled listener is likely to note this error. As the degree of distortion increases into the more severe range, the average listener will become aware of the error in production. Even though the phoneme is recognizable as a particular phoneme, it will call attention to itself. Further on the continuum of severity is substitution, in which another phoneme is used in place of the one that is intended. For example, a person may substitute a /t/ for a /k/. The most severe error is an omission, in which the sound is left out.

The order of progression of severity is based on the impact the error has on intelligibility and the knowledge the speaker has about the phoneme. In regard to intelligibility, a distortion of a phoneme in a word generally does not impair the listener's understanding of a word. A substitution or omission may make it difficult for the listener to identify the word being used. The knowledge a speaker has about the phoneme is also reflected in the type of error used. When the phoneme is distorted, the speaker knows that for example, it is an /s/ but they are unable to correctly execute the production. When the error is a substitution, for example /p/ for /s/, the speaker knows a sound is required in a particular location in a word but isn't sure which sound belongs there. In contrast, when a phoneme is omitted, the speaker doesn't realize a phoneme is needed. Thus, omission is the most severe type of error, followed by substitution and distortion.

The more common sources of articulation errors are (1) inaccurate learning, (2) incorrect speech models, (3) structural deficits of the speech and hearing mechanism, and (4) imprecise and/or poor coordination of motor movements. In the first instance, inaccurate learning, something interferes with the process as the child is acquiring a sound. For example, if a child has fluid in his or her ears or brain injury at a critical point in the acquisition of a phoneme, the child may not hear the sound or its replication accurately. It is thought that children rely heavily on the auditory modality when sounds are being learned, but later shift their focus to the proprioceptive/kinesthetic aspects for monitoring the accuracy of their productions. Thus, initially they focus on how their sound matches up auditorily to that produced by others, but later, once the phoneme is learned, they pay less attention to the auditory aspects and focus on how it feels both proprioceptively and kinesthetically. They then are thought to make the assumption that if the phoneme felt like last time, it must be correct. An erroneously learned production is thus maintained. Second, a child may have a family member or significant other who has an articulation error and is providing incorrect models for the child. Learning of faulty articulation is likely to occur because the child will imitate the errored phoneme and incorporate it into his or her repertoire. Third, structural abnormalities of the speech and hearing mechanism may be a contributing factor to articulation errors. Examples are teeth that do not occlude properly or inadequate velopharyngeal closure. The structure may interfere with the ability to produce acceptable phonemes. Fourth, imprecise motor movements and/or the coordination of these movements may cause articulation errors. Correct articulation requires precise placement, timing, and accurate movement of the articulators. Persons with cerebral palsy, dysarthria, or apraxia, for example, have difficulty in these domains, and their speech production is affected to varying degrees.

The treatment for articulation errors generally consists of teaching the phoneme in isolation, and then assisting the client in generalizing the new sound throughout their sound system. Traditional strategies, such as those suggested by Van Riper (1978) or Bankson and Bernthal (1998), may be used. Minimal pairs and co-articulation strategies may also be utilized. Typically, the prognosis for resolving the errors is good. The American Speech-Language-Hearing Association (2005) has an excellent website with current and helpful resources for articulation problems.

REFERENCES

American Speech and Language Association. (2005). *Articulation problems*. Retrieved from http://www.kidsource.com/ASHA/index.html

Bernthal, J., & Bankson, N. (1998). *Articulation and phonological disorders* (4th ed.). Boston, MA: Allyn & Bacon.

Sander, E. (1972). When are speech sounds learned? *Journal of Speech and Hearing Disorders, 37*, 55–63.

Van Riper, C. (1978). *Speech correction: Principles and methods* (6th ed.). Englewood Cliffs, NJ: Prentice Hall.

SUSANN DOWLING
University of Houston

See also Communication Disorders; Speech and Language Disabilities; Language Disorders

ARTS INTEGRATED WITH MATHEMATICS

All forms of arts are related with mathematics from various perspectives, and most of the connections between arts and mathematics could be developed as alternative mathematics instructional approaches to demonstrate and explain certain mathematics concepts, especially for students with special needs. In general, arts can facilitate mathematics learning from two aspects—provide a high motivational environment for students with mathematics anxiety and behavior problems to engage them in learning mathematics (Mansilla, 2005) and provide alternative approaches to understand mathematics for students who have difficulty understanding specific mathematics content as well as those students who do not possess intelligence strengths in mathematics (Gardner, 1993).

Emotion is essential in students' learning, because positive emotions may lead to higher levels of motivation facilitating students' ability to focus on attention to learning (Sylwester, 1995). In applying motivational theories, Miller and Mitchell (1994) suggested teachers should create a highly motivational environment for learning, free from tension and other possible causes of embarrassment or humiliation. Music, visual arts, dance and drama along with their aesthetical features, have the potential of creating highly motivational environments for students, in which they can discover and think about mathematical concepts in various ways and build fundamental understandings and appreciation for both mathematics and the arts. What is more, arts can provide students a highly motivational environment with less prejudice and violence, helping them becomes better risk takers and communicators (Trusty & Oliva, 1994). Arts not only can intrinsically motivate students to facilitate them to pursue more advanced mathematical knowledge based on their own initiative as well as accept more challenging task during learning but also can extrinsically motivate students to learn mathematics by increasing students' engagement in learning mathematics concepts and doing mathematical problems (Glastra, Hake, & Schedler, 2004).

Multiple intelligences theory has advocated that some students may have lower logical/mathematical intelligence than others, and some students might experience difficulties in learning mathematics through traditional instruction (Gardner, 1993). Using arts to enhance children's enjoyment and understanding of mathematical concepts and skills, can help students gain access to mathematics through new intelligences. For example, music (linked with musical intelligence), visual arts (linked with spatial intelligence), dance (linked with bodily-kinesthetic) and drama (linked with linguistic intelligence) all can be used to promote the development of intellectual domains of mathematics. Different form of arts can enable students to use different learning styles and prior knowledge, pulling together diverse cognitive and affective experiences and organizing them to assist understanding (Selwyn, 1993). As an application of multiple intelligence theory, teaching mathematics integrated with arts facilitates students to complete the process of knowledge transfer; as a result, students whose strengths lie in areas other than the logical-mathematical intelligence can learn mathematics more easily (Johnson & Edelson, 2003).

Teachers should take advantage of the opportunities that the variety of arts offers to help all students learn mathematics in challenging and enjoyable ways. By designing appropriate arts integrated into mathematics lessons, students can understand, analyze, and interpret mathematics through different routes (An & Capraro, 2010). Teaching mathematics linked to suitable arts elements is an effective strategy in designing and teaching mathematics in a pleasurable way with sense-making.

REFERENCES

An, S. A., & Capraro, M. M. (2011). *Music-math integrated activities for elementary and middle-grade students.* Irvine, CA: Education for All.

Gardner, H. (1993). *Multiple intelligences: The theory in practice.* New York: Basic Books.

Glastra, F. J., Hake, B. J.,& Schedler, P. E.(2004). Lifelong learning as transitional learning. *Adult Education Quarterly, 54,* 291–307.

Johnson, G., & Edelson, R. J. (2003). The integration of mathematics and music in the primary school classroom. *Teaching Children Mathematics, 4,* 475–479.

Mansilla, V. B. (2005). Assessing student work at disciplinary crossroads. *Change, 37*(1), 14–22.

Miller, L. D., & Mitchell, C. E. (1994). Mathematics anxiety and alternative methods of evaluation. *Journal of Instructional Psychology, 21,* 353–358.

Selwyn, D. (1993). *Living history in the classroom: Integrative arts activities for making social studies meaningful.* Tucson, AZ: Zephyr Press.

Sylwester, R. (1995) *A celebration of neurons: An educator's guide to the human brain.* Alexandria, Vancover, Canada: ASCD.

Trusty, J., & Oliva, G. (1994). The effects of arts and music education on students' self-concept. *Applications of Research in Music Education, 13*(1), 23–28.

SONG AN
Texas A&M University

ART THERAPY

The use of clients' artwork by psychiatrists and psychologists to understand their psychopathology has been around for many years. There have been instances as early as the 1900s, where psychiatrists used drawings to observe and understand the psychopathology of their clients. Despite this practice, the actual practice of art therapy has only existed since the mid 20th century (Malchiodi, 2005).

There have been two pioneers for art therapy in the United States: Margaret Naumburg and Edith Kramer (Ulman, 2001). Naumburg based her concept of art therapy on the psychoanalytic approach by Freud and Jung. Naumburg believed that artwork could be used as symbolic speech for the unconscious, uncovering deep emotions. Expressions of these unconscious emotions using artwork have been based on psychoanalytic and analytic techniques such as free association, transference between the client and therapist, and spontaneous art expression. About the same time Naumburg began to make advances in the area of art therapy, there was a second pioneer, Kramer, in the United States who brought her ideas and concepts to the area of art therapy (Ulman, 2001).

Kramer comprised her concept of art therapy using an emphasis on art in psychotherapy. Kramer believed that art is a means by which therapists can create human experiences. These experiences allowed the individuals to relive particular experiences in therapy as a way to resolve any conflicts that have arisen (Ulman, 2001). Both Naumburg and Kramer's concepts were used to help adults and children deal with depression and traumatic events.

Art therapy has been used to help juvenile offenders. Venable (2005) found that engaging juvenile offenders in artwork afforded them opportunities that gave them a better insight on life. For example, through a mural project the juvenile offenders were able to maintain positive relationships with teachers as well as learn various techniques pertaining to art.

Another population that art therapy has been used with is children with emotional disturbances. Graham (1994) believed that art could be a successful way for children with emotional problems to deal with the traumas or negative experiences in their lives. For example, through their paintings and drawings, children can express their feelings and thoughts that they may feel are hard to express to others. Although advances have been made in art therapy, there is still little research on outcome studies addressing the effectiveness of art therapy; however, the techniques and concepts of art therapy are still used by many in diverse professions.

REFERENCES

Graham, J. (1994). The art of emotionally disturbed adolescents: Designing a drawing program to address violent imagery. *American Journal of Art Therapy, 34*, 115–121.

Malchiodi, C. (2005). Expressive therapies. In C. Malchiodi (Ed.), *Art therapy* (pp. 16–45). New York, NY: Guilford Press.

Ulman, E. (2001). Art therapy: Problems of definition. *American Journal of Art Therapy, 40*, 16–26.

Venable, B. (2005). At risk and in need: Reaching juvenile offenders through art. *Art Education, 58*, 48–53.

TIA BILLY
Texas A&M University

See also Behavior Disorders; Emotional Disorders; Recreational Therapy

ASPERGER, HANS (FEBRUARY 18, 1906–OCTOBER 21, 1980)

Hans Asperger was a 20th-century Austrian pediatrician. He was best known for his work with a group of individuals with a constellation of symptoms that were both similar and distinct from autism as first described by Kanner in 1943. This constellation of symptoms was later called Asperger Syndrome (or Asperger Disorder)—named so after Hans Asperger. Currently, in the *Diagnostic and Statistical Manual of Mental Disorders–Fourth Edition–Text Revision* ([DSM-IV-TR], American Psychiatric Association [APA], 2000), Asperger Syndrome is considered one of the Pervasive Developmental Disorders.

Asperger was born in the Austrian countryside in 1906. He went to school in Vienna, eventually graduating with his medical degree in 1931. He worked at several hospitals and clinics over his career, most notably, the Children's Hospital of the University of Vienna and the University Pediatrics Clinic (Frith, 1991; Klin et al., 2000).

In 1944, Asperger published an article that described his work with a group of four youngsters that displayed characteristics of a condition that had not been described before. These children were cognitively bright but, most strikingly, had persistent social interaction difficulties. Other characteristics included intense obsessions and interests, nonverbal communication issues, sensory issues, and various repetitive behaviors (Asperger, 1944/1991). Asperger labeled these children as having "autistic psychopathy."

Coincidently at the same time in the United States, Leo Kanner (1943) was working with another group of children who he also called autistic. Unfortunately due to World War II, and because Asperger's (1944) work was published in German, it was not familiar in the west for decades, while Kanner's autism case studies became very well recognized. It was not until after Asperger died that his work became well known in the United States and subsequently important to several fields, including special education, psychology, and child health.

Lorna Wing (1981), a British physician and psychologist, brought the condition to a wider public and highlighted this disorder, which had both similarities to and differences from autism. Asperger Syndrome became an official diagnosis in the DSM-IV (APA) in 1994, distinct from autism due to lesser or nonexistent delays in communication, although individuals with AS have difficulty with pragmatics, or social use of communication. However, as of early 2013, with upcoming revisions to the DSM in progress, it was speculated that the Asperger diagnosis would be removed from the manual and that all autism related conditions be placed in one autism spectrum disorders category.

Asperger was a prolific writer with more than 300 publications (Lyons & Fitzgerald, 2007). His legacy in the areas of child health and education is evident in the hundreds of books, manuals, teaching guides, and personal stories that other authors have written about this syndrome. Based on accounts of his own behaviors and interests it has been speculated that perhaps Asperger himself had an autism spectrum disorder (Lyons & Fitzgerald, 2007). Asperger was married and had five children. He died in Vienna in 1980.

REFERENCES

Asperger, H. (1991). "Autistic psychopathy" in childhood. (U. Frith, Trans.) In U. Frith (Ed.), *Autism and Asperger syndrome* (pp. 37–92). Cambridge, UK: Cambridge University Press. (Original work published 1944).

Frith, U. (Ed.). (1991). *Autism and Asperger syndrome.* Cambridge, UK: Cambridge University Press.

Kanner, L. (1943). Autistic disturbances of affective contact. *The Nervous Child, 2,* 217–250.

Klin, A., Volkmar, F. R., & Sparrow, S. S. (2000). *Asperger Syndrome.* New York, NY: Guilford Press.

Lyons, V., & Fitzgerald, M. (2007). Did Hans Asperger (1906-1980) have Asperger syndrome? *Journal of Autism and Developmental Disorders, 37,* 2020–2021.

Wing, L. (1981). Asperger's syndrome: A clinical account. *Psychological Medicine, 11,* 115–129.

PAUL G. LaCava
Rhode Island College
Fourth edition

ASPERGER SYNDROME

In 1944 a Viennese physician, Hans Asperger, published a seminal paper that described four children with an unusual pattern of poor social skills and other atypical behavior (e.g., self-stimulatory responses and insistence on environmental sameness), albeit normal cognitive and language abilities. Asperger concluded that the condition was a unique and previously unidentified neurodevelopmental disorder that he termed "Autistic Psychopathy" in childhood (Asperger, 1944). Interestingly Hans Asperger made this discovery shortly after Leo Kanner identified children with early infantile autism (Kanner, 1943).

Following its identification in 1944 there was virtually no mention of Asperger syndrome (subsequently referred to as AS; also referred to as Asperger disorder) until 1981 when Lorna Wing wrote about Hans Asperger's work and Uta Frith translated Asperger's original paper in 1991 (Frith, 1991; Wing & Potter, 2002). Subsequent to the work of Wing and Frith there began a general and increasingly rapid acceleration and intensification of interest in AS; currently the condition is widely recognized by both professionals and the general public. The wide-scale awareness of the disorder has been accompanied by a dramatic increase in the number of individuals diagnosed with AS, including school-age children and youth. In spite of the extraordinary increase in interest in AS, the condition is generally poorly understood, including the unique and defining elements of the disability that distinguish it from other forms of higher-functioning autism. Identification and implementation of evidence-based methods that can assist individuals diagnosed with AS also significantly trail behind its recognition.

The dramatic increase in recognition and identification of individuals with AS correlates with addition of AS as a sub-classification of *Pervasive Developmental Disorder,* beginning in 1994, in the widely applied *Diagnostic and Statistical Manual of Mental Disorders–Fourth Edition–Text Revision* (DSM–IV–TR; American Psychiatric Association, 2000) and the parallel international classification system, *International Statistical Classification of Diseases and Related Health Problems* (World Health Organization, 2007). According to the current DSM–IV–TR, *Pervasive Developmental Disorder* is used as a diagnostic reference for persons who are "characterized by severe and pervasive impairment in several areas of development: reciprocal social interaction skills, communication skills, or the presence of stereotyped behavior, interests, and activities" (p. 69). Specific Pervasive Developmental Disorders identified in the DSM–IV–TR, in addition to AS, are Autistic Disorder, Childhood Disintegrative Disorder, Rett Disorder, and Pervasive Development Disorder–Not Otherwise Specified. The term "higher functioning autism spectrum disorders" is not a separate DSM classification; nevertheless this term is widely used to refer to a variety of children and youth who function at the higher end of the autism spectrum, i.e., relative to intellectual, cognitive, academic, language, and overall functioning. The increased acceptance and use of terms such as "higher functioning autism spectrum disorders" and "high functioning autism" is connected to the similarity in characteristics of children and youth with AS and other forms of higher-functioning autism.

In 2013, there will be a revision in the DSM classification system wherein the current subclasses of autism disorder, including AS, will likely be eliminated (Regier Narrow, Kuhl, & Kupfer, 2009). Those specific diagnostic elements will likely be replaced by *autism spectrum disorders* to account for autism-related disabilities falling on a continuum and in recognition that AS and higher functioning autism spectrum disorders make up similar and frequently indistinguishable conditions. The trend to reference AS and high-functioning autism as a similar entity is also related to recognition that the support and intervention methods and strategies for these individuals are often identical.

On the education front, AS was noted within the 1997 Individuals with Disabilities Education Act (IDEA) disability classification *Autism*. This education-policy amendment reflected the wide-ranging variability of the autism spectrum and that learners with AS and other forms of autism share core social, communication, and behavior characteristics that significantly affect educational performance and major life activities and functioning. As is the case with autism, AS is understood to be a biologically based disorder that causes impairments in social understanding and interactions, communication, and behavior. AS and other forms of autism spectrum disorders are not caused by poor parenting (Klin, Volkmar, & Sparrow, 2000; Thompson, 2007; Wing & Potter, 2001).

AS and other forms of autism spectrum disorders are approximately 5 times more common among boys than girls. These disorders have been identified throughout the world among all racial, ethnic, economic, and social groups. The Centers for Disease Control and Prevention (CDC, 2010) currently estimates that approximately 1 out of every 110 individuals will fall on the autism spectrum. That count is a striking increase when contrasted with the 4–5 per 10,000 prevalence estimate of past years (Lotter, 1996). It is also noteworthy that a number of professionals and professional organizations generally estimate that the current prevalence estimate is approximately 1 in 100 persons (Autism Society of America, 2010). It is difficult to precisely disaggregate the prevalence of AS and higher functioning autism spectrum disorders from all autism spectrum disorders. Brasic (2008) notes that "various studies indicate rates ranging from 1 case in 250-10,000 children"; and consequently that "additional epidemiologic studies are needed" (p. 1). Volkmar and Klin (2000) perceptively acknowledged that "the lack of a real consensus on the diagnosis of [AS] means that present data are, at best, 'guestimates' of its prevalence"

(p. 62). The DSM–IV–TR (2000) also withholds an exact prevalence estimate for AS, noting that "definitive data regarding the prevalence of Asperger Syndrome are lacking" (p. 82). Notwithstanding problems in knowing the exact prevalence of AS and higher functioning autism spectrum disorders, it appears that these disabilities are on the increase and are increasingly being documented.

Characteristics of Asperger Syndrome

As discussed below, common features of individual's diagnosed with AS fall in the areas of (a) social skills, (b) communication, (c) cognitive, academic, and learning, (d) behavior, emotion, and sensory characteristics; and (e) physical and motor skills.

Social Skill Considerations. First and foremost, AS is a social disorder (Frith, 1991; Klin, Volkmar, et al., 2000; Simpson & Myles, 2011). Individuals with AS are notable for their awkward and inept social behavior. Many children and adolescents with AS appear interested in interacting with others; however, their interactions tend to be unskilled or characterized by inability to engage in age-expected social interactions, including appropriate play. Indeed, the social deficits of many children and adolescents with AS and higher functioning autism spectrum disorders appear to primarily be due to a lack of recognizing and understanding appropriate social customs and poor skill in executing and participating in social interactions rather than a disinterest or fear of social contact and lack of motivation to interact with others. It is not unusual for children who appear motivated to interact with others to become less inclined to engage others socially in their teen and adult years, possible because of a lifetime of being rejected or snubbed. Individuals with AS may display emotional vulnerability and stress over not understanding social situations and how to apply social rules, especially when social circumstances, settings, and situations are variable and inconsistent. In this context it is common for individuals with AS to want environmental constancy and uniformity and strict application of rules (Williams, 2001).

A deficit in *theory of mind* capacity, wherein individuals with AS are thought to possess limited empathy and understanding of the internal thoughts, feelings, and beliefs of other people (Safran, 2001; cf. Frith, 1991; Klin, Volkmar, et al., 2000), is a commonly used explanation for these and related problems. Not surprisingly, many individuals with AS are poor incidental social learners. That is, they may attempt to learn appropriate social responses independent of context and without fully comprehending their meaning.

Communication and Language. Individuals with AS typically do not manifest clinically significant delays in language (American Psychiatric Association, 2000; Thompson, 2007). Frith (1991) observed that children with AS "tend to speak fluently by the time they are five" (p. 3).

However, she also noted that their language is frequently "odd in its use for communication" (p. 3). Without a doubt, children with AS tend to have a variety of unusual communication characteristics, especially with respect to standard pragmatic social and conversational standards. Voice quality, pitch and modulation characteristics may also be atypical. Common concerns include one-sided monologues, self-centered conversational styles, and narrowly focused interests. Nonverbal communication deficits and related social communication difficulties are also common, including eye contact and knowing how close to stand to another person while talking; making odd gestures or movements while talking; unusual body posture; and failing to use or understand gestures and facial expressions. It is not unusual for children with AS to experience problems in comprehending abstract concepts, figures of speech such as idioms and metaphors, and rhetorical questions (Shore, 2003).

Cognitive, Academic, and Learning Characteristics. Individuals diagnosed with AS are generally believed to have average or above-average intellectual abilities (World Health Organization, 2007), yet many of these learners experience academic performance problems (Attwood, 2007; Frith, 1991; Siegel, Minshew, & Goldstein, 1996). Obsessive and narrowly defined interests, concrete and literal thinking styles, inflexibility, poor problem-solving skills, poor organizational skills, and poor social abilities often result in poor classroom performance and educational outcomes that fall short of learners' potential. Children and youth with AS frequently experience difficulty in generalizing previously learned knowledge and skills and applying information and skills. Notwithstanding these challenges, many children and youth with AS attend college and there are a number of adults with AS who have successful professional careers and personal lives (Harpur, Lawlor & Fitzgerald, 2004).

Behavior, Emotion, and Sensory Characteristics. Behavioral problems are not universal among persons diagnosed with AS, though not uncommon (Barnhill et. al., 2000). Often these problems occur in response to disorganized, confusing, and unpredictable situations; related to stress, anxiety, loss of control or inability; and associated with social ineptness and obsessive and single-minded pursuit of idiosyncratic interests.

As individuals with AS get older, more significant social, emotional, and other mental health problems may develop (Attwood, 2007; Tantam, 2000). Studies of adolescents (Cesaroni & Garber, 1991; Ghaziuddin, Weidmer-Mikhail, & Ghaziuddin, 1998) suggest that a number of these individuals may experience heightened anxiety in social situations. Wing (1981) first noted that it is at this time that depression and anxiety tends to occur, a pattern that has been confirmed by others (Barnhill, 2001; Ghaziuddin et al., 1998; Tantam, 2000). It is also significant that individuals with AS are vulnerable to teasing and bullying across the lifespan.

Relative to sensory matters, individuals with AS are known for their hypersensitivity and hyposensitivity for sensory stimuli (Dunn, 2007). For instance, atypical responses to particular sounds, smells, visual stimuli, and food textures are common.

Physical and Motor Skill Abnormality. Wing (1981) observed that children with AS tended to have body balance and motor coordination problems. Others (Attwood, 2007; Smith, 2000; Smith & Bryson, 1994) have also observed that it is not unusual for individuals with AS to be clumsy and awkward. The significance of these problems can be far-reaching in that they can affect participation in games and activities calling for good motor skills. Because many school-related activities such as handwriting require fine motor dexterity these deficits can be associated with a number of significant problems (Todd & Reid, 2007).

Relative to matters related to characteristics it is also significant that individuals with AS have high rates of comorbidity (i.e., presence of related disorders and conditions). Attention-deficit/hyperactivity disorder, obsessive-compulsive disorder, mood disorders, and anxiety disorders are especially common in individuals with AS (American Psychiatric Association, 2000; Volkmar & Klin, 2000).

Assessment

As a general rule, assessment of individuals with AS falls within two major domains: (a) screening and diagnostic evaluations and (b) assessment for purposes of programming, instruction, and intervention planning (Simpson & Myles, 2011). Screening and diagnostic assessments may be undertaken by clinical professionals such as psychologists, psychiatrists, mental health teams, or by educational professionals. Clinical professionals typically use the diagnostic guidelines of the previously noted *Diagnostic and Statistical Manual of Mental Disorders* (DSM) (American Psychiatric Association, 2000). Educational diagnostic professionals, such as school psychologists, commonly rely on guidelines of the *Individuals with Disabilities Education Improvement Act.*

Accurate screening and diagnosis are fundamental and imperative. However these initial steps must be followed by assessments geared to intervention, program planning, and identifying individualized supports and accommodations (Simpson & Myles, 2011). Thus both clinical and educational screening and diagnostic evaluations must be followed by evaluations that are designed to understand students' needs and identify support programs and services. This second phase of the evaluation process will be the primary determinant of school and community success for children and youth with AS.

Screening, diagnostic assessments and evaluations focused on identifying individuals' unique learning, social, communication, adaptive, and other needs is based on both formal and informal assessment methods (Lord &

Bishop, 2009). *Formal assessment* generally refers to tests and other norm-referenced measures while *informal assessment* uses information and data based on record reviews, interviews, observations of students, curriculum-based assessments, and evaluation of informal learning traits. These methods are used to assess individuals' intellectual and cognitive abilities, academic skills and needs, language and communication, sensory and motor needs, adaptive behavior and independent living abilities and needs, behavior and emotional strengths and needs, and social abilities and challenges.

Screening and assessment scales specifically designed to evaluate children and youth for AS are limited. Two of the most widely used of these scales are the *Asperger Syndrome Diagnostic Scale* (Myles, Bock, & Simpson, 2000), a 50-item pencil-paper scale; and the *Gilliam Asperger Disorder Scale* (Gilliam, 2001), a 32-item scale that has four subscales (social interaction, restricted patterns of behavior, cognitive patterns, and pragmatic skills). The Australian Scale for Asperger's Syndrome (Garnett & Attwood, 1998) is another recognized screening tool. Another commonly used and well-accepted diagnostic tool appropriate for use with individuals suspected of having AS is the *Autism Diagnostic Interview–Revised* (ADI-R; Couteur, Lord & Rutter, 2003). The ADI-R uses a standardized, semi-structured clinical interview format that focuses on reciprocal social interaction; language and communication; and stereotyped, restricted, and repetitive interests and behaviors.

Interventions, Supports, and Accommodations

In spite of having a challenging disorder, individuals with AS typically have relatively strong cognitive, language, and learning abilities (Thompson, 2007). These assets generally bode well for school and post-school success. This optimistic note and corresponding potential, however, are contingent upon availability of appropriate supports and accommodations; and assistance, backing, and advocacy of knowledgeable and committed families, educators and other professionals. To be sure, it is extraordinary for individuals with AS to be successful in school and life without appropriate support services. Social impediments along with learning problems, unsupportive environments, and uninformed teachers, families, and others all too often result in significant problems and ultimately a failure on the part of individuals with AS to achieve on a plane with their potential. For this reason it is essential that persons connected to individuals with AS, especially teachers and related service educational personnel, use individualized and proven support methods and strategies.

First and foremost there is a need for social and behavioral supports for individuals with AS (Attwood, 2007). Social skills and social behavior affect and influence virtually every facet of life, including formation and maintenance of friendships and working relationships, employment, independent living, and overall quality of life throughout the life cycle. Particularly important are those skills that are foundational and essential to a number of areas, including development of social assets needed for peer and adult social interactions and positive and productive relationships; self-management, personal responsibility, and self-realization activities; and social skills specifically needed for school and academic success (Simpson & Myles, 2011). These domains can be developed using a variety of basic proven approaches, including explicit instruction of specific individualized social skills, programs that develop social understanding and social problem solving, social interpretation interventions, and intervention programs that rely on peer-mediated activities and supports (Simpson & Myles, 2011).

Academic and school-related supports are also essential. Strategies that assist learners with AS to deal with problems of distraction and inattention; narrow, obsessive, and unusual interests; atypical learning styles; fine and gross motor deficits; and poor motivation are especially important (Mesibov & Shea, 2010; Simpson & Myles, 2011). Supports that have proven to be generally effective include educational programs that provide strong structure, including predictable schedules and established routines, consistent assignment formats, clearly delivered and consistent expectations, and structured physical settings. Teachers and programs that provide ongoing assistance that facilitates learners' problem solving and development of skills needed to apply academic skills to address real-life problems and issues are also important. Academic and learning supports for students with AS include use of proven instructional support strategies such as priming, assignment modifications, and organizational methods such as visual supports, task organization programs, peer buddy programs, assignment notebooks, timelines, travel cards, and home base programs are also recommended (Myles & Simpson, 2001; Safran, 2001; Simpson & Myles, 2011; Williams, 2001).

REFERENCES

American Psychiatric Association. (2000). *Diagnostic and statistical manual of mental disorders* (4th ed., text rev.). Washington, DC: Author.

Asperger, H. (1944). Die 'Autistischen Psychopathen' im Kindesalter. ["Autistic Psychopathy" in Childhood]. *Archiv fur Psychiatrie und Nervenkrankheiten, 117*, 76–136.

Attwood, T. (2007). *The complete guide to Asperger syndrome*. Philadelphia, PA: Kingsley.

Autism Society of America. (2010). *What are autism spectrum disorders?* Retrieved from http://www.autism-society.org

Barnhill, G. P. (2001). Social attribution and depression in adolescents with Asperger Syndrome. *Focus on Autism and Other Developmental Disabilities, 16*, 46–53.

Barnhill, G., Hagiwara, T., Myles, B., Simpson, R., Brick, M., & Griswold, D. (2000). Parent, teacher, and self report of problems and adaptive behaviors in children and adolescents with Asperger syndrome. *Diagnostique, 25*, 147–167.

Brasic, J. R. (2010). Pervasive Developmental Disorder: Asperger Syndrome. Retrieved from e-medicine, from WebMD. http://www.medscape.com/

Centers for Disease Control and Prevention. (2010). *Autism information center*. Retrieved from http://www.cdc.gov/ncbddd/utism

Cesaroni, L., & Garber, M. (1991). Exploring the experience of autism through firsthand accounts. *Journal of Autism and Developmental Disorders, 21*, 303–313.

Couteur, A., Lord, C., & Rutter, M. (2003). *Autism Diagnostic Interview–Revised*. Los Angeles, CA: Western Psychological Services.

Dunn, W. (2007). A sensory processing approach to supporting students with autism spectrum disorders. In R. Simpson & B. Myles (Eds.), *Educating children and youth with autism* (pp. 299–356). Austin, TX: Pro-Ed.

Frith, U. (Ed.). (1991). *Autism and Asperger Syndrome*. Cambridge, UK: Cambridge University Press.

Garnett, M. S., & Attwood, A. J. (1998). The Australian Scale for Asperger's syndrome. In T. Attwood (Ed.), *Asperger's syndrome. A guide for parents and professionals* (pp. 17–19). London, UK: Kingsley.

Ghaziuddin, M., Weidmer-Mikhail, E., & Ghaziuddin, N. (1998). Comorbidity of Asperger Syndrome: A preliminary report. *Journal of Intellectual Disability Research, 42*, 279–283.

Gilliam, J. E. (2001). *Gilliam Asperger Disorder Scale*. Austin, TX: Pro-Ed.

Harpur, J., Lawlor, M., & Fitzgerald, M. (2004). *Succeeding in college with Asperger Syndrome: A student guide*. London, UK: Jessica Kingsley.

Kanner, L. (1943). Autistic disturbances of affective content. *The Nervous Child, 2*, 217–250.

Klin, A., Sparrow, S. S., Marans, W. D., Carter, A., & Volkmar, F. R. (2000a). Assessment issues in children and adolescents with Asperger Syndrome. In A. Klin, F. R. Volkmar, & S. S. Sparrow (Eds.), *Asperger Syndrome* (pp. 309–339). New York, NY: Guilford Press.

Klin, A., Volkmar, F. R., & Sparrow, S. S. (Eds.). (2000b). *Asperger Syndrome*. New York, NY: Guilford Press.

Lord, C. & Bishop, S. L. (2009). The autism spectrum: Definitions, assessment and diagnoses. *British Journal of Hospital Medicine, 70*, 234–237.

Lotter, V. (1996). Epideminilogy of autistic conditions in young children. *Social Psychiatry, 4*, 263–277.

Mesibov, G., & Shea, V. (2010). The TEACCH Program in the era of evidence-based practice. *Journal of Autism and Developmental Disorders, 40*, 570–579.

Myles, B. S., Bock, S. J., & Simpson, R. L. (2000). *Asperger Syndrome Diagnostic Test*. Austin, TX: Pro-Ed.

Myles, B. S., & Simpson, R. L. (2001). Effective practices for students with Asperger Syndrome. *Focus on Exceptional Children, 34*, 1–14.

Regier, D. A., Narrow, W., Kuhl, E., & Kupfer, D. (2009). Conceptual development of DSM-V. *American Journal of Psychiatry, 166*, 645–650.

Safran, S. P. (2001). Asperger Syndrome: The emerging challenge to special education. *Exceptional Children, 67*, 151–160.

Shore, S. (2003). My life with Asperger syndrome. In R. W. Du Charme & T. Gullotta (Eds.), *Asperger syndrome: A guide for professionals and families* (pp. 189–209). New York, NY: Kluwer Academic/Plenum Publishing.

Siegel, D., Minshew, N., & Goldstein, G. (1996). Wechsler IQ profiles in diagnosis of high-functioning autism. *Journal of Autism and Developmental Disorders, 26*, 389–406.

Simpson, R., & Myles, B. (2011). *Asperger Syndrome and high-functioning autism: A guide for effective practice*. Austin, TX: Pro-Ed.

Smith, I. (2000). Motor functioning in Asperger Syndrome. In A. Klin, F. Volkmar, & S. Sparrow (Eds.), *Asperger Syndrome* (pp. 97–124). New York, NY: Guilford Press.

Smith, I., & Bryson, S. (1994). Imitation and action in autism: A critical review. *Psychological Bulletin, 116*, 259–273.

Tantam, D. (2000). Adolescence and adulthood of individuals with Asperger syndrome. In A. Klin, F. Volkmar, & S. Sparrow (Eds.), *Asperger syndrome* (pp. 367–399). New York, NY: Guilford Press.

Thompson, T. (2007). *Making sense of autism*. Baltimore, MD: Paul Brookes.

Todd, T., & Reid, G. (2007). Increasing physical activity in individuals with autism. *Focus on Autism and Other Developmental Disabilities, 21*, 167–176.

U.S. Department of Education. (2009). IDEA 2004. Retrieved from http://idea.ed.gov/explore/search/p/,%20root,regs,300,A,300%252E8

Volkmar, F., & Klin, A. (2000). Diagnostic issues. In A. Klin, F. Volkmar, & S. Sparrow (Eds.), *Asperger Syndrome* (pp. 25–71). New York, NY: Guilford Press.

Williams, K. (2001). Understanding the student with Asperger Syndrome: Guidelines for teachers. *Intervention in School and Clinic, 36*, 287–292.

Wing, L., & Potter, D. (2002). The epidemiology of Autistic Spectrum Disorders: Is the prevalence rising? *Mental Retardation and Developmental Disabilities Research Reviews, 8*, 151–161.

World Health Organization. (2007). *International Statistical Classification of Diseases and Related Health Problems*. Geneva, Switzerland: Author.

RICHARD L. SIMPSON
University of Kansas
Fourth edition

ASPERGER SYNDROME DIAGNOSTIC SCALE

The Asperger Syndrome Diagnostic Scale (ASDS, 2000) is an individually administered measure used to identify children or adolescents ages 5 through 18 who manifest the characteristics of Asperger Syndrome. The scale contains 50 YES or NO items that are divided into five subscales of behavior including Language, Social, Maladaptive, Cognitive, and Sensorimotor. These items are summed to produce an Asperger Syndrome Quotient (ASQ), which indicates the likelihood that an individual has this disorder. Administration time usually takes between 10 to 15 minutes and the measure should be completed by an individual who has had direct, sustained contact with the child or adolescent for at least two weeks (e.g., parents, teachers). The record form provides the rater with instructions and contains a score summary section, a profile of scores, and an ASQ interpretation guide. There is also an additional section that provides the examiner with questions that may be used to obtain further diagnostic information.

This measure was normed on a sample of 115 children and adolescents between 5 and 18 years of age, who had been diagnosed with Asperger Syndrome. The sample was representative of the 1997 U.S. census data with respect to race and geographic region. There was a significantly larger percentage of males in the sample compared with females, which is appropriate, as it has been reported in research that males are four times more likely to be diagnosed with Asperger Syndrome than females (Kadesjo, Gillberg, & Hagberg 1999). The ASDS yields percentile ranks and standard scores (with a mean of 10 and a standard deviation of 3) for the subtests and a percentile rank and quotient score (with a mean of 100 and a standard deviation of 15) derived from the sum of the subscale scores.

The internal consistency of the items on the ASDS was determined to be adequate (Cronbach's coefficient alpha = .83), suggesting that the items measure the same construct as one another. Despite the criticism that some behavior rating scales have received regarding their lack of established interrater reliability (Reid, Maag, & Vasa, 1993) the ASDS has demonstrated an interrater reliability coefficient of .93. Item analysis of the ASQ has shown that the items have strong discriminating power and the ASDS has demonstrated an 85% accuracy rate in the identification of individuals with Asperger Syndrome. Research has shown that this measure can effectively discriminate individuals with Asperger Syndrome from other diagnostic groups such as autism, behavior disorders, attention-deficit hyperactivity disorder and learning disabilities.

Goldstein's review of the scale (2002) raised concerns about the validity of the ASDS, the population upon which it was normed, and the ability of the ASDS to provide accurate differential diagnoses. Goldstein noted that the scale may hold promise as a research tool, but there appeared to be little evidence that it could distinguish among the various types of pervasive developmental disorders or diagnose Asperger Syndrome specifically.

REFERENCES

Goldstein, S. (2002). Review of the Asperger Syndrome Diagnostic Scale. *Journal of Autism & Developmental Disorders, 32,* 611–614.

Kadesjo, B., Gillberg, C., & Hagberg, B. (1999). Brief report: Autism and AS in seven-year-old children: A total population study. *Journal of Autism and Developmental Disorders, 29,* 327–331.

Ron DUMONT
Fairleigh Dickinson University

JOHN O. WILLIS
Rivier College

KATHLEEN VIEZEL
Fairleigh Dickinson University

JAMIE ZIBULSKY
Fairleigh Dickinson University

ASPHYXIA

Asphyxia is a medical emergency requiring immediate intervention to prevent infant mortality and morbidity (Golden & Peters, 1985). Asphyxia occurs with inadequate oxygenation and cellular perfusion. This article deals specifically with asphyxia that occurs during the time of birth or shortly thereafter. Many terms are associated with oxygen deprivation during this period; pertinent information can be found in different sources under the headings of neonatal asphyxia, asphyxia neonatorium, perinatal asphyxia, intrapartum asphyxia, and hypoxic ischemic encephalopathy (HIE). Asphyxia has been hard to define accurately, which has caused difficulty in research on its effects and prognosis for recovery. The classical definition of asphyxia has been a low Apgar score with more emphasis on the 5- or even 10-minute scores than on the 1-minute (Fitzhardinge & Pape, 1981). As low Apgar scores are not necessarily associated with asphyxia, however, this definition is not always accurate and is a poor predictor for neurological outcome. Predicting outcome is very difficult. Even infants with 0 Apgar scores at birth have survived after efficient intervention with no serious handicaps (Rosen, 1985). Incidence of damage is generally overestimated when compared with actual findings (Brann, 1985). HIE, whose description follows, is predictive of later deficits.

Four basic mechanisms underlie asphyxia during the immediate perinatal period: (1) interruption of umbilical blood flow; (2) failure of placental exchange because of premature separation of the placenta from the uterus;

(3) inadequate perfusion or oxygenation of the maternal side of the placenta as in severe hypotension; and (4) infant failure to inflate the lungs and complete transition to extrauterine life. In early stages, asphyxia may reverse spontaneously if the cause is removed, but later stages require varying degrees of medical intervention because of circulatory and neurological changes (Fitzhardinge & Pape, 1981).

Asphyxia is a progressive yet potentially reversible process with severity and duration of the insult affecting later outcome. Severe asphyxia can result in death within 10 minutes without proper intervention (Fitzhardinge & Pape, 1981). Delayed intervention may exacerbate cellular injury in all organ systems, contributing to a poor outcome. The brain is the most vulnerable system and mediates the most pronounced effects on later life. Asphyxia not only affects the brain directly, but also impairs the autoregulation centers controlling cerebral blood flow, which may cause intraventricular hemorrhage with resultant complications (Golden & Peters, 1985). Premature infants appear to be particularly susceptible to this complication.

Cerebral palsy (CP) is the most frequent complication of asphyxia (Swaiman & Russman, 2006). Even then, risk is high only when the Apgar score is low. and can result in death within 10 minutes without proper intervention (Fitzhardinge & Pape, 1981). Delayed intervention is associated with intellectual disability in the absence of CP (Paneth & Stark, 1983).

HIE may result from severe asphyxia. Children diagnosed with HIE show signs of neurologic dysfunction within 1 week, and often within 12 hours, after birth. The major signs of dysfunction include seizures, altered states of consciousness, and abnormalities in tone, posture, reflexes, and respiration. Infants who exhibit seizures have a 30 to 75% likelihood of long-term sequelae. Mortality is high among infants who had definite neurologic abnormality at discharge. Full-term infants with a history of asphyxia and an abnormal neurologic exam during the first week of life show a 7% incidence of early death and a 28% incidence of neurological handicaps. The most common deficits seen in severely affected children include spastic quadriplegia (a form of CP), severe intellectual disability, seizures, hearing deficits, and microcephaly. Treatment for HIE is improving but research is difficult. Identification of infants at risk for neurological handicaps is becoming increasingly important as early intervention techniques improve (Brann, 1985).

Overall, the majority of asphyxiated infants suffer no detectable neurologic or intellectual sequelae. Prognosis is good even in relatively serious cases if neurologic examination is normal by 1 week of age. As would be expected, prognosis is poor when the asphyxia is long and severe or subsequent abnormal clinical features appear (Paneth & Stark, 1983). Much about asphyxia and its sequelae is still not well understood. However, adequate prenatal care, careful monitoring during labor and delivery with prompt obstetrical intervention, and immediate intervention after delivery by professionals skilled in resuscitation all contribute to lowering the incidence of asphyxia and lessening its long-term effects (Hill & Volpe, 2006; Phibbs, 1981).

REFERENCES

Brann, A., Jr. (1985). Factors during neonatal life that influence brain disorders. In J. Freeman (Ed.), *Prenatal and perinatal factors associated with brain disorders* (NIH Pub #85-1149, pp. 263–358). Bethesda, MD: National Institutes of Health.

Fitzhardinge, P. M., & Pape, K. E. (1981). Follow-up studies of the high risk newborn. In G. Avery (Ed.), *Neonatology: Pathophysiology and management of the newborn* (2nd ed., pp. 350–367). Philadelphia, PA: Lippincott.

Freeman, J. (1985). Summary. In J. Freeman (Ed.), *Prenatal and perinatal factors associated with brain disorders* (NIH Pub #85-1149, pp. 13–32). Bethesda, MD: National Institutes of Health.

Golden, S., & Peters, D. (1985). Delivery room care. In G. Merenstein & S. Gardner (Eds.), *Handbook of neonatal intensive care* (pp. 31–54). St. Louis, MO: Mosby.

Hill, A., & Volpe, J. J. (2006). Hypoxic-ischemic cerebral injury in the newborn. In K. F. Swaiman & S. Ashwal (Eds.), *Pediatric neurology* (4th ed., pp. 191–202). St. Louis, MO: Mosby.

Paneth, N., & Stark, R. I. (1983). Cerebral palsy and mental retardation in relation to indicators of perinatal asphyxia. *American Journal of Obstetrics & Gynecology, 146*, 960–966.

Phibbs, R. H. (1981). Delivery room management of the newborn. In G. Avery (Ed.), *Neonatology: Pathophysiology and management of the newborn* (2nd ed., pp. 350–367). Philadelphia, PA: Lippincott.

Rosen, M. G. (1985). Factors during labor and delivery that influence brain disorders. In J. Freeman (Ed.), *Prenatal and perinatal factors associated with brain disorders* (NIH Pub #85-1149, pp. 13–32). Bethesda, MD: National Institutes of Health.

Swaiman, K. F., & Russman, B. S. (2006). Cerebral palsy. In K. F. Swaiman & S. Ashwal (Eds.), *Pediatric neurology* (4th ed., pp. 312–324). St. Louis, MO: Mosby.

BRENDA M. POPE
New Hanover Memorial Hospital

See also Anoxia; Apgar Rating Scale; Cerebral Palsy; Low Birth Weight/Prematurity

ASSESSMENT OF BASIC LANGUAGE AND LEARNING SKILLS—REVISED (ABLLS-R)

The Assessment of Basic Language and Learning Skills– Revised (ABLLS-R) is a criterion-referenced assessment, curriculum guide, and progress monitoring tool (Partington, 2007). The *ABLLS-R* is designed for children with autism spectrum disorders or language delays between the ages of 3 and 9 years. This tool is designed for parents and professionals to gain information regarding the child's current skill repertoire and to facilitate the development of learning objectives, particularly as they relate to language skills. The assessment can be administered by parents, teachers, or therapists through direct observation of the child's skills and though interviews with persons familiar with the child.

The *ABLLS* was originally developed by Mark Sundberg, PhD, and James Partington, PhD (1998). In 2007 Partington released the *ABLLS-R* while Sundberg went on to develop the *VB-MAPP*, which was released in 2008 (see *VB-MAPP* entry). The *ABLLS-R* is based on the science of applied behavior analysis and B.F. Skinner's (1957) analysis of verbal behavior. Skinner's analysis of verbal behavior emphasizes the functional properties of language that are derived from environmental situations. According to Skinner, expressive language can be divided into different functional categories, or operants (e.g., echoics, mands, tacts, intraverbals) The *ABLLS-R* assesses each of these verbal operants separately.

The *ABLLS-R* is a criterion-referenced assessment, not a normed assessment (Partington, 2007). Therefore, the assessment does not compare the child's progress with the progress of groups of children. Additionally, the sequence of skills in the *ABLLS-R* is based upon observation of 100 children with language delays. Partington (2007) states that individual children may proceed through the skills differently and educators should not strictly adhere to a particular sequence when determining appropriate goals.

The *ABLLS-R* consists of two books: the *Assessment Protocol* and the *Scoring Instructions and IEP Development Guide* (Partington, 2007). The *Assessment Protocol* contains task analyses of 25 skill areas with a total of 544 discrete skills organized in a hierarchical manner to facilitate the development of appropriate target skills. While the primary focus of the *ABLLS-R* is on language development, skill areas also pertain to social, play/leisure, academic, daily living, and motor skills. For each discrete skill, information is presented regarding criteria for mastery, conditions under which skills are to be performed, and additional materials that pertain to demonstrating that skill. Data on the child's performance of specific skills are collected using direct observation or via caregiver interview and are entered by hand into the scoring booklet. The entire assessment can be completed in 10 to 14 hours and is designed to be administered every 6 to 12 months to monitor the child's progress toward specific goals. The *Scoring Instructions and IEP Development Guide* (Partington, 2007) presents instructions for administering and scoring the assessment along with procedures for updating the child's progress in the skills tracking log and the corresponding grid on which the child's progress

is visually represented. This manual also provides an overview of how to transfer information gathered from the assessment into measurable learning goals.

REFERENCES

Partington, J. W. (2007). *The Assessment of Basic Language and Learning Skills–Revised*. Pleasant Hill, CA: Behavior Analysts.

Partington, J. W., & Sundberg, M. L. (1998). *The Assessment of Basic Language and Learning Skills*. Pleasant Hill, CA: Behavior Analysts.

Skinner, B. F. (1957). *Verbal behavior*. Englewood Cliffs, NJ: Prentice Hall.

MANDY J. RISPOLI
Texas A&M University
Fourth edition

ASSESSMENT, CURRICULUM-BASED
(See Curriculum-Based Assessment)

ASSESSMENTS, ALTERNATE

Alternate assessments provide a vehicle for students to demonstrate their knowledge and skills through an alternative format to traditional testing. With the passage of the No Child Left Behind (NCLB) Act of 2001 (2002) and the reauthorization of the Individuals with Disabilities Education Improvement Act (2004), alternate assessments are most frequently defined in the context of statewide assessment programs. In a statewide test program, alternate assessments are used to evaluate the performance and progress of students with significant cognitive disabilities who are deemed unable to validly participate in a state's traditional assessment system. They are designed to capture a student's performance and progress toward grade-level content standards and are judged against a state's alternate achievement standards.

Typical statewide assessments are designed to allow educators to make broad inferences about what a student knows and can do in various settings and under various conditions; statewide alternate assessments do not allow for similar inferences. Because alternate assessments usually narrow the depth, breadth, or complexity of the content being assessed, inferences based on a student's score are restricted. In most cases, the data derived from alternate assessments will have limited generalizability to other contexts. Educators who interpret and use scores on alternate assessments should be aware of the limited generalizability of the data they provide.

Federal regulations make it clear that *all* students are to be assessed on a state's academic content standards (U.S. Department of Education, 2003). For example, a student who is expected to demonstrate knowledge of the critical features of biographies in the 10th grade may demonstrate their knowledge through a traditional statewide assessment or through an alternate assessment. The content remains the same regardless of assessment format. However, in an alternate assessment, the depth, breadth, or complexity of behaviors required on the test will be different from those expected of students on the traditional test. Differences between alternate assessments and traditional assessments, therefore, do not lie in their content standards but instead in the achievement standards associated with each type of assessment.

The format of alternate assessments varies from state to state. The majority of states use portfolio systems (Thompson & Thurlow, 2003), while a smaller number employ checklists or rating scales to measure the performance and progress of students with significant cognitive disabilities. A student's individualized education program (IEP) should not be used as an alternate assessment (U.S. Department of Education, 2003). Although the data obtained from an IEP is valuable and should be used to drive instructional programs for students with disabilities, it should not be used in a state accountability system. Empirical research into the effects of various formats on the technical adequacy of the test or the quality of inferences derived from test scores is limited. As states continue to refine their alternate assessments, the focus needs to be on creating assessments that accurately measure students' performance on grade-level content standards as well as contribute valid data to a state's accountability system (Johnson & Arnold, 2004).

Each student's IEP team decides how he or she will participate in a state's assessment system, and decisions are made on an individual basis. The federal government places only one parameter around this decision: Only those students with significant cognitive disabilities may participate (U.S. Department of Education, 2005). Once it is established that a student has a significant cognitive disability, his or her IEP team relies on various sources of information to inform their decision about the appropriateness of that student participating in an alternate assessment. Only if the student is unable to validly participate in a state's traditional assessment (with or without accommodations) is participation in an alternate assessment considered. The decision is not based on the student's disability per se but instead based on the student's ability to validly participate in a state's traditional assessment.

The percentage of students participating in an alternate assessment differs by state (Wiley, Thurlow, & Klein, 2005). No limits exist related to the number of students who may participate in an alternate assessment. However, according to NCLB, a school district may only include 1% of the total number of scores rated "proficient" or higher (on the alternate assessment) in their adequate yearly progress (AYP) calculations. All of the scores beyond the 1% cap are scored as "not proficient" regardless of the actual score.

In May 2005, the U.S. Department of Education released initial guidelines allowing states to include up to 2% of students measured against modified achievement standards. Unlike alternate achievement standards developed to measure students with significant cognitive disabilities, modified achievement standards are developed to measure progress and performance of students with persistent academic difficulties that challenge their ability to reach grade-level achievement standards even with research-based instruction. Release of these guidelines on the inclusion of an additional 2% of students in alternate assessments measured against modified achievement standards was due in part to research demonstrating that some students display persistent cognitive challenges that impede their ability to meaningfully participate in a state's traditional assessment. The decision was also in response to the concerns of many educators that including only 1% of students in an alternate assessment program leaves many students with no options for validly participating in a statewide test system. For these students, the alternate assessment has been shown to be too easy, while the traditional assessment is too hard. Other educators, however, are concerned that increasing the percentages allowable for AYP will result in lower expectations for those students with disabilities who are currently making progress toward passing the traditional assessment. This concern may be addressed at the level of the state department, as participation in an alternate assessment judged against modified achievement standards will not be mandated but instead will provide another option for educators as they strive for valid inclusion of all students in statewide accountability programs.

REFERENCES

Individuals with Disabilities Education Improvement Act of 2004, 20 U.S.C. § 1400, H.R. 1350.

Johnson, E., & Arnold, N. (2004, September). Validating an alternate assessment. *Remedial and Special Education, 25,* 266–275.

No Child Left Behind Act of 2001, Pub. L. No. 107-110, 115 Stat. 1425 (2002).

Thompson, S., & Thurlow, M. (2003). 2003 *State special education outcomes: Marching on.* Minneapolis: University of Minnesota, National Center on Educational Outcomes. Retrieved from http://education.umn.edu/NCEO/OnlinePubs/2003State Report.htm

U.S. Department of Education. (2003). *Title I—Improving the academic achievement of the disadvantaged; Final Rule, 68 Fed. Reg. 236* (December 9, 2003).

U.S. Department of Education. (2005). *Alternate achievement standards for students with the most significant cognitive disabilities: Non-Regulatory guidance* (August, 2005).

Wiley, H. I., Thurlow, M. L., & Klein, J. A. (2005). *Steady progress: State public reporting practices for students with disabilities after the first year of NCLB (2002–2003)* (Technical Report 40). Minneapolis: University of Minnesota, National Center on Educational Outcomes. Retrieved from http://education.umn.edu/NCEO/OnlinePubs/Technical40.htm

LINDY CRAWFORD
University of Colorado at Colorado Springs

See also Achievement Tests; Behavior Assessment System for Children–Second Edition; *g* Factor Theory; Individuals with Disabilities Education Improvement Act of 2004 (IDEIA); Intelligence Testing; Intelligent Testing; Kaufman Assessment Battery for Children–Second Edition; No Child Left Behind Act; Vineland Adaptive Behavior Scales—Second Edition; Wechsler Adult Intelligence Scale; Wechsler Intelligence Scale for Children—Fourth Edition

ASSESSMENT, TRANSITION

Transition assessment as a key component of the transition planning process was primarily a recommended practice in transition services literature until the Individuals with Disabilities Education Improvement Act of 2004 and its supporting regulations in 2006. While not defining transition assessment precisely, the Act used language that left no doubt of bipartisan Congressional intent. In the definition of transition services, the specific addition of the terms "improving the academic and functional achievement . . ." gave focus to a transition services process that addressed both academic and life-related competencies. The definition of transition services also qualifies the phrase, "a set of coordinated activities," with the caveat that those services ". . . shall be based on the individual child's needs, taking into account the child's strengths, preferences, and interests." (Authority: 20 U.S.C. § 1414 *et seq.*)

To further emphasize Congressional intent, the language of IDEA 2004 specified that the Individual Education Program (IEP) for all students 16 and older (and younger when appropriate) must have appropriate measurable postsecondary goals ". . . based upon age-appropriate transition assessments related to training, education, employment, and, where appropriate, independent living skills." The language in this section gives an assessment target for getting at academic and functional achievement or performance across the areas of education and training, employment, and independent living skills. These three areas may be generalized in terminology as the areas of learning, working, and living—the three primary areas of possible postsecondary outcome goals.

Without a legal definition of transition assessment, professionals are left to try to define it in terms of recommended practice. Sitlington, Neubert, Begun, Lombard, and Leconte (2007) propose this definition:

> Transition assessment is an ongoing process of collecting information on the student's strengths, needs, preferences, and interests as they relate to the demands of current and future living, learning, and working environments. This process should begin in middle school and continue until the student graduates or exits high school. Information from this process should be used to drive the IEP and transition planning process and to develop the SOP [Summary of Performance] document detailing the student's academic and functional performance and postsecondary goals. (pp. 2–3)

If one can agree to Clark's (2007) broad view of assessment as "question-asking," then it follows that transition assessment is a process of asking the important questions that every student and family should ask when planning for current and future learning, working, and living environments. That is, what are the postsecondary goals for continuing on for further education or training, for employment, and/or for living in the community? Once one or more of these dreams for the future translate into tentative postsecondary goal statements, they inform the school on the direction of next steps in question-asking. If the student or family chooses not to use school time or focus on all three of these goal areas, the nature and type of question-asking activities get more targeted in content. These questions can be raised in a variety of both formal and informal activities.

Typically, there are three general types of information needed in the transition planning process: (1) knowledge (information, facts, concepts, etc., related to adult learning, living, and working); (2) skills (performance of skills expected in learning, working, and living environments); and (3) intelligent application of knowledge and skills (functional achievement, including practical and social intelligence, self-determination, maintenance of physical and mental health and fitness, social and interpersonal relationships, community participation, etc.). Assessment activities that cut across all three of these general types of information for use in planning would include or be based on questions related to strengths, support needs, preferences, and interests.

Specific areas for question-asking vary with individual students and their postsecondary outcome goals but may include:

- Interests related to learning, living, and working
- Preferences related to learning, living, and working environments
- Physical health and fitness status
- Communication skills

- Current information on cognitive development and performance
- Adaptive behavior and skills
- Social and interpersonal relationship skills
- Emotional development and mental health
- Independent and interdependent living skills
- Recreation and leisure skills
- Employability and vocational skills
- Choice-making and self-determination skills
- Community participation and citizenship skills
- Needed supports or accommodations
- Needed linkages with current and future support services

IEP case managers, transition services personnel, IEP team members, special education support staff, and related services personnel may select from a variety of formal or informal assessment alternatives. Formal transition assessment instruments will have some evidence of validity and reliability and some might also have norms. Informal assessments do not have any demonstrated validity or reliability evidence, nor would they ever have norms.

Formal assessment instruments used in transition planning may include standardized tests or formal inventories or scales. Most of these are paper-and-pencil or computerized assessments that require varying degrees of reading comprehension and response capability. Accommodations may be appropriate for some of these (e.g., reading items to student, manual signing for student, extended time, adaptation of materials for blind students, etc.) but for others standardized administrations must be used. Formal transition instruments or scales may include general screening inventories of transition knowledge and skills or specific inventories of transition-related knowledge and skills. Most of the instruments directly pertaining to transition-related strengths, interests, or preferences do not require a highly skilled psychometrist or diagnostician, although those related to cognitive functioning, adaptive behavior, and emotional or behavioral functioning likely will. Administration of formal assessments is a matter of careful reading and administration procedure. Accurate interpretation and communication of results also require users to read and follow the instrument administration and interpretation guidelines in the manuals.

Informal assessment activities include curriculum-based assessments, interviews, surveys or questionnaires, checklists, rating scales, observation logs or observation protocols, commercially available or web-based instruments, environmental/ecological assessments, or person-centered planning. Each of these has its own advantages and disadvantages. Each also requires a set of skills for administration or interpretation that not all school personnel have without some training.

A practical issue in the transition assessment process is determining responsibility for coordinating the process.

That person is most often the IEP case manager, but in some cases a transition specialist may assume the role of transition assessment coordinator and case manager when a student reaches 16. Whoever does assume the coordination role draws on the assistance and collaboration of a range of possible contributors, starting with the student and his/her family. At school there will be special education personnel, paraprofessionals, general educators, career and technical educators, school administrators, guidance counselors, school psychologists and/or diagnosticians, related services personnel, and school building employees. Outside of school there are employers, work supervisors, extended family, community organizations and agencies, health care professionals, or disability advocates (adults or peers).

The most critical uses of transition assessment information are the IDEA mandates for developing a student's IEP annually and then as the basis for the Summary of Performance (SOP) for all students graduating or exiting after age eligibility expires. Other uses include course of study placement decisions, instructional decisions, guidance and counseling, referrals, curriculum planning, and documentation of procedures under IDEA.

REFERENCES

Clark, G. M. (2007). *Assessment for transitions planning* (2nd ed.). Austin, TX: Pro-Ed.

Sitlington, P. L., Neubert, D. A., Begun, W. H., Lombard, R. C., & Leconte, P. J. (2007). *Assess for success: A practitioner's handbook on transition assessment* (2nd ed.). Thousand Oaks, CA: Corwin.

GARY M. CLARK
University of Kansas

ASSIMILATION

Assimilation is one of two complementary processes of adaptation to the environment in Jean Piaget's theory of intellectual development; its counterpart is accommodation. Assimilation involves incorporating external elements (objects or events) into existing cognitive or sensorimotor schemes; incoming information is interpreted or adjusted in a manner consistent with current cognitive structures. In contrast, accommodation involves changing the structures that assimilate information (Brainerd, 1978).

The distinction between assimilation and accommodation can be illustrated by a physiological example: digestion of food (Ginsburg & Opper, 1969). Acids (or the body's current schemes or structures) transform the food into a form that can be used; thus elements of the external world are assimilated. Accommodation occurs in this example when, in order to deal with a foreign substance, stomach muscles contract, acids are released by certain organs, and so forth. Physical structures (the stomach and other organs) accommodate to an external element (food).

Assimilation involves both constraints on the nature and range of a child's interactions with the environment and the seeking out of new stimuli that can be assimilated into existing schemes (Gelman & Baillargeon, 1983). Piaget discusses three forms of assimilation: functional assimilation, which involves a basic tendency to use an existing structure such as a sucking reflex; recognitory assimilation, which involves recognizing particular situations in which the scheme should be applied; and generalizing assimilation, which involves a tendency to generalize a scheme to new objects and situations (Ginsburg & Opper, 1969).

REFERENCES

Brainerd, C. J. (1978). *Piaget's theory of intelligence*. Englewood Cliffs, NJ: Prentice Hall.

Gelman, R., & Baillargeon, R. (1983). A review of some Piagetian concepts. In P. H. Mussen (Ed.), *Handbook of child psychology*: *Vol. III. Cognitive development* (pp. 167–230). New York, NY: Wiley.

Ginsburg, H., & Opper, S. (1969). *Piaget's theory of intellectual development: An introduction*. Englewood Cliffs, NJ: Prentice Hall.

LINDA J. STEVENS
University of Minnesota

See also Accommodation; Piaget, Jean

ASSISTIVE TECHNOLOGY ACT

In 1998 Congress enacted the Assistive Technology Act (P.L. 105-394), commonly known as the *Tech Act*. Today, funding authorized by the Tech Act supports three general types of programs, which vary from state to state:

1. Assistive technology (AT) state grant programs, which provide a variety of services including demonstration centers to allow people to see different types of assistive technology, equipment loan and recycling programs, and information and referral services

2. Protection and advocacy services for persons needing legal assistance in obtaining services

3. Federal or state partnership alternative financing programs that provide low-interest loans to persons with disabilities to purchase assistive technology

On June 14, 2004, the House passed H.R. 4278, the Improving Access to Assistive Technology for Individuals with Disabilities Act of 2004, introduced on May 5, 2004. The bill amends the Assistive Technology Act of 1998 to support programs of grants to states to address the assistive technology needs of individuals with disabilities. The House and the Senate passed H.R. 4278, and it was signed into law by President Bush on October 25, 2004. To read the bill as signed into law, go to http://archives.republicans.edlabor.house.gov/archive/markups/108th/21st/hr4278/513main.htm

STAFF

ASSISTIVE TECHNOLOGY DEVICES

Whereas many people believe the term assistive technology is a recent development that applies only to computers, in reality, assistive technology devices (e.g., adaptive feeding instruments, wheelchairs, vision aids, etc.) have a long history in the field of special education and rehabilitation (Blackhurst, 1965, 1997; Office of Technology Assessment, 1982). Jacob (1999) provides an interesting historical timeline of devices that were originally developed for individuals with disabilities that subsequently became mainstream tools such as the typewriter, telephone, captioning, and talking books.

In the United States, the federal definition of assistive technology (AT) was first advanced in the 1988 Tech Act (P.L. 100-407) and has been subsequently cited in every federal and state law associated with technology use by people with disabilities:

§300.5 Assistive technology device.
... Assistive technology device means any item, piece of equipment, or product system, whether acquired commercially off the shelf, modified, or customized, that is used to increase, maintain, or improve the functional capabilities of a child with a disability. (20 U.S.C. 1401(1))

The definition is complex and therefore is worthy to be deconstructed into its four essential elements. First, AT is described as *any item, piece of equipment, or product system*. This broad statement is intended to cover a vast array of devices from a switch that is used to operate a computer by a person who cannot use a keyboard, to a powered wheelchair controlled by a person who is nonambulatory, to a talking cane that helps an individual who is blind independently navigate an environment. The second phrase, *whether acquired commercially off the shelf, modified, or customized*, speaks to the issue of how the assistive technology is obtained. When this definition was first written, assistive technology was generally created for an individual. Today the paradigm is reversed in that most assistive technology can be purchased off-the-shelf. The core issue here is that an array of interventions are needed to match the device with the unique capabilities and special needs of the individual. Third, the statement, *that is used to increase, maintain, or improve the functional capabilities*, addresses the purpose for using AT. The explicit goal is to enhance function (and presumably independence). Finally, the definition concludes with a focus on the user: *of a child with a disability*.

The value and significance of assistive technology can be understood in relation to a performance problem. That is, a person with a disability encounters a task that they are unable to successfully complete. Following the identification of an appropriate assistive technology device, acquisition of the product, training and support in its use, the person is subsequently able to complete the same task that was previously difficult or impossible. Thus, the motivation for locating appropriate assistive technology devices and services is to enhance the performance of individuals with disabilities by enabling them to complete tasks more effectively, efficiently, and independently than otherwise possible.

Edyburn (2001, 2009) has commented on several short-comings of the definition of AT that are impossible to revise because of its extensive citation within federal and state laws and policies. He argues that the definition of assistive technology is so broad that it could include anything. Indeed, that is a simple way to think about it: *Assistive technology is anything that improves the functional performance of an individual with a disability*. However, this statement is particularly problematic if it reveals that the definition of AT has no value in discerning what is and isn't AT.

Consider for example, the sensor above a store door that opens when a person approaches. If a person without a disability enters the stores, we cannot conclude that the device was a form of AT since the definition indicates that AT is only for people with disabilities. However, if a person using a power wheelchair enters the store, we must conclude that the sensor and door opener functioned as AT. How can the same sensor and door opener be AT in one situation and not AT in another?

Twenty-five years after the definition of AT was included in the Tech Act, we are still dealing with a legacy definition that does not clearly discern what AT is, and what AT is not. This problem is particularly disconcerting in the context of mild disabilities where technology performance-support tools take on the form of cognitive prostheses that may be useful to everyone, not just individuals with disabilities (Edyburn, 2006).

Concern over what is assistive technology and how to find the appropriate AT device has led to several important efforts within the field. Current estimates suggest that there are over 40,000 assistive technology devices designed to enhance the life functioning of individuals with

disabilities (AbleData, 2011). Another promising, but controversial, initiative has been created by Speech Language Therapist Debby McBride. *AAC Device Assistant* (http://www.aactechconnect.com/index.php/device-assistant) is a web-based decision-support system that guides users through a decision-making process based on key features (i.e., type of display, number of direct select cells, size of vocabulary) to yield a set of devices to explore from the more than 100 alternative and augmentative devices available in the marketplace. While the value of this system is that it allows nonexperts to explore the possibilities, experts decry the system as devoid of the clinical judgment needed to select the appropriate device. However, since such advanced product knowledge is not available in every community, such a system seems to have a place in helping the profession advance the systematic provision of assistive technology devices to those who could potentially benefit.

Edyburn (2001) has also argued that the federal definition of AT includes only two legs of a three-legged stool. That is, we have a definition of AT Devices, a companion definition of AT Services (see also Assistive Technology Services), but we lack a definition of AT outcome (see also Measurement of Assistive Technology Outcomes). That is, there is nothing in the existing definition of AT that involves collecting and evaluating evidence that AT actually produces enhanced functional outcomes in any measurable and meaningful way. Since federal law provides no guidance concerning how much benefit should be expected to accrue from the use of an AT device, the profession is woefully unprepared to answer questions concerning the outcome and benefit of AT device use (Edyburn, 2009).

DAVE EDYBURN
University of Wisconsin-Milwaukee
Fourth edition

ASSISTIVE TECHNOLOGY FOR HEARING IMPAIRMENTS

Telecommunication Device for the Deaf (TDD)/ Text Telephone (TTY)

This is a device that enables people who are deaf to communicate by phone via a typewriter that converts typed letters into electric signals through a modem. These signals are sent through the phone lines and then translated into typed messages and printed on a typewriter connected to a phone on the other end.

Assistive Listening Device (ALD)

The intelligibility of the human voice is degraded by poor room acoustics as well as hearing loss. Most assistive listening devices (ALDs) use a microphone or transmitter positioned close to the instructor's mouth to send the instructor's voice through the air or by cable to the receiver worn by the student. By placing the microphone close to the instructor's mouth, ALDs can provide clear sound over distances, eliminate echoes, and reduce surrounding noises. This is a distinct acoustic advantage of ALDs compared to personal hearing aids. The microphone location allows the level of the speaker's voice to stay constant to the listener regardless of the distance between the two.

There are different types of ALDs (FM, Soundfield Amplification, and Induction Loop Systems), each system having special features, capabilities, advantages, and disadvantages. No single technology is without limitations or can be expected to fulfill all the essential auditory needs of all users. It is important to find the one that is right for the individual with a hearing loss.

ANNE REBER
Texas A&M University

See also Assistive Devices; Assistive Technology Act

ASSISTIVE TECHNOLOGY IN HIGHER EDUCATION

Assistive technology is used extensively in higher education. Although the laws and statutes that govern the provision of services in higher education are somewhat different, the types of technologies used are very similar. As in the lower grades, alternative format production is a big issue. But unlike them, higher education has additional issues, especially with the textbook adoption process. Alternative format production is often the first step in the service provision process for a disability service office and therefore warrants some attention.

Textbook Adoptions and Alternative Format Production

Differences between the textbook adoption models of elementary and higher education contribute to major differences in the service provision model of the two systems. In the kindergarten through 12th grade (K–12) environment, it is typical for the textbook adoption process to take 2–3 years. Books are submitted by publishers to the state board of education for review. To even be considered, most publishers have to sign assurances that the book will be provided in accessible formats by the time of purchase. Publishers agree to this because they know that they will have sufficient time to produce such resources when and if the book is adopted. They further know that the quantities ordered will justify the time and expense of creating accessible formats. After a lengthy period of time, the book is officially adopted by the state, purchased in quantity, and shipped to the school districts for use. The average lifespan of a typical K–12 textbook is 2–3 years, but some states use books much longer.

In contrast to the K–12 model, textbook adoptions in higher education proceed much quicker as they are, in many cases, determined solely by the instructor. The instructors choose their course books, in many cases, independently of other instructors or departments. To keep current with this selection process, publishers focus more on variety and currency. Consequently, textbooks must be constantly updated in order for the publisher to keep competitive and make money. In general, institutional adoption policies in the higher education environment are loosely enforced, even if they exist. Many instructors feel strongly that institutional adoption policies are a blow to academic freedom, while others see utility in having some policies to insure consistency across the institution. The net result is a system of textbook adoption that has far more current textbooks than the K–12 system, but sacrifices process, consistency, and accessibility.

Given this model, there are three issues that affect format production in higher education when compared to that of K–12. The first issue relates to publishers. In most states, publishers have no legal responsibility to provide alternative formats to institutions of higher education. Some exceptions to this are California and Illinois. Moreover, publishers' infrastructures have been optimized to produce a final product that is physically printed on paper and distributed. Any other product format (such as a hypertext markup language [HTML] version of a textbook) must be produced from the print-optimized version. This leads to accessibility barriers. The bottom line is that publishers have little or no responsibility to provide accessible text materials in the higher education environment.

At this point in time, publishers cannot produce an accessible format without significant time and money. Recently, publishers have examined a change in process to produce digital formats of textbooks that transform gracefully into other formats. Slowly, publishers are moving in the digital direction. As more and more states approve statutes requiring accessible texts and national pressure mounts to address the issue in a legal manner, publishers are beginning to put the necessary changes into place.

This illustration is not meant to infer that publishers don't care about accessibility. On the contrary, they see accessibility as a means not only of assisting students with disabilities but also as a competitive advantage. After all, the same techniques that make information accessible to students with disabilities also make the information accessible to nondisabled students who may access the information using other means.

The second issue is related to the manner of provision of higher education. Higher education has evolved more and more into a customer-driven model of consumerism. This has led to a wide variety of classes and courses of study to meet the needs of the diverse student population. As a result, students can register for any course they are qualified to take at virtually any time. Because very few textbooks are available in an accessible format, accessible formats must be created ad hoc by the institution. This problem gives the disability services office little or no time to prepare.

The third issue is related to the selection of textbooks by instructors. It is not uncommon for the more populous courses to change textbooks annually or even each semester. Because staffing for courses is often delayed, instructors are sometimes assigned late to courses. In the absence of a textbook adoption policy, instructors may choose textbooks just before or even after a course begins. A recent survey of a major 4-year university revealed that 15% of textbook adoptions were given to the bookstores after the first day of class. This selection process provides little time for the disability services office to produce alternative formats.

Types of Assistive Technology in Higher Education

All of the major classes of assistive technology are represented in higher education, but some are less common than others. For example, augmentative communication technology, which is common in K–12, is generally not provided in higher education. Devices such as communication boards and speech synthesis microphones are generally provided by the student, not by the institution. Under the higher education model, augmentative communication in most cases would be considered a personal device and therefore not legally mandated to be provided, whereas in K–12, these devices were provided by the school district (under the Individuals with Disabilities Education Act [IDEA]). Once the student moves out of the K–12 system, their personal technology needs are handled in many cases by state vocational rehabilitation (VR) agencies. Thus assistive technology is split between VR and the college, with the college providing access to learning materials and VR supporting personal technology needs.

Many colleges offer alternative format production services to include recording text materials onto tape and textbook scanning. In some cases, braille and tactile graphic production services are provided. Modern braille printers are capable of combining tactile graphics with braille text and in some cases can even produce multi-height graphic embossing (see http://viewplustech.com/). Scanners are common and are usually equipped with optical character recognition software that is used to produce electronic versions of printed materials.

Getting the material converted into an accessible format is only the first step in giving the student access via assistive technology. Technologies commonly used to deliver the accessible material once it is converted include text-to-speech, print braille, refreshable braille, and screen magnification. Some student populations such as those with visual impairments may use a combination of technologies, such as text-to-speech and screen magnification. Increasingly, students with learning disabilities are using assistive technologies such as text-to-speech to listen to their text materials while reading them.

The advent of ubiquitous digital players such as MP3 players has given rise to a new alternative format process. Recently, some colleges have begun using textbook scanning combined with text-to-speech to output audio of scanned materials to digital files, such as MP3 files. These files can be burned to CD and played on a computer or downloaded to a portable digital audio player. The new technologies available greatly automate and speed this process to help disability services meet the tight turnaround requirements associated with higher education structures. For example, there is equipment readily available that removes a textbook's binding, and the pages are then scanned via an automatic feeder to provide an electronic version of the contents. The electronic text content is then converted to audio files for use in a digital audio player or integrated into special instructional resources.

Voice recognition software has been used in higher education for a number of years although it is not as common as other technologies. In the opinion of this reviewer, the technology is just now coming into its own, and it will be several years before voice recognition is as common as other assistive technologies. Currently, voice control over regular computer operations (e.g., open, close, send, print) is readily available on standard operating systems. Affordable dictation software is also available but requires extensive training for efficient use.

For students with hearing impairments, the use of wireless amplification systems (often termed *FM systems*) is a fairly common accommodation. Because this device offers access to the material presented in class, many colleges consider this device within their purview and will provide them. Computer-assisted captioning systems are also becoming more common. This accommodation consists of software usually used with a portable computer in the classroom that is used to record the audio portion of a class. Most systems do not produce a word-for-word transcript but rather an approximation or summary of what is said. Computer-assisted captioning requires a trained captionist in most cases. Although word-for-word, real-time captioning (e.g., courtroom type captioning) is sometimes used, it is less common than approximate dialog systems. As faculty more commonly use electronic formats for creation of their lecture materials, these materials may be made available to disability services offices for conversion to alternative formats. In keeping with the concept of universal design, such multiple formats are beginning to appear as part of the delivery format of many courses and will benefit all students, whether or not they have a disability.

REFERENCE

ViewPlus Technologies. (2005). *Braille printers and braille embossing hardware*. Retrieved from http://viewplustech.com/

DAVID SWEENEY
RONALD ZELLNER
Texas A&M University

See also Assistive Technology Act; Learning Disabled College Students

ASSISTIVE TECHNOLOGY, TRANSITION PLANNING

Assistive technology can play a vital role in supporting the transition from high school to adult life for youth with disabilities. IDEA 2004 defines assistive technology as, "any item, piece of equipment, or product system, whether acquired commercially off the shelf, modified, or customized, that is used to increase, maintain, or improve the functional capabilities of a child with a disability"(34CFR SS 300.5 [Authority: 20 USC §1401 (1)]). The purpose of assistive technology (AT) is to promote greater independence for people with disabilities, enabling their opportunity to perform tasks that they may have had difficulty performing or accomplishing. That purpose applies to the role that AT can provide in supporting the transition planning process: it can and should support the ability of youth with disability in meeting their goals for a preferred adult lifestyle.

As part of the development of a comprehensive annual Individualized Education Program or IEP, team members are required to consider whether assistive technology is needed to help support the acquisition of annual goals. During this annual planning meeting as goals are developed for students with disabilities, teams should consider whether there are AT devices and/or services that could help support a student in accessing the general education curriculum, participating in state and/or district-wide assessments, and/or achieving preferred postschool outcomes (for students who are required to have a transition plan as part of the IEP plan). Postschool outcomes include goals for a preferred adult lifestyle in one or more adult living domains including: employment, independent living, self-care, community involvement, recreation and leisure, postsecondary education, and/or transportation.

Not only must these various domains be taken into account, but teams must also think creatively to include consideration of a range of technology that can meet student transition goals. AT devices can be categorized along a continuum from low to high technology. Examples of low-tech equipment can include magnifying glasses, color-coding for keys or files, or large print. High technology examples can include computer equipment, environmental control systems, or insulin pumps. Most AT equipment serves a specific purpose, although some, like computer equipment, can be used for multiple purposes. Typically, AT devices are further categorized according to their purpose, including: positioning (assisting an individual in maintaining a body position/posture for a particular function); mobility; augmentative and alternative communication; computer access; adaptive toys and games; environmental control; instructional aides.

If a student with a disability could benefit from AT to support his or her transition plan, a comprehensive AT assessment might be necessary. AT assessments can be done in a number of different ways, but the processes that work the best use a team approach and consider not only the needs of the student and features of a specific AT device, but also the environment in which the device will be used, the support of others, and the preferences of the individual. For example, the SETT framework (Zabala, 1995) recommends that AT assessment focus on the **S**tudent, **E**nvironments, **T**ask, and **T**ools. Other similar AT protocols include the Matching Person and Technology (Craddock & Scherer, 2001) process and the Assistive Technology Protocol for Transition Planning (Reed & Canfield, 2001). Another option is the Adaptations Framework (Bryant & Bryant, 1988) which helps IEP teams consider a range of accommodations or adaptations including AT. Regardless of which assessment process is used, it is important that team members include individuals who know the individual best, the student himself or herself, as well as those who know enough about AT equipment to identify creative and useful options. And, when postschool outcomes are being considered, including those who understand the environments in which they will be used is also recommended.

Each of these AT assessment procedures include as a central feature the preferences and interests of the individual student. The most effective procedures for transition planning involve some level of student self-determination in the process (Wehmeyer, 1999), and AT assessment process is no different. Craddock & Scherer (2001) found that when the preference of individuals with disabilities is not considered as part of an AT assessment, there is a greater likelihood that the device will be unused. While one individual might enthusiastically embrace the use of a high-tech piece of equipment, another might prefer the support of a friend or aide.

The source of funding for AT devices is another important consideration for transition teams. While transition planning is a school-based process, the participation of adult service agencies is critical when AT devices are needed to support student postschool outcomes. Schools are required to provide AT to help students access the school learning, but these devices typically belong to the school and not to the student himself or herself. This can mean that funding from adult agencies will be necessary if an individual needs AT to meet a postschool outcome such as employment, community living, or transportation. It is important to identify the specific funding options, and to justify the expense given the mission of the funding agency. For example, justification for a communication device made to a local office of vocational rehabilitation should be made in reference to its necessity to secure and maintain employment while justification to Medicaid or to a health insurance agency should be made in reference to its necessity to secure and maintain medical care. Each state has agencies that can help provide more information about AT, including local, state, and national funding sources. Many of these also provide training for team members, parents, and individuals with disabilities as well as provide AT lending libraries that provide an option to practice with the device in the setting in which it will be used. In addition, AT device manufacturers often provide guidance and/or assistance in identifying and securing funding.

REFERENCES

Bryant, D. P., & Bryant, B. R. (1998). Using assistive technology adaptations to include students with learning disabilities in cooperative learning activities. *Journal of Learning Disabilities, 31*(1), 41–54.

Craddock, G., & Scherer, M. J. (2001). Assessing individual needs for assistive technology. In C. L. Sax & C. A. Thoma (Eds.), *Transition assessment: Wise decisions for quality lives* (pp. 105–121). Baltimore, MD: Paul H. Brookes.

Individuals with Disabilities Education Act. Pub.L. No. 104-17, 111 STAT.37.

Reed, P. & Canfield, T. (2001). *Assistive Technology in Transition Planning.* Oshkosh, WI: Wisconsin Assistive Technology Initiative.

Wehmeyer, M. L. (1999). Assistive technology and students with mental retardation: Utilization and barriers. *Journal of Special Education Technology, 14*(1), 48–58.

Zabala, J. (1995). *The SETT framework: Critical areas to consider when making informal assistive technology decisions.* Closing the Gap Conference on the Use of Assistive Technology in Special Education and Rehabilitation, Minneapolis, Minnesota.

COLLEEN THOMA
Virginia Commonwealth University
Fourth edition

ASSOCIATION FOR CHILDHOOD EDUCATION INTERNATIONAL

Founded in 1892, the Association for Childhood Education International (ACEI) is a not-for-profit professional education association of educators, parents, and other caregivers interested in promoting quality education practices for children. The organization was originally conceived to provide a formal organization to promote the interest and professionalism of the kindergarten movement throughout the world. With over 11,000 members in the United States and Canada, ACEI is the oldest organization of its kind. Members participate in local and state group activities, including meetings, workshops, and regional conferences. Annual Study Conferences have been held each year since 1896 to share ideas and contribute to the standard of excellence in teaching in all arenas, such as public and private day care centers, kindergartens, elementary schools, middle schools, high schools, and university-level teacher education programs.

The mission of ACEI is to promote the inherent rights, education, and well-being of all children, from infancy through early adolescence, in the home, school, and community. The organization is member-driven and is guided by a dynamic philosophy of education that is flexible and responsive to human needs in a changing society. Members are dedicated to a holistic, child-centered approach to education that considers the child's experiences in the home, school, community, and world.

ACEI is interested in promoting good educational practices for children. By acting as a facilitator for the sharing and dissemination of information through publications and conferences, the organization provides a service to its members and to the education community as a whole. This is accomplished through the regular publication of two refereed professional journals, *Childhood Education* and *Journal of Research in Childhood Education*. Additionally, the Association publishes books, newsletters, pamphlets, position papers, and position statements that relate to the welfare of children; recommend sound, developmentally appropriate educational practice; and include practical application guidelines for educators.

Other contributions of the organization include the publication of *Childhood Education*, a professional journal of theory and practice in the field. The journal has consistently sought to make a thoughtful, multifaceted contribution to the growing body of knowledge concerning children and the learning process. In 1986 an additional publication, *Journal of Research in Childhood Education*, was created as a vehicle for sharing research knowledge as it is acquired. A catalog containing information regarding ACEI publications is available free upon request.

Improved standards for teacher preparation and others involved with the care and development of children are among the association's goals. ACEI was appointed to serve as the organization responsible for overseeing the folio review process of elementary teacher preparation programs offered at U.S. colleges and universities seeking accreditation through the National Council for Accreditation of Teacher Education.

A library, including volumes on childhood and elementary education, is maintained at association headquarters. Association offices are located at 17904 Georgia Avenue, Suite 215, Olney, MD 20832. Tel.: (800) 423-3563 and (301) 570-2111.

TAMARA J. MARTIN
The University of Texas of the Permian Basin

ASSOCIATION FOR CHILDREN AND ADULTS WITH LEARNING DISABILITIES (*See Learning Disabilities Association*)

ASSOCIATION FOR PERSONS WITH SEVERE HANDICAPS (*See TASH*)

ASSOCIATION FOR POSITIVE BEHAVIOR SUPPORT (APBS)

The Association for Positive Behavior Support (APBS) is an international organization dedicated to promoting research-based strategies that combine applied behavior analysis and biomedical science with person-centered values and systems change to increase quality of life and decrease problem behaviors. The single subject research studies in applied behavior analysis beginning back in the 1960s have contributed to an applied science that describes how learning principles can be systematically applied to produce socially important changes in behavior (Baer, Wolf, & Risley, 1968; Cooper, Heron, & Heward, 1987). This research in applied behavior analysis provided an important foundation for what is now known today as positive behavior support (Dunlap & Horner, 2006), although positive behavior support also is known for employing concepts and methods from other disciplines and areas of study, including person-centered planning, wraparound and systems of care, self determination, systems change, physiological research and biomedical science (Carr et al., 2002).

One area of positive behavior support research that is growing at a very fast rate involves school-wide and organization-wide behavior prevention efforts. The school and/or organization is considered the unit of analysis, while the goal is to establish a positive "host" environment by teaching and reinforcing social behaviors in order to prevent the likelihood that problem behaviors will occur (Sugai et al., 2005). School-wide and organization-wide positive behavior support are currently being implemented in a variety of settings including elementary, middle, and high schools, early childhood organizations, and alternative settings (Fox & Hemmeter, 2009; Sugai & Horner, 2009; Simonsen, Britton, & Young, 2010; Stormont, Lewis, Beckner, & Johnson, 2007; Walker et al., 1996). New terms have emerged to describe the implementation of positive behavior support across larger scale systems change efforts, including *school-wide positive behavior support* in educational settings (Sugai et al., 2000), and *program-wide positive behavior support* in early childhood environments (Hemmeter, Fox, Jack, Broyles, & Doubet, 2007).

A major focus of positive behavior support is on the application of a research-validated technology in everyday home, school, and community settings with professionals and other individuals who do not have highly specialized degrees or training actively involved in implementing interventions to prevent the likelihood of problem behavior. The goal of positive behavior support is to provide families and professionals who work with children and adults both with and without disabilities with a set of systems, tools, and processes that can be used to prevent problem behavior in home, school, work, and community settings, and to respond to problem behavior if and when problem behaviors do arise. Problem behaviors such as aggression, self-injury, various forms of bullying, insubordination, disruption, vandalism, and withdrawal continue to be among the most common reasons why people with and without disabilities are excluded from typical home, school, work, and community contexts. Problem behaviors can serve as barriers to the development of meaningful social relationships, employment, academic achievement, functional life-skills, self-determination, health, and personal safety. Typical responses to problem behavior in society have historically been reactive since interventions tend to be implemented after problem behaviors have already occurred. The most common response to severe problem behavior has been to exclude individuals who engage in problem behaviors from local home, school, and community settings by placing them in alternative educational or institutional settings (Lane & Murakami, 1987). Furthermore, research indicates that the use of punishment alone without positive social instruction can actually have the counterintuitive result of increasing problem behavior (Mayer & Butterworth, 1981; Mayer, Butterworth, Nafpaktitis, & Sulzer-Azaroff, 1983; Mayer, Nafpaktitis, Butterworth, & Hollingsworth, 1987; Mayer & Sulzer-Azaroff, 1990).

Public policy in the areas of prevention, early intervention, education, adult services, and family support has increasingly emphasized the active inclusion of all individuals with disabilities in typical social and cultural contexts. However, problem behaviors remain a major barrier to achieving these public policy goals. Reducing problem behaviors in our schools and communities requires a fundamental shift that can be guided by the science of changing and influencing social and cultural practices (Biglan, 1995). Reduction of problem behavior will occur when *all* of the individuals in school and community settings place a stronger emphasis on prevention by teaching social skills, modeling appropriate behavior, providing reinforcement ratios for positive social behaviors that are higher than the negative interactions that occur when responding to problem behavior, and when more consistent and humane responses to problem behaviors set the stage for a positive and predictable social environment (Freeman et al., 2005; Sugai & Horner, 2009; Walker et al., 1996). The cultural shift toward prevention may occur only when families, professionals, policymakers, and other important stakeholder groups work together to implement positive behavior support on a large-scale basis. This cultural shift will be further enhanced by the creation of regional, national, and international networking to promote knowledge and awareness of positive behavior support and by establishing ways in which interagency collaboration can be enhanced in order to blend limited resources for positive behavior support implementation efforts.

The vision and mission of APBS is to assist in this effort by ensuring that: (a) information about the science (and associated practices) of positive behavior support is available on a wide-scale basis both nationally and internationally, (b) opportunities for networking across geographic areas as well as topical areas of interest are nurtured, and (c) information is made available for all stakeholders interested in advocating for research and practice in positive behavior support. APBS is an active organization, focusing its attention on dissemination, education, and public policy efforts. Specifically, APBS:

- Serves as an international forum for individuals interested in PBS
- Hosts an annual international conference
- Supports and promotes the *Journal of Positive Behavior Interventions*
- Publishes a quarterly newsletter
- Manages its website (www.apbs.org) and links to other important websites on PBS practices, systems, and examples
- Provides the resources and materials necessary for members to develop policy and practice related to positive behavior support at regional, national, and international levels
- Maintains a directory of members to facilitate interaction among individuals interested in positive behavior support practices
- Provides opportunities for informal collaborative groups to form by geographic and/or topical area in a loose affiliation with APBS through a network petition process that includes at least five or more

APBS members (each network submits an action plan and provides annual updates that are posted on the Association's website)
- Is working toward establishing national standards that define competency in the application of positive behavior support across various units of analysis (individual and systems levels)
- Encourages the training of professionals for various stakeholders in PBS practices through the development of training materials
- Promotes access to state-of-the-art books and literature pertaining to PBS

Membership, Products, and/or Publications

All members are given a variety of opportunities to become directly involved in outreach endeavors, pertinent business matters of the Association, and the election of members to the Board of Directors. In addition, members receive: a subscription to *The Journal of Positive Behavior Interventions (JPBI)* published by Hammill Institute on Disabilities, the quarterly *APBS Newsletter* included in *JPBI*, discounted registration for the annual APBS Conference, and access to valuable information and training materials posted in the Member's section of the apbs.org website. There are a variety of membership categories within APBS. The three most prevalent types of membership include: (1) Regular Membership: $80.00 annually or $200 for a 3-year membership; (2) Student or Family Membership: $35.00 annually; and (3) Agency Membership: $125.00 annually.

The Association for Positive Behavior Support (APBS) can be found at: P.O. Box 328, Bloomsburg, PA 17837. Website: www.apbs.org

REFERENCES

Association for Positive Behavior Support Website (2010). Retrieved November 19, 2010: http://www.apbs.org

Baer, D. M., Wolf, M. M., & Risley, T. R. (1968). Some current dimensions of applied behavior analysis. *Journal of Applied Behavior Analysis, 1,* 91–97. doi: 10.1901/jaba.1968.1-91

Biglan, A. (1995). *Changing cultural practices: A contextualist framework for intervention research.* Reno, NV: Context Press.

Carr, E. G., Dunlap, G., Horner, R. H., Koegel, R. L.,Turnbull, A. P., Sailor,W., et al. (2002). Positive behavior support: Evolution of an applied science. *Journal of Positive Behavior Interventions, 4,* 4–16. doi: 10.1177/109830070200400102

Cooper, J. O., Heron, T. E., & Heward, W. L. (1987). *Applied behavior analysis.* Upper Saddle River, NJ: Merrill.

Dunlap, G., & Horner, R. H. (2006). The applied behavior analytic heritage of PBS: A dynamic model of action-oriented research. *Journal of Positive Behavior Interventions, 8,* 58–60. doi: 10.1177/10983007060080010701

Fox, L., & Hemmeter, M. L. (2009). A programwide model for supporting social emotional development and addressing challenging behavior in early childhood settings. In W. Sailor, G. Dunlap, G. Sugai, & R. H. Horner (Eds.), *Handbook of positive behavior support* (pp.177–202). New York, NY: Springer.

Freeman, R., Smith, C., Zarcone, J., Kimbrough, P., Tieghi-Benet, M., & Wickham, D. (2005). Building a statewide plan for embedding positive behavior support in human service organizations. *Journal of Positive Behavior Interventions, 7*(2), 109–119.

Hemmeter, M. L., Fox, L., Jack, S., Broyles, L., & Doubet, S. (2007). A program-wide model of positive behavior support in early childhood settings. *Journal of Early Intervention, 29*, 337–355.

Lane, T. W., & Murakami, J. (1987). School programs for delinquency prevention and intervention. In E. K. Morris & C. J. Braukmann (Eds.), *Behavioral approaches to crime and delinquency: A handbook of application, research, and concepts* (pp. 305–330). New York: Plenum.

Mayer, M. J., & Leone, P. E. (1999). A structural analysis of school violence and disruption: Implications for creating safer schools. *Education and Treatment of Children, 22*(3), 333–356.

Mayer, G. R., & Butterworth, T. (1981). Evaluating a preventative approach to reducing school vandalism. *Phi Delta Kappan, 62*, 498–499.

Mayer, G. R., Butterworth, T., Nafpaktitius, M., & Sulzer-Azaroff, B. (1983). Preventing school vandalism and improving discipline: A three-year study. *Journal of Applied Behavior Analysis, 16*, 355–369. doi: 10.1901/jaba.1983.16-355

Mayer, G. G., Nafpaktitis, M., Butterworth, T., & Hollingsworth, P. (1987). A search for the elusive setting events of school vandalism: A correlational study. *Education and Treatment of Children, 10*, 259–270.

Mayer, G. R., & Sulzer-Azaroff, B. (1990). Interventions for vandalism. In G. Stoner, M. R. Shinn, & H. M. Walker (Eds.), *Interventions for achievement and behavior problems* (pp. 599–580) [Monograph]. Washington, DC: National Association for School Psychologists.

Simonsen, B., Britton, L., & Young, D. (2010). School-wide positive behavior support in an alternative school setting. *Journal of Positive Behavior Interventions, 12*, 180–191. doi: 10.1177/1098300708330495

Stormont, M., Lewis, T., Beckner, R., & Johnson, N. W. (2007). *Implementing positive behavior support systems in early childhood and elementary settings*. Thousand Oaks, CA: Corwin Press.

Sugai, G., & Horner, R. H. (2009). Defining and describing schoolwide positive behavior support. In W. Sailor, G. Dunlap, G. Sugai, & R. H. Horner (Eds.), *Handbook of positive behavior support* (pp. 307–326). New York, NY: Springer.

Sugai, G., Horner, R. H., Dunlap, G. Hieneman, M., Lewis, T. J., et al. (2000). Applying positive behavioral support and functional behavioral assessment in schools. *Journal of Positive Behavioral Interventions, 2*, 131–143.

Sugai, G., Horner, R., Sailor, W., Dunlap, G., Eber, L., et al. (2005). *School-wide positive behavior support: Implementers' blueprint and self-assessment*. Technical Assistance Center on Positive Behavioral Interventions and Supports.

Walker, H. M., Horner, R. H., Sugai, G., Bullis, M., Sprague, J. R., et al. (1996). Integrated approaches to preventing antisocial behavior patterns among school-age children and youth. *Journal of Emotional and Behavioral Disorders, 4*(4), 194–209.

RACHEL FREEMAN, PhD, PRESIDENT OF APBS
University of Kansas

TIM KNOSTER, EdD, EXECUTIVE DIRECTOR OF APBS
Bloomsburg University

ASSOCIATION FOR SPECIAL EDUCATION (See Center for Applied Technology)

ASSOCIATION FOR THE ADVANCEMENT OF BEHAVIOR THERAPY

The Association for the Advancement of Behavioral Therapies was founded in 1966 and renamed the Association for the Advancement of Behavior Therapy (AABT) in 1968. Headquartered in New York City, the AABT is a not-for-profit organization of over 4,500 mental health professionals and students who utilize and/or are interested in empirically based behavior therapy and cognitive behavior therapy. Membership is interdisciplinary and consists of psychologists, psychiatrists, social workers, physicians, nurses, and other mental health professionals who treat over 90 mental health problems. AABT does not certify its members.

Among its activities, the AABT sponsors training programs and lectures aimed at professionals and semiprofessionals, provides communication accessibility among behavior therapists interested in similar areas of research or specific problems, and maintains a speaker's bureau. Affiliates of the Association conduct training meetings, workshops, seminars, case demonstrations, and discussion groups. In addition, the AABT holds committees on continuing and public education and provides referrals to the general public upon request (a $5 postage and handling fee is required). A Fact Sheet regarding the problem for which help is being sought and the pamphlet, *Guidelines for Choosing a Behavior Therapist*, are included with mailed referrals. Referrals can be obtained by visiting AABT's website at www.aabt.org/aabt.

The Association's Media & Community Connection Program assists the media with background information and news of the latest developments in the behavioral therapies. The program also helps locate suitable experts in the field for interviews or speaking engagements. Providing membership services to mental health professionals and students seeking to network with like-minded colleagues and to remain current in the behavioral therapies is another activity of the AABT.

AABT offers Full and Associate professional memberships and sponsors an Annual Convention every November, attracting approximately 2,000 participants. One to three smaller educational seminars are held each year as well. Two peer-reviewed journals, *Behavior Therapy* and *Cognitive & Behavioral Practice*, are published by the organization in addition to its newsletter, *The Behavior Therapist*. For a list of AABT publications or for information regarding upcoming educational programs, please call (212) 647-1890 or visit the AABT website at www.aabt.org/aabt.

MARY LEON PEERY
Texas A&M University
First edition

TAMARA J. MARTIN
The University of Texas of the Permian Basin
Second edition

ASSOCIATION FOR THE GIFTED, THE

Founded in 1958, The Association for the Gifted is one of the 17 divisions of the Council for Exceptional Children. The five purposes of this association are to (1) promote the welfare and education of children and youth with gifts, talents, and/or high potential; (2) improve educational opportunities for individuals from all diverse groups with gifts, talents, and/or high potential; (3) sponsor and foster activities to develop the field of gifted education, such as the dissemination of information, the conduct of research, and other scholarly investigations; (4) support and encourage specialized professional preparation for educators of individuals with gifts, talents, and/or high potential, as well as for professional persons in related fields; and (5) work with organizations, agencies, families, or individuals whose purposes are consistent with those of the Association for the Gifted.

The Association distributes two publications to its membership. One, the *Journal for the Education of the Gifted*, is a forum for theoretical, descriptive, and research articles that analyze and communicate information about the needs of children and youth with gifts, talents, and/or high potential. The *Journal* also serves as a forum for the exchange of diverse ideas and points of view on the education of the gifted and talented. The second publication, *TAG Update*, is the Association's newsletter, containing brief, timely information on the Association's activities, upcoming events, workshops and institutes, reports on legislation, and relevant news from other organizations.

Membership inquiries should be made to the Association for the Gifted, The Council for Exceptional Children,

1110 N. Glebe Road, Suite 300, Arlington, VA 22201. Only members of the Council for Exceptional Children are eligible to join the Association for the Gifted. Special membership categories for students and parents and professionals are available for those who qualify for these discounted membership rates.

STAFF

ASSOCIATION OF BLACK PSYCHOLOGISTS

The Association of Black Psychologists (ABPsi) was founded in San Francisco in 1968 when a number of Black psychologists from across the country met to discuss the serious problems facing Black psychologists and the larger Black community. The founding members began building an organization through which they could confront the long-neglected needs of Black professionals. They also hoped to have a positive impact on the mental health of the Black community through programs, services, training, and advocacy. The Association is organized into four regions as well as a student division. From the original group, the membership of ABPsi has grown into an international organization of over 1,300 psychologists and mental health professionals, committed to addressing the mental health issues of individuals throughout the African diaspora.

The main offices of the Association of Black Psychologists can be reached at P.O. Box 55999, Washington, DC 20040-5999. Tel.: (202) 722-0808.

NADINE M. LAMBERT
University of California Berkeley,
First edition

KAY E. KETZENBERGER
The University of Texas of the Permian Basin
Second edition

ASSOCIATIVE LEARNING

Associative learning, as demonstrated in the classical conditioning experiments of Pavlov (1927), is based on the concept that events or ideas that are experienced at the same time tend to become associated with each other. When a new (conditioned) stimulus is presented with an old (unconditioned) stimulus, the conditioned stimulus assumes the capability of eliciting a (conditioned) response almost identical to the original (unconditioned) response. The conditioned stimulus should be presented about half a second before the unconditioned stimulus for maximum effectiveness.

Associative learning is routinely applied when students recognize words, spell, and recall math facts. A number of remedial techniques are also based on the associative principle. Multisensory approaches to reading, which presume the formation of associative bonds across sensory modalities, have been successful in remediating deficits in mildly and severely reading-disabled children and in intellectually disabled students (Sutaria, 1982). Visual imagery training, in which children learn to associate mental pictures with printed text, has been shown to improve learning-disabled students' reading comprehension (Clark, Warner, Alley, Deshler, & Shumaker, 1981).

Children with intellectual disability, for whom associative skills are often an area of relative strength, have improved their memory performance when taught to pair words according to their conceptual similarity (Lathey & Tobias, 1981). Associative learning is a fundamental principle of teaching, and children's associative learning skills can be corrected and compensated for by using a variety of techniques (Woolfolk, 1995).

REFERENCES

Clark, F., Warner, M., Alley, G., Deshler, D., Shumaker, J., Vetter, A., & Nolan, R. (1981). *Visual imagery and self questioning.* Washington, DC: Bureau of Education for the Handicapped. (ERIC Document Reproduction Service No. ED 217 655)

Lathey, J. W., & Tobias, S. (1981, April). *Associative and conceptual training of retarded and normal children.* Paper presented at the annual meeting of the American Educational Research Association, Los Angeles. (ERIC Document Reproduction Service No. ED 206 139)

Pavlov, I. P. (1927). *Conditioned reflexes.* London, UK: Oxford University Press.

Sutaria, S. (1982). *Multisensory approach to teaching of reading to learning disabled students.* Paper presented at the annual meeting of the World Congress on Reading, Dublin, Ireland. (ERIC Document Reproduction Service No. ED 246 600)

Woolfolk, A. E. (1995). *Educational psychology* (6th ed.). Boston, MA: Allyn & Bacon.

GARY BERKOWITZ
Temple University

See also Conditioning; Revisualization

ASTHMA

Asthma is the most prevalent chronic health problem among children (American Lung Association, 2005). In 2002, asthma was the third leading cause of hospitalizations among children under 15 years of age. An asthmatic episode is characterized by a series of events that conclude in narrowed airways within the lungs. Initially, the lining of the lungs swells, the muscle surrounding the bronchial tubes tightens, and mucus secretion is increased in the airway. As a consequence, wheezing, coughing, shortness of breath, and tightness in the chest is evident during an asthmatic episode and results from this narrowing of airways.

There are two types of asthma: extrinsic and intrinsic (Asthma and Allergy Foundation of America, 2005). Extrinsic (or allergic) asthma symptoms are related to a specific allergen. Extrinsic asthma is the most common form of asthma and can be triggered by the inhalation of dust mites, animal dander, pollen, mold, chemicals, and so on. Intrinsic (or nonallergic) asthma symptoms are not related to a specific allergic reaction. Triggers for intrinsic asthma include anxiety, stress, vigorous exercise, cold or dry air, smoke, environmental pollution, and other irritants.

Medical treatments in the form of prescription drugs for childhood asthma are separated into five groups: inhaled bronchodilator medications, anti-inflammatory medications, systemic bronchodilator medications, systemic corticosteroid medications, and leukotriene modifiers (American Lung Association, 2005). Inhaled bronchodilators are the most effective treatment for opening of airways constricted by asthma and are commonly used by children with mild asthma. This type of medication is only used when necessary, while anti-inflammatory medication is used on a daily basis. Anti-inflammatory medications are used for children with moderate to severe asthma to control airway inflammation. Neither inhaled bronchodilators nor anti-inflammatory medications have severe side effects. Systemic bronchodilators, on the other hand, can have unpleasant side effects that are rarely life-threatening. This type of medication is available in a slow-release form, which can be especially helpful for nocturnal asthmatics. Systemic corticosteroid medication is prescribed for children who have severe asthma attacks that are not effectively helped by the aforementioned medication groups. Systemic corticosteroids are used only for severe episodes and are not recommended for long-term use. However, because severe uncontrolled asthma is a potentially life-threatening illness, use of a corticosteroid may be the better option. Leukotriene modifiers are a new type of medication for long-term, everyday usage. They open the airways by preventing inflammation and swelling, and decreasing mucus in the lungs.

Children using medications containing corticosteroids decrease serotonin levels (Pretorius, 2005). There are researchers that argue that lower free serotonin levels in the plasma are advisable to reduce asthmatic symptoms. However, reduced serotonin levels in the brain can be linked to depressive symptoms, impulse control problems, and aggression. It is therefore plausible for a child prescribed with antidepressants, or medication for Attention-Deficit/Hyperactivity Disorder (ADHD) to display asthmatic symptoms, while, conversely, children utilizing corticosteroid medications may show depressive symptoms, behavior problems, or aggression.

Research aimed at pinpointing possible interventions to reduce asthma symptoms are commonly related to diet (Nafstad, Nystad, Magnus, & Jaakkola, 2003; Oddy, Klerk, Kendall, Mihrshahi, & Peat, 2004). Studies have shown that increasing food rich in omega-3 fatty acids (e.g., fresh or oily fish, whole grains) while decreasing intake of omega-6 fatty acids (e.g., margarines, processed food) can help with children's asthma symptoms (Oddy et al., 2004). Researchers hypothesize this phenomenon may be related to the anti-inflammatory effects of omega-3 fatty acids. In a related study research showed that fish consumption in the first year of life reduced the likelihood of asthma in children at risk for developing the disease (Nafstad et al., 2003).

Children with asthma should have an asthma-management plan on record in the administrative office (Madden, 2000). This plan is developed by the child's physician and should include such information as routine and emergency medications, symptoms of attack, emergency contact information, and whether the child should have an inhaler at all times. This point may conflict with certain schools' zero-tolerance drug policies and decrease a child's self-confidence to manage his or her chronic illness. Indoor air quality should be monitored on a regular basis to help avoid potential asthmatic reactions (DePaepe, Garrison-Kane, & Doelling, 2002). The Environmental Protection Agency (EPA) has published a guide to managing asthma in schools that includes such suggestions as controlling animal and cockroach allergens, controlling moisture and cleaning up any mold, eliminating secondhand smoke, reducing dust, developing asthma management plans, and providing school-based education (2000).

School teachers can easily be taught to recognize symptoms of respiratory distress in children with asthma (Sapien, Fullerton-Gleason, & Allen, 2004). In one study, after a 1-hour informational video, teachers were more accurate in identifying asthma symptoms. Teachers also expressed an increase in their comfort level in regard to general asthma knowledge and medication information. A greater improvement in asthma-related knowledge was related to the video intervention when compared to didactic intervention.

Approximately 20% to 25% of all school absences are accounted for by children with asthma (Sapien, Fullerton-Gleason, & Allen, 2004). The effects of absenteeism can commonly be seen in the child's academic performance. Asthmatic children may also display concentration problems, inattentiveness, problems with short-term memory, and decreased psychomotor functioning (Naudé & Pretorius, 2003).

REFERENCES

American Lung Association. (2005). *Asthma and children.* Retrieved from http://www.lungsusa.org

Asthma and Allergy Foundation of America. (2005). *Asthma overview.* From http://www.aafa.org

DePaepe, P., Garrison-Kane, L., & Doelling, J. (2002). Supporting students with health needs in schools: An overview of selected health conditions. *Focus on Exceptional Children, 35,* 1–14.

Environmental Protection Agency. (2000). *IAQ tools for schools: Managing asthma in the school environment,* EPA #402-K-00-003, 2–23.

Madden, J. (2000). Managing asthma at school. *Educational Leadership, 57*(6), 50–52.

Nafstad, P., Nystad, W., Magnus, P., & Jaakkola, J. (2003). Asthma and allergic rhinitis at 4 years of age in relation to fish consumption. *Journal of Asthma, 40*(4), 343–348.

Naudé, H., & Pretorius, E. (2003). Investigating the effects of asthma medication on the cognitive and psychosocial functioning of primary school children with asthma. *Early Child Development and Care, 173*(6), 699–709.

Oddy, W. H., Klerk, N. H., Kendall, G. E., Mihrshahi, S., & Peat, J. K. (2004). Ratio of omega-6 to omega-3 fatty acids and childhood asthma. *Journal of Asthma, 41*(3), 319–326.

Pretorius, E. (2005). Asthma medication and the role of serotonin in the development of cognitive and psychological difficulties. *Early Child Development and Care, 175*(2), 139–151.

Sapien, R. E., Fullerton-Gleason, L., & Allen, N. (2004). Teaching school teachers to recognize respiratory distress in asthmatic children. *Journal of Asthma, 41,* 739–743.

MIRANDA KUCERA
University of Colorado at Colorado Springs

See also Chronic Illness

ASTIGMATISM

Astigmatism is a refractive error that causes reduced visual acuity and a lack of sharply focused, clear vision. In astigmatism, the curve of the cornea is irregular. Because of this irregularity, some light rays may come to focus in front of the retina, some on the retina, and some at the theoretical point behind it. The result is distorted or blurred vision and headache or eye fatigue after intensive close work.

Astigmatism does not seem to be clearly related to difficulties in learning to read. However, astigmatism can be a component of amblyopia (lazy eye) which does have a serious effect on reading and near work in general (NEI, 2005).

The special educator should be aware of the symptoms of astigmatism (Rouse & Ryan, 1984): headaches; discomfort in tasks that demand visual interpretation; problems seeing far as well as near; red eyes; distortion in size, shape, or inclination of objects; frowning and squinting at desk tasks; and nausea in younger or lower-functioning students. Astigmatism is generally correctable with eyeglasses or contact lenses, which should be worn full-time by affected students. These students may be helped in the classroom by being moved closer to the front of the room and by a reduction in the amount of time spent on near tasks.

REFERENCES

NEI. (2005). *National Eye Institute: Childhood's most common eye disorder.* Retrieved from http://www.nei.nih.gov/news/press releases/041105.asp

Rouse, M. W., & Ryan, J. B. (1984). Teacher's guide to vision problems. *Reading Teacher, 38*(3), 306–317.

ANNE M. BAUER
University of Cincinnati

See also **Visual Acuity; Vision Training**

ASTROCYTOMAS

Astrocytomas are neoplasms of the stellate astrocytic neuroglia. Low-grade astrocytomas have a favorable prognosis in the pediatric age group. Slow-growing tumors, pediatric astrocytomas are far more benign than are those in adults. In children, astrocytomas usually occur in the posterior fossa (Brett & Harding, 1997).

The most widely used system for grading astrocytomas is the World Health Organization's four-tiered grading system. Grade I includes astrocytomas with an excellent prognosis following surgical excision, such as juvenile pilocytic astrocytomas of the cerebellum, the most common tumor of childhood (Sagar & Israel, 1998). Grade IV astrocytomas include glioblastoma multiforme, with the four features of endothelial proliferation, nuclear and cytoplasmic atypia, mitosis, and necrosis. Grade II tumors have two of the four features, whereas Grade III tumors are anaplastic, with three of the four features (Hanieh, 2000; Sagar & Israel, 1998). Unlike in adults, pediatric brain tumors are mostly infratentorial, representing 59% of all childhood neoplasms (Hanieh, 2000). The majority of cerebellar astrocytomas are histologically benign (B. Cohen & Garvin, 1996).

The histologically benign juvenile pilocytic astrocytoma of the cerebellum is the most common childhood brain tumor. Typically, this low-grade astrocytoma is well demarcated and is composed of compact, fibrillated cells alternating with looser, spongy areas (B. Cohen & Garvin, 1996; Sagar & Israel, 1998). Approximately 80% of cerebellar astrocytomas are cystic (M. Cohen & Duffner, 1999). The cyst contains straw-colored, proteinaceous fluid and has a mural nodule, the active portion of the tumor. Computerized tomography (CT) and magnetic resonance imaging (MRI) are equally sensitive in the diagnosis of cerebellar astrocytomas (B. Cohen & Garvin, 1996).

Astrocytomas affect males and females equally (Brett & Harding, 1997). They can occur at any age, with a peak incidence between ages 10 and 14 for both low- and high-grade astrocytomas, and a peak incidence between ages 5 and 9 for cerebellar astrocytomas (M. Cohen & Duffner, 1999). There is a lack of clear data regarding the link between ethnicity and incidence of low-grade astrocytomas, although malignant central nervous system (CNS) tumors are slightly more common in American Whites than in Blacks (Benardete & Jallo, 2000). Familial and genetic syndromes have been identified as most important risk factors for astrocytomas. These include the autosomal dominant conditions neurofibromatosis Types 1 and 2, tuberous sclerosis, and epidermal nevus syndrome (B. Cohen & Garvin, 1996; M. Cohen & Duffner, 1999). Environmental factors are believed to increase the risk of developing CNS tumors, including exposure to aromatic hydrocarbons, N-nitroso compounds, triazines, systemic hydrazines, and ionizing radiation (Benardete & Jallo, 2000; B. Cohen & Garvin, 1996; M. Cohen & Duffner, 1999).

Characteristics

1. There is no typical presentation of a child with an astrocytic CNS tumor. Signs and symptoms vary greatly, depending mostly on the location of the tumor and on the presence or absence of increased intracranial pressure (B. Cohen & Garvin, 1996).

2. The child is brought to the pediatrician most often due to headache. Other signs and symptoms include seizures, vomiting, weakness, dysmetria, gait disturbance, endocrinological dysfunction, decreased visual acuity, papilledema, nystagmus, abducens (sixth cranial nerve) palsy, behavioral abnormalities, confusion, memory loss, emotional lability, and declining school performance (Brett & Harding, 1997; B. Cohen & Garvin, 1996; M. Cohen & Duffner, 1999).

Diagnosis of a mass lesion is confirmed by MRI, with and without gadolinium enhancement, or by high-resolution CT scans with contrast. These have replaced other forms of imaging. Arteriography provides information regarding vascularity of the tumor and helps exclude vascular malformation (M. Cohen & Duffner, 1999).

The treatment of choice is gross total surgical resection (B. Cohen & Garvin, 1996). This intervention alleviates increased intracranial pressure, relieves local compression of the tumor on functional areas, and provides a tissue diagnosis (M. Cohen & Duffner, 1999). Total surgical removal is often possible in pediatric astrocytomas, especially in the case of cystic lesions. In more solid lesions and those involving the brain stem or midbrain, excision may be dangerous or impossible (Brett & Harding, 1997). There is no universally accepted approach to treatment of optic pathway gliomas (M. Cohen & Duffner, 1999). Drainage of the cyst may relieve blockage of cerebrospinal fluid (CSF) flow and the consequences of hydrocephalus. Ventriculostomy or shunting may be required (Hanieh, 2000). As many as 30% of patients with a posterior fossa mass will require CSF diversion via shunt (M. Cohen & Duffner, 1999).

In terms of adjuvant therapy, low-grade supratentorial astrocytomas and brain stem gliomas usually do not seed the CSF; therefore, radiation can be limited to the tumor bed alone (M. Cohen & Duffner, 1999). Radiation is not indicated for low-grade cerebellar astrocytomas. For some astrocytomas, radiation has been used only after partial removal or after partial removal of a recurrence (Brett & Harding, 1997). In some cases, chemotherapy is an alternative for patients who have progressive disease after surgery or who cannot undergo resection (B. Cohen & Garvin, 1996).

Special education services may be available to children with astrocytomas by qualifying under the Other Health Impairment handicapping conditions. The 504 plan is another alternative, allowing for classroom and learning modifications. Children with astrocytomas can expect to spend many days out of the classroom. Changes in intellectual functioning and academic performance may involve decrements in executive functioning, heightened sensitivity about performance, demoralization, and lower frustration tolerance, especially in cerebellar lesions with or without radiation therapy (Karatekin, Lazereff, & Asarnow, 2000).

Prognosis is excellent following gross total surgical resection without further treatment of low-grade astrocytomas, with a 5-year survival rate of 90–95%. Up to 85% of children with aggressive but subtotal resection will survive 5 years (Brett & Harding, 1997; B. Cohen & Garvin, 1996). In high-grade astrocytomas without postsurgical irradiation, the 5-year survival is 0–3%, compared with 15–20% in those who received radiotherapy (B. Cohen & Garvin, 1996; M. Cohen & Duffner, 1999).

REFERENCES

Benardete, E., & Jallo, G. (2000, July 10). Low-grade astrocytoma. In R. Kuljis, F. Talavera, J. Kattah, M. Baker, & N. Lorenzo (Eds.), *Medicine Journal* [Online]. Retrieved from http://emedicine.medscape.com/

Brett, E., & Harding, B. (1997). Intracranial and spinal cord tumours. In E. M. Brett (Ed.), *Paediatric neurology* (3rd ed., pp. 537–553). New York, NY: Churchill Livingstone.

Cohen, B., & Garvin, J. (1996). Tumors of the central nervous system. In A. M. Rudolph, J. E. Hoffman, & C. D. Rudolph (Eds.), *Rudolph's pediatrics* (20th ed., pp. 1900–1920). Stamford, CT: Appleton & Lange.

Cohen, M., & Duffner, P. (1999). Tumors of the brain and spinal cord including leukemic involvement. In K. F. Swaiman & S. Ashwal (Eds.), *Pediatric neurology: Principles and practice* (3rd ed., pp. 1049–1098). St. Louis, MO: Mosby.

Hanieh, A. (2000, November). Neoplasm: Pediatric brain tumors. Retrieved from http://www.health.adelaide.edu.au

Karatekin, C., Lazareff, J., & Asarnow, R. (2000). Relevance of the cerebellar hemispheres for executive functions. *Pediatric Neurology, 22*(2), 106–112.

Sagar, S., & Israel M. (1998). Tumors of the nervous system. In A. S. Fauci, J. B. Martin, E. Braunwald, D. L. Kasper, K. J. Isselbacher, S. L. Hauser, J. D. Wilson, & D. L. Longo (Eds.), *Harrison's principles of internal medicine* (14th ed., pp. 2398–2409). New York, NY: McGraw-Hill.

GRETA N. WILKENING
University of Colorado Health Sciences Center
The Children's Hospital

LAURIE L. FERGUSON
The Wright Institute
The Children's Hospital

ASYMMETRICAL TONIC NECK REFLEX

Asymmetric tonic neck reflex (ATNR) is one of a group of postural central nervous system reflexes that in the normal child is inhibited and incorporated into more sophisticated motor skills. The ATNR can be demonstrated easily in normal infants to about 40 weeks by placing the child on the back and turning the head to the left or right. As the face is turned to the left, the left arm extends and the right arm flexes, bringing the right hand flexed to the skull side of the head simultaneous with flexion of the leg on that and the opposite side. In the normal child with no pathology, this reflex is gradually inhibited; thus, children of 24 to 36 months can reach for toys in front of them, look to the side and still bring a cracker or spoon to the mouth when the head is in midposition, and cross the midline. Later on, the child can sustain weight on the arms and knees, and rotation of the head will not result in collapse or support on the skull side arm.

The child who has central nervous system damage above the level of the midbrain (usually considered to be in the basal ganglia, cerebral cortex, or both) will demonstrate a persistent ATNR well beyond the age of 1 year, with accompanying profound damage into adult life. The child with severe ATNR finds self-feeding impossible. Persistence of ATNR can interfere with sitting and standing balance and dressing and writing, and make voluntary motion difficult or impossible.

Some help can be provided to children with delayed inhibition of ATNR by positioning and adaptive motor responses in physical and occupational therapy. Proper classroom seating can help moderately to severely involved children learn to diminish uninhibited reflexive responses when they are relaxed and listening. Excitement, anxiety, and stress may override the child's ability to inhibit the reflexive movement, making controlled, purposeful movement difficult or impossible for the more severely involved young adult with persistent uninhibited ATNR.

RACHEL J. STEVENSON
Bedford, Ohio

See also Central Nervous System

ATAQUE DE NERVIOS

Ataque de nervios is a culture-bound idiom of mental distress principally reported among Latinos from the Caribbean but recognized among many Latin American and Latin Mediterranean groups (American Psychiatric Association [APA], 1994). Ataque de nervios has a very broad range of diagnosis and is apparently neither age nor gender specific (Cardenas et al., 1998).

Ataque de nervios first appeared in medical literature in 1955. The initial case study focused on extreme emotional reactions seen in Puerto Rican army recruits. From this initial study, the disorder has been documented as appearing in many Latin groups from Colombian Indians (Calderon, Pineros, & Rosselli, 1998) to Puerto Rican populations in Houston, Texas (Cardenas et al., 1998). In the incidence of immigrant Puerto Rican populations, "self-report of Ataque de Nervios was the central variable; 16% of all respondents reported having experienced an Ataque de Nervios at some point in their lives" (Cardenas et al., 1998, p. 233). When this rate is compared to the total population of Puerto Rico, the 16% positive responsive rate approximated a 13.8% overall prevalence. Typically, ataques de nervios are expressions of self-labels of psychiatric symptoms that have been shaped by cultural factors such that many cases are reported within family groups. Respectively, this disorder apparently affects all age groups, although cases are initially reported at adolescence (Calderon et al., 1998).

Characteristics

1. Uncontrollable shouting
2. Attacks of crying
3. Trembling
4. Heat in chest rising to head
5. Verbal or physical aggression
6. Asphyxia
7. Fear of dying

According to the Diagnostic and Statistical Manual of Mental Disorders–Fourth Edition, dissociative experiences are closely related to ataque de nervios. Seizure-like or fainting episodes and suicidal gestures are prominent in some attacks but absent in some others (APA, 1994). Ataque de nervios also seems to be stress related such that ataques have been known to occur typically at funerals, accidents, or family conflicts and "will call forth family or other social supports, suggesting that [ataques] may be culturally shaped and sanctioned responses to severe stress" (Cardenas et al., 1998, p. 234).

In treatment of this syndrome, diagnosticians created the Ataque de Nervios Questionnaire–Revised (ANQ-R). The ANQ-R is a "self-related questionnaire, which starts by asking subjects directly if they have ever experienced an Ataque de Nervios" (Cardenas et al., 1998, p. 234). Following completion of the questionnaire, a structured diagnostic interview is conducted with the Anxiety Disorders Interview Schedule–Revised (ADIS-R) or the Structured Clinical Interview for DSM-III (SCID) to detect the degree and frequency of the ataques (Cardenas et al., 1998). When treating and diagnosing children, a separate questionnaire is recommended, the Ataque de Nervios Questionnaire for the Child Study. Similarly, a semistructured diagnostic interview with a psychiatrist is recommended with child cases. Typically, ataque de nervios is treated with antidepressants.

When encountering a child exhibiting characteristics of ataque de nervios, utilizing the above methods of treatment is encouraged, and performing a proper family history to examine the degree of assimilation and family environment is recommended (Cardenas et al., 1998). Special education services may be needed if the condition is determined to be chronic and interfering with academic success at school.

There are no known studies of prognostic factors associated with ataque de nervios at this time. Clinicians working with students with this syndrome will need to be alert for culturally competent assessment and intervention methods in the school setting.

REFERENCES

American Psychiatric Association. (1994). *Diagnostic and statistical manual for mental disorders* (4th ed.). Washington, DC: Author.

Calderon, C., Pineros, M., & Rosselli, D. (1998). An epidemic of collective conversion and dissociation disorder in an indigenous group of Colombia: Its relation to cultural change. *Social Science and Medicine, 11,* 1425–1428.

Cardenas, D., Carrasco, J. L., Davies, S. O., Fyer, A. J., Guarnaccia, P. J., Jusino, C. M., ... Street, L. (1998). Subtypes of ataque de nervios: the influence of coexisting psychiatric diagnosis. *Culture, Medicine, and Psychiatry, 2,* 231–244.

KIELY ANN FLETCHER
Ohio State University

ATARAX

Atarax (hydroxyzine hydrochloride) may be used for short-term symptomatic relief of anxiety and tension and as an adjunct in organic disease states in which anxiety is manifested. It also may be used as a sedative; the most common manifestation of overdosage is extreme sedation. Other uses include treatment of pruritis owed to allergic conditions such as chronic urticaria and dermatoses. Although not a cortical depressant, its action may be due to suppression of activity in certain key regions of the subcortical area of the central nervous system with the effect of relaxing skeletal muscles (Konopasek, 2004). Adverse reactions may include dryness of mouth and drowsiness, with the possibility of tremor, involuntary motor activity, and convulsions reported in cases where higher than recommended doses have been used.

A brand name of Roeris Pharmaceuticals, it is available in tablets of 10, 25, 50, and 100 milligrams, and as a syrup. The recommended dosage for children under 6 years of age is 50 mg daily in divided doses, and for children over 6 years of age 50 to 100 mg daily in divided doses. When used as a sedative, dosage is recommended to be 0.6 mg/kg (milligram per kilogram of body weight) at all childhood ages, and 50 to 100 mg for adults.

REFERENCE

Konopasek, D. E. (2004). *Medication fact sheets.* Longmont, CO: Sopris West.

LAWRENCE C. HARTLAGE
Evans, Georgia

See also Antihistamines; Benadryl

ATAXIA

Ataxia is a type of cerebral palsy caused by the loss of cerebellar control. It is characterized by an unbalanced gait. An ataxic gait is often referred to as a drunken gait, as it resembles the walk of someone who is intoxicated.

According to Batshaw and Perret (1981), "The cerebellum coordinates the action of the voluntary muscles and times their contractions so that movements are performed smoothly and accurately" (p. 163). That is, the cerebellum senses where the limb is in space (based on input to the cerebellum), estimates where the target is, integrates the information, and then carries out the infinitesimal corrections necessary to compensate for inaccuracies in motor output, thereby maintaining fluid movement.

A child whose primary diagnosis is ataxia has poor righting and equilibrium reactions, and a staggering, lurching, irregular, and broad-based gait (Brown, 1973). According to Connor, Williamson, and Siepp (1978), the child has difficulty sustaining posture, as well as shifting posture in a coordinated manner. He or she often stumbles and falls. This postural instability may make the child overly cautious. The child may stiffen his or her trunk abnormally in order to increase stability. When walking, the child may visually fix on an object in the environment in an effort to maintain postural control. According to Walsch (1963), when an older child attempts purposeful reaching, he or she often overshoots the mark because of the presence of a distal, wavering tremor. Nystagmus is often present. The causes of ataxia are many. Extensive pediatric neurology texts such as Swaiman and Ashwal (2006) note ataxia in many common and rare disorders and diseases.

It is important that physical therapy begin as early as possible. According to Connor et al. (1978), early intervention should concentrate on the development of proximal control and stability. Repetition and reinforcement of movement is necessary so that responses become reliable. Activities that increase tremors or stiffening must be avoided. However, because children with ataxia demonstrate variations in their movement behavior, individual program planning is necessary.

REFERENCES

Batshaw, M. L., & Perret, Y. M. (1981). *Children with handicaps: A medical primer.* Baltimore, MD: Brookes.

Bobath, B., & Bobath, K. (1976). *Motor development in the different types of cerebral palsy.* London, UK: Heinemann Medical.

Brown, J. E. (1973). Disease of the cerebellum. In A. B. Baker & L. H. Baker (Eds.), *Clinical neurology, Vol. II.* New York, NY: Harper & Row.

Connor, F. P., Williamson, G. G., & Siepp, J. M. (1978). *Program guide for infants and toddlers with neuromotor and other developmental disabilities.* New York, NY: Teachers College Press.

Swaiman, K. F., & Right, F. S. (Eds.). (1982). *The practice of pediatric neurology* (2nd ed.). St. Louis, MO: Mosby.

Swaiman, K. F., & Ashwal, S. (2006). *Pediatric neurology* (4th ed.). St. Louis, MO: Mosby.

Walsch, G. (1963). *Cerebellum, posture, and cerebral palsy* (Clinics in Developmental Medicine, No. 8). London, UK: Heinemann Medical Books.

CAROLE REITER GOTHELF
Hunter College, City University of New York

See also Cerebral Palsy; Cerebellar Disorders

ATAXIA, FRIEDREICH

Friedreich ataxia is one of a set of inherited diseases resulting in degeneration of the spine and cerebellum. Friedreich ataxia is the most common of the hereditary ataxias (Evidente, Gwinn-Hardy, Caviness, & Gilman, 2000), with an estimated incidence of 1 in 20,000 and a prevalence of 1 in 50,000 people (Evidente et al., 2000). It is inherited in an autosomal recessive pattern, and the carrier rate, based on molecular data, is estimated at 1:60–1:90. The incidence of the disease in Asians and in those of African descent is low (Delatycki, Williamson, & Forrest, 2000). It affects males and females equally (Zoghbi & Swaiman, 1999).

Characteristics

1. Clinical manifestations are usually evident by late childhood. Mean age of onset is 10.52 years (Delatycki et al., 2000), with progression to loss of ambulation occurring at a mean age of 25 years.

2. The initial manifestation of the disease is most often progressive difficulty with gait, including widening, wavering, slowing, and gait disorganization.

3. Deep tendon reflexes in legs are absent.

4. There is progressive dysarthria (decreased pace, slurring, and rapid, uncontrolled changes in volume of speech) and a reduction in or loss of vibratory sense and proprioception.

5. Scoliosis and evidence of cardiomyopathy are common.

6. Bladder dysfunction may occur.

7. Diabetes mellitus is associated with Friedreich ataxia.

8. Higher cortical functions are generally intact, although auditory dysfunction is common, and limited eye movements, hand deformities, slow processing speed, and dysarthria progressing to ineffective speech may make school performance problematic.

9. Death occurs after progression, with an average age of death, most often related to cardiomyopathy, of 37.5 ± 14.4 years.

10. There is clinical variability in the presentation of the disease, even within sibships (Delatycki et al., 2000; Pandolfo, 1999; Zorghbi & Swaiman, 1999).

The symptoms are secondary to cellular damage and death, thought to be caused by mitochondrial iron accumulation, although the mechanism of damage continues to be debated (Evidente et al., 2000). Cellular death occurs primarily in the dorsal root ganglia, posterior columns of the spinal cord, corticospinal tracts, and the heart. There is mild cellular loss in the cerebellum (Delatycki et al., 2000). The disease is due to a genetic alteration that maps to Chromosome 9q13. In most cases the abnormality associated with Friedreich ataxia is a large expansion of a normal guanine-adenine-adenine (GAA) repeat. There is variability in the size of the expansion, with larger expansions associated with earlier onset and more severe pathology. The abnormality is unstable, and transmission from parent to child is accompanied by change in the size of the genetic abnormality. Maternal transmission may result in either a larger or smaller area of abnormality, whereas the GAA repeat size is generally diminished in paternal transmission (Delatycki et al., 2000). The abnormality causes a reduction in frataxin, a mitochondrial protein (Pandolfo, 1999).

There is currently no treatment for Friedreich ataxia, although identification of and cloning of the gene have offered new hope (Delatycki et al., 2000). The role of antioxidant therapy is being evaluated, and the results are said to be promising. Scientists have found that residual frataxin is present in all patients with Friedreich ataxia. This suggests that gene therapy may play a role in management of Friedreich ataxia, as the therapy could be delivered without the complications of an adverse immunologic response (Delatycki et al., 2000).

Few recent studies have looked at cognitive functioning in patients with Friedreich ataxia, and these have been conducted with adult populations. Patients with Friedreich ataxia appear to have a disturbance in the speed and efficiency of information processing, and this is independent of motor abnormalities. There is no consistent evidence of global cognitive impairment (Botez-Marquard & Boetz, 1993; Hart, Kwentus, Leshner, & Frazier, 1985).

Educational services to children with Friedreich ataxia should recognize the progressive nature of the disease, the sensory abnormalities that may develop, and the need for assistive technology. These children will require help with motor performance in all domains. They should be provided with alternative modes of response, such as dictation. Simple accommodations for the mildly affected, such as additional sets of books to decrease the need to carry, which makes ambulation yet more difficult, can help in the early stages of the disease. Additional time between classes is imperative. Allowances for bathroom breaks should be included in the individual education plan, or other educational plan. Teachers should be alerted to the need for extra processing time.

REFERENCES

Botez-Marquard, T., & Botez, M. I. (1993). Cognitive behavior in hereditodegenerative ataxias. *European Neurology, 33*(5), 351–357.

Delatycki, M. B., Williamson, R., & Forrest, S. M. (2000). Friedreich ataxia: An overview. *Journal of Medical Genetics, 37*, 1–8.

Evidente, V. G., Gwinn-Hardy, K. A., Caviness, J. N., & Gilman, S. (2000). Hereditary ataxias. *Mayo Clinic Proceedings, 75*, 473–490.

Hart, R. P., Kwentus, J. A., Leshner, R. T., & Frazier, R. (1985). Information processing speed in Friedreich's ataxia. *Annals of Neurology, 17*, 612–614.

Pandolfo, M. (1999). Molecular pathogenesis of Friedreich ataxia. *Archives of Neurology, 56*, 1201–1208.

Zoghbi, H. Y., & Swaiman, K. F. (1999). Spinocerebellar degeneration. In K. F. Swaimann & S. Ashwal (Eds.), *Pediatric neurology: Principles and practice* (3rd ed.). St. Louis, MO: Mosby.

GRETA N. WILKENING
*University of Colorado Health Sciences Center
The Children's Hospital*

ATAXIA, HEREDITARY

Hereditary ataxia is a designation for inherited disorders that involve incoordination of voluntary muscle movements as the result of spinocerebellar degeneration. There are several forms of hereditary ataxia, which are delineated according to how they are manifested genetically. Autosomal recessive forms of hereditary ataxia are expressed by means of a mutated recessive gene. For the disease to be expressed, children must inherit two affected genes, one from each parent (Evidente, Gwinn-Hardy, Caviness, Gilman, 2000). There are several identified autosomal recessive ataxias with heterogeneous etiologies and clinical features; however, the most common ataxia is

Friedreich ataxia. Friedreich ataxia has a prevalence of 1 in 50,000 persons. Onset of the disorder is usually before 20 years of age, and progression is continuous (Evidente et al., 2000). Late onset of Freidreich ataxia (this includes individuals older than 20 to 25 years) is characterized by a more benign course and lower incidence of skeletal deformities (Evidente et al., 2000).

Characteristics

Note: Symptoms for these disorders vary widely according to each specific disorder. The following are some common characteristics.

1. Incoordination of speech muscles and ataxia of all four limbs and of gait
2. Impaired eye movements
3. Sensory loss
4. Dementia
5. Swallowing difficulties
6. Motor neuron degeneration manifested as lack of coordination or muscle control
7. Skeletal abnormalities

Symptoms of Freidreich ataxia include gait and limb ataxia, dysarthria, absent muscle stretch reflexes in lower limbs, sensory loss, and skeletal abnormalities (Evidente et al., 2000). Diabetes and cardiac disease are also fairly common in persons with this disorder. Freidreich ataxia is thought to be the result of the expansion of a DNA trinucleotide repeat (guanine-adenine-adenine) that disrupts the normal assembly of amino acids into proteins (Evidente et al., 2000). This disruption eventually leads to cellular degeneration.

The autosomal dominant cerebellar ataxias (ADCAs) are the result of a mutated dominant gene. These disorders have been labeled as spinocerebellar ataxias (SCAs) and have been assigned numbers according to their chromosomal localization (Woods, 1999).

The incidence of ADCAs is 5 in 100,000 persons. Onset of these disorders occurs in childhood in only 10% of the cases, and progression is continuous. However, childhood onset is associated with a more rapid course. Similar to the autosomal recessive ataxias, genetic testing is required in order to diagnose ADCAs (Woods, 1999). Characteristics of the ADCAs differ according to genetic localization and are heterogeneous between and within affected families (Woods, 1999). In general, however, symptoms indicate involvement of peripheral nerves, spinal cord cell groups and tracts, cranial nerve nuclei, and basal ganglia (Evidente et al., 2000). These symptoms may include limb and gait ataxia, impaired eye movements, extrapyramidal tract and motor neuron degeneration, dementia, sphincter disturbances, and swallowing difficulties (Evidente et al., 2000; Woods, 1999). The ADCAs are thought to be caused by expansion of the DNA trinucleotide repeat (cytosine-adenine-guanine) that codes for polyglutamine (Woods, 1999).

The third type of hereditary ataxia is referred to as X-linked SCAs. These disorders are less common and have a heterogeneous presentation. Currently, they are not well characterized, and there is little genetic or molecular data (Evidente et al., 2000).

Presently, there is no cure for the hereditary ataxias and no effective treatments to slow the progression of the disease (Woods, 1999). Treatment may be focused on management of the symptoms and concomitant disorders such as diabetes and cardiac disease (Evidente et al., 2000). Physical therapy may prolong the use of the arms and legs.

Although inherited ataxias lead to tremendous loss of physical abilities, there is usually no impairment of cognitive functioning (Stevenson, 1987). For children enrolled in schools, special education programs should focus efforts on modifying the environment to accommodate the child's physical and emotional needs. This may involve providing close supervision, special seating arrangements, and devices such as a wheelchair or railings to increase safety for the child. Occupational, physical, and speech therapists may need to provide extensive support for the child, teachers, and family to maintain optimal functioning as long as possible. As children grow they gain insight into the progressive nature of their disease and may become vulnerable to significant depression and anxiety. Psychological counseling can be offered within the educational setting as a means of addressing these issues (Stevenson, 1987). Often, family therapy may also be warranted.

Future research will likely focus on determining the genetic and molecular substrates of these disorders as a means of developing methods of diagnosis, prevention, and treatment (Evidente et al., 2000).

REFERENCES

Evidente, V. G. H., Gwinn-Hardy, K. A., Caviness, J. N., & Gilman, S. (2000). Hereditary ataxias. *Mayo Clinic Proceedings, 75*(5), 475–490.

Stevenson, R. J. (1987). Cerebellar disorders. In C. Reynolds & L. Mann (Eds.), *Encyclopedia of special education: Reference for the education of the handicapped and other exceptional children and adults* (Vol. 1). New York, NY: Wiley.

Woods, B. T. (1999). The autosomal dominant spinocerebellar ataxias: Clinicopathologic findings and genetic mechanisms. In A. Joseph & R. Young (Eds.), *Movement disorders in neurology and neuropsychiatry* (2nd ed.). Boston, MA: Blackwell Science.

WILLIAM M. ACREE
THERESA KELLY
University of Northern Colorado

ATAXIA, MARIE'S

Ataxia is a disorder that involves incoordination of voluntary muscle movements. Marie's ataxia is a designation for hereditary conditions expressed through dominant genes and characterized by spinocerebellar degeneration. These conditions normally occur in adulthood, although the time of onset varies widely. The clinical features of Marie's ataxia are heterogeneous within and between families, so diagnosis and classification are difficult (Harding, 1982).

Marie's ataxia is thought to be a very rare condition, but there is little agreement as to its prevalence. Schoenberg (1978) estimated the prevalence of all inherited ataxias to be less than 6 cases per 100,000 people. The etiology of Marie's ataxia is thought to involve the expansion of an exonic DNA trinucleotide repeat (cytosine-adenine-guanine) that codes for polyglutamine (Woods, 1999).

Characteristics

1. Incoordination of speech muscles and ataxia of all four limbs and of gait
2. Most individuals becoming nonambulatory within 15 years of onset
3. Increased or decreased tendon reflexes
4. Impaired eye movements
5. Sphincter disturbances
6. Swallowing difficulties
7. Dementia
8. Optic atrophy

The presence of Marie's ataxia can be determined through genetic studies. Genetic counseling may allow people to prepare for the symptoms of the disease. However, at this point there is no effective treatment to reverse or halt its progression (Woods, 1999).

Early onset of Marie's ataxia can necessitate numerous environmental and educational modifications. This disorder may manifest itself as a physical handicap or as a health impairment. Special education programs need to modify the environment to accommodate the child's physical needs. This may include special seating arrangements, safety devices such as railings, and increased supervision. Occupational, physical, and speech therapists may provide support for the child, teachers, and family to maintain optimal functioning as long as possible. In addition, as children gain insight into the progressive nature of their disease, they become more vulnerable to significant anxiety and depression. Psychological counseling within the educational setting can be offered as a means of addressing these issues (Stephenson, 1987). Often, family therapy may also be warranted.

Marie's ataxia has a poor prognosis, as it is a progressive degenerative disease. With effective management of symptoms there may be 10 to 20 years of productivity following onset (Stephenson, 1987). Future research will likely focus on etiology, classification, and treatment.

REFERENCES

Harding, A. E. (1982). The clinical features and classification of the late onset autosomal dominant cerebellar ataxias: A study of 11 families, including descendants of "The Drew Family of Walworth." *Brain, 105,* 1–28.

Schoenberg, B. S. (1978). Epidemiology of the inherited ataxias. *Advances in Neurology, 21,* 15–30.

Stephenson, R. J. (1987). Cerebellar disorders. In C. Reynolds & L. Mann (Eds.), *Encyclopedia of special education: A reference for the education of the handicapped and other exceptional children and adults* (Vol. 1). New York, NY: Wiley.

Woods, B. T. (1999). The autosomal dominant spinocerebellar ataxias: Clinicopathologic findings and genetic mechanisms. In A. Joseph & R. Young (Eds.), *Movement disorders in neurology and neuropsychiatry* (2nd ed.). Boston, MA: Blackwell Science.

WILLIAM M. ACREE
THERESA KELLY
University of Northern Colorado

ATAXIA-TELANGIECTASIA (LOUIS-BAR-SYNDROME)

Ataxia-telangiectasia (A-T) is an autosomal recessive neurodegenerative genetic disorder characterized by progressive ataxia due to cerebellar degeneration, oculocutaneous telangiectasia, immunodeficiency with recurrent sinopulmonary infections, significant sensitivity to ionizing radiation, and increased risk of cancers, especially lymphoma and leukemia. Incidence is estimated as 1 in 40,000 births, although this may be an underestimate due to early deaths prior to diagnosis. There are between 500 and 600 cases of A-T in the United States. Occurrence has shown no bias on racial, gender, geographic, or other lines. It is estimated that 1% of the general population is a carrier for one of the mutated A-T genes, and carrier status itself is associated with lower than normal tolerance for radiation and an increased risk of cancer for both genders. For females, it is estimated that A-T carriers comprise approximately 6–9% of all breast cancer cases, and carrier status is associated with a 3- to 5-times greater risk of developing breast cancer (Lavin, 1998). Thus, this disorder carries health implications for both homozygote patients as well as heterozygote parent carriers. Well siblings have a two-thirds chance for being carriers.

Patients may appear normal at birth, and even though there may be early signs of cerebellar ataxia at infancy (e.g., abnormal swaying of the head and trunk) and later in toddlerhood (e.g., wobbly gait, clumsiness), the diagnosis is typically not established until ages 4 to 6. The appearance of telangiectasia may occur early but usually appears around age 4 or 5. A common early misdiagnosis because of the ataxia is cerebral palsy, and other children are often born into the family before an A-T diagnosis is established and genetic counseling is provided for the parents.

Earlier detection may occur with the use of routine serum alpha-fetoprotein testing in children with persistent ataxia, where elevated levels often distinguish A-T from other ataxia and immunodeficiency syndromes (Cabana, Crawford, Winkelstein, Christensen, & Lederman, 1998). Less established, but offering possible earlier diagnostic assistance, is the use of magnetic resonance imaging to pick up leukodystrophic changes in the brain that may predate the appearance of many clinical symptoms (Chung, Bodensteiner, Noorani, & Schochet, 1994).

Characteristics

1. Progressive cerebellar ataxia, with early signs such as head swaying, trunk instability, and clumsiness; by age 4 to 6 more apparent balance, coordination, and gait difficulties; use of a wheelchair typically by age 10

2. Related ocular ataxia, dysarthria, dysphagia, dystonia, choreoathetosis, and tremor

3. Reddish lesions on skin, mucosa, and conjunctivas (oculocutaneous telangiectasia)

4. Sensitivity to ionizing radiation

5. Immunodeficiencies, associated with recurrent sinopulmonary infections

6. Increased risk for cancers of all types, but especially lymphoma and leukemia

7. Normal range intelligence

8. A characteristic "sweet breath" in some cases

9. Abbreviated life expectancies, with most succumbing to cancer or respiratory illness before age 20

10. Elevated radiosensitivity and increased risk of cancers, including breast cancer, in single A-T gene carriers

---

A-T is not associated with intellectual disability. One study did report lower verbal IQ scores in A-T children (although this may be due to the indirect effects on learning from the symptoms of the disorder rather than direct effects limiting innate cognition) as well as reduced ability for judging duration of time intervals in A-T children (Mostofsky, Kunze, Cutting, Lederman, & Denckla, 2000). Cerebellar dysfunction has previously been linked to duration judgment deficits, and salient cognitive effects in A-T children may be identified as more is learned about the cerebellum's general role in cognition.

Nevertheless, the intelligence range of children with A-T is commensurate with that of the general population; thus, most A-T children should be appropriate for regular education classes, provided that appropriate accommodations related to their physical limitations and needs are made available. These would typically include speech, occupational, and physical therapies, as well as the use of classroom aids for handwriting, note taking, and even reading as progressive ocular apraxia can make reading functionally inadequate.

Although there is some variation in presentation of the disorder, progression of the ataxia is inexorable and prognosis is poor, typically leading to use of a walker by age 8, loss of writing ability by 8, wheelchair use by age 10, and loss of functional reading ability due to difficulties coordinating eye focus (e.g., fixation nystagmus). Death due to cancer or respiratory failure occurs frequently by age 20, although some patients may live into their 30s and very rarely into their 40s. Although there is no cure or treatment yet to correct the disorder, interventions have been directed toward the symptoms. These include neurorehabilitative oriented physical, occupational, and speech-swallowing therapies. Some symptoms can be managed to some degree pharmacologically (e.g., drooling with anticholinergics, basal ganglia–related movement disorders with dopamine agonists or antagonists as appropriate, weakness or fatigue with pyridostigmine; A-T Children's Project, 2000). Some benefits from nutritional supplements and diet changes for reducing symptoms have been reported.

A-T is a rare disorder. Research includes gene therapy and stem cell transplantation, as well as areas of nutrition and diet. For example, supplementation with myoinositol has shown some positive initial effects in improved coordination in some patients. B vitamins, fatty acids, antioxidants and coenzyme Q10 are also being investigated, as is an alcohol-avoidance diet, which may reduce the ataxic symptoms in some patients through avoidance of the ethanol and methanol in many foods and beverages (National Organization to Treat A-T, 2000).

REFERENCES

A-T Children's Project. (2000, November 1). *Managing the neurological symptoms of A-T with medications.* Retrieved from http://www.communityatcp.org/

Cabana, M., Crawford, T., Winkelstein, J., Christensen, J., & Lederman, H. (1998). Consequences of the delayed diagnosis of ataxia-telangiectasia. *Pediatrics, 102,* 98–100.

Chung, E., Bodensteiner, J., Noorani, P., & Schochet, S. (1994). Cerebral white-matter changes suggesting leukodystrophy in ataxia telangiectasia. *Journal of Child Neurology, 9*(1), 31–35.

Lavin, M. (1998, August 22). Role of the ataxia-telangiectasia gene (ATM) in breast cancer. *British Medical Journal, 317,* 486–487.

Mostofsky, S., Kunze, J., Cutting, L., Lederman, H., & Denckla, M. (2000). Judgment of duration in individuals with ataxia-telangiectasia. *Developmental Neuropsychology, 17*(1), 63–74.

National Organization to Treat A-T. (2000, November 1). *The nutritional approach.* Retrieved from http://www.treat-at.org/nutrition.aadietsupplement.html

VICKY Y. SPRADLING
Austin State Hospital

ATHETOSIS

Athetosis is a central nervous system disorder characterized by slow, writhing movements, most notable in the extremities. These involuntary muscle movements have been described also as wormlike or snakelike. The actual movements consist of alternating flexion–extension and supination–pronation of the limbs, and are usually associated with increased, though variable, muscle tone (Chow, Durard, Feldman, & Mills, 1979).

Athetosis is most commonly a form of cerebral palsy (CP) in childhood accounting for approximately 15% to 30% of children with that diagnosis; however, the overall incidence rate is declining, probably because of improved neonatal intensive care (Batshaw & Perret, 1981). The condition, also known as choreo-athetoid CP, often occurs in conjunction with other forms of CP, especially spasticity. As a form of cerebral palsy, athetosis is one of a group of nonprogressive neuromotor disorders caused by earlier brain damage. Unlike other common forms of CP, the athetoid type presents a problem of controlling movement and posture rather than a difficulty in initiating voluntary movement. The uncontrolled, purposeless, involuntary movements associated with athetosis are not evidenced during sleep. Although the precise nature of the central nervous system insult is often indeterminable, among known causes may be various prenatal factors (e.g., anoxia, blood group incompatibilities, excessive radiation dosage during gestation, physical injuries, various maternal infections); perinatal factors (e.g., prematurity, head trauma, asphyxia, kernicterus); and postnatal factors (e.g., head trauma, hemorrhage, infections of the brain or cranial linings). In the United States, one to two children per thousand may be affected by CP, including athetosis or mixed cerebral palsy with athetosis. It is believed that in the more pure athetoid type of CP, the site of lesion is generally in the basal ganglia or extrapyramidal track (Kandel, Schwartz, & Jessell, 1991; Vaughan, McKay, & Behrman, 1979).

Secondary problems important to the special educator frequently accompany athetosis. Early difficulties may be observed in sucking, feeding, chewing, and swallowing. Special techniques to deal with these problems may come from speech/language pathologists, occupational therapists, physical therapists, or physicians. Speech articulation is often impaired and drooling may be present. In addition, hearing loss, epilepsy, and intellectual disability may exist simultaneously. However, careful assessment of cognitive functioning is essential because both speech and motor skills are affected.

Little, if any, in the way of curative action is successful with cerebral palsy. Early intervention, special education, and vocational rehabilitation will be important, but the exact nature of the treatment approach will depend largely on the presence, nature, and degree of concomitant disorders. As many as 70% of children with the athetoid type of CP may function in the intellectually disabled range, so educational and habilitative services must take into account the child's developmental limitations. Because facial muscles are involved in athetosis, vision disorders, especially of the eye-muscle imbalance type, may be present in more than 40% of the affected group (Black, 1980). Hearing loss is also common, though less so than vision problems, necessitating early and continuous audiometric evaluations and the possible provision of amplification devices. Physical therapy, including bracing and splinting to help maintain balance and to control involuntary movements, may be indicated in many cases. Orthopedic surgery and neurosurgery, though sometimes helpful with other forms of CP, have not yet shown promise for children with athetosis (Kutz & Semrud-Clikeman, 2003).

REFERENCES

Batshaw, M. L., & Perret, Y. M. (1981). *Children with handicaps: A medical primer*. Baltimore, MD: Brookes.

Black, P. D. (1980). Ocular defects in children with cerebral palsy. *British Medical Journal, 281*, 487.

Chow, M. P., Durand, B. A., Feldman, M. N., & Mills, M. A. (1979). *Handbook of pediatric primary care*. New York, NY: Wiley.

Kandel, E., Schwartz, J., & Jessell, T. (1991). *Principles of neural science* (3rd ed.). New York, NY: Elsevier.

Kutz, A. S., & Semrud-Clikeman, M. (2003). Atheosis. In E. Fletcher-Janzen & C. R. Reynolds (Eds.), *Childhood*

disorders diagnostic desk reference (pp. 71–73). Hoboken, NJ: Wiley.

Vaughan, V. C., McKay, R. J., & Behrman, R. E. (1979). *Nelson textbook of pediatrics*. Philadelphia, PA: Saunders.

JOHN D. WILSON
Elwyn Institutes

See also **Central Nervous System; Cerebral Palsy**

ATRIOVENTRICULAR SEPTAL DEFECT

Atrioventricular septal defect (AVSD) is a congenital heart defect (present at birth). It is also known as cor biloculare. Additionally, there are several subdivisions depending on the size and location of the defect. Specifically, these subdivisions are atrial and septal and small ventricular septal defect, atrial septal defect primum, complete atrioventricular septal defect, incomplete atrioventricular septal defect, large atrial and ventricular defect, and transitional atrioventricular septal defect.

The heart is composed of four chambers, two atria and two ventricles. The atria are separated by a wall called the atrial septum, and the ventricles are also separated by a septum. The right atrium and right ventricle are connected by valves, as are the left atrium and ventricle. In the case of the presence of atrioventricular septal defects, the septa or valves either are not fully formed or are fully developed but are deformed. This causes the septa or valves to malfunction and blood to leak between chambers or be moved in incorrect directions within the heart. The severity of the defect ranges from mild, as in a cleft mitral valve, to severe, in which there are several deformities within both the valves and the chambers of the heart. The severity of the defect is categorized into three forms: cleft mitral valve, partial atrioventricular septal defect, and complete atrioventricular septal defect. The type of defect determines the symptoms and the type of medical care needed. However, medical care and surgery are almost always going to be needed in infancy. It is interesting to note that approximately half the cases of this defect occur in children with Down syndrome.

Depending on the type of defect, atrioventricular septal defects in infants can cause different types of irregular movement of blood within the heart. This can be as straightforward as left to right movement of blood (as opposed to vertical movement) or as complicated as movement of blood between the left ventricle and right atrium.

Infants with this defect are in danger of congestive heart failure at 4–12 weeks old because of abnormal blood flow levels. Infants whose hearts are able to function despite irregular movement of blood in the heart are at risk of pulmonary vascular obstructive disease at ages of less than 1 year. Defects must be repaired surgically, a difficult procedure because of the size, age, and lack of immunities in an infant. In some cases, surgeons may opt simply to stabilize the situation and fully correct the condition at a later date when the child is larger; however, this requires two surgeries and may also further deform the heart in the process.

Characteristics

1. Malformed septa or valves in heart
2. Inability to maintain blood flow through heart efficiently
3. Risk of congestive heart failure
4. Risk of pulmonary vascular obstructive disease

Because almost all cases of atrioventricular septal defect must be corrected in infancy (Kwiatkowska, Tomaszewski, Bielinacuteska, Potaz, & Ericinacuteski, 2000), surgical procedures are not likely to interrupt the life of a school child with this defect. However, this child may still need to be examined regularly and may not be able to participate in all activities that strain the heart or lungs. Many support, resource, and educational groups are available both locally and online, and it may be beneficial for a child with atrioventricular septal defects and his or her family to participate actively in one of these groups.

REFERENCE

Kwiatkowska, J., Tomaszewski, M., Bielinacuteska, B., Potaz, P., & Erecinacuteski, J. (2000). Atrioventricular septal defect: Clinical and diagnostic problems in children hospitalized in 1993–1998. *Medical Science Monitor*, *6*, 1148–1154.

ALLISON KATZ
Rutgers University

ATTACHMENT DISORDER

Attachment disorder derives from Bowlby's theoretical and process theory of attachment to caregivers or significant others in the course of normal development, a theory that also provides psychologists and special educators a framework for investigating atypical patterns of attachment in life (cf. Bowlby, 1982). Bowlby proposed that *attachments* (a) referred to a *pattern* of organized behavior within a relationship, not a static trait infants and children simply possessed. Attachments were not immutable and not independent of experience; (b) are framed by early experience, but are also transformed by later experience in life. This proposition is now referred to as a *dynamic systems theory of psychopathology*, based on the complex interactions experienced over life development; and (c) in early life (i.e., infancy or toddlerhood) often play a role in the developmental dynamic that produces pathology; however, this complex role depends on a surrounding context of sustaining environmental supports. Early experience influences later life outcomes, but the quality of those later life relationships also depends on the sustaining or supporting context in which those relationships are expressed (Carlson & Sroufe, 1995; Sroufe, Carlson, Levy, & Egeland, 1999).

If the developmental pathway model of attachment theory is conceptualized as a tree, then (a) there are more branches in the broad center of the large array of overall branches (i.e., owing to considerable diversity of experiences); (b) starting on any major trunk allows a large number of possible outcomes due to the complex number and diversity of subsequent branchings (i.e., due to circumstances, one can potentially and probabilistically deviate to the outward smaller branchings or continue along the main, normally developing branch); and (c) the longer the deviating offshoot branches are followed from the main branch, the more unlikely will there be a return to the main or central branch. Change or adaptations in attachments are more likely during infancy and toddlerhood, but if development continues to go awry well into adolescence, a return to a more healthy and organized form of attachment in relationships is viewed as quite difficult (Bowlby, 1973; Speltz, DeKlyen, & Greenburg, 1999; Sroufe et al., 1999). It must be kept in mind that Bowlby and his (and others') research does not support or suggest a linear pathway from early disruptions in attachment to later psychopathology; rather, (developmental) psychopathology will be the product of ongoing difficult challenges in life and the cumulative maladaptations to those challenges (Sroufe et al., 1999).

Assessment and Individual Differences in Quality of Attachment

Assessment of early dyadic relational patterns between infant and caregiver are drawn from (a) Ainsworth's Strange Situation procedure, developed from cross-cultural field research and home observations and used with most 12- to 18-month-old infants or toddlers; (b) the Attachment Q-Set; and (c) direct observations and perceptions of teacher-child relationships (Ainsworth, Blehar, Waters, & Wall, 1978; Carlson & Sroufe, 1995; Howes & Ritchie, 1999).

In the Strange Situation procedure, eight increasingly stressful analog episodes are presented: (1) caregiver and infant are introduced to an unfamiliar, sparsely furnished room containing a variety of attractive, age-appropriate toys; (2) the infant is allowed to explore with the caregiver present, seated in a chair; (3) a stranger enters, sits quietly, converses with the caregiver, then initiates interaction with the infant, taking cues from the baby; (4) the caregiver leaves; (5) the caregiver returns, and the stranger leaves unobtrusively; (6) the caregiver leaves the infant alone; (7) the stranger enters, attempts to comfort the infant if needed; and (8) the caregiver returns. The coder or observer seeks to classify behavioral organization during reunion episodes, those of proximity seeking, contact making, contact resistance, and avoidance (Ainsworth et al., 1978; Main & Solomon, 1990).

Based upon the outcome of the Strange Situation procedure, patterns of behavior are classified as either (a) *secure attachment*, where infants readily separate from caregivers and easily become absorbed in exploration. When wary of a stranger, threatened, or distressed by separation, the infant seeks contact and consolation until he or she is calm again. The infant's emotional regulation is considered to be smooth and well integrated; (b) *anxious/avoidant attachment*, which occurs when the caregiver's presence does not reduce distress or promote exploration. Such infants show little affective interaction with caregivers, show little suspicion of strangers, and are generally upset only if left alone. When the caregiver returns, such infants do not actively initiate interaction and are unresponsive to the caregiver's interactive attempts. As stress increases, so does avoidance of the caregiver. Emotional regulation for this type of infant is considered to be overly rigid; (c) *anxious/resistant attachment*, where infants show impoverished exploration and play and are wary of strangers and novel situations. They may cry even before being separated from the caregiver (i.e., are clingy), and upon reunion with the caregiver, they have tremendous difficulty settling down as if not reassured by their mother's presence or comforting. The emotional regulation of such infants is thought to come from intermittent caregiver responses to stress, producing a constant state of arousal in them. In their constant vigilant state, these infants may actually heighten their distress in order to elicit caregiver responses; and (d) *disorganized/disoriented attachment*, seen when infants and caregivers have no coherent relational strategies. There may be inconsistent or unusual behaviors such a hand-flapping, freezing, and other stereotypies that indicate seemingly undirected (disorganized) behavioral patterns to strange situations. It is hypothesized that incomprehensible or frightening caregiver behavior has interfered with the formation of coherent attachment strategies. For such infants, the caregiver serves as both a source of fear and a biologically based source of reassurance. No effective emotional regulation is thought to occur among these infants (Bowlby, 1973, 1980, 1982; Carlson & Sroufe, 1995).

The Strange Situation procedure used to arrive at these attachment classifications has been criticized for its lack of discriminant validity due to limited assessment ecology and restricted use with infant- or toddler-age children (Howes & Ritchie, 1999). The Attachment Q-Set (AQS; Waters & Deane, 1985), which has good validity with the Strange Situation procedure, is a viable alternative (Howe & Ritchie, 1999) because it can be used with a broader age range and is based on direct observations in the child's natural home environment. The AQS yields a continuous score, representing the degree of attachment security and now has subscales aimed at capturing the attachment organizations of insecure (avoidant or ambivalent or resistant) or secure (seeking comfort, proximity, and harmonious interactions). Speltz et al. (1999) also describe an observation coding system called the Preschool Attachment Assessment System (PAAS) for evaluating brief separation and reunion episodes between children and parents. The PAAS measures approach and avoidance behaviors as well as codes the content and affectivity of the child's verbal and nonverbal communication to the parent.

There is growing research support for the use of observations of teacher-child relationships in child care settings as well as gathering elementary school teacher perceptions of the teacher-child relationship. Research findings from both of these literature bases suggest that teachers can be successful in developing teacher-child relationships that are wholly different in quality from what they experience at home (Howes & Ritchie, 1999).

Bowlby's (1973, 1980, 1982) theory suggests that for individuals with impaired attachments, their stressful style of responding to others, themselves, and the environment might provide the basis for developing specific disorders. Expanding on these theoretical claims, Carlson and Sroufe (1995) explain that for individuals adopting an *avoidant/dismissing* strategy (because of insensitive or unpredictable parents), symptomatic behavior might include attempts to minimize attachment behavior and feelings. They might not only mask their own emotional expressions to avoid being hurt, but they may also view others as untrustworthy and overidealize attachment relationships to the point that when these ideals go unrealized, anger, resentment, and aggression are displayed. Conduct Disorders and antisocial personality styles are often associated with this pattern of emotional regulation and behavior (cf. Speltz et al., 1999), sometimes leading to depression because of continual failed relationships. Concerning individuals with *resistant/preoccupied* strategies of attachment, relational anxiety reduces exploration and increased attachment behavior (e.g., enmeshed, clingy relations). Such individuals have difficulty managing anxiety, manifest phobias and Conversion Disorders, and are preoccupied with personal suffering (Bowlby, 1973; Carlson & Sroufe, 1995) to the point of exaggerating their emotions and negative beliefs about themselves, which keep them confused about relationships. Bowlby (1973) further notes that a child's school refusal, psychosomatic symptoms, or phobias are often connected to family attachment patterns where the child is anxious about the availability or well-being of the parent(s). For individuals with *avoidant/dismissing* and *resistant/preoccupied* relationship strategies, death or major separations only serve to confirm their worst nightmare about the psychological availability of the attachment figure, leading to intense despair and anxiety (Bowlby, 1980). As a result, if one has a history of avoidant attachment behavior, mourning may be delayed for months or years, irritability and strain will be exhibited, and depression may occur long after the loss or separation was experienced. Resistant attachment issues may lead individuals to express intense anger or self-reproach with depression that lasts much longer than normal (Carlson & Sroufe, 1985).

Attachment disorders are best viewed as relational problems triggered as a result of dysfunctional or impaired parent-child transactions, which then become absorbed as part of the individual's unique psychological identity and functioning (Carlson & Sroufe, 1995; Sroufe et al., 1999). Considerable research has been conducted to examine the circumstances that affect or strain attachment relationships in infancy and toddlerhood as well as to investigate conditions in which maladaptive attachment patterns impact or effect psychological adjustment later in life. Such research issues related to attachment are commonly found in investigations of infant colic, infant failure to thrive, Feeding Disorders (e.g., Pica, Rumination Disorder, posttraumatic feeding problems), sleep disorders, Posttraumatic Stress Disorder, and Reactive Attachment Disorder. In addition, direct and collateral research on later psychiatric functioning has covered issues related to autism, Oppositional Defiant Disorder, Conduct Disorder, depression or anxiety, maltreatment, borderline and Dissociative Disorders, and adult pathology (cf. Carlson & Sroufe, 1995; Lyons-Ruth, Zeanah, & Benoit, 2003; Sroufe et al., 1999). As Carlson and Sroufe (1985) point out, a careful analysis of the current and longitudinal research on attachment in early care and later pathology supports a transactional multidetermined view of the development of psychopathology. What is less clear is the exact relationship between attachment and stressful life experiences, most likely due to variations in research design and methodology.

REFERENCES

Ainsworth, M. D. S., Blehar, M., Waters, E., & Wall, S. (1978). *Patterns of attachment.* Hillsdale, NJ: Erlbaum.

Bowlby, J. (1973). *Attachment and loss: Vol. 2. Separation.* New York, NY: Basic Books.

Bowlby, J. (1980). *Attachment and loss: Vol. 3. Loss.* New York, NY: Basic Books.

Bowlby, J. (1982). *Attachment and loss: Vol. 1. Attachment* (2nd ed.). New York, NY: Basic Books.

Carlson, E. A., & Sroufe, L. A. (1995). Contribution of attachment theory to developmental psychopathology. In D. Cicchetti & D. J. Cohen (Eds.), *Developmental psychopathology: Vol. 1. Theory and methods* (pp. 517–528). New York, NY: Wiley.

Howes, C., & Ritchie, S. (1999). Attachment organizations in children with difficult life circumstances. *Development and Psychopathology, 11,* 251–268.

Lyons-Ruth, K., Zeanah, C. H., & Benoit, D. (2003). Disorder and risk for disorder during infancy and toddlerhood. In E. J. Mash & R. A. Barkley (Eds.), *Child psychopathology* (2nd ed., pp. 589–631). New York, NY: Guilford Press.

Main, M., & Solomon, J. (1990). Procedures for identifying infants as disorganized/disoriented during the Ainsworth strange situation. In M. T. Greenburg, D. Cicchetti, & E. M. Cummings (Eds.), *Attachment in the preschool years* (pp. 121–160). Chicago, IL: University of Chicago Press.

Speltz, M. L., DeKlyen, M., & Greenburg, M. T. (1999). Attachment in boys with early onset conduct problems. *Development and Psychopathology, 11,* 269–285.

Sroufe, L. A., Carlson, E. A., Levy, A. K., & Egeland, B. (1999). Implications of attachment theory for developmental psychopathology. *Development and Psychopathology, 11,* 1–13.

Waters, E., & Deane, K. (1985). Defining and assessing individual differences in attachment relationships: Q-methodology and the organization of behavior in infancy and early childhood. In I. Brotherhood & E. Waters (Eds.), *Growing points of attachment theory and research* (pp. 41–65). *Monographs of the Society for Research in Child Development, 50*(1–2, Serial No. 209).

ROLLEN C. FOWLER
Eugene 4J School District, Eugene, Oregon

See also Emotional Disorders; Emotional Lability

ATTENTION-DEFICIT/HYPERACTIVITY DISORDER

Attention-Deficit/Hyperactivity Disorder (ADHD) is one of the most common disorders found among children. Children with ADHD exhibit more attention difficulties or hyperactive-impulsive behaviors than their same-age peers (American Psychiatric Association, 2000). Individuals with ADHD experience problems with sustained attention (i.e., maintaining attention to tasks with little intrinsic value) or selective attention (i.e., filtering essential from nonessential details), exhibit excessive motor movement, and demonstrate behavioral disinhibition (i.e., difficulty adjusting behavior to situational demands; Barkley, 1998). According to Barkley, behavioral disinhibition, overactivity, and inattention are the primary characteristics of ADHD.

Prevalence rates of ADHD among the school-age population have varied widely from about 1% to 9% (Bird, 1996), with 3% to 7% being the most common prevalence estimates reported among experts in the field (American Psychiatric Association, 2000). Attention-Deficit/Hyperactivity Disorder is reported to be more prevalent in males than in females, with the proportion of males to females manifesting the disorder ranging from 2:1 to 9:1 (American Psychiatric Association, 2000).

From a historical perspective, the conceptualization of ADHD and the terms used to describe the disorder have undergone a series of revisions. In the 1940s and 1950s, restless, impulsive, distractible, and inattentive behaviors currently associated with children with ADHD were attributed to brain damage. The term *Minimal Brain Damage* (MBD) was used during this period of time to describe these children whose greatest difficulty was their excessive activity levels (Strauss & Lehtinen, 1955). A lack of clear evidence supporting the link between organic impairment and excessive activity levels resulted in a change in terminology in the early 1960s. The term *Minimal Brain Damage* was replaced with a new label, *Minimal Brain Dysfunction*. Several years later, the term *minimal brain dysfunction* was replaced with a new label, *Hyperkinetic Reaction of Childhood*. The term *Hyperkinetic Reaction of Childhood* first appeared in the revised nomenclature of the American Psychiatric Association's *Diagnostic and Statistical Manual of Mental Disorders—Second Edition* (*DSM-II;* American Psychiatric Association, 1968). The primary feature of this disorder in the *DSM-II* was hyperactivity. Controversy surrounded the use of the *Hyperkinetic Reaction of Childhood* label in the late 1960s and 1970s because of the seemingly incompatible symptom presentation of this disorder. Some children with the disorder exhibited hyperactivity-impulsive behaviors, while other children with the disorder experienced attention difficulties (Wilmshurst, 2005). Along with the controversy, a shift in focus occurred during this period of time as inattentiveness was viewed as the most salient feature of this disorder (Douglas & Peters, 1979). As a result, the term and the description of the disorder changed from *Hyperkinetic Reaction of Childhood* to *Attention Deficit Disorder* (ADD) in the third revision of the *DSM*, the *DSM-III* (American Psychiatric Association, 1980). The *DSM-III* also recognized two distinct subtypes of ADD, Attention Deficit Disorder with Hyperactivity and Attention Deficit Disorder without Hyperactivity. Children with Attention Deficit Disorder with Hyperactivity exhibited inattention and hyperactive behavior, whereas children with Attention Deficit Disorder without Hyperactivity experienced only attention problems. Later in the 1980s, the *DSM* was revised again. In the *Diagnostic and Statistical Manual of Mental Disorders*, third edition, revised (*DSM-III-R;* American Psychiatric Association, 1987), the subtyping

was eliminated and Attention Deficit Disorder with Hyperactivity became known as Attention-Deficit Hyperactivity Disorder. In contrast, Attention Deficit Disorder without Hyperactivity was removed as a subtype.

The current conceptualization of ADHD and terms used to describe the disorder appear in the *Diagnostic and Statistical Manual of Mental Disorders*, fourth edition, text revision (*DSM-IV-TR;* American Psychiatric Association, 2000). In the *DSM-IV-TR*, three subtypes of ADHD are recognized, Attention-Deficit/Hyperactivity Disorder, Combined Type, Attention-Deficit/Hyperactivity Disorder, Predominately Inattentive Type, and Attention-Deficit/Hyperactivity Disorder, Predominately Hyperactive-Impulsive Type. These three subtypes are identified based on the degree to which a child exhibits the core features of ADHD (Wilmshurst, 2005). The three core features of the disorder include hyperactivity, impulsivity, and inattentiveness. The commonly seen, especially in lay publications, but unfortunately also in some professional publications, designation of ADD is archaic and no longer considered a valid diagnosis.

Children who meet the criteria for the most common subtype of ADHD, Attention-Deficit/Hyperactivity Disorder, Combined Type, display both inattentive and hyperactive-impulsive behaviors. Children with the Combined Type exhibit at least six of nine symptoms in the inattentive category (makes careless mistakes or does not attend to details in work, has problems sustaining attention, does not seem to listen, does not follow through on instructions or does not complete work, has problems organizing tasks, forgets things, is easily distracted, loses things, and is reluctant to engage in activities requiring mental effort) and at least six of nine symptoms in the hyperactive-impulsive category (fidgets with hands or feet or squirms in seat, has difficulty remaining seated, runs and climbs excessively in inappropriate places, has difficulty playing quietly, is extremely active, talks excessively, blurts out answers, has difficulty taking turns, and interrupts others; American Psychiatric Association, 2000). In contrast, children with Attention-Deficit/Hyperactivity Disorder, Predominately Inattentive Type exhibit at least six of nine symptoms in the inattentive category and less than six of nine symptoms in the hyperactive-impulsive category (American Psychiatric Association, 2000). These children experience attention difficulties, but they do not meet the diagnostic criteria for hyperactivity-impulsivity. Many children with the Predominately Inattentive type have concentration and academic difficulties and suffer from internalizing disorders such as depression or anxiety (Weiss, Worling, & Wasdell, 2003). Children with Attention-Deficit/Hyperactivity Disorder, Predominately Hyperactive-Impulsive Type exhibit at least six of nine symptoms in the hyperactive-impulsive category and less than six of nine symptoms in the inattentive category. Children with the Predominately Hyperactive-Impulsive Type demonstrate hyperactive-impulsive behaviors, but they do not meet the diagnostic criteria for inattentiveness (American Psychiatric Association, 2000). Many children who are diagnosed with this subtype experience social and academic problems due to their impulsive nature (Wilmshurst, 2005). The symptoms associated with the three subtypes of ADHD must (a) be present for at least 6 months, (b) cause significant impairment in social or academic functioning, and (c) occur across two or more settings (e.g., home and school). In addition, some of the symptoms associated with the different subtypes of ADHD must have been present before age 7 (American Psychiatric Association, 2000).

Most children with ADHD begin to exhibit symptoms of the disorder in early childhood. Around the age of 3 or 4, hyperactive-impulsive behaviors are first observed in children with ADHD. Hyperactive-impulsive behaviors are thought to come before inattention (Green, Loeber, & Lahey, 1991). Attention difficulties among children with ADHD are typically not detected until these individuals begin school (Wilmshurst, 2005) and experience learning difficulties (Applegate et al., 1997). When children with ADHD reach adolescence, many of these individuals display fewer hyperactive-impulsive behaviors and show improvement in their attention span (Hart, Lahey, Loeber, Applegate, & Frick, 1995). However, behavioral problems and cognitive difficulties persist with some of these individuals. In adulthood, many individuals with ADHD have reported an overall reduction in both hyperactive-impulsive and inattention symptoms (Shaffer, 1994), but for many, the disorder lasts a lifetime (Weiss & Hechtman, 1993).

Comorbid disorders are common among children with ADHD. According to Barkley (1998), more than 50% of children with ADHD have one or more co-occurring disorders. The most prevalent comorbid disorders are Conduct Disorders and Oppositional Defiant Disorders. Approximately 50% of children with ADHD have a Conduct Disorder, and 35% to 60% have an Oppositional Defiant Disorder (Szatmari, Boyle, & Offord, 1989). Other common, but less prevalent, comorbid disorders include Bipolar Disorders, Major Depressive Disorders, Anxiety Disorders, Learning Disorders, and Communication Disorders. Some children with ADHD have a Tic Disorder. However, the co-occurrence of a Tic Disorder occurs less frequently in children with ADHD (American Psychiatric Association, 2000).

Many children with ADHD have poor interpersonal relationships. Approximately 50% of children with ADHD experience peer rejection and have difficulty establishing and maintaining friendships (Landau, Milich, & Diener, 1998) due to their bossy, impulsive, intrusive, and argumentative nature. Some of these children demonstrate aggressive behavior toward peers because they misinterpret social cues from their environment (Barkley, 1998), which, in turn, leads to peer rejection. Few or no friends put these individuals at risk for future socioemotional

problems. Relationships with adults are also problematic for many of these children. Children with ADHD are less compliant to teacher and parent requests and receive more reprimands and punishment from significant adults in their lives (Barkley, 1998).

Besides poor interpersonal relationships, many children with ADHD experience academic and cognitive problems. Evidence suggests that children with ADHD score on average nine points below their peers on standardized measures of intelligence (Frazier, Demaree, & Youngstrom, 2004). Frazier and colleagues meta-analyzed 137 studies and found a statistically significant difference in overall cognitive ability between individuals with ADHD and controls. The weighted mean effect size was .61. According to the authors, this finding suggests that individuals with ADHD may have mild global cognitive inefficiencies or multiple specific deficits. Children with ADHD may also experience academic problems, with 30% of these children retained at least once in their academic careers (Barkley, 1998). Because many of these children struggle in the academic arena, approximately 30% will not finish high school (Barkley, 1998). Many students with ADHD struggle in a number of academic areas, including reading, mathematics, spelling, and writing (Barkley, 1998). Students who experience academic difficulties may qualify for special education and related services under the learning disability (LD) or other health impairment (OHI) category of the Individuals with Disabilities Education Act (IDEA) or for accommodations in the regular education classroom under Section 504 of the Rehabilitation Act. Approximately 30% of children with ADHD participate in special education programs (Barkley, 1998).

Significant controversy exists regarding the exact cause of ADHD (Wilmshurst, 2005), with a number of different etiologies offered to explain the disorder. However, neurobiological factors have received substantial empirical support in recent years as the greatest contributors to ADHD (Barkley, 1998). With modern technology, functional resonance imaging (FMRI) and single photon emission computed topography (SPECT) scans have revealed different activity levels in different regions of the brain of children with ADHD in comparison to children without ADHD. Children with ADHD have less activity in the frontal region of the brain and more activity in the cingulate gyrus than children without ADHD. The frontal region of the brain and the cingulate gyrus are responsible for executive functioning and focused attention, respectively (Wilmshurst, 2005). Another plausible explanation for the disorder is heredity (Edelbrock, Rende, Plomin, & Thompson, 1995). ADHD runs in families, with 50% of children with ADHD having a parent who also has the disorder (Biederman et al., 1995). Low levels of neurotransmitters have also been identified as a possible cause of ADHD. Research has shown that children with ADHD have lower levels of dopamine, epinephrine, and norepinephrine than children without ADHD and that these neurotransmitters are associated with attention and motor activity (Wilmshurst, 2005). Barkley (1997) cogently argued that deficits in the behavioral inhibition system provide an explanation for the disorder and the cognitive, behavioral, and social deficits observed in children with ADHD. Other possible neurological etiologies include prenatal and perinatal complications, exposure to environmental toxins, and infections. Environmental factors such as poor parenting, parental characteristics, chaotic home environment, and lower socioeconomic background have also been suggested as possible etiologies for the disorder. However, these factors have received little empirical support as causes of ADHD (Anastopoulos, Klinger, & Temple, 2001).

A multimethod approach in the assessment of children with ADHD has been recommended (Bradley & DuPaul, 1997). A multimethod assessment approach involves obtaining information from multiple informants (e.g., parent, teacher, child), measures, and settings (home, school) to pinpoint problematic areas of concern. Once the problematic areas are identified, intervention strategies are developed based on the assessment results to address these areas of concern.

A comprehensive evaluation of a child with ADHD in a clinical setting includes clinical interviews with the parent, teacher, and child; a medical examination consisting of a medical interview and a physical examination; and completion of behavioral rating scales by the parent, teacher, and child if applicable (Barkley & Edwards, 1998). Popular behavioral rating scales used in the assessment of children with ADHD includes the *Achenbach System of Empirically-Based Assessment* (ASEBA; Achenbach & Rescorla, 2001), the *Behavior Assessment System for Children–Second Edition* (BASC-2; Reynolds & Kamphaus, 2004), the *Brown Attention-Deficit Disorder Scales* (Brown ADD Scales; 2001), the *Conners' Rating Scale–Revised* (CRS-R; Conners, 1997), and the *Behavior Rating Inventory of Executive Function* (BRIEF; Gioia, Isquith, Guy, & Kenworthy, 2000). Additional behavior rating scales may be included to address other areas of concern. Behavioral observations, intelligence and academic achievement measures, neuropsychological tests, personality measures, and projectives may also be included to assess cognitive impairments or to aid in differential diagnosis (Gordon & Barkley, 1998).

Assessment of children with ADHD in a school setting may be conducted within a problem-solving model (see Hoff, Doepke, & Landau, 2002 for a discussion on the use of a problem-solving model in the assessment of children with ADHD). As part of the prereferral process, interviews with the parent, teacher, and child are conducted; behavior observations are performed; and behavior rating scales are completed by the parent, teacher, and child if applicable. A functional behavior assessment may also be performed to address behavioral concerns and curriculum-based measures may also be administered to assess academic problems. Based on these assessment results, intervention strategies are selected and implemented to address the issues of concern. If the intervention strategies prove to be ineffective, a comprehensive evaluation may be conducted and include standardized measures of intelligence and academic achievement and other measures, depending on the referral and information obtained in the assessment process. Based on the results of this comprehensive evaluation and a discussion among members of a multidisciplinary team consisting of school personnel, parents, and possibly the child, a child may be eligible for special education and related services under IDEA or for accommodations in the regular education classroom under Section 504 of the Rehabilitation Act (Lowe, 2005).

Many factors must be considered when providing treatment to children with ADHD. Because of the cross-situational pervasiveness of the disorder, comorbid and associative features, and symptoms, a multimodal approach has been used with many of these children (Anastopoulos et al., 2001). Medication, behavior modification techniques, counseling, and parent training have received empirical support (Pelham, Wheeler, & Chronis, 1998).

Stimulant medication has been reported to be the most effective single treatment in reducing the core symptoms of ADHD (MTA Cooperative Group, 1999). The rationale for the use of medication in the treatment of ADHD rests on the assumption that low levels of catecholamines (i.e., dopamine, epinephrine, and norepinephrine) are the cause of the disorder. Stimulant medication in current use to treat ADHD includes Ritalin, Concerta, Focalin, Metadate, Methylin, Adderall, Dexedrine, Dextrostat, and Cylert (Wilmshurst, 2005). Antidepressant medication has also been used to treat ADHD, including Imipramine and Wellbutrin. Antidepressant medication has been prescribed in many cases to reduce or eliminate motor tics, which can be a side effect associated with the ingestion of stimulant medication or to elevate a child's mood. A new nonstimulant medication, Strattera, received Food and Drug Administration (FDA) approval for use in the treatment of children with ADHD in 2003 (Wilmshurst, 2005). Collaboration among medical professionals, school personnel, and parents is needed to ensure thorough monitoring of the medication that an optimal dose is prescribed to children with ADHD.

Although medication has been effective in reducing hyperactive-impulsive behaviors and increasing attention in children with ADHD, there are side effects associated with the use of medication. Short-term side effects of stimulant medications include stomachaches; weight, height, and appetite suppression; and sleeping difficulties. Long-term side effects of stimulant medications include dysphoria, insomnia, increase in heart rate and blood pressure, and loss of appetite. The side effects associated with the long-term use of these medications across the life span are not known at the present time.

Nonpharmacological interventions have also been used in the treatment of children with ADHD. Parent training has been shown to be effective in reducing children's noncompliant behavior and increasing adults' parenting skills (Sonuga-Barke, Daley, Thompson, Laver-Bredbury, & Weeks, 2001). Parent training involves training adults in behavior modification techniques. Through training, parents learn ways to reduce their child's inappropriate behavior and to increase their child's appropriate behavior. A positive side effect of this training has been reduced levels of stress among parents (Sonuga-Barke et al., 2001).

Behavior modification techniques are effective intervention strategies to increase appropriate behavior and decrease inappropriate behavior among children with ADHD (Pfiffner & Barkley, 1998; Wilmshurst, 2005). Behavior modification strategies involve the manipulation of antecedents to modify the environment or task characteristics associated with a child's difficulties or the delivery of positive or negative consequences contingent upon the type of behavior demonstrated by the child. Modifications in the environment may include reducing the noise level in the classroom or moving a child's desk closer to the teacher and away from distractors to increase a child's attention. Praising or giving a child a tangible reward after the child sits quietly and completes his or her class work or taking away a privilege after a child runs around the classroom are examples of behavior modification strategies in which appropriate behavior is rewarded and inappropriate behavior results in negative consequences.

Home-school contingencies represent another group of behavioral strategies effective with children with ADHD (Pelham et al., 1998). Home-school contingencies represent one of the most widely used strategies with these children (Pfiffner & Barkley, 1998). The effectiveness of home-school contingencies is dependent upon collaboration between the home and school. An example of a home-school contingency is a daily report card that goes back and forth between the home and the school. Consequences are delivered in the home environment based on the child's behavior or academic performance in the school setting. Ratings of the child's behavior or academic performance are recorded on the report card, and the child carries the report to and from school on a daily basis. With home-school contingencies, generalization and maintenance of desired behavior are more likely to occur because the behavior is being addressed in two settings.

Peer strategies are a fourth group of strategies effective with children with ADHD. Peer tutoring and class-wide peer tutoring have been effective in improving academic performance and classroom behavior of children with ADHD (DuPaul & Henningson, 1993). Peer tutoring strategies are most effective when children with ADHD are paired with peers who serve as good role models (Pfiffner & Barkley, 1998).

Social skills training is another popular strategy used with children with ADHD. Many children with ADHD experience poor interpersonal relationships. The purpose of social skills training is to promote social competence. However, research has suggested that social skills training has not been extremely effective with high incidence populations, including children with ADHD (Gresham, Sugai, & Horner, 2001). Gresham and colleagues' meta-analysis revealed a weak effect for social skills training in improving the social competence of high incidence populations and problems with skill maintenance and generalization.

Self-management strategies have also been used with children with ADHD. Self-management strategies emphasize the development of self-control. Self-management strategies include self-instruction, self-monitoring, self-reinforcement, and problem-solving strategies. Overall, these strategies have fallen short of initial expectations (Braswell et al., 1997).

REFERENCES

Achenbach, T. M., & Rescorla, L. A. (2001). *Achenbach System of Empirically-Based Assessment*. Burlington: University of Vermont, Research Center for Children, Youth, and Families.

American Psychiatric Association. (1968). *Diagnostic and statistical manual of mental disorders* (2nd ed.). Washington, DC: Author.

American Psychiatric Association. (1980). *Diagnostic and statistical manual of mental disorders* (3rd ed.). Washington, DC: Author.

American Psychiatric Association. (1987). *Diagnostic and statistical manual of mental disorders* (3rd ed., rev. ed.). Washington, DC: Author.

American Psychiatric Association. (2000). *Diagnostic and statistical manual of mental disorders* (4th ed., text rev.). Washington, DC: Author.

Anastopoulos, A. D., Klinger, E. E., & Temple, E. P. (2001). Treating children and adolescents with Attention-Deficit/Hyperactivity Disorder. In J. N. Hughes, A. M. LaGreca, & J. C. Conoley (Eds.), *Handbook of psychological services for children and adolescents* (pp. 245–265). New York, NY: Oxford University Press.

Applegate, B., Lahey, B. B., Hart, E. L., Biederman, T., Hynd, G. W., Barkley, R. A., et al. (1997). Validity of the age-of-onset criterion for ADHD: A report from the DSM-IV field trials. *Journal of the American Academy of Child and Adolescent Psychiatry, 36*, 1211–1221.

Barkley, R. A. (1997). *ADHD and the nature of self-control*. New York, NY: Guilford Press.

Barkley, R. A. (1998). *Attention-Deficit Hyperactivity Disorder*. New York, NY: Guilford Press.

Barkley, R. A., & Edwards, G. (1998). Diagnostic interview, behavior rating scales, and the medical examination. In R. A. Barkley

(Ed.), *Attention-deficit hyperactivity disorder* (pp. 263–293). New York, NY: Guilford Press.

Biederman, J., Wozniak, J., Kiely, K., Ablon, S., Faraone, S., Mick, E.,...Kraus, I. (1995). CBCL clinical scales discriminate prepubertal children with structured interview-derived diagnosis of mania from those with ADHD. *Journal of the American Academy of Child and Adolescent Psychiatry, 34,* 464–471.

Bird, H. (1996). Epidemiology of childhood disorders in a cross-cultural context. *Journal of Child and Adolescent Psychiatry, 35,* 1440–1448.

Bradley, K. L., & DuPaul, G. J. (1997). Attention-Deficit/Hyperactivity Disorder. In G. G. Bear, K. M. Minke, & A. Thomas (Eds.), *Children's needs II: Development, problems and alternatives* (pp. 109–117). Bethesda, MD: National Association of School Psychologists.

Braswell, L., August, G. J., Bloomquist, M. L., Realmuto, G. M., Skare, S. S., & Crosby, R. D. (1997). School-based secondary prevention for children with disruptive behavior. *Journal of Abnormal Child Psychology, 25,* 197–205.

Brown, T. K. (2001). *Brown Attention-Deficit Disorder Scale.* San Antonio, TX: Harcourt Assessment.

Conners, C. K. (1997). *Conners Rating Scale* (rev. ed.). Toronto: Multi-Health Systems.

Douglas, V. I., & Peters, K. G. (1979). Toward a clearer definition of the attentional deficit in hyperactive children. In G. A. Hale & M. Lewis (Eds.), *Attention and the development of cognitive skills* (pp. 173–247). New York, NY: Plenum Press.

DuPaul, G. J., & Henningson, P. N. (1993). Peer tutoring effects on the classroom performance of children with Attention Deficit Hyperactivity Disorder. *School Psychology Review, 22,* 134–143.

Edelbrock, C. S., Rende, R., Plomin, R., & Thompson, L. (1995). A twin study of competence and problem behavior in childhood and early adolescence. *Journal of Child Psychology and Psychiatry, 36,* 775–786.

Frazier, T. W., Demaree, H. A., & Youngstrom, E. A. (2004). Meta-analysis of intellectual and neuropsychological test performance in Attention-Deficit/Hyperactivity Disorder. *Neuropsychology, 18,* 543–555.

Gioia, G. A., Isquith, P. K., Guy, S. C., & Kenworthy, L. (2000). *Behavior Rating Inventory of Executive Function.* Odessa, FL: Psychological Assessment Resources.

Gordon, M., & Barkley, R. A. (1998). Test and observational measures. In R. A. Barkley (Ed.), *Attention-Deficit Hyperactivity Disorder* (pp. 345–372). New York, NY: Guilford Press.

Green, S. M., Loeber, R., & Lahey, B. B. (1991). Stability of mothers' recall of the age of onset of their child's attention and hyperactivity problems. *Journal of the American Academy of Child and Adolescent Psychiatry, 38,* 503–512.

Gresham, F. M., Sugai, G., & Horner, R. H. (2001). Interpreting outcomes of social skills training for students with high incidence disabilities. *Exceptional Children, 67,* 331–334.

Hart, E. L., Lahey, B. B., Loeber, R., Applegate, B., & Frick, P. J. (1995). Developmental change in Attention-Deficit Hyperactivity Disorder in boys: A four-year longitudinal study. *Journal of Abnormal Child Psychology, 23,* 729–750.

Hoff, K. E., Doepka, K., & Landau, S. (2002). *Best practice in the assessment of children with Attention-Deficit/Hyperactivity Disorder.* In A. Thomas & J. Grimes (Eds.), *Best practices in school psychology* (Vol. 4, pp. 1129–1146). Washington, DC: National Association of School Psychologists.

Landau, S., Milich, R., & Diener, M. B. (1998). Peer relations of children with attention-deficit-disordered boys. *Journal of Abnormal Child Psychology, 16,* 69–81.

Lowe, P. A. (2005). Attention-Deficit/Hyperactivity Disorder. In S. W. Lee & P. A. Lowe (Eds.), *The encyclopedia of school psychology* (pp. 32–35). Thousand Oaks, CA: Sage.

MTA Cooperative Group. (1999). A 14-month randomized clinical trial of treatment strategies for Attention-Deficit/Hyperactivity Disorder. *Archives of General Psychiatry, 56,* 1073–1086.

Pelham, W. E., Jr., Wheeler, T., & Chronis, A. (1998). Empirically supported psychosocial treatments for Attention-Deficit/Hyperactivity Disorder. *Journal of Clinical Child Psychology, 27,* 190–205.

Pfiffner, L. J., & Barkley, R. A. (1998). Treatment of ADHD in school settings. In R. A. Barkley (Ed.), *Attention-Deficit Hyperactivity Disorder* (pp. 458–490). New York, NY: Guilford Press.

Reynolds, C. R., & Kamphaus, R. W. (2004). *Behavior Assessment System for Children* (2nd ed.). Circle Pines, MN: American Guidance Services.

Shaffer, D. (1994). Attention Deficit Hyperactivity Disorder in adults. *American Journal of Psychiatry, 151,* 633–638.

Sonuga-Barke, E. J., Daley, D., Thompson, M., Laver-Bredbury, C., & Weeks, A. (2001). Parent-based therapies for preschool Attention-Deficit/Hyperactivity Disorder: A randomized controlled trial with a community sample. *Journal of the American Academy of Child and Adolescent Psychiatry, 40,* 402–408.

Strauss, A. A., & Lehtinen, L. E. (1955). *Psychopathology and education of the brain-injured child.* New York, NY: Grune & Stone.

Szatmari, P., Boyle, M., & Offord, D. R. (1989). ADHD and Conduct Disorder: Degree of diagnostic overlap and differences among correlates. *Journal of the American Academy of Child and Adolescent Psychiatry, 28,* 865–872.

Weiss, G., & Hechtman, L. R. (1993). *Hyperactive children grown up* (2nd ed.). New York, NY: Guilford Press.

Weiss, M. D., Worling, D. E., & Wasdell, M. B. (2003). A chart review study of the inattentive and combined types of ADHD. *Journal of Attention Disorders, 7,* 1–9.

Wilmshurst, L. (2005). *Essentials of child psychopathology.* Hoboken, NJ: Wiley.

PATRICIA A. LOWE
University of Kansas

CECIL R. REYNOLDS
Texas A&M University

See also Attention Span; Ritalin; Stimulant Drugs; Traumatic Brain Injury

ATTENTION SPAN

Adequate attention span requires optimal arousal, selection of task-relevant information, maintenance of attention long enough to get a task done, and central processing of the task (Cohen, 1993; Posner & Boies, 1971). Arousal is assessed by heart rate, respiration, or other indicators of autonomic arousal, and there is a level that is optimal for learning. At very low levels of arousal, learning is inefficient and attention to environmental stimuli is diffuse; at very high levels, attention is narrowed but learning becomes inefficient, particularly for complex tasks. Teachers can increase arousal by increasing the novelty of classroom activities, by asking students questions to generate curiosity (Berlyne, 1960), by rotating students in and out of the "action zone" (the T-shaped front-row-and-center region of the classroom; Piontrowski & Calfee, 1979), or by directing questions to students outside the action zone.

Attention span in children can be negatively affected by sleep deprivation, attention-deficit disorder, depression, and many other disorders. Selective attention is assessed most frequently by use of incidental learning tasks. The child is instructed to recall a specific set of items (e.g., pictures of animals), but other incidental items (e.g., household items) are actually paired with the target (central) items during presentation. After being given tests of recall for central items, the child is tested for recall of the central-incidental pairs. The assumption is that only items that are attended to will be recalled. Recall for central items increases steadily from preschool age through adolescence, while memory for incidental items remains stable. The correlation between central and incidental recall becomes increasingly negative between ages 6 and 13 in normal children, indicating an increasing ability to screen out distractions with age. Adolescents and adults appear to screen out distractors by rehearsing central stimuli (Hagen & Stanovich, 1977). Hallahan et al. have found selective attention deficits to be common in children with learning problems. They also found that these children can be trained to improve their attention to central stimuli by using task-relevant self-talk and by being reinforced for recall of central items (Hallahan & Reeve, 1980).

Maintenance of attention can be assessed by observation, by interviewing, by self-monitoring, or through formal testing (see Reynolds & Bigler, 1997, 1994; Rossman, 2006). In observational methods, eye contact with assigned task materials, with the teacher during instruction, or during task-relevant interaction with peers, is scored as engaged (on-task); other activities are scored as nonengaged (Piontrowski & Calfee, 1979). Observed engaged time is related to achievement; for example, Leach reports that 58% of the variance in primary mathematics achievement is accounted for by academic engaged time (Leach & Dolan, 1985). Observed on-task attention increases from ages 5 to 11 (Higgins & Turnure, 1984), although students may become more adept at appearing to maintain attention with development (Hudgins, 1967). Self-monitoring of "paying attention" improved observed engaged time among second graders, and reinforcement for self-monitoring accuracy improved engaged time more than self-monitoring alone (Rooney, Hallahan, & Lloyd, 1984).

REFERENCES

Berlyne, D. (1960). *Conflict, arousal, and curiosity*. New York, NY: McGraw-Hill.

Cohen, R. A. (1993). *The neuropsychology of attention*. New York, NY: Plenum Press.

Hagen, J. W., & Stanovich, K. E. (1977). Memory: Strategies of acquisition. In R. V. Kail & J. W. Hagen (Eds.), *Perspectives on the development of memory and cognition*. Hillsdale, NJ: Erlbaum.

Hallahan, D. P., & Reeve, R. E. (1980). Selective attention and distractibility. In B. K. Keogh (Ed.), *Advances in special education, Vol. 1*. Greenwich, CT: JAI Press.

Higgins, A. T., & Turnure, J. E. (1984). Distractibility and concentration of attention in children's development. *Child Development, 55*, 1799–1810.

Hudgins, B. B. (1967). Attending and thinking in the classroom. *Psychology in the Schools, 66*, 29–32.

Leach, D. J., & Dolan, N. K. (1985). Helping teachers increase student academic engagement rate: The evaluation of a minimal feedback procedure. *Behavior Modification, 9*, 55–71.

Piontrowski, D., & Calfee, R. (1979). Attention in the classroom. In G. A. Hale & M. Lewis (Eds.), *Attention and cognitive development* (pp. 297–329). New York, NY: Plenum Press.

Posner, M. I., & Boies, S. J. (1971). Components of attention. *Psychological Review, 78*, 391–408.

Reynolds, C. R., & Bigler, E. D. (1994). *Test of memory and learning*. Austin, TX: PRO-ED.

Reynolds, C. R., & Bigler, E. D. (1997). Clinical neuropsychological assessment of child and adolescent memory with the Test of Memory and Learning. In C. R. Reynolds & E. Fletcher-Janzen (Eds.), *The handbook of clinical child neuropsychology* (3rd ed., pp. 296–319). New York, NY: Plenum Press.

Rooney, K. J., Hallahan, D. P., & Lloyd, J. W. (1984). Self-recording of attention by learning disabled students in the regular classroom. *Journal of Learning Disabilities, 17*, 360–364.

Rossman, N. P. (2006). Traumatic brain injury in children. In K. F. Swaiman & S. Ashwal (Eds.), *Pediatric neurology* (4th ed., pp. 873–895). St. Louis, MO: Mosby.

JOHN MACDONALD
Eastern Kentucky University

See also Attention-Deficit/Hyperactivity Disorder; Hyperkinesis; Test of Memory and Learning

ATTRIBUTION RETRAINING

Many pupils with disabilities perceive themselves to be incompetent in a variety of school-related activities. While these self-perceptions may accurately reflect limited skills in these areas, they may also affect youngsters' willingness to engage in learning tasks. When presented with school tasks, even tasks in which they have evidenced recent success, many pupils will state that they cannot do the work and as a consequence will not even try. To address the learning needs of their students, special education teachers need to focus on their students' cognitive and motivational characteristics. An intervention procedure entitled attributional retraining has been used to influence pupils' self-perceptions and their subsequent motivation to learn.

Attribution retraining may be defined as a systematic set of procedures designed to influence individuals' perceptions concerning the causes of their performance on tasks. Many of the procedures are derived from research in the area of cognitive behavior modification. In attributional retraining the focus is on modifying learners' thoughts concerning why they have succeeded or failed on a task. Although attributional retraining procedures have been used in treatment programs for a variety of problems including alcoholism, anxiety, depression, and diet management, the focus, here, will be on the use of these procedures with youngsters who evidence severe learning problems.

Most of the attributional retraining programs focus on the role of effort on student achievement. This emphasis is due, in part, to the fact that pupils can choose to change their levels of effort. In addition, high achieving students tend to attribute successes to their ability and effort and ascribe their failures to lack of effort. When students perceive that increased effort will result in success, they persist; this, in turn, enhances their performance. In contrast, children who have learning problems frequently attribute their failures to lack of ability, and fail to persist on academic tasks.

One of the first attributional retraining studies was conducted by Dweck (1975). In this investigation, children identified as learned helpless were asked to solve arithmetic problems. One group of pupils was given math tasks in which they continually succeeded; another group was given tasks that they occasionally failed at. When pupils did not correctly respond on an arithmetic task, they were given attributional feedback indicating that they should have tried harder. All the youngsters in the study were subsequently given difficult math problems. Pupils who received the attributional feedback maintained or improved their performances after failure, whereas the performances of children who continually succeeded deteriorated if they failed on a math problem. Chapin and Dyck (1976) and Fowler and Peterson (1981) subsequently reported that persistence on academic tasks was jointly affected by reinforcement procedures and attribution retraining. Fowler and Peterson also reported that reinforcement/attribution retraining that involved direct attributional feedback to pupils was more effective in increasing reading persistence than other treatment procedures. Recently, educational researchers have reported that attribution training procedures may influence students' use of learning strategies (Johnson & Winograd, 1985; Palmer & Goetz, 1984). Attribution training may affect both pupils' achievement outcomes and how they learn.

Related to the attributional retraining research, Decharms (1976) developed a two-part program to help teachers enhance personal causation of elementary-aged children. The project was designed to influence pupils' goal planning and ultimately produce a person who is in control of his or her achievements. The experiment involved two groups: one consisted of motivation-trained teachers using an experimental curriculum; a control group had untrained teachers and the regular curriculum. The first step involved a personal causation training course for all teachers in the experimental group, followed by a year-long implementation of a number of classroom exercises. Personal causation training did appear to affect pupil's self-confidence and their academic achievement scores. Four years later, a semi-structured interview revealed higher personal goals and responsibility orientation for those children in the trained group over those in the untrained group. Five years later, it was found that more pupils from the trained group had graduated. While there were a variety of components to the training program, one of the crucial elements was teaching the pupils that they had control over their achievement outcomes.

Although additional research is needed to determine how and when to most effectively use attributional retraining procedures, it appears that teachers' direct attributional feedback to children does influence students' willingness to learn and their school achievement. Teachers' systematic feedback to their pupils that effort is important in determining their successes or failures may affect youngsters' persistence on school tasks and ultimately their achievement.

Teachers who influence the class climate for assisting peers giving positive feedback to children with disabilities can positively affect attributions about self efficacy (Altermatt & Pomerantz, 2003). Siblings can also be utilized in this manner (Gnaulati, 2002). Praise from others (teachers, siblings, or peers) can have significant positive effects as long as it is directed to controllable causes and is perceived as sincere (Henderlong & Lepper, 2002).

REFERENCES

Altermatt, E. R., & Pomerantz, E. V. (2003). The development of competence-related motivational beliefs: An investigation of similarity and influence among friends. *Journal of Educational Psychology, 95*, 111–123.

Chapin, M., & Dyck, D. G. (1976). Persistence in children's reading behavior as a function of N length and attribution retraining. *Journal of Abnormal Psychology, 85,* 511–515.

Decharms, R. (1976). *Enhancing motivation: Change in the classroom.* New York, NY: Irvington.

Dweck, C. S. (1975). The role of expectations and attributions in the alleviation of learned helplessness. *Journal of Personality and Social Psychology, 31,* 674–685.

Fowler, J. W., & Peterson, P. L. (1981). Increasing reading persistence and altering attributional style of learned helpless children. *Journal of Educational Psychology, 73,* 251–260.

Gnaulati, E. (2002). Extending the uses of sibling therapy with children and adolescents. *Psychotherapy: Theory, Research, Practice, Training, 39,* 76–87.

Henderlong, J., & Lepper, M. R. (2002). The effects of praise on children's intrinsic motivation: A review and synthesis. *Psychological Bulletin, 128,* 774–795.

Johnson, P. H., & Winograd, P. N. (1985). Passive failure in reading. Unpublished manuscript.

Palmer, D. J., & Goetz, E. T. (1988). Selection and use of study strategies: The role of the studier's beliefs about self and strategies. In C. Weinstein, E. Goetz, & P. Alexander (Eds.), *Learning and study strategies: Issues and assessments, instructions and evaluations.* New York, NY: Academic Press.

DOUGLAS J. PALMER
NORMA GUERRA
Texas A&M University

See also Learned Helplessness; Motivation

ATTRIBUTIONS

By definition, many special education pupils experience a history of failure prior to being referred and ultimately placed in special education classes. It is this background of failure, current achievement problems, and the recognition that other pupils are doing well on classroom assignments that leads to perceptions of lack of competence. In turn, these perceptions concerning lack of ability influence pupils' expectancy for future performance and their willingness to try new tasks and persist on difficult ones.

Recently there has been considerable interest generated concerning the consequences of repeated academic failure and its effect on the motivation and achievement of special education children. The repeated academic failure experienced by these students may cause them to doubt their abilities and reduce their persistence and effort when exposed to novel or familiar tasks. Researchers have found that learning-disabled (LD) children are less likely than nondisabled children to attribute their failures to insufficient effort and more likely to attribute their failures

to their own inabilities. LD pupils also have exhibited less persistence on achievement tasks than nondisabled pupils. Investigators have found that LD pupils' tendency to attribute failure to ability is negatively related to persistence. It has also been reported that when LD children succeed at a task, they are less likely to attribute the success of their abilities and more likely to attribute the success to luck or ease of the task. These children appear to blame themselves when they fail and not give themselves credit when they succeed. Low levels of persistence and effort often result in additional failures, and the special education student, more frequently subjected to these difficulties, is caught in a vicious downward spiral of motivation and performance (Licht & Kistner, 1986). Measures of children's attributional styles are now included on several widely used assessment devices (Reynolds & Kamphaus, 1992).

REFERENCES

Heider, F. (1958). *The psychology of interpersonal relations.* New York, NY: Wiley.

Licht, B. G., & Kistner, J. A. (1986). Motivational problems of learning disabled children: Individual differences and their implications for treatment. In J. K. Torgesen & B. W. L. Wong (Eds.), *Learning disabilities: Some new perspectives.* Orlando, FL: Academic Press.

Reynolds, C. R., & Kamphaus, R. W. (1992). *Behavior assessment system for children.* Circle Pines, MN: American Guidance Service.

Weiner, B. (1972). *Theories of motivation: From mechanism to cognition.* Chicago, IL: Rand McNally.

Weiner, B. (1974). *Achievement motivation and attribution theory.* Morristown, NJ: General Learning.

Weiner, B. (1979). A theory of motivation for some classroom experiences. *Journal of Educational Psychology, 71,* 3–25.

DOUGLAS J. PALMER
MICHAEL L. STOWE
Texas A&M University

See also Locus of Control

ATYPICAL CHILD SYNDROME

Atypical child syndrome is a term borrowed from the medical profession and is no longer in common usage. The current term referring to this group is exceptional children. An exceptional child is one who deviates from the norm and could be categorized on the basis of a set of physical and/or behavioral characteristics. There are a variety of specific disorders in the area of special education that use the term syndrome as a part of the classification.

Hunter syndrome, Down syndrome, Turner syndrome, Lesch-Neyhan syndrome, Cornelin deLange syndrome, Sturge-Weber syndrome, and Klinefelter's syndrome are but a few that are discussed in the special education literature.

A wide range of disabilities contribute to the atypical child's condition. That condition may range from mild to severe, physical to intellectual, educational to social, or any combination of those conditions. It is difficult however, to fit an individual into a category. Disability classifications are set up according to the characteristics of the children that deviate from the average or normal child and were used to help educational programs meet the individual's needs. Kirk (1972) described five categories: (1) communication disorders (learning disabilities and speech handicaps); (2) intellectual deviations (gifted and disabled); (3) sensory handicaps (auditory and visual); (4) neurological, orthopedic, or other health problems; and (5) behavior disorders. Although these categories have been used by psychology, sociology, physiology, and the medical profession, they will be briefly addressed from the educational standpoint of this time period for historical purposes.

Learning disabilities was a classification for those individuals that have language difficulties, visual or auditory-perceptual problems, and memory or other cognitive disabilities. Learning problems sometimes contribute to behavior problems resulting from frustration with academic task demands. Although definitions have related these dysfunctions to the central nervous system (Clements, 1966), remediation is dealt with through educational intervention with a focus on academic, social, and emotional adjustment.

Intellectual disability involves below average intellectual functioning with social and behavioral deficits. Grossman (1973) describes five levels of individuals with intellectual disability, all of whom have IQs below 85 and engage in behaviors inappropriate for their age group. Using the terms from that time period to reflect his categories: individuals with borderline retardation (from 85 to 70 IQ) are frequently referred to as slow learners. Individuals with mild retardation (the educable mentally retarded) range from 69 to 55 IQs and have some potential to master basic academic skills. These individuals can live as independent or semi-independent adults. Moderately or trainable mentally retarded individuals with IQs of 54 to 40 have potential for learning self-help, social, and communication skills and simple occupational tasks. Severely mentally retarded individuals range from 39 to 25 IQs and need continual monitoring. They may be taught simple self-help skills, work tasks, and some type of communication system. The profoundly retarded, with IQs below 25, are totally dependent and require close supervision. Some may be able to perform self-help skills. Educational programs for the intellectually disabled have made great gains. Educational programs range from fully inclusive scheduling to self-contained classrooms to special schools and employ a great many management and instructional techniques (Snell, 1978). Generally speaking goals of access to the general curriculum, functional skills, and independence are prioritized.

Sensory disabilities range greatly from minimal visual defects and hard of hearing to blindness and deafness. Education can range from no special programming, to special part-time instruction from an itinerant teacher, to special schools. Focus in the public schools is on auditory and visual perception training.

Behavior disorders interfere with a child's growth and the development of relationships with others. Hewett and Jenkins (1945) defined three types of behavior disorders involving those having unsocialized aggression (participating with peers in misdemeanors and crime) or overinhibition (overdependent and withdrawn). All involve social maladjustments and emotional disturbances. Although they are dealt with through the mental health fields, education has taken on prevention and treatment. The interventions of the day, whether through resource rooms, itinerant teachers, special classes, special or residential schools, or hospitals, included psychodynamics, behavior modification, and developmental, ecological, or psychoeducational strategies (Kirk, 1972).

REFERENCES

Bleck, E. G., & Nagel, D. A. (1975). *Physically handicapped children: A medical atlas for teachers*. New York, NY: Grune & Stratton.

Clements, D. D. (1966). *Minimal brain dysfunction in children* (Public Health Service Publication No. 415). Washington, DC: Department of Health, Education, and Welfare.

Fliegler, I. A., & Bish, C. E. (1959, December). Summary of research on the academically talented student. *Review of Educational Research, 29*, 408–450.

Gloss, G. H., & Jones, R. L. (1968). *Correlates of school district provisions for gifted children: A statewide study*. Paper presented at the annual meeting of the Council for Exceptional Children, New York.

Grossman, H. J. (Ed.). (1973). Manual on terminology and classification in mental retardation. *American Journal of Mental Deficiency* (Special issue. Series No. 2).

Hewett, L. E., & Jenkins, R. L. (1945). *Fundamental patterns of maladjustment: The dynamics of their origin*. Springfield: State of Illinois.

Kirk, S. A. (1972). *Educational exceptional children*. Boston, MA: Houghton-Mifflin.

Snell, M. E. (1978). *Systematic instruction of the moderately and severely handicapped*. Columbus, OH: Merrill.

DONNA FILIPS
Steger, Illinois

***See also* Evaluation; Learning Disabilities; Mental Retardation**

AUDIOGRAM

An audiogram is a standardized graphic representation of hearing thresholds to discrete pure tones (American National Standards Institute [ANSI], 1996). The abscissa of the audiogram shows frequency in Hertz (Hz) from 25 to 8000 Hz. The ordinate shows hearing level (HL) in decibels (dB) from −10 to 120 dB. Audiometric zero was derived by taking an average of 100 healthy youths over a frequency range from 20 Hz to 10 KHz from 1971 to 1973 under the laboratory conditions (International Standards Organization [ISO], 1998). Air conduction thresholds are represented by a circle for the right ear and an *X* for the left ear. Air conduction thresholds reflect the integrity of the whole of the auditory system. Brackets represent bone conduction thresholds. Traditionally, the right ear was also represented by the color red and the left by the color blue, but this is less common now due to black-and-white copies, scanners, and printers (Katz, 2000).

Bone conduction bypasses the middle ear system and reveals the integrity of the auditory system at its most basic level. Sound presented at high enough intensity will cross over to the other ear, and another sound must be used to mask that ear. The level of 40 dB is the lowest signal known to cross, and this is the level where masking is to be implemented, for air conduction and masking should always be used for bone conduction (ANSI, 1996). In practice, it is not necessary to mask bone conduction thresholds if there is no difference in air conduction thresholds and the bone conduction scores and there is no air-bone gap (Katz, 2001). There are seven categories of hearing levels that are usually used: normal or no impairment, −10 to 15 dB; slight or minimal loss, 16 to 25 dB; mild loss, 26 to 30 dB; moderate loss, 31 to 50 dB; moderate or severe loss, 51 to 70 dB; severe loss, 71 to 90 dB; and profound loss, 91 dB or greater (VA National Center for Health Promotion and Disease Prevention, 2004).

REFERENCES

American National Standards Institute (ANSI). (1972). *Title of standard S3.13-1972. Catalogue of ANSI standards*. Retrieved from http://www.ansi.org/ansidocstore/product.asp?sku=ANSI +Catalog

American National Standards Institute (ANSI). (1996). *Title of standard s3.6-1996. Catalogue of ANSI standards*. Retrieved from http://www.ansi.org/ansidocstore/product.asp?sku=ANSI +Catalog

International Standards Organization (ISO). (1998). *Title of standard: 389-1:1988.*

Katz, J. (2001). *Handbook of clinical audiology*. Baltimore, MD: Williams & Wilkins.

VA National Center for Health Promotion and Disease Prevention. (2004). *Audiogram*. Retrieved from http://www.nchpdp .med.va.gov/MonthlyPreventionTopics/2004_08/DegreeOfHear ingLoss.doc

THOMAS A. FRANK
Pennsylvania State University
First edition

LISA WILDMO
Bryan, Texas

See also Auditory Discrimination; Auditory Perception; Deaf

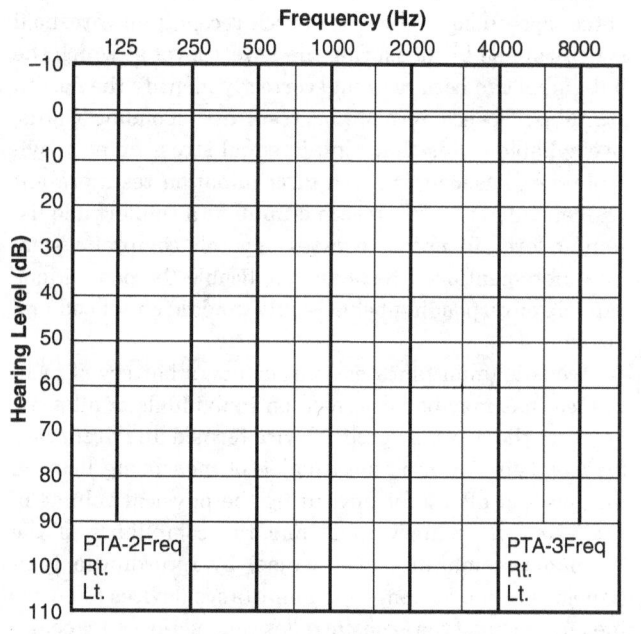

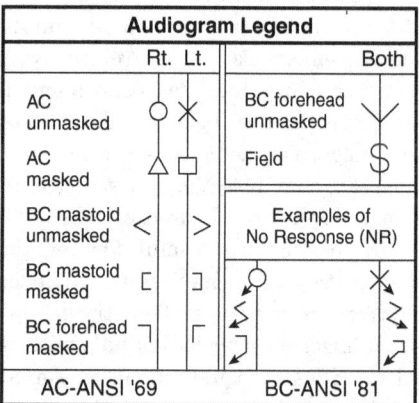

Figure A.5. Audiogram form and symbols.

AUDIOLOGY

Raymond Carhart (1947, as cited in Rintlemann, 1985) is credited with coining the term *audiology* for the new profession of hearing science. Soldiers returning from World

War II with service-connected hearing losses caused the rapid development of the field of audiology. Originally intended just to provide rehabilitation services, the scope of practice has increased to include the nonmedical management of hearing and balance disorders in children as well as adults such as tinnitus management, hearing aids, cochlear implants, assistive devices, hearing conservation programs, ototoxic drug management, interoperative monitoring, central auditory processing assessment, and cerumen removal.

Entry-level educational requirements for professionals in audiology include a master or doctoral degree. Licensure to practice audiology is required in all 50 states. The practice of audiology encompasses a comprehensive array of professional services related to the prevention of hearing loss and the audiological identification, assessment, diagnosis, and treatment of persons with impairment of auditory and vestibular function and to the prevention of impairments associated with them (American Academy of Audiology, n.d.). Audiologists serve in a number of roles, including clinician, therapist, teacher, consultant, researcher, and administrator (Martin & Greer, 1999).

Audiologists serve populations ranging from neonates to the geriatric populations. Audiologists can be found in diverse settings from private practice, schools, hospitals, universities, medical centers, and rehabilitation centers to government health care facilities (Martin & Greer, 1999).

REFERENCES

American Academy of Audiology. (n.d.). *What is an audiologist?* Retrieved September 13, 2005, from http://www.audiology.org/about/

Martin, F. N., & Greer, J. C. (1999). *Introduction to audiology* (7th ed.). Boston, MA: Allyn & Bacon.

Rintlemann, W. F. (Ed.). (1985). *Hearing assessment.* Baltimore, MD: University Park Press.

LISA WILDMO
Bryan, Texas

See also **Auditory Processing; Deaf**

AUDIOMETRY

Audiometry encompasses several techniques and procedures that effectively assess hearing. Routine and accurate calibration of the audiometer, a device used in the assessment of hearing, is critical in identifying hearing impairment. An audiological evaluation typically entails the use of pure-tone and speech audiometry in addition to acoustic immittance measurements, which assess the function of the middle ear, and otoacoustic emissions, which assess outer hair cell functioning.

Pure-tone audiometry requires an individual to respond to tones that are presented at various frequencies in order to determine threshold levels. There are two types of pure-tone measures: air conduction and bone conduction. Classification regarding the degree and type of hearing loss for each ear is possible by integrating the results of both measures. Air-conduction testing involves delivering a tone through the entire auditory pathway (outer, middle, and inner ear) by means of a headphone or insert transducer. Bone-conduction testing requires the use of a bone-conduction transducer, a vibrating device placed on the skull in order to stimulate fluids of the inner ear. Therefore, bone-conduction testing bypasses the outer and middle ear. The specific procedures for pure-tone audiometry have been specified by the American National Standards Institute (1997).

There are two types of speech audiometry: those that assess threshold and those that determine speech discrimination ability. Speech detection threshold is determined by measuring the lowest level at which an individual can detect speech sounds, while speech recognition threshold is determined by measuring the lowest level at which the individual can both hear and correctly identify the speech stimulus. Speech recognition tests use spondaic words, two syllable words that contain equal stress on each syllable (i.e., baseball). Speech discrimination tests present phonetically balanced speech stimuli at a comfortable listening level in order to assess speech comprehension. The aforementioned tests are applicable for populations capable of responding behaviorally (middle childhood and older).

Acoustic immittance measurements, a battery of techniques that may be performed on individuals of all ages, requires the use of a specific device termed an *immittance bridge*. This device is not capable of measuring hearing and instead allows for measuring the physical volume of the external auditory canal and the compliance of the tympanic membranes (ear drums) by recording a tympanogram. In addition, most immittance devices allow for measurement of the acoustic reflex contraction, a stapedial reflex that is elicited in response to loud stimuli.

Otoacoustic emissions is a relatively new and noninvasive technology that has been adopted into the general audiometric test battery. Similar to acoustic immittance, otoacoustic emissions are not a measure of hearing. Instead, they objectively assess the functioning of outer hair cells that reside on the cochlea. Otoacoustic emissions are particularly useful for individuals who are unable to respond behaviorally to air-conduction, bone-conduction, or speech audiometry tests, including newborns, malingerers, and individuals with physical or cognitive disabilities. Adequate identification and assessment of hearing impairments can be achieved through the application of various audiological techniques.

REFERENCES

American National Standards Institute. (1997). *Method for manual pure-tone threshold audiometry*. New York, NY: Author.

Hall, J. W. (2000). *Handbook of otoacoustic emissions*. Gainesville, FL: Singular.

Jacobson, J., & Jacobson, C. (2004). Evaluation of hearing loss in infants and young children. *Pediatric Annals, 33*(12), 811–821.

NICOLE NASEWICZ
CASSIE EIFFERT
University of Florida

See also Auditory Abnormalities

AUDITORY ABNORMALITIES

Auditory abnormalities or abnormalities that manifest as hearing loss may be sensory, neural, or both and may arise from differing causes. Although half of all auditory abnormalities are considered to be genetic in origin, 90% of all people with a congenital hearing loss have normal hearing parents, suggesting that this is a recessive trait (Toriellos, Reardon, & Gorlin, 2004). Karlsson, Harris, and Svartengren (1997) also found that 50% of all late onset hearing loss, or hearing loss in people over the age of 65, has a genetic component. Further, genetic conditions seem to have equal prevalence in all types of hearing loss.

Although hearing loss is usually associated with only the ear, auditory abnormalities can occur in any location through the entire auditory system. Hearing losses in the past have been classified using the interchangeable terms as *sensory-neural, sensorineural,* or *neurosensory*. Advances in clinical equipment and testing technique is allowing a more precise diagnosis and allow for the terms to be split. Otoacoustic emissions give us an indication of how the cochlea is functioning. Auditory brainstem response testing allows us to check the neural pathways to the auditory cortex. Acoustic reflexes check the auditory pathways to the level of the superior olivary complex. Impedance measures check the integrity of the middle ear system. Pure-tone testing checks the integrity of the whole of the system. Central auditory tests give us a glimpse of how the processing centers are working. With these advances, four main types of hearing loss can occur depending on location of the lesion. These types are conductive, sensory, neural, and vestibular.

Conductive hearing losses are caused by structural abnormalities such as atresia, otosclerosis, middle ear effusion, and eustachian tube dysfunction. This type of auditory abnormality accounts for the most common problem in children, with three out of four children having experienced an ear infection by the time they are 3 years old, and has the most educational significance (National Institute on Deafness and Communication Disorders [NIDCD], n.d.). Frequent ear infections put the child at risk for not only speech and language deficits but also for central auditory processing difficulties. Conductive hearing losses can be remediated medically and surgically.

Sensory auditory abnormalities are those caused by problems in the cochlea or auditory sense organ. Inner and outer hair cells can be damaged by ototoxic medications, excessive noise, obesity, and vascular problems that deprive the cochlea of blood supply and oxygen as well as by genetic conditions. Treatment options for this type of auditory abnormality include hearing aids and cochlear implants (NIDCD, n.d.).

Neural abnormalities are those that occur above the level of the cochlea in the auditory system. Acoustic neuromas, auditory neuropathy, and central auditory processing disorders are examples of neural abnormalities. Hearing aids are not usually the first choice of remediation for these types of difficulties but can be helpful in some instances. Remediation is dependent on the site of lesion and may include surgical options in the case of a tumor or auditory rehabilitation in the case of auditory processing difficulties (NIDCD, n.d.).

Vestibular disorders often are overlooked when thinking of auditory impairments. The vestibular system is located in the inner ear. Approximately 42% of the population will seek medical treatment for dizziness in their lifetime, and the majority of the causes will lie within the inner ear (Vestibular Disorders Association, n.d.). Causes of vestibular disorders include blows to the head; ototoxic medications, such as high-dose or long-term antibiotics; ear infections; or stroke. In many cases, however, cause of damage to the vestibular system cannot be determined. Treatment options include vestibular rehabilitation, mediation, and surgery (Vestibular Disorders Association, n.d.).

REFERENCES

Karlsson, K. K., Harris, J. R., & Svartengren, M. (1997). Description and preliminary results from an audiometric study of male twins. *Ear and Hearing, 18*, 114–120.

National Institute on Deafness and Communication Disorders (NIDCD). (n.d.). *Statistics and human communication*. Retrieved September 13, 2005, from www.nidcd.nih.gov/

Toriellos, H., Reardon, W., & Gorlin, R. (2004). *Hereditary hearing loss and its syndromes* (2nd ed.). Oxford, UK: Oxford University Press.

Vestibular Disorders Association. (n.d.). *Vestibular disorders*. Retrieved September 13, 2005, from www.vestibular.org

LISA WILDMO
Bryan, Texas

See also Auditory Discrimination; Auditory Perception; Deaf

AUDITORY DISCRIMINATION

Auditory discrimination is the ability to determine the differences between the speech sounds and sequencing. Auditory discrimination is the middle rung in the processing of sound. An acoustic signal must first be perceived, then discriminated, and, finally, processed. These three terms (*perception, discrimination, processing*) often are used interchangeably.

It has been demonstrated that speech discrimination scores cannot be predicted from pure-tone thresholds alone (Rintlemann, 1985). Speech discrimination scores give us an understanding of a higher level of processing than pure tones alone. Meaning can be attached to the different signals. Temporal processing or frequency, duration, and ordering must take place in order to understand the speech signal. In addition, auditory closure must take place in order to integrate the preceding information.

Discrimination tests conducted as part of a comprehensive audiological evaluation usually refer to speech discrimination testing. Generally, this is performed by presenting a standardized monosyllable word list like the NU6 or the CID W22 through headphones. Individuals may be asked to repeat words or may be asked if two words are the same or different. Monosyllabic words are used as they offer the least redundancy. The percentage correct is given as the speech discrimination scores. Difficulties at the discrimination level will lead to difficulties recognizing and using the prosodic aspects of speech, reading, and subtle changes in meaning as a result of prosodic changes (Bellis, 1996). Auditory discrimination of phonemes (single speech sounds) and tones has been linked to reading ability and disability (Lachmann, Berti, Kujala, & Schröger, 2005). Similarly, discrimination training has been found to result in better phonological processing in children (Moore, Rosenberg, & Coleman, 2005).

Auditory discrimination is a neural response and current research is looking into electroacoustic testing to help diagnose problems with discrimination. Electroacoustic testing is currently being used to calculate hearing thresholds in the infant and hard-to-test population, but it has been very difficult to determine discrimination abilities within this group as traditional testing has involved language and reasoning requirements. The Mismatched Negativity Test is one such electrophysiological test being studied (Cheour, Lappaenen, & Kraus, 2000).

REFERENCES

Bellis, T. J. (1996). *Assessment and management of central auditory processing disorders in the educational setting.* San Diego, CA: Singular.

Cheour, M., Leppaenen, P., & Kraus, N. (2000). Mismatched negativity (MMN) as a tool for investigating auditory discrimination and sensory memory in infants and children. *Clinical Neurophysiology, 111*, 4–16.

Lachmann, T., Berti, S., Kujala, T., & Schröger, E. (2005). Diagnostic subgroups of developmental dyslexic have different deficits in neural processing of tones and phonemes. *International Journal of Psychophysiology, 56*, 105–120.

Moore, D. R., Rosenberg, J. F., & Coleman, J. S. (2005). Discrimination training of phonemic contrasts enhances phonological processing in mainstream school children. *Brain and Language, 94*, 72–85.

Rintlemann, W. F. (1985). *Hearing assessment.* Baltimore, MD: University Park Press.

Lisa Wildmo
Bryan, Texas

See also **Auditory Perception; Developmental Dyslexia; Dyslexia; Reading Disorders**

AUDITORY PERCEPTION

Auditory perception is the ability to identify, interpret, and attach meaning to sound to make it meaningful phenomena (Garstecki & Erber, 1997). These abilities rely on several intact neurological processes such that sound must be heard and transmitted to appropriate structures within the brain. When these processes are not intact, difficulties in auditory perception occur.

Auditory perception follows a developmental trajectory (Moore, 2002; Boothroyd, 1997). Children at 6 months of age demonstrate the beginnings of auditory perception by contrasting phonemes, phoneme recognition, recognition of speech in noise, selective attention, and the use of linguistic content (Boothroyd, 1997). Complete maturation of the auditory system is not complete until later childhood—ages 5 to 12 years (Moore, 2002).

The terms *auditory perception* and *auditory processing* often are used interchangeably in the literature. Children with auditory perceptual problems and auditory processing disorders often exhibit language and learning disabilities (Garstecki & Erber, 1997). Auditory perception problems are found concomitantly with or misdiagnosed as Learning Disorders. Standard pure-tone and speech-discrimination evaluations are not sufficient to rule out an auditory perceptional problem (Katz & Wilde, 1985).

Fisher (1976) developed a checklist of 25 warning signs for which a child should be evaluated for an auditory perceptual problem. These included saying "what" in the absence of a hearing loss, inattentiveness, frequent middle ear infections, asking for repetitions, poor fine-motor coordination, difficulty following directions, poorer verbal than performance scores on intelligence tests, and inconsistencies in academic subjects.

REFERENCES

Boothroyd, A. (1997). Auditory development of the hearing child. *Scandinavian Audiology, 46*(Suppl.), 9–16.

Fisher, L. I. (1976). *Fisher auditory problems checklist.* Cedar Rapids, IA: Grant Wood Area Educational Agency.

Garstecki, D. C., & Erber, S. F. (1997). Hearing loss management in children and adults. In G. T. Menchers, S. E. Gerber, & A. McComve (Eds.), *Audiology and auditory dysfunction* (pp. 220–232). Needham Heights, MA: Allyn & Bacon.

Katz, J., & Wilde, L. (1985). Auditory perceptional disorders in children. In J. Katz (Ed.), *Handbook of clinical audiology* (3rd ed., pp. 664–668). Baltimore, MD: Williams & Wilkins.

Moore, J. K. (2002). Maturation of human auditory cortex: Implications for speech perception. *Annals Oto-Rhino-Larngology, 189*(Suppl.), 7–10.

LISA WILDMO
Bryan, Texas

See *also* Auditory Discrimination; Auditory Processing

AUDITORY PROCESSING

Although the terms *auditory perception* and *auditory processing* often are used interchangeably in the literature, auditory processing (or central auditory processing [CAP]) is the area we are most concerned about when we are dealing with children who are experiencing language and reading problems. In this context, *auditory processing* is an umbrella term used for the complex task of taking in all the auditory information and making it salient to the task at hand. According to the American Speech-Language-Hearing Association (ASHA; 1996) auditory processing involves mechanisms responsible for sound localization, lateralization, auditory discrimination, auditory pattern recognition, temporal aspects of audition, and auditory performance with competing acoustic signals. Given the multiple components, there is no wonder that Phillips (2002) concluded that "Central Auditory Processing Disorders (CAPD) are probably as idiosyncratic as the individuals they affect" (p. 256).

Due to the complexity of auditory processing, a multidisciplinary approach is recommended for assessment and management of auditory processing disorders (APDs). The team should include, but is not limited to, a speech language pathologist, audiologist, psychologist, parents, physicians, and classroom and special education teachers (Bellis & Ferre, 1996). Management of APD should focus on the range of listening and learning deficits experienced by the individual child. Recommended intervention is a combination of "auditory training, metalinguistic and metacognitive strategies designed to increase the scope and use of the auditory and central resources" (Wertz, Hall, & Davis, 2002, p. 282). Management also is focused on improving signal-to-noise ratios, improving listening skills, and the auditory behaviors of difficult listening situations for those with APD.

REFERENCES

American Speech-Language-Hearing Association (ASHA). (1996). Central auditory processing: Current status of research and implications for clinical practice. *American Journal of Audiology, 5*, 41–45.

Bellis, T., & Ferre, J. (1996). Assessment and management of central auditory processing disorders in children. *Educational Audiology Monograph, 6*, 23–27.

Phillips, D. (2002). Central auditory system and central auditory processing disorders: Some conceptual issues. *Seminars in Hearing, 23*, 251–261.

Wertz, D., Hall, J. W., & Davis, W. (2002). Auditory processing disorders: Management approaches past to present. *Seminars in Hearing, 23*, 277–285.

LISA WILDMO
Bryan, Texas

See *also* Auditory Discrimination; Auditory Perception; Central Auditory Dysfunction; Learning Disabilities

AUDITORY–VISUAL INTEGRATION

Auditory–visual perceptual integration is poorly understood; therefore, it is seldom measured and described in the psychoeducational diagnostic process. Instead, beginning in the 1920s with German psychology, and later (1930s) in clinical work, the focus fell almost solely on visual–motor perceptual development. Indeed, psychology in general, and Gestalt psychology in particular, drew heavily from the easily administered, easily scored visual motor tests. Bender's (1938) *Visual-Motor Gestalt Test*, an extension of Wertheimer's (1923) laboratory instrument, soon became the most commonly administered psychological test. Early on, these easily administered tests showed substantial correlations with intelligence (Armstrong & Hauck, 1960) as a diagnostic test for brain damage (Shaw & Cruickshank, 1956), academic achievement (Koppitz, 1958), emotional difficulties (Clawson, 1959), and perceptual development (Koppitz, 1962).

Auditory perception, which in many respects appears to be a sensory–perceptual corollary of visual perception, remains relatively unexplored. The reason may be that the auditory perceptual structures are less well understood than visual perception, and more difficult to ascertain. For example, it is difficult to identify precisely where auditory sensorial function stops, perception begins, auditory perception ends, and receptive language begins.

The result has been that psychologists and special educators have generally limited the theoretical scope to an explanation of auditory–visual perceptual integration as an operational construct important to human learning. However, that fact also conveys a certain ambience, as remedial educators have been tenacious about the importance of auditory–visual integration within the reading process. They believe that reading would be a slow, awkward instructional process in the absence of integrating perceptual symbolic information from the primary sensory channels. Many reading experts are convinced that perceptual integration is critical to early learning of letters and letter phonemic symbolism. For example, the visual perceptual system may neurally code a "B" and a "D" as distinct symbols based on luminancy differences. A "B" uses a different neuronal subsystem than a "D" because it draws on lateral inhibition and activation associated with on-center neurons; "D" draws on off-center neurons. Symbolic clarity in the visual perceptual realm may be influenced by these factors, all of which have been well investigated: extent and organization of retinal area activities; transformation of receptive-field organization; and estimates of size of receptive field.

In reading, as in most visual tasks, the eye gathers information during the pauses between saccadic movements. Ultimately, stimulus letters are recognized; that is, an appropriate subvocal or auditory response (saying a letter) occurs. The recognition (perceptual) memory can hold at least three letters for a period of about 1 second, until they have been rehearsed.

A scan component is needed to transform the visual information in very short-term visual perceptual memory into motoric information, and then auditory information. Actually, the visual scan component has at least three distinguishable functions: deciding which areas of the visual field contain information; directing processing capacity to the locations selected by the prescan ("attention"); and converting the visual input from the selected locations into the forms of motor memory units and ultimately auditory information.

In principle, although not in detail, the auditory scan is exactly analogous to the visual scan. The auditory scan selects some contents of auditory memory (e.g., the sound representation of one letter) and converts them into motor information. A street address is remembered by placing it into auditory–perceptual memory. By means of this short-term loop, information can be retained in auditory short-term memory. Subvocal rehearsal, the subvocal output of the rehearsal component, is entered into the auditory short-term memory just as though it had been a vocal output. Once that occurs, visual imagery results. The importance of visual–auditory or auditory–visual perceptual

integration becomes paramount when confronting remedial reading difficulties. Critchley (1964) noted that children with so-called congenital word blindness failed to develop visual perceptual memory, while their auditory perceptual memory was unaffected.

A great deal of literature from the mid and late 1960s suggested a close interrelationship between the short-term storage mechanisms of vision and audition. Conrad (1959) showed that subjects frequently make substitution errors when recalling lists of visually presented letters in which the letter substituted (e.g., ANQT) sounds similar to the correct letter (e.g., ANQE). Although these letters are highly dissimilar in appearance, they sound similar when spoken aloud. Thus, visual material, Conrad suggests, must have been translated and encoded in auditory storage.

Murray (1968) reported extensive studies of short-term storage for visual and auditory items. His results showed how the similarity of sounds affected recall of the list (acoustic similarity). In Murray's experiment, conditions enabling the auditory system to assist in the coding and storing of incoming information tend to produce superior performances; this may indicate that the auditory mechanism is generally superior to the visual mechanism in this respect. Such a superiority has also been demonstrated by Murdock (1968).

Wickelgren (1965) has demonstrated that the presence of acoustic elements in visually presented material can influence the accuracy of recall. Subjects listened to four random letters. Next, eight letters were visually presented and copied by the subject. Finally, a test of the first four aural letters was administered. Even though the interpolated material had to be copied rather than spoken, if the eight letters were similar in sound to the aural letters, performance on auditory recall was poorer than when the visual letters were quite dissimilar in sound.

Ross (1969) developed a logical test of the audio–visual interaction in short-term storage by measuring the retention of simple symbols (+ and −) either organized in patterns (e.g.,−++−+−+−) or unpatterned (e.g., +−+ +−+−−+). Blanton and Odom (1968) found a superiority in seeing and hearing children over deaf children in terms of the span of digits that could be recalled. However, this result may reflect greater experience with numbers on the part of the normal children.

In short, an integration of information from the visual and auditory perceptual channel seems to be occurring. How else, in fact, could a person read graphics, or listen to others read, and write the graphic symbol being received aurally? Reading is a dual process that, except for the learner with disabilities who may be missing one of the sensory channels or have perceptual deficits, is an integrated function. Current research is going toward a dual model of working memory that includes separate visual and auditory channels. On some tasks learners can integrate words and pictures more easily if the words are presented auditorily rather than visually (Mayer & Romano, 1998). With infants, for example, the synchronicity of visual and auditory stimuli are not as important as with older children and adults indicating developmental trends in integrating auditory and visual information presented at the same time (Lewkowicz, 1996).

In summary, auditory–visual integration would appear to be the internal stimulation of the opposite modality, for instance, visual perceptual information is received and a signal system translates the meaning to the auditory perceptual modality in reading. Information on the assumed trait is limited, and awaits much research. It does seem likely that this function holds promise as a predictor of what modality may be used as a unisensory or multisensory receiving mechanism in planning an intervention (Movellan & McClelland, 2001).

REFERENCES

Armstrong, R. G., & Hauck, P. A. (1960). Correlates of the Bender-Gestalt scores in children. *Journal of Psychological Studies*, *11*, 153–158.

Bender, L. (1938). *Visual Motor Gestalt Test and its clinical use*. American Ortho Psychiatry Association Research Monograph 3.

Birch, H. G., & Belmont, L. (1965). Auditory-visual integration in brain damaged and normal children. *Journal of Developmental Medicine and Child Neurology*, *7*, 135–144.

Blanton, R. L., & Odom, P. B. (1968). Some possible interferences and facilitation effects of pronounciability. *Journal of Verbal Learning Behavior*, *7*, 844–846.

Clawson, A. (1959). The Bender-Gestalt Visual Motor Gestalt Test as an index of emotional disturbance in children. *Journal of Project Technology*, *23*, 198–206.

Conrad, R. (1959). Errors of immediate memory. *British Journal of Psychology*, *50*, 349–359.

Critchley, M. (1965). *The dyslexic child*. London, UK: Heineman.

Koppitz, E. M. (1958). The Bender Gestalt Test and learning disturbances in young children. *Journal of Clinical Psychology*, *14*, 292–295.

Koppitz, E. M. (1962). Diagnosing brain damage in young children with the Bender Gestalt Test. *Journal of Consultative Psychology*, *26*, 541–546.

Lewkowicz, D. J. (1996). Perception of auditory visual temporal synchrony in human infants. *Journal of Experimental Psychology: Human Perception & Performance*, *22*, 1094–1106.

Mayer, R. E., & Romano, R. (1998). A split-attention effect in multimedia learning: Evidence for dual processing systems in working memory. *Journal of Educational Psychology*, *90*, 312–320.

Movellan, J. R., & McClelland, J. L. (2001). The Morton-Massaro law of information integration: Implications for models of perception. *Psychological Review*, *108*, 113–148.

Murdock, B. B., Jr. (1968). Modality effects in short-term memory: Storage or retrieval? *Journal of Experimental Psychology*, *78*, 70–86.

Murray, D. J. (1968). Articulation and acoustic confusability in short-term memory. *Journal of Experimental Psychology*, *78*, 679–684.

Ross, B. M. (1969). Sequential visual memory and the limited magic of the number seven. *Journal of Experimental Psychology*, *80*, 339–347.

Shaw, M. C., & Cruickshank, W. M. (1956). The use of the Bender-Gestalt Test with epileptic children. *Journal of Clinical Psychology*, *12*, 192–193.

Wertheimer, M. (1923). Untersuchanger zur Lehre von der Gestalt. II. *Psychol. forsch*, *5*, 301–350.

Wickelgren, W. A. (1965). Acoustic similarity and intrusion errors in short-term memory. *Journal of Experimental Psychology*, *70*, 102–108.

DAVID A. SABATINO
West Virginia College of Graduate Studies

See also Auditory Perception; Auditory Processing; Visual Perception and Discrimination

AUGMENTATIVE AND ALTERNATIVE COMMUNICATION

Augmentative and Alternative Communication (AAC) is a specialized area of research and clinical practice within the broader field of Speech-Language Pathology (American Speech-Language-Hearing Association, 2004). AAC research focuses on a range of issues related to the uses and effects of using nonspeech modes of communication by individuals with severe communication impairments. Clinical practice in AAC focuses on assessing individuals' communication needs, recommending AAC systems, and supporting effective use of AAC. Clinical practice in AAC also includes providing direct intervention to enable persons to communicate successfully through AAC.

AAC is often used by individuals with temporary or permanent speech impairment due to congenital or acquired conditions, such as acquired brain injury, cerebral palsy, severe aphasia, intellectual disability, and autism spectrum disorders (Beukelman & Mirenda, 2005). In cases where the condition results in unintelligible or dysfluent speech, AAC is primarily intended to augment the person's existing speech and language. In cases, where speech has largely failed to develop, AAC provides an alternative mode of communication. For individuals with autism spectrum disorders, AAC is most often indicated as an alternative mode of communication and is prescribed in cases where the individual has failed to acquire any appreciable amount of speech. This situation is usually found among individuals with the more severe symptoms of autistic disorder.

A range of alternative communication modes has been developed for individuals who require AAC. The various modes are typically classified as either aided or unaided (Beukelman & Mirenda, 2005). Aided AAC systems involve external materials, such as pictures, photographs, miniature objects, and electronic speech-generating devices. Unaided AAC options consist of sign language, manual signs, and formal or informal gestures.

The most commonly used AAC modes in communication interventions for individuals with autism spectrum disorders are manual signs, speech-generating devices and picture-exchange (Mirenda & Iacono, 2009). There is considerable debate as to which of these systems is best suited to individuals with autism spectrum disorders (Mirenda, 2003). However, research data show that all three modes have been successfully taught to individuals with autism spectrum disorders. In addition, comparative studies indicate few major or consistent differences in how quickly and easily individuals can learn to use each of these three AAC options (Wendt, 2009; Schlosser, Sigafoos, & Koul, 2009). Furthermore, the use of AAC does not appear to inhibit the emergence of speech and can have a moderately facilitative effect on speech development for some individuals (Millar, 2009). AAC intervention has also been associated with improvement in problem behavior (e.g., aggression, self-injury, extreme tantrums) associated with autism spectrum disorders (Sigafoos, O'Reilly, & Lancioni, 2009).

REFERENCES

American Speech-Language-Hearing Association (2004). Roles and responsibilities of speech-language pathologists with respect to augmentative and alternative communication. Technical Report. *ASHA Supplement, 24,* 1–17.

Beukelman, D. R., & Mirenda, P. (2005). *Augmentative and alternative communication: Supporting children and adults with complex communication needs* (3rd ed.). Baltimore, MD: Paul H. Brookes.

Millar, D. C. (2009). Effects of AAC on natural speech development of individuals with autism spectrum disorders. In P. Mirenda & T. Iacono (Eds.), *Autism spectrum disorders and AAC* (pp. 171–192). Baltimore, MD: Paul H. Brookes.

Mirenda, P. (2003). Toward functional augmentative and alternative communication for students with autism: Manual signs, graphic symbols, and voice output communication aids. *Language Speech and Hearing Services in Schools, 34,* 202–215.

Mirenda, P., & Iacono, T. (2009). *Autism spectrum disorders and AAC.* Baltimore, MD: Paul H. Brookes.

Schlosser, R. W., Sigafoos, J., & Koul, R. K. (2009). Speech output and speech-generating devices in autism spectrum disorders. In P. Mirenda & T. Iacono (Eds.), *Autism spectrum disorders and AAC* (pp. 141–169). Baltimore, MD: Paul H. Brookes.

Sigafoos, J., O'Reilly, M. F., & Lancioni, G. E. (2009). Functional communication training and choice-making interventions for the treatment of problem behavior in individuals with autism spectrum disorders. In P. Mirenda & T. Iacono (Eds.), *Autism spectrum disorders and AAC* (pp. 333–353). Baltimore, MD: Paul H. Brookes.

Wendt, O. (2009). Research on the use of manual signs and graphic symbols in autism spectrum disorders: A systematic review. In P. Mirenda & T. Iacono (Eds.), *Autism spectrum disorders and AAC* (pp. 83–139). Baltimore, MD: Paul H. Brookes.

JEFF SIGAFOOS
Victoria University of Wellington
Fourth edition

AUSTRALIA, SPECIAL EDUCATION IN

Historical Background and Context

The early 19th century in Australia saw the introduction of education for privileged children, as well as a very limited number of schools and institutions for some children (mainly boys) who were illiterate, those who were delinquent, and the destitute (Ashman, 2005). *The National Education Act of 1848* meant that some very few children with learning difficulties and intellectual disabilities began to be provided for (Ashman, 2005), and the first special schools for students with a hearing impairment were founded in Sydney and Melbourne in 1880 (Sweetman, Long & Smyth, 1992).

In 1901 a federation of states known as the Commonwealth of Australia was created. However, education remained a state responsibility with each jurisdiction developing its own Education Act with its own policies and programs related to compulsory education. During this time there was a increase in the provisions for children with mild intellectual disabilities (who were referred to as "educationally backward"), but other children, for example, those who were referred to as "educable" or "trainable" were not taught in public schools, although they may have been educated in private schools established by parents or charities (Ashman, 2005, Loreman, Deppler & Harvey, 2005). After World War II the terms educable and ineducable were discontinued, and some educational opportunities were offered to these children with disabilities in separate schools or classes, although many children received little additional support (Ashman, 2005).

From this point in time educational provisions for students with disabilities in Australia can be traced as movements from segregated schools for students with disabilities to mainstreaming to integration to inclusion. The negative responses to special schools and classes that were dominant in the United States in the 1960s also emerged in Australia, with calls for students with disabilities to be integrated into regular classrooms (Ashman, 2005). Children with disabilities were often placed in a special class in a regular school and participated occasionally in the mainstream setting (Forlin, 2006). Unlike their counterparts in the United States, students with learning difficulties (learning disabilities) in literacy and numeracy in Australia, historically, have not been enrolled in separate classes, but have participated in models of support in which they were withdrawn for one or more class lessons per week provided by a remedial, resource, or support teacher.

The movement toward inclusive education has been particularly apparent since the 1970s when there was a focus on the rights of people with disabilities and inclusive education was actively promoted at the Commonwealth, state and territory levels, especially following the Salamanca Statement (UNESCO, 1994). While there is still debate in Australia about what constitutes inclusive education (Graham & Slee, 2008), in general today there is a strong policy commitment to inclusive education in all states and territories and in all school systems, that is, in the government and nongovernment (specifically Catholic and Independent) systems. However, this commitment to inclusive education does not mean that the practices in the various educational systems are always consistent with their declared polices.

Commonwealth (Federal) Government Legislation and Initiatives

There are several pieces of Commonwealth (that is, federal) legislation that seek to protect the rights of Australia's citizens. One of the most important laws with respect to Australia's citizens with disabilities is the *Disability Discrimination Act 1992* (DDA) (Commonwealth Government, 1992). The DDA makes it unlawful to discriminate on the basis of disability. The DDA defines disability broadly (see Disability Discrimination Act 1992 (Cth), section 4, Commonwealth Government, 1992). Under the DDA students with various forms of disability (now referred to as impairment) have the same rights to education as nonimpaired students and they should be educated in the least restrictive environment possible.

The *Disability Standards for Education 2005* (Australian Government, Department of Education, Employment and Workplace Relations, 2005) were developed under the *Disability Discrimination Act 1992 (DDA)* and point to the obligations of education and training providers to ensure that students with disabilities can access and participate in education without discrimination (see Guthrie & Waldeck, 2008 for a discussion of the Standards and inclusiveness in education). The Standards also state that a range of measures must be used to identify children with disabilities and that these students must also receive specialised support.

Financial support for parents, carers and families of children with disabilities is provided for a range of services by the federal, state and territory governments. (See for example some of the funded services provided by the federal government [Australian Government, Department of Families, Housing, Community Services and Indigenous Affairs, 2011a]). Additional financial support is offered through new government initiatives from time to time. For example, funding for early intervention is provided for children under 6 years of age who have been diagnosed with Down syndrome, cerebral palsy, Fragile X syndrome, or a moderate or greater vision or hearing impairment, including deaf-blindness under the *Better Start for Children with Disability (Better Start)* initiative. The financial support can be used to access professionals such as speech pathologists and occupational therapists (Australian Government, Department of Families, Housing, Community Services and Indigenous Affairs, 2011b).

Consistent with the move toward inclusion, *The National Disability Strategy* launched in March 2011 refers to the vision of "an inclusive Australian society" (Australian Government, Department of Families, Housing, Community Services and Indigenous Affairs, 2011c). Amongst its six priority areas, in the coming years, the Strategy which will guide public policy at federal, state, and territory levels to develop an inclusive and high quality education system that is responsive to the needs of individuals with disabilities.

As part of bringing about a high quality education system, a national curriculum has been developed, with the Foundation to Year 10 Australian Curriculum for English, mathematics, science, and history available for use in schools (Australian Curriculum, Assessment and Reporting Authority (ACARA), 2011a). Other curriculum areas (e.g., geography) and other sections of the curriculum (e.g., for the senior years—Years 11 and 12) are being developed. This curriculum has been designed with the same objectives for all students and so schools and teachers can create programs that are inclusive of every learner. For a small percentage of students, especially those with a significant intellectual disability, a draft curriculum is being developed. This curriculum will allow the achievement of these students who are progressing to the Foundation level English and mathematics to be described in four overlapping and interrelated phases of learning progression, specifically Responsive, Exploratory, Active, and Purposeful (Australian Curriculum, Assessment and Reporting Authority, 2011b). In addition, ACARA is responsible for developing and administering national assessments and for analysing and reporting student assessment data in order for students' performance to be compared across the country (Australian Curriculum, Assessment and Reporting Authority, 2011c).

The Commonwealth government's initiative *Literacy, Numeracy and Special Learning Needs* (Australian Government, Department of Education, Employment and Workplace Relations, 2011) is an initiative that provides state and territory education systems with additional repources to support better learning outcomes in these two domains for students with special needs. These funds are typically distributed by education systems so schools and teachers can develop unique targeted programs in literacy and numeracy.

The Australian government also reaches out to other countries in the region. For example, underpinned by such documents as the *United Nations Convention on the Rights of Persons with Disabilities* (United Nations, 2006), the Commonwealth government is involved through its aid programs in supporting the governments of countries such as Samoa, Indonesia, and Papua New Guinea. In particular it is offering support as these governments move toward removing some of the barriers to education for students with disabilities, to developing initiatives to achieve universal primary education, and to creating policies and programs for inclusive education (Australian Government, AusAid, 2010).

Current State of Inclusive and Special Education

Eighty-nine percent of students in Australia with a diagnosed impairment between the ages of 5 and 14 attend regular schools, and only a small percent attend special schools (Australian Institute of Health and Welfare [AIHW], 2009). In particular, in 2010, there were 9468 schools in Australia, 416 of these were special schools and of those 332 were government schools and 84 were nongovernment schools (Australian Bureau of Statistics, 2011). An examination of trends in the proportion of students with a disability in Australian schools from 2000 to 2009 by Dempsey (2011) revealed an increase in the number of students with a disability and a more rapid increase in the identification of students with a disability in government than in nongovernment schools. In general the increase is due to enhanced professional awareness of various disabilities and school access to financial support for these students (Dempsey, 2011). However, there is no agreed-upon national definition of disability and this leads to some students being counted as having a disability in some states but not in others. Rather, the definition of disabilities is related to whether or not a child receives special education services and thus schools are responsible for assisting these students (Dempsey, 2011). Special educational services are determined through a process of appraisal that is undertaken at the school. The appraisal process determines the level of resources needed to make the adjustments for the students to access and participate in the educational programs and school activities.

All of Australia's state and territory departments of education provide a range of educational services and settings for students from around 3 years of age to school leaving age (in most states and territories this is around 18 years of age). As indicated earlier these government systems support and promote the enrollment of students in inclusive school settings. However, where special provisions are permitted under the *Disability Standards for Education 2005* (Australian Government, Department of Education, Employment and Workplace Relations, 2005), this may include placement (where parents/carers and professionals agree that such placements are in the best interests of the students) in special schools or special or support classes/units. Indeed some authors criticize the policies and practices of inclusive education in Australia, arguing that they represent a restructuring of the identification systems and of the roles of specialist staff. Instead they argue that what is needed is a rethinking of what is meant by disability, difference, and inclusion (Bourke, 2010, Graham, 2006). In addition, recent analyses of the data in some states (e.g., New South Wales) have revealed evidence of an increase in the enrollments of students with disabilities in segregated settings and in particular an increase in the numbers of students with emotional or behavioral difficulties who have been labeled and excluded from regular schools (Graham & Sweller, 2011).

In all states and territories, individual learning plans (ILPs), also known as individualized education plans (IEPs), are used to document the education programs of students with disabilities. These are typically written by a multidisciplinary assessment team that includes a student's parents, the teachers and an educational psychologist, guidance officer, or support teacher. The ILP/IEP identifies the adjustments that will be made to a student's curriculum, programs and activities in order for the student to be with his or her same age peers to the greatest extent possible. The adjustments most often refer to adjusting the curriculum and instruction, resources and the environment. With respect to curriculum, various means are used to make it more inclusive and meet the students' needs. For example, lessons are created using the principles of Universal Design for Learning and adapted using differentiated instruction (van Kraayenoord, 2007). Teachers are encouraged to develop a repertoire of practices that are inclusive and responsive and to use teaching adaptations and technology to support learning (Croser & Bridge, 2012; Shaddock, Giorcelli, & Smith, 2007a; van Kraayenoord & Elkins, 2012). The resources include both physical and human resources. For example, students with vision impairments who are typically in a regular classroom receive support from both the classroom teacher and an itinerant support teacher or advisor with expertise in vision. Each school's Special Needs Team or similar group monitors the educational progress of the student and in an ongoing way coordinates and reviews the support, as well as the review process itself. ILPs/IEPs are also formally reviewed annually. These reviews are to ensure that the programs and instruction offered are effective and appropriate. Indeed, increasingly, the effectiveness of the instructional programs that all students receive is becoming a priority area for schools and education systems in Australia (Rowe, 2007; van Kraayenoord, 2010).

Continuing Challenges

As schools strive to meet the needs of all students it has become apparent that particular groups of students fare less well than others. Providing culturally and linguistically appropriate and responsive education to Australia's indigenous students, including indigenous students with disabilities is a very serious challenge (de Courcy, 2010; Munro, 2012; Ministerial Advisory Committee: Students with Disabilities, 2003; Power & Hyde, 2002). In addition, Australia's geography has meant that students in rural and remote areas face isolation (Forlin, 2006), and rural and remote schools have difficulties attracting and retaining high-quality teachers (Reid, Green, Cooper, Hastings, Lock, & White, 2010). Thus meeting the needs of students with disabilities in rural and remote areas is also an ongoing challenge.

The issue of developing well-qualified teachers to work in inclusive contexts is a challenge for teacher preparation programs in Australian universities. There are a number of different approaches that tertiary educators use to prepare preservice teachers and the efficacy of these different approaches is still a topic for research (Forlin & Chambers, 2011; Furlonger, Sharma, Moore, & Smyth King, 2010). Nevertheless, it is important for both graduating teachers and for existing teachers to develop the appropriate knowledge and skills to work with students with disabilities and be able to develop supportive classroom environments. Some useful resources have recently been developed to meet this purpose (see Shaddock, Giorcelli, & Smith, 2007b).

Despite these challenges Australian teachers are striving to meet the needs of the diverse learners in their classrooms. With curricula, instruction, and assessment that is inclusive, responsive, and appropriate, the education that students with disabilities will receive will have a positive impact and will mean that these students lead fulfilling lives and make a valuable contribution to our country.

REFERENCES

Andersen, C., & Walter, M. (2010). Indigenous perspectives and cultural identity. In M. Hyde, L. Carpenter, & R. Conway (Eds.) Diversity and inclusion in Australian schools (pp. 63–87). South Melbourne, VIC: Oxford University Press Australia & New Zealand.

Ashman, A. (2005). Opportunities, rights, and the individual. In A. Ashman & J. Elkins (Eds.), Educating children with diverse abilities (pp. 65–95). Frenchs Forest, NSW: Pearson Education Australia.

Australian Bureau of Statistics. (2011). 4221.0-Schools, Australia, 2010. Retrieved from: http://www.abs.gov.au/AUSSTATS/abs@.nsf/DetailsPage/4221.02010?OpenDocument

Australian Curriculum, Assessment and Reporting Authority (ACARA). (2011a). Australian Curriculum. Retrieved from: http://www.acara.edu.au/curriculum/curriculum.html

Australian Curriculum, Assessment and Reporting Authority (ACARA). (2011b). Australian Curriculum: Progressing to Foundation—English and mathematics. Retrieved from: http://consultation.australiancurriculum.edu.au/

Australian Curriculum, Assessment and Reporting Authority (ACARA). (2011c). Assessment. Retrieved from: http://www.acara.edu.au/assessment/assessment.html

Australian Government, AusAID (2010). Development for all: Towards a disability-inclusive Australian aid program 2009-2104: Achievement highlights—the first two years. Retrieved from: http://www.ausaid.gov.au/publications/

Australian Government, Department of Education, Employment and Workplace Relations. (2005). Disability Standards for Education 2005. Retrieved from: http://www.deewr.gov.au/schooling/programs/pages/disabilitystandardsforeducation.aspx

Australian Government, Department of Education, Employment and Workplace Relations. (2011). Literacy, Numeracy and Special Learning Needs Programme. Retrieved from: http://deewr.gov.au/

Australian Government, Department of Families, Housing, Community Services and Indigenous Affairs. (2011a). Facts and Figures, October 2011. Retrieved from: http://www.fahcsia.gov.au/

Australian Government, Department of Families, Housing, Community Services and Indigenous Affairs. (2011b). Better start for children (Better Start) initiative. Retrieved from: http://www.fahcsia.gov.au/sa/disability/progserv/people/betterstart/Pages/better_start_early_intervention.aspx

Australian Government, Department of Families, Housing, Community Services and Indigenous Affairs. (2011c). National disability strategy launched. Retrieved from: http://www.fahcsia.gov.au/

Australian Institute of Health & Welfare. (2009). A picture of Australia's children. AIWH Cat. No. PHR 112. Canberra: Author.

Bourke, P. E. (2010). Inclusive education reform in Queensland: Implications for policy and practices. International Journal of Inclusive Education, 14(2), 183–193.

Commonwealth Government. (1992). Disability Discrimination Act, 1992. Canberra, Australia: Author.

Croser, R., & Bridge, D. (2012). Information and communication technologies. In A. Ashman & J. Elkins (Eds.), Education for inclusion and diversity (4th ed., pp. 162–187). Frenchs Forest, NSW: Pearson Australia.

De Courcy, M. (2010). Linguistic and cultural diversity. In M. Hyde, L. Carpenter, & R. Conway (Eds.) Diversity and inclusion in Australian schools (pp. 35–62). South Melbourne, VIC: Oxford University Press Australia & New Zealand.

Dempsey, I. (2011). Trends in the proportion of students with a disability in Australian schools, 2000-2009. Journal of Intellectual and Developmental Disability, 36(2), 144–145.

Forlin, C. (2006). Inclusive education in Australia ten years after Salamanca. European Journal of Psychology of Education, 25(3), 265–277.

Forlin, C., & Chambers, D. (2011). Teacher preparation for inclusive education: Increasing knowledge but raising concerns. Asia-Pacific Journal of Teacher Education, 39(1), 17–32.

Furlonger, B. E., Sharma, U., Moore, D. W., & Smyth King, B. (2009). A new approach to training teachers to meet the diverse learning needs of deaf and hard-to-hearing children within inclusive Australian schools. *International Journal of Inclusive Education, 14*(3), 289–308.

Graham, L. J. (2006). Caught in the net: A Foucaultian interrogation of the incidental effects of limited notions of inclusion. *International Journal of Inclusive Education, 10*(1), 3–24.

Graham, L. J., & Slee, R. (2008). An illusory interiority: Interrogating the discourse/s of inclusion. *Educational Philosophy and Theory, 40*(2), 247–260.

Graham, L. J., & Sweller, N. (2011). The inclusion lottery: Who's in and who's out? Tracking inclusion and exclusion in New South Wales government schools. International Journal of Inclusive Education, 1-13. DOI: 10.1080/13603110903470046. Retrieved from: http://www.tandfonline.com/doi/pdf/10.1080/13603110903470046

Guthrie, R., & Waldeck, E. (2008). Disability standards and inclusiveness in education: A review of the Australian landscape. *International Journal of Discrimination and the Law, 9*, 133–162.

Loreman, T., Deppeler, J., & Harvey, D. (2005). *Inclusive education: A practical guide to supporting diversity in the classroom.* Sydney, NSW: Allen & Unwin.

Ministerial Advisory Committee: Students with Disabilities. (2003). Aboriginal students with disabilities. Adelaide, SA: Author. Retrieved from: http://www.macswd.sa.gov.au/pages/default/publications/

Munro, J. (2012). Education systems that support inclusion. In A. Ashman & J. Elkins (Eds.), *Education for inclusion and diversity* (4th ed., pp. 99–123). Frenchs Forest, NSW: Pearson Australia.

Power, D., & Hyde, M. (2002). The characteristics and extent of participation of Deaf and hard-of-hearing students in regular classes in Australian schools. *Journal of Deaf Studies and Deaf Education, 7*(4), 302–311.

Reid, J-A., Green, B., Cooper, M., Hastings, W., Lock, G., & White, S. (2010). Regenerating rural social space? Teacher education for rural—regional sustainability. *Australian Journal of Education, 54*(3), 262–276.

Rowe, K. J. (2007). Educational effectiveness: The importance of evidence-based teaching practices for the provision of quality teaching and learning standards. In D. M. McInerney, S. van Etten & M. Dowson (Eds.), *Research on Sociocultural Influences on Motivation and Learning* (Volume 7, Standards in Education, pp. 59–92). Greenwich, CT: Information Age Publishing.

Shaddock, A., Giorcelli, L., & Smith, S. (2007a). Project to improve the learning outcomes of students with disabilities in the early, middle and post compulsory years of schooling. Part 1: Research objectives, methodology, analyses, outcomes and findings, and implications for classroom practice. Final research report. Canberra, ACT: Commonwealth of Australia. Retrieved from: http://www.ndco.stepscs.net.au/pdf/Strategies%20for%20teachers%20in%20mainstream%20classrooms%20booklet.pdf

Shaddock, A., Giorcelli, L., & Smith, S. (2007b). Students with disabilities in mainstream classrooms. A resource for teachers. Canberra, ACT: Commonwealth of Australia. Retrieved from: http://www.ndco.stepscs.net.au/pdf/Strategies%20for%20teachers%20in%20mainstream%20classrooms%20booklet.pdf

Sweetman, E., Long, C. R., & Smyth, J. (1992). *A history of state education in Victoria.* Melbourne, VIC: Education Department of Victoria/Critchley Parker.

United Nations. (2006). Convention on the Rights of Persons with Disabilities. Retrieved from: http://www.un.org/disabilities/default.asp?navid=14&pid=150

United Nations Educational, Scientific and Cultural Organization (UNESCO). (1994). Salamanca Statement. Retrieved from: www.unesco.org/education/

van Kraayenoord, C. E. (2007). School and classroom practices in inclusive education in Australia. *Childhood Education, 83*(6), 390–394.

van Kraayenoord, C. E. (2010). Response to Intervention: New ways and wariness. *Reading Research Quarterly, 45*(3), 363–375.

van Kraayenoord, C. E., & Elkins, J. (2012). Literacies and numeracy. In A. Ashman & J. Elkins (Eds.), *Education for inclusion and diversity* (4th ed., pp. 257–289). Frenchs Forest, NSW: Pearson Australia.

CHRISTINA E. VAN KRAAYENOORD
School of Education
The University of Queensland
Fourth edition

AUTISM

Autism, or autistic disorder, is one of five pervasive developmental disorders (PDD) and is usually diagnosed before 3 years of age (American Psychiatric Association, 2000). Diagnostic symptoms include: qualitative impairment in social interaction (e.g., failure to develop peer relationships), delays in the development of communication (e.g., limited or total lack of spoken language), and restrictive interests and/or repetitive body movements (e.g., rocking torso back and forth; American Psychiatric Association, 2000). In addition to the diagnostic symptoms, autism is also often associated with delays or difficulties in cognitive functioning, learning, attention, and sensory processing (Hess & Matson, 2010; Matson, Hess, Daniene, Mahan, & Fodstad, 2010). The term "spectrum" is often used to describe the heterogeneity within the population, because the symptoms associated with autism may range from mild to severe. The term "autism spectrum disorders" (ASD) has been used as an umbrella term to refer to all five PDDs (i.e., Rett syndrome, childhood disintegrative disorder, autistic disorder, Asperger syndrome, and Pervasive Developmental Disorder–Not Otherwise Specified [PDD-NOS]) or to refer only to autism, Asperger syndrome, and PDD-NOS (Lang, Regester, Rispoli, & Camargo, 2010). The function and validity of the term "ASD" and the practice of differentiating between the subtypes autistic disorder and Asperger syndrome are current subjects of debate (Matson, 2007; Sigafoos, O'Reilly, & Lancioni, 2009). The next revision of the Diagnostic and Statistical Manual of Mental Disorders (DSM-V) will likely clarify this issue.

Historical Overview

Although many historical accounts of individuals with autism have been subsequently identified (e.g., Koegel, 2008; Rutter & Schopler, 1978), Leo Kanner was the first to recognize autism as a unique diagnosis. In 1943, Kanner described the difficulty developing relationships, unusual or absent speech, unimaginative and repetitive play behaviors, and an insistence on sameness within their routines. Kanner also noted the absence of physical abnormalities and the presence of symptoms early in life. Kanner called the disorder "early infantile autism." Kanner used the word "autism," which was derived from the Greek word "auto," which means "self" to describe the state of extreme aloneness. However, the use of the word "autism" initially created confusion because the term had previously been used to refer to a withdrawal into fantasy by people with schizophrenia (Wing, 1976). Autistic disorder first appeared in the DSM-III in 1980. The diagnostic characteristics for autism have changed multiple times since Kanner's initial description.

Prevalence

The number of children diagnosed with ASD (i.e., autistic disorder, Asperger syndrome, and PDD-NOS) has increased substantially over several decades, and may be as high as 1 in 110 to 1 in 150 children (Fombonne, 2003; Rice, 2009). ASDs are 3 to 4 times more common in boys than in girls and 20 to 50 times more common in siblings of children with autism than in the general population (O'Roak & State, 2008). Currently, the cause of the increase in prevalence is being debated and researched (Matson & Kozlowski, 2010). Factors such as changing and broadening the diagnostic criteria (i.e., the inclusion of higher functioning individuals within the autism spectrum), increased awareness of autistic symptoms by pediatricians, diagnoses given earlier in life, recognition that ASD is a lifelong condition, and improved diagnostic methods account for at least some degree of the reported increase (Matson & Kozlowski, 2010). Another major contributing factor known to influence the prevalence

of autism is diagnostic substitution (Coo et al., 2008). Specifically, as the prevalence of autism increases, the number of other developmental disabilities seems to be decreasing, suggesting that diagnosticians may prefer to diagnose children with autism instead of with other disorders, such as intellectual impairments, or that children diagnosed with other disorders are having their diagnoses changed to autism. For example, in a study of school children in British Columbia, the prevalence of students with autism increased from 12.3 per 10,000 in 1996 to 43.1 per 10,000 in 2004. One-third of this increase was attributable to children originally given a different special education classification that were then reclassified as having autism (Coo et al., 2008). Currently, given the confounding variables listed above, the true increase in the prevalence of ASD is not known.

Etiology

The etiology of autism is also currently unknown. However, recent evidence supports a genetic cause (O'Roak & State, 2008). Several incorrect hypotheses regarding autism's etiology have been widely propagated before they were adequately researched (Metz, Mulick, & Butter, 2005; Offit, 2008). These etiological hypotheses have in some cases caused pain or damage to children with autism and their families (Baxter & Krenzelok, 2008; Metz et al., 2005; Offit, 2008). For example, in the 1960s it was widely believed that children with autism intentionally withdrew from social interaction because their mothers (i.e., "refrigerator mothers") had been cold and unloving (Bettelheim, 1967). This hypothesis was later discounted (Rutter, & Schopler, 1978). More recent etiological theories have involved potential gastrointestinal causes (i.e., a leaky intestinal wall allows wheat and dairy proteins to interrupt brain function; Mulloy et al., 2010), the presence of the measles virus in the blood stream introduced via the measles, mumps, and rubella (MMR) vaccine, and poisoning from Thimerosal (a mercury-based preservative) present in vaccines (Offit, 2008). However, repeated large-scale, scientifically rigorous research has not found sufficient evidence to support any of these theories (Offit, 2008).

Early Warning Signs of Autism

Treatment for autism is most effective early in life; therefore, early diagnosis is very important. The National Institute of Mental Health (2010) lists the following indicators as warning signs that a child might have autism.

- Does not babble, point, or make meaningful gestures by 1 year of age
- Does not speak one word by 16 months of age
- Does not combine two words by 2 years of age
- Does not respond to name

- Loses language or social skills that had previously developed
- Poor eye contact
- Does not play with toys
- Excessively puts objects in a line
- Is excessively attached to one particular toy or object
- Does not smile often
- May seem to be hearing impaired

Treatment

Many approaches to treatment are available to families of children with autism (Green et al., 2006). However, the majority of these treatments have not been rigorously evaluated by research and many make unsubstantiated claims to "cure" autism (Jacobson, Foxx, & Mulick, 2005). There is currently no known cure for autism (National Institute of Mental Health, 2010). However, intensive early intervention may result in significant improvements in language, socialization, and cognition for some children (Howlin, Magiati, & Charman, 2009; National Research Council, 2001; Reichow & Woolery, 2009).

Early intensive behavioral intervention should focus on teaching developmentally appropriate pivotal skills using instructional strategies based upon applied behavior analysis (ABA; Department of Health and Human Services, 1999; Howlin et al., 2009; National Research Council, 2001; Reichow & Woolery, 2009). Numerous ABA variations and procedures have been developed, for example, ABA interventions can be delivered systematically in a highly structured and controlled environment (e.g., discrete trial training: Lovaas, 1987) or embedded in play routines and delivered within the natural environment (e.g., Pivotal Response Training: Koegel, Koegel, Harrower, & Carter, 1999). ABA interventions target a wide variety of skills such as teaching functional communication via alternative and augmentative communication methods (e.g., Picture Exchange Communication System; Bondy & Frost, 2001), reducing challenging behavior (e.g., Functional Communication Training; Carr & Durand, 1985), increasing prosocial behaviors (Matson, & Swiezy, 1994), improving adaptive and self-help behaviors (Anderson, Jablonski, Thomeer, & Knapp, 2007), and improving academics (Dunlap, Kern, & Worcester, 2001). Additional skills targeted during early intervention include joint attention, play, and functional skills (e.g., toileting and dressing; Koegel, & Koegel, 2006; Lang, Machalicek, Rispoli, & Regester, 2009; National Research Council, 2001; Vismara & Rogers, 2008).

The National Research Council (2001) and the Department of Health and Human Services (1999) recommend that early intensive intervention begin as soon as possible. Treatment should occur between 25 and 40 hours per week and should involve direct instruction and reinforcement, occur within the child's natural environment (e.g., home and school), and involve parents and families in designing and implementing intervention.

REFERENCES

American Psychiatric Association. (2000). *Diagnostic and statistical manual of mental disorders* (4th ed., text rev.). Washington, DC: Author.

Anderson, S. R., Jablonski, A. L., Thomeer, M. L., & Knapp, M. V. (2007). *Self-help skills for people with autism: A systematic teaching approach*. Bethesda, MD: Woodbine House.

Baxter, A. J., & Krenzelok, E. P. (2008). Pediatric fatality secondary to EDTA chelation. *Clinical Toxicology, 46*, 1083–1084.

Bettelheim, B. (1967). *The empty fortress: Infantile autism and the birth of self*. New York, NY: The Free Press, Collier-Macmillian.

Bondy, A., & Frost, L. (2001). The Picture Exchange Communication System. *Behavior Modification, 25*, 725–744.

Carr, E. G., & Durand, V. M. (1985). Reducing behavior problems through functional communication training. *Journal of Applied Behavior Analysis, 18*, 111–126.

Coo, H., Oullette-Kuntz, H., Lloyd, J. E., Kasmara, L., Holden, J. J., & Lewis, S. (2008). Trends in autism prevalence: Diagnostic substitution revisited. *Journal of Autism and Developmental Disabilities, 38*, 1036–1046.

Department of Health and Human Services. (1999). *Mental health: A report of the Surgeon General*. Rockville, MD: Department of Health and Human services, Substance Abuse and Mental Health Services Administration, Center for Mental Health Services, National Institute of Mental Health.

Dunlap, G., Kern, L., & Worcester, J. (2001). ABA and academic instruction. *Focus on Autism and Other Developmental Disabilities, 16*, 129–136.

Fombonne, E. (2003). The prevalence of autism. *Journal of American Medical Association, 289*, 87–89.

Green, V. A., Pituch, K. A., Itchon, J., Aram, C., O'Reilly, M., & Sigafoos, J. (2006). Internet survey of treatments used by parents of children with autism. *Research in Developmental Disabilities, 27*, 70–84.

Jacobson, J. W., Foxx, R. M., & Mulick, J. A. (2005). *Controversial therapies for developmental disabilities: Fad fashion and science in professional practice*. Mahwah, NJ: Erlbaum.

Hess, J. A., & Matson, J. L. (2010). Psychiatric symptom endorsements in children and adolescents diagnosed with Autism Spectrum Disorders: A comparison to typically developing children and adolescents. *Journal of Developmental and Physical Disabilities, 22*, 485–496.

Howlin, P. Magiati, & Charman, T. (2009). Systematic review of early intensive behavioral interventions for children with autism. *American Journal of Intellectual and Developmental Disabilities, 114*, 23–41.

Koegel, A. (2008). Evidence suggesting the existence of Asperger Syndrome in the mid 1800s. *Journal of Positive Behavioral Interventions, 10*, 270–272.

Koegel, R. L., & Koegel, L. K. (2006). *Pivotal Response Treatments for autism: Communication, social, & academic development*. Baltimore, MD: Paul H. Brookes.

Koegel, L. K., Koegel, R. L., Harrower, J. K., & Carter, C. M. (1999). Pivotal response intervention I: Overview of approach. *Journal of the Association for Persons with Severe Handicaps, 24,* 174–185.

Lang, R., Machalicek, W., Rispoli, M. J., & Regester, A. (2009). Training parents to implement communication interventions for children with autism spectrum disorders: A systematic review of training procedures. *Evidenced-Based Communication Assessment and Intervention, 3,* 174–190.

Lang, R., Regester, A., Rispoli, M., & Camargo, S. H. (2010). Guest Editorial: Rehabilitation issues for children with Autism Spectrum Disorders. *Developmental Neurorehabilitation, 13,* 153–155.

Lovaas, O. I. (1987). Behavioral treatment and normal educational and intellectual functioning in young autistic children. *Journal of Consulting and Clinical Psychology, 55,* 3–9.

Matson, J. L. (2007). Current status of differential diagnosis for children with autism spectrum disorders. *Research in Developmental Disabilities, 28,* 109–118.

Matson, J. L., Hess, J. A., Daniene, N., Mahan, S., & Fodstad, J. C. (2010). Trend of symptoms in children with autistic disorders as measured by the Autism Spectrum Disorders Diagnostic for Children (ASD-DC). *Journal of Developmental and Physical Disabilities, 22,* 47–56.

Matson, J. L., & Swiezy, N. B. (1994). Social skills training with autistic children. In J. L. Matson (Ed.), *Autism in children and adults: Etiology, assessment and intervention.* Sycamore, IL: Sycamore.

Metz, B., Mullick, J., & Butter, E. (2005). Autism: A late-20th-century fad magnet. In J. Jacobson, R. Foxx, & J. Mullick (Eds.), *Controversial therapies for developmental disabilities: Fad, fashion, and science in professional practice* (pp. 237–263). Mahwah, NJ: Erlbaum.

Mulloy, A., Lang, R., O'Reilly, M., Sigafoos, J., Lancioni, G., & Rispoli, M. (2010). Gluten-free and casein-free diets in the treatment of autism spectrum disorders: A systematic review. *Research in Autism Spectrum Disorders, 4,* 328–329.

National Institute of Mental Health. (2010). *Autism spectrum disorders (pervasive developmental disorders).* Retrieved from: http://www.nimh.nih.gov/health/publications

National Research Council. (2001). *Educating children with autism.* Washington, DC: National Academy Press.

Offit, P. A. (2008). *Autism's false prophets: Bad science risky medicine and the search for a cure.* New York, NY: Columbia University Press.

O'Roak, B. J., & State, M. W. (2008). Autism genetics: Strategies, challenges, and opportunities. *Autism Research, 1,* 4–17.

Reichow, B., & Wolery, M. (2009). Comprehensive synthesis of early intervention behavioral interventions for young children with autism based on the UCLA Young Autism Project model. *Journal of Autism and Developmental Disorders, 39,* 23–41.

Rice, C. (2009). Prevalence of autism spectrum disorders. *Morbidity and Mortality, 58,* 1–20.

Rutter, M., & Schopler, E. (Eds.) (1978). *Autism: A reappraisal of concepts and treatment.* New York, NY: Plenum Press

Sigafoos, J., O'Reilly, M. F., & Lancioni, G. E. (2009) Does the ASD label have validity? *Developmental Neurorehabilitation, 12,* 63–65.

Vismara, L. A., & Rogers, S. J. (2008). The early start Denver model a case study of an innovative practice. *Journal of Early Intervention, 31,* 91–108.

Wing, J. K. (1976). Kanner's syndrome: A historical introduction. In L. Wing (Ed.). *Early childhood autism: Clinical, educational, and social aspects* (2nd ed.). Oxford, UK: Pergamon Press.

RUSSELL LANG
FARA EL ZEIN
BROOKE PFEIFFER
Texas State University–San Marcos
Fourth edition

See *also* Controversial and Noncontroversial Autism Treatments; Interventions for Autism Spectrum Disorders; Kanner, Leo

AUTISM BEHAVIOR CHECKLIST

The Autism Behavior Checklist (ABC) was originally published as one of five components of the Autism Screening Instrument for Educational Planning (ASIEP; Krug, Arick, & Almond, 1980). The ABC was designed as a screening instrument for use in educational settings with individuals ranging from 2 years, 0 months to 13 years, 11 months. The ABC has undergone two revisions since 1980, most recently in 2008 as part of the publication of the third edition of the Autism Screening Instrument for Educational Planning (ASIEP-3; Krug, Arick, & Almond, 2008). It has been used extensively in schools as a tool for universal screening assessments (Miranda-Linne & Melin, 2002).

The ABC is presented in a checklist format with a list of 47 observable, behavioral characteristics of autism, such as, "echoes (repeats) questions or statements made by others," and "has strong reactions to changes in routine or environment." The rater places a check next to each item that applies to the child. The ABC includes separate rating forms for parents and teachers, to enable comparison of behaviors in different settings and by different observers (Krug, Arick, & Almond, 2008).

Scoring the ABC is a relatively simple process. Individuals qualified to score the ABC include parents and educators, such as the school psychologist, teacher or speech-language pathologist. The previous version of the ABC included item weighting, however this has been removed in the most recent revision of the ASIEP-3 (Krug, Arick, & Almond, 2008). The current dichotomous scoring system (check or no check) has been found to enhance reliability. The Total Raw Score is computed by summing the number of checked items. The raw score is then converted into a standard score and a percentile rank. Standard scores are based on chronological age groups. Autism index scores are also provided to estimate the probability of the client having autism; probability designations include: very likely, possible, or unlikely (Krug et al., 2008).

The ABC parent forms were normed using a sample that included 342 children with autism in 21 states (Krug, Arick, & Almond, 2008). The teacher forms were normed based on a sample of 386 children with autism in 21 states (Krug et al., 2008). The sample was found to be representative of the population of school-age children as reported in *the Statistical Abstract of the United States*, except for gender distribution. The ASIEP manual reports satisfactory estimates of reliability and validity (Krug et al., 2008). The coefficient alpha was reported to be .88 with an SEM of .06. The test-retest reliability was reported as .99 for teacher raters and .76 for parent raters. The correlation for parent and teacher ratings is .55. Examination of construct validity indicated that the instrument satisfactorily discriminated between individuals with autism and those not diagnosed with autism. Additionally, the construct validity was found to be robust to differences in age or gender and ethnic group status (Krug et al., 2008). However, given the recent publication of the ASIEP-3 there is a need for further independent evaluation of the most recent edition of the assessment.

REFERENCES

Krug, D. A., Arick, J. R., & Almond, P. J. (2008). *Autism Screening Instrument for Educational Planning* (3rd ed.) (ASIEP-3). Austin, TX: Pro-Ed.

Miranda-Linne, F. M., & Melin, L. (2002). A factor analytic study of the Autism Behavior Checklist. *Journal of Autism and Developmental Disorders, 32,* 181–188.

MEREDITH JONES
Texas A&M University

AUTISM DIAGNOSTIC INTERVIEW—REVISED

The Autism Diagnostic Interview—Revised (ADI-R; Rutter, LeCouteur, & Lord, 2003) is a semistructured interview for use in the diagnosis of autism spectrum disorders. It is referred to as the gold standard for a clinical interview related to autism for individuals with a mental age of 18 months or higher (Constantino et al., 2003), particularly when combined with the Autism Diagnostic Observation

System (ADOS; Lord, Rutter, DiLavore, & Risi, 2001, 2008). The comprehensive interview provides information related to language and communication, reciprocal social interactions, and restricted/repetitive/stereotyped behaviors and interests. It includes 93 items, 37 of which are included in the diagnostic algorithm. Depending on the individual being assessed and the caregiver, the interview takes about 2 hours to complete (Rutter & LeCouteur, 2004; Rutter et al., 2003). Use of the ADI-R requires not only experience with the population and basic interviewing skills, but also training specific to the ADI-R. Responses are scored and interpreted based on either a diagnostic algorithm, current behavior algorithm or both, depending on the purpose of the assessment (Rutter et al., 2003). ADI-R does not have prescribed descriptive classifications; results are intended to provide information that would support the diagnosis of autism spectrum disorders and to identify needs of children and adults for intervention planning. The ADI-R is available in 11 languages and is used worldwide (Lord & Corsello, 2005).

Psychometric properties of the ADI-R are adequate; with appropriate training, interrater reliability for the scoring of the interview has been reported to be acceptable to excellent (.90 or higher; Constantino et al., 2003; de Bildt et al., 2004; Lecavalier et al., 2006). Statistical analysis was used in setting cut scores for the ADI-R (Lord et al., 1997). Discriminant evidence is provided in the manual. Bishop and Norbury (2002) concluded that results of the ADI-R were consistent with the child's actual diagnosis. Additional support for discriminant validity from the research literature was found for the ADI-R (e.g., Gray et al., 2008; Noterdaeme, Mildenberger, Sitter, & Amorosa, 2002). At the same time, Bishop and Norbury (2002) found a low level of agreement for the ADI-R and other parent interview information with the other specific measures of characteristics of autism. They concluded that this was in part because of the extent to which pragmatic language issues and age confound diagnosis. Recently, Matson, Hess, Mahan, and Fodstad (2010) also found a low level of agreement with current diagnosis, but did find a high level of agreement with another measure. In a study comparing the ADI-R with diagnostic decisions, de Bildt et al. (2004) found adequate agreement, but noted age effects.

REFERENCES

Bishop, D. V. M., & Norbury, C. F. (2002). Exploring the borderlands of autistic disorder and specific language impairment: A study using standardized diagnostic instruments. *Journal of Child Psychology and Psychiatry, 43,* 917–929.

Constantino, J. N., Davis, S. A., Todd, R. D., Schindler, M. K., Gross, M. M., Brophy, S. L.,...Reich, W. (2003). Validation of a brief quantitative measure of autistic traits: Comparison of the Social Responsiveness Scale with the Autism Diagnostic

Interview—Revised. *Journal of Autism and Developmental Disorders, 33,* 427–433.

de Bildt, A., Sytema, S., Ketelaars, C., Kraijer, D., Mulder, E., Volkmar, F., & Minderaa, R. (2004). Interrelationship between Autism Diagnostic Observation Schedule—Generic (ADOS-G), Autism Diagnostic Interview—Revised (ADI-R), and the Diagnostic and statistical manual of mental disorders (DSM-IV-TR) classification of children and adolescents with mental retardation. *Journal of Autism and Developmental Disorders, 34,* 129–137.

Gray, K. M., Tonge, B. J., & Sweeney, D. J. (2008). Using the Autism Diagnostic Interview—Revised and the Autism Diagnostic Observation Schedule with Young Children with Developmental Delay: Evaluating diagnostic validity. *Journal of Autism and Developmental Disorders, 38,* 657–667.

Lecavalier, L., Aman, A. G., Scahill, L., McDougle, C. J., McCracken, J. T., Vitiello, B.,...Kau, A. S. (2006). Validity of the Autism Diagnostic Interview—Revised. *American Journal on Mental Retardation, 111,* 199–215.

Lord, C., & Corsello, C. (2005). Diagnostic instruments in autistic spectrum disorders. In F. R. Volmar, R. Paul, A. Klin, & D. Cohen (Eds.), *Handbook of autism and pervasive developmental disorders* (Vol. 2, 3rd ed., pp. 730–771). Hoboken, NJ: Wiley.

Lord, C., Pickles, A., McLennan, J., Rutter, M., Bregman, J., Folstein, S.,...Minshew, N. (1997). Diagnosing autism: Analyses of data from the Autism Diagnostic Interview. *Journal of Autism and Developmental Disorders, 27,* 501–517.

Lord, C., Rutter, M., DiLavore, P., & Risi, S. (2001, 2008). *Autism diagnostic observation schedule (ADOS) manual.* Los Angeles, CA: Western Psychological Services.

Lord, C., Rutter, M., & LeCouteur, A. (1994). Autism Diagnostic Interview Revised: A revised version of a diagnostic interview for caregivers of individuals with possible pervasive developmental disorders. *Journal of Autism and Developmental Disorders, 24,* 659–685.

Matson, J. L., Hess, J. A., Mahan, S., & Fodstad, J. C. (2010). Convergent validity of the Autism Spectrum Disorder-Diagnostic for Children (ASD-DC) and Autism Diagnostic Interview—Revised. *Research in Autism Spectrum Disorders, 4,* 741–746.

Noterdaeme, M., Mildenberger, K., Sitter, S., & Amorosa, H. (2002). Parent information and direct observation in the diagnosis of pervasive and specific developmental disorders. *Autism, 6,* 159–168.

Rutter, M., & LeCouteur, A. (2004). *ADI-R: Autism diagnostic interview revised. Training guidebook.* Los Angeles, CA: Western Psychological Services.

Rutter, M., LeCouteur, A., & Lord, C. (2003). *Autism diagnostic interview revised*: Los Angeles, CA: Western Psychological Services.

CYNTHIA A. RICCIO
Texas A & M University
Fourth edition

See *also* Autism; Autism Diagnostic Observation System

AUTISM DIAGNOSTIC OBSERVATION SYSTEM

The Autism Diagnostic Observation System (ADOS; Lord, Rutter, DiLavore, & Risi, 2001, 2008) is a measure used in the assessment of autism spectrum disorders that combines direct observation in contrived situations, or "presses," with information obtained from parent interview. The assessment is semistructured and the activities provide opportunities to observe a range of social and communication behaviors. The ADOS has gained acceptance worldwide as the gold standard for assessment of autistic spectrum disorders (Lord & Corsello, 2005), particularly when administered in conjunction with the Autism Diagnostic Interview—Revised (ADI-R; Rutter, LeCouteur, & Lord, 2003).

The ADOS consists of four modules; the individual is administered the module that is best aligned with their overall language functioning from nonverbal to fluent and one module is designed for administration with adolescents and adults. Each of the modules is estimated to take 35 to 40 minutes; only one module is administered to each client. The activities and skills covered by the ADOS are intended to have direct implications for intervention (Lord et al., 2008). Although not appropriate for nonverbal adolescents or adults with autism, the ADOS is intended for use with all others who may have autism. Use of the ADOS requires experience, skills, and practice (Lord & Corsello, 2005); workshops are available on a regular basis to learn appropriate administration.

Following the observations, the results are considered in relation to cut-scores for autism and the general category of autism spectrum disorders (Lord et al., 1997). Psychometric properties (e.g., interrater reliability, internal consistency, temporal stability) are good (e.g., Lord et al., 2000). Content is appropriate for diagnosis with coverage of three domains essential for diagnosis of autistic spectrum disorders—communication, social behavior, and repetitive motor/stereotypy—included in each module. Discriminant evidence is provided in the manual, and supports the use of Modules 1, 2, and 3; less evidence is provided for Module 4. Additional support for discriminant validity from the research literature was found as well (e.g., de Bildt et al., 2004; Noterdaeme, Mildenberger, Sitter, & Amorosa, 2002).

In an effort to improve the diagnostic validity of the ADOS, Gotham, Risi, Pickles, and Lord (2007) developed revised algorithms for the ADOS, particularly Modules 1 through 3, to improve the sensitivity and specificity of the ADOS. In particular, the original ADOS algorithm does not include repetitive behaviors or restricted interests, although these behaviors are coded if they are observed (Lord et al., 2001). The revised algorithm includes a Social Affect factor (social and communication skills), a Restricted and Repetitive Behavior factor; these are then combined with differing cut-offs for autism and autism spectrum disorders, and differing algorithms for children younger and older than age 5 in Module 2. The revised algorithms have been validated in multiple studies (de Bildt et al., 2009; Gotham et al., 2008; Gray, Tong, & Sweeney, 2008; Noterdaeme et al., 2002; Oosterling et al., 2010; Overton, Fielding, & Garcia de Alba, 2008). There are indications of improved balance between sensitivity and specificity with the revised algorithms, but additional research is needed in this area.

REFERENCES

De Bildt, A., Sytema, S., Ketelaars, C., Kraijer, D., Mulder, E., Volkmar, F., & Minderaa, R. (2004). Interrelationship between Autism Diagnostic Observation Schedule—Generic (ADOS-G), Autism Diagnostic Interview—Revised (ADI-R), and the Diagnostic and statistical manual of mental disorders (DSM-IV-TR) classification of children and adolescents with mental retardation. *Journal of Autism and Developmental Disorders, 34*, 129–137.

De Bildt, A., Sytema, S., Van Lang, N. D. J., Minderaa, R. B., Van Engeland, H., & Dejonge, M. V. (2009). Evaluation of the ADOS revised algorithm: The applicability in 558 Dutch children and adolescents. *Journal of Autism and Developmental Disorders, 39*, 1350–1358.

Gotham, K., Risi, S., Dawson, G., Tager-Flusberg, H., Joseph, R., Carter, A.,...Lord, C. (2008). A replication of the Autism Diagnostic Observation Scale (ADOS) revised algorithms. *Journal of the American Academy of Child and Adolescent Psychiatry, 47*, 642–651.

Gotham, K., Risi, S., Pickles, A., & Lord, C. (2007). The Autism Diagnostic Observation Schedule: Revised algorithms for improved diagnostic validity. *Journal of Autism and Developmental Disorders, 37*, 613–627.

Gray, K. M., Tonge, B. J., & Sweeney, D. J. (2008). Using the Autism Diagnostic Interview—Revised and the Autism Diagnostic Observation Schedule with young children with developmental delay: Evaluating diagnostic validity. *Journal of Autism and Developmental Disorders, 38*, 657–667.

Lord, C., & Corsello, C. (2005). Diagnostic instruments in autistic spectrum disorders. In F. R. Volmar, R. Paul, A. Klin, & D. Cohen (Eds.), *Handbook of autism and pervasive developmental disorders* (Vol. 2, 3rd ed., pp. 730–771). Hoboken, NJ: Wiley.

Lord, C., Pickles, A., McLennan, J., Rutter, M., Bregman, J., Folstein, S.,...Minshew, N. (1997). Diagnosing autism: Analyses of data from the Autism Diagnostic Interview. *Journal of Autism and Developmental Disorders, 27*, 501–517.

Lord, C., Risi, S., Lambrecht, L., Cook, E. H. Jr., Leventhal, B. L., DiLavore, P. C.,...Rutter, M. (2000). The Autism Diagnostic Observation Schedule-Generic: A standard measure of social and communication deficits associated with the spectrum of autism. *Journal of Autism and Developmental Disorders, 30*, 205–223.

Lord, C., Rutter, M., DiLavore, P., & Risi, S. (2008). *Autism diagnostic observation schedule (ADOS) manual.* Los Angeles, CA: Western Psychological Services.

Noterdaeme, M., Mildenberger, K., Sitter, S., & Amorosa, H. (2002). Parent information and direct observation in the diagnosis of pervasive and specific developmental disorders. *Autism, 6*, 159–168.

Oosterling, I., Roos, S., de Bildt, A., Rommelse, N., de Jonge, M., Visser, J.,...Buitelaar, J. (2010). Improved diagnostic validity of the ADOS revised algorithms: A replication in an independent sample. *Journal of Autism and Developmental Disorders, 40*, 689–703.

Overton, T., Fielding, C., & Garcia de Alba, R. (2008). Brief report: Exploratory analysis of the ADOS revised algorithm: Specificity and predictive value with Hispanic children referred for autism spectrum disorders. *Journal of Autism and Developmental Disorders, 38*, 1166–1169.

Rutter, M., LeCouteur, A., & Lord, C. (2003). *Autism diagnostic interview revised.* Los Angeles, CA: Western Psychological Services.

CYNTHIA A. RICCIO
Texas A & M University
Fourth edition

See also Autism; Autism Diagnostic Interview—Revised

AUTISM SOCIETY OF AMERICA

The Autism Society of America (ASA) was founded in 1965 to help parents, family members, professionals, and caregivers learn about autism and how to effectively deal with the disability. ASA has over 24,000 members joined through a network of 225 chapters in 46 states across the country. The mission of ASA is to promote lifelong access and opportunities for persons within the autism spectrum and their families to be fully included, participating members of their communities through advocacy, public awareness, education, and research related to autism. ASA believes that each person with autism is a unique individual, and its policies promote the active and informed involvement of family members and those with autism in the planning of individualized, appropriate services and supports.

The ASA provides current information about autism through distribution of free packets of materials on a variety of topics; a comprehensive, bimonthly newsletter, the *Advocate*; and an annual national conference each July. An extensive library of information on issues affecting children and adults with autism, Pervasive Developmental Disorder—not otherwise specified (PDD-NOS), Asperger's, or other related disorders is maintained by the Society. In addition, ASA furnishes national legislators and government agencies with information about the needs of people with autism and their families and promotes medical research in the field.

Local chapters help families find trained professionals and service providers in their communities and organize parent support groups. Some chapters also host presentations by autism experts and advocate at the state level for improvements in programs and services specific to the disability.

A variety of information packets are available from the ASA national office, including materials dealing with general information about autism, facilitated communication, insurance, medications, education, and adult issues. Information provided assists families in appropriately matching the unique needs and potential of individuals with autism to treatments or strategies likely to be effective in moving the person closer to normal functioning. The Society promotes treatments supported by research while asserting that no one treatment exists which is equally effective for all persons. In doing so, they focus on important areas to consider when formulating a treatment plan, including social skill development, communication, behavior, and sensory integration. Additional information may be found at: Autism Society, 4340 East-West Highway, Suite 350, Bethesda, Maryland 20814. Tel.: (301) 657-0881 or (800) 3AUTISM (800-328-8476), website: http://www.autism-society.org/.

TAMARA J. MARTIN
The University of Texas of the Permian Basin
Third edition

AUTISM SPEAKS

History

Founded in 2005 by Bob and Suzanne Wright, Autism Speaks is currently the United States' largest science- and advocacy-focused autism organization. The Autism Speaks organization was created in response to the founders' grandchild's diagnosis of autism. Funding research to increase knowledge regarding the causes, prevention, treatments, and possible cures for autism is the organization's priority. Autism Speaks also serves as a resource for family and friends of those diagnosed with autism. Awareness and advocacy efforts are at the forefront of the organization's activities.

Mission

The mission of Autism Speaks is to improve the future for all who struggle with autism spectrum disorders. Dedicated to funding global biomedical research into the causes, prevention, treatments, and cure for autism; to raising public awareness about autism and its effects on individuals, families, and society; and to bringing hope to all who deal with the hardships of this disorder (Autism Speaks Inc., 2011).

Fundamental values reflected in the mission of Autism Speaks include "(1) recognition that individuals with autism spectrum disorders and their families are struggling, which inspires a sense of urgency and (2) commitment to discovery through scientific excellence; and the belief and commitment that parents are partners in this effort" (Autism Speaks Inc., 2011).

Services Provided

The services provided by the Autism Speaks organization include: information regarding the diagnosis of autism, legislation and rights for children in the public education system, early intervention services, and special education services. Autism Speaks also refers families toward community agencies, counseling services, and family services to address issues commonly dealt with by the autism community. Autism Speaks does not provide services that involve medical or legal advisory; rather, general information about community resources is promoted. The organization's website provides the following: information regarding the diagnosis, symptomology, basic facts, and child rights as they relate to Autism; policy statements, research initiatives, and news related to scientific findings; family services such as tool kits, resource libraries, community connections, grants, and projects for the future of Autism; advocacy related legislation, news, and ways to get involved; as well as opportunities to donate to the organization.

Contact Autism Speaks at the following addresses: New York office, 1 East 33rd Street, 4th floor, New York, NY 10016. Tel.: (212) 252-8584, fax: (212) 252-8676. Princeton, New Jersey office, 1060 State Road, 2nd floor, Princeton, NJ 08540. Tel.: (609) 228-7310, fax #1: (609) 430-9163, fax #2: (609) 430-9505. Los Angeles office, 5455 Wilshire Boulevard, Suite 2250, Los Angeles, CA 90036. Tel. (323) 549-0500, fax: (323) 549-0547.

E-mail: General Information: contactus@autismspeaks.org, website: http://www.autismspeaks.org/

Family Services: www.autismspeaks.org/community/family_services

All information retrieved on August 11, 2001, from: www.autismspeaks.org

BRITTANY LITTLE
The Chicago School of Professional Psychology
Fourth edition

AUTISM SPECTRUM RATING SCALES (ASRS)

The Autism Spectrum Rating Scales (ASRS; Goldstein & Naglieri, 2009) is intended to provide a brief assessment that measures behaviors associated with autism spectrum disorders (ASD) in children and adolescents ages 2 to 18 years old based on a questionnaire form completed by parents or teachers. The ASRS was designed to be used for diagnostic decision-making, progress monitoring, and in treatment evaluation. It is available in a short and full-length form, each with one version for children aged 2 to 5 and another for children and youth aged 6 to 18. All versions can be administered using either a pencil-and-paper method or through the ASRS Online Assessment Center.

The ASRS Short Form was designed to serve as a brief tool for screening purposes. This form contains a subset of 15 items from the full-length version of the ASRS and consists of just one form to be completed by both parents and teachers. Goldstein and Naglieri (2009) indicate that items included on the Short Form version differentiate between youth diagnosed with an ASD and those in the general population. The authors report a strong association between scores on the short and full-length version. They recommend use of the Short Form version in initial screenings of ASD and for progress monitoring. The full-length ASRS form provides a more comprehensive evaluation of ASD characteristics. This version includes 70 items for children aged 2 to 5 and 71 items for children aged 6 to 18. Separate parent and teacher rating forms are provided for each age group. The full-length ASRS provides a total score, separate scores for each of the ASRS scales, a score for the DSM-IV-TR scale, and treatment scale scores. For children aged 2 to 5, there are 2 ASRS scales, including Social/Communication and Unusual Behaviors. For children aged 6 to 18, there are three ASRS scales, including Social/Communication, Unusual Behavior, and Self-Regulation. Treatment scale scores provide information regarding specific items that pertain to treatment utility. The authors recommend use of the full-length ASRS in initial evaluations and full re-evaluations.

The ASRS was standardized and normed using a sample of 2,560 ratings from the general population and over 1,600 ratings from clinical samples (Goldstein & Naglieri, 2009). The clinical samples included approximately 700 ratings from individuals with an ASD diagnosis and over 500 ratings from individuals with other clinical diagnoses. The sample utilized a diverse group of individuals, found to be representative of the U.S. general population in relation to key demographic variables. This allows an assessor to compare an individual's standard score on the ASRS to his or her norm group. The authors report satisfactory reliability and validity regarding the psychometric properties of the scales. However, because the ASRS is a recently published instrument, there is limited research regarding the efficacy of this assessment tool; further independent evaluation is needed.

REFERENCE

Goldstein, S., & Naglieri, J. (2009). *Autism spectrum rating scales (ASRS): Technical manual.* Toronto, Canada: Multi-Health Systems.

MEREDITH JONES
Texas A&M University
Fourth edition

AUTISM: THE INTERNATIONAL JOURNAL OF RESEARCH AND PRACTICE (JOURNAL)

Autism: The International Journal of Research and Practice is an international, interdisciplinary, peer-reviewed research journal published six times per year. This interdisciplinary journal publishes interdisciplinary research on issues related to individuals with autism spectrum disorders. The journal spans the fields of medicine, education, psychology, neuroscience, epidemiology, and family services. Types of articles *Autism* publishes include research reports, research review articles, and letters to the editor. Manuscript submissions are accepted online and undergo double-blind peer review by at least two reviewers. *Autism's* 2010 Impact Factor was 2.606 (2010 5-year Impact Factor = 3.138) as determined in the *Journal Citation Reports®* (JCR), published by Thomson Reuters (formerly ISI). The current editor-in-chief of *Autism* is Dermot Bowler (City University, London, UK) and the editors are Dougal Julian Hare (University of Manchester, UK), David Mandell (University of Pennsylvania School of Medicine, USA), and Sarah Spence (Children's Hospital, Boston, USA). Individual and institutional subscriptions are available. The journal's website is: http://aut.sagepub.com/.

JENNIFER B. GANZ
Texas A&M University
Fourth edition

AUTOCORRELATION

In many types of research we think of our observations as independent such that one observation does not predict the next. For example, if we randomly sample 20 students we wouldn't expect the time on task of one randomly sampled student to predict the time on task of the next randomly sampled student. With time series data, however, we may expect one observation to be somewhat predictive of the next. For example, consider observing a student's time on task 20 days in a row. If we observed a relatively low time on task one day we may predict that student will have a relatively low time on task again the next day. It may be, for example, that the child is sick and that sickness impacts multiple observations in a row leading to greater similarities among observations that are close together in time. If so we would say the time series data are serially dependent, as opposed to independent. Autocorrelation is an index of the amount of dependence and is standardized like a correlation coefficient so that the possible values range from −1.0 to 1.0.

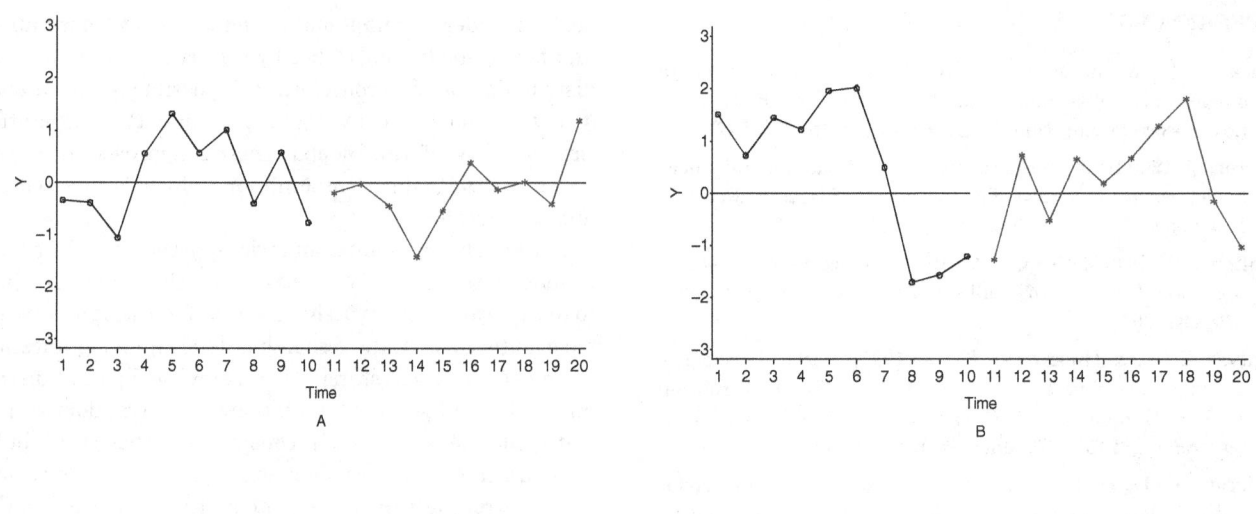

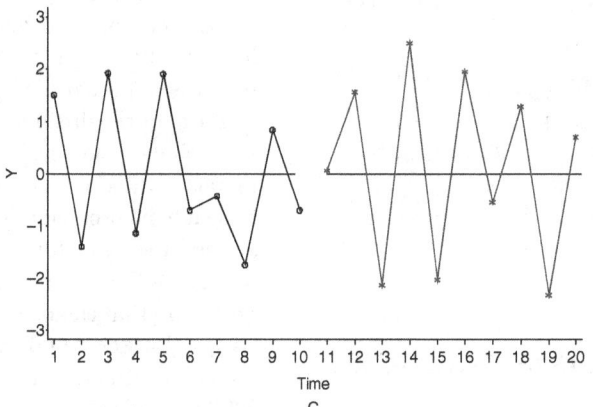

Figure A.6. Time series generated with a mean of 0 and no trend where errors were (A) independently sampled, (B) generated with positive autocorrelation, or (C) generated with negative autocorrelation.

Figure A.6 shows the data from three interrupted time series. In each panel the data from both the A and the B phase were generated from a process where the mean value was 0 and there was no trend. The panels differ from each other in the process used to generate the errors, which are the deviations from the trend line. In Panel A the errors were independently sampled, and thus the generation process had no autocorrelation. In Panel B the errors were generated to have positive autocorrelation ($\rho = .70$). Notice in this graph the observations that are close together tend to be more similar. For example, points 1 to 7 are on one side of the trend line, which indicates these points are more similar than typically seen in an independent process. In Panel C the errors were generated to have negative autocorrelation ($\rho = -.70$). In this time series we see the observations next to each other tend to be dissimilar and thus we see them jump back and forth across the trend line with great regularity than one would expect in an independent process (see points 1 to 6 as an example).

Given that time series data may be autocorrelated, several approaches have been developed for estimating the amount of autocorrelation. An estimate can focus on the

correlation between errors that differ by one point in time (first-order autocorrelation), or the correlation between errors that differ by two points in time (second-order autocorrelation), or more generally the correlation between errors spaced by n points in time. In addition there are multiple approaches for estimating an autocorrelation parameter (ρ) from the observed time series (see Huitema & McKean, 1991 for more information). The standard approaches are known to be biased (Huitema & McKean, 1991) and the bias is known to be more substantial when the series is short and the time series model complex (Ferron, 2002). In addition, estimates of autocorrelation tend to be imprecise with short series (Busk & Marascuilo, 1988), which makes it difficult to pinpoint the amount of autocorrelation in behavioral studies. Several surveys, analyses, and reanalyses have led to different conclusions about the amount of autocorrelation that is typical of behavioral time series, but small levels of positive autocorrelation seem plausible (Busk & Marascuilo, 1988; Matyas & Greenwood, 1997, Sideridis & Greenwood, 1997). Of interest, even small levels of autocorrelation have ramifications for analyses.

REFERENCES

Busk, P. L., & Marascuilo, L. A. (1988). Autocorrelation in single-subject research: A counterargument to the myth of no autocorrelation. *Behavioral Assessment, 10,* 229–242.

Ferron, J. (2002). Reconsidering the use of the general linear model with single-case data. *Behavior Research Methods, Instruments, & Computers, 34,* 324–331.

Huitema, B. E., & McKean, J. W. (1991). Autocorrelation estimation and inference with small samples. *Psychological Bulletin, 110,* 291–304.

Matyas, T. A., & Greenwood, K. M. (1997). Serial dependency in single-case time series. In R. D. Franklin, D. B. Allison, & B. S. Gorman (Eds.), *Design and analysis of single-case research* (pp. 215–243). Mahwah, NJ: Erlbaum.

Sideridis, G. D., & Greenwood, C. R. (1997). Is human behavior autocorrelated? An empirical analysis. *Journal of Behavioral Education, 7,* 273–293.

JOHN M. FERRON
JENNIE L. FARMER
University of Southern Florida
Fourth edition

AUTOCORRELATION EFFECTS IN SINGLE-CASE RESEARCH

Positive autocorrelation makes observations that are close together in time more similar than independently sampled observations. Consequently, a positively autocorrelated time series is more likely to appear to have a trend or shift than a time series resulting from an independent process. Negative autocorrelation makes observations close together more dissimilar than independently sampled observations, and thus makes it less likely to see chance trends or effects. With autocorrelation, visual analyses of time series become more difficult (Matyas & Greenwood, 1990). Specifically, positive autocorrelation makes it more likely to incorrectly conclude that an effect is present.

Researchers applying traditional ANOVA or regression models to interrupted time series data (e.g., data from AB, or ABAB type designs) assume the errors are independent. If the errors are positively autocorrelated the Type I error rates are inflated making it too likely that the researchers will falsely conclude there was a treatment effect (Toothaker, Banz, Noble, Camp, & Davis, 1983). If the errors are negatively autocorrelated the Type I error rate is decreased. This same pattern (i.e., an increase in Type I errors with positive autocorrelation and a decrease with negative autocorrelation) is seen if a permutation test is used to analyze the interrupted time series data. With the permutation test, significance is not determined by referring to a theoretical distribution (i.e., t or F)

derived under assumptions of independence, normality, and homogeneity, but rather by referring to an empirical distribution built by considering all possible permutations of observations into two groups (A and B). The statistical validity of this nonparametric approach is based on an exchangeability assumption, which is violated by autocorrelation.

An alternative nonparametric approach is offered by randomization tests. With these tests the researcher has to incorporate random assignment into the design. As with a permutation test, the researcher determines significance by comparing a test statistic to an empirically built distribution, but unlike the permutation test the randomization test limits the permutations considered to those that could have arisen from the random assignment. Randomization tests control the Type I error rate regardless of the level of autocorrelation (Edgington, 1980), but the autocorrelation impacts the power of these tests (for discussion of how power is impacted see Ferron & Ware, 1995).

Parametric alternatives to traditional regression models include time series models, which allow researchers to model autocorrelation. Complex time series models are known to be problematic with short series, however, there are short series alternatives including a double bootstrap procedure (McKnight, McKean, & Huitema, 2000) and a procedure that cleanses the autocorrelation and then bootstraps (Parker, 2006). Another option that is receiving increased attention is multilevel modeling (or hierarchical linear modeling), which is used to analyze interrupted time series data from multiple cases (Van den Noortgate, & Onghena, 2003). Multilevel models are flexible enough to model the autocorrelation and early studies have shown that when degrees of freedom are estimated using the small sample Kenward-Roger approach that confidence intervals for the average effect and for individual effects are accurate and thus Type I error rates can be controlled, at least for relatively simple interrupted time series models (Ferron, Farmer, & Owens, 2010). Although there currently is not agreement on which analysis method is best, there is agreement that autocorrelation complicates the analysis of single-case data.

REFERENCES

Edgington, E. S. (1980). Validity of randomization tests for one-subject experiments. *Journal of Educational Statistics, 5,* 235–251.

Ferron, J. M., Farmer, J. L., & Owens, C. M. (2010). Estimating individual treatment effects from multiple-baseline data: A Monte Carlo study of multilevel modeling approaches. *Behavior Research Methods, 42,* 930–943.

Ferron, J., & Ware, W. (1995). Analyzing single-case data: The power of randomization tests. *Journal of Experimental Education, 63,* 167–178.

Matyas, T. A., & Greenwood, K. M. (1990). Visual analysis of single-case time series: Effects of variability, serial dependence, and magnitude of intervention effects. *Journal of Applied Behavior Analysis, 23,* 341–351.

McKnight, S. D., McKean, J. W., & Huitema, B. E. (2000). A double bootstrap method to analyze linear models with autoregressive error terms. *Psychological Methods, 5,* 87–101.

Parker, R. I. (2006). Increased reliability for single-case research results: Is the bootstrap the answer? *Behavior Therapy, 37,* 326–338.

Toothaker, L. E., Banz, M., Noble, C., Camp, J., & Davis, D. (1983). N = 1 designs: The failure of ANOVA-based tests. *Journal of Educational Statistics, 4,* 289–309.

Van den Noortgate, W., & Onghena, P. (2003). Combining single-case experimental data using hierarchical linear models. *School Psychology Quarterly, 18,* 325–346.

JOHN M. FERRON
JENNIE L. FARMER
University of Southern Florida
Fourth edition

AUTOMATICITY

Automaticity is an aspect of perceptual and motor processing that occurs outside of conscious awareness. Factors such as stimulus novelty and response practice have been found to be related to automaticity in cognitive functioning (Neiser, 1976). When aroused by a novel or difficult stimulus, extensive cognitive processing occurs, forcing the event into conscious awareness. However, a habitual response elicited by an expected stimulus may be performed at an automatic level requiring little or no attention.

Humans have a limited attention capacity, therefore automatic functions add to the efficiency of the information processing system (Kutas & Hillyard, 1980). Many simple perceptual processes are innately automatic, while even complex activities such as reading can become automatic with sufficient practice. In fact, Hancock and Byrd (1984) state that reading efficiency is dependent on the extent to which decoding skills become automatized, and Garnett and Fleischner (1980) have related automatization to basic math facts acquisition.

Learning disabilities and intellectual have been discussed in terms of deficient automatization processes. Children with learning disabilities often take longer to produce acquired math facts than their nondisabled peers (Garnett & Fleischner, 1980). Their inability to perform this well-drilled task at an automatic level suggests that children with learning disabilities thinking processes are more circuitous and attention demanding. Severely disabled readers often demonstrate difficulty processing letters within words, while less impaired readers, who have automatized letter recognition, read whole words in a controlled, attention-demanding manner (Hancock & Byrd, 1984). Other research (Hurks et al., 2005) suggests that children with ADHD have no impairments in automatic preparations for visuomotor tasks but have great difficulty in visuomotor tasks that require planning and preparation.

Other researchers have suggested that automatic functions may be available to learning-disabled and intellectually disabled students, but that other factors impede their effects. Thus, children with disabilities have been found to perform as well as their nondisabled peers on a measure of perceptual memory automatization (Stein, Laskowski, & Trancone, 1982). The children with disabilities, however, had more difficulty organizing new skills, thereby preventing the automatization of more complex processes. In another study, learning-disabled children were found to produce the correct definitions of familiar words at a rate equal to that of nondisabled children, but showed a rapid decline in rate and accuracy when unfamiliar words were introduced (Ceci, 1983). As more purposeful processing was required, the learning-disabled students failed to decode the words, and instead substituted words that could be processed at an automatic level. Other skills must also become automatic and can be assessed in kindergarten (Schatschneider, Fletcher, Francis, Carlson, & Foorman, 2004).

REFERENCES

Ceci, S. J. (1983). Automatic and purposeful semantic processing characteristics of normal and language/learning disabled children. *Developmental Psychology, 19*(3), 427–439.

Garnett, K., & Fleischner, J. (1980). *Automatization and basic fact performance of normal and learning disabled children* (Technical Report No. 10). Washington, DC: Office of Special Education. (ERIC Document Reproduction Service No. ED 210 839)

Hancock, A. C., & Byrd, D. (1984, April). *Automatic processing in normal and learning disabled children.* Paper presented at the annual meeting of the Southwestern Psychological Association, New Orleans. (ERIC Document Reproduction Service No. ED 246 414)

Hurks, P. P., Adam, J. J., Hendrickson, J. G. M., Vles, J. S. H., Feron, F. J. M., Kaiff, A. C., ... Bolles, J. (2005). Controlled visuomotor preparation deficits in attention-deficit/hyperactivity disorder. *Neuropsychology, 19,* 66–76.

Kutas, M., & Hillyard, S. A. (1980). Reading senseless sentences: Brain potentials reflect semantic incongruity. *Science, 207,* 203–204.

Neiser, U. (1976). *Cognition and reality.* San Francisco, CA: Freeman.

Schatschneider, C., Fletcher, J. M., Francis, D. J., Carlson, C. D., & Foorman, B. R. (2004). Kindergarten prediction of reading skills: A longitudinal comparative analysis. *Journal of Educational Psychology, 96,* 265–282.

Stein, D. K., Laskowski, M. A., & Trancone, J. (1982). *Automatic memory processes in mentally retarded persons.* Paper presented at the annual meeting of the American Psychological Association, Washington, DC. (ERIC Document Reproduction Service No. ED 227 604)

GARY BERKOWITZ
Temple University

See also Cognitive Strategies; Conditioning; Transfer of Training

AUTOMUTISM (*See Elective Mutism*)

AUTONOMIC REACTIVITY

The autonomic nervous system consists of the sympathetic nervous system and the parasympathetic nervous system. The sympathetic nervous system, known as the fight-or-flight system, increases heart rate, adrenal secretions, sweating, and other responses that prepare the body for vigorous activity. The parasympathetic nervous system increases salivation, digestion, and other vegetative responses while antagonizing many effects of the sympathetic nervous system. Both systems are active at all times, although one or the other may predominate at the moment. The adrenal glands, sweat glands, muscles that erect the hairs, and muscles that constrict blood vessels receive only sympathetic input and no parasympathetic input.

Pain, sudden loud noises, and other intense stimuli activate the sympathetic nervous system, as do events that one interprets as threatening. People vary substantially in how strongly they react, and twin research indicates that much of the variation has a genetic contribution (Lensvelt-Mulders & Hettema, 2001). To a large extent, reactivity is consistent over time. Infants with an "inhibited" temperament react vigorously to novel sights and sounds. Most of them become shy children and anxious adults, showing a greater than average amygdala response to photographs suggesting fear (Schwartz, Wright, Shin, Kagan, & Rauch, 2003). Children with anxiety disorders tend to show greater-than-average sympathetic nervous system responses to loud noises, and most of their unaffected siblings do also, suggesting that the autonomic reactivity is a precursor to anxiety disorders, rather than a consequence (Bakker, Tijssen, van der Meer, Koelman, & Boer, 2009). In addition to the apparent influence of a biological predisposition, life experiences also influence autonomic reactivity. People who have endured a highly stressful experience show a temporarily increased sympathetic reactivity, and people with posttraumatic stress disorder show a more prolonged effect (Grillon, Morgan, Davis, & Southwick, 1998).

Although very high sympathetic reactivity correlates with anxiety, very low reactivity is not ideal, either. Low levels have been linked to impulsiveness, poor emotional regulation, and outbursts of anger and violence (Murray-Close, 2011; Stifter, Dollar, & Cipriano, 2011). Low reactivity correlates with antisocial behavior in both children and adults (Herpetz et al., 2007). The best level of reactivity varies across settings and situations, but is usually in an intermediate range.

Autonomic reactivity correlates with many behaviors. Researchers asked people a series of questions about their support for use of military and police powers, and their ownership of a gun. People with strong autonomic reactivity tended to endorse more use of force to combat possible threats (Oxley et al., 2008). Presumably they support strong interventions partly because of their strong fear of danger.

The sympathetic nervous system is generally most reactive in childhood (Shields, 1983). In old age, the resting level of the sympathetic nervous system increases, resulting in high blood pressure, but the reactivity of the system to change decreases (Hotta & Uchida, 2010). That is, reactivity and flexibility are greatest in the young, and least in the old.

REFERENCES

Bakker, M. J., Tijssen, M. A. J., van der Meer, J. N., Koelman, J. H. T. M., & Boer, F. (2009). Increased whole-body auditory startle reflex and autonomic reactivity in children with anxiety disorders. *Journal of Psychiatry and Neuroscience, 34,* 314–322.

Grillon, C., Morgan, C. A., III, Davis, M., & Southwick, S. M. (1998). Effects of darkness on acoustic startle in Vietnam veterans with PTSD. *American Journal of Psychiatry, 155,* 812–817.

Herpetz, S. C., Vloet, T., Mueller, B., Domes, G., Willmes, K., & Herpetz-Dahlmann, B. (2007). Similar autonomic responsivity in boys with conduct disorder and their fathers. *Journal of the American Academy of Child & Adolescent Psychiatry, 46,* 535–544.

Hotta, H., & Uchida, S. (2010). Aging of the autonomic nervous system and possible improvements in autonomic activity using somatic afferent stimulation. *Geriatrics Gerontology International, 10* (Suppl. 1), S127–S136.

Lensvelt-Mulders, G., & Hettema, J. (2001). Genetic analysis of autonomic reactivity to psychologically stressful situations. *Biological Psychology, 58,* 25–40.

Murray-Close, D. (2011). Autonomic reactivity and romantic relational aggression among female emerging adults: Moderating roles of social and cognitive risk. *International Journal of Psychophysiology, 80,* 28–35.

Oxley, D. R., Smith, K. B., Alford, J. R., Hibbing, M. V., Miller, J. L., Scalora, M., . . . Hibbing, J. R. (2008). Political attitudes vary with physiological traits. *Science, 321,* 1667–1670.

Schwartz, C. E., Wright, C. I., Shin, L. M., Kagan, J., & Rauch, S. L. (2003). Inhibited and uninhibited infants "grown up": Adult amygdalar response to novelty. *Science, 300,* 1952–1953.

Shields, S. A. (1983). Development of autonomic nervous system responsivity in children: A review of the literature. *International Journal of Behavioral Development, 6,* 291–319.

Stifter, C. A., Dollar, J. M., & Cipriano, E. A. (2011). Temperament and emotion regulation: The role of autonomic nervous system reactivity. *Developmental Psychobiology, 53,* 266–279.

JAMES KALAT
North Carolina State University
Fourth edition

AVERSIVE CONTROL

Aversive control employs the use of aversive stimuli to control behavior. Avoidance and punishment are two types of instrumental conditioning in which aversive stimuli are used. Avoidance procedures involve specific responses to prevent aversive stimuli. Punishment involves the use of aversive stimuli after a response is given (Domjan & Grau, 2009). The use of aversive stimuli to control behavior is one of the most controversial techniques employed by teachers, researchers, psychologists, therapists, and others. Applied research and those in clinical service must follow ethical guidelines in the use of less aversive interventions (Doughty, 2007). The effectiveness of this procedure is defined by its effect on behavior: It suppresses the behavior that it follows. This definition is similar to that for punishment. Indeed, aversive control is one form of punishment.

The controversy surrounding the use of aversive control is illustrated by Wood and Lakin (1982). They indicate that, although most states approve of the use of moderate corporal punishment, it is specifically forbidden by statutes in others (e.g., Maine and Massachusetts).

The use of aversive consequences for behavior control generally is viewed as a technique to be used only when other techniques have not been successful. Snell (1983) indicates that:

> Aversive conditioning using strong primary aversion (such as electric shock and slapping) to eliminate behavior is very defensible in two general instances: when the behavior is so dangerous or self-destructive that positive reinforcement and extinction are not feasible and when all other intervention methods (reinforce competing response, extinction, milder punishment forms) have been applied competently and have been documented as unsuccessful. (p. 140)

Despite the reservations that have been expressed regarding the use of aversives, aversives have been used to control behavior, particularly self-injurious behavior (SIB). Lemon juice (Sajwaj, Libet, & Agras, 1974), noxious odors (Baumeister & Baumeister, 1978), and electric shock are examples of aversive methods that have been used.

At times and under certain conditions, aversive procedures have been found to be the treatment of choice. However, aversive control should be reduced or eliminated when the desired behavior change has occurred or when the target behavior responds to less severe techniques. Suppression, and not elimination, of targeted behavior may result from using this technique. Unexpected and unintended results often occur whenever a punishment procedure is used; it is possible that similar side effects may occur when aversive control is used.

The use of aversives to control behavior raises many ethical questions. The basic rationale for the use of aversives is that other methods have failed, the child is at risk, and the aversive to be used is not as harmful as the behavior that is targeted for change.

REFERENCES

Baumeister, A., & Baumeister, A. (1978). Suppression of repetitive self-injurious behavior by contingent inhalation of aromatic ammonia. *Journal of Autism & Childhood Schizophrenia, 8,* 71–77.

Domjan, M., & Grau, J. W. (2009). *The principles of learning and behavior* (6th ed.). Belmont, CA: Cengage Learning.

Doughty, S. S., Anderson, C. A., Doughty, A. H., Williams, D. C., & Saunders, K. (2007). Discriminative control of punished stereotyped behavior in humans. *Journal of Experimental Analysis of Behavior, 87,* 325–336.

Sajwaj, T., Libet, J., & Agras, S. (1974). Lemon juice therapy: The control of life threatening rumination in a six-month old infant. *Journal of Applied Behavior Analysis, 1,* 557–566.

Snell, M. (Ed.). (1983). *Systematic instruction of the moderately and severely handicapped* (2nd). Columbus, OH: Merrill.

Wood, F. H., & Lakin, K. C. (Eds.). (1982). *Punishment and aversive stimulation in special education: Legal, theoretical and practical issues in their use with emotionally disturbed children and youth.* Reston, VA: Council for Exceptional Children.

PHILIP E. LYON
College of St. Rose
Third edition

See also Operant Conditioning; Punishment

AVERSIVE STIMULUS

Aversive stimuli are stimuli that function as punishers. An aversive stimulus whether unconditioned (e.g., bright lights) or conditioned (e.g., a frown or gesture) is "an unpleasant object or event" (Mayer, Sulzer-Azaroff, & Wallace, 2011) that can be used to decrease or increase a behavior. When presented as a consequence of, or contingent on, a specific behavior, it may be used to reduce or eliminate the rate of that behavior. However, when an aversive stimulus is removed contingent on the emission of a behavior, it may increase the rate of that behavior. In any case, an aversive stimulus is typically referred to as a punisher.

The application of aversive stimuli to effectively reduce or eliminate severe self-destructive behaviors and/or severe chronic behaviors has been demonstrated by several researchers including Lovaas and Simmons (1969), Risley (1968), and Rush (2011). However, the many disadvantages of applying aversive stimuli to reduce behaviors (e.g., withdrawal, aggression, generalization, imitation, negative self-statements; Mayer, Sulzer-Azaroff, & Wallace, 2011) seem to outweigh the advantages. Aversive stimuli to reduce behaviors should be reserved for serious destructive behaviors and employed only when other less aversive procedures have been tried. A more detailed presentation of the use of aversive stimuli may be found in Mayer, Sulzer-Azaroff, and Wallace (2011).

REFERENCES

Lovaas, O. I., Simmons, J. O. (1969). Manipulation of self-destruction in three retarded children. *Journal of Applied Behavior Analysis*, *2*, 143–157.

Mayer, G. R., Sulzer-Azaroff, B., & Wallace, M. (2011). *Behavior analysis for lasting change* (2nd ed.). Cornwall-on-Hudson, NY: Sloan.

Risley, T. (1968). The effects and side effects of punishing the autistic behaviors of a deviant child. *Journal of Applied Behavior Analysis*, *1*, 21–35.

Rush, K. S. (2011). An analysis of the selective effects of NCR with punishment targeting problem behavior associated with positive affect. *Behavioral Interventions*, *16*, 127.

ALLISON LEWIS
LOUIS J. LANUNZIATA
University of North Carolina at Wilmington
Third edition

See also **Behavior Modification; Punishment**

AVEYRON, WILD BOY OF (*See* Wild Boy of Aveyron)

AYLLON, TEODORO (1929–   )

Teodoro Ayllon obtained his PhD in clinical psychology in 1959 at the University of Houston. His special areas of interest are in behavior and condition therapy and applied behavior analysis. His major field of interest is in clinical

psychology. He has done extensive research in behavioral analysis and management and has published articles and books concerning this subject. He is currently working on a book on children and their families.

Some of his principal contributions include "Eliminating Discipline Problems by Strengthening Academic Performance," "The Elimination of Discipline Problems Through a Combined School-Home Motivational System," and "Behavioral Management of School Phobias." In these articles, Ayllon discusses a procedure in which discipline problems and school phobias can be remedied by having parents support the child with positive reinforcement to increase motivation to go to school and improve performance. Ayllon and Azrin (1968) wrote *The Token Economy: A Motivational System for Therapy and Rehabilitation*, which provides a glimpse into a system that often changes challenging behavior in both adolescents and adults and continues to be an implemented practice today.

He continues his research in clinical psychology and behavioral management and remains involved in the field of psychology. Ayllon's work has been recognized with honors. He retired as a professor of psychology and special education in the psychology department at Georgia State University in 1997. He is currently Professor Emeritus at Georgia State University and maintains offices in Atlanta and Duluth. Dr. Ayllon's current interests include problem-orientated, solution-focused, and time-limited behavioral family therapy for children and adolescents. Dr. Ayllon also serves on the board of advisors for the Cambridge Center for Behavioral Studies.

REFERENCES

Ayllon, T. (1974). Eliminating discipline problems by strengthening academic performance. *Journal of Applied Behavior Analysis*, *7*, 71–76.

Ayllon, T. (1999). *How to use token economy and point systems* (2nd ed.). Austin, TX: PRO-ED.

Ayllon, T., & Freed, M. (1989). *Stopping baby's colic*. New York, NY: Putnam.

Ayllon, T., Garber, S., & Pisor, K. (1975). The elimination of discipline problems through a combined school-home motivational system. *Journal of Behavior Therapy*, *6*, 616–626.

Ayllon, T., & Azrin, N. H. (1968). *The token economy: A motivational system for therapy and rehabilitation*. New York, NY: Appleton-Century-Crofts.

Ayllon, T., Smith, D., & Rogers, M. (1970). Behavioral management of school phobia. *Journal of Behavioral Therapy & Experimental Psychiatry*, *1*, 125–138.

REBECCA BAILEY
Texas A&M University

RACHEL M. TOPLIS
Falcon School District 49, Colorado Springs, Colorado

AYRES, A. JEAN (1920–1988)

A. Jean Ayres died on December 16, 1988 at the age of 68. Ayres obtained her BS in 1945 and MS in 1954 in Occupational Therapy, and went on to earn her PhD in 1961 in Educational Psychology from the University of Southern California. She worked as an occupational therapist in several California rehabilitation centers, and between 1955 and 1985, she taught and conducted research at the University of Southern California in the Departments of Occupational Therapy and Special Education, achieving the rank of emeritus professor after her retirement in 1985. Ayres was also in private practice in occupational therapy from 1977 to 1984.

Occupational therapy, particularly as related to perceptual and sensory integrative dysfunction and neuromuscular integration, was the focus of her work. From 1964 to 1966, she was a postdoctoral trainee at the University of California, Los Angeles Brain Research Institute, which led to her discovery of sensory integration dysfunction, a neurological disorder of the senses characterized by learning and behavioral problems as well as pain associated with the performance of even simple daily tasks. Ayres had struggled with learning problems similar to those caused by the disease, ultimately identifying an inefficient organization of sensory information received by the nervous system as its cause. Perhaps her greatest contribution was the development of sensory-integrative therapy, a neurologically based treatment for learning disorders widely used among occupational therapists. She is also credited with devising the Southern California Sensory Integration Tests and the Sensory Integration and Praxis Tests, tools used for identifying the disorder.

Distinguishing her work from others, Ayres (1972) used a neurological as opposed to an educational or psychodynamic approach to learning and behavior disorders, emphasizing the normalization of the sensory integration process in the brain stem while not excluding cortical integrative processes. Her research found that students with certain identifiable types of sensory integrative dysfunctions who received occupational therapy specifically for the integrative dysfunction, showed greater gains in academic scores than those who received an equal amount of time in academic work.

During her distinguished career, Ayres published over 50 tests, articles, and films. She was the recipient of the Eleanor Clarke Slagle Lectureship and the Award of Merit, the highest honors conferred by the American Occupational Therapy Association, and she was named to the 1971 edition of *Outstanding Educators of America*. Ayres was a charter member of the honorary Academy of Research of the American Occupational Therapy Association.

REFERENCE

Ayres, A. J. (1972). Improving academic scores through sensory integration. *Journal of Learning Disabilities, 5*, 338–343.

E. VALERIE HEWITT
Texas A&M University
First edition

TAMARA J. MARTIN
The University of Texas of the Permian Basin
Second edition

See *also* Occupational Therapy; Sensory Integrative Therapy

B

BABINSKI REFLEX

The Babinski reflex was first recognized in 1896 by a French neurologist of Polish descent, Joseph François Félix Babinski. Babinski was a pupil of Charcot and was the first to differentiate between a normal and pathologic response of the toes. The Babinski reflex is a phenomenon observed when the sole of the foot is stroked from below the heel toward the toes on the lateral (outside) side resulting in the big toe flexing toward the top of the foot and the other toes fanning out (Fletcher-Janzen, 2000). The Babinski sign, or extensor plantar response, is a phenomenon observed when the sole of the foot is stroked from below the heel toward the toes on the lateral (outside) side. The big toe turns upward or toward the head with the other toes fanned out and extended and the leg is withdrawn.

As the nervous system matures and the pyramidal tract gains more control over spinal motor neurons, the Babinski reflex will not be observed. Indeed, scratching the sole of the foot of a normal person with a dull object will produce a downward flexion of all toes. The presence of Babinski's reflex after the first year of life is an indication of damage to cortical motor neurons and a dysfunction of the pyramidal tract, and further neurological evaluation is required.

There has been controversy over the pathophysiologic interpretation of the Babinski sign or reflex; however, it is considered the single most important sign in clinical neurology because of its reliability. The clinical utility of the Babinski reflex has remained unchanged for more than 100 years after its initial description.

Characteristics

1. It is a reflex whereby the great toe flexes toward the top of the foot and the other toes fan out when the sole of the foot is firmly stroked.
2. It is a normal reflex in infants but is associated with a disturbance of the pyramidal or corticospinal tract in older children and adults.
3. Because the pyramidal tract is right- and left-sided, a Babinski reflex can occur on one side or both sides (Babinski's Reflex, 2013).
4. An abnormal Babinski reflex can be temporary or permanent (HealthCentral, 1998).
5. It is commonly characteristic of an upper motor neuron lesion (Walton, Beson, & Scott, 1986). But other common causes include amyotrophic lateral sclerosis, brain tumors, Friedreich ataxia, head injury, hepatic encephalopathy, meningitis, multiple sclerosis, pernicious anemia, rabies, spinal cord injury or tumor, stroke, and syringomeyelia (Babinski's Reflex, 2013).
6. Lack of coordination, weakness, and difficulty with muscle control are symptoms associated with an abnormal Babinski reflex (HealthCentral, 1998).

The Babinski reflex is symptomatic of a variety of disease processes. Common diseases that may result in an abnormal Babinski Reflex include amyotrophic lateral sclerosis, brain tumors of the corticospinal tract or cerebellum, head injury, meningitis, multiple sclerosis, spinal cord injury or tumor, and stroke (Babinski's Reflex, 2013). This list is not all-inclusive, and there are other causes of an abnormal Babinski reflex. The individual's health care provider usually finds the presence of an abnormal Babinski reflex during a medical examination. The individual is then referred for a comprehensive neurological examination, which may include computerized tomography scans of the head and spine, angiography of the head, or lumbar puncture and analysis of cerebrospinal fluid. Prognosis, treatment, and special education intervention or services are disease-specific and based on individual needs and are not necessarily related to the diagnosis of an abnormal Babinski reflex. All information in this entry is collected from and informed by the following works (Bassettti, 1995; Estanol, Huetta, & Garcia, 1997; Rothenberg & Chapman, 1994; Van Gijn, 1995)

REFERENCES

Babinski's reflex, 2013. Health Central.org. Retrieved from: http://www.healthcentral.com/

Bassetti, C. (1995). Babinski and Babinski sign. *Spine, 20*(23), 2591–2594.

Estanol, V. B., Huerta, D. E., & Garcia, R. G. (1997). 100 years of the Babinski sign. *Review Invest Clinical, 49*(2), 141–144.

Fletcher-Janzen, E., (Ed.). (2000). *Encyclopedia of special education* (2nd ed., Vol. 1). New York, NY: Wiley.

Rothenberg, M. A., & Chapman, C. F. (1994). *Dictionary of medical terms* (3rd ed.). Hauppauge, NY: Barron's.

Van Gijn, J. (1995). The Babinski reflex. *Postgraduate Medical Journal, 171*(841), 645–648.

ELAINE FLETCHER-JANZEN
Chicago School of Professional Psychology

DENISE E. MARICLE
DANA R. KONTER
University of Wisconsin-Stout

See *also* Apgar Rating Scale; Developmental Milestones; Plantar Reflex

BABY DOE

The term *Baby Doe*, traditionally used in legal pleadings and court proceedings to represent an infant the privacy and anonymity of whom the parties or the court wish to protect, has come to signify the issue of denying life-sustaining treatment to infants born with permanent handicaps combined with life-threatening but surgically correctible conditions. These infants are the focus of a debate that tests the limits of medical certainty in diagnosis and raises profound legal and ethical issues.

A major stimulus to the ethical and legal debate on foregoing lifesustaining treatment for newborns was provided by Duff and Campbell (1973). Their article describes how and why nontreatment was chosen for 43 out of 299 infants during a 30-month period in the intensive care nursery at Yale New Haven Hospital.

The term *Infant Doe* was first used on April 9, 1982, when a baby boy born with Down syndrome and esophageal atresia (a defect that prevents normal feeding) was born in Bloomington, Indiana. His parents refused to give consent for surgery to correct the tracheoesophageal defect. The courts refused to intervene, and Infant Doe died 6 days later. The Reagan administration responded by informing hospitals that Section 504 of the Rehabilitation Act of 1973, which prevents discrimination against individuals with handicaps in programs receiving federal funds, protects imperiled newborns. The administration issued an Interim Final Regulation in March 1983 that articulated this policy of nondiscrimination and established procedures to implement it. This regulation was overturned by a federal court because of the administration's failure to follow established notice and comment procedures in promulgating it.

In July 1983 the Reagan administration issued a second similar proposed rule. It stated that treatment of an infant with a disability was mandatory unless treatment was medically contraindicated. It provided that the denial of treatment on the basis of a potentially disabling condition constituted unlawful discrimination. It was also specified that this regulation was not intended to mandate futile therapies that would only prolong an infant's process of dying.

On October 11, 1983, Baby Jane Doe was born in Port Jefferson, New York. She was born with myelomeningocele, hydrocephaly, microcephaly, bilateral upper extremity spasticity, a prolapsed rectum, and a malformed brain stem. Her parents chose a course of conservative treatment as an alternative to surgery. Based on anonymous information, the Department of Health and Human Services filed a complaint with the state Child Protection Agency. The July 1983 ruling made it clear that the federal government was ready to step in if the decision of a state agency was considered insufficient. This case focused attention on the question of the federal government's right to intrude into the private realm of family decision making regarding treatment options.

In 1983, the President's Commission for the Study of Ethical Problems in Medicine and Biomedical Research issued, as part of its report, a statement on the decision to forgo life-sustaining treatment in critically ill newborns. It contrasted the presumption that parents are the appropriate decision makers for their infants with the *parens patriae* (literally, "parent of the country") power of the state. That is, while laws concerning the family protect a substantial range of discretion for parents, the state may supervise parental decisions before they become operative to ensure that the choices made are not neglectful or abusive to the child. It concluded that public policy should resist state intervention into family decisions unless serious issues are at stake and the intervention is likely to achieve better outcomes. Additionally, the commission suggested that infants with handicaps be treated no less vigorously than their peers without disability. However, it also suggested that futile therapies that merely delay death without offering a reasonable probability of saving a baby's life should be avoided. Finally, in ambiguous cases, where the course of action that would benefit the infant is not chosen by the parents, authorized persons acting for the state as *parens patriae* must step in.

On April 15, 1985, the Department of Health and Human Services issued the final rule and model guidelines that encouraged hospitals to establish infant care review committees (ICRCs). This was part of the child abuse and neglect prevention and treatment program included in the Child Abuse Amendments of 1984 (PL 98–457). This legislation attempted to protect the rights of infants with disabilities and limit governmental intervention into the practice of medicine and parental responsibilities. The purpose of the ICRCs was to educate hospital personnel and families of infants with disabilities and life-threatening conditions, to recommend guidelines concerning the withholding from infants of medically indicated treatment (including appropriate hydration, nutrition, and medication), and to offer counsel and review in cases involving infants with disabling and life-threatening conditions.

Later research (Carter, 1993) surveying military and civilian neonatologists found that, despite frequency of potential cases for review, ICRCs were seldom consulted. In fact, 67% of neonatologists surveyed indicated that the Baby Doe regulation has affected neither their thinking about ethical issues nor their practice.

The practice of decision making continues to be primarily led by the parents and neonatologist or by multidisciplinary conferences that typically do not include the nurses who deliver care (Martin, 1989). The use of multidisciplinary conferences predates the Baby Doe regulations.

The Child Abuse Amendments of 1984 (PL 98–45) state three circumstances under which treatment is not considered medically indicated: The infant is chronically and irreversibly comatose, the treatment would prolong dying but not be effective in ameliorating life-threatening conditions, and the treatment itself would be futile and inhumane. However, when even one of these three circumstances exists (and therefore failure to provide treatment would not be considered withholding medically indicated treatment), the infant must be provided with appropriate hydration, nutrition, and medication. Additionally, the law states that the withholding of treatment must not be based on subjective opinions about the future quality of life of such person but is to be based on the treating physicians' "reasonable medical judgment." These guidelines are advisory and not mandatory in any way because Congress did not make the rules binding on the states. Rather, it conditioned the receipt of federal funds on incorporation of the rule into each state's law. Most states have accepted the condition, largely through rulemaking by state child abuse agencies. The rules continue to be vigorously debated (Newman, 1989). (This entry uses and is informed by the additional sources: Federal Register, 1985; Presiedents Commission, 1983; Phoden & Arras, 1985; Vitello, 1984.)

REFERENCES

Carter, B. S. (1993). Neonatologists and bioethics after Baby Doe. *Perinatol, 13*(2), 144–150.

Duff, R. S., & Campbell, A. G. M. (1973). Moral and ethical dilemmas in the special-care nursery. *New England Journal of Medicine, 289*, 890–894.

Federal Register. (1985, April 15). Child abuse and neglect prevention and treatment program; final rule. *Model guidelines for health care providers to establish infant care review committees, 50*, 14878–14901.

Martin, D. A. (1989). Nurse's involvement in ethical decision-making with severely ill newborns. *Issues in Pediatric Nursing, 12*(6), 463–473.

Newman, S. A. (1989). Baby Doe, Congress and the states: Challenging the federal treatment standard for impaired infants. *American Journal of Law and Medicine, 15*(1), 1–60.

President's Commission for the Study of Ethical Problems in Medicine and Biomedical and Behavioral Research. (1983). *A report on the ethical, medical and legal issues in treatment decisions.* Washington, DC: Author.

Rhoden, N. K., & Arras, J. D. (1985). Withholding treatment from Baby Doe: From discrimination to child abuse. *Milbank Memorial Fund Quarterly / Health and Society, 63*, 27–50.

Vitiello, M. (1984). The Baby Jane Doe litigation and Section 504: An exercise in raw executive power. *Connecticut Law Review, 17*, 95–164.

CAROLE REITER GOTHELF
Hunter College, City University of New York
First edition

ELAINE FLETCHER-JANZEN
Chicago School of Professional Psychology
Second edition

KIMBERLY F. APPLEQUIST
University of Colorado at Colorado Springs
Third edition

BAER, DONALD M. (1931–2002)

Donald M. Baer received his BA degree in liberal arts from the University of Chicago in 1950 and his PhD in experimental psychology in 1957. At the time of his death he worked at the Department of Human Development of the University of Kansas at Lawrence.

He was most noted for his work with retarded children and reinforcement of appropriate behavioral imitativeness (Baer, Peterson, & Sherman, 1967). He has explored environmental situations in which retarded individuals can be taught imitation and language through the use of behavioral reinforcement and shaping techniques. He found that after reinforcement for appropriate imitation, generalization to similar situations was enhanced. Much of Baer's research focused on the learning process as it relates to social and personal adaptation in young children (Baer & Pinkston, 1997; Bijou & Baer, 1978).

He published more than 200 articles, chapters, and books, and made many more presentations. His published work addressed a variety of topics such as experimental methods and design, research in early childhood education, developmental disabilities and intellectual developmental disabilities, language development, self-regulation, and social development among other things. He also served as an expert witness, testifying on behalf of parents who sought the best possible education for their autistic children.

Between 1957 and 1965, with his colleague, Sidney W. Bijou, Baer established the "behavior analysis" approach to child development at the University of Washington (e.g., Bijou & Baer, 1961) where Don also contributed fundamentally to the experimental analysis of child behavior. In the late 1960s Baer, with Montrose Wolf and Todd Risley, founded the discipline of applied behavior analysis at the University of Kansas.

Don received many awards during his lifetime, among them the 1987 Don Hake Award from Division 25 (Behavior Analysis) of the American Psychological Association (APA) for work that bridges basic and applied research, APA's 1996 Division 33 (Intellectual Developmental Disabilities and Developmental Disabilities) Edgar A. Doll Award for his contributions to people with developmental disabilities, and the 1997 award for Distinguished Service to Behavior Analysis from the Society for the Advancement of Behavior Therapy. He also served as president of the Society for the Experimental Analysis of Behavior (1983–1984) and the Association for Behavior Analysis (1980–1981), as the editor of the *Journal of Applied Behavior Analysis* (1970–1971) and the associate editor of this and other journals (e.g., *American Journal of Mental Deficiency*), and as a reviewer of federal grants and for numerous additional scientific journals. Don was also widely invited to give colloquia, and was often an international distinguished visiting professor (e.g., in Australia, Brazil, Japan, New Zealand, Norway, Spain).

REFERENCES

Baer, D. M., & Pinkston, E. M. (Eds.). (1997). *Environment and behavior*. Boulder, CO: Westview.

Baer, D. M., Peterson, R. F., & Sherman, J. A. (1967). The development of imitation by reinforcing behavioral similarity to a model. *Journal of the Experimental Analysis of Behavior, 10*, 405–416.

Bijou, S. W., & Baer, D. M. (1961). *Child development, Vol. 1: A systematic and empirical theory*. New York, NY: Appleton-Century-Crofts.

Bijou, S. W., & Baer, D. M. (1978). *Behavior analysis of child development*. Englewood Cliffs, NJ: Prentice Hall.

RICK GONZALES
Texas A&M University
First edition

DEBORAH B. GUILLEN
University of Texas of the Permian Basin
Second edition

RACHEL M. TOPLIS
Falcon School District 49, Colorado Springs, Colorado
Third edition

BALLER-GEROLD SYNDROME (CRANIOSYNOSTOSIS-RADIAL APLASIA SYNDROME)

This is a rare, hereditary disorder characterized by premature fusion of the sutures between the skull bones (craniosynostosis) and various malformations of the bones in the forearm, hand, and fingers. Because of the paucity of cases (only about 20 appear in the literature), the prevalence of this syndrome is uncertain. A group of affected siblings was described a few years after the initial, unrelated case was reported in 1950. The pattern of inheritance appears to be autosomal recessive.

Characteristics

1. Craniosynostosis, malformed ears.
2. Complete absence or malformation of the radius (the bone on the thumb side of the forearm).
3. Short ulna (the other bone in the forearm).
4. Missing carpals (wrist bones), metacarpals (hand bones), phalanges (finger bones) and absent or very small thumb.
5. Prenatal and postnatal growth deficiency.
6. Fifty percent incidence of intellectual developmental disabilities in children followed beyond the first year.
7. Anal anomalies, including imperforate anus (no anal opening) and anteriorly placed anus (anal opening too far forward).
8. Kidney anomalies, including underdevelopment or complete absence of the organ.

Surgical treatment of craniosynostosis may be necessary to avoid disfiguring skull asymmetry. Premature fusion of all skull sutures requires operative intervention soon after the diagnosis is confirmed. Reopening the sutures allows for continuing expansion of cranial volume to accommodate brain growth. Repair of imperforate anus is undertaken soon after birth but may require two procedures. In some cases a colostomy is first done to provide an exit for fecal material. Some months later a "pull through and hook up" operation is performed, and the colostomy is taken down.

Because of a 50% incidence of intellectual developmental disabilities in children followed beyond the first year, there is an indication that children with Baller-Gerold syndrome will require special education support. However, the number of children who survive into school age is small, and therefore there is no research documenting specific educational strategies or behavioral problems.

The prognosis for this disorder is unfavorable. Twenty percent of affected infants die unexpectedly in the first year of life. There is a 50% incidence of intellectual developmental disabilities in those who survive beyond infancy. The anatomic abnormalities, although treatable, may need multiple surgeries before they are satisfactorily repaired. Occasional findings associated with this syndrome (conductive hearing loss and optic atrophy) may leave these children with significant sensory deficits (Jones, 1997).

REFERENCE

Jones, K. (1997). *Smith's recognizable patterns of human malformations* (5th ed.). Philadelphia, PA: Saunders.

BARRY H. DAVISON
Ennis, Texas

JOAN W. MAYFIELD
Baylor Pediatric Specialty Services, Dallas, Texas

BALO DISEASE

Balo disease, also known as *concentric sclerosis*, is a childhood neurological disorder characterized by brain demyelination. Rapid and progressive loss of the fatty covering around nerve fibers in the brain results in various neurological symptoms depending on the brain areas affected (Rowland, 1995; Thoene & Coker, 1995). The damage to the brain consists of irregular patches in a series of widening concentric circles. The cause of Balo disease is unknown, and symptoms can progress rapidly over several weeks or more slowly over 2 to 3 years. Balo disease may be the result of a slow virus or the involvement of autoimmune factors (Rowland, 1995). It may be a variant of multiple sclerosis or an unusual form of Schilder's disease (Thoene & Coker, 1995). Balo disease affects both male and female children.

Characteristics

1. Involuntary muscle spasms and gradual paralysis.
2. Possibly other neurological, intellectual, or physical symptoms may develop.
3. Possible impairment of regulation of physiologic functions.

Balo disease has no specific treatment; thus medical care is symptomatic and supportive (Thoene & Coker, 1995). Special education services for Balo disease may be available under the multiple handicapping condition of Other Health Impairment category or Physical Disability. Children may show neurological, physical, and intellectual deficits and thus need multiple interventions for all areas. Psychoeducational testing should occur annually to determine the ongoing educational need in these areas. Occupational and physical therapy may also be required services for children with Balo disease.

Balo disease is a life-threatening disorder. Most patients survive for less than a year (Rowland, 1995). Current research is aimed at determining the cause of this disease.

REFERENCES

Rowland, L. P. (Ed.). (1995). *Merritt's textbook of neurology* (9th ed.). Baltimore, MD: Williams & Wilkins.

Thoene, J. G., & Coker, N. P. (Eds.). (1995). *Physicians' guide to rare diseases* (2nd ed.). Montvale, NJ: Dowden.

JENNIFER HARGRAVE
University of Texas at Austin

See *also* Schilder's Disease

BANDURA, ALBERT (1925–   )

Albert Bandura received his bachelor's degree from the University of British Columbia in Vancouver. Later he began his doctorate at Iowa University and later joined the faculty at Stanford University where he remained throughout his career. He has served as the school's chairman of the Department of Psychology, and was honored by Stanford as the recipient of an endowed chair. He was named a David Starr Jordan Professor of Social Science in Psychology at Stanford University and is emeritus faculty at Stanford.

Influenced by K. L. Spence and the Hullian research tradition, Bandura is recognized as one of the developers of social cognitive theory. He proposes that human thought, affect, and behavior are strongly influenced by vicarious learning, and he is a proponent of social cognitive theory. This theory accords a central role to cognitive, vicarious, self-regulatory, and self-reflective processes in sociocognitive functioning. According to Bandura, psychology, through its research, bears an obligation to society for the betterment of humanity.

Bandura has authored nine books and countless articles on a wide range of issues in psychology. In addition, he serves on numerous editorial boards of journals and serials. His recent book, *Social Foundations of Thought and Action: A Social Cognitive Theory*, provides the conceptual framework for and analyzes the large body of knowledge bearing on social cognitive theory. *Self-Efficacy:*

The Exercise of Control, his latest book, presents efficacy belief as the foundation of action, and in it Bandura asserts that unless people believe they can produce desired effects by their actions, they have little incentive to act. Other publications include *Social Learning and Personality Development, Social Learning Theory, Aggression: A Social Learning Analysis; Principles of Behavior Modification;* and *Psychological Modeling, Conflicting Theories* (Bandura, 1969; Bandura, 1971; Bandura, 1973; Bandura, 1977; Bandura, 1986; Bandura, 1997; Bandura & Walters, 1963). Bandura's contributions to psychology have been recognized in the honors and awards he has received. He was elected to the presidency of the American Psychological Association (APA) in 1974 and the Western Psychological Association in 1980. His numerous awards included the Distinguished Scientific Contributions Award of the American Psychological Association; the Distinguished Scientist Award, Division 12 of the APA; the William James Award for outstanding achievements in psychological science of the American Psychological Society; the Distinguished Contribution Award of the International Society for Research on Aggression; and a Guggenheim Fellowship.

Bandura has been elected to the American Academy of Arts and Sciences and the Institute of Medicine of the National Academy of Sciences, and is the recipient of 11 honorary degrees. He has also served as chairman of the board of directors for the APA, trustee for the American Psychological Foundation, and chairman of the Western Psychological Association.

In 2001, he received the Lifetime Achievement Award from the Association for the Advancement of Behavior Therapy. In April 2004, he received an honorary degree from the University of Athens. In October 2004, he received an award from the University of Catama. In May 2004 he received the Lifetime Achievement Award from the Western Psychological Association as well as the coveted James McKeen Cattell Award from the American Psychological Society. In August 2004, Professor Bandura received the outstanding lifetime contribution to psychology award from the American Psychological Association (Pajares, 2004).

Bandura's research interests include investigating the power of psychological modeling in shaping human thought, emotion, and action. He is currently investigating "the mechanisms of human agency: how people exercise influence over their own motivation and behavior," and how an individual's perceptions of their ability to influence events affects their lives. Bandura is also researching how stress reactions and depressions are caused.

REFERENCES

Bandura, A. (1969). *Principles of behavior modification.* New York, NY: Holt, Rinehart, & Winston.

Bandura, A. (1971). *Psychological modeling, conflicting theories.* Chicago, IL: Aldine-Atherton.

Bandura, A. (1973). *Aggression: A social learning analysis.* Englewood Cliffs, NJ: Prentice Hall.

Bandura, A. (1977). *Social learning theory.* Englewood Cliffs, NJ: Prentice Hall.

Bandura, A. (1986). *Social foundations of thought and action: A social cognitive theory.* Englewood Cliffs, NJ: Prentice Hall.

Bandura, A. (1997). *Self-efficacy: The exercise of control.* New York, NY: Freeman & Company.

Bandura, A., & Walters, R. H. (1963). *Social learning and personality development.* New York, NY: Holt, Rinehart, & Winston.

Pajares, F. (2004). *Albert Bandura: Biographical sketch.* Retrieved from http://p20motivationlab.org/Bandura

MARY LEON PERRY
Texas A&M University
First edition

TAMARA J. MARTIN
University of Texas of the Permian Basin
Second edition

Rachel M. Toplis
Falcon School District 49, Colorado Springs, Colorado
Third edition

See *also* Social Learning Theory

BANNATYNE, ALEXANDER D. (1925–   )

Alexander Bannatyne received his BA in education and philosophy at Auckland University in New Zealand in 1949. He obtained his PhD in psychology at the Institute of Psychiatry at the University of London in 1953. As a professor, he taught on learning disabilities to doctoral students at the University of Illinois, 1966 to 1969.

Bannatyne's major areas of work are in dealing with learning-disabled children and their reading, writing, and spelling abilities. Bannatyne believes that to understand abnormal, one must be knowledgeable about what is normal. Only through presentation of the abnormal in conjunction with a knowledge of the normal can we work out what has gone wrong; only then do we have standards against which to measure degrees and types of abnormalities (Bannatyne, 1971). Bannatyne did studies on the relationships among learned and unlearned handedness, spelling ability, mirror imaging, motor functioning, balance, memory for designs, and auditory vocal sequencing in terms of hemispheric activity and dominance. He found that three types of brain functions may exist: (1) an efficient balanced brain associated with unlearned hand-edness, balance ability, and competent spelling; (2) a less verbally efficient right hemisphere dominant brain that seems to give mirror imaging, spatial competence, and left-handedness; and (3) a brain that is visuospatially inept even though it is not given to the drawing of mirror images.

Dr. Bannatyne was an associate professor at the Children's Research Center at the University of Illinois. He has authored many books. Some of his major works include *Language, Reading, and Learning Disabilities, Bannatyne System: Reading, Writing and Spelling, Body Image*, and *How Children Can Learn to Live Rewarding Lives* (Bannatyne, 1973a; Bannatyne, 1973b; Bannatyne, 1975).

REFERENCES

Bannatyne, A. D. (1971). *Language, reading, and learning disabilities.* Springfield, IL: Thomas.

Bannatyne, A. D. (1973a). *Body image: Communication program.* Lafayette, LA: Learning System.

Bannatyne, A. D. (1973b). *How children can learn to live rewarding lives.* Springfield, IL: Thomas.

Bannatyne, A. D. (1973c). *Reading: An auditory-vocal process.* San Rafael, CA: Academic Therapy.

Bannatyne, A. D. (1975). *Bannatyne system: Reading, writing, and spelling.* Lafayette, LA: Learning System.

ELIZABETH JONES
Texas A&M University

BARBITURATE ABUSE

Barbiturates are depressant drugs that were initially designed to induce sleep and relieve anxiety or tension by slowing down the central nervous system (Meeks, Heit, & Page, 1996). The sedative affect is much the same as alcohol's and normally lasts for 3 to 6 hours at a time (Information on barbiturates, 2002). Currently, there are more than 2,000 known legal and illegal barbiturates available. In small doses they are considered safe, and they may be prescribed by a physician for insomnia, anxiety, tension, or epilepsy (Information on barbiturates, 2002). Unfortunately, barbiturate dosage must continually be increased to maintain the same relaxation effect, and the use quickly establishes dependence in the user (Information on barbiturates, 2002). Higher levels of dosages are considered dangerous and may interfere with respiration (Information on barbiturates, 2002).

Legal use of barbiturates includes ingestion of a pill or tablet form; illegal use also includes pills or tablets and may include the use of a powder that is manufactured and injected. The use of barbiturates appears to have lessened

in recent years. In 1968, 24.7 million Americans used prescription barbiturates in comparison to 8.8 million in 1973 (DAWN barbiturates, 2002). A study dealing with workplace drug usage indicated that approximately 19% of the workers in the study had recently used barbiturates (News briefs, 1997).

Characteristics

Short-Term Use

1. Relief from tension, anxiety, and insomnia.
2. Behaviors consistent with intoxication: slurred speech, balance difficulties.
3. Memory problems.

Long-Term Use

1. Vision problems.
2. Slowed reflexes.
3. Menstrual problems.
4. Lack of coordination.
5. Sexual dysfunction.
6. Breathing problems.

The use of barbiturates is considered dangerous because of the potential for dependency. It is especially dangerous in infants born to barbiturate-dependent women. The treatment involves withdrawal from the effects and use of the drug. Because withdrawal can cause serious side effects, a physician should carefully monitor the period of withdrawal. Side effects can include irritability, nervousness, fainting, nausea, convulsions, and, in rare cases, death due to respiratory problems. The same potential side effects are possible with infants who must experience withdrawal (DAWN barbiturates, 2002).

In terms of special education, the use of barbiturates does not in itself render a student eligible for special education services. Students who are using (legal or illegal) drugs may be evaluated in all areas to determine whether there is a concomitant disability, such as a learning disability, emotional disability, or other health impairment. If the student is ineligible, the team may want to consider whether the student is eligible for a Section 504 plan because of possible chemical dependence.

Best practices for the future would be to institute effective preventative measures. For example, students who are at risk for drug use should be educated about the affects of barbiturates, and at-risk pregnant women should be educated regarding the effects on their unborn child.

REFERENCES

DAWN barbiturates. (2002). Retrieved from http://www.samhsa.gov/data/DAWN.aspx

Information on barbiturates. (2002). Retrieved from http://www.gwu.edu/~cade/barbiturates.htm

Meeks, L., Heit, P., & Page, R. (1996). *Comprehensive school health education: Totally awesome strategies for teaching health* (pp. 267–269). Blacklick, OH: Meeks Heit.

News briefs. (1997). Retrieved from http://www.ndsn.org/

DALENE M. MCCLOSKEY
University of Northern Colorado

BARDET-BIEDL SYNDROME

Bardet-Biedl syndrome is a rare disorder inherited as an autosomal recessive genetic trait. As with Laurence-Moon syndrome, Bardet-Biedl syndrome is characterized by intellectual developmental disabilities, hypogonadism, and progressive retinal dystrophy with vision failure. Renal failure also occurs, as does hypertension, and these represent the leading cause of death. Two symptoms specific to Bardet-Biedl syndrome include obesity and polydactyly. Alstrom syndrome and Prader-Willi syndrome exhibit similar symptoms to that of Bardet-Biedl and may be useful in terms of differential diagnosis.

Bardet-Biedl affects males and females in equal numbers. There have been more than 100 cases of this disorder reported in the medical literature with an increased number of incidences among the Arabs of Kuwait (Berg, 1996).

The primary symptom in this disorder is degeneration of the retina. This typically occurs in early childhood. The course of progression of sight deterioration differs in each individual. Impairments range from loss of central vision, to day-blindness, to lesions in the middle of the retina. In some cases, the degeneration of the retina may follow the course of retinitis pigmentosa with night blindness followed by tunnel vision (McKusick, 1992).

Besides obesity found in almost all individuals with Bardet-Biedl syndrome, many also suffer from abnormalities in their fingers and toes, such as additional fingers and/or toes, webbing of the digits, or abnormal shortness of the digits.

Another feature prevalent is mild to moderate retardation typically more apparent in males in early childhood than in females. Sexual maturation is often delayed or absent. Males tend to have small testes and genitalia and females are usually affected by menstrual irregularities and reproductive dysfunction. Other abnormalities include hypertension, diabetes mellitus, and short stature (McKusick, 1992).

Bardet-Biedl syndrome is inherited as an autosomal recessive genetic trait. In other words, the syndrome only affects the offspring if the defective gene is passed on by both the mother and the father. If the child receives only one defective gene from one parent, the child will be a carrier but will not display the symptoms. The risk of two parents carrying this gene and passing it on to their offspring is 25%. The risk of passing one of the defective genes is 50%, and there is a 25% chance of the parents passing on two normal genes. The risk is the same for each pregnancy (Berg, 1996).

Characteristics

1. Intellectual developmental disabilities.
2. Hypogonadism.
3. Progressive retinal dystrophy with vision failure.

Other symptoms may include hypertension, obesity, abnormal fingers and toes, and sexual maturation delay or absence and occasional hearing impairment.

Treatment and diagnosis of retinal degeneration found in Bardet-Biedl syndrome can be made by an ophthalmologist through various tests. Visual aids may help as vision decreases, and special eyeglasses can be used to protect the eye from excessive light. A variety of visual and nonvisual aids can help the individual to mediate visual deficits. Treatment also includes medical responses to symptoms, urinary cultures, measurement of blood pressure, and genetic counseling (Weidemann, Kunze, Grosse, & Dibbern, 1989).

Surgery may be helpful to remedy abnormalities found in the fingers and toes. Genetic counseling may be beneficial for patients and families. Additionally, psychological counseling can be a useful tool to help individuals and their families cope with the effects of Bardet-Biedl syndrome.

Finally, early educational intervention can be extremely critical in helping those affected by intellectual developmental disabilities. Indeed, the course and prognosis of this disorder is determined by the degree of intellectual developmental disabilities and by the progression of the retino- and neuropathy (Weidemann et al., 1989). Specialized classes addressing the child's strengths and mediating weaknesses will be useful in helping the child attain social and academic potential (Berg, 1996).

REFERENCES

Berg, B. (1996). *Principles of child neurology*. San Francisco, CA: McGraw-Hill.

McKusick, V. A. (1992). *Mendelian inheritance in man* (10th ed.). Baltimore, MD: Johns Hopkins University Press.

Weidemann, H. R., Kunze, J., Grosse, F. R., & Dibbern, H. (1989). *Atlas of clinical syndromes: A visual aid to diagnosis* (2nd ed.). St. Louis, MO: Mosby.

LISA A. FASNACHT-HILL
Keck University of Southern California School of Medicine,
University of Southern California / University Affiliated Program at Children's Hospital of Los Angeles

BARDON, JACK I. (1925–1993)

Jack I. Bardon earned his BA in psychology at Cleveland College of Western Reserve University in 1949, with a minor in education. He continued his professional education at the University of Pennsylvania, earning the MA in psychology in 1951 and a PhD in clinical psychology in 1956. From 1952 until 1958, Bardon was a school psychologist in the Princeton, New Jersey schools and served as coordinator of special education services from 1958 to 1960. In 1960 he became director of the Rutgers University doctoral program in school psychology with the academic rank of associate professor. He was promoted to professor in 1963 and became head of the department in 1968.

During his tenure at Rutgers, Bardon began to have an impact nationally on the delivery of school psychological services to handicapped children. His program in school psychology at Rutgers was one of the early pioneering programs in the field and, along with the University of Texas program, had a major influence on the development of doctoral schools of psychology. The Rutgers program reflected Bardon's own prominent, driving interest: to determine how the body of knowledge and the methods and techniques of psychology can be applied to the improvement of schooling generally, and to meeting the special needs of exceptional children in schools specifically. Bardon was instrumental in developing the primary role definitions of school psychologists (Bardon, 1982; Bardon & Bennett, 1974). Bardon was involved in work to help differentiate school psychology from other disciplines (Bardon, 1983). His work has benefited special education and regular education by improving the ability of school psychologists to provide services to children at all levels. In Bardon's most recent work (1992), he discussed the rationale for successes and failures in educational undertakings and how they relate to the field of school psychology.

Bardon left Rutgers in 1976 to accept a professorship at the University of North Carolina at Greensboro, where he became an Excellence Foundation Professor in 1983. Bardon was editor of the *Journal of School Psychology* from 1968 to 1971, was president of the Division of School Psychology of the American Psychological Association in 1969, and served on the board of directors of the American Orthopsychiatric Association from 1981 to 1984.

Jack Bardon retired from the University of North Carolina at Greensboro in 1991, and died in November, 1993. He worked hard throughout his career to apply psychological theory, principles, and practice to the field of education, and is credited by his colleagues with having made a substantial impact in the definition of school psychology, professional organizational issues, and in the debate over levels of training in school psychology.

REFERENCES

Bardon, J. I. (1982). The psychology of school psychology. In C. R. Reynolds & T. B. Gutkin (Eds.), *The handbook of school psychology*. New York, NY: Wiley.

Bardon, J. I. (1983). Psychology applied to education: A specialty in search of an identity. *American Psychologist, 38*, 185–196.

Bardon, J. I. (1992). Solving educational problems: Working across institutional, cultural and political differences. *School of Psychology Quarterly, 7*, 137–147.

Bardon, J. I., & Bennett, V. C. (1974). *School psychology*. Englewood Cliffs, NJ: Prentice Hall.

CECIL R. REYNOLDS
Texas A&M University
First edition

DEBORAH B. GUILLEN
University of Texas of the Permian Basin
Second edition

BARRAGA, NATALIE C. (1915–   )

Natalie C. Barraga obtained her BA in home economics from North Texas State University in 1938. She continued her education at the University of Texas in Austin and received her master's in 1957. In 1963, she earned her EdD in special education for the visually impaired from George Peabody College for Teachers. Barraga's entry into the field of the visually impaired originated from a prior interest in child development and an interest from her daughter, who had a severe visual impairment. She focused her years of teaching and research objectives on improving education for learners with visual impairments (Barraga, 1981; Barraga, 1989; Barraga, 1990; Barraga, 2007).

Barraga's research documented how vision is learned with a sequential progressive learning program to teach functional academic tasks. To further evolve and document her research in visual impairments, she developed visual assessment tools to help educators identify the sequential steps to teach academic tasks to learners with visual impairments. Support was given to her sequential learning program through the publication of a systematic instructional curriculum, *Development of Efficiency in Visual Functioning*.

Barraga continues to live in Austin, Texas, and is professor emerita at the University of Texas at Austin. She has published several books, monographs, assessment instruments, and articles as her contribution to the field of visual impairments. She continues to contribute to the field of visual impairments by consulting on both a national and international level and has interest in promoting interdisciplinary communication and an international exchange of information, especially with third-world countries to improve services for children and their families with visual impairments.

REFERENCES

Barraga, N. C. (1981). Innovations in teacher testing. *Journal of Visual Impairment & Blindness, 75,* 96–100.

Barraga, N. C. (1989). Perspectives on working with visually impaired persons worldwide: Looking forward. *Journal of Visual Impairment & Blindness, 83,* 84–87.

Barraga, N. C. (1990). Infusion of research and practice into personnel preparation. *Peabody Journal of Education, 67,* 10–21.

Barraga, N. C. (2007). *If anyone can, you can. The story of my life.* Texas School for the Blind and Visually Impaired. Austin, Texas. Retrieved from http://www.tsbvi.edu/curriculum-a-publications/3/1033-if-anyone-can-you-can-the-story-of-my-life-by-dr-natalie-carter-barraga

ELAINE FLETCHER-JANZEN
Chicago School of Professional Psychology
First edition

TAMARA J. MARTIN
University of Texas of the Permian Basin
Second edition

BARRIER-FREE EDUCATION

The delivery of special education services to all children with disabilities in the least restrictive environment, as required by the Individuals with Disabilities Act and related state and federal laws and regulations, means that school buildings and facilities must be designed or altered to make those services accessible. Barrier-free design standards typically give technical specifications that cover building entrances and exits, parking, curbs, stairs, elevators, lavatories, drinking fountains, hazard warnings, and building elements and fixtures. In both new construction and modifications of existing facilities, buildings may be subject to a variety of definitions and design standards (Redden, 1979). In 1973, the American National Standards Institute (ANSI) criteria were cited in the regulations for Section 504 of the Rehabilitation Act of 1973 as the minimum access standard to assure compliance with nondiscrimination provisions. The design standards set forth in the Uniform Federal Accessibility Standards (UFAS; 1984) generally were consistent with federal standards in effect, major model building codes, and most state and local codes; they were based on ANSI A117.1-1980. The 1984 UFAS criteria were geared to adult dimensions and anthropometrics. Some states, however, developed design guidelines for special education facilities that considered the total learning environment for children with all types of disabilities (Abend, Bedner, Froehlinger, & Stenzler, 1979). A barrier-free environment requires the removal of all architectural barriers to accessibility (Redden, 1979). It should be noted that the regulations for Section 504 (which were applicable to recipients of funds from the U.S. Department of Education or Health and Human Services) did not require barrier-free environments. Section 504 required *program accessibility*—that is, a recipient's program or activity, when viewed in its entirety, was to be readily accessible to and usable by persons with disabilities. Access to each facility was not required. Although the program accessibility standards could be achieved by a number of effective methods, including structural changes, priority was given intended to provide methods for the most integrated setting appropriate. Under Section 504, it was not permissible to isolate disabled students in a single accessible building.

The passage of the Americans with Disabilities Act of 1990 (ADA) substantially supported the intent of accessibility spelled out in Section 504. Title II of the ADA did not impose any major new requirements on school districts because school districts received federal funds and were required to provide accessibility under Section 504 as far back as 1973. However, as the ADA expanded nondiscriminatory protection to school students, it also took precedent over any lesser stringent rules in Section 504, the ADA reiterated that a school district must ensure that students with disabilities are not excluded from participation in, or denied the benefits of, its services, programs, and activities. It must also ensure that they are not subjected to discrimination by the school system (U.S. Department of Education, p. 45). The ADA provided new guidelines and self-evaluation surveys based on the Americans with Disabilities Act Accessibility Guidelines for Buildings and Facilities (ADDAG; U.S. Department of Education, 1996).

The Office for Civil Rights (OCR) enforces Title II of the ADA and Section 504 of the Rehabilitation Act of 1973. The OCR investigates complaints filed by individuals or their representatives, who believe that they have been discriminated against because of a disability. The OCR can be reached at U.S. Department of Education, Office for Civil Rights, 330 550 12th Street, S.W., Washington, DC 20202–1100. Tel.: (800) 421–3481, TDD number (877) 521–2172. The OCR can also be reached via e-mail at OCR@ed.gov, or through the Department of Education's website (http://www.ed.gov/).

In addition, one can find numerous Internet websites designed to provide information about the accommodation of specific disabilities, which can help teachers, parents, and students overcome educational obstacles.

REFERENCES

Abend, A. C., Bedner, M. J., Froehlinger, V. J., & Stenzler, Y. (1979). *Facilities for special educational services: A guide for planning new and renovated schools.* Reston, VA: Council for Exceptional Children.

Redden, M. R. (Ed.). (1979). *Assuring access for the handicapped.* San Francisco, CA: Jossey-Bass.

Uniform Federal Accessibility Standards (UFAS). (1984, August 7). 49 F.R. 31528–31621.

U.S. Department of Education, Office for Civil Rights. (1996). *Compliance with the Americans with Disabilities Act: A self-evaluation guide for public elementary and secondary schools.* Washington, DC: U.S. Government Printing Office.

SHIRLEY A. JONES
Virginia Polytechnic Institute and State University
First edition

ELAINE FLETCHER-JANZEN
Chicago School of Professional Psychology
Second edition

KIMBERLY F. APPLEQUIST
University of Colorado at Colorado Springs
Third edition

See also Americans with Disabilities Act; Rehabilitation Act of 1973, Section 504

BARRIERS, ARCHITECTURAL (See Architectural Barriers)

BARSCH, RAY H. (1917–2003)

Ray H. Barsch earned his BA in special education in 1950 and MEd in school psychology in 1952 from the University of Wisconsin, Milwaukee. He went on to receive his PhD in educational psychology from Northwestern University in 1959 under the direction of Claude Mathis, Paul Witty, and Helmer Myklebust.

Barsch was principally known for his development of a curriculum called *movigenics*, a theory of movement developed from "the study of origin and development of patterns of movement in man and the relationship of those movements to his learning efficiency." He regards movigenics as "orientation—a cognitive map to guide practitioners toward a goal of practical synthesis" (Barsch, 1976).

As an ardent supporter of interdisciplinary approaches to assessment and teaching in special education, Barsch defines learning disabilities as a concept that focuses on learning rather than "a frantic but seldom fruitful effort to delineate a uniform and specific set of characteristics" (Barsch, 1976).

Barsch worked as a professor in the department of special education at California State University, Northridge in 1970, and in the division for continuing education at the University of Santa Clara. Among other positions and consultantships, Barsch directed teacher preparation programs in the department of counseling and behavioral studies at the University of Wisconsin (1963–1966) and the Easter Seal Development Center in Milwaukee, Wisconsin (1950–1964).

From the early 1970s to the early 1980s, Barsch was a professor in the School of Education at the California State University, Northridge. He also directed the Ray Barsch Center for Learning, where he specialized in one-on-one therapy for children with specific learning problems and counseled parents. In addition, he has supervised the development of the Special Education Teacher Program in Ventura, California, as well as the training of graduate students in various evaluation and therapy techniques.

His (1995) book, *Fine Tuning: An Auditory-Visual Training Program*, describes exercises for developing students' listening skills, and a 1992 reprint in the *Journal of Learning Disabilities* of Barsch's article, "Perspectives on Learning Disabilities," has generated substantial debate, highlighting the absence of progress in defining, classifying, and providing appropriate interventions for learning disabilities. This piece, originally published in 1968, examines learning disabilities from the perspective of history, viewing them as a concept rather than a category, promoting interdisciplinary convergence, evaluating various delivery systems, and noting a new recognition of human divergence.

Of his many awards, in 1974 Barsch received the International Milestone Award of the International Federation of Learning Disabilities at its world congress in the Netherlands. Barsh continued to contribute to education throughout the Ray Barsch Center for Learning, which still exists today.

All information for the Ray Barsch Center for Learning was retrieved from http://www.corporationwiki.com/

California/Ventura/the-ray-barsch-center-for-learning-inc
/39837679.aspx.

REFERENCES

Barsch, R. H. (1976). *Achieving perceptual motor efficiency: A space oriented approach to learning* (Vol. *1*). Seattle, WA: Special Child.

Barsch, R. H. (1992). Perspectives on learning disabilities: The vectors of a new convergence. *Journal of Learning Disabilities*, *25*, 6–16.

Barsch, R. H. (1995). *Fine tuning: An auditory-visual training program*. Novato, CA: Academic Therapy.

ELAINE FLETCHER-JANZEN
Chicago School of Professional Psychology
First edition

TAMARA J. MARTIN
University of Texas of the Permian Basin
Second edition

BASAL READERS

Basal reader programs are comprehensive, meaningfully sequenced collections of stories, frequently arranged in groups according to a central theme or topic. Smith and Johnson (1980) described these programs as being based on the belief that a controlled vocabulary of high-frequency words, coupled with the presentation of easily decodable pattern words, facilitates learning to read and the improvement of reading skills.

Basal reader programs are intended to be used to instruct children from the stage of nonreading, through the acquisition of developing skills, to the level of mature, flexible reading. Typically, these programs include various correlated and supplementary materials including teachers' manuals, workbooks, skills sheets, activity boxes, criterion-referenced monitoring systems, and even computer software management programs. This self-contained aspect of basal reader programs is intended to provide all that is necessary for a core reading program. Teachers are carefully guided through instructional directed reading activities as outlined in the accompanying manuals. The structure of these lesson plans, explained by both Stauffer (1969) and Harris (1970), follows the sequence of pre-reading preparation, guided silent reading, oral rereading and comprehension assessment, skill development activities, and enrichment. In addition, teachers are usually provided with suggestions for choosing related books and other materials to use in conjunction with the basal reader. A survey of 500 educators by Bauman and Heubach in

1996 found that teachers believed that these materials have an empowering effect by providing additional instructional ideas to draw from, adapt, or extend (Bauman & Heubach, 1996).

The reading books themselves constitute the essential materials in any basal program. Usually there is a set of readiness materials for use with children at the beginning stages of reading instruction. These are followed by readers considered to be at the preprimer and primer levels of difficulty. The readers contain a limited number of frequently repeated words that assist in the development of a basic sight vocabulary. These basic reading books are followed by progressively more difficult readers extending through all the elementary grades and frequently into the middle and junior high grades as well. Many of these higher level basal readers consist of comprehensive literary anthologies and, according to Ringler and Weber (1984), may include a variety of narrative types such as realistic fiction, fantasy, science fiction, folklore, poetry, and plays.

In recent years basal readers have been analyzed in terms of cultural competence. Foley and Boulware (1996) found that gender equity reflected in basal readers has not essentially changed since the 1960s. In addition, analyses of basal readers regarding race and ethnicity indicate that these aspects of culture are omitted from the majority of basal texts. The omission of race and/or ethnicity from basal selections and teacher manuals may not meet the needs of many children (McDermott, 1997). Other criticisms of basal readers suggest that publisher censorship still exists and essential components of literary works are being eliminated by widespread anthologization (Reutzel & Larsen, 1995). However, others (Risner & Nicholson, 1996) applaud the addition of questions to the readers that support higher levels of comprehension than previously found. Therefore, research still suggests that basal readers support the development of additional teacher materials and engaging activities that, in turn, elevate student reading comprehension. Basal readers are currently being challenged by other approaches such as the workshop approach, which appears to be more flexible (Turner, 2004).

REFERENCES

Bauman, J. F., & Heubach, K. M. (1996). Do basal readers deskill teachers? A national survey of educator's use and opinions of basals. *Elementary School Journal*, *96*, 511–526.

Foley, C. L., & Boulware, B. J. (1996). Gender equity in 1990 middle school basal readers. *Reading Improvement*, *33*, 220–223.

Harris, A. J. (1970). *How to increase reading ability* (5th ed.). New York, NY: McKay.

McDermott, P. (1997). The illusion of racial diversity in contemporary basal readers: An analysis of teacher manuals. *Evaluative/feasibility report: speech/conference paper*. Abstract from: ERIC Item No. ED407473.

Reutzel, D. R., & Larsen, N. S. (1995). Look what they've done to real children's books in the new basal readers. *Language Arts, 72*, 495–507.

Ringler, L. H., & Weber, C. K. (1984). *A language-thinking approach to reading.* New York, NY: Harcourt Brace Jovanovich.

Risner, G. P., & Nicholson, J. I. (1996). *The new basal readers: What levels of comprehension do they promote? Evaluative/feasibility report.* (ERIC Item No. ED403546)

Smith, R. J., & Johnson, D. D. (1980). *Teaching children to read* (2nd ed.). Reading, MA: Addison-Wesley.

Stauffer, R. G. (1969). *Directing reading maturity as a cognitive process.* New York, NY: Harper & Row.

Turner, J. S. (2004). When teachers are readers. *National Association of Elementary School Principals Newsletter, 83*, 5.

JOHN M. EELLS
Souderton Area School District, Souderton, Pennsylvania
First edition

ELAINE FLETCHER-JANZEN
Chicago School of Professional Psychology
Second edition

See also High Interest–Low Vocabulary; Reading Disorders; Reading Remediation

BASC (*See* Behavior Assessment System for Children–2)

BASELINE DATA

Baseline data and/or baseline conditions are meant to represent the current state of the behavior and environment. A baseline is not simply the absence of a treatment or intervention condition; a baseline adequately, thoroughly, and descriptively details the condition prior to the first experimental condition. Baseline data may include direct observation counting, retrospective ratings, and inferential ratings. Baseline data sets the parameters for the range of data collected. Data collected in intervention sessions or conditions must be identical to that of the data collected baseline in order to make accurate comparisons. In pure applied behavior analysis (ABA) nomenclature baseline data must demonstrate stability prior to the initiation of intervention (Cooper, Heron, & Heward, 2007). Stability is said to have occurred when there is an absence of directionality or trend in the data and when there is restricted variation in the pattern of the data. Trend is said to occur when there are three or more data points pattern in a specific direction. This is also referred to as *celeration*

and is illustrated by data that increases or decreases. Baseline data that are either accelerating or decelerating are generally not useful as preintervention data in purely visual ABA interpretations. The trend in the data suggests that there is already something that is influencing the target behavior and therefore the environmental conditions are not under sufficient control. However, when the trend is countertherapeutic (i.e., moving in the undesired direction), the need for protracted baseline data collection is negated, because it may be assumed that these influences need to be overcome. Therefore, if the trend of the baseline data is therapeutic, continuation of the baseline is indicated until such time as the behavior becomes acceptable or until it levels off and becomes stable. If the data are countertherapeutic, this is not necessary and intervention can be begun in 5 to 10 sessions or days.

Variability in the data during baseline in the absence of a marked trend must be measured by examining its degree to determine its effect on the baseline. Baseline data should be stable so that the practitioner can say with reasonable certainty that the target behavior occurred in a specific condition prior to intervention. Stability is often measured as the degree of variability about the mean. A ±50% variability about the baseline mean (Alberto & Troutman, 2009) is sometimes discuss, so also is a 20% variability. For example, if we gathered 10 days of baseline data and then summed each day's score and divided by 10 we would have the mean of the baseline. If this mean were 40%, then all data should fall between 60% and 20% during the baseline as that is the range established by the ±50%. A single (or perhaps 2) data point(s) falling outside this range could be judged to be an oddity (sometimes called an *outlier*); it should not hamper the identification of these data as stable. However, more than this number would indicate a lack of stability and a longer baseline would be required. Baseline stability or countertherapeutic trend is a basic requirement prior to the initiation of intervention programming.

Recent advancements in the statistical analysis of baseline data are controversial in some circles but indicate different "rules" about baseline stability conditions (Horner et al., 2005; Kratchowill et al., 2010). Studies indicate three or more replications would be necessary to prevent chance occurrence to reasonably predict trend (Horner et al., 2005), however, relying on visual analysis of graphed data creates challenges in determining what the numerical values are and which phases should be compared (Parker & Brossart, 2006; Shadish et al., 2009).

REFERENCES

Alberto, P. A., & Troutman, A. C. (2009). *Applied behavior analysis for teachers* (8th ed.). Upper Saddle River, NJ: Pearson.

Cooper, J. O., Heron, T. E., & Heward, W. L. (2007). *Applied behavior analysis* (2nd ed.). Upper Saddle River, NJ: Pearson.

Horner, R. H., Carr, E. G., Halle, J., McGee, G., Odom, S., & Wolery, M. (2005). The use of single-subject research to identify evidence-based practice in special education. *Exceptional Children, 71*, 161–179.

Kratochwill, T. R., Hitchcock, J., Horner, R. H., Levin, J. R., Odom, S. L., Rindskopf, D. M., & Shadish, W. R. (2010). *Single-case designs technical documentation*. Retrieved from http://ies.ed.gov/ncee/wwc/pdf/wwc_scd.pdf

Parker, R. I., & Brossart, D. F. (2006). Phase contrasts for multiphase single case intervention designs. *School Psychology Quarterly, 21*, 531–563.

Shadish, W. R., Brasil, I. C. C., Illingworth, D. A., White, K. D., Galindo, R., Nagler, E. D., & Rindskopf, D. M. (2009). Using unGraph to extract data from image files: Verification of reliability and validity. *Behavior Research Methods, 41*, 177–183.

LYLE E. BARTON
Kent State University
First edition

KIMBERLY J. VANNEST
Texas A&M University
Fourth edition

BASE RATE

A base rate is a baseline measurement of a target behavior's rate of responding. This measurement is useful when the student's behavior of interest is one for which frequency recording is the appropriate recording strategy and for which rate of responding is the appropriate datum. The latter case is true when the response frequency dependent on duration of observation is important. For example, should the target behavior be either units of "X" assembled in a workshop or incidences of aggressive behavior, frequency would be an appropriate recording strategy. If, in addition, the issue of importance is this number within a specified time frame, then rate of response becomes the appropriate datum. If this period of observation tends to vary, then rate of response is the only appropriate datum. Therefore, the special education practitioner would record the frequency of student response and then divide the frequency by the number of minutes (or hours) of observation. The resultant figure (e.g., 1.56, 0.75, 0.05) would be indicative of the relative frequency of responding per unit of measurement (e.g., minutes, hours) and would be reported as rate per minute (rpm) or rate per hour (rph).

To determine the base rate, these data would be gathered over a period of days or sessions and would be examined to meet the criterion for stability for any baseline data; that is, the data must be stable (have limited variability) or countertherapeutic. Stability is said to occur when the data vary no more than ± 50% of the baseline mean (Alberto & Troutman, 1982). A countertherapeutic trend is said to occur when the data are not stable but moving in the opposite direction. Base-rate data are usually reported as a mean figure (e.g., "the mean base rate was…"); however, these data may be reported as including the range and the usual data display via a graph.

REFERENCE

Alberto, P. A., & Troutman, A. C. (1982). *Applied behavior analysis for teachers*. Columbus, OH: Merrill.

LYLE E. BARTON
Kent State University

See also Applied Behavior Analysis; Behavior Modification

BASIC SKILLS TRAINING

Historically, the term *"basic skills"* refers to the traditional disciplines of reading, writing, and arithmetic that are stressed in the early years of formal education. These areas of study are those that are seen as necessary for an individual to become a contributing member of society. Without at least a rudimentary proficiency in these basic areas, individuals experience difficulty in developing independence and self-esteem.

The exceptional child or adult, however, may require a completely different type of basic skill training than the traditional disciplines deemed necessary for normal functioning within society. Depending on the severity of the handicapping condition, basic skills for special education may vary little or greatly from those of regular students and adults. Basic skills training for exceptional children could best be termed those activities and subject areas that provide for each child's individual learning abilities (allowing for his or her weaknesses) in such a way that deviation from the norm is as limited as possible. This training allows children to accomplish what Blake (1981) refers to as *"cultural tasks,"* in which needs are met through means that are acceptable to society.

Specifically, basic skills for the exceptional child might include those skills noted by Berdine and Blackhurst (1981): training in attention skills, increased memory capacity, the ability to transfer and generalize recently learned skills, and language. In addition, study skills, self-management skills and computer competence are needed as basic skills. Therefore, for the special education student, the basic skills required for academic success are more process-orientated than for regular education students.

In recent years, inclusive programming has sought to assist the special education student in the acquisition of basic skills. Instead of pulling special education students out of the content classes, they have remained with specialized assistance (McCollum & Tindal, 1996). Unfortunately, little data exists to support the effectiveness of this programming for basic content skills at this time.

There is some evidence that computer-assisted learning takes place by online computer services. These services assist high school special education students enter career-focused activities that require basic processing skills that reflect organization, problem solving, and attention. Also, basic skills training can be melded with goals for appropriate behavior (Russell, 2005).

REFERENCES

Berdine, W. H., & Blackhurst, A. E. (1981). *An introduction to special education*. Boston, MA: Little, Brown.

Blake, K. A. (1981). *Educating exceptional pupils: An introduction to contemporary practices*. Reading, MA: Addison-Wesley.

McCollum, S., & Tindal, G. (1996). Supporting students in content areas classes using an outcome-based system of collaboration. *Special Services in the Schools, 12*, 1–17.

Russell, S. E. (2005). Information skills and the special needs student. *Academic Exchange Quarterly, 33*, 4–5.

JAMES H. MILLER
University of New Orleans
First edition

ELAINE FLETCHER-JANZEN
Chicago School of Professional Psychology
Second edition

See also Functional Domains; Functional Instruction

BATEMAN, BARBARA (1933–)

Barbara Bateman received her BA (1954) in psychology from the University of Washington, her MA (1958) from San Francisco State College, and her PhD in special education (1962) from the University of Illinois. In the early years of her professional career, she taught children with intellectual developmental disabilities and visual impairments at Washington State Hospital and a variety of exceptional children in the Oregon public schools. Bateman continued in the field teaching at the university level and became professor of education at the University of Oregon in 1969.

She retired from the University of Oregon in 1994 and is currently Professor Emeritus. Bateman maintains a private practice as a legal consultant in special education. Her interests currently include legally correct and

educationally useful implementation of IDEA and other special education law. Dr. Bateman has received many honors including *Who's Who of American Women, 6th Edition, Who's Who in the West, 12th Edition*, and *Community Leaders of America*. She was one of 53 individuals named as "Influential Person in the Development of the Field of Special Education" in *Remedial and Special Education 21* (November/December 2000).

She has always been a strong advocate of direct instruction, and has urged the field of education to accept the direct instructional philosophy, methods, and materials in publications such as *Essentials of Teaching* (1971) and *Teaching Reading to Learning Disabled and Other Hard-to-Teach Children* (1979). In the 1970s, Bateman's interests broadened to the legal aspects of special education; she received her JD from the University of Oregon Law School in 1976, and has published on law and special education including her influential publications, on IEPs (Bateman, 1996; Bateman & Linden, 2006; Bateman 2003; Herr & Bateman, 2005).

REFERENCES

Bateman, B. (1971). *Essentials of teaching*. Sioux Falls, SD: Adapt Press.

Bateman, B. (1979). Teaching reading to learning disabled and other hard-to-teach children. In L. Resnick & P. Weaver (Eds.), *Theory and practice of early reading*. Hillsdale, NJ: Erlbaum.

Bateman, B. D. (1996). *Better IEPs*. Longmont, CO: Sopris West.

Bateman, B. D., & Linden, M. A. (2006). *Better IEPs: How to develop legally correct and educationally useful programs* (4th). Verona, WI: Attainment.

Bateman, B. D., & Herr, C. M. (2003). *Writing measurable IEP goals and objectives*. Verona, WI: Attainment.

Herr, C. M., & Bateman, B. D. (2005). *Better IEP meetings*. Verona, WI: Attainment.

STAFF
First edition

RACHEL M. TOPLIS
Falcon School District 49, Colorado Springs, Colorado
Third edition

BATTEN DISEASE

Batten disease is one of a group of degenerative encephalopathic diseases known as the neuronal ceroid-lipofuscinoses (NCLs). Batten originally described the disease in 1903 (Cassedy & Edwards, 1993). In all the NCLs ceroid or lipofuscin accumulates within neurons and cells in other body systems. The cellular accumulations are autoflourescent, and the lipopigments distend the affected cells (Dyken, 1999). Multiple systems have been derived to categorize the set of NCLs. Although the term Batten disease sometimes is used to refer to the entire set of diseases, classically the term is used to refer only to the juvenile form of the disorder (classical juvenile NCL; Bennett & Hofmann, 1999).

Classical juvenile NCL is the most common of the NCLs, accounting for 49% of the patients with NCL (Dyken, 1999). It has an incidence of 1 in 25,000 in northern European populations (Munroe, 1996), but lower worldwide (1:100,000; Santavuori, 1988). The gene for classical juvenile NCL is located on Chromosome 16p11.2–12.1 (Bennett & Hofmann, 1999). Not all affected individuals have the classic deletion (Bennett & Hofmann, 1999). All of the NCLs have an autosomal recessive mode of inheritance. It is believed that the pathologic basis of the disorder is one of an inborn error in metabolism, leading to membrane instability (Dyken, 1999).

Characteristics

1. Slowly progressive dementia.
2. The usual age of onset is between 4 and 9 years of age (5.93 ± 1.35 years).
3. Initial symptoms are visual loss and behavioral changes. Initially, cognitive impairment is mild and is observable only at school.
4. By 10 to 15 years of age speech becomes indistinct, overly rapid, and dysarthric.
5. Psychomotor problems, including extrapyramidal, pyramidal, and cerebellar findings, develop.
6. Seizures develop later in the course of the disease.
7. Ocular exam demonstrates macular degeneration, optic atrophy, and retinal degeneration.
8. Death occurs by 20 years of age. (Dyken, 1999; Santavuori, 1988)

Educational interventions should be aimed at maintaining the highest level of functioning. The anticipated deterioration must be acknowledged in educational plans. There is no current, efficacious medical treatment (Percy, 1999). Future research will focus on understanding the basic pathophysiology of the disorder and its treatment. Treatment approaches using stem-cell transplantation or genetically engineered viruses for corrective gene therapy are anticipated (Percy, 1999).

REFERENCES

Bennett, M. J., & Hofmann, S. L. (1999). The neuronal ceroid-lipofuscinoses (Batten disease): A new class of lysosomal storage diseases. *Journal of Inherited Metabolic Diseases, 22,* 535–544.

Cassedy, K. J., & Edwards, M. K. (1993). Metabolic and degenerative diseases of childhood. *Topics in Magnetic Resonance Imaging, 5,* 73–95.

Dyken, P. R. (1999). Degenerative diseases primarily of gray matter. In K. Swaiman & S. Ashwal (Eds.), *Pediatric neurology: Principles and practice* (3rd ed.). St. Louis, MO: Mosby.

Munroe, P. B. (1996). Prenatal diagnosis of Batten's disease. *Lancet, 347,* 1014–1015.

Percy, A. K. (1999). Inherited neurodegenerative disease: The evolution of our thinking. *Journal of Child Neurology, 14*(4), 256–262.

Santavuori, P. (1988). Neuronal ceroidlipofuscinoses in childhood. *Brain and Development, 10,* 80–83.

GRETA N. WILKENING
University of Colorado Health Sciences Center
The Children's Hospital

See also Kufs Disease

BATTERED CHILD SYNDROME

In 1962, pediatrician C. Henry Kempe published an article entitled "The Battered Child Syndrome." This marked the first official recognition by the medical establishment of the problem of child abuse (Ellerstein, 2011). Kempe's article focused on abuse as a deliberate, violent attack on a child by a malicious adult and criticized the medical profession for failing to diagnose and report such cases. *Child abuse* is a broad term currently used to describe incidents of violent attack, neglect, or sexual abuse that may result in psychological and behavioral disturbances as well as physical or even life-threatening injury. Approximately 3.3 million child abuse allegations were made in 2009 and five children die per day due to abuse and neglect (www.childhelp.org, 2011; U.S. Department of Health and Human Services, 2010; United States Government Accountability Office, 2011). Indeed, the incidence of severe violence against children declined in the mid- to late 1980s. Possible reasons cited for the lower rate were an increased reluctance to report, differences in the methods of study, years of prevention and treatment efforts, and effects of changes in American society and family patterns that produce lower rates of violence toward children.

Researchers have investigated several factors associated with child abuse. Various models, each emphasizing the importance of particular factors, have been formulated to explain the phenomenon. The psychopathological model focuses on the personality characteristics of the perpetrator. Attributes such as personal history of abuse, low self-esteem, and inability to cope with frustration are seen as important contributing factors (Gil, 1975). The cognitive-behavioral model takes into account style of responding to stress and the belief systems of abusive parents (Green, 1984). A broader model encompassing the preceding elements and accounting for the significance of interactions between parents and children is referred to as the *ecological model* (Roscoe, Callahan, & Peterson, 1985).

Investigators have found that some children are more likely than others to become victims of child abuse. Children at increased risk for abuse often come from larger than average families, have low birth weights or were premature as infants, and fail to form attachment bonds with a caregiver. A comparison of incidence rates suggests that age, family income, and ethnicity were risk factors for both sexual and physical abuse. Gender was a risk factor for sexual abuse but not physical abuse (Cappelleri, Echenrode, & Powers, 1993). Males are more likely to be abused, as are disabled, retarded, and otherwise different or difficult children (Newberger, 1982).

Kempe's early article on the battered child syndrome achieved considerable public notoriety and drew the attention of legislators, resulting in the passage of mandatory reporting of child abuse in all 50 states. Physicians and other health professionals are legally required to report suspected child abuse. Additionally, most states require other professionals having contact with children to report suspected cases of abuse. These professionals include teachers, social workers, and child-care workers.

In 1997, child protection professionals were surveyed regarding their opinions about the best papers and chapters on child abuse available. Kempe's 1962 article was cited as one of the best resources on child abuse and a seminal work (Oates & Donnelly, 1997).

Although laws and service agencies fight to protect children against maltreatment and abuse, maltreatment of children continues. Barth (2011) found the following four common parental risk factors: substance abuse, mental illness, domestic violence, and severe behavior problems of children which often lead to the maltreatment of children. Barth further examines parent training programs to give parents who are identified as "at-risk" of child abuse the tools in finding and providing themselves with effective medical and mental health treatment. Evidence-based models should be considered in reducing and treating families and children involved in abuse and maltreatment.

Characteristics

1. Child's health is below average, and child shows poor skin hygiene, multiple soft tissue injuries, and malnutrition.

2. Parents' explanation for the injuries is not plausible according to clinical findings. When in care of a hospital or other protected environment, no new lesions emerge.

3. Injuries of the appendicular skeleton are the most common.

4. Subdural hematoma, failure to thrive, soft-tissue swellings or skin bruising, and multiple unexplained fractures and lesions at different healing stages may be apparent.

5. In the majority of sexual abuse cases, the perpetrator tends to be a relative or close family friend.

6. Battered children may exhibit self-injurious behavior or suicide attempts or ideation.

7. The first warning signs tend to be neglect and malnutrition.

8. Prematurity and low birth weight are risk factors concerning child battery.

REFERENCES

Barth, R. P. (2011). Preventing child abuse and neglect with parent training: Evidence and opportunities. *Future of Children, 19*(2), 95–118.

Cappelleri, J. C., Echenrode, J., & Powers, J. L. (1993). The epidemiology of child abuse: Findings from the second national incidence and prevalence study of child abuse and neglect. *American Journal of Public Health, 83*, 1622–1624.

Gil, D. (1975). Unraveling child abuse. *American Journal of Orthopsychiatry, 45*, 345–356.

Green, A. (1984). Child maltreatment: Recent studies and future directions. *Journal of the American Academy of Child Psychiatry, 23*, 675–678.

Kempe, C. H. (1962). The battered child syndrome. *Journal of the American Medical Association, 181*, 17–24.

Newberger, E. H. (Ed.). (1982). *Child abuse.* Boston, MA: Little, Brown.

Oates, R. K., & Donnelly, A. C. (1997). Influential papers in child abuse. *Child Abuse and Neglect, 21*, 319–326.

Roscoe, B., Callahan, J., & Peterson, K. (1985). Who is responsible? Adolescents' acceptance of theoretical child abuse models. *Adolescence, 20*, 188–197.

U.S. Department of Health and Human Services, Administration for Children and Families, Administration on Children, Youth and Families, Children's Bureau. (2010). Child *Maltreatment 2009.* Available from http://www.acf.hhs.gov/programs/cb/stats_research/index.htm#can

U.S. Government Accountability Office, 2011. Child maltreatment: Strengthening national data on child fatalities could aid in prevention (GAO-11–599). Retrieved from http://www.gao.gov/new.items/d11599.pdf

BERNICE ARRICALE
Hunter College, City University of New York
First edition

ELAINE FLETCHER-JANZEN
Chicago School of Professional Psychology
Second and third editions

See also Child Abuse

BAUMEISTER, ALFRED A. (1934–2011)

Born in Fairbanks, Alaska, Alfred A. Baumeister received his BA from the University of Alaska (1957) and his MA (1959) and PhD (1961) in psychology from George Peabody College. He is presently a professor at Vanderbilt University and George Peabody College, and directed the John F. Kennedy Center for Research on Education and Human Development at Vanderbilt University from 1983 to 1990.

Baumeister presented more than 150 papers and published more than 200 original investigations, literature reviews, and theoretical reports, many of which are concerned with learning and memory processes among mentally retarded children. He found that there are quantitative and structural differences in the short term information processing capabilities of retarded and nonretarded subjects (Baumeister, Runcie, & Gardepe, 1984). Another major effort of his was directed at understanding the treatment of aberrant behavior such as stereotyped movements and self-injurious actions.

Baumeister was active in the improvement of psychological services to students with intellectual developmental disabilities. He wrote about the role of the psychologist in public institutions (Baumeister & Hillsinger, 1984) and has served as a consultant to several state and federal agencies. He was a member of the Psychology Review Committee for the Joint Committee of the Accreditation of Hospitals.

Baumeister has been president of both the American Academy on Intellectual Developmental Disabilities and the Division of Intellectual Developmental Disabilities of the American Psychological Association. For several years, he served as a witness before the U.S. House and Senate appropriations subcommittees. He received awards for research contributions from the American Association on Mental Deficiency (1979) and the American Academy on Mental Retardation (1986). He continued to contribute to educational literature through publications on a variety of special education topics (Baumeister & Bacharach, 1996; Baumeister, Bacharach, & Baumeister, 1997).

REFERENCES

Baumeister, A. A., & Bacharach, V. R. (1996). A critical analysis of the infant health and development program. *Intelligence*, *23*(2), 79–104.

Baumeister, A. A., Bacharach, V. R., Baumeister, & Alan A. (1997). "Big" versus "little" science: Comparative analysis of program projects and individual research grants. *American Journal on Mental Retardation*, *102*(3), 211–227.

Baumeister, A. A., & Hillsinger, L. B. (1984). The role of psychologists in public institutions for the mentally retarded revisited. *Professional Psychology*, *15*, 134–141.

Baumeister, A. A., Runcie, D., & Gardepe, J. (1984). Processing of information in iconic memory: Differences between normal and retarded subjects. *Journal of Abnormal Psychology*, *93*, 433–447.

E. VALERIE HEWITT
Texas A&M University

BAYLEY SCALES OF INFANT AND TODDLER DEVELOPMENT, THIRD EDITION

The Bayley Scales of Infant and Toddler Development, Third Edition (Bayley-III, 2005) is an individually administered measure of developmental functioning of infants and children between 1 and 42 months of age across five domains: Cognitive, Language, Motor, Social-Emotional and Adaptive. It was designed to identify children with developmental delays and to guide treatment planning. The Bayley-III takes approximately 30 to 90 minutes to administer, depending on the age of the child. Scores for the Cognitive, Language, and Motor domains are obtained by administering items directly to the child, and the Social-Emotional and Adaptive domain scores result from caregiver responses. The Bayley-III also includes a Behavior Observation Inventory, completed by both the caregiver and the examiner.

The Cognitive Scale measures cognitive processes such as sensorimotor development, exploration, manipulation, object relatedness, concept formation and memory. This scale is based primarily on the Bayley Scales of Infant Development, Second Edition (BSID-II) Mental Scale, although efforts were made to reduce the receptive language skills required for responding to items on this scale. Indeed, many language-based items from the BSID-II Mental Scale were used to create the new Language Scale, which is comprised of Receptive and Expressive Communication subtests. The Receptive Communication subtest assesses preverbal skills, receptive vocabulary, understanding of morphological markers, and verbal comprehension. The Expressive Communication subtest measures preverbal communication behaviors, expressive vocabulary, and morpho-syntactic development. The Motor Scale is divided into Fine and Gross Motor subtests, with the Fine Motor subtest measuring skills including prehension, perceptual-motor integration, and motor planning and speed, and the Gross Motor subtest measuring movements of the limbs and torso.

Administration of these Bayley-III Scales requires several test items, manipulatives, and examiner-provided items (including coins and food pellets), which may engage young children. The manual provides clear descriptions of the use of these materials as well as administration of items. Examiners who are new to the Bayley-III should practice and become thoroughly familiar with the multitude of materials and varied methods of item scoring prior to administering the test.

The Social-Emotional and Adaptive Behavior Scales are included in a Questionnaire completed by a primary caregiver. Each of these Scales are adapted from other published measures. They are adapted from the Greenspan Social-Emotional Growth Chart: A Screening Questionnaire for Infants and Young Children (Greenspan, 2004) and the Adaptive Behavior Assessment System, Second Edition (ABAS-II; Harrison & Oakland, 2003), respectively. In the Bayley-III Questionnaire, the parent marks the behavioral frequency of several social-emotional and adaptive items. The Social-Emotional Scale includes measures of self-regulation, interest, communication of needs, engaging and establishing relationships with others, and using emotional signals and gestures in a purposeful or problem-solving manner. The Adaptive Behavior Scale includes measures of Communication, Community Health and Safety, Leisure, Self-Direction, Functional Pre-Academics, Home Living, Social and Motor skills, as well as a General Adaptive Composite.

The Bayley-III yields scaled scores, composite scores, percentile ranks, confidence intervals, developmental age equivalents and growth scores; however, not all scores are available for all subtests. The user is referred to the Bayley-III manual to determine which scores are available for particular subtests and Scales.

The Bayley-III was standardized on a demographically stratified sample of 1,700 children (aged 16 days to 43 months, 15 days). The sample had approximately equal number of boys and girls in each of the 17 created age groups. Stratification was guided by the 2000 U.S. Census Bureau and consideration was given to the following variables: parent education, race/ethnicity and geographic region. Approximately 10% of the overall sample included children from special groups, including those with Down syndrome, cerebral palsy, pervasive developmental disorder, premature birth, and language impairment. Overall, the standardization sample appears diverse

and representative. It should be noted for the Social-Emotional Scale, the Greenspan Social-Emotional Growth Chart standardization data was used. Similarly, for the Adaptive Behavior Scale, ABAS-II standardization data was utilized.

Internal consistency is generally high for the subtests and composites, with an average range of .86 to .93. Reliability coefficients for the special groups also were quite high, with averages ranging from .94 to .98. The internal consistency coefficients for the Social-Emotional Scale were also high (average range of .83 and .90). Finally, the Adaptive Behavior Scale reliability coefficients were adequate to high, with an average range of .79 to .97. As would be expected, these reliability coefficients were generally higher for older children. Test-retest reliability coefficients for the Cognitive, Language and Motor Scales were reported by age. In the youngest age group (2 to 4 months), the corrected subtest and composite coefficients were the lowest, ranging from .67 to .80. As would also be expected when testing very young children, the older age groups showed more robust test-retest coefficients: a range of .77 to .86 for the 9- to 13-month group, .71 to .88 for the 19- to 26-month group, and .83 to .94 for children aged 33- to 42 months. Test-retest reliability for the GAC was good, ranging from .88 to .92. No test-retest reliability was reported for the Social-Emotional Scale. Inter-rater reliability for the Adaptive Behavior Scale subtests ranged from .59 (Community Use) to .79 (Communication). The Adaptive domains were somewhat higher, ranging from .72 (Social Domain) to .86 (Conceptual Domain). The inter-rater reliability coefficient for the GAC was .82. Inter-rater reliability scores were not reported for the other Scales.

The manual provides good evidence for content, concurrent, and construct validity (Albers & Grieve, 2007; Fernandez, 2007). Confirmatory factor analysis yielded evidence for the 3-factor model, which fits the structure of the Bayley-III; specifically, the two Motor Scales on the first factor, the two Language subtests on the second scale, and the Cognitive Scale on the third factor. Additionally, the publishers note the measures on which the Social-Emotional and Adaptive Behavior Scales are based have an established research base supporting their validity. Overall, the Bayley-III is a sound and attractive instrument, and the latest *Mental Measurements Yearbook* reviews (Tobin, 2007; Venn, 2007) are quite complimentary.

REFERENCES

Albers, C., & Grieve, A. (2007). Review of 'Bayley scales of infant and toddler development (3rd ed.).' *Journal of Psychoeducational Assessment, 25*(2), 180–190.

Fernández, M., & Zaccario, M. (2007). Bayley III: A preliminary overview. *Journal of Early Childhood and Infant Psychology,* 3223–3233.

Harrison, P. L., & Oakland, T. (2003). *Adaptive Behavior Assessment System–Second Edition.* San Antonio, TX: Psychological Assessment Resources.

Tobin, R. M., & Hoff, K. E. (2007). Review of the Bayley scales of infant and toddler development (3rd ed.). In K. F. Geisinger, R. A. Spies, J. F. Carlson, & B. S. Plake (Eds.), *The seventeenth mental measurements yearbook.* Lincoln, NE: Buros Institute of Mental Measurements.

Venn, J. J. (2007). Review of the Bayley scales of infant and toddler development (3rd ed.). In K. F. Geisinger, R. A. Spies, J. F. Carlson, & B. S. Plake (Eds.), *The seventeenth mental measurements yearbook.* Lincoln, NE: Buros Institute of Mental Measurements.

KATHLEEN VIEZEL
Fairleigh Dickinson University

JAMIE ZIBULSKY
Fairleigh Dickinson University

RON DUMONT
Fairleigh Dickinson University

JOHN O. WILLIS
Rivier College
Fourth edition

BECHTEREV (BEKHTIAREV), VLADIMIR M. (1857–1927)

Vladimir M. Bechterev was born in Viatka province, Russia. He was a noted physiologist and neuropathologist and the founder of the School of Reflexology. He was also the founder of the first Russian experimental psychological laboratory at the University of Kazan. Bechterev obtained his PhD at the Military Medical Academy in St. Petersburg (Petrograd, now Leningrad) in 1881. He continued postgraduate studies at the universities of Leipzig, Berlin, and Paris. At Leipzig he became familiar with the work of Wilhelm Wundt, considered to be the founder of experimental psychology. In 1885 Bechterev became professor at the University of Kazan and in 1893, professor at the Military Medical Academy. The same year he began to publish a journal, *Neurological Review.* Bechterev was also interested in the education of exceptional children. His work in this area is referred to as pedagogical reflexology. In 1911 he addressed the International Congress of Pedology in Brussels, Belgium. His pioneering work contributed immensely toward the future development of Soviet defectology.

Bechterev made an important contribution to the knowledge of anatomy and physiology of the nervous system (Debus, 1968; Prokhorov, 1970). He conducted research on localization function of the brain and became famous for his work on nerve currents. He also identified the layer of fibers in the cerebral cortex known as Bechterev's fibers.

Bechterev was a prolific writer who produced over 135 publications and papers, including *General Principles of Reflexology* (1918) and *Objective Psychology* (1913).

REFERENCES

Bechterev, V. M. (1913). *Objective psychologie oder psychoreflexologia.* Leipzig/Berlin, Germany: Verlag Teubner.

Bechterev, V. M. (1918). *Obshtchie osnovi reflexologii* (General principles of reflexology). St. Petersburg, Russia: Issued in the U.S. by International Publishers.

Debus, A. G. (Ed.). (1968). *World who's who in science.* Chicago, IL: Marquis.

Prokhorov, A. M. (Ed.). (1970). *Bolshaya Sovetskay Entsyklopedia* (Major Soviet encyclopedia) (3rd ed.). Moscow, Russia: Soviet Encyclopedia.

IVAN Z. HOLOWINSKY
Rutgers University

BECKER, WESLEY C. (1928–2000)

A native of Rochester, New York, Wesley C. Becker received his BA (1951), MA (1953), and PhD (1955) from Stanford University in psychology, statistics, and learning theory, respectively. Originally a child clinical psychologist, Becker's initial research interest was in how behavior problems and personality characteristics develop as a function of parental child-rearing practices. His interest in parental child-rearing practices developed into an interest in applications of behavior analysis to changing parent and child behaviors (Becker, 1971). His book, *Parents Are Teachers,* has been published in German, Portuguese, and Spanish. Becker's interest shifted to applications of behavior analysis to teachers and problem students (Becker, 1986; Becker, Engelmann, & Thomas, 1975). In the late 1960s, Becker was interested in effective instructional practices, especially as they applied children who demonstrated challenging behavior in classrooms. Becker later became more active in disseminating research findings on effective instructional practices, such as the direct instruction (DI) follow-through model and its long-term effects on students (Becker, 1984; Gersten, Keating, & Becker, 1991).

Becker was a member of Phi Beta Kappa and a consultant to the Australian Association for Direct Instruction and was included in *Who's Who in America.*

REFERENCES

Becker, W. C. (1971). *Parents are teachers.* Champaign, IL: Research.

Becker, W. C. (1984, March 18–23). *Direct instruction—A twenty year review*. Paper presented at the 16th Annual Banff International Conference on Behavioral Science Honoring B. F. Skinner's 80th birthday, Banff, Canada.

Becker, W. C. (1986). *Applied psychology for teachers: A behavioral cognitive approach*. Chicago, IL: Science Research.

Becker, W. C., Engelmann, S., & Thomas, D. R. (1975). *Teaching 1: Classroom management*. Palo Alto, CA: Science Research.

Gersten, R., Keating, T., & Becker, W. C. (1991). The continued impact of the direct instructional model: Longitudinal studies of follow through students. *Education & Treatment of Children, 11*(4), 318–327.

E. Valerie Hewitt
Texas A&M University
First edition

Deborah B. Guillen
University of Texas of the Permian Basin
Second edition

BECKWITH-WIEDEMANN SYNDROME

Beckwith-Wiedemann syndrome (BWS) is a rare disorder recognized primarily by a consistent grouping of findings of unknown etiology (Genetics Home Reference, 2001) and is characterized by excessive size and height at birth. For instance, in many males, birth length may be at or above the 95th percentile. Typically, their height remains within this range throughout their adolescent years. Growth closely parallels the normal growth curve. Females, however, are usually born at or about the 75th percentile, and their height increases to the 95th percentile by 18 months of age. Their height then remains at this percentile throughout adolescence. Many infants also develop advanced bone age within the first 4 years of life. Other features include an unusually large tongue within a gaping mouth; enlarged organs, such as spleen, liver, and heart; umbilical hernias; and creases in the earlobes. Infancy is a very critical period because of the possibility of severe hypoglycemia, increased tumor growth, such as Wilm's, and gonadoblastoma (National Organization for Rare Disorders, 2001).

In most cases, BWS seems to result from a spontaneous genetic change. In rare cases, approximately 15%, it appears to be familial, suggesting autosomal dominant inheritance. The risk of transmitting the disorder from the affected parent to the offspring is 50% for each pregnancy regardless of the gender of the resulting child. This risk is the same for subsequent pregnancies (National Organization for Rare Disorders, 2001). The severity at which each child is affected is highly variable. The great majority of persons who carry the gene are only minimally affected (Beckwith-Wiedemann Support Network, 2001).

BWS seems to affect males and females equally. Since J. B. Beckwith and H. R. Wiedemann concurrently described the disorder in the early 1960s, more than 400 cases have been reported. The incidence of BWS has been difficult to determine because of the variance in the severity of the reported symptoms. Estimates range from 1 in 13,600 to 1 in 17,000 (National Organization for Rare Disorders, 2001).

Characteristics

1. Large newborn (large for gestational age, or LGA)
2. Large tongue, sometimes protruding
3. Large prominent eyes
4. Creases in earlobes
5. Pinna abnormalities and low-set ears
6. Umbilical hernia (omphalocele)
7. Separated abdominal muscles (diastasis recti)
8. Undescended testicles (cryptorchidism)
9. Hypoglycemia
10. Poor feeding
11. Lethargy
12. Seizures
13. Polyhydramnios
14. Enlargement of some organs and tissues

Source: Genetics Home Reference, 2000.

In families with a history of BWS, diagnostic screens can be performed prenatally. Ultrasound imaging may be used to determine fetal size or the size of the developing organs. Early detection of the syndrome allows for prompt treatment of some of the symptoms, especially neonatal hypoglycemia. The early treatment of hypoglycemia can prevent associated neurological complications, such as intellectual developmental disabilities. With early treatment, it seems that the hypoglycemia is usually temporary in infants, and the infant responds well to medical therapy during the first 4 months of life (National Organization for Rare Disorders, 2001). Intravenous glucose solutions and corticosteriods are used to treat the hypoglycemia. Treatment of other symptoms of BWS is directed toward the specific symptom. For instance, caregivers must pay careful attention to feeding and to the position of the child while he or she is sleeping to avoid problems with the enlarged tongue. In some children the umbilical hernias may disappear within the first year, but if the hernia becomes larger, surgery may be indicated (Ocean State Online, 2000). Medications and surgery may also be used in the cases with congenital heart defects. Tumors that develop require close observation to determine specific malignancy. Depending on the malignancy, treatment may include use of anticancer drugs, radiation therapy, or surgery (National Organization for Rare Disorders, 2001).

Children who survive infancy do well, although no long-term follow-up studies are available. Mental function seems to be normal to slightly below normal. Genetic counseling is strongly recommended for affected families. Although most treatment is symptomatic and supportive, special services such as speech therapy, social services, and vocational services may be beneficial to the affected children.

REFERENCES

Beckwith-Wiedemann Support Network. (2001, March 29). Retrieved from http://www.beckwith-wiedemann.org.future site.register.com/

Genetics Home Reference. (2004). http://ghr.nlm.nih.gov/condition/beckwith-wiedemann-syndrome.

National Organization for Rare Disorders, Inc. (2001, January 30). *Beckwith-Wiedemann syndrome*. Retrieved from http://www.rarediseases.org

VEDIA SHERMAN
Austin Neurological Clinic

BEERS, CLIFFORD W. (1876–1943)

Clifford W. Beers founded the mental hygiene movement following 3 years as a patient in mental hospitals in Connecticut in the early part of the 20th century. Because of the abuses that he suffered, he left the hospital determined to reform the system, to see harsh custodial care replaced with medical treatment. His book, *A Mind That Found Itself*, published in 1908, gives a vivid account of his experiences, and at the time created a public outcry against inhumane treatment of mental patients.

A gifted speaker and organizer, Beers obtained the support of eminent psychiatrists and other prominent people to form the Connecticut Society for Mental Hygiene in 1908, the National Committee for Mental Hygiene in 1909, and the International Committee for Mental Hygiene in 1930.

Beers's influence on the mental hygiene movement has been a lasting one, both through the work of the outstanding people he enlisted in the movement, and the continued popularity of *A Mind That Found Itself*, still in print after more than three-quarters of a century (Beers, 1981).

REFERENCE

Beers, C. W. (1981). *A mind that found itself* (5th ed.). Pittsburgh, PA: University of Pittsburgh Press.

PAUL IRVINE
Katonah, New York

BEERY-BUKTENICA DEVELOPMENTAL TEST OF VISUAL-MOTOR INTEGRATION, SIXTH EDITION

The Beery-Buktenica Developmental Test of Visual-Motor Integration, Sixth Edition (Beery VMI; 2010) is a measure of visual and motor integration for ages 2 through 100. With a focus on early childhood education, the sixth edition includes updated norms for ages 2 through 18 years. The Beery VMI presents individuals with drawings of geometric forms arranged in order of increasing difficulty, which they are asked to copy on the record form. The Full Form includes 30 items and can be completed in 10 to 15 minutes. A Short Form consisting of 21 items is available for children aged 2 through 7 years and usually takes less than 10 minutes to administer. The Beery VMI also includes optional standardized tests of visual perception and motor coordination that are generally administered when results show that further testing is necessary. With these supplemental tests, a comparison of the individual's ability to complete purely visual and purely motor tasks can be obtained. These tests can be administered individually or to groups, though individual administration is recommended for the supplemental tests. The authors suggest that these tests should be given in the order in which they were normed: VMI, Visual Perception, and Motor Coordination. The record form provides the examinee with instructions and the manual contains administration guidelines and examples of correct and incorrect responses for each item.

The sixth edition contains norms for children aged 2 through 18 from a sample gathered in 2010 (1,737 individuals), and for adults from a sample gathered in 2005 and 2006 (1,021 individuals). The sample was representative of the U.S. census data with respect to gender, ethnicity, residence (urban versus nonmetropolitan) and geographic location. Results are reported as standard scores (with a mean of 100 and a standard deviation of 15), scaled scores (with a mean of 10 and a standard deviation of 3), percentiles, and other equivalents including age equivalents. The VMI manual also provides a vast array of Stepping Stones, or milestones, derived from age-specific norms from birth through 6 years of age. References for teaching visual-motor integration skills also are included.

Because no new items were introduced, the sixth edition of the Beery VMI sometimes relies on preexisting studies examining its psychometrics. The internal consistency of the items on the Beery VMI was determined to be .96. For the sixth edition, a new test-retest study was completed for children aged 5 through 12. The overall coefficients were .88 for the Beery VMI, .84 for Visual Perception, and .85 for Motor Coordination. Test-retest coefficients for earlier versions were varied depending on the age of the children and the time between testing. However, as visual-motor skills are expected to change over time, this was expected. Inter-rater reliability coefficients for the sixth edition were impressive, ranging from .92 to .98. This could be owed to the clear and specific scoring guidelines presented in the manual.

The Beery VMI manual provides evidence for content, concurrent, construct and predictive validity. Past versions of the test have been frequently correlated with the original Bender-Gestalt, with a median correlation of .56. In particular, significant correlations have been demonstrated between the Bender Visual Motor Gestalt Test and the VMI with a sample of gifted elementary school students (Knoff & Sperling, 1986) and the VMI showed more developmental sensitivity than the Bender Visual Motor Gestalt Test when used in a sample of emotionally and behaviorally disturbed adolescents (Shapiro & Simpson, 1994). The Beery VMI has also demonstrated correlations ranging from .62 to .75 with the Copying, Position in Space and Eye-Hand Coordination subtests of the Developmental Test of Visual Perception (DTVP-2), whereas the correlation between the Beery VMI and the Drawing subtest of the Wide Range Assessment of Visual Motor Abilities (WRAVMA) was only .52. Past editions of the VMI have been found to be good predictors of academic or other problems when used in combination with other measures, though correlations decline as children progress through grade levels.

Although the Beery VMI appears to be a good screening instrument, more information is needed regarding the psychometric properties and utility of the sixth edition.

REFERENCES

Although no reviews of the Beery *VMI, Sixth Edition* were available at the time of this writing, the fifth edition was reviewed in: Geisinger, K. F., Spies, R. A., Carlson, J. F., & Plake, B. S. (Eds.), *The seventeenth mental measurements yearbook*. Lincoln, NE: Buros Institute of Mental Measurements.

Knoff, H. M. , & Sperling, B. L. (1986). Gifted children and visual-motor development: A comparison of Bender-Gestalt and VMI test performance. *Psychology in the Schools, 23*, 247–251.

Shapiro, S. K., & Simpson R. G. (1994). Patterns and predictors of performance on the Bender-Gestalt and the Developmental Test of Visual Motor Integration in a sample of behaviorally and emotionally disturbed adolescents. *Journal of Psychoeducational Assessment, 12*, 254–263.

KATHLEEN VIEZEL
Fairleigh Dickinson University

JAMIE ZIBULSKY
Fairleigh Dickinson University

RON DUMONT
Fairleigh Dickinson University

JOHN O. WILLIS
Rivier College
Fourth edition

BEHAVIOR

A behavior is a person's action or a reaction under specified conditions. Behaviors are monitored in order for teachers and researchers to determine their function, and how to control their frequency, intensity, duration, or latency. The behavior that is being analyzed is often referred to as the *target behavior*. Isolating a specific behavior and defining it in observable and measurable terms allows its antecedents and consequences to be identified. By manipulating either the antecedent that leads to the target behavior or the consequences of the behavior modifications can be made to the target behavior. A teacher or researcher may increase a desired behavior or decrease an undesirable behavior (Alvero & Austin, 2004; Haager & Klinger, 2005; Heward, 2006; McLoughlin & Lewis, 2005; Pierangelo & Giuliani, 2006; Taylor, 2006).

It is first necessary to define the target behavior in terms that are both observable and measurable. This definition needs to be specific enough so that consistency can be maintained both over time and between observers. Based on this definition, accurate measures of frequency, intensity, duration, or latency can be acquired as well as the antecedents and consequences of the behavior (Scott, Liaupsin, Nelson, & Jolivette, 2003).

The teacher or researcher must first decide what the behavior is that will be examined. It is not enough to say that the student is engaging in disruptive behaviors. The specific behavior must be described in such a way that all who are involved are using the same definition. For example, a behavior may be repetitively tapping a pencil against a desk or book with enough force to make a noise heard by the teacher at the front of the room. It may be necessary to further define the term repetitively, that is, three or more taps within 5 seconds. A clear definition of the behavior allows every person that is observing the student to focus on the same behavior. In addition, a clear definition maintains a consistency within the teacher or researcher's observation.

Behaviors can be divided into two broad categories, desirable and undesirable. Behaviors that are undesirable are those that should be decreased. To decrease undesirable behaviors, it should be arranged that antecedents that lead to the least likelihood of the behavior occurring are present and that after the behavior occurs those consequences that lead to the least likelihood of the behavior reoccurring should be presented. A person's use of a particular behavior has developed over time, therefore, to modify that behavior requires consistent and deliberate measures over time (Haager & Klinger, 2005; Heward, 2006; McLoughlin & Lewis, 2005; Pierangelo & Giuliani, 2006; Scott et al., 2003; Taylor, 2006).

The example used earlier of the pencil tapping student is an example of an undesired behavior. As described previously, a teacher or researcher who wished to reduce this behavior would first observe the student in the environment in which the behavior was occurring to identify the antecedents and consequences of the behavior. If, for example, the student pencil tapped more often during math class, the consequences for the tapping is to be told that he must put his pencil away. The function of the behavior may be to avoid the math work. By understanding how the antecedent—asking the student to do math increases the behavior—and the consequences of removing the pencil allows the student to avoid work, the teacher can manipulate these variables to reduce the frequency of the behavior.

Desirable behaviors are those that should be increased. To increase desirable behaviors, it should be arranged that antecedents that lead to the greatest likelihood of the behavior occurring are present and that after the behavior occurs those consequences that lead to the greatest likelihood of the behavior reoccurring should be presented (Haager & Klinger, 2005; Heward, 2006; McLoughlin & Lewis, 2005; Pierangelo & Giuliani, 2006; Scott et al., 2003; Taylor, 2006).

The example used earlier of a student's pencil tapping is an example of an undesired behavior. What we would like to see is the student using his pencil to solve the math problems. So the teacher or researcher observes when the desired behavior occurs, what antecedents trigger this behavior, and what consequences follow when the student performs the desired behavior. If, for example, when students are given basic addition problems they use their pencil to solve the problems without tapping (the desired behavior), the current consequences are that the teacher ignores the behavior and continues with the lesson. A teacher who is systematically observing and monitoring the student could identify that the antecedent of basic addition leads to the desired behavior and by manipulating

the consequences to include reinforcement, the desired behavior could be increased. In addition, through systematically manipulating the antecedent, the desired behavior could be shaped to occur more frequently across settings.

REFERENCES

Alvero, A. M., & Austin, J. (2004). The effects of conducting behavioral observations on the behavior of the observer. *Journal of Applied Behavior Analysis, 37*, 457–468.

Haager, D., & Klinger, J. K. (2005). *Differentiating instruction in inclusive classrooms: The special educator's guide*. New York, NY: Allyn & Bacon.

Heward, W. L. (2006). *Exceptional children: An introduction to special education* (8th ed.). Upper Saddle River, NJ: Pearson.

McLoughlin, J. A., & Lewis, R. B. (2005). *Assessing students with special needs* (6th ed.). Upper Saddle River, NJ: Pearson.

Pierangelo, R., & Giuliani, G. A. (2006). *Assessment in special education: A practical approach* (2nd ed.). New York, NY: Allyn & Bacon.

Scott, T. M., Liaupsin, C. J., Nelson, C. M., & Jolivette, K. (2003). Ensuring student success through team-based functional behavioral assessment. *Teaching Exceptional Children, 35*(5), 16–21.

Taylor, R. L. (2006). *Assessment of exceptional students: Educational and psychological procedures* (7th ed.). New York, NY: Allyn & Bacon.

WALTER A. ZILZ
Bloomsburg University

***See also* Adaptive Behavior; Emotional Disorders**

BEHAVIORAL AND EMOTIONAL RATING SCALE, SECOND EDITION, BERS-2

The Behavioral and Emotional Rating Scale (BERS2; Epstein, 2004) is an individually administered 52-item scale that assesses children's (ages 5:0 through 18:11) emotional and behavioral strengths in five-factor analytically derived subscales. The multimodal assessment measures the child's behavior using the Youth Rating Scale, Parent Rating Scale, and the Teacher Rating Scale. The first subscale, Interpersonal Strengths (e.g., "uses anger management skills," 15 items), assesses a child's ability to control emotions or behavior in a social situation. The second subscale, Family Involvement (e.g., "participates in family activities," 10 items), focuses on a child's participation and relationship with his or her family. The third subscale, Intrapersonal Strengths (e.g., "demonstrates a sense of humor," 11 items), assesses a child's outlook on his or her competence and accomplishments. Subscale four, School Functioning (e.g., "completes homework regularly," 9 items), focuses on a child's competence in school and classroom tasks. The fifth subscale, Career Strength (e.g., "asks for help," 7 items), addresses a child's ability to express feelings toward others and to accept affection from others.

A teacher, caregiver, or any adult knowledgeable about the child can complete the BERS-2 in approximately 10 minutes. The adult reads a statement (e.g., "participates in family activities") and chooses the number on a Likert-type scale from 0 to 3 (0 = not at all like the child; 1 = not much like the child; 2 = like the child; 3 = very much like the child) that best represents the child's emotions or behaviors in the past 3 months. Respondents are also asked to complete eight open-ended questions about the child's personal and situational resiliencies and protective factors (e.g., "What are the child's favorite hobbies or activities?" "Who is this child's favorite teacher?"). Information obtained from the BERS-2 is useful in the development of individualized education programs (IEPs), treatment or intervention planning, and evaluation of a program or treatment plan.

Raw scores from the five subscales can be converted to percentile ranks and to standard scores with a mean of 10 and a standard deviation of 3. Summing the standard scores of the five subscales and converting the sum into a quotient derives an overall "Strength Quotient" with a mean of 100 and a standard deviation of 15. BERS-2 is useful indentifying children in schools, mental health clinics, juvenile justice settings, and child welfare settings that demonstrate limited behavioral and emotional strengths, which may require further attention in providing evidence-based interventions to document the progress of each child in his or her emotional and behavioral well-being.

The BERS-2 scales were normed on representative samples of children without disabilities. The BERS-2 Teacher Rating Scale was normed on children with emotional and behavioral disorders. The manual reports demographics of this standardization sample based on age, gender, geographic location, race, ethnicity, and socioeconomic status. Based on these data, separate male and female norms for children without disabilities and separate male and female norms for children with emotional and behavioral disorders were calculated. Although the BERS-2 covers the age range of 5 to 18, there are no separate age-based norm tables in the manual.

Internal consistency of the BERS-2 subtest exceeds .80 for each subtest and .95 for the overall measure. More than 15 studies in the published literature has confirmed the BERS-2 content, construct, and criterion validity. The following sources were used in the creation of this entry (Achenbach, 1991; Durmont & Rauch, 2003; Epstein, 1998; Epstein & Sharma, 1998; Friedman, Friedman, & Weaver, 2003; Harter, 1985; Quay & Peterson, 1996; Trout, Tryan & LaVigne, 2003; Walker & McConnell, 1988).

REFERENCES

Achenbach, T. M. (1991). *Manual for the teacher report form and 1991 profile.* Burlington: University of Vermont, Department of Psychiatry.

Dumont, R., & Rauch, M. (2003). Test review: Behavioral and emotional rating scale by M. Epstein & J. Sharma (PRO-ED, 1998). *NASP Communiqué, 28,* article 7.

Epstein, M. H. (1998). Assessing the emotional and behavioral strengths of children. *Reclaiming Children and Youth, 6,* 250–252.

Epstein, M. H. (2004). *Behavioral and emotional rating scale—2nd edition: A strengths-based approach to assessment.* Austin, TX: PRO-ED.

Epstein, M. H., Harniss, M. K., Pearson, N., & Ryder, G. (1999). The behavioral and emotional rating scale: Test-retest and inter-rater reliability. *Journal of Child and Family Studies, 8,* 319–327.

Epstein, M. H., & Sharma, J. (1998). *Behavioral and emotional rating scale: A strength based approach to assessment.* Austin, TX: PRO-ED.

Friedman, P., Friedman, K. A., & Weaver, V. (2003). Strength-based assessment of African-American adolescents with behavioral disorders. *Perceptual & Motor Skills, 96,* 667–673.

Harter, S. (1985). *Manual for the self-perception profile for children.* Denver, CO: University of Denver.

Quay, H., & Peterson, D. R. (1996). *Revised behavior problem checklist: Professional manual.* Odessa, FL: Psychological Assessment.

Trout, A. L., Ryan, J. B., & La Vigne, S. P. (2003). Behavioral and emotional rating scale: Two studies of convergent validity. *Journal of Child and Family Studies, 12,* 399–410.

Walker, H. M., & McConnell, S. R. (1988). *Manual for the Walker-McConnell scale of social competence and school adjustment.* Austin, TX: PRO-ED.

RON DUMONT
Fairleigh Dickinson University

JOHN O. WILLIS
Rivier College

BEHAVIORAL ASSESSMENT

Behavioral assessment is an important component of evaluation and intervention planning by addressing a wide range of referral questions. Behavioral data can measure numerous actions that directly impede learning, such as withdrawal, defiance, or aggression. However, even when the referral concern is primarily academic rather than behavioral, behavioral components can indirectly affect learning ability (e.g., frustration tolerance, test anxiety, study habits). In fact, the Individuals with Disabilities Education Improvement Act of 2004 recommends classroom behavioral observations as a component of an assessment.

Various behavioral assessment methods may be used, including record reviews, interviewing, observations, rating scales, and adaptive behavior measures. Record reviews can yield insight on past trauma (e.g., abuse), major life-changing events (e.g., custody issues), school discipline actions, criminal history (e.g., adjudicated youth programs), and school attendance or achievement patterns. Interviewing parents, teachers, other caregivers, and students can provide information on medical concerns, family interaction patterns, events that precipitated behaviors, support networks, and student strengths outside of academics (e.g., altruistic deeds). An emphasis on identifying student strengths and positive behaviors can aid in designing strength-based interventions. When deriving hypotheses from interview information, one should consider the broader context of ethnic, cultural, and socioeconomic factors. Awareness of diversity issues can aid school personnel in better understanding children's behaviors and response styles (Kamphaus & Frick, 2000). Strengths of record review and interviewing techniques include information on past behavior patterns, perceptions, feelings, and home interaction styles. Limitations include lack of context for recorded events and possible weaknesses in children's self-perceptions or parental reporting bias.

Behavioral difficulties can be the result of complex interactions between risk factors, personality, academic frustrations, and environmental variables that reinforce behaviors (Evans et al., 2005; Frick, 1998; Mash & Barkley, 2003). Therefore, observational data often are crucial in behavioral assessments. The first step in behavioral observation is defining the behaviors to be monitored (e.g., withdrawn behaviors include diverting eye contact, self-isolation, not responding to direct questions). Observational data may be quantified to provide frequency, duration, latency, intensity, and time-of-day information. These data can be used to measure intervention efficacy by providing a baseline comparison for pre- and postintervention behavior frequency.

Observational data in the form of narrative recordings and anecdotal notes can be used to document children's verbal interactions and surrounding events in an effort to identify antecedent and consequent conditions that may impact behaviors. Knowledge of preceding events and outcomes for behaviors can provide data for functional analysis procedures that include changing antecedents or consequences to test hypotheses about their role in sustaining particular behaviors (Kaplan & Carter, 1995). An ecological approach to observation reviews physical, instructional, and interaction elements (e.g., noisy equipment, unclear rule expectations) in the classroom (Sattler, 2002). Based on ecological data, interventions may focus on

implementing environment changes or providing positive behavioral supports rather than academic remediation. Strengths of observational methods include their providing insights on antecedents and consequences of behaviors, revealing environmental variables, and frequency and duration data. Their limitations include providing no information on internal thoughts or moods, observer bias, and reactivity if the person is aware of being observed.

Behavior rating scales can provide an additional measure that incorporates teachers, parents, and student self-report data on the same behaviors (e.g., Behavior Assessment System for Children–II, Child Behavior Checklist). Rating scales may measure behaviors across a continuum, from internalizing to externalizing, and provide national norms that indicate at-risk and clinically maladaptive ranges. When omnibus rating scales indicate areas of significant concern, practitioners also may administer single construct rating scales that offer more in-depth information on specific symptoms (e.g., for depression, use the Children's Depression Inventory). Strengths of rating scales include cross-reference comparisons of multiple opinions and well-established national norms. Limitations include forms of rater bias and only modest correlations between various informant ratings (Kamphaus & Frick, 2000).

Adaptive scales also can provide additional objective measures of children's behavior in domains not typically addressed by behavior ratings scales. These skills include one's ability to function independently and to meet personal and social responsibility competencies (Sattler, 2002). Some instruments (e.g., Adaptive Behavior Assessment System–II) include norm references for skill areas recommended from the American Association of Intellectual Developmental Disabilities such as communication, home or school daily living, self-care, social interaction, health and safety, and work behaviors (Harrison & Oakland, 2003; Rust & Wallace, 2004). Other instruments (e.g., Battelle Developmental Inventory) can provide criterion-referenced information on skill hierarchies (Sattler, 2002). Adaptive behavior evaluation is required when diagnosing intellectual developmental disabilities. Additionally, these data can provide valuable insight as part of behavioral assessment batteries for children without cognitive deficits (e.g., lack of communication skills in aggressive children). Strengths of adaptive scales include insight for behavioral functioning at home and in the community as well as objective norm comparison of skills with other children the same age. Limitations include possible informant response distortions or limited ability to provide accurate answers and estimations of some behaviors not directly observed (Kamphaus & Frick, 2000; Sattler, 2002).

Because each assessment method has both strengths and limitations, best practices in assessment warrant including multiple sources of data when making decisions for children with consideration for the validity and reliability of each measure (American Educational Research

Association, 1999). Behavioral assessment that includes a broad spectrum of both quantitative and qualitative data can provide valuable insight to school personnel and students. Successful intervention for more extensive and serious behavioral difficulties can require a comprehensive behavioral assessment that requires a collaborative effort of teachers, parents, students, school psychologists, counselors, and social workers (Mash & Barkley, 2003).

REFERENCES

American Educational Research Association. (1999). *Standards for educational and psychological testing*. Washington, DC: Author.

Evans, D. L., Foa, E. B., Gur, R. E., Hendin, H., O'Brien, C. P., Seligman, M. E., & Walsh, B. T. (Eds.). (2005). *Treating and preventing adolescent mental health disorders: What we know and what we don't know*. New York, NY: Oxford University Press.

Frick, P. J. (1998). *Conduct Disorders and severe antisocial behavior*. New York, NY: Plenum Press.

Harrison, P. L., & Oakland, T. (2003). *Adaptive Behavior Assessment System* (2nd ed.). San Antonio, TX: Harcourt.

Individuals with Disabilities Education Improvement Act of 2004. 20 U.S.C. § 1400 et seq.

Kamphaus, R. W., & Frick, P. J. (2000). *Clinical assessment of child and adolescent personality and behavior*. Needham Heights, MA: Allyn & Bacon.

Kaplan, J. S., & Carter, J. (1995). *Beyond behavior modification: A cognitive-behavioral approach to behavior management in the school*. Austin, TX: PRO-ED.

Mash, E. J., & Barkley, R. A. (Eds.). (2003). *Child psychopathology* (2nd ed.). New York, NY: Guilford Press.

Rust, J. O., & Wallace, M. A. (2004). Test review: Adaptive behavior assessment system (2nd ed.). *Journal of Psychoeducational Assessment, 22*, 367–373.

Sattler, J. M. (2002). *Assessment of children: Behavioral and clinical applications* (4th ed.). La Mesa, CA: Author.

DIANA JOYCE
University of Florida

See also Behavior Assessment System for Children–2; Behavior Disorders;

BEHAVIORAL CONSULTATION

Consultation has proven to be a major approach to providing psychoeducational services to children in school settings. Three major models of consultation are used most frequently and include mental health consultation, organizational development consultation, and behavioral consultation. Bergan's (1977) original model of behavioral consultation has evolved and expanded over time. To reflect this evolution in research and practice, other names have been adopted, including *problem-solving, solution oriented*, and *ecobehavioral consultation*. Each can be traced to include features of behavioral consultation (Bergan & Kratochwill, 1990).

Several characteristics are associated with consultation services. Perhaps the most widely shared attribute of consultation activities is that they generally involve indirect service (Bergan, 1977). Typically, service is provided by a consultant (e.g., psychologist) to a consultee (e.g., teacher), who in turn provides services to one or more clients (e.g., students). The indirect approach to service characteristic of consultation is generally regarded as a major advantage of this form of service delivery. A consultant providing services to a number of consultees can bring expertise to many more clients than could be serviced by a direct-service approach. There is a multiplier effect in which the skills of the consultant can be brought to bear on client problems without the extensive time commitment required when the consultant provides direct services to the client.

A second attribute of consultation is that it is generally a problem-solving venture in which the consultant provides expert advice related to a problem presented by the consultee (Bergan, 1977). The consultant usually elicits a description of the problem from the consultee, assists in the development of a plan to solve the problem, and participates in an evaluation to determine the extent to which the problem has been solved.

A third feature of consultation is that it is typically assumed to involve a collegial relationship between the consultant and the consultee (Bergan, 1977). This means that the consultant has no direct authority over the consultee and the consultee has no direct authority over the consultant. Rather, each has an area of professional responsibility with respect to the services provided to the client. The consultant serves as an advisor. The consultee uses consultant advice in making and implementing decisions aimed at solving the problem(s) presented in consultation.

The three attributes discussed in the preceding paragraphs are not unique to behavioral consultation. Yet, they are a part of consultation provided from a behavioral perspective. What distinguishes behavioral consultation from other varieties of consultation is the use of a behavioral perspective in providing consultation services (Bergan, 1977; Feld, Bergan, & Stone, 1984). The behavioral viewpoint affects consultation in three important ways. First, it dictates that problems presented in consultation be conceptualized from a behavioral perspective. Second, it calls for the use of behavioral principles in designing interventions to solve problems. Third, it assumes an empirical approach to determining the effectiveness of consultation interventions.

Consultation services are usually provided in a series of stages, each of which is designed to address a particular aspect of the problem-solving process. Four stages are generally recognized in consultation (Bergan, 1977; Dorr, 1979; Goodwin & Coates, 1976; Tombari & Davis, 1979). They are (1) problem identification, (2) problem analysis, (3) plan implementation, and (4) problem evaluation.

Problem identification sets the direction that consultation will take. Within the behavioral perspective, a problem is defined in terms of a discrepancy between observed behavior and desired behavior. The problem is to eliminate the discrepancy. Determining the existence of a discrepancy between observed and desired behavior requires that the concerns communicated by the consultee be expressed in behavioral terms. During problem identification, the consultant assists the consultee to describe current client functioning and desired functioning in terms of current behaviors and desired behaviors. Data are generally collected to document the status of current behavior. A problem exists if the data reveal a difference between current and desired behavior that the consultee has identified as an issue.

Problem analysis follows problem identification. During this stage of consultation, the factors that may be influencing client behaviors of concern are identified and a plan is formulated to effect desired changes in behaviors. Behavioral principles are heavily relied on in determining influences on behavior. Problem analysis generally begins with the specification of antecedent and consequent environmental conditions that may be affecting behavior. However, client skills and behavioral patterns may also be the subject of analysis (Piersel, 1985). After hypothesized influences on client behavior have been identified, a plan is formulated to change client behavior. The consultant is generally responsible for specifying the strategies that may be used to achieve behavior change. However, the consultee often plays a major role in identifying specific tactics that may be useful in implementing a plan. For example, a consultant may determine that positive reinforcement may be useful in increasing a particular behavior of concern to the consultee. The consultee may then identify the type of reinforcement to be used with the behavior.

After a suitable plan has been formulated, it is implemented. Implementation is generally the responsibility of the consultee. However, the consultee may direct an implementation effort in which others actually carry out the plan. For instance, a teacher may direct a peer tutoring program designed to increase the reading skills of a group of children. The principal role of the consultant during the implementation is one of monitoring what is occurring and of assisting the consultee to make minor revisions in the plan in those instances in which the plans is not working as expected.

The final stage in consultation is problem evaluation. During this phase of consultation, the consultant and the consultee determine the extent to which the goals of consultation have been achieved and the extent to which the plan implemented to attain goals has been effective. Evaluation data guide the course of consultation. If the goals of consultation have not been achieved, consultation generally returns to problem analysis.

A large body of research supports behavioral consultation as an effective framework for delivering psychological services for children experiencing behavioral and academic problems (e.g., Bergan & Kratochwill, 1990; Reddy, Barboza-Whitehead, & Files, 2000; Sheridan, Welch, & Orme, 1996). In a large meta-analysis of outcomes studies between 1985 and 1995, Sheridan et al. (1996) concluded that 89% of the behavioral consultation studies reported positive results. Research on the model also shows that children are more likely to experience positive outcomes when the consultant is effective at defining the problem in behavioral terms at the close of the first interview (Bergan & Tombari, 1976); consultants use behavioral versus medical cues with consultees (Tombari & Bergan, 1978); consultants request consultee ideas regarding the resources needed to implement interventions plans (Bergan & Neumann, 1980); and consultants provide the consultee information about weekly and monthly performance data (Mortenson & Witt, 1998).

Behavioral consultation also been identified as the preferred consultative model among school psychologists (Gutkin & Curis, 1999), who are key educators trained in and expected to engage in consultation activities. Moreover, the relationship of the consultant and the consultee has been proven to play a more primary role than originally conceptualized (Gutkin & Curtis, 1999; Martin, 1978). That is, consultation is most effective when the consultant and consultee: (1) establish and maintain a sense of rapport, trust, and respect; (2) clarify expectations, roles, and responsibilities from the outset; (3) discuss relevant legal and ethical guidelines early in the process; (4) establish a preferred means of communication; (5) make certain that all members understand and support the problem solving process; (6) use language that is familiar to everyone; (7) share valuable information between team members; and (8) incorporate team members' perspectives and opinions (Colton & Sheridan, 1998; Sheridan & Kratochwill, 1992).

Behavioral consultation has withheld the test of time, evolving to adapt to new challenges and needs of schools and families over the past 35 years. The best example is Sheridan & Kratochwill's (2007) *conjoint behavioral consultation*, an expanded model of behavioral consultation that includes both teachers and parents in the problem-solving process. Furthermore, behavioral consultation is identified as a practice guideline for the delivery of evidence-based interventions (White & Kratochwill, 2005) and proves to be a primary vehicle for response to intervention (RtI) activities in U.S. schools (Kratochwill, Clements, & Kalymon, 2007).

REFERENCES

Bergan, J. R. (1977). *Behavioral consultation*. Columbus, OH: Merrill.

Bergan, J. R., & Kratochwill, T. R. (1990). *Behavioral consultation in applied settings*. New York, NY: Plenum Press.

Bergan, J. R., & Neumann, A. J. (1980). The identification of resources and constraints influencing plan design in consultation. *Journal of School Psychology, 18*, 317–323.

Bergan, J. R., & Tombari, M. L. (1976). Consultant skill and efficiency and the implementation of outcomes of consultation. *Journal of School Psychology, 14*, 3–13.

Colton, D., & Sheridan, S. (1998). Conjoint behavioral consultation and social skills training: Enhancing the play behaviors of boys with attention deficit hyperactivity disorder. *Journal of Educational and Psychological Consultation, 9*, 3–28.

Dorr, D. (1979). Psychological consulting in the schools. In J. J. Platt & R. J. Wicks (Eds.), *The psychological consultant*. New York, NY: Grune & Stratton.

Goodwin, D. L., & Coates, T. J. (1976). *Helping students help themselves*. Englewood Cliffs, NJ: Prentice Hall.

Gutkin, T. B., & Curtis, M. J. (1999). School-based consultation: The art and science of indirect service delivery. In C. R. Reynolds & T. B. Gutkin (Eds.), *The handbook of school psychology* (3rd ed., pp. 598–637). New York, NY: Wiley.

Feld, J. D., Bergen, J. R., & Stone, C. A. (1984) Behavioral approaches to school based consultation: current statust and future directions. In C. A. Maher (Ed.), *Behavioral Approaches to Providing Educational Services in Schools*. Hillsdale, NJ: Erlbaum.

Kratochwill, T. R., Clements, M. A., & Kalymon, K. M. (2007). Response to intervention: Conceptual and methodological issues in implementation. In S. R. Jimerson, M. K. Burns, & A. M. VanDerHeyden (Eds.), *Handbook of response to intervention: The science and practice of assessment and intervention* (pp. 25–52). New York, NY: Springer.

Martin, R. P. (1978). Expert and referent power: A framework for understanding and maximizing consultation effectiveness. *Journal of School Psychology, 16*, 49–55.

Mortenson, B. P., & Witt, J. C. (1998). The use of weekly performance data to increase teacher implementation of a prereferral academic intervention. *School Psychology Review, 27*, 613–627.

Piersel, W. C. (1985). Behavioral consultation: An approach to problem solving in educational settings. In J. R. Bergan (Eds.), *School psychology in contemporary society*. Columbus, OH: Merrill.

Reddy, L. A., Barboza-Whitehead, S., & Files, T. (2000). Clinical focus of consultation outcome research with children and adolescents. *Special Services in the Schools, 16*(1–2), 1–22.

Sheridan, S. M., & Kratochwill, T. R. (2007). *Conjoint behavioral consultation: Promoting family-school connections and interventions* (2nd ed.). New York, NY: Springer.

Sheridan, S. M., Welch, M., & Orme, S. F. (1996). Is consultation effective? A review of outcome research. *Remedial and Special Education, 17*, 341–354.

Tombari, M. L., & Bergan, J. R. (1978). Consultant cues and teacher verbalizations, judgments, and expectancies concerning children's adjustment problems. *Journal of School Psychology, 16*, 212–219.

White, J. L., & Kratochwill, T. R. (2005). Practice guidelines in school psychology: Issues and directions for evidence-based interventions in practice and training. *Journal of School Psychology, 43*, 99–115.

JOHN R. BERGAN
University of Arizona
Third edition

KRISTY K. KELLY
Chicago School of Professional Psychology
Fourth edition

BEHAVIORAL CONSULTATION, CONJOINT

Conjoint behavioral consultation (CBC) was developed as an extension of the well-known and accepted traditional model of behavioral consultation. Sheridan and Kratochwill (2007) conceptualized the model from an ecological-behavioral framework, with heavy consideration of the literature on family school partnerships. The model broadens traditional behavioral consultation, which is limited to only examining a child's functioning within a single environment (e.g., school), to consideration of a child's development and learning across multiple contexts and settings. The emphasis on parent involvement in this process is based on the theory that parents remain as the most constant variable in a child's life and development and are therefore a significant point of intervention and continuity over time. In their most recent work, Sheridan and Kratochwill (2007) have defined the model as "a strength-based, cross-system problem-solving and decision-making model wherein parents, teachers, and other caregivers or service providers work as partners and share responsibility for promoting positive and consistent outcomes related to a child's academic, behavioral and social-emotional development" (p. 25).

As previously noted, CBC is a partnership-centered model built on family-centered principles (Dunst, Trivette, & Deal, 1988) that strongly emphasizes relationship building throughout the process. Unlike other models of consultation, which often delineate relationship building as a formal stage, CBC promotes the development of relationships before problem-solving begins and encourages consideration of these factors throughout the consultation process. The development and strengthening of relationships throughout the process is seen as a critical aspect of the model. To underscore this point, CBC is viewed as (1) being concerned with both child outcomes and processes by which consultants and consultees work together, (2) responsive to the needs of consumers, (3) promoting competency acquisition in all those involved in the process, and (4) promoting partnership and collaboration among systems.

Three overarching goals guide the process of consultation in the model. The first goal is to promote academic, socioemotional, and behavioral outcomes for children, while the second and third goals relate to the promotion of culturally sensitive parent engagement in the process and the strengthening of relationships between systems within which the child is developing. A four-stage structured process of consultation has been designed to meet these goals. The stages include: (1) conjoint needs (problem) identification, (2) conjoint needs (problem) analysis, (3) plan implementation, and (4) conjoint plan evaluation (Sheridan, Kratochwill, & Bergan, 1996). The stages were designed to be dynamic, allowing for flexibility to move between various stages in response to client and consultee needs.

The first stage of CBC is conjoint needs (problem) identification. The main objective of this stage is for the consultant and the consultees to collaboratively prioritize needs, define target concerns, and establish procedures for collecting baseline data. This is accomplished largely through the conjoint needs (problem) identification interview (CNII), where the consultant works with consultees to prioritize areas of concern in the child's development across the home, school, and other natural settings. Once priorities are agreed on by all parties, the primary concern is operationally defined in terms that are clear, measurable, and manageable. Before the close of this interview, consultants work with parents and teachers to develop the most feasible and meaningful way to collect data that can be used in decision making and outcome monitoring throughout the process. A useful tool recognized for its ecological emphasis in assessment and comprehensive consideration of home and school factors is the *Functional Assessment of Academic Behavior* (FAAB; Ysseldyke & Christenson, 2002). Although most of the information is gathered during the CNII, it is likely that assessment and conceptualization of concerns begins prior to and on referral. For example, a teacher may flag a student for referral based on a high number of office referrals during the first month of school and have already collected information about reasons for the behavioral incidences.

The second stage of CBC is conjoint needs (problem) analysis and involves a structured interview called the conjoint needs analysis interview (CNAI). In this stage, parents and teachers conduct a functional assessment and develop intervention plans to be used across home and school settings. Baseline data are reviewed, behavioral goals for the child are identified, and hypotheses regarding environmental or functional conditions that may contribute to the occurrence of the problem behavior are developed. After analysis of the behavior, participants in

CBC work collaboratively to design effective intervention plans across settings. Typically, the consultant provides information on evidence-based strategies to address the functional features of the target behavior(s) and consultees make recommendations for how to shape the intervention to fit into existing structures, settings, and routines in relevant settings.

The third stage of CBC is plan implementation and consists of parents and teachers implementing the intervention procedures designed in the previous stage. This stage does not involve a structured interview; however, the consultant provides support to parents and teachers by maintaining close contact and offering assistance when necessary. The two most critical consultant roles in this stage include monitoring treatment integrity and assessing the child's response to the delivered intervention. Intervention integrity refers to the degree to which consultees implement plans as developed and intended (Gresham, 1989; Noell, 2008; Sanetti & Kratochwill, 2005). Assessment of the child's response to intervention is useful, as it provides opportunity to make adjustments and alterations to the designed intervention if the child is not responding as expected (e.g., progress is not in line with the goals identified during the conjoint needs analysis).

The final stage of CBC is conjoint plan evaluation, in which the conjoint plan evaluation interview (CPEI) is conducted. During this stage, consultants and consultees evaluate the effects of the intervention through review of the behavioral data gathered. This requires the consultant and consultees to determine whether the goals set forth in earlier stages of consultation have been met, whether there is overall treatment effectiveness, and to what extent the intervention has social validity.

To determine treatment effectiveness in consultation, it is necessary to collect data before the intervention is implemented (baseline), during the treatment period, as well as during follow-up. Consultants use a single case study design to analyze the treatment effects. Strength of intervention effects is greatest when they are repeated or replicated (Hayes, Barlow, & Nelson-Gray, 1999), which is why it is important to consider single case research designs beyond the simple A/B design (e.g., withdrawal design). Social validity is determined by examining the degree to which: (a) treatment goals are socially significant, (b) treatment procedure are considered socially appropriate, and (c) treatment effects are clinically meaningful (Sheridan & Kratochwill, 2007).

A large body of research, focusing primarily on outcomes, communication processes, and social validation, supports the use and effectiveness of CBC. Numerous studies have shown that CBC has positive effects on children's academic, social and behavioral outcomes (Clark, Burt, & Sheridan, 2007). In the first large scale review of CBC, Sheridan, Eagle, Cowan, and Mickelson (2001) found the average effect size for CBC case outcomes was 1.10. An effect size of .8 is considered *large or highly significant* in the literature (Cohen, 1992). Impact on child outcomes has also been replicated with diverse populations of students (Sheridan, Eagle, & Doll, 2006b). Using the *Procedural Coding Manual of the Division 16 Task Force on Evidence Based Interventions in School Psychology* (Kratochwill & Stoiber, 2002), Guli (2005) found CBC to hold promise as an evidence-based parent consultation model and provided the strongest evidence for effectiveness in comparison to other parent consultation models.

In addition to outcome research, support has been found for bidirectional and reciprocal communication patterns in the interactions between parents, teachers, and consultants during the CBC process (Erchul et al., 1999). This suggests that the process is collaborative in nature involving nonhierarchical and reciprocal relationships. Lastly, CBC has been recognized as an acceptable model of consultation (Freer & Watson, 1999; Sheridan & Steck, 1995) and the most preferred consultation approach (Freer & Watson, 1999) by parents and teachers.

REFERENCES

Clark, B. L., Burt, J. D., & Sheridan, S. M. (2007). Research on conjoint behavioral consultation. In S. M. Sheridan & T. R. Kratochwill (Eds.), *Conjoint behavioral consultation: Promoting family-school connections and interventions* (2nd ed.). New York, NY: Springer.

Cohen, J. (1992). Quantitative methods in psychology: A power primer. *Psychological Bulletin, 112*(1), 155–159.

Dunst, C. J., Trivette, C. M., & Deal, A. (1988). *Enabling and empowering families: Principles and guidelines for practice. Vol. 1. Methods, strategies and practices* (pp. 171–186). Cambridge, MA: Brookline Books.

Erchul, W. P., Sheridan, S. M., Ryan, D. A., Grissom, P. R., Killough, C. E., & Mettler, D. W. (1999). Patterns of relational communication in conjoint behavioral consultation. *School Psychology Quarterly, 14*, 121–147.

Freer, P., & Watson, T. S. (1999). A comparison on parent and teacher acceptability ratings of behavioral and conjoint behavioral consultation. *School Psychology Review, 2*, 672–684.

Gresham, F. M. (1989). Assessment of treatment integrity in school consultation and prereferral intervention. *School Psychology Review, 18*, 37–50.

Guli, L. A. (2005). Evidence-based parent consultation with school-related outcomes. *School Psychology Quarterly, 20*, 455–472.

Hayes, S. C., Barlow, D. H., & Nelson-Gray, R. O. (1999). *The scientist practitioner: Research and accountability in the age of managed care* (2nd ed.). Needham Heights, MA: Allyn & Bacon.

Kratochwill, T. R., & Stoiber, K. C. (2002). Evidence-based interventions in school psychology: Conceptual foundations of the procedural and coding manual for Division 16 and the Society for the Study of School Psychology Task Force. *School Psychology Quarterly, 17*, 341–389.

Noell, G. H. (2008). Research examining the relationships among consultation process, treatment integrity, and outcomes. In

W. P. Erchul & S. M. Sheridan (Eds.), *Handbook of research in school consultation: Empirical foundations for the field.* (pp. 323–342). Mahwah: NJ: Erlbaum.

Sanetti, L. H., & Kratochwill, T. R. (2005). Treatment integrity assessment within a problem-solving model. In R. Brown-Chidsey (Ed.), *Problem-solving based assessment for educational intervention* (pp. 304–325). New York, NY: Guilford Press.

Sheridan, S. M., Eagle, J. W., Cowan, R. J., & Mickelson, W. (2001). The effects of conjoint behavioral consultation: Results of a four-year investigation. *Journal of School Psychology, 39*, 361–385.

Sheridan, S. M., Eagle, J. W., & Doll, B. (2006). An examination of the efficacy of conjoint behavioral consultation with diverse clients. *School Psychology Quarterly, 21*, 396–417.

Sheridan, S. M., & Kratochwill, T. R. (2007). *Conjoint behavioral consultation: Promoting family-school connections and interventions* (2nd ed.). New York, NY: Springer.

Sheridan, S. M., Kratochwill, T. R., & Bergan, J. R. (1996). *Conjoint behavioral consultation: A procedural manual.* New York, NY: Plenum Press.

Sheridan, S. M., & Steck, M. (1995). Acceptability of conjoint behavioral consultation: A national survey of school psychologists. *School Psychology Review, 24*, 633–647.

Ysseldyke, J. E., & Christenson, S. L. (2002). *Functional assessment of academic behavior: A system for assessing individual student's instruction environments.* Longmont, CO: Sopris West.

KRISTY K. KELLY
Chicago School of Professional Psychology
Fourth edition

BEHAVIORAL DEFICIT

The terminology associated with behavioral deficit has become confused as a result of various incomplete usages. The original usage was associated with the 1961 American Association on Intellectual Developmental Disabilities inclusion of adaptive behavior in their definition of intellectual developmental disabilities. Adaptive behavior implies that many educational, psychological, sociological, and biological influences interact on the child, affecting function and performance. Principally, it is a term designed to offset the dependence the public schools, mental health agencies, and social welfare institutions had placed on measured intelligence.

The original concept was closely associated with developmental disabilities. Work in the late 1950s, and early 1960s with children with disabilities resulted in a description of developmental lag, placing the emphasis for the disability on irregular test protocols and subtest patterns clinically thought to reflect possible neurological insult.

The search had begun by psychoeducational researchers to specify the nature of these so-called behavioral deficits through the use of test and subtest patterns. In 1966, S. D. Clements placed into motion, through the committee he chaired on minimal neurological impairment, the search for neurological damage as an explanation of specific learning disabilities.

Tests designed to measure visual and auditory perceptual, perceptual-motor, and other cognitive abilities began to flood the market. The term specific added to learning disabilities accentuated that a deficit in one or more of the psychological processes was accountable for the condition.

In 1974, Gleason and Haring provided the first general behavioral definition of learning disabilities and in so doing used the term behavioral deficit as the principal construct associated with the concept learning disabilities: "We define a learning disability as a behavioral deficit almost always associated with academic performance and that can be remediated by precise, individualized instructional programming" (p. 226).

There are two major issues that surround the construct of behavioral deficits. The first is the possibility or utility of cognitive skills being broken into specific component parts. It should be remembered that all assumed cognitive behaviors are named, usually after a test or subtest designed to measure them. They are not occurrences in nature that are directly observable. The second issue is the reliability of most tests designed to ascertain or describe a basic behavior and therefore illustrate a behavioral deficit. As the reliability decreases, so does the validity.

A behavioral deficit then is a concept suggesting that human abilities are not all the same, and in some cases fall to a deficit level. Operationally defining a deficit has not been well done through the use of tests or subtests in terms of when a deficit statistically or clinically exists. Therefore, while the concept itself has driven several major thrusts (both diagnostic and treatment), including the term developmental disability to some degree, and theoretically is responsible for describing learning disability, it remains an incomplete term, less than fully developed by those who use it on a clinical basis.

REFERENCES

Clements, S. D. (1966). *Task force I: Minimal brain dysfunction in children. Monograph No. 3*. Washington, DC: U.S. Government Printing Office.

Gleason, C., & Haring, N. (1974). Learning disabilities. In N. G. Haring (Ed.), *Behavior of exceptional children* (pp. 245–295). Columbus, OH: Merrill.

DAVID A. SABATINO
West Virginia College of Graduate Studies

See also Ability Training, Early Efforts in; Behavioral
   Objectives

BEHAVIORAL DISORDERS, JOURNAL OF

The *Journal of Behavioral Disorders* is the official journal of the Council for Children with Behavioral Disorders (CCBD) of the Council for Exceptional Children. Founded in 1975, *Behavioral Disorders* serves as a resource for those professionals interested in the education and treatment of behaviorally disordered children and youth. *Behavioral Disorders* is the flagship journal of the organization.

With a quarterly distribution to the members of CCBD and hundreds of individual and institutional subscribers, *Behavioral Disorders* was developed under the editorships of Albert Fink of Indiana University (1975–1978), Denzil Edge of the University of Louisville (1978–1981), and Robert B. Rutherford Jr. of Arizona State University (1981–1987) into a forum for the publication of manuscripts derived from documented thought and empirical evidence. Current editors include: (a) Dr. Joe Gagnon, University of Florida, (b) Dr. Greg Benner, University of Washington, and (c) Dr. Tom Gumpel, the Hebrew University. These data-based articles are presented in several forms: experimental research (either original or replications), research and practice reviews and analyses, program or procedure descriptions, and scholarly reviews of texts, films, and other media. The editorial process of the journal is designed to thoroughly and professionally analyze submitted manuscripts in terms of originality, relevance of topic, importance of the findings or concepts, content organization, and documentation.

Historically, *Behavioral Disorders* evolved from an early dependence on cosponsored thematic issues and reliance on solicited manuscripts, but has evolved to an open journal relying on unsolicited manuscripts submitted by professionals in the field. *Behavioral Disorders* has contributed significantly to the professional literature on behavioral disorders of children and youths.

ROBERT B. RUTHERFORD JR.
Arizona State University

BEHAVIORAL MOMENTUM

Behavioral momentum is a metaphor applied to the observation that human (and animal) free-operant behavior possesses *momentum* under steady-state conditions of reinforcement and is resistant to change when the behavior experiences a change in the interval- or ratio-schedule of reinforcement (Mace et al., 1988; Nevin, 1988; Nevin, Mandell, & Atak, 1983). Steady-state conditions are synonymous with free-operant reinforcement where the individual is free to complete one response, receive reinforcement from the environment, and then go on to freely emit another response with the goal of receiving additional reinforcement. This is in contrast to more restricted discrete-trial learning situations where response emission is controlled by someone (or something) else other than the individual (e.g., a special education teacher teaching math to students in the learning center).

Nevin's observation that persistent, free-operant behavior possesses momentum was borne out of his experimental resistance-to-change research in the laboratory with pigeons, rats, and monkeys. To better communicate these observations, Newtonian mechanics was used as an analogy to help explain and understand the phenomenon, especially as it relates to human behavior in applied settings (Nevin et al., 1983). The Newtonian model describes momentum as the product of the velocity and mass of a moving body. The greater the mass of that moving body, the less impact any external force will have in altering its velocity. In relation to human learning, behavioral momentum can be thought of as the product of resistance to change (mass) and baseline response rate (velocity; Nevin, 1988). Behavioral *mass* is shaped by Pavlovian stimulus-reinforcer contingencies, while *velocity* of behavior is shaped by response-reinforcer contingencies (Plaud & Gaither, 1996). In theory, then, newly learned behavior moving at a particularly high velocity and mass will persist, or resist change, in the face of obstacles or interventions such as when reinforcement is no longer delivered for an emitted response (i.e., extinction procedures) or perhaps when a more demanding response is required of the person. Embedded within the behavioral momentum paradigm are issues related to the partial reinforcement effect, continuous reinforcement, establishing operations, and Herrnstein's matching law; however, due to space limitations, the reader is directed to the work of Brandon and Houlihan (1997), Houlihan and Brandon (1996), Nevin (1988), Nevin (1996), Plaud and Gaither (1996), and Strand (2000), for further independent study and analysis.

The first applied behavioral momentum research study with human subjects began with Mace and colleagues (1988) in which a series of three to five high-probability compliance requests (i.e., high-*p* requests) were issued to subjects with intellectual developmental disabilities just prior to the delivery of a low-probability compliance request (i.e., low-*p* request) the subject(s) rarely complied with. Mace et al. (1988) demonstrated that when a series of high-*p* requests are presented to these subjects, dramatic increases in compliance to low-*p* requests occur. Mace et al.'s (1988) initial study spawned a program of research in the field of applied behavior analysis aimed at using the behavioral momentum strategy to increase the frequency of compliance with individuals in clinical or applied contexts. Successful replications of behavioral momentum have since occurred across a variety of populations including children with autism, individuals with

self-injurious behavior, children with social skills deficits, individuals noncompliant with their medical regimens, and adult undergraduate students (Brandon & Houlihan, 1997; Plaud & Gaither, 1996). Behavioral momentum techniques have improved a variety of problematic behaviors such as decreasing vomiting, aggression, and stereotypic touching and increasing attempts to do difficult tasks and initiating social contacts (Strand, 2000). The apparent success of behavioral momentum techniques led Davis and Brady (1993) to suggest that the intervention should be utilized to improve language skills, motor skills, academic skills, and self-help skills. Strand (2000) also comments that behavioral momentum is a relevant heuristic for behavioral family therapy involving conduct disordered children, especially for increasing highly reinforcing reciprocal interactions between parents and their children and for helping to explain the effectiveness of parental *scaffolding* techniques designed to increase child social and cognitive skills beyond their present level of performance.

Although behavioral momentum research has enjoyed popularity and success, it has not been without its limitations and controversies. For example, while behavioral momentum is an interesting use of a metaphor to help explain and predict behavioral compliance, the procedures found in the high-*p* technique are not new to the experimental analysis of behavior. In fact, Houlihan and Brandon (1996), and Brandon and Houlihan (1997) trace functionally similar procedures in the behavioral compliance literature as far back as Weiss's (1934) study of factors affecting preschool children's compliance to commands and are concerned by the current tendency of researchers to cite pre-Nevin (i.e., before 1983) studies as evidence for behavioral momentum. Disquieting, according to Houlihan and Brandon (1996), is the fact that behavioral momentum bears a formal resemblance to Hull and Spence's *habit strength* concept that explained the strength of behavior as being based upon frequent stimulus-response pairings (i.e., drive) and motivation to engage in behavior based on reinforcement (i.e., incentive).

Houlihan and Brandon (1997) maintain that there has been an overextension of the behavioral momentum metaphor from the experimental animal literature to compliance research with human subjects, promoting the idea that the high-*p* sequence itself is the source of reinforcement responsible for behavioral change. What Houlihan and Brandon have pointed out (among other things) is that the high-*p* process may in fact be applying stimulus control and manipulating an establishing condition in which the person presenting the high-*p* prompts becomes the critical source of reinforcement, not the high-*p* prompt procedure itself. Such a possibility weakens the argument that what is in operation is *behavioral momentum*, but rather a *concurrent chain* schedule of reinforcement where two (or more) concurrently available sources of reinforcement exist for the subject to choose from. When using a high-*p* prompt strategy as one of the concurrent chains to increase the likelihood of compliance, the procedure functions as an *establishing operation* whereby all compliance behaviors reinforced by a therapist or teacher potentially compete against other concurrently available chains of reinforcement (see Brandon & Houlihan, 1997, for a fuller explanation).

Although Houlihan and Brandon (1996) and Brandon and Houlihan (1997) are concerned about researchers borrowing a metaphor from physics and applying it beyond its applicable boundaries with human behavior in applied settings, they acknowledge that behavioral momentum strategies are effective in increasing the frequency of behavior that are resistant to other conventional behavioral approaches. As such, the high-*p* procedure has demonstrated its utility and social validity. Research still needs to continue on its application and generalization beyond problems of noncompliance as well as investigate whether practitioners can effectively implement the strategy on their own in school or clinic settings; this would help determine if the efficacy of the high-*p* strategy is due to researcher effects or the potency and simplicity of the high-*p* strategy itself. Finally, behavioral momentum should be involved in analyzing more highly persistent free-operant behaviors such as gambling, smoking, or other health-related problem behaviors that are difficult to bring under stimulus control and decrease in incidence and prevalence (Brandon & Houlihan, 1997).

REFERENCES

Brandon, P. K., & Houlihan, D. (1997). Applying behavioral theory to practice: An examination of the behavioral momentum metaphor. *Behavioral Interventions, 12*, 113–131.

Davis, C. A., & Brady, M. P. (1993). Expanding the utility of behavioral momentum with young children: Where we've been, where we need to go. *Journal of Early Intervention, 17*, 211–223.

Houlihan, D., & Brandon, P. K. (1996). Compliant in a moment: A commentary on Nevin. *Journal of Applied Behavior Analysis, 29*, 549–555.

Mace, F. C., Hock, M. L., Lalli, J. S., West, B. J., Belfiore, P., Pinter, E., & Brown, D. K. (1988). Behavioral momentum in the treatment of noncompliance. *Journal of Applied Behavior Analysis, 21*, 123–141.

Nevin, J. A., Mandell, C., & Atak, J. R. (1983). The analysis of behavioral momentum. *Journal of the Experimental Analysis of Behavior, 39*, 49–59.

Nevin, J. A. (1988). Behavioral momentum and the partial reinforcement effect. *Psychological Bulletin, 103*, 44–56.

Nevin, J. A. (1996). The momentum of compliance. *Journal of Applied Behavior Analysis, 29*, 535–547.

Nevin, J. A., Mandell, C., & Atak, J. R. (1983). The analysis of behavioral momentum. *Journal of the Experimental Analysis of Behavior, 39*, 49–59.

Plaud, J. J., & Gaither, G. A. (1996). Human behavioral momentum: Implications for applied behavior analysis and therapy.

Journal of Behavior Therapy and Experimental Psychiatry, 27, 139–148.

Strand, P. S. (2000). A modern behavioral perspective on child Conduct Disorder: Integrating behavioral momentum and matching theory. *Clinical Psychology Review, 20*, 593–615.

Weiss, L. A. (1934). An experimental investigation of certain factors involved in the preschool child's compliance with commands. *Journal of Child Welfare, 9*, 127–157.

ROLLEN C. FOWLER
Eugene 4J School District, Eugene, Oregon

See also **Applied Behavior Analysis; Behavioral Assessment**

BEHAVIORAL OBJECTIVES

In the broadest sense, an objective is a statement of an aim or desired outcome. In an educational sense, an instructional objective may be a quantifiable and/or an observable academic or social achievement that specifies the enabling steps necessary to accomplish the objective in a stated period of time. All instructional or behavioral objectives must have observable or measurable outcomes. The difference between an instructional and a behavioral objective is the result to be achieved. The latter may be broader in scope and not confined to an educational effort; it may rather include a wide range of specified behavioral outcomes, for example, speech, language, perceptual development, motor training, and social skill development.

Behavioral objectives and instructional (teaching) objectives are frequently used interchangeably. Although each impacts on the other, these two sets of objectives address two different performances. A behavioral objective focuses on any visible activity displayed by a learner (student). It has at its core the terminal behavior, or what the learner can demonstrate has been learned. An instructional objective may include the desired learner outcomes; it will specify the criteria acceptable for success in attaining that outcome, but it focuses on what will be taught and how it will be taught.

The purpose for developing behavioral objectives is to increase teaching efficiency by having educators and behavioral scientists determine what it is that will be learned, how it will be taught, what materials will be used, and the length of time within which it should be learned against a predetermined criteria or standard. Behavioral objectives become targets to which teachers can direct their instruction. In the process of instruction, their use requires educators to determine whether outcomes or observations of performance are being effectively and efficiently provided and creating an exactness for what is learned and how it is taught. Thus, a teaching methodology may be used for a specified amount of time under conditions that will permit the educator to judge the amount of progress being made. Mager (1962) notes, "An instructor will function in a fog of his own making until he knows what he wants his students to be able to do at the end of the instruction" (p. 2).

Behavioral objectives must contain statements of concrete, measurable, or observable performances. In contrast, nonbehavioral goals are broad, abstract statements; they are not derived from previous observations or performance test data. They do not consider the skills necessary to enter into a next level of work. Nonbehavioral objectives are based on philosophy, ideology, and attitude, not the proficiency of task to be taught.

Popham and Baker (1970) note five different considerations necessary in the preparation and use of behavioral objectives:

1. *Systematic instructional decision making.* The use of behavioral objectives and the measured outcome to determine the most efficient method of instruction and how effective a specified method was in achieving an objective.

2. *Behavioral and/or educational objectives.* Determine what is to be accomplished, in what time period, and how it is to be accomplished.

3. *Selection of appropriate educational objectives.* Selecting significant and meaningful objectives is not easy; indeed, the task tends to be elusive and difficult. Educators must choose between the content (e.g., a math score, reading score from a formal or informal test, new words to be learned) and behaviors that are reasoned to influence the process of learning (e.g., time on task). Many times the two intersect and both become important elements in achieving a goal.

4. *Establishing performance standards.* One of the most difficult tasks is to set the criteria that denote whether a behavioral objective has been achieved successfully. There are no absolutes or clear rules for achieving that purpose. Some guidelines exist, such as the 80/80 criterion, which states that 80% of what has been taught must be demonstrated as a successfully learned outcome at an 80% minimal level of performance. Thus, if 10 words were taught, on measurement eight words must be learned before the next list of words is taught. Many educators use the 80% criterion as a minimal standard for instructional or subject matter content objectives. A large percentage of these same practitioners believe that a 90% criterion is useful with behavioral objectives. The establishment of performance standards addresses the sophistication or precision of the objective. While performance standards may largely be intuitive, a performance standard frequently addresses the knowledge the educator has of the learner.

5. *The curriculum rationale.* Educators spend their professional lives developing and implementing the curriculum. Countless hours are spent discussing curriculum questions each school year through school-district, building-level, and grade-level curriculum committees; in addition, thousands of curriculum guides exist in the United States. Combine those teacher-made curricula and guides with the innumerable commercially printed materials, and it would appear the curricular-planning process is complete. It is not. Despite all these efforts, 20% to 30% of schoolchildren fail academically or socially each year. Why?

A simple and clear explanation is that most curricula are targeted at theoretical learners who are ready to learn and have no disabilities. An educator using a general curricular guide or commercial material is exclusively concerned with determining the objectives for the educational system, and not any one typical or atypical youth in that system. There are basically two kinds of decisions that educators must make. First, they must decide what the objectives (the ends) of the instructional system should be; second, they must decide on the procedures (the means) for accomplishing those objectives. This is, the curricular rationale for using behavioral or instructional objectives. This point becomes critical when individualization of instruction is sought. The use of behavioral objectives suggests the teacher is selecting and evaluating instructional procedures to accomplish those objectives. Thus teachers are engaged in instructional decision making. Herein resides the critical difference between using a curriculum and an instructional objectives process. Instructional objectives require stated levels of success, and measured and/or observable outcomes. In short, they are empirical solutions requiring data. Curricular structures are generally value-based.

How then are behavioral objectives established? Usually by determining a behavioral characteristic such as inattentiveness, or a score on a test, or a set of facts or things to be learned, for example, words or numbers. Behavioral objectives specify what it is to be learned and place a comfortable floor beneath the learner by dropping below what the learner can do initially and ending with what the learner can comfortably learn in a given period of time. A sound behavioral objective does not test the learner's limit, unless designed to do so for good reason.

A behavioral objective is one activity in a series of, or sequence of, activities to be learned. That sequence can become the curriculum. The principal reason for having many small, tightly sequenced steps in the curriculum is that learner performance is examined frequently. More important, the learner is provided with corrective feedback after every trial. That point is critical. Prior knowledge is not an assumption. Behavioral or instructional objectives, once sequenced, become important interlocking steps. Because learning rates of children with disabilities varies widely, particularly when materials change, each objective permits the individual student the necessary time on tasks.

The three major advantages of a behavioral objective are:

1. Clear, explicit expectations.
2. Ability to progress monitor and provide feedback.
3. Ability to identify learning sequences for instruction.

REFERENCES

Mager, R. F. (1962). *Preparing instructional objectives*. Palo Alto, CA: Fearon.

Popham, W. J., & Baker, E. (1970). *Establishing instructional goals*. Englewood Cliffs, NJ: Prentice Hall.

DAVID A. SABATINO
West Virginia College of Graduate Studies
First edition

KIMBERLY J. VANNEST
Texas A&M University
Fourth edition

See also Age-Appropriate Curriculum; Positive Behavioral Support; Teaching Strategies

BEHAVIORAL OBSERVATION

Behavior observation, also known as *direct behavior observation*, is at the core of behavioral assessment. Behavior observation is a procedure for categorizing motor and verbal behavior into an organized permanent record. A behavior observation system meets three criteria (Jones, Reid, & Patterson, 1974). These include "recording of behavioral events in their natural settings at the time they occur, not retrospectively; the use of trained impartial observer-coders, and descriptions of behaviors which (sic) require little if any inference by observers to code the events" (p. 46). Excluded from this definition are narrative recordings, anecdotal records, checklists and rating scales, retrospective ratings, and procedures that require a person to observe and record his or her own behavior (i.e., self-recording).

Behavior observations occur in diverse settings and for numerous purposes. In educational settings, behavior observations are used for purposes of diagnosing individual students, planning an intervention to modify a pupil's behavior, evaluating interventions, consulting with teachers, and conducting research.

Although specific observational procedures and instruments vary in many important ways, they all require selectivity. The observation instrument structures the observer's attention to those selected aspects of behavior and the setting that are presumed to be most relevant to the purposes of the observation. Behavior occurs in a continuous stream, yet the observer must categorize behavior into objectively defined behavioral codes and encode it into an organized, permanent record. Care in defining what is to be observed is critical to measurable results. Narrative recordings and checklists can assist in selecting the most significant behavioral codes as well as the contextual, or environmental, events thought to be associated with the selected behaviors. Data on these antecedent and consequent events are useful in designing a plan for modifying the behaviors of concern.

To minimize observer subjectivity, the selected behaviors are defined as objectively as possible. "Aggressive behavior" is not as objective a definition as "hits, shoves, grabs, and tackles." Although aggressive behavior can serve as useful shorthand in coding behavior, the clear specification of the behaviors encompassed by this term gives the observer an objective definition of aggression. When the behavioral codes are objectively defined, any two trained observers should agree on the presence or absence of a behavior. Behavior observations can occur in natural settings (e.g., classroom, peer group, or home) or in simulated or role-playing settings.

Observational instruments vary in their degree of formality from homemade teacher-used instruments to published instruments requiring highly trained observers. Three major types of observational procedures are frequency recordings, duration recordings, and interval recordings (Barton & Ascione, 1984). In frequency recordings, the number of times a behavior occurs within the observational period is recorded. Frequency recordings are best suited to behaviors with a discrete beginning and end, which last approximately the same amount of time, and that do not occur so frequently within the duration that separating each occurrence becomes difficult. Hand raises, inappropriate noises, bed-wetting, and hitting are examples of frequency target behaviors. Figure B.1 shows the results of a frequency recording of a disruptive student's behavior. Each block represents 1 minute, and each observational period lasts 15 minutes. The totals at the end of each row are the frequencies of that target behavior in a 15-minute period. Observations should continue over enough time to obtain a reliable measure.

A duration recording is a direct measure of the amount of time an individual engages in the target behavior. Duration recordings are most appropriate for behaviors that have a clear beginning and ending and that last for more than a few seconds. If a child gets out of his or her

Observer: Cathy Snow (consultant)
Date: November 5, 1985
Student: Julie
Circumstance: Math seatwork

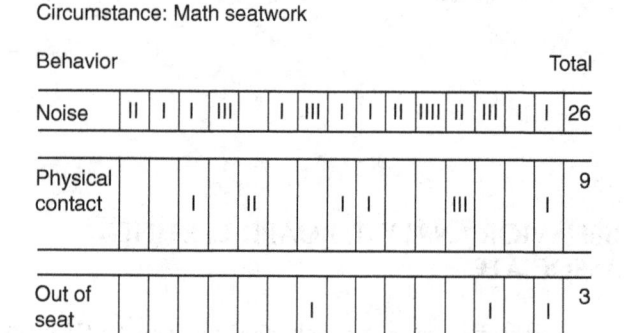

Figure B.1. Frequency recording sheet.
Source: Barton, C. J., & Ascione, F. R. (1984). Direct observation. In T. H. Ollendick & M. Hersen (Eds.), *Child behavioral assessment* (pp.166–194). New York, NY: Pergamon Press.

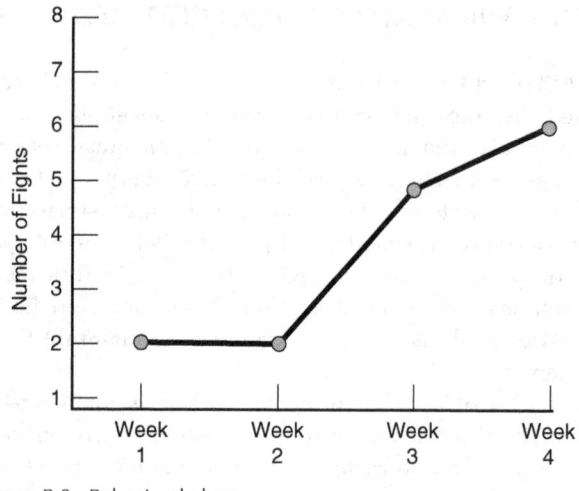

Figure B.2. Behavioral chart.

seat and stays out of the seat for periods of time ranging from 1 to 6 minutes, a duration count would indicate the percentage of time the child was out of the seat during the observational period.

In interval recordings, the occurrence or nonoccurrence of selected behaviors during a series of equal time intervals is recorded. Interval recording is recommended when several behaviors need to be observed, when behaviors occur at a high rate, or when behaviors do not have clear-cut beginnings and ends. There are several variations of interval recording procedures. Typically, some sort of signaling device (e.g., an audio timer) cues the observer to make a recording. The observer records which target behavior occurred during the preceding interval (usually 10 seconds).

Frequency, duration, and interval recordings can be adapted to a format that allows recording of selected antecedents and consequences of the behavioral codes. At the same time the observed child's behavior is coded, the antecedent and consequent circumstances are coded. Barton and Ascione (1984) provide examples of these different observational instruments.

Observational procedures are measurement procedures, and their reliability and validity need to be established. Direct observational measures can also include the use of categorical data such as a scale, although this is more inferential. An important part of establishing reliability is determining the extent to which two observers agree in their use of the instrument while observing the same behavior and context. Recent advances in computer technology have supported reliable data collection by the use of software.

Validity issues include the relationship of the behavioral code to the referral problem (face validity) and the normality of the observed behavior. One way of determining whether a child's behavior in particular settings (e.g.,

a classroom) is atypical is to observe other children in the same settings. If the observer alternates between observing the target child and observing other children in a classroom, the observer will have a composite observation of the typical child to compare with the referred child. The observer must also be culturally competent so as to include the sociocultural context to the observation process.

REFERENCES

Barton, C. J., & Ascione, F. R. (1984). Direct observation. In T. H. Ollendick & M. Hersen (Eds.), *Child behavioral assessment* (pp. 166–194). New York, NY: Pergamon Press.

Jones, R. R., Reid, J. B., & Patterson, G. B. (1974). Naturalistic observation in clinical assessment. In P. McReynolds (Ed.), *Advances in psychological assessment*. San Francisco, CA: Jossey-Bass.

JAN N. HUGHES
Texas A&M University

KIMBERLY J. VANNEST
Texas A&M University
Fourth edition

See also Applied Behavior Analysis; Behavior Therapy

BEHAVIORAL SUPPORT (*See* Support, Behavioral)

BEHAVIOR ANALYSIS (*See* Applied Behavior Analysis)

BEHAVIOR ANALYSIS, APPLIED (*See* Applied Behavior Analysis)

BEHAVIOR ANALYST, BOARD CERTIFIED

Board Certified Behavior Analysts (BCBAs) are certified by the Behavior Analyst Certification Board. Individuals who wish to become BCBAs must possess at least a master's degree, have 225 classroom hours of specific graduate-level coursework, meet supervised experience requirements, and pass the Behavior Analyst Certification Examination. Once certified, BCBAs must accumulate 36 hours of continuing education credit in behavior analysis over a 3-year period to maintain their credential.

The board certified behavior analyst is an independent practitioner who also may work as an employee or independent contractor for an organization. The BCBA conducts descriptive and systematic (e.g., analogue) behavioral assessments, including functional analyses, and provides behavior analytic interpretations of the results. The BCBA designs and supervises behavior analytic interventions. The BCBA is able to effectively develop and implement appropriate assessment and intervention methods for use in unfamiliar situations and for a range of cases. The BCBA seeks the consultation of more experienced practitioners when necessary. The BCBA teaches others to carry out ethical and effective behavior analytic interventions based on published research and designs and delivers instruction in behavior analysis. It is strongly recommended that the BCBA supervise the work of board certified associate behavior analysts and others who implement behavior analytic interventions. Additional information may be obtained at www.BACB.com. This entry has been informed by sources listed below.

REFERENCES

Johnston, J. M., & Shook, G. L. (2001). A national certification program for behavior analysts. *Behavioral Interventions, 16*(2), 77–85.

Moore, J., & Shook, G. L. (2001). Certification, accreditation and quality control in behavior analysis. *Behavior Analyst, 24,* 45–55.

Shook, G. L. (2005). An examination of the integrity and future of behavior analyst certification board credentials. *Behavior Modification, 29*(3), 562–574.

Shook, G. L., & Favell, J. E. (1996). Identifying qualified professionals in behavior analysis. In C. Maurice, G. Green, & S. C. Luce (Eds.), *Behavioral intervention for young children with autism: A manual for parents and professionals* (pp. 221–229). Austin, TX: PRO-ED.

Shook, G. L., Johnston, J. M., & Mellichamp, F. (2004). Determining essential content for applied behavior analyst practitioners. *Behavior Analyst, 27*(1), 67–94.

Shook, G. L., & Neisworth, J. (2005). Ensuring appropriate qualifications for applied behavior analyst professionals: The Behavior Analyst Certification Board. *Exceptionality, 13*(1), 3–10.

Shook, G. L., Rosales, S. A., & Glenn, S. (2002). Certification and training of behavior analyst professionals. *Behavior Modification, 26*(1), 27–48.

STAFF

BEHAVIOR ANALYST, BOARD CERTIFIED ASSOCIATE

Board certified associate behavior analysts (BCABAs) are certified by the Behavior Analyst Certification Board (BACB). Individuals who wish to be board certified associate behavior analysts (BCABAs) must have at least a bachelor's degree, have 135 classroom hours of specific coursework, meet supervised experience requirements, and pass the Associate Behavior Analyst Certification Examination. Once certified, BCBAs must accumulate 24 hours of continuing education credit in behavior analysis over a 3-year period to maintain their credential.

The BCABA conducts descriptive behavioral assessments and is able to interpret the results and design ethical and effective behavior analytic interventions for clients. The BCABA designs and oversees interventions in familiar cases (e.g., similar to those encountered during their training) that are consistent with the dimensions of applied behavior analysis. The BCABA obtains technical direction from a Board Certified Behavior Analyst (BCBA) for unfamiliar situations. The BCABA is able to teach others to carry out interventions once the BCABA has demonstrated competency with the procedures involved under the direct supervision of a BCBA. The BCABA may assist a BCBA with the design and delivery of introductory level instruction in behavior analysis. It is strongly recommended that the BCABA practice under the supervision of a BCBA, and that those governmental entities regulating BCABAs require this supervision. Additional information may be obtained at www.BACB.com. This entry has been informed by sources listed below. The references contain additional information regarding this topic.

REFERENCES

Johnston, J. M., & Shook, G. L. (2001). A national certification program for behavior analysts. *Behavioral Interventions, 16*(2), 77–85.

Moore, J., & Shook, G. L. (2001). Certification, accreditation and quality control in behavior analysis. *Behavior Analyst, 24,* 45–55.

Shook, G. L. (2005). An examination of the integrity and future of behavior analyst certification board credentials. *Behavior Modification, 29*(3), 562–574.

Shook, G. L., & Favell, J. E. (1996). Identifying qualified professionals in behavior analysis. In C. Maurice, G. Green,

& S. C. Luce (Eds.), *Behavioral intervention for young children with autism: A manual for parents and professionals* (pp. 221–229). Austin, TX: PRO-ED.

Shook, G. L., Johnston, J. M., & Mellichamp, F. (2004). Determining essential content for applied behavior analyst practitioners. *Behavior Analyst, 27*(1), 67–94.

Shook, G. L., & Neisworth, J. (2005). Ensuring appropriate qualifications for applied behavior analyst professionals: The behavior analyst certification board. *Exceptionality, 13*(1), 3–10.

Shook, G. L., Rosales, S. A., & Glenn, S. (2002). Certification and training of behavior analyst professionals. *Behavior Modification, 26*(1), 27–48.

STAFF

BEHAVIOR ANALYST CERTIFICATION BOARD, INC.

The Behavior Analyst Certification Board (BACB) is a nonprofit 501(c)(3) corporation established to meet professional credentialing needs identified by behavior analysts, government, and consumers of behavior analysis services. The BACB's mission is to develop, promote, and implement a national and international certification program for behavior analyst practitioners. The BACB has established uniform content, standards, and criteria for the credentialing process that are designed to meet:

- The legal standards established through state, federal, and case law.
- The accepted standards for national certification programs.
- The best-practice and ethical standards of the behavior analysis profession. The BACB enjoys the support of the Association for Behavior Analysis International.

The BACB program is based on the successful Behavior Analysis Certification Program developed by the state of Florida. Similar programs were established in California, Texas, Pennsylvania, New York, and Oklahoma. All of these programs transferred their certificants and credentialing responsibilities to the BACB and closed. The Behavior Analyst Certification Board credentials practitioners at two levels. Individuals who wish to become Board Certified Behavior Analysts (BCBAs) must possess at least a master's degree, have 225 classroom hours of specific graduate-level coursework, meet supervised experience requirements, and pass the Behavior Analyst Certification Examination. Persons wishing to be Board Certified Associate Behavior Analysts (BCABAs) must

have at least a bachelor's degree, have 135 classroom hours of specific coursework, meet supervised experience requirements, and pass the Associate Behavior Analyst Certification Examination. The BACB certificants must accumulate continuing education credit to maintain their credentials.

The Behavior Analyst Certification Board has developed:

- Eligibility standards to take the BACB certification examinations.
- Renewal and recertification standards to maintain certification.
- Guidelines for responsible conduct for behavior analysts.
- Professional disciplinary standards with review committee appeal procedures.
- A certificant registry.
- A process to approve university course sequences and university practica.
- Procedures to approve continuing education providers.
- Professionally developed and maintained certification examinations.

The Behavior Analyst Certification Board generally administers the examinations three times per year in more than 200 sites within the United States and more than 150 sites outside the United States. Additional information on the Behavior Analyst Certification Board may be obtained at www.BACB.com. This entry has been informed by sources listed below.

REFERENCES

Johnston, J. M., & Shook, G. L. (2001). A national certification program for behavior analysts. *Behavioral Interventions, 16*(2), 77–85.

Moore, J., & Shook, G. L. (2001). Certification, accreditation and quality control in behavior analysis. *Behavior Analyst, 24*, 45–55.

Shook, G. L. (2005). An examination of the integrity and future of Behavior Analyst Certification Board credentials. *Behavior Modification, 29*(3), 562–574.

Shook, G. L., & Favell, J. E. (1996). Identifying qualified professionals in behavior analysis. In C. Maurice, G. Green, & S. C. Luce (Eds.), *Behavioral intervention for young children with autism: A manual for parents and professionals* (pp. 221–229). Austin, TX: PRO-ED.

Shook, G. L., Johnston, J. M., & Mellichamp, F. (2004). Determining essential content for applied behavior analyst practitioners. *Behavior Analyst, 27*(1), 67–94.

Shook, G. L., & Neisworth, J. (2005). Ensuring appropriate qualifications for applied behavior analyst professionals: The behavior analyst certification board. *Exceptionality, 13*(1), 3–10.

Shook, G. L., Rosales, S. A., & Glenn, S. (2002). Certification and training of behavior analyst professionals. *Behavior Modification*, 26(1), 27–48.

STAFF

BEHAVIOR ASSESSMENT SYSTEM FOR CHILDREN-2

The Behavior Assessment System for Children-2 (BASC-2, 2004) is a multimethod, multidimensional system that is used to evaluate the behavior and self-perceptions of children of ages 2 years 6 months to 21 years 11 months. It is made up of five components, each of which may be used individually or in any combination:

The Teacher Rating Scales (TRS) is a comprehensive measure of both adaptive and problem behaviors in the school setting that is intended to be filled out by teachers or others who fill a similar role. The respondent rates descriptors of behaviors on a four-point scale of frequency, ranging from never to almost always. It takes 10 to 20 minutes to complete and has three forms with items targeted at three age levels: preschool (2½ to 5), child (6 to 11), and adolescent (12 to 21). The composite scores include Externalizing Problems, Internalizing Problems, School Problem, Adaptive Skills, and a broad composite, the Behavioral Symptoms Index (BSI). The TRS has various optional content scales that assist in the interpretation of the primary BASC-2 scales and also broaden the assessment to include recent concerns in behavioral assessment (e.g., bullying, anger control, evaluation of bipolar disorder). The TRS includes a validity check to detect a negative response set on the part of the teacher doing the rating.

The Parent Rating Scales (PRS) is a comprehensive measure of a child's adaptive and problem behaviors in community and home settings. The PRS uses the same four-choice response format as the TRS and also takes 10 to 20 minutes to complete. The PRS assesses the same clinical problems and adaptive behavior domains as the TRS; however, it does not include the school problems composite or the Learning Problems and Study Skills Scales. The PRS includes a validity check to assess the validity of the parent ratings.

The Self-Report of Personality (SRP) is a personality inventory that consists of true/false statements. It takes about 30 minutes to complete and has two forms: child (ages 6 to 7 or 8 to 11) and adolescent (ages 12 to 21). The composite scores include School Maladjustment, Clinical Maladjustment, Personal Adjustment, and on overall composite score, the Emotional Symptoms Index (ESI), which is composed of both negative (clinical) scales and positive (adaptive) scales. Indexes are incorporated to assess the validity of the child's responses. The SRP has various optional content scales to assist in the interpretation of the primary BASC-2 Scales and also broaden the assessment to include recent concerns in behavioral assessment (e.g., anger control, ego strength). The Structured Development History (SDH) is an extensive survey of a child's social and medical information. The SDH, completed by a clinician during an interview with parent or guardian, is useful in the diagnostic and treatment process.

The Student Observation System (SOS) is a form for recording a direct observation of the classroom behavior of a child. Children's positive and negative behaviors are recorded using the technique of momentary time sampling during 3-second intervals spaced 30 seconds apart over a 15-minute period. It can be used when initially assessing the child as part of the diagnostic process, and also repetitively to evaluate the effectiveness of treatment programs.

The BASC-2 Parent Ratings Scales, Self-Report of Personality, and the Structured Developmental History are available in Spanish as well as English.

The BASC-2 composite scores are converted to T-scores that have a mean of 50 and a standard deviation of 10. The manual that accompanies the BASC-2 contains instructions for administering and scoring the TRS, PRS, and SRP, and provides information for using the SDH and SOS. It also has information on the development, appropriate uses, validity, reliability, and interpretation of all components of the BASC-2. There are three formats available for the TRS, PRS, and SRP: hand-scoring, computer entry, and scannable forms. The hand-scoring forms allow the teacher, parent, or child to record their responses next to the items rather than on a separate answer sheet. These forms are printed in a convenient self-scoring format, which allows them to be scored rapidly without using templates or keys. The computer-entry forms are designed to allow users to key item responses into a personal computer in about 5 minutes. The scannable forms are designed for use with mark-read (bubble) scanners. There is also a Spanish edition of the Parent Rating Scales that is available in hand-scoring or computer-entry format. The BASC-2 Rating Scales Online offers a web-based system of data collection with forms that parents, caregivers, and teachers can complete online from any computer connected to the Internet.

The standardization sample used a total of 116 testing sites that were selected to provide diversity in geographic region, socioeconomic status, and culture and ethnicity. The sample included 3,065 individuals who completed the TRS, 4,042 individuals who completed the PRS, and 9,861 who completed the SRP. These samples were representative of the 1990 U.S. census. During data gathering, at each participating institution, two classrooms were selected per grade. Two male and two female children from each classroom were randomly selected for teacher ratings, and two of these four (one male and one female) were selected for parent ratings. All classroom members from grades 3 through 12 completed the SRP. This data gathering technique resulted in substantial overlap between the norm samples for the TRS, PRS, and SRP.

The internal consistency reliability for the TRS and SRP averaged about .80 for all three levels—preschool (P), child (C), and adolescent (A). The internal consistency was in the middle .80s to low .90s for the PRS. The test-retest reliability of the TRS had median values of .89, .91, and .92 and the PRS had median values of .85, .88, and .70 for the scales at the three age levels, respectively. The test-retest reliability for the SRP had a median value of .76 at each level.

Evidence of convergent validity of the BASC is based on its correlations with several other measures. The Behavior Symptoms Index (BSI) of the TRS correlates .92 and .90 with the Teacher's Report Form Total Problems score in the child and adolescent samples, respectively. There was a .76 correlation between the TRS Aggression scale and the Revised Behavior Problem Checklist Conduct Disorder Scale. Additionally, there was a .69 correlation between the TRS Depression scale and the Conners' Teacher Rating Scales Emotional Indulgent scale. Correlations between PRS scales and CBCL scales that have similar content are quite high. The level of correlation between PRS and PIC-R scales is moderate, with the highest values being in the .50s. The SRP Clinical Maladjustment composite correlates .89 with the anxiety factor, .82 with the Psychasthenia Scale, .78 with the Schizophrenia Scale, and .72 with the Psychopathic Deviate. The MMPI Anxiety Scale has high correlations with numerous SRP scales: .83 with the Social Stress Scale, .76 with the Anxiety and Sense of Inadequacy Scales, and .74 with the Depression Scale. This entry used data and information combined from Resorla, 2009; Stein, 2007; Tan, 2007; Waggoner, 2005; Watson & Wickstrom, 2007; Pearson.com.

REFERENCES

Rescorla, L. A. (2009). *Assessing childhood psychopathology and developmental disabilities*. I & M. L. Matson (Eds.), pp. 117–149. New York, NY: Springer.

Stein, S. (2007). Review of behavioral assessment system for children, second edition (BASC-2). In K. F. Geisinger, R. A. Spies, J. F. Carlson, & B. S. Plake (Eds.), *The seventeenth mental measurements yearbook*. Lincoln, NE: Buros Institute of Mental Measurements.

Tan, C. S. (2007). Test review: Reynolds, C. R., & Kamphaus, R. W. (2004). Behavior assessment system for children (2nd ed.). Circle Pines, MN: American Guidance Service. *Assessment for Effective Intervention 32*: 121–124.

Waggoner, C. E. (2005). Comparison of the BASC-2 PRS to the BASC PRS in a population of children and adolescents classified as HFA, Asperger disorder or PDD NOS including convergent validity. (Doctoral dissertation.)

Watson, T. S., & Wickstrom, K. (2007). *Review of the behavior assessment system for children* (2nd ed.). In Geisinger, K. F., Spies, R. A., Carlson, J. F., & Plake, B. S. (Eds.), *The seventeenth mental measurements yearbook*. Lincoln, NE: Buros Institute of Mental Measurements

Pearson Assessment.com http://www.pearsonassessments.com/HAIWEB/Cultures/en-us/Productdetail.htm?Pid=PAa30000

RON DUMONT
Fairleigh Dickinson University

JOHN O. WILLIS
Rivier College

KATHLEEN VIEZEL
Fairleigh Dickinson University

JAMIE ZIBULSKY
Fairleigh Dickinson University

BEHAVIOR CHARTING

Behavior charting is a term to describe a graphic or visual representation of behavioral data. Graphing behavioral data allows the special educator to see changes easily in target behaviors (behaviors that are to be increased or decreased in frequency or duration). The ordinate, or vertical line, of the graph is labeled with the behavioral measurement scale. This could be the number of occurrences of off-task behavior, the number of fights a child has, or the percentage of time that a child follows instructions. The abscissa, or horizontal line, is labeled with the unit of time. This could be treatment sessions, days, weeks, minutes, or other intervals over which changes in behavior can be measured (Sulzer-Azaroff & Mayer, 1977).

REFERENCE

Sulzer-Azaroff, B., & Mayer, G. R. (1977). *Applying behavior-analysis procedures with children and youth*. New York, NY: Holt, Rinehart, & Winston.

RANDY W. KAMPHAUS
Georgia State University

See also Applied Behavior Analysis

BEHAVIOR, DESTRUCTIVE (See Destructive Behaviors)

BEHAVIOR DISORDERS

Students with behavior disorders demonstrate a prolonged pattern of behavior that is considered maladaptive or problematic relative to age, cultural, and ethnic norms and across settings and interventions, to an extent that interferes with their ability to function in their environment (e.g., Kauffman, 2005). Students with behavior disorders may exhibit (1) *externalizing* behaviors (i.e., behaviors that are focused outward, including physical aggression, property destruction, self-injurious behavior, and verbal aggression), (2) *internalizing* behaviors (i.e., behaviors that are focused inward including social withdrawal), or (3) a *combination* of externalizing and internalizing behaviors. Although the label *behaviorally disordered* or BD is preferred by some school professionals, as it may be "more accurate" and "less stigmatizing" (Kauffman, 2005, p. 6), federal legislation uses the label *emotionally disturbed* or ED.

Federal Definition

The regulations for the Individuals with Disabilities Education Improvement Act of 2004 provide the federal definition for *emotional disturbance*.

(i) *Emotional disturbance* means a condition exhibiting one or more of the following characteristics over a long period of time and to a marked degree that adversely affects a child's educational performance:

  (A) An inability to learn that cannot be explained by intellectual, sensory, or health factors.
  (B) An inability to build or maintain satisfactory interpersonal relationships with peers and teachers.
  (C) Inappropriate types of behavior or feelings under normal circumstances.
  (D) A general pervasive mood of unhappiness or depression.
  (E) A tendency to develop physical symptoms or fears associated with personal or school problems.

(ii) Emotional disturbance includes schizophrenia. The term does not apply to children who are socially maladjusted, unless it is determined that they have an emotional disturbance under paragraph (c)(4)(i) of this section. (34 CFR Part 300.8(c)(4), Office of Special Education and Rehabilitative Services [OSERS], 2006)

This definition has been greatly criticized; as Cullinan (2004) discusses, arriving at an agreed on definition ED or BD is a complicated and currently unfinished process. As a result, the federal definition has remained unchanged since 1977 (Office of Special Education and Rehabilitative Services [OSERS], 2006).

Varying Labels

Various combinations of adjectives (e.g., *emotionally, behaviorally, socially,* and *personally*) and terms (*disturbed, disordered, maladjusted, handicapped, conflicted,*

impaired) are found in the research literature, legislation, and other materials (Kauffman, 2005). As a general rule, educators should use the federally accepted label (ED) when discussing eligibility for special education services and the preferred label (BD) when conversing with other professionals.

Etiology and Diagnosis of BD

Although the specific cause(s) have not been determined, most researchers suggest that BD results from interplay of biological and environmental factors (Kauffman, 2005). Behavior disorders are typically identified through a multistage assessment process (e.g., *Systematic Screening for Behavior Disorders;* Walker & Severson, 1990), and screening should begin as early as possible (Kauffman, 2005). In general, this process should involve multiple methods (e.g., interviews, observations, norm and criterion referenced assessments) and multiple informants (parents, school professionals, the child when appropriate) across multiple settings and time. Additionally, students must meet federal, state, and district eligibility criteria to receive special education services under the category of ED.

Evidence-Based Intervention Practices

Research shows that students with behavior disorders, like many students, benefit from a consistent, predictable, and positive environment. Schoolwide and setting-specific positive behavior interventions have produced positive effects (e.g., decreases in inappropriate and increases in appropriate behavior) for all students, including those with behavior disorders (e.g., Safran & Oswald, 2003). When individualized supports are necessary, students with behavior disorders benefit from function-based behavior intervention plans (e.g., Ingram, Lewis-Palmer, & Sugai, 2005). That is, plans that take into account (1) why the student is engaging in inappropriate behavior (e.g., to get access to or to escape from something), (2) teach the student new skills that meet the same function, and (3) ensure that the student is more successful in meeting their needs through appropriate skills than inappropriate behavior (Crone & Horner, 2003).

Further, Lane, Jolivette, Conroy, Nelson, and Benner (2011) provide four recommendations to support students with emotional or behavioral disorders: (1) implement evidence-based practices with integrity, (2) invest in a systems-level approach (e.g., schoolwide positive behavior support, response to intervention), (3) use applied and "service-based" research to continue to identify and document evidence-based practices, and (4) provide pre- and in-service professional development supports to develop the skills of teachers and other staff. By following these recommendations, services for students with emotional or behavioral disorders will be enhanced.

REFERENCES

Crone, D. A., & Horner, R. H. (2003). *Building positive behavior support systems in schools: Functional behavioral assessment.* New York, NY: Guilford Press.

Cullinan, D. (2004). Classification and definition of emotional and behavioral disorders. In R. B. Rutherford, M. M. Quinn, & S. R. Mathur (Eds.), *Handbook of research in emotional and behavioral disorders* (pp. 94–110). New York, NY: Guilford Press.

Ingram, K., Lewis-Palmer, T., & Sugai, G. (2005). Function-based intervention planning: Comparing the effectiveness of FBA indicated and contra-indicated intervention plans. *Journal of Positive Behavior Interventions, 7,* 224–236.

Kauffman, J. M. (2005). *Characteristics of emotional and behavioral disorders of children and youth* (8th ed.). Upper Saddle River, NJ: Pearson.

Lane, K. L., Jolivette, K., Conroy, M., Nelson, C. M., & Benner, G. J. (2011). Future research directions for the field of E/BD: Standing on the shoulders of giants. *Education and Treatment of Children, 34,* 423–443.

Office of Special Education and Rehabilitative Services, Department of Education. (2006). 34 CFR Parts 300 and 301: Assistance to states for the education of children with disabilities and preschool grants for children with disabilities; Final Rule. *Federal Register, 71,* 46756. Retrieved from http://idea.ed.gov/download/finalregulations.pdf

Safran, S. P., & Oswald, K. (2003). Positive behavior supports: Can schools reshape disciplinary practices? *Exceptional Children, 6,* 361–373.

Walker, H., & Severson, H. (1990). *Systematic screening for behavior disorders* (SSBD). Longmont, CO: Sopris.

BRANDI SIMONSEN

See also Behavior Assessment System for Children-2; Emotional Disorders; Emotional Lability

BEHAVIOR INTERVENTION PLANS

Behavior intervention plans are targeted plans for individual students to address problem behaviors and skills needed for improvement. They result from a process called *functional assessment*, which is a systematic way to determine the factors that reliably predict and maintain behavior over time. It is a multifaceted approach that utilizes data from teacher interviews, observations, and team meetings to establish the antecedents that predict the behavior, an operational definition of the behavior, and the consequences that occur after the behavior. With this information, teams can create behavior intervention plans that are matched to student need.

Behavior intervention plans are based on a number of premises. First, behavior is predictable and alterable, rather than unpredictable (Crone & Horner, 2000). With enough information about the antecedents and consequences for the behaviors, behavior intervention plans will be targeted and specific, so that the methods create positive behavior change in students. Second, approaches are proactive and preventative, rather than reactive and punitive. The focus is on promoting positive behavior, rather than punishing negative behavior. Students receive reinforcement for engaging in positive behaviors, in addition to receiving punishment as needed. Finally, interventions for high-risk students are individually tailored to what is promoting and sustaining the behavior (Crone & Horner, 2000). Educators engage in strategies specifically developed for the student in need, rather than selecting from a series of interventions previously tried with others. Students receive specifically what they need, so that behavior change is possible.

Comprehensive intervention plans are hypothesis driven, person-centered and uniquely tailored to an individual's typical daily routines across home, school, and community settings (Bambara & Knoster, 1998). The five component parts of behavior intervention plans include (1) antecedent strategies, (2) teaching strategies, (3) consequent strategies, (4) evaluation, and (5) generalization and maintenance strategies.

Antecedent Strategies

Effective teachers understand that the most successful classroom management procedures are proactive (e.g., establishing clear expectations and establishing rapport with students). In a similar sense, antecedent and setting event interventions address both the fast and slow triggers that set the stage for problem behavior with the student of concern. Specifically, interventions are put into place to eliminate or modify the fast and slow triggers to problem behavior as identified in the hypotheses formulated through the functional behavior assessment process. Manipulation of antecedents is powerful in that it (1) provides immediate relief from frustrating and problematic situations, and (2) expands opportunities to teach socially acceptable alternative skills. Antecedent intervention typically involves combinations of the following techniques: (1) removing a problem event (e.g., not asking a student to read aloud), (2) modifying a problem event (e.g., reducing the number of math problems on an independent worksheet), (3) interspersing difficult or unpleasant events with easy or pleasant events (e.g., having two mastery level problems for each instructional level problem on a worksheet), (4) adding events that promote desired behavior (e.g., building into activities things of interest to the student such as selecting reading on a topic of interest), and (5) blocking or neutralizing the impact of negative events (e.g., allowing for opportunities for the student to get up and get a drink on hot days).

Teaching Strategies

Effective behavior intervention plans teach socially acceptable alternative skills that enable the student to achieve desired outcomes. Typically individuals (students) engage in serious problem behavior because (1) they do not have the skills to meet their needs in a socially acceptable manner (i.e., skill deficit) or (2) they have learned that the problem behavior brings about the desired results more efficiently than socially acceptable alternatives. In either case, behavior intervention plans focus on teaching socially acceptable alternative skills that will enable the student to achieve the desired outcome (function). There are three types of alternative skills that should be targeted in behavior intervention plans: (1) functional equivalents that serve the exact same function as the problem behavior (e.g., raising hand in class to gain attention as opposed to yelling and jumping up and down out of seat), (2) general skills that help to alter problem situations and prevent the need for problem behavior (e.g., improve general reading skills so that when reading tasks are assigned they create less stress for the student), and (3) coping skills that teach students to cope or tolerate difficult situations (e.g., teach the student to take a cleansing breath and close his eyes to calm down when stressed). Each of these types of alternative skills should be part of teaching strategies in a behavior intervention plan.

Consequent Strategies

Consequent strategies are used to reinforce the acquisition and use of socially acceptable alternative skills as well as reduce the effectiveness of problem behavior. Reinforcement for the student's use of the functional equivalent is best delivered by providing access to the function (e.g., providing attention when appropriately requested as opposed to problem behavior). Reinforcement for general and coping skills may take many forms including verbal praise combined with stickers or points. When redirection for problem behavior occurs, the students of concern should be redirected to use their targeted alternative skills (e.g., saying "stop grabbing my arm; I want you to say help to get my attention"). Practitioners should strive to reinforce the student of concern for appropriate behavior five times for every one time that redirection for problem behavior occurs (Madsen & Madsen, 1974; Martin & Pear, 1999; Stuart, 1971).

Evaluation

The effects of the intervention plan are evaluated through the review of behavioral data gathered. Practitioners use a single case study design to analyze the treatment effects (e.g., A/B, withdrawal, multiple baseline). To determine treatment effectiveness, it is necessary to collect data before the intervention is implemented (baseline) during the treatment period, as well as during follow-up activities. In addition, practitioners identify measurable goals for the student with regard to progress toward the reduction in the problem behavior and acquisition of the replacement behavior. Measurable goals should identify the student, target behavior, conditions of the intervention, and criteria for acceptable performance. Behaviors should also be defined in concrete and observable terms, such that an independent observer would understand and interpret the behavior in the same way as the person writing the goal.

An important component of intervention implementation is the collection of formative evaluation data, as it allows a practitioner to make important decisions about how well the intervention is suited for the students' needs. Frequent and repeated monitoring of student progress over time is the most reliable way to evaluate an intervention (Batsche et al., 2005; Carter & Sugai, 1989). Progress monitoring should occur regularly over time to assess the student's responsiveness to the intervention. For example, if a student has not exhibited the use of the replacement behavior after 4 weeks of intervention, a practitioner may decide to increase the time the student spends in the intervention to improve skill acquisition.

Summative evaluation should also occur after a longer amount of time when students are expected to have reached their goal. Practitioners should analyze all of the data collected and decide how much the behavior changed due to the intervention and whether the student reached his or her goal. This will help to determine overall treatment effectiveness and is often calculated using an effect size statistic. The four-point rule has also been identified as a particularly helpful decision-making strategy for practitioners (Salvia et al., 2010). The strategy requires a practitioner to create a graphical representation of both the student goal and progress toward the goal. During data analysis, a goal or aimline is used as an indicator of success. Each data point collected after intervention implementation is plotted and the final four consecutive data points are examined. If the final four data points fall below the goal line (if the goal is in the positive direction), a change in the intervention is considered. If the data points fall above the goal line, the intervention is discontinued or conditions of the intervention are changed to begin generalization and maintenance procedures. If the final four data points are scattered above and below the goal line, the intervention is continued and progress is monitored for additional time.

Generalization and Maintenance Strategies

Generalization and maintenance strategies are used to help the students change their behavior in contexts outside of those that were used in the specific intervention. The goal is for the student to exhibit similar behaviors to those achieved through the intervention in other settings (generalization) and over extended lengths of time (maintenance). For example, students who learn to raise their hand in math class to answer questions after the implementation of an intervention should be expected to also learn to display this behavior in similar classroom settings (e.g., reading, social studies) and for months past the initiation of the intervention. Several strategies are related to the technology of generalization (Stokes & Bear, 1977).

Natural maintaining contingencies involves a strategy in which generalization can be achieved by introducing natural reinforcement in response to the presence of a desired behavior or absence of an undesired behavior. *Training sufficient exemplars* involves a strategy in which a behavior is generalized to other environments by training the individual with many examples of stimulus conditions and responses in the new environment. *Train loosely* is a technique in which control over the stimuli and responses involved is lessened and generalization is enhanced. *Indiscriminable contingencies* refers to a strategy where conditions are made less predictable for a student so that it becomes more difficult to discriminate when reinforcement should and should not occur. *Common stimuli* are used in generalization programming by incorporating social and physical stimuli in generalization settings into training sessions so as to familiarize the student with stimuli from other environments. *Mediated generalization* requires establishing a new response that is likely to be used in other problem situations. Finally, *training "to generalize"* refers to the concept of reinforcing generalization itself, as if it were a distinct behavior.

In summary, behavior intervention plans are specific and targeted plans that support promotion of positive behaviors. Students benefit from these plans because they are taught new skills and provided reinforcement and punishment as needed when engaging in behaviors. When designing these plans, the ultimate goal is to help the child, thus, plans should be individualized to meet each student's needs. The premise of using behavior intervention plans is that with these strategies in place, positive behavior change is possible. This perspective, along with targeted supports, allows students to alter their behavior in ways that are comprehensive, durable, and socially significant.

REFERENCES

Bambara, L. M., & Knoster, T. (1998). *Designing positive behavior support plans*. Washington, DC: American Association on Mental Retardation.

Batsche, G., Elliott, J., Graden, J. L., Grimes, J., Kovaleski, J. F., Prasse, D., et al. (2005). *Response to intervention: Policy considerations and implementation*. Alexandria, VA: National Association of State Directors of Special Education.

Crone, D. A., & Horner, R. H. (2000). Contextual, conceptual, and empirical foundations of functional behavioral assessment in schools. *Exceptionality*, 8(3), 161–172.

Carter, J., & Sugai, G. (1989). Survey on prereferral practices: Responses from state departments of education. *Exceptional children*, 55, 298–302.

Madsen, C. H., Jr., & Madsen, C. R. (1974). *Teaching discipline: Behavior principles towards a positive approach*. Boston, MA: Allyn & Bacon.

Martin, G., & Pear, J. (1999). *Behavior modification. 6th ed.* Upper Saddle River, NJ: Prentice Hall.

Salvia, J., Ysseldyke, J., & Bolt, S. (2010). *Assessment in special and inclusive education* (11th ed.). Belmont, CA: Wadsworth Cengage Learning.

Silberglitt, B., & Hintze, J. (2005). Formative assessment using CBM-R cut scores to track progress toward success on state-mandated achievement tests: A comparison of methods. *Journal of Psychoeducational Assessment*, 23, 304–325.

Stuart, R. B. (1971). Assessment and change of the communication patterns of juvenile delinquents and their parents. In R. D. Rubin, H. Fernsterheim, A. A. Lazarus, & C. M. Franks (Eds.), *Advances in behavior therapy* (pp. 183–196). NY: Academic Press.

Tim Knoster
Third edition

Kristy Kelly
Chicago School of Professional Psychology
Fourth edition

Kelly McGraw
Chicago School of Professional Psychology
Fourth edition

BEHAVIORISM

The root of behaviorism is the term *behavior*, which may be defined as the set or universe of things an organism can do, or more simply, what an organism does. Typically, behavior is a term used in the fields of psychology or sociology to describe human or animal activity, but it is important to note that the term can be, and is, applied to a wide range of other things, including plants, simple microorganisms, machines, and even subatomic particles. The critical attribute is that the activities or functions of the organism must be observable and therefore capable of being measured. Just as it is possible to speak of the behavior of single organisms of varying complexity and composition, it is also possible to examine the behavior of organisms in groups. The empirical emphasis of the term behavior is especially prominent in the United States, where the term is associated with a particular school of psychology known as *behaviorism*. Behaviorism has its philosophical roots in the radical empiricist traditions of early thinkers such as John Locke and David Hume in Europe and in the 20th-century movement known as *logical positivism*. The common thread philosophically is that behavior may be (and, for some, must be) understood purely as a lawful phenomenon in itself, without reference to intervening variables such as will, mind, volition, or motivation, which purport to explain why behavior occurs.

Early in the 20th century, the young discipline of psychology was quite concerned with such concepts as will and mind, notably in the work of introspectionists such as Titchner. However, when Pavlov and his colleagues demonstrated that learning was a process whose parameters could be empirically specified and whose results could be reliably predicted, psychologists such as John Watson saw that human behavior could be studied in a simpler, more elegant way, as other sciences were being studied. Watson articulated his position as follows: "Psychology, as the behaviorist views it, is a purely objective, experimental branch of science which needs introspection as little as do the sciences of chemistry and physics" (1913, p. 176). Watson's fervent rejection of the idea of introspection, mental states, or any other nonempirical behavior analysis has earned him general recognition as the founder of behaviorism.

It remained for later thinkers, notably Edward L. Thorndike and B. F. Skinner, to refine and clearly articulate behaviorism. Watson had emphasized stimulus conditions (following Pavlov's respondent conditioning principles) in his work; the most famous example was his introduction of the fear of a white rat in a young boy (Watson & Rayner, 1920). Thorndike (1935), through his Law of Effect, and Skinner (1953), through his Principle of Reinforcement, argued that the consequences of response determine much of what we learn. Skinner in particular has written extensively of the many ways in which this operant conditioning can be observed and applied in our daily affairs. Like Watson before him, Skinner adamantly rejects the need for a psychology of the mind or any other attempt to understand behavior in subjective terms. For Skinner, behavior is conditioned by external events, and as such it can be controlled, predicted, and studied by empirical methods. The wide range of studies of both human and animal learning (Kazdin, 1975; Kimble, 1961) as a function of behavioral methods demonstrate how powerful the principles of behaviorism can be when effectively applied.

More recently, behaviorists cautiously have begun to reexamine the role of mental processes in determining behavior. Members of this new school of thought, sometimes called *cognitive behaviorism*, include psychologists such as Albert Bandura (1977) and Donald Meichenbaum (1977). Reconsideration of the role of mental process in behavior has come about for two reasons. First, certain kinds of learning, such as modeling, occur in the absence of typical observable consequences. It is thought that in some cases a form of self-reinforcement (or perhaps self-punishment) through language is responsible for strengthening the behavior (Bandura, 1977). Others (e.g., Meichenbaum, 1977) have noted that traditional behavioral learning paradigms have been too simplistic to account for the wide array of individual differences in behavior, especially among humans. Even unyielding behavioral analyses such as Skinner's make use of variables such as reinforcement history, which imply some sort of cognitive process in mediating across gaps in time.

The influence of behavioristic thought in psychology is undeniable. The emphasis on empirical research conditions that seemed so strident and incongruous in Watson's time is now taught as the basis of good research, and the importance of both Pavlovian and Skinnerian conditioning has been observed even in popular literature. Behavioristic methods of treatment occupy a prominent place in the study of psychopathology, and behavioral principles are being applied in industrial/organizational settings. As the school of thought broadens its consideration of variables involved in behavior, it holds even brighter promise as a tool for understanding what we do and why we do it.

As the field continues to move forward and grow in understanding behavior and the multiple components that surround behavior, a move toward recognizing behaviorism as the field of cognitive science has emerged. Higher mental processes such as evaluation, motivation, goal-setting, and social judgment affect social interactions (Bargh & Ferguson, 2000). Behaviorists continue to focus on the external environment causes and cognitive psychologists continue to study the mental processes and their reaction to the environment in which they occur (Bargh & Ferguson, 2000). While automaticity seen in psychological processes may be influenced by the environment, further evaluation of executive processing and its relation to behavior and the environment research is needed to continue to discover the field.

REFERENCES

Bandura, A. (1977). Self-efficacy: Toward a unifying theory of behavioral change. *Psychological Review, 84*, 191–215.

Bargh, J. A., & Ferguson, M. J. (2000). Beyond behaviorism: On the automaticity of higher mental processes. *Psychological Bulletin, 126*(6), 925–945.

Kazdin, A. (1975). *Behavior modification in applied settings.* Homewood, IL: Dorsey.

Kimble, G. A. (1961). *Hilgard and Marquis' conditioning and learning* (2nd ed.). New York, NY: AppletonCentury-Crofts.

Meichenbaum, D. (1977). *Cognitive behavior modification: An integrative approach.* New York, NY: Plenum Press.

Skinner, B. F. (1953). *Science and human behavior.* New York, NY: Free Press.

Thorndike, E. L. (1935). *The psychology of wants, interests and attitudes.* New York, NY: Appleton-Century.

Watson, J. (1913). Psychology as the behaviorist views it. *Psychological Review, 20*, 1958–1977.

Watson, J., & Rayner, R. (1920). Conditioning emotional responses. *Journal of Experimental Psychology, 3*, 1–14.

JERRY L. SLOAN
Wilmington Psychiatric Associates

See also **Behavior Modification; Psychoanalysis and Special Education; Social Learning Theory**

BEHAVIOR MODELING

Modeling is a training intervention that was popularized by social learning theory and the works of Albert Bandura (1971). When using this procedure, the practitioner physically demonstrates the behavior for the student or shows a visual representation (e.g., photo sequence, video) of the production of the behavior (Charlop-Christy & Daneshvar, 2003). In essence, the practitioner shows the student the appropriate way to respond. The demonstration often includes secondary informational sources such as feedback about the model's success and the environmental and contextual cues that led the model to behave in the particular fashion demonstrated. Modeling, particularly video-based modeling, has been shown to be effective with a broad range target behaviors such as gymnastics skills (Boyer, Miltenberger, Batsche, & Fogel, 2009), discrete-trial instruction (Catania, Almeida, Liu-Constant & Digennaro Reed, 2009) and letter recognition (Marcus & Wilder, 2009).

The effectiveness of this procedure can be enhanced through attention to several variables. Of primary consideration are the characteristics of the person providing the model. In some cases the person who demonstrates the behavior could be another student. This would be appropriate when the other student is (1) competent to do the behavior; (2) someone with whom the student can identify (i.e., similar to themselves); (3) someone held in high esteem by the target student; (4) able to demonstrate the behavior clearly; (5) able to demonstrate novel responses that the target student has not yet learned to do; and (6) reinforced for the performance of the target behavior.

Target student factors are also important to the modeling process. First, the student must be sufficiently motivated to become an active participant in the modeling process. An absence of sufficient motivation will negate the qualities of the model and the modeling event. Second, the attention of the student must be keyed to the relevant properties of the modeled behavior. Third, the student must have sufficient motor abilities to replicate the modeled behavior. Finally, the ability of the student to remember and recall the modeled act will greatly affect the general and functional utility of the modeled behavior. This retention is based on two processes: memory and linguistic representation. In the first case, when stimuli are consistently paired, the occurrence of one of the paired stimuli will signal the other. In the second case, labeling of an event (through receptive or expressive means) lends saliency to the event.

Modeling, therefore, is a useful instructional procedure. As a technology for instruction, it requires that its users follow specific procedures to produce maximum results. These procedures are neither esoteric nor difficult to follow. Modeling is thought to be an evidence-based practice, and because it is usable in most environments, modeling should be considered to be an instructional procedure of choice under most circumstances.

REFERENCES

Bandura, A. (1971). Analysis of modeling processes. In A. Bandura (Ed.), *Psychological modeling: Conflicting theories*. Chicago, IL: Aldine-Atherton.

Boyer, E., Miltenberger, R. G., Batsche, C., & Fogel, V. (2009) Video modeling by experts with video feedback to enhance gymnastic skills. *Journal of Applied Behavior Analysis*, *42*, 855–860.

Catania, C. N., Almeida, D., Liu-Costant, B., & DiGennaro Reed, F. D. (2009). Video modeling to train staff to implement discrete-trial instruction. *Journal of Applied Behavior Analysis*, *42*, 387–392.

Charlop-Christy, M. H., & Daneshvar, S. (2003). Video modeling for individuals with autism: A perspective taking to children with autism. *Journal of Positive Behavior Intervention*, *5*, 12–21.

Cooper, J. O., Heron, T. E. & Heward, W. L (2007). *Applied behavior analysis* (2nd ed.). Upper Saddle River, NJ: Pearson.

Marcus, A., & Wilder, D. A. (2009). A comparison of peer video modeling and self video modeling to teach textual responses in children with autism. *Journal of Applied Behavior Analysis*, *42*, 355–341.

LYLE E. BARTON
Kent State University

BEHAVIOR MODIFICATION

Behavior modification is generally regarded as a term that encompasses the various methods derived from learning theory that are used to alter the response patterns of humans and other animals. The term has been used in this way by Bandura (1969); he and other behaviorists such as Skinner (1965) have enumerated a wide variety of learning principles that have been translated into methods for learning or changing behavior.

Although behavior modification is sometimes considered as a unitary position in discussions of certain issues in psychology, the techniques involved are derived from several different theoretical approaches to learning. Each approach tends to emphasize environmental determinants, as opposed to person-based determinants, of individual differences among organisms in the way in which they learn behavior. On the other hand, each approach also emphasizes the importance of determining the specific environmental variables that influence the behavior of an individual.

One such approach (Wolpe, 1982) is based on classical or respondent conditioning, which was studied extensively early in the 20th century by Ivan Pavlov, the Russian psychologist, and John Watson, the American sometimes known as the father of behaviorism. In this type of learning, a neutral stimulus is paired in time with another stimulus (called the *unconditioned stimulus*) already able to elicit a particular response, usually unlearned, from an organism's repertoire. Through repeated pairings, this neutral stimulus also acquires the capability of eliciting the original (or unconditioned) response; this neutral stimulus is called the conditioned stimulus. For example, Watson and Rayner (1920) performed a classic study in which a neutral stimulus (a white rat) took on fear-inducing properties for a young boy when it was presented to the child paired with a sudden loud noise (an unconditioned stimulus) that startled and frightened the child (the unconditioned response). Soon the child began attempting to avoid the white rat because of its newly acquired association with the loud noise. Classical conditioning is apparently important in establishing subtle types of learning such as attitudes, basic emotional states such as love, fear, and trust, and other similar behaviors acquired over long periods of time.

A second major approach to behavior modification (Skinner, 1965) is based on operant or instrumental conditioning. The basis of this approach is the so-called law of effect articulated by Thorndike (1935). He proposed that responses followed by pleasurable consequences would be strengthened, whereas responses followed by unpleasant consequences would be weakened. This formulation was refined and greatly expanded by others, notably Skinner, who had demonstrated that consequences (Thorndike would have called them *effects*) are important in learning a wide variety of behaviors. Most of these behaviors involve some activity or operation (hence the term *operant conditioning*) in the form of a skill the organism learns. An important derivative of operant conditioning has been described by Premack (1965). He showed that the opportunity to perform a desirable activity may be used as a consequence to reinforce or strengthen the performance of a less preferred activity. Thus a person may be willing to do something relatively unpleasant (perhaps balancing a checkbook or reading a boring book) if this activity is followed soon thereafter by a pleasurable activity (perhaps a movie or a golf outing).

The modification of behavior using the outlined principles of operant conditioning is sometimes called *applied behavior analysis*. Usually this involves detailed empirical specification of the behavior to be changed (or to be learned), careful observation of the contributing conditioning elements, and the development of a strategy (changing antecedent stimulus conditions, response consequences, or both) to achieve the desired results. It is important to note that the use of behavior modification techniques does not require the use of terms such as *normal* or *abnormal* to describe the behavior being examined. In fact, the learning theorists who have contributed to the development of behavior modification techniques assume that behavior is learned according to principles that operate nearly identically in all situations, even though a given observer may have a higher or lower value to place on a particular learned behavior. As a result, descriptive terms such as abnormal are frequently rejected because their use tempts us to infer that different laws of learning have governed the behavior so described.

REFERENCES

Bandura, A. (1969). *Principles of behavior modification*. New York, NY: Holt, Rinehart, & Winston.

Premack, D. (1965). Reinforcement therapy. In D. Levine (Ed.), *Nebraska symposium on motivation*. Lincoln: University of Nebraska Press.

Skinner, B. F. (1965). *Science and human behavior*. New York, NY: Free Press.

Thorndike, E. L. (1935). *The psychology of wants, interests and attitudes*. New York, NY: Appleton, Century.

Watson, J., & Rayner, R. (1920). Conditioning emotional response. *Journal of Experimental Psychology, 3*, 1–14.

Wolpe, J. (1982). *The practice of behavior therapy* (3rd ed.). New York, NY: Pergamon Press.

JERRY L. SLOAN
Wilmington Psychiatric Associates

See also **Applied Behavior Analysis; Operant Conditioning**

BEHAVIOR PROBLEM CHECKLIST, REVISED

The Revised Behavior Problem Checklist (RBPC; Quay & Peterson, 1993) is a widely researched rating scale for the clinical evaluation of deviant behavior. The original Behavior Problem Checklist (BPC) was developed in 1967 and the RBPC is the revised version of this scale. The RBPC consists of four major scales and two minor scales. The major scales include: Conduct Disorder (22 items), Socialized Aggression (17 items), Attention Problems–Immaturity (16 items), and Anxiety–Withdrawal (11 items). The two minor scales are Psychotic Behavior (6 items) and Motor Tension–Excess (5 items). In addition, 12 items are included for research purposes, and do not contribute to the overall score.

The revised version uses a weighted scoring system (2 = severe problem; 1 = mild problem; 0 = not a problem, no opportunity to observe, don't know). One problem associated with this scoring system is the failure to discriminate between the three possible zero responses (Roberts, 1986). Thus a score of zero does not necessarily indicate the absence of a behavior problem. Checklists and scoring templates are included with the manual. The checklists can be completed in approximately 15 minutes by any observer who is familiar with the subject. Scoring templates provide raw scores for each of the four major and two minor scales, and can be completed in 5 to 10 minutes.

Estimates of internal consistency reliability range from .68 to .95. Interrater reliabilities range from .52 to .85. Test-retest reliabilities (2-month interval) range from .49 to .83 ($N = 149$). Support for validity includes a substantial relationship between the RBPC and the BPC, discrimination between normal children and clinical groups, and support from numerous studies for many facets of validity (Dezolt, 1992; Hinshaw Morrison, Carte, & Cornsweet, 1987; Lahay & Piacentini, 1985). The authors do not provide representative norms based on U.S. Census data, but recommend developing local norms. However, the use of local norms without reference to a normative sample may be complicated by such things as cultural variation within communities and transient populations. The manual provides means and standard deviations for scale scores from clinical and nonclinical samples, and from parent and teacher ratings. However, little demographic information is included; thus, it is unclear whether these samples are representative.

The RBPC is a useful screening instrument for assessing behavior problems along four independent dimensions commonly associated with emotional disturbance (Quay, 1993).

REFERENCES

Cutchen, M. A., & Simpson, R. G. (1993). *Interrater reliability among teachers and mental health professionals when using the revised behavior problem checklist, 11*, 4–11. Reviewed in the Buros Institute, *Mental Measurements Yearbook*. Available at http://www.unl.edu/buros/

Dezolt, D. M. (1992). Review of the revised behavior problem checklist. In J. J. Kramer & J. C. Conoley (Eds.), *The eleventh mental measurements yearbook* (pp. 764–765). Lincoln, NE: Buros Institute of Mental Measurements.

Hinshaw, S. P., Morrison, D. C., Carte, E. T., & Cornsweet, C. (1987). Factorial dimensions of the revised behavior problem checklist: Replication and validation within a kindergarten sample. *Journal of Abnormal Child Psychology, 15*, 309–327.

Lahay, B. B., & Piacentini, J. C. (1985). An evaluation of the Quay-Peterson revised behavior problem checklist. *Journal of School Psychology, 23*, 285–289.

Quay, H. C., & Peterson, D. R. (1993). *The revised behavior problem checklist: Manual*. Odessa, FL: Psychological Assessment.

Roberts, T. (1986). Revised behavior problem checklist. In D. L. Keyser & R. C. Sweetland (Eds.), *Test critiques: Volume 5* (pp. 371–377). Kansas City, MO: Test Corporation of America.

Shapiro, E. S. (1992). Review of the revised behavior problem checklist. In J. J. Kramer & J. C. Conoley (Eds.), *The eleventh mental measurements yearbook* (pp. 765–766). Lincoln, NE: Buros Institute of Mental Measurements.

LIZANNE DESTEFANO
University of Illinois

BEHAVIOR RATING INVENTORY OF EXECUTIVE FUNCTION

The Behavior Rating Inventory of Executive Function (BRIEF, 2000) is a Likert-type questionnaire developed to assess a wide range of developmental and acquired neurological conditions in children ages 5 to 18 years. There are two rating forms: one for parents and one for teachers. Each form takes 10 to 15 minutes to complete and 15 to 20 minutes to score. The questionnaires consist of 86 items, although each form uses different questions. Both forms measure eight different aspects of executive functioning: Inhibit, Shift, Emotional Control, Initiate, Working Memory, Plan/Organize, Organization of Materials, and Monitor. In addition to the eight clinical scales, the BRIEF also contains two validity scales (Inconsistency and Negativity), and forms two broader indexes: Behavioral Regulation (three scales) and Metacognition (five scales) as well as a Global Executive Composite score. The BRIEF provides separate normative tables for both the parent and teacher forms with T scores, percentiles, and confidence intervals for four developmental age groups by gender.

Normative data was collected from 1,419 parents and 720 teachers from rural, suburban, and urban areas in Maryland consistent with the 1999 United States Census estimates of socioeconomic status, ethnicity, and gender distribution. Internal consistency is good, ranging from .80 to .98. Reliabilities were similar across teacher and parents forms. All of the clinical scales and composites have high reliability except the Initiate and Shift Scales, which tend to be the least reliable. Test-retest reliabilities were conducted on the parent form clinical and normative samples and the teacher normative sample and were reported in the mid to upper .80s. Inter-rater reliabilities for the parent and teacher raters were moderate ($r = .50$ or below). Divergent validity is reported as adequate; however, convergent validity was difficult to assess as there are few available measures that examine metacognitive functioning.

Reviewers found the materials easy for parents, teachers, and test administrators to use. The protocols are arranged in an efficient manner and are attractive. The rating scales are easy to score by hand and examiners have the option of purchasing a computer scoring program. The manual also includes six case illustrations that are helpful guides to interpretation. One problem is the lack of information regarding interpretation of the BRIEF. Three levels of interpretation are possible: Global Executive Composite, ("child's executive dysfunction level"), Behavioral Regulation Index ("child's ability to switch set"), and Metacognition Index (child's ability to "initiate, plan, organize, and sustain future oriented problem solving"; professional manual, p. 21). It is important to note that the manual does not note how the sites and participants in the pilot were chosen, why more fathers were not solicited to participate, and why the sample was not larger. Additionally, the fact that the sample was only drawn from Maryland may affect the normative data.

In addition to the original BRIEF, there are now several other versions, including: The Behavior Rating Inventory of Executive Function–Adult Version (BRIEF-A; Roth, Isquith, & Gioia, 2005), the Behavior Rating Inventory of Executive Function–Preschool Version (BRIEF-P; Gioia, Espy, & Isquith, 2003), and the Behavior Rating Inventory of Executive Function–Self-Report Version (BRIEF-SR; Guy, Isquith, & Gioia, 2004). The BRIEF-A is both a self- and informant-report measure designed for adults between 18 and 90 years of age. Nine clinical scales are included: Inhibit, Shift, Emotional Control, Self-Monitor, Initiate, Working Memory, Plan/Organize, Task Monitor, and Organization of Materials. Three validity scales also assess response style. The BRIEF-P is completed by parents or teachers of children aged 2 years to 5 years, 11 months. There are five clinical scales on this measure: Inhibit, Shift, Emotional, Control, Working Memory and Plan/Organize, as well as two validity scales. The BRIEF-SR is designed for youth aged 11 to 18 to report on their own executive functioning skills, and like the original BRIEF, generates eight clinical scales, except Task Completion replaces Initiate.

REFERENCES

Fitzpatrick, C. (2003). Review of the behavior rating inventory of executive function. In B. S. Plake, J. C. Impara, & R. A. Spies (Eds.), *The fifteenth mental measurements yearbook*. Lincoln, NE: Buros Institute of Mental Measurements.

Gioia, G. A, Isquith, P. K., Guy S. C., & Kenworthy, L. (2000). Test review behavior rating inventory of executive function. *Child Neuropsychology*, 3, 235–238.

Gioia, G. A, Isquith, P. K., Retzlaff, P. D., & Espy, K. A. (2004). Confirmatory factor analysis of the behavior rating inventory of executive function (BRIEF) in a clinical sample. *Child Neuropsychology*, 8, 249–57.

Gioia, G. A, & Isquith, P. K. (2004). Ecological assessment of executive function in traumatic brain injury. *Developmental Neuropsychology*, 25, 135–158.

Mahone, E. M., Cirino, P. T., Cutting, L. E., Cerrone, P. M., Hagelthorn, K. M., Hiemenz, J. R.,…Denckla, M. B. (2002).Validity of the behavior rating inventory of executive function in children with ADHD and/or Tourette syndrome. *Archives Clinical Neuropsychology*, 17, 643–662.

McAuley, T., Chen, S., Goos, L., Schachar, R., & Crosbie, J. (2010). Is the behavior rating inventory of executive function more strongly associated with measures of impairment or executive function? *Journal of the International Neuropsychological Society*, 16(3), 495–505.

Schraw, G. (2003). Review of the behavior rating inventory of executive function. In B. S. Plake, J. C. Impara, & R. A. Spies (Eds.), *The fifteenth mental measurements yearbook* (pp. 1024–1028). Lincoln, NE: Buros Institute of Mental Measurements.

Sherman, E., & Brooks, B. (2010). Behavior rating inventory of executive function-preschool version (BRIEF-P): Test review and clinical guidelines for use. *Child Neuropsychology*, 16(5), 503–519.

Walker, J. M., & D'Amato, R. C. (2006). Review of "behavior rating inventory of executive function—self-report version." *Journal of Psychoeducational Assessment*, 24(4), 394–398.

KATHLEEN VIEZEL
Fairleigh Dickinson University

JAMIE ZIBULSKY
Fairleigh Dickinson University

RON DUMONT
Fairleigh Dickinson University

JOHN O. WILLIS
Rivier College
Fourth edition

BEHAVIOR THERAPY

Behavior therapy is a term that is not frequently used in 2012. The term encompasses a broad range of philosophical, theoretical, and procedural approaches to the "alleviation of human suffering and the enhancement of human functioning" (Davison & Stuart, 1975, p. 755). An approach to assessment, therapy, ethics, and professional issues, it has been used successfully with a variety of populations (adults, children, adolescents, mentally retarded, etc.) in diverse settings (schools, hospitals, psychiatric facilities, mental health centers, etc.) and for various problems (anxiety, depression, addictive disorders, social skills deficits, psychotic behaviors, marital dysfunction, academic skills, parent-child problems, etc.). There are probably few human behaviors that have not been addressed by behavior therapists.

A number of terms with somewhat different origins and connotations have been used almost interchangeably to denote the field. These terms include *behavior therapy, behavior modification, applied behavior analysis, social learning theory, cognitive-behavior therapy, clinical behavior therapy,* and *multimodal behavior therapy*. Attempts to clarify or standardize the meaning of the various terms based on the populations served (e.g., individual or group), techniques used (e.g., systematic desensitization, contingency management), methodologies (e.g., single-subject designs), or theoretical bases (e.g., classical conditioning, operant conditioning) have failed to gain wide acceptance (Franzini & Tilker, 1972; Wilson, 1978).

Several formal definitions of behavior therapy have been proposed. For example, Wolpe (1982) defined behavior therapy as "the use of experimentally established principles and paradigms of learning to overcome unadaptive habits" (p. 1). Whereas Wolpe's definition emphasizes a theoretical basis of behavior therapy, other definitions stress the methods of inquiry used by behavior therapists. For example, Ross, in his presidential address to the Association for Advancement of Behavior Therapy, defined behavior therapy as "the empirically controlled application of the science of human behavior to the alleviation of psychological distress and the modification of maladaptive behavior" (Ross, 1985, p. 196). This definition reflects the growing acceptance of methodological behaviorism, which focuses on the methods used in obtaining psychological information. Such a definition, however, does not delineate behavior therapy from other construct systems that might also use empirical methods of inquiry.

The difficulty of arriving at a single definition of behavior therapy was well summarized by Kazdin and Wilson (1978):

Contemporary behavior therapy is marked by a diversity of views, a broad range of heterogeneous procedures with different theoretical rationales, and open debate about conceptual bases, methodological requirements, and evidence of efficacy. In short, there is no clearly agreed upon or commonly accepted definition of behavior therapy. (p. 1)

This lack of consensus reflects both the continuous development of behavior therapy and the various models within the behavioral construct system.

At least four major models within behavior therapy can be identified: (1) applied behavior analysis, (2) neobehavioristic mediational model, (3) social learning theory, and (4) cognitive-behavior therapy (Agras, Kazdin, & Wilson, 1979). The models differ on the bases of historical tradition, fundamental principles, and therapeutic procedures.

Applied behavior analysis draws heavily from the Skinner tradition of operant conditioning. Behavior is assumed to be under the control of environmental stimuli. These controlling stimuli include the consequences of behavior as well as the antecedent events that are associated with differential consequences. Intervention involves the manipulation of the controlling environmental stimuli in order to modify overt behavior. Therapeutic procedures are based on principles derived from operant conditioning such as reinforcement, punishment, extinction, and stimulus control. The token economy, in which appropriate behaviors earn tokens that later can be exchanged for desired activities, consumable goods, and privileges, is a procedure representative of applied behavior analysis.

The neobehavioristic mediational model is based primarily on the principles of classical conditioning derived from the learning theories of Pavlov, Hull, and Mowrer (Wolpe, 1982). The model emphasizes the role of anxiety as a conditioned emotional response. For example, the anxiety response can be elicited by previously neutral stimuli as a result of pairing those neutral stimuli with noxious stimuli. Therapeutic procedures such as systematic desensitization and flooding are designed to reduce the anxiety underlying behavioral disorders by exposing the individual to the conditioned, feared stimulus in the absence of the noxious stimulus.

According to the third model, social learning theory (Bandura, 1977), three interacting systems regulate behavior. The first system is external stimulus control, which regulates behavior either through the association of stimuli, as in classical conditioning, or through antecedent stimuli reliably predicting differential consequences of behavior. Response feedback, primarily in the form of reinforcing consequences, provides a second regulatory system. Finally, cognitive processes mediate the effect of external events by influencing which events are attended to and how those events are perceived and interpreted. An important cognitive mediator of behavior change is self-efficacy, the expectation that the behavior required to produce an outcome can be performed. Social learning theory further posits that human functioning is a result of the reciprocal interaction among behavior, the environment, and a person's cognitions (Bandura, 1981). That is, not only does the environment influence behavior, but a person's behavior also influences the environment. Modeling of the desired behavior by the therapist, either with or without the client's subsequent performance, is a therapeutic procedure derived from social learning theory's emphasis on cognitive processes such as the capacity to learn through observation.

The most recent development in behavior therapy is the emergence of cognitive-behavior therapy (Beck, 1976; Mahoney, 1974). According to this model, it is the perception of events rather than the events themselves that most influence behavior. Further, adaptive and maladaptive patterns are acquired through cognitive processes. Thus irrational beliefs, errors of logic, faulty self-talk, dysfunctional attributions, and mental representations of one's self and one's world contribute to behavioral and emotional disorders. Cognitive restructuring, in which clients are taught to examine and change faulty cognitions, is a representative procedure used in cognitive-behavior therapy. Cognitive-behavior therapy has become the treatment of choice for several adult and childhood disorders, including panic, phobic, and obsessive-compulsive disorders. It has also dominated outcome research on psychological therapy (Wilson, 1997).

Despite the diversity of models in the behavioral construct system and the inability to provide a single definition of behavior therapy, a number of characteristics and assumptions of behavior therapy can be delineated (Agras et al., 1979; Haynes, 1984; Kazdin & Hersen, 1980). No one of these characteristics is definitive of the field, nor does anyone necessarily differentiate behavior therapy from other systems. Nevertheless, taken together, they represent the common core of behavior therapy.

One set of characteristics concern five methods of inquiry:

1. There is a commitment to empiricism and scientific methodology as the primary basis for developing and evaluating concepts and therapeutic techniques.
2. There is a commitment to an explicit, testable, and falsifiable conceptual foundation.
3. Therapeutic procedures and hypotheses with sufficient precision to make evaluation, replication, and generalization possible are specified.
4. There are close ties to the experimental findings of the science of psychology.
5. There is a low level of inference about data so as to minimize biases.

These epistemological principles imply that behavior therapy will continue to evolve as new knowledge is gained from empirical findings.

A second set of seven characteristics concerns the assumptions about behavior and behavioral disorders.

1. There is a deterministic model of behavior in which environmental antecedents and consequences are assumed to have the greatest impact on behavior. Recently, interactional models have been introduced in which behavior, the environment, and the person (most notably cognitive events and physiological conditions) are all presumed to influence one another.
2. There is an emphasis on current determinants of behavior as opposed to historical determinants (i.e., early childhood experiences).
3. The same principles that govern normal behavior also govern abnormal behavior. That is, no qualitative difference separates normal from abnormal behavior.
4. There are multiple determinants of behavior. The determinants of behavioral disorders may vary from individual to individual and from one disorder to another.
5. Both the disease model of abnormal behavior and the implication that dysfunctional behavior is a sign or symptom of an underlying illness are rejected. Instead, dysfunctional behavior is construed as a "problem in living" or as learned, maladaptive behavior. Thus the dysfunctional behavior itself is targeted for behavior change.
6. Psychological disorders can be expressed in behavioral, cognitive, and affective modes. These modes can covary to differing degrees owing to situational factors and individual differences.
7. There is the relative specificity of behavior to the situation in which it occurs as opposed to the belief that behavior is consistent across situations.

A third set of six characteristics concerns the methods of behavior change:

1. Therapeutic procedures are derived from experimental-clinical psychology.
2. Therapy is conceptualized as an opportunity to unlearn maladaptive behaviors and to learn adaptive behaviors.
3. The importance of tailoring therapy to the individual based on an assessment of the idiosyncratic determinants of the individual's dysfunctional behavior is emphasized.
4. The importance of the therapist-client interaction as one source of behavior change is emphasized.
5. There is an ongoing evaluation of intervention results in order to modify procedures as needed.
6. Intervention results are generalized from the intervention setting to the client's natural environment.

In conclusion, behavior therapy is a multifaceted and diverse system linked by a common core of assumptions. It is a viable system that has withstood numerous criticisms to emerge as a major approach within the psychological treatment field.

REFERENCES

Agras, W. S., Kazdin, A. E., & Wilson, G. T. (1979). *Behavior therapy: Toward an applied clinical science*. San Francisco, CA: Freeman.

Bandura, A. (1977). *Social learning theory*. Englewood Cliffs, NJ: Prentice Hall.

Bandura, A. (1981). In search of pure unidirectional determinants. *Behavior Therapy, 12*, 30–40.

Beck, A. T. (1976). *Cognitive therapy and the emotional disorders*. New York, NY: International Universities Press.

Davison, G. C., & Stuart, R. B. (1975). Behavior therapy and civil liberties. *American Psychologist, 30*, 755–763.

Franzini, L. R., & Tilker, H. A. (1972). On the terminological confusion between behavior therapy and behavior modification. *Behavior Therapy, 3*, 279–282.

Haynes, S. N. (1984). Behavioral assessment of adults. In M. Hersen & G. Goldstein (Eds.), *Handbook of psychological assessment*. New York, NY: Pergamon Press.

Kazdin, A. E., & Hersen, M. (1980). The current status of behavior therapy. *Behavior Modification, 4*, 283–302.

Kazdin, A. E., & Wilson, G. T. (1978). *Evaluation of behavior therapy: Issues, evidence, and research strategies*. Cambridge, MA: Ballinger.

Mahoney, M. J. (1974). *Cognition and behavior modification*. Cambridge, MA: Ballinger.

Ross, A. O. (1985). To form a more perfect union: It is time to stop standing still. *Behavior Therapy, 16*, 195–204.

Wilson, G. T. (1978). On the much discussed nature of the term "behavior therapy." *Behavior Therapy, 9*, 89–98.

Wilson, G. T. (1997). Behavior therapy at century close. *Behavior Therapy, 28*(3), 449–457.

Wolpe, J. (1982). *The practice of behavior therapy* (3rd ed.). New York, NY: Pergamon Press.

JEFFREY L. PHILLIPS
University of North Carolina at Wilmington

See also Applied Behavior Analysis; Behavior Modification; Desensitization; Social Learning Theory

BELGIUM, SPECIAL EDUCATION IN

Belgium is composed of three regions (Flanders, Wallonia, and Brussels) and includes two linguistic communities (one French speaking and one Flemish speaking). Belgium's federal form of government recognizes and respects regional differences. For example, each linguistic community is responsible for education and health policies. Nevertheless, special education policies and organizational structures are somewhat similar in both linguistic communities. This discussion focuses only on the nature of special education services provided under laws and regulations enacted by the federal state and the French-speaking community of Belgium in order to avoid needless complexity.

Special education services are provided in self-contained schools, those specifically devoted to these programs. Special education students generally are not educated in regular education schools or mainstream classes. Special education programs are organized in reference to the following eight diagnostic categories (Conseil de la Communauté Française de Belgique, 2004). Type 1 addresses the needs of elementary and secondary level students with Mild Intellectual developmental disabilities. The following six categories address the needs of nursery-, elementary-, and secondary-level students who have Moderate Intellectual developmental disabilities (Type 2), behavioral or personality disorders (Type 3), physical disabilities (Type 4), diseases (Type 5), visual disorders (Type 6), and hearing disorders (Type 7). Type 8 is for elementary students who display instrumental disabilities. They include speech, perceptual, and spatial disorders that are assumed to underlie a learning disability. Students who display two or more disability types typically are placed in a program best suited to serve their most dominant disability type. At the secondary-school level, each of the seven types of special education programs is organized in four different forms that correspond to four disability levels. At one extreme, Form 1 is for the most severely disabled children; its goal is to develop adaptive skills. At the other extreme, Form

4 is for the least severely disabled children; its goal is to develop the abilities required for higher education.

During the 2002 to 2003 school year in the French-speaking region of Belgium, 0.6% of nursery school students, 4.6% of elementary school students, and 3.8% of secondary school students were enrolled in a special education program (Ministère de la Communauté Française, 2003). Among them, at the elementary school, 24.7% were enrolled in Type 1, 12.4% in Type 2, 11.2% in Type 3, 4.3% in Type 4, 2.9% in Type 5, 0.5% in Type 6, 2.0% in Type 7, and 42.0% in Type 8. Thus, students with an instrumental disability constitute the largest number of students served in special education at the elementary school. At the secondary school, 52.8% were enrolled in Type 1, 17.8% in Type 2, 19.9% in Type 3, 5.8% in Type 4, 1.3% in Type 5, 1.0% in Type 6, and 1.4% in Type 7. The Type 8 program being no longer organized at the secondary school, a part of the students are directed to Type 1, Type 2, or Type 3 programs, while the others are directed to an ordinary educational program. Thus, at the secondary school, students with Mild Intellectual Developmental Disabilities constitute, by far, the largest number of students served in special education.

Three services offer educational support to families with children who display severe levels of a disability: early assistance services, integration services, and housing services. Early assistance services are intended to help the child with disabilities and his or her family from birth to age 7. They provide educational, social, and psychological support, including educational counseling, coordination of care, and assessment of progress. Integration services provide similar services for children ages 6 through 20, including family guidance, collaborative support between them and special education schools, and other services designed to promote the child's autonomy and social integration. Housing services provide accommodation and educational support for children 24 hours a day when their families are unable to care for them for whatever the reason (e.g., the severity of the disability, distance between home and special education school, parent incompetence).

Special education programs are organized to meet children's special educational needs and to help them to reach their highest level of development. The rights of children and families to access special education resources are guaranteed by law. However, parents are not obligated to access them. Placement in a special education program always requires parental consent. The parents, a teacher, or a physician typically are the first persons to identify physical, behavioral, or learning problems. The children are then referred to a Centre Psycho-Medico-Social (Psychological Medical and Social Center), or a Service de Santé Mentale (Mental Health Service). Psychological Medical and Social Centers are independent bodies, subsidized by the education administration, and collaborate with schools to provide school-based guidance and counseling services. The Psychological Medical and Social Center director always is a psychologist and leads a team composed of several psychologists, social workers, and a nurse. The Mental Health Services comprise independent teams, subsidized by the health administration, who work to prevent mental disorders and provide ambulatory treatment for those with these disorders. The Mental Health Service director always is a psychiatrist and leads a team composed of several psychiatrists, psychologists, and social workers. The Psychological Medical and Social Centers and Mental Health Services are the only services that can authorize the enrollment of a child in a special education program. Authorization for Types 1, 2, 3, 4, and 8 special education programs require a multidisciplinary assessment that culminates in a report that includes medical, psychological, and social information that provides support for the enrollment.

Authorization for Types 5, 6, and 7 special education programs requires only a medical assessment. Policies governing this work discuss the child's personal characteristics to be assessed and diagnostic criteria; preferred methods and tests to be used are not specified (Ministère de l'Education de la Recherche et de la Formation, 1995). Consistent with the need for reports from the Psychological Medical and Social Centers and Mental Health Services, a certificate recommending a special education program must be issued. Parents then may select the school in which the desired program is provided.

A school can provide programs for one or more of the eight diagnostic types. A school's educational team always includes teachers trained in special education, paramedical professionals (e.g., speech-therapists, physical therapists, and nurses), psychologists, and social workers. This team and the associated Psychological Medical and Social Center form the classroom council, the goal of which is to specify an individualized educational program for each student and to appraise a student's development and achievement during the school year. This council also determines the child's specialized treatments (e.g., language, physical, or psychological services). The social workers ensure a relation between school and families, including linking them to their child's educational program.

The development of special education programs can be flexible, with each educational team able to define the program most suited to a child's needs. These programs are not restricted to the traditional school subjects (e.g., mathematics, reading) and may include the development of autonomy, communication skills, and social relationships. The main goal of all the special education programs is to help promote the best adaptation of a child to society.

Issues pertaining to the integration of students with special needs in the ordinary school system have been discussed for some time. Progress has been limited and not likely to increase soon. Only children enrolled in Types 4, 6, or 7 special education programs (and Form 3 or 4 in secondary schools) can be integrated either part time or full time in an ordinary school (Conseil de la Commuauté Française de Belgique, 2004) and will receive support from professionals working in the special school where they are coenrolled. Only a limited number of students with special needs are in integrated programs.

REFERENCES

Conseil de la Communauté Française de Belgique. (2004). *Décret organisant l'enseignement spécial*. Brussels, Belgium: Author.

Ministère de la Communauté Française. (2003). *Statistique des établissements, des élèves et des diplômes de l'enseignement de plein exercice. Annuaire 2001–2002*. Brussels, Belgium: Author.

Ministère de l'Education de la Recherche et de la Formation. (1995). *Circulaire ministérielle fixant la modèle de protocole justificatif à délivrer par les centres psycho-médico-sociaux et les organismes habilités à délivrer le rapport d'inscription dans un des types d'enseignement spécial*. Brussels, Belgium: Communauté Française de Belgique.

JACQUES GRÉGOIRE
Catholic University of Louvain, Belgium

See also **International Ethics and Special Education**

BELL, ALEXANDER GRAHAM (1847–1922)

Alexander Graham Bell, inventor of the telephone, educator, and spokesperson for the deaf, was born and educated in Scotland. Emigrating first to Canada and then to the United States, Bell's father and grandfather were authorities in the field of speech. Alexander Graham Bell specialized in the anatomy of the vocal apparatus, opened a school in Boston for the training of teachers for the deaf in 1872, and became a professor at Boston University. Bell later married one of his students, Mabel Hubbard, who was also deaf.

Widely acclaimed for his numerous inventions, Bell used his vast influence to foster his major interest to provide an education and support to individuals affected by partial or complete hearing loss. An avid proponent of oral methods of teaching the deaf, Bell became the acknowledged leader of the oral movement in the United States. He also campaigned tirelessly for the establishment of day schools to provide an alternative to residential school placement. Bell was a founder of the American Association to Promote the Teaching of Speech to the Deaf, later renamed the Alexander Graham Bell Association for the Deaf, and of the *Volta Bureau*, which he established for the dissemination of knowledge about Deaf individuals and educational strategies to enhance educational services for this community.

REFERENCE

Bruce, R. V. (1973). *Alexander Graham Bell and the conquest of solitude*. Boston, MA: Little, Brown.

PAUL IRVINE
Katonah, New York

BELLEVUE PSYCHIATRIC HOSPITAL

The history of psychiatric care at Bellevue Hospital Center and the history of psychiatric care in the United States are closely interwoven. Bellevue has been at the vanguard of treatment for the mentally ill since the 18th century, pioneering methods of identifying and categorizing patients, training psychiatrists and psychiatric nurses, and developing outpatient as well as inpatient courses of treatment.

The Public Workhouse and House of Correction, which opened in 1736, ultimately became Bellevue Hospital. It contained a six-bed unit designed to provide care for "the infirm, the aged, the unruly, and the maniac." By 1826, a total of 82 of the 184 patients were listed as insane. In 1879 a pavilion for the insane was erected within hospital grounds. The concept of including the care and treatment of psychiatric patients in a general hospital rather than entirely apart from the treatment of the physically ailing was revolutionary.

In 1902 the Department of Bellevue and Allied Hospitals appointed a resident physician, two assistants, and trained nurses to provide medical attention for psychiatric patients, thereby providing the framework for the development of a modern psychiatric service. During the early 1900s, the primary function of the department of psychiatry at Bellevue was to "afford temporary care and treatment for those patients who are to be transferred to the state hospital for mental diseases within 10 days." Perhaps a more important function than maintaining patients on remand was to "provide care for another group of patients which had hitherto been neglected, patients whose psychoses are of such a character that they are not suitable for commitment to a hospital for the insane nor are they acceptable in a general hospital, e.g., cases of mild mental disorders, psychoneuroses, epilepsy, deliria, transitory attacks of confusion or excitement." Simultaneously, in an effort to discourage long-term hospitalization, the department of psychiatry at Bellevue established mental health clinics and the practice of ongoing contact with patients' families.

The Children's Inpatient Psychiatric Service began at Bellevue in 1920. Separate male and female adolescent wards were maintained providing for 30 patients each. In 1935 the New York City Board of Education established a special school for emotionally disturbed children at Bellevue. Now designated as P.S. 106, the school continues to function at Bellevue.

In establishing itself as a psychiatric prison ward, Bellevue has contributed to forensic medicine via the Psychiatric Clinic of the Court of General Sessions, established in 1931. This psychiatric prison ward encouraged the development of rigid safeguards for the rights of all psychiatric patients, including prisoners.

Among many firsts at Bellevue, in 1936 Karl Murdock Bowman was the first physician in the country to use insulin shock therapy for treatment of mental illness. In 1939 David Wechsler developed the Wechsler-Bellevue Scale of Intelligence, later called the Wechsler Adult Intelligence Scale, a test still widely used today. Wechsler went on to develop a number of intelligence tests often used with handicapped children including the Wechsler Intelligence Scale for Children and the Wechsler Pre-School Scale of Intelligence. Loretta Bender, a pioneer in work with autistic children and youths, worked at Bellevue during the 1950s and 1960s. In 1984, when its facilities in the New Bellevue Hospital at 27th Street and East River Drive in New York City were completed, Bellevue's psychiatric department was united for the first time with the rest of Bellevue. Psychiatry was truly integrated into a full-service hospital setting.

In recent years, Bellevue has continued to lead the field of psychiatric treatment. In the 1990s Bellevue was innovative in developing treatment modalities for individuals with substance abuse and mental illness with peer-led milieu therapy. In addition, "social marketing" was promoted by developing educational print materials for immigrant, low-literate, and other hard-to-reach groups (Dooley, 1996). The institution also developed a model for hospital-based alcoholism outpatient treatment services for homeless alcoholics (Miescher & Galanter, 1996). A vivid portrait of the everyday life of the staff and patients at Bellevue is portrayed in the 1995 book by the chief psychologist at Bellevue, Frederick Covan, and is entitled *Crazy All the Time: Life, Lessons, and Insanity on the Psych Ward of Bellevue Hospital*.

REFERENCES

Bellevue Hospital Center. (n.d.). *Bellevue hospital center*. New York, NY: Author.

Covan, F. L., & Kahn, C. (1995). *Crazy all the time: Life, lessons, and insanity on the psych ward of Bellevue Hospital*. New York, NY: Simon & Schuster.

Dooley, A. R. (1996). A collaborative model for creating patient education resources. *American Journal of Health Behavior, 20*, 15–19.

Miescher, A., & Galanter, M. (1996). Shelter-based treatment of the homeless alcoholic. *Journal of Substance Abuse Treatment, 13*, 135–140.

New York City Health and Hospitals Corporation. (1984). *The nation's largest municipal health care system: Directory of services*. New York, NY: Author.

Walsh, J. (Ed.). (1982). *Bellevue*. New York, NY: Bellevue Hospital Center.

CATHERINE HALL RIKHYE
Hunter College, City University of New York
First edition

ELAINE FLETCHER-JANZEN
Chicago School of Professional Psychology
Second and third editions

BELL'S PALSY

Bell's palsy is an acute unilateral facial nerve paralysis resulting from injury or viral or spirochete infection (e.g., mumps, Lyme disease), or from postinfectious allergic or immune demyelinating facial neuritis that may have an abrupt onset of clinical manifestations about 2 weeks after infection. The age of onset can be anywhere from infancy to adolescence, and the incidence is common (Pedlynx, 2002).

Characteristics

1. Paresis of upper and lower face.
2. Drop of corner of mouth.
3. Unable to close eye leading to exposure keratitis at night.
4. Loss of taste on anterior two thirds of tongue in 50% of cases.
5. Possible signs of a neuropathy and regeneration of the facial nerve.

Supportive treatment includes the protection of the cornea with methylcellulose eye drops or an ocular lubricant, as well as medical assurances of the chances for recovery. Special education services would not likely be needed for this temporary condition because 85% of cases recover spontaneously. However, in 10% of cases mild facial weakness continues, and in 5% of cases severe facial weakness continues and may require cosmetic surgery (Rothenberg & Chapman, 1994).

REFERENCES

Pedlynx. (2002). Bell's palsy. Retrieved from http://www.icondata.com/health/pedbase/.les/Bell'spaHTM

Rothenberg, M., & Chapman, C. (1994). *Barron's dictionary of medical terms*. Hauppauge, NY: Barron's.

ELAINE FLETCHER-JANZEN
Chicago School of Professional Psychology

BELL, TERREL H. (1921–1996)

Terrel H. Bell died at his home in Salt Lake City on June 23, 1996, at the age of 74. Bell was born in Lava Hot Springs, Idaho, and received a master's degree from the University of Idaho in 1954 and a PhD in Educational Administration from the University of Utah in 1961. He was the recipient of 21 honorary doctorates conferred by various colleges and universities throughout the United States during his lifetime.

After serving in World War II as a U.S. Marine, Bell was a superintendent of schools in Idaho, Wyoming, and Utah. He was U.S. Commissioner of Education from 1974 to 1976 and secretary of the U.S. Department of Education from 1981 to 1984. He appointed members, wrote the national charter, and provided support and leadership for the work of the National Commission on Excellence in Education. The commission report, "A Nation At Risk," found serious flaws in the education system and concluded that schools were mired in mediocrity. Twelve national forums were sponsored to disseminate the commission report, which is credited with prompting a movement to overhaul education. More than 12 million copies of the report have been printed, reprinted, and widely distributed.

Bell's numerous honors and awards include the Department of Defense Distinguished Public Service Medal awarded by Secretary of Defense Caspar Weinberger in 1984. He authored numerous books and publications, and remained active in promoting education and learning after leaving the government. He subsequently taught Educational Administration at the University of Utah, and founded the educational consulting firm of T. H. Bell and Associates. In 1991, he wrote *How to Shape Up Our Nation's Schools: Three Crucial Steps for Renewing American Education*.

REFERENCES

Bell, T. H. (1956). *The prodigal pedagogue*. New York, NY: Exposition.

Bell, T. H. (1960). *A philosophy of education for the space age*. New York, NY: Exposition.

Bell, T. H. (1972). *Your child's intellect: A parent's guide to home based preschool education*. Salt Lake City, UT: Olympus.

Bell, T. H. (1974). *Active parent concern.* Englewood Cliffs, NJ: Prentice Hall.

Bell, T. H. (1984). *Excellence.* Salt Lake City, UT: Deseret.

ROBERTA C. STOKES
Texas A&M University
First edition

TAMARA J. MARTIN
University of Texas of the Permian Basin
Second edition

BENADRYL

Benadryl (diphenhydramine hydrochloride) is used for perennial or seasonal (hay fever) allergic rhinitis, motion sickness, and allergic conjunctivitis owed to inhalant allergens and foods. An antihistamine, it has anticholinergic (drying) and sedative side effects. In isolated cases, it has been used as a sedative for treatment of hyperactivity, and as a treatment for Parkinsonian symptoms associated with the side effects of antipsychotic medications (Konopasek, 2004). Adverse reactions include diminished mental alertness in both adults and children, with occasional excitation in the young child. A 1993 study (Vuurman, van Veggel, Uiterwijk, Leutner, & O'Hanlon, 1993) found that allergic reaction reduces learning ability in children. In addition, this effect is aggravated by diphenhydramine. Therefore, parents and educators should be aware that while Benadryl relieves some of the uncomfortable symptoms of allergies it increases problems in learning. Accommodations for the child with allergies should be specifically targeted to sedation if the child is taking Benadryl. These accommodations could include decreasing workload, increasing time for rehearsal of learning material and communications with parents on a daily basis to assist in the monitoring of side effects and learning retention.

A brand name of Parke-Davis Company, it is available in capsules of 25 and 50 mg; as an elixir for oral use; and in injectable syringes. Dosage for children (over 20 pounds) is 12.5 to 25 mg three to four times daily, with maximum daily dosage not in excess of 300 mg. For adults, dosage is 25 to 50 mg three to four times daily. Overdose with this or other antihistamines may cause hallucinations, convulsions, and death. Warnings of administering this medication to children younger than 4 have recently emerged. Children or adults who take other medications for allergies or who have been diagnosed with asthma or other lung diseases, heart disease, or an overactive thyroid should indicate these diagnoses to their physician or pharmacist to avoid harmful results that may occur (PubMedHealth, 2011).

REFERENCES

Konopasek, D. E. (2004). *Benadryl.* Longmont, CO: Sopris West.

Physician's desk reference. (1997). Oradell, NJ: Medical Economics.

PubMed Health [Internet]. Bethesda (MD): National Library of Medicine (US); [updated May 16th 2011; cited 2011 Oct 22]. Available from http://www.ncbi.nlm.nih.gov/pubmedhealth/

Vuurman, E. F., van Veggel, L. M., Uiterwijk, M. M., Leutner, D., & O'Hanlon, J. F. (1993). Seasonal allergic rhinitis and antihistamine effects on children's learning. *Annals of Allergy,* *71*(2), 121–126.

LAWRENCE HARTLAGE
Evans, Georgia
First edition

ELAINE FLETCHER-JANZEN
Chicago School of Professional Psychology
Second and third editions

BENDER, LAURETTA (1897–1987)

Born in Butte, Montana, in 1897, Lauretta Bender obtained her BS and MA degrees from the University of Chicago in 1922 and 1923, respectively. She obtained her MD degree at the State University of Iowa in 1926 and returned to Chicago (Billings Hospital) for her internship (1927–1928) and residency in neurology (1928). A residency in psychiatry at Boston's Psychopathic Hospital preceded another psychiatric residency, in 1929 to 1930, at Johns Hopkins' Phipps Clinic. She also received postgraduate training in neuroanatomy, physiology, and pathology at the University of Amsterdam on a Rockefeller grant in 1926 to 1927.

Bender held numerous appointments, including assistant instructor of neuropathology at Iowa (1923–1926) and several psychiatric positions in the New York City area. These include senior psychiatrist at Bellevue Hospital (1930–1956), director of the Child Guidance Clinic at the New York City Infirmary (1954–1960), principal research scientist of Child Psychiatry at New York State Department of Mental Hygiene (1956–1960), director of Psychiatric Research at the Children's Unit of Creedmoor State Hospital (1960–1969), and attending psychiatrist at the New York Psychiatric Institute (1969–1973). She held teaching positions at New York University, Adelphi College Graduate School, and Columbia University. She retired in 1973 and moved to Annapolis, Maryland, where she remained until her death on January 4, 1987, at the age of 89.

Bender received numerous awards during her career, among them the Adolph Meyer Award in 1953 for her contributions to the profession's knowledge base on schizophrenic children, and was named Medicine's Woman of the Year for New York in 1958. She was a fellow of the American Medical Association, American Psychiatric Association, American Neurological Association, and American Orthopsychiatric Association.

With more than 100 chapters and articles, Bender is widely published in the fields of child psychiatry, neurology, and psychology. She is best known for her Visual Motor Gestalt Test (1937), several books, including *Psychopathological Disorders of Children with Organic Brain Disease* (1956), and studies of learning disabilities (1970). Her theory of the role of brain pathology in the development of childhood schizophrenia is less known but also important. In addition, she developed the Face-Hand Test, which examines double simultaneous tactile sensation (face and hand). A variation of this test, the Fink-Green-Bender Test, has been used to discriminate between children with neurologic and schizophrenic disorders.

REFERENCES

Bender, L. (1937). *A visual motor gestalt test and its clinical use.* New York, NY: American Orthopsychiatric Association.

Bender, L. (1956). *Psychopathological disorders of children with organic brain disease.* Springfield, IL: Thomas.

Bender, L. (1970). Use of the visual motor gestalt test in diagnosing learning disability. *Journal of Special Education, 4,* 29–39.

ANTONIO E. PUENTE
University of North Carolina at Wilmington
First edition

KAY E. KETZENBERGER
University of Texas of the Permian Basin
Second edition

See also **Bender Visual-Motor Gestalt Test, Second Edition**

BENDER VISUAL-MOTOR GESTALT TEST, SECOND EDITION

The original Bender-Gestalt test was a frequently administered and thoroughly researched drawing test. Originally developed as a measure of visual-motor maturity in children, the test has come to be used as a projective tool for assessing personality, as well as an indicator of children's school readiness, emotional problems, and learning difficulties. It has also become widely used as screening measure for neurological impairment in both adults and children. The Bender-Gestalt II (2003) is an individually administered assessment used to quickly (in 10 to 20 minutes) evaluate visual-motor integration skills in children and adults ages 4 to 85. It consists of 16 geometric designs, printed on stimulus cards. These designs include the original nine designs from the Bender-Gestalt Test, and seven new designs that have been included to enhance its utility in educational, psychological, and neuropsychological assessment. The Bender-Gestalt II also includes an Observation Form as well as two supplemental tests, the Motor Test and the Perception Test, which aid in evaluating the examinee's performance on the Bender-Gestalt II. Administration of the primary measure involves two phases: the Copy phase and the Recall phase. In the Copy phase the examinee is asked to copy each of the designs onto a blank sheet of paper. In the Recall phase, the examinee is asked to redraw the designs from memory. Although the test has no time limits, the examiner records how long it takes the examinee to reproduce the designs. The Bender-Gestalt II Examiner's Manual contains administration and scoring guidelines; information on the standardization and norming process; normative tables; reliability and validity test data; and a new, easy-to-use global scoring system.

The standardization sample of the Bender-Gestalt II was based on a stratified, random sampling plan of 4,000 individuals, ages 4 to 85, devised to match the percentages of the stratification variables from the U.S. 2000 census (U.S. Census Bureau, 2001). The normative sample was designed to be nationally representative and matched to percentages of the U.S. population for demographic variables including age, sex, race/ethnicity, geographic region, and socioeconomic level (educational attainment). In addition, large numbers of individuals from clinical or special populations were collected to study the differential effects of group inclusion on test performance. These populations included individuals with intellectual developmental disabilities, specific learning disabilities, attention-deficit hyperactivity disorder, serious emotional disturbances, autism, Alzheimer's disease, and giftedness. After all normative data were collected, z scores were transformed into a standard score scale ($M = 100$, $SD = 15$). Scores were rounded and truncated to limit the standard score (SS) range to 4 standard deviations above and below the mean, providing a range of standard scores from 40 to 160.

A variety of methods was used to estimate the reliability of the Bender-Gestalt II Copy and Recall phases. When using the Global Scoring System, the average inter-rater reliability of the Copy phase was .90, and .96 for the Recall phase, both impressive given its ease of use and diverse applications. Using the split-half procedure to measure internal consistency, the overall reliability for the standardization group was .91 with an average standard error of measurement (SEM) of 4.55, indicating consistent and stable I. measurement. In test-retest reliability studies, the average corrected coefficient for the Copy phase was .85 and .83 for the Recall phase. These coefficients were well within the acceptable range. Evidence also suggests high validity. Several studies demonstrated a high correlation between the Bender-Gestalt II and intelligence, achievement, and visual-motor ability measures, which are often used in comprehensive psycho-educational assessment. The results also suggest that the Bender-Gestalt II is related to, yet distinct from, other constructs. The Bender-Gestalt II measures a single underlying construct that is sensitive to maturation and/or development, and scores are highly influenced and sensitive to clinical conditions. This dimensionality provides added utility to the test.

REFERENCES

Allen, R. A., & Decker, S. L. (2008). Utility of the Bender Visual-Motor Gestalt Test—Second Edition in the assessment of Attention-Deficit/Hyperactivity Disorder. *Perceptual and motor skills* (Vol. 107, 3), 663–675.

Brannigan, G. G., & Decker, S. L. (2003). *Bender visual-motor Gestalt test—Second edition: Examiner's manual.* Itasca, IL: Riverside.

Olmi, D. J., Sabers, D. L., & Bonner, S. (2006). *Review of the Bender-Gestalt test—Second edition.* In K. F. Geisinger, R. A. Spies, J. F. Carlson, & B. S. Plake, (Eds.), *The sixteenth mental measurements yearbook.* Lincoln, NE: Buros Institute of Mental Measurements.

Volker, M. A., Lopata, C., Vujnovic, R. K., Smerbeck, A. M., Toomey, J. A., Rodgers, ... Thomeer, M. L. (2010). Comparison of the Bender Gestalt-II and VMI-V in samples of typical children and children with high-functioning autism spectrum disorders. *Journal of Psychoeducational Assessment, 28*(3), 187–200.

RON DUMONT
Fairleigh Dickinson University

JOHN O. WILLIS
Rivier College

KATHLEEN VIEZEL
Fairleigh Dickinson University

JAMIE ZIBULSKY
Fairleigh Dickinson University

See also Visual-Motor and Visual-Perceptual Problems; Visual Perception and Discrimination

BENIGN ESSENTIAL TREMOR

Benign essential tremor (BET) is characterized by rapid rhythmic movements that are pronounced during active muscle innervation. The tremors are decreased or absent during rest and sleep. BET typically presents as a postural tremor that gets worse during action and sustained posturing. BET is also referred to as a *familial tremor, intention tremor,* and *hereditary BET* (senile tremor is used when the onset is much later in life).

In most cases the tremor begins in midlife (e.g., after 40 or 50 years of age) but can be found in children. The tremor has been reported to occur sporadically but is also familial. BET is considered an autosomal dominant disorder with approximately 50% of affected individuals having family members with a similar tremor (Williams, 1999). A specific gene has not been discovered, and the exact etiology of the disorder is still unknown. The tremor is suspected to be caused by a dysfunction of beta adrenergic receptors in the basal ganglia but is estimated to occur 20 times more frequently than Parkinson's disease (Marsden & Fowler, 1998). Incidence figures are difficult to obtain because many individuals are so mildly affected and do not seek medical opinions. Because the tremor is considered to be benign, it is not associated with other neurological abnormalities; however, it can be seen in cases of torsion dystonia, spasmodic torticollis, hereditary peripheral polyneuropathy, Parkinson's disease, and Charcot-Marie-Tooth disease.

Characteristics

1. Tremors tend to be bilateral and fairly symmetrical.
2. Tremors are most often present during volitional movements (e.g., holding cup) and are absent during rest.
3. In 50% of cases the head is involved, and in 33% legs are.
4. Tremors affect facial and oropharyngeal muscles causing chewing difficulty and vocal tremors.
5. Tremors are frequently exacerbated by stress and caffeine.
6. Coordination and walking are usually unaffected.

The severity of BET generally remains unchanged throughout an individual's life but in some instances worsens. Nearly half of individuals with BET respond to beta adrenoceptor blockers (e.g., propranolol and primidone; Williams, 1999). Postural arm tremors tend to respond best, whereas head tremors are more resistant to drug therapies. Drug response should be carefully monitored for side effects, including cardiac and respiratory complications. Like alcohol, benzodiazepines and barbiturates have been shown to reduce the tremor and relieve the embarrassment of having it. Drugs intended to treat Parkinson's disease have not been found to be effective with BET (Marsden & Fowler, 1998). When no drug works, deliberate lesioning of the thalamus, a procedure referred to as contralateral ventrolateral thalamotomy, has been used. Risks for this procedure are, however, serious (e.g., mutism).

Although referred to as a benign tremor, there are risks for serious social and psychological consequences, including social phobias and avoidance of potentially embarrassing situations, including eating and speaking in public (George & Lydiard, 1994). Some children also develop more generalized anxiety and mood disorders. Teachers and other professionals who are in contact with children who have BET need to be aware of this. Psychological help ranging from simple reassurance to counseling may be needed. Children with BET may qualify for special education services under Other Health Impairment if learning is affected. In most cases, however, this is not necessary, and regular classroom accommodations will suffice. Typical accommodations include allowing for oral examination and dictation of assignments and providing the child with written lecture notes. An occupational therapy evaluation, however, may help to ensure that accommodations are appropriate and that no other intervention is needed (this includes services under Section 504 of the Americans with Disabilities Act).

Further research is needed to determine more specifically the cause of BET and ways to prevent or effectively treat the tremor. Drug studies may be particularly beneficial.

REFERENCES

George, M. S., & Lydiard, R. B. (1994). Social phobia secondary to physical disability: A review of benign essential tremor (BET) and stuttering. *Psychosomatics, 35,* 520–523.

Marsden, C. D., & Fowler, T. J. (1998). *Clinical neurology* (2nd ed.). New York, NY: Oxford University Press.

Williams, A. C. (1999). *Patient care in neurology.* New York, NY: Oxford University Press.

JENISE JENSEN
ELAINE CLARK
University of Utah

Bennett worked in school psychology as both a practitioner and a trainer of school psychologists. Her primary interest was identification of children with learning problems, with emphasis on the remediation process, for those identified, through planning programs for teachers to implement within the regular classroom setting. She pioneered the mainstreaming of children identified for special educational resources in her practice in the New Jersey schools. With her doctoral students, she planned and implemented a program for the early identification (screening) of kindergarten children in the public schools of Trenton, New Jersey, a school district with a high proportion of minority group and Hispanic children.

Although always interested in the problems of schoolchildren, and always convinced that the public schools are the most effective milieu for dealing with those problems, Bennett's interests throughout 25 years as a school psychologist and a trainer in a highly urban state focused in later years on the problems of poor African-American children and youths, as well as on those of the increasing numbers of Hispanic children in the schools. These latter interests are exemplified in her publication of work with school-age parents and in the development of a doctoral program geared to the application of psychological knowledge and skills to the solution of educational problems.

Bennett was recognized for her leadership in school psychology, where she was perhaps best known for her work with Bardon (Bardon & Bennett, 1974; Bennett & Bardon, 1976). With Bardon, she pioneered the development of professional preparation programs for school psychologists. In 1977 the Division of School Psychology of the American Psychological Association recognized her with the Distinguished Service Award.

REFERENCES

Bardon, J. I., & Bennett, V. C. (1974). *School psychology.* Englewood Cliffs, NJ: Prentice Hall.

Bennett, V. C., & Bardon, J. I. (1976). Applied research can be useful. *Journal of School Psychology, 14,* 67–73.

CECIL R. REYNOLDS
Texas A&M University

BENNETT, VIRGINIA C. (1916–1998)

Virginia C. Bennett, a former nurse, studied elementary education at Rutgers University, earning a BA in this field in 1956. She subsequently was awarded an MEd in educational psychology (1961) and the EdD in school psychology (1963), both from Rutgers University, where she was on the faculty from 1963 until her retirement in 1983. During the years 1960 to 1963, Bennett was a W. S. Grant Foundation fellow.

BENZEDRINE

Benzedrine is a psychostimulant that acts on the central nervous system. It was the subject of widespread abuse and distribution under the slang term *"bennies"* until the 1970s. Its previous legitimate uses included, at times, the treatment of hyperactivity and obesity. Benzedrine gained popularity in the 1930s from psychiatrist Charles Bradley who administered the sulfate to children who demonstrated challenging behavior. Improvements were seen in school work, social relationships, and the child's emotional well-being. However, Bradley's studies were ignored for more than half a century.

Although Benzedrine is no longer used for the treatment of childhood or adolescent behavioral disorders, Bradley's findings over a century ago were an antecedent to the use of amphetamines to improve the challenging behavior often seen in children with behavior disorders.

REFERENCES

Bradley, C. (1937). The behavior of children receiving benzedrine. *American Journal of Psychiatry, 94*, 577–581.

Chiarello, R. J., & Cole, J. O. (1987). The use of psychostimulants in general psychiatry: A reconsideration. *Archives of General Psychiatry, 44*, 286–295.

Strohl, M. P. (2011). Bradley's benzedrine studies on children with behavior disorders. *Yale Journal of Biology and Medicine, 84*(1), 27–33.

STAFF

See also Attention-Deficit/Hyperactivity Disorder; Dexedrine

BEREITER, CARL (1930–)

Carl Bereiter received his BA (1951) and MA (1952) in comparative literature and his PhD (1959) in education from the University of Wisconsin. He was a research associate at Vassar College (1959–1961) and then joined the faculty at the University of Illinois (1961–1967). Since 1967, Bereiter has been a professor at the Ontario Institute for Studies in Education.

In the early 1960s, Bereiter and Siefried Engelmann taught reading, mathematics, and logical skills to young disadvantaged children. Out of this effort came the method they called *direct instruction*, an approach that was often misperceived as behavioristic rather than rational analysis of difficulties of understanding.

Bereiter and Marlene Scardamalia cofounded the Institute for Knowledge Innovation & Technology. Through research on composing and comprehension processes, they have identified an immature strategy that seems to reflect a general way of coping superficially with academic tasks. This discovery led to Bereiter's broadening his studies to intentional learning: how it develops, how it is influenced by school practices, and how a higher level of intentional control over learning can be fostered in students. His most recent work, in this area, has been in using Computer Supported Intentional Learning Environment (CSILE) software. CSILE is intended to create a knowledge-building society by linking diverse participants, including school children and parents, teacher education and medical students, project researchers, and software developers.

REFERENCES

Bereiter, C., & Engelmann, S. (1966). *Teaching disadvantaged children in the preschool.* Englewood Cliffs, NJ: Prentice Hall.

Bereiter, C., & Scardamalia, M. (1985). Cognitive coping strategies and the problem of "inert" knowledge. In S. S. Chipman, J. W. Segal, & R. Glaser (Eds.), *Thinking and learning skills: Research and open questions* (Vol. 2, pp. 65–80). Hillsdale, NJ: Erlbaum.

Scardamalia, M., & Bereiter, C. (1996). Engaging students in a knowledge society. *Educational Leadership, 54*(3), 6–10.

DEBORAH B. GUILLEN
University of Texas of the Permian Basin

BETA III

The Beta III (1999) provides a quick assessment of the nonverbal intellectual capabilities of adults, aged 16 to 89, including their abilities in the areas of visual information processing, spatial and nonverbal reasoning, processing speed, and aspects of fluid intelligence. It is easily administered and hand scored either individually or in a group and requires only 30 minutes to complete. It is useful for screening large populations of people for whom administering comprehensive test batteries would be difficult, including low-functioning or low-skilled individuals, and is ideal for use in prison systems, companies, and schools. Administration instructions for the Beta III are available in English or Spanish, making it one of the most comprehensive of language-free and culture-fair tests.

Beta III is the updated version of the *Revised Beta Examination, Second Edition*, which was published in 1974. It features new norms, contemporary and larger artwork, new items, new subtest (Matrix Reasoning), extended age range, low floors for individuals with average and lower cognitive abilities, and higher ceiling with more challenging items. Five subtests make up the Beta III: *Coding*, which contains code symbols with numbers that are assigned to the symbols at the top of the page; *Picture Completion*, which requires the subject to draw in what is missing to complete the picture; *Clerical Checking*, which entails circling an "equal" or a "not equal" symbol depending on whether pairs of pictures, symbols, or number are the same or different; *Picture Absurdities*, where the subject is asked to place an "X" on the one picture out of four that shows something wrong or foolish; and *Matrix Reasoning*, which requires the subject to choose the missing symbol or picture that best completes a set of symbols or pictures.

Extensive reliability and validity studies have been conducted with Beta III. The test was normed on a sample of 1,260 adults, including people with Intellectual Developmental Disabilities and more than 400 prison inmates. The sample was representative of the 1997 U.S. census data with respect to age, gender, race/ ethnicity, educational level, and geographic region. Beta III was validated using other well-known tests, including the WAIS-III, ABLE-II, *Raven's Standard Progressive Matrices, Revised Minnesota Paper Form Board Test* (RMPFBT), *Personnel Tests for Industry-Oral Direction Test* (PTI- ODT), *Bennett Mechanical Comprehensive Test* (BMCT), *and Revised Beta Examination, Second Edition* (Beta II).

REFERENCES

Reviews of this test by C. G. Bellah and Louise M. Soares are published in Geisinger, K. F., Spies, R. A., Carlson, J. F., Plake, B. S. (Eds.). (2006). *The Sixteenth mental measurements yearbook*. Lincoln, NE: Buros Institute of Mental Measurements.

McCallum, S., Bracken, B., & Wasserman, J. (2000). *Essentials of Nonverbal Assessment*. New York, NY: Wiley.

RON DUMONT
Fairleigh Dickinson University

JOHN O. WILLIS
Rivier College

KATHLEEN VIEZEL
Fairleigh Dickinson University

JAMIE ZIBULSKY
Fairleigh Dickinson University

BETTELHEIM, BRUNO (1903–1990)

Bruno Bettelheim received his doctoral degree from the University of Vienna in 1938. He was strongly influenced by Freudian thought. Bettelheim was a psychiatrist who gained his fame from work with emotionally disturbed children, particularly those with autism.

During his long association with the University of Chicago, Bettelheim acted as principal of the University of Chicago's Sonia Shankman Orthogeneic School, a residential treatment center for severely emotionally disturbed children. The philosophy and operation of the Shankman School are described in Bettelheim's book *Love Is Not Enough* (1950), and four case studies of the treatment there are covered in his *Truants From Life* (1955).

Bettelheim sought in his treatment of severely disturbed children to create a particular social environment, a society with its own definite set of mores, closely paralleling those of society at large. He believed that social norms and standards are important to the treatment of emotionally disturbed children just as they are important in normal populations.

Bettelheim published many books, including *Children of the Dream* (1969) and *The Empty Fortress* (1967). He died in 1990 at the age of 87.

REFERENCES

Bettelheim, B. (1950). *Love is not enough: The treatment of emotionally disturbed children*. Glencoe, IL: Free Press.

Bettelheim, B. (1955). *Truants from life: The rehabilitation of emotionally disturbed children*. Glencoe, IL: Free Press.

Bettelheim, B. (1967). *The empty fortress: Infantile autism and the birth of the self*. London, UK: Collier-Macmillan.

Bettelheim, B. (1969). *Children of the dream*. New York, NY: Macmillan.

REBECCA BAILEY
Texas A&M University

BIALER, IRVING (1919–2000)

Irving Bialer received his BA (1943) from Brooklyn College and his PhD (1960) in clinical psychology from George Peabody College, with a minor in education of exceptional children. His major field of interest was in clinical psychology; intellectual developmental disabilities and clinical child psychology were two special areas of interest.

His publications dealt with issues of assessment and diagnosis in the areas of intellectual developmental disabilities and neurological impairment, personality and motivational development in retarded individuals, and drug-related treatments for behavior problems in neuropsychiatrically impaired children. He had more than 30 publications to his credit, including books, articles, and book chapters. Some of his most significant publications include a chapter in *Social-Cultural Aspects of Mental Retardation*, discussing the relationship of intellectual developmental disabilities to emotional disturbance and physical disability, and *The Psychology of Mental Retardation: Issues and Approaches* (coedited with Manny Sternlicht), which focuses on the theoretical, practical issues and approaches to dealing with the psychology of mentally retarded people. Bialer and R. L. Cromwell (1965) wrote an article entitled "Failure as Motivation with Mentally Retarded Children," which was published in the *American Journal of Mental Deficiency*.

Bialer has held many academic positions in psychology and special education and was a consulting editor to the *American Journal of Mental Deficiency* as well as the journal's book review editor from 1971 to 1981.

REFERENCES

Bialer, I. (1970). Relationship of mental retardation to emotional disturbance and physical disability. In H. C. Haywood (Ed.), *Social-cultural aspects of mental retardation* (pp. 607–660). New York, NY: Appleton-Century-Crofts.

Bialer, I., & Cromwell, R. L. (1965). Failure as motivation with mentally retarded children. *American Journal of Mental Deficiency, 69*, 680–684.

Bialer, I., & Sternlicht, M. (Eds.). (1970). *The psychology of mental retardation: Issues and approaches.* New York, NY: Psychological Dimensions.

REBECCA BAILEY
Texas A&M University

BIBLIOTHERAPY

The bibliotherapy process is frequently summed into the three stages of identification, catharsis, and insight (Sridhar & Vaughn, 2000). *Bibliotherapy* is defined as "the use of reading materials for help in solving personal problems or for psychiatric therapy" (Merriam-Webster Online Dictionary, 2005). This description is broad, thus allowing for different interpretations and diverse application. Bibliotherapy can be used to explore and develop an individual's self-concept, increase understanding of human behavior, foster honest self-appraisal, relieve emotional or mental pressure, demonstrate that people encounter the same difficulties in life, provide various solutions to a problem, and assist in planning a constructive course of action (Aiex, 1993).

The bibliotherapy process as described by some practitioners (Orton, 1997; Pardeck, 1993) begins with identifying a person's needs. The second component involves matching these needs with appropriate reading materials. This process may entail consideration of the person's age, sex, race, reading level, and the nature of the themes. The next step is to establish the setting and time to engage in therapy. Other integral components include designing follow-up activities for the reading and motivating the client(s). The next step involves engaging the person in the reading, viewing, or listening phase. Time for

reflection and discussion is necessary to allow the individual to process the story and determine how it relates to his or her experiences. The final steps include the introduction of follow-up activities related to the story and assisting the person in achieving closure to the personal problems addressed in the story (Orton, 1997; Pardeck, 1993). Follow-up activities to reading the story may consist of retelling the story, an in-depth discussion of the book, engaging in art activities, creative writing, or dramatic activities, including the use of role playing and puppets.

Books are selected with themes that closely match the student's identified needs and have a desired therapeutic content. The books should be at the student's reading ability and interest level. The characters and themes should be believable to promote student empathy. The themes must be realistic and entail creativity in problem solving (Jackson, 2001; J. T. Pardeck & Pardeck, 1993). Books utilized in bibliotherapy include short stories of fiction, self-help, fairy tales, picture books, and nonfiction biographies (Orton, 1997).

The effectiveness of bibliotherapy is somewhat mixed. Bibliotherapy can be effective for cultivating assertiveness, changing attitudes, promoting self development, and achieving therapeutic benefits (Sridhar & Vaughn, 2000). In addition, bibliotherapy seems to have success in promoting self-esteem, problem-solving skills, interpersonal relationships, as well as improving academic achievement and reading comprehension (Borders & Paisley, 1992; Pardeck, 1993; Sridhar & Vaughn, 2000).

REFERENCES

Aiex, N. (1993). *Bibliotherapy. ERIC Digest.* (ERIC Document Reproduction Service No. ED357333).

Borders, S., & Paisley, P. O. (1992). Children's literature as a resource for classroom guidance. *Elementary School Guidance and Counseling, 27*(2), 131–140.

Jackson, S. A. (2001). Using bibliotherapy with clients. *Journal of Individual Psychology, 57*(3), 289–297.

Merriam-Webster Online Dictionary. (2005). Bibliotherapy. Retrieved from http://www.merriam-webster.com/

Orton, G. L. (1997). *Strategies for counseling children and their parents.* Pacific Grove, CA: Brooks/Cole.

Pardeck, J. T. (1993). *Using bibliotherapy in clinical practice: A guide to self-help books.* Westport, CT: Greenwood Press.

Pardeck, J. T., & Pardeck, J. A. (Eds.). (1993). *Bibliotherapy: A clinical approach to helping children.* Langhorne, PA: Gordon and Breach.

Sridhar, D., & Vaughn, S. (2000). Bibliotherapy for all: Enhancing reading comprehension, self-concept, and behavior. *Teaching Exceptional Children, 33*(2), 74–82.

LINDA RADBILL
University of Florida

See also Basal Readers; High Interest–Low Vocabulary; Recording for the Blind

BIELSCHOLWSKY SYNDROME (*See* Juvenile Cerebromacular Degeneration)

BIENNIAL DIRECTORY OF EDUCATIONAL FACILITIES FOR THE LEARNING DISABLED

The *Biennial Directory of Educational Facilities for the Learning Disabled* was last published by Academic Therapy Publications in 1979. It contained a listing of nonpublic educational facilities that specialize in programs for individuals with learning disabilities when this concept was more in vogue. The directory lists facilities in alphabetical order by state. Following the name, location, director, and number of staff members is coded information describing the following: type of facility—educational, related professional service (diagnostic, optometric, etc.), or summer camp; age ranges accepted; boys only, girls only, or coeducational; full day, part day, or residential; and fee information. A copy of the directory could at one time be obtained from Academic Therapy Publications: 20 Commercial Boulevard, Novato, CA 94949.

DANIEL R. PAULSON
University of Wisconsin at Stout
First edition

Staff
Fourth edition

BIJOU, SIDNEY W. (1908–2009)

Born in Baltimore, Maryland, Sidney W. Bijou received his BS in business administration from the University of Florida in 1933. He received his MS (1937) from Columbia University and his PhD (1941), both in psychology, from the University of Iowa. Bijou ended his career as professor emeritus at the University of Illinois, Bijou has been an adjunct professor of special education and psychology at the University of Arizona, and the University of Nevada.

Although he co-authored of the *Wide Range Achievement Test* (Bijou & Jastak, 1941), his major interest was in the behavioral analysis of child development (Bijou, 1978; Bijou & Baer, 1965, 1978). He also co-authored a book discussing behavior analysis and modification of children (Bijou & Ruiz, 1981). One of his major contentions he supported was that the child and the environment are always interacting and maintaining a symbiotic relationship. He emphasized the commonality of a general goal for children, both typical in development and delayed, in early childhood education, regardless of age or degree of the disability, while stressing individualization of education and treatment.

Bijou was a National Institute of Mental Health senior fellow, a Fulbright-Hays fellow, president of the Midwestern Association of Behavior Analysis, and president of the American Psychological Association's Division of Developmental Psychology. He also received the Research Award from the American Association of Mental Deficiency, and the G. Stanley Hall Award in child development from the American Psychological Association. The sum of Bijou's vast experience in the field continues to be reflected in his 1996 article, "Reflections on Some Early Events Related to Behavior Analysis of Child Development."

REFERENCES

Bijou, S. W. (1976). *Child development: The basic stage of early childhood.* Englewood Cliffs, NJ: Prentice Hall.

Bijou, S. W. (1996). Reflections on some early events related to behavior analysis of child development. *Behavior Analyst, 19*(1), 49–60.

Bijou, S. W., & Baer, D. M. (1965). *Child development: Universal stage of infancy* (Vol. 2). New York, NY: Appleton-Century-Crofts.

Bijou, S. W., & Baer, D. M. (1978). *Behavior analysis of child development.* Englewood Cliffs, NJ: Prentice Hall.

Bijou, S. W., & Jastak, J. F. (1941). *Wide range achievement test.* New York, NY: Psychological Corporation.

Bijou, S. W., & Ruiz, R. (Eds.). (1981). *Behavior modification: Contributions to education.* Hillsdale, NJ: Erlbaum.

E. VALERIE HEWITT
Texas A&M University

BILIARY CIRRHOSIS, PRIMARY

Primary biliary cirrhosis (PBC) is a disease of the bile ducts and liver. Primarily affecting women (Fanning et al., 2000), this condition may lie dormant for years and never cause a problem. However, once triggered, PBC acts as an autoimmune disorder in which the body attacks its own cells as if they were foreign. Specifically, the body attacks the cells that line the bile ducts. This causes damage to the ducts, allowing bile acids to corrode the liver. The condition of having this corrosion of the liver is called *cirrhosis.*

The triggers for PBC are unknown, but it is possible that pregnancy, infection, stress, or a hereditary factor may be involved. The incidence of PBC is 3 to 15 cases per million per year (Medline, 2002). Liver damage causes a number of serious side effects. Most common is the inability to break down toxins that enter the body. These toxins can be in the form of drugs, alcohol, and some foods. Damage can impair the liver's ability to balance the amounts of certain vitamins and minerals in the body.

Characteristics
1. Itching
2. Chronic fatigue
3. Discoloration of skin
4. Nausea, indigestion
5. Bone and joint pain
6. Aches in upper abdomen
7. Diarrhea
8. Dark urine, pale stools
9. Weakness in wrists and hands
10. Easy bruising
11. Dry eyes or mouth

There is no known cure for PBC, but doctors may prescribe drugs that decrease the activity of the immune system. PBC may also be controlled by diet: Eating small portions often will ensure that there is always some food for the bile ducts to be digesting, thus decreasing the amount of time that liver cells are attacked. Treatment basically is targeted at symptom reduction and prevention of complications (Medline, 2002).

In an educational setting, children may need special medical and dietary care that is specific to the liver problems and complications. They may also need to be absent more often due to symptoms that interfere with their ability to attend school; therefore, they will most likely qualify for special education under the Other Health Impairment category of services.

The course is variable, but untreated the average referral for liver transplantation occurs at 7 years. Statistical models are now used to predict the best timing of transplantation (Medline, 2002).

REFERENCES

Fanning, P. A., Jonsson, J. R., Clouston, A. D., Edwards-Smith, C., Balderson, G. A., Macdonald, G. A., ... Powell, E. E. (2000). Detection of male DNA in the liver of female patients with primary biliary cirrhosis. *Journal of Hepatology, 33,* 690–695.

Medline. (2002). Medline plus medical encyclopedia: Primary biliary cirrhosis. Retrieved from http://www.nlm.nih.gov/

ALLISON KATZ
Rutgers University

BILINGUAL ASSESSMENT AND SPECIAL EDUCATION

The assessment of children who are culturally and linguistically diverse for special education services has been a controversial issue for nearly 30 years. This controversy first received national attention via the case of *Diana v. California* in 1970 involving the identification of Spanish-speaking children as mentally retarded on the basis of being assessed in English. The safeguards decreed in this case had an impact on both legal requirements and professional ethical standards. Public Law 94-142 mandated that children be assessed in their primary language. Chapter 13 of the American Psychological Association's *Standards for Educational and Psychological Testing* (1985) acknowledges the need for assessing the native language of children.

Legal requirements and ethical standards, however, have not resolved the issue of disproportionate representation of culturally and linguistically diverse children in special education. The problem of disproportionate representation across different special education categories pertains both to overrepresentation (Artiles & Trent, 1994; Chinn & Hughes, 1987; Ortiz & Yates, 1983; Robertson, Kushner, Starks, & Drescher, 1994; Tucker, 1980; Wright & Cruz, 1983) and underrepresentation (Chinn & Hughes, 1987; Gersten & Woodward, 1994; Ortiz & Yates, 1983; Robertson et al., 1994).

There are many possible factors that contribute to the disproportionate representation of linguistically diverse students in special education. Ochoa, Powell, and Robles-Pina (1996) state that the following are among some of the reasons why this problem continues today: "(a) socioeconomic status of minorities students, (b) test bias associated with cultural differences, (c) factors associated with second language acquisition, and (d) inappropriate referrals" (p. 251).

In addition to these four aforementioned variables, the role of the school psychologist with respect to appropriately conducting and interpreting test results is a critical factor that can reduce the probability of misdiagnosing bilingual and/or limited-English-proficient (LEP) children. While experts (Barona & Santos de Barona, 1987; Caterino, 1990; Esquivel, 1988; Figueroa, 1990; Hamayan & Damico, 1991; Wilen & Sweeting, 1986) have provided the field of school psychology with recommended procedures and factors to consider when conducting bilingual assessment, recent research indicates that practitioners have not been exposed to this information. Ochoa, Rivera, and Ford (1997) found that 83% of the school psychologists who conducted bilingual assessment self-reported that they had not received adequate training in this area by their university training program. "Moreover, 56 percent stated that they [school psychologists] had received no or very little training on interpreting results of bilingual assessments" (Ochoa, Rivera, & Ford, 1997, p. 341).

Given this lack of training, it is critical that the assessment practices school psychologists use with bilingual and/or LEP children be reviewed. These include the following: (a) use of interpreters, (b) the extent to which and how language proficiency is assessed, (c) methods used to assess intellectual functioning, academic achievement, and adaptive behavior, and (d) compliance with Section Four of the exclusionary clause of Public Law 94-142.

Use of Interpreters

The use of interpreters is common practice in bilingual assessment. This is not surprising due to the many different low-incidence language groups school psychologists have to assess (Ochoa, Gonzalez, Galarza, & Guillemard, 1996). Ochoa, Gonzalez et al. (1996) reported that 53% of school psychologists use interpreters. They found that 77% of school psychologists who use interpreters self-reported that they were clearly not trained by their university training program on how to do so. Moreover, approximately two thirds of the interpreters used by the school psychologists did not have training to work in this capacity. Ochoa, Gonzalez et al. (1996) and Nuttall (1987) state the need for interpreter training. When school psychologists must resort to using interpreters, they should review the literature pertaining to the skills they should acquire in this situation (Figueroa, Sandoval, & Merino, 1984) as well as the skills that the interpreter should possess (Chamberlain & Medeiros-Landurand, 1991; Medina, 1982; Miller & Abudarham, 1984; Scribner, 1993; Wilen & Sweeting, 1986).

Language Proficiency Assessment

Language proficiency assessment is an essential component of bilingual assessment because it provides the school psychologist with information about (a) the appropriateness of the child's current educational placement with respect to his/her language development (Ochoa, Galarza, & Gonzalez, 1996) and (b) the child's native and second language development with respect to whether the student has achieved Cognitive Academic Language Proficiency (CALP). Cummins (1984) states that it is important to differentiate between CALP, which takes 5 to 7 years to acquire and is the type of proficiency that one needs to be successful in an academic context, and Basic Interpersonal Communication Skills (BICS), which is the proficiency one needs in social settings and only takes about two years to acquire. If bilingual students do not have CALP in English, they will find the linguistic demands of their instructional arrangement to be difficult, which could result in academic failure. Ochoa, Galarza, and Gonzalez (1996) concluded from their study of the language proficiency assessment practices of school psychologists when conducting bilingual assessment that they "are not implementing the following recommended language proficiency practices: (a) conducting their own testing rather than relying on external data, (b) obtaining information about the LEP child's CALP level, and (c) utilizing informal language assessment methods" (p. 33).

Intellectual Functioning, Academic and Adaptive Behavior Assessment

With respect to intellectual functioning, Ochoa, Powell, and Robles-Pina's (1996) study noted the following assessment trends used with bilingual and LEP students: (a) multiple measures are utilized; (b) nonverbal measures are commonly used; and (c) formally, informally translated tests and alternative/dynamic methods (i.e., Learning Potential Assessment Device and System of Multicultural Pluralistic Assessment) are often not used. In the area of academic assessment of second language learners, approximately 75% of school psychologists reported that they used the Woodcock instruments in both English and Spanish (Ochoa, Powell, & Robles-Pina, 1996). Moreover, the use of curriculum-based measurement (66% of school psychologists) and criterion reference testing (49% of school psychologists) in Spanish are also common practice to assess achievement (Ochoa, Powell, & Robles-Pina, 1996). With respect to adaptive behavior, the most commonly used measure with bilingual students is the Vineland Adaptive Behavior Scales–Survey Edition (Ochoa, Powell, & Robles-Pina, 1996).

Section Four of the Exclusionary Clause

Section Four of the exclusionary clause of Public Law 94-142 states that a student should not be identified as learning disabled if the "discrepancy between ability and achievement is primarily the result of environmental, cultural, or economic disadvantage" (U.S. Office of Education, 1977). Ochoa, Rivera, and Powell's (1997) study examined how school psychologists complied with this legal requirement. They identified 36 factors that school psychologists used which could be summarized by the following six major themes: "(a) family and home factors, (b) language instruction and language-related factors, (c) assessment instrument and procedural safeguards, (d) educational history factors, (e) general educational factors, and (f) other" (p. 163). Ochoa, Rivera, and Powell (1997) conclude that "the extent to which many of these factors are used, however, appears to be low. Moreover, many additional important factors are completely overlooked by school psychologists" (p. 163).

Conclusion

A review of the aforementioned research concerning the assessment practices used with bilingual and/or LEP students suggests that this area will continue to be controversial. Perhaps the words of Chinn and Hughes (1987) best summarize this situation: "The assessment of minority children for educational placement continues to be one of the more volatile issues in special education" (p. 45).

REFERENCES

American Psychological Association. (1985). *Standards for educational and psychological testing*. Washington, DC: Author.

Artiles, A. J., & Trent, S. C. (1994). Overrepresentation of minority students in special education: A continuing debate. *Journal of Special Education, 27*(4), 410–437.

Barona, A., & Santos de Barona, M. (1987). A model for assessment of limited English proficiency students referred for special education services. In S. H. Fradd & W. J. Tikunoff (Eds.), *Bilingual education and bilingual special education* (pp. 183–209). San Diego, CA: College Hill Press.

Caterino, L. C. (1990). Step-by-step procedure for the assessment of language minority children. In A. Barona & E. E. Garcia (Eds.), *Children at risk: Poverty, minority status, and other issues in educational equity* (pp. 269–282). Washington, DC: National Association of School Psychologists.

Chamberlain, P., & Medeiros-Landurand, P. (1991). Practical considerations in the assessment of LEP students with special needs. In E. V. Hamayan & J. S. Damico (Eds.), *Limiting bias in the assessment of bilingual students* (pp. 111–156). Austin, TX: PRO-ED.

Chinn, P. C., & Hughes, S. (1987). Representation of minority students in special classes. *Remedial and Special Education, 8*, 41–46.

Cummins, J. (1984). *Bilingual special education issues in assessment and pedagogy*. San Diego, CA: College-Hill.

Cummins, J. (1992). Bilingual education and English immersion: The Ramirez report in theoretical perspective. *Bilingual Research Journal, 16*, 91–104.

Esquivel, G. B. (1988). Best practices in the assessment of limited English proficient and bilingual children. In A. Thomas & J. Grimes (Eds.), *Best practices in school psychology* (pp. 113–123). Washington, DC: National Association of School Psychologists.

Figueroa, R. A. (1990). Best practices in the assessment of bilingual children. In A. Thomas & J. Grimes (Eds.), *Best practices in school psychology II* (pp. 93–106). Washington, DC: National Association of School Psychologists.

Figueroa, R. A., Sandoval, J., & Merino, B. (1984). School psychology and limited-English-proficient (LEP) children: New competencies. *Journal of School Psychology, 22*, 131–143.

Gersten, R., & Woodward, J. (1994). The language-minority student and special education: Issues, trends, and paradoxes. *Exceptional Children, 60*(4), 310–322.

Hamayan, E. V., & Damico, J. S. (Eds.). (1991). *Limiting bias in the assessment of bilingual students*. Austin, TX: PRO-ED.

Medina, V. (1982). *Issues regarding the use of interpreters and translators in a school setting*. (ERIC Reproduction No. ED 161191)

Miller, N., & Abudarham, S. (1984). Management of communication problems in bilingual children. In N. Miller (Ed.), *Bilingualism and language disability: Assessment and remediation* (pp. 177–198). San Diego, CA: College-Hill.

Nuttall, E. V. (1987). Survey of current practices in the psychological assessment of limited-English-proficiency handicapped children. *Journal of School Psychology, 25*, 53–61.

Ochoa, S. H., Galarza, A., & Gonzalez, D. (1996). An investigation of school psychologists' assessment practices of language proficiency with bilingual and limited-English-proficient students. *Diagnostique, 21*(4), 17–36.

Ochoa, S. H., Gonzalez, D., Galarza, A., & Guillemard, L. (1996). The training and use of interpreters in bilingual psychoeducational assessment: An alternative in need of study. *Diagnostique, 21*(3), 19–40.

Ochoa, S. H., Powell, M. P., & Robles-Pina, R. (1996c). School psychologists' assessment practices with bilingual and limited-English-proficient students. *Journal of Psychoeducational Assessment, 14*, 250–275.

Ochoa, S. H., Rivera, B., & Ford, L. (1997). An investigation of school psychology training pertaining to bilingual psychoeducational assessment of primarily Hispanic students: Twenty-five years after Diana v. California. *Journal of School Psychology, 35*, 329–349.

Ochoa, S. H., Rivera, B., & Powell, M. P. (1997). Factors used to comply with the exclusionary clause with bilingual and limited-English-proficient pupils: Initial guidelines. *Learning Disabilities Research & Practice, 12*, 161–167.

Ortiz, A., & Yates, J. (1983). Incidence of exceptionality among Hispanics: Implications for manpower planning. *National Association of Bilingual Education Journal, 7*, 41–54.

Robertson, P., Kushner, M. I., Starks, J., & Drescher, C. (1994). An update of participation rates of culturally and linguistically diverse students in special education: The need for a research and policy agenda. *The Bilingual Special Education Perspective, 14*(1), 3–9.

Scribner, A. P. (1993). The use of interpreters in the assessment of language minority students. *Bilingual Special Education Perspective, 12*(1), 2–6.

Tucker, J. A. (1980). Ethnic proportions in classes for the learning disabled: Issues in nonbiased assessment. *Journal of Special Education, 14*, 93–105.

U.S. Office of Education. (1977). Assistance to states for education of handicapped children: Procedures for evaluating specific learning disabilities. *Federal Register, 42*, 65083.

Wilen, D. K., & Sweeting, C. V. M. (1986). Assessment of limited English proficient Hispanic students. *School Psychology Review, 15*, 59–75.

Wright, P., & Cruz, R. S. (1983). Ethnic composition of special education programs in California. *Learning Disability Quarterly, 6*, 387–394.

HECTOR SALVIA OCHOA
Texas A&M University

See also Bilingual Special Education; Culturally/Linguistically Diverse Gifted Students

BILINGUAL SPECIAL EDUCATION

By the year 2025, approximately 40% of the total U.S. population will be African American, Hispanic, or Asian

American (Townsend, 1995) and by 2080, non-Hispanic Whites will be a minority. Every region of the country has experienced significant increases in the number of individuals from minority backgrounds, and schools are reporting dramatic increases in the number of language minority students they serve. "*Language minority*" refers to students who come from homes or communities where a language other than English is spoken. A subset of this population are limited English proficient (LEP) students, whose English skills are so limited they cannot profit from instruction delivered entirely in English and thus require the support of special language programs such as bilingual education or English as a second language instruction. LEP students represent some 200 language groups with Spanish being the most common language spoken (approximately 75%), followed by Vietnamese, Hmong, Cantonese, Cambodian, and Korean.

There is substantial evidence that educational services currently being provided to language minority students are not sufficient to meet their needs. These students experience higher rates of retention and school attrition, score poorly on standardized tests, are underrepresented in colleges and universities, and complete postsecondary studies at low rates. They are also disproportionately represented in special education.

Disproportionate Representation in Special Education

The prevalence of disabilities among language minority students is difficult to determine because local, state, and federal education agencies do not usually report disabilities by language proficiency level. Representation is affected by such factors as definitions, eligibility criteria, geographic location, percentage of minority enrollment, district size, and available program options. Consequently, in some states, LEP students are underrepresented, while in others they are seriously overrepresented in programs for students with special needs (Harry, 1992). Patterns of over- and underidentification suggest that some students are inappropriately placed in special education, but that others are neither being identified nor receiving the services they need and to which they are entitled. Because bilingual special education is a new field, research on second language learners with disabilities is limited and, consequently, when LEP students are identified as being eligible for special education, school districts struggle with how to best address disability- and language-related needs simultaneously.

Prevention and Prereferral

With increasing frequency, service delivery models such as the Assessment and Intervention Model for the Bilingual Exceptional Student (Ortiz & Wilkinson, 1991) emphasize proactive steps to ensure that all students are academically successful by creating school climates which reflect awareness and acceptance of diversity, high expectations

for all students, a challenging curriculum, quality bilingual education and ESL programs, and involvement of parents and communities. Prereferral interventions are designed to strengthen teachers' abilities to provide appropriate educational opportunities to a diverse student population. This is accomplished through professional development, which focuses on helping teachers understand the characteristics of language minority students, instructional practices known to be effective for these learners, and by giving teachers access to consultants or problem solving teams which help them design interventions to address students learning difficulties. If LEP students are ultimately referred for a comprehensive individual assessment, prereferral data help document that external factors such as limited English proficiency or lack of appropriate instruction have already been eliminated as possible causes of problems.

Assessment

Although inappropriate assessment is one of the primary causes of disproportionate representation of language minority students in special education, research on best practices in assessment of these students is still limited (Ortiz, 1997). Adaptation of standardized procedures is quite common (e.g., translations, use of interpreters, modification of test content). However, such adaptations invalidate the test, making scoring and interpretation of outcomes difficult and error-prone (Damico, 1991). Only those instruments that include appropriate samples of language minority students in the norming sample should be used in making eligibility decisions. If test norms are not appropriate, or if standardized administration procedures are violated, it is recommended that patterns of performance be described and used diagnostically to support eligibility decisions rather than reporting test scores. If performance on the formal and informal measures are positively correlated, multidisciplinary teams can be more confident that the student has a disability.

Students with disabilities demonstrate skills and abilities significantly deviant from those of students from similar language and cultural backgrounds. In the case of LEP students assessed only in English, assessments should document that the student's performance is discrepant with that of other LEP students who have had similar exposure to native language and/or English as a second language instruction. Behaviors are not deviant unless they are significantly different from the student's reference group.

Instruction

Individualized education programs (IEPs) for language minority students specify goals and objectives for native language and ESL instruction and include instructional recommendations that reflect understanding of cultural differences, socioeconomic background, preferred modalities, learning styles, and appropriate reinforcements (Yates & Ortiz, 1998). Because of the need to accommodate students' limited English proficiency, a combination of "reciprocal interaction" teaching approaches and basic skills instruction seem to be most beneficial for LEP students with disabilities (Cummins, 1984; Robertson-Courtney, Wilkinson, & Ortiz, 1991; Willig, Swedo, & Ortiz, 1987). Approaches that focus solely on teaching discrete skills in English are problematic for LEP students because activities that are simplified to focus on specific skills are frequently stripped of context and lose their meaning and purpose, becoming incomprehensible to the second language learner. Lessons which focus on specific skills (e.g., phonology or grammar) and accuracy may actually interfere with the second language acquisition process, since instruction attempts to correct "errors," which are, in reality, developmental. Reciprocal interaction approaches, on the other hand, are characterized by genuine dialogue between students and teacher, in both oral and written communication, opportunities for meaningful language use, collaborative learning groups, the teaching of basic skills in the context of lessons that focus on higher order thinking, and the incorporation of language use and development across the curriculum.

Service delivery models and alternative instructional arrangements are being explored in an effort to ensure that language minority students are served by special educators who have expertise in how language and culture influence learning (Yates & Ortiz, 1998). For example, students who are limited English proficient can be served by: (a) bilingual special educators (i.e., teachers whose certification program focused specifically on the education of language minority students with disabilities); (b) special education teachers with dual certification in special education and bilingual education or English as a second language; or (c) by bilingual education teachers with the support and consultation of the special education teacher. For effective service delivery, linkages between special education, special language programs, and general education must be established, instructional and related services must be coordinated, and the roles and responsibilities of all personnel who work with these students must be defined. Additionally, teacher education programs must prepare both monolingual and bilingual special educators to serve linguistically and culturally diverse learners. The content of preservice teacher education, which leads to licensure and certification, and perhaps even more importantly, professional development and graduate teacher training programs, must reflect competencies that promote the interface between linguistic and culturally diversity and disabilities.

REFERENCES

Cummins, J. (1984). *Bilingualism and special education: Issues in assessment and pedagogy.* Clevedon, Avon, England: Multilingual Matters.

Damico, J. S. (1991). Descriptive assessment of communicative ability in limited English proficient students. In E. V. Hamayan & J. S. Damico (Eds.), *Limiting bias in the assessment of bilingual students* (pp. 157–217). Austin, TX: PRO-ED.

Harry, B. (1992). *Cultural diversity, families, and the special education system: Communication and empowerment.* New York, NY: Teachers College Press.

Ortiz, A. A. (1997). Learning disabilities occurring concomitantly with linguistic differences. *Journal of Learning Disabilities, 30*(3), 321–332.

Ortiz, A. A., & Wilkinson, C. Y. (1991). Assessment and intervention model for the exceptional bilingual student (AIM for the BESt). *Teacher Education and Special Education, 14*(1), 11–18.

Robertson-Courtney, P., Wilkinson, C. Y., & Ortiz, A. A. (1991). Reciprocal interaction-oriented strategies for literacy development: Teacher training outcomes. *Journal of the New York State Association for Bilingual Education, 7*(1), 95–109.

Townsend, W. A. (1995). *Pocket digest: Digest of education statistics for limited English proficient students.* Washington, DC: Office of Bilingual Education and Minority Languages Affairs.

Willig, A. C., Swedo, J. J., & Ortiz, A. A. (1987). *Characteristics of teaching strategies which result in high task engagement for exceptional limited English proficient Hispanic students.* Austin: The University of Texas, Handicapped Minority Research Institute on Language Proficiency.

Yates, J. R., & Ortiz, A. A. (1998). Developing individualized educational programs for the exceptional bilingual student. In L. Baca & H. Cervantes (Eds.), *The Bilingual Special Education Interface* (3rd ed., pp. 188–212). Columbus, OH: Merrill.

HECTOR SALVIA OCHOA
Texas A&M University

ALBA ORTIZ
SHERNAZ B. GARCIA
University of Texas

See also Bilingual Assessment and Special Education; Culturally/Linguistically Diverse Students and Learning Disabilities

BILINGUAL SPEECH LANGUAGE PATHOLOGY

Bilingual speech language pathology is an emerging field within the profession of speech language pathology. It is recognized as an area of the field that serves individuals who are bilingual and have a communication disorder. There are graduate programs in the United States that train bilingual clinicians and adhere to the profession's position statement on academic and clinical competencies. The American Speech-Language Hearing Association approved a position statement that defines who can be a bilingual speech language pathologist and/or audiologist.

This position statement includes the language proficiency required in the minority language and also the academic competencies necessary to provide services (Kayser, 1995). The definition states (ASHA, 1989): "Speech-language pathologists or audiologists who present themselves as bilingual for the purposes of providing clinical services must be able to speak their primary language and to speak (or sign) at least one other language with native or near-native proficiency in lexicon (vocabulary), semantics (meaning), phonology (pronunciation), morphology/syntax (grammar), and pragmatics (uses) during clinical management" (p. 93). The academic requirements (ASHA, 1995) include the following: (a) language proficiency: native or near native fluency in both the minority language and the English language; (b) normative processes: the ability to describe the process of normal speech and language acquisition for both bilingual and monolingual individuals and how these processes are manifested in oral and written language; (c) assessment: the ability to administer and interpret formal and informal assessment procedures to distinguish between communication difference and communication disorders; (d) intervention: the ability to apply intervention strategies for treatment of communicative disorders; (e) intervention: the ability to apply intervention strategies for treatment of communicative disorders in the minority language; and (f) cultural sensitivity: the ability to recognize cultural factors that affect the delivery of speech-language pathology and audiology services to the minority language speaking community.

REFERENCES

American Speech-Language-Hearing Association. (ASHA). (1989). Definition: Bilingual speech-language pathologists and audiologists. *ASHA, 31*(3), 93.

American Speech-Language-Hearing Association. (ASHA). (1995). Clinical management of communicatively handicapped minority language populations. *ASHA, 27*(6), 29–32.

Kayser, H. (1995). An emerging specialist: The bilingual speech-language pathologist. In H. Kayser (Ed.), *Bilingual speech language pathology. An Hispanic focus* (pp. 1–14). San Diego, CA: Singular.

HORTENCIA KAYSER
New Mexico State University
Third edition

DIEGO MUÑOZ
Chicago School of Professional Psychology
Fourth edition

BILINGUAL VERBAL ABILITY TESTS

The Bilingual Verbal Ability Tests (BVAT; now published as the Bilingual Verbal Ability Tests [BVAT] Normative Update) is designed to provide a measure of overall verbal ability, and a unique combination of cognitive/academic language abilities for bilingual individuals aged 5 to adult.

The BVAT is comprised of three individually administered subtests: (1) picture vocabulary, in which the subject is required to name a pictured object with gradually increasing degrees of difficulty; (2) oral vocabulary—broken into two tasks: synonyms, where the subject is required to make a synonymous word association with difficulty increasing gradually; and antonyms, where the subject is required to make an opposite word association with gradually increasing degrees of difficulty; (3) verbal analogies, where the subject is required to recognize the analogous relationships between two words and to find a word that fits the same relationship to a third word.

All the subtests are administered first in the English language. Each item failed in English is readministered in the native language. If the children answer correctly in their native language, that score is added to the score for that subtest. The overall subtest score is based on the child's knowledge/reasoning skills using both languages, thus reflecting the nature of the bilingual ability.

These tests are drawn from the Woodcock-Johnson-Revised (1989) Cognitive Battery and translated into different languages, presumably the most widely used languages in the United States: Arabic, Chinese (Simplified and Traditional), English, French, German, Haitian-Creole, Hindi, Hmong, Italian, Japanese, Korean, Navajo, Polish, Portuguese, Russian, Spanish, Turkish, and Vietnamese. There are 10 separate test records for the BVAT depending on which languages you wish to assess. One test record is used for the following languages: Arabic, Chinese (Simplified and Traditional), German, Hindi, Korean, Polish, and Turkish. A second test record contains French and Russian. The other languages each have separate test records.

There are two basic options for the BVAT interpretation: age-based or grade-based. In addition to standard scores (the same indicator as the Relative Mastery Index in the WJ-R), and percentile ranks, the BVAT offers "instructional zones" index, five levels of English language proficiency (from Negligible through Very Limited, Limited, Fluent to Advanced), and aptitude/achievement discrepancies in relation to the WJ-R Achievement Tests. All scoring is automated through the "Scoring and Reporting Program" software, which is a standard feature of the BVAT kit. The *BVAT Comprehensive Manual* contains the "Examiner Training and Practice Exercises." A training videotape, prepared by the publisher, accompanies the test.

The BVAT provides an overall score (BVA), which can be used to determine an individual's overall level of verbal ability. Raw scores are converted to standard scores, percentile ranks, age and grade equivalents, relative proficiency index, instructional ranges, and cognitive-academic language proficiency (CALP) levels.

English language normative data for the BVAT Normative Update are the same data gathered from 8,818 subjects in more than 100 geographically diverse U.S. communities during the standardization of the Woodcock-Johnson III (WJ III).

The measure as presented in some of the languages may exclude particular items (sometimes up to four items) because of the "untranslatable" nature of these items (*Manual*, Table 8–5, p. 71). It is not clear what effect these omitted items may have on the scores obtained if those scores are based on norms that include all items. Another concern regarding content validity is the issue of "uneven" complexity (from a relatively easy naming task in picture vocabulary to a much more difficult verbal reasoning task in verbal analogies).

REFERENCES

Reviewed by Alan Garfinkel and Charles W. Stansfield in Plake, B. S., & Impara, J. C. (Eds.). (2001). *The fourteenth mental measurements yearbook*. Lincoln, NE: Buros Institute of Mental Measurements.

RON DUMONT
Fairleigh Dickinson University

JOHN O. WILLIS
Rivier College

KATHLEEN VIEZEL
Fairleigh Dickinson University

JAMIE ZIBULSKY
Fairleigh Dickinson University

BINET, ALFRED (1857–1911)

Alfred Binet, the founder of French experimental psychology, became director of the Laboratory of Physiological Psychology at the Sorbonne in Paris in 1895. In the same year, he and a colleague founded the first French journal of psychology, *Année psychologique*. He was cofounder of the Société Libre pour l'Étude Psychologique de l'Enfant, which after his death became the Société Alfred Binet.

Binet's investigations took him outside the laboratory. He observed children in schools and camps and used questionnaires and interviews to collect data. In 1904, the minister of public instruction appointed him to a commission created to formulate methods for identifying intellectual developmental disabilities in the public schools so that these children could be given a special school program. Out of Binet's work with this commission

came the first scale for measuring intelligence, based on the idea of classifying children according to individual differences in performance of tasks requiring thinking and reasoning. On the assumption that intelligence increases with age, he employed the concept of mental age. Results were expressed both as mental age and by a score obtained by subtracting mental age from chronological age. The German psychologist William Stern proposed an improved way of expressing the test results: dividing mental age by chronological age, yielding an intelligence quotient.

The scale was first published by Binet and Theodore Simon in 1905 and was revised in 1908 and 1911. It was translated into English by H. H. Goddard in the United States. In 1916, L. M. Terman at Stanford University published his *Stanford Revision of the Binet Scales*. For half a century dozens of translations and revisions of Binet's scales dominated the field of intelligence testing; they are still extensively used.

Alfred Binet had a variety of other interests in the field of psychology. One of his earliest works was a book on hypnosis. In addition, he developed, with Simon, a classification of mental disorders. He also used pictures and inkblots to study thought processes, foreshadowing later projective techniques.

REFERENCES

Varon, E. J. (1935). The development of Alfred Binet's psychology. *Psychological Monographs* (No. 207). Princeton, NJ: Psychological Review.

Watson, R. I. (1963). *The great psychologists*. New York, NY: Lippincott.

PAUL IRVINE
Katonah, New York

BIOCHEMICAL IRREGULARITIES

It has been long recognized that a large number of metabolic diseases have characteristic clinical, pathological, and biochemical irregularities that can be attributed to the congenital deficiency of a specific enzyme. This inadequacy is in turn owed to the presence of a particular abnormal gene. The identification and consequent understanding of such biochemical problems began in the early part of the 20th century with the first demonstration of Mendelian inheritance in humans. A. E. Garrod (Roberts, 1967) derived the basic concept of these disorders through studies on the rare condition known as *alcaptonuria* (Garrod, 1909). His classical investigation of this abnormality has provided an elegant and simple model for the interpretation of a great variety of different inherited diseases subsequently discovered.

Alcaptonuria is a condition in which large quantities of homogentisic acid are excreted into the urine, which turns black on standing. Under normal conditions, the amino acid tyrosine is converted through a series of enzymatic reactions to fumarate and acetoacetate (La Du, 1966). Garrod noted that when homogentisic acid, a normal intermediary metabolite of tyrosine, was fed to alcaptonuric subjects, it was excreted quantitatively in urine, whereas when given to normal subjects it appeared to be readily metabolized. Additionally, the administration of tyrosine or proteins containing it to alcaptonurics augmented the excretion of homogentisic acid.

The other striking feature of alcaptonuria to which Garrod drew attention was its familial distribution. After studying the characteristic pedigrees of these subjects, he concluded that they implied a hereditary or genetic basis for the condition. Garrod pointed out that the homogentisic acid must be derived from tyrosine and that the essential feature of alcaptonuria was a block in the metabolism of this substance, whereby breakdown could proceed only as far as homogentisic acid.

Eventually Garrod described a number of metabolic peculiarities of this kind and called them inborn errors of metabolism. He viewed the inborn errors as conditions in which the specific enzyme deficiency effectively blocked at a particular point a sequence of reactions that form part of the normal course of metabolism. As a result, metabolites immediately preceding the block would accumulate and metabolites subsequent to the block would not be formed (Harris, 1975). The various biochemical, clinical, and pathological manifestations of the condition could be regarded as secondary consequences of this primary metabolic defect. These secondary changes might be complex and widespread and would depend in general on the nature and the biochemical effects of the metabolites that tended to accumulate or whose formation was restricted (Harper, Rodwell, & Mayes, 1977).

It is now understood that the end products of gene action are proteins, either structural cell components, elements of extracellular matrices, or enzymes. Since genes are potentially mutable units, a change in a gene will disturb the synthesis of the specific protein for which it is responsible. This results in the formation of a different protein (or no protein at all), which alters the process or processes that depend on it. When the protein is absent or deficient, the normal process is impaired. The expression of such a mutation is a phenotypic effect of more or less consequence to the individual. Such defects in cellular enzyme formation are most often characterized by abnormal protein, carbohydrate, or fat metabolism.

All biochemical processes are under genetic control and each consists of a complex sequence of reactions. Part (a) of Figure B.3 schematically represents a portion of a normal

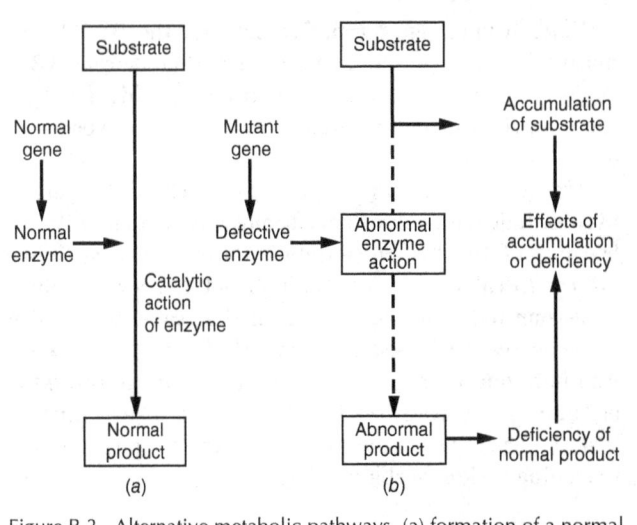

Figure B.3. Alternative metabolic pathways. (a) formation of a normal product. (b) accumulation of substrate or deficiency of product as a result of an abnormal metabolic pathway.
Source: Adapted from Whaley and Wong, 1983.

metabolic pathway. A substrate, the substance on which an enzyme acts, is converted into a product through the activity of a specific enzyme. A metabolic pathway consists of many such reactions or steps, each being dependent on the previous reaction and each catalyzed by a specific enzyme (Jenkins, 1983). Part (b) of the figure illustrates how a change in a gene that interferes with the synthesis of an essential enzyme interrupts this process. A block in the normal pathway may produce an accumulation of the substances preceding the block, such as the monosaccharide (simple sugar) galactose in classic galactosemia (Brown, 2003) or the amino acid phenylalanine in phenylketonuria (La Conte, 2003). In other cases, the block may create a deficiency in the normal product, such as the pigment melanin in albinism or the hormone thyroxine in familial cretinism. Sometimes alternative metabolic pathways are used that result in an increase in the products of these processes such as phenylketones in phenylketonuria. The effects of defective gene action are often observable in the individual as diseases.

There are many inherited disorders caused by an inborn error of metabolism that involves either the accumulation or degradation of metabolic processes. For the most part, they are rare diseases (National Organization of Rare Disorders [NORD], 2005), and the mode of transmission is almost always autosomal recessive genes. This may be best understood by considering the double-dose effect as it relates to the concept that one gene is responsible for one enzyme. If a specific gene controls the formation of an essential enzyme, and each individual has two such genes (the normal homozygote), then the enzyme is produced in normal amounts. The heterozygote, who has only one gene with a normal effect, is still capable of producing the enzyme in sufficient amounts to carry out the metabolic function under normal circumstances. However, the abnormal homozygote, who inherits a defective gene from each parent, has no functional enzyme and is, thus, clinically affected. It is becoming increasingly possible to detect and, therefore, to screen for a large variety of such inborn errors of metabolism. This should lead to the detection of the presence of the disease in the heterozygote (who is a carrier), the newborn, and the fetus before birth, thus allowing for proper genetic counseling of the parents and successful treatment of affected individuals (Goodenough, 1978).

REFERENCES

Brown, R. T. (2003). Galactosemia. In E. Fletcher-Janzen & C. R. Reynolds (Eds.), *Childhood disorders diagnostic desk reference*. Hoboken, NJ: Wiley.

Garrod, A. E. (1909). *Inborn errors of metabolism*. New York, NY: Oxford University Press.

Goodenough, U. (1978). *Genetics* (2nd ed.). New York, NY: Holt, Rinehart, & Winston.

Harper, H. A., Rodwell, V. W., & Mayes, P. A. (1977). *Review of physiological chemistry* (16th ed.). Los Altos, CA: Lange Medical.

Harris, H. (1975). *The principles of human biochemical genetics* (2nd ed.). New York, NY: American Elsevier.

Jenkins, J. B. (1983). *Human genetics*. New York, NY: Benjamin/Cummings.

La Conte, M. (2003). Phenylketonuria. In E. Fletcher-Janzen & C. R. Reynolds (Eds.), *Childhood disorders diagnostic desk reference*. Hoboken, NJ: Wiley.

La Du, B. N. (1966). Alcaptonuria. In J. B. Stanbury, J. B. Wyngaarden, & D. S. Fredickson (Eds.), *The metabolic basis of inherited diseases*. New York, NY: McGraw-Hill.

NORD. (2005). *National Organization of Rare Disorders*. Retrieved from http://www.rarediseases.org/

Roberts, J. A. F. (1967). *An introduction to medical genetics* (4th ed.). New York, NY: Oxford University Press.

Whaley, L. F., & Wong, D. L. (1983). *Nursing care of infants and children* (2nd ed.). St. Louis, MO: Mosby.

TIMOTHY A. BALLARD
University of North Carolina at Wilmington

See also Congenital Disorders; Cretinism; Inborn Errors of Metabolism; Phenylketonuria

BIOFEEDBACK

Biofeedback is a treatment technique in which people are trained to change bodily functions such as temperature or muscle tension based on signals from their own bodies.

The word *biofeedback* was first used in the late 1960s to describe laboratory procedures being used to train experimental research subjects to alter brain activity, blood pressure, heart rate, and other bodily functions that normally are not controlled voluntarily. Measuring a temperature with a thermometer or weight on a scale are both devices that provide feedback about the body's condition. Typically, however, biofeedback measurements used to enhance treatment are more complex and measure internal bodily function with sensitivity and precision. For example, machines designed to assess muscle tension translate electrical signals up the skin, converting them to something as simple as a flashing light that increases in intensity as muscles grow more tense to something more complex, such as a visual array on a computer screen.

At first, researchers believed that properly developed biofeedback techniques would make it possible to do away with drug treatments that often cause uncomfortable side effects in patients with serious conditions such as high blood pressure or even cancer. Today, most researchers and scientists agree that such hopes were not realistic. Biofeedback can help in the treatment of many diseases and painful conditions, but it is not a panacea. Biofeedback has shown that human beings have more control over so-called involuntary bodily functions than once thought possible. However, it has also been demonstrated that nature limits the extent of such control.

As with learning any skill, people receiving biofeedback attempts to monitor their performance and thus improve their ability to relax. With muscular feedback, when a light flashes or the screen demonstrates increased tension, the individual attempts to make internal adjustments that then alter the signals or feedback. Clinical biofeedback techniques used today include treatment of many conditions, including headache, disorders of the digestive system, blood pressure problems, cardiac arrhythmias, circulatory conditions, paralysis, and even epilepsy.

Scientific method has yet to completely explain the means by which biofeedback is effective. Individuals who benefit from biofeedback are trained to relax and modify their behavior. Most scientists believe that relaxation is a key component if biofeedback is to be effective. It is thought that stressful events produce strong emotions that arouse certain physical responses. Many of these responses are controlled by the sympathetic nervous system, the network of nerves that help prepare the body to meet emergencies. When an individual faces any type of physical threat or illness, this system is likely to be innervated. Pupils dilate to let in more light. Blood vessels near the skin contract to reduce bleeding. Those in the brain and muscles dilate to increase oxygen supply. The gastrointestinal tract, including the stomach and intestine, slows down to reduce the energy expended in digestion. The heart beats faster and blood pressure rises. As the stressful event passes, the body returns to normal. Researchers believe that when this system is innervated on a regular basis, relaxation becomes habitual. When the body is repeatedly aroused, one or more bodily functions may become permanently overactive. Biofeedback is aimed at changing habitual reactions to stress that cause pain or disease.

Biofeedback is not a passive process. Individuals must examine their behavior and the activities that contribute to distress and problems. They must recognize that they can, through their own efforts, remedy some physical ailments. They often have to practice relaxation exercises on a daily basis between biofeedback sessions. Biofeedback specialists include physicians, psychologists, dentists, and even physical therapists. The Association for Applied Psychophysiology and Biofeedback (formerly the Biofeedback Society of America) is a national membership association for professionals using biofeedback. The organization produces a journal, news magazine, and other biofeedback-related publications.

SAM GOLDSTEIN
University of Utah

See also **Biogenic Models; Magnetic Resonance Imaging; Spect, Single Photon Emission Computed Tomography**

BIOGENIC MODELS

Biogenic, or organic, models present causes of human actions in terms of the biological substrate that underlies behavior. Thus to predict, explain, and control behavior, the various activities of the nervous system and other bodily organs must be understood and manipulated. Implicit in this model is the notion that effective therapies will primarily involve biological interventions such as drugs or surgery. This approach can be contrasted with psychogenic models that emphasize psychological constructs as explanatory mechanisms of behavior (Butcher, Mineka, & Hooley, 2013; Franzblau, Kanadanian, & Rettig, 1995).

Contemporary models of behavior are rarely in absolutely biological or psychological terms, but when a model is primarily biogenic in nature there are important implications for the user's conceptual framework in understanding behavior and implementing behavioral change programs. Biogenic models place the locus of the cause of problem behavior squarely within the individual's biological status and give only minimal roles to other parts of the ecosystem such as family or school. Most contemporary biogenic models are reductionistic and pin their ultimate hopes on an understanding of the relationships among biological, biochemical, and behavioral phenomena. Alterations, which are observed in cognitions or social relations, can be viewed as symptoms of physiological actions. Although our current understanding of biological factors

may not allow for biochemical cures for all behavioral problems, the ultimate direction of the biogenic approach lies in biomedical interventions (Engel, 1977).

Critics of the biogenic model have difficulty denying that in a physical sense all behavior can ultimately be traced to biological processes. They do contend, however, that reductionist approaches may not always be the most fruitful guides to practice in education. Biogenic models tend to blame the victim by emphasizing changing the organism and not the environment or situation in which the individual exists (Albee, 1980; Millon & Davis, 1995). It is often the case that concepts of the biogenic model are confused with those of the medical or disease model. Engel (1977), however, proposed a disease model that replaced a biomedical with a biopsychosocial approach to the understanding of disordered behavior. This is now the norm (Suls & Rothman, 2004). However, research advances in such areas as neuroimaging and epigenetics have added a new emphasis on the biological component of the biopsychosocial model (Heussler & Oliver, 2011; Masterpasqua, 2009).

The organic (biogenic) model represents one of the major historical threads in the understanding of the etiology of abnormal behavior. This model has been advanced at least since the time of the Greek physician Hippocrates (Brown, 1986), and is still seen in the etiologic theories for autism spectrum disorder (Butcher et al., 2013). Indeed, for thousands of years, it was the only viable alternative to magical or supernatural explanations of exceptional behavior. It should be noted, however, that biogenic models have not always resulted in more humane treatment or exacting scientific research into the nature of behavior disorders. For example, the warehousing of patients in the late 19th- and early 20th-century psychiatric hospitals was the result in part of a belief that dealing with mental disease was hopeless until science found a biological cure (Erickson & Hyerstay, 1980).

Biogenic models may be of value to the classroom special education teacher as the basis for planning interventions. Wetherington and Hooper (2006) noted the importance of special education teachers' understanding of the role of early traumatic brain injury in managing classroom behaviors. In addition the biopsychosocial model takes into account aspects of chronic illness which are common to children in special education.

REFERENCES

Albee, G. (1980). A competency model to replace the deficit model. In M. Gibbs, J. Lachenmeyer, & J. Sigal (Eds.), *Community psychology: Theoretical and empirical approaches* (pp. 213–238). New York, NY: Gardner.

Brown, R. T. (1986). Etiology and development of exceptionality. In R. T. Brown & C. R. Reynolds (Eds.), *Psychological perspectives on childhood exceptionality: A handbook* (pp. 181–229). New York, NY: Wiley.

Butcher, J., Mineka, S., & Hooley, J. (2013). *Abnormal psychology* (15th ed.). Boston, MA: Pearson.

Engel, G. (1977). A need for a new medical model: A challenge for biomedicine. *Science, 96*, 129–136.

Erickson, R., & Hyerstay, B. (1980). Historical perspectives on treatment of the mentally ill. In M. Gibbs, J. Lachenmeyer, & J. Sigal (Eds.), *Community psychology: Theoretical and empirical approaches* (pp. 29–64). New York, NY: Gardner.

Franzblau, S. H., Kanadanian, M., & Rettig, E. (1995). Critique of reductionistic models of obsessive compulsive disorder. *Social Science and Medicine, 41*, 99–112.

Heussler, H. & Oliver, C. (2011). Behavioural phenotypes: From models to intervention. *Journal of Intellectual Disability Research, 55*(10), 945–947.

Masterpasqua, F. (2009). Psychology and epigenetics. *Review of General Psychology, 13*(3), 194–201.

Millon, T., & Davis, R. D. (1995). The development of personality disorders. In D. Cicchetti & D. J. Cohen (Eds.), *Developmental psychopathology* (Vol. 2). New York, NY: Wiley.

Suls, J., & Rothman, A. (2004). Evolution of biopsychosocial model: Prospects and challenges for health psychology. *Health Psychology, 23*, 119–125.

Wetherington, C., & Hooper, S. R. Preschool traumatic brain injury: A review for the early childhood special educator. *Exceptionality, 14*(3), 155–170.

LEE ANDERSON JACKSON JR.
University of North Carolina at Wilmington
Fourth edition

See also Biological Basis of Emotional Disorders; Biological Basis of Learning and Memory; Medical Model, Defense of

BIOLOGICAL BASIS OF EMOTIONAL DISORDERS

Biological factors contribute to emotional disorders in various ways. A genetic predisposition has been strongly implicated for schizophrenia, depression, and manic-depressive illness. There is at least moderate evidence of a genetic contribution to obsessive-compulsive disorder (Franzblau, Kanadanian, & Rettig, 1995), panic disorder, disability (Heubner & Thomas, 1995), and other conditions.

Whether because of genetics, improper nutrition, or other sources, certain areas of the nervous system can misfunction in ways that lead to behavioral abnormalities. For example, individuals who are subject to panic disorder have an overresponsive sympathetic nervous system. Even at rest, they have an elevated heart rate and blood epinephrine level compared with controls (Nesse, Cameron, Curtis, McCann, & Huber-Smith, 1984). They may respond with anxiety, agitation, and palpitations to injections that produce only mild signs of arousal in other people (Charney, Heninger, & Breier, 1984; Liebowitz et al., 1984). On the other hand, studies have documented a relationship between low physiological arousal and antisocial behavior (Susman, 2001).

Many types of emotional disorders have been linked to abnormalities affecting one or more synaptic transmitter systems in the brain. One example is depression. Most antidepressant drugs prolong the activity of the monoamine transmitters (dopamine, norepinephrine, and serotonin) in the brain. One interpretation of the effect of antidepressant drugs has been that they counteract an initial deficiency in the activity at monoamine synapses. That interpretation may be incorrect, however; a prolonged increase in the abundance of synaptic transmitter molecules at a synapse leads to a compensatory decline in the later release of that transmitter and to a decline in the number of receptors sensitive to that transmitter. Because of the multitude of effects, it is uncertain whether the antidepressant drugs help to repair an initial overactivity or underactivity of the monoamine synapses. Nevertheless, it is likely that some disorder of those synapses is responsible for many manifestations of depression.

Another probable example of a behavioral disorder linked to abnormalities at synapses is Gilles de la Tourette's syndrome. This uncommon condition affects mostly boys and has its onset in childhood. The symptoms include tics, repetitive movements, repetitive sounds, and learning disabilities (Golden, 1977). Although the cause is not known, the usual treatment is haloperidol and other drugs that block dopamine synapses in the brain.

The biological basis of an emotional disorder need not be a permanent chemical disorder of the brain, however, and drugs are not always the best remedy for a biological disorder. Many cases of depression have been linked to inadequate or poorly timed sleep. Occasionally, individuals suffer from winter depressions as a result of inadequate sunlight. Uncorrected visual problems may lead to headaches. Many adolescents experience moodiness and aggressive outbursts that may be triggered by hormonal changes. A lack of exercise may predispose the body to overreact to stress. Malnutrition can aggravate psychological disorders as well. In certain cases, emotional disorders can be alleviated by reducing stress, altering sleep, diet, exercise, and other habits without resorting to tranquilizers, antidepressant drugs, or other medical interventions (Kalat, 1984; Wickramasekera, Davies, & Davies, 1996).

REFERENCES

Charney, D. S., Heninger, G. R., & Breier, A. (1984). Noradrenergic function in panic anxiety. *Archives of General Psychiatry, 41*, 751–763.

Franzblau, S. H., Kanadanian, M., & Rettig, E. (1995). Critique of the reductionist models of obsessive compulsive disorder. *Social Science and Medicine, 41*, 99–112.

Golden, G. S. (1977). Tourette syndrome. *American Journal of Diseases of Children*, *131*, 531–534.

Heubner, R. A., & Thomas, R. (1995). The relationship between attachment, psychopathology, and childhood disability. *Rehabilitation Psychology*, *40*, 111–124.

Kalat, J. W. (1984). *Biological psychology* (2nd ed.). Belmont, CA: Wadsworth.

Liebowitz, M. R., Fyer, A. J., Gorman, J. M., Dillon, D., Appleby, I. L., Levy, G., . . . Klein, D. F. (1984). Lactate provocation of panic attacks: Vol. I. Clinical and behavioral findings. *Archives of General Psychiatry*, *41*, 764–770.

Nesse, R. M., Cameron, O. G., Curtis, G. C., McCann, D. S., & Huber-Smith, M. J. (1984). Adrenergic function in patients with panic anxiety. *Archives of General Psychiatry*, *41*, 771–776.

Susman, E. J. (2001). Mind-body interaction and development: Biology, behavior, and context. *European Psychologist*, *6*, 163–171.

Wickramasekera, I., Davies, T. E., & Davies, S. M. (1996). Applied psychophysiology: A bridge between the biomedical model and the biopsychosocial model in family medicine. *Professional Psychology: Research & Practice*, *27*, 221–233.

JAMES W. KALAT
North Carolina State University

See also Diagnostic and Statistical Manual of Mental Disorders (DSM-IV-TR); Emotional Disorders

BIOLOGICAL BASIS OF LEARNING AND MEMORY

To understand the biological basis of learning and memory, two largely independent questions must be dealt with: (1) How does a pattern of experience alter the future properties of cells and synapses in the nervous system? (2) How do populations of altered cells work together to produce adaptive behavior?

Striking progress has been made toward answering the first question. According to studies of invertebrates, short-term increases in behavior can be induced by chemical changes that block the flow of potassium across the presynaptic membrane of certain neurons. Longer lasting changes in behavior require the synthesis of proteins in the neurons to be changed (Kandel & Schwartz, 1982). Protein synthesis also appears to be necessary for learning by vertebrates, especially for long-term retention (Davis & Squire, 1984).

Certain of the brain changes associated with learning or the ability to learn are large enough to be visible under a light microscope. Enhanced learning ability is associated with a proliferation of glial cells and increased branching of dendrites (Uphouse, 1980). Impaired learning associated with the opposite anatomical changes. The extent of branching of dendrites is highly correlated with the number of synapses found in the brain.

Memory, on the other hand, is "attention" that leaves tracks or traces in the brain. Biologically, memory functions at two broad levels, one at the cellular level and one at a systems level. The creation of memories changes individual cell membranes and synaptic physiology (Reynolds & Bigler, 1997).

Investigators have not determined how the changed neurons operate together to produce the overall changes in behavior identified as learning. They have, however, identified areas of the mammalian brain that are necessary for certain aspects of learning. The famous neurological patient H. M. had most of his hippocampus removed as a treatment for severe epilepsy. He could recall very few events that occurred after the operation, although he was able to learn new skills such as reading material written in mirror fashion and working the Tower of Hanoi puzzle (Cohen & Squire, 1980; Milner, Corkin, & Teuber, 1968). Experiments with animals have indicated that amnesia is most severe if damage to the hippocampus is combined with damage to the amygdala. Damage to those two areas impairs animals' ability to store sensory information and respond to it a few minutes later (ZolaMorgan & Squire, 1985). Various other patterns of learning and memory loss occur after damage to the frontal lobes of the cerebral cortex and to numerous subcortical structures.

Majovski (1997) has suggested that:

> Data collected from studies of heredity and environment show that morphogenetic development of the brain's intellectual nature is attributable to both genetic and social environmental influences, the former having slightly greater effect than the latter. What this suggests is that several different cortical and cortical-subcortical systems are operative during the process of learning and information storage. What the infant senses, then, may be in part the result of what is neurally "set" to sense or competent to sense via a selective attention process. (p. 83)

The interactive process of learning and memory with the environmental and physical factors in childhood suggests a highly interactive biological set. A large-scale theory has been proposed for this set by Gerald Edleman (Edleman, 1992), a Nobel Prize winner, and coined as *"neural Darwinism,"* which suggests that the brain is context bound. Competition for advantage in the environment enhances the spread and strength of certain synapses, or neural connections, according to the value previously decided by evolutionary survival and therefore is self-organizing. Another term for this process is *"neuronal group selection."*

Overlapping the initial growth and development of the brain, and extending throughout an individual's life, a continuous process of synaptic selection occurs within the diverse repertoires of neuronal groups. This process may strengthen or weaken the connections between groups of neurons and it is constrained by value signals that arise from the activity of the ascending systems of the brain, which are continually modified by successful output. Experiential selection generates dynamic systems that can *"map"* complex spatio-temporal events from the sensory organs, body systems, and other neuronal groups in the brain onto other selected neuronal groups. Edelman argues that this dynamic selective process is directly analogous to the processes of selection that act on populations of individuals in species, and he also points out that this functional plasticity is imperative, since not even the vast coding capability of entire human genome is sufficient to explicitly specify the astronomically complex synaptic structures of the developing brain (Edelman, 1992, p. 224).

Large scale theories of learning and behavior have to interact with other scientific advances in environmental threats to healthy brain development. Exposure to alcohol and other toxins in utero can greatly impair neuronal health and development, as can severe malnutrition, or a chronic lack of social stimulation in early childhood. Evidence of long-term sequelae of prematurity and low birth weight are beginning to be discovered in the research literature that suggest neuropsychological outcomes for learning and memory extending into adulthood (Mulder, Pitchford, & Marlow, 2010; Raz, Debastos, Newman, & Batton, 2010). In addition, head injury leading to a temporary loss of consciousness and/or postconcussion syndrome is a commonly overlooked source of minor, diffuse brain damage (Bruce & Echemendia, 2003; Clay, 2011). These factors coupled with the acculturation and cross-cultural differences (Uomoto & Wong, 2000) makes the differential diagnosis of learning and memory problems very complex indeed.

REFERENCES

Bruce, J. M., & Echemendia, R. J. (2003). Delayed-onset deficits in verbal encoding strategies among patients with mild traumatic brain injury. *Neuropsychology, 17*, 622–629.

Clay, R. A. (2011). Giving a heads up on concussion. *American Psychologist, 42*(10), 54.

Cohen, N. J., & Squire, L. R. (1980). Preserved learning and retention of pattern-analyzing skill in amnesia: Dissociation of knowing how and knowing that. *Science, 210*, 207–211.

Davis, H. P., & Squire, L. R. (1984). Protein synthesis and memory: A review. *Psychological Bulletin, 96*, 518–559.

Edelmen, G. (1992). *Bright air, brilliant fire* (pp. 224). New York, NY: Penguin.

Kandel, E. R., & Schwartz, J. H. (1982). Molecular biology of learning: Modulation of transmitter release. *Science, 218*, 433–443.

Majovski, L. V. (1997). Development of higher brain functions in children: Neural, cognitive, and behavioral perspectives. In C. R. Reynolds & E. Fletcher-Janzen (Eds.), *Handbook*

of clinical child neuropsychology (2nd ed., pp. 63–101). New York, NY: Plenum Press.

Milner, B., Corkin, S., & Teuber, H. L. (1968). Further analysis of the hippocampal amnesic syndrome: 14-year follow-up study of H. M. *Neuropsychologia, 6*, 215–234.

Moscovitch, M. (1985). Memory from infancy to old age: Implications for theories of normal and pathological memory. *Annals of the New York Academy of Sciences, 444*, 78–96.

Mulder, H., Pitchford, N.J., & Marlow, N. (2010). Processing speed mediates executive function difficulties in very preterm children in middle childhood. *Journal of the International Neuropsychological Society, 17*, 445–454.

Raz, S., Debastos, A. K., Newman, J. B., & Batton, D. (2010). Extreme prematurity and neuropsychological outcome in the preschool years. *Journal of the International Neuropsychological Society, 16*, 169–179.

Reynolds, C. R., & Bigler, E. D. (1997). Clinical neuropsychological assessment of child and adolescent memory with the test of learning & memory. In C. R. Reynolds & E. Fletcher-Janzen (Eds.), *Handbook of clinical child neuropsychology* (2nd ed., pp. 296–329). New York, NY: Plenum Press.

Uomoto, J. M., & Wong, T. M. (2000). Multicultural perspectives on the neuropsychology of brain injury assessment and rehabilitation. In E. Fletcher-Janzen, T. L. Strickland, & C. R. Reynolds (Eds.), *Handbook of cross cultural neuropsychology* (pp. 169–184). New York, NY: Springer.

Uphouse, L. (1980). Reevaluation of mechanisms that mediate brain differences between enriched and impoverished animals. *Psychological Bulletin, 88*, 215–232.

Zola-Morgan, S., & Squire, L. R. (1985). Medial temporal lesions in monkeys impair memory on a variety of tasks sensitive to human amnesia. *Behavioral Neuroscience, 99*, 22–34.

JAMES W. KALAT
North Carolina State University
First edition

ELAINE FLETCHER-JANZEN
Chicago School of Professional Psychology
Fourth edition

BIPOLAR AFFECTIVE DISORDER

Bipolar affective disorder (BAD) is a mood disorder that is characterized by distinct periods of depression and manic episodes. Manic episodes are characterized by elevated mood, grandiosity, pressured speech, racing thoughts, distractibility, decreased need for sleep, increased goal-directed behavior, and extreme involvement in pleasurable (but reckless) activities. Depressive episodes are often characterized by diminished interest, sadness, disturbed sleep and appetite, feelings of guilt and hopelessness, and problems with concentration and performance. During periods of depression, suicidal thoughts are common. In fact, among adolescents diagnosed with BAD, around 20% make serious suicide attempts; males are more likely to complete these (American Psychiatric Association [APA], 2000).

According to the *Diagnostic and Statistical Manual of Mental Disorders, Fourth Edition*, Text Revision (*DSM-IV-TR*), there are two types of BAD, one that is characterized by a history of at least one manic episode (or mixed episodes) and depression (Bipolar I), and the other a history of one or more episodes of both major depression and hypomania (Bipolar II). *DSM-IV-TR* criteria are essentially the same for young people and adults. The overall risk of developing Bipolar I has been estimated to be .4% to 1.6%, and .5% for Bipolar II (APA, 2000). Twenty percent of individuals diagnosed as having BAD have their first episode during adolescence, with peak onset between 15 and 19 (and overall prevalence rate about 1%; McClellan & Werry, 1997). Sex differences have been reported, with more females being diagnosed with Bipolar II and presenting more often with depression as the first episode and the more frequent manifestation. Males are more likely to present with mania first but have equal occurrences of manic and depressive episodes over a lifetime. Compared to males, females and adolescents of both sexes are more likely to be rapid cyclers (i.e., 4 or more episodes a year).

Characteristics

1. There are distinct periods of abnormally elevated, expansive, or irritable mood lasting for at least one week (or requiring hospitalization).

2. If mood is elevated or expansive, the individual must have three or more prominent symptoms; if mood is irritable only, four or more (e.g., grandiosity, decreased need for sleep, racing thoughts, excessive involvement in reckless activities).

3. Symptoms must be distinguished from normal baseline behaviors, must have a fluctuating course, and must cause impairment in functioning (or significant distress).

4. Symptoms cannot be due to drug abuse, medication use, or medical condition.

5. Children tend to be more irritable and belligerent than euphoric, and adolescents more labile and psychotic (e.g., paranoia and frank hallucinations).

6. Long-term outcome for early versus later onset of BAD is about the same, but when occurring earlier, symptoms appear more chronic and resistant to treatment.

The risks for having an early onset of BAD include rapid onset of depression with psychomotor slowing or agitation, family history of affective disorders (especially BAD), and

report of mania-hypomania after treatment with antidepressant medications (McClellan & Werry, 1997). Mania is considered rare in young children; however, current thought suggests that chronic irritability, hypersensitivity, and belligerence may be symptomatic of BAD, and not just "normal" behaviors of childhood (Sach, Baldassano, Truman, & Guille, 2000). There is no known association between earlier onset and long-term outcome of the condition; however, the course appears more chronic and less responsive to treatment. This may be explained in part by the higher rate of mixed symptoms in earlier onset BAD and greater frequency of psychosis and comorbidity.

Frequently reported comorbid conditions include attention-deficit/hyperactivity disorder, conduct disorder, and substance abuse. The unusually high rate of comorbidity not only complicates treatment but also makes diagnosis more difficult (and the prognosis worse). Differential diagnosis is also complicated by conditions that have a number of shared features. This includes children with posttraumatic stress disorder who have unstable moods, irritability, sleep disturbance, and hypervigilance, as well as adolescents who have schizophrenia and present with disturbed thinking, paranoia, and hallucinations. Measures such as the Mania Rating Scale (Fristad, Weller, & Weller, 1990) can help to distinguish BAD from other conditions; however, a complete and reliable history is critical to ensure accurate diagnosis and treatment (e.g., data on baseline functioning and symptom stability of the child and family history of mood disorders, especially BAD).

Genetics plays a critical role in BAD; in fact, 15% of individuals with BAD have first-degree relatives with the disorder. The rate is even higher for early-onset BAD. Pharmacology is the most common treatment, and lithium is the drug of choice. Lithium has been found to be particularly effective in treating mania; however, when lithium is ineffective or contraindicated (e.g., females prone to developing ovarian cysts or children with renal problems), anticonvulsants such as valproate and carbamazepine have been used. Benzodiazepines and neuroleptics are also used as adjunctive therapies for agitation and psychotic symptoms. In addition to drug therapy, psychological interventions are needed to address certain behavior problems and psychosocial concerns. Research has demonstrated that individuals who experience significant negative life events and have fewer social supports take longer to recover than do those with positive attitudes and supports (Miklowitz & Alloy, 1999).

Children and adolescents with BAD are likely to require special accommodations at school, in some cases, special education (e.g., services under the category Emotional Disturbance). Regardless of the need for special service, the school psychologist should be contacted to ensure appropriate services, including home-school collaborations regarding behavior and schoolwork (e.g., implementing strategies such as home notes to improve work completion). Education about BAD is also important for the child, parent, and teacher.

BAD is considered a recurrent condition with relapse rates as high as 40% in the first year and 73% at year 5 (Gitlin, Swendsen, Heller, & Hammen, 1995). Research is therefore needed to identify treatments that will reduce the relapse rates and provide more effective symptom relief. Finding ways to identify at-risk infants and children is also needed to prevent associated problems such as school failure, substance abuse, and social-legal problems and to provide more effective symptom relief. Research is also needed to determine protective factors and the long-term consequence of early-onset BAD.

REFERENCES

American Psychiatric Association. (2000). *Diagnostic and statistical manual of mental disorders* (4th ed., Text rev.). Washington, DC: Author.

Fristad, M., Weller, E., & Weller, R. (1990). The mania rating scale: Can it be used in children? *Journal of the American Academy of Child and Adolescent Psychiatry, 34*(7), 867–876.

Gitlin, M., Swendsen, J., Heller, T., & Hammen, C. (1995). Relapse and impairment in bipolar disorder. *American Journal of Psychiatry, 152,* 1635–1640.

McClellan, J., & Werry, J. (1997). Practice parameters for the assessment and treatment of children and adolescents with bipolar disorder. *Journal of the American Academy of Child and Adolescent Psychiatry, 36*(10), 157–175.

Miklowitz, D., & Alloy, L. (1999). Psychosocial factors in the course and treatment of bipolar disorder: Introduction to the special section. *Journal of Abnormal Psychology, 108*(4), 555–557.

Sach, G., Baldassano, C., Truman, C., & Guille, C. (2000). Comorbidity of attention deficit hyperactivity disorder with early and late onset bipolar disorder. *American Journal of Psychiatry, 157*(3), 466–468.

ELAINE CLARK
REX GONZALES
University of Utah

BIRCH, HERBERT G. (1918–1973)

Herbert G. Birch was born in New York City on April 21, 1918. He graduated from New York University (NYU) in 1939, and received the PhD degree in psychology in 1944. In 1960 Birch received the MD degree from the New York College of Medicine. He served as a research associate at the Yerkes Laboratories for Primate Biology from 1944 to 1946, as an instructor in psychology at NYU the next year, and as an assistant and associate professor at the City College of New York from 1947 to 1955. For the following 2 years, Birch was research associate at Bellevue Medical

Center in New York City. From the time he received the MD degree in 1960 until his death, he was a member of the faculty of the Albert Einstein College of Medicine in New York City, first as an associate research professor and then as a full professor of pediatrics and director of the Center for Normal and Aberrant Behavioral Development. Concurrently, he was professor of psychology and education at the Ferkauf Graduate School of Humanities and Social Sciences, Yeshiva University.

An internationally known researcher in child development and brain injury, Birch was the author of 200 articles and coauthor of six books, the latter including *Brain Damage in Children* (1964), *Disadvantaged Children: Health, Nutrition, and School Failure* (1970), and *Children with Cerebral Dysfunction* (1971). He served in an editorial capacity for a number of journals, including the *Journal of Special Education*, the *American Journal of Mental Deficiency*, the *American Journal of Child Psychology and Human Development*, and the *International Journal of Mental Health*. In 1971 he received the Kennedy International Award for Scientific Research for outstanding scientific research contributing to the understanding and alleviation of intellectual developmental disabilities.

Birch died at his home in Suffern, New York, on February 4, 1973. In his eulogy, Dr. Leon Eisenberg said of Birch, "Those who knew Herbert Birch recognized that they were in the presence of authentic genius. His knowledge was encyclopedic; his intellect, prodigious; his productivity, unmatched." In May 1973, Birch was posthumously granted the Research Award of the American Association on Mental Deficiency.

REFERENCES

Birch, H. G. (Ed.). (1964). *Brain damage in children.* Baltimore, MD: Williams & Wilkins.

Birch, H. G., & Diller, K. (1971). *Children with cerebral dysfunction.* New York, NY: Grune & Stratton.

Birch, H. G., & Gussow, J. D. (1970). *Disadvantaged children: Health, nutrition and school failure.* New York, NY: Grune & Stratton.

Eisenberg, L. (1971). Herbert Birch 1918–1973. *International Journal of Mental Health, 1,* 80–81.

PAUL IRVINE
Katonah, New York

BIRCH, JACK W. (1915–1998)

A native of Glassport, Pennsylvania, Jack W. Birch began his career as an elementary education teacher after receiving a BS (1937) with majors in English and science and a minor in special education from California University of Pennsylvania. He later went on to earn his MEd from Pennsylvania State University (1941) and a PhD in Psychology from the University of Pittsburgh (1951).

Birch taught classes for educable mentally retarded children, and was a psychologist and supervisor of special education. From 1948 to 1958 he was director of special education for the Pittsburgh Public Schools, and spent the remainder of his career at the University of Pittsburgh as a professor of psychology and education, chairman of the Department of Special Education, and an associate dean in the School of Education. He was among the initial faculty organizers of the University Senate and served as its vice president. Birch became an emeritus professor in 1985 at the age of 70. He was active in the field of education and community service until his death on April 1, 1998.

As a young teacher in Eastern Pennsylvania in the 1930s, Birch was aghast at the ineptitude of a book about remedial reading he had purchased. He wrote the publisher, complaining of the money he had wasted buying the book and indicating that he could do a better job himself. The response from the publisher encouraged him to go ahead and try, so he did. His first book was published by that same company, beginning a long career combining his interests in research, writing, and special education. He published more than 120 articles and books on topics including gifted and talented persons and individuals with intellectual developmental disabilities, speech handicaps, blindness, deafness, and physical handicaps. *Teaching Exceptional Children in All America's Schools* and *Reports on the Implementation and Effects of the Adaptive Learning Environments Model in General and Special Education Settings* are two of his major books. His writings also included books related to aspects of academia, including writing better dissertations and how to make the best use of retired professors.

Believing that students with handicaps should have an opportunity to display skills society assumed they were incapable of developing, Birch was among early advocates of mainstreaming students with handicaps. In 1978 he reviewed the process of mainstreaming in a national sample of school systems, concluding that expansion of individualized education was a necessity and recommending ways to effectively implement mainstreaming. Four essential conditions were cited for successful mainstreaming: (1) regular educators must be oriented to the adaptation requirements for the inclusion of pupils with handicaps; (2) teachers must learn to use the specialized instructional materials exceptional children may need; (3) regular classroom teachers must be able, through an overt arrangement, to obtain help for pupils from special education teachers; and (4) regular classroom teachers must receive immediate assistance (with no loss of face) if a crisis in class or individual management occurs. Birch's research also indicated that many young people who were believed to have mental disabilities actually suffered from hearing problems, and that their ability to learn would be enhanced by first addressing the hearing problem.

During his lifetime, Birch traveled to numerous countries, frequently as a consultant in special education to various foreign governments and schools, and from 1985 to 1986, he was the Belle van Zuijlen professor of clinical child psychology and pedagogy at the University Utrecht, Netherlands. Among his memberships, he was a fellow of the American Psychological Association; regional chairman of the Commission on Psychology, Education, Nomenclature, and Standards of the American Association of Mental Deficiency; and president of both the Council for Exceptional Children and the Foundation for Exceptional Children. For his contributions to special education and rehabilitation, Birch received an award from the Pennsylvania Federation of the Council for Exceptional Children, and he was also honored for his service with an award from The National Accreditation Council of Services to the Blind and Visually Handicapped.

REFERENCES

Birch, J. W. (1978). Mainstreaming that works in elementary and secondary schools. *Journal of Teacher Education*, 29, 18–21.

Reynolds, M. C., & Birch, J. W. (1982). *Teaching exceptional children in all America's schools*. Reston, VA: Council for Exceptional Children.

Wang, M. C., & Birch, J. W. (1985). *Reports on the implementation and effects of the adaptive learning environments model in general and special education settings*. Pittsburgh, PA: University of Pittsburgh.

E. VALERIE HEWITT
Texas A&M University
First edition

TAMARA J. MARTIN
University of Texas of the Permian Basin
Second edition

BIRTH INJURIES

Birth injuries are the traumatic injuries to the brain, skull, spinal cord, peripheral nerves, and muscle of the newborn that occasionally occur during the birth process. These injuries include cephalohematoma, skull fracture, central nervous system hemorrhage, spinal cord injury, peripheral nerve injury, bony injury, abdominal injury, cerebral palsy, and seizure disorders. The frequency of these birth injuries has greatly decreased with the declining use of high and midforceps, better monitoring during labor, and decreased vaginal breech deliveries (Brann, 1985). However, the frequency of birth injuries may vary depending on the introduction of new techniques to assist delivery

BIRTH INJURIES

such as vacuum extraction (Hes, de Jong, Paz, & Avezaat, 1997).

Cephalohematoma usually refers to a benign traumatic lesion to the skull in which blood pools under the periosteum and is confined by suture boundaries. But 10% to 25% of all cephalohematomas are associated with an underlying skull fracture. These fractures rarely pose major problems but if depressed can result in compression of the skull (Menkes, 1984).

Central nervous system hemorrhage may be caused by mechanical trauma to the infant's brain during the birth process. The hemorrhage may occur in the subarachnoid space, the subdural space, or the dural space, or it may be intracerebral. The most common type of traumatic central nervous system hemorrhage is the subarachnoid hemorrhage resulting from tears in the meninges. Usually this is a benign condition unless it is associated with perinatal hypoxia or meningitis (Oxorn, 1986).

Subdural hemorrhage, now uncommon, may result in hydrocephalus and seizures. Intracerebral hemorrhage, one of the rarest types of traumatic central nervous system hemorrhage in the newborn, may result in increased intracranial pressure, hemiparesis, and convulsions. Hemorrhage into the dural space is also rare, but it usually results in massive hemorrhage and early neonatal death (Brann, 1985).

Traumatic spinal cord injuries are unusual. The most common sites of damage are the lower cervical and upper thoracic regions. These injuries can lead to stillbirth, respiratory failure, paralysis, or spasticity (Oxorn, 1986).

Peripheral nerve injuries can involve trauma to the brachial plexus, the phrenic nerve, the facial nerve, or the radial nerves. The nerve injuries are usually caused by traction or direct compression of the nerve itself. Trauma to the brachial plexus may cause muscle atrophy, contractures, and impaired limb growth (Menkes, 1984). The most common brachial plexus injury is Erb's palsy, which involves extension and paralysis of the arm, wrist and fingers. Although quick recovery may be observed, complete recovery can take months (Smith & Ouvrier, 2006).

Trauma to the phrenic nerve may cause diaphragm paralysis and mimic congenital pulmonary or heart disease, resulting in long-term ventilatory support. Damage to the facial nerve results in weakness of the muscles to the affected side of the face, causing failure on the affected side of the mouth to move and the eyelid to close. Radial nerve injury may result in wrist drop and the inability to extend the fingers and the thumb (Menkes, 1984).

Traumatic bony injuries include fractures of the clavicle, humerus, and femur. Fracture of the clavicle is the most common bony injury; it usually occurs in association with shoulder dystocia. Fractures of the humerus and femur are rare and result from traumatic delivery (Oxorn, 1986).

Traumatic abdominal injuries are uncommon but they can have serious consequences. The traumatic abdominal injuries include hepatic or splenic rupture; they result from traumatic delivery. These injuries are usually life-threatening conditions (Oxorn, 1986).

Cerebral palsy is a chronic nonprogressive disorder of the pyramidal motor system resulting in lack of voluntary muscle control and coordination. The cause is uncertain but cerebral anoxia during the perinatal period has been associated with the resulting cerebral damage (Rosen, 1985).

There are several types of cerebral palsy: spastic, dyskinetic, ataxic, and mixed-type. Spastic cerebral palsy, the most common clinical type, is characterized by hypertonicity, uneven muscle tone, persistent primitive reflexes, lack of normal postural control, and incomplete spastic paralysis (Whaley & Wong, 1983).

Dyskinetic cerebral palsy is characterized by slow, writhing movements that involve the entire body. There is also high-frequency deafness associated with this type of cerebral palsy. Ataxic cerebral palsy is manifested by irregular muscle action and failure of muscle coordination. Mixed-type cerebral palsy is manifested by a combination of spasticity and atethosis, the slow writhing movements (Whaley & Wong, 1983).

Disabilities associated with cerebral palsy include intellectual developmental disabilities, seizure disorders, impaired behavioral and interpersonal relationships, and impairment of other senses. Approximately two thirds of those diagnosed with cerebral palsy are also mentally retarded. About 50% of those with cerebral palsy have some type of seizure disorder. Those with impaired behavioral relationships usually have poor attention spans and hyperactive behavior. Impairment of the other senses include both visual and hearing defects (Batshaw & Perret, 1981). Cerebral palsy is a lifelong affliction. Most of those with the disorder live to adulthood but only 10% become self-supporting. The other 90% need support both medically and socially (Batshaw & Perret, 1981).

Seizure disorders may result from many causes, including perinatal asphyxia, intracranial hemorrhage, infection, congenital defects, metabolic disorders, drug withdrawal, inherited defects, and kernicterus. Perinatal asphyxia is the most frequent cause of seizures in the pre- and full-term infant. Perinatal asphyxia as the cause of neonatal seizures has the poorest prognosis. Approximately 60% of those infants with seizures caused by perinatal asphyxia have permanent neurologic sequelae and lifelong seizure disorders (Brann, 1985; Hill & Volpe, 2006).

REFERENCES

Batshaw, R. L., & Perret, Y. M. (1981). *Children with handicaps: A medical primer*. Baltimore, MD: Brookes.

Brann, A. W. (1985). Factors during neonatal life that influence brain disorders. In J. M. Freeman (Ed.), *Prenatal and perinatal factors associated with brain disorders* (NIH Publication

No. 85–1149, pp. 263–358). Bethesda, MD: U.S. Department of Health and Human Services.

Hes, R., de Jong, T. H., Paz, D. H., & Avezaat, C. J. (1997). Rapid evolution of a growing skull fracture after vacuum extraction. *Pediatric Neurosurgery, 26,* 269–274.

Hill, A., & Volpe, J. J. (2006). Hypoxic-ischemic cerebral injury in the newborn. In K. F. Swaiman & S. Ashwal (Eds.), *Pediatric neurology* (4th ed., pp. 191–204). St. Louis, MO: Mosby.

Menkes, J. H. (1984). Neurologic evaluation of the newborn infant. In M. E. Avery & H. W. Taeusch (Eds.), *Schaffer's diseases of the newborn* (5th ed., pp. 652–661). Philadelphia, PA: Saunders.

Oxorn, H. (1986). *Human labor and birth* (5th ed.). Norwalk, CT: Appleton-Century-Crofts.

Rosen, M. G. (1985). Factors during labor and delivery that influence brain disorders. In J. M. Freeman (Ed.), *Prenatal and perinatal factors associated with brain disorders* (NIH Publication No. 85-1149, pp. 359–440). Bethesda, MD: U.S. Department of Health and Human Services.

Smith, S. A., & Ouvrier, R. (2006). Peripheral neuropathies in children. In K. F. Swaiman & S. Ashwal (Eds.), *Pediatric neurology* (4th ed., pp. 1178–1201). St. Louis, MO: Mosby.

Whaley, L. F., & Wong, D. L. (1983). *Nursing care of infants and children* (2nd ed.). St. Louis, MO: Mosby.

ELIZABETH R. BAUERSCHMIDT
University of North Carolina at Wilmington

See also Absence Seizures; Brain Damage/Injury; Cerebral Palsy; Grand Mal Seizures

BIRTH ORDER

Birth order, or sibling status, refers to a child's ordinal position in the family. There has been much speculation about the effects of birth order on important variables such as personality characteristics, mental illness, intelligence, achievement, and occupational status; but consistent relationships have been difficult to establish unequivocally. The study of birth order can be traced at least as far back as *English Men of Science* (1874), in which Galton reported that firstborns were considerably overrepresented among the scientists of his day. Alfred Adler (1958) was also convinced of the influence of family position on development, and stated that "position in the family leaves an indelible stamp upon the style of life" (p. 154). In contrast, Craig (1996) concludes that there are no consistent personality characteristics associated with birth order.

There is an intuitive appeal to the view that each ordinal position is accompanied by unique family environments and patterns of family interactions. It is congruent with a social theory of personality development, one that emphasizes the interpersonal relationships that stem from the dynamics of a child's ordinal position. Over the course of childhood, any consistent differences in social learning experiences might well produce varied personality and achievement profiles or distinctive behavioral traits for children within the same family (Forer, 1976). For example, the amount of time that parents have available for a particular child is a function of birth order. Parents spend almost twice as much time in direct contact with firstborns as they do with succeeding children (White, Kaban, & Attanucci, 1979). Further, the older child in a typical U.S. family is accorded more opportunities to practice language skills and take responsibility for and teach younger siblings (Harris, 1973; Smith, 1984).

Harris (1973) describes the firstborn as being adult-civilized; parents are more actively involved in nurturing and guiding their firstborn child. Younger children in the family are more likely to be peer-civilized. Therefore, the firstborn or only child would be expected to identify more closely with the parents and hold more traditional values than laterborn children (Schacter, 1959; Sutton-Smith & Rosenburg, 1970). As subsequent children are added to the family, parents spend less and less time in direct care, and older siblings assume more responsibility for child care. The opportunity to teach younger siblings and assignment of more responsible roles within the family may enhance firstborns' intellectual development. It is also possible that firstborns receive more intellectual stimulation during infancy and more direct achievement training during the preschool years than laterborns do (Bradley & Caldwell, 1984; Rothbart, 1971).

Various personality profiles, though sometimes overlapping and inconsistent, have been suggested for prominent ordinal positions. The proposed profiles follow:

Firstborn. Firstborns are said to exhibit higher standards of moral honesty, have higher need for achievement, earlier social maturation, better work habits, and higher need for recognition and approval (Forer, 1976; Harris, 1973). Firstborns are also considered to rate higher in leadership, independence, and sensitivity to stress (Sutton-Smith & Rosenberg, 1970), and tend to be dominant, more aggressive, ambitious, and conservative (Koch, 1955).

Secondborn. Secondborns are believed to have good social skills, seek out group activities, and maintain better relationships in life than do firstborns. They also show more dependency behavior and seek more adult help and approval (Forer, 1976; McGurk & Grandon, 1979).

Middleborn. Middleborns, like secondborns, show better interpersonal skills and tend to express greater sensitivity to the feelings and needs of others (Falbo, 1981; Miller & Maruyama, 1976). Middle children generally have the fewest behavior problems, enjoy a healthier adjustment to life and as adults experience less anxiety in new or threatening situations

(Touliatos & Lindholm, 1980; Yannakis, 1976). They also show more concern for peer norms and consequently accept peer advice more readily (Harris, 1973).

Lastborn. The youngest child is more likely to exhibit dependency and be peer-oriented (Schacter, 1959). This birth order also has been associated with higher propensity to use alcohol and cigarettes (Ernst & Angst, 1983).

Onlyborn. Only children have a tendency to be leaders rather than joiners and show considerable affinity for independent behavior (Falbo, 1981). Schacter (1959) reports that only children experience more fear and anxiety during adolescence and adulthood than laterborn children. Conventional wisdom that singletons are selfish, lonely, and uncooperative is unsupported (Falbo, 1981).

Many factors affect a child's perception of ordinal position and associated family dynamics. Sex of siblings and spacing are important, as is the status of adopted children and stepchildren. For example, Adler (1958) has suggested that the male child with all female siblings may place more emphasis on his masculinity. A secondborn might assume the responsibilities of a firstborn who is developmentally delayed. With adopted children or stepchildren, previous family interactional patterns may have consequences for adjustment to new ordinal positions.

Several large-scale studies have found relationships between birth order and intelligence and achievement (Belmont & Marolla, 1973; Berbaum & Moreland, 1980; Zajonc & Markus, 1975). On the average, oldest children have higher IQs and have higher achievement in school and in careers. Only children also tend to be high achievers (Zajonc & Markus, 1975). However, a more recent study using a large data set from 1973 found that birth-order effects, when measured by educational attainment (i.e., total years of education), are negligible for small sib sizes, such as one to four children. For large families, it was found that lastborns and next-to-lastborns did considerably better than firstborns (Blake, 1989). Birth order and SAT data showed virtually no correlation. When these data were collected, presumably more resources were available for the lastborn child and more educational opportunities were afforded them.

Zajonc and Markus (1975) developed a model to make predictions concerning the relationship of birth order and intellectual ability. The confluence model uses an estimate of the average intellectual environment (AIE) of the family to predict the intelligence of each child, where AIE is equal to the total intellectual level of the family divided by the number of family members. According to the model, in a family with two children spaced only a few years apart, the second child is expected to have a lower IQ. In a family where the spacing between first and secondborn exceeds

7 years, the prediction would be reversed. The model also predicts that children from father-absent families and twins should have lowered IQs, as will laterborns from larger families.

There is no support in the literature for the confluence model. Reported birth order effects appear to be artifacts of sibship size or socioeconomic status; birth order is essentially random (Steelman, 1985). Furthermore, children raised in singleparent families do not show the poor intellectual performances that confluence theory predicts (Entwistle & Alexander, 1990).

Page and Grandon (1979) proposed the admixture theory as an alternative interpretation of the reported correlation of birth order with intellectual functioning. In their view, social class, race, and family size interact to determine birth order effects. Furthermore, their analysis indicates that social class and race are the dominant factors, while family size and birth order are actually negligible in their effects.

It must also be remembered that even the reported differences in IQ correlated with birth order are quite small and have been obtained only when large numbers of families are compared. It is therefore unwise to make predictions for individuals on the basis of birth order. Family size, family structure, and income have far greater effects on IQ than birth order. Wide spacing of siblings also tends to eliminate any evidence of birth order effects (Shaffer, 1993). To the degree that birth order may have consequences for achievement, it should not be assumed that such effects occur cross-culturally (LeVine, 1990).

As for personality, some research has found that firstborn infants, preschoolers, and adults are more socially outgoing and more interested in peer contacts than laterborns (Schachter, 1959; Snow, Jacklin, & Maccoby, 1981; Vandell, Wilson, & Whalen, 1981). There is some evidence that laterborn children tend to be somewhat more popular on average than firstborn children (Miller & Maruyama, 1976). And birth order may be a factor that contributes to children's acceptance by peers. One rationale offered is that laterborn children must learn to negotiate with older, more powerful siblings, and hence learn how to cooperate. Acquiring and using more conciliatory interpersonal skills may enable laterborns to be more popular than firstborns, who may use their greater power to dominate their younger siblings and use coercive ways with peers (Berndt & Bulleit, 1985).

However, as with correlations reported between birth order and measures of intelligence, ordinal position effects reported for sociability are quite small. Thus, one must conclude that birth order plays at best only a minor role in determining how sociable a child is likely to become. The same is true for effects on peer popularity. More research is needed before we can understand how children's experiences in their families are translated into patterns of behavior and social standing outside the family.

There is by no means unanimity of thinking about the value of birth order for understanding personality (Dunn & Plomin, 1990; Ernst & Angst, 1983; Schooler, 1972). That birth order may be significant for some individuals is not in dispute. Rather, the contention of critics of the birth order variable is that its significance is wholly unpredictable and certainly far less important than other social or genetic variables. Ernst and Angst concluded their extensive analysis of birth order and personality by saying:

> Birth order and sibship size do not have a strong impact on personality. The present investigation points instead to a broken home, an unfriendly educational style, and a premature disruption of relations with parents as concomitants of neuroticism and to higher income and social class...and an undisturbed home as concomitants of higher achievement.... Birth order influences on personality and IQ have been widely overrated. (p. 242)

And Dunn and Plomin (1990) assert that birth order "plays only a bit-part in the drama of sibling differences" (p. 85).

However, Frank Sulloway (1996), in his book *Born to Rebel*, marshals persuasive evidence for the contributions of birth order to personality development. His meta-analysis leads him to conclude that for the personality dimension of openness to experience, laterborns are more nonconforming, adventurous, and unconventional. And firstborns tend to be more responsible, achievement-oriented, and organized. They also tend to be more emotionally unstable, anxious, and fearful. In short, "firstborns tend to be dominant, aggressive, ambitious, jealous, and conservative" (p. 79). He also claims that birth order effects are 5 to 10 times greater for the key personality dimensions of openness to experience, conscientiousness, agreeableness, and neuroticism than they are for academic achievement and IQ.

It does appear that birth order, at certain times and in some cultures, has been a significant developmental variable. In societies where primogeniture has been important, the life experiences of firstborn males were vastly different from those of other siblings and were no doubt instrumental in promoting their success. There is also some evidence to support the influence of birth order, as mediated through the complex dynamics of family experience, on certain dimensions of human personality. Although birth order can affect developmental outcomes, its importance cannot be systematically predicted, and thus should be considered with reasonable caution as a potential contributor to personality development.

REFERENCES

Adler, A. (1958). *What life should mean to you.* New York, NY: Capricorn.

Belmont, L., & Marolla, F. A. (1973). Birth order, family size, and intelligence. *Science, 182,* 1096–1101.

Berbaum, M. L., & Moreland, R. I. (1980). Intellectual development within the family: A new application of the confluence model. *Developmental Psychology, 16,* 506–518.

Berndt, T. J., & Bulleit, T. N. (1985). Effects of sibling relationships on preschoolers' behavior at home and at school. *Developmental Psychology, 21,* 761–767.

Blake, J. (1989). *Family size and achievement.* Berkeley: University of California.

Bradley, R. H., & Caldwell, B. M. (1984). 174 children: A study of the relationship between home environment and cognitive development during the first 5 years. In A. W. Gottfried (Ed.), *Home environment and early cognitive development. Longitudinal research.* Orlando, FL: Academic Press.

Craig, G. J. (1996). *Human development.* Upper Saddle River, NJ: Prentice Hall.

Dunn, J., & Plomin, R. (1990). *Separate lives: Why siblings are so different.* New York, NY: Basic Books.

Entwistle, D. R., & Alexander, K. L. (1990). Beginning school math competence: Minority and majority comparisons. *Child Development, 61,* 454–471.

Ernst, C., & Angst, J. (1983). *Birth order: Its influence on personality.* Berlin, Germany: Springer-Verlag.

Falbo, T. (1981). Relationship between birth category, achievement, and interpersonal orientation. *Journal of Personality and Social Psychology, 41,* 121–131.

Forer, L. K. (1976). *The birth order factor.* New York, NY: McKay.

Galton, F. (1874). *English men of science.* London, UK: McMillan.

Harris, I. D. (1973). Differences in cognitive style and birth order. In J. C. Westman (Ed.), *Individual differences in children* (pp. 199–210). New York, NY: Wiley.

Koch, H. L. (1955). Some personality correlates of sex, sibling position, and sex of sibling among five- and six-year old children. *Genetic Psychology Monographs, 52,* 3–50.

LeVine, R. A. (1990). Enculturation: A biosocial perspective on the development of self. In D. Cicchetti & M. Beeghly (Eds.), *The self in transition: Infancy to childhood* (pp. 99–117). Chicago, IL: University of Chicago.

McGurk, H., & Grandon, G. M. (1979). Birth order: A phenomenon in search of an explanation. *Developmental Psychology, 7, 33,* 366.

Miller, N., & Maruyama, G. (1976). Ordinal position and peer popularity. *Journal of Personality and Social Psychology, 33,* 123–131.

Page, E. B., & Grandon, G. M. (1979). Family configuration and mental ability: Two theories contrasted with U.S. data. *American Educational Research Journal, 16,* 257–272.

Rogers, J. L. (1984). Confluence effects: Not here, not now! *Developmental Psychology, 20,* 321–331.

Rothbart, M. K. (1971). Birth order and mother-child interaction in an achievement situation. *Journal of Personality and Social Psychology, 17,* 113–120.

Schacter, S. (1959). *The psychology of affiliation.* Stanford, CA: Stanford University.

Schooler, C. (1972). Birth order effects: Not here, not now. *Psychological Bulletin*, 78, 161–175.

Shaffer, D. R. (1993). *Developmental psychology: Childhood and adolescence* (3rd ed.). Pacific Grove, CA: Brooks/Cole.

Smith, T. (1984). School grades and responsibility for younger siblings: An empirical study of the teaching function. *American Sociological Review*, 49, 248–261.

Snow, M. E., Jacklin, C. N., & Maccoby, E. E. (1981). Birth-order differences in peer sociability at thirty-three months. *Child Development*, 52, 589–595.

Stagner, R., & Katzoff, E. T. (1936). Personality as related to birth order and family size. *Journal of Applied Psychology*, 20, 340–346.

Steelman, L. C. (1985). A tale of two variables: A review of the intellectual consequences of sibship size and birth order. *Review of Educational Research*, 55, 353–386.

Sulloway, F. J. (1996). *Born to rebel: Birth order, family dynamics, and creative lives.* New York, NY: Pantheon.

Sutton-Smith, B., & Rosenberg, B. G. (1970). *The sibling.* New York, NY: Holt, Rinehart, & Winston.

Touliatos, J., & Lindholm, B. W. (1980). Birth order, family size, and children's mental health. *Psychological Reports*, 46, 1097–1098.

Vandell, D. L., Wilson, K. S., & Whalen, W. T. (1981). Birth-order and social experience differences in infant-peer interaction. *Developmental Psychology*, 17, 438–445.

White, B. L., Kaban, B. T., & Attanucci, J. S. (1979). *The origins of human competence.* Lexington, MA: Heath.

Yannakis, A. (1976). Birth order and preference for dangerous sports among males. *Quarterly Research*, 47, 42–67.

Zajonc, R. B., & Markus, G. B. (1975). Birth order and intellectual development. *Psychological Review*, 82, 74–88.

JAMES M. APPLEFIELD
University of North Carolina at Wilmington

See also Personality Assessment; Socioeconomic Status; Temperament

BIRTH TRAUMA

According to Freudian psychodynamic theory, early traumatic and painful events produce memories that, when repressed into the unconscious, may affect later life. Otto Rank (1929) elaborated on the proposition that birth is itself traumatic: It suddenly and painfully thrusts the infant from the warm, secure womb into a cold, hostile, and frustrating world. When frustrated later in life, people may in some ways behave as though they wished to return to the womb.

More recently, Leboyer (1975) has argued that birth should be as gentle as possible for both mother and infant. In his birthing technique, the shock of birth is reduced by, among other things, keeping light and noise levels in the delivery room low. At birth, the newborn is placed on the mother's breast, massaged to decrease initial crying, and placed in a warm bath. The father attends and assists in handling the newborn.

Although some physicians initially suggested that Leboyer's method put both newborn and mother at risk, research indicates that the procedure is safe. Relative to those conventionally delivered, Leboyer infants evidence normal physiological functioning (Kliot & Silverstein, 1984) and no differences in either maternal or infant morbidity or infant behavior (Nelson et al., 1980). At present, with the exception of shorter active labors among mothers expecting a Leboyer delivery (Nelson et al., 1980), advantages of the method appear more psychological than physiological (Grover, 1984). Indeed, evidence of long-term consequences of both conventional and Leboyer births are notably lacking, and the concept of birth trauma, particularly the Rankian version, is largely in disrepute.

Considering the other side of the issue, Handley et al. (1997) asked whether infants who had endured traumatic near-death births showed any later adverse effects. They longitudinally compared the development from 4 to 8 years of age of a group that had nearly suffocated during birth with a group that had experienced a normal birth. The two groups had comparable familial characteristics. The group that suffered the traumatic birth experience did not show meaningful deficits in cognitive and motor development, health, or general behavior.

Evidence of long-term effects of birth experiences, varying from Leboyer's gentle technique through traumatic ones, is notably lacking. Although it still has adherents, the concept of birth trauma, particularly the Rankian version, is largely in disrepute.

REFERENCES

Grover, J. W. (1984). Leboyer and obstetric practice. *New York State Journal of Medicine*, 84, 158–159.

Handley, D. M., Low, J. A., Burke, S. O., Wuarick, M., Killen, H., & Derrick, E. J. (1997). Intrapartum fetal asphyxia and the occurrence of minor deficits in 4 to 8 year old children. *Developmental Medicine and Child Neurology*, 39, 508–514.

Kliot, D., & Silverstein, L. (1984). Changing maternal and newborn care. *New York State Journal of Medicine*, 84, 169–174.

Leboyer, F. (1975). *Birth without violence.* New York, NY: Knopf.

Nelson, N. M., Enkin, M. W., Saigal, S., Bennett, K. J., Milner, R., & Sackett, D. L. (1980). A randomized clinical trial of the Leboyer approach to childbirth. *New England Journal of Medicine*, 302, 655–660.

Rank, O. (1929). *The trauma of birth.* New York, NY: Harcourt, Brace.

ROBERT T. BROWN
SHIRLEY PARKER WELLS
University of North Carolina at Wilmington
First edition

AIMEE R. HUNTER
University of North Carolina at Wilmington
Second edition

See also **Attachment Disorder; Child Abuse**

BLATT, BURTON (1927–1985)

Burton Blatt, widely known as a leader in the movement for deinstitutionalization of people with intellectual developmental disabilities, began his professional career as a special class teacher in the public schools of New York City. After earning the doctorate in special education at Pennsylvania State University in 1956, he served on the faculties of Southern Connecticut State College and Boston University before joining the faculty of Syracuse University in 1969, where he served as dean of the School of Education from 1976 until his death in 1985.

In 1971 he formed the Center on Human Policy at Syracuse University, devoted to the study and promotion of open settings for people with intellectual developmental disabilities and other disabilities. His work was characterized by an inspirational humanism that contributed greatly to his effectiveness as a leader.

REFERENCES

Blatt, B. (1984). Biography in autobiography. In B. Blatt & R. J. Morris (Eds.), *Perspectives in special education: Personal orientations* (pp. 263–307). Glenview, IL: Scott, Foresman.

Blatt, B., & Kaplan, F. (1966). *Christmas in purgatory: A photographic essay on mental retardation* (2nd ed.). Boston, MA: Allyn & Bacon.

Semmel, M. I. (1985). In memoriam: Burton Blatt, 1927–1985. *Exceptional Children, 52*, 102.

PAUL IRVINE
Katonah, New York

BLIND INFANTS

An increase in the birth of infants who are blind can be related to four major factors: (1) prematurity; (2) family history of a visual defect; (3) infection during pregnancy; and (4) difficult or assisted labor (Ellingham et al., 1976). With increasing medical advances in saving premature infants, the incidence of retinopathy of prematurity (previously termed *retrolental fibroplasia*) is rising (Morse & Trief, 1985).

The increase of visually impaired infants demands focused attention toward early intervention efforts. Unfortunately, many of the infants born prematurely are also born with deafness, intellectual developmental disabilities, and blindness (Morse & Trief, 1985). Early intervention services provide training and support to families of infants and toddlers diagnosed with a developmental delay or disability. Children with diagnosed with visual impairments qualify for early intervention services from birth to 3. Early intervention training of parents and caregivers is recommended to prevent developmental delays in cognitive development, language acquisition, and possible future problems with space acquisition (Ferrell, 1985). Parent training helps to increase the likelihood of early intervention to teach infants who are blind how to interact with their environments by making connections between movements and its yielded effects.

Vision allows for infants to acclimate themselves with environments to be able to understand and adapt to the environment. Lack of visual information can compromise infant development of personality and interactions between physical and social environments (Segond, Weiss, & Sampaio, 2007). Visuoauditory sensory systems have been used for older children with visual impairments, but were not implemented with visually impaired infants because of the lack of video resolution. However, with the increase in technological devices, further investigations continue by providing visuoauditory stimulation to infants with visual impairments to increase awareness of their environment and provide stimulation to avoid severe delays in critical developmental domains (Segond et al., 2007). While many practices continue to develop, empirical evidence supports early intervention programs and training for parents of visually impaired infants. Services focus on developmental therapies provided by law under the Early Intervention Program for Infants and Toddlers with Disabilities of the IDEIA Part-C. Each state varies on the implementation of services for infants and toddlers diagnosed with disabilities. For additional information on services for visually imparied infants visit http://www.ideainfanttoddler.org/.

REFERENCES

Aitken, K., & Trevarthen, C. (1997). Self/other organization in human psychological development. *Development and Psychopathology, 9*(4), 653–677.

Bigelow, A. (1995). The effect of blindness on the early development of the self. In P. Rochat (Ed.), *The self in infancy:*

Theory and research (Vol. *112*, pp. 327–347). Amsterdam, Netherlands: North Holland/Elsevier Science.

Chen, D. (1996). Parent-infant communication: Early intervention for very young children with visual impairment or hearing loss. *Infants and Young Children, 9*, 1–12.

Chen, D. (1999). Interactions between infants and caregivers: The context for early intervention. In D. Chen (Ed.), *Essential elements in early intervention: Visual impairment and multiple disabilities* (pp. 22–48). New York, NY: American Foundation for the Blind.

Council for Exceptional Children (CEC). (1992). *Visual impairments.* (ERIC Digest No. E511)

Dote-Kwan, J. (1995). Impact of mothers' interactions on the development of their young visually impaired children. *Journal of Visual Impairment & Blindness, 89*, 47–58.

Ellingham, T., Silva, P., Buckfield, P., & Clarkson, J. (1976). Neonatal at risk factors, visual defects and the preschool child: A report from the Queen Mary Hospital multidisciplinary child development study. *New Zealand Medical Journal, 83*, 74–77.

Erwin, E. J. (1994). Social competence in young children with visual impairments. *Infants and Young Children, 6*, 26–33.

Erwin, E. J., & Hill, E. W. (1993). Social participation of young children with visual impairments in specialized and integrated environments. *Journal of Visual Impairment & Blindness, 87*(5), 138–142.

Ferrell, K. (1985). *Reach out and teach: Meeting the training needs of parents of visually and multiply handicapped young children.* New York, NY: American Foundation for the Blind.

Hughes, M., Dote-Kwan, J., & Dolendo, J. (1998). A closer look at the cognitive play of preschoolers with visual impairments in the home. *Exceptional Children, 64*, 451–462.

Individuals with Disabilities Education Improvement Act of 2004, Part C-Infants and Toddlers with Disabilities. H.R. 1350, 108th Congress.

Kekelis, L. (1992). A field study of a blind preschooler. In S. L. Sacks, L. Kekelis, & R. Gaylord-Ross (Eds.), *The development of social skills by blind and visually impaired students.* New York, NY: American Foundation for the Blind.

Kekelis, L. (1996). Blind and sighted children with their mothers: The development of discourse skills. *Journal of Visual Impairment & Blindness, 90*(5), 423–436.

Moore, S. (1984). The need for programs and services for visually handicapped infants. *Education of the Visually Handicapped, 16*, 48–57.

Morse, A., & Trief, E. (1985). Diagnosis and evaluation of visual dysfunction in premature infants with low birth weight. *Journal of Visual Impairment & Blindness, 79*, 248–251.

Preisler, G. M. (1997). Social and emotional development of blind children: A longitudinal study. In V. Lewis & G. Collis (Eds.), *Blindness and psychological development in young children.* Leicester, England: British Psychological Society.

Sacks, S. Z., & Silberman, R. K. (2000). Social skills. In A. J. Koenig & M. C. Holbrook (Eds.), *Foundations of education: Instructional strategies for teaching children and youths with visual impairments* (Vol. 2, pp. 616–652). New York, NY: American Foundation for the Blind.

Segond, H., Weiss, D., Sampaio, E. (2007). A proposed tactile vision-substitution system for infants who are blind tested on sighted infants. *Journal of Visual Impairment and Blindness, 1*, 32–43.

VIVIAN I. CORREA
University of Florida
Third edition

HEATHER DAVIS
Texas A&M University
Fourth edition

BLINDISMS

Blindisms is a term used to describe a group of simple or complex stereotypical behaviors that involve both small movements of various parts of the body, such as eye rubbing and poking, head turning, and hand flapping, and large body movements such as rocking or swaying (Molloy & Rowe, 2011; Warren, 1984). The degree of behaviors exhibited are directly correlated to the degree of visual impairment of the child or adult (Molloy & Rowe, 2011). One of the most common mannerisms in children with visual impairments is pressing on one or both eyes. Pressure on the eyeball results in specific stimulation to the child with visual impairments. The most active eye pressers are children with retinal disorders (Scott, Jan, & Freeman, 1985).

There are several theories regarding the causes of stereotypic behaviors in children who are blind. One of them is that these behaviors are efforts to increase the level of sensory stimulation (Burlingham, 1967; Curson, 1979; Scott et al., 1985). It has also been suggested that stereotypic repetitive behaviors are pleasurable because of the motor discharge (Burlingham, 1965). Another theory related to cause of stereotypic behaviors is that the behaviors are a result of social rather than sensory deprivation (Warren, 1984). However, according to Webster (1983), one cannot separate the sensory stimulation factor from the social stimulation factor in the case of infants who are blind. Williams (1978) has indicated that mobility plays a role in inhibiting stereotypic behavior patterns, and that lack of early mobility causes these behaviors to perpetuate.

Stereotypic behaviors tend to decrease with the increase in child development (Molloy & Rowe, 2011). Children affected with more significant developmental disabilities are at risk of developing and maintaining the automatically reinforced behaviors (Molloy & Rowe, 2011). Research studies have shown that behavior modification approaches can reduce or eliminate some stereotypic behaviors in children with visual impairments (Brame, Martin, & Martin, 1998; Caetano & Kaufman, 1975; B. Miller & Miller, 1976; Williams, 1978).

Parents and teachers are advised to work together to help children with visual impairments develop positive exploratory and mobile behaviors. These efforts will enable this population to become more socially accepted by their peers, and to attend more to the outside environment.

REFERENCES

Brame, C. M., Martin, D., & Martin, P. (1998). Counseling the blind or visually impaired child: An examination of behavioral techniques. *Professional School Counseling, 1,* 60–62.

Burlingham, D. (1965). Some problems of ego development in blind children. *Psychoanalytic Study of the Child, 20,* 194–208.

Burlingham, D. (1967). Developmental considerations in the occupations of the blind. *Psychoanalytic Study of the Child, 22,* 187–198.

Caetano, A. P., & Kaufman, J. M. (1975). Reduction of rocking mannerisms in two blind children. *Education of the Visually Handicapped, 7,* 101–105.

Curson, A. (1979). The blind nursery school child. *Psychoanalytic Study of the Child, 34,* 51–83.

Eichel, V. J. (1979). A taxonomy for mannerisms of blind children. *Journal of Visual Impairment and Blindness, 72,* 125–130.

Jan, J. E., Freeman, R. D., & Scott, E. P. (1977). *Visual impairment in children and adolescents.* New York, NY: Grune & Stratton.

Miller, B. S., & Miller, W. H. (1976). Extinguishing "blindisms": A paradigm for intervention. *Education of the Visually Handicapped, 8,* 6–15.

Molloy, A. & Rowe, F. J. (2011). Manneristic behaviors of visually impaired children. *Strabismus, 19*(3), 77–84.

Scott, E. P., Jan, J. E., & Freeman, R. D. (1985). *Can't your child see?* Austin, TX: PRO-ED.

Smith, M. A., Chethik, M., & Adelson, E. (1969). Differential assessments of "blindisms." *American Journal of Orthopsychiatry, 39,* 807–817.

Warren, D. H. (1984). *Blindness and early childhood development.* New York, NY: American Foundation for the Blind.

Webster, R. (1983). What—No blindisms in African blind children? *Imfama, 7,* 16–18.

Williams, C. E. (1978). Strategies of intervention with the profoundly retarded visually-handicapped child: A brief report of a study of stereotypy. *Occasional Papers of the British Psychological Society, 2,* 68–72.

ROSANNE K. SILBERMAN
Hunter College, City University of New York

See also Blind; Self-Stimulation; Vision Training; Visual Impairment

BLIND LEARNING APTITUDE TEST

The Blind Learning Aptitude Test (BLAT) was developed in 1969 by T. Ernest Newland as a nonverbal, individually administered multiple aptitude battery for use with children and adolescents with visual impairments. The age range of BLAT is from 6 to 20 years, but it is most often recommended for use between the ages of 6 and 12. The test was designed to objectively measure learning process rather than learning product in children with visual impairments by minimizing the influence of experiences to which the sighted child is subjected. In fact, the majority of the items were taken from tests designed to minimize cultural bias. The BLAT items are presented in an embossed format involving dots and lines similar to those used in braille; however, no knowledge of braille is required to complete the test. The test consists of 61 tactile stimulus items, and 49 of those are scored while 12 are used for training purposes. The items measure abilities such as discrimination, generalization, and sequencing (Buros, 1978).

The BLAT manual (Newland, 1971) provides detailed directions for administering the test, including techniques for introducing the examinee to the test, guiding the examinee's fingers across stimulus items, and dealing with special situations that may arise. No formal time limits are provided, though the manual states that examinees typically respond to individual items within two minutes (Herman, 1985). The scoring procedure is deceptively simple. Items are scored right or wrong, and the number of correct items serves as the total raw score. Complications may arise, however, as the response sheet is laid out in such a way that training items are not clearly differentiated from actual test items. The BLAT yields a learning aptitude test quotient with a mean of 100 and a standard deviation of 15 points, making it similar to the IQ. The BLAT also yields a learning aptitude age, which is defined as the midpoint of an age range for a given score.

Standardized on a sample of 961 students with visual impairments in a number of residential and day schools for the children with visual impairments across the United States, the author reports reliability coefficients ranging from 0.86 to 0.93. However, much of the reliability data is indeterminate, as many tables lack information such as Ns, means, and standard deviations. Data on the validity of the BLAT is also incomplete. Factor analysis indicated some tendency for the items to fall into groups that relate to the six different items used in the test. However, information is not provided on the nature or size of the sample, nor how the factors were extracted or rotated.

While the BLAT pioneered test development for students with visual impairments, the norms tables are 30 years dated making the use of the assessment limited in education or research today.

REFERENCES

Buros, O. K. (1978). *The eighth mental measurements yearbook.* Highland Park, NJ: Buros Foundation.

Herman, D. O. (1985). Blind learning aptitude test. In D. L. Keyser & R. C. Sweetland (Eds.), *Test critiques* (Vol. 3, pp. 32–36). Kansas City, MO: Test Corporation of America.

Newland, T. E. (1971). *Manual for the Blind Learning Aptitude Test*: Experimental edition. Urbana, IL: Author.

LIZANNE DESTEFANO
University of Illinois

See also Blind; Visual Impairment; Visual Perception and Discrimination

BLINDNESS

The term used to describe an individual who cannot process stimuli through the visual system is *blindness*. Only a few people actually meet this criterion, and most individuals who are described as blind have some ability to perceive at least some information through the visual sense. Many people who call themselves blind actually are able to use vision to inform themselves about their environment, including those individuals who have light perception (i.e., they can tell that light is present) or have light projection (i.e., can tell from which direction a light is shining).

A legal definition of blindness exists that is based on an individual's performance during an assessment of visual acuity and range of visual field. Establishment of legal blindness qualifies an individual for special assistance from federal and state agencies. Individuals who qualify as legally blind, however, often have the capacity to use vision for informing themselves about the environment and, therefore, for learning. According to the American Printing House for the Blind (APH), there were approximately 59,400 legally blind children in the United States in 2009 (APH).

Within the educational system, students are identified as blind (or functionally blind) if they primarily use tactual, kinesthetic, or auditory means for learning. Braille, or a combination of print and braille, is the medium used for reading. Of particular relevance for educators is whether a student's blindness is congenital or adventitious. Students who acquire blindness after a period in which vision can be used for learning often have a well-developed understanding of the world. While they may experience some challenges related to learning, particularly with access to printed materials, the conceptual understanding of most of these students is not compromised. Students with congenital blindness, however, have difficulty learning through incidental visual observations of others and are challenged in their understanding of concepts, in part because they are only able to experience only a small part of their environment and the objects within it at a time (instead of having access to the "big picture").

Lowenfeld (1973) identified three basic limitations that are imposed by blindness: the range and variety of experiences, in the ability to get around, and in interactions with the environment. Although audition provides important social and directional information, it does not provide any information about the characteristics of an object. Only through touch can a child who is blind gain knowledge of the spatial qualities of objects. Because there are many objects that cannot be experienced directly (boiling water, skyscrapers, butterflies, etc.), the experiences of a child who is blind are necessarily restricted.

Further restricting the experiences of a child is the inherent limitation in moving around. Lowenfeld (1973) noted that the limitations on a child's mobility may present the most significant challenges to development. Vision provides a reason for movement (Ferrell, 2000), and without an incentive to discover what about an observed object is interesting, there is little reason to reach out beyond oneself and explore. Children who are blind are often encouraged to stay where they are safe, which further decreases exploratory behaviors.

The inability to move about with ease impacts the child in another area: social relationships. Because getting around is difficult, the individual who is blind may experience fewer opportunities for social engagement. In addition, restrictions in mobility can cause a person to become dependent on people with vision to provide assistance, which has the capacity to influence the sense of equality within a relationship. D. Tuttle and N. Tuttle (2006) noted that a strong relationship exists between the ability to travel independently and a person's self-esteem.

Challenges to self-determined behavior may be related to difficulties in the ability to move about the environment easily and safely. The child who is blind who does not know to reach for an object remains passive, as does the child who stays indoors because he is unaware that other children are playing in the neighborhood or does not have the skills to get to where they are. These types of self-directed experiences lay the foundation for self-determined behavior as children develop and must be purposefully encouraged in young children with blindness.

The development of self-determination is also threatened by the limitation in a child's interactions with—and inability to control—the environment. Children with unimpaired vision have the ability to use environmental activity to inform themselves about and to predict what is occurring around them. Children who are blind, however, cannot always know when they are being observed, who in the room is the focus of a reprimand, or the source of a loud sound. Social interactions are impacted by blindness, as when a child cannot see the facial expressions and gestures made by others and have difficulty imitating the social behaviors of adults and peers.

These limitations, first described by Lowenfeld (1973), are further impacted by the presence of additional disabilities, which are common among children and youth with congenital blindness and visual impairment. It is estimated that as many as many as 75% of students who are classified as visually impaired have additional disabilities (Silberman, 2000).

Children who are blind benefit from an educational program that is rich in concrete experiences, includes opportunities to learn by doing, and incorporates engagement in activities that provide an understanding of the totality of an event. Teachers must be prepared with specialized knowledge and skills that provide the foundation for designing instruction and adapting materials to meet students' educational needs. Among these educational needs are the skills collectively known as the Expanded Core Curriculum (ECC), which include: sensory efficiency skills, compensatory academic skills (including communication modes), assistive technology skills, orientation and mobility skills, career education skills, self-determination skills, independent living skills, recreation and leisure skills, and social interaction skills.

Most students who are blind are provided educational services in their local school program. Placed in either a general or special education classroom (based on the presence of other disabilities), the education of these students is supported by teachers of students with visual impairments and by orientation and mobility specialists. While teachers of students with visual impairments formerly provided academic support in the form of tutoring, these professionals now focus on assuring that students have the skills necessary to be successful in their current and future environments and are responsible for teaching the ECC. In addition, they modify materials and provide assistance to other educators to accommodate students who are blind in their classrooms. Approximately 10% of students are educated in specialized residential schools.

REFERENCES

American Printing House for the Blind. (2009). *2009 Annual Report*. Retrieved from http://www.aph.org/about/ar2009.html

Ferrell, K. A. (2000). Growth and development of young children. In M. C. Holbrook & A. J. Koenig, *Foundations of education (2nd ed.): Vol. 1: History and theory of teaching children and youths with visual impairments* (pp. 111–134). New York, NY: AFB Press.

Lowenfeld, B. (1973). Psychological considerations. In B. Lowenfeld (Ed.), *The visually handicapped child in school* (pp. 27–60). New York, NY: John Day.

Silberman, R. K. (2000). Children and youth with other exceptionalities. In M. C. Holbrook & A. J. Koenig, *Foundations of education (2nd ed.): Vol. 1: History and theory of teaching children and youths with visual impairments* (pp. 173–196). New York, NY: AFB Press.

Tuttle, D. W., & Tuttle, N. R. (1996). *Self-esteem and adjusting with blindness: The process of responding to life's demands* (2nd ed.). Springfield, IL: Thomas.

SANDRA LEWIS
Florida State University
Fourth edition

BLINDNESS, LEGAL

In 1935, Congress passed the Social Security Act, which included a special Aid to the Blind Program. To qualify for this program, the Act required that individuals meet the American Medical Association's definition of blindness (Koestler, 1972). Individuals who met these criteria, which were adopted as part of the legislation, were identified as "legally blind."

The definition of legal blindness has remained essentially unchanged since its first adoption, though it was rewritten in 1972, when the Supplemental Security Income Program was formed under Title XVI of the Social Security Act. It now reads:

> An individual shall be considered to be blind for purposes of this title if he has central visual acuity of 20/200 or less in the better eye with the use of a correcting lens. An eye that is accompanied by a limitation in the fields of vision such that the widest diameter of the visual field subtends an angle no greater than 20 degrees shall be considered for purposes of the first sentence of this subsection as having a central visual acuity of 20/200 or less.

Legal blindness must be certified by a competent authority, which includes doctors of medicine or osteopathy, ophthalmologists, optometrists, registered nurses, therapists, and other qualified professionals (National Library Service, 2010). The competent authority verifies distance visual acuity and visual field limitations with appropriate diagnostic tests. For the determination of visual acuity, a Snellen test is sufficient, which results in individuals with acuities poorer than 20/100 (the last line presented before the 20/200 line) categorized as legally blind.

The criterion for legal blindness is an arbitrary measure that provides little information about the ability of an individual to use vision for near or distance tasks. Nearly 80% of people who are classified as legally blind have some level of visual capacity (Barraga & Erin, 2001). Many of them read print without the use of magnification; some of them are eligible to apply for driver's licenses in some states. Because legal blindness does not describe functioning, it is of little value when identifying appropriate educational or rehabilitation services.

Individuals who have been identified as legally blind are eligible for certain government benefits and assistance, including entitlement to disability payments or to include an additional deduction when determining the amount of federal taxes owed. Many rehabilitation agencies that provide rehabilitation services to people with visual impairments restrict those services to people who have been certified as legally blind. Legal blindness is rarely used as the criterion for educational services (Barraga & Erin, 2001).

REFERENCES

Barraga, N. C., & Erin, J. N. (2001). *Visual impairments and learning* (4th ed.) Austin, TX: Pro-Ed.

Koestler, F. (1976). *The unseen minority.* New York, NY: David McKay.

National Library Service. (2010). *NLS: That all may read.* Retrieved from http://www.loc.gov/nls/eligible.html

Social Security Act. Sec. 1614. [42 U.S.C. 1382c] (a)(2). Retrieved http://www.ssa.gov/OP_Home/ssact/title16b/1614.htm

SANDRA LEWIS
Florida State University
Fourth edition

BLISSYMBOLS

Blissymbols, or Blissymbolics, is a graphic symbol system that was originally created by Charles K. Bliss in 1942 (Bliss, 1965). Blissymbols consist of 100 meaningful picture symbols that are combined in a logical manner for communication. Not simply a set of symbols, Blissymbolics is a language that has its own linguistic rule system. Blissymbolics was originally developed to be a language that could be easily learned and understood for international communication. In 1971, Blissymbols were first used as an augmentative communication symbol system for nonspeaking handicapped persons at the Ontario Crippled Children's Center in Toronto, Canada (Silverman, McNaughton, & Kates, 1978). Currently, Blissymbolics is one of many picture graphic symbol systems that have been developed for use with augmentative communication systems and is comprised of more than 3,000 symbols (BCI, 2012).

In Blissymbolics, the symbols are designed to depict the semantic concepts they represent. The meaning of the symbol can be pictographic, ideographic, or arbitrary (Figure B.4). Pictographic symbols physically look like the concept they represent. Ideographic symbols represent feelings or ideas about a concept. Arbitrary symbols are usually used only as semantic grammatical markers. Some symbols are mixed, with one or more categories of meaning combined.

House	Woman	Happy	Sad	Plural	Action
Pictographic		Ideographic		Arbitrary	

Figure B.4. Categories of Blissymbol concept representation.

thing marker	Happy		Toy

Figure B.5. Combining Blissymbols to create new word concepts.

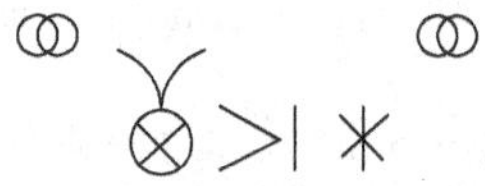

Spaceship
(combine) flying plane to (the) stars (combine)

Figure B.6. Use of the combined symbol to create new words.

By combining the basic 100 symbols together, many word concepts can be communicated. For example, the symbols for *happy* and *thing* are combined to create *toy*, a thing that can make someone happy (Figure B.5).

Blissymbolics uses semantic indicators to convey complex linguistic concepts such as plurality, action, number, and tense. In addition, the meaning of a symbol can change through changes in symbol size, orientation, position, or by adding pointers. The Blissymbolics Communication Institute (BCI), in Toronto, Canada, has developed an international standardized vocabulary of Blissymbols that is published in a user's dictionary (Hehner, 1980). New symbols are added after they are approved by BCI. Symbols that are newly created but are not approved should be designated with the combined symbol until they are approved (Figure B.6).

There are many methods of teaching the symbols. Shepard and Haaf (1995) distinguished that teaching the composite meaning of a symbol as well as the meaning of the elements from which it was comprised was superior to a paired association method.

Many studies have documented the effectiveness of using Blissymbols with individuals who are nonspeaking and who have physical disabilities (Silverman et al., 1978). In addition, they have been used with individuals who are mentally retarded, autistic (Kozleski, 1991), hearing impaired, and adults with aphasia. Blissymbols are best suited for persons who are unable to use traditional written language as an alternative communication method but are capable of learning large vocabularies. Blissymbols Communication International is a nonprofit, charitable organization that has the worldwide license for the use and publication of Blissymbols (BCI, 2012). Additional information on Blissymbols may be found at: http://www.blissymbolics.org/.

REFERENCES

BCI. (2012). *Blissymbols Communication International.* Retrieved from http://www.blissymbolics.org/

Bliss, C. K. (1965). *Semantography-Blissymbolics.* Sydney, Australia: Semantography.

Hehner, B. (1980). *Blissymbols for use*. Toronto, Canada: Blissymbolics Communication Institute.

Kozleski, E. B. (1991). Visual symbol acquisition by students with autism. *Exceptionality, 24*(4), 173–194.

Shepard, T. A., & Haaf, R. B. (1995). Comparison of two training methods in the learning and generalization of Blissymbolics. *Augmentative and Alternative Communication, 11*(3), 154–164.

Silverman, F., McNaughton, S., & Kates, B. (1978). *Handbook of Blissymbolics*. Toronto, Canada: Blissymbolics Communications Institute.

SHARON L. GLENNEN
Pennsylvania State University

BLOOM, BENJAMIN S. (1913–1999)

Bloom obtained his BA and MS degrees from Pennsylvania State University, and went on to earn his PhD from the University of Chicago in 1942. He was noted for his work with taxonomies of educational objectives, the impact of environment and heredity on intelligence, and mastery learning.

Bloom's *Taxonomy of Educational Objectives* (1956) classifies cognitive behaviors according to a hierarchy of domains, providing a framework for viewing the educational process, classifying goals of the educational system, and specifying objectives for learning experiences. The hierarchy includes knowledge, comprehension, application, analysis, synthesis, and evaluation.

Bloom's (1964) book, *Stability and Change in Human Characteristics*, refuted the commonly held assumption that learning occurs in a regular, ascending line, demonstrating the developing function of intelligence as well as the increased stability of measured intelligence with age. In terms of intelligence measured at the age of 17, his correlational data and absolute scale of intelligence development indicated that approximately 50% of IQ development occurs before age 4, with 80% of the development of adult IQ taking place by 8 years of age. His findings also demonstrated that changes in relevant environmental factors have the greatest effect on a specific characteristic during its most rapid period of change. Bloom's research in this area resulted in an educational shift, with increased focus on the early years of development.

His interest also included the identification and availability of highly favorable learning conditions. In his research, he found that mastery learning, including detailed trial tests and a variety of feedback correctives, can be used to improve levels of learning of groups of students, with trial test/feedback correctives helping students discover and correct learning errors (Brandt, 1979).

Bloom's career included positions as the Charles Swift Distinguished Service professor emeritus at the University of Chicago from 1970 and professor of education at Northwestern University, Evanston, Illinois from 1983 to 1989. He served as an education advisor to the governments of India and Israel and as vice chairman of the Meeting of Experts on Curriculum of General Education in Moscow in 1968. He was the recipient of the John Dewey award of the John Dewey Society (1968), the Teachers College medal for distinguished service of Columbia University (1970), and the award for distinguished contributions to education of the American Educational Research Association (1970). Bloom's numerous writings include *All Our Children Learning: A Primer for Parents, Teachers, and other Educators* (1980), *The State of Research on Selected Alterable Variables in Education* (1980), and *Developing Talent in Young People* (1985).

REFERENCES

Bloom, B. S. (Ed.). (1956). *Taxonomy of educational objectives. The classification of educational goals—Handbook I, cognitive domain*. New York, NY: McKay.

Bloom, B. S. (1964). *Stability and change in human characteristics*. New York, NY: Wiley.

Bloom, B. S. (1980). *The state of research on selected alterable variables in education*. Chicago, IL: University of Chicago.

Bloom, B. S., & Sosniak, L. A. (1985). *Developing talent in young people*. New York, NY: Ballantine.

Brandt, R. (1979). A conversation with Benjamin Bloom. *Educational Leadership, 37*(2), 157–161.

ANN E. LUPKOWSKI
Texas A&M University
First edition

TAMARA J. MARTIN
University of Texas of the Permian Basin
Second edition

BLUE DIAPER SYNDROME

Blue diaper syndrome is a metabolic disorder caused by the incomplete breakdown of the dietary nutrient and obligatory serotonin (5-HT) precursor tryptophan. Excessive amounts of tryptophan are broken down by intestinal bacteria, thus converting the excessive tryptophan into indican. The indican is then absorbed by the intestinal wall and excreted in urine, thus causing the bluish discoloration seen in infants' diapers. Blue diaper syndrome is believed to be an inherited, autosomal, possibly X-linked, recessive trait.

Blue diaper syndrome, often occurring in infancy, is rare and affects females and males equally. The actual prevalence of blue diaper syndrome is unknown, as it has been underreported. Because tryptophan is involved in the production of serotonin, a neurotransmitter involved in the regulation of mood and other cognitive processes, blue diaper syndrome has been known to be associated with cognitive sequelae.

Characteristics

1. Bluish discoloration of the infant's urine (and bluish stained diaper).

2. Craniostenosis (a congenital deformity of the skull resulting from premature closure of the sutures between the cranial bones) and osteoscerosis (abnormal increase in bone tissue density).

3. Dwarfism, intellectual developmental disabilities, hypercalcemia, failure to thrive, irritability, poor appetite, constipation, and vomiting.

4. Abnormally high levels of calcium in the blood (hypercalcemia), which could accumulate in the kidneys, eventually leading to possible kidney failure (nephrocalcinosis).

5. Impaired vision, as well as other ocular abnormalities, and frequent intestinal infections (Chen, Wu, & Xiong, 1991).

Treatment of blue diaper syndrome is predominantly symptomatic, revolving around dietary adjustments to minimize the side effects on the body. To reduce the likelihood of kidney damage, children's consumption of calcium should be restricted, as should their intake of protein and vitamin D. Antibiotics may be dispensed to control intestinal bacteria. Foods, such as turkey and milk, containing high levels of tryptophan should also be avoided. Genetic counseling also may be beneficial to families (Drummond & Michael, Ulstrom, & Good, 1961; McKusik, 1986).

Special education placement may become an issue; however, the range of mental deficiency is unknown at this time. Prognosis is highly dependent on individual symptomology and management via diet and medical intervention. Future research is aimed at genetic mapping, which could lead to prevention and treatment options for this rare disorder.

REFERENCES

Chen, Y., Wu, L., & Xiong, Q. (1991). The ocular abnormalities of blue diaper syndrome. *Metabolic, Pediatric, and Systemic Ophthalmology, 14,* 51–53.

Drummond, K. N., Michael, A. F., Ulstrom, R. A., & Good, R. A. (1964). The blue diaper syndrome: Familial hypercalcemia with nephrocalcinosis and indicanuria. *American Journal of Medicine, 37,* 928–947.

McKusick, V. A. (1986). *Online Mendelian inheritance in man, article 211000.* Retrieved from http://www.ncbi.nlm.nih.gov/pubmed/1818237

KIMBERLY M. ESTEP
University of Houston–Clear Lake

BOBATH METHOD

Karel Bobath, a neuropsychiatrist, and Berta Bobath, a physiotherapist, developed an assessment and treatment program in England based on central nervous system (CNS) functioning. Their approach focuses on the whole child and is referred to as *neurodevelopmental treatment* (NDT) (Bobath, 1980).

Central nervous system functioning is regarded as the basis of all motor functioning. It provides the individual with the ability to perform all posture and movement tasks, from the most simple to the most highly integrated complex ones. The individual is able to maintain the head and trunk in a midline or balanced position while pursuing a motor task because of the working of the CNS.

If for some reason—as in cerebral palsy, other developmentally delaying conditions of childhood, or stroke—the working of the CNS is impaired, a therapist trained to use the NDT method would work with the person to improve the quality of tone and movement. Problems related to tone, posture, and fluidity of movement are the focus of the therapy.

Treatment has two basic goals: (1) the inhibition of primitive and postural reflexes that are abnormally present, and (2) the facilitation of insufficiently developed normal postural reactions. All therapy is developmentally oriented and is determined by the unique, specific needs of the individual.

Through therapy the individual experiences the feeling of more normal movement patterns and works to maintain these new, more efficient motor patterns. The treatment is dynamic in that there is interaction as the therapist makes constant changes in handling to match the individual's postural and movement responses.

It is the normal postural reflex mechanism that provides the basis for the individual to exhibit normal postural tone and variety in movement patterns. Through the process of co-contraction, the trunk and head (proximal parts) are stabilized, thus allowing for more finitely graded motor activity to be performed by the arms, hands, legs, and feet (distal parts). It is important for the individual to develop a more normal postural reflex mechanism so that efficient, purposeful actions can increase. The righting and equilibrium reactions are the bases of the normal postural reflex mechanism.

A major emphasis of NDT when employed with children is that parents and teachers be taught appropriate handling techniques by the therapist with the physician's approval. For carryover and integration of new skills to occur, the same handling procedures used by the therapist should be used at home and in the classroom. The Bobath method has been criticized as being "insufficient in meeting the special cognitive, social, and emotional problems and integrating these variables into patient examination and physical rehabilitation" (Rasmussen, 1994). In addition, the National Center on Physical Activity and Disability (NCPAD; 2005) reports that there is no scientific evidence to support this form of therapy over any other or no therapy at all.

REFERENCES

Bobath, K. (1980). *A neurophysiological basis for the treatment of cerebral palsy*. Philadelphia, PA: Lippincott.

National Center on Physical Activity and Disability (NCPAD). (2005). A brief history of therapy in the treatment of cerebral palsy. Retrieved from http://ncpad.org/

Rasmussen, G. (1994). A new approach to physical rehabilitation. In A. L. Christensen & B. Uzzell (Eds.), *Brain injury and physical rehabilitation*. Hillsdale, NJ: Erlbaum.

Mary K. Dykes
University of Florida

See also **Cerebral Palsy; Occupational Therapy; Physical Therapy**

BODER TEST OF READING–SPELLING PATTERNS

The Boder Test of Reading-Spelling Patterns (the Boder Test) is subtitled "A diagnostic test for subtypes of reading disability," a designation that reflects the medical orientation of the test's senior author and the need for a typology of dyslexia. Boder and Jarrico (1982), in devising the Boder Test, relied on several assumptions about children and about reading.

The first assumption is that each dyslexic reader has a distinctive pattern of cognitive strengths and weaknesses across the two primary factors of the reading process: the visual gestalt and the auditory analytic functions. In Boder's scheme, the former underlies the development of a sight vocabulary and the latter the development of phonic word analysis or word attack. The Boder Test thus gives the following as its operational definition of developmental dyslexia:

> A reading disability in which the reading and spelling performance gives evidence of cognitive deficits in either the visual gestalt function or auditory analytic function, or both. A corollary of this definition is that when the reading-spelling pattern of poor readers gives no evidence of such cognitive deficits, the reading disability is regarded as nonspecific rather than dyslexic. (Boder & Jarrico, 1982, p. 5)

Accordingly, the Boder Test is intended to allow for differential diagnosis of developmental dyslexia by analyzing together a child's reading and spelling performances as interdependent functions. The manual describes what is offered as "a systematic sequence of simple reading and spelling tasks" giving "an essentially qualitative analysis of the ability to learn to read and spell, for which quantitative criteria are provided" (Boder & Jarrico, 1982, p. 5).

Four subgroups of reading disability are then identified: (1) *dysphonetic dyslexics*, children with strong visual-gestalt reading functions and weak phonic analysis; (2) *dyseidetic dyslexics*, children with strong phonic analysis functions and weak visual gestalt areas; (3) *mixed dysphonetic-dyseidetic*, children who are weak in visual gestalt and phonic analysis; and (4) *nonspecific reading disability*, children strong in visual gestalt and phonic analysis function but not reading well. According to Boder and Jarrico (1982, p. 6), these patterns exist only among reading-disabled children, for "strengths and deficits in the gestalt and analytic functions of dyslexic children are manifested in three characteristic reading-spelling patterns not found among good readers who are at or above grade level in both reading and spelling." Significant reading retardation is defined in the Boder Test as reading 2 or more years below normal expectancy for grade level or mental age, although it is noted that performance one year below may be diagnostically significant. The authors further assert (p. 9) that the "test can make a reliable early diagnosis of a reading disability and identify the child's preferred modality, either visual or auditory, in learning how to read."

The test proper consists of an oral reading test (word recognition) and a written spelling test. The spelling words are determined from the results of the reading test. The test is individually administered in not more than about 30 minutes. According to the manual, the test may be administered by teachers, reading specialists, psychologists, physicians, and speech therapists.

The reading test consists of 13 "graded" word lists of 20 words each; half of each list contains words that are phonetically regular and half words that are not phonetic. Word lists are presented twice, in timed (1 second) and untimed (10 seconds) conditions. Reading level is determined to be the grade level corresponding to the highest graded word list at which the students read 50% or more of the words correctly. A more precise reading level is obtained by giving 2 months of additional credit for each word read correctly from the flash presentation above this basal level. Two other scores are yielded by the Boder Test, reading age (reading level–5) and reading quotient (RA/CA) × 100; if the child's overall mental ability is substantially above or below average, this quotient is to be corrected for MA by use of the following formula: RQ = (2RA/(MA + CA)) × 100 or, by using RQ = (3RA/(MA + CA + Grade Age)) × 100. A set of rules is provided based on the RQ and the pattern of spelling errors to allow classification of each child as normal, dysphonetic, dyseidetic, mixed, or nonspecific in reading skill.

Although the Boder Test is the product of much clinical experience with children and reflects great insight into abnormal reading processes, the technical development of the Boder Test was inadequate to support its use in other than research settings. The use of antiquated quotients for scaling, the failure to collect normative data, and significant problems with the development of reliability and validity data (Flynn, 1992) all argue strongly against use of the scale. Boder's model of reading disabilities may still be useful in the conceptualization and treatment of children's reading difficulties, particularly in learning disabilities placements where differentiated instruction is possible, although the visual learner-auditory learner aspects of the approach are antiquated and have not been supported over the years (Reynolds, 1981). The use of the Boder Test in the diagnosis or evaluation of dyslexia or other reading difficulties is unsupportable at this time and other means of implementing Boder's model of dyslexia should be pursued.

REFERENCES

Boder, E., & Jarrico, S. (1982). *Boder Test of Reading-Spelling Patterns*. New York, NY: Grune & Stratton.

Flynn, J. M. (1992). Electrophysiological correlates of dyslexic subtypes. *Journal of Learning Disabilities, 25*(2), 133–141.

Reynolds, C. R. (1981). Neuropsychological basis of intelligence. In G. Hynd & J. Obrzunt (Eds.), *Neuropsychological assessment and the school aged child: Issues and procedures*. New York, NY: Grune & Stratton.

CECIL R. REYNOLDS
Texas A&M University

See also Grade Equivalents; Ratio IQ; Reading Disorders

BODY IMAGE

Body image refers to a person's conceptions of their body type and physical features. A person can hold either a positive body image or a negative body image (body dissatisfaction). People who possess a negative body image are at increased risk for low self-esteem, depression, and impaired social and sexual functioning (Davison & McCabe, 2005). Furthermore, body image dissatisfaction and eating disorder symptomatology, especially in females, are strongly linked (Lokken, Worthy, & Trautmann, 2004; McGee, Hewitt, Sherry, Parkin, & Flett, 2005).

A review of the literature on gender differences in body image dissatisfaction across the life span revealed specific developmental trends and several consistent patterns (McCabe & Ricciardelli, 2004). First, during childhood, males and females report similar levels of body dissatisfaction. Whereas females tend to report a desire for thinness, males tend to be split among a desire either to gain or lose weight. By adolescence, the gender gap among body dissatisfaction appears to increase as males report less body dissatisfaction than girls. As was reported for prepubescent males, adolescent males are divided in their desire either to gain or to lose weight. This decrease in body dissatisfaction among adolescent males may be because puberty brings males closer to the ideal body type, with the broadening of the chest and shoulders, whereas puberty often carries females further away from the ideal body type with the widening of the hips and increased fat deposits (McCabe, Ricciardelli, & Finemore, 2002).

The ideal body types presented in the media can create decreased body image satisfaction in females and males. An examination of male body types presented by the media to children (e.g., muscular models, movie stars, action figures) reveals that presented body types frequently have more muscular body types than can be achieved without the use of anabolic steroids (Labre, 2002). This impossible-to-reach ideal body type is presented to even very young children (Pope, Phillips, & Olivardia, 2000). For example, the G.I. Joe doll, a popular toy among young boys, has a physique more muscular than that of any known human. Males who possess a predisposition to internalize the ideal body images presented in the media reported increased body dissatisfaction due to repeated exposure to such images of the ideal male body type presented by the media (Humphreys & Paxton, 2004). In contrast, the media often portrays the female ideal body type as an extremely emaciated ectomorph type, one that cannot be healthily achieved by most females. The presentation of an extremely thin ideal body type has been linked to the formation of eating disorders in female children, adolescents, and adults (Lokken et al., 2004). Other conditions, including feedback from parents, also can contribute to the development of a positive or negative body image (McCabe & Ricciardelli, 2003).

Few studies have been conducted to determine factors that promote resilience to body image dissatisfaction, especially in males. However, Choate (2005) proposed a theoretical model of body image resilience in females. In her model she attributes feelings of holistic balance, which in turn encourage females to develop body image resilience, to supportive family relationships in which parents emphasize the importance of achievement in numerous domains, including satisfaction with gender role, confidence in physical and athletic abilities, and possession of effective skills to cope with the stress associated with development and transitions, instead of focusing only on appearance. Ethnicity has been found to have an effect on the perceptions of body image, with findings indicating that African American and Latina women are more satisfied with extra weight on their body, and one of the variables that contributes to this difference is cultural communities that are more accepting of body fat (Demarest & Allen, 2000; Poran, 2002). This finding is in contrast to Asian and white communities that have been found to not be not accepting of body fat (Barnett, Keel, & Conoscenti, 2001). Some research also suggests that because African American and Latino communities are more accepting of larger body types, the body image of African American and Latina women is less influenced by mainstream media than their white counterparts (Poran, 2002).

REFERENCES

Barnett, H. L., Keel, P. K., & Conoscenti, L. M. (2001). Body type preferences in Asian and Caucasian college students. *Sex Roles, 45*(11–12), 867–878. doi:10.1023/a:1015600705749

Choate, L. H. (2005). Toward a Theoretical model of women's body image resilience. *Journal of Counseling & Development, 83*(3), 320–330.

Davison, T. E., & McCabe, M. P. (2005). Relationships between men's and women's body image and their psychological, social, and sexual functioning. *Sex Roles, 52*(7–8), 463–475. doi:10.1007/s11199-005-3712-z

Demarest, J., & Allen, R. (2000). Body image: Gender, ethnic, and age differences. *The Journal of Social Psychology, 140*(4), 465–472. doi:10.1080/00224540009600485

Humphreys, P., & Paxton, S. J. (2004). Impact of exposure to idealised male images on adolescent boys' body image. *Body Image, 1*(3), 253–266. doi:10.1016/j.bodyim.2004.05.001

Labre, M. P. (2002). Adolescent boys and the muscular male body ideal. *Journal of Adolescent Health, 30*(4,Suppl), 233–242. doi:10.1016/s1054-139x(01)00413-x

Lokken, K. L., Worthy, S. L., & Trautmann, J. (2004). Examining the links among magazine preference, levels of awareness and internalization of sociocultural appearance standards, and presence of eating-disordered symptoms in college women. *Family and Consumer Sciences Research Journal, 32*(4), 361–381. doi:10.1177/1077727x04263837

McCabe, M. P., & Ricciardelli, L. A. (2003). Sociocultural influences on body image and body changes among adolescent boys and girls. *The Journal of Social Psychology, 143*(1), 5–26. doi:10.1080/00224540309598428

McCabe, M. P., & Ricciardelli, L. A. (2004). Body image dissatisfaction among males across the lifespan: A review of past literature. *Journal of Psychosomatic Research, 56*(6), 675–685. doi:10.1016/s0022-3999(03)00129-6

McCabe, M. P., Ricciardelli, L. A., & Finemore, J. (2002). The role of puberty, media and popularity with peers on strategies to increase weight, decrease weight and increase muscle tone among adolescent boys and girls. *Journal of Psychosomatic Research, 52*(3), 145–154. doi:10.1016/s0022-3999(01)00272-0

McGee, B. J., Hewitt, P. L., Sherry, S. B., Parkin, M., & Flett, G. L. (2005). Perfectionistic self-presentation, body image, and eating disorder symptoms. *Body Image, 2*(1), 29–40. doi:10.1016/j.bodyim.2005.01.002

Pope, H. G., Phillips, K. A., & Olivardia, R. (2000). *The Adonis Complex: The secret crisis of male body obsession.* New York, NY: The Free Press.

Poran, M. A. (2002). Denying diversity: Perceptions of beauty and social comparison processes among Latina, Black, and White women. *Sex Roles, 47*(1–2), 65–81. doi:10.1023/a:1020683720636

ALLISON G. DEMPSEY
University of Florida

See also Anorexia Nervosa; Eating Disorders

BODY TYPE

Body type refers to a person's overall body shape. Although body type is largely determined by one's genetic disposition, other conditions, including diet, exercise, and use of medications, may influence the body's appearance.

There are three different categories of body types: endomorph, ectomorph, and mesomorph. Rarely does a person embody one distinct body type; instead, most people display some combination of all three types, with one type being more dominant.

The endomorph body type is characterized by big bones, slow metabolism, and a high percentage of body fat. People who have a predominantly endomorph body type may experience greater difficulties controlling their weight through exercise and diet than do people with predominance for the ectomorph or mesomorph body types. The ectomorph body type is characterized by a linear physique, low percentage of body fat, and a high metabolism. The mesomorph body type is characterized by broad shoulders and a narrow waist, high metabolism, and large muscles.

Preference for specific body types varies by gender and ethnicity (Greenberg & LaPorte, 1996). However, many studies have found that the media frequently portrays an extreme mesomorph body type as the ideal body type for men, sometimes so extreme that it cannot be achieved without the use of anabolic steroids (Labre, 2002). In contrast, the media often portrays the female ideal body type as an extremely emaciated ectomorph body type, which cannot be healthily achieved by most females. This presentation of an extremely thin ideal body type has been linked to the formation of eating disorders in female adolescents and adults (Lokken, Worthy, & Trautmann, 2004).

A survey of adults indicated that men are more likely to specify a body type preference for dates than women (Glasser, Robnett, & Feliciano, 2009). African American and Latino males have a greater preference for larger female body types than white males, and African American men were the only race to be open to dating a variety of female body types when compared to white men. Glasser, Robnett, and Feliciano (2009) concluded that race and ethnicity are associated with how closely body type preference adheres to the dominant ideal body standards. The attribution of particular body types as attractive also varies by ethnicity (Jackson & McGill, 1996).

William Sheldon (Sheldon & Stevens, 1942) devised his somatotype theory, which designated that the same genes that determine a person's body type also affect the formation of a personality. Thus, he proposed that each body type was associated with a specific set of personality variables. For example, Sheldon postulated that endomorphs tend to be tolerant, extroverted, and extravagant. Ectomorphs tend to be shy and introspective. Mesomorphs tend to be assertive and energetic. However, this theory has been discredited due to a lack of findings that support a link between temperament and body type (Catell & Metzner, 1993).

REFERENCES

Catell, P., & Metzner, R. (1993). The body type/temperament mismatch and self-actualization. *Psychological Reports, 72,* 1165–1166.

Glasser, C. L., Robnett, B., & Feliciano, C. (2009). Internet daters' body type preferences: Race-ethnic and gender differences. *Sex Roles, 61*(1–2), 14–33. doi:10:1007/s11199-009-9604-x

Greenberg, D. R., & LaPorte, D. J. (1996). Racial differences in body type preferences of men for women. *International Journal of Eating Disorders, 19,* 275–278.

Jackson, L. A., & McGill, O. D. (1996). Body type preferences and body characteristics associated with attractive and unattractive bodies by African Americans and Anglo Americans. *Sex Roles, 35*(5–6), 295–307. doi:10.1007/BF01664771

Labre, M. P. (2002). Adolescent boys and the muscular male body ideal. *Journal of Adolescent Health, 30,* 233–242.

Lokken, K. L., Worthy, S. L., & Trautmann, J. (2004). Examining the links among magazine preference, levels of awareness and internalization of sociocultural appearance standards, and presence of eating-disordered symptoms in college women. *Family and Consumer Sciences Research Journal, 32,* 361–381.

Sheldon, W. H., & Stevens, S. S. (1942). *The varieties of temperament.* New York, NY: Harper & Row.

ALLISON G. DEMPSEY
University of Florida

BOEHM TEST OF BASIC CONCEPTS, THIRD EDITION

The Boehm Test of Basic Concepts, Third Edition (BTBC-3, 2000) was developed to assess the understanding of basic concepts in young children between the ages of 5 to 7 years. The test can be administered individually or in group format in kindergarten, Grade 1, and Grade 2 and takes approximately 30 to 45 minutes to administer. Children are asked to correctly identify a picture from among several choices when presented with verbal cues incorporating such terms as over, least, left, and so on (e.g., asked to identify the picture in which the ball is *over* the table). Based on these results, children's conceptual developmental and school readiness can be assessed.

The BTBC-3 assesses 50 basic concepts most frequently occurring in kindergarten, 1st, and 2nd-grade curriculum. These include size (i.e., medium-sized), direction (away), quantity (as many), time (first), classification (all), and general (other).

Two parallel forms, E and F, allow for pre- and posttesting to help determine if the student's comprehension of the concept is consistent across multiple contexts. The results can be used to demonstrate progress as a result of teaching or intervention. The manual includes directions for administration in English and Spanish.

Boehm-3 gives you raw scores and percentile ranks. It was normed on two samples in the fall 1999 (Form E $n = 2,866$; Form F $n = 3,189$) and in the spring 2000 (Form E $n = 2,348$; Form F $n = 2,196$). Reliability studies yielded coefficients alpha between .80 to .91. An alternate-forms reliability study showed that nearly 94% of students had a difference of 4 or fewer raw score points from one form to the other.

REFERENCES

Boehm, A. E. (2000). Assessment of basic relational concepts. In B. A. Bracken, *Psychoeducational assessment of preschool children* (3rd ed., pp. 186–203). Needham Heights, MA: Allyn & Bacon.

Geisinger, K. F., Spies, R. A., Carlson, J. F., & Plake, B. S. (Eds.). (2006). *The sixteenth mental measurements yearbook.* Lincoln, NE: Buros Institute of Mental Measurements.

RON DUMONT
Fairleigh Dickinson University

JOHN O. WILLIS
Rivier College

KATHLEEN VIEZEL
Fairleigh Dickinson University

JAMIE ZIBULSKY
Fairleigh Dickinson Univeristy

BONE ANCHORED HEARING DEVICE–BAHA

The bone anchored hearing device (BAHA) is a hearing system that works through bone conduction. It is an alternative system for other traditional bone and air conduction aids for a conductive hearing loss. The BAHA device is comprised of three components. The first component is a titanium screw; the second is a percutaneous abutment; and the third is a processor. To implant the BAHA it is surgically placed behind the hearing impaired ear and is allowed to osseointegrate into the skull. When this integration has taken place the percutaneous abutment is attached to the implant. After a period of time the sound processor is snapped on to the abutment and the procedure is then complete. When sound is presented it creates vibration in the titanium screw. The vibration causes transcranial compression of cochlear fluids causing transmission of sound to the auditory nerve. Although vibrations of the skull and the accompanying compression of cochlear fluids causes some lessening of high frequency sounds, that BAHA produces superior high frequency gain compared to conventional bone-conduction devices. The gain is usually between 7 and 17 decibels in frequencies between 3 and 8 K Hz.

Criteria for Selection of the BAHA

The BAHA is approved by the Food and Drug Administration for use by children 5 years of age and older and adults. It can be used for unilateral and bilateral conductive or mixed hearing loss and for a unilateral single-sided profound sensory neural hearing loss. In the incidence of profound deafness the BAHA acts as a bone conduction CROS (Contralateral Routing of the Offside Signal) device, which transmits the signal from the deaf side through the skull to the contralateral side. Conductive hearing loss is commonly caused by chronic otorrhea, otitis media, congenital aural atresia, external canal closure, and ossicular chain disorders (Battista & Ho, 2003). The criteria, which contraindicates a BAHA implant, includes a word recognition score <60% in the indicated ear, developmentally delayed children and adults, children younger than 5 years of age, and bone or skin disease at the site of the implant.

Since the BAHA procedure began recipients have expressed a 98% degree of satisfaction with the results in comparison to a 73% rate for conventional bone conduction aids.

REFERENCE

Battista, R. A., Ho, S. (2003). The bone anchored hearing device (BAHA). *Operative Techniques in Otolaryngology Head and Neck Surgery*, 272–276.

PATRICIA SCHERER
International Center on Deafness and the Arts
Fourth edition

BONET, JUAN P. (1579–1629)

Juan Pablo Bonet, a Spanish philologist, instructed students who were deaf in language and articulation, and taught them a manual alphabet and system of signs that he had developed. He wrote the first book on the education of the deaf, *Simplification of the Letters of the Alphabet and Method of Teaching Deaf-Mutes to Speak*. This work, which appeared in 1620, provided a basis for the developments relating to the education of the deaf in Europe and Great Britain during the 18th century (Lane, 1984).

REFERENCES

Bonet, J. P. (1890). *Reducción de las letras y arte para enseñar a ablar los mudos (Simplification of the letters of the alphabet and method of teaching deaf-mutes to speak)*. 1620. Reprint, Harrowgate: Farrar.

Lane, H. (1984). *When the mind hears*. New York, NY: Random House.

PAUL IRVINE
Katonah, New York

BORDERLINE PERSONALITY DISORDER

Borderline personality disorder is a diagnostic classification included in the *Diagnostic and Statistical Manual of Mental Disorders*, Fourth Edition, Revised (*DSM-IV-TR*; American Psychiatric Association, 2004). In the past, various borderline disorders were described in ambiguous terms as mild (or latent) forms of schizophrenia (falling somewhere between psychosis and neurosis). With the publication of the *DSM-III*, the disorder received official recognition as a distinct diagnostic entity, closer in form to the affective disorders than schizophrenia (Archer, Ball, & Hunter, 1985; NIMH, 2012).

The diagnosis of borderline personality disorder requires the presence of at least five of the following: impulsive or unpredictable behavior, unstable interpersonal relationships, difficulty in controlling anger or inappropriate anger, identity disturbance, unstable mood (including depression, anxiety, and irritability), physically self-damaging acts, chronic feelings of boredom, and intolerance of being alone. As is the case with other personality disorders, the borderline disorder represents a chronic, pervasive pattern of behavior that emerges during late childhood/adolescence and interferes with social and occupational functioning for much of the individual's adult life. Despite the presence of symptoms during adolescence, the *DSM-IV* recommends that this diagnosis be reserved for individuals 18 years of age and older. For those under 18, the diagnosis of identity disorder, characterized by a similar clinical picture (e.g., mild depression, anxiety, self-doubt, negative/oppositional behavior), is preferred. Identity disorder reflects an inability to establish an acceptable sense of self and includes uncertainty about such issues as career goals, sexual orientation or behavior, moral values, friends, and long-term goals. Contrary to *DSM-IV* recommendations, however, the borderline diagnosis is often used with children and adolescents (Bradley, 1981), a practice that has recently received some empirical support (Archer et al., 1985).

The advent of managed care companies has severely restricted the ability of the helping professions to give significant and long-term care to individuals with this condition. Consequently many individuals with borderline personality disorder are left to fend for themselves after short-term treatment. There is some research to support dialectic behavior therapy as a psychotherapeutic method for this disorder. In addition, frequent psychopharmacological treatment is used with BPD to reduce impulsivity, mood instability, and aggression (NIMH, 2012).

Characteristics

1. Pattern of unstable mood and conflicted interpersonal relationships.

2. Impulsive behavior including suicidal gestures and self-mutilating behavior.

3. Propensity to engage in high-risk behaviors such as promiscuity.

4. Identity disturbance marked by tenuous sense of self and feelings of emptiness.

5. Intense dependency on others as well as vulnerability to perceived separation from external sources of support.

6. Persistent feelings of emptiness, dysphoria, and intense, inappropriate anger.

REFERENCES

American Psychiatric Association. (2004). *Diagnostic and statistical manual of mental disorders* (4th ed.). Washington, DC: Author.

Archer, R. P., Ball, J. D., & Hunter, J. A. (1985). MMPI characteristics of borderline psychopathology in adolescent inpatients. *Journal of Personality Assessment, 49*, 47–55.

Bradley, S. J. (1981). The borderline diagnosis in children and adolescents. *Child Psychiatry & Human Development, 12*(2), 121–127.

NIMH. (2012). *National Institute of Mental Health: Borderline personality disorder*. Retrieved from http://www.nimh.nih.gov/health/topics/borderline-personality-disorder/index.shtml

ROBERT G. BRUBAKER
Eastern Kentucky University

See also **Childhood Psychosis; Childhood Schizophrenia; Diagnostic and Statistical Manual of Mental Disorders (DSM-IV-TR)**

BORJESON-FORSSMAN-LEHMANN SYNDROME

Borjeson-Forssman-Lehmann syndrome (BFLS) is an X-linked, possibly incompletely recessive, genetic disorder characterized by numerous dysmorphic anomalies, obesity, hypogonadism, epilepsy, and intellectual developmental disabilities. The full expression in males results in more severe symptoms, whereas penetrance in carrier females appears to be associated with variable X-chromosome inactivation (Kubota, Oga, Ohashi, Iwamoto, & Fukushima, 1999). In heterozygous women, the phenotypic effects vary widely between apparent normality to mild or moderately evident BFLS manifestations (Ardinger, Hanson, & Zellweger, 1984).

Characteristics

1. Facial anomalies: Enlarged but normally formed ears, hyperplastic supraorbital ridges, deep-set eyes, narrow palpegral fissures, ptosis, swollen subcutaneous facial tissue, microcephaly.

2. Extremities: Soft fleshy hands with tapering fingers; short, widely spaced, flexed toes.

3. Neurological problems: Seizures or epilepsy, mild to severe intellectual developmental disabilities (more severe in males), visual abnormalities and deficits.

4. Metabolic disorders: Hypometabolism, generalized obesity, hypotonia.

5. Endocrine abnormalities: Delayed bone age, short neck, hyperkyphosis; delayed sexual development, hypogonadism, micropenis, cryptorchidism, postpubertal gynecomastia in males.

Incidence is extremely rare, but BFLS is inherited with equal frequency in males and females. Three large families have been identified with the disorder, two from the United States and of European descent and one in Australia and originally from the United Kingdom. Although no more than a half-dozen families have been reported in the literature, there are also several smaller families identified with less certainty. Of these, three are from the United Kingdom, two from Australia, two located in the United States, one in Mexico, and two in Belgium. There has also been one unusual female case from Japan with an extremely skewed X-inactivation pattern. Genetic mapping has pointed to region Xq26q27, but the gene itself remains unidentified (Jones, 1997).

Hypotonia, obesity, and micropenis are often noted in infancy, along with the abnormalities of the face and extremities. The unusual facial appearance typically includes a coarse, fleshy face; enlarged but not deformed ears; and deep-set eyes with prominent supraorbital ridges and narrow palpebral fissures. Distal extremities are typically shortened, with tapering fingers and widely spaced, flexed toes. Other features include generalized obesity, epilepsy, intellectual developmental disabilities, stunted growth, and delayed sexual development. There may also be ophthalmologic abnormalities (e.g., nystagmus, cataract, poor vision), skeletal deformities (e.g., irregular end-plates to vertebrae, hyperkyphosis, short neck, thickened calvarium), and electroencephalogram disturbances. There are developmental delays including late walking. The degree of mental retardation varies from mild to severe. Common differential diagnoses include Prader-Willi, Noonan, Coffin-Lowry, and Bardet-Biedl syndromes. Occasional association with dilated cardiomyopathy suggests the importance of cardiovascular study in this syndrome (Kaplinsky et al., 2001).

Special education services are available for intellectual developmental disabilities, and the degree of intellectual impairment ranges from mild to severe. Intellectual deficits are more pronounced in males because of full expression. Depending on the degree of penetrance, female carriers may exhibit normal or borderline IQ or more mild to moderate retardation. Qualification for special education services may also be available for associated health problems (e.g., epilepsy, hypotonia) as well as for the behavioral problems and speech-language delays typically seen with mental retardation. Occupational therapy services may be useful depending on the degree of hypotonia, abnormalities of the distal extremities, hyperkyphosis, or other skeletal problems.

There is no cure for this genetic disorder. Life span is predicted to be normal. Treatment focuses on the symptoms, especially seizure control and management of metabolic and endocrine dysfunction, as well as on providing special education and other services. In some cases, testosterone supplementation may enhance intellectual performance and induce loss of weight when testosterone levels are low. Depending on the degree of impairment, a sheltered environment may be needed. Genetic counseling is recommended for patients and families.

REFERENCES

Ardinger, H., Hanson, J., & Zellweger, H. (1984). Borjeson-Forssman-Lehmann syndrome: Further delineation in five cases. *American Journal of Medical Genetics, 19*(4), 653–664.

Jones, K. (Ed.). (1997). *Smith's recognizable patterns of human malformation* (5th ed.). Philadelphia, PA: Saunders.

Kaplinsky, E., Perandones, C., Galiana, M., Fidelell, H., Favaloror, R., Carlos, V., & Perrone, S. (2001). Borjeson-Forssman-Lehmann syndrome and dilated cardiomyopathy: A previously unreported association. *Canadian Journal of Cardiology, 17*(1), 80–83.

Kubota, T., Oga, S., Ohashi, H., Iwamoto, Y., & Fukushima, Y. (1999). Borjeson-Forssman-Lehmann syndrome in a woman with skewed X-chromosome inactivation. *American Journal of Medical Genetics, 87*(3), 258–261.

Vicky Y. Spradling
Austin State Hospital

BOWER, ELI M. (1917–1991)

Eli M. Bower obtained a BS degree from New York University in 1937 and an MA from Columbia University in 1947. He continued his education at Stanford University, receiving his EdD in counseling psychology in 1954. He was professor emeritus and president of the American Orthopsychiatry Association at the University of California, Berkeley. Bower was a pioneer in the field of early childhood education of children with disabilities. Serving as a member of the California Governor's Advisory Committee on Children and Youth, he assumed an important role in the development of state policy on the education of children with emotional disorders and gifted children. He also held the position of deputy director of the California Department of Mental Hygiene in the early 1960s.

His major areas of study included orthopsychiatry, enhancing growth and learning for the disabled, and engaging children in the school setting with games. By bringing together mental health professionals and parents of disabled children, orthopsychiatry was founded in 1924. Orthopsychiatry is defined as the science of the study and treatment of behavior disorders, particularly those involving young people.

Bower's interest in this area was focused on behavioral and social problems and their daily resolution (Bower, 1971; Bower, 1974; Bower, 1974). He also believed that games should be encouraged as teaching devices, allowing children the freedom to be involved while learning to relate to the real world. Bower looked at the question of whether children with learning disabilities could be helped in an economical, effective, and institutionally acceptable manner early enough to change their course of school development.

Bower wrote several books and more than 100 articles. Some of his major works include *Games in Education and Development, Early Identification of Emotionally Handicapped Children in School,* and *Orthopsychiatry and Education.* Eli Bower died at his home in Alameda, California, on December 20, 1991 at the age of 74.

REFERENCES

Bower, E. M. (1971). *Orthopsychiatry and education.* Detroit, MI: Wayne State University Press.

Bower, E. M. (1974). *Early identification of emotionally handicapped children in school.* Springfield, IL: Thomas.

Bower, E. M., & Shears, L. M. (1974). *Games in education and development.* Springfield, IL: Thomas.

Elizabeth Jones
Texas A&M University
First edition

Tamara J. Martin
University of Texas of the Permian Basin
Second edition

BRACKEN BASIC CONCEPT SCALE: EXPRESSIVE

The Bracken Basic Concept Scale: Expressive (BBCS:E, 2006) is an individually administered measure of a child's ability to verbally label basic, educationally relevant concepts. It is appropriate for children aged 3 years through 6 years, 11 months. The BBCS:E was co-normed and can be used in conjunction with the receptive counterpart: the Bracken Basic Concept Scale, Third Edition: Receptive (BBCS-3:R, 2006). The conceptual categories in the BBCS:E include: Colors, Letters/Sounds, Numbers/Counting, Sizes/Comparisons, Shapes, Direction/Position, Self-/Social Awareness, Texture/Material, Quantity, and Time/Sequence. The first five subtests produce the School Readiness Composite (SRC), which can be used to assess preparation for early formal education. The entire test takes approximately 20 to 25 minutes to administer, and the SRC is estimated to take only 5 to 10 minutes. There is a Spanish version of the BBCS:E; however, the Spanish version was not normed and is intended to be used in a criterion-referenced or curriculum-based context.

The normative sample included more than 750 children and was based on the 2003 U.S. Census. There were 80 children per 6-month interval from ages 3:0 to 6:11 years. Reliability was estimated by means of test-retest stability, internal consistency, and interscorer reliability studies. The stability coefficients were in .80s through .90s based on a sample of 87 children who were retested between 2 to 30 days. Internal consistency coefficients for the overall normative sample were all above .80 for the subtests, and above .90 for the composite scores, and were equally reliable for children across gender and racial/ethnic groups. Coefficients for two clinical groups (52 children with language impairments and 64 with intellectual disabilities) also were high (in the .90s). Perhaps due to the relatively objective scoring procedures, interscorer agreement was excellent; ranging from .96 to .99. The manual provides good evidence for content and construct validity, and demonstrates clinical utility of the BBCS:E for those with language and intellectual impairment.

Like its receptive counterpart, the BBCS:E is appealing for its ease of use, brevity of administration, and appeal to young children. Initial psychometric evidence also appears sound. Because of its focus on expressive language, the BBCS:E should ideally be used as part of a more comprehensive evaluation. Finally, it is recommended further studies of its validity and clinical use be completed by independent researchers (Doggett, 2010; Snyder, 2010).

REFERENCES

Doggett, R. A. (2010). Review of the Bracken basic concept scale: Expressive. In R. A. Spies, J. F. Carlson, & K. F. Geisinger (Eds.), *The eighteenth mental measurements yearbook*. Lincoln, NE: Buros Institute of Mental Measurements.

Snyder, G. (2010). Review of the Bracken basic concept scale: Expressive. In R. A. Spies, J. F. Carlson, & K. F. Geisinger (Eds.), *The eighteenth mental measurements yearbook*. Lincoln, NE: Buros Institute of Mental Measurements.

KATHLEEN VIEZEL
Fairleigh Dickinson University

JAMIE ZIBULSKY
Fairleigh Dickinson University

RON DUMONT
Fairleigh Dickinson University

JOHN O. WILLIS
Rivier College
Fourth edition

BRAIDWOOD, THOMAS (1715–1806)

Thomas Braidwood, a Scottish teacher, established Great Britain's first school for children who were deaf in Edinburgh in 1760. Unaware of the methods of teaching children who were deaf that had been developed on Europe by Heinicke, Epée, and others, Braidwood developed his own techniques, through which his students learned to speak and lip read, and to read and write. Once he had established the effectiveness of his methods, Braidwood published a proposal for the provision of public funds for the education of those students who were deaf whose families could not afford to pay for schooling, and for the training of teachers in his methods. When public funding was not granted, Braidwood declared that the system would remain his property, and swore to secrecy the family members and others at the school who had learned his techniques (Bender, 1970).

Braidwood moved his school to Hackney, near London, in 1783. Because of his obsession with secrecy, it was not until after Braidwood's death that the details of his methods became known. The writings of his nephew, Joseph Watson, who assisted him at Hackney and later established England's first school for the indigent deaf, showed that Braidwood had developed an elaborate oral method of instruction that generally paralleled the development of the oral approach elsewhere. Braidwood's great contribution was the initiation of education for the deaf in Great Britain (Bender, 1970).

REFERENCE

Bender, R. (1970). *The conquest of deafness*. Cleveland, OH: Case Western Reserve University.

PAUL IRVINE
Katonah, New York

BRAILLE

Braille is a tactile system that individuals who are blind use to read and write. The basis of braille is a rectangular "cell" consisting of six raised dots, two vertical rows of three dots each. English Braille (American Edition) consists of alphabet letters, numbers, punctuation, composition signs, and 189 contractions and short-form words, both of which are abbreviations of whole words or parts of words to increase the speed of reading and writing braille. The Nemeth Code is used to transcribe mathematics and science; other codes are used to transcribe foreign languages, computer codes, and musical notation.

The first tactually perceptible code was developed in the early 19th century by Charles Barbier, a French army officer; its purpose was to send and receive messages at night. Louis Braille modified Barbier's code and published his system in 1829, while he was a professor at the Paris School for the Blind. Although Braille was permitted to teach his system outside of school hours, it was not officially accepted by the school until 1865, 2 years after he died. In the United States, the first school to adopt Braille's code was the Missouri School for the Blind, in 1869.

Reading and writing braille is taught to students who are blind by educators specifically trained to teach these skills to pupils with visual impairments for whom a learning media assessment has supported the braille as the most efficient reading medium. The majority of experienced braille readers use two hands. A skilled two-handed reader usually begins reading a line of braille by placing both hands at the beginning of the line; when the middle of the line is reached, the right hand continues across the line, while the left hand moves in the opposite direction and locates the beginning of the next line. After the entire first line has been read by the right hand, the left hand reads the first several words on the next line, while the right hand moves quickly back to meet he left hand (Wormsley, 1996). Important characteristics of braille readers include light finger touch, finger curvature, smooth independent hand movements, and page turning (Mangold, 1989). Typically, oral reading speeds of accomplished readers are reported around 90 wpm (Trent & Truan, 1997), though rates over 200 wpm have been reported in the literature (Millar, 1997).

Young children learn to write braille using a Perkins Brailler, a six-keyed device that has similarities to a typewriter. Once students become proficient in reading braille and in using the brailler, they are taught to use the slate and stylus, more complex tools that require that the user punch braille dots one at a time with a handheld stylus into paper that has been inserted into a frame. Although the brailler is easier to use, the slate and stylus is smaller, easier to carry, and more useful for taking short notes. Electronic braille notetakers, or personal data assistants (PDAs) are also used for many writing tasks. These devices permit the six-key entry familiar to users of the Perkins

Brailler, but provide for both auditory (and sometimes, braille) feedback of what is being written or what has been stored. They also allow manipulation of the text (editing, cutting, pasting, etc.), which is not possible with most manual braillers. PDAs can be connected to ink printers or to braille embossers for the preparation of written materials for both the teacher who doesn't know braille and for the student's use.

Wormsley (2004, 2011) recommends that a functional approach be used to teach braille to students who are blind and who have mild to moderate cognitive disabilities. This approach involves designing individualized literacy programs that are responsive to students, carefully selecting key vocabulary, teaching efficient hand movements, creating stories that use familiar vocabulary and that are meaningful to students, teaching phonics, slowly introducing contractions, integrating writing, expanding vocabulary as appropriate, and monitoring student progress.

REFERENCES

Mangold, S. S. (1989). *The Mangold developmental program of tactile perception and braille letter recognition*. Castro Valley, CA: Exceptional Teaching Aids.

Millar, S. (1997). *Reading by touch*. London, UK: Routledge.

Trent, S. D., & Truan, M. B. (1997). Speed, accuracy, and comprehension of adolescent Braille readers in a specialized school. *Journal of Visual Impairment & Blindness, 91*(5), 494–500.

Wormsley, D. (1996). Reading rates of young braille-reading children. *Journal of Visual Impairment & Blindness, 90*(3), 278–282.

Wormsley, D. P. (2004). *Braille literacy: A functional approach.* New York, NY: AFB Press.

Wormsley, D. P. (2011). A theoretical rationale for using the individualized meaning centered approach to braille literacy education with students who have mild to moderate cognitive disabilities. *Journal of Visual Impairment & Blindness, 105*(3), 145–156.

Rosanne K. Silberman
Hunter College,
  City University of New York
First edition

Sandra Lewis
Florida State University
Fourth edition

BRAILLE, LOUIS (1809–1852)

Louis Braille, who suffered an accident at the age of 3 causing blindness, developed his system of reading and writing for individuals who are blind while serving as a teacher at the Institution National des Jeunes Aveugles, the school for individuals who are blind in Paris (Kugelmass, 1951). Dissatisfied with earlier approaches that were cumbersome and difficult to read, Braille developed a code employing one or more raised dots in a cell three dots high and two wide. An accomplished musician, he also worked out an application of his system to musical notation. Ironically, his school did not accept his system and actually forbade its use. Braille feared that his invention would die with him, but it survived, although it did not immediately flourish. It was not until 1916 that braille was officially adopted by the schools for individuals who are blind in the United States. A universal braille code for the English-speaking world was adopted in 1932.

REFERENCE

Kugelmass, J. (1951). *Louis Braille: Windows for the blind.* New York, NY: Messner.

PAUL IRVINE
Katonah, New York

See also Braille

BRAIN DAMAGE/INJURY

The expression brain injury denotes a condition where extragenetic influences arrest or impair the normal structure, growth, development, and functioning of brain tissue (Cruickshank, 1980). Damage to the brain can be either congenital or acquired after birth, with acquired damage resulting most frequently from trauma (Rourke, Bakker, Fisk, & Strang, 1983). The severity of dysfunction and prognosis for recovery following trauma depend on many variables, including the nature, location, and extent of the injury, the developmental level, and demographic factors such as age and sex (Rourke et al., 1983).

Brain damage is but one of many important variables that influence behavior. To understand a child's learning problems, nonneurological factors must be investigated carefully. Even in a case of documented brain injury, learning impairment may reflect an impoverished home environment, problems in emotional adjustment, poor motivation, systemic health problems, developmental lags, and genetic predispositions (Figure B.7).

Brain damage may be the most important factor in a given case, but the label brain injury offers no clarification unless the nature, location, and extent of the damage are understood. There is also considerable danger in labeling a child *brain damaged*. To do so implies permanence, encourages drug treatment, minimizes the importance of education or remediation, and shifts responsibility to

Organic	Genetic
	Neurological
	Systemic
Individual	Cognitive
	Emotional
	Cultural
	Achievement
Social/Situational	Family
	Social
	Academic

Figure B.7. Factors that influence behavior.

physicians (Gaddes, 1980). Given such a label, important and remediable strengths may be ignored. However, the label of traumatic brain injury entered the official handicapping conditions list in 1990 with the advent of the Individuals with Disabilities Act (IDEA), a revision of Public Law 94-142 and subsequent revisions. The official label mandated that school personnel resist old nosology of "*damage*" and look more toward recovery and rehabilitation.

Clinical neuropsychological assessment of a child involves the elucidation of brain-behavior relationships in a developing human organism; consequently, this is a unique area of inquiry with problems quite different from those encountered in investigating the mature brain (Rourke et al., 1983). The developing brain undergoes rapid changes, and brain damage during childhood may impair future development of certain cognitive and behavioral capacities.

The brain of a child shows a capacity for development and recovery of function following brain injury. It has been argued (the Kennard principle) that early brain damage produces less dramatic behavioral effects and better prospects for recovery than damage in later life. This claim is only partially correct. The prognosis of early brain damage depends on many variables, including the type, location, and extent of the injury (Rourke et al., 1983). Most brain-injured children show some capacity for development of functions or recovery of functions, although it is difficult to predict the extent, rate, and degree of improvement because it depends on a number of neurological and psychological factors (Chronin, 2001; Kolb & Fantie, 1997; Rourke et al., 1983).

Early brain damage may produce permanent dysfunction, delayed onset of dysfunction, or no dysfunction, depending on the maturational status of the system (Teuber & Rudel, 1962). For example, the effect of brain damage initially may be mild until functions subserved by damaged tissue become crucial for behavioral performance during development.

The term growing into a deficit has been used to emphasize the importance of the maturational status of the brain area at the time of damage (Rourke et al., 1983). Rourke (1983) argues that attentional deficits are a special problem for the young brain-damaged child, while older brain-damaged children show cognitive deficits. Rourke contends the young brain-injured child also has cognitive deficits, but they may not be apparent because of the generalized effects of attentional deficits. As attentional deficits resolve, the previously masked cognitive deficits become evident. Part of the process of recovery may involve the brain-injured child's learning to solve old problems in new ways by reorganizing functional elements of the behavioral repertoire (Luria, 1973). Thus one important premise of neuropsychology is that if the nature and extent of the deficit can be identified early in life, effective remediation can be instituted to minimize the consequences of brain damage on future learning.

In summary, consequences of brain lesions must be assessed in light of the dynamic nature of the developing brain and its emerging anatomical and functional asymmetries. Only by looking at these factors can we hope to understand the apparent paradox that the immature brain is simultaneously characterized by both a greater vulnerability to cerebral impairment and an apparently enhanced potential for recovery of function (Chelune & Edwards, 1981).

There are few common behavior patterns characterizing brain damage. However, most changes suggest a loss of the normal inhibitory influence of the cortex on behavior (Rutter, 1983). There is also frequently a deficit in attention that can lead to perseveration, hyperactivity, and impaired sensory processing (Cruickshank, Bentzen, Ratzeburg, & Tannhauser, 1961; Gordon, White, & Diller, 1972; Haskell, Barrett, & Taylor, 1977).

Attention deficit disorders or hyperactivity represent early and common consequences of brain injury. Such behaviors may reflect a deficit in planning and regulation of behavior, a deficit in memory, or loss of inhibitory control on the brain stem reticular system. In cases where a major behavioral component of the dysfunction is attention deficits, other deficits may not be observable or may not be easily measured.

Deficits affecting primarily the diencephalon often produce impaired memory consolidation. Individuals with such deficits may be able to attend to a task but they do not benefit from their experiences. As with attentional deficits, memory deficits can be pervasive and lead to more generalized deficits unless effectively remediated.

Higher level functions involve more complex cortical processing of information. The left hemisphere processes verbal material and deals with material in a discrete manner. The right hemisphere deals with nonverbal and new material in a more global manner. Functions can be divided further in each hemisphere; thus cortical damage can have dramatically different effects on behavior and learning depending on the brain area damaged. Cognitive functions relate primarily to cortical processing and include a broad range of behaviors. Early deficits in acquired brain damage may be generalized, but most

pronounced recovery is noted in sensory and motor function and speech comprehension. Often recovery of language is given precedence and other functions may suffer. Left hemisphere damage is likely to impair syntactical functions, although with increasing severity, more general language processing may be involved. Furthermore, right-sided sensory and motor deficits may be observed as well as processing of verbally labeled material. Right hemisphere impairment results in deficits in visuo-spatial functions and spatial memory. Recovery of these functions is likely to lag behind language. Developmental changes appear to shift from right hemisphere global functions to left hemisphere linguistic functions. Rourke (1983) postulates that the left hemisphere functions in an automated manner, thus freeing the right hemisphere to deal with novelty, complexity, and intermodal integration.

Brain damage not only attenuates intellectual functions but also increases the chance of problems in emotional adjustment (Rutter, 1981). While brain damage can cause emotional lability, emotional problems are usually secondary or reactive to intellectual impairment, physical handicaps, or altered peer relations. The emotional consequences of brain injury are substantially influenced by the child's level of preinjury functioning as well as postinjury social support systems. Social learning is a complex cognitive function that involves learning social cues and gestures and modifying social behavior. Head-injured children are most likely to retain characterological deficits that limit full remediation (Lezak, 1976).

Neuropsychological assessment in the schools is a topic that has received much support during the last decade. Literature in the fields of special education, school psychology, and, recently, child neuropsychology has espoused understanding neuropsychological principles when assessing and planning educational intervention for children who are experiencing significant learning or behavioral problems in school (D'Amato, Fletcher-Janzen, & Reynolds, 2005; Hynd & Obrzut, 1981; Rourke et al., 1983).

Impaired learning may reflect the influence of multiple factors; therefore, an initial step in understanding the nature of learning impairment is to explore carefully the various potential contributing factors in each case. Once these factors are identified they can be prioritized in terms of their assumed significance (Long, 1985). In this way a framework is established for diagnosing the significance of brain-damage effects in each individual case.

An adequate evaluation involves assessing intelligence (verbal and nonverbal), memory, academic achievement, and emotional adjustment. In some cases more specific neuropsychological functions also must be tested (Figure B.8). In addition, consideration must be given to social/environmental factors and their contribution to overall performance. The assessment must produce a valid and reliable picture of the individual's strengths and weaknesses, and allow inferences about underlying brain functions to be made. It is important to differentiate

Basic sensory and motor functions
Perceptual and perceptual-motor functions
Attention
Language abilities
Intelligence
Problem-solving and abstract reasoing
Memory
Emotional adjustment

Figure B.8. Essential areas of neuropsychological assessment.

between behavioral problems that reflect structural lesions and behaviors having no direct relationship to the brain's continuity.

Determining the nature (e.g., acute versus chronic) and extent of brain damage of the child presents a much more difficult task for the neuropsychologist than the diagnosis of adult brain injury. The major difficulty concerns the role of age and development in children. Children change quickly in the kinds of skills we can expect them to acquire, and all children with the same chronological age are not at the same developmental level. It is necessary to take developmental factors into account. A basic rule in assessing children is to use multiple tests so that patterns and changes can be seen. The resulting profile then can be used to determine whether the hypothesis of delayed development is tenable (D'Amato et al., 2005; Golden & Anderson, 1979).

Assessment of intellectual and academic strengths and weaknesses for remedial or rehabilitative purposes, such as constructing an individual educational program (IEP), is maximally useful only when certain requirements are met (Hartlage, 1981). First, a majority of the child's educationally related cognitive abilities and methods of higher order information processing skills must be assessed in a quantifiable, replicable, and valid manner. Second, the assessment should be translated into a relevant and valid educational plan. Third, the assessment procedures should be reasonably efficient in terms of time and effort needed to administer and interpret them. In essence, the neuropsychological assessment process should be designed to test the specific referral problem and to provide the information needed to devise an appropriate program for the child in question (Fletcher-Janzen, 2005; Hartlage, 1981).

Comprehensive neuropsychological batteries developed for use with children such as the Reitan-Indiana Neuropsychological Battery and the Luria-Nebraska Neuropsychological Battery-Children's Revision add significantly to the evaluation and remedial planning process (Berg et al., 1984; Lezak, 1976). The major drawback to the use of these and similar batteries is the great deal of time and training required for administration and interpretation (Hartlage, 1981; Reynolds, 1981).

Hartlage (1981) suggests an alternative approach in the application of neuropsychological principles to the interpretation of developmental, behavioral, and test data that can provide a systematic framework for understanding

patterns of learning strengths and weaknesses and for making direct translations of the findings into intervention strategies that are uniquely relevant to the child's cerebral organization. By knowing the neuropsychological implications of common psychoeducational tests, such as the Wechsler Intelligence Scale for Children-IV (WISC-IV), and Bender-Gestalt, the neuropsychologist can determine which additional tests, if any, are needed to complete an adequate neuropsychological diagnostic profile (Hartlage, 1981). Detection with an accurate description of dysfunction leads to a remediation program to enhance the child's acquisition of skills using the child's intact areas and capitalizing on the child's neuropsychological strengths.

There are basically two approaches to the development of educational intervention based on psychoeducational test data: the strength model and the deficit model (Clark & Reynolds, 1984; Hartlage & Telzrow, 1984; Reynolds, 1981). The deficit model is the one most familiar to educators. This model is based on the premise that greater use of an impaired function will increase competency in that area (Hartlage & Telzrow, 1984) or restore dysfunctional neurological systems to their normal capacity (Clark & Reynolds, 1984). When neurological or genetic bases exist for the child's problem, the deficit approach to remediation is doomed to failure because it attempts to identify damaged or dysfunctional areas of the brain and focuses training specifically on those areas.

An academic intervention plan that focuses on deficits is not only ineffective, it is also more frustrating for the child, teacher, and parents (Hartlage & Telzrow, 1984). According to Reynolds (1981), this approach could be harmful to the child in that there is a high likelihood for failure and subsequent loss of self-esteem. To date there is limited empirical evidence to suggest any significant gains in academic or general behavioral functioning as a result of these efforts (Clark & Reynolds, 1984).

Remediation based on strengths has received little emphasis in educational settings primarily because eligibility for special education services is tied directly to the identification of deficits and treatments to restore those deficits (Hartlage & Telzrow, 1984). Reynolds (1981) has proposed the adoption of a habilitative or a strength model for the remediation of learning or behavioral problems. This approach involves designing instructional strategies that are based on or capitalize on the cognitive and neuropsychological strengths that are sufficiently intact so as to enable the child to successfully complete steps in an educational program (Clark & Reynolds, 1984; Reynolds, 1981). The strength model has been found to be effective in rehabilitation programs for adults, and preliminary research (Reynolds, 1981) shows great promise in its application with children.

To develop an individualized remediation strategy, careful attention must be given to the level of functioning and the role that various brain systems play in such functions. Luria's model of hierarchical systems is a convenient conceptual framework. The foundation for learning is based, at the lowest level, on attention. While the whole brain is involved in attention, in most cases the brain stem is of primary importance and brain-stem lesions can disrupt attention significantly. The child must be able to select salient cues and attend to them in order to learn effectively. When attention deficits are present, other intervention strategies may be ineffective. Attention deficits can be managed to some extent by (1) restricting distractors in the environment, (2) presenting more potent stimuli, and (3) dividing study into shorter periods of time. If these strategies are unsuccessful, consideration should be given to referral to pediatric neurology for psychopharmacological treatment.

Like attention, memory is related to total brain function and memory stores are located throughout the central cerebrum. However, the diencephalon and limbic system are particularly important for memory consolidation (storage of information). Deficits in memory obviously impair learning and severely limit acquisition of information. Intervention can be enhanced by (1) aiding the child in strategies for processing information by presenting it in discrete units, (2) increasing incentives, as most are strongly linked to memory consolidation, (3) sustaining practice, and (4) using multimodal sensory input. In memory rehabilitation in children, it is important to understand areas of weakness and assist in resorting to alternative methods of input and storage.

Remediation strategies must take into account strengths and deficits in higher level or cortical processing. With a comprehensive assessment, including neuropsychological assessment, not only modality but material specific weaknesses can be identified and remediation can be established to bypass such weaknesses.

Intervention and remediation in brain-impaired children involve standard procedures with adjustment in manner or mode of presentation. These children need sustained study on material where they receive effective feedback, and where material is interesting and presented on their level. Computer systems are an ideal tool for special education with such children, as they can provide individualized courses of study. Such systems should be viewed as an adjunct rather than a replacement for the educator.

REFERENCES

Berg, R. A., Bolter, J. F., Chien, L. T., Williams, S. J., Lancster, W., & Cummins, J. (1984). Comparative diagnostic accuracy of the Halstead-Reitan and Luria-Nebraska neuropsychology adult and children's batteries. *International Journal of Clinical Neuropsychology, 6,* 200–204.

Chelune, G. J., & Edwards, P. (1981). Early brain lesions: Ontogenetic-environmental consideration. *Journal of Consulting & Clinical Psychology, 49,* 777–790.

Chronin, A. F. (2001). Traumatic brain injury in children: Issues in community function. *American Journal of Occupational Therapy, 55,* 377–384.

Clark, J. H., & Reynolds, C. R. (1984, August). *Habilitation or rehabilitation: Strength versus deficit.* Paper presented at the meeting of the American Psychological Association, Toronto, Canada.

Cruickshank, W. M. (Ed.). (1980). *Psychology of exceptional children and youth.* Englewood Cliffs, NJ: Prentice Hall.

Cruickshank, W. E., Bentzen, F. A., Ratzeburg, E. H., & Tannhauser, M. T. (1961). *A teaching method for brain-injured and hyperactive children: A demonstration-pilot study.* Syracuse, NY: Syracuse University Press.

D'Amato, R., Fletcher-Janzen, E., & Reynolds, C. R. (2005). *School neuropsychology.* Hoboken, NJ: Wiley.

Fletcher-Janzen, E. (2005). School neuropsychological assessment. In R. D'Amato, E. Fletcher-Janzen, & C. R. Reynolds (Eds.), *School neuropsychology.* Hoboken, NJ: Wiley.

Gaddes, W. H. (1980). *Learning disabilities and brain function: A neuropsychological approach.* New York, NY: Springer-Verlag.

Golden, C. J., & Anderson, S. (1979). *Learning disabilities and brain dysfunction: An introduction for educators and parents.* Springfield, IL: Thomas.

Gordon, R., White, D., & Diller, L. (1972). Performance of neurologically impaired preschool children with educational material. *Exceptional Child, 38,* 428–437.

Hartlage, L. C. (1981). Neuropsychological assessment techniques. In C. R. Reynolds & T. Gutkin (Eds.), *Handbook of school psychology* (pp. 296–320). New York, NY: Wiley.

Hartlage, L. C., & Telzrow, C. F. (1984). Neuropsychological basis of educational assessment and programming. In P. E. Logue & J. M. Schear (Eds.), *Clinical neuropsychology: A multidisciplinary approach* (pp. 297–313). Springfield, IL: Thomas.

Haskell, S. H., Barrett, E. K., & Taylor, H. (1977). *The education of motor and neurologically handicapped children.* New York, NY: Wiley.

Hynd, G. W., & Obrzut, J. E. (1981). *Neuropsychological assessment and the school-age child.* New York, NY: Grune & Stratton.

Kolb, B., & Fantie, B. (1997). Development of the child's brain and behavior. In C. R. Reynolds & E. Fletcher-Janzen (Eds.), *Handbook of clinical child neuropsychology.* New York, NY: Plenum Press.

Lezak, M. D. (1976). *Neuropsychological assessment.* New York, NY: Oxford University Press.

Long, C. J. (1985). Neuropsychology in private practice: Its changing focus. *Psychotherapy in Private Practice, 3,* 45–55.

Luria, A. R. (1973). *The working brain: An introduction to neuropsychology.* New York, NY: Basic Books.

Reynolds, C. R. (1981). Neuropsychological assessment and the habilitation of learning: Considerations in the search for the aptitude × treatment interaction. *School Psychology Review, 10,* 343–349.

Rourke, B. P. (1983). Reading and spelling disabilities: A developmental neuropsychological perspective. In U. Kirk

(Ed.), *Neuropsychology of language, reading and spelling* (pp. 209–234). New York, NY: Academic Press.

Rourke, B. P., Bakker, D. J., Fisk, J. L., & Strang, J. D. (1983). *Child neuropsychology: An introduction to theory, research, and clinical practice.* New York, NY: Guilford Press.

Rutter, M. (1981). Psychological sequelae of brain damage in children. *American Journal of Psychiatry, 138,* 1533–1544.

Rutter, M. (1983). *Developmental neuropsychiatry.* New York, NY: Guilford Press.

Teuber, H. L., & Rudel, R. (1962). Behavior after cerebral lesions in children and adults. *Developmental Medicine & Child Neurology, 4,* 3–20.

CHARLES J. LONG
University of Memphis

TINA L. BROWN
Memphis State University

See also Neuropsychology; Traumatic Brain Injury

BRAIN DISORDERS (DEGENERATIVE MOTOR DYSFUNCTION)

Degenerative disorders of the central nervous system are a group of diseases of unspecified etiology leading to progressive deterioration and, eventually, death. Many of these disorders demonstrate a familial pattern and for some there is evidence of heritability (Gelbard, Boustany, & Shor, 1997; Slager, 1970). Recent studies that began with attempts to understand cell loss during normal development have now began to contribute to the understanding of the process of pathological cell loss (Gelbard et al., 1997). Specific degenerative disorders are characterized by their unique clinical and pathological features associated with age of onset and type and progression of symptoms (Alpers & Mancoll, 1971; Fletcher-Janzen & Reynolds, 2003; Slager, 1970).

Major degenerative brain disorders such as Alzheimer's disease, Pick's disease, and Creutzfeldt-Jakob disease have their onset during the middle to late adult years. The same is typically true of the major motor neuron disease, amyotrophic lateral sclerosis, and Huntington's chorea, a major, degenerative disease of the basal ganglia. The remainder of this section describes briefly several degenerative disorders that affect children and have relevance for special education.

Several genetically determined disorders are associated with progressive cerebral degeneration in children. Major types are the lipid storage disease, the leukodystrophies, and progressive degeneration of the gray matter (Fletcher-Janzen & Reynolds, 2003; Sandifer, 1967).

Tay-Sachs disease, a major example of cerebral lipidosis that is confined to children of Jewish descent, is an infantile variety of cerebromacular degeneration (Walton, 1971). Symptoms, which emerge during early infancy and result in death during the second or third year of life, include spastic paralysis, epilepsy, dementia, and optic atrophy leading to blindness (Sandifer, 1967). Alper's disease is an example of a disorder characterized by gray matter degeneration. Onset of symptoms occurs during infancy or early childhood. Symptoms include mental deficiency, cerebral palsy, ataxia, blindness, and epilepsy (Hargrave, 2003; Slager, 1970). Death typically occurs within a few months to several years (Sandifer, 1967). Hallervorden-Spatz disease encompasses a group of degenerative disorders that affect boys more than girls (Halliday, 1995; Plotts, 2003; Sandifer, 1967). Symptoms occur between the ages of 8 and 10 and include spastic paralysis, choreo-athetosis, and slowly developing dementia (Sandifer, 1967). The development of magnetic resonance imaging has increased the number of reports of this disease and the case-to-case variability is considerable. Demyelinating leukodystrophies are disorders associated with progressive paralysis and increased mental impairment (Conway, 1977). One example in metachromatic leukodystrophy, inherited as an autosomal recessive trait. Apparently normal development up until about two years is followed by onset of symptoms that include ataxia, impairment in swallowing and speaking, tonic seizures, and mental regression (Conway, 1977). Other examples of the demyelinating leukodystrophies include Krabbe's disease, Grienfield's disease, and Alexander's disease (Conway, 1977; Rollins, 2003).

Spinocerebellar ataxias are a group of degenerative disorders involving the cerebellum and associated pathways. Friedreich's ataxia is an autosomal recessive disorder with symptoms developing between ages 7 and 15 (Conway, 1977). Early symptoms include ataxia, gait disturbances, and poor coordination, including frequent falling (Rosenberg, 1979). Other cerebellar signs, including nystagmus, dysarthria, and sensory impairments distally may be evident. Other forms of progressive ataxia affecting children include Ramsay Hunt syndrome, hereditary cerebellar ataxia, and Louis-Bar syndrome (Conway, 1977).

Demyelinating encephalopathies are a group of progressive degenerative disorders resulting in death. One example is Leigh's disease (subacute necrotizing encephalopathy), an autosomal recessive condition with onset occurring during infancy. Characteristics of this disorder include hypotonia, ataxia, and spasticity. Respiratory or feeding problems may be associated with this condition, resulting in failure to thrive (Conway, 1977; Schnoebelen & Semrud-Clikeman, 2003; Slager, 1970). Schilder's disease is another example of the demeylinating encephalopathies. The progressive deterioration associated with this condition may result in significant behavioral disturbance in children during the middle years of childhood (Conway, 1977; Lahroud, 2003). More advanced symptoms of Schilder's disease include ataxia, cortical blindness, seizures, and deafness.

Some authors include among the degenerative diseases of the nervous systems neurocutaneous syndromes such as neurofibromatosis and tuberous sclerosis (Rosenberg, 1979; Walton, 1971). Such disorders may be expressed with wide degrees of severity, hence individual monitoring is essential. In summary, degenerative disorders of the nervous system are progressive, frequently hereditary conditions that produce significant mental, motor, and behavioral impairments that frequently result in death. Because of the genetic component associated with the transmission of many of these conditions, genetic counseling may be advisable for parents who have one affected child. Special education and related services may be required for children with degenerative disorders who survive to school age. The assistance of a variety of social service agencies may be of value to the families of afflicted children for counseling and group and individual support.

Characteristics

1. There is progressive deterioration in motor function with associated cognitive and emotional problems caused by abnormalities of the central nervous system.
2. Etiology varies, but genetic transmission is common.
3. The basal ganglia and cerebellum are often impacted by these diseases and explain the symptom manifestation (e.g., ataxia if cerebellar and chorea if basal ganglia).
4. Drug therapy provides symptom relief (i.e., motor and psychiatric).
5. Severity and life-span expectancy are associated with underlying cause and age at the time of onset (i.e., earlier onset equals worse prognosis).
6. As yet there is no cure for these diseases, and death is often inevitable.

REFERENCES

Alpers, B. J., & Mancoll, E. L. (1971). *Clinical neurology* (6th ed.). Philadelphia, PA: Davis.

Conway, B. L. (1977). *Pediatric neurologic nursing.* (2003). St. Louis, MO: Mosby.

Fletcher-Janzen, E., & Reynolds, C. R. (Eds.). (2003). *Childhood diagnostic desk reference.* Hoboken, NJ: Wiley.

Gelbard, H. A., Boustany, R. M., & Shor, N. F. (1997). Apoptosis in childhood neurologic disease. *Pediatric Neurology, 16,* 93–97.

Halliday, W. (1995). The nosology of Hallervorden-Spatz disease. *Journal of the Neurological Sciences, 134,* 84–91.

Hargrave, J. (2003). Alper's disease. In E. Fletcher-Janzen & C. R. Reynolds (Eds.), *Childhood disorders diagnostic desk reference* (p. 29). Hoboken, NJ: Wiley.

Lahroud, I. T. (2003). Schilder disease. In E. Fletcher-Janzen & C. R. Reynolds (Eds.), *Childhood disorders diagnostic desk reference* (p. 556). Hoboken, NJ: Wiley.

Plotts, C. (2003). Hallervodern-Spatz. In E. Fletcher-Janzen & C. R. Reynolds (Eds.), *Childhood disorders diagnostic desk reference* (p. 277). Hoboken, NJ: Wiley.

Rollins, D. A. (2003). Krabbe's disease. In E. Fletcher-Janzen & C. R. Reynolds (Eds.), *Childhood disorders diagnostic desk reference* (p. 353). Hoboken, NJ: Wiley.

Rosenberg, R. N. (1979). Inherited degenerative diseases of the nervous system. In P. B. Beeson, W. McDermott, & J. B. Wyngaarden (Eds.), *Cecil textbook of medicine* (15th ed., pp. 764–772). Philadelphia, PA: Saunders.

Sandifer, P. H. (1967). *Neurology in orthopaedics.* London, England: Butterworths.

Schnoebelen, S., & Semrud-Clikeman, M. (2003). Leigh's disease. In E. Fletcher-Janzen & C. R. Reynolds (Eds.), *Childhood disorders diagnostic desk reference* (p. 365). Hoboken, NJ: Wiley.

Slager, U. T. (1970). *Basic neuropathology.* Baltimore, MD: Williams & Wilkins.

Walton, J. N. (1971). *Essentials of neurology* (3rd ed.). Philadelphia, PA: Lippincott.

CATHY F. TELZROW
Kent State University

See also Congenital Disorders; Gait Disturbances; Neuropsychology; Physical Anomalies

BRAIN FAG

Brain fag, or brain fog, is a culture-bound psychiatric syndrome found in West Africa (American Psychiatric Association, 1994). This syndrome is a condition experienced by high school or university students in response to challenges of schooling (McCajor Hall, n/d). Brain fag is also termed brain fatigue in certain regions of Africa and is perceived as an idiom of distress in many cultures (McCajor Hall, n/d).

Behavioral manifestations of this disorder are closely related to, and in certain cases resemble, anxiety, depressive, and somatoform disorders. In fact, some authors and clinicians classify brain fag as "somatized anxiety with hysterical features" (Cherian, Cherian, & Peltzer, 1998, p. 1187).

This disorder primarily impacts students, and there appears to be a correlation between the frequency of brain fag and the degree of westernization within the culture area of the afflicted. According to Cherian et al. (1998), this correlation may support the hypothesis that children tend to develop distress disorders, such as brain fag, due to shifting from a collective and cooperative culture environment present in many African culture groups to the highly individualistic and competitive requirements of Western education systems.

There have been no reported epidemiological studies conducted on brain fag. However, Cherian et al. (1998, p. 1187), reports that "Brain Fag is a stereotyped psychiatric syndrome that affects 20% to 40% of secondary school and university students in diverse cultures across Africa south of the Sahara." The range tends to fall within 17 to 24 years. There appear to be four major clusters of symptoms of brain fag: unpleasant head symptoms, visual difficulties, fatigue, and sleepiness. This syndrome seems to have a direct relation to stress levels such that the student's life stress could give "rise to features of distress which are expressed as physiological disturbance and subsequent symptom of Brain Fag" (Cherian et al., 1998, p. 1192).

Characteristics

1. Difficulties in concentrating.
2. Difficulties in remembering.
3. Head and neck pain.
4. Pressure of tightness.
5. Blurring of vision.
6. Heat or burning sensations.
7. Complaints of "tired brain."

Incidents of brain fag could possibly be identified in the United States among immigrant African populations. For proper diagnosis of incidents of brain fag, medical and psychiatric professionals utilize the Cultural Orientation Scale (Bierbrauer, Meyer, & Wolfrandt, 1994), the General Self-Efficiency Scale (Schwarzer, 1993), and a Self-Reporting Questionnaire (World Health Organization, 1994) to determine socioeconomic status, cultural orientation, stress events, self-efficiency, perceived stress, and "neurotic" disorders (Cherian et al., 1998). Mental health professionals rather than cultural or traditional health care providers typically administer treatment for this disorder. Typically, treatment coincides with that of anxiety disorders.

It is unlikely that special education services would be needed or available for this syndrome. There is little information available on the treatment outcomes with brain fag; therefore, prevention efforts have not been noted.

REFERENCES

American Psychiatric Association. (1994). *Diagnostic and statistical manual of mental disorders* (4th ed.). Washington, DC: Author.

Bierbrauer, G., Meyer, H., & Wolfrandt, U. (1994). Measurement of normative and evaluative aspects in individualistic and collective orientations: The Cultural Orientation Scale (COS). In Kim, H. C. Triandis, C. Kagitcibasi, S. C. Choi, & G. Yoon (Eds.). *Individualism and collectivism: Theory, method, and applications* (pp. 189–199). London, UK: Sage.

Cherian, L., Cherian, V. I., & Peltzer, K. (1998). Brain fag symptoms in rural South African secondary school pupils. *Psychological Reports, 83*, 1187–1196.

McCajor Hall, T. (n/d). Glossary of culture-bound syndromes. http://mccajor.net/cbs_glos.html

Schwarzer, R. (1993). *Measurement of perceived self-efficacy: Psychometric scales for cross-cultural research.* Berlin, Germany: Freie Universitaet Berlin.

World Health Organization. (1994). *A user's guide to the Self-Reporting Questionnaire* (SRQ). Geneva, Switzerland: Author.

KIELY ANN FLETCHER
Ohio State University

BRAIN GROWTH PERIODIZATION

Brain growth periodization refers to the rapid unequal development of the central nervous system (CNS) in general and the brain in particular. Following the moment of conception, neuronal cells begin an accelerated developmental course of division and reorganization (Gardner, 1968). This process involves the sequence of neuronal cell proliferation, migration, differentiation, axonal growth, formation of synapses, process of elimination, and, finally, myelination. Complexity of this emerging system is immense, and it grows within the context of plasticity and modifiability that exists throughout prenatal, perinatal, and early postnatal development (Moore, 1985).

The formation of the neural plate, which is marked by rapid neuronal cell proliferation, is evident within 16 days following conception. This plate then folds over into a tube shape. After a month, it closes toward the front and rear. The majority of cells attach themselves to the front of the tube and eventually form the brain.

Cell differentiation occurs at variable rates, as dictated by the location of cells within the CNS, where the cortical areas change rapidly and other areas mature more slowly. Next, the axonal growth and dendritic formations of the cells expand to make synaptic connections to one another. This highly ordered circuitry, which links up the brain electrochemically, is controlled by genetic programming and is largely influenced by the environment. One function of the synapses is related to specificity of action, which changes relative to location in the CNS (Sidman & Rakic, 1982). The primary sensory and motor structures are examples of highly specific functioning areas.

Genetic programming initiates the processes of brain growth, but environmental influences modify its form and function. Myelination can be thought of as insulating the neuronal cells to increase the conductivity of sending or receiving electrochemical messages. Early influences of nutrition and mother's health and lifestyle impinge on prenatal development; social, cultural, and economic factors further refine brain growth through postnatal life (Avery, 1985; Freeman, 1985; Shore, 2002).

Epstein (1978) has postulated that periodic growth spurts of the brain occur at predictable ages, and that rapid growth periods are associated with increases in mental age. Further, complementary curricula employed during rapid growth periods would maximize the individual's biological capacities to facilitate learning. Although the theory appears logical, research has not yet decided its empirical efficacy. Indeed, studies challenging pace of growth (McCall, 1988), continuity as opposed to "spurts of growth" (Thornburg, Adey, & Finnis, 1986) and practicality of the concept to everyday academics (McCall, 1990) have been presented.

The observation of a growing and changing system that is adapting to environmental influences before and after birth complicates the prediction of any pathological outcome (i.e., early insult resulting in later specific learning disorders). Indeed, psychopathology and stressful environments can lead to enduring changes in brain structure and functioning (Carrey, 2001). Special educators should be aware of the periodic growth of the brain in the framework of a dynamic interaction between genetics and environment. Recognition of this complex process promotes understanding of students' individual differences and necessitates the development of unique perspectives for intervention.

REFERENCES

Avery, G. (1985). Effects of social, cultural and economic factors on brain development. In J. M. Freeman (Ed.), *Prenatal and perinatal factors associated with brain damage* (Publication No. 85-1149, pp. 163–176). Washington, DC: National Institutes of Health.

Carrey, N. (2001). Developmental neurobiology: Implications for pediatric psychopharmacology. *Canadian Journal of Psychiatry, 46*, 810–818.

Epstein, H. T. (1978). Growth spurts during brain development: Implications for educational policy and practice. In J. S. Chall & A. F. Mirsky (Eds.), *Education & the brain* (pp. 343–370). Chicago, IL: University of Chicago Press.

Freeman, J. M. (1985). *Prenatal and perinatal factors associated with brain damage* (Publication No. 85-1149). Washington, DC: National Institutes of Health.

Gardner, E. (1968). *Fundamentals of neurology*. Philadelphia, PA: Saunders.

McCall, B. (1988). Growth periodization in mental test performance. *Journal of Educational Psychology, 80*, 217–233.

McCall, B. (1990). The neuroscience of education: More research is needed before application. *Journal of Educational Psychology, 82*, 885–888.

Moore, R. Y. (1985). Normal development of the nervous system. In J. M. Freeman (Ed.), *Prenatal and perinatal factors associated with brain damage* (Publication No. 85-1149, pp. 33–51). Washington, DC: National Institutes of Health.

Shore, A. N. (2002). The neurobiology of attachment and early personality organization. *Journal of Prenatal and Perinatal Psychology and Health, 16*, 249–263.

Sidman, R. L., & Rakic, P. (1982). Development of the human central nervous system. In W. Haymaker & R. D. Adams (Eds.), *Histology and histopathology of the nervous system* (pp. 3–145). Springfield, MA: Thomas.

Thornburg, H. D., Adey, K. L., & Finnis, E. (1986). A comparison of gifted and nongifted early adolescents' movement toward abstract thinking. *Journal of Early Adolescence, 6*, 231–245.

Scott W. Sautter
Peabody College, Vanderbilt University

See also Brain Damage/Injury; Brain Disorders (Degenerative Motor Dysfunction); Neurological Organization

BRAIN INJURY ASSOCIATION OF AMERICA

The Brain Injury Association of America (BIAA), formerly the National Head Injury Foundation is the country's oldest and largest nationwide brain injury advocacy organization. It was founded in 1980 by concerned parents and professionals as the first national organization to advocate for persons who had sustained brain injuries and their families. The mission of BIAA is "to be the voice of brain injury. Through advocacy, education and research, they bring help, hope and healing to millions of individuals living with brain injury, their families and the professionals who serve them." The BIAA is dedicated to increasing access to quality health care and raising awareness and understanding of brain injury to help reduce incidence and improve outcomes for children and adults with brain injury. The BIAA is the only national nonprofit organization working on behalf of those with brain injury, maintaining a nationwide network of more than 40 chartered state affiliates and hundreds of local chapters and support groups.

The BIAA is an advocate for the 7 million individuals with brain injury, their family members, and the professionals who serve them. Each year an estimated 1.7 million children and adults in the United States sustain a traumatic brain injury (TBI) and another 795,000 individuals sustain an acquired brain injury (ABI) from non-traumatic causes. According to the Centers for Disease Control and Injury Prevention, the leading causes of TBI are: falls (35.2%), motor vehicle-traffic crashes (17.3%), struck by/against events (16.5%), and assaults (10%). The BIAA offers hope, healing, and care to those beginning the process of recovery. It works to ensure that those suffering from brain injuries, as well as their families, have access to the care that they need and deserve. The Council of Brain Injury Alumni is a support service that was organized with an initial focus on creating a platform for persons with brain injury to share their stories of hope and healing.

Increasing awareness, education, and prevention of brain injury is accomplished through the organization's work in conjugation with a diverse group of individuals, including persons with brain injury and their families, rehabilitation providers, physicians, attorneys, educators, therapists, case managers, counselors, government organizations, corporate partners, and citizens. Prevention and education is attained through publications, while advocacy results from work with government entities at all levels. One of the core services the Brain Injury Association of America provides is the National Brain Injury Information Center (NBIIC). It provides information, support and assistance and links each caller to the rehabilitation, legal, financial and other support services that are critical to maximizing recovery. The NBIIC can be reached at (800) 444-6443.

The BIAA also publishes the *Challenge!*, a quarterly magazine featuring news from Capitol Hill and across the country. Each issue focuses on a special topic of interest. The *Challenge!* is circulated free to members of BIAA's chartered state affiliates and to individuals who donate $25 or more to BIAA. Individuals and organizations may reproduce single copies of any article in its entirety to circulate for educational purposes. Articles may be reprinted in other publications with written permission from the BIAA. The Brain Injury Association of America main office is located at 1608 Spring Hill Road, Suite 110, Vienna, VA 22182. Tel.: (703) 761-0750; Fax: (703) 761-0755. The BIAA website is located at http://www.biausa.org/. Information for this entry was obtained from the BIAA website.

REFERENCE

Brain Injury Association of America. (2011). Retrieved from http://www.biausa.org/

Tamara J. Martin
University of Texas of the Permian Basin
Third edition

Jamie Slowinski
Chicago School of Professional Psychology
Fourth edition

BRAIN ORGANIZATION (*See Neurological Organization*)

BRAIN STEM AUDIOMETRY

Brain stem audiometry is an electrophysiologic measurement of hearing function currently known as auditory brain stem response (ABR) audiometry. As a diagnostic procedure, brain stem audiometry is used for the assessment of a peripheral hearing function (especially for high-risk infants; Durieux-Smith, Picton, Edwards, & MacMurray, 1987; Kaga, Yasui, & Yuge, 2002; individuals who are intellectually disabled, and those individuals who are unable to respond appropriately to traditional tests) and to determine the neurological integrity of the auditory nerve and brain stem (especially for adults suspected of having an auditory nerve or brain stem tumor or other neural pathology). Brain stem audiometry can be done when the patient is lightly sedated, asleep, or awake (Fria, 1980).

Brain stem audiometry is possible because the neural reaction of the brain stem is time-locked to an acoustic stimulus while higher-level ongoing brain stem neural activity is random. Consequently, with the use of an averaging computer, the time-locked brain stem neural response to an acoustic stimulus can be extracted from the random ongoing higher-level brain stem neural activity.

A brain stem audiometer contains an averaging computer that triggers stimulus-generating instrumentation that transduces an acoustic stimulus through an earphone, loudspeaker, or bone vibrator. The patient is fitted with an active surface electrode along the midline of the head (usually at the vertex) and reference surface electrodes (usually on each mastoid or earlobe). The output of the electrodes are amplified, filtered, and directed to the averaging computer, which is programmed to present many repetitions of the same stimulus and average the response of the neural activity for each stimulus for a period of about 10 milliseconds following the onset of the stimulus. The resultant pattern, known as the ABR waveform, is characterized by six to seven identifiable peaks having different latencies and amplitudes. Each peak is thought to originate from a neural generator starting with the auditory nerve through the brain stem. Peak I and especially Peak V are the most robust in reference to stimulus level and procedural variables (Davis, 1976).

If brain stem audiometry is done to determine the existence of a peripheral hearing impairment, an ABR waveform is obtained to high-level auditory stimuli and to the same stimuli at lower levels until an ABR waveform cannot be determined for each ear. Then the latency of Peaks I and V at each stimulus level (intensity) are usually plotted on an intensity-latency graph referenced to age-appropriate norms (Glasscock, Jackson, & Josey,

1981). This procedure allows for determining the degree and type of peripheral hearing loss. When used to determine neurological integrity, an ABR waveform is usually obtained for one or two high-level auditory stimuli for each ear (Jacobson, 1983). The amplitude and latency of the ABR peaks are analyzed individually and compared across ear and to norms to determine whether a pathologic condition exists.

REFERENCES

Davis, H. (1976). Principles of electric response audiometry. *Annals of Otology, Rhinology, & Laryngology, 85*(28), 1–96.

Durieux-Smith, A., Picton, T., Edwards, C. G., & MacMurray, B. (1987). Brainstem electric-response audiometry in infants of a neonatal intensive care unit. *Audiology, 26,* 284–297.

Fria, T. (1980). The auditory brain stem response: Background and clinical applications. *Maico Monographs in Contemporary Audiology, 2,* 1–44.

Glasscock, M. E., Jackson, G. G., & Josey, A. F. (1981). *Brainstem electric response audiometry.* New York, NY: Thieme-Stratton.

Kaga, K., Yasui, T., & Yuge, T. (2002). Auditory behaviors and auditory brainstem responses of infants with hypogenesis of cerebral hemispheres. *Acta Oto-Laryngologica, 12,* 16–20.

Jacobson, J. T. (1983). Auditory evoked potentials. In *Seminars in hearing* (Vol. 4). New York, NY: Thieme-Stratton.

THOMAS A. FRANK
Pennsylvania State University

See also Audiology; Audiometry

BRAIN TUMORS

Brain tumors are the most frequent type of childhood cancer, after leukemia. More than half of the brain tumors in childhood occur in the area of the cerebellum and brain stem; the rest occur higher in the brain, primarily in the cerebrum. Presenting symptoms for children with cerebellar tumors include early morning headaches, nausea and vomiting, vision problems, and loss of balance. Children with tumors located higher in the brain may experience more focal symptoms such as weakness on one side of the body or vision problems. For any child with a brain tumor, these symptoms are often accompanied by changes in mood and academic performance. These findings can easily lead parents or teachers to assume that the child is developing a school phobia or behavioral problems.

Many brain tumors are treated successfully with various combinations of surgery, radiation, and chemotherapy. Depending on the type and location of the tumor, and the treatment, most children are able to resume schooling (at least on a limited basis) within a few months following treatment. Teachers need to be aware of the treatment regimen and possible side effects for a child recovering from a brain tumor. For a period of 2 to 4 months following surgery, mood and behavior changes are frequently observed, presumably a result of cranial irradiation and the psychological impact of having been diagnosed with a severe illness (Katz, 1980; Mulhern, Crisco, & Kun, 1983; Richards & Clark, 2003). Some of these children will receive chemotherapy for 1 to 3 years following surgery. Most children experience at least one of the following side effects: hair loss (usually reversible), nausea, behavioral changes, and painful mouth sores. Cortisone, taken to reduce the traumatic effects of surgery, also may cause changes in mood and physical appearance.

A decline in academic performance following surgery (compared with their previous performance) can be expected for most of these children (Hirsch, Renier, Czernichow, Benveniste, & Pierre-Kahn, 1979; Radcliffe, Bunin, Sutton, & Goldwein, 1994; Walther & Gutjahr, 1982). There is some evidence to suggest that survivors also experience nonverbal learning disabilities (Carey, Barakat, Foley, Gyato, & Phillips, 2001). After returning to school, children may improve gradually in school performance. Other children experience a continued decline in academic performance as a result of the various treatment side effects. A continued decline also could signal a recurrence of the tumor. Regular communication with the child's primary physician is important to obtain information regarding the medical treatment and, in turn, to inform the physician about the child's functioning at school.

As these children resume school, they need regular, detailed assessment of their abilities and deficits. A complete neuropsychological assessment should be obtained every few years. There have not been enough studies to predict what specific deficits will occur; however, available data suggest that most children recovering from brain tumors suffer from at least one of the following: (1) poor coordination, (2) poor memory, (3) difficulty in acquiring and integrating new concepts, (4) a decline in overall IQ (ranging from only a few to 20 or more points), (5) emotional problems, especially somatic worries and low self-esteem (Mulhern et al., 1983). Most of these children will require either special education placement and a learning program that emphasizes gradual acquisition and practice of basic skills or placement in a regular classroom with the ready availability of additional resources. Parents can play a significant role in helping the child to perform at a maximal level.

Students who had previously done well in school often are frustrated by their inability to work as quickly and efficiently as before (Paviour, 1988). Teachers need to offer reassurance and encouragement, as well as extra time to learn and practice new material. Some students with impaired efficiency can continue to learn and use new information, but they may require more time than usually allowed on a timed exam to demonstrate their true levels of ability.

Characteristics

1. Intracranial pressure occurs in most types of brain tumors, with symptoms including papilledema, headache, and vomiting.
2. Depending on tumor location, seizures, hemiparesis, vision changes, endocrine problems, slurred speech, dysphagia, loss of appetite/weight, and ataxia occur.
3. Infants or young children are more likely to present with vague symptoms of irritability, crying, and failure to thrive.
4. Approximately 2,000 new pediatric cases are diagnosed in the United States each year.

Treatment options typically include surgery, radiation, and chemotherapy. Surgery is the treatment of choice; depending on tumor location, however, this may not be an option. Approximately 20% of brain tumors are successfully resected with surgery and do not require further treatment such as radiation and chemotherapy. Cancer cells tend to be responsive to radiation therapy; however, this treatment has been shown to cause serious cognitive deficits in young children. Currently, the standard practice is to use chemotherapy first and delay or avoid radiation therapy until the child gets older and brain development is less likely to be interrupted. If possible, no radiation should be used in children under 5 years of age. Medications used to treat brain tumors (e.g., chemotherapy) can also have negative long-term sequelae including kidney and liver toxicity, cataracts and glaucoma, ulcers, cardiac problems, growth retardation, and reproductive dysfunction. Neuropsychological problems are also common but to a lesser degree than when radiation is used. Common short-term side effects from chemotherapy include nausea, vomiting, diarrhea, abdominal pain, fever, chills, hair loss, jaw pain, and fluid retention. In addition, chemotherapy (and radiation) can increase the risk of developing future cancers.

Potentially life-threatening conditions such as a brain tumor cause significant stress to the family. Not only is the child's life changed, but so is the family's. Lengthy hospitalizations, the experience of pain and illness, and prolonged school absences can seriously impact the child's quality of life. Changes in physical appearance from hair loss, weight loss or gain, and surgical scars are just one of many adjustments that the child may have to make. Having to face peers, catch up on school work, and deal with cognitive changes (e.g., attentional difficulties and

diminished memory) may be more than the affected child can tolerate.

Children who have, or have had, a brain tumor often qualify for special education and related services under the category of Other Health Impairment. Services that are most often needed are intended to address various cognitive changes, attentional and memory difficulties, and language impairments.

Emotional concerns are also likely to arise and require counseling. Regular contact with the parents is critical to ensure that the child's progress is monitored and that adequate support is given. In addition, frequent parent contact can help to assess what their needs are, as well as those of the siblings. There are a number of community support services for children with brain tumors. In addition to brain tumor associations, there are special camp programs (e.g., Candlelighters). Providing opportunities for children and their families to interact with others who are faced with similar challenges is important. This provides not only opportunities for support but also resources for further (and future) assistance. Close monitoring and frequent assessment of the child is needed because many of the common difficulties of attention, cognitive changes, memory, language dificulties, and emotional concerns can vary greatly over time or show up years after treatment.

REFERENCES

Carey, M. E., Barakat, L. P., Foley, B., Gyato, K., & Phillips, P. C. (2001). Neuropsychological functioning and social functioning of survivors of pediatric brain tumors: Evidence of nonverbal learning disability. *Child Neuropsychology, 7,* 265–272.

Hirsch, J. F., Renier, D., Czernichow, R., Benveniste, L., & Pierre-Kahn, A. (1979). Medulloblastoma in childhood. Survival and functional results. *Acta Neurochirurgica, 48,* 1–15.

Katz, E. R. (1980). Illness impact and social reintegration. In J. Kellerman (Ed.), *Psychological aspects of childhood cancer* (pp. 14–46). Springfield, IL: Thomas.

Mulhern, R. K., Crisco, J. J., & Kun, L. E. (1983). Neuropsychological sequelae of childhood brain tumors: A review. *Journal of Clinical Child Psychology, 12*(1), 66–73.

Paviour, R. (1988). Walking in the valley of death: The impact of brain tumors on children. *Child & Adolescent Social Work Journal, 5,* 315–324.

Radcliffe, J., Bunin, G. R., Sutton, L. N., & Goldwein, J. (1994). Cognitive deficits in long term survivors of childhood medulloblastoma and other noncortical tumors age dependent effects of whole brain radiation. *International Journal of Developmental Neuroscience, 12,* 327–334.

Richards, L., & Clark, E. (2003). Brain tumor. In E. Fletcher-Janzen & C. R. Reynolds (Eds.), *Childhood disorders diagnostic desk reference* (pp. 94–95). Hoboken, NJ: Wiley.

Walther, B., & Gutjahr, P. (1982). Development after treatment of cerebellar medulloblastoma in childhood. In D. Voth, P. Gutjahr, & C. Langmaid (Eds.), *Tumours of the central nervous system in infancy and childhood* (pp. 389–398). Berlin, Germany: Springer-Verlag.

SAMUEL LEBARON
PAUL M. ZELTZER
University of Texas Health Science Center

LAURA RICHARDS
ELAINE CLARK
University of Utah

See also **Brain Disorders (Degenerative Motor Dysfunctions); Chemotherapy**

BRAZELTON, T. BERRY (1918–)

A native of Waco, Texas, Thomas B. Brazelton received his BA in 1940 from Princeton University and his MD from Columbia College of Physicians and Surgeons in 1943. He served his internship in 1944 at Roosevelt Hospital in New York City, and completed his residency (1947–1950) in child psychiatry at Putnam Children's Center, Roxbury, Massachusetts. Brazelton was an instructor in pediatrics (1951–1972) and clinical professor of pediatrics (1972–1986) at Harvard University Medical School, and served as director of the Child Development Unit, Children's Hospital Medical Center, Boston, Massachusetts from 1972 to 1992. Brazelton is currently Professor Emeritus at Harvard Medical School and President of Brazelton Touchpoints Center, Children's Hospital, Boston.

Brazelton's research has focused on early attachment of infants to their primary caregivers as well as cross-cultural research on child-rearing practices in Kenya, Guatemala, Mexico, and Greece. His comparison of interactional behaviors of African and American mothers' age-appropriate teaching tasks indicated that while techniques differed, both groups demonstrated positive interactions (Dixon, LeVine, Richman, & Brazelton, 1984). Brazelton views these findings as important in terms of culture-specific values, expectations for children, and goals and assumptions of the teaching process.

Brazelton (1973) developed the Brazelton Behavioral Assessment Scale, a tool for behavioral evaluation of newborn infants that measures interactions between the infant and social or potentially social stimuli, the infant's various reflexes, and physiologic responses to stress. Additional research led to his finding that term infants are more likely than preterm infants to lead interactions with their mothers, thus offering a possible explanation for later reported differences in children's development (Lester, Hoffman, & Brazelton, 1985).

For his work with infants, Brazelton received an award from the Child Study Association of America, and *Parent's Magazine* has awarded him a medal for outstanding service to children. He is the recipient of an Emmy award for Daytime Host (1994) for his cable television program, "What Every Baby Knows." Brazelton has served as president of the National Center for Clinical Infant Programs (1988–1991), president of Zero to Three (1989–1991), and member of the National Commission on Children (1989–1992). He has authored numerous books and articles, including *The Earliest Relationship* (1991), *Touchpoints: Your Child's Emotional and Behavioral Development* (1995), and *Going to the Doctor* (1996).

REFERENCES

Brazelton, T. B. (1973). *Neonatal behavioral assessment scale*. Philadelphia, PA: Lippincott.

Brazelton, T. B. (1995). *Touchpoints: Your child's emotional and behavioral development*. London, UK: Penguin.

Brazelton, T. B. (1996). *Going to the doctor*. Reading, MA: Addison-Wesley.

Brazelton, T. B., & Cramer, B. G. (1991). *The earliest relationship: Parents, infants, and the drama of early attachment*. London, UK: Karnac.

Dixon, S. D., LeVine, R. A., Richman, A., & Brazelton, T. B. (1984). Mother-child interaction around a teaching task: An African-American comparison. *Child Development, 55*(4), 1252–1264.

Lester, B. M., Hoffman, J., & Brazelton, T. B. (1985). The rhythmic structures of mother-infant interaction in term and preterm infants. *Child Development, 56*(1), 15–27.

E. VALERIE HEWITT
Texas A&M University
First edition

TAMARA J. MARTIN
University of Texas of the Permian Basin
Second edition

BRIDGMAN, LAURA DEWEY (1829–1899)

Laura Dewey Bridgman, diagnosed with deaf-blindness at the age of 2, entered the Perkins Institution and Massachusetts School for the Blind at the age of 7. The director of the institution, Samuel Gridley Howe, developed an educational program for Bridgman and she quickly learned to read from raised letters and to communicate with manual signs. She related well to people and developed into a cheerful, intelligent woman who used her talents to teach other students who were deaf-blind at Perkins (Ross, 1951).

Bridgman was the first person with deaf-blindness to become well educated, and her achievement received wide attention. Charles Dickens visited her and published an account of their meeting. That publication led Helen Keller's mother to appeal to Howe to find a teacher for Helen; the teacher he recommended was Anne Sullivan Macy, who, as a student at Perkins had lived in the same house as Bridgman. What Bridgman accomplished was later repeated by Helen Keller and others. But Bridgman was the first to demonstrate that proper education could enable a person with deaf-blindness to lead a happy and productive life.

REFERENCE

Ross, I. (1951). *Journey into light*. New York, NY: Appleton-Century-Crofts.

PAUL IRVINE
Katonah, New York

BRIGANCE DIAGNOSTIC INVENTORIES

The Brigance Inventories are a comprehensive set of individually administered criterion-referenced tests. There are several inventories, each covering a specific age range, that are used for assessment, diagnosis, record keeping, and instructional planning. The following paragraphs briefly describe the intended use of each of the inventories.

The Brigance Diagnostic Inventory of Early Development, II (Brigance, 2010) is designed to assess infants and children under age 7. In addition to being an assessment instrument, an instructional guide, a record-keeping tracking system, and a tool for developing individualized education programs, it can also serve as a resource for training parents and professionals. The Inventory of Early Development-II offers a variety of possible assessment methods: parent interview, teacher observation, group administration, or informal appraisal of the child's performance in the school setting. The goal of the assessment of the child under age 7 is to identify those segments of the curriculum objectives that have been mastered. The following skill areas are assessed: preambulatory motor skills and behaviors, gross-motor skills and behaviors, fine-motor skills and behaviors, self-help skills, speech and language skills, general knowledge and comprehension, social and emotional development, readiness, basic reading skills, manuscript writing, and basic math.

There are two Brigance measures that assess only kindergarteners and first graders. The Brigance K&1 Screen (Brigance, 1992) is designed for students in kindergarten and the 1st grade and assesses basic readiness and academic skills with the following subtests: readiness, reading, language arts, and math. The Brigance K and 1 Screen-Revised (Brigance, 1992) is designed for students in kindergarten and 1st grade and assesses pupils' basic skills in order to identify special service referrals, determine appropriate pupil placement, and assist in planning individual pupil programs. The following basic skills are evaluated with the K and 1 Screen–Revised: personal data response, color recognition, picture vocabulary, visual discrimination, visual motor skills, standing gross motor skills, ability to draw a person (body image), rate counting, identification of body parts, ability to recite alphabet, comprehension of verbal directions, numeral comprehension, recognition of lower and upper case letters, auditory discrimination, print personal data, syntax and fluency, and numerals in sequence. The Brigance Diagnostic Comprehensive Inventory of Basic Skills-II (Brigance, 2010) is designed to assess students in prekindergarten through the 9th grade. The Comprehensive Inventory of Basic Skills contains 203 skill sequences to be assessed in the areas of reading, listening, research and study skills, spelling, language, and mathematics.

Additional Brigance inventories assist special educators in more specific areas such as transition skills, and basic developmental readiness skills. The Brigance Life Skills (LSI) and Employability Skills Inventory (ESI) has been replaced with the Brigance Transition Skills Inventory (TSI) (2010). The new Transition Inventory measures skills in domains such as independent living, postsecondary opportunities, community participation, and academic skills needed to meet transition goals and monitor student progress towards postsecondary goals. The Brigance Readiness: Strategies and Practice (2005) provides activities to assess developmental readiness skills in 24 different areas for children ages 3 to 6.

Reviewers of the Brigance Diagnostic Inventories consistently have noted that the lack of reliability or validity data for these measures is troubling (Berk, 1995; Carpenter, 1995; Watson, 1995). Also questioned by one reviewer was the appropriateness of the instruments for students who do not speak English as a first language (Berk, 1995). The instruments are generally viewed as viable tool because of their flexibility and planning utility (Carpenter, 1995). One reviewer viewed the Brigance Inventories as positive methods for identifying a child's strengths and weaknesses (Penfield, 1995). Because of the lack of validity data, these inventories are perhaps best used as informal screening measures to provide assistance to teachers in planning curriculum objectives. Also because of the lack of data, placement decisions based on the inventories are inappropriate (Watson, 1995).

REFERENCES

Berk, R. (1995). Review of the revised Brigance K & 1 screen for kindergarten and first grade children–Revised. In J. C.

Conoley & J. C. Impara (Eds.), *The twelfth mental measurements yearbook* (pp. 133–134). Lincoln, NE: Buros Institute of Mental Measurements.

Brigance, A. H. (1992). *Brigance K and 1 screen–Revised*. North Billerica, MA: Curriculum Associates.

Brigance, A. H. (2005). *Brigance readiness: Stratagies and practice–Two*. North Billerica, MA: Curriculum Associates.

Brigance, A. H. (2010). *Brigance diagnostic inventory of early development–Two*. North Billerica, MA: Curriculum Associates.

Brigance, A. H. (2010). *Brigance transition skills inventory*. North Billerica, MA: Curriculum Associates.

Carpenter, C. D. (1995). Review of the revised Brigance diagnostic inventory of early development. In J. C. Conoley & J. C. Impara (Eds.), *The twelfth mental measurements yearbook* (pp. 852–853). Lincoln, NE: Buros Institute of Mental Measurements.

Penfield, D. A. (1995). Review of the revised Brigance diagnostic inventory of early development. In J. C. Conoley & J. C. Impara (Eds.), *The twelfth mental measurements yearbook* (pp. 853–854). Lincoln, NE: Buros Institute of Mental Measurements.

Watson, T. S. (1995). Review of the revised Brigance K & 1 screen for kindergarten and first grade children–Revised. In J. C. Conoley & J. C. Impara (Eds.), *The twelfth mental measurements yearbook* (pp. 134–135). Lincoln, NE: Buros Institute of Mental Measurements.

ELIZABETH O. LICHTENBERGER
Salk Institute

See also Criterion-Referenced Testing; Grade Equivalents

BRITTLE BONE DISEASE (OSTEOGENESIS IMPERFECTA)

Osteogenesis imperfecta (OI), commonly known as *brittle bone disease*, is a genetic disorder in which the production of collagen is inadequate or defective collagen is produced, leading to a susceptibility of bone fractures. An individual with OI may suffer as little as a few to several hundreds of bone fractures over a lifetime. The wide variation in the severity of OI has been described and categorized as four types of OI. The most mild and common form of OI is Type I (Moriwake & Seino, 1997).

The prevalence of OI in the United States remains unknown. Reports estimate that 1 in every 20,000 to 50,000 children born each year is affected (Osteogenesis Imperfecta Foundation [OIF], 2001). In general, frequent bone fractures in infancy and childhood, some even recognized before birth, are the cardinal symptoms of this disorder. The rate of fractures decreases during puberty

(Moriwake & Seino, 1997). Children with OI have bone deformities in their extremities and retarded growth, and they may experience chronic bone pain, although there can be wide variation in clinical features of OI across individuals. This holds true for individuals with OI within the same family as well. Thus, a combination of genes and environment influences the expression of the disorder.

Usually, clinical features of the different types of OI are used for diagnosis. In addition, DNA and collagen tests may be performed; however, several weeks are required to obtain the results, and the results are not always conclusive. OI patients have bones with less or poorer quality Type I collagen, the connective fibers of the bones, than of normal quality, either of which lead to bones that break easily (Moriwake & Seino, 1997). Children with OI Types I and IV often live normal life spans, and their deaths are due to unrelated causes. However, children with the most severe type of OI, Type III, are at higher risk for dying as a result of OI. Children with OI may be confined to a wheelchair and sometimes do not survive childhood. The severity of the OI contributes significantly to risk of death. Thus, minor injuries may have fatal consequences for a child with OI Type III (McAllion & Paterson, 1996).

Characteristics

1. Fragile bones leading to frequent fractures.
2. Growth retardation and deformities of the arms and legs.
3. Chronic bone pain.

No cure for OI exists. Increasing bone mass and preventing future fractures are goals of current treatments. Aggressive physical therapy and rehabilitation programs result in increased body control and replacement of the routine use of a wheelchair with physical supports, such as a brace, to enable children to walk more independently (Binder et al., 1993). Stimulating bone growth using growth hormones can be used during childhood. Rodding of the humeral bone (lower extremities) may also be used to prevent future bone deformities and fractures (Moriwake & Seino, 1997).

It is clear that a child with OI has a physical disability, but most children with OI do not have any cognitive disabilities. It is important that educational staff be aware of the child's increased susceptibility to injury. Thus, classroom modifications, physical assistance, adaptive physical education, and other arrangements to prevent injury should be taken into consideration (OIF, 2001). It is thought that each type of OI is due to different gene mutations, making gene therapy a potential avenue for future research (Moriwake & Seino, 1997).

REFERENCES

Binder, H., Conway, A., Hason, S., Gerber, L. H., Marini, J., Berry, R., & Weintrob, J. (1993). Comprehensive rehabilitation of the child with osteogenesis imperfecta. *American Journal of Medical Genetics, 45*, 265–269.

McAllion, S. J., & Paterson, C. R. (1996). Causes of death in osteogenesis imperfecta. *Journal of Clinical Pathology, 49*(8), 627–630.

Moriwake, T., & Seino, Y. (1997). Recent progress in diagnosis and treatment of osteogenesis imperfecta. *Acta Paediatrica Japonica, 39*, 521–527.

Osteogenesis Imperfecta Foundation. (2001). *OIF homepage.* Retrieved from http://www.oif.org

JENNIFER M. GILLIS
University of California Irvine

BROCA, PIERRE PAUL (1824–1880)

Pierre Paul Broca, a French surgeon and physical anthropologist noted for his studies of the brain and skull, was a member of the Academy of Medicine in Paris and professor of surgical pathology and clinical surgery (Talbott, 1970). Through postmortem examinations he learned that damage to the third convolution of the left frontal lobe of the brain (Broca's convolution) was associated with loss of the ability to speak; this was the first demonstration of a connection between a specific bodily activity and a specific area of the brain. His announcement of this finding in 1861 led to a vast amount of research on cerebral localization.

Broca was a key figure in the development of physical anthropology in France. He founded a laboratory, a school, a journal, and a society for the study of anthropology. He originated techniques and invented instruments for studying the skull, and helped to establish that the Neanderthal man discovered in his time was a primitive ancestor of modern man.

REFERENCE

Talbott, J. H. (1970). *A biographical history of medicine: Excerpts and essays on the men and their work.* New York, NY: Grune & Stratton.

PAUL IRVINE
Katonah, New York

BROCA'S APHASIA

Broca's aphasia is one of several subdivisions of nonfluent aphasia. Originally the symptoms associated with this acquired language disorder were believed to occur as a result of damage to Broca's Area, the posterior-inferior (third) frontal gyrus of the left hemisphere, also known as Broadman's area 44 (Hegde, 1994). Kearns (1997) reports that as modern neuroradiographic techniques obtain sophisticated data related to symptoms characteristic of damage to this area, it is often evident that many different parts of the brain may be damaged while still resulting in the type of symptoms classified as Broca's. Obviously, as our knowledge base expands, the model of brain function from a purely localized perspective is yielding to an overall view of brain function as a total system with localized areas and a myriad of vital pathways.

The major language characteristics most often associated with this diagnosis are: nonfluent and effortful speech, many inappropriate pauses, short mean length of utterance, telegraphic speech limited to nouns and verbs, omission of grammatical function words (articles, pronouns, auxiliary verbs, and some prepositions), impaired repetition of words and sentences, and impaired confrontation naming. Although these persons may have some problems in the area of auditory comprehension, silent reading comprehension, and writing, these persons most often have better skills in these areas than in their expressive communication (Hegde, 1994; Kearns, 1997). Other types of nonfluent aphasia include the following.

Transcortical Motor Aphasia

Originally the symptoms associated with this acquired language disorder were believed to occur as a result of damage to the watershed regions between the middle cerebral and anterior arteries and in the premotor area in front of the motor cortex. However, as Kearns reports (1997), as modern neuroradiographic techniques obtain sophisticated data related to symptoms characteristic of damage to this area, it is often evident that many different parts of the brain may be damaged while still resulting in the type of symptoms classified as transcortical motor aphasia.

The major language characteristics most often associated with this diagnosis are nonfluency, paraphasia, agrammaticisms, telegraphic (similar to those described in Broca's aphasia) and intact repetition (differing from Broca's aphasia), and echolalia. Comprehension may be impaired for complex speech but is generally good for simple conversation (Chapey, 1994; Hegde, 1994), with the individual focusing more on prearticulatory monitoring than post articulatory monitoring of speech (Oomen, Postma, & Kolk, 2001).

Global Aphasia

Originally, the symptoms associated with this acquired language disorder were believed to occur as a result of damage to the entire perisylvian region. All the so-called language centers are believed to be affected with destruction of the left fronto-temporoparietal regions. This disorder reflects a depth of neural destruction to the point that damage to cortical white matter was assumed even prior to the new view of systemic brain function (pathways versus localization; Hegde, 1994).

Persons with this diagnosis have profoundly impaired language skills in all ways, and fluency is greatly reduced (naming, repetition, auditory comprehension, reading, and writing are impaired). Language is limited to a few words, exclamations or automatic speech (Chapey, 1994; Hegde, 1994).

Isolation Aphasia

This is a rare type of nonfluent aphasia with severe impairment to all language functions except preservation of the skill to repeat words. It is this characteristic that discriminates between global aphasia and isolation aphasia. This subdivision is not acknowledged by all aphasiologists (Hegde, 1994).

REFERENCES

Chapey, R. (1994). *Language intervention strategies in adult aphasia* (3rd ed.). Baltimore, MD: Williams & Wilkins.

Hegde, M. (1994). *A coursebook on aphasia and other neurogenic language disorders*. San Diego, CA: Singular.

Kearns, K. P. (1997). Broca's aphasia. In L. L. LaPointe (Ed.), *Aphasia and related neurogenic language disorders* (pp. 1–41). New York, NY: Thieme.

Oomen, C. E., Postma, A., & Kolk, H. H. J. (2001). Prearticulatory and post-articulatory self-monitoring in Broca's aphasia. *Cortex, 37*, 627–641.

SHEELA STUART
George Washington University

BRONFENBRENNER, URI (1917–2005)

Uri Bronfenbrenner was born in Moscow, Russia, in 1917, and came to the United States at an early age. He received his BA degree from Cornell University in 1938, his EdM from Harvard in 1940, and his PhD in developmental psychology from the University of Michigan in 1942. After World War II, Bronfenbrenner returned to the University of Michigan as assistant professor. In 1948, he joined the faculty of Cornell as professor of psychology, child development, and family relationships, and ended his career at Jacob Gould Schurman, professor emeritus of Human Development and Family Studies and professor emeritus of Psychology.

Bronfenbrenner wrote extensively in the field of developmental psychology. He was perhaps best known for his ecological approach to developmental psychology (Bronfenbrenner, 1972; Bronfrenbrenner, McClelland, Wethington, Moen, & Ceci, 1996). The ecological environment, according to Bronfenbrenner, is like a set of nested Russian dolls in which one doll contains another that contains another and so forth. He recognized three levels of ecological environment in psychological development. "At the innermost level is the immediate setting containing the developing person. This can be the home, the classroom, or...the laboratory" (Bronfenbrenner, 1979).

Involving influences beyond the immediate setting and the relationships among them, the school and peer group exemplify the next level. Bronfenbrenner (1979) contends that a "child's ability to learn to read...may depend no less on how he is taught than on the existence and nature of ties between the school and the home." The third level consists of influences from events that occur in settings in which the child is not directly involved. According to Bronfenbrenner, our industrialized society, in which both parents are employed, has a direct influence on how children develop.

Bronfenbrenner was also well-known for his comparison of education in the United States and the former Soviet Union. He authored 15 books and countless articles. He also published several books including: *The State of Americans: This Generation and the Next, The Ecology of Human Development: Experiments by Nature* and *Design, and Two Worlds of Childhood: U.S. and USSR* (Bronfrenbrenner et al, 1996).

Bronfenbrenner's contributed to the field of psychology and human development by publishing on topics from developmental behavioral genetics to practical aspects of memory. He received numerous awards including six honorary doctorates from various colleges and universities, the Lifetime Contribution to Developmental Psychology in the Service of Science and Society Award of the American Psychological Association, Division 7; the James McKeen Cattell Award for Distinguished Scientific Contribution of the American Psychological Society; the Award for Distinguished Scientific Contributions in Child Development of the Society for Research in Child Development, and the Camille Cosby "World of Children" Award.

REFERENCES

Bronfenbrenner, U. (1972). *Two worlds of childhood: U.S. and USSR*. New York, NY: Simon & Schuster.

Bronfenbrenner, U. (1979). *The ecology of human development: Experiments by nature and design*. Cambridge, MA: Harvard University Press.

Bronfenbrenner, U., McClelland, P., Wethington, E., Moen, P., & Ceci, S. J. (1996). *The state of Americans: This generation and the next*. New York, NY: Free Press.

TAMARA J. MARTIN
University of Texas of the Permian Basin

BROWN, ANN L. (1943–1999)

Ann Brown received a BA in psychology with first-class honors in 1964 from Bedford College of the University of London, and her PhD in psychology in 1967, also from the University of London. She was a professor of Cognition and Development in the Graduate School of Education at the University of California, Berkeley, and was previously on the faculty at the University of Illinois.

Brown's research focused in the area of cognitive psychology, including cognition, metacognition, cognitive development, intentional learning, and transfer of learning. She distinguished between knowledge, or *cognition*, and how that knowledge is understood, or *metacognition*, and is an acknowledged leader in the field of metacognition. Major works include *Knowing When, Where, and How to Remember* (1978) and *Metacognition Reconsidered* (Reeve & Brown, 1984), the latter describing modifications Brown views as necessary for successful interventions based on metacognitive principles, including increased attention to pertinent developmental issues, and understanding transition from other-regulated to self-regulated thought. She was one of the founders and principal researchers of the Learning and Development Program, a research center within the Graduate School of Education at UC Berkeley. Her most recent articles focused on the integration of psychological theory and the design of innovative learning environments, and guided discovery.

Brown was highly active within the profession throughout her career. She was president of the National Academy of Education (1998), and a past president of the American Educational Research Association (1993–1994). Between 1976 and 1979, she was associate editor for the journal *Child Development*, and later a member of the Harvard University Press *Cognitive Science Series* and the MIT Press *Learning and Development and Conceptual Change Series*. Other editorial activities include serving as consulting editor for numerous scholarly journals, including the *Journal of Experimental Psychology, Developmental Psychology, American Journal of Mental Deficiency*, and the *American Journal of Psychology*. She also served as a member of the governing board of the Cognitive Science Society.

In 1997, Brown received the American Psychological Society James McKeen Catell Fellow Award for Distinguished Service to Applied Psychology, and was the recipient of AERA's Distinguished Research Award in 1991.

REFERENCES

Brown, A. L. (1978). Knowing when, where and how to remember: A problem in metacognition. In R. Glasser (Ed.), *Advances in instructional psychology*. Hillsdale, NJ: Erlbaum.

Reeve, R. A., & Brown, A. L. (1984). *Metacognition reconsidered: Implications for intervention research*. Champaign: University of Illinois.

Tamara J. Martin
University of Texas of the Permian Basin

BROWN, LOU (1939–)

Lou Brown received BA and MA degrees in Social Studies Education and Clinical Psychology from East Carolina University and a PhD degree in Special Education from Florida State University in 1969. Since 1969 he has been a professor in the Department of Rehabilitation Psychology and Special Education at the University of Wisconsin.

His efforts in the field of education have focused on the development of service delivery models, curricula, and values that prepare individuals with disabilities to live, work, and play in integrated society. His dream is that some day in the near future all such persons will live in decent family-style settings that contain no more than two unrelated persons with disabilities, perform real work in the real world next to nondisabled coworkers, enjoy rich and varied recreation and leisure lives with their nondisabled friends and neighbors, and have access to and use all community environments.

Brown's strong belief that individuals with disabilities can become productive members of integrated society, as well as his call for the termination of institutions, special schools and classes, sheltered workshops, activity centers, enclaves, group homes, and other manifestations of segregation, caused many in the past to consider his views radical and extreme. Such views are common today. He believes that many educational and vocational training programs do not adequately prepare persons with and without disabilities to function in integrated society. Thus, he contends that massive changes are needed in the ways we serve and prepare others to serve those with disabilities.

Brown has lectured, consulted, and served as a technical advisor for various organizations, school districts, colleges, and universities throughout the United States and abroad. He has written countless books and articles, and has been as a member of several editorial boards of publications including *The Journal of Special Education*, the *Encyclopedia of Special Education* (First Edition), *The Journal of the Association for Persons With Severe Handicaps, Journal of Applied Behavior Analysis, Exceptional Children, Teaching Exceptional Children, Education and Training of the Mentally Retarded*, and *Career Development for Exceptional Individuals*.

Recent publications by Brown include *Serving Formerly Excluded or Rejected Students With Disabilities in Regular Education Classrooms in Home Elementary Schools: Three Options* (Brown, Kluth, Suomi, Jorgensen, & Houghton, 2002), *The Buyout Option for Students With Significant Disabilities During the Transition Years* (Owens Johnson et al., 2002), and *Factors Affecting the Social Experiences of Students in Elementary Physical Education Classes* (Suomi, Collier, & Brown, 2003).

REFERENCES

Brown, L., Kluth, P., Suomi, J., Jorgensen, J., & Houghton, L. (2002). Serving formerly excluded or rejected students with disabilities in regular education classrooms in home elementary schools: Three options. In W. Sailor (Ed.), *Whole school success and inclusive education: Building partnerships for learning, achievement and accountability* (pp. 182–194). New York, NY: Teachers College Press.

Owens Johnson, L., Brown, L., Temple, J., McKeown, B., Ross, C., & Jorgensen, J. (2002). The buyout option for students with significant disabilities during the transition years. In W. Sailor (Ed.), *Whole school success and inclusive education: Building partnerships for learning, achievement and accountability* (pp. 106–120). New York, NY: Teachers College Press.

Suomi, J., Collier, D., & Brown, L. (2003). Factors affecting the social experiences of students in elementary physical education classes. *Journal of Teaching in Physical Education, 22*(2), 186–202.

TAMARA J. MARTIN
University of Texas of the Permian Basin

RACHEL M. TOPLIS
Falcon School District 49, Colorado Springs, Colorado

critical periods. In addition to being a consulting editor of the *Encyclopedia of Special Education*, he co-edited two books of relevance to special education, *Perspectives on Bias in Mental Testing* (Reynolds & Brown, 1984) and *Psychological Perspectives on Childhood Exceptionality: A Handbook* (Brown & Reynolds, 1986). He coedits, with Cecil R. Reynolds the Plenum Perspectives on Individual Differences, a series of professional books.

More publications include "Exercise Demonstrating a Genetic-Environment Interaction" (Brown, 1989), providing instruction for introducing and conducting an interaction between genetics and environment, and "Ex-huming an Old Issue" (Brown & Jackson, 1992), an article reviewing research on inductive reasoning errors.

REFERENCES

Brown, R. T., & Reynolds, C. R. (Eds.). (1986). *Psychological perspectives on childhood exceptionality: A handbook.* New York, NY: Wiley.

Brown, R. T. (1989). Exercise demonstrating a genetic-environment interaction. *Teaching Psychology, 16.*

Brown, R. T., & Jackson, L. A. (1992). Ex-huming an old issue. *Journal of School Psychology, 30,* 215–221.

Reynolds, C. R., & Brown, R. T. (Eds.). (1984). *Perspectives on bias in mental testing.* New York, NY: Plenum Press.

CECIL R. REYNOLDS
Texas A&M University
First edition

TAMARA J. MARTIN
University of Texas of the Permian Basin
Second edition

AMANDA C. CHOW
Texas A&M University
Fourth edition

BROWN, ROBERT T. (1940–   )

Born in 1940 in Greenwich, Connecticut, Robert T. Brown obtained his BA degree from Hamilton College in 1961 and his PhD in experimental psychology from Yale University in 1966. At Yale he worked with Allan R. Wagner and Frank A. Logan before conducting his dissertation research under the supervision of William Kessen. After a USPHS postdoctoral fellowship at the University of Sussex, he was on the faculty of William and Mary and then the University of North Carolina, Chapel Hill. He was a professor of psychology at the University of North Carolina, Wilmington, retiring in 2006.

His research on the effects of rearing environments on problem solving in rats and on imprinting in chicks and ducklings has influenced theories of early experience and

BROWN VERSUS BOARD OF EDUCATION

The landmark 1954 Supreme Court decision in *Brown v. Board of Education* (347 U.S. 483, 1954) reversed racially discriminatory segregation in public schools throughout the country and laid the groundwork for subsequent litigation and legislation that has had a tremendous impact on the field of education in general and special education in particular. The case, actually a consolidation of cases from four separate states, was brought to the Supreme Court by a Kansas African-American family, the Browns, along with African-American students from South Carolina, Delaware, and Virginia who sought admission to public schools that were at that time restricted to

Anglo-American students. The African-American students had been denied admission to these schools under the "separate but equal" doctrine outlined nearly 60 years earlier in the Supreme Court case *Plessy v. Ferguson* (1896), which held that the 14th Amendment's requirement for equal treatment of all citizens was fulfilled if different races were provided with facilities that were "substantially equal" though separate. The plaintiffs did not argue that the schools that they were attending were not of the same quality that other students attended, rather, they argued that, in fact, the "separate but equal" doctrine was inherently unequal and that by being denied access to the same educational facilities that Anglo-American students attended, they were being deprived of their right to an equal education.

Relying in part on behavioral science evidence, the Supreme Court ruled unanimously in favor of the plaintiffs, stating that the segregated schools violated the students' rights to an equal education under the Fourteenth Amendment to the U.S. Constitution. The justices found that segregated schools created irreparable harm to minority students, noting that state-sanctioned segregation created the impression that the segregated minority group was inferior to Anglo Americans. Justice Warren's opinion notes:

> Today...[education] is a principal instrument in awakening the child to cultural values, in preparing him for later professional training, and in helping him to adjust normally to his environment. In these days, it is doubtful that any child may reasonably be expected to succeed in life if he is denied the opportunity of an education. Such an opportunity, where the state has undertaken to provide it, is a right which must be made available to all on equal terms. (347 U.S. 483)

Ultimately, the *Brown* decision was important not only for outlawing school segregation, opening the door to a more open, less discriminatory educational system for all students, but also for opening the door to later cases relating to the provision of a free appropriate public education to students with disabilities. Almost 20 years later, attorneys cited the *Brown* decision in arguments in two important special education cases: *Pennsylvania Association for Retarded Citizens* (1972), and *Mills v. Board of Education of the District of Columbia* (1972). These court decisions played a major role in the enactment of the Education for All Handicapped Children Act of 1975 (P.L. 94–142), which in turn served as the predecessor for the Individuals with Disabilities Education Act (IDEA).

The Department of Education has stated that the "Brown decision was a crowbar for change, and we are all the better for it" (Riley, 1994). However, others (Ruiz, 1994) suggested that although 500 school districts were ordered to desegregate, 40 years after the *Brown* decision, very few of those schools were found by the courts to have completed the process. Ruiz (1994) suggested that

the central tenet of *Brown* is in danger of being lost amid "voluminous paperwork and clever legal arguments." Race discrimination issues are still prominent; however, the issues have evolved into conflicts about ability grouping, bilingual education, harassment, educational services for undocumented immigrants, and different kinds of educational remedies in school desegregation cases (Heubert, 1994).

REFERENCES

Heubert, J. P. (1994). *"Brown" at 40: The tasks that remain for educators and lawyers.* (ERIC Clearinghouse No. EA026514)

Riley, R. W. (1994). *Fulfilling the promise of Brown.* Washington, DC: Department of Education.

Ruiz, C. M. (1994). *Equity, excellence and school reform: A new paradigm for desegregation.* (ERIC Clearinghouse No. 026648)

EMILIA C. LOPEZ
Fordham University
Second edition

KIMBERLY F. APPLEQUIST
University of Colorado at Colorado Springs
Third edition

See also **Constitutional Law (in Special Education); Culture Fair Test; Disproportionality; Mills v. Board of Education of the District of Columbia; Pennsylvania Association for Retarded Citizens v. Pennsylvania; Socioeconomic Status**

BRUCELLOSIS

Brucellosis is an infectious disease that is transmitted from animals to humans through infected meat or animal products. The disease is rare in the United States, although it is more prevalent in Midwestern states and rural areas. Approximately 200 cases are found in the United States each year (Clayman, 1989). It is more frequently found in other countries where precautions in meat handling and pasteurization are not common practice, and it is sometimes carried to the United States by visitors or immigrants. Brucellosis is also known as *Cyprus fever, Gibraltar fever, Malta fever, Mediterranean fever, rock fever,* or *undulant fever* (Berkow, Beers, Bogin, & Fletcher, 1997).

Brucellosis is commonly caused by six types of gram-negative or rods of the Brucella genus of bacteria. Brucella abortus is carried by cattle, brucella suis by hogs, brucella melitensis by goats, brucella canis by dogs, brucella ovis by sheep and hares, and brucella neotomae by desert wood rats (Behrman, 1992). The disease is usually spread by contact with the excretions and secretions of infected animals (Anderson, Anderson, & Glanze, 1998). It may also be contracted by drinking infected, unpasteurized milk, eating cheese or other dairy products made from infected milk, or handling infected meat. It can also be transmitted by air (Clayman, 1989). Brucellosis is more commonly found in individuals who handle live animals or meat, such as veterinarians, farmers, and meat packers. It is rarely transmitted from person to person.

The symptoms of brucellosis can initially be subtle and mistaken for other diseases. The onset may also be acute. The patient can exhibit flu-like symptoms, with headache, fatigue, muscle and joint pain, insomnia, lack of appetite, sweating, irritability, and emotional instability. Intermittent fever may occur, which is usually higher at night and lower in the morning. Later, symptoms may include an enlarged spleen, liver, and lymph nodes. More severe complications include inflammation and infections of the heart, brain, nerves, testes, gallbladder, liver, and bones (Berkow et al., 1997).

Symptoms may become chronic, occurring in intervals followed by periods in which the patient may appear to be symptom-free, but then the symptoms will recur. Treatment is important to prevent complications and other infections such as encephalitis, pneumonia, and meningitis. Although the disease is rarely fatal, brucellosis can lead to chronic bad health, and the symptoms may persist.

Characteristics

1. Flu-like symptoms are experienced initially, with headache, fatigue, muscle and joint pain, insomnia, lack of appetite, sweating, irritability, and emotional instability.

2. Intermittent fever may occur, being higher at night and lower in the morning.

3. Later symptoms may include an enlarged spleen, liver, and lymph nodes.

4. More severe complications include inflammation and infections of the heart, brain, nerves, testes, gallbladder, liver, and bones.

5. Other symptoms may be severe constipation, profuse sweating, decreased body temperature, heart rate variability, and eye irregularities.

Incubation of brucellosis may be from a few days to several weeks, but it is usually 2 weeks after exposure. Often, patients do not seek treatment for some time after the disease has been contracted. The physician can detect brucellosis by checking the blood for high levels of antibodies to the bacteria. Brucellosis can also be detected in spinal fluid, urine, or bone marrow. Tissues may be sent

for culture to confirm the diagnosis; these cultures need be incubated for 21 days. Negative readings are common in chronic cases.

With treatment, patients usually recover from brucellosis in 2 to 3 weeks. Treatment with a single antibiotic for patients with the disorder may result in recurrence, so a combination of antibiotics is recommended. Tetracycline plus streptomycin with bed rest has been effective. Other combinations, such as doxycycline plus rifampin or streptomycin or both and trimethoprim-sulfamethoxazole plus rifampin or streptomycin (or both) have been found to be effective in doses over 21 days. Longer courses of treatment for several months may be needed in more severe or chronic cases (Tierney, McPhee, & Papadakis, 2001). Pain reliever may be needed to make the patient more comfortable.

Although brucellosis is treatable, children with chronic symptoms may need accommodations in school. Because the symptoms are similar to many common diseases, it may not be quickly diagnosed, and symptoms may persist over a long period of time. This may result in frequent absence from school. Students may fall behind in their work; tutoring or some kind of support may be necessary.

Research is currently being conducted to create vaccines to prevent human brucellosis (Cosivi & Corel, 1998). Prevention can be accomplished through the vaccination of young animals and the pasteurization of milk and milk products. Gloves and glasses should be worn when handling animals or animal products.

Brucellosis can be contracted through a break in the skin, so cuts in the skin should be covered. The practice of good hygiene can help to prevent spread of the bacteria that cause the disease.

REFERENCES

Anderson, K. N., Anderson, L. E., & Glanze, W. D. (Eds.). (1998). *Mosby's medical dictionary* (5th ed.). St. Louis, MO: Mosby.

Behrman, R. (Ed.). (1992). *Nelson's textbook of pediatrics* (14th ed.). Philadelphia, PA: W. B. Saunders.

Berkow, R., Beers, M. H., Bogin, R. M., & Fletcher, A. J. (Eds.). (1997). *The Merck manual of medical information*. Whitehouse Station, NJ: Merck.

Clayman, C. B. (Ed.). (1989). *The American Medical Association encyclopedia of medicine*. New York, NY: Random House.

Cosivi, O., & Corel, M. J. (1998). WHO consultation on the development of new/improved brucellosis vaccines. *Biologicals, 26,* 361–363.

Tierney, L. M., Jr., McPhee, S. J., & Papadakis, M. A. (Eds). (2001). *Current medical diagnosis and treatment* (40th ed.). New York, NY: Lange Medical Books, McGraw-Hill.

MICHELE WILSON KAMENS
Rider University

BRUININKS-OSERETSKY TEST OF MOTOR PROFICIENCY (BOT-2)

The Bruininks-Oseretsky Test of Motor Proficiency (R. Bruininks & Bruininks, 2005) is an individually administered test of gross and fine motor functioning of both typicall developing children and children with motor delays from ages 4 to 21 years of age. The test developed from the Oseretsky tests of motor proficiency published in Russia in 1903 (later translated into English by Edgar Doll in 1946) (Doll, 1946). The complete battery comprises 8 subtests with a total of 53 items: Fine Motor Precision (7 items) of cutting out objects and connecting dots, Fine Motor Integrations (8 items) of copying objects, Manual Dexterity (5 items) transferring objects, sorting and stringing beads, Bilateral Coordination (7 items) tapping foot and demonstrating jumping jacks, Balance (9 items) walking on a forward line and standing on a balance beam, Running Speed and Agility (5 items) shuttle run and one leg activities, Upper Limb Coordination (7 items) throwing and catching a ball, and Strength (5 items) standing long jump and sit-ups (R. Bruininks & B. Bruininks, 2005). In addition to subtest scores, composite scores are available for the gross motor subtest scores, the fine motor subtests, and the total battery. The complete form takes from 45 to 60 minutes to administer. There is also a 14-item short form, requiring 15 to 20 minutes, which provides a single index of general motor proficiency (Bruininks 1978).

Standardization occurred with a normative sample, which included 1,520 children and youth. Normative data are reported for 12 age groups. For ages 4 through 12, normative data are reported for 1-year intervals; for ages 13 through 14, normative data are reported for 2-year intervals; and for ages 17 through 21, a 5-year age interval is used. The normative sample for each age group was selected using stratified random sampling across sex, race/ethnicity, socioeconomic status, and disability status. Demographics were aligned with "the Current Population Survey (Bureau of the Census, 2001) and the Twenty-sixth Annual Report to Congress (U.S. Department of Education, 2004)" (Bruininks & Bruininks, 2005, p. 42). The normative sample included children varying disabilities, especially attention deficit hyperactivity disorder and the five highest incidence disability categories (emotional and behavioral disturbance; specific learning disability, mental retardation, developmental delay, and speech/language impairment) used by the U.S. Department of Education for children receiving special education services. Of the total sample, 168 (11.4%) had special education status (Deitz, Kartin, & Kopp, 2007).

Reliability was examined through inter-rater reliability (Anatstasi, 1997) with all subtests greater than .90, test-retest reliability with all subtests greater than .80, and internal consistency with correlations ranging from .60 to .92 (Deitz, Kartin, & Kopp, 2007). Validity of the BOT-2 was examined through content validity with developed by median subtest scores across age groups with the greatest increases occurring at early ages. When comparing the BOT-2 to other measures of motor development moderately strong results were found.

The Bruininks-Oseretsky Test, Second Edition (BOT-2) is a useful tool for measuring gross and fine motor delays, developing and evaluating motor training programs, and screening for special purposes (Deitz et al., 2007). Updated materials and cues diminish language demands for efficient administration and scoring, test items accurately reflect typical childhood activities, along with sound psychometric properties makes the BOT-2 an accurate measurement tool. Limitations in reliability scores of subtests and composite scores should be considered when diagnosing children with delays in motor development or determining a child's specific skill level in motor development. Additional limitations include the amount of time needed to accurately score the BOT-2 and difficulty of the items in specific age categories. Overall, the BOT-2 is useful in assessing children ages 6–21 suspected of having motor delays (Deitz et al., 2007).

REFERENCES

Anastasi, A. (1997). *Psychological testing* (7th ed.). Saddle River, NJ: Prentice Hall.

Bruininks, R. (1978). *Bruininks-Oseretsky test of motor proficiency: Examiner's manual*. Circle Pines, MN: American Guidance.

Bruininks, R., & Bruininks, B. (2005). *Bruininks-Oseretsky test of motor proficiency* (2nd ed.). Minneapolis, MN: Pearson.

Deitz, J. C., Kartin, D., & Kopp, K. (2007). Review of the Bruininks-Oseretsky test of motor proficiency, second edition (BOT-2). *Physical Occupational Therapy Pediatrics, 27,* 87–102.

Doll, E. A. (1946). *The Oseretsky tests of motor proficiency*. Minneapolis, MN: American Guidance.

Harrington, R. G. (1985). Bruininks-Oseretsky test of motor proficiency. In D. L. Keyser & R. C. Sweetland (Eds.), *Test critiques* (Vol. 3, pp. 99–110). Kansas City, MO: Test Corporation of America.

LIZANNE DESTEFANO
University of Illinois

HEATHER S DAVIS
Texas A&M University
Fourth edition

See also Visual-Motor Integration; Visual Perception and Discrimination

BRUNER, JEROME (1915–   )

Bruner obtained his BA from Duke University in 1937 and his PhD in Psychology from Harvard University in 1941. For almost three decades he was professor of psychology at Harvard University (1945–1972), and also served as director of the Center for Cognitive Studies there, founded by him in the 1960s. He was a professor at both Oxford and Cambridge Universities in England, and has held the positions of George Herbert Mead Professor at the New School for Social Research and fellow of the Institute for the Humanities at New York University. In 1991 Bruner was visiting professor at the New York University Law School and presently he continues at NYU as a university professor and research professor of psychology. Bruner's area of interest is the application of narrative principles to an understanding of legal processes.

Known by some as the only real intellectual in modern cognitive psychology, in his long career as a psychologist and teacher, Bruner has frequently rejected prevailing views, becoming a major influence in moving American psychology towards a more cognitive approach in the process. His principal areas of research have focused on the knowledge acquisition processes, including perception, memory, learning, thought, language, and literary and scientific creation.

In the 1950s Bruner demonstrated that perceptions are not merely mental photographs, but are actively shaped by the meaning to the individual of what is perceived. This research gave rise to the widely criticized "New Look" movement in psychology, which focused on factors such as how perception is affected by individual intentions or emotions. This movement was the precursor of cognitive psychology, a theory that continues to thrive today. Bruner's research in this area was later expanded to include studies conducted in Senegal in the 1960s of cultural influences on individual perception, an element he concluded was missing from Jean Piaget's child development model.

Another of Bruner's major contributions involved infant learning and the formerly prevalent notion that children's learning occurs entirely as a result of what they experience. This "blank slate" theory was challenged by his study indicating that infants could control whether slides of a woman's face were in or out of focus via their sucking patterns, suggesting a sense of intention as a factor in their intellectual development. These findings were the beginning of his conception for the development of the Head Start programs for preschool children in the United States.

Bruner's effort to bridge the gap between psychology and the humanities is reflected throughout his work. Believing that psychology, particularly cognitive psychology, has become excessively narrow, he has attempted to expand the discipline into the realms of philosophy, the arts, and literature, thus providing a broader perspective of the human mind. Some have criticized Bruner's (1990) call for a "renewed cognitive revolution," arguing that he fails to specify the direction of the movement as well as the obstacles that must be overcome for its success (Shanker, 1992).

His more recent work has focused on the study of narrative modes of thought, analyzing the words and construction used by individuals as they relate the story of their lives. Bruner argues that how the stories are told "becomes so habitual that they finally become recipes for structuring experience itself, for laying down routes into memory," therefore shaping the way people experience life itself.

His numerous publications include *A Study of Thinking* (1956), centering on problem-solving and thinking; *The Process of Education* (1961), a controversial study of the underlying structure of science curriculum; *Actual Minds, Possible Worlds* (1986), dealing with narrative modes of thought; and *Child's Talk* (1985), a summation of his findings and arguments regarding language learning. Bruner has served on two presidential commissions and received numerous awards and honorary degrees. In 1987 in Bern, Switzerland, he was awarded the prestigious Balzan Prize, previously given to Jean Piaget and Jorge Luis Borges, and only rarely presented to an American.

REFERENCES

Bruner, J. S. (1961). *The process of education*. Cambridge, MA: Harvard University Press.

Bruner, J. S. (1986). *Actual minds, possible worlds*. Cambridge, MA: Harvard University Press.

Bruner, J. S. (1990). *Acts of meaning*. Cambridge, MA: Harvard University Press.

Bruner, J. S., Goodnow, J. J., & Austin, G. A. (1956). *A study of thinking*. New York, NY: Wiley.

Bruner, J. S., & Watson, R. (1985). *Child's talk: Learning to use language*. New York, NY: Norton.

Shanker, S. (1992). In search of Bruner. *Language and Communications, 12,* 53–74.

TAMARA J. MARTIN
University of Texas of the Permian Basin
Second edition

RACHEL M. TOPLIS
Falcon School District 49, Colorado Springs, Colorado

BRUXISM AND THE STUDENT WITH DISABILITIES

Bruxism can be defined as the nonfunctional gnashing and grinding of teeth occurring during the day or night. The adverse effects of bruxism include severe dental wear, damage to the alveolar bone, temporomandibular joint disorders, and hypertrophy of masticatory muscles, as well as occasional infection. It can also result in significant pain, permanent damage to the structures of the mouth and jaw, and lost teeth (Rugh & Robbins, 1982). Dental wear is the most commonly used measure to determine the extent of bruxism.

Estimates of the frequency of bruxism in the non-retarded population have ranged between 5% (Reding, Rubright, & Zimmerman, 1966) to a high of 21% (Wigdorowicz-Makowerowa, Grodzki, & Maslanka, 1977), with no significant differences between sexes (Bober, 1982) or age groups (Lindqvist, 1971).

Investigators have reported more dental wear as a consequence of bruxism in severely mentally retarded children than in nonretarded children (Lindqvist & Heijbel, 1974). An informal survey by Blount, Drabman, Wilson, and Stewart (1982) indicated that 21.5% of a profoundly intellectually disabled group engaged in bruxism. The study of Richmond et al. of some 433 individuals with intellectual disabilities in a state institution revealed a rate of 41% to 59% in this group based on a questionnaire used with direct-care staff who were asked to observe the residents. Higher rates were reported for deaf-retarded individuals. Older patients were more likely to grind teeth and wear into the dentin than younger patients.

A variety of explanations for bruxism have been advanced. The etiology of bruxism has been approached along lines of local, psychological, neurophysiological, and systemic causes (Glaros & Melamed, 1992). An example of a local cause is occlusive abnormalities. Glaros and Rao (1977) believe that stress is a major cause. Systemic explanations include heredity factors and endocrinal or neurological dysfunction. It has been suggested (Lindqvist & Heijbel, 1974) that bruxism may be a form of stereotypy among retarded populations. It has also been suggested that bruxism can be the result of negative side effects of certain medications such as SSRIs (Bostwick & Jaffee, 1999).

Although such methods as deep muscle relaxation and massed practice have been found to assist individuals of typical intelligence, these methods require a certain level of cognitive ability to be successfully deployed and may not be suited for bruxists who have intellectual developmental disabilities. Behavioral methods to reduce bruxism have been favored in recent years (Rugh & Robbins, 1982). Thus positive reinforcement has been used to reduce its incidence in retarded individuals (i.e., to reinforce nonbruxist behaviors) and to encourage incompatible behaviors such as keeping the mouth open. Problems with positive reinforcers include the fact that social and tactile reinforcers usually do not have strong effects with intellectually developmentally delayed individuals. Edibles result in further chewing, thus reinforcing behaviors that are not compatible with efforts to reduce bruxism.

Hence behavioral treatment has sometimes been of an aversive nature (e.g., using a contingent sound blast) (Heller & Strage, 1973). Such treatment, however, involves expensive equipment. Blount et al. (1982) were able to use a much simpler method, known as *icing*, with two profoundly women with intellectual developmental dealys. They greatly reduced their bruxism and successfully generalized their improvements beyond the training sessions. In icing there is a brief contingent application of ice to cheeks or chin as an aversive stimulus. Another, similar method of aversive control of bruxism in an intellecutally developmentally delayed nonverbal child in a class for children with developmental delays was accomplished by Kramer (1981). The method involved the use of a contingent verbal "no" accompanied by the teacher's finger to the child's jaw. Unfortunately, the treatment ideology and modalities has been haphazard for bruxism; therefore, most treatment effects are short-lived (Glaros & Melamed, 1992).

Characteristics

1. The child reports mild headaches or earaches in the morning after waking up.
2. At night a grinding sound is heard while the child is sleeping.
3. In more extreme cases, the child may report temperature sensitivity along with severe pain in the jaw.
4. A popping or clicking sound in the jaw is heard.
5. The tips of the child's teeth appear flat and the tooth enamel appears worn down.
6. The child appears to have damage to the inside of the cheek.

REFERENCES

Blount, R. L., Drabman, R. S., Wilson, N., & Stewart, D. (1982). Reducing severe diurnal bruxism in two profoundly retarded females. *Journal of Applied Behavior Analysis, 15*, 565–571.

Bober, H. (1982). Cause and treatment of bruxism and bruxomania. *Dental Abstracts, 3*, 658–659.

Bostwick, J. M., & Jaffee, M. S. (1999). Buspirone as an antidote to SSRI-induced bruxism. *Journal of Clinical Psychiatry, 60*, 857–860.

Glaros, A. G., & Melamed, B. G. (1992). Bruxism in children, Etiology and treatment. *Applied and Preventive Psychology, 1*, 191–199.

Glaros, A. G., & Rao, S. M. (1977). Bruxism: A critical review. *Psychological Bulletin, 84*, 767–781.

Heller, R. F., & Strang, H. R. (1973). Controlling bruxism through automated aversive conditioning. *Behavior Research & Therapy, 11*, 327–328.

Kramer, J. J. (1981). Aversive control of bruxism in a mentally retarded child: A case study. *Psychological Reports, 49*, 815–818.

Lindqvist, B. (1971). Bruxism in children. *Odontologisk Revy, 22,* 413–424.

Lindqvist, B., & Heijbel, J. (1974). Bruxism in children with brain damage. *Acta Odontologica Scandinavica, 32,* 313–319.

Richmond, G., Rugh, J. D., Dolfi, R., & Wasilewsky, J. W. Survey of bruxism in an institutionalized mentally retarded population. *American Jounal of Mental Deficience, 88,* 418–21.

Reding, G. R., Rubright, W. C., & Zimmerman, S. O. (1966). Incidence of bruxism. *Journal of Dental Research, 45,* 1198–1204.

Rugh, J. D., & Robbins, W. J. (1982). Oral habit disorders. In B. Ingersoll (Ed.), *Behavioral aspects in dentistry* (pp. 179–202). New York, NY: Appleton-Century-Crofts.

Wigdorowicz-Makowerowa, N., Grodzki, C., & Maslanka, T. (1977). Frequency and etiopathogenes of bruxism (on the basis of prophylactic examinations of 1000 middle-aged men). *Czaopismo-Stomatologiczne, 25,* 1109–1112.

DAVID C. MANN
St. Francis Hospital

See also Dentistry and the Exceptional Child; Self-Injurious Behavior

BUCKLEY AMENDMENT (*See* Family Educational Rights and Privacy Act)

BULIMIA NERVOSA

Bulimia nervosa (a term of Greek origin meaning "*ox hunger*") is an eating disorder that is also referred to as the *binge-purge syndrome*. It is a condition in which an individual alternately binges (grossly overeats) and purges (rids the body of food or fluids). Although difficult to comprehend, bulimics apparently may ingest as many as 20,000 calories in one binge episode. Bulimics commonly chew and spit out food (Mitchell, Halsukami, Eckert, & Pyle, 1985). Bingeing is mainly on foods rich in carbohydrates; purging may be through vomiting, abuse of laxatives or diet tablets, or excessive exercise, regardless of fatigue (Garner & Garfinkel, 1985). No physical basis for the abnormal eating can be found. This disorder can be life-threatening, is increasing in occurrence, and is a serious problem for medical and psychological professionals who are attempting to treat it. Unlike anorexia, which has been known for centuries, bulimia is of relatively recent origin. Indeed, professional journals have commonly reported on bulimia only since the 1970s. This recency is partly responsible for the relatively little firm knowledge about bulimia and the absence of generally effective treatments. Incidence rates that vary with age, race, job status, and ethnic background further hamper general understanding of the disorder (Burch, 1975).

Bulimia nervosa is reported to have a 12-month prevelance in .3 % of the U.S. adult population with a lifetime prevelance of .6% of the U.S. adult population. The average age of onset was found to be around 20 years of age.

Although primarily affecting women, bulimia also is seen, and in some areas increasingly, in men. Reasons for the disorder appear to be quite different in men and women except in sports (e.g., gymnastics) or vocations (e.g., modeling or dancing) that impose comparable demands on members of both sexes. Those engaged in high-powered sports such as running and wrestling or vocations are particularly at risk. One study (McNulty, 1997) reported that Navy servicemen showed prevalence rates of 2.5% for anorexia and 6.8% for bulimia. In men, bulimia may be driven by individual competition where weight or appearance and goals of "perfection" are important. Male bulimics may need a high calorie intake for energy but at the same time fear not being able to burn off the fat. If a Naval officer wants high scores on body measurements and fitness tests, then he may find purging an effective means, in the short term.

Although bulimia is more common than anorexia, it is harder to recognize because affected individuals do not show severe weight loss and are usually of normal or slightly above normal weight. The stereotypical bulimic's physical appearance may not be apparent to anyone else, possibly not even the sufferer's spouse, as was the case of Princess of Wales, Diana.

However, some general etiological factors and occasionally effective treatments have been described. Bulimics share personality characteristics and have families with a particular complex of unhealthy attitudes and behaviors. Bulimics can suffer from gastrointestinal problems and serious potassium depletion and damage to their teeth due to the acid nature of the regurgitated food. In extreme cases, death may result. As is the case with anorexia, bulimia is viewed as a biopsychosocial disorder.

DSM-IV (American Psychiatric Association, 2000) criteria for bulimia include: (a) recurrent episodes of secretive binge eating (rapid consumption of a large amount of food in a short period of time); (b) termination of bingeing because of abdominal pain, sleep, or social interruptions; and (c) recurrent episodes of purging as an attempt to lose weight or avoid gaining weight through self-induced vomiting, severe diets, abuse of laxatives, cathartics, or diuretics, or excessive exercise. The bulimic suffers frequent weight fluctuations owing to alternating binges and fasts, awareness that the eating pattern is abnormal, and fear of not being able to stop eating voluntarily. Depression and self-deprecating thoughts may follow eating binges (American Psychiatric Association, 2000). *DSM-IV* distinguishes between purging and nonpurging types of bulimia. A purging type periodically engages in the act of self-induced vomiting or the use of laxatives, whereas a nonpurging type uses diets, exercise, and fasting instead of regular self-induced vomiting.

Considering biological aspects, bulimia leads to a variety of physiological complications, including cardiac irregularities, kidney dysfunction, neurological abnormalities, gastrointestinal pain, salivary gland enlargement (appearance of a chipmunk), edema and bloating, electrolyte imbalance, amenorrhea, dermatological disorders, and finger clubbing or swelling. Finger abnormalities result from the pressure against the mouth during self-induced vomiting. Abuse of laxatives can lead to permanent nerve damage in the colon, chronic stomach overloading, and potential of stomach rupture. Several of these complications can result in death.

Psychologically, bulimics share many behaviors and concerns. They are terrified of becoming obese, and measure their worth and self-esteem by how much they weigh and how little their stomachs protrude. They tend to be perfectionists, overdemanding of themselves, and very success-oriented. Low self-esteem and fear of rejection, especially by the opposite sex, are common. They are typically helpless, ineffective, nonassertive, have maturity fears, tension management problems, and difficulty in identifying or describing internal states (Johnson & Flach, 1985). Their relationships tend to be superficial and lack genuineness, as they have difficulty allowing others to become emotionally close to them. They are good at distancing themselves from people while seeming to be friendly and sociable. A common underlying fear is, "If this person really gets to know me, he or she won't like me." They frequently fear sexual rejection or not being good enough to please a sexual partner. Bulimics may additionally overidentify with femininity. Drug abuse among bulimics and their families occurs at a high rate (Herzog, 1982). Motivation for change is extremely difficult to maintain, making therapy difficult.

Bulimics commonly report that their disorder originated out of possible "comfort eating" stemming from loneliness, stress, or some other self-induced inadequacy, such as low self-esteem. Suicide can also be a fatal result of either lack of observation from family and friends, lack of support (as interpreted by the bulimia), or the lack of help from themselves or possibly from the therapist (Hsu, 1990). Not surprisingly, both depression and anxiety are comorbid conditions (Cooper & Fairburn, 1986).

The third aspect of the biopsychosocial triad model of bulimia is social factors. Many bulimics spend so much time in their eating rituals that they do not have time for a normal social life. In one study (Mitchell et al., 1985) 70% had interpersonal relations difficulties, 53% had family problems, and 50% had work-related interpersonal difficulties. Bulimics can also use their eating habits to shut out the world. They can avoid engaging with others or becoming involved in a situation that could potentially be out of their control. Eating rituals are one thing that bulimics (and anorexics as well) believe they can continue to control, even though it is evident to those who know

them that they have actually lost control. The specific etiology of bulimia is not known.

The biopsychosocial model suggests that unknown biological predispositions may interact with both individual psychological states and needs and society's emphasis, especially for women, on thinness as a desirable characteristic (S. Wooley & Wooley, 1985). Families of bulimics are characterized by a paradoxical combination of enmeshment and disengagement, showing high family conflict with little emphasis on self-expression, especially over conflict. Intellectual achievement is emphasized at the expense of social activities (Johnson & Flach, 1985).

Much of the bulimic's perceived control simply does not exist. The social world exposes vulnerable people to things that, depending on their perception, can exploit their fears. Mass communication can intensify people's low self-esteem and fear of rejection. Consider, for example, size 0 models in fashion shows, celebrities saying how easy it is to lose weight in advertisements for weight-loss programs. Supermodels or representatives of diet programs frequently suffer from serious eating disorders themselves. Numerous media messages instill an unrealistic view of the human form that may enhance fear of "fatness." At the same time, the average weight of American children and adults continues to increase with 66% of the U.S. population being overweight or obese while 16% of children and adolescents are overweight and 34% are at risk for becoming overweight or obese (Wang & Beydoun, 2007).

Treatment can be difficult. Usually, the longer bulimics have been ill, the more difficulty they will have in overcoming the disorder. Also, as mentioned previously, lack of motivation for change makes working with bulimics on an outpatient basis difficult (Bemis, 1978). The drive for a weight loss or the perfect body may outweigh the drive for being cured. Many therapists believe that treatment is likely to fail if this addictive quality is not addressed (Anderson, Morse, & Santmyer, 1985). Unfortunately, both bingeing and purging behaviors may have strong and immediate reinforcement qualities. Finally, continual dieting often results in compensatory overeating, which appears to have a physiological component. Whether inpatient treatment is necessary depends on factors as weight, self-harm tendencies, and other comorbid symptoms.

Cognitive behavior therapy has demonstrated improvements for patients diagnosed with bulimia. Effects from a recent study were significantly larger than those for medication in terms of binge frequency, purge frequency, and eating attitudes (medication ES_u's = 0.66, 0.39, and 0.71, respectively) (Butler, Chapman, Forman, & Beck, 2006). Although the initial findings are promising, further evaluation of cognitive behavior therapy in treating bulimia should be considered although CBT has the further advantage of being demonstrably effective in dealing with comorbid factors such as anxiety and depression. Family therapy has been discussed as another way of assisting patients with bulimia nervosa, but little research supports its effectiveness. As a recurring theme, no matter what kind of therapy is offered, whether cognitive behavioral, interpersonal, psychodynamic, or pharmacological, without sufficient and persistent motivation, bulimics will probably find treatment unsuccessful.

Certain beliefs and values seem to be important in the maintenance of these conditions. One of these is the belief that weight and shape are extremely important and need to be closely controlled at all costs. A change in these psychopathological beliefs and values concerning body weight and shape may be necessary for complete recovery. Self-help and support groups such as Overeaters Anonymous may be valuable.

Because eating-disordered individuals are usually perfectionists, teachers can help by advising and encouraging them to take fewer courses and to balance academic loads by combining difficult classes with classes that are less demanding. If hospitalization becomes necessary and the student expresses fear that she will be unable to maintain her academic standing, the teacher can point out that hospital personnel are usually more than willing to assist the patient by administering academic tests and by making arrangements to assist meeting other academic requirements. Major treatment centers, as well as many hospitals, have educational components and academic teachers on their staff.

Characteristics

1. Recurrent episodes of binge eating, each episode lasting approximately 1 to $1\frac{1}{2}$ hours, with consumption of approximately 3,500 calories per episode.
2. Feeling of lack of control overeating behavior during binges.
3. Regular desire to self-induce vomiting, use laxatives or diuretics, diet or fast, or vigorously exercise to prevent weight gain.
4. A minimum average of two binge eating episodes per week for at least the past 3 months.
5. Overly concerned with body shape and/or weight.

Additional sources listed below have been used for the writing of this entry.

REFERENCES

American Psychiatric Association. (2000). *Diagnostic and statistical manual of mental disorders-TR* (4th ed.). Washington, DC: Author.

Anderson, A. E., Morse, C., & Santmyer, K. (1985). Inpatient treatment for anorexia nervosa. In D. M. Garner & P. E. Garfinkel (Eds.), *Handbook of psychotherapy for anorexia nervosa and bulimia* (pp. 311–343). New York, NY: Guilford Press.

Bemis, K. M. (1978). Current approaches to the etiology and treatment of anorexia nervosa. *Psychological Bulletin, 35,* 593–617.

Bruch, H. (1985). Four decades of eating disorders. In D. M. Garner & P. E. Garfinkel (Eds.), *Handbook of psychotherapy for anorexia and bulimia* (pp. 7–18). New York, NY: Guilford Press.

Butler A. C., Chapman, J. E., Forman, E. M., & Beck, A. T. (2006). *The empirical status of cognitive-behavioral therapy: A review of meta-analyses. Clinical Psychology Review, 26,* 17–31.

Cooper, P. J., & Fairburn, C. G. (1986). The depressive symptoms of bulimia nervosa. *British Journal of Psychiatry, 148,* 234–246.

Garner, D. M., & Garfinkel, P. E. (Eds.). (1985). *Handbook of psychotherapy for anorexia nervosa and bulimia.* New York, NY: Guilford Press.

Goetestan, K. G., Erikson, L., Heggestad, T., & Neilson, S. (1998). Prevalence of eating disorders in Norwegian general hospitals 1990–1994: Admissions per year and seasonality. *International Journal of Eating Disorders, 23,* 57–64.

Halmi, K. A. (1983). Advances in anorexia nervosa. In M. Wolraich & D. K. Routh (Eds.), *Advances in development and behavioral pediatrics* (Vol. 4, pp. 1–23). Greenwich, CT: JAI Press.

Hart, K. J., & Ollendick, T. H. (1985). Prevalence of bulimia in working and university women. *American Journal of Psychiatry, 142,* 851–854.

Herzog, D. B. (1982). Bulimia: The secretive syndrome. *Psychosomatics, 23,* 481–487.

Hsu, T. (1990). *Eating disorders.* New York, NY: Guilford Press.

Johnson, C., & Flach, A. (1985). Family characteristics of 105 patients with bulimia. *American Journal of Psychiatry, 142,* 1321–1324.

Mitchell, J. E., Halsukami, D., Eckert, E. D., & Pyle, R. L. (1985). Characteristics of 275 patients with bulimia. *American Journal of Psychiatry, 142,* 251–255.

Neuman, P. A., & Halvorson, P. S. (1983). *Anorexia nervosa and bulimia: A handbook for counselors and therapists.* New York, NY: Van Nostrand Reinhold.

McNulty, P. A., (1997). Prevalence and contributing factors of eating disorder behavior in female athletes. *American Dietitic Association, 101,* 886–894.

Robin, A. L., Gilroy, M., & Dennis, A. B. (1998). Treatment of eating disorders in children and adolescents. *Clinical Psychology Review, 18,* 421–446.

Srinivasan, T. N., Suresh, T. R., & Jayaram, V. (1998). Emergence of eating disorders in India: Study of eating distress syndrome and development of a screening questionnaire. *International Journal of Social Psychiatry, 44,* 189–198.

Vandereycken, W., & Meermann, R. (1984). *Anorexia nervosa: A clinician's guide to treatment.* Berlin, Germany: de Gruyter.

Wang, Y., & Beydoun, M.A. (2007). The obesity epidemic in the United States—Gender, age, socioeconomic, racial/ethnic, and geographic characteristics: A systematic review and meta-regression analysis, *Epidemiological Review*, *29*, 6–28.

Wooley, S. C., & Wooley, O. W. (1985). Intensive outpatient and residential treatment for bulimia. In D. M. Garner & P. E. Garfinkel (Eds.), *Handbook of psychotherapy for anorexia nervosa and bulimia* (pp. 391–430). New York, NY: Guilford Press.

C. SUE LAMB
University of North Carolina at Wilmington

WENDY L. FLYNN
Staffordshire University

See also Anorexia Nervosa; Eating Disorders; Bullous Pemphigoid

BULLOUS PEMPHIGOID

Bullous pemphigoid is a skin disease in which the skin blisters severely. These blistered spots are most likely found in folds of skin such as the groin and armpit areas. Bullous pemphigoid is a rare disorder that is most often found in elderly persons, with the average age at onset being 65 to 75. However, it has recently been diagnosed in children along with other immunobullous diseases (Powell, Kirtschig, Allen, Dean, & Wojnarowska, 2001). Bullous pemphigoid is not a contagious condition.

Bullous pemphigoid is actually a disease of the immune system, in which the immune system begins to attack skin cells as if they were foreign cells. The reason for this immune response is not known, but it causes the layers of the skin to separate and thus form blisters.

Incidences of bullous pemphigoid begin as simple rashes on the skin but progress to itchy, inflamed areas. The skin condition is also often associated with fatigue and anxiety. Psychologically, the disease causes the patient to become lethargic and depressed. This in turn aggravates the skin condition more. A further aggravated condition may resemble other common skin diseases and thus is often mis-diagnosed.

Following the initial stages, blisters develop. These blisters are fluid filled and inflamed, causing the skin to feel itchy and painfully tender. These blisters have been found to be concentrated in folds of skin where movement occurs, as well as in mucous membranes in approximately one third of cases.

This disorder most often occurs in flare-ups: An affected person can be symptom free for a period of years before having an incidence. Additionally, the disease occurs in varying levels of severity. Between flare-ups affected persons are advised to keep the skin well hydrated. Various methods from bathing to lotions to oils may be suited for this purpose, but individuals report varying preferences and tolerances. Finally, those with bullous pemphigoid are advised to use caution in sunlight, as further skin damage can worsen the condition.

Characteristics

1. Itchy, inflamed rash in folds of skin.
2. Fatigue and anxiety.
3. Blisters (often large) that follow rash.
4. Possible blistering in the mouth.

There is no cure for bullous pemphigoid, but the symptoms are controllable. Treatment for this disorder when it is at its most severe involves hospitalization. Oral treatments often involve steroids or immunosuppressants, which decrease the activity of the immune system. However, as these are potent drugs with other side effects, they are usually administered in an initially large dosage, which is subsequently decreased until a minimum effective dose is reached. This then becomes a maintenance dose, which is continued for a set amount of time, possibly as long as several years. Additionally, the use of antibiotic ointment is strongly advised due to a high risk of infection, especially when dealing with blisters that have been broken.

This is a very rare disease in children (Baykal, Okan, & Sarica, 2001). However, it is undoubtedly a psychologically damaging one due to its outwardly visible nature. Children affected by bullous pemphigoid who are between flare-ups will be able to lead a routine life. However, children experiencing flare-ups will be subject to much teasing from peers. It may be necessary to educate classmates on the condition or to provide counseling for the affected child. Additionally, children with this disorder and their teachers will need to be aware of situations that may worsen the condition in order to avoid them.

REFERENCES

Baykal, C., Okan, G., & Sarica, R. (2001). Childhood bullous pemphigoid developed after the first vaccination. *Journal of American Academic Dermatology*, *44*, 348–350.

Powell, J., Kirtschig, G., Allen, J., Dean, D., & Wojnarowska, F. (2001). Mixed immunobullous disease of childhood: A good response to antimicrobials. *British Journal of Dermatology*, *144*(4), 769–774.

ALLISON KATZ
Rutgers University

BUREAU OF EDUCATION FOR THE HANDICAPPED

The Bureau of Education for the Handicapped (BEH) was created in 1966 to administer all U.S. Office of Education programs designed for individuals with disabilities. During the late 1960s and early 1970s, BEH administered newly created federal programs for individuals with disabilities, including regional resource centers that provided testing to determine the special education needs of disabled children. It also administered service centers for the deaf-blind; offered technical assistance on programs for the gifted and talented; provided funds for recruiting and training special education personnel; created experimental preschool and early education programs that could serve as models for school districts; and mounted research projects concerning individuals with disabilities. Eventually, BEH's responsibility was extended to include the provision of technical assistance, compliance monitoring, and evaluation of state education agency and local school district implementation of PL 93–380, the Education Amendments of 1974, and PL 94–142, the Education of All Handicapped Children Act of 1975. The BEH was succeeded in name but not in authority and responsibility by the Office of Special Education when the U.S. Department of Education was created in 1980. For a more detailed description of federal legislation and the role of BEH, see Weintraub, Abeson, Ballard, and LaVor (1976).

REFERENCE

Weintraub, F. J., Abeson, A., Ballard, J., & LaVor, M. L. (1976). *Public policy and the education of exceptional children*. Reston, VA: Council for Exceptional Children.

ROLAND K. YOSHIDA
Fordham University

BUREAU OF INDIAN EDUCATION

Formerly known as the Office of Indian Education Programs, the Bureau of Indian Education (BIE) supervises the policies and procedures of educating and appropriating funds for tribal families. The mission of the BIE is to provide opportunities and education to Indians by managing and staying abreast on policies and procedures of Indian education. Laws such as the No Child Left Behind Act of 2001 measure the accountability of schools for improving academic and behavior services with the U.S. Department of Education supplemental funds received through the Bureau.

The BIE fulfills its mission through its organization located in Washington, DC, as well as in 25 offices throughout the United States. Currently the BIE funds 183 schools serving approximately 42,000 Indian students.

The Bureau of Indian Education maintains an informative webpage http://www.bie.edu.

ELAINE FLETCHER-JANZEN
Chicago School of Professional Psychology

See also Cultural Bias in Testing

BURKS' BEHAVIOR RATING SCALES, SECOND EDITION (BBRS-2)

The Burks' Behavior Rating Scales (BBRS-2) is used to evaluate children ranging in age from preschool to 12th grade. Teacher and parent rating inventories are used to identify the type and severity of problem behaviors exhibited by referred children ages 4 to 18. The BBRS-2 is available in both teacher and parent rating forms using 100 items to measure how infrequent behaviors occur in typically developing children and having the teacher and parent rate the child on a 5-point scale of how often the child being evaluated demonstrates the behaviors. A nationally representative sample of 2,864 individuals was used to standardize the BBRS-3 demonstrating strong psychomeasurement scores in areas of reliability and validity.

This rating scale's practicality quickly helps educators identify children demonstrating problem behavior in schools (Burks, 1977). Outcome measures are divided into seven scale areas: disruptive behavior, attention and impulse control problems, emotional problems, social withdrawal, ability deficits, physical deficits, and weak self-confidence (Lerner, 1985). Scores obtained for the BBRS-2 can be used to define personality areas which require further evaluation, identify behaviors which are interfering with school performance, determine which children demonstrating behavior problems will benefit from special education services, and provide parents with objective information on creating and implementing intervention plans.

REFERENCES

Burks, H. F. (1977). *Burks' Behavior Rating Scales-2*. Los Angeles, CA: Western Psychological Services.

Lerner, J. V. (1985). Review of the Burks' behavior rating scales. In D. J. Keyser & R. C. Sweetland (Eds.), *Test critiques* (Vol. *2*, pp. 108–112). Kansas City, MO: Test Corporation of America.

GEORGE MCCLOSKEY
Philadelphia College of Osteopathic Medicine

See also Behavior Problem Checklist, Revised

BUROS MENTAL MEASUREMENTS YEARBOOK

There are 16 *Mental Measurements Yearbooks (MMYs)*. The yearbooks, which originated in 1938 (Buros, 1938), provide test users with factual information on all known tests published separately in the English-speaking countries of the world. In addition, the books contain test reviews written by professional people representing a variety of viewpoints. The volumes are also sources of comprehensive bibliographies for specific tests, and references relevant to the tests.

The purpose of all the *MMYs* is to provide a forum in which tests can be reviewed candidly to facilitate intelligent consumer choice and use of tests. The most recent *MMY* in its 17th Edition (Geisinger, Spies, Carlson, & Plake, 2007) contains descriptive information on new or revised tests, test reviews, extensive listings of test references and reviewer references, several indexes including indexes of test titles, classified subject areas, publishers, scores, and names of test authors and reviewers. In addition, the Buros Library of Mental Measurements provides qualitative reviews on computer-based test interpretation systems (Plake, Conoley, Kramer, & Murphy, 1989).

The books are published by the Buros Institute of Mental Measurements, located since 1979 at the University of Nebraska, Lincoln, Department of Educational Psychology. The institute, established originally by Oscar K. Buros, has published more than 20 volumes (edited by Buros) relating to test description and review. Online access to the *MMY* can be found at http://www.unl.edu/buros/bimm/html/17tests.html.

REFERENCES

Buros, O. K. (1938). *The 1938 mental measurements yearbook*. Highland Park, NJ: Gryphon.

Geisinger, K. F., Spies, R. A., Carlson, J. F., & Plake, B. S. (2007). *The seventeenth mental measurements yearbook*. Lincoln, NE: Buros Institute.

Plake, B. S., Conoley, J. C., Kramer, J. J., & Murphy, L. L. (1989). Buros bulletin. *Educational Measurement: Issues & Practices*, *8*, 20–21.

JANE CLOSE CONOLEY
University of Nebraska
First edition

ELAINE FLETCHER-JANZEN
Chicago School of Professional Psychology
Third edition

See also Buros, Oscar K.; Tests in Print

BUROS, OSCAR K. (1905–1978)

Oscar K. Buros is remembered internationally as the foremost proponent of critical analyses of educational and psychological tests. Buros attended the State Normal School in Superior, Wisconsin, from 1922 to 1924 and completed his undergraduate education at the University of Minnesota in 1925. Buros received his graduate degree from the Teachers College, Columbia University. He accepted a faculty appointment at Rutgers University in 1932 and was a member of that faculty until his retirement in 1965. During World War II, he was in charge of testing for the U.S. Army's specialized training program, and later an adviser on the assessment of leadership at West Point.

He married Luella Gubrud who, an accomplished artist in her own right, later shared with him the responsibilities for the famous *Buros Mental Measurements Yearbook* (*MMY*) series. It was she who saw the last edition through to its completion following his death on March 19, 1978. Buros published the first *MMY* in 1938. Seven other *Yearbooks* followed, as well as the *Mental Measurements Yearbook* monographs series (1968, 1970, and 1975a–i) and the *Tests in Print* series (1961, 1974).

He was the recipient of many professional honors and awards. Some of these were citations in 1953 from both the American Educational Research Association and the American Psychological Association for excellence in contributions to measurement; a senior Fulbright lectureship in statistics at Makerere University College, Uganda, 1956 to 1957; the 1965 Phi Delta Kappa research award; and in 1973 both an honorary Doctor of Science degree from Upsala College and the Distinguished Service to

Measurement Award from the Educational Testing Service. Buros was a fellow of the American Statistical Association and the American Psychological Association. Rutgers University's Graduate School of Applied and Professional Psychology established a professorship in Buros's honor in 1985.

In 1979, the Buros Institute of Mental Measurements was moved to the University of Nebraska-Lincoln. The institute has continued the Buros tradition by publishing *Tests in Print III* (Mitchell, 1983) and up to 12 *Mental Measurements Yearbooks* (Conoley, Impara, & Murphy, 1995).

REFERENCES

Buros, O. K. (1938). *The 1938 mental measurements yearbook*. Highland Park, NJ: Gryphon.

Buros, O. K. (1961). *Tests in print*. Highland Park, NJ: Gryphon.

Buros, O. K. (1968). *Reading tests and reviews I*. Highland Park, NJ: Gryphon.

Buros, O. K. (1970). *Personality tests and reviews I*. Highland Park, NJ: Gryphon.

Buros, O. K. (1974). *Tests in print II*. Highland Park, NJ: Gryphon.

Buros, O. K. (1975a). *Personality tests and reviews II*. Highland Park, NJ: Gryphon.

Buros, O. K. (1975b). *Reading tests and reviews II*. Highland Park, NJ: Gryphon.

Buros, O. K. (1975c). *Intelligence tests and reviews II*. Highland Park, NJ: Gryphon.

Buros, O. K. (1975d). *English tests and reviews*. Highland Park, NJ: Gryphon.

Buros, O. K. (1975e). *Foreign language tests and reviews*. Highland Park, NJ: Gryphon.

Buros, O. K. (1975f). *Mathematics tests and reviews*. Highland Park, NJ: Gryphon.

Buros, O. K. (1975g). *Science tests and reviews*. Highland Park, NJ: Gryphon.

Buros, O. K. (1975h). *Social studies tests reviews*. Highland Park, NJ: Gryphon.

Buros, O. K. (1975i). *Vocational tests and reviews*. Highland Park, NJ: Gryphon.

Conoley, J. C., Impara, J. C., & Murphy, L. L. (Eds.). (1995). *The twelfth mental measurements yearbook*. Lincoln, NE: Buros Institute of Mental Measurements.

Mitchell, J. V. Jr. (1983). *Tests in print III*. Lincoln, NE: Buros Institute of Mental Measurements.

Mitchell, J. V. Jr. (1985). *The ninth mental measurements yearbook*. Lincoln, NE: Buros Institute of Mental Measurements.

JANE CLOSE CONOLEY
University of Nebraska

See *also* Tests in Print

BURT, SIR CYRIL (1883–1971)

Sir Cyril Burt became the first psychologist in the world to be employed by a school system when he was appointed to the position of psychologist with the London County Council in 1913. Burt's career centered around the application of psychology to the study and education of children. He made pioneering investigations in the areas of intellectual developmental disabilities, delinquency, and the genetics of intelligence, and conducted studies that served as models of the application of the scientific method to the study of human characteristics. Burt developed numerous tests for use by school psychologists and published his influential *Factors of the Mind* in 1941. He was co-editor of the *British Journal of Statistical Psychology*.

From 1931 until his retirement in 1950, Burt was professor of psychology at University College, London, where he devoted most of his attention to the training of psychologists and the continuation of his research and writing. He was knighted in 1946.

Sadly, Burt's work and reputation are marred by findings that he deliberately fabricated data in some of his best-known studies. These acts of fraud cast doubt on his research findings, but do not erase his great contributions to psychology as a clinician, theoretician, and teacher (Hearnshaw, 1979).

REFERENCES

Burt, C. (1941). *The factors of the mind: An introduction to factor analysis in psychology*. New York, NY: Macmillan.

Hearnshaw, L. S. (1979). *Cyril Burt, psychologist*. Ithaca, NY: Cornell University Press.

PAUL IRVINE
Katonah, New York

C

CAFÉ AU LAIT SPOTS

Café au lait spots are areas of patchy pigmentation of skin, usually light brown in color. The long axis of the café au lait spot or oval is situated along a cutaneous (skin) nerve tract. The spots are usually present at birth but may become apparent in the first few years of life (Hull, 2000). They are so-named because of their resemblance in color to coffee with cream. They are of diagnostic significance because they may indicate the presence of serious disease such as neurofibromatosis, polyostotic fibrous dysplasia, or tuberous sclerosis (*Blakiston's*, 1979; Johnson, 1979). Café au lait spots may be found in normal individuals.

When six or more café au lait spots are present and they are larger than 1.5 cm in diameter, neurofibromatosis is suspected (Johnson, 1979; Steinman & Nussbaum, 2003). Neurofibromatosis, also known as Von Recklinghausen's disease, is a genetic disorder inherited as an autosomal dominant trait (Batshaw & Perret, 1981). In addition to the presence of café au lait spots, which exist at birth and hence aid in the diagnosis of this condition, other symptoms include multiple skin-colored tumors or nodules and freckles of the axillae (armpits), which represent the Crowe's sign of neurofibromatosis.

Neurofibromatosis may have numerous neurological, psychological, and educational implications. Tumors or neurofibromas typically develop prior to puberty. These tumors may be associated with the spinal or cranial nerves and hence may result in sensory deficits such as visual or hearing impairment. Enlargement and deformation of the bones and scoliosis (curvature of the spine) may occur. Hypertension may be present in young victims of this condition. There is reported to be an increased incidence of mental retardation (Johnson, 1979) and school problems associated with neurofibromatosis (Batshaw & Perret, 1981). In severe cases, the presence of multiple contiguous tumors produces elephantiasis neuromatosa, a cosmetically disfiguring condition. While skin tumors may be removed, there is some evidence these may recur and multiply (*Fact Sheet*, 1983).

In addition to neurofibromatosis, café au lait spots also have been observed in other neurocutaneous syndromes such as tuberous sclerosis (Bourneville's disease; Rosenberg, 1979). Also inherited as an autosomal dominant trait, tuberous sclerosis is characterized by nevi or moles on the face, epilepsy, and mental retardation (Rosenberg).

The course of tuberous sclerosis begins with the onset of epilepsy and declining mental ability during the first decade, with development of facial lesions around the cheeks and nose several years later (Rosenberg, 1979).

Café au lait spots occurring in the size and number as noted previously are considered diagnostically significant in neurofibromatosis. Ninety percent of afflicted individuals are reported to exhibit them at birth (Johnson, 1979). Because their presence is associated with serious medical conditions such as neurofibromatosis and tuberous sclerosis, identification of numerous café au lait spots in children without medical diagnoses warrants referral to a physician. Educational management of children who have been diagnosed as having neurofibromatosis or tuberous sclerosis should be conducted on an individual basis because the severity and expression of symptoms vary widely.

Characteristics

1. Flat, sharply demarcated oval patches
2. Light to medium-brown in color (coffee color)
3. Present at birth or emerge during childhood
4. Commonly benign, but possibly associated with neurofibromatosis

---

REFERENCES

Batshaw, M. L., & Perret, Y. M. (1981). *Children with handicaps: A medical primer*. Baltimore, MD: Brookes.

Blakiston's Gould medical dictionary (4th ed.). (1979). New York, NY: McGraw-Hill.

Fact sheet: Neurofibromatosis. (1983). Bethesda, MD: National Institute of Neurological and Communicative Disorders and Stroke.

Hull, J. (2000). *Parent's common sense encyclopedia*. National Organization for Rare Disorders. Retrieved from http://www.drhull.com/EncyMaster/C/cafe-au-lait.html

Johnson, M. (1979). Certain cutaneous diseases with significant systemic manifestations. In P. B. Beeson, W. McDermott, & J. B. Wyngaarden (Eds.), *Cecil textbook of medicine* (15th ed., pp. 2266–2312). Philadelphia, PA: Saunders.

Rosenberg, R. N. (1979). Inherited degenerative diseases of the nervous system. In P. B. Beeson, W. McDermott, & J. B. Wyngaarden (Eds.), *Cecil textbook of medicine* (15th ed., pp. 764–772). Philadelphia, PA: Saunders.

Steinman, D. R., & Nussbaum, N. (2003). In E. Fletcher-Janzen & C. R. Reynolds (Eds.), *Childhood disorders diagnostic desk reference* (p. 101). Hoboken, NJ: Wiley.

CATHY F. TELZROW
Kent State University

See also Minor Physical Anomalies; Neurofibromatosis

CALCULATORS

Calculators can be considered Mindtools rather than simply modification tools. A Mindtool functions as an intellectual partner that shares the cognitive load by carrying out the actual computations. Calculators become Mindtools for students when calculator choice and use is taught and guided by skillful instruction (Jonassen, 2006). "Since much of the mathematics of today is intricately interwoven with technology, the teacher must be able to understand and use the technology of mathematics in its instruction" (Grandgenett, 2008, p. 8). "Students benefit when their teachers receive professional development that is specific to calculator use in math instruction" (Heller, Curtis, Jaffe, & Verboncoeur, 2005, p. 20). Mathematics has moved from an era of hand computation practice to an age of sense-making (Woodward & Montague, 2002). Difficulties with mental math as well as problems with retention of math skills are symptoms of dyscalculia, which seems to affect males and females equally (James, 2007).

Some of these students have trouble learning the arithmetic tables; others never comprehend algorithms of addition, subtraction, multiplication, and division; still others either have problems understanding the concept of numbers or cannot write, read, or identify the correct word to the numeral (Shalev & Gross-Tsur, 2001).

Students with mild dyscalculia will benefit from the use of a calculator, particularly a graphing calculator that keeps track of what was keyed in (James, 2007). Construction calculators can also keep track of previous keystrokes. There are many types of calculators that can help students and teachers reason and make sense with quantities as well as calculate.

Four-Function Calculators

Calculators limited to the four basic functions of addition, subtraction, multiplication, and division are referred to as four-function calculators. These calculators can be purchased for about a dollar at many grocery stores, are built into many checkbooks, and differing versions can even be freely accessed on the web. Occasionally these calculators have percent keys and a limited memory function. The order of algebraic operations is not usually programmed into these simple calculators.

Construction Calculators

Calculators such as the Jobber 6 can perform unit conversions, and automatically solve triangles and compute slopes, as well as area and/or volume. These calculators perform addition, subtraction, multiplication, and division on any units in any format, giving the output in the user-specified format. Costing less than $100, and small enough to fit in a shirt pocket, these calculators are primarily built for tradespersons such as builders, carpenters, engineers, draftspersons, fabricators, shop employees, and contractors.

Scientific Calculators

Calculators able to carry out many scientific functions such as the six trigonometric functions, inverse trigonometric functions, exponents, reciprocals, statistical measures, as well as the four basic functions are referred to as scientific calculators. This type of calculator can be purchased for less than $50 at most office supply outlets, and versions can be accessed on the web or cell phone apps. The order of algebraic operations is not usually programmed into scientific calculators, although some scientific calculators use reverse Polish notation (RPN).

Graphing Calculators

Calculators able to carry out basic operations as well as operations on functions, perform scientific and statistical functions, build tables, find regression equations, and display many different types of graphs are referred to as graphing calculators. Graphing calculators are typically introduced in high school mathematics and science classes, although there are middle-grades versions of graphing calculators available. Most of these calculators use the order of algebraic operations, although some brands use reverse Polish notation (RPN). Some graphing calculators containing a Calculator Algebraic System (CAS) can actually carry out symbolic manipulation of variables such as factoring a polynomial. Some graphing calculators have a touchscreen as well as companion computer software. These calculators can be purchased for about $100 each and are powerful computing devices. There are many cell phone apps for graphing calculators.

Talking/Large Display Calculators

Many calculators can be procured with speech or tone features. Software for a talking graphics calculator includes graph displays as audio tones and costs about $350. Desktop four-function talking calculators cost under $20, or include an earpiece for another $10. These calculators can announce the result in either digits or units, as well as utilize a large digit display. These features can help special needs students with visual and/or auditory disabilities.

Students and teachers should make themselves aware of the type of calculators allowed on various assessments that face today's students as they seek entrance to the workforce, technical school, or higher education. In order to thrive quantitatively in today's technological world, students as well as teachers need to be well versed in the choice and use of available calculators.

REFERENCES

Grandgenett, N. F. (2008). Perhaps a matter of imagination: TPCK in mathematics education. In AACTE (Ed.), *Handbook of technological pedagogical content knowledge (TPCK) for educators* (pp. 145–165). New York, NY: Routledge.

Heller, J. I., Curtis, D. A., Jaffe, R., & Verboncoeur, C. J. (2005). *Impact of handheld graphing calculator use on student achievement in algebra.* Oakland, CA: Heller Research Associates.

James, A. N. (2007). Gender differences and the teaching of mathematics. *Inquiry, 12*(1), 14–25.

Jonassen, D. H. (2006). *Modeling with technology: Mindtools for conceptual change.* Upper Saddle River, NJ: Pearson Prentice Hall.

Shalev, R. S., & Gross-Tsur, V. (2001). Developmental dyscalculia. *Pediatric Neurology, 24,* 337–342.

Woodward, J., & Montague, M. (2002). Meeting the challenge of mathematics reform for students with LD. *Journal of Special Education, 36,* 89–101. doi:10.1177/00224669020360020401

ANNA PAT L. ALPERT
Texas A&M University
Fourth edition

CALDWELL, BETTYE M. (1924–   )

Bettye M. Caldwell received her BA (1945) from Baylor University, her MA (1946) from the University of Iowa, and her PhD (1951) in psychology from Washington University. Caldwell's career, which has spanned more than 30 years, reflects her interest in early childhood education and development. Currently, she is a Donaghey Distinguished Professor of Education at the University of Arkansas at Little Rock.

Since the late 1960s, when Caldwell was a member of the National Advisory Committee for Research and Evaluation for Project Head Start, she has maintained an interest in the impact of research on social policy. She has devoted her efforts to early intervention programs for very young handicapped children, demonstration day care centers, and training parents and others who work with young children. By studying the impact of day care on factors such as intellectual and social development and mother–child attachment, Caldwell has shown that day care can have a significant, positive impact on children, especially those from disadvantaged backgrounds (Caldwell, 1977).

One of Caldwell's major research interests has been the measurement of the quality of a child's home environment. The HOME (Home Observation for Measurement of the Environment) Inventory, which resulted from this work, is used worldwide as a measure of the learning environment within the home. Having such information available is vital both for the determination of the extent to which atypical development is due to inadequate or inappropriate environmental stimulation, and for the design of intervention programs (Bradley & Caldwell, 1984).

Caldwell has been involved as one of the major investigators in a large, 10-site study concerned with the effects of different patterns of child care during early infancy. She has also developed a unique training program for caregivers in educare settings that integrates knowledge and skills from both nursing and education. The training is based on contemporary research on brain development and early experience. Caregivers are taught to introduce learning activities that will meet the needs of the developing brain at each chronological age period and thereby facilitate emotional and cognitive advances in the children.

A leader in her field, Caldwell has been president of the National Association for the Education of Young Children (1982–1984) and editor of the journal *Child Development* (1968–1971). She has served on the editorial board and the board of directors for other journals and organizations. She also has earned international notice, serving as a U.S. delegate to the U.S.S.R. and the People's Republic of China to study early education programs in those countries.

Dr. Caldwell has published over 200 articles and books dating back to 1951. She has also written many articles for magazines and has written and produced several educational films and videos.

REFERENCES

Bradley, R. H., & Caldwell, B. M. (1984). 174 children: A study of the relation between home environment and mental development in the first five years. In A. Gottfried (Ed.), *Home environment and early cognitive development* (pp. 5–56). New York, NY: Academic Press.

Caldwell, B. M. (1977). Child development and social policy. In M. Scott & S. Grimmett (Eds.), *Current issues in child development.* Washington, DC: National Association for the Education of Young Children.

ANN E. LUPKOWSKI
Texas A&M University
First edition

TAMARA J. MARTIN
The University of Texas of the Permian Basin
Second edition

CALIFORNIA VERBAL LEARNING TEST, CHILDREN'S VERSION

The California Verbal Learning Test, Children's Version (CVLT-C, 1994) is an individually administered measure used to assess verbal learning and memory in children and adolescents ages 5 through 16.11 years. The test contains 30 items to recall from two lists. Administration time is 15 to 20 minutes, and a 20-minute time delay used to assess delayed recall. The CVLT-C uses two hypothetical shopping lists, the "Monday List" and the "Tuesday List." In the first five trials, the child is presented the "Monday List" and is asked to recall all 15 words from the list. The "Tuesday List," which contains 15 new words to be recalled, is then presented as an interference task. The Tuesday trial is followed by a short-delay free-recall trial and short-delay cued-recall trial of the Monday list (Ogletree & LeAdelle, 1998). After a 20-minute delay in which nonverbal intelligence can be assessed, a long-delay free-recall trial, long-delay cued-recall trial, and a recognition trial of the "Monday List" are administered. The CVLT-C requires an administration manual with verbal prompts for the instructor, and a record form to record the child's responses (Delis, Kramer, Kaplan, & Ober, 1994). The record form contains the items from both lists and gives space to record responses from each trial.

The CVLT-C was co-normed with the Children's Category Test (CCT). The standardization sample consisted of 920 children in 12 age groups ranging from 5 through 16 years of age. The test was standardized using a stratified random sample of children based on data from the March 1988 U.S. Bureau of Census. The data from the sample was stratified along the categories of age, gender, race/ethnicity, geographic region, and parent education level. For the stratification variables selected, the CVLT-C standardization sample strongly approximated the population of school-age children represented in the 1988 U.S. census data.

Reliability for the CVLT-C was evaluated using three separate indices. The first index assessed consistency of performance across trials. Odd–even reliability had an average coefficient of .88; the coefficient alpha was an average of .85. The second reliability index evaluated consistency of performance across semantically unrelated item sets. The average reliability coefficient was .72. The third reliability index measured across-word consistency. The average odd–even correlation was .83 and the average alpha coefficient was .81. These figures indicate that overall the trials show a high degree of internal consistency. Test–retest stability was assessed by retesting a group of 106 children. The median retest interval was 28 days. The correlations ranged from .38 to .90 for the 8-year-old group, .17 to .77 for the 12-year-old group, and .31 to .85 for the 16-year-old group. Although these are modest levels of reliability, they are within the expected limits given the kind of test. The CVLT-C was developed based on research

in cognitive science research and is therefore considered both content and criterion valid. Construct validity was evaluated using factor analysis. For the CVLT-C, factors whose eigenvalues were 1 or greater were retained, and loadings on a factor greater than .40 were considered significant. The factor analysis revealed that the CVLT-C corresponds to the Adult CVLT in terms of factor loading.

REFERENCES

Ogletree, B. T., & LeAdelle, P. (1998) in Impara, J. C., & Plake, B. S. (Eds.). *The thirteenth mental measurements yearbook*. Lincoln, NE: Buros Institute of Mental Measurements.

Delis, D., Kramer, J., Kaplan, E., & Ober, B. (1994). *California Verbal Learning Test—Children's Version manual*. New York, NY: Harcourt Brace.

Levin, H. S., Song, J., & Scheibel, R. S. (2000). Dissociation of frequency and recency processing from list recall after severe closed head injury in children and adolescents. *Journal of Clinical & Experimental Neuropsychology, 22*, 1–15.

Mahone, E. M., Koth, C. W., Cutting, L., Singer, H. S., & Denckla, M. B. (2001). Executive function in fluency and recall measures among children with Tourette syndrome or ADHD. *Journal of the International Neuropsychological Society, 7*, 102–111.

Yeates, K. O., Blumenstein, E., & Patterson, C. M. (1995). Verbal learning and memory following pediatric closed-head injury. *Journal of the International Neuropsychological Society, 1*, 78–87.

RON DUMONT
Fairleigh Dickinson University

JOHN O. WILLIS
Rivier College

KATHLEEN VIEZEL
Fairleigh Dickinson University

JAMIE ZIBULSKY
Fairleigh Dickinson University
Fourth edition

CALIFORNIA VERBAL LEARNING TEST, SECOND EDITION

The California Verbal Learning Test, Second Edition (CVLT-II, 2000) is an individually administered measure used to assess verbal learning and memory in adults ages 16 through 89 years. The Standard and Alternate Forms of the test contain 16 items to recall from two lists. The Short Form of the test contains two lists of nine words. Administration time for the Standard and Alternate Forms is 30 minutes and a 30-minute time delay used to assess delayed recall. The Short Form takes 15 minutes to administer, plus a 15-minute delay interval.

The CVLT-II uses two hypothetical shopping lists, the "Monday List" and the "Tuesday List." In the first five trials, the examinee is presented the "Monday List" and is asked to recall all 16 words from the list. The "Tuesday List," which contains 16 new words to be recalled, is then presented as an interference task. The Tuesday trial is followed by a short-delay free-recall trial and short-delay cued-recall trial of the Monday list. After a 30-minute delay in which nonverbal intelligence can be assessed, a long-delay free-recall trial, long-delay cued-recall trial, and a recognition trial of the "Monday List" are administered. An addition to the CVLT-II from the original version is a forced-choice recognition trial, which is designed to detect malingering. The Short Form can be used when administration time is limited and the Alternate Form can be used when it is necessary to retest an examinee. The CVLT-II contains an administration manual with verbal prompts for the instructor, and three versions of the record form to record the examinee's responses. The record forms contain the items from both lists and gives space to record responses from each trial.

The CVLT-II was co-normed with the Wechsler Abbreviated Scale of Intelligence (WASI) and the Delis-Kaplan Executive Function System (DKEFS). The test was standardized using a sample comprised of 1,087 adults matched to population data from the March 1999 U.S. Census. The data from the sample was stratified along the categories of age, gender, race/ethnicity, geographic region, and education level. The CVLT-II yields raw scores that are then transformed to standardized scores. Recall trials 1–5 were scaled using a normalized T-metric with a mean of 50 and a standard deviation of 10. All other scores on the test were normed on a linear z-score metric, with a mean of 0 and a standard deviation of 1.0. Norms were established for seven unique age groups ranging from 16 through 89 years of age (Stricker, Brown, Wixted, Baldo, & Delis, 2002).

Reliability for the CVLT-II was evaluated using three separate indices. The first index assessed consistency of performance across trials. Split-half reliability for the total sample was .94. The second reliability index evaluated consistency of performance in the four categories of words on the list across all five trials. The overall reliability for the total sample was .82. The third reliability index examined the number of times each of the words was recalled across the five initial trials. The split-half reliability for the total sample was .78. These figures indicate that overall the trials show a high degree of internal consistency. The reliability of the Alternate Form based on administration of both the Standard and Alternate Forms was evaluated by administering both forms to a sample of 288 adults with an average 21 days between administrations. Reliability coefficients for the key CVLT-II variables ranged from .72 to .79. Test–retest stability was assessed by retesting a group of 78 adults ranging in age from 16 to 88 years, with a median retest interval of 21 days. The correlation of scores between the two test administrations was .82. The validity of the CVLT-II was based on the validity information for the original CVLT. Construct validity for the original CVLT was examined in over 200 research studies. Since there is a great deal of concurrent validity between the CVLT and the CVLT-II, this is an indication of a comparable level of validity in the second version of the CVLT. Construct validity was evaluated using methods such as factor analysis to test the relationship between the test and variables known to account for variability in learning and memory and by correlating performance on the CVLT-II to verbal intelligence (Hubley & Cederick, 2005).

REFERENCES

Delis, D., Kramer, J, Kaplan, E., & Ober, B. (2000). *California Verbal Learning Test—Second Edition manual*. Harcourt Brace.

Hubley, A. M., & Lindskog, C. O. In Spies, R. A., & Plake, B. S. (Eds.). (2005). *The sixteenth mental measurements yearbook*. Lincoln, NE: Buros Institute of Mental Measurements.

Stricker, J. L., Brown, G. G., Wixted, J., Baldo, J. V., & Delis, D. C. (2002). New semantic and serial clustering indices for the California Verbal Learning Test—Second Edition: Background, rationale, and formulae. *Journal of the International Neuropsychological Society, 8*, 425–435.

RON DUMONT
Fairleigh Dickinson University

JOHN O. WILLIS
Rivier College

KATHLEEN VIEZEL
Fairleigh Dickinson University

JAMIE ZIBULSKY
Fairleigh Dickinson University
Fourth edition

CAMPBELL, SIR FRANCIS JOSEPH (1832–1914)

Francis J. Campbell was born on a farm in Tennessee on October 9, 1832. Blinded in an accident at the age of 3, he was educated at the newly opened Tennessee State Institution for the Blind, where he later served as a teacher of music while studying at the University of Tennessee. Following a period as a student at Harvard University and then as a teacher of the blind in Wisconsin, he became an instructor at Perkins Institution and Massachusetts Asylum for the Blind, where he served for 11 years as head of the music department.

A talented pianist, Campbell left Perkins to continue his music education in Europe and to study methods of teaching the blind. While in London he met Thomas Rhodes Armitage, a blind physician who had just completed joining together Britain's numerous organizations for the blind into a federation that ultimately became known as the Royal National Institute for the Blind.

Campbell's account of the large number of students at Perkins whom he had helped prepare for successful careers as professional musicians led Armitage to establish a music school to train blind children, with Campbell as headmaster. Starting in 1872 with two students, the school ultimately became the Royal Normal College and Academy of Music, with an enrollment, by 1885, of 170 students (Ross, 1951). Campbell's original faculty included a number of teachers from Perkins, and through the years he maintained a continuing exchange of teachers with Perkins and other schools in the United States. As a result, the Royal Normal College and Academy of Music probably had more influence on American teaching methods than any other foreign school. The institution, under Campbell, combined general education and physical training with careful vocational preparation, job placement, and follow-up after graduation. Between 80 and 90% of the graduates became self-supporting, mostly as musicians, teachers, and technicians trained in piano tuning and repair. This unprecedented achievement stimulated an emphasis on vocational preparation in schools for the blind throughout the world (Koester, 1976).

Campbell believed strongly in the value of physical exercise, and took great pride in his own physical prowess—he once scaled the formidable Mont Blanc, a feat that he considered one of the crowning achievements of his life. He viewed physical training as an essential ingredient in any educational program preparing the blind for active and productive lives and developed an extensive physical education program that greatly influenced other schools for the blind.

In recognition of his work on behalf of the blind, Campbell was knighted by King Edward VII in 1909. Campbell retired as headmaster in 1912. He died on June 30, 1914.

REFERENCES

Koestler, F. A. (1976). *The unseen minority: A social history of blindness in America.* New York, NY: McKay.

Ross, I. (1951). *Journey into light.* New York, NY: Appleton-Century-Crofts.

PAUL IRVINE
Katonah, New York

CAMP, BONNIE W. (1931–   )

Bonnie Camp received her BA from Mississippi State College for Women in 1948, and her MA and PhD in clinical psychology from Indiana University in 1954. She went on to receive her MD in 1965 from the University of Colorado School of Medicine and pediatric training from the University of Colorado Health Sciences Center. In 1972, she received a Research Career Award from NIMH for her studies on learning disabilities. She also served on the faculty of Pediatrics and Psychiatry at the University of Colorado School of Medicine, and was director of the JFK Child Development Center at the University of Colorado Health Sciences Center before retiring in 1993.

While employed as a pediatrician in the Denver Health and Hospitals Neighborhood Health Center, Camp organized a tutorial reading program for children with severe reading delay in the center's catchment area using community aides, older students, and volunteers. The program was eventually extended to schools throughout the Denver School District.

Camp is best known for her development of the Think Aloud Program (Bash & Camp, 1985a, 1985b, 1986; Camp & Bash, 1981, 1985). Think Aloud is a cognitive behavior modification program designed to improve social and cognitive problem-solving skills in young children. It was conceived as a training program to decrease impulsivity, encourage consideration of alternatives and plan a course of action. It emphasizes the use of cognitive modeling as a teaching tool whereby teachers model their own strategies for thinking through problems. Camp is currently professor emeritus of pediatrics and psychiatry at the University of Colorado School of Medicine.

REFERENCES

Bash, M. A. S., & Camp, B. W. (1985a). *The Think Aloud Classroom Program for grades 3 and 4.* Champaign, IL: Research Press.

Bash, M. A. S., & Camp, B. W. (1985b). *The Think Aloud Classroom Program for grades 5 and 6.* Champaign, IL: Research Press.

Bash, M. A. S., & Camp, B. A. (1986). Training teachers in the Think Aloud Classroom Program. In G. Cartledge & J. Milburn (Eds.), *Teaching social skills to children: Innovative approaches.* New York, NY: Pergamon Press.

Camp, B. W., & Bash, M. A. S. (1981). *Think Aloud: Increasing social and cognitive skills—A problem-solving program for children.* Champaign, IL: Research Press.

Camp, B. W., & Bash, M. A. S. (1985). *The Think Aloud Classroom Program for grades 1 and 2.* Champaign, IL: Research Press.

CAMPHILL COMMUNITY MOVEMENT

The Camphill Community (movement) was founded by Karl Koenig, a respected Viennese pediatrician (1902–1966) after he fled the Nazi powers of central Europe in 1939. The name Camphill refers to the group's first house in Aberdeen, Scotland (Baron & Haldane, 1991).

The Camphill Community is based on the writings of Rudolph Steiner (1861–1925). It works for a full understanding of people's spiritual being, eternal purpose, and earthly tasks. The goals of Steiner's work (known as *anthroposophy*) include allowing all human beings, disabled or not, to develop to their potential and to find a productive place in society. The fostering and development of individual human dignity is of paramount importance.

Camphill villages (there are 80) are currently found in countries worldwide, with 7 in the United States. Despite minor differences, village life centers around the family, community, and productive, meaningful work. The family typically consists of parents, children, and a number of individuals with intellectual developmental disabilities living and working together, free from labels and distinctions. Mutual responsibility is stressed; no salaries are paid but individuals have their needs met by the community.

The Camphill Special School, Glenmoore, Pennsylvania, provides services to both elementary and secondary school-age children and also provides transition services for adults moving into the community. Its program complements the philosophies of the larger Camphill Community and provides the "structure, rhythm, regularity, and consistency" needed for curative education. Each child works from an individual education program based on an adaptation of the Waldorf School movement. The education of the whole child is stressed; specific therapies (painting, speech, medicine, music) are provided depending on need. Older students are prepared vocationally for life after graduation through training in groundskeeping, woodwork, and household activities.

A 4-year training seminar is offered in the Beaver Run, Pennsylvania school. It is designed to train the individual in curative education using the Waldorf curriculum, as well as in all aspects of community living in the Camphill tradition.

Persons interested in joining or learning more about the Camphill communities are encouraged to contact them directly at their website (http://www.camphill specialschool.org).

REFERENCE

Baron, S., & Haldane, D. (1991). Approaching Camphill: From the boundary. *British Journal of Special Education*, 18(2), 75–78.

JOHN E. PORCELLA
Rhinebeck Country School

CAMPING FOR CHILDREN WITH DISABILITIES

Camping for children with disabilities is divided into two types—individual and organized camping. The camping areas used for individualized camping are either in developed or wilderness states. Developed campsites are usually near conveniences that facilitate their use by special needs campers (e.g., they offer amenities such as tent pads, electrical and water outlets, and restroom facilities). Their nature paths are wide and smooth to facilitate travel for children and youths who are wheelchair-bound or impaired in motor functioning (Gerstein, 1992; Sessoms, 1984).

Wilderness campgrounds have cruder facilities and fewer activity programs for the handicapped than developed camping areas. Most are designed for a low level of human use. They lack conveniences such as smooth paths and picnic facilities. As a rule, they are considered closed to the physically handicapped, though there are no limitations to other persons.

Organized camping has been defined as the merging of outdoor recreation and education in a campsite setting (Sessoms, 1984). Organized camping is carried out on day and residential bases. Activities at organized camps for disabled individuals range from general activities (such as sports and games, hobbies, arts and crafts, and drama) to special-purpose activities such as computer training and weight control. These camps are also likely to emphasize education and rehabilitation (Wiseman, 1982). Major emphases in organized camps are to foster socialization skills, the acceptance of responsibilities, and the learning of leisure skills, and to facilitate living in communal atmospheres.

Organized camping programs for children with disabilities are sponsored by the following types of agencies: (1) private or commercial campers agencies, whose fees come from their clients; (2) quasipublic agencies, some of whose funds come from donations and endowments while the balance is paid by the participants (e.g., Easter Seals and American Red Cross camps); and (3) public-camping programs supported and sponsored by either local or municipal parks and recreation systems, or by organizations serving the disabled and parent groups.

Four different types of organized camping programs may be distinguished. One type is camps that are located within communities where campers participate on a daily basis; these have accessible toilets, play, and eating areas. Another type is resident camps for children with special needs. These have cabins, dining halls, staff quarters, and indoor and outdoor recreation facilities. Their sessions last from 1 to 8 weeks. A third type is combination resident and daycamping opportunities that permit some campers to attend daily while others remain overnight. Finally, there are special-purpose camps that promote a single concept or activity such as a specific sport or religion (Wiseman, 1982).

Camps implement universal designs to meet the needs of all campers attending camp (i.e., involving all campers with disabilities in a normalized integrated camp program). Campers are evaluated for an integrated camping program on the basis of their level of functioning in camp activities. Campers with disabilities receive accomodations depending on their capabilities.

In integrative camping, campers with disabilities participate in all activities together with ablebodied campers. Camper's with disabilities often have the potential for regular group participation but may need additional modifications to camp activities in order to fully participate. Usually, children with disabilities engage in the same activities as typically developing campers and share the same facilities (Sessoms, 1984).

All camping activities are modified to the capabilities and interests to meet the individualized needs of students with disabilities. The American Camp Association (ACA) provides a very helpful website for persons searching for specific needs camps (http://www.acacamps.org/). This website creates a specific profile of the needs of the camper and possible opportunities.

REFERENCES

American Camp Association (ACA). (2012). *Search for camps for those with special needs*. Retrieved from http://www.acacamps.org/

American Camping Association standards for persons with special needs (Part IIC). (1980). Martinsville, IN: Bradford Woods.

Gerstein, J. (1992). *Direction of experiential therapy and adventure-based counseling programs*. (ERIC Clearinghouse No. ED39 80 21)

Sessoms, H. (1984). *Leisure services* (3rd ed.). Englewood Cliffs, NJ: Prentice Hall.

Wiseman, D. (1982). *A practical approach to adapted physical education*. Reading, MA: Addison-Wesley.

Thomas R. Burke
Hunter College,
City University of New York

See also **Equine Therapy; Recreational Therapy**

CANADA, SPECIAL EDUCATION IN

Canada is one of the few countries in the world that does not have a national education system; education is the exclusive jurisdiction of the 10 provinces and 3 territories[1]

that make up the country. These provinces/territories are unique in terms of political affiliation, population size, geographic area, proximity to urban centres, and linguistic and cultural representation. As a result, the legislation, regulations, and policies that guide education in general and special education in particular vary widely.

Within each province/territory, parents have the choice of publicly funded schools (Catholic or nondenominational), private schools, or home schooling for their children. While most students in Canada attend publicly funded schools, it is estimated that approximately 5% attend private schools (e.g., academic, religious, special needs) and a further 1–2% receive education at home (Basham, Merrifield, & Hepburn, 2007).

Canada also has a large and growing Aboriginal population (First Nations, Métis, and Inuit) comprising approximately 4% of the total population (Statistics Canada, 2008). Approximately 30% of Aboriginal people choose to live in Aboriginal communities (Statistics Canada, 2003), which include First Nations bands on reserves, Inuit communities in northern Canada, and Métis communities; these exist in every province/territory. Many of these communities have their own education system, including special education services, which may be run by the community leaders or by the federal government. As a multicultural country, Canada also includes students and families with a range of cultural and linguistic backgrounds other than Aboriginal, some of which are represented more strongly in some provinces than others. For example, in the Toronto District School Board over 80 languages are represented and 26% of students were born outside of Canada (TDSB, 2010). Meeting the needs of students who are learning English as a second language or those with varied cultural or educational backgrounds is part of the responsibility of provincial/territorial education systems.

Within each province and territory, there is a provincial/territorial act designed to regulate education. These acts are broad in scope and typically outline the ways in which education is delivered to students who are enrolled in publicly funded schools. Each province/territory also has specific policies and frameworks in place with respect to special education. These describe identification criteria for eligible students, funding models, available services, the roles of various personnel involved, and the key role of parents. While the specific approaches may vary, every province/territory has mandated the education of students with special education needs within the public school system and all have the regular education classroom as the preferred class placement for these students.

Current estimates of the number of students identified with special education needs in Canada are difficult to

---

[1]The provinces in Canada from east to west are Newfoundland and Labrador, Prince Edward Island, Nova Scotia, New

---

Brunswick, Quebec, Ontario, Manitoba, Saskatchewan, Alberta, and British Columbia. Currently there are three Canadian territories, from west to east the Yukon, the Northwest Territories, and Nunavut.

obtain, as each province/territory follows its own procedures for collecting this type of information. The largest group of students identified as having special education needs is those with learning disabilities (e.g., British Columbia Ministry of Education, 2011; Ontario Ministry of Education, 2005a). Students may also exhibit a range of emotional, behavioral, communicative, sensory, and/or physical needs that prevent them from experiencing their full academic potential without appropriate services. In 2010/2011, British Columbia reported that 10% of its students were identified as having special education needs, including 3.1% with learning disabilities, 2.4% with behavior disabilities (including mental illness), and 1.3% who were gifted (British Columbia, 2011). Other provinces have reported similar rates (Ontario Ministry of Education, 2011; Newfoundland and Labrador Department of Education, 2011).

The approaches adopted by the Canadian provinces/ territories to serving students with these varied needs have shifted over time. The history of Special Education of Canada can be seen as a progression from relative isolation to integration in regular schools and then to inclusion in regular classrooms with much of the change having taken place since the 1970s (Smith et al., 2011). Hutchinson (2010) provides the following description of the progression:

1800s:

- Segregated schools are established in Quebec, Ontario, Nova Scotia, and Manitoba for children who are blind and deaf.
- The Ontario Children's Aid Society is founded.

1900–1950:

- Elementary schools in urban areas begin to offer special education classes.
- Summer courses are offered for teachers of special classes.
- Many children with exceptionalities live in full-time residential schools.

1950–1970:

- Associations to support children with disabilities are created (Canadian Association for Retarded Children; Canadian Association for Children with Learning Disabilities).
- There is an increase in the number of segregated programs for students with special needs offered in schools, including children considered to be gifted.

1970–1980:

- Reports recommend integration of students with special needs into regular classes (Roberts & Lazure, 1970) and courses on children with special needs are included in teacher education programs.

- There is a push toward deinstitutionalization of individuals with special needs in favor of settings that are as close to normal as possible.

1980–1990:

- 1982: *Constitution Act of Canada* is adopted, including the *Charter of Rights and Freedoms*. The Charter includes *equality rights*, which specifically guarantee freedom from discrimination based on mental or physical disabilities. While provincial governments have authority over education, the laws and guidelines they create must be consistent with the Charter.
- By the mid-1980s, integration into regular schools becomes the prevailing approach and most provinces have begun to use Individual Education Plans (IEPs) to guide instruction for students with special needs.

1990–2000:

- Increasing demand by parents for inclusion of their children in regular classroom settings results in a number of court cases.
- One lengthy court case (*Eaton v. Brant County Board of Education*) initially results in a ruling that the first choice of placement should be the regular classroom with the wishes of the parents being the prime consideration. In 1996, the Supreme Court of Canada overturns the ruling and supports the provision of a variety of settings with the best interest of the child being paramount.

2000–present:

- There is a growing focus on creating environments that are inclusive and effective for all students drawing on instructional frameworks such as *differentiated instruction* and *universal design*.
- There is an increase in the number of students identified with autism and Asperger syndrome.
- A push toward collaboration among health care, education, social services, and justice to better meet the needs of students with special needs can be seen in a number of provinces (e.g., Alberta Education, 2009; Nova Scotia, 2010; Ontario Ministry of Children and Youth Services, 2009; Saskatchewan, 2002).
- Inclusion is given strong support by the Government of Canada in the 2006 report *Advancing the Inclusion of Persons with Disabilities*.

The focus of the past decade has been on educating students with a range of special educational needs within inclusive settings but with a focus beyond that of general class placements. The goal of inclusive education is to provide all students with the most appropriate learning environment that will allow the students to have equitable access to learning, achievement, and the pursuit of excellence; it includes meaningful participation and the promotion of interaction with others (Alberta Education, 2011; British Columbia Ministry of Education, 2006). This goal assumes that all students can experience success when they are given the opportunity and appropriate supports to do so. Inclusive education, in a broader sense, encompasses reaching all marginalized populations (Burnett, 2008).

In inclusive education, the regular classroom is deemed the most appropriate placement for most students with special education needs. According to the definitions adopted by most provinces/territories, however, this does not preclude students from being taught in flexible skills groupings or static small groups (either within the regular classroom or in a separate venue); being withdrawn for part of the day or for certain subjects, in order to remediate skills and/or provide extra support; or being provided with extra assistance when required. Students who are identified with special education needs will typically have an Individual Education Plan developed for them that outlines specific accommodations or modifications required for various subjects.

While general policies of inclusion are similar across provinces/territories, the attitudes, practices, and overall acceptance of the model by students, parents, and educators varies widely across the country. Issues such as insufficient teacher preparation, support and funding, accountability for high-stakes test results, and differing philosophies are presented as barriers to acceptance of inclusive education (Crawford & Porter, 2004; McBride, 2008; Winzer, 2008).

The provinces and territories that make up Canada have been implementing elements of inclusive education for almost 30 years (McIntosh et al., 2011). Differentiated Instruction, Universal Design for Learning, and the Tiered Approach are three interconnected teaching models that have been adopted by provinces/territories with the goal of facilitating success for most students within the regular classroom setting.

Differentiated Instruction (DI) is based on the premise that students have differing abilities, interests, prior experiences, learning styles, and needs and thus require varying teaching strategies, materials, and pacing in order to learn and demonstrate the knowledge and skills that have been acquired. DI is based on the belief that all students can learn, albeit in the students' own way and time (Alberta Education, 2011). Universal Design for Learning is the premise that a teaching strategy that is necessary for the success of one student may benefit most or all of the students in the class.

The three-tiered approach used in Saskatchewan in the 1970s (McIntosh et al., 2011) is currently in use in many provinces and territories in Canada. Tier I is class- and school-wide and includes approaches to instruction that have been proven effective for all students, such as differentiated instruction, encouragement toward personal

independence for the students, assessment of students, involvement of the students' caregivers, and participation of school personnel in team meetings regarding the progress of students. Tier I interventions are proactive, in that they are implemented with a view to preventing more serious learning difficulties in the future (O'Connor, 2000; Vaughn et al., 2003); learning challenges of students are often addressed as early as kindergarten or grade 1 (Vaughn et al., 2003). For those students who need extra assistance, there is Tier II of the Tiered Approach.

At Tier II, interventions are targeted and often delivered in small groups for short periods of time; such interventions include the use of assistive technology, multidisciplinary team meetings, and consultation with community agencies. A special education teacher or teacher assistant may be involved at this level of intervention (Ontario Ministry of Education, 2005a). The goal of Tier II interventions is to provide remediation of skills through supplemental instruction and strategically differentiated instruction. For those students who require more support, there is Tier III. At Tier III, intensive individual interventions are provided to the students. The support given is often one-to-one and of an enduring nature (McIntosh, Chard, Boland, & Horner, 2006; McIntosh, et al., 2011).

Within the Tiered Approach, there is constant monitoring of student progress. Should students receive support and then make sufficient progress as to be on par with age-level peers, the support may be considered to have been successful and the intervention discontinued. However, should students continue to have difficulties and demonstrate a lack of progress despite the extra help received, the supports implemented would incrementally become more intensive until student success was achieved.

In addition to instructional approaches, the provinces/ territories are developing policies and frameworks to facilitate the integration of education and community-based services for students, for example, with autism spectrum disorders, mental health issues, complex physical disabilities and developmental disabilities. For all students with special needs, however, the view is shared across provinces/territories that the responsibility for effectively including students with special needs in Canadian classrooms and ensuring positive outcomes for these students is shared by families, community-based professionals, and educators.

REFERENCES

Alberta Education. (2009). *Setting the direction framework.* Retrieved from http://education.alberta.ca/media/1082136/sc_settingthedirection_framework.pdf

Alberta Education. (2011). *Action on inclusion.* Retrieved from http://education.alberta.ca/department/ipr/inclusion.aspx

Basham, P., Merrifield, J., & Hepburn, C. R. (2007). *Home schooling: From the extreme to the mainstream* (2nd ed.). Toronto, ON: Fraser Institute.

British Columbia Ministry of Education. (2006). *Policy document: Special education*. Retrieved from http://www.bced.gov.bc.ca/policy/policies/special_ed.htm#

British Columbia Ministry of Education. (2011). *Student statistics*. Retrieved from http://www.bced.gov.bc.ca/reporting/

Burnett, N. (2008). Education for all. *Annals of the New York Academy of Sciences, 1136*(1), 269–275.

Crawford, C., & Porter, G. L. (2004). *Supporting teachers: A foundation for advancing inclusive education*. Toronto, ON: Roeher Institute.

Hardy, M. I., McLeod, J., Minto, H., Perkins, S. A., & Quance, W. R. (1971). *Standards for education of exceptional children in Canada: The SEECC Report*. Toronto, ON: Leonard Crainford.

Hutchinson, N. L. (2010). *Inclusion of exceptional learners in Canadian Schools: A practical handbook for teachers*. Toronto, ON: Pearson.

McBride, S. (2008). *A cross-Canada review of selected issues in Special Education*. Edmonton, AB: Alberta Education.

McIntosh, K., MacKay, L. D., Andreou, T., Brown, J. A., Mathews, S., Gietz, C., & Bennett, J. L. (2011). Response to intervention in Canada: Definitions, the evidence base, and future directions. *Canadian Journal of School Psychology, 26*(1), 18–43.

McIntosh, K., Chard, D. J., Boland, J. B., & Horner, R. H. (2006). Demonstration of combined efforts in school-wide academic and behavioral systems and incidence of reading and behavior challenges in early elementary grades. *Journal of Positive Behavior Interventions, 8*, 146–154.

Newfoundland and Labrador Department of Education. (2011). *Education statistics: Elementary–Secondary 2010–2011*. St. John's, NL: Author.

Nova Scotia Department of Education. (2010). *Nova Scotia Schools Plus*. Halifax, NS: Author. Retrieved from http://www.ednet.ns.ca/SchoolsPlus/

O'Connor, R. (2000). Increasing the intensity of intervention in kindergarten and first grade. *Learning Disabilities Practice, 15*(1), 43–54.

Ontario Ministry of Children and Youth Services. (2009). *Integrated services for Northern children*. Toronto, ON: Author. Retrieved from http://www.children.gov.on.ca/htdocs/English/topics/specialneeds/northern.aspx

Ontario Ministry of Education and Training. (2005). *Early school leavers: Understanding the lived reality of student disengagement from secondary school*. Toronto, ON: Author.

Ontario Ministry of Education. (2005a). *Education for all: The report of the expert panel on literacy and Numeracy instruction for students with special education needs, kindergarten to grade 6*. Toronto, ON: Queen's Printer for Ontario.

Ontario Ministry of Education. (2011). *School information finder*. Retrieved from http://www.edu.gov.on.ca/eng/sift/

Roberts, C. A., & Lazure, M. D. (1970). *One million children: A national study of Canadian children with emotional and learning disorders*. Toronto, ON: Crainford.

Smith, T. E. C., Polloway, E. A., Patton, J. R., Dowdy, C. A., & McIntyre, L. J. (2011). *Teaching students with special needs in inclusive settings* (4th ed.). Toronto, ON: Pearson Canada.

Saskatchewan Learning. (2002). SchoolPLUS. Regina, SK: Author. Retrieved from http://www.education.gov.sk.ca/SchoolPLUS

Statistics Canada. (2003). Aboriginal peoples survey 2001—Initial findings: Well-being of the non-reserve Aboriginal population. (Catalogue no. 89-589-XIE.) Ottawa, ON: Statistics Canada.

Statistics Canada. (2008). The Daily: Aboriginal Peoples in Canada in 2006: Inuit, Métis and First Nations, 2006 Census. Retrieved from http://www.statcan.gc.ca/daily-quotidien/080115/dq080115a-eng.htm

Toronto District School Board. (2010). *School matters: A parent's guide to the TDSB*. Toronto, ON: Author.

Vaughn, S., Linan-Thompson, S., Kouzekanani, K., Bryant, D., Dickson, S., & Blozis, S. (2003). Reading instruction grouping for students with reading difficulties. *Remedial and Special Education, 24*(5), 301–315.

Winzer, M. (2008). *Children with exceptionalities in Canadian classrooms* (8th ed.). Toronto, ON: Pearson Prentice Hall.

JESSICA WHITELY
SUZANNE GOODERHAM
CAROL WINDMILL
University of Ottawa
Fourth edition

CANCER, CHILDHOOD

Cancer is distinguished from other diseases by the rapid growth of abnormal cells in the body. When cancer cells travel to other parts of the body and invade tissues and organs, the process is referred to as *metastasis*. Many types of cancers form tumors; however, the most common type of childhood cancer, leukemia, does not form tumors. Leukemia is rather a disease of the blood-forming tissues in which immature lymphocytes and white blood cells proliferate while red blood cells decrease (Brown & Madan-Swain, 1993).

Cancer is the leading cause of death from disease in children under the age of 15. Fortunately, due to medical advances in childhood cancer research, death rates from childhood cancer have declined about 49% since 1975 (American Cancer Society, 2005). The treatment of cancer involves radiation, surgery, and/or chemotherapy. Children undergoing cancer treatment will often suffer from fatigue, weight loss, nausea, and irritability. Chemotherapy and radiation treatments have been shown to negatively affect children's cognitive abilities such as attention, memory, distractibility, visual-spatial function, visual-motor function, and executive functions (Kaemingk, Carey, Moore, Herzer, & Hutter, 2004). Such deficits are sometimes not evident until up to 2 years post diagnosis.

Children survivors of leukemia may have academic difficulties in reading, spelling, and more commonly, math

(Kaemingk et al., 2004). Math difficulties related to mathematical operations, mental calculations, and math applications have been found when compared to healthy peers or normative levels. Deficiencies have also been evident in the areas of verbal memory, auditory attention, basic reading skills, and psychomotor speed. Math performance among leukemia survivors has been shown to improve with individual tutoring; however, it is unknown whether this type of intervention will also aid in attention, memory, or other cognitive tasks.

Children who survive cancer may be at an increased risk of psychosocial difficulties related to the stress of disease and treatment as well as their isolation from peers (Shelby, Nagle, Barnett-Quenn, Quattlebaum, & Wuori, 1998). Peer relations and participation in school-related activities tend to decline, potentially leading to difficulties in specific developmental milestones (Stam, Grootenhuis, & Last, 2005). Recent research examining the course of life with survivors of childhood cancer shows significant differences between survivors and their peers in regard to developmental milestones. Young adult survivors tend to achieve fewer milestones than their healthy peers in areas such as autonomy development, psychosexual development, and social development. Fulfilling developmental milestones is important for adjustment in adult life; therefore, certain steps can be taken for the childhood survivor to aid in his or her development. For example, encouraging the child to be involved in peer activities, as well as encouraging independence, may aid the child's journey toward healthy development.

Recovering from cancer can be a lengthy process. For some children, referral to special education services may be an option when they are unable to cope with the demands of school. Under the guidelines of IDEA, cancer survivors are guaranteed appropriate educational services (Spinelli, 2002).

REFERENCES

American Cancer Society. (2005). *Children and cancer: Information and resources*. Retrieved from http://www.cancer.org/

Brown, R., & Madan-Swain, A. (1993). Cognitive, neuropsychological, and academic sequelae in children with leukemia. *Journal of Learning Disabilities, 26*(2), 74–90.

Kaemingk, K., Carey, M., Moore, I., Herzer, M., & Hutter, J. (2004). Math weaknesses in survivors of acute lymphoblastic leukemia compared to healthy children. *Child Neuropsychology, 10*(1), 14–23.

Shelby, M., Nagle, R., Barnett-Quenn, L., Quattlebaum, P., & Wuori, D. (1998). Parental reports of psychosocial adjustment and social competence in child survivors of acute lymphocytic leukemia. *Children's Health Care, 27*(2), 113–129.

Spinelli, C. (2002). Educational and psychosocial implications affecting childhood cancer survivors: What educators needs to know. *Journal of the Council for Exceptional Children, 11*(1), 49–64.

Stam, H., Grootenhuis, M. A., & Last, B. F. (2005). The course of life of survivors of childhood cancer. *Psycho-Oncology, 14*, 227–238.

MIRANDA KUCERA
University of Colorado at Colorado Springs

See also **Brain Disorders; Chemotherapy; Chronic Illness in Children**

CANDIDIASIS

The *Candida* genus is opportunistic in comparison to other fungal genera and is part of the normal gastrointestinal flora. Candidiasis is an opportunistic fungal infection. Symptoms of candidiasis may resemble bacterial sepsis or necrotizing enterocolitis (NEC; Witek-Janusek, Cusack, & Mathews, 1998). In its severest form, intramural intestinal gas, intrahepatic portal vein gas, and intestinal perforation characterize NEC (Hughes, Lepow, & Hill, 1993). The clinical diagnosis of disseminated fungal infection is usually associated with one or more of the following: respiratory deterioration, abdominal distention, guaiac-positive stools, carbohydrate intolerance, candiduria, endophthalmitis, meningitis, abscesses, erythematous rash, temperature instability, lethargy, and hypotension (Baley, 1991; Van den Anker, Popele, & Sauer, 1995).

The species most common in neonates with disseminated disease is *Candida albicans*, accounting for 75% of cases. *C. tropicalis* and *C. parapsilosis* account for 10% and 6%, respectively (Hughes et al., 1993).

Opportunistic microorganisms multiply in vulnerable infants; however, they are no threat to those with a noncompromised immune system (Witek-Janusek et al., 1998). Vulnerable infants are considered to be those in whom both inadequate immune defense mechanisms and risk factors associated with clinical management are present. Invasive *C. albicans* infection is generally difficult to manage and is associated with high morbidity and mortality (Witek-Janusek et al.). Neonatal systemic candidiasis is predominantly a disease of low-birth-weight infants (Hughes et al., 1993).

The placement of intravascular catheters and endotracheal tubes in premature infants interrupts the skin and mucous membranes as a defense against candidal invasion. Catheters provide an entryway for microorganisms and initiate a site of adherence for yeast (Hughes et al., 1993).

Infants usually become colonized with *Candida* soon after birth (Witek-Janusek et al., 1998). Colonization from the maternal vaginal tract during birth is a common path of *Candida* transmission. This is particularly the case for pregnant women with vaginal candidiasis. However, the interruption of initial colonization of the infant at birth may decrease the incidence of systemic *Candida* infections in high-risk infants (Witek-Janusek et al., 1998).

According to Hughes et al. (1993), the manifestations of candidiasis include oral, systemic, catheter-associated candidemia, urinary system, endocarditis, endophthalmitis, meningitis, and congenital.

Characteristics

1. Temperature instability
2. Respiratory distress
3. Abdominal distention

Other symptoms may include unstable vitals, apnea, bradycardia, lethargy, and decreased perfusion.

Systemic antifungal drugs used to treat candidiasis include amphotericin B, 5-flucytosine, miconazole, fluconazole, and itraconazole (Hughes et al., 1993). Despite good treatment, nosocomial fungal infections have become a cause of morbidity, extended hospitalization, and mortality in critically ill newborn babies (Khoory, Vino, Dall'Agnola, & Fanos, 1999). Furthermore, the high incidence of central nervous system involvement in septic newborns often results in serious neurological damage and psychomotorial sequelae (Khoory et al., 1999). *Candida* infection of the central nervous system has a significant impact on long-term neurodevelopmental outcome. Performance of cranial ultrasound examination is recommended as a part of the diagnostic investigation for these infants. Detection of brain parenchymal involvement might provide further information to predict outcome (Friedman, Richardson, Jacobs, & O'Brien, 2000).

Further research is needed to determine potential educational implications for infants with this serious infection.

REFERENCES

Baley, J. E. (1991). The current challenge. *Clinics in Perinatology, 18*, 263–280.

Friedman, S., Richardson, S. E., Jacobs, S. E., & O'Brien, K. (2000). Systemic candida infection in extremely low birth weight infants: Short-term morbidity and long term neurodevelopmental outcome. *Pediatric Infectious Disease Journal, 19*(6), 499–504.

Hughes, P. A., Lepow, M. L., & Hill, H. R. (1993). Neonatal can-didiasis. In G. P. Bodey (Ed.), *Candidiasis: Pathogenesis, diagnosis and treatment* (pp. 261–277). New York, NY: Raven Press.

Khoory, B. J., Vino, L., Dall'Agnola, A., & Fanos, V. (1999). Candida infections in newborns: A review. *Journal of Chemotherapy, 11*(5), 367–378.

Van den Anker, J. N., Popele, N. M., & Sauer, P. J. (1995). Antifungal agents in neonatal systemic candidiasis. *Antimicrobial Agents and Chemotherapy, 30*(7), 1391–1397.

Witek-Janusek, L., Cusack, C., & Mathews, H. L. (1998). Candida albicans: An opportunistic threat to critically ill low birth weight infants. *Dimensions of Critical Care Nursing, 17*(5), 243–255.

HELEN G. JENNE
*Alliant International University,
California School of Professional Psychology*

CANTRELL, ROBERT P. (1938–   )

Robert P. Cantrell received his BA in 1960 and MA in 1962 in psychology from Baylor University. He received his PhD in 1969 from George Peabody College for Teachers with a major in experimental child psychology and a minor in special education. Since 1980, he has been an adjunct professor in the department of special education, Kent State University, an adjunct professor in the department of specialized instructional programs, Cleveland State University, the co-director of the Institute for Ecological Study of Children and Youth, and the director of research, Positive Education Program, Cleveland, Ohio. He has remained at the Positive Education Program, and is currently a Research Fellow with them.

Early experiences as a psychologist on a special education diagnostic team taught him that teachers of special children demand practical solutions to their special teaching problems. Partly from these experiences, he became an advocate of a heuristic, ecological system of problem solving (Cantrell & Cantrell, 1977). Although many professionals learn over time to develop solutions to these practical problems, he recognized that there are inadequate means by which we transmit this knowledge of effective intervention strategies to the next generation of professionals.

Cantrell has worked toward the identification of intervention strategies that produce the most efficient and effective changes in the ecologies of behavior-disordered children (Cantrell & Cantrell, 1980) and continues to focus much of his research on the analysis of and interventions with troubled behavioral ecologies. His most recent published works describe an ecological treatment program for emotionally or behaviorally disordered children, with the goal of creating "a single, coordinated system of care of each child and family" (Cantrell, Cantrell, & Smith, 1998); underlying assumptions and implications for education; and treatment with an ecological perspective (Cantrell, Cantrell, Valore, Jones, & Fecser, 1999).

REFERENCES

Cantrell, M. L., Cantrell, R. P., & Smith, D. A. (1998). Coordinating care through connections' liaison staff: Services, costs, and outcomes. In M. Epstein & K. Kutash (Eds.), *Outcomes for children and youth with emotional and behavioral disorders and their families: Programs and evaluation best practices* (pp. 205–229). Austin, TX: PRO-ED.

Cantrell, M. P., Cantrell, R. P., Valore, T. G., Jones, J. M., & Fecser, F. A. (1999). *A revisitation of the ecological perspective on emotional and behavioral disorders: Underlying assumptions and implications for education and treatment.* Retrieved from http://www.ccbd.net/CCBD/Home/

Cantrell, R. P., & Cantrell, M. L. (1977). Evaluation of a heuristic approach to solving children's problems. *Peabody Journal of Education, 54*(3), 168–173.

Cantrell, R. P., & Cantrell, M. L. (1980). Ecological problem solving: A decision-making heuristic for prevention-intervention education strategies. In J. Hogg & P. Mittler (Eds.), *Advances in mental handicap research* (Vol. 1). New York, NY: Wiley.

E. Valerie Hewitt
Texas A&M University
First edition

Kay E. Ketzenberger
The University of Texas of the Permian Basin
Second edition

CARCINOID SYNDROME

Carcinoid tumors were first discovered in the 1800s, and the term *carcinoid* began being used by the medical profession in 1907. Tumors were found to arise from glandular endocrine-hormone-producing cells found commonly in the small intestine. To a lesser extent, these tumors may also be found in the appendix, the rectum, the lung, and the pancreas and very rarely in the ovaries, the testes, the liver, and the bile ducts. It was not until 1954 that carcinoid syndrome was recognized by medical professionals as a specific disease (Oats, 1996). Carcinoid syndrome is a rare, malignant disease affecting 8 out of every 100,000 persons. This rare disease affects males and females of all ages in equal numbers. The actual number may be underreported due to undetected tumors and the fact that some patients do not experience the three hallmark symptoms of carcinoid syndrome—flushing, wheezing, and diarrhea—leading to misdiagnosis (Oats, 1996). Carcinoid syndrome begins quietly with the absence of symptoms. It is not until the tumors have been growing for years that the symptoms are noticeable. Typically, the malignant tumors affect the small bowel, stomach, or pancreas. Eventually, the tumors can spread to the liver, lungs, and ovaries. As the disease progresses, congestive heart failure associated with the right-sided valvular heart disease develops. In addition, the carcinoid tumors make deadly hormones that are commonly found in the liver and cause the notorious symptoms of flushing of the face, asthma-like wheezing attacks, and diarrhea. These symptoms can become severe to the point of being life threatening. In the beginning stages of the disease, the "carcinoid crisis," as it is commonly referred to, may be infrequent and is usually associated with abrupt low blood pressure and fainting. As the disease progresses, the symptoms become more frequent and chronic (Thonene, 1995).

Characteristics

1. Flushing in the face
2. Diarrhea
3. Asthma-like wheezing
4. Loss of vital nutrients due to diarrhea
5. Stomach pain
6. Blocked arteries in the liver
7. Heart palpitations
8. Excessive peptide excretion in the liver

The first three characteristics are the hallmark symptoms of carcinoid syndrome.

At one time, the survival rate from onset of flushing was 3 years and only 2 years from the time of diagnosis with a range of 10 years. Seventy-five percent of the patients died from the potent substances released from the tumors, and 25% died from the tumor growth itself. Within the last 10 years, the prognosis of carcinoid syndrome has improved dramatically. This positive outlook is due to the effective combinations of treatments with Sandostatin, various surgeries, chemotherapy, hepatic artery injections, and biological response mediators. The average survival time from the start of treatment has increased by more than 5 years. The late diagnosis delays the start of treatment; thus, an early diagnosis may look even more favorable (Oats, 1996).

Although carcinoid syndrome does not directly affect the cognitive abilities of children, additional school services such as a private tutor may prove useful in helping the child maintain academic abilities while undergoing different life-saving procedures. Additional individual and family support can be useful to help the family cope with the symptoms and the side effects of treatment caused by this disorder.

REFERENCES

Oats, J. (1996). *Cecil textbook of internal medicine* (20th ed.). Philadelphia, PA: W. B. Saunders.

Thonene, J. G. (1995). *Physicians' guide to rare diseases*. Montvale, NJ: Dowden.

LISA A. FASNACHT-HILL
*Keck University of Southern California
School of Medicine,
University of Southern California /
University Affiliated Program at
Children's Hospital of Los Angeles*

CARCINOMA, RENAL CELL

Renal cell carcinoma is a type of cancer of the kidney that involves cancerous changes in the lining of renal tubule cells. Prevalence of this disorder is estimated to be .03%, with 18,000 new cases diagnosed each year in the United States and approximately 8,000 deaths (U.S. National Library of Medicine, 2000). The disorder is more common in men than in women, especially men over the age of 55. Among children, renal cell carcinoma is exceedingly rare, representing only 2.6% of all renal cancers in children under 15 years old (Bernstein, Liney, Smith, & Olshan, 1995). The National Cancer Institute reported just 32 cases of renal cell carcinoma in children under age 15 in the years between 1975 and 1995 (Bernstein et al., 1995).

Among the known risk factors for this disorder are a family history of kidney cancer, a kidney disease that requires dialysis, von Hippel-Lindau disease (an inherited condition that affects the capillaries of the brain), and smoking (U.S. National Library of Medicine, 2000). Occurrence of renal cell carcinoma in children is usually associated with tuberous sclerosis or von Hippel-Lindau disease (Henske, Thorner, Patterson, Zhuang, & Bernstein, 1999).

Characteristics

1. Evidence of blood in the urine or brown or rust-colored urine
2. Complaint of pain in the flank, back, or abdomen
3. Loss of more than 5% of body weight or an emaciated appearance
4. Enlargement of one testicle or swelling of the abdomen

The recommended treatment for this disorder is surgery to remove all or part of the kidney. The surrounding tissues, lymph nodes, and bladder also may be removed (U.S. National Library of Medicine, 2000). Renal cell carcinoma is known to metastasize quickly to the lungs and other organs. As a result, radiation therapy may be used either

prior to surgery to shrink the tumor or as a treatment to prevent metastasis (U.S. National Library of Medicine). However, renal cell carcinoma often does not respond to radiation. In some cases, hormone therapy and drugs such as alpha-interferon and interleukin have been successful in limiting the growth of the cancer (U.S. National Library of Medicine).

Due to its extremely low prevalence in children, little information is available on the educational implications of renal cell carcinoma. Henske et al. (1999) reported developmental delays in the two cases of childhood renal cell carcinoma that they studied. The need for surgery and radiation therapy associated with treatment for this disorder would lead to extended absences from school for children with renal cell carcinoma. These children may qualify for special education services under the Other Health Impairment handicapping condition.

When renal cell carcinoma is diagnosed in its early stages, 60–75% survival at 5 years is reported in adults (U.S. National Library of Medicine, 2000). This rate drops to 5–15% if the cancer has spread to the lymph nodes and to less than 5% if other organs show signs of carcinoma. In children, a 5-year survival rate of 83% was reported in cases diagnosed between 1985 and 1994 (Bernstein et al., 1995).

REFERENCES

Bernstein, L., Liney, M., Smith, M., & Olshan, A. (1995). Renal tumors. In *Cancer incidence and survival among children and adolescents: United States SEER program 1975–1995*. National Cancer Institute. Retrieved from http://seer.cancer.gov/

Henske, E., Thorner, P., Patterson, K., Zhuang, Z., & Bernstein, J. (1999). Renal cell carcinoma in children with diffuse cystic hyperplasia of the kidneys. *Pediatric and Developmental Pathology, 2*, 270–274.

U.S. National Library of Medicine. (2000). *Renal cell carcinoma*. Retrieved from http://medlineplus.adam.com/

NANCY K. SCAMMACCA
University of Texas at Austin

CARDIAC DISORDERS

Congenital cardiac disorders, with their subsequent physical impairments, constitute some of the most common and serious childhood illnesses. Congenital cardiac disorders are those in which defects in the structure of the heart and/or great vessels alter the normal flow of blood through the cardiorespiratory system. Whaley and Wong (1983) report the incidence of congenital heart disease to occur in approximately 8/1,000 to 10/1,000 live births, which amounts to approximately 40,000 children per year (American Heart Association [AHA], 2013). They also report that congenital anomalies are the major cause of death outside of prematurity. However, with the evolution of palliative and varied surgical techniques, the percentage of those infants who survive cardiac malformations/lesions in the neonatal period has dramatically increased; therefore, serious complex defects currently account for a large number of individuals passing through infancy and childhood into full maturity (AHA, 2013; Nelson, Behrman, & Vaughn, 1983). Surgically corrected congenital defects constitute the largest group of those surviving until adulthood.

There are two types of heart disease in children, acquired and congenital. Acquired cardiac disorders develop sometime during childhood and include Kawasaki disease, rheumatic fever, and infectious endocarditis (AHA, 20013). The cause of congenital cardiac anomalies is still relatively unknown at this time; however multifactorial patterns have been associated with an increased incidence of the disease. The following prenatal factors have been identified as having causal relationships of varying degrees: maternal rubella infection and other viruses such as cytomegalovirus, coxsackievirus B, and herpesvirus nomines B (Nelson et al., 1983; Nora, 1971); poor maternal nutrition (Reeder, Mastroianni, & Martin, 1983); alcohol, dextroamphetamine, lithium chloride, progesterone/estrogen, and warfarin, which are suspected teratogenic agents, as well as maternal overexposure to radiation (Taybi, 1971).

Genetic factors have also been associated with an increased incidence of cardiac disorders. Those parents who already have a child with a cardiac defect have a higher incidence of a second child with a cardiac malformation than parents with an unaffected child (King, 1975). Although this incidence is higher than the general population, it is still quite low (2 to 5%; King, 1975; Nelson et al., 1983). Other factors predisposing children to congenital heart disease are parents who have congenital cardiac disease themselves or chromosomal aberrations such as Down syndrome and/or other noncardiac anomalies. Between 30 and 40% of all children with Down syndrome have heart defects of some kind (Fletcher-Janzen & Reynolds, 2003; Rowe & Uchida, 1961).

The general signs and symptoms associated with congenital cardiac defects in children have been outlined by Miller (1985): (1) dyspnea, especially on exertion; (2) feeding difficulties or a general failure to thrive; (3) stridor or choking spells; (4) increased heart and respiratory rate (tachypnea) with retractions when the ribs show with each breath; (5) numerous respiratory tract infections; (6) in older children, delayed or poor physical and/or mental development with a decreased exercise tolerance; (7) cyanosis, posturing (particularly a squatting position and clubbing of fingers and toes); (8) heart murmurs; and (9) diaphoresis.

Cardiac lesions have been classified into two broad categories: acyanotic and cyanotic. "Acyanotic defects are those in which the blood flows from the arterial (left, oxygenated) side of the heart to the venous (right, deoxygenated) side as a result of a connection between the two sides and/or from a pressure gradient (left-to-right shunt)" (Carroll-Johnson & Neal, 1985, p. 605). Most acyanotic disorders are asymptomatic. There are six acyanotic defects demonstrating the left-to-right shunting of blood. The blood flows from the left ventricle to the right ventricle, where it mixes with venous blood with ventricular-septal defects (VSD). Watson (1968) has cited ventricular-septal defects as the most common cause of cardiac mortality. Atrial-septal defects (ASD) have blood flowing from the left atrium to the right atrium, then through the right ventricle before moving into the pulmonary artery and pulmonary circulation. Patent ductus arteriosus (PDA) is signified when the ductus arteriosus, which normally closes after birth, remains patent, thus recirculating blood repeatedly through the lungs, and, in essence, overoxygenating the blood. The fourth acyanotic lesion is a coarctation of the aorta. Narrowing of the aorta in this lesion manifests itself with an increased blood pressure in the upper extremities with a reciprocal decrease in pressure in the systemic circulation. Aortic stenosis is the narrowing or general inflexibility of the aortic valve, which increases the workload of the left ventricle with subsequent left ventricular hypertrophy resulting. Pulmonary stenosis in a like manner is the narrowing of the pulmonary valve. However, this narrowing results in decreased blood flow to the lungs and an increase in right ventricular pressure.

There are four cyanotic defects, with the outstanding clinical feature being cyanosis. The tetralogy of Fallot, with its four associated defects, has been described by Sacksteder, Gildea, and Dassy (1978, p. 267) as "(1) a large membranous ventricular septal defect; (2) right ventricular outflow obstruction; (3) right ventricular hypertrophy; and (4) dextroposition or overriding of the aorta." The outstanding clinical feature is cyanosis, along with associated features such as clubbing of nailbeds and squatting posture.

In addition to the tetralogy of Fallot, transposition of the great arteries is another cyanotic disorder. In this instance, the aorta arises from the right ventricle and the pulmonary artery from the left ventricle. Hence, two parallel and separate circulatory systems exist, one pulmonary and one systemic. This condition is incompatible with life unless coexisting lesions allow a mixture of blood to sustain life until the heart can be surgically repaired (Sacksteder et al., 1978).

The type of medical intervention or surgical treatment required for congenital heart disease depends on the type or severity of the cardiac lesion. The majority of children with mild congenital heart disease require no treatment. Children with severe heart defects may develop congestive heart failure, which is frequently treated with a cardiac glycoside (digoxin) and furosemide (Lasix). Selective palliative surgical procedures may be done to improve oxygenation temporarily until the child grows. Total correction of the heart defect is usually postponed until the benefits of surgery outweigh the risks, or until the child is between the ages of 3 and 5 years (Rowe, 1978).

Parents of children with congenital heart defects are encouraged to treat their children normally. In all but the most severe cases (Morris, 1993), a normal life can be expected. Restriction of the child's activities is rarely suggested, but it is often implemented as a control measure by parents. Discipline problems are common, and sibling rivalry is seen frequently because of the attention given the child with the cardiac disorder by parents, health-care workers, and educators. The best means of avoiding overprotection of the child is to have a functional knowledge of the child's unique disorder. Overprotection frequently results in increased anxiety in the child and interferes with a normal lifestyle. Parents are recommended to manage their child's heart condition by providing a well-balanced diet, prevention of anemia, and the usual childhood immunizations.

Those children whose lesions are moderate to severe need not severely restrict their activities. Nelson et al. (1983) suggest merely tailoring the child's activities to his or her ability to participate; however, rough competitive contact sports should be avoided. Generally, the child will establish his or her own limits. Nelson et al. (1983) also suggest that transportation to and from school may help school performance by eliminating excessive fatigue.

Additional, but imperative, guidelines for all children with cardiac lesions include treating bacterial infections vigorously but not prophylactically to prevent infective endocarditis. Specifically, cyanotic children should be alert for dehydration and iron deficiencies, which may interfere with activity tolerance. As maturity is achieved, women should be counseled regarding the risks of childbearing and the use of contraceptives.

The American Heart Association has an informative website for children with cardiac disorders (www.americanheart.org). In addition, the Health Resources and Services Administration of the federal government has online guidelines for health safety in the public schools that specifically mention cardiac disorders. The guidelines can be downloaded in printable form (www.nationalguidelines.org).

REFERENCES

American Heart Association (AHA) / Conditions Tab / Congenital Defects Children & Adults Tab. (2013). http://www .heart.org/HEARTORG/Conditions/CongenitalHeartDefects/ Congenital-Heart-Defects_UCM_001090_SubHomePage.jsp

Carroll-Johnson, R. M., & Neal, M. C. (Eds.). (1985). *American Journal of Nursing 1985 nursing boards review (pp. 605–607).* Pacific Palisades, CA: Nurseco.

Fletcher-Janzen, E., & Reynolds, C. R. (2003). *Childhood disorders diagnostic desk reference.* Hoboken, NJ: Wiley.

King, O. M. (Ed.). (1975). *Care of the cardiac surgical patient.* St. Louis, MO: Mosby.

Miller, A. (Ed.). (1985). *Mosby's comprehensive review of nursing* (11th ed., pp. 400–405). St. Louis, MO: Mosby.

Morris, R. D. (1993). Neuropsychological, academic, and adoptive functioning in children who survive in-hospital cardiac arrest and resuscitation. *Journal of Hearing Disabilities, 26*(1), 46–51.

Nelson, W. E., Behrman, R. E., & Vaughn, V. C. (Eds.). (1983). *Textbook of pediatrics* (12th ed., pp. 1121–1167). Philadelphia, PA: Saunders.

Nora, J. J. (1971). Etiologic factors in congenital heart diseases. In S. Kaplin (Ed.), *Pediatric clinics of North America* (Vol. 18, pp. 1059–1074). Philadelphia, PA: Saunders.

Reeder, S. J., Mastroianni, L., & Martin, L. (Eds.). (1983). *Maternity nursing* (15th ed.). Philadelphia, PA: Lippincott.

Rowe, R. D. (1978). Patent ductus arteriosus. In J. Keith, R. Rowe, & R. Vlad (Eds.), *Heart disease in infancy and children* (3rd ed.). New York, NY: Macmillan.

Rowe, R. D., & Uchida, I. A. (1961). Cardiac malformation in mongolism: A prospective study of 184 mongoloid children. *American Journal of Medicine, 31,* 726–735.

Sacksteder, S., Gildea, J. H., & Dassy, C. (1978, February). Common congenital cardiac defects. *American Journal of Nursing, 266–272.*

Taybi, H. (1971). Roentgen evaluation of cardiomegaly in the newborn period and early infancy. In S. Kaplin (Ed.), *Pediatric clinics of North America, 18*(4), 1031–1058. Philadelphia, PA: Saunders.

Watson, H. (Ed.). (1968). *Pediatric cardiology.* London, UK: Lloyd-Luke.

Whaley, L. F., & Wong, D. L. (1983). The child with heart disease. In L. F. Whaley & D. L. Wong (Eds.), *Nursing care of infants and children* (2nd ed., pp. 1279–1337). St. Louis, MO: Mosby.

MARY CLARE WILLIAMS
Ramey, Pennsylvania

See also **Physical Disabilities; Physical Education for Students With Disabilities**

CARDIOFACIOCUTANEOUS SYNDROME

Cardiofaciocutaneous (CFC) syndrome, also known as cardio-facial-cutaneous syndrome and facio-cardio-cutaneous syndrome, affects both males and females. It is a rare genetic disorder found in children that is diagnosed based on specific physical appearances of the head, face, chest, hands, skin, and/or heart, in addition to visual impairment, growth delays, and/or varying degrees of mental retardation.

This rare disorder has an autosomal dominant inheritance and, in circumstances where no family history of CFC syndrome is found, is thought to be the result of random sporadic mutations.

Many symptoms are associated with CFC syndrome. The head of a CFC patient may have one or more of the following characteristics: macrocephaly (unusually large in size); a prominent forehead with abnormal narrowing of both sides; a short, upturned nose with a low nasal bridge; and prominent external ears (pinnae) abnormally rotated toward the back of the head. Distinctive facial characteristics may consist of extremely sparse and brittle curly hair, a lack of eyebrows and eyelashes, palpebral fissures (downwardly slanting eyelid folds), ocular hypertelorism (widely spaced eyes), and esotropia (inward deviation of the eyes). There is also a greater chance of difficulties with oral motor/feeding/swallowing because of the increased incidence of craniofacial abnormalities.

Other symptoms include pectus carinatum or excavatum (protrusion or indentation of the breastbone), hands with pads on the fingertips, and opal-colored nails. There may also be a number of skin abnormalities, such as dermatitis (skin inflammation), generalized ichthyosis (unusually dry, thickened, scaly skin covering the entire body), generalized pigmentation, patchy hyperkeratosis (patches of thickened skin), keratosis plantaris (red skin in the soles of the feet), and keratosis pilaris (red skin surrounding the eyebrows).

Congenital heart defects are common among individuals with CFC syndrome. The defects include pulmonary stenosis (obstruction of the normal flow of blood from the lower-right chamber of the heart to the lungs due to a narrowing of a valve that connects the lungs to the heart), atrial septal defect (abnormal opening in the fibrous partition, or septum, that divides the left and right atria of the heart), and hypertrophic cardiomyopathy (enlarged heart).

Visual impairment as a result of strabismus (muscle imbalance), amblyopia (lazy eye), nystagmus (involuntary eye movements), ptosis (drooping eyelid), and optic atrophy (dysfunction of the optic nerve) are often seen in case studies done on children with CFC syndrome (Levack, 1991). In addition, most people with CFC syndrome have delayed growth, mild to severe mental retardation, and psychomotor retardation (delays in mastering the skills that require the coordination of muscular and mental activity).

To date, there is no laboratory test available to diagnose someone with CFC syndrome; diagnosis is dependent on a clinician's observations. For diagnosis to occur, a person must have several of the many symptoms of CFC syndrome. The majority of the physical features indicating that a patient has CFC syndrome are often not apparent until childhood, although in some cases a newborn may be diagnosed with CFC syndrome.

Characteristics

1. *Head*: large and oddly shaped head, forehead, nose, ears
2. *Face*: extremely sparse and brittle curly hair; lack of eyebrows and eyelashes; downward slanting, widely spaced, and inwardly deviated eyes; difficulties involving oral motor/feeding/swallowing
3. *Chest*: pectus carinatum or excavatum (protrusion or indentation of the breastbone)
4. *Hands*: pads on the fingertips, opal-colored nails
5. *Skin*: inflammation of skin; dry, thickened, scaly skin covering much of the body; red skin around eyebrows and/or on soles of the feet
6. *Heart*: narrowing of the valve that connects lungs and heart; abnormal opening in septum that divides the left and right atria; hypertrophic cardiomyopathy (enlarged heart)
7. *Vision*: muscle imbalance in eye, lazy eye, drooping eyelid or other involuntary eye movements; optic atrophy (dysfunction of the optic nerve)
8. *Other*: delayed growth; mild to severe mental or psychomotor retardation

---

Unfortunately, there is no cure for CFC syndrome. It is a genetic change and therefore affects every cell in the body. Science has not yet found a way to repair the gene coding for CFC syndrome, nor is there a way to treat every cell in a patient. As a result, clinicians must treat the symptoms and not the source of the CFC syndrome. Treatment should not be universal, but instead individual and based on each child's needs.

There are a multitude of support groups, foundations, and associations available for those who have children with CFC syndrome. The CFC Family Network is a group run strictly by parents who collect donations to supply CFC families with newsletters, family packets, contacts to other CFC families, articles, and photo albums. Currently, donations are being put toward helping families go to a CFC Research Program where doctors are examining children with CFC syndrome in the hope of learning more about this disorder (National Organization for Rare Disorders, Inc., 2000).

Children with CFC may need special care in the classroom. They may fall behind in their lessons due to mental retardation or to missing large amounts of classes. Additionally, these children may be on pain management techniques that interfere with their schooling.

REFERENCES

Levack, N. (1991). *Low vision: A resource guide with adaptations for students with vision impairments*. Texas School for the Blind.

National Organization for Rare Disorders, Inc. (2000). Retrieved from www.rarediseases.org

MARYANN TONI PARRINO
Montclair University

CAREER EDUCATION FOR STUDENTS RECEIVING SPECIAL EDUCATION SERVICES

Career education is an essential component of transition planning that moves the student from school to the working world. Career education is particularly important for those students receiving special education services. Although definitions vary, career education has two levels. The first level of career education is the general orientation to the working world. The next step in career education is personalization of knowledge and skill development for the individual. Career education generally includes three components: identifying interests and aptitudes; developing or increasing awareness and knowledge of occupational alternatives; and developing and supporting attitudes and habits related to work.

Attention to career education is part of the changes made to IDEIA 2004 (PL 108-446). In particular, the principles of career education are evident in the changes made to the definition of transitional services. Specifically, the law requires that transitional services be based on the individual child's strengths, preferences, and interests (NICHCY, 2005). This is essentially career education, although the term is not used in the law's language. "Transition services" is the most recent terminology.

While career education might be thought of as something that occurs in the later school years, in reality, the foundation for aptitude and interest, knowledge, and attitudes about the working world occurs throughout the child's school year. Identifying interests and aptitudes is an ongoing process, with looking at what the young student can do and expanding on potential. Developing awareness and knowledge of occupational alternatives can be initiated through activities such as career days and field trips in the community. Development of attitudes toward work begins in the earliest years of education, where children can learn about the value of working hard and having pride in their efforts. Identifying interests and aptitudes; developing or increasing awareness and knowledge of occupational alternatives; and developing and supporting attitudes and habits related to work must be purposely taught, trained, and observed. Having career- or transition-oriented curricula infused in the early school years can help students' knowledge and skill foundations for later training and may help decrease at-risk behaviors such as dropping out later (Razeghi, 1998).

As the student gets older, career education knowledge and skill sets may be part of the general curriculum available to all students. The Individualized Educational Plan (IEP) will set out specific goals and objectives that are linked to the student's working future. The student in special education may take classes that are in the general curriculum (e.g., industrial arts or agriculture science) that are related to future goals or interests. The student may be involved in activities such as work study that specially relate to career development. Paid employment for students in special education during high school can also be considered and may be one key predictor of future success (Eisenman, 2003). Other options, particularly for students with higher incidence of special education needs, may be school-wide activities such as career fairs, specific courses such as cooking, activities such as college nights, and outside employment. For students with more diverse learning needs, career education may be infused in the Life Skills curriculum or may be individualized to meet the needs of each student. This may include activities such as sheltered employment or work activities, where the work and support are tailored to the individual student.

For most students, formal career counseling will generally include three components: assessment, counseling, and planning (Roessler, Shearing, & Williams, 2000). Assessment can include standardized tests of interests and aptitude as well as interviews with the student, teachers, and parents about strengths, interests, and preferences. For students with greater cognitive or other challenges, the assessment process will also include careful assessment of overall life skills.

The assessment process will be followed by individualized counseling, which includes the student and parents. Parental involvement and support appears to be crucial (Eisenman, 2003). Assessment results are shared, and they can become the foundation of the counseling. Counseling includes understanding and sharing student and parent perspectives on the future, including career goals and living arrangements.

At this point, planning for the desired outcomes occurs. This includes involvement of community and/or state agencies, determining and following through on changes in legal standing such as managing conservator for the parents, and determination of future living arrangements. For all students, the goal of career education is to maximize their potential in the working world.

REFERENCES

Eisenman, L. T. (2003). Theories in practice: School-to-work-transitions-for-youth with mild disabilities. *Exceptionalities, 11*(2), 89–102.

NICHCY. (2005). *NICHCY Connections to Resources on IDEA 2004*. Retrieved from http://www.nichcy.org/resources/IDEA 2004resources.asp

PL 108-446. The Individuals with Disabilities Education Improvement Act of 2004.

Razeghi, J. A. (1998). A first step toward solving the problem of special education dropouts: Infusing career education into the curriculum. *Intervention in School & Clinic, 33*(3), 148–157.

Roessler, R., Shearing, A., & Williams, E. (2000). Three recommendations to improve transition planning in the IEP. *Journal for Vocational Special Needs, 22*(2), 31–36.

CONSTANCE J. FOURNIER
Texas A&M University

See also Learning Disabled College Students; Rehabilitation; Vocational Evaluation

CARIBBEAN, SPECIAL EDUCATION IN

Recognition of special education is a relatively recent phenomenon in the Caribbean. Although services for persons with special needs were evident in the first half of the 20th century, increased government involvement began in the second half of the century. Nongovernmental organizations and individuals with humanitarian concerns were the architects of special education services in the region, and these groups are still involved. Consequently, national associations for the deaf and local chapters of the Salvation Army, for example, continue to play indispensable roles in educating persons with hearing and visual impairments. Activities relating to physical disabilities, mental retardation, learning disabilities, and multiple disabilities have gained prominence over the years.

There is no island with a legislated policy exclusively for special education. However, interest groups use existing legislation relating to general education, as well as statements made by governments relating to "education for all," as fuel in their quest for appropriate support. Governments are committed, therefore, to the concept of equal educational opportunities for children with special needs in the school system. This commitment is displayed in special education units (departments responsible for national special education affairs) in the Education Ministries of the Republic of Trinidad and Tobago and Jamaica, and at least one special education officer in some of the other islands. Education officers work in close collaboration with special and mainstream schools and other relevant institutions. Most of the special education schools and institutions are incorporated into the public

system; therefore, governments are responsible for recurrent expenditure, including the payment of salaries. There are, however, some institutions operating independently by private sector and nongovernmental organizations.

In the Caribbean, most of the children with special needs are in mainstream schools without adequate support. For example, in the Republic of Trinidad and Tobago, the Ministry of Education (1993) reports a lack of services for the 13.1% of special needs children not in school; 5.8% in preschool; 5.1% attending special schools; 6.7% in other facilities, and 67.2% in mainstream schools. The implication is that only 2.1% of children with special needs are in the mainstream with adequate support.

A similar situation is also evident in Jamaica, where persons either attending government-aided special schools or enrolled in facilities operated by nongovernmental agencies comprise 0.64% of the 680,700 individuals in the mainstream preschool-to-secondary population (Planning Institute of Jamaica, 1996). However, using census data for 4 of 14 parishes, obtained from the Statistical Institute of Jamaica, Hall and Figueroa note that persons with disabilities comprised 4.8% of the population in these parishes, and that approximately 1.8% or 4,364 were in the 10–19 age group. From this group, 1,000 were attending secondary schools. A survey of secondary schools in the four parishes mentioned indicate that both students with special needs and their teachers believed that support was either absent or inadequate (Hall & Figueroa, 1998).

Overall, the support provided in the region is at varying levels of quality and organization, within both schools and institutions. In Jamaica, for example, there is a national Braille and large-print service, and over 400 texts have been printed and distributed to schools. Furthermore, at the Mona Campus of the University of the West Indies (UWI), there is a very active committee for students with special needs comprised of students and staff. Over the years, the committee has been acquiring resource materials to enhance the learning environment of the students. In January 1998, a member of the committee, who is blind and also a graduate student, created history when he was appointed Senator by the Jamaican Prime Minister.

Throughout the region, the current decade has witnessed intense efforts by persons with and without disabilities to pass local legislation relating to special needs. For example, in Jamaica, the Combined Disabilities Association finalized a draft of a policy for disabled persons in Jamaica for submission to the government. The basic tenets are grounded in the "Standard Rules on the Equalization of Opportunities," published by the United Nations. Education is one of the 11 policy issues addressed in the draft (Combined Disabilities of Jamaica, 1997).

The training of special education teachers began in 1971 with the introduction of a 1-year certificate program at UWI Mona Campus for teachers of the deaf. In 1976, Mico Teachers College began offering a 3-year program in mental retardation, learning disabilities, hearing impairment, and physical disabilities. These initial training program are still available, and recently visual impairment was included. In 1986, Mico, in collaboration with UWI, began a Bachelor in Education program in special education. Each of the programs mentioned has had large financial support from the Government of the Netherlands and regional governments, and is accessed by students throughout the region. In 1994, a B.Ed in "Managing Learning Difficulties" began at Mona, UWI. The program focuses on learners in mainstream classes. Graduate-level courses in special education are offered at Mona, and Cave Campus in Barbados introduced a Master in Education in special education during the 1997–98 academic year. In Trinidad and Tobago the local teachers' association, working in collaboration with a university in the United Kingdom, offers graduate-level training to its teachers.

There are other training programs throughout the region. For example, the Caribbean Association for the Mental Retarded or Developmental Disabilities (CAMRODD), a regional association, has a 3-year Parent Empowerment Program. Pairs of parents and professionals from several islands, including Antigua, Saba, St. Lucia, Barbados, St. Vincent, and Trinidad and Tobago, were involved (CAMRODD, 1997). The general plan is for participants involved in training to implement parent training workshops in their communities.

The major challenge in the region is economic constraint, and this manifests itself in part in limited resources, including personnel. Identifying persons without overt disabilities continues to be a challenge in the absence of appropriate assessment measures and in the inability of educators to employ nontraditional or alternative measures. There is also the need for general education for parents and professionals as well as urging agencies to collaborate so that limited resources can be maximized.

Future directions in the field must encompass aspects of early identification of special needs, more community involvement, inclusion, giftedness, and public education. In Barbados, for example, there are plans to assess annually children in the 3-to-7-year age group for visual, hearing, and speech impairments (Ministry of Education, Youth Affairs, & Culture, 1995). The Republic of Trinidad and Tobago has plans to establish regional diagnostic prescriptive centers. The Mico College Centre for Child Assessment and Research, a diagnostic and therapeutic center, is committed to intensifying its efforts in the area of research and its dissemination. The UWI, working with both governmental and nongovernmental agencies, is continuing to set standards and respond to needs with the delivery of relevant research and pedagogy. Finally, if work in progress in the area of special needs continues unabated, and plans articulated are implemented, interest groups within the region can greet the end of the millennium with optimism.

REFERENCES

Caribbean Association for the Mentally Retarded or Developmental Disabilities (CAMRODD). (1997). *CAMRODD's parent empowerment programme*. Jamaica: 3D's Documentation Unit.

Combined Disabilities of Jamaica. (1997). *Draft national policy for persons with disabilities*. Jamaica: Author.

Hall, W. M., & Figueroa M. (1998). Jamaican children with special needs: Concerns, realities and possibilities. *Disability and Society, 13*(2).

Ministry of Education. (1993). *Education policy paper: 1993–2003*. Trinidad and Tobago: Author.

Ministry of Education, Youth Affairs, & Culture. (1995). *White paper on education reform: Preparing for the 21st century*. Barbados: Government of Barbados.

Planning Institute of Jamaica. (1996). *Economic and social survey of Jamaica*. Jamaica: Author.

WINNIFRED M. HALL
University of the West Indies, Jamaica

COLLETTE LEYVA
KIMBERLY M. RENNIE
Texas A&M University

See also Ethics, International and Special Education

CARNINE, DOUGLAS W. (1947–   )

A native of Sullivan, Illinois, Douglas Carnine obtained his BS (1969) in psychology from the University of Illinois, Urbana, his MA (1971) in special education from the University of Oregon, Eugene, and his PhD (1974) in educational psychology from the University of Utah, Salt Lake City. In 1975, Carnine became an assistant professor in the Department of Education at the University of Oregon, Eugene, where he achieved the rank of full professor in 1987. Dr. Carnine was the director of the National Center to Improve Tools in Education (NCITE), which focused on state literacy initiatives, and also worked with legislative and state groups to support research-based educational tools for at-risk students.

As an undergraduate student, Carnine began working with Wesley Becker to conduct research on classroom management, and later assisted Siegfried Englemann in the development of DISTAR arithmetic (and still later, Connecting Math Concepts) as well as the implementation, in 10 school districts in eight states, of the Direct Instruction model of teaching (Silbert, Carnine, & Stein, 1981). These experiences led to his belief that curriculum, staff development, and administrative leadership must be addressed as effective interacting systems in any program intended to improve schools. Carnine argued that while administrators should take the lead in introducing school effectiveness programs, those program should be built on research on teaching variables (Engelmann & Carnine, 1982).

Discouraged about excessive demands on teachers' time, he has also investigated the effects of technology on the quality of instructional programs and improving teacher efficiency (Carnine, 1983).

Writing extensively on school-improvement programs, his publications range from *Theory of Instruction* (1982) to *Learning Pascal* (1988) as well as chapters in *School Improvement Programs: A Handbook for Educational Leaders* (1995), *Changing School Reading Programs* (1988), and *Teaching Struggling and At-Risk Readers* by Prentice Hall (Carnine & Silbert, 2005). His most recent book (with Siegfried Engelmann) is a historical analysis, *Could John Stuart Mill Have Saved Our Schools?* (2011). He was a featured speaker at the 1994 Summit on Learning Disabilities of the National Center for Learning Disabilities, Inc., and is recognized in *Who's Who in American Education*, third edition.

REFERENCES

Carnine, D. (1983). Direct institutional: In search of instructional solutions for educational problems. In D. Carnine & D. Elkind (Eds.), *Interdisciplinary voices in learning disabilities and remedial education* (pp. 1–66). Austin, TX: PRO-ED.

Carnine, D. (1988). How to overcome barriers to student achievement. In S. J. Samuels & P. D. Pearson (Eds.), *Changing school reading programs: Principles and case studies*. Newark, DE: International Reading Association.

Carnine, D. W., Grossen, B., & Silbert, J. (1995). Direct instruction to accelerate cognitive growth. In J. H. Block, S. T. Everson, & T. R. Guskey (Eds.), *School improvement programs: A handbook for educational leaders*. New York, NY: Scholastic.

Carnine, D. W., & Silbert, J. (2005). *Teaching struggling and at-risk readers: A direct instruction approach*. New York, NY: Prentice Hall.

Englemann, S., & Carnine, D. W. (1982). *Theory of instruction*. New York, NY: Irvington.

Englemann, S., & Carnine, D. W. (2011). *Could John Stuart Mill have saved our schools?* Madison, WI: Full Court Press.

Niedelman, M. S., & Carnine, D. (1988). *Learning Pascal*. Glenview, IL: Scott-Foresman.

Silbert, J., Carnine, D., & Stein, M. (1981). *Direct instruction mathematics*. Columbus, OH: Merrill.

E. VALERIE HEWITT
Texas A&M University
First edition

TAMARA J. MARTIN
The University of Texas of the Permian Basin
Second edition

CARNITINE PALMITOYLTRANSFERASE DEFICIENCY, TYPE I

Carnitine palmitoyltransferase deficiency (CPT) is an extremely rare genetic disorder of mitochondrial fatty-acid oxidation. Two forms of this genetic defect have been described: CPT-I and CPT-II. CPT-I is a more severe form (hepatocardiomuscular syndrome) associated with onset in infancy. CPT-II is a milder form of muscle disease associated with an adult presentation.

Of the two forms of this disorder, CPT-I, the hepatic form, has been documented the most. Ten patients (5 males and 5 females) with CPT-I have been reported in 8 families. Ethnic origins of patients with the hepatic form of the disease include Caucasian, Middle Eastern, Central American Indian, Inuit, and Asian Indian.

Characteristics

1. Initial onset usually in infancy (neonatal period to 18 months)
2. *CPT-I*: First presenting illness usually associated with fasting (viral infection, diarrhea) with attacks of vomiting, coma, seizures, hepatomegaly, and hypoglycemia
3. No evidence of chronic muscle weakness or cardiomyopathy
4. *CPT-II*: muscle pain after exhaustive exercise or fasting
5. Persistent neurological deficit, probably resulting from the initial insult
6. Developmental delays and cognitive deficits associated with neurological insult

A major element in management is avoidance of fasting. Recurrent episodes are common and have been successfully treated with glucose. Frequent feeding and special diet including reduction of fat appear to be beneficial. Children with mitochondrial disorders might have normal intelligence or static mental retardation or developmental delay. Children may have long periods with a stable neurologic picture simulating a static encephalopathy and later deteriorate either in an acute or in a slowly progressive manner (Nissenkorn et al., 2000). Of the 10 patients that have been reported, all but 1 are alive. Evaluation for special education needs is recommended. Many of these children will qualify for services under the classification of Other Health Impairment as a result of their medical condition. Future research should attempt to determine reasons behind the onset of CPT-I versus CPT-II.

REFERENCE

Nissenkorn, A., Zeharia, A., Lev, D., Watember, N., Fattal-Valevski, A., Barash, V.,...Lerman-Sagie, T. (2000). Neurologic presentations of mitochondrial disorders. *Journal of Child Neurology, 15,* 44–48.

VIRDETTE L. BRUMM
Children's Hospital Los Angeles Keck / USC School of Medicine

Characteristics

1. Usually found more frequently in individuals with diabetes and/or malnourishment
2. Detectable in adolescence or adulthood
3. Easy fatigue after prolonged periods of strenuous exercise or activity
4. Weak and disabling muscles lasting possibly for weeks after the onset
5. Red-brown urine

CARNITINE PALMITOYLTRANSFERASE DEFICIENCY, TYPE II

Carnitine palmitoyltransferase deficiency (CPT) is a very rare autosomal recessive genetic disease created from the interaction of one gene from the mother and one gene from the father. Thus, the condition does not appear in the child unless the same defective gene for the same trait from each parent is inherited. If only one normal and one gene with the disease are passed on, the child will be a carrier of the disease but usually will not show symptoms. If both parents are carriers of the recessive disease, the child has a 25% chance of demonstrating positive symptoms of the disease, a 50% chance of being of carrier, and a 25% chance of receiving both normal genes from each parent (Schaefer, Jackson, Taroni, Swift, & Turnbull, 1997).

The defective gene responsible for CPT Type I (CPT-I) regulates the production of the enzyme CPTase I. CPT Type II (CPT-II) is a milder form of the disorder that affects adults. CPT-I is located on the long arm of Chromosome 11, and CPT-II is located on the short arm of Chromosome 1. If a member of the family is diagnosed with CPT-II, each child in the family should be tested in order to take necessary precautions to avoid the symptoms of the illness.

CPT is very rare and observed in males more frequently than in females. This disease is seen more in individuals with diabetes and those who may be malnourished. The disorder is usually detectable in adolescence and adulthood. CPT is characterized by easy fatigability after prolonged periods of strenuous exercise. Weak and disabling muscles along with stiffness and pain may last for days. Destruction of the skeletal muscles may be followed by a passage of red-brown urine. The combination of these conditions can be life threatening (Schaefer, Jackson, Taroni, Swift, & Turnbull, 1997).

Related disorders with similar symptoms include Eaton-Lambert syndrome, scapuloperoneal myopathy, and fibromyalgia. Like CPT, these disorders are characterized by fatigue and muscle stiffness and deterioration of muscle tissue.

CPT is usually diagnosed by enzymatic studies and muscle biopsy. Persons diagnosed with metabolic problems should be cognizant of the types of foods eaten, specifically avoid high fatty foods, avoid a highly stressful lifestyle, and exercise in moderation (Schaefer et al., 1997). To aid in controlling the severity of the symptoms associated with this disease, supportive therapies include nutritional counseling, individual or family therapy, and frequent contact with school professionals to ensure that the ramifications from this disease are not hindering the child's learning. Additionally, genetic counseling is warranted for the affected individual and the family.

REFERENCE

Schaefer, J., Jackson, S., Taroni, F., Swift, P., & Turnbull, D. M. (1997). Characterization of carnitine palmitoyltransferases in patients with carnitine palmitoyltransferase deficiency: Implications for diagnosis and therapy. *Journal of Neurology Neurosurgery and Psychiatry, 62*(2), 169–176.

LISA A. FASNACHT-HILL
*Keck University of Southern California School of Medicine,
University of Southern California /
University Affiliated Program at Children's Hospital of Los Angeles*

CARPAL TUNNEL SYNDROME

Carpal tunnel syndrome (CTS) is a type of cumulative trauma disorder in the sense that it develops after protracted repetitive mechanical stress on musculoskeletal systems (Putz-Anderson, 1988). Musculoskeletal system disorders can subdivided into three classifications, namely nerve, neurovascular, and tendon disorders. CTS is considered a nerve compression disorder. Specifically, it is the resultant neuropathy associated with restriction of the median nerve passing through the carpal tunnel. Nerve compression disorders usually result in reduction or complete loss of motor, particularly fine motor skills, sensory, and sensory perception. In severe cases, complete autonomic nerve function is lost.

> ## Characteristics
>
> 1. Pain, numbness, reduced grip strength
> 2. Reduction or loss of fine motor skills in afflicted hand
> 3. Reduction or loss of sensation in afflicted hand
> 4. Weakness and tingling in hand
> 5. Dropping objects and reduced range of motion
> 6. Autonomic nerve function loss
> 7. Complete loss of hand function
> 8. History of prolonged, repetitive stress on afflicted hand

CTS has received special attention in recent years in children as a result of work-related injuries to children in underdeveloped countries. Children's hospitals and clinics have seen a proliferation of CTS and other nerve compression disorders associated with repeated and sustained work-related activities in the United States and abroad, but particularly in nations in which child labor laws are not enforced (Gross, 1988; U.S. Department of Labor, Bureau of Statistices, 1997).

Treatment for CTS varies from restriction of motion and medication to surgery in more severe cases. Future research should focus on the development of ergonomic methods capable of reducing these work-related injuries through human factor engineering and better surveillance. In the case of childhood injuries, the enforcement of child labor laws has been found to be a critical factor in reducing these injuries. Special education for these children should include the development of curriculum modification under an Other Health Impairment label. The application of technology as a way of reducing the use of the afflicted limb also is usually beneficial (Armstrong, 1986).

REFERENCES

Armstrong, T. J. (1986). Ergonomics and cumulative trauma disorders. *Hand Clinics, 2,* 553–565.

Gross, C. M. (1988). *Diagnostic criteria for cumulative trauma disorders of the upper extremity.* New York, NY: Melville.

Putz-Anderson, V. (Ed.). (1988). *Cumulative trauma disorders: A manual for musculoskeletal diseases of the upper limbs.* New York, NY: Taylor & Francis.

U.S. Department of Labor, Bureau of Statistics. (1997). *Worker injuries and illnesses by selected classification (1982–1996).* Washington, DC: U.S. Department of Labor.

ANTOLIN M. LLORENTE
Baylor College of Medicine,
Houston, Texas

CARPENTER SYNDROME (ACROCEPHALOPOLYSYNDACTYLY, TYPE II)

Carpenter syndrome (acrocephalopolysyndactyly, Type II) is a congenital condition that was first described in 1901 by George Carpenter, a British pediatrician (Islek, Kucuko-duk, Incesu, Selcuk, & Aygun, 1998). Although Carpenter syndrome presents with marked phenotypical variability (Islek et al.), defining characteristics of this disorder include acrocephaly (peaked head), craniosynostosis (premature closure of the cranial sutures), craniofacial asymmetry, soft tissue syndactyly (webbing of the fingers and toes), and preaxial polydactyly, primarily of the toes (Ashby, Rouse, & DeLange, 1994; National Organization for Rare Disorders, Inc. [NORD], 2000).

Carpenter syndrome occurs so rarely that only 43 cases, representing both isolated cases and recurrence in siblings, have been reported in the literature to date (Islek et al., 1998). There is significant intrafamilial variability as evidenced by affected siblings who present with very different profiles; in one instance, a female twin was affected while her twin brother was not (Ashby et al., 1994). Carpenter syndrome has been identified worldwide in males and females of various ethnicities. Affected individuals have ranged in age from a 20-week-old fetus to an adult male of 49 years (Balci, Onol, Eryilmaz, & Haytoglu, 1997). Parental age does not seem to be a factor in causation of Carpenter syndrome as the condition has been noted in children born to teens as well as to middle-aged parents. The fact that consanguinity of parents of affected children has been reported in six cases and suspected in one may be of potential significance (Al-Arrayed, 1999; Gershoni-Baruch, 1990).

The etiology of Carpenter syndrome is presently unknown. Although it is presumed to be the result of autosomal recessive inheritance, there is some speculation that it results from codominant or dominant inheritance, based on the fact that a father of four children with Carpenter syndrome also presented with some characteristics of the disorder (Al-Arrayed, 1999).

> ## Characteristics
>
> 1. Essential characteristics of Carpenter syndrome are acrocephaly; soft tissue syndactyly of the fingers and toes; craniosynostosis of the sagittal, lambdoid, and coronal cranial sutures; craniofacial asymmetry; and preaxial polydactyly, primarily of the toes (Islek et al., 1998; Taravath & Tonsgard, 1993).
> 2. Associated complications may include cardiovascular defects (seen in about a third of affected individuals), mild to moderate obesity, short stature, unusually short fingers and

toes, hypogenitalism, umbilical hernia, and cryptorchidism (NORD, 2000).

3. The most frequently occurring facial features include a flat nasal bridge; dysplastic, low-set ears; a small mouth with a hypoplastic maxilla or mandible; a narrow, high-arched palate; and abnormal and missing permanent teeth (NORD, 2000). About 50% of documented cases have abnormalities of the eyes, including corneal opacity and optic atrophy; other features include shallow orbits, palpebral fissures, epicanthic folds, and hypertelorism.

4. Some degree of intellectual impairment has been identified in approximately 75% of individuals with Carpenter syndrome; however, normal intelligence levels, with IQ scores of 103, have also been described. Mental retardation is common but is not necessary for a diagnosis; when it does occur, IQ scores have been reported in the mildly to profoundly retarded range (Islek et al., 1998).

5. Other problems include sensorineural hearing loss, visual impairments, delayed or impaired language, and speech problems in the areas of articulation, nasality, and resonance (Shprintzen, 1997).

6. Developmental milestones are generally acquired later than normal, and growth retardation is a constant feature of this condition.

A diagnosis of Carpenter syndrome is confirmed by examination of its phenotypic manifestations. Prenatal diagnosis has also been successfully attempted with the use of ultrasound in the second trimester and transabdominal embryoscopy in the first. The issue of differential diagnosis is particularly important because there is such variability in its expression and because there are a number of conditions that mimic this disorder. For example, Goodman and Summitt syndromes are considered to belong within the clinical spectrum of Carpenter syndrome but are associated with normal intelligence and often an absence of polydactyly (Gershoni-Baruch, 1990; Islek et al., 1998). The syndrome has also been diagnosed in individuals without acrocephaly, craniosynostosis, and congenital heart defects (Gershoni-Baruch, 1990).

Cranial computer tomography (CT) and magnetic resonance imaging (MRI) scans are used to indicate level of involvement, treatment plans, and prognosis. Treatment of Carpenter syndrome during the first year of life includes surgical intervention that is usually performed in stages. Such surgery is used mainly to correct cranial deformities, to support rapid growth of the brain, and to prevent mental retardation (Balci et al., 1997). Other treatment may include hand and foot surgery for release of syndactyly,

correction of cardiac defects, and midface advancement and jaw surgery (Shprintzen, 1997).

Psychoeducational interventions for the child with Carpenter syndrome will depend on the degree of involvement as well as on its severity. Most of these children will qualify for special educational services under the handicapping conditions of physical disabilities or multiple disabilities; as such, the Individualized Educational Plan (IEP) must offer comprehensive and aggressive treatment efforts designed to address the whole range of each child's needs. Such a child may need special educational services to remediate or compensate for cognitive and academic deficits and to develop social-behavioral skills. In addition, the IEP must outline the use of support services such as physical and occupational therapy to address gross and fine motor deficits, speech and language services, and assistance for hearing or visual impairments. Self-help and socialization skills may be limited because of retardation but also because of physical deficits. As children with Carpenter syndrome age, they may exhibit developmental delays and increasing difficulty with daily tasks. Personal and vocational counseling may be beneficial, particularly for older children and adults. In addition, because Carpenter syndrome appears to be inherited, it is strongly recommended that adults with this condition undergo genetic counseling prior to marriage and pregnancy. In general, intervention efforts for individuals of all ages should be directed toward increasing self-sufficiency and independence.

The prognosis for individuals with Carpenter syndrome is variable, given its expression. There is presently no cure for this condition, but individuals with Carpenter syndrome can learn to function adequately given early intervention and adequate support. Carpenter syndrome is thought to be associated with reduced life expectancy; however, no studies have been reported in this area. Given Carpenter's marked phenotypical variability and the contradictory information regarding inheritance, it is likely that future research efforts will be directed toward clarifying these issues and improving the quality of life for individuals affected by this serious condition.

REFERENCES

Al-Arrayed, S. S. (1999). *Carpenter syndrome in eight Arab patients, dominant inheritance suspected.* Retrieved from http://www.faseb.org/genetics/ashg99/f751.htm

Ashby, T., Rouse, F. A., & DeLange, M. (1994). Prenatal sonographic diagnosis of Carpenter syndrome. *Journal of Ultrasound in Medicine, 13,* 905–909.

Balci, S., Onol, B., Eryilmaz, M., & Haytoglu, T. (1997). A case of Carpenter syndrome diagnosed in a 20-week-old fetus with postmortem examination. *Clinical Genetics, 51*(6), 412–416.

Gershoni-Baruch, R. (1990). Carpenter syndrome: Marked variability of expression to include the Summitt and Goodman syndromes. *American Journal of Medical Genetics, 35*(2), 236–40.

Islek, I., Kucukoduk, S., Incesu, L., Selcuk, M. B., & Aygun, D. (1998, July). Carpenter syndrome: Report of two siblings. *Clinical Dysmorphology, 7*(3), 185–189.

National Organization for Rare Disorders, Inc. (2000). *Carpenter syndrome.* Retrieved from http://www.rarediseases.org

Shprintzen, R. J. (1997). *Genetics, syndromes, and communication disorders.* San Diego, CA: Singular.

Taravath, S., & Tonsgard, J. H. (1993). Cerebral malformations in Carpenter syndrome. *Pediatric Neurology, 9*(3), 230–234.

Mary M. Chittooran
Retha M. Edens
Saint Louis University

CARROW ELICITED LANGUAGE INVENTORY

The Carrow Elicited Language Inventory (CELI; Carrow, 1974) is a diagnostic test of expressive language, containing 51 sentences and one phrase that the child is required to repeat. The mean sentence length is six words. The sentences were selected to include basic sentence types, specific grammatical morphemes, and select transformational rules. The grammatical morphemes include nouns, plurals, verbs, adjectives, adverbs, pronouns, articles, negatives, prepositions, demonstratives, conjunctions, and contractions. The child's responses are audiotaped to assist the examiner in scoring errors on substitutions, omissions, additions, transpositions, and reversal. The manual provides mean total error scores and mean subcategory error scores for children between the ages of 3 years and 7 years 11 months at 1-year intervals. Percentile and stanine scores are also available.

The CELI was normed in 1973 on 475 White, middle-class Texans between 3 years and 7 years 11 months. Children who were identified with speech or language disorders were excluded from the normative sample. Validity of the CELI has been established by its ability to discriminate between children with and without language disorders and to identify children at high risk for learning disorders (Blau, Lahey, & Oleksiuk-Velez, 1984; Swift, 1984). Test–retest reliability at 2-week intervals is reported at .98, but this should be interpreted with caution because of the small sample size employed.

A major assumption underlying the CELI is that a child's imitations of model sentences will closely resemble his or her proficiency in spontaneous speech. However, numerous studies question the validity of the sentence imitation tasks as a valid measure of spontaneous language (Connell & Myles-Zitzer, 1982; Haniff & Seigel, 1981; Kuczaj & Maratsos, 1975; McDade & Simpson, 1983; Prutting, Gallagher, & Mulac, 1975). A weakness of this

test is that the normative data are limited (small sample size, restricted geographic region, and limited SES) and out of date.

REFERENCES

Blau, A. F., & Lahey, M., Oleksiuk-Velez, A. (1984). Planning goals for intervention: Language testing or language sampling? *Exceptional Children, 1,* 78–79.

Carrow, E. (1974). *Carrow Elicited Language Inventory.* Boston, MA: Teaching Resources Corporation.

Connell, P. J., & Myles-Zitzer, C. (1982). An analysis of elicited imitation as a language evaluation procedure. *Journal of Speech and Hearing Disability, 47,* 390–396.

Haniff, M. H., & Seigel, G. M. (1981). The effect of context on verbal elicited imitation. *Journal of Speech and Hearing Disability, 46,* 27–30.

Kuczaj, S., & Maratsos, M. (1975). What children can say before they will. *Merrill-Palmer Quarterly, 21,* 89–112.

McDade, H. L., & Simpson, M. A. (1983). Reply to Carrow-Woolfolk. *Journal of Speech and Hearing Disorders, 3,* 334–335.

Prutting, C. A., Gallagher, T. M., & Mulac, A. (1975). The expressive portion of the NSST compared to a spontaneous language sample. *Journal of Speech and Hearing Disabilities, 40,* 40–48.

Swift, C. (1984). Sentence imitation in kindergarten children at risk for learning disability: A comparative study. *Language, Speech, & Hearing Services in Schools, 1,* 10–15.

Margo E. Wilson
Lexington, Kentucky
First edition

Roseann Bisighini
The Salk Institute
Second edition

See also Language Delays; Language Disorders

CARTWRIGHT, G. PHILLIP (1937–)

G. Phillip Cartwright received his BS in 1960 in psychology and MS in 1962 in special education from the University of Illinois. He received his PhD in 1966 in special education and educational research from the University of Pittsburgh. Currently, he is professor and head of the Division of Special Education and Communication Disorders, Pennsylvania State University.

In the 1960s, Cartwright became convinced that the American education system was not providing an adequate education for children with disabilities. He attempted to implement the then-heretical idea of training regular educators to identify youngsters with disabilities in their early years and to help those youngsters to succeed in a regular classroom. Cartwright also proposed that the training of both regular and special education teachers be modified to include learning the use of alternative training approaches (Cartwright, 1977). One such approach is the use of computer technology in the process of training teachers (Cartwright, 1984). With this philosophy, Cartwright developed a series of computer-assisted instruction (CAI) courses (Cartwright, Cartwright, & Robine, 1972).

Cartwright continues his work in the field of computer-assisted instruction, writing pieces for *Change* promoting an increase in expertise and technology through partnerships between business and higher education (Barton & Cartwright, 1997) and outlining a technology program using a computer program to deliver courses at universities (Sedlak, 1997).

Cartwright has been recognized in *American Men and Women in Science, Who's Who in the East*, and *Leaders in Education*.

REFERENCES

Barton, L., & Cartwright, G. P. (1997). Reciprocal technology transfer: Changing partnerships. *Change, 29,* 44–47.

Cartwright, G. P. (1977). Educational technology. In S. Tarver & R. Kneedler (Eds.), *Changing perspectives in education.* Columbus, OH: Merrill.

Cartwright, G. P. (1984). Computer applications in special education. In D. F. Walker & R. D. Hess (Eds.), *Instructional software for design and use.* Belmont, CA: Wadsworth.

Cartwright, G. P., Cartwright, C. A., & Robine, G. C. (1972). CAI course in the early identification of handicapped children. *Exceptional Children, 38,* 453–459.

Sedlak, R. A. (1997). Two approaches to distance education: Lessons learned. *Change, 29,* 54–56.

E. Valerie Hewitt
Texas A&M University

CASCADE MODEL OF SPECIAL EDUCATION SERVICES

The Cascade Model of Special Education Services is a conceptualization of the range of placement and service options that used to be available for children with disabilities. The placement options were presented in hierarchical form and ranged from the least restrictive placement in the regular education classroom to the most restrictive placement in hospital or institutional settings. The Cascade Model was first proposed by Reynolds in 1962 and an amended version was proposed by Deno in 1970. Both proposals predated the passage of the Education of All Handicapped Children Act of 1975 (PL 94-142), a time

when placement and service options for the handicapped were scarce. Reynolds and Birch (1977) characterized the pre-PL 94-142 administrative arrangements as a two-box system in which parallel but separate educational programs for regular and special education were in operation within school buildings. Interaction and movement of children between the two systems was difficult at best, and more often, nonexistent. The Cascade Model helped create understanding of and support for a better system that "facilitates tailoring of treatment to individual needs rather than a system for sorting out children so they will fit conditions designed according to group standards not necessarily suitable for the particular case" (Deno, 1970, p. 235).

The Cascade Model visually appeared as a triangular form that contained two essential elements: the degree of placement specialization and the relative number of children in the various placement options. The base of the triangle coincided with regular classroom placement, the preferred placement for the largest number of students with disabilities. Progressively more specialized placements were included as the triangle extended toward the apex. The decreasing width of the triangle reflected the decreasing numbers of children to be placed in progressively more restrictive environments. Deno's Cascade Model was widely cited and reproduced; it has become a fundamental concept for the field of special education. (See Figure C.1 for an example of the Cascade Model.)

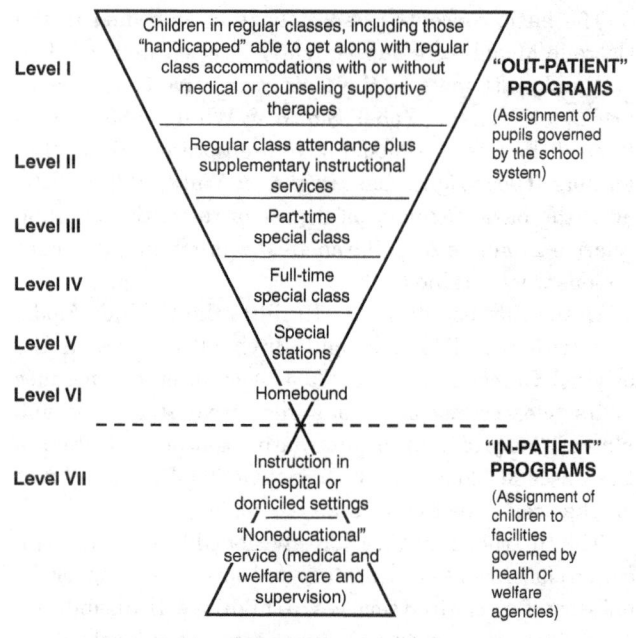

Figure C.1. The cascade system of special education service. The tapered design indicates the considerable difference in the numbers involved at the different levels and calls attention to the fact that the system serves as a diagnostic filter. The most specialized facilities are likely to be needed by the fewest children on a long-term basis. This organizational model can be applied to the development of special education services for all types of disabilities.

Source: Peterson, Zabel, Smith, and White (1983, pp. 404–408).

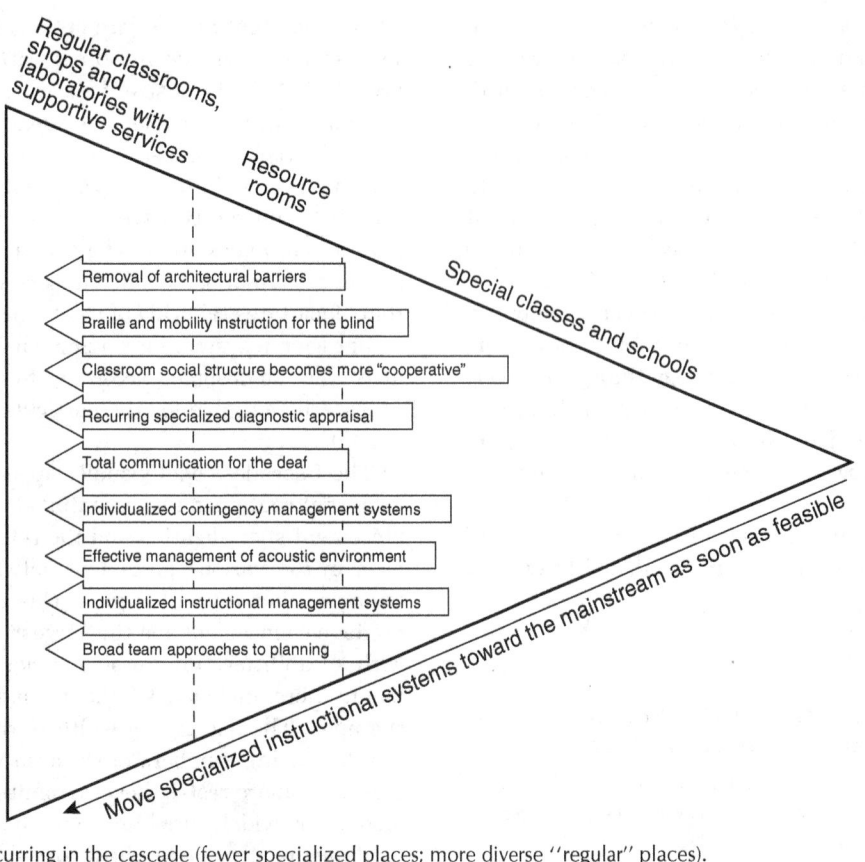

Figure C.2. Changes occurring in the cascade (fewer specialized places; more diverse ''regular'' places).
Source: Peterson, Zabel, Smith, and White (1983, pp. 404–408).

The basic concepts of specialization embodied in the Cascade Model were subsequently incorporated into federal and state laws as the least restrictive environment principle (Peterson, Zabel, Smith, & White, 1983). Variations of the Cascade Model have been presented by other authors (Cartwright, Cartwright, & Ward, 1985). However, the basic elements of degree of restrictiveness and relative numbers of children in the different placement options were retained.

Despite its popularity and utility, the Cascade Model was criticized. Reynolds and Birch (1977) viewed the original Cascade Model as "too place oriented" because of its "clearest focus on administrative structures and places." They offered an alternative conceptualization of the Cascade Model in which instructional diversity was emphasized. (See Figure C.2.)

The Instructional Cascade envisioned the regular education classroom as the primary and optimal setting for the delivery of specialized services to children with disabilities.

Children were seen as moving among the levels of the cascade for educational purposes. Ideally, a child would be moved to a more restrictive setting only for compelling educational reasons and was moved back as quickly as possible. The introduction of inclusive programming in the past few years has created a debate as to whether special education should abolish the Cascade Model. On one hand are conservative educators who believe in the original model that provided integration on a case-by-case method. On the other hand are abolitionists who believe in full inclusion for all special education students. At this time, federal law still supports individualization and many follow its lead (Fuchs, 1994). Retrospective studies in the next few years will probably determine the debate and also determine how the cascade of services will change. For example, Wolfe and Hall (2003) have devised a "cascade of integration options" for students with severe disabilities to receive full inclusion. This cascade includes options from unadapted participation in the general curriculum to functional curriculum outside the general education classroom. Regardless of names or labels, however, the determination of placement will always depend on the best interests of the student.

REFERENCES

Cartwright, G. P., Cartwright, C. A., & Ward, M. E. (1985). *Educating special learners* (2nd ed.). Belmont, CA: Wadsworth.

Deno, E. (1970). Special education as developmental capital. *Exceptional Children, 37*(3), 229–237.

Fuchs, D. (1994). *Best practices in school psychology: Peabody reintegration project.* (ERIC document No. ED378774.)

Peterson, R. L., Zabel, R. H., Smith, C. R., & White, M. A. (1983). Cascade of services model and emotionally disabled students. *Exceptional Children, 49*(5), 404–408.

Reynolds, M. C. (1962). A framework for considering some issues in special education. *Exceptional Children, 28*(7), 367–370.

Reynolds, M. C., & Birch, J. W. (1977). *Teaching exceptional children in all America's schools.* Reston, VA: Council for Exceptional Children.

Woffe, P. S., & Hall, T. E. (2003). Making inclusion a reality for students with severe disabilities. *Teaching Exceptional Children, 3*, 56–60.

LIBBY GOODMAN
Pennsylvania State University

See also Inclusion; Least Restrictive Environment; Philosophy of Education for Individuals With Disabilities; Special Class

CASE HISTORY

Case histories serve several purposes: to provide information about rare disorders, individual differences in treatment responsiveness, or the natural course for a disorder (Kratochwill, 1985); to provide information necessary to plan and monitor appropriate treatment; to provide data needed by external agencies; to illuminate pitfalls to be avoided; and to provide information for scientific, administrative, and instructional purposes.

Identification information in a complete case history should include client's name, date of birth, sex, ethnicity, dominant language, marital status, guardians' names if a minor, residence, phone number, persons to notify in an emergency, medical status, and current program status (e.g., grade or placement if an educational setting); this information should be in an easily located part of the record. Historical data, as determined relevant for client welfare by a multidisciplinary committee, should include developmental, health, and educational history; work history if an adult; and significant family events.

Specific statements of the concerns of the referral agent should be included. The client's status at the time of referral should include information about current health, including current medications; sensory or perceptual abilities; motor abilities; language skills; current adaptive behavior; intellectual abilities and academic skills; other cognitive data, such as current belief systems or attributions as may be pertinent to the referral problem; emotional behavior; social skills and behavior; family status; and vocational aptitudes, skills, and interests. A description of the client's current status with respect to the referring problem should always be included. The preintervention frequency of the problem behavior should be recorded to establish treatment effectiveness at a later time.

The case history should contain not only the treatment goals for a client, but the process by which those goals were determined, including dates of meetings for discussing goals, those who were present, alternative plans discussed, costs and benefits of alternative plans, and the final treatment plan agreed on. Records should also be maintained of the course of treatment implementation, including the goal to which the treatment session was directed, what was done during the session, and the clinician's notes about difficulties or unexpected results.

To establish intervention effectiveness, a record must be maintained of changes in the client's behavior or level of skill. Data from observations, self-monitoring, or other methods can be collected and recorded and effectiveness assessed by means of single-subject designs (Barlow & Hersen, 1984). These techniques have the advantage of demonstrating that specific treatments have been tried and have been effective or noneffective; of being sensitive to subtle changes in behavior; and of allowing the comparison of several alternative treatments.

REFERENCES

Barlow, D. H., & Hersen, M. (1984). *Single-case experimental designs: Strategies for studying behavior change* (2nd ed.). New York, NY: Pergamon Press.

Kratochwill, T. R. (1985). Case study research in school psychology. *School Psychology Review, 14*, 204–215.

JOHN MACDONALD
Eastern Kentucky University

See also Medical History; Mental Status Exams

CASTLEMAN DISEASE

Castleman disease (CD), also referred to as angiofollicular lymph node hyperplasia, is a heterogeneous group of lymphoproliferative disorders, characterized by abnormal growth of the lymph nodes. There are three histopathological variants of CD: hyaline-vascular type, which accounts for approximately 80–90% of reported cases; plasma cell type; and an intermediate, or mixed, histological type (Maslovsky & Lugassy, 1999). Clinical presentation of CD appears to be either localized or generalized (multicentric); however, there is controversy about whether the multicentric form is a distinct entity or simply a form of the plasma cell type (National Organization for Rare Disorders, Inc. [NORD], 2000; Parez, Bader-Meunier, Roy, & Dommergues, 1999). There is also some evidence that CD constitutes a spectrum of benign-to-malignant diseases (L. Malaguarnera, Pilastro, Vicari, Di Marco, M. Malaguarnera, & Messina, 1999) and that, if left untreated, the benign form of the disease may serve as a precursor to the malignant form (Parez et al., 1999).

Since it was first described in 1954, CD has been reported in fewer than 150 cases worldwide and appears to be more common in underdeveloped parts of Africa and southern Europe. Although the disease has been identified in both males and females, Smir, Greiner, and Weisenburger (1996) reported a male–female ratio of 1:3 in children. The disease occurs at all ages; however, its presentation in children tends to be localized, benign, and of the hyaline-vascular type (Parez et al., 1999). CD has a favorable clinical course in children, that is, low morbidity and mortality (Smir et al.). In adults, however, the disease tends to take an aggressive, often fatal course, and multicentric forms of the disease are common, particularly after age 50 (Malaguarnera et al., 1999).

The etiology of CD is presently unknown and somewhat controversial. Schulz (2000) speculated that genetic factors play an important role in this disorder. Malaguarnera et al. (1999) found that ornithine decarboxylase (ODC) gene expression varied between the localized and multicentric forms of the disease and suggested that aberrant ODC expression may be a critical factor in transforming a premalignant lesion into a malignant one. Researchers (e.g., Plaza & Gilbert-Barness, 2000) have suggested that certain environmental factors, as yet unidentified, could act as stimuli for the proliferation of lymph nodes. The association between HIV infection and multicentric CD in adults has been well established (Kumari, Schechter, Saini, & Benator, 2000), and Kaposi's sarcoma–associated herpesvirus (human herpes virus 8; HHV-8) is known to be involved in the pathogenesis of the plasma cell variant of multicentric CD in adults (Schulz, 2000). Elevated serum levels of Interleukin-6 (IL-6) have also been reported in patients with multicentric CD (Malaguarnera et al., 1999). Several medical conditions mimic CD; therefore, it is suggested that differential diagnoses of CD in children include consideration of microcytic anemia (De Heer-Groen, Prakken, Bax, & van Dijken, 1996), small round cell tumors of childhood (Fiel-Gan, Voytek, Weiss, Brown, & Joshi, 2000), and lymphoma.

Characteristics

1. Clinical presentation varies widely, but CD frequently manifests as a single mediastinal mass identified on radiographic examination. Although tumors develop most often in the chest and abdomen, they also occur in the axilla, pelvis, and pancreas. Tumors may represent abnormal enlargement of the lymph nodes normally found in these areas (lymphoid hamartoma).

2. The localized, hyaline-vascular type of CD is most common in children; affected individuals are frequently asymptomatic.

3. Multicentric, plasma cell CD, which is more common in adults, is characterized by fever, weight loss, chronic fatigue, general weakness, skin rash, and respiratory problems. Hepatosplenomegaly (abnormally large liver and spleen; NORD, 2000) may also be evident. Laboratory findings may include hemolytic anemia and hypergammaglobulinemia (increase of certain immune factors in the blood).

4. The intermediate type of CD may show features of both the hyaline-vascular and plasma cell variants.

5. Renal complications such as nephrotic syndrome have been infrequently reported.

The medical treatment of CD varies depending on its histologic variant, its clinical expression, and its severity. Surgical excision of localized tumors has been successful (Maslovsky & Lugassy, 1999) with the virtual disappearance of all symptoms following surgery; however, some recurrence of symptoms has been noted in adults (Tuerlinckx, Bodart, Delos, Remacle, & Ninane, 1997). Because multicentric CD is marked by a swift, often fatal course, treatment necessitates the use of aggressive chemotherapeutic regimens (Maslovsky & Lugassy, 1999). Some successes have been reported in the use of prednisone and retinoic acid (Parez et al., 1999; Rieu, Drooz, Gessain, Grunfeld, & Hermine, 1999), interferon-alpha (Kumari et al., 2000), and immunity-restoring methods such as HAART (Lanzafame, Carretta, Trevenzoli, Lazzarini, & Concia, 2000). Because patients present with immunosuppressive deficits, it has also been suggested (Maslovsky & Lugassy, 1999) that infections be treated promptly and that organ and blood donors be carefully screened.

Psychoeducational interventions for the child with CD depend on clinical presentation and degree of involvement. Children with localized CD may not have significant difficulties in a classroom other than those temporarily involved with surgery and postsurgical recovery. Children who present with the plasma cell multicentric variant may experience significant difficulties, particularly if the disease is not treated early or if it is inadequately managed. Many of these children will qualify for special educational services under Other Health Impairment; as such, the Individualized Educational Plan (IEP) must offer comprehensive efforts designed to address the whole range of needs, including academic, medical, social, and behavioral. As the disease progresses, children with multicentric CD may be hospitalized or homebound, and arrangements may have to be made for continued instruction as long as it is appropriate. Personal counseling may be beneficial for children and families, and vocational counseling should also be offered for adolescents.

Additional research studies are needed to clarify both the etiology and the pathophysiology of CD with a view to improving treatment options for affected individuals (Parez et al., 1999). Further, because CD has such variable clinical expression for age, it is anticipated that future research efforts will be directed toward differential management of the disease in children and adults.

REFERENCES

De Heer-Groen, T. A., Prakken, A. B. J., Bax, N. M. A., & van Dijken, P. J. (1996). Iron therapy resistant microcytic anemia in a 13-year old girl with Castleman disease. *European Journal of Pediatrics, 155*, 1015–1017.

Fiel-Gan, M. D., Voytek, T. M., Weiss, R. G., Brown, R. T., & Joshi, V. V. (2000). Castleman's disease of the left triceps in a child suspected to be a small round cell tumor of childhood. *Pedriatic and Developmental Pathology, 3*, 286–289.

Kumari, P., Schechter, G. P., Saini, N., & Benator, D. A. (2000). Successful treatment of human immunodeficiency virus–related Castleman's disease with interferon-alpha. *Clinical Infectious Diseases, 31*(2), 602–604.

Lanzafame, N., Carretta, G., Trevenzoli, M., Lassarini, L., & Concia, S. V. E. (2000). Successful treatment of Castleman's disease with HAART in two HIV-infected patients. *Journal of Infection, 40*(1), 90–91.

Malaguarnera, L., Pilastro, M. R., Vicari, L., Di Marco, R., Malaguarnera, M., & Messina, A. (1999). Ornithine decarboxylase gene expression in Castleman's disease. *Journal of Molecular Medicine, 77*, 798–803.

Maslovsky, I., & Lugassy, G. (1999). The management of Castleman's disease. *Blood, 94*(10), 4391.

National Organization for Rare Disorders, Inc. (2000). *Castleman's disease*. Retrieved from http://www.rarediseases.org

Parez, N., Bader-Meunier, B., Roy, C. C., & Dommergues, J. P. (1999). Paediatric Castleman disease: Report of seven cases and a review of the literature. *European Journal of Pediatrics, 158*(8), 631–637.

Plaza, M. C., & Gilbert-Barness, E. (2000). Castleman's disease: Pediatric pathology case. *Pediatric Pathology and Molecular Medicine, 19*(6), 487–490.

Rieu, P., Drooz, D., Gessain, A., Grunfeld, J. P., & Hermine, O. (1999). Retinoic acid for treatment of multicentric Castleman's disease. *Lancet, 354*(9186), 1262–1263.

Schulz, T. F. (2000). Kaposi's sarcoma–associated herpesvirus (human herpesvirus 8): Epidemiology and pathogenesis. *Journal of Antimicrobial Chemotherapy, 45*, 15–27.

Smir, B. N., Greiner, T. C., & Weisenburger, D. D. (1996). Multicentric angiofollicular lymph node hyperplasia in children:

A clinicopathologic study of eight patients. *Modern Pathology, 9*(12), 1135–1142.

Tuerlinckx, D., Bodart, E., Delos, M., Remacle, M., & Ninane, J. (1997). Unifocal cervical Castleman disease in two children. *European Journal of Pediatrics, 156*, 701–703.

MARY M. CHITTOORAN
Saint Louis University

CATALOG OF FEDERAL DOMESTIC ASSISTANCE

The *Catalog of Federal Domestic Assistance* (CFDA) is a compendium of over 2,197 programs, projects, and activities of the federal government that provide benefits or assistance to the public. The catalog provides basic descriptive information on each program or activity, such as the purposes of the program, eligible applicants, total funds available, examples and dollar range of prior awards, and person to contact. The catalog covers programs providing both financial and nonfinancial forms of assistance (e.g., information, technical assistance, transfer of real property). The catalog is now electronically disseminated through the CFDA website on the Internet. Printed copies of the catalog are no longer published for free, but may be obtained from the GPO (http://bookstore.gpo.gov) for $100.

Programs are organized by sponsoring agency, but are also indexed across all agencies by subject area, by the type of entity or individual eligible to apply for assistance, and even by application deadline (GSA, 2011). The indexes make the catalog a useful reference guide for someone trying to locate potential sources of assistance for a particular project or in a specific subject area (e.g., intellectual disability, early childhood education).

Users may call the Federal Service Desk by dialing (866) 606-8220 (national) or (334) 206-7828 (international) from 8:00 A.M. to 8:00 P.M. The website for the CFDA allows full free access to the catalog along with a user guide, search function, and additional resources (http://www.cfda.gov).

REFERENCE

General Services Administration. (2011). *Catalog of federal domestic assistance*. Washington, DC. Retrieved from https://www.cfda.gov/?s=generalinfo&mode=list&tab=list&tabmode=list&static=faqs

JAMES R. RICCIUTI
United States Office of Management and Budget

CATARACTS

A cataract is an imperfection in the clarity or a clouding of the lens of the eye. It will be experienced by a majority of people who live to an old age (Eden, 1978). In children, some cataracts are present at birth and others develop with metabolic or systemic abnormalities. In older children, cataracts are related to injuries or ocular inflammation due to juvenile arthritis (University of Minnesota, 2005).

Eden (1978) defines three types of cataracts. Senile cataracts are those that occur as part of the normal aging process. Cell layers form around the lens as people grow older; this is similar to rings forming in the trunks of trees. The lens becomes opaque and loses its resiliency. Secondary cataracts are those that result from some other trauma or disease. For example, persons with diabetes often develop cataracts. Secondary cataracts can also result from excessive radiation, electrical shock, and the side effects of some drugs. Excessive use of cortisone, for example, has been related to the development of lens opacity. Congenital cataracts are those that are present from birth. This type of cataract is very rare. Illnesses during pregnancy such as German measles (rubella) can cause congenital cataracts (Harley & Lawrence, 1977).

It was once thought that cataracts had to be "ripe" before the lens could be removed. For example, *Melloni's Illustrated Medical Dictionary* (Dox, Melloni, & Eisner, 1979) defines a mature cataract as one in which the entire lens substance has become opaque and thus easy to separate from its capsule. However, Eden (1978) reports that such ripening is not necessary before surgery is possible.

Some cataracts get progressively worse; others do not. Some cataracts involve only the periphery of the lens; others may be more centrally located (Harley & Lawrence, 1977). Therefore, the symptoms can vary a great deal from patient to patient, and, although surgery is the only cure, it is often not necessary.

Postoperative treatment of cataract removal involves the use of regular glasses or contact lenses, or the insertion of artificial plastic lenses in the eye itself. Such treatments are effective in restoring vision to the affected eye.

Characteristics

1. Vision becomes blurred during cataract development. Cataract size and density may remain stable or increase.
2. The lens may become swollen.
3. As the cataract matures, the lens may lose fluid and shrink.
4. In a final stage of development, the lens may either solidify or become filled with fluid.
5. Blindness may result if the cataract is left untreated.

REFERENCES

Dox, I., Melloni, B. J., & Eisner, G. (1979). *Melloni's illustrated medical dictionary*. Baltimore, MA: Williams & Wilkins.

Eden, J. (1978). *The eye book*. New York, NY: Viking.

Harley, R. K., & Lawrence, G. A. (1977). *Visual impairment in the schools*. Springfield, IL: Thomas.

University of Minnesota. (2005). *Cataracts in children*. Retrieved from http://www1.umn.edu/twincities/index.html

THOMAS E. ALLEN
Gallaudet College

See also Amblyopia; Blindness

CATECHOLAMINES

Epinephrine (adrenaline) and norepinephrine (noradrenaline) are hormones of the sympathetic division of the autonomic nervous system. Epinephrine was the first hormone to be isolated, and by 1897 Abel had separated it from the adrenal gland and found it to be represented by the formula $C_{17}H_{15}NO_4$. By 1905, the Japanese chemist Takamine treated Abel's abstract and named the product adrenaline, with the formula $C_9H_{13}NO_3$ (Krantz & Carr, 1961). Norepinephrine was not identified until 1942; it derives its name from the German expression *Nitrogen ohne radikal*, referring to the fact that the molecule is identical to that of epinephrine except for missing the methyl group on the nitrogen atom.

Epinephrine produces a variety of metabolic effects useful in an emergency: Increased epinephrine levels result in what is often called the "fight, flight, or fright" reaction (West & Todd, 1963). Epinephrine stimulates the effector cells of the pilomotor nerves to cause hair erection, and also causes pupillary dilation, giving rise to the picture of a fright reaction. By also causing a rapid rise in blood pressure and an increase in the rate and amplitude of respiration, it prepares for more effective fright or flight from danger. The metabolic behavioral effects of epinephrine and norepinephrine are in some ways opposite, in that while epinephrine is associated with tachycardia (rapid heartbeat), norepinephrine is associated with bradycardia (slow heart action; Eranko, 1955). In children, normal levels in plasma are 3–6 m/l for norepinephrine, and >1 m/l for epinephrine (Cone, 1968).

REFERENCES

Cone, T. E. (1968). The adrenal medulla. In R. Cooke & S. Levin (Eds.), *The biologic basis of pediatric practice* (pp. 1171–1177). New York, NY: McGraw-Hill.

Eranko, O. (1955). Distribution of adrenaline and noradrenaline in the adrenal medulla. *Nature, 88,* 175.

Krantz, R. C., & Carr, C. J. (1961). *The pharmacologic principles of medical practice* (5th ed.). Baltimore, MD: Williams & Wilkins.

West, E. S., & Todd, W. R. (1963). *Textbook of biochemistry* (3rd ed.). New York, NY: Macmillan.

LAWRENCE C. HARTLAGE
Evans, Georgia

See also Epinephrine; Phobias and Fears

CATEGORICAL EDUCATION

Categorical education was the practice of separating children with disabilities into subgroups representing different types of disability. Each subgroup had a specific categorical designation and its members were reviewed as a cohesive group for instructional purposes. The traditional categorical group structure presumed that there was significant homogeneity of student characteristics within each subgroup and that there was significant heterogeneity between the groups. That is, the members of one group shared common qualities that distinguished them from the members of all other groups. The assumptions of homogeneity within categories and heterogeneity between categories were not well founded (Hallahan & Kauffman, 1977; Iano, 1972; Kirk & Elkins, 1975; Leland, 1977), particularly for the mildly disabled.

Various categorical labels have been used to designate the separate subgroups of children with disabilities. Different labels were frequently used to apply to essentially the same children (e.g., *perceptually impaired, minimally brain damaged,* and *minimal cerebral dysfunction* were terms that have been subsumed under the term *learning disabilities*). *Dementia, feeblemindedness,* and *idiot* were terms that eventually gave way to the general label of mental retardation later known as *intellectual developmental disability*. The Education for All Handicapped Children Act of 1975 (PL 94-142) stipulated 11 handicapping conditions: intellectual developmental disability, hard of hearing, deaf, speech impaired, deaf-blind, learning disabled, visually handicapped, seriously emotionally disturbed, orthopedically handicapped, other health impaired, and multihandicapped. These categories became the prototype for the nation and were reflected in state and local plans for the education of handicapped children. They also continue to grow and change, such as with the inclusion of traumatic brain injury (TBI).

Although the categories of disabilities recognized by states and school districts were more consistent as a result of PL 94-142, the specific criteria actually used to identify handicapped children varied greatly from state to state and among local school districts. The variability in identification and placement criteria created the phenomenon that the same child could be placed in different categories in different states or school systems. Under a categorical system, the child invariably was, and still is, labeled with a disability designation. The process of labeling has been studied and the negative consequences of labeling for the child, family, and school community have been discussed at length. Discussions of the pros and cons of categorical labels are available in numerous works (Hewitt & Forness, 1977; Kirk & Gallagher, 1979; Lilly, 1979; Reschley, 1996).

A long-term disaffection with traditional categorical education has led to the development of alternative practices. Critics of traditional categorical labels such as *intellectually and developmentally delayed, learning disabled,* or *socially emotionally disturbed* emphasize that such labels are of little use to the teacher who must plan appropriate instructional programs. Therefore, the shift to inclusive practices of placement has placed emphasis on outcome rather than diagnosis or label. Alternative assessments (such as curriculum-based assessment) have also deemphasized labels and classification, and have attempted to individualize instructions to learner needs as opposed to label. Current educational qualifying categories are used to determine the level of supports and services in special education today (IDEA 2004, Part B).

REFERENCES

Hallahan, D. P., & Kauffman, J. M. (1977). Labels, categories, behaviors: ED, LD, and EMR reconsidered. *Journal of Special Education, 11*(2), 139–149.

Hewitt, F. M., & Forness, S. R. (1977). *Education of exceptional learners.* Boston, MA: Allyn & Bacon.

Iano, R. P. (1972). Shall we disband special classes? *Journal of Special Education, 6*(2), 167–177.

Individuals With Disabilities Education Improvement Act of 2004, 20 U.S.C. § 1400 et seq. (2004).

Kirk, S. A., & Elkins, J. (1975). Characteristics of children enrolled in the child service demonstration centers. *Journal of Learning Disabilities, 8*(10), 630–637.

Kirk, S. A., & Gallagher, J. J. (1979). *Educating exceptional children.* Boston, MA: Houghton Mifflin.

Leland, H. (1977). Mental retardation and adaptive behavior. *Journal of Special Education, 6*(1), 71–80.

Lilly, M. S. (1979). *Children with exceptional needs.* New York, NY: Holt, Rinehart & Winston.

Reschley, D. J. (1996). Identification and assessment of students with disabilities. *Future of Children, 6,* 1, 40–43.

LIBBY GOODMAN
Pennsylvania State University

See also Cascade Model of Special Education Services; Least Restrictive Environment

CAT EYE SYNDROME

Cat eye syndrome (CES) is a malformation involving an extra marker chromosome derived from Chromosome 22. CES shows characteristic features such as ocular coloboma of the iris, giving the appearance of a vertical pupil, hence the name. However, over half of the reported cases do not manifest this feature (Masukawa, Ozaki, & Nogimori, 1998). This chromosomal abnormality usually arises spontaneously, although there are reports of intergenerational family transmission. Transmission appears to be possible through both sexes. Some reports show the parents as mosaic for the marker chromosome but without phenotypic symptoms of the syndrome (McKusick, 1998).

CES is believed to be a very rare condition, but no reliable estimates are available. Estimates based on reported cases from northeast Switzerland during the past 20 years suggest incidence estimates ranging from 1:50,000 to 1:150,000. CES was first described in 1965 by Schachenmann and colleagues, and since then more than 40 cases have been reported in the literature (Liehr, Pfeiffer, & Trautmann, 1992). Variability in symptom manifestation is enormous, with the following characteristics listed in order of decreasing frequency. Rarer malformations can affect almost any organ, but the eyes are preferentially affected (McKusick, 1998).

Characteristics

1. Anal atresia (abnormal obstruction of the anus)
2. Unilateral or bilateral iris coloboma (absence of tissue from the colored part of the eyes)
3. Palpebral fissures (downward slanting openings between upper and lower eyelids)
4. Preauricular pits or tags (small depressions or growths of skin on outer ears)
5. Cardiac defects
6. Kidney problems (missing, extra, or underdeveloped kidneys)
7. Short stature
8. Scoliosis/skeletal problems
9. Mental retardation (mostly borderline normal to mildly retarded, a few of normal intelligence, rarely moderate to severe)
10. Micrognathia (smaller jaw)
11. Hernias
12. Cleft palate
13. Rarer malformations that can affect almost any organ

Treatment considerations include surgery for anal atresia and complex cardiac malformations. In addition, with intestinal problems, malrotation, Meckel diverticulum, and biliary atresia (related to passage of bile) must be considered. Further surgical procedures may be indicated if hernias or cleft palate are present. Patients with very short stature may have additional hypothalamic growth hormone deficiency and therefore be candidates for growth hormone therapy (McKusick, 1998). Orthopedic treatment for scoliosis may be a treatment issue as well. Genetic counseling will likely be recommended for families affected by CES.

Special education considerations include the possibility of growth retardation and other physical abnormalities that may require medical treatment and interfere with regular school attendance or progress. Mental retardation is possible. Most individuals with CES function in the borderline normal to mildly retarded range; a few are within the normal range of cognitive functioning; and some are moderately to severely retarded, although the latter condition is rare. Affected individuals may be eligible for special education services as Other Health Impairment, Mentally Retarded, or Orthopedically Handicapped, depending on specific symptoms and their severities. Behavioral problems have been reported in individual cases but are not characteristic of the disorder (Schinzel et al., 1981). Information regarding neuropsychological or educational functioning in individuals affected with CES is not available in the literature.

Life expectancy is not significantly reduced in patients who do not present with life-threatening abnormalities. However, a few patients die from multiple malformations during early infancy (Schinzel et al., 1981). Future research should focus on patterns of cognitive strength and weakness in children affected with CES, both through case studies and through collections of data across reported cases, to further inform educational interventions. Issues of psychosocial development, family adjustment, and effectiveness of medical and educational interventions are also important.

REFERENCES

Liehr, T., Pfeiffer, R. A., & Trautmann, U. (1992). Typical and partial cat eye syndrome: Identification of the marker chromosome by FISH. *Clinical Genetics, 42*, 91–96.

Masukawa, H., Ozaki, T., & Nogimori, T. (1998). Cat eye syndrome with hypogonadotropic hypogonadism. *Internal Medicine, 37*(10), 853–855.

McKusick, V. A. (1998, October 9). *Cat eye syndrome.* In Online Mendelian inheritance in man database [Online]. Retrieved from http://www.ncbi.nlm.nih.gov/htbin-post/Omim

Schinzel, A., Schmid, W., Fraccaro, M., Tiepolo, L., Zuffardi, O., Opitz, J. M., Lindsten, J., Zetterqvist, P., Enell, H., Baccichetti,

C., Tenconi, R., & Pagon, R. A. (1981). The "cat eye syndrome": Decentric small marker chromosome probably derived from a 22 associated with a characteristic phenotype. Report of 11 patients and delineation of the clinical picture. *Human Genetics, 57,* 148–158.

CYNTHIA A. PLOTTS
Texas State University at San Marcos

HEATHER HATTON
Texas A & M University
Fourth edition

CAT SCAN

Computerized axial tomography (CAT) scanning is an imaging technique (Binder, Haughton, & Ho, 1979) that permits visualization of many of the important landmarks and structures of the brain (see Figure C.3). This is a recent technique that did not become commercially available until 1973 (Hounsfield, 1973). The importance of this breakthrough in diagnostic neuroradiology is exemplified by the fact that the 1979 Nobel Prize in Medicine was awarded to the scientists G.N. Hounsfield and A.M. Cormack, who established the theoretical physics and radiographic basis for CAT scanning. The fascinating history behind these monumental breakthroughs is reviewed in the text by Oldendorf (1980).

CAT scanning is accomplished by passing a narrow X-ray beam directed toward a detector on the other side through the patient's head (or body). The detector is sensitive to the number of X-ray beam particles that pass through the tissue; this in turn is related to the density of the tissue (e.g., the greater the density the fewer the X-ray particles that pass through). The X-ray beam is passed through the head (or body) in numerous planes so as to examine the same point from multiple directions, thus allowing a specification of density for any given point on the surface of a plane. Next, each density point is color-coded depending on the degree of density; these various density points are used to computer-generate an "image" of the tissue being examined (see Figure C.4).

CAT scanning has numerous useful applications. The CAT image approximates an actual anatomic specimen taken in a similar plane; thus significant structural abnormalities can be detected. This is particularly true in cases of cerebral trauma, vascular infarctions, congenital and neoplastic disorders, and degenerative brain diseases (see Figure C.5). For children with developmental disorders, CAT scanning may reveal any major structural anomalies of the brain, but it has not been found to be routinely diagnostic in children in which the only problem is a learning disability (Denkla, LeMay, & Chapman, 1985). These observations suggest that, in general, there is no gross anatomic derangement associated with learning disorders.

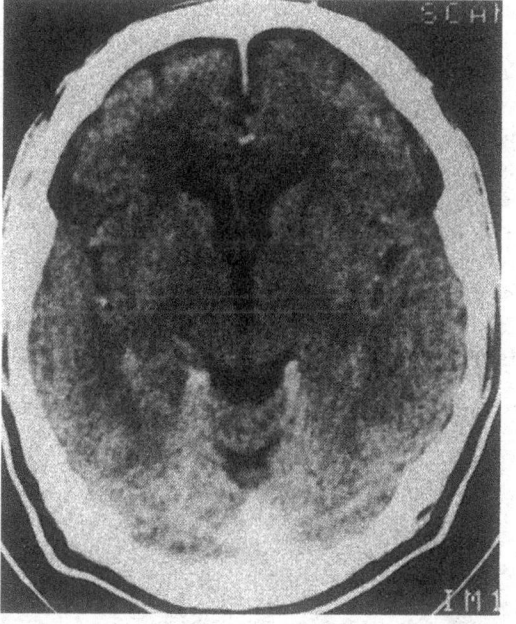

Figure C.3. CAT scan image of the brain in horizontal plane. The two upside-down L-shaped dark areas represent the anterior horns of the lateral ventricles. The light area just adjacent and lateral to these structures is the caudate nucleus. The centrally located dark area just below the anterior horns in this figure represents the third ventricle. On either side of the third ventricle is the thalamus. The angular, slightly darker area that runs from the outside top of the caudate nucleus down and adjacent to the outside of the thalamus is the internal capsule. Lateral to the internal capsule is the putamen-globus pallidus complex.

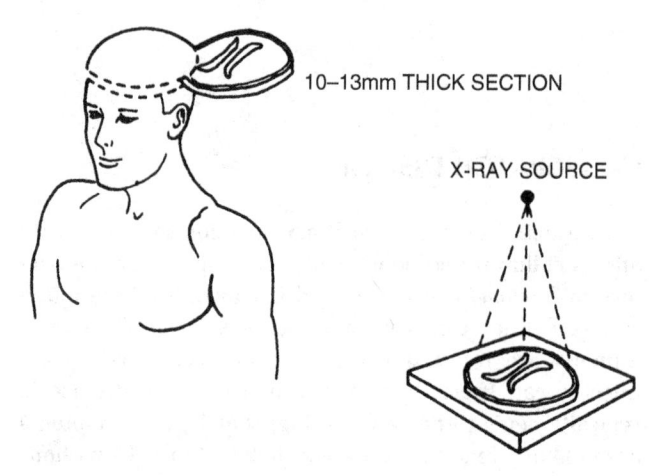

Figure C.4. Diagrammatic representation of the position of the view of the CAT image.

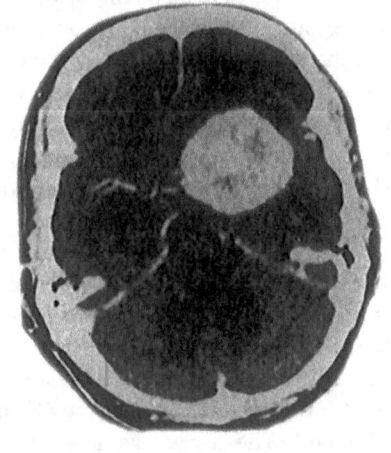 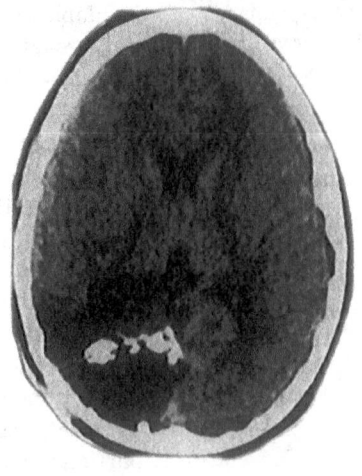 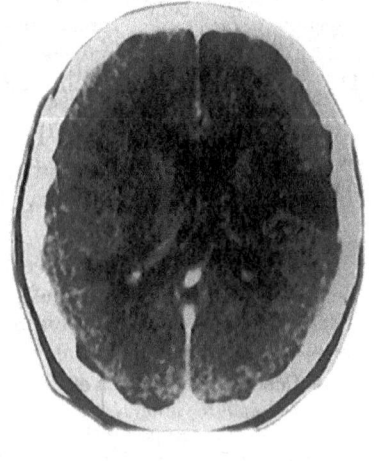

Figure C.5. Representative CAT scan depicting different types of organic pathology. Left: tumor (meningioma). Middle: gunshot wound. Right: stroke, dark area on right side.

REFERENCES

Binder, G. A., Haughton, V. M., & Ho, K-C. (1979). *Computed tomography of the brain in axial, coronal and sagittal planes* Boston, MA: Little, Brown.

Denkla, M. B., LeMay, M., & Chapman, C. A. (1985). Few CT scan abnormalities found ever in neurologically impaired learning disabled children. *Journal of Learning Disabilities, 18,* 132–135.

Hounsfield, G. N. (1973). Computerized transverse axial scanning (tomography): I. Description of system. *British Journal of Radiology, 46,* 1016–1022.

Oldendorf, W. H. (1980). *The quest for an image of brain.* New York, NY: Raven Press.

ERIN D. BIGLER
Brigham Young University

See also **Diffusion Tensor Imaging; Nuclear Magnetic Resonance; X-Ray Scanning Techniques**

CAT-SCRATCH DISEASE

Cat-scratch disease is a bacillary infection that primarily affects children and adolescents. It is caused by the bacterium *Bartonella henselae* and is transmitted via feline saliva. Felines contract the disease through fleas, and humans are infected when bitten or scratched by an infected cat, typically a very young cat. The disease is typically benign and self-limiting; that is, the symptoms are mild and tend to resolve within 2 to 4 months without treatment.

Serious complications are infrequent, that is, found in less than 10% of all cases (Busen & Scarborough, 1997). Although considered the least hazardous cause of encephalopathy (Carithers & Margileth, 1991), neurologic involvement occurs in about 2% of cases, including coma, seizures, temporary blindness, lethargy, and combative behavior (Wheeler, Wolf, & Steinberg, 1997). Other central nervous system problems include cranial and peripheral nerve palsy (e.g., facial weakness) and neuroretinitis (inflammation of the retina and optic nerve of the eye). Osteitis, which is a chronic bone infection, is another serious complication of cat-scratch disease.

Cat-scratch disease is estimated to affect 22,000 persons per year in the United States, resulting in hospitalization for 2,000 of those infected (Jackson, Perkins, & Wenger, 1993). In about 80% of cases, the age of onset is less than 21 years. Certain times of the year increase the risk factors for contracting the disease. For example, 75% of cases are reported from September through March. Males are slightly more likely to contract the disease than are females, with ratios reported to be about 3:2 (Carithers & Margileth, 1991).

Characteristics

1. Contracted through the saliva of a cat by a scratch or bite. Chronic lymphadenitis (i.e., swollen and tender lymph nodes) is the hallmark feature.

2. The disease is typically self-limiting, and symptoms remit spontaneously within 2 to 4 months without treatment except in cases of a compromised immune system.

3. Neurologic involvement such as encephalopathy may occur, but full recovery is expected.

4. The disease is considered nonfatal, but death has been implicated in .03% of cases.

Treatment depends on the severity of the sequelae. For example, in cases where fevers, conjunctivitis, and seizures occur, medications are likely to be used. Antibiotics are frequently prescribed to treat the disease (e.g., lymphadenopathy); however, there is considerable debate as to their effectiveness (Busen & Scarborough, 1997).

Prognosis for recovery is generally excellent. Even in cases where there is central nervous system involvement (e.g., seizures and blindness), recovery typically occurs within 12 months of onset (Wheeler et al., 1997). Although cat-scratch disease is considered nonfatal, some researchers have reported deaths. For example, Jackson et al. (1993) reported mortality in .03% of cases.

Special education is not likely to be required, except in cases where complications occur and achievement is affected. In these cases, services are likely to be provided under the category Other Health Impairment. Regular monitoring will be needed to determine how best to meet the child's educational needs. Because most recovery of neurologic problems occurs within the first year, short-term interventions are likely to be sufficient. In most cases, however, symptoms remit within the first few months; therefore, interventions need to be directed to facilitating recovery, including reduction of assignments and stimulation in and outside the classroom (e.g., playground). Parents should be involved so that information about the child's progress can be communicated among all professionals involved, including the child's treating physician.

Research is needed to increase understanding regarding the efficacy of antibiotic treatment. Further information about morbidity is also needed.

REFERENCES

Busen, N. H., & Scarborough, T. (1997, July 1). Diagnosis and management of cat-scratch disease in primary care. *Internet Journal of Advanced Nursing Practice, 1*(2). Retrieved from http://www.ispub.com/journals/IJANP/Vol1N2/catscratch.htm

Carithers, H., & Margileth, A. M. (1991). Cat-scratch disease. *American Journal of Diseases of Children, 145*(1), 98–101.

Jackson, L., Perkins, B., & Wenger, J. (1993). Cat scratch disease in the United States: An analysis of three national databases. *American Journal of Public Health, 83*(12), 1707–1711.

Wheeler, S., Wolf, S., & Steinberg, E. (1997). Cat-scratch encephalopathy. *Neurology, 49*(3), 876–878.

HEATHER EDGEL
ELAINE CLARK
University of Utah

THE CATTELL-HORN-CARROLL THEORY OF COGNITIVE ABILITIES

The Cattell-Horn-Carroll (CHC) theory of cognitive abilities is the most comprehensive and empirically supported psychometric theory of the structure of cognitive abilities to date. It represents the integrated works of Raymond Cattell, John Horn, and John Carroll (Alfonso, Flanagan, & Radwan, 2005; Horn & Blankson, 2005; McGrew, 2005; Schneider & McGrew, 2012). Because it has an impressive body of empirical support in the research literature (e.g., developmental, neurocognitive, outcome-criterion) it is used extensively as the foundation for selecting, organizing, and interpreting tests of intelligence and cognitive abilities (e.g., Flanagan, Alfonso, & Ortiz, 2012; Flanagan, Ortiz, & Alfonso, 2007). Most recently, it has been used for classifying intelligence and achievement batteries and neuropsychological tests to: (a) facilitate interpretation of cognitive performance; and (b) provide a foundation for organizing assessments for individuals suspected of having a learning disability (Flanagan, Alfonso, Mascolo, & Sotelo-Dynega, 2012; Flanagan, Alfonso, Ortiz, & Dynda, 2010; Flanagan, Ortiz, & Alfonso, in press). Additionally, CHC theory is the foundation on which most new and recently revised intelligence batteries were based (see Flanagan & Harrison, 2012 for comprehensive coverage of these batteries). A brief overview of the evolution of CHC theory follows.

Fluid–Crystallized (*Gf-Gc*) Theory

The original *Gf-Gc* theory was a dichotomous conceptualization of human cognitive ability put forth by Raymond Cattell in the early 1940s. Cattell based his theory on the factor-analytic work of Thurstone conducted in the 1930s. Cattell believed that Fluid Intelligence (*Gf*) included inductive and deductive reasoning abilities that were influenced by biological and neurological factors as well as incidental learning through interaction with the environment. He postulated further that Crystallized Intelligence (*Gc*) consisted primarily of acquired knowledge abilities that reflected, to a large extent, the influences of acculturation (Cattell, 1957, 1971).

In 1965, John Horn expanded the dichotomous *Gf-Gc* model to include four additional abilities, including visual perception or processing (*Gv*), short-term memory (Short-term Acquisition and Retrieval—SAR or *Gsm*), long-term storage and retrieval (Tertiary Storage and Retrieval—TSR or *Glr*), and speed of processing (*Gs*). Later he added auditory processing ability (*Ga*) to the theoretical model and refined the definitions of *Gv*, *Gs*, and *Glr* (Horn, 1968; Horn & Stankov, 1982).

In the early 1990s, Horn added a factor representing an individual's quickness in reacting (reaction time) and making decisions (decision speed). The acronym or code for this factor is *Gt* (Horn, 1991). Finally, quantitative (*Gq*) and broad reading-writing (*Grw*) factors were added to the model based on the research of Horn (e.g., 1991) and Woodcock (1994), respectively. Based largely on the results of Horn's thinking and research, *Gf-Gc* theory expanded into an eight-factor model that became known as the Cattell-Horn *Gf-Gc* theory (Horn, 1991; see Horn and Blankson, 2005, for a comprehensive review of Horn's contribution to *Gf-Gc* theory).

Carroll's Three-Stratum Theory

In his review of the extant factor-analytic research literature, Carroll differentiated factors or abilities into three strata that varied according to the "relative variety and diversity of variables" (Carroll, 1997, p. 124) included at each level. The various *G* abilities are the most prominent and recognized abilities of the model. They are classified as broad or stratum II abilities and include abilities such as *Gf* and *Gc*, the two original factors. According to Carroll (1993), *broad* abilities represent "basic constitutional and long standing characteristics of individuals that can govern or influence a great variety of behaviors in a given domain" and they vary in their emphasis on process, content, and manner of response (p. 634). Broad abilities, like *Gf* and *Gc*, subsume a large number of narrow or stratum I abilities of which approximately 70 have been identified (Carroll, 1993, 1997). *Narrow* abilities "represent greater specializations of abilities, often in quite specific ways that reflect the effects of experience and learning, or the adoption of particular strategies of performance" (Carroll, 1993, p. 634). The broadest or most general level of ability in the *Gf-Gc* model is represented by stratum III, located at the apex of Carroll's (1993) hierarchy. This single cognitive ability, which subsumes both broad (stratum II) and narrow (stratum I) abilities, is interpreted as representing a general factor (i.e., *g*) that is involved in complex higher-order cognitive processes (Gustaffson & Undheim, 1996; Jensen, 1997; McGrew & Woodcock, 2001).

It is important to note that the abilities within each level of the hierarchical *Gf-Gc* model typically display nonzero positive intercorrelations (Carroll, 1993; Gustafsson & Undheim, 1996). For example, the different stratum I (narrow) abilities that define the various *Gf-Gc* domains are correlated positively and to varying degrees. These intercorrelations give rise to and allow for the estimation of the stratum II (broad) ability factors. Likewise, the positive nonzero correlations among the stratum II (broad) *Gf-Gc* abilities allow for the estimation of the stratum III (general) *g* factor. The positive factor intercorrelations within each level of the *Gf-Gc* hierarchy indicate that the different *Gf-Gc* abilities do not reflect completely independent (uncorrelated or orthogonal) traits. However, they can, as is evident from the vast body of literature that supports their existence, be reliably distinguished from one another and therefore represent unique, albeit related, abilities (see Keith & Reynolds, 2012).

Similarities and Differences Between the Cattell-Horn Model and the Carroll Model

Simplified versions of the Cattell-Horn and Carroll models of the structure of abilities (i.e., where the narrow abilities are omitted) are presented together in Figure C.6, which shows a number of important similarities and differences between the two models. In general, these models are similar in that they both include multiple broad abilities with similar descriptions (e.g., *Gs*) and similar classification of

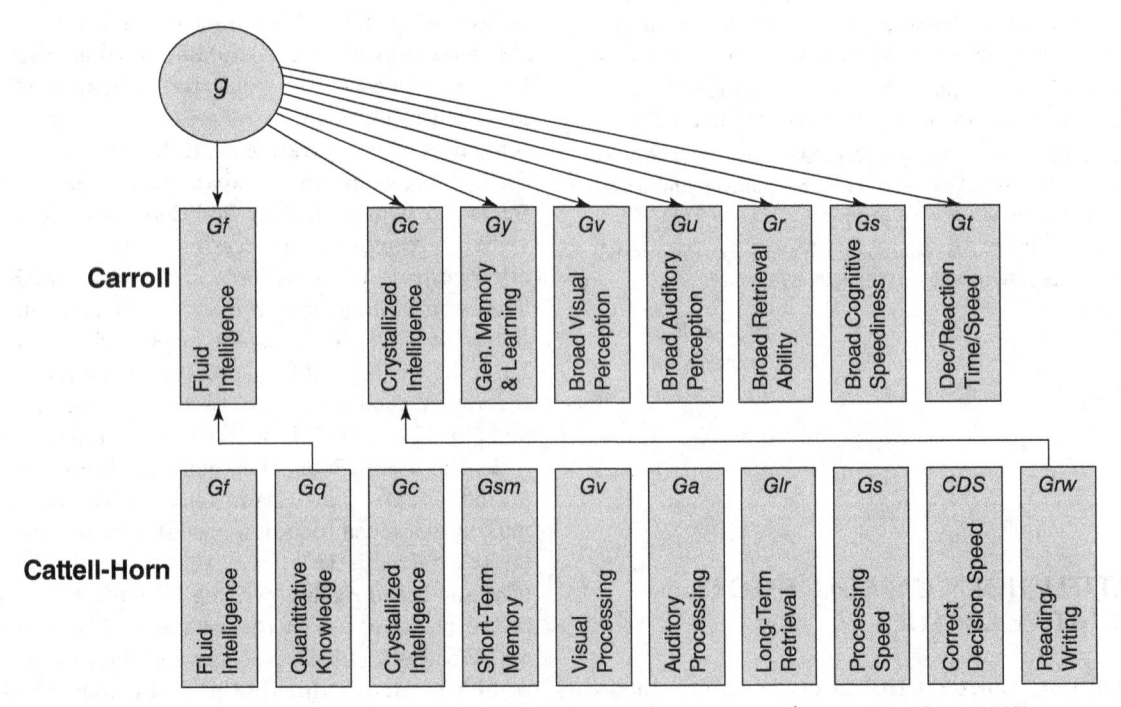

Figure C.6. Comparison of Cattell-Horn *Gf-Gc* theory and Carroll's Three-Stratum theory. *Source*: Flanagan & McGrew (1997).

narrow abilities. However there are four major structural differences between the Cattell-Horn and Carroll models.

First, Carroll's theory includes *g* (global or general ability) at stratum III and the Cattell-Horn theory does not, as these theorists disagreed over the existence of an overarching intellectual ability. This dispute is an ongoing debate in the field (see Schneider & McGrew, 2012 for a discussion on the existence of *g*). Second, in the Cattell-Horn model, *Gq* is comprised of quantitative knowledge and quantitative reasoning; however, Carroll classified quantitative reasoning as a narrow ability subsumed by *Gf*. Third, the Cattell-Horn theory includes a distinct broad reading/writing (*Grw*) factor, whereas Carroll's theory includes reading and writing as narrow abilities subsumed by *Gc*. Fourth, the Cattell-Horn and the Carroll models differ in their treatment of certain narrow memory abilities. Carroll combined both short-term memory and the narrow abilities of associative, meaningful, and free-recall memory with learning abilities under (*Gy*). Horn (1991) made a distinction between immediate apprehension (e.g., short-term memory span) and storage and retrieval abilities.

The First Generation of CHC Theory

Notwithstanding the important differences between the Cattell-Horn and the Carroll models, in order to realize the practical benefits of using theory to guide test selection, organization, and interpretation, it is necessary to define a single taxonomy—one that can be used to classify ability tests. A first effort to create a single taxonomy for this purpose was an integrated Cattell-Horn and Carroll model proposed by McGrew (1997). McGrew and Flanagan (1998) subsequently presented a slightly revised integrated model, which was further refined by Flanagan et al. (2000). The integrated model presented

by McGrew and colleagues was accepted by both John Horn and John Carroll and thus became known as the Cattell-Horn-Carroll (CHC) theory, reflecting the order in which these theorists made their contributions. The original integration of the Cattell-Horn *Gf-Gc* theory and Carroll's three-stratum theory, or simply CHC theory, is presented in Figure C.7. This figure depicts the original structure of CHC theory and reflects the manner in which the Cattell-Horn and Carroll models have been integrated. In this figure, CHC theory includes 10 broad cognitive abilities, which are subsumed by over 70 narrow abilities.

Latest Refinements to CHC Theory

A paramount feature of the CHC theory is that it is not static, but rather a dynamic model that is continuously reorganized and restructured based on current research. Recently, Schneider and McGrew (2012) conducted an extensive review on CHC theory by (1) analyzing the current theory and potential errors, (2) reviewing whether contemporary intellectual research validates or refutes the CHC model, (3) redefining constructs to be more meaningful for clinicians, (4) adding, deleting, and restructuring the broad and narrow abilities within the model, and (5) highlighting which aspects of the model are more central to CHC theory. While a thorough explanation and description of the changes made to CHC theory is beyond the scope of this entry, the interested reader is referred to Schneider and McGrew (2012).

The current model of CHC theory is presented in Figure C.8. In this model, CHC theory includes 16 broad cognitive abilities, which are subsumed by over 80 narrow abilities. The ovals represent broad abilities and rectangles represent narrow abilities. The darker rectangles represent those narrow abilities that are most consistently represented on tests of cognitive and academic abilities.

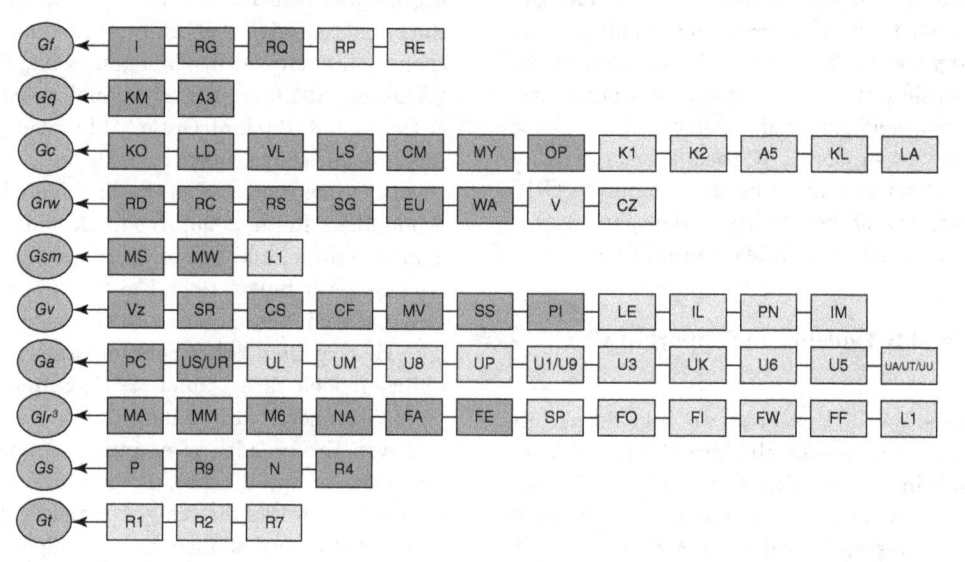

Figure C.7. Cattell-Horn-Carroll (CHC) theory. *Source*: Flanagan & McGrew (1997).

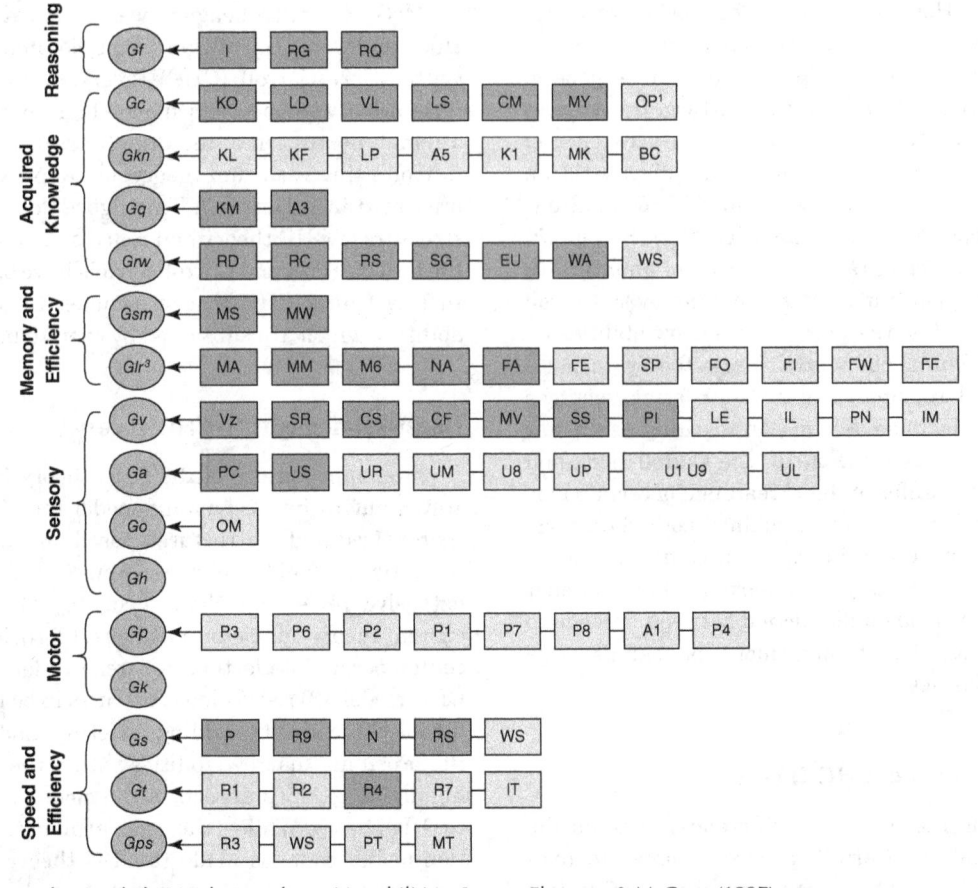

Figure C.8. Current and expanded CHC theory of cognitive abilities. *Source*: Flanagan & McGrew (1997).

Additionally, the overall *g* or general ability is omitted from this figure intentionally due to space limitations. The conceptual groupings of abilities (i.e., reasoning, acquired knowledge, memory and efficiency, sensory, motor, and speed and efficiency) were suggested by Schneider and McGrew and provide an integrated framework of both cognitive and neuropsychological perspectives (Flanagan et al., 2010). The CHC theory represented a culmination of more than 60 years of factor-analysis research in the psychometric tradition. However, in addition to structural evidence, there are other sources of validity evidence, some quite substantial, that support CHC theory. Prior to defining the broad and narrow abilities that comprise CHC theory, a brief overview of the validity evidence in support of this structure of cognitive abilities is presented.

A Network of Validity Evidence in Support of CHC Theory

It is beyond the scope of this entry to provide a fully detailed account and review of all the validity evidence currently available in support of the CHC structural model as well as the broad and narrow ability constructs it encompasses. The interested reader is referred to Carroll (1993, 2005), Flanagan and Harrison (2012), Horn and Blankson (2005), and Schneider & McGrew (2012) for a more thorough discussion.

Briefly, the CHC structure of abilities is supported by factor-analytic (i.e., structural) evidence as well as developmental, neurocognitive, and heritability evidence (see Horn & Blankson, 2005). Additionally, there is a mounting body of research available on the relations between the broad cognitive CHC abilities and many academic outcomes (summarized in Flanagan et al., 2006; McGrew & Wendling, 2010), and occupational outcomes (Ackerman & Heggestad, 1997; McGrew & Flanagan, 1998). Furthermore, studies have shown that the factor structure of CHC theory is invariant across the lifespan (Bickley, Keith, & Wolfe, 1995; Keith, 2005; Woodcock et al., 2001) and across gender, ethnic, and cultural groups (e.g., Carroll, 1993; Gustafsson & Balke, 1993; Keith, 1997, 1999). In general, CHC theory is based on a more extensive network of validity evidence than other contemporary multidimensional ability models (see Daniel, 1997; Schneider & McGrew, 2012; Sternberg & Kaufman, 1998).

Given the breadth of empirical support for the CHC structure of intelligence, it provides one of the most useful frameworks for designing and evaluating psychoeducational batteries, including intelligence, achievement, and neuropsychological tests (Flanagan et al., in press;

Keith & Reynolds, 2012). Moreover, in light of the well-established structural validity of CHC theory, external validity support for the various CHC constructs, derived through sound research methodology, can be used confidently to guide test interpretation (see Bensen, 1998; Evans, Floyd, McGrew, & Leforgee, 2002; Flanagan, 2000; Floyd, Evans, & McGrew, 2003; Vanderwood, McGrew, Flanagan, & Keith, 2002).

As previously mentioned, it is important to recognize that research related to CHC theory is not static. Rather, research on the hierarchical structure of abilities (within the *Gf-Gc* and now CHC framework) has been systematic, steady, and mounting for decades. Definitions of the broad and narrow abilities currently comprising CHC theory are presented in the next section.

Broad and Narrow CHC Ability Definitions

These definitions presented here were derived from an integration of the writings of Carroll (1993), Gustafsson and Undheim (1996), Horn (1991), McGrew (1997, 2005), and Schneider and McGrew (2012). The narrow ability definitions are presented in Tables C.1 through C.15.

Fluid Intelligence (*Gf*)

Fluid intelligence refers to mental operations that an individual uses when faced with a relatively novel task that cannot be performed automatically. These mental operations may include forming and recognizing concepts, perceiving relationships among patterns, drawing inferences, comprehending implications, problem solving, extrapolating, and reorganizing or transforming information. *Gf* can also be described as "deliberate but flexible control of attention to solve novel, 'on-the-spot' problems that cannot be performed by relying exclusively on previous learned habits, schemas, and scripts" (Schneider & McGrew, 2012, p. 111). Inductive and deductive reasoning are generally considered to be the hallmark narrow ability indicators of *Gf*. Although most practitioners would agree that this ability is typically not measured directly by individually administered achievement batteries, some tests of achievement clearly involve the use of specific *Gf* abilities. For example, many tests of reading comprehension require individuals to draw inferences from the text. Aside from general inductive and deductive reasoning abilities, *Gf* also subsumes more specific types of reasoning, most notably Quantitative Reasoning (RQ). Unlike the other narrow *Gf* abilities, RQ is more directly related to formal instruction and classroom-related experiences. Definitions of the narrow abilities subsumed by *Gf* are presented in Table C.1.

Crystallized Intelligence (*Gc*)

Crystallized intelligence refers to the breadth and depth of a person's acquired knowledge and skills that are valued by one's culture. This store of primarily verbal or language-based knowledge represents those abilities that have been developed largely through the "investment" of other abilities during educational and general life experiences (Horn & Blankson, 2005).

Gc includes both declarative (static) and procedural (dynamic) knowledge. Declarative knowledge includes factual information, comprehension, concepts, rules, and relationships, especially when the information is verbal in nature. Declarative knowledge is held in long-term memory and is activated when related information is in working memory (*Gsm*). Procedural knowledge refers to the process of reasoning with previously learned procedures in order to transform knowledge. For example, a child's knowledge of his or her street address would reflect declarative knowledge, whereas a child's ability to find his or her way home from school would require procedural knowledge (Gagne, 1985).

A rather unique aspect of *Gc* not seen in the other broad abilities is that it appears to be both a store of acquired knowledge (e.g., lexical knowledge, general information, information about culture) as well as a collection of processing abilities (e.g., communication ability, listening ability). The narrow ability of General Information (K0), for example, is clearly a repository of learned information, whereas the narrow Listening Ability (LS) appears to represent the ability to effectively comprehend and process information presented orally. Although research is needed to discern the nature of acquired knowledge versus processing abilities within the *Gc* domain, assessment of *Gc* should pay close attention to the narrow abilities that define this broad domain. Despite the interrelatedness of all narrow abilities under *Gc*, there may well be times when focus on the abilities that are more process oriented, as opposed to those that are knowledge oriented, is most important, and vice versa. Definitions of the narrow abilities subsumed by *Gc* are presented in Table C.2.

Table C.1. Narrow *Gf* Stratum I Ability Definitions

Narrow Stratum I Name (Code)	Definition
Fluid Intelligence (*Gf*)	
Induction (I)	Ability to discover the underlying characteristic (e.g., rule, concept, process, trend, class membership) that governs a problem or a set of materials.
General Sequential Reasoning (RG)	Ability to start with stated rules, premises, or conditions, and to engage in one or more steps to reach a solution to a novel problem.
Quantitative Reasoning (RQ)	Ability to inductively and deductively reason with concepts involving mathematical relations and properties.

Note. Definitions were derived from Carroll (1993) and Schneider and McGrew (2012).

Table C.2. Narrow *Gc* Stratum I Ability Definitions

Narrow Stratum I Name (Code)	Definition
Crystallized Intelligence (*Gc*)	
General (verbal) Information (*K0*)	Range of general knowledge.
Language Development (LD)	General development, or the understanding of words, sentences, and paragraphs (not requiring reading), in spoken native language skills.
Lexical Knowledge (VL)	Extent of vocabulary that can be understood in terms of correct word meanings.
Listening Ability (LS)	Ability to listen and comprehend oral communications.
Communication Ability (CM)	Ability to speak in real-life situations (e.g., lecture, group participation) in an adult-like manner.
Grammatical Sensitivity (MY)	Knowledge or awareness of the grammatical features of the native language.
Oral Production and Fluency (OP)	More specific or narrow oral communication skills than reflected by Communication Ability (CM).

Note. Definitions were derived from Carroll (1993) and Schneider and McGrew (2012).

Table C.3. Narrow *Gkn* Stratum I Ability Definitions

Narrow Stratum I Name (Code)	Definition
General (Domain-Specific) Knowledge (*Gkn*)	
Foreign Language Proficiency (KL)	Similar to Language Development (LD) but for a foreign language.
Knowledge of Signing (KF)	Knowledge of finger-spelling and signing (e.g., American Sign Language).
Skill in Lip-reading (LP)	Competence in the ability to understand communication from others by watching the movements of their mouths and expressions.
Geography Achievement (A5)	Range of geographic knowledge.
General Science Information (K1)	Range of scientific knowledge (e.g., biology, physics, engineering, mechanics, electronics).
Mechanical Knowledge (MK)	Knowledge about the function, terminology, and operation of ordinary tools, machines, and equipment.
Knowledge of Behavioral Content (BC)	Knowledge or sensitivity to nonverbal human communication/interaction systems (e.g., facial expressions and gestures).

Note. Definitions were derived from Carroll (1993) and Schneider and McGrew (2012).

General (Domain-Specific) Knowledge (*Gkn*)

General (domain-specific) knowledge (*Gkn*) is the "depth, breadth, and mastery of specialized knowledge (knowledge not all members of a society are expected to have)" (Schneider & McGrew, 2012, p. 123). This newly introduced broad ability was created from four narrow abilities previously accounted for in the *Gc* domain (i.e., Foreign Language [KL], Geography Achievement [A5], General Science Information [K1], and Knowledge of Culture [K2]) because they represent the acquired knowledge from specialized domains. This specialized knowledge is usually developed through an individual's work experience, hobbies, or passions. The *Gkn* broad ability is unique in that it is a domain that does not have a true *G* ability because the aggregates are of specific and distinct abilities. Furthermore, an individual should not be assessed in comparison with same age-peers in the general populations, but rather individuals who possess the same specialized knowledge base. For example, a sociologist's knowledge of human social behavior (i.e., *Gkn* narrow ability of sociology) should be compared only to other sociologists, not the general public. Since an almost infinite number of specialized areas of knowledge exist, the broad ability of *Gkn* contains an unlimited number of narrow abilities. However, several examples of *Gkn* narrow abilities are listed and defined below in Table C.3 (Schneider & McGrew, 2012).

Quantitative Knowledge (*Gq*)

Quantitative knowledge represents an individual's "depth and breadth of knowledge related to mathematics" (Schneider & McGrew, 2012, p. 127). The *Gq* store of acquired knowledge represents the ability to use quantitative information and manipulate numeric symbols. *Gq* abilities are typically measured by achievement tests. For example, most comprehensive tests of achievement include measures of math calculation, applied problems (or math problem solving), and general math knowledge. Although some intelligence batteries measure aspects of *Gq* (e.g., Arithmetic on the Wechsler Scales, Quantitative Reasoning on the SB5), they typically do not measure this ability comprehensively.

It is important to understand the difference between *Gq* and the Quantitative Reasoning (RQ) ability that is subsumed by *Gf*. On the whole, *Gq* represents an individual's store of acquired mathematical knowledge, including the ability to perform mathematical calculations (i.e., procedural knowledge). Quantitative Reasoning represents only the ability to reason inductively and deductively when solving quantitative problems. *Gq* is most evident when a task requires mathematical skills (e.g., addition, subtraction, multiplication, division) and general mathematical knowledge (e.g., knowing what the square-root symbol means). RQ, on the other hand, would be required to solve for a missing number in a number-series task (e.g., 3, 6,

Table C.4. Narrow *Gq* Stratum I Ability Definitions

Narrow Stratum I Name (Code)	Definition
Quantitative Knowledge (*Gq*)	
Mathematical Knowledge (*KM*)	Range of general knowledge about mathematics.
Mathematical Achievement (A3)	Measured mathematics achievement.

Note. Definitions were derived from Carroll (1993) and Schneider and McGrew (2012).

9, ___), for example. Three narrow abilities are listed and defined under *Gq* in Table C.4.

Reading/Writing Ability (*Grw*)

Reading/Writing ability is an acquired store of knowledge that includes basic reading, reading fluency, and writing skills required for the comprehension of written language and the expression of thought via writing. It includes both basic abilities (e.g., reading decoding and fluency, spelling) and complex abilities (e.g., comprehending written discourse, writing a story). Like *Gq*, *Grw* is considered to be an "achievement" domain and, therefore, has been measured traditionally (and almost exclusively) by tests of academic achievement. In Carroll's (1993) three-stratum model, eight narrow reading and writing abilities are subsumed by *Gc* in addition to other abilities. In the CHC model, six of the eight narrow abilities define the broad *Grw* ability (verbal language comprehension [V] and cloze ability [CZ] were dropped because they were not distinct abilities), and an additional measure (writing speed [WS]) was included. These *Grw* narrow abilities are defined in Table C.5.

Short-Term Memory (*Gsm*)

Short-term memory is the ability to apprehend and hold information in immediate awareness and then use it within a few seconds. *Gsm* is a limited-capacity system, as most individuals can retain only seven "chunks" of information (plus or minus two chunks) in this system at one time. An example of *Gsm* is the ability to remember a telephone number long enough to dial it. Given the limited amount of information that can be held in short-term memory, information is typically retained for only a few seconds before it is lost. As most individuals have experienced, it is difficult to remember an unfamiliar telephone number for more than a few seconds unless one consciously uses a cognitive learning strategy (e.g., continually repeating or rehearsing the numbers) or other mnemonic device. When a new task requires an individual to use his or her *Gsm* abilities to store new information, the previous

Table C.5. Narrow *Grw* Stratum I Ability Definitions

Narrow Stratum I Name (Code)	Definition
Reading/Writing (*Grw*)	
Reading Decoding (RD)	Ability to recognize and decode words or pseudowords in reading.
Reading Comprehension (RC)	Ability to comprehend connected discourse during reading.
Reading Speed (RS)	Time required to silently read a passage or series of sentences as quickly as possible.
Spelling Ability (SG)	Ability to spell. (Not clearly defined by existing research.)
English Usage Knowledge (EU)	Knowledge of writing in the English language with respect to capitalization, punctuation, usage, and spelling.
Writing Ability (WA)	Ability to write with clarity of thought, organization, and good sentence structure. (Not clearly defined by existing research).
Writing Speed (WS)	The ability to copy or generate text quickly.

Note. Definitions were derived from Carroll (1993) and Schneider and McGrew (2012).

information held in short-term memory is either lost or must be stored in the acquired stores of knowledge (i.e., *Gc*, *Gq*, *Grw*) through the use of *Glr*.

In the original CHC model, *Gsm* subsumes the narrow ability of working memory, which has received considerable attention in the cognitive psychology literature (see Kane, Bleckley, Conway, & Engle, 2001). However, in the recent revision of CHC theory, Schneider and McGrew renamed the narrow ability to Working Memory Capacity (MW), as it was more reflective of the tasks on cognitive and intelligence tests. Schneider and McGrew acknowledge that the current state of scientific literature on memory is immense, and therefore only relevant constructs are currently included in the CHC model. However, as research illuminates the correlations among different memory constructs and academic skills, it is likely that *Gsm* narrow abilities will continue to evolve. Definitions of the current narrow abilities subsumed by *Gsm* are presented in Table C.6.

Long-Term Storage and Retrieval (*Glr*)

Long-term storage and retrieval is the ability to store information in and fluently retrieve new or previously acquired information (e.g., concepts, ideas, items, names) from long-term memory. *Glr* abilities have been prominent in creativity research, where they have been referred to as

Table C.6. Narrow *Gsm* Stratum I Ability Definitions

Narrow Stratum I Name (Code)	Definition
Short-Term Memory (*Gsm*)	
Memory Span (MS)	Ability to attend to and immediately recall temporally ordered elements in the correct order after a single presentation.
Working Memory (MW)	Ability to temporarily store and perform a set of cognitive operations on information that requires divided attention and the management of the limited capacity of short-term memory.

Note. Definitions were derived from Carroll (1993) and Schneider and McGrew (2012).

idea production, ideational fluency, or associative fluency. It is important not to confuse *Glr* with *Gc*, *Gq*, and *Grw*, which represent to a large extent an individual's stores of acquired knowledge. Specifically, *Gc*, *Gq*, and *Grw* represent what is stored in long-term memory, whereas Glr is the efficiency by which this information is initially stored in and later retrieved from long-term memory.

It is also important to note that different processes are involved in *Glr* and *Gsm*. Although the word *long-term* frequently carries with it the connotation of days, weeks, months, and years in the clinical literature, long-term storage processes can begin within a few minutes or hours of performing a task. Therefore, the time lapse between the initial task performance and the recall of information related to that task is not necessarily of critical importance in defining *Glr*. However, the broad abilities of *Glr* and *Gsm* are highly interdependent, which is noted in the recent revisions of CHC theory. In the present CHC model, 11 narrow memory and fluency abilities are included under *Glr* (see Table C.7).

Visual Processing (*Gv*)

Visual processing (*Gv*) is the ability to generate, perceive, analyze, synthesize, store, retrieve, manipulate, transform, and think with visual patterns and stimuli (Lohman, 1994), or more succinctly, "the ability to make use of simulated mental imagery to solve problems" (Schneider & McGrew, 2012, p. 129). These abilities are measured frequently by tasks that require the perception and manipulation of visual shapes and forms, usually of a figural or geometric nature (e.g., a standard block design task). An individual who can mentally reverse and rotate objects effectively, interpret how objects change as they move through space, perceive and manipulate spatial configurations, and maintain spatial orientation would be regarded as having a strength in *Gv* abilities. *Gv* abilities are also related significantly to higher-level mathematics achievement (e.g., geometry and trigonometry; Casey, Nuttall, &

Table C.7. Narrow *Glr* Stratum I Ability Definitions

Narrow Stratum I Name (Code)	Definition
Long-Term Storage and Retrieval (*Glr*)	
Associative Memory (MA)	Ability to recall one part of a previously learned but unrelated pair of items when the other part is presented (i.e., paired-associative learning).
Meaningful Memory (MM)	Ability to recall a set of items where there is a meaningful relation between items or the items comprise a meaningful story or connected discourse.
Free-Recall Memory (M6)	Ability to recall as many unrelated items as possible, in any order, after a large collection of items is presented.
Naming Facility (NA)	Ability to rapidly produce names for concepts when presented with a pictorial or verbal cue.
Associational Fluency (FA)	The ability to rapidly produce a series of original or useful ideas related to a particular concept.
Expressional Fluency (FE)	The ability to rapidly think of different ways of expressing an idea.
Sensitivity to Problems/Alternative Solution Fluency (SP)	The ability to rapidly think of a number of solutions to particular practical problem.
Originality/Creativity (FO)	Ability to rapidly produce original, clever, and insightful responses (expressions, interpretations) to a given topic, situation, or task.
Ideational Fluency (FI)	Ability to rapidly produce a series of ideas, words, or phrases related to a specific condition or object. Quantity, not quality, is emphasized.
Word Fluency (FW)	Ability to rapidly produce words that have specific phonemic, structural, or orthographic characteristics (independent of word meanings).
Figural Fluency (FF)	Ability to rapidly draw or sketch several examples or elaborations when given a starting visual or descriptive stimulus.

Note. Definitions were derived from Carroll (1993) and Schneider and McGrew (2012).

Pezaris, 1997; Hegarty & Kozhevnikov, 1999). The various narrow abilities subsumed by *Gv* are listed and defined in Table C.8.

Auditory Processing (*Ga*)

In the broadest sense, auditory processing is the "ability to detect and process meaningful nonverbal information in sound" (Schneider & McGrew, 2012, p. 131). Specifically, auditory processing is the ability to perceive, analyze, and synthesize patterns among auditory stimuli, and to discriminate subtle nuances in patterns of sound (e.g.,

Table C.8. Narrow *Gv* Stratum I Ability Definitions

Narrow Stratum I Name (Code)	Definition
Visual Processing (*Gv*)	
Visualization (Vz)	The ability to perceive complex patterns and mentally simulate how they might look when transformed (e.g., rotated, changed in size, partially obscured).
Speeded Rotation (Spatial Relations; SR)	The ability to solve problems quickly by using mental rotation of simple images.
Closure Speed (CS)	Ability to quickly combine disconnected, vague, or partially obscured visual stimuli or patterns into a meaningful whole, without knowing in advance what the pattern is.
Flexibility of Closure (CF)	Ability to find, apprehend, and identify a visual figure or pattern embedded in a complex visual array, when knowing in advance what the pattern is.
Visual Memory (MV)	Ability to form and store a mental representation or image of a visual stimulus and then recognize or recall it later.
Spatial Scanning (SS)	Ability to accurately and quickly survey a spatial field or pattern and identify a path through the visual field or pattern.
Serial Perceptual Integration (PI)	Ability to apprehend and identify a pictorial or visual pattern when parts of the pattern are presented rapidly in serially or successive order.
Length Estimation (LE)	Ability to accurately estimate or compare visual lengths and distances without using measurement instruments.
Perceptual Illusions (IL)	Ability to resist being affected by perceptual illusions involving geometric figures.
Perceptual Alternations (PN)	Consistency in the rate of alternating between different visual perceptions.
Imagery (IM)	Ability to vividly mentally manipulate abstract spatial forms. (Not clearly defined by existing research.)

Note. Definitions were derived from Carroll (1993) and Schneider and McGrew (2012).

Table C.9. Narrow *Ga* Stratum I Ability Definitions

Narrow Stratum I Name (Code)	Definition
Auditory Processing (*Ga*)	
Phonetic Coding (PC)	Ability to hear phonemes distinctly. This ability is also referred to as phonological processing, phonological awareness, and phonemic awareness.
Speech Sound Discrimination (US)	Ability to detect differences in speech sounds under conditions of little distraction or distortion.
Resistance to Auditory Stimulus Distortion (UR)	Ability to understand speech and language that has been distorted or masked in one or more ways.
Memory for Sound Patterns (UM)	Ability to retain on a short-term basis auditory events such as tones, tonal patterns, and voices.
Maintaining and Judging Rhythm (U8)	Ability to recognize and maintain a musical beat.
Absolute Pitch (UP)	Ability to perfectly identify the pitch of tones.
Musical Discrimination and Judgment (U1 U9)	Ability to discriminate and judge tonal patterns in music with respect to melodic, harmonic, and expressive aspects (phrasing, tempo, harmonic complexity, intensity variations)
Sound Localization (UL)	Ability to localize heard sounds in space.

Note. Definitions were derived from Carroll (1993) and Schneider and McGrew (2012).

significantly in recent years, presumably as a result of the consistent finding that phonological awareness/processing appears to be the core deficit in individuals with reading difficulties (e.g., Morris et al., 1998; Vellutino, Scanlon, & Lyon, 2000; Velluntino & Scanlon, 2002). However, as can be seen from the list of narrow abilities subsumed by *Ga* (Table C.9), this domain is very broad, extending far beyond phonetic coding ability.

Olfactory Abilities (*Go*)

Olfactory abilities refer to the "abilities to detect and process meaningful information in odors" (Schneider & McGrew, 2012, p. 132). This broad ability does not account for how sensitive one is to smell, but rather the cognitive processes an individual uses to interpret information from the olfactory system. While the current CHC theory lists only one *Go* narrow ability (Olfactory Memory [OM], see Table C.10), research suggests that other narrow abilities (e.g., episodic odor memory, odor identification) may exist. *Go* was only recently added to the CHC model; therefore, more research is needed to identify additional narrow abilities or whether it is appropriately included in the model.

complex musical structure) and speech when presented under distorted conditions. Although *Ga* abilities do not require the comprehension of language (*Gc*) per se, they are important in the development of language skills (Liberman, Shankweiler, Fischer, & Carter, 1974; McGrew & Wendling, 2010; Wagner & Torgesen, 1987). *Ga* subsumes most of those abilities referred to as "phonological awareness/processing." Tests that measure these abilities (e.g., phonetic coding tests) are found typically on achievement batteries. In fact, the number of tests specifically designed to measure phonological processing has increased

Table C.10. Narrow *Go* Stratum I Ability Definitions

Narrow Stratum I Name (Code)	Definition
Olfactory Abilities (*Go*)	
Olfactory Memory (OM)	Ability to recognize previously encountered distinctive odors.

Note. Definition was derived from Carroll (1993) and Schneider and McGrew (2012).

Tactile Abilities (*Gh*)

Tactile abilities are defined as "the abilities to detect and process meaningful information in haptic (touch) sensations" (Schneider & McGrew, 2012, p. 133). Similar to *Go*, *Gh* is not how sensitive one is to touch, but how one uses cognitive processes to interpret touch. Due to limited operational definitions of tactile abilities, there is currently little evidence supporting *Gh* narrow abilities. However, it is likely that further research will identify narrow abilities, such as tactile memory or knowledge of textures. (See Table C.11.)

Psychomotor Abilities (*Gp*)

Psychomotor abilities are known as the "abilities to perform physical body motor movements (e.g., movement of fingers, hands, legs) with precision, coordination, or strength" (Schneider & McGrew, 2012, p. 134). Although *Gp* is not typically measured on cognitive and intelligence tests, psychomotor abilities are an important factor measured in neuropsychological assessments. For example, the Dean-Woodcock Neuropsychological Battery (Dean & Woodcock, 2003) includes several tasks designed to measure gross and fine motor skills (Flanagan et al., 2010). Psychomotor abilities are critical in understanding typical and atypical neuropsychological functioning, along with identifying any neurological or neuropsychological disorders. A list and definitions of current *Gp* narrow abilities can be found in Table C.12.

Kinesthetic Abilities (*Gk*)

Kinesthetic abilities are known as the "abilities to detect and process meaningful information in proprioceptive

Table C.11. Narrow *Gh* Stratum I Ability Definitions

Narrow Stratum I Name (Code)	Definition
Tactile Abilities (*Gh*)	
Note: There are no well-supported cognitive ability factors within *Gh* yet.	Tactile abilities (*Gh*) can be defined as the ability to detect and process meaningful information in haptic (touch) sensations.

Note. Description from Schneider and McGrew (2012).

Table C.12. Narrow *Gp* Stratum I Ability Definitions

Narrow Stratum I Name (Code)	Definition
Psychomotor Abilities (*Gp*)	
Static Strength (P3)	Ability to exert muscular force to move (push, lift, pull) a relatively heavy or immobile object.
Multilimb Coordination (P6)	Ability to make quick specific or discrete motor movements of the arms or legs.
Finger Dexterity (P2)	Ability to make precisely coordinated movements of the fingers (with or without the manipulation of objects).
Manual Dexterity (P1)	Ability to make precisely coordinated movements of a hand or a hand and the attached arm.
Arm–Hand Steadiness (P7)	Ability to precisely and skillfully coordinate arm–hand positioning in space.
Control Precision (P8)	Ability to exert precise control over muscle movements, typically in response to environmental feedback (e.g., changes in speed or position of object being manipulated).
Aiming (AI)	Ability to precisely and fluently execute a sequence of eye–hand coordination movements for positioning purposes.
Gross Body Equilibrium (P4)	Ability to maintain the body in an upright position in space or regain balance after balance has been disturbed.

Note. Definitions were derived from Carroll (1993) and Schneider and McGrew (2012).

sensations" (Schneider & McGrew, 2012, p. 133). Proprioception refers to one's awareness of body position and movement (Westen, 2002). Although there is currently a limited understanding of *Gk* narrow abilities, we can infer they may include abilities such as a yogi being able to feel the correct body position in a pose, or a swimmer being able to demonstrate an adjustment in arm position that improves technique.

Processing Speed (*Gs*)

Processing speed or mental quickness is often mentioned when talking about intelligent behavior (Nettelbeck, 1994). Processing speed is the "ability to perform simple, repetitive cognitive tasks quickly and fluently" (Schneider & McGrew, 2012, p. 119). These cognitive tasks often require maintained focused attention and concentration; therefore, "attentive speediness" encapsulates the essence of *Gs*. *Gs* is measured typically by fixed-interval timed tasks that require little in the way of complex thinking or mental processing (e.g., the Wechsler Animal Pegs, Symbol Search, Cancellation, and Digit Symbol/Coding tests).

Recent interest in information-processing models of cognitive functioning has resulted in a renewed focus on *Gs*

(Kail, 1991; Lohman, 1989, McGrew, 2005). A central construct in information-processing models is the idea of limited processing resources (e.g., the limited capacities of short-term and working memory): "Many cognitive activities require a person's deliberate efforts and people are limited in the amount of effort they can allocate. In the face of limited processing resources, the speed of processing is critical because it determines in part how rapidly limited resources can be reallocated to other cognitive tasks" (Kail, 1991, p. 492). Woodcock (1993) likens *Gs* to a valve in a water pipe. The rate at which water flows in the pipe (i.e., *Gs*) increases when the valve is opened wide and decreases when the valve is partially closed. Five different narrow speed-of-processing abilities are subsumed by *Gs* in the present CHC model (see Table C.13).

Decision Speed/Reaction Time (*Gt*)

In addition to *Gs*, both Carroll and Horn included a second broad speed ability in their respective models of the structure of abilities. Processing Speed or Decision Speed/Reaction Time (*Gt*), as proposed by Carroll, subsumes narrow abilities that reflect an individual's quickness in reacting (reaction time) and making decisions (decision speed). *Gt* is also considered as the "speed of making very simple decisions or judgments when items are presented one at a time" (Schneider & McGrew, 2012, p. 120). Correct Decision Speed (CDS), proposed by Horn as a second speed ability (*Gs* being the first), is typically measured by recording the time an individual requires

to provide an answer to problems on a variety of tests (e.g., letter series, classifications, vocabulary; Horn, 1988, 1991). Because Correct Decision Speed appeared to be a much narrower ability than *Gt*, it is subsumed by *Gt* in CHC theory.

It is important not to confuse *Gt* with *Gs*. *Gt* abilities reflect the immediacy with which an individual can react to stimuli or a task (typically measured in seconds or parts of seconds), whereas *Gs* abilities reflect the ability to work quickly over a longer period of time (typically measured in intervals of 2 to 3 minutes). Being asked to read a passage (on a self-paced scrolling video screen) as quickly as possible and, in the process, touch the word *the* with a stylus pen each time it appears on the screen, is an example of *Gs*. The individual's *Gs* score would reflect the number of correct responses (taking into account errors of omission and commission). In contrast, *Gt* may be measured by requiring a person to read the same text at his or her normal rate of reading and press the space bar as quickly as possible whenever a light is flashed on the screen. In this latter paradigm, the individual's score is based on the average response latency or the time interval between the onset of the stimulus and the individual's response. Table C.14 includes descriptions of the narrow abilities subsumed by *Gt*.

Psychomotor Speed (*Gps*)

Psychomotor speed is the "speed and fluidity with which physical body movements can be made" (Schneider & McGrew, 2012, p. 121). Psychomotor speed tasks are rarely measured on assessment batteries, with the exception of finger-tapping tasks in some neuropsychological tests. There are currently four narrow abilities of *Gps*, which are described in Table C.15.

Table C.13. Narrow *Gs* Stratum I Ability Definitions

Narrow Stratum I Name (Code)	Definition
Processing Speed (*Gs*)	
Perceptual Speed (P)	Ability to rapidly search for and compare known visual symbols or patterns presented side-by-side or separated in a visual field.
Rate-of-Test-Taking (R9)	Ability to rapidly perform tests which are relatively easy or that require very simple decisions.
Number Facility (N)	Ability to rapidly and accurately manipulate and deal with numbers, from elementary skills of counting and recognizing numbers to advanced skills of adding, subtracting, multiplying, and dividing numbers.
Reading Speed (Fluency) (RS)	Time required to silently read a passage or series of sentences as quickly as possible.
Writing Speed (Fluency) (WS)	The rate at which words or sentences can be generated or copied.

Note. Definitions were derived from Carroll (1993) and Schneider and McGrew (2012).

Table C.14. Narrow *Gt* Stratum I Ability Definitions

Narrow Stratum I Name (Code)	Definition
Decision/Reaction Time or Speed (*Gt*)	
Simple Reaction Time (R1)	Reaction time to the presentation of a single visual or auditory stimulus.
Choice Reaction Time (R2)	Reaction time to one of two or more alternative stimuli, depending on which alternative is signaled.
Semantic Processing Speed (R4)	Reaction time when the decision requires some encoding and mental manipulation of stimulus content.
Mental Comparison Speed (R7)	Reaction time where the stimuli must be compared for a particular attribute.
Inspection Time (IT)	The speed at which differences in stimuli can be perceived.

Note. Definitions were derived from Carroll (1993) and Schneider and McGrew (2012).

Table C.15. Narrow *Gps* Stratum I Ability Definitions

Narrow Stratum I Name (Code)	Definition
Psychomotor Speed (*Gps*)	
Speed of Limb Movement (R3)	The speed of arm and leg movement.
Writing Speed (Fluency) (WS)	The speed at which written words can be copied.
Speed of Articulation (PT)	Ability to rapidly perform successive articulations with the speech musculature.
Movement Time (MT)	The time taken to physically move a body part (e.g., a finger) to make the required response. MT may also measure the speed of finger, limb, or multilimb movements or vocal articulation (diadochokinesis; Greek for "successive movements") (Carroll, 1993).

Note. Definitions were derived from Carroll (1993) and Schneider and McGrew (2012).

Conclusion

The Cattell-Horn-Carroll theory is the most researched, empirically supported, and comprehensive hierarchical psychometric framework of the structure of cognitive abilities. It reflects a major review and reanalysis of the world's literature on individual differences in cognitive abilities, collected over most of a century (Carroll, 1993). The culmination of the monumental contributions of Raymond Cattell, John Horn, and John Carroll, know as CHC theory, will continue to define the taxonomy of cognitive differential psychology for decades to come.

REFERENCES

Ackerman, P. L., & Heggestad, E. D. (1997). Intelligence, personality, and interests: Evidence for overlapping traits. *Psychological Bulletin, 121*(2), 219–45.

Alfonso, V. C., Flanagan, D. P., & Radwan, S. (2005). The impact of the Cattell-Horn-Carroll theory on test development and interpretation of cognitive and academic abilities. In D. P. Flanagan & P. L. Harrison (Eds.), *Contemporary intellectual assessment: Theories, tests, and issues* (2nd ed., pp. 185–202). New York, NY: Guilford Press.

Bensen, J. (1998). Developing a strong program of construct validation: A test anxiety example. *Educational Measurement: Issues and Practice, 17*(1), 10–22.

Bickley, P. G., Keith, T. Z., & Wolfe, L. M. (1995). The three-stratum theory of cognitive abilities: Test of the structure of intelligence across the life span. *Intelligence, 20*, 309–328.

Carroll, J. B. (1993). *Human cognitive abilities: A survey of factor-analytic studies*. Cambridge, UK: Cambridge University Press.

Carroll, J. B. (1997). The three-stratum theory of cognitive abilities. In D. P. Flanagan, J. L. Genshaft, & P. L. Harrison (Eds.), *Contemporary intellectual assessment: Theories, tests, and issues* (pp. 122–130). New York, NY: Guilford Press.

Carroll, J. B. (2005). The three-stratum theory of cognitive abilities. In D. P. Flanagan & P. L. Harrison (Eds.), *Contemporary intellectual assessment: Theories, tests, and issues* (2nd ed., pp. 69–76). New York, NY: Guilford Press.

Casey, M. B., Nuttall, R. L., & Pezaris, E. (1997). Mediators of gender differences in mathematics college entrance test scores: A comparison of spatial skills with internalized beliefs and anxieties. *Developmental Psychology, 33*(4), 669–680.

Cattell, R. B. (1957). *Personality and motivation structure and measurement*. New York, NY: World Book.

Cattell, R. B. (1971). *Abilities: Their structure, growth, and action*. Boston, MA: Houghton Mifflin.

Daniel, M. H. (1997). Intelligence testing: Status and trends. *American Psychologist, 52*(10), 1038–1045.

Dean, R. S., & Woodcock, R. W. (2003). *Dean-Woodcock Neuropsychological Battery*. Itasca, IL: Riverside Publishing.

Evans, J., Floyd, R., McGrew, K. S., & Leforgee, M. (2002). The relations between measures of Cattell-Horn-Carroll (CHC) cognitive abilities and reading achievement during childhood and adolescence. *School Psychology Review, 3*(2), 246.

Flanagan, D. P. (2000). Wechsler-based CHC cross-battery assessment and reading achievement: Strengthening the validity of interpretations drawn from Wechsler test scores. *School Psychology Quarterly, 15*(3), 295–329.

Flanagan, D. P., Alfonso, V. C., Mascolo, J. T., Sotelo-Dynega, M. (2012). Use of ability tests in the identification of specific learning disabilities within the context of an operational definition. In D. P. Flanagan & P. L. Harrison (Eds.), *Contemporary intellectual assessment: Theories, tests, and issues* (3rd ed., pp. 643–669). New York, NY: Guilford Press.

Flanagan, D. P., Alfonso, V. C., Ortiz, S. O., & Dynda, A. M. (2010). Integrating cognitive assessment in school neuropsychological evaluations. In D. C. Miller (Ed.), *Best practices in school neuropsychology: Guidelines for effective practice, assessment, and evidence-based intervention* (pp. 101–140). Hoboken, NJ: Wiley.

Flanagan, D. P., & Harrison, P. L. (Eds.). (2012). *Contemporary intellectual assessment: Theories, tests, and issues* (3rd ed.). New York, NY: Guilford Press.

Flanagan, D. P., & McGrew, K. S. (1997). A cross-battery approach to assessing and interpreting cognitive abilities: Narrowing the gap between practice and cognitive science. In D. P. Flanagan, J. L. Genshaft, & P. L. Harrison (Eds.), *Contemporary intellectual assessment: Theories, tests, and issues* (pp. 314–325). New York, NY: Guilford Press.

Flanagan, D. P., McGrew, K. S., & Ortiz, S. O. (2000). *The Wechsler intelligence scales and CHC theory: A contemporary approach to interpretation*. Boston, MA: Allyn & Bacon.

Flanagan, D. P., Ortiz, S. O., & Alfonso, V. C. (in press). *Essentials of cross-battery assessment* (3rd ed.). Manuscript submitted for publication.

Flanagan, D. P., Ortiz, S. O., Alfonso, V. C., & Mascolo, J. T. (2002). *The achievement test desk reference (ATDR): Comprehensive assessment of learning disabilities*. Boston, MA: Allyn & Bacon.

Flanagan, D. P., Ortiz, S. O., Alfonso, V. C., & Mascolo, J. T. (2006). *The achievement test desk reference (ATDR), 2nd edition: A guide to learning disability identification.* Hoboken, NJ: Wiley.

Floyd, R. G., Evans, J. J., & McGrew, K. S. (2003). Relations between measures of Cattell-Horn-Carroll (CHC) cognitive abilities and mathematics achievement across the school-age years. *Psychology in the Schools, 40*(2), 155–171.

Gustafsson, J. E., & Balke, G. (1993). General and specific abilities as predictors of school achievement. *Multivariate Behavioral Research, 28*(4), 407–434.

Gustaffson, J. E., & Undheim, J. O. (1996). Individual differences in cognitive functions. In D. C. Berliner & R. C. Calfee (Eds.), *Handbook of educational psychology* (pp. 186–42). New York, NY: Macmillan.

Hegarty, M., & Kozhevnikov, M. (1999). Types of visual-spatial representations and mathematical problem solving. *Journal of Educational Psychology, 91*(4), 684–689.

Horn, J. L. (1968). Organization of abilities and the development of intelligence. *Psychological Review, 75*, 242–259.

Horn, J. L. (1988). Thinking about human abilities. In J. R. Nesselroade & R. B. Cattell (Eds.), *Handbook of multivariate psychology* (Rev. ed., pp. 645–685). New York, NY: Academic Press.

Horn, J. L. (1991). Measurement of intellectual capabilities: A review of theory. In K. S. McGrew, J. K. Werder, & R. W. Woodcock (Eds.), *Woodcock-Johnson technical manual* (pp. 197–232). Chicago, IL: Riverside.

Horn, J. L., & Blankson, N. (2005) Foundations for better understanding of cognitive abilities. In D. P. Flanagan & P. L. Harrison (Eds.), *Contemporary intellectual assessment: Theories, tests, and issues* (2nd ed., pp. 41–68). New York, NY: Guilford Press.

Horn, J. L., & Stankov, L. (1982). Auditory and visual factors of intelligence. *Intelligence, 6*, 165–185.

Jensen, A. R. (1997, July). *What we know and don't know about the g factor.* Keynote address delivered at the bi-annual convention of the International Society for the Study of Individual Differences. Aarhus, Denmark.

Jensen, A. R. (1998). *The g factor: The science of mental ability.* Westport, CT: Praeger.

Kail, R. (1991). Developmental changes in speed of processing during childhood and adolescence. *Psychological Bulletin, 109*, 490–501.

Kane, M. J., Bleckley, M. K., Conway, A. R. A., & Engle, R. W. (2001). A controlled-attention view of working-memory capacity. *Journal of Experimental Psychology General, 130*(2), 169–183.

Keith, T. Z. (1997). Using confirmatory factor analysis to aid in understanding the constructs measured by intelligence tests. In D. P. Flanagan, J. L. Genshaft, & P. L. Harrison (Eds.), *Contemporary intellectual assessment: Theories, tests, and issues* (pp. 373–402). New York, NY: Guilford Press.

Keith, T. Z. (1999). Effects of general and specific abilities on student achievement: Similarities and differences across ethnic groups. *School Psychology Quarterly, 14*(3), 239–262.

Keith, T. Z. (2005). Using confirmatory factor analysis to aid in understanding the constructs measured by intelligence tests.

In D. P. Flanagan & P. L. Harrison (Eds.), *Contemporary intellectual assessment: Theories, tests, and issues* (2nd ed., pp. 581–614). New York, NY: Guilford Press.

Keith, T. Z., & Kranzler, J. H. (1999). The absence of structural fidelity precludes construct validity: Rejoinder to Naglieri on what the cognitive assessment system does and does not measure. *School Psychology Review, 28*(2), 303–321.

Keith, T. Z., Kranzler, J. H., & Flanagan, D. P. (2001). What does the Cognitive Assessment System (CAS) measure? Joint confirmatory factor analysis of the CAS and the Woodcock-Johnson Tests of Cognitive Ability (3rd ed.). *School Psychology Review, 30*, 89–119.

Keith, T. Z., & Reynolds, M. R. (2010). Cattell-Horn-Carroll cognitive-achievement relations: What we have learned from the past 20 years of research. *Psychology in the Schools, 47*(7), 635–650.

Keith, T. Z., & Reynolds, M. R. (2012). Using confirmatory factor analysis to aid in understanding the constructs measured by intelligence tests. In D. P. Flanagan & P. L. Harrison (Eds.), *Contemporary intellectual assessment: Theories, tests, and issues* (3rd ed., pp. 758–799). New York, NY: Guilford Press.

Liberman, I., Shankweiler, D., Fischer, F. W., & Carter, B. (1974). Explicit syllable and phoneme segmentation in the young child. *Journal of Experimental Child Psychology, 8*, 201–212.

Lohman, D. F. (1989). Human intelligence: An introduction to advances in theory and research. *Review of Educational Research, 59*(4), 333–373.

Lohman, D. F. (1994). Spatial ability. In R. J. Sternberg (Ed.), *Encyclopedia of human intelligence* (pp. 1000–1007). New York, NY: Macmillan.

McGrew, K. S. (1997). Analysis of the major intelligence batteries according to a proposed comprehensive Gf-Gc framework. In D. P. Flanagan, J. L. Genshaft, & P. L. Harrison (Eds.), *Contemporary intellectual assessment: Theories, tests, and issues* (pp. 151–180). New York, NY: Guilford Press.

McGrew, K. S. (2005). The Cattell-Horn-Carroll theory of cognitive abilities: Past, present, and future. In D. P. Flanagan & P. L. Harrison (Eds.), *Contemporary intellectual assessment: Theories, tests, and issues* (2nd ed., pp. 136–182). New York, NY: Guilford Press.

McGrew, K. S., & Flanagan, D. P. (1998). *The Intelligence Test Desk Reference (ITDR): Gf-Gc cross-battery assessment.* Boston, MA: Allyn & Bacon.

McGrew, K. S., & Wendling, B. J. (2010). Cattell-Horn-Carroll cognitive-achievement relations: What we have learned from the past 20 years of research. *Psychology in the Schools, 47*(7), 651–675.

McGrew, K. S., & Woodcock, R. W. (2001). *Technical manual: Woodcock-Johnson III.* Itasca, IL: Riverside.

Morris, R. D., Stuebing, K. K., Fletcher, J. M., Shaywitz, S. E., Lyon, G. R., Shankweiler, D. P., . . . Shaywitz, B. A. (1998). Subtypes of reading disability: Variability around a phonological core. *Journal of Educational Psychology, 90*(3), 347–373.

Nettelbeck, T. (1994). Speediness. In R. J. Sternberg (Ed.), *Encyclopedia of human intelligence* (pp. 1014–1019). New York, NY: Macmillan.

Richardson, J. (1996). Evolving concepts of working memory. In J. Richardson, R. Engle, L. Hasher, R. Logie, E. Stoltzfus, & R. Zacks (Eds.), *Working memory and human cognition* (pp. 3–30). New York, NY: Oxford University Press.

Schneider, W. J., & McGrew, K. S. (2012). The Cattell-Horn-Carroll Model of Intelligence. In D. P. Flanagan, & P. L. Harrison (Eds.), *Contemporary intellectual assessment: Theories, tests, and issues* (3rd ed., pp. 99–144). New York, NY: Guilford Press.

Sternberg, R. J., & Kaufman, J. C. (1998). Human abilities. *Annual Review of Psychology, 49*, 479–502.

Vanderwood, M. L., McGrew, K. S., Flanagan, D. P., & Keith, T. Z. (2002). The contribution of general and specific cognitive abilities to reading achievement. *Learning and Individual Differences,13*, 159–188.

Vellutino, F. R., & Scanlon, D. M. (2002). The interactive strategies approach to reading intervention. *Contemporary Educational Psychology, 27*, 573–635.

Vellutino, F. R., Scanlon, D. M., & Lyon, G. R. (2000). Differentiating between difficult-to-remediate and readily remediated poor readers: More evidence against the IQ-achievement discrepancy definition of reading disability. *Journal of Learning Disabilities, 33(3)*, 223–238.

Wagner, R. K., & Torgesen, J. K. (1987). The nature of phonological processing and its causal role in the acquisition of reading skills. *Psychological Bulletins, 101(2)*, 192–212.

Westen, D. (2002). *Psychology: Mind, brain, & culture* (3rd ed.). Hoboken, NJ: Wiley.

Woodcock, R. W. (1993). An information processing view of Gf-Gc theory. *Journal of Psychoeducational Assessment Monograph Series, 11*, 80–102.

Woodcock, R. W. (1994). Measures of fluid and crystallized intelligence. In R. J. Sternberg (Ed.), *The encyclopedia of human intelligence* (pp. 452–456). New York, NY: Macmillan.

Woodcock, R. W., McGrew, K. S., & Mather, N. (2001). *Woodcock-Johnson III tests of achievement*. Itasca, IL: Riverside.

DAWN P. FLANAGAN
St. John's University

SHAUNA G. DIXON
St. John's University
Fourth edition

CATTELL, JAMES MCKEEN (1860–1944)

James McKeen Cattell was educated at Lafayette College in Pennsylvania and the University of Leipzig in Germany. He worked under Wilhelm Wundt at Leipzig and at Sir Francis Galton's psychological laboratory in London. He held the world's first professorship in psychology, at the University of Pennsylvania, and later was professor of psychology and head of the department of psychology at Columbia University (Woodworth, 1944).

A devoted researcher, Cattell conducted significant investigations in areas such as reaction time, perception, association, and individual differences. He developed numerous tests and coined the term *mental tests*. He studied the backgrounds and characteristics of eminent scientists, and published the widely used directory *Biographical Dictionary of American Men of Science*. To promote the practical application of psychology, he founded the Psychological Corporation and served as its president for many years. He also edited a number of influential journals, including the *American Journal of Psychology, Psychological Review*, and *Science*. Cattell, through his students, research, and writing and editing, was a major figure in the development of psychology as a profession in the United States (Watson, 1968).

REFERENCES

Watson, R. I. (1968). *The great psychologists*. New York, NY: Lippincott.

Woodworth, R. S. (1944). James McKeen Cattell, 1860–1944. *Psychological Review, 51*, 201–209.

PAUL IRVINE
Katonah, New York

AMANDA CHOW
Texas A&M University
Fourth edition

CAWLEY'S PROJECT MATH

Project MATH (Mathematics Activities for Teaching the Handicapped) is a comprehensive developmental mathematics program for children with special needs. The program was developed by Dr. John Cawley and his associates at the University of Connecticut under a federal grant operated from 1970 to 1975. The project was entitled "A Program Project Research and Demonstration Effort in Arithmetic among the Mentally Handicapped"; it is available commercially (Cawley, 1984; Cawley, 1985; Cawley, Goodstein, Fitzmaurice, Leport, Sedlak, & Althaus, 1976, 1977).

The teaching model used in the curriculum is called the *Interactive Unit* (IU). This teaching model allows for the presentation of information to the learner in four different ways and also allows the learner to respond to questions or information in four different ways. There are 16 possible interactions that can take place between the teacher and the learner for any concept being taught. No interaction is considered to be cognitively superior to another. The interactive unit teaching model offers several advantages for the instructor. Chief among these advantages is that the model allows an instructor to teach around a disability. Learners who have difficulty in reading or writing may be taught by any of the remaining nine interaction possibilities. The instructor components of the IU are state, construct, present, and graphically symbolize. The learner components are state, construct, identify, and graphically symbolize.

The goal of the curriculum is to give a balanced emphasis to the development of skills, concepts, and social growth. The content of the math strands addressed are patterns, numbers, operations, measurements, fractions, and geometry. There are multiple lessons and support materials for concepts taught in each strand. A math concept inventory accompanies each level of the curriculum. This inventory is essentially a criterion-referenced test used to make initial placement decisions in the curriculum and to measure growth.

The verbal-problem-solving component of the curriculum is unique in that problem solving is introduced at the lowest level of the curriculum (Level I) and is carried out in an increasingly complex manner in the remaining levels. Problem solving is viewed as the ultimate objective of the mathematics curriculum. Unlike most mathematics programs, reading is not an essential prerequisite for entry into the verbal problem-solving exercises; the need for computational skills is also minimized. The focus of the verbal problem-solving component is on the processing of information necessary for the solution, not on the practice of computational skills. Levels I and II use sets of pictures, cards, and prepared scripts to guide a teacher and learner through the problem-solving activities. In Level III, reading is required for the first time. The use of extraneous information and language plays a major role in the problem-solving activities.

The final component of the Cawley's Project MATH curriculum consists of *Social Utilization Units*. These units are real-life extensions of the verbal-problem-solving exercises; they require teams of learners to use mathematics to solve real-life problems. The units also stress social responsibility in that each member of the team is responsible for performing a task or gathering information so that the team's problem can be solved.

Two years of field testing, from 1972 to 1974, was undertaken. It involved 1,917 children instructed by 116 teachers in seven states. In addition to the curricular development thrust of the project, a large number of research studies were undertaken and published, primarily in the area of verbal problem solving. Cawley has continued to build on the Project MATH materials and to expand the basic model so that it can be used by a wide variety of special educators (Thornton, 1995).

Cawley continues to develop ways to reduce the inconvenience between special and general education mathematics instruction (Palmer & Cawley, 1995), and examines the MATH performance of students from different economic backgrounds (Pacer Center, 2005).

REFERENCES

Cawley, J. F. (Ed.). (1984). *Developmental teaching of mathematics for the learning disabled*. Rockville, MD: Aspen Systems.

Cawley, J. F. (Ed.). (1985). *Secondary school mathematics for the learning disabled*. Rockville, MD: Aspen Systems.

Cawley, J. F., Goodstein, H. A., Fitzmaurice, A. M., Lepore, A., Sedlak, R. A., & Althaus, V. (1976, 1977). *Project MATH: Mathematics activities for teaching the handicapped: Levels I–V*. Tulsa, OK: Educational Progress Corporation.

Pacer Center. (2005). *Standards-based reform*. Retrieved from http://www.pacer.org/

Palmer, R. S., & Cawley, J. F. (1995). Mathematics curricula frameworks: Goals for general and special education. *Focus on Learning Problems in Mathematics, 17*(2), 50–66.

Thornton, C. A. (1995). Promising research, programs, and projects. *Teaching Children Mathematics, 2*(2), 134–135.

ROBERT A. SEDLAK
University of Wisconsin at Stout

See also **Mathematics, Learning Disabilities in; Mathematics, Remedial**

CENTER FOR APPLIED SPECIAL TECHNOLOGY

The Center for Applied Special Technology (CAST) is a nonprofit organization founded in 1984, with the mission of expanding opportunities for people with disabilities through the development of and innovative uses of technology. Center activities include research, product development, and work within educational settings in the service of furthering universal design for learning. In its early years, CAST sought to help people with disabilities through the development and provision of assistive technology on the individual level; however, they realized that this approach by itself kept the burden of adapting to a disability on each individual, and failed to address systemically the many barriers that the vast majority of learners with disabilities encounter.

As a result, CAST now works from the premise that the most effective way to expand educational opportunities is for learning to be desigened for everyone, or Universal. The term *universal design* refers to the creation of technological devices and programs paired with learning models that are usable by everyone, including individuals of all ages, whether they are gifted, are typical learners, or have special needs" (CAST, 2010).

The CAST offices are located at 40 Harvard Mills Square, Suite 3, Wakefield, MA 01880-3233. Tel.: (781) 245-2212; e-mail: cast@cast.org

REFERENCE

Center for Applied Special Technology. (2012). *About CAST: Mission and history*. Retrieved from http://www.cast.org/index.html

KAY E. KETZENBERGER
University of Texas of the Permian Basin

CENTERS FOR INDEPENDENT LIVING

In discussing this select topic that addresses independent living for individuals who live with disabilities the author of this article would like to state that for more than four decades he has personally been involved as a classroom teacher with students who experience disabilities as well as in the preparation of special and general education credential students who themselves are preparing to be classroom teachers. Experience gained from working with and knowing numerous individuals over the years has left a significant mark not only in terms of being an educator but, also, in terms of how significant it is that individuals are viewed by others in terms of ability, prominence, stature, and self-worth. Indeed, the Independent Living Movement is a *civil rights movement* for individuals with disabilities. In its infancy, during the 1960s and 1970s, it was a time of protests, sit-ins, and media coverage. Newspapers, magazines, and the evening news on television told of these activities by college students living with disabilities and those who supported their efforts. These activities, taking place at the University of California at Berkeley in the West and at the University of Illinois in the East, were considered revolutionary in their nature. The movement represented human rights of persons with disabilities; however, more important than this was how, as a nation, all persons would be treated and respected by other individuals simply because they are human beings. If we trivialize the notion that some in society simply deserve to live more freely or openly and enjoy more individual rights than others, then perhaps we have played a trick on ourselves. In this case, we have lost our way. Instead, we should be members of a society in which we search for unity within a nation.

The three cornerstones of the independent living philosophy are consumer sovereignty, self-reliance, and political and economic rights. The philosophy rejects the supremacy of professionals as decision makers and views disability as an interaction with the society and the environment rather than as a medical condition or physical or mental impairment (DeJong, 1978). Models of service delivery that help foster independent living for persons with disabilities vary by region and locale. While Centers for Independent Living hold commonalities in services offered to individuals there is ample variance in how these services may be made available based on the type of disabilities encountered by individuals in a given locale. Also a good deal of variation in services available may depend on location, such as an urban environment as compared to a rural environment. Such locations play significantly into what and how services are delivered or made available. Ward produced an internationally acclaimed film titled: *A Little History Worth Knowing* (1998) that is a primer on disability and the vast stereotypes that individuals living with disabilities have endured over many centuries in society. Clearly indicated within the film is the necessary sweeping away of harmful stereotypes illustrated in print and other media while replacing such negativity with positive imagery of individuals with disabilities being active contributors within our communities. There are a number of essential features of the independent living service model discussed in the literature. These include consumer control, a cross-disability emphasis (inclusion of people with all types of disabilities—mental, physical, sensory), a community-based and community-responsive approach, peer role modeling, provision of a wide range of services, a community advocacy orientation, and open and ongoing access to services (Counts, 1978; Goodall, 1988; Lachat, 1988).

Centers for Independent Living (CILs) are designed to assist individuals with disabilities to achieve their maximum potential. Typically, CILs are nonresidential, private, nonprofit, community-based organizations providing services and advocacy by and for persons with disabilities. In discussing living options for those living with disabilities Goodall (1988) suggests that independent living philosophy calls for options and individual control. That is, when social and environmental options are available, persons with disabilities can live independently like other people in the community. To become fully independent, disabled persons must select their options, specify their goals, and take responsibility for achieving those goals. In this way, persons with disabilities can gain control of their lives and minimize reliance on others (Frieden, 1978). Moreover, Garboden (2011), suggests for people with disabilities the world of rents and benefits is a harsh one that may see them forced to live away from social networks. Local rents or housing availability may be prohibitive because of expense but, also, availability for suitable housing may cause hardship due to distance from support networks such as family and friends as well as transportation hampered by availability and cost. In their work dealing with models for independent living,

Nosek, Zhu, and Howard (1992), suggest that inequalities that existed could be remedied if consideration was given based on the uniqueness and individuality of people with disabilities along with provision of reasonable accommodations and appropriate services. Individuals living with severe disabilities were the real pioneers in the CIL movement because it afforded them options for living a more integrated life in their communities. Ironically it was individuals with some of the most serious as well as limiting disabilities that opened the door for other individuals with less serious disabilities to experience and enjoy models of living independence.

The term *severe disabilities* has been defined somewhat differently by various individuals and agencies. Generally, however, it implies a condition in which the development of typical abilities is in some way adversely affected (Sailor & Guess, 1983; Snell & Brown, 2011; Westling & Fox, 2009). Persons with severe disabilities are often challenged by significant weaknesses in general learning abilities, personal and social skills, and frequently, in areas of sensory and physical development.

According to Westling and Fox (2009), individuals who experience severe disabilities commonly do not demonstrate the general ability in skills necessary to maintain themselves independently. Most often these individuals require assistance and ongoing support from persons who do not experience disabilities, such as family members, friends, professionals, and care providers. The traditional categories of persons usually referred to as having a severe disability, as suggested by Westling and Fox (2009), include those who have been classified as having moderate, severe, or profound intellectual disabilities; some who have autism spectrum disorders (ASD); and those who have multiple physical or sensory disabilities as well as intellectual disabilities. Recent developments in defining the condition of severe disabilities and their impact on the lives of individuals as reported by Westling and Fox (2009) have focused on quality-of-life issues with regard to necessary support. TASH, an organization supporting equity, opportunity, and inclusion for people with disabilities, and the American Association on Intellectual and Developmental Disabilities (AAIDD) in its most recent characterization of intellectual disabilities, considered it as a human manifestation in which different levels of support are required. Since 1992, AAIDD ceased making distinctions using the traditional subclasses of intellectual disabilities, but instead proposed that an individual must be described within a multidimensional context that provides a comprehensive description of the person and the necessary supports (see Figure C.9).

The theoretical model of intellectual disabilities presented in Figure C.9 has five dimensions: (1) intellectual abilities, (2) adaptive behavior, (3) participation, interactions, and social roles, (4) health, and (5) context. These are mediated by a support system to affect an individual's functioning. Using this model the impact of all dimensions

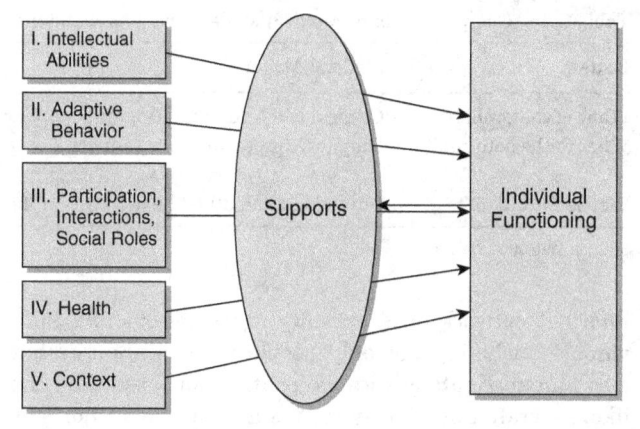

Figure C.9. Theoretical model of mental retardation.
Source: Westling & Fox (2009, p. 4).

on the individual is influenced by the support that buffers the person's life. The model implies that a person's functioning is due not solely to characteristics of the individual, but also to the supportive context in which the person must operate. Intellectual disabilities experienced by an individual as illustrated (see Figure C.9) is seen not as deficiency, but in terms of needed supports.

As suggested by Westling and Fox (2009), the AAIDD states five assumptions "essential" to the application of its definition:

1. Limitations in present functioning must be considered within the context of community environments typical of the individual's age peers and culture.
2. Valid assessment considers cultural and linguistic diversity, as well as differences in communication, sensory, motor, and behavioral factors.
3. Within an individual, limitations often coexist with strengths.
4. An important purpose of describing limitations is to develop a profile of needed supports.
5. With appropriate personalized supports over a sustained period, the life functioning of the person with intellectual disabilities generally will improve (pp. 3–4).

Although the AAIDD eliminated categories of intellectual disabilities based on levels of measured intelligence, these categories are still maintained in the American Psychiatric Association's (APA) *Diagnostic and Statistical Manual of Mental Disorders* (4th ed., Rev. text) (*DSM-IV-TR*, 2000). Stated levels and their corresponding approximate IQ ranges include mild (50–70), moderate (35–50), severe (20–35), and profound (below 20–25) intellectual disabilities.

DeJong (1978) and Wilson (1998) state that the independent living movement is characterized as the civil rights movement of people with disabilities. It was initiated by individuals, and quickly became a national,

Table C.16. Comparison of a "Medical Model" and "Independent Living Model" of Disability

Issue	Medical Model	Independent Living Model
What is the problem?	Clinical condition resulting in dependence and apathy	Discrimination and lack of supports
What is the solution?	Diagnose, prescribe, and support	Reasonable, appropriate accommodations, support services, and programs facilitating independence
Who is in control?	Physicians and allied health-care professionals	Consumers

Source: Wilson (1998, p. 2).

informal network of community organizations and individuals, including not only people with disabilities but also human rights advocates, political lobbyists, and the like. As stated previously in this article, the author saw and experienced first-hand the effects of this movement both in terms of educational implications for students with special needs receiving an education in public and private schools as well as adults with disabilities (and their advocates) demanding full accessibility for employment and living independently within their communities. Consumers (those living with disabilities) sought to live a more fulfilling life in the ablebodied world as well as the efforts of the rehabilitation professionals to reach disabled persons for whom a vocational goal was, until recently, unthinkable (Switzer, 2003). It was not until the early 1970s that the CIL movement gained greater visibility and recognition with the creation of the Center for Independent Living (CIL) in Berkeley, California.

Professionals in the field of rehabilitation have held common beliefs that rehabilitation programs are built upon the "medical model" of service delivery, while the disability rights and CIL movement promotes a completely different approach to service delivery. The approach is based on the principles of self-determination, choice, and consumer control (Nosek et al., 1992).

Self-determination refers to an individual's ability to express preferences and desires, make decisions, and initiate actions based on these decisions. Simply, self-determination refers to choice. Control focuses on the extent to which individuals are independent, self-sufficient, and capable of gaining access to the resources necessary to freely act on their choices and decisions (Wilson, 1998).

The medical model labeled people with disabilities as helpless, passive, dependent, unable, and perhaps disinterested in gaining or maintaining employment. The independent living model completely turned the medical model (and those who adhere to it) on its head. A comparison of these two divergent models of disability is illustrated vividly in Table C.16.

Contrasting the two models of disability illustrates the desired outcomes for CILs to assist individuals in decision making for taking control over one's daily life as paramount. The term *control* does not necessarily mean having the physical or mental capacity to do everyday tasks for oneself. Individuals who have worked or are in the process of initiating careers that bring them into contact with persons who live with disabilities understand first-hand the harsh realities of these individuals gaining full independence in their lives. What they ask for or request of us is the opportunity to experience as much independence and decision making in their lives as is feasible given the limitations they may live with. For some persons, complete control may not be possible but the CIL movement continues to work toward complete consumer control wherever and whenever possible.

In addition to established Independent Living Models in communities Garboden (2011) and Wilson (1998) both assert the requirement of every community needing the rehabilitation paradigm for the provision of adequate medical-based services. Equally important, however, is that each community needs an equal amount of service and advocacy stemming from the independent living paradigm. At this time, approximately 99% of all public dollars go into the rehabilitation paradigm while less than 1% goes into independent living.

The passage of PL 101-336, Americans with Disabilities Act of 1990 (ADA), creates a vision for equal opportunity and access for all persons. This vision according to Wilson (1998) is shared by people involved in both the traditional rehabilitation system and the newer disability rights and CIL movement. CILs enhance not only the lives of persons with disabilities, but also the individual communities where these centers are located. Additionally, CILs provide an advocacy voice on a wide range of national, state, and local issues. The more than 700 CILs in the United States are working to establish physical and programmatic access to housing, employment, communities, transportation, and recreational facilities, as well as health and social services. The movement for independent living has been evolving for well over four decades. The CIL movement will continue to grow because committed individuals will seek ways to assist all persons to feel that they are valued members of their community, whether they happen to live with or without disabilities.

REFERENCES

American Psychiatric Association. (2000). *Diagnostic and statistical manual of mental disorders* (4th ed., rev. text) (*DSM-IV-TR*, 2000). Washington, DC: Author.

Counts, R. (1978). *Independent living rehabilitation for severely handicapped people: A preliminary appraisal*. Washington, DC: Urban Institute.

DeJong, G. (1978, November 17). *The movement for independent living: Origins, ideology, and implications for disability research*. Boston: Medical Rehabilitation Institute, Tufts-New England Medical Center. Paper presented at the annual meetings of the American Congress of Rehabilitation Medicine, New Orleans, Louisiana.

Frieden, L. (1978). Independent living: Movement and programs. *American Rehabilitation*, 3(6), 6–9.

Garboden, M. (2011, November 24). Independence—at a price. *Community Care*. Retrieved from http://go.galegroup.com.ezproxylocal. Library.nova.edu/ps/

Goodall, J. (1988). Living options for physically disabled adults: A review. *Disability, Handicap & Society*, 3(2), 173–193.

Lachat, M. (1988). *The independent living service model: Historical roots, core elements and current practices*. Hampton, NH: Center for Resource Management.

Nosek, A., Zhu, Y., & Howard, C. (1992). The evolution of independent living programs. *Rehabilitation Counseling Bulletin*, 35(3), 175–189.

Sailor, W., & Guess, D. (1983). *Severely handicapped students: An instructional design*. Boston, MA: Houghton Mifflin.

Snell, M., & Brown, F. (2011). *Instruction of students with severe disabilities* (7th ed.). Upper Saddle River, NJ: Pearson Education.

Switzer, J. (2003). *Disabled rights: American disability policy and the fight for equality*. Washington, DC: Georgetown University Press.

Ward, I. (Director). (1998). *A little history worth knowing*. (Film). Cicero, NY: Program Development Associates.

Westling, D., & Fox, L. (2009). *Teaching students with severe disabilities* (4th ed.). Upper Saddle River, NJ: Pearson Education.

Wilson, K. (1998). Centers for independent living in support of transition. *Focus on Autism and Other Developmental Disabilities*, 13(3), 246–252.

PETER KOPRIVA
Fresno Pacific University
Fourth edition

CENTILE SCORES (See Percentile Scores)

CENTRAL AUDITORY DYSFUNCTION

Central auditory dysfunction is a term used to describe a broad spectrum of difficulties that may arise when an individual attempts to process an auditory signal. This disorder occurs even in people without measurable hearing loss. The term implies that when an individual has normal hearing status, but exhibits certain difficulties in correctly interpreting an auditory signal, there is some type of damage in the brain.

During the past three decades, a number of tests were devised to evaluate the integrity of the central auditory processing mechanism. These measures were used to evaluate the auditory processing of adults with anatomical lesions. Generally, these tests presented speech signals that reduced redundancy and made listening more difficult. It was found in a series of correlational studies that the performance of adults with known lesions was poorer than that of normal adults (Berlin & Lowe, 1972). It was then assumed that children who also performed poorly on similar tests suffered from some type of central auditory dysfunction (Keith, 1988). In the past 30 years, there have been attempts to determine whether children with language disorders also have a central auditory dysfunction. If they did, the question pertains to the relationship between the two and what remedial strategies could be used successfully. Language acquisition, language disorders of various types, and learning disabilities have all been considered to be directly related to various types of central auditory dysfunction (Cherry, 1992; Garstecki & Erler, 1997).

Two basic types of tests are given to evaluate the central auditory functioning of an individual. The first type is designed to evaluate the auditory neuromaturational level of the individual. Keith (1981) suggests that these tests should (1) not be loaded with language comprehension items; (2) not require linguistic manipulation of the signal; (3) not require, or least minimize, cross-modal input or response; (4) use nonlinguistic signal; and (5) be primarily a speech imitative task using nonmeaningful material or speech material so familiar that comprehension plays no role in the process. To that end, Keith (1986) developed a *central auditory processing disorder* (CAPD) assessment instrument called the SCAN: A Screening Test for Auditory Processing Disorders. The SCAN includes three subtests: a filtered word test, an auditory figure–ground test, and a competing word test. The SCAN was originally normed on children ages 3 to 11 (Cherry, 1992). Another CAPD test, the Selective Auditory Attention Test (SAAT), was developed by Cherry (1980). The SAAT is used to assess auditory distractibility and attention-deficit/hyperactivity disorder. The SAAT includes two subtests: a monosyllabic word test given in quiet and a similar monosyllabic word list with a semantic distractor. Keith (1988) also suggested that tests of CAPD include:

1. *Auditory localization.* Generally children are able to localize at a very early age so any normal child past infancy should be able to localize without difficulty.

2. *Binaural synthesis.* An example of this test is the Rapidly Alternating Speech Perception Test, where sentences are switched rapidly from one ear to the

other. If the child has difficulty with this test, there may be a lesion located in the brainstem.

3. *Binaural separation*. The Staggered Spondaic Word Test is used to determine whether the child shows ear dominance or whether the left ear score increases with age. Dichotic listening tests are also included in this category to determine whether children are establishing hemispheric dominance. A failure to do so may imply a neurological basis for a learning, reading, or language problem.

4. *Resistance to distortion*. Three types of tests are generally used in this category: speech in noise, filtered speech, and time-compressed speech. Individuals with normal central auditory functioning generally have no difficulty with these tasks, but when there is a specific lesion or other auditory abnormality, the individual will have difficulty in understanding speech with reduced redundancy.

Keith (1988) notes that these tests are to be used only after language has emerged. He also notes that the tests have substantial maturational effects up until about age of 12. Research has indicated that there are children with no apparent language or learning difficulties who perform poorly on these tests. Likewise, there are children with such difficulties who have no problems with the tests. Keith cautions that while these tests might find some indication of the neurologic status of a child, they do not indicate specific language, learning, or reading deficits. Further, they do not in themselves suggest any particular remediation strategy.

The second type of test can be categorized as auditory-language tests. These tests are heavily loaded both cognitively and linguistically. Examples are tests in which the child must point to a series of pictures in the order in which the words are heard. It should be noted that this task is not simply a single-factor auditory–perceptual test, but requires memory and comprehension. Another example of an auditory-language test is one that asks the child to listen to a word with a phoneme missing, and then identify the missing phoneme. This is a complex language-mediated task requiring the child to analyze a distorted signal. Another frequently administered test, the Goldman-Fristoe-Woodcock Test of Auditory Discrimination Noise Subtest, contains a similarly difficult task. The child must use visual perception, auditory–visual association, and an auditory–visual–motor response with a vocabulary that may not be familiar.

While noting that a number of children with language problems do poorly on tests of central auditory functioning, Rees (1981) observes that it is not at all clear whether the deficits actually produce the language disorders or whether they are simply behavioral correlates of these and other disabilities. She further criticizes these tests, stating that "no one has developed an intelligible account of how these central auditory processing skills, or the lack of them, relate to language acquisition or academic learning" (p. 118). She considers the tests that are heavily loaded with linguistic and cognitive material to be tests designed more to evaluate an individual child's metalinguistic ability (the ability to analyze and talk about language) than to measure directly the child's ability to learn language. While these tasks may be good indicators of the individual child's ability to function successfully in school, she questions whether they have a fundamental relationship with central auditory processing. Rees notes that in some ways all the phenomena that have been clustered under the rubric of central auditory functioning have only one thing in common. They all involve data taken in through the ear.

In summary, central auditory dysfunction refers to problems individuals may exhibit in processing an auditory signal even when they have no specific hearing loss. When adults with known brain lesions were asked to perform specific tasks related to auditory functioning, it was found that they exhibited specific problems. Some children with learning problems performed similarly on tests of auditory processing. It was presumed they also might have some kind of brain damage. Two types of tests are given to test auditory functioning. The first evaluates auditory maturational level. The second tests language-related auditory functions. It is not clear whether there is a cause-and-effect relationship between auditory functioning and learning disorders.

REFERENCES

Berlin, C., & Lowe, S. S. (1972). Temporary and dichotic factors in central auditory testing. In J. Katz (Ed.), *Handbook of clinical audiology* (4th ed.). Baltimore, MD: Williams & Wilkins.

Cherry, R. (1980). *Selective Auditory Attention Test (SAAT)*. St. Louis, MO: Auditec of St. Louis.

Cherry, R. (1992). Screening and evaluation of central auditory processing disorders in young children. In J. Katz, N. Steckler, & D. Henderson (Eds.), *Central auditory processing: A transdisciplinary view* (pp. 129–140). St. Louis, MO: Mosby.

Garstecki, D. C., & Erler, S. F. (1997). Hearing loss management in children and adults. In G. T. Mencher, S. E. Gerber, & A. McCombe (Eds.), *Audiology and auditory dysfunction* (pp. 220–232). Needham Heights, MA: Allyn & Bacon.

Keith, R. W. (1981). *Central auditory and language disorders in children*. San Diego, CA: College Hill.

Keith, R. W. (1986). *SCAN: A screening test for auditory processing disorders*. San Diego, CA: Psychology Corporation.

Keith, R. W. (1988). Central auditory tests. In L. N. McReynolds & D. Yoder (Eds.), *Handbook of speech language pathology and audiology* (pp. 1215–1236). Toronto, ON: B.C. Decker.

Rees, N. S. (1981). Saying more than we know: Is auditory processing a meaningful concept? In R. W. Keith (Ed.), *Central auditory and language disorders in children* (pp. 94–120). San Diego, CA: College Hill.

CAROLYN L. BULLARD
Lewis & Clark College
First edition

KATHLEEN M. CHINN
New Mexico State University
Second edition

See also Auditory Abnormalities; Auditory Discrimination; Auditory Perception; Auditory-Visual Integration

CENTRAL AUDITORY PROCESSING DISORDER

Central auditory processing disorder (CAPD) is the term used to describe audiological difficulties that are characterized by reduced abilities to process auditory information in individuals with normal peripheral hearing. CAPD includes difficulties in locating the source and direction of sounds, discriminating between sounds, recognizing patterns of sounds, ordering sounds that are presented in close temporal proximity, and discerning sounds in background noise (American Speech-Language-Hearing Association [ASHA], 1996).

Characteristics

1. Poor listening skills
2. Difficulty hearing in situations with background noise
3. Difficulty with localization of sounds
4. Difficulty following directions
5. High distractability by irrelevant noise
6. Inattention
7. History of ear infections
8. Academic difficulties, particularly in reading and spelling

(ASHA, 1996)

The incidence of CAPD is difficult to determine but is thought to be from 3% to 5% (Chermack & Musiek, 1997). Although CAPD is estimated to be more common than hearing loss, it is diagnosed less often. Children with CAPD are a heterogeneous group; not all children with CAPD have the same difficulties and are often misdiagnosed as having unrecognized comorbidity with attention-deficit/hyperactivity disorder (ADHD) and other language disorders (Riccio, Hynd, Cohen, Hall, & Molt,

1994). There is no evidence of differences in incidence by ethnic groups. The high comorbidity with language and learning problems suggests that CAPD may be more likely to occur in males, but this has not been documented.

A preliminary screening for CAPD may include information about cognitive functioning, speech-language development, peripheral hearing status, behavioral observations, and audiological screening (Bellis, 1996). An audiologist may use a test battery to gather information about the child's dichotic listening skills (different sounds presented to both ears simultaneously), temporal ordering abilities (sequencing of sounds), and binaural interactions (a method in which ears function together). The major challenge to identification of CAPD is the lack of acceptance on measures that should be included in the battery (Schow, Seikel, Chermak, & Berent, 2000).

There are no research-supported treatments at this time for CAPD, but there are some effective management techniques. Addressing the individual needs of a child with CAPD would include modifications to the environment, remediation, and development of compensatory abilities (Bellis, 1996). Each child's auditory profile would determine the most appropriate modifications; however, there are some general recommendations. Environmental changes can include decreasing background noise, improving the room's acoustics by covering hard floors and walls, using preferential seating, monitoring understanding frequently, using several modalities for learning, using advanced organizers for new information and vocabulary, providing lecture notes to the child, and using repetition and rephrasing during presentation of material (Bellis, 1996). It may be helpful to educate the older children about their disorder so individuals can help monitor their own needs for environmental modifications.

Special education or services under Section 504 of the Americans With Disabilities Act may be appropriate for a child with CAPD. Difficulty with the recognition of phonemes due to auditory processing deficits may affect receptive language development. The child's Individual Education Plan should include appropriate environmental modifications. The disorder may qualify the child for special education services under the learning disability or specific language impairments categories to the extent that the disorder can affect the child's ability to learn (Individuals with Disabilities Education Act, 1997).

Current research is examining the etiology of CAPD and its relationships to other disorders. Of particular interest has been the relation with ADHD and learning disabilities (Riccio et al., 1994). Genetic factors, neurological development, brain lesions, and reoccurring episodes of otitis media are indicated as risk factors for the auditory dysfunction that affects dichotic listening, temporal processing, and binaural integration of auditory information (Bellis, 1996).

Future research may focus on etiologies of CAPD to improve our ability to prevent and treat the disorder as well as on symptom management. Greater understanding of the etiology will aid in more accurate diagnoses of CAPD and comorbidities with other disorders.

REFERENCES

American Speech-Language-Hearing Association (1996). Report of the Task Force on Central Auditory Processing Consensus Development. *American Journal of Audiology*, 5(2), 41–54.

Bellis, T. J. (1996). *Assessment and management of central auditory processing disorders in the educational system: From science to practice*. San Diego, CA: Singular.

Chermack, G., & Musiek, F. (1997). *Central auditory processing disorders: New perspectives*. San Diego, CA: Singular.

Individuals with Disabilities Education Act. (1997). (Pub. L. No. 101–476). 20 U.S.C. Chapter 33. Amended by Pub.L. No. 105017.

Riccio, C. A., Hynd, G. W., Cohen, M. J., Hall, J., & Molt, L. (1994). Comorbidity of central auditory processing disorder and attention deficit hyperactivity disorder. *Journal of the American Academy of Child and Adolescent Psychiatry*, 33, 849–857.

Schow, R. L., Seikel, J. A., Chermak, G. D., & Berent, M. (2000). Central auditory processes and test measures: ASHA 1996 revisited. *American Journal of Audiology*, 9, 1–6.

MONICA E. WOLFE
CYNTHIA A. RICCIO
Texas A&M University

CENTRAL CORE DISEASE

Central core disease (CCD) is a relatively rare genetic disorder usually detected in infancy or early childhood. Central core disease tends to affect males and females in equal numbers. It is an autosomal dominant trait. Although less common, CCD has occurred spontaneously without a family history. This disease is characterized by abnormalities of skeletal muscles. Associated symptoms include diminished muscle tone, muscle weakness, delays in motor development, and musculoskeletal problems such as a dislocated hip at birth. In addition, CCD is associated with susceptibility to malignant hyperthermia. Malignant hyperthermia is a potentially life-threatening reaction to muscle relaxants and anesthetics. For this reason, it is essential that this risk be taken into consideration by surgeons, anesthesiologists, dentists, and other health-care providers when making decisions regarding medical or dental treatments (Online Mendelian Inheritance in Man, 2000).

Typically, CCD is detected in infancy; however, some cases can go undetected until childhood, adolescence, and even adulthood. Infants diagnosed with CCD have been reported to be delivered in breech position. In addition, the infant may demonstrate limited head support and poor muscle tone. Commonly, the muscle weakness is greater in muscles closest to the trunk such as the shoulders, upper arms, hips, and thighs. Mild muscle weakness may also be evident in the facial muscles. Central core disease is a nonprogressive disorder that usually does not continue to become more severe with time. However, as previously noted, infants with CCD may demonstrate difficulty reaching developmental milestones such as crawling, standing, walking, climbing stairs, and running. For this reason, a pediatric orthopedist is essential to monitor and mediate the delays (Online Mendelian Inheritance in Man, 2000; Wyngaarden, 1992).

Characteristics

1. Abnormalities of skeletal muscles
2. Diminished muscle tone
3. Delays in motor development
4. Dislocated hip at birth

Central core disease is symptomatically treated. The treatment specialists are dependent on the symptoms presented in the affected individual. In some cases orthopedic interventions are essential to help prevent and treat different musculoskeletal abnormalities associated with this disorder. Physical and occupational services may also be useful to help with mobility and exercise. With infants experiencing severe weakness, a feeding tube may be required; thus, nutritional counseling would be recommended to ensure that the infant is getting the proper nutrients. School professionals may also be needed to help with necessary physical or learning modifications for the child depending on the limitations experienced by the child.

Because of the chronicity of this disorder, psychological services can help the affected individual as well as the family develop strategies to cope with the impacts of CCD (Wyngaarden, 1992).

REFERENCES

Online Mendelian Inheritance in Man. (2000). Retrieved from http://www.ncbi.nlm.nih.gov/omim/

Wyngaarden, J. B. (1992). *Cecil textbook of medicine* (19th ed.). Philadelphia, PA: W. B. Saunders.

LISA A. FASNACHT-HILL
*Keck University of Southern California School of Medicine
University of Southern California/
University Affiliated Program at
Children's Hospital of Los Angeles*

CENTRAL HYPOVENTILATION SYNDROME (CONGENITAL)

Congenital central hypoventilation syndrome (CCHS) is a neurological disorder typically found in infants and children. It is characterized by normal respiration during waking hours but abnormal respiration during sleep. A diagnosis of CCHS should be considered when other brain-stem, lung, cardiac, or primary neuromuscular diseases have been ruled out. About 160–180 cases are identified in the world, but because it is so rare, many cases may go undiagnosed due to the physician's inability to diagnose the condition accurately (American Thoracic Society, 1999). CCHS is often mistaken for other diseases, so it is critical that the disorder be carefully diagnosed. CCHS is sometimes also known as congenital alveolar hypoventilation, congenital failure of autonomic control of respiration, idiopathic alveolar hypoventilation, Ondine's curse, primary alveolar hypoventilation, primary central hypoventilation syndrome, and idiopathic congenital central hypoventilation syndrome.

CCHS is frequently identified in newborns but may not be diagnosed until infancy. Symptoms may become manifested in the early adult years. It is characterized by ongoing difficulty with the control of breathing, particularly during sleep. As a result, the lungs do not get enough air, and tissues in the body are damaged from a lack of sufficient oxygen. CCHS may also result in feeding problems in infants. Other symptoms may be severe constipation, profuse sweating, and decreased body temperature (Hill & Goldberg, 1998). Patients with CCHS may also exhibit changes in the central nervous system (Gallina et al., 2000). If left untreated, this disorder may lead to serious complications such as organ damage and death.

In order to diagnose CCHS, it is necessary for the physician to perform a comprehensive history and physical examination. The patient should have a complete neurological evaluation, rectal biopsy, and ophthalmologic evaluation. A monitor should be used to determine patterns of spontaneous breathing while the patient is asleep and awake.

Characteristics

1. Normal respiration during waking hours, but abnormal respiration during sleep
2. May cause feeding problems in infants
3. Possibly severe constipation, profuse sweating, decreased body temperature, heart rate variability, eye irregularities, and changes in the central nervous system

Treatment of CCHS depends on the severity of the disorder. A mechanical ventilator may be used. It is critical that skilled caregivers closely monitor the patient. Parents of young children can be trained to operate the ventilator at home, but a trained nurse may also be needed. More serious cases may require a tracheostomy. In these cases, a one-way speaking valve called a Passy-Muir is used for the child to vocalize when awake (American Thoracic Society, 1999). Gozal and Simakajornboon (2000) have suggested that ventilation in children who are awake may be improved by passive motion of the feet and ankles.

Although the disorder may improve with age, CCHS is usually a lifelong diagnosis. Respiration, growth, speech, mental, and motor development should be monitored regularly. Infants and young children should be evaluated by a pediatrician and a pulmonologist every 1 to 2 months. After the age of 3 years, thorough checks should be conducted annually.

Children with CCHS must be watched closely for infections. They are not necessarily able to recognize or respond to hypoxemia (American Thoracic Society, 1999). Activity should be moderate with frequent periods of rest. Patients should participate in only noncontact sports; however, swimming is not recommended without constant supervision.

At school, children with CCHS may require special monitoring by the teacher and school nurse. They may also need to engage in limited and supervised activity. Specialized equipment may be necessary.

Tissue and organ damage may result in a variety of physical and cognitive difficulties. Depending on the individual situation, this may necessitate special education services. Some studies have found that CCHS frequently recurs in families. Ongoing research is being conducted to investigate the possibility of a genetic factor (Gozal, 1999).

If treated early and appropriately, chances of survival are good for patients with CCHS. Technological treatments can provide a good quality of life. The ultimate goal of treatment is to find the appropriate technology for each patient's lifestyle. As advances in technology occur, new methods of treatment for CCHS may be developed. Unfortunately, these types of treatments may be costly, and financial support may be inhibited by health-care providers.

REFERENCES

American Thoracic Society. (1999). Idiopathic congenital central hypoventilation syndrome. *American Journal of Respiratory and Critical Care Medicine, 160*(1), 368–373.

Gallina, S., Restivo, S., Cupido, G., Speciale, R., Giammanco, A. M., & Cimino, G. (2000). Otoneurological findings in a case of congenital central hypoventilation syndrome (Ondine's curse). *Acta Otorhinolaryngologica Italica, 20*(2), 121–124.

Gozal, D. (1999). Novel insights into congenital hypoventilation syndrome. *Current Opinions in Pulmonary Medicine, 5*(6), 335–338.

Gozal, D., & Simakajornboon, N. (2000). Passive motion of the extremities modifies alveolar ventilation during sleep in patients with congenital central hypoventilation syndrome. *American Journal of Respiratory and Critical Care Medicine*, *162*(2), 1747–1751.

Hill, N. S., & Goldberg, A. I. (1998). Mechanical ventilation beyond the intensive care unit: Report of a consensus conference of the American College of Chest Physicians. *Chest*, *113*(5), 298S–344S.

MICHELE WILSON KAMENS
Rider University

CENTRAL NERVOUS SYSTEM

The central nervous system (CNS) refers to the brain, including the cerebral cortex, cranial nerves, cerebellum, spinal cord, and other subcortical structures contained within the cranial vault. It consists of more than 100 billion neurons and approximately 10 times that number of glial cells. The cerebral cortex represents the CNS structure underlying most adaptive behavior, including sensation, perception, judgment, intellective functioning, and purposeful movement. Divided into two cerebral hemispheres, the respective cerebral cortices tend to be differentiated in terms of functions. As with other CNS structures that develop embryologically from the prosencephalon, the cerebral hemispheres have contralateral representation (i.e., the left side of the cortex controls the right side of the body, and vice versa). Each cerebral hemisphere is divided into anterior and posterior regions by the central sulcus or fissure of Rolando. Those cortical areas just anterior to the Rolandic fissure are specialized for motor functions, with motor enervation proceeding from superior areas of the motor strip, which control lower extremity movement, downward to more inferior areas, which control movement of the face. Just posterior to the Rolandic fissure is the sensory area, which controls such phenomena as sensitivity to stimulation for body areas corresponding to those enervated by the motor strip.

In addition to lateralized representation of motor and sensory functions, the cerebral cortex areas are also specialized for processing given types of information, and for processing information in given ways. In essentially all right-handed and in most left-handed individuals, the left cerebral hemisphere is more efficient in processing verbal or linguistic types of information, with the right hemisphere more specialized for the processing of spatial types of information. This specialization of function can be demonstrated in normal individuals by injecting fast-acting barbiturate types of drugs such as sodium amytal into a selected cerebral hemisphere. Following such an injection to the left cerebral hemisphere, for example, individuals will normally experience a brief period of aphasia, during which they are unable both to comprehend spoken language and to formulate verbalizations. Within a few minutes, all verbal functions return to preinjection levels. Similar temporary impairment of spatial function is demonstrated on right hemisphere injection (Hartlage & Flanigin, 1982).

In addition to specialization for type and process of cognitive information processing, the cerebral hemispheres also mediate differentiated emotional functions. Damage, deprivation of blood supply, unilateral electroconvulsive treatment, and depressant medication all have been shown to result in different emotional responses for each cerebral hemisphere. Insult to the right cerebral hemisphere produces what has been called the "la belle indifference syndrome," characterized by poor monitoring of behavior and euphoria. Insult to the left hemisphere produces the "catastrophic reaction," characterized by depression (Robertson & Inglis, 1973; Schwartz, Davidson, & Maer, 1975; Tucker, 1981).

Anatomically, the cerebral hemispheres are divided into four lobes. The frontal lobes are separated posteriorly from the parietal lobes by the central sulcus, and from the temporal lobes by the Sylvian fissure, which also separates the superiorly located parietal lobes from the temporal lobes. The occipital notch, at the posterior end of the parietal lobes, divides the parietal lobes from the occipital lobes. An approach to further subclassification of the cerebral hemispheres is the cytoarchitectural system of Brodmann, in which discrete areas of the cerebral cortices are divided into 52 Brodmann areas (Krieg, 1957) and are referred to and identified by numbers corresponding to those locations. For example, "Brodmann's area 8" corresponds to the frontal eye fields.

There is good evidence that in most individuals the cerebral hemispheres are not symmetrical (Geschwind & Levitsky, 1968; Von Bonin, 1962). This asymmetry has been related to differences in facility with processing certain types of information and other psychological characteristics (Lansdell & Smith, 1975; Levy, 1974; Reynolds, 1981; Reynolds, Kamphaus, Rosenthal, & Hiemenz, 1997). This hemispheric asymmetry has been postulated as being etiologic in certain mental disorders such as schizophrenia (Gruzelier, 1984; Newlin, Carpenter, & Golden, 1981), autism (Colby & Parkinson, 1977; Dawson, Warrenburg, & Fuller, 1982), and a number of other maladaptive behaviors (Sandel & Alcorn, 1980).

Separating the right and left cerebral hemispheres is the corpus callosum, which contains many fibers that convey impulses between the hemispheres. Right-handed individuals have a somewhat smaller corpus callosum than do individuals who are left handed or with mixed hand dominance. This phenomenon may be related to greater hemispheric specialization in strongly right-handed individuals (Witelson, 1985).

Although much adaptive behavior is attributed to the cerebral hemispheres, other portions of the central nervous system mediate behaviors of crucial importance to the individual. The 12 cranial nerves (olfactory, optic, oculomotor, trochlear, trigeminal, abducens, facial, acoustic, glossopharyngeal, vagus, accessory, and hypoglossal) control such functions as smell, visual acuity, eye movement, facial sensation and movement, and hearing.

The cerebellum, located posteriorly and partially under the occipital lobe, with connections to many portions of the cerebral cortex, is involved with balance and with coordination of some motor activities (because some areas of the cerebellum are uniquely sensitive to the effects of alcohol, law enforcement officers often check some aspects of cerebellar function when screening drivers suspected of intoxication). A number of brain areas often referred to as subcortical (e.g., amygdala, hippocampus, thalamus), because of their location under the cortex, have been identified as playing important roles in such behaviors as emotion, memory, movement, and the integration of information from diverse cortical areas (Riklan & Levita, 1965). The medulla, that portion of the central nervous system that bridges with the spinal cord, is more involved with lower sensory and motor functions than with higher cognitive abilities.

Although some areas of the CNS have been shown to be crucial for the performance of given tasks, the CNS functions in an interrelated way for the execution of most complex tasks. Damage to the CNS will almost always result in a complex disorder requiring special educational services.

REFERENCES

Colby, K. M., & Parkinson, C. (1977). Handedness in autistic children. *Journal of Autism and Childhood Schizophrenia, 7,* 3–9.

Dawson, G., Warrenburg, S., & Fuller, D. (1982). Cerebral lateralization in individuals diagnosed as autistic in early childhood. *Brain and Language, 15,* 353–368.

Geschwind, N., & Levitsky, W. (1968). Human brain: Left–right asymmetries in temporal speech region. *Science, 161,* 186–187.

Gruzelier, J. H. (1984). Hemispheric imbalances in schizophrenia. *International Journal of Psychophysiology, 1,* 227–240.

Hartlage, L. C., & Flanigin, H. (1982, October). *An abbreviated intracarotical amytal testing procedure.* Paper presented at the annual meeting of the National Academy of Neuropsychologists, Atlanta, GA.

Krieg, W. J. S. (1957). *Brain mechanisms in diachrome* (2nd ed.). Evanston, IL: Brain Books.

Lansdell, H., & Smith, F. J. (1975). Asymmetrical cerebral function for two WAIS factors and their recovery after brain injury. *Journal of Consulting and Clinical Psychology, 43,* 931.

Levy, H. (1974). Psychological implications of bilateral asymmetry. In S. J. Dimond & J. G. Beaumont (Eds.), *Hemispheric function in the human brain.* London, UK: Elek Science.

Newlin, D. B., Carpenter, B., & Golden, C. (1981). Hemispheric asymmetries in schizophrenia. *Biological Psychiatry, 16,* 561–581.

Reynolds, C. R. (1981). The neuropsychological basis of intelligence. In G. Hynd & J. Obrzut (Eds.), *Neuropsychological assessment of the school aged child: Issues and procedures.* New York, NY: Grune & Stratton.

Reynolds, C. R., Kamphaus, R. W., Rosenthal, B. L., & Hiemenz, J. R. (1997). Applications of the Kaufman Assessment Battery for Children (K-ABC) in neuropsychological assessment. In C. R. Reynolds & E. Fletcher-Janzen (Eds.), *Handbook of clinical child neuropsychology* (2nd ed.). New York, NY: Plenum Press.

Riklan, M., & Levita, E. (1965). Laterality of subcortical involvement and psychological functions. *Psychological Bulletin, 64,* 217–224.

Robertson, A. D., & Inglis, J. (1973). Cerebral asymmetry and electroconvulsive therapy. *Proceedings of the 81st Annual Convention of the American Psychological Association, 8,* 431–432.

Sandel, A., & Alcorn, J. (1980). Individual hemispherity and maladaptive behaviors. *Journal of Abnormal Psychology, 9,* 514–517.

Schwartz, G. E., Davidson, R. J., & Maer, F. (1975). Right hemisphere lateralization for emotion in the human brain: Interactions with cognition. *Science, 190,* 286–288.

Tucker, D. M. (1981). Lateral brain function emotion, and conceptualization. *Psychological Bulletin, 89,* 19–46.

Von Bonin, G. (1962). Anatomical asymmetries of the cerebral hemispheres. In V. B. Mountcastle (Ed.), *Interhemispheric relations and cerebral dominance* (pp. 1–6). Baltimore, MD: Johns Hopkins Press.

Witelson, S. F. (1985). The brain connection: The corpus callosum is larger in left handers. *Science, 229,* 665–668.

Lawrence C. Hartlage
Evans, Georgia

See also Aphasia; Brain Organizations; Cerebral Dominance; Cerebral Function, Lateralization of; Left Brain/Right Brain

CENTRAL PROCESSING DYSFUNCTIONS IN CHILDREN

The world is a colorful, noisy, and interesting place. To learn and respond to the world around them, infants, children, adolescents, and adults receive information about their world through the senses of vision, hearing, smell, touch, and bodily movement.

The brain serves as a center for: (a) receiving incoming sensations from the eyes, ears, skin, muscles, and internal organs; (b) analyzing and organizing sensory information; (c) interpreting or giving meaning to the sensory information that is being received; (d) generating messages to send to all parts of the body for purposes of responding; and (e) storing information for later use (Chalfant & Scheffelin, 1969).

When the brain does not function properly in receiving, analyzing, and storing sensory information or sending messages to the bodily parts, a dysfunction is said to exist. Because the brain is part of the central nervous system, which processes sensory information, a breakdown in this system is often referred to as a central processing dysfunction.

Central processing dysfunctions can be caused by damage to the brain, but brain damage is not always the cause. There are many cases in which individuals behave as if they had a central processing dysfunction, but show no evidence of brain damage. All of the causes of central processing dysfunctions are not yet known.

There are three major systems in which a central processing dysfunction might occur: the visual processing system, the auditory processing system, and the haptic processing system. Symptoms of dysfunctions in these systems follow.

With visual processing dysfunctions, a student may have normal visual acuity but have difficulty processing and obtaining meaning from visual information. Some of the major characteristics of visual processing dysfunctions are difficulty in (a) attending to or focusing on what is seen; (b) seeing the difference between printed numbers, letters, and words; (c) learning spatial relationships such as left–right, up–down, far–near; (d) distinguishing a figure or object from the background within which it is embedded; (e) reorganizing a whole when one or more of its parts are missing, as in constructing a puzzle; (f) remembering what has been seen; and (g) responding quickly to visual stimuli. Visual processing dysfunctions may result in academic learning disabilities in reading, writing, and arithmetic (Kirk & Chalfant, 1984).

In auditory processing dysfunctions, a student may have normal hearing, but have difficulty in processing what is heard. Auditory processing dysfunctions are characterized by difficulty in (a) listening or attending to sound; (b) locating the origin or source of sound; (c) hearing the differences or similarities between pitch, loudness, rhythm, melody, rate, or duration of sounds; (d) listening to a teacher's instructions are processed through the interferences of classroom noises (background); (e) reorganizing a spoken word when only part of the word is heard, e.g., "telepho—"; (f) remembering what has been heard; and (g) associating sounds to experiences such as *ding-dong* to a bell. Dysfunctions in auditory processing may result in learning disabilities in understanding spoken language, expressing oneself through oral language, forming concepts, and developing abstract thinking skills (Kirk & Chalfant, 1984).

In the haptic processing system, the term *haptic processing* refers to the information received from both touch and movement. Dysfunctions in the haptic system will result in difficulty in performing fine motor tasks such as writing, manipulating tools and equipment, or learning motor performance skills. There are two subsystems for haptic processing (Gibson, 1965). The first subsystem is the tactile or cutaneous one. If a dysfunction exists in the tactile system, difficulties may be experienced in (a) being sensitive to the presence of pressure or textures on the skin; (b) reorganizing objects through the sense of touch; (c) perceiving information about surface areas, sizes, shapes, boundaries, angles, and so on; and (d) being sensitive to pressure or aware of pain. Children with difficulties in the tactile system will have difficulty performing any task that requires the coordinated use of fingers such as learning to button or use a knife, fork, or spoon, or writing.

The second subsystem is the kinesthetic one. Bodily movement such as the movement of fingers, toes, arms, legs, head, lower jaw, tongue, and trunk, provides information about the body itself. Movement also provides information about direction and the location of objects in the environment in relation to the body itself. Muscular efforts such as lifting, pulling, and pushing objects give information about the weight of objects and gravity. Dysfunctions in the kinesthetic system result in difficulty in learning movement patterns such as crawling, walking, eating, dressing, undressing, writing, and riding a bicycle, or those needed for competing in sports activities (Kirk & Chalfant, 1984).

In summary, central processing dysfunctions can have a wide range of impact on a child or student. Young children often will be delayed in developing an understanding of and the use of oral language, visual–motor coordination, and/or cognitive abilities such as attention, discrimination, memory, conceptualization, and problem-solving skills. Students of school age may present academic disabilities in reading, writing, spelling, or arithmetic.

REFERENCES

Chalfant, J. C., & Scheffelin, M. A. (1969). *Central processing dysfunction in children: A review of research* (NINDS Monograph No. 9). Washington, DC: U.S. Department of Health, Education, and Welfare.

Gibson, J. J. (1965). *The senses considered as perceptual systems*. Boston, MA: Houghton Mifflin.

Kirk, S. A., & Chalfant, J. C. (1984). *Academic and developmental learning disabilities*. Denver, CO: Love.

JAMES C. CHALFANT
University of Arizona

See also Brain Damage/Injury; Learning Disabilities; Learning Disabilities, Problems in Definition of; Learning Styles

CENTRAL TENDENCY

Measures of central tendency are used to describe the typical or average score in a sample or population of scores. Many measures of central tendency exist, but the three most popularly used in the behavioral sciences are the *mean*, the *median*, and the *mode* (Glass & Hopkins, 1984).

The mean is the most widely used measure of central tendency. It is the arithmetic average of a given set of scores. For example, given the set of scores 87, 96, 98, 110, 113, 114, 119, the mean is 105.29, the sum of the seven scores divided by the number of scores, seven.

The median of a set of scores is the score that divides the set into two groups with each group containing the same number of scores. To compute the median, first rank the set of scores from smallest to largest (Hays, 1981; Kirk, 1984). When the number of scores is odd and there are no ties, the median is the middle score. For example, the median of the above scores is 110. When the number of scores is even, with no ties, the median is the average of the two middle scores. Thus, the median score of 87, 96, 98, 110, 113, 114, 119, 120 is 110 + 113/2 = 111.50.

The mode is the score that occurs most frequently in a set of scores. For the scores 87, 96, 98, 98, 98, 110, 113, 114, 119, the mode is 98. When there are two modes, the distribution of scores is said to be bimodal. All three measures may be used when the data are quantitative. The median and mode are used with ranked data, whereas only the mode is applicable to nominal data (MacGillivray, 1985).

The mean is the preferred measure of central tendency when the variable measured is quantitative and the distribution is relatively symmetric. It is relatively stable and reflects the value of every score in the distribution and, unlike the median and the mode, it is amenable to arithmetic and algebraic manipulations. These qualities make the mean useful not only for describing the average of a set of scores, but also for making inferences about population means. We can infer the value of the population mean from the sample mean, and also make inferences about the differences between population means for the same or different groups of individuals on one or more variables. When the distribution of scores is skewed, or the variable being measured is qualitative, the mean is not the preferred measure of central tendency.

For skewed distributions, the median is used. This is because the median is not affected by the scores falling above and below it. For example, the median of the scores 109, 108, 107, 106, 60 is 107; it more accurately reflects the typical score than the mean of 98. Inferences about the population median may also be concluded (see Marascuilo & McSweeney, 1977).

When the distribution is symmetric and unimodal, the median, mean, and mode are the same. When the distribution is skewed, however, the median and mean are unequal with median > mean in negatively skewed distributions and mean > median in positively skewed distributions. This entry has been informed by the following references.

REFERENCES

Glass, G. V., & Hopkins, K. D. (1984). *Statistical methods in education and psychology* (2nd ed.). Englewood Cliffs, NJ: Prentice Hall.

Hays, W. L. (1981). *Statistics* (3rd ed.). New York, NY: Holt, Rinehart & Winston.

Kirk, R. E. (1984). *Elementary statistics* (2nd ed.). Monterey, CA: Brooks/Cole.

MacGillivray, H. L. (1985). Mean, median, mode, and skewness. In S. Kotz, N. L. Johnson, & C. B. Read (Eds.), *Encyclopedia of the statistical sciences* (Vol. 5). New York, NY: Wiley.

Marascuilo, L. A., & McSweeney, M. (1977). *Nonparametric and distribution-free methods for the social sciences*. Monterey, CA: Brooks/Cole.

GWYNETH M. BOODOO
Texas A&M University

See also Standard Deviation

CEREBELLAR DISORDERS

The cerebellum is an oval-shaped portion of the brain under the occipital lobe of the cerebrum and behind the brain stem. It has a right and left hemisphere and a central section. The cerebellum integrates information vital to the control of posture and voluntary movement. The cerebellum is responsible for maintaining equilibrium and trunk balance; regulating muscle tension, spinal nerve reflexes, posture, and balance of the limbs; and regulating fine movements initiated by the frontal lobes.

Persons with cerebellar dysfunction may show any or all of the following deficits: wide-based clumsy gait; tremor on attempted motion; clumsy, rapid alternating movements; inability to control the range of voluntary movements with overshooting the goal most common; low muscle tone; and scanning speech with inappropriate accenting of syllables. Rapid alternating eye movements (nystagmus) may be observed as a component of closely associated vestibular involvement.

Tumors of the cerebellum, heavy metal poisoning, repeated high fever or head trauma, and hypothyroidism can affect the cerebellum directly. The cerebellum receives postural and movement information from many parts of the brain, integrates them, and sends information out to motor coordinating areas; therefore, the function of the cerebellum may be impaired by a wide range of neurological conditions. Multiple sclerosis, blood clots, and congenital anomalies of other parts of the brain can influence the cerebellum via input/output tracts as well. The spinocerebellar diseases are a family of degenerative hereditary diseases that affect (to varying degrees) the cerebellum, spinal cord, brain stem, and other parts of the nervous system. Most of these diseases have their onset in childhood, are slowly progressive, and have no known specific inheritance patterns, cause, or treatment, although in some individual family studies clinical findings and inheritance patterns are consistent. It is believed that inherited biochemical abnormalities are causal, and some have been identified. Some diseases in this category with early onset, rapid progression, and strong familial tendencies are Marie's ataxia, Roussy-Levy syndrome, and Friedreich's ataxia. Although progression results in clumsiness, poor balance, later use of a wheelchair for safety, slurred speech, and loss of skilled hand function, there is usually no related impairment to intelligence.

Friedreich's ataxia is a hereditary disease of unknown origin with symptoms of frequent falling, clumsiness, and incoordination (ataxia) beginning between age 5 and 25 (Berkow, 1982). Slurred speech, swallowing difficulty, contractures, deformities, and weakness typically result in the need to use a wheelchair within 5 to 10 years. The lack of intellectual impairment is often in considerable contrast to the severity of the physical impairments, a circumstance that represents a challenge to educators to provide stimulating instruction within the limitations presented by the child's deteriorating physical condition. Occupational, physical, and speech therapists can provide useful adaptive support techniques to the child's teachers and family so that optimal function can continue as long as possible. Clinical experience has shown that these children are vulnerable because of their insight into the progressive nature of their disease. Anxiety, anger, and depression may occur, and such feelings may be exacerbated by observing the struggles and deaths of elder siblings. The impact on family life when several siblings have Friedreich's ataxia is profound. Since the average onset age is 13 years, a family may have a number of children before the eldest has symptoms and is diagnosed. Clinical experience suggests that early admission of all symptomatic family members to special education programs where supportive related services are available can help normalize adaptive responses and provide maximum comfort, safety, deformity prevention, and learning opportunities while prolonging activity. Estimates suggest that with proper management there may be 10 to 20 years of productivity following onset (Clark, 2003). Death frequently is due to progressive heart failure, medical complications, or effects of inactivity rather than the disease itself (Stolov and Clowers, 1981).

Dr. John C. Eccles (1973), a recognized authority on the cerebellum, believes that the relative simplicity of neuronal design, together with its well-defined action in control of movement, will result in the cerebellum becoming one of the first parts of the brain where linkage between structure and function can be documented. The rapid growth of specific knowledge about cerebellar diseases suggests that differential diagnosis by a skilled neurologist together with genetic studies when indicated are imperative in children with cerebellar disorders, as there are treatable conditions that may present symptoms similar to the degenerative disorders.

Characteristics

1. Uncoordinated muscle movements (sometimes jerky) and poor balance
2. Dysmetria, or difficulty judging distances
3. Headaches, vomiting, seizure, vision changes, drowsiness, and confusion

Special education, if needed at all, is typically provided under the category Other Health Impairment. If a brain injury, however, is the cause of the cerebellar abnormality, a classification of TBI may be more appropriate. Regardless of the need for special education, children with cerebellar disorders are likely to need some classroom accommodations and services from a physical or occupational therapist. Speech and language services and psychological consultation (including counseling) may also be appropriate. Like the treatment, the prognosis for a child with a cerebellar disorder depends on the underlying cause and severity of symptoms and disability.

REFERENCES

Berkow, R. (Ed.). (1982). *The Merck manual of diagnosis and therapy* (14th ed.). Rahway, NJ: Merck, Sharp & Dohme.

Clark, E. (2003). Brain disorders and degenerative motor diseases. In E. Fletcher-Janzen & C. R. Reynolds (Eds.), *Childhood disorders diagnostic desk reference* (pp. 91–92). Hoboken, NJ: Wiley.

Eccles, J. C. (1973). *The understanding of the brain.* New York, NY: McGraw-Hill.

Stolov, W. C., & Clowers, M. R. (Eds.). (1981). *Handbook of severe disability* (stock #017-090-00054-2). Washington, DC: U.S. Government Printing Office.

RACHAEL J. STEVENSON
Bedford, Ohio

LAURA RICHARDS
ELAINE CLARK
University of Utah From CDDR

See also Ataxia; Brain Organizations; Friedreich's Ataxia

CEREBRAL DOMINANCE

Cerebral dominance refers to the asymmetrical lateralization of language and perceptual functions in the human brain. Cerebral dominance, or hemispheric specialization, was initially applied to language functions that are served by the left hemisphere in most individuals. However, the term was later expanded to include cognitive functions of nonverbal reasoning and visual–spatial information processing that are associated with the right hemisphere. In short, functions associated with the left hemisphere involve processing linguistic, analytical, and sequential information while the right hemisphere is responsible for processing nonlinguistic or spatial information in a holistic fashion (see Witelson, 1976).

Early reference to cerebral dominance can be traced back to Dax in 1836 and Broca in 1861; they found that damage to the left hemisphere results in disorders of speech and language. They believed that the left hemisphere is the dominant side for most people in that it controls the functions of language (Gaddes, 1980). The notion of cerebral dominance was further delineated by the writings of Jackson, who postulated that the left hemisphere is the dominant or the leading side and right hemisphere is the automatic and minor side (Dean, 1984). The emphasis in determining cerebral dominance for language was also noted by Orton (1937). He speculated that delayed or incomplete lateralization for linguistic functions by the left hemisphere results in the types of language disorders often seen in children.

Methods for assessing specializations of each hemisphere have employed invasive techniques such as direct electrical stimulation of the brain, hemispheric anesthetization, and split-brain studies. *Noninvasive procedures* have involved dichotic listening and split-visual field research.

Research using direct electric stimulation of the brain was pioneered by Penfield (Penfield & Roberts, 1959). This technique was developed to map the centers of the brain that controlled specific functions prior to surgical procedures. Since the brain does not contain pain receptors, the patient was conscious when a small electrical current was applied to the surface of the brain to determine areas of the brain associated with such functions as vision, hearing, olfaction, or haptic sensations. Applications of electrical stimulation to areas believed to control speech would be verified by the patient's inability to talk. These "aphasic arrests" would occur only when areas of the brain associated with speech were electrically stimulated. In this way, hypotheses about other functions of the brain could also be verified if responses associated with those functions were absent during stimulation.

Another invasive technique to study brain functioning has been to anesthetize one hemisphere by injecting sodium amytal in the carotid artery located on either the right or left side of the patient's neck. This procedure, known as the Wada test, quickly anesthetized that side of the brain. For example, if the left side or the side dominant for language was infused, the individual would become speechless while the drug was in effect, while the functions of the right hemisphere would remain intact. Wada and Rasmussen (1960) hypothesized that the left hemisphere is dominant for processing verbal information and the right hemisphere for nonverbal information. To demonstrate this, Wada and his associate injected sodium amytal into the left hemisphere and asked the patient to sing "Happy Birthday"; the patient was able to hum the tune without producing the words. When the right hemisphere was anesthetized and the patient was required to perform the same task, the patient was only able to recite the words of "Happy Birthday" in a monotone without producing a tune. Using this procedure, Milner (1974) found that 95% of right-handed and 70% of left-handed individuals are left hemisphere dominant for language.

Split-brain surgery or commissurotomy is another invasive technique used to study cerebral dominance. A commissurotomy is a surgical procedure used to stop the spread of seizure activity from a focal point in one hemisphere to the other hemisphere via the corpus callosum. This procedure involves the severing of the corpus callosum, a large band of nerve fibers that connects the left and right hemispheres, thereby preventing any communication between the hemispheres.

Much research was conducted by Speery in the 1950s. Researchers were able to localize functions of language, motoric control of the same or opposite sides of the body, and visual discrimination (Hacaen, 1981). In one study that examined visual perception, Levy and her associates (Levy, Trevarthen, & Speery, 1972) used stimulus figures in which the left half of one face was joined with the right half of another. The patient was required to gaze at a dot on the center of the screen before a figure was flashed on the screen. The presentation was such that each half of the face would be projected to only one hemisphere. When the patient was asked to respond by pointing to the correct picture from available alternatives, the left sides of faces, which are processed by the right hemisphere, were correctly chosen more often than the right sides regardless of the hand used for pointing. However, when the patient was required to verbally identify the picture, the face on the right side (left hemisphere) was chosen, although the number of errors made by this response mode was much higher. These results were subsequently replicated using other stimuli, suggesting that the right hemisphere is superior in processing nonverbal visual stimuli.

A noninvasive technique in the study of brain–behavior relationships has been dichotic listening. This procedure involves the simultaneous presentation of verbal or nonverbal information to each ear. Similar but different information is presented to each ear and the subject's task is to identify or recall what was heard. This technique was initially developed by Broadbent (1954) to study auditory attention and later adapted by Kimura (1961) to study cerebral lateralization. Studying normal individuals, Kimura found that subjects were more able to identify correctly verbal information when it was presented to the right ear (left hemisphere). If the information was nonverbal, however, a left-ear advantage (right hemisphere) was found. Kimura also showed that if patients having neurological disorders were found to be left hemisphere dominant for language (via the Wada test), a right-ear advantage was noted for verbal information. Similarly, if the patient was right hemisphere dominant for language, a left-ear advantage (right hemisphere) was found for verbal information. These findings suggested that superiority for each ear varies with the specialization in function for the opposite hemisphere.

Studies that have examined language lateralization for dyslexic children using a dichotic listening paradigm have found mixed results. Dyslexic or reading-disabled children are usually characterized by a significant lag in reading achievement despite average intelligence and an absence of any sensory-motor, neurological, or emotional difficulties (Hynd & Cohen, 1983). Some studies (e.g., Witelson & Rabinovitch, 1972) have reported that children with dyslexia show a left-ear advantage for verbal information. Other researchers (e.g., Leong, 1976) have demonstrated a right-ear advantage for verbal information for both dyslexic and normal readers. Differential findings may be partially due to differences in methodology, criteria of subject selection, and age and attention.

Another noninvasive technique in studying cerebral dominance has been split-visual field research. This involves a tachistoscopic presentation of verbal or spatial information to either the right-half or left-half visual fields. The visual pathways are such that information perceived in the left-visual field is processed by the right hemisphere while right-visual field information is processed by the left hemisphere. Studies have demonstrated that while word recognition levels were lower for the dyslexic children when compared with normal readers, both readers showed a right-visual field superiority for words (Marcel & Rajan, 1975). However, when pictures were presented to either visual field, Witelson (1976) reported that while normal readers had a significant left visual-field advantage, this difference was not significant for a dyslexic group. These results suggest that while dyslexic readers, like normal readers, have a left-hemisphere representation for language, the dyslexic group appears to lack right-hemisphere specialization for visual-spatial information.

In sum, invasive and noninvasive techniques have made significant contributions in mapping functions of the brain. However, our knowledge of hemispheric specializations is far from complete. Given the interindividual differences in cognitive processing, the brain's ability to compensate for damage, and developmental factors, the assessment of hemispheric specializations remains a complex and sometimes chaotic (Reynolds, Kamphaus, Rosenthal, & Hiemenz, 1997) endeavor.

REFERENCES

Broadbent, D. E. (1954). The role of auditory localization in attention and memory. *Journal of Experimental Psychology*, *47*, 191–196.

Dean, R. S. (1984). Functional lateralization of the brain. *Journal of Special Education*, *18*, 239–256.

Gaddes, W. H. (1980). *Learning disabilities and brain function: A neuropsychological approach*. New York, NY: Springer-Verlag.

Hacaen, H. (1981). Apraxias. In S. B. Filskov & T. J. Boll (Eds.), *Handbook of clinical neuropsychology*. New York, NY: Wiley.

Hugdahl, K., Carlsson, G., & Eichele, T. (2002). Age effects in dichotic listening to consonant–vowel syllables: Interactions with attention. *Developmental Neuropsychology*, *20*, 445–457.

Hynd, G., & Cohen, M. (1983). *Dyslexia: Neuropsychological theory, research, and clinical differentiation*. New York, NY: Grune & Stratton.

Jackson, J. H. (1874). On the duality of the brain. *Medical Press Circulator*, *1*, 19, 41, 63.

Kimura, D. (1961). Cerebral dominance and the perception of verbal stimuli. *Canadian Journal of Psychology*, *15*, 166–171.

Leong, C. K. (1976). Lateralization in severely disabled readers in relation to functional cerebral development and synthesis of information. In R. M. Knights & D. J. Bakker (Eds.), *Neuropsychology of learning disorders: Theoretical approaches*. Baltimore, MD: University Park Press.

Levy, J., Trevarthen, C., & Speery, R. W. (1972). Perception of bilateral chimeric figures following hemispheric disconnection. *Brain*, *95*, 61–78.

Marcel, T., & Rajan, P. (1975). Lateral specialization of recognition of words and faces in good and poor readers. *Neuropsychologia*, *13*, 489–497.

Milner, B. (1974). Hemispheric specialization scope and limits. In F. O. Schmitt & F. G. Warden (Eds.), *The neurosciences: Third study programme*. Cambridge, MA: MIT Press.

Orton, S. T. (1937). *Reading, writing, and speech problems in children*. New York, NY: Norton.

Penfield, W., & Roberts, L. (1959). *Speech and brain mechanisms*. Princeton, NJ: Princeton University Press.

Reynolds, C. R., Kamphaus, K. W., Rosenthal, B. L., & Hiemenz, J. R. (1997). Applications of the Kaufman Assessment Battery for Children in neuropsychological assessment. In C. R. Reynolds & E. Fletcher-Janzen (Eds.), *Handbook of clinical child neuropsychology* (2nd ed.). New York, NY: Plenum Press.

Wada, J. A., & Rasmussen, T. (1960). Intracarotid injection of sodium amytal for lateralization of cerebral speech dominance: Experimental and clinical observations. *Journal of Neurosurgery*, *17*, 266–282.

Witelson, S. F. (1976). Abnormal right hemisphere specialization in developmental dyslexia. In R. M. Knights & D. F. Bakker (Eds.), *Neuropsychology of learning disorders: Theoretical approaches*. Baltimore, MD: University Park Press.

Witelson, S. F. & Rabinovitch, M. S. (1972). Hemispheric speech lateralization in children with auditory-linguistic deficits. *Cortex 8*, 412–426.

GURMAL RATTAN
Indiana University of Pennsylvania

RAYMOND S. DEAN
Ball State University,
Indiana University School of Medicine

CEREBRAL FUNCTION, LATERALIZATION OF

The human brain is divided longitudinally into two distinct hemispheres. Research over the past century has confirmed early speculations (Broca, 1861; Dax, 1865) that each of these cerebral hemispheres serves specialized functions (Dean, 1984). Although anatomical differences have been identified between hemispheres at birth, more complex patterns of functional specialization may well continue to develop throughout childhood (Dean, 1985).

Our present understanding of the lateralization of functions in the cerebral cortex owes much to the early efforts of investigations of the late 19th century (e.g., Broca, 1861; Dax, 1865; Jackson, 1874). Based on case studies of patients with confirmed brain damage, a number of researchers (e.g., Broca, 1861) argued in favor of the localization of individual functions (e.g., speech) to specific structures of the brain. Moreover, it was generally reported during this time that with damage to the left cerebral hemisphere, one could expect impaired language functions (Broca, 1861; Dax, 1865). These early underpinnings of the notion of lateralization were further extended by Jackson (1874), who suggested that a lateralization of functions corresponds to the two hemispheres of the brain. Jackson (1874) argued that the left cerebral hemisphere is responsible for language-related functions, while the right hemisphere is the more automatic side, responsible for sensation and perception. The notion of hemispheric dominance grew out of such early arguments, which equated language lateralization in the left hemisphere with control functions. Although rather naive some hundred years later, the idea of hemispheric dominance continues in the literature. Clearly, these early case studies, which attempted to draw conclusions concerning the neuropsychology of normal individuals based on observations of patients with brain damage, were limited. However, the scientific interest stimulated by these reports in tandem with increasingly sophisticated approaches in research is responsible for the wealth of our present knowledge about the functioning of the brain.

While the differences in hemispheric functioning are acknowledged by most neuroscientists, the specific mechanism underlying these differences continues to be debated. At this point, it is not clear whether functional lateralization is related to differences in processing (e.g., Geschwind & Levitsky, 1968), storage (e.g., Dean, 1984), or attention (e.g., Kinsbourne, 1975). However, most researchers have found the arguments attributing observed differences to processing predisposition for the individual hemispheres compelling. From this point of view, the differences in functioning for the sides of the brain are due to biological differences in processing information that implicate the left hemisphere in language-related tasks and the right side in nonverbal elements.

Although communication between hemispheres is acknowledged, specific functional differences may be attributed to the individual hemispheres. Indeed, it is rather well established that the left hemisphere of the brain best processes information in a sequential, temporal, and analytic fashion. This may be likened to a verbal-sequential mode of thought in which information is represented, processed, and encoded with the aid of linguistic units (Dean, 1983; Paivio, 1971).

A second mode of thought may be seen to correspond to the functions of the right hemisphere. This mode is most clearly oriented toward processing visual information in a concrete, simultaneous, or holistic fashion (e.g., Sperry, 1974). Rather primitive when compared with the left, the right hemisphere seems predisposed to represent, reorganize, and encode visual-spatial elements (e.g., Dimond & Beaumont, 1974). Indeed, the use of imagery seems to be the most idiosyncratic expression of its processing (Seamon & Gazzaniga, 1973).

Hemispheric lateralization has been argued to be an interactive process in which the mode is dependent on the degree of cognitive reformulation, constraints of attention, and actual hemispheric differences in function (Dean, 1984; Gordon, 1974; Kinsbourne, 1997; Paivio, 1971). It has been suggested that normal individuals can employ different strategies that make differential use of one hemisphere or the other regardless of the form of the original stimulus (Dean, 1984). Clearly, information presented in a visual fashion may be encoded almost entirely in semantic terms (Conrad, 1964). So, too, it has been shown that verbal stimuli may be encoded and recalled as visual memory traces (Bower, 1970; Dean, 1983). As Dean (1984) points out, "even young learners can generate visual or verbal encoding strategies which correspond to hemispheric specific abilities regardless of the form of the original stimulus array" (p. 249). This point of view acknowledges independent cognitive processes served by each hemisphere while it stresses the importance of interhemispheric communication. It seems, therefore, that the verbal–nonverbal or left-right hemispheric differences may well be an exaggeration of reality. That is, cerebral lateralization may be more heuristically attributed to modes of processing information than to lateralization for specific stimuli. Therefore, the total task demands for the process of a given bit of information are necessary prior to assuming hemispheric lateralization.

The lateralization of functions is dependent in part on the degree to which cognitive processing is necessary for interpretation and encoding (e.g., Gordon, 1974). Indeed, few differences have been found between hemispheres for lower-level information processing. For example, in the discrimination of sensory elements such as brightness, color, pressure, sharpness, pitch, and contour, little lateralization exists in processing (e.g., Dean, 1984; Rabinowicz, 1976). However, when learners are required to form generalizations, categorize, reorder, or integrate, or when they are called on to abstract common elements, clear hemispheric differences emerge. As would be expected, cerebral lateralization is dependent on the amount of interpretation or prior knowledge that the subject must draw on in dealing with the incoming information. Such cognitive processing enhances the degree to which functionally lateralized abilities are relied on (e.g., Moscovitch, 1979).

Although less than complete agreement exists among neuroscientists, it would seem that functional lateralization of cerebral hemispheres of the brain corresponds to the developmental pattern of consolidation that occurs from birth and progresses through adolescence (Dean, 1985). Dean (1984) argues that the rate of lateralization in the child varies with the specific function being examined. In keeping with this hypothesis, Krashen (1973) has offered data favoring a progressive decrease in the role played by the right cerebral hemisphere in verbal-analytic tasks with the child's increasing neurological development. The progressive lateralization of cerebral functions seems concomitant with the rate and variable progression in the maturation of the commissure-association cortex (Sperry, 1969).

Gender differences have been reported for the lateralization of cerebral functions. The force of the data in this area suggests less secure hemispheric specialization for females than for males (e.g., Witelson, 1976). Although anatomical gender differences exist (e.g., MacLusky & Naftolin, 1981), the functional differences found for males and females seem more heuristically attributed to organizational factors than differences in structure (e.g., Kolata, 1979). However, language lateralization develops and is localized similarly in males and females and does not seem to address cognitive differences usually found (Sommer, Aleman, Bouma, & Kahn, 2004). A convincing argument may be made for a genetic-hormonal cultural locus for observed gender differences (Dean, 1984).

In sum, the functioning of the left hemisphere seems predisposed to process information in a sequential, temporal, or analytic fashion; as such, language is an excellent tool for such forms of cognition. The right hemisphere, in contrast, is best prepared to function in a more simultaneous, holistic, or nonverbal fashion, with spatial reasoning and imagery being the most consistently reported mode of thought. This pattern corresponds with a large body of research in both cognitive psychology and the neurosciences. A good deal of interhemispheric communication should be recognized and functional lateralization is exhibited only as the individual must employ higher-order cognitive skills in an attempt to comprehend or learn the incoming information.

REFERENCES

Bower, G. H. (1970). Analysis of a mnemonic device. *American Scientist, 58*, 496–510.

Broca, P. (1861). Nouvelle observation d'aphemie produite par une lesion de la moite posterieure des deuxieme et troiseme circonvolutions frontales. *Bulletin de la Society Anatomique de Paris, 36*, 398–407.

Conrad, R. (1964). Acoustic confusions in immediate memory. *British Journal of Psychology, 55*, 75–83.

Dax, G. (1865). Lesions de la moitie gauche de l'encephale coincident avec l'oubli des signes de la pensee. *Gazette Hebdomadaire de Medicine et de Chirurgie, 2*, 259–262.

Dean, R. S. (1983, February). *Dual processing of prose and cerebral laterality*. Paper presented at the annual meeting of the International Neuropsychological Society, Mexico City, Mexico.

Dean, R. S. (1984). Functional lateralization of the brain. *Journal of Special Education, 18*(3), 239–256.

Dean, R. S. (1985). Foundation and rationale for neuropsychological bases of individual differences. In L. C. Hartlage & C. F. Telzrow (Eds.), *The neuropsychology of individual differences: A developmental perspective*. New York, NY: Plenum Press.

Dimond, S., & Beaumont, J. (1974). *Hemisphere function in the human brain*. London, UK: Elek Scientific Books.

Geschwind, N., & Levitsky, W. (1968). Human brain: Left–right asymmetries in temporal speech region. *Science, 161*, 186–187.

Gordon, H. W. (1974). Auditory specialization of the right and left hemispheres. In M. Kinsbourne & W. L. Smith (Eds.), *Hemispheric disconnection and cerebral function*. Springfield, IL: Thomas.

Jackson, J. H. (1874). On the duality of the brain. In J. Taylor (Ed.), *Selected writings of John Hughlings Jackson* (Vol. 2). London, UK: Hodder & Stoughton.

Kinsbourne, M. (1975). Cerebral dominance, learning, and cognition. In H. R. Myklebust (Ed.), *Progress in learning disabilities*. New York, NY: Grune & Stratton.

Kinsbourne, M. (1997). Mechanisms and development of cerebral lateralization in children. In C. R. Reynolds & E. Fletcher-Janzen (Eds.), *Handbook of clinical child neuropsychology* (2nd ed.) New York, NY: Plenum Press.

Kolata, G. B. (1979). Sex hormones and brain development. *Science, 205*, 985–987.

Krashen, S. D. (1973). Lateralization, language learning, and the critical period: Some new evidence. *Language Learning, 23*, 63–74.

MacLusky, N. J., & Naftolin, F. (1981). Sexual differentiation of the central nervous system. *Science, 211*, 1294–1302.

Moscovitch, M. (1979). Information processing and the cerebral hemispheres. In M.S. Gazzaniga (Ed.), *Handbook of behavioral neurobiology: Vol. 2. Neuropsychology*. New York, NY: Plenum.

Paivio, A. (1971). *Imagery and verbal processes*. New York, NY: Holt, Rinehart, & Winston.

Rabinowicz, B. H. (1976). *A non-lateralized auditory process in speech perception*. Unpublished master's thesis, University of Toronto.

Seamon, J. G., & Gazzaniga, M. D. (1973). Coding strategies and cerebral laterality effects. *Cognitive Psychology, 5*, 249–256.

Sommer, E. C., Aleman, A., Bouma, A., & Kahn, R. S. (2004). Do women really have more bilateral language representation than men? A meta-analysis of functional imaging studies. *Brain, 8*, 1845–1852.

Sperry, R. W. (1969). A modified concept of consciousness. *Psychological Review, 76*, 532–536.

Sperry, R. W. (1974). Lateral specialization in the surgically separated hemispheres. In F. O. Schmitt & F. G. Worden (Eds.), *The neurosciences: Third study program*. New York, NY: Wiley.

Witelson, S. F. (1976). Early hemisphere specialization and inter-hemisphere plasticity: An empirical and theoretical review. In S. Segalowitz & F. Gruber (Eds.), *Language and development and neurologic theory*. New York, NY: Academic Press.

RAYMOND S. DEAN
Ball State University,
Indiana University School of Medicine

See also Hemispheric Functions; Cerebral Dominance; Left Brain/Right Brain; Neuropsychology

CEREBRAL INFARCTION

Cerebral infarction refers to the death of brain tissues resulting from a sudden onset of a circulation disorder that often leads to a neurological deficit. Infarction is caused by conditions of anoxia, hypoglycemia, or ischemia (Toole, 1984; Toole & Patel, 1974). Anoxic infarction results from a lack of oxygen to the brain, whereas hypoglycemic infarction occurs when an insufficient level of blood glucose exists for a prolonged period of time despite normal circulation. The most prevalent of the infarctions, however, is ischemic infarction, which results from a sudden interruption of blood supply owed to an obstruction in an artery. Cerebral infarction can occur in any of the cerebral blood vessels of the carotid (anterior portion of the brain) or vertebral basilar (posterior portion of the brain) systems. It may be confused with symptomology resulting from cerebral hemorrhage, tumor, or other space-occupying lesions. Because ischemic infarctions are the most common, they will be the focus of the remaining discussion.

Transient ischemic attack (TIA) refers to a temporary obstruction of blood vessels; this is frequently caused by platelet-fibrin emboli or blood clots (de Veber, 1999). An embolus is an aggregate of blood particles and tissue overgrowth (thrombus), fatty deposits, clumps of bacteria, or obstructive gas bubbles that block the blood vessels. Other causes of TIAs are acute high blood pressure and vasospasm or spasmodic constriction of blood vessels.

Transient ischemic attacks always have a sudden onset and peak in intensity within 2 to 5 minutes. Symptoms quickly disappear, within 30 minutes, but if symptoms persist past 24 hours, the diagnosis changes to a complete stroke or a cardiac vascular accident. Causes of TIAs are numerous and can be from intravascular disorders of the metabolic, hematologic, or prothrombotic states; trauma, vasculitis, and heart disease (de Veber, 1999). The extent to which TIAs result in temporary or permanent neurological damage in unclear. Symptoms of carotid TIA include monocular blindness or blurring of vision in a previously normal eye; aphasic reactions such as difficulty with writing, reading, arithmetic, and receptive and expressive language; and contralateral weakness and numbness of the face, arm, and leg, which may occur either simultaneously or separately. Weakness is characterized by heaviness or clumsiness of the extremities, while numbness can be described as a numbing sensation or a pins-and-needles sensation. These sensations do not spread or "march" to the various anatomical parts, but occur simultaneously. Vertebral basilar TIAs, however, have the following symptomology: vertigo (spinning movement of the environment); intermittent diplopia (double vision); visual blurring of both eyes; episodic ataxia (gait problems); and spells in which sudden loss of strength in the lower extremities causes the patient to fall to the ground without loss of consciousness.

Transient ischemic attacks may occur sporadically or regularly, either in a short time span or over several months or years. More than one-third of the patients with diagnosed TIAs sustain a complete stroke within one year, while more than one-half of these patients eventually sustain a major stroke during their lifetime. Patients with TIAs may suffer mild cognitive impairments, especially on delayed-recall tasks (Lezak, 1983). Patients suspected of having a TIA can have the diagnosis confirmed by an angiography, which enables a radiological visualization of the blood vessels.

Medical therapy usually involves a regimen of drugs that have the properties of inhibiting the formation or aggregation of red blood cells and the narrowing of arteries. Such drugs consist of aspirin, Anturane, Persantine, and Coumadin (Lubic & Palkovitz, 1979).

REFERENCES

de Veber, G. (1999). Cerebrovascular disease in children. In K.F. Swaiman & S. Ashwal (Eds.), *Pediatric neurology* (3rd ed., p. 1101). St. Louis, MO: Mosby.

Lezak, M. D. (1983). *Neuropsychological assessment* (2nd ed.). New York, NY: Oxford University Press.

Lubic, L. G., & Palkovitz, H. P. (1979). *Discussions in patient management: Stroke.* New York, NY: Medical Examination.

Toole, J. F. (1984). *Cerebrovascular disorders* (3rd ed.). New York, NY: Raven.

Toole, J. F., & Patel, A. N. (1974). *Cerebrovascular disorders* (2nd ed.). New York, NY: McGraw-Hill.

GURMAL RATTAN
Indiana University of Pennsylvania

RAYMOND S. DEAN
Ball State University,
Indiana University School of Medicine

See also Anoxia

CEREBRAL LESION, CHRONIC

A chronic cerebral lesion is one that has been in existence beyond what might be considered to be the amount of time required for recovery of lost function.

Chronic cerebral lesions, much like acute cerebral lesions, are likely to influence behavior in ways related to their location and extent or size. Unlike acute cerebral lesions, however, chronic cerebral lesions may have greater effects on behavior than effects related to their location and extent. Increased effects on behavior can result from two conditions. The primary behavioral loss can be due to the interruption of developmental schemata, whereby a child who sustains a chronic cerebral lesion at an early age may be precluded from development of the normal repertoire of behaviors dependent on the integrity of the area of lesion. The normal sequence of ontogenetic recapitulation of phylogenetic phenomena is interrupted. Therefore, not only is there limitation of the behavior dependent on the specific area of cerebral tissue that sustains a lesion, but also of the subsequent behaviors dependent on the development of that initial behavior. The secondary loss from a chronic cerebral lesion results from a disuse atrophy phenomenon, whereby deterioration of muscle tissue or degeneration of neurotransmitter receptor sites, resulting secondary to the lesion, inhibits the development, performance, or acquisition of given behavioral skills.

Chronic cerebral lesions, especially those acquired after the developmental sequence is completed, may have lesser behavioral effects than those of acute lesions, in that the individual over time may acquire compensatory skills that help overcome some of the behavioral limitations imposed by the lesion.

Although chronic cerebral lesions can have onset at any age, many such lesions of congenital or prenatal onset result in death or profound developmental handicap. Onset age appears to be related to the severity of the handicap imposed by the lesion. Although it has been traditional to believe that the effects of chronic brain lesions are less severe in children because of presumed greater plasticity in the organization of their central nervous systems (Lyons & Matheny, 1984), there is accumulating evidence that a chronic cerebral lesion acquired early in childhood may have more severely debilitating effects (Cermak, 1985; Levin, Benton, & Grossman, 1982). There is also evidence that such lesions limit the development of memory and intellectual ability to a greater extent with early age onset than with later age onset (Levin, Eisenberg, Wigg, & Kobayashi, 1982). Further, there is evidence to suggest a greater likelihood of emotional problems resulting from chronic cerebral lesions at an early age (Rutter, 1981). These problems may interact with cognitive problems, depending on the age at which the lesion was acquired (Lyons & Matheny, 1984). The selective results of unilateral cerebral lesions on such specific aspects of behavior as language development, previously thought to be less specific when acquired at an early age, have been found to be similar in early childhood onset to those of later age onset (Aram, Ekelman, Rose, & Whitaker, 1985). Even for those children who appear to show good recovery from early onset chronic cerebral lesions, there is a strong likelihood that special educational placement may be necessary (Lehr, 1984). The etiology of the chronic cerebral lesion, whether from head injury, brain tumor, or radiation therapy, appears to be unrelated to the neuropsychological outcome (Bruce, 1982).

Although developments in neurochemistry suggest that neurochemical adaptations at surviving synapses may mediate behavioral changes over time, which would account for frequent observations that behavioral consequences of chronic cerebral lesions change as time following the injury increases (Marshall, 1984), there is no generally accepted explanation for why this change over time should occur.

Characteristics

1. Approximately one-half of the chronic cerebral lesions resulting from traumatic brain injuries (TBIs) yield concomitant motor, cognitive, communication, behavioral, and social problems.

   a. The most commonly affected cognitive domains in children with TBIs include attention, executive functions, processing speed, and learning and memory for new information.

b. Increased fatigue is commonly associated with TBIs.

c. Children with TBIs are 5 to 13 times more likely to have seizures compared to normal populations.

d. Personality changes are observed in the majority of head injury victims.

2. The cognitive, behavioral, and social consequences of neurological diseases are less known. Localization of the pathology is strongly associated with observed functional deficits. The deficits can also involve consequences similar to those associated with TBIs.

3. The courses of recovery from either TBIs or neurological diseases also vary with most children with TBIs achieving maximal recovery within 2 years of the injuries.

a. Factors associated with the course of recovery include severity of injury, length of posttraumatic amnesia, premorbid intellectual and behavioral status, and social support.

A variety of considerations must be made in reintegrating a child with a chronic cerebral lesion to an academic environment. Because a cerebral lesion may affect one or many functional domains (e.g., motor, social, cognitive), successful reintegration requires a multidisciplinary approach. Children may vary in the degree of services required depending on factors such as severity of the lesion. Some children may need minimal or no assistance, whereas other children may need specialized alternative school placements.

Recommendations for successful school reentry should be based on early identification, assessment, and intervention based on individualized assessment results. General recommendations for reintegration include a gradual introduction to the school program, quiet instructional settings, and methods to accommodate fatigue (e.g., reducing length of school day; Gans, Mann, & Ylvisaker, 1990).

The prognosis for children with chronic lesions also is variable depending on the severity of the lesion and environmental factors such as social support. An important consideration is the finding that school difficulties may not appear immediately after the injury. Because a common consequence of childhood chronic lesions includes impairments in learning new information, these children can initially rely on previous acquired knowledge to maintain previous levels of performance in school. As they progress through grades, they are less able to succeed based on the knowledge they acquired before the injury. Furthermore, because speed of processing and executive functions may also be impaired, children with chronic lesions also face difficulties in the transition to middle school and high school where independent learning of increased quantities of material is required.

REFERENCES

Aram, D. M., Ekelman, B. L., Rose, D. F., & Whitaker, H. A. (1985). Verbal and cognitive sequelae following unilateral lesions acquired in early childhood. *Journal of Clinical and Experimental Neuropsychology*, 7, 55–78.

Bruce, D. A. (1982). Comment. *Neurosurgery*, 11, 672–673.

Cermak, L. A. (1985, February). *The effects of age at onset and causal agent of brain injury on later adaptive functioning in children*. Paper presented at the International Neuropsychological Society, San Diego. Abstract in *Proceedings* (p. 10).

Gans, B., Mann, N., & Ylvisaker, M. (1990). Rehabilitation management approaches. In M. Rosenthal, E. Griffith, M. Bond, & J. D. Miller (Eds.), *Rehabilitation of the adult and child with traumatic brain injury* (2nd ed., pp. 593–615). Philadelphia, PA: F. A. Davis.

Lehr, E. (1984, August). *Good recovery from severe head injury in children and adolescents*. Paper presented at American Psychological Association meeting, Toronto, Ontario.

Levin, H. S., Benton, A. L., & Grossman, R. G. (1982a). *Neurobehavioral consequences of closed head injury*. New York, NY: Oxford University Press.

Levin, H. S., Eisenberg, H. M., Wigg, N. R., & Kobayashi, K. (1982b). Memory and intellectual ability after head injury in children and adolescents. *Neurosurgery*, 11, 668–672.

Lyons, M. J., & Matheny, A. P. (1984). Cognitive and personality differences between identical twins following skull fracture. *Journal of Pediatric Psychology*, 9, 485–494.

Marshall, J. F. (1984). Brain function: Neural adaptations and recovery from injury. *Annual Review of Psychology*, 35, 277–308.

Rutter, M. (1981). Psychological sequelae of brain damage in children. *American Journal of Psychiatry*, 138, 1533–1544.

LAWRENCE C. HARTLAGE
Evans, Georgia

LATHA V. SOORYA
*Binghamton University and
Institute for Child Development from CDDR*

See also Birth Injuries; Brain Damage/Injury; Cerebral Infarction; Traumatic Brain Injury

CEREBRAL PALSY

Cerebral palsy (CP), sometimes called congenital spastic paralysis, is characterized by varying degrees of disturbance of voluntary movements caused by damage to the brain. Cerebral refers to the brain and palsy refers to weakness or lack of control. Cerebral palsy was originally called Little's disease after the English surgeon William John Little, who first described it. Later, Winthrop Phelps, an orthopedic surgeon, coined the term *cerebral palsy* and brought it into common usage as a result of his extensive work with this population in the United States.

There is agreement among experts in the field that cerebral palsy is a complex of characteristics attributed to brain injury. It has been defined by the United Cerebral Palsy Research and Educational Foundation as having the following elements: (a) being caused by injury to the brain; (b) causing motor disturbance, including paralysis, weakness, and uncoordination; (c) consisting of a cluster of symptoms; (d) usually originating in childhood; and (e) perhaps including learning difficulties, psychological problems, sensory defects, convulsions, and behavioral disorders of organic origin. In addition to these elements, cerebral palsy is nonprogressive, static, and unamenable to treatment.

There are two major types of CP: spastic, characterized by sudden, violent, involuntary muscular contractions, and athetosic, characterized by ceaseless, involuntary, slow, sinuous, writhing movements. The physical symptoms of CP can be so mild that they are detected only with difficulty, or they can be so profound that the affected individual is almost completely physically incapacitated. It is not unusual for a cerebral palsied individual to function normally intellectually. However, this intelligence is often masked (at least to the layperson) by uncontrolled physical characteristics, involuntary movements of the body and extremities, speech disorders, and drooling. Cerebral palsy is not a disease, and it is not curable.

The incidence of cerebral palsy varies; a conservative estimate of its occurrence is 1.5 to 2.0 cases per 1,000 live births. It has been estimated that the incidence may be higher in areas where there is inadequate prenatal care and accompanying prematurity. It is estimated that there are 750,000 individuals with cerebral palsy in the United States. While CP occurs at every socioeconomic level, it is more prevalent among lower socioeconomic groups. Children born in poverty situations have a greater chance of incurring brain damage from factors such as malnutrition, poor prenatal and postnatal care, and environmental hazards during infancy. Cerebral palsy occurs slightly more frequently in males than in females, and more white than black children are affected. Cerebral palsy makes up the largest category of physical disabilities, representing 30 to 40% of all children in programs for the physically disabled.

In most cases, cerebral palsy is congenital (approximately 90% of all cases; UCP, 2005), meaning damage to the brain occurs during pregnancy or at birth. However, infectious diseases or severe head injuries can cause cerebral palsy at any time in life. Postnatal causes are said to be acquired, whereas those present at birth are congenital. It is generally agreed that CP cannot be inherited.

Prenatal causes of CP include German measles in the mother, pH incompatibility, maternal anoxia, use of drugs, and metabolic disorders such as maternal diabetes. Faulty growth of the fetal brain may occur if the mother is malnourished during pregnancy. In addition, maternal exposure to the toxic substances in X-rays may also damage the brain of the fetus. Perinatal (birth process) causes include prolonged labor, breech delivery, anoxia, and prematurity. High fever, poisonings, and other related factors may cause harm immediately following birth. After birth (postnatal) causes include anoxia, direct trauma to the brain, and infection. Poisonings also may contribute to brain damage during the postnatal period. In some cases, severe and consistent child beating has caused CP.

It is estimated that as many as three-quarters of all persons with CP have additional disabilities such as retardation, seizures, auditory and visual impairments, or communication disorders (UCP, 1998, 2005). Approximately 50 to 60% of CP children are retarded. Mental retardation has been difficult to diagnose in the population since intelligence tests were standardized on children with adequate speech, language, and motor abilities. Seizures are associated with approximately 25 to 35% of individuals with cerebral palsy and are much more prevalent with spastic CP persons. Strabismus (squinting) occurs in approximately 30 to 35% of cerebral-palsied individuals. Some athetotic CPs experience farsightedness while spastic CPs are nearsighted. Visual field reduction also can occur in some types of CP (Capute, 1978).

Speech and/or language problems can range from normal speech and reception processing and expression to that which is nonfunctional. Speech in the two major types of CP has been characterized by Berry and Eisenson (1956) as (1) spastic speech, for example, "slow, labored rate, lack of vocal inflection, gutteral or breathy quality of voice, uncontrolled volume, and, most important, grave articulatory problems which reflect the inability to secure graded, synchronous movement of the tongue, lips, and jaw"; and (2) athetoid speech, for example, "varying gradations of a pattern of irregular, shallow, and noisy breathing; whispered or hoarse phonation, and articulatory problems varying from the extremes of complete mutism of extreme dysarthria (impaired articulation) to a slight awkwardness in lingual movement."

Speech disorders are found in 70% of cerebral-palsied children. It has been reported that speech defects are found in 88% of persons with athetosis, 85% of those with ataxia, and 52% of those who are spastic. Most of the speech problems are caused by problems controlling the muscles used to make speech sounds.

Minear (1956) developed a classification scheme for cerebral-palsied individuals based on motor characteristics as well as the area of the body where the problem is located. The six types within the motor component were adopted by the American Academy for Cerebral Palsy and have been described by others (Bleck, 1975; Denhoff, 1978; Healy, 1983). The six types include spasticity, athetosis, ataxia, rigidity, tremor, and mixed.

Spasticity is the most common type of CP, occurring in approximately 40 to 60% of the total. Stiffness of the muscles in spastic children occurs when the injury is on the brain surface or when it involves those nerves leading from the surface through the substance of the brain and onto the spinal cord. The spastic type is characterized by a loss of voluntary motor control. When the child initiates voluntary movement, it is likely to be jerky, with lack of control in the body extremities. This disability may affect any or all limbs. Involvement in the upper extremities may include varying degrees of flexing of the arms and fingers, depending on the severity of the disability. When lower extremities are involved, there may be a scissoring movement of the legs, caused by muscle contractions.

Athetosis is the second largest group in the CP population, occurring in approximately 15 to 20% of the total. This type is caused by injury to the brain's motor switchboard. Athetoid children are characterized by involuntary jerky, writhing movements, especially in the fingers and wrists. The head is often drawn back with the neck extended and mouth open. There are generally two types of athetosis: tension and nontension. The tension athetoid's muscles are always tense; this reduces contorted movement of limbs. The nontension athetoid has contorted movements without muscle tightness. Unlike the spastic child, all movements cease during sleep. The movements occur only in a conscious state; when emotionality increases, athetosis movements become intensified. Athetoids are usually higher in intelligence than spastic CP victims.

Ataxia is less prevalent than spasticity and athetosis. Together with tremor and rigidity, it makes up approximately 8% of the total CP population. The injury is in the cerebellum. Ataxic children are characterized by a lack of coordination and sense of balance. The eyes are often uncoordinated and the child may stumble and fall frequently.

Rigidity and tremor types of CP are extremely rare. Rigidity is unlike the other types in that the lower level of muscles stiffen and a rigid posture is maintained. The rigid type is usually severely retarded with a high incidence of convulsions. In tremor, there is involuntary movement in one extremity, usually one hand or arm. The motion may vary in its consistency and pattern. In intention tremor, the involuntary movement happens only when the child attempts an activity while in constant tremor. The involuntary movement is continuous.

Mixed is another variation of CP. It is a combination of the other five types with one type predominating. Approximately 30% of individuals with CP have more than one type.

The movement or motor component of the clinical classification system is composed of two types, pyramidal and extrapyramidal. The pyramidal type refers to the spastic cerebral-palsied group because the usual nerve cell involved in this disorder is shaped like a pyramid. Extrapyramidal refers to all other types of CP, athetosis, rigidity, tremor, ataxia, and mixed, in which the area of the brain affected is composed of conglomerates of nerve cells (Capute, 1978).

In addition to describing CP by type of neuromuscular or motor involvement, Denhoff (1978) also characterized this multihandicapped population by the body parts that are affected. This is also known as topographical classification, with (generally) seven types. With hemiplegia, one half, either the right side or left side, of the body is involved. Of cerebral-palsied individuals 30 to 40% fall into this category. The legs are involved to a greater extent than the arms with diplegia. Of all cerebral-palsied children 10 to 20% are diplegic. Quadriplegia involves all four limbs and accounts for 15 to 20% of the total CP population. With paraplegia, occurring in 10 to 20% of all cerebral cases, only the legs are involved. Monoplegia involves only one limb and triplegia involves three limbs. These two types rarely occur. With double hemiplegia, both halves of the body are involved, but unlike quadriplegia, the two sides are affected differently. This type, too, rarely occurs.

Also CP can be classified by the severity of the motor involvement. Deaver (1955) described the CP child based on the mild, moderate, and severe classification scheme. Even though the descriptions were formulated several years ago, they are still useful today because of the explicitness of the activity level included in each category. In the mild category, no treatment is needed. The individual has no speech problem, is able to care for himself or herself, and can walk without the aid of appliances. In the moderate category, treatment is needed for speech problems and/or difficulties in ambulation and self-care. Braces and other equipment are needed. In the severe category, treatment is needed, but the degree of involvement is at a level wherein the prognosis for speech, self-care, and ambulation is poor.

Educational programs for children with cerebral palsy in the public schools gained momentum in the early 1970s with the emphasis on deinstitutionalization and normalization. Prior to this, many of these children, with multiple handicaps and not adequately diagnosed, remained in institutions for the mentally retarded.

It is generally agreed by experts in the field that treatment and educational considerations are extremely important and more complicated because cerebral-palsied children are multihandicapped. Not only must special equipment and facilities be provided to accommodate their physical disabilities, but additional special education techniques are needed to accommodate other handicaps (mental retardation, learning disabilities, auditory and visual disabilities).

When planning and implementing educational programs for cerebral-palsied individuals, a cadre of persons working in a multidisciplinary approach must be used. Many educators and physicians (Capute, 1978; Gearheart, 1980; Healy, 1983) have delineated the specific roles of the individuals who must work together in the education of cerebral-palsied children. The degree of CP and physical characteristics will determine the extent of participation by the physician. The physician may prescribe drugs for the patient to relax and to control the convulsions as well as treat overall health problems. Braces and other mechanical devices that provide support and allow children to walk are usually prescribed by medical doctors. The physical therapist works to facilitate motor development, to prevent or slow orthopedic problems, and to improve posture and positioning so that the child may benefit from other intervention activities. The occupational therapist uses creative, educational, and recreational activities to enhance self-help skills and teach parents to handle the child's daily living activities. The speech pathologist will monitor the child's progress in speech and language and provide therapy if the child is able to benefit from it. The speech therapist also may work with parents and other educational personnel on how to stimulate language development. An audiologist, learning disabilities specialist, and teacher of the mentally retarded may be needed to provide some direct and indirect services to the primary teacher when required. Biofeedback clinicians may be useful in teaching the individual what muscle groups are voluntarily affected (UCP, 2012).

A variety of specialized equipment is available to teachers, including adapted typewriters, pencil holders, book holders, page turners, and special desks to make cerebral-palsied individuals more self-sufficient.

The success achieved by the cerebral-palsied child depends largely on the extent of his or her physical and mental disability. While some cerebral-palsied people will need constant care in a protected environment, many can lead relatively normal lives and become productive citizens if given the opportunity.

Special education issues will vary widely depending on the severity of CP symptoms. These services will be available to children with CP under the handicapping condition of Other Health Impairment or Physical Disability. Some children with CP can be mainstreamed with minimal special education services, as needed, whereas others will need to utilize comprehensive services due to the severity of motor and cognitive impairments. Approximately 30 to 40% of children with CP have significant neurological involvement, resulting in mental retardation. These children require special education services to address limited cognitive capacity and its effect on learning. Children with CP are also at increased risk for learning disabilities, behavioral difficulty, and attentional impairments. Special education assistance may be necessary to deal with these complications of CP. Adaptations to the classroom may be necessary due to motor dysfunction. Many children with CP can participate in adapted physical education classes.

Physical therapy, occupational therapy, and speech and language therapy are often necessary to meet an individual child's educational needs. A child with CP may also require assistive technology to communicate or complete academic work. Devices such as communication boards and keyboards may be useful.

When working with a child with CP, it is important to have good communication with parents and medical professionals. The child may have many absences due to surgery, medical appointments, or private therapies. He or she may have difficulty catching up with work and may require additional tutoring to keep up with these demands.

CP is a lifelong disorder. Improvement can be expected with medical and allied health intervention. There continue to be new investigational treatments to help alleviate symptoms including surgery and new medications. Many children can learn to cope with physical disabilities associated with CP and live productive lives.

Characteristics

1. Motor dysfunction
2. Abnormal muscle tone (most often spasticity but sometimes hypotonia)
3. Developmental delays (especially motor and language)
4. No evidence for progressive disease or loss of previously acquired skills
5. Often vision or hearing impairment
6. Possibly seizure disorder

REFERENCES

Berry, M. F., & Eisenson, P. (1956). *Speech disorders*. New York, NY: Appleton-Century-Crofts.

Bleck, E. E. (1975). Cerebral palsy. In E. E. Bleck & D. A. Nagel (Eds.), *Physically handicapped children: A medical atlas for teachers*. New York, NY: Grune & Stratton.

Capute, A. J. (1978). Cerebral palsy and associated dysfunctions. In R. H. Haslam & P. G. Valletutti (Eds.), *Medical problems in the classroom*. Baltimore, MD: University Park Press.

Deaver, G. G. (1955). Cerebral palsy: Methods of evaluation and treatment. *Institute of Physical Medicine & Rehabilitation, 9*.

Denhoff, E. (1978). Medical aspects. In W. M. Cruickshank (Ed.), *Cerebral palsy: A developmental disability* (3rd ed.). Syracuse, NY: Syracuse University Press.

Gearheart, B. R. (1980). *Special education for the 80s*. St Louis, MO: Mosby.

Healy, A. (1983). Cerebral palsy. In J. A. Blackman (Ed.), *Medical aspects of developmental disabilities in children—birth to three*. Iowa City: University of Iowa Press.

Minear, W. L. (1956). A classification of cerebral palsy. *Pediatrics*, *18*, 841–852.

United Cerebral Palsy (UCP). (2012). *Comments on biofeedback.* Retrieved from www.ucp.org

United Cerebral Palsy (UCP). (2012). *Cerebral palsy facts and figures.* Retrieved from http://www.ucp.org/uploads/media_items/ucp-fact-sheet-1.original.pdf

CECELIA STEPPE-JONES
North Carolina Central University

MELISSA R. BUNNER
Austin Neurological Clinic

DILIP KARNIK
'Specially for Children Children's Hospital of Austin from CDDR

See also Habilitation of Individuals With Disabilities; High-Incidence Disabilities; Multiple Handicapping Conditions; Physical Disabilities; United Cerebral Palsy

CEREBRO-HEPATO-RENAL SYNDROME

Cerebro-hepato-renal syndrome, sometimes called Zellweger syndrome, is a rare genetically determined disorder identified as one of the leukodystrophies in which the area affected is the growth of the myelin sheath, which is the fatty covering that acts as insulation on nerve fibers in the brain. It is characterized by the absence or reduction of cell structures that rid the body of toxic substances called peroxisomes. It has a prenatal onset and may be identified by physical characteristics such as unusual craniofacial features, enlarged liver, and a lack of muscle tone. There may also be developmental delays, jaundice, gastrointestinal bleeding, seizures, and an inability to suck (Nelson, Behrman, Kliegman, & Arvin, 1996).

Zellweger syndrome is autosomally recessive, so both parents must be carriers. It is found equally in males and females. Diagnosis is made through biochemical blood analyses to detect an accumulation of very long fatty acid chains and reduced or absent peroxisomes (Jones, 1997). It is one of the most severe forms of the leukodystrophies and is typically fatal within six months of diagnosis, which usually occurs at birth. Like most other peroxismal disorders, it can be diagnosed prenatally in the first or second trimester of pregnancy. The same techniques used postnatally to diagnosis the disorder can be used to find it prenatally (Nelson et al., 1996).

Characteristics

1. Prenatal and postnatal growth failure and failure to thrive
2. Craniofacial anomalies including low-set ears, high forehead, large fontanels, epicanthic folds in the skin extending from the root of the nose, slanted or "Mongoloid"-type eyes, hypertelorism (abnormal distance between the eyes), a shallow orbital ridge, broad nasal ridge, cataracts or cloudy corneas, a redundant neck skin fold, and cleft palate
3. Limb anomalies including the lateral deviation of the forearm (cubitus valgus), campodactyly or the permanent flexation of fingers or toes, transverse palmar crease and talipes equinovarus (clubfoot)
4. Hypotonia or poor muscle tone and poor or no sucking ability
5. Enlarged liver and jaundice
6. Postnatal seizures
7. Severe mental and motor developmental delays

There is currently no cure for Zellweger syndrome, so treatment is symptomatic and supportive. Death is usually the result of gastrointestinal bleeding, liver failure, or respiratory distress.

There is no research on educational implications of this disorder, as few of its victims survive long enough to attend school.

REFERENCES

Jones, K. L. (1997). *Smith's recognizable patterns of human malformation* (5th ed.). Philadelphia, PA: W. B. Saunders.

Nelson, W. E., Behrman, R. E., Kliegman, R. M., & Arvin, A. M. (1996). *Nelson textbook of pediatrics* (15th ed.). Philadelphia, PA: W. B. Saunders.

CAROL SCHMITT
San Diego Unified School District

CERTIFICATION/LICENSURE ISSUES

With only a few exceptions, the issues and standards involving special education programs do not differ from those that apply to teacher education programs nationwide. These issues include teacher testing, the use of teaching personnel having college degrees but lacking teacher preparation courses, standards used to approve teacher education programs, and state certification requirements.

These issues are now magnified with the concept of "highly qualified special education teacher" mandates put forth in the revision of IDEA, the Individuals with Disabilities Education Improvement Act of 2004 (IDEIA).

A number of states have moved toward, or implemented, the use of tests as part of the certification process. Some states require a test of basic skills prior to entering a teacher education program (e.g., California, Missouri) while other states require teachers to achieve a passing score on a content area test. It has been suggested that such tests will have a significant impact on the qualifications of individuals desiring to become teachers, particularly minority populations (Feistritzer, 1983). Feistritzer (1983) has suggested that the number of minority candidates entering teacher preparation programs has declined considerably in recent years. The Center for Minority Research in Special Education (COMRISE; 1998, 2005) is attempting to increase the number and research capacity of minority scholars in institutions of higher education with high minority enrollments and is trying to improve the quality and effectiveness of these programs.

An issue that has importance to special education is that of appropriate certification in the actual field of teaching. While most teachers are certified to teach in some field, not all teachers have been trained and certified to teach in the field to which they are assigned. For example, large numbers of special education teachers are not certified in special education or are not teaching the types of disabled children and youths for which they hold a special education certificate. Thus teachers who are qualified to teach nondisabled children in elementary schools may be teaching learning-disabled, emotionally disturbed, or some other type of disabled children. While emergency, temporary, or provisional certificates permit regular education teachers to teach disabled learners, there is some question as to whether this constitutes the most appropriate and effective instruction for these students. An analysis of the changes made in the past 25 years to special education coursework for regular educators seeking recertification shows dramatic advances (Patton & Braithwaite, 1990).

Many teacher-training programs are competency based and result in program graduates receiving generic teaching licenses or endorsements. While this affords local school districts considerable flexibility for serving students, there is concern that distinct differences exist among differing handicapping conditions that cannot be met through the preparation of a generic teacher. While the needs of some students with disabilities can be served using generic teaching personnel, the use of resource rooms for some learners (learning disabled, etc.) often results in placement with a noncategorically certified teacher rather than a teacher who holds a categorical (learning disabled, etc.) certificate.

Certification and licensure are also affected by supply and demand. In the past, special education teachers have been in short supply and the use of temporary or provisional certificates, as noted earlier, became common. This led to the development of teacher preparation programs that prepare teachers to meet temporary endorsement requirements as well as to meet full certification requirements. In many respects, programs become defined by the certification standards they parallel and are not being designed to promote excellence. Teachers, or prospective teachers, tend to enroll in programs that most expeditiously meet the minimum standards necessary for them to maintain or gain employment. For this reason, preparation programs in competitive situations (i.e., with other institutions of higher education) may feel compelled to meet minimum training requirements, which in turn become maximum training requirements.

The development of inclusionary education has changed the requirements of teacher preparation from a focus of individual mastery to a consultation/collaboration format. The inclusion of special education students in the regular classroom has mandated teacher preparation to prepare students for collaborative teaching arrangements (Campbell & Fyfe, 1995). Programs that involve students in practicum supervision involving regular-education cooperating teachers, special-education cooperating teachers, and university supervisors are growing in number (Ludlow, Wienke, Henderson, & Klein, 1998). The reflection of educational service delivery trends such as inclusion in teacher preparation, however, is not uniform and assessing competency is difficult at best.

Current issues now remain with the fulfillment of IDEIA requirements that require a bachelor's degree, a state special education license non-waived licensure (not temporary or provisional), responsibility to provide consultative services to a care-content highly qualified teacher, and passing of a state test in subjects of the basic school curriculum (NEA, 2005).

REFERENCES

Campbell, D. M., & Fyfe, B. (1995, February 12). *Reforming teacher education: The challenge of inclusive education.* Paper presented at the Annual Meeting of the Association of Independent Liberal Arts Colleges for Teacher Education, Washington, DC.

COMRISE. (1998). *Center for Minority Research in Special Education.* Charlottesville: University of Virginia, Curry School of Education.

COMRISE. (2005). *Center for Minority Research in Special Education.* Retrieved from http://curry.virginia.edu/

Feistritzer, C. E. (1983). *The condition of teaching.* Lawrenceville, NJ: Princeton University Press.

Ludlow, B. L., Wienke, W. D., Henderson, J., & Klein, H. (1998, March 25–28). A collaborative program to prepare mainstream teachers: Using peer supervision by general and special educators. In American Council on Rural Special Education Conference Proceedings, *Coming together: Preparing for Rural Special Education in the 21st Century.*

National Education Association (NEA). (2005). Highly qualified definition for special education teachers. Retrieved from http://www.nea.org/home/19162.htm

Patton, J. M., & Braithwaite, R. (1990). Special education certification/recertification for regular educators. *Journal of Special Education, 24*, 117–124.

PATRICIA ANN ABRAMSON
*Hudson Public Schools,
Hudson, Wisconsin*

See *also*; Professional Standards for Special Educators

CHALFANT, JAMES C. (1932–   )

A native of Fremont, Ohio, James Chalfant obtained his BS in 1954, MS in 1958, and Ed.D in 1965 from the University of Illinois. Early in his career, Chalfant's interest focused on an integrated training program for children with Down syndrome. Made available by the state of Illinois to all teachers of children with Down syndrome, the program involved intensive behavior shaping of self-help skills and the development of language, motor, and social skills (Chalfant, Silikovitz, & Tawney, 1977).

Chalfant is also noted for his extensive work on the development of teacher assistance teams, a team problem-solving model designed to assist and support individual teachers in managing situations for which the teacher needed additional help that was otherwise unavailable (Chalfant & Pysh, 1982). This work is detailed in a chapter written by Chalfant in *Critical Issues in Gifted Education: Programs for the Gifted in Regular Classrooms* (1993).

During his distinguished career, Chalfant has been head of the Division of Special Education, Rehabilitation, and School Psychology at the University of Arizona, where he remains an active researcher and teacher with the rank of full professor. His most current research involves the study of self-concept in the visually impaired, and he teaches courses in learning disabilities, program development/service delivery, self-esteem, and cognitive abilities.

Chalfant was a member of a U.S. Department of Education task force focusing on issues and practices related to the identification of students with learning disabilities, and he was honored with a Presidential Citation for Outstanding Services for his work with the U.S. Office of Education's Division of Handicapped Children and Youth. Chalfant is also the recipient of the Award of Honor of the South African Association for Children with Learning Disabilities as "the international educator who has most influenced the field of learning disabilities in South Africa."

REFERENCES

Chalfant, J. C. (1993). Teacher assistance teams: Implications for the gifted. In C. J. Maker (Ed.), *Critical issues in gifted education: Programs for the gifted in regular classrooms*. Austin, TX: PRO-ED.

Chalfant, J. C., & Pysh, M. V. (1982). *Teacher assistance teams: A procedure for supporting classroom teachers* (filmstrip; audiocassette; handout). New Rochelle, NY: Pem Press/Pathescope Educational Media.

Chalfant, J. C., Silikovitz, R. G., & Tawney, J. W. (1977). *Systematic instruction for retarded children: The Illinois program*. Danville, IL: Interstate.

E. VALERIE HEWITT
*Texas A&M University
First edition*

TAMARA J. MARTIN
*University of Texas of the Permian Basin
Second edition*

CHALL, JEANNE S. (1921–1999)

Jeanne S. Chall earned her BBA from the City College of New York in 1941. She went on to do her graduate work at Ohio State University, receiving her PhD in 1952. Chall taught at the City College of the City University of New York for 15 years. She joined the faculty at Harvard in 1965.

Chall became a leading expert in reading research and instruction during her time there. Dr. Chall was professor emerita at the Graduate School of Education (GSE) when she died on November 27, 1999. At Harvard, she founded the Harvard Reading Laboratory in 1966 and directed the lab for more than 20 years. She trained legions of researchers, reading teachers, and policy experts. Chall was called upon by a succession of U.S. presidents and secretaries of education to bring her wisdom to national literacy efforts.

Chall served on numerous national committees and acted in a consulting capacity to various government education agencies. In addition, she was a member of the editorial boards of several journals in the fields of reading, education, and educational psychology, including *Reading Research Quarterly* and the *Journal of Educational Psychology*. Three major books on reading have been authored by Chall, one currently in its third edition (1967, 1983a, 1983b, 1996a, 1996b). In earlier work, she authored two columns on the readability of instructional materials. She also published diagnostic instruments to aid in the diagnosis of reading and other language-related disorders. The *Roswell-Chall Diagnostic Reading Test of Word Analysis Skills* (1997) is the most notable of these instruments.

Chall published widely on readability of instructional materials and other texts, co-authoring the Dale-Chall formula in 1948 and the New Dale-Chall formula in 1996. In 1996, she wrote a book entitled *Qualitative Assessment of Text Difficulty: A Practical Guide for Teachers and Writers*.

In addition to her diagnostic instruments, Chall's major contributions to the field of special education were her research in reading and learning disabilities and in teacher training in these closely related areas. She received many honors for her outstanding achievements. In 1979, Chall was elected to the Reading Hall of Fame and the National Academy of Education. In 1982, Chall received both the American Educational Research Association Award for Distinguished Contributions to Research in Education and the American Psychological Association Edward L. Thorndike Award for Educational Psychology. In 1996, she received the Samuel T. Orton Award from the Orton Dyslexia Society. In the weeks before passing away, Chall completed her final volume, *The Academic Achievement Challenge: What Really Works in the Classroom?*, which was published in 2000 by Guilford Press.

REFERENCES

Chall, J. S. (1967, 1983a, 1996a). *Learning to read: The great debate* (3rd ed.). Fort Worth, TX: Harcourt Brace.

Chall, J. S. (1983b, 1996b). *Stages of reading development* (2nd ed.). Fort Worth, TX: Harcourt Brace.

Chall, J. S. (2000). *The academic achievement challenge: What really works in the classroom?* New York, NY: Guilford.

Chall, J. S., Bixxes, G., Conard, S., & Harris-Sharples, S. (1996). *Qualitative assessment of text difficulty: A practical guide for teachers and writers*. Cambridge, MA: Brookline Books.

Chall, J. S. & Dale, E. (1995). *Readability revisited and the New Dale-Chall Readability Formula*. Cambridge, MA: Brookline Books.

Chall, J. S., Jacobs, V. A., & Baldwin, L. E. (1990). *The reading crisis: Why poor children fall behind*. Cambridge, MA: Harvard University Press.

Jeanne Chall, Reading Expert and Psychologist, Dies at Age 78. *Harvard Gazette* archives. Retrieved August 4, 2005, from http://hpac.harvard.edu/

Roswell, F. G., & Chall, J. S. (1997). *Roswell-Chall Diagnostic Test of Word Analysis Skills* (4th ed.). Cambridge, MA: Educators Publishing Company.

KATHRYN A. SULLIVAN
Texas A&M University
First edition

TAMARA J. MARTIN
University of Texas of the Permian Basin
Second edition

RACHEL M. TOPLIS
Falcon School District 49,
   Colorado Springs, Colorado
Third edition

CHANGING CRITERION DESIGN (*See Single Case Research Design*)

CHARCOT-MARIE-TOOTH DISEASE

Charcot-Marie-Tooth disease (CMT) is a genetically heterogeneous group of neuromuscular disorders characterized by slow progressive atrophy; wasting and weakness of the distal limb muscles; sensory loss in the feet, lower legs, and hands; skeletal deformities (i.e., pes cavus); and reduced tendon reflexes (Tabaraud et al., 1999). The disease was named after three physicians who simultaneously commented on the characteristics in 1886, Howard Henry Tooth of England and Jean Martin Charcot and Pierre Marie from France. Individuals with CMT have difficulty walking and often fall and sprain their ankles. This is often the result of leg weakness. Hand weakness often results in problems with fine motor control, causing difficulty in writing, buttoning clothes, and manipulating small objects. Tendon atrophy further causes problems with foot drop and exaggerated leg lifting (i.e., to clear the ground). Pain is uncommon, but loss of sensation is frequently reported.

CMT is usually divided into two types in which the neuropathy is either demyelinating (CMT Type 1) or axonal (CMT Type 2; Birouk et al., 1998). Three major subtypes of CMT Type 1 have been identified and located on Chromosomes 1 and 17 and the X chromosome. As yet, no gene locus has been identified for CMT Type 2. Onset is typically in the first two decades of life; however, CMT Type 2 is usually diagnosed later than Type 1, and Type 1 is diagnosed in late childhood and adolescence. Severity is highly variable, and severe impairment is rare. Unlike many other neuromuscular diseases CMT has no effect on intellectual functioning and does not shorten life expectancy.

CMT is one of the most common hereditary neuromuscular disorders with an estimated frequency of 1 in 2,500. CMT Type 1 and CMT Type 2 are autosomal dominant disorders, whereas CMT Type 1, resulting from a defect in a gene located on the X chromosome, is an X-linked dominant disorder (Pareyson, 1999).

Characteristics

1. Onset is typically in the first 2 decades of life.
2. Initial feature of disease is foot abnormalities such as a high arch and flexed toes.
3. Foot muscle weakness causes falls, ankle sprains, and skeletal deformity.
4. Foot drop results in a steppage gait in which the foot must be raised.

5. Hand weakness results in poor fine motor control.
6. CMT has no known effect on intellectual functioning or life span expectancy.

There is no cure for CMT, and treatment is limited to symptom relief. Physical therapy, braces, shoe inserts, and surgery are some treatment options. Physical therapy focuses on heel cord stretching exercises to prevent the Achilles tendon from shortening. Braces and shoe inserts help maintain proper foot and leg alignment and can hold the foot at a 90-degree angle in order to help keep toes from dragging when walking. If the entire lower leg is affected, braces that extend above the knee are used to give adequate support. When foot deformity is severe, surgery is used. Surgery is also an option for correcting scoliosis of the spine. Occupational therapy, like vocational therapy, may be appropriate for some individuals to maximize independent functioning.

Educational considerations for children afflicted with CMT should focus on the physical impairments of the disease. Although special education is rarely needed, classroom accommodations may be necessary to address problems with small motor coordination and mobility. Amelioration of poor small motor coordination due to weakness or tremors of the hands may be achieved through the use of assistive technology devices. Physical education would likely require monitoring and possible modification due to the high probability of injury. In the case of a severe impairment, physical education may have to be eliminated or significantly adapted.

Most individuals diagnosed with CMT live a relatively normal life; however, depending on the severity and age of onset, the disease can cause eventual disability. Long-term prognosis is therefore poor due to the slow, progressive nature of the disease.

Research on the genetic transmission of the disease is ongoing, including the locus of CMT subtypes. Further information is needed to better understand the process of myelin formation and demyelination in the peripheral nervous system. Work is also being done in developing techniques for early diagnosis in order to develop drug therapies to preserve and restore structure and function of nerve fibers (and their myelin sheaths).

REFERENCES

Birouk, N., LeGuern, E., Maisonobe, T., Rouger, H., Gouider, R., Tardieu, S., ... Bouch, P. (1998). X-linked Charcot-Marie-Tooth disease with connexin 32 mutations. *Neurology, 40*(10), 1061–1067.

Pareyson, D. (1999). Charcot-Marie-Tooth disease and related neuropathies: Molecular basis for distinction and diagnosis. *Muscle and Nerve, 22*(11), 1498–1509.

Tabaraud, F., Lagrange, E., Sindou, P., Vandenbuerghe, A., Levy, N., & Vallat, J. M. (1999). Demyelinating X-linked Charcot-Marie-Tooth disease: Unusual electrophysiological findings. *Muscle and Nerve, 22*(10), 1442–1447.

LORI DEKEYZER
ELAINE CLARK
University of Utah

See also Neuropathy, Hereditary Motor and Sensory, Type I; Neuropathy, Hereditary Motor and Sensory, Type II

CHC CROSS-BATTERY APPROACH, THE

The Cattell-Horn-Carroll (CHC) Cross-Battery approach (hereafter referred to as the XBA approach) was introduced by Flanagan and her colleagues in the late 1990s (Flanagan & McGrew, 1997; Flanagan, McGrew, & Ortiz, 2000; McGrew & Flanagan, 1998; Ortiz & Flanagan, 2002). The XBA approach provides practitioners with the means to make systematic, valid, and *up-to-date* interpretations of intelligence batteries and to augment them with other tests in a way that is consistent with the empirically supported CHC theory of cognitive abilities. Moving beyond the boundaries of a single intelligence *test kit* by adopting the psychometrically and theoretically defensible XBA principles and procedures represents a significantly improved method of measuring cognitive abilities (Carroll, 1998; Kaufman, 2000).

According to Carroll (1997), the CHC taxonomy of human cognitive abilities "appears to prescribe that individuals should be assessed with respect to the *total range* of abilities the theory specifies" (p. 129). However, because Carroll recognized that "any such prescription would of course create enormous problems," he indicated that "[r]esearch is needed to spell out how the assessor can select what abilities need to be tested in particular cases" (p. 129). Flanagan and colleagues' XBA approach was developed specifically to "spell out" how practitioners can conduct assessments that approximate the total range of broad cognitive abilities more adequately than what is possible with most single intelligence batteries. In a review of the XBA approach, Carroll (1998) stated that it "can be used to develop the most appropriate information about an individual in a given testing situation" (p. xi). In Kaufman's (2000) review of the XBA, he stated that the approach is based on sound assessment principles, adds theory to psychometrics, and improves the quality of the assessment and interpretation of cognitive abilities and processes.

Noteworthy is the fact that the "crossing" of batteries is not a new method of intellectual assessment.

Neuropsychological assessment has long adopted the practice of crossing various standardized tests in an attempt to measure a broader range of brain functions than that offered by any single instrument (Lezak, 1976, 1995). Nevertheless, several problems with crossing batteries have plagued assessment-related fields for years. Many of these problems have been circumvented by Flanagan and colleagues' XBA approach (see Table C.17 for examples). But unlike the XBA model, the various so-called "cross-battery" techniques applied within the field of neuropsychological assessment, for example, are not grounded in a systematic approach that is both psychometrically and theoretically defensible. Thus, as Wilson (1992) cogently pointed out, the field of neuropsychological assessment is in need of an approach that would guide practitioners through the selection of measures that would result in more specific and delineated patterns of function and dysfunction—an approach that provides more clinically useful information than one that is "wedded to the utilization of subscale scores and IQs" (p. 382). Indeed, all fields involved in the assessment of cognitive functioning have some need for an approach that would aid practitioners in their attempt to "touch all of the major cognitive areas, with emphasis on those most suspect on the basis of history, observation, and on-going test findings" (Wilson, 1992, p. 382). The XBA approach represents a quantum leap in this direction. The definition of XBA assessment as well as the *foundation* and *rationale* for and *application* of this approach are described briefly in the following paragraphs.

Definition

The XBA approach is a time-efficient method of cognitive assessment that is grounded in CHC theory and research. It allows practitioners to reliably measure a wider range (or a more in-depth but selective range) of cognitive abilities than that represented by most single intelligence batteries. The XBA approach is based on three foundational sources of information, or three pillars (Flanagan & McGrew, 1997; Flanagan & Ortiz, 2001; Flanagan, Ortiz, & Alfonso, 2006; McGrew & Flanagan, 1998). Together, these pillars provide the knowledge base necessary to organize theory-driven, comprehensive, reliable, and valid assessments of cognitive abilities and processes.

Foundations of the XBA Approach

The first pillar of the XBA approach is CHC theory. This theory was selected to guide assessment and interpretation because it is based on a more thorough network of validity evidence than other contemporary multidimensional ability models of intelligence (see McGrew & Flanagan, 1998; Messick, 1992; Sternberg & Kaufman, 1998). According to Daniel (1997), the strength of the multiple (CHC) cognitive abilities model is that it was arrived at "by synthesizing hundreds of factor analyses conducted over decades by independent researchers using many different collections of tests. Never before has a psychometric ability model been so firmly grounded in data" (pp. 1042–1043). Because the broad and narrow abilities that comprise CHC theory have been defined elsewhere in this book (see Flanagan, this volume), these definitions will not be reiterated here.

The second pillar of the XBA approach is the CHC broad (stratum II) classifications of cognitive and academic ability tests. Specifically, based on the results of a series of cross-battery (or joint) confirmatory factor-analysis studies of the major intelligence batteries and task analyses conducted by many test experts, Flanagan and colleagues classified all the subtests of the major cognitive and achievement batteries according to the particular CHC broad abilities they measured. To date, over 500 CHC broad ability classifications have been made based on the results of these studies. These classifications of cognitive and academic ability tests assist practitioners in identifying measures that assess various aspects of the *broad* abilities represented in CHC theory, such as Fluid Intelligence (*Gf*), Crystallized Intelligence (*Gc*), Short-Term Memory (*Gsm*), and Quantitative Knowledge (*Gq*). Classification of tests at the broad ability level is necessary to improve upon the validity of cognitive assessment and interpretation. Specifically, broad ability classifications ensure that the CHC constructs that underlie assessments are minimally affected by *construct irrelevant variance* (Messick, 1989, 1995). In other words, knowing what tests measure what abilities enables clinicians to organize tests into *construct relevant* clusters—clusters that are less "contaminated" by other constructs because they contain only measures that are *relevant* to the construct or ability of interest.

The third pillar of the XBA approach is the CHC narrow (stratum I) classifications of cognitive and academic ability tests. These classifications were originally reported in McGrew (1997). Subsequently, Flanagan and colleagues provided content validity evidence for the narrow ability classifications underlying the major intelligence and achievement batteries (Flanagan & Ortiz, 2001; Flanagan, Ortiz, & Alfonso, 2006; Flanagan, Ortiz, Alfonso, & Mascolo, 2002, 2006). Use of narrow ability classifications was necessary to ensure that the CHC constructs that underlie assessments are well represented. That is, the narrow ability classifications of tests assist practitioners in combining qualitatively different narrow ability indicators (or tests) of a given broad ability into clusters so that appropriate inferences can be made from test performance. Taken together, the three pillars underlying the XBA approach provide the necessary foundation from which to organize assessments of cognitive and academic abilities that are theoretically driven, comprehensive, and valid.

Table C.17. Parallel Needs in Cognitive Assessment-Related Fields Addressed by the XBA Approach

Need Within Assessment-Related Fields	Need Addressed by the XBA Approach
School Psychology, Clinical Psychology, and Neuropsychology have lagged in the development of conceptual models of the assessment of individuals. There is a need for the development of contemporary models.	The XBA approach provides a contemporary model for measurement and interpretation of cognitive and academic abilities and neuropsychological processes.
It is likely that there is a need for events external to a field of endeavor to give impetus to new developments and real advances in that field.	Carroll and Horn's *Fluid-Crystallized* theoretical models (and more recently Schneider and McGrew's CHC model) and research in cognitive psychology and neuropsychology provided the impetus for and continued refinements to the XBA approach and led to the development of better assessment instruments and interpretive procedures.
There is a need to utilize a conceptual framework to direct any approach to assessment. This would aid in both the selection of instruments and methods, and in the interpretation of test findings.	The XBA approach to assessment is based mainly on CHC theory, but also neuropsychological theory. Since the XBA approach links all the major intelligence and achievement batteries as well as selected neuropsychological instruments to CHC theory, in particular, both selection of tests and interpretation of test findings are made easier.
It is necessary that the conceptual framework or model underlying assessment incorporate various aspects of neuropsychological and cognitive ability function that can be described in terms of constructs that are recognized in the neuropsychological and cognitive psychology literature.	The XBA approach incorporates various aspects of neuropsychological and cognitive ability functions that are described in terms of constructs that are recognized in the literature. In fact, a consistent set of terms and definitions within the CHC literature) and the neuropsychology literature underlie the XBA approach.
There is a need to adopt a conceptual framework that allows for the measurement of the full range of behavioral functions subserved by the brain. Unfortunately, in neuropsychological assessment there is no inclusive set of measures that is standardized on a single normative population.	XBA assessment allows for the measurement of a wide range of broad and narrow cognitive abilities specified in CHC theory and neuropsychological processes specified by neuropsychology theory and research. Although an XBA norm group does not exist, the crossing of batteries and the interpretation of assessment results are based on sound psychometric principles and procedures.
Because there are no truly unidimensional measures in psychological assessment, there is a need to select subtests from standardized instruments that appear to reflect the neurocognitive function of interest. In neuropsychological assessment, the aim, therefore, is to select those measures that, on the basis of careful task analysis, appear mainly to tap a given construct.	The XBA approach is defined in part by a CHC classification system. The majority of subtests from the major intelligence and achievement batteries as well as selected neuropsychological instruments were classified empirically as measures of broad and narrow CHC constructs (either via CHC within- or cross-battery factor analysis or expert consensus or both). In addition, the subtests of intelligence and neuropsychological batteries were classified according to several neuropsychological domains (e.g., attention, visual-spatial, auditory-verbal, speed and efficiency, executive). Use of evidence-based classifications allows practitioners to be reasonably confident that a given test taps a given construct.
It is clear that an eclectic approach is needed in the selection of measures, preferably subtests rather that the omnibus IQs, in order to gain more specificity in the delineation of patterns of function and dysfunction.	The XBA approach ensures that two or more relatively pure, but qualitatively different, indicators of each *broad* cognitive ability are represented in a complete assessment. Two or more qualitatively similar indicators are necessary to make inferences about specific or *narrow* CHC abilities. This process is eclectic in its selection of measures.
There is a need to solve the potential problems that can arise from crossing normative groups as well as sets of measures that vary in reliability.	In the XBA approach, one can typically achieve baseline data in cognitive functioning across seven to nine CHC broad abilities through the use of only two well-standardized batteries, which minimizes the effects of error due to norming differences. Also, since interpretation of both broad and narrow CHC abilities is made at the cluster (rather than subtest) level, issues related to low reliability are less problematic in this approach. Finally, because cross-battery clusters are generated using estimated median reliabilities and intercorrelations, the data yielded by this approach are psychometrically sound.

Information obtained in part from Wilson (1992, pp. 377–394).

Rationale for the CHC Cross-Battery Approach

The XBA approach has significant implications for practice, research, and test development. A brief discussion of these implications follows.

Practice

The XBA approach provides "a much needed and updated bridge between current intellectual theory and research and practice" (Flanagan & McGrew, 1997, p. 322). The results of several joint factor analyses conducted over the past 10+ years demonstrated that none of our intelligence batteries contained measures that sufficiently approximated the full range of *broad* abilities that define the structure of intelligence specified in contemporary psychometric theory (e.g., Carroll, 1993; Horn, 1991; Keith, Kranzler, & Flanagan, 2001; McGrew, 1997; Phelps, McGrew,

Knopik, & Ford, 2005; Woodcock, 1990). Indeed, the joint factor analyses conducted by Woodcock (1990) suggested that it may be necessary to "cross" batteries to measure a broader range of cognitive abilities than that provided by a single intelligence battery.

The findings of these joint factor analyses of intelligence batteries that were published before 1998 are presented in Table C.18. As may be seen in this table, most batteries fall far short of measuring all seven of the broad cognitive abilities listed. Of the major intelligence batteries in use prior to 1998, most failed to measure three or more broad CHC abilities (viz., *Ga, Glr, Gf, Gs*) that were (and are) considered important in understanding and predicting school achievement. In fact, *Gf*, often considered to be the *essence* of intelligence, was either not measured or not measured adequately by most of the intelligence batteries included in Table C.18 (i.e., WISC-III, WAIS-R, WPPSI-R, K-ABC, and CAS).

Table C.18. Comparing the Representation of Broad CHC Abilities on Nine Intelligence Batteries Published Before and After 2000

Test before 2000/ Test after 2000	Gf		Gc		Gv		Gsm		Glr		Ga		Gs	
	< 2000	2000 >	< 2000	2000 >	< 2000	2000 >	< 2000	2000 >	< 2000	2000 >	< 2000	2000 >	< 2000	2000 >
WISC-III/ WISC-IV	✗	✓	✓	✓	✓	✓	●	✓	✗	✗	✗	✗	✓	✓
WAIS-R/ WAIS-IV	✗	✓	✓	✓	✓	✓	●	✓	✗	✗	✗	✗	●	✓
WPPSI-R/ WPPSI-III	✗	●	✓	✓	✓	✓	●	✗	✗	✗	✗	✗	●	✓
KAIT	✓		✓		●		✗		✓		✗		✗	
K-ABC/ KABC-II	●	✓	✗	✓	✓	✓	●	✓	✗	✓	✗	✗	✗	✗
CAS	✗		✗		✓		●		✗		✗		✓	
DAS/ DAS-II	✓	✓	✓	✓	✓	✓	●	✓	●	✓	✗	●	●	✓
WJ-R/ WJ-III	✓	✓	●	✓	✓	✓	●	✓	●	✓	●	✓	●	●
SB:FE/ SB5	✓	✓	✓	✓	✓	✓	●	✓	✗	✗	✗	✗	✗	✗

✓ – Adequately measured
● – Underrepresented
✗ – Not measured

Note. WISC-III = Wechsler Intelligence Scale for Children-Third Edition (Wechsler, 1991); WAIS-R = Wechsler Adult Intelligence Scale-Revised (Wechsler, 1981); WPPSI-R = Wechsler Preschool and Primary Scale of Intelligence-Revised (Wechsler, 1989); KAIT = Kaufman Adolescent and Adult Intelligence Test (Kaufman & Kaufman 1993); K-ABC = Kaufman Assessment Battery for Children (Kaufman & Kaufman, 1983); CAS = Cognitive Assessment System (Das & Naglieri, 1997); DAS = Differential Ability Scales (Elliott, 1990); WJ-R = Woodcock-Johnson Psycho-Educational Battery-Revised (Woodcock & Johnson, 1989); SB:FE = Stanford-Binet Intelligence Scale-Fourth Edition (Thorndike, Hagen, & Sattler, 1986).

The finding that the abilities *not measured* by the intelligence batteries listed in Table C.18 are *important in understanding children's learning difficulties* provided the impetus for developing the XBA approach. In effect, the XBA approach was developed to systematically replace the dashes in Table C.18 with tests from another battery. As such, this approach guides practitioners in the selection of tests, both core and supplemental, that together provide measurement of abilities that is considered sufficient in both breadth and depth for the purpose of addressing referral concerns.

Another benefit of the XBA approach is that it facilitates communication among professionals. Most scientific disciplines have a standard nomenclature (i.e., a common set of terms and definitions) that facilitates communication and guards against misinterpretation. For example, the standard nomenclature in chemistry is reflected in the *Periodic Table;* in biology, it is reflected in the classification of animals according to phyla; in psychology and psychiatry, it is reflected in the *Diagnostic and Statistical Manual of Mental Disorders;* and in medicine, it is reflected in the *International Classification of Diseases.* Underlying the XBA approach is a standard nomenclature or *Table of Human Cognitive Abilities* that includes classifications of over 500 tests according to the broad and narrow CHC abilities they measure (see also Flanagan & Ortiz, 2001; Flanagan, Ortiz, & Alfonso, 2006; Flanagan et al., 2006). The XBA classification system has had a positive impact on communication among practitioners, has improved research on the relations between cognitive and academic abilities, and has resulted in substantial improvements in the measurement of cognitive constructs, as may be seen in the design and structure of current intelligence tests.

Finally, the XBA approach offers practitioners a psychometrically defensible means to identifying population-relative (or normative) strengths and weaknesses. According to Brackett and McPherson (1996), "the limited capacity of standardized instruments to assess isolated cognitive processes creates a major weakness in intracognitive discrepancy models. Although analysis of [Wechsler] subtests typically report measures of distinct cognitive abilities, such abilities may not emerge by individual subtests but rather in combination with other subtests" (p. 79). The XBA approach addresses this limitation. By focusing interpretations on cognitive ability clusters (i.e., combination of subtests) that contain qualitatively different indicators of each broad CHC cognitive ability (or process), the identification of normative processing strengths and weaknesses via XBA procedures is both psychometrically defensible and theoretically sound. In sum, the XBA approach addresses the longstanding need within the entire field of assessment, from learning disabilities to neuropsychological assessment, for methods that "provide a greater range of information about the ways individuals learn—the ways individuals receive, store, integrate, and express information" (Brackett & McPherson, 1996, p. 80).

Research

The XBA approach was also developed to promote a greater understanding of the relationship between cognitive abilities and important outcome criteria. Because XBA assessments are based on the empirically supported CHC theory and constructed in a psychometrically defensible manner, they represent a valid means of measuring cognitive constructs (Flanagan, 2000; Phelps et al., 2005). It is noteworthy that when second-order constructs are composed of (moderately) correlated but qualitatively distinct measures, they will tend to have higher correlations with complex criteria (e.g., academic achievement), as compared to lower-order constructs, because they are broader in what they measure (Comrey, 1988). Predictive statements about different achievements (i.e., criterion-related inferences) that are made from XBA clusters are based on a more solid foundation than individual subtests (and perhaps some global scores from single intelligence batteries) because the predictor constructs are represented by relatively pure and qualitatively distinct measures of broad CHC abilities. Thus, improving the validity of CHC ability measures has further elucidated the relations between CHC cognitive abilities and processes and different achievement and vocational/occupational outcomes (e.g., Flanagan, 2000; McGrew, Flanagan, Keith, & Vanderwood, 1997).

Test Development

Although there was substantial evidence of at least eight or nine broad cognitive CHC abilities by the late 1980s, the tests of the time did not reflect this diversity in measurement. For example, Table C.18 shows that the WPPSI-R, K-ABC, KAIT, WAIS-R, and CAS batteries only measured 2 to 3 broad CHC abilities adequately. The WPPSI-R primarily measured *Gv* and *Gc*. The K-ABC primarily measured *Gv* and *Gsm*, and to a much lesser extent *Gf*, while the KAIT primarily measured *Gc* and *Glr*, and to a much lesser extent *Gf* and *Gv*. The CAS measured *Gs, Gsm,* and *Gv*. Finally, while the DAS, SB:IV, and WISC-III did not provide sufficient coverage of abilities to narrow the gap between contemporary theory and practice, their comprehensive measurement of approximately four CHC abilities was nonetheless an improvement over the aforementioned batteries. Table C.18 shows that only the WJ-R included measures of all broad cognitive abilities listed in the table. Nevertheless, most of the broad abilities were not measured adequately by the WJ-R (Alfonso, Flanagan, & Radwan, 2005; McGrew & Flanagan, 1998).

In general, Table C.18 shows that *Gf, Gsm, Glr, Ga,* and *Gs* were not measured well by the majority of intelligence tests published prior to 1998. Therefore, it is clear that most test authors did not use contemporary psychometric theories of the structure of cognitive abilities to guide the development of their intelligence tests. As such, a substantial *theory–practice gap* existed—that is, theories of the structure of cognitive abilities were far in advance of the instruments used to operationalize them. In fact, prior to the mid-1980s, theory seldom played a role in intelligence-test development. The numerous dashes in Table C.18 exemplify the theory–practice gap that existed in the field of intellectual assessment at that time (Alfonso et al., 2005).

In the past decade, *Gf-Gc* theory, and more recently CHC theory, has had a significant impact on the revision of old and development of new intelligence batteries. For example, a wider range of broad and narrow abilities is represented on current intelligence batteries than that represented on previous editions of these tests. Table C.19 provides several salient examples of the impact that CHC theory and XBA classifications has had on intelligence-test development over the past 2 decades. This table lists the major intelligence tests in the order in which they were revised, beginning with those tests with the greatest number of years between revisions (i.e., KABC) and ending with newly developed tests and tests that have yet to be revised (e.g., WRIT and DAS, respectively). As is obvious from a review of Table C.19, CHC theory and XBA classifications have had a significant impact on recent test development.

Of the seven intelligence batteries (including both comprehensive and brief measures) that were published since 1998, the test authors of three clearly used CHC theory and XBA classifications as a blueprint for test development (i.e., WJ III, SB5, KABC-II); and the test authors of two were obviously influenced by CHC theory (i.e., RIAS and WRIT). Only the authors of the Wechsler Scales (i.e., WPPSI-III, WISC-IV, and WAIS-III) did not state explicitly that CHC theory was used as a guide for revision. Nevertheless, these authors acknowledged the research of Cattell, Horn, and Carroll in their most recent manuals (Wechsler, 2002, 2003). Presently, as Table C.19 shows, nearly all intelligence batteries that are used with some regularity subscribe either explicitly or implicitly to CHC theory.

Convergence toward the incorporation of CHC theory is also seen clearly in Table C.20. This table is identical to Table C.18 except it also includes the subtests from the most recent revisions of the tests from Table C.19. A review of Table C.20, which includes all intelligence batteries that were published after 1998, shows that many of the gaps in measurement of broad cognitive abilities have been filled. Specifically, the majority of tests published after 1998 now measure four to five broad cognitive abilities adequately (see Table C.20), as compared to two to three (see Table C.18). For example, Table C.20 shows that the WISC-IV, WAIS-III, WPPSI-III, KABC-II, and SB5 measure four to five broad CHC abilities. The WISC-IV measures *Gf, Gc,*

Gv, Gsm, and *Gs,* while the KABC-II measures *Gf, Gc, Gv, Gsm,* and *Glr.* The WAIS-III measures *Gc, Gv, Gsm,* and *Gs* adequately, and to a lesser extent *Gf,* while the WPPSI-III measures *Gf, Gc, Gv,* and *Gs* adequately. Finally, the SB5 measures four CHC broad abilities (i.e., *Gf, Gc, Gv, Gsm;* cf. Alfonso et al., 2005).

Table C.20 shows that the WJ III continues to include measures of all the major broad cognitive abilities and now measures these abilities well, particularly when it is used in conjunction with the Diagnostic Supplement (DS; Woodcock, McGrew, & Schrank, 2003). Third, a comparison of Tables C.18 and C.19 indicates that two broad abilities not measured by many intelligence batteries prior to 1998 are now measured by the majority of intelligence batteries available today: that is, *Gf* and *Gsm.* These broad abilities may be better represented on revised and new intelligence batteries because of the accumulating research evidence regarding their importance in overall academic success (see Flanagan et al., 2006, for a review). Finally, Table C.20 reveals that intelligence batteries continue to fall short in their measurement of three CHC broad abilities: specifically, *Glr, Ga,* and *Gs.* Thus, although there is greater coverage of CHC broad abilities now than there was just a few years ago, the need for the XBA approach to assessment remains (Alfonso et al., 2005).

Application of the XBA Approach

Guiding Principles

In order to ensure that XBA procedures are psychometrically and theoretically sound, it is recommended that practitioners adhere to several guiding principles. These principles are defined briefly in the following paragraphs.

First, select a comprehensive intelligence battery as your core battery in assessment. It is expected that the battery of choice will be one that is deemed most responsive to referral concerns. These batteries may include, but are certainly not limited to the Wechsler Scales, WJ III, SB5, and KABC-II. It is important to note that the use of co-normed tests, such as the WJ III tests of cognitive ability and tests of achievement and the KABC-II and KTEA-II, may allow for the widest coverage of broad and narrow CHC abilities and processes.

Second, use subtests and *clusters/composites* from a single battery whenever possible to represent broad CHC abilities. In other words, best practices involve using actual norms whenever they are available in lieu of arithmetic averages of scaled scores from different batteries. In the past, it was necessary to convert subtest scaled scores from different batteries to a common metric and then average them (after determining that there was a nonsignificant difference between the scores) in order to build construct-relevant broad CHC ability clusters. Because the development of current intelligence batteries benefited greatly from current theory and research, this practice is

Table C.19. Impact of CHC Theory and XBA CHC Classifications on Intelligence Test Development

Test (Year of Publication) CHC and XBA Impact	Revision (Year of Publication) CHC and XBA Impact
K-ABC (1983) No obvious impact.	KABC-II (2004) Provided a second global score that included fluid and crystallized abilities; included several new subtests measuring reasoning; interpretation of test performance may be based on CHC theory or Luria's theory; provided assessment of five CHC broad abilities.
SB:FE (1986) Used a three-level hierarchical model of the structure of cognitive abilities to guide construction of the test; the top level included general reasoning factor (*g*); the middle level included three broad factors called crystallized abilities, fluid-analytic abilities, and short-term memory; the third level included more specific factors including verbal reasoning, quantitative reasoning, and abstract/visual reasoning.	SB5 (2003) Used CHC theory to guide test development; increased the number of broad factors from 4 to 5; included a Working Memory Factor based on research indicating its importance for academic success.
WPPSI-R (1989) No obvious impact.	WPPSI-III (2002) Incorporated measures of Processing Speed that yielded a Processing Speed Quotient based on recent research indicating the importance of processing speed for early academic success; enhanced the measurement of fluid reasoning by adding the Matrix Reasoning and Picture Concepts subtests.
WJ-R (1989) Used modern *Gf-Gc* theory as the cognitive model for test development; included two measures of each of eight broad abilities.	WJ III (2001; Normative Update, 2007) Used CHC theory as a blueprint for test development; included two or three qualitatively different narrow abilities for each broad ability; the combined cognitive and achievement batteries of the WJ III include 9 of the 10 broad abilities subsumed in CHC theory.
WISC-III (1991) No obvious impact.	WISC-IV (2003) Eliminated Verbal and Performance IQs; replaced the Freedom from Distractibility Index with the Working Memory Index; replaced the Perceptual Organization Index with the Perceptual Reasoning Index; enhanced the measurement of fluid reasoning by adding Matrix Reasoning and Picture Concepts; enhanced measurement of Processing Speed with the Cancellation subtest.
DAS (1990) No obvious impact.	DAS-II (2007) CHC broad abilities are represented in the DAS-II subtests and composites.
WAIS-III (1997) No obvious impact.	WAIS-IV (2008) Eliminated Verbal and Performance IQs; replaced the Perceptual Organization Index with the Perceptual Reasoning Index; enhanced the measurement of fluid reasoning by adding the Figure Weights and Visual Puzzles subtests; enhanced measurement of Processing Speed with the Cancellation subtest; enhanced measurement of memory with the Working Memory Index.
WPPSI-III (2002) Incorporated measures of Processing Speed that yielded a Processing Speed Quotient based on recent research indicating the importance of processing speed for early academic success; enhanced the measurement of fluid reasoning by adding the Matrix Reasoning and Picture Concepts subtests.	WPPSI-IV (2012) Eliminated Verbal and Performance IQs; enhanced measures of working memory, processing speed, and inhibitory control; updated studies on the relationship to other measures, including WPPSI–III, WISC–IV, Bayley-III, DAS-II, WIAT-III, and select NEPSY-2 subtests, indicating the importance of understanding how these abilities are interrelated.

Note. K-ABC = Kaufman Assessment Battery for Children (Kaufman & Kaufman, 1983); KABC-II = Kaufman Assessment Battery for Children-Second Edition (Kaufman & Kaufman, 2004); SB:FE = Stanford-Binet Intelligence Scale-Fourth Edition (Thorndike, Hagen, & Sattler, 1986); SB5 = Stanford-Binet Intelligence Scales-Fifth Edition (Roid, 2003); WAIS-III = Wechsler Adult Intelligence Scale-Third Edition (Wechsler, 1997); WAIS-IV = Wechsler Adult Intelligence Scale-Fourth Edition (Wechsler, 2008); WPPSI-R = Wechsler Preschool and Primary Scale of Intelligence-Revised (Wechsler, 1989); WPPSI-III = Wechsler Preschool and Primary Scale of Intelligence-Third Edition (Wechsler, 2002); WJ-R = Woodcock-Johnson Psycho-Educational Battery-Revised (Woodcock & Johnson, 1989); WJ III = Woodcock-Johnson III Tests of Cognitive Abilities (Woodcock, McGrew, & Mather, 2001); WISC-III = Wechsler Intelligence Scale for Children-Third Edition (Wechsler, 1991); WISC-IV = Wechsler Intelligence Scale for Children-Fourth Edition (Wechsler, 2003); KAIT = Kaufman Adolescent and Adult Intelligence Test (Kaufman & Kaufman, 1993); DAS = Differential Ability Scales (Elliott, 1990); DAS-II = Differential Ability Scales-Second Edition (Elliott, 2007).

Table C.20. Narrow *Gq* Stratum I Ability Definitions

Narrow Stratum I Name (Code)	Definition
Quantitative Knowledge (*Gq*)	
Mathematical Knowledge (KM)	Range of general knowledge about mathematics.
Mathematical Achievement (A3)	Measured mathematics achievement.

Note. Definitions were derived from Carroll (1993) and Schneider and McGrew (2012).

seldom necessary at the broad ability level. It continues to be necessary at the narrow ability level and when testing hypotheses about aberrant performance within broad ability domains (see Flanagan, Ortiz, & Alfonso, 2006; Flanagan et al., 2006 for details).

Third, when constructing CHC broad and narrow ability clusters, select tests that have been classified through an acceptable method, such as through CHC theory-driven factor analyses or expert consensus content-validity studies. All test classifications included in the works of Flanagan and colleagues have been classified through these acceptable methods (Flanagan & Ortiz, 2001; Flanagan, Ortiz, & Alfonso, 2006; Flanagan et al., 2006). For example, when constructing broad (stratum II) ability composites or clusters, *relatively pure CHC indicators* should be included (i.e., tests that had either *strong* or *moderate* [but not mixed] loadings on their respective factors in theory-driven within- or cross-battery factor analyses). Furthermore, to ensure appropriate construct representation when constructing broad (stratum II) ability composites, *two or more qualitatively different* narrow (stratum I) ability indicators should be included to represent each domain. Without empirical classifications of tests, constructs may not be adequately represented and, therefore, inferences about an individual's broad (stratum II) ability cannot be made. Of course, the more broadly an ability is represented (i.e., through the derivation of composites based on *multiple* qualitatively different narrow ability indicators), the more confidence one has in drawing inferences about that broad ability underlying a composite. A minimum of two qualitatively different indicators per CHC composite is recommended in the XBA approach for practical reasons (viz., time efficient assessment).

Fourth, when at least two qualitatively different indicators of a broad ability of interest are not available on the core battery, then supplement the core battery with at least two qualitatively different indicators of that broad ability from another battery. In other words, if an evaluator is interested in measuring Auditory Processing (*Ga*), and the core battery includes only one or no *Ga* subtests, then select a *Ga cluster* from another battery to supplement the core battery.

Fifth, when crossing batteries (e.g., augmenting a core battery with relevant CHC clusters from another battery)

or when constructing CHC broad or narrow ability clusters using tests from different batteries (e.g., averaging scores when the broad ability cluster of interest is not available), select tests that were developed and normed within a few years of one another to minimize the effect of spurious differences between test scores that may be attributable to the "Flynn effect" (Flynn, 1984). The XBA worksheets developed by Flanagan and colleagues include only those tests that were normed within 10 years of one another.

Sixth, select tests from the smallest number of batteries to minimize the effect of spurious differences between test scores that may be attributable to differences in the characteristics of independent norm samples (McGrew, 1994). In most cases, using select tests from a single battery to augment the constructs measured by any other major intelligence battery is sufficient to represent the breadth of broad cognitive abilities adequately, as well as to allow for at least three qualitatively different narrow ability indicators of most broad abilities.

Noteworthy is the fact that when the XBA guiding principles are implemented systematically and the recommendations for development, use, and interpretation of clusters are adhered to, the potential error introduced through the crossing of norm groups is negligible (Flanagan & Ortiz, 2001; McGrew & Flanagan, 1998). Furthermore, although there are other limitations to crossing batteries, this systematic approach to the assessment and interpretation of cognitive abilities has far *fewer* implications with regard to the potential for error than those associated with the improper use and interpretation of cognitive performance inherent in traditional assessment approaches (e.g., subtest analysis, discrepancy analysis, atheoretical approaches to assessment and interpretation; see Flanagan, Ortiz, & Alfonso, 2006).

Step-by-Step Process

The XBA approach can be carried out, using any intelligence battery as the core instrument in assessment, following six simple steps. These steps are described in detail in Flanagan and Ortiz (2001); Flanagan, Ortiz, and Alfonso (2006); and Flanagan et al. (2002, 2006), and, therefore, will only be highlighted here.

The first step of the XBA approach involves selecting a battery that is most conducive to a number of variables, including the age of the child, his or her developmental level and proficiency in English, the specific referral concerns, and so forth. As such, while a test like the WJ III may be appropriate for a relatively bright and articulate seventh-grader who is struggling in math and science, it may not be the best instrument of choice for a third-grader who is an English-language learner and who is significantly behind her classmates in all academic areas, despite the fact that the WJ III provides the most comprehensive coverage of CHC abilities. This is because many of the WJ III tests have relatively high and particularly receptive language demands. In the case of this third-grader, an intelligence battery such as the KABC-II may be more appropriate because its language demands and cultural loadings are generally quite low.

The second step of the XBA approach required that the examiner identify the CHC broad abilities that are adequately measured by the core battery. Table C.19 may be useful in this regard. If the battery does not allow for adequate measurement of the broad and narrow abilities considered most germane in light of the referral, then it will be necessary to supplement the core battery.

The third step requires that the examiner select a supplemental battery that includes measurement of all or nearly all of the abilities that are deemed necessary to assess vis-a-vis the referral but are not measured by the core battery. Several examples of how to supplement each of the major intelligence tests to gain a better or more in-depth understanding of CHC broad and narrow abilities can be found in Flanagan, Ortiz, and Alfonso (2006) and Flanagan et al. (2002, 2006).

Step four requires that the examiner administer and score the core and supplemental tests. Step five involves completing the XBA worksheets. While these worksheets may be completed manually, most users prefer the auto-mated versions. Therefore, after administering and scoring the cross-battery assessment, the examiner need only enter scaled scores into an automated worksheet. The many benefits of such a worksheet are described in detail in Flanagan, Ortiz, and Alfonso (2006). The final step, step six, requires that the examiner follow the XBA interpretive guidelines outlined by Flanagan and her colleagues.

Although a step-by-step approach to XBA assessment is available, it is important to understand that the XBA approach is not a "cookbook" method for assessment. The XBA principles, procedures, and steps, as well as the XBA automated worksheets, are intended to guide practitioners *systematically* through the process of test selection and test interpretation in order to maximize the implementation of psychometrically and theoretically defensible evalua-tions. Thus, clinical ingenuity, judgment, and experience remain important and necessary components of compe-tent, defensible, and sound assessment and interpretation practices.

Extending the XBA Approach to Culturally and Linguistically Diverse Populations

As a natural result from efforts to classify tests according to the broad and narrow ability constructs they mea-sure, XBA assessment was extended along additional dimensions that provide applicability to culturally and lin-guistically diverse populations (Flanagan & Ortiz, 2001; Flanagan, Ortiz, & Alfonso, 2006; Ortiz & Flanagan, 2002).

These dimensions, now known as the Culture-Language Test Classifications (C-LTC) and Culture-Language In-terpretive Matrix (C-LIM), center around additional classification of intelligence and special-purpose (i.e., sup-plemental) tests according to two important variables—cultural loading and linguistic demand. *Cultural loading* refers to the degree or extent to which any given test requires culture-specific knowledge that is inherently embedded in tests. Tests vary widely on this basis ranging from those that have high cultural loadings (e.g., Wechsler Information) to those that have relatively low cultural loadings (e.g., KABC-II Triangles).

Similar to cultural loading, *linguistic demand* repre-sents a classification based on the degree or extent to which language or communication is required in order for a given test to be administered to, comprehended by, or responded to by the examinee. Some tests have high language demands (e.g., Wechsler Vocabulary), whereas others have low language demands (e.g., UNIT Cube Design). Note that although some tests can be adminis-tered in a completely nonverbal manner (e.g., pantomime, gestures), some degree of communication is required in order for the examinee to comprehend what is expected (e.g., the nature of the task, when to start, when to stop, when to work quickly) and in what manner an acceptable response is to be given. Thus, all tests have some degree of language (or communication) demands and all tests are culturally loaded to some extent (Sattler, 1992).

Note that test performance is not adversely influenced or biased merely because tests are culturally loaded or make particular language demands. Rather, test perfor-mance may reflect bias only when children are tested who do not meet particular assumptions that accompany psy-chometric testing. Chief among these is the assumption of comparability, which specifies that "the students we test are similar to those on whom the test was standard-ized" (Salvia & Ysseldyke, 1991, p. 18). In other words, we assume that the level of acculturation and linguis-tic history of the students we test are comparable to the students included in the test's normative sample. Differences in experiential histories, particularly those related to level of acculturation and English-language proficiency, represent the greatest threats to the valid-ity of this assumption and thus the validity that may be ascribed to any inferences drawn from test data. For example, because a growing number of school-age chil-dren in the United States are being raised in culturally different or bicultural environments and because they are frequently bilingual (nonnative English speakers), they cannot be presumed to be "comparable" to the individu-als on whom any current tests have been normed. When norms are used that do not control for the effect of cultural and linguistic differences, test performance may be more of a reflection of an individual's level of acculturation or English-language proficiency than the constructs of inter-est (e.g., auditory processing, intelligence) for individuals who are English-language learners and who are not fully acculturated. Thus, careful attention must be paid to these inherent qualities of tests that directly affect performance, and thereby threaten the validity of findings, for individuals whose cultural and linguistic backgrounds differ from the mainstream (Valdés & Figueroa, 1994).

Classifying tests according to degree of cultural loading and degree of linguistic demand and providing a matrix to assist in interpretation of test findings have three fundamental benefits. First, the C-LTC provides a systematic method for the deliberate and careful selection of tests that are low on these dimensions (i.e., cultural loading and linguistic demand), allowing for a better approximation of the true performance of diverse children. In other words, practitioners can use the classifications to select tests that are likely to result in fairer and more accurate estimates of the ability being measured in an individual from a diverse background. Second, the C-LIM organizes obtained data in a way that makes use of the known "pattern" of performance for diverse individuals established over many decades of research. Historically, a pattern of attenuated performance as a function of a test's cultural loading and linguistic demand has been observed (Valdes & Figueroa, 1994). The C-LIM is designed to evaluate the degree to which an individual's test performance follows this historical pattern. When it does, it can be presumed that cultural and linguistic factors were the primary influences on performance and thus the results are not valid and cannot be interpreted as reflections of true intellectual capabilities. When the pattern is absent, it can be presumed that cultural or linguistic factors did not influence test performance adversely and that the findings represent reliable and valid estimates of performance. Thus, the basic question in assessment of diverse individuals (i.e., Is low performance due to differences in culture/language or to a disorder of cognitive deficiency?) can be addressed directly. And third, when it is deemed that culture or language were not the primary factors that affected test performance, subsequent test interpretation continues to be based on current science and modern conceptualizations of intelligence. We do not propose, however, that these extensions of the XBA approach by themselves are sufficient to evaluate the performance of diverse children fairly. On the contrary, we view these extensions as supplemental to the broader assessment process, guiding test selection and interpretation in a manner that may more appropriately meet the needs of diverse populations within the context of a comprehensive, defensible system of nondiscriminatory assessment.

The XBA Approach in Perspective

Although not without its limitations, since its formal introduction to the field, the XBA approach has been well received (e.g., Borgas, 1999; Carroll, 1998; Daniel, 1997; Esters, Ittenbach, & Han, 1997; Genshaft & Gerner, 1998; Kaufman, 2000), and has grown in popularity because of the need for such an approach, particularly in the evaluation of suspected learning disability (e.g., Kavale &

Mostert, 2005). However, like any new approach, especially one that differs markedly from traditional methods, there are often a variety of questions and misconceptions (e.g., practical, psychometric, theoretical, logistical) that arise with respect to its implementation. Table C.20 includes a sampling of a few misconceptions about XBA assessment that have emerged within the past few years along with corresponding clarifications. After reviewing Table C.20 and the many commentaries and articles that have been written about this approach, it should be clear that the XBA approach is a viable and time-efficient method of measuring and interpreting cognitive and academic abilities and processes. More recently, the XBA approach has been used within the context of an operational definition of learning disability that is consistent with current federal and legal mandates (Flanagan et al., 2006).

Conclusions

The XBA approach is a method that allows practitioners to augment or supplement any major intelligence battery to ensure measurement of a wider range of broad cognitive abilities in a manner consistent with contemporary theory and research. The foundational sources of information upon which the XBA approach was built (i.e., the classifications of the major intelligence batteries according to CHC theory) provide a way to systematically construct a more theoretically driven, comprehensive, and valid assessment of cognitive abilities. When the XBA approach is applied to the Wechsler Intelligence Scales, for example, it is possible to measure important abilities that would otherwise go unassessed (e.g., *Ga, Glr*)—abilities that are important in understanding school learning and a variety of vocational and occupational outcomes (e.g., Flanagan & Kaufman, 2004; Flanagan et al., 2006).

The XBA approach allows for the measurement of the major cognitive areas specified in CHC theory with emphasis on those considered most critical on the basis of history, observation, and available test data. The CHC classifications of a multitude of cognitive ability tests bring stronger content- and construct-validity evidence to the evaluation and interpretation process. As test development continues to evolve and becomes increasingly more sophisticated (psychometrically and theoretically), batteries of the future will undoubtedly possess stronger content and construct validity. (A comparison of Tables C.18 and C.20 illustrates this point.) Notwithstanding, it is unrealistic from an economic and practical standpoint to develop a battery that operationalizes contemporary CHC theory fully (Carroll, 1998). Therefore, it is likely that the XBA approach will become increasingly important as the empirical support for CHC theory mounts.

With a strong research base and a multiplicity of CHC measures available, XBA procedures can aid practitioners in the selective measurement of cognitive abilities that are important with regard to the examinee's presenting problem(s). In particular, because the XBA approach was developed following important psychometric and validity principles, practitioners are able to address the "disorder in a basic psychological process" component of learning disability more reliably and validly.

In the past, the lack of theoretical clarity of widely used intelligence tests (e.g., the Wechsler Scales) confounded interpretation and adversely affected the examiner's ability to draw clear and useful conclusions from the data. The XBA approach has changed the direction of intellectual assessment in several ways. It has aided test authors and publishers in clarifying the theoretical underpinnings of their instruments. It has influenced the interpretation approaches of several commonly used intelligence batteries (e.g., KABC-II, WISC-IV). It has provided a means for understanding the relations between specific cognitive and academic abilities, thereby aiding significantly in the design and interpretation of assessments of individuals suspected of having a learning disability. And, it has assisted in narrowing the gap between theory and practice in assessment-related fields. As a result, measurement and interpretation of human cognitive abilities is guided more by science than clinical acumen.

REFERENCES

Alfonso, V. C., Flanagan, D. P., & Radwan, S. (2005). The impact of the Cattell-Horn-Carroll theory on test development and interpretation of cognitive and academic abilities. In D. P. Flanagan & P. L. Harrison (Eds.), *Contemporary intellectual assessment: Theories, tests, and issues* (2nd ed., pp. 185–202). New York, NY: Guilford Press.

Borgas, K. (1999). Intelligence theories and psychological assessment: Which theory of intelligence guides your interpretation of intelligence test profiles? *The School Psychologist, 53*, 24–25.

Brackett, J., & McPherson, A. (1996). Learning disabilities diagnosis in postsecondary students: A comparison of discrepancy-based diagnostic models. In N. Gregg, C. Hoy, & A. F. Gay (Eds.), *Adults with learning disabilities: Theoretical and practical perspectives* (pp. 68–84). New York: Guilford.

Carroll, J. B. (1993). *Human cognitive abilities: A survey of factor-analytic studies*. Cambridge, UK: Cambridge University Press.

Carroll, J. B. (1997). The three-stratum theory of cognitive abilities. In D.P. Flanagan, J.L. Genshaft, & P.L. Harrison (Eds.), *Contemporary intellectual assessment: Theories, tests, and issues* (pp. 122–130). New York, NY: Guilford Press.

Carroll, J. B. (1998). Foreword. In K.S. McGrew & D.P. Flanagan, *The intelligence test desk reference: Gf-Gc cross-battery assessment* (pp. xi–xii). Boston, MA: Allyn & Bacon.

Comrey, A. L. (1988). Factor-analytic methods of scale development in personality and clinical psychology. *Journal of Consulting and Clinical Psychology, 56*, 754–761.

Daniel, M. H. (1997). Intelligence testing: Status and trends. *American Psychologist, 52*, 1038–1045.

Das, J. P., & Naglieri, J. A. (1997). *Das-Naglieri Cognitive Assessment System*. Itasca, Il: Riverside Publishing.

Elliott, C. D. (1990). *Differential Ability Scales*. San Antonio, TX: The Psychological Corporation.

Esters, E. G., Ittenbach, R. F., & Han, K. (1997). Today's IQ tests: Are they really better than their historical predecessors? *School Psychology Review, 26*, 211–223.

Flanagan, D. P. (2000). Wechsler-based CHC cross-battery assessment and reading achievement: Strengthening the validity of interpretations drawn from Wechsler test scores. *School Psychology Quarterly, 15*, 295–329.

Flanagan, D. L., & Kaufman, A. S. (2004). *Essentials of the WISC-IV*. Hoboken, NJ: Wiley.

Flanagan, D. P., & McGrew, K. S. (1997). A cross-battery approach to assessing and interpreting cognitive abilities: Narrowing the gap between practice and cognitive science. In D. P. Flanagan, J. L. Genshaft, & P. L. Harrison (Eds.), *Contemporary intellectual assessment: Theories, tests, and issues* (pp. 314–325). New York, NY: Guilford Press.

Flanagan, D. P., McGrew, K. S., & Ortiz, S. O. (2000). *The Wechsler intelligence scales and Gf-Gc theory: A contemporary approach to interpretation*. Needham Heights, MA: Allyn & Bacon.

Flanagan, D. P., & Ortiz, S. O. (2001). *Essentials of cross-battery assessment*. New York, NY: Wiley.

Flanagan, D. P., Ortiz, S. O., & Alfonso, V. C. (2006a). *Essentials of cross-battery assessment* (2nd ed.). Hoboken, NJ: Wiley.

Flanagan, D. P., Ortiz, S. O., Alfonso, V. C., & Mascolo, J. T. (2002). *The achievement test desk reference (ADTR): Comprehensive assessment and learning disabilities*. Boston, MA: Allyn & Bacon.

Flanagan, D. P., Ortiz, S. O., Alfonso, V. C., & Mascolo, J. T. (2006b). *The achievement test desk reference (ADTR): A guide to learning disability identification*. Boston, MA: Allyn & Bacon.

Floyd, R. G., Keith, T. Z., Taub, G., & McGrew, K. S. (in press). Cattell-Horn-Carroll cognitive abilities and their effects on reading decoding skills g has indirect effects, more specific abilities have direct effects. *School Psychology Quarterly*.

Flynn, J. R. (1984). The mean IQ of Americans: Massive gains 1932 to 1978. *Psychological Bulletin, 95*, 29–51.

Genshaft, J. L., & Gerner, M. (1998). CHC cross-battery assessment: Implications for school psychologists. *Communique, 26*(8), 24–27.

Horn, J. L. (1991). Measurement of intellectual capabilities: A review of theory. In K. S. McGrew, J. K. Werder, & R. W. Woodcock (Eds.), *Woodcock-Johnson technical manual* (pp. 197–232). Chicago, IL: Riverside.

Kaufman, A. S. (2000). Forward. In Flanagan, D. P., McGrew, K. S., & Ortiz, S. O. (Eds.), *The Wechsler intelligence scales and Gf-Gc theory: A contemporary approach to interpretation*. Needham Heights, MA: Allyn & Bacon.

Kaufman, A. S., & Kaufman, N. L. (1983). *Kaufman Assessment Battery for Children*. Circle Pines, MN: American Guidance Service.

Kaufman, A. S., & Kaufman, N. L. (1993). *Kaufman Adolescent and Adult Intelligence Test*. Circle Pines, MN: American Guidance Service.

Keith, T. Z., Kranzler, J. H., & Flanagan, D. P. (2001). Independent confirmatory factor analysis of the Cognitive Assessment System (CAS): What does the CAS measure? *School Psychology Review, 28,* 117–144.

Lezak, M. D. (1976). *Neuropsychological assessment.* New York, NY: Oxford University Press.

Lezak, M. D. (1995). *Neuropsychological assessment* (3rd ed.). New York, NY: Oxford University Press.

McGrew, K. S. (1994). *Clinical interpretation of the Woodcock-Johnson Tests of Cognitive Ability* (Rev. ed.). Boston, MA: Allyn & Bacon.

McGrew, K. S. (1997). Analysis of the major intelligence batteries according to a proposed comprehensive CHC framework. In D. P. Flanagan, J. L. Genshaft, & P. L. Harrison (Eds.), *Contemporary intellectual assessment: Theories, tests, and issues* (pp. 151–180). New York, NY: Guilford Press.

McGrew, K. S., & Flanagan, D. P. (1998). *The intelligence test desk reference (ITDR): CHC cross-battery assessment.* Boston, MA: Allyn & Bacon.

McGrew, K. S., Flanagan, D. P., Keith, T. Z. & Vanderwood, M. (1997). Beyond *g*: The impact of CHC specific cognitive abilities research on the future use and interpretation of intelligence tests in the schools. *School Psychology Review, 26,* 189–210.

Messick, S. (1989). Validity. In R. Linn (Ed.), *Educational measurement* (3rd ed., pp. 104–131). Washington, DC: American Council on Education.

Messick, S. (1992). Multiple intelligences or multilevel intelligence? Selective emphasis on distinctive properties of hierarchy: On Gardner's *Frames of Mind* and Sternberg's *Beyond IQ* in the context of theory and research on the structure of human abilities. *Psychological Inquiry, 3,* 365–384.

Messick, S. (1995). Validity of psychological assessment: Validation of inferences from persons' responses and performances as scientific inquiry into score meaning. *American Psychologist, 50,* 741–749.

Ortiz, S. O., & Flanagan, D. P. (2002). Best practices in working with culturally and diverse families. In A. Thomas & J. Grimes (Eds.), *Best practices in school psychology IV* (pp. 337–352). Washington, DC: National Association of School Psychologists.

Phelps, L., McGrew, K. S., Knopik, S. N., & Ford, L. (2005). The general (*g*) broad and narrow CHC stratum characteristics of the WJ III and WISC-III tests: A confirmatory cross-battery investigation. *Journal of School Psychology, 320,* 66–58.

Salvia, J., & Ysseldyke, J. E. (1991). *Assessment* (5th ed.). New York, NY: Houghton Mifflin.

Sattler, J. M. (1992). *Assessment of children* (3rd ed.). San Diego, CA: Author.

Sternberg, R. J., & Kaufman, J. C. (1998). Human abilities. *Annual Review of Psychology, 49,* 479–502.

Valdés, G., & Figueroa, R. A. (1994). *Bilingualism and testing: A special case of bias.* Norwood, NJ: Ablex.

Vanderwood, M., McGrew, K. S., & Flanagan, D. P. (2001). Examination of the contribution of general and specific cognitive abilities to reading achievement. *Learning and Individual Differences, 13,* 159–188.

Wechsler, D. (1981). *Wechsler Adult Intelligence Scale-Revised.* San Antontio, TX: The Psychological Corporation.

Wechsler, D. (1989). *Wechsler Preschool and Primary Scale of Intelligence-Revised.* San Antonio, TX: The Psychological Corporation.

Wechsler, D. (2002). *Wechsler Preschool and Primary Scale of Intelligence* (3rd. ed.). San Antonio, TX: Psychological Corporation.

Wechsler, D. (2003). *Wechsler Intelligence Scale for Children* (4th ed.). San Antonio, TX: Psychological Corporation.

Wilson, B. C. (1992). The neuropsychological assessment of the preschool child: A branching model. In I. Rapin & S.I. Segalowitz (Vol. Eds.), *Handbook of neuropsychology: Vol. 6. Child neuropsychology: Vol. 6* (pp. 377–394). San Diego, CA: Elsevier.

Woodcock, R. W. (1990). Theoretical foundations of the WJ-R measures of cognitive ability. *Journal of Psychoeducational Assessment, 8,* 231–58.

Woodcock, R. W., McGrew, K. S., & Schrank, F. A. (2003). *Diagnostic supplement to the Woodcock-Johnson III Tests of Cognitive Abilities.* Itasca, IL: Riverside.

DAWN P. FLANAGAN
St. John's University

VINCENT C. ALFONSO
Fordham University

SAMUEL O. ORTIZ
St. John's University

CHEMICALLY DEPENDENT YOUTHS

Chemically dependent youths are children and adolescents who want and need continued use of a psychoactive substance to sustain or maintain a chronic state of euphoria or intoxication. Alcohol and drug use by young people must be viewed not in isolation but in concert with that period of life known as adolescence. Substance use and addiction have profound effects on development and have serious implications for the future functioning of the abuser (Cohen, 1983).

The period of life commonly referred to as adolescence generally runs from 12 to 22 years of age. Adolescents are often described by age groupings: early (12 to 15), middle (15 to 18), and late (18 to 22). Although these divisions are convenient, they do not adequately describe the complex period of adolescence. More important are the biological, emotional, social, academic, and intellectual changes that young people undergo as they move from childhood to adulthood. Because these phases vary widely across adolescents and even within the same adolescent, no one variable, including age, is sufficient. The complex interplay of these dynamic phases in youth and the distinct stages of movement from drug use to chemical dependency best explain chemical dependency. Newman and Newman (1975) note that the physical development that accompanies puberty leads to a heightened awareness of body sensations. Drugs, especially marijuana and the hallucinogens, accentuate pleasurable bodily sensations and may be used by adolescents in an attempt to increase the sense of physical arousal. Cohen (1984) warns that adolescence, a period of critical psychosocial development when adaptive responses are being learned, is much more vulnerable to the loss of learning time than is adulthood.

Two types of chemical dependency occur, physical and psychological. Some substances induce tolerance and create a physical craving and addiction cycle, whereas others create a psychological dependency in which the user experiences changes in mood. Further, some compounds create both a physical and psychological dependency. In the latter case, chemically dependent youths may undergo detoxification to treat the physical craving and resultant withdrawal symptoms, but may continue to experience a craving or felt need to use again. This process sets up a cycle of dependency, detoxification, and return to use that accounts for the recidivism rate among addicted youths.

Psychological dependence is characterized by a drive to continue taking a drug when the user feels the effects of the drug are needed to maintain his or her sense of well-being at an optimal level. The complex interaction of drug effects, personality, and stage of development constitute the degree of psychic craving or compulsion the user may experience. Drug-seeking behavior or compulsive drug use develops when the user comes to believe that the drug can produce pleasure and deter discomfort such that continuous or periodic administration of the drug is required. This mental state is the most powerful of all the factors involved in chronic intoxication with psychoactive drugs (Adesso, 1985).

Physiological dependence is characterized by reliance of body tissue on the continued presence of a drug within the user's system. Its presence is unknown to the user as long as the drug continues to be taken and is of no immediate consequence until the drug is withdrawn or no longer available. The magnitude of the dependence and the severity of the withdrawal symptoms vary directly with the type, amount, frequency, and duration of the drug use. Physiological dependence manifests itself as severe and immediate physical pain and discomfort, commonly referred to as withdrawal symptoms or abstinence syndrome. Symptoms may include fever, chills, gastrointestinal cramps, watery eyes, runny nose, and muscle cramping or spasms. They are frequently accompanied by psychological dependence. For drugs like alcohol, barbiturates, narcotic analgesics (morphine, Percodan, heroin) and cocaine, withdrawal symptoms and accompanying psychological dependence are so uncomfortable and threatening that they motivate young drug users to continue to seek and administer the drug. For drugs like stimulants (speed), and to a lesser degree marijuana and hallucinogenics (LSD, mescaline, psilocybin, peyote), the primary disturbance is psychological rather than physiological. But it should be noted that although the symptoms are not as severe as with physiological withdrawal, the user does experience discomfort of a mental or emotional nature (Bardo & Risner, 1985).

Different drug compounds act on different youths in different ways, both psychologically and physiologically. A 13-year-old pubescent male who is smoking two to three joints of high-grade (THC potent) marijuana daily over a 5- to 6-month period is likely to develop a psychological compulsion while not experiencing physical withdrawal symptoms on cessation. However, evidence suggests that THC lowers levels of the male hormone testosterone in the young male's system, retarding development of secondary sexual characteristics. Additionally, an amotivational syndrome from chronic cannabis intoxication results in lethargy, restlessness, and increased irritability (Cohen, 1984). Conversely, the same male drinking 1 to 3 ounces of alcohol (beer, wine, or hard liquor) over the same period of time will most likely experience both psychological and physiological withdrawal symptoms. Although medical complications may be more severe in the latter case, emotional, social, and intellectual complications occur in both.

Kandel (1984) proposes that culturally determined developmental stages of drug behavior are observed in adolescents. Initiation, progression, and regression in drug behavior are related to factors like prior delinquent behavior, high levels of drug-using peer affiliations, and parental models who use or abuse alcohol and drugs. The role of genetics in the development of substance abuse is also a major area of concern (Crabbe, McSwignan, & Belknap, 1985). Extensive research, primarily using animal models, indicates a strong predisposition to addiction in the offspring of addicted parents, particularly those using alcohol and sedative compounds. In sum, environment, psychosocial variables, and genetics are important concepts for consideration in adolescent substance abuse.

A single episode of intoxication does not produce either physical or psychological dependency. Several stages occur in the move from no use to dependency. The initial reason to try any drug depends more on the value the youth places on its use than on its pharmacological properties. Curiosity and availability, key factors at this stage, are influenced by the social factors of peer pressure and acceptance, adult role models, and family norms or values. Adolescents with learning disabilities are at particularly high risk for chemical dependency (Karacostas & Fisher, 1993) as are those with a history of physical and emotional abuse (Grella & Joshi, 2003). The majority of youthful experimenters do not proceed through all stages to dependence because of the drug effects themselves not being valued and the fact that most peer-group norms do not support continued use (Kandel, Kessler, & Margulies, 1978).

Experimental use may proceed to casual or occasional use, frequently referred to as sociorecreational use. This pattern usually involves imitation of adult role models who drink during social gatherings or use other drugs as mood enhancers. The youthful user may use drugs while at a party once or twice a month, or while attending a movie or listening to music with friends. Such use tends to be spontaneous and in a social context where drugs are readily available. Reasons for use are primarily social in that friends use and approve of use. Also, the drugs enhance self-confidence and social interaction during the identity phase of adolescence. The youthful user does not avidly seek drugs at this stage but will participate with a group if drugs are available.

The third stage, regular use, is distinguished from sociorecreational use by several features. The user at this stage actively seeks drugs, and is rarely seen in a social context without being intoxicated. Psychological dependence occurs. The user perceives that he or she functions better in social gatherings while intoxicated. Regular use also may involve physiological dependence if the user develops tolerance to a drug and experiences physical discomfort with cessation. The pharmacological properties of the drug become critical at this point. Whether the user proceeds into the final stage, dependency, is partly a function of what the drug does for the user's personality and the user's stage in adolescence.

The final stage is physical and/or psychological reliance on the drug to produce the user's desired effect. Heavy or compulsive use implies daily intoxication, although the user may indulge in binge-type use. Although only a minority of users become chemically dependent youths, the central factor is the degree to which use dominates the life of the adolescent. Intoxication may avoid other critical issues of adolescence (e.g., responsibilities of school and family, stress, lack of self-confidence) or mask the pain and discomfort of other pathological personality or mental disorders. Psychological and physical dependence are critical at this stage because regardless of reasons for continued use, the youthful user will have to continue to take the drug in order to avoid the newly acquired set of symptoms and difficulties associated with chemical dependency (Kandel, 1984). Although chemical dependency is not an official handicapping condition under federal legislation, it has been considered (Williams, 1990), and specialized programs for individuals with disabilities have been developed (Campbell, 1994), such as the Mental Health/Chemical Dependency/Mental Retardation Certificate at the Columbus State Community College (CSCC; 2005).

REFERENCES

Adesso, V. J. (1985). Cognitive factors in alcohol and drug use. In M. Galizio & S. A. Maisto (Eds.), *Determinants of substance abuse* (pp. 179–208). New York, NY: Plenum Press.

Bardo, M. T., & Risner, M. E. (1985). Biochemical substrates of drug abuse. In M. Galizio & S. A. Maisto (Eds.), *Determinants of substance abuse* (pp. 65–99). New York, NY: Plenum Press.

Campbell, J. (1994). Issues in chemical dependency treatment and aftercare for people with learning differences. *Health and Social Work, 19*, 1, 63–70.

Cohen, S. (1983). *The alcoholism problems.* New York, NY: Haworth.

Cohen, S. (1984). Adolescence and drug abuse: Biological consequences. In D. J. Lettieri & J. P. Ludford (Eds.), *Drug abuse and the American adolescent* (pp. 104–109). Rockville, MD: National Institute on Drug Abuse.

Crabbe, J. C., McSwignan, J. D., & Belknap, J. K. (1985). The role of genetics in substance abuse. In M. Galizio & S. A. Maisto (Eds.), *Determinants of substance abuse* (pp. 13–54). New York, NY: Plenum Press.

Columbus State Community College (CSCC). (2005). *MH/CD/MR Program.* Retrieved from http://cscc.edu/

Grella, C. E., & Joshi, V. (2003). Treatment processes and outcomes among adolescents with a history of abuse who are in drug treatment. *Child Maltreatment, 8*, 7–18.

Kandel, D. B. (1984). Drug use by youth: An overview. In D. J. Lettieri & J. P. Ludford (Eds.), *Drug abuse and the American adolescent* (pp. 1–24). Rockville, MD: National Institute on Drug Abuse.

Kandel, D. B., Kessler, R. C., & Margulies, R. (1978). Adolescent initiation into stages of drug use: A developmental analysis. In D. B. Kandel (Ed.), *Longitudinal research in drug use: Empirical findings and methodological issues* (pp. 73–99). Washington, DC: Hemisphere.

Karacostas, D. D., & Fisher, G. L. (1993). Chemical dependency in students with and without hearing disabilities. *Journal of Hearing Disabilities, 26*, 491–495.

Newman, B. M., & Newman, P. R. (1975). *Development through life: A psychosocial approach.* Homewood, IL: Dorsey.

Williams, R. W. (1990). Adolescent chemical dependency as a handicapping condition: An analysis of state regulations. *Journal of Chemical Dependency, 1*(1), 69–82.

L. WORTH BOLTON
Cape Fear Substance Abuse Center

See also Alcohol and Drug Abuse Patterns; Drug Abuse; Substance Abuse

CHEMOTHERAPY

The treatment of cancer in children usually includes chemotherapy, which consists of drugs that are administered to the child intravenously, intramuscularly, or orally on a repeated schedule (e.g., every 10 days or every month). The purpose of chemotherapy is to poison the cancer cells. Unfortunately, it also is toxic to healthy cells of the body. As a result, many children receiving chemotherapy experience unpleasant side effects.

Two common side effects of chemotherapy are nausea and vomiting. Children differ in the extent to which they have these symptoms. Furthermore, the degree of nausea and vomiting for a given child may vary widely from one course of chemotherapy to the next, even when there are no changes in chemotherapy. Many children feel intensely ill during the days they receive chemotherapy and for a few days afterward. Other children are able to carry on with play and other normal activities to varying degrees (Kidshealth, 2005; Zeltzer, LeBaron, & Zeltzer, 1984).

Another possible side effect is a temporary susceptibility to bacterial infection or excessive bleeding. During such a period, physicians usually will advise the child not to participate in any contact sports or activities (e.g., gymnastics) that might increase the risk of bleeding. Because children on chemotherapy also are sometimes at risk for severe illness with certain viral infections, doctors often advise these children to stay home from school for a period of time if there is an outbreak of chicken pox. However, for the majority of time the child is receiving chemotherapy, the doctor usually will permit the child to engage in all normal school activities, including sports.

Another problem related to chemotherapy is that total hair loss may occur. Baldness is the most troublesome side effect of chemotherapy for many children. Bald children may feel so embarrassed that they refuse to go to school. Many children cope with this problem by wearing a cap, kerchief, or wig; others explain to their friends the reason for the baldness. Fortunately, in almost all cases, the hair grows back once chemotherapy is completed.

What are the effects of chemotherapy on the child's behavior and academic performance? Many of these children are absent from school at regular intervals because of medical appointments and chemotherapy side effects. Some children also stay home because of embarrassment over hair loss and fear of being rejected by peers. A further reason for school absence is a fear of failure because of the large amount of school material missed (Deasy-Spinetta, 1981; Deasy-Spinetta & Spinetta, 1980; Katz, Kellerman, Rigler, Williams, & Siegle, 1977; Kidshealth, 2005).

For some children, radiation to the head produces cognitive deficits, especially when combined with injections of chemotherapy into the spinal canal. Many children with cancer show little or no evidence of cognitive deficits, but these are problems that can occur gradually and may be long-lasting. During the acute phase of radiation therapy, there often is transient swelling of the brain, which could produce additional temporary cognitive deficits.

There are several ways educators can be helpful to the student who is receiving chemotherapy. A teacher or counselor needs to contact the student's parents to discuss ways in which the student's educational needs can be met. For example, if the student is in the hospital, a few books and short assignments could be sent. If the child is likely to be at home for some time, homebound education may be indicated. A student who would not otherwise qualify for special education can qualify on the basis of the illness and can benefit greatly from both home and hospital teacher visits combined with regular school attendance.

With the permission of the child's parents, it usually is helpful to contact the student's physician to learn about the doctor's expectations regarding the student's capabilities during the period of treatment. The teacher also can ask the student how he or she feels about returning to school. A discussion of the student's needs and feelings with classmates can give the class an opportunity to discuss their misconceptions and worries about the student, as well as to ask questions. Children who are unable to return to school for a period of time usually appreciate receiving cards, drawings, or letters from classmates at school.

Educators need to be aware that hospitalization or confinement to bed at home because of nausea and vomiting does not necessarily preclude school work. On the contrary, involvement in school work, at least at a minimal level, can have therapeutic value. By attending school a few hours a day, having a homebound teacher, or doing some school work in the hospital, children can be distracted from unpleasant physical symptoms or worries. Some adolescents who receive chemotherapy in the morning prefer to come to school in the afternoon rather than to spend the rest of the day at home feeling sick. If the student experiences some nausea, he or she may need to leave the class abruptly. If these considerations are discussed in advance, then involvement in school can be therapeutic for many children and may reduce the severity of nausea and vomiting.

Teachers can be most helpful to children receiving chemotherapy by maintaining a flexible attitude and realistic expectations. Most children receiving chemotherapy can maintain a normal educational load. However, specific expectations regarding homework and exams need to be flexible because of the intermittent nature of treatment-related problems. Frequent consultation with the student and parent will help to define reasonable and appropriate education goals. An excellent website for teachers is provided by Kidshealth.org. The information on this website explains the use of chemotherapy and its effects (Kidshealth, 2005).

REFERENCES

Deasy-Spinetta, P. (1981). The school and the child with cancer. In J. J. Spinetta & P. Deasy-Spinetta (Eds.), *Living with childhood cancer* (pp. 153–168). St. Louis, MO: Mosby.

Deasy-Spinetta, P. M., & Spinetta, J. J. (1980). The child with cancer in school: Teachers' appraisal. *American Journal of Pediatric Hematology/Oncology, 2,* 89–94.

Katz, E. R., Kellerman, J., Rigler, D., Williams, K., & Siegle, S. E. (1977). School intervention with pediatric cancer patients. *Journal of Pediatric Psychology, 2*, 72–76.

Kidshealth. (2005). *Chemotherapy.* Retrieved from http://kids health.org/

Zeltzer, L. K., LeBaron, S., & Zeltzer, P. M. (1984). The adolescent with cancer. In R. Blum (Ed.), *Chronic illness and disabilities in childhood and adolescence* (pp. 375–395). Orlando, FL: Grune & Stratton.

SAMUEL LeBARON
LONNIE K. ZELTZER
University of Texas Health Science Center

See also Cancer, Childhood; Homebound Instruction

CHESS, STELLA (1914–2007)

Stella Chess was born and educated in New York City. She received her BA from Smith College in 1935 and MD from New York University School of Medicine in 1939. She served several internships, including psychoanalytic training, and became a diplomate of the American Board of Psychiatry and Neurology in Child Psychiatry in 1959. A member of the staff at New York Medical College from 1945, she became professor and director of the Division of Child Psychiatry in 1964. In 1966, Chess moved to a full professorship at New York University.

Chess is best known for her collaboration (1956–present) with her husband, Alexander Thomas, and Herbert Birch (deceased) on a longitudinal study of the individual characteristics of children. This study found early differentiable temperament factors that persist and strongly influence child–environment interaction and later behavior. Additional longitudinal studies by Chess include behavioral patterns and child-care practices of Puerto Rican families in New York City (1956–1970), children with multiple handicaps and congenital rubella (1970–1981), and children with mild mental retardation (1963–1968).

For her book, *How to Help Your Child Get the Most Out of School* (1974), Chess was awarded the Family Life Book Award of the Child Study Association of America. Her many awards and honors include the Honors Award from the Society for Research in Child Development for Distinguished Contributions to Psychiatric Theory (1993), the Adolph Myers Award of the American Psychiatric Association for Scientific Contributions to Psychiatric Theory and Practice (1996), and the George Tarjan Award from the American Academy of Child and Adolescent Psychiatry for Significant Contributions to Mental and Developmental Disabilities.

Chess and Thomas were editors of the series *Annual Progress in Child Psychiatry and Child Development* from 1968 to 1970. Other books include *Origins and Evolution of Behavior Disorders: From Infancy to Early Adult Life* (1984/1987) and *Temperament: Theory and Practice* (1996). With well over 50 publications spanning 25 years, including journal articles, authored books, and edited books, Chess remains highly active and productive in her fields of interest.

REFERENCES

Chess, S., & Thomas, A. (1974). *Annual progress in child psychiatry and child development.* New York, NY: Brunner/Mazel.

Chess, S., & Thomas, A. (1987). *Origins and evolution of behavior disorders: Infancy to early adult life.* Cambridge, MA: Harvard University Press.

Chess, S., & Thomas, A. (1996). *Temperament: Theory and practice.* New York, NY: Brunner/Mazel.

Chess, S., & Whitbread, J. (1974). *How to help your child get the most out of school.* Garden City, NY: Doubleday.

ELAINE FLETCHER-JANZEN
Chicago School of Professional Psychology
First edition

TAMARA J. MARTIN
University of Texas of the Permian Basin
Second edition

CHILD ABUSE

The age-old phenomenon of child maltreatment only formally attracted the attention of mental health professionals in the 1960s. Psychiatric and psychological exploration of child battering has lagged two decades behind the pioneering efforts of pediatricians and radiologists in establishing medical diagnostic criteria for physical abuse in children. Between 1963 and 1965, the passage of laws by all 50 states requiring medical reporting of child abuse ultimately subjected the abusing parents to the legal process; these laws were also the catalyst for the formation of child protective services throughout the nation. The first psychological studies of abusing parents were carried out during this period.

Child abuse is currently regarded as the leading cause of death in children and a major public health problem. The National Child Abuse and Neglect Data System (NCANDS) reported an estimated 1,400 child fatalities in 2002, and many believe this figure to be an underrepresentation. Young children are the most frequent targets of child abuse and approximately one-third of their deaths are a result of neglect alone (NCANDS, 2005). The proliferation of child abuse and neglect might bear some relationship to the alarming general increase of violence in our society demonstrated by the rising incidence of violent crimes, delinquency, suicide, and lethal accidents. In the past 30 years, child abuse has become a major focus of research and clinical study. A concerted effort is being made by federal, state, and local governments to develop programs for the study, prevention, and treatment of child abuse.

Owing to its complexity and far-reaching consequences, the problem of child abuse has attracted the attention of professionals from widely divergent backgrounds. Contributions to this area have come from the fields of pediatrics, psychiatry, psychology, social work, sociology, nursing, education, law, and law enforcement. Such multidisciplinary involvement has been essential in tracking down cases, locating medical treatment, and arranging for protective intervention and long-term planning with families. At the same time, it has become a source of confusion as a result of the differing roles, frames of reference, and terminology of each specialty. Exclusively cultural, socioeconomic, psychodynamic, and behavioral interpretations of the child abuse syndrome have failed to present the full picture.

The definition of child abuse has been continually expanding in recent years. A classic paper, "The Battered Child Syndrome" (Kempe, Silverman, Steele, Droegemueller, & Silver, 1962), described child abuse as the infliction of serious injury on young children by parents or caretakers. The injuries, which included fractures, subdural hematoma, and multiple soft tissue injuries, often resulted in permanent disability and death. Fontana's (1964) concept of the "maltreatment syndrome" viewed child abuse as one end of a spectrum of maltreatment that also included emotional deprivation, neglect, and malnutrition. Helfer (1975) recognized the prevalence of minor injuries resulting from abuse and suspected that abuse might be implicated in 10% of all childhood accidents treated in emergency rooms. Gil (1974) extended the concept of child abuse to include any action that prevents a child from achieving his physical and psychological potential.

Child protective services are specialized agencies existing under public welfare auspices; they are responsible for receiving and investigating all reports of child abuse or maltreatment for the purpose of preventing further abuse, providing services necessary to safeguard the child's well-being, and strengthening the family unit. These agencies are responsible for maintaining service until the conditions of maltreatment are remedied. They also have the mandate to invoke the authority of the juvenile or family court to secure the protection and treatment of children whose parents are unable or unwilling to use their services.

The wide variety of behavior and personality traits observed in abusing parents suggests that a specific abusive personality does not exist. Rather, individuals with a certain psychological makeup operating in combination with the burden of a painfully perceived childhood and immediate environmental stress might be likely to abuse the offspring who most readily elicits the unhappy childhood imagery of the past. Frequently the perpetrator is a young adult in his or her mid-20s, without a high school diploma, living at the poverty level, with depression (NCANDS, 2005).

While environmental stress has often been suggested as a prominent etiological factor in child abuse, the precise definition of this relationship has eluded most investigators. One author has attributed child abuse almost exclusively to socioeconomic determinants (Gil, 1968, 1970), but most researchers agree that environmental stress is only the catalyst, in many instances, for an abuse-prone personality.

The stress argument has at least in part been predicated on the high percentage of low socioeconomic status (SES), multiple-problem families in child abuse registers throughout the country. It is probable that reporting procedures themselves have led to the greater emphasis on socioeconomic determinants. Any controlled study that matches for SES is compelled to look beyond such variables as family income for the origins of child abuse. The conclusion that Spinetta and Rigler (1972) reach in their review of the literature is far more likely—that environmental stress is neither necessary nor sufficient for child abuse but that it does, in some instances, interact with other factors such as parent personality variables and child behaviors to potentiate child battering.

Environmental stress includes current events that widen the discrepancy between the limited capacity of the parents and increased child-rearing pressures. The stress may consist of a diminution of child-rearing resources owing to a spouse's illness or desertion, or to the unavailability of an earlier caretaker such as a neighbor or some other family member.

Environmental stress also includes the actual or threatened loss of a key relationship that provides the parent with emotional security and dependency gratification. This may occur when the spouse becomes physically or emotionally unavailable or when ties with parents or important relatives are severed owing to estrangement, illness, or death. Additional child-rearing pressures such as the birth or illness of another child, or the assumption of temporary care of other children, create environmental stress that may also lead to child abuse.

Justice and Duncan (1975) described the contribution of work-related pressures to environmental stress in situations of child abuse. They cited four types of work-related situations: unemployed fathers caring for children at home; working mothers with domestic obligations; overworked husbands who neglect their wives; and traumatic job experiences resulting in undischarged tension. Justice and Justice (1979) were able to document the importance of stress in terms of excessive life changes in child-abusing families by means of the *Social Readjustment Rating Scale* developed by Holmes and Rahe (1967).

The greatest area of agreement in the field of child abuse has pertained to the history and background of the abusive parents themselves. These individuals have usually experienced abuse, deprivation, rejection, and inadequate mothering during childhood. As children they were subjected to unrealistic expectations and premature demands by their parents. Parents with these characteristics are said to have "abuse-prone" personality traits.

The psychodynamics in a given case of child abuse are largely determined by the abuse-prone personality traits of the parent. The relationship between the abusing parent and his or her child is distorted by the cumulative impact of the parent's own traumatic experiences as a child reared in a punitive, unloving environment. Individuals who abuse their children cannot envision any parent–child relationship as a mutually gratifying experience. The task of parenting mobilizes identifications with the parent-aggressor, child-victim dyad of the past. The key psychodynamic elements in child abuse are role reversal, excessive use of denial and projection as defenses, rapidly shifting identifications, and displacement of aggression from frustrating objects onto the child.

Role reversal occurs when the unfulfilled abusing parent seeks dependency gratification, which is unavailable from his or her spouse or family, from the "parentified" child. It is based on an identification with the child-victim. The child's inability to gratify the father or mother causes the youngster to be unconsciously perceived as the rejecting mother. This intensifies the parent's feelings of rejection and worthlessness, which further threaten his or her narcissistic equilibrium. These painful feelings are denied and projected onto the child, who then becomes the recipient of the parent's self-directed aggression.

Any plan for the prevention or treatment of child abuse must be designed to create a safe environment for the child and to modify the potentiating factors underlying abuse. Therefore, an effective treatment program must deal specifically with the parental abuse proneness, those characteristics of the child that make him or her vulnerable for scapegoating, and the environmental stresses that trigger the abusive interaction.

A wide range of psychotherapeutic and educational techniques have proven successful in reducing the symptoms and problems of abused children. In general, these children present with ego deficits and cognitive impairment to such a degree that an emphasis on ego integration, reality testing, containment of drives and impulses, and strengthening of higher level defenses (similar to those techniques applied to borderline and psychotic children) proves necessary.

The ideal objective in studying and treating child abuse on a nationwide scale is, as with any major public health problem, the development of a strategy for prevention. Thus far, early case findings and protective intervention

in abusing families have been the primary areas of interest for workers in this field. As more basic knowledge is accumulated about the child-abuse syndrome, through clinical experience and research, one can envision a logical shift in focus from treatment and rehabilitation (secondary prevention) to primary intervention. The National Clearinghouse on Child Abuse and Neglect (NCANDS; 2005) has an extensive website with multiple topics, resources, and links.

REFERENCES

Fontana, V. (1964). *The maltreated child*. Springfield, IL: Thomas.

Gil, D. (1968). Incidence of child abuse and demographic characteristics of persons involved. In R. E. Helfer & C. H. Kempe (Eds.), *The battered child*. Chicago, IL: University of Chicago Press.

Gil, D. (1970). *Violence against children*. Cambridge, MA: Harvard University Press.

Gil, D. (1974). *A holistic perspective on child abuse and its prevention*. Paper presented at the Conference on Research on Child Abuse, National Institute of Child Health and Human Development, Washington, DC.

Helfer, R. E. (1975). *The diagnostic process and treatment programs*. Washington, DC: U.S. Department of Health, Education and Welfare, National Center for Child Abuse and Neglect.

Holmes, T., & Rahe, R. (1967). The social readjustment rating scale. *Journal of Psychosomatic Medicine, 11*, 213–218.

Justice, B., & Duncan, D. (1975). *Child abuse as a work-related problem*. Paper presented at American Public Health Association, Chicago.

Justice, B., & Justice, R. (1979). *The broken taboo: Sex in the family*. New York, NY: Human Science Press.

Kempe, C. H., Silverman, F., Steele, B., Droegemueller, W., & Silver, H. (1962). The battered child syndrome. *Journal of the American Medical Association, 181*, 17–24.

NCANDS. (2005). *National Clearinghouse on Child Abuse and Neglect Information*. Retrieved from https://cbexpress.acf.hhs.gov/index.cfm?event=website.viewArticles&issueid=46&articleid=715

Spinetta, J., & Rigler, D. (1972). The child abusing parent: A psychological review. *Psychological Bulletin, 77*, 296–304.

CHARLES P. BARNARD
University of Wisconsin at Stout

See also **Abused Children, Psychotherapy With; Battered Child Syndrome**

CHILD DEVELOPMENT

Since its inception in 1930, *Child Development* was published six times per year by the University of Chicago

Press. It is a professional journal sponsored by the Society for Research in Child Development. As an interdisciplinary group, the Society for Research in Child Development uses the *Child Development* journal to publish manuscripts from all academic and professional disciplines that study developmental processes. The articles range from empirical and theoretical to reviews of previous research. The scholarly papers that appear in *Child Development* focus on the growth and development of children from conception through adolescence, including the development of language, thinking and reasoning, moral judgment, social skills, and family relationships.

The distribution of the journal, while primarily North American, is international. The editorial board is made of world-renowned scholars. *Child Development*, clearly the most comprehensive journal in this field, is read by psychologists, pediatricians, anthropologists, social workers, and others who wish to obtain information related to research in child development.

The editor of *Child Development* is Lynn S. Liben and subscription information can be obtained online from Blackwell Publishing at www.blackwellpublishing.com (now merged with John Wiley & Sons).

MICHAEL J. ASH
JOSE LUIS TORRES
Texas A&M University

CHILD FIND

Child find is a federal requirement for states to identify, locate, and evaluate all children, from birth to age 21, in need of special education services as mandated through Part C of the Individuals with Disabilities Education Act (IDEA) of 1997 and the Individuals with Disabilities Education Improvement Act (IDEIA) of 2004. The term *child find* has been in use since 1974. In 1986, Congress authorized support for the Infants and Toddlers with Disabilities Program under Part H of the Education for All Handicapped Children Act, which is now known as "child find" through the IDEA. This legislation represents an effort to promote the importance of early intervention for children with disabilities and to provide services for their family's functioning abilities. In addition, the federal definition of *child find* includes a requirement for states to find nontraditional or highly mobile children (such as migrant and homeless children). There are two programs providing services to children who are eligible under the IDEA guidelines: the Early Intervention Program (Part C) and the Preschool Special Education Program (Part B/619). Through these programs, each state is required to have a comprehensive child find system. A comprehensive system includes a definition of the target population, public awareness, referral and intake, screening and identification of young children who may be eligible for IDEA services, eligibility determination, tracking, and interagency coordination. Unfortunately, the states differ on their systems for identifying children (Dynamic Community Connections Project, 2005).

The research supports early intervention as the best way to help children with disabilities. The number of children served under Part C of IDEA has increased by 25% from 1994 to 1999 (Dynamic Community Connections Project, 2005). However, the National Early Intervention Longitudinal Study (Hebbeler, Wagner, Spiker, Scarborough, Simeonsson, & Collier, 2004) estimated the average age of identifying children with a developmental delay is 15.5 months. Furthermore, children of color represented 44% of the early intervention population, which is greater than their representation in the general population (37%).

Due to health disparities and unequal access to health care, there is an effort to improve access to services for children. Therefore, states coordinate a variety of child find strategies to notify the public and improve program participation, especially among diverse groups. Methods such as door-to-door visits, brochures, and contacting pediatricians were useful in notifying the public (Karnes & Shaunessy, 2004). Pavri (2001) proposed several guidelines in an attempt to develop culturally sensitive programs. A study conducted in Hawaii examined equity of access to referrals and enrollment and found promising results with low-income and immigrant households, but improvements for access to resources were needed for military families and families whose children lacked health insurance (Shapiro & Derrington, 2004). One of the few nationwide studies examined families' experiences with determining their child's eligibility, interaction with professionals, and satisfaction with services (Bailey, Hebbeler, Scarborough, Spiker, & Mallik, 2004). Interestingly, some states, including Kansas, Louisiana, Pennsylvania, Tennessee, and West Virginia, incorporate "gifted" in their child find eligibility definitions and further initiatives to develop a national child find plan to identify this group are occurring (Shapiro & Derrington, 2004).

The U.S. Office of Special Education Programs is funding studies from six states for the early childhood child find demonstration projects. These feasibility projects are the *Interagency Collaboration for Colorado Part C Child Find*, Denver, CO; *Enhanced Child Find through Newborn Hearing Screening*, Farmington, CT; *Strategies for Effective and Efficient "Keiki" (Child) Find (Project SEEK)*, Honolulu, HI; *Dynamic Community Connections: A Process Model for Enhancing Child Find in Rural Areas*, Missoula, MT; *Promoting Early Identification and Support for Families of Young Children: The Early Connections Project*, Durham, NH; and *Creating Partnerships between Pediatric Practitioners and Early Developmental Interventionists for Child Find (PEDI-Link)*, Burlington, VT

(Dynamic Community Connections Project, 2005). Furthermore, there are national reports on the success of child find. The Office of Special Education collects annual data and provides data fact sheets on Part C of IDEA (U.S. Office of Special Education Programs, 2005). In addition, there are annual reports to Congress about the effectiveness of IDEA (Twenty-fifth Annual Report, 2003).

REFERENCES

Bailey, D., Hebbeler, K., Scarborough, A., Spiker, D., & Mallik, S. (2004). First experiences with early intervention: A national perspective. *Pediatrics, 113*, 887–897.

Dynamic Community Connections Project. (2005). *Child find.* Retrieved from www.childfindidea.org

Hebbeler, K., Wagner, M., Spiker, D., Scarborough, A., Simeonsson, R., & Collier, M. (2004). A national look at children and families entering early intervention. *Exceptional Children, 70,* 469–484.

Individuals with Disabilities Education Act (IDEA) PL 105-17. (1997). [Electronic version]. Retrieved from http://www.cec.sped.org/

Individuals With Disabilities Education Improvement Act (IDEIA) PL 108-446. (2004). [Electronic version]. Retrieved from http://www.ed.gov/

Karnes, F. A., & Shaunessy, E. (2004). A plan for child find in gifted education. *Roeper Review, 26,* 229–233.

Pavri, S. (2001). Developmental delay or cultural difference? Developing effective child find practices for young children from culturally and linguistically diverse families. *Exceptional Children, 4,* 2–9.

Shapiro, B. J., & Derrington, T. M. (2004). Equity and disparity in access to services: An outcome-based evaluation of early intervention child find in Hawai'i. *Topics in Early Childhood Special Education, 24,* 199–213.

Twenty-fifth annual report to Congress on the implementation of the IDEA. (2003). *Washington,* DC: U.S. Department of Education.

U.S. Office of Special Education Programs. (2005). *Individuals with Disabilities Education Act (IDEA) data: Part C annual report tables.* Retrieved from http://www.ed.gov/

Krystal T. Cook
Texas A&M University

See also Developmental Delay; Early Identification of Children With Disabilities

CHILD GUIDANCE CLINIC

Child guidance clinics are the result of the blending of several historical forces. The feminist movement was instrumental in opening the way for the *Century of the Child* (Key, 1909). This was precipitated by a new interest in child psychology that occurred at the turn of the century. Concern for children was also evidenced at this time in the passage of child labor laws. Also, as compulsory education gained momentum, problem children could no longer be hidden away at home and school-related problems became more prominent. In fact, the first clinic created for children (Lightner Witmer, at the University of Pennsylvania in 1896) was primarily concerned with the adaptation of children to the school situation. In 1891, America's earliest child psychologist of renown, G. Stanley Hall, designed the first journal devoted to child psychology; it served as a record of educational literature, institutions, and progress.

A second major force in the development of child clinics was the mental hygiene movement that was stimulated by the publication of *The Mind That Found Itself* (Beers, 1908). Beers and his associates set out to disprove the age-old dictum that suggested once insane, insane forever. This proved to be a significant step in the direction of acknowledging that if mental hygiene held value for adults, the same must hold true for children.

Another significant force was the influence of the psychiatrists that came to be known as the Boston Group. They viewed mental disorders as maladjustments of the personality rather than as diseases of the nervous system. Adolf Meyer (1928), a member of this group, believed that all possible factors should be considered, including original endowment, personality traits, home influences, habits, bodily ailments, and environmental stresses. Meyer is also believed to be the initiator of psychiatric social work as his wife visited the homes of his patients to determine emotional histories and information about their personalities and other illnesses. Meyer's wife was also concerned with preparing families for the return of the patient to the home setting. This interest in families and the childhood experiences of adult patients established a precedent for similar interest in the families and experiences of child patients.

By 1921, there were a number of clinics for children that were attached to mental hospitals, social agencies, schools, and colleges. Child guidance clinics were formally organized under that name in 1922 by the National Committee for Mental Hygiene and the Commonwealth Fund. These early clinics emphasized a team approach to the diagnosis and treatment of children's problems. A social worker and psychologist (under the supervision of a psychiatrist) constituted the treatment team. Thus, the interdisciplinary team concept was initiated, and it was revolutionary for its time. While interdisciplinary teams today have considerable overlap in role and function, the early teams were regimented so that the psychologist did the necessary testing, the social worker dealt with the parents (typically just the mother), and the psychiatrist worked with the child.

The Philadelphia Child Guidance Clinic was one of these early clinics; it has survived the years and seems reflective of the changes that have evolved. This is the clinic that is identified strongly with one of the major orientations to working with families: primarily structural family therapy as developed by Salvador Minuchin (1974). As Minuchin was an employee of the Philadelphia-based clinic, so were other influential persons in the development of family therapy such as Jay Haley, Harry Aponte, and Braulio Montalvo. This clinic also demonstrates the great overlap of functioning by various disciplines; social workers, psychologists, and psychiatrists all share equally in the delivery of services. In fact, a project supervised by Haley and Minuchin in the early 1970s focused on the training of laypeople as significant helpers with troubled families. The Philadelphia Child Guidance Clinic, with its emphasis on one-way mirrors, live supervision, and videotaping, has also distinguished itself as a significant training institution. While not on the same scale as the Philadelphia clinic, many other clinics have followed the lead and developed themselves as centers of treatment and training (Chandra, Srinath, & Kinshore, 1993). Certainly, the early child guidance clinics initiated the development of a far more elaborate treatment delivery system, but their influence still seems easily distinguishable as one considers the many community mental health centers that feature the multidisciplinary treatment teams that are now considered standard practice.

REFERENCES

Beers, C. (1908). *The mind that found itself*. New York, NY: Longmans, Green.

Chandra, P. S., Srinath, S., & Kinshore, A. (1993). Disturbed children grown up: Follow-up of a child guidance clinic population into adulthood. *NIMHANS Journal, 11*(1), 43–47.

Key, E. (1909). *The century of the child*. New York, NY: Putnam.

Meyer, A. (1928). Presidential address: 35 years of psychiatry in the United States and our present outlook. *American Journal of Psychiatry*, LXXXV, 1–32.

Minuchin, S. (1974). *Families and family therapy*. Cambridge, MA: Harvard University Press.

CHARLES P. BARNARD
University of Wisconsin at Stout

See also Child Psychiatry; Child Psychology

CHILDHOOD APHASIA

Childhood aphasia, a label used in the pediatric and neurologic literature to describe disorders of speech and language in children, covers various disorders of communication. It is applied to children who have impairment of previously normal language and to children who failed in the normal acquisition of language.

The term *aphasia* derives from adult pathology in which an acute or progressive lesion produces a characteristic language disorder; it is "a clinical term that denotes the loss or impairment of language following brain damage and therefore, by definition, aphasia is a neurologic disorder" (Benson, 1979). When the brain has reached maturity, all the cerebral areas have their specialized activities. The language function is localized in the left hemisphere in right-handed people but also in the majority of left-handed persons. The cerebral hemispheres are not symmetrical anatomically or functionally. The asymmetry is already present in the fetus, but it becomes more marked in adult life. The planum temporale (superior temporal cortex) is larger on the left side of the brain and corresponds to an auditory association area that, in the adult, is included in the receptive area for language, called Wernicke's area. The left hemisphere is preponderant for language but its activities result from relations with different areas of the same hemisphere and also with the right hemisphere, which participates in language function.

An exhaustive study of cerebral lateralization, cerebral dominance, and asymmetrical functions in the nervous system was reviewed by Geschwind and Galaburda (1985). Many classifications of the adult aphasias are known. Benson (1979) describes in detail eight different types of acquired aphasia that are based on the possibility of the patient expressing himself or herself in a fluent way or not, of understanding spoken language or not, and of repeating, reading, and writing. In the adult there are mainly two groups of aphasia. The first, in which the patient is more affected in the comprehension of oral language, is called receptive, sensory, or Wernicke's aphasia. The patient is able to speak fluently but speech may have no connection with the questions asked. The pathology involves the posterior-superior portion of the first temporal gyrus (Wernicke's area). In the second group, the aphasic patient has great difficulties with speech but is able to write or to show the answers indicating that comprehension is correct. This is expressive, motor, or Broca's aphasia. The underlying pathology affects mainly the prerolandic region of the brain (frontal operculum or Broca's area).

Acquired aphasia in children is defined as impairment of previously normal language. Even in similar pathologic processes, as in adults, the clinical symptoms of aphasia in children depend on the degree of language development prior to cerebral insult. Childhood aphasia is characterized by an absence of spontaneous expressive language (oral, written, and gestural), producing a clinical syndrome of nonfluent speech or mutism (Wright, 1982). In all cases, the lexicon is reduced and the syntax is simplified; there is no logorrhea and even the lesion is temporal. Recovery is more frequent and rapid than in the adult, but when children regain language they rarely return to the premorbid level. Guttmann (1942) showed that disorders of language are mainly a reduction of the verbal expression of speech (thus, mainly a motor disorder). The prognosis is good unless there are simultaneous expressive and comprehension disorders.

Basser (1962) supported hemispheric equipotentiality because pre- or perinatal hemiplegia does not produce language impairment if the lesion is left or right; there is a possible transfer to the other hemisphere of the processes responsible for language when the damage is early, before language development. But if language is already acquired at the time of the hemiplegia, there is a persistent language deficit. Alajouanine and Lhermitte (1965) studied acquired aphasia in 32 children ages 6 to 15 years. The lesion was always in the left hemisphere, either traumatic or vascular. In all cases, they observed a reduction in expression in oral language, written language, or gestures; spontaneous language was nearly absent. Lenneberg (1967) suggested that up to age 11, language function could be assumed by the right hemisphere. However, Hecaen (1976) showed that 88% of acquired aphasias in children are due to left hemisphere lesions, while only 33% have right hemisphere lesions. Woods and Teuber (1978) confirmed that less than 10% of acquired aphasia results from right hemisphere lesions; if left-handedness is excluded, only 5% are due to right hemispheric lesions. Recovery, more frequent than in adults, is less evident if there are bilateral lesions. Recovery is better and more likely to occur with early lesions, before age 8. The recovery is never complete in comparison with normal controls, even when the child is no longer aphasic. In children with an injury prior to 12 months, there is no deficit in language, but the verbal IQ is significantly lower than that of sibling controls, showing that hemispheric specialization for language is very early. If the injury to the left hemisphere is made after 1 year, there is a persistent aphasic deficit as well as impaired cognitive function (Woods & Carey, 1979).

A syndrome of aphasia with convulsive disorders has been described in childhood by Landau and Kleffner (1957; GAPS, 2005). This syndrome occurs in children who have had normal language development. It may begin between 18 months of age and 13 years, but the peak is reached between 3 and 7 years. The affected children may develop acutely or progressively (over days to months) a severe impairment of verbal comprehension as well as a loss of expressive language. At times, they appear deaf. The deficit has been ascribed to a verbal auditory agnosia (Rapin, Mattis, Rowan, & Golden, 1977) or autism, developmental disorder, hearing impairment, childhood schizophrenia, attention-deficit/hyperactivity disorder, mental retardation, or emotional/behavioral disorders (GAPS, 2005). The aphasic disorder may fluctuate with complete recovery and relapse. Intelligence remains normal. Outcome is variable with complete recovery or persistence of a mild or moderate deficit. Epileptic fits usually precede the language disorder, but they are not always present even though the electroencephalogram (EEG) always shows paroxysmal epileptic activity. The clinical fits usually disappear before 15 years and the EEG also becomes normal. No organic lesion has been shown in this syndrome.

Developmental language disorders or dysphasias are seen in children who have never acquired normal language function. They have been described under various terms: congenital or developmental aphasias, specific language disorders, and dysphasias. From the literature it appears that the capability for human language is partially an innate cognitive skill (Mayeux & Kandel, 1985). The process of acquisition of normal language function (Rapin, 1982; Wright, 1982) starts at birth. Infants with normal hearing are sensitive to sounds and react to them; they progressively become able to discriminate the acoustically subtle phonetic cues crucial for the comprehension of human language. This sensitivity is lost as language is acquired. Children learn to associate meaningful visual precepts (visual memory) with discriminable auditory ones (auditory memory), and to demonstrate this by pointing to objects on verbal command. Therefore, language acquisition is not a passive operation based on imitation. The child will only start to repeat syllables and words when he or she is able to segment speech sounds and elemental units of meaningful language extracted from the casual conversation all around. Auditory comprehension precedes speaking. An infant understands the meaning of a word before vocalizing it and initially learns to comprehend the spoken symbol of a word (decoding). When the child comprehends the word, he or she is able to express the language symbol (encoding; Wright, 1982). Children progressively acquire the rules of grammar and form sentences by age 4. It will take a child much longer to perfect articulatory skills and to learn to produce highly complex sentences. The addition of new words throughout the vocabulary continues throughout life. The process of acquisition follows a progression related to the overall maturation and development of the infant, but it also requires normal functioning and control of the structures involved in sound production.

The acquisition of language by children in all cultures follows a similar series of stages. Some children progress through these stages faster than others, but the average age for each stage is the same for all cultures, with peaks of development at certain ages. At 3 to 6 months, an infant is able to do cooing, then babbling at 6 to 9 months. At 9 to 12 months, the baby imitates sounds and says the first intelligible words. By 14 months, the first word is given in a specific sense, usually "mommy" and "daddy." By 18 months, the vocabulary has 10 to 15 words. At 2 years, the child is able to make some sentences containing two or three words. At 3 years, speech contains questions and statements, as well as some emotional tone. Questions are of importance as they show the interest of the child in the surrounding world. At 4 years, complex sentences of a few words are used and the child knows his or her first and last names.

Developmental language disorders traditionally have been divided into two groups. The first is disorders of receptive language, in which impaired comprehension is the essential feature; however, one may find some degree of verbal language and articulation dysfunction. The second group is expressive language disorders, characterized by delayed talking; poverty of words (especially in naming); and agrammatical spontaneous speech but normal comprehension, provided the child has no deafness, no mental retardation, no cerebral palsy, and is not psychiatrically disturbed and did not suffer from environmental deprivation. As this type of classification has not satisfied clinicians or linguists, other subgroups have been proposed (Aram & Nation, 1975; Bishop & Rosenbloom, 1987; Rapin, 1982, 1985). The classification presented by Rapin (1985) takes into account the input–central processing–output stages of language operation as well as the level of language most severely affected; it is based on the various levels of acquisition of language. The levels are phonology (concerned with sounds used as linguistic symbols), grammar (syntax and morphology, or the arrangement of words into meaningful sentences), semantics (the representation of meaning in language), pragmatics (how language is used).

In verbal auditory agnosia (word deafness), one is incapable of decoding the sounds around him or her (phonologic level, first necessary step to comprehension of language). The child does not understand phonemes or verbal words; therefore, he or she cannot reproduce them, is mute, or utters single words with phonologic distortion. The syntax is poor. These children learn gestural language and can express themselves through drawings. Their comprehension of symbols and cognitive functions is good and is expressed through games. They will benefit from teaching techniques for deaf children.

In semantic-pragmatic syndrome, the child has an impaired comprehension of the meaning and intent of communication but has good phonology and syntax. The child has a fluent language and often reproduces what is said, but is echolalic for even well-constructed sentences. As the deficit affects comprehension and use of language, the syndrome will be mainly observed with sophisticated questions. If these are put in a simply way, the child can answer yes or no, showing the deficit is not a cognitive one. These children have good auditory memory and are able to repeat long sentences, but their spontaneous speech often lacks precision. As pragmatics is affected in this syndrome, the subject cannot read facial expression or recognize tone of voice, so speech can be unadapted to the situation, creating difficulties in social contacts and behavioral problems. These children also can learn to read, but they do not totally understand what they read.

In semantic-syntactic-organizing syndrome, the deficit lies at two levels: syntax, necessary to organize words into meaningful sentences, and semantics, which is concerned with the meaning of sentences. Therefore, children are dysfluent, using incorrect words in an inadequate order. The repetition of words is better than spontaneous speech.

Mixed receptive-expressive (phonologic-syntactic) syndrome is the most frequently seen syndrome of the developmental dysphasias. Comprehension is always better than expression, and can even be normal. The children are dysfluent and have a reduced vocabulary and an elementary syntax. The phonology is also impaired, producing some distortions of poorly articulated words. Speech may be telegraphic.

In severe expressive syndrome (verbal apraxial), children with normal comprehension have a deficiency in coding language symbols into words. Their speech is extremely poor; often the children are mute. They learn to read and sign.

Phonological programming deficit syndrome is a subgroup of severe expressive syndrome. Children have a good comprehension, are fluent, and are able to speak in sentences. Phonologic disorder produces distorted pronunciation with substitutions or omissions in words; speech is incomprehensible to other than family members. This can be further confounded when bilingualism is present (Paradis, 1995).

The classifications used in developmental language disorders are still descriptive and the anatomic clinical correlations are less well understood than in adult or childhood acquired language disorders. The mechanisms involved are not only dependent on the left hemisphere, they have still to be elucidated.

REFERENCES

Alajouanine, T., & Lhermitte, F. (1965). Acquired aphasia in children. *Brain, 88,* 653–662.

Aram, D. M., & Nation, J. E. (1975). Patterns of language behavior in children with developmental language disorders. *Journal of Speech & Hearing Research, 18,* 229–241.

Basser, L. S. (1962). Hemiplegia of early onset and the faculty of speech with special reference to the effects of hemispherectomy. *Brain, 85,* 427–460.

Benson, D. F. (1979). Aphasia. In K. M. Heilman & E. Valenstein (Eds.), *Clinical neuropsychology* (pp. 22–58). New York, NY: Oxford University Press.

Bishop, D. V. M., & Rosenbloom, L. (1987). Childhood language disorders: Classification and overview. In W. Yule, M. Rutter, & M. Bax (Eds.), *Language development and disorders. Clinics in developmental medicine.* Philadelphia, PA: Blackwell Scientific & Lippincott.

Genetic Information and Patient Services (GAPS). (2005). Landau-Kleffner syndrome. Retrieved from http://non-profit-organizations.findthebest.com/l/1349590/Genetic-Information-and-Patient-Services-Inc

Geshwind, N., & Galaburda, A. M. (1985). Cerebral lateralization. Biological mechanisms, associations and pathology. *Archives of Neurology, 42*-I, 428–459; 42-II, 521–552; 42-III, 634–654.

Guttmann, E. (1942). Aphasia in children. *Brain*, *65*, 205.

Hecaen, H. (1976). Acquired aphasia in children and the ontogenesis of hemispheric functional specialization. *Brain & Language*, *3*, 114–134.

Landau, W. M., & Kleffner, F. R. (1957). Syndrome of acquired aphasia with convulsive disorder in children. *Neurology*, *7*, 523–530.

Lenneberg, E. H. (1967). *Biological foundations of language*. New York, NY: Wiley.

Mayeux, R., & Kandel, E. R. (1985). Natural language, disorders of language, and other localizable disorders of cognitive functioning. In E. R. Kandel & J. H. Schwartz (Eds.), *Principles of neural science*. New York, NY: Elsevier.

Paradis, M. (1995). *Aspects of bilingual aphasia*. New York, NY: Pergamon Press.

Rapin, I. (1982). *Children with brain dysfunction: Neurology, cognition, language and behavior*. New York, NY: Raven.

Rapin, I. (1985). Communication disorders in children. In H. Szliwowski & J. Bormans (Eds.), *Progrès en neurologie pédiatrique*. Brussels, Belgium: Prodim.

Rapin, I., Mattis, S., Rowan, A. J., & Golden, G. G. (1977). Verbal auditory agnosia in children. *Developmental Medicine & Child Neurology*, *19*, 192–207.

Woods, B. T., & Carey, S. (1979). Language deficits after apparent clinical recovery from childhood aphasia. *Annals of Neurology*, *6*, 405–409.

Woods, B. T., & Teuber, H. L. (1978). Changing patterns of childhood aphasia. *Annals of Neurology*, *3*, 273–280.

Wright, F. S. (1982). Disorders of speech and language. In K. F. Swaiman & F. S. Wright (Eds.), *The practice of pediatric neurology*. St. Louis, MO: Mosby.

Henri B. Szliwowski
Catherine Wetzburger
Hôpital Erasme, Université Libre de Bruxelles, Belgium

See also Aphasia; Language Disorders; Left Brain/Right Brain; Mutism

CHILDHOOD AUTISM RATING SCALE, SECOND EDITION

The Childhood Autism Rating Scale, Second Edition (CARS2, 2010) is a rating scale completed by an examiner (on the basis of direct observations of the child, parent interviews, record review, etc.) in order to identify behaviors associated with *autism spectrum disorders* (ASDs) in children ages 2 and older, and to differentiate between children exhibiting mild symptoms of ASDs and children exhibiting severe symptoms of ASDs. The CARS2 includes three different forms, one of which is consistent with the older edition of the CARS (i.e., Standard Version Rating Booklet; CARS2-ST). Whereas the original CARS focused specifically on the diagnosis of autism, this new version of the instrument includes a separate form for assessing verbally fluent individuals, children 6 years of age and older, and children with IQ scores above 80 (i.e., High-Functioning Version Rating Booklet; CARS2-HF), as well as an unscored Questionnaire for Parents or Caregivers (CARS2-QPC), used to assist examiners in making their ratings and in structuring follow-up interviews.

The CARS2-ST is comprised of 15 items on which a child's behavior is rated on a Likert scale ranging from within normal limits (1) to severely abnormal (4) for the child's chronological age. The behaviors rated include: (1) Relating to People, (2) Imitation, (3) Emotional Response, (4) Body Use, (5) Object Use, (6) Adaptation to Change, (7) Visual Response, (8) Listening Response, (9) Taste/Smell/Touch Response and Use, (10) Fear or Nervousness, (11) Verbal Communication, (12) Nonverbal Communication, (13) Activity Level, (14) Level and Consistency of Intellectual Response, and (15) General Impressions. The CARS-HF is structured very similarly, although many of the scales are altered slightly to reflect aspects of ASDs not captured in the other scale. The behaviors rated include: (1) Social-Emotional Understanding, (2) Emotional Expression and Regulation of Emotions, (3) Relating to People, (4) Body Use, (5) Object Use in Play, (6) Adaptation to Change/Restricted Interests, (7) Visual Response, (8) Listening Response, (9) Taste/Smell/Touch Response and Use, (10) Fear or Anxiety, (11) Verbal Communication, (12) Nonverbal Communication, (13) Thinking/Cognitive Integration Skills, (14) Level and Consistency of Intellectual Response, and (15) General Impressions.

This instrument was first published in 1988, and the norm data were collected on a sample of 1,606 individuals who had been referred for ASD evaluation in the early 1980s. Two updated studies, both a verification sample used to assess the reliability and validity of the CARS2-ST ($N = 1,034$) and a CARS2-HF development sample ($N = 994$), were conducted in order to evaluate the psychometric properties of the revised instrument. For the CARS2-ST, the sample is predominantly male (78%) and all participants' IQ scores are 85 or lower (and in these ways, the sample is representative of the population diagnosed with ASDs). In contrast, all participants who were administered the CARS2-HF instrument had IQs of 80 or higher. Again, this sample was predominantly (78%) male, and participants in this group had a variety of clinical diagnoses (e.g., PDD-NOS, ADHD).

Internal consistency estimates for both instruments are high (i.e., CARS2-ST = .93, CARS2-HF = .96). Because the CARS instruments require examiners to use their clinical judgment in scoring, interrater reliability is a particularly important construct to consider when assessing the instrument. The authors rely on the original interrater reliability data from the CARS when discussing the reliability of the CARS2-ST; this measure has a median correlation of .71. On the CARS2-HF, data was collected on 239 individuals. Total scores across two raters were correlated .95, and interrater reliability estimates for particular items range from .53 (for Level and Consistency of Intellectual Response) to .93 (for General Impressions), indicating an overall acceptable level of agreement across raters. The authors again rely on the original CARS data when discussing interrater reliability of professionals in different professions (e.g., school psychologists, audiologists, medical students) and from different sources of clinical information; reevaluating interrater reliability in these areas using the more recent samples would be helpful.

The validity of these instruments is discussed in depth in the examiner's manual, and includes a discussion of the varied factor analyses that have been conducted using these measures. The authors also discuss the convergent and divergent validity of these scales by comparing child performance on the CARS-ST and CARS2-HF to performance on other measures such as the Autism Diagnostic Observation Schedule and the Social Responsiveness Scale. Globally, the authors demonstrate that these measures have the potential to accurately identify students with ASDs and to adequately differentiate between children exhibiting varying levels of symptoms. This updated version of the CARS has not yet been reviewed in the *Mental Measurements Yearbook*. However, past reviewers endorsed the original measure strongly (although noting concerns about the potentially outdated normative sample, even at that time).

JAMIE ZIBULSKY
Fairleigh Dickinson University

KATHLEEN VIEZEL
Fairleigh Dickinson University
Fourth edition

CHILDHOOD AUTISM SPECTRUM TEST (CAST)

The Childhood Asperger Syndrome Test (CAST; Scott, Baren-Cohen, Bolton, & Brayne, 2002) was originally designed by a group of researchers at the University of Cambridge for use in a prevalence study of Asperger syndrome in childhood. Specifically it was designed as a screening measure for Asperger syndrome and related social and communication disorders (Scott et al., 2002). It has since been renamed the Childhood Autism Spectrum Test to indicate a broader range of use (Williams et al., 2008). The CAST has primarily been studied and used in the United Kingdom with children aged 5–11 as a screening measure for epidemiological research. It was developed to be sensitive to autism spectrum disorders in the general education school population where children typically have cognitive ability within the normal range (Williams et al., 2005). This instrument screens autism spectrum conditions in primary school children by measuring social and communication skills through a 37-item parent questionnaire asking Yes/No questions. Development of the measure was based on behavioral descriptions from the International Classification of Diseases, ninth edition (WHO, 1993), and the *Diagnostic and Statistical Manual of Mental Disorders*, fourth edition (American Psychiatric Association, 1994), of the core features of autism (Scott et al., 2002). The self-completion questionnaire is comprised of skills from the following areas: initiation and maintenance of conversation and specific language difficulties, social interaction with adults and peers, choice of play activities, presence of rigid or repetitive behaviors, choice of interests, and sharing interests with others (Williams et al., 2008).

The CAST has a maximum score of 31; six items are control questions that are not scored (Scott et al., 2002). A cut-point of 15 and above is used to indicate concerns of possible autism spectrum disorder. The sensitivity of the CAST has been demonstrated to be 100%, specificity 97%, and positive predictive value 50% (Williams et al., 2005). The low positive predictive value may be a function of the low prevalence of Asperger syndrome in the general population (Williams et al., 2005). Due to the low positive predictive value, the CAST is not generally recommended for screening in the general population in a public health or educational setting, but is recommended for epidemiological studies (Willimas et al., 2005). The CAST has a test–retest reliability of 0.83 (Spearman's rho), with 97% of children not moving past the cut-point upon retest (Williams et al., 2006). The test–retest reliability in a high-scoring sample has a correlation of 0.67 (Allison et al., 2007). A free downloadable copy of the CAST questionnaire and scoring key is available through the Autism Research Center website at the University of Cambridge (www.autismresearchcenter.com).

REFERENCES

Allison, C., Williams, J., Scott, F., Stott, C., Bolton, P., Baron-Cohen, S., & Brayne, C. (2007). The Childhood Asperger Syndrome Test (CAST): Test-retest reliability in a high scoring sample. *Autism, 11*, 173–85.

American Psychiatric Association. (1994). *Diagnostic and statistical manual of mental disorders* (4th ed.). Washington, DC: Author.

Scott, F. J., Baron-Cohen, S., Bolton, P., & Brayne, C. (2002). The CAST (Childhood Asperger Syndrome Test): Preliminary development of UK screen for mainstream primary-school children. *Autism, 6*, 9–31.

Williams, J., Scott, F., Stott, F., Allison, C., Bolton, P., Baron-Cohen, S., Brayne, C. (2005). The CAST (Childhood Asperger Syndrome Test): Test accuracy. *Autism*, *9*, 45–68.

Williams, J., Scott, F., Stott, F., Allison, C., Bolton, P., Baron-Cohen, S., & Brayne, C. (2006). The Childhood Asperger Syndrome Test (CAST): test retest reliability. *Autism*, *10*, 415–27.

Williams, J. G., Allison, C., Scott, F. J., Bolton, F., Baron-Cohen, S., Matthews, F. E., & Brayne, C. (2008). The Childhood Autism Spectrum Test (CAST): Sex differences. *Journal of Autism and Developmental Disorders*, *38*, 1731–1739.

World Health Organization (1993). *The ICD-10 Classification of Mental and Behavioural Disorders: Diagnostic Criteria for Research*. Geneva: WHO.

DEANNA CLEMENS
College Station Independent School District,
College Station, TX
Fourth edition

CHILDHOOD DISINTEGRATIVE DISORDER

Childhood disintegrative disorder (CDD) is classified as a pervasive developmental disorder and is characterized by at least 2 years of normal early development followed by profound loss of previously acquired skills in the areas of cognition, communication, motor control, and bowel and bladder control. Once established, behaviors manifested as a result of CDD are indistinguishable from those of autism. Previously, CDD has been referred to as Heller's syndrome, dementia infantilis, and disintegrative psychosis (Filipek et al., 1999).

Etiology of the disorder is unknown; however, marked disintegration of functioning after a normal period of development suggests that the underlying mechanism is organic (e.g., neurobiological disorder or medical condition). Neurologic conditions such as tuberous sclerosis, neurolipidoses, and metachromatic leucodystrophyas have been implicated with the disorder, as have pertussis and measles (Volkmar, 1992). Children with CDD have been shown to have abnormal epileptiform electroencephalograms; however, if seizures occur, they are rarely the first sign. More often than not, seizures occur after the onset of CDD (Malhotra & Gupta, 1999).

CDD is a rare condition with prevalence rates reported to be about 1 per 100,000 children (Malhotra & Gupta, 1999). Because CDD shares a number of features with other pervasive developmental disorders, it is often indistinguishable. Children with CDD have impaired communication (verbal and nonverbal), poor social interactions, and stereotypic behaviors and interests, like children with autism. There is some indication that CDD may be more common in males than females; given how rare the disorder is, however, this remains unclear. Critical to the diagnosis of CDD is a history of normal development up to the age of 2 years followed by a marked decline. This "normal" period of development distinguishes CDD from infantile autism.

Characteristics

1. Normal early development until at least 2 years of age, followed by loss of functioning prior to age 10
2. Loss of previously acquired skills in the areas of cognitive functioning, verbal and nonverbal communication, social skills, motor skills, and bowel and bladder control
3. Intellectual functioning ranging from moderate to profound mental retardation
4. Emergence of restricted, stereotypic behavior or resistance to change (compulsive behavior)
5. Affective symptoms such as excessive fearfulness and anxiety
6. Overactivity

Treatment of CDD is typically with psychotropic medication such as antipsychotics (e.g., haloperidol), benzodiazepenes, antidepressants, lithium, and clozapine. Comorbid seizure disorders are treated with antiepileptics (e.g., carbamazepine). Behavior management is also commonly required. Children with CDD require comprehensive services, including treatment that encourages the reacquisition of cognitive and adaptive skills and speech and motor control. Most children with CDD will be served in self-contained special education classrooms. Speech and language pathology services, as well as occupational and physical therapy, will typically be required. School nurses may also be involved in the care of these children.

Prognosis is poor given that 75% of all cases have profound mental retardation. Despite treatment efforts, the course tends to be static with limited recovery of skills. The outcome in fact is much worse than autism, as children with CDD tend to be lower functioning and more aloof and to have higher rates of epilepsy. Life expectancy appears normal; however, due to the severe nature of the disorder, most individuals are cared for at home or in residential settings. Further research is needed to investigate the various causes of CDD and ways to prevent this unfortunate condition from occurring.

REFERENCES

Filipek, P. A., Accardo, P. J., Baranek, G. T., Cook, E. H., Jr., Dawson, G., Gordon, B., ... Volkmar, F. R. (1999). The screening and diagnosis of autistic spectrum disorders. *Journal of Autism and Developmental Disorders*, *29*(6), 439–484.

Malhotra, S., & Gupta, N. (1999). Childhood disintegrative disorder. *Journal of Autism and Developmental Disorders, 29*(6), 491–498.

Volkmar, F. R. (1992). Childhood disintegrative disorder: Issues for *DSM-IV*. *Journal of Autism and Developmental Disorders, 22*(4), 625–642.

LORI DEKEYZER
ELAINE CLARK
University of Utah

See also Pervasive Developmental Disorder

CHILDHOOD NEUROSIS (See Psychoneurotic Disorders)

CHILDHOOD PSYCHOSIS

Researchers in child psychology and psychiatry agree that there exist identifiable-clinical syndromes where children are out of touch with reality, withdraw from the social world around them, and show unusual and bizarre behaviors. These psychotic children present great challenges to their caretakers: parents who try to provide for the psychotic child's needs and integration into the family system; teachers who try to educate the child and provide basic social skills training; and mental health professionals who try to treat the child clinically.

Consider the following case that the author supervised at a community mental health center. A 9-year-old boy was referred by foster parents following a sudden onset of bizarre destructive behavior and hallucinations. He thought monsters lurked behind doors, heard voices, and displayed bizarre speech during psychotic episodes. This child had been placed in several different foster homes since being abused and neglected as an infant. Two of his siblings were being legally adopted by one set of foster parents, but this child's behavior had led them to decide not to adopt him. He showed poor social skills, was intrusive with others (i.e., did not keep his hands to himself), and had a short attention span. He tolerated stress poorly and would sometimes lash out at others in a violent manner when frustrated. Several psychiatric hospitalizations had only temporarily stabilized self-control and reality orientation. This child was psychotic.

Other clinical cases make the important point that highly unusual and even bizarre behavior does not necessarily imply that a child is psychotic. During the clinical evaluation, for example, one 8-year-old boy freely launched into colorful descriptions of monsters and secret fantasy worlds. His conversation was marked by bizarre verbalizations with little distinction between reality and illusion.

He mixed grandiose and paranoid ideas with characters of fantasy and real significant others from his life. Taken out of context, these verbalizations might be construed to reflect an active psychotic delusional state. However, on other occasions, the child was able to perceive reality accurately and to describe his delusions as a fantasy game. This child was not psychotic, but used fantasy as a retreat from high conflict and turmoil in his life. His family history did suggest that he was at risk for developing a psychotic state under stress since his mother had been diagnosed as schizophrenic.

Incidence of childhood psychosis is estimated to be approximately .01 to .05 per 1,000 children and increasing with age (Dekeyzer & Clark, 2003). Unfortunately, methodological difficulties impede accurate estimates of incidence. However, research consistently shows that more boys than girls are diagnosed for each of the psychotic disorders. Estimated differences vary considerably, but it appears that at least twice as many boys are diagnosed as psychotic (Wing, 1968).

Early interest in psychotic states in children appeared near the turn of the 20th century in the writings of Kraepelin and Bleuler, who introduced the terms *dementia praecox* (early insanity) and *schizophrenia* (split mind), respectively. Both of these pioneers felt that the onset of many of their adult patients' psychotic disorders had been in their childhood. Thus childhood psychosis was seen as essentially identical symptomatically to adult schizophrenia. The concept of childhood psychoses gained greater acceptance as a result of articles by Potter (1933), Bender (1942), and Bradley and Bowen (1941) on childhood schizophrenia; Kanner (1943) on early infantile autism; Rank (1949) on atypical child psychosis; Mahler (1952) on symbiotic psychosis. These early writings were uniformly based on medical model or disease conception of mental abnormality and were marked by conceptual ambiguity and a lack of specific diagnostic criteria (Wing, 1968).

The evolution of theoretical syndromes points to three general types of childhood psychosis: (1) childhood schizophrenia, (2) early infantile autism, and (3) atypical or symbiotic psychosis.

Interest in childhood schizophrenia followed Potter's (1933) paper. The schizophrenic child was seen as someone who was disinterested in the environment, manifested disturbed thought processes and frequently poor verbal skills, had difficulty in forming emotional attachments to others, and showed bizarre behaviors with a tendency to perseverate in various activities. This view of childhood schizophrenia was modeled after adult schizophrenia.

Research on childhood autism was pioneered by Kanner (1943), who described autistic children as generally having a limited ability to relate to other people beginning in infancy, a language disturbance making it difficult to communicate with others, and conspicuous and obsessive behavior for repetition and maintaining sameness.

Symbiotic psychosis is a rare subtype described by Mahler (1952) as a disturbance owed to intense resistance by the child to becoming psychologically independent of the mother. The number of cases reported is small. The syndrome may be due to repeated early traumatic events and also may stem from a constitutional predisposition to fail to see the mother as a separate object (Mahler, 1965). The onset of this syndrome occurs between 2½ and 5 years of age, preceded by fairly normal development during the first 2 years of life. The onset of symptoms can be set off by such events as illness of a mother, birth of a sibling, or the beginning of school. Figure C.10 shows the general distribution of cases (not necessarily according to Mahler's theory) of childhood psychoses given by age of onset.

The child manifests the behaviors of extreme separation anxiety, emotional withdrawal, and distortions of reality similar to autism. Threats of separation create panic. Frustration tolerance is low, and even minor disruptions in routine create panic. There is a craving for sameness. This type of environmental disinterestedness diminishes contact with reality. This syndrome produces hypoactivity or hyperactivity, peculiar thoughts and abnormal speech, and aggressive behavior such as biting and hitting. The central symptom is profound anxiety to the point of panic over the possibility of separation from the mother. When this bond is threatened, the symbiotic child may show excessive screaming and temper tantrums. These episodes may be followed by disturbed thinking and the expression of bizarre ideas. Following the onset of the psychotic state, the child may show regression in previously acquired habits such as toilet training and disturbances in other behaviors such as eating and sleeping.

The *Diagnostic and Statistical Manual of Mental Disorders, Fourth Edition Text Revision* (*DSM-IV-R*; American Psychiatric Association, 2000) attempted to integrate the various approaches to childhood psychosis. This was not an easy task because of the complexity of the subject matter and the distinct points of view on such disorders as childhood schizophrenia. The resulting classification system is organized under the concept of pervasive developmental

disorders, with separate subcategories for infantile autism and childhood onset pervasive developmental disorder. This latter category is very general and appears to reflect early research on childhood schizophrenia represented by the work of Lauretta Bender; it excludes work on symbiotic psychosis by Mahler. A separate, less specifically defined category, atypical pervasive developmental disorder, allows the clinician to use diagnostic flexibility in describing the individual case, including a symbiotic psychotic child. The clinician can draw on the diagnostic criteria for adult schizophrenia in determining the appropriateness of this category for a child. The *DSM-IV* represents the most current thinking of the mental health profession on these disorders, and contains specific criteria for each psychotic disorder.

Treatment Approaches

Psychotherapy

Individual psychotherapy has been widely used in the treatment of childhood psychosis. Treatment approaches differ depending on the clinician's theory of the causes of the disorder, but they have in common an attempt to resolve psychic turmoil. Psychoanalytic-based approaches focus on the individual child and the presumed intrapsychic conflicts created by a fractured mother–child relationship (Mahler, 1965). Other approaches focus more on interpersonal skills and involve other family members in the treatment (Reiser, 1963).

Research on the effectiveness of psychotherapy with psychotic children has produced differing estimates of improvement. Most writers agree that it often helps to improve symptoms, but there is disagreement on how much it contributes beyond an untreated recovery rate. Some reported recovery rates have been astoundingly high, but the research is difficult to evaluate because of differing criteria used to measure success and lack of untreated control groups.

Milieu and Educational Therapy

This approach manipulates the total environment in a residential setting. It addresses impairments to all areas of functioning and employs multiple treatments (individual, educational, and group therapy). Children referred for these programs are usually the most disturbed; this may partly explain why clinical improvement occurs in a high percentage of cases. Milieu therapy often focuses on improving adaptive self-care skills and improving reality orientation to facilitate better relatedness to others (Zimmerman, 1994). Research on the effectiveness of such programs is difficult to evaluate owing to lack of experimental controls, diverse groups of psychotic children, and small sample sizes. However, more structured programs appear to be more effective (Schopler, 1974).

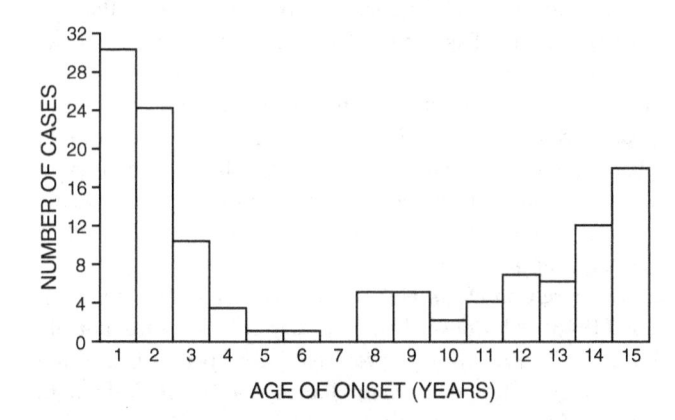

Figure C.10. Distribution of cases of childhood psychosis given by age of onset (first detection).

Behavior Therapy

Principles of learning theory have been successfully applied to treating the symptoms of psychotic children, especially autism (Ferster, 1961). The application of behavioral contingencies has helped child-care workers and parents to shape the behavior of disturbed children in positive ways, but research suggests that the effects are not easily generalizable across settings.

Organic Treatments

A wide variety of physical treatments have been attempted. Electroconvulsive shock therapy, sensory deprivation, vitamin therapy, hallucinogenic drugs (LSD), and antipsychotic drugs all have been used. Campbell (1973) concluded that little success can be attributed to any of these treatments though antipsychotic drugs are effective in alleviating the worst of some symptoms such as aggressiveness and hallucinations.

Summary

Biological, genetic (Crow, Done, & Sacker, 1995), and family factors combine to produce psychotic disturbance in children. A small percentage of children appear to be at risk of developing psychotic symptoms owed to these etiological factors when exposed to extreme environmental stress. Although a variety of treatments may produce some positive changes, long-term prognosis is generally poor for psychotic children. A high percentage continue to show psychotic symptoms or minimal social adjustment over time. With onset before age 10, the prognosis appears to be particularly poor. When a therapist and/or parent demonstrates a high degree of emotional involvement over time, the prognosis improves.

Characteristics

1. Prominent auditory (sometimes visual and tactile) hallucinations, delusions (reflecting developmental issues such as monsters), magical thinking, and thought disturbance
2. Social impairment, including trouble making and keeping friends
3. Odd, stereotypic behavior
4. Anxiety and mood disturbance (often mood-congruent with children)
5. In some adolescents, psychosis resembling adult schizophrenia

REFERENCES

American Psychiatric Association. (2000). *Diagnostic and statistical manual of mental disorders* (4th ed., Text Revision). Washington, DC: Author.

Bender, L. (1942). Schizophrenia in childhood. *Nervous Child, 1,* 138–140.

Bradley, C., & Bowen, M. (1941). Behavior characteristics of schizophrenic children. *Psychiatric Quarterly, 15,* 296–315.

Campbell, M. (1973). Biological interventions in psychoses of childhood. *Journal of Autism & Childhood Schizophrenia, 3,* 347–373.

Crow, T. J., Done, D. J., & Sacker, A. (1995). Childhood precursors of psychosis as clues to its evolutionary origins. *European Archives of Psychiatry & Clinical Neuroscience, 245*(2), 61–69.

Dekeyzer, L., & Clark, E. (2003). Childhood psychosis. In E. Fletcher-Janzen & C. R. Reynolds (Eds.). *Childhood disorders diagnostic desk reference* (pp. 123–124). Hoboken, NJ: Wiley.

Ferster, C. (1961). Positive reinforcement and behavioral deficits of autistic children. *Child Development, 32,* 437–456.

Kanner, L. (1943). Autistic disturbances of affective contact. *Nervous Child, 2,* 217–250.

Mahler, M. (1952). On child psychosis in schizophrenia: Autistic and symbiotic infantile psychosis. *Psychoanalytic Study of the Child, 7,* 286–305.

Mahler, M. (1965). On early infantile psychosis: The symbiotic and autistic syndromes. *Journal of the American Academy of Psychiatry, 4,* 554–568.

Potter, H. W. (1933). Schizophrenia in children. *American Journal of Psychiatry, 12,* 1253–1270.

Rank, B. (1949). Adaptation of the psychoanalytic technique in the treatment of young children with atypical development. *American Journal of Orthopsychiatry, 19,* 130–139.

Reiser, D. (1963). Psychosis of infancy and early childhood. *New England Journal of Medicine, 269,* 790–798, 844–850.

Schopler, E. (1974). Changes of direction with psychotic children. In A. Davids (Ed.), *Child personality and psychopathology: Current topics* (Vol. 1). New York, NY: Wiley.

Werry, J. S. (1972). Childhood psychosis. In H. D. Quay & J. S. Werry (Eds.), *Psychopathological disorders of childhood.* New York, NY: Wiley.

Wing, J. (1968). Review of B. Bettelheim, *The empty fortress. British Journal of Psychiatry, 114,* 788–791.

Zimmerman, P. D. (1994). Bruno Bettelheim: The mysterious other: Historical reflections on the treatment of childhood psychosis. *Psychoanalytic Review, 81*(3), 411–413.

WILLIAM G. AUSTIN
Cape Fear Psychological Services

See also Autism; Borderline Personality Disorder; Depression, Childhood and Adolescent; Emotional Disorders; Mental Status Exams; Psychoneurotic Disorders

CHILDHOOD SCHIZOPHRENIA

The term *childhood schizophrenia* is one that is the subject of considerable dispute among authorities in the fields of child psychiatry and psychology. The dispute has mainly to do with the boundaries of this term and the validity of the concept of a childhood onset schizophrenic disorder. As a result of the uncertainty and differences of opinion, firm conclusions have not been reached, and the variation in interpretation of the term *childhood schizophrenia* has made compilation of a database problematic.

A large part of the current confusion about childhood schizophrenia results from changes in the definition of the term itself. As Walk (1964) has noted, most authors prior to 1930 tended to diagnose schizophreniclike disorders in children much as they would have diagnosed them in adults. Typical of this literature is De Sanctis's (1906) use of the term *dementia precocissima*, which apparently was a variant of Kraepelin's concept of *dementia praecox* in adults.

By about 1935, several major clinics had been established in the United States for the study and treatment of severe children's disorders. The directors of these clinics (Bender, 1947; Kanner, 1943; Potter, 1933) all published descriptions of their samples of children and follow-up studies delineating the children's progress. Throughout the period 1930 to 1960, the terms *infantile psychosis*, *autism*, and *childhood schizophrenia* tended to be used interchangeably, although Kanner and his colleagues (Kanner, 1949; Kanner & Eisenberg, 1955) tended to define autism as a separate category that was seen as the earliest form of schizophrenia. Most of these early authors also agreed that schizophrenic disorders closely resembling the adult disorder could occur in childhood, although adult symptoms such as delusions and hallucinations did not occur before about age 6. Creak (1961) provided a working definition of childhood schizophrenia that included nine basic characteristics. However, this definition included a substantial overlap into both the autistic and schizophrenic syndromes. Early analytic writers such as Bettelheim (1950) and Szurek (1956) also tended to lump a wide variety of disorders under the rubric of childhood psychosis. In contrast to earlier authorities who were uncertain about etiology, psychoanalytic writers felt that the etiology of the disorder was always psychogenic.

By the end of the period 1965 to 1980, it became clear that some important and distinct subpopulations were emerging. Barbara Fish and her colleagues (Fish, Shapiro, & Campbell, 1968) developed a classification system based on language and the ability to integrate basic functions in infancy, and Rutter (1978) presented his findings from long-term studies at Maudsley Hospital in London. In addition, Kolvin (1971), Vrono (1974), and others had published epidemiological data that demonstrated that two major peaks occurred in the distribution of cases across age. The first, at about 2 to 3 years, consisted of cases of autism and autisticlike disorders. The second, occurring in early adolescence, consisted of cases resembling adult schizophrenia with delusions, hallucinations, and a thought disorder of form or content. It was also clear

that a mixed or residual group with unclear symptoms existed, and most writers clearly acknowledged that some crossover cases existed that did not follow the age-of-onset distinction. This tripartite division of severe childhood disorders is the basis of the third edition of the *Diagnostic and Statistical Manual of Mental Disorders*, Fourth Edition, Text Revision (*DSM-IV-TR;* American Psychiatric Association, 2000) classification of pervasive developmental disorders.

In *DSM-IV*, childhood schizophrenia is not set apart as a separate category, but is diagnosed using the adult criteria for schizophrenia. These include:

A. *Characteristic symptoms*: Two (or more) of the following, each present for a significant portion of time during a 1-month period (or less if successfully treated):
   (1) Delusions
   (2) Hallucinations
   (3) Disorganized speech (e.g., frequent derailment or incoherence)
   (4) Grossly disorganized or catatonic behavior
   (5) Negative symptoms (i.e., affective flattening, alogia, or avolition)

B. *Social/occupational dysfunction*: Major areas of life are extensively affected for a significant amount of time.

C. *Duration*: Continuous signs of the disturbance for at least 6 months.

D. *Schizoaffective and mood disorder exclusion*: Signs of depressive and manic states in personality.

E. *Substance/general medical condition exclusion*: The disturbance is not due to effects of a substance (e.g., a drug of abuse, a medication, or a general medical condition).

F. *Relationship to a pervasive developmental disorder*: If there is a history of autistic disorder or another pervasive developmental disorder, the additional diagnosis of schizophrenia is made only if prominent delusions or hallucinations are also present for at least a month (or less if successfully treated).

DSM-IV suggests that this approach is controversial. Part of the problem involves the inherent difficulty in identifying delusions, hallucinations, and thought disorders in children whose language abilities are very limited. Another shortcoming involves the inability to diagnose organic disorders in children, especially at an early age. Finally, a number of authors (e.g., Fish & Ritvo, 1979) have noted the crossover of children from one category to another. This crossover does not occur often in samples of more retarded children, who tend to show more autistic symptoms, but it occurs often enough among samples with average intelligence to prompt concern about the diagnostic criteria.

Demographic data using the *DSM-IV* criteria for schizophrenia in children are virtually nonexistent except insofar as they may be inferred from data obtained for adults. The overall incidence of schizophrenia is thought to range between 15 and about 1% of the population, with an equal sex distribution and a higher incidence rate in lower-socioeconomic classes. It also appears to have a higher incidence in some families, but the concordance rate, even in monozygotic twins, is not perfect, implying intervening environmental and/or biological factors. The lower limit for the age of onset using the *DSM-IV* criteria appears to be 8 or 9 years, but there are isolated reports of much earlier onset. As Rutter (1974) notes, the differences in age of onset between autism and schizophrenia and the low incidence of any severe disorder between age 3 and early adolescence suggest that both autism and schizophrenia are etiologically distinct and valid syndromes. Unfortunately, little of substance can be said regarding the prognosis or etiology of schizophrenia in children or adults. Whereas autism has been linked to a number of organic and/or genetic conditions, the changing definition of childhood schizophrenia has prevented the compilation of a large enough database to permit inferences about etiology. The same general state of affairs exists concerning prognosis, although in adults, schizophrenia is thought to have a very poor outcome and a high relapse rate, as noted in *DSM-IV*.

As noted, early in the previous century it was common to lump all severe childhood disorders together diagnostically; it was assumed that these were earlier forms of adult schizophrenia. In the past 30 years, however, it has become clear that distinctions should be made among these disorders. The most important differential diagnoses are between schizophrenia and disorders such as autism, mental retardation, and pervasive developmental disorders or disintegrative diseases of organic origin such as Heller's syndrome. Some of these disorders are documented in *DSM-IV* and some are not, but delineation of the differences among them may illuminate the nature of schizophrenia in children.

Both schizophrenia and mental retardation may coexist in the same individual, and *DSM-IV* is careful to point out that some of the social isolation and odd behavior seen in retarded children, especially at a very early age, may be mistaken for symptoms of schizophrenia. In general, however, among the retarded one may expect to find a steady, unremitting course to the disorder, whereas schizophrenics will usually show a prolonged period of normal development. In addition, many retarded persons have physical (particularly facial) stigmata that permit their identification into basic syndromes, but the presence of such stigmata is rare in child schizophrenia of later onset. Goldfarb (1967) has noted stigmata present in early onset psychoses and Bender (1947) also noted their presence among psychotic children, but it is not clear how their samples correspond to current *DSM-IV* categories. Hallmarks

of schizophrenia such as delusions and hallucinations are rarely found in individuals who are diagnosed only as retarded. It is generally possible to distinguish between retardation and schizophrenia when careful psychological testing is done to establish the subject's mental age as a baseline for judging the appropriateness of language and social behavior.

By far the most effort has been expended to differentiate schizophrenia from infantile autism. Kanner (1943) initially described autism as the earliest form of schizophrenia, but it has become clear that there are marked differences between the two disorders. First, Rutter (1974) points out that there is a great difference in the distribution of the age of onset between the two disorders, with a peak at 2 to 3 years for the onset of autism and a much later peak in adolescence for schizophrenia. In addition, the course of the two disorders differs sharply, with schizophrenic children having a period of normal development followed by an uneven course, whereas autistic children show deviant development from birth and a consistent course. The symptoms themselves differ: Schizophrenic symptoms such as delusions and hallucinations are rare in autism, whereas the autistic child's need for sameness and frequent seizures (in about 25% of cases) are not usual features of schizophrenia. Although most major studies of schizophrenia show a familial loading for schizophrenia and an equal sex distribution, schizophrenia is rare in the families of autistic children and autism occurs more frequently in boys than girls by a ratio of about 4:1 (Rutter, 1985). In most cases (a few exceptions have been reported) children who are diagnosed as autistic do not resemble schizophrenics as adults (Kanner & Eisenberg, 1955).

Some authorities have noted that distinguishing between autism and other disorders is particularly difficult when the child is of average intelligence and does not show many of the characteristic language and behavior peculiarities of the younger and/or more limited autistic child. Asperger (1944) proposed that these children constitute a separate diagnostic group characterized by normal intellect, restricted and obsessive interests in certain subjects or activities, and constricted emotional and social responses. However, this description also applies to many children who have been diagnosed as autistic at an earlier age, especially those with better intelligence and/or language skills.

Schopler (1985) has pointed out that until some behavior distinction between higher level autism and so-called Asperger's syndrome can be demonstrated, confusion might be reduced if Asperger's syndrome were not regarded as a distinct diagnostic category. Most cases could adequately be classified as autistic or as schizoid disorders of adolescence (Rutter & Schopler, 1985). Both high-level autism and the adolescent schizoid disorder differ from schizophrenia, however, because the former disorders do not have hallucinations as a major feature and have an earlier age of onset with a fairly even course marked by the failure to develop normal social relationships.

Heller (1930) described a disorder in which an initial period of 3 to 4 years of apparently normal development is followed by a gradual and widespread disintegration of behavior involving areas as diverse as receptive and expressive language and bowel and bladder training. Social impairment and a general loss of interest in the outside world follow. Other disorders such as tuberous sclerosis may, in the early stages, show some features similar to schizophrenia. However, the early onset age of these latter disorders and the broad deterioration (including social skill areas such as toileting), accompanied in some cases by seizures and other physical problems, are the distinguishing features for differential diagnosis. The etiology is thought to be organic.

Because of the heterogeneity of the cases that have been labeled as schizophrenia, a wide variety of treatments have been employed, as has been the case with autism. Insofar as schizophrenic children may have more intact intellectual/language skills than children with other severe disorders, the traditional play, insight-oriented, and "talking" therapies might be expected to be more effective. Unfortunately, no good studies documenting the utility of this approach are available, again owing in part to differences in diagnostic terminology over the years. The most common form of treatment today involves parental support, counseling, and special psychoeducational strategies, much as with autistic children. In fact, many classes for severely disturbed or psychotic children contain a mix of autistic, schizophrenic, and other types of children. The prognosis for children with schizophrenia is one of a lifelong course and the need for supportive structures (George, 2003). Treatment often includes psychoactive medications and research has supported the use of clozapine (George, 2003).

Characteristics

1. Disorganized hallucinations of a visual type (and sometimes auditory)
2. Delusions
3. Disorganized and incoherent speech (which can involve echolalia)
4. Disorganized or catatonic behavior
5. Flat affect
6. Loss of interest in current activities
7. Cognitive skills problems
8. Motor skills problems
9. Memory loss
10. Social skills deficits

REFERENCES

American Psychiatric Association. (2000). *Diagnostic and Statistical Manual of Mental Disorders* (4th ed., Text Revision). Washington, DC: Author.

Asperger, H. (1944). Die autistischen psychopathen im kindersalter. *Archives Fur Psychiatrie und Nervenkrankheiten, 117,* 76–136.

Bender, L. (1947). Childhood schizophrenia. Clinical study of one hundred schizophrenic children. *American Journal of Orthopsychiatry, 17,* 40–56.

Bettelheim, B. (1950). *Love is not enough.* Glencoe, IL: Free Press.

Campbell, M. (1975). Pharmacotherapy in early infantile autism. *Biological Psychiatry, 10,* 399–423.

Creak, M. (1961). Schizophrenia syndrome in childhood: Progress report of a working party. *Cerebral Palsy Bulletin, 3,* 501–504.

DeSanctis, S. (1906). On some varieties of dementia praecox. Translated and reprinted in J. G. Howells (Ed.), *Modern perspectives in international child psychiatry.* Edinburgh: Oliver & Boyd, 1969.

Fish, B., & Ritvo, E. (1979). Psychoses of childhood. In J. Noshpitz (Ed.), *Basic handbook of child psychiatry.* New York, NY: Basic Books.

Fish, B., Shapiro, T., & Campbell, M. (1968). A classification of schizophrenic children under five years. *American Journal of Psychiatry, 124,* 1415–1423.

George, C. (2003). Childhood schizophrenia. In E. Fletcher-Janzen & C. R. Reynolds (Eds.), *Childhood disorders diagnostic desk reference* (pp. 125–126). New York, NY: Wiley.

Goldfarb, W. (1967). Factors in the development of schizophrenic children: An approach to subclassification. In J. Romano (Ed.), *The origins of schizophrenia.* New York, NY: Excerpta Media Foundation.

Heller, T. (1930). About dementia infantilis. Reprinted in J. G. Howell (Ed.), *Modern perspectives in international child psychiatry.* Edinburgh, UK: Oliver & Boyd.

Kanner, L. (1943). Autistic disturbances of affective contact. *Nervous Child, 2,* 219–230.

Kanner, L. (1949). Problems of nosology and psychodynamics of early infantile autism. *American Journal of Orthopsychiatry, 19,* 416–426.

Kanner, L., & Eisenberg, L. (1955). Notes on the follow-up studies of autistic children. In P. Hoch & J. Zubin (Eds.), *Psychopathology of childhood.* New York, NY: Grune & Stratton.

Kolvin, I. (1971). Psychoses in childhood: A comparative study. In M. Rutter (Ed.), *Infantile autism: Concepts, characteristics and treatment.* London, UK: Churchill-Livingstone.

Potter, H. (1933). Schizophrenia in children. *American Journal of Psychiatry, 12,* 1253–1270.

Rutter, M. (1974). The development of infantile autism. *Psychological Medicine, 4,* 147–163.

Rutter, M. (1978). Diagnosis and definition. In M. Rutter & E. Schopler (Eds.), *Autism: A reappraisal of concepts and treatment.* New York, NY: Plenum Press.

Rutter, M. (1985). Infantile autism and other pervasive developmental disorders. In M. Rutter & L. Hersov (Eds.), *Child and adolescent psychiatry: Modern approaches.* Oxford, UK: Blackwell Scientific.

Rutter, M., & Schopler, E. (1985). Autism and pervasive developmental disorders: Concepts and diagnostic issues. Paper prepared for National Institute of Mental Health Research Workshop, Washington, DC.

Schopler, E. (1985). Convergence of learning disability, higher-level autism, and Asperger's syndrome. *Journal of Autism and Developmental Disabilities, 15*(4), 359.

Szurek, S. (1956). Childhood schizophrenia symposium 1955: Psychotic episodes and psychotic maldevelopment. *American Journal of Orthopsychiatry, 25,* 519–543.

Vrono, M. (1974). Schizophrenia in childhood and adolescence. *International Journal of Mental Health, 2,* 7–116.

Walk, A. (1964). The pre-history of child psychiatry. *British Journal of Psychiatry, 110,* 754–767.

ERIC SCHOPLER
University of North Carolina at Chapel Hill

JERRY L. SLOAN
Wilmington Psychiatric Associates

See also Autism; Childhood Psychosis; Psychoneurotic Disorders

CHILD MALTREATMENT AND DISABILITIES

Child maltreatment is the general term used to describe all forms of child abuse and neglect. The federal government defines child abuse and neglect in the Child Abuse Prevention and Treatment Act (2003) as "the physical and mental injury, sexual abuse, negligent treatment, or maltreatment of a child under the age of 18 by a person who is responsible for the child's welfare under circumstances which indicate that the child's health or welfare is harmed or threatened." Each state elaborates on the federal definition of child maltreatment and specifically defines what constitutes each type of abuse for residents of that state.

Relationships between disabilities and child maltreatment have been known for several decades. Children diagnosed with disabilities are several times more likely than their nondisabled peers to have a confirmed history of maltreatment. In addition, children with a history of maltreatment are more likely to be diagnosed with a disability. While researchers have determined this strong link exists, the nature of this relationship is not clear.

In 1962, the importance of child maltreatment was heightened when Kempe introduced the termed *battered child syndrome.* His scholarship and that of others helped raise awareness and spearheaded legislation in the fight against child abuse and neglect (Kempe, Silverman, Steele, Droegemueller, & Silver, 1962). One of the first studies directly exploring relationships between child maltreatment and children with disabilities analyzed the maltreatment histories of 3,881 hospitalized children using records from child protection services, foster care, and law enforcement to determine if there was a history of maltreatment (Sullivan & Knutson, 2000). Children with disabilities were found to be at risk for maltreatment.

A follow-up study (Sullivan & Knutson, 2000) dispelled any doubts of the previous findings. A review of records from 50,278 students enrolled in public and Archdiocese schools in Omaha, Nebraska, found that children placed in special education were 3.4 times more likely to be maltreated than their classmates without disabilities. In addition, 22% of children with a history of maltreatment were receiving special education services.

Most children suffered from more than one form of maltreatment. Neglect was the most common form of abuse. Compared to their classmates without disabilities, children with disabilities were 3.88 times more likely to be emotionally abused, 3.79 times more likely to be physically abused, 3.76 times more likely to be neglected, and 3.14 times more likely to be sexually abused. Among children who had confirmed histories of abuse, 50% were diagnosed with a behavioral disorder, 30% as having speech and language disorders, and 25% with mental retardation or health impairments. Thus, there is no question that a strong relationship exists between child maltreatment and disability.

Instances in which child abuse directly causes the disability were examined. The shaken baby syndrome (SBS) was one of the most common. Among children who survive this type of attack, approximately 60% suffer from severe disabilities. A study tracing the histories of 25 shaken baby syndrome infants found only 10 survived and only one was discharged without a diagnosed disability (Fischer & Allasio, 1994). In addition to shaken baby syndrome in infants, approximately one-fourth of serious brain injury in young children results from child abuse. For example, Reece and Sege (2000) found that child abuse was the cause of 19% of the cases where children under the age of 6.5 were admitted to the hospital with brain injury. Cases of brain injury suffered as a result of physical abuse are the clearest link that abuse causes disability.

Child maltreatment can have adverse behavioral and psychological effects. Learning and behavior problems may be one of the most common effects of child maltreatment (Mansell & Sobsey, 2001). Children who suffer horrific forms of child maltreatment may develop *post-traumatic stress disorder* (PTSD) for which the more common forms of complications are withdrawal, aggression, sexually inappropriate behavior, depression, and low self-esteem (Mansell & Sobsey). Regression in learning also is common because children become preoccupied with the traumatic events they experienced. Given these conditions, children can respond to stress with intense neurological and neuropsychological reactions that can block their ability to learn in the classroom.

Current research is focusing on neurological effects and brain development during the first years of life. Children who experience severe and ongoing trauma are more likely to develop a host of neurological deficits, including mental illness, vulnerability to addictions, damage to the structure of the hippocampus, seizures, attention deficits (Brownlee, 1996), as well as damage to the limbic system, one essential to attention in young children (Teicher, Glod, Surrey, & Swett, 1993).

Various conditions may increase the risk for children to develop disabilities along with becoming victims of child maltreatment. Substance abuse during pregnancy is one of the most common forms. Approximately 2% of women reportedly consumed more than five drinks in one day during their pregnancy (Batshaw & Conlon, 1997). Approximately 2 babies out of 1,000 are born with fetal alcohol syndrome, and 4 out of 1,000 are born with a milder condition. These children account for nearly 10 to 20% of the population with mental retardation (Batshaw & Conlon).

Drug abuse also plays a major role in contributing to disabilities in prenatal children. Approximately 1% of pregnant women report using cocaine at some time during their pregnancy (Sobsey, 2002). These babies are more likely to be born premature and display developmental problems and numerous other complications. Parental drug use is highly correlated with the occurrence of child abuse within the home (Thyen, Leventhal, Yazdgerdi, & Perrin, 1997).

Spousal abuse and domestic violence also increases the risk for children to develop disabilities along with becoming victims of child maltreatment. Approximately 10% of women report violence during pregnancy. Mothers experiencing both physical and nonphysical abuse are more than twice as likely to deliver premature and low-birthweight babies. Their higher level of anxiety increases the risk of decreased blood flow to the uterus (Fernandez & Krueger, 1999), thus increasing the likelihood of the fetus being born with a disability. A child who witnesses domestic violence also becomes more likely to develop a disability or suffer from violence-invoked injury. High levels of stress in children may result in such medical problems as asthma, diarrhea, ulcers, and intestinal problems (Horton & Cruise, 2001). Children also run the risk of regressing in their development in such areas as toileting, language, eating, and sleeping patterns (Margolin, 1998).

Educators can expect 10% of their students to display both a history of maltreatment and a diagnosed disability (Sullivan & Knutson, 2000). These students are likely to display various learning, behavioral, and academic challenges. Teachers, school psychologists, and other early interventionists constitute a large faction of frontline professionals who should become engaged in preventing, intervening, and providing treatment for this population. Regardless of the dangers their home environment

presents, most children attend on a daily basis a public school system that is committed to serving the needs of all children. Thus, educators and other school personnel should be vigilant in identifying and serving this large and vulnerable population.

REFERENCES

Batshaw, M. L., & Conlon, C. J. (1997). Substance abuse: A preventable threat to development. In M. L. Batshaw (Ed.), *Children with disabilities* (4th ed., pp. 143–162). Baltimore, MD: Brookes.

Brownlee, S. (1996, November 11). Fear can harm a child's brain: Is it reversible? *U.S. News and World Report.*

Child Abuse Prevention and Treatment Act (CAPTA) as amended by Keeping Children and Families Safe Act of 2003, 42 U.S.C. § 5106(g). (2003).

Fernandez, F. M., & Krueger, P. M. (1999). Domestic violence: Effect on pregnancy outcome. *Journal of the American Osteopathic Association, 99,* 254–256.

Fischer, H., & Allasio, D. (1994). Permanently damaged: Long-term follow-up of shaken babies. *Pediatrics, 33,* 696–698.

Horton, C., & Cruise, T. (2001). *Child abuse & neglect: The school's response.* New York, NY: Guilford Press.

Kempe, C. H., Silverman, F. N., Steele, B. F., Droegemueller, W., & Silver, H. K. (1962). The battered child syndrome. *Journal of the American Medical Association, 181,* 17–24.

Mansell, S., & Sobsey, D. (2001). *Counseling people with developmental disabilities who have been sexually abused.* Kingston, NY: NADD Press.

Margolin, G. (1998). Effects of domestic violence on children. In *Violence against Children in the Family and the Community* (pp. 57–102). Washington, DC: American Psychological Association.

Reece, R. M., & Sege, R. (2000). Childhood head injuries: Accidental or inflicted? *Archives of Pediatric and Adolescent Medicine, 154,* 11–15.

Sobsey, D. (2002). Exceptionality, education, and maltreatment. *Exceptionality, 10*(1), 29–46.

Sullivan, P. M., & Knutson, J. F. (1998). The association between child maltreatment and disabilities in a hospital-based epidemiological study. *Child Abuse & Neglect, 22,* 271–278.

Sullivan, P. M., & Knutson, J. F. (2000). Maltreatment and disabilities: A population-based epidemiological study. *Child Abuse & Neglect, 24,* 1257–1273.

Teicher, M., Glod, C., Surrey, J., & Swett, C. (1993). Early childhood abuse and limbic system ratings in adult psychiatric outpatients. *Journal of Neuropsychiatry and Clinical Neurosciences, 5,* 301–306.

Thyen, U., Leventhal, J. M., Yazdgerdi, S. R., & Perrin, J. M. (1997). Concerns about child maltreatment in hospitalized children. *Child Abuse & Neglect, 21,* 187–198.

DANIELLE MADERA
University of Florida

See also Battered Child Syndrome; Child Abuse

CHILD PSYCHIATRY

Child psychiatry is a subdiscipline of psychiatry, a branch of medicine focusing on human emotional development and pathology. As a subspecialty, child psychiatry is approximately 75 years old, with Freud's treatment of a young boy in 1909 marking its genesis (Jones, 1959). The practitioner of child psychiatry must have comprehensive training both in general psychiatry and child development. This includes a firm understanding of trends in cognitive, language, and motor development. Training in neurology is also essential in understanding which developmental delays may be attributed to organic as opposed to psychogenic etiology (AACAP, 2005).

Initial involvement of the child psychiatrist is focused on the mentally retarded and an assessment of them for the purpose of deciding on entrance to state schools and hospitals for the mentally retarded. This may have been influenced by European trends in determining which children were able to benefit from a public education and which were ineligible as a result of deficient mental abilities (Wolman, 1972). This focus has been greatly expanded to areas of treatment and prevention, with assessment being regarded as the role of a multidisciplinary team.

While the earliest child psychiatrists often acted in a unitary fashion, more contemporary approaches have included psychiatrists as team members. This has also been reflected in their involvement in a larger variety of agencies than traditionally noted. Earlier trends in child psychiatry have placed the psychiatrist in medically oriented facilities such as hospitals, state homes for the retarded, and pediatric services. Recent trends have included child psychiatric services in child-guidance clinics, community mental health facilities, and, with the introduction of PL 94-142, in community-based schools.

Along with this shift in orientation, child psychiatrists have attained more of a consultant status (Knapp & Harris, 1998); they are no longer seen as the sole practitioner for the young child. Their presence is observed throughout the progression from the mainstream classroom to the residential facility. For example, if the child with special needs is educated within the mainstream class, resource room, or special education class, the child psychiatrist may consult to assist in determining developmental needs requiring medical attention. This assessment is made in conjunction with other members of the multidisciplinary team. As the placement shifts to a more restrictive milieu, as with residential placement, the multidisciplinary team remains the functional unit for developing the individual education plan (IEP), with the child psychiatrist maintaining a consultant and team-member status and contributing from his or her area of expertise.

Another domain of child psychiatry includes participation on recommendations of Committees for the Handicapped (COH) and school-based guidance and support teams. Within his or her area of expertise, this new consultant to the educational system contributes in a unique manner, evaluating the child for possible psychopharmacological intervention to assist in the learning process. With the advent of medications focusing on attentional-deficit disorders, disruptive behaviors, and childhood depression syndromes, new tools interface the educational and the medical approaches with child development and treatment. This required the special knowledge that the child psychiatrist is trained to possess. Transcending traditional training in dynamic psychotherapy, the knowledge of more contemporary behavioral management techniques has also become part of the armamentarium of this profession, thus allowing for additional assistance in structuring the child's environment for facilitating growth. In conjunction with significant school personnel and the family, the child psychiatrist may assist in developing treatment plans geared to maximize the child's educational experience. To carry out this role, the practitioner must have a sound foundation of knowledge about child development, assessment of personality and its pathology, child neurology, therapeutic intervention, and prevention (AACAP, 2005; Noshpitz, 1979).

REFERENCES

AACAP. (2005). *Facts for families*. Retrieved from http://www.aacp.org/Pages/Default.aspx

Jones, E. (Ed.). (1959). *Sigmund Freud: Collected papers (5 vols.)*. New York, NY: Basic Books.

Knapp, P. K., & Harris, E. S. (1998). Consultation–liaison in child psychiatry: A review of the past 10 years. *Journal of the American Academy of Child and Adolescent Psychiatry, 37*(2), 139–146.

Noshpitz, J. D. (1979). *Basic handbook of child psychiatry (4 vols.)*. New York, NY: Basic Books.

Wolman, B. B. (Ed.). (1972). *Manual of child psychopathology*. New York, NY: McGraw-Hill.

Ellis I. Barowsky
Hunter College,
City University of New York

See also Cascade Model of Special Education Services; Mental Status Exams; Multidisciplinary Team

CHILD PSYCHOLOGY

Child psychology is concerned with answering two basic questions: How do children change as they develop, and what are the determinants of these developmental changes? (Hetherington & Parke, 1979). Modern child psychology is particularly concerned with understanding the processes that produce and account for age-related changes in children. Child psychology is concerned with development from conception to adolescence.

Historically, child psychology can be traced to the work of G. Stanley Hall, president of Clark University and one of the founders of the American Psychological Association (Kessen, 1965). In 1893, Hall published *The Contents of Children's Minds*, the first systematic study of large groups of children using a questionnaire method to obtain information about children's and adolescents' behaviors, attitudes, and interests. During the early years of this century, research in child psychology was primarily atheoretical and focused on the description of age changes in physical, psychological, and behavioral characteristics. Child psychologists in the past several decades, however, have been primarily interested in studying the basic processes underlying development. Some of the earliest researchers and theorists who had great impact on the expansion of the field of child psychology were Binet, who developed the first test of intelligence, Gesell, who investigated perceptual–motor abilities in young children, Freud, who proposed a theory of personality development, and Piaget, who published an influential theory of children's cognitive development.

Biologists and geneticists have made important contributions to an understanding of some of the processes and mechanisms related to development (Mash & Dozois, 2003). Behavior geneticists have been concerned with the mechanisms by which genetic factors contribute to a wide range of individual differences observed in human behavior across the entire life span. Research suggests that genetic factors play a role in the development of many physical and physiological characteristics, in intelligence, sociability, emotional responsiveness, and in some types of psychopathology.

Developmental changes in sensory capacities, visual-perceptual abilities, and fine and gross motor skills are major areas of study by child psychologists during the period of infancy. Among the specific areas studied are sound discrimination, visual stimulus preferences, and depth perception. Another important focus of child psychologists during infancy has been the effects of early experiences on their cognitive, motor, and social-emotional development. Among the issues addressed are the timing of experiences (i.e., early versus later experiences; the existence of critical periods) and concerns with the plasticity of development (i.e., will previously acquired behavior patterns be modified by later experience?; Bower, 1977).

Child psychologists recognize the influence of heredity on setting the foundation for the course of development. These genetic factors interact with the child's learning experiences to determine actual developmental outcomes. Learning processes (e.g., conditioning mechanisms, imitation) are therefore an important area of study by child psychologists.

During the past three decades, five areas of development have received considerable attention by child psychologists. These areas are emotional development, language development, cognitive development, moral development, and the development of sex role behaviors (Mussen, 1970).

In the area of emotional development, research has focused on the manner in which positive and negative emotions originate and how the expression of emotions changes with age (Yarrow, 1979). Another area that has attracted considerable interest is the development of attachment, in which infants show a specific desire to be near particular caretakers in their environment. Related to this issue is the study of the development of fears in the young child, particularly the fear of strangers. Child psychologists also have been interested in the ways that children learn to label and recognize their own and other people's emotions. Resiliency is also a new area of interest in child development. Researchers are examining the positive attributes of children that allow them to withstand negative experiences and thrive (Goldstein & Brooks, 2005).

Language development represents one of the most significant achievements of childhood because of its importance in communication, thinking, and learning. Child psychologists differ on their views of the mechanisms underlying the development of language. Some argue that language is innate while others contend that language can be accounted for by traditional principles. A third view, which is held by most current theorists, is that both genetic and learning factors play a role in language development (Dale, 1977; Lyon, Fletcher, & Barnes, 2003).

Research in children's cognitive development has dominated the field of child psychology. The area of cognition pertains to the mental activity and behavior through which knowledge is acquired and processed, including learning, perception, memory, and thinking. The psychological processes that underlie cognitive development are of particular interest to the child psychologist, including the operations involved in receiving, attending to, discriminating, transforming, storing, and recalling information.

Piaget (1952) developed the most comprehensive and influential theory of cognitive development. His theory emphasized developmental changes in the organization and structure of intelligence, and how differences in those structures are reflected in the learning of children at different ages. Another component of Piaget's theory involved his approach to the development of social cognition, that is, the way in which children perceive, understand, and think about themselves, other people, and social interactions. Piaget's provocative theory probably has stimulated more research by contemporary child psychologists than any other theory.

In addition to investigating the basic processes by which children learn, researchers also have investigated how children retain information and recognize, recall, and use it when needed. A distinction is made between two types of memory: short term and long term. Developmental changes in various strategies used by children to facilitate memory such as rehearsal, mental imagery, and organization, also have been investigated by child psychologists.

Child psychologists have noted individual differences in the cognitive styles that children use to process information. One of the most frequently studied dimensions of cognitive style is reflectivity–impulsivity. Reflectivity–impulsivity is associated with a number of intellectual, social, and personality factors.

Cognitive problem-solving abilities, as reflected in the concept of intelligence, have attracted the attention of psychologists for nearly a century. Child psychologists have addressed such issues as whether intelligence is a unitary, generalized ability, or a group of relatively separate abilities. There have been debates between those groups who argue that intelligence is genetically determined and, therefore, not alterable, and those who suggest that intelligence is more dependent on learning experiences. Similarly, the development and use of intelligence tests has generated considerable controversy within the field, with some investigators arguing that such tests are culturally biased toward white middle-class experiences. Intelligence tests, based on the concept of global intelligence, yield a single IQ score and continue to be widely used by practicing psychologists in clinical and academic settings.

The development of sex roles also has been an area of study in child psychology. Sex-role typing is the process by which children acquire the values and behaviors that are regarded as appropriate to either males or females in a specific culture. Characteristics of masculinity and femininity appear to be developed very early in life and are stable over time. Research indicates that the development of sex roles and sex differences in behavior is a complex phenomenon that involves the interaction of biological, social, and cognitive factors (Maccoby & Jacklin, 1974).

One component of the socialization process of children that has been of particular interest to child psychologists is the development of moral values and moral behaviors. Psychological research has focused on three basic aspects of morality: (1) cognitive factors, including knowledge of ethical rules and judgments about whether various acts are right or wrong; (2) behavioral factors involving negative acts such as cheating, lying, resisting temptation, and controlling aggression, and behaviors involved in prosocial acts such as sharing, cooperation, altruism, and helping; and (3) emotional factors of morality, such as feelings of guilt following a transgression (Hoffman, 1979).

Children are intimately involved in a number of social systems, including the family, peer group, and school. Child psychologists have investigated the influence of these social systems on various aspects of the development of children (Hartup, 1979).

There is a long history of interest by child psychologists in the family's role in the socialization process.

Of particular interest has been the relationship between child-rearing attitudes and practices and children's cognitive, personality, and social development. Contemporary issues pertaining to the family that have been investigated by child psychologists include the effects of child abuse, divorce, single-parent families, and maternal employment on the child's development.

Relationships with age mates are another important influence on the development of children. Age-related changes in peer interactions and the role of play behaviors have been the focus of much research. The influence of peers as models for negative and prosocial behaviors, and factors affecting peer group acceptance, also have been investigated.

Finally, child psychologists have studied the influence of the school as a socializing agent with children. In particular, the effects of teachers on children's academic achievement as well as social and emotional development have been examined. One area of interest has been an investigation of the impact of teacher expectations on children's performance in the classroom.

The major research interests in child psychology have changed over the course of time, often in response to social and historical pressures. Much of the knowledge that has accumulated in this field has been used to meet the needs of children in today's society and improve their well-being through the implementation of various programs and services. In recent years, child psychologists have become increasingly interested and influential in the formulation of social policies affecting children (Seitz, 1979). A review of development in child psychology from the 1960s to 1990s can be found in Reese (1993).

REFERENCES

Bower, T. G. R. (1977). *A primer of infant development*. San Francisco, CA: Freeman.

Dale, P. S. (1977). *Language development: Structure and function* (2nd ed.). New York, NY: Holt, Rinehart, & Winston.

Goldstein, S., & Brooks, R. B. (2005). *Resilience in children*. New York, NY: Springer.

Hartup, W. W. (1979). The social worlds of childhood. *American Psychologist, 34*, 944–950.

Hetherington, E. M., & Parke, R. D. (1979). *Child psychology: A contemporary viewpoint* (2nd ed.). New York, NY: McGraw-Hill.

Hoffman, M. L. (1979). Development of moral thought, feeling, and behavior. *American Psychologist, 34*, 958–966.

Kessen, W. (1965). *The child*. New York, NY: Wiley.

Lyon, G. R., Fletcher, J. M., & Barnes, M. C. (2003). Learning disabilities. In E. J. Mash & R. A. Barkley (Eds.), *Child psychopathology* (pp. 520–574). New York, NY: Guilford Press.

Maccoby, E. E., & Jacklin, C. N. (1974). *The psychology of sex differences*. Stanford, CA: Stanford University Press.

Mash, E. J., & Dozois, D. J. A. (2003). Child psychopathology. In E. J. Mash & R. A. Barkley (Eds.), *Child psychopathology* (pp. 3–74). New York, NY: Guilford Press.

Mussen, P. H. (Ed.). (1970). *Carmichael's handbook of child psychology*. New York, NY: Wiley.

Piaget, J. (1952). *The origins of intelligence in children*. New York, NY: International Universities Press.

Reese, H. W. (1993). Developments in child psychology from the 1960s to the 1990s. *Developmental Review, 13*(4), 503–524.

Rosenthal, D. (1970). *Genetic theory and abnormal behavior*. New York, NY: McGraw-Hill.

Seitz, V. (1979). Psychology and social policy for children. *American Psychologist, 34*, 1007–1008.

Yarrow, L. J. (1979). Emotional development. *American Psychologist, 34*, 951–957.

LAWRENCE J. SIEGEL
*University of Texas Medical Branch,
Galveston*

See also Child Psychiatry; Clinical Psychology; Pediatric Psychologist

CHILDREN OF A LESSER GOD

Children of a Lesser God is a play by Mark Medoff that was a hit on the Broadway stage in 1980. It is about the meeting, courtship, and marriage of James Leeds, a speech teacher at a state school for the deaf, and Sarah Norman, a maid at the school who has been deaf from birth and who refuses to lip-read or speak. Sarah wishes to be left alone in her silent world. James insists that she learn to lip-read and speak if she is to achieve first-class citizenship in the hearing, speaking world. He repeats aloud everything he and Sarah sign in an attempt to teach Sarah to lip-read. The two cannot reconcile their differences, and, in the end, they separate. James asks Sarah to return, but it is left unclear whether the marriage will be successful (Guernsey, 1980).

Mark Medoff, the author of *Children of a Lesser God (1980)*, found sign language an interesting theatrical device, and used deafness as a symbol for the problems inherent in all human communication. He wrote the play for Phyllis Frelich, a founding member of the National Theater of the Deaf, in response to her difficulty in finding roles (Kakutani, 1980). The play was developed based on situations suggested by Medoff and improvised by Frelich and her husband Robert Steinberg, who originally played the role of James in workshop and regional productions of the play.

REFERENCES

Guernsey, O. L., Jr. (Ed.). (1980). *The best plays of 1979–1980*. New York, NY: Dodd, Mead.

Kakutani, M. (1980, April 1). Deaf since birth, Phyllis Frelich became an actress and now a star. *New York Times, III*, 7:1.

Medoff, M. (1980). *Children of a lesser god*. New York, NY: Dramatists Play Service.

CATHERINE O. BRUCE
*Hunter College,
City University of New York*

See also Deaf Education; Sign Language

CHILDREN'S DEFENSE FUND

The Children's Defense Fund (CDF) is an advocacy organization for poor, minority, and handicapped children. The mission of the CDF is to "Leave No Child Behind" (CDF, 1999). Efforts are undertaken on behalf of large numbers of children as opposed to individual children. Relevant to special education, the organization has addressed exclusion of children from school as well as the labeling and treatment of children with special needs (Staff, 1974). The CDF maintains a lobbying organization, pursuing an annual legislative agenda in the U.S. Congress; works with state and local child advocates, providing information, technical assistance, and support; monitors the development and implementation of federal and state policies; and litigates selected cases (CDF, 1999).

The CDF also develops information on key issues affecting children. It has published books and handbooks of interest to special education, including *94-142 and 504: Numbers that Add Up to Educational Rights for Handicapped Children, How to Help Handicapped Children Get an Education*. A monthly newsletter, *CDF Reports*, is also published.

The CDF was founded in 1973. Until 1978, CDF was known as the Children's Defense Fund of the Washington Research Project. It is a private organization, with its main office in Washington DC at 25 E. Street NW, Washington DC 20001. The CDF has a very informative website (www.childrensdefense.org).

REFERENCES

Children's Defense Fund (CDF). (1999). *About the Children's Defense Fund*. Washington, DC: Author.

Staff. (1974). An interview with Marian Edelman Wright. *Harvard Educational Review, 44*, 53–73.

DOUGLAS L. FRIEDMAN
Fordham University

CHILDREN'S MANIFEST ANXIETY SCALE

Originally published in 1956 by Castaneda, McCandless, and Palermo as a downward extension of Taylor's Manifest Anxiety Scale for adults (Taylor, 1951), the Children's Manifest Anxiety Scale (CMAS) was substantively revised in 1978 (Reynolds & Richmond). The *Revised Children's Anxiety Scale* (RCMAS) was published in 1985 (Reynolds & Richmond). Since its first publication, more than 150 articles using the CMAS or the RCMAS have been published in various scholarly journals. These scales have been used in studies of the effects of anxiety on children's learning, behavior in the classroom, and response to a variety of treatment programs, and in descriptive studies of anxiety and its relationship to behavior, gender, ethnicity, age, socioeconomic status, and other variables.

Designed to measure anxiety of longstanding duration (i.e., trait as opposed to state or situational anxiety), the RCMAS has four empirically derived subscales titled: Concentration/Social, Worry and Oversensitivity, Physiological Anxiety, and Lie or Social Desirability. Standard scores are provided for a total anxiety score and for each subscale. Reliability data are good with most studies reporting internal consistency estimates in the .80s across age (5 to 19 years), gender, and race (Black, White, and Hispanic). Extensive validity data are provided in the test manual (Reynolds & Richmond, 1985).

The RCMAS is used principally by school, child clinical, and pediatric psychologists in the screening and diagnosis of various anxiety-related emotional disorders in children, and by researchers interested in children's anxiety. Learning-disabled and other groups of children in special education programs have been shown to display higher-than-normal levels of anxiety on the RCMAS (Paget & Reynolds, 1984), while students in programs for the intellectually gifted demonstrate lower-than-average anxiety levels when compared with the normal population (Scholwinski & Reynolds, 1985). The RCMAS is currently being revised.

REFERENCES

Castaneda, A., McCandless, B., & Palermo, D. (1956). The children's form of the Manifest Anxiety Scale. *Child Development, 27*, 327–332.

Paget, K. D., & Reynolds, C. R. (1984). Dimensions, levels, and reliabilities on the Revised Children's Anxiety Scale with learning disabled children. *Journal of Learning Disabilities, 17*, 137–141.

Reynolds, C. R., & Richmond, B. O. (1978). What I think and feel: A revised measure of children's manifest anxiety. *Journal of Abnormal Psychology, 43*, 281–283.

Reynolds, C. R., & Richmond, B. O. (1985). *Revised Children's Manifest Anxiety Scale*. Los Angeles, CA: Western Psychological Services.

Scholwinski, E., & Reynolds, C. R. (1985). Dimensions of anxiety among high IQ children. *Gifted Child Quarterly, 29*, 125–130.

Taylor, J. A. (1951). The relationship of anxiety to the conditioned eyelid response. *Journal of Experimental Psychology, 41*, 18–92.

CECIL R. REYNOLDS
Texas A&M University

See also Anxiety; Anxiety Disorders

CHILDREN'S RIGHTS INTERNATIONALLY

The concept of children's rights evolved from being minimally and unevenly valued to near universally recognized by governments at the end of the 20th century. During the 19th and 20th centuries, societal concern for children moved from longstanding consideration of them as the property of parents, without protection, genuine personal identity, or rights (Aries, 1962; de Mause, 1975), to being viewed as potential resources to present and future societies, and progressively, although as yet incompletely, to being valued as rights-bearing persons with individual personalities. This evolution of thinking increasingly recognizes children's *being* and *becoming* states. Although they are vulnerable, malleable, and en route to higher levels of development, they also are fully human at each point in their lives and with views and capacities deserving respect and support (Verhellen, 1994).

The formalization of international rights standards and requirements occurs through legal instruments, known as treaties, that are legally binding, specify implementation mechanisms, hold ratifying states parties (i.e., officially committed national governments) accountable, and contain nonbinding declarations, standards, and rules.

Knowledge of the history of attempts to establish international legal instruments relevant to children provides some clarification of progress in conceptualizing and respecting children's rights. Among nonbinding instruments are the 1924 Declaration of Geneva, which is protection and development oriented; the Universal

Declaration of Human Rights, a comprehensive document applying to the child indirectly by implication (United Nations General Assembly, 1948); and the 1959 U.N. Declaration of the Rights of the Child, including 10 principles on the right to care, protection, and development. Other instruments dealing with children in conflict with the law, including the United Nations Rules for the Protection of Juveniles Deprived of their Liberty, the United Nations Standard Minimum Rules for Administration of Juvenile Justice, and the United Nations Guidelines for the Prevention of Juvenile Delinquency, were adopted in the 1980s and 1990s.

The rights of persons with disabilities have been the topic of two U.N. declarations and one set of rules: the 1971 Declaration on the Rights of Mentally Retarded and the 1975 Declaration on the Rights of Disabled Persons, both of which should be applicable to children but neither of which contains language making this clear; and the 1993 Standard Rules on the Equalization of Opportunities for Persons With Disabilities, covering preconditions, target areas, and implementation measures for equal participation, and affirming its relevance to children by citing the Convention on the Rights of the Child (described below) in its preamble.

Among the treaties or binding instruments, some indirectly and/or directly focus on children. Treaties that are more indirect, yet applicable to children, include four U.N. treaties: the International Covenant on Economic, Social, and Cultural Rights (adopted 1996, in force 1976) that protects against economic and social discrimination and exploitation; the International Covenant on Civil and Political Rights (adopted 1996, in force 1976) that protects children even more directly and prohibits a sentence of death for those under 18 years of age; the International Convention on the Protection of the Rights of All Migrant Workers and Members of their Families (adopted 1990, in force 2003) that prohibits discrimination, protects identity, and encourages education; and the International Labor Organization Convention (No. 169) on Indigenous and Tribal Peoples in Independent Countries (adopted 1989, in force 1991) that refers to children as it outlines fair and secure working conditions and the need for indigenous education.

Treaties directly focused on children include international labor conventions, which are child protection treaties. Among them are the 1919 International Labor Organization Conventions Nos. 5 and 6, which is the earliest of child rights treaties dealing with age minimums for work and protection from dangerous work; the United Nations Convention on the Rights of the Child (Convention on the Rights of the Child; United Nations General Assembly, 1989), the first comprehensive treaty on children's rights (discussed in upcoming sections); the 1990 Charter on the Rights and Welfare of the African Child, a comprehensive treaty strongly influenced by the Convention on the Rights of the Child; the European Convention

on the Exercise of Children's Rights, adopted by the Council of Europe in 1996, basically dealing with enabling procedures; and treaties of the Hague Conference on Private International Law, harmonizing conflicts between differing national family laws, such as the 1980 Convention on the Civil Aspects of International Child Abduction and the Convention on Protection of Children and Co-Operation in Respect of Intercountry Adoption (concluded 1993, in force 1995).

The Convention on the Rights of the Child represents the hallmark in the ascendance of recognition and support for children's rights. In conjunction with the 1979 International Year of the Child, the Polish government proposed a treaty be drafted that would give legally binding rights to children. Representatives of the U.N.'s member nations deliberated 10 years on the development of this Convention (Detrick, Doek, & Cantwell, 1992). It was adopted by the United Nations General Assembly without dissent in 1989, entered into force in 1990, and ratified by 191 of the 193 recognized nations by 1997, making it, in these terms, the most successful human rights treaty in history.

The Convention on the Rights of the Child has three parts: Part 1 includes 41 articles on substantive rights themes (clarified below), and parts 2 and 3 include 13 articles discussing implementation mechanism (reports to the Committee on the Rights of the Child by States Parties; Articles 43–45) and procedural matters (e.g. ratification, entry into force, amending procedures; United Nations General Assembly, 1989).

The Convention on the Rights of the Child has become the preeminent international guiding framework and set of standards for children's rights. Its importance as the central rallying point for child advocacy work internationally can be argued with at least six reasons: a high level of international participation occurred in the drafting of the treaty; its comprehensive range, including both minimum standards and aspirational goals; its ratification by nearly all nations has raised it to the height of universal standards; states parties (nations that have ratified) are required to periodically and publicly report their progress in achieving its standards to the United Nations Committee of the Child (the official monitoring mechanism for the Convention, hereafter referred to as the Committee) and are expected to pursue further improvements; opinions and expertise of nongovernmental bodies and experts are welcomed and applied by the Committee in its processes to support effective implementation; and progress is promoted primarily through public accountability, guidance, and moral persuasion.

Human rights generally are categorized as civil, political, economic, social, and cultural for adults. For children, and particularly in the Convention, human rights more often are organized under themes of survival, protection, development, and participation. The following are illustrative examples: Article 6 acknowledges the right to life, survival, and development; Article 19 acknowledges the right to protection from all forms of physical and mental violence, injury, abuse, neglect, or exploitation; Articles 28 and 29 acknowledge the rights to education on the basis of equal opportunity and to education directed to full development of personality, talents, and mental and physical abilities; and Articles 12, 13, 14, 15, and 17 acknowledge the rights to express one's views and have them given due weight, access to and exchange of information, freedom of belief, and freedom of association.

Some of the Convention's rights and imperatives are particularly relevant to children with disabilities, including the expectation that the child's maturity and evolving capacities will be considered in the exercise of rights, as specifically supported in Articles 5, 12, and 14. Two articles have been drawn out for special consideration regarding persons with disabilities by the Committee in its guidelines for the development of reports to it by states parties (Committee on the Rights of the Child, 1996): Article 2 requires nondiscrimination in application of rights and in which disability is a specifically identified category for which discrimination is prohibited, and Article 23 states the special measures needed to ensure the rights of children with disabilities (Hodgkin & Newell, 1998), as follows:

Article 23

1. States Parties recognize that a mentally or physically disabled child should enjoy a full and decent life, in conditions which ensure dignity, promote self-reliance and facilitate the child's active participation in the community.

2. States Parties recognize the right of the disabled child to special care and shall encourage and ensure the extension, subject to available resources, to the eligible child and those responsible for his or her care, of assistance for which application is made and which is appropriate to the child's condition and to the circumstances of the parents or others caring for the child.

3. Recognizing the special needs of a disabled child, assistance extended in accordance with paragraph 2 of the present article shall be provided free of charge, whenever possible, taking into account the financial resources of the parents or others caring for the child, and shall be designed to ensure that the disabled child has effective access to and receives education, training, health care services, rehabilitation services, preparation for employment and recreation opportunities in a manner conducive to the child's achieving the fullest possible social integration and individual development, including his or her cultural and spiritual development.

4. States Parties shall promote, in the spirit of international cooperation, the exchange of appropriate information in the field of preventive health care and of medical, psychological and functional treatment of disabled children, including dissemination of and access to information concerning methods of rehabilitation, education and vocational services, with the aim of enabling States Parties to improve their capabilities and skills and to widen their experience in these areas. In this regard, particular account shall be taken of the needs of developing countries.

Work to further address the international rights of children with disabilities continues internationally. In 1997 the Committee on the Rights of the Child devoted its annual Day of General Discussion to Children with Disabilities. It focused specifically on the right to life, development, self-representation, full participation, and full participation in education. The Committee's recommendations are available on its website (http://www.ohchr.org/english/bodies/crc/discussion.htm). Strong support was expressed for the right to inclusion in everyday life, including education, which the Committee has continued to support in its communications with governments.

The first International Conference on Children's Rights in Education (Hart, Cohen, Erickson, & Flekkoy, 2001; *Prospects*, 1999) gave specific attention to the rights of children with disabilities (Saleh, 2001). The Committee currently is drafting another of its General Comments (an expanded commentary and guideline for the Convention on the Rights of the Child commissioned by the Committee) that will address the rights of children with disabilities. This General Comments was to be considered at the September 2005 meeting of the Committee and made available following its adoption. Related developments can be found on the Committee's website (http://www.ohchr.org/EN/Pages/WelcomePage.aspx). In addition, an international review of human rights standards for children with disabilities has been developed that assists in assessing progress in implementing the Convention on the Rights of the Child internationally. This document is found in a report to the United Nations General Assembly Session on Children in 2001 (see Lansdown, 2001; http://daa.org.uk/).

As promulgated in the Convention, children's rights primarily address issues for which governments are responsible. However, this emphasis does not usurp the rights and responsibilities of parents. They are specifically considered in 19 articles of the Convention. Nor does this emphasis suggest that governments and laws alone can achieve the full intentions of the spirit of the rights it embodies. The Convention both explicitly and implicitly refers at numerous points to the responsibilities of private as well as public institutions and bodies, and, in so doing, recognizes that children's rights must become a part of the fabric of everyday living if they are to be realized. The Committee has appreciated the importance of going beyond law in implementing children's rights, as exhibited in its repeated encouragement for child rights education for professionals serving children so that their practices will be duly influenced and influencing. At its 37th Session, held September 2004, the Committee endorsed the international program Child Rights Education for Professionals, coordinated by the International Institute for Child Rights and Development (www.iicrd.org).

State party implementation reports to the Committee on the Rights of the Child, alternative nongovernmental reports, together with critiques, responses, and recommendations of the Committee itself can be found on the website of the Office of the United Nations High Commissioner for Human Rights (www.ohchr.org).

REFERENCES

Aries, P. (1962). *Centuries of childhood*. New York, NY: Vintage Books.

Committee on the Rights of the Child. (1996). *Reporting guidelines to governments: General guidelines regarding the form and contents of periodic reports to be submitted by States Parties under Article 44, Paragraph 1(b), of the Convention.* Geneva, Switzerland: Office of the United Nations High Commissioner of Human Rights (www2.ohchr.org/english/bodies/crc).

De Mause, L. (1975). *The history of childhood*. New York, NY: Harper & Row.

Detrick, S., Doek, J., & Cantwell, N. (Eds.). (1992). *The United Nations Convention on the Rights of the Child: A guide to the "Travaux Preparatoires."* Dordrecht, The Netherlands: Martinus Nijhoff.

Hart, S. N., Cohen, C. P., Erickson, M. F., & Flekkoy, M. (Eds.). (2001). *Children's rights in education*. London, UK: Jessica Kingsley.

Hodgkin, R., & Newell, P. (1998). *Implementation handbook for the Convention on the Rights of the Child*. New York, NY: UNICEF.

Lansdown, G. (2001). *It's our world too! A report on the lives of disabled children*. London, UK: Disability Awareness in Action.

Prospects. (1999, June). 110 Open File: Children's rights in education. *Prospects 110, 29*(2) (Brussels), pp. 181–266.

Saleh, L. (2001). The rights of children with special needs: From rights to obligations and responsibilities. In S. N. Hart, C. P. Cohen, M. F. Erickson, M. F., & M. Flekkoy (Eds.), *Children's rights in education* (pp. 110–135). London, UK: Jessica Kingsley.

United Nations (U.N.) General Assembly. (1948, December 10). *Adoption of a universal declaration of human rights*. New York, NY: Author.

United Nations (U.N.) General Assembly. (1989, November 20). *Adoption of a convention on the rights of the child*. New York, NY: Author.

Verhellen, E. (1994). *Convention on the Rights of the Child: Background, motivation, strategies, and main themes*. Garant, The Netherlands: Leuven-Apeldoorn, Garant.

STUART N. HART
University of Victoria,
Victoria, British Columbia

CYNTHIA PRICE COHEN
Child Rights International
Research Institute

See also **International Ethics and Special Education; International School Psychology Association**

CHILD SERVICE DEMONSTRATION CENTERS

Child Service Demonstration Centers (CSDCs) (1971–1980) were federally funded operations that, in their totality, represented the largest single national commitment specifically made to the education of the learning disabled (Mann, Cartwright, Kenowitz, Boyer, Metz, & Wolford, 1984).

Their beginnings are to be found in several pieces of legislation. PL 88-164, passed in 1963, which predated the introduction of the modern term *learning disabilities* (LD), provided assistance to learning-disabled children in a bill directed at the educational needs of handicapped children under the rubric of "crippled and other health impaired." Then, under PL 91-230, passed in 1969, the U.S. commissioner of education was enjoined by Congress "to seek to make equitable geographic distribution of training programs, and train personnel throughout the nation, and . . . to encourage the establishment of a model training center in each of the states." This was to be done by making grants or contracts available to public schools, state educational agencies, nonprofit organizations, and colleges and universities. Such model centers for the learning disabled were then authorized, and ultimately created, under PL 91-230, Title VI-G.

This law made possible Child Service Demonstration Centers to serve learning-disabled students. Under the law, the to-be-created centers were to: (1) provide testing and educational evaluation to identify learning-disabled students; (2) develop and conduct model programs designed to meet their special educational needs; (3) assist appropriate educational agencies, organizations, and institutions "in making such model programs available to other children with learning disabilities"; and (4) disseminate new methods or techniques for overcoming learning disabilities and evaluate their effectiveness.

From 1971 to 1980, 97 CSDCs were created in all, with each of the 50 states being served by at least one during that time. The majority operated under the auspices of state educational agencies (SEAs). A good number also operated out of universities, and sometimes out of local educational agencies (LEAs), often on the basis of their serving as agencies of the states. The private sector was only minimally represented.

Many of the CSDCs were to carry out state as well as federal mandates. Often they were supported by state and local funds and resources that allowed them to augment their efforts far beyond the limits allowed by their relatively meager funds. Thus the hopes of the federal government that state and local education agencies would contribute to the support of the CSDCs with their own funds were realized.

The federal government had high hopes for the CSDCs. They were expected to assume major responsibility for trailblazing in the creation of service models, programs, and technologies; the identification, diagnosis, and remediation of learning disabilities; and the training of regular as well as special education teachers, specialists, and administrators. They were also expected to play a major role in research on the learning disabled. Furthermore, they were cast as both transformation instigators and partners for state educational agencies. In these roles they were expected to help the state agencies to plan and implement statewide learning disabilities programs and services; indeed, the initial CSDCs were granted to state educational agencies to further this expectation.

While every state had at least one project, as did the Commonwealth of Puerto Rico, some states had multiple centers operating at the same time under their state educational departments (e.g., California, New York). Most centers operated for 3 years; reapplication and competition for further funding was needed for subsequent years. The strategy was that the first year would involve planning, the second year the actual operation of the center, and the third year replication and dissemination. Some states, however, put projects together to create longitudinal efforts of some duration.

During their tenure, the CSDCs served a mix of urban, suburban, and rural areas. Most of the services were rendered, however, to rural children. This was in large part the result of the federal government's insistence that unserved and underserved learning-disabled students, who were in greatest abundance in rural areas at the time, be given priority in the provision of services.

For much the same reason, the racial composition of the learning-disabled students served by the CSDCs included a disproportionate number of minority students. Two projects were directed to American Indians and two to Puerto Rican students, while many of the urban and rural centers were oriented to the needs of black students. This is an interesting point in light of the fact that some advocacy groups at the time were claiming that learning disabilities were a white-middle-class syndrome, with minority students being consigned to classes for the mentally retarded or having their academic problems neglected.

The CSDCs emphasized elementary school-aged children since the LD movement is generally oriented to this stage of education. There were some preschool and secondary efforts as well. Interest and efforts in the latter accelerated during the later years of funding as the federal government increased its emphasis on secondary school programming.

The CSDCs were in the vanguard of mainstreaming and the provision of special education services in the least restrictive environment. They also did much to relate special education services for learning-disabled pupils to those of general education. In these respects they clearly fulfilled the federal government's expectations. Their major service delivery models were those of resource rooms, consulting teachers, and regular classrooms.

The assessment and diagnostic efforts of the CSDCs were traditional. They were strictly secondary to the service and training functions assumed by the centers. Furthermore, they eventually resulted in controversies that still percolate in education. Although the CSDCs were expected to identify appropriately handicapped children who had specific learning disabilities, as per federal definitions, their screening and identification efforts were such as to assign children to their services on the basis of academic failure and other school problems rather than on the basis of any precise learning disability criteria. It was on such bases that a position was taken by some critics that the concept of learning disabilities, as a defensible independent diagnostic entity apart from and different from school failure, could not be sustained.

The intervention models stressed by the CSDCs were strongly academic, as might be expected since students receiving services from the CSDCs usually had been referred because of academic problems. Remedial reading was the treatment of choice, on similar grounds. Perceptual motor training, including ITPA-based interventions, held the second highest priority, particularly in the early projects, when perceptual motor training was still the vogue. Surprisingly, the behavioral movement that so dominated special education during much of the CSDCs' sway does not appear to have greatly influenced most of the CSDCs, though some had strong behavioral emphases. While only several projects have averred ecological orientations, there was an ecological shift over the course of CSDC operations. Earlier projects were committed to overcoming learning disabilities through direct intervention, whereas later ones were more likely to emphasize helping learning-disabled students to adjust to academic and school environments and assisting schools in their accommodations to the special needs of learning-disabled students.

One of the major efforts made by CSDCs was in respect to training. Some of this was at the college and university level. Most, often representing an introduction to LD concepts and practices, was of an in-service nature directed at regular as well as special education teachers, administrators, paraprofessionals, and parents.

The CSDCs' efforts at replication were considerable. Most of the replications were at the local level, with far fewer at the state level. Impressive is the fact that there were 16 national replications. The CSDCs generated an extraordinary number of screening, remedial, and curricular materials and training manuals for teachers and parents. Because these were in the public domain, many were adapted by schools subsequent to the CSDCs' close, though often without awareness of their origins.

While there were some exemplary research efforts, the CSDCs remained essentially service agencies and, generally speaking, did not assume the research leadership originally expected of them. This was not surprising since neither their funding, nor their personnel capabilities, nor the nature of local conditions were such as to encourage earnest research. The Learning Disability Institutes, funded in 1977, were created in response the federal government's recognition of these facts and a desire to seek wider research efforts from other sources.

Public Law 91-239 also authorized the creation of the Leadership Training Institute (LTI) at the University of Arizona (1971–1974). The institute was supposed to assist the CSDCs in addition to carrying out its own research and training missions. It was later replaced by the National Learning Disabilities Assistance Project (1975–1979), which was entirely devoted to providing support functions for the CSDCs.

The federal government clearly expected the CSDCs to have a major national impact on LD practices. That they did not fulfill such expectations can be attributed to a variety of causes. One was the fact that their allocation of funds was far below original authorizations. Another was that individual centers came on line too slowly and irregularly; thus any collaborative thrust on their part was weakened. Still another reason was that they did not affect state educational policies as had been hoped, the states usually pursuing their own LD agendas rather than those of the federal government or of the CSDCs. Furthermore, the demands made on the CSDCs regularly changed as a consequence of changes in federal direction and because of disagreements among recognized LD specialists as to the nature of learning disabilities and the goals of intervention. Finally, most of the projects were funded for only 3 years, and several were funded for 2 or less, hardly time to create forceful and enduring efforts. Nevertheless, they did sensitize many areas of the nation and its schools to the needs of learning-disabled children and provided them with guidance, training, programs, materials, and direct services during a period when the field of learning disabilities was still emerging as an area of educational concern in the United States. Undoubtedly, they also shaped current concepts and services.

The CSDCs were subject to a number of external evaluations. A study of the CSDCs' intervention efforts was carried out by Kirk and Elkin in 1975. In 1976, a major yearlong effort was made by the American Institute of Research to examine the operations of the CSDCs. In 1979, Ysseldyke et al. began their studies of the CSDCs' assessment approaches (Thurlow & Ysseldyke, 1979). At the final closing of the CSDCs, Mann et al. published several summative articles reviewing the status and contributions of the CSDCs (Boyer, Mann, Davis, Metz, & Wolford, 1982; Mann, Davis, Boyer, Metz, & Wolford, 1983; Mann et al., 1984).

REFERENCES

Boyer, C. W., Mann, L., Davis, C. H., Metz, C. M., & Wolford, B. (1982). The Child Service Demonstration Centers: Retrospective of an age. *Academic Therapy*, 18, 171–177.

Kirk, S. A., & Elkin, V. (1975). Characteristics of children enrolled in the Child Service Demonstration Centers. *Journal of Learning Disabilities*, 16, 63–68.

Mann, L., Cartwright, G. P., Kenowitz, L. A., Boyer, C. W., Metz, C. M., & Wolford, B. (1984). The Child Service Demonstration Centers: A summary report. *Exceptional Children, 50*, 532–540.

Mann, L., Davis, C. H., Boyer, C. W., Metz, C. M., & Wolford, B. (1983). LD or not LD, that was the question: A retrospective analysis of the Child Service Demonstration Centers' compliance with the federal definition of learning disabilities. *Journal of Learning Disabilities, 16*, 14–17.

Thurlow, M. L., & Ysseldyke, J. E. (1979). Current assessment and decision making practices in model LD programs. *Learning Disability Quarterly, 4*, 15–24.

JONI J. GLEASON
University of West Florida

See also **Diagnosis in Special Education; Learning Disabilities**

CHILD VARIANCE PROJECT

The Conceptual Project in Child Variance was undertaken from 1970 to 1972 at the University of Michigan under the direction of William C. Rhodes. It was funded as a special project by the (then) Bureau of Education for the Handicapped to "order and organize the vast but scattered literature on emotional disturbance and other types of variance in children" and to "serve as a prototype for combining the functions of graduate training and professional research" (Rhodes & Tracy, 1974, p. 1). The product of this prodigious undertaking is a series of five volumes in which the literature on explanations of variance, intervention with variant children, and service provision are integrated and synthesized.

The first volume, *Conceptual Models* (Rhodes & Tracy, 1974d), has had a significant impact on subsequent treatments of childhood emotional disturbance and the education of disturbed children. The volume is comprised of papers in which explanatory models from five perspectives are presented. These models include biological, behavioral, psychodynamic, sociological, and ecological accounts of deviance. A paper on countertheoretical perspectives is included, as is a paper by Rhodes establishing a framework for understanding and synthesizing these diverse accounts.

The organization of the second volume, *Interventions* (Rhodes & M. L. Tracy, 1974b), derives from the first. In it, intervention with variant children is considered from biophysical, behavioral, psychodynamic, environmental, and countertheoretical perspectives. (The paper on environmental intervention explores approaches derived from both the sociological and ecological perspectives.) Of course, the rapid and multifaceted advance in the treatment of disturbed children in the decade since the publication of this volume has limited its usefulness. Nonetheless, the logic of its organization has endured. The idea that intervention must be understood in the context of the explanatory system has influenced scholars and teacher trainers to this day.

In the third volume, *Service Delivery Systems* (Rhodes & M. W. Tracy, 1974e), the development of contemporary services for deviant children provided by educational, correctional, mental health, and social welfare systems and religious institutions is analyzed from a historical perspective. The current services provided by these systems in a representative American community are examined and evaluated through a series of case studies. The fourth volume, *The Future* (1974c), is a treatise by Rhodes on the somewhat profound cultural and philosophical changes that must be realized for our society to fulfill its caretaking role. The fifth volume, *Exercise Book* (Rhodes, 1975), presents a series of exercises through which the sometimes complex and abstract content of the previous volumes may be brought to life for students.

Although the project has not yet realized the ultimate and far-reaching goals set forth by Rhodes in *The Future*, its impact on our thinking about emotional disturbance, the education of emotionally disturbed children, and the training of teachers of the emotionally disturbed has been significant and enduring. The organization of explanatory theory and its application to the understanding of intervention approaches are legacies of the Child Variance Project. Furthermore, its emphasis on the understanding of problems in their broadest context provided impetus to the subsequent development of ecological theory and intervention approaches.

REFERENCES

Rhodes, W. C. (1975). *A study of child variance: Vol. 5. Exercise book*. Ann Arbor, MI: University of Michigan Press.

Rhodes, W. C., & Tracy, M. L. (1974a). Preface. In W. C. Rhodes & M. L. Tracy (Eds.), *A study of child variance: Vol. 2. Interventions* (pp. 1–15). Ann Arbor, MI: University of Michigan Press.

Rhodes, W. C., & Tracy, M. L. (1974b). *A study of child variance: Vol. 2. Interventions*. Ann Arbor, MI: University of Michigan Press.

Rhodes, W. C., & Tracy, M. L. (1974c). *A study of child variance: Vol. 4. The future*. Ann Arbor, MI: University of Michigan Press.

Rhodes, W. C., & Tracy, M. W. (Eds.). (1974d). *A study of child variance: Vol. 1. Conceptual models*. Ann Arbor, MI: University of Michigan Press.

Rhodes, W. C., & Tracy, M. W. (Eds.). (1974e). *A study of child variance: Vol. 3. Service delivery systems*. Ann Arbor, MI: University of Michigan Press.

PAUL T. SINDELAR
Florida State University

See also Affective Education; Emotional Disorders

CHILD WITH A DISABILITY, DEFINITION OF

The Education for All Handicapped Children Act of 1975 (PL 94-142) originally defined the disability conditions that are eligible for services that are reimbursable by the federal government. Early versions of the Individuals With Disabilities Education Act (IDEA) maintained essentially the same wording in the definition of *handicapped*. More recent iterations of the IDEA and its implementing regulations have adopted the now preferred term *child with a disability* when referring to children eligible for certain types of assistance under the IDEA. The regulations currently in effect to implement the IDEA define a child with a disability as a child evaluated in accordance with the regulations who is found as "having mental retardation, a hearing impairment including deafness, a speech or language impairment, a visual impairment including blindness, serious emotional disturbance, an orthopedic impairment, autism, traumatic brain injury, an other health impairment, a specific learning disability, deaf-blindness or multiple disabilities, and who, by reason thereof, needs special education and related services" (34 C.F.R. 300.7(a)(1)). Children requiring only "related services" under the IDEA who do not need special education services are not included in this definition, although if the service that is considered a related service under federal law is considered a special education service under applicable state standards, the child is still considered a child with a disability (34 C.F.R. 300.7(a)(2)). Proposed regulations issued June 21, 2005, to implement the most recent version of the IDEA, which was passed in 2004, make only minor, nonsubstantive changes to this definition.

The terms used in the definition of *child with a disability* are further defined by the current regulations as follows:

(1) (i) *Autism* means a developmental disability significantly affecting verbal and nonverbal communication and social interaction, generally evident before age 3, that adversely affects a child's educational performance. Other characteristics often associated with autism are engagement in repetitive activities and stereotyped movements, resistance to environmental change or change in daily routines, and unusual responses to sensory experiences. The term does not apply if a child's educational performance is adversely affected primarily because the child has an emotional disturbance, as defined in paragraph (b)(4) of this section.

(ii) A child who manifests the characteristics of "autism" after age 3 could be diagnosed as having "autism" if the criteria in paragraph (c)(1)(i) of this section are satisfied.

(2) *Deaf-blindness* means concomitant hearing and visual impairments, the combination of which causes such severe communication and other developmental and educational needs that they cannot be accommodated in special education programs solely for children with deafness or children with blindness.

(3) *Deafness* means a hearing impairment that is so severe that the child is impaired in processing linguistic information through hearing, with or without amplification, that adversely affects a child's educational performance.

(4) *Emotional disturbance* is defined as follows:

　(i) The term means a condition exhibiting one or more of the following characteristics over a long period of time and to a marked degree that adversely affects a child's educational performance:

　　A. An inability to learn that cannot be explained by intellectual, sensory, or health factors.

　　B. An inability to build or maintain satisfactory interpersonal relationships with peers and teachers.

　　C. Inappropriate types of behavior or feelings under normal circumstances.

　　D. A general pervasive mood of unhappiness or depression.

　　E. A tendency to develop physical symptoms or fears associated with personal or school problems.

　(ii) The term includes schizophrenia. The term does not apply to children who are socially maladjusted, unless it is determined that they have an emotional disturbance.

(5) *Hearing impairment* means an impairment in hearing, whether permanent or fluctuating, that adversely affects a child's educational performance but that is not included under the definition of deafness in this section.

(6) *Mental retardation* means significantly subaverage general intellectual functioning, existing concurrently with deficits in adaptive behavior and manifested during the developmental period, that adversely affects a child's educational performance.

(7) *Multiple disabilities* means concomitant impairments (such as mental retardation–blindness, mental retardation–orthopedic impairment, etc.), the combination of which causes such severe educational needs that they cannot be accommodated in special education programs solely for one of the impairments. The term does not include deaf-blindness.

(8) *Orthopedic impairment* means a severe orthopedic impairment that adversely affects a child's educational performance. The term includes impairments caused by congenital anomaly (e.g., clubfoot, absence of some member, etc.), impairments caused by disease (e.g., poliomyelitis, bone tuberculosis, etc.), and impairments from other causes (e.g., cerebral palsy, amputations, and fractures or burns that cause contractures).

(9) *Other health impairment* means having limited strength, vitality, or alertness, including a heightened alertness to environmental stimuli, that results in limited alertness with respect to the educational environment, that—

　(i) Is due to chronic or acute health problems such as asthma, attention-deficit disorder or attention-deficit/hyperactivity disorder, diabetes, epilepsy, a heart condition, hemophilia, lead poisoning, leukemia, nephritis, rheumatic fever, and sickle cell anemia; and

　(ii) Adversely affects a child's educational performance.

(10) *Specific learning disability* is defined as follows:

　(i) *General.* The term means a disorder in one or more of the basic psychological processes involved in understanding or in using language, spoken or written, that may manifest itself in an imperfect ability to listen, think, speak, read, write, spell, or to do mathematical calculations, including conditions such as perceptual disabilities, brain injury, minimal brain dysfunction, dyslexia, and developmental aphasia.

　(ii) *Disorders not included.* The term does not include learning problems that are primarily the result of visual, hearing, or motor disabilities, of mental retardation, of emotional disturbance, or of environmental, cultural, or economic disadvantage.

(11) *Speech or language impairment* means a communication disorder, such as stuttering, impaired articulation, a language impairment, or a voice impairment, that adversely affects a child's educational performance.

(12) *Traumatic brain injury* means an acquired injury to the brain caused by an external physical force, resulting in total or partial functional disability or psychosocial impairment, or both, that adversely affects a child's educational performance. The term applies to open or closed head injuries resulting in impairments in one or more areas, such as cognition; language; memory; attention; reasoning; abstract thinking; judgment; problem-solving; sensory, perceptual, and motor abilities; psychosocial

behavior; physical functions; information processing; and speech. The term does not apply to brain injuries that are congenital or degenerative, or to brain injuries induced by birth trauma.

(13) *Visual impairment including blindness* means an impairment in vision that, even with correction, adversely affects a child's educational performance. The term includes both partial sight and blindness.

(34 C.F.R. 300.7(c)). The proposed regulations issued in June 2005 make only minor, nonsubstantive changes to these definitions.

KIMBERLY F. APPLEQUIST
University of Colorado at Colorado Springs,
Kimberly Lund
Fourth edition

See *also* Disability; Disability Etiquette; Individuals With Disabilities Education Improvement Act of 2004 (IDEIA)

CHINA, SPECIAL EDUCATION IN

History of Special Education Services

China has a history of civilization exceeding 5,000 years. The description of disabled people (deaf and blind) was first documented in the fourth century B.C. in Zuo. The progressive thought that all people with disabilities should be well taken care of was explicitly stated in the *Book of Rites*, in the second century B.C. In 1859, Hong Rengan proposed that institutions for disabled people be established. However, the first school for the blind was founded by a British missionary named William Murray in Beijing, in 1874. Thirteen years later (1887), an American, C. R. Mills, became the founder of the first school for the deaf in Shandong. It was not until 1916 when the first Chinese, Zhang Jian, opened Nantong School for the Deaf in Jiangsu, which is still in operation. By 1948, there were a total of 42 special schools for the deaf and blind, with an enrollment of 2,380 students and 360 faculty/staff members. Among these schools, eight were funded by the public. At that time, special education was categorized as social education.

After the People's Republic of China was founded in 1949, the government integrated special education into the general educational system and new special education programs were created in the Department of Education. The number of schools for the deaf and blind increased significantly from 64 to 253 between 1953 and 1963. According to statistics in 1984, the enrollment of deaf and blind students was 33,055, served by 8,000 faculty and staff. Meanwhile, four schools for students with other disabilities came into existence. In 1997, there were a total of 1,440 special education schools—27 higher education institutions, 845 schools for the deaf, 143 schools for the deaf and blind, and 425 schools for children with disabilities. The number of disabled students enrolled also increased to 340,621, along with 43,296 faculty and staff members.

In 1987, the survey results showed that there were 52 million disabled people in China, 4.9% of the national population. It was estimated that 60 million people were handicapped out of 1.2 billion Chinese; among them 12.3 million were under 18, which was 2.58% of the total population. The enrollment rate of school-age children with visual, hearing, speech, and mental disabilities increased from 20% (1991) to nearly 60% (1995).

Legal Rights and Public Policy

A legal regulation system regarding special education has been developing since 1980. Provision No. 45 of the Constitution of People's Republic of China (1982) states that all disabled persons have the right to be educated. In response to the Constitution, provincial governments support special education through various ways to meet their local needs. Special education is also touched upon in specific legal regulations. It is stipulated in Provision No. 9 of the Law of Compulsory Education (1986) that the government is obligated to set up and support special education schools or classes for disabled children, and any individuals are encouraged to found schools. Special law—Law of the PRC on the Protection of Disabled Persons—was constituted in 1990. This law declares that the educational rights of the disabled are protected, and classifies special education as one of the components of general education. Nine provisions in Regulation No. 3 of the 1990 law stipulate the responsibilities, policies, funding, approaches, adult education, training of faculty/staff, and so on in special education. Rules and regulations were also established for various departments in the government, specifying how they comply with the laws. Fifty-two provisions in Educational Regulations for the Disabled Persons specifically define the education of the disabled at different stages. In addition, other relevant laws, such as Law of Teachers and Law of Vocational Education, also relate to special education.

The following aspects are highlighted in the laws and regulations. It is clearly stated that teaching disabled children is one of the most important components in compulsory education, which must be insured and enforced by the government. The educational policy regarding disabled people observes the principle of keeping a balance of popularization and advancement, with the former as the focus. While the priority is to improve compulsory and vocational education, preschool education should be strengthened and secondary and higher education should gradually be developed. It is stipulated that multiple methods should be applied in the education of disabled children. The guiding principle in special education is that general education schools function as the backbone, and learning in regular classrooms and special education classes/programs constitutes the main body. The training of faculty and staff should be emphasized and the supply for special education should be assured.

Present Structure

Special education can be defined in the following two ways: (1) In a broad sense, it may indicate the education of all children who have special needs, including the gifted and talented and juvenile criminals, or (2) in a narrow sense, it may imply the education of all kinds of mentally and physically disabled people. Currently, the emphasis in special education is placed on the training of people, especially children, with various disabilities, though the study of all who need special care in education is being conducted simultaneously.

China is developing a special education system with its own characteristics, responding to the situation of a large number of disabled children, a developing economy, and a developing educational foundation. This system is neither complete segregation nor mainstreaming and inclusiveness; it is a combination of general education and special education—each is independent but also integrated. Special education is in one of three forms: special education schools, special education programs, and learning in regular class. However, the majority of the students are enrolled in either special programs or regular classes in general education schools.

The focus of special education is within the 9-year compulsory education. Early childhood education is considered critical and the early intervention and training of deaf and mentally disabled children have received a great deal of attention. Meanwhile, disabled adult vocational education also grows rapidly. In 1997, 610 adult vocational education institutions were registered and 1.5 million disabled people were trained. In addition to advancing their education in regular higher educational institutions, disabled people also enjoy the privilege of attending two universities founded exclusively for them. Although the national educational department established standard curriculum and instruction materials in special education, local educational institutions are encouraged to make any changes to accommodate their specific needs.

Financing

As is the general 9-year compulsory primary and secondary education, special education is run and supported by local governments. On the other hand, noncompulsory early childhood and higher education is supported by the central government and by individuals. The central government has increased its budget to improve and further develop special education in the past decade. In 1994, the national financial budget for special education reached ¥28 million, a 142% increase of the budget in 1990. A special allowance was provided by relevant central government departments for the purpose of enhancing special education in 1989—¥14 million were allocated between 1989 and 1995. Consequently, local governments followed the example, creating their special allowance for special education. Another financial source for special education is donations and fund raising. Economically disadvantaged students are supported with assistantship and scholarship awarded by the government.

Education and Training of Educators

There was no special institution where faculty and staff were trained for special education in P.R. China until 1980. Special education majors received their training at secondary normal schools in several provinces in the early 1980s. The special education program was created at Beijing Normal University in 1986. At present, there are 34 secondary special education normal schools in operation. Special education programs are offered in five nationally and two provincially affiliated normal universities, where teacher candidates pursue bachelor's degrees. Graduate programs are also available at institutions such as Beijing Normal University. Bachelor's degrees can be completed in four years, and master's degrees in three years. Special education classes are opened in general secondary normal schools to train special education candidates in a regular classroom setting. Various workshops and long-distance learning also are part of the overall training system. In addition, the National Educational Committee often entrusts relevant institutions with seminars for different types of education professionals, such as principals and special education administrators. Experts from home and abroad are invited to lecture and teach at these seminars. Moreover, professional special education research institutions and mass research organizations have been developed. Journals such as *Modern Special Education* and *Special Education in China* are published periodically. Lastly, special educators are entitled to a special allowance that equals 15–25% of their base salary.

Relationship to Other Social Services

Special education touches all walks of life. In 1993, the State Council Coordinating Committee on Disability was organized, with chief officers from 34 departments as its members. The central government issued *Work Program for Disabled Persons During the Ninth Five-Year Plan Period, 1996–2000*. Specific requirements and implementation plans have been proposed in early intervention community services, compulsory education, vocational education, employment, culture, appliances for the handicapped, immunization, legality, reduction of expenses, and organization. A series of special regulations are also included in laws and policies. For instance, Electoral Law states that disabled people have equal rights to vote, Inheritance Law stipulates that the disabled have equal property and civil rights, and Criminal Law and Civil Law insure that the disabled are protected in human rights and lawsuits. In employment, a quota of 1.5–2% is assigned for any institution to hire the disabled. Nontax or tax deduction is applicable to any enterprise whose employees are handicapped. The blind enjoy free reading materials and free urban transportation. It is also regulated that the third Sunday of May each year is the national Individuals with Disabilities Day.

Trends and Goals for the Present and Near Future

A Chinese-style special education system is being established on the basis of adapting models from other countries to serve the needs of China. The national government has set the following five priorities in developing special education for the near future:

1. The expansion of special education in rural areas will be emphasized. For those places where special education has been available, the focus will be placed on educational improvement and reform. The goal is to increase the enrollment rate of disabled children to that of regular children. Approximately 80% of all blind, deaf, and mentally handicapped children are expected to attend schools.
2. Early childhood special education will be improved considerably, and families and communities are encouraged to participate in early intervention.
3. Vocational training for the disabled will be strengthened, with short-term training as the primary means.
4. Promotions systems will be established for special education teachers to improve their benefits.
5. Further research will be conducted on the education of children with learning disability, autism, and other disabilities.

Due to historical reasons, special education in Taiwan, Hong Kong, and Macao shares similar cultural tradition and background with that in P.R. China. However, each has formed its own characteristics in classification, standards, and educational methods in their process of development. In December 1997, a symposium was held at Taibei Normal University to discuss special education in mainland China and Taiwan. The theme of the conference was to create a brand-new world of special education with love and wisdom. The interaction among Chinese and international special education professionals has increased significantly in recent years. These educators' interactions enhance mutual understanding and advance the knowledge of special education by all nations.

REFERENCES

Law of the People's Republic of China on the Protection of Disabled Persons. (1991). *Beijing*, China: Hua Xia.

Mao, Y. (1993). Viewpoints gleaned from participating early intervention in China. *Early Child Development and Care, 84,* 59–74.

Piao, Y. (Ed.). (1995). *Special pedagogy*. Fuzhou: Fujian Education Press.

Piao, Y. (1987). China, People's Republic of. In J. Van Cleve (Ed.), *Gallaudet encyclopedia of deaf people and deafness* (Vol. 1, pp. 181–184). New York, NY: McGraw-Hill.

Piao, Y., Gargiulo, R., & Yun, X. (1995). Special education in the People's Republic of China: Characteristics and practices. *International Journal of Special Education, 10*(1), 52–65.

State Council. (1994, August 27). The provisions on the education of disabled persons. *People's Daily*.

State Education Commission. (1995). *Documents of special education, 1990–1995*. Beijing: Author.

State Statistics Bureau. (1987). *First national sampling of the handicapped*. Beijing, China: Author.

Work Program for Disabled Persons During the Ninth Five-Year National Development Plan (1996–2000). (1992). *Beijing*, China: Hua Xia.

Yang, H., & Wang, H. (1994). Special education in China. *Journal of Special Education, 28*(1), 93–105.

Yun, X. (1994), China. In K. Mazurek & M. Winzer (Eds.), *Comparative studies in special education* (pp. 163–178). Washington, DC: Gallaudet University Press.

YONGXIN PIAO
Beijing Normal University

PING LIN
Elmhurst College

See also Hong Kong, Special Education in; Japan, Special Education in

CHLAMYDIA TRACHOMATIS, ADOLESCENT ONSET

Chlamydia is the most common sexually transmitted bacterial infection in the United States. Its full name is *chlamydia trachomatis*. This kind of bacteria can infect the penis, vagina, cervix, anus, urethra, or eye (Planned Parenthood, 2000a, 2000b). Chlamydia specifically targets the mucosal membranes of these areas. In addition, the mucosal surface of the pharynx is susceptible to infection.

It is estimated that more than 4 million people are infected with chlamydia each year (National Institute of Allergy and Infectious Diseases, 2000). Chlamydia is four times as common as gonorrhea, more than 30 times as common as syphilis, and most common among women and men under age 25. For every person with herpes, there are six with chlamydia. Adolescents and young adults are at greater risk more than likely due to behavioral factors such as unprotected intercourse, multiple sex partners, and a lack of information for accurately assessing level of risk. Furthermore, chlamydia easily infects the immature cervix (specifically the tissue covering the cervix in women younger than 20 years old), making teenage girls more susceptible to infection than adult women (Kaiser Family Foundation, 1998). In some studies, up to 30–40% of sexually active teenage girls were infected (Eng & Butler, 1997).

The long-term ramifications of untreated chlamydia are serious for both women and men. In women, when transmission occurs during vaginal sex, the infection usually begins on the cervix. From the cervix it can spread to the fallopian tubes and ovaries. Untreated chlamydia can result in pelvic inflammatory disease (PID), which is a root cause of infertility in many women. At least 15% of all infertile American women are infertile because of tubal damage caused by PID (American Social Health Association, 2001). In men, when chlamydia is transmitted from an infected sexual partner to the penis, the infection can spread from the urethra to the testicles. When untreated the subsequent damage from the infection can result in a condition known as epididymitis, which can lead to sterility. Chlamydia causes more than 250,000 cases of acute epididymitis in the United States every year.

Characteristics

1. It is estimated that up to 75% of women and 50% of men with chlamydia have no symptoms or symptoms so mild that they do not seek medical attention (U.S. Food & Drug Administration, 1999).

2. When symptoms do occur, they usually appear between 1 and 3 weeks after exposure.

3. In women, signs of infection may include unusual vaginal discharge or bleeding, burning during urination, urge to urinate more frequently, abdominal pain, low-grade fever, cervical inflammation, pain during vaginal sex, inflamed rectum, or inflamed urethra.

4. In men, signs of infection may include burning and itching around the penis, unusual discharge from the penis, pain or burning during urination, pain or swelling of the testicles, inflamed rectum, or inflamed urethra.

5. The infection is transmitted primarily during anal or vaginal sex. However, transmission via oral sex is possible.

6. The infection can be transmitted even if bodily fluids are not exchanged.

7. Chlamydia can infect the eyes when discharge from an infected partner enters the eye during sex or hand-to-eye contact. If infection occurs, chlamydia may cause redness, itching, and possibly discharge.

The only accurate way to determine if chlamydial infection exists is through screening from a health center or clinic, doctor's office, or health department—most of which offer both testing and treatment. Testing is done via sending a sample of pus or discharge from the vagina or penis to a laboratory that will look for the bacteria, or a urine test that does not require a pelvic exam or swabbing of the penis. Results from the urine test are usually available within 24 hours. The following antibiotic prescriptions are most commonly given to individuals infected with chlamydia: azithromycin (taken for 1 day only), doxycycline (taken for 7 days), erythromycin, or ofloxacin. If the symptoms do not disappear after the prescribed dosage of antibiotic, or if they return, the individual should return to her or his health care provider. In addition, any current and past sexual partners should be examined and treated if necessary.

All adolescents, whether developmentally challenged or not, need to receive accurate, sensitive, and thorough information regarding the risks of transmission for chlamydia and other sexually transmitted diseases (STDs), as well as ways and means to prevent the spread of these diseases. Although often considered asexual by many medical or social work professionals, individuals who are mentally handicapped are also at risk for chlamydial infection if they are sexually active. Additional factors to consider when assessing risk for adolescents in particular include the multitude of psychosocial issues dealt with by adolescents, creative sexual exploration that may not fall under adult definitions of sexual activity, previous sexual assault or abuse, and the practice of "serial" monogamy among many adolescents—the practice of engaging in a series of short-term monogamous relationships.

Although even "protected" sex with a condom cannot completely prevent transmission of chlamydia or other STDs, correct and consistent condom use significantly reduces the chances of getting chlamydia or other STDs. When reducing risk, latex and polyurethane condoms as well as oral barriers for vaginal, anal, and oral sex offer protection. Many doctors recommend that individuals who have more than one sex partner, and especially women under 25 years of age, be tested for chlamydial infection regularly, even if they do not exhibit any symptoms. Furthermore, scientists are constantly seeking out better ways to diagnose, treat, and prevent chlamydial infections. Recently, the completed sequence for the chlamydia trachomatis genome was identified, thus providing scientists with invaluable information as they try to develop a safe and effective vaccine. Another area of research is in developing topical microbicides (preparations that can be inserted into the vagina to prevent infection) that are effective and easy for women to use. Left untreated, the "silent epidemic" of chlamydia threatens to cause reproductive damage and infertility in many of the individuals who contract the disease each year. In response, effective sexual health education and access to means for prevention, screening, and treatment provide the best course of action.

REFERENCES

American Social Health Association. (2001). *STD statistics & "Information to live by: Chlamydia."* Retrieved from http://www.asha.org

Eng, T., & William, B. (Eds.). (1997). *The hidden epidemic: Confronting sexually transmitted diseases.* Washington, DC: National Academy Press.

Kaiser Family Foundation. (1998). *Sexually transmitted diseases in America: How many cases and at what cost?* Pittsburgh, PA: Kaiser Family Foundation and American Social Health Association.

National Institute of Allergy and Infectious Diseases, National Institutes of Health. (2000, October). *Chlamydial infection.* Retrieved from http://www.niaid.nih.gov/factsheets/stdclam .htm

Planned Parenthood. (2000a, April). *Chlamydia: Questions and answers.* Retrieved from http://www.plannedparenthood.org

Planned Parenthood. (2000b). Fact sheet prepared by the Katharine Dexter McCormick Library. Retrieved from http:// www.plannedparenthood.org

U.S. Food and Drug Administration. (1999). *Chlamydia's quick cure.* Retrieved from http://www.fda.gov

LESLIE BURKHOLDER
Idea Infusion Consulting and Contracting Denver, Colorado

CHLAMYDIA TRACHOMATIS INFECTIONS

Chlamydia trachomatis is the most prevalent sexually transmitted infection in the United States today. The annual incidence is estimated to be as high as 2.8 million infections occur annually (CDC, 2011; Washington, Gove, Schachter, & Sweet, 1985).

Chlamydia is spread by intimate and/or sexual contact, and affects both women and homosexual/heterosexual men in all socioeconomic classes. The disease is especially alarming because it is often silent, having no symptoms. Up to 70% of women and 25% of men with chlamydia may be relatively asymptomatic (CDC, 2011; Washington et al., 1985).

The bacteria can cause painful urination and pelvic urinary, eye, and respiratory infections in both sexes. Additional symptoms in women may include vaginal discharge, lower abdominal pain or sensitivity, abnormal Pap smear (often described as heavy or moderate inflammation), vaginal bleeding between periods even when taking birth-control pills regularly, and uterine infection. Symptoms in men may include penile discomfort and/or discharge.

If silent or not correctly diagnosed and treated, the disease can lead to such serious complications as pelvic inflammatory disease, ectopic (tubal) pregnancy, infertility, and, possibly, cervical cancer in women and urethritis and sterility in men. Though common, the disease may not be recognized among individuals with mental retardation, often thought of as asexual by many medical or social work personnel. Mentally retarded adolescents, and young adults in particular, should receive education in the recognition of chlamydia and other venereal diseases.

There is some evidence that in pregnant women chlamydia infections may lead to prematurity. It is the leading cause of early infant pneumonia and conjunctivitis (CDC, 2011). Chlamydia infections are curable with a full 21-day treatment with tetracycline. A 7-day treatment may be effective for men, but not for women. Sulfisoxazole and erythromycin are also effective, but penicillin is not.

REFERENCES

Centers for Disease Control and Prevention (CDC). (2011). *What is chlamydia?* Retrieved from http://www.cdc.gov/ std/chlamydia/stdfact-chlamydia.htm

Fraser, J., Rettig, P., & Kaplan, D. (1983). Prevalence of cervical chlamydia trachomatis and *Neisseria gonorrheae* in female adolescents. *Pediatrics, 71,* 333–336.

Washington, E., Gove, S., Schachter, J., & Sweet, R. (1985). Oral contraceptives, chlamydia trachomatis infection, and pelvic inflammatory disease. *Journal of the American Medical Association, 253,* 2246–2250.

C. SUE LAMB
GINGA L. COLCOUGH
University of North Carolina at Wilmington

See *also* Herpes Simplex I and II

CHLORPROMAZINE

Chlorpromazine (CPZ) is the generic name for Thorazine, a phenothiazine used in the treatment of psychoses and other psychiatric disorders (Conley et al., 1998). Though CPZ was synthesized by Charpentier in 1950 during research intended to produce an antipsychotic medication, the endeavor began in 1949 with a French surgeon Laborit, who was seeking a medication to reduce shock during surgery (Leavitt, 1982). Chlorpromazine is used primarily in the treatment of schizophrenia, but also has been used at low dosages to treat nausea and seasickness.

Though the actions of CPZ on the central nervous system (CNS) are not completely understood, it tends to produce the following behavioral changes: decreases apparent agitation, decreases perceptions of anxiety, decreases reports of hallucinatory experiences, produces mild to moderate sedating effects that appear to be both dosage and clinical condition dependent, and decreases spontaneous motor activity.

Because CPZ and all phenothiazines appear to block dopamine receptors in the CNS, a number of motor-related adverse effects are noted, especially during initial usage, chronic usage, or at high dosages. Three general reactions may be observed: dystonic reactions (most often with children, especially during acute infections or while dehydrated; these include spasms of neck muscles, rigidity with extension of back muscles, jaw tics, difficulty in swallowing or talking, and facial spasms with tongue protrusion, and may be accompanied by sweating or pallor); feelings of motor restlessness (e.g., agitation, inability to sit still, tapping of feet, insomnia, strong desire to move about without reported anxiety; often occurs within 2 to 3 days of initiating treatment); and parkinsonlike symptoms (most frequent with elderly persons; include masked facial appearance, increased salivation/drooling, motor slowing, including slowed speech, swallowing difficulties, and cogwheel rigidity; McEvoy, 1985). In addition, blurred vision and dry mouth are reported during early stages of treatment. A persistent motor syndrome called tardive dyskinesia, characterized by rhythmic involuntary movements of facial and oral musculature and occasionally the limbs, may develop in conjunction with CPZ administration (Konopasek, 2004). The elderly, especially females, on high dosages are reported as most at risk for this condition.

REFERENCES

Conley, R. R., Tamminga, C. A., Bartro, J. J., Richardson, C., Peske, M. Lingle, J.,...Zaremba, S. (1998). Olanzapine compared with chlorpromazine in treatment-resistant schizophrenia. *American Journal of Psychiatry, 155*(7), 914–920.

Konopasek, D. E. (2004). *Medication fact sheets.* Longmont, CO: SoprisWest.

Leavitt, F. (1982). *Drugs and behavior.* New York, NY: Wiley.

McEvoy, G. K. (1985). *American hospital formulary service: Drug information 85.* Bethesda, MD: American Society of Hospital Pharmacists.

ROBERT F. SAWICKI
Lake Erie Institute of Rehabilitation

See also Phenothiazines

CHOLINESTERASE

Neurons are the basic information processing and transmitting elements of the central nervous system. The transmission of impulses across these nerve cells is a biochemical process. As such, a neurochemical process is the foundation of all human behavior.

Impulses travel from one neuron to another across a biochemical junction (synapse). Specifically, when an impulse reaches the terminal button of a neuron, it releases a transmitter substance called acetylcholine (ACh), which causes a temporary change in the membrane of the receiving neuron. If there is sufficient chemical stimulation, the second neuron will subsequently fire. Following the alteration of the membrane potential, the enzyme *cholinesterase* (ChE) neutralizes (destroys) the transmitter substance and thus restores the synapse to a resting state. In this way a single impulse is transmitted through the nervous system.

Neuroscientists have long hypothesized that this biochemical process underlies learning and memory functioning in the brain (Hillgard & Bower, 1975). While a clear relationship has not been established between cholinesterase activity and memory functioning, a number of investigators have consistently found a cholinergic deficit in dementia patients (e.g., Giacobini, Gracon, Smith, & Hoover, 1997; Perry et al., 1978). Based on postmortem examination, these investigators found reduced cholinesterase levels in those areas of the brain typically associated with memory (e.g., the hippocampus). Thus, it appears that a reduction in cholinesterase activity may be related to memory dysfunctions. Research efforts are presently under way that examine the relationship between increased cholinergic activity and memory and learning functions, and the role of cholinesterase in obsessive-compulsive disorder (Erzegovesi, Bellodi, & Smeraldi, 1995). Interestingly, cholinesterase inhibitors are being used to treat mild to moderate symptoms of Alzheimer disease as they increase levels of acetylcholine in the brain (Alzheimer's Association, 2005).

REFERENCES

Alzheimer's Association. (2005). *Fact sheet: About FDA-approved cholinesterase inhibitors.* Retrieved from http://www.alz.org/

Erzegovesi, S., Bellodi, L., & Smeraldi, E. (1995). Serum cholinesterase in obsessive-compulsive disorder. *Psychiatry Research*, *58*(3), 265–268.

Giacobini, E., Gracon, S., Smith, F., & Hoover, T. (1997). Cholinesterase inhibitors in Alzheimer disease treatment. In R. E. Becker & E. Giacobini (Eds.), *Alzheimer disease: From molecular biology to therapy*. Boston, MA: Birkhauser.

Hillgard, E. R., & Bower, G. H. (1975). *Theories of learning*. Englewood Cliffs, NJ: Prentice Hall.

Perry, E. K., Tomlinson, B. E., Blessed, G., Bergmann, K., Gibson, P. H., & Perry, R. H. (1978). Correlation of cholinergic abnormalities with senile plaques and mental test scores in senile dementia. *British Medical Journal*, *2*, 1457–1459.

JEFFREY W. GRAY
Ball State University

RAYMOND S. DEAN
Ball State University,
Indiana University School of Medicine

See also **Neurological Organizations; Synapses**

CHOMSKY, NOAM (1928–   )

Noam Chomsky was born on December 7, 1928, in Philadelphia, Pennsylvania. His undergraduate and graduate years were spent at the University of Pennsylvania, where he received his BA in 1949 and his PhD in Linguistics in 1955. From 1951 to 1955, Chomsky was a Junior Fellow of the Harvard University Society of Fellows. It was during this time that he completed his doctoral dissertation entitled *Transformational Analysis*. The major theoretical viewpoints of the dissertation were published in the monograph, *Syntactic Structure*, in 1957, which was later expanded in a more extensive work published in 1975, *The Logical Structure of Linguistic Theory*.

Chomsky joined the staff of the Massachusetts Institute of Technology (MIT) in 1955, and in 1961 was appointed full professor in the Department of Modern Languages and Linguistics, currently the Department of Linguistics and Philosophy. From 1966 to 1976, he was the Ferrai P. Ward Professor of Modern Languages and Linguistics, and he was appointed Institute professor in 1975.

Chomsky is famous for the construction of a system of generative programs developed out of his interest in modern logic and mathematics. His theory proposes that the grammatical rules for any given language are, in general, similar in all languages. He is best known for his work on the "Chomsky hierarchy," which classifies language groups according to the different types of grammars that generate them. In particular, he was the first linguist to identify what are today thought of as "context-free" grammars. Among his earlier works are *Cartesian Linguistics* (1966) and *Language and Mind* (1968).

Chomsky became interested in politics and the dynamics of governmental power during the Vietnam War, and has subsequently written much on language, politics, philosophy, and the media. Among the best known are *Manufacturing Consent* (1988), *Necessary Illusions* (1989), and *Deterring Democracy* (1992). He has also written and lectured widely on contemporary issues, international affairs, intellectual issues, and U.S. foreign policy.

From 1958 to 1959, Chomsky was in residence at the Institute for Advanced Study at Princeton, New Jersey. He delivered the John Locke Lectures at Oxford in 1969, the Bertrand Russell Memorial Lecture at Cambridge University in 1970, the Nehru Memorial Lecture in New Delhi in 1972, and the Huizinga Lecture in Leiden in 1977. His numerous honors include honorary degrees from the University of London, University of Pennsylvania, Georgetown University, and Cambridge University. He is a Fellow of the American Academy of Arts and Sciences as well as a member of other professional and learned societies, including the National Academy of Science. In addition, he is a recipient of the Distinguished Scientific Contribution Award of the American Psychological Association (APA). Chomsky remains on the faculty at MIT, and continues to be actively involved in the wide variety of interests that have marked his career as a highly productive scholar and citizen.

REFERENCES

Chomsky, A. N. (1957). *Syntactic structures*. 'S-Gravenhage: Mouton.

Chomsky, A. N. (1966). *Cartesian linguistics: A chapter in the history of rationalist thought*. New York, NY: Harper & Row.

Chomsky, A. N. (1968). *Language and mind*. New York, NY: Harcourt, Brace & World.

Chomsky, A. N. (1975). *Logical structure of linguistic theory*. New York, NY: Plenum Press.

Chomsky, N. (1992). *Deterring democracy*. New York, NY: Hill & Wang.

IVAN Z. HOLOWINSKY
Rutgers University
First edition

KAY E. KETZENBERGER
TAMARA J. MARTIN
The University of Texas of
the Permian Basin
Second edition

CHOREA

Choreiform movement is a term used to describe a disorder characterized by quick, sudden, random, purposeless, jerky, irregular, spasmodic movement. Choreiform movement can occur in any body part and often is observed in shoulders, arms, and hands, or in the tongue and face as grimaces. Chorea often occurs with writhing and twisting movements that are called *atheosis*. Chorea can be induced by drugs, metabolic and endocrine disorders, and vascular incidents (NINDS, 2005).

Two major kinds of chorea are of primary interest to school personnel because of their possible school-age onsets and their markedly different outlook for recovery or prognosis. Sydenham's chorea (also known as chorea minor, rheumatic chorea, or St. Vitus's dance) is a disease of the central nervous system that usually occurs following streptococcal inflammation. Its slow start, often several months after the initial infection, begins with choreiform movements after the initial infection, begins with choreiform movements involving all muscles except those of the eyes, and may involve obsessive-compulsive symptoms (Swedo & Leonard, 1994). There are seldom any specific laboratory findings. There is no specific treatment except for sedation and protection from injury, together with prophylactic follow-up for identified residual infection. Recovery is slow and spontaneous, usually within 3 to 6 months, with no permanent damage to the central nervous system. Medical follow-up is recommended, and return to regular school is encouraged as soon as the transitory motor symptoms permit. The disease is reported to be more common in girls, with onset most frequent in summer and early fall (Berkow, 1982).

The second major type of chorea is Huntington's chorea (also known as chorea degenerative, progressive, or hereditary). The age of insidious onset of Huntington's chorea is reported by most sources to be between 30 and 50 years (Barr, 1979; Chusid, 1976; Clark, 1975; NINDS, 2005). However, a subtype of this disease has been described with onset in childhood, with initial symptoms of stiffness (rigidity), slowed movement (bradykinesia), and later choreiform movement (Berkow, 1982). The disease is characterized by progressive choreiform movement, progressive mental deterioration, and marked personality changes. Swallowing becomes difficult, walking impossible, and dementia profound with progression. Death usually follows within 10 to 15 years. Treatment is symptomatic for motor symptoms. There is no known treatment for the dementia.

Huntington's chorea is transmitted as an autosomal dominant trait, which means that half of the children of an affected parent are at risk for developing the disease. Those who do not have the disease do not transmit it. In cases where the family history is not known, affected individuals with onset after childbearing years may transmit the disease to offspring before their own onset. Research has been directed toward a chemical identification of those with the disease, but at present the only conclusive evidence is family history, and *all* potential known carriers are advised not to have children. Chusid (1976) suggests that most American cases have been traced to two brothers who emigrated from England.

Clinical experience suggests that the subtypes with early childhood onset appear to progress more rapidly to early death. The presence of several children with the disorder in one family is a devastating experience. The serious implications of Huntington's chorea should serve to reinforce the importance of differential diagnosis of choreiform movement disorders by a skilled neurologist with appropriate medical follow-up. Supportive special education services should be provided.

Characteristics

1. Irregular, involuntary movements that flow from one body part to another
2. Irregular movements in the upper and lower facial areas
3. Irregular movements in the trunk and limb areas
4. Motor inefficiency
5. Difficulty with eating or swallowing

REFERENCES

Barr, M. L. (1979). *The human nervous system* (3rd ed.). Hagerstown, MD: Harper & Row.

Berkow, R. (Ed.). (1982). *The Merck manual of diagnosis and therapy* (14th ed.). Rahway, NJ: Merck, Sharp & Dohme.

Chusid, J. G. (1976). *Correlative neuroanatomy and functional neurology* (16th ed.). Los Angeles, CA: Lang Medical.

Clark, R. G. (1975). *Manter and Gatz's essentials of clinical neuroanatomy and neurophysiology* (5th ed.). Philadelphia, PA: Davis.

National Institute of Neurological Disorders and Stroke (NINDS). (2005). *NINDS chorea information page.* Retrieved from http://www.ninds.nih.gov/

Swedo, S. E., & Leonard, H. (1994). Childhood movement disorders and obsessive compulsive disorder. *Journal of Clinical Psychiatry, 55*(3), 32–37.

RACHAEL J. STEVENSON
Bedford, Ohio

See also Genetic Counseling; Huntington's Chorea

CHORIONIC VILLUS SAMPLING

Chorionic villus sampling (CVS), sometimes called chorionvillus biopsy, is a relatively new technique that allows diagnosis of chromosomal abnormalities, many inborn errors of metabolism, and other disorders, in the first trimester of pregnancy. Most women who have CVS are over 35 years of age (CDC, 2005). Conducted before organogenesis is complete, it cannot reliably detect disorders such as neural tube defects; these may be assessed with later maternal serum alpha-fetoprotein (AFP) screening.

CVS has clear advantages over amniocentesis as a technique for antenatal (prenatal) diagnosis. It can be performed optimally at 9 weeks of pregnancy as opposed to 16 to 18 weeks, and results, including chromosomal analyses, are available about a week after testing, as opposed to the 2 to 4 weeks for amniocentesis (*Lancet*, 1986). Thus genetic counseling can be provided early in pregnancy in cases where disorders are identified, avoiding some of the ethical and emotional concomitants of later abortion.

In CVS, 10–50 mg of placental tissue are removed. Enzyme assay and DNA analysis are performed directly on this tissue; chromosomal analysis is generally done on cultures of the CVS tissue. Most CVS assays are done transcervically, with a small percentage conducted abdominally (*Lancet*, 1986).

Risk of CVS is not established, although the likelihood of it infecting the embryo appears low. Of particular concern is the suggestion of greater risk of test-induced abortion following CVS than following amniocentesis (Clarke, 1985), although at least one study has found no difference between the two techniques (Jahoda, Vosters, Sacks, & Galjaard, 1985). A number of questions, particularly regarding safety, remain unanswered (*Lancet*, 1986) but risk factors appear to be relatively low at 0.5% to 1.0% (CDC, 2005). Widespread availability of CVS will depend on the outcome of large-sample controlled studies of risk and accuracy. Research reports are appearing frequently, and coordinated evaluation studies in Europe, Canada, and the United States began in 1985 (Clarke, 1985). In 1990, more than 200,000 procedures were performed in the United States (CDC, 2005).

REFERENCES

Centers for Disease Control and Prevention (CDC). (2005). *Chorionic villus sampling: Recommendations for prenatal counseling*. Retrieved from http://www.cdc.gov/

Clarke, M. (1985). Fetal diagnosis trial. *Nature, 315*, 269.

Jahoda, M. G., Vosters, R. P. L., Sacks, E. S., & Galjaard, H. (1985). Safety of chorionic villus sampling. *Lancet, 2*, 941–942.

Staff. (1986). The potential of chorionic villus sampling. *Lancet, 1*, 76.

ROBERT T. BROWN
University of North Carolina at Wilmington

BRENDA M. POPE
New Hanover Memorial Hospital

See also **Amniocentesis; Chromosomes, Human Anomalies, and Cytogenetic Abnormalities; Maternal Serum Alpha-Fetoprotein (AFP) Screening**

CHOROIDEREMIA

Choroideremia is also known as choroidal sclerosis, progressive choroidal atrophy, progressive tapetochoroidal dystrophy, or TCD (National Organization for Rare Disorders [NORD], 2000). It is a rare, inherited disorder that causes progressive loss of vision due to degeneration of the choroid and retina (PDR Medical Dictionary, 2000; Sebra, 1999).

Choroideremia usually affects males. Female carriers may have mild symptoms without loss of vision (NORD, 2000; *PDR Medical Dictionary*, 2000). Choroideremia is genetically passed through families by the X-linked pattern of inheritance. Females have two X chromosomes and can carry the disease gene on one of their X chromosomes. Females typically are not affected by X-linked diseases such as choroideremia because they have a healthy version of the gene on their other X chromosome. Males, however, have only one X chromosome and are therefore genetically susceptible to X-linked diseases. Males cannot be carriers of X-linked diseases. Males affected with an X-linked disease always pass the gene on the X chromosome to their daughters. Affected males never pass an X-linked disease gene to their sons because fathers pass the Y chromosome to their sons. Female carriers have a 50% chance of passing the X-linked disease gene to their daughters. They also have a 50% chance of passing the gene to their sons, who are then affected by the disease. By 1980, about 58 cases had been identified in Finland. Almost all of them came from the northern part of the country (McKusick, 2000).

Characteristics

1. Night blindness during childhood
2. Progressive constriction of visual fields
3. Complete loss of vision

Choroideremia is one the few degenerative diseases that might be detected prenatally in some cases. Female carriers are recommended to seek information about this testing from a medical geneticist. All members of affected families are encouraged to consult an ophthalmologist and genetic counselor. Recently, the exact location of the gene on the X chromosome that causes choroideremia was found. However, at present there is no effective treatment or cure. Until a treatment is discovered, help is available through low-vision aids that include optical, electronic, and computer-based devices. In addition, personal, educational, and vocational counseling, as well as adaptive training skills, job placement, and income assistance, are available through community resources (Choroideremia Research Foundation, Inc., 2000). Patients with peripheral vision loss may benefit from a rehabilitation program that combines low-vision training with amorphic lenses in a bioptic configuration (Szlyk, Seiple, Laderman, Kelsch, Ho, & McMahon, 1998).

Services for this disorder range depending on the severity of the visual impairment. For mild impairments, modifications to the regular curriculum including assistive technology under the 504 Act are appropriate. For more severe impairment, the child qualifies for services as visually impaired.

Recent research on choroideremia has progressed steadily since the early 1980s. This results in a good understanding of the genetics of the disorder. This understanding may lead to a treatment for choroideremia in the coming years. Recently, a practical new test to detect choroideremia was developed. Better testing methods will help confirm the clinical suspicion of the disease. Thus, important information on the course of the disease, the likelihood of functional blindness, and the probability of maintaining useful vision can be provided to the patients and family members.

REFERENCES

Choroideremia Research Foundation, Inc. (2000, May). *Choroideremia disorder*. Retrieved from http://choroideremia.org/

McKusick, V. A. (2000). *Choroideremia disorder*. Retrieved from http://www.ncbi.nlm.nih.gov/htbin-post/Omim/dispmim?303100

National Organization for Rare Disorders. (2000). *Choroideremia disorder*. Retrieved from http://www.rarediseases.org/

PDR medical dictionary (2nd ed.). (2000). Montvale, NJ: Medical Economics.

Szlyk, J. P., Seiple, W., Laderman, D. J., Kelsch, R., Ho, K., & McMahon, T. (1998). Use of bioptic amorphic lenses to expand the visual field in patients with peripheral loss. *Optometry & Vision Science, 75*, 518–524.

NINA CHENG
University of Texas at Austin

CHROMOSOME 9, TRISOMY 9P (MULTIPLE VARIANTS)

In Chromosome 9, Trisomy 9p, a rare chromosomal disorder, part of Chromosome 9 appears three times (trisomy) rather than twice in body cells. Location of the trisomy varies and may be part or all of the short arm (p) or the short arm and part of the long arm (q) of the chromosome. Effects are often similar regardless of which and how much extra chromosomal material is present, although those with large amounts of extra long-arm material may be more severely affected (National Organization for Rare Disorders [NORD], 2001). Virtually all Trisomy 9p individuals show severe mental retardation, and most show growth retardation and characteristic facies. Other effects are more variable and depend in part on the amount and location of extra material. Some 5–10% die in infancy or early childhood (Jones, 1997; NORD, 2001). Cause may be a balanced translocation error in parental germ cell or a spontaneous error very early in the germinal stage (NORD, 2001). About 100 cases had been identified at the time of publication of Jones (1997).

Characteristics

1. Severe mental retardation and language deficiency
2. Growth retardation and delayed puberty
3. Facies: microcephaly, hypertelorism, deep-set eyes, down-turned palpebral fissures and corners of the mouth, large nose
4. Numerous skeletal abnormalities, including short fingers and toes, scoliosis, deformities of bones in fingers and toes
5. Occasional congenital heart disease

Initial tentative diagnosis may be on the basis of clinical signs, but confirmation will be through cytogenetic analysis. If Trisomy 9p is confirmed, the parents should also undergo cytogenetic analysis. If one is a carrier of the translocation error, risk of reoccurrence greatly increases, and genetic counseling and subsequent antenatal testing may be appropriate.

No effective treatment is currently available. Lifelong care will be needed. Special education in a separate classroom or institutionalization are likely placements. In cases where the affected individual will live at home, family counseling should be made available. A Trisomy 9 parental support group can be reached at http://www.trisomy9.org/.

REFERENCES

Jones, K. L. (1997). *Smith's recognizable patterns of human malformation* (5th ed.). Philadelphia, PA: Saunders.

National Organization for Rare Disorders. (2001). Chromosome 9, Trisomy 9p (Multiple Variants). Retrieved from http://www.rarediseases.org

ROBERT T. BROWN
University of North Carolina, Wilmington

CHROMOSOME 18P SYNDROME

Chromosome 18p syndrome occurs when any piece of the short arm of Chromosome 18 is missing. There are three classes of Chromosome 18 deletion syndromes; 18q, 18p, and Ring 18. Deletion syndromes of Chromosome 18 are the second most common of the autosomal deletion syndromes. Most deletions occur very early in the embryonic stage of development. There are several ways that this deletion can occur. Most children with 18p syndrome have parents who have normal chromosomes. The parent may also have a deletion on the chromosome, but the deleted piece is attached to another chromosome. As a result, the parent still has all of his or her genetic information; it is just arranged differently. This parent will not show any symptoms. Cases have also been reported in which a parent with 18p syndrome has a child with the same syndrome. Therefore, the chromosomal abnormality has been genetically passed on to the child. Because the genes that are missing vary and the content of the normal chromosome (the unaffected in the pair) can vary, the symptoms vary as well. Due to these variances, it is not possible to have a clear-cut list of symptoms. It is possible that a child might look a little different and has made it through school with Cs and Ds and actually has a chromosomal abnormality that was never diagnosed (Chromosome 18 Registry and Research Society, 1991). A belief exists that there are some people with 18p who are so mildly affected that they do not know they have a chromosomal abnormality until they have a child who is 18p and is more severely affected. There exists no evidence that this syndrome can be caused by environmental agents. It is important to note that most descriptions of this syndrome come from medical case reports. Due to the diagnostic nature of information available, very little is known about the outcomes for the affected individual (Chromosome 18 Registry and Research Society, 1991).

As of 1991, the frequency of Chromosome 18 deletion syndromes was estimated to be 1 in every 46,000. However, this included all three classes of Chromosome 18 deletion syndromes. The incidence for 18p alone is unknown. The female-to-male ratio of 18p is 2 to 1 (Chromosome 18 Registry and Research Society, 1991). Birthweight averages 2,600 g (5 lb, 11 oz), which falls at the low end of normal. Nineteen percent of 18p newborns die from severe brain malformations.

Characteristics

1. Mental retardation occurs in 98% of patients.
2. Average IQ is around 59.
3. Other common characteristics include short stature, abnormal external ears (low set, floppy, and/or large), webbed neck, holoprosencephaly (developmental malformation of the brain that has a large range of severity and can be fatal), IgA (an infection-fighting protein) deficit, which can cause upper respiratory problems, small jaw, and excessive cavities.
4. Most doctors mentioned that the patient was originally brought in for evaluation because of failure to thrive.
5. Speech is often delayed along with a dissociation between language skills and practical (nonverbal) performance (Thompson, Peters, & Smith, 1986).
6. Behavior problems such as restlessness, emotional lability, fear of strangers, poor concentration, and inability to form relationships have been reported.
7. Case studies also indicate delayed articulation (speech sound production) skills (Thompson et al., 1986).

It has been recommended that children be seen at least once by the following specialists: a pediatric neurologist, a developmental pediatrician, a dentist, and a geneticist and genetic counselor (Chromosome 18 Registry and Research Society, 1991).

Early intervention programs have been found to benefit a young child with 18p, which suggests that there is a potential for progress with remediation (Thompson et al., 1986). For children as young as 3 years old, special education programs are usually available through the public school system. Speech therapy would also likely be beneficial.

As mentioned before, reviews of literature lack outcome data of most patients. Due to the variability in symptoms, exact prognoses are difficult to determine. Although no cure exists, therapies aimed at specific problems can and will be developed (Chromosome 18 Registry and Research Society, 1991).

REFERENCES

Chromosome 18 Registry and Research Society. (1991). *Deletion syndromes of chromosome 18* [Brochure]. San Antonio, TX: Author.

Thompson, R. W., Peters, J. E., & Smith, S. D. (1986). Intellectual, behavioral, and linguistic characteristics of three children with 18p syndrome. *Journal of Developmental and Behavioral Pediatrics, 7*(1), 1–7.

CATHERINE M. CALDWELL
University of Texas at Austin

CHROMOSOME 18Q SYNDROME

Chromosome 18q syndrome occurs when any piece of the long arm of Chromosome 18 is missing. Deletion syndromes of Chromosome 18 are the second most common of the autosomal deletion syndromes. Most deletions occur very early in the embryonic stage of development. There are several ways that this deletion can occur. Most children with 18q syndrome have parents who have normal chromosomes. The parent may also have a deletion on the chromosome, but the deleted piece is attached to another chromosome. As a result, the parent still has all of his or her genetic information; it is just arranged differently. This parent will not show any symptoms and probably has no idea that he or she has the chromosomal abnormality. Cases have also been reported in which a parent with 18q syndrome has a child with the same syndrome. Therefore, the chromosomal abnormality has been genetically passed on to the child. Because the genes that are missing vary and the content of the normal chromosome (the unaffected in the pair) can vary, the symptoms vary as well. Moreover, the clinical picture is variable and does not always correspond to the size and site of the deletion (Miller, Mowrey, Hopper, Frankel, & Ladda, 1990). Due to these variances, it is not possible to have a clear-cut list of symptoms. There exists no evidence that this syndrome can be caused by environmental agents. It is important to note that most descriptions of this syndrome come from medical case reports. Due to the diagnostic nature of information available, very little is known about the outcomes for the affected individual (Chromosome 18 Registry and Research Society, 1991).

The frequency of Chromosome 18 deletion syndromes is estimated to be 1 in every 46,000. However, this includes all three classes of chromosome 18 deletion syndromes, including 18q, 18p, and Ring 18. Females are 1.7 times more likely than males to have this disorder (Chromosome 18 Registry and Research Society, 1991).

Characteristics

1. Mental retardation occurs in 96% of patients.
2. In one study, intelligence ranged from borderline to severely deficient (IQ, 73 to below 40; Mahr et al., 1996).
3. Other common characteristics include short stature, flat midface, hypotonia (poor muscle tone), prominent antihelix (outer curl of the ear), microcephaly (small head and brain), carp mouth (downturned corners), abnormal male genitals, abnormal female genitals, and foot deformity.
4. Impaired hearing occurs in 26% of patients.
5. In a study of a mother and son with 18q syndrome, both were found to have hearing loss, borderline cognitive functioning, and idiopathic tremor actions that progressively worsened (Miller et al., 1990).
6. Performance in specific neuropsychological functions, including attention, novel problem solving, memory, language, visuomotor integration, and fine motor dexterity, was consistently in the moderately to severely impaired range (Mahr et al., 1996).
7. Aggression, hyperactivity, and temper tantrums are common behavior problems in both males and females (Mahr et al., 1996).

It has been recommended that children be seen at least once by the following specialists: a pediatric ophthalmologist, a pediatric neurologist, a developmental pediatrician, an audiologist, an otolaryngologist, and a geneticist and genetic counselor. The child's poor muscle tone will require years of occupational and physical therapy (Chromosome 18 Registry and Research Society, 1991). Special education services will also be needed due to the high incidence of mental retardation. Audiological services would also be beneficial for possible hearing impairments.

An early intervention program would likely benefit a young child with 18q. For children as young as 3 years old, special services are typically available through the public school system. For those children with hearing impairments, speech will likely be delayed, which necessitates years of speech therapy (Chromosome 18 Registry and Research Society, 1991).

As mentioned before, reviews of literature lack outcome data of most patients. One study, however, did find an IQ from 25 years prior and found that there had been no cognitive change. However, this patient did develop a progressive and debilitating tremor (Mahr et al., 1996). Due to the variability in symptoms, exact prognoses are difficult to determine. Research is currently being conducted to see the effect of growth hormone treatment. Although no cure exists, therapies aimed at specific problems can and will be developed (Chromosome 18 Registry and Research Society, 1991).

REFERENCES

Chromosome 18 Registry and Research Society. (1991). *Deletion syndromes of Chromosome 18* [Brochure]. San Antonio, TX: Author.

Mahr, R. N., Moberg, P. J., Overhauser, J., Strathdee, G., Kamholz, J., Loevner, L. A.,...Shapiro, R. M. (1996). Neuropsychiatry of 18q syndrome. *American Journal of Medical Genetics, 67,* 172–178.

Miller, G., Mowrey, P. N., Hopper, K. D., Frankel, C. A., & Ladda, R. L. (1990). Neurologic manifestations in 18q syndrome. *American Journal of Medical Genetics, 37,* 128–132.

CATHERINE M. CALDWELL
University of Texas at Austin

CHROMOSOMES, HUMAN ANOMALIES, AND CYTOGENETIC ABNORMALITIES

Chromosomal (cytogenetic) abnormalities are the most frequent cause of congenital (present at birth) malformations, affecting some 1 in 200 newborns (Moore, 1982). Their importance is reflected in the fact that they account for at least 10 to 15% of individuals with mental retardation severe enough to require institutionalization (Moore, 1982; Pueschel, 1983) and for about 8 to 10% of newborn and early infant deaths (Sperling, 1984). Further, some 30% of spontaneously aborted embryos/fetuses had a chromosomal abnormality, an incidence 50 times higher than that in live births, meaning that incidence in all pregnancies must be about 5% (Sperling, 1984).

Because chromosomal abnormalities involve disruption in the action of many genes, most are associated with severe and varied effects (Brown, 1986). These frequently, but not always, involve general and specific intellective deficits, particular facial anomalies, and cardiovascular, digestive, and pulmonary defects. Further, people with chromosomal abnormalities usually have such characteristic phenotypes (physical appearance and physiological and behavioral functioning) that they frequently look more like unrelated persons with the same chromosomal abnormality than like their own siblings (Dobyns, 1999; Moore, 1982). The common characteristics that differentiate individuals with one abnormality from normal people or those with a different abnormality are called syndromes. Some two-dozen chromosomally based syndromes have been identified. Although some, particularly the familiar Down, Klinefelter, and Turner syndromes are relatively common, others are so rare that only 50 or so cases have been reported (Smith, 1982).

This entry will address general issues about abnormalities, provide background information for more specialized reading, and address similarities and differences among currently identified syndromes. As is the case with other genetically based disorders and congenital and perinatal abnormalities, new research routinely leads to significant changes in knowledge.

Vogel and Motulsky (1979, p. 18) elegantly describe human cytogenetics as "a successful late arrival." Although the chromosome theory of inheritance had been proposed in 1902, cytogenetics really began in 1956 with the discovery that the diploid number of human chromosomes was 46 instead of the commonly accepted 48. To give an idea of past attitudes toward the handicapped and their behavior, the diploid number 48 had been found by Painter (1923) in studies of spermatogenesis in testes of three inmates of the Texas State Insane Asylum who had been castrated because of, among other things, their excessive masturbation. When in 1959 researchers discovered chromosomal bases for three common and well-established human syndromes (Down, Klinefelter, and Turner), human cytogenetics really came into its own.

Since then, a variety of chromosomally based syndromes have been discovered on the basis of now-routine cytogenic analysis of spontaneously aborted fetuses, early death newborns and infants, and individuals with physical and behavioral abnormalities. A number of children traditionally labeled by diagnosticians as "syndromish in appearance" (something looks wrong but no etiology is known) now are identified as having a chromosomal abnormality. In most cases, the description of the physical and behavioral characteristics of the syndrome has followed, rather than preceded, chromosomal analysis. Further, subsequent studies have identified multiple chromosomal bases for syndromes such as Down, Klinefelter, and Turner that help to account for high variability among and even within affected individuals. A variety of technical advances account for much of our knowledge about these abnormalities (Dobyns, 1999; Sperling, 1984; Vogel & Motulsky, 1979).

Normal and Abnormal Karyotypes

Normal humans have 23 pairs of chromosomes in all body cells, 22 pairs of autosomes, and one pair of sex chromosomes. Females normally have two long X sex chromosomes and males one long X and one shorter Y sex chromosome. Chromosomes (colored bodies) are visible only early in mitosis, when cell samples are subjected to certain stains. A *karyotype* is a picture of chromosomes arranged by pair. The 22 autosomal pairs are arranged from the longest (1) to the shortest (22), followed by the sex chromosomes. A karyotype, showing chromosomal bands, of a normal human male is shown in Figure C.11. Figure C.12 shows a typical chromosome pair; the short arm is termed "p" and the long arm, "q"; the two arms are held together at the centromere, or primary constriction. Cohen and Nadler (1983) suggest the useful mnemonic of associating "p" with petite. Chromosomes are grouped into three types: metacentric (e.g., numbers 1 and 3), where the arms are nearly equal in length; submetacentric (e.g., numbers 4 and 5), where the p arm is distinctly shorter than the q; and acrocentric (e.g., numbers 14 and 21), which have a secondary constriction and abbreviated and apparently genetically inactive satellite p arms.

Normal Cell Division

During mitosis, the process of duplication of body cells, each of the 46 chromosomes divides and one member of each migrates to a pole of the cells. When the cell divides, each offspring cell contains the same 23 pairs of chromosomes. Thus mitosis is a process of chromosome duplication. In meiosis, the process of production of germ cells (sperm and eggs), each of the 23 chromosome pairs divides and one member of each pair migrates to a pole of the cell. When the cell divides, each offspring has 23 chromosomes. Thus each germ cell has 23 chromosomes.

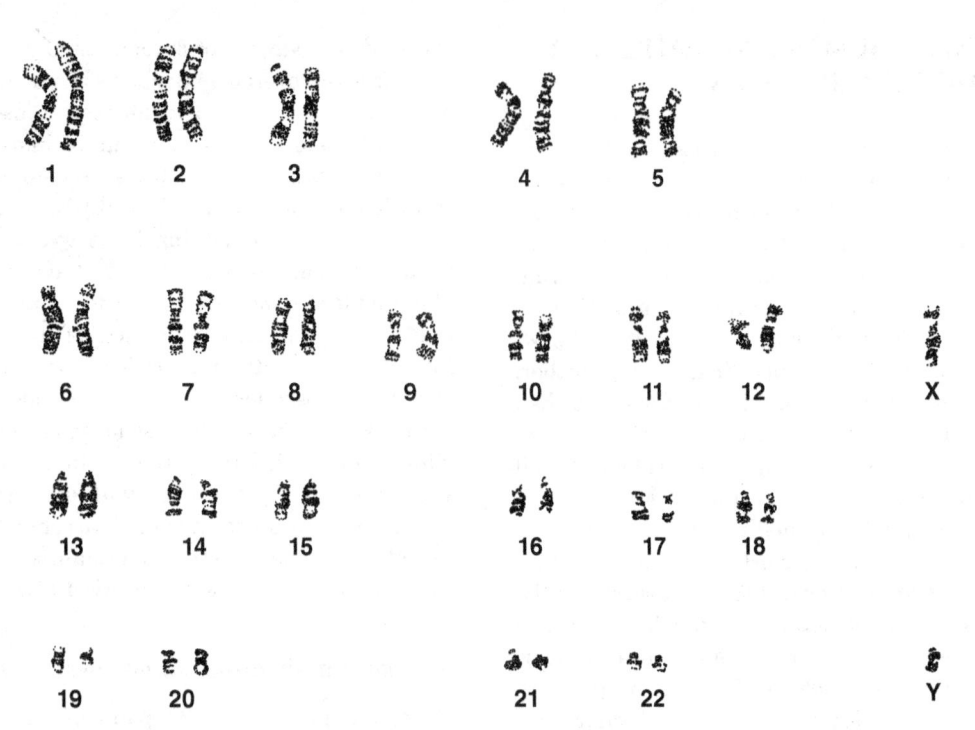

Figure C.11. Karyotype for a normal human male. Twenty-two pairs of autosomes have been ordered and numbered according to convention from largest to smallest. Sex chromosomes are labeled X and Y.
Source: Cohen and Nadler (1983).

— SHORT (p) ARM

— CENTROMERE

— LONG (q) ARM

Figure C.12. Standard nomenclature for describing parts of a chromosome, after Cohen and Nadler (1983).
Source: Cohen and Nadler (1983).

Meiosis is a process of chromosome reduction. Women's eggs will all have 22 autosomes and an X chromosome; men's sperm all have 22 autosomes and can have either an X or a Y. In sexual recombination, when a sperm penetrates an egg, the resulting zygote normally has the appropriate 46 chromosomes. Thus, gender of offspring is determined by the father's sperm.

Abnormal Karyotypes

Abnormalities can be: (1) an abnormal total number of chromosomes in an individual's body cells; (2) structural aberrations resulting from breakage in one or more chromosomes; or (3) populations of cells of different chromosome numbers in the same individual (mosaicism).

Aneuploidies refers to deviations, greater or fewer, in number of chromosomes from the normal 46. The most common aneuploidy is trisomy 21, which accounts for the greatest number of chromosomal abnormalities in spontaneous abortions as well as in live births. Trisomies on most

pairs are prenatally lethal. Similarly, monosomy, absence of one of a pair, resulting in fewer than 46 chromosomes, is virtually always prenatally lethal, except for Turner's syndrome, in which one X chromosome is missing (45,X). Even then, only one in 150 to 200 45,X embryos survives to full-term birth. The most common cause of aneuploidy is nondisjunction, the failure of a chromosome pair to split during formation of germ cells in meiosis. Thus, one offspring germ cell will have a "double dose" of one chromosome and the other will have none. Anaphase lag can also produce monosomy.

Mosaicism results from nondisjunction occurring mitotically in a cell in an embryo in an early stage of development. As a result, if the embryo survives and continues to develop, it will have both normal and abnormal, generally trisomic, cell populations. Because of the presence of normal cells, individuals with mosaicism will generally show less severe symptoms than those with the pure syndrome.

The basis for nondisjunction is not known, but is presumed to be manifested biochemically. In nondisjunction Down syndrome, approximately 80% of the cases result from maternal and 20% from paternal nondisjunction (Sperling, 1984). Since all autosomal trisomies (not just Down syndrome) increase dramatically with maternal age, research focuses on factors that correlate with aging, including potential problems with aging oocytes themselves. Hypothesized links with irradiation, chemical agents, methods of birth control, and endocrine factors have not been fully confirmed, but some evidence suggests they play a role (Hassold & Jacobs, 1984).

Chromosomes may break, with material being either lost or attached to another chromosome. The most common structural aberrations are translocations, which result when two chromosomes break and parts of one are transferred to another. A reciprocal translocation occurs when two nonhomologous chromosomes exchange pieces. Individuals with such translocation chromosomes themselves have an appropriate balance of chromosomes and are phenotypically normal. Since they are carriers of a translocation chromosome, their offspring may suffer from duplication-deficiency syndromes, notably partial trisomies.

Important because of clinical implications are centric fusions, or Robertsonian translocations. Centric fusion occurs when two acrocentric chromosomes each break near the centromere and rejoin. Generally, the short arms of both and the centromere of one are lost. Again, individuals may be unaffected, although they have one-fewer-than-normal chromosome, but they are carriers. Their offspring may have a trisomy syndrome. Monosomies are also possible, but appear to be prenatally lethal. The best-known translocation is Down syndrome, resulting from centric fusion of chromosome 21 with chromosome 14 or, less frequently, 15.

Several other structural aberrations also may occur. Simple loss of part of a chromosome may result in a deletion syndrome. Isochromosomes occur when instead of a chromosome pair dividing longitudinally through the centromere, it divides horizontally, producing two chromosomes with identical arms. Fertilization will produce a cell with three p or q arms and only one of the other. When the segment between two breaks in a chromosome becomes inverted, reversing the gene order, an inversion results. Ring chromosomes occur when both ends of a chromosome break off and the tips of the centric segment rejoin. The resulting circular chromosome is unstable and has material from both ends deleted.

Standard Nomenclature

Normal and abnormal human karyotypes are described using a standard system, general aspects and examples of which are given here. More detailed descriptions are in Cohen and Nadler (1983), Smith (1982), Vogel and Motulsky (1979), and most human genetics textbooks.

The order of information is (1) total number of chromosomes; (2) sex chromosomes; and (3) any abnormalities. Extra or missing chromosomes are indicated by "+" and "−", respectively, before the affected chromosome's number; extra or missing parts are indicated by "+" and "−", respectively, after the affected part. Structural aberrations are indicated by a standard abbreviation followed, parenthetically, by the number of the affected chromosome(s). Then, also parenthetically, the affected arm(s) and, if known, the chromosomal band numbers, are stated.

Mosaics are indicated by a (/) mark separating descriptions of the two cell populations.

Abnormalities and Their Characteristics

Although chromosomal syndromes vary widely in their effects, the various types share some characteristics. Because much genetic material either has been added or is missing, many are lethal and most of the rest involve multiple and severe complications. However, as normal individuals vary in their physical and behavioral characteristics, so do those affected by chromosomal abnormalities. Not all will show even all of the major effects.

It is important that different sources vary in their estimates of incidence and specification of major characteristics. In a number of cases, subsequent cases have led to changes in what were initially thought to be defining characteristics. For example, Cat-eye syndrome (trisomy 22p) was named for the striking coloboma of the iris seen originally. However, it has occurred only in a minority of the 40 cases that had been reported at the time of Smith's summary (1982).

Chromosomal Aneuploidies

The most common abnormalities are aneuploidies, involving an added or missing chromosome. Multiple forms of some may occur. By far the most common is Down syndrome (trisomy 21), but several others have been reported. Early death is common in all, and in some types virtually all die in early infancy. Although each has individual characteristics, all involve brain damage generally resulting in moderate to severe mental retardation, congenital heart disease, and malformed ears. Specific facial, limb, and digit abnormalities are also common. All increase dramatically in incidence with maternal age (Vogel & Motulsky, 1979).

Turner and Klinefelter syndromes have clear phenotypic characteristics and were described before the development of modern cytogenic techniques. Both are associated with absence of puberty and sterility. Unfortunately, as pointed out by Brown (1986), textbook authors have frequently described sex-chromosome aneuploidies in chapters on mental retardation. However, standard forms are associated with low average intelligence (IQ > 90), not mental retardation, although incidence of mental retardation is higher than among the normal population. Many affected individuals will complete high school and college. Mosaic Turner females and Klinefelter males will be less affected. Klinefelter males and Poly-X females with extra X chromosomes above trisomy for sex chromosomes are much more adversely affected and likely to be retarded (Korf, 1999).

Klinefelter and Poly-X syndromes increase with maternal age (Hassold & Jacobs, 1984). However, incidence of neither Turner nor XYY syndrome correlates with maternal age, consistent with largely paternal origin (Hassold & Jacobs, 1984; Simpson, 1982).

Abnormal Parts of Chromosomes

Several partial trisomy syndromes, involving extra chromosomal material, and deletion syndromes are known. Mental retardation of some degree is common to all. Low birthweight and specific facial and digital anomalies are also frequent.

Of particular current interest is Fragile X syndrome, resulting from a constriction in the X chromosome, which cytogenic studies reveal to be relatively common. Associated with mental retardation in affected males, it appears to be second only to Down syndrome as a cytogenic cause of mental retardation.

Human Genome Project

The Human Genome Project (HGP) was the international, collaborative research program whose goal was the complete mapping and understanding of all the genes of human beings. All our genes together are known as our *genome*. The HGP was the natural culmination of the history of genetics research.

The HGP has revealed that there are probably somewhere between 30,000 and 40,000 human genes. The completed human sequence can now identify their locations. This ultimate product of the HGP has given the world a resource of detailed information about the structure, organization, and function of the complete set of human genes. This information can be thought of as the basic set of inheritable "instructions" for the development and function of a human being.

The International Human Genome Sequencing Consortium published the first draft of the human genome in the journal *Nature* in February 2001 with the sequence of the entire genome's 3 billion base pairs some 90% complete. A startling finding of this first draft was that the number of human genes appeared to be significantly fewer than previous estimates, which ranged from 50,000 genes to as many as 140,000. The full sequence was completed and published in April 2003.

Upon publication of the majority of the genome in February 2001, Francis Collins, the director of the National Human Genome Research Institute (NHGRI), noted that the genome could be thought of in terms of a book with multiple uses. The tools created through the HGP also continue to inform efforts to characterize the entire genomes of several other organisms used extensively in biological research, such as mice, fruit flies, and flatworms. These efforts support each other, because most organisms have many similar, or *homologous*, genes with similar functions. Therefore, the identification of the sequence or function of a gene in a model organism, for example, the roundworm *C. elegans*, has the potential to explain a homologous gene in human beings, or in one of the other model organisms.

This ambitious project required a variety of new technologies that made it possible to construct a first draft of the human genome relatively rapidly. These techniques included: DNA Sequencing, the Employment of Restriction Fragment-Length Polymorphisms (RFLP), Yeast Artificial Chromosomes (YAC), Bacterial Artificial Chromosomes (BAC), the Polymerase Chain Reaction (PCR), and Electrophoresis.

Of course, information is only as good as the ability to use it. Therefore, advanced methods for widely disseminating the information generated by the HGP to scientists, physicians, and others is necessary to ensure the most rapid application of research results for the benefit of humanity. Biomedical technology and research are particular beneficiaries of the HGP.

However, the momentous implications to individuals and society from possessing the detailed genetic information made possible by the HGP were recognized from the outset. Another major component of the HGP—and an ongoing component of NHGRI—is, therefore, devoted to the analysis of the ethical, legal, and social implications of the newfound genetic knowledge and the subsequent development of policy options for public consideration (National Human Genome Research Institute, 2005).

Implications for Special Educators

As cytogenic analyses become more standard, increasing numbers of children will be identified as having some chromosomal disorder. Many minor ones will have few implications for teachers. Others will be associated with general and specific intellectual deficits, coordination problems, and emotional disorders. Special educators and others in education generally may need to become familiar with the syndrome and standard nomenclature. Further, research will doubtless render some current knowledge incorrect and we must be ready to accept new information. It should be kept in mind that syndromes can induce stereotypes, and that affected children should be treated on the basis of their individual characteristics, not the general ones of a syndrome.

REFERENCES

Brown, R. T. (1986). Etiology and development of exceptionality. In R. T. Brown & C. R. Reynolds (Eds.), *Psychological perspectives on childhood exceptionality: A handbook* (pp. 181–229). New York, NY: Wiley.

Cohen, M. M., & Nadler, H. L. (1983). Chromosomes and their abnormalities. In R. E. Behrman & V. C. Vaughn, III (Eds.), *Nelson textbook of pediatrics* (12th ed., pp. 288–310). Philadelphia, PA: Saunders.

Dobyns, W. B. (1999). Introduction to genetics. In K. F. Swaiman, & S. Ashwal (Eds.), *Pediatric neurology* (pp. 325–353). St. Louis, MO: Mosby.

Hassold, T. J., & Jacobs, P. A. (1984). Trisomy in man. *Annual Review of Genetics, 18*, 69–97.

Korf, B. R. (1999). Chromosomes and chromosomal abnormalities. In K. F. Swaiman & S. Ashwal (Eds.), *Pediatric neurology* (pp. 354–376). St. Louis, MO: Mosby.

Moore, K. L. (1982). *The developing human* (3rd ed.). Philadelphia, PA: Saunders.

National Human Genome Research Institute. (2005). Retrieved from http://www.genome.gov/

Painter, T. S. (1923). Studies in mammalian spermatogenesis: II. *The spermatogenesis of man. Journal of Experimental Zoology, 37*, 291–321.

Pueschel, S. M. (1983). The child with Down syndrome. In M. D. Levine, W. B. Carey, A. C. Crocker, & R. T. Gross (Eds.), *Developmental-behavioral pediatrics* (pp. 353–362). Philadelphia, PA: Saunders.

Simpson, J. L. (1982). Abnormal sexual differentiation in humans. *Annual Review of Genetics, 16*, 193–224.

Smith, D. W. (1982). *Recognizable patterns of human malformation* (2nd ed.). Philadelphia, PA: Saunders.

Sperling, K. (1984). Frequency and origin of chromosome abnormalities in man. In G. Obe (Ed.), *Mutations in man* (pp. 128–146). Berlin, Germany and New York, NY: Springer-Verlag.

Vogel, F., & Motulsky, A. G. (1979). *Human genetics*. Berlin, Germany and New York, NY: Springer-Verlag.

ROBERT T. BROWN
University of North Carolina at Wilmington
First and second editions

STAFF
Third edition

See also Cri du Chat Syndrome; Down Syndrome; Etiology; Fragile X Syndrome; Klinefelter's Syndrome; Turner Syndrome; XYY Syndrome

CHRONIC FATIGUE SYNDROME

Chronic fatigue syndrome (CFS) or chronic fatigue immune dysfunction syndrome in children and adolescents is characterized by debilitating fatigue, neurological problems, and a variety of symptoms (Chronic Fatigue Immune Dysfunction Syndrome Association of America, Inc., 1996–2000). It is defined by a thorough medical examination that excludes other medical and psychiatric diagnoses and by unexplained, persistent chronic fatigue that exists for at least 6 months and is of new onset, resulting in reduced occupational, educational, social, or personal activities. Second, at least four of the following symptoms co-occur: substantial impairment in short-term memory or concentration, multijoint pain without swelling or redness, headaches, sore throat, tender lymph nodes, muscle pain, unrefreshing sleep, and postexertional malaise lasting for more than 24 hours (Bell, 1995).

Etiology is unconfirmed (Swenson, 2000) but has been attributed to several theories. Persistent viral infection associated with Epstein-Barr virus, influenza-type viruses, varicella zoster, and rubella have been reported by patients; often, however, CFS patients show no laboratory evidence of these infections. Primary muscle disorder has been proposed, but no metabolic abnormality in skeletal muscle in patients has been shown. Chronic immune dysfunction has been proposed secondary to a broad range of abnormalities in the immune system by CFS patients. Often, a high association with allergies coincides with a precipitating infection. Neuroendocrine disorder has been suggested because patients with CFS have a functional abnormality of the hypothalamic-pituitary system, contributing to a secondary impairment of the adrenal system. Primary sleep disorder has also been put forth, as most CFS patients experience daytime fatigue due to a disruption in the circadian rhythm. Finally, primary depression, somatization, and stress have been cited as possible causative factors, although it is difficult to determine whether these are contributing factors or results of CFS, especially in children where depression is so much a part of any chronic illness.

Prevalence rates for CFS in children and adolescents (ages 12 to 17), as indicated by physician referrals, are 8.7 cases per 100,000 (Dobbins, Randall, Reyes, Steele, Livens, & Reeves, 1997). School nurse referrals, on the other hand, suggest 52.9 cases per 100,000.

Characteristics

1. Unexplained, persistent chronic fatigue for at least 6 months that is not alleviated by rest
2. Significant reduction in previous levels of occupational, educational, social, or personal activities
3. Impaired short-term memory and concentration
4. Sore throat, tender lymph nodes, muscle pain, headaches
5. Multijoint pain without joint swelling or redness
6. Unrefreshing sleep and postexertional malaise lasting more than 24 hours

Treatment for CFS is generally symptomatic, resulting in medical-oriented therapies and pharmacological enhancement of symptoms. Physical therapy is often employed to reduce pain through gentle stretching techniques, myofascial release, and heat or cold applications.

Therapeutic massage can also help in pain reduction. Exercise may be an eventual goal, but it has proven controversial because it may contribute to further relapse. Initially, walking or pool therapy may be safely included. Alternative therapies have been tried with adults, but their efficacy in randomized trials has not been proven.

Physicians may prescribe medications to help manage depression and anxiety symptoms. Other medications may help musculoskeletal complaints, flu-like symptoms, and muscle aches. Antiviral and immunodilatory drugs have also been used. Cognitive behavior therapy (CBT) has been used successfully in adults to reduce depression, stress, and fatigue severity with treatment focusing on acquisition of cognitive and behavioral coping skills, identification of symptom relapse stimuli, activity modification to minimize setbacks, and stress reduction and relaxation techniques.

Special education placement under Other Health Impairment may be warranted if students are diagnosed with CFS by a physician and if it is educationally significant. Students may benefit from a modified schedule that allows for some social periods during the day at school but also accommodates their fatigue. Homebound instruction may help minimize academic difficulties and provide ongoing tutorial support. Physical therapy services may help alleviate painful symptoms and facilitate some physical exercise to guard against negative consequences of deconditioning. Adaptive physical education (PE) may help meet PE requirements in the school. Cognitive impairments may be documented and monitored by ongoing evaluation. Occupational therapy may help with adaptations to physical roadblocks, especially related to physical output necessary for academic performance. Accommodations and adaptations may be implemented to help students be successful with state standards assessments.

Most children do recover from CFS with a mean out-of-school duration of one year. Some cycle through periods of recovery and relapse over a prolonged period of time, however, with few reports of worsening of symptoms. Future research is focusing on exact etiology and combinations of treatments, such as CBT with children combined with medical regimens.

REFERENCES

Bell, D. S. (1995). Chronic fatigue syndrome in children and adolescents. *Focus and Opinions: Pediatrics, 1*, 412–420.

Chronic Fatigue Immune Dysfunction Syndrome Association of America, Inc. (1996–2000). *Chronic fatigue syndrome.* Retrieved from http://www.cfids.org/

Dobbins, J. G., Randall, B., Reyes, M., Steele, L., Livens, E. A., & Reeves, W. C. (1997). Prevalence of chronic fatigue illness among adolescents in the United States. *Journal of Chronic Fatigue Syndrome, 3*, 15–28.

Swenson, T. S. (2000). Chronic fatigue syndrome. *Journal of Rehabilitation, 1*, 37–42.

R. Brett Nelson
Diana L. Nebel
University of Northern Colorado

CHRONIC GRANULOMATOUS DISEASE

Chronic granulomatous disease (CGD) is a rare genetic syndrome characterized by susceptibility to recurrent severe infections and associated with immune dysfunction. It is inherited as either an X-linked or an autosomal recessive genetic disorder. At least eight subtypes are recognized, but one X-linked subtype accounts for the majority of CGD cases. Most patients present with CGD before 2 years of age. Prevalence is approximately 1 in 500,000 individuals (Nelson, Behrman, Kliegman, & Arvin, 1996).

Characteristics

1. Onset is usually in the first few months of life with at least one unusual or severe infection during the first year of life.
2. Eighty percent are identified with unusual susceptibility to serious infections before their second birthday.
3. Diagnosis may be delayed until adolescence or adulthood.
4. Abscess formation is the hallmark symptom and may occur in any organ of the body, including the brain.
5. Pulmonary disorders occur in nearly all children.

The primary aim of therapy for patients with CGD is prevention and cure of infection. Prophylaxis with antibiotic is standard. Steroids, and surgery in more severe cases, are required to treat granulomas affecting the gastrointestinal or genitourinary tract. Bone marrow transplantation and gene therapy have been used effectively.

CGD is a lifelong disease (Stiehm, 1996). Susceptibility to serious bacterial and fungal infection is a hallmark of CGD; however, the quality of life of patients has improved dramatically over the past three decades. Survival beyond the fourth decade occurs frequently. Special education services or accommodation may be required due to the long-term impact of the medical illness on school achievement. Many children with CGD qualify for services under the classification of Other Health Impairment.

REFERENCES

Nelson, W. E., Behrman, R. E., Kliegman, R. M., & Arvin, A. M. (1996). *Nelson textbook of pediatrics* (15th ed.). Bangalore, India: Prism Books.

Stiehm, E. R. (Ed.). (1996). *Immunologic disorders in infants and children* (4th ed.). Philadelphia, PA: W. B. Saunders.

VIRDETTE L. BRUMM
*Children's Hospital Los Angeles Keck /
USC School of Medicine*

CHRONIC ILLNESS IN CHILDREN

Approximately 6 to 15% of children and adolescents live with a chronic illness such as diabetes, asthma, cancer, cystic fibrosis, epilepsy, muscular dystrophy, sickle cell anemia, migraines, and many others (Powers, Patton, Hommel, & Hershey, 2003; Thies & McAllister, 2001). Special education programs were designed with developmentally disabled children in mind; therefore, children with chronic illness do not have a special program designed around their educational and health needs.

Children with chronic illness have multiple professionals involved in supporting their well-being in the health-care setting as well as the academic setting. Professionals such as teachers, doctors, school nurses, school administrators, medical consultants, therapists, and learning support staff all have important roles in the child's life. Collaboration and communication among the professionals involved is imperative to the child's well-being. However, research has indicated that this communication is lacking, especially between health-care providers and school staff (Lightfoot, Muckherjee, & Sloper, 2001). School teachers are often cognizant of specific children in their school or class who have a chronic health condition; however, educators commonly lack the information necessary to adequately aid the child (Clay, McCarthy, Kelly, Johnson, Roman, & Zimmerman, 2004). Issues surrounding confidentiality on the part of the health-care staff contributes to the educators' lack of knowledge surrounding the health condition of the child, which leads to inadequate educational support. Educators, administrators, and support staff may benefit from educational programs to assist in recognition of certain chronic health conditions, such as asthma (Sapien, Fullerton-Gleason, & Allen, 2004).

Children born with extremely low birthweight have three times the chance of developing chronic health conditions compared to normal birthweight children (Mayor, 2005). Chronic health conditions linked to low birthweight include asthma, cerebral palsy, and visual difficulties. In addition, these children are at a higher risk for certain cognitive and social difficulties, such as decreased cognitive ability and school achievement as well as poor motor skills and social adaptive functioning.

Cognitive effects have been researched among specific chronic health conditions such as diabetes and cancer. Ferguson et al. (2005) examined neurodevelopment among early onset type 1 diabetes with results indicating lower nonverbal intelligence and slower psychomotor speed in adults who developed diabetes before the age of seven. The researchers also found structural brain abnormalities among the same population, possibly supporting the hypothesis that early onset of type 1 diabetes could be harmful to normal brain development. Similarly, cancer survivors often show declines in memory, attention, reading skills, and psychomotor speed (Kaemingk, Carey, Moore, Herzer, & Hutter, 2004). Cognitive deficits and problems in school functioning have also been shown in children with sickle cell disease (Schatz, Finke, & Kellett, 2002), Lyme disease (Tager, Fallon, Keilp, Rissenberg, Jones, & Liebowitz, 2001), chronic migraines (Powers et al., 2003), and epilepsy (Sanyal & Rajagopalan, 2005).

School absenteeism is common among children with chronic health conditions. Frequent and/or chronic absence can potentially affect the child's schoolwork and learning process. The majority of students will be able to catch up on their work with minimal help; however, some children will experience anxiety as a result of the workload, which will thereby drain their already exhausted bodies, further interfering with their cognitive abilities (Shiu, 2001).

A minority of students will have significant impairments related to the illness or subsequent medical treatment. These students would benefit from an individualized educational program to assist in their academic endeavors. The challenges the student will face on return to school can be lessened to a certain degree with school programs designed to ease the transition, thereby alleviating anxiety and positively affecting performance and attendance. Children with chronic illness are served under the "other health impaired" category in the Individuals With Disabilities Education Act.

REFERENCES

Clay, D. L., McCarthy, A., Kelly, M. W., Johnson, S., Roman, J., & Zimmerman, M. (2004). Changes in medications administered in schools. *Journal of School Nursing, 22,* 102–107.

Ferguson, S., Blane, A., Wardlaw, J., Frier, B., Perros, P., McCrimmon, J., & Deary, I. J. (2005). Influence of an early-onset age of type 1 diabetes on cerebral structure and cognitive function. *Diabetes Care, 28,* 1431–1438.

Kaemingk, K., Carey, M., Moore, I., Herzer, M., & Hutter, J. (2004). Math weaknesses in survivors of acute lymphoblastic leukemia compared to healthy children. *Child Neuropsychology, 10*(1), 14–23.

Lightfoot, J., Muckherjee, S. & Sloper, P. (2001). Supporting pupils with special health needs in mainstream schools: Policy and practice. *Children & Society, 15,* 57–69.

Mayor, S. (2005). Extremely low birth weight is linked to risk of chronic illness. *British Medical Journal, 331,* 180.

Powers, S., Patton, S., Hommel, K., & Hershey, A. (2003). Quality of life in childhood migraines: Clinical impact and comparison to other chronic illness. *Pediatrics, 112*(1), 1–5.

Sanyal, N. & Rajagopalan, N. (2005). A comparative cognitive profile of epileptic and non-epileptic normal preadolescents. *Journal of Projective Psychology & Mental Health, 12*(2), 129–140.

Sapien, R., Fullerton-Gleason, L., & Allen, N. (2004). Teaching school teachers to recognize respiratory distress in asthmatic children. *Journal of Asthma, 41*(7), 739–743.

Schatz, J., Finke, R., & Kellett, J. (2002). Cognitive functioning in children with sickle cell disease: A meta-analysis. *Journal of Pediatric Psychology, 27*(8), 739–748.

Shiu, S. (2001). Issues in the education of students with chronic illness. *International Journal of Disability, Development, and Education, 48*(3), 269–281.

Tager, F., Fallon, B., Keilp, J., Rissenberg, M., Jones, C., & Liebowitz, M. (2001). A controlled study of cognitive deficits in children with chronic Lyme disease. *Journal of Neuropsychiatry & Clinical Neuroscience, 13*(4), 500–507.

Thies, K., & McAllister, J. (2001). The health and education leadership project: A school initiative for children and adolescents with chronic health conditions. *Journal of School Health, 71*(5), 167–172.

MIRANDA KUCERA
University of Colorado at Colorado Springs

CHRONIC INFLAMMATORY DEMYELINATING POLYNEUROPATHY

Chronic inflammatory demyelinating polyneuropathy (CIDP) is a rare neurological disorder that results in swelling of the nerve roots and the destruction of the myelin sheath, the fatty covering that surrounds the axon of nerves in the body (National Organization for Rare Disorders, Inc. [NORD], 2001). The presentation, course, and severity of this disorder vary from case to case. To receive a diagnosis of CIDP, an individual must have been free from viral infections for at least three months prior to the presentation of symptoms (NORD, 2001). Most cases do not exhibit a family history of CIDP or related disorders (NORD, 2001).

CIDP can affect all ages, and the onset of the disorder can begin at any age. The average age of onset of CIDP is 50, with twice as many males diagnosed as females.

The prevalence rate of CIDP in the United States is 1 in 100,000 individuals (NORD, 2001).

Characteristics

1. A child usually visits the doctor complaining of progressive muscle weakness or sensory dysfunction in the upper or lower extremities, usually apparent within a few months of the onset of the disease (NORD, 2001).

2. The child may also complain of a loss of sensation, abnormal sensations, or impaired motor control (NORD, 2001).

3. The course of the disease varies greatly from case to case; some individuals have symptoms that progress slowly, whereas others have symptoms that get worse, better, and then worse again (NORD, 2001).

4. Symptoms of CIDP include fatigue, numbness, burning, and tingling sensations affecting the upper and lower extremities; weak or absent reflexes in the face or upper and lower extremities; paralysis or lack of sensation of the upper and lower extremities; weakness of the torso muscles; respiratory problems; and difficulty walking (NORD, 2001).

The exact etiology of CIDP is not known. Although it has not been proven, CIDP is thought to be a disorder of the autoimmune system (NORD, 2001). Diagnosing CIDP can be difficult because of the wide range of symptoms and the differences the presentation and course of the disorder have in each individual (NORD, 2001).

Recommended treatments include glucocorticoid drugs, although side effects are common, especially at high doses. Glucocorticoid drugs are also often used in conjunction with immunosuppressive drugs (NORD, 2001). Intravenous immunoglobulin treatment, increasing immunoglobulin through intravenous injections, is also a treatment used with CIDP as a way to increase immune functioning that has been successful in some trials (Hahne, Bolton, Zochodne, Feasby, 1996: NORD, 2001). However, acute meningitis has been identified as a serious side effect of intravenous immunoglobulin treatment (King Faisal Specialist Hospital and Research Centre, Annals of Saudi Medicine, 2001). Experimental treatments include plasma transfusions and the use of alpha 2a, although the effectiveness of these treatments is currently under investigation (NORD, 2001).

Children with chronic inflammatory demyelinating polyneuropathy may need academic modifications in order to attend and function at school. If the child's symptoms are severe enough that they interfere with one or more of the major life activities, they qualify as Other Health Impairment under Section 504. Once qualified, the school is required to provide modifications, depending on the type and severity of symptoms the child is experiencing. For a child experiencing motor weakness or paralysis in the upper and lower extremities, for example, occupational therapy and wheelchair access are modifications that may be required for the child to continue in mainstream education.

REFERENCES

Hahne, A. F., Bolton, C. F., Zochodne, D., & Feasby, T. E. (1996). Intravenous immunoglobulin treatment in chronic inflammatory demyelinating polyneuropathy: A double-blind, placebo-controlled, cross-over study. *Brain, 119*(4), 1067–1077.

King Faisal Specialist Hospital and Research Centre, Annals of Saudi Medicine. (2001, March 18). Acute aseptic meningitis associated with administration of immunoglobulin in children: A case report and review of the literature. Retrieved from http://www.kfshrc.edu.sa

National Organization for Rare Disorders, Inc. (2001, March 20). Chronic inflammatory demyelinating polyneuropathy. Retrieved from http://www.rarediseases.org/

MOANA KRUSCHWITZ
MARGARET SEMRUD-CLIKEMAN
University of Texas at Austin

CITIZEN ADVOCACY GROUPS (*See* Advocacy Groups, Citizen)

CIVIL RIGHTS OF INDIVIDUALS WITH DISABILITIES

A person with a disability has certain rights guaranteed by law that relate to education, employment, health care, senior citizen activities, welfare, and any other private services, programs, or activities that receive federal assistance.

Diamond (1979) has summarized the need for services and the specific rights of individuals with disabilities from a personal perspective. She reports that persons with disabilities have a right to private and public education at the elementary, secondary, and postsecondary levels. In addition to the education curriculum, supportive or rehabilitative services should be made available. When requiring a service (e.g., when dining out or shopping) the same courtesies should be extended to individuals with disabilities as to others.

People with disabilities have the right to travel assisted or unassisted on airplanes, trains, buses, and taxi cabs. Persons with disabilities have a right to gain entrance to public facilities without being inconvenienced, and buildings should be free of architectural barriers. Individuals with disabilities have a right to receive equal treatment by doctors and hospitals. This will require that medical personnel acquire understanding and knowledge of disabilities. Individuals with disabilities have a right to apply for any license (e.g., marriage, fishing) made available to nondisabled individuals without additional requirements or embarrassment. It is unlawful to discriminate against individuals with disabilities regarding employment practices. It is also unlawful for the owner of commercial property to refuse to sell, rent, or lease, or in any way discriminate because of a disability. As important as the services needed is the right to feel assured that the members of society will look on individuals with disabilities as responsible people capable of making a contribution to society.

It is the responsibility of the Office of Civil Rights in the Department of Education and the Office of Civil Rights in the Department of Health and Human Services to enforce federal laws prohibiting discrimination against persons on the basis of race, color, national origin, sex, age, or disability in federally assisted programs or activities, and to investigate discrimination complaints brought by individuals under a variety of statutes guaranteeing the rights of individuals with disabilities, including in particular the Americans with Disabilities Act (Office of Civil Rights, 2009).

REFERENCES

Diamond, S. (1979). Developmentally disabled persons: Their rights and their needs for services. In R. Weigerink & J. Pelosi (Eds.), *Developmental disabilities: The DD movement* (pp. 15–25). Baltimore. MD: Brookes.

Office of Civil Rights. (2009). Frequently asked questions about Section 504 and the education of children with disabilities. Washington, DC: U.S. Department of Education. Retrieved from http://www2.ed.gov/about/offices/list/ocr/504faq.html

CECILIA STEPPE-JONES
North Carolina Central University
Second edition

KIMBERLY F. APPLEQUIST
University of Colorado at Colorado Springs
Third edition

See also Americans With Disabilities Act; Individuals With Disabilities Education Improvement Act of 2004 (IDEIA); Rehabilitation Act of 1973, Section 504 of; Social Behavior of Individuals With Disabilities

CLASS-ACTION LAWSUITS

Class actions are lawsuits in which a class of persons is represented by one or more of its members. In federal and in most state courts, groups of persons who have similar interests in the law and fact of the lawsuit can sue or be sued through a representative who acts on their behalf. A class action offers the following: the benefits of a clear resolution of a specific issue; the convenience of a useful method to assert legal rights in cases that have common interest where small individual claims might otherwise preclude judicial relief; and the saving of time, money, and effort by eliminating repetitious lawsuits (Redden & Vernon, 1980).

General requirements of a class action are as follows: The representative class must be large, although no specific number has been determined, so that it would be impractical to name each individual as a party to be brought before the court; the court must be able to clearly recognize the group as a class by virtue of its well-defined interests; and members of the class must raise the same questions of law and fact. The existence of an ascertainable class is evidenced by its certification by the court, which is necessary for the maintenance of a class action. All persons who will be affected by a judgment in a class action must be notified that such an action has commenced; each is provided an opportunity to present his or her side of the case. The court's ruling in a class-action suit applies to all members of that class unless a member has requested an option indicating that he or she does not wish to be bound by the specified court action (Redden & Vernon, 1980).

Court rulings in class-action suits have stimulated both litigation and legislation on behalf of individuals with disabilities. During the 1950s, courts were confronted with class actions concerning the civil rights of handicapped children and adults. The majority of the actions were focused on the public's responsibility to provide education and treatment for handicapped citizens. The legal doctrines that courts have relied on to substantiate the right to an education for the handicapped stem in part from the Supreme Court ruling in *Brown v. Board of Education*. The Supreme Court ruled in this landmark decision that all children are constitutionally entitled to an equal educational opportunity (Abeson & Bolick, 1974; Kirp, 1976). Subsequent class-action suits addressed the enforcement of the ruling in *Brown v. Board of Education* (Martin, 1980). Handicapped children were no longer denied a public education; however, many issues remained unresolved, and new issues surfaced in the courts as well. For example, several state laws still regarded the severely handicapped as uneducable and thereby excluded this group from public schools. Questions regarding racial overrepresentation in special programs were also subjects of extensive litigation (Kirp, 1976).

The major legislation that governs our present delivery of services to exceptional children, the Individuals with Disabilities Education Act (IDEA), precipitated litigation that was more diverse and more individualized, thereby decreasing the numbers of representative classes. With the advent of the earlier version of IDEA, the Education for All Handicapped Children Act of 1975 (PL 94-142), class-action suits declined and individual legal claims were filed in matters of due process, Individualized Education Plan (IEP) challenges, placement, and related services.

REFERENCES

Abeson, A., & Bolick, N. (1974). *A continuing summary of pending and completed litigation regarding the education of handicapped children.* Reston, VA: Council for Exceptional Children.

Kirp, D. (1976). *Trends in education: The special child goes to court.* Columbus, OH: University Council for Educational Administration.

Martin, R. (1980). *Educating handicapped children: The legal mandate.* Champaign, IL: Research Press.

Redden, K., & Vernon, E. (1980). *Modern legal glossary.* Charlottesville, VA: Michie.

FRANCES T. HARRINGTON
Radford University
Second edition

KIMBERLY F. APPLEQUIST
University of Colorado at Colorado Springs
Third edition

See also Brown v. Board of Education; Individuals With Disabilities Education Improvement Act of 2004 (IDEIA); Larry P.

CLASSROOMS, POSITIVE BEHAVIOR SUPPORTS

Class-wide positive behavior interventions and supports (PBIS) is a proactive and preventative approach to classroom and behavior management. Teachers design positive classroom environments that promote the success of all students, and they organize class-wide PBIS practices along a continuum to support students with varying social skills and behavioral needs. Thus, class-wide PBIS shares many features with school-wide PBIS (SWPBIS; see entry in this encyclopedia), including a clear focus on practices, data, systems, and outcomes—the critical elements of PBIS (Sugai et al., 2010). These elements should be considered within and across classrooms.

Practices

Teachers should implement a continuum of proactive practices to support the social behavior and academic needs of all students. This continuum is typically conceptualized as a three-tier model, applied at the school- or setting-wide level (e.g., Walker et al., 1996), that employs response-to-intervention logic (e.g., Fairbanks, Sugai, Gauardino, & Lathrop, 2007). This model can also be applied within individual classroom environments (e.g., Fairbanks et al., 2007; Fairbanks, Simonsen, & Sugai, 2008), with tier 1 supports provided to all students in the classroom; tier 2 supports provided to a small, targeted group of students whose behaviors have not been responsive to tier 1; and tier 3 supports provided to individual students who require even more intensive and individualized supports to successfully participate in the classroom environment.

Tier 1

The first tier of class-wide PBIS includes empirically supported and proactive classroom management practices (e.g., Conroy, Sutherland, Snyder, & Marsh, 2008; Fairbanks et al., 2007). Simonsen, Fairbanks, Briesch, Myers, & Sugai (2008) identified five critical features of evidence-based classroom management. First, teachers maximize structure by establishing and teaching predictable routines and arranging their classroom environment to minimize distraction. Second, teachers select, teach, prompt, and review a few (i.e., three to five) positively stated expectations. If a school is implementing SWPBIS, class-wide expectations are the same as the school-wide expectations (e.g., Be Safe, Be Responsible, Be Respectful). In addition to establishing expectations, teachers actively supervise students' expectation-following behavior (e.g., DePry & Sugai, 2002).

Third, teachers actively engage students by designing instruction to increase students' opportunities to respond. Teachers may choose to implement a variety of evidence-based instructional practices that (a) promote active engagement and (b) are associated with desired student outcomes, including direct instruction (e.g., Becker & Gersten, 1982; Carnine, Silbert, Kame'enui, & Tarver, 2004), class-wide peer tutoring (e.g., Greenwood, Delquadri, & Hall, 1989), computer-assisted instruction (e.g., Ota & DuPaul, 2002), choral responding or response cards (e.g., Christle & Schuster, 2003), and guided notes (Lazarus, 1993).

Fourth, teachers implement a continuum of strategies to reinforce appropriate student behavior, including specific and contingent praise, behavior contracts, group contingencies, and token economies (see descriptions presented in Cooper, Heron, & Heward, 2007).

Finally, teachers implement a continuum of strategies to correct inappropriate student behavior. This continuum may include: specific, contingent, and brief error corrections; differential reinforcement strategies; planned ignoring; response cost procedures; and timeout procedures (see Cooper et al., 2007). In addition, Conroy and colleagues (2008) recommend implementing the Good Behavior Game to increase appropriate and decrease inappropriate classroom behaviors.

When implemented with fidelity, teachers should expect most (≥80%) students' behavior to respond to these tier 1 class-wide PBIS practices. Students who require additional support to be successful may be benefit from tier 2 supports in the classroom.

Tier 2

Although tier 2 practices are ideally implemented, coordinated, and evaluated school-wide, a teacher may implement the practices within his or her classroom. A common approach to tier 2 intervention is a check-in/check-out (CICO) or behavior education program (BEP; Crone, Horner, & Hawken, 2010). When implementing CICO in a classroom, the teacher checks-in with targeted students at the beginning of the day to remind them of the class-wide expectations, routines, and required materials. The teacher also gives the students a point card that includes written prompts of the expectations and opportunities for students to receive positive comments and points at predetermined checkpoints throughout the day. The teacher(s) then check in with the students throughout the day to provide feedback and award points on the point sheet. At the end of the day, the teacher checks-out with the targeted students, helping them calculate their point totals for the day and awarding reinforcement, if appropriate. The teacher sends a copy of the point sheet home and reminds the students to have their parents review, sign, and provide feedback on the their performance. Although CICO interventions are often effective (e.g., Hawken & Horner, 2003; Hawken, MacLeod, & Rawlings, 2007; Simonsen, Myers, & Briere, in press), a small percentage of students will require additional support to be successful and may benefit from tier 3 interventions.

Tier 3

The intensive and individualized interventions implemented in tier 3 should be coordinated at the school-wide level, where additional expertise, resources, and support are typically available; however, teachers should actively participate in designing and implementing tier 3 supports for students in their classrooms (along with a behavioral expert, the student's guardians, and other individuals knowledgeable about the student's behavior). In particular, a teacher may provide records, give an interview, and collect basic behavioral data to assist with completion of a functional behavioral assessment (FBA); a teacher may provide input and guidance with selecting preventative, individualized interventions that are documented in a positive behavior intervention plan (BIP; e.g., Crone & Horner, 2003).

Data

To monitor and evaluate the effectiveness of class-wide PBIS practices, teachers should collect, review, and evaluate data. As part of the school-wide system, teachers may document serious behavioral incidents on office discipline referrals (ODRs). In addition, teachers should collect data on behaviors that are more sensitive to change in the classroom. For example, if teachers employ a class-wide token economy, they may track the number of tokens earned as an indicator of students' appropriate behavior. Teachers may also choose to tally minor disruptive behaviors (e.g., talk-outs) and specific appropriate behaviors (e.g., hand raises). These simple data collection techniques allow teachers to (a) track the overall responsiveness of students to class-wide PBIS practices; (b) make data-based decisions about modifications to intervention approaches, including when to re-teach class-wide expectations, intensify reinforcement, and so forth; and (c) identify students who require additional tier 2 or 3 support. In addition to the data sources applied class-wide, teachers may collect data for students participating in tier 2 or tier 3 interventions (e.g., points earned on the point sheet or progress toward individualized behavior goals, respectively).

Systems

To promote teachers' implementation of class-wide PBIS with fidelity, supportive school-wide systems need to be in place. Often, teachers require additional training and support to implement class-wide PBIS practices effectively. Researchers have documented that training alone is ineffective (e.g., Fixsen, Naoom, Blasé, Friedman, & Wallace, 2005). Instead, training must be supplemented with mentoring, coaching, performance feedback, or some combination thereof (e.g., Abbott, O'Donnell, Hawkins, Hill, Kosterman, & Catalano, 1998; Allen & Forman, 1984; Jeffrey, McCurdy, Ewing, & Polis, 2009; Simonsen, Myers, & DeLuca, 2010b). In addition to comprehensive professional development, schools should consider implementing a staff reinforcement system to recognize teachers who excel in one or more areas of class-wide PBIS.

Outcomes

When evidence-based class-wide PBIS practices are implemented effectively, as indicated by data, and supported by school-wide systems, desired outcomes are likely to be achieved. At the classroom level, teachers should expect most ($\geq$ 80%) students to respond to tier 1 practices, as evidenced by increases in prosocial behavior and decreases in classroom level disruptions, and receive one or fewer ODRs. At the school level, desired outcomes may include (a) decreases in the number or proportion of ODRs generated in classroom settings and (b) increases in the percentage of staff implementing class-wide PBIS with fidelity.

Summary

Class-wide PBIS practices are conceptualized along a three-tier continuum, with teachers involved in designing and implementing practices in each tier. To measure the effectiveness of class-wide PBIS practices, teachers should collect, review, and evaluate data on students' behavior. In addition, schools should invest in comprehensive professional development and staff reinforcement systems to promote teachers' fidelity of implementation. When these three elements (practices, data, and systems) are established, desired outcomes are likely.

REFERENCES

Abbott, R. D., O'Donnell, J., Hawkins, J. D., Hill, K. G., Kosterman, R., & Catalano, R. F. (1998). Changing teaching practices to promote achievement and bonding to school. *American Journal of Orthopsychiatry, 68,* 542–552.

Allen, C. T., & Forman, S. G. (1984). Efficacy of methods of training teachers in behavior modification. *School Psychology Review, 13,* 26–32.

Becker, W. C., & Gersten, R. (1982). A follow-up of Follow Through: The later effects of the Direct Instruction Model on children in fifth and sixth grades. *American Educational Research Journal, 19*(1), 75–92.

Carnine, D. W., Silbert, J., Kame'enui, E. J., & Tarver, S. G. (2004). *Direct instruction reading.* (4th ed.). Upper Saddle River, NJ: Merrill Prentice Hall.

Christle, C. A., & Schuster, J. W. (2003). The effects of using response cards on student participation, academic achievement, and on-task behavior during whole-class, math instruction. *Journal of Behavioral Education, 12,* 147–165.

Conroy, M. A., Sutherland, K. S., Snyder, A. L., & Marsh, S. (2008). Class-wide interventions: Effective instruction makes a difference. *Teaching Exceptional Children, 40,* 24–30.

Cooper, J. O., Heron, T. E., & Heward, W. L. (2007). *Applied behavior analysis* (2nd ed.). Upper Saddle River, NJ: Prentice Hall.

Crone, D. A., & Horner, R. H. (2003). *Building positive behavior support systems in schools: Functional behavioral assessment.* New York, NY: Guilford Press.

Crone, D. A., Horner, R. H., & Hawken, L. S. (2010). *Responding to problem behavior in schools: The Behavior Education Program* (2nd ed.). New York, NY: Guilford Press.

DePry, R. L., & Sugai, G. (2002). The effect of active supervision and pre-correction on minor behavioral incidents in a sixth grade general education classroom. *Journal of Behavioral Education, 11,* 255–264.

Fairbanks, S., Simonsen, B. M., & Sugai, G. (2008). Class-wide secondary and tertiary tier practices and supports. *Teaching Exceptional Children, Special Issue: Positive Behavior Interventions and Supports, 40,* 44–52.

Fairbanks, S., Sugai, G., Guardino, D., & Lathrop, M. (2007). Response to intervention: Examining classroom behavior support in second grade. *Exceptional Children, 73,* 288–310.

Fixsen, D. L., Naoom, S. F., Blasé, K. A., Friedman, R. M., & Wallace, F. (2005). *Implementation research: A synthesis of the literature.* Tampa, FL: University of South Florida, Louis de la Parte Florida Mental Health Institute, The National Implementation Research Network (FMHI Publication #231).

Greenwood, C. R., Delquadri, J. C., & Hall, R. V. (1989). Longitudinal effects of class-wide peer tutoring. *Journal of Educational Psychology, 81*(3), 371–383.

Hawken, L. S., & Horner, R. H. (2003). Evaluation of a targeted intervention within a school-wide system of behavior support. *Journal of Behavioral Education, 12*, 225–240.

Hawken, L. S., MacLeod, K. S., & Rawlings, L. (2007). Effects of the behavior education program on office discipline referrals of elementary school students. *Journal of Positive Behavior Interventions, 9*, 94–101.

Jeffrey, J. L., McCurdy, B. L., Ewing, S., & Polis, D. (2009). Class-wide PBIS for students with EBD: Initial evaluation of an integrity tool. *Education and Treatment of Children, 32*, 537–550.

Lazarus, B. D. (1993). Guided notes: Effects with secondary and postsecondary students with mild disabilities. *Education and Treatment of Children, 16*, 272–289.

Ota, K., & DuPaul, G. J. (2002). Task engagement and mathematics performance in children with attention-deficit hyperactivity disorder: Effects of supplemental computer instruction. *School Psychology Quarterly, 17*, 242–257.

Simonsen, B., Fairbanks, S., Briesch, A., Myers, D., & Sugai, G. (2008). Evidence-based practices in classroom management: Considerations for research to practice. *Education and Treatment for Children, 31*, 351–380.

Simonsen, B., Myers, D., & Briere, D. (in press; prepublished April 20, 2010a). Comparing a behavioral check-in/check-out (CICO) intervention with standard practice in an urban middle school using an experimental group design. *Journal of Positive Behavior Interventions.* doi:10.1177/1098300709359026

Simonsen, B., Myers, D., & DeLuca, C. (2010b). Providing teachers with training and performance feedback to increase use of three classroom management skills: Prompts, opportunities to respond, and reinforcement. *Teacher Education in Special Education, 33*, 300–318. doi: 10.1177/0888406409359905

Sugai, G., Horner, R. H., Algozzine, R., Barrett, S., Lewis, T., Anderson, C.,...Simonsen, B. (2010). *School-wide positive behavior support: Implementers' blueprint and self-assessment.* Eugene: University of Oregon.

Walker, H. M., Horner, R. H., Sugai, G., Bullis, M., Sprague, J. R., Bricker, D., & Kaufman, M. J. (1996). Integrated approaches to preventing antisocial behavior patterns among school-age children and youth. *Journal of Emotional and Behavioral Disorders, 4*, 194–209.

BRANDI SIMONSEN
University of Connecticut
Fourth edition

CLAUSEN, JOHS (1913–)

Johs Clausen was born in Bergen, Norway. He is a psychophysiologist and researcher in mental retardation. In 1939 he obtained his MA at the University of Oslo and in 1956 his PhD at the Faculty of Medicine, University of Oslo. Between 1949 and 1951, Clausen was a research fellow at Columbia University. He participated in the Columbia Greystone Project and the New York State Brain Research Project. He was also a research fellow with the Norwegian Research Council from 1953 to 1955; an associate scientist at the New York Psychiatric Institute from 1955 to 1966; and research psychologist, chief of psychological research, and research administrator at the Training School at Vineland (American Institute of Mental Studies). Clausen conducted research on ability structures and autonomic nervous functions in mentally retarded individuals. From 1966 to 1984, Clausen was chief research scientist, department of psychology, New York State Institute for Basic Research in Mental Retardation.

Among his numerous professional affiliations, Clausen has been a member of the American Psychological Association, Eastern Psychological Association, American Association for the Advancement of Science, American Association on Mental Deficiency, and the American Academy on Mental Retardation. He is the author of *Ability Structure and Subgroups in Mental Retardation* (1966) as well as more than 55 scientific studies.

REFERENCE

Clausen, J. (1966). *Ability structure and subgroups in mental retardation.* Washington, DC: Spartan.

IVAN Z. HOLOWINSKY
Rutgers University

CLEFT LIP/PALATE

The phenomenon of cleft lip and palate is a rather frequent one all over the world: 0.1% of all neonates are born with a more or less severe cleft, ranging from a cleft uvula or a partly cleft upper lip to a two-sided complete cleft of upper lip, jaw, and hard and soft palate. Normally, three main groups are discerned: cleft lip only (CL), cleft palate only (CP), and cleft lip and palate combined (CLP). Cleft lip and palate malformations are congenital and originate in the 4th to 7th week (CL) and in the 7th to 12th week (CP) of embryonic development. Although in some cases viral, medical, and X-ray influences may play a role in causing these malformations, they are generally believed to have a hereditary basis. The chance of cleft lip and palate increases accordingly as the occurrence of clefts in a family are more frequent and more severe, and with the closeness of the relationship (mother or father). The occurrence of clefts is more frequent in boys than in girls, and, moreover, types of clefts are not equally divided between the sexes. One in 1,000 babies are born with cleft palate per year with the condition being more common in Asians and specific groups of American Indians while occurring less frequently in African American populations. Other birth defects are present in up to 13% of the reported cleft lip and palate cases (American Academy of Otolaryngology, 2011).

Problems arising from being born with a cleft lip and palate are highly dependent on the part of the world in which the baby is born. In Third World countries, where no surgery is done on cleft lip and palate children, the main problem is survival and nourishment. In highly developed countries, the problems for cleft lip and palate children mainly concern communication and socialization. But even in these countries, a large differentiation can be found in the treatment of children with cleft lip and palate depending on the scientific ideas and theories of the treating medical team. However, for all newborn babies with cleft lip and palate, the first problem encountered is the feeding, because of the difficulties in sucking and swallowing. In Third World countries, infants depend entirely on breast feeding; if the baby is kept in a somewhat deviant feeding position (almost vertically sitting on the mother's lap or nearly horizontally held against the body of the mother), breast feeding is generally considered to be successful. Breast feeding is advisable in highly developed countries as well, because apart from other advantages, it is highly beneficial to the mother–child bond. In case of insurmountable breast feeding problems, feeding by means of special spoons and cups is preferred to bottles with long nipples (so-called lamb's nipples). Sometimes the infant will be provided with an obturator, a small plastic plate covering the cleft in the palate. This may help normal sucking, but it must be frequently renewed and readjusted because of the growing of the infant's mouth.

In most countries where surgery is applied, the child passes through a whole program of treatment and rehabilitation during the first years of life, often starting with healing of the lip followed by closure of the soft palate some months later, and sometimes the hard palate as well. The schedule and type of treatment depends to a large extent on the philosophy of the medical team. For example, the plastic surgeon will stress the aesthetic and visible aspects, the orthodontist the dental aspects, the speech pathologist the importance of the development of language and speech, and so on. Nevertheless, it will be clear that the best results are achieved by an interdisciplinary team of experts in close cooperation, all aiming to establish normal appearance, normal dental function, and good language and communication skills. As for the intellectual abilities of cleft lip and palate children, many prejudices have to be disproved. Visible congenital deformations, especially of the head, are often wrongly associated with poor intellectual capacities. In recent research, children with cleft lip and palate were found to have at least average general intelligence, with no intellectual differences between boys and girls. The lowest-scoring group are children with cleft palate only (CP), the group with no visible abnormalities.

As for the speech and language development and related verbal expression abilities of children with cleft lip and palate, a clear delay is found compared with the average population. One of the causes might be hearing problems, since children with cleft lip and palate have increased chances of inflammation of the middle ear combined with hearing impairment. Nevertheless, these possible hearing losses are not considered to be the main cause of the speech and language delays. Nor are the pronunciation problems that result from the abnormalities of the speech production mechanism, although a thorough speech training program will nearly always be necessary. No one-to-one relationship can be found between the severity of the malformation or the proportions of the cleft and the degree of delay in language and speech development. More and more, the psychosocial development of the child is believed to be a ground for speech and language problems (Moller & Star, 1993).

Because interaction between parent and child is the cradle of the development of communication, it is clear that acceptance of the infant and his or her difficulties is a must. The birth of a child with a cleft lip and palate will undoubtedly cause the parents a degree of concern. The questions of the parents, their anxieties and concerns, require immediate professional counseling to create safe and adjusted surroundings for the child (Brookshire, Lynch, & Fox, 1984). Well-balanced interaction between parents and infant provides the possibility for the cleft palate child to develop normal linguistic, communicative, and social skills.

Characteristics

1. Cleft lip is identified when the two sides of the upper lip do not join together properly.
2. Cleft palate, harder to detect visually, may be first suspected when the infant regurgitates fluid from the nose during nursing.
3. Infants may have difficulty feeding because they cannot suck effectively.
4. Affected children may have hypernasal speech and articulation problems.
5. Middle ear dysfunction and resulting hearing impairment may occur.

REFERENCES

American Academy of Otolaryngology. (2011). *Cleft lip and cleft palate fact sheet*. Retrieved from http://www.entnet.org/HealthInformation/cleftLipPalate.cfm

Brookshire, B. L., Lynch, J. I., & Fox, D. R. (1984). *A parent–child cleft palate curriculum*. Tigard, OR: C. C. Publications.

Moller, K., & Starr, C. (1993). *Cleft palate: Interdisciplinary issues and treatment: For clinicians by clinicians*. Austin, TX: PRO-ED.

F. J. Koopmans-Van Beinum
Amsterdam, The Netherlands
First edition

Robert L. Rhodes
New Mexico State University
Second edition

See also Language Disorders; Physical Anomalies

CLELAND, CHARLES C. (1924–   )

Charles Cleland received his BS in political science in 1950, and his MS in educational psychology in 1951, from Southern Illinois University. Cleland's doctoral work in educational psychology and general and industrial management at the University of Texas, Austin (1957), presented a theme that has been reflected in most of his work.

After a year as chief psychologist at the Lincoln State School (Illinois), Cleland returned to Texas to the Austin State School. In 1959, he was promoted to superintendent of the Abilene State School, where he stayed for 4 years until joining the faculty in the educational psychology department at the University of Texas, Austin.

Since that time, Cleland has been a professor of special education and educational psychology, teaching courses primarily in the areas of mental retardation, residential care, and management of service facilities. Although Cleland does not view himself as researcher (personal communication, June 26, 1985), his 250 articles, chapters in books, monographs, and books on a wide variety of subjects may prove otherwise. His principal publications include *Mental Retardation: A Developmental Approach* (1978), *Exceptionalities Through the Lifespan* (Cleland & Schwartz, 1982), *Mental Retardation Approaches to Institutional Change* (Cleland & Schwartz, 1969), and *Mental Retardation* (1992).

Dr. Cleland is Professor Emeritus in the department of special education at the University of Texas at Austin.

REFERENCES

Cleland, C. C. (1978). *Mental retardation: A developmental approach*. Englewood Cliffs, NJ: Prentice Hall.

Cleland, C. C. (1992). *Mental retardation*. New York, NY: Wiley.

Cleland, C. C., & Schwartz, J. D. (1969). *Mental retardation approaches to institutional change*. New York, NY: Grune & Stratton.

Cleland, C. C., & Schwartz, J. D. (1982). *Exceptionalities through the lifespan*. New York, NY: Macmillan.

Elaine Fletcher-Janzen
Chicago School of Professional Psychology

CLERC, LAURENT (1785–1869)

Laurent Clerc, deaf from the age of 1, was educated at the Institution Nationale des Sourdes Muets in Paris and following graduation served as a teacher there. He traveled to the United States with Thomas Hopkins Gallaudet to open the nation's first school for the deaf, now the American School for the Deaf, at Hartford, Connecticut, in 1817. Schooled in the teaching methods of Epée and Sicard, Clerc was the school's first teacher and was responsible for the training of new teachers (Turner, 1871).

Clerc was the first educated deaf person to be seen in the United States. He exemplified the potential of education for the deaf, and was influential in the movement to establish public responsibility for the education of the deaf (Lane, 1984).

REFERENCES

Lane, H. (1984). *When the mind hears*. New York, NY: Random House.

Turner, W. W. (1871). Laurent Clerc. *American Annals of the Deaf*, *15*, 14–25.

Paul Irvine
Katonah, New York

CLINICAL EVALUATION OF LANGUAGE FUNDAMENTALS, FOURTH EDITION

The Clinical Evaluation of Language Fundamentals, Fourth Edition (CELF-4, 2003) is an individually administered battery of tests that can be used to diagnose language disorders. The basic battery is designed to be administered to individuals ages 5 through 21 and takes approximately 30 to 60 minutes to administer, although administration time may vary based on which subtests are administered. There are two spiral-bound stimulus easels that contain visual stimuli for many subtests. Examinee responses are recorded on the provided record form, and there are separate record forms for 5- to 8-year-olds and 9- to 21-year-olds. A computer scoring and report generation program is available for this instrument, and a variety of scores—including standard scores, percentile ranks, and age equivalents—are reported.

The CELF-4 consists of 18 subtests that are utilized in four stages. The first stage of testing requires assessing general language ability, and deriving a Core Language Score (CLS) based on performance on several foundational subtests. Based on these initial results, examiners can go on to assess the nature of the language disorder (i.e., receptive and expressive language ability), granular skills associated with the disorder (i.e., phonological awareness, rapid automatic naming, working memory), and the effect of the disorder on classroom functioning (through the completion of an Observational Rating Scale and pragmatic profile).

Core subtests include Concepts and Following Directions (on which the student identifies pictured objects in response to orally presented directions), Word Structure (on which the student completes orally presented sentences), Recalling Sentences (on which the student imitates orally presented sentences), Formulated Sentences (on which the student is given target word and picture stimulus and asked to form a sentence), Word Classes (on which the student picks orally presented words that go together and describes their relationship), and Word Definitions (on which the student defines a word that is used in a sentence). Although several of these subtests are used with all examinees, the specific subtests that make up the core (and therefore, CLS) differ slightly for 5- to 8- versus 9- to 21-year-olds.

Additional subtests are administered as appropriate to better understand a student's profile of strengths and weaknesses. These additional subtests include Sentence Structure (on which the student points to a picture that depicts the orally presented sentence), Expressive Vocabulary (on which the student describes presented pictures), Understanding Spoken Paragraphs (on which the student responds to inferential and deductive questions about orally presented paragraphs), Sentence Assembly (on which the student produces two semantically and syntactically intact sentences from visually and orally presented words or word clusters), Semantic Relationships (on which the student listens to a sentence, then selects two of four visually presented options to answer a target question), Number Repetition 1 and 2 (on which the student repeats a series of numbers forward and backward), Familiar Sequences 1 and 2 (on which the student provides simple pieces of information, such as the days of the week, under time constraints), Rapid Automatic Naming (on which the student names colors, shapes, and color-shape combinations, under time constraints), Word Associations (on which the student lists as many words within a given category as possible in 1 minute), and

Phonological Awareness (on which the student identifies, rhymes, blends, and segments sounds and syllables in words).

Finally, two supplemental measures can be administered to better understand the impact of a language disorder on classroom functioning. The Pragmatics Profile provides a parent or teacher report of a student's social language skills in three areas: Rituals and Conversational Skills; Asking For, Giving, and Responding to Information; and Nonverbal Communication Skills. Similarly, the Observational Rating Scale is a 4-point Likert scale used to measure the frequency with which a student may have problems in listening, speaking, reading, and writing and can be administered to parents, teachers, or students.

The norms are based on a sample of 2,650 students that ranged in age from 5 to 21 years. The sample was representative of U.S. population in 2000 with respect to sex, race, geographic region, highest education achieved by primary caregiver, and children with identified conditions. A notable change from earlier versions of the CELF, which were normed using only typically developing children, is that "about 9% of children in the CELF-4 normative sample were receiving special services and 7% were diagnosed with speech and/or language disorders" (Langlois, 2005).

Globally, this measure meets standards for reliability. Internal consistency tests for the composite scores ranged from .87 to .95 and from .69 to .91 for the subtests (Semel, Wiig, & Secord, 2003). Test–retest reliability was calculated using 320 individuals from the norming sample with an average administration interval of 16 days, and Semel et al. (2003) found that it ranged from .88 to .92 for composite scores and from .71 to .86 for subtests (although coefficients for particular age groups on particular subtests were found to be in the .6 range). Interrater reliability scores ranged from .88 to .99, indicating that scoring rules for subtests that require clinical judgment are adequately interpreted by test administrators.

Validity of this measure was also assessed in a variety of ways. The newly designed and revised subtests comprehensively address the developing language skills of 5- to 21-year-olds as described by other researchers in this area, and the measure appears to have strong content validity. Observations of response process during test administration provided additional evidence that the subtests functioned as intended. A factor analysis conducted by the authors supported the idea of a general language factor, and the examiner's manual provides details about the relationships between composite and subtest scores.

Validity was also examined by determining the relationship between the CELF-4 and other measures. Correlations between the CELF-3 and CELF-4 are moderate, which is likely due to the number of revisions made to this new version of the instrument. Correlations between the CELF-4 and the Wechsler Intelligence Scale for Children (WISC-IV Integrated) were conducted using a small sample of 55 children ages 6:0 to 16:11 who had been diagnosed with language disorders. The correlation between a student's CLS on the CELF-4 and full-scale IQ score on the WISC-IV Integrated was .59, and the correlation between a student's CLS on the CELF-4 and Verbal Comprehension composite score on the WISC-IV Integrated was .69 (*Technical Report*, 2005). The CELF-4 has high sensitivity and specificity, making it an appropriate instrument to utilize in differentiating between students with language disorders and other learning or developmental issues.

The CELF-4 provides a more comprehensive assessment of overall language functioning than past versions of this instrument, as well as updated and stronger normative data. Several new subtests have been added to this edition, and many other subtests have been revised. Testing in four stages is a new concept, introduced in this version of the examiner's manual, and allows for the instrument to be used flexibly, for multiple purposes, and in ways consistent with testing requirements set by the reauthorization of the Individuals with Disabilities Education Act and other recent reform efforts.

REFERENCES

Langlois, A. (2005). Review of the Clinical Evaluation of Language Fundamentals, Fourth Edition. In R. A. Spies, and B. S. Plake, (Eds.), *The sixteenth mental measurements yearbook*. Lincoln, NE: Buros Institute of Mental Measurements.

Semel, E. M., Wiig, E. H., & Secord, W. A. (2003). *Clinical evaluation of language fundamentals* (3rd ed.). San Antonio, TX: The Psychological Corporation.

Technical Report: Correlations between the CELF-4 and WISC-4 Integrated. (2005). Retrieved from http://psychcorp.pearson assessments.com/hai/images/resource/techrpts/CELF4_WISC 4_TechReport.pdf

JAMIE ZIBULSKY
Fairleigh Dickinson University

KATHLEEN VIEZEL
Fairleigh Dickinson University
Fourth edition

CLINICAL INTERVIEW

Assessment interviews are conducted to identify and define current problems, to collect information concerning why current problems exist, or to make a diagnostic decision. The focus can be on information the client provides directly (content interviews), or on information that the client's behavior provides (process interviews, also known as mental status exams), or both. Manuals for conducting process interviews with children include Beiser's (1962), Goodman and Sours' (1967),

and Greenspan's (1981). Content interviews have been emphasized in the literature on behavioral assessment of adult disorders (e.g., Haynes, 1978); prior to 1975, however, there were few references to content interviews with children. Since then, a number of studies have demonstrated that children can directly provide reliable information (e.g., Abu-Saad & Holzemer, 1981; Herjanic & Campbell, 1977), particularly when describing publicly observable events.

As with any assessment instrument, the quality of an interview depends on getting accurate information with the least amount of error. Three major sources of error are present in the interview: the interviewer, the interviewee, and the interview setting. One obvious interviewer error is the failure to ask for necessary information. It is unlikely that information that is not specifically asked for will be obtained; thus the information needed from an interview should be well planned. Some interviews are highly structured (e.g., the Vineland Adaptive Behavior Scales); others use rough organizing frameworks such as BASIC ID (Lazarus, 1973) or S-O-R-K-C (Kanfer & Saslow, 1969). The interview also may be organized ad hoc by the clinician. Several structured interviews for the assessment of child psychopathology exist (e.g., Edelbrock & Costello, 1984; Orvaschel, Sholomskas, & Weissman, 1980; Structured Clinical Interview for the *DSM-IV-TR*, 2004 by First, Gibbon, Spitzer, & Williams, 2005). The specific plan an interviewer uses will depend on the interviewer's purpose and theoretical model (Ventura, Liberman, Green, Shaner, & Mintz, 1998). The interviewer, however, must be careful not to lead the client's responses; only information to which the client has access should be asked for, and it should be clear to the client that no one response is favored by the interviewer. A second information-gathering error is the failure to recognize and clarify ambiguous responses. This source of error can be reduced by asking questions that clarify contradictory information.

A great deal of information can be given during interviews; thus, the storage and retrieval system used by the clinician is a third potential source of error. Audio or video recording ensures that all information given is stored, but recordings are cumbersome to review, may have adverse effects on rapport, and are not readily available in some settings. Notetaking is more efficient and can be more easily organized, but notetaking can also detract from rapport with some clients. Notetaking also has the effect of implicitly reinforcing clients for giving specific types of information, an advantage if this is information that the clinician needs. The interviewer may decide to neither record nor take notes; but the interviewer then needs to rely more heavily on specific memory strategies (e.g., making frequent summary statements of known information), and later writing notes.

An interviewer may use tactics that initially result in accurate information, but the information quality will deteriorate throughout the interview if the interviewer does not maintain a relationship in which the client continues to want to give accurate information. Maintaining warmth, empathy, genuineness, and personal reinforcement may help maintain rapport. The interviewer must remain alert to changes in affect and change tactics to maintain an appropriate and culturally competent (Lesser, 1997) relationship.

Sources of interviewee error fall into categories of effects of developmental deficits, client perceptions of the nature and consequences of the interview, and fatigue. To the extent that the effects of these sources of error are under some control by the interviewer, they represent interviewer errors of control. Clinicians should be alert to signs of fatigue and other physiological effects. Interview sessions should be as short as possible and conducted at times when the client is rested and least distractible. Children and developmentally delayed adults have deficits in their knowledge of vocabulary and conversational conventions (Conti & Camras, 1984; Dickson, 1981), in their understanding of what a listener needs to know (Flavell, Botkin, Fry, Wright, & Jarvis, 1968), and in the facility with which they can meet the cognitive demands of answering questions (Shatz, 1977). These sources of error can be partly controlled by ensuring that vocabulary used by the interviewer is familiar to the client, by keeping cognitive demands low (e.g., by asking for single bits of information at once rather than multiple bits), and by clearly explaining what information the interviewer knows and what information is needed. There is evidence that closed-ended or multiple-response format questions (e.g., "When the other kids call you that name, do you feel angry, sad, or something else?") obtain more reliable responses from developmentally younger persons than open-ended questions (e.g., "How do you feel when they call you that name?"), and some evidence that open-ended questions produce more refusals and less complete information than closed-ended ones (Ammons, 1950; Miller & Bigi, 1979). However, there is a tendency for developmentally delayed adults and children to give acquiescent responses to Yes/No questions, and to give the last choice in multiple-response formats (Sigelman et al., 1981). There is also a tendency for normal children under six to assume that they understand ambiguous questions and not ask clarifying questions (Robinson & Robinson, 1984). These deficits imply that when interviewing young children and developmentally delayed older persons, clinicians need to ask closed-ended questions, but avoid Yes/No formats; clinicians should also be alert to a possible response bias. Sigelman et al. (1981) found a picture-choice format to be the most reliable, but nonverbal formats for interviewing may not always be available.

The interviewee's expectations about the interview and about what will be done with the information obtained is also likely to affect validity. Clinicians should ensure that clients understand what will happen during the interview, why the interview is being conducted, and how the information will be used, and should elicit any concerns the client has about the interview. In interpreting data, the clinician should consider the likelihood that the client may have been giving biased responses because of the demands of the setting; for example, when interviewing a client in a dormitory about involvement in an incident of stealing, it is likely that the client will give biased information, particularly if the client believes such information will be shared with houseparents. Bias owed to ecological demand characteristics can be reduced if the interview is designed so that the client believes the interview will be ecologically helpful. If the clinician begins the interview by asking whether there are problems in the setting that the client would like to have ameliorated, the client is more likely to be cooperative in sharing information.

The interview setting influences the interview, and can therefore be a source of error. Interviewer and interviewee should generally be alone unless the presence of other persons is expected to enhance the quality of the interview (e.g., a young child may be very fearful unless mother is present). The clinician needs to consider how the presence of other persons may affect the demand characteristics of the interview when interpreting the results. The client's prior experience with the clinician may also bias results; this problem is minimal in situations in which interviewer and interviewee have never met. The location of the interview may also affect the information that is elicited; interviewing a child in a classroom, for example, may generate a client expectation that the interviewer is a teacher; on the other hand, the setting can be used to prompt information that may not be normally accessible. It's possible, for example, that a child will give more reliable information about what has occurred in a classroom when the child is interviewed alone in the classroom. The setting for the interview should be carefully planned by the clinician.

The building blocks of a good clinical interview have been described as respect, curiosity, listening, searching for patterns and hypotheses, and supporting competence (Pennsylvania Public Welfare, 2005). These building blocks appear to summarize the goals of a competent clinical interview that complements special education objectives and goals.

REFERENCES

Abu-Saad, H., & Holzemer, W. L. (1981). Measuring children's self-assessment of pain. *Issues in Comprehensive Pediatric Nursing, 5*, 337–349.

Ammons, R. B. (1950). Reactions in a projective doll-play interview of white males two to six years of age to differences in skin color and facial features. *Journal of Genetic Psychology, 76*, 323–341.

Beiser, H. R. (1962). Psychiatric diagnostic interviews with children. *Journal of the American Academy of Child Psychiatry, 1*, 656–670.

Conti, D. J., & Camras, L. A. (1984). Children's understanding of conversational principles. *Journal of Experimental Child Psychology, 38,* 456–463.

Dickson, W. P. (1981). Introduction: Toward an interdisciplinary conception of children's communication abilities. In W. P. Dickson (Ed.), *Children's oral communication abilities* (pp. 1–10). New York, NY: Academic.

Edelbrock, C., & Costello, A. J. (1984). *A review of structured psychiatric interviews for children.* Unpublished manuscript.

First, M. B., Gibbon, M., Spitzer, R. L., & Williams, J. B. W. (2005). *SCID web page.* Retrieved from http://scid4 .org/

Flavell, J. H., Botkin, P. T., Fry, C. L., Wright, J. W., & Jarvis, P. E. (1968). *The development of role-taking and communication skills in children.* New York, NY: Wiley.

Goodman, J., & Sours, J. (1967). *The child mental status examination.* New York, NY: Basic Books.

Greenspan, S. I. (1981). *The clinical interview of the child.* New York, NY: McGraw-Hill.

Haynes, S. N. (1978). The behavioral interview. In S. N. Haynes (Ed.), *Principles of behavioral assessment.* New York, NY: Gardner Press.

Herjanic, B., & Campbell, W. (1977). Differentiating psychiatrically disturbed children on the basis of a structured interview. *Journal of Abnormal Child Psychology, 5,* 127–134.

Kanfer, F. H., & Saslow, G. (1969). Behavioral diagnosis. In C. M. Franks (Ed.), *Behavior theory: Appraisal and status.* New York, NY: McGraw-Hill.

Lazarus, A. (1973). Multimodal behavior therapy: Treating the BASIC ID. *Journal of Nervous and Mental Disease, 156,* 404–411.

Lesser, I. M. (1997). Cultural considerations using the Structured Clinical Interview for *DSM-III* for mood and anxiety disorder assessment. *Journal of Psychopathology & Behavioral Assessment, 19,* 149–160.

Miller, P. H., & Bigi, L. (1979). The development of children's understanding of attention. *Merrill-Palmer Quarterly, 25,* 235–250.

Orvaschel, H., Sholomskas, D., & Weissman, M. M. (1980). *The assessment of psychopathology and behavioral problems in children: A review of epidemiological and clinical research (1967–1979).* Rockville, MD: National Institute of Mental Health, Division of Biometry and Epidemiology (DHHS Publication No. [ADM]80-1037).

Pennsylvania Public Welfare. (2005). *Building blocks of the clinical interview.* Retrieved from http://www.dpw.state.pa.us/

Robinson, E. J., & Robinson, W. P. (1984). Realizing you don't understand: A further study. *Journal of Child Psychology and Psychiatry, 25,* 621–627.

Shatz, M. (1977). The relationship between cognitive processes and the development of communication skills. *Nebraska Symposium on Motivation, 25,* 1–42.

Sigelman, C. K., Schoenrock, C. J., Winer, J. L., Spanhel, C. L., Hromas, S. G., Martin, P. W., . . . Bensberg, G. J. (1981). In R. H. Bruininks, C. E. Meyers, B. B. Sigford, & K. C. Lakin (Eds.), *Deinstitutionalization and community adjustment of mentally retarded people.* Washington, DC: American Association of Mental Deficiency.

Ventura, J., Liberman, R. P., Green, M. F., Shaner, A., & Mintz, J. (1998). Training and quality assurance with Structured Clinical Interview for *DSM-IV* (SC ID-I/P). *Psychiatry Research, 19,* 2, 16–17.

JOHN MACDONALD
Eastern Kentucky University

See also Assessments, Alternative; Mental Status Exams

CLINICAL PSYCHOLOGY

Clinical psychology is the branch of psychology devoted to the scientific study, assessment, diagnosis, and treatment of mental disorders. Clinical psychology has its origins in 1896 with the construction of the first psychological clinic by Lightner Witmer at the University of Pennsylvania (Benjamin, 1997). In 1907, Witmer founded and served as editor of *The Psychological Clinic,* a journal describing the types of problems and work performed at the clinic. Witmer wrote the initial article in the new journal and described his work with a child referred for treatment of bad spelling in school (Witmer, 1907). The article was titled "Clinical Psychology," wherein Witmer applied this name to his work, and became known as the founder of clinical psychology (Benjamin, 1997).

Initially, clinical psychology was most interested in the development and assessment of human abilities, and provided the government the means to test intelligence, achievement, vocational interests, and personality characteristics of recruits during both world wars. After World War II, the Veterans Administration hired large numbers of clinical psychologists to work with disabled veterans, and the psychologists' roles expanded beyond assessment to psychotherapy (Phares, 1979). During this time, clinical psychology gained professional status by obtaining licensure in most states, and establishing independent practice activities.

Training for clinical psychology is normally 4 years of graduate coursework followed by a full-time year of internship. Courses taken for the degree include basic psychological areas such as social, learning, methodology, and biological with advanced coursework in assessment and psychopathology (Matthews & Walker, 1997). The PhD (Doctor of Philosophy) degree is the traditional degree for clinical psychology and usually involves a scientist-practitioner model of training. The PsyD (Doctor of Psychology) is a newer degree focusing more on practitioner training with less emphasis on research productivity. Current requirements for licensure usually involve both a written and oral examination followed by a year of postdoctoral supervision. Additionally, the American Psychological Association provides accreditation for clinical psychology programs, allowing for common goals and training among diverse graduate programs.

At the present time, clinical psychologists are in ever-expanding positions committed to the advancement and promotion of mental health and human well-being. They serve in the traditional roles of providing diagnosis and assessment functions and psychotherapy, but are increasingly called upon to provide consultation and supervision, or to assume administrative positions (Matthews & Walker, 1997). Current theoretical perspectives include psychodynamic, behavioral, cognitive, humanistic, and systemic. Clinical psychologists work with all age groups from infants to the elderly; and they are also developing specialty areas such as forensic psychology, health psychology, children, the aging, scientific research, psychology of women, child health problems, and ethnic minority issues. Finally, clinical psychologists work in a wide range of settings such as individual practice, mental health clinics, hospitals, schools, universities, counseling centers, legal systems, government organizations, and the military services.

REFERENCES

Benjamin, L. T., Jr. (1997). *A history of psychology: Original sources and contemporary research* (2nd ed.). New York, NY: McGraw-Hill.

Matthews, J. R., & Walker, C. E. (1997). *Basic skills and professional issues in clinical psychology*. Boston, MA: Allyn & Bacon.

Phares, E. J. (1979). *Clinical psychology: Concepts, methods, and profession* (Vols. 1–2). Homewood, IL: Dorsey Press.

Witmer, L. (1907). Clinical psychology. *The Psychological Clinic, 1*, 1–9.

LINDA M. MONTGOMERY
The University of Texas of the Permian Basin

See also Clinical Interview; Diagnostic and Statistical Manual of Mental Disorders (*DSM-IV*); Mental Status Exams

CLINICAL TEACHING

Clinical teaching is teaching prescriptive (diagnosis + prescription = remediation), with the intent of matching the student's strengths and weaknesses to a specific type of instruction. Clinical teaching is therefore often called diagnostic-prescriptive teaching. It is a continuous test-teach-test process. This process was influenced by Johnson and Myklebust (1967), Smith (1968, 1974), Learner (1985), and many others. Teaching strategies in clinical teaching include task analysis and applied behavior analysis.

Learner (1985) views the clinical teaching process as a five-stage repetitive cycle of decision making that consists of assessment, planning, implementation, evaluation, and modification of the assessment. She further adds that the clinical teacher considers the student's ecological, home, social, and cultural environments.

Smith (1983) offers eight steps in the clinical teaching process: (1) The clinical teacher should objectively observe and analyze the student's classroom abilities; (2) the teacher should objectively observe and analyze the nature of the student's successes and difficulties on different types of tasks; (3) the teacher should scrutinize the characteristics of alternative tasks and settings; (4) the teacher should compare and contrast how information gained from step (3) might interact with the observations in steps (2) and (1) so as to result in more favorable achievement; (5) the teacher should consult with the student whenever possible, present the choices for modification, and together decide which ones to try; (6) the teacher should set short-term goals and make the modifications; (7) teach; and (8) evaluate progress after a reasonable time interval and, if successful, continue teaching similar but higher level objectives, or, if unsuccessful, retrace steps 1–7 (p. 361).

Recently there has been a shift away from clinical teaching toward educational design that includes variables associated more with potential and diversity (Duke, 2000).

REFERENCES

Duke, D. L. (2000). *A design for Alana: Creating the next generation of American schools*. Bloomington IN: Phi Delta Kappa International.

Johnson, D., & Mykelbust, H. (1967). *Learning disabilities: Educational principles and practices*. New York, NY: Grune & Stratton.

Learner, J. (1985). *Learning disabilities: Theories, diagnosis, and teaching strategies* (4th ed.). Boston, MA: Houghton Mifflin.

Smith, C. R. (1983). *Learning disabilities: The intervention of learner, task and setting*. Boston, MA: Little, Brown.

Smith, R. M. (1968, 1974). *Clinical teaching: Methods of instruction for the retarded*. New York, NY: McGraw-Hill.

MARIBETH MONTGOMERY KASIK
Governors State University

See also Diagnostic Prescriptive Teaching

CLOSED CIRCUIT TELEVISION

Closed circuit televisions (CCTVs) are assistive devices used by people with low vision to magnify print media. Similar to microfiche readers, CCTVs consist of a camera, viewing screen, and movable media platform. Conventional CCTVs utilize these three components in an integrated device, usually designed to fit on a desktop. Print media is placed on the movable platform, which is located directly below the camera and viewing screen, and can be moved two-dimensionally along the X and Y axes. Clutches on both axes allow the media to be maneuvered smoothly in one axis without jitter in the second axis, thus making the task of reading text easier. Viewing screens, or monitors, are large (usually 21 inches or bigger) and, in modern devices, display color images more often than black-and-white. Integrated circuitry provides convenience features, such as automatic focus, zoom, reverse video, color filtering, and masking controls to display only one line of text at a time.

Hybrid devices have been developed, which provide a mobile solution. For example, a small handheld camera may be paired with a battery-operated viewing screen for easy portability. The technology has even paired handheld cameras with tiny display screens placed in goggles or visors. The user points the mobile camera at the object to be viewed and the image is displayed inside the wearable visor. Lens systems can be used in conjunction with CCTV visors to create a custom solution for the user.

DAVID SWEENEY
Texas A&M University

See also Assistive Technology Act

CLOZE TECHNIQUE

The cloze technique is a procedure that is used for both the assessment and instruction of reading comprehension skills. Based on the psychological construct of closure, the technique was first developed by Taylor (1953), who believed that a person reading a narrative or expository selection psychologically endeavors to complete a pattern of thought and language that is left incomplete. With the cloze technique, such a language pattern is typically a reading passage from which words have been deleted. Typically, in a reading selection of approximately 250 words, every tenth lexical word would be deleted and it would be the reader's task to fill in the missing words.

According to Rye (1982), the cloze technique may be more appropriately considered a construction procedure, whereby the reader uses both linguistic knowledge and past experience to complete sentences in appropriate ways. Experience and language are used to choose the correct grammatical class of words.

Cloze exercises may be developed from basal reader texts, trade books, content area materials, and any other reading selections that are appropriate for a given population of readers. Often, the cloze procedure has been used as a device for the assessment of reading comprehension. As described by Smith and Johnson (1980), it may involve the use of a variety of cloze passages taken from the same reading material. For example, three different passages of approximately 100 words in length may be taken from the beginning, middle, and end of a selection. Then, certain words are deleted (e.g., every 5th or 10th lexical word). The reader's task is to read the passage and write in the missing word on a blank. Ekwall (1985) elaborated on this procedure by stating that the first and last sentences of the selection should be left intact, with every fifth word omitted to be replaced with a blank of 10 spaces in length. Again, the reader is required to read the selection and fill in blank spaces with a word that would seem to fit.

Cloze exercises can be used with either individual students or groups of students. As an assessment tool, there is usually no time limit for the completion of a cloze exercise. The evaluation or scoring of a cloze passage is usually based on a percentage of blank spaces that have been completed correctly. Furthermore, according to Smith and Johnson (1980), only the exact deleted word should be counted as correct. If a student is able to complete approximately 45 to 50% of the omitted spaces correctly, the reading material is judged to be at the reader's instructional level. If 60% or more of the blanks have been filled in correctly, the selection is probably at the reader's independent reading level. If fewer than 45% of the blanks are completed correctly, the material is at the reader's frustration reading level.

In addition to being used as a diagnostic measure, the cloze technique can also be used to improve reading comprehension in an instructional setting. In this manner, the technique can be used as a prereading activity to determine the reader's ability to deal with certain material, and as a postreading activity to develop certain comprehension skills and to practice various comprehension strategies (e.g., the use of context clues in understanding what has been read).

The cloze technique, therefore, based on the construct of perception and closure as defined by the gestalt psychologists, assumes the ability of a fluent reader to predict or anticipate what is coming next in a reading passage. This requires the use of various reading skills, including context clues, knowledge of linguistic patterns, and the ability to comprehend in general what is being read. As Rye (1982) describes, the activity involves a sampling of information from a contextual setting and the formation of hypotheses, a prediction of what will appear subsequently in the selection both linguistically and conceptually. The value of the cloze technique as both a diagnostic and instructional device lies in its demand on the reader's comprehension abilities and a variety of language skills.

REFERENCES

Ekwall, E. E. (1985). *Locating and correcting reading difficulties* (4th ed.). Columbus, OH: Merrill.

Rye, J. (1982). *Cloze procedure and the teaching of reading*. Exeter, NH: Heinemann.

Smith, R. J., & Johnson, D. D. (1980). *Teaching children to read* (2nd ed.). Reading, MA: Addison-Wesley.

Taylor, W. L. (1953). Cloze procedure: A new tool for measuring readability. *Journalism Quarterly, 30*, 415–433.

JOHN M. EELLS
*Souderton Area School District,
Souderton, Pennsylvania*

CLUBFOOT

Clubfoot is a descriptive term for a number of congenital deformities of one or both feet that vary in severity and etiology (Clubfoot.net, 2001). Involving both the soft tissues and the bone of the leg and foot, clubfoot generally occurs in isolation with no known cause, but it may also occur with chromosomal abnormalities and neurological disorders such as cerebral palsy and spina bifida (Dietz, Rebbeck, Blake, & Mathews, 1996; Dormans & Batshaw, 1997). Milder deformations of the foot that apparently arise from the fetus's position in the womb and may correct themselves or need minimal intervention are generally not described as clubfoot (Clubfoot.net, 2001). Most cases of true clubfoot are talipes equinovarus. This is where the joints, tendons, and ligaments incorrectly develop in the foot and ankle. It is characterized by a drawn up heel and pointed downward toes so that the bottom of the foot points straight back. (Clubfoot.net, 2001). This complex disorder affects twice as many boys as girls and has an incidence of 1 in 1,000 children.

Characteristics

1. The child is born with one or both feet turned inward.
2. No pain is associated with the feet.
3. The child also has spina bifida or cerebral palsy.
4. The child is born with any deformity involving solely the feet and ankles.

Clubfoot requires treatment, and early treatment is the most successful. If uncorrected, an affected child will walk on the outside-top surface of the foot, leading to other problems (Clubfoot.net, 2001). Type and timing of treatment vary with severity of the disorder. In mild cases, the only treatment that may be needed is a regimen of regular stretching of foot muscles that parents can be taught to do at home. In most cases, orthopedists use casting as the first treatment, and the cast is put on soon after birth or at a few weeks of age. In casting, the foot is twisted into the correct position and held so that the bones and muscles grow appropriately. This can be mildly painful, but the pain usually lasts only during the casting itself. Casting can take from 3 to 6 months, with the casts changed weekly or biweekly. A splint or special shoes may then be used to prevent regression (Clubfoot.net, 2001). In about 50% of cases, manipulation and casting alone are sufficient to correct the deformity, but regular checkups are required to ensure that the foot does not return to the deformed shape. In the remaining cases, corrective surgery, performed between 3 and 12 months of age, is needed to release all tight tendons and ligaments. The surgery is complex and difficult, with recurrences of the deformity occasionally occurring. Again, regular checkups are called for.

With early and effective treatment, prognosis is good, and those born with clubfoot can have normal or near-normal foot appearance and mobility. If untreated, the foot will continue to grow in its twisted position and cause permanent mobility problems. No further intervention is generally needed, but parents should consult with their orthopedist concerning sports and physical education activities.

REFERENCES

Clubfoot.net (2001, March 20). *Clubfoot*. Retrieved from http://www.clubfoot.net/clubfoot.php3

Dietz, F. R., Rebbeck, T. R., Blake, D. D., & Mathews, K. D. (1996). An idiopathic clubfoot family does not show linkage to the chromosome region linked to distal arthrogryposis I. *Pediatrics, 98*, 560–561.

Dormans, J. P., & Batshaw, M. L. (1997). Muscles, bones, and nerves. In M. L. Batshaw (Ed.), *Children with disabilities* (4th ed., pp. 315–332). Baltimore, MD: Paul H. Brookes.

ROBERT T. BROWN
AMY M. MORROW
University of North Carolina

CLUTTERING

Cluttering is a speech disorder—or, more specifically, a fluency disorder—related to stuttering. Importantly, the two disorders are not the same. Cluttering is characterized by excessive breaks in the normal flow of speech that result from disorganized speech planning, talking too fast or in a jerky fashion, or simply being unsure of what one wants to say. By contrast, the person who stutters typically knows exactly what he or she wants to say but is temporarily unable to say it, thus repeating or prolonging sounds or syllables, blocking, and/or using accessory (secondary) devices (e.g., eye-blinks, synonyms for difficult words, or abnormal facial postures; Daly, 1992; St. Louis & Myers, 1997). Because cluttering is not well-known, there is much ambiguity about the disorder. For example, the speech of many people who clutter is often described by themselves or others as stuttering. Moreover, cluttering frequently coexists with stuttering and some authorities question whether a reliable definition of cluttering has been established (e.g., Curlee, 1996).

The definition of cluttering recently adopted by the fluency disorders division of the American Speech-Language-Hearing Association is "a fluency disorder characterized by a rapid and/or irregular speaking rate, excessive disfluencies, and often other symptoms such as language or phonological errors and attention deficits" (St. Louis, Hanley, & Hood, 1998). Clutterers' speech does not sound fluent; in other words, they do not appear to be clear about either what they want to say or how to say it. They manifest excessive levels of normal disfluencies, such as interjections (e.g., "um," or "you know") and revisions (e.g., "We went over . . . we started to go to Grandma's . . ."; St. Louis, Hinzman, & Hull, 1985). They manifest little or no physical struggle in speaking and they have few, if any, accessory behaviors. A rapid and/or irregular speaking rate would be present in a speaker who shows symptoms of speaking too fast, whether based on actual syllable-per-minute counts or simply an overall impression; sounding jerky; or using pauses during speech that are too short, too long, or improperly placed.

These fluency and rate deviations are often considered to be the essential symptoms of cluttering (St. Louis, 1992). Other characteristics may also be present but are not mandatory. These include confusing, disorganized language or conversational skills, often with word-finding difficulties; limited awareness of fluency or rate problems; temporary improvement when asked to slow down or to pay attention to speech (or when being tape recorded); specific sound misarticulations, slurred speech, or deleting nonstressed syllables in longer words (e.g., "ferchly" for "fortunately"); speech that is difficult to understand; a family history of stuttering and/or cluttering; social or vocational problems; learning disabilities; attention-deficit/hyperactivity disorder; sloppy handwriting; difficulty with organizational skills for daily activities; and/or auditory perceptual difficulties (Daly, 1992; St. Louis & Myers, 1995, 1997; Weiss, 1964).

A team approach to assessment and diagnosis with cluttering is often necessary. In addition to a standard speech evaluation by a speech-language pathologist (SLP), contributions or reports from classroom teachers, special educators, psychologists, or (possibly) neuropsychologists may also be warranted. The SLP evaluation will carefully assess the fluency problem, but also any coexisting oral-motor, language, or articulation problems. If the suspected clutterer is in school, special education personnel may be asked to provide information on learning, social problems, and attention or behavioral problems, and psychologists could be requested to provide test information on academic achievement or intelligence. The eventual diagnosis should specify whether cluttering is present and also what other problems are present, such as stuttering, a language disorder, or a learning disability (St. Louis & Myers, 1997).

Therapy for clutterers generally addresses the contributing problems before focusing directly on fluency. Ordinarily, one of the first goals of therapy is to reduce the speaking rate, although this may not be easy for the clutterer to achieve. Some clutterers respond well to "timing" their speech to a delayed auditory feedback (DAF) device; some do not. Another technique that has been found helpful with younger clutterers is to use the analogy of a speedometer wherein rapid speech is above the speed limit, and "speeding tickets" are given for exceeding the limit (St. Louis & Myers, 1995, 1997).

Articulation and language symptoms are often reduced if the clutterer can achieve a slower rate. Sometimes, however, these problems need to be addressed directly. One technique involves practice first in using short, highly structured utterances. It may also be helpful for clutterers to learn to exaggerate stressed syllables in longer words while being sure to include all the unstressed syllables (e.g., "par-tic'u-lar," "con-di'-tion-al," or "gen-er-o'-si-ty"; St. Louis & Myers, 1997).

Some clutterers benefit from planning both the content (the *what*) of a message as well as the delivery (the *how*). For example, the *what* can be taught as formulating a telegram (e.g., "Car won't start. I pump accelerator. Carburetor gets flooded."). The *how* then focuses on filling in the appropriate small words (e.g., "My car often won't start after it sits for a few minutes. I pump the accelerator a few times before trying again. Often, the carburetor gets flooded."; Myers & Bradley, 1992).

As noted, many clutterers also stutter, and often the cluttering is masked by the stuttering. In some of these individuals, the cluttering emerges as the individual gets control of the stuttering or begins to stutter less (Van Riper, 1992). Yet, whether or not the clutterer also stutters (or previously stuttered), any therapy techniques that focus attention on fluency targets, such as easy onset of the voice, more prolonged syllables, or correct breathing, can also help the person to manage many of the cluttering symptoms. The important thing is that the clutterer learn to pay attention to—or monitor—his or her speech and do anything that makes it easier to remember to do so (Craig, 1996; Langevin & Boberg, 1996).

Lack of awareness is a particularly difficult clinical problem, for many clutterers are genuinely unaware of the extent of their cluttering behaviors. They must be taught to be careful observers of listener feedback. Some older clutterers are better able to monitor if they listen daily to a tape with a short sample of their disorganized cluttered speech and, immediately following, a sample of their clear, monitored speech (Daly, 1992).

It is currently impossible to predict with accuracy whether a clutterer will benefit from speech therapy. Most who benefit have become convinced from friends, family, or employers (or on their own) that they do have a significant speech problem. Also, motivation is a key element; successful clients typically have good reason for working hard to change, such as the likelihood of a job promotion. On the other hand, clutterers who are not sure that they have a problem, or are relatively unconcerned about it, tend not to improve as much or as easily from therapy (Daly, 1992; St. Louis & Myers, 1997).

REFERENCES

Craig, A. (1996). Long-term effects of intensive treatment for a client with both a cluttering and stuttering disorder. In K. O. St. Louis (Ed.), *Research and opinion on cluttering: State of the art and science*, Special issue of the *Journal of Fluency Disorders, 21*, 329–335.

Curlee, R. F. (1996). Cluttering: Data in search of understanding. In K. O. St. Louis (Ed.), *Research and opinion on cluttering: State of the art and science*, Special issue of the *Journal of Fluency Disorders, 21*, 315–327.

Daly, D. A. (1992). Helping the clutterer: Therapy considerations. In F. L. Myers & K. O. St. Louis. *Cluttering: A clinical perspective* (pp. 107–124). Kibworth, UK: Far Communications. (Reissued in 1996 by Singular Press, San Diego, California.)

Langevin, M., & Boberg, E. (1996). Results of intensive stuttering therapy with adults who clutter and stutter. In K. O. St. Louis (Ed.), *Research and opinion on cluttering: State of the art and science*, Special issue of the *Journal of Fluency Disorders, 21*, 315–327.

Myers, F. L., & Bradley, C. L. (1992). Clinical management of cluttering from a synergistic framework. In F. L. Myers & K. O. St. Louis (Eds.), *Cluttering: A clinical perspective* (pp. 85–105). Kibworth, UK: Far Communications. (Reissued in 1996 by Singular Press, San Diego, California.)

St. Louis, K. O. (1992). On defining cluttering. In F. L. Myers & K. O. St. Louis (Eds.), *Cluttering: A clinical perspective* (pp. 37–53). Kibworth, UK: Far Communications. (Reissued in 1996 by Singular Press, San Diego, California.)

St. Louis, K. O., Hanley, J. M., & Hood, S. B. (1998). *Terminology pertaining to fluency and fluency disorders*. Final report of the Terminology Task Force of the Special Interest Division on Fluency and Fluency Disorders of the American Speech-Language-Hearing Association.

St. Louis, K. O., Hinzman, A. R., & Hull, F. M. (1985). Studies of cluttering: Disfluency and language measures in young possible clutterers and stutterers. *Journal of Fluency Disorders, 10*, 151–172.

St. Louis, K. O., & Myers, F. L. (1995). Clinical management of cluttering. *Language, Speech, and Hearing Services in Schools, 25*, 187–195.

St. Louis, K. O., & Myers, F. L. (1997). Management of cluttering and related fluency disorders. In R. Curlee & G. Siegel (Eds.), *Nature and treatment of stuttering: New directions* (pp. 313–332). New York, NY: Allyn & Bacon.

Van Riper, C. (1992). Foreword. In F. L. Myers, & K. O. St. Louis, *Cluttering: A clinical perspective* (pp. vii–ix). Kibworth, UK: Far Communications. (Reissued in 1996 by Singular Press, San Diego, California.)

Weiss, D. (1964). *Cluttering*. Englewood Cliffs, NJ: Prentice Hall.

KENNETH O. ST. LOUIS
West Virginia University

COACHING/FACILITATING, POSITIVE BEHAVIOR SUPPORT

Technical Assistance Centers across the nation have initiated development of coaching curriculum and technical support at the primary, secondary, and tertiary tiers. In particular, the Office of Special Education Programs Technical Assistance Center on Positive Behavioral Interventions and Supports (OSEP TA Center on PBIS) curriculum embeds the skills necessary to implement PBIS while allowing school personnel to take ownership in systems change by aligning it with their school's needs and culture. One critical element to the curriculum and support provided is the development of a leadership team to oversee PBIS activities through an established coaching network. While capacity building maintains the goal of starting a coach's network, current research on the definitions, dimensions, and assumptions underlying effective coaching have recently grown across education and human services. According to Fixsen, Blasé, Horner & Sugai, (2009), as this new knowledge increases, and as coaches/facilitators providing technical assistance will need to be supported with best practices, there will be a need to integrate this knowledge into action. It is clear that coaching is an integral part of initiating and sustaining PBIS implementation, particularly when districts and states start "scaling up."

A PBS District Leadership Team's primary function is to engage in leadership and coordination functions that support and sustain integrity in implementation of a continuum of evidence-based School-wide Positive Behavior Support (SWPBS) practices. The Leadership Team's activities are configured around guiding principles in the SWPBS Implementation Blueprint: (a) capacity building for training, coaching, evaluation, and coordination; (b) administrative participation for political support, visibility, funding, and policy; and (c) demonstrations of school and district implementation (George & Kincaid, 2008; George, Kincaid, & Pollard-Sage, 2009; Sugai et al., 2010). Coaching is one of the critical components for the District Leadership Team to develop in order to achieve fidelity and sustain efforts. As such, these coaches or facilitators are highly qualified technical assistance providers positioned to coach, facilitate, and evaluate implementation of PBIS across states, districts, and schools. Preliminary research has indicated that without a well-developed and implemented coaching network, schools experience low implementation fidelity (e.g., George & Kincaid, 2008).

Definition and Functions

According to the *SWPBS Implementors' Blueprint*: To support school team implementation of SWPBS, an overt and formalized network is needed to link training experiences and actual use of the SWPBS systems and practices. Coaching, or facilitation, capacity refers to the system's ability to organize personnel and resources for facilitating, assisting, maintaining, and adapting local school training implementation efforts (Sugai et al., p. 84). Coaching can be defined as a set of responsibilities, actions, and activities that bridge the gap between training and implementation. Individuals possess the skills to coach when fluent with the trained curriculum, and experienced with implementation, and engage adults in the learning process. Functions of a coach include guidance and technical assistance in the application of PBIS practices, resource access, problem solving, data-based decision making, positive reinforcement, prompting, and providing an ongoing communication network (Sugai, 2010).

Individuals who assume coaching responsibilities must have technical skills as well as facilitation skills. Technical skills focus on fluency with the systems, data, and practices of PBIS. A coach must be able to adapt the trained concepts/skills to local contexts and challenges, redirect misapplications, and increase fidelity and improve sustainability of overall implementation. Coaching is done by someone with credibility and experience with the target skill(s), within natural settings and over a period of time. In addition to technical skills, facilitation skills are necessary to build capacity of implementation by enhancing group work. Coaches need to be skilled at constructing and posing questions, using nonjudgmental responses, as well as facilitating appropriate nonverbal behaviors to establish and maintain rapport (Horner, 2009).

Coaching Activities

Coaching includes activities related to developing the organizational capacity of whole schools. Activities include: helping principals and teachers reallocate their resources, improving administration's use of data for improved instruction, one-on-one observations, feedback of teachers' instructional strategies, and small-group training (Neufeld & Roper, 2010). Examples of coaches' training curriculum can be found by following training links on the www.pbis.org website. Local, regional, state, and national coaches' training and technical assistance offer professional development courses and ongoing opportunities to refine and practice skill development. Coaching skill areas emphasize basic PBIS coaching at all three tiers, classroom-based application of PBIS, developing Tier Two/Three systems, and use of data for decision making at the school-wide and advanced tier levels. Annual leadership conferences with sessions provided by state and national PBIS leadership, APBS members, and district and school leaders are readily available across the country. These conferences help coaches acquire and maintain skills to better support PBIS implementation. Audience-specific conferences, forums, and summits (including alternative schools, early childhood centers, middle school, high school, and coaches) are being developed.

Types of Coaches

Coaching involves school-based professional development designed within the district's strategic plan and is guided by the goal of meeting schools' specific instructional learning needs as outlined in their school improvement plans. Although there are many different people that may serve in a coaching capacity, Neufeld and Roper (2010) describe two main areas of coaches: change and content. *Change coaches* address whole-school, organizational improvement. They help schools investigate existing resources (e.g., time, money, personnel, etc.), assist in effective reorganization, and develop the leadership skills of both teachers and principals. *Content coaches* focus almost exclusively on improving teachers' instructional strategies in specific content areas (e.g., math, literacy, etc.). These coaches work directly with teachers rather than with principals. Regardless of how a district decides to use coaches whose work is directly tied to instruction, or supports the collaborative learning environment of the school (i.e., systems change), or both, all coaches must address issues of instructional capacity.

Others have outlined various coaching functions and responsibilities depending upon their location: external (offsite or district-level) or internal (site-based or school-level). These types of coaches also provide the energy and expertise needed to explore, implement, and sustain tiered behavioral supports for all students that include the following: a district-level administrator, a district skills coach, a building-based skills coach, and coaches for advanced tiers of support (e.g., Illinois PBIS Network District Readiness Checklist, v. 10.3.08).

District PBIS Administrator

The District PBIS Administrator or Coordinator is a central office administrator who has the authority to support

PBIS implementation. The District PBIS Administrator has a good understanding of school improvement, including Response to Intervention (RtI) three-tier models for academic and behavioral supports, and an operational knowledge of all tiers of PBIS, and can apply data-based decision making as it applies to school improvement. Similar to a change coach, the district administrator coaches/facilitates the district decision makers (i.e., leadership team) to invest in the change process to produce quality implementation and sustainability of the implementation. Recommended description of duties includes:

Convene and conduct regularly scheduled meetings of the District PBIS Leadership Team.

Facilitate district strategic/action planning for PBIS.

Ensure that PBIS is consistent with the District's Strategic Plan and School Improvement Plan.

Develop district budget for PBIS.

Make presentations to the District Board of Education on the status of PBIS in the district.

Develop a process for recognizing schools for their accomplishments with PBIS.

Facilitate the development and maintenance of a district website for PBIS.

Develop a system and schedule of staff development for PBIS.

Facilitate the sustainability and expansion of PBIS in the district.

Support attendance of district staff at related trainings and conferences.

Facilitate visibility of PBIS within the district and in the community.

Act as a liaison between the District Leadership Team and the Board of Education.

Facilitate district coach's meetings.

Provide support to the district external and internal coaches.

Attend yearly PBIS state-wide booster trainings (i.e., conferences, forums, etc.).

Keep the district superintendent abreast of the progress and barriers to implementing PBIS within the district.

Work collaboratively with principals to ensure PBIS implementation fidelity.

Facilitate the "working smarter" concept of PBIS by helping to blend PBIS with other similar district initiatives.

District External Coaches/Facilitators

District External Coaches/Facilitators support PBIS schools through their existing roles in districts, or other professional service providers such as Special Education Cooperatives, Intermediate Service Centers, and Regional Offices of Education. The responsibilities of individuals in existing positions (i.e., school psychologist, counselor, special education consultant, behavior specialist) can be modified to include PBIS external coaching functions. They are members of the District PBIS Leadership Team, have experience and training with PBIS, including school-wide, classroom, and individual plans, and ability to coach multiple school teams. They guide the school-based coaches and serve as a conduit for communication between the building-level teams and the District Leadership Team. Recommended description of duties includes:

Participate in district and building-level team meetings.

Identify schools, get administrative support, help schools identify team members for initial training.

Become familiar with district's and/or schools' policies/procedures (e.g., handbooks, budgets, staff development).

Support building-level team meetings by providing technical assistance (e.g., meeting dates, calendar tasks, agenda, communication with staff and others—community, parents, news) and assist with action plan development at all three tiers.

Provide ongoing support and technical assistance to internal coaches through district-level coaches' meetings.

Oversee progress of district teams (e.g., faculty, team, district, and principals)

Insure school-wide data collection systems are established.

Collect process and impact data from schools and resource to decision makers, as needed.

Collaborate with state-wide PBIS projects/centers to utilize and analyze data collected.

Provide technical assistance on school-wide data analysis and secondary and tertiary interventions.

Assist schools in sustaining PBIS.

Participate in subregion, statewide, and national trainings for PBIS.

Provide school-based trainings.

Internal Coaches/Team Leaders

Internal Coaches/Team Leaders are building-based personnel who have been identified to provide PBIS leadership within their building, such as a content coach. They have attended PBIS trainings with their team and work to ensure that PBIS is implemented with integrity in their building. As a faculty member, they know the school's systems, data, and practices and maintain communication with the School Improvement Process. Internal coaches know the research and practices related to SWPBS, including applied behavior analysis, and ability to use a variety of observational and interviewing skills. They may be in the position of social worker, classroom teacher, or tiered interventionist. Time is allotted for them to lead the building-level PBIS team in the implementation process. Recommended description of duties includes:

Data collection in building (i.e., big five and academic data).

Ensure expectations are taught, reinforced, and monitored at the school-wide level.

Ensure proper implementation of celebrations/boosters.

Facilitation of monthly Tier 1/Universal Team meetings, including creating an agenda, following an efficient and effective teaming model.

Communication of PBIS activities at faculty meetings.

Collect and analyze PBIS specific data.

Communicate with parent/parent liaison/PTA/PTO.

Annual report shared with district team (i.e., District Leadership Team, Board of Education).

Network with other internal coaches, external coaches, and subregion coordinators

District Tiers Two/Three Coach/Facilitator

District Tiers Two/Three (Secondary/Tertiary) Coaches/ Facilitators are building or district-based personnel who have been identified to provide PBIS leadership to one or more buildings around individual student supports. Counselors, social workers, and behavior specialists often emerge as the site leaders at this level. Recommended description (includes both change and content coach levels) of Tier Two/Three coaches includes:

Co-facilitate and coach Tier 2/Secondary and Tier 3/Tertiary Team process meetings in each building.

Provide technical assistance and support to Tiers 2/3 team members and Wraparound Facilitators.

Assist with data collection and data-based decision-making process.

District-level support

Data collection and reporting to state PBIS center/project.

Co-facilitate district Tier 3/Tertiary team meetings.

Facilitate district-level data analysis, review.

Facilitate expansion and sustainability of practices district-wide.

Trainings

Actively participate in all Tier 3/Tertiary trainings provided by state center/project.

Assist building and district staff in training readiness and participation during trainings.

Technical assistance regarding:

Effective team meetings

Support to students & families

Full continuum of Tiers 2/3 supports, including FBA/BIP and wraparound

Wraparound facilitation

Data-based decision making

Liaison

To/from state PBIS center/project

To/from building Tier 3/Tertiary teams

To/from district Tier 3/Tertiary team

To/from district staff (not involved with selected schools)

Effects on the Classroom

To improve teachers' and students' learning requires professional development that is closely and explicitly tied to teachers' ongoing work in the classroom through coaching. Research has shown the positive effect that coaching support has on teacher practice. Coaching has been linked to increased teacher efficacy, one of the most vital factors in the successful implementation of change (Fullan, 2003). Teachers who possess more self-efficacy approach their work with more energy, persevere when faced with challenges, and generally have a more positive attitude toward teaching; they are the teachers desired in the classrooms. Similarly, teachers who are coached consistently have increased self-efficacy (Costa & Garmston, 2002; Fullan, 2003; Joyce & Showers, 2002; Wong, 2008). Even more striking than the research on efficacy is the evidence that coaching dramatically increases teachers' capacity to implement new instructional practices in the classroom. When all training components are included and teachers are provided with ongoing coaching support upon return to their classrooms, 95% of participants demonstrate thorough content knowledge and demonstrate skill and proficiency with the materials following training. With the addition of coaching, Joyce & Showers (2002) demonstrated that 95% of participants successfully transferred their new knowledge and skills into classroom application.

Coaching Capacity

Strengthening the coaching network continues to be a major focus of scaling-up PBIS. With the support of both building-level and district-level technical assistance, the complex endeavor of developing PBIS systems along a continuum can be created by local expertise and augmented by network proficiency (Eber, 2010). In fact, the transfer of knowledge to the arena of practice would be impossible without the influence of these highly trained technical assistance providers, both change and content coaches, at the state, district, and building level.

Successful coaching depends not only on the knowledge and skill of individual coaches but also on a number of district- and school-level factors that may enhance or impede a coach's efforts. Coaching activities are highly localized (e.g., onsite at a school) and the principal plays a key role in the program, but success ultimately depends on district support for coaching at the school level. Districts need to shape the coaches' role, focus the coaches' work around the district's strategic goals, and articulate the connection between that work and schools' overall improvement plan. Creating and supporting effective professional development through coaching is a complex responsibility that requires careful planning. Challenges can be overcome provided that the following areas are addressed during the strategic planning: (a) allocating coaches, (b) finding time to do the work, (c) changing teachers' practices, and (d) measuring the quality and impact of coaches' work (Neufeld & Roper, 2003).

The importance of coaching is directly tied to sustainability. Unless district-level ownership of PBIS systems, processes, and data are nurtured through training and state-level technical assistance, the support for school-level PBIS systems will not be maintained independently over time (Eber, 2010). The *OSEP TA Center on PBIS* has provided an *Implementors' Blueprint* where three of the 38 critical features (items 25–27) focus on coaching: (25) leadership team that has developed a coaching network that establishes and sustains SWPBS, (26) individuals who are available to provide coaching and facilitation supports on a monthly basis with each emerging school team and at least quarterly with established teams, and (27) coaching functions are identified and established for internal (school-level) and external (district/regional-level) coaching supports (Sugai et al., 2010). The *Blueprint* is designed to guide large-scale implementation of specific systems or an organizational approach, such as SWPBS.

Future Directions

The practical skill sets that coaches need to guide PBIS implementation are being refined and practiced across the country, and research is expanding. The collaborative facilitation skills of coaches are emerging and identified as a core feature to sustain evidence-based practices. The emphasis on coaching will continue to increase as the State Implementation of Scaling-up Evidence-based Practices (SISEP) Center advances research in the implementation of effective educational practices. Collaborative culture training is taking place through this initiative and being delivered at the coaching level. PBIS implementers are adapting and adopting resources from the Center for Adaptive Schools and Cognitive Coaching to develop coaches who are highly skilled as facilitators. This implementation research is guiding the process for improvement in scaling-up evidence-based practices, and includes emphasis on coaching recruitment, training, technical assistance, and accountability (SISEP, 2008; Fixsen, 2009). Districts interested in implementing PBIS need to establish a district leadership team, build coaching expertise within their district, and provide training and technical assistance in PBIS systems, data, and practices to support all tiers of interventions.

REFERENCES

Costa, A., & Garmston, R. (2002). *Cognitive coaching: A foundation for renaissance schools*. Norwood, MA: Christopher-Gordon.

Eber, L. E. (2010). *Illinois PBIS Network, FY10 Annual Report*. Retrieved from http://www.pbisillinois.org/Online_Library/Downloads/Reports/FY10_Annual_Rpt

Fixsen, D. L., Blasé, K. A., Horner, R. & Sugai, G. (2009). *Intensive technical assistance. Scaling up Brief #2*. Chapel Hill: The University of North Carolina, FPG, SISEP.

Fullan, M. (2003). *Change forces with a vengeance*. New York, NY: Routledge Falmer.

George, H. P., & Kincaid, D. (2008). Building district-wide capacity for positive behavior support. *Journal of Positive Behavioral Interventions, 10*, 20–32.

George, H. P., Kincaid, D., & Pollard-Sage, J. (2009). Primary tier interventions and supports. In W. Sailor, G. Dunlap, G. Sugai, & R. Horner (Eds.), *Handbook of positive behavior support* (pp. 375–394). Lawrence, KS: Issues in Clinical Child Psychology.

Horner, R. (2009) *Importance of coaching in implementation of evidence-based practices* [PowerPoint slides]. Retrieved from http:www.pbis.org

Joyce, B., & Showers, B. (2002). Student achievement through staff development. *ASCD* (3).

Neufeld, B., & Roper, D. (2010). *Coaching: A strategy for developing instructional capacity*. Cambridge, MA: Education Matters.

State Implementation & Scaling-up of Evidence-based Practices. (2008). Retrieved from http://scalingup.org

Sugai, G. (2010). *Coaching considerations* [PowerPoint slides]. Retrieved from http:www.pbis.org

Sugai, G., Horner, R. H., Algozzine, R., Barrett, S., Lewis, T., Anderson, C.,...Simonsen, B. (2010). *School-wide positive behavior support: Implementers' blueprint and self-assessment*. Eugene: University of Oregon.

Wong, H. (2008). *Academic coaching produces more effective teachers*. Retrieved from www.teachers.net

MARLA RAE DEWHIRST
Illinois PBIS Network
Fourth edition

COATS' DISEASE

Coats' disease, or exudative retinitis, is a rare eye disorder that is characterized by a white or yellowish matter called telangiectatic malformations in the macular area or peripheral retina. The abnormal enlargement of the retinal blood vessels results in leakage of the yellow matter into the retina. This disease usually occurs within the first 10 years of life and may result in loss of vision or detachment of the retina (National Organization for Rare Disorders, Inc. [NORD], 1999). The specific etiology of Coats' disease is unknown, but it is believed to be an anomaly in the embryologic development of retinal blood vessels (Thoene & Coker, 1995).

Coats' disease affects more males than females and usually occurs in childhood. When Coats' disease occurs in the adult population it is called hyperlipemic retinitis (NORD, 1999).

Characteristics

1. Early signs consisting of large yellowish areas in and below the retina
2. Dilated telangiectatic blood vessels in the peripheral retina
3. Usually occurs only in one eye and affects central vision or peripheral vision
4. Subretinal bleeding if retinal detachment occurs
5. May cause strabismus (squinting)

Coats' disease is sometimes treated by photocoagulation (surgery) or cryotherapy (freezing) in order to destroy the yellowish areas or telangiectatic malformations. Removal of abnormal blood vessels will not necessarily restore vision if too much fluid leaked into the retina (Thoene & Coker, 1995). Corticosteroid drugs may also be used to alleviate symptoms.

Special education services may be available for children with Coats' disease under vision problems if the disorder results in vision loss.

Treatment that is applied early may be successful in preventing progression of Coats' disease and improving vision. Coats' disease may progress to other severe symptoms such as retinal detachment, secondary cataracts, fibrous mass in the retina, rubeosis iridis, swelling of the membrane covering the back of the eyeball (secondary uveitis), secondary glaucoma, or shrinkage of the eyeball (Thoene & Coker, 1995).

REFERENCES

National Organization for Rare Disorders, Inc. (1999). *Coats' disease*. Retrieved from http://www.rarediseases.org

Thoene, J. G., & Coker, N. P. (Eds.). (1995). *Physicians guide to rare diseases* (2nd ed.). Montvale, NJ: Dowden.

JENNIFER HARGRAVE
University of Texas at Austin

COCAINE ABUSE

Cocaine is a powerfully addictive stimulant that became extremely popular and widely used in the 1980s and 1990s. It is typically sold on the street as a fine, white, crystalline powder. Cocaine can be sniffed or snorted, injected, or smoked. Street names include *coke*, *C*, *snow*, *flake*, or *blow* (National Institute on Drug Abuse, 2001a).

Cocaine makes the user feel instantly alert and creates a false sense of joy or a high that generally wears off within 30 minutes. As the effects of the drug wear off, the user may feel anxious, depressed, and tired (American Academy of Pediatrics, 2000). Cocaine appears to block the normal flow of dopamine, a neurotransmitter, in the brain. It carries messages from one nerve cell to another and is associated with awareness, motivation, body movement, judgment, and pleasure. Dopamine appears to be responsible for the addictive effects of cocaine (Swan, 1998).

Crack, the street name for the freebase form of cocaine, is made by processing powdered cocaine so that it is smokable. It is called crack because of the crackling sound heard when the substance is smoked. Crack is inexpensive both to produce and to buy. Smoking cocaine allows extremely high doses of the drug to reach the brain very rapidly, resulting in an intense and immediate high, generally within 10 seconds (National Institute on Drug Abuse, 2001b). As a result, crack is said to be almost instantly addictive (American Medical Association, 1999).

Research examining the extent of cocaine use among adolescents in this country indicates that approximately 4.7% of 8th graders, 7.7% of 10th graders, and 9.8% of 12th graders have used cocaine at least once in their lifetimes. Data indicate increases in this area during the 1990s, although the extent of use for high school seniors is significantly less than its peak of 17.3% in 1985 (National Institute on Drug Abuse, 2001b). Factors that appear to increase the risk for substance abuse include previous treatment with therapeutic drugs, low achievement, low self-esteem, and having an alcoholic parent (Fox & Forbing, 1991).

Short-Term Effects

1. Increased energy
2. Euphoria
3. Decreased appetite

4. Mental alertness

5. Increased heart rate and blood pressure

6. Constricted blood vessels

7. Increased temperature

8. Dilated pupils

Cocaine's effects appear almost immediately after taking the drug. In addition to the short-term effects, cocaine may cause anxiety, irritability, confusion, and tremors. Some users experience hallucinations, including what is known as coke bugs, or a sensation of insects crawling over the skin (American Medical Association, 1999). Taking large amounts of the drug (several milligrams or more) not only intensifies the high but also can result in erratic, bizarre, and violent behavior (National Institute on Drug Abuse, 2001a).

Long-Term Effects

1. Addiction

2. Irritability and mood disturbances

3. Restlessness

4. Paranoia

5. Auditory hallucinations

A discernible tolerance to cocaine tends to develop with regular and continued use. Many users report that successive highs are not as pleasurable as the first one, and they increase their doses to intensify and prolong the euphoric effects. Taking the drug repeatedly and at high doses (a binge) can result in a full-blown paranoid psychosis (National Institute of Drug Abuse, 2001a).

A number of serious medical complications are also associated with cocaine use. These include abdominal pain and nausea, disturbances in heart rhythm, heart attack, chest pain, respiratory failure, and neurological problems that range from headaches to seizures and strokes. In rare instance, sudden death can occur. Other adverse effects are related to the manner in which the cocaine is used. Nose-bleeds, loss of smell, problems swallowing, and a chronically inflamed, runny nose can all result from snorting cocaine. Injecting the drug can result in puncture marks and tracks, and sometimes an allergic reaction (National Institute on Drug Abuse, 2001a).

Treatment of cocaine abuse and addiction tends to be rather complex, and it must address a variety of problems because abuse and addiction involve not only biological changes in the brain but a number of social, familial, and environmental factors as well. Behavioral treatments, especially cognitive-behavioral therapy, can be effective in decreasing drug use. Generally, this approach involves helping users recognize, avoid, and cope with problems and dysfunctional behaviors associated with drug use. The use of a token economy or contingency management can also be effective with cocaine abusers and addicts. With

this type of system, the user receives positive rewards for continuing treatment and remaining drug free (National Institute on Drug Abuse, 2001a). Crisis intervention may also be helpful in addressing some of the acute problems associated with abuse and addiction (Newcomb & Bentler, 1989). In addition, a number of medications are currently being evaluated in clinical trials to examine their safety and effectiveness in treating cocaine addiction (National Institute on Drug Abuse, 2001b).

Research indicates that students receiving special education services, such as those with learning disabilities and emotional or behavior disorders, may demonstrate higher rates of substance abuse and chemical dependence than do regular education students (e.g., Elmquist, Morgan, & Bolds, 1992; Karacostas & Fisher, 1993). Because of these risks, it is important that special education programs include preventive efforts such as drug education, affective skill building, and coping skills training. Research also indicates that the effects of substance abuse can result in behaviors similar to those exhibited by youth with learning problems (Fox & Forbing, 1991). Comprehensive and appropriate assessment is necessary to differentiate students with learning disorders and students abusing drugs. Future research is focusing on developing effective medications to treat addiction, as well as evaluating the efficacy of various prevention programs and therapeutic interventions.

REFERENCES

American Academy of Pediatrics. (2000). *Cocaine*. Retrieved from http://www.ama.org

American Medical Association. (1999). *Substance abuse: Types of drugs and their effects*. Retrieved from http://www.ama.org

Elmquist, D. L., Morgan, D. P., & Bolds, P. K. (1992). Alcohol and other drug abuse among adolescents with disabilities. *International Journal of the Addictions, 27*(12), 1475–1483.

Fox, C. L., & Forbing, S. E. (1991). Overlapping symptoms of substance abuse and learning handicaps: Implications for educators. *Journal of Learning Disabilities, 24*(1), 24–31.

Karacostas, D. D., & Fisher, G. L. (1993). Chemical dependency in students with and without learning disabilities. *Journal of Learning Disabilities, 26*(7), 491–195.

National Institute on Drug Abuse. (2001a). *Cocaine abuse and addiction*. Retrieved from http://www.nida.nih.gov/Research Reports/Cocaine/cocaine3.html#short

National Institute on Drug Abuse. (2001b). *Crack and cocaine*. Retrieved from http://www.nida.nih.gov/Infofax/cocaine.html

Newcomb, M. D., & Bentler, P. M. (1989). Substance use and abuse among children and teens. *American Psychologist, 44*, 242–248.

Swan, N. (1998). *Brain scans open window to view cocaine's effects on the brain*. Retrieved from http://165.112.78.61/NIDA_Notes /NNVol13N2/Brain.html

M. FRANCI CREPEAU-HOBSON
University of Northern Colorado

COCKAYNE SYNDROME

Cockayne syndrome (CS) is rare genetic disorder, autosomally recessive, of unknown prevalence. Males and females are equally affected. In CS, growth and development are normal for at least the first year followed by neurodevelopmental retardation that may not become especially prominent in many cases until 4 or 5 years of age.

In the early stages of CS, these children are often misdiagnosed with ADHD or with various coordination disorders. Typically, mental retardation develops in the childhood years and may be mild to severe. Photosensitivity is common and peripheral neuropathy develops. Small stature with large ears occurs routinely. Leukodystrophy occurs in all cases along with premature death. There is no cure, and the only treatment is symptom management. Diagnosis is by physical examination and CT or MRI (Gillberg, 1995). Symptoms are usually well-expressed by age 10 years.

Special education will typically be required for intellectual impairment and externalizing behavior problems. Dwarfism and emotional symptoms may occur as well, and may require special assistance. Thorough psychoeducational evaluations on a yearly basis are required due to the severity of the disorder and the rapid changes that may occur in behavior, intellect, and motor skills.

Characteristics

1. Growth deficiency and microcephaly following a period of normal growth, with severe dwarfism as the final result. There is also a loss of subcutaneous fat and adipose tissue that results in a precociously senile appearance.

2. Mental retardation that is progressive. The decrease in mental abilities appears to be related to atrophy of brain tissue and demyelination of nerves. There are also accompanying language delays with more than 20% of cases never progressing beyond the single-word stage.

3. Severe sensitivity to sunlight. Minimal exposure generally results in a red, scaly rash that is followed by scarring, excessive pigmentation, and atrophies of the skin.

4. Cataracts and retinal atrophy are common with increasing age, and there is a risk of blindness. In addition, the eyes often have a hollow, sunken appearance, and lid closure tends to be poor.

5. Malformed or prominent ears and sensorineural deafness.

6. Decreased muscle tone and reflexes resulting in a gait disturbance.

REFERENCE

Gillberg, C. (1995). *Clinical child neuropsychiatry*. Cambridge, UK: Cambridge University Press.

CECIL R. REYNOLDS
Texas A&M University

CODE OF FAIR TESTING PRACTICES IN EDUCATION

The Code of Fair Testing Practices in Education (Code) is a guide for professionals in fulfilling their obligation to provide and use tests that are fair to all test takers regardless of age, gender, disability, race, ethnicity, national origin, religion, sexual orientation, linguistic background, or other personal characteristics. Fairness is a primary consideration in all aspects of testing. Careful standardization of tests and administration conditions helps to ensure that all test takers are given a comparable opportunity to demonstrate what they know and how they can perform in the area being tested. Fairness implies that every test taker has the opportunity to prepare for the test and is informed about the general nature and content of the test, as appropriate to the purpose of the test. Fairness also extends to the accurate reporting of individual and group test results. Fairness is not an isolated concept, but must be considered in all aspects of the testing process.

The Code applies broadly to testing in education (admissions, educational assessment, educational diagnosis, and student placement) regardless of the mode of presentation, so it is relevant to conventional paper-and-pencil tests, computer-based tests, and performance tests. It is not designed to cover employment testing, licensure or certification testing, or other types of testing outside the field of education. The Code is directed primarily at professionally developed tests used in formally administered testing programs. Although the Code is not intended to cover tests made by teachers for use in their own classrooms, teachers are encouraged to use the guidelines to help improve their testing practices.

The Code addresses the roles of test developers and test users separately. Test developers are people and organizations that construct tests, as well as those that set policies for testing programs. Test users are people and agencies that select tests, administer tests, commission test development services, or make decisions on the basis of test scores. Test-developer and test-user roles may overlap, for example, when a state or local education agency commissions test development services, sets policies that control the test development process, and makes decisions on the basis of the test scores.

Many of the statements in the Code refer to the selection and use of existing tests. When a new test is developed, when an existing test is modified, or when the administration of a test is modified, the Code is intended to provide guidance for this process.

The Code is not intended to be mandatory, exhaustive, or definitive, and it may not be applicable to every situation. Instead, the Code is intended to be aspirational and is not intended to take precedence over the judgment of those who have competence in the subjects addressed.

The Code provides guidance separately for test developers and test users in four critical areas:

A. Developing and Selecting Appropriate Tests
B. Administering and Scoring Tests
C. Reporting and Interpreting Test Results
D. Informing Test Takers

The Code is intended to be consistent with the relevant parts of the Standards for Educational and Psychological Testing (American Educational Research Association [AERA], American Psychological Association [APA], and National Council on Measurement in Education [NCME], 1999). The Code is not meant to add new principles over and above those in the Standards or to change their meaning. Rather, the Code is intended to represent the spirit of selected portions of the Standards in a way that is relevant and meaningful to developers and users of tests, as well as to test takers and/or their parents or guardians. States, districts, schools, organizations, and individual professionals are encouraged to commit themselves to fairness in testing and safeguarding the rights of test takers. The Code is intended to assist in carrying out such commitments.

The Code has been prepared by the Joint Committee on Testing Practices, a cooperative effort among several

Table C.A. Developing and Selecting Appropriate Tests

Test Developers	Test Users
Test developers should provide the information and supporting evidence that test users need to select appropriate tests.	Test users should select tests that meet the intended purpose and that are appropriate for the intended test takers.
A-1. Provide evidence of what the test measures, the recommended uses, the intended test takers, and the strengths and limitations of the test, including the level of precision of the test scores.	A-1. Define the purpose for testing, the content and skills to be tested, and the intended test takers. Select and use the most appropriate test based on a thorough review of available information.
A-2. Describe how the content and skills to be tested were selected and how the tests were developed.	A-2. Review and select tests based on the appropriateness of test content, skills tested, and content coverage for the intended purpose of testing.
A-3. Communicate information about a test's characteristics at a level of detail appropriate to the intended test users.	A-3. Review materials provided by test developers and select tests for which clear, accurate, and complete information is provided.
A-4. Provide guidance on the levels of skills, knowledge, and training necessary for appropriate review, selection, and administration of tests.	A-4. Select tests through a process that includes persons with appropriate knowledge, skills, and training.
A-5. Provide evidence that the technical quality, including reliability and validity, of the test meets its intended purposes.	A-5. Evaluate evidence of the technical quality of the test provided by the test developer and any independent reviewers.
A-6. Provide to qualified test users representative samples of test questions or practice tests, directions, answer sheets, manuals, and score reports.	A-6. Evaluate representative samples of test questions or practice tests, directions, answer sheets, manuals, and score reports before selecting a test.
A-7. Avoid potentially offensive content or language when developing test questions and related materials.	A-7. Evaluate procedures and materials used by test developers, as well as the resulting test, to ensure that potentially offensive content or language is avoided.
A-8. Make appropriately modified forms of tests or administration procedures available for test takers with disabilities who need special accommodations.	A-8. Select tests with appropriately modified forms or administration procedures for test takers with disabilities who need special accommodations.
A-9. Obtain and provide evidence on the performance of test takers of diverse subgroups, making significant efforts to obtain sample sizes that are adequate for subgroup analyses. Evaluate the evidence to ensure that differences in performance are related to the skills being assessed.	A-9. Evaluate the available evidence on the performance of test takers of diverse subgroups. Determine to the extent feasible which performance differences may have been caused by factors unrelated to the skills being assessed.

Table C.B. Administering and Scoring Tests

Test Developers	Test Users
Test developers should explain how to administer and score tests correctly and fairly.	Test users should administer and score tests correctly and fairly.
B-1. Provide clear descriptions of detailed procedures for administering tests in a standardized manner.	B-1. Follow established procedures for administering tests in a standardized manner.
B-2. Provide guidelines on reasonable procedures for assessing persons with disabilities who need special accommodations or those with diverse linguistic backgrounds.	B-2. Provide and document appropriate procedures for test takers with disabilities who need special accommodations or those with diverse linguistic backgrounds. Some accommodations may be required by law or regulation.
B-3. Provide information to test takers or test users on test question formats and procedures for answering test questions, including information on the use of any needed materials and equipment.	B-3. Provide test takers with an opportunity to become familiar with test question formats and any materials or equipment that may be used during testing.
B-4. Establish and implement procedures to ensure the security of testing materials during all phases of test development, administration, scoring, and reporting.	B-4. Protect the security of test materials, including respecting copyrights and eliminating opportunities for test takers to obtain scores by fraudulent means.
B-5. Provide procedures, materials, and guidelines for scoring the tests, and for monitoring the accuracy of the scoring process. If scoring the test is the responsibility of the test developer, provide adequate training for scorers.	B-5. If test scoring is the responsibility of the test user, provide adequate training to scorers and ensure and monitor the accuracy of the scoring process.
B-6. Correct errors that affect the interpretation of the scores and communicate the corrected results promptly.	B-6. Correct errors that affect the interpretation of the scores and communicate the corrected results promptly.
B-7. Develop and implement procedures for ensuring the confidentiality of scores.	B-7. Develop and implement procedures for ensuring the confidentiality of scores.

Table C.C. Reporting and Interpreting Test Results

Test Developers	Test Users
Test developers should report test results accurately and provide information to help test users interpret test results correctly.	Test users should report and interpret test results accurately and clearly.
C-1. Provide information to support recommended interpretations of the results, including the nature of the content, norms or comparison groups, and other technical evidence. Advise test users of the benefits and limitations of test results and their interpretation. Warn against assigning greater precision than is warranted.	C-1. Interpret the meaning of the test results, taking into account the nature of the content, norms or comparison groups, other technical evidence, and benefits and limitations of test results.
C-2. Provide guidance regarding the interpretations of results for tests administered with modifications. Inform test users of potential problems in interpreting test results when tests or test administration procedures are modified.	C-2. Interpret test results from modified test or test administration procedures in view of the impact those modifications may have had on test results.
C-3. Specify appropriate uses of test results and warn test users of potential misuses.	C-3. Avoid using tests for purposes other than those recommended by the test developer unless there is evidence to support the intended use or interpretation.
C-4. When test developers set standards, provide the rationale, procedures, and evidence for setting performance standards or passing scores. Avoid using stigmatizing labels.	C-4. Review the procedures for setting performance standards or passing scores. Avoid using stigmatizing labels.
C-5. Encourage test users to base decisions about test takers on multiple sources of appropriate information, not on a single test score.	C-5. Avoid using a single test score as the sole determinant of decisions about test takers. Interpret test scores in conjunction with other information about individuals.
C-6. Provide information to enable test users to accurately interpret and report test results for groups of test takers, including information about who were and who were not included in the different groups being compared, and information about factors that might influence the interpretation of results.	C-6. State the intended interpretation and use of test results for groups of test takers. Avoid grouping test results for purposes not specifically recommended by the test developer unless evidence is obtained to support the intended use. Report procedures that were followed in determining who were and who were not included in the groups being compared and describe factors that might influence the interpretation of results.
C-7. Provide test results in a timely fashion and in a manner that is understood by the test taker.	C-7. Communicate test results in a timely fashion and in a manner that is understood by the test taker.
C-8. Provide guidance to test users about how to monitor the extent to which the test is fulfilling its intended purposes.	C-8. Develop and implement procedures for monitoring test use, including consistency with the intended purposes of the test.

Table C.D. Informing Test Takers

Under some circumstances, test developers have direct communication with the test takers and/or control of the tests, testing process, and test results. In other circumstances the test users have these responsibilities.

Test developers or test users should inform test takers about the nature of the test, test taker rights and responsibilities, the appropriate use of scores, and procedures for resolving challenges to scores.

D-1. Inform test takers in advance of the test administration about the coverage of the test, the types of question formats, the directions, and appropriate test-taking strategies. Make such information available to all test takers.

D-2. When a test is optional, provide test takers or their parents/guardians with information to help them judge whether a test should be taken—including indications of any consequences that may result from not taking the test (e.g., not being eligible to compete for a particular scholarship)—and whether there is an available alternative to the test.

D-3. Provide test takers or their parents/guardians with information about rights test takers may have to obtain copies of tests and completed answer sheets, to retake tests, to have tests rescored, or to have scores declared invalid.

D-4. Provide test takers or their parents/guardians with information about responsibilities test takers have, such as being aware of the intended purpose and uses of the test, performing at capacity, following directions, and not disclosing test items or interfering with other test takers.

D-5. Inform test takers or their parents/guardians how long scores will be kept on file and indicate to whom, under what circumstances, and in what manner test scores and related information will or will not be released. Protect test scores from unauthorized release and access.

D-6. Describe procedures for investigating and resolving circumstances that might result in canceling or withholding scores, such as failure to adhere to specified testing procedures.

D-7. Describe procedures that test takers, parents/guardians, and other interested parties may use to obtain more information about the test, register complaints, and have problems resolved.

Source: Joint Committee on Testing Practices. The Joint Committee on Testing Practices (JCTP) was established in 1985 by the American Educational Research Association (AERA), the American Psychological Association (APA), and the National Council on Measurement in Education (NCME). In 2007 the JCTP disbanded, but JCTP publications are still available. http://www.apa.org/science/programs/testing/committee.aspx

professional organizations. The aim of the Joint Committee is to act, in the public interest, to advance the quality of testing practices. Members of the Joint Committee include the American Counseling Association (ACA), the American Educational Research Association (AERA), the American Psychological Association (APA), the American Speech-Language-Hearing Association (ASHA), the National Association of School Psychologists (NASP), the National Association of Test Directors (NATD), and the National Council on Measurement in Education (NCME).

COFFIN-LOWRY SYNDROME

Coffin-Lowry syndrome is a rare genetic disorder characterized by craniofacial and skeletal abnormalities, mental retardation, short stature, characteristic hands, and hypotonia (Weidemann, Kunze, Grosse, & Dibbern, 1989). Characteristic facial features may include an underdeveloped upper jaw bone (maxillary hypoplasia), an abnormally prominent brow, downslanting eyelid folds (palpebral fissures), widely spaced eyes (hypertelorism), large ears, and unusually thick eyebrows. Skeletal abnormalities may include abnormal front-to-back and side-to-side curvature of the spine (kyphoscoliosis), unusual prominence of the breastbone (pectus carinatum), and short, tapered fingers. Additional abnormalities may also be present. Other features may include feeding and respiratory problems, developmental delay, hearing impairment, awkward gait, flat feet, and heart and kidney involvement.

The disorder affects males and females in equal numbers, but symptoms may be more severe in males. The disorder is caused by a defective gene, which was found in 1996 on the X chromosome (National Institute of Neurological Disorders and Stroke [NINDS], 2002).

Characteristics

1. Narrow, rectangular protruding forehead appearing bitemporally compressed; hypertelorism, antimongoloid slant of the palpebral fissures, thick upper eyelids, broad nasal root and short, broad pug nose with a thick septum; pouting lower lip, mouth usually open; and unusual ears.

2. Mental retardation; IQ usually below 50 in males.

3. Small stature, variously severe, height possibly below the third percentile.

4. "Full" forearms; plumpish, lax, soft hands with tapered, hyperextensible fingers.

There is no cure and no standard course of treatment for Coffin-Lowry syndrome. Treatment is symptomatic and supportive and may include physical and speech therapy and genetic counseling. Educational support from special education will definitely be needed for these students, and placement in the least restrictive environment may be difficult to ascertain and may also change during development.

The prognosis for individuals with Coffin-Lowry syndrome varies depending on the severity of symptoms. Early intervention may improve the outlook for patients. NINDS supports and conducts research on genetic disorders, such as Coffin-Lowry syndrome, in an effort to find ways to prevent, treat, and, ultimately, cure this disorder (NINDS, 2002).

Families may obtain support and information from the Coffin-Lowry Syndrome Foundation, 3045 255th Avenue SE, Sammamish, WA 98075. Tel.: (425) 427-0939; e-mail: CLSFoundation@yahoo.com; web address: http://clsfoundation.tripod.com

REFERENCES

Gilbert, P. (1993). *The A–Z reference book of syndromes and inherited disorders: A manual for health, social and education workers.* London, UK: Chapman & Hall.

National Institute of Neurological Disorders and Stroke. (2002). *MedlinePlus Coffin-Lowry information page.* Retrieved from http://www.nlm.nih.gov/medlineplus/geneticdisorders.html

Weidemann, H. R., Kunze, J., Grosse, F. R., & Dibbern, H. (1989). *Atlas of clinical syndromes: A visual aid to diagnosis.* St. Louis, MO: Mosby.

ELAINE FLETCHER-JANZEN
Chicago School of Professional Psychology

COGENTIN

Cogentin is the proprietary name of benztropine mesylate, a skeletal muscle relaxant used in the treatment of Parkinson's disease (Modell, 1985). Cogentin acts on the basal ganglia of the brain. By restoring more normal chemical balance in the basal ganglia, specific movement disorders associated with parkinsonism are relieved. Cogentin reduces tremors, gait disturbances, and rigidity in afflicted individuals (Ellis & Speed, 1998; Long, 1982). Common side effects, especially during initial drug use, include blurred vision, nervousness, constipation, and dryness of the mouth. On rare occasions more serious side effects may occur, including confusion, hallucinations, nausea, and vomiting (Long, 1982). Common cold and cough remedies may interact unfavorably with Cogentin. The drug is not recommended for use in children under 3 years of age, and should be used with caution in older children (Konopasek, 2003; Long, 1982; *Physician's Desk Reference*, 1983).

REFERENCES

Ellis, K. L., & Speed, J. (1998). Pharmacologic management of movement disorder after midbrain haemorrhage. *Brain Injury, 12*(7), 623–628.

Konopasek, D. E. (2003). *Medication fact sheets.* Longmont, CO: Sopris West.

Long, J. W. (1982). *The essential guide to prescription drugs.* New York, NY: Harper & Row.

Modell, W. (Ed.). (1985). *Drugs in current use and new drugs* (31st ed.). New York, NY: Springer.

Physician's desk reference (37th ed.). (1983). Oradell, NJ: Medical Economics.

CATHY F. TELZROW
Kent State University

See also Medication

COGNITIVE ASSESSMENT SYSTEM

The Cognitive Assessment System (Naglieri & Das, 1997a) is a test of cognitive ability. It is administered individually, and created for children ages 5 years through 17 years and 11 months. The test is comprised of a total of 12 subtests, and can be administered in two forms. The Standard battery consists of all 12 subtests, while the Basic battery is made up of 8 subtests. Administration time is 60 minutes and 45 minutes, respectively.

The CAS was created as a tool for professionals to complete clinical, psychoeducational, and neuropsychological evaluations and is based on the PASS model. The PASS theory is represented by four scales on the CAS specifically, Planning, Attention, Simultaneous, and Successive cognitive processes (PASS). The first process, Planning, is the ability for an individual to conceptualize and then apply the proper strategies to successfully complete a novel task. Essentially the individual must be able to determine, select, and then use a strategy to efficiently solve a problem. Attention is a cognitive process by which an individual focuses on one cognitive process while excluding extraneous competing stimuli. The third process, Simultaneous processing, is the integration of stimuli into a coherent whole. Fourth is Successive processing, which involves organizing various things into a specific sequential order. A Full Scale score can also be obtained from the data.

Standard scores are provided for all subtests, with a mean of 10 and a standard deviation of 3. The four scales, along with the Full Scale score, are also reported as standard scores, and have a mean of 100 and a standard deviation of 15.

The CAS was standardized on a stratified random sample of 2,200 American children and adolescents aged 5 years 0 months to 17 years 11 months, using the 1990 census data. Strata included race, gender, region, community setting, educational classification, classroom placement, and parent education. A total of 240 examiners were utilized for standardization, along with 68 sites.

Reliability data are impressive. Median internal consistency reliabilities for the Full Scale are .96 on the Standard battery and .87 on the Basic battery. Internal consistency for the scales is also very good; reliability coefficients range from .88 to .93. Median test–retest reliability coefficients for the Basic and Standard batteries are .82. Studies investigating the criterion validity of the CAS have generally shown that the CAS does not sufficiently correlate with other measures of cognitive ability. As many of these measures are based on the Cattell-Horn-Carroll theory, these results are seen by some as lending evidence to the assertion that the CAS is an alternative way of validly conceptualizing intelligence.

Overall, the CAS is a well-standardized instrument. Because the test is based on the PASS theory, and differs from other assessment tools, it may offer a different context through which intelligence can be measured and thought of. It has also been suggested that the CAS has implications that are important in the learning environment. Although the CAS demonstrates assets, it does have limitations. In particular, caution must be exercised when using the data for interpretation. There is much overlap within the Attention scale and the Planning scale. As such, it may be difficult to separately interpret their results. Despite the fact that Naglieri and Das provide factor-analytic evidence to support the CAS and the PASS model, further validation is needed. This entry has been informed by the sources listed below.

REFERENCES

Hildebrand, D. K., & Sattler, J. M. (2001). Cognitive Assessment System. In J. M. Sattler, *Assessment of children: Cognitive applications* (4th ed., pp. 548–550). San Diego, CA: Jerome M. Sattler.

Keith, T. Z., Kranzler, J. H., & Flanagan, D. P. (2001). What does the Cognitive Assessment System (CAS) measure? Joint confirmatory factor analysis of the CAS and the Woodcock-Johnson Tests of Cognitive Ability (3rd ed.). *School Psychology Review, 30*, 89–119.

Kranzler, J. H., & Keith, T. Z. (1999). Independent confirmatory factor analysis of the Cognitive Assessment System (CAS): What does CAS measure? *School Psychology Review, 28*, 117.

Naglieri, J. A. (1999). How valid is the PASS theory and CAS? *School Psychology Review, 28*, 145.

Naglieri, J. A., & Conway, C. (2009). The Cognitive Assessment System. In J. A. Naglieri & S. Goldstein (Eds.), *Practitioner's guide to assessing intelligence and achievement*. Hoboken, NJ: Wiley.

Naglieri, J. A., & Das, J. P. (1997a). *Cognitive Assessment System*. Chicago, IL: Riverside Publishing.

Naglieri, J. A., & Das, J. P. (1997b). *Cognitive Assessment System: Interpretive handbook*. Chicago, IL: Riverside.

Plake, B. S., & Impara, J. C. (Eds.). (2001). *The fourteenth mental measurements yearbook*. Lincoln, NE: Buros Institute of Mental Measurements.

RON DUMONT
Fairleigh Dickinson University

JOHN O. WILLIS
Rivier College

KATHLEEN VIEZEL
Fairleigh Dickinson University

JAMIE ZIBULSKY
Fairleigh Dickinson University
Fourth edition

COGNITIVE BEHAVIOR THERAPY

The term *cognitive behavior therapy* refers to a diverse assemblage of theoretical and applied orientations that share three underlying assumptions. First, a person's behavior is mediated by cognitive events (i.e., thoughts, images, expectancies, and beliefs). Second is a corollary to the first; it states that a change in mediating events results in a change in behavior. Third, a person is an active participant in his or her own learning. The third assumption recognizes the reciprocal relationships among a person's thoughts, behavior, and environment and runs counter to the behaviorist's unidirectional view of the individual as a passive recipient of environmental influences.

During the reign of behaviorism in American psychology, cognitions were banned from investigation because the earlier methods used in their investigation were methodologically unsound and because cognitions, which are not directly observable, were considered inappropriate subject matter for the scientific study of psychology. During the 1960s, an explosion of research into such cognitive processes as attention, memory, problem solving, imagery, self-referent speech, beliefs, attributions, and motivation heralded a cognitive revolution in American psychology. Behaviorists impressed with the rigor of experimental cognitive psychologists and alert to the limitations of traditional behaviorism increasingly considered the role of cognitive variables in the development of behavior and in the treatment of maladaptive behavior. Because Bandura's research in observational learning was couched in a learning theory framework, it provided a timely bridge between the cognitivists and behaviorists. Bandura's explanations for modeling became more cognitive as he introduced such cognitive constructs as attention, retention, and expectancies to explain observational learning. Bandura's view of the reciprocal relationships among cognitions, behavior, and environment remains a basic tenet of cognitive behavior therapy. The widely discussed *controversy* between the cognitivists and the behaviorists that was prevalent in the 1960s and early 1970s quieted. The compatibility of the two perspectives has been recognized and the advantages of the joint consideration of cognitions and behaviors in modifying behaviors have been demonstrated.

A variety of therapies derived from research in cognitive psychology and taking advantage of the broadened behavioral perspective were developed and subjected to empirical test. These therapies attempt to modify thinking processes as a mechanism for effecting cognitive and behavioral changes. Particular therapeutic approaches that are closely identified with cognitive behavior therapy include modeling, self-instructional training, problem-solving training, rational emotive therapy, cognitive therapy, self-control training, and cognitive skills training. Because self-instructional training and problem-solving training illustrate the dual focus on cognitions and behavior, have been researched in schools, and are particularly well suited to classroom application, they will be briefly described in this entry.

In self-instructional training, the child is taught to regulate his or her behavior through self-talk. The child is taught to ask and to answer covertly questions that guide his or her own performance. The questions are of four types:

1. Questions about the nature of the problem ("Okay, now, what is it I have to do? I have to find the two cars that are twins.")
2. Plans, or self-instructions for solving the task ("How can I do it? I could look at each car carefully, looking at the hood first, and then the front wheels, until I get to the end.")
3. Self-monitoring ("Am I using my plan?")
4. Self-evaluation ("How did I do? I did fine because I looked at each car carefully and I found the twins.")

The particular self-statements vary according to the type of task.

The steps in teaching children to use self-speech to guide problem-solving behavior are derived from research in the developmental sequence by which language regulates one's behavior. First, an adult talks out loud while solving a task, and the child observes (modeling). Next, the child performs the same task while the adult verbally instructs the child. Next, the child performs the task while instructing himself or herself out loud. Then the child performs the task while whispering. Finally, the child performs the task while talking silently to himself or herself, with no lip movements.

Research in self-instructional talk has demonstrated that it helps impulsive children to think before acting (Meichenbaum & Goodman, 1971). While treated children have improved on novel problem-solving tasks and academic performance (Camp, Blom, Hebert, & Van Doorninck, 1977; Meichenbaum & Goodman, 1971), results of treatment on classroom behavior have been inconclusive (Camp, 1980; Camp et al., 1977).

Problem-solving training is similar to self-instructional training in that the child is taught to think through problems following a systematic problem-solving process. In a series of studies, Spivack and Shure (1974; Spivack, Platt, & Shure, 1976) taught preschool children the following interpersonal cognitive problem-solving skills: problem identification, means–end thinking, alternative thinking, and consequential thinking. Means–end thinking includes the ability to plan, step-by-step, ways to reach an interpersonal goal. Alternative thinking includes the ability to generate different plans for solving a given interpersonal problem. Consequential thinking is the ability to anticipate and evaluate consequences of a given interpersonal solution. These skills are taught in game-type interactions involving pictures, puppets, and stories depicting interpersonal problem situations. Research on problem-solving training has demonstrated improvement on teacher ratings, academic performance, and behavior observations (Shure, 1981).

In terms of psychotherapeutic intervention, cognitive behavior therapy has been shown to be very helpful with pain control (Tan & Leucht, 1997), depression, body dysmorphic disorder (Neziroglu, McKay, Todaro, & Yaryura-Tobias, 1996), and eating disorders (Eldredge et al., 1997). However, there are two caveats for using cognitive behavior therapy with school-aged populations. The first is including both the assessment of logical/analytical thought structures *and* social perspective-taking abilities of the child when planning a course of cognitive behavior therapy (Kinney, 1991). The second, which pertains to any age of client/subject, is that multicultural influences and diversity must be taken into account and formally addressed if the course of treatment is to be successful (Hays, 1997).

REFERENCES

Camp, B. W. (1980). Two psychoeducational treatment programs for young aggressive boys. In C. K. Walen & B. Henker (Eds.), *Hyperactive children: The social psychology of identification and treatment*. New York, NY: Academic.

Camp, B. W., Blom, G. E., Hebert, F., & Van Doorninck, W. J. (1977). "Think Aloud": A program for developing self-control in young aggressive boys. *Journal of Abnormal Child Psychology*, *5*, 157–169.

Eldredge, K. L., Agras, W. S., Arnow, B., Telch, C. F., Bell, S., Castonguay, L., & Marnell, M. (1997). The effects of extending cognitive-behavior therapy for binge eating disorder among initial treatment nonresponders. *International Journal of Eating Disorders*, *21*(4), 347–352.

Hays, P. A. (1997). Multicultural applications of cognitive behavior therapy. *Professional Psychology: Research & Practice*, *26*(3), 309–315.

Kinney, A. (1991). Cognitive-behavior therapy with children: Developmental considerations. *Journal of Rational-Emotive & Cognitive Behavior Therapy*, *9*(1), 51–61.

Meichenbaum, D. H., & Goodman, J. (1971). Training impulsive children to talk to themselves: A means of developing self-control. *Journal of Abnormal Psychology*, *77*, 115–126.

Neziroglu, F., McKay, D., Todaro, J., & Yaryura-Tobias, J. A. (1996). Effect of cognitive behavior therapy on persons with body dysmorphic disorder and comorbid Axis II diagnosis. *Behavior Therapy*, *27*(1), 67–77.

Shure, M. B. (1981). Social competence as a problem-solving skill. In J. D. Wine & M. D. Smyne (Eds.), *Social competence* (pp. 158–185). New York, NY: Guilford Press.

Spivack, G., Platt, J. J., & Shure, M. B. (1976). *The problem-solving approach to adjustment*. San Francisco, CA: Jossey-Bass.

Spivack, G., & Shure, M. B. (1974). *Social adjustment of young children: A cognitive approach to solving real-life problems*. San Francisco, CA: Jossey-Bass.

Tan, Siang-Yang, & Leucht, C. A., (1997). Cognitive-behavioral therapy for clinical pain control: A 15-year update and its relationship to hypnosis. *International Journal of Clinical & Experimental Hypnosis*, *45*(4), 396–416.

JAN N. HUGHES
Texas A&M University

See also **Cognitive Retraining; Cognitive Strategies; Self-Control Curriculum**

COGNITIVE DEVELOPMENT

Cognitive development consists of numerous overlapping conceptual and theoretical processes involving changes that occur in mental capacity and facility between birth and death. Cognition, the product of cognitive development, refers to mental processes by which individuals acquire knowledge. Moreover, cognition is the process of acquiring a conscious awareness that helps us to "know" and "understand" in a wide spectrum of activities such as remembering, learning, thinking, and attending. As a human phenomenon, cognition is comprised of unobservable events, their subsequent comprehension, and resultant response (Flavell, 1982). These covert behaviors characterize the activities of human thought processes.

In an effort to present general parameters of childhood cognitive development as it pertains to special education, several cognitive perspectives must be addressed. The human is an active problem solver who attempts to discriminate, extract, and analyze information; subsequently, directed planful action undergoes developmental change. Three contemporary theoretical orientations are consistent with the theme of the child as an active problem solver: Piaget's theory of cognitive development, information-processing approaches, and social learning theory.

One of the most influential descriptors of how development occurs is Piaget's theory of cognitive development (Piaget, 1970). In his work, cognitive structures are represented in the symbolic medium of formal logic, where each structure is regarded as a broad system of logical operations that mediates and unites a whole range of more specific intellectual behaviors and characteristics. Even though research with large samples of infants has confirmed Piaget's theories, certain aspects of his developmental accounts have come under scrutiny (Flavell, 1980; Gelman, 1978) and warrant revision or reinterpretation. Nevertheless, the Piagetian approach remains an important scientific paradigm on human intellectual development. The formative phases of the domain of study known as cognitive development are rooted in Piaget's theoretical formulations.

Piaget defines intelligence as a basic life function through which an individual adapts to the environment. In Piaget's view, children do not simply receive information from the environment; they actively seek and achieve knowledge through their own efforts. This interaction, from Piaget's biological perspective, is viewed as adaptation. Organisms adapt by using their newly acquired information by processing and gaining understanding of the environment. Thus adaptation and construction of reality depend on a child's level of cognitive development.

Piaget views cognitive development as a process of the development of cognitive structures and intellectual functions. He uses the term *schema* to describe mental structures used by the individual to represent, organize, and interpret experience. Therefore, a schema is defined as a pattern of thought or action by which an individual constructs an "understanding" of some aspect of the environment. Three types of intellectual structures have been defined by Piaget: sensorimotor (organized behavior patterns used to represent or respond to objects or experiences), symbolic (internal cognitive images used to represent past experiences), and operational (internal cognitive images that organize thoughts logically).

According to Piaget's theory, cognitive development depends on maturation (genetically transmitted) and the child's interactions with the environment. Contingent on normal maturation is the organism's ability to adapt to environmental changes and demands. Thus, with maturation, assimilation, and accommodation (Piaget, 1970), the human organism tries to interpret new experiences in terms of existing information.

Analogously, through accommodation, the child modifies an existing schema to suit a novel experience. Hence, Piaget describes intellectual growth as an active process whereby children are repeatedly assimilating new experiences and accommodating their cognitive structures to their new experiences. The cognitive operations of adaptation and organization facilitate children's ability to construct a progressively better understanding of the world. A child's formulation of self and external world depend on the knowledge base acquired up to the particular point in time at which a response is necessary. Consequently, the greater the immaturity of the child's cognitive system, the more limited the interpretation of environmental events.

Age ranges designated for each of Piaget's four stages are average estimates; nonetheless, the sequential emergence of hierarchical "stages" is believed to be absolutely constant or invariant. Piaget felt that earlier developmental stages are not skipped en route to later stages. Accomplishments for each stage are said to accumulate (i.e., skills achieved in earlier stages are not lost with the advent of latent stages).

Sensorimotor Stage

During the sensorimotor stage of development, birth to about 2 years of age, cognitive development originates with ability to organize and coordinate bodily sensations and perceptions with the child's own physical movements and actions. Throughout sensorimotor development, an infant progresses from instinctual reflexive actions at birth to symbolic reflexive actions toward the end of the second year.

Initial means of coordinating sensation and action are accomplished through instinctual reflexive behaviors such as sucking and rooting. These behaviors are exhibited during substage 1, simple reflexes (ages birth to 1 month).

Substage 2, first habits and primary circular reactions, is comprised of first acquired adaptations. For example, when orally stimulated by a bottle during the first substage (simple reflexes), an infant might suck; conversely, during the second substage, repetitions of sucking may commence when no bottle is present.

During substage 3 (4 to 8 months), secondary circular reactions, behaviors are also repetitious and pleasurable; however, they focus on events and objects in the external environment that occur by chance.

Throughout substage 4 (8 to 12 months), coordination of secondary schemata, cognitive thought is comprised of intentionally combining previously unrelated stimuli, producing simple feats, solving simple problems, and

imitating the behavior of others. Piaget suggests that throughout substage 4, an infant is applying known cognitive structures to new situations to produce coordinated, goal-directed, and independent imitative actions with his or her own body or environment.

Substage 5 (12 to 18 months), tertiary circular reactions, is evidenced by exploratory trial-and-error schematas in which the infant purposely discovers new procedures to solve problems or reproduce interesting outcomes. Piaget refers to this period as the developmental starting point for human curiosity and interest in novelty.

Finally, during the last sensorimotor substage (18 to 24 months), internalization of cognitive structures begins to develop. Mental functioning shifts from a purely sensorimotor plane to a symbolic plane in which infants develop the ability to use primitive symbols.

Object Permanence

Object permanence, considered one of the infant's most significant cognitive development achievements during the sensorimotor stage, is the idea that people, places, and things continue to exist when they are no longer visible or detectable through the senses. According to Piaget, the object concept first appears during substage 4, coordination of secondary schemata. During substage 5, tertiary circular reactions, an infant searches for and locates hidden objects in novel and familiar locations; nonetheless, this occurs only if movement of the objects is visible. In the final sensorimotor substage, object permanence is complete; invisible movement of objects can be followed in the imagination by means of mental representations. Thus the infant searches for and finds objects that have been hidden through visible displacements.

Contrary to Piaget, Bower's (1982) research suggests that infants understand object permanence earlier, during primary circular reactions, even though they will not search for objects during this substage. Evidence of object permanence in Bower's research is indicated by the infant's surprise or anticipation of perceived object location. Bower suggests that errors in spatial reasoning, rather than absence of the object concept, account for younger infants' failure to search in Piagetian tasks.

Preoperational Stage

In the preoperational stage (ages 2 to 7 years), a period when symbolic schemata predominates, a young child's symbolic system expands such that use of language and perceptual images moves well beyond abilities at the end of the sensorimotor period. The preoperational stage consists of two phases: the preconceptual period (ages 2 to 4 years) and the intuitive period (ages 5 to 7 years).

According to Piaget, deficits in logical reasoning are evident throughout the preconceptual period. For example, egocentrism, the most salient feature of preconceptual thought, is evidenced by an inability to distinguish easily between a child's own perspective and that of someone else. Another deficit exhibited during the preconceptual period is animism; the young child believes that inanimate objects have human qualities and are capable of human action. During the preconceptual period, pretend play develops to a level in which children are capable of creating fantasy worlds, inventing imaginary playmates, participating in role playing, and using play as a vehicle for coping with emotional crises.

The second phase of the preoperational stage, the intuitive period, is an extension of preconceptual thought where the use of symbolic thought improves. Perceptually based logic appears in class inclusion problems such as "a string of beads that has both blocks and beads," whereby the child focuses on one feature only. According to Piaget, the child has a hard time thinking about the subset.

To aid in the use of symbolic thought, two main systematic capabilities are necessary during the preoperational period: centration and irreversibility. Fundamentally, centration is a child's tendency to focus on a single aspect of a problem while ignoring other information that helps the child to answer correctly. Irreversibility is the inability to reverse or to undo an action mentally.

Research (Flavell, Everett, Croft, & Flavell, 1981; Mossler, Marvin, & Greenberg, 1976) suggests that preoperational children are less egocentric, take another's point of view, and can conserve, contrary to what Piaget found. Gelman (1978) found that preschoolers are capable of causal reasoning. Additional research (Beilin, 1980) indicates that conservation problems can be taught to preoperational children by methods such as identity training (i.e., objects or substances transformed in a conservation task are still the same regardless of their new appearance). Finally, the work of Acredolo and Acredolo (1979) suggests that reversibility and compensation are not absolutely necessary for conservation.

Concrete Operations Stage

Piaget's concrete operations stage, a period between ages 7 and 11 years, is a stage during which the child's thinking crystallizes into a coherent organization of cognitive operations. Cognitive deficits most evident in the preoperational stage completely fade during the concrete operations stage.

Cognitive operations shift to a more refined system of thought that leads to levels that facilitate previously unattainable competencies. During concrete operations development, children often display *horizontal decalage*, meaning the child can solve some conservation problems but not others. For example, conservation skills such as reversibility develop such that the child can mentally reverse flow of action and thereby realize that a column of

water can look the same when poured back into its original container. Ability to classify and reverse enables linguistic humor to develop. Another shift is the move from egocentrism to relativism. The child can now decenter, or operate with two or more aspects of a problem simultaneously.

Formal Operations Stage

The formal operations stage, the final stage of Piaget's cognitive development theory, is characterized by the ability to reason abstractly and hypothetically. Abstract quality of thought can be seen primarily in the adolescent's use of verbal propositions in problem solving. For example, the concrete thinker (sensorimotor stage) needs to see concrete elements A, B, and C to be able to make the logical inference that if A > B and B > C, then A > C. Conversely, formal thinkers can solve the previous problem merely by having it presented as a verbal puzzle.

Although the transition to formal operations takes place gradually over several years, systematic and abstract thinking builds a foundation for considering morality, justice, beliefs, and values. Socially, the formal thinker no longer need rely on concrete experiences with people to form complex judgments about them.

Formal Thought in Adolescence

Since Piaget's classic experiments, many researchers have delved into the nature of adolescent thought. Their objective has been to specify the characteristics that distinguish this form of reasoning and problem solving from other, more primitive forms.

One important characteristic of formal thought involves seeking explanations rather than mere descriptions of what has been observed. Another characteristic of formal thought involves the ability to remove oneself from the immediate context of a problem in order to get an additional perspective. One of the most socially significant characteristics of formal thought is the metacognitive ability to think about thinking (i.e., the ability to reflect on the thought process itself). In sum, formal thought is characterized by a relative freedom from the immediate constraints of a problem, which results in flexibility.

Late Adolescence and Adulthood

During this stage the most pronounced changes in cognitive development have taken place. Nonetheless, small but observable changes are still evident later in life. Young adults, from Erikson's (1963) theory of psychosocial development, experience a crisis of identity versus role confusion. Moreover, sex and romance influence the role of young adults.

Cognitive development continues to refine in its development as the young adult attempts to conceptualize a lifelong role in society by selecting an occupation. This mature realism about one's occupation is seen as a process that remains throughout one's life, sometimes leading to midlife career changes.

Information-Processing Approach to Cognitive Development

As a model of human cognitive development, information processing explains decision making, knowing, and remembering as processes. In this approach to the study of cognitive development, the mind is conceived of as a complex cognitive system, analogous in some ways to a computer. In essence, human cognition becomes what the computer must know in order to produce behavior y. Information from the environment is abstracted from sensory systems and "flows" through a variety of proposed information-processing components (Moynahan, 1977). Information is transformed and analyzed at each step; feedback and feedforward loops among the components influence these transformations and analyses. Planning and purposeful thinking are derived by executive functions. The executive system contains sets of elementary information-processing rules that construct, execute, and monitor the flow of information to achieve objectives.

Most of the information-processing research builds directly on Piaget's contributions to the understanding of cognitive development. Contrary to Piaget's structural explanation underlying the thought structure of logic in thought processes and operational reversibility, information processing accounts for and identifies specific mental processes by which cognition is processed. Some researchers, such as Pascual-Leone (1980) and Case (1978), have modified Piagetian theory to take into account information-processing considerations (also called neo-Piagetian theories). One such approach is Siegler's (1981) rule-assessment approach. In essence, Siegler's work examines a child's problem-solving skills within a domain at different ages. A child's pattern of responses across problems helps to determine which of the information-processing rules the child is using.

Several other information-processing perspectives have examined cognitive development. For example, researchers have found that young children have limited attention and persistence at tasks (Wellman, Ritter, & Flavell, 1975) and that their curiosity interferes with systematic problem solving. Thus, contrary to Piagetian theory, very young children may fail to solve many problems because they are unable to sustain their attention long enough to gather the necessary information. By about age 5 children become more persistent in their attempts to solve problems. Hence younger children may know to look first at relevant stimuli and label them; whereas, older children are better at selectively attending without special training.

Social Learning Theory

Social learning theorists (Bandura, 1977b) suggest that cognitive development is much more than a result of some combination of individual characteristics and environmental influences. They view all three as existing within a mutually interdependent network; they exist as a set of reciprocal determinants. Thus cognitions, beliefs, and expectations influence behavior and vice versa. Behavior partially determines the nature of the environment, whereas cognitions determine the psychological definitions of the environment.

Learning takes place either directly (through association of behaviors and consequences) or through modeling. The direct consequences of behavior, or reinforcements, are not conceptualized in the more traditional fashion that ignores awareness of the contingencies on the part of the child. Hence consequences of behavior explicitly carry information and function to provoke the individual into formulating and testing hypotheses. Thus reinforcement influences whether a response will elicit cognitions or thoughts about stimulus associations.

Learning is thought to be acquired through modeling. All new behaviors are observed along with their consequences. Inherent symbolic abilities facilitate abstraction and representation of information and provide an efficient means for retaining that information. From a social learning perspective, the anticipation of reinforcement may serve as a stimulus to direct attention to a model's behavior; hence, reinforcement may facilitate learning.

In summary, social learning theory places a great deal of emphasis on symbolic and self-regulatory processes. Cognitive development is important to the extent that changes in cognitive functioning influence changes in those processes. In children, development becomes more refined with experience and actual manipulation and, consequently, children are better able to represent efficiently and retain observational experiences. Additionally, symbolic processes, attentional processes, and motivational processes change with observational learning.

Implications for Special Education

Traditional stages of cognitive development apply to individuals with and without disabilities alike. Handicapping conditions, however, may result in irregularities or delays in cognitive development, particularly in profoundly mentally retarded or multiply impaired persons. Some profoundly mentally retarded individuals never progress into the higher stages of cognitive development such as preoperational or operational thought. Other children acquire skills by rote or through carefully structured instruction, but have difficulty in applying them to new situations (Brown, Campione, & Murphy, 1977).

Most mildly and moderately retarded children do progress through Piaget's lower stages of cognitive development; however, their rate of skill acquisition is much slower. As the child gets older, the gap between the age at which specific skills are expected to be learned and the age at which they are actually learned increases. The retarded child also performs cognitive tasks with less efficiency than the nonretarded child (Campione & Brown, 1978).

Individuals with learning disabilities (LD) represent the largest percentage of the disabled population (U.S. Office of Special Education, 1996); they evidence a broad array of cognitive dysfunctions. These deficits emerge when academic learning lags with age. Children who are learning disabled may not exhibit specific cognitive problems early in development; however, skills acquired during Piaget's preoperational stage (intuitive thinking) are learned at a slower pace. Thus, problems in areas such as mathematics, reading, and memory are more prevalent.

During the primary years, children with LD have problems with seriation and classification tasks that are essential for mathematics. They cannot sort objects by size, match objects, or grasp the concept of counting and addition. In reading, LD children evidence word recognition errors (omissions, insertions, substitutions, reversals, and transpositions) and comprehension errors (inability to recall facts, sequences, or main ideas).

Word recognition difficulties suggest that LD children are unable to make a word or a letter stand for or represent something else. These are preconceptual skills (ages 2 to 7) of cognitive development in which symbolic thought develops. Problems with centration may inhibit reading comprehension.

Students with learning disabilities generally have problems with recalling auditory and visual stimuli. They also have problems with tasks requiring production or generation of specific learning or memorization strategies that influence the efficient organization of input for retrieval and recall. Bauer (1979) found that poor readers perform poorly on memory tasks that require complex organizational and retrieval strategies. Kauffman and Hallahan (1979) suggest that LD students fail to engage in strategies that enhance attention and recall. These deficits are evident when applied to academic tasks.

Cognitive development may be viewed from numerous perspectives and subsequently applied to academic problems encountered in the field of special education. The information-processing approach to cognitive development is still in the early stage. It is best described as a complement to, rather than a replacement for, Piaget's earlier framework. However, recent research suggests that infants and young children are more competent and adults less competent than once thought (Flavell, 1992). Growth and extension of the cognitive development literature continues and quite often fills in some of the gaps in Piaget's

model (Siegler & Crowley, 1991); hence, advances in empirical findings will eventually aid in the development of successful school-based interventions.

REFERENCES

Acredolo, L., & Acredolo, L. T. (1979). Identity, compensation, and conservation. *Child Development, 50,* 524–535

Bandura, A. (1977). Self-efficacy: Toward a unifying theory of behavioral change, *Psychological Review (84)2,* 191–215.

Bauer, R. H. (1979). Memory, acquisition, and category clustering in learning disabled children. *Journal of Experimental Child Psychology, 217,* 365–383.

Beilin, H. (1980). Piaget's theory: Refinement, revision, or rejection? In R. Kluwe & H. Spada (Eds.), *Developmental models of thinking.* New York, NY: Academic.

Bower, T. G. R. (1982). *Development in infancy.* San Francisco, CA: Freeman.

Brown, A., Campione, J., & Murphy, M. (1977). Maintenance and generalization of training meta-mnemonic awareness of educable retarded children. *Journal of Experimental Child Psychology, 24,* 191–211.

Campione, J. C., & Brown, A. (1978). Toward a theory of intelligence: Contributions from research with retarded children. *Intelligence, 2,* 279–304.

Case, R. S. (1978). Intellectual development from birth to adulthood: A neo-Piagetian interpretation. In R. W. Siegler (Ed.), *Children's thinking: What develops?* Hillsdale, NJ: Erlbaum.

Erikson, E. H. (1963). *Childhood and society* (2nd ed.). New York, NY: Norton.

Flavell, J. (1980, Fall). A tribute to Piaget. *Society for Research in Child Development Newsletter.*

Flavell, J. (1982). On cognitive development. *Child Development, 53,* 1–10.

Flavell, J. (1992). Cognitive development. *Developmental Psychology, 28,* 998–1005.

Flavell, J., Everett, B. A., Croft, K., & Flavell, E. R. (1981). Young children's knowledge about visual perception: Further evidence for the Level 1–Level 2 distinction. *Developmental Psychology, 15,* 95–120.

Gelman, R. (1978). Cognitive development. *Annual Review of Psychology, 29,* 297–332.

Kauffman, J. M., & Hallahan, D. P. (1979). Learning disabled and hyperactivity. In B. B. Lahey & A. E. Kazdin (Eds.), *Advances in clinical child psychology* (Vol. 2). New York, NY: Plenum Press.

Mossler, D. G., Marvin, R. S., & Greenberg, M. T. (1976). Conceptual perspective taking in 2- to 6-year-old children. *Developmental Psychology, 12,* 85–86.

Moynahan, E. D. (1973). The development of knowledge concerning the effect of categorization upon free recall. *Child Development, 44,* 238–246.

Pascual-Leone, J. (1980). Constructive problems for constructive theories: The current relevance of Piaget's work and a critique of information-processing simulation psychology. In

R. H. Kluwe & H. Spada (Eds.), *Developmental models of thinking*. New York, NY: Academic.

Piaget, J. (1970). Piaget's theory. In P. H. Mussen (Ed.), *Carmichael's manual of child psychology* (Vol. 1). New York, NY: Wiley.

Siegler, R. S. (1981). Developmental sequences within and between concepts. *Monographs for the Society for Research in Child Development, 46* (Serial No. 189).

Siegler, R. S., & Crowley, K. (1991). The microgenetic method. *American Psychologist, 46*(6), 606–620.

U.S. Office of Special Education. (1996). *Eighteenth annual report to Congress on the implementation of Public Law 94-142: The Education for All Handicapped Children Act*. Washington, DC: U.S. Department of Education.

Wellman, H. M., Ritter, K., & Flavell, J. (1975). Deliberate memory in the delayed reactions of very young children. *Developmental Psychology, 11*, 780–787.

JOSE LUIS TORRES
MICHAEL J. ASH
Texas A&M University

See also Cognitive Strategies; Cognitive Styles; Information Processing; Intelligence; Piaget, Jean; Social Learning Theory

COGNITIVE IMPAIRMENT AND METAL POLLUTANTS

It is well known that children who are exposed to high doses of lead and other metal pollutants may suffer permanent neurological sequelae and cognitive impairments (Hartman 1995; Moon, Marlow, Stellern, & Errera, 1985). The causes of metal pollution are often associated with substandard living conditions (e.g., living in dilapidated substandard housing with peeling lead-based paints or plaster, living with household dust carrying metal pollutants, and living in proximity to heavy traffic or factories with noxious emissions). Inadequate nutrition also contributes to the effects of metal pollution.

Some of the physical difficulties associated with metal pollution are loss of appetite, chronic abdominal pain, headache, and anemia. Reported behavior difficulties associated with high levels of such poisoning are decreased learning performance, deficient attention, irritability, and clumsiness. Investigators have implicated metal toxicity in nonadaptive behavior as manifested in classroom situations (Marlowe, Moon, Errera, Cossairt, McNeil, & Peak, 1985), associated with learning-disabled children (Marlowe, Errera, Cossairt, & Welch, 1985) and with emotional disturbances in children (Marlowe, Errera, & Jacoby, 1983).

The assessment of metal concentrations in humans is easily carried out through various bodily analyses (e.g., of blood, teeth, and hair). The study of hair is both easy and noninvasive: Samples are subjected to the study of atomic absorption spectroscopy (Laker, 1982). Trace elements such as metals accumulate in hair at concentrations that are usually higher than in the blood serum. Hair thus can provide a record of a child's nutrient and mineral status. A method appropriate to classroom use to help teachers identify children who are potentially suffering from metal pollution is the Metal Exposure Questionnaire (Marlowe et al., 1983). This provides quantitative information about the possibility that a schoolchild is suffering significantly from metal pollutants.

Many studies of metal pollutant effects suffer from methodological errors. One of the more significant of these is that while investigators study the effects of one toxic metal, they often fail to take into account the effects of other toxic metals on a child's behavior (Hartman, 1995; Moon et al., 1985).

While there is clear evidence indicating that high doses of metal pollution are physically and cognitively deleterious, there is less certainty as to whether low doses of such metals have significant effects. A number of studies have suggested that they do. Low levels of arsenic, cadmium, mercury, aluminum, and lead have been implicated in cognitive, perceptual, and behavioral childhood developmental deficits (Winneke et al., 1983). Some investigators also have hypothesized that metal combinations have interactive effects, thereby increasing the total toxicity in a child (Moon et al., 1985).

Among the more comprehensive reviews of literature concerning the behavioral effects of metal pollutants is that of Rimland and Larson (1983), who summarized studies of the relationship between incidence of learning disabilities and long-term, low-level metal exposure as measured through hair analysis. They found a total of nine studies. In five of the studies, learning-disabled subjects were found to have significantly more lead and/or cadmium than their controls. In the four remaining studies, the learning-disabled students were found to be somewhat higher in lead, cadmium, and/or aluminum concentrations.

The potential widespread nature of metal pollutants' toxic effects has been demonstrated by Moon et al. (1985). These investigators, studying a randomly selected sample of elementary school children, found significant relationships between low metal concentrations and diminished performance on a variety of cognitive and academic tasks. They also discovered interactive effects. Thus, both increases in arsenic and its interaction with lead were significantly related to decreased reading and spelling achievement. Increases in aluminum and the interaction of aluminum with lead were associated with decreased visual-motor performance. An excellent review of the neuropsychological sequelae of toxic substance exposure can be found by Hartman (1995). Readers may also wish to access the National Institute of Neurological Disorders and Stroke for resources on neurotoxicology (http://www.ninds.nih.gov/disorders/neurotoxicity).

REFERENCES

Hartman, D. E. (1995). *Neuropsychological toxicology* (2nd ed.). New York, NY: Plenum Press.

Laker, M. (1982). On determining trace element levels in man: The uses of blood and hair. *Lancet, 12*, 260–263.

Marlowe, M., Errera, J., Cossairt, A., & Welch, K. (1985). Hair mineral content as a predictor of learning disabilities. *Journal of Learning Disabilities, 40*, 221–225.

Marlowe, M., Errera, J., & Jacoby, J. (1983). Increased lead and cadmium levels in emotionally disturbed children. *Journal of Orthomolecular Psychiatry, 12*, 260–267.

Marlowe, M., Moon, C., Errera, J., Cossairt, A., McNeil, A., & Peak, R. (1985). Main and interaction effects of metallic toxins on classroom behavior. *Journal of Abnormal Child Psychology, 13*, 185–198.

Moon, C., Marlowe, M., Stellern, J., & Errera, J. (1985). Main and interaction effects of metallic pollutants on cognitive functioning. *Journal of Learning Disabilities, 18*, 217–220.

Rimland, B., & Larson, G. E. (1983). Hair mineral analysis and behavior: An analysis of 51 studies. *Journal of Learning Disabilities, 16*, 279–285.

Winneke, G., Kramer, U., Brockhaus, U., Evers, U., Kujanek, G., Lechner, H., & Janke, W. (1983). Neuropsychological studies in children with elevated tooth-lead concentrations. *International Archives of Occupational Environmental Health, 51*, 231–252.

LESTER MANN
*Hunter College,
City University of New York*

See also **Lead Poisoning; Poverty, Relationship to Special Education**

COGNITIVE MAPPING SOFTWARE

Cognitive mapping software refers to a computer program that can visually map compositional ideas, thoughts, and concepts using symbols and graphics rather than text. Cognitive mapping has its roots, and is very similar to, flowcharting. However, unlike flowcharts, cognitive mapping software has evolved with robust sets of symbols and graphics encompassing more than just procedural symbols. Furthermore, the software can convert a cognitive

map into a linear textual document similar to an outline. For example, consider the following cognitive map:

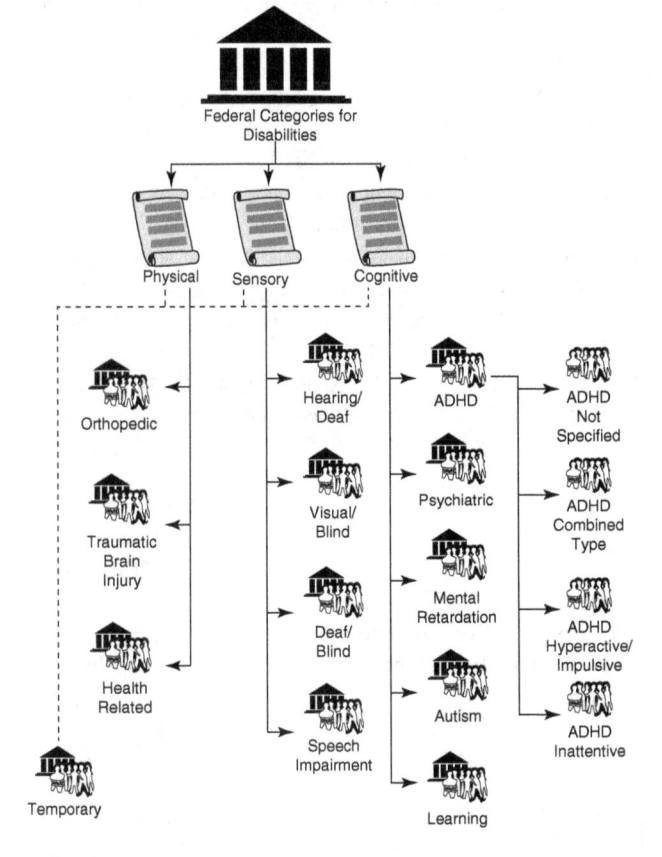

Cognitive mapping software may render this map into the following outline:

I. Physical
   A. Orthopedic
   B. Traumatic Brain Injury
   C. Health Related
   D. Temporary
II. Sensory
   A. Hearing/Deaf
   B. Visual/Blind
   C. Deaf/Blind
   D. Speech Impairment
   E. Temporary
III. Cognitive
   A. ADHD
      1. ADHD—Not Specified
      2. ADHD—Combined Type
      3. ADHD—Hyperactive/Impulsive
      4. ADHD—Inattentive
   B. Learning
   C. Psychiatric
   D. Mental Retardation
   E. Autism
   F. Temporary

This process has been found to be useful for some students with learning disabilities and ADHD as it provides a visual-spatial method of composition that some students find easier to do. Because the software can create a linear outline of the symbol map, a student may use this to jumpstart a composition. An example of cognitive mapping software is Inspiration (2011). This software comes in different versions, some targeted for early childhood while others are targeted with specific symbol sets at later grades and even professional endeavors such as engineering.

REFERENCE

Inspiration Software. (2011). Retrieved from http://www.inspiration.com/

STAFF

COGNITIVE RETRAINING

Cognitive retraining, or cognitive training, is used to describe various intervention or treatment efforts that are intended to promote positive adaptive functioning in individuals with neurologically based cognitive deficits (Barrett & Gonzalez-Rothi, 2002). Historically, cognitive retraining has been considered in the context of intense program development in head injury rehabilitation. In this context, cognitive retraining is associated with restoration of function through process-specific interventions. The objectives of cognitive approaches involve restoration, or development of, specific skills and abilities, or compensatory training with the ultimate goal of optimizing adjustment and outcome (Eslinger & Oliveri, 2002). Research specific to cognitive retraining is done within the fields of pediatric neuropsychology, rehabilitation psychology, or cognitive psychology as opposed to school psychology. Cognitive training programs have received the most attention in the context of rehabilitation for individuals who have sustained traumatic brain injury (TBI; Mateer & Mapou, 1996; Park & Ingles, 2000; Sbordonne, 1986). The underlying rationale is that behavior results from the action and interaction of neurons and the related presumption that this action and interaction can be altered (or bypassed) by changing the associated neurological processes (for additional detail see Barrett & Gonzalez-Rothi, 2002).

Rehabilitation approaches generally either target underlying impairments as in deficit models or use intact processes or external means to address those functional areas affected (Glisky & Glisky, 2002). The exclusive emphasis on the underlying impairment ignores those intact functions of the individual, and, as suggested by the aptitude by treatment interaction studies, there is no evidence of progress with a focus on remediation of deficits. As such, a preferred approach focuses on optimizing the remaining function in the area of the deficit. Although there is a continued goal of restoring or developing that functional ability to the extent feasible, there is more of a focus on refining how the functional capacities that remain can be used (Anderson, 2002). Instead of drill and practice, the emphasis is on strategy instruction and metacognitive training. These methods may be most appropriate for individuals with mild to moderate impairments, who have sufficient intact abilities to master the strategies. Compensation approaches identify ways to bypass deficit skills through the use of intact functions or external aids or substitute methods of reaching the same goal (Anderson, 2002).

Ylvisaker and Szekeres (1996) identified goals of cognitive approaches to intervention as follows: (1) the restoration or development of cognitive processes or systems that were delayed or impaired by the injury or disorder; (2) acquisition of new knowledge that increasingly facilitates effective information processing; (3) increasing the strategic approaches of individuals and equipping them with strategic procedures that enable them to accomplish goals; (4) identification of ways in which academic, social, and vocational environments can be modified to promote success despite ongoing cognitive challenges; (5) identification of instructional strategies that are consistent with the child's profile of cognitive strengths and weaknesses that can be used with greatest effectiveness in school; and (6) heightening children's understanding of their needs so that they are increasingly active participants in the process of solving the many problems caused by their cognitive deficits. Regardless of whether the child has sustained a head injury, has a learning disability, or has some other neurological disorder, these goals would be appropriate and would improve the overall adjustment and functioning of the child.

With cognitive retraining, intervention involves implementation of environmental manipulations, training in compensatory activities, and use of activities designed to restore or improve underlying abilities (Mateer, 1999). The major methods used in cognitive retraining include: (1) metacognitive interventions; (2) strategy instruction; (3) computer-assisted training; (4) biofeedback; (5) use of external aids and environmental supports; and (6) domain-specific learning. When impairments or disabilities are viewed in the context of cognitive deficits, cognitive approaches seem like a logical approach (Mateer, Kerns, & Eso, 1996). Further, cognitive mechanisms such as working memory capacity, inhibition, and strategic problem solving are important for a broad range of intellectual and social behaviors (Welsh, 2002).

Unfortunately, critical evaluation of cognitive retraining or training programs is limited to general reviews and discussions of methodological problems specific to a given population (e.g., see McCaffrey & Gansler, 1992, for strategies with traumatic brain injuries). Park and Ingles' (2000) meta-analysis indicated that the majority of studies yielded small effect sizes (−0.01 to 0.41; $X = 0.15$). Suslow, Schonauer, and Arolt (2001) concurred with regard to small effect sizes and also pointed to the low power and contradictory results of available studies. More extensive research is needed to determine the extent of generalizability, maintenance, and efficacy of the varying cognitive approaches for specific populations and neurocognitive profiles.

REFERENCES

Anderson, S. W. (2002). Visuospatial impairments. In P. J. Eslinger (Ed.), *Neuropsychological interventions: Clinical research and practice* (pp. 163–181). New York, NY: Guilford Press.

Barrett, A. M., & Gonzalez-Rothi, L. J. (2002). Theoretical bases for neuropsychological interventions. In P. J. Eslinger (Ed.), *Neuropsychological interventions: Clinical research and practice* (pp. 16–37). New York, NY: Guilford Press.

Eslinger, P. J., & Oliveri, M. V. (2002). Approaching interventions clinically and scientifically. In P. J. Eslinger (Ed.), *Neuropsychological interventions: Clinical research and practice* (pp. 3–15). New York, NY: Guilford Press.

Glisky, E. L., & Glisky, M. L. (2002). Learning and memory impairments. In P. J. Eslinger (Ed.), *Neuropsychological interventions: Clinical research and practice* (pp. 137–162). New York, NY: Guilford Press.

Mateer, C. A. (1999). The rehabilitation of executive disorders. In D. T. Stuss, G. Winocur, & I. H. Robertson (Eds.), *Cognitive rehabilitation* (pp. 314–322). Cambridge, UK: Cambridge University Press.

Mateer, C. A., Kerns, K. A., & Eso, K. L. (1996). Management of attention and memory disorders following traumatic brain injury. *Journal of Learning Disabilities, 29,* 618–632.

Mateer, C. A., & Mapou, R. L. (1996). Understanding, evaluation, and managing attention disorders following traumatic brain injury. *Journal of Head Trauma Rehabilitation, 11,* 1–16.

McCaffrey, R. J., & Gansler, D. A. (1992). The efficacy of attention-remediation programs for traumatically brain-injured survivors. In C. J. Long & L. K. Ross (Eds.), *Handbook of head trauma: Acute care to recovery* (pp. 203–217). New York, NY: Plenum Press.

Park, N. W., & Ingles, J. L. (2000). Effectiveness of attention training after an acquired brain injury: A meta-analysis of rehabilitation studies. *Brain Cognition, 44,* 5–9.

Sbordonne, R. (1986). Does computer assisted cognitive rehabilitation work? A case study. *Psychotherapy in Private Practice, 4*(4), 51–61.

Suslow, T., Schonauer, K., & Arolt, V. (2001). Attention training in the cognitive rehabilitation of schizophrenic patients: A review of efficacy studies. *Acta Psychiatrica Scandinavica, 103,* 15–23.

Welsh, M. C. (2002). Developmental and clinical variations in executive functions. In D. L. Molfese & V. J. Molfese (Eds.), *Developmental variations in learning: Applications to social, executive function, language and reading skills* (pp. 139–185). Mahwah, NJ: Erlbaum.

Ylvisaker, M., & Szekeres, S. F. (1996). Cognitive rehabilitation for children with traumatic brain injury. In P. W. Corrigan & S. C. Yudkfsky (Eds.), *Cognitive rehabilitation for neuropsychiatric disorders*. Washington, DC: American Psychiatric Press.

CYNTHIA A. RICCIO
Texas A&M University

See also Biofeedback; Cognitive Strategies; Metacognition; Traumatic Brain Injury

COGNITIVE STRATEGIES

Cognitive strategies are cognitive processes that we use to monitor, control, and manage our cognitive functioning. They mediate both learning and performance. While cognitive strategies have been studied under various names for a long time, credit should probably go to Bruner, Goodnow, and Austin (1956) for first using the construct in the modern-day sense of the term. During recent years, there has been considerable interest in the training and remediation of such strategies.

All of us, whether child, adult, gifted, or mentally retarded, constantly use cognitive strategies to control and direct our thinking and behavior. Word attack skills are strategic in nature, as are the carrying processes used in arithmetic. The ways students take notes or check test responses for accuracy are determined strategically. The manner in which an individual comports himself or herself during a job interview is strategically controlled.

While a variety of cognitive theories have influenced work on cognitive strategies, information processing theories have been the most influential of all. Defining cognitive strategies from an information processing point of view, Young has pointed out that most tasks and problems can be carried out and solved in a variety of different ways and that individuals "have at their command a number of different strategies from which to choose for these purposes . . . there is an analogy between strategies and the subroutines used by computer programmers to organize [their programs]" (1978, pp. 357–358).

Cognitive strategies are theoretically distinguished from cognitive capacities (abilities) and knowledge (information). They are regarded as cognitive techniques that guide the ways our capacities are exercised and our knowledge is used. Strategies are learned both informally and formally. Most important from the standpoint of special education is that they are susceptible to training and improvement.

Apropos of this susceptibility is the distinction that has been made between fixed and modifiable cognitive characteristics (Baron, 1978). Fixed cognitive characteristics (i.e., cognitive capacities or abilities such as intelligence and memory) are difficult to influence environmentally or to change to any significant degree. Modifiable cognitive characteristics, such as cognitive strategies, however, are usually amenable to change and may be significantly improved by education and remediation. While fixed cognitive characteristics ultimately set limits on the development and expression of all cognitive processes, including cognitive strategy, some cognitive researchers believe that effective use of cognitive strategies can overcome "hardwired" cognitive limitations to a great degree: that students with mental retardation, for example, can approach normal cognitive achievement in certain areas if they are taught how to use strategies properly. One of the most important of intervention studies with the mentally retarded was carried out in the area of strategic training by Belmont and Butterfield (1979). These investigators found that with strategic training, mentally retarded learners were able to function on levels equivalent to those of non-retarded individuals in particular tasks.

Some cognitive strategies are general and can be applied across a broad spectrum of activities (e.g., checking one's work for accuracy on completion is a general strategy that is useful in most tasks). Other strategies are applicable only to specific situations (e.g., applying the processes of single-column addition).

There are short-term cognitive strategies and there are long-term ones. A student will apply certain strategies when taking a particular multiple-choice quiz and these strategies serve a short-term purpose. The same student may develop a plan for gaining entry to professional school and, in such a case, long-term strategies will be involved.

Cognitive strategies are sometimes used with full awareness of their application. At other times they operate automatically and with little or no consciousness of their use. We are usually most conscious of using them and laborious in their application when we are first learning them or when we attempt to correct or improve on them. As a rule, the more automatically cognitive strategies operate, and the less aware we are of their operations, the smoother and more effortless they will be. They are also likely to be more effective from the standpoint of freeing up our cognitive apparatuses to work on other aspects of a task or problem. Thus a concert pianist's efforts at interpreting music is at first consciously strategic in nature. The pianist plays with conscious intent to give the music certain nuances while practicing it. During the concert, however, such strategies, while still directing the pianist's playing, work at lower levels of awareness or entirely in an automatic fashion. Indeed, a high degree of awareness of any strategic intentions on the pianist's part would make it impossible to sustain smooth playing, particularly during passages of high velocity.

The particular cognitive strategies that an individual acquires and uses depend on that individual's experiences and instruction. They also depend on the individual's abilities and maturity. An adult will usually use more sophisticated and effective strategies than a 10-year-old child. A gifted child uses more complex strategies and has access to a wider range of strategies than does a child with intellectual disability. A deaf child will be limited in the use of certain strategies because of limited language capabilities but may learn to use still others more effectively than hearing children (Mann & Sabatino, 1985).

Not all cognitive strategies have the same degree of effectiveness. Some are effective for an appropriate age level or handicap but not for others (e.g., a first-grader uses counting strategies that are effective for that age but may actually have negative effects if used in later grades). A child with learning disabilities may be ineffective at strategies that a good learner uses with ease.

Some strategies may even be harmful. A child who is a social isolate may use strategic approaches to other children that are intended to make friends but instead result in rejection. A child who is having trouble with advanced mathematics keeps using calculation strategies that are cumbersome and that interfere with understanding. If remedial cognitive strategy training is to succeed with such children, it will often require the unlearning of "bad" strategies prior to the acquisition of good ones.

Furthermore, it is not enough to know how to use a particular strategy well. It also is required that the user be skilled in its application and know when the strategy is appropriate or when another strategy should be used instead. Regular practice under varied conditions appears essential for most new strategies to become effective. Mentally retarded students will almost always be found to be deficient in their use of cognitive strategies and to require a great deal of rehearsal to master new strategies (Baron, 1978).

Success in school may ultimately depend on the number of effective strategies that a student can appropriately employ. Children with good abilities may fail academically because they do not know enough effective strategies to deal with their schoolwork, or because they rely on inadequate or inappropriate strategies, or because they fail to effectively use the good strategies at their disposal. On the other hand, children with limited abilities may succeed academically because they have learned to use cognitive strategies to compensate for and minimize the impact of their deficiencies.

A number of classification systems have been suggested for cognitive strategies. Baron (1978) has suggested that we categorize them in three ways: (1) central strategies that are basic to the development of others' strategies; (2) general strategies applicable to a variety of situations; and (3) specific strategies pertaining to particular types of applications.

Newell (1979) has addressed the classification of strategies using an analogy of an inverted cone of strategic skills. At the bottom of the cone are a large number of strategies that apply only to certain problems or situations (e.g., a carrying strategy for two-column addition). Such narrow strategies may be powerful and, if properly used, should effectively solve the problems to which they are applied. They are, however, limited to specific types of problems or work only under particular conditions.

As we move up Newell's inverted cone to its tip we find more generalizable but less effective strategies; there is a tradeoff between generalizability and effectiveness. At the very tip of the cone we find a few highly general strategies that are applicable to almost any problem or situation but that are weak and by themselves unable to solve any specific problem. Checking one's schoolwork to see that it is accurate is an example of a general beneficial cognitive strategy, but it has weak effects and by itself can solve no specific problem. In between lie a variety of intermediate-level strategies that vary in specificity and power. It has been suggested that the most useful approach to cognitive strategy training from a general remedial standpoint might be to address such intermediate-level strategies (Brown & Palincsar, 1982). Thus scanning written pages in a systematic left-to-right fashion is a strategy that has some specificity (i.e., it applies to reading); it also has some generality in that it applies to a wide range of reading.

In determining what type of strategies to use with special education students, the cognitive trainer is confronted with decisions as to optimal training programs. Teachers engaged in the cognitive training of learning-disabled children might well stick to specific and intermediate-level strategies that are directly applicable to particular types of schoolwork. Psychologists might be interested in more general types of cognitive strategic training such as is involved in problem solving, test taking, and so forth (Borkowski & Kornarski, 1981).

A distinction has been made between blind and informed cognitive strategy training. Blind training programs are ones in which the subjects do not know the purpose of the training they are receiving. Informed cognitive strategy training not only trains the pupils strategically but helps them to understand the purpose of the training and the benefits to be derived from it. There is evidence that both types of training programs can be effective. However, students trained under informed conditions are likely to use their strategies more effectively and to continue to use them after their formal training is over (Kendall, Borkowski, & Cavanaugh, 1980).

A number of researchers have offered recommendations to guide cognitive strategy training with handicapped students (Belmont & Butterfield, 1979; Brown & Palincsar, 1982; Borkowski & Cavanaugh, 1981; Kreiner, 1992). Some investigators have advised that teachers of handicapped students may wish to use cognitive strategy curricula (Borkowski & Cavanaugh, 1979; Winschel & Lawrence, 1975).

The most active interest in cognitive strategies currently is in metacognition, which represents a supraordinate realm of executive cognitive strategies that monitor and regulate lower-level strategies, and in cognitive behavioral interventions, which involve strategic training.

REFERENCES

Baron, J. (1978). Intelligence and general strategies. In G. Underwood (Ed.), *Strategies of information processing* (pp. 403–450). London, UK: Academic.

Belmont, J. M., & Butterfield, E. C. (1979). Learning strategies as determinants of memory deficiencies. *Cognitive Psychology*, *2*, 411–420.

Borkowski, J. G., & Cavanaugh, J. C. (1979). Maintenance and generalization of skills and strategies by the retarded. In W. R. Ellis (Ed.), *Handbook of mental deficiency* (2nd ed.). Hillsdale, NJ: Erlbaum.

Borkowski, J. G., & Kornarski, E. A. (1981). Educational implications of efforts to change intelligence. *Journal of Special Education*, *15*, 289–306.

Brown, A. C., & Palincsar, A. S. (1982). Inducing strategic learning from texts by means of informed, self control training. *Topics in Learning & Learning Disabilities*, *2*, 1–17.

Bruner, J. S., Goodnow, J. J., & Austin, G. A. (1956). *A study of thinking*. New York, NY: Wiley.

Kendall, C. R., Borkowski, J. G., & Cavanaugh, J. C. (1980). Metamemory and the transfer of an interrogative strategy by EMR children. *Intelligence*, *4*, 255–270.

Kreiner, D. S. (1992). Reaction times measures of spelling. *Journal of Experimental Psychology: Learning, Memory, & Cognition*, *18*, 4, 765–776.

Mann, L., & Sabatino, D. A. (1985). *Foundations of cognitive processes in remedial and special education*. Rockville, MD: Aspen.

Newell, A. (1979). One final word. In D. T. Tuma & F. Reid (Eds.), *Problem solving and education: Issues in teaching and research*. Hillsdale, NJ: Erlbaum.

Winschel, J. F., & Lawrence, E. A. (1975). Short-term memory: Curricular implications for the mentally retarded. *Journal of Special Education*, *9*, 395–408.

Young, R. M. (1978). Strategies and the structure of a cognitive skill. In G. Underwood (Ed.), *Strategies of information processing* (pp. 357–401). London, UK: Academic.

JONI J. GLEASON
University of West Florida

See also **Cognitive Styles; Information Processing; Metacognition**

COGNITIVE STYLES

Cognitive styles are constructs that help to explain the ways that personality variables affect cognition. Kogan has defined them as reflecting "individual variations in *modes* of attending, perceiving, remembering and thinking" (1980, p. 64). Two individuals who score identically on intelligence and other cognitive aptitude or achievement tests and are the same in information processing capabilities may nevertheless differ significantly in schoolwork, success on the job, and other behaviors because they differ in their cognitive styles (Mann & Sabatino, 1985).

The study of cognitive styles began in earnest following World War II, urged on by concern about the psychiatric casualties of that war and postwar interest in personal self-development and psychotherapy. Personality assessment had become exceedingly popular. Thus interest developed respecting the ways that personality variables affect cognitive variables. Studies of what came to be known as cognitive styles emerged.

Interest in cognitive styles first appeared most prominently in the work of George Klein and associates at the Menninger clinic. While the original work was conceptualized in terms of perceptual attitudes (perceptual types of tests being used as the most prominent way of assessing cognitive styles), later research emphasized the cognitive aspects of the research and the term *cognitive controls* became the dominant descriptor applied to work seeking to determine how personality factors interact with and influence cognitive skills.

Many definitions of cognitive styles have been offered (Kane, 1984). They generally agree that cognitive styles should be thought of as personality characteristics or traits that are related to other personality characteristics. Furthermore, while cognitive styles cannot always be distinguished or separated from cognitive skills, they are distinct from cognitive contents.

A considerable number of different types of cognitive styles have been distinguished through research. Some are similar, but others are clearly different in their implications for cognitive functioning. It is not unusual to study children and adults from the standpoint of several different cognitive styles.

While the assessment of cognitive styles of schoolchildren is usually done through paper-and-pencil questionnaires and tests, problem-solving tasks and perceptual types of apparatus are also used. Among the most ingenious of the latter has been the tilting-room chair test (Goldstein & Blackman, 1977). In this test, the subjects sit in a chair that is suspended in a small room. Both the chair and the room may be tilted either left or right in varying degrees. In one version, the Room-Adjustment Test (RAT), the room is tilted 56 degrees and chair 22 degrees. There are eight trials; in four of these trials the room and chair are tilted in the same direction; in the other four they are tilted in opposite directions. The object of the test is to determine the degree of effectiveness with which the subject can direct the examiner to reorient the room to an upright position under these circumstances. In the Body Adjustment Test (BAT), the room remains tilted and the subject directs the examiner to move him or her to an upright position. The degree to which the subjects succeed on these orientation tasks was originally used to assess an individual's ability at field articulation and later to assess an individual's degree of field independence–dependence.

The scores assigned an individual on the basis of performance on cognitive-style assessments are usually used to place the subject somewhere on a bipolar continuum whose poles represent opposing stylistic types (e.g., leveling–sharpening, scanning–focusing). The more the individual's score is oriented toward one pole or another, the more he or she is characterized as being typified by the particular cognitive style associated with that pole. In the case of some cognitive styles, however, an individual will be characterized as belonging to one of several cognitive style categories, according to the means by which questions were answered or problems solved. This category is presumed to identify the way that an individual characteristically perceives, thinks, solves problems, and so on. An example of this is provided by conceptual styles tasks that categorize children as to whether they tend to be analytic, categorical, or relational in their thinking.

Though there has been disagreement on the issue, Kogan has suggested that cognitive styles can be classified on the basis of whether the results obtained are judgmental (i.e., have positive or negative implications attached to particular styles and their scores). Thus certain cognitive styles clearly suggest good or poor cognitive performance (e.g., Witkin's field dependence–independence continuum). Other cognitive styles, however, only indirectly imply cognitive strength or weakness, while still others appear to be truly stylistic (i.e., imputing neither cognitive strength nor weakness but rather suggesting different ways of thinking). Still other cognitive styles can be interpreted either in terms of cognitive strengths and weaknesses or in purely stylistic terms, depending on the circumstances of usage and interpretation.

While the study of cognitive styles began with adult populations, it gradually moved over to juvenile populations as well, including those of children with learning problems and disabilities. This has been more for research rather than diagnostic purposes. The two most popular of cognitive-style study approaches to schoolchildren and special education students are those of field independence–dependence and conceptual tempo. Blackman and Goldstein (1982) have suggested that a major reason for their popularity is the easy availability of instruments to assess them. Another reason seems to be that they appear to be cognitive styles that may have particular relevance to schoolwork.

There have been many studies suggesting that field-independent students are better and more self-dependent learners than field-dependent ones; that they are better decoders in reading than field-dependent students; and that they are better at math and science as well. Field-independent students have been found to do better in "discovery" types of learning situations, while field-dependent students are benefited by structured learning situations. Gifted children are more likely to be field independent than mentally retarded ones (Mann & Sabatino, 1985). Learning-disabled pupils are more likely to be field dependent than normal readers.

In respect to conceptual tempo, this cognitive-style dimension characterizes children on the basis of their placement on a reflection–impulsivity dimension, according to their performance on problem-solving tests, and so on. As might be expected, reflective children are usually better students, while impulsive ones are more likely to read inaccurately and to manifest behavior problems.

While the research into cognitive styles has been very active, and results are regularly found indicating that cognitive styles are significantly related to school and academic variables that are important to both disabled and nondisabled children, the sum and substance of this research does not appear to support a position that knowledge of a disabled child's particular cognitive style, in and of itself, is particularly helpful in respect to predicting school achievement (Swanson, 1980) or in guiding day-to-day instruction or management. Socioeconomic and general cognitive factors play roles of far greater importance in the school lives of special education students. Indeed, many of the significant differences found in the school performances of special education students who differ in cognitive style appear to be the result of consequences of investigators confounding their variables.

The most popular variants or offshoots of cognitive styles currently are identified as learning styles based on objective imaging and EEG examinations (Riding, Glass, Butler, Pleydell-Pearce, 1997). Since learning styles tend to be educationally oriented, they have received a great deal of attention in educational circles. Learning style constructs, which emphasize learning preferences rather than personality characteristics, have taken much of the attention away from other types of cognitive styles among researchers concerned with school and academic achievement.

REFERENCES

Blackman, S., & Goldstein, K. M. (1982). Cognitive styles and learning disabilities. *Journal of Learning Disabilities, 15,* 106–113.

Goldstein, K. M., & Blackman, S. (1977). *Cognitive styles: Five approaches to theory and research.* New York, NY: Wiley.

Kane, M. (1984). Cognitive styles of thinking and learning: Part one. *Academic Therapy, 19,* 527–536.

Klein, G. S., & Schlesinger, H. J. (1949). Where is the perceiver in perceptual theory? *Journal of Personality, 18,* 32–47.

Kogan, N. (1980). Cognitive styles and reading performance. *Bulletin of the Orton Society, 39,* 63–77.

Mann, L., & Sabatino, D. A. (1985). *Foundations of cognitive processes in remedial and special education.* Rockville, MD: Aspen.

Riding, R. J., Glass, A., Butler, S. R., & Pleydell-Pearce, C. W. (1997). Cognitive style and individual differences in EEG alpha during information processing. *Educational Psychology, 17,* 219–234.

Swanson, L. (1980). Cognitive style, locus of control, and school achievement in learning disabled females. *Journal of Clinical Psychology, 36,* 964–967.

EMILY WAHLEN
LESTER MANN
Hunter College,
City University of New York

See also Learning Styles; Sperry, Roger W.; Split-Brain Research; Temperament

COHEN SYNDROME

Cohen syndrome is characterized by truncal obesity, hypotonia, mental retardation, and ocular and craniofacial abnormalities. Characteristic craniofacial features include microcephaly, small jaw, prominent incisors, small philtrum, and high-arched palate.

Cohen syndrome is a rare disorder. Approximately 100 cases have been documented. It appears to occur with greater frequency in people of Eastern European Jewish decent. Females and males are affected equally. It is primarily an autosomal recessive genetic disorder that is present from birth. The gene responsible for the syndrome has been mapped to the long arm of Chromosome 8 (Thomaidis, Fryssira, Katsarou, & Metaxotou, 1999).

Characteristics

1. Low birthweight, delayed growth, delayed puberty, hypotonia, and obesity occurring in middle childhood.

2. Prominent lips, downslant of eyelids, hyperextensible joints, narrow hands and feet, and possibly webbed feet and seizures (Jones, 1988).

3. Ocular abnormalities, including diminished vision in bright light, degeneration of the retina (retina pigmentosa), optic atrophy, decreased visual acuity, and possibly total blindness.

4. Mild to moderate mental retardation in 82% of cases (Gandy, 1994).

Treatment of Cohen syndrome depends on the individual's symptoms, but it may include surgery to correct abnormal facial features, visual problems, or webbed feet. Physical therapy may be necessary for children with hypotonia. Developmental delays and childhood obesity should be monitored. The child may need services from an ophthalmologist to care for visual abnormalities. Families often benefit from genetic counseling to better understand the disorder (Gandy, 1994).

The services required in school depend on the child's symptoms and needs. Children with Cohen syndrome usually qualify for special education services due to mental retardation, health problems, or visual impairments that affect learning. For children with developmental delays or hypotonia, early intervention programs are appropriate.

Individuals may require physical therapy. Periodic assessments help school personnel develop appropriate individual educational plans that maximize the student's learning potential (Plumridge, Bennett, Dinno, & Branson, 1993).

The prognosis of an individual with Cohen syndrome is variable, depending on the person's symptoms. Adults with mild mental retardation, for example, may be able to function with minimum supportive services. Future research is focused on understanding the etiology and genetics of the disorder.

REFERENCES

Gandy, A. (1994, December 4). *Cohen syndrome*. Retrieved from http://www.icondata.com/health/pedbase/.les/cohensyn.htm

Jones, K. (1988). *Smith's recognizable patterns of human malformation*. Philadelphia PA: W. B. Saunders.

Plumridge, D., Bennett, R., Dinno, N., & Branson, C. (Eds.). (1993). *The student with a genetic disorder*. Springfield, IL: Charles C. Thomas.

Thomaidis, L., Fryssira, H., Katsarou, E., & Metaxotou, C. (1999). Cohen syndrome: Two new cases in siblings. *European Journal of Pediatrics, 158*, 838–841.

SUSANNAH MORE
University of Texas at Austin

COLITIS

Ulcerative colitis is a chronic inflammatory disease of the colon (large intestine). It is a progressive disease, spreading to include part or all of the colon and rectum (Goodman & Sparburg, 1978). It is characterized by alternating remissions and relapses. The disease is usually more severe in children than adults, carrying an increased risk of malignancy because of the greater severity and duration of the disease (Dixon & Walker, 1984). A disease closely related to ulcerative colitis is Crohn's disease, which involves the small intestine as well as the large. Symptomatology and progression in Crohn's closely resembles that in ulcerative colitis (Hanauer, 1984).

The cause of ulcerative colitis is unknown (Goulston & McGovern, 1981). Symptoms of the disease include diarrhea with blood and mucus, abdominal pain preceding defecation, anemia, and rectal urgency. Weight loss is apparent in some children owing to reduced caloric intake or to limitation of food eaten to avoid discomforts of the disease (Dixon & Walker, 1984).

Treatment of colitis varies with severity and extent of the disease. The goal of treatment for children is to bring about remission to allow normal growth and development. Medical therapy includes use of corticosteroids to control inflammation and sulfasalazine to control flare-ups (Bokey & Shell, 1985). Undesirable side effects of the two precipitate cautious use with children. Corticosteroids interfere with growth, increase susceptibility to infection, and cause temporary alterations in physical appearance. Sulfasalazine can cause headaches, nausea, vomiting, anorexia, and rash.

If the disease does not respond to medical therapy, or if it involves complications, surgery is required. Part or all of the colon is removed and then resected together or attached to the abdominal wall. If attached to the abdominal wall, a stoma is formed to allow excretion of waste products into an external collecting apparatus. With surgery, the effects of the disease disappear.

Children and their families need a great deal of emotional support and understanding in dealing with the manifestations of the disease and the effects of treatment (Burke, Neigut, Kocoshis, & Chandra, 1994; Melvin, 2003). Children need special understanding and encouragement when dealing with side effects of steroid treatment or adjusting to the use of an external collecting apparatus. Advances in development of collection apparatus now make it possible for most children to participate in many activities and sports. Most individuals with colitis live a normal life under prolonged medical care.

REFERENCES

Bokey, E. L., & Shell, R. (1985). *Stomal therapy: A guide for nurses, practitioners and patients*. Sydney, Australia: Pergamon.

Burke, P. M., Neigut, D., Kocoshis, P. R., & Chandra, R. (1994). Correlates of depression in new onset pediatric bowel disease. *Child Psychiatry and Human Development, 24*, 4, 275–283.

Dixon, M. L., & Walker, W. A. (1984). Ulcerative colitis and Crohn's disease. In S. S. Gellis & B. M. Kagan (Eds.), *Current pediatric therapy* (pp. 195–198). Philadelphia, PA: Saunders.

Goodman, M. J., & Sparberg, M. (1978). *Ulcerative colitis*. New York, NY: Wiley.

Goulston, S. J., & McGovern, V. J. (1981). *Fundamentals of colitis*. Oxford, UK: Pergamon Press.

Hanauer, S. B. (1984). Ulcerative colitis. In R. E. Rakel (Ed.), *Conn's current therapy* (pp. 410–415). Philadelphia, PA: Saunders.

Melvin, B. (2003). Crohn's disease. In E. Fletcher-Janzen & C. R. Reynolds (Eds.), *Childhood disorders diagnostic desk reference* (pp. 156–157). Hoboken, NJ: Wiley.

CHRISTINE A. ESPIN
University of Minnesota

See also **Family Response to a Child With Disabilities; Physical Disabilities**

COLITIS, COLLAGENOUS

Collagenous colitis is a rare but treatable inflammatory disorder of the mucous membranes lining the colon. It is a poorly understood disorder that has not received much attention in the research (Microscopic/Collagenous Colitis FAQ, 1999). Collagenous colitis is often referred to as a form of microscopic colitis because it can be detected only by a pathologist using a microscope after a biopsy; with this condition during an endoscope procedure (colonoscopy or sigmoidoscopy), the colon looks normal. Collagenous colitis is also often referred to as lymphocytic colitis because it is characterized by a thickening of the subepithelial collagen layer and increased lymphocytes in the lining of the colon.

Despite controversy over the syndrome's name, the treatment and symptoms are virtually identical (Mayo Clinic Rochester, 2000). Symptoms are characterized by watery, nonbloody diarrhea that may be severe and explosive, requiring up to 30 bathroom visits per day. Episodes are extremely sudden and may be persistent or intermittent over a period of months or years. In rare cases, the diarrhea may cause dehydration; other symptoms include weakness and fatigue, difficulty eating, abdominal bloating or pain, weight loss, and nausea. Dietary factors alone do not seem to influence the sudden bouts of diarrhea although certain foods such as high fiber, fat, milk products, spices, wheat, or uncooked fruits and vegetables may exacerbate symptoms, especially diarrhea (Cleveland Clinic, 1999).

Characteristics

1. Sudden and explosive fecal incontinence up to 30 times a day
2. Watery, nonbloody diarrhea
3. Persistent or intermittent episodes that can lead to dehydration and weight loss
4. Associated with secondary symptoms of weakness and fatigue and nausea
5. Associated with secondary symptoms of abdominal bloating, pain, and poor eating abilities
6. Can be aggravated by specific foods
7. Often originates as an elusive form of arthritis

Patients sometimes seek treatment for an elusive form of arthritis as much as 10 years prior to problems controlling diarrhea (National Organization for Rare Disorders, 1998). The arthritis typically affects the back, hips, and sometimes ribs. Other associated problems with this illness may include iritis, purpura, thyroid disease, pernicious anemia, idiopathic pulmonary fibrosis, fibromyalgia, unexplained severe itching, mouth sores, fatigue, depression, mitral valve prolapse, and celiac sprue (Mayo Clinic Rochester, 2000). There does not seem to be an association with Crohn's disease, ulcerative colitis, or cancer.

The typical patient is a middle-aged woman, and the rate of onset increases after the age of 40. It is also seen in men and in children as young as 7 years, with a reoccurrence of likelihood in older individuals. Many patients diagnosed are Caucasians in Northern Europe, Canada, the United States, Australia, and New Zealand (Microscopic/Collagenous Colitis FAQ, 1999). Many patients report a close family member with the same or similar intestinal symptoms, giving the appearance of a hereditary factor. Other possible causes are unidentified chronic gastrointestinal infections such as dysentery or giardia; immune disturbances, including autoimmune disease; and medications such as some nonsteriodal anti-inflammatory agents (i.e., ibuprofen, ranitidine, carbemazepine).

Diagnosis is often made through a process of elimination. There is no proven cure, but medications can arrest the syndrome (Mayo Clinic Rochester, 2000). Traditionally, treatment is started with sulfasalazine, but if patients cannot tolerate it, Asocal is typically prescribed. Anti-diarrheal medications such as Imodium and Lomotil are also used for temporary relief but tend merely to delay the diarrhea. Other medications that can help are aminosalicylate, metronidazole, cholestyramine, and bismuth sub-salicylate. Prednisone is also often prescribed but cannot be used long-term due to the side effects of cataract formation, high blood pressure, and increased rate of diabetes that are associated with its use. Antibiotics have shown excellent short-term results. Surgical removal of the colon by ileostomy is a radical approach that is seldom used.

Children experiencing this condition may need to engage in stress-reduction activities to eliminate anxiety over illness and social stigma created from required frequent bathroom breaks. Other services may also need to be provided by the school to accommodate the child, such as conveniently located restrooms and provision of educational material when the child is unable to be in the classroom. Although special education services are typically not warranted, in rare occasions children are served under the classification of Other Health Impairment.

REFERENCES

Cleveland Clinic. (1999, September). *Gastrointestinal center: Treatments for collagenous colitis.* Retrieved from http://onhealth.webmd.com/conditions/condctr/gasrto/item,49305.asp

Mayo Clinic Rochester. (2000). *Inflammatory bowel disease interest group: Collagenous / microscopic colitis.* Retrieved from http://www.mayo.edu/int-med/gi/ibd.htm

Microscopic/Collagenous Colitis FAQ. (1999, October). Retrieved from http://www.malinowski.com/faq.htm

National Organization for Rare Disorders. (1998). *Colitis, collagenous.* Retrieved from http://www.rarediseases.org

WALTER R. SCHAMBER
RIK CARL D'AMATO
University of Northern Colorado

COLITIS, ULCERATIVE

Ulcerative colitis is an inflammatory bowel disease, often chronic, that affects the mucus of the colon. It usually begins in the rectum and sigmoid colon and spreads to the entire colon, but rarely affects the small intestine. The ulcerated areas of the large intestine become inflamed and may cause abscesses leading to episodes of bloody diarrhea, abdominal pain, urgent bowel movements, fever, weight loss, joint pain, and skin lesions (Larson, 1990). The etiology of this disease is unknown.

The epidemiology and demographic incidence of this condition is 50–150 cases per 100,000 individuals, primarily affecting women between the ages of 14 and 38 years. A second increase in incidences occurs between the ages of 55 and 70 (Ferri, 1999). It also seems more prevalent among Jewish and high-socioeconomic groups (Weinstock, Andrews, & Cray, 1998). Causes are unknown but may be related to stress, alcohol use, smoking, genetic factors, and diet.

Characteristics

Early symptoms

1. Pain in the left side of the abdomen that improves after bowel movements

2. Episodes of bloody diarrhea with mucus or pus, alternating with symptom-free intervals

Acute symptoms

1. Increased bloody diarrhea of up to 10–20 bowel movements a day
2. Severe cramps and abdominal pain, especially around the rectum
3. High fever of up to 104°F (40°C)
4. Sweating, dehydration
5. Nausea and irritability
6. Bloated abdomen
7. Joint pain
8. Skin lesions

Treatment goals consist of controlling inflammation, replacing nutritional losses and blood volume, and preventing complications. Bed rest is necessary with intravenous fluid replacement and a clear liquid diet to reduce stool volume. Blood transfusions or iron supplements may be needed to correct anemia.

Minimal symptoms are corrected with an antidiarrheal medication prescribed by a doctor. For mild or moderate conditions, the disease can be treated orally with an aminosalicylate, usually sulfasalazine, at 500 mg twice a day until a therapeutic dose of 4 to 6 g a day is reached. In addition, medicated enemas such as hydrocortisone can be effective. For severe disease, oral, enema, or suppository corticosteroids such as prednisone (40–60 mg/day) are useful (Ferri, 1999). Approximately 20–25% of patients afflicted will require surgery if they do not respond to medication therapy. The operation most commonly performed is the ileoanal anastomosis, in which the diseased colon and large intestine are removed but the rectum is left intact. The small intestine is then stitched to the rectum, allowing for normal passage of stool rather than a permanent use of an ileostomy bag (Larson, 1990).

Psychotherapy is useful in most patients due to the chronicity of the disease and the young age of patients. Referral to self-help groups is recommended and especially important when the illness may be related to anorexia nervosa (Ferri, 1999).

Colonoscopic surveillance and multiple biopsies should be instituted yearly after diagnosis to prevent the increased risk of colon cancer (10–20% of patients develop it after 10 years of the disease). Furthermore, 75% of patients treated medically will experience relapse and need further medical attention. Consultation for suspected cases should be brought to the attention of a gastrointestinal physician for a sigmoidoscopy or colonoscopy (Griffith, 1995).

REFERENCES

Ferri, F. (1999). *Ferri's clinical advisor: Instant diagnosis and treatment*. St. Louis, MO: Mosby.

Griffith, H. (1995). *Complete guide to symptoms: Illness and surgery* (3rd ed.). New York, NY: Body Press/Perigee.

Larson, D. (1990). *The Mayo Clinic family health book*. New York, NY: William Morrow.

Weinstock, D., Andrews, M., & Cray, J. (1998). *Professional guide to disease* (6th ed.). Springhouse, PA: Springhouse.

WALTER R. SCHAMBER
RIK CARL D'AMATO
University of Northern Colorado

COLLABORATION (See Inclusion)

COLLABORATIVE PERINATAL PROJECT

The main purpose of the Collaborative Perinatal Project was to evaluate factors in pregnancy that may relate to cerebral palsy and other abnormalities of the central nervous system. The project was sponsored by the National Institute of Neurological and Communicative Disorders and Strokes. Over 50,000 pregnant women were recruited (from January 1959 to December 1965) for the largest prospective study of its kind. Although readers of the study are urged to regard conclusions as tentative, it is generally agreed that this massive undertaking adds substantially to what is known about the general epidemiology of birth defects.

Data collected at the 14 university-affiliated hospitals included information on the mother's social and medical background; coexisting diseases; complications of pregnancy; current drug/medication use; and previous use of drugs (extending beyond the mother's last menstrual period). Each participant was interviewed at least monthly throughout pregnancy, at scheduled intervals during the infant's first 2 years, and annually until the child reached 8 years. Records on each child until the age of 8 years include birth and developmental history, diseases, noted congenital defects, and information on siblings and father. Infants received daily examinations for the first 7 days of life (and weekly for prolonged postnatal hospitalizations), with an extensive, standard pediatric exam at age 1. Of the mortality rate (4.4% or 2,227 stillborn or died before age 4), 81% came to autopsy.

A tangential purpose of this project was the epidemiological investigation of the possible teratogenic role of drugs (or those drugs that cause malformations)—in other words, the relationship between drugs taken during pregnancy and malformations in offspring. Although frequent hypotheses are suggested, only a few such relationships are accepted universally as causal. Potent teratogens (e.g., thalidomide) are identified relatively easily. Less potent drugs with less dramatic outcomes are equally important but more difficult to isolate and detect. The Collaborative Perinatal Project provided the opportunity to use a battery of epidemiological and statistical methods to screen a variety of drugs against a variety of malformation outcomes.

The study (1) provided quantitative information, much not previously available, on relationships among birth defects; (2) confirmed and elaborated on, in quantitative terms, factors such as single umbilical artery and birth defects; (3) raised, in quantitative terms, hypotheses concerning risk factors, some previously suspected but without quantitative information and some not previously suspected; and (4) concluded that birth defects are rarely attributable to a single cause and that many malformation outcomes appear to have multiple risk factors that are interrelated.

Heinonen et al. (1977) were commissioned by the National Institutes of Health to document all findings. Their text contains detailed information on methods, malformations, drugs used, and so on. The data from the project continue to be analyzed (Friedman, Granick, Bransfield & Kreisher, 1995) and debated (Hardy, 2003; James, 1996).

REFERENCES

Friedman, H. S., Granick, S., Bransfield, S., & Kreisher, C. (1995). Gender difference in early life risk factors for substance use/abuse: A study of an African-American sample. *American Journal of Drug & Alcohol Abuse, 21*(4), 511–531.

Hardy, J. B. (2003). The collaborative perinatal project: Lessons and legacy. *Annuals of Epidemiology, 13*(5), 303–311.

Heinonen, O. P., Slone, D., & Shapiro, J. (1977). *Birth defects and drugs in pregnancy*. Littleton, MA: Publishing Sciences Group.

James, W. H. (1996). Debate and argument: The sex ratio of the sibs of neurodevelopmentally disordered children. *Journal of Child Psychology & Psychiatry & Allied Disciplines, 37*(5), 619.

C. MILDRED TASHMAN
College of St. Rose

See also Congenital Disorders

COLLEGE PROGRAMS FOR DISABLED COLLEGE STUDENTS

Following the end of World War II, the majority of colleges and universities in the United States became more sensitive to the needs of students who would have been financially disabled without the original G.I. bill. This same sensitivity, however, on the part of colleges and universities for those who were physically, socially, and/or academically disabled did not manifest itself to any major degree until the 1970s.

In April 1978, the Association on Handicapped Student Service Programs in Post-Secondary Education (AHSSPPE) came into existence. This organization, along with others, provided professional support for full implementation of the Architectural Barriers Act of 1968 as upgraded and expanded on by Section 504 of the Vocational Rehabilitation Act of 1973, which became operational in April 1977. The net effect of this Act and its revisions was to ensure the access and use of public schools (elementary through college) by the physically disabled through assurance that the schools would be constructed to accommodate the handicapped person.

Similarly, by the late 1970s, a few colleges and universities began formal programs to serve college-bound students who had academic deficits resulting from either some innate and formal learning (language) disability and/or environmentally induced one. Those higher education institutions having programs for this population were identified in part by research projects sponsored by the National Association of College Admission Counselors (NACAC; Mangrum & Strickhart, 1984). Two agencies that contributed to the development of the NACAC directory of college programs were the Post-Secondary School Committee of the Association for Children with Learning Disabilities (ACLD) and the Loyola Academy of Wilmette, Illinois. Other references that identify colleges and universities having academic support services are Liscio's (1984) *A Guide to Colleges for Learning Disabled Students;* Mangrum and Strichart's (1984) *College and the Learning Disabled Student;* the *FCLD Guide for Parents of Children with Learning Disabilities* (1984); and *Peterson's Guide to Colleges with Programs for Learning Disabled Students* (1985). These references suggest that the prospective user ask certain questions, as identified by Liscio (1984):

1. Is there a special program for learning-disabled students?
2. How many full-time learning-disabled students are enrolled in the program?
3. Is there a brochure or written description of the program available?
4. Do learning-disabled students in special programs take regular college courses?
5. Are special courses required of learning-disabled students? Do they carry college credit? Can credit be used toward graduation?
6. Are there additional tuition or fee requirements for learning-disabled students? (p. 12)

Additionally, the prospective users of these references and others like them, following a personal onsite examination of the institution and its services as listed, will probably determine that the primary thrust or intent of the institution's services falls into one of two categories: (1) assistance and support that is not necessarily remedial, and (2) assistance and support that is intended to be remedial. The former is specifically characterized by the use of books on tape (the same service used by blind students); oral presentations instead of written exams; cassette tapes in lieu of written papers; readers for reading textbooks and exams; and notetakers. These services allow the language-handicapped student to cope and to graduate in spite of unremediated reading and spelling deficits.

The college-aged learning-disabled student who is looking for a school to attend will find that the majority of two- and four-year higher-education institutions (both public and private) that offer support services will be of the type just depicted, for example, those that provide assistance and support that is not necessarily intended to be remedial. The student who wishes to become language independent, academically as well as socially, might want to consider the other major type of service.

Those institutions that intend to remediate the student's language disabling and his or her accompanying social and psychological deficits will be characterized by instruction that is designed to remediate the student's reading, spelling, written expression, and arithmetic deficits. The kind of instruction that would be most commonly used would directly reteach the basic or requisite information that must be known to read, spell, write, and carry out mathematical operations. Other probable aspects of this second service posture would be the use of tutors who have been trained to carry out direct remediation of the student's academic deficits and formal support programs that deal directly with the student's social habilitation and psychological needs. Both types of schools offer their learning-disabled students the opportunity to take exams in a private setting without time constraints, use tape recorders to record lectures, take a reduced load as necessary, and partake in the institution's traditional student support services. Beyond the traditional academic assistance and/or remediation, most institutions of higher learning also offer counseling and testing support services. The University of Washington provides some helpful resources for college funding strategies for students with disabilities (http://www.washington.edu/doit/Brochures/Academics/financial-aid.html).

REFERENCES

The FCLD guide for parents of children with learning disabilities. (1984). New York, NY: Foundation for Children with Learning Disabilities.

Liscio, M. A. (1984). *A guide to colleges for learning disabled students.* Orlando, FL: Academic.

Mangrum, C. T., & Strichart, S. S. (1984). *College and the learning disabled student*. Orlando, FL: Grune & Stratton.

Peterson's guide to colleges with programs for learning disabled students. (1985). Princeton, NJ: Peterson's Guide.

ROBERT T. NASH
University of Wisconsin Oshkosh

COLORADO TICK FEVER

Colorado tick fever is an acute viral infection transmitted by the bite of a tick. This disease is characterized by a sudden onset of symptoms including fever, severe muscle aches (myalgia), joint stiffness, headache, sore throat, sensitivity to light (photophobia), nausea, vomiting, fatigue, and occasionally a raised rash. More severe symptoms include sequelae such as meningoencephalitis, an inflammation of the membranes covering the brain and spinal cord. Extensive involvement of the respiratory system is rarely seen with Colorado tick fever (Byrd, Vasquez, & Roy, 1997); however, infection has been associated with vascular instability, circulatory disturbance (hemorrhagic disease), cardiac inflammation (myocarditis), and other pulmonary problems.

The prevalence of Colorado tick fever is estimated to be 200 to 300 cases annually. The infection is limited to mountainous areas in the Western United States and is most frequently reported to occur from early spring to late summer. The incubation period lasts from 3 to 6 days, and the period of illness lasts 7 to 10 days. The course of illness, however, tends to be biphasic; that is, symptoms present, remit, and then reoccur (Harrison's Principles of Internal Medicine, 2000). For example, common symptoms such as fever and muscle soreness may continue for three days and then remit, only to recur one to three days later.

Characteristics

1. This acute viral infection is transmitted by the bite of a tick in the Western United States.
2. Fever and muscle aches are the most common symptoms.
3. Full recovery is usually expected, but complications can occur (e.g., meningoencephalitis, hemorrhagic disease, myocarditis, and pulmonary involvement).
4. Permanent neurological complications can be manifest as seizures, motor abnormalities, language disturbance, and intellectual deficits.

Blood tests can be used to make the diagnosis at any stage of the disease (Attoui, Billoir, Bruey, de Micco, & de

Llamballerie, 1998). Prognosis is generally good; that is, symptoms remit within the first couple of weeks. Treatment is typically focused on symptom relief after successful removal of the tick. Aspirin should not be given to infants or children who have recently had a tick bite as this treatment may exacerbate the condition (e.g., increase vascular instability).

In cases where Colorado tick fever causes the marrow cells to become infected by the virus, symptoms are likely to persist, and hospitalization may even be required. In these and other cases of complicated tick fever (e.g., encephalitis, respiratory difficulties, and hemorrhagic fevers), extended school absences may occur. It is rare, however, for children to require special education services as a result of this infection. When services are required, they are likely to be under the category of Other Health Impairment. If significant cognitive sequelae persist, it may be necessary to serve the child in classrooms for students with intellectual disabilities. In any case, a comprehensive psychological evaluation should be conducted before providing services. In addition, consultations should be obtained from the speech and language pathologist when language deficits are noted, and from occupational or physical therapists when motor abnormalities are observed.

Future research needs to address immune response to Colorado tick fever. It remains unclear why some individuals are affected adversely and others are not. Better understanding of the mechanism of the disease will hopefully result in greater prevention and more effective intervention (e.g., vaccines).

REFERENCES

Attoui, H., Billoir, F., Bruey, J. M., de Micco, P., & de Llamballerie, X. (1998). Serologic and molecular diagnosis of Colorado tick fever viral infections. *American Journal of Tropical Medicine and Hygiene*, 59, 763–768.

Byrd, R., Vasquez, J., & Roy, T. (1997). Respiratory manifestations of tick-borne diseases in the Southeastern United States. *Southern Medical Journal*, 90, 1–4.

Harrison's Principles of Internal Medicine. (2000, December). Retrieved from http://www.harrisonsonline.com

HEATHER EDGEL
ELAINE CLARK
University of Utah

COLOR BLINDNESS

The inability to perceive or discriminate colors is known as color blindness. There are four main types of color blindness, each containing a number of subtypes. The most rare type is known as *achromotopsia*. In this condition, the subject sees no color; everything is perceived as black, white, or shades of gray. This condition can result from a degenerative process. In the absence of such pathology, the condition is due to an autosomal recessive gene and is extremely rare.

The more common types of color vision disturbances are closely related to retinal physiology, specifically, to the structure and function of the cones. Since the cones are not evenly distributed in the retina, color vision in the visual field is somewhat variable. Color perception is not possible in the periphery of the visual field and diminishes as the object moves away from the point of fixation (Wald, 1968). The perception of color is dependent on the presence not only of different types of cone cells, but of complex chemical pigments thought to respond selectively to the different wavelengths of light.

Protanopia refers to the condition in which the individual has difficulty in distinguishing red. *Deuteranopia* is the condition in which the individual has difficulty in distinguishing green. *Tritanopia* is the condition in which the individual cannot distinguish blue; it is a severe and rare form of colorblindness, affecting less than .1% of the population. Tritanopia is considered to be an autosomal dominant trait.

Red-green color disturbances occur in both protanopia and deuteranopia. The former is more severe and less common than the latter. Both are sex-linked (X) recessive traits, explaining their nearly exclusive presence in males. The prevalence of protanopia is about 1:100; deuteranopia about 1:20 (Linksz, 1964).

Determination of the condition is easily made using pseudoisochromatic plates (Isihara test) that present colored patterns or numbers to the individual. The normal person sees one pattern or number and those with color disturbances see the stimulus differently (Thuline, 1972). Color perception can be diminished by papillitis, a condition where the optic disk becomes inflamed. The causes of papillitis are numerous and can include toxins, tumors, or syphillis (Riccio, 2003).

Color blindness is not generally considered to be a significant handicap. Some authors (Cooley, 1977) feel that the tests are far too sensitive and that some persons have been needlessly denied employment. The classroom teacher, especially in the early grades, should expect to find at least one color-blind male in the classroom. Tasks involving color discrimination must be eliminated. The literature is replete with retinal changes owed to phenothiazine (Mellaril, Thorazine) administration (Apt, 1960; Weekly, Potts, Rebotem, & May, 1960). Color vision anomalies may occur if a youngster is under phenothiazine therapy.

REFERENCES

Apt, R. (1960). Complications of phenothiazine tranquilizers ocular side effects. *Survey Ophthalmology, 5,* 550.

Cooley, D. (Ed.). (1977). *Family medical guide.* New York, NY: Better Homes & Gardens.

Linksz, A. (1964). *An essay on color vision and clinical color vision tests.* New York, NY: Grune & Stratton.

Riccio, C. (2003). Papillitis. In E. F. Janzen, & C. R. Reynolds (Eds.), *Childhood disorders diagnostic desk reference* (pp. 448–449). Hoboken, NJ: Wiley.

Thuline, H. (1972). Color blindness in children: The importance and feasibility of early recognition. *Clinical Pediatrics, 11*(5), 295–299.

Wald, G. (1968). The receptors of human color vision. *Science Magazine, 145,* 1007.

Weekly, R., Potts, A., Rebotem, J., & May, R. (1960). Pigmentary retinopathy in patients receiving high doses of a new phenothiazene. *Archives of Ophthalmology, 64,* 65.

JOHN E. PORCELLA
Rhinebeck Country School

See also Mellaril; Thorazine; Visual Impairment; Visual Perception and Discrimination

COMMUNICATION AIDS, ELECTRONIC COMMUNICATION BOARDS

Communication boards are simple, nonelectronic, augmentative communication systems used by nonspeaking persons. They are usually made individually according to the skills and needs of the nonspeaking user. The advantages of communication boards are their flexibility and low cost. Any symbol system ranging from objects and pictures to written alphabet letters can be used as message symbols. The communication board can be accessed by direct selection, through scanning, or by an encoding process. As the nonspeaking person's skills change over time, the communication board can be easily adapted to reflect those changes.

The major disadvantage of communication boards is the lack of spoken or written output from the system. The listener who interacts with a nonspeaking communication board user must be able to physically see the communication board to receive a message. For long messages, the listener must remember each symbol selected and mentally sequence the symbols back together to understand the message. Communication boards are used frequently with children and adults who have limited vocabularies. In addition, they are often used as a secondary backup communication device for nonspeaking persons who rely primarily on sophisticated electronic augmentative systems.

REFERENCES

Goossens, C., Crain, S. S., & Elder, P. S. (1995). *Engineering the preschool environment for interactive symbolic communication.* Birmingham, AL: Southeast Augmentative Communication Conference Publications.

Musselwhite, C. R., & St. Louis, K. O. (1982). *Communication programming for the severely handicapped: Vocal and nonvocal strategies.* Houston, TX: College-Hill.

SHARON GLENNEN
Pennsylvania State University
First edition

SHEELA STUART
George Washington University
Second edition

See also Computer Use With Students With Disabilities; Robotics

COMMUNICATION DISORDERS

Communication disorders are defined as an observed disturbance in the normal speech, language, or hearing processes as determined by (1) objective signs (i.e., measurable characteristics that can be observed by other persons), (2) social signs (i.e., failing to understand a speaker's meaning and responding inappropriately, resulting in mutual embarrassment), and (3) personal signs (i.e., a person's reactions to a self-perceived disorder; Plante & Beeson, 1999). Communication disorders may involve the processes of listening, speaking, reading, writing, and thinking. The American Speech-Language-Hearing Association (ASHA) estimates that about 10% of the population in the United States (approximately 25 million individuals of all ages) has some form of communication disorder involving speech, language, and/or hearing (Shames, Wiig, & Secord, 1994). Severity of communication disorders ranges from mild to severe/profound across different levels of communication (prelinguistic, sounds and letters, words, phrases and sentences, oral and literate discourse [conversation, narration, exposition] plus [nonliteral language, math language (including time and money), computer language, foreign language, and career or employment language]). Communication disorders are categorized as impairment (abnormality of structure or function at the organ level), disability (functional consequences of an impairment), or handicap (social consequences of impairment or disability; Gelfer, 1996).

Communication disorders may be caused by: (a) physical conditions (e.g., oral facial anomalies, cerebral palsy), (b) physiological conditions (e.g., neurological impairment), (c) psychological conditions (e.g., emotional/behavioral disorders such as neuroses and psychoses; learning, motivation), or (d) social conditions (e.g., lack of stimulation or communicative interaction with other humans; Boone & Plante, 1993; Pressley & McCormick, 1995). Communication disorders affect not only the individuals who have the disorder, but others (family, peers, caregivers, colleagues) with whom the individuals need to communicate.

Because the purposes of communication are to regulate social interactions or interpersonal functions, as well as to transmit scientific or logically based knowledge and skills, communication disorders have a far-reaching effect on society. Communication rules and use vary from culture to culture and, therefore, differentiation is made among communication differences, communication delays, and communication disorders. It is generally recognized that to progress through life, humans must be able to understand and use, with some degree of competence, the cognitive, linguistic, and contextual conventions associated with oral, literate, and manually coded communication systems.

Speech Disorders

Speech disorders are variations from commonly used acoustic characteristics of the utterances one makes, rather than of the meaning of the utterances (Hegde, 1995; Silverman, 1995). Speech disorders include articulation (the process of producing vowels and consonants that result in meaningful language morphemes, words, phrases, sentences, and discourse), stuttering (the interruption of the flow of speech, characterized by sound or word repetitions, prolongations, and blocking of sound), and voice (production of the frequency and intensity of speech sounds that is atypical of sex, physical maturity, and age, resulting in disorders of phonation and resonance). Associated features of speech disorders may be rate of speaking (too fast or too slow for communicative purposes) and dysphagia (disordered swallowing because of inflammation, compression, paralysis, weakness, or hypertonicity of the esophagus).

Language Disorders

Language disorders involve the impaired ability to receive, process, and use auditory, visual, and haptic (touch and movement) symbols in order to negotiate meaning for social interaction and/or academic/professional communication learning. Language disorders may involve nonverbal symbols or verbal language (phonologic, semantic, syntactic, morphologic, and pragmatic linguistic rule systems). Language disorders are often classified as receptive (watching, listening, reading), expressive (moving/gesturing, speaking, writing), or a combination of receptive and expressive (Palmer & Yantis, 1990). Language disorders include the problems associated with understanding and use of oral-aural language, Braille, and manually coded communication systems (Nelson, 1998).

Auditory language disorders include problems making sense of speech sounds, single words, phrases, sentences, thoughts, concepts, and ideas. Visual language disorders include problems making sense of the nonverbal dimensions of communication that are critical in the pragmatic dimensions of communication (i.e., who can communicate what, with whom, how, when, where, and why), as well as decoding and encoding the graphemic and geometric visual symbols used for Augmentative/Alternative Communication (AAC) systems, reading, writing, mathematics, and the physical and technological sciences. Haptic language disorders include problems receiving, interpreting, and using nonverbal symbols involved in pragmatics, the linguistic symbols and motor acts associated with cursive and manuscript writing, and with specialized systems such as Braille and manually coded communication.

Language disorders and learning disabilities are integrally related. Preschool-aged children with a diagnosed language disorder (learning to communicate) will likely encounter problems with academic language (communicating to learn) when they enter a formal education system. Although the underlying problem is the encoding and decoding of symbols (language disorder), the disorder may be termed a learning disability because of the problems encountered learning academic material. The preferred term is *language-learning disorder* (Gelfer, 1996; Nelson, 1998; Plante & Beeson, 1999). Because individuals do not outgrow language-learning disorders, they continue to encounter social or academic problems as adults. The communication-learning deficits that are evident at the adult level are referred to as adaptive communication-learning disorders (Weller, Crelly, Watteyne, & Herbert, 1992).

Hearing Disorders

Hearing disorders stem from problems within the auditory system. Although this is usually associated with the ear, it may also be located in the areas of the peripheral and central nervous system where the perception of word meanings and associations occurs. Individuals with ear infections or allergy/cold-related symptoms may have temporary or chronic problems with hearing. Hearing impairments may slowly develop with advancing age. Irreversible impairment can occur following unusual levels of noise exposure, or from ototoxic drugs. Hearing impairments can easily lead to serious difficulties in the ability to perceive and understand the speech and language of others, resulting in speech and/or language disorders (Gelfer, 1996; Minifie, 1994; Plante & Beeson, 1999).

Early identification and intervention are important to maximize the successful management of both individuals with communication disorders and their families. Communication disorders should be assessed and treated by speech-language pathologists and audiologists who hold state licensure or who hold the certificate of clinical competence in speech-language pathology (CCC-SLP) or audiology (CCC-A) from ASHA. Speech-language pathologists and audiologists work in schools, hospitals, rehabilitation centers, long-term care facilities, through contract healthcare companies, and in private practice (Boone & Plante, 1993; Gelfer, 1996; Hegde, 1995; Minifie, 1994; Palmer & Yantis, 1990; Shames et al., 1994; Silverman, 1995).

ASHA promotes aggressive prevention practices: primary (e.g., prenatal care to prevent a disorder from occurring), secondary (e.g., early identification and intervention to eliminate or minimize the effects of a disorder) and tertiary (decrease the possibility of further problems occurring because of an existing disorder, such as aspiration pneumonia related to dysphagia; Plante & Beeson, 1999). The American Speech-Language-Hearing Association provides information through print and broadcast media. Contact can be made at 10801 Rockville Pike, Rockville, MD 20852; (301) 897-5700 voice or TTY; fax (301) 571-0481; or on the Internet at www.asha.org.

REFERENCES

Boone, D. R., & Plante, E. (1993). *Human communication and its disorders* (2nd ed.). Englewood Cliffs, NJ: Prentice Hall.

Gelfer, M. P. (1996). *Survey of communication disorders: A social and behavioral perspective.* New York, NY: McGraw-Hill.

Hegde, M. N. (1995). *Introduction to communicative disorders* (2nd ed.). Austin, TX: PRO-ED.

Minifie, F. D. (Ed.). (1994). *Introduction to communication sciences and disorders.* San Diego, CA: Singular Publishing Group.

Nelson, N. W. (1998). *Childhood language disorders in context: Infancy through adolescence* (2nd ed.). Boston, MA: Allyn & Bacon.

Palmer, J. M., & Yantis, P. A. (1990). *Survey of communication disorders.* Baltimore, MD: Williams & Wilkins.

Plante, E., & Beeson, P. M. (1999). *Communication and communication disorders: A clinical introduction.* Boston, MA: Allyn & Bacon.

Pressley, M., & McCormick, C. B. (1995). *Advanced educational psychology: For educators, researchers, and policymakers.* New York, NY: HarperCollins.

Shames, G. H., Wiig, E. H., & Secord, W. A. (1994). *Human communication disorders: An introduction* (4th ed.). New York, NY: Merrill/Macmillan.

Silverman, F. H. (1995). *Speech, language, & hearing disorders.* Boston, MA: Allyn & Bacon.

Weller, C., Crelly, C., Watteyne, L., & Herbert, M. (1992). *Adaptive language disorders of young adults with learning disabilities.* San Diego, CA: Singular Publishing Group.

STEPHEN S. FARMER
New Mexico State University

See also Aphasia; Audiology; Auditory Abnormalities; Language Disorders

COMMUNICATION SPECIALIST

A communication specialist is any one of a number of professionals who deal with aspects of both normal and disordered human communication. Such an individual may have expertise in communication theory, small-group communication, organizational communication, or rhetoric. This individual may call himself or herself a linguist, a psycholinguist, a sociolinguist, a cultural linguist, or a rhetorician. The specialist is concerned with the influence of such diverse disciplines as linguistics, psychology, and sociology on human communication in general and language and speech in particular. In addition, these professionals study the development of normal communication theories and processes.

The study of disordered communication can also be considered in the realm of the communication specialist. The individual typically has expertise in communication disorders, education of the hearing impaired, or neurolinguistics. Speech and language disorders in children and adults can be studied from an organic (anatomic and physiologic) or functional (psychological, learning) perspective. The specialist in disordered communication may be concerned with such problems as language delay in children from multiple articulation errors or delay in (or loss of) the acquisition of morphologic, syntactic, or semantic rules of language. The communication specialist will also be concerned with language disorders owed to neurologic factors (e.g., brain damage).

HARVEY R. GILBERT
Pennsylvania State University

See also **Communication Disorders; Speech-Language Pathologist**

COMMUNITY-BASED INSTRUCTION

Community-based instruction refers to the delivery of skills training for students in the natural setting where those skills would be utilized (Kluth, 2000). With the legal mandate of education in the least restrictive environment for all students with disabilities, community-based instruction has been implemented in many special education programs, especially in those that serve students with moderate to severe disabilities. Students with disabilities may have difficulty generalizing skills taught in the classroom to real-world situations (Tekin-Iftar, 2008). Indeed, community-based instruction is a more powerful predictor

of education/adaptive gains than intelligence quotient, level of ambulation, or presence of behavior problems (McDonnell, 1993).

Community-based instruction may be implemented in a variety of ways (Walker, Uphold, Richter, & Test, 2010). These include consecutive instruction, whereby skills are taught in a simulated setting within the school facility until a certain skill level is reached; instruction in a non-school setting (community) then follows. Concurrent instruction can occur where instruction takes place in both school and the community setting at daily or weekly intervals. Non-school instruction can be implemented with direct training in community settings only.

The purpose of community-based instruction is to teach students functional skills in natural environments (Hamill, 2002). Community-based instruction may involve instruction in a number of areas. Ordering, purchasing, and eating food in a restaurant may be taught. Use of consumer services such as public transportation, banks, and laundromats may be emphasized during training. Recreation skills may be taught in natural community sites, including parks, community gymnasiums, and aerobics/fitness centers. Students may be taught to use stores and shops such as grocery stores, pharmacies, and department stores. Vocational skills may be taught in community vocational sites. Selection of community-based training sites can be determined by examining the current and future needs of particular students in community-referenced activities (Glasenapp, 1992). Certain skills such as street crossing, appropriate social interaction with non-disabled peers and adults, and nonverbal or verbal communication may be taught in more than one community-based training activity.

A number of advantages in using community-based instruction with students who have moderate to severe disabilities have been cited by professionals in the field of special education. If training takes place in heterogeneous, non-school environments, student adaptive functioning will be more likely in current and subsequent community settings. Transfer and generalization of community skills will be more likely to occur when taught in natural rather than simulated settings (Council for Exceptional Children, 1990; Tekin-Iftar, 2008; Wehmeyer, 2002). In addition, students with disabilities participating in community-based instruction will have frequent access to peers without disabilities who may serve as role models. In turn, the awareness by people without disabilities of their peers with disabilities will be enhanced. This will enable the peers without disabilities to be cognizant of the abilities of individuals with disabilities, thus promoting a smoother transition to post-school environments on the part of individuals with disabilities. Parent and teacher expectations of student abilities may be increased when community-based instruction occurs. Finally, the opportunity for students to sample the reinforcing aspects of activities in the community can be an advantage in achieving acquisition of functional skills (Csapo, 1991; Walker et al., 2010).

A number of factors need to be taken into account when considering community-based instruction. These include staffing, transportation, scheduling, costs, necessary curriculum changes and modifications for students with severe physical disabilities, and legal issues such as liability coverage (Boethel, 2000). Considerations such as these require careful planning on the part of teachers and administrators to facilitate adequate community-based programming.

REFERENCES

Boethel, M., & Southwest Educational Development Lab. (2000). Adapting to community-based learning. (Benefits)[2]: *The exponential results of linking school improvement and community development, 4.* Austin, TX: Southwest Educational Development Lab.

Council for Exceptional Children. (1990). *Designing community-based instruction.* (Research brief for teachers.) Reston, VA: Author.

Csapo, M. (1991). *Community-based instruction: Its origin and description.* In D. A. Baine (Ed.), *Instructional environments for learners having severe handicaps* (pp. 15–33). Edmonton: Alberta University.

Glasenapp, G., & Teaching Research Infant and Child Center. (1992). Community-based inservice model. Teaching Research. Monmouth: Western Oregon State College.

Hamill, L. B. (2002). *Teaching students with moderate to severe disabilities: An applied approach for inclusive environments.* Upper Saddle River, NJ: Merrill Prentice Hall.

Kluth, P. (2000). Community-referenced learning and the inclusive classroom. *Remedial and Special Education, 21,* 19–26.

McDonnell, J. (1993). Impact of community-based instruction on the development of adaptive behavior of secondary-level students with mental retardation. *American Journal on Mental Retardation, 97*(5), 575–584.

Tekin-Iftar, E. (2008). Parent-delivered community-based instruction with simultaneous prompting for teaching community skills to children with developmental disabilities. *Education and Training in Developmental Disabilities, 43*(2), 249–265.

Walker, A. R., Uphold, N. M., Richter, S., & Test, D. W. (2010). Review of the literature on community-based instruction across grade levels. *Education and Training in Autism and Developmental Disabilities, 45*(2), 242–267.

Wehmeyer, M. L. (2002). *Teaching students with mental retardation.* Baltimore, MD: Paul H. Brookes.

CORNELIA L. IZEN
George Mason University

DAVID LOJKOVIC
George Mason University
Fourth edition

COMMUNITY RESIDENTIAL PROGRAMS

There is an array of community residential options available. Foster homes, also known as personal care homes or family care homes (McCoin, 1983), are private homes rented or owned by a family with one or more persons with disabilities living as family members (Hill & Lakin, 1984). The number of residents rarely exceeds six (Miller & Intagliata, 1984). These residences are licensed by a state agency or a local facility (e.g., a hospital). Foster homes are available for both children and adults. They tend to be homelike, with the person with the disability being "one of the family."

Group homes are residences with staff to provide care and supervision of one or more persons with disabilities (Hill & Lakin, 1984). Financial support comes from a variety of sources, including churches, states, private nonprofit organizations, and private for-profit organizations (Miller & Intagliata, 1984). It is not uncommon to find group homes staffed with house parents (a man and a woman who live in the residence, with one having an additional outside job) and one or two additional staff members for the hours when the majority of residents are home. The number of residents living in groups varies from home to home. Most of the research conducted has involved group homes serving under 20 residents (Miller & Intagliata).

Semi-independent-living facilities are facilities having separate units or apartments with staff members living in one unit or apartment; however, staff members live in the same building to provide support services to those in need. Services might include assistance with budgeting or managing money, housework, or laundry. Currently, these facilities are mainly supported by nonprofit organizations (Hill, Lakin, & Bruininks, 1984).

Domiciliary care facilities are community-based facilities whose primary function is to provide shelter and protection to the residents. There are no training or rehabilitation activities conducted (Miller & Intagliata, 1984). Since there is a lack of emphasis on training or rehabilitation, these types of facilities are deemed most appropriate for persons with high levels of independent living skills who need little or no additional training, or for those persons who, because of severe medical or physical needs or age, would not benefit from additional skill training (Miller & Intagliata). The number of residents in these facilities ranges from 5 to 200. Most of these facilities are operated by individual proprietors (Hill et al., 1984).

Although there are a variety of names given to domiciliary care facilities, there are generally two broad categories. Board-and-care facilities are also known as boarding homes and adult homes. As a general rule, these facilities provide a room and meals to the residents. Some also provide limited supervision. The major source of support for most residents is Social Security (Miller & Intagliata, 1984). Health-care facilities are also known as convalescent care homes, nursing homes, skilled nursing facilities, intermediate care facilities, and health-related facilities (Miller & Intagliata). In addition to providing a room and meals, these facilities also provide some level of nursing care to the residents. Generally, these facilities are funded through Medicare and Medicaid.

Halfway houses are short-term residential options available to persons leaving institutional settings (Katz, 1968). The setting is supervised with emphasis on facilitating the person's reentry into the community. The number of residents ranges from 12 to 25. An extensive report on residential services can be found by Prouty and Lakin (1997).

REFERENCES

Hill, B. K., & Lakin, K. C. (1984). *Classification of residential facilities for mentally retarded people* (Brief No. 24). Minneapolis: Center for Residential and Community Services, University of Minnesota, Department of Educational Psychology.

Hill, B. K., Lakin, K. C., & Bruininks, R. H. (1984). Trends in residential services for people who are mentally retarded 1977–1982. *Journal of the Association for Persons with Severe Handicaps, 9*(4), 243–251.

Katz, E. (1968). *The retarded adult in the community*. Springfield, IL: Thomas.

McCoin, J. M. (1983). *Adult foster homes: Their managers and residents*. New York, NY: Human Sciences.

Miller, B., & Intagliata, T. (1984). *Promises and realities for mentally retarded citizens: Life in the community*. Baltimore, MD: University Park Press.

Prouty, R., & Lakin, K. (1997). *Residential services for persons with development disabilities: Status and trends through 1996, Report #49*. Minneapolis: University of Minnesota.

SUE ANN MORROW
EDGE, Inc.

LONNY W. MORROW
Northeast Missouri State University

See also Independent Living Centers; Residential Facilities

COMPAZINE

Compazine (prochlorperazine) is used for the short-term treatment of generalized nonpsychotic anxiety, the control of severe nausea and vomiting (Konopasek, 2004), and the management of the manifestations of psychotic disorders (Servis & Miller, 1997). Compazine may impair mental or physical abilities, especially during the first few days of therapy. Adverse reactions can include drowsiness, dizziness, blurred vision, restlessness, agitation,

jitteriness, insomnia, and motor dysfunctions such as muscle spasms, pseudoparkinsonism, and tardive dyskinesia. Overdose can produce coma. (See also pages 1874–1877 in *Physician's Desk Reference*, published in 1984 by Medical Economics, Oradell, NJ.)

A brand name of Smith Kline and French, Compazine is available in tablets of 5, 10, and 25 mg, in sustained-release capsules of 10, 15, and 30 mg in injectible ampules, and in suppositories of 2 1/2, 5, and 25 mg. Dosage may vary, ranging from 2 1/2 mg, according to the symptom being treated. It is given one or two times per day for severe nausea and vomiting in young children to a maximum of 25 mg per day in children 6 to 12 years of age being treated for psychosis.

REFERENCES

Konopasek, D. E. (2004). *Medication fact sheets*. Longmont, CO: Sopris West.

Servis, M., & Miller, B. (1997). Treatment of psychosis with prochlorperazine in the ICU setting. *Psychosomatics, 38*(6), 589–590.

LAWRENCE C. HARTLAGE
Evans, Georgia

See also Benadryl; Navane

COMPENSATORY EDUCATION

Compensatory education usually refers to supplemental educational services provided through federal, state, or local programs to educationally disadvantaged children in schools with concentrations of children from low-income families. The largest such program is that authorized by Chapter 1 of the Education Consolidation and Improvement Act, formerly known as Title I of the Elementary and Secondary Education Act (ESEA). Federal grants are made through state education agencies to local school districts based on the number of children from families in poverty. About 90% of all districts receive Chapter 1 funds. Local educational agencies then allocate funds to schools based on poverty and educational criteria. Schools provide services to children based not on family income, but on extent of educational deprivation. This determination is made at the local level within broad federal guidelines. In general, schools with the greatest concentrations of children from poor families and children most in need of services receive priority in program delivery.

Additional children receive services from state and local compensatory education programs, and some Chapter 1 participants receive additional services from such programs. Participants are concentrated in lower-achievement quartiles; as the achievement quartile increases, percent participation in Chapter 1 decreases (White, 1984).

The law allows for a wide range of services to be provided: instructional services, purchase of materials and equipment, teacher training, construction, and social and health services. Historically, about 80% of funds were spent on instructional services (White, 1984), with particular emphasis on reading and math. About three-fourths of participants receive compensatory reading and almost one-half receive compensatory math, with language arts the next most common service (Carpenter & Hopper, 1985). Almost two-thirds of districts pull students out of regular classrooms to provide services in classes that are likely to be smaller and more personnel-intensive than regular classes. Title I average class size was about 10 children, with a student-to-instructor ratio of 4.5 to 1 (White, 1984).

Compensatory education programs resemble special education programs for learning-disabled children in several ways. They attempt to address a similar symptom: low or lower-than-expected achievement. There is a special concentration on attacking difficulties with reading and mathematics skills. Children are often removed from regular classrooms for part of the school day for more personnel-intensive services in smaller classes. That is not to suggest that children served, educational needs, or instructional content of programs for learning-disabled children and compensatory education are identical, or that learning-disabled children are interchangeable with children receiving compensatory education. They are not. But in terms of difficulty addressed, administrative design, or general approach to service delivery, there are important similarities.

Given the Chapter 1 eligibility criterion of educational disadvantagement, nothing prohibits a child with a disability who receives special education and related services from also being served as an educationally deprived child through compensatory education. Anecdotal evidence suggests this may not be common.

It is important to note that the No Child Left Behind Act (NCLB), passed in 2001, introduced sweeping changes to the ESEA, and in particular to Chapter 1 programs. Under NCLB, the focus has shifted from the income levels of families of students at a school to the performance of the school, as measured by statewide academic requirements for adequate yearly progress, without regard to the socioeconomic status of the students attending it. Although funding for older Chapter 1 programs was authorized under NCLB through 2007, the ultimate fate of such programs remains unclear, as does the ultimate impact on the children who are in such programs. The true consequences, in terms of educational outcomes, will probably not be known for many years.

It is also important to remember that many compensatory education programs run by state and local educational agencies complement and extend Chapter 1. Information on children served, services provided, and evaluation results of these programs is available from state and local education agencies.

REFERENCES

Carpenter, M., & Hopper, P. (1985). *Synthesis of state Chapter 1 data: Draft summary report*. Washington, DC: Advanced Technology.

White, B. F. (1984). *Compensatory education*. Washington, DC: Office of Management and Budget.

JAMES R. RICCIUTI
United State Office of Management and Budget
Second edition

KIMBERLY F. APPLEQUIST
University of Colorado at Colorado Springs
Third edition

See also No Child Left Behind Act

COMPETENCY TESTING FOR TEACHERS (*See Highly Qualified Teachers*)

COMPETING BEHAVIOR PATH ANALYSIS

Competing behavior path analysis and its related principles and procedures has typically been used in the context of situations in which students are exhibiting problem behaviors, including aggression toward others, self-injurious behavior (e.g., head-hitting), destruction of materials, and other disruptive behaviors (e.g., talking out in the classroom). Completing a *competing behavior path analysis* (CBA) is a step in the process of developing a *behavior support plan* (BSP) for a student engaging in such behaviors (Chafouleas, Riley-Tillman, & Sugai, 2007; O'Neill, Horner, Albin, Storey, Sprague, & Newton, 1997).

The conceptual foundation for this type of analysis was presented by Billingsley and Neel (1985) and Horner and Billingsley (1988). They discussed how, in various situations, desired appropriate student behaviors can be thought of as being in competition with problem behaviors. That is, in a given situation a student may be able to exhibit a variety of problematic or appropriate behaviors. For example, in a situation in which a student is asked to complete an academic task or activity, she or he could either begin working on the task or could exhibit disruptive or aggressive behavior. Horner and Billingsley (1988) outlined a number of factors that may influence which types of behaviors might occur, including the presence or absence of stimuli that influence the different behaviors, and the likelihood of reinforcing consequences for them. For example, a student may learn through experience that a certain teacher or staffperson is very likely to allow the student to escape from non-preferred academic tasks if disruptive or aggressive behavior occurs. Thereafter, the presence of that teacher or staffperson may substantially increase the likelihood that such problem behavior will occur versus more appropriate work activity. In such a case, the problem behavior "won the competition" in relation to the desired appropriate behavior (i.e., work completion).

A practical process for applying these concepts to analyze problem situations was presented by O'Neill et al. (1997). They discussed a competing behavior analysis as a transitional step between a functional behavioral assessment (FBA) and the development of a behavior support plan for an individual student. The FBA should produce a variety of information, including: (a) description of the full range of problem behaviors of concern, (b) identification of the setting and antecedent events that predict the occurrence of the behaviors, and (c) identification of the reinforcing outcomes that are maintaining the behaviors (i.e., the functions they are serving for the student). This information is used to generate hypotheses or summary statements that succinctly pull together the information. An example of a summary statement would be: "When Mario has had little sleep, and he is asked to do difficult academic activities, he will curse, throw materials, and/or spit at the teacher in order to escape the task demands." Such a statement identifies a setting event (lack of sleep), a more immediate antecedent (difficult task demands), the behaviors that might occur, and the apparent function of the behaviors, or the reinforcing outcome maintaining them (escape from difficult/aversive tasks). An FBA may result in multiple such statements for a given student, depending on the range of behaviors he or she exhibits and the functions they may be serving.

A competing behavior analysis (CBA) provides a framework for a three-step process in moving from the results of an FBA to the details of developing a behavior support plan (Crone & Horner, 2003; O'Neill et al., 1997). First, the summary statement or hypothesis is diagrammed on a

Competing Behavior Analysis Form. Figure C.13 presents a version of this form. The components of the summary statement presented above for Mario are laid out on the middle line of the form (setting event, antecedent, behavior, maintaining consequence). The second step involves identifying two things: (1) the general desired behavior appropriate for that situation, and (2) an appropriate alternative or replacement behavior that will produce the same outcome that the problem behaviors currently produce. In the example of Mario in Figure C.13, the general desired behavior was for Mario to complete his assigned work, which would lead to a grade or other evaluation, and presumably some kind of positive recognition from the teacher. An alternative replacement behavior would be for Mario to request assistance with the difficult work. This would be functionally equivalent to the problem behaviors in allowing him to escape the aversive aspects of the difficult tasks. (*Note*: This diagram/format illustrates the different possible behavior "paths" that might be followed in particular situations; hence the term *competing behavior path analysis*.)

Once the competing behavior path analysis is completed, the third main step in the process is to identify behavioral support strategies that will increase the probability of the desired and replacement behaviors, and decrease the likelihood of the problem behaviors. One function of the CBA format is to encourage consideration of a comprehensive range of strategies to influence problem behavior situations. That is, it is important to consider potential changes that could be made in each component of the framework (i.e., setting events, antecedents, teaching alternative behaviors, and consequences for appropriate and problem behaviors). It is beyond the scope of this entry to provide more detail on intervention strategies. However, there are an increasing number of resources available for teachers and other practitioners that provide more detail in this area (e.g., Bambara & Kern, 2005; Crone & Horner, 2003). In addition, the competing behavior analysis logic and format is being adopted and used by practitioners in the field (e.g., Chandler & Dahlquist, 2002; Condon & Tobin, 2001; Scott & Nelson, 1999). Finally, it is worth noting that the CBA method is frequently a component of

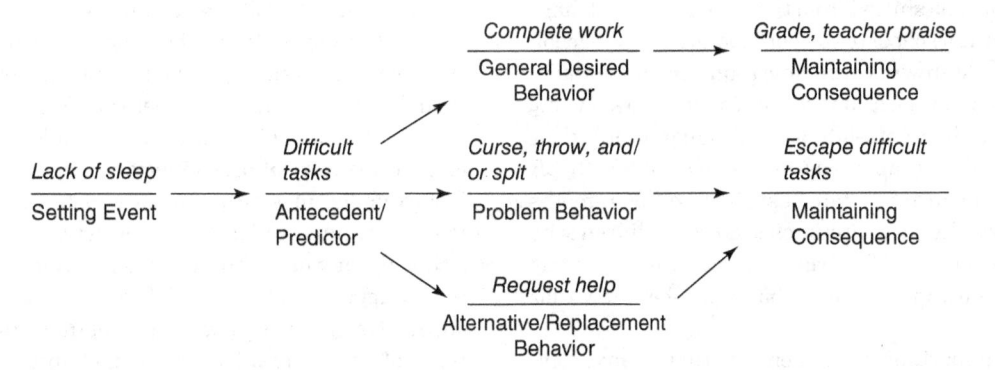

Figure C.13. Example of a competing behavior analysis diagram. *Source*: O'Neill, Horner, Albin, Storey, Sprague, & Newton (1997).

a more comprehensive general approach known as *positive behavior support* (PBS; Chafouleas, Riley-Tillman, & Sugai, 2007; Bambara, Dunlap, & Schwartz, 2004).

REFERENCES

Bambara, L. M., Dunlap, G., & Schwartz, I. (Eds.). (2004). *Positive behavior support: Critical articles on improving practice for individuals with severe disabilities.* Austin, TX: PRO-ED.

Bambara, L. M., & Kern, L. (2005). *Individualized supports for students with problem behaviors: Designing positive behavior plans.* New York, NY: Guilford Press.

Billingsley, F. F., & Neel, R. S. (1985). Competing behaviors and their effects on skill generalization and maintenance. *Analysis and Intervention in Developmental Disabilities, 5,* 357–372.

Chafouleas, S., Riley-Tillman, T. C., & Sugai, G. (2007). *School-based behavioral assessment: Informing intervention and instruction.* New York, NY: Guilford Press.

Chandler, L. K., & Dahlquist, C. M. (2002). *Functional assessment: Strategies to prevent and remediate challenging behavior in school settings.* Columbus, OH: Merrill.

Condon, K. A., & Tobin, T. J. (2001). Functional behavioral assessment at work. *Teaching Exceptional Children, 33,* 44–51.

Crone, D. A., & Horner, R. H. (2003). *Building positive behavior support systems in schools.* New York, NY: Guilford Press.

Horner, R. H., & Billingsley, F. F. (1988). The effect of competing behavior on the generalization and maintenance of adaptive behavior in applied settings. In R. H. Horner, G. Dunlap, & R. L. Koegel (Eds.), *Generalization and maintenance: Life-style changes in applied settings* (pp. 197–220). Baltimore, MD: Paul H. Brookes.

O'Neill, R. E., Horner, R. H., Albin, R. W., Storey, K., Sprague, J. R., & Newton, J. S. (1997). *Functional assessment and program development for problem behavior: A practical handbook* (2nd ed.). Belmont, CA: Wadsworth.

Scott, T. M., & Nelson, C. M. (1999). Using functional behavioral assessment to develop effective intervention plans: Practical classroom applications. *Journal of Positive Behavior Interventions, 1,* 242–251.

Rob O'Neill
University of Utah

Leslie C. Neely
Texas A&M University
Fourth edition

See also **Behavioral Assessment; Applied Behavior Analysis**

COMPREHENSIVE ASSESSMENT OF SPOKEN LANGUAGE

The Comprehensive Assessment of Spoken Language (CASL, 1999) is an individually administered, norm-referenced test that provides an assessment of the oral language skills of children and young adults (ages 3-0 through 21-11). Only a verbal or nonverbal (pointing) response is required of the examinee and reading or writing ability is not needed to respond to test items. Each of the 15 CASL tests is a highly reliable, stand-alone test. The clinician is free to give one test or several tests and can report the score(s) with confidence. Subtest must be given in conjunction with other subtests to form a composite score.

The CASL provides an in-depth assessment of four language categories:

1. **Lexical/Semantic Language**: assessed using the following tests:

   Basic Concepts: Examiner reads a sentence aloud while examinee looks at four pictures and points to the picture or part of the picture that represents the correct response.

   Antonyms: Examiner says a stimulus word and the examinee must respond orally with a single word that means the opposite of the stimulus word.

   Synonyms: Examiner says a stimulus word and four synonym options, then repeats the stimulus word. The examinee chooses the option that means the same as the stimulus.

   Sentence Completion: Examiner reads the stimulus sentence, which is missing the last word, and the examinee must respond with a single word that meaningfully completes the sentence.

   Idiomatic Language: Examiner reads the stimulus idiom, which is missing its final part, and the examinee must complete the phrase with an acceptable form of the idiom.

2. **Syntactic Language**: assessed using the following tests:

   Syntax Construction: Examiner reads the stimulus item while the examinee looks at a picture. The examinee must respond with a word, phrase, or sentence that is grammatically and semantically appropriate.

   Paragraph Comprehension: Examiner reads a stimulus paragraph twice, then reads a series of items relating to the paragraph while the examinee looks at a set of pictures for each item and responds by pointing to or giving the number of the correct response.

   Grammatical Morphemes: Examiner reads one pair of words or phrases that demonstrates an analogy, then reads the first word or phrase of a second pair. The examinee must complete the analogy of the second pair.

Sentence Comprehension: For each item, examiner reads two pairs of stimulus sentences, one pair at a time. The examinee must determine whether both sentences in each pair mean the same thing.

Grammaticality Judgment: Examiner reads a stimulus sentence that is grammatically either correct or incorrect. The examinee must judge the correctness of the sentence and, if it is incorrect, must correct it by changing only one word.

3. **Supralinguistic Language**: assessed using the following tests:

Nonliteral Language: Examiner reads the stimulus item and the accompanying question and the examinee must answer by explaining the nonliteral meaning of the item.

Meaning from Context: Each item contains a very uncommon word. The examiner reads the item and the examinee must explain the meaning of the uncommon word by using context clues.

Inference: Examiner describes a situation in which part of the information is omitted, then asks an accompanying question. The examinee must answer the question using world knowledge to infer the missing information.

Ambiguous Sentences: Examiner reads the stimulus item and examinee must respond with two possible meanings for the item.

4. **Pragmatic Language**: assessed using the following test:

Pragmatic Judgment: Examiner reads a situation that represents some aspect of everyday life that requires communication or a pragmatic judgment on the part of the examinee. The examinee responds with the appropriate thing to say or do in the situation.

The CASL was standardized on 1,700 children between 3-0 and 21-11 selected to match the 1994 U.S. census data. The manual provides evidence for strong reliability. Internal reliability ranged from .64 to .94 depending on subtest. Core composites and indexes also showed high reliability, with most being in the low to middle .90s. Test–retest reliability is reported as ranging from .92 to .93 for core composites and .88 to .96 for indexes. The manual also provides adequate evidence for content, construct, and criterion-related validity. Intercorrelations among the test components ranged from .30 to .79 and provide evidence to suggest that each test is measuring something unique but high enough to support their combination to produce the Core Composite and Index scores. Age-based and grade-based standard scores (M = 100, SD = 15),

grade and test-age equivalents, percentiles, normal curve equivalents (NCEs), and stanines are available.

REVIEWED IN

Plake, B. S., Impara, J. C., & Spies, R. A. (Eds.). (2003). *The fifteenth mental measurements yearbook*. Lincoln, NE: Buros Institute of Mental Measurements.

Elizabeth Carrow-Woolfolk. (1999). *Comprehensive Assessment Spoken Language*. Circle Pines, MN: American Guidance Service, Inc.

RON DUMONT
Fairleigh Dickinson University

JOHN O. WILLIS
Rivier College

KATHLEEN VIEZEL
Fairleigh Dickinson University

JAMIE ZIBULSKY
Fairleigh Dickinson University

COMPREHENSIVE RECEPTIVE AND EXPRESSIVE VOCABULARY TEST, SECOND EDITION

The Comprehensive Receptive and Expressive Vocabulary Test, Second Edition (CREVT-2), provides an efficient measure of both receptive and expressive oral vocabulary. It is used predominantly to identify students who fall significantly below their age group in oral vocabulary proficiency, and to note discrepancies between levels of receptive and expressive skill.

Administration of the CREVT-2 takes about 20 to 30 minutes. All words in the CREVT-2 are appropriate for children and adults and were found to be unbiased. The Receptive Vocabulary Subtest requires the examinee to point to the picture of the word said by the examiner. The 61 items are thematic, full-color photographs representing concepts with which most people are familiar, such as animals, transportation, household appliances, recreation, and clerical materials. The Expressive Vocabulary Subtest asks the examinee to define words said by the examiner, encouraging the individual to discuss in detail each stimulus word. The 25 items of this subtest relate to the same 10 common themes used in the Receptive Vocabulary Subtest (i.e., animals, transportation, occupations, etc.), allowing for easy transition from subtest to subtest. The applications of basals and ceilings allow this test to be given quickly and make it appropriate for a wide age range (4-0 through 89-11).

To quantitatively measure performance, the raw scores obtained on each subtest are converted to standard scores and percentile ranks. Age equivalents are also given.

The CREVT-2 was normed on a representative sample of 2,545 persons, ages 4-0 through 89-11. Norms were stratified by age according to gender, socioeconomic standing, disability, ethnicity, and other critical variables. This sample reflected the 2000 United States Census data.

Reliability coefficients are provided for the normative sample and its subgroups.

REVIEWED IN

Plake, B. S., Impara, J. C., & Spies, R. A. (Eds.). (2003). *The fifteenth mental measurements yearbook.* Lincoln, NE: Buros Institute of Mental Measurements.

Smith, T., Smith, B. L., & Eichler, J. B. (2002). Validity of the Comprehensive Receptive and Expressive Vocabulary Test in assessment of children with speech and learning problems. *Psychology in the Schools, 39,* 613–619.

Wallace, G., & Hammill, D. D. (1994). *Comprehensive Receptive and Expressive Vocabulary Test.* Austin, TX: PRO-ED.

RON DUMONT
Fairleigh Dickinson University

JOHN O. WILLIS
Rivier College

KATHLEEN VIEZEL
Fairleigh Dickinson University

JAMIE ZIBULSKY
Fairleigh Dickinson University
Fourth edition

COMPREHENSIVE TEST OF NONVERBAL INTELLIGENCE, SECOND EDITION

The Comprehensive Test of Nonverbal Intelligence (CTONI-2; 2009) measures nonverbal reasoning abilities of individuals aged 6 through 90 for whom other tests may be inappropriate or biased. Because CTONI-2 contains no oral responses, reading, writing, or object manipulation it is particularly appropriate for students who are bilingual, speak a language other than English, or are socially/economically disadvantaged, deaf, language disordered, motor impaired, or neurologically impaired. The CTONI-2 should not be administered to people with vision problems. It is easy to administer and score and requires only 1 hour to complete. The CTONI-2 instructions can be administered orally to students who speak English or in pantomime for those who speak languages other than English or who are deaf, aphasic, or neurologically impaired. During standardization data collection, approximately 95% of those assessed were tested using English oral instructions; the remaining were tested using the pantomime instructions.

The CTONI-2 measures analogical reasoning, categorical reasoning, and sequential reasoning in two different contexts: pictures of familiar objects (people, toys, and animals) and geometric designs (unfamiliar sketches, patterns, and drawings). There are six subtests in total. Three subtests use pictured objects while three use geometric designs. Each subtest contains 25 items. Examinees indicate their answers by pointing to alternative choices. In addition to raw scores, scaled and standard scores, percentiles, and age equivalents, CTONI-2 also provides three Composite Index scores; Full Scale, Pictorial Scale, and Geometric Scale. Items have been carefully reviewed to protect against bias in regard to race, gender, ethnicity, and language.

The CTONI-2 was normed on a sample of over 2,827 individuals from 10 states, tested in the fall and winter of 2007 and spring 2008, and is representative of the U.S. population with respect to age, gender, race/ethnicity, educational level, and geographic region. Reliability studies of the CTONI-2 provide evidence for content sampling, time sampling, and interscorer reliability and have yielded reliability coefficients of .80 or greater. Studies have reported content, criterion-related, and construct validity as well.

ADDITIONAL INFORMATION

Hammill, D. D., & Pearson, N. A. The Comprehensive Test of Nonverbal Intelligence, Second Edition. (2009). In J. A. Naglieri & S. Goldstein (Eds.), *Practitioner's guide to assessing intelligence and achievement.* Hoboken, NJ: Wiley.

Hammill, D. D. Pearson, N. A., & Wiederhold, J. L. (2009) Comprehensive Test of Nonverbal Intelligence. Mayer-Johnson. Pittsburg, PA.

RON DUMONT
Fairleigh Dickinson University

JOHN O. WILLIS
Rivier College

KATHLEEN VIEZEL
Fairleigh Dickinson University

JAMIE ZIBULSKY
Fairleigh Dickinson University
Fourth edition

COMPREHENSIVE TEST OF PHONOLOGICAL PROCESSING

The Comprehensive Test of Phonological Processing (CTOPP, 2001) assesses phonological awareness, phonological memory, and rapid naming. The CTOPP's principal uses are to identify individuals who are significantly below their peers in important phonological abilities, to determine strengths and weaknesses among developed phonological processes, and to document an individual's progress in phonological processing as a result of special intervention programs.

Because the test spans such a wide range of ages and abilities, it was necessary to develop two versions of the test. Version 1 is designed primarily for kindergarteners and first-graders (ages 5–6) and contains seven core subtests and one supplemental test. Version 2 is designed for persons in second grade through college (ages 7–24) and contains six core subtests and eight supplemental tests.

The CTOPP contains the three composites: Phonological Awareness Quotient (PAQ), measuring awareness of and access to phonological structure of oral language; Phonological Memory Quotient (PMQ), measuring the ability to code information phonologically for temporary storage in working or short-term memory; and Rapid Naming Quotient (RNQ), measuring efficient retrieval of phonological information from long-term or permanent memory, as well as the examinee's ability to execute a sequence of operations quickly and repeatedly. The test also allows for the computation of an Alternative Phonological Awareness Composite (based on nonword stimuli) and an Alternative Rapid Naming Composite (based on stimuli that are not part of the alphabetic script).

The test contains the following subtests: Elision, Blending Words, Sound Matching, Memory for Digits, Nonword Repetition, Rapid Color Naming, Rapid Digit Naming, Rapid Letter Naming, Rapid Object Naming, Blending Nonwords, Phoneme Reversal, Segmenting Words, and Segmenting Nonwords.

Composite scores are reported by combining scores from the following tasks for each construct listed:

Ages 5 and 6:

Phonological Awareness: Elision, Blending Words, and Sound Matching

Phonological Memory: Memory for Digits and Nonword Repetition

Rapid Naming: Rapid Color Naming and Rapid Object Naming

Ages 7–24:

Phonological Awareness: Elision and Blending Words

Phonological Memory: Memory for Digits and Nonword Repetition

Rapid Naming: Rapid Digit Naming and Rapid Letter Naming

All subtests begin with item #1. The ceilings are uniform on all subtests: three missed items in a row, except for the sound matching (4 out of 7 items are missed) and the rapid naming tasks (measure time, if incorrectly names more than 4 items, no score for the subtest). If items are given above the ceiling and any of these items are passes, they are scored as incorrect.

Scores provided include percentiles, standard scores, and age and grade equivalents. Subtest standard scores have a mean of 10 and a standard deviation of 3. The composite quotients have a mean of 100 and a standard deviation of 15. The manual also provides information relating the CTOPP standard scores to NCE scores, *T*-scores, *z*-scores, and stanines.

The CTOPP was normed on 1,656 individuals ranging in age from 5 through 24 and residing in 30 states. The total school-age population was 1,544. Over half of the norming sample came from children in elementary school (through grade five), where the CTOPP is expected to have its widest use. The demographic characteristics of the normative sample are representative of the U.S. population as a whole with regard to gender, race, ethnicity, residence, family income, educational attainment of parents, and geographic regions. The sample characteristics were stratified by age and keyed to the demographic characteristics reported in the 1997 Statistical Abstract of the United States.

Most of the average internal consistency or alternative forms reliability coefficients exceed .80. The test–retest coefficients range from .70 to .92.

At the time this review was written the CTOPP-2 was being prepared for publication. Along with updating the normative sample, a new phonological awareness subtest, based on phoneme isolation, will be added. The lower age limit will drop from age 5 to age 4.

ADDITIONAL INFORMATION

Bhat, P., Griffin, C. C., & Sindelar, P. (2003). Phonological awareness instruction for middle school students with learning disabilities. *Learning Disability Quarterly*, *26*, 73–87.

Haight, S. L. (2006). Reviews of the Comprehensive Test of Phonological Processing (CTOPP). *Assessment for Effective Intervention*, *31*, 81–84.

Havey, J. M., Story, N., & Buker, K. (2002). Convergent and concurrent validity of two measures of phonological processing. *Psychology in the Schools*, *39*, 507–514.

Hintze, J. M., Ryan, A. L., & Stoner, G. (2003). Concurrent validity and diagnostic accuracy of the dynamic indicators of basic early literacy skills and the Comprehensive Test of Phonological Processing. *School Psychology Review*, *32*, 541–556.

Lennon, J. E., & Slesinski, C. (2001). Comprehensive Test of Phonological Processing (CTOPP): Cognitive-linguistic assessment of severe reading problems. Torrance, CA: Western Psychological Services.

http://naspoline.org/

RON DUMONT
Fairleigh Dickinson University

JOHN O. WILLIS
Rivier College

KATHLEEN VIEZEL
Fairleigh Dickinson University

JAMIE ZIBULSKY
Fairleigh Dickinson University
Fourth edition

COMPREHENSIVE TRAIL MAKING TEST

The Comprehensive Trail Making Test (CTMT, 2002), designed for ages 11 through 74, is a standardized set of five visual search and sequencing tasks that are heavily influenced by attention, concentration, resistance to distraction, and cognitive flexibility (or set-shifting). This quick test (which takes 5 to 10 minutes to complete) may be especially useful in the detection of brain compromise and in tracking progress in rehabilitation. It may also be used to detect frontal lobe deficits; problems with psychomotor speed, visual search and sequencing, and attention; and impairments in set-shifting.

The basic task of the CTMT is to connect a series of stimuli (numbers, expressed as numerals or in word form, and letters) in a specified order as fast as possible. The test includes five trails, each administered in numerical order:

Trail 1: The examinee draws a line to connect the numbers 1 through 25 (each contained in a plain circle) in order.

Trail 2: The examinee draws a line to connect the numbers 1 through 25 in order. Each numeral is contained in a plain circle and 29 empty distractor circles also appear on the page.

Trail 3: The examinee draws a line to connect in the numbers 1 through 25 in order. Each is contained in a plain circle. On the same page there are also 13 empty distractor circles and 19 distractor circles containing irrelevant line drawings.

Trail 4: The examinee draws a line to connect the numbers 1 through 21 in order. Twelve of the numbers are presented as Arabic numerals, (e.g., 1, 7) and each is contained in a plain circle; 9 numbers

are spelled out (e.g., Ten, Four) and contained in rectangular boxes.

Trail 5: The examinee draws a line to connect in alternating sequence the numbers 1 through 13 and the letters A through L. The examinee begins with 1 and then draws a line to A, then proceeds to 2, then B, and so on until all the numbers and letters are connected. Each of the numbers and letters is contained in a plain circle. Fifteen empty distractor circles appear on the same page.

The score derived for each trail is the number of seconds required to complete the task. Errors made by the examinee are not counted or scored, but they are corrected by the examiner and thus add to the completion time. Normative scores are provided in the form of T-scores, having a mean of 50 and a standard deviation of 10, along with their accompanying percentile ranks. Z scores and stanines are also available. The composite score is obtained by summing the T-scores from the individual trails and looking up that sum in the manual.

The CTMT is standardized on a nationwide sample of 1,664 persons from 19 states. Demographic characteristics of the sample included geographic area, gender, race, ethnicity, family income, parent education, and disability, and each matched fairly closely (within 0 to 7 percentage points) the U.S. 1998 Census data. Norms were collected for 13 age groups: full year from ages 11 to 16, combined ages 17–19, 10-year groups for ages 20 to 69 (e.g., 20–29), and a 5-year age group for 70–75. For the full-year age groups (11–16) the number of participants in each group ranged from 79 to 106. For the remaining combined age groups, the number ranged from 104 to 205. Internal reliability coefficients for each individual trail ranged from .67 to .83 across all ages while the composite score has a reliability coefficient of .90 or higher at all ages. Test–retest reliabilities for a sample of 30 individuals tested 1 week apart ranged from .70 to .78 for the 5 trails and .84 for the Composite. Validity evidence provided in the manual shows strong, consistent evidence for the CTMT.

REVIEWED IN

Allen, D. N., Haderlie, M., Kazakov, D., & Mayfield, J. (2009). Construct and criterion validity of the Comprehensive Trail Making Test in children and adolescents with traumatic brain injury. *Child Neuropsychology, 15*, 543–553.

Gray, R. (2006). Review of "Comprehensive Trail Making Test." *Journal of Psychoeducational Assessment, 24.*

Plake, B. S., Impara, J. C., & Spies, R. A. (Eds.). (2003). *The fifteenth mental measurements yearbook*. Lincoln, NE: Buros Institute of Mental Measurements.

Reynolds, C. R. (2002) Comprehensive Trail Making Test. Torrance, CA: Western Psychological Services.

Smith, S. R., Servesco, A. M., Edwards, J. W., Rahban, R., Barazani, S., Nowinski, L. A., ... Green, J. G. (2008). Exploring the validity of the Comprehensive Trail Making Test. *Clinical Neuropsychologist, 22*, 507–518.

RON DUMONT
Fairleigh Dickinson University

JOHN O. WILLIS
Rivier College

KATHLEEN VIEZEL
Fairleigh Dickinson University

JAMIE ZIBULSKY
Fairleigh Dickinson University
Fourth edition

COMPULSORY ATTENDANCE (AND STUDENTS WITH DISABILITIES)

Compulsory school attendance laws have been in effect in nearly every state and in most other parts of the western world for the bulk of the twentieth century. These laws require the parents or legal guardians of all children to send them to school or to provide an equivalent education. The ages of children for whom school attendance is compulsory varies as well, but includes children between the ages of 7 and 16 years in the vast majority of states. The courts have exempted some religious groups from the enforcement of compulsory attendance laws, notably the Amish nationwide and in some states the Mennonites. The states differ greatly in what constitutes a legal school under their compulsory attendance laws. Some states recognize only state-certified and supervised schools (public or private), while some allow children to attend noncertified church-supported schools. Others are even more liberal and allow home schooling accomplished by lay parents. Compulsory attendance laws have been the subject of much litigation since their initial enactment.

Many consider compulsory attendance laws to be an infringement on various rights granted to the general population in the first 10 amendments to the U.S. Constitution (the Bill of Rights). However, the courts have held, with minor religious exceptions, that the state has a compelling interest in the welfare of all children within its jurisdiction and that the provision for education under compulsory circumstances is an acceptable part of this compelling interest and is a legal extension of the police powers of the state. The full extent of the state's compelling interest in education has yet to be defined in adequate detail by the courts, but it is related to the provision of an education that allows individuals to become contributing members of society, preventing them from becoming burdens on the state.

Prior to the passage of the Education for All Handicapped Children Act of 1975 (PL 94-142), which required the states to make available to all disabled children a free, appropriate, public education, few states enforced their compulsory attendance laws where disabled children were involved. Many school districts throughout the country would not allow many children with disabilities to attend, and in many such instances, encouraged parents to keep these children at home. Many states remain lax in the enforcement of compulsory attendance statutes with regard to the handicapped. With the growing problem of delinquency in the United States, there has been a recent trend away from strict enforcement of truancy laws.

In most states, children with disabilities are included in the compulsory attendance laws and the failure (or refusal) of the parents or legal guardians to present these children for school attendance is likely actionable on civil and/or criminal bases in most states. However, school officials or child welfare workers will, in the typical case, have to take the lead in seeking the enforcement of compulsory attendance laws for children with disabilities. It is clear, however, that unless specifically exempted by the wording of the state statute, disabled children are required to attend school. What constitutes a school or an equivalent educational program may be different for the disabled than the nondisabled given the broad authority granted to multidisciplinary teams to diagnose and prescribe educational plans.

CECIL R. REYNOLDS
Texas A&M University
Second edition

KIMBERLY F. APPLEQUIST
University of Colorado at Colorado Springs
Third edition

See also Individuals With Disabilities Education Improvement Act of 2004 (IDEIA)

COMPUTERIZED AXIAL TOMOGRAPHY (*See* CAT Scan)

COMPUTERS AND EDUCATION, AN INTERNATIONAL JOURNAL

Computers and Education is a scholarly journal published by the Pergamon division of Elsevier Publishing. Since 1977, the journal has provided a forum for communication in the use of all forms of computing. *Computers and Education* publishes papers in the language of the academic computer user on educational and training system development using techniques from and applications in many knowledge domains including: graphics, simulation, computer-aided design, computer-integrated manufacture, and artificial intelligence and its applications. The journal is published eight times a year and subscriptions can be ordered online (http://www.elsevier.com/).

COMPUTERS IN HUMAN BEHAVIOR

Computers in Human Behavior is a scholarly journal devoted to research that attempts to articulate the relationship between psychology, the science of human behavior, and technological advances in computer science. Articles are concerned with advances in research design and the technology of research, but also with the effects of computers on the topics chosen for study by psychologists, such as the use of health promotion programs to promote behavioral change, and use of virtual reality programs (Riva, 1998). Changes in clinical practice, ethics, and standards related to computers are also examined. Articles appearing in the journal have also included studies of the equivalence of testing conditions (computerized vs. standard administration), and computerized interpretation of tests (Bosworth, Gustofson, & Hawkins, 1994). The latter two areas are of interest to special educators as several articles have addressed placement decisions and educational diagnosis using computer programs to interpret tests. *Computers in Human Behavior* is a Pergamon Press journal; it began publication in 1985.

REFERENCES

Bosworth, K., Gustafson, D. H., & Hawkins, R. P. (1994). The BARN system and impact of adolescent health promotion via computer. *Computers in Human Behavior, 10*(4), 467–482.

Riva, G. (1998). Virtual environment for body image modification: Virtual reality system for the treatment of body image disturbances. *Computers in Human Behavior, 14*(3), 477–490.

CECIL R. REYNOLDS
Texas A&M University

COMPUTER USE WITH STUDENTS WITH DISABILITIES

For disabled persons, computers have three main functions: compensation for disabilities, management, and instructional delivery.

In terms of compensation for disabilities, one of the most exciting aspects of computer technology is the use of augmentative devices for communication and control. Computers help users overcome communication problems associated with limited mobility and sensory impairment. To increase the speed and accuracy of using computers, engineers and educators have developed special input and output devices. Innovative input devices include voice recognition, speech synthesizers (Schery & Spaw, 1993), the mouse, joysticks and game paddles, mechanical keyboard aids such as guards, mouths, headsticks, and splints. Examples of computer output devices are synthetic speech, Blissymbols, tactile display (Opticon), Braille, and portable computer printers (Brady, 1982).

For individuals with cerebral palsy, amyotrophic lateral sclerosis, or severe paralysis, one of the biggest problems of computer usage is the multiple simultaneous key strokes required to run many pieces of standard software. To take advantage of a computer's capacity to control the environment, a person with limited mobility must have an adaptive firmware card. The card is a device that enables a person with limited mobility to run software by activating a single switch (Schwedjda & Vanderheiden, 1982). Single switches and expanded keyboards require only slight movement, such as the blinking of an eye.

Access to standard software allows disabled individuals to use computers for information management. The four primary areas of information management are word processing, database management, financial management, and telecommunications. Word processing programs allow users to draft, edit, and print text with relative ease. Changing margins and moving sentences or paragraphs are a matter of a few keystrokes. Learning-disabled students can use word processing programs to overcome some of the problems associated with writing and spelling (Arms, 1984). Database management programs are used to store, sort, and retrieve large amounts of information. In special education, administrators and teachers use database management programs to file information such as students' names, addresses, birthdates, disabilities, and test scores. Financial management programs such as spreadsheets allow users to create, monitor, and change budgets. Other programs help with checkbook balancing and income tax preparation.

With the use of the Internet, computer users have access to virtually limitless sources of information. Subscribers can access stock market reports, make travel reservations, obtain up-to-the-minute weather reports, or search through large bibliographic databases and websites for information on a given topic.

Word processing, database management, financial management, and telecommunications packages have reached a high level of sophistication. Users can now take the information from one program and load it into another. If, for example, a user wanted to include a budget in a manuscript, he or she could load the information from a spreadsheet program into the text of a word processing program. Or, for example, a homebound individual could compose text on the word processor and send it to a teacher or other interested party by e-mail.

In addition to the functions that allow computers to aid in communication and information management, computers have certain characteristics that enhance the delivery of instruction. Interaction means that computers can perform many of the functions that are typically performed by the teacher, such as providing immediate feedback. Software can be designed so that rates of response and levels of difficulty can be varied according to the student. One of the characteristics that tends to motivate students is branching capability (i.e., the capability of moving from one part of a program to another). Branching allows learners to decide whether they need to repeat material or move on to new material. Moreover, computers are tireless; they do not become irritated when asked to repeat information or activities.

REFERENCES

Arms, V. M. (1984). A dyslexic can compose a computer. *Educational Technology, 24,* 39–41.

Brady, M. (1982). The Trace Center International Hardware/Software Registry: Programs for handicapped students. *Journal of Special Education Technology, 5,* 16–21.

Schery, T., & Spaw, L. (1993, December 14). *Computer talk: Helping young handicapped children communicate.* Paper presented at the Council for Exceptional Children Conference, San Diego, CA.

Schwejda, P., & Vanderheiden, G. (1982). Adaptive-firmware card for the Apple II. *Byte, 7,* 276–314.

ELIZABETH MCCLELLAN
Council for Exceptional Children

CONCEPT FORMATION

The term *concept* is used to describe one of the ways the human mind organizes the tremendous amounts of data with which it is bombarded. As Ausubel (1968) points out:

> Anyone who pauses long enough to give the problem some serious thought cannot escape the conclusion that man lives in a world of concepts, rather than a world of objects, events, and situations.... Reality, figuratively speaking, is experienced through a conceptual or categorical filter. (p. 505)

A concept would appear to be a mental construct that serves to group together similar entities. Having knowledge of a concept means having at least knowledge of the common elements that define inclusion or exclusion of an entity from a category. The presence of a concept is tested by observing which objects are placed in the same category or are acted on similarly. The individual carrying out such an activity may or may not have any idea what the concept is that he or she is using for categorization, nor what the common elements may be.

There are often confusions between the ideas of concept and language. It is not an uncommon approach to define a concept as "something about an idea expressed in words of our language" (Platt, 1963, p. 21). However, it is clear that animals as well as humans have concepts (Humphrey, 1984). A dog does not react to an unfamiliar cat each time it sees one as if it were a unique object. Rather, it behaves toward the cat based on its past experiences with other cats. The dog, then, must have some concept of cats.

The relationship between a concept and language is a culturally contextual and problematical one, however. Gagne (1970), for example, has argued that there are two types of concepts, concrete ones such as "dog," which are based on direct empirical experience, and those such as "uncle" or "democracy," which cannot exist without language. It is further argued by some that the way language organizes and categorizes information actually affects the way one perceives incoming data. For example, different languages break up the color spectrum differently. A number of studies have been conducted to determine whether individuals from different cultures actually perceive colors differently, based on their language.

Two general approaches for concept formation have been described (Martorella, 1972). The first is inductive, the second deductive. Concepts learned inductively start with a group of facts, data, or concepts that are already understood. Through the use of certain intellectual skills, new, more abstract concepts are developed. For example, to assist a child in learning the rule that *e* in a VCVe word usually makes the vowel long, the child could compare two lists of similar words, one containing the final *e*, the other not. The deductive approach, on the other hand, begins by presenting the more abstract principle. The learner develops an understanding of the principle through repeated mental operations on examples pertinent to the concept. In this case, a child would be presented with the rule about the final *e* first, and then would be shown a number of examples. Research has not yet determined that teaching using either type of model is clearly superior. There is in fact some indication in cognitive-style research that the success of one method over the other is at least to some degree dependent on a person's individual learning style (Witkin, Moore, Goodenough, & Cox, 1977).

Vygotsky (1962) made a similar distinction between two types of conceptual learning. He described two methods for learning concepts depending on whether the concept is spontaneous or scientific. Spontaneous concepts are learned from day-to-day concrete exposure to specific examples of the concept. An example of this type of concept would be that of *dog*. The individual learns what a dog is by living with a dog and by seeing pictures of many different kinds of dogs. However, a term like *exploitation* is probably learned through a mediated situation in a formal learning environment. The individual is presented with only the beginning schematics of the term's meaning. A fuller understanding is gained over time with examples not directly experienced by the learner, but learned through discussion and reading.

In a sense, the development of spontaneous concepts is an upward process, the development of scientific ones a downward one. Concepts learned through an upward process start with a number of concrete examples, with the learner developing a general notion of the essence of "dogginess." Concepts learned through a downward process tend to start with definitions, with the learner gradually determining which specific instances are examples of the general notion.

Behaviorists have attempted to explain the development of concepts in strict stimulus–response terms. Vygotsky and others have objected to this explanation on the grounds that while the mental processes described by behaviorists are necessary, they are not sufficient for explaining how external phenomena become categorized into conceptual frameworks. These thinkers find the stimulus–response paradigm an inadequate explanation for how the brain arrives at the essence of concepts such as dogginess or exploitation.

Festinger (1957), in describing the process of concept formation, borrowed from the Piagetian notion of equilibrium. Festinger stated that if an organism has two cognitions that are perceived as being dissonant with one another, there is a tendency to attempt a modification of the cognitive structures to reduce the dissonance. This process, he states, creates new concepts. For example, if a child calls all animals "doggie" but notices others call some of those "cats," the child will in time modify his or her notion of what characteristics identify members of the class of dogs.

DeCecco (1968) has proposed the following general model for teaching concepts:

1. Describe what performance is expected after the concept is taught.
2. For complex concepts, reduce the number of attributes to be taught; emphasize dominant attributes.
3. Provide clear verbal associations.
4. Give positive and negative examples of the concept.
5. Present the examples either in close succession or simultaneously.
6. Present a new positive example, asking the student to identify it.
7. Verify the student's understanding of the concept.
8. Ask the student to define the concept.

9. Provide opportunities for the student to practice the concept with appropriate reinforcement (p. 58).

There was considerable interest in the process of concept formation during the late 1960s and early 1970s, when new mathematics and social studies curricula were being developed. The back-to-basics movement led to a declining interest in this field of inquiry. Recently, with the introduction of problem solving into the curriculum, a renewed interest in concept formation has developed. The hope is that, particularly for students with special needs, understanding how concept formation occurs in a culturally competent context (Gonzales & Schallert, 1993) will guide teachers in helping their students become more effective learners.

REFERENCES

Ausubel, D. P. (1968). *Educational psychology: A cognitive view*. New York, NY: Holt, Rinehart, & Winston.

DeCecco, J. P. (1968). *The psychology of learning and instruction*. Englewood Cliffs, NJ: Prentice Hall.

Festinger, L. (1957). The motivating factor of cognitive dissonance. In R. C. Harper et al. (Eds.), *The cognitive processes*. Englewood Cliffs, NJ: Prentice Hall.

Gagne, R. M. (1970). *The conditions of learning* (2nd ed.). New York, NY: Holt, Rinehart, & Winston.

Gonzales, V., & Schallert, D. (1993, April 12–16). *Influence of linguistic, and cultural variables on conceptual learning in second language situations*. Paper presented at the Annual Meeting of the American Educational Research Association, Atlanta, GA.

Humphrey, N. (1984). *Consciousness regained: Chapters in the development of the mind*. Oxford, England: Oxford University Press.

Martorella, P. H. (1972). *Concept learning: Designs for instruction*. Scranton, PA: Intext Educational.

Platt, M. M. (1963). Concepts and the curriculum. *Social Education, 27*, 21.

Vygotsky, L. S. (1962). *Thought and language*. Cambridge, MA: MIT Press.

Witkin, H. A., Moore, C. A., Goodenough, D. R., & Cox, P. W. (1977). Field-dependent and field-independent cognitive styles and their educational implications. *Review of Educational Research, 47*, 1–64.

CAROLYN L. BULLARD
Lewis & Clark College

See also Abstract Thinking, Impairment in; Thought Disorders; Vygotsky, Lev S.

CONCEPT OF ACTIVITY (*See* Theory of Activity; Vygotsky, Lev S.)

CONCRETE OPERATIONS

Concrete operations is the third of four invariant stages of Piaget's theory of cognitive development. According to Piaget, the distinctive features of children's thought occurring during the period of concrete operations are logic and objectivity that includes the ability to perform mental manipulations directly related to objects and events. These manipulations, which emerge between the ages of approximately 7 to 11 years, are termed *operations* by Piaget. To qualify as an operation, an action must be internalizable, reversible, and part of an overall system of actions. By *internalizable* Piaget meant that a child can think about the action "without losing their original character of actions" (1953, p. 8). An example of internalization during the concrete operations stage is the performance of mental arithmetic. Essential to understanding number and size relationships are transitivity and associativity. Transitivity, the basis for seriation, is the ability to arrange a series of events or objects in a continuum such as "less than," "greater than," "fewer than," or "more than." Associativity is demonstrated by understanding that parts of a whole may be combined in different ways without effecting a change on the whole.

Reversibility is another ability that characterizes a child's thought during the concrete operations stage. The child is able to reverse actions mentally (e.g., the child learns that the number of fingers on a hand counted sequentially from thumb to little finger is the same as counted from little finger to thumb, or the child imagines the effect weights will have when placed on or taken off a scale). Actions cannot be isolated manipulations. Instead, they are part of a coherent system of thinking. Concrete operational children develop a capacity to think about concept classes in equivalent and hierarchic forms; for example, oranges and bananas are both fruit, fruit is food, but all food is not fruit.

The classic measure of whether a particular child is capable of concrete operational thinking is provided by the task of conservation. There are more than 1,000 published studies on conservation (Yussen & Santrock, 1982). In a classic study, a child is seated before two same-size beakers, equally filled with water, and a taller, empty beaker. The experimenter pours one of the beakers into the tall, empty one and asks the child if the amounts in the tall beaker and the unpoured beaker are the same or different. The conserver (i.e., the concrete operational thinker) knows that the amount of liquid has not changed and that if it were poured back into the original container (internalization of a reversible action) it would be the same.

In recent years, several aspects of Piaget's theory of cognitive development have been challenged (Flavell, 1992). As early as 1964, Jerome Bruner showed that children who should not be able to conserve, according to Piaget,

could do so if the transformation of the object (pouring the beaker of water) were hidden from view. Since then, there has been considerable debate as to the accuracy of Piaget's four-stage model. It now seems clear that many specifics of Piaget's theory, such as the age of onset of concrete operations, are in doubt. Nonetheless, the elegance and insight that Piaget brought to the study of children's thinking was immense.

REFERENCES

Bruner, J. S. (1964). The course of cognitive growth. *American Psychologists*, *19*, 1–15.

Flavell, J. H. (1992). Cognitive development: Past, present, and future. *Developmental Psychology*, *28*(6), 998–1005.

Piaget, J. (1953). *Logic and psychology*. Manchester, UK: Manchester University.

Yussen, S. R., & Santrock, J. W. (1982). *Child development: An introduction*. Dubuque, IA: Brown.

MICHAEL ASH
JOSE LUIS TORRES
Texas A&M University

See also Cognitive Development

CONDITIONED REINFORCER

A *conditioned reinforcer* is a concept found and used primarily within the field of Applied Behavior Analysis. In essence, this concept relates to when a reinforcing event has acquired its efficacy because of an individual's life history or strong association with certain environmental stimuli (Pierce & Epling, 1995). Conditioned, or secondary, reinforcers are not related to any biological need or desire; rather, they are a result of each individual's unique social history, and as a result, these conditioned reinforcers are always changing or evolving. When a neutral stimulus is "conditioned," it implies that a learning process has occurred between the presentation or withdrawal of a stimulus and the consequences on behavior. The end result of this process is that it strengthens a target behavior; that is, there will be concomitant increases in the desired behavior when the conditioned reinforcer is presented to, or withdrawn from, the person. This process of developing a conditioned reinforcer occurs by repeatedly and contingently pairing a neutral consequence with another stimulus that is already reinforcing to the individual (Skinner, 1953). Social attention and approval (and disapproval) are powerful human conditioned reinforcers because of how much control they have in manipulating or effecting behavioral change in people.

Perhaps the best example of a conditioned reinforcer is money. Money is inherently neutral, either just a slip of colorful paper or small piece of metal. However, when a person learns that money can purchase many highly valuable things or events, it quickly becomes a powerful tool for increasing behavior in people. In school settings, many things can take on conditioned reinforcer status if such repeated and contingent pairing is made (e.g., computer time, recess, peer relations, social praise from adults, etc.); however, a conditioned reinforcer is only "reinforcing" if increases in target behaviors are associated with it. Whether by presenting or withdrawing a conditioned reinforcer, concomitant increases in behavior must occur. If the target behavior decreases when the reinforcer is presented or withdrawn, then it is quite likely that the stimulus being presented or withdrawn was actually a punisher (i.e., an aversive) and involves the process called "punishment," which is a behavioral technique designed to weaken the occurrence of a particular behavior (Bijou, 1993).

Conditioned reinforcers can be subcategorized as either tangible, activity-oriented, social, or generalized reinforcers (Cooper, Heron, & Heward, 1987). *Tangibles* could include trinkets, stickers, toys, gel-pens; *activity* reinforcers might include board games, computer games, going to the movies or a baseball game; *social* reinforcers might include hugs, kisses, positive statements/comments, proximity to a person. A *generalized* reinforcer, on the other hand, provides individuals with access to a wide variety/range of primary or secondary (conditioned) reinforcers. Token economy systems are a good example of how conditioned reinforcers can be used to increase target behaviors, a behavioral system that is well established in the research literature (e.g., Kazdin, 1977; Kazdin & Bootzin, 1972). Basically, when a consequence is successfully paired with several unconditioned or conditioned reinforcers, it is called a generalized conditioned reinforcer. Due to the fact that a generalized conditioned reinforcer is tied to many different reinforcing events or stimuli, it is useful for avoiding satiation because a menu of reinforcing possibilities is available instead of just one (Wolery, Bailey, & Sugai, 1988).

When a stimulus is paired with a reinforcer to become a conditioned reinforcer, the stimulus is not what has changed, but rather the person, because it is his or her behavior that has been modified. It must be kept in mind that while it is convenient to speak of a conditioned reinforcer as a real "thing" that has an assumed reinforcing effect on a person, the person's behavioral response to the conditioned reinforcer is not arbitrary. A conditioned reinforcer may lead to a reinforcing event, but the reinforcing effect of an event is not the specific property of the event itself. Rather, it belongs to the actual changes in ongoing behavior. The defining characteristic of a conditioned (secondary) reinforcer is how it changes behavior (Morse & Kelleher, 1977).

REFERENCES

Bijou, S. W. (1993). *Behavior analysis of child development* (2nd rev. ed.). Reno, NV: Context Press.

Cooper, J. O., Heron, T. E., & Heward, W. L. (1987). *Applied behavior analysis*. New York, NY: Macmillan.

Kazdin, A. E. (1977). *The token economy: A review and evaluation.* New York, NY: Plenum Press.

Kazdin, A. E., & Bootzin, R. R. (1972). The token economy: An evaluative review. *Journal of Applied Behavior Analysis, 5,* 343–372.

Morse, W. H., & Kelleher, R. T. (1977). Determinants of reinforcement and punishment. In W. K. Honig & J. E. R. Staddon (Eds.), *Handbook of operant behavior* (pp. 174–200). Englewood Cliffs, NJ: Prentice Hall.

Pierce, W. D., & Epling, W. F. (1995). *Behavior analysis and learning*. Englewood Cliffs, NJ: Prentice Hall.

Skinner, B. F. (1953). *Science and human behavior*. New York, NY: Macmillan.

Wolery, M., Bailey, D. B. Jr., & Sugai, G. M. (1988). *Effective teaching: Principles and procedures of applied behavior analysis with exceptional students*. Boston, MA: Allyn & Bacon.

ROLLEN C. FOWLER
Eugene 4J School District,
Eugene, Oregon

See also **Behavioral Assessment; Behavior Disorders**

CONDITIONING

Conditioning is a general term that describes a strengthening (through a predictive relationship) of an association between a stimulus and a response or between two stimuli. With conditioning, responses become increasingly likely to occur under appropriate circumstances. In operant conditioning, the probability of a response that has been followed by reinforcement increases. In Pavlovian (or respondent or classical) conditioning, the probability of a response to an initially neutral stimulus increases when that neutral stimulus is followed by one that reliably elicits a response in reflex fashion. Pavlovian conditioning is named after the great Russian physiologist Ivan Pavlov (1927), whose research established the basic phenomena associated with this type of conditioning. However, the phenomenon itself had been discovered and described some years earlier by an American psychologist, E. B. Twitmeyer.

Basic Aspects for Pavlovian Conditioning

The paradigm for Pavlovian conditioning is:

CS → UCS →UCR   (before conditioning)
CS → CR   (after conditioning)

Pairing of an initially neutral conditional stimulus (CS) with an unconditional stimulus (UCS) that reliably elicits a response (UCR) leads to a conditional response (CR) occurring to the CS. Frequently, but not always, the CR is similar to the UCR in form. For example, Pavlov would sound a bell (CS) and then give a dog food (UCS), which elicited salivation (UCR). After several pairings of the bell with food, the bell itself elicited salivation. Using the paradigm:

CS → UCS → UCR   (before conditioning)
(bell) (food)   (salivation)
CS → CR   (after conditioning)
(bell) (salivation)

we can see that through pairing, a response can occur to a stimulus that never occurred to it before.

Watson (1916) made Pavlovian conditioning the basic form of learning in his formulation of behaviorism. In 1920, Watson and Rayner published a classic article on conditioning of an emotional response in a human infant. While one experimenter held a white rat (CS) toward 11-month-old Albert, the other experimenter hit a bar with a hammer, making a very loud noise (UCR) that elicited crying (UCS) from Albert. After only five pairings, the rat itself elicited crying (CR).

The basic aspects of conditioning can be briefly described:

Acquisition. With repeated trials, strength of the CR increases to some maximum level.

Extinction. Presentation of the CS without the UCS leads to a decrease in intensity of the CR until no response is observed.

Spontaneous Recovery. Presenting the CS after some delay following extinction may revoke a CR, although it will be of relatively low intensity.

Reacquisition. Repairing of the CS and UCS generally leads to more rapid reconditioning than original conditioning.

Generalization. After conditioning, a CR will tend to occur, but at lower intensity, to similar stimuli.

Discrimination. Presentation of one CS (CS^1) followed by a UCS and of another (CS^2) not followed by a UCS will generally result in the subject developing a discrimination such that it produces a CR to CS^1 but not CS^2.

Some Important Issues

The Nature of the CR

Pavlov proposed that the CS came to take the place of the UCS—stimulus substitution—in a mechanical process. Thus, the CR should be similar in form to the UCR. However, although dogs salivate to both bells and food, they do not try to eat the bell. Indeed, they look at and move toward the food dish, behaviors that suggest that conditioning produces a CR that anticipates the UCS (Zener, 1937). Research (Rescorla, 1966; Siegel, 1975) suggests that in at least some cases, conditioning indeed leads to the CS eliciting a CR that reflects expectancy of the UCS. For example, Siegel gave rats a series of insulin injections in which the hypodermic needle was the CS, the insulin was the UCS, and insulin-elicited hypoglycemia was the UCS. In response to a CS-only test, the rats showed hyperglycemia, as though they were compensating for the anticipated UCS, insulin. The influential Rescorla and Wagner (1972) model proposes that conditioning will occur only when the CS provides information ("expectancy") about the UCS.

Biological Constraints on Learning

Although early theorists felt that all stimuli and responses should be equally conditionable, research shows that they are not. In their now-classic study, Garcia and Koelling (1966) gave rats either "sweet water" or "bright-noisy water" (water paired with flashing lights and noise) and then either shocked them or made them ill. Of rats given sweet water, only those made ill subsequently avoided drinking the water; of rats given bright-noisy water, only those shocked subsequently avoided drinking. Similar results appear to hold in humans (Seligman, 1970). The specificity of "cue–consequence relations" is a topic of current interest. The implication is that some types of associations have particularly important adaptive value, and have been selected through evolution.

Consideration of biological factors helps to resolve the controversial question of whether young infants demonstrate classical conditioning. Although the existence of such conditioning had been generally accepted, Sameroff (1971) concluded that positive studies either could not be replicated or suffered from methodological problems, and that conditioning in newborns had not clearly been demonstrated. Sameroff and Cavenaugh (1979) later suggested that studies published since the initial review, which successfully demonstrated conditioning, had used CS and UCS pairings of biological relevance to the newborn. Indeed, by pairing biologically relevant stimuli, Blass, Ganchrow, and Steiner (1984) have obtained conditioning in infants of 2 to 48 hours of age. Tactile stimulation (CS) was followed by presentation of sucrose solution (UCS) that elicited sucking (UCR). Newborns sucked during CS in conditioning and showed extinction of sucking during subsequent CS-only trials. Further, seven of eight experimental infants cried during extinction trials at a time when the sucrose had been presented, suggesting an affective component of the conditioning.

Long-Delay Learning

Initially, research indicated that the CS and UCS had to be closely linked in time for conditioning to occur. However, in some circumstances, particularly where the UCS elicits illness, an association may be formed with a novel taste or olfactory CS encountered over 12 hours earlier (Revusky & Garcia, 1970). Thus, under circumstances such as food poisoning, a CR can occur to a stimulus removed in time from the UCS. Some have suggested that aversions to food that develop in cancer patients undergoing chemotherapy may be classically conditioned since most chemotherapeutic agents induce intense symptoms of food poisoning (Braveman & Bronstein, 1985).

Higher-Order Conditioning

The potential role of Pavlovian conditioning is greatly extended by higher-order conditioning, originally described by Pavlov and studied in detail by Rescorla (1980). In such conditioning, a first CS (CS^1) is paired with a UCS to establish a CR to CS^1. Then, a second CS (CS^2) is paired only with CS1, leading to the response conditioned to CS1 now occurring to CS2. Thus, once a response has been conditioned to a CS, other CSs may be tied to it that are not themselves directly associated with the UCS but are remote from it. If the original link between CS1 and the UCS is broken, as in extinction, the higher-order CRs also diminish.

Applications to Children's Development

Development of Emotions

Since the time of Watson, Pavlovian conditioning has played an important role in accounting for the association of positive and negative emotional reactions with particular stimuli. Watson and Rayner demonstrated how conditioning could lead to negative emotions such as fear. Indeed, conditioning is viewed as a major process underlying the development of severe fears or phobias.

As conditioning may induce phobias, so it may be used to reduce them. As early as 1924, Jones "countercondi-tioned" a severe fear of rabbits in a child, Peter, by pairing a rabbit with pleasurable stimuli such as peer play and ice cream cones. By the end of the process, Peter no longer feared rabbits and, indeed, was petting them. This procedure, now called *desensitization*, is one of the most effective means of treating phobias in children and adults. Conditioning may also produce positive emotional responses, as shown, for example, in children's excitement at the sight of a favored food, person, or toy.

Development of Meaning

Conditioning is one process thought to underlie the attachment of meaning to words (Mowrer, 1954). Pairing a word (CS) with the object (UCS) signified by the word will result in responses elicited by the object becoming attached to the word as a CR. Thus, pairing the word *doll* with an actual doll leads to responses elicited by the doll becoming associated with *doll*. Although a conditioning model cannot deal with all meaning, particularly that involving abstract concepts, it does provide a framework for understanding how reactions to stimuli can become attached to symbols for them. If an object comes to elicit an emotional response, then the word for the object may also elicit that response. If a child who has been painfully knocked to the ground by a large dog now fears all large dogs, he or she may show fear at the phrase *large dog*. On the other hand, a child who likes ice cream cones might well show positive anticipation to the phrase *ice cream cone*.

Also important is the related concept of mediated or semantic generalization. Once a CR occurs to a word, it will occur to words similar in meaning if the individual has developed a concept involving that word. Thus, if conditioned to respond to the word *shoe*, an individual will respond more to *boot*, or other words similar in meaning, than to *shoot*, a word similar in physical characteristics. Already apparent by at least age 8, semantic generalization becomes stronger with age (Osgood, 1953).

Implications for Educators

Those dealing with children need to be sensitive to the fact that they and the situation they are in are paired with what they say and do to the children. So is the situation paired with peers' reactions to children. Thus, teachers who use aversive means of classroom management may condition children to be anxious about them and their classrooms. Similarly, children who are ridiculed in class or on the playground or who experience much failure and little success may become conditioned to fear school itself and teachers generally. In the extreme, a school phobia may result.

We should also be aware that children will arrive at school with conditioned likes and dislikes and emotional responses. Some may have been specifically food poisoned or have had gastric distress after eating and may have strong aversions to certain foods. Others may have strong fears. However controversial it may be, those in special education should consider the roles of conditioning when predicting the effects of inclusion on children with disabilities. Those children who succeed socially and academically will have a positive conditioning experience, whereas those who are not accepted and/or fail academically may suffer from negative conditioning and develop conditioned responses associated with anxiety and fear of failure.

REFERENCES

Blass, E. M., Ganchrow, J. R., & Steiner, J. E. (1984). Classical conditioning in new born humans 2–48 hours of age. *Infant Behavior and Development, 7*, 223–235.

Braveman, N. S., & Bronstein, P. (Eds.). (1985). Experimental assessments and clinical applications of conditioned food aversions. *Annuals of the New York Academy of Sciences, 443.*

Garcia, J., & Koelling, R. A. (1966). Relation of cue to consequence in avoidance learning. *Psychonomic Science, 4*, 123–124.

Jones, M. C. (1924). A laboratory study of fear: The case of Peter. *Pedagogical Seminary and Journal of Genetic Psychology, 31*, 308–315.

Mowrer, O. H. (1954). The psychologist looks at language. *American Psychologist, 9*, 660–694.

Osgood, C. E. (1953). *Method and theory in experimental psychology.* New York, NY: Oxford University Press.

Pavlov, I. P. (1927). *Conditioned reflexes* (translated by G. V. Anrep). New York, NY: Oxford University Press.

Rescorla, R. A. (1966). Predictability and number of pairings in Pavlovian fear conditioning. *Psychonomic Science, 4*, 383–384.

Rescorla, R. A. (1980). *Pavlovian second-order conditioning.* Hillsdale, NJ: Erlbaum.

Rescorla, R. A., & Wagner, A. R. (1972). A theory of Pavlovian conditioning: Variations in the effectiveness of reinforcement and nonreinforcement. In A. H. Black & W. F. Prokasy (Eds.), *Classical conditioning II: Current research and theory.* New York, NY: Appleton-Century-Crofts.

Revusky, S. H., & Garcia, J. (1970). Learned associations over long delays. In G. H. Bower & J. T. Spence (Eds.), *The psychology of learning and motivation* (Vol. 4). New York, NY: Academic.

Sameroff, A. J. (1971). Can conditioned responses be established in the newborn infant? *Developmental Psychology, 5*, 1–12.

Sameroff, A. J., & Cavenaugh, P. J. (1979). Learning in infancy: A developmental perspective. In J. D. Osofsky (Ed.), *Handbook of infant development* (pp. 344–392). New York, NY: Wiley.

Seligman, M. E. P. (1970). On the generality of the laws of learning. *Psychological Review, 77*, 406–418.

Siegel, S. (1975). Conditioning insulin effects. *Journal of Comparative and Physiological Psychology, 89*, 189–199.

Watson, J. B. (1916). The place of the conditioned reflex in psychology. *Psychological Review, 23*, 89–116.

Watson, J. B., & Rayner, R. (1920). Conditioned emotional reactions. *Journal of Experimental Psychology, 3*, 1–14.

Zener, K. (1937). The significance of behavior accompanying conditioned salivary secretion for theories of the conditioned reflex. *American Journal of Psychology, 50*, 384–403.

Robert T. Brown
University of North Carolina at Wilmington

See also **Behavior Modification; Operant Conditioning**

CONDUCT DISORDER

Conduct disorder is a behavioral disorder in youth characterized by a "repetitive and persistent pattern of behavior in which the basic rights of others or major age-appropriate societal norms or rules are violated" (American Psychiatric Association, 1994, p. 85). The behaviors fall into four basic groups: (1) aggressive behaviors that cause or threaten physical harm to people or animals; (2) nonaggressive behaviors that cause harm to property; (3) deceitfulness or theft; and (4) serious violations of rules. Three or more of the characteristics must have been present for 12 months or more, and at least one of the characteristics for 6 months for a diagnosis to be made. Overall, the disturbance in conduct must significantly impair the youth's social, academic, or occupational functioning. The prevalence of conduct disorder has increased over the past few decades: For males under the age of 18, rates changed from 6 to 16%, and females from 2 to 9% (American Psychiatric Association, 1994).

Individuals with conduct disorder may not be the best informants about their own behavior; therefore, it is important that diagnosticians conduct assessments that are multi-setting, multimodal, and multimethod to accurately assess functioning (Sommers-Flanagan & Sommers-Flanagan, 1998). Many individuals with conduct disorder have little empathy for the feelings of others, and may negatively distort the positive intentions of others. The disorder is also highly correlated with early and risky sexual behavior, substance abuse, recklessness, and illegal acts. The onset of conduct disorder may occur as early as age 5, but it usually begins in late childhood or early adolescence. Many youth diagnosed with this disorder continue to show similar behaviors in adulthood (Storm-Mathisen & Vaglum, 1994) and meet the criteria for Antisocial Personality Disorder (American Psychiatric Association, 1994). There is a significant overlap of other psychiatric disorders (such as depression) with conduct disorders (Offord, Boyle, & Racine, 1994), especially in incarcerated juvenile populations (Eppright, Kashani, Robison, & Reid, 1993). Substance abuse is a significant precursor for disorders of conduct (Storm-Mathisen & Vaglum 1994), especially in Hispanic populations (Stewart, Brown, & Myers, 1997).

There is a great deal of research activity devoted to the treatment of youth with conduct disorders, and there are constant calls citing the need for new models of treatment delivery (Kazdin, 1997). Treatments include problem-solving skills training, parent management training, functional family therapy, and multisystemic therapy (Kazdin, 1997). The treatments are usually delivered in residential facilities and are subject to the common criticism of not being amenable to demonstrating clinically significant change that generalizes to every patient's situation. In addition, research about the treatments is not longitudinal in nature (Kazdin, 1993, 1997), which compromises the certainty of results. There have been some promising psychopharmacological treatments that are being researched (Shah, Seese, Abikoff, & Klein, 1994), but no conclusive results are available because of the multiple etiologies of conduct disorder (Stoewe, Kruesi, & Lelio, 1995). An exciting line of research stems from the field of neuropsychiatry where organic etiologies, such as early traumatic brain injury, are being studied with reasonable treatment success (Wood & Singh, 1994). Some researchers of conduct disorders, after reviewing treatment effectiveness, suggest that prevention is a far more effective and economical use of resources (Dodge, 1993; Offord, 1994.)

Special education services may be available to students with conduct disorders usually because of the comorbidity with handicapping conditions such as serious emotional disturbance, attention-deficit/hyperactivity disorder, and learning disabilities. However, far too many of these students are underidentified and they subsequently enter the juvenile justice system where specific treatments that are linked to the etiology of the disorder are seldom available. School psychologists and support personnel can best serve these students by using multiple sources of information and assessment, not only for diagnosis, but also for treatment. Success in the demands of everyday living for these students requires that the school, community, and home work in unison.

REFERENCES

American Psychiatric Association. (1994). *Diagnostic and statistical manual of mental disorders* (4th ed.). Washington, DC: Author.

Dodge, K. A. (1993). The future of research on the treatment of conduct disorder. *Development and Psychopathology, 5*(1–2), 311–319.

Eppright, T. D., Kashani, J. H., Robison, B. D., & Reid, J. C. (1993). Comorbidity of conduct disorder and personality disorders in an incarcerated juvenile population. *American Journal of Psychiatry, 150*(8), 1233–1236.

Kazdin, A. E. (1993). Treatment of conduct disorder: Progress and directions in psychotherapy research. *Development & Psychopathology, 5*(1–2), 277–310.

Kazdin, A. E. (1997). Practitioner review: Psychosocial treatments for conduct disorder in children. *Journal of Child Psychology & Psychiatry & Allied Disciplines, 38*(2), 161–178.

Offord, D. R., & Bennett, K. J. (1994). Conduct disorder: Long-term outcomes and intervention effectiveness. *Journal of the American Academy of Child & Adolescent Psychiatry, 33*(8), 1069–1078.

Offord, D. R., Boyle, M. H., & Racine, Y. A. (1991). *The epidemiology of antisocial behavior in childhood and adolescence.* Hillsdale, NJ: Erlbaum.

Shah, M. R., Seese, L. M., Abikoff, H., & Klein, R. G. (1994). Pemoline for children and adolescents with conduct disorder: A pilot investigation. *Journal of Child & Adolescent Psychopharmacology, 4*(4), 255–261.

Sommers-Flanagan, J., & Sommers-Flanagan, R. (1998). Assessment and diagnosis of conduct disorder. *Journal of Counseling & Development, 76*(2), 189–197.

Stewart, D. G., Brown, S. A., & Myers, M. G. (1997). Antisocial behavior and psychoactive substance involvement among Hispanic and non-Hispanic Caucasian adolescents in substance abuse treatment. *Journal of Child and Adolescent Substance Abuse, 6*(4), 1–22.

Stoewe, J. K., Kruesi, M. J. P., & Lelio, D. F. (1995). Psychopharmacology of aggressive states and features of conduct disorder. *Child & Adolescent Psychiatric Clinics of North America, 4*(2), 359–379.

Storm-Mathisen, A., & Vaglum, P. (1994). Conduct disorder patients 20 years later: A personal follow-up study. *Acta Psychiatrica Scandinavica, 89*(6), 416–420.

Wood, I. K., & Singh, N. N. (1994). The impact of neuropsychiatry upon forensic issues related to children and adolescents. In L. F. Koziol & C. E. Stout (Eds.), *The neuropsychology of mental disorders: A practical guide.* Springfield, IL: Charles C. Thomas.

ELAINE FLETCHER-JANZEN
Chicago School of Professional Psychology

See also Antisocial Personality; Emotional Disorders; Substance Abuse

CONDUCTIVE HEARING LOSS

Auditory functioning can be altered at several levels: the ear, the auditory nerve, or the brain. In the ear, there are two types of anatomical structures—those concerned with the mechanical transmission of sound (a physical process) and those concerned with the transformation of the sound waves into nervous impulses (a biological process). Conductive hearing loss (CHL) applies to the condition resulting from an alteration of the former in opposition to sensory-neural hearing loss, which results from pathology of the latter. The combination of CHL with sensory-neural hearing loss is called mixed hearing loss. For more details about terms and causes of the different types, see Davis and Silverman (1960).

The mechanical transmission of the sound vibrations obeys the laws of acoustics. It is effected by the external and middle ear, the fluids of the inner ear, and the combined displacements of the cochlea's basilar and tectorial membranes. These bring the vibrations to bear on the sensory cells of the organ of Corti, the hair cells. There the conduction process ends; the hair cells are the transducers that transform the acoustic phenomenon into a biochemical and bioelectrical event. The CHL alone is never greater than 60 dB hearing loss, for higher-intensity sounds reach the inner ear directly through the skull (von Békésy,

1948). In small children, it is often superimposed on sensoryneural hearing loss, thereby producing an additional deficiency.

Interference with the conduction process most commonly occurs at the level of external or middle ear structures.

One of the most frequent causes of temporary CHL is the external obstruction of the external ear canal (the auditory meatus) by cerumen, a waxlike secretion, especially in individuals with mental retardation (Crandell & Roesner, 1993). Obstruction by foreign bodies is also relatively frequent, especially in children. Various malformations of the external ear can affect hearing, the most serious being nondevelopment of the external auditory meatus.

The tympanic membrane, or eardrum, located between the external and middle ear, is linked with the malleus, incus, and stapes. With these ossicles it constitutes the tympano-ossicular chain, which transmits the sound arriving through the external ear to the oval window, an orifice in the bony wall separating middle and inner ear. Numerous pathological processes can affect these structures and thus produce conductive hearing loss. The eardrum can be swollen by inflammation, stiffened by sclerosis, or perforated (Nicholls & Pelletier, 2003). The ossicles may be partly or totally absent or malformed. The mobility of the chain may be reduced by fixation of the stapes in the oval window owing to abnormal bone proliferation at that level. This occurs in otosclerosis (otospongiosis), a frequent condition in adults and a rare one in children.

The accumulation of fluid in the ear occurs in several different forms of otitis media. One of them, serous otitis media, is a frequent chronic or semichronic disease of small children up to 5 or 6 years of age. It is often associated with obstruction of the eustachian tube. These conditions can usually be alleviated or cured relatively easily by medical and/or surgical treatment. However, since the CHL caused by them is mild or moderate, it is often ignored or neglected. This could have serious consequences in later life. Animal studies by Webster and Webster (1979) have shown that temporary moderate auditory restriction in the rat produces changes in the auditory brain stem nuclei. Studies reviewed by Ruben (1984) indicate that language-related skills may be durably impaired, even after restoration of normal hearing, in children who had prolonged CHL during the early years of life. This is because the early years are a particularly sensitive period for language development.

Because CHL affects only the mechanical part of the auditory channel, it produces a decrease in the sound pressure level reaching the inner ear, but no qualitative deformation of that sound. Therefore, a hearing aid that amplifies the sound waves, inasmuch as it does not itself introduce distortions, is capable of restoring a practically normal hearing sensation. While most causes of CHL can be efficiently corrected by medical and/or surgical treatment, the latter may have to be delayed, especially in children where plastic reconstruction surgery can only be done at a certain age level. For these patients, as well as for those where surgical therapy has failed or is contraindicated, is impossible for practical reasons, or is refused by the patient, a well-adapted hearing aid is an excellent solution.

While CHL alone does not prevent spoken language development, it may severely slow down its progression and affect speech skills if undiagnosed or inadequately treated. In the latter case, speech and hearing therapy, following the appropriate medical and/or surgical treatment and/or hearing aid fitting, may be required. Special education may also be necessary as a temporary measure for those children whose speech and language deficiencies prevent them from holding their own in a school for those who hear normally. The great majority of children with CHL, however, can follow their whole curriculum in a mainstream situation, for instance, in ordinary schools with hearing children.

REFERENCES

Crandell, C. C., & Roesner, R. J. (1993). Incidence of excessive/impacted cerumen in individuals with mental retardation: A longitudinal study. *American Journal on Mental Retardation, 97*(5), 568–574.

Davis, H., & Silverman, S. R. (1960). *Hearing and deafness*. New York, NY: Holt, Rinehart & Winston.

Nicholls, J., & Pelletier, S. (2003). Conductive hearing loss. In E. Fletcher-Janzen & C. R. Reynolds (Eds.), *Childhood disorders diagnostic desk reference* (pp. 146–147). Hoboken, NJ: Wiley.

Ruben, R. J. (1984). An inquiry into the minimal amount of auditory deprivation which results in a cognitive effect in man. *Acta Oto-Laryngological* (Suppl. 414), 157–164.

von Békésy, G. (1948). Vibration of the head in a sound field and its role in hearing by bone conduction. *Journal of the Acoustical Society of America, 20*, 749–760.

Webster, D. B., & Webster, M. (1979). Effects of neonatal conductive hearing loss on brain stem auditory nuclei. *Annals of Otology, Rhinology and Laryngology, 88*, 684–688.

OLIVIER PÉRIER
*Université Libre de Bruxelles,
Centre Comprendre et Parler,
Belgium*

See also Deaf Education; Deprivation, Bioneural Results of

CONFIDENTIALITY OF INFORMATION (See Buckley Amendment; Individuals With Disabilities Education Improvement Act of 2004 [IDEIA])

CONGENITAL DISORDERS

Two concepts are joined together in the expression *congenital disorders*, making it pertinent to begin this entry with a short comment on each. *Congenital* stands for present at birth. This definition does not imply any causal relationship. Nevertheless, for a long time, the terms *congenital* and *hereditary* have been confused. Indeed, some congenital disorders may be hereditary, but in many others heredity is not involved. Thus the clear recognition of the absence of any familial factor allows many couples to be reassured concerning the possible recurrence of congenital disorders.

Disorder (*malformation* or *anomaly* are also used) means any defect when compared with the normal. Earlier, mainly visible anomalies were detected; today, disorders are described at any level, on the surface or inside the organism, with the aid of sophisticated technical procedures. Therefore, according to Warkany (1971), "Congenital malformations are structural defects present at birth. They may be gross or microscopic, on the surface of the body or within it, familial or sporadic, hereditary or non-hereditary, single or multiple." Only the molecular level must be added to this definition to include all congenital disorders.

Estimations of the incidence of congenital disorders vary from report to report, depending heavily on the mode of ascertainment: external examination only at birth, X-rays, microscopic analyses of tissues, functional tests, inclusion or exclusion of stillbirths, distinction between major and minor defects, and even the personal interest of the examiner in charge at the birth of the child. Thus in a Belgian study, significantly more congenital heart anomalies were observed in two maternity wards participating in a concerted action project of the European Economic Community, probably because the neonatologist pediatricians had special training in cardiology (Borlée-Grimée, De Wals, & Vinçotte-Mols, 1985). Nevertheless, a mean figure could be 2 to 3%. This may seem very high, but it is well established that stillbirths show more congenital anomalies than live births, and that at least 50% of abortions of the first trimester show severe chromosome defects that are likely linked with expulsion (Boué, Boué, & Lazar 1975). Therefore, the figure of 2 to 3% represents only a small proportion of all malformed embryos. Moreover, all disorders are included, from severe congenital heart malformations incompatible with life, to the partial fusion of two small toes. On the other hand, it is important to point out that congenital disorders are not so exceptional in our species and, fortunately, not all are associated with a severe handicap. To our knowledge, there is no particular definition of major and minor anomalies; the interpretation is usually left to reporting authors.

There are many causes of congenital disorders. It is possible to distinguish three broad categories: (1) disorders genetically transmitted following classical Mendelian modes (McKusick, 1983), (2) disorders owed to anomalies of the genetic material but usually not transmitted (e.g., chromosome anomalies), and (3) disorders owed to environmental factors. Many can be recognized at birth by at least one characteristic symptom and some others are detected only later in life.

Dominant heredity is most frequently observed in the case of minor anomalies that do not impair normal life (e.g., supernumerary or fused fingers or toes). A dominant congenital defect is theoretically transmitted to half the offspring, and may be followed through many generations. Sometimes, one generation seems skipped over, or, on the contrary, more severely affected: This is due to variations in penetration or expressivity of the gene. However, severe congenital disorders can be transmitted through a dominant mode. This is the case in Huntington's chorea, a disease of the nervous system (for a recent review, see Robert, 1985). Strictly speaking, Huntington's chorea is a congenital disorder, the gene responsible for it being present at birth. However, carriers of the mutation enjoy a normal life until 30 or 40 years of age and in reproduction transmit the gene to half their offspring. The onset of the disease is observed with a progressive neurological symptomatology (involuntary movements), and often a psychiatric component (depression, sometimes ending in suicide). Death usually follows 10 to 15 years after the onset of symptoms.

Recessive heredity is characterized by the birth of affected children to normal parents. Indeed, the father and the mother are heterozygous for a common mutant gene, and 25% of their offspring are homozygous and affected. Hundreds of examples are found in McKusick's catalog of Mendelian diseases in man (1983). When the disorder is severe, people with the disease usually do not reproduce and the genes are eliminated: The reservoir of the disease is thus found in the heterozygous carriers. Many recessive disorders are rare: Consanguineous marriages are a well-known favoring factor, as is a common ethnic background (e.g., Tay-Sachs disease is more frequent in Ashkenazi Jews, sickle-cell anemia in blacks, thalassemia in Mediterranean populations). However, this is not a general rule, and unrelated parents from different ethnic backgrounds may be heterozygous for a common recessive gene (a well-known example is mucoviscidosis). When a recessive disorder is suspected, the diagnosis must first be firmly established with the use of appropriate techniques: X-rays, laboratory tests, pathologic and molecular studies. Genetic counseling then becomes possible.

Congenital disorders may be sex-linked, either dominant or recessive. In the first case, females and males are affected, in the second, only males. Some common congenital malformations such as cleft lip and palate, clubfoot, spina bifida cystica, anencephaly, and pyloric stenosis are not transmitted through simple Mendelian inheritance, but nevertheless show a clear familial aggregation (Carter, 1976). In these cases, a particular genetic mechanism, called polygenism, is involved. In short, the anomaly is determined by more than one gene, all acting in the same direction and possibly interacting with environmental factors. Beyond a given threshold, the malformation is present. For instance, let us suppose a birth defect associated with the presence of five specific genes acting together in a specific environment. The intact father may possess four of them and the intact mother three. Unpredictably, they can transmit to one of their children five or more deleterious genes. Of course, they may also have non-affected children. The risk is not of the monogenic type (i.e., 50%, 25%), or sex-linked. Empirical tables have been proposed after tabulating direct observations. For example, in a determined population, the risk of having a child with a cleft lip is 1 in 1,000 births. A couple who already has one affected child will have a risk increase of 40 times (4%; Carter, 1976). If one of the two parents is affected, the risk before any pregnancy is around 3%. If one of the parents is affected and one child is also affected, the risk is 11%. A major cause of congenital anomalies, usually associated with mental retardation, is chromosome anomalies. The malformations are undoubtedly of genetic origin, owed to anomalies of genetic material, but even if they are genetic and congenital, they are usually not hereditary.

A number of congenital disorders are due to environmental factors. The term *environmental* must, however, be understood in a broad sense: everything that alters the normal parameters of the body, the body being considered a conglomerate of cells. Clearly, this means that environmental factors can originate from the surrounding area in which the patient lives (e.g., radiation, viruses, drugs), or inside his or her own body (e.g., diabetes, hypothyroidism). This creates abnormal environmental conditions for the cells and, if the patient is a pregnant woman, for the fetus.

In experiments with animals, many agents are known to cause congenital disorders when they are administered to pregnant females (Warkany, 1971). The systematic study of these effects is called teratology. A catalog of teratogenic agents is regularly published and kept up to date (Shepard, 1983). Many drugs are known to be associated with fetal malformations. Pregnant women are usually warned to seek medical advice before taking any medication. Nevertheless, some compounds, although carefully tested before marketing, escape detection and are responsible for the birth of malformed babies. The case of thalidomide is well known. This sedative drug, used also by pregnant women for nausea and vomiting, was found to induce severe anomalies in the human fetus when ingested between the 35th and the 50th day after the last menstrual period (the 23rd to 38th day after conception). Rat and mouse embryos did not seem to suffer from thalidomide administered to pregnant females. However, when the relationship between human malformations and thalidomide was established, the effect of the drug was studied again on macaques. They showed the same sensibility as man. Rabbits also suffered, but to a lesser degree. This demonstrates the importance of selecting a good experimental model. All teratogenic agents cannot be reviewed here; only a few will be discussed.

Ionizing radiations have a well-known teratogenic effect. However, fear of congenital malformations in the fetus must not stop pregnant women from having examinations needed for their health (and thus for their baby's health). The teratogenic effect is dose-dependent; it also depends on the site of irradiation and the advancement of the pregnancy. As all this has been extensively demonstrated, it is best to advise the radiologist about a pregnancy or to perform a pregnancy test in case of doubt. Some viruses, but not all, also present with teratogenic activity. The example of rubella is well known; however, the risk is not the same throughout pregnancy. The maximum fetal sensitivity is during the first trimester. Alcohol ingestion may be harmful and cause fetal alcohol syndrome. Heavy smoking is also responsible for fetal damage and low birthweight. Diseases of the mother may affect the fetus if not corrected. Diabetes causes the birth of large infants, higher mortality at birth, and a tendency to hypoglycemia and respiratory distress after delivery (Delaney & Ptacek, 1970). Moreover, some authors are convinced that congenital malformations are more frequent in children of diabetic mothers or at least that some diabetic mothers are more at risk than others. However, if the ingestion of some drugs is known to be teratogenic, the absence of other elements, like vitamins, is harmful. Nutritional deficiencies as a cause of congenital malformations in experimental animals are well documented (Warkany, 1971). These situations are seldom encountered under normal human living conditions, but they explain why a vitamin supplement is advised for pregnant women.

The prevention of congenital malformations has many aspects. An important and simple means of prevention is regular medical surveillance during pregnancy. Another mode of prevention is to avoid any known teratogenic agent and to have balanced nutritional intake. If the birth of a child with severe congenital disorder is followed by death, necropsy is of paramount importance to determine the recurrence risk for the parents. However, sophisticated means of surveillance have been developed for the at-risk mother to be. Prenatal diagnosis is offered, including chromosome analysis of the fetus, research on abnormal genes at the molecular level with recombinant DNA techniques, blood sampling or biopsy of the fetus, follow-up of the anatomical growth of the fetus with ultrasound, various biochemical dosages in the amniotic fluid, and direct viral research on fetal tissues. For some defects, no known treatment is possible, and interruption of pregnancy may appear as the most appropriate solution. For others, treatment is possible either directly with the fetus or just after birth. Thus if a curable congenital heart malformation is diagnosed before birth, the mother can be delivered in a hospital specializing in the correction of such an anomaly.

Neonatal screening is important in some metabolic or endocrine disorders. For instance, hypothyroidism at birth is responsible for future mental retardation of the child, known as cretinism. Nevertheless, after delivery, hypothyroidic children are potentially normal, the maternal thyroid having supplemented the fetus. Immediate substitution treatment allows normal intellectual development. Hypothyroidism can be diagnosed just after birth by the increase of the hormone stimulating the thyroid activity (the thyreostimulating hormone [TSH]) in the blood. Testing is possible on a few drops of blood taken in the perinatal period, and the affected babies, duly treated, enjoy normal development (Delange, Beckers, Höfer, König, Monaco, & Varrone, 1979). Many other disorders can be detected by neonatal screening (Bickel, Guthrie, & Hammersen, 1980), and progress in this area is promising. This compensates for the high incidence of congenital disorders at birth.

REFERENCES

Bickel, H., Guthrie, R., & Hammersen, G. (1980). *Neonatal screening for inborn errors of metabolism* (Vol. 1). Berlin, Germany: Springer-Verlag.

Borlée-Grimée, I., De Wals, P., & Vinçotte-Mols, M. (1985). Problems in the ascertainment of congenital heart disease: Review of 308 cases registered in Hainaut from 1979 to 1982. In P. De Wals, J. A. C. Weatherall, & M. F. Lechat (Eds.), *Registration of congenital anomalies in Eurocat Centers, 1979–1983*. Louvain-la-Neuve, Cabay.

Boué, J., Boué, A., & Lazar, P. (1975). The epidemiology of human spontaneous abortions with chromosome anomalies. In R. J. Blondau (Ed.), *Aging gametes*. Basel, Switzerland: Karger.

Carter, C. O. (1976). Genetics of common single malformations. *British Medical Bulletin, 32*, 21–26.

Delaney, J. J., & Ptacek, J. (1970). Three decades of experience with diabetic pregnancies. *American Journal of Obstetrics & Gynecology, 106*, 550.

Delange, F., Beckers, C., Höfer, R., König, M. P., Monaco, F., & Varrone, S. (1979). Neonatal screening for congenital hypothyroidism in Europe. *Acta Endocrinologica, 90*(Suppl. 223), 1–27.

McKusick, V. (1983). *Mendelian inheritance in man* (6th ed.). Baltimore, MD: Johns Hopkins University Press.

Robert, J. M. (1985). La chorée de Huntington: Histoire naturelle de la maladie. *Journal de Genetique Humaine, 33*, 83–90.

Shepard, T. H. (1983). *Catalog of teratogenic agents* (4th ed.). Baltimore, MD: Johns Hopkins University Press.

Warkany, J. (1971). *Congenital malformations* (Vol. 1). Chicago, IL: Year Book Medical.

L. KOULISCHER
*Institut de Morphologie Pathologique,
Belgium*

See also Genetic Counseling; Genetic Variations

CONGENITAL WORD BLINDNESS

Congenital word blindness was the first term used to describe poor readers. It was first used by W. P. Morgan (1896) in the late 19th century to explain unexpected reading failures in otherwise intelligent children. Morgan assumed that the disorder was congenital rather than acquired by postnatal injury or assault. As an analogy to describe the condition, however, he used adults who demonstrated reading problems following acquired brain lesions. Congenital word blindness was first thought to be caused by a defect in the angular gyrus of the left cerebral hemisphere, an area of the brain associated with visual memory of words (Doehring, Backman, & Waters, 1983). The condition, however, was later viewed as a problem with left–right orientation and stephosymbolia (i.e., twisted word imagery) caused in part by a lack of cerebral dominance (Wallin, 1968).

The incidence of congenital word blindness was reported to be between 0.05% and 25%, but most studies reported closer to 10% (Hagger, 1968). It was generally believed that the disorder was genetic, as it was often found in first- and second-degree relatives and in three or four times more males than females (Hagger, 1968).

Characteristics

1. Specific difficulties in the area of reading despite normal visual included the following:
   a. Inability to perceive and remember the shapes of printed letters
   b. Difficulty in figure–ground discrimination in both visual and auditory fields
   c. Reversals and translocations of letters and words
   d. Mirror writing
   e. Confusion between pairs of letters (e.g., m/w; n/h; b/d)
   f. Misaligned capital letters and letters that are uneven sizes and positions
2. Spelling and writing were also frequently affected.
3. Individuals otherwise had normal intelligence.
4. The difficulty is not due to mental retardation, sensory deprivation, environmental deprivation, or emotional or social problems.

Treatment methods developed to address the visual perceptual problems believed to be inherent in congenital word blindness frequently emphasized early motor training and improving eye–hand coordination to develop learning patterns better. Specifically, materials were developed to help address the child's difficulties with figure–ground discrimination, visual closure, visual-motor speed, position in space, and form constancy. Methods that emphasized the simultaneous stimulation of several modes of sensory input (e.g., placing finger on larynx while speaking, tracing fingers over largely written words, and handling cut-out letters and words) were also popular. Although the effectiveness of these interventions in improving reading lacked support, they made an important contribution to education.

The work done by these early researchers and educators highlighted the importance of early intervention and small teacher-to-student ratio for reading remediation and increased awareness that these children were not simply unmotivated, disobedient, or lacking in intellectual prowess: They had a specific reading problem. This work also stimulated further research in the area of reading disabilities.

REFERENCES

Doehring, D. G., Backman, J., & Waters, G. (1983). Theoretical models of reading disabilities, past, present, and future. *Topics in Learning and Learning Disabilities*, 3(1), 84–94.

Hagger, T. D. (1968). Congenital word blindness or specific developmental dyslexia: A review. *Medical Journal of Australia*, 1(19), 783–789.

Morgan, W. P. (1896). A case of congenital word blindness. *British Medical Journal*, 2, 1378–1379.

Wallin, J. E. (1968). An historical conspectus on the existence of congenital word blindness. *Journal of Special Education*, 2(2), 203–207.

JENISE JENSEN
ELAINE CLARK
University of Utah

CONJUNCTIVITIS, LIGNEOUS

Ligneous conjunctivitis is a chronic disorder characterized by the growth of thick, wood-like lesions on mucous membranes. Lesions often begin in the eyes and later develop in other areas such as the nose, vocal cords, larynx, trachea, sinuses, and female genital tract. The etiology of this disease is unknown, but there is some evidence of an autosomal recessive inheritance (Kanai & Polack, 1971; Ligneous conjunctivitis, 1990; National Organization for Rare Disorders [NORD], 1999).

This condition begins in early childhood, during the first 3 years of life, and generally continues throughout the life course (Kanai & Polack, 1971; Schuster, Mingers, Seidenspinner, Nussgens, Pukrop, & Kreth, 1997). It is a rare disorder with a prevalence rate of approximately 60 to 70 reported cases (Firat, 1974; Ligneous conjunctivitis,

1990), and it is more common in females than in males with a ratio of 3:1 (Cohen, 1990).

Characteristics

1. Recurring growth of tough, thick, wood-like lesions on mucous membranes begins in early childhood (ages 0 to 3) and continues into adulthood.

2. Chronic infections of the upper respiratory tract are common; eyes may be perforated or lost (Firat, 1974); and death from pneumonia or airway obstruction may occur (Cohen, 1990).

3. Removal of lesions causes hemorrhaging and the regrowth of thicker lesions at the removal site (Firat, 1974).

No successful treatment for ligneous conjunctivitis has been found at this time (Cohen, 1990; Ligneous conjunctivitis, 1990); however, improvement was reported for some individuals who were treated with Kinaden and chymotrypsin eye drops over a 12-month period (Firat, 1974). Antibiotics may be used to treat upper respiratory infections that are common in individuals with this disease.

Children with ligneous conjunctivitis may qualify for special education services under Other Health Impairment due to possible visual impairments and medical needs. Students with visual impairment may require an orientation and mobility instructor to help them successfully navigate their surroundings at school. It is also important for visually impaired students to learn organizational skills so that they can easily find materials needed to complete schoolwork (Bradley-Johnson, 1995).

Modifications in the classroom may be necessary as well. For example, students should be provided with materials written in braille or large print. They should also be allowed more time to complete assignments as reading braille or large type takes longer than reading standard print. Students may also require a braille typewriter or a voice-activated computer. Real objects should be used for teaching math concepts and arithmetic operations (Bradley-Johnson, 1995). In addition to classroom modifications, students with ligneous conjunctivitis may require social skills training, as their social development may be delayed. In addition, the need for frequent medical attention may require children with the disorder to be absent from school often; therefore, home visits or home schooling may be necessary.

Prognosis is poor because ligneous conjunctivitis is a chronic condition with no cure (Cohen, 1990; Ligneous conjunctivitis, 1990). Individuals with the disease will continue to experience complications over the life span such as the loss of their eyes or voice, and death from pneumonia or airway obstruction may occur (Cohen, 1990; Firat,

1974). Etiology and treatment are the focus of further research.

REFERENCES

Bradley-Johnson, S. (1995). Best practices in planning effective instruction for students who are visually impaired or blind. In A. Thomas & J. Grimes (Eds.), *Best practices in school psychology* (pp. 1133–1140). Washington, DC: National Association of School Psychologists.

Cohen, S. R. (1990). Ligneous conjunctivitis: An ophthalmic disease with potentially fatal tracheobronchial obstruction. *Annals of Otology, Rhinology, and Laryngology, 99*, 509–512.

Firat, T. (1974). Ligneous conjunctivitis. *American Journal of Ophthalmology, 78*(4), 679–688.

Kanai, A., & Polack, F. M. (1971). Histologic and electron microscope studies of ligneous conjunctivitis. *American Journal of Ophthalmology, 72*(5), 909–916.

Ligneous conjunctivitis. (1990). *Lancet, 335*(8681), 84.

National Organization for Rare Disorders. (1999). *Conjunctivitis, ligneous.* Retrieved from http://www.rarediseases.org

Schuster, V., Mingers, A. M., Seidenspinner, S., Nussgens, Z., Pukrop, T., & Kreth, H. W. (1997). Homozygous mutations in the plasminogen gene of two unrelated girls with ligneous conjunctivitis. *Blood, 90*(3), 958–966.

STACEY L. BATES
University of Texas at Austin

CONNERS 3RD EDITION

The Conners 3rd Edition (Conners-3) is a revision of the popular Conners Rating Scales, Revised (CRS-R; Conners, 1997) and continues to focus on the assessment of *attention-deficit/hyperactivity disorder* (ADHD) and common associated difficulties. The Conners-3 has many similarities to previous versions, while making improvements such as utilizing new normative data, the addition of validity scales, and increased alignment with *DSM-IV-TR* and IDEA 2004. Several forms are available for the assessment of children aged 6 to 18 years. The full-length forms contain every Connors-3 item and index, and are available in Parent, Teacher, and Self-Report forms. Briefer versions, including the Short Forms, Index Forms, Conners-3-AI, and Conners-3-GI, are also available; however, this review will focus on the full-length forms, each of which takes approximately 20 minutes to complete.

The long forms include several types of scales. The Conners-3 Content Scales include: Inattention, Hyperactivity/Impulsivity, Learning Problems/Executive Functioning (Teacher form only), Learning Problems, Executive Functioning (Parent and Teacher forms), Aggression, Peer Relations (Parent and Teacher forms),

and Family Relations (Self-Report only). The *DSM-IV* Symptom Scales include: ADHD Inattentive, ADHD Hyperactive-Impulsive, ADHD Combined, Conduct Disorder, and Oppositional Defiant Disorder. The Validity scales are: Positive Impression, Negative Impression, and the Inconsistency Index. All three full-length forms have the Conners-3 ADHD Index, and the Parent and Teacher Forms also contain the Conners-3 Global Index. Screener items include Anxiety and Depression, and Critical Items assess Severe Conduct. Impairment Items include Schoolwork/Grades, Friendship/Relationships, and Home Life (Parent and Self-Report Forms). Finally, Additional Questions assess for Other Concerns and Strengths/Skills.

There are multiple administration and scoring options for the Conners-3. Raters can complete a paper-and-pencil version of the test, or complete the forms online. Paper-and-pencil protocols can be hand scored, scored via computer software, or scored online. Those forms that are completed online are scored automatically. When completing the forms, respondents are asked to consider how often behaviors have occurred within the past month, and rate their responses along a Likert scale ranging from 0 (Not true at all; Never, Seldom) to 3 (Very much true, Very often, Very frequently). If necessary, administrators are permitted to read items aloud to the respondent. Scored forms yield *T*-scores and percentile ranks. When calculating scores, age is taken into account, and the evaluator has a choice as to whether to use gender-based or combined norms. The manual provides clear and thorough step-by-step guides for interpretation. A nice feature of the Conners-3 manual is an additional chapter on developing and implementing interventions.

The large and representative norm sample is a strength of the Conners-3. The test was normed on a population of 3,400 individuals, with approximately two-thirds of the sample having multiple informants across the various scales. Both general population and clinical samples were collected. When considering individual forms, the Conners-3-P included 2,300 children (including 731 from a clinical population) and the Conners-3-T sample included 2,437 individuals (including 694 clinical) aged 6 to 18 years. The Conners-3-SR included 2,088 individuals (718 clinical). All samples included comparable numbers of males and females and were ethnically and geographically diverse. The manual includes a thorough description of each normative sample. Effects of demographic variables were analyzed, which led to creation of norms for separate age and gender groups.

The manual summarizes studies conducted by Gallant et al. (2007) and Gallant (2008), which provide evidence for internal consistency, test–retest reliability, and standard error of measurement (SEM) measurement. The mean internal consistency coefficients for all scales across all forms ranged from .77 to .95, and the test–retest coefficients ranged from .71 to .98, indicating that the measure has moderate to strong reliability. It should be noted the internal consistency for the validity scales was sometimes lower, which could be explained by the small number of items associated with each scale and lack of item variance. Interrater reliability between parent and teacher report also appears strong; however, no evidence was given for interrater reliability utilizing the self-report form. Good evidence for validity was presented via factor analysis, across-informant correlations, convergent and divergent validity, and discriminative validity.

Overall, the Conners-3 appears to be an easy-to-use, psychometrically sound and valuable tool for the assessment of ADHD in children. It is a welcome revision of the Conners, Revised forms, and preliminary reviews are complimentary (i.e., Arffa, 2010; Dunn, 2010).

REFERENCES

Arffa, S. (2010). Review of the Conners 3rd Edition. In R. A. Spies, J. F. Carlson, & K. F. Geisinger (Eds.), *The eighteenth mental measurements yearbook*. Lincoln, NE: Buros Institute of Mental Measurements.

Conners, C. K., (1997). Multi Health Systems (MHS) Assessments: Toronto, ON, Canada.

Dunn, T. M. (2010). Review of the Conners 3rd Edition. In R. A. Spies, J. F. Carlson, & K. F. Geisinger (Eds.), *The eighteenth mental measurements yearbook*. Lincoln, NE: Buros Institute of Mental Measurements.

Gallant, S. (2008, February). *Conners 3: Psychometric properties and practical applications*. Paper presented at the annual meeting of the National Association of School Psychologists, New Orleans, LA.

Gallant, S., Conners, C. K., Rzepa, S. R., Pitkanen, J., Marocco, M., & Sitarenios, G. (2007, August). *Psychometric properties of the Conners 3*. Poster presented at the annual meeting of the American Psychological Association, San Francisco, CA.

KATHLEEN VIEZEL
Fairleigh Dickinson University

JAMIE ZIBULSKY
Fairleigh Dickinson University

RON DUMONT
Fairleigh Dickinson University

JOHN O. WILLIS
Rivier College

CONRADI-HUNERMANN SYNDROME

This disorder is one of three clinically, genetically, and biochemically distinct forms of chondrodysplasia punctata, which is a rare hereditary bone disease. The hallmarks of Conradi-Hunermann syndrome (CHS) are mild to moderate short stature, asymmetric limb shortening, pinpoint calcifications of epiphyses (the areas of active bone growth), and large skin pores (Jones, 1997).

CHS is rare. No data are available about its incidence in the general population. The pattern of inheritance is X-linked dominant. Affected individuals are all female. The presence of the abnormal gene in the male embryo is apparently lethal.

Characteristics

1. Mild to moderate growth deficiency, failure to thrive in infancy
2. Low nasal bridge, flat face, downward slanting eyelids, cataracts
3. Asymmetric limb shortening, joint contractures of varying severity
4. Scoliosis (lateral curvature of the spine), related to abnormal mineralization of vertebrae (may be present at birth)
5. Sparse, coarse hair and patchy hair loss
6. Almost all newborns covered with a thick, yellow, scaling rash, with extremely red underlying skin
7. In older children, large skin pores resembling an orange peel; scattered areas of dry, scaly skin
8. Various degrees of mental deficiency

Treatment of children with CHS addresses their orthopedic problems. Scoliosis may require bracing, casting, or surgery. Children with CHS require modifications and cognitive support through special education services based on the degree of intellectual disability (Darmastadt, 2000). A comprehensive neuropsychological evaluation to determine cognitive strengths and weaknesses would provide the individual's educators with valuable information in developing an educational plan.

Poor weight gain and recurrent infections are common during infancy. Children who make it through this period have a favorable prognosis for continued survival. Orthopedic problems persist, however, and the incidence of cataract formation is high.

REFERENCES

Darmstadt, G. L. (2000). Disorders of keratinization. In R. E. Behrman, R. M. Kleigman, & H. B. Jenson (Eds.), *Nelson's textbook of pediatrics* (16th ed., pp. 2007–2011). Philadelphia, PA: W. B. Saunders.

Jones, K. (1997). *Smith's recognizable patterns of human malformations* (5th ed.). Philadelphia, PA: W. B. Saunders.

BARRY H. DAVISON
Ennis, Texas

JOAN W. MAYFIELD
*Baylor Pediatric Specialty Services,
Dallas, Texas*

CONSCIENCE, LACK OF IN INDIVIDUALS WITH DISABILITIES

Society is particularly concerned that children develop the skills to regulate their own behavior or, stated differently, internalize moral principles. Situations often arise that pose a conflict between the individual desires of the person and the requirements of society. These circumstances call for the exercise of self-control as the person suppresses self-interested behavior in favor of actions that serve the needs of others. Two areas of research bear directly on this problem—altruism and resistance to temptation.

Altruism

Altruism refers to behavior that is carried out to benefit another in the absence of threat or expected reward. Altruism entails self-control since the helper must weigh the costs of helping (e.g., material loss or physical danger) against the benefits (e.g., self-satisfaction) of helping (Kanfer, 1979). Research with children has relied on several measures of altruism, including donating possessions to a charity or another child, willingness to rescue someone in trouble, peer ratings, and naturalistic observations of helping and sharing.

Most children show an increase in sharing during the period of middle childhood. This change parallels children's decreasing egocentrism and increasingly sophisticated moral reasoning abilities. However, the relationship among these variables is not clearly understood. At least with children of average IQ, general level of cognitive development is unrelated to various measures of altruism (Rushton & Wiener, 1975). There does appear to be a weak relationship between generosity and level of moral reasoning among 7- to 11-year-old children, but it is not known if moral reasoning directly affects moral behavior (Rushton, 1975). Most studies fail to find a relationship between sex and altruism, but when differences are noted they tend to show females as more altruistic (Krebs, 1970). Finally, investigators have found a substantial degree of behavioral specificity across situations that offer an opportunity for altruistic behavior. For example, a child may donate a toy to a needy stranger but fail to volunteer time to help a peer. The correlation across measures is about .30

and may reflect the weak effect of an underlying personality variable or experimental or psychometric artifacts (Rushton, 1976).

One research finding that is unequivocal is that the altruistic behavior of children can be modified. Numerous studies have shown that children will imitate an altruistic model (Harris, 1971). In fact, the influence of a model was shown in one study to extend up to 4 months, even though posttesting was conducted under very different circumstances (Rushton, 1975). These results have obvious implications for child-rearing practices.

Resistance to Temptation

Resistance to temptation is another example of self-control. Here the child is required to exercise self-restraint in the absence of immediate surveillance. Several studies have examined variables that promote this form of self-control. From a developmental perspective, the emergence of language is important in that it allows the child to regulate his or her behavior by stating rules of conduct (Kanfer & Phillips, 1970). The ability to verbalize rules may be necessary but usually is not sufficient for resisting temptation.

Children who score high on resistance to temptation often make use of cognitive strategies (i.e., self-control techniques). A body of work by Kanfer (Hartig & Kanfer, 1973; Kanfer & Zich, 1974) and Mischel (Mischel, Ebbesen, & Zeiss, 1972; Mischel & Patterson, 1978) has shown that resistance to temptation is enhanced when children distract themselves (e.g., singing songs or thinking of a "fun activity"), repeatedly state a rule (e.g., "I'm a good girl if I don't look at the hampster"), or engage in mental transformations (e.g., "The pretzel is really just a log of wood"). The fact that older children are more successful in such situations is in part attributed to a greater facility in the use of language and a larger repertoire of cognitive strategies.

Researchers have just recently begun to extend these findings to individuals with intellectual disabilities. It has been noted that adolescents with intellectual disability prefer immediate rewards even though by waiting they could receive twice as many of those rewards (Franzini, Litrownik, & Magy, 1978). In one study, training in self-instruction ("I am gonna get more money if I wait to get paid . . . I sure am a good worker") reinforced practice and the provision of successful models led to a fivefold increase in the delay of gratification (Franzini, Litrownik, & Magy, 1980).

The importance of verbal controlling strategies in resistance to temptation is underscored by a study comparing children with Down syndrome to nondisabled children matched for level of cognitive development. On the average, the children were less able to resist temptation than were the nonretarded children, a finding consistent with the Franzini et al. (1980) study. Interestingly, those children who were most successful were observed to spontaneously engage in verbal and nonverbal behaviors that served to distract them from the desired object (Kopp, Krakow, & Johnson, 1983).

In considering the research in both the areas of altruism and resistance to temptation, a clear directive for teachers and parents is evident. In order to enhance self-control one should not think in terms of building the child's character. Instead, the child should be taught specific verbal and nonverbal behavioral skills that can be used for self-regulation in tempting situations.

REFERENCES

Franzini, L. R., Litrownik, A. J., & Magy, M. A. (1978). Immediate and delayed reward preferences of TMR adolescents. *American Journal of Mental Deficiency, 82,* 406–409.

Franzini, L. R., Litrownik, A. J., & Magy, M. A. (1980). Training trainable mentally retarded adolescents in delay behavior. *Mental Retardation, 18,* 45–47.

Harris, M. (1971). Models, norms and sharing. *Psychological Reports, 29,* 147–153.

Hartig, M., & Kanfer, F. H. (1973). The role of verbal self-instructions in children's resistance to temptation. *Journal of Personality & Social Psychology, 25,* 259–267.

Kanfer, F. H. (1979). Personal control, social control, and altruism: Can society survive the age of individualism? *American Psychologist, 34,* 231–239.

Kanfer, F. H., & Phillips, J. S. (1970). *Learning foundations of behavior therapy.* New York, NY: Wiley.

Kanfer, F. H., & Zich, J. (1974). Self-control training: The effects of external control on children's resistance to temptation. *Developmental Psychology, 10,* 108–115.

Kopp, C. B., Krakow, J. B., & Johnson, K. L. (1983). Strategy production by young Down syndrome children. *American Journal of Mental Deficiency, 88,* 164–169.

Krebs, D. L. (1970). Altruism: An examination of the concept and a review of the literature. *Psychological Bulletin, 73,* 258–302.

Mischel, W., Ebbesen, E. B., & Zeiss, A. R. (1972). Cognitive and attentional mechanisms in delay of gratification. *Journal of Personality & Social Psychology, 21,* 204–218.

Mischel, W., & Patterson, C. J. (1978). Effective plans for self-control. In W. A. Collins (Ed.), *Minnesota symposia on child psychology* (Vol. 2). Hillsdale, NJ: Erlbaum.

Rushton, J. P. (1975). Generosity in children: Immediate and long term effects of modeling, preaching, and moral judgment. *Journal of Personality & Social Psychology, 31,* 459–466.

Rushton, J. P. (1976). Socialization and the altruistic behavior of children. *Psychological Bulletin, 83,* 898–913.

Rushton, J. P., & Wiener, J. (1975). Altruism and cognitive development in children. *British Journal of Social & Clinical Psychology, 14,* 341–349.

LAURENCE C. GRIMM
University of Illinois

See also Attachment Disorder; Impulse Control; Moral Reasoning; Self-Control Curriculum

CONSENT DECREE

A consent decree is a legal mandate or court order issued by a judiciary authority that has jurisdiction over the particular civil matter resolved in the decree. It is a legally enforceable order of that court. Consent decrees derive from the agreement of the adversarial parties to a civil lawsuit to end their disagreement provided that certain acts are performed by one or both parties and agreed to in order to avoid continuing litigation. The agreement is drawn up by the two parties, signed by the appropriate legal representatives, and submitted to the court for review. If the court decides the agreement is fair and entered into with appropriate understanding and representation by both parties, the court will then mandate and enforce the decree by court order.

Many special education cases are decided by consent agreements that become enforceable court decrees. Among the best known and most influential are *Diana v. State Board of Education* (1970) and *Guadalupe v. Tempe Elementary School District* (1972). Consent decrees are binding only on the parties to the decree and do not constitute case law that may be cited as true legal precedent. However, they can influence policymakers in the legislative process, prompting new laws that address the substantive issues underlying the consent decrees.

CECIL R. REYNOLDS
Texas A&M University
Second edition

KIMBERLY F. APPLEQUIST
University of Colorado at Colorado Springs
Third edition

See also Diana v. State Board of Education

CONSENT, INFORMED

Informed consent is founded on the ethical responsibility of researchers and diagnosticians to disclose the potential risks and benefits associated with participation in a research study or in educational and psychological testing (American Educational Research Association, American Psychological Association, & National Council on Measurement in Education, 1985; Schloss & Smith, 1999). Informed consent, as public policy, is linked to historical human rights violations in medical, social, and psychological research. The National Commission (1979) describes two important examples of human rights violations in the 20th century: "[T]he exploitation of unwilling prisoners as research subjects in Nazi concentration camps was condemned as a particularly flagrant injustice. In this country, in the 1940s, the Tuskegee syphilis study used disadvantaged, rural black men to study the untreated course of a disease that is by no means confined to that population. These subjects were deprived of demonstrably effective treatment in order not to interrupt the project, long after such treatment became generally available" (p. 7). A number of other high-profile examples, including the infection of children with disabilities with hepatitis, introduction of cancer cells into chronically ill patients with dementia, secret radiation experiments with human subjects, and intentionally deceiving research subjects as part of psychological research (see Brody, Gluck, & Aragon, 1997; Jacobs & Zonnenberg, 2004) led to the passage of the *National Research Act* in 1974 (PL 93-348).

The National Commission for the Protection of Human Subjects of Biomedical and Behavioral Research was created as a result of the passage of PL 93-348. The National Commission was tasked with developing guidelines and principles for research involving human participants. The dissemination of *The Belmont Report* (National Commission, 1979) was the result of this work and serves as a seminal document in guiding the practice of researchers nationally. Specific guidelines for ethical research practice, as outlined in *The Belmont Report*, include respect for persons, beneficence, and justice, and are discussed below.

Respect for persons includes two important principles: the principle of the autonomy of individuals and the principle of protection for those with "diminished autonomy" (National Commission, 1979, p. 5). The acknowledgment of personal autonomy suggests that most persons are capable of making choices and decisions regarding their lives, including participation in research. Brody et al. (1997) write: "*Personal autonomy* refers to a respect for the integrity of the individual. It is recognized legally as the right of self-determination and constitutionally as the right of privacy. In the research context, autonomy is honored and preserved through the participant's right to consent or refuse participation" (p. 286). Protection of those with diminished autonomy suggests that additional protections and safeguards are needed for those who might not be in a position to provide informed consent to participate in research. Examples of persons who may need additional safeguards include children, persons with cognitive disabilities, persons with chronic illnesses, and prisoners. *The Belmont Report* concludes that "the extent of protection afforded should depend upon the risk of harm and the likelihood of benefit. The judgment that any individual lacks autonomy should be periodically reevaluated and will vary in different situations" (p. 5).

Beneficence refers to an obligation of researchers to make every effort to "maximize possible benefits" (National Commission, 1979, p. 6) by not engaging in research activities that could potentially cause physical or psychological harm. Beneficence is a principle that receives careful scrutiny when a researcher presents a proposal to his or her Institutional Review Board (IRB). The IRB is typically charged with reviewing all research proposals that involve human participants and determining if the proposals comply with federal regulations (Gall, Borg, & Gall, 1996). In terms of beneficence, the IRB is obligated to determine if the risk-to-benefit ratio is reasonable given the nature of the study.

The principle of justice suggests that all persons should be treated equally, including how potential participants are selected to participate in a research study, the availability of treatment, and the provision of informed consent. This principle is rooted in the history of marginalized populations (e.g., the disabled, prisoners, economically disadvantaged) that have been the subject of research abuses. In other words, "the selection of research subjects needs to be scrutinized in order to determine whether some classes" (e.g., welfare patients, particular racial and ethnic minorities, or persons confined to institutions) are being systematically selected simply because of their easy availability, their compromised position, or their manipulability, rather than for reasons directly related to the problem being studied (National Commission, 1979, p. 7). In addition to outlining ethnical principles, *The Belmont Report* provides specific standards for the application of these principles within the context of conducting biomedical and behavioral research, including standards for providing informed consent, standards for the assessment of risk and benefits, and standards for the selection of potential participants.

Informed consent, by definition, "ensures that research participants enter the research of their free will and with understanding of the nature of the study and any possible dangers that may arise. It is intended to reduce the likelihood that participants will be exploited by a researcher persuading them to participate without fully knowing what the study's requirements are" (Gay & Airasian, 2003, p. 81). *The Belmont Report* (National Commission, 1979) uses the following benchmarks to guide how informed consent should be obtained, including how and what information is communicated, comprehension of that information by the potential participant, and the provision of voluntariness and choice of participation throughout the research study. Information refers to a complete disclosure of what the researcher intends to do and stating (verbally and in writing) any anticipated risks and benefits associated with the study. The standard of comprehension suggests that the researcher has taken into account the potential subject's capabilities and has presented all information in a manner that is easily understood. Voluntariness refers to the exercise of a person's free will to participate or not participate in the absence of coercion or undue influence. This standard also suggests that a person can withdraw from a research study at any time without penalty.

Fisher (2004) outlines important considerations for obtaining informed consent as part of the Revised American Psychological Association's Ethics Code and the Health Insurance Portability and Accountability Act (HIPAA). These standards provide guidelines for obtaining informed consent from adolescents with adult legal status; standards for working with persons who are English-language learners, including the appropriate use of interpreters; standards for obtaining assent from minors who are potential participants in a research project; and standards for working with legal guardians, in particular, guardians of foster children and juvenile detainees.

According to the National Commission (1979), the IRB must determine if the risks, as stated in the proposal, are justified, thereby giving the potential participant(s) the opportunity to carefully determine if they would like to participate in the proposed study. In describing what constitutes a risk, *The Belmont Report* writes: "Many kinds of possible harms and benefits need to be taken into account. There are, for example, risks of psychological harm, physical harm, legal harm, social harm and economic harm and the corresponding benefits. While the most likely types of harms to research subjects are those of psychological or physical pain or injury, other possible kinds should not be overlooked" (p. 10).

Finally, procedures for subject selection must be carefully reviewed. All efforts should be maintained that will protect against bias and knowingly imposing an undue burden on potential classes of participants. Moreover, vulnerable populations that may need additional safeguards should be carefully reviewed following the principles of informed consent, beneficence, and justice as described above (National Commission, 1979).

Informed consent as public policy has been well defined and articulated. However, informed consent is also part of a larger research ethic that is intended to fully disclose the risks and benefits associated with participation in a research study and eliminate the potential for physical, social, and psychological harm that may occur from participation in biomedical and behavioral research. *The Belmont Report* (National Commission, 1979) provides principles for ethical research, including demonstrating respect for all potential participants, beneficence, and social justice. Application of these principles is found in the standards of informed consent, assessment of risk and benefits, and the selection of participants.

REFERENCES

American Educational Research Association, American Psychological Association, & National Council on Measurement in Education. (1985). *Standards for educational and psychological testing*. Washington, DC: Author.

Brody, J. L., Gluck, J. P., & Aragon, A. S. (1997). Participants' understanding of the process of psychological research: Informed consent. *Ethics and Behavior, 7*, 285–298.

Fisher, C. B. (2004). Informed consent and clinical research involving children and adolescents: Implications for the revised APA ethics code and HIPAA. *Journal of Clinical Child and Adolescent Psychology, 33*, 832–839.

Gall, M. D., Borg, W. R., & Gall, J. P. (1996). *Educational research: An introduction* (6th ed.). White Plains, NY: Longman.

Gay, L. R., & Airasian, P. (2003). *Educational research: Competencies for analysis and applications* (7th ed.). Upper Saddle River, NJ: Prentice Hall.

Jacobs, F., & Zonnenberg, A. (2004). Tangible and intangible cost of "protecting human subjects": The impact of the National Research Act of 1974 on university research activities. *Education Policy Analysis Archives, 12*, 1–12.

National Commission for the Protection of Human Subjects of Biomedical and Behavioral Research (National Commission). (1979). *Belmont report: Ethical principles and guidelines for the protection of human subjects of research*. Washington DC: U.S. Department of Health, Education, & Welfare.

Schloss, P. J., & Smith, M. A. (1999). *Conducting research*. Upper Saddle River, NJ: Prentice Hall.

RANDALL L. DE PRY
University of Colorado at Colorado Springs

See *also* Research in Special Education

CONSEQUENCES

Consequences are the events that occur as a result of a particular behavior. Consequences are monitored to help teachers and researchers determine the function of a particular behavior, and how to control the frequency, intensity, duration, or latency of that specific behavior. The behavior that is being analyzed is often referred to as the target behavior (Pierangelo & Giuliani, 2006; Taylor, 2006). Isolating a specific behavior and defining it in observable and measurable terms allows the antecedent and consequences to be identified (Scott, Liaupsin, Nelson, & Jolivette, 2003). Manipulating either an antecedent that leads to the target behavior or a consequence of the behavior, modifications can be made to the target behavior. In this way the teacher or researcher may increase a desired behavior or decrease an undesirable behavior (Haager & Klinger, 2005; Heward, 2006; McLoughlin & Lewis, 2005; Pierangelo & Giuliani, 2006; Scott et al., 2003; Taylor, 2006).

If a teacher or researcher wishes to modify a student's behavior, he or she must define the behavior in specific terms so that it is recognized by all people who will observe the student, and to insure that consistency is maintained. For example, a student may engage in disruptive behaviors, defined as striking his hand against the desk with enough force to create a noise that is heard in all areas of the classroom. Systematic observations of not only the behavior, but the events preceding the behavior (antecedents) and the events that occur as a result of the behavior (consequences) are then recorded.

Consequences should be recorded using measurable and observable terms. It is important to separate what you believe or feel is happening from what is physically happening. Everything that occurs as a result of the target behavior is a consequence; use of class time to resolve the issue, giving of a reward, attention of peers, attention of the teacher, loss of these attentions, or any other change that occurs in the environment due to the target behavior are consequences (Friend, 2005; Scott et al., 2003). These consequences can be divided into two categories, punishment and reinforcement (Heward, 2006; Haager & Klinger, 2005).

Punishment reduces the likelihood that the behavior will occur again. The intent of the teacher or researcher does not determine if a consequence is a punishment. If the frequency, intensity, duration, or latency of the target behavior is reduced after the consequence occurs, then that consequence is by definition a punisher for that behavior (Alberto & Troutman, 1990).

If the student in the aforementioned example strikes his hand against the desk and the teacher takes time out of class to tell him to stop, but the overall frequency of the behavior is not reduced, then telling him to stop is not a punisher. In fact, if the behavior increases (perhaps the student is seeking attention), the behavior is actually being reinforced.

Reinforcement increases the likelihood that the behavior will occur again. By carefully monitoring the consequences that are occurring and the patterns of future behaviors, researchers and teachers can manipulate the consequences that occur as a result of a behavior and thus influence the likelihood that that behavior will occur again (Alberto & Troutman, 1990; Haager & Klinger, 2005; Heward, 2006; McLoughlin & Lewis, 2005; Pierangelo & Giuliani, 2006; Scott et al., 2003; Taylor, 2006). The teacher or researcher can arrange for reinforcing consequences to occur for desirable behaviors and punishing consequences to occur for undesirable behaviors.

In the example used so far, the teacher or researcher would need to determine the behavior they would like to have the student perform instead of striking the desk. This is often referred to as a replacement behavior (Alberto & Troutman, 1990; Taylor, 2006). The researcher would then manipulate the antecedents to generate the desired behavior, such as asking the student to lace his fingers together and rest them on the desk. Immediately after the student complies (performing the desired target behavior), the teacher could praise, reward, or in any other way create a reinforcing consequence for the student. Through the use of reinforcement (manipulating the consequences), the frequency of the student demonstrating the desired behavior can be increased.

REFERENCES

Alberto, P. A., & Troutman, A. C. (1990). *Applied behavior analysis for teachers* (3rd ed.). Columbus, OH: Merrill.

Friend, M. (2005). *Special education: Contemporary perspectives for school professionals*. New York, NY: Pearson Education.

Haager, D., & Klinger, J. K. (2005). *Differentiating instruction in inclusive classrooms: The special educator's guide*. New York, NY: Allyn & Bacon.

Heward, W. L. (2006). *Exceptional children: An introduction to special education* (8th ed.). Upper Saddle River, NJ: Prentice Hall.

McLoughlin, J. A., & Lewis, R. B. (2005). *Assessing students with special needs* (6th ed.). Upper Saddle River, NJ: Prentice Hall.

Pierangelo, R., & Giuliani, G. A. (2006). *Assessment in special education: A practical approach* (2nd ed.). New York, NY: Allyn & Bacon.

Scott, T. M., Liaupsin, C. J., Nelson, C. M., & Jolivette, K. (2003). Ensuring student success through team-based functional behavioral assessment. *Teaching Exceptional Children, 35*(5), 16–21.

Taylor, R. L. (2006). *Assessment of exceptional students: Educational and psychological procedures* (7th ed.). New York, NY: Allyn & Bacon.

WALTER A. ZILZ
Bloomsburg University

See also Behavioral Assessment; Behavior Disorders

CONSORTIUM FOR CITIZENS WITH DISABILITIES

The Consortium for Citizens With Disabilities (CCD) is a coalition of approximately 100 national disability organizations working together to advocate for national public policy on behalf of the 54 million children and adults with disabilities and their families living in the United States. CCD's Chairman is currently Curt Decker of National Disability Rights Network (NDRN).

The CCD's goal is to achieve federal legislation that ensures that all Americans with disabilities are fully integrated into the mainstream of society. To achieve this goal CCD engages in advocacy efforts that:

- Ensure the self-determination, independence, empowerment, integration, and inclusion of children and adults with disabilities in all aspects of society.
- Enhance the civil rights and quality of life of all people with disabilities and their families.
- Reflect the values of the Americans With Disabilities Act.

CCD was originally formulated in the late 1960s and early 1970s on an ad-hoc basis to advocate support for the Developmental Disabilities Act, legislation to provide grants to states to coordinate and plan services for people with developmental disabilities, and grants to train professionals in various developmental disabilities service fields. In 1975, the coalition became more formalized and officially became the Consortium Concerned With the Developmentally Disabled. Over time, the coalition grew and the focus expanded to federal legislation and legal issues affecting people with disabilities, including education, employment, rights, housing, and long-term services and supports. CCD played a significant role in the enactment of the 1990 Americans With Disabilities Act. The coalition voted in the mid-1980s to change its name to the Consortium for Citizens With Disabilities to reflect the reality of its membership and focus. Today CCD has almost 100 member organizations working through 15 task forces. CCD achieves its goals by:

- Identifying and researching public policy issues, developing testimony and policy recommendations, and encouraging innovative solutions to public policy concerns
- Educating members of Congress in an effort to improve public policies and programs on behalf of individuals with disabilities
- Encouraging people with disabilities and their families to advocate for themselves and coordinating grassroots efforts to support them

CCD envisions an American society in which all individuals, aided by an enabling government, have the freedom and opportunity to exercise individual decisions concerning their own lives, welfare, and personal dignity. This society would be fully accessible to all individuals with disabilities and their families, and they would be included and able to fully participate in all aspects of community life. The consortium has been formulated to make this vision a reality for all Americans.

The organization is based in Washington, DC, at The Consortium for Citizens with Disabilities, 1331 H Street, NW, Suite 301, Washington, DC 20005. Tel.: (202) 783-2229; fax: (202) 783-8250; e-mail: Info@c-c-d.org; web address: http://c-c-d.org/.

STAFF

CONSTITUTIONAL LAW (IN SPECIAL EDUCATION)

Judicial interpretations of the Constitution and its amendments have played a major role in the comparatively recent efforts to obtain and maintain appropriate special education programs and services for children and youth with disabilities and their families. The groundwork for this role was laid in the 1954 Supreme Court decision in *Brown* v. *Board of Education;* the decision made clear that separate education facilities for children of different races are inherently not equal (Lippman & Goldberg, 1973). This decision affirmed that, because of the importance of education today, education "is a right which must be available to all on equal terms" (*Brown* v. *Board of Education*, 347 U.S. 483). Citing this decision almost 20 years later, attorneys in two class-action suits built their arguments for landmark special education cases that were resolved in federal district courts (*Pennsylvania Association for Retarded Citizens v. Commonwealth of Pennsylvania*, 334 F. Supp. 1257, E.D. Pa., 1971), which made clear that mentally retarded children in Pennsylvania are entitled to free education programs appropriate for their needs; and *Mills v. Board* (*Mills v. Board of Education, District of Columbia*, 348 F. Supp. 866, 1972), which extended free and appropriate education to all children with disabilities in the District of Columbia.

Both the *PARC* and *Mills* cases have been cited in subsequent litigation involving similar and related principles that eventually were incorporated into federal legislation. Of particular importance to special education are the Rehabilitation Act of 1973, which requires access to programs and facilities, and more recently the Individuals with Disabilities Education Act (IDEA) and subsequent amendments, the latest being in 2004. They embody the principles of zero project, nondiscriminatory testing, individualized and appropriate education planning and programming, least restrictive alternative as preferred educational placement, and procedural due process. All of these principles can be found in the guarantees of the Fifth and Fourteenth amendments to the Constitution (Turnbull & Fiedler, 1984) which state:

- No person shall...be deprived of life, liberty, or property, without due process of law (Constitution of the United States, Amendment V, 1791).
- No State shall make or enforce any law which shall abridge the privileges or immunities of citizens of the United States; nor shall any State deprive any person of life, liberty or property without due process of law, nor deny to any person within its jurisdiction the equal protection of the laws (Constitution of the United States, Amendment XIV, 1868).

For a detailed discussion of litigation in special education and its reliance on constitutional guarantees and interpretations of the Supreme Court, see Turnbull and Fiedler (1984). Recent litigation has focused on the constitutionality of state financing systems (Verstegen, 1998).

REFERENCES

Lippman, L., & Goldberg, I. (1973). *Right to education: Anatomy of the Pennsylvania case and its implications for exceptional children.* New York, NY: Teachers College Press.

Turnbull, J. R., III, & Fiedler, C. R. (1984). *Judicial interpretation of the Education for All Handicapped Children Act.* Reston, VA: Council for Exceptional Children.

Verstegen, D. A. (1998). *Landmark court decisions challenge state special education funding. Center for Special Education Brief.* Palo Alto, CA: American Institutes for Research.

MARJORIE E. WARD
Ohio State University
Second edition

KIMBERLY F. APPLEQUIST
University of Colorado at Colorado Springs
Third edition

See also **Brown v. Board of Education; Larry P.; Mills v. Board of Education of the District of Columbia; Pase v. Hannon; Pennsylvania Association for Retarded Citizens v. Pennsylvania**

CONSULTATION

Consultation refers to a professional relationship in which a specialist attempts to improve the functioning of another professional. Although there are many models of school consultation, each with different sets of assumptions, techniques, and goals, Bergan and Tombari's definition (1976) is general enough to encompass the idiosyncrasies of these various models. "Consultation refers to services rendered by a consultant (e.g., school psychologist) to a consultee (e.g., teacher) who functions as a change agent with respect to the learning or adjustment of a client (e.g., a child) or a group of clients" (p. 4).

Consultation in school settings is an indirect model of providing broadly defined mental health services to children. The consultant attempts to effect a change in children's behavior and learning by attempting to change the teacher's (or administrator's) attitudes, perceptions, and behaviors. One of the rationales for consultation is the economy of resources it offers. By improving teacher and administrator functioning, the psychologist can affect many more children than possible in the traditional counseling and testing models of service delivery.

Certain key elements distinguish consultation from other professional activities. First, consultation is a professional-to-professional relationship that is focused on helping the consultee to do a job. Consultation is a voluntary relationship; thus the consultee is free to accept or reject the consultant's help and recommendations. In turn, the consultee is expected to contribute to the problem-solving process and is responsible for implementing action plans that result from the consultation. Finally, the consultant respects the confidential nature of the relationship.

One professional activity that shares similarities with consultation is supervision; however, consultation differs from supervision in several important ways. Because the supervisor is administratively responsible for the supervisee's work, the supervisee is obligated to accept the supervisor's advice. A supervisor is usually a senior professional in the same discipline as the supervisee, whereas the consultant is usually trained in a discipline different from that of the consultee. Thus supervision involves a hierarchical obligatory relationship, while consultation involves an egalitarian voluntary relationship.

Consultation has both remedial and preventive goals, but different consultation models emphasize one or the other goals. Thus when consulting with a teacher, the consultant attempts to improve both the learning and adjustment of the child about whom the teacher is concerned and the teacher's ability to cope effectively with similar children in the future. This latter, preventive goal of consultation allows psychologists to broaden their impact beyond the target child.

The goals of consultation listed by Conoley and Conoley (1982) are relevant to several consultation models and include: (1) providing an objective point of view; (2) increasing problem-solving skills; (3) increasing coping skills; (4) increasing freedom of choice; (5) increasing commitment to choices made; and (6) increasing available resources.

The different models of school consultation do not have identical conceptual bases. For example, behavioral consultation is based on social learning theory, and the technology of applied behavioral analysis is used to change students' and teachers' behaviors. Process consultation is based on social, psychological, and general systems theory and assumes interpersonal and group processes affect educational outcomes. There are certain assumptions, or concepts, that are common to the various models. Two shared assumptions are that children's classroom behaviors and learning are determined by variables in the child and in the classroom setting and that the consultant must work jointly with the consultee to solve problems.

Considerable attention in the consultation literature is given to the task of entry as a consultant into an organization. Entry tasks include: (1) obtaining approval for consultation from administrators; (2) establishing a shared set of expectations with administrators and teachers regarding consultation's purposes, the roles and responsibilities of the consultant and consultees, confidentiality, and the types of problems to be discussed in consultation; and (3) establishing the consultant as a credible and trustworthy resource person. If teachers are accustomed to receiving recommendations from psychologists, and the psychologist-consultant does not carefully lay the groundwork for the consultative relationship, the teacher and the psychologist will find themselves working at cross purposes, based on their differing expectations for the interaction.

Consultation involves two jobs: working on the content, or specific problem brought to consultation, and working on the process of helping the consultee improve his or her job-related performance. It is important for the consultant to have specialized knowledge that is relevant to the consultation content (e.g., the particular behavior, learning, or programmatic concern). Indeed, the reason the consultee asked for the consultant's help is that the consultee believes the consultant has such relevant knowledge. Knowledge bases the psychologist-consultant might draw from in teacher consultation include child development, theories of learning, childhood psychopathology, tests and measurements, diagnosis of learning and behavior, group processes, individual instructional programming, and treatment of childhood learning and behavioral disorders.

In addition to content skills, the consultant must have skills necessary for establishing and maintaining rapport with the consultee and for facilitating the consultee's professional growth. Thus the consultant: (1) seeks clarification, encouraging consultees to see problems from new or broader perspectives; (2) supports the consultee while he or she is grappling with the problem, boosting consultee motivation and self-confidence; (3) asks questions that require consultees to validate information; (4) probes for feelings to help consultees accept their emotional reactions to children; (5) provides choices to increase consultee freedom to choose and commitment to choices made; and (6) confronts consultees either directly or indirectly to increase consultee objectivity. An example of an indirect confrontation is telling a female teacher who is inappropriately "mothering" a young girl that the girl is expecting the teacher to do too much for her and the girl needs to learn that the teacher cannot be her mother. An example of a direct confrontation is telling a male teacher that he seems to be apologizing to his students when he assumes an authoritative role, and that perhaps students are misbehaving because they are picking up on his discomfort in the authoritarian role.

Five models of school consultation are described with respect to their primary purpose and the roles and skills required of the consultant. Psychoeducational consultation is the type of consultation most frequently practiced in schools. After the psychologist has evaluated a child, the psychologist interprets the evaluation results to the teacher, presents recommendations to the teacher, and engages the teacher in a discussion of these recommendations so that the teacher will be able to choose and implement one or more recommendations. The primary purpose is remedial. The consultant's primary role is to diagnose the problem and recommend treatment.

Behavioral consultation is based on social learning theory. The behavioral consultant applies the technology of applied behavior analysis to the task of changing student and teacher behavior. The consultant observes the child as well as the teacher in the classroom to identify and count target behaviors, determine antecedents and consequences of those target behaviors, and recommend changes expected to result in a change in target behaviors. Because the teacher is ultimately responsible for making any changes that are recommended by the consultant, the consultant needs to establish a collaborative working relationship with the teacher. The primary goal in behavioral consultation is remedial; however, the consultant expects consultees will improve their skills in applied behavior analysis and will apply their new skills to similar problems in the future.

In educational consultation, the consultant presents new information or teaches new skills to consultees by conducting in-service workshops. The effective consultant-trainer carefully assesses educational needs of the workshop audience as well as the expectations of the administrators, and provides training that matches those needs and expectations. It is important, in cases of individual student consultation, that the question of needing informed consent from the parents is considered (Heron, 1996).

The mental health consultant's primary purpose is to improve the consultee's ability to effectively cope with similar problems in the future without the consultant's continued help. The particular problem discussed in consultation acts as leverage for changing the consultee's behavior. A secondary goal is to change the child's behavior. Because the focus is on the consultee, the consultant's process skills are especially important. The mental health consultant uses clinical interviewing skills to determine the reason a teacher is experiencing difficulty and employs different consultation approaches depending on the presumed reason for the consultee's difficulty. When the consultee's problem is presumed to be a lack of objectivity, the consultant uses specialized skills that require specialized training in consultation techniques. The consultant attempts to minimize the teacher's displacement of personal problems onto the work setting.

In program consultation, the consultant is requested by the administration to design or to evaluate a specific program such as a gifted education program, a race relations program, or a truancy program. The consultant must have experience and skills relevant to the particular program. The consultant issues a written report that contains recommendations for the school to implement.

Process consultation, like program consultation, is initiated by an administrator. It attempts to effect a change in the system rather than in the individual teacher or child. Process consultation is based on social psychological and general systems theory. The process consultant attempts to improve interpersonal and group processes used by administrators, teachers, parents, and students to reach educational objectives. Thus the consultant will involve the administrators and teachers in a mutual problem-solving effort aimed at diagnosing and changing such human processes as communication, leadership, decision making, and trust. The process consultant does not deal directly with the subject matter of the interactions of an organization. Rather, the consultant provides help with the methods of communication, problem solving, planning, and decision making (Schmuck, 1976).

Consultation is a term that encompasses a diverse set of models for delivering psychological services to a school (or other organization). The common thread is that the psychologist attempts to effect change in clients of the organization (e.g., students) by influencing the behaviors of persons who have a responsibility for client care.

REFERENCES

Bergan, J. R., & Tombari, M. L. (1976). Consultant skill and efficiency and the implementation and outcomes of consultation. *Journal of School Psychology, 14*(1), 3–14.

Conoley, J. C., & Conoley, C. W. (1982). *School consultation: A guide to practice and training*. New York, NY: Pergamon Press.

Heron, T. E. (1996). Ethical and legal issues in consultation. *Remedial and Special Education, 17*(6), 377–385.

Schmuck, R. A. (1976). *Process consultation and organization development*. Reading, MA: Addison-Wesley.

JAN N. HUGHES
Texas A&M University

See also **Consultation, Mental Health; Multidisciplinary Team; Prereferral Intervention; Preschool Screening; Professional School Psychology**

CONSULTATION, INCLUSION AND (See Inclusion)

CONSULTATION, MENTAL HEALTH

Mental health consultation is an indirect mode of providing mental health services to clients served by some agency. The mental health consultant attempts to improve the psychological adjustment of persons in the community (i.e., students, parishioners, probationers, or patients) by consulting with professional caregivers in the community (i.e., teachers, clergymen, probation officers, or doctors). Gerald Caplan's seminal book, *The Theory and Practice of Mental Health Consultation* (1970), summarized his most important writings on the subject and offered the first comprehensive coverage of this mode of providing mental health services. Caplan defined mental health consultation as "a process of interaction between two professional persons—the consultant, who is a specialist, and the consultee, who invokes the consultant's help in regard to a current work problem with which he is having some difficulty and which he has decided is within the other's area of specialized competence" (p. 19). Other persons have broadened this definition to include consultation with more than one consultee and consultation with nonprofessionals (Altrocchi, 1972).

The mental health consultant may be a psychiatrist, psychologist, or social worker, and the consultee may be any person whose ministrations to lay persons in the community have mental health implications. Mental health consultation is more prevalent in schools than in other settings. Reasons for its prevalence in schools include the opportunity provided in schools to affect the mental health of large numbers of children through consultation with a small number of teachers, the recognition of the importance of schooling on children's mental health, the presence of psychologists in schools, and the demonstrated relevance of psychological theories and knowledge to educational goals and practices. Consistent with the focus of this work, the following discussion of consultation will be specific to mental health consultation in schools.

There are several key elements in the previous definition of consultation that distinguish consultation from other professional activities. First, the consultee (teacher, principal, other administrator) invokes the consultant's help. Because consultation is a professional-to-professional interaction, the consultee is responsible for determining whether the assistance of the consultant would be helpful.

Second, the consultee retains responsibility for the problem. Thus, when teachers or administrators ask for a consultant's help, they do not diminish their responsibility for instructing the child or administering the program. Because the consultee retains responsibility for the problem and its handling, the consultee is an active participant in a joint problem-solving process. Responsibility for problem formulation and solution is shared between the consultant and consultee. Thus, consultation is different from referral of a child to a psychologist who then assumes sole responsibility for diagnosing the problem and prescribing treatment. In the referral model, the treatment may or may not be the teacher's responsibility to implement. By contrast, any recommendations that result from the consultation process are the responsibility of the consultee to implement. Moreover, the consultee is free to accept or to reject the consultant's advice, and the consultee may terminate the relationship at any point.

The consultant has no authority over the consultee except the authority of the consultant's good ideas.

Consultation is a confidential relationship. By the time a teacher seeks a consultant's help, he or she may feel discouraged. Teachers would be reluctant to reveal their perceived failures in consultation if the relationship were not confidential. The active role of the teacher-consultee requires the teacher to communicate openly and honestly, with no fear that the consultant will disclose aspects of the communication to third parties. The active role is necessary because the consultant depends on the teacher's wealth of information regarding the problem, including past efforts to solve it. Furthermore, the teacher's values, beliefs, role constraints, resources for solving the problem, instructional methods, interactional style, knowledge base, and skills are important variables for the consultant to consider in jointly designing a plan for solving the problem brought to consultation. If the consultation plan is not compatible with the unique characteristics of the teacher's work situation, either it will not be implemented as intended or it will result in a disruption of the teacher's functioning. The confidential nature of the consultation relationship enables the consultee to play the active role required in consultation.

Consultation is a collaborative relationship. The consultant's role is that of a facilitator. Although consultation includes giving expert advice, the consultant's primary method of assisting teachers includes offering observations, asking questions that clarify the problem or place the problem in a new perspective, suggesting information that needs to be obtained in order to understand the problem, serving as a springboard for the teacher's own ideas, and sharing pertinent knowledge from such fields as child development, learning theory, group processes, behavior analysis, child psychopathology, tests and measurements, or family systems theory.

The problems discussed in consultation are work-related problems. The consultant does not help the consultee solve personal problems. Although personal problems influence work performance, the professional-to-professional nature of consultation requires a focus on work-related concerns. When personal problems are brought up by the teacher, the consultant conveys an accepting attitude but refocuses the discussion on the teacher's professional functioning.

Caplan categorized mental health consultation as to the kind of problem dealt with (a case or an administrative problem) and as to the focus (the client or program on the one hand or the consultee on the other). This resulted in four categories of consultation.

In *client-centered case* consultation, the focus is on a child's problems. The goal of change in the teacher is secondary to the goal of formulating the problem. A written report to the teacher summarizes the diagnostic findings and recommendations for the teacher's handling of the problem.

In *consultee-centered case* consultation, the focus is on the student; however, the consultant's primary goal is change in the teacher's knowledge, skills, self-confidence, or objectivity. The problem case is a leverage point for effecting a change in the teacher that will enable the teacher to work more effectively, not only with the particular child who is the focus of consultation, but also with similar children in the future. This expected ripple effect in consultation extends the impact of consultation to an indefinite number of children. Because a change in the teacher is the primary goal, the consultant spends considerable time with the teacher, helping the teacher gain new perspectives, insights, knowledge, and skills that will generalize to similar problems in the future. Rather than offering an expert formulation of the problem and strategy for change, the consultant engages the teacher as a peer professional in a problem-solving process, facilitating the teacher's ability to solve the problem independently. As assumption in consultee-centered case consultation is that the teacher will generalize new learnings to future cases if the teacher accepts responsibility for the problem formulation and action plans in consultation. In this type of consultation, the task of assessing the child's problem is secondary to the task of assessing the nature of the teacher's work difficulty, which may involve a lack of knowledge, skills, self-confidence, or professional objectivity. The consultant's expertise is directed primarily to the task of helping the teacher remedy whichever of these shortcomings is present. It is this type of consultation about which the most has been written, and it is this type of consultation that has become nearly synonymous with the term *mental health consultation.*

In *program-centered administrative* consultation, the focus is on a particular program for which the administrator-consultee has responsibility. The primary goal is the assessment of obstacles to achieving goals of a particular program. After a site visit and interviews with persons in the school, a written report summarizing the consultant's findings and recommendations is prepared. As in client-centered case consultation, the goal of educating administrators to handle similar problems in the future is secondary.

In *consultee-centered administrative* consultation, the focus is on the administrator's skills in areas such as group processes, leadership, and interpersonal relationships. This model of consultation is frequently referred to as organizational development consultation. It assumes that change in social structures and human processes within a school will result in the greatest positive impact on the mental health of students and teachers.

Typically, the consultant has no line authority over consultees. Two sources of influence over consultees available to consultants are expert and referent power (Meyers, Parsons, & Martin, 1979). Expert power is the influence the consultant has with a consultee based on the consultee's attribution of expertise to the consultant. Teachers seek out a consultant's help because they believe the consultant has special expert knowledge relevant to the problem for which consultation is sought. Referent power is influence the consultant has with consultees based on the consultee's identification with the consultant. When a consultee admires the consultant and identifies with the consultant's values, attitudes, and behaviors, the consultant is attributed referent power. Much of the consultation literature focuses on methods of building rapport, or referent power. While not using the term *referent power*, Caplan recommends such identification techniques as emphasizing the peer-professional relationship, "one-downsmanship," empathic listening, conveying respect for the consultee, accepting the consultee, emphasizing commonalities, being approachable, and engaging in informal social contacts with consultees.

Although consultation is different from teaching, the consultant has an educational role. As teacher, the consultant instructs, shares information, translates psychological theories into educationally relevant practices, models approaches, offers ideas, and interprets data. As facilitator, the consultant provides a model of professional objectivity, guides teachers in problem solving, encourages, helps consultees deal with affect that may decrease their ability to deal effectively with a problem, and helps consultees avoid displacement of personal problems into the work setting. The consultant also facilitates communication among different organizational units within the school (i.e., regular and special education teachers, grade-level teachers, and administrators).

Empirical evidence derived from over 60 studies on the effectiveness of consultation services in alleviating special problems brought to consultation is positive (Mannino & Shore, 1975; Medway, 1979). Fewer studies on the preventive goals of consultation have been published; however, the results of these studies are positive (Gutkin & Curtis, 1982).

REFERENCES

Altrocchi, J. (1972). Mental health consultation. In S. Golann & C. Eisdorfer (Eds.), *Handbook of community mental health* (pp. 477–507). New York, NY: Appleton-Century-Crofts.

Caplan, G. (1970). *The theory and practice of mental health consultation*. New York, NY: Basic Books.

Gutkin, T. B., & Curtis, M. J. (1982). School-based consultation: Theory and techniques. In C. R. Reynolds & T. B. Gutkin (Eds.), *The handbook of school psychology* (pp. 796–828). New York, NY: Wiley.

Mannino, F. V., & Shore, M. F. (1975). Effecting change through consultation. In F. V. Mannino, B. W. MacLennan, & M. F. Shore (Eds.), *The practice of mental health consultation*. New York, NY: Gardner.

Medway, F. J. (1979). How effective is school consultation: A review of recent research. *Journal of School Psychology, 17*, 275–282.

Meyers, J., Parsons, R. D., & Martin R. (1979). *Mental health consultation in the schools*. San Francisco, CA: Jossey-Bass.

JAN N. HUGHES
Texas A&M University

See also Consultation; Psychology in the Schools; School Psychology

CONTINGENCY CONTRACTING

A contingency contract is a behavior management technique designed to decrease unwanted behaviors or increase desired behaviors. These specific behaviors may be academic or social in nature. The contract is a written agreement signed by all parties that details the expected behaviors and the various consequences associated with the degree of compliance with its terms. Although contingency contracts have been used extensively in the special education environment, they have become increasingly popular management alternatives in inclusive settings for both students with disabilities and gifted students who require individualized programs.

Contingency contracts have been demonstrated to decrease unwanted behaviors such as school tardiness (Din, Isaac, & Rietveld, 2003), disruptive behavior in the general education classroom (Wilkinson, 2003), and suspensions among middle school students (Novell, 1994). Examples of using this technique to develop desired academic behaviors include increasing assignment completion in sixth-grade students (Poston, 1991) and increasing proper capitalization and punctuation (Newstrom, McLaughlin, & Sweeney, 1999).

Stuart (1971) recommends incorporating five components into an ideal contract. First, a precise explanation of the behaviors, penalties, rewards, and privileges must be provided. For example, if a teacher wanted a student to remain in his or her seat in exchange for extra time at the computer, the time of in-seat behavior that must be exhibited before earning a specified amount of computer time needs to be detailed. Closely related, the second component necessitates that all behaviors are observable and measurable and all terms are specified. For example, once computer time has been earned, one should be able to refer to the contract to learn when this time may be claimed. While "in-seat behavior" can be operationally defined and accurately measured, behaviors such as "attending" or "listening" are more nebulous and would be difficult (though not impossible) to measure reliably enough for use in a contract. Third, contingencies for failure to meet the terms of the contract should be specified for both parties. Just as the child must experience the consequences if he or she does not perform as required, the teacher must also be willing to experience consequences (e.g., double reinforcement for the student) if his or her part of the agreement is not fulfilled. Fourth, a bonus clause for consistent performance may be included if the student or teacher feels it may be beneficial. This addition would emphasize the positive aspects of the contract. Finally, either the contract or the teacher should provide a means of monitoring the contract's effectiveness. By providing for this feedback, the contract can help to induce more positive comments on the part of the involved parties when each is in compliance with the contract terms.

Contingency contracts have also been used to increase both academic skills and autonomous learning behaviors in gifted students by describing independent projects and structuring working conditions for such students in the regular classroom. By offering optional assignments at varying degrees of challenge and clearly articulating the expected behaviors during completion of a project, such agreements enable highly capable learners to receive appropriate support without disrupting regular classroom activity (Hishinuma, 1996). Winebrenner (2000) not only incorporates these two components of the contract but also recommends that it detail the level of participation expected in the regular educational program. By including these provisions, gifted students will know when they are expected to work without their teacher's assistance, when they can receive help, and when they are expected to join their classmates.

One of the major features of contingency contracts is that they tend to develop a more collaborative relationship between student and teacher, since the student generally has an active role in formulating the plan. Kohn (1993) supports the use of contracts if the agreement is jointly constructed and recommends that the student be an integral part of the process.

Contingency contracting has demonstrated great promise as a useful management tool for both special and regular educators. Because contracts enhance communication by specifying expectations on the part of both parties, compliance with the terms and performance can be measured easily and contingencies can be enforced. As with any behavioral strategy, however, the procedure is only as effective as its consistent application. For information on implementation and examples of contracts, see Winebrenner (1996, 2000) and Downing (1990).

REFERENCES

Din, F. S., Isaak, L. R., & Rietveld, J. (2003). *Effects of contingency contracting on decreasing student tardiness.* (ERIC DRS No. 474642)

Downing, J. A. (1990). Contingency contracts: A step-by-step format. *Intervention in School and Clinic, 26,* 111–113.

Hishinuma, E. S. (1996). Motivating the gifted underachiever: Implementing reward menus and behavioral contracts within an integrated approach. *Gifted Child Today Magazine, 19,* 30–35, 43–48.

Kohn, A. (1993). *Punished by rewards.* New York, NY: Houghton Mifflin.

Newstrom, J., McLaughlin, T. F., & Sweeney, W. J. (1999). The effects of contingency contracting to improve the mechanics of written language with a middle school student with behavior disorders. *Child and Family Behavior Therapy, 2,* 39–48.

Novell, I. (1994). *Decreasing school suspensions among middle school children by implementing a rehabilitation in-room suspension.* (ERIC DRS No. ED371833)

Poston, R. (1991). *Increasing assignment completion of sixth grade students through behavior modification.* (ERIC DRS No. ED339455)

Stuart, R. B. (1971). Behavioral contracting within the families of delinquents. *Journal of Behavior Therapy and Experimental Psychiatry, 2,* 1–11.

Wilkinson, L. (2003). Using behavioral consultation to reduce challenging behavior in the classroom. *Preventing School Failure, 47,* 100–105.

Winebrenner, S. (1996). *Teaching kids with learning difficulties in the regular classroom: Strategies and techniques every teacher can use to challenge and motivate struggling students.* Minneapolis, MN: Free Spirit.

Winebrenner, S. (2000). *Teaching gifted kids in the regular classroom: Strategies and techniques every teacher can use to meet the academic needs of the gifted and talented.* Minneapolis, MN: Free Spirit.

ANDREW R. BRULLE
JILLIAN N. LEDERHOUSE
Wheaton College

See also Behavioral Assessment; Behavior Disorders

CONTINUOUS REINFORCEMENT

Positive reinforcement is the increase in the frequency of a response following the presentation of something pleasant or desirable. For example, teachers often praise and provide points for work completion to increase the likelihood that students will engage in this behavior in the future. A reinforcement schedule refers to how frequently a reinforcer will be delivered and there are two basic schedules of reinforcement: continuous and intermittent. Continuous reinforcement involves reinforcing an individual's behavior or response each time it occurs whereas intermittent reinforcement involves reinforcing the behavior or response on some occasions but not others (Chance, 1999). In schools and in the community, the majority of behavior is reinforced on intermittent schedules as it is typically impossible to reinforce each appropriate academic or social behavior that an individual exhibits.

The use of continuous reinforcement schedules is important to establish the association between engaging in a certain behavior and receiving a reinforcer (Alberto & Troutman, 2003). For example, students learn that each time their teacher points to a letter and they identify the letter name correctly, they receive verbal praise. Often, once the association between engaging in a certain behavior and receiving a reinforcer has been established, it is important to switch to a more intermittent schedule of reinforcement to effectively maintain behavior over time. In some cases, continuous schedules of reinforcement will always be appropriate such as when solving crossword puzzles, using vending machines, or ordering food at a restaurant (Pryor, 1999). If we did not obtain the food we wanted when ordering at a restaurant, this behavior (i.e., food ordering) would cease very quickly.

In general, continuous schedules of reinforcement should be used when individuals are learning new behaviors or responses (Kazdin, 2000). When an individual is learning a new behavior, such as riding a bike, the final behavior as well as the responses that are close to the final behavior (e.g., putting feet on the pedals, keeping hands positioned correctly on the handlebars) should be reinforced on a continuous basis. Once the behavior is learned, it no longer needs to be reinforced on a continuous schedule. There are often reinforcers in the natural environment that take over and reinforcement from teachers and/or caregivers is no longer needed to maintain the behavior. In the example of riding a bike, a child receives reinforcement from caregivers during the learning process, but once he or she has learned the behavior other reinforcers, such as being able to get to the park quickly via bike riding, help maintain the behavior over time.

There are several problems associated with the use of continuous reinforcement schedules (Alberto & Troutman, 2003). To begin with, when using this type of schedule, once the reinforcer is withdrawn or no longer provided, the desired behavior will rapidly decline and cease to occur (i.e., extinguish). Second, an individual who is reinforced on a continuous basis may become satiated or tired of the reinforcer, especially when food is used as a reinforcer. Finally, individuals may begin to expect a reinforcer for every appropriate behavior exhibited or may only engage in an appropriate behavior when a reinforcer is desired. For these reasons, it is important to switch to intermittent schedules of reinforcement as soon as the individual has learned the desired behavior.

REFERENCES

Alberto, P. A., & Troutman, A. C. (2003). *Applied behavior analysis for teachers* (6th ed.). Upper Saddle River, NJ: Pearson Education.

Chance, P. (1999). *Learning and behavior*. Pacific Grove, CA: Brooks/Cole.

Kazdin, A. E. (2000). *Behavior modification in applied settings*. Belmont, CA: Wadsworth.

Pryor, K. (1999). *Don't shoot the dog*. New York, NY: Bantam Books.

LEANNE S. HAWKEN
University of Utah

See also Behavioral Assessment; Behavior Disorders

CONTINUUM OF SPECIAL EDUCATION SERVICES (*See* Inclusion)

CONTINUUM OF SUPPORT (*See* Positive Behavioral Support, School-wide)

CONTRACT PROCUREMENT

Contract procurement is a term used in vocational rehabilitation facilities, sheltered workshops, and work activities centers. The term is simply defined; however, the concept and process are more complex. The word *contract* refers to jobs that are used in the cited facilities to teach work-habit skills or trade skills, or provide activities that result in reimbursement to persons with disabilities. The term *procurement* refers to the act of attaining contracts. The term *contract procurement*, as it relates to programs for the disabled, refers to the process of attaining work from businesses to be done by persons with disabilities. Subcontracts and prime manufacturing are two categories of contracts.

Subcontracts are jobs that are attained from businesses and that involve no purchases of materials or equipment. An example would be assembling circuit boards for microcomputers. Company A manufactures the parts to be assembled on the circuit boards. They purchase the boards and the boxes for shipping, and send a truck once a week to pick up the assembled and packaged product. The contract involves only labor; on completion of the contract, all surplus parts are returned to Company A.

Prime manufacturing contracts necessitate the purchase and inventory of materials to create a product. Attaining work is a sales function. In the process of selling the abilities of a work program, not only the equipment available but the manpower require legal protection. For example, Company A subcontracts the assembly of circuit boards to Work Program B. All assembly and packaging is done at Work Program B's site. However, Company A gets a special order for microcomputers with an additional resistor on the circuit boards that are already assembled into the microcomputers and boxed. The deadline is such that delivery and pickup of changes is too costly between Company A and Work Program B. Consequently, a labor force must be procured and attained by Company A if their business is to complete the work. They must open the boxes and add the resistor to each microcomputer circuit board, and then repackage the unit.

Understanding that sales is a key concept in contract procurement is important. Often work programs fail to understand that attaining work is a process of identifying, attaining, working, and delivering. Some programs still use non-sales people to attain work and deliver a product, thus causing contract procurement for persons with disabilities to be thought of as cheap, subsidized labor.

The process of attaining work is subdivided into time-and-motion studies, and submitting a bid for subcontract or setting a price for prime manufacturing. Time-and-motion refers to setting up the work in the most efficient manner and then timing the steps in completing the work. The federal Department of Labor publications explain the rules for time-and-motion studies. A bid should include the following information: labor rate, overhead, materials, handling and waste, freight, and profit.

The bid also should include any conditions that may need to be included in the subcontract that concern the workshop regulations.

JEFF HEINZEN
Indianhead Enterprise

See also **Habilitation of Individuals With Disabilities; Rehabilitation**

CONTROL GROUPS

Control groups are aggregates of subjects who do not receive the treatment of interest in an experimental or quasi-experimental intervention. They are used in research and program evaluation to provide baselines against which to measure the impact of an experimental manipulation and as a means to rule out alternative explanations of "treatment" effects. Control groups are useful particularly in field settings, where there may be a number of plausible rival accounts for the meaning of the researcher's observations. Whether the study is an elaborate investigation or the simple introduction of classroom innovation, control groups are often crucial to the interpretation of results.

The logic of the use of control groups centers around the ability to equate subjects in the "treatment" (experimental) and control groups on all factors except the treatment of interest. Many studies are limited because the assignment of subjects to experimental and control groups is such that the assumption of equivalence is not tenable. In addition, the nature of the research setting may result in the contamination of the control groups by such factors as rivalries with the experimental group or imitation of the treatment by the control group (Cook & Campbell, 1979).

Control groups often involve a no-treatment control, where members engage in their activities with no intervention by the experimenter. Cook, Leviton, and Shadish (1985) note that rather than a no-treatment control group, it might be preferable to use a control that allows for comparison between the treatment of interest and another intervention. This might particularly be the case where practitioners are concerned with the relative efficacy of approaches or where ethical constraints prohibit withdrawal or denial of treatment.

Particularly in the case of quasiexperimental designs, where random assignment of subjects is not possible, a number of control groups are often used to rule out different competing interpretations. For example, members of a placebo control group receive an irrelevant treatment that gives an amount of time and attention similar to that of the experimental group (Cook & Campbell, 1979).

It is commonplace to introduce innovative programs in special education. By following proper control group design, one can judge the effectiveness of "reforms as experiments" and make policy decisions on a more rational basis (Campbell, 1969).

REFERENCES

Campbell, D. T. (1969). Reforms as experiments. *American Psychologist, 24,* 409–429.

Cook, T. D., & Campbell, D. T. (1979). *Quasiexperimentation: Design and analysis issues for field settings.* Chicago, IL: Rand McNally.

Cook, T. D., Leviton, L. C., & Shadish, W. R. (1985). Program evaluation. In G. Lindzey & E. Aronson (Eds.), *Handbook of social psychology* (3rd ed., Vol. 1, pp. 699–777). New York, NY: Random House.

LEE ANDERSON JACKSON JR.
University of North Carolina at Wilmington

See also **Measurement; Research in Special Education**

CONTROVERSIAL AND NON-CONVENTIONAL AUTISM TREATMENTS

The terms *controversial* and *non-conventional* are often used to describe unestablished or unvalidated treatments for which there is little or no scientific evidence to support the effectiveness and safety of the intervention (Simpson, Myles, & Ganz, 2008; Volkmar & Weisner, 2009). Many of these therapies promise extraordinary results or a cure for autism (Simpson, 2005; Simpson & Myles, 1998; Volkmar & Weisner, 2009). Controversial and non-conventional autism treatments that are noted in the literature include antifungal medication, such as Flagyl, Diflucan, and Nystatin; aquatic therapy; art therapy; auditory integration training; biofilm protocol; chelation; craniosacral and chiropractic therapy; dolphin therapy; facilitated communication; FastForWord; Feingold diet; Gentle Teaching; gluten-free-casein-free (GFCF) diets; hippotherapy; holding therapy; hyperbaric oxygen therapy; iridology; Irlen Lenses; Lindamood-Bell; the Miller method; music therapy; Options Son Rise Program; patterning; plasmapheresis; rapid eye therapy; rhythmic entrainment interventions; secretin; sensory integration; vision therapy; vitamin and supplemental therapy (vitamins A, B6, B12, C, and D, magnesium, dimethylglycerine, omega-3 fatty acids); and yoked prisms (Association for Science in Autism Treatment, n.d.; Heflin & Simpson, 1998; Volkmar & Wiesner, 2009).

There are numerous reasons the aforementioned interventions are considered controversial or non-conventional. The primary reason relates to minimal or lack of rigorous research that supports the use of these interventions with children and youth with autism. Some treatments, such as Gentle Teaching, holding therapy, facilitated communication, auditory integration training, and FastForWord, have provided evidence of effectiveness; however, these outcomes have primarily been reported by the developers of these treatments and have not been replicated by other researchers. Other interventions, such as the Irlen Lenses, Options Son Rise Program, secretin, and gluten-free-casein-free (GFC) diets, have demonstrated effectiveness through case studies and testimonials; however, such evidence is difficult to evaluate and lacks scientific rigor.

Safety is another consideration; for example, very high doses of vitamins as recommended in some mega-vitamin therapy protocols can cause liver damage and high doses of vitamin B6 can cause nerve damage, ulcers, and seizures (Volkmar & Wiesner, 2009). There are also medical risks with plasmapheresis and hyperbaric oxygen therapy (Volkmar & Wiesner, 2009) and some forms of chelation therapy have been associated with life-threatening reactions and even death (Kane, 2006). Finally, interventions such as facilitated communication (FC) have resulted in legal actions (Gorman, 1999). Allegations of sexual abuse were made against parents, caretakers, and teachers based on alleged messages made by FC users (*Autism Research Review International*, 1993; Seligmann & Chideya, 1992). Additionally, civil suits were filed against facilitators who may have inadvertently influenced these messages (*Autism Research Review International*, 1993). Volkmar and Wiesner (2009) discuss other negative outcomes of FC, including parents removing children from their special education placements and terminating the use of other interventions to enroll their children in likely inappropriate settings that would access their "true" abilities, and some physicians prescribing medications based upon alleged communication using FC.

Due to the large number of controversial or non-conventional treatments available and the potential for harm from some, Simpson, Myles, and Ganz (2008) developed a list of questions to assist parents, educators, and other professionals in evaluating and determining to use a controversial method. These questions include the following:

Will the intervention impair or detract from the overall educational and treatment program?

Will it cause frustration or regression?

What happens if the method proves ineffective?

Is the controversial method balanced with other program components?

Have appropriate outcomes and assessment methods been identified, and can these methods be maintained in the long term with appropriately trained personnel and other resources?

Does the method lead to increased independence?

What is the impact of the method on an individual's general quality of life? (p. 498)

Parents and practitioners are urged to use extreme caution when considering these and other unproven treatments.

REFERENCES

Autism Research Review International 1993 Free Quarterly Newsletter available from http://autism.com/ari/newsletter/subscribe.htm

Association for Science in Autism Treatment. (n.d.). *Summaries of scientific research on interventions on autism.* Retrieved from http://www.asatonline.org/intervention/treatments_desc.htm

Gorman, B. J. (1999). Facilitated communication: Rejected in science, accepted in court—a case study and analysis of the use of FC evidence under *Frye* and *Daubert. Behavioral Sciences and the Law, 17,* 517–541.

Heflin, L. J. & Simpson, R. L. (1998). Interventions for children and youth with autism: Prudent choices in a world of exaggerated claims and empty promises: Part 1. Intervention and treatment options. *Focus on Autism and Other Developmental Disabilities, 13,* 194–211.

Kane, K. (2006, January 6). Death of 5-year-old boy linked to controversial chelation therapy. *Pittsburgh Post Gazette.* Retrieved from http://www.post-gazette.com/pg/06006/633541-85.stm

Seligmann, J., & Chideya, F. (1992, September 21). Horror story or big hoax? *Newsweek.* Retrieved from http://www.newsweek.com/1992/09/20/horror-story-or-big-hoax.html#

Simpson, R. L. (2005). Evidence-based practices and students with autism spectrum disorders. *Focus on Autism and Other Developmental Disabilities, 20*, 140–149.

Simpson, R., & Myles, B. (1995). Effectiveness of facilitated communication with children and youth with autism. *Journal of Special Education, 28*, 424–439.

Simpson, R., & Myles, B. (1998). Controversial therapies and interventions with children and youth with autism. In R. L. Simpson & B. S. Myles (Eds.), *Educating children and youth with autism* (pp. 315–331). Austin, TX: PRO-ED.

Simpson, R., Myles, B., & Ganz, J. B. (2008). Efficacious interventions and treatments for learners with autism spectrum disorders. In R. L. Simpson & B. S. Myles (Eds.), *Educating children and youth with autism: Strategies for effective practice* (2nd ed., pp. 447–512). Austin, TX: PRO-ED.

Volkmar, F. R. & Wienser, L. A. (2009). *A practical guide to autism: What every parent, family member, and teacher needs to know*. Hoboken, NJ: Wiley.

THERESA EARLES-VOLLRATH
University of Central Missouri

CONVERGENT AND DIVERGENT THINKING

Emerging from Guilford's structure of intellect model of human intelligence, the concepts of convergent and divergent thinking are often applied to the education of gifted children. Both are viewed as high-level cognitive operations that individuals use when making decisions (Guilford, 1966, 1984).

Convergent thinking requires a narrowing process by which an individual develops classification rules that explain the relationships among objects and concepts. Essential to this process is the invocation of recall and recognition strategies. As such, the products of convergent thinking tend to be in the form of single "correct" answers. Critics have argued that typical school instruction demands an inappropriate proportion of convergent thinking at the expense of more creative (divergent) processes (Steffin, 1983).

Divergent thinking involves a broad scanning operation, enabling an individual to generate multiple possible solutions. It has received a major share of research attention in creativity, problem solving, and critical thinking (Steffin, 1983).

Guilford (1984) has discussed three aspects of divergent thinking. One aspect, fluency, relates to the breadth of associations available to an individual regarding a particular stimulus. A second, flexibility, is defined as the simultaneous consideration of multiple classes of information. In contrast to convergent processes, flexibility allows the individual to develop novel combinations. The third aspect, elaboration, is an integrative process that results in the formation of a broad theory. Here the thinker, demonstrating insight, is able to make predictions based on incomplete information.

Several studies have shown that young children's divergent productions can be increased by the use of open-ended questions in class discussions (Pucket-Cliatt, Shaw, & Sherwood, 1980; Thomas & Holcomb, 1981). These studies have also suggested that teachers can become increasingly comfortable using open-ended questions and that they can decrease their reliance on rote memory activities.

Steffin (1983) suggests that computers offer new opportunities for fostering divergent thinking. Increasingly sophisticated computer simulations, with their capacity for user-controlled interaction and variability in presentation, can teach students to develop algorithms that can be generalized across learning situations.

While learning-disabled (Jaben, 1983) and language-deficient (Burrows & Wolf, 1983) children have shown gains in creativity following training in divergent thinking, the observation and development of creative thinking in gifted students continues to dominate the research literature at the present time (Hildebrand, 1991; Kaufman, 2005).

REFERENCES

Burrows, D., & Wolf, B. (1983). Creativity and the dyslexic child: A classroom view. *Annals of Dyslexia, 33*, 269–274.

Guilford, J. P. (1966). Basic problems in teaching for creativity. In C. W. Taylor & F. E. Williams (Eds.), *Instructional media and creativity*. New York, NY: Wiley.

Guilford, J. P. (1984). Varieties of divergent production. *Journal of Creative Behavior, 18*, 1–10.

Hildebrand, V. (1991). Young children's care and education: Creative teaching and management. *Early Child Development and Care, 71*, 63–72.

Kaufman, J. (2005). Creativity and the special education student. In E. Fletcher-Janzen & C. R. Reynolds (Eds.), *The special education almanac* (pp. 369–390). Hoboken, NJ: Wiley.

Jaben, T. H. (1983). The effects of creativity training on learning disabled students' creative written expression. *Journal of Learning Disabilities, 16*, 264–265.

Pucket-Cliatt, M. J., Shaw, J. M., & Sherwood, J. M. (1980). Effects of training on the divergent thinking abilities of kindergarten children. *Child Development, 51*, 1061–1064.

Steffin, S. A. (1983). Fighting against convergent thinking. *Childhood Education, 59*, 255–258.

Thomas, E., & Holcomb, C. (1981). Nurturing productive thinking in able students. *Journal of General Psychology, 104*, 67–79.

GARY BERKOWITZ
Temple University

See also Creative Problem Solving; Teacher Expectations; Teaching Strategies

See Febrile Convulsions

CONVULSIVE DISORDERS (*See Seizure Disorders*)

COOPERATIVE GROUPING, MATHEMATICS

Cooperative learning is an instructional method where students work in academically heterogeneous small groups accomplishing shared goals, seeking outcomes beneficial to each group member, and having discussions to ensure everyone understands the assigned material (Johnson & Johnson, 1999). Success of cooperative learning hinges on the inclusion of five essential elements: positive interdependence, individual accountability, face-to-face promotive interaction, coaching in social skills, and group processing (Johnson & Johnson, 1989). Effectiveness of cooperative learning in improving student achievement depends on the emphasis on incentivized intergroup competition and individual accountability (Reid, 1992). These features distinguish cooperative learning groups from noncooperative learning groups where students are often evaluated individually and within-group competition exists. Overall student performance, therefore, tends to be lower and students would achieve more working individually (Johnson & Johnson, 1999).

Group investigations, Student Teams–Achievement Divisions, and Jigsaw II are typical strategies of cooperative learning (Balkcom, 1992). Group investigations are meant to help develop students' problem-solving skills and students may help identify a topic for a group project. With Student Teams–Achievement Divisions (STAD), students of varying academic abilities, gender, and racial/ethnic background study teacher-presented content in teams of four or five members. Although each team member is tested individually, scores are combined to form a team score. This necessitates the need for team members to help each other. With the Jigsaw II approach, each team member is responsible for learning a specific part of a topic. Students from different teams who are focused on learning the same part of a topic meet for discussions. They then go and report back to their groups. This provides all team members with the opportunity to discuss the topic and ask questions. This may be followed by class discussions and individual assessments.

Research has shown that cooperative learning results in students performing academically higher than they would working individually (Johnson & Johnson, 1999). Other positive outcomes include increased student self-esteem (Slavin, 1980), students actively learning mathematics at a comfortable pace, students becoming more confident as problem solvers, enhanced social skills (Davidson, 1990), and reduced peer competition and isolation (Rivera, 1996). Because of the demonstrated benefits cooperative learning has shown with students in general education classrooms,

researchers (for example, Malmgren, 1998) have recommended using cooperative learning with students with disabilities.

In a comparative study involving students with disabilities (Kuntz, McLaughlin, & Howard, 2001), students' math scores were higher when cooperative learning or individualized instruction was used in place of traditional instruction. Additionally, students' work was found to be more accurate when cooperative learning was used instead of individual instruction. Cooperative grouping can help students understand mathematics concepts better and improve students' oral and written communication of mathematics (Snyder, 2006). Special and regular education students working cooperatively promotes peer acceptance (Putnam, Markovchick, Johnson, & Johnson, 1996). Although success of special education students when using cooperative learning may be influenced by students' characteristics, such as attention problems and low motivation, and how their peers respond to these characteristics, with selection of suitable partners, teachers reported special education students having improved self-esteem and greater success on classroom tasks (Jenkins, Antil, Wayne, & Vadasy, 2003). Benefits of cooperative learning are most likely to be realized by students with disabilities when small, academically heterogeneous groups are used, assigned tasks are truly cooperative in nature, positive interdependence exists, there is individual accountability, students with disabilities make contributions without undue hardships, teachers ensure students can be present during time set aside for group work, and ground rules are in place and clearly communicated to the students (Malmgren, 1998).

REFERENCES

Balkcom, S. (1992). *Cooperative learning*. Office of Educational Research and Improvement (ED), Washington, DC. Retrieved from http://www.proteacher.com/redirect.php?goto=1461

Davidson, N. (Ed.) (1990). *Small-group cooperative learning in mathematics: 1990 year book (pp. 52–61)*. Reston, VA: National Council of Teachers of Mathematics.

Jenkins, J. R., Antil, L. R., Wayne, S. K., & Vadasy, P. F. (2003). How cooperative learning works for special education and remedial students. *Exceptional Children, 69*, 279–292.

Johnson, D. W., & Johnson, T. (1989). Cooperative learning: What special education teachers need to know. *The Pointer, 33*(2), 5–10.

Johnson, D. W., & Johnson, T. (1999). Making cooperative learning work. *Theory into Practice, 38*(2), 67.

Kuntz, K. J., McLaughlin, T. F., & Howard, V. F. (2001). A comparison of cooperative learning and small group individualized instruction for math in a self contained classroom for elementary students with disabilities. *Educational Research Quarterly, 24*(3), 41.

Malmgren, K. W. (1998). Cooperative learning as an academic intervention for students with mild disabilities. *Focus on Exceptional Children, 31*, 1–8.

Putnam, J., Markovchick, K., Johnson, D. W., & Johnson, R. T. (1996). Cooperative learning and peer acceptance of students with learning disabilities. *Journal of Social Psychology, 136*, 741–752.

Reid, J. (1992). The effects of cooperative learning with intergroup competition on the math achievement of seventh grade students. (ERIC Document Reproduction Service No. ED355106)

Rivera, D. P. (1996). Using cooperative learning to teach mathematics to students with learning disabilities. *LD Forum: Council for Learning Disabilities, 21*(3), 29–33.

Slavin, R. E. (1980). Cooperative learning. *Review of Educational Research, 50*, 315–342.

Snyder, S. S. (2006, July). *Cooperative learning groups in the middle school mathematics classroom.* A report on an action research project submitted in partial fulfillment of the requirements for participation in the Math in the Middle Institute, University of Nebraska at Lincoln.

MICHAEL T. MUZHEVE
*Texas A&M University,
Kingsville*
Fourth edition

COOPERATIVE TEACHING (*See* Inclusion)

COPROLALIA

Coprolalia is a condition characterized by an irresistible urge to utter obscene words and phrases and uncontrollable performance of obscene gestures (Singer, 1997), which are frequently observed together. Obscenities are interspersed randomly within a dialogue, interrupting the normal flow of conversation. The cursing is usually uttered during a break between sentences and in a loud, sharp tone in contrast to normal voice. The frequency of obscene utterances has a tendency to vary from low to high frequencies for extended periods of time. Coprolalic episodes are positively associated with periods of anxiety and anticipation.

Coprolalia is most often associated with Gilles de la Tourette's syndrome (TS) and is evident in some patients following a stroke (Slappey & Brown, 2003). As with other tics associated with TS, coprolalia can be controlled by TS patients for brief intervals. Lees, Robertson, Trimble, and Murray (1984) report that TS patients exhibiting coprolalia attempt to substitute euphemisms or somewhat disguised neologisms for obscenities. Early estimates of the prevalence of coprolalia in Tourette syndrome patients were approximately 60%, but have been revised to approximately 33% (Lees et al., 1984). Coprolalia tends to peak in adolescence and to wane in adulthood (Singer, 1997).

Both medical and behavioral treatments have been used successfully to control coprolalic expressions. Erenberg, Cruse, and Rothner (1985) report that the preferred medical treatment is the use of dopamine-blocking agents such as haloperidol, a drug used in treating hyperkinetic and manic disorders. Comings and Comings (1985) recommend starting with low doses of haloperidol (.05 mg daily for 1 week) and increasing the dosage by .05 mg at weekly intervals until a 70 to 90% reduction of symptoms occurs. Because of the sedative side effects of haloperidol, stimulant drugs may be given simultaneously. Price, Leckman, Pauls, Cohen, and Kidd (1986) report, however, that stimulant drugs appear to be associated positively with increases in the frequency of tics.

Behavioral treatments have included the use of self-management and negative practice techniques. Friedman (1980), for instance, had a patient substitute socially acceptable utterances for obscenities whenever she had the urge to curse. Evans and Evans (1983) decreased the rate of utterances of an expletive using a self-counting procedure. The patient simply recorded each frequency of his use of the target expletive. Storms (1985) had patients practice their tics until they were tired, had them rest, and then repeated the practice.

Medical and behavioral treatments of coprolalia have been used in combination with each other as well as in isolation. Storms (1985), for instance, used doses of haloperidol in combination with negative practice to reduce the frequency of tics. Medical marijuana is also being researched and preliminary results at the reduction and overall symptom relief are good (Slappey & Brown, 2003).

Characteristics

1. Coprolalia is a complex vocal tic.
2. Obscenities and elaborate sexual and aggressive statements are uttered at inappropriate times.
3. Use of racial slurs in public situations is common.
4. Coprolalia may occur less frequently than simple motor tics, such as eye blinking or grimacing.
5. Coprolalia is more disruptive than simple motor tics.
6. When in the presence of a doctor or therapist, affected children may temporarily "lose" their tics. However, as soon as they leave, their symptoms may become more severe.
7. Coprolalia is more frequent in stressful situations.

REFERENCES

Comings, D. E., & Comings, B. G. (1985). Tourette syndrome: Clinical and psychological aspects. *Human Genetics, 37*, 435–450.

Erenberg, G., Cruse, R. P., & Rothner, A. D. (1985). Gilles de la Tourette's syndrome: Effects of stimulant drugs. *Neurology, 35*, 1346–1348.

Evans, W. H., & Evans, S. S. (1983). Self-counting in the treatment of Gilles de la Tourette syndrome. *Journal of Precision Teaching, 4*, 14–17.

Friedman, S. (1980). Self-control in the treatment of Gilles de la Tourette's syndrome: Case study with 18-month follow-up. *Journal of Consulting & Clinical Psychology, 48*, 400–402.

Lees, A. J., Robertson, M., Trimble, M. R., & Murray, N. M. F. (1984). A clinical study of Gilles de la Tourette syndrome in the United Kingdom. *Journal of Neurology, Neurosurgery, & Psychiatry, 47*, 1–8.

Price, R. A., Leckman, J. F., Pauls, D. L., Cohen, D. J., & Kidd, K. K. (1986). Gilles de la Tourette syndrome: Tics and central nervous system stimulants in twins and non-twins. *Neurology, 36*, 232–237.

Singer, C. (1997). Coprolalia and other coprophenomena. *Neurologic Clinics, 15*(2), 299–308.

Slappey, J., & Brown, R. T. (2003). Coprolalia. In E. F. Janzen & C. R. Reynolds (Eds.), *Childhood disorders diagnostic desk reference* (pp. 150–151). Hoboken, NJ: Wiley.

Storms, L. (1985). Massed negative practice as a behavioral treatment for Gilles de la Tourette's syndrome. *American Journal of Psychotherapy, 39*, 277–281.

LAWRENCE J. O'SHEA
University of Florida

See also **Stimulant Drugs; Tic Disorder; Tourette Syndrome**

COPROPRAXIA (*See* Coprolalia)

CORE SCHOOL

The term *core* refers to an educational concept that first emerged in the United States in the 1930s and 1940s. The core school tries to provide a common background for all students and engineer a course of study that combines basic topics from school subjects that are usually taught separately. The intention of this concept was to make education more meaningful for students. Most popular in the 1950s, its popularity has declined in recent years, but it is still operational (Manning, 1971).

The core concept has two basic components: time and philosophy (Oliver, 1965). Time is usually administered through a "block time class," for example, two or more class periods are joined together in order to study a wide range of related subjects. The philosophy of core involves the breaking down of strict boundaries between disciplines. Thus, students may study a topic from literary, historical, mathematical, and artistic viewpoints concurrently rather than as separate topics in isolated classes (Manning, 1971; Oliver, 1965).

Beyond these two basic components, cores are identified as having the following characteristics (Hass, Wiles, & Bondi, 1970; Manning, 1971; Oliver, 1965):

1. They are problem centered.
2. Learning is done through firsthand experiences by the learner.
3. Students are involved in the planning, teaching, and evaluation processes.
4. Students are provided with opportunities for total growth by way of lifelike environments.
5. The instruction is more personal, allowing for individual guidance.
6. There are opportunities for integrated knowledge across subject lines.

The core concept, when practiced, will probably be more student-oriented than may occur in other settings. The organization and overlapping of classes can be especially beneficial to the special education student needing structure and concentrated study. Student-oriented classes provide motivation for paying attention and becoming an active participant in the learning process.

REFERENCES

Hass, G., Wiles, K., & Bondi, J. (1970). *Reading in curriculum* (2nd ed.). Boston, MA: Allyn & Bacon.

Manning, D. (1971). *Toward a humanistic curriculum*. New York, NY: Harper & Row.

Oliver, A. I. (1965). *Curriculum improvement: A guide to problems, principles, and procedures*. New York, NY: Dodd, Mead.

ROBERT T. NASH
University of Wisconsin Oshkosh

See also **Ecological Education for Children With Disabilities; Holistic Approach and Learning Disabilities; Test-Teach-Test Paradigm**

CORNEAL DYSTROPHY

The cornea is the transparent outer layer of the eye. Corneal tissue consists of five layers: the epithelium, the Bowman's layer, the stroma, the Descemet's membrane, and the endothelium. A corneal dystrophy is a condition in which one or more parts of the cornea lose their normal clarity due to the accumulation of abnormal material (Sowka, Gurwood, & Cabat, 1998). Corneal dystrophies generally affect both eyes.

There are over 20 corneal dystrophies. Most corneal dystrophies have a genetic link and are primarily autosomal dominant; that is, only one parent needs to be a carrier of the gene in order for a child to inherit the disease (Bevan, 1997). Males and females are equally affected (National Eye Institute [NEI], 2000). With the exception of a few subtypes that predominantly affect older adults, most individuals will be diagnosed with the disease before they turn 20 years of age. However, although children may be born with a corneal dystrophy, they are more likely to be diagnosed during adolescence, and the disease usually progresses slowly throughout the patient's lifetime (Trattler & Clark, 2000).

Corneal dystrophies are classified based on the layer of the cornea that is affected. An individual is diagnosed with an anterior corneal dystrophy when the epithelium is affected. Corneal dystrophies that affect the central layer of the cornea are stromal dystrophies. These include lattice, granular, and macular dystrophies. Corneal dystrophies in the posterior layers of the cornea affect the Descemet's membrane and the endothelium (Trattler & Clark, 2000).

Characteristics

1. Some corneal dystrophies may produce no symptoms and are detected only through a routine eye exam. Other corneal dystrophies may cause repeated episodes of pain and may or may not affect vision.
2. Child may complain of eye irritation or severe eye pain.
3. Child may experience blurry vision or the sensation of a foreign object in the eye.
4. Eyes may be especially sensitive to light.
5. Although most individuals do experience some vision loss, visual impairment often does not occur until years after diagnosis.

Symptoms and prognosis vary according to the type of corneal dystrophy an individual has. Four main subtypes that would be most likely to be identified in children in their first decade are lattice-type corneal dystrophy (presents prior to age 10, and vision loss is probable by age 50; Klintworth, 1999); macular corneal dystrophy (autosomal recessive, presents prior to age 10, intense pains, visual impairment by age 30; Trattler & Clark, 2000); juvenile epithelial corneal dystrophy of Meesmann (presents by age 2, eye irritation, vision loss is not probable); and Reis-Buckler's corneal dystrophy (early childhood onset of recurrent, painful corneal erosion, rapid loss of visual acuity as child ages; National Organization for Rare Disorders, 1988).

For patients who experience pain as a result of the corneal dystrophy, doctors can prescribe ointments and eye drops (NEI, 2000) or eye patches with antibiotic ointment (Trattler & Clark, 2000). Sunglasses can help alleviate photophobia (sensitivity to light). Treatment may consist of corneal grafting to repair the cornea (Bevan, 1997). If there is a severe loss of vision, a corneal transplant may be needed. In most cases, the surgery restores sight (NEI, 2000).

Because corneal dystrophies vary greatly in their effects on vision, professionals need to evaluate each child's individual needs. In most cases, children will not experience any permanent vision loss during their school years. Nonetheless, because vision loss may be gradual, teachers need to monitor a child's responses to visual stimuli, paying careful attention to whether the child squints his or her eyes, turns his or her head to focus, or loses visual attention easily. Depending on the nature of the presenting symptoms, teachers can maximize a child's functional use of vision by incorporating visual aids that are varied in the size of the print, color contrast, and lighting and are tailored to each individual child. Teachers should also present instructional material through other sensory modalities, such as tactile and auditory. Children with vision loss may also benefit from orientation and mobility training, in which the child develops increased spatial awareness in order to move successfully around in his or her environment. Children with limited functional vision will also need instruction in Braille literacy. In rare cases where there is substantial loss of vision, it may be necessary for a child to attend programs for the visually impaired or blind (Heller, Alberto, Forney, & Schwartzman, 1996).

REFERENCES

Bevan, V. (1997). *Corneal dystrophy factsheet*. Royal National Institute for the Blind. Retrieved from http://www.rnib.org.uk

Heller, K. W., Alberto, P. A., Forney, P. E., & Schwartzman, M. N. (1996). *Understanding physical, sensory, and health impairments: Characteristics and educational implications*. Pacific Grove, CA: Brooks/Cole.

Klintworth, G. K. (1999). Perspective: Advances in molecular genetics of corneal dystrophies. *American Journal of Ophthalmology, 128*(6), 747–754.

National Eye Institute. (2000). *The cornea and corneal disease*. Retrieved from http://www.medhelp.org/

National Organization for Rare Disorders. (1988). *Topic: Corneal dystrophy*. Retrieved from http://www.rarediseases.org/

Sowka, J. W., Gurwood, A. S., & Cabat, A. G. (1998). *Handbook of ocular disease management*. Review of *Ophthalmology Online*. Retrieved from http://www.revoptom.com/

Trattler, W., & Clark, W. (2000). *Dystrophy, macular*. eMedicine: Ophthalmology. Retrieved from http://www.emedicine.com

MICHELLE PERFECT
University of Texas at Austin

CORNELIA DE LANGE SYNDROME

Cornelia de Lange syndrome (CdLS) is a rare genetic disorder that is characterized by prenatal and postnatal growth retardation, facial abnormalities, cognitive deficits or mental retardation, and developmental delays. In the United States, the disorder occurs in approximately 1 in 10,000 births and appears to affect males and females equally. Recurrence within affected families appears to be estimated at less than 1% (National Organization for Rare Disorders [NORD], 2000). Physical characteristics and symptoms vary in severity and presentation from case to case.

Characteristics

1. Craniofacial abnormalities
2. Mild to severe retardation
3. Unusually long vertical groove between the upper lip and nose, a depressed nasal bridge, anteverted nares, and a protruding upper jaw
4. Facial abnormalities such as thin down-turned lips; low-set ears; arched, well-defined eyebrows that grow together across the base of the nose; and abnormally curly, long eyelashes
5. Possible limb malformations such as small hands and feet, inward deviation of the fifth fingers, or webbing of certain toes
6. For infants, possible feeding and breathing difficulties, increased respiratory problems, heart defects, a low "growling" cry, hearing deficits, or other physical abnormalities

The abnormalities characteristic of CdLS may be detected prenatally through the use of ultrasound imaging; in most cases, however, it is diagnosed at birth (Aitken, Ireland, Crossley, Macri, Burn, & Conner, 1999). A diagnosis of CdLS should be considered if the child exhibits the distinctive facial characteristics listed along with the limb anomalies, mental retardation, and growth retardation. Associated abnormalities include cardiac defects, gastroesophogeal reflux, glue ear, intestinal obstruction due to gastrointestinal problems, and respiratory infection (NORD, 2000). Associated behavioral characteristics include hyperactivity, self-injury, aggression, and sleep disturbances (Berney, Ireland, & Burn, 1999).

Treatment is directed toward the noted symptoms and may involve the collaborative efforts of numerous healthcare professionals, including pediatricians, orthopedic surgeons, heart specialists, urologists, speech pathologists, and occupational therapists. Surgery may be performed to correct cleft palate, and orthopedic techniques may be used to treat limb deformities. Plastic surgery may also be helpful in reducing excessive hair. Antibiotic drug therapy may help fight associated respiratory infection. Anticonvulsant medication may be needed for patients who experience seizure episodes.

Early intervention is important in ensuring that children with CdLS reach their highest potentials. Special education services may be available to children with CdLS under the handicapping condition of Other Health Impairment. Services that may be beneficial include special remedial education, vocational training, speech therapy, and other medical and social services. Because of the numerous health issues associated with the disorder, children may need to spend a great deal of time in treatment and away from the classroom. Therefore, tutoring services or home-based instruction may also be required. In addition, patients may also benefit from counseling services designed to help them psychologically adjust to their illnesses. Medication side effects should be considered when formally assessing the patients' cognitive, social, or academic functionings (NORD, 2000).

Research on CdLS and its cause is ongoing. There is no known cure for CdLS, but there is hope that the Human Genome Project, sponsored by the National Institutes of Health, may shed light on why genes sometimes malfunction (NORD, 2000).

REFERENCES

Aitken, D. A., Ireland, M., Crossley, B. E., Macri, J. N., Burn, J., & Conner, J. M. (1999). Second trimester pregnancy associated plasma protein-A levels are reduced in Cornelia de Lange syndrome pregnancies. *Prenatal Diagnosis, 19*(8), 706–710.

Berney, T. P., Ireland, M., & Burn, J. (1999). Behavioural phenotype of Cornelia de Lange syndrome. *Archives of Disease in Childhood, 81*(4), 333–336.

National Organization for Rare Diseases. (2000, March). *Cornelia De Lange syndrome*. Retrieved from http://www.rarediseases .org

MARY CORLETT
University of Texas at Austin

CORRECTIONAL EDUCATION

The Correctional Education Association (1983) defined *correctional education* as a coordinated system of individualized learning services and activities conducted within the walls of a correctional facility. Services are provided by certified educational staff and are designed to meet the identified needs of the inmate population in the areas of basic education leading to a high-school credential; vocational training geared toward obtaining entry-level skills and maintaining competitive employment; and development of attitudes, skills, and abilities in the context of sociopersonal development.

It is difficult to summarize the types of correctional education programs available in institutions because services vary among and within states. Few states provide comprehensive educational services to meet the identified educational needs. Usually, a state will focus on just a few program areas such as higher education or adult education.

Estimates indicate that 85 to 95% of incarcerated adults do not have high-school diplomas. Many of them can neither read nor write after completing their sentences (Loeffler & Martin, 1982). From a survey conducted by Bell (1979), it was found that 50% of the adults in federal and state institutions were illiterate. Researchers such as Roberts (1973) state that the average inmate is unable to complete a job application, read and understand newspapers, or apply for an automobile operator's license (Day & McCane, 1982). In addition, 70% of the inmates have had no vocational training prior to sentencing. The National Advisory Council on Vocational Education found that the typical inmate is male, poor, and with less than 10 years of schooling. Gehring (1980) described correctional students as frequently afflicted by special learning and/or drug-related problems, accustomed to violence, and lacking in academic skills.

According to the U.S. Department of Justice (1983), the incarceration rate for individuals not completing elementary school is 259 per 1,000 for males between the ages of 20 to 29 years; for elementary school graduates, it is 83 per 1,000; for those completing 9 to 11 years in school, it is 70 per 1,000; for high-school graduates, it decreased to 11 per 1,000; and for persons with 16 years of schooling, the rate drops to 1 per 1,000.

Numerous research studies on correctional education programs have documented the effectiveness of both juvenile and adult correctional programs (Correctional Education Association, 1983). Correctional education programs have resulted in increased employment and improved quality of life for released inmates.

A major difficulty facing correctional educational administrators stems from the fact that the quantity of existing correctional education programs is insufficient to meet the needs of the hundreds of thousands of men, women, and children who are incarcerated in correctional institutions throughout the United States. The lack of public support and financial resources for correctional education programs severely limit the extent of correctional program effectiveness.

REFERENCES

Bell, R. (1979, June). *Correctional education program for inmates* (National Evaluation Programs, Phase I). Washington, DC: U.S. Department of Justice.

Correctional Education Association. (1983). *Lobbying for correctional education: A guide to action.* (Available from Correctional Education Association, 1400 20th Street, NW, Washington, DC 20009)

Day, S. R., & McCane, M. R. (1982). *Vocational education in corrections* (Information Series 237, 11–12). Columbus, OH: State University, National Center for Research in Vocational Education.

Gehring, T. (1980, September). Correctional education and the U.S. Department of Education. *Journal of Correctional Education, 35*(4), 137–141.

Loeffler, C. A., & Martin, T. C. (1982, April). *The functional illiterate: Is correctional education doing its job?* Huntsville, TX: Marloe Research.

Roberts, A. R. (1973). *Readings in prison education.* Springfield, IL: Thomas.

U.S. Department of Justice. (1983, October). *Report to the nation on crime and justice. The data* (NCJ-87060, p. 37). Rockville, MD: Bureau of Justice Statistics.

STAN A. KARCZ
University of Wisconsin at Stout

See also **Correctional Special Education; Juvenile Delinquency; Right to Education**

CORRECTIONAL SPECIAL EDUCATION

Over 500,000 criminal offenders are currently housed in the nation's 559 state and federal prisons and 3,493 local jails. Of this population, approximately 72,000 are incarcerated in state juvenile correctional facilities, jails, and group homes. In addition, almost 3 million persons are under community supervision instead of in confinement (Bureau of Justice Statistics, 1998). This rate of incarceration is among the highest in the world.

A large portion of the incarcerated population have educational disabilities. For example, Morgan's (1979) survey indicated that 42% of incarcerated juveniles met IDEA definitional criteria as handicapped. Surveys of adult correctional facilities in Oregon (Hurtz & Heintz, 1979) and Louisiana (Klinger, Marshall, Price, & Ward, 1983) suggest similar proportions of persons with disabilities in adult prisons, for example, between 30 and 50%.

Correctional education, which consists of formal educational programs ranging from basic literacy training to postsecondary vocational and university education, is offered in the vast majority of correctional facilities in the United States. Such programs typically are voluntary in adult facilities, but mandatory for juveniles. The administrative regulations for IDEA specifically include correctional education programs in the mandate for a free and appropriate public education for persons with disabilities 21 years of age and under; however, less than 10%

of the state departments of juvenile and adult corrections are in compliance (Coffey, 1983). States not in compliance are experiencing heightened pressure through litigation (Wood, 1984) and administrative sanctions to provide special education programs. Increased interest in correctional special education is reflected in federally funded demonstration and training projects, receipt of PL 94-142 state flow-through monies by correctional education programs, and the development of training programs for correctional special educators.

In 1984 the Correctional/Special Education Training (C/SET) Project staff (Rutherford, Nelson, & Wolford, 1985) surveyed the 85 state departments of juvenile and/or adult corrections and the 50 state departments of education to determine the number of offenders in juvenile and adult correctional facilities with disabilities.

There are 33,190 individuals incarcerated in state juvenile correctional facilities. Of this number, 30,681, or 92%, are in correctional education programs. The estimated number of juvenile offenders with disabilities is 9,443, or 28% of the total incarcerated population. The number of juveniles receiving special education services is 7,750, or 23% of the number of juveniles in corrections. Thus, according to state administrators' estimates, approximately 80% of juvenile offenders with disabilities are being served.

In addition to the data collected concerning offenders with disabilities in juvenile corrections, data were also collected relative to services for inmates with disabilities in state adult correctional facilities. An estimated 117,000 of those in adult corrections are under the age of 22 (Gerry, 1985) and thus potentially eligible for special education services under IDEA.

Of the 399,636 adults in state corrections programs, approximately 118,158, or 30%, are receiving correctional education services. Based on data reported by 31 states, the estimated number of offenders with disabilities in adult corrections is 41,590, or 10%, 4,313 of whom, or less than 1%, are receiving special education services.

Currently a need exists for correctional special education services in juvenile and adult correctional institutions, raising the question of what constitutes an effective correctional special education program. Some researchers (e.g., Gerry, 1985; Smith & Hockenberry, 1980; Smith, Ramirez, & Rutherford, 1983) have delineated essential compliance issues with regard to implementation of IDEA in correctional education programs. There are six factors that are important to the implementation of meaningful correctional special education programs. These are (1) procedures for conducting functional assessments of the skills and learning needs of handicapped offenders; (2) the existence of a curriculum that teaches functional academic and daily living skills; (3) the inclusion of vocational special education in the curriculum; (4) the existence of transitional programs and procedures between correctional programs and the public schools or the world of work;

(5) the presence of a comprehensive system for providing institutional and community services to handicapped offenders; and (6) the provision of in-service and preservice training for correctional educators in special education.

REFERENCES

Bureau of Justice Statistics. (1998). *Justice statistics.* Washington, DC: U.S. Department of Justice.

Coffey, O. D. (1983). Meeting the needs of youth from a corrections viewpoint. In S. Braaten, R. B. Rutherford, & C. A. Kardash (Eds.), *Programming for adolescents with behavioral disorders* (pp. 79–84). Reston, VA: Council for Children with Behavioral Disorders.

Gerry, M. H. (1985). *Monitoring the special education programs of correctional institutions.* Washington, DC: U.S. Department of Education.

Hurzt, R., & Heintz, E. I. (1979). *Incidence of specific learning disabilities at Oregon State Correctional Institution.* Paper presented at the National Institute of Corrections Conference, Portland, OR.

Klinger, J. H., Marshall, G. M., Price, A. W., & Ward, K. D. (1983). A pupil appraisal for adults in the Louisiana Department of Corrections. *Journal of Correctional Education, 34*(2), 46–48.

Morgan, D. J. (1979). Prevalence and types of handicapping conditions found in juvenile correctional institutions: A national survey. *Journal of Special Education, 13,* 283–295.

Rutherford, R. B., Nelson, C. M., & Wolford, B. I. (1985). Special education in the most restrictive environment: Correctional/special education. *Journal of Special Education, 19,* 60–71.

Smith, B. J., & Hockenberry, C. M. (1980). Implementing the Education for All Handicapped Children Act, PL 94-142, in youth corrections facilities: Selected issues. In F. J. Weintraub, A. Abeson, J. Ballard, & M. L. LaVor (Eds.), *Public policy and the education of exceptional children* (pp. 1–36). Reston, VA: Council for Exceptional Children.

Smith, B. J., Ramirez, B., & Rutherford, R. B. (1983). Special education in youth correctional facilities. *Journal of Correctional Education, 34,* 108–112.

Wood, F. J. (1984). *The law and correctional education.* Tempe, AZ: Correctional Special Education Training Project.

ROBERT B. RUTHERFORD JR.
Arizona State University

See also Correctional Education; Juvenile Delinquency

CORTICAL VISUAL IMPAIRMENT

Cortical visual impairment (CVI) is a disorder in which the structures of the visual system (i.e., orb, lens, retina, optic nerve, etc.) may appear normal, but the brain does not correctly interpret visual information. CVI is often present in students with brain injury, especially when such damage occurs in the optic radiations, visual cortex, and other areas associated with visual processing (Schwartz, 2011). Other terms that are used or have been used to refer to this condition are neurological visual impairment, cerebral visual impairment, and brain-injury-related visual impairment (Ferrell, 2011).

CVI is a complex condition, as it refers to disruptions in visual processing in the brain, rather than in the structure of the eye. Children with CVI may exhibit all or a combination of the following visual characteristics: poor visual attention, restricted visual field attention, difficulty discriminating complex patterns or foreground from background, poor distance vision, poor depth perception, light gazing, attention to movement, looking away when reaching, color preference, prolonged fixation, and delayed visual responses (Ferrell, 2011; Roman et al., 2008). Many, but not all, children with CVI have additional disabilities that may affect their motor control, cognition, and overall development (Morse, 1999).

Although a diagnosis of CVI does not refer to the structure of the visual system, CVI can coexist with other ocular disorders. When no other ocular disorder can explain the child's apparent vision loss, CVI may be the cause. Overall, to best identify and diagnose CVI, a doctor's eye exam should show a lack of vision that cannot be explained by an ocular condition, past or current neurological problems or trauma, and the presence of the aforementioned visual and behavioral characteristics (Roman et al., 2008; Roman-Lantzy, 2007).

Obtaining a standardized visual acuity to determine eligibility for services can be difficult with students with CVI, as their vision fluctuates and they frequently have additional disabilities. Field deficits are also common, including central field loss, random blind spots in the visual field, or loss of half of the visual field in each eye (hemianopsia) (Schwartz, 2010). Furthermore, when the testing environment is not familiar (as when conducted in the office of an eye medical doctor), the visual performance of students may be unreliable. Other methods to obtain a visual acuity may include electrophysiological imaging, such as visual evoked potential acuities, preferential looking (i.e. Teller Cards), or functional exams that record the smallest size of a seen object and, based on that performance, determine an equivalent acuity (Roman et al., 2008).

Although CVI refers to the neurological processes of the visual system, it is critical to investigate the ocular structures and pathways to be sure that no other issues are present and that correction has been made when possible. The presence of a muscle imbalance (such as nystagmus), strabismus, or other refractive errors in addition to CVI can significantly change the child's visual abilities and responses. Therefore, if lenses or other corrections may help, they should be provided before further assessment and intervention take place (Hyvärinen, 2001). Lens correction is especially important for infants, as corrective lenses may help their under-developed visual system. Many students with multiple impairments and CVI may never develop normal accommodation and convergence skills (ability to focus on an object at different distances and shift that focus from near and far distances) and develop strabismus (Hyvärinen, 2001).

Students with CVI are served in a variety of educational settings and require services provided by a teacher of students with visual impairments (TVI). As with all students with a diagnosed visual impairment, a complete functional vision assessment should be conducted. Within this assessment, the student's visual behaviors and CVI characteristics should be reported. CVI and its characteristics should be considered and treated as a spectrum of severity (Roman-Lantzy, 2007). An important educational consideration for students with CVI is the environment and the child's visual performance in various environments should be recorded as part of the functional vision assessment. Environmental challenges that are commonly considered are noise level, visual complexity, and familiarity (of people and materials).

Once a functional vision assessment (FVA) has been completed and the student's performance related to each of the common visual characteristics of CVI has been considered (some children may not exhibit issues with all characteristics), a learning media assessment (LMA) should be conducted. Many students with CVI are nonverbal and have cognitive deficits; these traits, combined with fluctuating visual abilities, challenge TVIs to identify the appropriate media in which to provide educational materials. Only after both the FVA and the LMA are completed, however, can appropriate educational programming occur and effective adaptations be recommended (Roman-Lantzy, 2007).

Due to the increased plasticity of the brain and developmental window of the visual cortex in infancy, early intervention can increase visual functioning of very young children with CVI with permanent results (Roman-Lantzy, 2007). However, CVI is often not diagnosed until 6 months of age (Ferrell, 2011), making this window of opportunity shorter. Older children with CVI are still able to increase their use of vision, though it may be at a slower rate (Roman-Lantzy, 2007). Because visual skills associated with CVI are often learned at a slower rate, practice and repetition are important to strengthen the visual processing pathways in the brain. Starting with simple, high-contrast materials in a quiet environment gives the child time to concentrate and respond. As the activity is repeated, the student becomes more familiar with the materials and visual tasks that are required, thus becoming more successful. With the refinement of the student's visual processing skills within that particular activity or routine, more complex materials may be added. For example, when working on visual fixation, a teacher or parent may start with simply holding a bright, single-colored toy (i.e. a pompom, ball, or Elmo) within 6 inches of the student's face. After repeated exposure (maybe several minutes, trials, days, or even months), it may take less time for the child to fixate on the toy; she may be able to fixate longer, and (if able) may even reach for the toy. As responses become more mature, complexity can be added; perhaps two toys can be presented, the environment changed, the distance of presentation increased, or a different color of the same toy introduced. Further refinement of visual processing skills is likely to occur as more materials are introduced and become familiar to the student. This kind of discrete trial training should always be accompanied by opportunities for the student to practice the skill within naturally occurring activities.

In order to implement activities, the TVI must be responsible for communicating the visual and environmental adaptations that may be needed to optimize a student's functional vision. In conjunction with other team members, the TVI must also determine appropriate interventions and implement them within the natural environment and within functional contexts and routines. Since students with CVI require practice throughout the day, the TVI must also educate and train other team members and parents in appropriate strategies, activities, and adaptations. As the student's visual processing skills change and evolve, the TVI must provide ongoing assessment and programming changes to continually meet the needs of the child (Roman et al., 2008). Therefore, the TVI needs time to continually assess the student and collaborate with the team.

The population of students diagnosed with CVI is increasing, making it the most frequent cause of visual impairment in children in the United States (Ferrell, 2011). There are several theoretical perspectives that have been developed over the years, but there is not yet a worldwide consensus as to how to define CVI and whether CVI should include other perceptual and cognitive processing issues (Hyvärinen, 2001; Roman et al., 2008). As TVIs attempt to meet the complex needs of students with this unique visual condition, there is an increased need for valid and research-based practices (Roman et al., 2008). It is important for TVIs to stay current of emerging best practices as described in the literature in order to provide meaningful and effective interventions.

KITTY (CATHERINE) GREELEY-BENNETT
Florida State University
Fourth edition

COR TRIATRIUM

Cor triatrium is a birth defect in which the left atrium of the heart is doubled. The atrium is formed with a perforated membrane separating the two chambers. Severity of this condition is dependent on the degree of separation and the presence or absence of a shunt between the two sections (Dauphin et al., 1998).

Cor triatrium is often diagnosed in early childhood by echocardiography, but it has also been detected in adults who have been asymptomatic. It is a congenital heart defect, defined as being present at birth. About .8% of all children are born with some kind of heart defect, although the seriousness of the defect varies greatly.

Characteristics

1. Left atrium of the heart divided by perforated membrane
2. Infants sometimes born with a blue color
3. Difficulty breathing and exercising

Occasionally, children born with congenital heart defects have impaired learning. Cor triatrium is a serious defect, but it is potentially repairable. Children who have undergone corrective surgery may need to be restricted in some of their activities, especially in recess and physical education. Additionally, they may be subject to missing abnormal amounts of school due to monitoring of the heart.

REFERENCE

Dauphin, C., Lusson, J. R., Motreff, P., Lorillard, R., Justin E. P., Briand, F., ... Cassagnes, J. (1998). Left intra-atrial membrane without pulmonary vein obstruction: Benign condition of progressive evolution? Apropos of 7 cases. *Archives des Maladies du Coeur et des Vaisseaux*, *91*, 615–621.

ALLISON KATZ
Rutgers University

COSTA RICA, SPECIAL EDUCATION IN

Costa Rica has the strongest public education system in Central America. The 1869 constitution mandated a free, obligatory, and state-supported educational system, making Costa Rica one of the first countries in the world to pass such legislation (Biesanz, Biesanz, & Biesanz, 1999; Creedman, 1991). Approximately 23% of the national budget is dedicated to education (UNESCO, 2011) and schools can be found even in the most isolated regions of the country. As a result, Costa Rica's literacy rate of 96% is one of the highest in Latin America and high school graduation rates are effectively equal for girls and boys (UNESCO, 2011).

Costa Rica is equally progressive in educating children with disabilities. Special education services were first established in 1940 when the Fernando Centeno Güell School was created near the capital city of San José (Centeno, 1941). The founding of the school, which initially provided services for students with intellectual disabilities, was a significant educational milestone for the country (Dengo Obregón, 2000). Costa Rica passed one of the first pieces of special education legislation in the world in 1957, the Fundamental Law of Education. The Fundamental Law of Education established the constitutional right of students with disabilities to receive a special education, including special didactic techniques and materials, and the right of parents to receive information on assisting their child with special educational needs. Today in Costa Rica, special education services are functioning throughout the country under the direction of the Department of Special Education within a nationally centralized Ministry of Public Education.

Special education in Costa Rica has become increasingly inclusive. Through the 1960s, students with disabilities in Costa Rica typically received instruction at one of 20 segregated special education campuses (Bulgarelli, 1971). Beginning in the early 1970s, however, special education professionals trained in Europe and the U.S. embraced inclusionary theory and pedagogy that fundamentally changed special education service delivery (Meléndez, 2000). The Ministry of Education began to place special education classrooms on regular education campuses in 1974 when the need for special education was increasing at a rate disproportionate to what services were available at the time (Meléndez, 2000). By 1984, 118 special education classrooms were in existence on general education campuses in Costa Rica (Stough, 1990). The Ministry of Education rapidly expanded the number of resource rooms during the 1980s by hiring teachers to instruct recargo, or an extra shift, each day (Stough & Aguirre-Roy, 1997). Special education students, especially those with learning disabilities, attended school for additional instructional hours in the afternoon and were taught by trained recargo teachers. By 1988, the recargo classroom was the predominant special education service delivery model with over 600 elementary classrooms staffed across the country.

Costa Rica changed from a diagnostic model for determining eligibility for services to a needs-based model in 1990. This shift in philosophical approach emphasized the type of instructional modifications required by a student rather than using categorical diagnoses to drive educational diagnosis and service delivery (Stough, 2003). The Ministry of Public Education now uses three categories to describe modifications required by students: (1) modifications of access, which include adaptations such as ramps, sign language, or braille required to access the general education system; (2) nonsignificant modifications, which involve modifications to didactic methods such as calculators or assistive devices that do not affect the level of academic expectation; and (3) significant modifications, which require changes in objectives, methodology, or evaluation that clearly differentiate students in terms of expectations (Ministerio de Educación Pública, 2010a). During the 2009 school year, of the 170,859 students enrolled in Costa Rica's public education system, 1.7% (11,178) received an accommodation of access, 12.0% (113,027) received non-significant modifications, while 1.6% (12,237) received some type of significant instructional modification (Ministerio de Educación Pública, 2010a). The Ministry of Education has divided Costa Rica into 23 educational service regions, each of which is served by a Regional Special Education Advisor and a Regional Itinerant Team. Eligibility for special education services is determined through local Educational Assistance Committees, in coordination with Regional Special Education Advisor and Regional Itinerate Team (Stough, 2003).

Costa Rica has a diverse educational service system that delivers special education through teaching hospitals, home schooling, special education centers, integrated classrooms, resource rooms, instructional aides, consulting teachers, and co-teaching (Meléndez, 2005). Children with disabilities are eligible to receive educational services beginning at birth and these services continue through age 18, which is the age at which most Costa Ricans finish high school. Early stimulation classes are provided for children who have disabilities or were born at risk in special education centers, preschools, and within nutrition and education centers overseen by the Ministry of Health in most large towns. Students with mild disabilities usually receive services in a general education classroom but sometimes receive support from a special education assistant. Students with significant disabilities usually receive services in segregated special education classrooms located in general public education schools or in special education centers (Ministerio de Educación Pública, 2010). At the high school level, special education students usually attend a vocational, rather than academic, high school. Students who attend academic high schools are eligible to receive services through modifications or through the support of teaching assistants. In rural areas, such as in the province of Guanacaste, itinerant teachers are hired to travel intermittently to schools that have small numbers of students with special needs. Special education students may also receive support services from a physical therapist, language therapist, occupational therapist, psychologist, or orientation and mobility specialist, among others. Students older than 18 can enroll in centers for adults with disabilities, attend special courses offered by the National Learning Institute or the Helen Keller Institute, or attend institutions of higher education with curricular modifications or technical assistance (Meléndez, 2005).

The Ministry of Education embraced the Schools for All movement in the early 1990s, which was based on the principles of normalization, integration, and self-advocacy, and ratified during the 1992 World Conference on Special Education as part of the Salamanca Agreement (Marin Arias, 2000). Costa Rica passed further progressive legislation for individuals with disabilities in 1996 through the Equal Opportunity Law 7600 for Persons with Disabilities, which guaranteed equal rights for individuals with disabilities across all sectors of public life. Special education was redefined in this law as "the combination of assistance and services at the disposal of students with special education needs, whether they be temporary or permanent" (Sección VI, Artículo 27). The Equal Opportunity Law also strongly advised that students with disabilities be integrated into regular education classrooms that were "preferentially in the educational center closest to their home" (Capítulo I, Artículo 18). The Ministry of Public Education, together with the National Board on Rehabilitation and Special Education, implements the Equal Opportunity Law and Law 8661, a ratification of the International Convention of the Rights of People with Disabilities of 2007 (Asamblea Legislativa de Costa Rica, 2007).

Recent educational initiatives following the passing of this legislation have exponentially increased movement toward a more inclusive educational system. The National Resource Center for Inclusive Education was established in 2002 by the Ministry of Education with the mission of making inclusive education a reality in Costa Rica. The Center supports inclusive training and pedagogy for teachers and other personnel who educate students with disabilities. In 2007, the Universidad Estatal a Distancia established an inclusive education project in three primary education schools following the guidelines of the Index of Inclusion (Booth and Ainscow, 2000). This model has been subsequently replicated by the National Commission on Inclusive Education of the Ministry of Public Education in nine primary and secondary schools in the province of Heredia.

Special education is offered as a major in three of the five public universities and as a program at 12 private universities, which has increased both the quality and the quantity of professionals in the field (CONARE, 2011). The Equal Opportunity Law (1996) stipulated that teachers who instruct students with disabilities should receive special training; however, requirements for teacher certification vary and inclusive pedagogy is not evenly addressed in all special education teacher training programs. Special education programs are less common in rural areas of the country and the shortage of trained special education professionals has remained an ongoing challenge for Costa Rica (Stough, 2002).

Special education in Costa Rica confronts many challenges shared by other developing countries: limited material resources, geographic isolation of segments of the population, and few teacher training programs. However, for over 70 years Costa Rica has supported undeniably progressive legislation that has established the rights of individuals with disabilities to be educated, to work, and to receive public health services. Costa Rica has also historically allocated over 20% of its national budget to education. Special education services are consequently widely available and integrated into the very fabric of the Costa Rican educational system.

REFERENCES

Asamblea Legislativa de Costa Rica [Legislative Assembly of Costa Rica]. (2007). Ley 8661 de aprobación y ratificación de la Convención Internacional de los Derechos de las Personas con Discapacidad y Protocolo de Acción [Law 8661 of Endorsement and Ratification of the International Convention on the Rights of Persons with Disabilities and a Protocol for Action]. San José: Imprenta Nacional.

Biesanz, M. H., Biesanz, R., and Biesanz, K. Z. (1999). *The Ticos*. Boulder, CO: Lynne Rienner.

Booth, A., & Ainscow, M. (2000). *Index for inclusion*. Santiago, Chile: OREALC/UNESCO.

Bulgarelli, O. A. (Ed.). (1971). *El desarrollo nacional en 150 años de vida independiente* [National development in 150 years of independent life]. San José, Costa Rica: Publicaciones de la Universidad de Costa Rica.

Centeno, F. (1941). *La Escuela de Enseñanza Especial: Su origen, finalidad, organización y funcionamiento*. Costa Rica: Secretaría de Educación Nacional.

CONARE (2011). *Directorio en línea de carreras*. Retrieved from http://www.coneau.edu.ar/riaces/costarica.html

Creedman, T. S. (1991). *Historical dictionary of Costa Rica* (2nd ed.). Metuchen, NJ: Scarecrow Press.

Dengo Obregón, M. E. (2000). Educación Costarricense [Costa Rican education], San José, Costa Rica: Editorial Universidad Estatal a Distancia.

Ley de Igualdad de Oportunidades para las Personas con Discapacidad [Equal Opportunity Law for Persons With Disabilities]. (1996).

Ley Fundamental de Educación de Costa Rica, Capítulo IV, Artículos 27, 28 y 29 [Costa Rican Fundamental Law of Education, Chapter IV, Articles 27, 28, and 29]. (1957).

Marin Arias, M. G. (2000). *Atención del niño excepcional* [Treatment of the exceptional child]. San José, Costa Rica: Editorial Universidad Estatal a Distancia.

Meléndez, L. (2000). Aspectos históricos de la atención a las personas con necesidades educativas especiales en Costa Rica y el mundo [Historical aspects of the attention of persons with special education needs in Costa Rica and the world]. In G. Aguilar Montoya, F. Arias Núñez, C. Conejo Solera, M. Masís Muñoz, G. Monge Chavarría, O. Mora Moreira,...B. Páez Vargas (Eds.), *Módulo de inducción para funcionarios de equipos itinerantes regionales de educación especial* [Training manual for members of regional itinerate special education teams]. San José, Costa Rica: Ministry of Public Education.

Meléndez, L. (2005). *La Educación Especial en Costa Rica: Fundamentos y evolución* [Special education in Costa Rica: Fundamentals and development]. Costa Rica: EUNED.

Ministerio de Educación Pública. (2010). *Boletín 05-10: Adecuaciones curriculares en educación tradicional 2009* [Curricular modifications in traditional education, 2009]. Costa Rica: MEP.

Ministerio de Educación Pública. (2010). *Boletín 11-10: Necesidades educativas especiales en centros que brindan educación tradicional* [Special education needs in traditional education centers]. Costa Rica: MEP.

Ministerio de Educación Pública. (2011). *Matrícula inicial en Educación Especial* [Initial enrollment in special education]. Retrieved from educacion.gob.ec/inscripcion-y-matriculacion-educacion

Stough, L. M. (1990). *Special education and teacher training in the third world: Costa Rican and Honduran rural education programs*. Paper presented at the annual meeting of the Southwest Educational Research Association, Austin, TX.

Stough, L. M. (2002). Teaching special education in Costa Rica. *Teaching Exceptional Children, 34*(5), 34–39.

Stough, L. M. (2003). Special education and severe disabilities in Costa Rica: Developing inclusion in a developing country. *Research and Practice for Persons with Severe Disabilities, 28*(1), 7–15.

Stough, L. M., & Aguirre-Roy, A. R. (1997). Learning disabilities in Costa Rica: Challenges for "an army of teachers." *Journal of Learning Disabilities, 30*(5), 566–571.

United Nations Educational, Scientific, and Cultural Organization [UNESCO] Institute for Statistics. (2011). *World development indicator*. Retrieved from http://data.worldbank.org/indicator/SE.XPD.TOTL.GB.ZS

Laura M. Stough
Texas A&M University

COSTELLO SYNDROME

Costello syndrome is an extremely rare genetic disorder marked by growth delay, excessive skin, tumor growth, and mild mental retardation. There have been approximately 150 cases reported to date of Costello syndrome, and over 30 published cases. J. M. Costello first reported this syndrome and described it in 1977 (Costello, 1977, 1996). Der Kaloustian, Moroz, McIntosh, Watters, and Blaichman (1991) identified additional children with the disorder and proposed that it be called Costello syndrome.

Children with Costello syndrome tend to be of average birthweight but then experience a postnatal growth deficiency; as a result, they tend to be of very short stature. They frequently develop benign tumors in their noses or mouths. Infants may also vomit frequently and have difficulty with being fed (Kerr et al., 1998).

The distinctive facial and body appearance associated with Costello syndrome includes a large head, a coarse face, thick lips and ears, a short neck, curly hair, a depressed bridge of the nose, thick palms and soles, and excessive skin (Martin & Jones, 1993). Costello syndrome is a genetic disorder present from birth that has been found in approximately 150 individuals (see http://www.costellokids.org.uk). Most cases are isolated cases in families, with no other family members having the disorder. Costello Syndrome is similar to both Noonan syndrome and cardiofaciocutaneous syndrome. Although most published reports focus on children with Costello syndrome, there have been published studies of adults (van Eeghen, van Gelderen, & Hennekam, 1999).

Characteristics

1. Growth delay
2. Benign tumor growth
3. Excess skin around neck and palms
4. Possible mental retardation

Children suffering from Costello syndrome are also likely to have mental retardation, and the same special education services that would be needed for mental retardation would be needed for children with Costello syndrome. In addition, children may need possible assistance for pain management or depression resulting from a serious illness.

Future research is continually being conducted on genetic disorders such as Costello syndrome; one broad example is the Human Genome Project.

REFERENCES

Costello, J. M. (1977). A new syndrome: Mental subnormality and nasal papillomata. *Australian Paediatric Journal, 13*, 114–118.

Costello, J. M. (1996). Costello syndrome: Update on the original cases and commentary. *American Journal of Medical Genetics, 62*, 199–201.

Der Kaloustian, V. M., Moroz, B., McIntosh, N., Watters, A. K., & Blaichman, S. (1991). Costello syndrome. *American Journal of Medical Genetics, 41*, 69–73.

Kerr, B., Eden, O. B., Dandamudi, R., Shannon, N., Quarrell, O., Emmerson, A.,...Donnai, D. (1998). Costello syndrome: Two cases with embryonal rhabdomyosarcoma. *American Journal of Medical Genetics, 35*, 1036–1039.

Martin, R. A., & Jones, K. L. (1993). Faciocutaneous-skeletal syndrome is the Costello syndrome. *American Journal of Medical Genetics, 47,* 169.

van Eeghen, A. M., van Gelderen, I., & Hennekam, R. C. (1999). Costello syndrome: Report and review. *American Journal of Medical Genetics, 82,* 187–193.

JAMES C. KAUFMAN
Educational Testing Service Princeton, New Jersey

COUNCIL FOR EXCEPTIONAL CHILDREN

The Council for Exceptional Children (CEC) is the world's largest professional organization dedicated to the welfare of exceptional children. The CEC was founded in 1922 at Teachers' College, Columbia University. The organization is further divided into special interest groups, including 17 specialized divisions focusing on issues and legislation for specific disability categories.

CEC members include educators, parents, students, and others concerned with the education of children with disabilities and gifted and talented children and youth. The CEC's membership is dedicated to increasing educational opportunities for all exceptional children and youth and to improving conditions for the professionals who work with them. The CEC advocates for appropriate governmental policies, sets professional standards, provides continual professional development, advocates for newly and historically underserved individuals with exceptionalities, and helps professionals obtain conditions and resources necessary for effective professional practice.

CEC has been highly visible as an advocate for federal legislation and funding for the gifted and the disabled. The organization issues two respected periodicals, *Exceptional Children* and *Teaching Exceptional Children*. The former is more research and policy oriented, while the latter is geared more toward practitioners' needs. In addition, several hundred books, multimedia packages, bibliographies, and fact sheets are available from CEC. Access to nearly half a million references on children with disabilities and gifted children can be obtained from ERIC (Educational Resources Information Center) and CEC Information Services. Each year, a national convention sponsored by CEC attracts thousands of professionals, paraprofessionals, and parents. In the past few years, CEC has sponsored successful topical workshops devoted to areas such as microcomputer use in special education, black exceptional children, and early childhood special education. Periodic international conferences are also sponsored by CEC.

The CEC's founding in 1922 was predated by other organizations concerned with the disabled: Convention of American Instructors of the Deaf, 1850; American Association of Instructors of the Blind, 1853; Conference of Executives of American Schools for the Deaf, 1863; American Association on Mental Deficiency, 1876; American Association to Promote the Teaching of Speech to the Deaf, 1890; and National Education Association's Department of Special Education, 1897. The CEC was founded the same year that a related organization, the National Association for the Study and Education of Exceptional Children, was disbanded. Four years earlier, the National Education Association (NEA) discontinued its Department of Special Education.

Elizabeth E. Farrell, who had been active in NEA's special education activities earlier, other Teachers' College faculty, and advanced students in the 1922 summer session at Columbia, formed CEC at a meeting on August 10 in a downtown New York restaurant. The early years found an organization without a true central office, limited funds, and a heavy reliance on volunteers for its existence. Various internal and external problems nearly ended CEC in its first two decades.

A sense of the *whole child* developed among members since CEC's interests were broader than early groups with single-category interests (Council for Exceptional Children, 2012). After the 1930s depression, CEC began to stabilize with the nation. Reorganization of the council's internal structure and a better financial situation allowed for expansion of CEC's role and activities. Today, despite some decline in membership from its peak in the 1970s, CEC is respected as a leader and advocate in its field. It works cooperatively with other organizations to promote the education and welfare of all exceptional children and youth. The Council for Exceptional Children's headquarters are now located at 1920 Association Drive, Reston, VA 20191, and may be reached by phone at (703) 620-3660.

REFERENCE

Council for Exceptional Children. (2012). *About CEC*. Retrieved from http://www.cec.sped.org/AM/Template.cfm?Section=About_CEC

JOHN D. WILSON
Elwyn Institutes

COUNCIL FOR EXCEPTIONAL CHILDREN, COUNCIL FOR CHILDREN WITH BEHAVIORAL DISORDERS

The Council for Children with Behavioral Disorders (CCBD) is the division of the Council for Exceptional Children (CEC) that according to their website is dedicated "to supporting the professional development and enhancing the expertise of those who work on behalf of children with challenging behavior and their families. CCBD is committed to students who are identified as having emotional and behavioral disorders and those whose behavior puts them at risk for failure in school, home, and/or community. CCBD supports prevention of problem behavior and enhancement of social, emotional, and educational well-being of all children and youth." For over 50 years, the division has worked to promote evidence-based educational practices and services; advocated for children and youth with emotional and behavioral disorders; and disseminated research and policy information through journals, professional conferences, publications, websites, and social media outlets.

CCBD is open to all members of CEC. The division provides the peer-reviewed research journal, *Behavioral Disorders*, a practitioner-oriented peer-reviewed publication titled *Beyond Behavior*, and the *CCBD Newsletter* to all members. In addition, members can access position papers, policy recommendations, and online articles from the CCBD website. The CCBD Foundation has four interrelated priorities that include "Supporting classroom practitioners; Supporting professional development activities; Recognizing leaders in the field; and Providing scholarships for undergraduate and graduate study." CCBD sponsors an international conference and has strands and networking opportunities at the CEC Convention & Expo each year. For additional information on the programs and services that CCBD offers to its members, go to the division's website (http://ccbdning.ning.com/).

RANDALL L. DE PRY
Portland State University
Fourth edition

COUNCIL FOR EXCEPTIONAL CHILDREN, COUNCIL FOR EDUCATIONAL DIAGNOSTIC SERVICES

The Council for Educational Diagnostic Services (CEDS) is the division of the Council for Exceptional Children (CEC) that seeks to integrate diagnostic and prescriptive services across disciplines to support exceptional children, promote research on the use and application of psychoeducational assessments, and support research and practices that will directly benefit members in applied settings.

CEDS is open to all members of CEC. Members receive the peer-reviewed journal, *Assessment for Effective Intervention*. According to their website, the journal includes "articles that describe the relationship between assessment and instruction; introduce innovative assessment strategies; outline diagnostic procedures; analyze

relationships between existing instruments; and review assessment techniques, strategies, and instrumentation." In addition, CEDS publishes *Communiqué*, the division newsletter. CEDS also sponsors an annual conference for its members and others interested in educational assessment. Additional information on the services that CEDS provides to its members can be found on its website (http://www.ceds.us/).

RANDALL L. DE PRY
Portland State University
Fourth edition

COUNCIL FOR EXCEPTIONAL CHILDREN, DIVISION FOR COMMUNICATIVE DISABILITIES AND DEAFNESS

The Division for Communicative Disabilities and Deafness (DCDD) is one of 17 divisions of the Council for Exceptional Children (CEC). The primary mission of the Division for Communicative Disabilities and Deafness is to promote the welfare, development, and education of infants, toddlers, children, and youth with communicative disabilities or who are deaf or hard of hearing. In addition, DCDD seeks to promote growth in professionals and families as a means to better understand the development of communicative abilities and the prevention of communicative disabilities.

DCDD plans a large segment of the annual CEC Convention & Expo each year to provide professional development for its members and others who attend the convention. The annual meeting is held at the convention within a social gathering called the MemberFest. The division maintains a membership of at least 700 paid members who meet the membership qualifications established by CEC.

All members of the division must hold concurrent membership in the CEC. Although membership varies from year to year, the division maintains approximately 1,500 members. Membership in the division consists of regular and student members. Regular membership is open to professional personnel engaged in the education or provision of services for infants, toddlers, children, and youth with developmental communication needs or communication disorders and to other individuals interested in the purpose of the division. Student membership is available for preservice students and students continuing their education who are in full-time attendance during the academic year at a regionally accredited college or university. All members must pay annual dues to both the division and the CEC.

Officers of the division include president, president-elect, past president, secretary, financial officer, and chairs of six constituent committees. The president appoints other executive board members for 3-year terms, including chairs of the Knowledge and Skills committee and the Professional Development committee, and the newsletter editor. Ad-hoc committees are appointed for special topics and projects.

DCDD's Publication Board oversees its many publications. The past president chairs the Publication Board. *Communication Disorders Quarterly* (CDQ) is the division's journal, published by Pro-ED in Austin, Texas. Prior to 1999, the journal was called *Journal of Communication Disorders and Deafness* (JCCD). To review these articles go to JCCD's website (http://cdq.sagepub.com/search/results?fulltext=journal+of+communication+disorders+and+deafness&submit=yes&journal_set=spcdq&src=selected&andorexactfulltext=and&x=0&y=0.

The *DCDD New Times* is the division's newsletter, with copies available online on the DCDD website four times a year. The newsletter is distributed to the membership inside the journal, *Communication Disorders Quarterly*. The listserv is an interactive feature of the organization's website and enables members to exchange valuable information about communication disability, evidence-based assessment and intervention, and special education programs and services in all 50 states and Canada. DCDD has representation on the Council of Educators of the Deaf, National Joint Committee on Learning Disabilities, and the National Joint Committee for the Communication Needs of Persons with Severe Disabilities.

JUDY K. MONTGOMERY
Chapman University

COUNCIL FOR EXCEPTIONAL CHILDREN, DIVISION FOR CULTURALLY AND LINGUISTICALLY DIVERSE EXCEPTIONAL LEARNERS

The Division for Culturally and Linguistically Diverse Exceptional Learners (DDEL) is the division of the Council for Exceptional Children (CEC) that strives to "improve, through professional excellence and advocacy, the education and quality of life for individuals with exceptionalities from diverse racial, ethnic, cultural, and linguistic communities." According to the DDEL website, DDEL advocates for policies and procedures that support the needs of diverse learners; promotes collaboration across disciplines; disseminates research to members and other interested parties using a variety of methods; promotes the

recruitment and retention of personnel from diverse populations; provides technical assistance at the preservice and inservice levels; and supports the policies, procedures, and activities of CEC.

DDEL is open to all members of CEC. The division provides the peer-reviewed research journal, *Multiple Voices for Ethnically Diverse Exceptional Learners*, to all members. The editors actively seek scholarly work "that explicitly addresses the interrelationships between culture, language, and exceptionality in educational systems, policy, research, and/or practice." DDEL also publishes the *DDEL Newsletter*, which highlights recent developments in the field, training opportunities, information on political action, and information on conferences for members. DDEL sponsors sessions for members at the annual CEC Convention & Expo and provides ongoing networking opportunities at the conference. For additional information on DDEL, go to its website (http://www.ddelcec.org/).

RANDALL L. DE PRY
Portland State University
Fourth edition

COUNCIL FOR EXCEPTIONAL CHILDREN, DIVISION FOR EARLY CHILDHOOD

The Division for Early Childhood (DEC) is one of 17 divisions of the Council for Exceptional Children (CEC), the largest international professional organization dedicated to improving educational outcomes for individuals with exceptionalities, students with disabilities, and/or the gifted. DEC is especially for individuals who work with or on behalf of children with special needs and their families. Founded in 1973, the division is dedicated to promoting policies and practices that support families and enhance the optimal development of children from birth to age 8. Children with special needs include those who have disabilities, developmental delays, are gifted/talented, or are at risk of future developmental problems.

DEC is committed to promoting parent–professional collaboration in all facets of planning, designing, and implementing early childhood intervention services and is devoted to advocating for policy, planning, and best practice in prevention and intervention. DEC supports full access for young children with special needs and their families to natural settings and service delivery options, and respect for family values, diverse cultural and linguistic backgrounds, and family circumstance, and supports those who work with or on behalf of infants and young children with special needs and their families.

DEC provides specific services to its members through collaboration and communication among organizations, practitioners, and family members; innovations in research and the development of new knowledge; dissemination and use of information about research, resources, best practices, and current issues; and professional development through an array of activities and strategies. More information can be obtained by visiting DEC's website (http://www.dec-sped.org/).

BETH ROUS
University of Kentucky

COUNCIL FOR EXCEPTIONAL CHILDREN, DIVISION FOR LEARNING DISABILITIES

The Division for Learning Disabilities (DLD) is the division of the Council for Exceptional Children (CEC) that according to their website seeks to "To promote the education and general welfare of persons with learning disabilities; to provide a forum for discussion of issues facing the field of learning disabilities; to encourage interaction among the many disciplinary groups whose research and service efforts affect persons with learning disabilities; to foster research regarding the varied disabilities subsumed in the term 'learning disabilities' and promote dissemination of research findings; to advocate exemplary professional training practices to insure the highest quality of services in the field of learning disabilities; and to promote exemplary diagnostic and teaching practices in a context of tolerance for new and divergent ideas."

DLD is open to all members of CEC. The division publishes the peer-reviewed journal, *Learning Disabilities Research & Practice*. In addition, members receive *Current Practice Alerts* that provide a synopsis of evidence-based instructional practices. The alerts are co-sponsored by DLD and the CEC Division for Research. Members also receive *New Times for DLD*, the division's newsletter. The Teaching LD website provides public and member-only resources, including current research, teacher guides, lesson plans that can be downloaded, listings of professional organizations and technical assistance centers, and general information about learning disabilities. DLD also sponsors a conference titled "Bridging the Gap between Research and Practice" for educators and researchers on an annual basis. Additional information on DLD can be found at the Teaching LD website (http://teachingld.org/).

RANDALL L. DE PRY
Portland State University
Fourth edition

COUNCIL FOR EXCEPTIONAL CHILDREN, DIVISION FOR PHYSICAL, HEALTH, AND MULTIPLE DISABILITIES

The Division for Physical, Health, and Multiple Disabilities (DPHMD), formerly the Division for Physical and Health Disabilities, is the division of the Council for Exceptional Children (CEC) that according to their website "advocates for quality education for all individuals with physical disabilities, multiple disabilities, and special health care needs served in schools, hospitals, or home settings." DPHMD promotes the development of resources and programs, disseminates research and effective practices, provides technical assistance, and advocates for policies and legislation that support persons with physical, health, and multiple disabilities.

DPHMD is open to all members of CEC. The division provides the peer-reviewed research journal, *Physical Disabilities, Education and Related Services*, to all members. In addition, members receive the *DPHMD Newsletter*, which highlights current division information and news, including information on conferences and political action. The division also sponsors sessions and activities for members at the annual CEC Convention & Expo. Additional information on DPHMD can be found at its website (http://web.utk.edu/~dphmd/).

RANDALL L. DE PRY
Portland State University
Fourth edition

COUNCIL FOR EXCEPTIONAL CHILDREN, DIVISION FOR RESEARCH

The Division for Research (CEC-DR) is the division of the Council for Exceptional Children (CEC) that according to their official website is "devoted to the advancement of research related to the education of individuals with disabilities and/or who are gifted. The goals of CEC-DR include the promotion of equal partnership with practitioners in designing, conducting and interpreting research in special education." The division seeks to advance the use of evidence-based strategies as it relates to programs and practices for children and youth with disabilities and those who are gifted through special education research.

CEC-DR is open to all members of CEC. Members of CEC-DR receive the peer-reviewed *Journal of Special Education* and *Focus on Research*, the division newsletter. These publications provide research and important information for members on projects, funding, and current issues facing the field. CEC-DR also sponsors two major awards: the Early Career Award and the

Kauffman-Hallahan Distinguished Researcher Award. The division website includes position papers, article reprints, practice alerts, and other publications of interest to members, as well as additional information on CEC-DR (http://cecdr.org/).

RANDALL L. DE PRY
Portland State University
Fourth edition

COUNCIL FOR EXCEPTIONAL CHILDREN, DIVISION OF INTERNATIONAL SPECIAL EDUCATION AND SERVICES

In June 1978, the Council for Exceptional Children held the first World Congress on Future Special Education in Stirling, Scotland (Fink, 1978). Following that meeting, in order to preserve the momentum created by this Congress, some university faculty members organized a special-interest group within the CEC's Teacher Education Division. This group was concerned primarily with the international aspects of delivery of special education services to children with disabilities. Since the scope of interest went beyond teacher education, a separate division of the CEC, known as the Division of International Special Education and Services (DISES), was formed in 1990 with the mission of assisting in the improvement of the quality of special education and services to individuals with disabilities throughout the world.

With the breakup of the USSR and the movement away from communism in the former Soviet republics, DISES established relations with several organizations serving children with disabilities, especially in St. Petersburg and Moscow, Russia; Latvia; Lithuania; and Kazakhstan. In 1993, working with Project Concern International, DISES identified special educators to assist adolescents who had been institutionalized in Romania to function independently. Also during 1993, DISES served as the international portion of a COSMOS Corporation project to identify trends in the delivery of special education services, and to anticipate how educational technology could be used effectively for students with disabilities throughout the world. In 1995, DISES, working with the Citizen Ambassador Program of People to People International, led a special education delegation visiting programs in China.

DISES has also been active in disseminating information about special education programs worldwide through its newsletter and special publications. Four monographs have been published, and a professional journal, *The Journal of International Special Needs Education* (*JISNE*), began publication in 1998. The editors of the DISES newsletter are Bob Henderson of the University of Illinois (bob-h@uiuc.edu), Lisa Dieker of the University of Wisconsin, Milwaukee (dieker@csd.uwm.edu), and Yash Bhagwanj (bhagwanj@students.uiuc.edu); and the editor of *JISNE* is Robert Michael (michaelr@npvm.newpaltz.edu).

Another major activity of DISES has been the organization of the Special Education World Congress 2000 (SEWC, 2000), held in Vancouver, British Columbia, during April 2–5, 2000. Building on previous conferences, SEWC 2000 involves partnerships with the other CEC divisions; professional organizations dealing with various disabilities, such as the American Association on Mental Retardation and the American Foundation for the Blind; international groups such as UNESCO, the World Health Organization, the International Association of Special Education, and Rehabilitation International; and special education offices in various Ministries of Education. A unique feature of SEWC 2000 has been the use of the Internet to conduct "cyber-seminars," in which participants read and commented on professional papers that were published on the SEWC 2000 website (http://cecdr.org/).

REFERENCE

Fink, A. H. (1978). *International perspectives on future special education*. Reston, VA: Council for Exceptional Children.

STAFF

COUNCIL FOR EXCEPTIONAL CHILDREN, DIVISION ON AUTISM AND DEVELOPMENTAL DISABILITIES (DADD)

The Division on Autism and Developmental Disabilities (DADD), Council for Exceptional Children (CEC), is dedicated to enhancing the quality of life for children and youth with autism and intellectual and developmental disabilities. DADD, previously known as the Division on Developmental Disabilities (DDD), is committed to working toward positive life outcomes and continuing education of professionals in the field. Key areas such as academic learning, behavior management, independent living, and vocational preparation are a focus of the division. Training materials on educational and proactive practices that are published by DADD maximize the knowledge base of special education professionals and DADD members working with children diagnosed with autism and intellectual disabilities.

DADD is open to all CEC members, who also have access to annual conference sessions related directly to educating students with autism and intellectual disabilities. Biannual or annual conferences held by DADD focus on targeting specific areas of need for students with autism and developmental delays, in addition to the annual CEC convention. *Education and Training in Autism and Developmental Disabilities*, a publication of DADD, is a peer-reviewed journal that provides members with solid, research-based evidence for educating and providing effective practices for students with autism and intellectual and developmental disabilities. Other publications include a newsletter that appears in the journal *Focus on Autism and Other Development Disabilities*. A critical-issues committee through DADD creates scholarly works on topics of high interest to members. Active committees on Diversity, Professional Standards, and Critical Issues continue to represent topics of concern for DADD members. An archive has been created on the website to locate past articles of interest and a video, book, and monograph series is available for members in which access to evidence-based strategies and implementation ideas would be beneficial. Additional information on DADD can be found at http://daddcec.org/ and http://www.cec.sped.org/.

RANDALL L. DE PRY
University of Colorado at Colorado Springs
Third edition

HEATHER S. DAVIS
Texas A&M University
Fourth edition

COUNCIL FOR EXCEPTIONAL CHILDREN, DIVISION ON CAREER DEVELOPMENT AND TRANSITION

The Division on Career Development and Transition (DCDT) is the division of the Council for Exceptional Children (CEC) that according to their website seeks to "promote national and international efforts to improve the quality of and access to career/vocational and transition services, increase participation of education in career development and transition goals and to influence policies affecting career development and transition services for persons with disabilities."

DCDT is open to all members of CEC. The division provides the peer-reviewed research journal, *Career Development of Exceptional Individuals*, to all members. In addition, the division publishes the *DCDT Network* newsletter three times per year. The DCDT website offers a wide variety of resources, including division news, leadership information, transition resources from a variety of state and national sources, and professional development

opportunities. DCDT also hosts an annual conference that serves as a venue for researchers and practitioners alike to present their current research and promising practices to members and others interested in career development and transition. Additional information on DCDT is available at its website (http://www.dcdt.org/).

RANDALL L. DE PRY
Portland State University
Fourth edition

COUNCIL FOR EXCEPTIONAL CHILDREN, DIVISION ON VISUAL IMPAIRMENTS

The Division on Visual Impairments (DVI) is the division of the Council for Exceptional Children (CEC) that advocates for "effective policies, practices, and services that address the unique educational needs of children and youth who have visual impairments, including those with additional exceptionalities." The division engages in a wide range of activities, including advocating for federal, state, and local policies that support the education of children and youth with visual impairments; curriculum and resource development; connecting research to practice at the pre-service and inservice levels; and career and transition planning.

DVI is open to all CEC members. Members receive the *DVI Quarterly* newsletter four times per year as part of their membership. In addition, members have access to position papers that address issues in the areas of professional practice, curriculum development, and adaptations. Additional information on DVI can be found at its website (http://www.cecdvi.org/).

RANDALL L. DE PRY
Portland State University
Fourth edition

COUNCIL FOR EXCEPTIONAL CHILDREN, PIONEERS DIVISION

The Council for Exceptional Children's Pioneers Division (CEC-PD) is available to CEC members who have maintained 20 or more years of membership in the organization. Membership is also open to life members, retired members, and past presidents of CEC. According to the division website, the goals for CEC-PD are focused on "serving the general community by increasing awareness of the educational needs of children with disabilities and/or who are gifted and the services available to them; serving the professional community by organizing volunteers willing to donate time, effort, and expertise to activities that promote the education and welfare of exceptional children; supporting the activities, policies, and procedures of CEC and other CEC divisions."

For over 4 years, CEC-PD has provided an innovative mentoring program for student members of CEC at the preservice, student teaching, graduate program, and transition phases of their membership. Over 100 students have benefited from this program. CEC-PD also has six subdivisions in the United States and one in Canada. Subdivisions work on local activities that align with the mission of CEC-PD. Members of CEC-PD receive the *Pioneers Press* newsletter, which is published three times per year. In addition, the division sponsors sessions, activities, and a dinner at the annual CEC Convention & Expo. For additional information on the Pioneers Division of CEC, go to its website (http://tedcec.org/.

RANDALL L. DE PRY
Portland State University
Fourth edition

COUNCIL FOR EXCEPTIONAL CHILDREN, TEACHER EDUCATION DIVISION

The Teacher Education Division (TED) is the division of the Council for Exceptional Children (CEC) that according to their website "is a diverse community of professionals who lead and support teacher education on behalf of students with exceptional needs and their families. We accomplish this through research, professional and leadership development, and advocacy." The division's membership is made up of persons who are interested in research and effective practices related to special education teacher preparation, including the ongoing professional development of those who train and support teachers at the preservice and inservice levels.

TED is open to all CEC members. Members of TED receive the peer-reviewed journal, *Teacher Education and Special Education*, and the *TED Newsletter*. These publications provide members with information on research, practice, and general information on current initiatives, division news, and conferences. The division holds an annual conference where teacher educators, researchers, and other interested professionals meet to discuss issues such as teacher preparation, research, technology, and

service delivery. Additional information on TED can be found at its website (http://tedcec.org/).

RANDALL L. DE PRY
Portland State University
Fourth edition

COUNCIL FOR EXCEPTIONAL CHILDREN, TECHNOLOGY AND MEDIA DIVISION

The Technology and Media Division (TAM) is the division of the Council for Exceptional Children (CEC) that according to their website seeks to support "educational participation and improved results for individuals with disabilities and diverse learning needs through the selection, acquisition, and use of technology. The secondary purpose is to provide services to members and other units of CEC, to federal, state, and local education agencies, and to business and industry regarding the current and future uses of technology and media with individuals with exceptionalities."

TAM is open to all CEC members. Members of TAM receive the peer-reviewed journal, *The Journal of Special Education Technology* (*JSET*), the *TAM Connector*, and *Technology in Action*. These publications provide members with current research, preferred practices, legislative updates, information on advocacy, and division information. *JSET* holds the distinction of being the top publisher of research related to assistive technology. The division holds an annual conference for its members and other interested professionals. Conference presentations focus on research and practical applications of assistive technology across disciplines for supporting persons with exceptional learning needs. Additional information about TAM can be found at its website (http://www.tamcec.org/).

RANDALL L. DE PRY
Portland State University
Fourth edition

COUNCIL FOR LEARNING DISABILITIES

In 1968, educators formed the Division for Children with Learning Disabilities (DCLD) within the Council for Exceptional Children (CEC; Hallahan, Kauffman, & Lloyd, 1985). Both groups believed that without a name to identify a group of children who did not fit into any other handicapping condition, there would be difficulty in obtaining needed funds for special services.

During the early 1980s there emerged the realization that not only did children have learning disabilities but so did adults. Consequently, the Division for Children with Learning Disabilities became the Council for Learning Disabilities (CLD). Besides this change of name, CLD changed its affiliation as it seceded from the Council for Exceptional Children (Lerner, 1985). The majority of CLD's membership voted to become a separate and independent organization.

Conferences and newsletters sponsored by CLD provide a valuable means of sharing information and serve as a stimulus for research, program development, and advocacy. In addition, CLD formed a strong national lobbying group to promote legislative recognition of learning disabilities.

REFERENCES

Hallahan, D. P., Kauffman, J. M., & Lloyd, J. W. (1985). *Introduction to learning disabilities*. Englewood Cliffs, NJ: Prentice Hall.

Learner, J. W. (1985). *Learning disabilities*. Dallas, TX: Houghton Mifflin.

Joseph M. Russo
Hunter College,
City University of New York

COUNCIL OF ADMINISTRATORS OF SPECIAL EDUCATION

The Council of Administrators of Special Education (CASE) was founded in 1952 as a division of the Council for Exceptional Children (CEC). The CASE membership of 5,200 includes administrators, directors, supervisors, and coordinators of local private and public special education programs, schools, or classes serving children and youth with special needs. There are also a number of members who are state department personnel as well as those who are university faculty engaged in the preparation of special education administrators. The purpose of CASE is to promote professional leadership, to provide opportunity for the study of problems common to its members, and to provide information for developing improved services to exceptional children. CASE has 41 subdivisions in the United States and Canada.

CASE provides six newsletters and two issues of its refereed journal, *CASE in Point*, to its members annually. Through its publications program the Council also offers publications of interest to administrators. CASE provides professional development opportunities to its members. Among those are an annual institute devoted to the study of a specific topic and an annual conference offering a wide range of topics for discussion and study. CASE maintains a website (http://www.casecec.org/) where members may obtain current information on a variety of topics and activities of the Council.

The office may be contacted at Fort Valley State University, 1005 State University Drive, Fort Valley, GA 31030. E-mail/web address: http://www.casecec.org/.

Jo Thomason
Executive Director, CASE

COUNSELING INDIVIDUALS WITH DISABILITIES

With so much emphasis placed on disabled individuals' educational, adaptive behavior, and social skill needs, their emotional needs are often forgotten. Indeed, disabled individuals often have issues that affect their lives that could be addressed and resolved through the counseling process. A child/adolescent counselor or therapist needs to have an expanded knowledge base of the human condition and what constitutes counseling or therapy. Children and adolescents do not require a scaled-down version of adult therapy; they require their own, so the therapist must be open and creative. For example, some mentally retarded individuals experience feelings of frustration because of their disability and its limitations and could benefit from counseling in several different ways. Learning-disabled students, given the peer rejection sometimes associated with their academic difficulties, would also benefit. Counseling should be a central intervention for behaviorally and emotionally disturbed persons.

While the need for counseling with the disabled is apparent, the specific counseling techniques or approaches that are most effective under defined circumstances are not empirically evident. From a comprehensive diagnostic and treatment perspective, the multimodal approach of Lazarus (1976) has been used with disabled children. Using Lazarus's *BASIC ID* modalities (behavior, affect, sensation, images, cognition, interpersonal relationships, and drugs/biological functioning), disabled children's comprehensive social-emotional needs are analyzed and a counseling and psychotherapy program is developed to address the modalities most critical to the identified issues. In 1996, Keat expanded Lazarus's BASIC ID modalities, making it BASIC IDEAL, the E being for *education*, A for *adult*, and L for *learning* (Keat, 1979). Again, primary concerns in the modality areas are identified and then targeted for counseling support.

From a purely counseling perspective, a number of therapeutic approaches are available. Prout and Brown (1983) identified six major theoretical approaches to counseling and psychotherapy that can be adopted when handicapped individuals are the primary clients: behavior therapy, reality therapy, person-centered therapy, rational-emotive therapy, Adlerian therapy, and psychoanalytic/psychodynamic therapy. Behavior therapy has been especially useful with behaviorally disturbed individuals. Using operant or classical conditioning, cognitive, or social learning behavioral approaches, positive behaviors are taught and/or reinforced while disruptive or disturbing behaviors are altered or extinguished. The other psychotherapeutic approaches have been used, in addition to the behavioral, for emotionally disturbed individuals who manifest an assortment of affectively based difficulties and issues. Additionally, all of these approaches can be applied to the emotional issues that often coexist or result from other handicapping conditions.

Besides the psychotherapeutic approaches, a number of more specialized approaches are available when counseling disabled individuals. Briefly reviewed in Reynolds and Gutkin (1982), these include family therapy approaches, sociodrama, developmental therapy, art therapy, music therapy, and holistic or milieu therapy. Again, these approaches often become part of a comprehensive program that addresses disabled children's educational, social-emotional, affective, family, and adaptive needs. In many cases, the use of counseling occurs only as an afterthought to what is otherwise a comprehensive program. Clearly, the possibility that disabled children have related or separate counseling needs must be emphasized in research programs and in applied settings.

REFERENCES

Keat, D. B. (1979). *Multimodal therapy with children.* New York, NY: Pergamon Press.

Lazarus, A. A. (1976). *Multimodal behavior therapy.* New York, NY: McGraw-Hill.

Prout, H. T., & Brown, D. T. (1983). *Counseling and psychotherapy with children and adolescents.* Tampa, FL: Mariner.

Reynolds, C. R., & Gutkin, T. B. (1982). *The handbook of school psychology.* New York, NY: Wiley.

HOWARD M. KNOFF
University of South Florida

CRACK, PRENATAL EXPOSURE

A child who is crack affected is one whose mother used crack or cocaine during pregnancy (Waller, 1993). The Office of the Inspector General estimates that 100,000 children are born prenatally exposed to crack in the United States each year (Berger & Waldfogel, 2000). Prenatal crack exposure significantly increases the number of children who have significant problems in learning and require special education services to be successful (Twohey, 1999).

The effects of prenatal crack exposure vary greatly, from children with severe damage to children that are apparently perfect (Humphries, 1999). Medical effects in the perinatal stage include strokes, neurological dysfunction, and hypoxia, which is low oxygenation of the brain that can result in brain damage. Infants born exposed to crack might be inconsolable and hypersensitive. They may demonstrate attachment problems, be emotionally cold, and have jerky movements or rigid bodies. As toddlers, they may be slow to crawl and walk, be easily distractible, and lack skills necessary to plan, initiate, and follow through with tasks (Hoerig & D'Amato, 1994). As children reach preschool and school age, they may demonstrate additional behavioral symptoms of prenatal crack exposure. The child might appear to be in constant motion, with a low frustration level and lack of persistence. Children may also be oversensitive to stimuli, disorganized, demonstrate limited adaptability, and have difficulties with emotional attachment. A child exposed to crack can also be clumsy in gross motor activities and experience deficits in fine motor skills. Children might have difficulty with memory, concentration, speech, and language deficits (Hoerig & D'Amato, 1994).

Characteristics

The effects of prenatal crack exposure vary from greatly damaged to seemingly perfect. These characteristics may not be present in every case.

1. Hypoxia, strokes, and neurological dysfunction
2. Delayed development of gross motor skills
3. Deficits in fine motor skill
4. Distractibility
5. Appearance of constant motion
6. Low frustration level
7. Lack of persistence
8. Oversensitivity to stimuli
9. Limited adaptability
10. Speech problems and language deficits

Most children will require the use of specific interventions. Children with severe impairments often require special education services in the classroom. For children with speech and language disorder, other health impaired, multiple handicaps, or emotional disorder, recommended interventions include allowing children to be with one teacher for more than 1 year; training teachers to work with and assess the behavioral symptoms of neuropsychological and neurological impairment; using multidisciplinary teams for evaluation; low teacher–child ratios; and traditional behavioral management techniques (Hoerig & D'Amato, 1994). These children learn more effectively if they are specifically taught academic and social skills rather than learning through observations (Waller, 1993). Routines are important; only one skill should be taught at a time; groups should be small; and choices and number of activities should be limited. In addition to academic instruction, appropriate facial expressions and body language should be taught (Waller, 1993). Although there can be serious consequences of prenatal crack exposure, current research is finding a greater impact on children's social development than on their medical condition, and its effects are often subtle (Twohey, 1999).

REFERENCES

Berger, L. M., & Waldfogel, J. (2000). Prenatal cocaine exposure: Long-run effects and policy implications. *Social Service Review, 74*(1), 28–62.

Hoerig, D. C., & D'Amato, R. C. (1994). Cracked but not broken: Understanding and serving crack children. *Communiqué, 23,* 33–34.

Humphries, D. (1999). *Crack mothers.* Columbus: Ohio State University Press.

Twohey, M. (1999). The crack-baby myth. *National Journal, 31*(46), 3340–3345.

Waller, M. B. (1993). *Crack affected children: A teacher's guide.* Newbury Park, CA: Corwin Press.

Jessica L. Singleton
Rik Carl D'Amato
University of Northern Colorado

CRATTY, BRYANT J. (1929–   )

As an assistant, associate, and full professor of kinesiology at the University of Southern California since 1961, Bryant Cratty has done research on perceptual and motor development and its relationship to the human personality. He developed programs for the neurologically impaired in the early 1960s that expanded to research of learning games to aid slow learners to acquire academic skills.

In 1970, Cratty published the first edition of *Perceptual and Motor Development in Infants and Children,* which traced motor development from infancy to adolescence and gave specific teaching suggestions. In *Motor Activity and the Education of Retardates* (1975), Cratty offered detailed curriculum guides, including relaxation and motor activities that would assist a child in gaining self-confidence. In 1991, Cratty, with Iranide Deoliveira,

examined and assessed infants who had been exposed to cocaine prenatally: Measurable delays were noted.

Cratty has published over 55 books and monographs (many translated into 15 languages and Braille) that range from graduate texts in motor development and learning to applied sports psychology (Cratty, 1980; Cratty, 1985; Cratty, 1986). He has also published over 100 articles in domestic and foreign journals and lectured in 20 countries. Presently Dr. Cratty is Professor Emeritus at the Physiological Sciences Department of the University of California Los Angeles.

REFERENCES

Cratty, B. J. (1975). *Motor activity and the education of retardates* (2nd ed.). Philadelphia, PA: Lea and Febiger.

Cratty, B. J. (1980). *Adapted physical education for handicapped children and youth.* Denver, CO: Love.

Cratty, B. J. (1985). *Active learning* (2nd ed.). Englewood Cliffs, NJ: Prentice Hall.

Cratty, B. J. (1970). *Perceptual and motor development in infants and children* (1st ed.). Englewood Cliffs, NJ: Prentice Hall.

Deoliveira, I. J., & Cratty, B. J. (1991). Survey of ten infants exposed prenatally to maternal cocaine use. *International Journal of Rehabilitation Research, 14*(3), 265–274.

Elaine Fletcher-Janzen
Chicago School of Professional Psychology

CREATIVE PROBLEM SOLVING

Creative problem solving (CPS) is a structured model for using knowledge and imagination to arrive at a creative, innovative, or effective solution to a problem. CPS occurs when one of several conditions is satisfied: The product is novel or has value, the thinking used is unconventional and requires rejection or modification of previous ideas, thinking requires motivation or perseverance over a length of time, or the initial problem is vague or poorly defined, so problem formulation is part of the solution (Kletke, Mackay, Barr, & Jones, 2001).

Developed by Alex F. Osborn (1953), the original process consisted of three steps: fact finding, including problem definition and preparation; idea finding, including idea production and idea development; and solution finding, including evaluation and adoption. This process was refined by Parnes in 1967 and evolved into a five-step comprehensive model that incorporated findings from applied and theoretical research on creative thinking and behavior. The five steps are fact finding, problem finding, idea finding, solution finding, and acceptance finding.

CPS, also known as the Osborn-Parnes Model, is the most widely used method to encourage the application of creative thinking skills in the solving of problems. Deferred judgment is fundamental to the CPS process. This principle is based on Osborn's original notion that when judgment is withheld during ideation, at least 70% more good ideas are produced (1953). Throughout the process both divergent and convergent thinking constantly occur as the problem solver moves from one step to the next. Prior to the first step of CPS, there is the "mess" or preparation stage in which the identification or recognition of a situation of personal importance is determined. In fact finding, the emphasis is on gathering all possible background information that may help to define the real problem. Data are collected, facts about the situation are explored, and what is known about the situation is sought out and analyzed. Judgment is withheld until all alternatives have been exhausted. The next step focuses on the problem.

In problem finding, the emphasis is on restating the problem for solution. The problem is examined from a wide variety of perspectives and is redefined, narrowed, and analyzed. As the problem is being defined, it is recommended that the phrase "In what ways might I ..." (IWWMI) be used to encourage more ideas and further elaborations. Again, it is important that judgment be deferred so that thoughts about the problem may flow freely. Sometimes new facts or data will cause a return to step one for more fact finding.

Once the problem has been satisfactorily defined, the third step, called idea finding, occurs. The intent is to generate ideas and possible solutions. Deferred judgment is important for idea finding as well. Many techniques may be used to generate ideas. The most popular is brainstorming, to generate new and frequently innovative ideas. Application of the four cardinal rules of brainstorming are a must to ensure that ideas flow freely before they are judged for their merits. The rules of brainstorming are (1) rule out criticism; (2) welcome freewheeling or wild ideas; (3) seek quantity; and (4) seek combination and improvement. Other techniques that may be used here and throughout the five steps to encourage the production of ideas are idea-spurring questions, morphological analyses, synectics, attribute listing, scampering, and free association.

In step four, solution finding, the goal is to choose those alternatives that seem to provide the greatest potential for solving the problem. Criteria for evaluating solutions are developed and applied to each possible solution. The best idea or combination of ideas to solve the problem is chosen. Those ideas not chosen should not be discarded for they may be used later.

The final step, acceptance finding, involves preparations to put the idea into use. The challenge is to make it acceptable. This involves developing a plan for carrying out an idea and to sell and promote it. Considerations must be given to all factors that may aid or hinder the implementation of the plan.

Parnes (1967) has emphasized the importance of knowledge and imagination in creative productivity. Through the Creative Problem Solving Institute, in university classes, and other settings, he has successfully demonstrated that the process is easy to learn and applicable to many situations. College students, government officials, business persons, artists, educators, parents, and children are among those who have learned to apply the set of skills in CPS to the solution of practical problems.

Brophy (1998) constructed a matching theory regarding CPS. This theory maintains that creatively solvable problems differ in levels of complexity, levels of knowledge needed, and amounts of convergent and divergent thought needed. Thus, problem solvers best match the needs of particular problems based on their preferences, abilities, knowledge, and work plans.

The literature on CPS is extensive. Reviews of the CPS process have been completed by Parnes (1981) and Noller (1977), among others. Edwards (1986) has provided an extensive review of information on approaches to enhance creative thinking and ideation during the CPS process. Researchers have taken an interest in the link between CPS and computers. It has been postulated that incorporating creativity-enhancing techniques into computer systems may improve some outcomes of CPS (Kletke et al., 2001). These systems have come to be known as Computerized Creativity Support Systems (CCSSs). Another topic of interest for CPS researchers is individual versus group performance (Mumford & Gustafson, 1988). Mumford, Feldmen, Hein, and Nagao (2001) indicated that more available ideas led to better individual performance, and in group settings, providing information about the problem content led to more elaboration and refinement of solutions to problems.

REFERENCES

Brophy, D. R. (1998). Understanding, measuring, and enhancing individual creative problem solving effects. *Creativity Research Journal*, *11*(2), 123–150.

Edwards, M. O. (1986). *Idea power: Time tested methods to stimulate your imagination*. Buffalo, NY: Bearly.

Kletke, M. G., Mackay, J. M., Barr, S. H., & Jones, B. (2001). Creativity in the organization: The role of individual creative problem solving and computer support. *International Journal of Human-Computer Studies*, *55*(3), 217–237.

Mumford, M. D., Feldmen, J. M., Hein, M. B., & Nagao, D. J. (2001). Tradeoffs between ideas and structure: Individuals vs. group performance in creative problem solving. *Journal of Creative Behavior*, *35*(1), 1–23.

Mumford, M. D., & Gustafson, S. B. (1988). Creativity syndrome: Integration, application, and innovation. *Psychological Bulletin*, *103*, 27–43.

Noller, R. B. (1977). *Scratching the surface of creative problem solving*. Buffalo, NY: D.O.K.

Osborn, A. F. (1953). *Applied imagination*. New York, NY: Scribner.

Parnes, S. J. (1967). *Creative behavior guidebook*. New York, NY: Scribner.

Parnes, S. J. (1981). *The magic of your mind*. Buffalo, NY: Bearly.

KRISTIANA POWERS
*California State University,
San Bernadino*

See also Creativity; Creativity Tests

CREATIVE PROBLEM SOLVING INSTITUTE

The Creative Problem Solving Institute (CPSI) is a multidisciplinary, multilevel program designed to familiarize participants with the principles and techniques of creative problem solving (CPS). Founded in 1955 by Alex Osborn, the institute is sponsored by the Creative Education Foundation. In its first years, the institute's program was based on brainstorming, a procedure introduced by Osborn to facilitate creative thinking in a group. Osborn's (1953) notion was that "most of us can work better creatively when teamed up with the right partner because collaboration tends to induce effort, and also to spur our automatic power of association" (p. 72). His conceptualization of the creative problem-solving process included three steps: (1) fact finding, (2) idea finding, and (3) solution finding (Osborn, 1953).

Sidney J. Parnes, who succeeded Osborn as the director of the institute, retained the basic principles of the original model while extending the process to encompass a more eclectic approach. Kitano and Kirby (1986) summarized Parnes's approach as follows: "The Model consists of six steps and incorporates a variety of research-supported techniques for stimulating creativity, including brainstorming, synectics, incubation, imaging, deferred judgment, forced relationships and practice" (p. 205). The six steps as outlined by Parnes (1977) are objective finding, fact finding, problem finding, idea finding, solution finding, and acceptance finding. Each step can be thought of as having two phases, a divergent phase (coming up with many ideas) and an evaluative phase (selecting best candidate ideas). A model of the process is shown in Figure C.14 (adapted from Baer, 1997). The current model retains its earlier elements but continues to evolve (Isaksen, Dorval, & Treffinger, 2000).

The annual summer institute—the longest-running creativity conference in the world—has a range of programs, including ones for participants new to CPS training and extension programs for participants who have experience working with the CPS model. In addition to annual summer institutes, regional Creative Problem Solving institutes, symposiums, and workshops are held throughout the year. The CPSI attracts people from business, education, and government to its summer institutes and other programs. Participants receive training from specialists with varied experiences in fields associated with creativity.

DIVERGENT PHASE	CPS STAGE	EVALUATIVE PHASE
• Opportunities are explored • Situations are searched for possible opportunities	OBJECTIVE FINDING	• Challenge is accepted • Systematic effort is taken to respond to challenge
• Data are gathered • Situation is examined from many viewpoints • Info, impressions, feeling are collected	FACT FINDING	• Most important data are identified and analyzed
• Many possible problem statements are generated in the form "In what ways might I (we)...?"	PROBLEM FINDING	• A working problem statement is chosen
• Many different ways of responding to the problem statement are developed and listed	IDEA FINDING	• Ideas that seem most promising or interesting are selected for further examination
• Many possible criteria are formulated for use in reviewing and evaluating ideas	SOLUTION FINDING	• The most imporant criteria are selected • These criteria are used to evaluate, refine, and strengthen ideas
• Possible sources of assistance and implementation steps are identified	ACCEPTANCE FINDING	• Specific plans are formulated • Roles are assigned • Timeline is set

Figure C.14. CPS model of creative problem solving. *Source*: http://www.cpsb.com

REFERENCES

Baer, J. (1997). *Creative teachers, creative students*. Boston, MA: Allyn & Bacon.

Isaksen, S. G., Dorval, K. B., & Treffinger, D. J. (2000). *Creative approaches to problem solving: A framework for change* (2nd. ed.). Williamsville, NY: Creative Problem Solving Group, Buffalo.

Kitano, M. K., & Kirby, D. F. (1986). *Gifted education: A comprehensive review*. Boston, MA: Little, Brown.

Osborn, A. F. (1953). *Applied imagination: Principles and procedures of creative problem-solving* (Rev. ed.). New York, NY: Scribner.

Parnes, S. J. (1977). Guiding creative action. *Gifted Child Quarterly, 21*(4), 460–476.

JOHN BAER
Rider University

CREATIVE STUDIES PROGRAM

The Creative Studies Program was started with graduate-level courses in 1967 by Stanley J. Parnes at Buffalo State College in New York to enhance various aspects of college students' present and future behaviors both in college and the general community (Parnes & Noller, 1972a). Parnes and his colleagues developed the Creative Studies Program curriculum based on an earlier project, Creative Problem Solving.

The Creative Problem Solving curriculum is a five-step process: (1) fact finding, (2) problem finding, (3) idea finding, (4) solution finding, and (5) acceptance finding. It emphasizes the generation of a variety of alternatives prior to selecting or implementing a solution (Maher, 1982). The general purposes of the Creative Problem Solving Model are, first, to provide a sequential process that will enable an individual to work from an accumulation of information to arrive at a creative, innovative, or effective solution, and, second, to improve students' overall creative behavior (Maher, 1982).

In implementing the Creative Studies Project curriculum at Buffalo State College, Noller and Parnes (1972) developed a two-year, four-semester curriculum. The first year of the curriculum provided the students with hands-on experience in creativity. Such experiences were provided through a variety of instructional procedures, including the use of discussions, creative media (e.g., sculpture, art, dance), films, and guest leaders (Noller & Parnes, 1972). The second year of the project provided the students an opportunity to lead others through the project's curriculum.

The Creative Studies Program appears to be a successful method to increase the creative performance of college students (Maher, 1982; Parnes & Noller, 1972b). These students do better in school, perform better on three out of five mental operations (cognition, divergent production, and convergent production) in Guilford's Structure of Intellect Model (Guilford, 1967), and are more productive in nonacademic settings calling for creative performance. Torrance (1972) notes that the Creative Problem Solving curriculum or its modifications (e.g., the Creative Studies Program) is successful in teaching children to think creatively 91–92% of the time.

Buffalo State College was the first college to establish such a program; there are now at least 39 different programs and courses that have similar missions. Buffalo State College has five full-time professors in the program, led by Gerald Puccio (Xu, McDonnell, & Nash, 2005).

REFERENCES

Guilford, J. P. (1967). *The nature of human intelligence*. New York, NY: McGraw-Hill.

Maher, C. J. (1982). *Teaching models in the education of the gifted*. Rockville, MD: Aspen.

Noller, R. B., & Parnes, S. J. (1972). Applied creativity: The Creative Studies Project: Part III. The curriculum. *Journal of Creative Behavior, 6*, 275–294.

Parnes, S. J., & Noller, R. B. (1972a). Applied creativity: The Creative Studies Project: Part I. The development. *Journal of Creative Behavior, 6*, 11–22.

Parnes, S. J., & Noller, R. B. (1972b). Applied creativity: The Creative Studies Project: Part II. Results of the two-year program. *Journal of Creative Behavior, 6*, 164–186.

Torrance, E. P. (1972). Can we teach children to think creatively? *Journal of Creative Behavior, 6*, 114–143.

Xu, F., McDonnell, G., & Nash, W. R. (2005). A survey of creativity courses at universities in principal countries. *Journal of Creative Behavior, 39*, 75–88.

ROJA DILMORE-RIOS
*California State University,
San Bernardino*

See also Creativity; Creativity Tests

CREATIVITY

Creativity is a complex and multifaceted phenomenon of human behavior. Early philosophers conceptualized creativity as a mystical characteristic, resulting from divine intervention. The psychodynamic approach viewed creativity as an "unconscious process through which libidinal or aggressive energies are converted into culturally sanctioned behaviors" (Freud, 1924).

Today, the creative *person, process, product*, and *environment* are the vantage points from which creativity is most often discussed. Psychologists taking the person-centered view focus on individual differences in people's creativity, as well as the distinctive attributes of creative people. The psychometric approach has made a significant contribution to the measurement of creativity in individuals. This approach originated with Guilford (1950) when he urged psychologists to open up research on creativity, which he saw as a long-neglected but important attribute of humans. Psychometric researchers developed various measures to assess creativity, but have traditionally focused on divergent thinking ability. The most frequently used measure of creativity is the Torrance Tests of Creative Thinking (1974), which measures divergent thinking by scoring along the dimensions of originality, fluency, flexibility, and elaboration. Other measures of creativity that focus on divergent thinking are batteries developed by Guilford (1959), Getzels and Jackson (1962), and Wallach and Kogan (1965). Critics have emphasized the need to measure processes of creativity other than divergent thinking, such as evaluative thinking and problem identification.

The distinctive characteristics of creative individuals have also been investigated. Consistent among the many descriptions of creative persons are traits and behaviors such as unusual sensitivity to their environment, independence in thinking, nonconformance in their behaviors, and persistence at tasks. Creative people also tend to be open to new ideas and experiences and less accepting of traditional points of view. Exploring ideas for their own sake, a marked sense of humor, a high tolerance for ambiguity, and strong self-confidence in their own work are other common traits of highly creative people.

What happens in the creative process? Wallas (1926) described the process as consisting of four stages: preparation, incubation, illumination, and verification. Torrance defined the process as "one of becoming sensitive to or aware of problems...bringing together available information...searching for solutions...and communicating the results" (Torrance & Myers, 1970, p. 22).

Other psychologists have used experimental and computer-simulation methodologies to investigate the creative process. Such approaches usually take place in controlled laboratory environments, rely on quantitative measurement, and seek to determine causality by manipulating variables and measuring its effects on creativity.

Some of the earliest experimental studies focused on the nature of insight (Sternberg & Davidson, 1995). Today, an active area of research is based on the Creative Cognition approach (Smith, Ward, & Finke, 1995), which adopted the experimental methodologies of cognitive psychology to elucidate the creative thinking process. Creative Cognition researchers have identified two main phases of creative invention that occur in a cyclical fashion in ordinary individuals. During the *generative phase*, the individual generates numerous candidate ideas or solutions and forms a mental representation (referred to as a preinventive structure). Then, during the *exploratory* stage, the individual examines the candidate mental representations and ideas and works out their implications. A number of mental processes enter into the generative phase, including retrieval, association, synthesis, transformation, analogical transfer, and categorical reduction. Computer simulations have been conducted to simulate the creative problem-solving process, using heuristics derived from the cognitive task analysis of people solving creative problems (Langley, Simon, Bradshaw, & Zytkow, 1987).

Leading proponents of the search for methods to teach creative cognitive processing have been Parnes (1967) and Torrance (1979). Parnes developed the Creative Problem Solving Process, a five-step method combining knowledge and imagination in problem solving. Torrance (1979) created a three-stage instructional model—the Incubation Model—that integrates creativity objectives with content objectives. More recently, Sternberg has viewed creativity as a decision and has proposed strategies to develop creativity (Sternberg & Grigorenko, 2000). Nickerson (1999) provides further information on different methods to enhance creativity.

Creative products may be ideas, works of art, or scientific theories, provided certain criteria are met. There is a general consensus that creative products must be novel and relevant to a problem, situation, or goal. A relatively recent product assessment method is the Consensual Assessment Technique (CAT) developed by Amabile (1982). According to the CAT, participants are asked to complete some task in a specific domain (such as poetry), and experts in that domain (such as poets) independently rate the creativity of the products. If the interrater agreement is high, then the mean rating of the judges is used as a dependent measure of creativity (Hennessey & Amabile, 1988).

Psychologists taking the biographical approach to studying creativity have tended to focus on famous real-world creators and the personal and environmental factors that affect the quality and quantity of their products. The biographical approach has its roots in Galton (1869), Terman (1925), and Cox (1926). Current biographical researchers apply both qualitative case-study methodologies (Gardner, 1993; Wallace & Gruber, 1989) as well as historiometric quantitative measurement (Simonton, 1999).

An environment or situation that is open and accepting is critical for the release and development of creative potential. Csikszentmihalyi (1999) argues for a systems model of creativity that focuses on the interrelation of the *domain, field*, and *individual*. The domain consists of a set of rules, procedures, and instructions for action. The field includes all the individuals who act as gatekeepers to the domain. According to the systems model, creativity occurs when an individual makes a change in the information contained in a domain, and that change is selected by the field for inclusion in the domain. Torrance (1962) has suggested that other important variables are those that encourage unusual questions and ideas and those that allow performance to occur without constant threat of evaluation.

The debate regarding the nature of the relationship between creativity and intelligence has not been conclusively resolved. Kitano and Kirby (1986) contend that creativity is distinguishable from general intelligence. That is, "an individual can be extremely bright but uncreative, or highly creative but not necessarily intellectually gifted" (p. 192). Other researchers view intelligence as a subset of creativity. According to the Investment Theory of Creativity (Lubart & Sternberg, 1995), creativity requires a combination of six distinct but interrelated resources: intellectual abilities, knowledge, styles of thinking, personality, motivation, and environment. It has been estimated that an IQ of at least 120 is generally necessary for high creativity. IQ levels may vary according to the nature of the creative act.

REFERENCES

Amabile, T. M. (1982). Social psychology of creativity: A consensual assessment technique. *Journal of Personality and Social Psychology, 43*, 997–1013.

Csikszentmihalyi, M. (1999). Implications of a systems perspective for the study of creativity. In R. J. Sternberg (Ed.), *Handbook of creativity* (pp. 313–339). New York, NY: Cambridge University Press.

Cox, C. (1926). *The early mental traits of three hundred geniuses.* Stanford, CA: Stanford University Press.

Freud, S. (1924). *The relations of the poet to day-dreaming.* In collected papers (Vol. 2). London, UK: Hogarth. (Original work published 1908)

Galton, F. (1869). *Hereditary genius: An inquiry into its laws and consequences.* London, UK: Macmillan.

Gardner, H. (1993). *Multiple intelligences: The theory in practice.* New York, NY: Basic Books.

Getzels, J. W., & Jackson, P. W. (1962). *Creativity and intelligence: Explorations with gifted students.* New York, NY: Wiley.

Guilford, J. P. (1950). Creativity. *American Psychologist, 5*, 444–454.

Guilford, J. P. (1959). Three faces of intellect. *American Psychology, 14*, 469–479.

Hennessey, B. A., & Amabile, T. M. (1988). The conditions of creativity. In R. J. Sternberg (Ed.), *The nature of creativity: Contemporary psychological perspectives* (pp. 11–38). Cambridge, UK: Cambridge University Press.

Kitano, M. K., & Kirby, D. F. (1986). *Gifted education: A comprehensive view.* Boston, MA: Little, Brown.

Langley, P., Simon, H. A., Bradshaw, G. L., & Zytkow, J. M. (1987). *Scientific discovery: Computational explorations of the creative process.* Cambridge, MA: MIT Press.

Lubart, T. J., & Sternberg, R. J. (1995). An investment approach to creativity: Theory and data. In S. M. Smith, T. B. Ward, & R. A. Finke (Eds.), *The creative cognition approach* (pp. 269–302). Cambridge, MA: MIT Press.

Nickerson, R. S. (1999). Enhancing creativity. In R. J. Sternberg (Ed.), *Handbook of creativity* (pp. 392–431). New York, NY: Cambridge University Press.

Parnes, S. J. (1967). *Creative behavior guidebook.* New York, NY: Scribner.

Simonton, D. K. (1999). Creativity from a historiometric perspective. In R. J. Sternberg (Ed.), *Handbook of creativity* (pp. 116–137). New York, NY: Cambridge University Press.

Smith, S. M., Ward, T. B., & Finke, R. A. (Eds.). (1995). *The creative cognition approach.* Cambridge, MA: MIT Press.

Sternberg, R. J., & Davidson, J. E. (Eds.). (1995). *The nature of insight.* Cambridge, MA: MIT Press.

Sternberg, R. J., & Grigorenko, J. L. (2000). *Teaching for successful intelligence.* Arlington Heights, IL: Skylight Training and Publishing.

Terman, L. M. (1925). *Mental and physical traits of a thousand gifted children.* Stanford, CA: Stanford University Press.

Torrance, E. P. (1962). *Guiding creative talent.* Englewood Cliffs, NJ: Prentice Hall.

Torrance, E. P. (1974). *Torrance Tests of Creative Thinking.* Bensonville, IL: Scholastic.

Torrance, E. P., & Myers, R. E. (1970). *Creative learning and teaching.* New York, NY: Dodd, Mead.

Torrance, E. P. (1979). *The search for Satori and Creativity.* Buffalo, NY: Creative Education Foundation.

Wallace, D. B., & Gruber, H. E. (Eds.). (1989). *Creative people at work: Twelve cognitive case studies.* New York, NY: Oxford University Press.

Wallach, M. A., & Kogan, N. (1965). *Modes of thinking in young children.* New York, NY: Holt, Rinehart & Winston.

Wallas, G. (1926). *The art of thought.* New York, NY: Harcourt Brace Jovanovich.

SCOTT BARRY KAUFMAN
Yale University

See also Creativity, Theories of; Creativity Tests

CREATIVITY, AMUSEMENT PARK THEORY (APT MODEL) OF

The APT model uses the metaphor of an amusement park to explore the process of creativity (Baer & Kaufman, 2005; Kaufman & Baer, 2004a, 2005a). First there are *initial requirements* (intelligence, motivation, and environment) that must be present at some level for all creative work—much as you need certain basic requirements in order to go to an amusement park (e.g., transportation, a ticket). Next, there are *general thematic areas* in which someone could be creative (e.g., the arts, science); this level is like deciding which type of amusement park to visit (e.g., a water park, a zoo). The next level focuses on more specific *domains*—within the general thematic area of "the arts," for example, could be such varied domains as dance, music, visual arts, and so on. Similarly, once you have selected the type of amusement park you want to visit, you must then choose a particular park. Finally, once you have settled on a domain, there are *micro-domains* that represent specific tasks associated with each domain—much as there are many individual rides to select from once you are at an amusement park.

The APT model attempts to integrate both domain-general and domain-specific views of creativity. The first level (initial requirements) is very general, and each subsequent level gets more and more domain specific. By the final level (micro-domains), the theory is very domain specific.

Initial requirements are things that are necessary, but are not by themselves sufficient, for any type of creative production. They include such things as intelligence, motivation, and suitable environments. Each of these factors is a prerequisite to creative achievement in any domain, and if someone lacks the requisite level of any of these initial requirements, then creative performance is at best unlikely.

Every field of creative endeavor is part of a large, general thematic area, all of whose component fields share an underlying unity. General thematic areas are similar in nature to what some people call domains (Feist, 2004) or intelligences (Gardner, 1999).

Within each of the general thematic areas are several more narrowly defined creativity domains. Knowledge plays a large role at the domain level. For example, although psychology, sociology, criminal justice, and political science all may require many skills in the general thematic area of Empathy/Communication, the knowledge bases for these four social-science subjects are strikingly different, with only modest overlap, as are the knowledge bases that are foundational for work in the life sciences, chemistry, and physics, even though all will require skill in the Math/Science general thematic area.

Although there are many commonalities among all the tasks that are part of a domain, there are still big differences in what one needs to know, and what one needs to know how to do, in order to be creative when undertaking different tasks in that domain. This is rather like the transition from undergraduate to graduate education. Everyone in a graduate program in psychology, for example, may be preparing for a career as a psychologist, but future clinical psychologists, social psychologists, and cognitive psychologists likely take very few of the same courses. Similarly, studying fruit flies intensively for 5 years may help one develop creative theories in one of biology's micro-domains but be of little use in another, and practicing on a 12-string guitar may help one perform creatively in some micro-domains of the music world but not others.

The APT model provides a hierarchical model that makes it possible to accommodate both the domain-general aspects of creativity and the many levels of domain specificity of creativity that research (Baer, 1993, 2010; Kaufman & Baer, 2004b, 2004c, 2005b) has demonstrated.

REFERENCES

Baer, J. (1993). *Divergent thinking and creativity: A task-specific approach.* Hillsdale, NJ: Erlbaum.

Baer, J. (2010). Is creativity domain specific? In J. C. Kaufman & R. J. Sternberg (Eds.), *Cambridge handbook of creativity* (pp. 321–341). New York, NY: Cambridge University Press.

Baer, J., & Kaufman, J. C. (2005). Bridging generality and specificity: The Amusement Park Theoretical (APT) model of creativity. *Roeper Review, 27,* 158–163.

Feist, G. J. (2004). The evolved fluid specificity of human creative talent. In R. J. Sternberg, E. L. Grigorenko, & J. L. Singer (Eds.), *Creativity: From potential to realization* (pp. 57–82). Washington, DC: American Psychological Association.

Gardner, H. (1999). *Intelligence reframed: Multiple intelligences for the 21st century.* New York, NY: Basic Books.

Kaufman, J. C., & Baer, J. (2004a). The Amusement Park Theoretical (APT) model of creativity. *Korean Journal of Thinking & Problem Solving, 14*(2), 15–25.

Kaufman, J. C., & Baer, J. (2004b). Hawking's haiku, Madonna's math: Why it's hard to be creative in every room of the house. In R. J. Sternberg, E. L. Grigorenko, & J. L. Singer (Eds.), *Creativity: From potential to realization* (pp. 3–19). Washington, DC: American Psychological Association.

Kaufman, J. C., & Baer, J. (2004c). Sure, I'm creative—but not in math!: Self-reported creativity in diverse domains. *Empirical Studies of the Arts, 22*(2), 143–155.

Kaufman, J. C., & Baer, J. (2005a). The Amusement Park Theory of Creativity. In J. C. Kaufman & J. Baer (Eds.), *Creativity across domains: Faces of the muse* (pp. 321–328). Hillsdale, NJ: Erlbaum.

Kaufman, J. C., & Baer, J. (Eds.). (2005b). *Creativity across domains: Faces of the muse.* Hillsdale, NJ: Erlbaum.

JOHN BAER
Rider University

See *also* Creativity, Theories of; Gifted Children

CREATIVITY, CONSENSUAL ASSESSMENT OF

The Consensual Assessment Technique (CAT; Amabile, 1982, 1996; Baer, Kaufman, & Gentile, 2004; Kaufman, Plucker, & Baer, 2008) is widely used in creativity research. In the CAT, subjects are asked to create something, and experts are then asked to evaluate the creativity of those products. Poems, collages, and stories have been widely used in CAT studies, and the potential range of creative products that might work using the CAT is quite wide. In the CAT, rather than trying to measure some skill that is theoretically linked to creativity, it is the actual creativity of things subjects have produced that is assessed.

The basic procedure when using the CAT is to provide subjects with some instruction for creating some kind of product and then have experts independently assess the creativity of those artifacts. For example, in one study "students were given a line drawing of a girl and a boy . . . [and] asked to write an original story in which the boy and the girl played some part" (Baer, 1994a, p. 39). Experts in the area of children's writing were then asked to rate the creativity of the stories on a scale of 1.0 to 5.0. These expert judges were not asked to explain or defend their ratings in any way. They were simply asked to use their expert sense of what is creative in the domain in question to rate the creativity of the products in relation to one another. Interrater reliabilities among expert judges are generally quite good, typically in the .70-to-.90 range (Amabile, 1996; Baer, 1993, 1998; Hennessey & Amabile, 1999; Runco, 1989).

The key issue regarding the validity of any test is whether the test is measuring what it's supposed to measure, and one of the great strengths of the CAT is how clearly and directly it can respond to this question. The CAT assesses the creativity of a variety of products (poems, collages, etc.) of psychological studies the same way creativity is assessed at the genius level—by experts in that field. While it is true that experts don't always agree and expert opinion may change over time, at a given point in time there is no more objective or valid measure of the creativity of a work of art than the collective judgments of artists and art critics, just as there is no more valid measure of the creativity of a scientific theory than the collective opinions of scientists working in that field (Kaufman, Baer, & Cole, 2009).

CAT ratings of poems, stories, and collages have been shown to be valid measures of poetry-writing, story-writing, and collage-making creativity. It is less clear whether these measures also assess more general creativity-relevant skills, a topic about which there has been much debate (Amabile, 1982, 1996; Baer, 1993, 1994a, 1996; Conti, Coon, & Amabile, 1996); but for experimental studies designed to determine the impact of a wide variety of interventions, training, or experimental constraints, CAT ratings have been shown to work quite well. The CAT is not tied to any one theory of creativity, and so its validity does not rise or fall with one's opinion of any particular theory. Unlike most creativity-assessment techniques, the CAT is totally uncommitted (and therefore unbiased) regarding most of the big questions in creativity research. For example, it can be used equally well by those who believe that creativity has a significant domain-transcending, general component (e.g., Amabile, 1982, 1996), those who argue for a more domain-specific understanding of creativity (e.g., Baer, 1994a, 1996), or even those who wish to separate domain-general and domain-specific variance in creativity (e.g., Baer, 1993; Conti et al., 1996). This would be impossible with most creativity tests (such as the widely used divergent-thinking tests) because such tests assume a high level of generality of creativity. CAT ratings are also generally stable across time (Baer, 1994b), but they respond quite well to real within-subject changes in motivation (e.g., Amabile, 1996) or skill (e.g., Baer, 1994a).

CAT ratings can also be used within a classroom to assess creativity (Baer & McKool, 2009). CAT ratings can be used to compare one student's creativity on a particular task to the creativity of other students on the same task, but because creativity varies a great deal from domain to domain (and even on tasks in the same domain; Baer, 1993), CAT ratings cannot be used to compare students' creativity more generally. It is also not possible to devise any meaningful norms for CAT-based assessments, and therefore the use of the CAT has been primarily in creativity research, not in classroom applications.

REFERENCES

Amabile, T. M. (1982). Social psychology of creativity: A consensual assessment technique. *Journal of Personality and Social Psychology, 43*, 997–1013.

Amabile, T. M. (1996). *Creativity in context: Update to the social psychology of creativity*. Boulder, CO: Westview.

Baer, J. (1993). *Creativity and divergent thinking: A task-specific approach*. Hillsdale, NJ: Erlbaum.

Baer, J. (1994a). Divergent thinking is not a general trait: A multi-domain training experiment. *Creativity Research Journal, 7*, 35–46.

Baer, J. (1994b). Performance assessments of creativity: Do they have long-term stability? *Roeper Review, 7*(1), 7–11.

Baer, J. (1996). The effects of task-specific divergent-thinking training. *Journal of Creative Behavior, 30*, 183–187.

Baer, J. (1998). The case for domain specificity in creativity. *Creativity Research Journal, 11*, 173–177.

Baer, J., Kaufman, J. C., & Gentile, C. A. (2004). Extension of the consensual assessment technique to nonparallel creative products. *Creativity Research Journal, 16*, 113–117.

Baer, J., & McKool, S. (2009). Assessing creativity using the consensual assessment. In C. Schreiner (Ed.), *Handbook of assessment technologies, methods, and applications in higher education*. Hershey, PA: IGI Global.

Conti, R., Coon, H., & Amabile, T. M. (1996). Evidence to support the componential model of creativity: Secondary analyses of three studies. *Creativity Research Journal, 9*, 385–389.

Hennessey, B. A., & Amabile, T. M. (1999). Consensual assessment. In M. A. Runco & S. R. Pritzker (Eds.), *Encyclopedia of creativity* (Vol. 1, pp. 346–359). San Diego, CA: Academic Press.

Kaufman, J. C., Baer, J., & Cole, J. C. (2009). Expertise, domains, and the Consensual Assessment Technique. *Journal of Creative Behavior, 223–233*.

Kaufman, J. C., Plucker, J. A., & Baer, J. (2008). *Essentials of creativity assessment*. Hoboken, NJ: Wiley.

Runco, M. A. (1989). The creativity of children's art. *Child Study Journal, 19*, 177–190.

JOHN BAER
Rider University

See also Creativity, Theories of; Creativity Tests

CREATIVITY, FAIRNESS AND

Standardized tests are often criticized as being biased, and these criticisms can come in two main forms. A common lay approach to criticizing tests as biased is to point to significant differences that occur between males and females and among ethnic groups on various tests of aptitude or ability. Indeed, a wide variety of measures of intelligence and ability have shown lower scores for African Americans and Latinos (see Loehlin, 1999, for an overview).

Psychometric approaches to bias in testing take a more sophisticated view of the problem and do not accept the view that just because two groups may perform differently on a mental test, the test itself must be in error or biased (Kauffman, 2006). Current approaches evaluate content statistically that may be inappropriate because it unfairly favors one group over another. Methods are commonly applied as well to determine whether different constructs may be measured across nominal groups by the same test (e.g., a test may measure verbal ability in Caucasians, but may be measuring something quite different in a Hispanic population; Reynolds, Lowe, & Saenz, 1999).

One approach to seeking out nonbiased assessment is to supplement traditional assessment with additional measures of constructs that may be influencing a score on a traditional test of ability or achievement (Kaufman, 2005). Creativity is a prime candidate to be such a supplement. One reason is that creativity is related to intelligence and academic ability, yet not so closely related as to not account for additional variance. Indeed, creativity is an important, if not essential, part of most major theories of intelligences (see Kaufman & Plucker, in press, for an overview). Another promising reason is the reduction in gender and ethnicity differences.

Studies of ethnicity and divergent thinking typically show no differences between Caucasians and African Americans (Glover, 1976) or a slight advantage for African Americans (Torrance, 1971, Troiano & Bracken, 1983). When actual creative performance is measured, there are either no differences (Kaufman, Niu, Sexton, & Cole, 2010), or Caucasians score slightly higher (Sternberg, 2009). Comparisons of Caucasians and Hispanics typically find Caucasians scoring higher on verbal measures but no differences on figural/drawing tests (Argulewicz & Kush, 1984). There are many additional constructs that may be used as part of such a supplemental approach to nonbiased testing (e.g., emotional intelligence, motivation, thinking styles), but creativity serves as a good exemplar of this approach. There are multiple ways of measuring creativity, extensive studies have examined creativity across many different possible groups, the relationship between intelligence and creativity has been well explored, and the field is still actively studied. Kaufman (2010) specifically outlines the case for creativity to be included in college and graduate school admissions.

REFERENCES

Argulewicz, E. N., & Kush, J. C. (1984). Concurrent validity of the SRBCSS Creativity Scale for Anglo-American and Mexican-American gifted students. *Educational and Psychological Research, 4*, 81–89.

Glover, J. A. (1976). Comparative levels of creative ability in Black and White college students. *Journal of Genetic Psychology, 128*, 95–99.

Kaufman, J. C. (2005). Non-biased assessment: A supplemental approach. In C. L. Frisby & C. R. Reynolds (Eds.), *Children's Handbook of Multicultural School Psychology* (pp. 824–840). Hoboken, NJ: Wiley.

Kaufman, J. C. (2006). Self-reported differences in creativity by gender and ethnicity. *Journal of Applied Cognitive Psychology, 20*, 1065–1082.

Kaufman, J. C. (2010). Using creativity to reduce ethnic bias in college admissions. *Review of General Psychology, 14*, 189–203.

Kaufman, J. C., Baer, J., & Gentile, C. A. (2004). Differences in gender and ethnicity as measured by ratings of three writing tasks, *Journal of Creative Behavior, 38*(1), 56–69.

Kaufman, J. C., Niu, W., Sexton, J. D., & Cole, J. C. (2010). In the eye of the beholder: Differences across ethnicity and gender in evaluating creative work. *Journal of Applied Social Psychology, 40*, 496–511

Kaufman, J. C., & Plucker, J. A. (in press). Intelligence and creativity. To appear in R. J. Sternberg & S. B. Kaufman (Eds.), *Cambridge handbook of intelligence*. New York, NY: Cambridge University Press.

Loehlin, J. C. (1999). Group differences in intelligence. In R. J. Sternberg (Ed.), *Handbook of intelligence* (pp. 176–193). Cambridge, UK: Cambridge University Press.

Reynolds, C. R., Lowe, P. A., & Saenz, A. L. (1999). The problem of bias psychological assessment. In C. R. Reynolds & T. B. Gutkin (Eds.), *The handbook of school psychology* (pp. 549–596). New York, NY: Wiley.

Sternberg, R. J. (2009). The Rainbow and Kaleidoscope projects: A new psychological approach to undergraduate admissions. *European Psychologist, 14,* 279–287

Torrance, E. P. (1971). Are the Torrance Tests of Creative Thinking biased against or in favor of the "disadvantaged" groups? *Gifted Child Quarterly, 15,* 75–80.

Troiano, A. B. & Bracken, B. A. (1983). Creative thinking and movement styles of three culturally homogeneous kindergarten groups. *Journal of Psychoeducational Assessment, 1,* 35–46.

JAMES C. KAUFMAN
MARIA J. AVITIA
Learning Research Institute,
California State University,
San Bernardino
Fourth edition

See also **Creativity; Culturally/Linguistically Diverse Gifted Students**

CREATIVITY, THEORIES OF

Creativity is a complex phenomenon that involves a combination of individual and social factors. Galton (1869) was the first to focus on creative genius as the subject of scientific investigation (Tannenbaum, 1986) and psychoanalysts like Sigmund Freud (1856–1939) and Carl Jung (1875–1961) established a connection between science, the humanities, and creativity (Weiner, 2000). However, it was J. P. Guilford's (1897–1988) keynote address at the American Psychological Association in 1950 that marked the beginning of a greater interest in creativity research (Weiner, 2000). In the address, he emphasized the importance of creativity research and called the neglect of creativity "appalling" (Weisberg, 1986, p. 55).

There are three broad categories under which theories of creativity fall: theories focusing on the personality of the creative individual, theories focusing on the cognitive aspect of the creative process, and theories focusing on sociocultural factors that impact creativity (Csikszentmihalyi, 1990; Ryhammar & Brolin, 1999).

Earlier studies of creativity focused on the creative individual and theories were built on the assumption that personality was the only determinant of creativity. For example, Galton (1869) suggested that genius was inherited and that social obstacles could not hinder the creative

genius from excelling. Guilford (1950) stated that creativity was "a set of traits that are characteristic of creative persons" (as cited by Feldhusen & Goh, 1995, p. 232). Later researchers such as Renzulli (1986), Dabrowski (1972), Gardner (1983), and Kirton (1976) continued the focus on the individual without excluding the possible impact of sociocultural factors. Renzulli's (1986) Three-Ring Conception of Giftedness focuses on three characteristics of the individual: above-average ability, task commitment, and creativity. Dabrowski (1972) supported the idea that highly creative individuals had specific, above-average abilities, as well as components of psychic life that contained heightened levels of energy, called overexcitabilities (Ngara & Porath, 2004). Gardner (1983) extended the idea of specific abilities and suggested there were different kinds of creativity or "intelligences": linguistic, musical, logical-mathematical, spatial, bodily-kinesthetic, interpersonal, and intrapersonal (and later, naturalistic). Kirton (1976) presented his theory of two creativity styles: Adaptors exercised their creativity within established paradigms, while innovators created new paradigms and frameworks. While slightly different, all of these theories focused mainly on the creative individual's personality.

Models that fall under the cognitive approach focus on the creative thinking process. For example, Dewey (1910) suggested that creative problem solving is a basic cycle of perceiving and defining a problem, devising solutions, weighing consequences, and accepting a solution. Wallas (1926) suggested that the creative process had four stages: preparation, incubation, illumination, and verification. Building on these models, Parnes (1962) introduced brainstorming as a commonsensical individual and group approach based on deferred judgment to produce a range of ideas. According to Osborn (1963), creativity depended on the following brain functions: absorbing (gaining knowledge), retaining, imagining, and judging (Basadur & Gelade, 2003). Csikszentmihalyi (1991, 1996) suggested that while exercising their creativity, individuals experience "flow," during which they become completely absorbed with the task at hand. Torrance (1962) studied developmental aspects of creativity, focusing on developing imagination and fostering a sense of individuality among gifted and talented children. Together, this body of creativity research helped to launch interest in creativity-oriented classroom instruction and programs. According to Torrance and Safter (1990, 1999), one's creative insights could occur when one redirects one's attention to a task completely unrelated to the creative endeavor, which is called the incubation process.

It was during the 1980s that a sociocultural approach to creativity emerged, which was a shift from "the earlier almost exclusive focus on creative persons" (Ryhammar & Brolin, 1999, p. 269). Until then, creativity had been expressed as a talent that is within the boundaries of the individual (Cropley, 2006) and the focus had been solely on internal causes, while external causes were mostly excluded (Amabile, 1996). After sociocultural factors became an important focus of creativity research, which has indicated that such factors indeed have a great impact on creativity (e.g., Albert & Runco, 1999; Gardner, 1993; Harrington, 1990; Lubart & Georgsdottir, 2004; Mumford & Gustafson, 1988; Simonton, 1992; Sternberg & Lubart, 1991; Vass, 2004), various theories that united all three approaches—sociocultural factors, personal characteristics, and cognitive processes—have emerged. For example, Sternberg's (1986) Triarchic Theory of Intellectual Giftedness is composed of three subtheories that emphasize both creative individuals and their relationships with the environment: (1) "a componential subtheory" relating intelligence to the person's internal world; (2) "an experiential subtheory" relating intelligence to the person's internal and external worlds; and (3) "a contextual subtheory" relating intelligence to the person's external world (p. 240). Amabile's (1996) componential model, which suggests that creativity results from individual skill, domain knowledge, task motivation, and extrinsic motivation (e.g., rewards or constraints), has been used to study creativity in social systems (e.g., parenting, schooling, families, teams, and organizations). According to Csikszentmihalyi's (1990, 1996, 1999) systems model, creativity is the result of the interaction among well-defined domains with rules and procedures within a specific field, social institutions including "gatekeepers" to the domain who decide whether a new product or idea should be included in the domain, and the individual's talent and personality traits. Gardner's (1988) holistic model of creativity considers four areas: the subpersonal (genetic), the personal (cognition, motivation, personality), the extrapersonal (knowledge domain), and the multipersonal (the field).

Taken together, these theories and system models provide a set of useful frameworks for considering creativity, creative individuals, creative processes, and outcomes in educational institutions and organizations.

REFERENCES

Albert, R. S., & Runco, M. A. (1999). A history of research on creativity. In R. J. Sternberg (Ed.), *Handbook of creativity* (pp. 13–31). Cambridge, UK: Cambridge University Press.

Amabile, T. M. (1996). *Creativity in context: Update to the social psychology of creativity*. Boulder, CO: Westview.

Basadur, M., & Gelade, G. (2003). Using the creative problem solving profile (CPSP) for diagnosing and solving real-world problems. *Emergence, 5*(3), 22–47.

Cropley, A. (2006). Creativity: A social approach. *Roeper Review, 28*(3), 125–130.

Csikszentmihalyi, M. (1990). The domain of creativity. In M. A. Runco & R. S. Albert (Eds.), *Theories of creativity* (pp. 190–212). Newbury Park, CA: Sage.

Csikszentmihalyi, M. (1991). *Flow: The psychology of optimal experience*. New York, NY: Harper Perennial.

Csikszentmihalyi, M. (1996). *Creativity: Flow and the psychology of discovery and invention*. New York, NY: HarperCollins.

Csikszentmihalyi, M. (1999). Implications of a systems perspective for the study of creativity. In R. J. Sternberg (Ed.), *Handbook of human creativity* (pp. 313–338). New York, NY: Cambridge University Press.

Dewey, J. (1910). *How we think*. Boston, MA: Heath.

Dabrowski, K. (1972). *Psychoneurosis is not an illness*. London, UK: Gryf.

Feldhusen, J. F., & Goh, B. E. (1995). Assessing and accessing creativity: An integrative review of theory, research, and development. *Creativity Research Journal, 8*(3), 231–247.

Galton, F. (1869). *Hereditary genius: An inquiry into its causes and consequences*. London, UK: Macmillan.

Gardner, H. (1983). *Frames of mind*. New York, NY: Basic Books.

Gardner, H. (1988). Creative lives and creative works: A synthetic scientific approach. In R. J. Sternberg (Ed.), *The nature of creativity: Contemporary psychological perspectives* (pp. 125–147). New York, NY: Cambridge University Press.

Gardner, H. (1993). *Creating minds: An anatomy of creativity seen through the lives of Freud, Einstein, Picasso, Stravinsky, Eliot, Graham, and Gandhi*. New York, NY: Basic Books.

Guilford, J. P. (1950). Creativity. *American Psychologist, 5*(9), 444–454.

Harrington, D. M. (1990). The ecology of human creativity: A psychological perspective. In M. A. Runco & R. S. Albert (Eds.), *Theories of creativity* (pp. 143–169). Newbury Park, CA: Sage.

Kirton, M. J. (1976). Adaptors and innovators: A description and measure. *Journal of Applied Psychology, 61*, 622–629.

Lubart, T. I., & Georgsdottir, A. (2004). Creativity: Developmental and cross-cultural issues. In S. Lau, A. N. N. Hui, & G. Y. C. Ng (Eds.), *Creativity: When East meets West* (pp. 23–54). River Edge, NJ: World Scientific.

Mumford, M. D., & Gustafson, S. B. (1988). Creativity syndrome: Integration, application, and innovation. *Psychological Bulletin, 103*, 27–43.

Ngara, C., & Porath, M. (2004). Shona culture of Zimbabwe's views of giftedness. *High Ability Studies, 15*(2), 189–209.

Osborn, A. F. (1963). *Applied imagination* (3rd rev. ed). Buffalo, NY: Creative Education Foundation Press.

Parnes, S. J. (1962). Do you really understand brainstorming? In S. J. Parnes & H. F. Harding (Eds.), *A source book for creative thinking* (pp. 283–290). New York, NY: Charles Scribner's Sons.

Renzulli, J. S. (1986). *Three-ring conception of giftedness: A developmental model for creative productivity*. In Sternberg & Davidson (Eds.), Conceptions of giftedness (pp. 53–92). New York, NY: Cambridge University Press.

Ryhammar, L., & Brolin, C. (1999). Creativity research: Historical considerations and main lines of development. *Scandinavian Journal of Education Research, 43*(3), 259–273.

Simonton, D. K. (1992). The social context of career success and course for 2,026 scientists and inventors. *Personality and Social Psychology Bulletin, 18*(4), 452–463.

Sternberg, R. J. (1986). A triarchic theory of intellectual giftedness. In R. J. Sternberg & J. E. Davidson (Eds.), *Conceptions of giftedness* (pp. 223–246). New York, NY: Cambridge University Press.

Sternberg, R. J., & Lubart, T. I. (1991). An investment theory of creativity and its development. *Human Development, 34,* 1–31.

Tannenbaum, A. J. (1986). *Giftedness: A psychosocial approach.* In Sternberg & Davidson (Eds.), Conceptions of giftedness (pp. 21–53). New York, NY: Cambridge University Press.

Torrance, E. P. (1962). Ten ways of helping young children gifted in creative writing and speech. *Gifted Child Quarterly, 6,* 121–127.

Torrance, E. P., & Safter, H. T. (1990). *The incubation model of teaching.* Buffalo: NY: Bearly.

Torrance, E. P., & Safter, H. T. (1999). *Making the creative leap beyond.* Buffalo, NY: Creative Education Foundation Press.

Vass, E. (2004). Understanding collaborative creativity: Young children's classroom-based shared creative writing. In D. Miell & K. Littleton (Eds.), *Collaborative creativity: Contemporary perspectives* (pp. 79–95). London, UK: Free Association Books.

Wallas, G. (1926). *The art of thought.* New York, NY: Harcourt Brace.

Weiner, R. (2000). *Creativity and beyond: Cultures, values, and change.* Albany: State University of New York Press.

Weisberg, R. W. (1986). *Creativity: Genius and other myths.* New York, NY: Freeman.

ADALET B. GUNERSEL
Temple University
Fourth edition

See also Creativity, Fairness and; Creativity Tests

CREATIVITY TESTS

History of Creativity Testing

Creativity testing to assess and identify individuals with creative abilities and talents has a history in the measurement field for at least the past 50 years. Creativity test development gained momentum and started to expand during the 1950s under E. Paul Torrance as he was deeply influenced by J. P. Guilford. Perhaps the most important contribution Guilford made to the understanding of creativity was the distinction between convergent and divergent thinking, the former requiring a single, correct solution, and the latter allowing many different, "creative" solutions (Guilford, 1967). Torrance expanded upon this theory by measuring creativity using a number of solutions and infrequency of responses as the metric of choice. This distinction provided a substrate for creativity test development as researchers now had a basis by

which to build from the ground up. Getzels and Jackson's book, *Intelligence and Creativity* (1962), and Torrance's threshold hypothesis (Guilford, 1967), which stipulated that intelligence is necessary, but not sufficient, for creative abilities, subsequently influenced the trajectory of creative test development. Following the formulation of this theory, the relationship between intelligence and creativity became much more defined and empirically understood.

Models of Creativity

In order to measure creativity, there was a need to understand the theory based on a model. With a model, psychologists and the like could build measurement criteria with the model serving as a proxy for the construct creativity. Graham Wallas first proposed a model in 1926 that portrayed the creative process in five steps: preparation, incubation, intimation, illumination, and verification (Wallas, 1926). Guilford's model was premised on the idea of convergent/divergent thinking, and the best way to capture creativity was to measure this abstract phenomenon as it occurs through items requiring the extraction of that creative power (Guilford, 1962). Torrance (1974, p. 8) defined creativity as "a process of becoming sensitive to problems, deficiencies, gaps in knowledge, missing elements, disharmonies, and so on; identifying the difficulty; searching for solutions, making guesses, or formulating hypotheses and possibly modifying and retesting them; and finally communicating the results." In his American Psychological Association's President's Column of the *American Psychologist,* Sternberg (2003, p. 5) summarized his proposal that "creativity is a decision," and itemized a number of activities ("not abilities") that represent choices that can be made, ranging from defining "problems in ways different from those in which their colleagues define them" to overcoming "the numerous and often difficult obstacles placed in their paths" to deciding "to tolerate ambiguity," and so forth. Arthur Koestler proposed the idea of *bisociation,* where creativity arises out of an intersection of two different frames of reference (Koestler, 1964). Finke et al. advocated for a *geneplore* model, which consists of a generative phase where an individual constructs mental representations, and an exploratory phase where the individual uses those representations to come up with creative ideas (1992). More recently, a wave of cognitive science has culminated in the idea that creativity can be understood via the theory of conceptual blending. Conceptual blending is a theory in cognitive science that is defined by elements and vital relations from disparate scenarios blended in a subconscious process much akin to everyday thought and language (Fauconnier & Turner, 2002).

How Do We Measure Creativity?

Guilford's battery of tests was based on his model, the Structure of the Intellect (1962). This psychometric model utilized concepts such as divergent thinking and transformation to assess creativity. Today, the *Torrance Tests of Creative Thinking* (TTCT) are perhaps the most highly regarded creativity tests in use (Torrance & Ball, 1984), and they may flow from his definition of creativity. One could even envision the tests including some sort of measure of some of the "decision" activities that Sternberg lists, that is, tolerating ambiguity may be related to Torrance's measure of resistance to closure (see above for mention of Torrance and Sternberg). Of course, Sternberg's activities of choice seem also to include a social-personality approach, that is, creativity may be measured by self-confidence, independent judgment, or even openness to experience (Sternberg & Lubart, 1999). Creativity is a complex construct and the measurement theory behind it is still forming as empirically testable models are explored.

REFERENCES

Fauconnier, G., & Turner, M. (2002). The way we think: Conceptual blending and the mind's hidden complexities. New York, NY: Basic Books.

Finke, R. A., Ward, T. B., & Smith, S. M. (1992). *Creative cognition: Theory, research, and applications.* Cambridge, MA: MIT Press.

Getzels, J. W., & Jackson, P. W. (1962). *Creativity and intelligence.* New York, NY: Wiley.

Gilles, F., & Mark, T. (2002). *The way we think: Conceptual blending and the mind's hidden complexities.* New York, NY: Basic Books.

Guilford, J. P. (1962). Potentiality for creativity. *Gifted Child Quarterly, 6,* 87–90.

Guilford, J. P. (1967). *The nature of human intelligence.* New York, NY: McGraw-Hill.

Koestler, A. (1964). *The act of creation.* London, UK: Pan Books.

Sternberg, R. J. (2003). Creativity is a decision. *American Psychologist, 57*(5), 376.

Sternberg, R. J., & Lubart, T. I. (1999). The concept of creativity: Prospects and paradigms. In R. J. Sternberg (Ed.), *Handbook of creativity.* New York, NY: Cambridge University Press.

Torrance, E. P. (1974). *Torrance Tests of Creative Thinking: Norms—Technical manual (p. 8).* Bensenville, IL: Scholastic Testing Service.

Torrance, E. P., & Ball, O. E. (1984). *Torrance tests of creative thinking: Streamlined.* Bensonville, IL: Scholastic.

Wallas, G. (1926). *Art of thought.* New York, NY: Harcourt Brace.

DANNY B. HAJOVSKY
University of Kansas

WILLIAM R. NASH, ED. D
*Professor Emeritus of Educational Psychology,
Texas A&M University
Fourth edition*

See also Welsh Figure Preference Test

CRETINISM

Cretinism is a syndrome caused by hypothyroidism (underactivity of the thyroid gland) at birth. Two types of cretinism have been distinguished. Endemic cretinism is essentially an iodine deficiency disorder. Insufficient levels of iodine cause maternal hypothyroidism, which increases the incidence of fetal hypothyroidism in the neonate (Dussault, 1997). Endemic cretinism is characterized by severe developmental delays, deaf-mutism, and spasticity of the arms and legs (Hetzel, 2000). The second form, sporadic cretinism or congenital hypothyroidism, is most commonly caused by a developmental defect of the thyroid gland, in which the thyroid gland fails to develop (aplasia) or is underdeveloped (hypoplasia; Vanderbilt University Medical Center, 1998). Developmental delays and stunted growth are the most common complications associated with sporadic cretinism.

Endemic cretinism has been virtually eradicated in the United States and in many developed nations with the addition of iodine to table salt. In iodine-deficient areas, such as Zaire, Ecuador, India, China, and mountainous areas of the Andes and Himalayas, severe hypothyroidism can be found in 5–15% of the population. The incidence of sporadic cretinism is approximately 1 in 4,000 Caucasian infants and 1 in 30,000 African American infants. In addition, congenital hypothyroidism is twice as common in girls as in boys (Vanderbilt University Medical Center, 1998).

Characteristics

Endemic cretinism

1. Fetal hypothyroidism, which can occur as early as the fourth month of gestation
2. Severe iodine deficiency
3. Severe developmental delays and mental deficiency, particularly with marked impairment for abstract thought
4. Deafness, with up to 50% of individuals showing complete loss and subsequent mutism (those with partial hearing may or may not have intelligible speech)
5. Motor disorders characterized by proximal rigidity in both lower and upper extremities

Sporadic cretinism

1. Severe hypothyroidism
2. Markedly delayed bone maturation and short stature
3. Delayed sexual maturation
4. Mental deficiency, though often not as severe as that associated with endemic cretinism

Treatment involves a substantial preventative component. Restored maternal iodine levels prior to pregnancy, either with iodized salt or by injection of iodized oil, can eliminate maternal hypothyroidism and subsequent fetal hypothyroidism (Dussault, 1997). Screening programs in the United States (and many developed nations) test all newborn babies for congenital hypothyroidism. If hypothyroidism is detected, thyroid hormone replacement therapy with L-thyroxine can be initiated as early as 1 month of age (Dussault, 1997). Frequent clinical examination is recommended every few months through age 3, and at least yearly thereafter, to monitor growth and development.

For individuals with frank cretinism, special education placement will most likely be necessitated. Admission under the qualifying condition of multiply handicapped may be appropriate to address the hearing impairments, mutism or speech difficulties, and mental retardation that are associated with this disorder. Occupation and physical therapies may also be necessary to address coordination and gait disorders, as well as spasticity.

With early detection and intervention, the prognosis for infants with congenital hypothyroidism is good. Recent studies emphasize that early treatment is essential and have demonstrated that most optimal development is achieved if thyroid deficiencies are corrected before the third week of life (Bongers-Scholkking, Koot, Wiersma, Verkerk, & de Muink Keizer-Schrama, 2000). Children who receive early treatment can achieve normal mental and psychomotor development. The World Health Organization has identified endemic cretinism as the most common preventable cause of brain damage in the world and has launched a global effort to eliminate this disorder through national iodization programs. Current research has studied the effectiveness of such iodization programs. Other trends in research focus on identifying treatment protocols to optimize outcomes in children with chronic hypothyroidism.

REFERENCES

Bongers-Scholkking, J. J., Koot, H. M., Wiersma, D., Verkerk, P. H., & de Muink Keizer-Schrama, S. M. P. F. (2000). Influence of timing and dose of thyroid hormone replacement on development in infants with congenital hypothyroidism. *Journal of Pediatrics, 136*, 292–297.

Dussault, J. H. (1997). Childhood primary hypothyroidism and endemic cretinism. *Current Therapy in Endocrinology and Metabolism, 6*, 107–109.

Hetzel, B. S. (2000). Iodine and neuropsychological development. *Journal of Nutrition, 2S*, 493S–495S.

Vanderbilt University Medical Center. (1998, June 16). *Endocrinology: Congenital hypothyroidism.* Retrieved from http://mc.vanderbilt.edu/

HEIDI A. McCALLISTER
University of Texas, Austin

See also **Hypothyroidism**

CRI DU CHAT SYNDROME (CAT CRY SYNDROME)

Discovered by Jerome Lejeune, director of the department of genetics at the University of Paris, and his coworkers, Gautier and Turpin, in 1963, cri du chat syndrome is associated with a partial deletion of one of the chromosomes in the B group; specifically, there is a deletion of the short arm of chromosome 5 (5p–). Cri du chat syndrome is the most frequently reported of the autosomal deletion syndromes. The name was derived from the characteristic high-pitched, mewing cry, closely resembling the cry of a kitten, that is heard in the immediate newborn period, lasts several weeks, and then disappears with the exception of some cases, in which the catlike cry persists into adulthood. Incidence is estimated at 1:50,000 births (Hynd & Willis, 1987).

Affected infants show low birthweight, failure to thrive, hypotonia, microcephaly, a round or moon-faced appearance with hypertelorism (wide-set eyes), antimongoloid or downward sloping palpebral fissures with or without epicanthal folds, strabismus, and a broad-based nose. Ears are low-set and abnormally shaped with malformations, including narrow external canals and preauricular tags. Micrognathia, a short neck, and varying degrees of syndactyly are present. Various types of congenital heart defects and abnormal dermatoglyphics are frequently noted. Major diagnostic features include severe mental retardation and markedly delayed motor development.

A significant number of cri du chat infants survive to adulthood and continue to demonstrate microcephaly. They also have short stature, facial asymmetry, dental malocclusions, skeletal problems such as scoliosis, eye defects, and a waddling gait. These individuals are at or below the trainable level. As school-aged children, they are found in classes for the moderately and severely retarded. According to Gearheart and Litton (1975), the incidence of cri du chat is not known. Berg et al. (1970) found that 7 of the 744 patients with IQs below 35 had this defect. Goodman and Gorlin (1970) reported that a preponderance of patients were female.

No treatment is presently available for this syndrome. As with other chromosome defects, prevention is associated with amniocentesis and genetic counseling. The possibility of a recurrence of the syndrome in another member of the family is rare unless the condition is due to a translocation chromosome. Most cases of cri du chat syndrome are sporadic, with about 13% originating from a balanced carrier parent who is phenotypically normal.

Future research will focus on earlier identification of the syndrome and effective intervention strategies (Guy & Nussbaum, 2003).

Characteristics

1. Catlike cry during the first few weeks following birth

2. Low birthweight

3. Abnormal facial features, including small head, round, asymmetric face, improperly closing mouth, wide-set eyes, wide nose, and low-set, abnormally shaped ears

4. Webbed fingers

5. Microcephaly

6. Poor muscle tone

This article was informed by the following references.

REFERENCES

Berg, J. M., McCreary, B. D., Ridler, M. A., & Smith, G. F. (1970). *The deLange syndrome.* Oxford, UK: Pergamon Press.

Berkow, R. (Ed.). (1982). *The Merck manual of diagnosis and therapy* (14th ed.). Rahway, NJ: Merck Sharp & Dohme Research Laboratories.

Cegelka, P. T., & Prehn, H. J. (1982). *Mental retardation: From categories to people.* Columbus, OH: Merrill.

Gearheart, B. R., & Litton, F. W. (1975). *The trainable retarded: A foundations approach.* St. Louis, MO: Mosby.

Goodman, R. M., & Gorlin, R. J. (1970). *The face in genetic disorders.* St. Louis, MO: Mosby.

Guy, K. L., & Nussbaum, N. L. (2003). Cri du chat syndrome. In E. Fletcher-Janzen & C. R. Reynolds (Eds.), *Childhood disorders diagnostic desk reference* (pp. 156–157). Hoboken, NJ: Wiley.

Holmes, L. B., Moses, H. W., Halldorsson, S., Mack, C., Pavt, S. S., & Matzilevich, B. (1972). *Mental retardation: An atlas of diseases with associated physical abnormalities.* New York, NY: Macmillan.

Hynd, G., & Willis, G. (1987). *Pediatric neuropsychology.* Boston, MA: Allyn & Bacon.

Lejuene, J., Gautier, M., & Turpin, R. (1959). *Les chromosomes humains en culture des tissues: Competes rendus hebdomadaires des seances de l'Academie des Sciences* (pp. 248–602). Paris, France: l'Academie des Sciences.

Zellweger, H., & Ionasescu, V. (1978). Genetics of mental retardation. In C. H. Carter (Ed.), *Medical aspects of mental retardation* (2nd ed.). Springfield, IL: Thomas.

CATHERINE HALL RIKHYE
Hunter College,
City University of New York

See also **Chromosomes, Human Anomalies, and Cytogenetic Abnormalities; Mental Retardation**

CRIME AND INDIVIDUALS WITH DISABILITIES

Public Law 94-142 first mandated that educational services be provided to all youths with disabilities no matter where they reside, a mandate continued by its successor, the Individuals With Disabilities Education Act (IDEA). Johnson (1979) indicates that about one-third of incarcerated youths are thought to have serious learning disabilities, in contrast to only 16% of the unincarcerated population.

Morgan (1979) conducted a study to produce a national profile of disability conditions. He sent questionnaires to administrators of juvenile correctional facilities in 50 states and 5 U.S. territories. Among the respondents, only 6 did not provide most of the requested information; 204 institutions responded. Among the findings, Morgan reports that:

1. Compared to the national incidence of children with disabilities (12.3%), 42.4% of delinquent children committed to correctional institutions were found to have some type of disability.

2. The disabilities with the highest incident rates in correctional facilities were emotional disturbance (16.23%), learning disabilities (10.59%), and educable mental retardation (7.69%).

Morgan (1979) indicates that the figure 42% is inflated, while other studies put the figure between 28 and 43% (Fink, 1991; Rutherford, 1985). Keilitz and Miller (1980) combined results of several studies, including Morgan's (1979), and concluded that those studies suggest that (a) prevalence estimates of the major categories of emotional disorders, learning disabilities, and mental retardation are of greater magnitude than expected on the basis of estimates of prevalence among the general student population; and (b) the great difference in prevalence of disabilities between those youths outside and inside the justice system remains even when study design problems and bias are minimized.

Much speculation exists as to the relationship between criminal behavior and disability. Siegel and Senna (1981) assign theories that attempt to determine the cause of delinquency into four categories: individualized, social structure, social process, and social reaction. Unfortunately, the variables and factors that impact on these theories are the same that are used to describe the educable mentally retarded and emotionally disabled.

Keilitz and Miller (1980) present three rationales as the most prominent explanations of the disproportionate prevalence of disabilities among youths in the justice system. The three are school failure, susceptibility, and differential treatment.

Despite these attempts to account for unexpectedly high prevalence, there is no definitive explanation for the disproportionate number of youths with disabilities in the justice system. There is clear evidence that services (Johnson, 1979) mandated under PL 94-142 and the IDEA must be provided and that these services have not been fully implemented. The problem of disabilities as they relate to crime is serious and needs much more attention, especially in the areas of research, programs, and prevention (Brown & Robbins, 1979).

REFERENCES

Brown, S., & Robbins, M. (1979). Serving the special education needs of students in correctional facilities. *Exceptional Children, 45,* 574–579.

Fink, C. M. (1991). Special education in service for correctional education. *Journal of Correctional Education, 41*(4), 186–190.

Johnson, J. (1979). An essay on incarcerated youth: An oppressed group. *Exceptional Children, 45,* 566–571.

Keilitz, I., & Miller, S. L. (1980). Handicapped adolescents and young adults in the justice system. *Exceptional Education Quarterly, 1*(2), 117–126.

Morgan, D. I. (1979). Prevalence and type of handicapping conditions found in juvenile correctional institutions: A national survey. *Journal of Special Education, 13,* 283–295.

Rutherford, R. B., Jr. (1985). Special education in the most restrictive environment: Correctional/special education. *Journal of Special Education, 19,* 59–71.

Siegel, L. J., & Senna, J. J. (1981). *Juvenile delinquency: Theory, practice, and law.* St. Paul, MN: West.

PHILIP E. LYON
College of St. Rose
First edition

KIMBERLY F. APPLEQUIST
University of Colorado at Colorado Springs
Third edition

See also **Educationally Disadvantaged; Juvenile Delinquency**

CRISIS INTERVENTION

Crisis intervention is a service spontaneously available to individuals and students who are in need of immediate assistance (Kelly & Vergason, 1978). Caplan defines a crisis as a sudden onset of behavioral imbalance in a child where previous function was stable (Caplan, 1963). The intent of intervention in a crisis is to provide knowledge of coping behaviors of enduring value. According to Swanson and Reinert (1976), a child in conflict is one "whose manifested behavior has a deleterious effect on his/her personal or educational development and/or the personal or educational development of his peers" (p. 5).

Intervention at the point of disruption or crisis is not new. Traditionally, the crisis was handled by an administrator or teacher. According to Long, Morse, and Newman (1976):

> [T]he problem is these are usually of a reflexive and haphazard type. From our analysis of acts and reactions in the school setting it appears that a good many leave much to be desired. Since they usually lack an awareness of the underlying conditions, they are reactions to symptoms, often with a curbing intention [p. 232]. Also these crisis situations may be only "a crisis to the teacher who is the consumer of the behavior." (p. 325)

The crisis concept has changed in four ways. The first is in consultation, which has gone from supervisory to strategic planning. In other words, clinicians and teachers work together toward resolution. The second is in the use of the helping teacher, who becomes responsible for the disturbed child. The third change is in the style of interviewing proposed by Redl called life space interviewing (LSI). The fourth change occurs in a system to manage the confrontation situations that are found in secondary education.

The holding of crisis meetings is one way to develop a positive, success-oriented classroom. When disruptions such as fights, serious arguments, misunderstandings, and expressions of angry feelings (verbal or physical) occur, impromptu crisis meetings help students understand and resolve serious conflicts (Redl, 1959). These meetings, which involve only those students who were actually involved in the problem situation, can take place in the classroom, lunchroom, or playground. To conduct a crisis meeting, the following steps are usually taken:

1. *Cooling off.* Students should be given a few minutes to cool off if they are very upset and not ready to engage in thoughtful discussion. If necessary, students can be sent to their desks, a quiet area, or the principal's office.

2. *Setting rules.* The meeting is initiated by speaking in a calm manner. Ground rules for the discussion are set. These may include avoiding arguing and listening to what each person has to say.

3. *Listening actively.* The student is asked to describe the incident, what led up to the incident, and how he or she feels. After listening carefully, the listener rephrases what the student has said to show

understanding. Other students may be asked to summarize or repeat what the first student said. Then the second student is asked to give his or her recollection of the incident. During the active listening phase, the main goal is to obtain a clarification of what happened and how the participants are feeling. Helping students clarify their feelings may also serve to drain off some anger or frustration.

4. *Exploring the problem.* At this step, the problem is considered at length. Questions such as how the problem could have been avoided, what can be done the next time the problem begins, and what consequences should be expected (Glass, Christiansen, & Christiansen, 1982) can be addressed.

Another resource is the crisis or helping teacher. Gearheart and Weishahn (1980) find that this teacher

provides temporary support and control to troubled students when they are unable or unwilling to cope with the demands of the regular classroom. The type of service the Crisis Teacher provides requires that he/she be available at the time of the crisis. Working closely with the regular classroom teachers, he/she provides support, reassurance, and behavioral management strategies. Troubled students come and go on either a regular or an episodic basis, depending on the needs of the students. When the teacher is not dealing with a crisis, he/she can be helping less troubled students academically and behaviorally. He/she can make referrals to supportive services, provide the needed intensive assistance for the more severely troubled students, and follow up on specific recommendations. The crisis teacher becomes an active partner with the teacher, mental health personnel, and parents in helping this student. (p. 223)

Another form of crisis intervention is the LSI method, which was developed to help teachers become effective in talking to children and to help teachers use these skills as a specific management tool (L'Abate & Curtis, 1975). There are two main goals: clinical exploitation of life events and immediate emotional first aid. There are both long-range and immediate goals. This kind of therapy may help the student to express hostility, frustration, or aggression; provide support while helping the student to avoid panic or guilt; help the student to maintain relationships; allow teachers to supervise behavior and ensure conformity to rules; and help teachers in settling complex situations (L'Abate & Curtis, 1975). Bernstein (1963) in L'Abate and Curtis (1975) provides some guidelines for LSI:

1. Be polite.
2. Do not tower above a child; bend down to him.
3. Be sure of yourself.
4. Use "why" sparingly.
5. Encourage talk about the actual situation.
6. Help the child to avoid being overwhelmed by shame or guilt by minimizing the problem.

7. Help the child to express his or her feelings about the situation.
8. Be aware of the kind of thinking demanded by a particular situation.
9. Work with the child to make the situation better.
10. Allow the child time to ask questions.

L'Abate and Curtis (1975) list some limitations of LSI:

1. It requires the teacher to have an ability to understand human behavior in more of an art than a science form.
2. It often requires more time than a regular classroom teacher with 30 students has to spare; this is where the helping teacher could assist.
3. It requires education and cooperation among all members of the school staff.

The resource classroom is yet another way to help exceptional children. Here the child is provided with instruction and emotional support by the resource teacher for part of the day. The child may move between the classrooms and receive instruction from both teachers. It is even possible that the child can be placed on a limited day schedule in cases where he or she cannot handle either the resource or regular classroom. In summary, crisis intervention can be the most appropriate kind of action if all psychological, sociological, and educational knowledge is applied at the correct moment in time.

REFERENCES

Caplan, G. (1963). Opportunities for school psychologists in the primary prevention. *Mental Hygiene, 47*(4), 525–539.

Gearheart, B. R., & Weishahn, M. W. (1980). *The handicapped student in the regular classroom.* St. Louis, MO: Mosby.

Glass, R., Christiansen, J., & Christiansen, J. L. (1982). *Teaching exceptional students in the regular classroom.* Boston, MA: Little, Brown.

Kelly, L. J., & Vergason, G. A. (1978). *Dictionary for special education and rehabilitation.* Denver, CO: Love.

L'Abate, L., & Curtis, L. T. (1975). *Teaching the exceptional child.* Philadelphia, PA: Saunders.

Long, H. J., Morse, W. C., & Newman, R. G. (1976). *Conflict in the classroom: The education of emotionally disturbed children.* Belmont, CA: Wadsworth.

Redl, F. (1959). Concept of the life space interview. *American Journal of Orthopsychiatry, 29*(1), 1–18.

Swanson, L. H., & Reinert, H. R. (1979). *Teaching strategies for children in conflict curriculum methods, and materials.* St. Louis, MO: Mosby.

RICHARD E. HALMSTAD
University of Wisconsin at Stout

See also **Life Space Interviewing; Redl, Fritz**

CRISIS TEACHER

The concept of the crisis teacher/helping teacher was initiated, according to Long, Morse, and Newman (1976), as the result of the efforts of a staff of elementary teachers in a highly problematic school. The crisis teacher was first an educator trained in psychoeducational theory and practice who provided direct assistance to regular classroom teachers and students that might exhibit disruptive (crisis) behaviors. Ultimately, this educator would enhance the learning environment by providing a liaison between the crisis teacher and the regular classroom teacher. This brought to the classroom teacher immediate peer help as opposed to the consultants, such as the school psychologist, school counselor, or principal, ordinarily sought out.

Historically, crises had been met by sending the students involved to the principal's office. Frequently, this procedure would yield less-than-adequate results for various reasons. First, the principal was often uninformed of the events leading up to the classroom crisis. Second, the principal's administrative responsibilities may make him or her unavailable when needed most. Third, the repressive nature of being sent to the principal's office could have, in some instances, exacerbated the problem. In addition, resorting to this method of crisis resolution in some instances resulted in an inadvertent reinforcer being applied to the situation.

Regular classroom teachers were cognizant of the needs expressed by all students in their classrooms and as such understood that not all children manifested disruptive behaviors at all times. However, teachers were aware that every child in the classroom had the right to an equal share of his or her time. Since disruptive children could not always be physically removed from the classroom and other students had educational needs to be met, the crisis teacher concept seemed to meet the purpose of addressing the one who needed help while keeping the classroom teacher in continuing interaction with other students.

Immediate help from a crisis teacher was also seen as an effort to interject a process that would promote a more expedient method of handling psychoeducational problems manifested by the disruptive student. Prior to such a process being developed, regular classroom teachers resorted to punishment and then waited until a staffing could be arranged to receive advice from a psychologist, nurse, counselor, special education teacher, or other team member. Again, the regular classroom teacher was faced with receiving well-meaning but delayed corrective suggestions that proved inappropriate to their needs. As cited by Reynolds and Birch (1977), such advice was often impractical. Teachers knew what to do but did not have the resources to implement the course of action advocated by a team to which the teacher was not always a contributing member.

Due to changes in special education over the years, the crisis teacher model is no longer popular.

REFERENCES

Long, N. J., Morse, W. C., & Newman, R. G. (1976). *Conflict in the classroom: The education of emotionally disturbed children* (3rd ed.). Belmont, CA: Wadsworth.

Reynolds, M. C., & Birch, J. W. (1977). *Teaching exceptional children in all America's schools*. Reston, VA: Council for Exceptional Children.

RICHARD E. HALMSTAD
University of Wisconsin at Stout

See also Crisis Intervention; Resource Room; Special Class

CRISSEY, MARIE SKODAK (1910–2000)

Born in Lorain, Ohio, Marie Skodak Crissey obtained her BS and MA degrees from Ohio State University in 1931. She was an Institute of International Education fellow at the University of Budapest in 1931–1932. Crissey became interested in factors influencing development of intelligence and school achievement partly through the influence of Henry H. Goddard and Sidney Pressey. Her PhD was in developmental psychology from the University of Iowa in 1938.

She was well known for her still frequently cited classic research (Skodak, 1939; Skodak & Skeels, 1949) on the heredity–environment issue, which countered the then-widely held concept of genetically determined and fixed IQ. She found that the IQs of adopted children correlated more highly with the estimated intelligence of their biological rather than their adoptive parents, but that their actual level of intelligence was closer to that of their adoptive parents. Thus her research showed both hereditary and environmental influences on intelligence, and demonstrated that favorable home environment could raise levels of intelligence. From an applied standpoint, she emphasized the potential effectiveness of environmental intervention programs to stimulate the development of children from deprived backgrounds.

During her professional career, Crissey developed special education programs, intervention programs for disabled and deprived children, vocational guidance programs for high school students, and vocational rehabilitation services for the disabled. She was at the Child Guidance Center at Flint, Michigan, from 1938 to 1946 and was director of school psychology and special education at Dearborn, Michigan, from 1949 to 1969. She had a private practice in psychology (Anonymous, 1984). She was a fellow of the American Association of Mental Deficiency and of five divisions of the American Psychological Association. Among her numerous awards were the Joseph P. Kennedy

International Award for research in mental retardation in 1968 and a citation for distinguished service from the American Psychological Association in 1972.

REFERENCES

Anonymous. (1984). Crissey, Marie Skodak. In R. Corsini (Ed.), *Encyclopedia of psychology* (Vol. 2). New York, NY: Wiley.

Skodak, M. (1939). Children in foster homes: A study of mental development. *University of Iowa Studies in Child Welfare, 16*(1).

Skodak, M., & Skeels, H. M. (1949). A final follow-up study of one hundred adopted children. *Journal of Genetic Psychology, 75,* 85–125.

ROBERT T. BROWN
University of North Carolina at Wilmington

CRITERION-REFERENCED TESTING

Criterion-referenced testing is a method for examining a person's performance with respect to a standard or criterion. It is commonly contrasted with norm-referenced testing, in which a person's performance is compared with that of other persons who make up a norm group. While this concept has been used in pedagogy for millennia, it was formalized by Glaser and Klaus (1962). In their conception, a criterion is a level of performance achieved only when the person being examined is able to perform certain tasks. These tasks have been determined to be necessary for learning. During the course of study there may be many criteria, which may be viewed as stages or intermediate steps. The assessment of the performance on the tasks necessary to achieve criteria is commonly called criterion-referenced testing (CRT). A criterion-referenced test is thus a test constructed to assess the performance level of examinees in relation to a well-defined domain of content (Hambleton, 1999).

In the late 1960s, criterion referencing became commonly associated with mastery (Glass, 1978; Popham & Husek, 1969), especially with minimum-competency testing. In this variant, CRT is intended to classify persons into those who can and those who cannot perform at some minimally acceptable level. Nearly all states in the United States require some form of minimum-competency testing (Hambleton, 1999). Purposes for the testing include issuing of high-school diplomas, passage to high school from junior high, and comparison of classes and schools for various political purposes. While the latter reason is almost never formally stated, it is common practice in many states to publish building- or district-level average test performance. These are then compared with state "competitors." There have been numerous proposals to link teacher salaries to their classrooms' performance on such tests. In only a few isolated school districts have such procedures been established.

The major issues in CRT are definition of the content, development of the tests, evaluation of test characteristics, standard setting and test results use (National Education Association [NEA], 2006). A useful text on these issues has been compiled by Berk (1984a); more current thinking by researchers in the CRT field is reviewed by Hambleton (1999).

Definition of the content for criterion-referenced tests is closely tied to instruction. If one uses the Glaser and Husek concept of CRT, a careful analysis of the tasks being required of the students forms the basis for the test. Those tasks are separated either hierarchically or organizationally into stages or steps. Tests are constructed that sample the behaviors the student must exhibit to demonstrate knowledge or mastery for each step. In hierarchical content, the student must know certain content or be able to perform certain tasks before the next content or task can be attempted. Many courses in mathematics exhibit such structure. Other content may have an organizational sequence that is not inherent to it, such as English literature. It may be studied historically, thematically, or by type, such as poetry, novel, and essay. Criterion-referenced testing may be used to indicate level of achievement for each part. Nitko (1984) refers to ordering and definition for domains. A domain may be ordered or unordered and well-defined or ill-defined. He asserts that CRT should be used only with well-defined content domains.

There has been relatively little research on developing items or questions for CRTs, and most test developers have used item-writing technology developed for norm-referenced achievement tests. Roid and Haladyna (1980) have attempted to develop an item-writing technology using algorithms for sentence writing. Other proposed approaches are based on mapping and on factor analysis (Roid, 1984). Future efforts are certain to use computers in the generation of items for CRTs.

Analysis of item and test characteristics has received considerable attention from psychometricians. Both classical reliability theory and item characteristic curve theory have been applied to the analysis of items and of the entire test. Reliability of CRT tests has been derived for test scores (Berk, 1984b) and for the classification decision (Hambleton, 1999; Subkoviak, 1984).

A major debate erupted in the latter 1970s over the issue of standards setting: Can standards be set, and who sets them? Glass (1978) argued that the arbitrariness of standard setting results in poor educational practice and that test scores should be interpreted in other, unspecified ways. Numerous authors argued for standard setting, and several techniques, notably owed to Nedelsky, Angoff, and Ebel, have been developed. Hambleton (1999), Shepard (1984), and the NEA (2006) give overviews of the issues and the techniques.

REFERENCES

Berk, R. A. (Ed.). (1984a). *A guide to criterion-referenced test construction*. Baltimore, MD: Johns Hopkins University Press.

Berk, R. A. (1984b). Conducting the item analysis. In R. A. Berk (Ed.), *A guide to criterion-referenced test construction* (pp. 97–143). Baltimore, MD: Johns Hopkins University Press.

Glaser, R. (1963). Instructional technology and the measurement of learning outcomes: Some questions. *American Psychologist, 18*, 519–521.

Glaser, R., & Klaus, D. J. (1962). Proficiency measurement: Assessing human performance. In R. M. Gagne (Ed.), *Psychological principles in systems development* (pp. 419–474). New York, NY: Holt, Reinhart & Winston.

Glass, G. V. (1978). Standards and criteria. *Journal of Educational Measurement, 59*, 602–605.

Hambleton, R. (1999). Criterion-referenced testing: Principles, technical advances, and evaluation guidelines. In C. R. Reynolds & T. B. Gutkin (Eds.), *The handbook of school psychology* (3rd ed., pp. 409–433). New York, NY: Wiley.

National Education Association (NEA). (2006). *Standardized testing*. Retrieved from http://www.nea.org/

Nitko, A. J. (1984). Defining "Criterion-Referenced Test." In R. A. Berk (Ed.), *A guide to criterion-referenced test construction* (pp. 8–28). Baltimore, MD: Johns Hopkins University Press.

Popham, W. J., & Husek, T. R. (1969). Implications of criterion-referenced measurement. *Journal of Educational Measurement, 6*, 1–9.

Roid, G. H. (1984). Generating the test items. In R. A. Berk (Ed.), *A guide to criterion-referenced test construction* (pp. 49–77). Baltimore, MD: Johns Hopkins University Press.

Roid, G. H., & Haladyna, T. M. (1980). The emergence of an item-writing technology. *Review of Educational Research, 50*, 293–314.

Shepard, L. A. (1984). Setting performance standards. In R. A. Berk (Ed.), *A guide to criterion-referenced test construction* (pp. 169–198). Baltimore, MD: Johns Hopkins University Press.

Subkoviak, M. J. (1984). Estimating the reliability of mastery nonmastery classifications. In R. A. Berk (Ed.), *A guide to criterion referenced test construction* (pp. 267–291). Baltimore, MD: Johns Hopkins University Press.

Victor L. Willson
Texas A&M University

See also Minimum Competency Testing; Norm-Referenced Testing

CROHN'S DISEASE

Crohn's disease is an idiopathic, chronic inflammatory bowel disorder. The disease may be controlled through management of symptoms, but no cure is now available. Crohn's disease is very similar to ulcerative colitis, and together they belong to a category of disorders referred to as inflammatory bowel disease. Although similar, they are distinct in important ways. Crohn's disease may involve any part of the alimentary tract—mouth, esophagus, stomach, small and large intestine—but most frequently involves the small bowel and colon. Gastrointestinal involvement is transmural, meaning that all layers of the bowel wall are affected. The inflammatory process is segmental and erratic, often skipping sections of bowel with little predictability of where it will strike next (KidsHealth, 2001). On the other hand, ulcerative colitis is continuous in nature, primarily involves the large intestine and rectum with inflammation limited to the inner mucosal bowel lining, and puts individuals at high risk for developing colon cancer.

Characteristics

Presenting symptoms

1. Persistent diarrhea, abdominal pain, and rectal bleeding
2. Fever and fatigue
3. Weight loss, dehydration, and malnutrition

Later symptoms

1. Skin or eye irritations
2. Growth retardation and delay of sexual maturation
3. Malnutrition
4. Extraintestinal manifestations

The incidence of Crohn's disease is 3–4 in 100,000 and has increased over the past 10 years. In the United States, incidence in Whites and Blacks is 3–10 times greater than in Hispanics and Asians. Crohn's disease is diagnosed most often during adolescence but may also appear again at around age 40. Earlier onset is more severe and leads to more complications and involvement of other organ systems. Cause is unknown, but the disease is believed to be autoimmune in nature and to have familial tendencies. Family history is positive in 10–20% of affected individuals (Behrman, Kliegman, & Jenson, 2000).

Manifestations of Crohn's disease depend on the area of involved bowel, severity of inflammation, and presence of complications. Symptoms often resemble those of other conditions. Initially, Crohn's disease and ulcerative colitis may be hard to distinguish. Thorough history, physical exam, blood tests and radiological studies, and endoscopic exam are important for accurate diagnosis. Symptoms may not appear for years and range from mild to severe (Crohn's and Colitis Foundation of America [CCFA], 2001). Crohn's is characterized by periods of exacerbation and remission. Diagnosis may not be made until 1 to 2 years after onset of symptoms.

The goal of treatment in Crohn's disease is to alleviate symptoms. Owing to the complexity of this illness, treatment may involve a variety of medications and interventions. The two most commonly used categories of drugs are anti-inflammatory drugs (such as Asacol, Dipentum, Pentasa, and Balasalazide) and immunosuppressive agents (such as steroids, cyclosporin, azothioprine, and anti-TNF antibodies). Over time, the inflammatory process causes complications such as bowel strictures, fistulas, perianal disease, intra-abdominal abscess, and increased risk of cancer (CCFA, 2001). Generally, the better the inflammatory process is controlled, the longer complications are delayed. One promising focus of current study is on the role of the autoimmune process and extraintestinal complications (CCFA, 2001). In spite of good medical management, almost all those with Crohn's disease will eventually require surgery. Surgery is avoided as long as possible because the incidence of recurrence is greater than 50% at 5 years, and the risk of additional surgery increases with each operation (Behrman et al., 2000).

Aggressive nutritional therapy is beneficial as a primary treatment. Enteral feedings of elemental formula may be considered in the presence of weight loss, malnutrition, poor appetite, malabsorbtion, growth failure, and poor response to conventional therapy (Behrman et al., 2000).

Emotional stress does not cause Crohn's disease, but stress may trigger flare-ups. Use of relaxation and stress management techniques is often helpful. Although poor diet does not cause Crohn's disease, high-fat and -sodium foods can intensify symptoms. Thus, dietary modifications and maintenance of adequate nutrition may reduce symptoms. Frequent, small, nutritionally balanced meals are generally tolerated better than are infrequent, larger meals (KidsHealth, 2001).

Children with Crohn's disease face challenges similar to all children with a chronic disease: psychosocial issues of being different, concerns over body image, restriction of activity, missed days of school, daily medications, and increased family stress. They may have further self-concept and social interaction problems owing to delayed growth and puberty. Counseling may help children and adolescents deal with the consequences of the disorder. Management of diarrhea during school is of great concern to children. Crohn's is a chronic disorder with high morbidity but low mortality. Periods of remission, during which the child is symptom free, can often be achieved. Most children with Crohn's disease lead active, full lives. Special camps sponsored by CCFA are available; information is available at http://ccfa.org/.

REFERENCES

Crohn's and Colitis Foundation of America. (2001). *New insight into autoimmunity*. Retrieved from http://ccfa.org/

Behrman, R. E., Kliegman, R. M., & Jenson, H. B. (2000). *Nelson textbook of pediatrics* (16th ed.). Philadelphia, PA: W. B. Saunders.

KidsHealth. (2001). *Inflammatory bowel disease*. Retrieved from http://www.kidshealth.org/parent/medical/digestive/ibd.html

BRENDA MELVIN
*New Hanover Regional Medical Center,
Wilmington, North Carolina*

CRONBACH, LEE J. (1916–2001)

Lee J. Cronbach attended Fresno College, gaining his BA degree in 1934. After completing his MA degree at the University of California, Berkeley, in 1937, he attended the educational psychology program at the University of Chicago, gaining his PhD in 1940.

In 1940, Cronbach went to the State College of Washington as instructor in the department of psychology. He stayed there until 1946, advancing to the rank of assistant professor. During World War II, he was involved with the University of California division of War Research at San Diego, serving as research psychologist. After the war, Cronbach spent three years (1946–1948) as assistant professor of education at the University of Chicago. In 1948, Cronbach went to the University of Illinois, where he remained until 1964. Cronbach was also a professor of education at Stanford University for 16 years. He served the American Psychological Association as chairman of its Committee on Test Standards (1950–1953) and served on the Committee on Psychological Tests. His book, *Essentials of Psychological Testing* (1960), is considered a classic in the field.

Cronbach is well known for his work as co-investigator on the Terman Study of Children of High Ability, a project he joined in 1963. That study was a long-term longitudinal study of intellectually gifted students. The study has demonstrated much of what we know of the lives and productivity of the intellectually gifted. It has dispelled many of the common stereotypes surrounding the intellectually gifted. Cronbach is also well known for his work on measurement theory, program evaluation, and instruction. He developed the most frequently used measure of reliability for psychological and educational assessments, known as "Cronbach's alpha." At the time of his death, Cronbach was working on a paper commemorating the fiftieth anniversary of the publication of the alpha paper. Lee Cronbach died of congestive heart failure in his Palo Alto home on October 1, 2001.

This article was informed by the following references.

REFERENCES

Cronbach, L. J. (1951). Coefficient alpha and the internal structure of tests. *Psychometrika*, 16, 297–334.

Cronbach, L. J. (1960). *Essentials of psychological testing* (2nd ed.). New York, NY: Harper & Brothers.

Cronbach, L. J., & Gleser, G. C. (1965). *Psychological test and personnel decisions* (2nd ed.). Champaign: University of Illinois Press.

RAND B. EVANS
Texas A&M University

JESSI K. WHEATLEY
*Falcon School District 49,
Colorado Springs, Colorado*

CROSS-CULTURAL ADAPTABILITY INVENTORY

The Cross-Cultural Adaptability Inventory (CCAI; Kelly & Meyers, 1992) is a 50-item self-scored inventory that measures the ability of an individual to live and work in a cross-cultural environment. The CCAI is a self-assessment inventory. The instrument was first developed in 1987 by Dr. Colleen Kelly, a human resource specialist, and Dr. Judith Meyers, a clinical psychologist with a specialty in diagnostics. The instrument met the needs of cross-cultural specialists who needed a training tool to promote cross-cultural understanding and insight. The CCAI focuses on four skill areas that research has shown to be critical in adapting to other-cultures. The CCAI is based on a cultural general approach, which purports that there are certain commonalities to all areas across cultural transitions, regardless of the culture of origin. It provides a frame of reference for evaluating individuals adapting from one culture to another or working in a multicultural setting.

The inventory is a self-report instrument that requires individuals to respond along a six-point Likert scale. Because of its high face validity, the questions can be transparent: Individuals who want to place themselves in a favorable light can slant their answers. However, respondents are encouraged to be honest about their responding style so that the information will be useful. The instrument stanine scores on four dimensions associated with cross-cultural adaption. Scores are plotted on a circle graph,

and the individual compares his or her four scores to one another. Follow-up training focuses on skill development in needed areas.

The Emotional Resilience scale is the largest of the four, with 18 items. The content focus involves coping with stress and ambiguity, rebounding from imperfections and mistakes, trying new things and experiences, and interacting with people in new or similar situations. People who are emotionally resilient tend to have a positive attitude, resourcefulness, and the ability to modulate negative emotions.

The next dimension, Flexibility/Openness, has 17 items and assesses the extent to which a person enjoys the different ways of thinking and behaving that are usually encountered in a cross-cultural experience. The items deal with openness toward those who are different from oneself, tolerance of others, and flexibility with regard to new experiences. It involves a nonjudgmental approach and flexibility in behavior.

The Perceptual Acuity scale has 10 items and deals with attention to communication cues and the accurate perception of cues across cultures. It assesses behaviors as well as perceptions. Perceptual acuity is synonymous with cultural empathy. It is the ability to distinguish the logic and coherence of other cultures, and involves the ability to interpret nonverbal and social cues.

The final scale is Personal Autonomy, which has seven items. It deals with personal identity, confidence in one's values and beliefs, and a sense of empowerment in the context of an unfamiliar environment with different values. It measures a person's sense of identity and adherence to a strong set of cultural values, as well as respect for the values and traditions of another culture.

The CCAI is a popular instrument among trainers and cross-cultural specialists because it is research based, easy to understand and administer, self-scoring, inexpensive, and easily available. It was normed on a population of 653 cross-cultural specialists, foreign students, educators, missionaries, and businesspeople. The test underwent two revisions where factor analysis, principal components analysis, and item analysis were performed. The final version was published by NCS in 1992. The instrument has excellent alpha reliability, face validity, and construct validity. Predictive validity has not been established, and it is not recommended that the CCAI be used for selection purposes.

The CCAI is used to develop insight into the adaption process, increase awareness of cross-cultural issues, and provide training for individuals living and working in other cultures. It also has application for multicultural work groups. The CCAI has been used to train foreign students and to prepare businesspeople and their families for relocation abroad. The CCAI has trained volunteer groups working abroad (such as missionaries) and has assisted social-services groups working with immigrant populations. The CCAI is also an excellent tool for training counselors, teachers, and principals in the issues of cross-cultural competency. Psychotherapists have found the CCAI useful in working with foreign-born patients as a feedback tool.

The CCAI has a manual that provides thorough information on the development of the instrument, the theories underlying the instrument, and the statistical data supporting it. Training tools are available that provide a full-day training design, as well as follow-up materials in the form of action planning. A feedback form is also available.

REFERENCE

Kelly, C., & Meyers, J. (1992). *The Cross-Cultural Adaptability Inventory (CCAI)*. Minneapolis, MN: National Computer Systems.

JUDITH MEYERS
San Diego, California

CROSS-CULTURAL SPECIAL EDUCATION (*See* Culturally/Linguistically Diverse Students and Learning Disabilities)

CROSS-MODALITY TRAINING

Cross-modality training refers to teaching the neurological process of converting information received through one input modality to another system within the brain. The process is also referred to as intersensory integration, intermodal transfer, and transducing. Cross-modality integration problems have been linked historically to learning disabilities. It has been hypothesized that certain learners may process visual and auditory information accurately when each type of information is presented distinctly but be deficient in tasks requiring them to shift or cross information between sensory systems (Chalfant & Scheffelin, 1969).

Reading, where the learner must relate visual symbols to auditory equivalents, is one academic domain for which cross-modal integration is required. Johnson and Myklebust (1978) proposed that some reading disorders are due to an inability to make such conversions within the neurosensory system. It also has been proposed that disabilities such as apraxia, or the inability to plan and execute appropriate motor action, are related to inadequate cross-modality integration because the child must convert an auditory memory of a word into motor output (Lerner, 1985).

Cross-modality training programs have been devised to address intersensory integration problems. For example, Frostig (1965, 1968) advocated cross-modality exercises, including activities such as describing a picture (visual to auditory), following spoken directions (auditory to motor), and feeling objects through a curtain and drawing their shapes on paper (tactile to visual-motor). Scant research is available to support the use of cross-modality training as a strategy to improve students' academic skills. Additionally, few, if any, tests are designed to assess cross-modal perception. However, cross-modality training for a speaking-writing connection has recently became popular, but lacks a theoretical base (Weissburg, 2006).

REFERENCES

Chalfant, J., & Scheffelin, M. (1969). *Central processing dysfunction in children* (NINDS Monograph NO. 9). Bethesda, MD: U.S. Department of Health, Education, and Welfare.

Frostig, M. (1965). Corrective reading in the classroom. *Reading Teacher, 18,* 573–580.

Frostig, M. (1968). Education for children with learning disabilities. In H. Myklebust (Ed.), *Progress in learning disabilities.* New York, NY: Grune & Stratton.

Johnson, D., & Myklebust, H. (1967). *Learning disabilities: Educational principles and practices.* New York, NY: Grune & Stratton.

Lerner, J. W. (1985). *Learning disabilities: Theories, diagnosis, and teaching strategies.* Boston, MA: Houghton Mifflin.

Weissburg, R. (2006). *What cross-modality studies (don't) tell us about L2 writing.* Retrieved from www.symposium:slw.org/2006/

DOUGLAS FUCHS
LYNN S. FUCHS
Peabody College,
Vanderbilt University

See *also* Developmental Test of Visual Perception—Second Edition; Frostig Remedial Program; Multisensory Instruction

CROUZON SYNDROME

Crouzon syndrome, also known as craniofacial dysostosis, is characterized by premature closure of the cranial sutures between certain bones in the skull and distinctive facial abnormalities. Crouzon syndrome can be evident at birth or during infancy. Crouzon syndrome is a rare disorder that can be inherited as an autosomal dominant trait or, in some cases, results possibly from mutation, as there is no family history. Both male and female are thought to be equally affected with as many as 1 in 25,000 found at birth. Due to the variability in associated symptoms, this number may be a low estimate of the actual number of cases (Kreiborg, 1981a).

Crouzon syndrome is commonly characterized by facial features, including a flat, broad forehead, widely spaced eyes with a reversed slant, a high palate, a beak-like nose, and occasionally malformations of auditory canals. The cranial and facial malformations can vary in severity from case to case, including differences seen among individuals within the same family. The degree of cranial malformation may be variable depending on the specific cranial sutures involved as well as the order and rate of progression. Limb abnormalities are rarely seen. Often, however, individuals with Crouzon syndrome experience dental abnormalities due to underdevelopment of the upper jaw. The degree of cranial malformation may be variable, depending on the specific cranial sutures involved as well as the order and rate of progression. Often there is a premature fusion of the sutures between the bones forming the forehead and the upper sides of the skull (Kreiborg, 1981a).

Studies have shown that neurological deficits include as many as 30% affected by headaches and about 12% affected by uncontrolled seizures. Mental retardation was present only in approximately 3% of the cases (Berg, 1996).

As previously stated, Crouzon syndrome can be inherited as an autosomal dominant trait; thus, the one gene from the mother or father will be expressed dominating the other, normal gene and resulting in the appearance of the disease. The risk of transmitting this disease from the affected parent to the offspring is 50% for each pregnancy regardless of the sex of the child (Berg, 1996).

On rare occasions, Crouzon syndrome can occur with a skin disease known as acanthosis nigricans, which is characterized by a velvety thickening of the skin with hyperpigmentation. These skin disorders usually emerge around puberty and can occur on the neck, abdomen, chest, breasts, eyelids, and nostrils as well as under the arms and around the mouth. In addition, unlike Crouzon syndrome alone, with acanthosis nigricans individuals may suffer from hydrocephalus (impaired flow or absorption of cerebrospinal fluid, potentially leading to increasing fluid pressure within the skull) and choanal atresia (bony tissue blocks the passageway between the nose and throat; Kreiborg, 1981b).

Other syndromes similar to Crouzon syndrome include Pfeiffer, Apert, Saethre-Bhotzen, and Jackson-Weiss syndromes. These disorders share the commonality of craniofacial malformations or abnormalities. Similar disorders are helpful for a differential diagnosis.

Characteristics

1. Facial abnormalities include a wide, broad forehead, beak-like nose, and widely spaced eyes.

2. Although rare, limb abnormalities can occur.
3. Neurological deficits include as many as 30% headaches and 12% uncontrolled seizures.
4. In 3% of the cases, mental retardation was present.
5. A skin disease known as acanthosis nigricans occurred in a few cases.

Early intervention is important with infants diagnosed with Crouzon syndrome. Diagnosis is often based on a variety of clinical evaluations, identification of characteristic physical findings, and specialized tests. Treatment will depend on the specific symptoms affecting the individual. A team of medical professionals including pediatricians, surgeons, orthopedists, neurologists, ophthalmologists, and other health-care professionals can address the defects. In addition, to help children suffering from Crouzon syndrome reach their fullest potential, special social support, speech therapy, psychological treatment, and other vocational services may also be useful. Although only a small percentage are affected by mental retardation, special educational services may prove useful to mediate any potential learning disabilities as well as help the child maintain studies due to potential frequent absences from doctors' appointments and other medical interventions.

REFERENCES

Berg, B. (1996). *Principles of child neurology*. San Francisco, CA: McGraw-Hill.

Kreiborg, S. (1981a). Crouzon syndrome. *Scandinavian Journal of Dental Research, 81*, 170–198.

Kreiborg, S. (1981b). Variable expressivity of Crouzon's syndrome within a family. *Scandinavian Journal of Dental Research, 85*, 175–184.

Lisa A. Fasnacht-Hill
*Keck University of Southern California
School of Medicine,
University of Southern California/
University Affiliated Program at
Children's Hospital of Los Angeles*

CROUZON SYNDROME (CRANIOFACIAL DYSOSTOSIS)

Crouzon syndrome (CS) is believed to be a congenital disability that follows a pattern of autosomal dominance. The major physical characteristics are a result of premature closing of the skull, which causes cranial deformity, widely spaced eyes (which may protrude), and a misshapened face. The nasal bridge may be flat and the nose beaked with underdeveloped nasal sinuses. Malformation of the ear canals and eyes as a result of hypertension and orbital deformity is said to occur in 70 to 80% of the cases (along with optic atrophy); this may cause visual and hearing problems. The upper jaw and bones of the midface may be underdeveloped and the lower jaw may be prominent. Crowding, misalignment of upper teeth, and an enlarged tongue may cause some problems with eating and speech development. Higher incidence of infections also may occur, and in some cases congenital heart disease has been reported. Mental retardation may be noted in some children, but most have average mental abilities. In rare instances, spina bifida may be present (Carter, 1978).

Some related services may be necessary if visual, aural, and motor problems exist. Speech therapy will probably be required. In addition, psychological and guidance counseling may be required because of the physical appearance of the child. Mainstreamed placement with support services is often the proper educational approach for CS children (Fasnacht-Hill, 2003).

REFERENCES

Carter, C. (Ed.). (1978). *Medical aspects of mental retardation* (2nd ed.). Springfield, IL: Thomas.

Fasnacht-Hill, L. (2003). Crouzon syndrome. In E. Fletcher-Janzen & C. R. Reynolds (Eds.), *Childhood disorders diagnostic desk reference* (pp. 157–158). Hoboken, NJ: Wiley.

Goodman, R., & Gorlin, R. (1977). *Atlas of the face in genetic disorders* (2nd ed.). St. Louis, MO: Mosby.

SALLY L. FLAGLER
University of Oklahoma

CRUICKSHANK, WILLIAM M. (1915–1992)

William M. Cruickshank received his BA in 1937 from Eastern Michigan University, his MA in 1938 from the University of Chicago, and his PhD in 1945 from the University of Michigan.

Cruickshank was the founder and director of the Division of Special Education and Rehabilitation and distinguished professor at Syracuse University from 1946 to 1967. He subsequently became director of the Institute for the Study of Mental Health and Related Disabilities and professor of child and family health, psychology, and education at the University of Michigan from 1967 until his retirement.

Since 1937, Cruickshank's main interests were in the area of brain-injured children, neurologically handicapped children, and the neurophysiological characteristics of accurately defined learning-disabled children. Author of over 200 books, articles, and edited books (some of which are translated in several languages), Cruickshank's major publications include *Teaching Methods for Brain-Injured and Hyperactive Children* (1961), *Learning Disabilities in Home, School, and Community* (1977), and *Psychoeducational Foundations of Learning Disabilities* (1973).

Holder of six honorary degrees, he taught in many countries and remained active as a visiting professor and lecturer for a number of years following his retirement from the University of Michigan. As the founder, first president (1975–1985), and executive director of the International Academy for Research in Learning Disabilities, he was an international authority on the problems of learning-disabled children and youths. Dr. William Cruickshank passed away in 1992, after a long and productive career.

REFERENCES

Cruickshank, W. M. (1973). Psychoeducational foundations of learning disabilities. Upper Saddle River, NJ: Prentice Hall.

Cruickshank, W. M. (1977). *Learning disabilities in home, school, and community* (Rev. ed.). Syracuse, NY: Syracuse University.

Cruickshank, W. M., et al. (1961). *Teaching methods for brain-injured and hyperactive children*. Syracuse, NY: Syracuse University.

KAY E. KETZENBERGER
The University of Texas of the Permian Basin

CRYPTOPHASIA

Cryptophasia is a language disorder characteristic of twins. It occurs in 40–47% of all twin pairs in early childhood (Caldwell, 2003). Cryptophasia was historically described as a secret language between twins that they invent themselves and that is unintelligible to others. It has been found that some words are indeed invented, but for the most part the words come from the adult language to which they are exposed (Bakker, 1987). Twins often have delayed language development accompanied by what appears to be a jargon that only the twins understand. This jargon is a form of imitation of adult language with its own syntax, a type of "pidgin." The language may become elaborate and complex but remains, for the most part, understandable only to the twins. The language develops as they attempt to imitate the speech sounds of adults. Since twins spend an inordinate amount of time together, they begin to understand approximations of mature language and reinforce each other for use of this lesser form of communication. Cryptophasia retards normal language development and therefore twins may need speech/language services in special education (Caldwell, 2003).

Characteristics

1. The words spoken lack morphology, present in a different word order, and have deviant articulation and a different syntax to the point that the language may be completely unintelligible to adult speakers.

2. Cryptophasia not only occurs in twins but also can emerge in two siblings or close friends in the same stage of language development.

3. The language is thought to stem entirely from the environment, not genetics, and is based on reinforcement from the other child or twin.

4. The unintelligible language disappears soon.

5. One source stated that nearly 5% of twins develop language difficulties.

6. Cryptophasia can restrain intellectual development—more specifically, language development in terms of grammatical structure and richness of vocabulary.

7. Children with cryptophasia tend to be slower in language acquisition than other children, particularly in articulation.

REFERENCES

Bakker, P. (1987). Autonomous languages of twins. *Acta Geneticae Medicae et Gemellologiae, 36,* 233–238.

Caldwell, C. M. (2003). Cryptophasia. In E. Fletcher-Janzen & C. R. Reynolds (Eds.), *Childhood disorders diagnostic desk reference* (pp. 158–159). Hoboken, NJ: Wiley.

CECIL R. REYNOLDS
Texas A&M University

See also **Language Delays; Language Disorders; Twins**

CRYSTALLIZED VERSUS FLUID INTELLIGENCE (*See* Cattell-Horn-Carroll Theory of Cognitive Abilities)

CUED SPEECH

Cued speech was developed in 1967 by R. Orin Cornett at Gallaudet College in Washington, DC. It was designed to clarify ambiguity experienced by severely and profoundly hearing-impaired individuals relying on lipreading as a means of comprehending speech (Evans, 1982; NCSA, 2006). During speechreading, hearing-impaired individuals may confuse many sounds such as /p/, /m/, and /b/, because they are visually similar. Users of cued speech attempt to overcome this confusion by providing a visual supplement to information presented through speechreading.

This system includes 12 hand signals or cues (presented in Figure C.15). Four cues are hand positions that differentiate between groups of vowel sounds. A hand can be placed at the side of the face, the throat, the chin, or the corner of the mouth. Eight cues, based on American Sign Language (ASL) hand shapes, are hand configurations used to visually differentiate between groups of consonants (Wilbur, 1979; NCSA, 2006). For example, a full hand represents the /m/, /f/, and /t/ sounds, whereas the extension of only the index finger represents the /d/, /p/, and /zh/ sounds. An auditory signal is visually supplemented by superimposing a consonant hand configuration on a vowel hand position. For example, the words *mitt* and *bit* may appear similar to the hearing-impaired speech reader; however, these words are cued differently. *Mitt* is cued with a full hand positioned at the throat, whereas *bit* is cued by placing a *b* hand shape at the throat.

Use of cued speech requires training for both the sender and the hearing-impaired individual. Cornett (1967) reports that an average of approximately 12 to

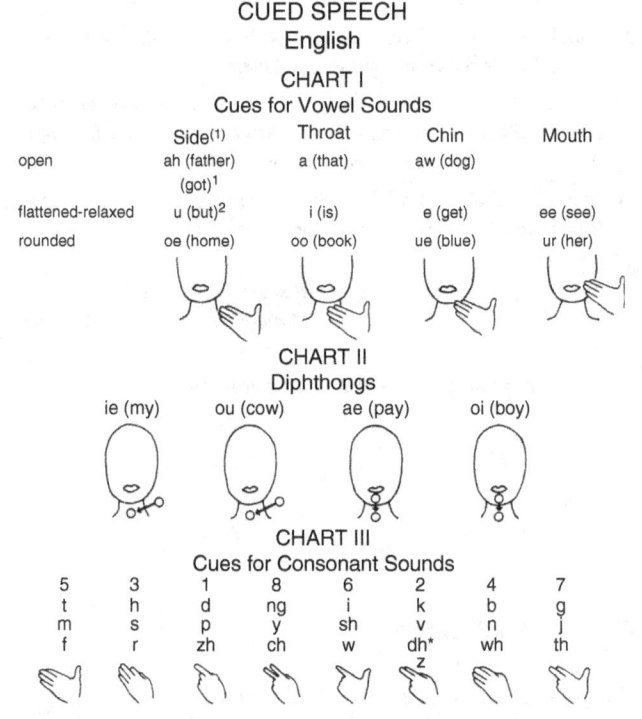

Figure C.15. Cued speech—English.
Source: Wilbur (1979).

20 hours is required to develop proficient use of cued speech. Actually, time will vary with the individual learner and fluency comes with practice.

There are advantages and disadvantages associated with the use of cued speech. Its advantages include an adherence to the philosophy of oralism. Cued speech supplements information presented through speechreading; however, it cannot be used and understood in the absence of speech. In addition, use of cued speech has been associated with increases in speechreading accuracy (Clarke & Ling, 1976; Ling & Clarke, 1975; NCSA, 2006), vocabulary, and intelligibility (Rupert, 1969). Disadvantages include the questionable phonetic competence of users, lack of transfer potential to reading (Wilbur, 1979), and an overdependence on cues (Clarke & Ling, 1976). The National Cued Speech Association (NCSA) can be found online (http://cuedspeech.org/).

REFERENCES

Clarke, B. R., & Ling, D. (1976). The effects of using cued speech: A follow-up study. *Volta Review*, *78*, 23–34.

Cornett, R. O. (1967). Cued speech. *American Annals of the Deaf*, *112*, 3–13.

Evans, L. (1982). *Total communication: Structure and strategy*. Washington, DC: Gallaudet College Press.

Ling, D., & Clarke, B. R. (1975). Cued speech: An evaluative study. *American Annals of the Deaf*, *120*, 480–488.

National Cued Speech Association (NCSA). (2006). *Cued speech index*. Retrieved from http://cuedspeech.org/

Rupert, J. (1969). Kindergarten program using cued speech at the Idaho School for the Deaf. *Proceedings of the 44th Meeting of American Instructors of the Deaf*, Berkeley, CA.

Wilbur, R. B. (1979). *American Sign Language and sign systems*. Baltimore, MD: University Park Press.

MAUREEN A. SMITH
Pennsylvania State University

See also Sign Language; Total Communication

CUISENAIRE RODS

Cuisenaire rods are a set of colored rods of different lengths used to aid in the instruction and learning of important mathematical fundamentals primarily at the elementary level, including seriation, arithmetic, measurement, fractions, and variables (Davidson, 1977).

Cuisenaire rods were invented by Belgian teacher Georges Cuisenaire, who wrote about using the rods

Color	Length (in cm)	Visual Representation	Number of rods per set
White	1		22
Red	2		12
Light Green	3		10
Lavender	4		6
Yellow	5		4
Dark Green	6		4
Black	7		4
Brown	8		4
Blue	9		4
Orange	10		4

Figure C.16. Length and number of Cuisenaire rods in a complete set.

in teaching in his 1952 book, *Les nombres en couleurs* (*Numbers in Color*). Although there are 10 different rods, a complete set includes multiples of each rod for various mathematical applications. Figure C.16 shows the length in centimeters and number of each rod in a complete set of Cuisenaire rods.

Both Friedrich Froebel and Maria Montessori used sets of rods to teach mathematics concepts. Froebel's consisted of 12 wooden rods of lengths 1 through 12 inches. Montessori's consisted of 10 rods with lengths 1 through 10 units with alternating blue and red segments. Both Froebel and Montessori emphasized a developmentally appropriate approach to learning that included physical objects as concrete representations of mathematical concepts. Cuisenaire shared a similar pedagogical approach to learning mathematics.

The National Council of Teachers of Mathematics (NCTM) recommends students "develop and deepen their understanding of mathematical concepts and relationships as they create, compare, and use various representations" (2000, p. 280). Manipulatives such as Cuisenaire rods can serve to guide students on a pathway from concrete to abstract representations of mathematics. An effective strategy for mathematics education for students with learning disabilities is the Concrete-to-Representational-to-Abstract (CRA) instruction model (Cass, Case, Smith, & Jackson, 2003). The CRA model is comprised of three levels of learning where each level is based on the previous level. Cuisenaire rods provide an environment where learners begin with a concrete, hands-on representation of mathematics ideas and move to static representations, before proceeding to the final abstract stage where symbols and standard mathematical notation is used. Using manipulatives such as Cuisenaire rods can help students

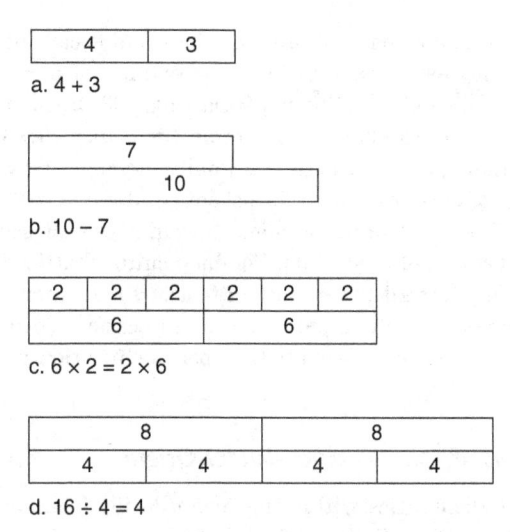

Figure C.17. Using Cuisenaire rods to model (a) addition, (b) subtraction, (c) multiplication, and (d) division.

develop a deep understanding of the target concept and reduce the need for teachers to review concepts (Piel & Green, 2010).

Figure C.17 shows examples of ways Cuisenaire rods can model arithmetic at a conceptual level. Figures C.17 (a) and (b) show how addition and subtraction can be modeled. Figure (c) incorporates different concepts behind multiplication, including a way to model six groups of two, two groups of six, and the Commutative Property of Multiplication, which states that the products of both multiplications will be equal. Figure (d) shows both measurement and partitive division using the Cuisenaire rods. For learning fractions, Cuisenaire rods can be used as a measurement model, in addition to or instead of the more traditional area model used to represent fractions (McNamara, 2007). Students with learning disabilities have also been shown to benefit from the use of Cuisenaire rods when solving word problems (Marsh & Cook, 1996).

There also exist computer-based versions of the Cuisenaire rods, available either as a Web-based application or stand-alone software for a computer. A virtual manipulative has been defined as "an interactive, Web-based visual representation of a dynamic object that presents opportunities for constructing mathematical knowledge" (Moyer, Bolyard, & Spikell, 2002, p. 373). The NRICH Project by a group of mathematics educators from the University of Cambridge hosts a website that has a large number of online games and applications based on the Cuisenaire rods (http://nrich.maths.org). Other sites, such as Math Playground (http://www.mathplayground.com), offer their version of the online Cuisenaire rods called Number Bars.

[References omitted by the author.]

ADAM P. HARBAUGH, PhD
University of North Carolina at Charlotte
Fourth edition

CULTURAL ATTITUDES TOWARD SPECIAL EDUCATION

The children and youth of the United States represent an increasingly diverse variety of cultural and linguistic groups. Between 1995 and 2050, the overall U.S. population is forecast to grow by almost 50%, with the Anglo (White, Not of Hispanic Origin) population experiencing the smallest proportional increase (approximately 7% percent; U.S. Bureau of the Census, 1994). This is in sharp contrast to the proportional increase forecast for the African American population (70%), Native American population (83%), Hispanic population (258%), and the Asian/Pacific Islander population (269%) during the same time period.

In order to provide appropriate educational services for such a heterogeneous population, an understanding of cultural affiliation and corresponding cultural attitudes as related to special education is necessary. A cultural group, for the purpose of this entry, is defined as a group set apart from others because of its national origin or distinctive cultural patterns (Schaefer, 1990). It is furthermore recognized that although members of a cultural group may have common values, beliefs, and behaviors, no individual member exemplifies all of the group's modal practices (Wehrly, 1995). The following sections include a discussion of the literature related to cultural attitudes toward special education, a summary of common attitudes reported for various cultural groups, and an analysis of the benefits and limitations of our current knowledge base.

The present body of literature related to cultural attitudes toward special education is largely focused on suggestions for practice in the special education arena and can be generally categorized as either (a) theory based (e.g., "best practice" papers in which general knowledge of specific cultural groups is applied to the school setting), or (b) research based (i.e., the presentation of data to demonstrate specific relationships between cultural attitudes and educational strategies). Thus, cultural attitudes toward special education are presented within the framework of these two categories.

Theory-Based Literature

Throughout the previous century, two main theoretical perspectives have been employed when working with culturally and linguistically diverse children within the school setting (Bowman, 1994). These two perspectives may be simplistically categorized as uniformity and diversity. The theoretical perspective of uniformity, labeled by Kohlberg and Mayer (1972) as "cultural transmission," places an emphasis on socializing children into a uniform culture through standardized curricula, educational experiences, and achievement expectations. In contrast, the theoretical perspective of diversity emphasizes the uniquely individual nature of education and the need for schools to address the cultural, linguistic, and intellectual heterogeneity of children.

Special education service delivery as mandated by public law (e.g., PL 94-142, IDEA, IDEIA) is based upon the theoretical perspective of diversity. In order to effectively meet the legal requirements set forth within the public law, it is necessary for school personnel to have a basic understanding of the attitudes and beliefs common to the different culturally and linguistically diverse groups that they serve. Numerous special education theorists have attempted to provide such an understanding through the application of specific cultural knowledge to the interpersonal interactions that take place within a school setting (e.g., Banks, 1994; Harry, 1992; Lynch & Hansen, 1992). The following is a synopsis of theory-based literature regarding the attitudes of culturally and linguistically diverse parents toward special education.

Parental Attitudes

The topic of parental attitudes toward special education as discussed in theory-based literature is typically focused on specific cultural groups.

Parents of African American Origin

Literature regarding the attitudes of African American parents is limited and thus far suggests that parents may emphasize the role of immediate and extended family members (Seligman & Darling, 1989) and that attitudes toward severe disability may be often be related to a traditionally fatalistic interpretation of events (Harry, 1992). Common to many cultural groups, this fatalistic perception is described by Seligman and Darling (1989) as a seemingly passive acceptance of life circumstances that may in turn assist in the acceptance of a child's disability. African American parents of children with more mild forms of disability may display attitudes of caution and skepticism due to a well-documented history of group misdiagnosis and inappropriate special education service delivery (Harry, 1992).

Parents of Hispanic Origin

Hispanic parents may also emphasize the role of immediate and extended family members and may be strongly tied to familism. This traditional view of the child as a reflection of the family unit may make acceptance of a severe disability more difficult for many Hispanic parents (Harry, 1992). A common cultural perception, in which developmental and intellectual disabilities are indistinguishable from mental disorders and mental illness, may add to the difficulty of acceptance (Adkins & Young, 1976). As a result of these two factors, the stigma associated with severe disabilities may be quite personal and significant for many Hispanic parents. On the other hand, a cultural emphasis on family relations and social interactions may assist parents in the acceptance of more mild forms of disability (Seligman & Darling, 1989). The mildly disabled child's ability to maintain his or her social role with immediate and extended family members may be a source of encouragement for parents and may even serve as a foundation for questioning the validity of the school's classification of their child. Common cultural attitudes of deference toward and respect for teachers and other school personnel may inhibit parental communication of concerns and expectations related to the special education process (Harry, 1992).

Parents of Asian/Pacific Islander Origin

Severe disabilities within the Asian/Pacific Islander culture have typically been viewed as the result of previous actions of parents or ancestors, the influence of spiritual forces (as in the case of some Southeast Asian groups), specific behaviors of the mother during pregnancy, or the imbalance of physiological functions (Chan, 1986). The potential cause of a disability may therefore be a source of shame for parents in that it is thought to reflect on the past or present behavior of family members. In addition, the inability of a child with a severe disability to represent the family through academic or occupational success may serve as a secondary source of embarrassment for some parents (Yano, 1986, as cited in Harry, 1992). A traditional Asian social structure that places the needs of the group before the needs of the individual may help influence acceptance of the situation and parental attitude toward special education service delivery (Dao, 1991). Asian/Pacific Islander parents of children with more mild forms of disability may tend to interpret the source of difficulty as "laziness" or ineffective training at home (Chan, 1986).

Parents of Native American Origin

In accordance with traditional beliefs, many Native American parents view disabilities as having both a spiritual and physical etiology. The singular biological/psychoeducational viewpoint of the public schools in regard to disabilities may limit the course of action preferred by many Native American parents (Harry, 1992). Likewise, the public school procedure of interacting directly with parents may bypass the complex system of extended family communication shared by many Native Americans (Huang & Gibbs, 1992). The attitude of parents toward special education may also be influenced by the emphasis placed on childhood independence and the use of extended family members as caregivers. The extended support system available to the child and the child's freedom to find his or her own place in community relations is exemplified by the absence of words such as "disabled" and "handicapped" from most Native American languages (Harry, 1992).

Benefits and Limitations

The benefit of theory-based literature within this area is the increased awareness and improved communication that results from a basic understanding of a group's common beliefs and practices. Flanagan and Miranda (1995) note that the specific information generated about a given culture through theory-based literature aids in understanding the values, beliefs, and behaviors that are expressed in cross-cultural interactions. Unfortunately, the tendency to generalize cultural attitudes to all members of a particular group to the exclusion of individual traits and preferences may serve as its greatest limitation. This concern sparked Lynch and Harry (1992) to caution against the use of theory-based literature as a cross-cultural "recipe book" that stereotypes individuals rather than providing a foundation for better understanding.

Research-Based Literature

There are a limited number of research-based studies addressing the attitudes of culturally and linguistically diverse groups within the United States toward special education. The few studies that are available tend to be ethnographic in nature and are focused on parental and teacher attitudes regarding (a) meanings attached to disabilities or special education labels, (b) the role of language and culture in special education placements, (c) special education instruction format, and (d) parental participation in the special education process. The majority of researchers within this area employed naturalistic research methodologies such as interviews, surveys, or both, with not all studies including a quantitative analysis of results. The results from a sample of exemplary research-based studies are included in this section.

Parental Attitudes

Research-based studies regarding culturally and linguistically diverse parental attitudes toward special education have addressed various topics.

Meanings Attached to Labels

Studies on the meanings attached to special education labels by culturally and linguistically diverse parents reveal that (a) their concept and boundaries of "normal" may be different from those of the educational system (Bennett, 1988; Danseco, 1997; Harry, 1992; Rodriguez, 1995; Zetlin, Padron, & Wilson, 1996); (b) they are often confused by the specific terminology or labels common to special education (e.g., handicapped, disabled, impaired, retarded) and may associate these labels with more severe, as opposed to mild, manifestations of impairments (Danseco, 1997; Harry, 1992); (c) they may perceive the label as somehow reflective of family inadequacies (Harry, 1992); and (d) they may attach biomedical and sociocultural (e.g., spiritual) causes to the labels (Danseco, 1997; Rodriguez, 1995).

Perceived Role of Language and Culture

Several studies (e.g., Harry, 1992; Rodriguez, 1995; Zetlin et al., 1996) revealed parental perceptions that their child was placed in special education as a result of a language and cultural difference and not because of a true handicapping condition. This sentiment was reported by parents from various cultural and linguistic backgrounds (e.g., Hispanic and Southeast Asian).

Instructional Format Concerns

While parents tend to report positive feelings regarding the smaller group size for instruction found in special education, they also expressed concern that the slower pace and lack of actual individualization of instruction might hinder, rather than help, their children (Harry, 1992; Zetlin et al., 1996). Confusion seems to exist among some parents as to how native language and culture should be utilized in their child's instruction (Zetlin et al., 1996), while others felt that instruction should focus on English and reading (Harry, 1992; Rodriguez, 1995).

Factors Affecting Parental Participation

Parental opportunities for participation in the special education process were often reported by parents as (a) impersonal and one-sided (e.g., during meetings), with school personnel underestimating parental capabilities and limiting parental voice and power in decision making; (b) overwhelming with regard to the number of letters and forms involved; (c) constrained by the parents' limited knowledge of the special education process (e.g., legal rights and necessity of attendance at meetings; Bennett, 1988; Danseco, 1997; Harry, 1992; Rodriguez, 1995); and (d) permeated with distrust (Bennett, 1988; Harry, 1992).

School Personnel Attitudes

Research-based studies within this area are generally focused on the attitudes of culturally and linguistically diverse school personnel, primarily teachers, toward special education. Two recent studies provide an example of this type of research. Rodriguez (1995) and Paez, Flores, and Trujillo (in press) surveyed culturally and linguistically diverse teachers employed in bilingual education programs. Both studies revealed that the teachers' knowledge of special education services and processes were limited and that the older the age group (Rodriguez, 1995) or the longer the time since college graduation (Paez et al., in press) the less informed they generally were.

According to Rodriguez (1995), there was significant variation among 100 teachers of Southeast Asian origin with regard to the belief that spiritual forces or destiny cause a child's disability with approximately one-third agreeing, over one-third disagreeing, and the rest being ambivalent on this point. Many of these teachers felt that children were often misplaced in special education and were discriminated against because of lower English proficiency. Moreover, they reported that lower levels of English proficiency among some students of Southeast Asian origin resulted in lower expectations for these students on the part of other school personnel.

Benefits and Limitations

The benefits of research-based literature in this area are that it provides for data-based decision making, often validates best practices literature, and supports a naturalistic or personalized approach to research. However, the current methodological approach in which surveys, interviews, or a combination of both are utilized is limited by subjectivity (e.g., in the generation of questions and consolidation of results) and the possible intrusion of the interviewer in the process. In addition, when the attitudes surveyed are those of culturally and linguistically diverse groups, the studies are ethnographic and have additional constraints, such as language and sociocultural barriers that are encountered regardless of whether the researcher is a member of the cultural group.

Conclusion

It is clear that cultural attitudes play an important role in a family's adjustment to a child with a disability and the impact the situation has on the family's responsiveness and receptivity to sources of help (Fine & Gardner, 1994). The work of Harry (1992) serves as an example of the use of theory-based knowledge to construct data-based research. It is this type of application that will allow accurate and pertinent knowledge regarding cultural attitudes to be applied to the special education setting. Regardless of the informational source, whether it be theory- or research-based literature, the attitudes of culturally and linguistically diverse parents toward special education must be viewed within the context of the current life situation of the individual caregiver (Fracasso & Busch-Rossnagel, 1992). Dennis and Giangreco (1996) expand on this sentiment by noting that contextual considerations that should be considered include the emotional climate of racial or ethnic discrimination experienced by the individual, the implications of poverty, the neighborhood and living environment, and the degree and duration of acculturation into the dominant cultural group. Added to this list is the universal and very individual experience of caring for a child with special needs (Lynch & Hansen, 1992).

REFERENCES

Adkins, P. G., & Young, R. G. (1976). Cultural perceptions on the treatment of handicapped school children of Mexican-American parentage. *Journal of Research and Development in Education, 9*(4), 83–90.

Banks, J. A. (1994). *An introduction to multicultural education.* Boston, MA: Allyn & Bacon.

Bennett, A. T. (1988). Gateways to powerlessness: Incorporating Hispanic deaf children and families into formal schooling. *Disability, Handicap, and Society, 3*(2), 119–151.

Bowman, B. T. (1994). The challenge of diversity. *Phi Delta Kappan, 76,* 218–224.

Chan, S. Q. (1986). Parents of exceptional Asian children. In M. K. Kitano & P. C. Chinn (Eds.), *Exceptional Asian children and youth* (pp. 36–53). Reston, VA: Council for Exceptional Children.

Danseco, E. R. (1997). Parental beliefs on childhood disability: Insights on culture, children development, and intervention. *International Journal of Disability, Development and Education, 44,* 41–52.

Dao, M. (1991). Designing assessment procedures for educationally at-risk Southeast Asian–American students. *Journal of Learning Disabilities, 24,* 594–601.

Dennis, R. E., & Giangreco, M. F. (1996). Creating conversation: Reflections on cultural sensitivity in family interviewing. *Exceptional Children, 63*(1), 103–113.

Fine, M. J., & Gardner, A. (1994). Collaborative consultation with families of children with special needs: Why bother? *Journal of Educational and Psychological Consultation, 5,* 283–308.

Flanagan, D. P., & Miranda, A. H. (1995). Best practices in working with culturally different families. In A. Thomas & J. Grimes (Eds.), *Best practices in school psychology III* (pp. 1049–1060). Washington, DC: NASP.

Fracasso, M., & Busch-Rossnagel, N. (1992). Parents and children of Hispanic origin. In M. Procidano & C. Fisher (Eds.), *Contemporary families: A handbook for school professionals* (pp. 83–98). New York, NY: Teachers College Press.

Harry, B. (1992). *Cultural diversity, families and the education system: Communication and empowerment.* New York, NY: Teachers College Press.

Huang, L. N., & Gibbs, J. T. (1992). Partners or adversaries? Home–school collaboration across culture, race, and ethnicity. In S. L. Christenson & J. C. Conoley (Eds.), *Home–school collaboration* (pp. 81–109). Silver Spring, MD: National Association of School Psychologists.

Kohlberg, L., & Mayer, R. (1972). Development as the aim of education. *Harvard Educational Review, 42,* 449–469.

Lynch, E. W., & Hansen, M. J. (1992). *Developing cross-cultural competence: A guide for working with young children and their families.* Baltimore, MD: Brookes.

Paez, D., Flores, J., & Trujillo, T. (in press). Rural school personnel's conceptions of issues of diversity. *Rural Special Education Quarterly, 17.*

Rodriguez, J. (1995). *Southeast Asian's conception of disabilities and special education intervention in American schools.* Lowell: University of Massachusetts, College of Education. (ERIC Document Reproduction Service No. 388 740)

Schaefer, R. T. (1990). *Racial and ethnic groups* (4th ed.). Glenview, IL: Scott Foresman.

Seligman, M., & Darling, R. B. (1989). *Ordinary families, special children.* New York, NY: Guilford Press.

U.S. Bureau of the Census. (1990). *1990 United States census.* Washington, DC: U.S. Department of Commerce, Economics and Statistics Administration.

U.S. Bureau of the Census. (1994). *Population projections of the United States by age, sex, race, and Hispanic origin: 1995–2050.* Washington, DC: U.S. Department of Commerce, Economics and Statistics Administration.

Wehrly, B. (1995). *Pathways to multicultural counseling competence: A developmental journey.* Pacific Grove, CA: Brooks/Cole.

Zetlin, A., Padron, M., & Wilson, S. (1996). The experience of five Latin American families with the special education system. *Education and Training in Mental Retardation and Developmental Disabilities, 31,* 22–28.

ROBERT L. RHODES
DORIS PAEZ
New Mexico State University

CULTURAL BIAS IN TESTING

The cultural test bias hypothesis is the contention that racial and ethnic group differences in mental test scores are the result of inherent flaws in the tests themselves. These flaws bias, or cause systematic error, in a manner that causes ethnic minorities to earn low scores. Mean differences in scores among groups are then interpreted as artifacts of the test and not as reflecting any real differences in mental abilities or skills.

Mean differences in mental test scores across race are some of the most well-established phenomena in psychological research on individual differences. One of the primary explanations of these differences is that they are produced by people who are reared in very different environments, with lower scoring groups having been relatively deprived of the quantity and quality of stimulation received in the formative years by higher scoring groups. Another explanation is that lower scoring groups reflect a difference in the genetic potential for intellectual performance. Most contemporary views take an environment × genetic interaction approach.

Cultural bias in testing has existed as a potential explanation at least since it was raised by Sir Cyril Burt (1921), with occasional papers on the issue appearing over the years. It was not widely accepted as a serious hypothesis until the late 1960s, when the Association of Black Psychologists (ABP) called for a moratorium on the use of psychological tests with minorities and disadvantaged students, particularly with regard to placement in special education programs. In 1969 the ABP issued an official policy statement encouraging parents of black children to refuse to allow their children or themselves to be evaluated on any achievement, intelligence, aptitude, or performance test.

The primary objections to the testing of minorities on the basis of race or cultural bias in the tests have been classified by Reynolds (1982a) into six categories as follows:

1. *Inappropriate content.* Black or other minority children have not been exposed to the material on the test questions or other stimulus materials. The tests are geared toward white middle-class homes and values.

2. *Inappropriate standardization samples.* Ethnic minorities are underrepresented in the collection of normative reference group data. In the early years, it was not unusual for standardization samples of major tests to be all white.

3. *Examiner and language bias.* Since most psychologists are white and primarily speak only standard English, they intimidate blacks and other minorities. They are also unable to communicate accurately with minority children. Lower test scores for minorities, then, are said to reflect this intimidation and difficulty in the communication process, not lower ability levels.

4. *Inequitable social consequences.* As a result of bias in educational and psychological tests, minority group members, who are already at a disadvantage in the educational and vocational markets because of past discrimination, are disproportionately relegated to dead-end educational tracks and thought unable to learn. Labeling effects also fall into this category.

5. *Measurement of different constructs.* Related to item (1), this position asserts that the tests are measuring significantly different attributes when used with children from other than the white, middle-class culture.

6. *Differential predictive validity.* While tests may accurately predict a variety of outcomes for white, middle-class children, they fail to predict at an acceptable level any relevant criteria for minority group members. Corollary to this objection are a variety of competing positions regarding the selection of an appropriate, common criterion

against which to validate tests across cultural groupings. Scholastic or academic attainment levels are considered by a variety of black psychologists to be biased as to criteria.

Additionally, it has been argued (see Reynolds, Lowe, & Saenz, 1999, for a discussion) that minority and majority groups have qualitatively distinct forms of intelligence and personality and thus cannot be assessed with the same methods, negating any attempt to compare groups or test performance.

The actions by the ABP had several positive effects. Prior to the call for a moratorium on testing of minorities, little actual research existed in the area. Much research was prompted by the ABP position as it brought the race bias hypothesis to the forefront of explanations of race differences in intelligence. Also in response to this call for a moratorium, the American Psychological Association Board of Scientific Affairs had a committee appointed to study the use of tests with disadvantaged students. The committee, headed by T. Anne Cleary, gave its official report in the form of an article in *American Psychologist* (Cleary, Humphreys, Kendrick, & Wesman, 1975).

Research on race bias in testing was, and continues to be, of major importance to psychology as well as to society. The cultural test bias hypothesis is probably one of the most crucial scientific questions facing psychology (Reynolds, 1981). If this hypothesis ultimately is accepted as correct, then the past 100 years or so of research into the psychology of individual differences (or differential psychology, the basic psychological science underlying all fields of applied psychology) must be dismissed as artifactual, or at least as confounded, since such research is based on standard psychometric methodology. Race bias in testing is being tested in the judicial courts as well as in the scholarly court of open inquiry. Two major court decisions, known as *Larry P.* (1979) and *Pase* (1980), have given conflicting opinions regarding the issues. Of two federal district courts, one decided that intelligence tests are racially biased and the other decided they are not biased.

Contrary to the position of the late 1960s, considerable research is now available regarding race bias in testing. For the most part, this research has failed to support the test bias hypothesis, revealing that (1) well-constructed, well-standardized educational and psychological tests predict future performance in an essentially equivalent manner across race for U.S.-born ethnic minorities; (2) the internal psychometric structure of the tests is essentially invariant with regard to race; and (3) the content of these tests is about equally appropriate across these groups (Reynolds, 1982a; Reynolds et al., 1999; Reynolds & Carson, 2005).

Race bias in testing is one of the most controversial and violently emotional issues in psychology. It will not be resolved entirely on the basis of research and data,

as tests have unquestionably been abused in their past use with minority groups. Much of the controversy centers around the placement of minority children in special education programs. Thus, special consideration must be given to ensure that the misuses and abuses of the past are thwarted by "intelligent testing" (Kaufman, 1979). A general review of race bias in testing can be found in Jensen (1980). Specialty reviews of race bias in employment testing have been done by Hunter et al. (1979), and of bias in the testing of children by Reynolds (1982a; Reynolds et al., 1999; Reynolds & Carson, 2005). A book-length debate of the issues can be found in Reynolds and Brown (1984). Methodology for investigating most aspects of cultural bias in testing relevant to special education is reviewed in Reynolds (1982b) and Reynolds et al. (1999).

REFERENCES

Burt, C. (1921). *Mental and scholastic tests*. London, UK: P. S. King.

Cleary, T. A., Humphreys, L. G., Kendrick, S. A., & Wesman, A. (1975). Educational uses of tests with disadvantaged students. *American Psychologist, 30*, 15–41.

Hunter, J. E., Schmidt, F. L., & Hunter, R. (1979). Differential validity of employment tests by race: A comprehensive review and analysis. *Psychological Bulletin, 86*, 721–735.

Jensen, A. R. (1980). *Bias in mental testing*. New York, NY: Free Press.

Kaufman, A. S. (1979). *Intelligence testing with the WISC-R*. New York, NY: Wiley.

Reynolds, C. R. (1981). In support of bias in mental testing and scientific inquiry. *Behavioral & Brain Sciences, 3*, 352.

Reynolds, C. R. (1982a). The problem of bias in psychological assessment. In C. R. Reynolds & T. B. Gutkin (Eds.), *The handbook of school psychology*. New York, NY: Wiley.

Reynolds, C. R. (1982b). Methods for detecting construct and predictive bias. In R. A. Berk (Ed.), *Handbook of methods for detecting test bias*. Baltimore, MD: Johns Hopkins University Press.

Reynolds, C. R., & Brown, R. T. (1984). *Perspectives on bias in mental testing*. New York, NY: Wiley.

Reynolds, C. R., & Carson, A. D. (2005). Methods for assessing cultural bias in testing. In C. L. Frisby & C. R. Reynolds (Eds.), *Comprehensive handbook of multicultural school psychology* (pp. 795–823). Hoboken, NJ: Wiley.

Reynolds, C. R., Lowe, P., & Saenz, A. (1999). The problem of bias in psychological assessment. In C. R. Reynolds & T. B. Gutkin (Eds.), *The handbook of school psychology* (3rd ed., pp. 549–595). New York, NY: Wiley.

CECIL R. REYNOLDS
Texas A&M University

See also Larry P.; Marshall v. Georgia; Pase v. Hannon

CULTURALLY/LINGUISTICALLY DIVERSE GIFTED STUDENTS

The immortal words of Harry Passow (1986) express concerns for the exclusion of various cultural and linguistic populations in gifted education programs:

> [T]hese populations constitute the largest reservoir of untapped and underdeveloped talent available in our society. There is clear evidence that talent is not the prerogative of any racial or ethnic group, any social class, or any residential area. It may lie untapped in some situations under some conditions, but no population has either a monopoly or an absence of giftedness. (p. 27)

The fact is that students with special gifts and talents come from all populations, and as society becomes increasingly diverse, educators are faced with a challenge in meeting the needs of students who have special gifts from all populations represented in society. However, government and media reports indicate that educators are not effectively identifying and serving minority students, particularly those who are either considered limited English proficient, or those who are from low socioeconomic status (SES) backgrounds and/or from other cultures out of the mainstream middle-class Anglo American culture. In fact, these groups are not fairly represented in programs for the gifted and talented (Irby, 1993; Ortiz & González, 1989; USDE, 1993).

In the early 1970s, the term *culturally different* was used to refer to children who were from low-SES backgrounds and/or who were not members of the hegemonous society; however, in the latter part of that decade, the term *culturally diverse* began to be used (Frasier, 1977). Zuke (1983) defined culturally diverse gifted children as those "who by reason of cultural identification and socioeconomic status have not been able to assimilate themselves into the dominant culture"; *assimilation* was a key term used in this definition. Later, Sheehy (1986) and Goffin (1988) suggested that cultural diversity is evidenced through any of an individual's traditional customs and sex-role behaviors that are different from those observed in the mainstream culture. Additionally, cultural differences may be found in learning styles, listening behaviors (Trueba, 1983), and response patterns (Cohen, 1988; Harris, 1988) that are typically associated with mainstream giftedness.

Because cultural diversity, as it has been defined, is closely associated with the language(s) one speaks (García, 1994; Lara-Alecio & Irby, 1996), it is difficult to view cultural diversity apart from linguistic diversity when identifying and serving the gifted student. Linguistically and culturally diverse gifted students must then be defined within their own socio-linguistic-cultural context. Typically, school district personnel base definitions on the mainstream, Anglo middle-class gifted student, without taking into consideration cultural and linguistic diversity

(Bermúdez & Rakow, 1990; Cohen, 1988). Borrowing from Renzulli's (1986) original definition of giftedness, a simple definition of the linguistically and culturally diverse gifted could be individuals who possess above-average intelligence, task commitment, and creativity, with these three components being viewed solely within the individual's socio-linguistic-cultural context (Lara-Alecio & Irby, 1993). Other definitions, such as the multiple intelligence model promoted by Gardner (1983), may be applied, but all must be set within the same socio-linguistic-cultural context. Definitions of giftedness must be far more inclusive than they currently are, and far more adapted to a society defined by cultural and linguistic diversity.

There are a number of reasons that have been posed for the inequities in services provided to culturally and linguistically diverse gifted student populations. The challenge of providing appropriate services is particularly complex when native language and culture are conflicting with the child's new cultural and language environment. The exclusion of the culturally and linguistically diverse groups of underidentified and underserved children in programs for the gifted has at least three main implications. First, such exclusion sends a negative message to underrepresented populations and implies that they are somehow less able than those in mainstream populations. Many teachers hold opinions that there are just no gifted minorities, or that minority children are in need of academic remediation, particularly those who are limited English proficient (Davis & Rimm, 1989). Additionally, when teachers equate giftedness with an IQ score of 130 (García, 1994), it further denigrates the diverse child's true abilities. Being fluent in English does not mean that the child has the same cultural experiences as the mainstream child; thus, identifying a limited-English-proficient child with standardized test scores based on majority culture may not be valid (González, Bauerie, & Félix-Holt, 1994).

Because of the misunderstandings among educators regarding this population (García, 1994), and furthermore, because Borland and Wright (1994) suggested that the potential for giftedness is present in roughly equal proportions in all groups of our society, there is a need to develop valid and reliable methods of screening and identifying culturally and linguistically diverse potentially gifted students (Irby, Hernandez, Torres, & González, 1997). Additionally, with increasing reliance on nominations from teachers who are guided by a checklist of behaviors commonly attributed to exceptional children (Strom, Johnson, Strom, & Strom, 1992), it becomes important for teachers to have valid, defining characteristics with which to screen culturally and linguistically diverse populations.

Several formal instruments or techniques for identifying potentially gifted individuals who are culturally and linguistically diverse have surfaced over the past three decades and include the child's cultural context. Among those are the Baldwin Matrix (Baldwin, 1977), the System of Multicultural Pluralistic Assessment (SOMPA; Mercer

& Lewis, 1978), the Kranz Talent Identification Instrument (KTII; Kranz, 1981), the Structure of the Intellect Test (Meeker, 1985), Torrance Tests of Creative Thinking (TTCT; Torrance, 1970, 1977), the Group Inventory for Finding Talent (Rimm, 1976), and Fraiser's Talent Assessment Profile (1990). For screening purposes, the Hispanic Bilingual Gifted Screening Instrument (Irby & Lara-Alecio, 1996) is under development and has been specifically designed for Hispanic linguistically and culturally diverse students. Eleven characteristic aspects of gifted students have been determined to be significant for identifying potential within the population of diverse students: Motivation for Learning, Social and Academic Language, Cultural Sensitivity, Familial, Collaboration, Imagery, Achievement, Creative Performance, Support, Problem Solving, and Locus of Control (Lara-Alecio, Irby, & Walker, 1997).

A second implication for the culturally and linguistically diverse populations' underrepresentation in gifted programs is that the very exclusion of these groups is contradictory to the American principles of egalitarianism (Gintis, 1988). The task of providing equitable services for the gifted is made more difficult by the lack of uniformity in objective identification procedures and in appropriate needs-based curriculum services (Kaufman, 2005). Uniformity does not preclude the use of a multidimensional approach to identification of giftedness (Frasier, 1992; Irby & Lara-Alecio, 1996; Kitano, 1991; Maker & Scheiver, 1989; Zappia, 1989). Furthermore, a study conducted by Irby, Henderson, and Berry (1992) determined that in many cases there was little or no match between the programmatic services being provided and a district's plan of gifted identification.

The third implication is that practitioners must learn how to change the programmatic services and/or the identification plans that merge at a point that responds to their particular populations within their communities. Curriculum cannot be discussed or developed in isolation from the definition of giftedness and identification of the particular cultural and language minority group. There is a sufficient amount of theoretical claims regarding who these children are and what type of curricular programming they need, but there are few empirical data to support these claims (Frasier, 1978; Irby & Lara-Alecio, 1996; Zappia, 1989), and few teachers are trained at a level to make data-based decisions regarding the program structure for the culturally and linguistically diverse gifted child (Ford & Harris, 1990).

In summary, there are several principles that may be followed to improve the numbers of culturally and linguistically diverse students served in gifted education programs.

1. The definition used in the school district should be inclusive. Renzulli (1986) noted that the definition of giftedness must be based on research about characteristics of gifted individuals; in this case, those individuals would be representative of the diverse group to be served. Furthermore, researchers should identify ecological characteristics of the diverse group.

2. Definitions should be connected to the identification procedures and those identification procedures should be diverse (Frasier, 1990). Look for the diversity.

3. Identification procedures should be multifaceted or multidimensional, including objective and subjective data. Data should also be gathered from those who know the child on a personal/cultural level (Frasier, 1990). Additionally, the instruments used should be based on sociocultural and linguistic characteristics of the referent population; seek out valid and reliable instruments in the child's native language or use nonverbal measures.

4. Implement an identification program early that includes a screening phase, an evaluation phase, and a recommendation phase (Frasier, 1990).

5. Make sure that all relevant information on a student has been reviewed prior to making a decision (Frasier, 1990).

6. Train teachers in general and specific diverse population characteristics of giftedness (Lara-Alecio & Irby, 1993; Rogers, 1986). Use a send-in model with the teachers of the gifted—send them into the classrooms and have them observe functional levels of children within the classrooms on various types of activities. When observing, have them focus on products and performance. Additionally, have the teachers solicit products and performances demonstrated away from school.

7. Program options must match district definitions and identification procedures (Frasier, 1990; Lara-Alecio & Irby, 1993). The best learning environment should be provided for the student (Frasier, 1990).

8. Bilingual/bicultural instruction should be provided in early programming, in particular, which suggests a two-way bilingual campus program. Trained bilingual, biliterate, and bicultural teachers are needed for the gifted program (Lara-Alecio & Irby, 1993). Curriculum for the general education program should have a multicultural perspective, which would urge educators to modify their opinions regarding cultural diversity (Kitano, 1991).

9. Include staff development for mainstream and gifted education teachers with a suggested model that includes workshops on research in this field, exploration of negative myths about the culturally and linguistically diverse, how to develop supportive environments, how to help

alter attitudes about specific diverse populations, and how to utilize bilingualism in the classroom.

10. Come to a point of viewing cultural and linguistic diversity as an asset, not as a liability or as a need for remediation. Educators need to celebrate differences and develop a secure communicative environment in which the diverse gifted can thrive.

REFERENCES

Baldwin, A. Y. (1977). *Baldwin identification matrix inservice kit for the identification of gifted and talented students.* East Aurora, NY: Trillium.

Bermúdez, A., & Rakow, S. (1993). Analyzing teachers' perception of identification procedures for gifted and talented Hispanic limited English proficient students at risk. *Journal of Educational Issues of Language Minority Students, 7,* 21–31.

Borland, J. H., & Wright, L. (1994). Identifying young, potentially gifted, economically disadvantaged students. *Gifted Child Quarterly, 38,* 164–171.

Cohen, M. (1988). Immigrant children need aid, study says. *Boston Globe,* p. 25.

Davis, G., & Rimm, S. (1989). *Education of the gifted and talented* (2nd ed.). Englewood Cliffs, NJ: Prentice Hall.

Ford, D. Y., & Harris, J. J. (1990). On discovering the hidden treasure of gifted and talented African American children. *Roeper Review, 13*(1), 27–37.

Frasier, M. (1977). *Help for organizing productive experience (HOPE) for the culturally diverse gifted and talented.* Reston, VA: Council for Exceptional Children. (ERIC Document Reproduction Service No. ED 141 981 & EC 101 227)

Frasier, M. (1978). Culturally different gifted/talented: Educational implications: Cognitive. In H. N. Rivlin (Ed.), *Advantage: Disadvantaged gifted.* Presentations from the Third National Conference on Disadvantaged Gifted (53–57). Ventura, CA: Ventura County Superintendent of Schools Office.

Frasier, M. (1990). *Frasier's Talent Assessment Profile.* Athens: University of Georgia.

Frasier, M. (1992). Ethnic/minority children: Reflections and directions. In *Challenges in gifted education: Developing potential and investing in knowledge for the 21st century.* Columbus: Ohio State Department of Education. (ED 344 402)

García, E. (1994). *Understanding and meeting the challenge of student cultural diversity.* Boston, MA: Houghton Mifflin.

García, J. H. (1994). Nonstandardized instruments for the assessment of Mexican-American children for gifted/talented programs. In S. H. García (Ed.), *Addressing cultural and linguistic diversity in special education: Issues and trends.* Reston, VA: Council for Exceptional Children.

Gardner, H. (1983). *Frames of mind: The theory of multiple intelligences.* New York, NY: Basic Books.

Gintis, H. (1988). Education, personal development, and the human dignity. In H. Holtz (Ed.), *Education and the American dream: Conservatives, liberals and radicals debate the future of education.* Granby, MA: Bergin & Garvey.

Goffin, G. (1988). Putting our advocacy efforts into a new context. *Journal of the National Association for the Education of Young Children, 43*(3), 52–56.

Gonzalez, V., Bauerle, P., & Felix-Holt, M. (1994). A qualitative assessment method for accurately diagnosing bilingual gifted children. NABE '92–'93 Annual Conference Journal, 37–52. Washington, DC: NABE.

Harris, R. (1988). *Cultural conflict and patterns of achievement in gifted Asian-Pacific children.* Paper presented at the meeting of the National Association for Asian and Pacific American Education.

Irby, B. (1993, May). Hispanic LEP gifted students. *Education Week.*

Irby, B., Henderson, D., & Berry, K. (1992). *State of gifted education in Texas.* Unpublished manuscript submitted to the Texas Association of Gifted and Talented for a Grants in Excellence project. Huntsville, TX: Sam Houston State University.

Irby, B., Hernández, L., Torres, D., & González, C. (1985). *The correlation between teacher perceptions of giftedness and the Hispanic bilingual screening instrument.* Unpublished manuscript, Sam Houston State University, Huntsville, TX.

Irby, B., & Lara-Alecio, R. (1996). Attributes of Hispanic gifted bilingual students as perceived by bilingual educators in Texas. *NYSABE Journal, 11,* 120–142.

Kaufman, J. (2005). Nonbiased assessment: A supplemental approach. In C. L. Frisby & C. R. Reynolds (Eds.), *Comprehensive handbook of multicultural school psychology* (pp. 825–840). Hoboken, NJ: Wiley.

Kitano, M. K. (1991). A multicultural education perspective on serving the culturally diverse gifted. *Journal for the Education of the Gifted, 15*(1), 4–19.

Kranz, B. (1981). *Kranz talent identification instrument.* Moorhead, MN: Moorhead State College.

Lara-Alecio, R., & Irby, B. (1993). *Reforming identification procedures for the bilingual gifted child.* Paper presented at BEAM, The Ninth Annual Bilingual/ESL Spring Conference, Denton, TX.

Lara-Alecio, R., & Irby, B. (1996). Bilingual education & multicultural education: An inclusively oriented educational delivery system. *Journal of Educational Issues of Language Minority Students, 17,* 11–24.

Maker, C. J., & Scheiver, S. W. (Eds.). (1989). *Critical issues in gifted education: Defensible programs for cultural and ethnic minorities.* Austin, TX: PRO-ED.

Meeker, M. (1985). Structure of the intellect test. SOI Systems. Vida, Oregon.

Meeker, M. N., Meeker, R., & Roid, G. (1985). *Structure-of-intellect learning abilities test (SOI-LA).* Los Angeles: Western Psychological Services.

Mercer, J. R., & Lewis, J. F. (1978). Using the system of multicultural pluralistic assessment (SOMPA) to identify the gifted minority child. In A. Y. Baldwin, G. H. Gear, & L. J. Lucito (Eds.), *Educational planning for the gifted* (pp. 7–14). Reston, VA: Council for Exceptional Children.

Ortíz, V., & González, A. (1989). Validation of a short form of the WISC-R with accelerated and gifted Hispanic students. *Gifted Child Quarterly, 33,* 152–155.

Passow, H. (1986, February 6). *Educational programs for minority/disadvantaged gifted students*. Paper prepared for presentation in the Distinguished Lecture Series of the San Diego Unified School District, California.

Renzulli, J. S. (1986). The three-ring conception of giftedness: A developmental model for creative productivity. In R. J. Sternberg & J. E. Davidson (Eds.), *Conception of giftedness*. New York, NY: Cambridge University Press.

Rimm, S. B. (1976). *GIFT: Group Inventory for Finding Creative Talent*. Watertown, WI: Educational Assessment Service.

Rogers, K. (1986). *Review of research on the education of intellectually and academically gifted students*. St. Paul: Minnesota State Department of Education.

Sheehy, G. (1986). *Spirit of survival*. New York, NY: Bantam.

Strom, R., Johnson, A., Strom, S., & Strom, P. (1992). *Educating gifted children: Genetic studies of genius* (Vol. 1). Stanford, CA: Stanford University Press.

Torrance, E. P. (1970). *Encouraging creativity in the classroom*. Dubuque, IA: William C. Brown.

Torrance, E. P. (1997). *Discovery & nurturance of giftedness in the culturally different*. Reston, VA: Council for Exceptional Children.

Torrance, E. P. (1974). *Torrance Tests of Creative Thinking: Norms—Technical manual*. Bensenville, IL: Scholastic Testing Service.

Trueba, H. (1983). Adjustment problems of Mexican and Mexican-American students. An anthropological study. *Learning Disability Quarterly, 6*(4), 395–415.

U.S. Department of Education, Office of Educational Research and Improvement. (1993). *National excellence: A case for developing America's talented*. Washington, DC: U.S. Government Printing Office.

Zappia, I. A. (1989). Identification of gifted Hispanic students: A multidimensional view. In C. J. Maker & S. W. Schiever (Eds.), *Critical issues in gifted education: Vol. 2. Defensible programs for cultural and ethnic minorities* (pp. 19–26). Austin, TX: PRO-ED.

Zuke, M. (1983). *Building bridges for culturally diverse gifted students*. (ERIC Document Reproduction Service No. ED 234570)

RAFAEL LARA-ALECIO
Texas A&M University

BEVERLY J. IRBY
Sam Houston State University

See also Creativity; Disproportionality; Gifted and Learning Disabilities; Gifted and Talented Children

CULTURALLY/LINGUISTICALLY DIVERSE STUDENTS AND LEARNING DISABILITIES

Students who are culturally and linguistically diverse (CLD) who experience academic difficulties are often misidentified, misplaced, and misinstructed. Historically, these students been overrepresented in special education (Mercer & Rueda, 1991), although for many, their academic problems were more a result of limited English proficiency than a learning disability. More recently, some CLD students have been denied special education services as a reaction to the previous trend of misidentification, resulting in an underrepresentation of CLD students (Frisby & Reynolds, 2005; Gersten & Woodward, 1994).

One critical issue for providing appropriate services for CLD students with learning disabilities is first determining if a student's academic difficulties are the result of a specific learning disability or other causal factors. Has the student had sufficient educational opportunity? Is the student literate in his or her native language? Does the student have the requisite English proficiency to successfully complete academic tasks in English? Is the student familiar with the content presented in academic subject areas? Is the student's behavior significantly different from peers from the same language and/or cultural group?

If the answer to any of these questions is *no*, then prereferral interventions are in order. Prereferral interventions are systematic, documented modifications suggested by a site-based team, often called a Student Study Team, to ensure student success. Such interventions may include adapting assignments in ways that capitalize on the student's strengths, involving parents in the teaching and learning process, and using teaching approaches known to be effective with CLD learners.

If difficulties persist after appropriate interventions have been exhausted, a referral for special education services may be in order. Assessment of CLD students includes testing in the student's native language as well as English, to ensure the problem is evident in both languages. Also, informal measures should be used to support or refute the findings of standardized measures.

Once a learning disability has been diagnosed, a linguistically appropriate Individualized Education Plan (IEP) is developed to reflect the student's cultural and language needs. The IEP addresses areas (such as language support options) that meet students' cultural and linguistic needs, including primary language support, ESL, and/or sheltered instruction. The IEP should also specify the language of instruction for each instructional goal, the specifics of the systematic development of English-language skills, and how progress in these language-related areas will be measured.

Primary language support is best provided by the special education teacher who is proficient in the student's native language; however, shortage of bilingual special education teachers is critical. Other options for primary language support include a bilingual paraprofessional, a community volunteer, or a peer from the same cultural group. Sheltered instruction is an effective instructional approach for students who have intermediate proficiency in English, or when primary language support is not available.

Sheltered instruction takes into account linguistic needs of CLD learners by modifying the curriculum and delivery of instruction to make it understandable for them. CLD students with learning disabilities need extra support in acquiring content area concepts as well as developing English-language skills (Echevarria & Graves, 1998).

The following issues in the education of CLD students with learning disabilities should be considered:

- Special educators must address the cognitive and language needs of English-language learners who have learning disabilities.
- Instruction, including ESL teaching, may need to be more explicit for students with learning disabilities since they tend not to learn incidentally.
- Instruction must be meaningful and relevant to students' cultural and educational experiences.
- Learning environments must be culturally responsive, accommodating the learning needs of culturally diverse learners.
- Assessing whether students acquired the academic concepts and language development objectives of lessons is essential. This can be done by establishing relevant goals, carefully analyzing and documenting the student's progress, or reteaching the lesson, based on the needs of the student.
- Modifications may include adapting the curriculum, using visuals to accompany oral presentation of information, and embedding activities in meaningful experiences that are linguistically and educationally rich.

Finally, special educators and paraprofessionals working with students with learning disabilities often are overlooked or excluded from general education professional development sessions that deal with culturally and linguistically diverse students. Special educators and paraprofessionals must be trained in current instructional practices in working with CLD students. Moreover, little interface occurs between special educators and those professionals who have expertise in working with CLD students (Gersten & Woodward, 1994). The focus needs to be on meeting the individual student's needs, not on purview. Increased communication and collaboration between programs and service providers, as well as support from administrators, would alleviate some of the issues relative to educating CLD students with learning disabilities.

REFERENCES

Echevarria, J., & Graves, A. (1998). *Sheltered content instruction: Teaching English-language learners with diverse abilities.* Boston, MA: Allyn & Bacon.

Frisby, C., & Reynolds, C. R. (2005). *Comprehensive handbook of multicultural school psychology.* Hoboken, NJ: Wiley.

Gersten, R., & Woodward, J. (1994). The language minority student and special education: Issues, trends and paradoxes. *Exceptional Children, 60*(4), 310–322.

Mercer, J., & Rueda, R. (1991, November). *The impact of changing paradigms of disabilities on assessment of special education.* Paper presented at the Council for Exceptional Children Topical Conference on At-Risk Children & Youth, New Orleans, LA.

JANA ECHEVARRIA
AMITA EDRAN
*California State University,
Long Beach*

See *also* Disproportionality; Learning Disabilities

CULTURALLY/LINGUISTICALLY DIVERSE STUDENTS IN SPECIAL EDUCATION, FAMILIES OF

School involvement by culturally and linguistically diverse families of children with disabilities should be seen in the context of the way parental roles have been conceptualized by professionals over the past four decades (for a comprehensive review, see Turnbull & Turnbull, 1997). Prior to the 1970s, the emphasis was on psychoanalytic approaches that (a) promoted a pathological view of families of children with disabilities, presenting the mother as victim or patient in severe psychological crisis, and (b) completely omitted the impact of differential cultural beliefs and practices on family reactions. The early 1970s saw the advent of the "parent as teacher" approach, which sought to promote positive parental involvement through behavioral training programs, based predominantly on the childrearing practices and personal interaction styles prevalent among white, middle-class families. While some professionals failed to recognize or give credence to non-mainstream family patterns and practices, others interpreted parenting patterns that deviated from the mainstream as evidence of "deprivation" of culture.

The advent of PL 99-142 in 1975 brought into focus the ideal of the parent as collaborator with professionals. This concept of parent participation was based on the model of the middle-class advocate who would participate in formal conference and, if necessary, draw on the availability of due process of law. Early studies of parent participation revealed that the advocacy role expected of parents was an ideal very difficult to achieve, even for middle-class parents. For low-income and minority parents, the challenge has been even more difficult.

The first direct attention to adaptations that might be needed for particular minority groups to participate effectively in the IEP process came from Marion (1979). Marion advocated adaptations that ought to have been considered basic requirements for interactions with all families, such as a personalized approach, respectful verbal and nonverbal interactions, simplification of educational jargon, and full, comprehensible explanation of rights, procedures, and test results. Overall, Marion's main point was that poor and minority parents stood at a disadvantage in terms of the stigma that had traditionally been attached to their ethnicity, culture, and social status, and that careless, even disrespectful, treatment of such parents was common. Marion's concerns have been echoed by researchers who studied the perceptions and experiences of families from various cultural backgrounds, such as American Indians (Connery, 1987), Chinese Americans (Smith & Ryan, 1987; Tran, 1982; Trueba, Jacobs, & Kirton, 1990), Mexican Americans (Lynch & Stein, 1987). African Americans (Harry, Allen, & McLaughlin, 1995; Patton & Braithwaite, 1984; Redding & Arrigo, 2005; Tomlinson, Acker, Canter, & Lindborg, 1977), Puerto Rican Americans (Harry, 1992), and a mixed-nationality Hispanic group (Bennett, 1988). Other researchers have pointed to culturally based differences in interaction styles and levels of information, which tend to serve as barriers to effective parent–professional communication (Chan, 1986; Correa, 1989; Cunningham, Cunningham, & O'Connell, 1987; Harry, 1992; Leung, 1988; Sontag & Schact, 1994; Tran, 1982; Zetlin, Padron, & Wilson, 1996). Studies show that low levels of parental awareness of available services and their perceptions of their eligibility for such services are highly correlated with low income and geographic location (Huang & Van Horne, 1995; Sontag & Schact, 1994). Further, school personnel's strong identification with the culture of professionalism tends to dominate their interactions with parents (Bailey, Buysse, Edmondson, & Smith, 1992; Katz & Scarpati, 1995), contributing to a "we–they posture by which parents are seen as adversaries rather than allies" (Harry, Allen, & McLaughlin, 1995, p. 374). Parental participation may also be negatively affected by differing cultural constructions of disability and developmental norms (Barnwell & Day, 1996; Harry & Kalyanpur, 1994). These differences often affect parental understanding of the assessment and diagnosis process as well as the setting of educational goals for students (Linan-Thompson & Jean, 1997). With regard to more severe disabilities, cross-cultural studies indicate unequivocally that while all groups recognize gross developmental, behavioral, or sensory impairments, the attributions for their etiology or importance differ widely, as do the extent of the stigma or value attached to the condition (Fadiman, 1997; Scheer & Groce, 1988). For children with milder disabilities, research reveals that culture and acculturation are strong predictors of parental expectations of children's cognitive and social development (Goodnow, Cashmore, Cotton, & Knight, 1984; Hess, Kashigawi, Azuma, Price, & Dickson, 1980; Quirk et al., 1986; Rosenthal, 1985). These variances in parental beliefs on children's development

have implications for the classification of children as "mildly retarded," "behavior disordered," or "learning disabled." Studies show that many culturally diverse parents hold broader parameters of normalcy than allowed by the school-based evaluations by which children are classified (Harry, 1992; Harry et al., 1995).

In summary, attempts to examine parental participation among ethnic minorities reveal the following patterns: (a) lower levels of involvement than White counterparts, (b) lower awareness of procedures, rights, and services, (c) expressed sense of isolation and low self-confidence in dealing with professionals, (d) stressful life circumstances and lack of logistical supports such as transportation, child care, and respite, (e) culturally based assumptions of deference to and/or mistrust of school personnel, (f) professionals' implicit or explicit discouragement of parents' participation in the special education process, and (g) culturally based dissonance between parental and professional understandings of the meanings and importance of disabilities.

Since the mid-1980s, because of PL 99-457, the ideal of parental participation has evolved into a vision of family-centered practice with issues of diverse family beliefs and practices becoming a crucial focus in the effort to address the problems listed above. Family-centered practice revolves around the concept of family empowerment, or the process of helping families increase control over their lives and take action to get what they want. Empowerment occurs when professionals (a) give families information about services and their rights; (b) facilitate their participation; for instance, by arranging transportation and/or childcare and scheduling meetings at times convenient to parents; and (c) develop collaborative relationships with families by affirming and building on family strengths, honoring cultural diversity and creative and cooperative problem-solving, and establishing trust and respect (Dunst & Trivette, 1987; Lynch & Hanson, 1992; Salend & Taylor, 1993; Turnbull & Turnbull, 1996). Evidence for the continuing centrality of this ideal is the 1997 reauthorization of IDEA. This current focus has generated the need for reconceptualizing culture—whether it is perceived as a static or discrete phenomenon—in order to prevent families from being presented in stereotypical ways. The original notion of culture as a process of stages (for instance, from traditional to bicultural to assimilation) through which individuals from minority groups might move has gradually been superseded by a less discrete view of culture, where boundaries are variable according to different dimensions of individual identity, thus acknowledging that an individual may assume multiple group memberships simultaneously (Banks & Banks, 1992).

This definition has also provided a need for context, which brings the focus of study to the precise realm of the individual family, rather than assuming that a generalized concept of the family's cultural tradition will be adequate. By applying Bronfenbrenner's theory of nested systems and Vygotsky's concept of the zone of proximal development, all development is seen as being based in participation in specific social and cultural settings or an individual's "ecocultural niche" (Tharp & Gallimore, 1988), combining the family's ecology and culture. This perspective takes into account more than just the ethnic status of the family by including contextual variables, such as education, acculturation, socioeconomic status, or geographic location, and the effects of these on the daily routines of families to describe a family in all its individuality, as opposed to generalizations about what a family from "this" or "that" cultural group would be expected to look like. The importance of examining contextual influences to avoid cultural stereotypes is well-illustrated, for instance, by Mardiros' (1989) study of Mexican-American parents, which demonstrated that parents from a relatively homogeneous cultural group, who held similar beliefs regarding the causation of a disability, still displayed a range of responses, some very proactive and creative, others passive and resigned. Similarly, Harry et al. (1995) offer evidence of effective single parenting when they note that the six "living alone" mothers were the most proactive advocates in a sample of 24 African American families of preschoolers with mild disabilities.

Several writers have identified strategies that specifically accommodate this new concept of contextualized culture toward increasing the participation of culturally and linguistically diverse parents in the special education process.

1. *Developing self-awareness as a first step toward understanding one's personal and professional values* (Caple, Salsido, & di Cecco, 1995). This can involve examining genealogical records and asking oneself questions like "When I was growing up, what did my family say about people from different cultures?" (Hyun & Fowler, 1995), or "Why do I want 21-year-old Husain to move into a group home?" to recognize the cultural value that underlies one's professional recommendation (Kalyanpur & Harry, 1997).

2. *Engaging in conversations with families to learn about their culture and values.* This involves using naturalistic means for collecting information about families' situations, including open-ended interviewing (Harry, 1992), and identifying and involving key and/or extended members of the family (Linan-Thompson & Jean, 1997). Professionals should identify and accommodate the family's preferred method of communication, whether written or verbal, English or native language (Barnwell & Day, 1996); make time to listen to parents' stories (Caple, Salsido, & di Cecco, 1995; Kalyanpur & Rao, 1991; Thorp, 1997); and respect their input in the decision-making process (Correa, 1987; Harry, 1992).

3. *Making available services and professional recommendations that are compatible with families' values.* This involves working with the family to identify their resources and supports and modifying service options or developing creative, individualized alternatives (Correa, 1989; Harry, 1992; Rueda & Martinez, 1994). Comer and Haynes (1991) describe the successful efforts of the Yale Child Study Center Team to "change the ecology of a school" and empower low-income parents by improving parental status and meaningful collaboration between parents and professionals in special education. The program contained three mechanisms for change: (1) a governance mechanism, the school planning and management team, which represented all the adult stakeholders in the school, to develop a plan for restructuring the school; (2) a mental health team to address the developmental and behavioral needs of students; and (3) a parent program that focused on supporting the social program of the school restructuring plan and on the academic program as needed. The parent program created social occasions for families and professionals to meet, developing a sense of community, and encouraged parent volunteers to participate in a broad range of school activities from helping in classrooms to participation on the school planning and management team. The authors attribute the success of the entire program to allowing parents to participate in the way they were comfortable and effective and to play meaningful roles, with staff support, with a clear direction and purpose. Unfortunately, efforts to replicate this model have not been as successful in involving special education teachers and parents (Ware, 1994).

In conclusion, school involvement by families from culturally and linguistically diverse backgrounds continues to be problematic. However, parental participation can be enhanced when professionals use naturalistic collection of information about families' situations in order to find out where a family stands on a given issue, are aware of their own cultural influences in the decision-making process, and are committed to flexibility and responsiveness to the need for change.

REFERENCES

Bailey, D. B., Jr., Buysse, V., Edmondson, R., & Smith, T. (1992). Creating family-centered services in early intervention: Perceptions of professionals in four states. *Exceptional Children, 58*, 298–309.

Banks, J., & Banks, C. A. (1992). *Multicultural education: Issues and perspectives* (2nd ed.). Boston, MA: Allyn & Bacon.

Barnwell, D. A., & Day, M. (1996). Providing support to diverse families. In P. J. Beckman (Ed.), *Strategies for working with families of young children with disabilities* (pp. 47–68). Baltimore, MD: Brooks.

Bennett, A. T. (1988). Gateways to powerlessness: Incorporating Hispanic deaf children and families into formal schooling. *Disability, Handicap & Society, 3,* 119–151.

Caple, F. S., Salsido, R. M., & di Cecco, J. (1995). Engaging effectively with culturally diverse families and children. *Social Work in Education, 17*(3), 159–170.

Chan, S. (1986). Parents of exceptional Asian children. In M. K. Kitano & P. C. Chinn (Eds.), *Exceptional Asian children and youth* (pp. 36–53). Reston, VA: Council for Exceptional Children.

Comer, J. P., & Haynes, N. M. (1991). Parent involvement in schools: An ecological approach. *The Elementary School Journal, 91*(3), 271–277.

Connery, A. R. (1987). *A description and comparison of Native American and Anglo parents' knowledge of their handicapped children's rights.* Doctoral dissertation, Northern Arizona University.

Correa, V. I. (1989). Involving culturally diverse families in the educational process. In S. H. Fradd & M. J. Weismantel (Eds.), *Meeting the needs of culturally and linguistically different students: A handbook for educators* (pp. 130–144). Boston, MA: College-Hill.

Cunningham, K., Cunningham, K., & O'Connell, J. C. (1987). Impact of differing cultural perceptions on special education service delivery. *Rural Special Education Quarterly, 8*(1), 2–8.

Dunst, C. J., & Trivette, C. M. (1987). Enabling and empowering families: Conceptual and intervention issues. *School Psychology Review, 16,* 443–456.

Fadiman, A. (1997). *The spirit catches you and you fall down: A Hmong child, her American doctors, and the collision of two cultures.* New York, NY: Farrar, Strauss & Giroux.

Goodnow, J. J., Cashmore, J., Cotton, S., & Knight, R. (1984). Mothers' developmental timetables in two cultural groups. *International Journal of Psychology, 19,* 193–205.

Harry, B. (1992). *Cultural diversity, families, and the special education system: Communication and empowerment.* New York, NY: Teachers College.

Harry, B., Allen, N., & McLaughlin, M. (1995). Communication versus compliance: African American parents' involvement in special education. *Exceptional Children, 61*(4), 364–377.

Harry, B., & Kalyanpur, M. (1994). The cultural underpinnings of special education: Implications for professional interactions with culturally diverse families. *Disability & Society, 9*(2), 145–165.

Hess, R. D., Kashigawi, K., Azuma, H., Price, G. G. & Dickson, W. P. (1980). Maternal expectations for the mastery of developmental tasks in Japan and the United States. *International Journal of Psychology, 15,* 259–271.

Huang, G. G., & Van Horne, P. (1995). Using child care services: Families with disabled children in nonmetropolitan areas. *Rural Special Education Quarterly, 14*(4), 27–36.

Hyun, J. K., & Fowler, S. A. (1995). Respect, cultural sensitivity, and communication: Promoting participation by Asian families in the Individualized Family Service Plan. *Teaching Exceptional Children, 28*(1), 25–28.

Kalyanpur, M., & Harry, B. (1997). A posture of reciprocity: A practical approach to collaboration between professionals and parents of culturally diverse backgrounds. *Journal of Child and Family Studies, 6*(4), 485–509.

Kalyanpur, M., & Rao, S. S. (1991). Empowering low-income, black families of handicapped children. *American Journal of Orthopsychiatry, 61,* 523–532.

Katz, L., & Scarpati, S. (1995). A cultural interpretation of early intervention teams and the IFSP: Parent and professional perceptions of roles and responsibilities. *The Transdisciplinary Journal, 5*(2), 177–192.

Leung, E. K. (1988). Cultural and acculturational commonalties and diversities among Asian Americans: Identification and programming considerations. In A. A. Ortiz & B. A. Ramirez (Eds.), *Schools and the culturally diverse student* (pp. 86–95). Reston, VA: ERIC.

Linan-Thompson, S., & Jean, R. E. (1997). Completing the parent participation puzzle: Accepting diversity. *Teaching Exceptional Children, 52*(6), 46–50.

Lynch, E. W., & Hanson, M. J. (1992). *Developing cross-cultural competence: A guide for working with young children and their families.* Baltimore, MD: Brooks.

Lynch, E. W., & Stein, R. (1987). Parent participation by ethnicity: A comparison of Hispanic, Black, and Anglo families. *Exceptional Children, 54,* 105–11.

Mardiros, M. (1989). Conception of childhood disability among Mexican-American parents. *Medical Anthropology, 12,* 55–68.

Marion, R. (1979). Minority parent involvement in the IEP process: A systematic model approach. *Focus on Exceptional Children, 10*(8), 1–16.

Patton, J. M., & Braithwaite, R. L. (1984, August). Obstacles to the participation of black parents in the educational programs of their handicapped children. *Centering Teacher Education, 34–37.*

Quirk, M., Ciottone, R., Minami, J., Wapner, S., Yamamoto, S., Ishii, S., . . . Pacheco, A. (1986). Values mothers hold for handicapped and nonhandicapped preschool children in Japan, Puerto Rico, and the United States Mainland. *International Journal of Psychology, 21,* 463–485.

Redding, R. E., & Arrigo, B. (2005). Multicultural perspectives on delinquency among African-American youth: Etiology and intervention. In C. L. Frisby & C. R. Reynolds (Eds.), *Comprehensive handbook of multicultural school psychology* (pp. 710–743). Hoboken, NJ: Wiley.

Rosenthal, D. (1985, July). *Child-rearing and cultural values: A study of Greek and Australian mothers.* Paper presented at the meeting of the International Society for the Study of Behavioural Development, Tours, France.

Rueda, R., & Martinez, I. (1994). Fiesta educativa: One community's approach to parent training in developmental disabilities for Latino families. *JASH, 17*(2), 95–103.

Salend, S. J., & Taylor, L. (1993). Working with families: A cross-cultural perspective. *Remedial and Special Education, 14*(5), 25–32.

Scheer, J., & Groce, N. (1988). Impairment as a human constant: Cross-cultural and historical perspectives on variation. *Journal of Social Issues, 44*(1), 23–37.

Smith, M. J., & Ryan, A. S. (1987). Chinese-American families of children with developmental disabilities: An exploratory study of reactions to service providers. *Mental Retardation, 25*(6), 345–350.

Sontag, J. C., & Schacht, R. (1994). An ethnic comparison of parent participation and information needs in early intervention. *Exceptional Children, 60*(5), 422–433.

Tharp, R. G., & Gallimore, R. (1988). *Rousing minds to life: Teaching, learning and schooling in social context*. Cambridge, MA: Cambridge University Press.

Thorp, E. K. (1997). Increasing opportunities for partnership with culturally and linguistically diverse families. *Intervention in School and Clinic, 32*(5), 261–269.

Tomlinson, J. R., Acker, N., Canter, A., & Lindborg, S. (1977). Minority status, sex and school psychological services. *Psychology in the Schools, 14*(4), 456–460.

Tran, X. C. (1982). *The factors hindering Indochinese parent participation in school activities*. San Diego, CA: San Diego State University, Institute for Cultural Pluralism. (ERIC Document Reproduction Service No. ED 245-018)

Trueba, H., Jacobs, L., & Kirton, E. (1990). *Cultural conflict and adaptation: The case of Hmong children in American society*. New York, NY: Falmer Press.

Turnbull, A. P., & Turnbull, H. R. (1997). *Families, professionals, and exceptionality: A special partnership* (3rd ed.). Upper Saddle River, NJ: Merrill.

Ware, L. P. (1994). Contextual barriers to collaboration. *Journal of Educational and Psychological Consultation, 5*(4), 339–357.

Zetlin, A., Padron, M., & Wilson, S. (1996). The experience of five Latin American families with the special education system. *Education and Training in Mental Retardation and Developmental Disabilities, 31*, 22–28.

BETH HARRY
University of Miami

MAYA KALYANPUR
Towson University

See *also* Family Counseling

CULTURALLY/LINGUISTICALLY DIVERSE STUDENTS, REPRESENTATION OF

Special educators have debated for decades about the disproportionate representation of ethnic and linguistic minority students in special and gifted education programs. This phenomenon refers to unequal proportions of culturally diverse students in these special programs. Two patterns are associated with disproportionality, namely over- and underrepresentation of minority students. The former tends to occur in special education, specifically, in the mild disability categories—such as mild mental retardation (MMR), specific learning disabilities (SLD), and serious emotional disturbances (SED). Underrepresentation is generally observed in programs for students with gifts and talents (G&T). Historically, certain ethnic minority groups (particularly African American) and poor and male students have been most affected by disproportionality.

Litigation (particularly placement bias cases) has been at the center of disproportionality discussions. For instance, some of the most important rulings in *Diana v. California Board of Education* (1970) and *Larry P. v. Riles* (1979) (which involved Latino and African American students, respectively) included (a) intelligence tests were culturally and linguistically biased, (b) biased assessment resulted in the overrepresentation of Latino and African American students in MMR programs, (c) alternative procedures were needed to assess students' abilities (e.g., nonverbal tests, assessment in native language), and (d) many students needed to be retested and reclassified. These cases were very influential in the passage of federal legislation designed to protect the rights of individuals with disabilities, specifically in the inclusion of a requirement that identification and assessment procedures must be nondiscriminatory.

Although disproportionality patterns persisted throughout the 1970s and 1980s (Artiles & Trent, 1994), it was not until the 14th Report that the U.S. Department of Education (USDOE) provided enrollment data in disability programs by ethnic group. Interestingly, disproportionate representation has received more attention in the 1990s. For instance, the USDOE authorized the National Academy of Sciences to conduct a study on disproportionality (B. Ford, personal communication, November 1997). It is ironic that this interest has emerged at a time when societal attitudes toward culturally diverse people are hostile and intolerant, two compelling examples being the anti-immigrant and the anti-Affirmative Action discourse, litigation, and policymaking.

Causes of Disproportionate Representation

The most widely used explanation of this problem is based on the deficit thinking that has characterized theories about minority students' educational performance (Trent, Artiles, & Englert, 1998). It has been concluded that many of these students lack the abilities and skills needed to succeed in the general educational system; hence, they need to receive specialized services. The most favored argument to explain minority students' deficits is the nefarious effects of poverty, which is rampant among these groups. Because of their higher levels of poverty, the argument follows, we should expect a higher incidence of negative developmental outcomes (e.g., disabilities) among these groups. In this vein, research has linked poverty to placement in special education; however, we need more inquiries to understand (a) the complex nature of this association, (b) minorities' resilience to the negative effects of poverty, and (c) the role of structural factors in the production of higher rates of poverty among minority groups.

An alternative position posits that deficit explanations oversimplify this complex problem by blaming the student and disregarding the significant impact of contextual, technical, structural, and ideological factors. For example, a critical technical factor is related to the procedures used in the special education field. Also, such patterns seem to vary according to school location. For example, it has been found that the psychometric profiles of students with LD in urban and suburban schools differ to the point that many identified students in urban schools did not fit the established eligibility criteria for LD (e.g., in terms of ability levels; Gottlieb, Alter, Gottlieb, & Wishner, 1994).

Furthermore, we must be mindful of the nature of the disproportionality data. Many of these analyses draw from the Office for Civil Rights (OCR) survey data, which purportedly have several methodological limitations. For instance, the data are not based on a nationally representative sample, different surveys have sampled school districts with distinct demographic profiles, and distinct sampling procedures have been used over the different surveys, which complicates longitudinal and comparative analyses (Reschly, 1997). Hence, the question arises as to how we can assess the magnitude and causes of disproportionality given the potential confounding effect of the aforementioned technical aspects.

Another factor that complicates disproportionality analyses is our limited understanding of the role of culture in human development. For instance, an analysis of 22 years of research in four major special education journals showed a paucity of studies on ethnic minority students, a narrow scope of research topics, and a disregard for potential interactions between sociocultural variables (e.g., ethnicity and language, gender, or social class; Artiles, Trent, & Kuan, 1997; Oakland & Gallegos, 2005). How, then, can educators discern the influence of language, cognitions, social class, and ethnicity on students' competence and performance? How can educators make decisions about students' competence based on culturally insensitive criteria? Indeed, this paucity of knowledge has enormous implications for the identification of students' needs and the provision of adequate educational services.

Other factors could impinge upon this predicament, though they have received scant attention by the research community. For instance, we need to investigate how disproportionality can be exacerbated, masked, or reduced in distinct contexts by (a) the quality of the instructional context, (b) the role of racism and discrimination, (c) the dismissal of alternative ways of knowing in the design and implementation of school rules, curricula, assessment practices, and expectations, (d) the inattention to the influence of sociocultural variables in researchers' labor (e.g., investigators' beliefs or values about cultural diversity), (e) the disregard for within-cultural-group variability, (f) the failure to include minority students' perspectives in investigations, and (g) the availability of alternative services (e.g., prereferral, bilingual education, and Chapter 1 programs).

Looking Ahead: Risks and Possibilities

We must transcend oversimplification of this problem so that we do not debate endlessly whether special education is harmful to minority students, whether disabilities exist or are social constructions, or whether minority students' poverty is the cause of the problem. By focusing on these oversimplifications we run the risk of losing generations of culturally diverse students, the future of our nation. At the same time, this multidimensional problem affords us the possibility to rethink the meaning and place of special education in our increasingly diverse society. For this purpose, we must acknowledge that implicit in this predicament are assumptions about human difference and about the role of education in a heterogeneous society. Hence, we must undertake two crucial tasks in the immediate future. First, we must conduct more and better studies that address the limitations of past research. Second, we must strengthen the theoretical grounding of the disproportionality discourse to begin grappling with equity issues in the education of culturally diverse students and with how our educational system meets the needs of an increasingly diverse society.

REFERENCES

Artiles, A. J., & Trent, S. C. (1994). Overrepresentation of minority students in special education: A continuing debate. *Journal of Special Education, 27,* 410–437.

Artiles, A. J., Trent, S. C., & Kuan, L. A. (1997). Learning disabilities research on ethnic minority students: An analysis of 22 years of studies published in selected refereed journals. *Learning Disabilities Research & Practice, 12,* 82–91.

Gottlieb, J., Alter, M., Gottlieb, B. W., & Wishner, J. (1994). Special education in urban America: It's not justifiable for many. *Journal of Special Education, 27,* 453–465.

Oakland, T., & Gallegos, E. M. (2005). Selected legal issues affecting students from multicultural backgrounds. In C. R. Frisby & C. R. Reynolds (Eds.), *Comprehensive handbook of multicultural school psychology* (pp. 1048–1078). Hoboken, NJ: Wiley.

Reschly, D. J. (1997). *Disproportionate minority representation in general and special education: Patterns, issues, and alternatives.* Des Moines: Iowa Department of Education.

Trent, S. C., Artiles, A. J., & Englert, C. S. (1998). *From deficit thinking to social constructivism: A review of special education theory, research and practice.* Review of Research in Education.

ALFREDO J. ARTILES
*University of California,
Los Angeles*

STANLEY O. TRENT
University of Virginia

CULTURAL PERSPECTIVES ON BEHAVIORAL DISORDERS

Children with behavioral disorders constitute one of the major national issues confronting the schools and society. There is increasing concern about the academic failure and school dropout rate of U.S. children and adolescents identified with behavioral disorders (BD). Observation, diagnosis, and intervention strategies for these students are poorly defined nationally (Sabatino, 1987). The current definition of BD may encourage the underidentification of students with behavioral disorders from the entire school-age population, while promoting an overrepresentation of students identified as BD from culturally diverse groups (Algozzine, Ruhl, & Ramsey, 1991). The rates of identification, placement, and achievement of children and adolescents with BD are strongly correlated with gender, race, and other cultural dimensions. However, these issues are often neglected in our educational system (Singh, Ellis, Oswald, Wechsler, & Curtis, 1997).

In 1990, about one-third of school-age children in the United States were children from nondominant cultures (Maag & Howell, 1992). The growing diversity in student population has increased the potential and practice for inappropriate educational placement of students. For example, in 1987, African Americans were 16% of the total enrollment in the nation's school system. However, in the same year, African Americans made up 27% of the students identified as having a behavioral/emotional disorder in the public schools. There is concern by many in this country that this 11% discrepancy is based on faulty thinking, biases, and inappropriate identification of culturally diverse students (Harry, 1992). Anglo American students are less likely to be identified as BD or placed in restrictive settings than are students from other cultures, particularly African American students. Hispanic American students are underrepresented in BD across most of the nation.

Overrepresentation of Culturally Diverse Students

Unfortunately, many culturally diverse groups of students are being misidentified as behaviorally disordered. This phenomenon is causing a misuse of services for other students who may need them but are not yet identified. Minority groups, other than ethnic minority children, are also affected by this situation. Students with limited English proficiency (LEP) are frequently misplaced in programs for students with BD. Students from nondominant cultural backgrounds should not be at risk for being labeled as BD simply for displaying traits reflecting their cultural upbringing.

The mismatch between schools and culturally diverse homes is a factor influencing the misidentification of students as BD. A home culture exists for all students, and this culture may be discrepant with the traditional Anglo middle-class public school culture. This discrepancy is often viewed by school personnel as a problem within the individual student instead of a cultural mismatch. The student may then be identified as having a behavioral problem and assigned a label, with a resulting loss of self-esteem (Algozzine et al., 1991).

Children of immigrant families and children from wartorn and politically repressive countries are vulnerable to being mislabeled as BD, yet often do not have their needs recognized by school personnel. Additionally, many students who are lesbian, gay, or bisexual are at risk for being identified as BD when they have no disability. The same scenario holds true for children raised in families with same-sex partners (McIntyre, 1996).

Preservice Training and Recruitment

Improved preservice training for future educators and improved recruitment of teachers of students with behavioral disorders may help solve the problem of inadequate education of culturally diverse students.

Preservice Training

Most teachers do not have a solid grounding in multicultural education. Those that did receive multicultural training in college were trained about "culture within a cultural literacy model." This model teaches cultural diversity within the limited framework of race and ethnicity. Preservice teachers are often taught general characteristics and stereotypes regarding different minority groups. Research demonstrates that teacher sensitivity and general knowledge about a student's culture is correlated to student achievement; therefore, reevaluation of instructing preservice teachers needs to occur (Harry, 1992). In addition to preservice training, continued training inservice in the profession should also be provided on this topic.

Recruiting Preservice Teachers

Recruitment and retention of culturally diverse preservice teachers also needs to be addressed by colleges and universities. In special education classrooms, a disparity often exists between cultural background of students and teachers. This difference is even greater in programs involving students with BD. Gender issues are also important to consider. Female teachers refer students, particularly boys, for behavioral problems more often than male teachers. This problem will continue to increase as fewer males and culturally diverse individuals choose teaching as a career. This shortage of professionals from culturally diverse backgrounds leads to problems of isolation of majority students from teachers of culturally diverse backgrounds, reduces role models for culturally diverse students, and yields inadequate expertise in recommending multicultural changes and training to other school colleagues.

Aggressive recruitment of culturally diverse preservice teachers is necessary. While it is recognized that one's cultural background does not guarantee the ability to relate and work effectively with students exhibiting BD, the need for the recruitment of professionals from culturally diverse backgrounds is evident (McIntyre, 1996). Unfortunately, states such as California, Texas, and Michigan have been court-ordered to reduce or stop opportunities that would recruit underrepresented groups to meet a particular professional need. Practices such as these are hurting attempts to increase the cultural diversity of educators to serve students with BD.

Inadequately Prepared Professionals

To ensure that students with BD have access to a free appropriate public education, there must be an adequate supply of teachers and other instructional and noninstructional staff with appropriate training or certification (USDOE, 1996). There are 331,392 special education teachers in the United States, yet many of these teachers are not professionally certified (6.3%). In addition, there are inadequate numbers of teachers of special education, with a reported 3,643 special education teachers needed. These problems increase when we look at instructing students with BD. Many of the teachers ($n = 30,151$) who work with students with BD are not certified or not adequately trained to work with students with BD (Katsiyannis, Landrum, Bullock, & Vinton, 1997).

Cultural Mismatch of Teachers and Students

Behavioral patterns and values are often defined by and vary by culture. Also, behaviors and actions viewed as aberrant often vary by culture. Teachers who are unaware of cultural differences often misinterpret and judge culturally determined behavior as being evidence of BD. In such a subjective climate, culturally diverse students identified as BD are set up for failure (Harry, 1992). Far too few educators realize that many culturally different youth view the school environment as alienating. Also, many African American, Mexican American, Native American, and Native Hawaiian students feel great pressure from their peers not to achieve (Ogbu, 1992). Due to numerous factors, such as historical oppression and an emphasis on cultural cohesion and cooperation rather than competition, individual success in schooling is often viewed as rejection of one's cultural group.

Cultural Diversity Misidentified as a Behavioral Disorder

The cultural mismatch between the teacher and the student often results in students from some cultures being misidentified as BD by teachers who are not aware or culturally competent. Educators generally have a more negative attitude toward students with BD, as a group, than toward students with other disabilities such as learning disabilities (Algozzine et al., 1991). By adding cultural diversity along with BD, the bias against these students by many teachers is exaggerated (Algozzine et al., 1991). Because some teachers discriminate against students because of their racial, ethnic, political, or socioeconomic backgrounds, it is obvious that the coupling of BD with any of these traits has the potential for heightening the imbalance (Singh et al., 1997).

A continuation of this practice is present in the data collected in the area of student discipline. Some teachers' differential use of disciplinary practices with Anglo American students and those from other cultures is well-documented (Harry, 1992). African American students experience the most severe forms of discipline. The educational system is in the unfortunate position of having culturally inexperienced teachers from the dominant culture (over 80% European American females) teaching students of increasing diversity.

Cultural Competence

Culturally competent teachers acknowledge, accept, and value cultural differences in their students. Teachers must be aware of their own culture as well as the culture of others and must acknowledge how it could bias their service toward students (Singh et al., 1997). A teacher should assess students with BD through their students' cultural backgrounds while acknowledging the expectations of the dominant culture.

Educators teach students prosocial norms for the public school setting usually from a middle-class, European-American perspective. Educators need to also incorporate values and behavioral standards from other cultural groups. Teachers must ensure that students have pride in their original culture as well as observing the determined norms for a particular setting. Modification of classroom practices can promote self-esteem and motivation for all students (McIntyre, 1996).

Biased Assessment Practices

Most individuals truly understand only their own culture and frequently find it difficult to appreciate behavior that is different from their own. This fact influences not only the way educators teach, but also the way students are assessed. Culturally based behavioral patterns often differ from what is considered normative on assessment instruments (Harry, 1992). Cultural biases and prejudices are often acknowledged to exist in many standardized instruments, particularly those measuring self-concept (McIntyre, 1996).

Complexity of Cultural Diversity and BD

The assessment of students for the possible presence of BD is a complex process that becomes more difficult when students are from a culturally diverse background. It has been demonstrated that assessment tools reflect cultural as well as school learning, but the invisible quality of many central aspects of culture makes the identification of cultural bias a challenging task (Harry, 1992). For example, it is easy to see that testing an LEP student in English would be unfair, but it is less obvious to many that standard English testing can be unfair to speakers of nonstandard varieties of the language. There is a pressing need for the development and implementation of more appropriate and accurate methods of assessment for culturally diverse students. This need is particularly noticeable in the area of behavioral disorders, since students who display culturally different behaviors are particularly susceptible to this diagnosis.

Assessment Changes

The entire approach to assessment may need to change for students with BD who are culturally diverse. A more holistic method of assessment could be incorporated and framed within the context of a student's culture. The practice of using norm-referenced tests is problematic because these tests have often been shown to be based on middle-class Anglo American values and experiences (Singh et al., 1997). Assessment procedures should help to differentiate BD from cultural differences in behavior. Also, a diverse multidisciplinary team reviewing students' assessments can help increase cultural awareness and decrease misidentification of students as BD.

The public school system needs to continue to move away from a cultural deficit model to a cultural difference model. A cultural difference model accepts that the cognitive, learning, and motivational styles of students are different from those often expected by the teacher, who is usually from the dominant culture (Singh et al., 1997) while a cultural deficit model uses the culture as the explanation for school failures. The idea that all students should assimilate and fit into the majority culture has been successfully challenged by the concept of cultural pluralism.

The United States is becoming a country where minority groups are becoming the majority (Robinson & Bradley, 1997). These demographic changes require adaptations in assessment and teaching in our public schools. Current trends lead to an overrepresentation of culturally diverse students being misidentified as emotionally or behaviorally disordered. In most cases, culturally divergent behaviors can be respected (McIntyre, 1996). Acknowledging culture as a predominant factor in shaping behaviors and values and respecting culturally defined traits will yield a more productive learning and teaching environment for culturally diverse students, students with BD, and teachers. This change also should result in more accurate identification of all students and more appropriate support for students who have BD, and it potentially will decrease the misdiagnosis of culturally diverse students (Singh et al., 1997).

REFERENCES

Algozzine, B., Ruhl, K., & Ramsey, R. (1991). *Behaviorally disordered? Assessment for identification and instruction.* Reston, VA: Council for Exceptional Children.

Harry, B. (1992). *Cultural diversity, families, and the special education system: Communication and empowerment.* New York, NY: Teachers College.

Katsiyannis, A., Landrum, T. J., Bullock, L., & Vinton, L. (1997). Certification requirements for teachers of students with emotional or behavioral disorders: A national survey. *Behavioral Disorders, 22*(3), 131–140.

Maag, J. W., & Howell, K. W. (1992). Special education and the exclusion of youth with social maladjustments: A cultural-organizational perspective. *Remedial and Special Education, 13*(1), 47–54, 59.

McIntyre, T. (1996). Guidelines for providing appropriate services to culturally diverse students with emotional and/or behavioral disorders. *Behavioral Disorders, 21*(2), 137–144.

Ogbu, J. U. (1992). Understanding cultural diversity and learning. *Educational Researcher, 21*(8), 5–14.

Robinson, B., & Bradley, L. J. (1997). Multicultural training for undergraduates: Developing knowledge and awareness. *Journal of Multicultural Counseling and Development, 25*(4), 281–289.

Sabatino, D. A. (1987). Behavior disorders. In C. R. Reynolds & L. Mann (Eds.), *The encyclopedia of special education* (Vol. 1). New York, NY: Wiley.

Singh, N. N., Ellis, C. R., Oswald, D. P., Wechsler, H. A., & Curtis, W. J. (1997). Value and address diversity. *Journal of Emotional and Behavioral Disorders, 5*(1), 24–35.

U.S. Department of Education. (1996). *Eighteenth annual report to Congress on the implementation of the Individuals with Disabilities Education Act.* Washington, DC.

NANCY E. ALGERT
LINDA H. PARRISH
Texas A&M University

CULTURAL SENSITIVITY DURING TRANSITION PLANNING

Providing appropriate special education services for culturally and linguistically diverse (CLD) students with disabilities is an emerging concern in the field of special education (Murtadha-Watts & Stoughton, 2004; Skiba, Poloni-Staudinger, Gallini, Simmons, & Feggins-Azziz, 2005). The U.S. Census in 2006 indicated that in the public school system 38% of the children are CLD, which is a 7% increase since 2000 (Landmark, Zhang, & Montoya, 2007). Such changing demographics mean that secondary special educators are likely to be planning for transition with families and youth whose cultures do not reflect their own (Blue-Banning, Turnbull, & Pereira, 2002).

Given recent data regarding postschool outcomes, it would appear that schools have an especially difficult time meeting the transition needs of youth with disabilities who are from CLD groups (Artiles, Klinger, & Tate, 2006; Wagner et al., 2005). Addressing the multiplicity of postschool outcomes for CLD youth with disabilities requires secondary special educators to better understand the diverse strengths and needs of these youth as well their families and cultural values (Trainor, Lindstrom, Simon-Burroughs, Martin, & Sorrells, 2008). A lack of attention to the cultural aspects of transition is troubling, especially when views of adult outcomes can vary considerably among ethnic groups (Geenen, Powers, & Lopez-Vasquez, 2001; Kim & Morningstar, 2005). If transition professionals apply a single standard for transition without considering how this might impact CLD youth and their families, postschool outcomes will be inhibited. Unfortunately, many educators have not considered these specific circumstances and how they might affect the CLD families' involvement in transition planning. As a result, CLD.

Given limited attention to culturally responsive transition planning, it is no surprise that CLD youth with disabilities lag considerably behind their European American peers in postschool outcomes. For example, African American and Hispanic American youth with disabilities experience significantly lower postsecondary educational enrollment and employment rates than their Euro-American peers with disabilities (Wagner, Newman, Cameto, & Levine, 2005). In addition, African American youth are less likely than European American youth to find employment or have a driver's license or a checking account. Furthermore, African American, Hispanic, and all other racial/ethnic students with disabilities scored lower on academic achievement measures than European Americans (Wagner, Newman, Cameto, Levine, & Garza, 2005). Targeted attention is needed to address the needs of CLD families and their adolescents during transition.

Transition planning is most successful when it involves the family and considers cultural values and beliefs (Artiles, Trent, & Palmer, 2004; Kim & Morningstar, 2005; Wehmeyer, Morningstar, & Husted, 1999). Professional understanding of family cultural norms can influence family involvement and satisfaction with transition planning (Geenen, Powers, & Lopez-Vasquez, 2001). Acknowledging the family's values and beliefs promotes increased cultural reciprocity because professionals take steps toward identifying their own beliefs as well as those of the family when planning for transition (Gil-Kashiwabara, Hogansen, Geenen, Powers, & Powers, 2007; Harry, Rueda, & Kalyanpur, 1999).

Although it has long been advocated that family participation is a particularly important strategy for including students from historically marginalized populations (Greene, 1996; Harry, 1992), CLD parents are less actively participating in school-based activities than their European American counterparts (Geenen et al., 2001). The tendency of CLD parents to seek support outside of school may be partially explained by the obstacles placed on CLD parents. These groups of parents were more likely to encounter barriers to school participation, including: (a) professional's negative attitudes, (b) insensitivity and discrimination, (c) poverty and byproducts of poverty, and (d) bureaucratic barriers, including lack of information and knowledge regarding their rights, the process and procedures of the education system, and the system policies that affect them and their children (Garriott, Wandry, & Snyder, 2000; Geenen, Powers, Lopez-Vasquez, & Bersani, 2003). Such barriers lead to disenfranchisement and disinterest in the normative culture of levels of participation considered appropriate by public schools (Klinger, Blanchett, & Harry, 2007; Trainor, 2008). Consequently, CLD families tend to withdraw from or take a more passive role in school-based planning and decision-making processes. Furthermore, discrimination and cultural insensitivity may have caused CLD families to give up formal supports and increase their reliance on informal supports from the ethnic communities to which they belong (Geenen et al., 2003; Kim & Morningstar, 2005; Nix-Williams, 2010).

Implementation of certain transition activities may represent the standards of European American values and may not reflect CLD families, thus causing disparity during transition (Trainor, 2005; Zhang, 2005; Zhang, Wehmeyer, & Chen, 2005). In fact, cultural values may influence expectations for the future, which may impede involvement in transition planning if different from those of transition professionals (Geenen et al., 2003; Rueda, Monzo, Shapiro, Gomez, & Blacher, 2005). Cultural views also impact how families and youth use information, particularly when securing access to transition resources (Morningstar & Mutua, 2003; Trainor, 2008). In one recent study, it was determined that families from diverse cultural backgrounds use a variety of strategies for obtaining information, yet traditional methods most often used by schools, such as brochures and written materials, were not highly utilized (Nix-Williams, 2010).

One way to support CLD families and youth during transition is by using the informal community networks with which CLD families have already established a trusting relationship (Leake & Cholymay, 2004). Research indicates that many CLD families turn to their community during their children's transition rather than to formal institutions and service systems (Kim & Morningstar, 2005). In fact, Kim and Morningstar (2005) maintained that existing supports such as faith-based organizations (FBO) and cultural centers may be underutilized. It would benefit transition if professionals learned about informal cultural organizations and resources that are supporting families and youth in order to gain a richer understanding of the needs, experiences, and strengths of CLD students and families. Nix-Williams (2010) recently explored the utility of approach by interviewing staff from informal cultural networks (i.e., faith-based organizations, community cultural centers). The results indicated that informal cultural networks can offer rich perspectives on unique ways to support families and youth during transition. Establishing partnerships with informal cultural networks can support transition professionals to develop culturally responsive transition planning and services.

Transition planning is fundamental to the success of students with disabilities. The lack of attention to cultural aspects of transition may cause difficulties, especially when views of successful adulthood vary among and between ethnic groups and professional views. To provide culturally responsive transition services, professionals have to involve youth and parents as partners in transition planning and decision making. To work together toward mutual goals leading to successful postschool outcomes for CLD students with disabilities, both professionals and families should be willing to share their attitudes, behaviors, and values in collaborative and respectful ways. Professionals and families will empower each other through trust and encouragement. Above all, professionals must accept cultural differences as strengths, and CLD families must be aware that they are important sources for their children and be willing to share their cultural values and information with professionals.

REFERENCES

Artiles, A. J., Klinger, J. K., & Tate, W. F. (2006). Representation of minority students in special education: Complicating traditional explanations. *Educational Researcher, 35*(6), 3–5.

Artiles, A. J., Trent, S. C., & Palmer, J. D. (2004). Culturally diverse students in special education: Legacies and prospects. In J. A. Banks, & C. A. McGee Banks (Eds.), *Handbook of research on multicultural education* (pp. 716–735). San Francisco, CA: Jossey-Bass.

Blue-Banning, M., Turnbull, A. P., & Pereira, L. (2002). Hispanic youth/young adults with disabilities: Parents' visions for the future. *Research and Practice for Persons with Severe Disabilities, 27,* 204–219.

Garriott, P. P., Wandry, D., & Snyder, L. (2000). Teachers as parents, parents as children: What's wrong with this picture? *Preventing School Failure, 45,* 37–43.

Geenen, S., Powers, L., & Lopez-Vasquez, A. (2001). Multicultural aspects of parent involvement in transition planning. *Exceptional Children, 67,* 265–282.

Geenen, S., Powers, L., Lopez-Vasquez, A., & Bersani, H. (2003). Understanding and promoting the transition of minority adolescents. *Career Development for Exceptional Individuals, 26,* 27–46.

Greene, G. (1996). Empowering culturally and linguistically diverse families in the transition planning process. *Journal for Vocational Special Needs Education, 19,* 26–30.

Gil-Kashiwabara, E., Hogansen, J., Geenen, S., Powers, K., & Powers, L. (2007). Improving transition outcomes for marginalized youth. *Career Development for Exceptional Individuals, 30*(2), 80–91.

Harry, B. (1992). *Cultural diversity, families, and the special education system: Communication and empowerment.* New York, NY: Teachers College Press.

Harry, B., Rueda, R., & Kalyanpur, M. (1999). Cultural reciprocity in socioculture perspectives: Adapting the normalization principle of family collaboration. *Exceptional Children. 66*(1), 123–136.

Kim, K., & Morningstar, M. (2005). Transition planning involving culturally and linguistically diverse families. *Career Development for Exceptional Children, 28*(2), 92–103.

Klinger, J. K., Blanchett, W. J., & Harry, B. (2007). Race, culture, and developmental disabilities. In S. L. Odom, R. H. Horner, M. E. Snell, & J. Blacher (Eds.) *Handbook of developmental disabilities* (pp. 55–75). New York, NY: Guilford Press.

Landmark, L., Zhang, D., & Montoya, L. (2007). Culturally diverse parents' experiences in their children's transition: Knowledge and involvement. *Career Development for Exceptional Individuals, 30*(2), 68–79.

Leake, D., & Cholymay, M. (2004, February). Addressing the needs of culturally and linguistically diverse students with disabilities in postsecondary education, *Information Brief, 3.*

Morningstar, M. E., & Mutua, K. (2003). Transitions to adulthood for youth with disabilities. In C. Utley & F. Obiakor (Eds.), *Psychology of effective education for learners with disabilities: Vol. 15. Advances in special education.* Stamford, CT: JAI Press.

Murtadha-Watts, K., & Stoughton, E. (2004). Critical cultural knowledge in special education: Reshaping the responsiveness of school leaders. *Focus on Exceptional Children 37*(2), 1–8.

Nix-Williams, T. R. (2010). *Providing outreach to families of youth with disabilities from culturally and linguistically diverse backgrounds by working with cultural groups and community organizations.* (Unpublished doctoral dissertation). University of Kansas, Lawrence, KS.

Rueda, R., Monzo, L., Shapiro, J., Gomez, J., & Blacher, J. (2005). Cultural models of transition: Latina mothers of young adults with developmental disabilities. *Exceptional Children, 71,* 401–414.

Skiba, R. J., Poloni-Staudinger, L., Simmons, A. B., Feggins-Azziz, L. R., & Chung, C.-G. (2005). Unproven links: Can poverty explain ethnic disproportionality in special education? *Journal of Special Education, 39*, 130–144.

Trainor, A. A. (2005). Self-determination perceptions and behaviors of diverse students with LD during the transition planning process. *Journal of Learning Disabilities, 38*, 233–249.

Trainor, A. A. (2008). Using cultural and social capital to improve postsecondary outcomes and expand transition models for youth with disabilities. *Journal of Special Education, 42*(3), 148–162.

Trainor, A. A., Lindstrom, L., Simon-Burroughs, M., Martin, J. E., & Sorrells, A. (2008). From marginalized to maximized opportunities for diverse youth with disabilities: A position paper of the Division on Career Development and Transition. *Career Development for Exceptional Individuals, 31*, 56–64.

Wagner, M., Newman, L., Cameto, R., Garza, N., & Levine, P. (2005). *After high school: A first look at the postschool experiences of youth with disabilities.* Menlo Park, CA: SRI International.

Wagner, M., Newman, L., Cameto, R., & Levine, P. (2005). *Changes over time in the early postschool outcomes of youth with disabilities.* Menlo Park, CA: SRI International.

Wehmeyer, M. L., Morningstar, M. E., & Husted, D. (1999). *Family involvement in transition planning and program implementation.* Austin, TX: PRO-ED.

Zhang, D. (2005). Parent practices in facilitating self-determination skills: The influences of culture, socioeconomic status, and children's special education status. *Research & Practice for Persons with Severe Disabilities, 30*(3), 154–162.

Zhang, D., Wehmeyer, M., & Chen, L. (2005). Parents and teachers engagement in fostering the self-determination of students with disabilities: A comparison between the United States and the Republic of China. *Remedial and Special Education, 26*(1), 55–64.

MARY E. MORNINGSTAR
University of Kansas
Fourth edition

CULTURE-FAIR TEST

Education and processes of socialization teach individuals cultural knowledge. Many standardized tests measure how well one has learned the information specific to a particular culture. The development of culture-fair tests was begun to neutralize the culturally loaded information found in standardized tests (Lewis, 1998). A test used to assess diverse cultural groups cannot contain items specific to any one particular culture; otherwise, it would not be considered to have content validity.

The Culture Fair Intelligence Test (Cattell, 1973) is a measure virtually devoid of verbal content (the test uses a paper-and-pencil format). It consists of novel problem-solving items that do not occur in any particular culture. The test format is multiple choice and includes four

subtests: Series Completion, Classification, Matrices, and Conditions. Different levels are administered depending on the subject's age: 4 to 8 years, 8 to 14 years, or 14 to adult. Similar to other standardized tests, the results of the Culture Fair Intelligence Test are expressed as deviation IQs with a mean of 100 and a standard deviation of 16.

Lewis (1998) notes that there are some weaknesses of the Culture Fair Intelligence Test. One is that it uses fairly extensive verbal instructions during administration of the test. This causes difficulty for linguistically different clients. Therefore, although the test does not have culturally loaded information items or verbal components, the verbal nature of the directions themselves are problematic. Also, the subtests emphasize speed. This emphasis on speed can differ cross-culturally, and thereby reduces the cultural fairness of the instrument. These potential problems should be taken into account when assessing clients of different cultural backgrounds. Anastasi (1988) has noted that the interpretation of test scores are "by far the most important considerations in the assessment of culturally diverse groups" (p. 66). Misinterpretation of scores with these groups is a serious concern.

REFERENCES

Anastasi, A. A. (1988). *Psychological testing* (6th ed.). New York, NY: Macmillan.

Cattell, R. B. (1973). *Technical supplement for the Culture Fair Intelligence Tests Scales 2 and 3.* Champaign, IL: Institute for Personality and Ability Testing.

Lewis, J. E. (1998). Nontraditional uses of traditional aptitude tests. In R. J. Samuda, R. Feurerstein, A. S. Kaufman, J. E. Lewis, & R. J. Sternberg (Eds.), *Advances in cross cultural assessment.* Thousand Oaks, CA: Sage.

ELIZABETH O. LICHTENBERGER
The Salk Institute

See also **Cultural Bias in Testing**

CULTURE FREE SELF-ESTEEM INVENTORIES, THIRD EDITION

The Culture Free Self-Esteem Inventories, Third Edition (CFSEI-3) is a set of self-report inventories used to measure self-esteem in a culturally fair manner. It is to be administered individually or in groups to children and adolescents between the ages of 6.0 and 18.11 years. Administration takes approximately 15 to 20 minutes and requires individuals to write or respond verbally to a series of Yes/No questions. It is composed of three age-appropriate forms: Primary, Intermediate, and Adolescent. All three forms provide a Global Self-Esteem Quotient and a defensive measure to assess the degree to which an individual's response may be guarded. In addition, the Intermediate and Adolescent forms provide self-esteem scores in the following categories: Academic, General, Parental/Home, and Social. The Adolescent Form also includes a score for Personal Self-Esteem. An Examiner's Manual and easy-to-use Profile and Scoring Forms are provided. The CFSEI-3 is easy to administer and score. Responses (simple Yes/No answers) can be either written or spoken. Conversion tables provide subscale standard scores based on a mean of 10 and a standard deviation of 3 and quotient scores based on a mean of 100 and a standard deviation of 15.

The CFSEI-3 was standardized on a sample of 1,727 school-age individuals from 17 states. The sample was representative of the 2000 U.S. Census with respect to geographic region, gender, race, rural or urban residence, ethnicity, family income, parent education, and disability.

Content, criterion-prediction, and construct-identification were used to investigate validity. The CFSEI-3 correlates strongly with other self-esteem and self-concept measures. Information regarding differential item functioning analyses and separate reliability and validity information for seven subgroups (male, female, European American, African American, Hispanic American, gifted and talented, and learning disabled) is provided with the test kit. In addition, a full chapter in the Examiner's Manual is devoted to the CFSEI-3's absence of bias.

Content sampling and time sampling estimates were used to assess reliability. For the Global Self-Esteem Quotient scores, the average internal consistency coefficients range from .81 to .93 while the average time sampling coefficients range from .72 to .98.

For more information on the CFSEI-3, see Plake, Impara, and Spies (2003), and the James Battle website (http://www.jamesbattle.com/cfsei.htm).

REFERENCE

Plake, B. S., Impara, J. C., & Spies, R. A. (Eds.). (2003). *The fifteenth mental measurements yearbook.* Lincoln, NE: Buros Institute of Mental Measurements.

Ron Dumont
Fairleigh Dickinson University

John O. Willis
Rivier College

Kathleen Viezel
Fairleigh Dickinson University

Jamie Zibulsky
Fairleigh Dickinson University
Fourth edition

CURRICULUM

Educational curriculum is what students learn, or the content of instruction. Historically, the curriculum of U.S. public education was specified in broad, global terms, addressing abstract notions such as Americanization and instilling of democratic values in youths (Mulhern, 1959). In the 20th century, however, developments in learning theory such as Thorndike's demonstration of the specificity of transfer promoted a reconceptualization of learning from concurrent strengthening of global faculties to sequential mastery of numerous, definite, and particularized skills and knowledge (Fuchs & Deno, 1982). This reconceptualization has led to alternative ways of specifying school curricula for distinct behavioral outcomes (Bloom, Hastings, & Mandaus, 1981). Current curriculum statements typically represent carefully sequenced, calibrated, and organized sets of tasks, regularly called objectives (Johnson, 1967).

In special education, as in regular education, curriculum is derived from an analysis of the needs of society. This analysis, however, renders considerably different instructional focuses for mildly and severely disabled students. For the mildly disabled, analysis of the needs of society results in a curriculum similar, if not identical, to that of normally developing pupils; it includes curricular tasks such as reading, writing, and mathematics. For the more severely disabled, this analysis results in a curriculum that addresses basic survival skill requirements. These alternative educational focuses often are referred to as developmental curriculum (which identifies tasks for normally performing children; Snell, 1983) and functional curriculum (which addresses skills necessary for ultimate attainment of self-sufficiency; Holvoet, Guess, Mulligan, & Brown, 1980).

For the mildly disabled student, the curriculum may be resequenced, broken down into smaller tasks, reorganized, or taught via dramatically different instructional strategies. Two alternative ways of addressing curriculum for the mildly disabled have been referred to as the task analytic approach and the ability training model (Ysseldyke & Salvia, 1974). With the task analytic approach, the curriculum is approached by breaking down terminal tasks into sets of subskills, which are addressed separately and sequentially and ultimately synthesized into final tasks of the curriculum (Howell, 1986). With the ability training model, hierarchies of abilities that are prerequisite to mastery of basic reading, writing, and mathematics skills such as perceptual-motor or psycholinguistic abilities are hypothesized. These abilities are addressed before the standard school curriculum is taught. In both cases, however, the ultimate curriculum, or the final educational objective, remains constant and is consonant with the curricular goals of the mainstream educational environment.

In contradistinction, the functional curriculum of the more severely disabled population is determined more individually. It addresses objectives that (1) represent the practical or functional skills most likely to be needed currently or in the near future; (2) span the four instructional domains of domestic, leisure/recreational, community, and vocational skills; (3) are suitable for the student's chronological age; and (4) address the pupil's current performance levels and are reasonably thought to be attainable (Snell, 1983). The basic assumption of a functional curriculum for individuals with severe disabilities is that the school's responsibility is to teach skills that optimize a person's independent and responsible functioning in society (Hawkins & Hawkins, 1981). For individuals with severe disabilities, these skills must be chosen from a group of tasks and activities that have a high probability of being required and that increase self-sufficiency (Brown, Branston, Hamre-Nietupski, Pumpian, Certo, & Gruenewald, 1979).

REFERENCES

Bloom, B. S., Hastings, J. T., & Mandaus, G. F. (1981). *Handbook on formative and summative evaluation of student learning.* New York, NY: McGraw-Hill.

Brown, L., Branston, M. B., Hamre-Nietupski, S., Pumpian, I., Certo, N., & Gruenewald, L. (1979). A strategy for developing chronological age appropriate and functional curricular content for severely handicapped adolescents and young adults. *Journal of Special Education, 13,* 81–90.

Fuchs, L. S., & Deno, S. L. (1982). *Developing goals and objectives for educational programs.* Washington, DC: American Association of Colleges for Teacher Education.

Hawkins, R. P., & Hawkins, K. K. (1981). Parental observation on the education of severely retarded children: Can it be done in the classroom? *Analysis & Intervention in Developmental Disabilities, 1,* 13–22.

Holvoet, J., Guess, D., Mulligan, M., & Brown, F. (1980). The Individualized Curriculum Sequencing model (II): A teaching strategy for severely handicapped students. *Journal of the Association for the Severely Handicapped, 5,* 337–351.

Howell, K. W. (1986). Direct assessment of academic performance. *School Psychology Review, 15,* 324–335.

Johnson, M. (1967). Definitions and models in curriculum theory. *Educational Theory, 7,* 127–140.

Mulhern, J. (1959). *A history of education* (2nd ed.). New York, NY: Ronald.

Snell, M. E. (1983). *Systematic instruction of the moderately and severely handicapped* (2nd ed.). Columbus, OH: Merrill.

Ysseldyke, J. E., & Salvia, J. (1974). Diagnostic prescriptive teaching: Two models. *Exceptional Children, 41,* 181–185.

Lynn S. Fuchs
Peabody College,
Vanderbilt University

See also Annual Goals

CURRICULUM, AGE-APPROPRIATE

An age-appropriate curriculum is a special-educational curriculum that consists of activities that are matched to both the students' chronological ages and their developmental or skill levels. This match has been difficult to achieve, especially for older trainable and severely disabled students who continue to function on preschool levels. The older students with severe disabilities often need continued training in fine motor, cognitive, and language skills, but also need to acquire skills that can be used immediately and will transfer to later community and vocational placements (Drew, Logan, & Hardman, 1984).

The Education for All Handicapped Children Act (PL 94-142), and its successor, the Individuals with Disabilities Education Act, have mandated an appropriate education for all students with disabilities, but wide differences remain when defining this term. The justification for using an age-appropriate education lies in the principle of normalization, which Nirje (1979) has defined as follows: "Making available to all mentally retarded people patterns of life and conditions of everyday living which are as close as possible to the regular circumstances of society" (p. 73). Although it may appear unrealistic to teach age-appropriate behaviors to students with severe developmental delays, Larsen and Jackson (1981) argue that this is the mission of special education: "No, we will not be completely successful (but)...our goals for students will stress skills relevant to the general culture, rather than skills that have a proven value only in special-education classrooms" (p. 1).

Our current knowledge of developmental milestones, task analysis procedures, and behavior modification principles can be used in adopting this approach if we also examine the "age-appropriateness" of the materials, skills, activities, environments, and reinforcers used during instruction. For example, in learning visual discrimination of shapes, elementary-age students may use form boards and shape sorters, while older students use community signs and mosaic art activities. For other skills, calculators may be used instead of number lines; colored clothing can be sorted rather than colored cubes; and the assembly of vocational products may replace pegboards and beads (Bates, Renzaglia, & Wehman, 1981).

Because there are many skills that older severely disabled youths will never acquire (e.g., reading a newspaper, buying groceries), the curriculum focuses on those abilities that can be learned (e.g., reading survival signs, following directions). To identify these skills for each group of students, Brown et al. (1979) employ an ecological inventory approach listing the environments and subenvironments where the students currently (or will eventually) function. An inventory of the activities in each environment and a listing of skills needed to participate in those activities provide the framework for selecting curriculum goals. In this approach, for example, the basic skill of matching pictures leads to finding grooming items in a drugstore, and identifying different foods leads to ordering in a fast-food restaurant.

Classroom design and décor also should reflect the chronological age of the students. For older youths, pictures of teen activities and movie celebrities are more age-appropriate decorations than cartoon characters. Many special-education classrooms have moved into secondary buildings, opening up opportunities to use age-appropriate training sites such as home economics rooms.

Severely handicapped students may have extremely slow learning rates and much difficulty in generalizing learning skills to new situations. Therefore, their education must include the teaching of critical skill clusters and opportunities to practice functional skills in natural settings, such as sheltered workshops, supermarkets, and public transportation. For a more detailed description of curricular approaches to teaching functional skill clusters see Guess and Noonan (1982).

REFERENCES

Bates, P., Renzaglia, A., & Wehman, P. (1981). Characteristics of an appropriate education for severely and profoundly handicapped students. *Education & Training of the Mentally Retarded, 16,* 142–149.

Brown, L., Branston, M. B., Homre-Nietupski, S., Pumpian, I., Certo, N., & Grunewald, L. (1979). A strategy for developing chronological age appropriate and functional curriculum content for severely handicapped adolescents and young adults. *Journal of Special Education, 13,* 81–90.

Drew, C. J., Logan, D. R., & Hardman, M. L. (1984). *Mental retardation: A life cycle approach* (3rd ed.). St. Louis, MO: Times Mirror/Mosby.

Guess, D., & Noonan, M. J. (1982). Curricula and instructional procedures for severely handicapped students. *Focus on Exceptional Children, 14,* 9–10.

Larsen, L. A., & Jackson, L. B. (1981). Chronological age in the design of educational programs for severely and profoundly impaired students. *PRISE Reporter, 13,* 1–2.

Nirje, B. (1979). Changing patterns in residential services for the mentally retarded. In E. L. Meyen (Ed.), *Basic readings in the study of exceptional children and youth.* Denver, CO: Love.

KATHERINE D. COUTURIER
Pennsylvania State University

KIMBERLY F. APPLEQUIST
University of Colorado at Colorado Springs

CURRICULUM-BASED ASSESSMENT

Curriculum-based assessment (CBA), defined as a procedure for determining the instructional needs of a student based on the student's ongoing performance with existing course content, comprises a broad category of assessment procedures that are tied to curriculum (Tucker, 1985). CBA includes a range of testing procedures that may or may not be standardized. These procedures are intended to directly assess a student's performance on the curriculum that is being taught so as to evaluate student progress on specific as well as general goals and provide an analysis of the skills a student has and has not mastered. Knowledge of the skills and objectives a student has attained facilitate the placement of the student at a proper instructional level and the teachers' and parents' ability to make decisions about the suitable instructional goal (Salvia & Ysseldyke, 2004).

Within an instructional decision-making model, CBA is thought to improve instruction by providing corrective feedback (Thomas & Grimes, 2002). CBA seeks to answer the following five questions: (1) What does the student know? (2) What can the student do? (3) How does the student think? (4) How does the student approach difficult tasks? (5) What does the teacher do next? (See Gickling, 1998.) CBA provides direct measurement of student performance on the curriculum and evaluates student progress on specific as well as general goals. Frequent administrations (e.g., three to four times per year) are thought to provide sensitive information about discreet yet important changes in student performance (Salvia & Hughes, 1990).

CBA may involve administering tests in each academic subject that was, is, and will be taught. A student's performance generally is compared to that of his or her peers or the expected level of attainment based on the student's curriculum. For example, when assessing reading of a student beyond grade two, CBA may involve administering short (150 to 200 words) oral-reading passages taken from the reading series in which the student is being taught. Reading fluency is measured as the number of words read correctly per minute, and comprehension is measured by the number of questions passed. CBA in mathematics may involve administering approximately 30 math problems per grade level. Probes assess single skills (e.g., single-digit addition or subtraction) or multiple skills (e.g., adding two- and three-digit numbers). When assessing writing, CBA may use a "story starter" that provides a student with an initial idea on which to write. After some time period (e.g., 3 minutes), the number of words correctly written is counted. When assessing spelling, CBA may require the student to write three sets of 20 words from successive grade level probes taken randomly from the text used in the spelling curriculum (Shapiro, 1996).

The CBA process is based on established research and helps educational professionals, students, and parents gain an accurate picture of a student's current knowledge and skills. CBA's advantages over norm-referenced achievement tests include a more direct examination of student performance on current curricula, improved content validity by examining student performance on products related to the curriculum, and directly linking assessment and instruction. Its disadvantages include an inability to compare a student's performance with the performances of a large, national sample of same-age peers and an inability to describe performance in reference to a normal distribution. Also, short test sessions prohibit professionals from making observations that facilitate adjustments to match student learning style and temperament.

REFERENCES

Gickling, E. E. (1998). *Instructional assessment training manual.* Unpublished manuscript.

Salvia, J., & Hughes, C. (1990). *Curriculum-based assessment: Testing what's taught.* New York, NY: Macmillan.

Salvia, J., & Ysseldyke, J. E. (2004). *Assessment in special and inclusive education* (9th ed.). Boston, MA: Houghton Mifflin.

Shapiro, E. S. (1996). *Academic skills problems: Direct assessment and intervention* (2nd ed.). New York, NY: Guilford Press.

Thomas, A., & Grimes, J. (Eds.). (2002). *Best practices in school psychology IV.* Bethesda, MD: National Association of School Psychologists.

Tucker, J. (1985). Curriculum-based assessment: An introduction. *Exceptional Children, 52,* 199–204.

JEFFREY DITTERLINE
University of Florida

See also Assessment, Curriculum-Based; Curriculum, Age-Appropriate; Norm-Referenced Testing; Response to Intervention

CURRICULUM-BASED MEASUREMENT

Curriculum-based measurement (CBM) refers to a specific set of procedures for measuring student growth in basic skills that were developed by Dr. Stanley L. Deno and his colleagues at the University of Minnesota through the Institute for Research on Learning Disabilities (Deno, 1985). The procedures were developed as a larger research effort directed toward designing a practically feasible and effective formative evaluation system that special education teachers could use to build more effective instructional programs for their students. To develop such a system Dr. Deno sought to create a simple, reliable, and valid set of measurement procedures that teachers could use to frequently and repeatedly measure the growth of their students in the basic skills of reading spelling and written expression.

Dr. Deno sought to address the following three key questions in developing the CBM procedures: (1) What are the outcome tasks on which performance should be measured, (2) how should the measurement activities be structured to produce technically adequate data, and (3) could the data be used to improve educational programs? The questions were answered through systematic examination of the technical adequacy of the measures, the treatment validity or utility of the measures, and the feasibility of the measures. The results of this research on progress monitoring led to the development of CBM. Subsequent research on CBM has shown that using CBM to measure progress in student growth in basic skills areas results in improved student achievement (Fuchs & Fuchs, 1986; Reschly, Busch, Betts, Deno, & Long, 2009).

Continued development of CBM led to the finding that the generic measurement procedures of CBM could provide technically adequate, instructionally relevant data even when the materials used for measurement had been drawn from sources other than a school's curriculum. For that reason, researchers began to use the term *general outcome measurement* to refer to the generic procedures of using these measures to monitor student growth (Fuchs, Deno, & Mirkin, 1984).

The use of CBM has also been extended to new areas such as secondary reading, written expression, and other subjects, early literacy, English-language learners, and response to intervention (RtI) systems. Yell and Steckert (2003) asserted that by using CBM to conduct assessments, develop measurable annual goals, and monitor student programs IEP teams can ensure the development of educationally meaningful and legally sound IEPs.

REFERENCES

Deno, S. L. (1985). Curriculum-based measurement: The emerging alternative. *Exceptional Children, 52,* 219–232.

Fuchs, L. S., Deno, S. L., & Mirkin, P. K. (1984). The effects of frequent curriculum-based measurement and evaluation on pedagogy, student achievement, and student awareness of learning. *American Educational Research Journal, 21,* 449–460.

Fuchs, L. S., & Fuchs, D. (1986). Effects of systematic formative evaluation on student achievement: A meta-analysis. *Exceptional Children, 53,* 199–208.

Reschly, A. L., Busch, T. W., Betts, J., Deno, S. L., & Long, J. (2009). Curriculum-Based Measurement Oral Reading as an indicator of reading achievement: A meta-analysis of the correlational evidence. *Journal of School Psychology, 47,* 427–469.

Yell, M. L., & Steckert, P. M. (2003). Developing legally correct and educationally meaningful IEPs using curriculum-based measurement. *Assessment for Effective Intervention, 28,* 73–88.

MITCHELL YELL
University of South Carolina
Fourth edition

CURRICULUM FOR STUDENTS WITH MILD DISABILITIES IN SPECIAL EDUCATION

The definition of curriculum varies in the literature, but in the broadest sense it is used in the field in two ways: (1) to indicate a plan for the education of learners, and (2) to identify a field of study. The word *curriculum* comes from a Latin root meaning racecourse; it can be regarded as the standardized ground covered by students in their race for a diploma (Zais, 1976).

Special education curriculum for the mildly disabled learner consists of learning tasks, activities, or assignments that are directed toward increasing a student's knowledge or skills in a specific content or subject area. It is the special educator's task to identify the differences between the regular and special education curriculum and to make educational decisions based on available assessment data.

The decision to provide variation in content may be less significant in educating learners with mild disabilities than the decision to provide variation in the conditions under which learning can be best facilitated. A critical issue involves the determination of the need for compensatory versus remedial curricula (Case, 1975). Many of the strategies and techniques used with mildly handicapped learners in special education overlap with Chapter I, other remedial programs, and regular education.

Mainstreaming and inclusion has encouraged efforts to help the over 70% of special education students who spend at least part of the day in regular classrooms to master the regular curriculum or "face curricular isolationism" (O'Connell-Mason & Raison, 1982).

This special education curriculum must be coordinated with regular education curriculum, which in turn must be modified or changed at times to accommodate students with different learning styles. The curricula must be designed to meet the particular needs and characteristics of the individuals who are to learn various contents.

Howell, Kaplan, and O'Connell (1979) indicate that to date, the research has not demonstrated the superiority of one type of curriculum modification over another. However, there are a number of general types of modifications that have been found useful: (1) Eliminate or reduce the subjects in the student's curriculum; (2) develop or identify an alternative curriculum; (3) alter expectations for the quantity or quality of work; (4) teach subject matter more slowly; (5) teach only the most essential subject matter; (6) develop a parallel curriculum; (7) provide a supplemented curriculum; or (8) adjust materials and/or response modes.

Growth in the field of special education curricula for mild disabilities has become an integral part of regular education. It is clear that the similarities are greater than the differences. The same principles and procedures, with some modifications, can be used to instruct all children. All children can reach their potential given the opportunity, effective teaching, and proper resources (Berdine & Blackhurst, 1985).

REFERENCES

Berdine, W. H., & Blackhurst, A. E. (1985). *An introduction to special education*. Boston, MA: Little, Brown.

Case, R. (1975). Gearing the demands of instruction to the developmental capacities of the learner. *Review of Educational Research, 45*, 3–9.

Howell, K. W., Kaplan, J. S., & O'Connell, C. Y. (1979). *Evaluating exceptional children: A task analysis approach*. Columbus, OH: Merrill.

O'Connell-Mason, C., & Raison, S. B. (1982). *Curriculum assessment and modification*. Washington, DC: American Association of Colleges for Teacher Education.

Zais, R. S. (1976). *Curriculum: Principles and foundations*. New York, NY: Harper & Row.

DEBORAH A. SHANLEY
*Medgar Evers College,
City University of New York*

See also Curriculum, Age-Appropriate; Mainstreaming; Task Analysis

CURRICULUM FOR STUDENTS WITH SEVERE DISABILITIES

Educational curriculum is what students learn, or the content of instruction. Historically, the curricula of U.S. public education was specified in broad, global terms, addressing abstract notions such as Americanization and instilling of democratic values in youths (Mulhern, 1959). In the 20th century, however, developments in learning theory such as Thorndike's demonstration of the specificity of transfer promoted a reconceptualization of learning from concurrent strengthening of global faculties to sequential mastery of numerous, definite, and particularized skills and knowledge (Fuchs & Deno, 1982). This reconceptualization led to alternative ways of specifying school curricula for distinct behavioral outcomes (Bloom, Hastings, & Mandaus, 1981). Current curriculum statements typically represent carefully sequenced, calibrated, and

In special education, as in regular education, curriculum is derived from an analysis of the needs of society. For the severely disabled individual, this analysis results in curriculum that addresses basic survival skill requirements. This educational focus, which represents an alternative to the normal or developmental educational curriculum (Snell, 1983), is referred to as a functional curriculum. The basic assumptions of a functional curriculum for the severely disabled are that the school's responsibility is to teach skills that optimize a person's independent and responsible functioning in society (Hawkins & Hawkins, 1981) and that, for children with severe disabilities, these skills must be chosen from a group of tasks and activities that have a high probability of being required and that increase self-sufficiency (Brown, Branston, Hamre-Nietupski, Pumpian, Certo, & Gruenewald, 1979).

This functional curriculum is determined individually and addresses objectives that (a) represent practical or functional skills most likely to be needed currently or in the near future; (b) are suitable for the student's chronological age; (c) address the pupil's current performance levels and are reasonably thought to be attainable; and (d) span four instructional domains (Snell, 1983).

The four domains of instructional content are domestic, leisure/recreational, community, and vocational. The domestic domain includes skills performed in and around the home, including self-care, clothing care, housekeeping, cooking, and yard work. In the leisure/recreational domain are skills needed to engage in spectator or participant activities performed for self-pleasure. Skills required in the community domain include street crossing, using public transportation, shopping, eating in restaurants, and using other public facilities such as parks. The vocational domain addresses skills necessary for employment, such as appropriate work dress and demeanor, assembly line behavior, interviewing for jobs, completing work applications, and punctuality.

The process of determining appropriate functional curricula on an individual basis has been conceptualized as comprising five steps (Brown et al., 1979): (1) selecting curriculum domains; (2) identifying and surveying current and future natural environments; (3) dividing the relevant environments into subenvironments; (4) inventorying these subenvironments for the relevant activities performed there; and (5) examining the activities to isolate the skills required for their performance.

To address the functional curriculum for individuals with severe disabilities, instructional strategies typically have been based on behavioral methodology. The instructional process begins with a descriptive analysis of the environmental events subsequent to, antecedent to, or during recurring behavioral events, with the purpose of identifying possible discriminative and reinforcing stimuli. Then, a task analysis of terminal objectives is conducted; in it subskills necessary for successful mastery of the final objectives are identified. Next, subskill instructional objectives are established and initial teaching strategies are specified. Then ongoing assessments of pupils' progress toward goals are collected as the instructional hypothesis is implemented. Finally, ongoing assessment data are evaluated and employed formatively to redesign instructional procedures in order to increase the probability of goal attainment.

REFERENCES

Bloom, B. S., Hastings, J. T., & Mandaus, G. F. (1981). *Handbook on formative and summative evaluation of student learning.* New York, NY: McGraw-Hill.

Brown, L., Branston, M. B., Hamre-Nietupski, S., Pumpian, I., Certo, N., & Gruenewald, L. (1979). A strategy for developing chronological age appropriate and functional curricular content for severely handicapped adolescents and young adults. *Journal of Special Education, 13,* 81–90.

Fuchs, L. S., & Deno, S. L. (1982). *Developing goals and objectives for educational programs.* Washington, DC: American Association of Colleges for Teacher Education.

Hawkins, R. P., & Hawkins, K. K. (1981). Parental observation on the education of severely retarded children: Can it be done in the classroom? *Analysis & Intervention in Developmental Disabilities, 1,* 13–22.

Holvoet, J., Guess, D., Mulligan, M., & Brown, F. (1980). The Individualized Curriculum Sequencing Model (II): A teaching strategy for severely handicapped students. *Journal of the Association for the Severely Handicapped, 5,* 337–351.

Johnson, M. (1967). Definitions and models in curriculum theory. *Educational Theory, 7,* 127–140.

Mulhern, J. (1959). *A history of education* (2nd ed.). New York, NY: Ronald.

Snell, M. E. (1983). *Systematic instruction of the moderately and severely handicapped* (2nd ed.). Columbus, OH: Merrill.

LYNN S. FUCHS
*Peabody College,
Vanderbilt University*

See also Curriculum; Functional Instruction; Functional Skills Training

CURRICULUM IN EARLY CHILDHOOD INTERVENTION

Early intervention curricula vary depending on the needs of the individual child; however, a substantial literature base exists supporting the use of curriula that occur in natural enviornments with inclusive learning activities (Bruder, 2001; Campbell, Sawyer, & Muhlenhaupt, 2009). Curricula provided in natural environments allow the instructor and child the advantage of enhancing behavioral and developmental skills through play and other typical day activities (Bruder, 2001). Skills known to enhance the child's psychological and behavioral maturation emphasize motor, cognitive, language, social, and self-help skill development areas through the teaching of curriculum in natural settings. Individualized instruction can be provided to the child and family throughout the day in all environments to take advantage of learning opportunities (Campbell, 2004). The purposes of early intervention curricula are to develop, habilitate, or accelerate young children's development. For children with disabilities, the intent is to minimize the effects of the disability and increase development and learning for future school success. The Division for Early Childhood and National Association for the Education of Young Children recommend creating high expectations for every child and developing a program of inclusive practices, which is delivered with dimensions of high quality as the driving principle for all supports and services provided to young children with disabilities (DEC/NAEYC; 2009).

REFERENCES

Bruder, M. B. (2001). Infants and toddlers: Outcomes and ecology. In M. J. Guralnick (Ed.), *Early childhood inclusion: Focus on change* (pp. 203–228). Baltimore, MD: Paul H. Brookes.

Campbell, P. H. (2004). Participation-based services: Promoting children's participation in natural settings. *Young Exceptional Children, S*(I), 20–29.

Campbell, P. H., Sawyer, L. B., & Muhlenhaupt, M. (2009). The meaning of natural environments for parents and professionals. *Infants and Young Children, 22*(4), 264–278.

Division for Early Childhood and the National Association for the Education of Young Children (DEC/NAEYC). (2009). *Early childhood inclusion: A joint position statement of the Division for Early Childhood (DEC) and the National Association for the Education of Young Children (NAEYC).* Chapel Hill: University of North Carolina, FPG Child Development Institute.

MARY MURRAY
Journal of Special Education

HEATHER S. DAVIS
Texas A&M University
Fourth edition

See also Early Identification of Children With Disabilities; Preschool Assessment; Preschool Special Education

CUSHING'S SYNDROME

Cushing's syndrome, or hypercortisolism, is a hormonal disorder that is caused by an excess of the hormone cortisol. The syndrome is relatively rare, and its etiology has been traced to an abnormal functioning of the pituitary gland. Other causes may be as the result of high doses of cortisol or other glucocorticoid (steroid) hormones taken for prolonged periods of time for the treatment of asthma, rheumatoid arthritis, lupus, or certain allergies (Shin, 1999). The syndrome is distinguishable from Cushing's disease in that the latter involves tumors in the pituitary that cause the excessive amounts of cortisol.

This condition most commonly affects adults ages 20 to 50 (Shin, 1999). Although the condition has been found to occur up to 5 times more frequently in females of reproductive age, there have been reports of occurrence at all ages in both males and females (Krieger, 1982).

Characteristics

1. The child experiences obesity noticeable especially in the abdomen, face (moon face), neck, and upper back (buffalo hump) and growth retardation.
2. The child may complain of weak muscles in the upper arms and legs and has a tendency to bruise easily.
3. Other physical characteristics may include thinning of the skin and pink or purple stretch marks (striae) on the abdomen, thighs, breasts, and shoulders.
4. The child or adolescent commonly experiences increased acne, facial hair growth, and scalp hair loss in women.
5. High blood pressure and menstrual difficulties are common.

If the syndrome occurs as the result of taking hormonal steroids, withdrawing the steroids allows the body eventually to go back to normal. For Cushing's disease, in which tumors are present in the pituitary gland, surgery or radiation therapy have been found to be successful in the majority of cases. Several drugs (Mitotane, aminoglutethimide, metyrapone, and ketoconazole) help inhibit cortisol production (National Organization for Rare Disorders [NORD], 1999). Most of the clinical manifestations, and particularly growth arrest in children, are reversible with the correction of the adrenocortical hyperfunction (Binder & Hall, 1972). Treatment may last anywhere from 2 to 18 months (Shin, 1999).

Children who develop Cushing's syndrome may be eligible for special education services under the handicapping condition of Other Health Impairment or Physical Disability. Because frequent visits to the doctor are necessary during treatment, the child will most likely have many absences from school. Counseling that is sensitive to chronic illnesses should be considered, especially in light of the length of treatment and the physically undesirable characteristics associated with the disease. There is a possibility that the child will suffer from depression. Occupational therapy may also be considered for students whose symptoms include weak muscles.

The National Institutes of Health are currently researching use of the drug RU 486, a glucocorticoid antagonist, for treatment. Research is also being conducted with the drug octreotide acetate, which may shrink the tumors associated with Cushing's syndrome. Scientists are also conducting better testing methods for diagnosis. Such methods include studying fluids that have been drained from the pituitary gland to detect hormone levels that relate to the presence of pituitary tumors (NORD, 1999).

REFERENCES

Binder, C., & Hall, P. (Ed.). (1972). *Cushing's syndrome: Diagnosis and treatment*. London, UK: William Heinemann Medical Books.

Krieger, D. (1982). *Cushing's syndrome*. New York, NY: Springer-Verlag.

National Organization for Rare Disorders. (1999). *Cushing syndrome*. Retrieved from http://rarediseases.org

Shin, L. (Ed.). (1999). *Endocrine and metabolic disorders sourcebook: Basic information for the layperson about pancreatic and insulin-related disorders*. Detroit, MI: Omnigraphics.

CHRISTINE D. CDE BACA
University of Northern Colorado

CUSTODIAL CARE OF INDIVIDUALS WITH DISABILITIES, HISTORY OF

Organized care for individuals with disabilities goes back no more than 150 years. If we consider the disabled to include the insane, mentally infirm, orphans, the poor, and those found to be criminal in nature, then we can easily locate the second American Revolution as during the Jackson presidency (Rothman, 1971). Prior to this period, care of individuals with disabilities was managed primarily by families, neighbors, and friends of the disabled. In the case of criminals, the offenders were put to death.

During the Jacksonian period large institutions were constructed in Boston, New York, and Philadelphia. Almshouses for the poor were constructed in smaller communities. Governmental agencies and the wealthy provided funds for the erection of insane asylums. Soon the medical profession was actively using the asylums as an integral part of care for the insane. It was also during this time that penitentiaries proliferated throughout the East Coast states. In addition, homes built with public funds and other types of asylums were constructed for orphans and delinquent children. In Rothman's (1971) *Discovery of the Asylum*, we find ample documentation of reform during the Jacksonian period. As Rothman has stated, this period could appropriately be referred to as "the age of the asylum."

Interested investigators have claimed that the growth of institutions in America for the insane, orphans, poor, criminals, and, one could hypothesize, the mentally retarded, paralleled the growth of psychiatry. It was 300

years prior to the advent of the first U.S. institutions that we find King Henry VIII taking the old monastery of St. Mary of Bethlehem in London, England, and reserving it solely for the care of the mentally ill. One can assume that at that time little was known about any differentiation of diagnosis between the mentally disturbed and the mentally retarded. Thus, the idiot and the insane were probably treated much the same. St. Mary's provided deplorable conditions and inadequate care for the infirm. Other asylums soon appeared in Mexico (1566), France (1641), Moscow (1764), and Vienna (the famous Lunatics' Tower, 1784). All of these institutions were the forerunners of similar edifices in America. Many of the first institutions were nothing more than a modification of a penal institution. An example of such early primitive care can be seen in the description of Lunatics' Tower:

> It was an ornately decorated tower within which were square rooms. The doctors and keepers lived in the square rooms, while the patients were confined in the spaces between the walls of the square rooms and the outside of the tower. The patients were put on exhibit to the public for a small fee. (Coleman, Butcher, & Carson, 1984)

An account (Coleman, Butcher, & Carson, 1984) of the LaBicetre Hospital in Paris is said to be representative of most institutions for the insane throughout the 18th century:

> The patients were ordinarily shackled to the walls of their dark, unlighted cells by iron collars which held them flat against the wall and permitting little movement. Oftimes, there were also iron hoops around the waists of the patients and both their hands and feet were chained. Although these chains usually permitted enough movement that the patients could feed themselves out of bowls, they often kept them from being able to lie down at night. Since little was known about dietetics, and the patients were presumed to be animals anyway, little attention was paid to whether they were adequately fed or to whether the food was good or bad. The cells were furnished only with straw and were never swept or cleaned; the patient remained in the midst of all the accumulated ordure. No one visited the cells except at feeding time, no provision was made for warmth, and even the most elementary gestures of humanity were lacking. (modified from Selling, 1943)

What is striking to the reader is the never-ending stream of trends in the care of the disabled, often instituted in the name of progress. In fact, care was generally for profit, coercion, incarceration, or medical validation. Historical accounts indicate that while benevolence was the primary motivation for the creation of institutional care, society also needed to seek stability from social disruption.

Humanitarian reform of institutions both in Europe and America occurred on a small scale during the 18th century. Pinel's experiments at LaBicetre included removing the chains, adding sunlit rooms, extending kindness, and including freedom to exercise. Reactions by patients were recorded as overwhelmingly positive by even the most seriously disturbed (Zilboorg & Henry, 1941). William Tuke, an English Quaker, also provided a humane environment at the York Retreat in England, while in America, Benjamin Rush, the founder of American psychiatry, provided care in a more benevolent manner. Such examples of humane treatment, however, are isolated, as most institutions continued to treat their residents much like animals and such labels as "snake pits" and "schools for unimprovable or unteachable idiots" were not uncommon.

Notable among Americans who created a moral cognizance of existing deplorable conditions was Dorothea Dix (1802–1887). In her famous *Memorial*, submitted to the U.S. Congress in 1848, she remarked that she had observed

> more than 9000 idiots, epileptics, and insane in the United States, destitute of appropriate care and protection...bound with galling chains; bowed beneath fetters and heavy iron balls attached to drag chains, lacerated with ropes, scourged with rods, and terrified beneath storms of execration and cruel blows; now subject to jibes and scorn and torturing tricks; now abandoned to the most outrageous violations. (Zilboorg & Henry, 1941, pp. 583–584)

This message was repeated often as Dix and her followers became instrumental in improving conditions throughout the United States, Canada, and Scotland. She is credited with establishing 32 hospitals. Unfortunately, most asylums continued to be unfit for humans.

It was not until the late 1800s that the mentally retarded were beginning to be seen as a group separate, at least in name, from other of society's deviant groups. There is reason to suspect that the mentally retarded had often been punished severely and in some instances hanged for criminal activities beyond their comprehension. The first institutions constructed solely for the mentally retarded seem to have been built for educational purposes. These temporary boarding school–type facilities were established primarily for the "improvables." The schools rejected admittance to those who could not be cured and returned to their families. Even the famed Fernald State School sought to create an institution that would not serve uncurables. When the effort to educate the mentally retarded and return them to society failed, retarded individuals' care deteriorated. The retarded were viewed as subhuman and unable to be taught productive skills. The failure was probably due to the unrealistically high expectations of complete recovery.

The perception of failure and disappointment prevailed after these early attempts at cure failed. Along with this perception came a dramatic change in the care of retarded individuals. People who had the potential to be developmentally changed were treated accordingly, while those thought of as having subhuman qualities were treated as animals.

State schools and institutions soon gave way to asylums. In 1893, the Custodial Asylum for Unteachable Idiots was founded in Rome, New York. Governor Butler of Massachusetts said:

> A well-fed, well-cared for idiot is a happy creature. An idiot awakened to his condition is a miserable one.... It is earnestly urged that the best disposal to be made of this large class of the permanently disabled is to place it in custodial departments of institutions for the feebleminded persons...under the same merciful system that inspires hope and help for the lowest of humanity. (Kerlin, 1888, quoted in Kugel & Shearer, 1976)

It was also during this time (1885) that Illinois built a facility to provide for custodial care; the states of Iowa and Connecticut followed. Intentions were noble. There was an implied protectiveness associated with each state's appropriation for an asylum (Kugel & Shearer, 1976). History, however, has recorded the opposite to have been the case.

In the early 1900s, perceptions of the mentally retarded again changed and custodial care was said to have deteriorated. The moron and imbecile were soon made the source of all social ills. Leaders in the field, such as M. W. Barr, a past president of the American Association for Mental Retardation (AAMR), issued indictments of imbeciles as a threat to home and community. Calling for action, Johnson (1901) spoke bluntly when he stated that in order to prevent the propagation of idiocy and imbecility it might be "necessary to kill them or to resort to the knife" (Kugel & Shearer, 1976, p. 57). With attitudes such as these, it is little wonder that retarded individuals received deplorable care for the next 50 years.

The severely retarded were gradually dehumanized and moved to the back wards. These wards as well as other asylum cells were filthy and overcrowded. Such facilities were often referred to as the land of the living dead. In the fall of 1965, Senator Robert Kennedy visited several of his state's institutions; he was appalled at the conditions he encountered. Additional investigations by Blatt (1970) further delineated the horrors: "[I]n toilets, I frequently saw urinals ripped out, sinks broken and toilet bowls backed up...I found incredible overcrowding" (p. 13). The national average cost of caring for the mentally retarded in 1962 was less than $5 per day per patient. Some states managed to lower that to less than $2.50 per day.

Blatt (1970) further described conditions in several institutions. He saw 7-foot-by-7-foot isolation cells that seldom included beds, washstands, or toilets. Restraints were common. There were alarming shortages of staff and one supervisor for each 100 severely retarded individuals was not uncommon. It is small wonder that patients were locked up, restrained, or sedated. The odors of the wards and dayrooms were overpowering even though rooms were hosed down daily to move the human excretions to sewers located in the center of the rooms.

Blatt's (1966) photographic essay, *Christmas in Purgatory*, did much to alert professionals and the general public to the deplorable conditions existing for the institutionalized retarded. Those pictures of the stark gray, high walls, barred windows, beds pushed head to head, patients lying unclothed in feces, and rooms full of young children left their mark. The ensuing years have seen a movement away from those custodial conditions. Even in the 1960s, many institutions such as the Seaside, also chronicled by Blatt, were providing residential treatment that encouraged more and better trained staff, family participation, fewer closed wards, sunlit areas, medical and dental attention, and daily hygienic care. Within the past 30 years, the mentally retarded have been part of a deinstitutionalization movement unlike that of any era in U.S. history. Residential homes for individuals with disabilities are commonplace and the U.S. educational system now provides especially designed curricula to teach basic independent-living skills. In addition, government-supported projects have proliferated throughout the United States and now include not only programs for assessment and training but opportunities in employment that were nonexistent only a few years ago.

REFERENCES

Blatt, B. (1970). *Exodus from pandemonium*. Boston, MA: Allyn & Bacon.

Blatt, B., & Kaplan, F. (1966). *Christmas in purgatory*. Boston, MA: Allyn & Bacon.

Coleman, J. C., Butcher, J. N., & Carson, R. C. (1984). *Abnormal psychology and modern life* (7th ed.). Glenview, IL: Scott, Foresman.

Inge, K. J. (2006). Customized employment: A growing strategy for facilitating inclusive employment. *Journal of Vocational Rehabilitation, 24*, 191–193.

Johnson, A. Discussion on care of feeble-minded and epileptic. *Proc. Nat. Conf. Charities & Correction*. 1901, 410–411.

Kugel, R. B., & Shearer, A. (Eds.). (1976). *Changing patterns in residential services for the mentally retarded*. Washington, DC: President's Committee on Mental Retardation.

Rothman, D. J. (1971). *The discovery of the asylum*. Boston, MA: Little, Brown.

Selling, L. S. (1943). *Men against madness*. New York, NY: Garden City Books.

Targett, P., Young, C., Revell, G., Williams, S., & Wehman, P. (2007). Customized employment in the One Stop Centers. *Teaching Exceptional Children, 40*(2), 6–11.

Zilboorg, G., & Henry, G. W. (1941). *A history of medical psychology*. New York, NY: Norton.

Richard E. Halmstad
University of Wisconsin at Stout

See also **Deinstitutionalization; Institutionalization**

CUSTOMIZED EMPLOYMENT

Customized employment means tailoring an employment relationship to meet both a job seeker and an employer's needs. It is an ideal match between a job candidate's strengths, preferences, and needs, and an employer's hiring demands (ODEP, 2005). The term *customized employment* was introduced in 2001 by the Office of Disability Employment Policy (ODEP). It was derived from the establishment of the Investment Act of 1998 (WIA), which authorizes the development of a statewide one-stop system to increase all clients' employment outcomes. Under this background, the ODEP, which is on a mission to improve employment of people with disabilities, established grant initiatives to build the One Stops' capacity to serve all people, such as the Training and Technical Assistance for Providers (T-TAP) program, through which a number of principles and strategies for customized employment were developed (Targett, Young, Revell, Williams, & Wehman, 2007).

Customized employment is suggested as an alternative to supported employment and it involves up-front negotiation and individualized job development that benefit both parties. Very similar to supported employment, customized employment also provides competitive employment in integrated settings and ongoing support for individuals with significant disabilities. However, individuals with significant disabilities may need modifications in job responsibilities, so that they are able to perform the job and meet the employer's expectation. Therefore, customized employment makes it possible for individuals with disabilities to choose a job based on their own preferences and abilities (Inge, 2006).

Customized employment may include the following activities: (a) assessing and deciding the strengths, needs, and interests of a job seeker with a disability; (b) developing an employment plan and setting up the individual's employment goals; (c) negotiating with potential employers about their expectations and job responsibilities; (d) presenting a proposal about an individualized job that meets both parties' needs to employers who voluntarily agree to negotiate; (e) offering necessary representation during the negotiation process; (f) securing supports and funding sources; and (g) developing employment from self-employment (Griffin, Hammis, Geary, & Sullivan, 2008). One key principle of customized employment is that individuals with disabilities control the job-seeking direction and planning process based on preferences and abilities. It is also fundamental in customized employment that the employment is individualized through negotiation with employers or based on business demands (OSEP).

There is a variety of ways to customize a job, including job carving, job negotiation, job sharing, job creation, resource ownership, and self-employment (Griffin, Hammis, & Geary, 2007). Job carving is creating a new job description by removing one or more unsuitable tasks from the original job description for a traditional job. Job negotiation is to decide a new job description by selecting suitable tasks from all available tasks in the workplace that belong to different jobs. Job creation is creating a new job from unmet workplace needs. Resource ownership is to create an individualized job position along with provided technical resources or equipment that expand or enhance the business (Griffin, Hammis, & Geary). Employers, especially smaller businesses, benefit from hiring an individual along with the resources she or he brings to the job. Self-employment is also considered as one form of customized employment. Individuals with disabilities can create employment for themselves by owning and operating a small business, usually a microenterprise. This self-employment is developed through personal planning and the matching of individual and market needs.

Customized employment is a growing strategy. Improvements are needed with regard to implementation regulations, staff training, negotiation strategies, conflict resolution, and funding sources (Inge, 2006). It is considered as an innovation of employment options for individuals with significant disabilities in the 21st century. More research is needed to examine the efficacy of this option.

REFERENCES

Griffin, C., Hammis, D., & Geary, T. (2007). *The job developer's handbook: Practical tactics for customized employment.* Baltimore, MD: Brookes Publishing.

Griffin, C. C., Hammis, D., Geary, T., & Sullivan, M. (2008). Customized employment: Where we are; Where we're headed. *Journal of Vocational Rehabilitation. 28*(3), 135–139.

Office of Disability Employment (2005). Retrieved from http://www.dol.gov/odep/

Song Ju
Texas A&M University
Fourth edition

CUTIS MARMORATA TELANGIECTATICA CONGENITA

Cutis marmorata telangiectatica congenita (CMTC), also known as Van Lohuizen's syndrome, is a rare genetic skin disorder. First written about by Van Lohuizen (1922), CMTC occurs when dilated surface blood vessels result in patches of discolored skin. Often this discoloration is blue or purple and presents in a mottled pattern (Devillers, de Waard-van der Spek, & Oranje, 1999).

Cutis marmorata translates to "marbled skin," a reference to the patterns on the skin. Skin lesions and ulcers may also be present. CMTC is more likely to occur in girls than in boys. The skin discolorations usually are present only on part of an individual's body, and one side may be much more affected than the other side.

CMTC is a relatively moderate condition that usually improves by adulthood; the skin discoloration and lesions often disappear within 2 years. More worrisome are other congenital difficulties that sometimes are associated with CMTC, including lesions around the eyes and atrophy (Shield, Shield, Koller, Federman, Koblenzer, & Barbera, 1990). One variant of CMTC, megalencephaly cutis marmorata telangiectatica congenita syndrome (M-CMTC), is much more serious than CMTC. With M-CMTC, prenatal overgrowth and macrocephaly are present. Infants born with M-CMTC are at an increased risk of early death (Bottani, Chevallier, Dahoun, Cossali, & Pfister, 2000).

Characteristics

1. Discolored skin
2. Possible skin lesions and ulcers

Some infants with CMTC will be successfully treated by the time they reach school age. Others may need counseling to help with having a different appearance than other children.

Future research is continually being conducted on genetic disorders and skin disorders such as CMTC; one broad example is the Skin Federation in the Netherlands.

REFERENCES

Bottani, A., Chevallier, I., Dahoun, S., Cossali, D., & Pfister, R. (2000). Macrocephalycutis marmorata telangiectatica congenita (M-CMTC) syndrome can be caused by diploidy/tetraploidy skin mosaicism. *European Journal of Human Genetics, 8,* 66.

Devillers, A. C. A., de Waard-van der Spek, F. B., & Oranje, A. P. (1999). Cutis marmorata telangiectatica congenita: Clinical features in 35 cases. *Archives of Dermatology, 135,* 34–38.

Shield, J. A., Shield, C. L., Koller, H. P., Federman, J. L., Koblenzer, P., & Barbera, L. S. (1990). Cutis marmorata telangiectatica congenita associated with bilateral congenital retinal detachment. *Retina, 10,* 135–139.

Van Lohuizen, C. H. J. (1922). Ueber eine seltene angeborene Haut-anomalie (Cutis marmorata telangiectatica congenita). *Acta Dermatology Venerology, 3,* 202–211.

James C. Kaufman
Educational Testing Service Princeton, New Jersey

CYCLIC VOMITING SYNDROME

Cyclic vomiting syndrome (CVS) is a rare childhood disorder characterized by recurrent, prolonged episodes of severe vomiting, nausea, and prostration. The etiology of this disease is unknown.

The onset of symptoms commonly occurs between 3 and 7 years of age. Males and females alike are affected without regard to family situation or geographic location (Cyclic Vomiting Syndrome Association, 1998).

Characteristics

1. Episodes almost always begin at night or when waking in the morning.
2. Symptoms include forceful, repeated vomiting, as often as 5–6 times an hour.
3. Vomiting persists from hours to several days or more and often leads to dehydration.
4. The episodes may recur several times a year to several times a month.
5. Infection, distress, and excitement are the most commonly reported triggers, but most episodes occur without an identifiable trigger.
6. There is often a family history of migraines.
7. There is no apparent cause of vomiting.
8. There are intervals of normal health between episodes.

CVS is seldom seen in clinical practice and has been difficult to diagnose because vomiting may be caused by a large number of other disorders. There are no laboratory tests, X-rays, or other technical procedures for identifying this disorder. Diagnosis is made by careful review of the patient's history, a physical examination, and tests to rule out other diseases.

Emphasis should be placed on early intervention and providing a supportive environment. It is critical to create a dark, quiet environment for sleep, and hospitalization with intravenous fluid replacement may be needed during episodes. Antimigraine agents may help prevent episodes, and HT3 blocking antiemetic agents are the most successful treatments to abort episodes (Li, 2000). Sedatives are used to attenuate symptoms during episodes. A family history of migraine headaches renders the patient more likely to respond to antimigraine therapy (Li, 2000). The value of using stress management techniques should also be recognized.

Successful management of CVS involves a responsive, collaborative doctor–patient relationship. Medical professionals must be sensitive to circumstances that may predispose the child to attacks and to stresses caused by the illness. Other important components of long-term management include the use of antiemetic agents to abort or shorten attacks, the use of prophylactic agents in patients experiencing severe and frequent episodes, and treatment of complications (Fleisher & Matar, 1993). Common complications of cyclic vomiting episodes are esophagitis, hematemesis, depletion of intracellular electrolytes, hypertension, and secretion of an inappropriate antidiuretic hormone.

Special education services may be available to children with CVS under the handicapping condition of Other Health Impairment. In severe cases, significant periods of time away from the classroom may be involved, and home visits from special educators might be necessary. Side effects of medications should be taken into account when formally assessing the cognitive, social, emotional, and academic abilities of children suffering from CVS.

CVS is a self-limited disorder, but the duration cannot be predicted. The disorder frequently diminishes during adolescence and also may begin to manifest as migraine headaches. More studies are needed to determine the long-term safety and effectiveness of treatments for CVS.

REFERENCES

Cyclic Vomiting Syndrome Association. (1998). *CVS facts*. Retrieved from http://www.healthboard.com/websites/Detailed /9533.html

Fleisher, D. R., & Matar, M. (1993). The cyclic vomiting syndrome: A report of 71 cases and literature review. *Journal of Pediatric Gastroenterology and Nutrition*, *17*(4), 361–369.

Li, B. U. K. (2000). Cyclic vomiting syndrome. *Current Treatment Options in Gastroenterology*, *3*(5), 395–402.

CAREY E. COOPER
University of Texas at Austin

CYCLOTHYMIA

Cyclothymia refers to a chronic mood disorder that involves numerous hypomanic and depressive episodes that do not meet criteria for a bipolar affective disorder (BAD). The term was first used in the late 1800s and is credited to Kahlbaum, who described the condition as cyclical insanity. It was Kraepelin, however, who described cyclothymia as a temperament that predisposed individuals to more severe (and cyclical) episodes of mania and depression. More recently, cyclothymia has been described as a chronic subsyndromal mood disorder (e.g., Lovejoy & Steuerwald, 1995; Marneros, 2001). It is distinguished from BAD in terms of duration and severity (i.e., shorter duration and less severe symptoms). Studies of individuals diagnosed with BAD, however, indicate that in about a third of the cases there was a history of cyclothymia (Howland & Thase, 1993).

Characteristics

1. Numerous periods of persistent hypomanic and depressive symptoms last 1 year if a child or adolescent and 2 years if an adult.
2. During the 1- or 2-year period, the individual has not been without symptoms for more than two months at a time.
3. During the initial 1- or 2-year period, there has not been a major depressive episode or a manic episode (this can occur after the first 1 or 2 years).
4. Functioning is impaired or significant distress is caused by the condition.

Hypomanic episodes are characterized by distinct periods of abnormally expansive, elevated, or irritable mood with associated symptoms such as distractibility, increased energy, reduced need for sleep, psychomotor agitation, racing thoughts, pressured speech, grandiosity, and excessive involvement in pleasurable activities, especially those that pose risks. Depressive episodes are characterized by decreased energy, diminished interest, difficulty concentrating, problems with sleep, fatigue, problems with appetite (and sometimes weight), and loss of pleasure in previously enjoyed activities (American Psychiatric Association [APA], 2000).

Prevalence rates indicate that cyclothymia occurs in about .4–3.5% of the general population (APA, 2000). Cyclothymia is typically diagnosed during adolescence and early adulthood. The disorder is more prevalent in families with a history of BAD, with rates being particularly high in first-degree relatives (APA, 2000). There is evidence that individuals with cyclothymia may also have biological markers (e.g., endocrine problems such as hypothyroidism; Howland & Thase, 1993); however, the studies are inconclusive.

The course of cyclothymia is chronic and the prognosis unfavorable. This may be due in part to the fact that individuals are often diagnosed with other conditions that have poor response to treatment (e.g., borderline personality disorder). Lithium has been used for treating cyclothymia; however, the response rate has been poorer than that found among individuals diagnosed with BAD. Studies have, however, shown that lithium may have a prophylactic effect in terms of the development of major depressive episodes (Howland & Thase, 1993). Antidepressants have also been used with cyclothymia patients, and certain drugs (e.g., imipramine) have provided symptom relief. Psychological therapies may prove beneficial in helping the individual manage symptoms (e.g., cognitive-behavioral treatments). School psychologists may be an appropriate resource for this. Designing programs that help ensure maximal performance at school may also be helpful, and is a service that school psychologist can provide. Special education is not likely to be needed because marked impairment is not typically found among individuals with cyclothymia. If services through the Individuals With Disabilities Education Act are needed, however, it would likely be under the category Emotional Disturbance. In these cases, it may be necessary to refer the child for a psychiatric consultation to determine what, if any, medications are needed.

Cyclothymia has not received the same amount of attention in the literature as have other disorders from the *Diagnostic and Statistical Manual of Mental Disorders, Fourth Edition*, including BAD. There is a pressing need for information that will improve understanding about the condition, including its etiology, course, and long-term outcome. Further research is also needed to determine how best to treat cyclothymia and prevent the development of more severe symptomatology, including BAD. Drug studies that examine the efficacy of lithium, anticonvulsant medications used for BAD (e.g., carbamazepine and valproate), and antidepressants are also needed.

REFERENCES

American Psychiatric Association. (2000). *Diagnostic and statistical manual of mental disorders* (4th ed., text rev.). Washington, DC: Author.

Howland, R., & Thase, M. (1993). A comprehensive review of cyclothymic disorder. *Journal of Nervous and Mental Disease, 181*(8), 485–493.

Lovejoy, M., & Steuerwald, B. (1995). Subsyndromal unipolar and bipolar disorders: Comparisons on positive and negative affect. *Journal of Abnormal Psychology, 104*(2), 381–384.

Marneros, A. (2001). Expanding the group of bipolar disorders. *Journal of Affective Disorders, 62*(1), 139–141.

ELAINE CLARK
REX GONZALES
University of Utah

CYLERT

Cylert (Pemoline) is a mild central nervous system stimulant medication that is used in the management of hyperactive children. While the onset of effectiveness of Cylert has been found to be slower than that of some other central nervous system stimulants, it also has been found to have a longer half-life, 12 hours compared with 4 hours for other stimulants (Ross & Ross, 1982). Because of this longer half-life, Cylert need be administered only on a once-daily basis. For hyperactive children, this eliminates the social stigma associated with taking medication at school. In addition, parents are better able to supervise drug administration, thereby reducing the possibility of drug abuse and increasing the probability of compliance. Another advantage of Cylert therapy over other psychostimulants in pediatric populations is its long duration of therapeutic action without sympathomimetic cardiovascular effects. In fact, therapeutic effects of Cylert have been found to be similar to those of amphetamines and methylphenidate (Ross & Ross, 1982). Clinical trials have yielded data to indicate that Cylert enhances short-term memory, attentiveness to cognitive and academic tasks, and social functioning (Ross & Ross, 1982).

As with other psychostimulants, one concern with Cylert administration has been the occurrence of side effects. While mild side effects, including insomnia, headaches, anorexia, abdominal pains, dizziness, and nausea have been reported, of greater concern is the elevation of liver enzymes, which often necessitates the withdrawal of medication. Severe dysphoric effects following the cessation of Cylert also have been reported in some isolated cases (Brown, Borden, Spunt, & Medenis, 1985).

REFERENCES

Brown, R. T., Borden, K. A., Spunt, A. L., & Medenis, R. (1985). Depression following Pemoline withdrawal in a hyperactive child. *Clinical Pediatrics*, *24*, 174.

Ross, D. M., & Ross, S. A. (1982). *Hyperactivity: Current issues, research and theory* (2nd ed.). New York, NY: Wiley-Interscience.

RONALD T. BROWN
Emory University School of Medicine

See also Hyperactivity; Medical Management

CYSTIC FIBROSIS

Cystic fibrosis (CF) is one of the most common genetic diseases to affect Caucasian populations, affecting approximately 1 in 3,400 live births. CF rarely affects other ethnic populations. For example, the incidence in the African American population is only 1 in 17,000 live births. CF is an autosomal recessive disease—thus, both parents must be carriers of the defective gene to produce an affected child (FitzSimmons, 1993).

CF is primarily a disease of the respiratory and digestive systems, resulting from a genetic defect that disrupts the way salt and water move in and out of the body's cells. In CF patients, the body develops thick, sticky mucus

secretions that clog airways in the lungs, leading to frequent infections and inflammation (Quittner, Modi, & Roux, 2004). Lung disease in patients with CF is progressive; respiratory failure accounts for more than 85% of mortality (FitzSimmons, 1993). The respiratory effects of CF often result in a chronic cough. Because CF has such a profound impact on respiratory function, treatment for CF generally attempts to keep the lungs cleared of mucus and minimize lung infection and inflammation. This is accomplished through a variety of means, including airway clearance to help physically loosen the secretions, medications to help thin the sticky mucus, and antibiotics (oral or inhaled). Many of these treatments are managed on a daily basis by the child's parents at home. Sometimes, a child with CF will need to be hospitalized to receive intravenous antibiotics and other more intensive treatments. The frequency of these hospitalizations varies from child to child, and each hospitalization may last 2 or more weeks (Quittner et al., 2004).

In addition to respiratory complications, the digestive system also is affected by the thick, sticky secretions, which block the pancreas during the prenatal developmental period. This blockage prevents the release of enzymes needed to digest food, resulting in malabsorption of nutrients and fat, digestive difficulties, and diminished growth. As a result, children with CF must consume more calories than their typical peers (125 to 150% of the Recommended Daily Allowance) and also must take pancreatic enzyme replacements (in pill or powder form) with every meal and snack. Despite these treatments, children with CF are often shorter and thinner than their peers (Quittner et al., 2004).

Recent scientific advances in the treatment of CF include more powerful antibiotics, new methods of delivering antibiotics to the lungs, and earlier diagnosis. Thus, the life span of children with CF has increased. In the 1960s, most individuals with CF died during childhood. Today, children born with CF can expect to reach adulthood; the median survival age is approximately 31 (FitzSimmons, 1993).

Aggressive treatment of CF has enabled most children with CF to attend school regularly. Children and adolescents with CF are not at increased risk for cognitive or academic problems (Thompson, Gustafson, Meghdadpour, Harrell, Johndrow, & Spock, 1992). However, other challenges at school may arise. School problems for children with CF are more likely to concern management of CF symptoms and treatments, absenteeism, and interaction with peers (DiGirolamo, Quittner, Ackerman, & Stevens, 1997). For example, children with CF may resist taking medication at school because they are worried about looking different in front of their peers. Children with CF may be absent from school more often because of hospitalizations or clinic visits and may fall behind in their schoolwork if plans are not set up ahead of time to deal with absences (Quittner et al., 2004). Thus, professionals involved in the education of a child with CF should be well-informed about the child's medical condition and maintain frequent communication with the child's parents in order to facilitate adjustment in the school setting.

Characteristics

1. Genetic disorder that impacts respiratory function
2. Can also impact gastrointestinal, pancreatic, hepatic, and reproduction systems, causing megacolon, liver cirrhosis, and sterility
3. Initial symptoms consisting of chronic cough and upper respiratory infection
4. Shortness of breath, decreased activity, poor appetite, and weight loss
5. Can cause progressive and irreversible lung damage and death

---

REFERENCES

DiGirolamo, A. M., Quittner, A. L., Ackerman, V., & Stevens, J. (1997). Identification and assessment of ongoing stressors in adolescents with chronic illness: An application of the behavior-analytic model. *Journal of Clinical Child Psychology*, *26*, 53–66.

FitzSimmons, S. C. (1993). The changing epidemiology of cystic fibrosis. *Journal of Pediatrics*, *122*, 1–9.

Quittner, A. L., Modi, A. C., & Roux, A. L. (2004). Psychosocial challenges and clinical interventions for children and adolescents with cystic fibrosis: A developmental approach. In R. Brown (Ed.), *Handbook of pediatric psychology in school settings* (pp. 333–61). Mahwah, NJ: Erlbaum.

Thompson, R. J., Gustafson, K. E., Meghdadpour, S., Harrell, E., Johndrow, D. A., & Spock, A. (1992). The role of biomedical and psychosocial processes in the intellectual and academic functioning of children and adolescents with cystic fibrosis. *Journal of Clinical Psychology*, *48*(1), 3–10.

AMY LOOMIS ROUX
University of Florida

See *also* Adapted Physical Education; Cystic Fibrosis Foundation; Health Maintenance Procedures

CYSTIC FIBROSIS FOUNDATION

The Cystic Fibrosis Foundation is a voluntary, nonprofit health organization that actively supports research and treatment for cystic fibrosis. Founded in 1955 by a small group of parents of children with cystic fibrosis, it was originally conceived to raise money for research to find a cure and improve the quality of life for individuals with the disease. With the help of more than 250,000 volunteers operating in 65 chapters and branch offices across the United States, the organization depends on public support to implement its programs.

The Foundation actively supports the advancement of medical science by funding research centers at leading universities and medical centers throughout the United States and providing a variety of grants to scientists for research on the disease. It also offers comprehensive diagnosis and treatment for people with cystic fibrosis through a nationwide network of 113 cystic fibrosis care centers. In addition to the research, diagnostic, and treatment services provided, the centers also offer professional medical education and training and conduct clinical trials testing new drug therapies. The Therapeutic Development Program, which provides matching funds to biotechnology companies to stimulate development of new therapies, furnishes the infrastructure needed to conduct these clinical trials in the early phases.

The Cystic Fibrosis Foundation influences public policy related to the disease by working closely with the U.S. Congress, the Food and Drug Administration, and pharmaceutical companies to speed the development of drugs to treat the disorder. The organization's efforts in this area also include advocating for increased funding for the National Institutes of Health and testifying before Congress to encourage more money for research.

Information on a variety of subjects related to cystic fibrosis, including updates on research, clinical trials, public policy issues, and ways to become involved with the Cystic Fibrosis Foundation, may be obtained through its website (http://www.cff.org/AboutCF/). The Foundation may be contacted at its national offices at 6931 Arlington Road, Bethesda, MD 20814. Tel.: (800) FIGHTCF, (301) 951-4422, or fax at (301) 951-6378.

All information retrieved from http://www.cff.org/ on January 9, 2012.

HEATHER DAVIS
Texas A&M University
Fourth edition

CYSTIC HYGROMA

Cystic hygromas are cystic lesions that are usually found in the neck. They are caused by dilated, or enlarged, lymphatic tissue that becomes malformed, resulting in a type of benign tumor. Cystic hygromas develop at approximately 40 days of gestation because of a failure of the embryonic lymphatics to connect with the venous system (PedLine, 2001). Cystic hygromas can be present at birth or can develop in early childhood. These cysts are filled with lymphatic fluid and lymph cells and may be inherited as through an autosomal recessive trait (National Organization for Rare Disorders [NORD], 2001). They are most frequently located in the posterior lower area of the neck (Tibesar, Rimell, & Michel, 1999), and they occur twice as often on the left side (NORD, 2001; PedLine, 2001).

The onset of cystic hygromas usually occurs at birth or within the first year of life. The incidence of this disorder is 1 out of every 12,000 births, and it is equally prevalent in males and females (NORD, 2001; PedLine, 2001).

Characteristics

1. The child sees the pediatrician because of the detection of a mass or masses on the base of the neck, face, mouth, tongue, or other areas of the upper torso.

2. The masses may also be identified by ultrasound, and they can be a unilocular or multilocular cyst with a thin or thick wall, filled with a clear or tan fluid, or a blood-tinged liquid if infected (PedLine, 2001).

3. Small to medium-sized hygromas are often asymptomatic (PedLine, 2001).

4. Especially when located in the throat and chest area, large hygromas can cause complications such as upper-airway obstruction (stridor, apneas, cyanosis), dysphagia, mandibular maldevelopment, nerve palsies, hemorrhage, and infection (PedLine, 2001).

An ultrasound of the suspected area of the child, or an ultrasound of the suspected area of the fetus, is used to detect cystic hygromas (NORD, 2001; PedLine, 2001). Testing for elevated levels of alpha-1-fetoprotein in the water sac surrounding the fetus is also a method being used to detect hygromas in vitro (NORD, 2001). Genetic testing is recommended for families with a history of hygromas (NORD, 2001). Sclerosing agents have been used with patients with cystic hygromas but have had varying results (Tibesar et al., 1999).

The recommended treatment of cystic hygromas is immediate surgical removal (NORD, 2001) or immediate removal for those that are large and symptomatic (PedLine, 2001). Multiple surgeries may be required, although some hygromas may resolve untreated (PedLine, 2001).

The prognosis of patients with cystic hygromas depends greatly on the complications that occur, which depends on the location and size of the hygromas. Recurrence of the hygromas is common (Tibesar et al., 1999), and the

hygromas are often unpredictable in their growth and spread to surrounding tissue (PedLine, 2001). Patients with cystic hygromas are expected to have a normal life span and intelligence (PedLine, 2001).

Children with cystic hygromas may qualify as Other Health Impairment under Section 504, depending on the severity of their symptoms. The affected child may require home schooling during recovery time after surgeries needed to remove the hygromas. The child may also need speech and occupational therapy if the tumor interferes with these functions. Although cystic hygromas are often present without noticeable symptoms, school modifications may be necessary in specific cases.

REFERENCES

National Organization for Rare Disorders. (2001, March 20). *Cystic hygroma.* Retrieved from http://www.rarediseases.org

PedLine; (2001, March 8). Cystic hygroma. Retrieved from http://icondata.com.searchnut.com/index.php?y=10296994&r=c%3E bXOwcnSieHFvZ3%3Au%27f%3Ebtl%3Cvt%3C33%3C2%3C2 %3C213%3A7%3A%3A5%3Ctuzmf2%6033%2Fdtt%3C3%3Cjo ufsdptnpt%60bggjmjbuf%60xq%60e3s%60efsq%3Cxizqbsl%3C xizqbsl%3C87227%3C87227%3Ccboofe%3C%3Cbtl%3Cqbslfe %2Ftzoejdbujpo%2Fbtl%2Fdpn%27jqvb%60je%3Ebf4c81g68% 3Afb7c3%3A3fd11%3Ab5fc468949%27enybsht%3Eg219b43c1 %3Aec8fc8dg9c951e8e8%3A9bc%3A&rd=3

Tibesar, R. J., Rimell, F. L., & Michel, E. (1999). Cystic hygroma of the skull space. *Archives of Otolaryngol Head and Neck Surgery, 125,* 1390–1393.

MOANA KRUSCHWITZ
MARGARET SEMRUD-CLIKEMAN
University of Texas at Austin

CYTOMEGALOVIRUS

The cytomegalovirus is a filterable DNA virus in the family of herpes viruses. It is responsible for the infectious disease known as cytomegalic inclusion disease. The virus is not easily eliminated and persists in host tissues for months, years, or even a lifetime. It produces a chronic infection with a variable incubation period, outcome, and course. The infection may be a significant form of congenital disease in newborns whose immune system is incompletely developed or in adults who are immunosuppressed, such as individuals with AIDS (Sessoms, & Brown, 2003).

There are two patterns of infection: localized and generalized. In the localized form, inclusion bodies are found only in the salivary glands; this clinical entity sometimes is referred to as generalized salivary gland disease. The second, generalized, form is represented in two principal types: that accompanied by necrotizing and calcifying encephalitis and that associated with enlargement of the spleen and the liver, lymphadenopathy, and blood dyscrasias. There is increasing recognition of the association of this infection with acquired immune deficiency syndrome (AIDS). Where there is significant cerebral damage, there is often ocular involvement.

It is generally agreed that the virus is widespread; the localized form of the disease is both frequent in occurrence and asymptomatic. Ten to 32% of autopsied infants show evidence of localized disease. Although the generalized form of the disease may occur in adults, it is characteristically seen in infants and children, occurring in up to 1% of children. Cytomegalovirus has been detected in up to 90% of immunosuppressed kidney transplant patients; active infection may predispose these patients to bacterial superinfection and transplant rejection. The virus also alters the immune system, although apparently only during the acute phase of infection; the mechanism for immunosuppression is not fully understood.

Because many organs may be affected in generalized disease, the clinical features are variable. Usually there is an acute or subacute febrile illness, and infants are likely to have been premature. There may be severe jaundice and bleeding tendencies, and enlargement of the spleen and liver is frequent. Pneumonia and renal involvement often are present. In the encephalitic form, hydrocephalus and chorioretinitis occur. Most infected infants succumb to encephalitic disease. Among those who survive, mental or motor retardation, microcephaly, seizures, and ocular involvement are common. Ocular lesions include microcornea, chorioretinitis, pseudocolobomas of the retina, retinal hemorrhage, pale optic discs, uveitis, keratoconjunctivitis, and dacryoadenitis.

The diagnosis is best established by recovery of the virus from the urine, saliva, or aqueous humor of the eye. Congenital toxoplasmosis is difficult to differentiate, but radiologic evidence of periventricular calcification suggests cytomegalic inclusion disease. Other diseases to be differentiated include generalized bacterial infection, herpes simplex encephalitis, congenital liver deformities, and diseases of the reticuloendothelial system. No treatment has been effective in controlling this disease. Several antiviral medications used to control the herpes virus have been tried with minimal success.

This article was informed by the following references.

REFERENCES

Friedlaender, M. H. (1963). Immunology of infections systemic diseases that affect the eye. In T. D. Duane & E. A. Jaeger (Eds.), *Biomedical foundations of ophthalmology*. Hagerstown, MD: Harper & Row.

Sessoms, A., & Brown, R. T. (2003). Cytomegalovirus, congenital. In E. Fletcher-Janzen & C. R. Reynolds (Eds.), *Childhood disorders diagnostic desk reference* (pp. 164–165). Hoboken, NJ: Wiley.

Walsh, F. B., & Hoyt, W. F. (1969). *Clinical neuro-ophthalmology*. Baltimore, MD: Williams & Wilkins.

GEORGE R. BEAUCHAMP
Cleveland Clinic Foundation

See also **Chronic Illness in Children; Herpes Simplex I and II**

CYTOMEGALOVIRUS, CONGENITAL

Cytomegalovirus (CMV) is a communicable DNA virus in the herpes family that when contracted in later childhood or adulthood is generally either asymptomatic or causes a short, mild illness with a fever and other flulike symptoms. It may remain in infected individuals' systems throughout life and be excreted in their urine, saliva, breast milk, cervical secretions, and semen, even if they have never experienced symptoms (e.g., Beauchamp, 2000; Graham & Morgan, 1997). In individuals with AIDS and other patients with weakened immune systems, CMV and other viruses may cause serious and pervasive problems.

If contracted by a pregnant woman, CMV may cross the placental barrier and cause fetal death or serious deformities in her offspring. It is a member of the STORCH (syphilis, toxoplasmosis, varicella, and other infections, rubella, cytomegalovirus, and herpes) complex, a group of maternal infections that have similar effects on offspring. It is the most common such infection, occurring in some 5–25 per 1,000 births. As with other herpes viruses, exposure prior to pregnancy prevents neither recurrence nor congenital infection.

Characteristics

Symptomatic newborns

1. Petechiae (small hemorrhage spot on skin or other surface)
2. Enlargement of liver and spleen
3. Jaundice
4. Microcephaly
5. Intrauterine growth retardation

Developmental characteristics in symptomatic or asymptomatic newborns

1. Sensorineural hearing loss
2. Psychomotor retardation
3. Mental retardation
4. Dental abnormalities
5. Chorioretinitis

About 10% of fetuses infected in early prenatal development will be born with CMV and show symptoms at birth. In the rare case of severe, life-threatening CMV infection, infants may be treated with intravenous and then oral antiviral medication. Antiviral medication may be put directly into the eyes of those with CMV retinitis. However, antiviral medicines have serious side effects and are used only in extreme situations.

Of infants asymptomatic at birth, about 5–15% will develop hearing loss, low intelligence, or behavior problems during the first few years of life. Later prenatal exposure may lead to hearing loss (e.g., Graham & Morgan, 1997). Congenital CMV is more likely to occur in the offspring of women who contracted CMV for the first time during pregnancy and themselves had symptoms. Other maternal risk factors include low socioeconomic status, age over 30 years, non-White, and having been breast-fed (Roizen & Johnson, 1996).

Rarely, infants can contract CMV during or after delivery when they pass through the birth canal of, or consume breast milk from, an infected mother. Transmission through blood transfusion contaminated with CMV has been virtually eliminated through screening procedures. Most infants affected by such perinatal CMV are asymptomatic at birth but may develop lung and blood problems, poor weight gain, swollen glands, rash, and hepatitis during development. Those born prematurely are at higher risk to develop symptoms (KidsHealth, 2001).

Diagnosis must be through laboratory testing of a urine or saliva sample to identify the virus because symptoms of congenital infections are similar. Testing must be conducted early to differentiate congenital from postnatal infection, but it is often delayed in asymptomatic infants, precluding accurate diagnosis (Roizen & Johnson, 1996).

No effective treatment is available for congenital or perinatal CMV. A variety of supportive care and special education services will be required, depending on the extent and variety of symptoms. Adaptive technology for sensory impairments, speech therapy, and special education may be needed. In addition, no vaccine is available, so prevention of spread of the virus is important. Common practices such as thorough hand washing, especially in day-care centers where children and staff come into contact with infected children's saliva or urine, can prevent the virus from being spread from unwashed hands and shared toys.

REFERENCES

Beauchamp, G. R. (2000). Cytomegalovirus. In C. R. Reynolds & E. Fletcher-Janzen (Eds.), *Encyclopedia of special education* (2nd ed., Vol. 1, p. 528). New York, NY: Wiley.

Graham, E. M., & Morgan, M. A. (1997). Growth before birth. In M. L. Batshaw (Ed.), *Children with disabilities* (4th ed., pp. 53–69). Baltimore, MD: Brooks.

KidsHealth. (2001). *Cytomegalovirus (CMV)*. Retrieved from http://www.kidshealth.org/parent/infections/bacterial_viral/cytomegalovirus.html

Roizen, N. J., & Johnson, D. (1996). Congenital infections. In A. J. Capute & P. J. Accardo (Eds.), *Developmental disabilities in infancy and childhood: Vol. 1. Neurodevelopmental diagnosis and treatment* (2nd ed., pp. 175–193). Baltimore, MD: Brooks.

AMY SESSOMS
ROBERT T. BROWN
University of North Carolina,
Wilmington